gotow|ać (*-uję*) ⟨*u-, z-,* (*się* v/i.); *obiad* cook ; *fig* *się* seethe; → **przygotow**

... na różne ...gorie gramatyczne

Entries divided into grammatical categories

aresztowa|ć ⟨*za-*⟩ (*-uję*) arr (*-a*) arrest; *~ny* **1.** arrested, in **2.** *m* (*-ego; -i*), *~na* *f* (*-ej; -e*) pe der arrest, detainee

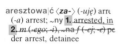

awans *m* (*-u; -e/-y*) promotion; *~ spo-* *łeczny* social advancement; *otrzymać* *~em* get in advance; *~ować* (*im*)*pf* (*-uję*) *v/t.* promote; *v/t.* be promoted (**na** *A* to), (*też w sporcie*) move up

Różnice w rekcji między językiem polskim i angielskim

Differences in grammar governing usage

bycz|ek *m* (*-czka; -czki*) bull-calf; *~y* bull's; F (*fajny*) great, terrific; *~y chłop* F hell of a guy

Kwalifikatory stylistyczne

Register labels

podać *pf.* → **podawać, dymisja**

Odsyłacz do innego hasła

Mark of reference

autostrada *f* (*-y*) *Brt.* motorway; *Am.* expressway; (*płatna*) *Am.* turnpike

Angielski brytyjski i angielski amerykański

British and American variants

Polish
Compact Dictionary

Polish – English
English – Polish

Berlitz Publishing
New York · Munich · Singapore

Original edition edited by the Langenscheidt editorial staff

Based on a dictionary compiled by Prof. Tadeusz Piotrowski in collaboration with Dr. Adam Sumera

Book in cover photo: © Punchstock/Medioimages

© 2007 Berlitz Publishing/APA Publications GmbH & Co. Verlag KG
Singapore Branch, Singapore

Berlitz Publishing
193 Morris Avenue
Springfield, NJ 07081
USA

Printed in Germany
ISBN 978-981-268-056-3

07
08
09
10
11
5.
4.
3.
2.
1.

Preface

Here is a new dictionary of Polish and English, a tool with some 50,000 references for those who work with the Polish and English languages at beginner's or intermediate level.

Focusing on modern usage, the dictionary offers coverage of everyday language – and this means including vocabulary from areas such as computer use and business. English means both American and British English.

The editors have provided a reference tool to enable the user to get straight to the translation that fits a particular context of use. Indicating words are given to identify senses. Is the *mouse* you need for your computer, for example, the same in Polish as the *mouse* you don't want in the house? Is *flimsy* referring to furniture the same in Polish as *flimsy* referring to an excuse? This dictionary is rich in sense distinctions like this – and in translation options tied to specific, identified senses.

Vocabulary needs grammar to back it up. So in this dictionary you'll find English irregular verb forms, irregular English plural forms, inflectional endings of Polish nouns or verbs.

Since some vocabulary items are often only clearly understood when contextualized, a large number of idiomatic phrases are given to show how the two languages correspond in particular contexts.

All in all, this is a book full of information, which will become a valuable part of your language toolkit.

Przedmowa

Słownik praktyczny polsko-angielski i angielsko-polski zawiera około 50 000 haseł i zwrotów na 672 stronach. Niewielki format, a pomimo to bogaty i rzetelny materiał językowy ujęty w słowniku przesądzają o jego przydatności zarówno na lekcjach, jak i w codziennej komunikacji językowej.

Przy wyborze haseł kierowano się przede wszystkim częstotliwością ich występowania we współczesnym języku polskim i angielskim.

Charakterystyczną i najważniejszą cechą słownika jest staranny dobór haseł. W słowniku uwzględniono, poza słownictwem ogólnym, także terminy fachowe z takich dziedzin, jak: szkolnictwo, kultura, turystyka, gospodarka, biznes i technika.

Precyzyjnie zredagowane hasła, objaśnione znaczenia główne, poboczne i idiomatyczne wyrazów decydują o tym, że słownik jest przydatny dla początkujących i zaawansowanych.

Aby ułatwić użytkownikom poprawne odczytanie informacji zawartych w artykułach hasłowych, na stronach wewnętrznych okładki umieszczono przejrzyste objaśnienia wszystkich elementów stosowanych przy opisie hasła.

Ważną częścią słownika, decydującą o jego przydatności na kursach szkolnych jest dodatek gramatyczny, zawierający najważniejsze dla użytkownika informacje gramatyczne, np. wykaz czasowników nieregularnych.

Słownik polecany jest uczniom oraz osobom samodzielnie uczącym się języka do codziennego użytku w szkole, w pracy lub w podróży po Europie XXI wieku.

Spis treści
Contents

Wskazówki dla użytkownika
Guide to Using the Dictionary

Porządek alfabetyczny i dobór haseł
Wszystkie wyrazy hasłowe podane są w porządku alfabetycznym. Do ich opisu stosowane są odpowiednie kwalifikatory dziedzinowe – przedstawiające ich przynależność do poszczególnych dziedzin oraz kwalifikatory stylistyczne – wskazujące na różne style danego wyrazu.

akuszer *m* (*-a; -rzy*) *med.* obstetrician; **~ka** *f* (*-i; G -rek*) midwife

Użycie tyldy (~) i dywizu
Tylda zastępuje cały wyraz hasłowy lub jego część, znajdującą się po lewej stronie kreski pionowej.

cierpliw|ość *f* (*-ści; 0*) patience; **u-zbroić się w ~ość** exercise one's patience; **~ie** patiently

bawić ⟨**po- za-**⟩ (*-ę*) *v/i.* stay; be on a visit (*u G* to); *v/t.* entertain; amuse; **~ się** (*dobrze itp.*) have a good time; enjoy o.s.; **~ się** play (**z dziećmi** with children, **lalką** with a doll); *fig.* **nie ~ się w** (*A*) not waste too much time on

W formach gramatycznych, podawanych w nawiasach okrągłych lub w nawiasach trójkątnych wyrazy hasłowe lub ekwiwalenty wyrazów hasłowych zastąpiono dywizem.

cierpliw|ość *f* (*-ści; 0*) patience

Hasła mające kilka odpowiedników
Odpowiedniki bliskoznaczne wyrazu hasłowego podano obok siebie oddzielając je przecinkami.

administrować (*-uję*) (*I*) administer, manage

Jeżeli wyraz hasłowy ma kilka odpowiedników dalekoznacznych, w takim przypadku na pierwszym miejscu podano znaczenie bliższe lub pierwotne, a potem kolejno znaczenia dalsze lub pochodne, oddzielone średnikiem.
Różnice znaczeniowe objaśniane są za pomocą:
– kwalifikatorów działowych,
– poprzedzających synonimów, podawanych w nawiasach okrągłych,

Alphabetical order and the choice of entries
The entries are given in a strictly alphabetical order. Special labels are used to help to describe them. There are also labels for words that are restricted to specific fields of usage.

akuszer *m* (*-a; -rzy*) *med.* obstetrician; **~ka** *f* (*-i; G -rek*) midwife

The use of the swung dash (~) and the hyphen The swung dash replaces the headword or the part of it that appears to the left of the vertical bar.

cierpliw|ość *f* (*-ści; 0*) patience; **u-zbroić się w ~ość** exercise one's patience; **~ie** patiently

bawić ⟨**po- za-**⟩ (*-ę*) *v/i.* stay; be on a visit (*u G* to); *v/t.* entertain; amuse; **~ się** (*dobrze itp.*) have a good time; enjoy o.s.; **~ się** play (**z dziećmi** with children, **lalką** with a doll); *fig.* **nie ~ się w** (*A*) not waste too much time on

In grammatical forms given in round or angle brackets the entries or their equivalents are replaced with a hyphen.

cierpliw|ość *f* (*-ści; 0*) patience

Entries with more than one meaning
Translations of the headword that are used synonymously are given next to each other and are separated by commas.

administrować (*-uję*) (*I*) administer, manage

If the Polish headword has more than one English equivalent, it is the basic or original meaning that is presented first. Further or derivative meanings come later and are separated by a semicolons.
Differences in meaning are explained by the use of:
– labels,
– preceding synonyms, given in round brackets,

– poprzedzających lub następujących po odpowiedniku dopełnień, podmiotów lub innych wskazówek objaśniających.

– objects, subjects or other explanatory notes preceding or following the translation.

ciąć ⟨ś-⟩ v/t. cut; impf. drzewa fell; (piłą) saw; v/i. deszcz wiatr. lash

ciąć ⟨ś-⟩ v/t. cut; impf. drzewa fell; (piłą) saw; v/i. deszcz wiatr. lash

Jeżeli wyraz hasłowy należy do różnych kategorii gramatycznych, oddzielono je cyfrą arabską oraz oznaczono odpowiednim kwalifikatorem gramatycznym.

If the Polish headword is used as more than one part of speech, it is separated by Arabic numerals and marked with a suitable grammatical label.

bez|ustanny 1. adj. incessant, unstopping; 2. adv. ~ustannie incessantly; ~usterkowy (-wo) trouble-free; ~użyteczny useless

bez|ustanny 1. adj. incessant, unstopping; 2. adv. ~ustannie incessantly; ~usterkowy (-wo) trouble-free; ~użyteczny useless

Homonimy podano w osobnych hasłach oznaczonych kolejnymi cyframi arabskimi, podanymi w indeksie.

Homonyms are presented under separate entries marked with exponent numerals.

ciepło¹ n (-a; 0) warmth, heat
ciepło² adv. warm

ciepło¹ n (-a; 0) warmth, heat
ciepło² adv. warm

Hasła rzeczownikowe
Hasła rzeczownikowe opatrzone są zawsze skrótem rodzaju gramatycznego m, f, n.
W nawiasach okrągłych podano końcówki drugiego przypadka l. poj., pierwszego przypadka l. mn. oraz sporadycznie drugiego przypadka l. mn.

Nouns
Noun entries are always assigned an abbreviation of grammatical gender: m, f or n.
The endings of the second case singular, the first case plural and sometimes the second case plural are given in round brackets.

cierń m (-nia; -nie -ni) thorn, spine

cierń m (-nia; -nie -ni) thorn, spine

Hasła przymiotnikowe
Jako hasła główne występują przymiotniki w mianowniku liczby poj. w rodzaju męskim w stopniu równym. Przymiotniki występujące tylko w rodzaju żeńskim podane są jako oddzielne hasła. Formy stopnia wyższego i najwyższego przymiotników stopniowanych nieregularnie podawane są w nawiasach okrągłych. Dodatkowo formy te zostały ujęte w liście haseł.

Adjectives
Adjectives are given in the singular, masculine nominative of the simple form. Adjectives that are only feminine are given as separate entries. When the comparative and superlative forms of an adjective are irregular, these have been given in round brackets. Additionally, these forms have been included in the list of entries.

ładny adj. (comp. -niejszy) pretty, nice

ładny adj. (comp. -niejszy) pretty, nice

Hasła czasownikowe
Jako wyrazy hasłowe występują z reguły czasowniki niedokonane. Przy czasownikach niedokonanych, posiadających aspekt dokonany podano w nawiasach trójkątnych przedrostek lub przyrostek, za pomocą których tworzony jest ich aspekt dokonany. Czasowniki niedokonane, nieposiadające odpowiednika dokonanego pozostają nieoznaczone. Cza-

Verbs
As a rule imperfect verbs appear as entries. Imperfect verbs that have the perfect aspect are followed by angle brackets in which a prefix or a suffix that is used to form the perfect aspect of the verb is given. Imperfect verbs that do not have their perfect aspect are unmarked. Verbs that have only the perfect aspect are marked pf. Verbs that

9

sowniki, posiadające tylko aspekt dokonany zostały opatrzone kwalifikatorem
pf. Czasowniki dwuaspektowe natomiast oznaczone kwalifikatorem *(im)pf.*

jechać *(-dę)* ⟨**po-**⟩ go (**koleją** by train);
ride (**rowerem** (on) a bike, **konno** (on) a
horse)
minąć *pf.* *(-nę -ń)* go by
kazać *(im)pf* *(każę każ!)* order, command

W nawiasach okrągłych z dywizem podano końcówki pierwszej osoby l. poj.

lamentować *(-uję)* lament (**nad** *I* over)

can be used in both aspects are marked
(im)pf.

jechać *(-dę)* ⟨**po-**⟩ go (**koleją** by train);
ride (**rowerem** (on) a bike, **konno** (on) a
horse)
minąć *pf.* *(-nę -ń)* go by
kazać *(im)pf* *(każę każ!)* order, command

The endings of the first person singular
are given in round brackets with a hyphen.

lamentować *(-uję)* lament (**nad** *I* over)

Skróty
Abbreviations

biernik	*A*	accusative
przymiotnik	*adj.*	adjective
przysłówek	*adv.*	adverb
rolnictwo	*agr.*	agriculture
amerykański angielski	*Am.*	American English
anatomia	*anat.*	anatomy
architektura	*arch.*	architecture
astronomia	*astr.*	astronomy
przydawka	*attr.*	attributive
lotnictwo	*aviat.*	aviation
bezokolicznik	*bezok.*	infinitive
biologia	*biol.*	biology
botanika	*bot.*	botany
brytyjski angielski	*Brt.*	British English
budownictwo	*bud.*	building
chemia	*chem.*	chemistry
spójnik	*cj.*	conjunction
stopień wyższy	*comp.*	comparative
pogardliwy	*cont.*	contemptuously
celownik	*D*	dative
dialekt	*dial.*	dialect
ekonomia	*econ.*	economics
elektronika	*electr.*	electrical engineering
rodzaj żeński	*f*	feminine
potoczny, pospolity	*F*	familiar, colloquial
przenośnie	*fig.*	figuratively

dopełniacz	*G*	genitive
gastronomia	*gastr.*	gastronomy
gerundium	*ger.*	gerund
gramatyka	*gr.*	grammar
historia	*hist.*	history
humorystyczny	*hum.*	humorous
łowiectwo	*hunt.*	hunting
narzędnik	*I*	instrumental
nieodmienny	*idkl*	indeclinable
aspekt niedokonany i dokonany	*(im)pf*	imperfective and perfective
wykrzyknik	*int.*	interjection
i tym podobnie	*itp.*	et cetera
prawniczy	*jur.*	legal
kogoś	*k-ś*	*somebody's*
miejscownik	*L*	locative
językoznawstwo	*ling.*	lingustics
literatura, literacki	*lit.*	literature, literary use
rodzaj męski	*m*	masculine
rodzaj męski lub rodzaj żeński	*m/f*	masculine or feminine
matematyka	*math.*	mathematics
medycyna	*med.*	medicine
meteorologia	*meteor.*	meteorology
wojskowość	*mil.*	military term
między innymi	*min.*	among other things
motoryzacja	*mot.*	motoring
muzyka	*mus.*	music
rodzaj nijaki	*n*	neuter
żeglarstwo	*naut.*	nautical
mianownik	*N*	nominative
ogólnie	*ogóln.*	generally
optyka	*opt.*	optics
parlamentarny	*parl.*	parliamentary term
partykuła	*part.*	particle
imiesłów czasu przeszłego	*p.p.*	past participle
pedagogika	*ped.*	pedagogy
pejoratywny	*pej.*	pejorative
farmacja	*pharm.*	pharmacy
fotografika	*phot.*	photography
fizyka	*phys.*	physics
fizjologia	*physiol.*	physiology
liczba mnoga	*pl.*	plural
poetycki	*poet.*	poetic
polityka	*pol.*	politics
czas przeszły	*pret.*	preterit(e)
drukarstwo	*print.*	printing
zaimek	*pron.*	pronoun
przyimek	*prp.*	preposition
przestarzały	*przest.*	obsolete
psychologia	*psych.*	psychology

kolejnictwo	*rail.*	railroad, railway
religia	*rel.*	religion
patrz	*see*	refer to
liczba pojedyncza	*sg.*	singular
slang	*sl.*	slang
sportowy	*sport.*	sports
stopień najwyższy	*sup.*	superlative
szkocki angielski	*Szkoc.*	Scottish
technika	*tech.*	technology
telekomunikacja	*teleph.*	telephony
zastrzeżony znak towarowy	*TM*	trademark
teatr	*theat.*	theatre
tylko	*t-ko*	only
uniwersytecki	*univ.*	university
wulgarny	V	vulgar
czasownik posiłkowy	*v/aux.*	auxiliary verb
czasownik nieprzechodni	*v/i.*	intransitive verb
czasownik momentalny	*v/s.*	instantaneous verb
czasownik przechodni	*v/t.*	transitive verb
weterynaria	*vet.*	veterinary medicine
w złożeniach	*w złoż.*	compound
wyraz zbiorowy	*zbior.*	collective noun
zoologia	*zo.*	zoology
zwykle	*zw.*	usually
zwłaszcza	*zwł.*	especially
patrz	→	see, refer to

Notes on Polish Pronunciation

Polish vowels

letter	sound	pronunciation	example
a	a	similar to English *a* in luck	mama
ą	ɔ̃	similar to English *ow*, in know	mąż
e	ε	between English *a* in man and *e* in men	chleb
ę	ε̃	similar to English *en* in ten	męski
i	i	as English *i* in he	mina
	ĭ	as English *y* in year	talia
o	ɔ	as English *o* in boy	okno
ó	u	as English *oo* in moon, but shorter	ósmy
u	u	as English *u* in put	suma
y	i	between English *i* in sit and *e* in set	syn

Pronunciation of nasalised vowels

1. When used at the end of a word the vowels **ą, ę** lose their nasality
ę → /e/, ą → /o/, e.g.:
daję → /daje/, *gazetę* → /gazete/, *są* → /so/, *dają* → /dajo/
2. Pronunciation of nasalised vowels **ą, ę** before consonants
before **p, b** – ą, ę → /om/, /em/, e.g.:
skąpy → /skompy/, *kąpie* → /kompie/, *trąba* → /tromba/
następny → /nastempny/, *tępy* → /tempy/, *zęby* → /zemby/
before **t, d, c, dz, cz** – ą, ę → /on/, /en/, e.g.:
piąty → /pionty/, *kąty* → /konty/, *gorąco* → /goronco/
piętro → /pientro/, *chętnie* → /chentnie/, *więc* → /wienc/
before **ć, dź** – ą, ę → /oń/, /eń/, e.g.:
płynąć → /płynońć/, *bądź* → /bońć/, *mąci* → /mońci/
pięć → /pieńć/, *zdjęcie* → /zdjeńcie/, *wszędzie* → /fszeńdzie/
before **k, g** – ą, ę → /oŋ/, /eŋ/, e.g.:
rąk → /roŋk/, *strąk* → /stroŋk/, *drągiem* → /droŋgiem/
ręka → /reŋka/, *węgiel* → /weŋgiel/, *tęgi* → /teŋgi/
before **l, ł** – ą, ę → /o/, /e/, e.g.:
zaczął → /zaczoł/, *zaczęli* → /zaczeli/
before **w, w, f, f, s, ś, z, ź, ż (rz), ch (h), ch, h** – ą, ę do not lose their nasality, e.g.:
wąs → /vąs/, *kęs* → /kęs/.

Polish consonants

letter	sound	pronunciation	example
c	ts	as English *ts* in its	cały
ch	x	as English *h* in hand	chyba
cz	tʃ	as English *tch* in itch	czas

ć (ci)	tç	as softly *tch*	bić, ciocia
dz	dz	as in English red <u>z</u>one	chodzę, dzwon
dź (dzi)	ðž	as softly *dz*	dźwig, działo
dż, drz	dʒ	as English *j* in just	dżem, drzwi
h	x	as English *h* in hand	herbata
ł	w	as English *w* in wet	stół, miło
ń (ni)	ŋ	as English *ni* in onion	koń, koniec
r	r	as English *r* in red	rak
rz	ʃ	as English *s* in ship	krzak
	ʒ	as English *s* in pleasure	rzeka
s	s	as English *s* in yes	sala
sz	ʃ	as English *sh* in show	szal
ś (si)	ç	as softly *s*	świt, siwy
w	v	as English *v* in voice	woda
z	z	as English *z* in zebra	zadanie
ź (zi)	ž	as softly *z*	późno, zimno
ż	ʒ	as English *s* in pleasure	żaba

Pronunciation of consonants

Most voiced consonants have voiceless equivalents, e.g. **b p, w f, d t, z s, dz c, ż sz, dż cz, ź ś, dź ć, g k.**
Voiced consonants become voiceless in the following contexts:
– at the end of a word, e.g.: *klub* → /klup/, *bagaż* → /bagasz/
– before voiceless consonants, e.g.: *babka* → /bapka/, *brzydki* → /brzytki/, *wszyscy* → /fszyscy/
The consonant **ł** is not pronounced when situated between 2 consonants, e.g. *jabłko* → /japko/.

on, om, en, em are pronounced **ą, ę,** before the following consonants: **f, w, s, z, t, d, dz, n, ł,** e.g.: *sens* → /sęs/, *konsul* → /kąsul/, *komfort* → /kąfort/.

Stress in Polish

Stress in Polish is regular and usually falls on the penultimate syllable, e.g.: *gotowa-nie, przemówienie, robotnik, klasówka.* Stressed syllables are pronounced longer than unstressed syllables.
Exceptions:
a) The third syllable from the end is stressed in the first and second person plural, e.g: *czytaliśmy, zwiedzaliście,* as well as in all singular forms and third person plural of the conditional, e.g.: *zrobiłabym, widzieliby.*
b) The third syllable from the end is stressed in nouns ending in *-yka, -ika,* e.g.: *matematyka, turystyka, polemika.*
c) The fourth syllable from the end is stressed in the first and second person plural of the conditional, e.g.: *zrobilibyśmy, widzielibyście.*

Zestawienie symboli fonetycznych
w języku angielskim

Samogłoski i dwugłoski

znak fonetyczny	zbliżony polski odpowiednik	przykłady
iː	*i*	s<u>ee</u>, r<u>ea</u>d
ɪ	*y*	<u>i</u>n, ch<u>i</u>ps
e	*e*	b<u>e</u>d, h<u>ea</u>d
ɜː	*e (długie)*	f<u>ir</u>st, n<u>ur</u>se
ə	*a (zanikowe)*	<u>a</u>bout, butt<u>er</u>
æ	*a*	b<u>a</u>d, c<u>a</u>t
ʌ	*a (krótkie)*	m<u>u</u>ch, l<u>o</u>ve
ɑː	*a (długie)*	f<u>a</u>ther, st<u>ar</u>t
uː	*u (długie)*	t<u>oo</u>, tw<u>o</u>
ʊ	*u (krótkie)*	g<u>oo</u>d, p<u>u</u>t
ɔː	*o (długie)*	d<u>oo</u>r, l<u>aw</u>
ɒ	*o (krótkie)*	sh<u>o</u>p, l<u>o</u>t
aɪ	*ay (łączne)*	r<u>i</u>de, tr<u>y</u>
eɪ	*ey (łączne)*	d<u>ay</u>, f<u>a</u>ce
ɔɪ	*oy (łączne)*	b<u>oy</u>, ch<u>oi</u>ce
ɪə	*ya (łączne)*	h<u>ere</u>, b<u>ee</u>r
eə	*ea (łączne)*	h<u>air</u>, p<u>ear</u>
ʊə	*ua (łączne)*	p<u>oor</u> t<u>our</u>
aʊ	*au (łączne)*	n<u>ow</u>, m<u>ou</u>th
əʊ	*ou (łączne)*	h<u>o</u>me, n<u>o</u>

Spółgłoski

znak fonetyczny	zbliżony polski odpowiednik	przykłady
p	*p*	<u>p</u>en, ha<u>pp</u>en
b	*b (rozdźwięcznione)*	<u>b</u>ody, jo<u>b</u>
t	*t*	<u>t</u>oy, be<u>tt</u>er
d	*d (rozdźwięcznione)*	o<u>dd</u>, <u>d</u>ay
k	*k*	<u>k</u>ey, s<u>ch</u>ool
g	*g (rozdźwięcznione)*	<u>gh</u>ost, <u>g</u>o
f	*f*	<u>c</u>offee, <u>ph</u>ysics

v	w	heavy, very
θ	f *(wymawiane międzyzębowo)*	think, path
ð	z *(wymawiane międzyzębowo)*	this, other
s	s lub z *(po dźwięcznej spółgłosce)*	sister, glass, dogs
z	z *(rozdźwięcznione)*	zero
ʃ	sz	shop, fish
ʒ	ż *(rozdźwięcznione)*	pleasure, television
tʃ	cz	church, much
dʒ	dż *(rozdźwięcznione)*	age, just
h	h *(wymawiane wydechowo)*	hot, whole
m	m	more, hammer
n	n	nice, sun
ŋ	n *(jak np. w bank)*	thing, long
l	l	light, feel
r	r *(bryt. ang. wymawiane tylko przed samogłoskami)*	right, hurry
j	j	yes, use
w	ł	one, when

Alfabet angielski

	wymowa			wymowa
a	[eɪ]		**n**	[en]
b	[biː]		**o**	[əʊ]
c	[siː]		**p**	[piː]
d	[diː]		**q**	[kjuː]
e	[iː]		**r**	[ɑː]
f	[ef]		**s**	[es]
g	[dʒiː]		**t**	[tiː]
h	[eɪtʃ]		**u**	[juː]
i	[ai]		**v**	[viː]
j	[dʒeɪ]		**w**	['dʌbljuː]
k	[keɪ]		**x**	[eks]
l	[el]		**y**	[waɪ]
m	[em]		**z**	[zed]

The Polish Alphabet

	Pronunciation		Pronunciation
a	[a]	p	[pɛ]
ą	[ɔ̃]	r	[ɛr]
b	[bɛ]	s	[ɛs]
c	[tsɛ]	ś	[ɛɕ]
ć	[tɕɛ]	t	[tɛ]
d	[dɛ]	u	[u]
e	[ɛ]	w	[vu]
ę	[ɛ̃]	x	[iks]
f	[ɛf]	y	[i grɛk]
g	[gɛ]	z	[zɛt]
h	[xa]	ź	[ɛt]
i	[i]	ż	[ʒɛt]
j	[jɔt]	**Compound letters**	
k	[ka]	ch	[xa]
l	[ɛl]	cz	[tʃɛ]
ł	[ɛw]	dz	[dzɛ]
m	[ɛm]	dź	[dzɛ]
n	[ɛn]	dż	[dʒɛ]
ń	[ɛɲ]	rz	[ɛrzɛt]
o	[ɔ]	sz	[ɛʃ]
ó	[ɔ krɛskɔvanɛ]		

Polish – English

A

a *cj.*, *part* and; *~! int.* oh!, ah!; *nic ~ nic* nothing at all

a. *skrót pisany: albo* or

abażur *m* (*-u/-a*; *-y*) lampshade

abdykacja *f* (*-i*; *-e*) abdication

abecadło *n* (*-a*; *G -deł*) alphabet; (*podstawy*) the ABC

abonament *m* (*-u*, *-y*) (*teatralny itp.*) season ticket; *tel.* rental charge; *RTV: Brt.* licence (*Am.* license) fee

abonent *m* (*-a*; *-ci*), *~ka f* (*-i*; *G -tek*) *tel. itp.* subscriber

abonować (*-uję*) subscribe to

aborcja *f* (*-i*; *-e*) abortion

abp *skrót pisany: arcybiskup* Abp, Arch. (*Archbishop*)

absencja *f* (*-i*; *-e*) absence; (*chorobowa*) absenteeism

absolutny absolute; *cisza* complete

absolwent *m* (*-a*, *-ci*), *~ka f* (*-i*; *G -tek*) graduate, school-leaver

absorbować ⟨*za-*⟩ (*-uję*) absorb (*też fig.*)

abstrahować (*-uję*): *~ od* (*G*) ignore, take no notice of

absurd *m* (*-u*; *-y*) absurdity

absurdalny absurd

aby *cj.* (in order) to, in order that; *~ tylko* let's (just) hope (that)

acetylen *m* (*-u*; *0*) acetylene

ach *int.* oh

aczkolwiek although

adamaszek *m* (*-szku*; *-szki*) damask

adaptacja *f* (*-i*; *-e*) adaptation; *bud.* conversion (*na biuro* into offices)

adapt|er *m* (*-a/-u*; *-y*) F record-player; *~ować* (*im*)*pf* (*-uję*) *dzieło* adapt; *bud.* convert (*na A* into); *~ować się* adapt (o.s.) (*do* to)

adekwatny (*do G*) commensurate (with *lub* to), adequate (to)

adidasy F *m/pl.* (*-ów*) sports shoes *pl.*, *Brt.* trainers *pl.*

adiunkt *m* (*-a*; *-nci*) (senior) lecturer

adiutant *m* (*-a*; *-nci*) aide-de-camp

administra|cja *f* (*-i*;*-e*) administration; *~cyjny* administrative; *kara ~cyjna* penalty for contempt of court; *~tor m*

(*-a*; *-rzy*), *~torka f* (*-i*; *G -rek*) administrator

administrować (*-uję*) (*I*) administer, manage

admirał *m* (*-a*; *-owie*) admiral

adnotacja *f* (*-i*; *-e*) note

adoptować ⟨*za-*⟩ (*-uję*) adopt

adorator *m* (*-a*; *-rzy/-owie*), *~ka f* (*-i*; *G -rek*) admirer

adres *m* (*-u*; *-y*) address; *pod jej ~em* to her address; *fig.* to her; *~at m* (*-a*; *-ci*), *~atka f* (*-i*) addressee; *fig.* receiver; *~at nieznany* address unknown

adresować ⟨*za-*⟩ (*-uję*) address; (*do G*) address (to); *fig.* direct (at)

Adriatyk *m* (*-u*; *0*) Adriatic Sea

adwent *m* (*-u*; *-y*) Advent; *~owy: okres ~owy* time of Advent

adwoka|cki lawyer's; *zespół ~cki* lawyer's office; *~t m* (*-a*; *-ci*), *~tka f* (*-i*; *G -tek*) lawyer; *Brt.* solicitor, *Am.* attorney; (*przed sądem*) *Brt.* barrister, *Am.* attorney(-at-law); *~tura f* (*-y*; *0*) legal profession

aero|- aero-, air-; *~bik m* (*-u*; *-i*) aerobics *sg.*; *~dynamiczny* aerodynamic; *~zol m* (*-u*; *-e*) aerosol, spray

afektowany affected

afera *f* (*-y*) scandal

aferzyst|a *m* (*-y*; *-ści*, *-ów*), *~ka f* (*-i*; *G -tek*) confidence trickster; F con-man

afgański Afghan

afisz *m* (*-a*; *-e*) poster; *zejść z ~a theat.* not to be performed any longer; *~ować się* (*-uję*) (*I*, *z I*) make a show (of), parade (s.th.)

Afryka *f* (*-i*) Africa

Afrykan|in *m* (*-a*; *-anie*; *-ów*), *~ka f* (*-i*; *G -nek*) African

afrykański African

agat *m* (*-u*; *-y*) agate

agen|cja *f* (*-i*; *-e*) agency; *~cja towarzyska* escort agency; *~cyjny* agency; *~da f* (*-y*) branch; (*terminarz*) agenda; *~t m* (*-a*; *-ci*), *~tka f* (*-i*; *G -tek*) agent; *~tura f* (*-y*) → *agencja*; *coll.* agents *m/pl.*

agitac|ja *f* (*-i*; *zw. 0*) agitation; *pol.* canvassing; **~ja wyborcza** election propaganda; **~yjny** propaganda

aglomeracja f (*-i; -e*) conurbation

agonia f (*GDL -ii; 0*) agony

agrafka f (*-i; G -fek*) safety pin

agrarny agrarian, agricultural

agresja f (*-i; -e*) aggression

agresor m (*-a; -rzy/-owie*) aggressor

agrest m (*-u; zw. 0*) *bot.* gooseberry

agresywny aggressive

agro|nom m (*-a; -owie/-i*) agronomist; **~technika** f agricultural technology

AIDS m (*idkl.*) AIDS; **chory na ~** person suffering from AIDS

airbus m (*-a; -y*) *aviat.* airbus

akacja f (*-i; -e*) *bot.* acacia; F robinia

akademia f (*GDL -ii; -e*) academy; (*zebranie*) ceremony

akademick|i academic; student; **dom ~i** student hostel; students' (hall of) residence; **młodzież ~a** students *pl.*; student body; **rok ~i** academic year

akademik m **1.** (*-a; -i*) F student hostel; students' (hall of) residence; **2.** (*-a; -cy*) (*członek akademii*) academic

akcent m (*-u; -y*) accent; stress; **~ować** ⟨*za-*⟩ (*-uję*) accent, stress; *fig.* emphasize

akcept m (*-u; -y*) *econ.* acceptance

akceptować ⟨*za-*⟩ (*-uję*) accept

akces m (*-u; zw. 0*) accession; **zgłaszać ~ do** (*G*) affirm one's wish to become

akcesoria *n/pl.* accessories *pl.*

akcj|a f (*-i; -e*) action; *econ.* campaign; **~a powieści** plot of the novel; **~a wyborcza** canvassing; **~a policyjna** police operation; **wprowadzić do ~i** put into action; **miejsce ~i** scene; **~e** *pl.* shares *pl.*

akcjonariusz m (*-a; -e*), **~ka** f (*-i; G -szek*) shareholder

akcyjn|y unsystematic; *econ.* share; **spółka ~a** *econ.* joint-stock company; **kapitał ~y** *econ.* share capital

aklamacj|a f (*-i; 0*); **przez ~ę** by acclamation

akompani|ament m (*-u; zw. 0*) (*fortepianowy*) (piano) accompaniment; **~ować** accompany

akord m (*-u; -y*) *econ.* piece-work; *mus.* chord; **pracować na ~** be on piece-work

akordeon m (*-u; -y*) accordion

akordow|o *adv.*: **pracować ~o** be on

piece-work; **~y** piece-work; **robotnik ~y** pieceworker

akredytować (*-uję*) accredit

akredytywa f (*-y*) *econ.* letter of credit

akrobat|a m (*-y; -ci*), **~ka** f (*-i; G -tek*) acrobat; **~(k)a na trapezie** trapeze artist

akrylow|y acrylic; **żywica ~a** acrylic resin

aksamit m (*-u; -y*) velvet; **~ka** f (*-i; G -tek*) velvet ribbon; *bot.* marigold; **~ny** velvet; **głos itp.** velvety

akt m **1.** (*-u; -y*) act (*też jur.*); (*uroczystość*) ceremony; (*dokument*) act, deed; (*malarstwo*) nude; **2.** (*pl. -a*) file; **~ kupna** bill of sale; (*domu*) title deed; **~ oskarżenia** indictment; **~ otwarcia** opening ceremony; **~ zgonu** death certificate; **~a** *pl.* **osobowe** personal file *lub* dossier; **odkładać do ~** file away; *fig.* lay to rest

aktor m (*-a; -rzy*), **~ka** f (*-i; G -rek*) actor; **~ski** acting; **~sko** like an actor; **~stwo** n (*-a; 0*) acting; (*sztuka*) dramatic art

aktówka f (*-i; G -wek*) briefcase, attaché case

aktualn|izować (*-uję*) update; **~nie** *adv.* at present, currently; **~ność** f (*-ści*) relevance (to the present); (*wiadomości itp.*) topicality; **~ny** current; **problemy ~ne** topical

aktywizować (*-uję*) activate; *ludzi* mobilize

aktywn|ość f (*-ści*) activity; **~y** active

akumu|lacja f (*-i; 0*) accumulation; **~lator** m (*-a; -y*) *Brt.* accumulator, *Am.* storage battery; **~lować** ⟨*z-*⟩ (*-uję*) accumulate

akupunktura f (*-y; 0*) acupuncture

akurat *adv.* (*teraz*) at this very moment; (*dokładnie*) exactly; **~!** no way!

akustyczny acoustic(al)

akuszer m (*-a; -rzy*) *med.* obstetrician; **~ka** f (*-i; G -rek*) midwife

akwa|planacja f (*-i; -e*) aquaplaning; **~rela** f (*-i; -e*) water-colo(u)r; **~rium** n (*idkl.; -ia, -ów*) aquarium

al. *skrót pisany*: **aleja** Ave. (*Avenue*)

alarm m (*-u; -y*) alarm; (*stan*) alert; **bić na ~** sound the alarm; **~ować** ⟨*za-*⟩ (*-uję*) alarm; *policję itp.* call out; **~owy** alarm

Alaska f (*-i; 0*) Alaska

Alban|ia f (-ii; 0) Albania; ~ka f (-i; G -nek) Albanian

Albań|czyk m (-a; -cy) Albanian; Ωski Albanian; **mówić po Ωsku** speak Albanian

albatros m (-a; -y) albatross

albinos m (-a; -y/m-os -i) albino

albo cj. or; ~ ..., ~ ... either ... or ...; ~-~ alternative; ~ też or else; ~wiem cj. because, for

album m (-u; -y) album

ale cj. but; however; ~ **jesteś duży!** aren't you tall!; ~ **gdzie tam!** of course not!; **bez żadnego ~** no ifs and buts

alegoria f (-ii; -e) allegory

alegoryczny allegoric

aleja f (-ei; -e, -ei/-ej) alley; (droga) avenue

alergi|a f (GDL -ii; zw. 0) allergy; ~czny allergic (**na** A to)

ależ part. but; ~ **tak!** why, yes!

alfabet m (-u; -y) alphabet; ~ **Braille'a** Braille

alfabetyczny alphabetic(al)

alfons F m (-a; -i/-y) pimp

algebra f (-y; 0) algebra

Algier|ia f (-ii; 0) Algeria; ~czyk m (-a; -cy), ~ka f (-i; G -rek) Algerian; Ωski Algerian

alian|cki allied; ~t m (-a; -ci) ally

alibi n (idkl.) alibi

alienacja f (-i; 0) alienation

aligator m (-a; -y) zo. alligator

alimenty pl. (-ów) (po rozwodzie) maintenance payment sg.; (w separacji) alimony sg.

alkaliczny alkaline

alkohol m (-u; -e) alcohol; (napój) (alcoholic) drink; ~ik m (-a; -cy), ~iczka f (-i; G -czek) alcoholic; ~owy alcoholic

alleluja n (idkl.) hallelujah; **Wesołego** Ω**!** Happy Easter!

alpejski Alpine

alpinist|a m (-y; -ści, -ów), ~ka f (-i; G -tek) mountaineer, climber

Alpy pl. (G -) the Alps

alt m (-u; -y) alto

altan|a f (-y;), ~ka f (-i; G -tek) arbo(u)r; summerhouse

alternat|or m (-a; -y) mot. alternator; ~ywa (-y) alternative; ~ywny alternative

altowiolist|a m (-y; -ści), ~ka f (-i; -ki) viola player

altówka f (-i; G -wek) mus. viola

alumini|owy Brt. aluminium, Am. aluminum; ~um n (idkl.) Brt. aluminium, Am. aluminum

aluzj|a f (-i; e) allusion, hint; **czynić ~e** (**do** G) hint (at)

aluzyjnie adv. in the form of a hint

alzacki Alsatian

ałun m (-u; -y) alum

AM skrót pisany: **Akademia Medyczna** Medical Academy

amalgamat m (-u; -y) amalgam (też fig.)

amant m (-a; -ci), ~ka f (-i; G -tek) theat. lover

amarantowy amaranthine

amator m (-a; -rzy), ~ka f (-i; G -rek) amateur (też sport.); lover; (reflektujący) potential buyer (**na** A of); ~ski amateurish; **teatr ~ski** amateur Brt. theatre (Am. theater) group; ~sko adv. in an amateurish way

ambasa|da f (-y) pol. embassy; ~dor m (-a; -rzy) ambassador

ambicja f (-i; e) też pej. ambition; (poczucie godności) sense of hono(u)r

ambitny ambitious

ambona f (-y) rel. pulpit

ambulans m (-u; -e) ambulance; ~ **pocztowy** mail coach

ambula'to|rium n (idkl.; -ia, -ów) med. out-patient(s') department; ~ryjny med. out-patient

amen n (idkl.) amen; **pewne jak ~ w pacierzu** you can bet your bottom dollar on it; **na ~** totally, utterly

Ameryka f (-i; G -) America; ~nin m (-a; -anie, -ów), ~nka f (-i; G -nek) American; Ω**nka** sofa, bed; Ω**ński** American; **po** Ω**nsku** like an American

ametyst m (-u; -y) amethyst

amfibia f (GDL -ii; -e) tech. amphibious vehicle; zo. amphibian

aminokwas m (-u; -y) amino acid

amne|stia f (GDL -ii; -e) amnesty; ~zja f (-i; 0) amnesia

amoniak m (-u; 0) ammonia

amoralny amoral

amorty|zacja f (-i; 0) econ. (maszyn) depreciation; (aktywów) amortization; tech. shock absorption; ~zator m (-a; -y) shock absorber; ~zować (-uję) wstrząsy cushion, absorb; econ. amortize, depreciate (też **się**)

ampero|godzina *f* ampere-hour; **~mierz** *m* (*-a*; *-e*) ammeter
ampułka *f* (*-i*; *G -lek*) ampoule
amputować (*im*)*pf* (*-uję*) amputate
amunicja *f* (*-i*; *0*) ammunition, F ammo
anabolicz|ny: **~ne** anabolic drugs *pl.*
anachroniczny anachronic
analfabet|a *m* (*-y*; *-ci*), **~ka** *f* (*-i*; *G -tek*) illiterate (person); **~yzm** *m* illiteracy
analiz|a *f* (*-y*) analysis; *med.* test; → **ba-danie**; **~ować** ⟨*prze-*⟩ (*-uję*) analyze
analogiczny analogical
analogowy analog(ue)
ananas *m* (*-a*; *-y*) pineapple; *fig.* good--for-nothing; **~owy** pineapple
anarchia *f* (*-i*; *0*) anarchy
anarchi|czny anarchic; **~sta** *m* (*-y*; *-ści*, *-ów*), **~stka** *f* (*-i*; *G -tek*) anarchist; **~styczny** anarchistic
anatomi|a *f* (*GDL -ii*; *0*) anatomy; **~czny** anatomic(al)
androny *pl.* (*-ów*) rubbish, nonsense; **pleść ~** F drivel
andrut *m* (*-a*; *-y*) waffle
anegdota *f* (*-y*) anecdote
anek|s *m* (*-u*; *-y*) supplement, *Brt.* annexe, *Am.* annex; *bud.* extension; **~to-wać** ⟨*za-*⟩ (*-uję*) annex
anemiczny an(a)emic
aneste|tyk *m* (*-u*; *-i*) anesthetic, *Brt.* anaesthetic; **~zja** *f* (*-i*; *-e*) anesthesia, *Brt.* anaesthesia; **~zjolog** *m* (*-a*; *-dzy/-owie*) *Brt.* anaesthetist, *Am.* anesthesiologist
ang. *skrót pisany:* **angielski** Eng. (*English*)
angażować ⟨*za-*⟩ (*-uję*) take on, employ; *theat.* engage; → **wplątywać**; **~** ⟨*za-*⟩ **się** become involved (**w** *A/I* in)
Angiel|ka *f* (*-i*; *G -lek*), English, English girl; **2ski** English; **mówić po 2sku** speak English; **ziele 2skie** *bot.* allspice; **2szczyzna** *f* (*-y*; *0*) English
angina *f* (*-y*; *0*) throat infection; **~ pec-toris** angina (pectoris)
Anglia *f* (*-i*; *0*) England
Anglik *m* (*-a*; *-cy*) Englishman, English boy
anglikański Anglican
anglistyka *f* (*-i*; *0*) (*studia*) English studies *pl.*; (*instytut*) English department
anglo|języczny English-speaking; **~saski** Anglo-Saxon
angorski *zo., włók.* angora

ani 1. *cj.*: **~ ... ~, nie ... ~ nie** neither ... nor ...; **2.** *part.* not a; **~ chybi** without fail; **~ razu** not once; **~ rusz** not at all; **~ kropli** not a (single) drop; **~ odrobiny** not a bit; **~ śladu** (*G*) not a trace (of)
aniels|ki angelic; **~ko** angelically
animowany: **film ~** (animated) cartoon
anioł *m* (*-a*; *aniele!*, *-y/-owie/anieli*) angel; **~ stróż** guardian angel
aniżeli *cj.* than
ankiet|a *f* (*-y*) questionnaire; (*akcja*) survey; **~owany** *m* (*-ego*; *-i*), **~owana** *f* (*-ej*; *-e*) person questioned
ano *part.* well
anonim *m* **1.** (*-a*; *-owie*) anonymous person; **2.** (*-u*; *-y*) anonymous letter; **~owo** anonymously; **~owy** anonymous
anons *m* (*-u*; *-e*) advertisement, F ad; (*ogłoszenie*) announcement; **~ować** ⟨*za-*⟩ (*-uję*) advertise; announce
ans|a: mieć ~ę do kogoś bear s.o. ill will
antagonistyczny antagonistic
antałek *m* (*-łka*; *-łki*) small barrell
Antarkty|da *f* (*-y*; *0*) Antarctica; **2czny** Antarctic
antena *f* (*-y*) aerial, antenna
antenat *m* (*-a*; *-ci*), **~ka** *f* (*-i*; *G -tek*) forefather, ancestor
antenowy aerial; **czas ~** broadcasting time
antologia *f* (*-ii*; *-e*) anthology
antrakt *m* (*-u*; *-y*) (*przerwa*) intermission
antresola *f* (*-i*; *-e*) mezzanine
antropologiczny anthropological
antrykot *m* (*-u*; *-y*) *gastr.* entrecôte
anty- *w złoż.* anti-
antyaborcyjn|y: ustawa ~a anti-abortion law
anty|biotyk *m* (*-u*; *-i*) antibiotic; **~cyklon** *m* anticyclon, F high
antyczny antique
anty|datować (*-uję*) antedate; **~demokratyczny** anti-democratic; **~do-pingowy: kontrola ~dopingowa** doping control
antyk *m* (*-u*; *-i*) (*okres*) classical antiquity; (*rzecz*) antique
antykoncepcyjny: środek ~ *med.* contraceptive
antykwa|riat *m* (*-u*; *-y*) (*z książkami*) second-hand bookshop; (*z antykami*) antique shop; **~riusz** *m* (*-a*; *-e*) sec-

ond-hand bookseller; ~rski, ~ryczny second-hand; (*cenny*) antiquarian

antylopa *f* (-y) antelope

anty|narkotykowy: wydział służb ~narkotykowych narcotics squad; ~naukowy unscientific; ~niemiecki anti-German; ~patia *f* (-*i*; -*e*) antipathy; ~patyczny antipathetic(al); ~polski anti-Polish; ~semicki anti-Semitic; ~septyczny antiseptic; ~wojenny anti-war, antimilitaristic

anulowa|ć (-*uję*) annul; *dokument* cancel; ~nie *n* (-*a*) annulment

anyż *m* (-*u*; -*e*) aniseed; ~owy aniseed

Apacz *m* (-*a*; -*e*) Apache

aparat *m* (-*u*; -*y*) (*techniczny, państwowy*) apparatus; (*w domu*) appliance; (*radiowy*) radio; (*telewizyjny*) TV set; (*telefoniczny*) phone; ~ura *f* (-*y*) apparatus (*też fig.*); (*sprzęt*) equipment

apartament *m* (-*u*; -*y*) apartment; (*hotelowy*) suite

apaszka *f* (-*i*; *G* -*szek*) scarf

apatyczny apathetic

apel *m* (-*u*; -*e*, -*i*/-*ów*) roll call; (*odezwa*) appeal (**o** *A* for)

apelacj|a *f* (-*i*; -*e*) *jur.* appeal; **wnosić ~ę** appeal, lodge an appeal

apel|acyjny *jur.* of appeal; ~ować ⟨za-⟩ (-*uję*) appeal (**do** *G* to)

apety|czny appetizing; ~t *m* (-*u*; -*y*) appetite (*też fig.* **na** *A* for); **pobudzać ~t** stimulate the appetite

aplauz *m* (-*u*; -*e*) applause, cheer

aplika|cja *f* (-*i*; -*e*) *jur.* (practical) training for the bar; ~nt *m* (-*a*; -*ci*), ~ntka *f* (-*i*; *G* -*tek*) *jur.* trainee lawyer, *Brt.* articled clerk; ~ntura *f* (-*y*) → **aplikacja**

aplikować ⟨za-⟩ (-*uję*) administer

apoplektyczny apoplectic; **atak** ~ stroke

aposto|lski apostolic; ~ł *m* (-*a*; -*owie*) apostle (*też fig.*), disciple

apostrof *m* (-*u*; -*y*) apostrophe

Appalachy *pl.* (*G* -*ów*) Appalachian Mountains *pl.*

aprob|ata *f* (-*y*; 0/-*y*) approval; ~ować ⟨za-⟩ (-*uję*) approve of

aprowizacja *f* (-*i*; 0) food supply; ~yjny food

aptecz|ka *f* (-*i*; *G* -*czek*) (*w domu*) medicine cabinet; first-aid kit (*pierwszej pomocy*); ~ny pharmaceutical

apteka *f* (-*i*) *Brt.* chemist's (shop), *Am.*

drugstore; (*szpitalna*) dispensary; ~rka *f* (-*i*; *G* -*rek*), ~rz *m* (-*a*; *e*, *G* -*y*) *Brt.* (dispensing) chemist, *Am.* druggist

Arab *m* (-*a*; -*owie*) Arab; Ω *f* (*pl.* -*y*) (*koń*) Arab; ~ia *f* (-*ii*; 0) Arabia; ~ka *f* (-*i*; *G* -*bek*) Arab; Ωka (*koń*) Arab; Ωski **1.** (*narody itp.*) Arab; (*półwysep itp.*) Arabian; (*język, cyfra itp.*) Arabic; **mówić po Ωsku** speak Arabic; **2.** *m* (-*ego*; 0) Arabic

aranż|er *m* (-*a*; -*owie*/-*rzy*) organizer; *mus.* arranger; ~ować ⟨za-⟩ (-*uję*) arrange (**na** *A* for)

arbitraż *m* (-*u*; -*e*, *y*/-*ów*) arbitration

arbitrażow|y: sąd ~y arbitration tribunal; **wyrok sądu ~ego** verdict of the arbitration tribunal

arbuz *m* (-*a*; -*y*) watermelon

archanioł *m* (-*a*; -*y*) archangel

archeologi|a *f* (*GDL* -*ii*; 0/-*ie*) arch(a)eology; ~czny arch(a)eological

archipelag *m* (-*u*; -*i*) archipelago

architekt *m* (-*a*; -*ci*), ~ka *f* (-*i*; *G* -*tek*) architect; ~oniczny architectural; ~ura *f* architecture

archiwum *n* (*idkl.*; -*wa*; *G* -*wów*) archives *pl.*

arcy|biskup *m* archbishop; ~ciekawy fascinating; ~dzieło *n* masterpiece; ~nudny extremely boring, F deadly; ~zabawny hilarious

areał *m* (-*u*; -*y*) area

arena *f* (-*y*) (*sportowa*) arena; (*w cyrku*) ring

areszt *m* (-*u*; -*y*) arrest; (*budynek*) prison; ~ **śledczy** (*stan*) detention while awaiting trial; (*budynek*) prison (for people awaiting trial); → *jur.* **zajęcie**

aresztowa|ć ⟨za-⟩ (-*uję*) arrest; ~nie *n* (-*a*) arrest; ~ny **1.** arrested, in custody; **2.** *m* (-*ego*; -*i*), ~na *f* (-*ej*; -*e*) person under arrest, detainee

Argent|yna *f* (-*y*) Argentina; ~ynka *f* (-*i*; *G* -*nek*), ~yńczyk *m* (-*a*; -*cy*) Argentinian; Ωyński Argentinian, Argentine

argumentować (-*uję*) argue; → **uzasadniać**

aria *f* (*GDL* -*ii*; -*e*) aria

ark. *skrót pisany:* **arkusz** sht (*sheet*)

arka *f* (-*i*; *G* ark) ark; ~ **przymierza** *rel.* Ark of the Covenant

arkada *f* (-*y*) arcade

arktyczny Arctic

arkusz *m* (-*a*; -*e*, -*y*) sheet

armat|a f (-y) gun, *hist.* cannon; ~**ni** gun, cannon

armator m (-ra, -rzy) shipowner

armatura f (-y) fittings *pl.*

armeńs|ki Armenian; **mówić po ~ku** speak Armenian

armia f (GDL -ii; -e) army; ♀ **Zbawienia** Salvation Army

aroganc|ki arrogant; ~**ko** arrogantly

aromat m (-u; -y) aroma, scent; (*przyprawa*) flavo(u)ring

aromatyczny aromatic

arras m (-u; -y) tapestry

arsenał m (-u; -y) arsenal

arszenik m (-u; 0) arsenic

arteri|a f (GDL -ii; -e) artery (*med., mot.*); *fig.* vein; ~**o-** arterio-

artretyzm m (-u; -y/0) arthritis

artykuł m (-u; -y) article; (*w gazecie też*) piece; ~ **wstępny** editorial; ~**y** pl. **spożywcze** food (stuffs pl.), (*w sklepie*) groceries *pl.*

artyle|ria f (GDL -ii; 0) artillery; ~**ryjski** artillery

artyst|a m (-y; -ści, -ów), ~**ka** f (-i; G -tek) artist; ~**a malarz** painter

artystyczn|y artistic; (*harmonijny*) exquisite; **rzemiosło ~e** arts and crafts *pl.*

artyzm m (-u; -y) artistic skill, artistry

arystokrat|a m (-y; -ci), ~**ka** f (-i) aristocrat

arystokratyczny aristocratic

arytmety|czny arithmetic(al); **działanie ~czne** arithmetical operation; ~**ka** f (-i; 0) arithmetic

as m (-a; -y) ace (*też fig.*)

ascetyczny ascetic

asekurac|ja f (-i; -e) (*zabezpieczenie*) safeguard (**przeciw(ko)** against); (*ubezpieczenie*) insurance; ~**yjny** security; insurance

asekurować się ⟨**za- się**⟩ (-uję) protect o.s.; *fig.* cover o.s. (two ways)

asesor m (-a; -rzy, -ów) assistant judge

asfaltowy asphalt

askorbinowy: kwas ~ ascorbic acid

asocjacja f (-i; -e) association

asortyment m (-u; -y) range

ASP *skrót:* **Akademia Sztuk Pięknych** Academy of Fine Arts

aspekt m (-u; -y) aspect

aspiracje f/pl (-ji) aspirations pl.; → **ambicja**

aspołeczny antisocial, asocial

astma f (-y; 0) asthma; ~**tyczny** asthmatic

astro|logia f (GDL -ii; 0) astrology; ~**nauta** m (-y; -ci), ~**nautka** f (-i; G -tek) astronaut; ~**nautyka** f (-i; 0) astronautics; ~**nomia** f (GDL -ii; 0) astronomy; ~**nomiczny** astronomical

asygnować ⟨**wy-**⟩ (-uję) *sumę* allocate; *środki* award (**na** A for)

asyst|a f (-y) company; ~**ent** m (-a; -ci), ~**entka** f (-i; G -tek) assistant; ~**ować** (-uję) (*pomagać*) assist (**przy** L with); (*towarzyszyć*) accompany

atak m (-u; -i) attack (*też fig.*); *mil.* assault; (*w sporcie*) forward line; *med.* attack, fit

atakować ⟨**za-**⟩ (-uję) attack; *mil.* assault

ateistyczny atheistic

atelier n (*idkl.*) studio; ~ **filmowe** film studio

Ateny pl. (G -) Athens *sg.*

atest m (-u; -y) certificate

atlantycki Atlantic

Atlantyk m (-u; 0) (the) Atlantic

atlas m (-u; -y) atlas

atlet|a m (-y; -ci), ~**ka** f (-i; G -tek) athlete; (*w cyrku*) strongman; ~**yczny** athletic; ~**yka** f (-i; 0) athletics; **lekka ~ yka** track-and-field events

atłas m (-u; -y) satin; **jak ~** velvety; ~**owy** of satin; *fig.* velvety

atmosfer|a f (-y) atmosphere (*też fig.*); ~**yczny** atmospheric

atol m (-u; -e) atoll

atom m (-u; -y) atom; ~**owy** atomic; *okręt itp.* nuclear; **energia ~owa** nuclear energy

atrakc|ja f (-e; -i) attraction; ~**yjny** attractive

atrament m (-u; -y) ink; ~ **do stempli** stamp-pad ink; ~**owy** ink

atut m (-u; -y) trump (card) (*też fig.*)

audiowizualny audio-visual

audyc|ja f (-i; -e) RTV: programme; broadcast; **cykl ~i** series (of programmes)

audytorium n (*idkl.*; -ria, -ów) (*pomieaszczenie*) auditorium; (*słuchacze*) audience

aukcja f (-i; -je) auction

aura f (-y; 0) weather; *fig.* aura

auspicj|e pl: **pod ~ami** (G) under the auspices (of)

Australia f (-ii; 0) Australia

Australij|czyk m (-a; -cy), ~ka f (-i; G -jek) Australian; **2ski** Australian

Austria f (G -ii; 0)Austria; **2cki** Austrian; ~czka f (-i; -czek), ~k m (-a; -cy) Austrian

aut m (-u; -y) (w sporcie) out

autentyczny authentic

auto n (-a; G aut) Brt. car, Am. automobile; **autem** by car; ~alarm m mot. alarm (device)

autobiograficzny autobiographic(al)

autobus m (-a; -y) bus; coach; ~em by bus, (między miastami) by coach

autocasco (idkl.) → casco

autochton m (-a; -ni), ~ka f (-ki; G -nek) native

auto|geniczny: trening ~geniczny autogenic training; autogenics; ~graf m (-u; -y) autograph; ~kar coach; ~mat m (-u; -y) automatic (też mil.); (sprzedający) vending machine; ~mat **telefoniczny** Brt. pay phone, Am. pay station; ~matyczny automatic

automatyz|acja f (-i; 0) automatization; ~ować ⟨z-⟩ (-uję) automatize, automate

autonomi|a f (-ii; 0) autonomy; ~czny autonomous

autoportret m self-portrait

autopsj|a f (-i; -e) med. autopsy; post-mortem (examination); **z ~i** from experience

autor m (-a; -rzy), ~ka f (-i; G - rek) author;(pisarz)writer;(sprawca)originator; ~ski authorial; author's; ~stwo n (-a; 0) authorship

autory|tatywny authoritative; ~tet m (-u; -y) authority; prestige; ~zowany authorized

auto|sanie pl. motorized sledge; ~serwis m service station

autostop m: jechać ~em hitch-hike

autostopowicz F m, ~ka f (-i; G -czka) hitch-hiker

autostrada f (-y) Brt. motorway; Am. expressway; (płatna) Am. turnpike

autowy: sędzia ~ linesman

awangarda f (-y) avant-garde

awans m (-u; -e/-y) promotion; ~ **społeczny** social advancement; **otrzymać ~em** get in advance; ~ować (im)pf (-uję) v/t. promote; v/i. be promoted (**na** A to), (też w sporcie) move up

awantur|a f (-y) row, fracas; ~niczo adventurously; ~niczy adventure; adventurous; (kłótliwy) quarrelsome; ~nica f (-y; -e) quarrelsome woman; ~nik m (-a; -cy) rowdy, troublemaker; ~ować **się** (-uję) make a row; cause trouble (**z** I with)

awari|a f (GDL -ii; -e) (zwł. mot.) breakdown; ~jny emergency; **wyjście** ~**yjne** emergency exit

awers m (-u; -y) obverse; ~ja f (-i; 0) aversion

AWF skrót: **Akademia Wychowania Fizycznego** Academy of Physical Education

awizować ⟨za-⟩ (-uję) send notification (A of)

azalia f (GDL -ii; -e) azalea

azbest m (-u; 0) asbestos; ~owy asbestos

Azja f (-i; 0) Asia; ~ta m (-y; -ci), ~tka f (-i; G -tek) Asian; **2tycki** Asian

azot m (-u; 0) nitrogen; ~owy nitrogen, nitrogenous, nitric; **kwas ~owy** nitric acid

azyl m (-u; -e) asylum; **prawo ~u** right of asylum; **udzielić ~u** grant asylum

azylant m (-a; -ci), ~ka f (-i; G -tek) (mający azyl) person granted asylum; (szukający azylu) person seeking asylum

aż cj., part. till, until; ~ **do** (G) till, up to; ~ **do wczoraj** until yesterday; ~ **po kolana** up to the knees; ~ **pięć** as many as five; ~ **miło słuchać** it is nice to hear of it; ~ **nadto** more than enough; ~ **strach pomyśleć** one shudders to think of it

ażeby → aby

ażurowy open-work

B

b. skrót pisany: *były* former; *bardzo* very

bab|a f (-y; G -) (old, peasant *itp.*) woman; **~cia** f (-i; -e) grandmother, F granny; **~i: ~ie lato** (*pora*) Indian summer; **~ka** → *babcia*; *gastr.* (ring) cake; F chick

babrać się (-rzę; -am) slosh about, *fig.* dirty one's hands

bab|ski female; **~unia** f, **~usia** f (-i; -iu!/-e) → *babcia*

bachor m (-a; -y) brat

baczki m/pl. (-ków) whiskers pl.

baczn|ość f (-ści; 0): **stać na ~ość** stand at attention; **mieć się na ~ości** stand at one's guard, look out; **~y** vigilant, attentive

bacz|yć: nie ~ąc na (A) regardless of

bać się be afraid, be worried (*o* A about)

bada|cz m (-a; -e), **~czka** f (-ki; G -czek) researcher, student; **~ć ⟨z-⟩** (-am) (*przestudiować*) research, study; *chorych* examine; *świadka* interrogate; *puls* feel; **~nie** n (-a) study, examination; interrogation; (*opinii publicznej* public) opinion poll; **~wczo** inquisitively; **~wczy** searching; *pracownik* **~wczy** researcher

bagatela f (-i; -e) trifle

bagaż m (-u; -e) *Brt.* luggage, *Am.* baggage; **~nik** m (-a; -i) *mot. Brt.* boot, *Am.* trunk; (*dachowy*) (roof) rack; **~owy 1.** luggage, baggage; **2.** m (-ego; -i) porter

bagnet m (-u; -y) bayonet

bagnisty swampy, marshy

bagno n (-a; G -gien) swamp, marshes pl.

bajeczny fairy-story, magical

bajka f (-i; G -jek) fairy tale

bajoro n (-a) muddy pool

bak m (-u; -i) tank

bakalie pl. (-ii) nuts and raisins pl.

bakier: na ~ at a slant

bakłażan m (-u; -y) *bot. Brt.* aubergine, *Am.* eggplant

bakterio|bójczy (-czo) germicidal; **~logiczny** bacteriological

bal¹ m (-a; -e, -i) balk

bal² m (-u; -e, -ów) (*maskowy* masked) ball

balast m (-u; -y) ballast

baleron m (-u; -y) rolled smoked ham

balet m (-u; -y) ballet; **~nica** f (-y; -e), **~nik** m (-a; -cy) ballet-dancer; **~owy** ballet

balkon m (-u; -y) balcony; *theat.* gallery

balon m (-u; -y), **~ik** m (-a; -i) balloon

balowy ball

balustrada f (-y) balustrade

bała|gan F m (-u; -y) muddle; mess; *na~robić* **~ganu** (*w* L) mess up (in); **~mu-cić ⟨z-⟩** (-cę) v/t. chat up

Bałka|ny pl. (G -ów) the Balkans pl.; **2ński** Balkan

Bałty|k m (-u; 0) (the) Baltic Sea; **2cki** Baltic

bałwan m (-a; -y) F dimwit; (*bożek*) idol; (*śniegowy*) snowman; **~y** pl. też breakers pl., whitecaps pl.

bambosz m (-a; -y/-ów) slipper

bambus m (-a; -y) bamboo; **~owy** bamboo

banalny banal; (*trywialny*) trivial

banał m (-u; -y) banality; commonplace

banan m (-a/-u; -y) banana

banda f (-y) gang

bandaż m (-a; -e) *med.* bandage; **~ować ⟨o-⟩** (-uję) bandage

bandera f (-y) *naut.* flag

bandy|cki vicious; **~ta** m (-y; -ci, -ów) bandit, robber; **~tyzm** m (-u; 0) crime

bank m (-u; -i) bank

bankiet m (-u; -y) banquet

bank|not m (-u; -y) *zwł. Brt.* banknote, *Am.* bill; **~omat** cash dispenser; **~ruc-two** n (-a) bankruptcy; **~rutować ⟨z-⟩** (-uję) go bankrupt

bańka f (-i; G -niek) (*mydlana* soap) bubble; (*naczynie*) can; *med.* cuppping glass

bar¹ m (-u; -y) bar; **~ samoobsługowy** snack bar

bar² m (-u; 0) *chem.* barium

barak m (-u; -i) shack; (*na budowie itp.*) hut

baran m (-a; -y) ram; F *nosić kogoś na* **~a** carry s.o. piggyback; 2 *znak Zodia-*

ku: Aries; **on(a)** *jest spod znaku Ba-rana* he/she is (an) Aries; ~ek *m* (*-nka*; *-nki*) lamb (*też rel.*); ~i mutton; ~ina *f* (*-y*; *0*) mutton

barbarzyńca *m* (*-y*; *G -ów*) barbarian

barczysty broad-shouldered

bardz|iej more; **coraz** ~*iej* more and more; **tym** ~*iej że* the more so that; **tym** ~*iej nie* all the more not; ~o *adv.* very; **nie** ~*o* not much

bariera *f* (*-y*) barrier; ~ **dźwiękowa** sound barrier; ~ **ochronna** (*przy drodze*) crash barrier

bark *m* (*-u*; *-i*) *anat.* shoulder

barka *f* (*-i*; *G -rek*) barge

barłóg *m* (*-ogu*; *-ogi*) (*dla zwierzęcia*) litter; (*dla człowieka*) pallet

barman *m* (*-a*; *-i*) *Brt.* barman, bartender, *Am.* barkeeper; ~ka *f* (*-i*; *G -nek*) barmaid

barokowy Baroque

barometr *m* (*-u*; *-y*) barometer

barowy bar; *chem.* barium, baric

barszcz *m* (*-u*; *-e*) *Brt.* beetroot soup, *Am.* beet soup, bortsch (borsch)

barw|a *f* (*-y*) colo(u)r; ~ **głosu** timbre; ~ić ⟨*u-*, *za-*⟩ colo(u)r (**na czerwono** red); *się* dye; ~inek *m* (*-nka*; *-nki*) periwinkle; ~nik *m* (*-a*; *-i*) dye; pigment; ~ny (*oddający kolory*) colo(u)r; (*barwny*) colourful

barykad|a *f* (*-y*) barricade; ~ować ⟨*za-*⟩ barricade

baryłka *f* (*-i*; *G -łek*) (*piwa itp.*) keg; (*ropy*) barrel

baryton *m* (*-u/os. -a*; *-y*) baritone

bas *m* (*-u/os. -a*; *-y*) bass

basen *m* (*-u*; *-y*) (**pływacki** swimming) pool; (*dla chorych*) bedpan

baskij|ka *f* (*-i*; *G -jek*) beret; ~ski Basque; **mówić po** ~**sku** speak Basque

baszta *f* (*-y*) tower

baśniowy fairy-tale, fable

baśń *f* (*-ni*; *-nie*) fable

bat *m* (*-a*; *D -owi*; *-y*) whip; **dostać** ~**y** get a hiding

bateria *f* (*GDL -ii*; *-e*) *electr.* battery

bateryjka *f* (*-i*; *G -jek*) *electr.* battery

batut|a *f* (*-y*) baton; **pod** ~**ą** (*G*) *mus.* conducted by

batyst *m* (*-u*; *-y*) batiste

Bawar|czyk *m* (*-a*; *-cy*), ~ka *f* (*-i*; *G -rek*) Bavarian; 2ski Bavarian; **po** 2**sku** like a Bavarian

bawełn|a *f* cotton; ~niany cotton

bawić ⟨*po-*, *za-*⟩ (*-ę*) *v/i.* stay; be on a visit (**u** *G* to); *v/t.* entertain; amuse; ~ ⟨*po-*, *za-*⟩ **się** (*dobrze itp.*) have a good time; enjoy o.s.; ~ **się z dziećmi** play with children; ~ **się lalką** play with a doll; *fig.* **nie** ~ **się w** (*A*) not waste too much time on

baw|oli buffalo; ~ół *m* (*-ołu*; *-oły*) buffalo

baza *f* (*-y*) base; (*podstawa*) basis; (*transportowa itp.*) depot; ~ **danych** database; ~ **pływająca** mother ship

bazar *m* (*-u*; *-y*) bazaar; (*targ*) market-place

bazgrać ⟨*-rzę*; *-rz/-raj!*⟩ ⟨*na-*⟩ scribble, scrawl; ⟨*po-*⟩ scribble on

bazgranina *f* (*-y*) scribble, scrawl

bazia *f* (*-i*; *- e*, *-i*) willow catkin

bazować ⟨*-uję*⟩ base (**na L** on)

Bazylea *f* (*-i*; *-0*) Basle, Basel

bazylia *f* (*GDL -ii*; *-e*) *bot.* (sweet) basil

bazylika *f* (*-i*) *arch.* basilica

bażant *m* (*-a*; *-y*) pheasant

bąbe|l *m* (*-bla*; *-ble*) (*na pięcie itp.*) blister; (*na wodzie*) bubble; ~lek *m* (*-lka*; *-lki*) (small) blister; (small) bubble

bądź *cj.* or; ~ ... ~ ... either ... or ...; ~ **co** ~ after all; **co** ~ anything; **kto** ~ anybody; → **być**

bąk *m* (*-a*; *-i*) *zo.* (*owad bydlęcy*) horsefly, (*trzmiel*) bumble-bee, (*ptak*) bittern; (*zabawka*) top; F (*dziecko*) toddler, tot; **zbijać** ~**i** hang around the streets; ~**ać** (*-am*) mumble, mutter; (*czytać*) read in a halting way; (*napomykać*) hint

beatyfikacja *f* (*-i*; *-e*) beatification

beczeć ⟨*za-*⟩ (*-ę*) *owca, koza*: bleat; F (*płakać*) whinge, whimper

beczk|a *f* (*-i*; *G -czek*) barrel; (*drewniana, na wino*) cask; *aviat.* roll; ~owy barrell, cask; **piwo** ~**owe** draught beer

beczułka *f* (*-i*; *G -łek*) (small) barrel, (small) cask

bednarz *m* (*-a*; *-e*) cooper

befsztyk *m* (*-a*; *-i*) beefsteak; ~ **po tatarsku** steak tartar(e)

bejc|a *f* (*-y*; *-e*, *-y*) wood-stain; ~ować (*-uję*) stain

bek *m* (*-u*; *-i*) bleat; blubber, whimper; → **beczeć**

bekas *m* (*-a*; *-y*) *zo.* snipe

bekhend *m* (*-u*; *-y*) (*w sporcie*) backhand

beknąć v/s. (-nę) → **beczeć**

bekon m (-u; -y) (wędzonka) bacon

beksa F f/m (-y; G -/-ów) cry-baby

bela f (-i; -e) (drewniana) beam; (materiału) bale; **pijany jak ~** blind drunk

belfer F m (-fra; -frowie/-frzy), ~ka f (-rek; -rki) teacher

Belg m (-a; -owie, -ów) Belgian; ~ia f (-ii; 0) Belgium; ~ijka f (-i; G -jek) Belgian; £ijski Belgian

belka f (-i; G -lek) beam; F mil. stripe; ~ **nośna** supporting beam

bełkot m (-u; -y) gibberish, babble; ~ać ⟨**wy-**⟩ gibber, babble

bełtać ⟨**z-**⟩ (-am) stir up

beniaminek m (-nka; -nki/-nkowie) darling, pet

benzoesowy: **kwas ~** benzoic acid

benzyn|a f (-y) Brt. petrol, Am. gasoline, Am. F gas; ~owy Brt. petrol, Am. gas; **stacja ~owa** filling station

berbeć F m (-cia; -cie, -ci/-ciów) tot

beret m (-u; -y) béret

Berl|in m (-a; 0) Berlin; £iński Berlin

berło n (-ła; G -reł) Brt. sceptre, Am. scepter

bernardyn m (-a; -y) (pies) St. Bernard (dog)

Berno n (-a; 0) Bern(e)

bessa f (-y) econ. fall (na giełdzie) bear

besti|a f (GDL -ii; -e) beast; ~alski bestial, savage; ~alsko bestially, savagely

besztać ⟨**z-**⟩ (-am) tell off, scold

Betlejem n (idkl) Bethlehem

beton m (-u; -y) concrete; ~ować ⟨**za-**⟩ (-uję) concrete; **drogę** surface with concrete; ~owy concrete

bez[1] m (bzu; bzy) lilac; **czarny ~** elder

bez[2] prp. without; **~ potrzeby** unnecessarily; **~ ustanku** incessantly; **~ wad** faultless

beza f (-y) meringue

bez|alkoholowy non-alcoholic, alcohol-free; **napój** soft; ~awaryjny trouble-free; ~barwny colo(u)rless; ~błędny perfect, faultless; ~bolesny painless; ~bronny defenceless; ~brzeżny boundless (też fig.); ~celowość pointlessness; ~celowy pointless

bezcen: **za ~** dirt cheap; ~ny invaluable, priceless

bez|ceremonialny unceremonious; ~chmurny cloudless; ~czelność impudence; ~czelny impudent; ~czyn-

ność inactivity; idleness; ~czynny inactive; idle; ~darny, ~denny bottomless; fig. incredible; ~domny **1.** homeless; **2.** (m-os -ni) vagrant; **bezdomni** the homeless; ~droże n (-a; G -y): zwł. pl. **~droża** wilderness

bez|drzewny treeless; **papier** woodfree; ~duszny heartless; soulless; ~dzietność f (-i; 0) childlessness; ~dzietny childless; ~dźwięczny soundless; jęz. voiceless

beze → **bez**; ~cny lit. heinous

bez|gorączkowy free from fever; ~gotówkowo without cash; ~gotówkowy cashless; ~graniczny boundless; ~imienny nameless; ~interesowny unselfish, selfless; ~karnie unpunished; with impunity; ~kofeinowy decaffeinated; ~kompromisowy uncompromising; ~konkurencyjny unrivalled; ~kresny limitless; ~krwawo bloodlessly; ~krwawy bloodless; ~krwisty bloodless; ~krytyczny uncritical; ~kształtny shapeless; ~leśny unwooded

bez liku adv. countless, innumerable

bez|litosny merciless; ~litośnie mercilessly; ~ludny desolate; **wyspa** uninhabited, desert; ~ład disorder, F mess; ~ładny disorderly

bez mała almost, nearly

bez|miar m (-u; -y) huge expanse; ~mierny immeasurable, immense; ~mięsny gastr. without meat; ~miłosierny → **bezlitosny**; ~myślny thoughtless; ~nadziejny hopeless; ~namiętny dispassionate, detached; ~nogi (bez jednej) one-legged; (bez obu) legless; ~objawowy (**-wo**) med. without symptoms, asymptomatic(ally); ~oki eyeless

bezokolicznik m (-a; -i) jęz. infinitive

bez|ołowiowy unleaded, lead-free; ~osobowo impersonally; ~osobowy impersonal; ~owocny fruitless; ~pański abandoned; pies stray; ~partyjny independent; ~pestkowy bot. seedless

bezpieczeństw|o n (-a; 0) security, safety; **~o i higiena pracy** protection of health and safety standards at work; **~o ruchu** road safety; **pas ~a** safety belt, seat belt; **Rada £a** Security Council

bezpiecz|nik m (-a; -i) electr. fuse; (ka-

rabinu) safety-catch; ~ny safe; ~**ny w użyciu** (operationally) safe

bez|planowo aimlessly, unsystematically; ~**planowy** aimless, unsystematic; ~**płatny** free (of charge); ~**płciowy** sexless; (*roślina itp.*) asexual; ~**płodność** bareness, sterility; ~**płodny** bare, sterile; *fig.* → **bezowocny**

bez|podstawny baseless; ~**pośredni** direct, immediate; just (**po** *L* after); ~**pośrednio** directly, immediately; ~**powrotny** irretrievable

bezpraw|ie *n* (*-a*; *0*) lawlessness; illegality; ~**ny** lawless; illegal

bez|precedensowy unprecedented; ~**problemowy** unproblematic; ~**procentowy** (*kredyt itp.*) interest-free; ~**przedmiotowo** baselessly; ~**przedmiotowy** unfounded, baseless; ~**przewodowy** cordless; ~**przykładny** unparalleled, outrageous; ~**radny** helpless

bezręki (*bez jednej*) one-armed; (*bez obu*) armless

bezrobo|cie *n* (*-a*) unemployment; ~**tny** 1. unemployed; 2. *m* (*-ego*; *-ni*), ~**tna** *f* (*-ej*; *-e*) unemployed person; **bezrobotni** *pl.* the unemployed *pl.*; **zasiłek dla** ~**tnych** unemployment benefit, F dole

bezrolny landless

bezruch *m* (*0*): **w** ~**u** immobility, stillness

bez|senność *f* sleeplessness; ~**senny** sleepless; ~**sens** *m* senselessness; ~**sensowny** senseless; ~**silny** powerless (**wobec** *G* in the face of)

bezskutecz|nie *adv.* vainly; ~**ny** vain, futile

bez|słoneczny sunless; ~**sporny** doubtless; ~**sprzeczny** unquestionable; ~**stronny** impartial; ~**szelestnie** *adv.* noiselessly; ~**śnieżny** snowless; ~**terminowy** (*-wo*) for an unlimited period; ~**treściowy** empty

beztros|ka *f* (*-i*; *0*) carelessness, carefreeness; ~**ki** careless, carefree; ~**ko** carelessly

bez|ustanny 1. *adj.* incessant, unstopping; 2. *adv.*: ~**ustannie** incessantly; ~**usterkowy** (*-wo*) trouble-free; ~**użyteczny** useless

bez|wartościowy valueless; ~**warunkowo** unconditionally; ~**warunkowy** unconditional; ~**wiedny** unconscious; (*niezamierzony*) unintentional; ~**wi-**

zowy without a visa

bezwład *m* (*-u*; *0*) inertia; (*kończyny itp.*) paralysis; ~**ność** *f* (*-ci*; *0*) inertia, inactivity; **siła** ~**ności** *phys.* inertia; ~**ny** inert, inactive

bez|włosy hairless; ~**wodny** waterless; ~**wolny** passive, without will; ~**wonny** odo(u)rless

bezwstyd *m* (*-u*; *0*) shamelessness, impudence; ~**ny** shameless, impudent

bez|wyznaniowy non-denominational, not belonging to any denomination; ~**względność** *f* ruthlessness; ~**względny** ruthless; absolute; ~**zakłóceniowy** trouble-free; ~**załogowy** unmanned; ~**zasadny** groundless; unfounded; ~**zębny** toothless; ~**złocz**ny immediate; ~**zwrotny** non-returnable; ~**żenny** celibate

beż *m* (*idkl*), ~**owy** (*-wo*) beige

bęb|en *m* (*-bna*; *-bny*) drum; **grać na** ~**nie** play the drum; ~**enek** *m* (*-nka*; *-nki*) drum; *anat.* ear-drum; ~**nić** (*-ę*; *-nij!*) drum

bęcwał *m* (*-a*; *-y*) → **próżniak**

będę, będzie → **być**

bękart *m* (*-a*; *-y*) bastard (*też fig.*)

BHP *skrót pisany:* **bezpieczeństwo i higiena pracy** protection of health and safety standards at work

biad|a! woe betide you/him *itp.*; ~**ać** (*-am*), ~**olić** (*-lę*) lament (**nad czymś** s.th.)

biała|czka *f* (*-i*; *0*) *Brt.* leukaemia, *Am.* leukemia; ~**wy** (*-wo*) whitish

białko *n* (*-a*; *G* -*łek*) (*jajka, oka itp.*) white; *biol.*, *chem.* protein

biało *adv.* white; **ubrany na** ~ dressed in white; ~-**czerwony** white-red; ⁹**ru**-**sin** *m* (*-a*; *-i*), ⁹**rusinka** *f* (*-i*; *G* - *nek*) B(y)elorussian; ~**ruski** B(y)elorussian; **mówić po** ~**rusku** speak B(y)elorussian; ⁹**ruś** *f* (*-si*; *0*) B(y)elarus; ~**ść** *f* (*-i*; *0*) whiteness

biał|y white; ~**a kawa** *Brt.* white coffee, coffee with milk; **w** ~**y dzień** in broad daylight; **czarno na** ~**ym** in black and white

bibka F *f* (*-i*) party, F bash

biblia *f* (*GDL -ii*; *-e*) (the) Bible

biblijny Biblical

bibliotecz|ka *f* (*-i*; *G* -*czek*) (*zwł. podręczna*) reference library; (*mebel*) bookcase; ~**ny** library

B

biblioteka f library; ~rka f (-ki; G -rek), ~rz m (-a; -e, -y) librarian; ~rski library

bibuła f (-y) blotting paper; ~a filtracyjna filter paper; ~ka f (-i; G -łek) tissue paper; cigarette-paper

bicie n (-a) striking (**zegara** of the clock); ringing (**w dzwony** of the bells); (pobicie) beating; **z ~m serca** with a pounding heart

bicz m (-a; -e) whip; fig. scourge; **jak zá~aátrzasł** in no time

bić (-ję; bij!) v/t. hit (**po twarzy, w twarz** in the face), beat; rywala, rekord itp. beat; drób slaughter; kartę take; medal strike; ~ **brawo** applaud; v/i. zegar. strike; serce: beat; źródło: gush; działo: shoot; ~ **w dzwony** ring the bells; **to bije w oczy** it is as clear as daylight; ~ásię fight, beat; ~ **się z myślami** be in two minds; → **uderzać**

biec ⟨po-⟩ (→**biegnąć**) run; fig. (życie itp.) pass

bied|a f (-y) poverty; fig. trouble; (nieszczęście) bad luck; ~a z nędzą abject poverty; **klepać ~ę** suffer poverty; **zá~ą, od ~y** with difficulty; **pół ~y** it's not as bad as all that; **mieć ~ę** have great difficulty (**z** I in); ~actwo n (-a) poor thing; ~aczka f (-i; G -czek) poor woman; ~aczysko m/n (-a) poor devil; ~ak m (-a; -cy) poor (wo)man; **biedacy** pl. the poor pl.; ~nieć ⟨z-⟩ (-eję) become poor; ~ny 1. adj (też fig.); (nędzny) poor, shabby; 2. → **biedak**; ~ota f (-y) zbior. the poor pl.; ~ować ⟨-uję⟩ suffer poverty

biedronka f (-i; G -nek) zo. Brt. ladybird, Am. ladybug

biedzić się ⟨**na-się**⟩ ⟨-dzę⟩ slave away (**z, nad** I at)

bieg m (-u; i) run (też fig., hunt.); (pociągu itp.) motion; mot. gear; (w sporcie) race; ~ **krótkodystansowy** short-distance race; ~ **zjazdowy** downhill racing; ~ **przełajowy** cross-country; **w pełnym ~u** at full speed; **dolny/górny** ~ lower/upper reaches pl.; **z ~iem rzeki** downstream; **z ~iem czasu/lat** in the course of time; **zmiana ~ów** gear change; ~acz m (-a; -e), ~aczka f (-i; G -czek) runner

biega|ć ⟨-am⟩ run; ~ć **po sklepach** doáthe rounds of all the shops; ~ć **za**

(D) run lub chase after; ~nina f (-y) running around

bieg|le adv. mówić: fluently; ~ły **1.** adj. (comp. -lejszy) skilful (**w L** at); **2.** m (-ego; -li) expert; ~nąć ⟨po-⟩ (-nę, -ł) run; → **biec**; ~owy (narty) cross-country; ~un m (-a; -y) phys., geogr. pole; **koń na ~unach** rocking horse

biegunka f (-i; G -nek) Brt. diarrhoea, Am. diarrhea

biegunow|o diametrally; ~y Polar; **koło ~e** polar circle

biel f (-i; -e) (**cynkowa** Chinese) white; **w ~i** in white; ~eć ⟨-eję⟩ ⟨po-, z-⟩ whiten, go white; ~ej comp. od adv. → **biało**; ~ić ⟨po-, wy-⟩ ściany whitewash; materiał bleach; ⟨za-⟩ make white; zupę add cream to

bielizna f (-y) (**pościelowa, stołowa** bed-, table-) linen; ~ **osobista** underwear

bieliźnia|ny linen; ~rka f (-i; G -rek) chest of drawers

biel|mo n (-a) med. leukoma; film (też fig.); ~ony whitewashed; ~szy adj. comp. od → **biały**

bielutki F quite white, white all over

bier|nik m (-a; -i) gr. accusative; ~ność f (-ści; 0) passivity; ~ny passive (też chem.); **strona ~na** the passive (voice)

bierzmowanie n (-a) rel. confirmation

bies m (-a; -y) devil

biesiada f (-y) banquet

bież. skrót pisany: **bieżący** ct (current)

bież|ąco: prowadzić na ~ąco (A) keep up-to-date; ~ący running; actual, current; **rachunek ~ący** current account; ~nia f (-i; -e) (w sporcie) track; ~nik m (-a; -i) (na stół) runner; mot. tread

bigamista m (-y; -ci) bigamist

bigos m (-u; y) bigos (stew made with meat and cabbage); F fig. **narobić ~u** make a mess

bijak m (-a; -i) (w sporcie) batter

bijatyka f (-i) brawl

bila f (-i; -e, -/-i) sport: billiard-ball

bilans m (-u; -e) balance (też fig.); ~ować ⟨z-⟩ ⟨-uję⟩ balance

bilard m (-u; -e) billiards

bile|t m (-u; -y) (**powrotny, lotniczy** return, plane) ticket; ~t **miesięczny** monthly season-ticket; ~t **wstępu** entrance ticket; ~t **do teatru** Brt. theatre (Am. theater) ticket; ~ter m (-a; -rzy)

bliższy

usher; **-rka** f (-i; G -rek) usherette; **~towy: kasa ~towa** ticket window; (w teatrze, kinie) box office

bilon m (-u; 0) coins pl.; small change

bimber m (-bru; 0) Brt. poteen, zwł. Am. moonshine

biochemia f biochemistry

biodro n (-a) hip; **~wy** hip

bio|'grafia f (GDL -ii; -e) biography; **~'logia** f (GDL -ii; e) biology; **~logiczny** biological; **~technologia** f biotechnology

biorą(c) → **brać**

biorca m (-y; G -ów) recipient

biorę → **brać**

biret m (-u; -y) (duchownego itp.) biretta; (profesora, prawnika) cap

bis m (-u; -y) theat. encore

biskup m (-a; -i) bishop; **~i** bishop's, episcopal; **~stwo** n (-a) bishopric

biskwit m (-u; -y) gastr. biscuit

biszkopt m (-u; -y) gastr. sponge biscuit; **~owy** sponge-biscuit; **tort ~owy** sponge-biscuit gateau

bit m (-u; -y) komp. bit

bitka f (-i) brawl, fight; zwł. pl. **bitki** chops pl.

bit|ny brave, courageous; **~wa** f (-y) battle; **~y** (szlak itp.) beaten; (drób) slaughtered; **~a godzina** a whole hour; **~a śmietana** whipped cream

biuletyn m (-u; -y) bulletin

biurko n (-a) desk

biuro n (-a) office; (podróży itp.) agency; (matrymonialne itp.) bureau; **~ meldunkowe** local government office for registration of residents; F **po biurze** after office hours; **~kracja** f (-i; -e) bureaucracy; **~kratyczny** bureaucratic; **~wiec** m (-wca; -wce) office building; **~wość** f (-ści; 0) office work; **~wy** office

biust m (-u; -y) bust, bosom; → **popiersie**; **~onosz** m (-a; -e) bra, brassière

biwak m (-u; -i) bivouac, camp; **~ować** (-uję) bivouac, camp

bizmut m (-u; 0) chem. bismuth

biznes m (-u; y) business; **~men** m (-a; -i) businessman; **~menka** f (-i) businesswoman

bizon m (-a; -y) buffalo; bison

biżuteria f (GDL -ii; 0) (**sztuczna** costume) jewellery

blacha f (-y) sheet metal; (do ciasta)

baking tray; (kuchenna, węglowa) top, (elektryczna) hotplate; **~rka** f (-ki) metalwork; **~rski** tin; **~rz** m (-a; -e) tinsmith

blad|ł(a, -o) → **blednąć**; **~o** adv. pale(ly); w złoż. pale-; **~ość** f (-i; 0) paleness, pallor

blady (jak trup deathly) pale; white

blag|a F f (-i) tall story, hoax; **~ier** m (-a; -rzy), **-rka** f (-i; G -rek) hoaxer; **~ować** F (-uję) talk rubbish, humbug

blaknąć ⟨**wy-**⟩ (-nę; -kł/-nął) fade, pale (też fig.)

blamować się ⟨**z- się**⟩ (-uję) make a fool of o.s.

blankiet m (-u; -y) form

blanszować (-uję) gastr. blanch

blask m (-u; -i) (rażący) glare; (nie rażący) shine, (klejnotów) sparkle

blaszan|ka f (-i; G -nek) can, Brt. tin; **~y** tin, metal

blaszka f (-i; G-szek) a piece of metal

blat m (-u; -y) (table-)top

blednąć ⟨**z-**⟩ (-nę; -nął/bladł) go lub turn pale; fig. pale, fade

blef m (-u; 0) bluff; **~ować** (-uję) bluff

blenda f (-y) arch. blind window; chem. blende

blezer m (-a/-u; -y) blazer

blichtr m (-u; 0) gaudiness, tawdriness

blisk|i 1. near; close (też fig.); → **pobliski, bliższy**; **~a przyjaźń** close friendship; **2.** (m-os -scy) relative, member of one's family; **~o** adv. near, close (G, od G to) (też w czasie); (prawie) almost; **z ~a** at close quarters; from a short distance; → **bliżej**

bliskość f (-ści; 0) closeness (też fig.); proximity

blisko|wschodni Middle-Eastern; **~znaczny** synonymous

blizna f (-y) scar

bliź|ni m (-ego; i) fellow human being; rel. neighbo(u)r; **~niaczka** f (-i; G -czek) twin sister; **~niaczo: być ~niaczo podobnym do** (G) be the spitting image of; **~niaczy** twin; **~niak** m (-a; -i) twin brother; **~nięta** n/pl. (-niąt) twins pl.; znak Zodiaku: **Bliźnięta** Gemini; **on(a) jest spod znaku Bliźniąt** he/she is (a) Gemini

bliż|ej adv. (comp. od → **blisko**) nearer; **~ej nieznany** little known; **~szy** adj. (comp. od → **najbliższy**) nearer,

closer; ~**sze dane** more precise information

bloczek *m* ⟨*-czka; -czki*⟩ notepad

blok *m* ⟨*-u; -i*⟩ block; *tech.* ~ **rysunkowy** sketch-pad; ~ **mieszkalny** block (of flats); ~ **cylindrów** cylinder block; ~**ada** *f* ⟨*-y*⟩ blockade; (*w sporcie*) blocking; ~**ować** ⟨*za-*⟩ ⟨*-uję*⟩ block; *państwo itp.* blockade; *ruch* stop; ~**owisko** *n* ⟨*-a*⟩ prefab housing estate

blond *idkl.* blond(e); **włosy** ~ (**męż-czyzny**) blond, (*kobiety*) blonde; ~**yn** *m* ⟨*-a; -i*⟩ fair-haired *lub* blond man; ~**ynka** *f* ⟨*-i; G -nek*⟩ blonde

bluszcz *m* ⟨*-u; -e*⟩ *bot.* ivy

bluz|a *f* ⟨*-y*⟩ (*żołnierza itp.*) tunic; (*sportowca itp.*) sweatshirt; ~**ka** ⟨*-i*⟩ blouse

bluz|gać ⟨*-am*⟩ ⟨~**nąć**⟩ ⟨*-nę*⟩ *błoto, itp.*: spout, splash; F (*przekleństwami itp.*) hurl

bluźnierstwo *n* ⟨*-a*⟩ blasphemy

błaga|ć ⟨*-am*⟩ plead, implore; ~**lny** imploring; ~**nie** *n* ⟨*-a*⟩ plea, entreaty

błah|ostka *f* ⟨*-i; G -tek*⟩ trifle; ~**y** trivial; unimportant

bławatek *m* ⟨*-tka; -tki*⟩ *bot.* cornflower, bluebottle

błaz|en *m* ⟨*-na; -zny/-źni*⟩ clown; *fig.* fool; ~**eński** foolish; ~**eńsko** foolishly; ~**eństwo** *n* ⟨*-a*⟩ folly; stupidity; ~**nować** ⟨*-uję*⟩ F fool (around)

błaźnić się ⟨*z- się*⟩ ⟨*-nę, -nij!*⟩ make a fool of o.s.

błąd *m* ⟨*błędu; błędy*⟩ mistake, error; ~**d maszynowy** typing error, F typo; ~**d w rachunku** arithmetical error; **być w błędzie** be wrong *lub* mistaken; **wprowadzić w** ~**d** mislead, deceive; ~**dzić** ⟨*-dzę*⟩ wander (**po** L, **wśród** G around); ⟨**po-, z-**⟩ go wrong (**w** L with); *tylko pf* lose one's way; ~**kać się** ⟨*-am*⟩ wander about *lub* around

błęd|nie *adv.* mistakenly; ~**ny** mistaken; *wzrok itp.* vague; ~**ne koło** vicious circle; ~**y** *pl.* → **błąd**

błękit *m* ⟨*-u; -y*⟩ blue; ~**nooki** blue-eyed; ~**ny** blue

błocić ⟨*na-, za-*⟩ ⟨*-cę*⟩ get dirty (with mud)

bło|gi blissful, delightful; ~**go** blissfully, delightfully

błogosła|wić ⟨*po-*⟩ ⟨*-ę*⟩ bless; ~**wień-stwo** *n* ⟨*-a*⟩ blessing (*też iron.*); ~**wiony** blessed

błon|a *f* ⟨*-y*⟩ membrane; *phot.* film; ~**a śluzowa** mucous membrane; ~**a dzie-wicza** hymen; ~**ica** *f* ⟨*-y; -0*⟩ diphtheria

błonka *f* ⟨*-i; G -nek*⟩ membrane

błot|nik *m* ⟨*-a; -i*⟩ *Am.* fender, *Brt. mot.* wing, (*rowerowy*) mudguard; ~**nisty** muddy; ~**ny** muddy, marshy; (*roślina itp.*) marsh; ~**o** *n* ⟨*-a*⟩ mud, dirt; *fig.* dirt, filth, F muck; ~**a** *pl.* swamp; **zmieszać z** ~**em** *fig.* drag through the mud

błysk *m* ⟨*-u; -i*⟩ flash; ~**ać** ⟨*-am*⟩ flash, sparkle; **błysnęło** there was a flash of lightning; ~**a się** there are flashes of lightning

błyskawi|ca *f* ⟨*-y; -e*⟩ lightning; **jak** ~**ca** as fast as lightning; ~**czny** (*szybki*) lightning; (*zupa*) instant; → **zamek**

błyskot|ka *f* ⟨*-i; G -tek*⟩ trinket; ~**ki** *pl.* tinsel; ~**liwie** glitteringly; *fig.* brilliantly; ~**liwy** glittering; *fig.* brilliant

błys|kowy flash; ~**nąć** *v/s.* ⟨*-nę*⟩ → **bły-skać**

błyszcz|ący shining, shiny; *papier itp.* glossy; **wypolerować coś na** ~**ąco** polish s.th. until it shines; ~**eć** ⟨*-ę*⟩ shine (*też fig.*); glitter, sparkle; ~**ka** *f* ⟨*-i; G -czek*⟩ (*na ryby*) spoon(-bait)

błyśnięcie *n* ⟨*-a*⟩ → **błysk**

bm. *skrót pisany:* **bieżącego miesiąca** inst. (*instant: this month*)

bo *cj.* because, or (else)

boazeria *f* ⟨*GDL -ii; -e*⟩ wainscoting, wood panelling

bobas F *m* ⟨*-a; -y*⟩ baby

bobkowy: listek ~ bay leaf

bobslej *m* ⟨*-a; -e*⟩ bobsleigh; ~**owy: tor** ~**owy** bobsleigh run

bochen *m* ⟨*-chna; -chny*⟩, ~**ek** *m* ⟨*-nka; -nki*⟩ loaf (of bread)

bocian *m* ⟨*-a; -y*⟩ *zo.* stork; ~**i** stork

bocz|ek *m* ⟨*-czku; -czki*⟩ *gastr.* bacon; ~**nica** *f* ⟨*-y; -e*⟩ *rail.* siding; (*ulica*) side-street; ~**ny** side

boczyć się ⟨*-ę*⟩ (**na** A) be cross with

boćwina *f* ⟨*-y; 0*⟩ → **botwina**

bodaj, ~**że** *part.* at least; perhaps; → **chyba, pewnie**

bodziec *m* ⟨*-dźca; -dźce*⟩ stimulus; (*też materialny*) incentive

boga|cić ⟨*wz-*⟩ ⟨*-cę*⟩ enrich; ~**cić** ⟨*wz-*⟩ **się** get rich; ~**ctwo** *n* ⟨*-a*⟩ wealth, riches *pl.*

bogacz *m* ⟨*-a; -e*⟩ rich man; ~**ka** *f* ⟨*-i; G -czek*⟩ rich woman

Bogarodzica f (-y; 0) Mother of God
bogat|o richly, fig. abundantly; ~y rich, fig. abundant (**w** A in)
bogini f (GDL -ni; -e, -iń) goddess
boginka f (-ki; G -nek) goddess, nymph
bogobojny god-fearing
bohater m (-a; -erzy/-owie) hero; ~ka f (-i; G -rek) heroine; ~ski heroic; ~sko heroically; ~stwo n (-a; 0) heroism
bohomaz m (-u/-a; -y) fig. F daub; (na papierze) doodle
boi się → **bać się**
boisko n (-a) sports field; ~ **do piłki nożnej** football ground lub field
boja f (GDL boi; -e) naut. buoy
bojaź|liwie timidly; ~liwy timid, fearful, fainthearted; ~ń f (-ni; 0) fear; **z ~ni** (G) for fear of
boj|ą, ~ę się → **bać się**
bojkot m (-u; -y) boycott
bojkotować ⟨z-⟩ (-uję) boycott
bojler m (-a; -y) boiler; (w domu) (electric) water heater
bojow|niczka f (-i; G- czek), ~nik m (-a; -cy) fighter; (**o prawa człowieka** for human rights); ~o (zaczepnie) belligerently; ~y fighting, (patrol itp.) battle; (buty itp.) combat; (zaczepny) belligerent; **organizacja ~a** military organization
bojówka f (-ki; G -wek) raiding part; (partyjna itp.) hit-squad
bok m (-u; -i) side; **na** ~ to one side; **na ~u** at the side; (w odległości) away; **przy/u ~u** (G) at the side (of); **w ~** in the side; away; **z ~u** at the side; **pod ~iem** near (at hand); **robić ~ami** fig. (z wysiłku) slave away; **zarabiać na ~u** earn on the side; **zrywać ~i ze śmiechu** split one's sides; ~ami, ~iem adv. sidewise; ~iem (G) sideways; ~obrody pl. (-ów) (side) whiskers pl.; Brt. sideboards pl., Am. sideburns pl.
boks¹ m (-u; -y) (dla koni) loosebox; (w garażu) (partitioned off) (parking-)space
boks² m (-u; 0) boxing; **uprawiać ~** practise boxing; ~erski boxing; ~ować (-uję) fight (**się** v/i.)
bola|cy → **bolesny**; ~czka f (-i; G -czek) fig. difficulty, problem
bolec m (-lca; -lce) pin, bolt
bole|ć¹ też fig. hurt, ache; **boli mnie ząb**

I have a toothache; my tooth hurts me; **nie mogę na to patrzeć** fig. I am not able to stand the sight of it any more
bole|ć² (-eję) (**nad** I) lament; ~sny (-śnie) painful (też fig.), aching; F sore; ~ści f/pl. (G -ści) pain (zwł. abdominal)
Boliw|ia f (GDL -ii) Bolivia; 2ijski Bolivian
bom|ba f (-y) bomb; fig. sensation, bombshell; ~bardować (-uję) bomb; (silnie) blitz; ~bastyczny bombastic; ~bka f (-i; G -bek) glass ball
bombow|iec m (-wca; -wce) aviat. bomber; ~y bomb; F (kapitalny) super
bon m (-u; -y) coupon
bonifikata f (-y) price reduction, discount; sport: handicap
boraks m (-u; 0) borax
bordo¹ n, też **Bordeaux** (idkl.) wino: Bordeaux
bordo² adj. (idkl.), ~wy (-wo) wine-red
borny: kwas ~ boric acid
borowik m (-a; -i) cep
borowin|a f (-y; G -in) mud; ~owy: **kąpiel ~owa** mud bath
borowy → **borny**
borów|ka f (-i; G -wek): ~ **brusznica** cowberry; ~ **czernica** bilberry, blueberry, whortleberry
borsu|czy badger; ~k m (-a; -i) badger
borykać się (-am) contend (**z** I with)
bosak¹: na ~a barefoot
bosak² m (-a; -i) boat-hook
bosk|i God's, divine; **na litość ~ą** for God's sake; **rany ~ie!** for heaven's sake
bosko adv. fig. heavenly
bosman m (-a; -i) naut. boatswain
boso adv. barefoot; ~nogi, **bosy** barefoot
Bośnia f (-i; 0) Bosnia; 2cki Bosnian
bot m (-a; -y) → **boty**
botani|czny botanic(al); ~ka f (-i; 0) botany
botwin|a f (-y), ~ka f (-i; G -nek) beetroot leaves pl.; (soup from beetroot leaves)
boty m/pl. (-ów) snow-boots pl.
bowiem cj. as, since; → **bo**
boy m (-a; -e. -ów) (w hotelu) Brt. page, Am. bellboy
Bozia f F (-i; 0) sweet God
Boże → **bóg**; 2ek m (-ka; -ki) god, idol; 2onarodzeniowy Christmas; 2y

God's; **Boże Narodzenie** Christmas; **Boże Ciało** Corpus Christi

bożyszcze n (-a) idol

bób m (bobu; boby) bot. broad bean

bóbr m (bobra; bobry) zo. beaver

bóg m (boga, bogu, boże!; bogowie/bogi, rel. Bóg) god, rel. God; **~ wojny** god of war; **jak Boga kocham!** I swear on God!; **broń Boże, Boże uchowaj** Heaven forbid!; **jak 2 da** God willing; **Bogu ducha winien/winna** innocent; **szczęść Boże!** God bless you!

bójka f (-i; G -jek) skirmish, fight

ból m (-u, -e; -ów) (głowy, zęba) head-, tooth-) ache; **~ gardła** sore throat; **~e porodowe** pl. labo(u)r pains pl.; **z ~em serca** with a heavy heart

bór m (boru; bory) forest

bóstwo n (-a; G -) deity; fig. good-looker

bóść v/i. gore

bóżnica f (-y; -e) rel. (żydowska) synagogue

bp skrót pisany: **biskup** Bp (Bishop)

br. skrót pisany: **bieżącego roku** ha (of/in this year)

brac|ia → **brat**; (firma) brothers pl. (skrót: **Bros**); **~iszek** m (-szka; -szkowie) little brother; (zakonny) brother; **~two** n (-a) brotherhood

brać v/t. take; **~ kogoś do wojska** call s.o. up; **~ na serio** take seriously; **~ na siebie** take on; **~ ze sobą** take with o.s.; → **rachuba, uwaga, zły** itp.; **~ się** (do (robienia) czegoś) set about ((doing) s.th.); v/i. ryba: bite

brak¹ m (-u; -i) lack; (niedostatek, wada) shortcoming; (produkt) reject; **z ~u czasu** owing to lack of time; **~i w wykształceniu** gaps pl. in education; **~ w kasie** cash deficit; **cierpieć na ~** (G) suffer for lack of; **odczuwać ~** (G) (czegoś) lack, (zwł. kogoś) miss

brak² pred. s.o./s.th. lacks s.o./s.th.; **~ mi ciebie** I miss you; **~ mi słów** I am lost for words; **nie ~ mu odwagi** he does not lack courage; **~nąć** (-nę) → **brakować¹**; **~óróbstwo** n (-a; 0) slipshod work, sloppiness

brakow|ać¹ (-uję) (G) lack; **komuś brakuje ... s.o.** lacks...; **tego tylko ~ało** that was all we needed; → **brak²**

brakować² (-uję) → **wybrakowywać**

bram|a f (-y) gate, (do garażu itp.) door; (przejazdowa, też fig.) gateway; **~ka** f (-i; G -mek) little gate/door; (w sporcie) goal; **strzał w ~kę** shot (at goal); **~karz** m (-a; -e) (w sporcie) goalkeeper; (przy drzwiach) F bouncer, chucker-out; **~kowy** (w sporcie) goal

bramofon m (-u; -y) intercom, Brt. entryphone

Brandenbur|gia f (-ii; 0) Brandenburg; **2ski** Brandenburg

bransoletka f (-i; G - tek) bracelet

branż|a f (-y; -e) (przemysłowa) (branch of) industry; (biznesu) line (of business); **~owy** trade; **sklep ~owy** specialist shop

brat m (-a; D -tu, L -cie; -cia, -ci, I -ćmi) brother (też rel.); **być za pan ~** be close friends (**z** I with); → **cioteczny**

bratan|ek m (-nka; -nki/-nkowie) nephew; **~ica** f (-y; -e), **~ka** f (-i; G -nek) niece

bratek m (-tka; -tki) bot. pansy

braters|ki brotherly, fraternal; **po ~ku** like brothers; **~two** n (-a; 0) (broni) brotherhood (-in-arms)

bratni brotherly, fraternal

bratobój|czy: wojna ~cza fratricidal war; **~stwo** n (-a) fratricide

bratowa f (-wej, -wo!; -e) sister-in-law

Bratysława f (-y; 0) Bratislava

brawo n (-a) cheer(ing); **~!** bravo!; **~ bić**

brawurow|o daringly, courageously; **~y** daring, courageous

Brazyli|a f (-ii) Brazil; **~jczyk** m (-a; -ycy), **~jka** f (-i) Brazilian; **2jski** Brazilian

brąz m (-u; -y) brown; (metal) bronze; **opalić się na ~** be sun-tanned; **~owy** (-wo) brown; (z metalu) bronze

bre|dnie f/pl. (-i) nonsense, F balderdash; **~dzić** (-dzę) (w gorączce) rave; babble

breja f (brei; 0) mush

brew f (brwi; brwi) (eye-)brow

brewerie f/pl. (-ii) row, fuss; **wyprawiać ~** scrap

brewiarz m (-a; -e) breviary

brezent m (-u; -y) canvas

brnąć (-nę) tramp, plod (**przez błoto** through mud; **w śniegu** through the snow)

broczyć (-czę): **~ krwią** bleed

broda f (-y; G bród) chin; (zarost)

beard; **zapuścić brodę** grow a beard;
~ty bearded; ~wka f (-i; G -wek) *med.*,
bot. wart

brodz|ić ⟨-dzę⟩ wade; ~ik m (-a; -i) (*ba-sen dla dzieci*) paddling-pool; (*w ła-zience*) shower base

broić ⟨**na-, z-**⟩ ⟨-ję; -isz, brój!⟩ act up,
frolic

brona f (-y) harrow

bronchit m (-u; -y) bronchitis

bronić ⟨-ę⟩⟨**o-**⟩ (G) defend (A; **się** o.s.);
protect, guard (**przed** I against); ~ **się**
też defend o.s. (**przed** I against); ⟨**za-**⟩
(G) prevent, prohibit

bronować ⟨**za-**⟩ ⟨-uję⟩ harrow

broń[1] → **bronić, bóg**

broń[2] f (-ni; -ie) weapon, arms *pl.*;
~ **krótka** small arms *pl.*; ~ **masowego**
rażenia weapon(s *pl.*) of mass destruc-
tion; ~ **biała** cutting weapon(s *pl.*); **po-**
wołać pod ~ call to arms; **złożyć** ~ lay
down one's arms

broszka f (-i; G -szek) brooch

broszura f (-y) brochure, leaflet

browar m (-u; -y) brewery

bród m (-odu; -ody) ford; **przejść w** ~
ford, wade; *fig.* **w** ~ in abundance

bródka f (-i; G -dek) (*zarost*) (little)
beard

brud m (-u; -y) dirt; → **brudy**; ... **od**
~**u** ... with dirt; ~**as** m (-a; -y) F (*dirty*)
pig; (*dziecko*) dirty brat; ~**no** *adv.* →
brudny; **pisać na ~no** make a rough
copy; ~**nopis** m (-u; -y) rough copy;
~**ny** dirty (*też fig.*); ~**y** *m/pl.* (-ów)
(dirty) laundry; *fig.* dirty linen; → **brud**

brudzić ⟨**po-, za-**⟩ ⟨-dzę⟩ make dirty,
dirty; ~ ⟨**po-, za-**⟩ **się** get dirty

bruk m (-u; -i) paving; **wyrzucić kogoś**
na ~ (*z pracy*) give s.o. the sack; (*z miesz-*
kania) turn s.o. out on to the street

brukać ⟨-am⟩ lit. defile

brukiew f (-kwi; -kwie) swede

brukow|ać ⟨**wy-**⟩ ⟨-uję⟩ surface; ~**iec**
m (*nieregularny*) cobble(stone); (*czwo-*
rokątny) set(t); ~**y** paving; **prasa** ~**a**
gutter press

Bruksel|la f (-i; 0) Brussels; 2ka f (-i)
Brussels sprout(s *pl.*); 2ski Brussels

brulion m (-u; -y) notebook

brunatny ⟨**-no**⟩ dark brown

brunet m (-a; -ci) dark-haired man; ~ka
f (-i; G -tek) brunette

brusznica f (-y; -e) *bot.* cowberry

brutal m (-a; -e, -i/-ów) brute, brutal
person; ~**ność** f (-ści; 0) brutality; ~**ny**
brutal

brutto (*idkl.*) gross

bruzda f (-y) (*zwł. w ziemi*) furrow;
groove

bruździć ⟨-żdżę; -isz⟩ furrow; *fig.* make
difficulties (**w** I in), put obstacles in
s.o.'s way

brwi → **brew**; ~**owy** brow

bryczesy *pl.* (-ów) (riding) breeches *pl.*

brydż m (-a; 0) bridge

brygada f (-y) *mil.* brigade; (*pracowni-*
ków work) team

brygadzist|a m (-y; -ści) foreman; ~**ka**
f (-i; G -tek) forewoman

bryk F m (-a; -i) crib

brykać ⟨-am⟩ romp about

brykiet m (-u; -y) briquette

bryknąć *pf* (-nę) F (*zwiać*) scram;
scarper

brylant m (-u; -y) diamond

brył|a f (-y) (*ziemi itp.*) lump, clod; ~**ka** f
(-i) (*złota itp.*) nugget

brył(k)owaty lumpy

bryndza f (-y; -e) sheep's cheese

brytan m (-a; -y) mastiff

Brytania f (-ii; 0) Britain; **Wielka** ~
Great Britain

brytfanna f (-y) baking pan

Brytyj|czyk m (-a; -ycy) Briton; ~**czycy**
pl. the British *pl.*; ~**ka** f (-i; G -jek)
Briton; 2ski British

bryza f (-y) breeze

bryz|g m (-u; -i) splash; ~**gać** ⟨-am⟩
⟨~**nąć**⟩ ⟨-nę⟩ splash, splatter

bryzol m (-u; -e, -i/-ów) *gastr.* (fried)
piece of loin

brzask m (-u; -i) dawn; **o** ~**u, z** ~**iem** at
dawn

brzdąc m (-a; -e) *Brt.* nipper, kid

brzdą|kać, ~**ękać** ⟨-am⟩ *v/t.* melodię
plunk out; *v/i.* strum (**na gitarze** on
the guitar); ~**ąkanie, ~ękanie** n (-a)
plunking

brzeg m (-u; -i) edge; (*naczynia itp.*)
rim; (*rzeki itp.*) bank; (*morza*) coast;
na ~**u** *fig.* on the verge; **po** ~**i** (*naczy-*
nie) brimful; (*sala itp.*) chock-full; **nad**
~**iem morza** by the sea; **wystąpić**
z ~**ów** overflow

brzemienny pregnant; ~ **w skutki** fate-
ful

brzemię n (-enia; -iona) burden (*też fig.*)

B

brzezina f (-y) (drewno) birch(wood); (zagajnik) birch grove

brzeżek m (-żka; -żki) edge, rim

brzę|czeć ⟨za-⟩ (-ę, -y) mucha, dzwonek: buzz; szkło, szyba: ring; naczynia: clink; ~czyk m (-a; -i) buzzer; ~k m (-u; -i) buzz; ringing; clinking

brzmie|ć (-ę; -mij!) sound; słowa itp.: read; ~nie n (-a) sound

brzoskwinia f (-i; -e) bot. peach

brzoz|a f (-y) bot. birch; ~owy birch

brzuch m (-a; -y) stomach, F belly; na ~u on one's stomach; taniec ~a belly dance; ~acz F m (-a; -e) potbelly, F fatso; ~aty potbellied; (dzbanek) bulbous

brzuchomów|ca m (-y;-y), ~czyni f (-yni; -ynie) ventriloquist

brzuszny belly; ból itp. abdominal; dur ~ typhus

brzyd|actwo n (-a) fright, frump; ~al m (-a; -e) ugly man; ~ki (m-os -dsi) ugly; ~ko in an ugly way; ~nąć ⟨z-⟩ (-nę, -/-nął) become ugly; ~ota f (-y) ugliness; ~ula f (-i; -e) ugly woman

brzydzić się (-dzę) (I) find s.th. repulsive

brzydziej adv. comp. od → brzydki

brzytwa f (-y; G -tew) razor

bubek m (-bka, -bki) pej. (modniś) dandy; (głupek) Am. jerk, Brt. twit

buble F m/pl. (-i) trash sg., inferior merchandise sg.

buchać (-am) v/i. płomieniem, dym: belch (out); krew, woda: gush; v/t. smrodem, zapachem: give off; ~ żarem → buchnąć

buchalteria f (GDL -ii; -e) accountancy

buchnąć v/s. (-nę) v/i. → buchać; v/t. F pilfer, snitch

buci|k m (-a; -i) shoe; ~or m (-a; -y) heavy shoe lub boot

bucze|ć (-ę) syrena: sound; dziecko: blubber; ~k m (-czka; -czki) siren; buzzer

buczyna f (-y; 0) (drewno) beech(wood), (drzewa) beech wood

buda f (-y) shed; (na targu) booth, stall; mot. canvas cover; F (szkoła) school; psia ~ kennel

Budapeszt m (-u; 0) Budapest

buddyjski Buddhist

budka f (-i; G -dek) kiosk; small shed;

(schronienie) shelter; tel. (tele)phone booth, Brt. (tele)phone box

budow|a f (-y) building; (czynność) construction; plac/teren ~y construction/building site; ~ać ⟨po-, wy-, z-⟩ (-uję) build; fig. construct, create; ~ać ⟨po-⟩ się be under construction; (dla siebie) be building a house for o.s.; ~la f (-i; -e) building, structure; ~lany 1. building, construction; 2. m/zbior.: ~lani pl. construction workers; pl.; ~nictwo n (-a; 0) building and construction industry; ~nictwo mieszkaniowe housing construction; ~niczy m (-ego; -czowie) builder

budu|jący edifying; ~lec m (-lca; 0) building material(s pl.)

budynek m (-nku; -nki) building, house; ~ mieszkalny dwelling house

budyń m (-nia; -nie, -ni/-niów) pudding

budzi|ć ⟨o-, z-⟩ (-dzę) wake; fig. ⟨o-, roz-⟩ arouse; ~ć ⟨o-, roz-⟩ się wake up; ~k m (-a; -i) alarm clock

budżet m (-u; -y) budget; ~owy budget, budgetary

bufet m (-u; -y) buffet; (na dworcu itp.) (station) bar; zimny ~ cold buffet

bufiasty (rękaw itp.) puff

bufonada f (-y) bragging

bufor m (-u-/-a; -y) buffer; ~owy buffer

buhaj m (-a; -e, -ów) breeding bull

buja|ć (-am) v/i. fly, hover (też fig.); (wędrować) romp about (po L in); ⟨z-⟩ (kłamać) fib, tell fibs; v/t. ⟨po-⟩ rock (się v/t.); ~k m (-a; -i) rocking-chair

bujda f (-y) (kłamstwo) fib; (oszustwo) humbug

bujn|y roślinność luxuriant; włosy thick; życie eventful; ~a fantazja lively imagination

buk m (-a/-u; -i) bot. beech

bukiet m (-u; -y) (kwiaty) bunch, (oficjalny) bouquet; (aromat) bouquet

bukiew f (-kwi; 0) beech-nut(s)

bukinista m (-y; -ści, -stów) secondhand bookseller

bukmacher m (-a; -rzy) bookmaker, F bookie

bukowy beech

buksować (-uję) v/i. koło: spin

bukszpan m (-u; -y) box(-tree)

bulaj m (-a/-u; -e) naut. (circular) porthole

buldog m (-a; -i) bulldog

buldożer m (-a; -y) bulldozer

bulgotać (-czę/-ocę) *strumień itp.*: gurgle; (*w czajniku*) bubble

bulić F ⟨**wy-**⟩ (-lę) cough up

bulion m (-u; -y) stock; (*zupa*) broth; ~ **w kostkach** stock cube(s *pl.*)

bulwa f (-y) tuber

bulwar m (-u; -y) boulevard; ~**owy** boulevard; *prasa itp.* gutter

bulwersować ⟨**z-**⟩ (-uję) shock

bulwiasty bulbous

buława f (-y): ~ **marszałkowska** marshal's baton (*też fig.*)

bułeczka f (-i; G -czek) → **bułka**

Bułgar m (-a; -rzy) Bulgarian; ~**ia** f (-ii; 0) Bulgaria; ~**ka** f (-i; G- rek) Bulgarian; ⊇**ski** Bulgarian; **mówić po** ⊇**sku** speak Bulgarian

bułka f (-i; G -łek) (bread) roll

bumel|anctwo n (-a; 0) dawdling; ~**ować** (-uję) dawdle

bumerang m (-u; -i) boomerang

bunkier m (-kra; -kry) *mil.* bunker; (*dla cywilów*) shelter; ~**przeciwlotniczy** air-raid shelter

bunt m (-u; -y) revolt, rebellion (*też fig.*); (*na statku*) mutiny

buntow|ać ⟨**pod-, z-**⟩ (-uję) incite to rebel; ~**ać** ⟨**z-**⟩ **się** rebel *lub* revolt; ~**niczo** rebelliously; ~**niczy** rebellious; ~**nik** m (-a; -cy) rebel

buńczuczny cheeky, impertinent

bura f (-y) bawling-out

bura|czany beet(root); ~**czki** m/pl. (-ów) boiled beetroots; ~**k** m (-a; -i) beet; (*ćwikłowy*) beetroot

burczeć (-czę) mumble, mutter; *żołądek*: rumble

burda f (-y) row

burdel m (-u; -e, G -i) F brothel; *fig.* (*bałagan*) mess

burgund m (-a; -y) burgundy

burkliwy sullen, sulky

burmistrz m (-a; -e) mayor

buro adv. → **bury**

bursztyn m (-u; -y) amber; ~**owy** amber

burt|a f *naut.*: **lewa** ~**a** port; **prawa** ~**a** starboard; **wyrzucić za** ~**ę** throw overboard

bury (**-ro**) mousy

burz|a f (-y; -e) storm (*też fig.*); (*z piorunami*) thunderstorm; ~**liwie** *fig.* tempestuously; ~**liwy** stormy; *fig.* tempes-

tuous; ~**yć** (-ę) ⟨**z-**⟩ destroy; *dom, mur, też* pull down; ⟨**wz-**⟩ **wodę** churn up; ~**yć** ⟨**z-**⟩ **się** seethe, churn

burżuaz|ja f (-i; 0) bourgeoisie; ~**yjny** bourgeois

burżuj m (-a; -e) bourgeois

busola f (-i; -e) compass

buszować (-uję) rummage (**po** L through, around)

but m (-a; -y) shoe; (*z cholewką*) boot; **takie** ~ **y** that's the way things stand; **głupi jak** ~ as thick as two short planks

butan m (-u; 0) → **propan**

butelk|a f (-i) bottle; ~**a od wina, po winie** wine bottle; ~**a wina** bottle of wine; ~**owy** bottle; **piwo** ~**owe** bottled beer

butik m (-u; -i) boutique

butla f (-i; -e) large bottle; (*na wino*) flask; ~ **tlenowa** oxygen cylinder

butny overbearing; imperious

butonierka f (-i; G -rek) buttonhole

butwieć ⟨**z-**⟩ (-eję) rot, decay

buzia F f (-i; -e, -zi/-i) face; (*usta*) mouth; ~**k** m (-a; -i) (*całus*) little kiss, F peck

by 1. *cj.* (in order) to, in order that; **2.** *part.*: (*trybu warunkowego*) **napisałbym to** I would write it

by|cie n (-a; 0): **sposób** ~**cia** manner

bycz|ek m (-czka; -czki) bull-calf; ~**y** bull's; F (*fajny*) great, terrific; ~**y chłop** F hell of a guy

być be; (*istnieć też*) exist; ~ **może** perhaps, maybe; **nie może** ~**!** this cannot be!; **bądź zdrów!** farewell!; **będę pamiętał** I will remember; **był naprawiony ...** it has been repaired; **było już późno** it was already late; **niech i tak będzie** let it be so; F if you like; **co z nim będzie?** what will happen with him?; **jest mu zimno** he is cold; → **jest, są**

bydlę n (-ęcia; -ęta) cow, bull, calf; ~**ta** *pl.* cattle *pl.*; (*człowiek*) beast, animal; ~**cy** cattle; *fig.* animal, savage

bydło n (-a; 0) *zbior.* cattle *pl.*

byk m (-a; -i) bull; ⊇ *znak Zodiaku:* Taurus; **on(a) jest spod znaku** ⊇**a** he/she is (a) Taurus; F (*gafa*) goof; **strzelić** ~**a** *Brt. sl.* boob; *Am. sl.* make a boo-boo

byle *adv.* any-; ~ **co** anything; ~ **gdzie**

anywhere; **~ jak** anyhow; **~ jaki** any; (*lichy*) shoddy; **~ kto** anybody, anyone; **~by** *cj.* in order to, in order that

byli → **być, były**

bylina *f* (-*y*) *bot.* herbaceous perennial

były (*m-os byli*) former; ex-; *mój ~ my* ex; → *być*

bynajmniej (**nie**) not at all, not in the least; **~!** not in the slightest!

bystr|ość *f* (-*ści; 0*) rapidity; speed; **~ość umysłu** astuteness; **~y** *adj.* (*comp.* -*rzejszy*), **~o** *adv.* (*comp.* -*rzej*) *adv.* fast; *nurt itp.* swift; *człowiek, uczeń* bright, sharp

byt *m* (-*u*; -*y*) (*istnienie*) existence; (*istota*) being; **~ność** *f* (-*ści*; *0*) presence; (*odwiedziny*) stay; **~owy** social; **wa-**

runki ~owe living conditions, conditions of life

bywa|ć (-*am*) visit (*u kogoś s.o., w czymś s.th.*); *bywa*(, *że*) it happens (that); **~łczyni** *f* (-*ni*; -*nie, G* -*ń*), **~lec** *m* (-*lca*; -*lcy*) regular visitor, (*w sklepie itp.*) regular customer; **~ły** experienced

b.z. *skrót pisany: bez zmian* no changes; *med.* NAD (*no abnormality detected; no appreciable difference*)

bzdet F *m* (-*u*; -*y*) rubbish

bzdur|a *f* (-*y*) nonsense; **~ny** nonsensical, absurd

bzik F *m* (-*a*; *0*) fad; *mieć ~a* be mad about *s.th.*

bzów, bzu, bzy → *bez²*

bzykać (-*am*) hum, buzz

C

cack|ać się F (-*am*) fuss (*z I* over); **~o** *n* (-*a; G* -*cek*) *fig.* trinket, knick-knack

cal *m* (-*a*; -*e*, -*i*) inch; *w każdym ~u* every inch

calówka *f* (-*i*; *G* -*wek*) folding rule

całka *f* (-*i*; *G* -*łek*) *math.* integral; **~kiem** *adv.* quite, wholly, completely

całkow|icie entirely, completely; wholly; **~ity** complete; (*suma też*) total; whole; (*liczba*) integral; **~y: rachunek ~y** *math.* integral calculus

cało *adv.* (*niezraniony*) undamaged, unhurt

cało|dobowy round the clock, twenty--four-hour; **~dzienny** all-day; (*praca itp.*) full-time; **~kształt** *m* the whole; general picture; **~nocny** all-night; **~roczny** yearlong, all the year round; (*dochód*) full year's

całoś|ciowo completely, in an integrated way; **~ciowy** complete, integrated; **~ć** *f* (-*ści*) whole; completeness; *w ~ci* as a whole; entirely, in its entirety

całotygodniowy all-week, for the whole week

całować ⟨*po-*⟩ (-*uję*) kiss (*się też* each other)

całus *m* (-*a*; -*y*) kiss

cał|y *adj.* (*kompletny*) complete; (*zdrowy*) unhurt; → *cało*; *z ~ej siły* with full force; with all one's might;

~ymi godzinami for hours

camping → *kemping*

Cambridge (*idkl.*) Cambridge

cap *m* (-*a*; -*y*) *zo.* (billy)goat

capnąć *pf.* (-*nę*) F grab; (*aresztować*) nab

capstrzyk *m* (-*a*; -*i*) tattoo

car *m* (-*a*; -*owie*) tsar; **~owa** → *caryca*; **~ski** tsar; **~yca** *f* (-*y*; -*e*) tsarina

casco *n* (*idkl.*) vehicle insurance, *naut.* hull insurance

cążki *pl.* (-*ów*) clippers *pl.*, F clips *pl.*

CBOS *skrót pisany: Centrum Badania Opinii Społecznej* Public Opinion Research Centre

cdn., c.d.n. *skrót: ciąg dalszy nastąpi* to be continued

ceb|er *m* (-*bra*; -*bry*) tub; *leje jak z ~ra* it's raining cats and dogs

cebul|a *f* (-*i*; -*e*) *bot.* onion; **~ka** *f* (-*i*; *G* -*lek*) *bot.* onion; (*tulipana itp.*) bulb; **~(k)owaty** bulbous, bulb-shaped; **~owy** onion; *wzór ~owy* onion pattern

cech *m* (-*u*; -*y*) guild, fraternity

cecha *f* (-*y*) feature; characteristic; (*znak*) mark; (*probiercza*) hallmark; **~ charakteru** characteristic

cechować (-*uję*) mark; label; *obrączkę itp.* hallmark; *przyrząd* standardize; **~ się** be marked (*I* by)

cedować ⟨*s-*⟩ (-*uję*) *jur.* cede

cedr *m* (*-u; -y*) cedar

cedu|ła *f* (*-y*) *fin.*: ~ **giełdowa** exchange list

cedz|ak *m* (*-a; -i*) colander, strainer; ~**ić** (*-dzę*) ⟨**prze-**⟩ strain; ⟨**wy-**⟩ *napój* sip; *słowa* drawl, mince

ceg|ielnia *f* (*-i; -e*) brickworks *sg.*; ~**iełka** *f* (*-i*) (small) brick; *fig.* contribution; ~**lasty** (*-to*) brick-red; ~**ła** *f* (*-y; G -gieł*) brick

cekaem *m* (*-u; -y*) machine gun

cel *m* (*-u; -e, -ów*) aim, goal; (*tarcza, obiekt, też fig.*) target; (*podróży*) destination; **bez ~u** aimlessly; **do ~u** to the target/aim; **u ~u** at the end; **na ten ~, w tym ~u** for this purpose; **w ~u** for the purpose of; **wziąć na ~** take aim; **mieć na ~u/za ~** aim at, aim to achieve; → **celem**

cela *f* (*-i; -e*) (**klasztorna, więzienna** monastery, prison) cell

celibat *m* (*-u; -0*) celibacy

celni|czka *f* (*-i; G -czek*), ~**k** *m* (*-a; -cy*) customs officer

celn|ość *f* (*-ści; 0*) (*strzału*) accuracy; (*uwagi itp.*) relevance, aptitude; ~**y**[1] *strzał, strzelec* accurate; *uwaga* relevant, apt

celny[2] customs; **opłata ~a** (customs) duty; **urząd ~y** customs office

celny[3] *proza* eminent, distinguished

celow|ać[1] ⟨**wy-**⟩ (*-uję*) aim (**do** *G* to, **w** *A* at)

celow|ać[2] (*-uję*) distinguish o.s. (**w** *L* in); ~**nik** *m* (*-a; -i*) backsight; *phot.* viewfinder; *gr.* dative; ~**nik lunetowy** telescopic sight; ~**ość** *f* (*-ości; 0*) appropriateness; ~**o** appropriately, relevantly; ~**y** appropriate, relevant

celują|co excellent; ~**y** eminent, distinguished; (*ocena*) excellent

celuloza *f* (*-y; 0*) cellulose

cement *m* (*-u; -y*) cement; ~**ownia** *f* (*-i; -e*) cement plant; ~**owy** cement

cen|a *f* (*-y; -ów*) price; **po tej ~ie** at this price; **za wszelką ~ę** at any price; ~**ić** (*-ę*) *fig.* value; ~**nik** *m* (*-a; -i*) price list; ~**ny** valuable; ~**owy** price

centnar → **cetnar**

central|a *f* (*-i; -e*) head/central office; (*policji, partii*) headquarters *sg./pl.*; (*sterowania*) control room; *tel.* ~**a międzymiastowa** telephone exchange; (*w biurze itp.*) switchboard; ~**izacja** *f* (*-i; -e*) centralization; ~**ny** central

centrum *n* (*idkl.; -ra. -ów*) *Brt.* centre; *Am.* center; ~ **handlowe** shopping centre/center; ~ **obliczeniowe** computer centre/center

centymetr *m* *Brt.* centimetre, *Am.* centimeter; (*taśma*) (centimetre) measuring-tape

cenzur|a *f* (*-y*) censorship; ~**ować** (*-uję*) censor; object to

cep *m* (*-u-a; -y*) flail

cera[1] *f* (*-y; 0*) complexion

cera[2] *f* (*-y*) (*w tkaninie*) darn

cerami|czny ceramic; ~**ka** *f* (*-i*) ceramics *pl.*; pottery; ~**ka szlachetna** ceramic whiteware

cerata *f* (*-y*) oilcloth

ceregiel|le F *pl.* (*-i*) fuss; **bez ~i** without ceremony

cere'monia *f* (*GDL -ii; -e*) ceremony; F *pl.* fuss

cerkiew *f* (*-kwi; -kwie, -kwi*) (*wyznanie*) the Orthodox Church; (*budynek*) orthodox church; ~**ny** orthodox

cerować ⟨**za-**⟩ (*-uję*) darn

certować się (*-uję*) make a fuss (**z** *I* about)

certyfikat *m* (*-u; -y*) certificate; ~ **pochodzenia** certificate of birth

cesa|rski imperial; ~**rstwo** *n* (*-a; G -*) empire; ~**rz** *m* (*-a; -e/-owie*) emperor; ~**rzowa** *f* (*-wej, -wo!; -we*) empress

cesja *f* (*-i; -e*) *jur.* cession

cetnar *m* (*-a; -y*) centner; metric hundredweight

cewka *f* (*-i; G -wek*) *tech.* coil; *anat.* ~ **moczowa** urethra; *electr.* ~ **zapłonowa** spark coil

cez *m* (*-u; 0*) *chem.* caesium

cęgi *pl.* (*-ów*) pliers *pl.*, pincers *pl.*

cętk|a *f* (*-i; G -tek*) dot, (*większa*) spot; ~**owany** mottled; speckled

chaber *m* (*-bra; -bry*) *bot.* cornflower

chadec|ja *f* (*-i; -e*) Christian Democratic Party, Christian Democratics; ~**ki** Christian Democratic

chała *f* (*-y*) *fig.* trash

chałka *f* (*-i; G -łek*) F (*bułka*) plait

chałupa *f* (*-y*) hut; (*biedna*) shack; (*z drewna*) (log) cabin

chałupni|ctwo *n* (*-a; 0*) outwork, home work; ~**czka** *f* (*-i; G -czek*), ~**k** *m* (*-a; -cy*) outworker, home worker

cham *m* (*-a; -y*) lout, boor; ~**ka** *f* (*-i*)

loutish woman; ~ski loutish

chao|s m (-u; 0) chaos; ~tyczny chaotic

charakte|r m (-u; y): ~r pisma handwriting; bez ~ru unprincipled; (miasto itp.) characterless; w ~rze gościa as a guest; ~rystyczny characteristic (dla G of); ~'rystyka f (-i) characterization; ~ryzacja f (-i) theat. make-up; ~ryzator m (-a; -rzy), -rka f (-i) make-up artist

charakteryzować (-uję) ⟨s-⟩ characterize; ~ ⟨s-⟩ się be characterized by (I); ⟨u-⟩ make up; ~ się put make-up

char|czeć (-czę, -y) rasp; ~kać (-am) ⟨~knąć⟩ spew

charkot m (-u; -y) rattle; med. stertor

chart m (-a; -y) zo. greyhound; ~ afgański Afghan hound

charter m (-u; -y) charter; ~owy charter(ed)

charytatywny charitable

chaszcze pl. (-y/-ów) thicket, (w lesie) dense undergrowth

chata f (-y) → chałupa

chcieć ⟨ze-⟩ want; (nie) chce mi się czegoś zrobić I (don't) feel like doing s.th.; nie chce mi się też I can't be bothered; chciał(a)bym I would like

chciw|ie adv. ~iec m (-wca; -wcy) miser, niggard; ~ość f (-ści; 0) greed, avarice; ~y greedy, avaricious; ~y wiedzy eager for knowledge; dziecko eager to learn

chełbia f (-i; -e) aurelia

chełp|ić się (-ię, -e) boast, brag (I about); ~liwość f (-ści; 0) boastfulness; ~liwie boastfully; ~liwy boastful

chemi|a f (GDL -ii; 0) chemistry; ~czka f (-i) chemist; ~czny chemical; ołówek ~czny indelible pencil; ~k m (-a; -cy) chemist

cherlawy frail, sickly

cherubinek m (-a; -i) putto; (dziecko) cherub

chę|ć f (-i) desire; (zamiar) intention; mieć ~ć feel like (do zrobienia doing, na coś s.th.); dobre ~ci goodwill; z mi-łą ~cią with pleasure

chęt|ka f (-i; E -tek) desire; mieć ~kę F be really keen (na A on); ~nie adv. willingly; ~ny willing; on jest ~ny do nauki he is an eager student

chichot m (-u; -y) giggle; ~ać (-czę/-oczę) giggle

Chil|e n (idkl.) Chile; ~ijczyk m (-a; -ycy), ~ijka f (-i) Chilean; 2ijski Chilean

chimer|a f (-y) fig. chimera, illusion; ~y pl. moods pl.

chinina f (-y; 0) quinine

Chin|ka f (-i; G -nek) Chinese; ~y pl. (G -) China

Chiń|czyk m (-a; -cy) Chinese; 2ski 1. Chinese; mówić po 2sku speak Chinese; 2. m (-ego) Chinese (language); 2szczyzna f (-y; 0) Chinese; fig. double Dutch

chiromancja f (-i; 0) palmistry

chirurg m (-a; -dzy/-owie) surgeon; ~ia (GDL -ii; 0) surgery; ~iczny surgical

chlać ⟨-am/-eję⟩ F booze

chlap|a f (-y) slush; (pogoda) slushy weather; ~ać (-ię) v/i. splash (po L about); v/t. ⟨też ~nąć⟩ (-nę) splay; głupstwo itp. babble

chlas|tać (-am-szczę) v/i. deszcz: beat; v/t. ⟨też ~nąć⟩ whip

chleb m (-a, -y) bread (też fig.); ~ z ma-słem bread and butter; zarabiać na ~ earn one's daily bread; ~odawca m (-y) employer; ~owy bread

chlew m (-a/-u; -y) pigsty; ~ny: trzoda ~na zbior pigs pl., swine pl.

chlipać (-pię) sob, whimper

chlor m (-u; 0) chlorine; ~ek m (-rku; -rki): ~ek (bielący) bleaching powder; tech. chloride of lime; ~owodór m hydrogen chloride; ~owy chloric

chlub|a f (-y; 0) fame, esteem; (pl. -y) pride; ~ić się pride o.s. (I on); ~ny glorious; (świadectwo) outstanding, excellent

chlup|ać (-ię) v/i. splash; rzeka itp.: bubble, gurgle; ~ać się splash about; ~nąć do v/s. (-nę) splash into

chlus|tać (-am) ⟨~nąć⟩ gush, spurt; → chlastać, chlupnąć

chłam F m (-u; 0) trash, rubbish

chłeptać (-czę/-cę) kot: lap

chłod|ek m (-dku; -dki) cool, coolness; ~nia f (-i; -e) refrigerator, cool store; wagon ~nia refrigerator car lub Brt. wagon; ~nica f (-y; -e) mot. radiator; ~niczy refrigeration; ~nieć ⟨po-⟩ (-eję) get colder; ~nik m (-a; -i) (cold beetroot soup); ~no coldly; jest ~no it is cold; ~ny cold (też fig)

chłodz|iarka refrigerator, F fridge; ~ić

⟨o-⟩ (-dzę) cool (down); ~ić ⟨o-⟩ się cool; ~ony wodą water-cooled

chłoną|ć ⟨w-⟩ (-nę) absorb; ~ka f (-i) →*limfa*; ~ny absorptive, absorbent; *fig.* receptive, responsive; **węzeł ~ny** *anat.* lymphatic node

chłop m (-a, -u; -i) peasant; F (pl. -y) guy, chap; ~ak m (-a; -cy/-i) boy; ~czyk m (-a; -i) (young) boy

chłopiec m (-pca, -pcy) → **chłopak**; (*adorator*) boyfriend; ~ **do wszystkie-go**, ~ **na posyłki** errand boy

chłop|ięco boyishly; ~ięcy boyish; *odzież itp.* boy's(); ~ka f (-i; G -pek) peasant woman; ~ski peasant; **po ~sku** in a peasant way; ~stwo n (-a; 0) *zbior.* peasantry

chłost|a f (-y) whipping, lashing; **kara ~y** corporal punishment; ~ać (-szczę) whip, lash; *fig.* castigate

chłód m (-odu; -ody) cold; chill

chmara f (-y) (*owadów*) swarm; (*ludzi*) crowd

chmiel m (-u; 0) *bot.* hop; (*kwiatostan*) hops *pl.*

chmur|a f (-y), ~ka f (-i; G -rek) cloud; ~nie with clouds; *fig.* sullenly, gloomily; ~ny cloudy; *fig.* sullen, gloomy

chmurzyć (-ę) ⟨na-⟩ *czoło* frown; *brwi* knit; ~ się cloud over; *fig.* darken

chochla f (-i; -e, -i/-chel) soup-ladle

chochlik m (-a; -i) brownie, sprite

cho|ciaż, ~ć *cj.* although; though; → ~ćby 1. *cj.* even if; 2. *part.* at least

chod|ak m (-a; -i) clog; ~nik m (-a; -i) *Brt.* pavement, *Am.* sidewalk; (*dywan*) (long narrow) carpet; (*w kopalni*) gallery, gangway; ~y *pl* → **chód**

chodzić (-dzę) walk, go; *pociąg*: run; *maszyna*: work, run; look after (**koło czegoś** s.th.); ~ **do szkoły** go to school; ~ **o lasce** walk with a stick; ~ **o kulach** go about on crutches; ~ **w sukni** wear a dress; **chodzi o ...** it is about ...; **nie chodzi o ...** the point is not that ...; **o co chodzi?** what is the matter?; **o ile o mnie chodzi** as far as I am concerned; ~ **z** (*narzeczonym itp.*) go out with, go steady

choink|a f (-i; -nek) Christmas tree; (*za-bawa*) Christmas party; **dostać pod ~ę** to get as a Christmas present; ~owy: **zabawki** f/pl. ~owe Christmas-tree ornaments

cholera f (-y; 0) *med.* cholera; F ~**!** damn!

cholerny F damned

cholesterol m (-u; -e) cholesterol

cholewa f (-y) boot-leg; **buty** m/pl. **z ~mi** high boots

chomąto n (-a) (horse-)collar

chomik m (-a; -i) *zo.* hamster

chorą|giew f (-gwi; -gwie) flag, banner; *hist.* cavalry company; (*harcerzy*) troop; ~giewka f (-i; -wek) (little) flag; ~giew-ka na dachu (weather-)vane; ~ży m (-ego; -owie) standard-bearer, ensign

choro|ba f (-y) disease, illness; ~ba morska seasickness; ~ba zawodowa occupational disease; ~ba Heinego--Medina poliomyelitis, polio; ~ba! damn!, shit!; ~bliwie morbidly (*też fig.*); ~bliwy morbid (*też fig.*); ~botwórczy pathogenic; ~bowy 1. *adj.* disease; 2. ~bowe n F (-ego; -owe) sickness benefit; ~wać (-uję) be ill, *Am.* be sick; (*na A*) suffer (from); ~**wać na serce** have a heart condition

chorowity sickly

Chorwa|cja f (-i; 0) Croatia; 2cki Croatian; **mówić po 2cku** speak Croatian; ~t m (-a; -ci), ~tka f (-i) Croatian

chor|y 1. ill, sick; *organ itp.* bad, diseased; *fig.* sick, ailing; ~**y na wątro-bę** suffering from a liver complaint; ~**y umysłowo** mentally ill; 2. m (-ego, -rzy), ~a f (-ej; -e) patient; sick person

chować (-am) ⟨s-⟩ (*ukrywać*) hide (*też się*); conceal; → **wkładać**; ⟨po-⟩ bury; ⟨wy-⟩ bring up; *impf* (*hodować*) raise; **zdrowo się** ~ flourish, prosper

chowan|y m (-ego; 0) *podwozie itp.* retractable; **bawić się w ~ego** play hide and seek

chód m (-odu; -ody) walk, gait; (*chód sportowy*) walking; F **mieć chody** have connections

chór m (-u; -y) choir, (*w operze itp.*) chorus; ~em *adv.* in chorus

chórzyst|a m (-y; -ści, -stów), ~ka f (-i; G -tek) member of the choir/chorus

chów m (-owu; 0) breeding, raising

chrabąszcz m (-a; -e) *zo.* cockchafer; ~ **majowy** May beetle, May bug

chrapać (-pię) snore; → **charczeć**

chrapliwy hoarse

chrapy f/pl. (-/ów) nostrils

chrobotać (-czę/-cę) *v/i.* grate, scratch

chrobry brave, heroic

chrom *m* (-*u*; *0*) *chem.* chromium; ~**owy** chromium

chroniczny chronic

chronić (-*ę*) ⟨*u*-⟩ protect (**się** o.s., **od** *G* from, **przed** *I* against); ~ ⟨**s**-⟩ **się** take shelter (**przed** *I* against)

chroniony protected

chronometraż *m* timekeeping

chrop|awo roughly; *głos* hoarsely; ~**awy** rough; *głos* hoarse; ~**owato** roughly; *głos* hoarsely; ~**owaty** rough; *głos* hoarse

chrup|ać ⟨**s**-⟩ (-*ię*) crunch; ~**ki** crunchy; ~**ki chleb** crispbread

chrust *m* (-*u*; *0*) brushwood

chryja F *f* (-*yi*; -*e*) trouble

chryp|a *f* (-*y*; -*pek*), ~**ka** *f* (-*i*; *G* -*pek*) hoarseness; huskiness; ~**liwie** hoarsely, huskily; ~**liwy** hoarse, husky; ~**nąć** ⟨*o*-⟩ get *lub* become hoarse

Chrystus *m* (-*a*, -*sie*/**Chryste!**; *0*) Christ; **przed ~em, przed narodzeniem ~a** before Christ (**skrót:** BC)

chrzan *m* (-*u*; *0*) horse-radish

chrząk|ać (-*am*) ⟨~**nąć**⟩ clear one's throat; *zwł. zwierzęta:* grunt; ~**anie** *n* (-*a*), ~**nięcie** *n* (-*a*) grunting

chrząstka *f* (-*i*; *G* -*tek*) *anat.* cartilage; (*w jedzeniu*) gristle

chrząszcz *m* (-*a*, -*e*) *zo.* beetle

chrzcić ⟨*o*-⟩ (-*czę*) *rel.* christen, baptize

chrzcielnica *f* (-*y*; -*e*) *rel.* font

chrzciny *pl.* (*chrzcin*) *rel.* christening, baptism

chrzest *m* (*chrztu*; *chrzty*) baptism; ~**ny 1.** baptismal; **2.** *m* (-*ego*, -*i*) godparent; (*mężczyzna*) godfather; ~**na** *f* (-*ej*; -*e*) godmother; *rodzice m/pl.* ~**ni** godparents *pl.*; ~**ny syn** *f* godson; ~**na córka** *f* goddaughter

chrześcijan|in *m* (-*a*; -*anie*, -), ~**ka** *f* (-*i*; *G* -*nek*) Christian

chrześcijańs|ki Christian; **po ~ku** in a Christian way, like a Christian; ~**two** *n* (-*a*; *0*) Christianity

chrześni|czka *f* (-*i*; *G* -*czek*), ~**k** *m* (-*a*; -*cy*) godchild

chrzę|st *m* (-*u*; -*y*) crunching; scraping, grating; ~**ścić** (-*szczę*) rustle; crunch; scrape, grate

chuch|ać (-*am*) ⟨~**nąć**⟩ (-*nę*) breathe, blow; ~**ać na** (A) breathe on

chu|derlawy slight; ~**dnąć** ⟨**s**-⟩ (-*nę*, -*dł*) become thin, lose weight; (*celowo*)

slim; ~**dość** *f* (-*ści*; *0*) thinness; ~**dy** thin; *fig. Brt.* meagre, *Am.* meager; *mięso itp.* lean; ~**dzielec** F *m* (-*lca*; -*lcy*; -*lce*) bag of bones

chuligan *m* (-*a*; -*i*) hooligan

chuligaństwo *n* (-*a*) hooliganism

chust|a *f* (-*y*) shawl; ~**eczka** *f* (-*i*; *G* -*czek*) handkerchief, F hanky; ~**eczka higieniczna** tissue, Kleenex TM; → ~**ka** *f* (-*i*; *G* -*tek*): ~**ka do nosa** handkerchief; ~**ka na głowę** headscarf

chwa|lebny praiseworthy; laudable; ~**lić** ⟨*po*-⟩ (-*lę*) praise; laud; ~**lić** ⟨*po*-⟩ **się** (*I*) boast (about), brag (about); ~**ła** *f* (-*y*; *0*) glory; ~**ła Bogu** thank goodness

chwast *m* (-*u*; -*y*) (*zielsko*) weed

chwiać (-*eję*) rock; sway; ~ **się** sway; (*jak pijany*) totter; *ząb:* be loose

chwiej|ność *f* (-*ści*; *0*) instability; *fig.* inconstancy, fickleness; ~**y** instable; *fig.* inconstant, fickle

chwil|a *f* (-*i*; -*e*) moment, instant; while; ~**e** *pl. też* time; ~**a wytchnienia** breathing space; ~**ami** from time to time, occasionally; **co ~a** all the time; **lada ~a** any moment; **na ~ę** for a moment; **od tej ~i** from this moment, from now on; **po ~i** after a while; **przed ~ą** a minute ago; **przez ~ę** for a moment or so; **w danej ~i** in this very moment; **w tej ~i** instantly; immediately; at once; **za ~ę** in a minute; in a short while; **z ~ą** the moment

chwilow|o momentarily; temporarily; ~**y** momentary; temporary; short-lived

chwy|cić *pf* (-*cę*) → **chwytać**; ~**t** *m* (-*u*; -*y*) hold; grip, grasp; → **uchwyt**; ~**tać** (-*am*) *v/t.* grasp, grip (**za** *A*); take hold (**za** *A* of); *piłkę itp.* catch; *żal, gniew* seize; ~**tać powietrze** gasp for breath *lub* air; ~**tać za pióro** take up one's pen; *mróz* ~**ta** it is freezing; ~**tać się** catch; ~**tać się za głowę** throw up one's hands in despair

chyba 1. *part.* maybe, probably; **2.** *cj.*: ~ **że** unless; ~ **nie** hardly

chybi|ać (-*am*) ⟨~**ć**⟩ (-*ę*) miss (*celu* the target); **na ~ł trafił** at random; ~**ony** missed; *fig.* ineffective

chylić ⟨*po*-, **s**-⟩ (-*lę*) (**się**) lean, bend

chyłkiem *adv.* furtively; surreptitiously

chytro *adv.* → **chytry**; ~**ść** *f* (-*ści*) shrewdness, cunning

chytry clever, shrewd, cunning; → **chcIwy**

chytrzej(szy) *adv. (adj.), comp. od* → **chytro, chytry**

ci *m-os* → **ten**

ciałko *n (-a; G -łek) biol.* corpuscle; **czerwone ~ krwi** erythrocyte; **białe ~ krwi** leucocyte

ciało *n (-a) body (też fig.); (tkanka)* flesh; *(zwłoki)* corpse; **~o pedagogiczne** teachers, teaching staff; **spaść z ~a** F waste away; → **boży**

ciarki *f/pl. (-rek)* creeps; **przeszły mnie ~** cold shivers ran down my spine

ciasn|ota *f (-y; 0)* lack of space; *fig.* narrow-mindedness; **~o** tightly; narrowly; **~y** **ubranie** tight, close-fitting; *pomieszczenie* cramped, restricted; narrow *(też fig.)*

ciast|ko *n (-a; G -tek)* cake; *(suche) Brt.* biscuit, *Am.* cookie; *(nadziewane)* tartlet; **~o** *n (-a, L cieście; -a)* cake; *(do nadziewania)* pastry; **~o francuskie** puff pastry

ciaśniej(szy) *adv. (adj.) comp. od* → **ciasno, ciasny**

ciąć ⟨**ś-**⟩ *v/t.* cut; *impf. drzewa* fell; *(piłą)* saw; *v/i. deszcz, wiatr* lash; ⟨**po-**⟩ *komary:* sting

ciąg *m (-u; -i)* pull, *tech.* traction; **~ powietrza** draught; **~ uliczny** street; *(czasu)* course; **~ dalszy** continuation; *(odcinek)* instalment; **w ~u** *(G) (za)* within, in; *(w trakcie)* in the course *(of);* **w dalszym ~u** still; **~le** *adv.* constantly, permanently; continuously; **~łość** *f (-ści; 0)* continuity; **~ły** continuous, constant; → **stały, ustawiczny**; **~nąć** *(-nę)* pull *(też za A* at, *do G* to); *(wlec) drag; samochód itp.* tow; → **pociągać**; *v/t.* pull; **~nąć dalej** continue, go on; *tu ~nie* there is a draught here; **~nąć się** drag, *(w czasie)* go on and on; **~nienie** *n (-a) (loterii)* draw; *tech.* drawing; **~nik** *m (-a; -i)* tractor

ciąż|a *f (-y)* pregnancy; **być w ~y** be pregnant; **zajść w ~ę** become pregnant; **~enie** *n (-a; 0)* gravity; **~yć** *(-ę)* be a burden; weigh heavily *(na L* on); tend *(ku D* towards)

cichaczem *adv.* secretly, in secret

cich|nąć ⟨**u-**⟩ *(-nę; też -ł)* fall silent; *(stopniowo)* die away; *wiatr:* die down; **~o** *(po -chu, z -cha)* silently, quietly;

bądź ~o! be quiet!; **~y** silent, quiet; *partner itp.* sleeping

ciebie *(GA →* **ty**) you; **u ~** with you, at your place

ciec → **cieknąć**

ciecz *f (-y; -e)* fluid

ciekaw|ić *(-ę)* interest; **~ie** *adv.* → **ciekawy**; **~ostka** *f (-i; G -tek) (przedmiot)* curio; *(fakt)* interesting fact; **~ość** *f (-ści; 0)* curiosity; **przez ~ość, z ~ości** out of curiosity; **~ie** curiously; interestingly, excitingly; **~y** curious (G of); interesting, exciting; **~(a) jestem, czy ...** I am keen to know whether...

ciek|ły fluid; **~nąć** *(-nę; też -ł)* flow; *rura itp.* leak; → **przeciekać**

cielesny *(-śnie)* bodily

cielę *n (-ęcia; -ęta)* calf; **~cina** *f (-y; 0)* veal; **~cy** *skóra itp.* calf; *mięso itp.* veal

cieliczka *f (-i; G -czek) (young)* heifer

cielić się ⟨**o- się**⟩ *(-lę)* calf

cielisty flesh-colo(u)red

ciem *G/pl.* → **ćma**

ciemię *n (-enia; -iona) anat.* top of one's head

ciemku: po ~ in the dark

ciemni|a *f (-i; -e)* darkroom; **~eć** ⟨**po-**⟩ *(-eję)* get dark; darken

ciemno → **ciemny**; **robi się ~** it is getting dark; **~blond** light brown; **~czerwony** dark red; **~granatowy** dark blue; **~skóry** dark-skinned

ciemność *f (-ści)* darkness

ciemn|o dark; **~y** dark; *pokój, zarys itp.* dim; *(zacofany)* outdated; antiquated

cieniej *adv. comp. od* → **cienko**

cienist|o *adv.* shadily; **~y** shady

cien|iutki *materiał itp.* gossamer-thin; *plasterek* paper-thin; **~ki** thin; *książka itp.* slim; *herbata itp.* weak; **~ko** thinly; **~kość** *f (-ści; 0)* thinness

cień *m (-niu; -nie)* shadow; *(miejsce zacienione)* shade

cieńszy → **cienki**

ciepl|arnia *f (-i; -e, -i/-ń)* greenhouse; **~eć** ⟨**po-**⟩ *(-eję)* get warm; **~ej(szy)** *adv. (adj.) comp. od* → **ciepło, ciepły**; **~ica** *f (-y; -e)* thermal spring; **~ny** heat; **ciep|ławo** tepidly; **~ławy** lukewarm, tepid

ciepło¹ *n (-a; 0)* warmth, heat

ciep|ło² *adv.* warm; **robi się ~ło** it is getting warm; **~łownia** *f (-i; -e)* heat-generating plant; **~ły** *adj.* warm *(też fig.)*

cierni|owy, ~sty thorny

cierń m (-nia; -nie, -ni) thorn, spine

cierpiący suffering (**na** A from)

cierpie|ć ⟨-ę, -i⟩ suffer; (**głód** hunger; **z powodu** G because of; **na** A from); (znosić) tolerate; put up with; **nie ~ć** (G) hate; ~nie n (-a) suffering

cierpk|i sour → **kwaśny**; ~o sourly → **kwaśny**

cierpliw|ość f (-ści; 0) patience; **u-zbroić się w ~ość** exercise one's patience; ~ie patiently; ~y patient

cierpn|ąć ⟨ś-⟩ (-nę; też -ł) (drętwieć) become numb, go to sleep; **aż skóra ~ie** so that a cold shiver runs down one's spine

ciesielski carpenter

cieszyć ⟨u-⟩ (-ę) please; ~ ⟨u-⟩ **się** be pleased (**z** G, **na** A with), take pleasure in, enjoy; ~ **zdrowiem** enjoy the best of health

cieśla m (-li; -le) carpenter

cieśnina f (-y) straits pl.; ♀ **Kaletańska** Strait of Dover

cietrzew m (-wia; -wie) black grouse

cię (A → **ty**) you; por. **ciebie**

cię|cie n (-a) cut; (też czynność) cutting; med. incision; (cios) blow; ~ciwa f (-y) (łuku) bow; math. chord

cięgi pl. (-ów) beating, hiding

cięty cut; fig. incisive; **uwaga** biting, cutting

ciężar m (-u; -y) weight; (też fig.) burden; **być ~em** be a burden (**dla** G on); **podnoszenie ~ów** weight-lifting; ~ek m (-rka; -rki) weight; ~na **1.** adj. pregnant; **2.** f (-nej; -ne) pregnant woman, expectant mother; ~owy (transport) zwł. Brt. goods, freight; (**w sporcie**) weightlifting

ciężarówka f (-i; G -wek) mot. Brt. lorry, Am. truck

cięż|ej adv. comp. od → **ciężko**; ~ki adj. heavy (też fig.); (trudny) difficult, hard; szok, sztorm itp. severe; **choroba** itp. serious

ciężko adv. heavily; (trudno) hard; ~**chory** seriously ill; ~ **ranny** badly wounded

ciężkość f (-ści; 0) weight; phys. gravity; **punkt/środek ~ci** Brt. centre (Am. center) of gravity; fig. main focus

ciocia f (-i; -e) aunt, F auntie

cios m (-u; -y) blow (też fig.); (pięścią) punch

ciosać ⟨o-⟩ (-am) hew

ciota f (-y) F queen, queer

cioteczn|y: **brat ~y, siostra ~a** cousin

ciotka f (-i; G -tek) aunt

cis m (-u/a; -y) yew(-tree)

ciskać (-am) fling, hurl; ~ **obelgi na** A hurl insults at

cisnąć[1] pf (-nę) → **ciskać**

cisną|ć[2] (-nę) press; **ubranie** pinch; ~**ć się** press, push (forward)

cisz|a f (-y; 0) silence; calm (też naut.); fig. quiet, calm; **proszę o ~ę!** silence, please!; ~ej adv. comp. od → **cicho**; ~kiem → **cichaczem**

ciśnienie n (-a) (**powietrza** air, **krwi** blood) pressure

ciuchy F m/pl. (-ów) togs pl., clobber

ciuciubabk|a f: **bawić się w ~ę** play blind man's buff

ciułać ⟨u-⟩ (-am) save up, salt away

ciupaga f (-i) alpenstock

ciurkiem: **płynąć ~** dribble, trickle

ciż m-os → **tenże**

ciżba f (-y) crowd, throng

ckliw|ie maudlinly; ~y maudlin, F tear-jerking; **robi mi się ~ie** I am getting sick → **mdły**

clić ⟨o-⟩ (-lę; clij!) pay duty on; clear (s.th. through) customs

cło n (cła; G ceł) duty; **wolny od cła** duty-free; **podlegający cłu** dutiable

cmenta|rny cemetery, graveyard; ~rz m (-a; -e) cemetery, (**przy kościele**) graveyard

cmentarzysko n (-a) (large) cemetery; ~ **starych samochodów** car dump

cmok|ać (-am) ⟨~nąć⟩ smack one's lips; (**całować**) smack; **fajkę, palec** suck

cnot|a f (-y) virtue; ~liwie virtuously; righteously; ~liwy virtuous; (**pełen cnót** też) righteous

c.o. skrót pisany: **centralne ogrzewanie** c.h. (central heating)

co pron. (G czego, D czemu, I czym; 0) what; (który) that; ~ **za** ... what (a)...; ~ **innego** something else; ~ **do** as to; ~ **do mnie** as for me; ~ **mu jest?** what is the matter with him?; ~ **to jest?** what is this?; **czego chcesz?** what do you want?; **w razie czego** if need be, if necessary; **czym mogę służyć?** what can I do for you?; ~ **gorsza** what is worse; **o czym** about what; **po czym** after which; (idkl.) ~ (**drugi**) **tydzień** every (second) week; ~ **krok** every step; → **czas, bądź**

codzien|nie adv. everyday; ~ny adj. everyday; gazeta daily; (nie świąteczny) everyday, workaday

cof|ać (-am) ⟨~nąć⟩ (-nę) rękę, wojska itp. pull back; samochód move back; reverse; back; zegar put back; słowo, obietnicę take back; zlecenie, zamówienie cancel, withdraw; ~ać ⟨~nąć⟩ się retreat, move back (**przed** I against)

co|godzinny hourly; ~kolwiek (G czego-, D czemu-, I czymkolwiek; 0) anything; (nieco) some, a little

cokół m (-ołu; -oły) plinth, pedestal

comber m (-bra; -bry) gastr. saddle

conocny nightly, every night

coraz more and more; ~ **cieplej** warmer and warmer; ~ **więcej** more and more; ~ **to** again and again

coroczny yearly, annual

coś pron. (G czegoś, D czemuś, I czymś; 0) something, anything; ~ **takiego!** would you believe it!; ~kolwiek → **cokolwiek**

cotygodniowy weekly

córka f (-i; G -rek) daughter

cóż pron. (G czegoż, D czemuż, I czymże; 0) well; **no i ~?** so what? ~ **dopiero** let alone

cuchnąć (-nę) stink

cucić ⟨o-⟩ (-cę) revive, bring round

cud m (-u; -a/-y, -ów) wonder; rel. miracle; ~**em** by a miracle; ~aczny → **dziwaczny**; ~ny pleasing; beautiful

cudo n (-a) marvel; ~twórca m, ~twórczyni f wonder-worker; ~wnie adv. → **cudem**; też ~**wny** wonderful; (piękny) exquisite, marvellous

cudzo|łóstwo n (-a; 0) adultery; ~ziemiec m (-mca; -mcy), ~ziemka f (-i; G -mek) foreigner; ~ziemski foreign; **po ~ziemsku, z ~ziemska** in a foreign way/manner

cudzy foreign; (nie mój) other people's; of others; (nieznany) strange; ~słów m (-owu; -owy, -owów) quotation marks pl., inverted commas pl.

cugle pl. (-i) reins pl.

cukier m (-kru; -kry) sugar; ~ek m (-rka; -rki) sweet, Am. candy; ~nia f (-i; -e, -i) cake-shop; (lokal) café; ~nica f (-y; -e, -i) sugar bowl; ~nik m (-a; -cy) confectioner, pastry cook

cu'kinia f (GDL -ii; -e) Brt. courgette; Am. zucchini

cukrownia f (-i; -e) sugar factory

cukrzyca f (-y; 0) diabetes

cukrzyć ⟨o-, po-⟩ (-ę) sugar

cumować (-uję) naut. moor

cwał m (-u; 0) gallop; ~**em, w ~** at a gallop; ~ować ⟨po-⟩ gallop

cwan|iaczka F f (-i; G -czek), ~iak F m (-a; -cy/-i) sly lub cunning person; ~y cunning, sly

cycek m (-cka, -cki) teat; **cycki** pl. pej. tits pl.

cyfr|a f (-y) digit, figure; ~owy digital

Cygan m (-a; -anie), ~ka f (-i; G -nek) Gypsy; 2ić F (-ę) cheat, fib

cygańs|ki: po ~ku Gypsy; (język) Romany

cygar|niczka f (-i; G -czek) cigarette-holder; ~o n (-a) cigar

cyjanek m (-nka; -nki) cyanide

cykać (-am) tick; świerszcz: chirp

cykata f (-y; 0) candied lemon-peel

cykl m (-u; -e) cycle

cyklamen m (-u; -y) cyclamen

cykliczny cyclic, periodic

cyklistówka f (-i; G -wek) baseball cap

cyklon m (-u; -y) cyclone, hurricane

cykuta f (-y) bot. hemlock

cylinder m (-dra; -dry) cylinder; (kapelusz) top hat

cymbał m (-a; -y) F fool; **cymbały** pl. dulcimer, (węgierskie) cimbalom

cyna f (-y; 0) chem. tin

cynaderki f/pl. (-rek) gastr. kidneys pl.

cynamon m (-u; 0) cinnamon; ~owy cinnamon

cynfolia f (GDL -ii; 0) tinfoil

cyniczny cynical

cynk m (-u; 0) zinc; F tip; ~ować ⟨o-⟩ (-uję) galvanize; ~owy zinc

cynować ⟨o-⟩ (-uję) tin, plate with tin

cypel m (-pla; -ple) headland, spit

Cypr m (-u) Cyprus; 2yjski Cyprus

cyprys m (-a; -y) cypress

cyrk m (-u; -i) circus (też fig.)

cyrkiel m (-kla; -kle) compasses pl.

cyrk|owiec m (-wca; -wce); ~ówka f (-i; G -wek) circus artist; ~owy circus

cyrkul|acja f (-i; -e) circulation; ~ować (-uję) circulate

cysterna f (-y) tank, cistern

cysterski Cistercian

cytadela f (-i; -e) citadel

cytat *m* (*-u*; *-y*), ~a *f* (*-y*) quotation, citation

cytować ⟨za-⟩ (*-uję*) quote

cyt|rusowe: owoce *m/pl.* ~owe citrus fruit; ~ryna *f* (*-y*) lemon; ~rynowy lemon

cyw. *skrót pisany:* cywilny civ. (*civil*)

cywil *m* (*-a; -e, -ów*): w ~u civilian; w ~u (*ubraniu*) in civilian clothes, F in mufti; (*w życiu*) F in civilian life; ~izacja *f* (*-i; -e*) civilisation; ~noprawny civil law, of civil law; ~ny civilian; civil; stan ~ny marital status; → urząd

cz. *skrót pisany:* część pt (*part*)

czad *m* (*-u; -y*) carbon monoxide; (*woń spalenizny*) smell of burning

czaić się ⟨przy-, za-się⟩ (*-ję*) lie in wait

czajnik *m* (*-a; -i*) kettle

czambuł *m*: w ~ wholesale, without exception

czap|eczka *f* (*-i; G -czek*) (little) cap; ~ka *f* (*-i; G -pek*) cap

czapla *f* (*-i; -e*) zo. heron

czaprak *m* (*-a; -i*) saddle-cloth

czar *m* (*-u; -y*) magic; (*oczarowanie*) magic spell; (*urok*) charm; ~y *pl.* magic

czarno *adv.*: na ~ black; → biały; ~-biały black and white; ⟨góra *f* (*-y; 0*) Montenegro; ~księżnia *m* (*-a; -y*) sorcerer; ~oki black-eyed; ~rynkowy black-market; ~skóry black; ~włosy black-haired

czarn|y black; *fig.* gloomy; ~a jagoda bilberry, blueberry; *pół* ~ej, *mała* ~a a cup of black coffee; na ~ą godzinę in case of emergency

czarodziej *m* (*-a; -e, -i/-ów*), ~ka *f* (*-i*) magician; ~ski magic, magical; ~stwo *n* (*-a*) magic

czarow|ać (*-uję*) do *lub* work magic, *fig.* ⟨o-⟩ bewitch, enchant; ~nica *f* (*-y; -e*) witch; ~nik *m* (*-a; -cy*) wizard; ~ny enchanting, charming

czart *m* (*-a, D -u/-rcie; -y*) devil

czarter *m* (*-u; -y*) charter; ~ować (*-uję*) charter; ~owy charter

czar|ująco charmingly; ~ujący charming; ~y → czar

czas *m* (*-u; -y*) time; ~ odjazdu time of departure; ~ pracy working time; working hours *pl.*; *już* ~ (*+bezok.*) it is (high) time we went; *mieć* ~ na (*A*) to have time to; ~ przeszły *gr.* the past tense; ~ przyszły *gr.* the future tense; ~ teraź-

niejszy *gr.* the present tense; (*przez*) jakiś ~ for some time; co jakiś ~, od ~u do ~u from time to time; do tego ~u until then; na ~ in time; na ~ie up to the minute, topical; (*od* ~u) (*jak*) since the time (when); od tego ~u from that time on, since then; po ~ie too late; przed ~em too early, (*przedwcześnie*) prematurely; w ~ie (*G*) when; w krótkim ~ie shortly, soon; swego ~u at that time; in those days; w sam ~ just in time; z ~em with time; za moich ~ów in my times; ~ami now and again; at times; ~em → czasami; (*przypadkiem*) perhaps

czaso|chłonny time-consuming; ~pismo *n* periodical; (*zwł. codzienne*) newspaper; ~wnik *m* (*-a; -i*) *gr.* verb; ~wo *adv.* temporarily; ~wy temporal, temporary

czaszka *f* (*-i; G -szek*) *anat.* skull; trupia ~ (*jako symbol*) death's head

czat|ować (*-uję*) lie in wait (na *A* for); ~y *f/pl.* (-) lookout; stać na ~ach be on the lookout

cząst|eczka *f* (*-i; G -czek*) *phys.* molecule; ~ka *f* (*-i; G -tek*) particle; small part; ~kowy partial

czci → cześć, czcić; ~ciel *m* (*-a, -e*), ~cielka *f* (*-i; G -lek*) worshipper, adorer; ~ć worship, adore; ~godny venerable, esteemed

czcionka *f* (*-i; G -nek*) type; font, *Brt.* fount

czcz|ą, ~ę → czcić; ~o *adv.* → czczy; na ~o on an empty stomach; ~y (*płonny, pusty*) idle, futile; żołądek, *też fig.* empty

Czech *m* (*-a; -si*) Czech; ~y *pl.* (*G -*) (*region*) Bohemia; (*państwo*) Czech Republic

czego, ~kolwiek, ~ś → co(kolwiek)

czek *m* (*-u; i*) *Brt.* cheque, *Am.* check; ~ gotówkowy open *lub* uncrossed cheque/check; ~ podróżny *Brt.* traveller's cheque, *Am.* traveler's check; ~iem by cheque/check

czekać ⟨po-, za-⟩ (*-am*) wait (*G*, na *A* for; *impf. też* być udziałem) expect

czekolad|a *f* (*-y*) chocolate; ~ka *f* (*-i; G -dek*) chocolate; ~ka nadziewana filled chocolate; ~owy chocolate

czekowy *Brt.* cheque, *Am.* check

czeladnik *m* (*-a; -cy*) journeyman

czel|e → czoło; ~ny arrogant

czeluść f (-ści; -ście) abyss, chasm

czemu → co; (dlaczego) why; F **po ~** how much; ~kolwiek, ~ś; ~ż → **cokolwiek, coś, cóż**

czepek m (-pka; -pki) (pielęgniarki, dziecka itp.) cap; (dawniej) bonnet; ~**kąpielowy** swimming lub bathing cap

czepi|ać się (-am) ⟨~ć się⟩ (-ę) cling (G to), hang (G to); fig. (G) find fault (with), carp (at)

czepiec m (-pca; -pce) cap

czeremcha f (-y) bot. bird cherry

czerep m (-u; -y) head; (odłamek) piece, fragment

czereśnia f (-i; -e) bot. sweet cherry

czerni|ak m (-a; -i) med. melanoma; ~**ca** f (-y; -e) → **borówka**; ~**ć** (-ę, -ń/-nij/) blacken; ~**eć** (-eję) appear in black; ⟨**po-, s-**⟩ get lub become black, turn black

czernina f (-y) gastr. (soup made of blood)

czerń f (-ni) black; blackness

czerp|ać (-ię) wodę, zasoby, fig. itp. draw; (czerpakiem) scoop (up); ~**ak** m (-a; -i) scoop; tech. dredge, bucket

czerstw|o adv. robustly; ~**y** chleb itp. stale; fig. hale (and hearty), robust

czerw m (-wia; -wie, -wi) maggot

czerw|cowy June; ~**iec** June; ~**ienić się** ⟨**za- się**⟩ (-ę), ~**ienieć** ⟨**po-**⟩ (-eję) redden (na twarzy), become red

czerwonka f (-i; 0) med. dysentery

czerwono adv.: **na ~** red; ~**skóry** pej. redskin; ~**ść** f (-ści; 0) red, redness, blush

czerwony adj. red

czesać ⟨**u-**⟩ (-szę) comb (**się** też one's hair)

czesankow|y: wełna ~a worsted

czeski (**po -ku**) Czech

Czeszka f (-i; G -szek) Czech

cześć f (czci, czcią; 0) deference, hono(u)r; **otaczać czcią** venerate; revere; (zmarłego) hono(u)r s.o.'s memory; **na ~, ku czci** (G) in hono(u)r of; ~**l** bye!, so long!

często adv., ~**kroć** adv. often, frequently

częstotliwość f (-ści) frequency

częstować ⟨**po-**⟩ (-uję) offer (I to), treat (I to); ~ **⟨po-⟩ się** help o.s. (I to)

częsty adj. (m-os części, comp. -tszy) often

częś|ciej adv. more often; ~**ciowo** adv. partly; ~**ciowy** partial; ~**ć** f (-ci) part; ~**ć składowa** component, element; **większa ~ć** larger part; **lwia ~ć** lion's share; ~**ć mowy** gr. part of speech; **po/w ~ci** partly

czka|ć (-m) hiccup; ~**wka** f (-i; G -wek) hiccup

człapać (-pię) clump, trudge

człek m (-a, -owi/-u, -u/-ecze!, I -kiem; 0) → **człowiek**

człon m (-a/-u; -y) section, part

członek[1] m (-nka; -nki) anat. (penis) penis; (kończyna) limb

człon|ek[2] m (-nka; -nkowie), ~**kini** f (-; -inie) member; **być ~kiem komitetu** sit on a committee; ~**kostwo** n (-a) membership; ~**kowski** member('s)

człowie|czeństwo n (-a; 0) humanity; ~**k** m (-a; ludzie) human being, (zwł. mężczyzna) man; (bezosobowo) one; **szary ~k** the man in the street; ~**k interesu** (zwł. mężczyzna) businessman, (kobieta) businesswoman; → **czyn**

czmychać (-am) make off

czołg m (-u; -i) tank

czołgać się (-am) crawl, creep

czoł|o n (-a, L -czele; -a, czół) anat. forehead; (przód) front; (pochodu) head; (burzy) front(line); **stawić ~o** stand lub face up to; **na czele** at the head; ~**em!** hallo!

czołowy forehead; med. frontal; zderzenie itp. head-on; fig. foremost

czołówka f (-i; G -wek) forefront; (artykuł) leading article; (na filmie) opening credits pl.; sport: lead, top

czop m (-a; -y) bung; ~**ek** m (-pka; -pki) plug; med. suppository

czosn|ek m (-nku; 0) garlic; ~**kowy** garlic

czół|enka n/pl. (-nek) pumps pl.; ~**no** n (-na; G -łen) boat, canoe; (z pnia) dug-out

czterdzie|sta f (-i; G -tek) forty; ~**stoletni** forty-year-long, -old; ~**stu** m-s, ~**sty**, ~**ści(oro)** → **666**

czter|ech (też w zł.); ~**ej** four; ~**nastka** f (-i; G -tek) fourteen; (linia) number fourteen; ~**nastu** m-os, ~**nasty**, ~**naście**, ~**naścioro** → **666**

cztero- w zł. four; ~**krotny** fourfold; ~**letni** four-year-long, -old; ~**motoro-**

wy four-engine; ~osobowy for four persons; ~pasmowy *droga* four-lane; ~suwowy *Brt.* four-stroke, *Am.* four-cycle; ~ścieżkowy *zapis (na ścieżce)* four-track

cztery four; ~sta, ~stu *m-os* four hundred

czub *m* (-*a*; -*y*) (*włosów*) shock of hair; (*piór*) crest; z ~em heaped; *fig.* with interest; ~ato *adv.* with a heap; ~aty *zo.* crested; ~ek *m* (-*bka*; -*bki*) tip; (*szczyt*) top; ~ek głowy top of one's head; ~ek palca fingertip

czu|cie *n* (-*a*; -*a*) feeling; bez ~cia (*odrętwiały*) numb, insensitive; (*nieprzytomny*) unconscious; ~ć ⟨po-, u-⟩ (-*uję*) feel (się też o.s.); Polakiem o.s. to be a Pole); ~ć miłość do (*G*) feel love for; *impf.* (*I*) smell of)

czuj|ka *f* (-*i*; *G* -*jek*) *tech.* detector; ~nik *m* (-*a*; -*i*) *tech.* sensor; ~ny watchful, vigilant, alert; *sen* light

czule *adv.* → czuły

czuło|stkowo (over-)sentimentally; ~stkowy (over-)sentimental; ~ść *f* (-*ści*) tenderness; affection; (*pieszczota*) *zwł. pl.* caress(es *pl.*); (*wagi, instrumentu*) sensitivity; (*filmu*) speed

czuły tender, affectionate; (*uczulony*) sensitive (*też przyrząd itp.*); *słuch* acute; ~ na światło sensitive to light; *tech.* photosensitive

czupiradło *n* (-*a*; *G* -*deł*) *fig.* scarecrow

czupryna *f* (-*y*) hair

czuwać (-*am*) be awake, sit up (przy *I* at); (*pilnować*) watch (nad *I* over)

czw. *skrót pisany:* czwartek Thur(s). (Thursday)

czwart|ek *m* (-*tku*; -*tki*) Thursday; ~kowy Thursday; ~y fourth; ~a godzina four o'clock; po ~e fourthly

czwora|czki *m/pl.* (-*ów*) quadruplets *pl.*, F quads *pl.*; ~ki four-fold; na ~kach on all fours

czworo four; we ~ in a foursome, in a group of four; złożyć we ~ fold in four; ~bok *m* (-*u*; -*i*), ~kąt *m* (-*a*; -*y*) quadrangle; ~nożny four-legged

czwór|ka *f* (-*i*; *G* -*rek*) four; (*linia*) number four; *szkoła: jakby:* B; we ~ge in a foursome, in a group of four; ~ami in fours

czy 1. *part.* if, whether; ~ to prawda? is it true?; ~ wierzysz w to? do you be-

lieve in this?; nie wiem ~ to dobrze I don't know if it is OK; 2. *cj.* or; tak ~ inaczej one way or the other

czyhać (-*am*) lie in wait (na *A* for)

czyj *m*, ~a *f*, ~e *n* whose; ~kolwiek anyone's, anybody's; ~ś someone's, somebody's

czyli that is

czym → co; ~ ... tym the ... the ...; ~ prędzej as soon as possible; ~kolwiek → cokolwiek; ~ś → coś; ~że → cóż

czyn *m* (-*u*; -*y*) act, deed, action; człowiek ~u man/woman of action; ~ić ⟨u-⟩ (-*ę*) do; *postępy, ustępstwa* make; *cuda* work; (*wynosić*) constitute, make; ~nie → czynny; ~nik *m* (-*a*; -*i*) factor; *zwł. pl.* organ(s *pl.*); ~ność *f* (-*ści*) activity; action; (*organu itp.*) function; ~ny active; *mechanizm* operating, functioning; *sklep* open; *napad* physical; ~ny zawodowo working, in paid employment; *gr.* strona ~na the active voice

czynsz *m* (-*u*; -*y*) rent

czyrak *m* (-*a*; -*i*) *med.* boil, *med.* furuncle

czyst|a 1. *f* (-*ej*; -*e*) F (clear) vodka; 2. *adj. f* → czysty; ~o *adv.* clean(ly); (*bez domieszek*) purely; (*schludnie*) tidily, neatly; *śpiewać* in tune; przepisać na ~o make a fair copy; wyjść na ~o break even

czystość *f* (-*ści*; 0) tidiness, cleanness; (*chemikalia itp.*) purity; (*skóry*) clearness

czyst|y clean, tidy, neat; (*bez domieszek*) pure; *dochód* net(t); *niebo* clear; *przyjemność itp.* sheer; do ~a completely, entirely

czyszczenie *n* (-*a*) cleaning, cleansing; (*w pralni chemicznej*) dry-cleaning

czyś|cibut *m* shoe-cleaner; ~cić ⟨o-, wy-⟩ (-*szczę*) clean, cleanse, tidy; ~cić szczotką brush; ~ciej(szy) *adv.* (*adj.*) *comp. od* → czysto, czysty

czytać (-*am*) read (głośno aloud)

czytan|ie *n* (-*a*) reading; do ~ia to be read; ~ka *f* (-*i*) reader

czyteln|ia *f* (-*i*; -*ie*) reading room; (*wypożyczalnia*) (lending) library; ~iczka *f* (-*i*; *G* -*czek*), ~ik *m* (-*a*; -*cy*) reader; ~y readable, legible

czytnik *m* (-*a*; -*i*) *komp.* reader

czyż → czy

czyżyk *m* (-*a*; -*i*) siskin

Ć

ćma f (-y; G ciem) zo. moth

ćmić (-ę; ćmij!) v/i. (boleć) ache; (też **się**) smo(u)lder, burn without fire; v/t. (palić) F puff (away) at; → **przyćmiewać**

ćpać f (-am) (brać) take, F do; (regularnie) be an addict.

ćpun F m (-a; -y) drug addict, F junkie

ćwiartka f (-i; G -tek) quarter; F quarter Brt. litre (Am. liter); (butelka) Brt. quarter-liter, Am. liter bottle; **~ papieru** slip of paper

ćwicze|bny drill, practice; (ubiór) training; **~nie** n (-a) exercise; **~nie domowe** homework; **~nia** pl. mil. exercise(s pl.); **~nia** pl. (na uniwersytecie itp.) classes

ćwiczyć (-ę) ⟨**wy-**⟩ train; drill; opanowanie itp. exercise; pamięć practise; **~** ⟨**wy-**⟩ **się** (w L) practise; ⟨**o-**⟩ flog

ćwiek m (-a; -i) tack

ćwierć f (-ci; -ci) quarter; **~finałowy** quarterfinal; **~litrowy** Brt. quarter-litre (Am. -liter); **~nuta** f mus. Brt. crotchet, Am. quarter note; **~wiecze** n (-a) quarter of a century

ćwierkać (-am) chirp

ćwikła f (-y; G -kieł) red-beet salad; **~owy: burak ~owy** Brt. beetroot, Am. red beet

D

da → **dać**

dach m (-u; -y) roof; **bez ~u nad głową** homeless; **~ówka** f (-i) (roof) tile

dać pf (dam, dadzą, daj!) → **dawać**; **~ się** (być możliwym) be possible; **da się zrobić** it can be done; **co się da** whatever is possible; **gdzie się da(ło)** somewhere, anywhere; **jak się da** somehow or other; **dajmy na to** let's say; **daj spokój!** come off it!

daktyl m (-a; -e) date

dal f (-i; -e) distance; **w ~i** in the distance; **z ~a** at a distance (**od** G from)

dale|ce adv.: **jak ~ce** to what extent, how far; **tak ~ce** so much (**że** that); **~j** adv. (comp. od → **daleko**) further; farther; **i tak ~j** and so on; **nie ~j jak tydzień temu** a week or so ago; **~ki** distant (też fig.); far-off, faraway; **z ~ka** from a distance; **~ko** adv. far; **~ko idący** far reaching; **~ko lepiej** far better; **~ko więcej** far more

daleko|bieżny rail. long-distance; **~morski statek** oceangoing; połowy deep-sea; **~pis** telex; **~siężny** far-reaching; **~wzroczność** f (-ści; 0) long-sightedness; fig. far-sightedness

dalia f (GDL -ii; -e) dahlia

dal|mierz m (-a; -e) range-finder; **~szy** adj. (comp. od → **daleki**) farther, further; **~szy plan** background; → **ciąg**

dam → **dać**

dam|a f (-y) lady; (szlachcianka) Dame; (w kartach) queen; **~ski** lady('s), women('s), female, feminine

dan|e¹ → **dany**; **~e²** pl. (-ych) data sg./pl.; **baza ~ych** data base; **przetwarzanie ~ych** data processing; **~ie** n (-a; 0) giving; (pl. -a, G -ń) gastr. dish, meal; **bez ~ia racji** without an explanation

Dania f (-ii; 0) Denmark

daniel m (-a; -e) zo. fallow deer sg./pl.

danina f (-y) hist. fig. tribute

dansing m (-u; -i) dancing; (lokal) café/ restaurant with dancing

dany given; **w ~m razie** in this case; **w ~ch warunkach** given these circumstances

dar m (-u; -y) gift (też fig.), present

daremny futile, vain

darmo adv. free; (bezpłatnie) free of charge; **za pół ~** for a song; **~wy** free; **~zjad** m (-a; -y) sponger, scrounger

dar|nina f (-y), **~ń** f (-ni; -nie) sod, turf

darow|ać pf (-uję) ⟨też **po-**⟩ give, present; karę remit; winy, urazę forgive;

~izna f (-y) donation, gift; **akt ~izny** deed of gift

da|rzyć ⟨ob-⟩ (-ę) give, favo(u)r; ~sz → **dać**

daszek m (-szka; -szki) (small) roof; (nad drzwiami itp.) canopy; (czapki) peak

dat|a f (-y) date; F **pod dobrą ~ą** tipsy

datek m (-tka; -tki) donation, contribution

datow|ać (-uję) date; (się) be dated; ~nik m (-a; -i) date-stamp; **~nik okolicznościowy** special postmark

dawać (-ję) give; podarunek też present; dowód provide; okazję offer, give; zysk bring in; zezwolenie grant; cień afford, give; ~ **coś do naprawy** have s.th. repaired; ~ **k-ś spokój** let s.o. alone; ~ **się słyszeć** could be heard; **tego nie da się otworzyć** it cannot be opened; → **dać**

daw|ca m (-y; G -ów), ~czyni f (-i; -e) donor; ~ca, ~czyni krwi blood-donor; ~ka f (-i; G -wek) dose; ~kować (-uję) dose; fig. uczucia itp. dispense in small doses

dawn|iej adv. (comp. od → **dawno**); earlier; formerly; ~o adv. a long time ago; **jak ~o** how long; ~y (były) former; earlier; **od ~a** for a long time; **po ~emu** (the same) as before

dąb m (dębu; dęby) bot. oak; **stawać dęba** koń: rear up; włosy: stand on end

dąć (dmę) blow; ⟨na-⟩ też **się** puff up

dąs|ać **się** (-am) sulk, be cross (na A with); ~y pl. (-ów) sulk

dąż|enie n (-a) aspiration; ~ność f (-ści) effort, attempt; tendency; ~yć (-ę) (**do** G) strive (for), aspire (to), (do celu) pursue, ⟨też **po-**⟩ make (for), go (to)

dba|ć (-am) (**o** A) chorego care (for), nurse; wygląd take care (of), maszynę itp. look after; ~le adv. carefully; considerately, thoughtfully; ~łość f (-ści; 0) care (for, of); ~ły careful; considerate, thoughtful

dealer m (-a; -rzy) dealer; (też sprzedawca) retailer

debat|a f (-y) debate, discussion; ~ować (-uję) debate (**nad** I)

debel m (-bla; -ble) (w sporcie) double

debil m (-a; -e), ~ka f (-i; G -lek) moron (też med.); ~ny moronic

debiut m (-u; -y) debut, first appearance; ~ować ⟨za-⟩ (-uję) debut, make a debut

decentraliz|acja f (-i; -e) decentralisation; ~ować (-uję) decentralize

dech m (tchu, tchowi, dech, tchem, tchu; 0) breath; (powiew) breeze; **nabrać tchu** take lub draw a breath; **bez tchu** breathless; **co/ile tchu** F for all one's worth; **jednym tchem** at once

decy- w złoż. deci-

decyd|ent m (-a; -ci) decision-maker; ~ować ⟨za-⟩ (-uję) decide; make decisions (**o** L about); ~ować ⟨z-⟩ **się** (**na** A, bezok.) decide (on, bezok.), settle (on)

decy|dująco decisively; ~dujący decisive; ~zja f (-i; -e) decision; (sędziego itp.) ruling; verdict; **powziąć ~zję** make a decision

dedyk|acja f (-i; -e) dedication; ~ować ⟨za-⟩ (-uję) dedicate

defekt m (-u; -y) defect, fault; (usterka) breakdown, malfunction; **z ~em** faulty; defective

defensyw|a f (-y) defensive; ~ny defensive

deficyt m (-u; -y) deficit; (niedobór) shortage, lack; ~owy: **towar ~owy** (brakujący) product in short supply, (niezyskowny) unprofitable product

defil|ada f (-i; -e) parade, march; ~ować ⟨prze-⟩ parade, march

defini|cja f (-i; -e) definition; ~tywny definitive, definite, conclusive

deformować ⟨z-⟩ (-uję) deform; ~ **się** become deformed

de|fraudacja f (-i; -e) embezzlement; ~generacja f (-i; 0) degeneration; ~generować się (-uję) degenerate; (w pracy) degrade

degradacja f (-i; 0) degradation; (w pracy) demotion; ~ **środowiska** environmental degradation; med., chem. breakdown; fig. decline, deterioration

deka F n (-idkl.) decagram; w zł. deca-; ~da f (-y) decade

dekarstwo n (-a; 0) roofwork

dekarz m (-a; -e) roofer

dekla|mator m (-a; -rzy) reciter; ~mować (-uję) recite, declaim

deklaracja f (-i; -e) declaration; ~ **celna** customs declaration; (blankiet) form; ~ **podatkowa** tax return deklarować ⟨**za-**⟩ (-*uję*) declare; state

deklin|acja *f* (-*i*; -*e*) *gr.* declension; ~ować (-*uję*) decline

dekolt *m* (-*u*; -*y*) low(-cut) neckline; **sukienka z dużym ~em** very low-cut dress; ~ować się (-*uję*) wear low-cut dresses; put on a low-cut dress

dekora|cja *f* (-*i*; -*e*) decoration; (*wystawa*) window-dressing; (*w teatrze, filmie*) set, scenery; ~cyjny (-*nie*) decorative; ~tor *m* (-*a*; -*rzy*), ~torka *f* (-*i*; *G* -*rek*) (*wystaw*) window-dresser; (*wnętrz*) interior decorator; *teatr.* scene-painter; ~tywny decorative

dekorować ⟨**u-**⟩ (-*uję*) decorate (*też odznaczeniem*); *wystawę* dress

dekować F (-*uję*) cover up for; ~ się dodge (service), shirk

dekret *m* (-*u*; -*y*) decree; ~ować ⟨**za-**⟩ (-*uję*) decree

delega|cja *f* (-*i*; -*e*) (*wysłannicy*) delegation; (*wyjazd służbowy*) business trip; ~t *m* (-*a*; -*ci*), ~tka *f* (-*i*; *G*- *tek*) delegate; ~tura *f* (-*y*) agency, branch

delegować ⟨**wy-**⟩ (-*uję*) send as a delegate/delegates; (*służbowo*) send on a business trip; *odpowiedzialność* delegate

delektować się (-*uję*) savo(u)r

delfin *m* (-*a*; -*y*) *zo.* dolphin; (*w sporcie*) (*pływanie*) butterfly (stroke)

delicje *f/pl.* (-*i*-*cyj*) delicacy

delikatesy *m/pl.* (-*ów*) (*sklep*) delicatessen, F deli

delikatn|ość *f* (-*ści*; 0) delicacy; (*skóry*) softness; (*porcelany*) fragility; (*zdrowia, dziecka*) frailty; ~y delicate; soft; fragile

delikwent *m* (-*a*; -*ci*), ~ka *f* (-*i*; *G* -*tek*) offender

demaskować ⟨**z-**⟩ (-*uję*) expose; ~ ⟨**z-**⟩ się give o.s. away

demen|tować ⟨**z-**⟩ (-*uję*) deny; ~ti *n* (*idkl.*) denial

demilitaryzacja *f* (-*i*; 0) demilitarisation

demobilizować (-*uję*) demobilize

demokra|cja *f* (-*i*; -*e*) democracy; ~ta *m* (-*y*; -*ci*), ~tka *f* (-*i*; *G* -*tek*) democrat (*też pol.*); ~tyczny democratic

demolować ⟨**z-**⟩ (-*uję*) wreck, smash up

demonstra|cja *f* (-*i*; -*e*) demonstration, manifestation; (*manifestacja itp.*) de-

monstration, F demo; ~cyjny demonstrative

demon|strować (-*uję*) demonstrate; ~tować ⟨**z-**⟩ (-*uję*) take apart, dismantle, disassemble

demoralizować ⟨**z-**⟩ (-*uję*) deprave, debase; ~ ⟨**z-**⟩ się become depraved *lub* debased

den → **dno**

denat *m* (-*a*; -*ci*), ~ka *f* (-*i*; *G* -*tek*) victim, casualty; (*samobójca*) suicide

denaturat *m* (-*u*; 0) methylated spirits

denerwować ⟨**z-**⟩(-*uję*) irritate, annoy; ~ ⟨**z-**⟩ się get excited, get worked up

denerwująco : **działać ~ na kogoś** get on s.o.'s nerves

den|ko *n* (-*a*) bottom; ~ny bottom

dentyst|a, *m* (-*y*; -*ści*); ~ka *f* (-*i*; -*tek*) dentist; ~yczny dentist; ~yka *f* (-*i*; 0) dentistry

de|nuklearyzacja *f* (-*i*; -*e*) denuclearisation; ~nuncjator *m* (-*a*; -*rzy*), **-rka** *f* (-*i*; *G*-*rek*) informer

denuncjować ⟨**za-**⟩ (-*uję*) inform (**kogoś** on s.o.)

departament *m* (-*u*; -*y*) department, (*ministerialny Brt. też*) office; **♀ stanu** *Am.* Department of State

depesza *f* (-*y*; -*e*) telegram, *Brt.* Telemessage; (*kablem podmorskim*) cable

deponować ⟨**z-**⟩ (-*uję*) deposit (**u** *A* with)

deport|acja *f* (-*i*; -*e*) deportation; ~ować (-*uję*) deport

depozyt *m* (-*u*; -*y*) deposit; **oddać do ~u** *u* deposit with

de|prawować ⟨**z-**⟩ (-*uję*) deprave, corrupt, debase; ~precjacja *f* (-*i*; -*e*) depreciation; ~presja *f* (-*i*; -*e*) depression (*też fin., psych.*); ~prymować ⟨**z-**⟩ (-*uję*) depress; ~prymująco depressingly, dishearteningly; ~prymujący depressing, disheartening

depta|ć ⟨**po-, roz-**⟩ (-*pczę/-cę*) (*A*, **po** *L*) (*nieumyślnie*) step (on), tread (on); (*umyślnie*) stamp (on); *też fig.* trample (on); *impf.* ~**ć komuś po piętach** follow at s.o.'s heels; ~k *m* (-*a*; -*i*) promenade, public walk

deput|at *m* (-*u*; -*y*) payment in kind; ~owany *m* (-*ego*, -*i*), ~owana *f* (-*ej*; -*e*) delegate, deputy

derka *f* (-*i*; *G* -*rek*) (horse-) blanket

dermatolog *m* (-*a*; -*dzy*) dermatologist

desant m (-u; -y) landing; **~ powietrz-ny** air landing operation; **~owiec** m (-wca; -wce) (urządzenie) landing craft

deseń m (-niu/-nia; -nie) pattern

deser m (-u; -y) dessert, Brt. F afters; **na ~** as a lub for dessert; **~owy** dessert

deska| f (-i; G -sek) board; (długa, gruba) plank; pl. **deski** (narty) skis; **~a do prasowania** ironing board; **ostatnia ~a ratunku** the last hope; **od ~i do ~i** from cover to cover; → **tablica**

desko|rolka f (-i) skateboard; **~wanie** n (-a) bud. formwork, Brt. shuttering; (deski) board

desperac|ki desperate; **~ko** adv. desperately

despotyczny despotic

destruk|cyjny, ~tywny destructive

de|stylacja f (-i; -e) destilation; **~stylować ⟨prze-⟩** (-uję) destilate; **~sygnować** (-uję) designate (**na** A as)

deszcz m (-u/rzadk. dżdżu; -e) rain; **drobny ~** drizzle, fine rain; **ulewny ~** downpour; → **padać; ~ownia** f (-i; -e) sprinkler; **~owy** rainy; **~ówka** f (-i; 0) rainwater

deszczułka f (-i; G -łek) board

deszczyk m (-u; -i) light rain

detal m (-u; -e) detail; (szczegół) particular; F econ. retail (trade); **nie wchodząc w ~e** without going into (the) details; **~iczny** retail; **cena ~iczna** retail price

detektyw m (-a; -i) detective; (prywatny) private detective/investigator; **~istyczny** detective

deton|ator m (-a; -y) detonator; **~ować ⟨z-⟩** (-uję) detonate, explode; kogoś confuse, disconcert

dewaluacja f (-i; -e) devaluation

dewast|acja f (-i; -e) vandalism, destruction; **~ować ⟨z-⟩** (-uję) vandalize

dewiz|a f (-; -y) motto, maxim; → **dewizy**; **~ka** f (-i; G -zek) watch-chain; **~y** pl. (-) foreign currrency

dewocjonalia pl. (-ów) devotional objects pl.

dezaprobata f (-y; 0) disapproval

dezer|cja f (-i; -e) desertion; **~terować ⟨z-⟩** (-uję) desert

dezodorant m (-u; -y) deodorant; **~ do pach** underarm deodorant; **~w sprayu/ kulce** spray/roll-on deodorant

dezodoryzator m (-a; -y) (do po-

mieszczeń) deodorant

dezorganiz|acja f (-i; -e) lack of organisation; **~ować ⟨z-⟩** (-uję) disorganize

dezorientować ⟨z-⟩ (-uję) confuse, disorientate; **~ ⟨z-⟩ się** get confused

dezyderat m (-u; -y) claim

dezynfekcja f (-i; -e) disinfection

dęb|ina f (-y) (drewno) oak(-wood); **~owy** oak(en); **~y → dąb**

dęt|ka f (-i; G -tek) mot. inner tube; **~y** wind; **orkiestra ~a** brass band

dia|belny F damned; **~belski** diabolic(al); fiendish, devilish; **~belsko** fiendishly, devilishly; **~beł** m (-bła, D -błu, -ble; -bły/-bli, -ów) devil; **do ~bła!** damn it!

diab|lica f (-y; -e) she-devil; **~oliczny** diabolical

dia|gnoza f (-y) diagnosis; **~gnozować** (-uję) diagnose; **~gonalny** diagonal; **~gram** m (-u; -y) diagram; **~lekt** m (-u; -y) gr. dialect; **~lektyczny** dialectical; gr. dialectal

dializacyjny dialysis; **ośrodek ~** med. dialysis Brt. centre (Am. center)

di'alog m (-u; -i) Brt. dialogue, Am. dialog

di'ament m (-u; -y) diamond; **~owy** diamond

diecezja f (-i; -e) diocese; **~lny** diocesan

dies|el m (-sla; -sle) diesel (engine); **~lowski** diesel

di'e|ta f (-y) diet; **~ty** pl. (parlamentarzysty) parliamentary allowance; (na delegacji) travelling (traveling Am.) expenses pl.; **być na ~cie** diet; **~tetyczny** diet; dietary; **napój ~tetyczny** diet drink

dla prp. (G) for; **~ dorosłych** for adults; **miły ~ rąk** kind to the hands; **przyjazny ~ zwierząt** animal-friendly; **~ nabrania tchu** in order to take a breath of air; **~czego** why; **~ń = dla niego**; **~tego** for that reason; because of that; **~tego, że** because

dł. skrót pisany: **długość** (length)

dławić ⟨z-⟩ (-ę) choke, strangle; fig. sup press, hold back; **~ ⟨z-⟩ się** (I) choke (on)

dławik m (-a; -i) electr. choking coil

dło|ń f (-ni; -nie) palm; hand; **jasne jak na ~ni** it is obvious

dłubać (mieszać się) fiddle (**przy** L with); **~ ⟨wy-⟩** (-bię) (w nosie, zębach)

dobry

pick; (*w jedzeniu*) pick (**w** *L* at)

dług *m* (*-u*; *-i*) debt, (*też moralny*) obligation

dług|awy longish; ~i long; ~o long; *jak* ~o? how long?; *na* ~o for a long time; *tak* ~o *aż* so/as long that

długo|dystansowiec *m* (*-wca*; *-wcy*) long-distance runner; *falowy* long-term; ~*falowo* on a long-term basis, in the long term; ~letni long-standing; of many years' standing; ~pis *m* (*-u*; *-y*) ball-point (pen); ~ść *f* (*-ci*) length; (*okres też*) duration; ~terminowo long-term; ~terminowy long-term; ~trwały long-lasting; *choroba itp.* lengthy, prolonged; ~wieczny long-lived; ~włosy long-haired

dłuto *n* (*-a*) chisel

dłużej *adv.* (*comp. od* → *długo*); ~ *nie* no longer

dłużn|iczka *f* (*-i; G -czek*); ~ik *m* (*-a; -cy*) debtor; ~y: *być* ~*ym* owe to

dłuż|szy *adj.* (*comp. od* → *długi*); *na* ~*szy czas, od* ~*szego czasu* for a longer time; ~yć się (*-ę*) drag

dmą, dmę → *dąć*

dmuch|ać (*-am*) blow; ~awa *f* (*-y*) blower; ~awiec *m* (*-wca*; *-wce*) bot. dandelion; ~nąć → *dmuchać* F (*ukraść*) pinch, swipe

dn. *skrót pisany: dnia* on; *też* d.n. *dokończenie nastąpi* to be cont'd (*to be continued*)

dna, dnem → *dno*

dni, ~a, ~e → *dzień*; ~eć: ~*eje* it is dawning; ~*ało* the day broke

dniów|ka *f* (*-i; G -wek*) working day; (*zapłata*) daily *lub* day's wage(*s pl.*); *pracować na* ~*ę* work as a day-labo(u)rer

dniu → *dzień*

dno *n* (*-a*; *G den*) bottom; *pójść na* ~ go down; *do góry dnem* bottom up

do *prp.* (*G*) to; till, until; into ; ~ *niego* to him; ~ *szkoły* to school; ~ *piątku* until Friday; (*aż*) ~ *rana* until the morning; ~ *pudła* into the box; *pół* ~ *drugiej* half past one **od** *...* ~ *...* from ... to ...; (*często nie tłumaczy się, zwłaszcza w złożeniach*); *łańcuch* ~ *drzwi* door chain; *beczka* ~ *wina* wine barrel; *lekki* ~ *strawienia* easily digestible

dob|a *f* (*-y; G dób*) day (and night); 24 hours; *fig.* age; *przez całą* ~*ę* round the clock

dobić *pf.* → *dobijać, targ*

dobie|gać ⟨~*c*, ~*gnąć*⟩ (*-gam*) (**do** *G*) run (to); (*do celu*) reach; (*o dźwiękach*) reach, come; ~*ga godzina ...* it is almost ... o'clock; *to* ~*ga końca* it is drawing to an end

dobierać (*-am*) take more; (*wybierać*) choose, select; ~ *się* get (**do** *G* at); (*majstrować*) fiddle (**do** *G* with)

dobijać *pf.*) *v/t.* deal the final blow to; finish off (*też fig.*); *fig.* destroy, ruin; *v/i.* ~ *do celu* reach the goal; ~ *do brzegu* reach the shore; ~ *się do drzwi* rap at the door

dobit|ek: *na* ~*ek*, ~ka: *na* ~*kę* on top of that; ~ny *głos* stentorian, resonant; *żądanie* insistent, urgent

doborowy excellent; *oddziały* elite

dobosz *m* (*-a*; *-e*) drummer

dobowy day-and-night; → *doba*

dobór *m* (*-boru*; *0*) selection

dobrać *pf.* → *dobierać* (*się*); ~ *się* (*pasować*) make a good match

dobranoc (*idkl.*) good night; ~ka *f* (*-i*)- (*bedtime TV feature for children*)

dobrany *adj.* well-matched

dobre *n* (*-ego*; *0*) → *dobro, dobry*; *na* ~ for good; *po* ~*mu* in an amicable way; *wszystkiego* ~*go!* all the best!

dobrnąć *pf.* (**do** *G*) get (to), reach (with difficulty)

dobr|o *n* (*-a*; *G dóbr*) good; ~*o społeczne* public *lub* common good; ~*a pl. rodzinne* (*majątek*) property; ~*a pl.kulturalne* cultural possessions *pl.*; *dla* ~*a* (*G*) for the good (of); *na* ~*o* in favo(u)r of; *zapisać* (*A*) *na* ~*o k-ś/rachunku* *econ.* credit s.o./s.o.'s account with

dobro|byt *m* (*-u*) prosperity, affluence; ~*czynność* *f* charity; ~*czynny* *skutek itp.* beneficial, agreeable; *akcja itp.* charitable

dobro|ć *f* (*-ci*; *0*) goodness, kindness; *po* ~*ci* amicably; ~*duszny* good-natured; ~*dziejstwo* good deed, favo(u)r; *pl. rel.* blessings *pl.*; ~*tliwość* *f* (*-ści*) goodness, kindness; ~*tliwie* kindly, good-naturedly; ~*tliwy* good, kind, good-natured; *med.* benign; ~*wolnie* voluntarily, of one's own will; ~*wolny* voluntary

dob|ry good; (*na A*, **do** *G*) good (for); (*w L*) good (at); ~*ra!* OK!; *a to* ~*re!* I like that!; *na* ~*rą sprawę* actually;

na ~rej drodze on the right track; *przez ~re dwie godziny* for two solid hours, F for two hours solid; → *dobre*

dobrze well; *wyglądać, czuć się* good; *~ ubrany* well-dressed; *~ wychowany* well brought-up; *on ma się ~* he is fine; *~ mu tak!* (it) serves him right!

dobudow(yw)ać (-[w]uję) *skrzydło* build on, add

dobudówka *f* (-*i; G* -*wek*) extension

doby|ć *pf.* → **dobywać**; *~tek m* (-*tku; 0*) possessions *pl.*, belongings *pl.*; (*bydło*) cattle; *~wać* (G) draw; (*wytężyć*) exert, call on; *~wać się* appear

docelowy destination; *port ~* destination

doceni|ać (-*am*) ⟨*~ć*⟩ appreciate, acknowledge; *nie ~ć* underestimate

docent *m* (-*a; -ci*) lecturer

dochodow|ość *f* (-*ści; 0*) profitability; *~y* profitable; → *podatek*

dochodz|enie *n* (-*a*) investigation; *jur. też* assertion; *~enie sądowe jur.* preliminary inquiry; *~ić* (*do* G) approach, come up to (to); (*nadchodzić*) come; (*sięgać*) (*do* G) reach (to), get (to); (*dociekać*) investigate; *prawa* claim; *gastr.* be coming along; *owoce:* ripen; *~ić swego* assert one's rights; *~ić do głosu* get a chance to speak; *fig.* come to the fore; *~i ósma* it is almost eight (o'clock); → *dojść*

dochow|ywać (-*wuję*) ⟨*~ać*⟩ (G) preserve; *~ać słowa* keep one's word; *~(yw)ać się* remain in good condition; *~ać się* manage to bring up

dochód *m* (-*chodu; -chody*) income; *czysty ~* net income; *dochody pl.* returns *pl.*

docią|ć → *docinać*; *~gać* (-*am*) ⟨*~gnąć*⟩ draw (do *G* as far as); *pas, śrubę* tighten

docie|kać (-*am*) ⟨*~c*⟩ *fig.* (G) make inquiries about; *~kliwie* inquisitively; *~kliwy* inquisitive; *~rać* (-*am*) *v/i.* (*do*) get as far as (to), reach; *v/t. mot.* run in

docin|ać (-*am*) *fig.* (D) tease, gibe (at); *~ek m* (-*nka; -nki*) gibe, dig

docis|kać ⟨*~nąć*⟩ (-*am*) tighten; *~kać* ⟨*~nąć*⟩ *się* force one's way through

do cna completely

doczekać (się) *pf.* (G) wait until; live to; *~ się* receive at last; *nie móc się ~* be impatient for

doczepi(a)ć attach

doczesny earthly, worldly

dod. *skrót pisany:* **dodatek** sup. (*supplement*)

dodać *pf.* → **dodawać**

dodat|ek *m* (-*tku; -tki*) addition; (*budynek*) annex, extension; (*do pensji*) extra pay, additional allowance; (*do gazety*) supplement; (*do książki*) supplement, appendix; *~ek mieszkaniowy* housing benefit; *~ek nadzwyczajny* special edition, extra; *z ~kiem* (G) with; *na ~ek, w ~ku* in addition, additionally; *~ki pl.* ingredients *pl.*

dodatkow|o *adv.* additionally; *~y* additional; *wartość ~a* value added

doda|tni positive; *fig.* advantageous, beneficial; *znak ~tni* plus (sign); *bilans* favourable; *~nio* *adv.* positively; *fig.* advantageously, beneficially; *~(wa)ć* (-*ję*) (*do* G) add (to); *fig.* give, lend; *math.* add (up); *~ć otuchy* (D) encourage; *~ć gazu* F step on it; *~wanie* addition

dodzwonić się *pf* (*do* G) get through (to); *nie mogę się ~* nobody answers

doga|dać *się pf* (*z* I) (*porozumieć się*) make o.s. understood (to); (*uzgodnić*) come to terms (with); *~dywać* (-*uję*) → *docinać*; *~dzać* (-*am*) (D) pamper; coddle; satisfy (*zachciankom* whims); *to mu nie ~dza* that does not appeal to him; *~niać* catch up with; *~snąć* go out

doglądać (-*am*) (G) supervize, care for; look after

dogmat *m* (-*u; -y*) dogma

dogo|dny convenient; *na ~dnych warunkach* on favo(u)rable conditions; *~dzić pf.* → *dogadzać*; *~nić pf.* → *doganiać*; *~rywać* *cam* be in agony; *~towywać się* (-*wuję*) ⟨*~tować się*⟩ finish cooking

do|grywać (-*am*) ⟨*~grać*⟩ (*mecz*) play extra time; *~grywka* (-*i; -wek*) extra time; *~gryzać* (-*am*) ⟨*~gryźć*⟩ *fig.* (D) tease; *~grzewać* (-*am*) warm (up)

doić ⟨*wy-*⟩ (-*ję; dój!*) milk

dojadać finish eating; *resztki* finish; *nie ~* not eat enough

dojarka *f* (-*i; G* -*rek*) milkmaid; *~ mechaniczna* milking machine

dojazd *m* (-*u; -y*) journey, way; (*droga*) approach, drive; *~owy droga* access; *kolejka ~owa rail.* local (train) do|jąć *pf* (-*jmę*) → **dojmować**; ~jechać *pf.* (**do** *G*) arrive (at, in), reach; ~jeść → **dojadać**; ~jeżdżać (-*am*): ~**jeżdżać do pracy** commute (to work)

dojm|ować (-*uję*) *v/t.* get through to, pierce; ~**ujący** piercing; acute

dojn|y: **krowa ~a** dairy cow

dojrzale *adv.* in a mature way, *owoc itp.* ripely

dojrzał|ość *f* (-*ści; 0*) maturity; (*owocu itp.*) ripeness; **egzamin ~ości** *jakby*: Brt. GCSE, Am. high school diploma; ~y mature, *owoc itp.* ripe

dojrze|ć[1] *pf* (-*ę; -y*) catch sight of, see; ~wać ⟨~*ć*[2]⟩ -*eję*) *człowiek*: mature, *ser, owoc*: ripen

dojście *n* (-*a*) way, approach (**do** *G* to); ~ **do skutku** coming into effect

dojść *pf.* (-*dę*) → **dochodzić**; *fig.* (**do** *G*) come to, approach; ~ **do zdrowia** regain one's health; ~ **do skutku** come into being *lub* effect; ~ **do władzy** come to power

dok *m* (-*u; -i*) *naut.* dock

dokańczać (-*am*) finish, complete, bring to an end

dokazywać[1] (-*uję*) romp around

doka|zywać[2] accomplish, achieve; ⟨~**zać**⟩ ~**ywać swego** assert o.s.

dokąd where; (*czas*) as long as; ~ **bądź** → **bądź**; ~kolwiek, ~ś anywhere

doker *m* (-*a; -rzy*) dock-worker; docker

dokład|ać (-*am*) add; (*szczodrobliwie*) throw in; ~**ność** *f* (-*ci; 0*) precision; ~**ny** precise, exact, accurate

dokoła *adv.* all around; *prp.* (*G*) (a)round; ~ **siebie** (a)round o.s.

dokon|any finished, accomplished; *gr.* perfect, perfective; ~ywać *i* *wać* ⟨~**ać**⟩ *wyczynu itp.* accomplish; *zbrodni* commit; *wyboru* make; ~(**yw**)**ać się** take place, occur

dokończenie *n* (-*a*) ending; end; ~ **nastąpi** to be continued

dokończyć *pf.* → **dokańczać**

dokształcać (-*am*) ⟨-**ić**⟩ provide further education; ~ **się** continue one's education

dokształcający further education

doktor *m* (-*a; -rzy/-owie*) doctor; (*lekarz też*) medical doctor; ~ant *m* (-*a; -nci*) post-graduate student; ~at *m* (-*u; -y*) doctorate; ~ski doctor's, doctoral;

~yzować się (-*uję*) obtain a/one's doctorate (**z** *G* in)

dokucz|ać (-*am*) ⟨~**yć**⟩ (*D*) tease, annoy; *ból, głód*: torment, plague; ~liwie *adv.* pesteringly, tiresomely; plaguingly; ~liwy pestering, tiresome; plaguing

dokument *m* (-*u; -y*) document; ~**y** *pl. też* F (identity) papers; ~**acja** *f* (-*i; -e*) documentation; ~**alny**, ~**arny** documentary; ~**ować** ⟨*u*-⟩ (-*uję*) document

dokup|ywać (-*uję*) ⟨~**ić**⟩ buy additionally

dola *f* (-*i; zw. 0*) fate, destiny

do|lać → **dolewać**; ~latywać (-*uję*) ⟨~**lecieć**⟩ (**do** *G*) approach (by plane) (to); *pf.* reach; *fig.* get through (to), come through (to) (**z** *G* from)

doleg|ać (-*am*; *t-ko bezok. i 3. os.*) (*D*) trouble, bother; (*boleć*) hurt; **co ci/Panu ~a?** what seems to be the matter?; ~**liwość** *f* (-*ści*) trouble; (*ból*) pain

dolewać (-*am*) (*G*) fill up

dolicz|ać (-*am*) ⟨~**yć**⟩ add; ~**yć się** count (up); **nie ~yć się** be … short

dolin|a *f* (-*y*) valley; **dno ~y** valley floor

doliniarz *m* (-*a; -e*) pickpocket

dolno- *w zł.* lower, low

dolnoniemiecki Low German

doln|y lower, bottom; ~**a część** lower part

dołącz|ać (-*am*) ⟨~**yć**⟩ (**do** *G*) add (to); (*z listem*) enclose; join (**się** to)

doł|ek *m* (-*łka, -łki*) hole; *med.* pit; (*w brodzie*) dimple; *fig.* F **być w ~ku** have a crisis, be depressed; ~**em** below, underneath

do|łożyć *pf.* → **dokładać**; ~**ły** *pl.* → **dół**

dom *m* (-*u; -y*) (*budynek*) house; (*rodzinny*) *fig.* home; ~ **dziecka** children's home; **do ~u** home; **w ~u** at home; **z ~u** *kobieta*: née; **czuć się jak u siebie w ~u** feel like at home; **pan(i) ~u** host

domagać się (-*am*) (*G*) demand

domek *m* (-*mku; -mki*) (small) house; ~**letniskowy** (summer) holiday house; ~ **jednorodzinny** (one-family) house

domiar *m* (-*u; -y*) *econ.* back tax; **na ~ złego** to make matters worse

domiesz|ać *pf.* (*G do G*) add (to); ~**ka** *f* (-*i; G -szek*) addition

domięśniow|o *adv. med.* intramuscularly; ~**y** *med.* intramuscular

dominować (-*uję*) (**nad** *I*) dominate

(over); ~ujący dominating

domknąć pf. → **domykać**

domniemany alleged, purported

domo|fon m (-u; -y) intercom, Brt. entryphone; ~**krążca** m (-y; G -ów) pedlar, hawker; ~**stwo** n (-a) (rolne) farmstead; house; ~**wnik** m (-a; -cy) member of the household; ~**wy** home; domestic; household; **porządki** m/pl. ~**we** clean-out, (wiosenne) spring-clean; ~**wej produkcji** domestic

domy|kać (-am) shut, push to; **drzwi nie ~kają się** the door won't shut; ~**sł** m (-u; -y) supposition, conjecture; ~**ślać się** (-am) ⟨~**ślić się**⟩ (-lę) (G) suspect, presume; pf. guess, find out (**że** that); ~**ślny** perceptive, shrewd

doni|ca f (-y; -e) (na kwiaty) large flowerpot; (kuchenna) pot; ~**czka** f (-i; G -czek) flowerpot; ~**czkowy**: **kwiaty** m/pl. ~**czkowe** potted flowers

donie|sienie n (-a; G -ń) report; → **donos**; ~**ść** pf. → **donosić**

donikąd nowhere

doniosł|ość f (-ści; 0), significance, importance, moment; ~**y** significant, important, momentous

donos m (-u; -y) denunciation; ~**iciel** m (-a; -e), ~**lka** f (-i) informer; ~**ić** (-szę) ⟨**na** A) report (against, on); (**o** L) report (about)

donośny stentorian, resonant

doń = **do niego**; → **on**

dookoła → **dokoła**

dopa|dać (**do** G) lay hands (on), seize; smutek itp.: come over; → **dopaść**; ~**lać** (-am) ⟨~**lić**⟩ cygaro finish (smoking); węgiel burn; ~**lać się** ogień: burn low; budynek: burn down

dopa|sow(yw)ać (-[w]uję) fit; (do otoczenia) adapt (**się** o.s.; **do** G to); ~**ść** pf. → **dopaść**; (dogonić) catch (up with); ~**trywać się** (-uję) ⟨~**trzyć się**⟩ (**w kimś** G) see (in s.o.)

dopełni|acz m (-a; -e) gr. genitive; ~**ać** (-am) ⟨~**ć**⟩ fill up, refill; (uzupełnić) complete; fig. fulfill; ~**ający** completing; ~**enie** n (-a) completion; gr. object

dopędz|ać (-am) ⟨~**ić**⟩ catch up with

dopiąć pf. fig. (G) achieve; ~ **swego** have one's will; → **dopinać**

do|pić pf. → **dopijać**; ~**piekać** (-am) ⟨~**piec**⟩ v/i. słońce: be scorching, be burning down; fig. (D) nettle, sting

dopiero only, just; ~**co** just now; **a to ~ !** well, well!

dopi|jać (-am) drink up; ~**lnować** pf. (G, **aby**) look (to it that); ~**nać** (-am) button up, fix; → **dopiąć**

dopingować (-uję) spur on, encourage, cheer

doping|owy, ~**ujący**: **środek** ~**owy**/ ~**ujący** stimulant drug

dopis|ek m (-sku; -ski) comment, note; ~**ek na marginesie** marginal note fig. comment; ~**ywać** (-uję) ⟨~**ać**⟩ v/t. add (in writing); v/i. (-3. os.) be good, be favourable; **pogoda ~uje** the weather is fine; **zdrowie mu nie ~uje** he is in poor health; **szczęście mu nie ~ało** he had bad luck

dopła|cać (-am) ⟨~**cić**⟩ (**do** G) pay extra (to), pay an additional sum (to); porto pay additionally (to); ~**ta** f (-y) additional payment; extra payment; (w pociągu) excess (fare)

dopły|nąć pf. → **dopływać**; ~**w** m (-u; 0) (energii) supply, (kabel) line; fig. influx; (pl. -y) feeder stream; (rzeka) tributary

dopływ|ać (-am) (**do** G) reach; statek, łódź: approach; ~**owy** kabel itp. supply; rzeka itp. tributary, feeder

dopo|magać (-m) (**w** L) help out (with), be helpful (with); ~**minać się** (-am) ⟨~**mnieć się**⟩ (-nę, -nij!) (**o coś** A) **u kogoś** claim (s.th. from s.o.), demand (s.th. from s.o.); ask (for)

dopó|ki cj. as/so long as; ~**ty: ~ty ... aż, ~ty ... dopóki** as long as

doprawdy adv. really

doprowadz|ać (-am) ⟨~**ić**⟩ (**do** G) lead (to), result (in); tech. convey (to), supply (to); prąd, gaz connect (to); ~**ić do końca** bring to an end; ~**ić do ruiny** ruin; ~**enie** n supply; connection; electr. lead

dopuszcza|ć (-m) (**do** G) allow, permit; **nie możemy do tego ~ć** we cannot let it happen; ~**ć się** (G) commit, make; ~**lny** permissible

dopuścić pf. → **dopuszczać**; ~ **do głosu** let s.o. speak

dopyt|ywać się (-uję) ⟨~**ać się**⟩ (G, **o** A) ask (about), inquire (about)

dorabiać (-am) prepare; klucz duplicate; też ~ **sobie** (I) earn on the side, earn extra; ~ **się** (G) make one's way;

(*wzbogacać*) get rich, do all right for o.s.

dorad|ca *m* (*-y*; *-y*),**~czyni** *f* (*-*; *-e*, *-yń*) advisor *lub* adviser; consultant; **~czy** advisory, consultative

doradz|ać (*-am*) ⟨*~ić*⟩ advise; **~two** *n* (*-a*; *0*) consultation; (*usługi*) consultancy (services *pl.*)

dorasta|ć (*-am*) grow up (*też fig.*) (**do** *G* (in)to); → **dorównywać**; **~jący** growing up

doraźn|ie *adv.* (*na razie*) for the time being; temporarily; (*karać*) summarily; **~y** summary; temporary; **pomoc ~a** emergency relief; (*medyczna*) first aid; **sąd ~y** summary court

doręcz|ać (*-am*) ⟨*~yć*⟩ hand over; *list itp.* deliver; **~enie** *n* (*-a*) delivery

dorob|ek *m* (*-bku*; *0*) (*niematerialny*) achievements *pl.*, (*materialny*) property; (*utwory itp.*) work; **~ek kulturalny** cultural possessions *pl.*; **być na ~ku** make one's way; **~ić** *pf.* → **dorabiać**

doroczny annual

dorodny well-built, good-looking; *zboże itp.* ripe

doros|ły 1. *adj.* adult, grown-up; **2.** *m* (*-ego*; *-śli*) adult, grown-up; **~nąć** → **dorastać**

do|rożka *f* (*-i*; *G -żek*) cab; **~róść** *pf.* → **dorastać**

dorówn|ywać (*-uję*) ⟨*~ać*⟩ (*D*) equal, match; **~ywać komuś** be s.o.'s equal/match

dorsz *m* (*-a*; *-e*) *zo.* cod

dorysow(yw)ać (*-[w]uję*) finish drawing; (*dodać*) add

dorywcz|o *adv.* occasionally, from time to time, incidentally; **~y** occasional, incidental; *praca* odd

dorzecze *n* (*-a*) *geogr.* basin

dorzeczny reasonable

dorzuc|ać (*-am*) ⟨*~ić*⟩ (**do** *G*) throw (as far as); add (*też fig.*); *węgla itp.* put more

dosadny *dowcip itp.* earthy, crude

do|salać (*-am*) add salt; **~siadać** ⟨*~siąść*⟩ mount (**konia** the horse), get on; **~siąść się** (**do k-ś**) join (s.o.)

do siego: **~ roku!** happy New Year!

dosięg|ać ⟨*~nąć*⟩ (*G*, **do** *G*) reach (to) (*też fig.*)

doskona|le *adv.* → **doskonały**; **~lenie** (**się**) *n* (*-a*; *0*) perfecting; (*nauka*) further education; **~lić** ⟨*u-*⟩ (*-lę*) per-

fect; **~lić się** improve; **~łość** *f* (*-ci*; *0*) perfection; **~ły** *adj.* perfect; (*znakomity*) excellent, first-rate

do|słać → **dosyłać**; **~słowny** literal; **~słyszeć** *pf.* hear; **on nie ~słyszy** he is hard of hearing; **~solić** *pf.* → **dosalać**; **~spać** *pf.* → **dosypiać**; **~stać** *pf.* → **dostawać**

dostarcz|ać ⟨*~yć*⟩ (*A*, *G*) deliver (to), supply (with); *świadka*, *dowody* produce; *fig.* (*dawać*) provide

dostat|ecznie *adv.* sufficiently, (*dobry itp.*) acceptably; **~eczny** sufficient, acceptable; *ocena* fair; **~ek** *m* (*-tku*; *0*) prosperity; **pod ~kiem** in abundance, in plenty; **~ni** prosperous, comfortable; **~nio** *adv.* prosperously, comfortably

dostaw|a *f* (*-y*) delivery, supply; **termin ~y** delivery time; **~ać** get, obtain, receive; (*wyjmować*) take out; (*dosięgać*) get, reach (**do** *G* to); **~ać się** (**do** *G*) get (to, into); **~ać się w ... ręce** get into the hands of ...; **nagroda dostała się** (*D*) the price was given to; **~ca** *m* (*-y*; *G -ów*) supplier; (*bezpośredni*) delivery man; **~czy** delivery; **~i(a)ć** *stół itp.* add; *więźnia itp.* deliver, bring; → **przystawiać**, **dostarczać**

dostąpić *pf.* (*-ę*) → **dostępować**

dostęp *m* (*-u*; *zw.* *0*) admission; *też fig.* access; **~ny** accessible; *cena też* reasonable; *tekst też* clear; **~ować** (*-uję*) (*dochodzić*) (**do** *G*) approach, go up (to); *fig.* → **dostąpić**

dostoj|eństwo *n* (*-a*) dignity; **~nik** *m* (*-a*; *-cy*) dignitary; **~ny** dignified; → **czcigodny**

dostosow|anie *n* (*-a*; *0*) adaptation, adjustment; **~(yw)ać** adapt, adjust (**do** *G* to; **się** o.s.); **~awczy** adaptative

do|strajać (*-am*) ⟨*~stroić*⟩ *mus.*, *RTV*: tune; *fig.* adjust (**się do** o.s. to); **~strzegać** (*-am*) ⟨*~strzec*⟩ notice

dostrzegalny noticeable; **~ ledwo** hardly noticeable

dosu|wać ⟨*~nąć*⟩ move up closer, push (**do** *G* to)

dosyć *adv.* quite, fairly; **~ dobrze** quite good; **mieć ~** (*G*) be sick *lub* tired of

dosy|łać (*-am*) send on, send after; **~piać** (*-am*): **nie ~piać** sleep too little; **~pywać** (*-uję*) ⟨*~pać*⟩ (**do** *G*) pour in more, *węgla itp.* put on more

do|szczętny (adv. też do szczętu) complete, total; ~szkalać (-am) ⟨~szkolić⟩ → dokształcać; ~sztukow(yw)ać (-[w]uję) (do G) dywanu itp. add a piece to; sukienkę itp. lengthen

doszuk|ać się pf. (G) find, come across; ~iwać się (-uję) (G) suspect

dościg|ać ⟨~nąć⟩ (-am) catch up with

dość n ⟨też dosyć⟩; ~ na tym, że ... in a word; od ~ dawna for quite a long time

dośpiewać pf.: ~ sobie guess

dośrodkow(yw)ać (-[w]uję) (w sporcie) Brt. centre, Am. center; ~o adv. centripetally; ~y centripetal

doświadcz|ać (-am) (G) experience; bólu itp. go through, endure; los go ciężko ~ył fate has been very unkind to him; ~alny experimental; ~enie n (-a) experiment (na zwierzętach on animals), (próba też) test; experience; brak ~enia lack of experience; z ~enia from experience; ~ony experienced; (wypróbowany) (tried and) tested; ~yć pf. → doświadczać

dot. skrót pisany: dotyczy Re:

dotacja f (-i; -e) subvention

dotąd (w czasie) until now; up to now; (w przestrzeni) so far; → dopóty

dotk|liwie adv. sharply, severely; ~liwy sharp, severe; ~nąć pf. → dotykać; fig. hurt, wound; ~nięcie (się) n (-a) touch, contact; ~nięty (I) (urażony) upset, hurt; (spustoszony itp.) stricken

dotować (-uję) subsidize

do|trwać pf. (do G) remain (until), hold out (until), last (until); ~trzeć pf. → docierać; ~trzymywać (-uję) ⟨~trzymać⟩ słowa, kroku, towarzystwa keep; warunków keep to

dotychczas adv. until now; ~owy previous

doty|czyć (G) concern, apply to; co ~czy ... as to lub for; to mnie nie ~czy that does not concern me; ~czące ciebie ... concerning you; ~k m (-u; -i) touch; na ~k to the touch; być szorstkim w ~ku be rough to the touch; zmysł ~ku sense of touch; ~kać (-am) (G) touch (się o.s., each other); ~kalny palpable, tangible; ~kowy touch

doucz|ać (-am) ⟨~yć⟩ continue (się one's) education; ~yć się learn

doustny oral

doważ|ać (-am) ⟨dowaźyć⟩: nie ~ cheat on the weight

dowcip m (-u; -y) joke; ~kować (-uję) joke; ~ny witty

dowiadywać się (-uję) enquire (o A about); → dowiedzieć się

dowidzieć: nie~ have poor eyesight

dowie|dzieć się pf. learn, hear (o A about); ~dziony proved, proven; ~rzać (-am) trust; nie~rzać mistrust; ~ść pf. → dowodzić; ~źć pf. → dowozić

dowlec pf. drag (się o.s.)

dowodow|y: jur. wartość ~a value as evidence; postępowanie ~e jur. hearing of evidence

dowodz|enie n (-a) command; (wykazywanie) argumentation, reasoning; jur. presentation of the case; ~ić (-dzę) argue (for), prove; mil. have command of, be in command of

dowoln|y free; ćwiczenia ~e (w sporcie) free Brt. programme (Am. program), optional exercises

dowozić v/t. (do G) bring (to), drive (to), rzeczy transport (to); (dostarczać) supply

dowód m (-odu; -ody) (też jur.) proof, evidence; (dokument) certificate, receipt; ~ osobisty identity card; ~ nadania certificate of posting; ~ rzeczowy jur. (piece of) material evidence; na/w ~ (G) in token of; ~ca m (-y; G -ów) commander; mil. commanding officer; ~ca plutonu mil. platoon commander

dowództwo n (-a) command; (miejsce) command post; (siedziba) headquarters sg./pl.

dowóz m supply

doza f (-y) dose

dozbr|ajać (-am) ⟨~oić⟩ rearm

dozgonny lifelong, for life

dozna|wać (-ję) ⟨~ć⟩ (G) feel; złego experience; straty, kontuzji suffer; ~ć zawodu feel disappointment; ~ć wrażenia get an impression

dozor|ca m (-y; -y, G -ów), ~czyni f (-ni; -e, G -yń) (domu) caretaker, janitor (zwł. Am.); (w więzieniu) Brt. warder, Am. (prison) guard; ~ować (-uję) (G) supervize, oversee

dozować (-uję) dose, measure out (a dose)

dozór *m* (*-oru*; *0*) supervision; ~ **techniczny** technical inspection/supervision

dozw|alać (*-am*) ⟨~**olić**⟩ (*-lę*; *-wól!*) allow; permit; ~**olony dla młodzieży** suitable for persons under 18

dożyć *pf.* (*G*) live (to); ~ **stu lat** live to be a hundred; ~ **późnego wieku** live to a ripe old age

dożylny *med.* intravenous

dożynki *pl.* (*-nek*) harvest festival

doży|wać (*-am*) → **dożyć**; ~**wać swoich dni** reach the twilight of one's life; ~**wiać się** (*-am*) take additional food; ~**wotni** lifelong; *jur.* life; ~**wotnio** *adv.* lifelong; for life

dójka *f* (*-i*; *G* -*jek*) milkmaid; (*cycek*) teat

dób *G pl.* → **doba**; ⟨~**r** *G pl.* → **dobro**

dół *m* (*dołu*, *doły*) hole, pit; (*dolna część*) bottom part; under-side; bottom; **w/na** ~ down; **na** ~ (*domu*) downstairs; **iść w** ~ *fig.* go down; **w** ~ **rzeki** downstream; **z/od dołu** from below; **w/na dole, u dołu** (down) below; **płatny z dołu** payment on delivery

dr *skrót pisany:* **doktor** Dr, PhD, MedD

drab F *m* (*-a*; *-y*) ruffian, thug

drabin|a *f* (*-y*) ladder; ~**iasty: wóz ~iasty** open-frame wooden cart; ~**ka** *f* (*-i*) ladder; ~**ka linowa, sznurowa** rope ladder; ~**ka szwedzka** (*w sporcie*) wall bars *pl.*

dragi *f/pl. sl.* (*narkotyki*) drugs

draka *f* (*-i*) F row

drakoński draconian

dramat *m* (*-u*; *-y*) drama (*też fig.*)

drama|topisarz *m* (*-a*; *-e*), **-rka** *f* (*-i*) playwright; ~**tyczny** dramatic

drań *m* (*-nia*; *-nie*, *-ni[ów]*) *pej.* scoundrel, swine; ~**stwo** *n* (*-a*) meanness; nastiness

drapa|cz *m* (*-a*; *-e*): ~**cz chmur** skyscraper; ~**ć** ⟨**po-**⟩ (*-ię*) scratch (**się** (o.s.), **w** *A* on); ~**ć się pod górę** clamber up; ~**k** *m* (*-a*; *-i*) old comb; **dać** ~**ka** → **drapnąć**

drapieżn|ik *m* (*-a*; *-i*) predator (*też fig.*), (*ptak*) bird of prey, (*ssak*) beast of prey; ~**ość** *f* (*-ci*; *0*) rapacity; ~**y** predacious, predaceous

drapn|ąć *v/s.* (*-nę*) scratch; F make o.s. scarce; ~**ięcie** *n* (*-a*; *G* -*ć*) scratch

drapować ⟨**u-**⟩ (*-uję*) drape

drasnąć *v/s.* (*-nę*) scratch, scrape; *kula:* graze; *fig.* hurt, wound

drastyczny drastic

draśnięcie *n* (*-a*; *G* -*ć*) scratch

drażetka *f* (*-i*; *G* -*tek*) med. dragée

draż|liwość *f* (*-ści*; *0*) irritability; ~**liwie** *adv.* irritably; ~**liwy** irritable; touchy; *sytuacja* risky; ~**niąco** *adv.*: **działać** ~**niąco** →; ~**nić** (*-ę*, *-ń/-nij!*) irritate

drą → **drzeć**

drą|g *m* (*-a*; *-i*) pole, rod; ~**żek** *m* (*-żka*; *-żki*) (*w sporcie*) horizontal bar, high bar; **na** ~**żkach ...** on the horizontal bar; ~**żyć** ⟨**wy-**⟩ (*-żę*) hollow out; *tunel* bore

drelować → **drylować**

drelich *m* (*-u*; *-y*) *teh.* drain pipe; *med.* drain; ~**ować** ⟨**-uję**⟩ drain

dreptać ⟨**po-**⟩ (*-czę/-cę*) toddle, patter

dres *m* (*-u*; *-y*) sweat suit, (*cieplejszy*) tracksuit

dreszcz *m* (*-u*; *-e*) shudder, shiver; ~**e** *pl.* shivers; *fig.* F kick, buzz; ~**yk** *m* (*-u*; *-i*) shiver, shudder; *fig.* F kick, buzz; **opowieść z** ~**ykiem** horror story

drew|niak *m* (*-a*; *-i*) timber house; (*but*) clog; ~**niany** wooden (*też fig.*); ~**nieć** ⟨**z-**⟩ (*-eję*) *fig.* stiffen; ~**no** *n* (*-a*; *0*) wood; (*kawałek*) piece of wood

drę → **drzeć**; ~**czący** tormenting, torturing; ~**czyć** (*-ę*) torment, torture; ~**czyć się** worry, agonize (*I* about)

drętw|ieć ⟨**o-**, **z-**⟩ (*-eję*) stiffen (**z zimna** from cold); *noga*, *ręka*: go numb, go to sleep; be paralysed (**na myśl** by the thought of); ~**o** *adv.* drearily, boringly; ~**y** (*ścierpnięty*) numb; *fig.* dull, dreary

drg|ać (*-am*) tremble, shiver; (*nerwowo*) twitter, jerk; *urządzenie:* vibrate; ~**ania** *n/pl.* (*-ń*) *phys.* vibrations *pl.*; ~**awki** *f/pl.* (*-wek*) spasms *pl.*, convulsions *pl.*; ~**nąć** *v/s.* (*-nę*) → **drgać**; **ani** (*nie*) ~**nąć** not budge

drobiazg *m* (*-u*; *-i*) trifle; small thing, minor detail; **to** ~**!** don't mention it!; ~**owość** *f* (*-ści*; *0*) pedantry, punctiliousness; ~**owo** *adv.* pedantically, punctiliously; ~**owy** pedantic, punctilious

drobi|ć ⟨**roz-**⟩ (*-ę*) *chleb* crumble, break into crumbs; (*nogami*) toddle; ~**na** *f*

(-y) particle; *chem., phys.* molecule

drobn|e *pl.* (-ych) small change; ~ica *f* (-y; *0*) *econ.* general cargo; ~icowiec *m* (-wca; -wce) *econ.* general cargo ship

drobno *adv.* → **drobny**; ~mieszczański petit(e) bourgeois; ~stka *f* (-i; *G* -tek) trifle; small thing, minor detail; ~stkowy pernickety, small-minded; ~ustrój *m* microorganism; ~ziarnisty fine, fine-grained

drobny small; petty; *szczegół* petty; *(miałki)* fine; *(delikatny)* delicate; → **drobne, deszcz**

droczyć się F (-ę) (**z** *I*) tease

droga[1] *adj. f* → **drogi**

drog|a[2] *f* (-i; *G* dróg) way (*też fig.*); (*szosa*) road; (*podróż*) journey; ~**a szybkiego ruchu** expressway; ~**a startowa** (take-off) runway; **wybrać się w** ~**ę** set off; **zejść k-ś z** ~**i** get out of s.o.'s way; ~**ą urzędową** through the official channels; **swoją** ~**ą** at any rate, anyhow; **po/w drodze** on one's way; **szczęśliwej** ~**i!** have a good journey!

dro'geria *f* (*GDL* -ii; -e) *Brt.* chemist's (shop), *Am.* drugstore

drogi expensive; *fig. też* dear; *pl.* → **droga**[2]

drogo *adv.* expensively, dearly; ~cenny precious, valuable

drogo|wskaz *m* (-u; -y) signpost; ~wy road; traffic; *kodeks* ~**wy** rules of the road, *Brt.* Highway Code

drogówka F *f* (-i; *0*) traffic police

drozd *m* (-a; -y) *zo.* thrush

drożdż|e *pl.* (-y) yeast; ~owy yeast

droż|eć ⟨**po-, z-**⟩ (-eję) get more expensive, go up; ~ej *adv.* (*comp. od* → **drogo**), ~szy *adj.* (*comp. od* → **drogi**) more expensive; ~yzna *f* (-y; *0*) high prices *pl.*

drób *m* (*drobiu*; *0*) poultry

dró|g *G pl.* → **droga**[2]; ~żka *f* (-i; *G* -żek) path; ~żnik *m* (-a; -cy) *rail. Brt.* linesman, *Am.* trackman

druci|any wire; ~k *f* (-a; -i) little wire

druczek *m* (-czka; -czki) form

drugi second; (*inny*)(*the*)other;(*z dwóch*) (the) latter; ~**e danie** main course; **co** ~ every second; **po** ~**e** secondly; ~**e tyle** twice as much; **jeden po/za** ~**m** one after the other; **po** ~**ej stronie** on the other side; **z** ~**ej strony** on the other hand; **z** ~**ej ręki** second-hand;

druga (**godzina**) two o'clock

drugo|planowy secondary; ~rzędny second-rate;

druh *m* (-a; -owie/-y) friend; (*harcerz*) scout; ~na *f* (-y; *G* -hen) (*na weselu*) bridesmaid; (*harcerka*) *jakby*: *Brt.* (Girl) Guide, *Am.* Girl Scout

druk *m* (-u; *0*) print; (*pl. -i*) form; (*na poczcie*) printed matter; **wyjść** ~**iem** appear in print

drukar|ka *f* (-i) printer; ~**ka igłowa/laserowa/atramentowa** dot-matrix/laser/ink-jet printer; ~**nia** *f* (-ni; -e) printing-works; (*firma*) printing-house; printer's; ~**ski** print; **błąd** ~**ski** misprint

druk|arz *m* (-a; -e) printer; ~ować (-uję) print

drut *m* (-u; -y) wire; ~**y** *pl. też* knitting-needles *pl.*; **robić na** ~**ach** knit

druzgotać ⟨**z-**⟩ (-czę/-cę) crush, smash

druż|ba *m* (-y; -owie) best man; ~ka *f* (-i; *G* -żek) bridesmaid

druży|na *f* (-y) (*w sporcie*) team; *mil.* squad; (*harcerzy*) troop; ~owo *adv.* in a group, together; ~owy **1.** group, team; **2.** *m* (-ego; -i), ~owa *f* (-ej; -e) Scouter, scout leader

drwa *pl.* (*drew*) wood

drwalnia *f* (-i; -e) wood-shed

drwi|ąco *adv.* sneeringly, mockingly; ~**ący** sneering, mocking; ~**ć** (-ę; -ij!) (**z** *G*) sneer (at), mock (at); ~**ny** *f/pl.* (-) sneer(ing), mocking

dryblas F *m* (-a; -y) beanpole, strapper

dryblować (-uję) (*w sporcie*) dribble (the ball)

dryfować (-uję) *v/i.* drift

dryl *m* (-u; *0*) *mil. zwł. pej.* drill, training

drylować (-uję) stone

drzazga *f* (-i) splinter; **rozbić na/w** ~**i** splinter, shatter

drzeć ⟨**po-**⟩ *v/t.* tear (to pieces); *ubranie* wear out; ~ **się ubranie**: wear out; (*krzyczeć*) shout

drzem|ać (-mię) doze, snooze, nap; *fig.* lie dormant; ~ka *f* (-i; *G* -mek) nap, snooze; ~**ka poobiednia** after-lunch nap

drzew|ce *n* (-a) shaft; (*flagi*) pole, staff; ~**ko** *n* (-a; *G* -wek) small tree; (*młode*) young tree; ~**ny** tree, timber; ~**o** *n* (-a) *bot.* tree; ~**o iglaste/liściaste/owocowe** deciduous/coniferous/fruit tree; (*drewno*) wood; ~**oryt** *m* (-u; -y): ~**oryt**

wzdłużny woodcut; **~oryt sztorcowy** wood engraving

drzwi pl. (*drzwi*) door; **rozsuwane ~** sliding door; **~ oszklone/przeszklone** French window; **~ami** through the door; **przy ~ach zamkniętych** jur. in camera; fig. behind closed doors; **~czki** pl. (*-czek*) (small) door; (*klapa*) (hinged) lid; **~owy** door

drże|ć (*-ę*) tremble, shiver, shake; **~nie** n (*-a; zw. 0*) tremble, shiver, shaking; med. tremor

d/s, d.s. skrót pisany: **do spraw** for

dubbing m (*-u; 0*) dubbing; **~ować** (*-uję*) dub

dubeltówka m (*-i; G -wek*) double-barrelled shotgun

dubler m (*-a; -rzy*), **~ka** f (*-i; G -rek*) stand-in, (*w filmie też*) double

Dublin m (*-a/-u; 0*) Dublin

dublować ⟨z-⟩ (*-uję*) double; *kogoś* stand in for; (*w sporcie*) lap

duch m (*-a; -y*) spirit, (*też zjawa*) ghost; (*odwaga*) spirit, mettle; **~ czasu** spirit of the age; **wierzyć w ~y** believe in ghosts; **w ~u** in spirit; **nabrać ~a** cheer up; **podnieść k-ś na ~u** cheer s.o. up

duchow|ieństwo n (*-a; 0*) clergy; **~ny 1.** spiritual, religious; **2.** m (*-ego; -i*) clergyman; **~o** adv. mentally, intellectually; **~y** mental, intellectual

dud|ka f (*-i; G -dek*) → **fujarka**; **~nić** (*-ę*) deszcz: drum, batter; grzmot, czołg: rumble, grumble; **~y** pl. (*dud/dudów*) mus. bagpipes pl.

duet m (*-u; -y*) (*wokalny*) duet; (*instrumentalny*) duo

dum|a f (*-y 0*) pride; (*w Rosji*) duma; **~ać** (*-am*) (*o L*) think (of, about), muse (on), ponder (on); **~ka** f (*-i; G -mek*) (*romantic Ukrainian folk song*); **~ny** proud (**z** G of)

Du|naj m (*-u; 0*) Danube; **~nka** f (*-i; G -nek*), **~ńczyk** m (*-a; -cy*) Dane; 2**ński** Danish; **mówić po** 2**ńsku** speak Danish

dup|a ∨ f (*-y*) Brt. arse, Am. ass; **do ~y** lousy, shitty

dur¹ m (*-u; 0*) med. typhus; **~ plamisty** typhoid fever

dur² (*idkl.*) major; **C-dur** C major

dur|eń m (*-rnia; -rnie, -rni[ów]*) fool; **~ny** foolish, dense

---

durszlak m (*-a; -i*) → **cedzak**

du|rzyć się (*-ę*) F have a crush (**w** L on); **~sić** (*-szę*) ⟨**u-, za-**⟩ strangle, choke; fig. suppress, quell; gastr. ⟨**u-**⟩ stew; **~sić się** suffocate; gastr. stew

dusz|a f (*-y; -e*) soul (*też fig.*); tech. core; **zrobiło jej się lekko na ~y** a weight was lifted from her heart; **czego ~a zapragnie** everything one's heart desires; **~kiem** adv. wypić at one gulp; **~nica** f (*-y; -e*): **~nica bolesna** angina pectoris; **~ność** f (*-ści*) shortness of breath; **~ny** (*parny*) sultry, close; **~pasterski** pastoral; **~pasterz** m (*-a; -e*) priest

duż|o adv. much; many; **~y** big, large; deszcz, mróz, zachmurzenie heavy

dw. skrót pisany: **dworzec** Stn (*Station*)

dwa two; **~ słowa** a word or two; → **666**; **~dzieścia** twenty; **~j** m-os two; **~naście** twelve

dwie f/pl. two; **~ście** two hundred

dwo|ić się (*-ję; dwój!*) → **podwajać**; **~i mi się w oczach** I see everything double; **~isty** dual, double; **~jaczki** m/pl. (*-ów*) twins pl.; **~jaki** double, two different; **~jako** adv. doubly; **~je** two; **jedno z ~jga** one of the two; **na ~je** in two; **za ~je** for two

dwom D → **dwa**

dwo|rcowy (railway) station; **~rski** court, courtly; **~ry, ~rze** → **dwór**; **~rzec** m (*-rca; -rce*) station; **~rzec lotniczy** airport

dwóch m-os two

dwój|k|a f (*-i; G -jek*) two; (*linia*) number two; (*łódź*) pair-oar, double-scull; (*ocena*) unsatisfactory; **we ~ę** in two; **~ami** two by two

dwójnasób: w ~ doubly

dwóm D → **dwa**

dwór m (*-oru; -ory*) (*królewski*) court, (*magnacki*) manor; **na ~** out, outdoors; **na dworze** in the open

dwu 1. m-os two; **2.** w zł. two, double; **~aktówka** f (*-i*) two-act play; **~bój** m (*-boju; -boje*) biathlon; **~cyfrowy** two-figure, two-digit; **~częściowy** two-part; ubiór two-piece; **~daniowy** two-course; **~dniowy** two-day

dwudziest|ka f (*-i; G -tek*) twenty; (*banknot*) twenty-zloty itp. note; (*linia*) number twenty; **~o-** w zł. twenty-; **~y**

twentieth; *lata* ~e the twenties

dwu|głoska *f (-i) gr.* diphthong; ~**go-
dzinny** two-hour (long); ~**języczny**
bilingual; ~**kierunkowy** bidirectional;
two-way; ~**kropek** *m (-pka; -pki)*
colon

dwukrotn|ie *adv.* twice, **wzrosnąć ~ie**
grow twice as much; ~**y** twofold

dwu|letni two-year-long, -old; *roślina
~letnia* biennial; ~**licowy** duplicitous;
~**mian** *m (-u; -y) math.* binomial;
~**miejscowy** two-seat, for two people;
~**miesięcznik** *m (-a; -i)* bimonthly;
~**miesięczno** bimonthly

dwunast|ka *f (-i; G- tek)* twelve; *(linia)*
number twelve; ~**nica** *f (-y; -e)* duo-
denum; ~**o-** *w zł.* twelve; ~**y** twelfth;
~**a** twelve (o'clock); → *666*

dwu|nogi, ~**nożny** bipedal; ~**osobowy**
two-person; double; ~**piętrowy** two-
-floor, two-stor(e)y; ~**pokojowy** two-
-room

dwu|rodzinny two-family; ~**rzędowy**
double-breasted; ~**rzędówka** F *f
(-i)* double-breasted suit/coat/jacket;
~**setny** two-hundredth; ~**silnikowy**
two-engine; ~**stopniowy** two-stage;
~**stronny** bilateral; two-sided; ~**su-
wowy** *Brt.* two-stroke, *Am.* two-cycle;
~**szereg** *m (-u; -i)* double-line; ~**tlenek** *m (-nku; -nki)* dioxide; ~**tlenek
węgla** carbon dioxide; ~**tomowy**
two-volume; ~**torowy** double-track,
double-line; ~**tygodnik** *m (-a; -i)* biweekly; ~**tygodniowy** biweekly

dwuwęglan *m:* ~ *sodu* sodium bicarbonate, bicarbonate of soda

dwu|wymiarowy two-dimensional;
~**zakresowy** *RTV:* with two wave-
bands; ~**zmianowy** two-shift; ~**znaczny** ambiguous, equivocal; ~**żeństwo** *n
(-a; 0)* bigamy

dybel *m (-bla; -ble)* dowel

dychawica *f (-y; -e)* asthma

dydaktyczny didactic

dyfteryt *m (-u; -y)* diphtheria

dygnitarz *m (-a; -e)* dignitary

dygotać *(-czę/-cę)* tremble, shiver (*z G*
from)

dykcja *f (-i; -e)* pronunciation

dykta *f (-y)* plywood

dykta|fon *m (-u; -y)* Dictaphone *TM,*
dictating machine; ~**ndo** *n (-a; G -nd)*
dictation; *pisać pod ~ndo* take dicta-

tion; ~**tor** *m (-a; -rzy/-owie)* dictator;
~**tura** *f (-y)* dictatorship

dyktować *(-uję)* dictate

dyl *m (-a; -e, -i/ów)* floor-board; thick
plank

dylemat *m (-u; -y)* dilemma

dyletanck|i dilettant, amateurish;
po ~u in an amateurish way

dym *m (-u; -y)* smoke; *pójść z ~em*
go up in smoke; *puścić z ~em* lay in
ashes; *rozwiać się jak ~ fig.* go up in
smoke; ~**ić (-ę)** smoke; ~**ić się** be
smoking

dymisj|a *f (-i; -e) komuś* dismissal;
(własna) resignation; *udzielić ~i (D)*
dismiss; *podać się do ~i z* resign from;
~**onować** dismiss; ~**onowany** retired,
in retirement

dymny smoke

dynamiczny dynamic

dy'nastia *f (GDL -ii; -e)* dynasty; house

dynia *f (-i; -e) bot.* pumpkin

dyplom *m (-u; -y)* diploma, certificate;
(wyższej szkoły) degree; ~**acja** *f (-i; 0)*
diplomacy; ~**ata** *m (-y; -ci)*, ~**atka** *f (-i)*
diplomat; ~**atyczny** diplomatic; ~**owany** qualified; ~**owy** degree, diploma

dyr. *skrót pisany: dyrektor* dir. *(director)*

dyrek|cja *f (-i; -e)* management, admin-
istration; ~**tor** *m (-a; -rzy/-owie)*, ~**tor-
ka** *f (-i)* director, manager; *(szkoły)*
head teacher; ~**torski** director's; ~**ty-
wa** *f (-y)* directive, instruction

dyrygent *m (-a; -ci)* conductor

dyrygować *(-uję)* conduct

dyscyplina *f (-y)* discipline; ~**rny** discip-
linary

dysertacja *f (-i; -e)* dissertation, thesis

dysfunkcja *f (-i; -e)* malfunction

dysk *m (-u; -i) Brt.* disc, *Am.* disk;
~ *twardy komp.* hard disk; *(w sporcie)*
discus; *rzut ~iem* the discus

dyskietka *f (-i; G -tek)* floppy disk,
diskette

dyskobol *m (-a; -e)*, ~**ka** *f (-i)* discus
thrower

dys|komfort *m (-u; 0)* discomfort, un-
easiness; ~**konto** *n (-a)* discount;
~**kontowy** discount

dyskotek|a *f (-i)* discotheque, F disco;
~**owy: muzyka ~owa** disco music

dyskre|cja *f (-i; -e)* discretion; ~**dyto-
wać** *⟨z-⟩ (-uję)* discredit

dyskrymin|acja f (-i; 0) discrimination; ~ować (-uję) discriminate

dysku|sja f (-i; -e) discussion, debate; **poddać ~sji/pod ~się** put forward to discussion; ~syjny controversial,debatable; ~tować ⟨**prze-**⟩ (-uję) discuss

dyskwalifik|acja f (-i; -e) disqualification; ~ować ⟨**z-**⟩ (-uję) disqualify

dysponować (-uję) have at one's disposal

dyspozy|cja f (-i; -e) right of disposal; **mieć do ~cji** have at one's disposal

dysproporcja f (-i; -e) disproportion, disparity

dystans m (-u; -e) distance; **trzymać na ~** keep at long range

dystrybu|cja f (-i; 0) distribution; ~tor m (-a; -y) mot. Brt. petrol-pump, Am. gas(oline) pump

dystynkcje f/pl. (-i) insignia (of rank)

dysydent m (-a; -ci), ~ka f (-i) dissident

dysz|a f (-y; -e) nozzle, jet; ~eć (-ę, -y) pant, puff

dyszel m (-szla, -szle) pole

dywan m (-u; -y) carpet

dywersja f (-i; -e) sabotage

dywidenda f (-y) dividend

dywiz|ja f (-i; -e) mil. division; ~jon m (-u; -y) aviat., naut. squadron

dyżur m (-u; -y) duty; ~ **nocny** night duty; ~ny **1.** adj. duty; on duty; ~na zupa soup of the day; ~ny temat current topic; **2.** m (-ego; -i), ~na f (-ej; -e) duty officer, (w szkole) monitor; ~ny ruchu rail. train controller; ~ować (-uję) be on duty

dz. skrót pisany: **dzień** d. (day); **dziennie** dly (daily); **dziennik** J. (journal)

dzban m (-a; -y) jug, (wiekszy lub Am.) pitcher; ~ gliniany clay jug; ~ek m (-nka; -nki) pot, jug

dziać[1] **dzieję**; **dział** knit

dziać[2] się (t-ko 3. os. dzieje, działo się) go on, happen, be; be the matter (z I with); **co się tu dzieje?** what's going on here?

dziad m (-a, -dzie-/du!; -y) beggar; (starzec) old man; pej. chap, bloke; (pl. -owie) → ~ek m (-dka; -dkowie) grandfather; F grandpa; pl. grandfathers pl., grandparents pl.; ~ek do orzechów nutcracker; ~owski trashy, poor; (nędzny) pitiful; dreadful, appalling; ~y pl. (-ów) hist. memorial service

dział m (-u; -y) department, section (też część czasopisma); (część własności) share; ~ kadr personnel department; ~ wód watershed

działacz m (-a; -e) activist; ~ partyjny cadre-party member; ~ polityczny politician; ~ rewolucyjny professional revolutionist; ~ ruchu robotniczego workers' leader; ~ka f (-i) activist; → **działacz**; ~ka społeczna socially committed woman; ~ka podziemia underground fighter

działać (-am) function, work, operate; (oddziaływać) act; ⟨**po-**⟩ have an effect; ~ć na nerwy get on one's nerves; ~lność f (-ci; 0) activity; ~nie n (-a) operating, functioning, working; effect; mil. operation; → **arytmetyczny**

dział|ka f (-i; G -lek) plot (of land), (ogródek) small garden, Brt. allotment; ~owicz m (-a; -e), ~owiczka f (-i) allotment-holder

działo[1] n (-a) gun

działo[2] się → **dziać się**

działow|a: ścianka ~a a partition

dzia|nina f (-y) (tkanina) jersey; (ubiór) jersey clothes pl.; ~ny knitted

dziarsk|i (-ka (and hearty); robust, vigorous; ~o adv. robustly, vigorously

dziąsło n (-a) anat. gum

dzicz f (-y; 0) (miejsce) wilderness, back country; fig. zbior. (ludzie) mob, rabble; ~eć ⟨**z-**⟩ (-eję) go wild; fig. brutalize; ~yzna f (-y; 0) venison, game

dzida f (-y) spear

dzie|ci pl. → **dziecko**; ~ciak m (-a; -i) child, F kid; ~ciarnia f (-i; 0) zbior. children pl.; ~ciątko n (-a; G -tek) baby; ℒ**ciątko Jezus** Baby Jesus; ~cięco like a child; ~cięcy children's; childlike; ~cinada f (-y; 0) childish behavio(u)r; ~cinny → **dziecięcy**; fig. childish; **po ~cinnemu** like a child; ~ciństwo n (-a; 0) childhood; ~ciobójstwo n (-a) child murder, (własnego) infanticide; ~ciuch F m (-a; -y) child; ~cko n (-a; dzieci, I) child; **od ~cka** from childhood

dziedzi|c m (-a; -e) heir; hist. squire; ~ctwo n (-a; 0) heritage, inheritance; ~czka f (-i; G -czek) heiress; hist. lady of the manor; ~czny hereditary; ~czyć ⟨**o-**⟩ (-czę) inherit (**po** L from)

dziedzina f (-y) domain, area, field

dziedziniec m (-ńca; -ńce) courtyard

dziegieć m (-ciu; 0) tar

dzieje pl. (-ów) history, fig. story; ~ się → **dziać się**

dziejowy historical, (przełomowy) historic

dziekan n (-a; -i) dean; (dyplomatów) doyen; ~at m (-u; -y) dean's office

dziel|enie n (-a; 0) division (też math.); ~ić ⟨**po-, roz-**⟩ (-lę) divide (też math. **przez** by, **się**); share (out) (**między** A among, between); (rozdzielać) separate; ~ić ⟨**po-**⟩ **się** (I) share; (sekretami) confide (**z kimś** in s.o.); math. be divisible; ~na 1. f (-ej; -e) math. dividend; **2.** → **dzielny**

dziel|nica f (-y; -e) region, province; (miasta) district, part; ~nicowy regional, provincial; district; ~nie → **dzielny**; ~nik m (-a; -i) math. divisor; ~ność f (-ści; 0) bravery, boldness; ~ny brave, bold

dzieł|o n (-a) work; ⟨**za**⟩**brać się/przystąpić do** ~a set to work

dzien|nie daily; (na dzień) a day; ~nik m (-a; -i) (gazeta) daily; (pamiętnik) diary; (wiadomości) news; ~nik urzędowy official gazette; ~nik klasowy jakby: class-register; ~nikarka f (-i; G -rek), ~nikarz m (-a; -e, -y) journalist; ~ny daily; (w ciągu dnia) daytime

dzień m (dnia; dni/dnie, G dni) day; ~ świąteczny holiday, (religijny) feast-day; ~ **dobry!** hello!; ~ **w** ~, ~ **po dniu** day after day; **za dnia** in daylight; **z dnia na** ~ from one day to the next; **w ciągu dnia** during the day (time); **co** (drugi) ~ every other day; **na drugi** ~ next day; **do dziś dnia** until today

dzierżaw|a f (-y) lease, tenancy; ~ca f (-y) leaseholder, tenant; ~czy leasing; gr. possessive; ~czyni f (-, -e) leaseholder, tenant; ~ić ⟨**wy-**⟩ (-ę) lease, rent; ~ne n (-ego; 0) rent; ~ny: **czynsz** ~ny rent; **umowa** ~na lease contract

dzierżyć (-ę) wield, hold

dziesiąt|ek m (-tka; -tki) decade; też → ~**ka** f (-tki; G -tek) ten; (linia) number ten; (banknot itp.) F tenner; ~kować ⟨**z-**⟩ (-uję) decimate; ~y tenth; **jedna** ~a a tenth

dziesięcio|- w zł. deca-, ten-; ~**boista** m (-y; -ści, -ów) decathlete; ~**krotny** tenfold; ~**lecie** n (-a) tenth anniversary

dziesię|ć, m-os. ~ciu ten → **666**; ~ćkroć adv. tenfold; ~tnik m (-a; -cy) hist. decurion; ~tny decimal

dziewcz|ę n (-ęcia; -ęta) girl; ~ęco adv. girlishly; ~ęcy girlish; ~yna f (-y) girl; ~ynka f (-i) little girl

dziewiąt|ka f (-i; G -tek) nine; (linia) number nine; ~y ninth → **666**

dziewica f (-y; -e) virgin

dziewiczy virginal, virgin (też fig.)

dziewięcio|- w zł. nine-; ~**krotny** ninefold; ~**letni** nine-year-long, -old

dziewię|ć m-os. ~ciu nine → **666**; ~**ćdziesiąt** ninety; ~**ćset** nine hundred; ~**tnastka** f (-i; G -tek) nineteen; (linia) number nineteen; ~**tnasto-** w zł. nineteen; ~**tnaście** nineteen → **666**

dziewucha f (-y) girl, żart. wench

dzieża f (-y; -e) kneading trough

dzięcioł m (-a; -y) zo. woodpecker

dzięk|czynny thankful, thank-you; ~i **1.** pl. thanks pl. (**za** A for); **2.** prp. thanks (to); ~i **Bogu** thank God!; ~ować ⟨**po-**⟩ (-uję) thank (**k-u za** A s.o. for)

dzik m (-a; -i) zo. wild boar (też odyniec); ~i wild; fig. (dziwny) odd, peculiar; ~o adv. wildly; fig. (dziwnie) oddly, peculiarly; ~us m (-a; -y), -ska f (-i; G -sek) savage

dziob|ać (-ię), ⟨**~nąć**⟩ (-nę) peck; ~aty pock-marked; ~y pl. → **dziób**

dziób m (-obu/-oba; -oby) bill; (drapieżcy) beak; (statku) bow, (samolotu) nose; F gob; **dzioby** pl. (na twarzy) pock-marks

dzi|siaj → **dziś**; ~**siejszy** today's; contemporary; **po dzień** ~**siejszy** until the present day; ~ś **1.** adv. today; **2.** n (idkl.) today; ~ś **rano** this morning; **od** ~ś from now on; **na** ~ś for today

dziupla f (-i; -e) hollow

dziura f (-y) hole; (w zębie) cavity; F (miejsce) dump, hole; ~**wić** ⟨**prze-**⟩ (-ę) puncture, pierce, perforate; ~**wy** full of holes (też fig.); **garnek** broken

dziur|ka f (-i; G -rek) hole; ~**ka od klucza** keyhole; ~**ka na guzik** buttonhole; ~**kacz** m (-a; -e) punch; ~**kować** (-uję) punch; perforate

dziw m (-u; -y) wonder, (natury itp.) curio; **nie** ~ no wonder; ~**actwo** n (-a) oddity; ~**aczeć** ⟨**z-**⟩ (-eję) become odd; ~**aczka** f (-i; G -czek) eccentric,

F oddity;~**aczny** odd, eccentric;~**ak** *m*
(*-a*; *-cy/-i*) eccentric, F oddity;~**ić** ⟨**z-**,
za-⟩ (*-ę*) surprise, astonish; ~**ić** ⟨**z-**⟩
się (*D*) be surprised (**z** *A* at)

dziwka *f* (*-i*; *G -wek*) *pej.* slut

dziwn|y strange, odd;~**a rzecz** strangely
enough; *nic* ~**ego**, **że** no wonder that

dziwo *n* (*-a*) → **dziw**; ~**ląg** *m* (*-a*; *-i*)
freak, curiosity

DzU, **Dz.U** *skrót pisany:* **Dziennik
Urzędowy** (*law gazette*)

dzwon *m* (*-u*; *-y*) bell; ~**ek** *m* (*-nka*;
-nki) bell; (*dźwięk*) ringing; *bot.* bell-
flower, campanula; ~**ić** ⟨**za-**⟩ (*-ę*)
ring (the bell); (*szkłem itp.*) clink; F
(**do** *G*) call, *Brt.* ring up; ~**ko** *n* (*-a*;
G -nek) slice (**śledzia** of herring);~**ni-**
ca *f* (*-y*; *-e*) belfry

dźwięk|czeć ⟨**za-**⟩ (*-czę*) sound; ring;
~**czny głos** sonorous; *gr.* voiced;~**k** *m*
(*-u*; *-i*) sound; *mus.* tone; **barwa** ~**ku**
tone colo(u)r;**zapis** ~**ku** sound record-

ing; ~**koszczelny** soundproof; ~**kowy**
ścieżka, *film:* sound

dźwig *m* (*-u*; *-i*) (*winda*) *Brt.* lift, *Am.*
elevator; *tech.* crane; ~**ać** (*-am*) *impf.*
lift up; (*nosić*) carry; ~**ar** *m* (*-a/-u*; *-y*)
supporting beam; ~**nąć** *pf.* lift (up);
~**nąć z gruzów** rebuild; ~**nąć się** rise
up; ~**nia** *f* (*-i*; *-e*) *tech.* lever; ~**owy 1.**
adj. crane; lift, elevator; **2.** *m* (*-ego*;
-i), ~**owa** *f* (*-ej*; *-e*) crane-operator

dżdż|ownica *f* (*-y*; *-e*) *zo.* earthworm;
~**u** → **deszcz**; ~**ysty** rainy

dżem *m* (*-u*; *-y*) jam; (*z cytrusów*) marmalade

dżentelmen *m* (*-a*; *-i*) gentleman

dżersej *m* (*-u*; *-e*) jersey

dżez → *jazz*

dżins|owy denim, jean;~**y** *pl.* (*-ów*)jeans

dżokej *m* (*-a*; *-e*) jockey

dżul *m* (*-a*; *-e*) *phys.* joule

dżuma *f* (*-y*; *0*) *med.* (bubonic) plague

dżungla *f* (*-i*; *-e*) jungle

E

echo *f* (*-a*) echo; *fig.* response, reper-
cussions *pl.*; ~**sonda** *f* (*-y*) echo-
-sounder; sonic depth finder

Edynburg *m* (*-a*; *0*) Edinburgh

edukac|ja *f* (*-i*; *0*) education; ~**cyjny**
educational

edycja *f* (*-i*; *-e*) edition

efek|ciarstwo *f*(*-a*;*0*) showiness, flash-
iness; ~**t** *m* (*-u*; *-y*) effect; (*skutek*) result, outcome; **zrobić wielki** ~**t na** leave
a great impression on; ~**towny** effective; ~**tywny** efficient, effective

egi|da *f* (*-y*; *0*): **pod** ~**dą** (*G*) under the
auspices of

Egipcjan|in *m* (*-a*; *-nie*, *-*), ~**ka** *f* (*-i*)
Egyptian

egipski (**po -ku**) Egyptian

Egipt *m* (*-u*; *0*) Egypt

egoist|a *m* (*-y*; *-ści*), ~**ka** *f* (*-i*) egoist;
~**yczny** egoistic(al)

egz. *skrót pisany:***egzemplarz** co.(*copy*)

egzaltowany affected, pretentious

egzamin *m* (*-u*;*-y*)examination, F exam;
~ **z polskiego** examination in Polish, ~ **na prawo jazdy** driving test;
~ **wstępny** entrance examination;

→ **zda**(**wa**)**ć**; ~**acyjny** examination;
~**ować** (*-uję*) examine

egzekuc|ja *f* (*-i*; *-e*) execution; ~**yjny**
nakaz itp. enforcement; **pluton** ~**yjny**
firing squad

egzekwować ⟨**wy-**⟩ (*-uję*) (*wymagać*)
demand, insist on; (*wykonywać*) extort, exact

egzema (*-y*) *med.* eczema

egzemplarz *m* (*-a*; *-e*) copy; **w trzech**
~**ach** in three copies

egzotyczny exotic

egzys|tencja *f* (*-i*; *-e*) existence; **mini-
mum** ~**tencji** subsistence level; ~**to-**
wać (*-uję*) (*istnieć*) exist; (*utrzymywać*
się) subsist

ekierka *f* (*-i*; *G -rek*) set square

ekipa *f* (*-y*) team; (*pracowników*) crew

ekler *m* (*-a*; *-y*) *gastr.* éclair; (*zamek*) zip
(fastener); ~**ka** *f* (*-i*) *gastr.* éclair

ekologi|a *f*(*GDL -ii*; *0*) ecology;~**czny**
ecological

ekonomi|a *f* (*GDL -ii*; *0*) economy;
(*nauka*) economics; → **oszczędność**;
~**czny** economic; (*oszczędny*) economi-
cal; ~**ka** *f* (*-i*; *0*) economics; manage-

ment; **~ka przedsiębiorstwa** business management

ekonomist|a *m* (*-y*; *-ści*), **~ka** *f* (*-i*) economist

eko|system *m* (*-u*; *-y*) ecosystem; **~turystyka** *f* ecotourism

ekran *m* (*-u*; *-y*) screen (*też RTV*); *tech.* shield; **~ kinowy** cinema screen; **szeroki ~** wide screen; **~izacja** *f* (*-i*; *-e*) filming (**powieści** of a novel)

eks|- *w zł.* ex-, former; **~centryczny** eccentric; **~cesy** *m/pl.* (*-ów*) act of violence *pl.*, disturbances *pl.*; **~humacja** *f* (*-i*; *-e*) exhumation, disinterment; **~kluzywny** exclusive; (*luksusowy*) luxurious; **~komunikować** (*-uję*) excommunicate; **~misja** *f* (*-i*; *-e*) eviction; **~mitować** (*-uję*) evict; **~pansja** *f* (*-i*; *0*) expansion; **~patriacja** *f* (*-i*; *-e*) expatriation; **~patriować** (*-uję*) expatriate

ekspedient *m* (*-a*; *-ci*), **~ka** *f* (*-i*) (shop) assistant

eksped|iować ⟨**wy-**⟩ (*-uję*) ship, dispatch, forward; **~ycja** *f* (*-i*; *-e*) expedition; (*towar*) shipment; **~ycja bagażowa** dispatch office; **~ycyjny** expeditionary; dispatch

ekspert *m* (*-a*; *-ci*) expert, specialist, authority; **~yza** *f* (*-y*) expert opinion, expert's report

eksperyment|alny experimental; **~ować** (*-uję*) experiment

eksploat|acja *f* (*-i*; *-e*) use; utilisation; exploitation; *górnictwo*: mining; **być w ~acji** be in use; **oddać do ~acji** put into service; **~ować** (*-uję*) use; utilize; *ludzi* exploit

eksplozja *f* (*-i*; *-e*) explosion

ekspon|at *m* (*-u*; *-y*) exhibit, display item; **~ować** ⟨**wy-**⟩ (*-uję*) display, exhibit; (*podkreślać*) make prominent

eksport *m* (*-u*; *0*) export; **na ~** to be exported; **~ować** ⟨**wy-**⟩ (*-uję*) export; **~owy** export

ekspozy|cja *f* (*-y*; *-e*) exposition, display; **~tura** *f* (*-y*) branch office, agency

ekspres *m* (*-u*; *-y*) (*pociąg itp.*) express; (*pocztowy*) special delivery; **~ do kawy** coffee-maker; **~owy** express; **herbata ~owa** tea bags

ekstaza *f* (*-y*) ecstasy, rapture

eksterminacja *f* (*-i*; *0*) extermination

ekstra (*idkl.*) extra; F first-class, great; **~dycja** *f* (*-i*; *-e*) extradition

ekstrakt *m* (*-u*; *-y*) extract

ekstrawagancki extravagant

ekstrem|alny extreme; **~ista** *m* (*-y*; *-ści*), **~istka** *f* (*-i*) extremist

ekwi|punek *m* (*-nku*; *0*) equipment, gear, outfit; **~walent** *f* (*-u*; *-y*) equivalent

elastyczn|ość *f* (*-ci*; *0*) elasticity; *fig.* flexibility; **~y** elastic; *fig.* flexible

elegan|cki elegant; **~tować się** ⟨**wysię**⟩ F (*-uję*) doll up, dress up

elektor *m* (*-a*; *-rzy*) elector (*też hist.*); **~at** *m* (*-u*; *zw. 0*) electorate; voters *pl.*; **~ski** electoral

elektro|ciepłownia *f* (*-i*; *-e*) heat and power plant; **~da** *f* (*-y*) electrode; **~kardiogram** *m* (*-u*; *-y*) electrocardiogram; **~liza** *f* (*-y*; *0*) electrolysis; **~magnes** *m* (*-u*; *-y*) electromagnet; **~mechanik** *m* (*-a*; *-cy*) electrical engineer; **~monter** *m* (*-a*; *-rzy*) electrician; **~niczny** electronic; **poczta ~niczna** e-mail, email; **~nowy** electron, electronic; **~technika** *f* (*-i*; *0*) electrical engineering

elektrownia *f* (*-i*; *-e*) power station; **~ cieplna/wodna** thermal/hydroelectric power station

elektrowóz *m* (*-wozu*; *-wozy*) electric locomotive

elektry|czność *f* (*-ci*; *0*) electricity; **~czny** electric; **~k** *m* electrician; **inżynier ~k** electrical engineer; **~zować** ⟨**na-, z-**⟩ (*-uję*) electrify

element *m* (*-u*; *-y*) element, component; F shady elements *pl.*; **~y** *pl.* elements *pl.*, rudiments *pl.*

elementarz *m* (*-a*; *-e*) primer

elewa|cja *f* (*-i*; *-e*) façade, frontage; **~tor** *m* (*-a*; *-y*) elevator (*zwł. Am.*), grain silo

eliminac|ja *f* (*-i*; *-e*) elimination; (*w sporcie*) qualifier, qualifying round; **~yjny** qualifying

eliminować ⟨**wy-**⟩ (*-uję*) eliminate; (*wyłączać*) exclude

elip|sa *f* (*-y*) ellipsis; **~tyczny** elliptical

elita *f* (*-y*) élite; **~rny** elitist, select

emali|a *f* (*GDL -ii*; *-e*) enamel; **~owany** enamel(l)ed

emancyp|antka *f* (*-i*) woman emancipation activist, suffragist; **~ować się** ⟨**wy- się**⟩ (*-uję*) emancipate o.s.

emblemat *m* (*-u*; *-y*) emblem

embrion *m* (*-a/-u*; *-y*) embryo

ementalski: *ser* ~ Emmenthal(er)

emeryt *m* (*-a*; *-ci*), **~ka** *f* (*-i*) old-age pensioner; retired person; **~owany** retired; **~ura** *f* (*-y*) retirement; (*pieniądze*) pension; **wcześniejsza ~ura** early retirement; **przejść na ~urę** retire; **pobierać ~urę** receive pension

emigr|acja *f* (*-i*; *-e*) emigration; **na ~acji** in exile; **~acyjny** émigré; in exile; **~ować** (*im)pf* **<wy-**) (*-uję*) emigrate

emi|sja *f* (*-i*; *-e*) (*znaczków itp.*) issue; (*gazów itp.*) emission; (*radiowa lub telewizyjna* broadcast; **~tować** (*-uję*) emit

emocja *f* (*-i*; *-e*) emotion

emocjonalny emotional

emocjonujący (-co) exciting

emulsja *f* (*-i*; *-e*) emulsion; (*kosmetyk*) lotion

encyklika *f* (*-i*) *rel.* encyclical

encyklopedia *f* (*GDL -ii*; *-e*) *Brt.* encyclopaedia, *Am.* encyclopedia; **~yczny** encyclopedic

energety|czny energy; **surowce** *m/pl.* **~czne** energy sources *pl.*; **~ka** *f* (*-i*; *0*) energy sector; (*przemysł*) power industry

energi|a *f* (*GDL -ii*; *0*) energy; power; **~czny** energetic

energo|chłonny energy-consuming; **~oszczędny** energy-saving

entuzja|styczny enthusiastic; **~zmować się** (*-uję*) (*I*) be enthusiastic about

epatować (*-uję*) impress, amaze

epi|cki (-ko), **~czny** epic

epi|demia *f* (*GDL -ii*; *-e*) epidemic; **~lepsja** *f* (*-i*; *-e*) epilepsy

episkopat *m* (*-u*; *-y*) episcopate

epi|tafium *n* (*pl. -fia*, *-fiów*) epitaph; memorial plaque; **~tet** *m* (*-u*; *-y*) epithet; F epithet, abusive word

epizod *m* (*-u*; *-y*) episode

epo|ka *f* (*-i*) epoch, age, time; **~ka kamienna** Stone Age; **~kowy** historic, epoch-making; **~peja** *f* (*-ei*; *-e*, *-ei*) epic, epos

era *f* (*-y*) era; **naszej ery** AD, **przed naszą erą** BC

erekcja *f* (*-i*; *-e*) erection

eremita *m* (*-y*; *-ci*) hermit

erka F *f* (*-i*; *-rek*) emergency ambulance

eroty|ka *f* (*-i*;0) eroticism; **~czny** erotic

erudycja *f* (*-i*; *0*) erudition

erupcja *f* (*-i*; *-e*) eruption

esej *m* (*-u*; *-e*, *-ów*) essay

esencja *f* (*-i*; *-e*) essence; (*herbaciana*) brew

eskadra *f*(*-y*) *aviat.* flight; *naut.* squadron

eskalacja *f* (*-i*; *0*) escalation

Eskimos *m* (*-a*; *-i*), **~ka** *f* (*-i*) Eskimo; **2ki** Eskimo

eskort|a *f* (*-y*) escort; **pod ~ą** under escort; **~ować** (*-uję*) escort

estetyczny esthetic, *Brt.* aesthetic

Esto|nia *f* (*GDL -ii*; *0*) Estonia; **~nka** *f* (*-i*); **~ńczyk** *m* (*-a*; *-cy*) Estonian; **2ński (po -ku)** Estonian

estrad|a *f* (*-y*) platform, podium, dais; **~owy** cabaret

etap *m* (*-u*; *-y*) stage; (*podróży*) leg; **~owo** by stages

eta|t *m* (*-u*; *-y*) permanent position, full-time job; **pracować na pół ~tu** work part-time; **być na ~cie** have a full-time job; have a permanent position; **~towy** permanent, regular

etażerka *f* (*-i*; *G -rek*) shelf unit

eter *m* (*-u*; *0*) *chem.*, *phys.* ether; **na falach ~u** on the air

Etiop|czyk *m* (*-a*; *-cy*) Ethiopian; **~ia** *f* (*GDL -ii*) Ethiopia; **2ski** Ethiopian

etiuda *f* (*-y*) *mus.* etude

etniczny ethnic

ety|czny ethical; **~kieta** *f* (*-y*), **~kietka** *f* (*-i*; *G -tek*) label

etylina *f* (*-y*) *Brt.* leaded petrol, *Am.* ethyl gasoline

eukaliptus *m* (*-a*; *-y*) *bot.* eucalyptus; **~owy** eucalyptus

euroczek *m* (*-u*; *-i*) *Brt.* Eurocheque, *Am.* Eurocheck

Europa *f* (*-y*; *0*) Europe

Europej|czyk *m* (*-a*; *-cy*), **~ka** *f* (*-i*) European; **2ski** European

ewakuac|ja *f* (*-i*; *-e*) evacuation; **~yjny** evacuation

ewakuować (*-uuję*) evacuate

ewan'geli|a *f* (*GDl -ii*; *-e*) (*rel.* 2) Gospel; **~cki** Protestant

ewenement *m* (*-u*; *-y*) sensation

ew(ent). *skrót pisany:* **ewentualnie** alternatively

ewentual|ność *f* (*-ci*; *0*) eventuality; **~ny** possible; **~nie** *adv. też* if applicable, if possible

ewidencja *f* (*-i*; *-e*) registration; (*wykaz*) record(s *pl.*)

ewidencjonować (*-uję*) register; record

ewolucja *f* (*-i*; *-e*) evolution

F

fabryczny factory

'fabryka f (-i) factory; works sg.

fabrykować (-uję) fabricate

fabularny: film ~ feature film

facet F m (-a; -ci) guy, fellow; **~ka** f (-i) pej. female

fach m (-u; -y) trade; **kolega po ~u** fellow-worker by trade; professional colleague; **~owiec** m (-wca; -wcy) F fixer, repairman; (ekspert) specialist, expert; **~owy** professional; expert

facjata f (-y) attic (room); F (twarz) gob

faja F f (GDL -fai; -e, -) pipe

fajansowy faience; earthenware

fajdać F ⟨za-⟩ (-am) shit

fajerwerk m (-u; -i) firework; **~i** pl. (pokaz) fireworks pl.

fajk|a f (-i) pipe; F (papieros) fag; (znaczek) Brt. tick, Am. check; **~owy** pipe

fajny F (-no, -nie) super, great

fajtłapa m/f (-y; G f: -/m: -ów) bungler, duffer

faks m (-u; -y) fax; **~ować** fax

fak|t m (-u; -y) fact; **~t ~tem** it is true; **po ~cie** afterwards, belatedly; **~tyczny** actual; **stan ~tyczny** facts of the matter

fakultatywny optional

fakultet m (-u; -y) faculty

fal|a f (-i; -e) wave (też phys., fig.); fig. flood; **~a zimna** cold wave; **~e pl. średnie** medium waves pl.; **~ami** in waves

falban|a f (-y), **~ka** f (-i; G -nek) frill

falisty ruch, linia, włosy wavy; (-ście, -to) ruch wavelike

falo|chron m (-u; -y) breakwater; **~wać** (-uję) morze, tłum: surge; zboże: wave; **~wanie** n (-a) surge, waving

falstart m (-u; -y) (w sporcie) false start

falsyfikat m (-u; -y) fake, forgery

fałd m (-u; -y), **~a** f (-y) fold; **~ować** ⟨po-, s-⟩ (-uję) fold

fałsz m (-u; -e) (kłamstwo) falsity, falsehood; (obłuda) falseness; **~erka** f (-i; G -rek) forger; counterfeiter; **~erstwo** n (-a; G -tw) forgery; **~erz** m (-a; -e) forger; counterfeiter

fałszowa|ć ⟨s-⟩ (-uję) forge, counterfeit; fakty falsify; melodię sing/play out of tune; **~ny** counterfeit, forged

fałszyw|ość f (-ci; 0) (cecha) duplicity; (stan) falseness; **~y** (-wie) false

fanaty|czny fanatic(al); **~czka** f (-i; G -czek), **~k** m (-a; -cy) fanatic

fanfara f (-y) fanfare; flourish

fant m (-u/-a; -y) forfeit; prize; (w zabawie) forfeit; **gra w ~y** (game of) forfeits

fantastyczny fantastic

fantazj|a f (-i; -e) fantasy; (wymysł) fancy; (animusz) panache, flair; mus. fantasia; **~jować** (-uję) fantasize; **~yjny** imaginative

fantow|y: loteria ~a prize lottery

faraon m (-a; -i/-owie) pharaoh

farb|a f (-y) paint; **~a kryjąca** hiding paint; **~a olejna** oil paint; **~ować** ⟨po-, u-⟩ (-uję) dye

farma f (-y) farm

farma|ceutyczny pharmaceutical; **~cja** f (-i; 0) pharmacy

farmer m (-a; -rzy) farmer

farsa f (-y) farce, burlesque

farsz m (-u; -e) gastr. stuffing, (mięsny) forcemeat

fart F m (-u; 0) luck, break

fartu|ch m (-a; -y) apron; (mechanika) overall; (lekarza) white coat; **~szek** m (-szka; -szki) apron

fasada f (-y) façade; fig. front

fascyn|ować ⟨za-⟩ (-uję) fascinate; **~ujący** (-co) fascinating

fasol|a f (-i; -e) bot. bean(s pl.); **~owy** bean; **zupa ~owa** bean soup; **~ka** f (-i; G -lek) bot. bean; **~ka szparagowa** string bean; **~ka po bretońsku** baked beans pl.

fason m (-u; -y) pattern, cut; fig. style; F **trzymać ~** stand fast

fastryg|a f (-i) tack; **~ować** ⟨s-⟩ (-uję) baste, tack

faszerowa|ć ⟨na-⟩ (-uję) gastr. stuff; **~ć (się)** ⟨na-⟩ pump (o.s.) full of; **~ny** stuffed; warzywa filled

faszystowski Fascist

fatalny skutki itp. unfortunate, fatal; pogoda awful

fatałaszki *m/pl.* (-ów) frippery, finery

fatyg|a *m* (-i) trouble, bother; (*zmęczenie*) fatigue; *nie żałować ~i* spare no effort; *szkoda ~i* it is not worth the trouble; ~ować ⟨*po*-⟩ (-uję) trouble; ~ować ⟨*po*-⟩ *się* (*bezok.*) make an effort (to do)

faul *m* (-a; -e) (*w sporcie*) foul

fawo|ryt *m* (-a; -ci), -tka *f* (-i; *G* -tek) favo(u)rite; ~ryzować (-uję) favo(u)r

faza *f* (-y) stage, phase

febra *f* (-y) *med.* fever

federa|cja *f* (-i; -e) federation; ~cyjny, ~lny federal

feler F *m* (-u; -y) fault, flaw, defect

felieton *m* (-u; -y) column

feministka *f* (-i) feminist, F libber

fenig *m* (-a; -i) pfennig

fenol *m* (-u; -e) *chem.* phenol

fenomenalny phenomenal, extraordinary

feralny unlucky, fatal

ferie *pl.* vacation (*zwł. Am.*), *Brt.* holiday

ferma *f* (-y) farm

fermentować (-uje) ferment

fertyczny spry

festiwal *m* (-u; -e) festival

festyn *m* (-u; -y) feast, festival; ~ *ludowy* public festival; (*w ogrodzie*) garden party

fetor *m* (-u; -y) stink, fetor

fetyszyst|a *m*(-y,-ści),~ka*f*(-i) fetishist

feudalny feudal

fig|a *f* (-i) fig; ~*i pl.* (*majtki*) panties *pl.*

fig|iel *m* (-gla; -gle) joke; ~*le pl.* fooling around; *o mały ~iel* almost, nearly; ~larka *f* (-i) → ~larz; ~larny playful; *uśmiech też.* coquettish; ~larz *m* (-a; -e) trickster, prankster; ~lować (-uję) play jokes; (*wygłupiać się*) fool around

figow|iec *m* (-wca; -wce) fig tree; ~y fig; *listek ~y* fig leaf (*też fig.*)

figur|a *f* (-y) figure; (*postać też*) form; *szachowa:* piece; *iron.* sort, character; ~*a myślowa* hypothesis; F *do ~y* without a coat; ~ować (-uję) figure; (*na spisie*) be, appear; ~owy: *jazda ~owa na lodzie* figure skating

fikać (-am): ~ *nogami* kick one's feet; → *koziołek*

fikcyjny fictional

fikus *m* (-a; -y) *bot.* rubber plant

Filadelfia *f* (-ii; 0) Philadelphia

filar *m* (-a/-u; -y) pillar (*też fig.*); (*mostu*) pier

filatelistyka *f* (-i; 0) philately, stamp collecting

filcowy felt

filet *m* (-u; -y) fillet; ~ *rybny* fish fillet

filharmoni|a *f* (*GDL -ii; -e*) (*budynek*) (philharmonic) concert hall; (*instytucja*) philharmonic society; ~czny philharmonic

filia *f* (*GDL -ii; -e*) branch

Filipi|ny *pl.* (*G* -) Philippines; ~ńczyk *m* (-a; -cy), ~nka *f* (-i; -nek) Filipino

filiżanka *f* (-i) cup

film *m* (-u; -y) film; ~ *oświatowy* documentary film; → *animowany, fabularny, błona,* ~ować ⟨*s*-⟩ (-uję) film, shoot; ~owy film

filologi|a *f* (*GDL -ii; -e*) philology; ~*a angielska* English department; ~czny philological; *studia pl.* ~*czne* foreign language studies *pl.*

filozof *m* (-a; -owie) philosopher; ~ia *f* (*GDL -ii; -e*) philosophy; ~iczny philosophical; ~ka *f* (-i) philosopher; ~ować (-uję) philosophize

filtr *m* (-a/-u;-y) filter; ~ować(-uję) filter

fluterny roguish; mischievous

Fin *m* (-a; -owie) Finn

finali|sta *m* (-y; -ści), ~stka *f* (-i; *G* -tek) finalist; ~zować ⟨*s*-⟩ (-uję) finalize, complete, make final

finał *m* (-u; -y) ending; (*w sporcie*) final; *mus.* finale; ~owy final

finans|e *pl.* (-ów) finances *pl.*; funds *pl.*; ~ować ⟨*s*-⟩ (-uję) finance; ~owy financial

fingować ⟨*s*-⟩ (-uję) fake

Finka *f* (-i; *G* -nek) Finn; ⚥ (*nóż*) sheath knife

Finlandia *f* (*GDL -ii*) Finland

fiński Finnish; *mówić po ~u* speak Finnish

fioletowy (-*wo*) purple; violet

fioł|ek *m* (-*łka; -łki*) violet; ~ek *alpejski* cyclamen; ~ek *trójbarwny* pansy; ~kowy (-*wo*) violet

firanka *f* (-i; *G* -nek) (net) curtain

fircyk *m* (-y; -i) dandy, fop

firm|a *f* (-y) firm, business; ~owy company; *danie ~owe Brt.* speciality, *Am.* specialty; *papier ~owy* letterhead

fiskalny fiscal

fistuła *f* (-y) *med.* → *przetoka*

fito- w zł. phyto

fizjologi|a f (GDL -ii; 0) physiology; **~czny** physiological

fizjonomia f (GDL -ii; -e) physiognomy, countenance

fizyczn|y physical; corporal; (ręczny) manual; **wychowanie ~e** (skrót **WF**) physical education

fizyk m (-a; -cy) physicist; **~a** f (-i; 0) physics

f-ka skrót pisany: **fabryka** factory

flaczki m/pl. (-ów) gastr. tripe

flag|a f (-i) flag; **~owy** flag

flaki m/pl. (-ów) intestines, F guts; gastr. → **flaczki**

flakon m (-u; -y), **~ik** m (-a; -i) bottle; (na kwiaty) vase

Flaman|d m (-a; -owie), **~dka** f (-i) Fleming; 2dzki (**po -ku**) Flemish

flamaster m (-a; -y) felt-tip pen

flaming m (-a; -i) zo. flamingo

flanca f (-y; -e) seedling

flanel|a f (-i; -e) flannel; **~owy** flannel

flanka f (-i; G flank) flank

flaszka f (-i) bottle

flądra f (-y) zo. flounder

flecist|a m (-y; -ści), **~ka** f (-i) flutist

flegma f (-y; 0) phlegm; (opanowanie też) sluggishness; **~tyczny** phlegmatic

flejtuchowaty (**-to**) slobbish

flesz m (-a; -e) phot. flash

flet m (-u; -y) (poprzeczny) flute; (prosty) recorder

flirtować (-uję) flirt

flisak m (-a; -cy) raftsman

florecist|a m (-y; -ści); **~ka** f (-i) foil fencer

Florencja f (-i; 0) Florence

floret m (-u; -y) foil

Floryda f (-y; 0) Florida

flota f (-y) fleet; **~a dalekomorska** deep-sea fleet; **~a wojenna** navy

flower m (-u; -y) small-bore rifle

fluktuacja f (-i; -e) fluctuation

fluor m (-u; 0) chem. fluorine

fochy F pl.(-ów) whims pl.

fok|a f (-i) seal; **~i** pl. (futro) sealskin

fokstrot m (-a; -y) foxtrot

folgować (-uję) (D) be lenient; **~ sobie** take it easy; indulge (**w** in)

foli|a f (GDL -ii; -e) (z metalu) foil; (plastik) plastic; **~owy** foil; plastic

folwark m (-u; -i) estate

fon|etyczny phonetic; **~etyka** f (-i)

phonetics; **~ia** f (-i; 0) sound; **~o-w** zł. phono-

fonoteka f (-i) sound archive

fontanna f (-y) fountain

for m (-a; -y) handicap; **mieć ~y u** find favo(u)r with

foremka f (-i) (do ciasta) (baking) tin; (do zabawy) Brt. mould, Am. mold; → **forma**

foremny shapely

form|a f (-y; G form) shape, form; **nie być w ~ie** be out of form, **być w ~ie** be in (good) form; **~y towarzyskie** good manners; → **foremka**

forma|cja f (-i; -e) formation; **~listyczny** formal; **~lność** f (-ci) formality; **~lny** formal; **w kwestii ~lnej** point of order; **~t** m (-u; -y) format (też komp.); (rozmiar) size; **~tować** ⟨**s-**⟩ (-uję) komp. format

formować ⟨**u-**⟩ (też się v/i.) form, build up; ⟨**s-**⟩ form, group

formu|larz m (-a; -e) form; **~ła** f (-y), **~łka** f (-i) formula; **~łować** ⟨**s-**⟩ (-uję) formulate, express

fornir m (-u; -y) veneer

forsa F f (-y; 0) dough

forsow|ać (-uję) force (też mil.), step up; ⟨**s-**⟩ strain; **~ać się** overstrain; **~ny** forced, intensive

forteca f (-y; -e) fortress

fortel m (-u; -e) trick, scheme

fortepian m (-u; -y) piano; **na ~** for the piano; też. → **~owy** piano

fortun|a f (-y; 0) fortune; **koło ~y** wheel of fortune

fortyfikacja f (-i; -e) fortifications pl.

fosa f (-y) moat

fosfor m (-u; 0) chem. phosphorus; **~yzować** (-uję) phosphoresce

fotel m (-a; -e) armchair; **~ wyrzucany** ejector seat

fotka f (-i; G -tek) snapshot

fotogeniczny photogenic

fotogra|f m (-a; -owie) photographer; **~fia** f (GDL -ii; -e) (sztuka) photography; (zdjęcie) photo(graph); **~ficzny** photographic; **~fować** ⟨**s-**⟩ (-uję) photograph

foto|komórka f photo-electric cell; **~kopia** f photocopy; **~montaż** m photomontage; **~reporter(ka** f) m news reporter

fotos F m (-u; -y) still; (zdjęcie) snapshot

fracht *m* (*-u*; *-y*) freight; **~owiec** *m* (*-wca*; *-wce*) freighter; **~owy** freight

fragment *m* (*-u*; *-y*) fragment; (*tekstu*) excerpt

frajda *f* (*-y*) fun

frajer *m* (*-a*; *-rzy/-y*) nincompoop; **zrobić ~a** (**z k-ś**) take (s.o.) for a ride; **~ka** *f* (*-i*; *G -rek*) silly goose

frak *m* (*-a*; *-i*) tail coat, F tails *pl*.

frakcja *f* (*-i*; *-e*) fraction; *pol*. faction

Fran|cja *f* (*-i*; *0*) France; **2cuski** (**po -ku**) French; **2cuszczyzna** *f* (*-y*; *0*) French language; **~cuz** *m* (*-a*; *-i*) Frenchman; **~zi** the French; **~cuzka** *f* (*-i*) Frenchwoman

frank *m* (*-a*; *-i*) franc

frankować ⟨*o-*⟩ (*-uję*) frank

frapujący (**-co**) astonishing

fraszka *f* (*-i*; *G -szek*) trifle; (*wiersz*) epigram

frazes *m* (*-u*; *-y*) phrase, hackneyed phrase

frekwencj|a *f* (*-i*; *0*) attendance; turn-out; **cieszyć się ~ą** be popular

fresk *m* (*-u*; *-i*) fresco

frez *m* (*-u*; *-y*) cutter; **~arka** *f* (*-i*; *G -rek*) (*do drewna*) mo(u)lding machine; (*do metalu*) milling machine

frędzla *f* (*-i*; *-e*) tassel; **frędzle** *pl*. fringe

fron|t *m* (*-u*; *-y*): **na ~cie** at the front; **~towy** front

froterować ⟨*wy-*⟩ (*-uję*) polish

frotté *n* (*idkl*) terry (towel(l)ing); **ręcznik ~** terry towel

frunąć *pf*. (*-nę*) → **fruwać**

frustrować (*-uję*) frustrate; ⟨*s-*⟩ **~ się** get frustrated

fruwać (*-am*) fly

frycowe F *n* (*-wego*; *0*): **płacić ~** learn the hard way

frykasy *m/pl*. (*-ów*) titbits *pl*., *zwł. Am*. tidbits *pl*.

frytki *f/pl*. *Brt*. chips, *Am*. (French) fries

fryzjer *m* (*-a*; *-rzy*) hairdresser, (*męski*) barber; **~ka** *f* (*-i*; *G -rek*) → **fryzjer**; **~ski: zakład ~ski** hairdresser's

fryzura *f* (*-y*) hairstyle

fujarka *f* (*-i*; *G -rek*) pipe

fund|acja *f* (*-i*; *-e*) foundation; **~ament** *m* (*-u*; *-y*) foundation(s); **~ować** (*-uję*) ⟨*u-*⟩ found, grant; ⟨*za-*⟩ *napój itp*. stand; **~usz** *m* (*-u*; *-e*) fund(s *pl*.); **~usz powierniczy** trust fund

funkc|ja *f* (*-i*; *-e*) function; **~jonalny** functional; **~jonariusz** *m* (*-a*; *-e*), **~jonariuszka** *f* (*-i*) functionary, officer

funkcjonować (*-uję*) function

funt *m* (*-a*; *-y*) pound

fura *f* (*-y*) cart; F (*G*) a heap of

furgonetka *f* (*-i*) van

furi|a *f* (*GDl -ii*; *-e*) fury, rage; **wpaść w ~ę** fly into a rage

furkotać ⟨*-czę/-cę*⟩ *Brt*. whirr, *Am*. whir

furman *m* (*-a*; *-i*) carter, driver; **~ka** *f* (*-i*; *G -nek*) cart

furt|a *f* (*-y*), **~ka** *f* (*-i*; *G -tek*) gate, door

fusy *m/pl*. dregs *pl*.; (*kawy też*) grounds *pl*.; (*herbaty*) tea leaves

fuszer|ka *f* (*-i*) botch, bungle; **~ować** → **partaczyć**

futbolowy soccer, football

futerał *m* (*-u*; *-y*) case; étui

futerkow|y fur; **zwierzę ~e** fur-bearing animal

futro *f* (*-a*) fur

futryna *f* (*-y*): **~ drzwiowa/okienna** door/window frame

futrzany fur

fuzja[1] *f* (*-i*; *-e*) (*strzelba*) shotgun

fuzja[2] *f* (*-i*; *-e*) *econ*. fusion, merger

G

g. *skrót pisany*: **godzina** hr (*hour*)

gabinet *m* (*-u*; *-y*) office; (*pokój w domu*) study; *pol*. cabinet; **~ lekarski** consulting-room; **~ kosmetyczny** beauty salon; **~owy** cabinet

gablotka *f* (*-i*; *G -tek*) display case; show-case

gad *m* (*-a*; *-y*) *zo*. reptile

gada|ć (*-am*) talk, chat, chatter; **~nie** *n* (*-a*), **~nina** *f* (*-y*) chatter; **~tliwy** (**-wie**) talkative

gadzina *f* (*-y*) *pej. fig*. reptile

gaf|a *f* (*-y*) faux pas; gaffe; **popełnić ~ę** make a gaffe

gaj *m* (*-u*; *-e*) grove

gajowy *m* (*-ego*, *-i*) forester

gala f (-i; -e) gala

galaktyka f (-i; G -) galaxy

galanteria f (GDL -ii; 0) gallantry; zbior. fashion accessories pl.

galare|ta f (-y) jelly; (do ryby, mięsa) aspic; **w ~cie** in aspic; **~tka** f (-i) jelly

galeria f (GDl -ii; -e) gallery

galimatias m (-u; 0) → **bałagan**

galon[1] m (-u; -y) (miara) gallon

galon[2] m (-u; -y) braid; (na mundurze) stripe

galop m (-u; 0) gallop; **~em** at a gallop; **~ować** (-uję) gallop

galowy gala; **w stroju ~m** in gala dress; (wojskowy) in full uniform

gałą|zka f (-i) twig; **~ź** f (-ęzi) branch

gałgan m (-a; -y) rag; fig. (pl. -i/-) (łobuz) scamp

gałka f (-i; G -łek) ball; (do drzwi itp., w radiu itp.) knob; **~ oczna** eyeball

gama f (-y) mus. scale; (zakres) range

gamoń m (-nia; -nie) nitwit

ganek m (-nku; -nki) veranda, porch

gang m (-u; -i) gang; **~ samochodowy** gang of car thieves; **~sterski** criminal, gangster

gani|ać (-am) run around/about; (za I) run after; **~ć** ⟨z-⟩ criticize (za A for)

gap m (gapia; -pie, -piów) onlooker; bystander; **~a** F m/f (-y; G -) scatterbrain; → **oferma**; **jechać na ~ę** dodge paying the fare; **~ić się** ⟨za- się⟩ (-ię) gape (**na** A at); **~iostwo** n (-a; 0) absent-mindedness; **~iowaty** (-to) foolish, simple-minded

garaż m (-u; -e) garage

garb m (-u; -y) hunchback, hump (też zo.)

garbarnia f (-i, -e) tannery

garb|aty (-to) hunchbacked; **~ić się** ⟨-ię⟩ stoop

garbować ⟨wy-⟩ tan; fig. **~ komuś skórę** tan s.o's hide

garbus m (-a; -i/-y) hunchback; F (samochód) beetle; **~ka** f (-i) hunchback

garderoba f (-y) (pokój) dressing-room; (szatnia) Am. check-room, Brt. cloak-room; (ubrania) clothes pl., wardrobe

gard|ło n (-a, L -dle; G -deł) throat; **wąskie ~ło** bottleneck; **ból ~ła** sore throat; **na całe ~ło** at the top of one's voice; **~łować** (-uję) clamo(u)r; **~łowy** głos throaty

gardzić ⟨po-, wz-⟩ (I) (-dzę) despise

gardziel f(-i;-e)→**gardło**;fig.bottleneck

garkuchnia f soup kitchen

garmaże|ria f (GDL -ii; -e) delicatessen pl.; **~ryjny** delicatessen pl.

garnąć ⟨**przy-**⟩ (-nę): **~ się** cuddle up (**do** G to); **~ się do nauki** be eager to learn

garn|carnia f (-i; -e) pottery, potter's workshop; **~carz** m (-a; -e) potter

garnek m (-nka; -nki) pot

garnirować (-uję) gastr. garnish

garnitur m (-u; -y) suit; (komplet) set, (mebli) suite

garnuszek m (-szka; -szki) small pot; (kubek) mug

garsonka f (-i; G -nek) woman's suit

gar|stka f (-i; G -tek) fig. handful; **~ść** f (-ści, -ście) hand; (ilość) handful; **wziąć się w ~ść** pull o.s. together

gas|ić ⟨**wy-, z-**⟩ (-szę) put out, extinguish; światło turn off; silnik switch off; (**u-**) pragnienie quench; zapał kill; **~nąć** ⟨**z-**⟩ (-nę) go out; silnik: stall

gastro'nomi|a f (GDL -ii; 0) gastronomy; (restauracje) restaurant trade; **~czny** gastronomic; restaurant

gaszenie n (-a) extinguishing

gaśnica f (-y; -e) fire-extinguisher

gatun|ek m (-nku; -nki) sort, type, brand; biol. species; (jakość) high quality; **~kowy** high-quality; select

gawęda f (-y) tale, chat

gawędzić ⟨**po-**⟩ (-ę) chat

gaworzyć (-rzę) niemowlę: babble

gawron m (-a; -y) zo. rook

gaz m (-u; -y) gas; **~ łzawiący** tear gas; **~ rozweselający** laughing gas; **~ ziemny** natural gas; **pełnym ~em, na pełnym ~ie** at full speed; **pod ~em** drunk; **~y** pl. (jelitowe) wind

gaza f (-y) gauze

gazda m (-y; -owie) jakby: mountain farmer

gaze|ciarka f (-i), **~ciarz** m (-a; -e) (sprzedawca)newspaper-seller,(roznosiciel) newspaper-deliverer; **~ta** f (-y) newspaper, paper; **~towy** newspaper

gazo|ciąg m (-u; -i) gas pipeline; **~mierz** m (-a; -e) gas meter; **~wany** napój sparkling; **~wnia** f (-i; -e) gasworks sg.; **~wy** gas; chem., phys. gaseous

gaździna f (-y) jakby: mountain farmer

gaźnik m (-a; -i) carburettor, Am. carburetor

gaża *f* (*-y*; *-e*) fee, honorarium

gąb|czasty (*-to*) spongy; **~ka** *f* (*-i*) sponge (*też zo.*)

gąsienic|a *f* (*-y*; *-e*) *zo.*, *tech.* caterpillar; *tech.* caterpillar (track); **~owy** caterpillar

gąsior *m* (*-a*; *-y*) *zo.* gander; (*naczynie*) demijohn

gąska *f* (*-i*, *-sek*) *zo.* young goose; gosling; *bot.* blewits *sg.*; **głupia ~** a silly goose

gąszcz *m* (*-u*; *-e*) thicket; dense undergrowth; *fig.* tangle

gbur *m* (*-a*; *-y*) oaf; **~owaty** (*-to*) oafish

gdakać (*-czę*) *kura:* cackle

gderać (*-am*) grumble, carp

gdy *cj.* when; as; **~ tylko** as soon as; **podczas ~** when, during; **~by** *cj.* if

gdynki

gdyż *cj.* because

gdzie where; **~ indziej** somewhere else; → **bądź**; **~kolwiek** anywhere; **~'nie-gdzie** here and there; **~ś** some place (or other); **~ż** where else

gej F *m* (*-a*; *-e*) gay

gem *m* (*-a*; *-e*) (*w sporcie*) game

gen *m* (*-u*; *-y*) gene

gencjana *f* (*-y*) gentian

genealogiczn|y:**drzewo ~e** family tree

genera|cja *f* (*-i*; *-e*) generation; **~lny** general, overall; **~lne porządki** thorough cleaning

generał *m* (*-a*; *-owie*) general

gene|tyczny genetic; **~tyka** *f* (*-i*; *0*) genetics *sg.*; **~za** *f* (*-y*; *0*) genesis

geni|alny brilliant; of genius; **~usz** *m* (*-a*; *-e*) genius

genowy *biol.* gene

geo|'grafia *f* (*GDL -ii*; *0*) geography; **~graficzny** geographical; **~logia** *f* (*GDL -ii*; *0*) geology; **~logiczny** geological; **~metria** *f* (*GDL -ii*; *-e*) geometry; **~metryczny** geometrical

germa'nistyka *f* (*-i*) (*studia*) German studies *pl.*; (*instytut*) German department

gest *m* (*-u*; *-y*) gesture (*też fig.*)

getto *n* (*-a*) ghetto

gęb|a F *f* (*-y*; *G gąb/gęb*) (*usta*) trap, *Brt.* gob; (*twarz*) mug; *zo.* mouth; **zamknij ~ę!** shut your trap!; **dać w ~ę** smack in the ~; **~owy** oral

gę|gać (*-am*) gaggle; **~si** goose; **~siego** in single *lub* Indian file; **~si-**

na *f* (*-y*; *0*) goose

gest|nieć ⟨*z-*⟩ (*-eję*) ciecz, mgła: thicken, get thicker; *tłum:* become more dense; **~ość** *f* (*-ści*) thickness; density; **~wina** *f* (*-y*) thicket, dense undergrowth; **~y** (*-to*) thick; dense

gęś *f* (*-si*; *I -siami/-śmi*) goose

giąć (*gnę*) ⟨**się** *v/i.*⟩ bend

gibki (*-ko*) lithe, supple

gicz *f* (*-y*; *-e*): **~ cielęca** knuckle of veal

gieł|da *f* (*-y*) *econ.* exchange; **~dowy** exchange; **~dziarz** *m* (*-a*; *-e*) stock-market speculator

giemza *f* (*-y*; *0*) kid

gier *G pl.* → **gra**

giermek *m* (*-mka*; *-mkowie*) *hist.* shield-bearer

giętk|i elastic; *fig.* flexible; **~ość** (*-ści*; *0*) elasticity; flexibility

gigantyczny gigantic

gil *m* (*-a*; *-e*) *zo.* bullfinch

gimnasty|czny gymnastic; **~k** *m* (*-a*; *-cy*), **~czka** *f* (*-i*; *G -czek*) gymnast; (*nauczyciel*) PE teacher; **~ka** *f* (*-i*; *0*) gymnastics *sg.*; (*ćwiczenia*) gymnastics *pl.*; **~kować się** (*-uję*) do gymnastics, exercise

gimna|zjalny *Brt.* grammar-school, *Am.* high-school; **~zjum** *n* (*idkl.*; *-a*, *-ów*) *Brt.* (*a three-year school between primary school and secondary school*)

ginąć (*-nę*) ⟨*z-*⟩ die (*też fig.* *z G* of), perish; (*niknąć*) disappear, vanish; (*gubić się*) ⟨*też za-*⟩ get lost

ginekolog *m* (*-a*; *-owie/-dzy*) gynecologist, *Brt.* gynaecologist; **~ia** *f* (*GDl -ii*; *0*) gynecology, *Brt.* gynaecology

gips *m* (*-u*; *-y*) plaster; *chem.* gypsum; **~owy** plaster; gypsum

girlsa *f* (*-y*) chorus-girl

giro- w *zł.* → **żyro-**

gisernia *f* (*-i*; *-e*) *tech.* foundry

gita|ra *f* (*-y*) *mus.* guitar; **~rzysta** *m* (*-y*; *-ści*), **~rzystka** *f* (*-i*) guitar player, guitarist

glansowany shining, gleaming, polished

glazur|a *f* (*-y*) glaze, glazing; (*kafelki*) tiling; **~ować** ⟨*po-*⟩ (*-uję*) glaze; (*kafelkami*) tile

gleba *f* (*-y*) soil; *fig.* ground

ględzić F (*-dzę*) blather, zwł. *Am.* blether; prattle

gliceryna *f* (*-y*; *0*) glycerine

glin *m* (*-u*; *-0*) *chem. Brt.* aluminium, *Am.* aluminum

glina *f* (*-y*) clay

glinian|ka *f* (*-i*; *G -nek*) (*zagłębienie*) clay-pit; **~y** clay; (*naczynie itp.*) earthen

gliniarz *m* (*-a*; *-e*) F cop

gliniasty clayey

glinka *f* (*-i*; *G -nek*) clay; **~ kaolinowa** kaolin

glista *f* (*-y*; *-y, glist*) ascarid; F earthworm

glob *m* (*-u*; *-y*) globe; **~alny** global; (*suma itp.*) total

globus *m* (*-a/-u*; *-y*) globe

glon *m* (*-u*; *-y*) *bot.* alga

glosa *f* (*-y*) gloss

gł. *skrót pisany:* **główny** main

gładk|i smooth (*też fig.*); (*bez ozdób*) simple; **~o wygolony** clean-shaven; **~ość** *f* (*-ci*; *0*) smoothness; simplicity

gładzić (*-dzę*) ⟨**wy-**⟩ smooth out/down; ⟨**po-**⟩ → **głaskać**

głaskać ⟨**po-**⟩ (*-szczę/-am*) stroke; **~ się** stroke o.s.

głaz *m* (*-u*; *-y*) boulder

głąb[1] *m* (*-a*; *-y*) (*kapusty*) heart; F *fig.* fool

głąb[2] *f* (*głębi*; *-ębie*) interior; **w ~ kraju** inland, toward the interior

głęb|ia *f* (*-i*; *-e*) depth; *phot.* **~ia ostrości** depth of focus; **w ~i** deeply, profoundly; **z ~i serca** from the bottom of the heart; **~iej** *adv.* (*comp. od* → **głęboki**) deeper; *stopn.* abyssal; **studnia ~inowa** deep well; **~oki** deep; profound (*też fig.*); *głos* low; *sen* sound; **~oko** deep(ly); **~oko idący** far-reaching; **~okość** *f* (*-ści*) depth; **~szy** *adj. comp. od* → **głęboki**

głodny (*-no*) hungry; F **strasznie ~ jestem** I'm famished

głodow|ać (*-uję*) starve; **~y** hunger; *dieta itp.* starvation; **umrzeć śmiercią ~ą** starve to death

głodówka *f* (*-i*) (*leczenie*) starvation diet; (*strajk*) hunger strike

głodzić ⟨**wy-**⟩ (*-dzę*) starve; **~ się** go hungry, starve

głos *m* (*-u*; *-y*) voice; (*ptaka*) call; (*prawo głosu*) say; (*w wyborach*) vote; *mus.* part; **prosić o ~** ask to speak; **zabrać ~** take the floor; **na cały ~** loud(ly); **~ić** (*-szę*) preach; **~ka** *f* (*-i*; *G -sek*) *gr.* sound

głosow|ać (*-uję*) vote (*nad I* on; **za** *I*, **na** *A* for; **przeciwko** *D* against); **~anie** *n* (*-a*) voting; **~y** (*-wo*) vocal; *gr.* sound

głoś|nik *m* (*-a*; *-i*) loudspeaker; **~ność** *f* (*-ci*; *0*) loudness; **~ny** (*-no*) loud; (*sławny*) famous

głow|a *f* (*-y*) head; **~a państwa/rodziny** head of state/the family; **bez ~y** *fig.* panic-stricken; **na ~ę, od ~y** per head/ capita; **uderzyć k-ś do ~y** go to s.o.'s head; **strzelić do ~y** suddenly occur to, come to mind; **łamać ~ę, zachodzić w ~ę** rack one's brains; **chodzić komu po ~ie** have *s.th.* on the brain; **wbić sobie do ~y** get it into one's head; **mieć ~ę na karku** have one's head screwed on; **włos mu z ~y nie spadnie** (*D*) nobody will harm a hair on his head; **to stoi na ~ie** it is wrong side up; **~ą w dół** headlong; **~a do góry!** cheer up!; **od stóp do głów** from head to toe

głowiasty *bot.* head

głowi|ca *f* (*-y*; *-e*) *tech., mil.* head; *arch.* capital; **~ć się** (*-ię*; *głów!*) rack one's brains (*nad I* over); **~zna** *f* (*-y*) pig's head

głód *m* (*-łodu*; *0*) hunger; **~ mieszkaniowy** housing crisis; **klęska głodu** famine

głóg *m* (*-ogu*; *-ogi*) *bot.* hawthorn

głów|ka *f* (*-i*) (*fajki*) bowl; (*młotka*) head; (*w sporcie*) header; **~ka maku** poppyhead; **~ka czosnku** bulb of garlic

głów|nie *adv.* mainly, chiefly; **~odowodzący** *m* (*-ego*; *-y*) commander in chief; **~y** main, chief

głuchnąć (*-nę*) ⟨**o-**⟩ go deaf; (*cichnąć*) die away

głucho *adv.* hollowly, dully; quietly; **zamknięty na ~** locked up; **~niemy** deaf-mute, *pej.* deaf and dumb; **~ta** *f* (*-y*; *0*) deafness

głuchy 1. deaf (*też fig. na A* to); (*dźwięki*) hollow; (*cisza, prowincja*) deep; **~ jak pień** stone-deaf; **2.** *m* (*-ego*; *-si*) deaf man; **głusi** the deaf *pl.*

głupi 1. foolish, stupid; **udawać ~ego** act stupid; **2.** *m* (*-ego*; *-*) → fool; **~ec** *m* (*-pca*; *-pcy*) fool; **~eć** ⟨**z-**⟩ (*-eję*) go stupid, get daft

głup|io *adv.* stupidly; foolishly; **czuć się ~io** feel stupid; **~ota** *f* (*-y*; *0*) foolishness, stupidity; **~stwo** *n* (*-a*) nonsense; (*drobnostka*) trifle, nothing

głusz|a *f* (-*y*; -*e*) wilderness; ~ec *m* (-*szca*, -*szce*) *zo.* capercaillie, wood grouse; ~yć (-*szę*) ⟨**o-**⟩ stun; ⟨**za-**⟩ drown out; (*chwasty*) overgrow

gm. *skrót pisany:* **gmina** commune

gmach *m* (-*u*; -*y*) building, edifice

gmatwać ⟨**po-**⟩ tangle; (*też* ⟨**za-**⟩) (-*am*) confuse; ~ **się** get confused

gmatwanina *f* (-*y*) tangle

gmerać (-*am*) rummage around/about

gmin|a *f* (-*y*) commune; ~**ny** communal

gnać (*gnam*) rush

gnat F *m* (-*a*; -*y*) bone

gną, gnę → **giąć**

gnębić (-*ę*) suppress, oppress; *fig.* worry, pester

gniazd|kon (-*a*) *electr.* socket, *Am.* outlet; → ~**o** *n* (-*a*) nest; → **wtyczkowy**

gnicie *n* (-*a*; 0) decay, rotting

gnić ⟨**z-**⟩ (-*ję*) decay, rot

gnida *f* (-*y*) *zo.* nit; *fig. pej.* blighter

gnie|sz → **giąć**, ~**ść** press; *gastr.* mash, *ciasto* knead; *fig.* weigh on; → **miąć**; ~**ść się** crowd, throng

gniew *m* anger; **wpaść w** ~ get angry; ~**ać** (-*am*) anger, enrage; ~**ać** ⟨**po-**⟩ **się** get angry (**na** *A* with); ~**ny** angry, cross

gnieździć się (-*żdżę*) nest *fig.* live (in a cramped space)

gnij → **giąć, gnić**

gno|ić (-*ję*) fertilize; (*upokarzać*) F slag off, put down; ~**jowisko** *n* (-*a*) manure heap; ~**jówka** *f* (-*i*; *G* -*wek*) liquid manure

gnój *m* (*gnoju*; 0) manure, dung; (*gnoju*; -*e*) V asshole

gnuśn|ieć ⟨**z-**⟩ (-*eję*) get sluggish; ~**y** sluggish

go *pron.* (*ściągn. jego*) → **on**

godło *n* (-*a*; *G* -*deł*) emblem; ~ **państwowe** national emblem

godn|ie *adv.* fittingly; (*z godnością*) with dignity; ~**ość** *f* (-*ci*; 0) dignity; (*pl.* -*ści*) high position/rank; *jak Pana*/ *Pani* ~**ość?** what is your name?; ~**y** worthy; suitable; *podziwu* ~**y** admirable; ~**y zaufania** trustworthy; ~**y pogardy** despicable; ~**y polecenia** recommendable; *nic* ~**ego uwagi** nothing noteworthy

gody *pl.* (-*ów*) *biol.* mating period; *weselne* ~ wedding; *złote* ~ golden wedding (anniversary)

godz. *skrót pisany:* **godzina** hr (*hour*)

godzi|ć (-*dzę*, *gódź!*) ⟨**po-**⟩ reconcile, conciliate; ~**ć się** become reconciled; *v/i.* (**w** *A*) aim (at); *v/r.* ~**ć** ⟨**po-**⟩ **się** (**z** *I*) agree (to); resign o.s. (to); → **zgadzać się, przystawać**[1]; ~**en** *pred.* → **godny**

godzin|a *f* (-*y*) hour; *która* ~**a?** what time is it? *jest* (~**a**) *druga* it is two (o'clock); *o której* ~**ie?** at what time?; *za* ~**ę** in an hour; *z* ~**y na** ~**ę** from hour to hour, hourly; ~**ami** for hours and hours; ~**y otwarcia** opening hours; → **przyjęcie, nadliczbowy**; ~**ny** one--hour; ~**owy** (-**wo**) hour(ly)

gogle *pl.* (-*i*) (protective) goggles *pl.*

goić ⟨**wy-, za-**⟩ (-*ję*, *gój!*) heal; ~ ⟨**wy-, za-**⟩ **się** heal up/over

golarka *f* (-*i*; *G* -*rek*) shaver

goleni|e (**się**) *n* (-*a*) shaving, shave; *maszynka do* ~**a** electric shaver; *płyn po* ~**u** shaving lotion

goleń *f* (-*ni*; -*nie*) shank

golf[1] *m* (-*a*; 0) golf

golf[2] *m* (-*u*; -*y*) polo neck, turtleneck; ~**y** *pl.* (*spodnie*) knickerbockers *pl.*

golić ⟨**o-**⟩ (-*lę*, *gól!*) (**się** *v/i.*) shave

golonka *f* (-*i*; *G* -*nek*) *gastr.* knuckle of pork

gołąb *m* (-*ębia*; -*ębie*, -*bi*) pigeon, dove; ~ *pocztowy* carrier pigeon; ~**ki** *m/pl.* (-*bków*) *gastr.* stuffed cabbage

gołęb|i pigeon; *fig.* dovelike; ~**iarz** *m* (-*a*; -*e*) pigeon keeper; ~**ica** *f* (-*y*; -*e*) pigeon; ~**nik** *m* (-*a*; -*i*) pigeon-loft

goło *adv.* → **goły**; ~**ledź** *f* (-*dzi*; -*dzie*) black ice; ~**słowny** groundless; ~**wąs** F *m* callow youth

goły naked, bare; *drut, ręce, drzewa* bare; *pod* ~**m niebem** in the open (air); ~**mi rękoma** with bare hands; ~**m okiem** with the naked eye

gondola *f* (-*i*; -*e*) gondola

goni|ć (-*ę*) (*A*, **za** *I*) chase (after); → **poganiać**; *v/i.* hurry, hasten; ~**ć się** race; ~**ec** *m* (-*ńca*; -*ńcy*, -*ńców*) office boy, (*dziewczyna*) office girl; (*pl.* -*ńce*) *szachy*: bishop; ~**twa** *f* (-*y*; *G* -) race; chase

gont *m* (-*a*/-*u*; -*y*) shingle

gończy (*pies*) hunting; *list* ~ 'wanted' poster

GOPR *skrót:* **Górskie Ochotnicze Pogotowie Ratunkowe** mountain rescue service

gorąco¹ n (-a; 0) heat

gorąco² adv. warmly; hot; **~o (jest)** it is hot; **na ~o** fig. live; **parówki** f/pl. **na ~o** sausages served hot

gorącokrwisty warm-blooded

gorący hot; fig. hot-blooded; **złapać k-ś na ~m uczynku** catch s.o. red-handed

gorączk|a f (-i) fever (też fig.); fig. excitement; F (człowiek) hothead; **biała ~a** delirium tremens; **~ować** (-uję) run a fever; **~ować się** get excited; **~owy** feverish (też fig.)

gorczyca f (-y; 0) bot. mustard

gorę|cej adv. comp. od → **gorąco**; **~tszy** adj. comp. od → **gorący**

gorliw|iec m (-wca; -wcy) zealot, fanatic; **~ość** f (-ści; 0) zeal, enthusiasm; **~y** (-wie) zealous

gors m (-u; -y) bust; (koszuli) shirt-front; **~et** m (-u; -y) corset

gorsz|ący (-co) offensive, objectionable; **~y** adj. (comp. od → **zły**); **co ~a** what is worse; **~yć** ‹z-› (-ę) give offence (**k-o** to s.o.), scandalize (I with); **~yć** ‹z-› **się** (I) be offended (at), be scandalized (at)

gorycz f (-y; 0) bitterness (też fig.); **~ka** f (-i; G -czek) bitter taste; bot. gentian

goryl m (-a; -e) zo. gorilla

gorzej adv., adv. comp. od → **źle** worse

gorzelnia f (-i; -e) distillery

gorzk|i (-ko) bitter (też fig.); **~nąć** (-nę), **~nieć** ‹z-› (-eję) grow bitter, fig. become embittered

gospoda f (-y) inn, restaurant

gospodar|czy (-czo) economic; **~ka** f (-i; G -rek) economy; (rolna) farm, farming; (zarządzanie) management; **zła ~ka** mismanagement; **~ny** economical; **~ować** (-uję) (I) manage; (**na** L) farm; **~ski** economic; **~stwo** n (-a) farm; **~stwo domowe** household

gospo|darz m (-a; -e) farmer; (pan domu) host; (wynajmujący) landlord; **~darz schroniska** warden; **~dyni** f (-i; -e, -ń) (pani domu) hostess; (wynajmująca) landlady; → **~sia** f (-i; -e) housekeeper

gościć (-szczę) v/t. be host to, entertain; v/i. stay (**u G** with); **zbyt długo u k-ś ~** overstay one's welcome

gościec m (-śćca; 0) med. rheumatism; F rheumatics pl.

gościn|a f (-y; 0) visit; **w ~ie/~ę** on a visit; **~iec** m (-ńca; -ńce) (droga) country road; **~ność** f (-ści; 0) hospitality; **~ny** hospitable; **pokój ~ny** guest lub spare room

gość m (-ścia; -ście, ści, I -śćmi) guest; visitor; F guy, chap; → **facet, klient**; **mieć ~ci** have visitors

gotow|ać (-uję) ‹u-, z-, za-› wodę boil (**się** v/i.); obiad cook ; fig. **~ać** ‹u-, za-› **się** seethe; → **przygotowywać**; **~any** boiled; **~ość** f (-ści; 0) readiness; **~y** ready (**do** G for; **na** A to do); **~y do użycia** ready to be used; **~e ubrania** ready-made clothes

gotów pred. → **gotowy**; **~ka** f (-i; 0) cash; **zapłacić ~ką** pay cash; **za ~kę** for cash; **~kowy** cash

goty|cki Gothic; **~k** m (-u; i) Gothic

goździk m (-a; -i) bot. (kwiat) pink, carnation; (przyprawa) clove; **~owy** pink, carnation; clove

gór|a f (-y) mountain; (sukni) top; (fartucha) bib; (budynku) (the) upstairs; **do ~y, na/w ~ę** up(wards), (budynku) upstairs; **na górze** up (here/there), (budynku) upstairs; **od ~y do dołu** from top to bottom; **pod ~ę** uphill; **u ~y** at the top; **z ~y** from above; fig. condescendingly; (płacić) in advance; **z ~ą** (ponad) with interest; **iść w ~ę** fig. go up; **brać ~ę** gain the upper hand

góral m (-a; -e), **~ka** f (-a; -i) highlander

górka f (-i; G -rek) mountain

górni|ctwo n (-a; 0) mining; **~czy** mining; **~k** m (-a; -cy) miner

gór|nolotny high-flown; **~ny** upper; high; **~ny Śląsk** Upper Silesia; **~ować** (-uję) (**nad** I) dominate, overlook; be superior (**~ować siłą nad** in power to); → **dominować, przodować**; **~ski** mountain; **choroba ~ska** med. mountain sickness

Góry Skaliste pl. Rocky Mountains pl., Rockies pl.

górzysty mountainous

gówniarz m (-a; -e) F squirt

gówno V n (-a; G -wien) shit; **~ prawda** bullshit

gr skrót pisany: **grosz(y)** gr (grosze)

gra f (gry; G gier) play (też fig.); mus. playing, performance; (w sporcie) game; (aktora) acting, performance; **~ na fortepianie** piano performance; **~ w kar-**

groszek

ty card game, *nie wchodzić w grę* be out of the question

grab *m* (*-u/-a*; *-y*) *bot.* hornbeam

grabarz *m* (*-a*; *-e*) grave-digger

grabi|ć (*-ę*) rake; ⟨*tupić*⟩ rob; *~e pl.* (*-i*) rake; *~eć* ⟨*z-*⟩ (*-eję*) grow numb (*z zimna* from cold)

grabież *f* (*-y*; *-e*) robbery, plunder; *~ca* *m* (*-y*; *G -ów*) robber; plunderer

grabina *f* (*-y*) hornbeam (wood)

graca *f* (*-y*; *-e*) hoe

gracj|a *f* (*-i*; *-e*) grace; *z ~ą* gracefully

gracować (*-uję*) hoe

gracz *m* (*-a*; *-e*) player

grać (*-am*) ⟨*za-*⟩ play (*na flecie* the flute; *w koszykówkę* play basketball); → *gra*; *~ na nerwach* get on *s.o.*'s nerves; *~ na zwłokę* play for time; *co grają w kinie?* what's on at the cinema?

grad *m* (*-u*; *0*) hail; *fig.* storm; *pada ~* it is hailing; *~obicie* *n* (*-a*) hailstorm

gradzina *f* (*-y*) hailstone

grafi|czny graphic; *karta ~czna* *komp.* graphics card; *~k* *m* (*-a*; *-cy*) graphic designer; *~ka* *f* (*-i*; *0*) graphics *sg.*

grafit *m* (*-u*; *0*) *chem.* graphite; (*-u*; *-y*) (*do ołówka*) lead

grafologiczny graphologic(al)

graham *m* (*-a*; *-y*) whole-wheat bread

grajek *m* (*-jka*; *-jki*, *-jkowie*) player

gram *m* (*-a*; *-y*) gram

gramaty|czny grammatical; *~ka* *f* (*-i*) grammar

granat *m* (*-u*; *-y*) *bot.* pomegranate; (*mineral*) garnet; (*kolor*) navy blue; *mil.* grenade; *~ ręczny* hand grenade; *~owy* (*-wo*) navy blue

grand|a *f* (*-y*) row; *na ~ę* by force, unceremoniously

graniastosłup *m* (*-a*; *-y*) prism

graniasty sharp-edged, angular

grani|ca *f* (*-y*; *-e*) (*państwowa*) border, frontier; (*majątku itp.*) boundary; (*rozgraniczenie*) borderline; (*zakres*) limit; *za ~cą/za ~cę* abroad; *na ~cy* at the border; *~czny* border, frontier; *~czyć* (*-ę*) border (*z A* on); *fig.* verge (*z A* on)

granit *m* (*-u*; *-y*) granite; *~owy* granite

granulowany granulated

grań *f* (*-ni*; *-nie*, *-ni*) ridge

grasica *f* (*-y*; *-e*) *anat.* thymus (gland)

grasować (*-uję*) stalk, prowl; *choroba*: rage

grat *m* (*-a*; *-y*) a piece of junk; (*pojazd*) F

heap; *~y pl.* junk, trash

gratis(owy) free, complimentary

gratka *f* (*-i*) (dead) bargain; windfall

gratul|acje *pl.* (*-i*) congratulations *pl.*; *~ować* ⟨*po-*⟩ congratulate (*czegoś* on s.th.)

gratyfikacja *f* (*-i*; *-e*) gratuity, bonus

grawerować ⟨*wy-*⟩ engrave

grawerunek *m* (*-nku*; *-nki*) engraving

grążel *m* (*-a*; *-e*) *bot.* water-lily

grdyka *f* (*-i*) Adam's apple

Gre|cja *f* (*-i*; *0*) Greece; **2cki** (*po -cku*) Greek; *~czynka* *f* (*-i*; *G -nek*), *~k* *m* (*-a*; *-cy*) Greek; **2ka** *f* (*-i*; *0*) Greek (language)

gremi|alnie *adv.* in a body, en masse; *~alny* joint, unified

Grenlandia *f* (*-ii*; *0*) Greenland

grobla *f* (*-i*; *-e*, *G -el*) dike, embankment

grobow|iec *m* (*-wca*; *-wce*) tomb; *~iec rodzinny* family vault; *~o* gravely; gloomily; *~y* grave; sepulchral; (*ponury*) gloomy; *cisza* dead; *do ~ej deski* till death

groch *m* (*-u*; *0*) *bot.* pea(s *pl.*); *~ z kapustą* mishmash; *~owy* pea; *~ówka* *f* (*-i*, *G -wek*) *gastr.* pea soup

grodzi|ć (*-dzę*) → **ogradzać, zagradzać**; *~sko* *n* (*-a*) castle

grodzki municipal, city, town

grom *m* (*-u*; *-y*) thunder; *jak ~ z jasnego nieba* like a bolt from the blue

gromad|a *f* (*-y*) crowd, group; *~nie* *adv.* in a group, in droves; *~ny* group, (*liczny*) numerous

gromadzi|ć ⟨*na-, z-*⟩ (*-dzę*) accumulate (*też się* v/i.); (*o ludziach*) group together, gather (*też się* v/i.)

gromić ⟨*z-*⟩ (*-ę*) rebuke, scold

gromki loud; *oklaski itp.* thunderous

gromni|ca *f* (*-y*; *-e*) votive candle; *~czny*: (*dzień*) **Matki Boskiej 2cznej** Candlemas

gron|kowce *m/pl.* (*-ów*) staphylococci; *~o* *f* (*-a*; *G -*) (*winne*) bunch, (*porzeczek itp.*) cluster; (*grupa*) bunch

gronostaj *m* (*-u*; *-e*) *zo.* stoat; *~e pl.* (*futro*) ermine

gronowy grape

grosz *m* (*-a*; *-e*) grosz; (*austriacki*) groschen; *fig.* penny; F (*pieniądze*) *zbior.* money, F *~a* dough; *bez ~a* without a penny; *co do ~a* down to a penny

grosz|ek *m* (*-szku*; *-szki*) green pea-

(s pl.); (deseń) polka-dot; **w ~ki** polka-dot

groszowy grosz, fig. penny

grot m (-u; -y) head; **~ strzały** arrowhead

grota f (-y) cave

groteskowy grotesque; (śmieszny) ridiculous

grotołaz m (-a; -i/-y) speleologist; (sportowy) caver

groz|a f (-y) awe; terror; **zdjęty ~ą** overawed, intimidated; **~ić** (-żę) terrify (I with); endanger; **za ... ~i mu więzienie** he is liable to imprisonment for ...

groź|ba f (-y; G gróźb) threat; danger; **~ba pożaru** danger of fire; **pod ~bą** (G) under threat of; **~ny** dangerous; mina itp. threatening

grożący impending, threatening: **~ śmiercią** mortally dangerous; **~ zawaleniem** in imminent danger of collapsing

grób m (-obu; -oby) grave

gród m (-odu; -ody) castle; town

grub|as m (-a; -y), **~aska** f (-i) fatty, F fatso; **~ieć** (**po-, z-**) (-eję) grow fat; głos: become lower; **~iej** adv. comp. od → **grubo**

grubo adv. thickly; (z miarami) thick; podkreślać heavily; (mało subtelnie) coarsely, roughly; → **gruby**; **~skórny** fig. thick-skinned; **~ść** f (-ści; 0) thickness; (ludzi) fatness; **~ziarnisty** coarse

grub|y thick; człowiek fat; płótno, ziarno coarse; głos deep; **~e pieniądze** F heaps of money; **z ~sza** roughly; **w ~szych zarysach** in rough outline

gruch|ać (-am) coo; fig. bill and coo; **~nąć** v/s. (-chnę) v/i. crash; wieść: break; → **grzmotnąć (się** v/i.); **~ot** m (-u; -y) rattle; F (rzecz) museum-piece, (samochód) heap; **~otać** (-ocze-/-cę) v/i. rattle, clatter; (**po-, z-**) shatter, smash

gruczoł m (-u; -y) anat. gland; **~ dokrewny** endocrine gland; **~owy** glandular

gru|da f (-y; G -) clod, clump; **jak po ~dzie** with great difficulty; **~dka** f (-i; G -dek) small clod; **~dniowy** December; **~dzień** m (-dnia; -dnie) December

grunt m (-u; -y) ground; soil; land; F **~ to ...** the main thing is ...; **do ~u** totally, utterly; **z ~u** at heart; in fact; **w gruncie rzeczy** in fact, at bottom

gruntow|ać (**za-**) (-uję) prime; (zmie-

rzyć) też fig. fathom; **~ny** fundamental; basic; **~y** soil; warzywa outdoor

grup|a f (-y) group; **~ować** (**z-**) (-uję) group, gather (też **się** v/i.); **~owo** in a group; **~owy** group

grusz|a f (-y; -e) anat. pear (tree) → **~ka** f (-i; G -szek) pear; **~(k)owy** pear

gruz m (-u; -y) rubble; **~y** pl. ruins pl.; **zamienić w ~y** devastate, ravage

gruzeł m (-zła; -zły) lump

Gruz|ja f (-i; 0) Georgia; **~in** m (-a; -i), **~inka** f (-i; G -nek) Georgian; Ω**iński** (**po -ku**) Georgian

gruzowisko n (-a) heap of rubble

gruźli|ca f (-y; -e) med. tuberculosis, TB; **~czy** tubercular; **~k** m (-a; -cy), **~czka** f (-i; G -czek) tubercular

gry G pl. → **gra**

gryczan|y buckwheat; **kasza ~a** buckwheat (grits)

gryf m (-a; -y) griffin; (-u; -y) (gitary itp.) neck

gryka f (-i) buckwheat

gryma|s m (-u; -y) grimace; **~sy** pl. whims pl.; **~sić** (-szę) be finicky; dziecko: give trouble, Brt. play up; **~śny** capricious, whimsical

gryp|a f (-y) influenza, F flu; **~owy** influenza, F flu

gryps F m (-u; -y) secret message

grysik m (-u; 0) semolina

grywać (-am) play occasionally

gryzący biting (też fig.); zapach sharp; dym acrid

gryzmolić (-lę) scrawl, scribble

gryzoń m (-nia; -nie) rodent

gryźć bite; kość gnaw (at); orzechy crack; dym, osy: sting; pchły, komary: bite; sumienie: gnaw at; **~ się** kolory: clash; (martwić się) worry (I about); F be at loggerheads (**z I** with)

grza|ć (-eję) heat, warm; słońce itp.: beat down; F (bić) belt; **~ć się** warm o.s.; warm up; → **ogrzewać**; **~łka** f (-i; G -łek) heater; **~łka nurkowa** immersion heater; **~nka** f (-i; G -nek) toast; (w zupie) crouton

grządka f (-i; G -dek) (kwiatów) bed, (warzyw) patch, plot

grząski marshy

grzbiet m (-u; -y) back; (górski) ridge

grzebać (-ię) (**w L**) (w ziemi) root (in); fig. rummage (in); kury: scratch; F **~ się** (**z I**) dawdle (over); → **pogrzebać**

grzebień m (-nia; -nie) comb; (zwierząt) crest

grzebyk m (-a; -i) comb

grzech m (-u; -y) sin

grzechot|ać (-czę/-cę) rattle; ~**kać** f (-i; G -tek) rattle; ~**nik** m (-a; -i) rattlesnake

grzeczn|ościowy courtesy; ~**ość** f (-ci; 0) politeness, courtesy; (przysługa) favo(u)r, courtesy; **z ~ości, przez ~ość** out of kindness; ~**ny** polite, courteous

grzej|nik m (-a; -i) heater; (kaloryfer) radiator; ~**nik elektryczny** electric heater, Brt. electric fire; ~**nik wody** hot-water heater, Brt. geyser; ~**ny** heating

grzesz|nica f (-y; -e), ~**nik** m (-a; -cy) sinner; ~**ny** sinful; ~**yć** ⟨z-⟩ (-ę) sin

grzę|da f (-y; G -ród) patch, plot, bed; (dla kur) roost, perch; ~**znąć** ⟨u-⟩ (-nę, grzązł) sink, swamp; pf. też get stuck

grzmi|ąco adv. boomingly; ~**eć** (-ę; -mij!) thunder; głos: boom; **grzmi** nieos it is thundering

grzmo|cić (-cę) beat, belt; ~**t** m (-u; -y) thunder; ~**tnąć** v/s. (-nę) v/t. F clout s.o. one; (rzucić) smash; F ~**tnąć się** (o A) bump o.s. (on)

grzyb m (-a; -y) bot., med. fungus; bot. (z kapeluszem) mushroom; (na ścianie) mould; ~ **trujący** toadstool; ~**ica** f (-y; -e) med. mycosis; ~**owy** mushroom

grzywa f (-y; G -) mane

grzywna f (-y; G -wien) fine

gubern|ator m (-a; -rzy) governor; ~**ia** f (-i; -nie) province

gubić ⟨z-⟩ (-ę) lose; ~ ⟨z-⟩ **się** get lost; lose one's way

guma f (-y) rubber; gum; ~ **do żucia** chewing gum; F (prezerwatywa) rubber

gumisie m/pl. jelly babies

gumka f (-i; G-mek) (do ubrania) elastic; (do wycierania) eraser, Brt. rubber

gumowy rubber; fig. rubbery

GUS skrót pisany: **Główny Urząd Statystyczny** Main Statistical Organization

gusła n/pl. (-seł) sorcery; superstition

gust m (-u; -y/-a) taste; **w tym guście** of this type; ~**ować** ⟨-uję⟩ (**w** L) take pleasure (in); ~**owny** tasteful, in good taste

guz m (-a; -y) bump; knob; med. tumo(u)r

guzdrać się F (-am) dawdle

guzik m (-a; -i) button

gwał|cić (-cę) ⟨po-⟩ prawo violate; ⟨z-⟩ kobietę rape; ~**t** m (-u;-y) violation; rape; (przemoc) force; **zadać** ~**t** force; ~**tem** by force; ~**t** immediately, at once; ~**towny** violent; (nagły) abrupt

gwar m (-u; 0) clatter, hum

gwara f (-y; G -) gr. dialect

gwaran|cja f (-i; -e) guarantee; (zwł. na towar) warranty; ~**cyjny** guarantee; warranty; ~**tować** ⟨za-⟩ (-uję) guarantee, warrant

gwardia f (GDl -ii; -e) guard; ♀ **Narodowa** Am. National Guard

gwarny noisy

gwiazd|a f (-y) star; ~**ka** f (-i; D -dek) star; (znak) asterisk; (aktorka) starlet; (24-26.XII) Christmas; ~**kowy: podarunek** ~**kowy** Christmas gift; ~**or** m (-a; -rzy) star; ~**ozbiór** m (-oru; -ory) constellation

gwiaździsty (-ście) starry; kształt star-shaped

gwiezdny stellar, star

gwint m (-u; -y) thread

gwizd m (-u; -y) whistle; ~**ać** (-żdżę) whistle; ~**ek** m (-dka; -dki) whistle; ~**nąć** v/s. (-nę) whistle; F (ukraść) pinch

gwóźdź m (gwoździa; -oździe, I -oździami/-oźdźmi) nail

gzyms m (-u;-y) arch. cornice; →**karnisz**

H

habit m (-u; -y) habit

haczyk m (-a; -i) hook

hafciarka f (-i; G -rek) embroiderer

haft m (-u; -y) embroidery; ~**ka** f (-i; G -tek) hook and eye; ~**ować** ⟨wy-⟩ (-uję) embroider; F (wymiotować) puke

Haga f (-i) The Hague

hak m (-u; -i) hook

hala[1] f (-i; -e) hall; (w fabryce) workshop; ~ **targowa** covered market

hala[2] f (-i; -e) mountain pasture

halibut m (-a; -y) zo. halibut

halka f (-i; G -lek) slip

halogenowy halogen

halowy indoor

hałas *m* (*-u; -y*) noise; ~**ować** (*-uję*) make a noise, be noisy

hałaśliwy (*-wie*) noisy

hałda *f* (*-y; G hałd*) slag-heap; *fig.* heap

hamak *m* (*-a; -i*) hammock

hamować (*-uję*) ⟨**za-**⟩ brake; *fig. też* hinder, hamper; ⟨**po-**⟩ łzy hold back, keep in; *gniew itp.* curb, restrain; ~ **się** control o.s.

hamul|cowy brake, braking; ~**ec** *m* (*-ca; -e, -ów*) brake; *fig.* inhibition

hand|el *m* (*-dlu; -0*) trade, commerce; **prowadzić** ~**el, zajmować się** ~**lem** (*I*) trade (in), deal (in); do business; ~**larz** *m* (*-a; -e*) (**używanymi samochodami, narkotykami** used-car, drug) dealer; (**uliczny** street) vendor; ~**larka** *f* (*-i; G -rek*) dealer, vendor

handlow|ać (*-uję*) (*I*) trade (in), deal (in); ~**iec** *m* (*-wca; -wcy*) trader; salesperson; ~**y** trade, commercial

hangar *m* (*-u; -y*) hangar

haniebny disgraceful, disreputable

hań|ba *f* (*-y; 0*) dishono(u)r, disgrace; ~**ić** ⟨**z-**⟩ (*-ę*) dishono(u)r, disgrace

haracz *m* (*-u; -e*) tribute; (*okup*) ransom

haratać ⟨**po-**⟩ (*-am/-czę*) mangle, cut up (**się** *o.s.*)

harce|rka *f* (*-i; G -rek*) *Brt.* (Girl) Guide, *Am.* Girl Scout; ~**rz** *m* (*-a; -e*) Scout; ~**rski** Scouting, Scout(s *pl.*); ~**rstwo** *n* (*-a; 0*) Scouting

hard|ość *f* (*-ści; 0*) imperiousness; (*dziecko itp.*) unruliness; ~**y** (*-do*) overbearing; imperious; *dziecko itp.* unruly

harfa *f* (*-y; G -*) *mus.* harp

har'mo|nia *f* (*GDL -ii; 0*) harmony; (*GDL -ii; -e*) *mus.* (*ręczna*) concertina; ~**nijka** *f* (*-i; G -jek*) *mus.* harmonica, mouth organ; ~**nijny** harmonious; ~**nizować** (*-uję*) ⟨**z-**⟩ *też mus.* harmonize (**z** *I* with); ~**nogram** *m* (*-u; -y*) chart, diagram

harować F (*-uję*) slave, slog away

harówka *f* (*-i; G -wek*) slaving away; slog

harpun *m* (*-a; -y*) harpoon

hart *m* (*-u; 0*) power, strength; ~ **ducha** will-power; ~ **fizyczny** stamina, staying-power; ~**ować** ⟨**za-**⟩ (*-uję*) *stal* temper; *plastik* cure; *fig.* harden (**się** o.s.); ~**ow(a)ny** tempered; cured; hardened

haski Hague

hasło *n* (*-a; G -seł*) motto, slogan; *mil.*,

komp. password; (*w słowniku*) entry

haszysz *m* (*-u; 0*) hashish

haust *m* (*-u; -y*) swallow, (*duży*) gulp; **jednym** ~**em** at a gulp

Hawaje *pl.* (*G -ów*) Hawaii

hazardow|y gambling; **gra** ~**a** gambling; **grać** ~**o w karty** gamble at cards

heban *m* (*-u; 0*) ebony

heb|el *m* (*-bla, -ble*) plane; ~**lować** (*-uję*) plane

hebrajski (**po -ku**) Hebrew

Hebrydy *pl.* (*G -ów*) Hebrides *pl.*

hec|a *f* (*-y; -e*) farce, fuss; **urządzić** ~**ę** make a fuss; **to ci** ~**a!** what a farce!

hejnał *m* (*-u; -y*) bugle-call

hektar *m* (*-a; -y*) hectare

hel *m* (*-u; 0*) *chem.* helium

helikopter *m* (*-a; -y*) helicopter

hełm *m* (*-u; -y*) helmet; (*na wieży*) steeple

hemo|filik *m* (*-a; -cy*) *med. Brt.* haemophiliac, *Am.* hemophiliac; F bleeder; ~**roidy** *pl.* (*-ów*) *med. Brt.* haemorrhoids *pl.*, *Am.* hemorrhoids *pl.*, F piles *pl.*

hen:~**daleko** faraway; ~**wysoko** high up

hera *f* (*-y; 0*) *sl.* (*heroina*) junk

herb *m* (*-u; -y*) coat of arms; ~ **rodowy** family coat of arms

herba|ciany tea; ~**ciarnia** *f* (*-i; -e*) tea-shop, tearoom; ~**ta** *f* (*-y*) tea; ~**ta ekspresowa** tea bag; ~**tniki** *pl.* (*-ów*) *Brt.* biscuits, *Am.* cookies

herbowy armorial

herc *m* (*-a; -e*) *phys.* hertz

here|tycki heretic; ~**zja** *f* (*-i; -e*) heresy

hermetycz|ny hermetic; *fig.* opaque, dense; ~**nie** air-tight

herod-baba F *f* (*-y*) dragon

heroi|czny heroic, valiant; ~**na** *f* (*-y; 0*) *chem.* heroin; ~**nowy** heroin

herszt *m* (*-a; -ci/-y*) ringleader

heteroseksualny heterosexual

hetman *m* (*-a; -i/-owie*) *hist.* hetman; (*w szachach*) queen

hiena *f* (*-y*) *zo.* hyena

hieroglif *m* (*-u; -y*) hieroglyph (*też fig.*)

higi'ena *f* (*-y; 0*) hygiene; ~ **osobista**, ~ **ciała** personal hygiene

higieniczny hygienic, healthy

higroskopijny hygroscopic

Himalaje *pl.* (*G -jów/-ai*) Himalayas *pl.*

Hindus *m* (*-a; -si*), ~**ka** *f* (*-i; G -sek*) (*narodowość*) Indian, Hindu; ~**m**, ~**ka** *f* (*przynależność do religii*) Hindu; 2**ki** Indian

hymn

hiobow|y: *wieść* ~*a* dismal news

hipiczny: *konkurs* ~ riding event

hipis *m* (*-a*; *-i*), ~**ka** *f* (*-i*) hippie *lub* hippy

hipno|tyzować ⟨*za-*⟩ (*-uję*) hypnotize; ~**za** *f* (*-y*; *0*) hypnosis

hipopotam *m* (*-a*, *-y*) *zo.* hippopotamus

hipo|teczny hypothetical; ~**teka** *f* (*-i*) mortgage; ~**teza** *f* (*-y*) hypothesis

histeryczny hysterical

hi'stor|ia *f* (*GDL -ii*; *-e*) history; ~**yk** *m* (*-a*; *-cy*) historian; (*nauczyciel*) history teacher; ~**yczny** historical; (*przełomowy*) historic

Hiszpan *m* (*-a*; *-ie*) Spaniard; ~**ia** *f* (*GDl -ii*; *0*) Spain; ~**ka** *f* (*-i*; *G -nek*) Spaniard

hiszpańsk|i Spanish; *mówić po* ~*u* speak Spanish

hodow|ać (*-uję*) breed; *rośliny* cultivate, grow; ⟨*wy-*⟩ bring up; raise; rear; ~**ca** *m* (*-y*; *G -ów*), ~**czyni** *f* (*-*; *-e*) breeder; (*roślin*) grower; ~**la** *f* (*-i*; *-e*) breeding; growing; ~**lany** breeding

hojn|ie *adv.* generously, copiously; ~**y** generous, copious

hokej *m* (*-a*; *0*) hockey; ~ *na lodzie* ice hockey

hol[1] *m* (*-u*; *-e*, *-ów/-i*) foyer, hall, entrance

hol[2] *m* (*-u*; *-e*, *-ów*) tow; *brać na* ~ take in tow

Holandia *f* (*-ii*; *0*) Holland

Holender *m* (*-dra*; *-drzy*, *-rów*), Dutchman; *Holendrzy pl.* the Dutch *pl.*; ~**ka** *f* (*-i*; *G -rek*) Dutch woman; ⟨**ski** (*po-ku*) Dutch

holow|ać ⟨*-uję*⟩ ⟨*od-*⟩ tow; ~**niczy** towing; *lina* ~**nicza** towrope; ~**nik** *m* (*-a*; *-i*) tug(boat)

hołd *m* (*-u*; *-y*) tribute, homage; *złożyć* ~ *pamięci* (*G*) commemorate; ~**ować** (*-uję*) *fig.* (*D*) indulge in

hołota *f* (*-y*) mob, rabble

homar *m* (*-a*; *-y*) *zo.* lobster

homeopatyczny homeopathic

homoseksual|ny homosexual; ~**ista** *m* (*-y*; *-ści*) homosexual

honor *m* (*-u*) hono(u)r; *słowo* ~*u* word of hono(u)r; → *honory*; ~**arium** *n* (*-a*; *G -ów*) (*adwokata itp.*) fee; (*autorskie*) royalty; ~**ować** (*-uję*) hono(u)r; ~**owy** hono(u)rable; *pozycja itp.* honorary; ~**y** *pl.* (*-ów*) salute; ~**y domu** the hono(u)rs *pl.*

hormon *m* (*-u*; *-y*) hormone; ~**alny** hormonal

horyzont *m* (*-u*; *-y*) horizon (*też fig.*)

hossa *f* (*-y*) *econ.* boom; (*na giełdzie*) bull market

hostia *f* (*GDL -ii*; *-e*) the Host

hotel *m* (*-u*; *-e*) hotel; ~ *robotniczy* workers' hostel; ~**owy** hotel

hoży (*-żo*) well-built; *cera itp.* fine

hrabi|a *m* (*GA -ego/-i*, *D -iemu/-i*, *V -io!*, *I -ią/-im*, *L -i*; *-iowie*, *GA -iów*, *D -iom*, *I -iami*, *L -iach*) count; ~**anka** (*-i*; *G -nek*) count's (unmarried) daughter; ~**na** *f* (*-y*) countess; ~**owski** count's, of the count

hreczka *f* (*-i*; *G -czek*) → *gryka*

hucz|eć (*-ę*, *-y*) *bom*; *morze*, *wiatr*, *maszyna*: roar; ~**nie** *adv.* loud(ly); ~**ny** *impreza* lively, exuberant; *oklaski* thunderous; *śmiech* booming

hufiec *m* (*-fca*; *-fce*): ~ *harcerski* troop unit

huk *m* (*-u*; *-i*) boom; roar

hulać (*-am*) F live it up

hulajnoga *f* scooter

hulanka *f* (*-i*; *G -nek*) booze-up

humanitarny humanitarian; (*ludzki*) humane

humo|r *m* (*-u*; *0*) humo(u)r; (*-u*; *-y*) (*nastrój*) mood; whim; *w złym* ~*rze* in a bad mood; ~**rystyczny** humorous, comic(al)

huragan *m* (*-u*; *-y*) hurricane; (*wiatr*) gale; ~**owy** hurricane; *fig.* thunderous

hurt *m* (*-u*; *0*) *econ.* wholesale; ~**em** wholesale; F *en bloc*

hurtow|nia *f* (*-i*; *-e*) wholesale business; ~**nik** *m* (*-a*; *-cy*) wholesaler; ~**o** *adv.* wholesale; ~**y** wholesale

huśtać ⟨*po-*⟩ (*-am*) swing; (*w krześle*) rock; (*się* *v/i.*)

huśtawka *f* (*-i*; *G -wek*) swing; (*pozioma*) seesaw

hut|a *f* (*-t*) works *sg./pl.*; ~*a stali* iron (and steel) works; ~*a szkła* glassworks; ~**nictwo** *n* (*-a*; *0*) iron and steel industry; ~**nik** *m* (*-a*; *-cy*) ironworker, steelworker

hydrauli|czny hydraulic; ~**k** *m* (*-a*; *-cy*) plumber

hydro|elektrownia *f* water power station; ~**energia** *f* water power; ~**plan** *m* hydroplane; ~**terapia** *f* hydrotherapy

hymn *m* (*-u*; *-y*) (*kościelny*) hymn; (*państwowy*) anthem

I

i *cj.* and; ~ ... ~ ... both ... and ..., ~ as well as ...; ~ **tak** anyway

ich 1. *pron. D → one, G, A → oni;* **2.** *poss.* ~ **rzeczy** their things

idą *3. os. pl →* **iść**

idea *f (GDL idei; -ee, -ei, -eom)* idea; ~**alny** ideal; ~**ał** *m (-u; -y)* ideal

identyczny identical, the same; ~**fikować** *(-uję)* identify (**się** *v/i.* **z** with)

ideo|logiczny ideological; ~**wy** ideological

idę *1. os. sg. →* **iść**

idiot|a *m (-y; -ci),* ~**ka** *f (-i; G -tek)* idiot *(też med.),* fool; ~**yczny** foolish, stupid; ~**yzm** *m (-u; -y)* stupidity, idiocy; nonsense

idyll|a *f (-i; -e)* idyll; ~**iczny** idyllic

idzie|my, ~sz, idź → **iść**

igie|lny needle; ~**łka** *f (-i; G -łek)* (little) needle; ~**łkowy** needle(-shaped)

iglast|y coniferous; *drzewo* ~**e** conifer

ig|lica *f (-y; -e) tech.* pin; *(w broni)* firing pin; *(na wieży)* spire; ~**liwie** *n (-a; 0)* needles *pl.;* ~**ła** *f (-y; G -ieł)* needle; *(kaktusa itp.)* spine; ~**ła do szycia** sewing needle; *jak z ~ły* spick and span

ignorować *⟨z-⟩ (-uję)* ignore

igra|ć *(-m)* play *(z I* with); ~**szka** *f (-i; G -szek)* plaything

igrzyska *n/pl.* games *pl.;* ⚲ *Olimpijskie* the Olympic Games

i in. *skrót pisany:* **i inni, i inne** et al. *(and others)*

ikr|a *f (-y; 0)* roe, spawn; *składać* ~**ę** spawn; *z* ~**ą** with nerve, with guts

ile *(m-os ilu, I iloma) (niepoliczalne)* how much, *(policzalne)* how many; ~ *razy* how often; ~ *masz lat?* how old are you?; *o ~ bardziej* how much more; *o ~ wiem* as far as I know; *o ~ ... o tyle* ... in so far as; *o ~ nie* unless; *~kroć* whenever; ~**ś** *(m-os iluś)* some; ~**ś** *lat temu* some years ago

ilo|czyn *m (-u; -y) math.* product; ~**ma** → **ile;** ~**raz** *m (-u; -y) math.* quotient; ~**ściowy** quantitative; ~**ść** *f (-ci)* quantity

ilu *m-os →* **ile**

iluminacja *f (-i; -e)* illumination;

(festive) illuminations *pl.;* ~**tor** *m (-a; -y)* (circular) porthole

ilustracja *f (-i; -e)* illustration; *(obrazek)* picture

ilustrowany illustrated; *magazyn* ~ glossy

iluz|ja *f (-i; -e)* illusion; ~**jonista** *m (-y; -ści),* -**tka** *f (-i)* conjurer; ~**oryczny** illusory; pointless

ił *m (-u; -y)* clay; ~**owaty** clay, clayey

im. *skrót pisany:* **imię** n. *(name)*

im 1. *pron. (D → one, oni)* **2.** *adv.* the; ~ *prędzej, tym lepiej* the sooner the better

imadło *n (-a)* vice

imaginac|ja *f (-i; 0)* imagination; ~**yjny** imaginary

imbir *m (-u; 0)* ginger; ~**owy** ginger

imbryk *m (-a; -i)* kettle

imien|iny *pl. (-in)* name-day; ~**niczka** *f (-i; G -czek),* ~**nik** *m (-a; -cy)* namesake; ~**ny** name; *gr.* nominal; *(-nie)* by name

imiesłów *m (-u; -y) gr.* participle

imię *n* name; *gr.* noun; *fig. też* **dobre** ~ good reputation; *mieć na* ~ be called; *jak ci na* ~? what is your name?; *po imieniu* by name; *w* ~ *(G),* *w imieniu (G)* in the name of, on behalf of; *szkoła imienia NN* NN school

imigracja *f (-i; -e)* immigration

imiona *pl. →* **imię**

imit|acja *f (-i; -cje)* imitation; ~**ować** *(-uję)* imitate

im|matrykulacja *(-i; -e)* matriculation; ~**munizować** *(-uję)* immunize

impas *m (-u; -y) fig.* impasse, stalemate

imperialistyczny imperialistic

imperium *n (-a; G -ów)* empire

impertynen|cja *f (-i; -e)* impertinence, impudence; *(wyzwisko)* a piece of impertinence; ~**cki** impertinent, impudent; ~**t** *m (-a; -ci),* ~**tka** *f (-i; G -tek)* impertinent *lub* impudent person

impet *m (-u; 0)* momentum, impetus, drive

imponować *⟨za-⟩ (-uję)* impress *(czymś* with s.th.); ~**ujący** *(-co)* impressive, imposing

import *m (-u; -y)* import; ~**ować** *(-uję)*

import; ~owy imported

impotencj|a f (-i; 0) med. impotence; **cierpieć na ~ę** be impotent

im|pregnować (-uję) impregnate, waterproof; ~preza f (-y) (*sportowa* sporting) event; (*przyjęcie*) party; ~prowizować (-uję) improvize; ~pulsywny impulsive, impetuous

in. *skrót pisany: inaczej* differently

inaczej differently (*niż* than); (*w przeciwnym razie*) otherwise; **tak czy ~** either way; **jakże ~** how else

inaugur|acja f (-i; -cje) inauguration; opening; ~acyjny inaugural; inauguration; ~ować ⟨za-⟩ (-uję) inaugurate; open

incydent m (-u; -y) incident, event

indagować (-uję) ask (**o** *A* about)

indeks m (-u; -y) index; (*studenta*) student's credit book; **~ rzeczowy** subject index

indeksacja f (-i; -e) econ. indexation, index-linking

Indi'a|nin m (-a; -ie), ~nka f (-i; G -nek) Indian; ♀ński Indian

Indie pl. (GDL -ii; 0) India

Indonezj|a f (-i; 0) Indonesia; ♀yjski Indonesian

indor m (-a; -y) turkey (cock)

indos m (-a; -y) econ. endorsement

indosować (-uję) endorse

indukc|ja f (-i; -e) induction; ~yjny inductive

indycz|ka f (-i; G -czek) turkey (hen); ~y turkey; ~yć się F (-ę) get annoyed

indyjs|ki (po -ku) Indian

indyk m (-a; -i) turkey

indywidu|alność f (-ści; 0) individuality; ~alny individual; personal; single; ~um n (idkl.; -ua, -duów) individual; character

indziej → gdzie, kiedy, nigdzie

inercj|a f (-i; 0) inertia; **siła ~i** inertia

infekcja f (-i; -e) infection

inflacja f (-i; -e) inflation

informa|cja f (-i; -e) information; (*jedna*) piece of information; (*okienko itp.*) information desk/office *etc.*; ~cyjny information; ~tor m (-a; -ry) (*książka*) guide (**po** *L* to); (*pl. -rzy*) informer ~tyka f (-i; 0) computer science

informować ⟨po-⟩ (-uję) inform; **~ się** inquire (**o** *L*, **w sprawie** *G* about); ask (**u** *G* s.o.)

infuła f (-y) Brt. mitre, Am. miter

ingerować ⟨za-⟩ (-uję) interfere, intervene

inhalować (-uję) inhale

inicjator m (-a; -rzy), ~ka f (-i; G -rek) initiator, originator

inicjatyw|a f (-y) initiative; **z ~y** on s.o.'s own initiative

inicjować ⟨za-⟩ (-uję) initiate, originate

iniekcja f (-i; -e) med. injection

inkas|ent m (-a; -ci) collector; ~ent gazowni gas-meter reader; ~o n (-a) econ. collection

inkrustowany inlaid

inkubacyjny: **okres ~** med. incubation period

inkubator m (-a; -y) incubator

in|na, ~ne, ~ni → inny; ~no- *w zł.* differently

innowacja f (-i; -e) innovation

inny another, other; **co innego** something else; **kto ~** someone else; → między

inscenizacja f (-i; -e) theat. staging

inspek|cja f (-i; -e) inspection, checking; ~tor m (-a; -rzy), inspector; superintendent; **~tor szkolny** schools inspector; ~torat m (-u; -y) inspectorate; ~towy hothouse; ~ty m/pl. (-ów) (cold) frame

instal|acja f (-i; -e) installation; (*zakładanie*) fitting; (*urządzenia*) zw. pl. installations pl., facilities pl.; ~ować ⟨za-⟩ (-uję) install; put in, put up, fit in; **~ować się** make o.s. at home

instruk|cja f (-i; -e) instruction; **~cja obsługi** operating instructions pl.; ~tor m (-a; -rzy), ~rka f (-i; G -rek) (*jazdy, pilotażu* driving, flying) instructor; ~tywny instructive

instrument m (-u; -y) instrument

instynktowny instinctive

instytucja f (-i; -e) institution

instytut m (-u; -y) institute; department

insynuacja f (-i; -e) insinuation

insynuować (-uję) insinuate

integra|cja f (-i; 0) integration; ~lny integral

integrować ⟨z-⟩ (-uję) integrate

intelektual|ista m (-y; -ści), ~istka f (-i; G -tek) intellectual; ~ny intellectual

inteligen|cja f (-i; 0) intelligence; (*klasa*) intelligentsia; ~cki of intelligentsia; ~tny intelligent

intencj|a f (-i; -e) intention; plan; **w ~i** on behalf of

intencyjny: *list* ~ letter of intent

intensyfikować ⟨z-⟩ (-uję) intensify

intensywn|ość f (-ci; 0) intensity; **~y** intensive; *światło, kolor itp.* intense

intonacja f (-i; -e) intonation

interes m (-u; -y) business; (*sprawa*) interest; (*transakcja*) dealings pl.; **nie twój ~** none of your business; **w twoim ~ie** in your (best) interest(s pl.); *ładny ~!* a pretty kettle of fish!

interesant m (-a; -ci), **~ka** f (-i; G -tek) client, customer; *econ.* potential buyer

interesow|ać ⟨za-⟩ (-uję) v/t. interest; v/i. (**~ać się**) be interested (*I* in); **~ny** self-interested, selfish

interesujący (-co) interesting

inter|na F f (-y; 0) internal medicine; **~nat** m (-u; -y) dormitory bloc; (*prywatna*) **szkoła z ~natem** boarding school; **~nować** (-uję) intern; **~pretować** (-uję) interpret; **~punkcja** f (-i; 0) punctuation

interwen|cja f (-i; -e) intervention; **~cyjny:** *prace f/pl.* **~cyjne** job-creation measures; **~iować** (-uję) intervene; F step in

intonować ⟨za-⟩ (-uję) *pieśń* start singing

intratny lucrative, profitable

introligatornia f (-i; -e) bindery

intruz m (-a; -i/-y) intruder

intry|ga f (-i) intrigue, scheme; **~gancki** scheming; **~gować** ⟨za-⟩ (-uję) scheme; **~gujący** intriguing

intymn|ość f (-ci; 0) intimacy; (*odosobnienie*) privacy; **~y** intimate; (*osobny*) private

inwali|da m (-y; -dzi), **~dka** f (G -dek) invalid; **~da wojenny** war invalid; **~dzki** invalid; **wózek ~dzki** wheelchair

in|wazja f (-i; -e) invasion; **~wentaryzacja** f (-i; -e) stock-taking; **~wentarz** m (-a; -e) stock, inventory

inwersyjny: *film* ~ *phot.* reversal film

investor m (-a; -rzy) investor

inwestować ⟨za-⟩ (-uję) invest

inwestyc|ja f (-i; -e) (*działalność*) investment; (*przedsięwzięcie*) investment project; **~yjny** investment

inwigilacja f (-i; -e) surveillance

inż. *skrót pisany:* **inżynier** Eng., Engr. (*Engineer*)

inżynie|r m (-a; -owie) engineer; **~ria** f (GDL -ii; 0) engineering; **~ria genetyczna** genetic engineering; **~ria lądowa** (building) construction and civil engineering

ira|cki Iraqi; **Ǝk** (-a; 0) Iraq; **Ǝkijczyk** m (-a; -cy), **Ǝkijka** f (-i; G -jek) Iraqi; **Ǝn** (-u; 0) Iran; **Ǝnka** f (-i; -nek), **Ǝńczyk** m (-a; -cy) Iranian; **~ński** Iranian

Irlan|dczyk m (-a; -cy) Irishman; **~dczycy** pl. the Irish; **~dia** f (GDL -ii; 0) Ireland; **~dka** f (-i; G -dek) Irishwoman; **Ǝdzki** Irish

ironiczny ironic

irygacyjny irrigation

irys m (-a; -y) *bot.* iris

iryt|acja f (-i; 0) annoyance, irritation; **~ować** ⟨po-, z-⟩ (-uję) annoy; **~ować** ⟨z-⟩ **się** get annoyed

isk|ra f (-y; G -kier) spark; **~rzyć** (-ę) spark (**się** v/i.)

islam m (-u; 0) Islam; **~ski** Islamic

Islan|dia f (GDL -ii; 0) Iceland; **~dczyk** m (-a; -cy), **~dka** f (-i; G -dek) Icelander; **Ǝdzki** Icelandic

istnie|ć (-eje) exist; be; → **być, trwać**; **~nie** n (-a) existence, being

istny veritable, virtual

isto|ta f (-y) creature, being; (*sedno*) essence; **w ~cie** in fact; **~tny** essential, fundamental

iść go, (do G to); (*pieszo*) walk; (*pojazdy*) run; ~ **po** fetch, get; ~ **za** (*I*) follow; ~ **za mąż** (**za** *I*) get married (to); ~ **dalej** go on, continue; *idzie o ...* all this is about..., what is at stake is...; **co za tym idzie** what follows from this is ...; → ⟨**przy**⟩**chodzić, pójść**

itd. *skrót:* **i tak dalej** etc. (*and so on*)

itp. *skrót:* **i tym podobne** etc. (*and so on*)

izba f (-y) room; (*instytucja itp.*) chamber; *pol.* house; **Ǝ Gmin** the House of Commons; **~ przyjęć** (*w szpitalu*) admissions office

izola|cja f (-i) isolation; (*kabla, pokoju itp.*) insulating, insulation; **~cyjny** isolating; insulating; **~tka** f (-i; G -tek) (*dla chorego*) isolation ward; (*w szkole itp.*) sickbay

izolować ⟨za-, od-⟩ (-uję) isolate; *kabel itp.* insulate

Izrael m (-a; 0) Israel; **~czyk** m (-a; -cy), **~ka** f (-i; G -lek) Israeli; **Ǝski** Israeli

iż *cj.* that; → **że**

J

ja *pron.* I; *kto tam? to ~* who is it?
- that's me; *własne ~* one's own self
jabłeczn|ik *m* apple pie; (*wino*) cider;
~y apple
jabłko *n* (*-a; G -łek*) apple
jabło|ń *f* (*-ni, -nie*) apple-tree; *kwiat ~ni*
apple blossom
jacht *m* (*-u; -y*) yacht; *~ kabinowy*
cabin cruiser
jacy *m-os* → **jaki**
jad *m* (*-u; -y*) venom (*też fig.*); (*trucizna*)
poison; *~ kiełbasiany* botulin
jada|ć (*-am*) → **jeść**; *~lnia* *f* (*-i, -e, -i*)
dining-room; (*meble*) dining-room
suite; *~lny* edible, eatable; *sala ~lna*
dining-room
ja|dą, ~dę → jechać; ~dł(a) → jeść
jadło|dajnia (*-i; -e, -i*) restaurant, *Am.*
diner; *~spis* *m* (*-u; -y*) menu
jado|wity venomous (*też fig.*), poison-
ous; *~wy* *zo.* venomous
jaglan|y: kasza ~a millet gruel
jagły *f/pl.* (*-gieł*) millet; millet gruel
jagnię *n* (*-cia; -ta, G -niąt*) lamb
jagnięcy lamb
jagod|a *f* (*-y; G -gód*) *bot.* berry; *czar-
na ~a → borówka brusznica*; *~y pl.*
też soft fruit; *~owy* bilberry, blueberry,
whortleberry
jajeczkowanie *n* (*-a*) *biol.* ovulation
jajecznica *f* (*-y; -ce*) scrambled eggs *pl.*
jaj|ko *n* (*-a; G -jek*) egg; *~ka pl. sadzone*
fried eggs *pl.*; *~nik* *m* (*-a;-i*) *anat.* ovary
jajo egg; *biol.* ovum; *~waty* egg-shaped;
biol. ovoid
jak 1. *pron.* how; as; *~ się masz?* how
are you?; **2.** *cj.* as; like; *~ gdyby* as if;
~ na owe czasy for those times; **3.** *part.*
as; *nic innego ~* nothing else but; *~ najwięcej* as much as possible; *~ najlepszy* best of all; → *byle, tylko*
jakby as if, as though; F something like;
→ *gdyby*
jaki *(m-os jacy)* what; which; how;
~ bądź whichever; *~ taki* so so; *~m prawem* by what right; *~m cudem* by a
miracle or what; *za ~ rok* in a year or
so; F *po ~emu* how, in what language;
~'kolwiek any; *~ś* some; about; *~eś*

trzy metry about three meters; *~ś*
dziwny sort of strange
jak'kolwiek however; (*chociaż*)
although
jako as; *~ taki* as such; *~ tako* to some
extent, F a bit; *~ że* because, as; *~by* *adv.*
supposedly, allegedly; *~ś* somehow
jakoś|ciowy (*-wo*) qualitative; *~ć* *f*
(*-ci; 0*) quality
jakże how; → *jak*
jałmużna *f* (*-y; zw. 0*) alms *pl.*; *fig.* pit-
tance
jałow|cowy juniper; *~iec* *m* (*-wca/-wcu;*
-wce) juniper
jałowy arid, barren; *biol.* infertile, barren; *electr., tech.* neutral; *tech.* idle;
bieg ~ neutral
jałówka *f* (*-i; G -wek*) heifer
jama *f* (*-y*) pit, hole; *anat.* cavity
jamnik *m* (*-a; -i*) *zo.* dachshund
janowiec *m* (*-wca; -wce*) broom
Japo|nia *f* (*GDL -ii; 0*) Japan; *~nka* *f*
(*-i; G -nek*), *~ńczyk* *m* (*-a; -cy*) Japanese; 2ński (*po -ku*) Japanese
jarmar|czny fair, market; *fig.* cheap-
jack; *~k* *m* (*-u; -i*) fair, market
jarosz *m* (*-a; -e*) vegetarian
jar|ski vegetarian; *~y* *agr.* spring
jarząb *m* (*-rzębu/-ęba; -rzęby/-ębie,*
-ębiów) *bot.* mountain ash; *~ek* *m*
(*-bka; -bki*) *zo.* hazelhen
jarzeniówka *f* (*-i; G -wek*) strip light
jarzębina *f* (*-y*) *bot.* rowan, European
mountain ash
jarzmo *n* (*-a; G -/-rzem*) yoke
jarzyć się (*-ę*) glow; (*lśnić*) glisten
jarzyn|a *f* (*-y*) vegetable; *~owy* veget-
able
jasełka *n/pl.* (*-łek*) *rel.* nativity play
jasiek *m* (*-śka; -śki*) little pillow; *bot.*
(*type of large white bean*)
jaskini|a *f* (*-i; -e*) cave, cavern; *~nio-
wiec* *m* (*-wca; -wcy*) caveman (*też fig.*);
~niowy cave
jaskół|czy swallow; *~ka* *f* (*-i; G -łek*)
zo. swallow; (*w sporcie*) arabesque
jaskra *f* (*-y; 0*) *med.* glaucoma
jaskraw|o- glaringly; bright; *~y* (*-wo*)
glaring (*też fig.*); bright

jasno light; ~**blond** (*idkl.*) very fair; (*o kobiecie*) light blonde, ~**ść** *f* (*-ści*; *0*) brightness; *fig.* clarity, lucidity; ~**widz** *m* (*-a*; *-e*) clairvoyant; ~**żółty** light yellow

jasn|y light; *fig.* clear, lucid; **rzecz ~a**, F ~**e** it is clear; **w ~y dzień** in broad daylight

jastrząb *m* (*-rzębia*; *-ębie*, *-ębi*) hawk (*też pol.*)

jaszczur *m* (*-a*; *-y*) zo. reptile; ~**ka** *f* (*-i*; *G* *-rek*) zo. lizard

jaśmin *m* (*-u*; *-y*) *bot.* jasmine

jaśnie|ć (*-eję*) be shining (*też fig.* with); glow; ⟨*po-*⟩ brighten, become lighter; ~**j(szy)** *adv.* (*adj.*) *comp. od → jasno*, **jasny**

jatka *f* (*-i*; *G* *-tek*) slaughter house; *fig.* slaughter, butchery

jaw: **wyjść na ~** come to light; **wydobyć na ~** bring to light; ~**ić się** (*im*)*pf* (*-ę*) appear (**k-ś** to s.o.); ~**nie** *adv.* openly, in the open; ~**ny** open; undisguised

jawor *m* (*-a*; *-y*) *bot.* sycamore (maple)

jaz *m* (*-u*; *-y*) dam, *Brt.* weir

jazda *f* (*-y*) travel, journey; ~ **koleją** journey by train; ~ **na rowerze** bike ride; ~ **na nartach** skiing; ~ **konna** → **prawo, rozkład**

jazz *m* (*-u*; *0*) *mus.* jazz; ~**ować** (*-uję*) play jazz; ~**owy** jazz, F jazzy

jaź|ń *f* (*-ni*; *-nie*) ego, the I; **rozdwojenie ~ni** split personality

ją *pron. → ona*

jądr|o *f* (*-a*; *G* *-der*) core; nucleus (*też phys., biol., fig.*); (*orzecha*) kernel; *anat.* testicle; ~**owy** nuclear;

jąkać się (*-am*) stutter, stammer

jątrzyć (*-ę*) foment, stir up; ~ **się** fester, ulcerate

je *pron. A*; *→ one, ono*; *v/t., v/i. → jeść*

jechać (*-dę*) ⟨*po-*⟩ go (**koleją** by train); ride (**rowerem** (on) a bike; **konno** (on) a horse); (*samochodem*) *kierowca*: drive, *pasażer*: ride in; travel; **windą** take; ~ **jeździć**

jeden → **666**; one; ~ **raz** once; ~**drugiego/drugiemu** one another; ~ **do zera** one-nil; **ani ~** not a single one; **sam ~** all alone; ~ **i ten sam** the same; **jednym słowem** in a word; **z jednej strony** on the one hand; **co to za ~?** who is he?

jedena|stka *f* (*-i*; *G* *-tek*) eleven; (*w sporcie*) penalty kick; (*drużyna*) team; ~**sty** eleventh; ~**ście**, ~**stu** *m-os* eleven

jedlina *f* (*-y*) → **jodła**; fir sprigs *pl.*

jedn. *skrót pisany* **jednostka** unit

jedna *f* → **jeden**; ~**ć** ⟨*z-*⟩ (*-am*) gain, win (*też sobie*); → **pojednać**; ~**k** nevertheless, however; ~**kowo** *adv.* identically; in the same way; equally; ~**kowy** identical

jedni *m-os pl.* → **jeden**

jedno *n* (*jednego*; *jedni*) one; the same; → **jeden**; ~**barwny** unicolo(u)r; monochromatic; ~**brzmiący** identical (in sound); ~**czesny** (*-śnie*) simultaneous; ~**czyć** ⟨*z-*⟩ (*-ę*) unite (**się** *v/i.*); ~**dniowy** one-day; ~**głośnie** unanimously; ~**imienny** of the same name

jednokierunkow|y one-way; **ruch ~y** one-way traffic; **ulica ~a** a one-way street

jedno|kondygnacyjny one-stor(e)y, single-stor(e)y; ~**konny** one-horse; ~**krotny** single; ~**lity** uniform; homogeneous; ~**myślny** unanimous; ~**oki** one-eyed; ~**osobowy** single; single-person; ~**piętrowy** two-stor(e)y; ~**pokojowy** one-room

jednoraz|owy single; **do ~owego użycia** disposable; ~**ówka** *f* (*-i*; *G* *-wek*) disposable

jedno|ręki one-handed; ~**roczny** one-year; ~**rodny** homogeneous; ~**rodzinny** one-family, single-family; ~**rzędowy** *marynarka* single-breasted; ~**silnikowy** one-engine; ~**stajny** monotonous

jednost|ka *f* (*-i*; *G* *-tek*) unit; (*osobnik*) individual; ~**ka miary** unit of measure; ~**ka wojskowa** army unit (*też math.*); ~**kowy** unique; individual, single

jednostronny one-sided, unilateral

jedność *f* (*-ći*; *0*) unity; unit

jedno|tlenek *m* monoxide; ~**torowy** one-track; ~**zgłoskowy** *gr.* monosyllabic; ~**znaczny** unambiguous, unequivocal

jedwab *m* (*-iu*; *-ie*) silk; ~**isty** silky, silken; ~**ny** silk, silken, silky

jedyna|czka *f* (*-i*; *G* *-czek*) only daughter; ~**k** *f* (*-a*; *-i*) only son

jedyn|ie *adv.* only, merely; ~**ka** *f* (*-i*; *G* *-nek*) one; (*linia*) number one; **szkoła:** jakby: F, failing; ~**y** only, single; ~**y w swoim rodzaju** unique

jedz|(ą) → **jeść**; ~enie n (-a; 0) food; eating

jedzie(cie, -sz), jedź → **jechać**

je|go **1.** *pron.* (GA → **on**) him; (G → **ono**) it; **2.** *poss.* his; ~j *pron.* (GD → **ona**) her; *poss.* her, hers

jeleń m (-nia, -nie) zo. deer, *(samiec)* stag

jelito n (-a) anat. intestine, bowel; ~ **grube** large intestine; ~wy intestinal

jełcze|ć ⟨z-⟩ (-eję) grow rancid, go bad

jem *1. os. sg.* → **jeść**

jemioła f (-y) bot. mistletoe

jemu *pron.* (D → **on, ono**) him

jeniec m (-ńca; -ńcy) prisoner; ~ki prisoner

Jerozolima f (-y; 0) Jerusalem

jesie|nny autumn(al); fall; ~ń f (-ni; -nie) Brt. autumn, Am. fall; ~nią in autumn/fall

jesion m (-u; -y) bot. ash

jesionka f (-i; G -nek) coat

jesiotr m (-a; -y) zo. sturgeon

jest (he, she, it) is; ~**em** (I) am; ~**eś** (you) are; ~**eśmy** (we) are; ~**eście** (you) are; → **być**

jesz *2. os. sg.* → **jeść**

jeszcze yet, still; ~ **jak!** and how!; ~ **nie** not yet; ~ **dłuższy** even longer

jeść ⟨z-⟩ eat; have; ~ **c-ś** have s.th. to eat; ~ **śniadanie** have breakfast; **dać c-ś** ~ give s.th. to eat; **chce mi się** ~ I am hungry

jeśli *cj.* if, when

jez. *skrót pisany:* **jezioro** L., *lub* l. (lake)

jezdnia f (-i; -e) roadway

jezioro n (-a) lake; ~ **sztuczne** artificial lake

jezuicki Jesuit

jeździć ⟨-żdżę⟩ go (**na urlop** on holiday); travel (**po kraju** all over the country); *autobus, pociąg:* run; ~ **na nartach** ski; ~ **samochodem** kierowca: drive; → **jechać**

jeździec m (-dźca -dźcy, jeźdźce!) rider; ~ki riding; ~two n (-a; 0) riding

jeż m (-a; -e) zo. hedgehog; **włosy** m/pl. **na** ~**a** crew-cut

jeżeli → **jeśli**

jeżyć ⟨na-⟩ (-ę) bristle (**się** v/i.)

jeżyna f (-y) bot. blackberry, bramble

jęczeć (-ę, -y) moan, groan

jęczmie|nny barley; ~ń m (-nia; -nie) barley; *med.* sty(e)

jędrny husky; *styl* expressive

jędza f (-y; -e) termagant, shrew; *(czarownica)* witch

jęk m (-u; -i) moan, groan; ~liwy (-**wie**) moaning; ~nąć v/s. (-nę) give a groan

jęzor m (-a; -y) tongue

języ|czek m (-czka; -czki) tongue; *anat.* uvula; ~k m anat. tongue (*też fig.*); ~k **ojczysty** mother tongue; **kaleczyć** ~k **polski** speak broken Polish; **mleć** ~**kiem** waffle about; ~kowy linguistic; ~koznawstwo n (-a; 0) linguistics

jidysz m (-u; 0) Yiddish

j.n. *skrót pisany:* **jak niżej** as below

jod m (-u; 0) chem. iodine

jod|ełka f (-i; G -łek): **garnitur w** ~**ełkę** a herringbone suit; ~ła f (-y; G -deł) bot. fir

jodyna f (-y; 0) iodine

jogurt m (-u; -y) yoghurt

jonowy ionic

Jowisz m. (-a; 0) astr. Jupiter

jubilat m (-a; -ci), *(man celebrating his anniversary/birthday)*; ~ka f (-i; G -tek) *(woman celebrating her anniversary/birthday)*

jubiler m (-a; -ów) jeweller; ~ka F f (-i; 0) *(rzemiosło)* jewellery; ~ski jeweller's

jubileusz m (-a; -e) anniversary

juczny *zwierzę* pack

juda|istyczny Judaistic; ~izm m (-u) Judaism

judasz m (-a; -e) *fig.* Judas; *(w drzwiach)* peep-hole, judas; ~owski, ~owy judas

judzić (-dzę) goad (**do** G into)

juhas m (-a; -i) junior sheep herder (*in the Tatras*); ~ka f (-i; G -sek) junior sheep woman herder (*in the Tatras*)

junacki daring, audacious

junior m (-a; -rzy), ~ka f (-i; G -rek) junior

juror m (-a; -rzy) juryman; ~ka f (-i; G -rek) jurywoman, juryperson

jutr|o **1.** *adv.* tomorrow; **2.** n (-a; 0) tomorrow; **od** ~**a** from/since tomorrow

jutrze|jszy tomorrow; ~nka f (-i; G -nek) dawn; 2nka Morning Star

już already; yet; ~ **nie** no longer; ~ **nigdy** never again; ~! OK; (I'm) coming

K

kabaczek m (-czka; -czki) Brt. marrow, Am. squash

kabał|a f (-y; G -) cabbala; **stawiać ~ę** tell fortunes (from the cards); **wpaść w ~ę** F get into a mess

kabaret m (-u; -y) cabaret

ka|bel m (-bla; -ble, -bli) cable; **~bina** cabin; tel. phone booth; (przepierzenie) cubicle; lotn. **~bina pilota** cockpit; **~blowy: telewizja ~blowa** cable TV

kabłąk m (-u; -i) bow; bail; tech. pantograph, bow; **~owaty (-to)** bent

kabura f (-y) holster

kabz|a f: F **nabić ~ę** make a pile

kac F m (-a; -e) hangover; **mieć ~a** be hung over

kacyk m (-a; -i) chieftain

kaczan m → **głąb**¹; corncob

kacz|ka f (-i; G -czek) zo. duck; **~ka pieczona** roast duck; **~or** m (-a; -y) zo. drake; **~y** duck

kadencja f (-i; -e) term (of office); parl. legislative period; mus. cadence

kadłub m (-a; -y) body; (samolotu) fuselage; (statku) hull

kadr m (-u; -y) frame

kadr|a f (-y; G -) personnel, staff, cadre; **~y kierownicze** management; **~owy 1.** (zawodowy) cadre; (personalny) personnel; **2.** m (-ego; -wi), **~owa** f (-wej; -we) personnel officer

kadzi|ć (-dzę) incense; fig. honey up; **~dło** n (-a; G -deł) incense

kadź f (-dzi; -dzie) tub

kafar m (-u) bud. pile-driver

kafejka f (-ki; G -jek) cafe/café

kafel m (-fla; -fle, -fli), **~ek** m (-ka; -ki) tile

kaflowy tile, tiled

kaftan m (-a; -y): **~ bezpieczeństwa** strait-jacket; **~ik** m (-a; -i) (niemowlęcia) shirt, Brt. vest

kaganiec m (-ńca; -ńce) muzzle

Kair m (-u; 0) Cairo

kajak m (-a; -i) kayak, canoe; **~ składany** collapsible kayak/canoe; **~arstwo** n (-a) canoeing

kajdan|ki pl. (-nek/-nków) handcuffs pl.; **~y** pl. (-) fetters pl., shackles pl.

kajuta f (-y) cabin

kajzerka f (-i; G -rek) bread roll

kakao n (idkl.) cocoa

kaktus m (-a; -y) cactus

kalać ⟨po-, s-⟩ (-am) defile

kalafior m (-a; -y) bot. cauliflower

kalambur m (-a; -y) pun

kalarepa f (-y) kohlrabi

kale|ctwo n (-a) disability; **~czyć** ⟨po-, s-⟩ (-ę) cut (**się** o.s.; **sobie rękę** one's hand); → **język**; **~ka** m/f (-i; -i/-cy, G -/-ów) disabled person, pej. cripple (też fig.); **~ki** disabled, cripple(d)

kalendarz m (-a; -e) calendar; (podręczny) Brt. diary, Am. (pocket) calendar

kalenica f (-y; -e) (roof-)ridge

kalesony pl. (-ów) underpants; (długie) long underwear, F long johns pl.

kaliber m (-bru; -y) Brt. calibre, Am. caliber (też fig.)

Kalifornia f (-ii; 0) California

kalina f (-y) bot. snowball

kalk|a f (-i; G -/-lek) carbon paper; **~omania** m (GDL -ii; -e) Brt. transfer, Am. decalc(omania)

kalkula|cja f (-i; -e) calculation; **~cyjny: arkusz ~cyjny** spreadsheet; **~tor** m (-a; -y), **~torek** m (-rka; -rki) calculator

kalkulować ⟨s-, wy-⟩ (-uję) calculate; **~ się** F pay, pay off

kaloryczny caloric; (pożywny) high-calorie

kaloryfer m (-u; -y) radiator

kalosz m (-a; -e) Brt. wellington (boot), Am. rubber (boot)

kal'waria (GDL -ii; -e) calvary (też fig.)

kalwiński Calvinist

kał m (-u; 0) Brt. faeces pl., Am. feces

kałamarz m (-a; -e) ink-pot

kałuża f (-y, -e) puddle; (krwi, oleju) pool

kambuz m (-a; -y) naut. galley

kameleon m (-a; -y) zo. chameleon

kamer|a f (-y) camera; **~alny** mus. chamber; **~ton** m (-u; -y) tuning fork

kamerzysta m (-y; -ści) cameraman

kamfora f (-y; 0) camphor

kamica f (-y; -e) med. lithiasis; **~ nerkowa** med. urolithiasis

kamieni|arka f (-i) masonry; stonework; **~arski: zakład ~arski** (nagrobkowy) monumental mason's workshop; marble mason's workshop; **~arz** marble mason; (nagrobków) monumental mason; **~ca** f (-y; -e) house; **~ca czynszowa** block of (rented) Brt. flats lub Am. apartments; **~eć** ⟨s-⟩ (-eję) turn to stone, petrify (też fig.); **~ołom** m (-u; -y) quarry; **~sty** (-ście) stony

kamie|nny stone; **~ń** m (-nia; -nie) stone; (pojedynczy też) pebble; (kotłowy) scale, Brt. fur; **~ń węgielny** corner-stone (też fig.); **~ń do zapalniczki** flint; **~ń obrazy** a bone of contention; **jak ~ń w wodę** without a trace; F **jak z ~nia** with a difficulty

kamionkowy stoneware

kamizelka f (-i; G -lek) Brt. waistcoat, Am. vest

kam'pania f (GDL -ii; -e) campaign; **~ promocyjna** advertising lub promotion campaign; **~ wyborcza** election campaign

kamrat m (-a; -ci) pal, mate, buddy

kamy|czek m (-czka; -czki), **~k** m (-ka; -ki) stone; pebble

Kanad|a f (-y) Canada; **~yjczyk** m (-a; -cy), **~yjka** f (-i; G -jek) Canadian; **2yjka** (kajak) Canadian canoe; **2yjski** Canadian

kanaliza|cja f (-i; -e) (urządzenia) sewage system; (kanalizowanie) installation of a sewage system; **~cyjny** sewage

kanał m (-u; -y) naturalny channel; sztuczny canal; (ściekowy) sewer; (rów) ditch; TV: channel; **2 La Manche** English Channel; **~owy: leczenie ~owe** med. root(-canal) therapy

kanap|a f (-y) sofa, couch; **~ka** f (-i; G -pek) settee, sofa; (przekąska) sandwich

kanarek m (-rka; -rki) zo. canary

kance'laria f (GDL -ii; -e) office; **~ryjny** office; **papier ~ryjny** (large-size) writing paper

kancia|rstwo F n (-a) swindling; **~rka** f (-i; G -rek), **~rz** m (-a; -e) swindler

kanciasty (-to) angular

kanc|lerski chancellor's; **~lerz** m (-a; -e) chancellor

kand. skrót pisany: **kandydat** cand. (candidate)

kandy|dat m (-a; -ci), **~datka** f (-i; G -tek) candidate (**na** A, **do** G to); **~do-**

~wać (-uję) apply (**na** A for), stand (as a candidate) (**na** A for)

kandyzowany glacé, candied

kangur m (-a; -y) zo. kangaroo

kanikuła f (-y) dog days pl.; (upał) heat wave

kanonada f (-y) bombardment, cannonade

kanoni|k m (-a; -cy) canon; **~zować** (-uję) canonize

kant m (-u; -y) edge; (po zaprasowaniu) crease; F swindle

kantor¹ m (-u; -y) office; **~ walutowy** exchange office

kantor² m (-a; -rzy) cantor

kantować F ⟨o-⟩ (-uję) swindle, cheat

kantówka f (-i; G -wek) bud. square timber; ruler

kantyna f (-y) (sklep) canteen

kapa f (-a; -y) bedspread; rel. cope

kapać (-ię) drop, drip

kapary m/pl. (-ów) capers pl.

kapeć m (-pcia; -pcie, -pci[ów]) slipper; (stary but) old worn-out slipper/shoe

kapela f (-i; -e) mus. F band; (ludowa) folk group

kapel|an m (-a; -i/-owie) rel. chaplain; mil. army chaplain; **~mistrz** m (-a; -e/-owie) mus. bandmaster, band leader; (dyrygent) conductor

kapelusz m (-a; -e) hat

kaper|ować ⟨s-⟩ (-uję) capture, seize; (w sporcie) entice; **~unek** m (-nku; -nki) capturing; enticing

kapiszon m (-a; -y) → **kaptur, spłonka**

kapitali|sta m (-y; -ści) capitalist; **~styczny** capitalist; **~zm** m (-u; -y) capitalism

kapital|ny F splendid, wonderful; **remont ~lny** general overhaul; **~ł** m (-u; -y) capital; **~ł zakładowy** registered lub nominal capital; **~ł akcyjny** joint stock

kapitan m (-a; -owie) mil., naut., (w sporcie) captain; **~at** m (-u; -y) naut. port authority

kapitański: mostek ~ bridge

kapitu|lacja f (-i; -e) capitulation, surrender; **~lować** ⟨s-⟩ (-uję) capitulate, surrender; fig. give up

kapituła f (-y) rel. chapter

kapli|ca f (-y; -e, G -czek) rel. chapel; **~czka** rel. chapel; wayside shrine

kapła|n m (-a; -i) priest; **~nka** f (-i; G

-nek) priestess; **~ński** clerical, priestly, sacerdotal

kapnąć *v/s.* *(-nę)* drip

kapota *f (-y)* coat, jacket

kapować **‹s-›** F *(-uję)* get, understand

kapral *m (-a; -e)* corporal

kapry|s *m (-u; -y)* whim; caprice; *mus.* capriccio; **~sić** → **grymasić**; **~śny** capricious, whimsical

kapsel *m (-sla; -sle, -sli)* (crown) cap

kapsuł|a *f (-y; G -)* capsule; *astr.* (space) capsule; **~ka** *f (-i; G -łek) med.* capsule

Kapsztad *m (-u; 0)* Cape Town

kaptować **‹s-›** *(-uję)* entice; buy

kaptur *m (-a; -y)* hood; *tech.* cover

kapucyn *m (-a; -i) rel.* Capuchin (friar)

kapu|sta *f (-y; G -) bot.* cabbage; **biała ~sta** white cabbage; **główiasta ~sta** headed cabbage; **włoska ~sta** savoy cabbage; **~ściany** cabbage; **~śniak** *m (-a; -i) gastr.* cabbage soup; *(deszcz)* drizzle

kar|a *f (-y; G -)* punishment *(za A* for); penalty; **~a pozbawienia wolności** imprisonment; *pod* **~ą więzienia** punishable by prison; *za* **~ę** as a punishment

karabin *m (-u; -y)* gun, *mil. zwł.* rifle; **~ek** *m (-nka; -nki)* small-bore rifle; snap hook, karabiner, **~owy** rifle, gun

karać **‹u-›** *(-rzę)* punish *(za A* for; *więzieniem* with imprisonment)

karafka *f (-i; G -fek)* decanter

karakułowy astrakhan

karalny punishable; *czyn* **~** *jur.* criminal offence

karaluch *m (-a; -y) zo.* cockroach

karambol *m (-u; -e) mot.* pile-up

karaś *m (-sia; -sie) zo.* crucian

karawan *m (-u; -y)* hearse; **~a** *f (-y; G -)* caravan

karb *m (-u; -y)* notch, score; *kłaść na* **~** *(G)* put down to, set down to; *trzymać w* **~ach** curb, restrain

karbidówka *f (-i; G -wek)* carbide lamp

karbowa|ć *(-uję)* notch, score; *włosy* → **kręcić**; **~ny** notched, scored

karcąco *adv.* reproachfully

karciany card

karcić **‹s-›** *(-cę)* rebuke; → **ganić**

karczma *f (-y; G -czem)* inn

karczoch *m (-a; -y) bot.* artichoke

karczow|ać **‹wy-›** *(-uję)* grub; **~isko** *n (-a)* clearance

kardio|gram *m (-u; -y) med.* cardiogram; **~stymulator** *m (-a; -y) med.* pace-maker

kardynalny fundamental, basic, cardinal

kardynał *m (-a; -owie) rel.* cardinal

karet|a *f (-y)* carriage, coach; **~ka** *f (-i; G -tek)*: **~ka pogotowia (ratunkowego)** ambulance; **~ka więzienna** *Brt.* prison van, *Am.* patrol wagon

kariera *f (-y)* career; success

kark *m (-u; -i) anat.* neck; *nadstawiać* **~u** risk one's neck; *zima na* **~u** the winter is approaching; **~ołomny** breakneck, headlong

karłowaty dwarfish, dwarf

karmazyn *m (-a; -y) zo.* rose-fish; **~owy** crimson

karmel *m (-u; -e)* caramel; **~ek** *m (-ka; -ki)* caramel (toffee)

karmelicki Carmelite

karmi|ć *‹na-›* give food to; *niemowlę* breast-feed; *zwł. zwierzę* feed; **~ się** live on; **~enie** *n (-a)* feeding

karnawał *m (-u; -y)* carnival

karn|ość *f (-ści; 0)* discipline; **~y** disciplined

karo *n (-a lub idkl.; -a)* gra w karty: diamond(s *pl*).; *as* **~** ace of diamonds; *wyjść w* **~** play diamonds

karoseria *f (GDL -ii; -e) mot.* bodywork

karowy gra w karty: diamond

karp *m (-ia; -ie) zo.* carp

kart|a *f (-y; G -)* (kredytowa, do gry) card; *(papieru)* sheet; *komp.* expansion card; **~a tytułowa** title page; **~a łowiecka** game licence; **~a wyborcza** ballot-paper; **~a telefoniczna** zwł. *Brt.* phonecard; *zielona* **~a** *Brt.* green card, certificate of motor insurance; *grać w (otwarte)* **~y** put one's cards on the table; *z* **~y** à la carte; **~ka** *f (-i; G -tek)* (w książce) leaf; *(luzem)* sheet; **~ka pocztowa** postcard

kartof|el *m (-fla; -fle)* potato; **~lanka** *m (-i; G -nek)* potato soup

karton *m (-u; -y)* cardboard; *(pudło)* box; **~owy** cardboard

kartoteka *f* card file *lub* index

karuzela *f (-i -e) Brt.* merry-go-round, *Am.* carousel

karygodny criminal

karykatu|ra *f (-y)* cartoon; *(portret)* caricature; **~rować** **‹s-›** *(-uję)* caricature;

~rzysta *m* (-y; -ści), ~rzystka *f* (-i; *G* -tek) cartoonist, caricaturist

karzeł *m* (-rła; -rły) dwarf

kasa *f* (-y) cash-box, (*urządzenie*) cash register; (*miejsce*) pay desk, (*w supermarkecie*) check-out; (*w teatrze itp.*) box-office; F (*pieniądze*) money; **~ pancerna** safe, strongbox

kasacja *f* (-i; -e) *jur.* annulment, cassation

kaset|a *f* (-y; *G* -) (*na pieniądze*) cash--box; *RTV:* cassette, tape; *phot.* cartridge; ~ka *f* (-i; *G* -tek) box; ~owy cassette

kasjer *m* (-a; -rzy), ~ka *f* (-i; *G* -rek) cashier, teller

kask *m* (-u; -i) (*motocyklisty itp.*) helmet, (*robotnika itp.*) hard-hat

kaskader *m* (-a; -rzy) stuntman

kasłać (-am) → **kaszlać**

kasow|ać ⟨s-⟩ (-uję) *wyrok* annul; *zapis* cancel; *bilet* cancel, punch; *nagranie* erase; *komp.* delete, erase; ~ość *f* (-ści; *0*) success at the box-office; ~y wpływy cash; *sukces* box-office

kastet *m* (-u; -y) *Brt.* knuckle-duster, *Am.* brass knuckles *pl.*

kastrować ⟨wy-⟩ (-uję) *samca* castrate; *samicę* spay

kasyno *n* (-a) casino; *mil.* mess

kasza *f* (-y; -e) (*sypka*) groats *pl.*; (*przyrządzona*) gruel; ~nka *f* (-i; *G* -nek) *Brt.* black pudding, *Am.* blood sausage

kaszel *m* (-szlu; -szle) cough

kaszkiet *m* (-u; -y) peaked cap

kaszl|ać, ~eć (-lę, -l!) ⟨~nąć⟩ *v/s.* (-nę) cough

kasztan *m* (-a; -y) (*jadalny*) chestnut; (*kasztanowiec*) horse chestnut, (*owoc*) conker; (*koń*) chestnut; ~owy chestnut

kat *m* (-a; -ci/-y) hangman, executioner

kata|klizm *m* (-u; -y) cataclysm, catastrophe, (natural) disaster; ~lizator *m* (-a; -y) *chem.*, *mot.* catalyst; ~log *m* (-u; -i) catalog(ue); *komp.* directory; ~logować ⟨s-⟩ (-uję) catalog(ue)

katar *m* (-u; -y) cold (in the head), catarrh

katarakta *f* (-y) cataract (*też med.*)

katarynka *f* (-i; *G* -nek) barrel organ

katastrofa *f* (-y) catastrophe; **~ kolejowa/lotnicza** train/air crash; **~ samochodowa** car accident

katechizm *m* (-u; -y) catechism

katedra *f* (-y) cathedral; (*uczelnia*) chair

(*historii* of history); ~lny cathedral

kategor|ia *f* (*GDL* -ii; -e) category; ~yczny categorical; ~yzować (-uję) categorize

katoli|cki (**po -ku**) (Roman) Catholic; ~cyzm (Roman) Catholicism; ~czka *f* (-i; *G* -czek), ~k *m* (-a; -cy) (Roman) Catholic

katować (-uję) torment, torture

kaucja *f* (-i; -e) (*w sklepie itp.*) deposit; *jur.* bail

kauczukowy caoutchouc, rubber

Kauk|az *m* (-u; *0*) the Caucasus; 2aski Caucasus, Caucasian

kawa *f* (-y) coffee; **~ naturalna** real coffee; → **biały, zbożowy**

kawalarz F *m* (-a; -e) joker

kawaler *m* (-a; -rzy/-owie) bachelor, unmarried man; (*amant*) boyfriend, beau; (*pl.* -owie) Knight (**Orderu ...** of the Order...); (*na dworze*) chevalier; ~ia *f* (*GDL* -ii; -e) *mil.* cavalry; ~ka *f* (-i; *G* -czek) *Brt.* bachelor flat, *Am.* studio apartment; ~ski bachelor; ~yjski cavalry

kawał *m* (-u; -y) lump, chunk; F joke; **~ drogi** a long way; **~ chłopa** a fine figure of a man; **zrobić komuś ~** play a joke on s.o.; ~eczek *m* (-czka; -czki) a little bit, piece; ~ek *m* (-ka; -ki) a bit, piece; **na ~ki** to pieces

kawiarnia *f* (-i; -e) café/cafe, coffee shop

kawior *m* (-u; *0*) caviar(e)

kawka *f* (-i; *G* -wek) jackdaw

kawowy coffee

kaza|ć (*im*)*pf* (każę, każ!) order, command; **~ł mi na siebie czekać** he made me wait for him, he kept me waiting; ~lnica *f* (-y; -e) *rel.* pulpit; ~nie *n* (-a) *rel.* sermon; *fig.* lecture

kazirodztwo *n* (-a; *0*) incest

kaznodzieja *m* (-i; -e, *G* -jów) *rel.* preacher

kaźń *f* (-ni; *0*) torture

każdorazowo *adv.* each/every time

każd|y (~a, ~e) every, each; everybody, everyone; **w ~ej chwili** (at) any moment; **o ~ej porze** (at) any time; **za ~ym razem** every time; **na ~ym kroku** at every step

kącik *m* (-a; -i) → **kąt**; (*zakątek*) nook

kąpać ⟨wy-⟩ (-ię) *v/t.* *Brt.* bath, *Am.* bathe; ~ ⟨wy-⟩ (-ię) *v/i.*; (*myć*) take *lub* have a bath; (*pływać*) swim; **~ się w słońcu** soak up the sun

kąpiel f (-i; -e) (mycie) bath; (pływanie) swim;~isko n (-a) bathing place; bathing beach; ~**isko morskie** seaside resort; ~owy bathing; **strój** ~owy bathing suit; ~ówki f/pl. (-wek) bathing trunks pl.

kąs|ać (-am) bite; ~ek m (-ska; -ski) morsel, bit, chunk

kąśliwy (-wie) biting, sharp

kąt m (-a; -y) math. angle; (pokoju itp.) corner; F place to stay; ~ **widzenia** point of view; **pod ostrym** ~**em** at an acute angle; **pod** ~**em** at an angle; (G) from the point of; **po** ~**ach** secretly; ~omierz m (-a; -e) protractor; ~ownik m (-a; -i) tech. angle (iron), angle (bar); ~owy angle, angular

kc skrót pisany: **kodeks cywilny** civil code

kciuk m (-a; -i) thumb

keczup m (-a; 0) ketchup

kefir m (-u; -y) kefir

keks m (-u; -y) fruit cake

kelner m (-a; -rzy) waiter; ~ka f (-i; G -rek) waitress

kemping m (-u; -i) camping site; ~owy camping; **przyczepa** ~**owa** Brt. caravan, Am. trailer

kędzierzawy curly, curling

kędzior m (-a; -y) lock

kęp|a f (-y) (drzew) clump, cluster; (trawy) tuft, bunch; (wyspa) islet, Brt. holm; ~ka f (-i; G -pek) little cluster

kęs m (-a; -y), ~**ek** (-ska; -ski) bite, mouthful

kibel F m (-bla; -ble) (toaleta) Brt. loo, Am. john

kibic m (-a; -e) fan, supporter

kibuc m (-a; -e) kibbutz

kich|ać (-am) ⟨~nąć⟩ (-chnę) sneeze; fig. think nothing (na A of)

kicia m (-i; -e) F pussy

kiczowaty (-to) kitschy, trashy, cheap

kić F (-cia, -cie; -ciów) Brt. nick, zwł. Am. slammer

kiecka f (-i; G -cek) skirt; **kiecki** pl. F togs pl.

kiedy 1. pron. when; **2.** cj. when; as; ~ **indziej** another time; ~**kolwiek** whenever; at any time; ~**ś** sometime, (at) some time (or other); ~**ż** when at last

kielich m (-a; -y) goblet; rel. chalice; bot. calyx; **iść na** ~**a** go for a drink

kieliszek m (-a; -szki) glass; ~ **do wódki** vodka glas; ~ **do jaj** egg cup

kielnia f (-i; -e) bud. trowel

kieł m (-kła; -kły) canine tooth; (drapieżcy) fang; (słonia, dzika) tusk

kiełbas|a f (-y; G -) sausage; ~**iany** sausage; **jad** ~**iany** botulin. ~**ka** f (-i; G -sek) sausage; frankfurter

kiełkować ⟨wy-⟩ (-uję) germinate; sprout; fig. stir, awaken

kiepski bad; poor

kier. skrót pisany: **kierownik** man., mngr (manager); **kierunek** dir. (direction)

kier m (-a; -y) gra w karty: heart's (pl.); **as** ~ ace of hearts; → też **kra**; **wyjść w** ~**y** play hearts

kierat m (-u; -y) treadmill (też fig.); fig. drudgery, dreary routine

kiermasz m (-u; -e) fair, bazaar

kierować (-uję) ⟨s-⟩ (do G, na A) direct (to, towards, też fig.), aim (at); spojrzenie turn (towards); broń point (at); ⟨po-⟩ (I) (autem itp.) drive (też v/i.); (zakładem) manage, run; ~ **się** (I) be guided (by)

kierow|ca m (-cy; G -ów) driver; ~**nica** m (-y; -e) steering wheel; (roweru) handlebars pl.

kierowni|ctwo n (-a) management; supervision; ~**czka** f (-i; G -czek) manager, director, head; (szkoły) headmistress; ~**czy** managerial, executive; ~**k** m (-a; -cy) manager, director, head; (szkoły) headmaster

kierowy heart(s)

kierun|ek m (-nku; -nki) direction; **pod** ~**kiem** under the direction lub supervision of; ~**kowskaz** m (-y; G -ów) (drogowskaz) signpost; mot. Brt. indicator, Am. turn signal; ~**kowy** directional; **numer** ~**kowy** tel. dialling code, Am. area code

kieszeń f (-ni; -nie) (spodni, wewnętrzna) trouser, inside) pocket

kieszonkow|e n (-ego) pocket money; ~**iec** m (-wca; -wcy) pickpocket; (pl. -wce) (książka) pocket book; ~**y** pocket

kij m (-a; -e, -ów) stick; ~ **golfowy** golf club; F ~**e** pl. beating, caning, hiding

kijanka f (-i; G -nek) tadpole

Kijów m (-jowa; 0) Kiev

kikut m (-a; -y) stump, stub

kilim m (-a; -y) kilim

kilka (m-os kilku) several, some; F a

couple (of); ~dziesiąt a few dozen; ~krotny repeated; -nie *adv.* repeatedly; ~naście a dozen or so; ~set several hundred

kilk|oro, ~u *m-os* → *kilka*

kilku|dniowy lasting several days; several days long; ~godzinny lasting several hours, of several hours; ~letni lasting several years, of several years; ~miesięczny lasting several months, of several months; ~nasto- *w zł.* → *kilkanaście*; ~nastoletni lasting over ten years; in one's teens; ~osobowy for several people; ~rodzinny for several families; multifamily; ~set → *kilkaset*; ~tysięczny of several thousand

kilof *m* (-*a*; -*y*) pick mattock, *Brt.* pickaxe, *Am.* pickax

kilo|gram *m* kilogram; ~metr *m Brt.* kilometre, *Am.* kilometer; ~wy one-kilogram; *naut.* keel

kiła *m* (-*y*; *0*) *med.* syphilis

kim(że) (*IL* → *kto, któż*): z ~ with who(m); o ~ about who(m)

kimać (-*am*) F nap, doze off

kinkiet *m* (-*u*; -*y*) wall lamp

kino *n* (-*a*) (*budynek*) *Brt.* cinema, *Am.* movie theater; (*seans*) *Brt.* the cinema, *Am.* the movies; (*sztuka*) cinema; ~operator *m* (-*a*; -*rzy*) projectionist; ~wy cinema

kiosk *m* (-*u*; -*i*) kiosk; newsagent('s); ~arka *f* (-*i*; *G* -*rek*), ~arz *m* (-*a*; -*e*) newsagent

kipi|ący boiling, seething; ~eć (-*ę*, -*i*) boil, seethe (*też fig.* z *G* with)

kir *m* (-*u*; *0*) crepe; *fig.* mourning

kis|ić ⟨*za-*⟩ (-*szę*, -*ś!*) pickle; ~ić się pickle; *fig.* ferment; ~iel *m* (-*ślu*; -*śle*) jelly-like dessert; ~nąć ⟨*s-*⟩ (-*nę*, -[*ną*]*ł*) turn sour

kiszka *f* (-*i*; *G* -*szek*) F gut, bowel; **ślepa** ~ F *med.* appendix; ~ **pasztetowa** *gastr.* liver sausage

kiszon|ka *f* (-*G* -*nek*) *agr.* silage; ~y: ~a **kapusta** sauerkraut; ~y **ogórek** pickled cucumber/gherkin

kiść *f* (-*ci*; -*cie*) bunch

kit *m* (-*u*; -*y*) putty; ~a *f* (-*y*) plume, (*ogon*) brush, brushy tail

kitel *m* (-*tla*; -*tle*) overall; (*lekarza itp.*) white coat

kitować (-*uję*) ⟨*za-*⟩ putty, fix with putty; ⟨*wy-*⟩ F *Brt.* croak, peg out

kiw|ać (-*am*) ⟨~*nąć*⟩ (-*nę*) (*głową*) nod (one's head); (*ręką*) wave (**na k-oś** to s.o.); ~ać **się** move about, be loose; *meble*: be rickety; → *kołysać się*

kiwi *n* (*idkl.*) *zo.*, *bot.* kiwi

kk *skrót pisany:* **kodeks karny** criminal code

kl. *skrót pisany:* **klasa** cl. *lub* Cl. (*class*)

klacz *f* (-*y*; -*e*) mare

klajster *m* (-*tra*, -*try*) paste; (*paćka*) goo

klakson *m* (-*u*; -*y*) *mot.* horn

klam|ka *f* (-*i*; *G* -*mek*) door-handle, (*gałka*) doorknob; ~ra *f* (-*y*; *G* -*mer*) clasp; buckle

klap|a *f* (-*y*; -) hinged lid, trapdoor; (*marynarki*) lapel; ~a **bezpieczeństwa** safety valve; **zrobić** ~ę fall flat; ~ać (-*ię*) *chodaki*: click; *kapcie*: pad; *deska*: rattle; ~nąć *v/s.* (-*nę*) fall *lub* sit with a bump

klarnet *m* (-*u*; -*y*) *mus.* clarinet

klarow|ać ⟨*wy-*⟩ (-*uję*) *wino* clear; clarify, make clear; ~ny clear

klas|a *f* (-*y*; *G* -) class (*też uczniów*); (*oddział uczniów w szkole*) *Brt.* form, *Am.* grade, (*sala*) classroom; ~kać (-*szczę-/kam*) ⟨~*nąć*⟩ (-*nę*) clap (one's hands); applaud; ~owy class; classroom; ~ówka *f* (-*i*; *G* -*wek*) test; ~yczny classical, classic

klasy|fikować ⟨*za-*⟩ (-*uję*) classify; ~fikować **się** be classified, be grouped; ~ka *f* (-*i*; *0*) classics *pl.*

klasztor *m* (-*u*; -*y*) *rel.* (*męski*) monastery, (*żeński*) convent; ~ny monastery, monastic; convent, conventual

klatka *f* (-*i*; *G* -*tek*) cage; (*zdjęciowa*) frame; ~ **piersiowa** chest, *med.* thorax; ~ **schodowa** staircase

klauzula *f* (-*i*; -*le*) *jur.* clause

klawiatura *f* (-*y*) keyboard

klawisz *m* (-*a*; -*e*) key; ~owy *instrument* keyboard

kląć (*klnę*) (**na** *A*) swear (at), curse; ~twa *f* (-*y*; *G* -) curse

klecić ⟨*s-*⟩ (-*cę*) *meble itp.* knock together; *wypracowanie itp.* knock off

kleić ⟨*s-*, *za-*⟩ (-*ję*) glue (together), stick (together); ~ **się** be sticky; stick; (*do kogoś*) cling (**do** *G* to); F *fig.* **nie** ~ **się** not work out (all right)

kle|ik *m* (-*u*; -*i*) gruel; ~isty sticky; *ręce itp.* clammy

klej *m* (-*u*; -*e*) glue; paste

klejnot *m* (-u; -y) jewel

klekotać (-cę/-czę) rattle, clatter; → **paplać**

klep|ać (-ię) ⟨**po-**⟩ slap, pat (**się** o.s., each other); ⟨**wy-**⟩ (*mówić*) patter; *ko-* **się** strickle; *metal* chase; **~isko** *n* (-a) (*w stodole*) thrashing floor; **~ka** *f* (-i; *G* -pek) (*w beczce*) stave; (*na podłodze*) flooring strip *lub* block; F **brak mu piątej ~ki** he has got a screw loose; **~nąć** → **klepać**

klepsydra *f* (-y; *G* -) hourglass; (*nekrolog*) obituary (notice)

kler *m* (-u; 0) (the) clergy; **~ykalny** clerical

kleszcz *m* (-a; -e) zo. tick; **~e** *m/pl.* (-y/-ów) *tech.* pliers *pl.* pincers *pl.*; *med.* forceps *pl.*; zo. pincers *pl.*; **~owy**: **poród ~owy** *med.* forceps delivery

klęcz|eć (-ę) kneel; **~ki** *pl.*: **na ~kach** on knees; **~nik** *m* (-a; -i) prie-dieu

klęk|ać ⟨-am⟩ ⟨**~nąć**⟩ (-nę, *też* -kła, -kli) kneel down

klę|li, ~łam → **kląć**

klęsk|a *f* (-i; *G* -) defeat; disaster, catastrophe; **~a pożaru** fire, conflagration, **~a głodu** hunger, famine; **ponieść ~ę** suffer defeat

klient *m* (-a; -ci) client; customer; **~ela** *f* (-i; *G* -el) clientele, customers *pl.*; **~ka** *f* (-i; *G* -tek) client; customer

klika *f* (-i; *G* -) clique

klikać (-nę) *komp.* (A) click (on)

klimat *m* (-u; -y) climate; **~yczny** climatic; **stacja ~yczna** climatic health resort; **~yzacja** *f* (-i; 0) air-conditioning; **~yzator** air-conditioner

klin *m* (-a; -y) wedge; (*w ubraniu*) (wedge-shaped) gusset; **zabić ~(a) między** drive a wedge between

klinga *f* (-i; *G* -) blade

klini|czny clinical; **~ka** *f* (-i) teaching hospital; clinic

klinow|aty wedge-shaped; **~y**: **pas ~y** *tech.* V-belt; **pismo ~e** cuneiform writing

klisza *f* (-y; -e) plate; film

kln|ą, ~ę, ~iecie, ~iesz → **kląć**

kloc *m* (-a; -e) block, (*pień*) log; **~ek** *m* (-cka; -cki) block

klomb *m* (-u; -y) flowerbed

klon *m* (-u; -y) *bot.* maple; *biol.* clone; **~ować** (-uję) clone

klops *m* (-a; -y) meat loaf; (*mały*) meat-

ball; F washout; **~ik** *m* (-a; -i) meatball, rissole

klosz *m* (-a; -e) lampshade; (*na ser itp.*) bell-shaped cover; (*na rośliny*) cloche; **w ~** → **~owy** (widely) flared

klown *m* (-a; -y/-i) clown

klozet *m* (-u; -y) WC, toilet; **~owy** toilet

klub *m* (-u; -y) club; **~ poselski** parliamentary group; **~owy** club

klucz *m* (-a; -e) key (*też* fig.); *mus.* clef; *tech.* Brt. spanner, Am. wrench; **pod ~em** under lock and key; (*w więzieniu*) behind bars; **~owy** key

kluć się (-ję) hatch

klusk|a *f* (-i; *G* -sek) dumpling; **~i** *pl. też* pasta

kła → **kieł**

kłaczkowaty fluffy

kła|dą, ~dę → **kłaść**; **~dka** (-i; *G* -dek) foot-bridge, *naut.* gangplank; **~dziesz** → **kłaść**

kłak *m* (-a; -i) flock, tuft; **~i** *pl. pej.* shock, mop

kłam *m* (-u; 0): **zadać ~** (*D*) give the lie to; **~ać** ⟨**s-**⟩ (-ię) lie; **~ca** *m* (-y; *G* -ów) liar; **~liwy** (-wie) lying; **~stwo** *n* (-a) lie

kłania|ć się (-am) bow; nod (**znajomym** to acquaintances); **~j się im od nas** remember us to them

kłaść lay; (*do łóżka*) lay down; put (**do kieszeni** (in)to the pocket); **~ się** lie down; → **wkładać**

kłąb *m* (kłębu; kłęby) ball, tangle; zo. withers *pl.*; **kłęby** clouds (**dymu, kurzu** of smoke, of dust)

kłęb|ek *m* (-ka; -ki) ball, tangle; *fig.* **~ek nerwów** a bundle of nerves; **zwinąć się w ~ek** curl up; **~ić się** (-ę) get up (in clouds), hang (in clouds); mill about

kłoda *f* (-y; *G* kłód) log

kłonić ⟨**s-, po-**⟩ bow down (**się** v/i.)

kłopot *m* (-u; -y) trouble, problem, worry; **~y pieniężne** financial difficulties *pl.*; **~y z sercem** heart trouble; **wprawić w ~** embarrass; **~ać się** (-czę/-cę) worry (**o** A about); **~liwy** troublesome, difficult

kłos *m* (-a; -y) ear

kłócić się (-cę) quarrel, argue (**o** A about); *kolory*: clash

kłódka *f* (-i; *G* -dek) padlock

kłót|liwy (-wie) quarrelsome; **~nia** *f* (-i; -e) quarrel, argument

kłu|ć (-ję/kolę, kolesz, kole, kłuj!) prick;

ból: stab; ~jący prickling; stabbing

kłus m (-a; 0) trot; ~em at a trot; ~ak m (-a; -i) trotter

kłusować¹ (-uję) trot

kłusow|ać² (-uję) poach; ~nictwo n (-a; 0) poaching; ~nik m (-a; -cy) poacher

kły pl. → kieł

KM skrót pisany: **koń mechaniczny** HP (horse power)

kminek m (-nku; 0) caraway (seed)

knajpa F f (-y) joint, Brt. dive, boozer, Am. beanery

knedle m/pl. dumplings

knocić F ⟨na-, s-⟩ (-cę) → partaczyć

knot m (-a; -y) wick; F (partactwo) botch-up

knowania pl. (-ń) intrigues pl.

knuć ⟨u-⟩ (-ję) scheme, intrigue

koalic|ja f (-i -e) coalition; ~yjny coalition

kobiałka f (-i; G -łek) basket

kobie|ciarz m (-a; -e) womanizer; ~cy (-co, po -cemu) feminine; female; ~ta f (-y) woman

kobyła f (-y) mare

koc m (-a; -e) blanket; wełniany ~ woollen blanket

kocha|ć (-am) love (się o.s.); ~ć się (w I) be in love (with); (z I) make love (to); ~m cię I love you; jak mamę ~m cross my heart; ~nek m (-nka; -nkowie) lover; ~nka f (-i; G -nek) mistress; ~ny dear

kocher m (-u; -y) stove

koci catty, catlike; biol. feline; ~ak m (-a; -i), ~ę n (-ęcia; -ęta) kitten, kitty

kocioł m (kotła; -tły) vat, pot, cauldron; tech. boiler; kotły pl. mus. (kettle)-drums pl.

kocur m (-a; -y) tom(cat)

koczow|ać (-uję) lead a nomadic existence; F squat, park (o.s.); ~nik m (-a; -cy) nomad

kod m (-u; -y) code; ~ banku sorting code number; ~ pocztowy Brt. post-code, Am. zip code

kodeks m (-u; -y) code; ~ karny criminal code; ~ postępowania cywilnego civil procedure

kodować ⟨za-⟩ (-uję) code

kogo(ż) (GA → kto, któż) who(m); do ~ to who(m); od ~ from who(m)

kogu|ci: waga ~cia bantam weight; ~t m (-a; -y) cock, zwł. Am. rooster

koić ⟨u-⟩ (-ję) soothe, comfort, calm

kojarzyć ⟨s-⟩ (-ę) associate; ~ się be associated (z I with)

kojący (-co) soothing, calming

kojec m (-jca; -jce) (dla kur) coop; (dla dziecka) playpen

kok m (-a; -i) bun

kokain|a f (-y; 0) cocaine; ~izować się (-uję) take cocaine, snort (cocaine)

kokarda f (-y) bow

kokiet|eryjny coquettish, flirtatious; ~ować (-uję) flirt (A with)

koklusz m (-u; 0) med. whopping cough

kokos m (-a; -y) bot. coconut; ~owy coconut; ~owy interes gold mine

kokoszka f (-i; G -szek) brood-hen

koks m (-u; 0) coke; na ~ie F doped

koksownia f (-i; -e) coking plant

koktajl m (-u; -e) (alkohol) cocktail; (mleczny) milk shake

kol. skrót pisany: **kolega, koleżanka** colleague; **kolejowy** rail. (railway); **kolegium** college

kolacj|a f (-i; -e) supper; (późny obiad) dinner; jeść ~ę have supper/dinner

kolano n (-a) knee; ~wy knee, med. genual

kola|rski cycle; ~rstwo n (-a; 0) cycling; ~rz m (-a; -e) cyclist

kolaż m (-u; -e) collage

kolą → kłuć; ~y → kłujący

kolba f (-y; G -) mil. butt; bot. cob

kol|ce → kolec; ~czasty (-to) prickly, ~czyk m (-a; -i) earring; agr. earmark

kolebka f (-i; G -bek) cradle (też fig.)

kol|e → kłuć; ~ec m (-lca, -lce) thorn, spine; ~ce (w. sporcie) spikes pl.

kolega m (-i; -dzy) colleague, friend; ~ z pracy workmate, fellow worker; ~ szkolny schoolmate; → fach

kole|gialny collective; ~giata f (-y) rel. collegiate church; ~gować (-uję) be friends (z I with)

kole'ina f (-y) rut

kole|j f (GDl -i; -e, -ei) rail. railway, Am. railroad; order, sequence; ~j rzeczy course of events; pracować na ~i work on the railway; spóźnić się na ~j miss the train; po ~i one by one, by turns; ~j na mnie it is my turn; z ~i in turn

kolejarz m (-a; -e, -y) Brt. railwayman, Am. railroader

kolej|ka f (-i; G -jek) train; (do skle-

pu) Brt. queue, *Am.* line; **~ka górska** mountain railway/railroad; **stać w ~ce** queue up *(po A* for); **wejść poza ~ką** jump the queue; **stawiać ~kę** *(G)* buy a round of ...

kolej|nictwo *n (-a; 0)* railway/railroad system;**~no** in turn;**~ność** *f (-ci; 0)* sequence, order; **według ~ności** one after the other;**~ny** next

kolejowy *Brt.* railway, *Am.* railroad

kolek|cjonować *(-uję)* collect;**~tura** *f (-y)* lottery-ticket selling point

kolektyw *m (-u; -y)* collective, body; **~ny** collective

koleż|anka *f (-i; G -nek)* → **kolega**; **~eński** comradely; **~eństwo** *n (-a; 0)* friendship, comradeship

kolę *1. os. sg.* → **kłuć**

kolęda *f (-y)* carol

kolidować *(-uję)* clash **(z** *I* with)

kolisty *(-to)* circular

kolizja *f (-i; -e)* collision; → **zderzenie**

kolka *f (-i; G -lek)* stitch; *med., wet.* colic

kolokwium *n (idkl.; -a, G -ów)* test

koloni|a *f (GDL -ii; -e)* colony; **~e (letnie)** *pl.* holiday camp; **~zować** ⟨**s-**⟩ *(-uję)* colonize

kolońsk|i: woda ~a (eau de) cologne

kolor *m (-u; -y)* colo(u)r; *(w grze w karty)* suit; **pod ~** colo(u)r-coordinated; **~y** *pl.* colo(u)reds *pl.*; → **barwa, barwnik**;**~owy** colo(u)red, colo(u)rful

koloryzować *(-uję)* embellish, whitewash

kolos *m (-a; -y)* colossus;**~alny** colossal

kolpor|taż *m (-u; 0)* distribution; **~ter** *m (-a; -rzy)*, **-rka** *f (-i; G -rek)* distributor;**~tować** *(-uję)* distribute

kolumna *f (-y)* column; *(głośnik)* loudspeaker; **~da** *f (-y)* colonnade

kołatać *(-czę)* knock **(do** *G* on); beat; **~ się** shake, rattle *v/i.*

kołczan *m (-u; -y)* quiver

kołdra *f (-y; G -der)* blanket, quilt

kołduny *m/pl. (-ów)* meat-filled dumplings *pl.*

kołek *m (-łka; -łki)* peg

kołnierz *m (-a; -e)*,**~yk** *m (-a; -i)* collar; **~yk koszuli** shirt collar

koło¹ *n (-a; G kół)* circle *(też fig., math.); (pojazdu)* wheel; **~em, w ~o** all around; → **grono, kółko**

koło² *prp. (G)* near, close to, next to;

~ Wrocławia near Wrocław; → **niedaleko, około**

kołow|acizna *f (-y; 0)* wet. staggers *sg./pl.*; F confusion; **~ać** *(-uję)* circle; *(po lotnisku)* taxi; **~rotek** *m (-tka; -tki)* spinning-wheel; *wędkarstwo:* reel; **~rót** *m (-rotu; -roty)* winch; *(przy wejściu itp.)* turnstile; *(w sporcie)* circle; **~y** circular; *pojazd* wheeled

kołpak *m (-a; -i)* cap, helmet; *mot.* hubcap

kołtun *m (-a; -y) fig.* bourgeois, philistine; **~y** *pl.* matted hair *sg.*

koły|sać *(-szę)* rock, *(biodrami itp.)* sway; **~sać się** rock; sway; → **bujać (się)**; **~sanka** *f (-i; G -nek)* lullaby; **~ska** *f (-ski; G -sek)* cradle

koman|dorski: Krzyż ~dorski Grand Cross; **~dos** *m (-a; -i)* commando

komandytow|y: spółka ~a limited partnership

komar *m (-a; -y)* mosquito, gnat

kombajn *m (-u; -y) agr.* combine harvester; *(górniczy)* cutter loader

kombina|cja *f (-i; -e)* combination; *fig.* **~cje** *pl.* wheeling and dealing; **~tor** *m (-a; -rzy)*,**~torka** *f (-i; G -rek)* swindler

kombi|nerki *pl. tech.* (a pair of) combination pliers *pl.*; **~nezon** *m (-u; -y) Brt.* overalls, *Am.* coveralls; jump suit; *(astronauty)* space suit; **~nować** *(-uję)* combine, join together; F think; **~nować jak** *inf.* how to *bezok.*; F be up to

ko'media *f (GDL -ii; -e)* comedy;**~nt** *m (-a; -ci)*, **~ntka** *f (-i; G -tek)* comedian, comic

komediowy comedy

komenda *f (-y)* command; **~ policji/ straży pożarnej** police/fire brigade headquarters *pl.*; **~nt** *m (-a; -ci)* commandant; *mil.* commander, commanding officer

komenderować *(-uję)* command, be in command of

komentarz *m (-a; -e)* commentary

komentować ⟨**s-**⟩ *(-uję)* comment

komercyjny commercial

komet|a *f (-y; G -)* comet; **~ka** *f (-i; G -tek) sport:* badminton

komfortowy comfortable

komi|czny comical, funny; **~k** *m (-a; -cy)* comic, comedian; **~ks** *m (-u; -y)* comic strip; *(książeczka)* comic

komin *m (-a; -y)* chimney, *(wysoki)*

smokestack; (*statku*) funnel; ~ek *m* (*-nka*; *-nki*) (w pokoju) fireplace; ~iarz *m* (*-a*; *-e*) chimney sweep; ~kowy fireplace

komis F *m* (*-u*; *-y*) commission shop

komi|'**sariat** *m* (*-u*, *-y*) police station; ~**saryczny**: **zarząd ~saryczny** receivership; ~**sarz** *m* (*-a*; *-e*) commissioner; (*policji*) *Brt.* superintendent, *Am.* captain; (*komunistyczny*) commissar; ~**sja** *f* (*-i*) committee, commission; board; ~**tet** *m* (*-u*; *-y*) committee

komityw|**a** *f* (*-y*; 0): **żyć w ~ie** be good friends (**z** *I* with); **wejść w ~ę** become good friends (**z** *I* with)

komiwojażer *m* (*-a*; *-owie*/-*rzy*) (travelling) salesman/saleswoman, commercial travel(l)er

komnata *f* (*-y*) chamber

komoda *f* (*-y*) chest of drawers

komor|**a** *f* (*-y*) *biol.*, *med.*, *tech.* chamber; *anat.* ventricle; ~**ne** *n* (*-ego*; 0) rent; ~**nik** *m* (*-a*; *-cy*) *jur.* bailiff; ~**owy** *tech.* chamber

komórk|**a** *f* (*-i*; *G -rek*) *biol.*, *tech.* cell; (*pomieszczenie*) closet; F (*telefon komórkowy*) mobile; ~**owiec** mobile; ~**owy** cellular; → **telefon**

kompakt *m* (*-u*; *-y*) CD, *Brt.* compact disc, *Am.* compact disk; CD player; ~**owy** CD, compact

kompan *m* (*-a*; *-i*) mate, buddy

kom'pania *f* (*GDL -ii*; *-e*) *mil.*, *econ.* company

kompas *m* (*-u*; *-y*) compass

kompatybilny compatible

kompensa|**cyjny** compensatory; ~**ta** *f* (*-i*; *-e*) compensation

kompensować (*-uję*) compensate

kompeten|**cja** *f* (*-i*; *-e*) competence; ~**tny** competent

kompleks *m* (*-u*; *-y*) complex

komplement *m* (*-u*; *-y*) compliment

komple|**t** *m* (*-u*; *-y*) set; (*mebli itp.*) suite; ~**t widzów** full house; **w ~cie** in full force; **do ~tu** to make complete

komplet|**ny** complete; F utter; ~**ować** ⟨*s-*⟩ (*-uję*) complete, make complete

komplik|**acja** *f* (*-i*; *-e*) complication; ~**ować** ⟨*s-*⟩ (*-uję*) complicate

kompo|**nent** *m* (*-u*; *-y*) component, constituent; ~**nować** ⟨*s-*⟩ (*-uję*) compose

kompost *m* (*-u*; 0) *agr.* compost; ~**ować** ⟨*za-*⟩ (*-uję*) compost

kompot *m* (*-u*; *-y*) stewed fruit; compote

kompozy|**cja** *f* (*-i*; *-e*) composition; ~**tor** *m* (*-a*; *-rzy*), ~**torka** *f* (*-i G -rek*) composer

kompres *m* (*-u*; *-y*) compress; ~**ja** *f* (*-i*; *-e*) compression

kompromi|**s** *m* (*-u*; *-y*) compromise; ~**tacja** *f* (*-i*; *-e*) discredit; ~**tować** ⟨*s-*⟩ (*-uję*) discredit, compromise; ~**tujący** discrediting, compromising

komputer *m* (*-a*, *-y*) computer; ~ **osobisty** personal computer (*skrót*: *PC*); ~**owy** computer; ~**owiec** F *m* (*-wca*; *-wcy*) computer wizard; ~**ować** ⟨*s-*⟩ (*-uję*) computerize

komu (*D → kto*) to whom

komuch F *m* (*-a*; *-y*) commie

komu|**na** *f* (*-y*) *hist.* commune; *pej.* communist system, commies *pl.*; ~**nalny** municipal; *bud.* *Brt.* council, *Am.* low-cost; ~**nał** *m* (*-u*; *-y*) commonplace; ~**nia** *f* (*GDl -ii*; *-e*) communion; ~**nikacja** *f* (*-i*; 0) communication; (*transport*) communications *pl.*, *Brt.* transport, *Am.* transportation; ~**nikacyjny** communication; *Brt.* transport, *Am.* transportation; ~**nikat** *m* (*-u*; *-y*) (*rządowy itp.*) communiqué; announcement; (**o stanie pogody**, **radiowy**) weather, radio) report

komunikować (*-uję*) ⟨*za-*⟩ communicate, announce; ~ **się** *t-ko impf.* be in touch; ⟨*s-*⟩ get in touch

komunistyczny Communist

komuż (*D → któż*) to who(m)

komża *f* (*-y*; *-e*, *-y/-mez*) surplice

kona|**ć** (*-am*) be dying; ~**ć ze śmiechu** die laughing; ~**jący** dying

konar *m* (*-a*; *-y*) bough

koncentra|**cja** *f* (*-i*; 0) concentration; ~**cyjny** concentration

koncentrować ⟨*s-*⟩ (*-uję*) concentrate, focus (**się na** *L* on)

koncep|**cja** *f* (*-i*; *-e*) idea, conception; ~**t** *m* (*-u*; *-y*) idea; **ruszyć ~tem** think of s.th.

koncern *m* (*-u*; *-y*) concern

koncert *m* (*-u*; *-y*) performance, concert

conces|**ja** *f* (*-i*; *-e*) *Brt.* licence, *Am.* license; ~**jonować** (*-uję*) license

koncha *f* (*-y*; *G -*) conch

kondensowa|**ć** ⟨*s-*⟩ (*-uję*) condense; **mleko ~ne** (*słodzone*) condensed milk, (*niesłodzone*) evaporated milk

kondolenc|je *f/pl.* (*-i*): **składać ~je** offer one's condolences (*D* to); **~yjny** condolence

kondom *m* (*-u*; *-y*) condom, F rubber

kondukt *m* (*-u*; *-y*): **~ żałobny** funeral procession

konduktor *m* (*-a*; *-rzy*), **~ka** *f* (*-i*; *G -rek*) (*w autobusie*) conductor; *rail. Brt.* guard, *Am.* conductor; **~ka** *też* satchel

kondy|cja *f* (*-i*; *-e*) condition, fitness; **~cyjny** fitness; **~gnacja** *f* (*-i*; *-e*) stor(e)y, level

konewka *f* (*-i*; *G -wek*) watering-can

konfederacja *f* (*-i*; *-e*) confederation

konfekcyjny ready-made

konfe|ransjer *m* (*-a*; *-rzy*), **~ransjerka** *f* (*-i*; *G -rek*) *Brt.* compère, master of ceremonies (*skrót:* **MC**); **~rencja** *f* (*-i*; *-e*) conference; **~rować** (*-uję*) confer

konfesjonał *m* (*-u*; *-y*) *rel.* confessional

konfiden|cjonalny confidential; **~t** *m* (*-a*; *-ci*), **~tka** *f* (*-i*; *G -tek*) informer

konfirmacja *f* (*-i*; *-e*) confirmation (*też rel.*)

konfisk|ata *f* (*-y*) confiscation; **~ować** ⟨**s-**⟩ (*-uję*) confiscate

konfitury *f/pl.* (*-*) jam

konfliktowy provocative

konfront|acja *f* (*-i*; *-e*) confrontation; comparison; **~ować** ⟨**s-**⟩ (*-uję*) (**z** *I*) confront (with), compare (with)

kongres *m* (*-u*; *-y*) congress

koniak *m* (*-u*; *-i*) *gastr.* brandy, (*francuski*) cognac

koniczyna *f* (*-y*) clover

koniec *m* (*-ńca*; *-ńce*) ending, end; (*szpic też*) tip; **~ świata** end of the world; **i na tym ~** and that will do; **bez końca** infinite, interminable; **do (samego) końca** to the very end; **na/w końcu** in the end, finally; **od końca** from the end, from back; **pod ~** at the end; **~ końców** in the end, finally; → **kres, dobiegać**

koniecz|nie *adv.* absolutely; necessarily; **~ność** *f* (*-ści*; *0*) necessity; **z ~ności** of necessity; **~ny** necessary, obligatory

koni|k *m* (*-a*; *-i*) pony; *fig.* hobby; (*w szachach*) knight; **~k polny** grasshopper; **~na** *f* (*-y*) horse-meat; **~okrad** *m* (*-a*; *-y*) horse thief; **~uch** *m* (*-a*; *-y/-owie*) groom, stableman

koni|ugacja *f* (*-i*; *-e*) *gr.* conjugation; **~unktura** *f* (*-y*) economic trend; (*do-*

bra) economic boom

koniuszek *m* (*-szka*; *-szki*) tip

konkluzja *f* (*-i*; *-e*) conclusion

konkret|ny concrete; specific; **człowiek** practical, down-to-earth; **~yzować** ⟨**s-**⟩ (*-uję*) put in concrete terms

konkubina *f* (*-y*) *jur.* concubine; cohabitant

konkur|encja *f* (*-i*) competition; (*wsporcie*) event; **~encyjny** competitive; **~ent** *m* (*-a*; *-ci*), **~entka** *f* (*-i*; *G -tek*) competitor, rival; **~ować** (*-uję*) compete (**o** for)

konkurs *m* (*-u*; *-y*) competition, contest; **otwarty ~** open competition (**na** A for); **brać udział poza ~em** take part as an unofficial competitor; **~owy** competition, contest

kóń|no *adv.* on horseback; → **jechać**; **~ny** horse; horse-drawn; mounted

konopie *f/pl.* (*-pi*) *bot.* hemp, cannabis

konosament *m* (*-u*; *-y*) *econ.* bill of lading

konował *f* (*-a*; *-y*) *pej.* quack

konsekwen|cja *f* (*-i*; *-e*) consequence; logicality, consistency; **~tny** consequent; consistent, logical

konserwa *f* (*-y*) *Brt.* tinned food, *Am.* canned food; **~cja** *f* (*-i*; *-e*) maintenance; conservation; **~'torium** *n* (*idkl.*; *-ia, -iów*) conservatory, music school; **~tysta** *m* (*-y*; *-ści*), **~tystka** *f* (*-i*; *G -tek*) conservative; **~tywny** conservative

konserwo|wać ⟨**za-**⟩ (*-uję*) preserve, conserve; maintain; **~wy** *Brt.* tinned; *Am.* canned

kon|solidacja *f* (*-i*; *-e*) consolidation; **~sorcjum** *n* (*idkl.*; *-ja, -ów*) consortium; **~spekt** *m* (*-u*; *-y*) outline, draft

konspira|cja *f* (*-i*; *-e*) conspiracy; underground movement; underground organisation; **~cyjny** conspiratorial; underground

kon|spirować (*-uję*) conspire; ⟨**za-**⟩ hide, camouflage (**się** o.s.); **~statować** ⟨**s-**⟩ (*-uję*) state

konsternacja *f* (*-i*; *0*) consternation, dismay

konstru|kcja *f* (*-i*; *-e*) construction; structure; **~kcyjny** constructional; structural; **~ktor** *m* (*-a*; *-rzy*), **~ktorka** *f* (*-i*; *G -rek*) constructor; designer; **~ktywny** constructive; **~ować** ⟨**s-**⟩ (*-uję*) construct, design

koparka

konsty|tucja f (-i; -e) constitution;~**tucyjny** constitutional; ~**tuować** ⟨**u-**⟩ (-uję) constitute

konsul m (-a; -owie, -ów) consul;~**at** m (-u; -y) consulate

konsul|tacja f (-i;-e) consultation;~**tant** m (-a; -nci),~**tantka** f (-i; G -tek) consultant; specialist; ~**tingowy** consulting; firma consultancy; ~**tować** (-uję) consult; discuss; give advice; ~**tować się** (u A) consult (with), take advice (from)

konsum|encki consumer; ~**ent** m (-a; -nci), ~**entka** f (-i; G -tek) consumer; ~**ować** ⟨**s-**⟩(-uję) consume;~**pcja** f (-i; 0) consumption;~**pcyjny** consumer;**artykuły** pl. ~**pcyjne** consumer goods pl.

konsygnacja f (-i; -e) econ. delivery note

konsystorz m (-a; -e) rel. consistory

konszachty pl. (-ów) underhand dealings pl.

kontakt m (-u; -y) contact; electr. (przełącznik) switch, (gniazdko) socket, Am. outlet; ~**ować** ⟨**s-**⟩ (-uję) bring into contact (**k-o z** I s.o. with); ~**ować** ⟨**s-**⟩ **się** (**z** I) come into contact (with); stay in contact (with); ~**owy** friendly, approachable

kontener m (-a; -y) container; ~**owiec** m (-wca; -wce) naut. container ship

konto n (-a; G -) account; **na** ~ on account

kontra¹ f (-y) (w kartach) double; (boks) counter-blow

kontra² against; versus; ~**banda** f contraband → **przemyt**

kontrahent m (-a; -nci), ~**ka** f (-i; G -tek) econ. contractor

kontrakt m (-u; -y) contract;~**owy** contractual

kontrargument m (-u; -y) counter-argument

kontrasygnować (-uję) countersign; ~**atak** m counterattack;~**kandydat** m, ~**kandydatka** f opponent;~**ofensywa** f counteroffensive

kontrol|a f (-i; -e) control; inspection; check; (punkt) checkpoint; ~**er** m (-a; -rzy),~**erka** f (-i; G -rek) inspector;~**ny** controlling; check; ~**ować** ⟨**s-**⟩ (-uję) control; inspect, check

kontro|wać (-uję) counter; (w kartach) double; ~**wersyjny** controversial

kontr|propozycja f counterproposal; ~**rewolucja** f counterrevolution;~**uderzenie** n counterstroke; counterattack; ~**wywiad** m counterintelligence

kontuar m (-u; -y) counter

kon|tur m (-u; -y) outline, conto(u)r; ~**tuzja** f (-i; -e) med. contusion; F injury

konty|nent m (-u; -y) continent; ~**nentalny** continental, mainland; ~**ngent** m (-u; -y) quota; mil. contingent; ~**nuacja** f (-i; 0) continuation; ~**nuować** (-uuję) continue

kon'walia f (GDL -ii; -e) bot. lily of the valley

konwen|anse m/pl. (-ów) conventions pl., propriety;~**cja** f (-i; -e) convention; ~**cjonalny** conventional; ~**t** m (-u; -y) council of elders; ~**t seniorów** parl. advisory parliamentary committee

konwersacja f (-i; -e) conversation

konwersja f (-i; -e) conversion

konwo|jent m (-a; -nci) escort;~**jować** (-uję) escort; convoy

konw|ój m (-oju; -oje) convoy; **pod ~ojem** też under guard

konwuls|je f/pl. (-i) convulsions pl.; ~**yjny** convulsive

koń m (-nia; -nie, I -ńmi) zo. horse; (w szachach) knight; ~ **mechaniczny** tech. horsepower; **na koniu** on horseback

kończ|a G,~**e** pl. → **koniec**;~**owy** final, end; ~**ówka** f (-i; G -wek) ending (też gr.); (reszta) remainder; (w sporcie) final; (w szachach) endgame; tech. tip, end, terminal

kończy|ć (-ę) ⟨**s-, u-**⟩ end, finish, complete; v/i. stop (**z czymś** s.th.); ~**ć** ⟨**s-**⟩ **się** end; (zużywać się) come to an end; run out; (kończyć ważność) expire; ~**na** f anat. limb, extremity

koński horse; biol. equine

kooper|acja f (-i; -e) co-operation; ~**ant** m (-a; -ci) co-operating partner; ~**ować** (-uję) co-operate

koordynować ⟨**s-**⟩ (-uję) co-ordinate

kopa|czka f (-i; G -czek) agr. digger;~**ć** (-pię) piłkę itp. kick; ⟨**wy-**⟩ dół dig out/up; studnię sink; ziemniaki lift; węgiel excavate; ~**lnia** f (-ni; -nie) mine (też fig.), pit; ~**lniany** mine; ~**lny** fossil; ~**nie** n (-a; 0) digging; kicking; excavating;~**rka** f (-i; G -rek) excavator; digger

kop|cić (*-cę, ć!*) give off clouds of smoke; F *papierosy* puff away (at); *~eć* f (*-pcia/-pciu; 0*) soot

Kopenhaga f (*-i; 0*) Copenhagen

koper m (*-pru; -pry*), *~ek* (*-rku; -rki*) bot. dill; *~kowy* dill

koperta f (*-y; G -*) envelope

kopi|a f (*GDL -ii; -e*) copy; duplicate; *~ał m* (*-u; -y*) duplicate pad; *~arka* f (*-i; G -rek*) copier; (*kserograficzna*) photocopier

kopiec m (*-pca; -pce*) heap; *~ mogilny* grave mound; agr. clamp

kopiow|ać (*-uję*) ⟨*s-*⟩ copy, duplicate; ⟨*prze-*⟩ trace; *~y: ołówek ~y* indelible pencil

kopn|ąć v/s. (*-nę*) → **kopać**; *~iak* m (*-a; -i*) kick

kopu|lacja f (*-i; -e*) copulation; *~lacyj-ny* copulative; *~lować* (*-uję*) copulate; *~la* f (*-y; G -*) cupola, dome

kopyto n (*-a; G -*) hoof

kora f (*-y; G -*) bark

koral m (*-a; -e*) zo. coral; *~e szklane* glass beads; *~owy* coral

korb|a f (*-y; G -*) crank (handle), handle; *~owód* m (*-odu; -ody*) connecting-rod

korcić (*t-ko 3.os.*) tempt, attract; *~ło go|ją, by* he/she was tempted to

kordon m (*-u; -y*) cordon

Korea f (*-ei; 0*) Korea; *~nka* f (*-i; G -nek*), *~ńczyk* m (*-a; -cy*) Korean; ℒński (**po -ku**) Korean

kor|ek m (*-rka; -rki*) bot. cork; (*do butelki itp.*) cork, stopper; (*do wanny itp.*) plug; F electr. fuse; F (*na jezdni*) jam, Brt. tailback, Am. backup; *~ek wlewu paliwa* filler cap; *~ki* pl. cork heels pl.

kore|kta f (*-y; G-*) correction; revision; (*publikacji itp.*) proof-reading; F (*materiał do korekty*) the proofs; *~petycje* f/pl. (*-i; G -cji*) private lessons pl.

koresponden|cja f (*-i; 0*) correspondence; letters pl., Brt. post, Am. mail; *~cyjny* correspondence; *studia pl. ~cyjny* correspondence course, Brt. Open University course; *~t* m (*-a; -ci*), *~tka* f (*-i; G -tek*) correspondent

korespondować (*-uję*) correspond

korko|ciąg m (*-u; -i*) corkscrew; *~wać* ⟨*za-*⟩ (*-uję*) cork

kornet m (*-u; -y*) mus. cornet

kornik m (*-a; -i*) zo. bark beetle

korniszon m (*-a; -y*) gherkin

Kornwalia f (*-ii; 0*) Cornwall

koron|a f (*-y; G -*) crown; *~acja* f (*-i; -e*) crowning; *~ka* f (*-i; G -nek*) med. tooth cap; lace; *~kowy* lace; *~ować* ⟨*u-*⟩ (*-uję*) crown (*kogoś na króla* s.o. king)

korozja f (*-i; 0*) corrosion

korowód m (*-wodu;-wody*) round dance

korporacja f (*-i;-e*) corporation, corporate body

korpu|lentny corpulent, obese; *~s* m (*-u; -y*) trunk; mil. corps sg.

Korsyka f (*-i; 0*) Corsica; *~ńczyk* m (*-a; -cy*) Corsican; ℒński Corsican

kort m (*-u; -y*) (*w sporcie*) court

korup|cja f (*-i; -e*) corruption; *~cyjny* corrupt

korygować ⟨*s-*⟩ (*-uję*) correct, revise

koryntka f (*-i; G -tek*) bot. currant

koryt|arz m (*-a; -e*) hall, hallway, corridor; *~o* n (*-a; G -*) (*rzeki*) bed; (*świni*) trough

korze|nić się (*-nię*) take root; *~nny* spicy; *~ń* m (*-nia; -nie*) root; *~nie* pl. (*przyprawa*) spices pl.

korzon|ek m (*-nka, -nki*) med. radicle; **zapalenie** *~ków* med. radiculitis; → **korzeń**

korzyst|ać ⟨*s-*⟩ (*-am*) (*z G*) use; make use (of); take advantage (of); *~ny* useful; favo(u)rable; profitable

korzyś|ć f (*-ści*) advantage; profit; **na twoją** *~* in your favo(u)r, to your benefit

kos m (*-a; -y*) zo. blackbird

ko|sa f (*-y; G -*) agr. scythe (*też fig.*); *~siarka* f (*-i; G -rek*) mower; *~sić* ⟨*s-*⟩ (*-szę*) mow

kosmaty (*-to*) shaggy; hirsute

kosmety|czka f (*-i; G -czek*) beautician, cosmetician; (*torebka*) vanity bag, Brt. sponge bag; *~czny* cosmetic (*też fig.*); *~k* m (*-u; -i*) cosmetic; *~ka* f (*-i; 0*) fig. cosmetic procedures pl.

kosm|iczny cosmic; *~os* m (*-u; -y*) cosmos

kosmyk m (*-a; -i*) wisp, stray lock

koso: patrzeć *~* (**na** A) look askance (at); *~drzewina* f (*-y; 0*) bot. (*sosna*) dwarf pine; *~oki* slit-eyed; → **zezowaty**

kostium m (*-u; -y*) costume; → **kąpie-lowy**

kost|ka f (*-i; G -tek*) small bone; anat. ankle; (*cukru*) lump; (*brukowa*) cobble

(stone); (*do gry*) die, *pl.* dice; **krajać
w ~kę** *gastr.* dice; **po ~ki** ankle-deep;
~nica *f* (*-y; -e*) mortuary, morgue;
~nieć ⟨**s-**⟩ (*-eję*) grow stiff (**z zimna**
with cold); ~ny bone

kosy slanting; scowling

kosz *m* (*-a; -e*) basket; F (*w sporcie*) basketball; *mot.* sidecar

koszar|owy barrack(s); ~y *pl.* barracks
sg.

koszerny kosher

koszmar *m* (*-u; -y*) nightmare; horror;
~ny nightmarish; horrible

koszt *f* (*-u; -y*) cost, expense; (*rozcho-
dy*) *pl.* expenses *pl.*; ~**em** (*G*) at the cost
(of); **narazić na ~y** put s.o. to expense

koszto|rys *m* (*-u; -y*) cost estimate;
~wać (*-uję*) cost; ~wności *pl.* precious
objects *pl.*, jewel(le)ry; ~wny expensive

koszul|a *f* (*-i; -e*) shirt; ~**a nocna** night-
dress; ~ka *f* (*-i; G -lek*) singlet, T-shirt;
tech. mantel; → **podkoszulek**

koszyk *m* (*-a; -i*) basket; ~arka *f* (*-i; G
-rek*), ~arz *m* (*-a; -e*) basketball player;
~ówka *f* (*-i; 0*) basketball

kościec *m* (*-śćca; -śćce*) bone structure;
fig. backbone

kościelny 1. church; **2.** *m* (*-nego; -ni*)
sexton

kościotrup *m* (*-a; -y*) skeleton

kościół *m* (*-cioła; -cioły*) church

koś|cisty bony; ~ć *f* (*-ści; -ści, I śćmi*)
bone; **kości** *pl.* **do gry** dice; ~**ć słoniowa** ivory; ~**ć strzałkowa** *anat.* fibula;
~**ć niezgody** a bone of contention;
do (**szpiku**) ~**ci** to the bone; ~ławy
crooked, lopsided; *meble* wobbly; *styl*
halting

kot *m* (*-a; -y*) *zo.* cat

kotara *f* (*-y; G -*) curtain, drape

ko'teria *f* (*GDL -ii; -e*) coterie, clique

kotka *f* (*-i; G -tek*) *zo.* (she-)cat, tabby

kotlet *m* (*-a; -y*) cutlet, chop; ~ **mielony**
hamburger, beefburger; ~ **siekany** rissole

kotlina *f* (*-y; G -*) valley

kot|ła, ~em → **kocioł**; ~ować się
(*-uję*) churn, seethe; ~ownia *f* (*-i; -e*)
boiler room; boiler-house; ~owy boiler;
kamień ~owy fur; ~y *pl.* → **kocioł**

kotny pregnant

kotwi|ca *f* (*-y; -e*) *naut.* anchor; **rzucać
~cę** anchor, drop anchor; ~czny anchor

kowa|dło *n* (*-a*) anvil; ~l *m* (*-a; -e*)
blacksmith; ~lik *m* (*-a; -i*) *zo.* nuthatch;
~lski blacksmith

kowboj *m* (*-a; -e*) cowboy

koz|a *f* (*-y; G kóz*) *zo.* goat, (*samica*)
nanny-goat; **siedzieć w ~ie** *przest.*
be in clink

kozetka *f* (*-i; G -tek*) couch, day bed

kozi goat, *biol.* caprine; ~**ca** *f* (*-y; -e*)
chamois; ~**na** *f* (*-y; 0*) goat (meat)

kozioł *m* (*-zła; -zły*) *zo.* buck; (*kozy*)
billy goat; ~ **ofiarny** scapegoat; ~**ek** *m*
(*-łka; -łki*): **fikać ~ki** turn somersaults

koziorożec *m* (*-żca; -żce*) *zo.* ibex; &ec
znak Zodiaku: Capricorn; **on**(**a**) **jest
spod znaku** &**ca** he/she is (a) Capricorn

koź|lątko *n* (*-a; G -tek*), ~**ę** *n* (*-ecia;
-ęta*) kid

kożuch *m* (*-a; -y*) sheepskin; (*do ubrania*) sheepskin coat; (*na mleku*) skin

kół *m* (*kołu; koły*) stake; → **koło**

kółko *n* (*-a; G -lek*) ring; circle (*też fig.*);
~ **do kluczy** key-ring; **w ~** in a circle, in
circles; *fig.* over and over; → **koło**

k.p.a. *skrót pisany:* **kodeks postępowania administracyjnego** code of
administrative proceedings

kpi|ąco mockingly; ~ć *m* (*-e; kpij!*) (**z** *G*)
mock, ridicule, poke fun (at); ~na *f* (*-y*)
jeer; *zwł. pl.* ~**ny** mockery, ridicule

kpt. *skrót pisany:* **kapitan** Capt. (*captain*)

kra *f* (*-y; G kier*) ice floe

krab *m* (*-a; -y*) *zo.* crab

krach *m* (*-u; -y*) collapse; (*giełdowy*)
crash

kraciasty checked, *Am.* checkered

kra|dli, ~dł *itp.* → **kraść**; ~**dzież** *f* (*-y;
-e*) theft; (*z włamaniem*) robbery;
(*w sklepie*) shoplifting; ~**dziony** stolen

kraj *m* (*-u; -e*) country; ~ **rodzinny**
homeland; **tęsknota za ~em** home-
sickness; **do ~u** home

krajać ⟨**na-, po-**⟩ (*-ę*) cut; *mięso* carve

krajo|braz *m* (*-u; -y*) landscape, scenery;
~**braz miejski** cityscape; ~**wiec** *m*
(*-wca; -wcy*) native; ~**wy** native; *produkt* domestic; ~**znawczy** sightseeing

krakać ⟨*-czę*⟩ *zo.* fig. croak

Krak|ów *m* (*-owa; 0*) Cracow, Krakow;
&**owski** Cracow

krakers *m* (*-a; -y*) cracker

kraksa *f* (*-y; G -*) collision, crash, smash

kram m (-u; -y) stall; (rzeczy) stuff, junk; → kłopot

kran m (-u; -y) (kurek) Brt. tap, Am. faucet; **woda z ~u** tap-water; → żuraw

kra|niec m (-ńca; -ńce) end; **na ~ńcu** at the end; **~ńce** pl. **miasta** outskirts; ~ńcowy extreme

krasić ⟨o-⟩ (-szę) gastr. add fat to

kras|nal m (-a; -e), ~noludek m (-dka; -dki) dwarf, brownie; gnome; ~omówca m (-y) orator

kraszanka f (-i; G -nek) → pisanka

kraść ⟨s-, u-⟩ (-dnę) steal

krat|a f (-y; G -) grating, bars pl.; (deseń) check; ~a: **za ~kami** behind bars; **w ~kę** checked; ~kowany checked; papier squared; ~kować (-uję) square

kraul m (-u; -e) (w sporcie) crawl

krawat m (-a; -y) neck-tie

kra|wcowa f (-wej; -e) (damski) dressmaker; → ~wiec; ~wędź f (-dzi; -dzie) edge, brink; (łyżki) rim; (filiżanki) lip; ~wężnik m (-a; -i) Brt. kerb, Am. curb; ~wiec m (-wca; -wcy) dressmaker, (męski) tailor; ~wiectwo n (-a; 0) dressmaking; tailoring

krą|g m (kręgu; kręgi) circle (też fig.); ring; ~żek m (-żka; -żki) Brt. disc, Am. disk; (w hokeju) puck; tech. roller; ~żenie n (-a) (też med.) circulation; ~żownik m (-a; -i) naut. cruiser; ~żyć (-żę) go (dokoła (a)round) circle; circulate

krea|cja f (-i; -e) creation; ~tura f (-y; G -) pej. wretch; ~tywny creative

kreci mole; ~a robota ruse, scheme

kreda f (-y) chalk

kredens m (-u; -y) dresser, sideboard

kredka f (-i; G -dek) crayon; (rodzaj ołówka) colo(u)red pencil; ~ do ust lipstick

kredow|o- w zł. chalk; ~o-biały as white as sheet; ~y chalk

kredyt m (-u; -y) credit, loan; **na ~** on credit; ~ować (-uję) credit, extend credit to; ~owy credit

krem m (-u; -y) cream

kremacja f (-i; -e) cremation

kremowy (-wo) cream, creamy

kreować (-uję) create; perform

krepa f (-y) crepe

kres m (-u; -y) limit; end; **być u ~u** (G) be at the end of; **położyć ~** (D) put an end (to)

kreskla f (-i; G -sek) line; (w rysunku)

---

stroke; (na skali) mark; ~ować (-uję) shade; ~owany shaded; ~owy line; ~ówka f (-i; G -wek) (animated) cartoon

kreśl|arka f (-i; G -rek) Brt. draughtswoman, Am. draftswoman; ~arz m (-a; -e) Brt. draughtsman, Am. draftsman; ~enie n (-a) tech. drawing; ~ić (-lę) ⟨na-⟩ draw; ⟨s-, wy-⟩ cross out, strike out

kret m (-a; -y) zo. mole; ~owisko n (-a) molehill

kret|yn m (-a; -i/-y) moron, cretin (też med.); ~yński moronic

krew f (krwi; 0) blood; ~ **go zalała na to** it made him see red; **z krwi i kości** flesh and blood; **czystej krwi** purebred, pure-blooded; **z zimną krwią** in cold blood

krewet|ka f (-i; G -tek) zo., gastr. shrimp, prawn; ~ki panierowane scampi pl.

krew|ki hot-blooded, rash; ~na f (-nej; -ne), ~ny m (-nego; -ni) relative, relation; najbliższy ~ny next of kin

kręc|ić (-cę) turn; włosy curl; wąsa twirl; F (kłamać) tell fibs; ~ić głową shake one's head; ~ić nosem na turn up one's nose at; ~ić się spin; turn; włosy curl; twitch, fidget; ~ić się koło (G) hover about; **w głowie jej się ~i** her head is spinning; ~ony włosy curly; **schody ~one** spiral staircase

kręg m (-u; -i) anat. vertebra; → krąg; ~arstwo n (-a; 0) chiropractic; ~ielnia f (-i; -e) bowling alley; ~le m/pl. (-i) skittles pl.; **grać w ~le** bowl

kręgo|słup m (-a; -y) anat. spinal column; backbone; spine (też fig.); ~wce m/pl. (-wców) vertebrates pl.

krępować ⟨s-⟩ (-uję) tie up; fig. limit; (żenować) embarrass; ~⟨s-⟩ się be ashamed

krępujący (-co) embarrassing; awkward

krępy stocky

kręta|ctwo n (-a; G -) crookedness, guile; ~cz m (-a; -e), ~czka f (-i; G -czek) crook

kręty (-to) droga winding; wyjaśnienie devious

krnąbrny unruly

krochmal m (-u; 0) starch; ~ić ⟨na-, wy-⟩ (-ę) starch

krocze n (-a) anat. crotch, med. perineum

kroczyć (-ę) pace, *(dużymi krokami)* stride; *(dumnie)* strut

kroić (-ję, krój!; -ją) ⟨**po-**⟩ cut, slice; ⟨**s-**⟩ cut out

krok m (-u; -i) step *(też fig.)*; *(krocze)* crotch; **~i** pl. measures pl.; **~ za ~iem** step by step; **podejmować ~i, aby** take steps to; **na każdym ~u** at everystep

krokiet m (-a; -y) gastr. croquet

krokodyl m (-a; -e) zo. crocodile

kromka f (-i; -mek) slice (of bread)

kronika f (-i; G -) chronicle; **~ filmowa** newsreel

krop|elka f (-i; G -lek) → **kropla**; **~ić** ⟨**po-, s-**⟩ (-ę) sprinkle; **~i** it is spitting; **~idło** n (-a; G -deł) aspersorium, aspergillum; **~ielnica** f (-y; -e) aspersorium; **~ka** f (-i; G -pek) dot, spot; *(w interpunkcji)* Brt. full stop, Am. period; **w ~ki** dotted; **~kowany** dotted; **~la** f (-i; -e, -i/-pel) drop; *(potu)* bead; **~lów-ka** f (-i; G -wek) med. drip (infusion)

krosno n (-a; G -sen) loom

krosta f (-y) spot, pimple; med. pustule

krotochwila f (-i; -e) farce

krow|a f (-y; G krów) zo. cow; **~i** cow(s')

króc|ej adv. *(comp. od → **krótki***) shorter; **~iutki** very short

krój m (-oju; -oje, -ojów) cut

król m (-a; -owie) king; **Święto Trzech Śli** rel. Epiphany

królestwo n (-wa; G -tw) kingdom

królew|na f (-ny; G -wien) princess; **~ski** royal, regal

królik m (-a; -i) zo. rabbit; **~arnia** f (-i; -e) rabbit hutch

królowa f (-ej, -wo!; -e) queen; **~ć** (-uję) reign, rule *(nad I* over); *fig. też* predominate

krótki short; brief; *rozmowa tel., spacer* quick

krótko adv. briefly; **~dystansowiec** m *(-wca; -wcy)* short (film); **~falowy** short-wave; **~metrażówka** f (-i; G -wek) *(w sporcie)* sprint; **~ść** f (-ści; 0) brevity; shortness; **~terminowy** short-term; **~trwały** short-lived; **~widz** m (-a; -e) short-sighted person; **~wzroczny** short-sighted

krótszy adj. *(comp. od → **krótko***) shorter *(od G* than, from)

krówka f (-i; G -wek) → **krowa**; fudge; **boża ~** Brt. ladybird, Am. ladybug

krtań f (-ni; -nie) anat. larynx; **zapale-** **nie ~ni** med. laryngitis

krucho adv. → **kruchy**; F terribly, badly

kruchta f (-y; G -) porch

kruch|y fragile *(też fig.)*, brittle; *mięso* tender; *ciastko, sałata* crisp; **~e ciasto** short pastry

krucjata f (-y; G -) crusade

krucyfiks m (-u; -y) crucifix

kruczek m (-czka; -czki) snag, catch

kru|czy raven; **~k** m (-a; -i) zo. raven

krup m (-u; -0) med. croup; **~a** f (-y), zwł. pl. **~y** grains pl.; *meteo.* soft hail pellet, graupel; **~nik** m (-u; -i) gastr. barley soup

krusz|ec m (-szca; -szce) ore; precious metal; **~eć** ⟨**s-**⟩ (-eję) become brittle; *mięso:* become tender; **~on** m (-u; -y) gastr. punch; **~onka** f (-i; G -nek) gastr. crumbly topping, Am. streusel

kruszy|ć ⟨**po-, s-**⟩ (-ę) crumble **(się** v/i.); → **drobić**; **~na** f (-y; G -) crumb; *(dziecko)* a little one; **~wo** n (-a; G -) bud. aggregate, ballast

kruż|ganek m (-nka; -nki) cloister

krwawią|cy bleeding; **~czka** f (-i; 0) h(a)emophilia

krwawi|ca f (-y; -e) back-breaking work; hard-earned money; **~ć** (-ję) bleed

krwa|woczerwony blood-red; **~wy** bloody, bloodstained; *praca* hard

krwi|ak m (-a; -i) med. h(a)ematoma; **~a** → **krew**; **~nka** f (-ki; G -nek) med. blood cell; **czerwona ~nka** erythrocyte

krwio|bieg m (-u; -i) blood circulation; bloodstream; **~dawca** m (-y), **~daw-czyni** f (-i; G -yń) blood donor; **~noś-ny: naczynie ~nośne** blood vessel; **~żerczy** bloodthirsty

krwisty *oczy itp.* bloodshot; *kiszka* blood; *befsztyk* rare; *rumieniec* ruddy

krwotok m (-u; -i) h(a)emorrhage

kry|ć (-ję) ⟨**u-**⟩ conceal, hide *(też się v/i.)*; *(tuszować)* cover up; *(w sporcie)* cover, mark; ⟨**po-**⟩ cover **(się** o.s.); **~jówka** f (-i; G -wek) hiding place, hideaway

Krym m (-u; 0) the Crimea

kryminal|ista m (-y; -ści), **~istka** f (-i; G -tek) criminal; **~ny** criminal; **policja ~na** criminal police

kryminał F m (-u; -y) nick; *(utwór)* thriller, detective story; *(czyn)* criminal activity

krynica f (-y; -e) fount

krystali|czny crystal; *fig.* crystal clear; **~zować się** *(-uję)* crystallize

kryształ *m (-u; -y)* crystal; **~owy (-wo)** crystal

kryterium *n (idkl.; -a)* criterion

kryty covered; roofed

kryty|czny critical; **~k** *m (-a; -cy)* critic; reviewer; **~ka** *f (-i; G -)* criticism; critique; **~kować** ⟨**s-**⟩ *(-uję)* criticize (**za** *A* for)

kryzys *m (-u; -e)* crisis; **~owy** crisis

krza|czasty (-to) bushy; **~k** *m (-a; -i)** bush, shrub

krzątać się bustle *(koło G, przy L* about); **~nina** *f (-y; 0)* bustle

krze|m *m (-u; 0) chem.* silicon; **~mian** *m (-u -y)* silicate; **~mień** *m (-nia; -nie)* flint; **~mionka** *f (-i; G -nek)* siliceous earth

krzepić ⟨**po-**⟩ *(-ę)* fortify; refresh *(się* o.s.); **~ki** robust, vigorous; *(silny)* hefty; **~nąć** ⟨**s-, za-**⟩ *(-ę; -[ną]ł, -pła)* set, solidify; *krew:* coagulate, congeal

krzesać ⟨**wy-**⟩ *(-szę) iskry* strike

krzesełkowy: wyciąg ~ chair lift

krzesło *n (-a; G -seł)* chair

krzew *m (-u; -y)* shrub

krzewić *(-ę)* spread *(się v/i.)*

krzt|a: ani ~y not an ounce

krztusić się ⟨**za- się**⟩ *(-szę)* choke *(I* on); → **dławić się**

krztusiec *m (-śca; 0) med.* whooping cough

krzy|czący (-co) crying; **~czeć (-ę)** cry *(z G* with); shout *(na kogoś* at s.o.); scream; **~k** *m (-u; -i)* cry, shout; scream; **~kliwy** noisy; loud *(też fig.)*; *kolory* garish, lurid; *(-wie)* **~kliwy dzieciak** bawler

krzywa *f (-wej; -e) math.* curve

krzyw|da *f (-y; G -)* harm, injustice; wrong; **~dzić** ⟨**po-, s-**⟩ *(-dzę)* harm, hurt; do injustice to, do *s.o.* wrong

krzywi|ca *f (-y; 0) med.* rickets *pl.*; **~ć** ⟨**s-, wy-**⟩ *(-ę)* bend *(się v/i.)*; **~ć** ⟨**s-**⟩ **się** make faces *(na A* at); *(z bólu)* wince; **~zna** *f (-y; G -)* curvature

krzywo *adv.* not straight, crookedly; **spojrzeć ~** frown *(na A* on); **~nogi** bandy-legged; **~przysięstwo** *n (-a) jur.* perjury

krzywy bent; crooked; uneven; *uśmiech* wry; **w ~m zwierciadle** distorted; → **krzywo**

krzyż *m (-a; -e)* cross *(też rel.)*; *anat.* small of the back; **na ~** across, crosswise; **bóle w ~u** pain in the small of the back; **~ak** *m (-a; -i) tech.* cross; *zo.* cross spider; **2ak** *(-a; -cy)* knight of the Teutonic Order; **~ować** *(-uję)* ⟨**u-**⟩ cross; *rel.* crucify; ⟨**u-**⟩ upset; ⟨**s-**⟩ cross *(się v/i.)*; **~ować się** intersect; **~owy** cruciform; *anat.* sacral; **wojny ~owe** Crusades; **wziąć w ~owy ogień pytań** cross-examine; **~ówka** *f (-i; G -wek)* intersection; *(w gazecie)* crossword *(puzzle)*; **~yk** *m (-a; -i)* cross; **oznaczyć ~ykiem** cross; *mus.* sharp

ks. *skrót pisany:* **książę** duke, prince, **ksiądz** the Rev. *(reverend)*

kserokopia *f* photocopy; **~rka** *f (-i; G -rek)* photocopier

ksiądz *m (księdza, -ędzu, -eże!; księża, -ęży, -ężom; I -ężmi)* priest; *(tytuł)* Father *(skrót:* the Rev.)

książeczka *f (-i; G -czek)* book, booklet; **~ oszczędnościowa** saving book; **~ czekowa** *Brt.* chequebook, *Am.* checkbook

książę *m (GA księcia, DL księciu, I księciem, książę!; książęta, -żąt)* prince, duke; **~cy** ducal, princely

książk|a *f (-i; G -żek)* book; **~owy** book; **mól ~owy** bookworm

księcia, ~dza → **książę, ksiądz**

księga *f (-i; G ksiąg)* book; **księgi** *pl. (rachunkowe)* the books; **~rnia** *f (-i; -e) Brt.* bookshop, *Am.* bookstore; **~rz** *f (-a; -e)* bookseller

księgo|susz *m (-u; 0) wet.* rinder pest; **~wa** *f (-ej; -e)* accountant; **~wać** ⟨**za-**⟩ *(-uję)* enter; **~wość** *f (-ci; 0)* accountancy, bookkeeping; **~wy** *m (-ego; -i)* accountant; **~zbiór** *m (-oru; -ory)* library

księ|stwo *n (-a; G -)* dukedom, duchy; **~żna** *f (-nej/-ny; DL księż-nie, A -nę!/-ną, -no!/; -ne, -nych, -nym/-nom)* duchess, princess; **~żniczka** *f (-i)* princess

księżyc *m (-a; -e)* moon; **światło ~a** moonlight; **~owy** moon(lit), lunar

ksylofon *m (-u; -y)* xylophone

ksywa *F f (-y)* nickname, F moniker

kształc|enie *n (-a; 0)* education; → **doskonalenie; ~ić** ⟨**wy-**⟩ *(-cę)* educate; *umysł itp.* train, discipline, develop; **~ić się** learn, study; **~ić się** study *(na A* to be)

kupujący

kształt *m* (*-u*; *-y*) shape, form; **coś na ~** (*G*) something like; **~ny** shapely; **~ować** ⟨*u-*⟩ shape; form; **~ować się** *ceny, liczby*: be established, stand

kto *pron.* who; → **bądź**; **~'kolwiek** anyone, anybody; whoever; **~ś** someone, somebody

któr|ędy where, which way; **~y** *pron.* which, that, who; what; → **godzina**; **~ego dziś mamy?** what day is it today?; **dom, w ~ym ...** the house in which...; **ludzie, ~zy ...** the people who/that

który|'kolwiek, **~ś** any, either (**z was** of you)

któż who; **kogóż ja widzę?** who do I see here?

ku *prp.* (*D*) to; towards; for, → **cześć**

Kuba *f* (*-y; 0*) Cuba; 2ński Cuban; **~ńczyk** *m* (*-a; -cy*), **~nka** *f* (*-i; G -nek*) Cuban

kubatura *f* (*-y; G -*) cubature, capacity

kubek *m* (*-bka; -bki*) mug

kubeł *m* (*-bła; -bły*) bucket, pail; (*na śmieci*) *Brt.* dustbin, *Am.* trash can

kubiczny cubic

kucha|rka *f* (*-i; G -rek*) cook; **~rski** cookery, cooking; **książka ~rska** *Brt.* cookery book, *Am.* cookbook; **~rz** *m* (*-a; -e*) cook

kuchen|ka *f* (*-i; G -nek*) cooker, stove; **~ny** kitchen

kuchmistrz *m* (*-a; -e*), **~yni** *f* (*-; G -yń*) chef

kuchnia *f* (*-i; -e, -i/-chen*) kitchen; (*styl*) cookery

kuc|ać (*-am*) ⟨**~nąć**⟩ squat, croach; **~ki** *pl.* (*-cek*): **siedzieć w ~ki** squat, crouch; **~nąć** (*-nę*) → **kucać**

kucyk *m* (*-a; -i*) pony

kuć (*kuję, kuj!, kuł*) *metal* forge, hammer; *dziurę* chisel; F *Brt.* cram, *Am.* bone up on; → **podkuwać, w(y)kuwać**

kudłaty shaggy

kufel *m* (*-fla; -fle*) mug

kufer *m* (*-fra; -fry*) trunk; → **bagażnik**

kuglarz *m* (*-a; -e*) conjurer

kuk *m* (*-a; -owie*) *naut.* cook

kukanie *n* (*-a*) cuckooing

kuk|iełka *f* (*-i; G -łek*) puppet; **~iełkowy** puppet; **~ła** *f* (*-y; G -kieł*) dummy

kukuł|czy cuckoo; **zegar z ~ką** cuckoo clock

kukurydza *f* (*-y; -e*) *Brt.* maize, *Am.* corn; **~ prażona** popcorn

KUL *skrót pisany:* **Katolicki Uniwersytet Lubelski** Lublin Catholic University

kul|a[1] *f* (*-i; -e*) ball; *math.* sphere; (*nabój*) bullet; **pchnięcie ~ą** (*w sporcie*) shot put

kul|a[2] *f* (*-i; -e*) crutch; **chodzić o ~ach** walk on crutches; **~awy** lame

kule|czka *f* (*-i; G -czek*) → **kulka, kula**; **~ć** (*-ję*) limp, hobble; *fig.* ail

kulić (*-lę*) *nogi itp.* curl up; **~** ⟨**s-**⟩ **się** huddle, curl up; (*ze strachu*) cower

kulig *m* (*-u; -i*) sleigh ride

kuli|s *m* (*-a; -i*) coolie; **~sty** spherical; **~sy** *pl.* (*-*) wings *pl.*

kul|ka *f* (*-i; G -lek*) → **kula**; **~a szklana** marble; **~owy** ball

kuloodporny bullet-proof

kulszowy: **nerw ~** schiatic nerve

kult *m* (*-u; -y*) cult; **~ jednostki** personality cult

kultur|a *f* (*-y; G -*) culture; (*osobista*) good manners; **~alny** cultural; polite; **~owy** cultural, culture; **~ystyka** *f* (*-i; 0*) body-building

kultywować (*-uję*) cultivate, nourish

kuluary *m/pl.* (*-ów*) lobby

kułak *m* (*-a; -i*) fist

kum *m* (*-a; -y/-owie*) godfather; **~a** *f* (*-y; G -*) godmother; **~kać** (*-am*) croak

kumo|szka *f* (*-i; G -szek*) gossip; **~ter** *m* (*-tra; -trzy/-trowie*) mate; **~terstwo** *n* (*-a; 0*) nepotism

kumpel F *m* (*-pla; -ple*) pal, buddy, mate

kuna *f* (*-y; G -*) *zo.* marten

kundel *m* (*-dla; -dle*) mongrel

kunsztowny ornate, elaborate

kup|a *f* (*-y; G -*) heap, pile (*też fig.*); F (*odchody*) turd; **do ~y, na ~ę, na ~ie** together; **trzymać się ~y** stick together

kuper *m* (*-pra; -pry*) rump (*też* F)

kupić *pf* (*-ę*) → **kupować**

kupiec *m* (*-pca, -pcze/-pcu!; -pcy*) trader, merchant; (*w sklepiku*) shopkeeper; (*nabywca*) buyer, purchaser; **~ki** (**po -ku**) businesslike

kupka *f* (*-i; G -pek*) → **kupa**

kupn|o *n* (*-pna; 0*) purchase, buying; **~y** F bought

kupon *m* (*-a; -y*) coupon; national-lottery coupon; voucher

kup|ować (*-uję*) buy; purchase; **~ujący**

K

m (*-ego; -y*), **-ca** *f* (*-ej; -e*) buyer, purchaser

kur *m* (*-a; -y*): **czerwony ~** fire; **~a** *f* (*-y; G -*) hen

kurac|ja *f* (*-i; -e*) cure, treatment; **na ~ji, na ~ję** on a cure, to a health resort; **~jusz** *m* (*-a; -e*), **-szka** *f* (*-i; G -szek*) visitor, patient; **~yjny** health

kuranty *m/pl.* (*-ów*) *mus.* glockenspiel

kurat|ela *f* (*-i; -e*) *jur.* guardianship; **~or** *m* (*-a; -rzy*), **-rka** *f* (*-i; G -rek*) guardian; (*szkolny*) superintendent of schools; **~orium** *n* (*idkl.; -ia, -iów*) education authority

kurcz *m* (*-a; -e*) spasm, cramp

kurcz|ak *m* (*-a;-i*), **~ę** *n* (*-cia; -ta*) chicken

kurcz|owy spasmodic, convulsive; **~yć się** ⟨**s- się**⟩ (*-ę*) *muskuł:* contract; *materiał:* shrink

kurek *m* (*-rka; -rki*) *tech., mil.* cock; (*z wodą*) *Brt.* tap, *Am.* faucet

kurenda *f* (*-y; G -*) circular (letter)

kurewski ∨ whorish, whore, bitch

kuria *f* (*GDL -ii; -e*) *rel.* curia

kurier *m* (*-a; -rzy*) courier, messenger; **~ski** courier

kuriozalny odd

kurnik *m* (*-a; -i*) *agr.* hen house

kuropatwa *f* (*-y; G -*) *zo.* partridge

kurs *m* (*-u; -y*) course (*też fig.*); *econ.* rate, price; (*wykład*) course, class; (*jazda*) ride; → **obieg**; **~ant** *m* (*-a;-ci*),**-tka** *f* (*-i; G -tek*) course participant; **~ować** (*-uję*) run

kursywa *f* (*-y; G -*) italics *pl.*

kurtka *f* (*-i; G -tek*) jacket

kurtuazyjny courteous

kurtyna *f* (*-y; G -*) curtain

kurwa ∨ *f* (*-y; G -*) whore, bitch, hooker

kurz *m* (*-u; -e*) dust; **~ajka** *f* (*-i; G -jek*) flat wart, *med.* verruca; **~awa** *f* (*-y; G -*) cloud of dust

kurz|y hen, chicken; **~e łapki** crow's feet

kurzyć (*-ę*) dust; raise dust; **kurzy się** there is a lot of dust; **kurzy się z** (*G*) there is smoke from

kusi|ciel *m* (*-a; -e*), **~cielka** *f* (*-i; G -lek*) temptress; **~ć** ⟨**s-**⟩ (*-szę*) tempt; lure

kustosz *m* (*-a; -e*) curator

kusy ⟨**-so**⟩ short; skimpy, scanty

kusza *f* (*-y; G -*) crossbow

kuszący ⟨**-co**⟩ tempting, alluring

kuszetka *f* (*-i; G -tek*) couchette

kuśnierz *m* (*-a; -e*) furrier

kuśtykać ⟨**po-**⟩ (*-am*) limp, walk with a limp

kutas ∨ *m* (*-a; -y*) prick, cock

kuter *m* (*-tra; -try*) fishing boat, cutter

kutia *f* (*GDL -ii;-e*) (*Christmas sweet dish*)

kutwa *m/f* (*-y; -ów/-*) skinflint

kuty wrought; **koń** shod

kuzyn *m* (*-a; -i*),**~ka** *f* (*-i; G-nek*) cousin; **~ostwo** *n* (*-a*) cousin with his wife

kuźnia *f* (*-ni; -nie*) smithy

kw. *skrót pisany:* **kwadratowy** (*square*); **kwartał** q. (*quarter*)

kwadra *f* (*-y; G -*) *astr.* quarter; **~ns** *m* (*-u; -e*) quarter; **za ~ns druga** a quarter to two; **~ns po drugiej** a quarter past two *Brt.*

kwadrans *m* (*-a; -e*) quarter; **za ~ns druga** a quarter to two; **~ns po drugiej** a quarter past two *Brt.* past two *lub Am.* after two; **~t** *m* (*-u; -y*) *math.* square; **~towy** square; **metr ~towy** square *Brt.* metre (*Am.* meter) (*skrót:* **sq. m**)

kwakać (*-czę*) quack

kwakier *m* (*-a; -rzy*), **~ka** *f* (*-i; G -rek*) Quaker

kwalifikacja *f* (*-i; -e*) qualification

kwalifikowa|ć ⟨**za-**⟩ (*-uję*) qualify; **~ć** ⟨**za-**⟩ **się** (**na** *A*) be suitable (as); qualify (as); **~ny** qualified

kwantowy quantum

kwapić się (*-ę*): **nie ~** (**z** *I*) not be in any hurry (with)

kwarantanna *f* (*-y; G -*) quarantine

kwarc *m* (*-u; -e*) *chem.* quartz; **~ówka** *f* (*-i; G -wek*) sun lamp

kwart|a *f* (*-y; G -*) quart; **pół ~y piwa** pint of beer

kwarta|lnik *m* (*-a; -i*) quarterly; **~lny** quarterly; **~ł** *m* (*-u; -y*) quarter

kwartet *m* (*-u; -y*) *mus.* quartet

kwas *m* (*-u; -y*) *chem.* acid; (*zaczyn*) leaven; **~y** *pl.* quarrels *pl.*, arguments *pl.*; **~ić** ⟨*-szę*⟩ → **kisić**; **~kowaty** (**-to**) sharp

kwa|soodporny acid-resistant; **~sowy** acid; **~szony** → **kiszony**; **~śnieć** ⟨**s-**⟩ (*-ję*) turn acid, turn sour; **~śno** *fig.* sourly, wryly; **~śnosłodki** sweet and sour; **~śny** acid, sour

kwater|a *f* (*-y; G -*) *mil.* quarters *pl.*; accommodation(s *pl.*); lodgings *pl.*; **~a główna** headquarters (*skrót:* HQ); **~ować** (*-uję*) house, take lodgings; **~unkowy** *Brt.* municipal

kwes|ta *f* (*-y*) collection; **~tia** *f* (*GDl -ii; -e*) question; **~tionariusz** *m* (*-a; -e*) questionnaire; **~tionować** ⟨**za-**⟩

(-*uję*) question, challenge, dispute
kwestować (-*uję*) collect
kwękać (-*am*) be ailing
kwiacia|rka *f* (-*i*; *G* -*rek*) flower girl,
florist; ~**rnia** *f* (-*i*; -*e*) florist('s), flower
shop; ~**sty** → **kwiecisty**
kwiat *m* (-*u*, *L* kwiecie; -*y*) flower (*też*
fig.), bloom, blossom; ~**ek** *m* (-*tka*; -*tki*)
→ **kwiat**; ~**owy** *bot.* flowering; flowery
kwiczeć (-*czę*) squeal
kwie|cień *m* (-*tnia*; -*tnie*) April; ~**cisty**
(-*to*, -*ście*) flowery; flowered; ~**tnik** *m*
(-*a*; -*i*) flower bed; ~**tniowy** April
kwik *m* (-*u*; -*i*) squeal
kwilić (-*ę*) whimper

kwint|al *m* (-*a*; -*e*) quintal; ~**et** *m* (-*u*; -*y*)
mus. quintet
kwit *m* (-*u*; -*y*) receipt; ~ **bagażowy**
Brt. luggage ticket, *Am.* baggage check;
~ **zastawny** pawn ticket; ~**a** F (*idkl.*):
być ~a z kimś be quits with s.o.;
~**ariusz** *m* (-*a*; -*e*) receipt block
kwitnąć (-*nę*) flower, bloom, blossom;
fig. flourish
kwitować ⟨*po*-⟩ (-*uję*) acknowledge
receipt of
kwiz *m* (-*u*; -*y*) quiz
kwoka *f* (-*i*; *G* -) hen
kworum *n* (*idkl.*) quorum
kwota *f* (-*y*; *G* -) amount, sum

L

laborato|rium *n* (*idkl.*; -*ia*, -*iów*) la-
boratory, F lab; ~**ryjny** laboratory
l. *skrót pisany:* **liczba** n. (*number*)
lać (*leję*) pour; F (*bić*) shower blows
(on), hit; ~ **się** pour; stream; run; **leje**
(**jak z cebra**) it's pouring buckets; →
nalewać, rozlewać, wylewać
lada[1] *f* (-*y*; *G* -) counter; ~ **chłodnicza**
cold shelves *pl.*
lada[2] *part.*(+ *rzecz.*): ~ **trudność** any
(small) difficulty; ~ **chwila** any moment; (+ *pron.*) → **byle**; **nie** ~ not to
be scoffed at
lafirynda *f* (-*y*; *G* -) *pej.* slut
lai|cki lay; ~**k** *m* (-*a*; -*cy*) lay person, lay-
man
lak *m* (-*u*; -*i*) sealing wax; *bot.* wall flower
lakier *m* (-*u*; -*y*) varnish, lacquer; ~ **do**
paznokci nail polish; ~**ować** ⟨*po*-⟩
(-*uję*) varnish; polish; ~**owany** var-
nished; lacquered; *skóra* patent
lakować ⟨*za*-⟩ (-*uję*) seal
lal|a *f* (-*i*; -*e*), ~**ka** *f* (-*i*; *G* -*lek*) doll; *teatr*
~**ek** puppet *Brt.* theatre (*Am.* theater)
lamentować (-*uję*) lament (**nad** *I* over)
lamówka *f* (-*i*; *G* -*wek*) binding
lampa *f* (-*y*; *G* -) lamp; → **błyskowy**
lampart *m* (-*a*; -*y*) *zo.* leopard
lampka *f* (-*i*; *G* -*pek*) lamp; ~ **nocna**
bedside lamp; ~ **kontrolna** control
lamp; ~ **wina** a glass of wine
lamus *m* (-*a*; -*y*) junk room; **złożyć do**
~**a** discard, scrap

landrynk|a *f* (-*i*; *G* -*nek*) fruit drop;
~**owy** sweet
lan|ie *n* (-*a*; *G* lań) pouring; (*bicie*) beat-
ing, hiding; ~**e wody** *fig.* waffle; ~**y**
poured; *metal* cast
Lap|onia *f* (*GDL* -*ii*; *0*) Lapland; ~**oń-
czyk** *m* (-*a*; -*cy*), ~**oka** *f* (-*i*; *G* -*nek*)
Lapp; ⸨**oński** Lapp
larwa *f* (-*y*; *G* -) *zo.* larva
laryngolog *m* (-*a*; -*owie*/-*dzy*) laryngo-
logist, ENT specialist
las *m* (-*u*; -*y*) wood, forest
lase|cznik *m.* (-*a*; -*i*) *biol.* bacillus; ~**k** *m*
(-*sku*; -*ski*) → **las**
laser *m* (-*a*; -*y*) laser; ~**owy** laser
lask|a *f* (-*i*; *G* -*sek*) walking stick, cane;
F chick, *Brt.* bird; *tech.* rod; ~**owy** stick;
orzech ~**y** hazelnut
lasować (-*uję*) slake
lata *pl.* years *pl.*; → **lato**; *1. sg. od* **latać**
ile masz lat? how old are you?; ~ **dzie-
więćdziesiąte** the 1990's; **sto lat!**
many happy returns!; **na swoje** ~ for
his/her age
lata|ć (-*am*) fly; F (*biegać*) run (**do** *G* to);
(**za** *I*) run (after); ~**ć po zakupy** go
shopping in a hurry; ~**nina** *f* (-*y*; *G* -)
running around
latar|ka *f* (-*i*; *G* -*rek*) *Brt.* torch, *Am.*
flashlight; ~**nia** *f* (-*i*; -*e*) lamp, *naut.* lantern; ~**nia morska** lighthouse; ~**nio-
wiec** *m* (-*wca*; -*wce*) lightship
latawiec *m* (-*wca*; -*wce*) kite

lato n (-a; G -) summer; *latem*, *w lecie* in summer; *na ~* for the summer; *~rosł f (-i; -e)* offspring

lau|r m (-u; -y) laurel; *~reat* m (-a; -ci), *~reatka f (-i; G -tek)* laureate; *~rowy* laurel, bay

lawa f (-y) lava

lawenda f (-y) zo. lavender

lawin|a f (-y; G -) avalanche (*też fig.*); *~owy (-wo)* like an avalanche

lawirować (*-uję*) Brt. manoeuvre, Am. manoeuver

laz|ł(a), *~łam*, *~łem* → **leźć**

lazurowy (-wo) azure

ląd m (-u; -y) land; *~ stały* mainland, dry land; *~em* overland; *zejść na ~* go on shore; *~owa ⟨wy-⟩ (-uję)* land; *samolot:* touch down; *~owanie* n (-a; G -ń) landing; (*samolotu*) touchdown; *~owisko* n (-a; G -) airfield, landing strip; (*helikoptera*) pad; *~owy* land; *przesyłka* overland; *biol.* terrestrial; *poczta ~owa* surface mail

lecieć ⟨po-⟩ (*-cę, -ci, leć!*) fly; *ciecz:* run; F run, hurry; → *przelatywać*; *jak leci?* how are you?; *co leci w telewizji wieczorem?* what's on TV tonight?

leciutki lightweight

leciwy aged

lecz but; yet; *nie tylko ..., ~ także ...* not only ... but also ...

lecz|enie n (-a) treatment; *~nica f (-y; G -)* hospital, clinic; *~nictwo* n (-a; 0) health care; *~niczy* therapeutic; *kosmetyk* medicated; *~yć ⟨-cze⟩* treat, cure; *~yć się* be under medical treatment; *rana itp.:* heal

ledw|ie, ~o hardly, scarcely; *~ie/~o nie* almost, nearly; *~ie żywy* nearly dead

legal|izować ⟨za-⟩ (-uję) legalize; *~ny* legal, lawful

legawy: *pies ~* pointer

legenda f (-y; G -) legend; (*mapy*) key

legi|a f (GDL -ii; -e) legion; *~onista* m (-y; -ści) legionnaire

leginsy pl. (-ów) leggings pl.

legislacyjny legislative

legitym|acja f (-y; -e) identification, identity card; (*członkowska*) membership card; *~ować (-uję)* ask to see identification; *~ować ⟨wy-⟩ się* establish one's identity (*I* by); check

legowisko n (-a; G -) bedding; → *barłóg*

legumina f (-y; G -) pudding

lej m (-a; -e) crater; → *lać*

lejce pl. (-y/-ów) reins pl.

lejek m (-ka; -ki) funnel

lek. *skrót pisany:* **lekarz** MD (*Doctor of Medicine*)

lek m (-u; -i) med. medicine, drug; *fig.* cure

lekar|ka f (-i; G -rek) doctor, physician; *~ski* medical; doctor's; *~stwo* n (-a; G -) → *lek*

lekarz doctor, physician; *~ specjalista* consultant

lekceważ|ący (-co) disdainful, disrespectful; neglecting (*obowiązków*); *~enie* n (-a; 0) disdain, disrespect; *~yć ⟨z-⟩* disdain, disrespect; *obowiązki* neglect

lekcj|a f (-i) lesson, class; (*godzina*) period; *prowadzić ~e* teach; *odrabiać ~e* do homework

lekk|i light (*też fig.*); slight; *herbata* weak; *szum* faint; *z ~a* lightly; *~o* adv. light; lightly; slightly

lekko|atletyczny track; *~myślny* careless; irresponsible; *~ść f (-ści; 0)* lightness; → *łatwość*; *~strawny* light, easily digestible

lekooporny med. drug-resistant

lek|sykon m (-u; -y) lexicon; *~tor* m (-a; -rzy) instructor; *~tura f (-y; G -)* reading; text; *~tura obowiązkowa* set book

lemiesz m (-a; -e) agr. Brt. ploughshare, Am. plowshare

lemoniada f (-y; G -) lemonade

len m (*lnu, G lnie/lny*) bot. flax; (*materiał*) linen

leni|ć się (-ę) be lazy (*do G* to, *z I* with); → *linieć*; *~stwo* n (-a; 0) laziness

leniuch m (-a; -y) layabout; idler; *~ować (-uję)* laze (away)

leniw|iec m (-wca; -wce) zo. sloth; (*-wcy*) → *leniuch*; *~y* lazy, idle

leń m (-nia; -nie, -ni/-niów); → *leniuch*

lep m (-u; -y) glue; *~ na muchy* fly paper; *~ić (-pię) ⟨u-⟩* shape, model; *⟨przy-⟩* stick, glue; *~ić się (być lepkim)* be sticky

lepiej adv. (*comp. od* → *najlepiej*) better

lepki sticky, tacky

lepsz|y adj. (*comp. od* → *dobry*; *m-os lepsi*) better; *zmienić się na ~e* turn for the better

lesbijka f (-i; G -jek) Lesbian

lesisty woody

leszcz m (-a; -e) zo. bream

leszczyna f (-y; G -) bot. hazel

leśni|ctwo n (-a; G -) forestry; **~czów-ka** f (-i; G -wek) forester's house; **~czy** m (-ego; G -ych) forester

leśn|ik m (-a; -cy) forester; **~y** woodland, forest

letni tepid, lukewarm; summer, summery; **~czka** f (-i; G -czek), **~k** m (-a; -cy) holiday-maker; **~o** adv. → **letni**; **~sko** n (-a; G -) summer resort

lew m (lwa; lwy, G lwów) zo. lion; ♌ znak Zodiaku: Leo; **on(a) jest spod znaku Lwa** he/she is (a) Leo

lew|a f (-y) (w kartach) trick; **~acki** leftist

lewar|ek m (-rka; -rki) jack; **podnosić ~kiem** jack up

lewatywa f (-y; G -) med. enema

lewic|a f (-y; -e) zwł. pol. left; left wing; **~owy** left, leftist

lew'konia f (GDL -ii; -e) bot. stock

lewo adv.: **na ~, w ~** to the left; left; **na ~** under the table, on the sly; **~ręczny** left-handed

lewostronny: ruch ~ driving on the left

lew|y left; F fig. też fake, pseudo; **po ~ej (stronie)** on the left; **z ~a** from the left; → **lewo**

leźć F climb; **(do G)** get (into)

leż|ak m (-a; -i) deck-chair; **~anka** f (-i; G -nek) couch; **~ąco: na ~ąco** when lying, lying down; **~eć** (-żę, -y) lie (też fig.); suknia: fit

lędźwie pl. (-dźwi) loins pl.

lęgnąć się ⟨**wy- się**⟩ (-nę, lągł) (z jaja) hatch; fig. breed

lęk m (-u; -i) fear, anxiety; **~ać się** (-am) fear, dread; **~liwy** fearful, apprehensive

lgnąć (-nę) **(do G)** cling (to)

libacja f (-i; -e) binge, F booze-up

Liba|n m (-u; 0) Lebanon; **~ńczyk** m (-a; -cy) Lebanese; ♀**ński** Lebanese

liberalizować (-uję) liberalize; **~lny** liberal; **~ł** m (-a; -owie) liberal

Libi|a f (GDL -ii; 0) Libya; **~jczyk** m (-a; -cy), **~jka** f (-i; G -jek) Libyan; ♀**jski** Libyan

licealist|a m (-y; -ści), **~ka** f (-i; G -tek) secondary-school student

licenc|ja f (-i; -e) Brt. licence, Am. license; **~jat** m (-u; -y) Bachelor's degree

liceum n (idkl.; -a, -ów) Brt. grammar school, Am. high school, lycée; **~zawodowe** vocational secondary school

licho[1] adv. → **lichy**

lich|o[2] n (-a) devil; **~o wie** God knows; **co u ~a** what on earth; **mieć do ~a** (G) have in plenty

lichota f (-y; G -) trash

lichtarz m (-a; -e) candlestick

lichwia|rski extortionate; **~rstwo** n (-a) usury; **~rz** m (-a; -e) usurer

lichy crummy, paltry, poor

lico n (-a; G lic) lit. face, countenance; **~wać** (-uję) **(z I)** v/i. fit, be suitable, be appropriate; v/t. arch. face; **~wy** facing

licyt|acja f (-i; -e) auction; (w kartach) bidding; **~ator** m (-a; -rzy) auctioneer; **~ować** (-uję) auction; (w kartach) bid

liczb|a f (-y) number; **~a mnoga** the plural; **~a pojedyncza** the singular; **w ~ie gości** among the guests; **przeważać ~ą** outnumber, exceed in number; **~a ofiar śmiertelnych** death toll; **~owo** adv. numerically; in numbers; **~owy** numerical

licze|bnik m (-a; -i) gr. numeral; **~bnik porządkowy** ordinal; **~bnik główny** cardinal; **~bny** numerical; **stan ~bny** number, size; **~nie** n (-a; 0) counting

licz|nik m (-a; -i) meter, (w taksówce) clock; tech. counter; math. numerator; **~nik gazowy** gas meter; **~ny** numerous

liczyć ⟨**po-**⟩ (-ę) count (impf też v/i.) calculate; number; → **obliczać, wyliczać**; fig. **(na A)** depend (on), rely (on); on **~ł sobie ... lat** he was ... years old; **~ć się** count v/i.; **(z I)** reckon (with), take s.o./s.th. into account; **to się nie ~** it does not count; **~dło** n (-a; G -deł) abacus

lider m (-a; -rzy) leader

liga f (-i; G -) league

lignina f (-y; G -) med. wood-wool

ligow|iec m (-wca; -wcy) league player; **~y** league

likier m (-u; -y) liqueur

likwid|acja f (-i; -e) liquidation; elimination; **~ować** ⟨**z-**⟩ (-uję) liquidate; eliminate

lili|a f (GDL -ii; -e) lily; **~owy** lilac

liliput m (-a; -ci), **~ka** f (-i; G -tek) Lilliputian

limfa f (-y; 0) lymph; **~tyczny** lymphatic

limit m (-u; -y) limit; **~ować** (-uję) limit, restrict

lin m (-a; -y) zo. tench

lina f (-y; G -) rope, line; (w cyrku) tightrope

linczować ⟨z-⟩ (-uję) lynch
lingwistyczny linguistic
lini|a f (GDL -ii; -e) line (też fig.); **~a polityczna** platform; **dbać o ~ę** watch one's weight; → **kreska**; ~ał m (-u; -y) ruler
linieć (-eję) Brt. moult, Am. molt
lini|jka f (-i; G -jek) ruler; ~owany ruled; ~owy linear
linka f (-i; G -nek) →**lina**
lino|leum n (idkl.) linoleum; ~ryt m (-u; -y) linocut
lino|skoczek m (-czka; -czkowie/-czki) tightrope-walker; ~wy rope, cable
lip|a f (-y; G -) lime, linden; ~cowy July; ~iec m (-pca; -pce) July; ~ny F fake; → **lichy**; ~owy lime, linden
liry|czny lyrical; lyric; ~ka f (-i; G -) lyric poetry
lis m (-a; -y) zo. fox
lisi fox; foxlike; ~ca f (-y; G -) zo. vixen; bot. chanterelle
list m (-u; -y) letter; ~a f (-y; G -) list, register; ~ek m (-tka; -tki) → **liść**
listonosz m (-a; -e) Brt. postman, Am. mailman, mail carrier; ~ka f (-i; G-szek) Brt. postwoman, Am. mail carrier
listo|pad m (-a; -y) November; ~padowy November; ~wie n (-wia; 0) leaves pl., foliage
listow|ny, ~y letter
listwa f (-y; G -tew) strip; batten; slat; **~ zasilająca** power strip
liszaj m (-a; -e) med. lichen
liszka f (-i; G -szek) zo. caterpillar
liś|ciasty deciduous; ~ć m (-cia; -cie) leaf
lit m (-u; 0) chem. lithium
li'tania f (GDL -ii; -e) litany
litera f (-y; G -) letter; ~cki **(-ko, po -ku)** literary; ~lny literal; ~t m (-a; -ci); ~tka f (-i; G -tek) writer; ~tura f (-y; G -) literature
literować ⟨prze-⟩ (-uję) spell
litewski (po -ku) Lithuanian
litoś|ciwy merciful, compassionate; ~ć f (-ści; 0) mercy, pity
litować się ⟨u-, z- się⟩ (-uję) have mercy **(nad I** on), pity
litr m (-a; -y) Brt. litre, Am. liter; ~aż m (-u; 0) mot. cubic capacity; ~owy Brt. litre, Am. liter
li'turgia f (GDL -ii; -e) liturgy
Lit|wa f (-y; 0) Lithuania; ~win m (-a; -i), ~winka f (-i; G -nek) Lithuanian

lity solid
liz|ać (-żę, liż!) lick; ~ak m (-a; -i) lollipop
Lizbona f (-y; 0) Lisbon
liznąć v/s. (-nę) → **lizać**
lizus m (-a; -y) pej. bootlicker, toady, creep; ~owski toady
lm skrótpisany:**liczba mnoga** pl. (plural)
ln|iany bot. flaxen; linen; ~u, ~y → **len**
loch m (-u; -y) dungeon
locha f (-y; G -) zo. wild sow; (młoda) gilt
loczek m (-czka; -czki) → **lok**
lodo|łamacz m (-a; -e) naut. icebreaker; ~waty **(-to)** icy; glacial, ice-cold; ~wiec m (-wca; -wce) glacier; ~wisko n (-a; G -) ice rink; ~wnia f (-i; -e) cold room
lo|dowy ice; ice-cream; ~dówka f (-i; G -wek) fridge; ~dy m/pl. (-ów) ice-cream; → **lód**; ~dziarnia f (-i; -e) ice-cream parlo(u)r; ~dziarka f (-i; G -rek), ~dziarz m (-a; -e) ice-cream seller, Am. iceman
logarytm m (-u; -y) logarithm
logi|czny logical, coherent; ~ka f (-i; -) logic; coherence
logować się (-uję) komp. log in
lojaln|ość f (-ści; 0) loyalty; ~y loyal
lok m (-a; -i) curl, lock
lokaj m (-a; -e) lackey (też fig.), valet
lokal m (-u; -e) place; accommodation; restaurant; **~ nocny** night club; ~ **wyborczy** polling station; ~izować ⟨z-⟩ (-uję) localize, locate; ~ny local
lokata f (-y; G -) place, position; (w banku) deposit; (kapitału) investment
lokator m (-a; -rzy), ~ka f (-i; G -rek) lodger, tenant, occupant
lokaut m (-u; -y) econ. lockout
lokomo|cja f (-i; -) vehicle; ~ **środek ~cji** means of Brt. transport, Am. transportation; ~tywa f (-y; G-) locomotive, engine
lokować ⟨u-⟩ (-uję) place, position **(się** o.s.); econ. invest
lokówka f (-i; G -wek) curler
lombard m (-u; -y) pawnshop
Londyn m (-u; 0) London; ~ńczyk Londoner; 2ński London
lont m (-u; -y) fuse
lord m (-a; -owie) Lord, lord
lornetka f (-i; G -tek) binoculars pl., glasses pl.; ~ **teatralna** opera-glasses pl.
los m (-u; -y) fate, lot; (w grze) ticket; **dobry ~** good luck; ~ **loteryjny** lottery ticket; **rzucać ~y** cast lots; **na ~ szczęścia** hit-or-miss

losow|ać (-uję) draw (lots v/i.); ~anie n
(-a; G -ań) drawing; ~y random; **wybrany ~owo** chosen at random

lot m (-u; -y) flight; **w ~** immediately,
at once; → **ptak**; ~**em błyskawicy** like
lightning

lo'ter|ia f (GDL -ii; -e) lottery; ~**ia fan-
towa** raffle

lot|ka f (-i; G -tek) zo. flight feather;
(w sporcie) shuttlecock; ~nia f (-i; -e)
hang-glider; ~niarz m (-a; -e) hang-
-glider; ~nictwo n (-a; 0) aviation;
(wojskowe) air force; ~niczy air, aerial;
~nik m (-a; -cy) aviator, airman; ~ni-
sko n (-a; G -) airport; (małe) airfield;
~niskowiec m (-wca; -wce) mil. aircraft carrier; ~niskowy airport

lotn. skrót pisany: **lotniczy** airline

lotny airborne; ciecz volatile; człowiek
quick, alert

loża f (-y; G lóż) theat. box

lód (lodu; lody) ice; → **lody**

lp. **liczba porządkowa** No. (number);
liczba pojedyncza sing. (singular)

lśni|ący (-co) glistening, glittering; ~ć
(się) (-ę) glisten, glitter

lub cj. or

lubić (-ę) like, enjoy

lubieżny lewd, lascivious; **czyn ~** jur.
immoral act

lubować się (-uję) (I) take pleasure
(in)

lud m (-u, -u/-dzie!; -y) people, nation;
~ność f (-ści; 0) population, inhabit-
ants pl.; ~ny populated

ludo|bójstwo n (-a; G -) genocide; ~wy
folk; (wiejski) rural, peasant; pol.
people's; ~znawczy ethnographic;
~żerca m (-y) cannibal

ludz|ie pl. (-i, I -dźmi) people; ~ki (**po-
-ku**) human; (dobry) humane; ~kość f
(-ści; 0) humanity, mankind, humankind

lufa f (-y; G -) barrel

lufcik m (-a; -i) air vent (in a window)

luft F **do ~u** good-for-nothing

luk m (-u; -i) hatch; ~a f (-i; G -) gap

lukier m (-kru; 0) icing

lukrecja f (-i; -e) bot. liquorice

lukrować ⟨po-⟩ ice

luksusowy (-wo) luxurious

luna|tyczka f (-i; G -czek), ~k m (-a;
-cy) sleepwalker

lunąć pf. (-nę, -ń!) v/i. beat down, pelt
down

luneta f (-y; G -) telescope

lupa f (-y; G -) magnifying glass

lust|erko n (-rka; G -rek) pocket mir-
ror; ~racja f (-i; -e) inspection, review;
~ro n (-a; G -ter) mirror; ~rować ⟨z-⟩
(-uję) inspect, review

lustrzan|ka f (-i; G -nek) reflex camera;
~y mirror

lut m (-u, -y) solder

Lutera|nin m (-a; -e), ~nka f (-i; G
-nek) Lutheran; ~nizm m (-u; 0)
Lutheranism; 2ński Lutheran

lutnia f (-i; -e) mus. lute

lutow|ać (-uję) solder; ~nica f (-y; -e)
soldering iron; ~niczy soldering

lut|owy February; ~y m (-ego; 0) Febru-
ary

luz m (-u; -y) room; tech. play, slackness;
mot. neutral (gear); F ~em loose;
wóz empty; fig. free; **na ~ie** mot. in
neutral; **na (pełnym) ~ie** fig. easy-
going, carefree; ~ować ⟨z-⟩ (-uję) re-
lieve, take over from (**się** v/i.); ⟨**ob-,
po-**⟩ loosen

luźny (**-no**) loose; lina slack; sweter baggy

lw|a → **lew**; ~i lion; ~ica f (-y; -e) zo.
lioness; ~y pl. → **lew**

lżej(szy) adv. (adj.) comp. od → **lekki,
lekko**

lżyć ⟨ze-⟩ (-ę, lżyj!) scold, abuse

Ł

Łaba f (-y; 0) Elbe

łabę|dzi swan; ~dź m (-dzia; -dzie, -dzi)
zo. swan

łach(man) m (-a; -y) rag; ~y pl. też F
togs pl., things pl.

łachudra f/m (-y; G -der/-drów) pej.

sloven, bum; → **szubrawiec**

łaciaty koń roan

łaci|na f (-y; 0) Latin; ~ński Latin

ład m (-u; -y) order; **dojść do ~u**
straighten out (**z** I)

ładny adj. (comp. -niejszy) pretty, nice

ładow|ać (*-uję*) ⟨*za-, wy-*⟩ load; ⟨*na-*⟩ **broń** load; *akumulator* charge; *~nia f* (*-i; -e*) hold; *~ność f* (*-ści; 0*) load capacity; *~ny → pakowny*

ładunek *m* (*-nku; -nki*) load, cargo; *electr.* charge; *~ wybuchowy* (explosive) charge

łago|dnieć ⟨*z-*⟩ (*-ję*) soften; *ból, wiatr*: subside; *~dność f* (*-ści; 0*) gentleness, mildness; *~dny* gentle, mild, soft; *med.* benign; *~dzić* ⟨*z-*⟩⟨*z-*⟩ ease, appease; relieve; **okoliczności** *f/pl.* *~dzące* mitigating (*lub* extenuating) circumstances *pl.*

łajać ⟨*z-*⟩ (*-am*) scold, rap

łajda|cki villainous; *~ctwo n* (*-a; G -*) rascality, villainy; *~czka f* (*-i; G -czek*), *~k m* (*-a; -i/-cy*) scoundrel

łajno *n* (*-a; G -jen*) dung; F turd, crap

łakocie *pl.* (*-i*) *Brt.* sweets *pl.*, *Am.* candy

łakom|ić się ⟨*po- się*⟩ (*-ę*) (*na A*) crave (for); be greedy (for); *~y* greedy (*też* **na** *A* for); (*na słodycze*) sweet-toothed

łam *m* (*-u; -y*) *print.* column; *~ać* (*-ię*) ⟨*po-, z-*⟩ break; *~ać* ⟨*po-*⟩ *się* break, give way; *fig.* crack up; *~anie n* (*-a; G -ń*) *med.* pains *pl.*; *~any* broken

łami|główka *f* (*-i; G -wek*) puzzle; *~strajk m* (*-a; -i*) strike-breaker, scab

łamliwy fragile, breakable

łan *m* (*-u; -y*) field

łania *f* (*-ni; -e*) *zo.* doe

łańcu|ch *m* (*-a; -y*) chain; (*gór*) ridge; **przykuwać** *~chem* chain; *~chowy* chain; **pies** *~chowy* watchdog; *~szek m* (*-szka; -szki*) chain

łapa *f* (*-y; G -*) paw (*też fig.*)

łapa|ć ⟨*z-*⟩ (*-pię*) catch (*też fig.*); get hold of; get; (*nagle*) grab; *~ć się na cz-ś* catch o.s. doing s.th.; *~nka f* (*-i; G -nek*) raid

łap|czywy greedy, avid; *~ka f* (*-i; G -pek*) (**na myszy** mouse)trap

łapówk|a *f* (*-i; G -wek*) bribe; **dawać** *~kę* bribe; *~arski* bribery; *~arstwo n* (*-a; 0*) bribery

łasica *f* (*-y; G -*) *zo.* weasel

łasić się (*-szę*) fawn (**do** *G* on)

łas|ka *f* (*-i; G -*) favo(u)r; mercy, clemency; *rel.* grace; **prawo** *~ki* the right of reprieve; **niech pan** *z ~ki swojej* would you be so kind as to; **z** *~ki* condescend-

ingly; *~kawy* gracious; favo(u)rable; kind; **bądź** *~kaw* be so kind

łaskot|ać ⟨*po-*⟩ (*-am*) tickle; *~ki f/pl.*: **mieć** *~tki* be ticklish; *~liwy* ticklish

łas|owy *m* treat o.s. to; *~y → łako-my*

łata[1] *f* (*-y; G -*) slat

łata[2] *f* (*-y; G -*) patch; *~ć* ⟨*za-*⟩ (*-am*) patch (up); *~nina f* (*-y*) botch, patch-work

łatka *f* (*-i; G -tek*) → **łata**

łatwo *adv.* (*comp. -wiej*) easily; readily; *~ść f* (*-ści; 0*) easiness, ease; readiness; *~wierny* credulous, gullible

łatwy *adj.* (*comp. -wiejszy*) easy; simple

ław|a *f* (*-y; G -*) bench; coffee table; *~a oskarżonych* dock; *~a przysięgłych* jury; *~ica f* (*-y; G -*) school; (*piasku*) drift, shoal; *~ka f* (*-i; G -wek*) bench; (*w kościele*) pew; *~niczka f* (*-i; G -czek*), *~nik m* (*-a; -cy*) juror

łazanki *f/pl.* *jakby*: lasagne

łazić (*-żę*) (*po I*) F trudge, walk; climb

łazienka *f* (*-i; G -nek*) bathroom

łazik *m* (*-a; -i*) *Brt.* tramp, *Am.* hobo; *mot.* jeep; *~ować* (*-uję*) roam, hang around (**po ulicach** the streets)

łaźnia *f* (*-i; -e*) baths *sg./pl.*

łącz|nica *f* (*-y; G -*) *tel.* switchboard; *~niczka f* (*-i; G -czek*) courier, messenger; *~nie* together (**z** *I* with); including; *~nik m* (*-a; -cy*) courier, messenger; *mil.* liaison officer; *print.* hyphen; *tech.* coupling; *~ność f* (*-ści; 0*) connection (*też tel.*), contact; *tel.* (tele)communications *pl.*; *fig.* (sense of) community; *~ny* all-in, inclusive; joint; *~yć* ⟨*po-, z-*⟩ (*-czę*) **się**) connect, link; join; combine, merge; unite; *tel.* put through; *~ymy się z* (*I*) we are going over to

łąk|a *f* (*-i; G -*) meadow; *~owy* meadow

łeb *m* (*łba; łby*) head, F nut; **na** *~*, **na szyję** headlong; **kocie** *łby* *pl.* cobbles *pl.*; *~ek m* (*-bka; -bki*) head (**gwoździa** of the nail); **od** *~ka* per head; **po** *~kach* cursorily, slapdash

łechta|czka *f* (*-i; F -czek*) *anat.* clitoris; *~ć* (*-am*) tickle

łga|ć F lie; tell fibs; *~rz m* (*-a; -e*) liar

łkać (*-am*) sob

łobuz *m* (*-a; -y/-i*) hooligan, yob; (*chłopiec*) rascal; *~erski* roguish; **spojrzenie** arch; *~ować* (*-uję*) go wild, charge about

łodyga *f* (*-i*; *G* -) stalk, stem

łodzi *G* → **łódź**

łojo|tok *m* (*-u*; *0*) seborrh(o)ea; ~**wy** seborrh(o)eal, seborrh(o)eic

łok|ciowy elbow; ~**ieć** *m* (*-kcia*; *-kcie*) elbow

łom *m* (*-u*; *-y*) crowbar

łomot *m* (*-u*; *-y*) thud, bang, crash; ~**ać** (*-czę/-cę*) crash, bang, thud

łon|o *n* (*-a*; *G* -) womb; (*piersi*) bosom (*też fig.*); *anat.* pubis; *fig.* **w ~ie** (*G*) inside; in the bosom of; ~**owy** pubic

łopat|a *f* (*-y*; *G* -) shovel; (*śmigła*) blade; ~**ka** *f* (*-i*; *G -tek*) (small) shovel; *anat.* (shoulder) blade; *gastr.* (*przyrząd*) spatula; (*potrawa*) shoulder of ham

łopian *m* (*-u*; *-y*) *bot.* burdock

łopotać (*-czę/-cę*) flutter, flap

łosi|ca *f* (*-y*; *-e, G* -) *zo.* elk; ~**ca amerykańska** moose

łoskot *m* (*-u*; *-y*) din; bang, crash

łoso|siowy salmon; ~**ś** *m* (*-sia*; *-sie*) *zo.* salmon

łoś *m* (*-a*; *G łosi*) *zo.* elk; ~ **amerykański** moose

Łot|wa *f* (*-y*; *0*) Latvia; ℤ**ewski** (**po -ku**) Latvian; ℤ**ysz** *m* (*-a*; *-e*), **-szka** *f* (*-i*; *G -szek*) Latvian

łot|r *m* (*-a*; *-y/-trzy*), ~**rzyca** *f* (*-y*; *G* -) villain, scoundrel

łow|ca *m* (*-y*; *-cy*), ~**czyni** *f* (*-ń, -nie*) hunter; ~**czy** **1.** hunting; **2.** *m* (*-ego; -owie*) master of the hunt; ~**ić** ⟨**z-**⟩ (*-ię*) catch; hunt; ~**ić ryby** fish; ~**iecki** hunting; ~**ny**: **zwierzyna ~na** game; ~**y** *pl.* (*-ów*) hunt

łoza *f* (*-y*; *łóz*) *bot.* willow

łoże *n* (*-a*; *G łóż*) (**małżeńskie, śmierci** marital, death) bed

łoży|ć (*-żę*) (**na** *A*) finance, pay (for); ~**sko** *n* (*-a*; *G* -) (**kulkowe** ball) bearing

łó|dka *f* (*-i*; *G -dek*), ~**dź** *f* (*łodzi; łodzie, -dzi*) boat

łój *m* (*łoju*; *0*) (*jadalny*) suet, (*na mydło itp.*) tallow

łóż|eczko *n* (*-a*; *G -czek*): ~**eczko dziecięce** *zwł. Brt.* cot, crib; → **kołyska**; ~**ko** *n* (*-a*; *G -żek*) bed; **do ~ka** to bed; ~**kowy** bed

łubin *m* (*-u*; *-y*) *bot.* lupin

łuczni|ctwo *n* (*-a*; *0*) archery; ~**czka** *f* (*-i*; *G -czek*), ~**k m** (*-a*; *-cy*) archer

łudz|ący (**-co**) *podobieństwo* remarkable, striking; ~**ić** ⟨**z-**⟩ (*-dzę*) deceive, delude; (**nie**) ~**ić się, że** (not) be under the illusion that; ~**ić się nadzieją** entertain the hope

ług *m* (*-u*; *-i*) *chem.* lye

łuk *m* (*-u*; *-i*) curve; *math.* arc; *arch.* arch; (*broń*) bow; ~**owy** *tech.* arc; *arch.* arch

łuna *f* (*-y*; *G* -) glow

łup *m* (*-u*; *-y*) loot, plunder; **paść ~em** (*D*) fall prey (to)

łup|acz *m* (*-a*; *-e*) *zo.* haddock; ~**ać** ⟨**roz-**⟩ (*-pię*) split; *orzech* crack; ~**ek** *m* (*-pka*; *-pki*) slate; ~**ić** (*-pię*) loot, plunder

łupież *m* (*-u*; *0*) dandruff

łupin|a *f* (*-y*; *G* -) (*owoców*) skin, (*ziemniaków*) peel; (*orzecha, też arch.*) shell; ~**owy** *arch.* shell

łupnąć F *v/s.* (*-nę*) hit, smash

łuska *f* (*-i*; *G -sek*) scale; (*grochu itp.*) pod, hull; *mil.* shell; → **łupina**; ~**ć** (*-am*) shell

łuszczy|ca *f* (*-y*; *0*) *med.* psoriasis; ~**ć** (*-szczę*) → **łuskać**; ~**ć się** peel, flake

łut *m* (*-u*; *-y*): ~ **szczęścia** a piece of luck

Łużyc|e *pl.* (*-c*) Lusatia; ℤ**ki** Lusatian

łydk|a *f* (*-i*; *G -dek*) calf

łyk *m* (*-a/-u*; *-i*) swallow, mouthful; ~**ać** (*-am*) swallow; ~**nąć** *v/s.* (*-nę*) (*G*) take a swallow

łyko *n* (*-a*) *bot.* phloem; ~**waty** *gastr.* stringy

łys|ieć ⟨**wy-**⟩ (*-eję*) bald, go bald; ~**ina** *f* (*-y*; *G* -) bald patch; (*cała głowa*) bald head; ~**y** bald

łyż|eczka *f* (*-i*; *G -czek*) (tea)spoon; ~**ka** *f* (*-i*; *G -żek*) (**stołowa** soup-)-spoon; ~**ka do nabierania** table-spoon

łyżwa *f* (*-y*; *G -żew*) skate

łyżwia|rstwo *n* (*-a*; *0*) skating; ~**rka** *f* (*-i*; *G -rek*), ~**rz** *m* (*-a*; *-e*) skater

łyżworolki *f/pl.* (*G -lek*) Rollerblades *pl.*, in-line skates *pl.*

łza *f* (*łzy*; *łzy, G łez*) tear; **śmiać się do łez** laugh till the tears come; **przez łzy** through tears; ~**wiący** *oczy* watering; **gaz ~wiący** teargas; ~**wić** (*-wię*) water; ~**wy** tear-jerking, maudlin

łzowy *anat.* lachrymal, lacrimal

łżą, łże(sz) → **łgać**

Ł

M

m. *skrót pisany*: **miasto** town; **miesiąc** month; **mieszkanie** flat; apt. (*apartment*)

ma¹ *3. os. sg.* → **mieć**; *econ.* credit

ma² *pron.* (*ściągn.* **moja**) → **mój**

macać ⟨**po-**⟩ (*-am*) feel, finger; feel up

Macedo|nia *f* (*GDL -ii; 0*) Macedonia; ~nka *f* (*-i; G -nek*), ~ńczyk *m* (*-a; -cy*) Macedonian; 2ński Macedonian

machać (*-am*) wave (**do G** to); (*skrzydłami*) flap; ~ **ogonem** wag

machin|a *f* (*-y; G -*) machine; *fig.* machinery; ~acje *f/pl.* (*G -i*) machinations *pl.*

machlojka F *f* (*-i; G -jek*) fraud, *Brt.* fiddle, wangle

machnąć *v/s.* (*-nę*) → **machać**; ~ **ręką** (**na** *A*) give up

maci|ca *f* (*-y; -e, G -*) *anat.* uterus; ~**ca perłowa** mother of pearl; ~czny uterine

macie *2. os. pl.* → **mieć**

macierz *f* (*-y; -e*) *math.* matrix

macierzanka *f* (*-i; G -nek*) *bot.* thyme

macierzy|ński maternal; motherly; **urlop ~ński** maternity leave; ~ństwo *n* (*-a; G -*) maternity, motherhood; ~sty native, indigenous

maciora *f* (*-y; G -*) sow

mac|ka *f* (*-i; G -cek*) feeler, tentacle; ~nąć *v/s.* (*-nę*) → **macać**

maco|cha *f* (*-y; G -*) stepmother; ~szy (**po-szemu**) *fig.* unfeeling, uncompassionate

maczać (*-czam*) dip

mać V: **psia ~!** shit!, *Brt.* bloody hell!; **kurwa ~!** fucking hell!

madera *f* (*-y*) Madeira

Madryt *m* (*-u; 0*) Madrid

mafia *f* (*GDL -ii; -e*) the Mafia

mag *m* (*-a; -owie*) magician

magazy|n *m* (*-u; -y*) store(-room), warehouse; (*pismo*) magazine; ~nek *m* (*-nku; -nki*) *mil.* magazine; ~nier *m* (*-a; -rzy*) warehouseman; ~nować ⟨**z-**⟩ (*-uję*) store (up)

magi|a *f* (*GDL -ii; -e*) magic; ~czny magic(al)

magiel *m* (*-gla; -gle*) mangle; ~ **elektryczny** electric ironer

magik *m* (*-a; -cy*) magician; conjurer

magi|ster *m* (*-a; -trzy*) person with a Master's degree; ~stracki municipal; ~strala *f* (*-i; -e*) main road; *rail.* main line; (*gazowa itp.*) main; *komp.* bus

maglować ⟨**wy-**⟩ (*-uję*) mangle, iron, press; *fig.* mangle

magnes *m* (*-u; -y*) magnet (*też fig.*)

magnetofon *m* (*-u; -y*) tape-recorder; (*bez wzmacniacza*) tape deck; ~ **kasetowy** cassette recorder; ~owy tape-recorder

magne|towid *m* (*-u;-y*) video cassette recorder (*skrót:* VCR); ~tyczny magnetic

magnez *m* (*-u; -y*) *chem.* magnesium

mahometa|nizm *m* (*-u; 0*) Islam; ~ański Islamic, Muslim; 2anin *m* (*-a; -e*), 2anka *f* (*-i; G -nek*) Muslim

maho|ń *m* (*-niu; -nie*) *bot.* mahogany; ~niowy mahogany

maj *m* (*-a; -e*) May; **1 2a** May Day

majacz|enie *n* (*-a; G -ń*) delirium; ~yć (*-ę*) be delirious, rave; → **bredzić**; (**się**) appear, loom

mają *3. os. sg.* → **mieć**; ~tek *m* (*-tku; -tki*) fortune, possessions *pl.*; (*ziemski*) landed property; ~tkowy financial

majeranek *m* (*-nku; -nki*) *bot.* marjoram

majestat *m* (*-u; 0*) majesty

majętny wealthy, affluent

majonez *m* (*-u; -y*) *gastr.* mayonnaise

major *m* (*-a; -rzy*) *mil.* major

majowy May

majster *m* (*-tra; -trzy, -trowie*) (**w** *fabryce*) foreman; (*rzemieślnik*) master craftsman; (*mistrz*) master; ~ **do wszystkiego** handyman

majsterkow|ać (*-uję*) *Brt.* do DIY, *Am.* fix things; ~anie *n* (*-a*) DIY; ~icz *m* (*-a; -e*) *Brt.* DIY enthusiast, *Am.* do-it-yourselfer

majstrować (*-uję*) tinker (**przy** *I* with); ⟨**z-**⟩ build, make; *fig.* tinker

majtać (*-am*) nogami dangle; ogonem wag

majt|eczki *pl.* (*-czek*) → **majtki**; ~ki *pl.* (*-tek*) briefs *pl.*, (*damskie*) panties *pl.*

mak *m* (*-u; -i*) *bot.* poppy

makabryczny ghastly, grusome

makaron *m* (*-u*; *-y*) pasta; **~ nitki** vermicelli *pl.*; **~ paski** noodles *pl.*; **~ rurki** macaroni; **~owy** pasta

makata *f* (*-y*; *G* -) wall-hanging

makieta *f* (*-y*; *G* -) model; *tech.* mock-up; *print.* dummy

makijaż *m* (*-u*, -*e*) make-up

makler *m* (*-a*, -*rzy*) *econ.* stock-broker

makow|iec *m* (*-wca*; *-wce*), **~nik** *m* (*-a*; -*i*) poppyseed cake; **~y** poppyseed

makówka *f* (*-i*; *G* -*wek*) poppy-head

maksyma *f* (*-y*; *G* -) maxime, saying; **~lny** maximum, maximal

Malaj *m* (*-a*; -*e*) Malay; **♀ski** Malay

malaria *f* (*GDL* -*ii*; -*e*) *med.* malaria

malar|ka *f* (*-i*, *G* -*rek*) painter; **~ski** painting; painter's; **sztuka ~ska** painting; **~stwo** *n* (*-a*; *0*) painting

malarz *m* (*-a*; -*e*) painter

male|c *m* (*-lca*; *-lce*) little one, F kid; **~ć** ⟨*z-*⟩ (-*eje*) diminish; *siły*: decline; **~ńki** tiny; **~ństwo** *n* (*-a*; *G* -) baby

Malezja *f* (*-i*; *0*) Malaysia

mali *m-os pl.* → **mały**

malign|a *f* (*-y*; *0*): **w ~ie** in fever

malin|a *f* (*-y*; *G* -) raspberry; **~owy** raspberry

malkontenctwo *n* (*-a*; *G* -) grumbling

malow|ać (-*uję*) ⟨*na-*, *po-*⟩ paint (**się** o.s.; **na biało** white); ⟨*u-*, *po-*⟩ **~ać się** make up; **~anki** *f/pl.* (*-nek*) colo(u)ring-book; **~idło** *n* (*-a*; *G* -*deł*) painting; **~niczy** ⟨*-czo*⟩ picturesque; scenic

maltańs|ki (**po -ku**) Maltese

maltretować (-*uję*) maltreat, ill-treat; (*bić*) batter

malu|ch *m* (*-a*; -*y*) kid, toddler; **~tki** tiny

malwa *f* (*-y*; *G* -) *bot.* mallow

malwersacja *f* (*-i*; -*e*) embezzlement

mała, małe → **mały**

mało *adv.* little, few; **~ kto** few people; **~ co, o ~ nie** nearly, almost; **~ kiedy** hardly ever; **~ tego** that's not all; **~ ważny** insignificant; **~duszny** mean; **~kaloryczny** low-calorie; **~lat** *m* (*-a*; -*y*) F teenager; **~letni** teenage; *jur.* juvenile; **~mówny** taciturn; **~obrazkowy** 35 mm; **~rolny**: **chłop ~rolny** smallholder; **~stkowy** mean, petty; **~wartościowy** low-quality, inferior

małp|a *f* (*-y*; *G* -) monkey; (*człekokształtna*) ape; **~i** (**-pio**) monkey; ape; **~ować** (-*uję*) ape

mał|y 1. small, little; **bez ~a** almost, nearly; **od ~ego** from childhood; **2.** *m* (*-ego*, -*li*), **~a** *f* (*-ej*; -*e*), **~e** *n* (*-ego*; -*e*) baby, little one

małż *m* (*-a*; -*e*) *zo.* clam; (*jadalny*) mussel

małżeńs|ki marital, matrimonial, married; **~two** *n* (*-a*; *G* -) (*związek*) marriage; (*mąż i żona*) couple

małżon|ek *m* (*-ka*; -*kowie*) spouse, partner; (*mąż*) husband; **~ka** *f* (*-i*; *G* -*nek*) wife

małżowina *f* (*-y*; *G* -) *anat.* external ear, auricle

mam *1. os. sg. pres.* → **mieć**

mama *f* (*-y*; *G* -) mother, mum

mamer F *m* (*-mra*; -*mry*) clink

mamić ⟨*z-*⟩ (-*ę*) → **wabić, zwodzić**

maminsynek *m* (*-a*; -*i*) mother's boy

mam|lać, ~leć (*-ę*, -*i*), **~rotać** (-*czę*/-*cę*) ⟨*wy-*⟩ mumble, mutter

mamy *1. os. pl. pres.* → **mieć**

manatki F (*-tków*) stuff

mandarynka *f* (*-i*; *G* -*nek*) mandarin, tangerine

mandat *m* (*-u*, -*y*) fine, ticket; (*parlamentarny*) seat

manekin *m* (*-a*; -*y*) dummy

manewr *m* (*-u*; -*y*) *Brt.* manoeuvre, *Am.* maneuver; **~ować** (-*uję*) *Brt.* manoeuvre, *Am.* maneuver

mango *n* (*-a*) *bot.* mango

mania *f* (*GDl* -*ii*; -*e*) mania; **~ prześladowcza** persecution mania; **~cki** maniac(al); **~czka** *f* (*-i*; *G* -*czek*), **~k** *m* (*-a*; -*cy*) maniac

manicurzystka *f* (*-i*; *G* -*tek*) → **manikiurzystka**

maniera *f* (*-y*; *G* -) manner; mannerism

manierka *f* (*-i*; *G* -*rek*) canteen

manifest|acja *f* (*-i*; *G* -*e*) demonstration; rally; manifestation; **~ować** (-*uję*) demonstrate (**na rzecz** *G* in support of)

manikiurzystka *f* (*-i*; *G* -*tek*) manicurist

manipul|acja *f* (*-i*; -*e*) manipulation; **~ować** (-*uję*) manipulate; handle; *niepotrzebnie* tamper

mankament *m* (*-u*; -*y*) defect, shortcoming

mankiet *m* (*-u*; -*y*) cuff; **~ u spodni** *Brt.* turn-up, *Am.* cuff

manna *f* (*-y*; *0*) *fig.* manna; **kasza ~** semolina

manowce *m/pl.* (*-ów*) wrong track; **zejść na ~** go astray mańkut *m* (-*a*; -*ci*/-*y*) left-hander

mapa *f* (-*y*; *G* -) map

mara|tończyk *m* (-*a*; -*cy*) marathon runner; ~toński: *bieg ~toński* marathon (race)

marc|a *G*, ~*e* *pl.* → *marzec*

marcepan *m* (-*a*; -*y*) marzipan

marchew *f* (-*wi*; -*wie*), ~ka *f* (-*i*; *G* -*wek*) carrot

marc|owy March; ~u *DL* → *marzec*

margaryna *f* (-*y*; *G* -) margarine, F marge

margines *m* (-*u*; -*y*) margin; *uwaga na ~ie* marginal note, comment in passing; ~owy marginal

marihuana *f* (-*y*; *0*) marijuana *lub* marihuana

marionetka *f* (-*i*; *G* -*tek*) marionette; *fig.* puppet

marka¹ *f* (-*i*; *G* -*rek*) mark

marka² (-*i*; *G* -*rek*) brand, make

marketingowy marketing

marko|tny (-*nie*, -*no*) glum, morose; ~wać (-*uję*) feign, pretend

marmolada *f* (-*y*; *G* -) jam, (*z cytrusów*) marmalade

marmur *m* (-*u*; -*y*) marble; ~owy marble

marnie *adv.* → *marny*; ~ć ⟨*z*-⟩ (-*ję*) wither, fade

marnotraw|ić ⟨*z*-⟩ (-*ię*) squander, waste; ~stwo *n* (-*a*; *G* -) waste

marnować ⟨*z*-⟩ (-*uję*) waste; *okazję* lose; ~ ⟨*z*-⟩ *się* go to waste

marn|y poor; bad; worthless; *pójść na ~e* go to waste

marskość *f* (-*ci*; *0*) *med.* cirrhosis

marsz *m* (-*u*/*mus.* -*a*; -*e*) march; ~ *stąd!*, ~ *za drzwi!* out you go!

marszałek *m* (-*łka*; -*łkowie*) *mil.* marshal; ~ *sejmu* speaker

marszczyć ⟨*na*-, *z*-⟩ (-*czę*) wrinkle (*się v/i.*); *woda*: ripple; ~ *się* shrivel; crease

marszruta *f* (-*y*; *G* -) itinerary

martwi|ca *f* (-*y*; *0*) *med.* necrosis; ~ć ⟨*z*-⟩ (-*ę*) trouble, worry; ~ć *się* worry (*o A* about); ~eć ⟨*z*-⟩ (-*eję*) *fig.* be paralysed (*z G* by)

martw|y dead; ~*a natura* still life; *utknąć w ~ym punkcie* come to a standstill

martyro'logia *f* (*GDL* -*ii*; *0*) martyrdom

maru|dny peevish, sulky; ~dzić (-*dzę*) dawdle; → *guzdrać się*

maryjny *rel.* Marian, Lady

maryna|rka *f* (-*i*; *G* -*rek*) jacket; (-*i*; *0*) *naut.* (*wojenna*) navy, (*handlowa też*) marine; ~rski nautical, naval; ~rz *m* (-*a*; -*e*) *naut.* sailor, seaman

mary|nata *f* (-*y*; *G* -) marinade, pickle; ~nować ⟨*za*-⟩ (-*uję*) pickle, marinade

marzec March

marzenie *n* (-*a*; *G* -*eń*) dream, day--dream

marznąć [-r·z-] (-*nę*, -*ł*) ⟨*z*-⟩ freeze; ⟨*za*-⟩ freeze to death; *roślina*: be damaged by frost

marzyciel *m* (-*a*; -*e*), ~ka *f* (-*i*; *G* -*lek*) dreamer; ~ski dreaming; ~stwo *n* (-*a*; *0*) dreaming

marzyć (-*ę*) dream (*o L* about); *fig.* be dying (*o L* for)

marża *f* (-*y*; *G* -) *econ.* margin

masa *f* (-*y*; *0*) *phys.* mass; *fig.* F heaps *pl.*; (*do ciasta*) paste

masakra *f* (-*y*; *G* -*kr*) massacre, slaughter

masarski meat, butcher

masaż *m* (-*u*; -*e*) massage; *salon ~u* massage parlo(u)r; ~ysta *m* (-*y*; -*ści*), ~ystka *f* (-*i*; -*tek*) masseur

maselniczka *f* (-*i*; *G* -*czek*) butter dish

maska *f* (-*i*; *G* -*sek*) mask; *mot. Brt.* bonnet, *Am.* hood; ~rada *f* (-*y*; *G* -) masquerade

maskotka *f* (-*i*; *G* -*tek*) mascot, charm

maskow|ać ⟨*za*-⟩ (-*uję*) mask, *mil.* camouflage; ~ać ⟨*za*-⟩ *się* disguise o.s.; ~y mask

masło *n* (-*a*; *G* -*seł*) butter; ~ *maślane* tautology

mason *m* (-*a*; -*i*) Freemason

masować ⟨*po*-, *wy*-⟩ (-*uję*) massage

masow|o *adv.* in masses; ~y mass

mass 'media *pl.* (*G* -*ów*) mass media *pl.*, the media *pl.*

masturb|acja *f* (-*i*; -*e*) masturbation; ~ować się (-*uję*) masturbate

masyw *m* (-*u*; -*y*) massif; ~ny massive, solid

masz 2. *os. sg. pres.* → *mieć*

maszerować (-*uję*) march

maszkara *f* (-*y*; *G* -) nightmare

maszt *m* (-*u*; -*y*) mast

maszyn|a *f* (-*y*; *G* -) machine, device; ~*na do pisania* typewriter; ~*na do szycia* sewing-machine; ~nista *m* (-*y*; -*ści*) *rail. Brt.* engine-driver, *Am.* engineer; ~nistka *f* (-*i*; *G* -*stek*) typist

maszynka *f* (-*i*; *G* -*nek*): ~ *do kawy*

coffee-maker; ~ *do mięsa* mincer; ~ *spirytusowa* spiritus stove

maszyno|pis *m* (*-u*; *-y*) typescript, manuscript; ~**wy** machine; automatic

maść *f* (*-ci*) ointment

maśli|k *m* (*-a*; *-i*) boletus luteus; ~**nka** *f* (*-i*; *-nek*) buttermilk; ~**ny** butter

mat *m* (*-u*; *0*) matt; (*-a*; *0*) *w szachach* checkmate; *dać ~a* checkmate

mata *f* (*-y*; *G* -) mat

matactwo *n* (*-a*; *G* -) cheating, fraud

matczyn(y) motherly

matema|tyczny mathematical; ~**tyk** *m* (*-a*; *-cy*) mathematician; ~**tyka** *f* (*-i*) mathematics *sg.*

materac *m* (*-a*; *-e*) mattress

ma'teri|a *m* (*GDL -ii*; *0*) matter; ~**alny** material; ~**ał** *m* (*-u*; *-y*) fabric, textile; (*surowiec*) material

matka *f* (*-i*; *G* -*tek*) mother; ♀ *Boska* Mother of God; ~ *chrzestna* godmother; ~ *zastępcza* surrogate mother

matnia *f* (*-i*; *-e*) *fig.* trap

matołek *m* (*-łka*; *-łki*) simpleton, dimwit

matowy (*-wo*) matt; frosted

matryca *f* (*-y*; *G* -*) Brt.* mould, *Am.* mold; pattern

matrymonialny matrimonial

matu|ra *f* (*-y*; *G* -) (*secondary-school leaving examination; secondary-school examination certificate*); ~**rzysta** *m* (*-y*; *-ści*), ~**rzystka** *f* (*-i*; *G* -*tek) Brt.* (*secondary school leaver*); *Am.* graduate

mawiać (*-am*) say

maza|ć (*-żę*) smear; ~**k** *m* (*-a*; *-i*) felt-tip pen; ~**nina** *f* (*-y*; *G* -) scribble

mazgaj *m* (*-a*; *-e*) cry-baby

maznąć *v/s.* (*-nę*) → *mazać*

Mazowsze *n* (*-a*; *0*) Mazovia

mazurek *m* (*-rka*; *-rki*) *mus.* mazurka; *gastr.* Easter cake

Mazury *pl.* (*G* -) Masuria

maź *f* (*-zi*; *-zie*) grease; F gook, goo

mącić ⟨*z-*⟩ (*-cę*) make cloudy, cloud; ~ *się* become cloudy; *fig.* get confused

mącz|ka *f* (*-i*; *G* -*czek) Brt.* flour; ~**ny** flour; ~**ysty** (*-to*) powdery

mądro|ść *f* (*-ci*; *0*) wisdom; ~**ry** (*-rze*) wise; ~**rzeć** ⟨*z-*⟩ (*-ję*) become wiser; ~**rzej(szy)** *adv.* (*adj.*) (*comp. od* → *mądrze, mądry*) wiser

mąka *f* (*-i*; *G* -) flour; ~ *ziemniaczana* potato starch

mątwa *f* (*-y*; *G* -) *zo.* cuttlefish

mąż *m* (*męża, mężowie, mężów*) husband; *wyjść za* ~ (*za A*) marry, get married (to); *wydać za* ~ marry; ~ *stanu* statesman

m.b. *skrót pisany:* **metr bieżący** m. (*metre*)

m-c *skrót pisany:* **miesiąc** m. (*month*)

mchu *DL*, **mchy** *pl.* → **mech**

mdleć ⟨*ze-*⟩ (*-ję*) faint, pass out

mdlić: *k-ś mdli* s.o. feels sick

mdł|ości *pl.* (-) nausea; *mieć ~ości* feel sick; ~**y** (*-ło*) bland, tasteless

me *pron.* (*ściągn.* **moje**) → *mój*

mebel *m* (*-bla*; *-ble*, *-bli*) piece of furniture; *meble pl.* furniture

meblo|wać ⟨*u-*⟩ (*-uję*) furnish; ~**wóz** *m* furniture van

mecenas *m* (*-a*; *-si*) Maecenas; (*adwokat*) lawyer

mech *m* (*mchu*; *mchy*) moss

mechani|czny mechanical; ~**k** *m* (*-a*; *-cy*) mechanic; ~**zm** *m* (*-u*; *-y*) mechanism; ~**zm zegara** clockwork; ~**zować** ⟨*z-*⟩ (*-uję*) mechanize

mecz *m* (*-u*; *-e*) match, game

meczet *m* (*-u*; *-y*) *rel.* mosque

meda|l *m* (*-a*; *-e*) medal; ~**lik** *m* (*-a*; *-i*) locket; ~**lista** *m* (*-y*; *-ści*), ~**listka** *f* (*-i*; *G* -*tek*) (*w sporcie*) medal winner, medallist, title holder

medi'ator *m* (*-a*; *-rzy*) mediator

Mediolan *m* (*-u*; *0*) Milan

meduza *f* (*-y*; *G* -) *zo.* jellyfish

medy|cyna *f* (*-y*; *0*) medicine; ~**czny** medical

medytować (*-uję*) meditate

mega|bajt *m* (*-u*; *-y*) megabyte (*skrót:* MB); ~**lo'mania** *f* (*GDL -ii*; *0*) megalomania; ~**tona** *f* megaton

mego *pron.* (*ściągn.* **mojego**), **mej** *pron.* (*ściągn.* **mojej**) → *mój*

Meksy|k *m* (*-u*; *0*) Mexico; ~**kanka** *f* (*-i*; *G* -*nek*), ~**kańczyk** *m* (*-a*; *-cy*) Mexican; ♀**kański** Mexican

melancholijny melancholic

meld|ować ⟨*za-*⟩ (*-uję*) report (*się* v/i.); *zamieszkanie* register (*się* v/i.); ~**unek** *m* (*-nku*; *-nki*) report; ~**unkowy** registration

melin|a F *f* (*-y*; *G* -) hide-out; den; *z alkoholem* after-hours joint; ~**ować** ⟨*za-*⟩ (*-uję*) F hide (*też się* v/i.)

melioracja *f* (*-i*; *-e*) *agr.* melioration

me'lodia *f* (*GDL -ii*; *-e*) melody

melo|dyjny melodious; musical, tuneful; **~man** *m* (*-a; -i*); **~manka** *f* (*-i; G -nek*) music-lover

melon *m* (*-a; -y*) *bot.* melon; **~ik** *m* (*-a; -i*) bowler (hat)

meł|li, **~ł(am, -em)** → **mielić**

me'moriał *m* (*-u; -y*) memorandum; F (*w sporcie*) memorial contest

Men *m* (*-u; 0*) Main

menażka *f* (*-i; G -żek*) *Brt.* mess tin, *Am.* mess kit

menedżer *m* (*-a; -rzy*) manager

mennica *f* (*-y; G -*) mint

mentalność *f* (*-ci; 0*) mentality

mentolowy menthol

menu *n* (*idkl.*) menu

merdać ⟨**po-**⟩ (*-am*) wag

mereżka *f* (*-i; G -żek*) hem-stitch

merla *f* gauze

merynos *m* (*-a; -y*) *zo.* merino

merytoryczn|y substantial; *w sprawie ~ej* to the point

Mesjasz *m* (*-a*) *rel.* Messiah

meszek *m* (*-szka; -szki*) down

met|a *f* (*-y; G -*) finish; *na bliższą/ dalszą ~ę* in the short/long run

metal|l *m* (*-u; -e*) metal; *mus.* heavy-metal; **~liczny** metallic; **~lowiec** *m* (*-wca; -wcy*) metalworker; **~lowy** metal

metan *m* (*-u; -y*) methane

meteorologiczny meteorologic(al)

meteor *m* (*-u; -y*) meteor; **~yt** *m* (*-u; -y*) meteorite

metka[1] *f* (*-i; G -tek*) (soft) sausage

metka[2] *f* (*-i; G -tek*) label, tag

meto|da *f* (*-y; G -*) method; **~dyczny** methodical; **~dysta** *m* (*-y; -ów*), **~dystka** *f* (*-i; G -tek*) *rel.* Methodist

metr *m* (*-a; -y*) *Brt.* metre, *Am.* meter

metraż *m* (*-u; -e*) area (in metres); *krótki ~ zbior.* short film

metro *n* (*-a, 0*) *Brt.* underground, *Am.* subway

metrowy *Brt.* metre, *Am.* meter

metryka *f* (*-i; G -*) (*ślubu, urodzenia, zgonu, chrztu*) wedding, birth, death, baptismal) certificate

metylowy methyl

Metys *m* (*-a; -i*) mestizo; **~ka** *f* (*-i*) mestiza

mewa *f* (*-y; G -*) gull; **~ śmieszka** black-headed gull

męcz|arnia *f* (*-i; -e*) agony, torment, torture; **~ący** (*-co*) tiring; *fig.* trying;

~ennik *m* (*-a; -cy*), **~ennica** *f* (*-e; G-*) martyr (*też rel.*); **~eński** martyr's; **~yć** (*-ę*) torment; **~yć się** suffer; ⟨**z-**⟩ tire, make tired; *oczy itp.*: strain; **~yć się** get tired; *też* **~yć się** slave away (**nad** *I* over)

mędr|ek *m* (*-rka; -rki/-rkowie*) F smart aleck; **~rzec** *m* (*-drca, -drcy/-drcowie*) sage, savant

męka *f* (*-i; G mąk*) torment, torture, agony

męs|ki male; masculine, manly; *gr.* masculine; *po ~ku* like a man; **~kość** *f* (*-ci; 0*) masculinity, manhood, virility; **~two** *n* (*-a; 0*) bravery, valo(u)r

męt|lik *m* (*-a; -i*) confusion, mess; **~nieć** ⟨**z-**⟩ (*-eję*) become cloudy/opaque; **~ny** cloudy; opaque; **~y** *pl.* (*-ów*) dregs *pl.*

mężatk|a *f* (*-i; G -tek*) married woman; *ona jest ~ą* she is married

mę|czyzna *m* (*-y; G -*) man, male; **~ny** brave, valiant, valorous; **~owski** husband's

mglisty (*-ście*) foggy, misty; *fig.* vague, hazy

mgła *f* (*-y, DL mgle; -y, G mgieł*) fog, mist; *zajść mgłą* mist up; **~wica** *f* (*-y; G -wic*) nebula

mgnieni|e *n* (*-a; G -eń*): *na ~e* for a moment; *w ~u oka* in no time

mgr *skrót pisany:* **magister** MA (*Master of Arts*)

mi *pron.* (*ściągn. D*) → **mnie**

miał[1], **~a**, **~o** → **mieć**

miał[2] *m* (*-u; -y*) dust, powder; **~ki** fine

miano *n* (*-a; G -*) *lit.* name; → **nazwa**; **~wać** (*-uję*) appoint (*I* as), nominate; **~wicie** namely; *a ~wicie* to be precise; **~wnik** *m* (*-a; -i*) *gr.* nominative; *math.* denominator

miar|a *f* (*-y; G -*) measurement, measure; *bez ~y* boundless; *szyty na ~ę* made to measure; *nad ~ę* beyond measure; *w ~ę* moderately; *w ~ę jak* as; *w ~ę możliwości/potrzeby* as the need arises; *w pewnej mierze* to some extent; *w dużej mierze* to a great extent; *ze wszech miar* by all means; *żadną ~ą* by no means; **~ka** *f* (*-i; G -rek*) measure

miarkować (*-uję*) (*się*) contain (o.s.), restrain (o.s.), control (o.s.)

miaro|dajny authoritative; **~wy** rhythmic

miasteczko *n (-a; G -czek)* → *miasto*; **wesołe ~** amusement park, *Brt.* funfair

miast|o *n (-a, L mieście; G -)* town, city; **jechać do ~a** go to town; **~o portowe** port

miauczeć *(-czę)* meow

miazga *f (-i; G -)* pulp

miażdży|ca *f (-y; 0) med.* sclerosis, *zwł.* arteriosclerosis; **~ć ⟨z-⟩** *(-ę)* crush, squash; *fig.* overwhelm

miąć ⟨wy-, z-⟩ *(mnę)* crumple, crease **(się** *v/i.)*

miąższ *m (-u; 0)* pulp, flesh

miech *m (-u; -y)* bellows *sg. lub pl.*

miecz *m (-a; -e)* sword; *naut. Brt.* centreboard, *Am.* centerboard; **~nik** *m (-a; -i) zo.* swordfish; *(orka)* orc, killer whale; **~yk** *m (-a; -i) bot.* gladiolus

mieć have, possess; *(+ bezok.)* be going to; *(tu)* **masz, macie ...** here is, here are ...; **nie ma** there is not; **~ na sobie** have on, wear; **~ 40 lat** be 40 years old; **nie ma za co** you are welcome; **~ miejsce** take place; **~ za złe** take amiss; **masz ci los!** there we are!; **ja miałbym to zrobić?** I am supposed to do it?; **miano tu budować dom** a house was to be built here; **nie ma jak ...** there is nothing like ...; **on ma się dobrze** he is fine; **jak się masz?** how are you?; **nie ma się czego wstydzić** there is nothing to be ashamed of; **ma się na deszcz** it looks like rain; **on ma się za artystę** he considers himself an artist; **~ się ku** it is going to; → **baczność, lata**

miednic|a *f (-y; G -)* bowl; *anat.* pelvis; **~owy** *anat.* pelvic

miedza *f (-y; G -)* balk

miedziany copper

miedzioryt *m (-u; -y)* copperplate engraving

miedź *f (-dzi; 0) chem.* copper

miej|cie → **mieć**

miejsc|e *n (-a; G -)* place **(na** *A,* **do** *G* for); position, location; space, room; seat *(też fig.)*; **~e pracy** workplace; **~e zbrodni** scene of the crime; **~e spotkania** meeting place, rendezvous; **na ~u** there and then; on the spot; **na twoim ~u** if I were you; **w ~e** in place of; **w tym ~u** at this place; **z ~a** at once; **ustąpić ~a** make room; *fig.* give way; → **pobyt, przeznaczenie; ~ami** in place

miejscownik *m (-a; -i) gr.* locative

miejscow|ość *f (-ści)* locality, place; **~y** local; *(w sporcie)* home

miejs|cówka *f (-i; G -wek) rail.* seat reservation (ticket); **~ki** urban, municipal; *(po -ku)* town; **rada ~ka** town council

miel|ą, ~e(sz), ~ę, ~i → **mleć**

mielisz|cie, ~my → **mieć**

mielizna *f (-y; G -)* shallow; **osiąść na ~źnie** run aground

mielon|y minced; **mięso ~e** minced meat, *Brt.* mince

mienić się *(-nię)* shimmer

mienie *n (-a; 0)* property; **~ społeczne** common property

miern|iczy 1. measuring; **2.** *m (-ego; -owie)* land surveyor; **~ik** *m (-a; -i)* measure; *tech.* measuring instrument; *fig.* yardstick; **~ik wartości** standard; **~ość** *f (-ści; 0)* mediocrity; **~y** mediocre

mierz|eja *f (-i; -e)* sandbar

mierzić *[-rz-] (t-ko 3. os. -i)* feel with digust

mierzwić ⟨z-⟩ *(-wię)* tousle, ruffle

mierzy|ć ⟨z-⟩ *(-ę)* measure; *suknię* try on; **~ wzrokiem** eye; **nie móc się ~ z** be no match for; *v/i.* take aim **(do** *G* at)

mies. *skrót pisany:* **miesiąc** m. *(month)*; **~ięczny** monthly; **~ięcznik** *m* monthly

miesiąc *m (-a; -e)* month; **raz na ~** once a month; **za ~** in a month; **~ami** for months on end

miesiączk|a *f (-i; G -czek)* menstruation, period; **mieć ~ę** have a period, menstruate

miesić ⟨wy-⟩ *(-szę)* knead

miesięcz|nik *m (-a; -i)* monthly; **~y** monthly

miesza|ć *(-am)* **⟨za-⟩** stir; **⟨z-⟩** mix together, blend; **⟨w-⟩** add **(do** *G* to); *fig.* drag into; involve; **~ć się** interfere **(do** *G* in), intervene; **~dło** *n (-a; G -del)* mixer; **~niec** *m (-ńca; -ńce/-ńcy)* mongrel; *(też -ńcy)* half-caste; **~nina** *f (-y; G -)* mixture; **~nka** *f (-i; G -nek)* mixture; blend, assortment

mieszczań|ski middle-class; **~stwo** *n (-a; G -)* middle class, bourgeoisie

mieszka|ć *(-am)* live; inhabit; **~lny** inhabitable, habitable; **~nie** *n (-a; G -ań) Brt.* flat, *Am.* apartment; home; **~niec** *m (-ńca; -ńcy),* **~nka** *f (-nki; G -nek)* inhabitant, resident; **~niowy** housing;

M

dzielnica residential; → **głód**

mieśc|ić (-*szczę*) contain, hold; accommodate; **~ć się** fit; ⟨*po-*, *z-*⟩ fit in; *budynek*: house; **~na** *f* (-*y*; *G* -) little town

miewać (-*am*) have from time to time

mię (*ściągn. GA*) → **mnie**

mięczak *m* (-*a*; -*i*) *pej.* softy, pushover; *zo. Brt.* mollusc, *Am.* mollusk

międlić F (-*lę*) → **miąć, ględzić**

między *prp.* (*I*, *A*) between, among; **~ innymi** among other things; **~czas** *m*: **w ~czasie** in the meantime; **~kontynentalny** intercontinental; **~ludzki** interpersonal; **~miastowy: rozmowa ~miastowa** long-distance call, trunk call; **~narodowy** international; **~wojenny** interwar

mięk|czyć ⟨*z-*⟩ (-*ę*) make soft; soften (*też fig.*); *gr.* palatalize; **~isz** *m* (-*a*; -*e*) (bread)crumb; *biol.* parenchyma; **~ki** (*m-os -kcy*) soft; *mięso* tender; *fig.* wet; *gr.* palatalized; **jajko na ~ko** soft-boiled egg; **~kość** *f* (-*ści*; 0) softness; **~nąć** ⟨*z-*⟩ (-*nę*) become soft, soften

mię|sień *m* (-*śnia*; -*śnie*) muscle; **~sisty** meaty; *fig.* brawny; **~sny** meat; **~so** *n* (-*a*; *G mięs*) meat, flesh; **~sożerny** carnivorous; **~śniowy** muscular

mię|ta *f* (-*y*; *G mięt*) mint, (*zwł. pieprzowa*) peppermint; **~tosić** (-*szę*) → **miąć**; **~towy** mint, peppermint

mig *m* (-*u*; -*i*): **na ~i** by signs, in sign language; **w ~** in an instant; **~acz** *mot. Brt.* indicator, *Am.* turn signal; **~ać** (-*am*) flash; *lampa*: flicker; → **przemykać**

migawk|a *f* (-*i*; *G* -*wek*) *phot.* shutter; *fig.* **~i** *pl.* scenes *pl.*; **~owy** shutter

migdał *m* (-*a*; -*y*) *bot.* almond; **~ek** *m* → migdał; *anat.* tonsil; **~owy** almond

mig|nąć *v/s.* (-*nę*) → **migać**; **~otać** (-*czę/-cę*) flicker, waver; **~owy** sign

migracja *f* (-*i*; -*e*) migration

migrena *f* (-*y*; *G* -) migraine

mija|ć (-*am*) *v/t.* pass; *v/i.* pass by, go by; **~ć się** pass each other; *listy*: cross; *fig.* (**z** *I*) miss; **~ć się z prawdą** depart from the truth; **... go nie minie** he will not escape ...; **~nka** *f* (-*i*; *G* -*nek*) passing place; *rail.*, *mot.* turnout

mika *f* (-*i*; 0) mica

Mikołaj *m* (-*a*; -*e*) *też* **św(ięty)** ~ *jakby*: Santa Claus, Father Christmas

mikro|bus *m* (-*u*; -*y*) minibus; **~element** *m* (-*u*; -*y*) trace element; **~fala** *f* (-*i*; -*e*) microwave; **~falowy** microwave; **~falówka** *f* (-*i*) F microwave (oven); **~fon** *m* (-*u*; -*y*) microphone; **~komputer** *m* (-*a*; -*y*) *komp.* microcomputer; **~procesor** *m* (-*a*; -*y*) *komp.* microprocessor; **~skop** *m* (-*u*; -*y*) microscope; **~skopijny**, **~skopowy** microscopic

mikrus *m* (-*a*; -*y*) little one

mikser *m* (-*a*; -*y*) mixer; *gastr. też* liquidizer; *Brt.* blender; *RTV*: mixing desk

mila *f* (-*i*; -*e*) mile; **~ morska** nautical mile

milcz|ący silent; implicit; **~eć** (-*czę*) be silent; **~enie** *n* (-*a*; 0) silence; **chwila ~enia** minute's silence; **pominąć ~eniem** pass over in silence; **~kiem** *adv.* stealthily, secretively

mile *adv.* kindly; (*ładnie*) pretty; **~ widziany** welcome

miliard *m* (-*a*; -*y*) billion, *Brt. też* milliard; **~owy** billionth; **jedna ~owa** one billionth

milicja *f* (-*i*; 0) (Communist) police; **~nt** *m* (-*a*; -*nci*) policeman

mili|gram *m* (-*u*; -*y*) milligram; **~metr** *m* (-*a*; -*y*)*Brt.* millimetre, *Am.* millimeter; **~on** *m* (-*a*; -*y*) million; **~oner** *m* (-*a*; -*rzy*), **~onerka** *f* (-*i*; *G* -*rek*) millionaire; **~onowy** millionth **jedna ~onowa** one millionth

militarystyczny militaristic

milk|nąć ⟨*za-*⟩ (-*nę*, -[*ną*]*ł*) fall silent; *fig.* calm down

milowy mile

mil|szy *adv. comp. od* → **miły**; **~uchny**, **~utki** nice

miło *adv.* pleasantly, agreeably; kind(ly); **~ mi** pleased to meet you; **~sierdzie** *n* (-*a*; 0) mercy, charity; **~sierny** merciful, charitable; **~sny** love; **~stka** *f* (-*i*; *G* -*tek*) (love) affair; **~ść** *f* (-*ści*) love; **~śniczka** *f* (-*i*; *G* -*czek*), **~śnik** *m* (-*a*; -*cy*) (*sztuki*) lover; (*sportu*) fan; **~wać** (-*uję*) *lit.* love

miły (-*le*, -*ło*) kind; pleasant, agreeable; (*drogi*) dear

mimo *cj.* (*G*) in spite of; despite; **~ to** nevertheless; **~ wszystko** all the same; **~ że**, **~ iż** though, although; → **pomimo, wola**; **~chodem** *adv.* in passing; **~wolny** involuntary

m.in. *skrót pisany:* **między innymi** among others

mina[1] *f* (-*y*; *G* -) face

mina² *f* (*-y*; *G* -) *mil.* mine

miną*ć pf.* (*-nę, -ń*) go by, pass by → **mijać**

minera|lny mineral; *~ł m* (*-u, -y*) mineral

mini *f* (*idkl.*) *w złoż.* mini; F mini(skirt); *~*aturowy (*-wo*) miniature; *~*malny minimum, minimal; *~*mum **1.** *n* (*idkl.*; *-a, -mów*) minimum; **2.** *adv.* at least

miniony last; past

mini|**ówa** F *f* (*-wy*) mini; *~*spódniczka *f* (*-i*; *G -czek*) miniskirt

minister *m* (*-tra*; *-trowie*) minister, secretary; *rada ministrów* Council of Ministers; *~*alny ministerial; *~*stwo *n* (*-a*; *G* -) (*sprawiedliwości*) ministry (of justice)

minorowy *mus.* minor; (*-wo*) gloomy

minować ⟨*za-*⟩ (*-nuję*) *mil.* mine

minus *m* (*-a*; *-y*) *math.* minus (sign); (*-u*; *-y*) minus; *plus ~* give or take; *2 ~ 1 2* minus/less 1; *~*owy minus; negative; below zero

minut|a *f* (*-y*; *G* -) minute; *za ~ę* in a minute; *co do ~y* to a minute; *~*owy minute; *wskazówka* big

miodow|nik *m* (*-a*; *-i*) *gastr.* honey cake; *~y* honey; *miesiąc ~y* honeymoon

miot *m* (*-u*; *-y*) *zo.* litter; *~*acz *m* (*-a*; *-e*), *~*aczka *f* (*-i*; *G -czek*) thrower; *~acz kulą* (*w sporcie*) shot putter; *~acz gazu* (Chemical) Mace; *~acz płomieni* flame thrower; *~*ać (*-am*) hurl, throw; *~*ła *f* (*-y*; *G -teł*) broom, brush

miód *m* (*miodu*; *miody*) honey; *~ pitny* mead

miraż *m* (*-u*; *-e*) mirage; *fig.* illusion

mirt *m* (*-u*; *-y*) *bot.* myrtle

misja *f* (*-i*; *-e*) mission

miska *f* (*-i*; *G -sek*) bowl; *~ klozetowa* toilet bowl

Missisipi (*idkl.*) Mississippi

misterny elaborate, delicate

mistrz *m* (*-a*; *-owie, -ów*) master; (*w sporcie*) champion; *~ Polski* Polish champion

mistrzo|stwo *n* (*-a*; *G* -) mastery; (*w sporcie*) championship; *~*wski masterful, masterly; champion; *po ~wsku* expertly

mistrzyni *f* (*-ni*; *-nie, -ń*) master; (*w sporcie*) champion

misty|fikować (*-uję*) deceive; mystify; *~*czka *f* (*-i*; *G -czek*), *~*k *m* (*-a*; *-cy*) mystic; *~*ka *f* (*-i*; *0*) mysticism

misyjny missionary

miś *m* (*-sia*; *-sie*) (*zabawka*) teddy-bear; (*w bajkach*) bruin

mit *m* (*-u*; *-y*) myth; *~*ologiczny mythological

mitręga *f* (*-i*; *G* -) waste of time

mityczny mythical

mitygować (*-uję*) calm, mollify

mizdrzyć się F (*-rzę*) (*do* G) letch after

mi'zer|ia *f* (*GDL -ii*; *-e*) *gastr.* cucumber salad; *~*nieć ⟨*z-*⟩ (*-nję*) waste away; grow thin; *~*ny poor; paltry

m-ka *skrót pisany:* **marka** make; mark

mknąć (*-knę*) hurry (along)

MKOl *skrót pisany:* **Międzynarodowy Komitet Olimpijski** IOC (*International Olympic Committee*)

mkw. *skrót pisany:* **metr kwadratowy** sq. m. (*square metre*)

mlas|kać (*-skam*) F slurp; ⟨*~nąć*⟩ (*-nę*) click one's tongue

mld *skrót pisany:* **miliard** billion

mlecz *m* (*-a*; *-e*) *bot.* sow-thistle; F (*mniszek*) dandelion; *zo.* milt, soft roe; *~*ar-nia *f* (*-i*; *-e*) dairy; *~*arstwo *n* (*-a*; *0*) dairy industry; dairying; *~*arz *m* (*-a*; *-e*) milkman; *~*ko *n* (*-a*; *G -czek*) milk; *~*ny milk; milky

mleć ⟨*ze-*⟩, mielić grind, mill; *~ językiem* chatter

mleko *n* (*-a*; *0*) milk; *~ pełne* full-cream milk; *~ w proszku* powdered milk; *na mleku* *gastr.* milk; *~*dajny dairy

mln *skrót pisany:* **milion** m (*million*)

mł. *skrót pisany:* **młodszy** the younger

młocarnia *f* (*-i*; *-e*) threshing machine

młocka *f* (*-i*; *G -cek*) threshing

młod|e *n* (*-ego*; *-e*) young, baby; → *młody*; *~*nieć (*-eję*) get younger

młodo *adv.* young; *~*ciany *jur.* **1.** juvenile; **2.** *m* (*-nego*; *-ni*), *~ciana f* (*-nej*; *-ne*) juvenile; *~*ść *f* (*-ci*; *0*) youth; *nie pierwszej ~ści* not young any more

młod|szy *adj.* (*comp. od* → *młody*; *m-os -dsi*) younger; *~*y young; *ziemniak, wino* new; *mięso* tender; *pan ~y* (*bride*)groom; *panna ~a* bride; *za ~u* in one's youth

młodzie|j *adv. comp. od* → *młodo*; *~*niec *m* (*-ńca*; *-ńcy*) youth, boy, young man, adolescent; *~*ńczy (*-czo, po -czemu*) youthful; *~*ż *f* (*-y*; *0*) the young *pl.*; *~ż szkolna* school children; *~*żowy youth

młodzik *m* (*-a*; *- i*) youngster

młodziutki very young

młokos *m* (*-a; -y*) *pej. Brt.* pup

młot *m* (*-a; -y*) hammer; **~ pneuma- tyczny** pneumatic drill; **walić jak ~em** pound; **~ek** *m* (*-tka; -tki*) hammer

młócić ⟨**wy-**⟩ (*-cę*) thresh

młyn *m* (*-a; -y*) mill; **~arka** *f* (*-i; G -rek*), **~arz** *m* (*-a; -e*) miller; **~ek** *m* (*-nka; -nki*) mill; **~ek do kawy** coffee grinder

młyński mill; **koło ~e** millstone

mną[1] *pron.* (*I → ja*); **ze ~** with me

mną[2] *3. os. pl. pres.* → **miąć**

mnich *m* (*-a; -si*) monk

mnie[1] *pron.* (*GA → ja*) me; (*DL → ja*) me; **o ~** about me; **u ~** with me

mnie[2] *3. os. pl. sg.* → **miąć**

mniej *adv.* (*comp. od → mało*) less, fewer; **~ więcej** more or less; **~szość** *f* (*-ści*) minority; **~szy** *adj.* (*comp. od → mały*) smaller (*od G* than); lesser; **~sza o to/z tym** never mind

mniema|**ć** (*-am*) believe; **~nie** *n* (*-a*) belief; **w ~niu** też on the assumption

mni|**si** → **mnich**; *adj.* monastic; **~szek** *m* (*-szka; -szki*) *bot.* dandelion; **~szka** *f* (*-i; G -szek*) nun; *zo.* nun moth

mnog|**i** (*m-os mnodzy*) numerous; → **liczba**; **~ość** *f* (*-ści; 0*) multitude

mnoż|**enie** *n* (*-a*) reproduction; *math.* multiplication; **~na** *f* (*-nej; -ne*) *math.* multiplicand; **~nik** *m* (*-a; -i*) *math.* multiplier; **~yć** ⟨**po-**⟩ (*-żę*) multiply (też *math.*; **się** *v/i.*)

mnóstwo *n* (*-a; 0*) lots of

mobil|**izacja** *f* (*-i; -e*) mobilisation; **~izować** ⟨**z-**⟩ mobilize; **~ny** mobile

moc *f* (*-y; -e*) power; *jur.* force; F lots of; **nabierać ~y** take effect; **wszystko, co w jego ~y** all in his power; **na ~y** (*G*) on the strength (of), in virtue (of); **~ą** (*G*) by virtue (of); **~ alkoholu** proof; **~arstwo** *n* (*-a; G -*) power; **wiel- kie ~arstwo** superpower; **~niej(szy)** *adv.* (*adj.*) (*comp. od → mocno, moc- ny*) more powerful, stronger; **~no** *adv.* very, hard; **~ny** powerful, strong; *ból* sharp; *chwyt itp.* firm, tight

mocować ⟨**przy-, u-**⟩ (*-uję*) attach, fix (*do G* to); **~ się** wrestle (też *fig.*)

mocz *m* (*-u; -e*) urine

moczary *m/pl.* (*-ów*) marsh, swamp

mocznik *m* (*-a; 0*) *chem.* urea

moczo|**pędny** diuretic; **~wód** *m* (*-odu; -ody*) *anat.* ureter; **~wy** uretic

moczyć (*-czę*) ⟨**z-**⟩ wet; ⟨**za-**⟩ soak; wa- ter; *impf.* **~ się** soak; (*moczem*) water

mod|**a** *f* (*-y; G mód*) fashion, vogue; **wyjść z ~y** go out of fashion

model *m* (*-u; -e*) model; *tech.* mock-up; **~arstwo** *n* (*-a; G -*) model making; **~ka** *f* (*-i; G -lek*) model; **~ować** (*-uję*) model; *włosy* style

modem *m* (*-u; -y*) modem; **~owy** modem

moderni|**zacja** *f* (*-i; -e*) modernisation; **~zować** ⟨**z-**⟩ (*-uję*) modernize, update

modli|**ć się** ⟨**po- się**⟩ (*-ę; módl!*) pray (*do G* to); **~twa** *f* (*-y; G -*) prayer

modł|**a** *f* (*-y; -deł*); **na ~ę** (*G*) after the fashion (of); **~y** *pl.* (*-ów*) prayers *pl.*

modrzew *m* (*-ia; -ie*) *bot.* larch; **~iowy** larch

moduł *m* (*-u; -y*) module (też *math.*); unit; *phys.* modulus; **~owy** modular

modyfik|**acja** *f* (*-i; -e*) modification; **~ować** ⟨**z-**⟩ (*-uję*) modify

modzel *m* (*-a; -e*) *med.* callus

mogił|**a** *f* (*-y; G -*) grave; **~ wspólna** mass grave

mog|**ą, ~ę, ~li, ~łam, ~łem** → **móc**

mohair, moher *m* (*-u; 0*) mohair

moi, moja, moje → **mój**

mojżeszowy Mosaic

mok|**nąć** ⟨**z-**⟩ (*-nę, nął/mókł*) get wet; *impf.* soak; **~ry** (*-ro*) wet

moll *m* (*idkl.*) *mus.* minor; **c-moll** C- -minor

molo *n* (*idkl./-a; G mol*) pier, jetty

moloodporny moth-resistant

moment *m* (*-u; -y*) moment; **za ~** in a moment; **~alnie** at once, immediately, instantaneously; **~alny** immediate, in- stantaneous

Monachium *n* (*idkl.*) Munich

monarch|**a** *m* (*-y; -owie*) monarch; **~ia** *f* (*GDL -ii; -e*) monarchy; **~istyczny** monarchist

monet|**a** *f* (*-y; G -*) coin; **brać coś za dobrą ~ę** take s.th. at its face value

Mongo|**lia** *f* (*GDL -ii; 0*) Mongolia; **~lski** Mongolian

monit *m* (*-u; -y*) reminder; **~ować** (*-uję*) remind

mono (*idkl.*) mono, *w złoż.* mono-; **~'grafia** *f* (*GDl -ii; -e*) monograph; **~gram** *m* (*-u; -y*) monogram; **~partyj- ny** mono-party; **~pol** *m* (*-u; -e*) *econ.*, *pol.* monopoly; **~polowy: sklep ~po- lowy** *Brt.* off-licence, *Am.* liquor store;

~tonny monotonous

monstrualny monstrous

monsun m (-u; -y) monsoon

montaż m (-u; -e) tech. assembly, installation; phot. editing; ~owy editing; assembly; ~ysta m (-y; -ści), ~ystka f (-y; G -tek) phot., RTV: editor

monter m (-a; -rzy) mechanic; fitter; ~ instalacji wodociągowych plumber

montować (-uję) ⟨z-⟩ assemble; install; erect; phot., RTV: edit; ⟨za-⟩ fix, put up, build in

mora|lność f (-ci; 0) morality; ~lny moral; ~l m (-u; -y) moral, maxim

mord m (-u; -y) murder

morda f (G -; -y) muzzle; F gob, mug

morder|ca m (-y; G -ów), ~czyni f (-i; -nie, -ń) murderer; ~czy (-czo) murderous; ~stwo n (a; G -) murder

mordęga F f (-i G -) toil; drudgery

mordować (-uję) ⟨po-, za-⟩ murder; ⟨z-⟩ exhaust, tire, strain; ~ (na-, z-) się get tired; struggle (z I, przy I with); ⟨z-⟩ pf. też be dead tired

morel|a f (-i; -e) bot. apricot; ~owy apricot

morfin|a f (-y; 0) morphine; ~izować się (-uję) take morphine

morfo'logia f (GDl -ii; 0) bot., gr. morphology

morowy pestilential; ~ chłop Brt. great bloke, Am. great chap

mors m (-a; -y) bot. walrus

mor|ski sea; naval; maritime; marine; drogą ~ską by sea; ~szczuk m (-a; -i) zo. hake; ~świn m (-a; -y) zo. porpoise

morwa f (-y; G morw) bot. mulberry

morz|e n (-a; G mórz) sea; pełne ~e the high seas; nad ~em (wakacje itp.) at the seaside; wyjść w ~e put to sea; na ~u at sea; → poziom

Morze Karaibskie n the Caribbean Sea

Morze Śródziemne n the Mediterranean Sea

morzyć (-ę) v/i. ⟨z-⟩ sen: overcome; v/t. ~ głodem ⟨za-⟩ starve

mosiądz m (-u; 0) brass

mosiężny brass

moskit m (-a; -y) mosquito; ~iera f (-y; G -) mosquito net

Moskwa f (-y; 0) Moscow

most m (-u; -y) bridge; ~ zwodzony drawbridge; prosto z ~u without beating about the bush; ~ek m (-a -ku; -tki) bridge; → kapitański; ~owy bridge

moszcz m (-u; 0) new wine

moszn|a f (-y; G -) anat. scrotum; ~owy scrotal

mot|ać (-am) wind, entangle; ~ać się get entangled; ~ek m (-a -tka; -tki) skein

motel m (-u; -e) motel

motłoch m (-u; -y) mob, rabble

motocykl m (-a; -e) motorcycle; ~ista m (-y; -ści), ~istka f (-i; G -tek) motorcyclist; ~owy motorcycle

motor m (-u; -y) engine, motor; F cycle, bike; ~niczy m (-ego; -owie), -cza f (-ej; -e) tram-driver

motorow|er m (-u; -y) moped, light motorcycle; ~iec m (-wca; -wce) motor ship; ~y motor, engine

motorówka f (-i; G -wek) motor boat

motory|zacyjny motor, automobile, automotive; ~zować ⟨z-⟩ (-uję) motorize; być zmotoryzowanym have a car, have wheels; ~zować się get a car, get o.s. wheels

motyka f (-i; G -) hoe

motyl m (-a; -e) butterfly

motyw m (-u; -y) (postępku) motive; (literacki) motif; theme; ~ować ⟨u-⟩ (-uję) coś give a reason for; kogoś motivate

mow|a f (-y; G mów) speech; language; tongue; wygłosić ~ę deliver a speech; ~a ojczysta mother tongue; w ~ie orally; nie ma ~y! F no way!

mozaika f (-i; G -) mosaic; fig. patchwork

mozol|ić się (-lę, -zól!) (nad I) labo(u)r (over), toil (over); ~ny laborious

moździerz m (-a; -e) mil., gastr. mortar

może 3. os. sg. pres. → móc; adv. maybe; być ~ perhaps; ~ byśmy usiedli why don't we sit down?; ~cie, ~my, ~sz → móc

możliw|ie adv. possibly; ~ość f (-ści; 0) possibility, chance; ~y possible, likely; F not too bad, fair enough; ~y do (G) -able; ~y do realizacji implementable, realisable; robić wszystko co ~e do whatever is possible

można one can/may...; nie ~ one must not..., one cannot...; ~ by one could...; jak ~ najlepiej as good as possible

możność f (-ci; 0) possibility, opportunity, chance

możny affluent, opulent

móc can, may; be able to; be allowed to

M

mój (*moja f, moje n, moi m-os/pl., moje f/pl.*) my, mine; **to moje** that's mine; **moi** my family

mól *m* (*mola; mole*) moth

mów|ca *m* (*-y; G -ów*), **~czyni** *f* (*-i; -e*) speaker; **~ić** (*-ę*) speak, say; talk, tell; **~ić po angielsku** speak English; **~ią, że** they say that, it is said that; **szcze-rze ~iąc** to be frank; **szkoda ~ić** it is not even worth talking about; **nie ma o czym ~ić** don't mention it; **to ~i samo za siebie** it speaks for itself; **~ienie** *n* (*-a; 0*) speaking; **~nica** *f* (*-y; -e*) rostrum, platform

mózg *m* (*-u; -i*) brain (*też fig.*); F **padło mu na ~** he is off his rocker; **~owy** cerebral (*też fig.*)

MPK *skrót: Miejskie Przedsiębiorstwo Komunikacyjne* Municipal Transport Company

mro|czny (*-no*) dark; *fig.* gloomy; **~k** *m* (*-u; -i*) dark, darkness; *fig.* gloom; **za-pada ~k** dusk is falling

mrowi|ć się (*-ę*) swarm, teem; **~e** *n* (*-a; 0*) → **mnóstwo**; **~sko** *n* (*-a; G-*) ant-hill

mrozić (*-żę*) ⟨**z-**⟩ freeze (*też fig.*), chill

mrozoodporny frost-resistant

mroźn|o *adv.*: **jest ~o** it is freezing; **~y** frosty, icy

mrożon|ki *f/pl.* (*-nek*) frozen food; **~ka warzywna** frozen vegetables *pl.*; **~y** frozen, deep-frozen

mrówk|a *f* (*-i; G -wek*) *zo.* ant; **~owiec** *m* (*-wca; -wce*) F high-rise block

mróz *m* (*-ozu; -y*) frost

mru|czeć (*-ę, -y*) murmur; mutter; *kot:* purr; **~gać** (*-am*) ⟨**~gnąć**⟩ blink; *gwiazda:* twinkle; (**do** *G*, **na** *A*) wink (to, at); **~k** *m* (*-a; -i*) grouch, grumbler; **~kliwy** (*-wie*) grumpy, grouchy; **~knąć** *v/s.* (*-nę*) → **mruczeć**

mrużyć (*-żę*) ⟨**z-**⟩: **~ oczy** squint

mrzonka *f* (*-i; G -nek*) pipe-dream, daydream

m.st. *skrót: miasto stołeczne* capital city

MSW *skrót: Ministerstwo Spraw Wewnętrznych* Ministry of Interior; *Brt.* HO (*Home Office*)

MSZ *skrót: Ministerstwo Spraw Zagranicznych* Ministry of Foreign Affairs; *Brt.* FO (*Foreign Office*)

msz|a *f* (*-y; msze*) *rel.* Mass, service; **słu-żyć do ~y** serve at Mass; **dać na ~ę**

have a Mass said; **iść na ~ę** go to Mass; **~ał** *m* (*-u; -y*) *rel.* missal

mszcząą, ~ę → **mścić**

mszyca *f* (*-y; -e*) *zo.* aphid, greenfly

mści|ciel *m* (*-a; -e*), **-lka** *f* (*-i; G -lek*) avenger; **~ć** ⟨**po-**⟩ avenge, take revenge for; **~ć się** take one's revenge (**za** *A* for); **~wość** *f* (*-ci; -*) revengefulness, vindictiveness; **~wy** (*-wie*) revengeful, vindictive

MTP *skrót pisany: Międzynarodowe Targi Poznańskie* International Poznan Fair

mu *pron.* (*ściągn. jemu*) → **on**

much|a *f* (*-y; G -*) *zo.* fly; bow-tie; **~a nie siada** tip-top; **być pod ~ą** be tipsy

muchomór *m* (*-ora; -ory*) toadstool

mularski → **murarski**

mulisty muddy, slimy

multimedialny multimedia

muł[1] *m* (*-a; -y*) *zo.* mule

muł[2] *m* (*-u; -y*) mud, slime

mumia *f* (*-i; -e*) mummy

mundur *m* (*-u; -y*) uniform; **~owy** uniform

mur *m* (*-u; -y*) wall (*też fig.*); **~ pruski** half-timbering; **na ~** F for sure; **~arski** mason's; **~arstwo** *n* (*-a; 0*) bricklaying, masonry; **~arz** *m* (*-a; -e*) mason, bricklayer; **~ować** ⟨**wy-**⟩ (*-uję*) lay bricks; *budynek* build; **~owany** brick, stone; F dead-certain

Murzy|n *m* (*-a; -i*), **~nka** *f* (*-i; G -nek*) African; (*w USA*) Afro-American, Black; **£ński** Black

mus[1] *m* (*-u; -y*) *gastr.* mousse

mus[2] *m* (*-u; 0*) necessity; **z ~u** out of necessity; **~ieć** (*-szę*) have to, must

muskać (*-am*) brush

muskularny muscular

musnąć *v/s.* (*-nę*) → **muskać**

mus|ować (*-uję*) effervesce, fizz; **~ująą-cy** effervescent, fizzy; *wino* sparkling

muszk|a *f* (*-i; G -szek*) → **muskać**; *mil.* foresight; **wziąć na ~ę** take aim at

muszkat *m* (*-u; -y*) nutmeg; **~ołowy**: **gałka ~ołowa** nutmeg

muszla *m* (*-i; -e, -i/-szel*) shell; **~ kloze-towa** toilet bowl

musztard|a *f* (*-y; G -*) mustard; **~owy** mustard

musztr|a *f* (*-y; G -*) drill; **~ować** (*-uję*) drill

musz|y fly; **waga ~a** flyweight; **~e śla-**

dy fly droppings *pl.*
muśnięcie *n* (*-a*; *G -ęć*) brushing
muza *f* (*-y*) muse
muze|um *n* (*idkl.*; *-a, -ów*) museum; **~alny** museum
muzułma|nin *m* (*-a; -anie, -ów*), **~nka** *f* (*-i*; *G -nek*) Muslim; **~ński** Muslim
muzy|czny music(al), melodious; **~ka** *f* (*-a; -cy*) musician; **~ka** *f* (*-i; 0*) music; **~kalny** musical; **~kować** (*-uję*) play music, make music; **~kować na ulicy** *Brt.* busk
my *pron.* (*GAL nas*, *D nam*, *I nami*) we; *o* **nas** about us; *z* **nami** with us
myć (*-ję*) ⟨*u-*⟩ wash ⟨*się v/i. lub o.s.*⟩; *warzywa*, *kafelki* clean
myd|lany soap; **~lić** ⟨*na-*⟩ (*-lę*) soap ⟨*się o.s.*⟩; *mydło*: lather; **~lić oczy** dupe; **~liny** *pl.* (*G -*) suds *pl.*; **~ło** *n* (*-a*; *G -deł*) soap
myjnia *f* (*-i; -e*) car wash
myl|ić (*-lę*) ⟨*po-, z-*⟩ confuse, mix; **~ić** ⟨*o-, po-*⟩ **się** get confused, go wrong; be wrong; **~ny** mistaken, wrong

mysi mouse; *fig.* mousy
mysz *f* (*-y*), **~ka** *f* (*-i*; *G -szek*) mouse; **~kować** (*-uję*) snoop about, nose about
myśl *f* (*-i*) thought; idea; *w* **~** according to; **mieć na ~i** have in mind; *w* **~i** in mind; **wpaść na ~** hit on an idea; **przyjść na ~** come to mind; **być dobrej ~i** be in good spirits; **~ący** thinking; **~eć** ⟨*po-*⟩ (*-lę, -i*) think (*o L* of, about); **niewiele ~ąc** without thinking too much; **~enie** *n* (*-a; 0*) thinking; **sposób ~enia** way of thinking, mentality; **~iciel** *m* (*-a; -e*) thinker
myśli|stwo *n* (*-a; 0*) hunting; **~wiec** *m* (*-wca; -wce*) *mil.* fighter; (*-wca; -wcy*) hunter; **~wski** hunting; *mil.* fighter; **~wy** hunting
myśl|nik *m* (*-a; -i*) dash; **~owy** intellectual
MZK *skrót:* **Miejskie Zakłady Komunikacyjne** Municipal Transport Company
mżawka *f* (*-i; G -wek*) drizzle
mżyć: (*deszcz*) *mży* it is drizzling

N

n. *skrót pisany:* **nad** over, above
na *prp.* (*L*) *pozycja* on (**~ półce** on the shelf); in (**~ łóżku** in bed); **~ Litwie** in Lithuania); *istnienie* in (**~ piśmie** in writing); (*A*) *ruch*: on(to), on (**~ łóżko** on the bed), to (**~ Ukrainę** to (the) Ukraine); *okres*, *termin* in (**~ wiosnę** in spring), for (**~ Wielkanoc** for Easter; **~ dwa dni** for two days), on (**~ drugi dzień** on the next day); *miara* per (**raz ~ miesiąc** once a/per month); *cel* to, on, for (**iść ~ spacer** go for a walk); *skutek*, *przyczyna* at, with, about (**zachorować ~** be taken ill with; **skarżyć się ~** complain about); *przeznaczenie* for (**lekarstwo ~ kaszel** medicine for coughing); *rezultat* into (**dzielić ~ części** divide into parts); **~ końcu** ... in the end; finally; ...; *często nie tłumaczy się*: *miara* **głęboki ~ dwa metry** two metres deep; **~ dole** downstairs; *gra* **grać ~ flecie** play the flute; *przeznaczenie* **pojemnik ~ chleb** bread--bin; **złapać ~ kradzieży** catch steal-ing; → *odnośne rzeczowniki i czasowniki*
nabawi|ać się (*-am*) ⟨**~ć się**⟩ (*G*) catch, contract
nabiał *m* (*-u; 0*) dairy products *pl.*; **~owy** dairy
na|bić → **bić**, **nabijać**; **~biegać** ⟨**~biec, ~biegnąć**⟩ (*I*) *łzy*: well up; *rumieniec*: spread
nabierać (*-am*) (*G, A*) take; *powietrza*, *tchu* take in; *F* (*oszukiwać*) take in, kid; **~ znaczenia** gain importance; → **nabrać, siła**
nabijać (*-am*) (*wypełniać*) stuff full; *broń* load; **~ gwoździami** stud with nails; **~ się** (*z G*) → **drwić**
nabożeństwo *n* (*-a; G -w*) divine service; **~ny** pious
nabój *m* (*-boju; -boje, -boi*) charge; (*kula*) bullet; **ślepy ~** blank
nabrać *pf.* → **nabierać**; *F* **~ na kawał** take in; **dać się ~** fall for
nabrzeże *n* (*-a; G -y*) quay, wharf; embankment

na|brzmiały swollen; ~brzmiewać ⟨~mieć⟩ (-am) swell

naby|tek m (-tku; -tki) purchase, acquisition; ~wać ⟨~ć⟩ (-am) buy, purchase, acquire; ~wca m (-y) buyer, purchaser; ~wczy: siła ~wcza econ. purchasing power

na|chalny F cheeky, brazen; ~chmurzony frowning, grim

nachodzić (opanować) overcome; (odwiedzać) descend (up)on; ~ się tire o.s. by walking

nachy|lać (-am) ⟨~lić⟩ bend (się down); ~lony bent

nacią|ć → nacinać; ~gać (-am) ⟨~gnąć⟩ v/t. draw lub pull tight; koszulę itp. pull on; mięsień strain; F fig. → nabierać; v/i. herbata draw, brew

nacie|k m (-u; -i) med. (o)edema; ~kać (-am) ⟨~c, ~knąć⟩ leak in(to), flow in(to); ~rać (-am) v/t. run in; v/i. (na A) attack, assault

na|cięcie n (-a; G -ęć) score, notch, incision; ~cinać (-am) cut, incise

nacis|k m (-u; -i) pressure (też fig.); gr. stress; fig. z ~kiem with emphasis; ~kać ⟨~nąć⟩ press; guzik push; fig. pressurize

nacjonali|styczny nationalistic; ~zować (-uję) nationalize

nacz. skrót pisany: naczelny chief

naczeln|ik m (-a; -cy) head; chief; ~ik urzędu pocztowego postmaster; ~ik stacji stationmaster; ~ik urzędu policyjnego Am. marshal; ~y head; chief, foremost; supreme

naczyni|e n (-a; G -yń) vessel (też anat.); dish; ~a pl. crockery

nać f (-ci; -cie) tops pl.

naćpany F high (I on)

nad prp. (I) miejsce over, above; (przy) on, by (~ Wisłą on the Vistula, ~ morzem by the sea); ~ ranem towards morning; (A) kierunek to; ~ podziw astonishingly; →miara, wyraz, wszystko

nad. skrót pisany: nadawca sender

nada|ć pf. → nadawać; ~jnik m (-a; -i) transmitter

nadal adv. still

nada|remnie adv. to no effect, fruitlessly; ~remny futile, fruitless; ~rzać się (-am) ⟨~rzyć się⟩ okazja: occur

nadaw|ać list send; imię, kształt give; tytuł confer, bestow; RTV: broadcast;

~ać się (do G, na A) be fit (for); be suitable (for, to); ~anie n (-a; G -ań) RTV: broadcast; (tytułu) conferral; ~ca m (-y; G -ców), ~czyni f (-i; -e) sender; ~czy: zespół ~czy transmitter unit

nadą|ć pf. → nadymać; ~sany sulky; ~żać (-am) ⟨~żyć⟩ (za I) keep pace (with); nie ~żać też fall behind; fig. not be with s.o.

nad|bagaż m excess baggage; ~bałtycki Baltic; ~biegać ⟨~biec, ~biegnąć⟩ come running up; ~bity talerz chipped; ~brzeże n (-a; G -y) seafront

nadbudow|a f superstructure; ~(yw)ać (-uję) build on

nadchodz|ący approaching; ~ić (-dzę) approach, come up

nad|ciąć pf. → nacinać; ~ciągać (-am) ⟨~ciągnąć⟩ v/i. arrive; come up; burza: approach; ~cięcie n (-a; G -ć) incision, cut; ~cinać (-am) → nacinać; ~ciśnienie n (-a; G -ń) excess pressure; med. hypertension; ~czuły hypersensitive; ~czynność f (-ści; 0) med. hyperfunction; ~ciągać (-am) → nadrywać; ~dźwiękowy supersonic

nade → nad; ~drzeć pf., ~rwać → nadrywać

nadejś|cie n (-a) approach, coming; oncoming; ~ć pf. come, approach; → nadchodzić

na|deptać pf. (na A) tread (on), niechcący step (on); ~der adv. extremely, very, greatly; ~derwać pf. → nadrywać; F ~derwać się overstrain, sprain; ~desłać pf. → nadsyłać

nadetatowy supernumerary

nadęty → nadąsany, napuszony

nad|fioletowy ultraviolet; ~garstek m (-tka; -tki) wrist; ~godzina f (-y; G -) one hour's overtime; ~godziny f/pl. overtime; ~gorliwy officious; ~graniczny border, frontier; ~gryzać (-am) ⟨~gryźć⟩ bite into, take a bite of; ~jeżdżać (-am) ⟨~jechać⟩ come, arrive; ~latywać (-uję) ⟨~lecieć⟩ come flying up, arrive

nadleśni|ctwo n (-a; G -) forestry administration (office); ~czy m senior forestry officer

nadliczbow|y overtime; godziny f/pl. ~e overtime

nad|ludzki superhuman; ~łamywać (-uję) ⟨~łamać⟩ v/t. crack; ~miar m

nagromadzenie

(-*u*; *0*) (*G*) excess; surplus; *w ~miarze* in excess

nadmie|niać (-*am*) ⟨*~nić*⟩ mention

nadmierny excessive, surplus

nadmorski seaside

nadmuch|iwać (-*uję*) ⟨*~ać*⟩ blow up, inflate; *~iwany* inflated

nad|naturalny supernatural; *~obowiązkowy* optional; *~palać* (-*am*) ⟨*~palić*⟩ singe; *~pijać* (-*am*) ⟨*~pić*⟩ start drinking; *~piłow(yw)ać* (-[*w*]*uję*) start to saw; *~płacać* (-*am*) ⟨*~płacić*⟩ overpay; *~pływać* (-*am*) ⟨*~płynąć*⟩ → *przypływać*; *~produkcja* f (-*i*; *0*) overproduction, surplus

nadprogram *m* supporting program(me); *~owy* additional, surplus

nad|przyrodzony supernatural; → **nadnaturalny**;*~psuty* slightly spoiled; *mięso bad*; *~rabiać* (-*am*) ⟨*~robić*⟩ *czas* make up; *zaległości* catch up on, make up for; *~rabiać miną* put on a show of bravery; *~robić drogi* go a long way round

nadruk *m* (-*u*; -*i*) imprint

nad|rywać (-*am*) rip, tear; *~rywać się* strain o.s., overstrain; *~rzędny* overriding; higher; *~skakiwać* (-*uję*) (*D*) pay court to, toady; *~słuchiwać* (-*uję*) listen out for; *~spodziewany* surprise, startling, unanticipated; *~stawi(a)ć* (-*am*) hold out, *uszy* prick up (*też* fig.); *~stawi(a)ć głowy* take risks; *~stawka* f (-*i*; *G* -*wek*) top *lub* upper part; *~syłać* (-*am*) send in; *~szarpnąć* pf. fig. shatter; *zdrowie* ruin; *~tlenek* *m chem.* peroxide

nadto *adv.* moreover

naduży|cie *n* (-*cia*; *G* -*ć*) abuse, misuse; *jur.* embezzlement; *~cie podatkowe* tax evasion; *~(wa)ć* (*G*) abuse; *~wać alkoholu* drink too much

nad|waga f overweight, excess weight; *~wątlony* impaired, weakened

nadweręż|ać (-*am*) ⟨*~yć*⟩ (-*ę*) impair, weaken

nadwodny aquatic; above water level

nadworny court

nadwozie *n* (-*a*; *G* -*i*) *mot.* body

nad|wrażliwy hypersensitive;*~wyżka* f (-*i*; *G* -*żek*) surplus

na|dymać (-*am*) inflate, blow up; *~dymać się* puff o.s. up; *~dziać* pf. → *nadziewać* (-*am*)

nadzie|ja f (-*ei*; -*e*, -*ei*) hope; *mieć ~ję* hope; *w ~i/z ~ją, że* in the hope that; *przy ~i* with child

nadziemny above ground, overhead

nadziemski ethereal; supernatural

nadzie|nie *n* (-*a*; *G* -*ń*) *gastr.* filling, stuffing; *~wać* (-*am*) *gastr.* (*nadzieniem*) fill, stuff (*I* with); impale (*się na* o.s. on); *~wany* filled

nadzor|ca *m* (-*y*; *GA* -*ców*), *~czyni* f (-*i*; -*nie*, -*ń*) warder, supervisor; *~czy* supervising, supervisory; *~ować* (-*uję*) supervize, oversee, control

nadzór *m* (-*oru*; *0*) supervision, overseeing, control

nadzwyczaj(nie) *adv.* unusually, remarkably; *~ny* unusual, remarkable; *profesor* extraordinary; extra

nadzy *m-os pl.* → **nagi**

naft|a f(-*y*;*0*) *Brt.* paraffin (oil), *Am.* kerosene;*~owy* paraffin, kerosene; →*ropa*

nagab|ywać (-*uję*) ⟨*~nąć*⟩ (-*nę*), pester, solicit; bother (*o A* about)

nagana f (-*y*; *G* -) rebuke, reprimand

nag|i (-*go*) naked, *też drzewo itp.* bare; *do ~a* naked

na|ginać (-*am*) ⟨*~giąć*⟩ bend (down), bow; *~ginać się* bend; *~ chylić*; *~glący* urgent, pressing; *~gle* suddenly; abruptly, all at once; → *nagły*; *~glić* (-*lę*) → *przynaglać*; *czas ~gli* time presses; *~głaśniać* (-*am*) ⟨*~głośnić*⟩ (-*ę*, -*nij!*) fig. make public; *~głość* f (-*ści*;*0*) suddenness, urgency; *~główek* *m* (-*wka*, -*wki*) headline; letter-heading; *~gły* sudden, abrupt; *~gminny* common, wide-spread; *~gniotek* *m* (-*tka*; -*tki*) corn

nago *adv.* → *nagi*

nagonka f (-*ki*; -*G* -*nek*) battue; fig. witch-hunt

nagość f (-*ści*; *0*) nudity, nakedness, bareness

nagra|ć pf. → *nagrywać*; *~dzać* (-*am*) reward; *~nie* *n* (-*a*; *G* -*ań*) recording

nagrob|ek *m* (-*bka*; -*bki*) tomb; tombstone, gravestone; *~kowy*, *~ny* tombstone, gravestone

nagro|da f (-*y*; *G* -*ród*) award, reward; prize; *~da pocieszenia* consolation prize; *w ~dę za* (*A*) in reward for; *~dzić* pf. → *nagradzać*; *~dzony* awarded

nagromadz|enie *n* (-*a*) accumulation,

amassing; ~ać (-*am*) → **gromadzić**

na|grywać (-*am*) record; ~**grywać na taśmę** tape, put on tape; ~**grzewać** (-*am*) ⟨~**grzać**⟩ (-*eję*) heat, warm (**się** *v/i.*)

nagusieńki stark-naked, F starkers

naigrawać się (-*am*) → **kpić, drwić**

naiwn|ość *f* (-*ci; 0*) naivety *lub* naïveté, ingenuousness; ~**y** naive *lub* naïve, ingenuous

najadać się (-*am*) eat one's fill

najazd *m* (-*u; -y*) invasion; raid

najać *pf.* (-*jmę*) → **najmować**

naj|bardziej *adv.* (*sup. od* → **bardzo**) most; ~**bliższy** ⟨~**bliżej**⟩ (*sup. od* → **bliski**); nearest, closest; *czas* next; ~**bliższa rodzina** next of kin; ~**częściej** *adv.* (*sup. od* → **często**); most frequently, most often; mostly; ~**dalej** *adv.* (*sup. od* → **daleki**) farthest, furthest; *czas* at the latest; ~**dalszy** *adv.* (*sup. od* → **daleko**) farthest, furthest; ~**dłużej** *adv.* (*sup. od* →**długo**) longest; *fig.* at the most; ~**dłuższy** *adj.* (*sup. od* → **długi**) longest

najechać *pf.* → **najeżdżać**

najem *m* (-*jmu; 0*) hire, lease; **umowa o** ~ tenancy agreement; ~**ca** *m* (-*y; GA -ów*), ~**czyni** *f* (-*ń; -nie*) tenant; ~**nik** *m* (-*a; -cy*) *mil.* mercenary; ~**ny** hired; **praca ~na** hired labo(u)r; **wojsko ~ne** mercenary troops *pl.*

naje|ść się *pf.* → **najadać się**; ~**źdźca** *m* (-*cy; GA -ców*) invader, aggressor; ~**żać** (-*am*) → **jeżyć**; ~**żdżać** (-*am*) (**na** *A*) drive (into), run (into); (*na kraj*) invade; ~**żony** (*I*) bristling (with)

naj|gorszy *adj.* (*sup. od* → **zły**) worst; **w ~gorszym razie** at (the) worst; ~**gorzej** *adv.* (*sup. od* → **źle**) worst

naj|lepiej *adv.* (*sup. od* → **dobrze**) best; ~**lepszy** *adj.* (*sup. od* → **dobry**) best; **w ~lepszym razie** at best, at most; **wszystkiego ~lepszego!** all the best!

najmniej *adv.* (*sup. od* → **mało**) least, smallest; **co ~** at least; **jak ~** as little as possible; ~**szy** *adj.* (*sup. od* → **mały**) least, smallest; **w ~szym stopniu** not in the least

najmować (-*uję*) hire, rent; *osobę* engage, hire; ~ **się** become engaged, get a job

naj|niżej *adv.* (*sup.* → **nisko**) lowest; right at the bottom; ~**niższy** *adj.* (*sup. od* →**nisko**) lowest; ~**nowszy** *adj.* (*sup.*

od →**nowy**) latest, most recent; ~**pierw** *adv.* at first; first; to begin with; ~**prawdopodobniej** *adv.* (*sup. od* → **prawdopodobnie**) most probably; ~**prędzej** *adv.* (*sup. od* → **prędko**) at the earliest; **jak ~prędzej** as soon as possible; ~**starszy** *adj.* (*sup. od* → **stary**) oldest, eldest; ~**ście** *n* (-*a*) intrusion, trespass; ~**ść** *pf.* (→ **-jść**) → **nachodzić**; ~**ważniejszy** *adj.* (*sup. od* → **ważny**) most important; uppermost, paramount; ~**wcześniej** *adv.* (*sup. od* → **wcześnie**) earliest; **jak ~wcześniej** as soon as; ~**wyżej** *adv.* (*sup. od* → **wysoko**) highest; (**co - żej**) at (the) most; ~**wyższy** *adj.* (*sup. od* → **wysoki**) highest, tallest; *sąd itp.* supreme; **stopień ~wyższy** *gr.* (the) superlative; ~**zupełniej** *adj.* (*sup. od* → **zupełny**) totally, utterly

nakarmić *pf.* → **karmić**

nakaz *m* (-*u; -y*) order; *fig.* dictate; *jur.* warrant; *jur.* ~ **sądowy** writ, injunction; ~**ywać** (-*uję*) ⟨~**ać**⟩ order, impose; *dietę itp.* prescribe; *szacunek* command

nakle|jać (-*am*) ⟨~**ić**⟩ stick on, paste on; ~**jka** *f* (-*i; G -jek*) sticker

nakład *m* (-*u; -y*) expenditure, expense; *print.* print run, circulation; ~**em** (*G*) published by; ~**ać** (-*am*) put on; *krem, lekarstwo* apply; *obowiązek, podatek, karę itp.* impose; *podatek też* levy; ~**any**: *kieszeń* ~**ana** patch-pocket

nakł|aniać ⟨~**onić**⟩ → **skłaniać**

nakra|- *pf.* → **kra-**, ~**piany** speckled

nakre- *pf.* → **kre-**

nakrę|cać (-*am*) ⟨~**cić**⟩ *zegarek* wind up; *numer* dial; *film* shoot, tape; ~**tka** *f* (-*i; G -tek*) *tech.* nut; (*butelki*) cap

nakry|cie *n* (-*a; G -yć*) cover; ~**cie głowy** headgear, head covering; ~**wać** (-*am*) ⟨~**ć**⟩ cover (**się** o.s.); ~**wać stół**, ~**wać do stołu** lay the table; ~**wać się nogami** do a head over heels

nakup|ować ⟨~**ić**⟩ buy a lot of things

nalać *pf.* → **nalewać**

nale|gać (-*am*) (**na** *A*) insist (on), demand; ~**piać** (-*am*) ⟨~**pić**⟩ stick on, paste on; ~**pka** *f* (-*i; G -pek*) sticker; ~**śnik** *m* (-*a; -i*) pancake; ~**wać** (-*am*) pour; ~**wka** *f* (-*i; G -wek*) fruit liqueur

należ|eć (**do** *G*) belong (to); ~**eć się** (*D*) be due (to); ~**y**(**się**)…one should…, it is necessary to…; ~**ałoby…** it would be necessary to…; **jak ~y** correctly, properly; *ile się panu/pani ~y?* how much do I owe you?; ~ność *f* (-*ści*) charge, amount due, outstanding amount; ~ny due; *zapłata* outstanding; ~y → *należeć*; ~yty appropriate

nalot *m* (-*u*; -*y*) raid; *med.* coating, (*na języku*) fur; ~ **bombowy** *mil.* bomb attack, bombing raid

nała|-*pf.* → *ła*-; ~dowany loaded (*też* F)

nałogow|**iec** *m* (-*wca*; -*wcy*) addict; ~y *palacz* habitual; *pijak* compulsive

nałożyć *pf.* → *nakładać*

nałóg *m* (-*łogu*; -*łogi*) addiction; *fig.* (bad) habit

nam *pron.* (*D pl.* → *my*) us

namaca|**ć** *pf.* make out by touch; *drogę* feel one's way; ~lny tangible; *med.* palpable

namal-, **namar**- *pf.* → *mal*-, **mar**-

namaszczenie *n* (-*a*; *G* -*eń*) *rel.* unction; *z* ~*m* solemnly; *ostatnie* ~ *rel.* anointing of the sick, extreme unction

namawiać (-*am*) persuade (*do kupna G* to buy; *kogoś na spacer* s.o. to go for a walk)

nami *pron.* (*I pl.* → *my*); *z* ~ with us

namiastka *f* (-*i*; *G* -*tek*) substitute, surrogate

namięk|**ać** (-*am*) ⟨~*nąć*⟩ become soft

namiętn|**ość** *f* (-*ści*) passion; ~ypassionate

namiot *m* (-*u*; -*y*) tent

namo|- *pf.* → *mo*-; ~knąć *pf.* become soft; soak through; ~wa *f* (-*y*; *G* -*mów*) persuasion, instigation; *za jego* ~wą at his instigation

namówić → *namawiać*

namy|**dlać** (-*am*) → *mydlić*; ~sł *m* (-*u*; *0*) reflection, consideration; *bez* ~*słu* without thinking; (*od razu*) without a moment's thought; *po* ~*śle* on reflection; *czas do* ~*słu* time for reflection; ~ślać się (~*ślić się*) reflect, think (*nad I* about)

na|**nosić** (*im*)*pf* ⟨~*nieść*⟩ (*G*) *błota itp.* track; *wiatr:* drift; *woda:* wash up; *na mapę* plot; ~nosić poprawki make corrections

naoczn|**ie** *adv.* with one's own eyes; ~y visible *fig.* apparent, obvious; → *świadek*

naokoło *prp.* (*G*) (a)round

naówczas *lit.* at that time

napad *m* (-*u*; -*y*) attack, assault; (*na*

państwo) invasion; (*kradzież*) robbery; *med. fig.* attack, fit; ~ać (-*am*) (*na A*) attack, assault; ~ało dużo śniegu there has been a heavy snowfall

napalić *pf.* (*w L*) heat, stoke; ~ się na (*A*) F get hooked on

na|**par** *m* (-*u*; -*y*) infusion; ~parstek *m* (-*tka*; -*tki*) thimble; ~parzać (-*am*) → **parzyć**; ~paskudzić F *pf.* (-*dzę*) mess up, make filthy

napast|**liwy** ⟨-*wie*⟩ aggressive; → *złośliwy*; ~nik *m* (-*a*; -*cy*) attacker, assailant; (*w sporcie*) forward, striker; ~ować (-*uję*) bother, pester; (*seksualnie*) molest; *owady:* plague

na|**paść** (*paść¹*) → **napadać**; ~paść² → **paść²**; *f* (-*ści*; -*ści*) attack, assault; → **napad**; ~pawać (-*am*) fill with (**dumą** pride); ~*pawać się* (*I*) feast (on), delight (in); ~pchać *pf.* → **napychać**; ~pchać się (*do G*) push one's way (into)

napełni|**ać** (-*am*) ⟨~*ć*⟩ fill up (*I* with; *się v/i.*); *fig.* fill (*I* with)

napę|**d** *m* (-*u*; -*y*) drive (*też mot., komp.*); *mot.* transmission; ~dowy driving, drive; ~dzać (-*am*) *tech.* drive, propel; *też* ⟨~*dzić*⟩ (*G*) herd into; ~dzać do *fig.* set to; ~dzać komuś strachu give s.o. a fright

na|**pić** *pf.* → **napinać**; ~pić się *pf.* (*G*) drink, have a drink; ~piec *pf.* → **piec²**; ~pierać (-*am*) (*na A*) press (against); *fig.* assail (with)

napię|**cie** *n* (-*a*; *G* -*ęć*) tension, strain; suspense; *electr.* voltage; ~tek *m* (-*tka*; -*tki*) (*buta*) heel; ~tnować *f* → *piętnować*; ~ty tense (*też fig.*); *uwaga* close; *nerwy* taut; *sytuacja* fraught

napinać (-*am*) tighten, tauten; *muskuły* tense, flex; ~ się become *lub* go taut; *muskuły* tense

napis *m* (-*u*; -*y*) inscription; (*kwestii na filmie*) subtitles *pl.*, (*na zakończenie*) credits *pl.*; ~ać *pf.* → *pisać*

napiwek *m* (-*wku*; -*wki*) tip

napletek *m* (-*tka*; -*tki*) *anat.* prepuce, foreskin

napływ *m* (-*u*; -*y*) flow, inflow; (*też fig.*) influx, rush; *med.* inflow, afflux; ~ać ⟨*napłynąć*⟩ flow in; (*w dużych ilościach*) flood in; *ludzie:* come in crowds, (*na stałe*) immigrate; ~owy immigrational

napo|cić się *pf.* sweat (*też fig.* ***przy** I* over); **~czynać** ⟨**~cząć**⟩ *chleb* start (eating); *butelkę* open; **~minać** (*-am*) admonish, reprimand; **~mknąć** *pf.* → ***napomykać***; **~mnienie** *n* (*-a*) admonition, reprimand; **~mnieć** *pf.* (*-nę; -nij*) → ***napominać***; **~mykać** (*-am*) (**o** *L*) mention, hint; **~t(y)kać** (*-am*) encounter; come across

na|pój *m* (*-poju; -poje*) beverage, drink; ***~pój bezalkoholowy*** soft drink; ***~pój gazowany*** pop; **~pór** *m* (*-poru; 0*) pressure; *fig.* power, weight

napraw|a *f* (*-y; G -*) repair; renovation; *fig.* recovery; ***dać do ~y*** have repaired; **~czy** repair; *fig.* recovery

naprawdę *adv.* really, actually

napraw|iać (*-am*) ⟨**~ić**⟩ repair, renovate; *fig.* improve (**się** *v/i.*); *zło, krzywdę* right, undo

naprędce *adv.* hastily, rashly

napręż|ać (*-am*) ⟨**~yć**⟩ (*-ę*) (**się** *v/i.*) tighten, tauten; tense; *mięśnie* flex; **~enie** *n* (*-a*) tension; *fig.* strain, stress; **~ony** → ***napięty***

napro|mieniować (*-uję*) *phys.* irradiate; **~mieniowanie** *n* (*-a; G -ań*) irradiation, exposure; **~wadzać** (*-am*) ⟨**~wadzić**⟩ guide; direct; ***~wadzać na właściwy ślad*** put on the right track

naprze|ciw 1. *prp.* (*G*) against, opposite (to); in front of; **2.** *adv.* towards; ***wyjść ~ciw*** (*D*) *fig.* meet halfway; **~ć** *pf.* → ***napierać***

N

naprzód *adv.* forward(s), ahead

naprzykrz|ać się (*-am*) ⟨***~yć się***⟩ (*D*) bother, hassle

na|pso- *pf.* → ***pso-***; **~puchnięty** swollen; **~puszony** pompous; **~pychać** (*-am*) (**do** *G*) stuff (into); → ***napchać***

nara|da *f* (*-y; G -*) meeting, conference; **~dzać się** (*-am*) ⟨***~dzić się***⟩ discuss, consult, confer

naramien|nik *m* (*-a; -i*) shoulder-strap; **~ny** shoulder

narastać (*-am*) grow, mount up

naraz *adv.* at once, suddenly

nara|żać (*-am*) ⟨**~zić**⟩ risk, jeopardize; (***na** A*) subject (to) ***~zić się*** (*D*) run the risk of; F displease; **~żenie** *n* (*-a; 0*): ***z ~żeniem życia*** at the risk of one's life

narcia|rka *f* (*-i; G -rek*) skier; **~rski** ski, skiing; **~rstwo** *n* (*-a; 0*) skiing; **~rz** *m* (*-a; -e*) skier

narcyz *m* (*-a; -y*) *bot.* narcissus, daffodil

nareszcie *adv.* at last, finally

naręcze *n* (*-a; G -y*) bunch, armful

narko|man *m* (*-a; -i*), **~manka** *f* (*-i; G -nek*) drug addict; F junkie; **~mania** *f* (*GDL -ii; 0*) drug addiction; **~tyk** *m* (*-u; -i*) (hard) drug; narcotic; **~tyzować się** (*-uję*) take drugs; **~za** *f* (*-y; G -*) sedation, an(a)esthesia

narobić *pf.* (*G*) make, do, cause

narodow|ość *f* (*-ci; 0*) nationality; **~y** national

naro|dzenie (**się**) *n* (*-a; G -eń*) birth; ***Boże ≈dzenie*** Christmas; **~dziny** *pl.* (*-*) birth; **~snąć** *pf.* → ***narastać***; **~śl** *f* (*-i; -e*) growth; *med.* excrescence, tumo(u)r; **~wisty** *koń* vicious

naroż|nik *m* (*-a; -i*) corner; **~ny** corner; ***dom ~ny*** house on the corner

naród *m* (*-odu; -ody*) nation

narta *f* (*-y; G -*) ski; ***jeździć na ~ch*** ski

narusz|ać *prawo, granicę* violate; *umowę* breach; *słowo* break; *równowagę* upset; *zapasy, kapitał* make inroads in; *prywatność* trespass on; **~enie** *n* (*-a; G -ń*) (*też prawa*) violation, breach, infringement

narwany F *fig.* crazy

narybek *m* (*-bku; -bki*) *zo.* fry; *fig.* new blood, new recruits *pl.*

narząd *m* (*-u; -y*) organ

narzecze *n* (*-a; G -y*) dialect

narzeczon|a *f* (*-ej; -e*) fiancee *lub* fiancée; **~y** *m* (*-ego; -czeni*) fiancé

na|rzekać (*-am*) complain (***na** A* about); **~rzędnik** *m* (*-a; -i*) *gr.* instrumental; **~rzędzie** *n* (*-a; G -*) tool, implement

narznąć *pf.* → ***narzynać***

narzu|cać ⟨**~cić**⟩ *płaszcz* throw on *lub* over; *fig.* force (***na** A* on); ***~cać się*** impose o.s. on (*A*); **~t** *m* (*-u; -y*) *econ.* mark-up; **~ta** *f* (*-y; G -*) bedspread; **~tka** *f* (*-i; G -tek*) cape

narżnąć *pf.* → ***narzynać***

nas *pron.* (*GA* → ***my***) us

nasa|da *f* (*-y; G -*) butt, handle; *anat.*, *bot.* base; ***~da włosów*** hairline; **~dka** *f* (*-i; G -dek*) cap; **~dzać** ⟨**~dzić**⟩ put on, pin on

nasenny: ***środek ~*** soporific; sleeping pill

nasercowy: ***środek~*** cardiac, F heart pill

nasi *pron. m-os* → ***nasz***

nasiadówka *f* (*-i; G -wek*) hip-bath

nasiąk|ać (*-am*) ⟨**~nąć**⟩ (*-nę*) (*I*) soak through, absorb

nasien|ie *n* (*-a; -siona, -sion*) *bot.* seed; *zo.* sperm, semen; **~ny** seed

nasilenie *n* (*-a; G -eń*) intensification; escalation

nasiona *pl.* → **nasienie**

na|skoczyć *pf.* → **naskakiwać**; **~skórek** *m* (*-rka; -rki*) *anat.* cuticle; **~stać** *pf.* → **nasyłać**; **~słuchiwać** (*-uję*) listen in; **~sma-** *pf.* → **sma-**; **~so-** *pf.* → **so-**; **~srożony** angry; **~stać** *pf.* → **nastawać**; **~stanie** *n* (*-a; 0*) start, onset; **~starczyć** *pf.*: **nie móc ~starczyć** (*G*) not be able to satisfy the needs (of)

nasta|wać come; (**po** *L*) follow (after); **~wać na czyjeś życie** threaten s.o.'s life; **~wiać** *budzik* set; *mechanizm* adjust, regulate; *RTV*: tune in; *uszy* cock; *med.* set; **~wiać wodę na herbatę** put the kettle on; **~wienie** *n* (*-a; G -eń*) setting (*też med.*); (*umysłowe*) attitude; **~wnia** *f* (*-i; -e*) *rail.* *Brt.* signal box, *Am.* switch tower

nastąpić *pf.* → **następować**

następ|ca *m* (*-y; G -ców*) successor; **~ca tronu** crown prince; **~czyni** *f* (*-i; -nie,-ń*) successor; **~nie** *adv.* next, then; **~ny** next, following; **~nego dnia** next day; **~ować** (*-uję*) step (**na** *A* on); follow (**po sobie** one after the other); **jak ~uje** as follows; → **nastawać**; **~stwo** *n* (*-a; G -*) succession; consequence, after-effect; **~ująco** *adv.* as follows, in the following way; **~ujący** following

nastolat|ek *m* (*-tka; G -tków*), **~ka** *f* (*-i; G -tek*) teenager

nastoletni teenage

nastra|jać (*-am*) → **stroić**; **~szyć** *pf.* → (**prze**)**straszyć**

nastręcz|ać (*-am*) ⟨**~yć**⟩ present, offer (**się** o.s.)

nastro|ić *pf.* → **stroić**; **~jowy** atmospheric; **~szony** bristled; *ptak, pióra*: ruffled up; → **stroszyć**

nastr|ój *m* (*-oju; -oje, -ojów*) spirit, mood; atmosphere, climate; **w dobrym ~oju** in good spirits

nasturcja *f* (*-i; -e*) nasturtium

nasu|wać ⟨**~nąć**⟩ *czapkę* pull (**na oczy** over one's eyes); draw (**na** *A* on); *fig.* *wątpliwości*: give rise to; *pomysł* suggest; **~wać** ⟨**na-**⟩ **się** arise, occur, *pomysł*: come

nasy|cać (*-am*) → **sycić**; **~cony** *chem.* saturated; satiated, satisfied; **~łać** (*-am*) *F* put s.o. on (to)

nasyp *m* (*-u; -y*) embankment; **~ywać** (*-uję*) ⟨**~ać**⟩ pour (**do** *G* into)

nasz *pron.* (*m-os nasi*) our, ours; *F* **po ~emu** like we do; like we speak

na|szki- *pf.* → **szki-**; **~szukać się** search for hours

naszy|ć *pf.* → **naszywać**; **~jnik** *m* (*-a; -i*) necklace; **~wka** *f* (*-i; G -wek*) *mil.* stripe; **~wać** (*-am*) sew on(to)

naśladow|ać (*-uję*) imitate, copy; mimic; **~ca** *m* (*-y; G -ów*), **~czyni** *f* (*-i; -nie, -ń*) imitator; mimic; **~czy** imitative; **~nictwo** *n* (*-a; G -*) imitation

na|śmiewać się (*-am*) (**z** *G*) mock, ridicule; **~świetlać** (*-am*) ⟨**~świetlić**⟩ (*-lę*) *phys.* irradiate; *med.* use radiation treatment; *phot,* expose (*też fig.*)

natar|cie *n* (*-a; G -ć*) *mil.,* (*w sporcie*) attack; *mil.* advance; **~czywy** (**-wie**) insistent

natchnąć *pf.* inspire (**do** *G* to); **~ienie** *n* (*-a; G -ń*) inspiration

natęż|ać (*-am*) ⟨**~yć**⟩ (*-ę*) *wzrok* *itp.* strain, exert; **~enie** *n* (*-a; G -eń*) intensity (*też phys.*); (*dźwięku*) volume

na|tknąć *pf.* → **natykać** **się**; **~tłoczony** crowded, packed; **~tłok** *m* (*-u; 0*) crowd, crush; *fig.* flood, influx

natomiast *adv.* however

natrafi(a)ć (**na** *A*) encounter, come across; (*na złoto*) strike

natręc|two *n* (*-a; G -w*) pushiness, insistence; *med.* compulsion, obsession; **~tny** pushy, insistent

natrysk *m* (*-u; -i*) shower; **~iwać** (*-uję*) spray, sprinkle; **~owy** shower

na|trząsać się (*-am*) (**z** *G*) mock, ridicule; **~trzeć** *pf.* → **nacierać**

natu|ra *f* (*-y; G -*) nature; **z ~ry** by nature; **w ~rze** in nature; **~ralizacja** *f* (*-i; -e*) naturalisation; **~ralny** natural

natychmiast *adv.* immediately, instantly; **~owy** immediate, instant

natyka|ć się (*-am*) (**na** *A*) meet, come across

naucz|ać (*-am*) teach; **~anie** *n* (*-a; G -ń*) teaching, instruction; **~ka** *f* (*-i; G -czek*) *fig.* lesson; **dać k-š ~kę** give s.o. a lesson

nauczyciel *m* (*-a; -e*), **~ka** *f* (*-i; G -lek*) teacher; **~ski** teacher

N

nau|czyć pf. → **nauczać, uczyć**; **~czyć się** (G) teach; **~ka** f (-i; G -) (przyrodnicza) science, (humanistyczna) scholarship; (szkolna) teaching; (teoria) teaching(s pl.); (morał) lesson; (nauczanie zawodu) apprenticeship; **~kowiec** m (-wca; -wcy) (przyrodnik) scientist, (humanista) scholar; **~kowy** academic, scientific, scholarly

naumyślnie adv. on purpose

nausznik m (-a; -i) ear-flap

nawa f (-y; G -): **~ główna** nave; **~ boczna** aisle

nawadniać (-am) irrigate

nawa|lać (-am) ⟨**~lić**⟩ v/t. pile up, heap up; v/i. F fail, crash; pf. też be broken down

nawał m (-u; 0) barrage, spate; **~a** f (-y; G -) mil. barrage; **~nica** f (-y; -e) thunderstorm

nawet adv. even; **~ gdyby** even if; **~ nie** not even

nawia|ć pf. → **nawiewać**; **~s** m (-u; -y) parenthesis, (zwł. kwadratowy) bracket; **~sem mówiąc** incidentally; **wyłączyć poza ~s** exclude; **~sowy** parenthetic(al), bracket

nawiąz|ywać (-uję) ⟨**~ać**⟩ kontakty, establish; negocjacje open, start; stosunki form; znajomość strike up; take (**do** G up); **~ując do** (G) with reference (to), referring (to)

nawiedz|ać (-am) ⟨**~ić**⟩ (-dzę) nieszczęście afflict, strike, plague; (we śnie) appear; (myśl, wspomnienia: haunt

nawierzchnia f (-i; -e, -i) surface

nawietrzn|y: strona ~a windward

na|wiewać (-am) ⟨**~wiać**⟩ (-eję) blow (in); F scram

nawi|jać (-am) wind up, reel up, roll up **(się** v/i.) fig. okazja come up, crop up; **~nąć** pf. (-nę; -ń!) → **nawijać**

na|wlekać (-am) ⟨**~wlec**⟩ igłę thread; paciorki string; **~wodnić** pf. (-ę; -nij!) → **nawadniać; ~wodny: budowla ~wodna** lacustrine dwelling

nawoływać (-uję) call; fig. call (**do** G up(on))

na|wozić fertilize; **~wóz** m (-ozu; -ozy) dung, manure; **~wóz sztuczny** fertilizer

na|wracać (-am) ⟨**~wrócić**⟩ v/i. mot. do an about-turn; → **wracać**; v/t. mot. turn; rel. convert (**na** A to); **~wracać**

~wrócić) się become converted (**na** A to); **~wrócenie** n (-a; G -eń) rel. conversion; **~wrót** m (-otu; -oty) return, recurrence; med. relapse

nawyk m (-u; -i) habit; **~ać** (-am) ⟨**~nąć**⟩ (-nę) (**do** G) get used (to), get accustomed (to)

nawzajem adv. each other, one another; **dziękuję, ~!** thank you, the same to you!

nazajutrz adv. (on) the next day

nazbyt adv. too, excessively

na|zębny dental; **kamień ~zębny** dental plaque; **~ziemny** zo. terrestrial; astr., aviat. ground

naznacz|ać (-am) ⟨**~yć**⟩ mark; termin fix, establish

nazw. skrót pisany: **nazwisko** n. (name)

nazwa f (-y; G -) name; **~ć** pf. → **nazywać**

nazwisk|o n (-a) (family) name, surname; **~iem, o ~u ...** by name; **znać z ~a** know by name

nazyw|ać (-am) call, name; **~ać się** be called; **to się ~a ...!** that's what I call...; **jak się ~a?** what's its name?; **jak się ~asz?** what's your name?

nażreć się pf. (fig.) stuff o.s.

NBP skrót: **Narodowy Bank Polski** Polish National Bank

n.e. skrót pisany: **naszej ery** AD (Anno Domini)

Neapol m (-u; 0) Naples

negatyw m (-u; -y) negative; **~ny** negative

negliż m (-u; -e, -y) undress; **w ~u** in a state of undress

negocja|cje f/pl. (-i) negotiations pl.; **~tor** m (-a; -rzy), **~torka** (-i; G -rek) negotiator

ne|gocjować (-uję) negotiate; **~gować** (-uję) negate; **~krolog** m (-u; -i) obituary; (w gazecie) death notice

nenufar m (-u/-a; -y) bot. water lily, (zwł.) yellow water lily

neo- w zł. neo-

neon m (-u; 0) chem. neon; (-u; -y) neon light; **~ówka** f (-i; G -wek) strip light

nerk|a f (-i; G -rek) anat., gastr. kidney; **~owaty** kidney-shaped, reniform; **~owy** kidney; renal

nerw m (-u; -y) anat. nerve; **działać na ~y** get on nerves; **~ica** f (-y; G -) med. neurosis; **~ica lękowa** anxiety neurosis; **~oból** m med. neuralgia; **~owy** nervous; nerve; **~owo chory** mentally ill

neseser *m* (*-u*, *-y*) *Brt.* sponge-bag, *Am.* toilet bag; *też* briefcase, attaché case

neska F *f* (*-i; 0*) instant (coffee)

netto (*idkl.*) net

neuro- *w zł.* neuro-

neutral|izować ⟨*z*-⟩ (*-uję*) neutralize; **~ny** neutral

newralgiczny sore, touchy

nęc|ący tempting, enticing; **~ić** ⟨*z*-⟩ (*-cę*) tempt, entice

nędz|a *f* (*-y; -e*) poverty; misery, destitution; **cierpieć ~ę** suffer poverty; **~arka** *f* (*-i; G -rek*), **~arz** *m* (*-a; -e*) pauper; **~ny** poor, destitute, miserable; → **nikczemny**

nękać ⟨*z*-⟩ (*-am*) plague; *fig.* pester

ni *cj.* → **ani**; **~ stąd**, **~ zowąd** without reason; **~ to** ..., **~ owo** ... neither fish nor fowl; **~ w pięć**, **~ w dziewięć** without rhyme or reason

niań|czyć (*-ę*) nurse; **~ka** *f* (*-i; G -niek*) nurse

nią *pron.* (*AI* → **ona**); **z ~** with her

niby 1. *part.* (*A*) as though, as it were; of a kind; **małżeństwo na ~** sham marriage; **~ śpi** ... he is apparently sleeping; **2.** *w złoż.* pseudo-, quasi-, sham

nic *pron.* nothing; **~ a ~** not a thing; **jak gdyby ~** as if nothing (had) happened; **na ~** for nothing; a waste of time; **~ z tego** (**nie będzie**) nothing will come of it; **tyle co ~** next to nothing; **~ ci do tego** that's none of your business; **za ~ w świecie** not for anything; **niczego nie brakuje** there's nothing missing; **być do niczego** be of no use; **zostać bez niczego** be left with nothing; **z niczym** empty-handed; **na niczym mu nie zależy** he doesn't care about anything; **skończyć się na niczym** come to nothing; **w niczym** not at all

nich *pron.* (*GL* → **oni, one**; *A* → **oni**); **o ~** about them

nici *pl.* → **nić**

nicować ⟨*prze*-⟩ (*-uję*) *ubranie* turn over

nicpoń *m* (*-nia; -nie, -i/-ów*) god-for-nothing

nicz|ego (*G*) → **nic**; F **~ego sobie** not bad; **~emu** (*D*) → **nic**; **~yj** no-one's; **ziemia ~yja** no man's land; **bez ~yjej pomocy** on one's own; **~ym** (*IL* → **nic**) *prp. lit.* (*A*) like

nić *f* (*-ci; -ci, I -ćmi*) thread; *med.* suture

niderlandzki Netherlandic, Netherlandian

nie 1. *part.* no; (+ *verb*) not; **jeszcze ~** not yet; **to ~ żarty** no joking; **~ płacąc** without paying; **~ zapytany** not asked; **no ~?** isn't it so?; **~ ma** there isn't; → **już, mieć, nic**; **2.** *w złoż.* un-, in-, non-

nie|aktualny out of date; invalid; **~apetyczny** unappetizing; **~baczny** careless, inconsiderate; **~bawem** soon, before long

niebezpiecz|eństwo *n* (*-a; G* -) danger; threat; **~ny** dangerous, hazardous; perilous

niebiesk|awy (**-wo**) bluish; **~i**[1] (**-ko**) blue; **~i**[2] heavenly; **Królestwo ~ie** Kingdom of Heaven; **~ooki** blue-eyed

niebiosa *pl.* (**-os**, *L* -osach) heavens *pl.*

nieb|o *n* (*-a; -a*, → **niebiosa**) sky; *rel.* heaven; **na ~ie** in the sky; **w ~ie** *rel.* in heaven

niebora|czka *f* (*-i; G* -czek) → **biedaczka**; **~k** *m* (*-a; -cy/-i*) → **biedak**

nieboszcz|ka *f* (*-i; G* -czek), **~yk** *m* (*-a; -cy/-i*) the deceased; **moja babka ~ka** my late lamented Grandmother

niebotyczny sky-high, lofty

nie|brzydki not bad; **~bywały** unbelievable, unheard-of; **~całkowity** incomplete, not complete; **~cały** not quite; **~cały tydzień** less than a week, under a week; **~celny** imprecise; **~celowy** inadvisable; **~cenzuralny** indecent, obscene; unprintable

niech *part.* let; **~ zaczeka** let him wait; **~ sobie jadą** let them go; **~ pan(i) po-zwoli** allow me; **~ żyje demokracja!** long live democracy; **~ żyje Jan!** hurray for John!; **~ przypuszczam** suppose; even though

niechcący unwittingly, incidentally

niechę|ć *f* (*-ci*) dislike (**do** *G* towards); reluctance; **~tnie** *adv.* reluctantly; **~tny** reluctant; averse (**do** *G* to); hostile

niecierpliw|ić ⟨*z*-⟩ (*-ę*) *v/t.* make impatient; **~ić** ⟨*z*-⟩ **się** be impatient, grow impatient; **~ość** *f* (*-ci*) impatience; **~y** impatient

niecka 132

niecka *f* (*-i*; *G -cek*) trough; *geol.* hollow

niecny dastardly, heinous

nieco *adv.* somewhat; **~ za mały** on the small side; **~dzienny** unusual; **~ś →
nieco**; **coś ~ś** a little bit

nie|często *adv.* infrequently, now and then; **~czuły** insensitive (**na** A to); **~czynny** inactive; out of order; *zakład* closed; *wulkan* extinct; *chem.* inert; **~czysto** *adv.* → **nieczysty**

nieczyst|ość (*-ści*; *0*) untidiness; *tylko pl.* **~ości** waste; *Brt.* refuse, *Am.* garbage; **~y** (*-to*) untidy, unclean; *chem.* impure (*też fig.*); dirty; **~e sumienie** guilty conscience

nie|czytelny illegible; **~daleki →
pobliski; ~dalеко** near (to), not far (from); (*w czasie*) at hand; **~daleko** *adv.* (*G, od* G) not far (from)

niedawn|o *adv.* recently; **~o temu** not long ago; **~y** recent; **od ~a** for a short time; **do ~a** until recently

niedba|lstwo *n* (*-a*; *0*) carelessness, negligence; **~ły** careless, negligent

nie|delikatny indelicate; tactless; **~długo** *adv.* before long; (*wkrótce*) soon

niedo|bór *m* (*-boru*; *-ory*) lack, shortage; deficiency; **~brany** ill-matched, mismatched; **~bry** bad; wrong; *czyn* bad, wicked, nasty; *smak, pogoda* bad, foul, nasty; (*niezdrowy*) unwell; **~brze mi** I feel sick; **~ciągnięcie** *n* (*-a*) shortcoming; **~czas** *m* (*-u*; *-y*): **być w ~czasie** be pressed for time

niedogod|ność *f* (*-ści*) inconvenience; **~ny** inconvenient

niedojadanie *n* (*-a*) malnutrition

niedojrzały immature

niedo|kładny imprecise, inaccurate; **~konany** *gr.* imperfect(ive); **~krwistość** *f* (*-ści*; *0*) *med.* an(a)emia; **~kształcony** half-educated

niedola *f* (*-i*; *-e*) adversity, misfortune

niedołę|ga *f/m* (*-i*; *G -/-ów*) failure; →
niezdara; ~stwo *n* (*-a*; *0*) infirmity, frailty; **~żny** infirm, frail

niedomag|ać (*-am*) be ailing; be ill (**na** A with); **~anie** *n* (*-a*) illness, complaint; *fig.* shortcoming; defect

niedo|moga *f* (*-i*; *G -móg*) *med.* insufficiency; *fig.* shortcoming; **~mówienie** *n* (*-a*; *G -eń*) hint, suggestion; vague hint; **~myśleny** slow to understand; **~pałek** *m* (*-łka*, *-łki*, *-łków*) butt, stub;

~patrzenie *n* (*-a*; *-eń*) inattentiveness, carelessness; **przez ~patrzenie** by oversight; **~płata** *f* (*-y*; *G -*) underpayment; **~powiedzenie** *n* (*-a*; *G -eń*) **~niedomówienie**; **~puszczalny** inadmissible

niedorajda *f/m* (*-y*; *G -*) bungler; →
niedołęga

niedoręczeni|e *n* (*-a*; *G -eń*): **w razie
~a ...** if undelivered ...

niedo|rosły immature; **~rostek** *m* (*-tka*, *-tki*) adolescent, teenager; **~rozwinięty** retarded, (**umysłowo** mentally-)-handicapped; **~rozwój** underdevelopment; (*psychiczny*) mental deficiency; **~rzeczny** absurd, ridiculous; **~sięgły** unattainable, beyond grasp; **~skonały** (*m-os -li*) imperfect

niedosłysz|alny inaudible; **~eć** (*-ę*) be hard of hearing; **~enie** *n* (*-a*; *0*) hardness of hearing

niedo|smażony underdone; **~solony** insufficiently salted; **~spać** *pf.* → **niedosypiać; ~stateczny** insufficient, *ocena* unsatisfactory; **~statek** *m* (*-tku*, *-tki*) shortage, lack; **~stępny** inaccessible, unattainable; **~strzegalny** indiscernible, imperceptible; **~sypiać** (*-am*) sleep too short *lub* too little; **~szły** would-be, potential, unfulfilled

niedo|ścigły **~ścigniony** unequalled; unmatched; **~świadczony** inexperienced; **~trzymanie** *n* (*-a*) non-compliance, breach; **~tykalny** untouchable; **~uczony** half-educated; → **niedokształcony; ~waga** *f* underweight; **~warzony** *fig.* unripe, immature; **~wiarek** *m* (*-rka*; *-rki/-rkowie*) sceptic, disbeliever; **~widzieć** (*-dzę*) be short-sighted

niedowierza|jąco disbelievingly, incredulously; **~nie** *n* (*-a*) disbelief, doubt

nie|dowład *m* (*-u*; *-y*) *med.* paresis; **~dozwolony** forbidden, prohibited; **~dożywiony** undernourished; **~drogi** (*-go*) inexpensive, low-priced; **~dużo** *adv.* not much, little; not many, few; **~duży** small; **~dwuznaczny** unambiguous, unequivocal; **~dyskrecja** *f* indiscretion; **~dysponowany** unwell; **~dyspozycja** *f* indisposition

niedz. *skrót pisany:* **niedziela** Sun. (*Sunday*)

niedziel|a *f* (*-i*; *-e*) Sunday; **~ny** Sunday

niedźwiadek *m* (*-dka*, *-dki*) *zo.* → **miś,
niedźwiedź**

niedźwiedzi bear, *biol.* ursine; ~ca *f* (-*y*; -*e*, -) *zo.* she-bear; **Wielka &ca** Ursa Major, (Great) Bear

niedźwiedź *m* (-*dzia*; -*dzie*) *zo.* (**biały, brunatny** polar, brown) bear

nie|efektowny unattractive; ~**ekonomiczny** uneconomical; ~**estetyczny** unsightly, disagreeable; ~**efektywny** ineffective

nie|fachowy unprofessional, incompetent; ~**foremny** ungainly, shapeless; ~**formalny** informal; ~**fortunny** unfortunate; luckless, unhappy; ~**frasobliwy** (-*wie*) carefree, free and easy; ~**gazowany** still; ~**głęboki** shallow, superficial; ~**głupi** clever, sensible

niego *pron.* (*GA → on*; *G → ono*); *dla/od/do/u* ~ for/from/to/with him

niego|dny, *pred.* ~**dzien** (*G*) unworthy, undeserving; ~**dziwy** (-*wie*) → *niecny*

nie|gospodarny uneconomic; ~**gościnny** inhospitable; ~**gotowy**, ~**gotów** *pred.* unfinished, not ready; ~**groźny** harmless; ~**grzeczność** *f* impoliteness, unkindness, rudeness; ~**grzeczny** impolite, unkind, rude; ~**gustowny** tasteless; ~**higieniczny** insanitary, unhealthy; ~**ingerencja** non-intervention; ~**istotny** insignificant, inconsiderable

niej *pron.* (*GDL → ona*); *dla/od/do/u* ~ for/from/to/with her

nieja|dalny inedible; ~**dowity** non-poisonous

nieja|ki certain; some; *od ~kiego czasu* for some time; ~*ki pan ...* a certain Mr; ~*ko* *adv.* as it were; ~**sny** (-*no*) unclear, vague; ~**wny** closed, classified

niejed|en, ~**na**, ~**no**[1] many a, many; ~**na kobieta** many a woman, many women

niejedno[2] all kinds of, all sorts of; *przeżył* ~ he has seen a lot of life; ~**krotnie** *adv.* several times, repeatedly; ~**krotny** repeated; ~**lity** non-uniform; ~**znaczny** ambiguous

niekar|alny exempt from punishment; ~**ność** *f* (-*ści*) exemption from punishment; ~**ny** **1.** without criminal record; **2.** *m* (-*ego*) person without criminal record

niekiedy sometimes, occasionally; *kiedy* ~ now and then

nie|kłamany sincere, honest; ~**koleżeński** unhelpful to one's colleagues; ~**kompetentny** incompetent; ~**kompletny** incomplete; ~**koniecznie** *adv.* not necessarily; ~**konsekwentny** inconsistent

niekorzy|stny unfavo(u)rable; ~**ść** *f*: *na* ~**ść** (*G*) to disadvantage, to detriment

nie|kształtny shapeless, ungainly; ~**które** *pl.*, ~**które** *f/pl.* some; ~**którzy z nich** some of them; ~**kulturalny** uncultured, uncultivated; ~**legalny** illegal; ~**letni** under age; ~**liczny**: *~liczni*, *~liczne* few; ~**litościwy** unmerciful; ~**logiczny** illogical; ~**lojalny** disloyal; ~**ludzki** inhuman

nieła|d *m* (-*u*; 0) disorder, disarray, mess; *w ~dzie* disordered

nie|ładny plain; wrong; ~**łamliwy** unbreakable; ~**łaska** (-*i*; 0); *być w ~łasce* be out of favo(u)r; ~**łatwy** not easy; *~łatwe zadanie* not an easy task

nie|mal(że) *adv.* almost, nearly; ~**mało** *adv.* quite a lot; ~**mały** quite big; ~**mądry** (-*rze*) unwise

niemczyzna *f* (-*y*; 0) German, the German language

nie|męski unmanly; effeminate; ~**miara** *f* f: *co ~miara* a heap of

Niemcy *pl.* (-*iec*) Germany

Niemiec *m* (-*mca*; -*mcy*, -*mców*) German; &**ki** (*po -ku*) German

nie|mieszkalny non-residential; ~**mile** *adv.*; ~**miło** *adv.* → *niemiły*; ~**miłosierny** unmerciful; *F* terrible, awful; ~**miły** unkind, unpleasant

Niemka *f* (-*i*; *G -mek*) German (woman/girl *itp.*)

niemnący non-crease

niemniej nevertheless, even so

niemo *adv.* silently, speechlessly

niemoc *f* (-*y*; 0) weakness; ~ *płciowa* impotence; ~**ny** weak (*też* F *fig.*)

nie|modny unfashionable; ~**moralny** immoral; *czyn ~moralny* *jur.* sexual offence (*Am.* offence); ~**mowa** *f/m.* (-*y*; *G -mów/-owów*) mute

niemowlę *n* (-*cia*; -*ta*, *G -ląt*) baby, infant; ~**ctwo** *n* (-*a*; 0) infancy; ~**cy** infant, baby

niemoż|liwie *adv.* F impossibly, awfully, terribly; ~**liwy** impossible; awful, terrible; *to ~liwe* that's impossible; ~**liwy do opisania** indescribable, beyond

N

niemożność 134

description; ~ność *f* (*-ci; 0*) lack of ability, impossibility

niemrawy sluggish, languid

niemu *pron.* → *jemu*; **ku** ~ to him

niemy mute, dumb; *fig.* speechless,-wordless; → **niemowa**

niena|ganny beyond reproach; ~**prawialny** irreparable, beyond repair; ~**ruszalny** inviolable, sacred; ~**ruszony** intact; ~**sycony** insatiable, quenchless; ~**turalny** unnatural; ~**umyślnie** *adv.* unintentionally

nienawi|dzić (*-dzę*) hate, detest (**się** each other); ~**stny** hateful, detestable; ~**ść** *f* (*-ści; 0*) hatred, hate, loathing

nie|nawykły unaccustomed (**do** *G* to); ~**normalny** abnormal; ~**nowy** not new, used; ~**obcy** not strange

nieobecn|ość *f* (*-ści; 0*) absence; **pod ~ość** (*G*) in the absence (of); ~**y** absent; **być ~ym** be absent (**na** *L* at)

nie|obliczalny incalculable; *fig.* unpredictable; ~**obowiązkowy** *osoba* negligent; ~**obrobiony** rough; untreated; ~**obsadzony** vacant; ~**obywatelski** unsocial, antisocial; ~**oceniony** inestimable; ~**oczekiwany** unexpected; ~**odczuwalny** indiscernible, imperceptible

nieod|gadniony inscrutable; ~**łączny** inseparable; ~**mienny** unalterable, unchangeable; *gr.* uninflected; ~**party** irresistible; **chęć** irrepressible; *argument* irrefutable; ~**płatny** free (of charge); ~**powiedni** inappropriate, inadequate, improper; ~**powiedzialny** irresponsible; ~**stępny** → **nieodłączny**; ~**wołalny** irrevocable, unalterable; ~**wracalny** irreversible; ~**zowny** indispensable, essential; ~**żałowany** *strata* irretrievable, irrecoverable

nie|oficjalny unofficial; ~**oględny** careless, rash; ~**ograniczony** (*-czenie*) unlimited; limitless; ~**okiełznany** *fig.* rampant; uncontrolled; ~**określony** indefinite (*też gr.*); nondescript; ~**okrzesany** *fig.* loutish; ~**omal** → **niemal**; ~**omylny** infallible, unerring; ~**opanowany** uncontrollable, unruly; ~**opatrzny** unguarded; ~**opisany** indescribable; ~**opłacalny** unprofitable, uneconomic; ~**organiczny** inorganic; ~**osiągalny** unattainable, beyond reach; ~**osobowy** impersonal

nieostrożn|ość *f* (*-ści; 0*) carelessness, rashness; ~**y** careless, rash

nie|ostry not sharp, blunt; *phot.* out of focus; *zdjęcie* fuzzy; *zima* mild; ~**oświecony** unenlightened, backward; ~**ożywiony** inanimate

niepalą|cy 1. non-smoking; **2.** *m* (*-ego; -y*), ~**a** *f* (*-ej; -e*) non-smoker; **jestem ~y** I don't smoke; **wagon dla ~ych** non-smoker

niepalny non-flammable, not flammable

niepamię|ć *f*: **puścić w ~ć** forgive and forget; **wydobyć z ~ci** rescue from oblivion; ~**tliwy** forgiving, relenting; ~**tny**: **od ~tnych czasów** from time immemorial

nieparzysty odd

niepełno|letni 1. under age; **2.** *m* (*-ego; -ni*), ~**letnia** *f* (*-ej; -e*) minor; ~**prawny** without full legal capacity; ~**sprawny** disabled

nie|pełny incomplete; deficient; ~**pewność** uncertainty, incertitude; ~**pewny** uncertain, doubtful; ~**pijący** *m* (*-ego; -y*) non-drinker; ~**piśmienny** illiterate; ~**planowy** unplanned; unscheduled; ~**płodny** sterile; fruitless; ~**pochlebny** unfavo(u)rable; ~**pocieszony** disconsolate, inconsolable; ~**poczytalny** not responsible for one's actions, of unsound mind

niepodległ|ość *f* (*-ci; 0*) independence; ~**y** independent

niepodob|ieństwo *n* imposibility; ~**na** (*nieos.*) it is impossible; ~**ny** (**do** *G*) unlike

niepo|dzielny indivisible; *fig.* absolute; ~**goda** (*-y; 0*) bad weather; ~**hamowany** unrestrained, uncontrollable; ~**jętny** untalented, ungifted; ~**jęty** incomprehensible; ~**kalany** *rel.* immaculate; ~**kaźny** inconspicuous; ~**koić** (**za-**) (*-ję*) bother, worry, disturb; ~**koić się** worry (**o** *A* about); ~**kojący** (*-co*) worrying; disturbing; ~**konany** invincible, unconquered; ~**kój** *m* (*-koju; -koje*) anxiety, worry, disquiet; ~**liczalny** uncountable

nie|pomierny excessive; ~**pomny** (*G*) forgetful (of), unmindful (of); ~**pomyślny** unfavo(u)rable, adverse; ~**potłatny** unprofitable; ~**poprawny** incorrect, inaccurate; *winowajca* incorrigible; ~popularny unpopular; ~poradny → **niezaradny**; ~poręczny unwieldy, cumbersome; ~porozumienie n (-a; G -eń) misunderstanding; zw. pl. (spory) difference of opinion

nieporów|nany incomparable, inimitable; ~nywalny incomparable

niepo|ruszony immovable, still; spojrzenie fixed; ~rządek m → **nieład**; ~rządny → **niechlujny**; ~skromiony → **niepohamowany**

nieposłusz|eństwo n disobedience, insubordination, ~ny disobedient, insubordinate

niepo|spolity uncommon; ~strzeżenie unnoticed; ~szanowanie disrespectfulness; lack of respect; ~**szanowanie prawa** disregard for law; ~szlakowany impeccable, irreproachable; ~trzebny unnecessary, needless

niepo|ważny frivolous, flippant; ~wetowany irreparable, irrecoverable; ~wodzenie n failure, misadventure; ~wołany unauthorized; ~wstrzymany irrepressible, unrestrained; ~wszedni not everyday; → **niepospolity**; ~wtarzalny unique, single, one-off; ~znawalny fig. unfathomable; ~zorny inconspicuous; ~żądany undesirable

niepraktyczny impractical, unpractical

niepraw|da f untruth, untruthfulness; **to ~da** that's not true; **jest duży, ~da?** it is big, isn't it?; **był duży, ~da?** it was big, wasn't it?; ~dopodobny improbable; ~dziwy (-wie) untrue; (sztuczny) false

nieprawidłow|ość f (-ści) irregularity; ~y incorrect, wrong, improper

niepra|wny unlawful, illegal; ~womocny jur. not final; invalid; ~wowity unlawful, illegal

nie|prędko adv. not soon; ~produktywny unproductive; ~profesjonalny unprofessional, amateur

nieproliferacj|a f (-i; 0): **układ o ~i** nonproliferation treaty

nie|proporcjonalny disproportionate (**do** G to); ~proszony uninvited, unwelcome, unbidden

nieprze|brany innumerable, immeasurable; ~byty impassable, impenetrable; ~chodni gr. intransitive; ~ciętny uncommon, above average; ~jednany irreconcilable; ~jezdny impassable

nieprzejrzany tłum enormous, immense; mrok impenetrable

nieprze|konujący, ~konywujący unconvincing; ~kraczalny impassable; termin latest possible; ~kupny incorruptible; ~makalny waterproof; ~mijający piękno unchanging; sława immortal; ~nikniony impenetrable; ~pisowy (-wo) against the rules; ~puszczalny impermeable, impervious

nieprzerwany incessant, ceaseless

nieprze|ścigniony unsurpassable; ~tłumaczalny untranslatable; ~widziany unforeseen; ~zorny careless; inadvertent; ~zroczysty opaque; ~zwyciężony insurmountable

nieprzy|chylny unfavo(u)rable; ~datny useless (**do** G, **na** A to, for); → **bezużyteczny**; ~jaciel m (-a; -e, G -ciół), ~jaciółka f (-i; G -łek) enemy; ~jacielski enemy, hostile; ~jazny unfriendly, inimical; ~jemność f trouble; ~jemny unpleasant; ~padkowy not accidental; purposeful, deliberate; ~stępny unapproachable; cena prohibitive; ~tomny unconscious; wzrok absent-minded; ~**tomny ze strachu** frightened out of one's wits; ~tulny cheerless, unfriendly; ~zwoity indecent; wyrazy obscene

nie|punktualny unpunctual; ~racjonalny irrational

nierad (m-os -dzi) (D) unwilling; **rad ~** willy-nilly

nieraz adv. frequently; sometimes

nierdzewny stainless

nie|realny unreal; ~regularny irregular; ~rentowny unprofitable; ~rogacizna (-y; 0) zbior. swine; ~rozdzielny inseparable; ~rozerwalny indissoluble

nieroz|garnięty slow-witted; ~łączka f (-i; G -czek) zo. budgerigar, F budgie; ~łączny inseparable; ~poznawalny unrecognizable; ~puszczalny insoluble; ~sądny unreasonable; thoughtless; ~strzygalny unsolvable, insoluble; ~tropny → **nierozsądny**; czyn unthinking, ill-considered; rash

nierozumny irrational

nierozwa|ga f (-i; 0) thoughtlessness; rashness; ~żny thoughtless, rash

nieroz|wiązalny insoluble, insurmountable; ~winięty undeveloped; immature; pąk unopened

nieróbstwo n (-a; 0) idleness

N

nierów|no *adv.* → **nierówny**; ~**no-mierny** uneven; ~**ność** *f (-ści)* inequal-ity; ~**ny** *(statusem)* unequal; *powierz-chnia, droga* uneven; *teren* rough

nieruch|awy, ~**liwy** slow, lethargic; ~**omo** → **nieruchomy**; ~**omość** *f (-ści)* *Brt.* real property, *Am.* real estate; ~**omy** motionless, immobile, immovable

nierzadk|i frequent, often; ~**o** *adv.* fre-quently, often

nierząd *m (-u; 0)* prostitution; ~**ny**: **czyn ~ny** *jur.* indecent assault

nierze|czowy pointless, futile; ~**czywi-sty** unreal; ~**telny** dishonest, unreliable

nie|samowity weird, uncanny; ~**sforny** unruly; ~**skalany**, ~**skazitelny** impec-cable *fig.* immaculate; ~**skłonny** *(do G)* averse (to), unwilling (to); ~**skom-plikowany** uncomplicated, simple; ~**skończony (-czenie)** infinite, end-less; ~**skromny** immodest; indecent; ~**skuteczny** ineffective, inefficient; ~**sławny** inglorious, obscure; ~**słony** unsalted; ~**słowny** unreliable; ~**słusz-nie** *adv.* unjustly; ~**słuszny** unjust *(też jur.)*; unfair; ~**słychany** unheard of; unbelievable; ~**smaczny** tasteless *(też fig.)*; ~**smak** *m (-u; 0)* nasty after-taste

niesnaski *f/pl. (-sek)* quarrelling, dis-putes *pl.*

nie|solidny unreliable; ~**specjalnie** *adv.* not really; ~**spełna** less than; ~**spełna rozumu** out of one's mind; ~**spo-dzianka** *f (-i; G -nek)* surprise; ~**spo-dzi(ew)any** unexpected; ~**spokojny** uneasy; *wzrok itp.* restless; ~**sporo** *adv.* slowly, slow; ~**spożyty** robust, vigorous

niesprawiedliw|ość *f (-ści; 0)* unjust-ness, injustice; ~**y** unjust, unfair *(wo-bec, dla G* on)

niesprawny *urządzenie* out of order

niesta|ły unstable; changeable, vari-able; ~**ranny** careless; slapdash; messy; ~**stateczny** fickle, unstable

niestety *adv.* unfortunately, regrettably

nie|stosowny inappropriate; unsuit-able; ~**strawność** *f (-ści; 0) med.* indi-gestion, dyspepsia; ~**strawny** indiges-tible; ~**strudzony** restless, tireless, unflagging; ~**stworzony** F incredible; ~**sumienny** → **nierzetelny, niesta-ranny**; ~**swojo** *adv.* uneasily, uncom-fortably; ~**swój (→ swój)** unwell

nie|symetryczny asymmetric(al); ~**sympatyczny** disagreeable, unpleas-ant; ~**systematyczny** unsystematic, haphazard; ~**syty** insatiable; ~**szablo-nowy** → **niepospolity**; ~**szczególny** insignificant, nondescript, uninterest-ing; ~**szczelny** leaky; ~**szczery** insin-cere

nieszczę|sny unfortunate; F wretched; ~**ście** *n (-cia; G -ść)* bad luck; **na ~ście** unfortunately; ~**śliwy** unlucky; un-happy

nieszkodliwy safe; harmless *(dla zdrowia* to health); ~ **dla środowiska** environment-friendly

nieszpory *pl. (-ów) rel.* vespers *pl.*

nieścisł|ość *f (-ci; 0)* inaccuracy, im-precision; ~**y** inaccurate, imprecise

nieść *v/t.* carry; bring *(też sprawiać)*; *ja-ja* lay; ~ **się** *dźwięki, woń:* carry; *kura:* lay eggs

nie|ślubny *dziecko* illegitimate; ~**śmia-ły** timid, shy; ~**śmiertelny** immortal

nieświado|mość *f* unawareness, un-consciousness; ignorance; ~**my** *(pred. m ~m)* unaware; unconscious; ignor-ant

nie|świeży off, not fresh; ~**takt** *m* tact-lessness; discourtesy; ~**taktowny** tact-less; discourteous; ~**terminowy (-wo)** after the closing date; ~**tęgi (-go)** F weak; ~**tknięty** → **nienaruszony**; ~**tłu-kący** unbreakable; ~**tolerancyjny** in-tolerant

nietoperz *m (-a; -e) zo.* bat

nie|towarzyski unsociable; ~**trafny** → **chybiony**; ~**trudny** easy, effortless; ~**trwały** non-durable, short-lived; *ko-lor* not fast, fast-fading; ~**trzeźwość** *f* insobriety, intoxication; ~**trzeźwy** in-toxicated, drunk; ~**tutejszy** strange, not local

nietykaln|ość *f (-ści; 0)* inviolability; *pol.* immunity; ~**y** inviolable; *pol.* pos-sessing immunity

nie|typowy atypical; ~**ubłagany** im-placable; ~**uchronny** inevitable; ~**u-chwytny** difficult to catch; *fig.* imper-ceptible; ~**uchwytny dla ucha** inaud-ible; ~**uctwo** *n (-a; 0)* ignorance; ~**u-czciwy** dishonest, fraudulent; ~**udany** unsuccessful, failed

nieudoln|ość *f (-ści; 0)* incompetence, ineptitude; ~**y** incompetent, inept

nie|ufność f distrust, mistrust; ~**ufny** distrustful, mistrustful, suspicious; ~**ugaszony** inextinguishable, fig. unquenchable; ~**ugięty** unyielding

nieuk m (-a; -cy) ignorant

nie|ukojony inconsolable; ~**uleczalny** incurable; ~**ulękły** intrepid, fearless; ~**umiarkowany** intemperate; unrestrained; ~**umiejętny** inept, incompetent; ~**umyślny** unintentional; ~**unikniony** unavoidable; ~**uprzedzony** unbiased; ~**uprzejmy** unkind, impolite

nieurodzaj m (-u; -e) bad harvest; ~**ny** *ziemia* infertile, barren; ~**ny rok** bad year

nieusta|jący, ~**nny** incessant, ceaseless

nie|ustępliwy (-wie) unyielding; ~**ustraszony** intrepid, fearless; ~**usuwalny** *plama* indelible; ~**uwaga** f inattentiveness, carelessness; **przez ~uwagę** because of carelessness; ~**uważny** inattentive; ~**uzasadniony** unfounded, groundless; ~**użyteczny** useless; ~**użytki** m/pl. (-ów) agr. fallow land, uncultivated land

niewart (m-os -rci) not worth; **nic ~ ...** worth nothing

nieważ|kość f (-ści; 0) weightlessness; ~**ny** unimportant, insignificant

niewątpliw|ie adv. undoubtedly, without doubt; ~**y** undoubted, certain

nie|wczas m: **po ~wczasie** afterwards, after the event; ~**wdzięczny** unthankful, ungrateful; ~**wesoły (-ło)** joyless, sad

niewiadom|y unknown; ~**a** f (-ej; -e) *math.* unknown; **w ~e** to nowhere in particular

niewiar|a f (-y; 0) disbelief, unbelief; ~**ogodny**, ~**ygodny** incredible, unreliable

niewiasta f (-y; G -) woman, fair

niewido|czny invisible; ~**my** **1.** blind, visually impaired; **2.** m (-ego;-mi), ~**ma** f (-ej; -e) blind person; ~**mi** the blind

nie|widzialny invisible; ~**wiedza** f ignorance

niewiel|e 1. (m-os -lu) not much, little; not many, few; **2.** adv. little; ~**e brakowało** all but, nearly; → **myśleć**; ~**ki** small, little, low

niewie|rność f infidelity, unfaithfulness; ~**rny** unfaithful; ~**rzący 1.** unbelieving; **2.** m (-ego; -cy), ~**rząca** f

(-ej; -e) unbeliever

niewin|iątko n (-a; G -tek) iron. innocent; ~**ność** f (-ści; 0) innocence; ~**ny** innocent

niewłaściwy (-wie) improper, inappropriate

niewol|a f (-i; -e) captivity, slavery; ~**nica** f (-y; -e) slave; ~**nictwo** n (-a; G -) slavery; ~**niczy (-czo)** slavish, servile; ~**nik** m (-a; -cy) slave

niewód m (-wodu; -wody) dragnet

nie|wprawny unskilful; ~**wrażliwy (na** A) insensitive (to); insensible (to); ~**wskazany** inadvisable; ~**współmierny** disproportionate, incommensurate; ~**wybaczalny** inexcusable, unforgivable; ~**wybredny** undemanding, not fussy; iron. tasteless; ~**wybuch** m blind, F dud; ~**wyczerpany** inexhaustible; ~**wydolny** med. insufficient

niewy|goda f discomfort, inconvenience; ~**godny** uncomfortable, inconvenient; ~**konalny** impracticable; ~**kwalifikowany** unqualified, unskilled; ~**magający** undemanding; ~**mierny** immeasurable; ~**mowny** unspeakable; ~**muszony** natural, unaffected; ~**myślny** simple, plain

niewy|pał m misfired shell, F dud; F fiasco, flop; ~**płacalny** insolvent, bankrupt; ~**powiedziany** unuttered, unspoken; ~**raźny** indistinct; *kształt* blurred; *mowa* inarticulate; F *mina itp.* strange; ~**robiony** unpractised; inexperienced; ~**spany: być ~spanym** be sleepy; ~**starczająco** adv. insufficiently; inadequately; ~**szukany** homely, plain; ~**tłumaczalny** inexplicable; ~**tłumaczony** unexplained; ~**trzymały (na** A) not resistant (to), sensitive (to); ~**żyty** unsated, unsatisfied

nie|wzruszony (-szenie) adamant, imperturbable; ~**zaangażowany** pol. non-aligned; ~**zachwiany** unshaken, steadfast; ~**zadługo** adv. shortly, soon; ~**zadowolenie** n discontent, displeasure; ~**zadowolony** discontented, displeased **(z** G with)

niezależn|ość f independence; ~**y** independent **(od** G of); **mowa ~a** gr. direct speech; → **samodzielny**

nieza|mącony imperturbable, unruffled; ~**mężny** single, unmarried; ~**możny** impecunious; ~**pominajka** f

(*-i*; *G -jek*) *bot.* forget-me-not; ~pomniany unforgettable; ~przeczalny undeniable, indisputable; ~radny helpless, unenterprising; ~służenie *adv.* unjustly, undeservedly; ~stąpiony irreplaceable; ~tarty indelible; ~uważalny inconspicuous; ~uważony unnoticed

niezawisł|ość *f* (*-ści*; *0*) independence; ~y (*-śle*) independent

niezawodn|ie *adv.* without fail; reliably; ~ość *f* (*-ści*; *0*) reliability, dependability; ~y reliable, dependable

nie|zbadany unstudied, unexplored; *fig.* unfathomable; ~zbędny indispensable, necessary; ~zbity irrefutable

niezbyt *adv.* not very (much)

nie|zdarny clumsy, awkward; ~zdatny (*do G*, *na A*) unfit (to); → **niezdolny**

niezdecydowa|nie¹ *n* indecision, hesitation; ~nie² *adv.*, ~ny undecided, indecisive, hesitant

niezdoln|ość *f* (*-ści*; *0*) inability, incompetence; ~y (*do G*) unable (to), incapable (of), unfit (for); ~**y do służby wojskowej** unfit for military service; ~**y do pracy** unable to work

nie|zdrowy unwell, indisposed; ~zdyscyplinowany undisciplined; ~zgłębiony unfathomed

niezgod|a *f* (*-y*; *0*) discord; ~ność *f* incompatibility, conflict; ~ny incompatible, inconsistent; ~**ny z przepisami** against the regulations, irregular

nie|zgrabny ungainly, shapeless; → **niezdarny**; ~ziszczalny unrealizable; ~zliczony innumerable; ~złomny steadfast, inflexible; unbroken; ~zły not bad; ~zmienny unchangeable, immutable; ~zmiernie *adv.* extremely, exceedingly; ~zmierny immense; ~zmordowany indefatigable, untiring; ~zmywalny indelible

niezna|czny slight; ~jomość *f* (*-ści*; *0*) ignorance; ~jomy **1.** *adj.* unfamiliar, unknown; **2.** *m* (*-ego*; *-i*),~joma *f* (*-ej*; *-e*) stranger; ~ny unknown; **w ~ne** to nowhere in particular

nie|znośny unbearable; ~zręczny clumsy, awkward; → **niezdarny**; ~zrozumiały incomprehensible; ~zrozumienie *n* (*-a*; *0*) incomprehension; ~zrównany unmatched, unequalled; ~zupełny *adv.* not quite; incompletely;

~zupełny incomplete; ~zwłoczny prompt, immediate; ~zwyciężony inconquerable, invincible; ~zwykły uncommon, unusual; extraordinary

nieźle *adv.* not bad

nie|żonaty single, unmarried; ~życiowy unrealistic; ~życzliwy (*-wie*) unkind; ~żyjący dead; the late

nieżyt *m* (*-u*; *-y*) *med.* infection, inflammation; ~ **żołądka** gastritis

nieżyw|otny inanimate; ~y dead

nigdy never; ~ **więcej** never more *lub* again; **jak** ~ as never before

nigdzie nowhere, anywhere; ~ **indziej** nowhere else

nijak F in no way, nowise; ~i nondescript, commonplace; *gr.* neuter; ~o *adv.* indefinably, F awkward; **czuć się** ~**o** feel unpleasant

NIK *skrót:* **Najwyższa Izba Kontroli** Supreme Chamber of Control

nikczemny vile, mean, wicked

nikiel *m* (*-klu*; *0*) *chem.* nickel

nikim (*IL* → **nikt**); **z** ~ **innym** with nobody else

niklow|ać ⟨*po-*⟩ (*-uję*) nickel, plate with nickel; ~any nickel-plated; ~y nickel

nik|ły (*-le*, *-ło*) faint; ~nąć (*-nę*) fade, die away

niko|go (*G* → **nikt**); ~**go tam nie ma** there's no-one there, there isn't anyone there; ~mu (*D* → **nikt**): **nie ufam** ~**mu** I do not trust anybody

nikotyna *f* (*-y*; *0*) nicotine

nikt *pron.* nobody, no-one; anyone, anybody; → **nikim, nikogo, nikomu**

nim¹ *cj.* before

nim² (*IL* → **on**[o]); **z** ~ with him; (*D* → **oni, one**); **dzięki** ~ thanks to them; ~**i** (*I* → **oni, one**); **z** ~**i** with them

nin. *skrót pisany:* **niniejszy** this

niniejszy present; ~**m** hereby; **wraz z** ~**m** enclosed

niski low; *wzrost* short; *głos*, *ukłon* deep; → **niższy**; ~**o** *adv.* low; deep; → **niżej**

nisko|gatunkowy low-quality, low--grade; ~**kaloryczny** low-calorie

nisza *f* (*-y*; *G* -) niche

niszcz|ący ⟨*-co*⟩ destructive; ~**eć** ⟨*z-*⟩ (*-eje*) decay, become ruined; fall to pieces; ~**yciel** *m* (*-a*; *-e*) *mil.* destroyer; ~**yć** ⟨*z-*⟩ (*-ę*) destroy, ruin; ~**yć się** → **niszczeć**

nit *m* (*-u; -y*) rivet; **~ka** *f* (*-i; G -tek*) thread; **~ować** (*-uję*) rivet

niuans *m* (*-u; -e*) nuance, subtlety

niuch *m* (*-a; -y*) pinch of snuff; F smell; **~ać** (*-am*); **~ać tabakę** snuff

niwa *f* (*-y; G -*) *lit.* field; *fig.* area, field

niweczyć ⟨*z-*⟩ (*-ę*) thwart, shatter; → **niszczyć, udaremniać**

niwelować ⟨*z-*⟩ (*-uję*) level

nizać ⟨*na-*⟩ (*-żę*) thread

nizin|a *f* (*-y; G -*) lowland; **~ny** lowland

niziutki → **niski**

niż[1] *cj.* than; **więcej ~** more than

niż[2] *m* (*-u, -e*) → **nizina**; *meteo.* depression; **~ej** *adv.* (*comp. od* → **nisko**) lower, below; **~ej podpisany** the undersigned; *comp.* **zatoka ~owa** *meteo.* trough; **~szość** *f* (*-ści; 0*) inferiority; **~szy** *adj.* (*comp. od* → **niski**); lower; *fig.* inferior; junior

no *part.* well; now; **patrz ~!** well, I never!; **~ proszę!** well, well!; **~ dobrze** well, all right; **~, mówże!** fire away!

noc *f* (*-y; -e*) night; **po ~y, w ~y** by night; **~ w ~, całymi ~ami** night after night; **do późna w ~y** until late at night; **przez ~, na ~** overnight; **~leg** *m* (*-u; -i*) accommodation for the night; **~legowy: dom ~legowy** hostel; **miejsce ~legowe** place to sleep; **~nik** *m* (*-a; -i*) chamber pot, F potty; **~ny** night, nightly; **~ować** ⟨*prze-, za-*⟩ (*-uję*) spend the night; *kogoś* put up

nog|a *f* (*-i; G nóg*) leg; (*stopa*) foot; **zerwać się na równe ~i** jump up; **walić się z nóg** hardly stand up; **wstawać lewą ~ą** get out on the wrong side of the bed; **do góry ~ami** upside down, head over heels; **stanąć na ~i** find one's feet; **do ~i!** heel!; **w ~i!** F let's hop it!

nogawka *f* (*-i; G -wek*) (*trouser itp.*) leg

nokaut *m* (*-u; -y*) knockout, k.o.; **~ować** ⟨*z-*⟩ (*-uję*) knock out

nomada *m* (*-y; -dzi/-owie, -ów*) nomad

nomina|cja *f* (*-i; -e*) nomination, appointment; **~cyjny** appointment; **~lny** nominal; **~ł** *m* (*-u; -y*) denomination

nonsens *m* (*-u; -y*) nonsense, absurd; **~owny** nonsensical

nora *f* (*-y; G -*) (*lisia*) burrow; (*mysia*) hole; *fig.* hole

nork|a *f* (*-i; G -rek*) → **nora**; *zo.* mink; **~i** *pl.* mink coat

norma *f* (*-y; G -*) norm; **~ prawna** legal norm; **~lizować** (*-uję*) normalize (**się** *w/i.*); **~lny** normal

normować ⟨*u-*⟩ standardize; **~** ⟨*u-*⟩ **się** be standardized

Norwe|gia *f* (*-ii*) Norway; **~g** *m* (*-a; -dzy/-owie*), **~żka** *f* (*-ki; G -żek*) Norwegian; **2ski** (**po -ku**) Norwegian

nos *m* (*-a; -y*) nose (*też fig.*); **przez ~** through the nose; F **mieć w ~ie** (*A*) not care (about); **~ kręcić, sprzątnąć, wodzić; ~acizna** *f* (*-y; 0*) *wet.* glanders *sg.*; **~ek** *m* (*-ska; -ski*) → **nos**; (*buta*) toe

nosi|ciel *m* (*-a; -e*), **~cielka** *f* (*-i; G -lek*) carrier; **~ć** (*-szę*) carry (**przy sobie** on o.s.); bear; *ubranie* wear; **~ć się** dress; be contemplating, think (**z** *I* of)

noso|rożec *m* (*-żca; -żce*) *zo.* rhinoceros, F rhino; **~wy** nasal, nose

nostalgiczny nostalgic, romantic

nosze *pl.* (*-y*) stretcher; **~nie** *n* (*-a; 0*) carrying, bearing; **~nie się** style of dress

nośn|ik *m* (*-a; -i*) *tech., econ.* medium; vehicle; **~ość** *f* (*-ści; 0*) capacity; (*broni*) range; **~y** carrying; *food.* load-carrying; **kura ~a** laying hen; **rakieta ~a** carrier vehicle

nota *f* (*-y; G -*) note; memorandum, F memo; **~bene** (*idkl.*) incidentally, by the way

notari|alny notarial; notarized; **~usz** *m* (*-a; -e*) notary

notat|ka *f* (*-i; G -tek*) note; **~nik** *m* (*-a; -i*) notepad

notes *m* (*-u; -y*) notebook

notoryczny notorious

notowa|ć ⟨*za-*⟩ (*-uję*) take down, take notes; *fig.* note, notice; **być źle ~nym u kogoś** be in s.o.'s bad books; **~nie** *n* (*-a; G -ań*) *econ.* quotation

nowa|lie *pl.*(*-ii/-ij*), **~lijki** *pl.* (*-jek*) early vegetables *pl.*; **~tor** *m* (*-a; -rzy*), **~torka** *f* (*-i; G -rek*) innovator; **~torski** innovative

Nowa Zelandia *f* New Zealand

nowela *f* (*-i; -e*) short story

nowelizacja *f* (*-i; -e*) *jur.* amendment

nowicjusz *m* (*-a; -e*), **~ka** *f* (*-i; G -szek*) novice, recruit

nowin|a *f* (*-y; G -*) piece of news; **~y** *pl.* news *sg.*; **to nie ~a** that is nothing new; **~ka** (*-i; G -nek*) → **nowina**

nowiut(eń)ki brand new

nowo|czesny (**-śnie**) modern; ~mod-
ny newfangled; ~roczny New Year's;
~rodek *m* (**-dka**; *-dki*) newborn baby
nowość *f* (**-ści**) novelty
nowo|twór *m* (**-woru**; *-wory*) *med.* tu-
mo(u)r; ~żeniec *m* (**-ńca**; *-ńcy*) newly-
wed; ~żytny modern
now|y new; **♀y Rok** New Year; **od ~a,
na ~o** anew, afresh; **po ~emu** in a new
way; ~**e** *n* (**-ego**; *0*) the latest; **co ~ego?**
what's new?
Nowy Jork *m* New York
Nowy Orlean *m* New Orleans
nozdrze *n* (**-a**; **-y**) nostril
noż|e *pl.* → **nóż**; ~ny foot; ~ownik *m*
(**-a**; *-cy*) knifeman; ~yce *f/pl.* (**-**), ~ycz-
ki *f/pl.* (**-czek**) scissors *pl.*
nów *m* (*GL nowiu*; *0*) new moon
nóż *m* (**noża**, *noże*, *noży*) knife; ~ **do
(otwierania) konserw** *Brt.* tin opener,
Am. can opener; **być na noże** (**z** *I*)
be in conflict (with), fight (with *lub*
against); **mieć ~ na gardle** be pinned
into a tight corner
nóżka *f* (**-i**; *G -żek*) → **noga**; (grzyba,
kieliszka) stem
np. *skrót pisany:* **na przykład** e.g. (*for
example*)
n.p.m. *skrót pisany:* **nad poziomem
morza** a.s.l. (*above sea level*)
nr *skrót pisany:* **numer** No (*number*)
NSA *skrót pisany:* **Naczelny Sąd Administracyjny** Chief Administrative
Court

nucić (**-cę**) hum
nud|a *f* (**-y**; *-y*, *-ów*) boredom; **z ~ów** out
of boredom; ~ności *f/pl.* nausea; ~ny
boring, dull
nudyst|a *m* (**-y**; *-yści*), ~ka *f* (**-i**; *G -tek*)
nudist; ~yczny nudist
nudzi|ara *f* (**-y**; *G -*), ~arz *m* (**-a**; *-e*)
bore, nuisance; ~ć (**-dzę**) bore; ~ć
się be bored; → **mdlić**
numer *m* (**-u**; *-y*) number (*skrót:* No.);
(*butów itp.*) size; (*czasopisma*) issue;
(*w kabarecie*) act; ~ **rejestracyjny** *mot.*
registration number; ~ować ⟨**po-**⟩
(**-uję**) number;
nuncjusz *m* (**-a**; *-e*) *rel.* nuncio
nur *m* (**-a**; *-y*): **dać ~a** a dive; ~ek *m* (**-rka**;
-rkowie) diver; **dać ~ka → nur**; ~ka *f*
(**-i**; *G -rek*) → **norka**
nurkow|ać (**-uję**) dive; ~y diving; **lot ~y**
nose-dive
nurt *m* (**-u**; *-y*) current; trend; ~**y**
pl. *też* waters *pl.*; ~ować (**-uję**; *t-ko
3. os.*) be on *s.o.'s* mind; (*dręczyć*) torment
nurzać (**-am**) immerse; dip; ~ **się** (**w** *L*)
wallow (in); revel (in)
nut|a *f* (**-y**; *G -*) *mus.* note (*też fig.*); **cała
~a** *Brt.* semibreve, *Am.* whole note;
~owy note
nuż: **a ~** what if
nuż|ący (**-co**) tiring, tiresome; ~yć ⟨**z-**⟩
(**-ę**) tire, exhaust
nygus F *m* (**-a**; *-i*) loafer
nylon *m* (**-u**; *-y*) nylon; ~owy nylon

O

o[1] *prp.* (*L*, *A*) about, on; **mówił ~ tobie**
he was talking about you; **niepokoić
się ~ dzieci** worry about the children;
pytać ~ drogę ask about the way; *godzina, pora:* at; ~ **świcie** at dawn; *cecha:* with; ~ **jasnych włosach** with fair
hair; *styczność:* against; **oprzeć ~ ścianę** lean against the wall; *sposób:* on,
with; **chodzić ~ lasce** walk with a stick;
~ **kulach** on crutches; ~ **własnych
siłach** by one's own efforts; **może być
tłumaczony przez złożenie:** ~ **napędzie silnikowym** motor-driven
o[2] *int.* oh; ~ **tak!** oh, yes!

oaza *f* (**-y**; *G -*) oasis
ob. *skrót pisany:* **obywatel(ka)** citizen
oba, ~**j** *num.* both
obal|ać (**-am**) ⟨~**ić**⟩ (**-lę**) *v/t.* knock down;
władzę overthrow; *prawo, zwyczaje* abolish; *teorię* disprove; ~enie *n* (**-a**; *G -ń*)
fig. overturn, overthrow; *jur.* abolition
obandażowany *med.* bandaged
obarcz|ać (**-am**) ⟨~**yć**⟩ (**-ę**) (**k-o** *I*) bur-
den (with), overburden (with); ~**ać**
⟨~**yć**⟩ **się** (*I*) burden (o.s.); ~**ony rodziną** with a family
obaw|a *f* (**-y**; *G -*) fear, anxiety; *pl. też*
doubt; **z ~y przed** (*I*) for fear of; **mieć**

lub **żywić** ~**y** fear, be afraid; ~iać się (*-am*) (*G*) be afraid (of); (*o A*) be worried (about)

obcas *m* (*-a; -y*) heel

obcesowo brusquely, bluntly; ~**y** brusque, blunt

obcęgi *pl.* pincers *pl.*

obcho|dzenie się *n* (*-a; 0*) (**z** *I*) handling (of); dealing (with); ~**dzić** pace out, walk around; *przeszkodę, prawo* go round; (*interesować się*) concern, interest, care; *rocznicę* celebrate, commemorate; ~**dzić sklepy** do the rounds of the shops; ~**dzić się** (**z** *I*) treat, handle; use, operate; (**bez** *G*) go (without), do (without)

obchód *m* round; patrol; **obchody** *pl.* celebrations *pl.*, festivities *pl.*

obcią|ć *pf.* → **obcinać**; ~**gać** (*-am*) ⟨~**gnąć**⟩ (*I*) cover (with); *suknię itp.* straighten; ~**żać** (*-am*) ⟨~**żyć**⟩ load (*I* with; **się** o.s.); weight, weigh down; *fig.* burden; (*też fin., jur.*) charge; *jur.* incriminate; → **obarczać**; ~**żenie** *n* (*-a; G -eń*) load; drain; *electr.* load; *tech.* ballast; ~**żenie dziedziczne** inherited susceptibility to a disease

ob|cierać (*-am*) wipe off/away; rub; ~**cierać się** wipe; ~**cięcie** *n* cutting; clipping; (*zarobków*) (*G*) cut (in); ~**cinać** (*-am*) cut off; clip; *fig.* restrict; F (*na egzaminie*) fail, *Am.* flunk; ~**ciosywać** (*-uję*) → **ciosać**; ~**cisły** skin-tight

obco *adv.* (*czuć się*) foreign, strange; ~**języczny** foreign-language; ~**krajowiec** *m* foreigner; ~**ść** *f* (*-ści; 0*) strangeness, foreignness; ~**wać** (*-uję*) (**z** *I*) associate (with); mix (with); ~**wanie** *n* (*-a; 0*) (**z** *I*) association (with), mixing (with); dealings *pl.* (with)

ob|cy 1. somebody else's, other people's; strange; foreign; **2.** *m* (*-ego; -cy*), ~**ca** *f* (*-ej; -ce*) stranger; outsider; ~**czyzna** *f* (*-y; 0*) foreign lands *pl.*; **na** ~**czyźnie** in exile

obdarow(yw)ać (*-[w]uję*) present

obdarty shabby, ragged

obdarzać (*-am*) → **darzyć**

obdrapany scratched

obdukcja *f* (*-i; -e*) *jur.* autopsy, post-mortem

obdzie|lać (*-am*) ⟨~**lić**⟩ (**k-o** *I*) distribute (to); hand out (to); ~**rać** (*-am*) (*ze skóry*) skin; *skórę* graze; *korę* bark; *fig.* (**k-o**

z *G*) rob (of); F ~**rać ze skóry** (*A*) fleece

obecn|ie *adv.* at present, now; ~**ość** *f* (*-ści; 0*) presence; **lista** ~**ości** attendance list; ~**y** present (**przy** *L* at; **na** *L* in); current; ~**i** *pl.* those *pl.* present

obedrzeć *pf.* → **obdzierać**

obejmować (*-uję*) embrace, hug (**się** *v/i.*); (*zawierać, włączać*) include; *urząd, rządy* take; *okres* span; *lęk:* overcome; *płomienie:* catch; *umysłem* grasp; *wzrokiem* take in

obej|rzeć *pf.* → **oglądać**; ~**rzenie** *n:* **do** ~**rzenia** for inspection; **2.** ~**ście** *n* **1.** (*-a; G -ść*) *dom* farmstead; **2.** (*-a; 0*) manner *pl.*; **miły w** ~**ściu** charming, pleasant; ~**ść** *pf.* (→ **-jść**) → **obchodzić**

obel|ga *f* (*-i; G-*) insult, offence; ~**gi** *pl.* abuse; ~**żywie** *adv.* insultingly; offensively; abusively; ~**żywy** insulting; offensive; abusive

oberwać *pf.* → **obrywać**; ~**nie** *n:* ~**nie** (**się**) **chmury** cloudburst; ~**ny** ragged; → **obdarty**

oberża *f* (*-y; G -*) inn

oberżnąć *pf.* → **obrzynać**

oberżyna *f* (*-y; G -*) → **bakłażan**

obe|schnąć *pf.* → **obsychać**; ~**trzeć** *pf.* → **obcierać**; ~**znany** familiar (**z** *I* with)

obezwładni|ać (*-am*) ⟨~**ć**⟩ (*-ę, -nij!*) overpower; *uczucie:* overwhelm, overcome

obeżreć *pf.* → **obżerać**

obfi|cie *adv.* → **obfity**; ~**tość** *f* (*-ści; 0*) abundance; **róg** ~**tości** horn of plenty, *fig.* cornucopia; ~**tować** (*-uję*) (**w** *A*) abound (with), teem (with); ~**ty** abundant; plentiful; *porcja* generous

obgryzać ⟨~**źć**⟩ → **ogryzać**

obiad *m* (*-u; -y*) (*wieczorem*) dinner; (*w południe*) lunch; **jeść** ~ have dinner/lunch; ~**owy** dinner, lunch

obibok *m* (*-a; -i*) loafer

obi|cie *n* (*-a; G -ć*) upholstery; ~**ć** *pf.* → **obijać**; ~**e** *num. f/pl.* → **oba**

obiec|ać *pf.* (*-am*) → **obiecywać**; ~**anka** *f* (*-i; G -nek*) empty promise; ~**ująco** promisingly; ~**ujący** promising; ~**ywać** (*-uję*) promise; ~**ywać sobie po** (*L*) hope for

obieg *m* (*-u; 0*) *astr., phys.* rotation, revolution; (**krwi** blood) circulation; **czas** ~**u** *astr.* period; **puścić w** ~ circulate; **wycofać z** ~**u** withdraw from circulation; ~**ać** ⟨~**nąć**⟩ (*-am*) circulate, go (a)round; *astr.* revolve; *sklepy itp.* do the rounds of; ~owy current; **pieniądz ~owy** currency

obiek|cja *f* (-i; -e) objection; reservation; ~tyw *m* (-u; -y) *phot.* lens *sg.*; ~tywny objective

obie|rać (-*am*) *warzywa* peel; *owoce* skin; *os., zawód* go into; *(na stanowisko)* choose, appoint; ~ralny elected; ~rki *f/pl.* (-*rek*), ~rzyny *f/pl.* (-) peelings *pl.*

obietnica *f* (-y; *G* -) promise

obieżyświat F *m* (-*a*; -*y*) globetrotter

obijać (-*am*) *(młotkiem itp.)* knock off; *kubek itp.* chip; *krzesło* upholster; ~ **się o uszy** come to one's ears; ~ **się** F loaf about/around

objadać się F gorge o.s., stuff o.s.

objaśni|ać (-*am*) ⟨~*ć*⟩ (-*ę, nij!*) explain; ~enie *n* (-*a*) explanation

obja|w *m* (-*u*; -*y*) symptom *(też med.)*; ~wiać (-*am*) ⟨~*wić*⟩ manifest; show, reveal (**się** o.s.); ~wienie *n* (-*a*; *G* -*eń*) revelation *(też rel.)*

objazd *m* (-*u*; -*y*) detour; diversion; *(artystyczny)* tour; ~owy itinerant; *wysta-wa itp.* touring; **droga ~owa** bypass

ob|jąć *pf.* (-*ejmę*) → **obejmować**; ~jeść *pf.* → **objadać**; ~jeżdżać (-*am*) ⟨~*je-chać*⟩ *przeszkodę, plac* go round; *kraj* travel around; ~jęcie *n* (-*a*; *G* -*ęć*) embrace, hug; beginning; taking over; takeover; **w ~jęciach** (*G*) in the arms (of); → **obejmować**

objętość *f* (-*ści*; *0*) volume; capacity; size

ob|juczony (*I*) loaded (with), laden (with); ~kła-, ~ko-, ~kra- → **okła-, oko-, okra-**; ~lać *pf.* → **oblewać**; ~la-tany F *fig.* knowledgeable, well-versed; ~latywać (-*uję*) ⟨~*lecieć*⟩ *v/t.* fly (a)round; *(wypróbować samolot)* test-fly; ~**latywać sklepy** F do the rounds of the shops; ~legać (-*am*) ⟨~*lec, ~legnąć*⟩ besiege

oble|piać (-*am*) ⟨~*pić*⟩ stick all over *(ścianę itp.)*; ~śny lecherous; lascivious; ~wać (-*am*) douse; *wody:* wash; *fig.* *(ogarnąć)* flood; F *egzamin* fail; ~**wać się potem** be bathed in sweat; ~wanie *n* *(mieszkania)* house-warming (party); ~żć *pf.* → **obłazić**

oblężenie *n* (-*a*) siege

obli|cow(yw)ać (-[*w*]*uję*) *bud.* face; ~czać (-*am*) count; calculate; ~czalny calculable

oblicz|e *n* (-*a*; *G* -) *lit.* countenance, face; **w ~u** (*G*) in the face (of), in view (of); ~enie *n* (-*a*) calculation; count; ~eniowy computational; ~yć *pf.* → **obliczać**

obligacja *f* (-i; -*e*) *econ.* bond, stock

oblizywać (-*uję*) ⟨~*ać*⟩ lick

ob|lodzić ⟨-*dzę*⟩ ice up; ~lodzony icy; ~luzowany loose

obła|dow(yw)ać (-[*w*]*uję*) load; weigh; ~mywać (-*uję*) ⟨~*mać*⟩ break (**się** *v/ i.*); ~piać F (-*am*) ⟨~*pić*⟩ (-*ę*) neck; ~skawiony tame(d); ~wa *f* (-*y*; *G* -) hunt; *(na człowieka)* manhunt; ~zić *robaki:* cover (with); *farba:* peel off

obłąka|nie *n* (-*a*; *0*) → **obłęd**; ~niec F (-*ńca*; -*ńcy*) madman *m*, madwoman *f*; ~ny, ~ńczy mad, insane

obłęd *m* (-*u*; -*y*) madness, insanity; ~ny F terrific

obłok *m* (-*u*; -*i*) cloud

obło|wić się *pf.* F (**na** *L*) make a profit (from); ~żny: **~żna choroba** serious illness; **~żnie chory** bed-ridden; ~żyć *pf.* → **okładać**

obłożony: **~ język** coated tongue

obłud|a *f* (-*y*; *0*) hypocrisy; ~nica *f* (-*y*; *G* -), ~nik *m* (-*a*; -*cy*) hypocrite; ~ny hypocritical, false

obłu|pywać (-*uję*) ⟨~*pać*⟩ peel; *jajko* shell; ~skiwać (-*uję*) shell; → **łuskać**

obły oval

obmac|ywać (-*uję*) ⟨~*ać*⟩ → **macać**

obmarz|ać [-r·z-] (-*am*) ⟨~*nąć*⟩ ice up; freeze over

ob|mawiać (-*am*) slander, backbite; ~mierzać (-*am*) ⟨~*mierzyć*⟩ measure; ~mierzły [-r·z-] nasty; ~mowa *f* (-*y*; *G* -*mów*) slander, backbiting; ~mówić *pf.* → **obmawiać**; ~murow(yw)ać (-[*w*]*uję*) wall, surround with a wall; ~myć *pf.* → **obmywać**; ~myślać ⟨~*myślić*⟩ (-*am*) ⟨~*myślić*⟩ devise, think out; ~mywać (-*am*) bathe, wash; *fale:* wash

obnaż|ać (-*am*) ⟨~*yć*⟩ (-*ę*) bare, uncover; *fig.* reveal; ~**ać się** take one's clothes off; *fig.* expose o.s.; ~ony bare; naked; *fig.* reveal

obniż|ać (-*am*) ⟨~*yć*⟩ lower; *econ. też* reduce; ~**ać się** sink, come down; subside; ~ka *f* (-*i*; *G* -*żek*) *(cen, kosztów price, cost)* reduction; ~**kapłac** wage cut

obnosić pass round, show round

obojczyk *m* (-*a*; -*i*) *anat.* collar-bone, clavicle

obrywać

oboje → *obaj*

obojętn|ieć ⟨z-⟩ (-eję) become indifferent (**na** A to); ~ość f (-ści; 0) indifference; ~y indifferent; (*nijaki*) bland; **to mi ~e** I do not care

obojnak m (-a; -i) hermaphrodite

obok **1.** *adv.* nearby, next to, past; **tuż ~, ~ siebie** side by side; **2.** *prp.* beside, by, near

obolały sore, painful, aching

OBOP *skrót*: **Ośrodek Badania Opinii Publicznej** Centre for Research of Public Opinion

obopólny mutual, reciprocal

obor|a f (-y; G obór) cowshed, *Am.* barn; ~nik m (-a; 0) manure

obosieczny double-edged

obostrz|ać (-am) ⟨~yć⟩ make more severe, tighten; ~enie n (-a; G -eń) tightening; greater severity

obowiąz|any obliged (**do** G to); ~ek m (-zku; -zki) obligation; **poczuwać się do ~ku** feel obliged; **pełniący ~ki** (G) acting, deputy; ~kowo *adv.* obligatorily; → **obowiązkowy**; ~kowość f (-ści; 0) sense of duty; ~kowy obligatory, compulsory; **człowiek** conscientious; ~ujący valid, in force, binding; **nadać moc ~ującą** bring into force; ~ywać (-uję, t-ko 3. os.) be in force, hold

obozow|ać (-uję) camp (out); ~isko n (-a; G -) camping site, campsite; ~y camp, camping

obój m (-boju; -boje) *mus.* oboe

obóz m (-bozu; -bozy) camp; **stanąć obozem** set up camp

obrabia|ć (-am) work; machine; *ziemię* cultivate, till; *brzeg* hem; ~rka f (-i; G -rek) machine tool

obra|bow(yw)ać (-[w]uję) rob; ~cać (-am) turn; use; ~cać **na kupno** use for buying; reduce ~cać **w gruzy** reduce to rubble; ~cać **się** turn, rotate, spin; revolve; ~chow(yw)ać (-[w]uję) → **obliczać**; ~chunek m reckoning

obrać *pf.* → **obierać**

obrad|y *pl.* (G -) proceedings *pl.*, debate; ~ować (-uję) (**nad** I) debate

obra|dzać (-am) *roślina*: produce a good crop; ~mow(yw)ać (-[w]uję) border; frame; ~stać (-am) (I) grow over (with); be overgrown (with)

obraz m (-u; -y) picture; painting; film, *Am.* movie

obraza f (-y; *zw.* 0) offence, *Am.* offense; outrage; ~ **moralności publicznej** indecency

obrazek m (-zka; -zki) → *obraz*

obrazić *pf.* → *obrażać*

obraz|kowy picture; ~ować ⟨z-⟩ (-uję) portray; depict; ~owo graphically; ~owy graphic, vivid

obra|źliwie *adv.* offensively, insultingly; ~źliwy offensive, insulting; ~żać (-am) offend, insult; ~żenie n (-a; G -eń) injury; ~żony offended, insulted

obrąb|ywać (-uję) ⟨~ać⟩ chop off

obrączka f (-i; G -czek) (*ślubna*) ring; → **obręcz**

obręb m (-u; -y) area; **w ~ie** within, inside; **poza ~em** outside; ~ek m (-bka; -bki) hem; ~iać (-am) ⟨~ić⟩ (-ę) hem

obręcz f (-y; -e, -y) hoop, ring; (*koła*) (wheel) rim

obr/min *skrót pisany*: **obrotów na minutę** rpm (*revolutions per minute*)

obro|bić *pf.* → **obrabiać**; ~dzić *pf.* → **obradzać**; ~k m (-u; -i) horse feed, provender

obro|na f (-y; G -) defence, *Am.* defense; ~**na własna** self-defence; **stawać w ~nie** (G) stand up (for); → **bronić**; ~ność f (-ści; 0) defence capability; ~nny defence; ~ńca m (-y; G -ów); ~ńczyni f (-ni; -e, G -yń) defender (*też sport*); *fig.* protector; ~ńcy *pl.* (*w sporcie*) defence; ~ńczy *jur.*: **mowa ~ńcza** final speech, speech for the defence

obro|snąć *pf.* → **obrastać**; ~śnięty (I) overgrown (with)

obrotn|ość f (-ści; 0) resourcefulness, ingenuity; ~y resourceful, ingenuous

obrotomierz m (-a;-e) *mot.* tachometer, rev counter

obrotow|y revolving; *krzesło* swivel; *econ.* sales, turnover; **środki** *pl.* ~**e** active assets *pl.*

obroża f (-y; -e) collar

obróbka f (-i; G -bek) processing; *tech.* working

obró|cić *pf.* → **obracać**; ~t m (-rotu; -roty) turn; revolution; rotation; *econ.* turnover; *fig.* turn (**na** A for); **wziąć w obroty** (A) F give a talking-to

obrumieni|eć (-am) ⟨~ć⟩ *gastr.* brown

obrus m (-a; -y) tablecloth

obrys m (-u; -y) outline

obrywać (-am) tear down; *owoce* pick; ~ **się** come off

obryzgiwać (-uję) ⟨~ać⟩ splash

obrządek m (-dku; -dki) ritual; rite

obrzez|ać (-am) circumcise; ~anie n (-a; G -ań) circumcision

obrzeże n (-a; G -y) edge

obrzęd m (-u; -y) ceremony; → obrządek; ~owy ceremonial; ritual

obrzęk m (-u; -i) med. (o)edema; ~ać (-am) ⟨~nąć⟩ (-nę) med. swell (up); ~ły swollen

obrzmi|ałość f (-ści),~enie n (-a; -eń) swelling;~ały bloated; → obrzękły

obrzuc|ać (-am) ⟨~ić⟩ throw; pelt (się at each other); ~ić wzrokiem (A) cast a glance (at)

obrzyd|listwo n (-a; G -) disgusting thing; repulsiveness; ~liwiec m (-wca; -wcy) scoundrel; ~liwość f (-ści; 0) abomination;~liwy (-wie),~ły disgusting, repulsive;~nąć (-nę) pf:: ~ł(a)/~ło mi ... I am sick of...; → brzydnąć

obrzydz|ać (-am) ⟨~ić⟩ spoil, put off; ~enie n (-a; 0) disgust; loathing; revulsion; do ~enia until one has wearied

obrzynać (-am) cut off

obsa|da f (-y; G -) theat. cast, casting; (załoga) crew; personnel; tech. holder, mounting; ~dka f (-i; G -dek) holder; ~dzać (-am) ⟨~dzić⟩ (I) plant (with); fig. fill; cast; → osadzać

obserwa|cja f (-i; -e) observation;~cyjny observational; ~tor m (-a; -rzy) observer; ~torium n (idkl.; -ia, -iów) observatory; ~torka f (-i) observer

obserwować (-uję) ⟨za-⟩ watch; observe

obsług|a f (-i; G -) service; handling; (personel) staff; ~iwać (-uję) serve, deal with

obstaw|a f (-y; G -) zbior. F guard;~ać (-ję) (przy L) insist (on), persist (in); ~i(a)ć (I) surround; pieniądze bet (on), stake (on)

obst|ępować (-uję) ⟨~ąpić⟩ surround, ring

obstrukcja f (-i; -e) obstruction; med. constipation

obstrz|ał m (-u; -y) shelling, shooting; ~eliwać (-wuję) ⟨~elać⟩ (A) shoot (at), fire (at)

obsu|wać się ⟨~nąć się⟩ slip

obsy|chać (-am) dry; ~pywać (-uję) ⟨~pać⟩ scatter, sprinkle; fig. heap, shower; ~p(yw)ać się crumble away

obszar m (-u; -y) area, region; territory; ~nik m (-a; -cy) big landowner

obszarpany ragged

obszerny large, extensive;~ubranieloose

obszy|cie n (-a; G -yć) trimming, edging; ~wać (-am) ⟨~ć⟩ (I) trim (with), edge (with)

obt|aczać ⟨~oczyć⟩ roll; ~aczać w mące toss in flour; tech. turn

obtarcie n (-a; G -rć) med. abrasion, graze; (szmatą itp.) swell

obu num. → oba; w złoż. bi-, di-, two-

obuch m (-a; -y) poll

obudow|a f (-y; G -dów) casing, housing;~(yw)ać (-[w]uję) (I) build up; encase

obudzić pf. → budzić

obukierunkowy two-way

oburącz adv. with both hands

oburz|ać (-am) ⟨~yć⟩ outrage, incense; ~ać się become outraged lub indignant (na A about); ~ająco adv. outrageously; ~ający outrageous; ~enie n (-a; 0) outrage; indignation; ~ony indignant, incensed

obustron|nie adv. mutually; bilaterally; ~ny mutual; bilateral

obuwie n (-a; 0) shoes pl., footgear; sklep z ~m shoe shop/store

obwa|łow(yw)ać (-[w]uję) rzekę embank; ~rowanie n (-a; G -ań) embankment

obwarzanek m (-nka; -nki) pretzel

obwąch|iwać (-uję) ⟨~ać⟩ sniff

obwiąz|ywać (-uję) ⟨~ać⟩ (I) tie up (with); wrap (with)

obwie|szczać (-am) ⟨~ścić⟩ announce; make public; ~szczenie n (-a; G -eń) announcement; public notice; ~źć pf. → obwozić

obwi|jać → owijać; ~niać (-am) ⟨~nić⟩ (k-o o A) blame (s.o. for); ~sać (-am) ⟨~snąć⟩ droop, sag

obwo|dnica f (-y; -e) Brt. ring road; bypass, Am. belt(way); ~dowy peripheral; district; ~luta f (-y; G -) dust jacket; ~ływać (-uję) ⟨~łać⟩ (I) proclaim; ~zić drive round (po mieście the town)

obwód m (-odu; -ody) perimeter; math. circumference; (obszar) district; electr. circuit; ~ scalony integrated circuit; ~ka f (-i; G -dek) border, edge

oby *part.* may it be so; **~ był szczęśliwy!** may he be happy!

obycie *n* (*-a; 0*) good manners *pl.*; **~ w świecie** worldliness

obyczaj *m* (*-u; -e, -ów*) custom; *pl. też* morals *pl.*; **starym ~em** in accordance with an old custom; **zepsucie ~ów** moral decline; **~owość** *f* (*-ści; 0*) custom, customs *pl.*; morals *pl.*; **~owy** moral; *policja:* vice

obyć się *pf.* → **obywać się**

obydw|**a**(**j**), **~ie**, **~oje** → **oba, oboje**

oby|**ty** polite, well-bred; (**z** *I*) experienced (with), familiar (with); **~wać się** (**bez** *G*) do without, go without; (*I*) make do (without), content o.s. (with)

obywatel *m* (*-a; -e*), **~ka** *f* (*-i; G -lek*) citizen; national; **~ski** civic; civil; **~stwo** *n* (*-a; G -*) citizenship; nationality

obżar|**stwo** *f* (*-a; 0*) gluttony; **~tuch** *m* (*-a; -y*) F pig, glutton

OC *skrót pisany:* **ubezpieczenie OC (odpowiedzialności cywilnej)** *mot* third party insurance

ocal|**ać** (*-am*) → **ocalić**; **~eć** (*-eję*) (**z** *G*) survive (from); **~eć od śmierci** escape death; **~enie** *n* (*-a*) rescue; salvation; saving; **~ić** *pf.* (*-ę*) (**od** *G*) save (from)

ocean *m* (*-u; -y*) ocean

ocen|**a** *f* (*-y; G -*) assessment, valuation; estimate; (*w szkole*) *Brt.* mark, *Am.* grade; **~iać** (*-am*) ⟨**~ić**⟩ assess, evaluate; estimate; *Brt.* mark, *Am.* grade

ocet *m* (*octu; octy*) vinegar

ochładzać (*-am*) → **chłodzić**

ochłap *m* (*-u; -y*) scrap of meat

och|**łodzenie** *n* (*-a; G -eń*) cooling; **~onąć** *pf.* cool down; calm down; **~onąć z szoku** recover from shock

ocho|**czo** *adv.* willingly; eagerly; **~czy** eager; cheerful; (**do** *G*) **~chętny**; **~ta** *f* (*-y; 0*) desire, willingness; **mieć ~tę na** (*A*) feel like doing; → **chęć**

ochotni|**czka** *f* (*-i; G -czek*) volunteer; **~czo** *adv.* voluntarily; **~czy** voluntary; **~k** *m* (*-a; -cy*) volunteer

ochra *f* (*-y; 0*) ochre

ochrania|**cz** *m* (*-a; -e*) guard; pad; **~ć** (*-am*) protect, shelter (**od** *G* from, against)

ochron|**a** *f* (*-y; G -*) protection; (*osoba*) bodyguard; **~a środowiska naturalnego** conservation; **~iarz** *m* (*-a; -e*) F

bodyguard; **~ić** *pf.* (*-nię*) → **ochraniać, chronić**; **~ny** protective

ochryp|**le** hoarsely; **~ły** hoarse, husky; → **chrypnąć**

ochrzanić F *pf.* (*-ę*) rap

ociąg|**ać się** (*-am*) (**z** *I*) dawdle (over)

ocie|**kać** (*-am*) (*I*) be dripping wet; drip (with); **~lić się** *pf.* calf

ociemniały (*m-os -li*) blind; **związek ~ch** organization of the blind

ociep|**lać** (*-am*) ⟨**~ić**⟩ (*-lę*) warm; *budynek itp.* insulate; **~ać się** get warm; **~enie** *n* (*-a; 0*) warming up; insulation

ocierać (*-am*) → **obcierać**; *skórę* chafe

ocię|**żale** heavily; **~ły** heavy

ocios|**ywać** (*-uje*) ⟨**~ać**⟩ hew

ocknąć się *pf.* (*-nę*) wake up; (*po omdleniu itp.*) come round

oclen|**ie** *n* payment of duty; **podlegający ~u** dutiable; **nie mieć nic do ~a** have nothing to declare

oclić *pf.* → **clić**

oct|**an** *m* (*-u; -y*) *chem.* acetate; **~owy** vinegar

o|**cukrzyć** *pf.* → **cukrzyć**; **~cyganić** F *pf.* con, diddle; **~czarow(yw)ać** (*-[w]uję*) charm, enthral(l)

oczekiw|**ać** (*-uję*) expect (**po kimś** from s.o.); wait (**na** *A* for); **~anie** *n* (*-a*) expectation; waiting; **wbrew ~aniom** contrary to expectation

oczerni|**ać** (*-am*) ⟨**~ć**⟩ *fig.* blacken; defame

ocz|**ko** *n* (*-a; G -czek*) → **oko**; (*na karcie*) pip; (*gra w karty*) blackjack; (*w pończosze*) *Brt.* ladder, *Am.* run; (*przy dzierganiu*) stitch; (*w pierścionku*) stone; (*w sieci*) mesh; **~ny** eye; *anat.* ocular; optic; **~odół** *m anat.* eye-socket, orbit; **~y** *pl.* → **oko**

oczyszcza|**ć** (*-am*) (**z** *G*) clean (from/off), clear (from), *fig.* exonerate (from); *por. czyścić*; **~lnia** *f* (*-i; -e*) (*ścieków*) sewage treatment plant; **~nie** *n* (*-a; G -ań*) cleaning; clearing

oczy|**tany** well-read; **~wisty** obvious, evident; **~wiście** *adv.* obviously, evidently

od *prp.* (*G*) from; (*czasu*) since, for; (*niż*) than; (*przeciw*) against, for; **~ morza** from the sea; **~ rana** since the morning; **~ 2 godzin** for 2 hours; **starszy ~e mnie** older than me; **~ kaszlu** for coughing, against coughing; *często nie* *tłumaczy się*: **dziurka ~ klucza** keyhole; **~ ręki** right away; *por.* **dla, do**

odb. *skrót pisany*: **odbiorca** addressee

odbarwi|ać (*-am*) ⟨**~ć**⟩ discolo(u)r (**się** *v/i.*)

odbezpiecz|ać (*-am*) ⟨**~yć**⟩ (*-ę*) *broń* release the safety catch

odbi|cie *n* reflection; image; (*piłki*) hitting off; (*kraju*) reconquest; (*uwolnienie*) release; **~cie od brzegu** *naut.* cast-off; **kąt ~cia** angle of reflection; **~ć** *pf.* → **odbijać**

odbie|c *pf.*, **~gać** ⟨**~gnąć**⟩ (*od A*) run away (from); *fig.* differ (from), deviate (from); **~gł go sen** he was unable to sleep; **~gła ją chęć na to** she no longer took pleasure in it; **~rać** (*-am*) (**od** *G*) take away (from); *paczkę* collect (from), reclaim; *dziecko* pick up; *przysięgę, towar, RTV*: receive (from); *telefon* answer; → **odebrać**

odbijać (*-am*) *v/t. światło* reflect, throw back; *pieczęć* imprint; *deseń* print; (*na kopiarce*) run off; *tynk itp.* knock off; *atak* fend off; *piłkę* return; *jeńców* rescue; *miasto itp.* win back; (*w tańcu*) cut in; *sympatię* steal; *v/i. łódź*: cast off; **~ się** be reflected; *głos*: echo, resound; *piłka*: bounce; *narciarz*: push off; *ślad*: leave marks; *fig.* have an effect (**na** *A* on); F (*po jedzeniu*) belch, *dziecko*: burp

odbior|ca *m* (*-y*; *G -ców*), **~czyni** *f* (*-i*; *-e*) receiver; recipient; **~czy** receiving; **~nik** *m* (*-a*; *-i*) *RTV*: receiver, set

od|biór *m* (*-oru*; *0*) reception; **~bitka** *f* (*-i*; *G -tek*) *phot.*, *print.* copy; **~bity** *światło* reflected; **~błask** *m* reflection; **~błaskowy** *tech.* reflective; **~błyśnik** *m* (*-a*; *-i*) reflector

odbudo|wa *f* restoration; re-building; **~w(yw)ać** (*-[w]uję*) restore, re-build

odby|cie *n* (*-a*; *0*): **~cie kary** serving of sentence; **w celu ~cia rozmów** to carry out negotiations; **~ć** *pf.* → **odbywać**

odbytnica *f* (*-y*; *-e*, *G -*) *anat.* rectum

odbywać *zebranie* hold; *studia* pursue; *służbę*, *karę* serve, go through; *podróż* make; **~ się** take place

odc. *skrót pisany*: **odcinek** sector

odcho|dy *pl.* (*-ów*) excrements *pl.*, f(a)eces *pl.*; **~dzić** go away; *pociąg itp.*: leave, depart; *ulica*: branch (off), diverge; (*z pracy*) (**z** *G*) quit, leave; (**od** *G*) leave; (*umrzeć*) depart from this

world; *fig.* leave; **~dzić od zmysłów** be out of one's senses

od|chrząknąć *pf.* clear one's throat; → **chrząkać**; **~chudzać się** (*-am*) slim

odchyl|ać (*-am*) ⟨**~ić**⟩ deflect (**się** *v/i.*); (**do tyłu**) bend back (**się** *v/i.*); *firankę* draw back; **~ać się** deflect; deviate (**od** *G* from); **~enie** *n* (*-a*) deviation; departure

odcią|ć *pf.* → **odcinać**; **~gać** (*-am*) ⟨**~gnąć**⟩ *v/t.* draw back; pull away; *fig.* dissuade (**od** *G* from); *uwagę* divert; **mleko ~gane** *Brt.* skimmed milk, *Am.* skim milk; **~żać** (*-am*) ⟨**~żyć**⟩ lighten, relieve

odcie|kać (*-am*) ⟨**~c**⟩ drain away

od|cień *m* (*-nia*; *-nie*) shade; tone; nuance; **~cierpieć** *pf.* (**za** *A*) suffer (for); *rel.* atone (for)

odcię|cie *n* (*-a*; *G -ęć*) cutting off; *med.* amputation; **~ty** cut off; **~ta** *f* (*-ej*; *-e*) *math.* abscissa

odcin|ać (*-am*) cut (off); *med.* amputate; *dostęp* seal off; *gaz* disconnect; *połączenia* sever (*też fig.*); **~ać się** answer back; (**od** *G*) separate (from), distance (from); stand out, contrast (**na tle** against); **~ek** *m* (*-nka*; *-nki*) section; *math.* segment; stub, (*biletu itp.*) counterfoil; (*podróży*) leg; (*filmu*) episode; **~ek czasu** period; **powieść w ~kach** serialized novel

odcis|k *m* (*-u*; *-i*) impression, imprint; (*stopy*) print; *med.* corn; **~k palca** fingerprint; **~kać** (*-am*) ⟨**~nąć**⟩ *pieczęć* impress; *ser* squeeze; *ślad* make; **~nąć się** leave an imprint

od|cyfrować *pf.* (*-uję*) decode; decipher; **~czekać** *pf.* wait; **~czepi(a)ć** (*-am*) detach, remove; unfasten; undo; **~czepić się** lay off (**od** *G*)

odczu|(wa)ć feel; (*wyczuwać*) sense; perceive; **dać się ~ć** be felt; **~walny** perceivable, perceptible

odczyn *m* (*-u*; *-y*) *chem.* reaction; *med.* **~ Biernackiego** (*skrót*: OB) erythrocyte sedimentation rate (*skrót*: ESR); **~nik** *m* (*-a*; *-i*) *chem.* reagent

odczyt *m* (*-u*; *-y*) lecture, talk; **~ywać** (*-uję*) ⟨**~ać**⟩ read out

oddać *pf.* → **oddawać**

odda|lać (*-am*) ⟨**~lić**⟩ (*-lę*) drive away; (*ze szkoły*) expel; *wniosek* reject; *jur.* dismiss; **~lać** ⟨**~lić**⟩ **się** go away; (**z** *G*) leave; ~**lenie** n (-a; -leń) distance; jur. rejection, dismissal; (ze szkoły) expulsion; ~**lony** distant, remote; ~**nie** n (-a; G -ń) return; fig. devotion, dedication; ~**nie do eksploatacji** bringing into service; ~**ny** devoted, dedicated

oddaw|**ać** (-ję) give back, return; give; cześć pay; usługę do; ukłony return; (do instytucji) send; broń, miasto surrender; ~**ać mocz** pass water; ~**ać pod sąd** bring to court; ~**ać się** give o.s. up; komuś give o.s. to; ~**ca** m (-y), ~**czyni** f (-i; -e) bearer

oddech m (-u; -y) breath; ~**owy** breathing

oddolny fig. grass-roots

oddycha|**ć** (-am) breathe; ~**nie** n (-a; 0) breathing, respiration; **sztuczne ~nie** artificial respiration, resuscitation

oddz. skrót pisany: **oddział** department

oddział m (-u; -y) department, section; mil. troop, unit; med. ward; ~**owy** departmental; med. ward; ~**ywać** (-uję/ -am) ⟨-**ać**⟩ (**na** A) affect, act (on)

oddziel|**ać** (-am) ⟨-**ić**⟩ separate (**się** v/i.); ~**ny** separate

oddzwaniać (-niam) ⟨-**dzwonić**⟩ (-nię) (**do k-ś**) call back s.o.

oddźwięk m (-u; -i) repercussion; fig. response, reaction

ode pf. → **od**; ~**brać** pf. → **odbierać**

ode|**chcie(wa)ć** się: ⟨~**chciewa**⟩ ⟨~**chciało**⟩ **mu się** (G, bezok.) he is not eager (to bezok.) any more; ~**gnać** pf. → **odganiać**; ~**grać** pf. → **odgrywać**

odejmowa|**ć** (-uję) math. subtract; (zabierać) deduct; (odłączać) take away; ~**nie** n (-a; 0) math. subtraction

odejś|**cie** n (-a; G -ść) departure; ~**ć** pf. → (-**jść**) → **odchodzić**

ode|**mknąć** → **odmykać**; ~**pchnąć** pf. → **odpychać**; ~**przeć** pf. → **odpierać**; v/i. retort, reply; ~**rwać** pf. → **odrywać**; ~**rwanie** n (-a; 0) detachment; **w ~rwaniu** (**od** G) in isolation (from); ~**rznąć** pf., ~**rżnąć** pf. → **odrzynać**; ~**słać** pf. → **odsyłać**; ~**tchnąć** pf. breathe (**swobodnie** freely); fig. have a breather; ~**tkać** pf. (-am) → **odtykać**; ~**zwa** f (-y; G -dezw) proclamation; ~**zwać się** pf. (-ę, -ie, -wij!) → **odzywać się**

odęty puffed up; grumpy, surly; → **nadąsany**

odfajkow(yw)ać (-[w]uję) Brt. tick

off, Am. check off

odfru|**wać** (-am) ⟨~**nąć**⟩ (-nę) fly away, take flight

odga|**dywać** (-uję) ⟨-**dnąć**⟩ (-nę) guess; ~**łęziać się** ⟨-**łęzić się**⟩ (-żę) branch off; ~**łęzienie** f (-a; G -eń) branching, forking; ~**niać** → **odpędzać**; ~**rniać** (-am) ⟨-**rnąć**⟩ rake aside, push aside; śnieg scrape away

od|**ginać** (-am) ⟨~**giąć**⟩ (-egnę) bend (up, back itp.); ~**głos** m (-u; -y) echo; zw. pl. sound, noise; ~**gniatać** (-am) ⟨~**gnieść**⟩ mark; ~**gniatać się** make marks; ~**gonić** pf. → **odpędzić**; ~**gradzać** (-am) fence off

odgranicz|**ać** (-am) ⟨~**yć**⟩ bound, enclose

odgrażać się (-am) threaten; ~**grodzić** pf. → **odgradzać**; ~**gruzow**(**yw**)**ać** (-[w]uję) remove the rubble; ~**grywać** (-am) play; głupiego play, act; ~**grywać się** get one's revenge; ~**gryzać** (-am) ⟨~**gryźć**⟩ bite off; ~**gryzać się** hit back; ~**grzać** pf. → **odgrzewać**

odgrze|**bywać** (-uję) ⟨~**bać**⟩ dig up; fig. rake up; ~**wać** (-am) re-warm, warm up

od|**gwizdać** pf. whistle; blow the whistle; ~**holować** pf. tow away; ~**izolowywać** (-wuję) → **izolować**

od|**jazd** m (-u; -y) departure; ~**jąć** pf. (-ejmę) → **odejmować**; ~**jemna** f (-ej; -e) math. minuend; ~**jemnik** m (-a; -i) math. subtrahend; ~**jeżdżać** (-am) ⟨~**jechać**⟩ (I, **na** L) depart (in/on), drive off (in/on); leave (**do** G for); ~**karmiony** well-fed; ~**każać** (-am) ⟨~**kazić**⟩ (-żę) disinfect, teren decontaminate; ~**każający** disinfecting, antiseptic

odkąd pron. from/since when; since; from; (from) where

odkła|**dać** (-am) put away, put back, replace; słuchawkę hang up; (oszczędzać) put aside, put by; (odraczać) put off, postpone; ~**dać się** being kept, be deposited; ~**niać się** ⟨**odkłonić się**⟩ (D) return s.o.'s greetings

odkodować (-uję) szyfrogram decode; RTV: unscramble

od|**komenderować** pf. send, detail (**do** G to/for); ~**kopywać** (-uję) ⟨~**kopać**⟩ dig up; ~**korkow(yw)ać** (-[w]uję) uncork; ~**krajać** ⟨~**krawać**⟩ (-am) cut off; ~**kręcać** (-am) ⟨~**kręcić**⟩ unscrew; twist off; kurek turn on; ~**kroić** pf. → **odkrajać**

odkry|cie n (-a; G -yć) discovery; ~wać (-am) ⟨~ć⟩ ląd discover; ramię, twarz uncover; fig. reveal, expose; ~wać ⟨~ć⟩ się throw off one's covers; ~ty uncovered; ląd discovered; ~wca m (-y; G -ów), ~wczyni f (-i; G -yń) discoverer; ~wczy of discovery; fig. revealing; ~wka f (-i; G -wek) Brt. opencast mine, Am. strip mine

odkup|iciel m (-a; -e) rel. redeemer; ~ywać (-uję)⟨~ić⟩(od G) buy back (from), repurchase (from); winę compensate, expiate; rel. redeem; → okupywać

odkurz|acz m (-a; -e) vacuum, vacuum cleaner, Brt. Hoover; ~ać (-am) ⟨~yć⟩ vacuum

od|lać pf. → odlewać; ~latywać (-uję) ⟨~lecieć⟩ fly away; samolot: depart; obcas itp.: come off

odległ|ość f (-ści) distance; range; ~y adj.(comp. -glejszy)remote;distant;far-away; ~y o pięć kroków 5 steps away

odlepi|ać (-am) ⟨~ć⟩ remove, unstick

odlew m (-u; -y) cast; ~ać (-am) pour off; tech. cast; ~ać się V take a leak; ~nia f (-i; -e) foundry

odleż|eć się pf. owoce: mature; fig. wait one's turn; ~yny pl. (G -yn) med. bedsores

odlicz|ać (-am) ⟨~yć⟩ count (out); (odjąć) deduct; ~enie n (-a) count; deduction; (czasu) countdown

odlot m departure; czas ~u departure time

odludny secluded, isolated

odłam m (-u; -y) fig. fraction; pol. faction; ~ek m (-mka; -mki) splinter; chip; fragment; ~ywać (-uję) ⟨~ać⟩ break (off) (się v/i.)

od|łączać (-am) ⟨~łączyć⟩ disconnect; isolate (się v/i.); → odczepiać; ~łożyć pf. → odkładać; ~łóg m (-ogu; -ogi) fallow land; leżeć ~łogiem lie fallow; ~łu-pywać (-uję)⟨~łupać⟩chip off,split off

odma|czać soak off; ~low(yw)ać (-[w]uję) repaint; fig. depict; → malować; ~rzać [-r·z-] (-am) ⟨~rznąć⟩ thaw out (v/i.); defrost; ~wiać (G) refuse, deny (sobie o.s.), (k-o od G) talk s.o. out of s.th.; (A) pacierz say; wizytę cancel; ~wiać przyjęcia reject; ~wiać wstępu turn away

odmęt m (-u; -y) lit. zw. pl. waters pl., fig. whirls pl.

odmian|a f (-y; G -) change; agr., biol. variety; (odmianka) variant; gr. inflection; dla ~y, na ~ę for a change

odmien|iać (-am)⟨~ić⟩change (się v/i.); transform; gr. inflect; ~ić się change; ~ność f (-ści; 0) difference; different nature; ~ny different; gr. inflectional

od|mierzać (-am)⟨~mierzyć⟩measure; ~mładzać (-am) ⟨~młodzić⟩ rejuvenate, make younger; ~młądzać ⟨~młodzić⟩ się become younger; grow young again; ~młodnieć pf. → młodnieć; ~moczyć pf. → odmaczać; ~mowa f (-y; G -mów) refusal, denial; ~mowny negative; ~mówić pf. → odmawiać; ~mrażać (-am) ⟨~mrozić⟩ defrost, de-ice; ~mrażać sobie uszy lose ears through frostbite; ~mrożenie n (-a; G -eń) frostbite; ~myć pf. → odmywać; ~mykać pf. (-am) open, unlock; ~mywać (-am) wash off; naczynia wash up

odna|jdować, ~jdywać (-uję) find again (się each other); fig. regain; ~jmować ⟨~jąć⟩ hire, rent; ~leźć pf. (→ -naleźć) → odnajdować; ~wiać (-am) renovate; ~wiać się renew itself

odnie|sienie n (-a): w ~sieniu do (G) with reference to; ~ść pf. → odnosić

odno|ga f→odgałęzienie; arm, branch; (górska) offset, spur; (rzeki) river) arm, branch; ~sić (-szę) carry back, take back; wrażenie from: sukces, zwycięstwo achieve; korzyść reap; szkodę, rany suffer; ~sić się (do G) apply (to), refer (to); relate (to); feel (about); ~śnie ~śnie do (G) with respect to; ~śny concerning, appropriate

odno|tow(yw)ać (-[w]uję) take down; fig. note; ~wić pf. (-ę, -nów!) → odnawiać

odos|abniać (-am) ⟨~obnić⟩ (-ę, -nij!) isolate (się v/i.); ~obnienie n (-a; 0) isolation; (zamknięcie) confinement; ~obniony isolated; confined

odór m (-oru; -ory) bad smell, stench

odpad|ać (-am) fall off, come off; fig. be inapplicable, be inappropriate; sport: be eliminated; ~ek m (-dka; -dki) zw. pl. ~ki refuse, Brt. rubbish, Am. garbage; (na ulicy) litter; ~(k)owy waste; ~y m/pl. (G -ów) (przemysłowe) waste

odpa|rcie n (-a; 0) (ataku) repulsion; (zarzutu) refutation, rebuttal; ~row(yw)ać (-[w]uję) evaporate; fig.

parry, fend off; **~rzać** (*-am*) ⟨**~rzyć**⟩
chafe; **~ść** *pf.* → **odpadać**

od|pędzać (*-am*) ⟨**~pędzić**⟩ chase
away; ward off; **~piąć** *pf.* (*-epnę*) → **od-
pinać**; **~pić** *pf.* → **odpijać**; **~pieczęto-
w(yw)ać** (*-[w]uję*) unseal; **~pierać**
(*-am*) *atak*, *wroga* repel, drive back; *cios*
parry, ward off; *zarzut* refute, disprove

odpi|jać (*-am*) drink off; **~łow(yw)ać**
(*-[w]uję*) saw off; **~nać** (*-am*) undo, un-
fasten; *guzik* unbutton; **~nać** ⟨**~ąć**⟩
się get undone

odpis *m* (*-u*; *-y*) copy; *econ.* deduction;
~ywać (*-uję*) ⟨**~ać**⟩ copy; *econ.* write
off; deduct

odpła|cać (*-am*) ⟨**~cić**⟩ (*za A*) pay
back (*też fig.*), repay; **~ta** *f* (*-y*; *G* -) repayment (*też fig.*); **~tny** paid

odpły|nąć *pf.* → **odpływać**; **~w** *m* (*-u*;
-y) outlet; (*morza*) ebb, low tide; *fig.*
migration, departure; **~wać** (*-am*) *ludzie*: swim away; *statek*: sail out; *ciecz*:
flow away; *ludność*: emigrate; **~wowy**
kratka drain

odpocz|ynek *m* (*-nku*; *-nki*) rest; peace;
~ywać (*-am*) ⟨**~ąć**⟩ rest, have a rest

odpo|kutow(yw)ać (*-[w]uję*) atone
for; *rel.* redeem; **~mpow(yw)ać** (*-[w]u-
ję*) pump out

odporn|ość *f* (*-ści*) resistance; resili-
ence (*też biol.*); *med.* immunity, resistance; **~y** (*na A*) resistant (to); **~y na
wpływy atmosferyczne** weather-res-
istant

odpowi|adać (*-am*) answer (**na** *A* to;
za *A* for); reply, respond; (*być odpowiednim*) be appropriate, be suitable;
match; **~edni** (**do** *G*) suitable (to),
suitable (to); adequate (to); **~ednik** *m*
(*-a*; *-i*) counterpart, equivalent; **~ednio**
adv. appropriately, suitably

odpowiedzialn|ość *f* (*-ści*; *0*) responsi-
bility; accountability; *econ.* liability;
spółka z ograniczoną ~ością limited
liability company; **~y** responsible (*za*
A for)

od|powiedzieć *pf.* → **odpowiadać**;
~powiedź *f* (*-dzi*) answer, reply; response

odpowietrzyć *pf.* (*-ę*) bleed

odpór *m* (*-poru*; *0*) resistance

odpra|cow(yw)ać (*-[w]uję*) work out;
~wa *f* (*-y*; *G* -) briefing; (*odmowa*) re-
buff; (*zapłata*) compensation; *aviat.*

check-in; **~wa celna** customs *pl.*; **~wiać**
(*-am*) ⟨**~wić**⟩ *towar* dispatch; *rel.*
celebrate, officiate; → **odsyłać**

odpręż|ać (*-am*) ⟨**~yć**⟩ (*-ę*) relax (**się**
v/i.); **~enie** *n* (*-a*; *G -eń*) relaxation;
pol. détente

odprowadz|ać (*-am*) ⟨**~ić**⟩ accomany,
escort; *ścieki itp.* carry (away); **~ać do
drzwi** show to the door; **~ać do domu**
see home; **~ać na dworzec** see off

odpru|wać (*-am*) ⟨**~ć**⟩ unseam, rip

odprys|kiwać (*-uję*) ⟨**~nąć**⟩ flake off

odprzeda|wać (*-ję*) ⟨**~ć**⟩ (*-am*) resell

odpu|st *m* (*-u*; *-y*) *rel.* indulgence; (*fes-
tyn*) fête; **~szczać** (*-am*) ⟨**~ścić**⟩ par-
don, forgive

odpycha|ć (*-am*) push away, shove
away; *fig.*, *phys.* repel; **~jąco** *adv.* repulsively; **~jący** repulsive

odpyl|ać (*-am*) ⟨**~ić**⟩ dust

odra *f* (*-y*; *0*) *med.* measles *sg.*; ♀ *f* (*-y*; *0*)
(the) Oder, Odra

odra|biać (*-am*) *dług* work off; *lekcje*
do; *zaległości*, *błędy* make up for; *zaległości też* catch up with; **~czać** (*-am*)
put off, postpone; *jur.* suspend; **~dzać¹**
(*-am*) ⟨**~dzić**⟩ (*A*) advise (against)

odra|dzać² → **odrodzić**; **~pywać**
(*-uję*) ⟨**~pać**⟩ scratch; **~stać** (*-am*)
grow again; → **podrastać**; **~tow-
(yw)ać** (*-[w]uję*) rescue; *fig.* revive; **~za**
f (*-y*; *0*) repulsion, aversion; **~żająco**
adv. repulsively, disgustingly; **~żający**
repulsive, disgusting

odrąb|ywać (*-uję*) ⟨**~ać**⟩ chop off

odre- *pf.* → **re-**

odrę|bny different; distinct, special;
~czny hand-written; *rysunek* free-
-hand; *naprawa* on the spot, immediate

odrętwie|ć *pf.* → **drętwieć**; **~nie** *n* (*-a*)
numbness; *fig.* lethargy

odro|bić *pf.* → **odrabiać**; **~bina** *f* (*-y*;
G -) particle; (*G*) a bit (of); **~czenie** *n*
(*-a*; *G -eń*) postponement, adjourn-
ment; (*wyroku*) reprieve; **~czyć** *pf.* →
odraczać; **~dzenie** *n* (*-a*; *0*) renas-
cence, rebirth, renaissance; ♀**dzenie**
Renaissance; **~dzić** *pf.* revive, renew;
~dzić się revive; **~snąć** *pf.* → **odrastać**

odróżni|ać (*-am*) ⟨**~ć**⟩ distinguish (**od**
G from); **~ać się** differ (**od** *G* from);
~enie *n* (*-a*) distinction; **w ~eniu**
(**od** *G*) in contrast (to), unlike; **nie do
~enia** indistinguishable

O

odruch m (-u; -y) biol. reflex; fig. emotion, prompting; **~owo** adv. involuntarily; **~owy** involuntary

odry|głow(yw)ać (-[w]uję) unbolt; **~wać** (-am) tear off; *wzrok* turn away; **~wać się** come off, break off; fig. wrench o.s. away (**od** G from)

odrzec pf. say

odrzu|cać (-am) **⟨~cić⟩** discard, cast off; *prośbę* turn down; (*w głosowaniu*) overrule; *skargę, warunki* reject; **~t** m mil. recoil; econ. reject; **~towiec** m (-wca; -wce) jet (plane); **~towy** jet

odrzwia pl. door frame

od|rzynać (-am) cut off; **~salanie** n (-a; 0) desalination; **~salutować** (-uję) salute; **~sapnać** (-nę) have a breather; **~sądzać** (-am) **⟨~sądzić⟩** (*kogoś od* G) deny

odset|ek m (-tka; -tki) percentage; **~ki** pl. interest (**za zwłokę** for late payment)

odsia|ć pf. → **odsiewać**; **~dywać** (-uję) sit out, F *wyrok* do

odsie|cz f (-y; -e) mil. relief; **~dzieć** pf. → **odsiadywać**; **~wać** (-am) sift; fig. sift through

od|skakiwać (-uję) **⟨~skoczyć⟩** (**od** G) jump aside/back; *piłka:* bounce (off); **~skocznia** f (-i; -e) springboard; **~słaniać** (-am) uncover; *pomnik* unveil; *prawdę* reveal; *głowę* bare; *zasłonę* draw (back); **~słaniać się** appear; **~słona** f (-y; G -) theat. act; **~słonić** pf. → **odsłaniać**; **~słonięcie** n (-a; G -ęć) unveiling; revelation

odsprzedawać → **odprzedawać**

odsta|wać **⟨~ć⟩** (→ **stać²**) come off; *uszy:* stick out; (*wyróżniać się*) stand out; **~wi(a)ć** put away, put aside; deliver; *lekarstwo* stop taking; **~wiać dziecko od piersi** wean the baby

odstąpi|ć pf. → **odstępować**; **~enie** n (-a) (*praw, ziemi*) cession; relinquishment, renunciation (**od** G of)

odstęp m (-u; -y) interval, distance; space, gap; **~ne** n (-ego; -e) compensation; **~nik** m (-a; -i) space-bar; **~ować** (-uję) v/i. step aside; cede; waive; econ. dispose; transfer; withdraw (**od umowy** from the agreement); mil. retreat, move away (**od** G from); v/t. cede, transfer; **~stwo** n (-a; G -) departure; rel. dissent

odstrasz|ać (-am) **⟨~yć⟩** scare away (**od** G from); deter; **~ająco** adv. frighteningly; **~ający** deterrent; frightening

odstręcz|ać (-am) **⟨~yć⟩** (-ę) fig. repel, put off; (*zniechęcać*) (**od** G) prevent (from)

odstrzał m (-u; -y) hunt. shooting down

odsuwać (-am) **⟨odsunąć⟩** push away, move away; *zasuwę, firankę* draw back; **~ od władzy** remove from power; **~ ⟨odsunąć⟩ się** move away; fig. withdraw, retire

odsyła|cz m (-a; -e) reference; **~ć** (-am) (**do** G) send back (to), return (to); refer (to)

odsyp|ywać (-uję) **⟨~ać⟩** pour away

odszkodowani|e n (-a; G -ań) compensation, recompense; jur. damages pl.; **~a wojenne** reparations pl.

od|szraniać (-am) **⟨~szronić⟩** (-ę) defrost; **~szukać** (-am) trace, find (again) (**się** v/i.); **~szyfrow(yw)ać** (-[w]uję) decipher, decode; **~śpiewać** pf. sing; **~środkowy** centrifugal

odśwież|ać (-am) **⟨~yć⟩** (-ę) refresh; *mieszkanie* renew; fig. brush up on; **~yć się** freshen o.s. up, refresh o.s.

od|świętny festive; **~tajać** pf. thaw

odtąd since; from… on…; *przestrzeń:* from here

odtłuszczon|y: *mleko* **~e** skimmed milk

od|transportować pf. take away, remove; **~trącać** (-am) **⟨~trącić⟩** push away, shove away; fig. reject; → **potrącać**; **~trutka** f (-i; G -tek) antidote (*też* fig.); **~twarzacz** m (-a; -e): **~twarzacz płyt kompaktowych** CD player; **~twarzać** (-am) **⟨~tworzyć⟩** reconstruct, reproduce; *taśmę* play; *rolę* play, act; **~twarzać się** biol. regenerate

odtwór|ca m (-y; G -ców), **~czyni** f (-i; -e) interpreter, performer

od|tykać (-am) unblock, unstop; **~uczać** (-am) **⟨~uczyć⟩**: **~uczać kogoś od** (G) teach s.o. not to; (*zwyczaju*) break s.o. of; **~uczać się** unlearn

odurz|ać (-am) **⟨~yć⟩** intoxicate; **~ać ⟨~yć⟩ się** become intoxicated; fig. become carried away; **~ająco** adv. intoxicatingly; **~ający** intoxicating, heady; **~enie** n (-a; G -eń) intoxication

odwadniać drain

odwag|a f (-i; 0) courage; **~a cywilna**

courage of one's convictions; **nabrać ~i, zebrać się na ~ę** muster up courage; **dodać ~** encourage

odwal|ać (*-am*) ⟨**~ić**⟩ remove; F (*wykonać*) get s.th. over and done with; (*wykonać źle*) bungle; **zostać ~onym** be given the brush-off; F **~ się!** get lost!

odwar *m* (*-u*; *-y*) *med.* decoction

odważ|ać (*-am*) weigh out; **~ać się → odważyć**; **~nik** *m* (*-a*; *-i*) weight; **~ny** courageous; brave; **~yć** *pf.* → **odważać**; **~yć się** (**na** *A*) dare (to); have the courage (to)

odwdzięcz|ać się ⟨**~yć się**⟩ (*-ę*) (**za** *A*) repay (for), return (for)

odwet *m* (*-u*; *0*) retaliation, reprisal; **w ~ za** in reprisal/retaliation for; **~owiec** *m* (*-wca*; *-wcy*) revanchist

od|wiązywać (*-uję*) ⟨**~wiązać**⟩ untie, undo; **~wiązać się** get untied, get undone; **~wieczny** perennial

odwiedz|ać (*-am*) ⟨**~ić**⟩ (*-dzę*) visit; **~iny** *pl.* (*-*) visit; **przyjść w ~iny** (**do** *G*) visit, come to visit

odwiert *m* (*-u*; *-y*) *tech.* well

od|wieźć *pf.* → **odwozić**; **~wieźć** *pf.* → **odwozić**; **~wijać** (*-am*) unwind, reel off; **rękaw** turn up; **~wijać się** unwind o.s.; **~wilż** *f* (*-y*; *-e*) thaw (*też fig.*); **~winąć** *pf.* → **odwijać**

od|wirow(yw)ać (*-[w]uję*) spin; *pranie też.* spin-dry; **~wlekać** (*-am*) ⟨**~wlec**⟩ drag away, pull away; *fig.* put off, delay; **~wodnić** *pf.* (*-ę*, *-nij!*) → **odwadniać**; **~wodzić** lead away, take away; *kurek* cock; **~wodzić od** (*G*) dissuade from

odwoła|ć *pf.* → **odwoływać**; **~nie** *n* cancellation; *jur.* repeal; **aż do ~nia** until further notice; **~nie alarmu** all-clear (signal); **~nie się** (**do** *G*) call (to), appeal (to); **~wczy** *jur.* appeal

odwoływać (*-uję*) call off, cancel; *urzędnika* recall, call back; *rozkaz, zamówienie* cancel, revoke; **~ się** (**do** *G*) turn (to), appeal (to)

odwozić (*samochodem*) drive off; cart away

odwraca|ć turn (round) (**się** *v/i.*); *głowę, klęskę* turn away; **~ć uwagę** distract; **~lny** reversible; **film ~lny** reversal film

odwrot|nie *adv.* conversely, vice versa; inversely; the other way round; **~ność** *f* (*-ści*; *0*) the opposite; reversal; *math.*

reciprocal; **~ny** opposite; reverse; **~na strona** back, reverse, the other side

odwró|cenie *n* (*-a*; *0*) reversal; **~cić** *pf.* → **odwracać**; **~t** *m* (*-otu*; *-oty*) *mil.*, *fig.* retreat; withdrawal; **na ~t → odwrotnie**; **na odwrocie** (*strony*) overleaf

odwyk|ać (*-am*) ⟨**~nąć**⟩ (*-nę*) (**od** *G*) lose the habit (of); **~owy** withdrawal

odwzajemni|ać (*-am*) ⟨**~ć**⟩ (*-ę*, *-nij!*) return; **~a(ć)ć się** repay (**k-u za** *A* s.o. for)

odyniec *m* (*-ńca*; *-ńce*) wild boar

odzew *m* (*-u*; *-y*) *mil.* password; *fig.* response

odziedziczony inherited

odzież *f* (*-y*; *0*) clothing, clothes *pl.*; **~owy** clothing, clothes

odzna|czać (*-am*) (*orderem*) decorate; single out, distinguish; **~czać się** stand out; **~czenie** *n* (*-a*; *G -eń*) decoration; (*wyróżnienie*) award; **~czyć** *pf.* → **odznaczać**; **~ka** *f* (*-i*; *G -*) badge

odzwierciedl|ać (*-am*) ⟨**~ić**⟩ (*-lę*, *-lij!*) reflect, mirror; **~ać się** be reflected; **~enie** *n* (*-a*; *G -eń*) reflection

odzwycza|jać (*-am*) ⟨**~ić**⟩ (*-ję*, *-j!*) break (**k-o od** *G* s.o. of) a habit, wean (**od** *G* from); **~jać** ⟨**~ić**⟩ **się** (**od** *G*) lose the habit (of)

odzysk|anie *n* (*-a*; *0*) recovery, recuperation; **~(iw)ać** (*-[w]uję*) recover; regain; *zdrowie* recuperate; *surowce* recycle; **~ać przytomność** regain consciousness

odzyw|ać się (*-am*) say, speak; *dzwonek*: sound, be heard; *gry w karty*: bid; (**do** *G*) speak (to); **nikt się nie odzywa** *tel.* nobody answers; F **nie odezwał się jeszcze** we haven't heard from him yet; **~ka** *f* (*-i*) *gry w karty*: bid

odźwierny *m* (*-ego*; *-ni*) porter, doorman, gatekeeper

odżałować *pf.* get over

odżyw|ać (*-je*) ⟨**odżyć**⟩ come (back) to life; *fig.* revive, rejuvenate; **~czo** *adv.* nutritiously; **~czy** nutritious, nourishing; **~iać** (*-am*) ⟨**~ić**⟩ feed; nourish **~iać się** *zw. zwierzęta*: feed (on); live on; **~ianie** nutrition, nourishment; **~ka** *f* (*-i*; *G -wek*) nutrient; (*do włosów*) conditioner; **~ka dla dzieci** formula feed, baby food

ofensyw|a *f* (*-y*; *G -*) offensive; *sport*: attack; **~ny** offensive

ofer|ent *m* (*-a*; *-ci*) bidder; **~ować** (*-uję*)

⟨**za-**⟩ (-uję) offer; **~ta** f (-y; G -) offer; **złożyć ~tę** make an offer

ofiar|a f (-y, DL ofierze; -y, G -) sacrifice; osoba itp.: victim; casualty (wypadku); datek: offering, donation; F oferma: loss-loser; **paść ~ą** (G) fall victim (to); **~ność** f devotion; **~ny** devoted; **~odawca** m, **~odawczyni** f contributor, donor, donator; **~ow(yw)ać** (-[w]uję) give, też (**się z** I) offer; donate, (poświęcać) sacrifice

ofi|cer m (-a; -owie) officer; **~cerski** officer; **~cjalny** official, formal

oficyna f (-y; G -) (building) wing; wydawnicza publishing house

ofsajd m (-u; -y) (w sporcie) offside

ofuk|iwać ⟨**~nąć**⟩ (- nę) snub

oganiać (się) → **opędzać (się)**

ogarek m (-rka; -rki) stump

ogarn|iać ⟨**~ąć**⟩ take in, include; (pojąć) grasp, catch; por. **obejmować**, **otaczać**

ogie|ń m (ognia; ognie, -ni) fire; **w ~niu** on fire; **puścić z ~niem** set on fire; **otwierać ~ień (na** A) open fire (at)

ogier m (-a; -y) zo. stallion

oglądać (-am) watch (**się** o.s.; **w** I in); view, see; **~ się** look round (**na** A at)

oglę|dność f (-ści; 0) prudence; **~dny** cautious, guarded; **~dnie mówiąc** putting it mildly; **~dziny** pl. (-) inspection; **~dziny zwłok** post-mortem, autopsy

ogłada f (-y; 0) polish, politeness; **bez ~y** unrefined, uncouth; → **obycie**

ogłaszać (-am) announce, make public; **~ drukiem** publish; **~ się** advertise

ogło|sić pf. → **ogłaszać**; **~szenie** n (-a; G -eń) announcement; notice; advertisement; **~szeniowy** notice

ogłuchnąć pf. grow deaf

ogłupi|ały stupefied; **~eć** pf. lose one's head; go soft in the head

ogłusz|ać (-am) → **głuszyć**; **~ająco** adv. deafeningly

ognie pl. → **ogień**; **sztuczne ~e** pl. fireworks pl.; **zimne ~e** pl. sparklers pl.; **~k** m (-a; -i) flame; **błędny ~k** will o' the wisp; jack o' lantern

ognio|odporny, **~trwały** fire-proof; **~wy** fire; **straż ~wa** Brt. fire brigade, Am. fire department

ognisko n (-a; G -) (bon)fire; fig. Brt. centre, Am. center; phys., phot. focus; **~ domowe** hearth (and home); **~wa** f

(-ej; -e) phys. focal length; **~wać** (-uję) ⟨**z-**⟩ (-uję) focus (**się** v/i.)

ogni|sto- w złoż. fire; **~ście** adv. passionately; **~sty** fiery; fig. fiery, passionate; flaming red

ogniwo n (-a; G -) link; electr. cell

ogołoc|ić pf. (-cę) denude; take away (**z pieniędzy** one's money); **~ony z liści** bare, without leaves

ogon m (-a; -y) tail; **wlec się w ~ie** bring up the rear; **~ek** m (-nka; -nki) → **ogon**; (kucyk) ponytail; (kolejka) Brt. queue, Am. line; **ustawić się w ~ku** Brt. queue up, Am. line up; **~owy** tail; biol. caudal

ogorzały tanned

ogólni|e adv. generally; **~k** m (-a; -i) → **komunał**; **~kowo** adv. generally, vaguely; **~kowy** general, vague

ogólno|europejski European, pan-European; **~kształcący** all-round education; **~polski** Polish, all-Polish; **~światowy** world-wide, world

ogólny general

ogół m (-u; 0) general public, public at large; **dobro ~u** public welfare lub good; **~em** in all; **na ~** usually; on the whole; **w ogóle** by and large; **w ogóle nie** not at all

ogór|ek m (-rka; -rki) bot. cucumber; **~kowy** cucumber; **sezon ~kowy** the silly season

ogra|biać (-am) → **grabić**; **~ść** pf. → **ogrywać**; **~dzać** (-am) fence off/in

ogranicz|ać (-am) limit, restrict; **~ać się** (**do** G) restrict o.s. (to), confine o.s.(to); **~enie** n (-a; G -eń) restriction, limit; **~oność** f (-ści; 0) limited intelligence; **~ony** limited, restricted; fig. dull-witted, narrow-minded; **~yć** pf. → **ograniczać**

ograny dowcip itp. hackneyed, trite

ogrod|nictwo n (-a; 0) gardening; horticulture; **~niczka** f (-ki; G -czek) **~nik** m (-a; -icy) gardener; **~owy** garden, gardening; horticultural

ogrodz|enie n (-a; G -eń) fence; **~ić** pf. → **ogradzać**

ogrom m (-u; 0) enormity; immensity; magnitude; **~ny** enormous; immense; magnitude

ogród m (-odu; -ody) garden; **~ owocowy** orchard; **~ek** m. → **ogród**; (działka) Brt. allotment; **~ek przed domem** front garden

ogród|ka *f*: **bez ~ek** without beating about the bush

ogry|wać (-*am*) win all *s.o.'s* money (**w pokera** at poker); beat (**w** *A* at); ~zać (-*am*) ⟨~źć⟩ gnaw at; ~zek *m* (-*zka; -zki*) (*owocu*) core

ogrzewa|ć (-*am*) ⟨ogrzać⟩ heat, warm; ~ć ⟨ogrzać⟩ się get warm; ~nie *n* (-*a; G -ń*) (**centralne** central) heating

ogumienie *n* (-*a; G -eń*) *mot.* set of Brt. tyres, *Am.* tires

ohydny hideous

OI *skrót pisany*: **Ośrodek Informacyjny** information centre

oj oh

ojciec *m* (-*jca; -jców*) father; **~ chrzestny** godfather; **po ojcu** paternal; **bez ojca** fatherless

ojco|stwo *n* (-*a; G -tw*) fatherhood, paternity; ~wizna *f* (-*y; G -zn*) patrimony; ~wski fatherly, paternal; **po ~wsku** like a father

ojczy|m *m* (-*a; -y*) stepfather; ~sty native; → **język**; ~zna *f* (-*y; G -zn*) homeland, motherland, mother country

ok. *skrót pisany*: **około** c. (*around*)

okalać (-*am*) surround, encircle

okalecz|enie *n* (-*a; G -eń*) injury; ~yć (-*ę*) injure, hurt

okamgnieni|e *n* (-*a*): **w ~u** in a flash

okap *m* (-*u; -y*) *bud.* eaves *pl.*; (*wyciąg*) hood

okaz *m* (-*u; -y*) specimen; ~ać się *pf.* → **okazywać się**; ~ale *adv.* spectacularly; ~ały spectacular, impressive; ~anie *n* (-*a; 0*) (*dowodu*) production, demonstration; ~anie pomocy assistance; **za ~aniem** on production *lub* presentation; ~iciel *m* (-*a; -e*), ~icielka *f* (-*i; G -lek*) bearer; **czek na ~iciela** Brt. bearer cheque, *Am.* bearer check

okazj|a *f* (-*i; -e*) occasion; (*kupna*) bargain, good buy; **przy ~i, z ~i** (*G*) on the occasion (of)

okaz|owy specimen; ~yjny bargain; ~yjna cena special price; ~ywać (-*uję*) present, demonstrate; (*dać wyraz*) express; ~ywać pomoc help; ~ywać się (*I*) turn out, prove; **jak się ~ało** as it turned out

okien|ko *n* (-*nka; G -nek*) window; (*w urzędzie też*) counter; ~nica *f* (-*y; -e*) shutter; ~ny window

oklapnąć *pf.* F *fig.* wilt, sag

oklaski *m/pl.* (-*ów*) applause; ~wać (-*uję*) applaud

okle|ina *f* (-*y; G -*) veneer; ~jać (-*am*) ⟨~ić⟩ stick (all over *s.th.*)

oklepany hackneyed, trite

okład *m* (-*u; -y*) *med.* compress, (*ciepły*) poultice; F **sto ... z ~em** a good hundred ...; ~ać (-*am*) cover; (*kompresem*) apply; *tech.* face, (*metalem*) clad; ~ać **kijem** thrash with a stick; ~ka *f* (-*i; G -dek*) (*książki*) cover; (**na książkę**) jacket; (*płyty*) sleeve

okładzina *f* (-*y; G -*) overing, lining; facing

okłam|ywać (-*uję*) ⟨~ać⟩ lie (*A* to)

okno *n* (-*a; G okien*) window; **~ wystawowe** shop window; **przez ~, z okna, oknem** out of the window

oko *n* (*oka; oczy, oczu, oczom, oczami/ oczyma, o oczach*) *anat.* eye; (*oka; oka, ok, okami*) mesh; → **oczko**; **mieć ~ na** (*A*) have an eye (on); **nie rzucać się w oczy** keep a low profile; **~ za ~** eye for eye; **na ~** approximately; **na oczach** in full view; **w cztery oczy** face to face; **na własne oczy** with one's own eyes; **w oczach** visibly

okolic|a *f* (-*y; G -*) area; neighbo(u)rhood; **w ~y** round about

okolicz|nik *m* (-*a; -i*) *gr.* adverbial; ~nościowy occasional; ~ność *f* (-*ści*) *zw. pl.* circumstances *pl.*, conditions *pl.*; **w tych ~nościach** under these circumstances; ~ny local; neighbo(u)ring; ~ni mieszkańcy *pl.* locals *pl.*

oko|lić *pf.* (-*lę*) → **okalać**; ~ło *prp.* (*G*) about, around

okoń *m* (-*nia; -nie*) *zo.* perch

okop *m* (-*u; -y*) trench; ~ywać (-*uję*) ⟨~ać⟩ *agr.* earth up

oko|stna *f* (-*nej; 0*) *anat.* periosteum; ~wy *f/pl.* (-*wów*) fetters *pl.*, chains *pl.*

okóln|ik *m* (-*a; -i*) circular; ~y circular; → **okręžnie**

ok|piwać (-*am*) ⟨~pić⟩ F lead on

okradać (-*am*) rob

okra|jać → **okrawać**; ~kiem astride; ~sa *f* (-*y; -*) fat; ~szać (-*am*) → **krasić**; ~ść *pf.* → **okradać**; ~tować (-*uję*) put bars over; ~wać (-*am*) trim, cut; *fig.* shorten; ~wek *m* (-*wka; -wki*) paring, scrap

okrąg *m* (*okręgu; okręgi*) *math.* circle; ~lak *m* (-*a; -i*) round timber; ~ły round; circular

okrąż|ać (-am) go round; enclose; surround; ~**enie** n (-a; G -eń) circuit; (w sporcie) lap; ~yć pf. → **okrążać**

okres m (-u; -y) (**próbny, ochronny** trial, close) period; szkoła: term; (u kobiety) period, menstruation; season (świąt itp.); ~**owo** adv. periodically; ~**owy** periodic; tymczasowy temporary; **bilet ~owy** season ticket

określ|ać (-am)⟨~**ić**⟩ determine, define; (nazywać) call, describe; ~**enie** n (-a; G -eń) determination, definition; description, label; ~**ony** specific; gr. definite

okręc|ać (-am) ⟨~**ić**⟩ (I) bind (with), wind (with), wrap (with); (obracać) twist; ~**ać** ⟨~**ić**⟩ **się** (wokół) coil (around); (obracać się) turn (a) round

okręg m (-u; -i) district, region; ~**owy** district; regional

okręt m (-u; -y) naut. warship; ~**ownic-two** n (-a; 0) shipbuilding; ~**ować** ⟨**za-**⟩ (-uję) embark; ~**owy** ship, naval, marine; **linia ~owa** shipping line; **dziennik ~owy** log

okręż|ny roundabout; circular; **droga** ~**a** roundabout way, detour; **drogą** ~**ą** fig. indirectly; → **skrzyżowanie**

okroić pf. → **okrawać**

okrop|ieństwo n (-a; G -) horror, atrocity; ~**ność** f (-ści; 0) horror; ~**ny** horrible, atrocious; ból itp. awful, terrible

okruch m (-a; -y) crumb; fig. piece, bit

okrucieństwo n (-a; G -) cruelty

okruszyna f (-y; G -) crumb; → **okruch**

okrutny cruel

okry|cie n (-a; G -yć) cover; (płaszcz) coat; ~**wać** (-am) ⟨~**ć**⟩ (-ję) cover (**się** o.s.; I with); envelop (też fig.)

okrzepnąć pf. → **krzepnąć**

okrzy|czany famous; (złej sławy) notorious; ~**k** m (-u; -i) shout, cry; ~**ki radości** shouts of joy

Oksford m (-u; 0) Oxford

oktawa f (-y; G -) mus. octave

oku|cie n (-a; G -uć) fitting; (laski itp.) ferrule; ~**ć** pf. → **okuwać**; ~**lary** pl. (-ów) glasses (pl.; (końskie) blinkers pl.; **on nosi ~lary** he wears glasses

okulist|a m (-y; -ów), ~**ka** f (-i; G -tek) med. eye doctor; ophthalmologist; ~**yczny** ophthalmological

okup m (-u; -y) ransom; ~**acja** f (-i; -e) occupation; ~**acyjny** occupation; ~**ant** m (-a; -nci) occupant; ~**ować** (-uję) kraj

occupy; fig. hog, monopolize; ~**ywać** (-uję) pay (**życiem** with one's life); krzywdę redeem; ~**ywać się** buy o.s. off, buy one's freedom

okuwać (-am) fit; konia shoe

olbrzym m (-a; -i/-y) giant; ~**i** giant, colossal; ~**ka** f (-i; G -ek) giant

olch|a f (-y; G -) bot. alder; ~**owy** alder

ole|isty oily; ~**j** m (-u; -e) (**jadalny, opałowy, napędowy** cooking, heating, diesel) oil; ~**jarka** f (-i; G -jek) oiler, oilcan; ~**jarnia** f (-i; -e) oil-mill; ~**jek** m (-jku; -jki) (**do opalania** suntan) oil; ~**jny**, ~**jowy** oil; ~**odruk** m (-u; -i) oleograph

olicowanie n (-a) bud. facing

olimpi|ada f (-y; G -) Olympics pl.; ~**jczyk** m (-a; -cy), ~**jka** f (-i; G -jek) Olympic competitor, Am. Olympian; ~**jski** Olympic

oliw|a f (-y; zw. 0) (olive) oil; ~**ić** (**na-**⟩ (-ę) oil, lubricate; ~**ka** f (-i; G -wek) olive; ~**kowy** olive/kolor olive-green; ~**ny** olive; **gałązka ~na** też fig. olive branch

olsz|a f (-y; G -) bot., ~**yna** f (-y; G -) → **olcha**

olśnić pf. → **olśniewać**

olśnie|nie n (-a; G -eń) fig. flash of inspiration, brain wave; ~**wać** (-am) dazzle (też fig.); ~**wająco** adv. stunningly, brilliantly; ~**wający** stunning, glamorous, brilliant

ołowi|any, ~**owy** lead; fig. leaden

ołów m (-łowiu; 0) chem. lead; ~**ek** m (-wka; -wki) pencil; ~**ek do brwi** eyebrow pencil; ~**ek kolorowy** colo(u)red pencil; ~**ek automatyczny** Brt. propelling pencil, Am. mechanical pencil

ołtarz m (-a; -e) rel. altar; **wielki ~** high altar

omac|ek: iść po ~ku, ~kiem grope one's way; **szukać po ~ku** grope for; ~**ywać** (-uję) → **macać**

omal: ~ (**że**) **nie** almost, nearly

omam m (-u; -y) delusion, illusion; ~**iać** (-iam) ⟨~**ić**⟩ (-ię) beguile, deceive

omawiać go over, discuss; treat

omdl|ały faint, limp; ~**enie** n (-a; G -eń) faint; ~**ewać** (-am)⟨~**eć**⟩ faint, pass out

omiatać (-am) sweep

omieszkać (-am): **nie ~** not fail, not forget

omi|eść pf. → **omiatać**; ~**jać** ⟨~**nąć**⟩ v/t. go round, bypass; trudność, prob-

lem, zakaz get round; (*t-ko impf.*) avoid;
nie ~nie go kara he will not escape
punishment; **~nął ją awans** she was
passed over for promotion; → *mijać*

omlet *m* (*-u; -y*) *gastr.* omelette

omłot *m* (*-u; -y*) *agr.* threshing; **~owy**
threshing

omomierz *m* (*-a; -e*) *tech.* ohmmeter

omot|ywać (*-uję*) ⟨**~ać**⟩ wrap (*I* with);
fig. ensnare (**w** *A* in)

omówi|ć *pf.* → **omawiać**; **~enie** *n* (*-a;*
G -eń) discussion, treatment; **bez ~eń**
openly

omszały mossy

omułek *m* (*-łka; -łki*) *zo.* (edible) mussel

omy|ć *pf.* → **omywać**; **~lić** *pf.* → **mylić**;
~lny fallible; **~łka** *f* (*-i; G -łek*) error,
mistake; → **błąd, pomyłka**; **~łkowo**
adv. erroneously; **~łkowy** erroneous

on *pron.* (*G [je]go, D [je]mu, A [je]go, IL*
nim) he; *rzecz.*: it; **~a** *pron.* (*GD jej, A ją,*
I nią, L niej) she; *rzecz.*: it

onanizować się (*-uję*) masturbate

ondulacja *f* (*-i; -e*): **trwała** **~** perm

on|e *pron.* *ż-rzecz* (*G [n]ich, D [n]im,*
A je, nie, I nimi, L nich), **~i** *pron.*
m-os (*A [n]ich*; → **one**) they

oniemiały (**z** *G*) dumbfounded, speechless (with)

onieśmiel|ać (*-am*) ⟨**~ić**⟩ (*-lę*) discour-
age, overawe

ono *pron.* (*A je*; → **on**) it

ONZ *skrót pisany:* **Organizacja Naro-**
dów Zjednoczonych UN (*United Na-*
tions)

opactwo *n* (*-a; G -w*) abbey

opaczn|ie *adv.* wrong, falsely; **~y** wrong,
false

opad *m* (*-u; -y*) fall; (*w sporcie*) bend
from the hips; **~ krwi** F *med.* EST, sedimentation test; *zw. pl.* **~y** *meteo.*
showers *pl.*; **~y śnieżne** snowfall;
~ać *v/i.* fall, drop (*też fig.*); *głowa,*
głos itp.: droop; *teren*: sink down;
gorączka: subside; (*ze zmęczenia*)
collapse; *v/t. owady itp.* besiege,
swarm around; *fig.* disgage, persecute;
on ~a z sił he is losing his strength

opak: **na ~** the other way round, amiss

opakowa|nie *n* (*-a; G -ań*) packaging,
wrapping, packet; **w ładnym ~aniu** *fig.*
in nice packaging; **w (próżniowym)**
~aniu vacuum-packed; **~ywać** (*-uję*)
→ *pakować*

opala|cz *m* (*-a; -e*) bikini top; **~ć** (*-am*)
pokój heat; *sierść* singe; (*część ciała*)
tan; **~ć się** tan, sunbathe

opal|enizna *f* (*-y; G -zn*) suntan; **~ić** *pf.*
→ *opalać*; **~ony** (sun)tanned

opał *m* (*-u; -y*) fuel; **skład ~u** coal merchant's; **~owy**: **drewno ~owe** firewood

opamięt|ywać się (*-uję*) ⟨**~ać się**⟩
come to one's senses

opancerzony armo(u)red;→**pancerny**

opanowa|nie *n* composure; calmness;
~any calm, self-controlled; **~(yw)ać**
(*-[w]uję*) control (**się** o.s.); *pożar, sytua-*
cję bring under control; (*o uczuciach*)
overcome, seize

opar *m* (*-u; -y*) veil of mist; **~y** *pl.* fumes
pl., vapo(u)rs *pl.*; → *wyziewy*

opar|cie *m* (*-a; G -rć*) (*krzesła itp.*)
back; support; *fig.* reliance; **~cie dla**
głowy headrest; **punkt ~cia** hold; **~ty**
based (**na** *L* on)

oparz|elina *f* (*-y; G -in*) *med.* scalding;
~enie *n* (*-a; G -eń*) burning; **~yć** *pf.* →
parzyć

opas|ać *pf.* → **opasywać**; **~ka** *f* (*-i; G*
-sek) band; **~ka żałobna** mourning-
band; **~ły** obese; **~ywać** (*-uję*) (*I*) belt
(with), bind (with), gird (with); **~ywać**
się gird

opaść *pf.* → **paść¹, opadać**

opat *m* (*-a; -ci*) abbot

opatentować *pf.* (*-uję*) patent

opatrun|ek *m* (*-nku; -nki*) *med.* dres-
sing; **~kowy** dressing

opatrywać (*-uję*) get ready; *ranę* dress;
(*pieczęcią, kratą*) (*D*) provide (with);
~ datą date

opatrznoś|ciowy providential; **~ć** *f*
(*-ści; 0*) providence

opa|trzyć *pf.* → **opatrywać**; **~tulać**
(*-am*) ⟨**~tulić**⟩ (*-lę*) wrap up

opcja *f* (*-i; -e*) option

opera *f* (*-y; G -er*) opera; (*budynek*)
opera house

opera|cja *f* (*-i; -e*) operation (*też mil.,*
med.); *med.* surgery; **~cja handlowa**
transaction; **~cyjny** operating; surgical; **system ~cyjny** *komp.* operating
system; **~tor** *m* (*-a; -rzy*), **~torka** *f*
(*-i; G -rek*) operator; **~tywny** efficient

operetk|a *f* (*-i; G -tek*) operetta; **~owy**
operetta

operować (*-uję*) ⟨**z-**⟩ *v/i.* operate; *v/t. med.* operate on; manipulate

operowy opera, operatic

opędz|ać (-*am*) ⟨-*ić*⟩ (*też się od G*) chase away; *wydatki* meet; *potrzeby* satisfy; **nie móc się ~ić** not be able to get rid of

opęt|ać *pf.* → **opętywać**; ~**anie** *n* (-*a*) possession; *fig.* obsession; ~**ańczy** like one possessed; ~**ywać** (-*uję*) possess; **być ~anym przez** (*A*) be possessed by, *fig.* be obsessed with

opić *pf.* → **opijać**

opie|c *pf.* → **opiekać**; ~**czę-** *pf.* → **pie-czę-**; ~**ka** *f* (-*i; G -*) care; ~**ka społeczna** social security, welfare; ~**ka lekarska** medical care; ~**ka nad zabytkami** preservation of historic monuments; **być pod ~ką** (*G*) be under the care (of)

opieka|cz *m* (-*a; -e*) toaster; ~**ć** (*am*) *chleb* toast; (*na ruszcie*) grill; (*w tłuszczu*) braise

opiek|ować ⟨*za-*⟩ **się** -*uję*) (*I*) look (after), take care (of); (*chorym*) nurse; (*dziećmi dorywczo*) baby-sit; ~**un** *m* (-*a; -owie/-i*),~**unka** *f* (-*i; G -nek*) (*starszych itp.*) social worker; (*dzieci, stały*) (*child*) minder, (*dorywczy*) baby-sitter; (*studentów*) tutor; *jur.* guardian; ~**uńczo** protectively; ~**uńczy** protective, caring; **państwo ~uńcze** welfare state

opieprz|ać (-*am*) ⟨-*yć*⟩ F *Brt.* tear a strip, *Am.* chew out

opierać (-*am*) (**o** *A*) lean (against) (**się** *v/i.*), prop (against); rest (on) (**się** *v/i.*); (**na** *A*) *fig.* base (on); ~ **się** *fig.* resist, withstand

opiesza|le *adv.* negligently, inertly; ~**łość** *f* (-*ści; 0*) negligence; ~**ły** slow-moving, negligent, inert

opiewać (-*am*) extol, glorify; (**na** *A*) amount to; *wyrok* come to

opięty tight, close-fitting

opij|ać (-*am*) celebrate with a drink; ~**ać się** (*I*) drink too much, F sink; ~**lstwo** *n* (-*a; 0*) alcoholism; **w stanie ~lstwa** when drunk

opił|ki *m/pl.* filings *pl.*; ~**ow(yw)ać** (-*[w]uję*) file

opini|a *f* (*GDl -ii; -e*) opinion, view, belief; (*sława*) reputation; *szkoła:* school report; → **ocena**; ~**ować** ⟨*za-*⟩ (-*uję*) (*A*, **o** *L*) express opinion (about)

opis *m* (-*u; -y*) description; ~**ywać** (-*uję*) ⟨-*ać*⟩ describe

o|platać (-*am*) entwine (**się** *v/i.*); fold

around; ~**platywać** (-*uję*) ⟨~**plątać**⟩ entangle (*też fig.*); ~**pleść** *pf.* → **oplatać**; ~**pluwać** (-*am*) ⟨~**pluć**⟩ (**na** *A*) spit (at)

opłac|ać (-*am*) pay; ~**ać się** pay (*też fig.*); *szantażyście* pay off; **nie opłaca się** it's no use; ~**alny** profitable, lucrative; *fig.* worthwhile, rewarding; ~**ić** *pf.* →**opłacać**; ~**ony** paid; *koperta* stamped

opłak|any sorry, pitiful; ~**iwać** (-*uję*) lament, mourn (*też fig.*)

opłat|a *f* (-*y; G -*) charge, fee; (*opłacenie*) payment; ~ **za przejazd** fare; ~ **pocztowa** postage

opłatek *m* (-*tka; -tki*) *rel.* wafer

opłucna *f* (-*ej; -e*) *anat.* pleura

opłuk|iwać (-*uję*) ⟨~**ać**⟩ rinse, flush

opły|wać ⟨~**nąć**⟩ *v/t.* *człowiek:* swim-round; *okręt:* sail round; *woda:* wash round; ~**wać w dostatki** be rolling in money; ~**wowy** streamlined

opodal 1. *adv.* (*też* **nie** ~) nearby; **2.** *prp.* (*G*) nearby

opodatkow|anie *n* (-*a; G -ań*) taxation; ~**(yw)ać** (-*[w]uję*) tax

opona *f* (-*y; G -*) *mot.* *Brt.* tyre, *Am.* tire; *anat.* ~ **mózgowa** meninx

oponować ⟨*za-*⟩ (-*uję*) (**przeciw** *D*) protest, oppose

opończa *f* (-*y; G -cz*) cape

opor|nie *adv.* reluctantly; *przesuwać* with difficulty; ~**nik** *m* (-*a; -i*) *electr.* resistor; ~**ność** *f* (-*ści; 0*) *electr.* resistance; ~**ny** (*niegrzeczny*) disobedient; resistant

oportunistyczny opportunistic

oporządz|ać (-*am*) ⟨-*ić*⟩ *bydło* look after; *gastr.* gut

opowiada|ć (-*am*) narrate, tell; ~**ć się** (**za** *I*) declare o.s. in favo(u)r (of); ~**nie** *n* (-*a; G -ań*) tale; story

opowie|dzieć *pf.* → **opowiadać**; ~**ść** *f* tale

opozyc|ja *f* (-*i; -e*) opposition; ~**yjny** opposition

opór *m* (-*oru; -ory*) resistance; opposition; **ruch oporu** the Resistance

opóźni|ać (-*am*) ⟨-*ić*⟩ delay, hold up; ~**ać** ⟨-*ić*⟩ **się** be late (**z** *I* with); ~**enie** *n* (-*a; G -eń*) delay; hold-up; ~**ony** late, delayed; *fig.* retarded (**w** *I* in)

opracow|anie *n* (*dzieła*) treatise, study; working out; ~**(yw)ać** (-*[w]uję*) work out, develop, prepare; *dzieło* prepare, make up opraw|a f (-y; G -) setting (*też theat.*, *fig.*); *print.* binding; **w ~ie** *print.* bound; **w twardej ~ie** hardback; → **oprawka**; **~iać** (*-am*) ⟨**~ić**⟩ bind; *obraz* frame; *klejnot* set, mount; *tuszę* dress, skin; **~ka** f (*-i; G -wek*) → **oprawa**; *okularów* frame, rim; *żarówki* socket; *tech.* holder; **~ny** bound; framed; set, mounted

opresj|a f (*-i; -e*) predicament, F fix; **w ~i** in dire straits

oprocentowanie n (*-a; G -ań*) interest

oprogramowanie n (*-a; G -ań*) *komp.* software

opromieniony *fig.* bright

oprowadz|ać (*-am*) ⟨**~ić**⟩ show around

oprócz *prp.* (G) besides, aside from

opróżni|ać (*-am*) ⟨**~ć**⟩ (*-ę, -nij!*) empty (**się** *v/i.*); *pokój* vacate, move out of; *teren* evacuate; **~ać** ⟨**~ć**⟩ **się** become empty

oprysk|iwać (*-uję*) ⟨**~ać**⟩ sprinkle, spatter; **~liwie** *adv.* gruffly, brusquely; **~liwy** gruff, brusque

opryszczka f (*-i; G -ek*) *med.* herpes

opryszek m (*-szka; -szki/-szkowie*) thug, mugger, hudlum

oprzeć *pf.* → **opierać**

oprzęd m (*-u; -y*) cocoon shell, floss

oprzytomnieć *pf.* (*-eję*) regain consciousness; collect o.s.; → **opamiętywać się**

optować (*-uję*) opt (**na rzecz** G in favo(u)r of, for)

opty|czny optical; **~k** m (*-a; -ycy*) optician; **~ka** f (*-i; G -tek*) optics *sg.*

opty|malizować (*-uję*) optimize; **~malny** optimal, optimum; **~mista** m (*-y; G -tów*), **~mistka** f (*-i; G -tek*) optimist; **~mistyczny** optimistic

opuch|li(z)na f (*-y; G -(z)n*) swelling; **~ły, ~nięty** swollen; → **puchnąć**

opuk|iwać (*-uję*)⟨**~ać**⟩ tap; *med.* percuss

opust *econ.* → **upust**

opustosz|ały deserted, empty; **~eć** *pf.* (*-eję*) become deserted; **~yć** *pf.* → **pustoszyć**

opuszcz|ać leave; *wyraz* omit, skip; *wykład* miss, skip; *rodzinę* desert; *por.* **spuszczać**; **~ać się** come down; (*w pracy*) become disorderly/untidy; **~enie** n (*-a; 0*) desolation; neglect; (*rodziny itp.*) desertion; (*pl. -a*) (*tekstu*) omission; **~ony** left; deserted; omitted; skipped

opuszka f (*-i; G -szek*) fingertip

opuścić *pf.* → **opuszczać**

opyl|ać (*-am*) ⟨**~ić**⟩ dust; F sell

orać ⟨**z-, za-**⟩ *Brt.* plough, *Am.* plow; (*t-ko impf.*) F *fig.* work like hell

oranżada f (*-y; G -ad*) orangeade

oraz *cj.* and

orbi|ta f (*-y; G -*) orbit; **na ~cie** in orbit

orchidea f (*-dei; -dee*) *bot.* orchid

orczyk m (*-a; -i*) swingletree, *Am.* whiffletree; *aviat.* rudderbar; (*w sporcie*) tow bar; **~owy: wyciąg ~owy** tow lift

order m (*-u; -y*) medal, decoration

ordy|nacja f: **~nacja wyborcza** voting regulations *pl.*; **~nans** m (*-a; -i*) *mil.* orderly; **~narny** vulgar, gross; **~nator** m (*-a; -rzy*) consultant; **~nować** (*-uję*) administer, prescribe

orędowni|czka f (*-i; G -czek*), **~k** m (*-a; -cy*) advocate, champion

orędzie n (*-a; G -*) speech, address

oręż m (*-a; zw. 0*) weapons *pl.*

organ m (*-u; -y*) organ; **~y** *pl. mus.* organ; **~iczny** organic; **~ista** m (*-y; -ści, -stów*), **~istka** f (*-i; G -tek*) organist

organiza|cja f (*-i; -e*) organization; institution; **~cyjny** organizational; **~tor** m (*-a; -rzy*), **~torka** f (*-i; G -rek*) organizer

organizm m (*-y*) organism

organizować ⟨**z-**⟩ (*-uję*) organize; *spotkanie* arrange; *przyjęcie* hold

organ|ki *pl.* (*-ków*) *mus.* mouth organ; **~owy** *pl.* **~y** → **organ**

orgazm m (*-u; -y*) orgasm

orgia f (*GDl -ii; -e*) orgy

orienta|cja f (*-i; -e*) orientation; *fig.* view; **zmysł ~cji** sense of direction; **~cja seksualna** sexuality; **~cyjny** guiding; (*przybliżony*) approximate; **~lny** Oriental

orientować ⟨**z-**⟩ (*-uję*) inform; (**w** *terenie, kościół*) orient, orientate; **~ się** orientate o.s.; be familiar (**w** L with); understand

orka f (*-i; 0*) *Brt.* ploughing, *Am.* plowing

Orkady *pl.* (G *-ów*) Orkneys *pl.*

orkiestra f (*-y; G -*) orchestra; **~ symfoniczna** symphony orchestra

orli aquiline

Ormianin m (*-a; -nie*), **~ka** f (*-i; G -nek*) Armenian

ormiańs|ki Armenian; **mówić po ~ku** speak Armenian

ornament m (*-u; -y*) ornament

ornat m (*-u; -y*) *rel.* chasuble

O

ornitologi|a f (GDL -ii; 0) ornithology;
~czny ornithological

orny arable; **grunt** ~ arable land

orszak m (-u; -i) entourage; (**ślubny,
żałobny** wedding, funeral) procession

ortodoksyjny orthodox

ortograficzny spelling

ortodontyczny orthodontic

ortopedyczny orthop(a)edic

oryginaln|ie originally; ~y original

oryginał m (-u; -y) original, (m-os a,
-y/-owie) original, nonconformist

orzec pf. → **orzekać**

orzech m (-a; -y) bot. nut; ~ **włoski** wal-
nut; ~owy nut; zapach nutty; kolor hazel

orzecz|enie n (-a; G -eń) decision; jur.
judg(e)ment, verdict, ruling; gr. predic-
ate; med. expert (medical) opinion

orzeka|ć (-am) decide, judge; jur. rule,
adjudicate; ~jący: **tryb ~jący** indic-
ative mood

orzeł m (orła; orły) eagle; → **reszka**

orzeszek m (-szka; -szki) → **orzech**

orzeźwi|ać (-am) ⟨~ć⟩ refresh (**się**
o.s.); ~ająco adv. refreshingly; ~ający
refreshing; fig. invigorating; **napoje** pl.
~ające refreshments pl.

os. skrót pisany: **osoba, osób** person;
osiedle estate, settlement

osa f (-y; G os) zo. wasp

osacz|ać (-am) ⟨~yć⟩ encircle, beset

osad m (-u; -y) sediment, deposit; ~a f
(-y; G -) settlement; ~niczka f (-i; G
-czek), ~nik m (-a; -cy) settler; ~owy
sedimentation, sedimentary

osadz|ać (-am) ⟨~ić⟩ (w miejscu, też
osad) settle (**się** v/i.); łopatę fix; mount;
fig. establish; ~ić w areszcie put under
arrest

osamotni|eć pf. (-eję) become lonely;
~enie n (-a; G -eń) loneliness, solitude;
~ony lonely

osącz|ać (-am) ⟨~yć⟩ drip off

osą|d m (-u; -y) estimation; judg(e)-
ment; ~dzać (-am) ⟨~dzić⟩ estimate;
czyny adjudge

osch|le adv. stiffly, crisply; ~łość f (-ści;
0) stiffness; ~ły stiff, crisp

oscyla-, oscylo- w złoż. oscilla-, oscil-
lo-

osełka f (-i; G -łek) whetstone

oset m (ostu; osty) bot. thistle

osiad|ać settle down; budynek, teren
subside, sink; osad settle, deposit (**na**

L on); → osadzać **się**; ~ty settled

osiąg|ać (-am) ⟨~nąć⟩ (-nę) reach,
achieve; cenę fetch; ~alny within
reach; available, attainable; ~i m/pl.
(-ów) tech. performance; ~nięcie n
(-a) achievement, attainment; accom-
plishment

osiąść → **osiadać, mielizna**

osie pl. → **oś**

osiedl|ać (-am) settle (**się** v/i.); ~e n (-a;
G -i) Brt. housing estate, Am. housing
development; ~eńczy settling; ~ić pf.
(-lę) → **osiedlać**; ~owy estate

osiem eight; ~dziesiąt eighty; → **666**;
~nasto- w złoż. eighteen-; ~nastka f
(-i; G -tek) eighteen; (**linia**) number
eighteen; ~nasty eighteenth; ~naście
eighteen; → **666**; ~set eight hundred;
→ **666**; ~setny eight hundredth

osierdzie n (-a; G -dź) anat. pericardium

osieroc|ać (-am) ⟨~ić⟩ orphan

osi|ka f (-i; G -) bot. aspen; ~na f (-y;
G -) aspen wood

osioł m (osła; osły) zo. donkey, ass (też
fig.)

osiow|y axial; ~e n (-ego; 0) rail. stall fee

oskarż|ać (-am) accuse (**o** A of); jur.
też. impeach, charge (**o** A with);
~ać **przed sądem** sue, take to court;
~enie n (-a; G -eń) accusation; charge;
wnieść ~**enie** (**przeciw** D) sue
(against); **akt** ~**enia** indictment; ~ony
m (-ego; -żeni, G -żonych), ~ona f (-ej;
G -ych) jur. the accused, defendant;
ława ~**onych** the dock; ~yciel m (-a;
-e), ~cielka f (-i; G -lek) jur. prosecutor; ~yć pf. (-am) → **oskarżać**

oskrob|ywać (-uję) ⟨~ać⟩ scrape; (z łu-
sek) scale

oskrzel|e n (-a; G -i) anat. bronchus,
bronchial tube; **zapalenie/nieżyt** ~ł
bronchitis

oskubywać (-uję) pluck; → **skubać**

osłab|iać (-am) ⟨~ć⟩ (-ę) lessen,
weaken; krytykę, **argumenty** tone
down, moderate; ~enie n (-a; 0)
weakening, lessening; moderation;
~ony weakened; moderated

osła|bnąć pf. → **słabnąć**; ~dzać (-am)
sweeten, sugar (też fig.); ~niać (-am)
cover; protect; (**przed światłem**) shade;
fig. shield; ~wiony notorious

osło|dzić pf. → **osładzać**; ~na f (-y;
G -) cover, shield; shelter; fig. protec-

tion; *mil.* covering (fire); (*w sporcie*) covering, guard; ~nić *pf.* → **osłaniać**; ~nka *f* (*-; G -nek*) (*kiełbasy*) skin; **bez ~nek** openly

osłuch|iwać (*-uję*) ⟨*~ać*⟩ listen to; *med.* auscultate

osłupie|ć *pf.* (*-eję*) be flabbergasted; ~nie *n* (*-a; 0*) amazement, bewilderment; **wprawić w ~nie** amaze, bewilder

osma|lać (*-am*) → **smalić**; ~row(yw)ać (*-[w]uję*) daub; besmear (*też fig.*); ~żać (*-am*) ⟨*~żyć*⟩ brown

osnowa *f* (*-y; G -nów*) *włók.* warp; *fig.* fabric

osob|a *f* (*-y; G osób*): **~a fizyczna/prawna** natural/legal person; individual; **na ~ę, od ~y** per person; **starsza ~a** older person; ~istość *f* (*-ści*) personage, notable; ~isty personal; individual; → **dowód**; ~iście in person, personally, individually

osobliw|ie *adv.* peculiarly; unusually; ~ość *f* (*-ści*) curiosity; rarity; peculiarity; ~y peculiar; unusual; **nic ~ego** nothing peculiar

osob|nik *m* (*-a, -i; m-os pl. -cy*) individual; ~o *adv.* separately, individually; ~y separate, individual; → **oddzielny, odrębny; każdy z ~a** each individual

osobow|ość *f* (*-ści*) personality; **~ość prawna** *jur.* legal capacity; ~y personal; **akta** *pl.* **~e** personal files/dossiers *pl.*; **pociąg ~y** slow train

osowia|le *adv.* dejectedly; ~ły depressed, downcast

ospa *f* (*-y; 0*) *med.* smallpox, variola; **~ wietrzna** chickenpox

ospa|le *adv.* sluggishly; lethargically; ~ły sluggish; lethargic

ospowaty pock-marked

osprzęt *m* (*-u; -y*) equipment; *zwł. komp.* hardware

ostateczn|ie *adv.* finally, after all; ~ość *f* (*-ści*) extremity; finality; **w ~ości** as a last resort; in an emergency; ~y final; extreme → **sąd**

ostat|ek *m* (*-tku; -tki*) rest; *t-ko pl.* **~ki** Shrovetide, Mardi Gras; **do ~ka** to the end; **na ~ek** at the end; ~ni last; final; (*najnowszy*) latest; ~**nimi czasy** → ~nio *adv.* recently, lately; → **namaszczenie**

ostentacyjny ostentatious, F splashy

ostoja *f* (*-oi; -oje, -oi*) *fig.* bastion, mainstay

ostro *adv.* sharply, sharp; keenly; → **ostry**; ~ga *f* (*-i; G ostróg*) spur; ~kątny acute-angled; ~słup *math.* pyramid; ~ść *f* (*-ści, 0*) sharpness; *phot.* focus; (*nauczyciela itp.*) harshness

ostrożn|ie *adv.* carefully; cautiously; ~ość *f* (*-ści, 0*) care, caution; carefulness; **środki** *pl.* **~ości** precautions *pl.*, precautionary measures *pl.*; ~y careful, cautious; *wyliczenia* conservative

ostr|y sharp; *światło* dazzling; *głos* shrill; *nauczyciel itp.* harsh; *zdjęcie* in focus; *zapach* pungent; *jedzenie* hot; *med.* acute; **~e pogotowie** alert; **~y dyżur** *med.* emergency service, emergency *Brt.* centre (*Am.* center)

ostryga *f* (*-i; G -*) *zo.* oyster

ostrze *n* (*-a; G -y*) blade

ostrze|gać (*-am*) ⟨*~c*⟩ warn (**przed** *I* against); ~gawczy warning; ~liwać (*-wuję*) ⟨*~lać*⟩ shell, bombard; ~żenie *n* (*-a; G -eń*) warning

o|strzyc *pf.* → **strzyc**; ~strzyć ⟨*na-*⟩ (*-ę*) sharpen, (*na szlifierce*) grind; *fig.* whet; ~studzać (*-am*) cool; ~stygać (*-am*) → **stygnąć**; ~sunąć się *pf.* → **osuwać**

osusz|ać (*-am*) ⟨*~yć*⟩ dry; *bagno itp.* drain; F *butelkę* empty

osuw|ać się slip, slip off; *ziemia*: give way, slide; *ktoś*: sink (down); ~isko *n* (*-a; G -*) landslide, landslip

oswa|badzać (*-am*) → **oswobadzać**; ~jać (*-am*) (**się z** *I*) get used (to), get accustomed (to); *zwierzę* tame

oswo|badzać (*-am*) ⟨*~bodzić*⟩ (*-dzę*; *też -bódź!*) free (**się** *o.s.*; **od** *G* from), liberate; ~bodzenie *n* (*-a; 0*) freeing; liberating; ~ić *pf.* → **oswajać; ~ić się** *zwierzę*: become tame; ~jony tame

osyp(yw)ać → **obsypywać**

osza|cować *pf.* → **szacować**; ~leć go mad

oszał|amiać (*-am*)stun;*fig.*daze,dazzle; ~miająco *adv.* stunningly; bewileringly; ~miający stunning; dazzling, bewildering

oszczep *m* (*-u; -y*) (*w sporcie*) javelin

oszczepni|ctwo *n* (*-a; 0*) (*w sporcie*) javelin-throwing; ~czka *f* (*-i; G -czek*) ~k *m* (*-a, -cy*) *sport:* javelin-thrower

oszczer|ca *m* (*-y; G -ców*) slanderer; ~czo *adv.* slanderously; libellously; ~czy slanderous; libellous; ~stwo *n* (*-a; G -*) slander; libel

oszczę|dnościowy *rachunek itp.* savings; *poczynania* economy; **~dność** *f* (*-ści; 0*) economy; thriftiness; (*pl.* **~dności**) savings *pl.*; **~dny** economical; sparing; *osoba* thrifty; **~dzać** (*-am*) ⟨**~dzić**⟩ (*na A*) save (up for); (*na L*) be sparing (with); *światło, materiały* save, economize on; *k-uś* save, spare; (*żyć oszczędnie*) economize

oszk|- *fig.* → **szk-**; **~lony** glazed

oszołomi|ć *pf.* → **oszałamiać**; **~enie** *n* (*-a; 0*) daze; *fig.* bewilderment

oszpecać *pf.* → **szpecić**

oszroniony frosted

oszuka|ć *pf.* → **oszukiwać**; **~ńczo** *adv.* deceitfully; **~ńczy** deceitful; deceptive; **~ństwo** *n* (*-a; G-*) deceit; deceptiveness

oszukiwać (*-uję*) deceive; *v/i.* cheat; **~ się** deceive o.s.

oszust *m* (*-a; -ści*), **~ka** *f* (*-i; G -tek*) cheat, fraud, impostor; **~wo** *n* (*-a; G-*) deceit, deception; fraud

oś *f* (*osi; osie*) *mot.* axle; *math. itp.* axis

ościenny neighbo(u)ring

oścież: na ~ wide open

ość *f* (*ości*) fishbone

oślep: na ~ blindly, blind; **~iać** (*-am*) ⟨**~ić**⟩ (*-ę*) blind; (*światłem*) daze; **~iająco** *adv.* dazzlingly; **~iający** dazzling; **~nąć** (*-nę*) *pf.* go blind

oś|li donkey; asinine (*też fig.*); **~e uszy** *fig.* dog ears; **~ica** *f* (*-y; G-*) *zo.* she-donkey; jenny-ass

ośliz(g)ły slimy

ośmie|lać (*-am*) ⟨**~lić**⟩ (*-lę*) encourage; **~lić się** take heart; dare; **~szać** (*-am*) ⟨**~szyć**⟩ (*-szę*) ridicule; **~szać** ⟨**~szyć**⟩ **się** make a fool of o.s.

ośmio- *w złoż.* eight-; *math., chem. itp.* octo-, octa-; **~bok** *m* (*-u; -i*) *math.* octagon; **~dniowy** eight-day(-long); **~krotny** eightfold; **~letni** eight-year-long, -old

ośmiornica *f* (*-y; G-*) *zo.* octopus

ośmi|oro, ~u *m-os* eight → **666**

ośnieżony snow-covered

ośr. *skrót pisany:* **ośrodek** *Brt.* centre, *Am.* center

ośrodek *m* (*-dka; -dki*) *Brt.* centre, *Am.* center

oświadcz|ać (*-am*) ⟨**~yć**⟩ state, declare; **~yć się** (*D*) propose (to); **~enie** *n* (*-a; G -eń*) statement, declaration; **~yny** *pl.* (*-*) proposal

oświat|a *f* (*-y; 0*) education; **~owy** educational; **film ~owy** educational film

oświec|ać (*-am*) ⟨**~ić**⟩ *zwł. fig.* enlighten; **~enie** *n* (*-a; 0*) enlightenment; **2enie** Enlightenment; **~ony** enlighted

oświetl|ać (*-am*) ⟨**~ić**⟩ (*-lę*) light, light up; illuminate; **~enie** *n* light (s*pl.*); lighting; illumination; **~eniowy** lighting

Oświęcim *m* (*-ia*) (*miejsce obozu koncentracyjnego*) Auschwitz; **2ski** Auschwitz

otaczać (*-am*) surround, encircle; **~ się** (*I*) surround o.s. (with)

otchłań *f* (*-ni; -nie*) abyss, chasm

otępi|ały stupefied, torpid; *wzrok* vacant; **~eć** (*-eje*) deaden, become stupefied; **~enie** *n* (*-a; 0*) stupefaction; *med.* dementia

oto here, there; **~ wszystko** that's all; **~ nasz dom** here is our house; **~ oni/ one** here they are

otocz|ak *m* (*-a; -i*) pebble; **~enie** *n* (*-a; G -eń*) surrounding(s *pl.*); environment; **w ~eniu** (*G*) surrounded (by); **~yć** *pf.* → **otaczać**

otok *m* (*-u; -i*) round; **~ czapki** cap band

otomana *f* (*-y; G-*) ottoman

otóż → oto; **~ to** to that is it

otręby *pl.* (*-rąb/-bów*) bran

otru|cie *n* (*-a; G -uć*) poisoning; **~ć** *pf.* poison; **~ty** poisoned

otrzaska|ć się F *pf.* (*z I*) get the knack (of); **~ny** F → **obyty**

otrząs|ać ⟨**~nąć**⟩ (*-nę*) (*też* **się z** *G*) shake off; **~ać** ⟨**~nąć**⟩ **się** shake o.s.; *fig.* recover (*po I* after)

otrze|ć *fig.* → **ocierać**; **~pywać** ⟨**~pać**⟩ knock off, tap off

otrzewna *f* (*-ej; -e*) *anat.* peritoneum

otrzeźwi|ać (*-am*) ⟨**~ć**⟩ (*-ę*) refresh (**się** o.s.); *fig.* sober up

otrzym|anie *n* (*-a; 0*) receipt; reception; **~ywać** (*-uję*) ⟨**~ać**⟩ receive, get, obtain; *tech.* produce

otuch|a *f* (*-y; 0*) comfort; **pełen ~y** confident

otul|ać (*-am*) ⟨**~ić**⟩ (*I*) wrap (with); *v/i. fig.* shroud

otumaniać (*-am*) → **tumanić**

otwar|cie 1. *adv.* openly; **2.** *n* (*-a; G -rć*) opening; → **godzina**; **~tość** *f* (*-ści; 0*) openness; *cando(u)r*; **~ty** open; *ktoś* candid, frank

otwier|acz m (-a; -e) opener; **~ać** (-am)
open; (zaczynać) open, start; parasol
put up; **~ać się** open

otwo|rek m (-rka; -rki) → **otwór**; **~rem**:
stać ~rem be open; **~rzyć** pf. → **otwierać**

otwór m (-woru; -wory) opening; hole;
gap

otyłość f (-ści; 0) obesity

otyły obese

owa f → **ów**; **~cja** f (-i; -e) ovation, applause; **~cyjny** enthusiastic

owad m (-a; -y) zo. insect

owado|bójczy: środek ~bójczy in-
secticide, insect poison; **~żerny** insect-
ivore

owak(i) → **tak(i)**

owal m (-u; -e) oval; **~ny** oval

owca f (-y; -e, G -wiec) zo. sheep sg./pl.

owcza|rek m (-rka; -rki) sheepdog,
shepherd dog; **~rek niemiecki** Alsatian; **~rek szkocki** collie; **~rnia** f (-i;
-e, -i/-ń) sheep-fold; **~rstwo** f (-a; 0)
sheep-breeding; **~rz** m (-a; -e) shepherd

owczy sheep; **~ pęd** herd instinct

owdowi|eć (-eję) kobieta: become
a widow; mężczyzna: become a
widower; **~ały** widowed

owdzie → **ówdzie**

owe ż-rzecz → **ów**

owędy: tędy i ~ here and there

owi pl. m-os → **ów**

owieczka f (-i; G -czek) zo. → **owca**

owies m (-wsa; -wsy) bot. oat, (nasiona)
oats pl.

owi|ewać (-am) blow on; fig. envelope;
~jać (-am) **⟨~nąć⟩** (-nę, -ń!) wrap
(round), bind (round); **~jać ⟨~nąć⟩ się**
wind o.s., wrap o.s. (**wokół** G round)

owładnąć pf (-nę) → **zawładnąć**

owłosiony hairy

owo n → **ów**

owoc m (-u; -e) bot. fruit (też fig.); **~ar-**

ski fruit; **~ny** fruitful; **~ować** fruit;
~owy fruit

owrzodz|enie n (-a; G -eń) med. ul-
ceration; **~ony** ulcerated

owsian|ka f (-i; G -nek) porridge; **~y** oat

owszem adv. of course, without a
doubt; on the contrary

ozdabiać (-am) decorate, embellish; →
zdobić

ozdob|a f (-y; G -dób) decoration, or-
nament; **~ić** pf. → **ozdabiać**; **~ny** orna-
mental, decorative; (przeładowany) ornate

ozdrowie|niec m (-a; -y) convalescent;
~ńczy convalescent; econ. redevelop-
ment, rehabilitation

ozięb|iać (-am) **⟨~ić⟩** cool down (**się**
v/i.); **~enie** n (-a; G -eń) cooling

ozięb|le adv. coldly; **~ły** cold; chilly;
(seksualnie) frigid

ozim|ina f (-y; G -) agr. winter seed;
winter grain; **~y** agr. winter

oznacz|ać (-am) mean, signify; symbol-
ize, represent; **⟨~yć⟩** też mark, label

oznajmi|ać (-am) **⟨~ć⟩** (-ę, -mij!) de-
clare, state, announce; **~enie** n (-a) announcement; → **obwieszczenie**

oznajmujący:tryb~gr.indicativemood

oznaka f (-i; G -) symptom, sign, indica-
tion; (znaczek) badge

ozon m (-u; 0) chem. ozone; **~owy**
ozone; **warstwa ~owa** ozone layer

ozór m (-zoru; -zory) tongue (też gastr.)

ożaglowanie n (-a; G -ań) naut. rig

ożen|ek m (-nku; -nki) marriage; **~ić
się** → **żenić się**; **~iony** married (**z I** to)

oży|wać (-am) **⟨~ć⟩** come alive; fig. re-
vive; **~wczo** adv.in a stimulating way;
~wczy stimulating,invigorating; **~wiać**
(-am) **⟨~wić⟩** enliven, F liven up;
stimulate; **~wiać⟨~wić⟩ się** oczy: light
up; gospodarka: revive; **~wiony** lively,
animated

Ó

ósemka f (-i; G -mek) eight; (linia itp.)
number eight; mus. Brt. quaver, Am.
eighth note

ósm|y eighth; **~a** eight (o'clock); →

ów (**owa** f, **owo** n, **owe** ż-rzecz, **owi** m-
os) this; **to i owo** this and that; **ni z tego i z owego** out of the blue

ów|czesny the then; **~dzie: tu i ~dzie**
here and there

P

p. *skrót pisany:* **pan** Mr; **pani** Mrs, Ms; **panna** Miss; **patrz** see; **piętro** floor; **porównaj** cf. *(compare)*; **punkt** point; **po** after

pach|a *f* (*-y*) armpit; *(w ubraniu)* armhole; **pod ~ą** under the arm

pach|nąco *adv.* fragrantly; **~nący** fragrant, scented; **~nieć** (*-nę; -nij!*) smell; *(I)* smell, pick up the scent

pachołek *m* (*-łka; -łki-łkowie*) *(słupek)* *naut.* bollard

pachwina *f* (*-y; G -*) *anat.* groin

pacierz *m* (*-a; -e, -y*) prayer; **odmawiać ~** pray, say prayers

paciorek *m* (*-rka; -rki*) bead

pacjent *m* (*-a; -nci*), **~ka** *f* (*-i; G -tek*) patient

packa *f* (*-i; G -cek*) fly swat

Pacyfik *m* (*-u; 0*) the Pacific Ocean

pacz|ka *f* (*-i; G -czek*) parcel; packet; *(papierosów)* *Brt.* packet, *Am.* package; F *(ludzi)* bunch, crowd; **~kowany** packaged; **~yć** ⟨**s-, wy-**⟩ (*-ę*): **~yć** ⟨**s-, wy-**⟩ **się** warp

padaczka *f* (*-i; 0*) epilepsy

padać (*-am*) fall, drop; **pada deszcz/śnieg** it is raining/snowing

padalec *m* (*-lca; -lce*) *zo.* slow-worm

padlina *f* (*-y; 0*) rotten carcass; *(mięso)* carrion

pagaj *m* (*-a; -e*) paddle

pagór|ek *m* (*-rka; -rki*) hillock; **~kowaty** hilly

pajacyk *m* (*-a; -i*) *(zabawka)* jumping jack; *(ubranie)* rompers *pl.*, play-suit

pająk *m* (*-a; -i*) *zo.* spider; **~ęczyna** *f* (*-y; G -*) cobweb

paka *f* (*-i; G -*) box, chest; → **paczka**; F *(więzienie)* clink

pakie|cik *m* (*-a; -i*) → **pakiet**; **~t** *m* (*-u; -y*) packet

pakow|ać (*-uję*) ⟨**za-**⟩ pack; ⟨**o-**⟩ wrap (up); ⟨**w-**⟩ put into; *(siłą)* cram into; **~ać** ⟨**s-**⟩ **się** pack up; **~ny** roomy; **~y:** *papier ~y* manila paper, wrapping paper

paktować (*-uję*) pact

pakunek *m* (*-nku; -nki*) package; bundle; *tech.* packing

pal *m* (*-a; -e, -i/-ów*) stake, post; *bud.* pile

---

palacz *m* (*-a; -e*), *(w piecu)* stoker; *(papierosów)* smoker; **~ka** *f* (*-i; G -czek*) smoker

palarnia *f* (*-i; -e*) smoking room

palący burning *(też fig.)*; smoking; *słońce* scorching; **dla ~ch** smoker

pal|ec *m* (*-lca; -lce*) *(ręki)* finger, *(stopy)* toe; *anat.* digit; **~ec wskazujący** index finger; **~ec serdeczny** ring finger; **duży ~ec** big toe; **na ~cach** tip-toe; **sam jak ~ec** all alone

pale|nie *n* (*-a; G -eń*) burning; *(w piecu)* heating; *(tytoniu)* smoking; *(kawy)* roasting; **~nisko** *n* (*-a; G -*) hearth

Palestyna *f* (*-y; 0*) Palestine

paleta *f* (*-y; G -*) *(malarza)* palette; *tech.* pallet

pali|ć (*-lę*) *v/i.* *(w piecu)* heat, stove; *(rana, w gardle)* burn; *papierosy* smoke; *papiery* burn; *lampę* have on, keep on; ⟨**s-**⟩ burn; **~ć się** burn; *budynek:* be on fire; *lampa:* be on; F be burning to do; **~wo** *n* (*-a; G -*) fuel

palm|a *f* (*-y; G -*) *bot.* palm (tree); **~owy** palm

paln|ąć F *v/s* (*-nę*) *(trzasnąć)* bash; **~ąć sobie w łeb** blow one's brains out; **~ik** *m* (*-a; -i*) burner; **~y** inflammable, combustible; **broń ~a** firearm

palto *n* (*-a; G -*) overcoat

palu|ch *m* (*-a; -y*) *anat.* big toe; **~szek** *m* (*-szka; -szki*) → **palec**; **~szki** *pl.* **rybne** *gastr.* fish fingers *pl.*

pałac *m* (*-u; -e*) palace

pałać (*-am*) *oczy:* blaze; **~ nienawiścią** be burning with hatred

pał|ąk *m* (*-a; -i*) bail; bow; **~eczka** *f* (*-i; G -czek*) → **pałka**; *gastr.* chopstick; **~ka** *f* (*-i; G -łek*) stick; *(policjanta)* club, *Brt.* truncheon, *Am.* night stick

pamiąt|ka *f* (*-i; G -tek*) memento, souvenir *(~a po matce* of the mother); *(z wczasów)* souvenir; **na ~ę** to remember; **~owy** commemorative

pamię|ć *f* (*-ci; 0*) memory *(też komp.)*; *(wspomnienie)* remembrance; **na ~ć** by heart; **świętej ~ci** of blessed memory; **ku ~ci** (*G*) in memory (of); **~tać** (*-am*) *(A)* remember; *(o L)* not forget (about);

~tnik *m* (-*a*; -*i*) diary; *pl.* ~tniki memoirs *pl.*; ~tny memorable, unforgettable

PAN *skrót pisany:* **Polska Akademia Nauk** Polish Academy of Sciences

pan *m* (-*a*; *DL* -*u*; -*owie*) gentleman; (*psa itp.*) master; (*przy zwracaniu się: z nazwiskiem*) Mr, (*bez nazwiska*) sir; ~ **Nowak** Mr Nowak; ~ie doktorze Doctor (*skrót:* Dr); czy ~ ma ...? do you have...?; ~ domu (*gospodarz*) host, landlord; ~ młody bridegroom

pan|cerni *m* (-*a*; -*i*) battleship; *zo.* armadillo; ~cerny armo(u)red; ~cerz *m* (-*a*; -*e*) armo(u)r

panel *m* (-*a*; -*e*) panel; (*dyskusja*) panel discussion

pani *f* (*A* -*q*, *G* -; -*e*) woman, lady; (*psa, władczyni*) mistress; (*przy zwracaniu się, z nazwiskiem*) Ms, zamężna Mrs, niezamężna Miss; (*bez nazwiska*) madam; czy ~ ma ...? do you have...?; ~ domu hostess, landlady

paniczny panic

panienka *f* (-*i*; *G* -*nek*) young woman, young lady; (*przy zwracaniu się*) Miss

panień|ski: nazwisko ~skie maiden name

panierować ⟨*o*-⟩ (-*uję*) bread

panika *f* (-*i*; *0*) panic

pann|a *f* (-*y*; *G* -*nien*) girl, maiden; (*w dowodzie*) unmarried woman; (*przy zwracaniu się*) Miss; *Ω* znak Zodiaku: Virgo; on(a) jest spod znaku *Ωy* (s)he is (a) Virgo; stara ~a spinster; ~a młoda bride; → pani

panowa|ć (-*uję*) rule, reign (*też* nad *I* over); ⟨*za*-⟩ (nad sobą) control (o.s.), be in control of (o.s.); panuje ... there is ...; ~nie *n* (-*a*; *0*) rule, ruling, mastery; control (nad sobą of o.s.)

pantera *f* (-*y*; *G* -) *zo.* panther

panterka *f* (-*i*; *G* -*rek*) camouflage jacket

pantof|el *m* (-*la*; -*fle*, -*fli*) shoe; ~le *pl.* damskie ladies' shoes *pl.*; ~le *pl.* domowe slippers *pl.*; ~larz F *m* (-*a*; -*e*) henpecked husband

pantomima *f* (-*y*; *G* -) mime

pańsk|i gest lordly, grand; your, yours; ~i list your letter; po pańsku gentlemanly

państw|o *n* (-*a*; *G* -) (*kraj*) country, state; you, (*z nazwiskiem*) Mr and Mrs; proszę ~a ... Ladies and Gentleman; ~o pozwolą please allow me; ~o mło-

dzi *pl.* the newlyweds *pl.*

państwowy state

PAP *skrót pisany:* **Polska Agencja Prasowa** Polish Press Agency

papa *f* (-*y*; *G* -): ~ dachowa roofing-felt

papier *m* (-*u*; -*y*) (maszynowy, toaletowy typing, toilet) paper; F ~y *pl.* documents *pl.*, identity papers *pl.*; ~ek *m* (-*rka*; -*rki*) a piece of paper

papiero|s *m* (-*a*; -*y*) cigarette; ~śnica *f* (-*y*; *G* -) cigarette-case; ~wy paper

papieski papal

papież *m* (-*a*; -*e*) *rel.* pope

papk|a *f* (-*i*; *G* -*ek*) mash, pap; ~owaty mashy

paplanina *f* (-*y*; *G* -) chatter

papra|ć -*przę*) smear; ~ się rana: fester

paproć *f* (-*oci*; -*ocie*) *bot.* fern

papryka *f* (-*i*; *G* -) *bot.* (w strączkach) pepper, (proszek) paprika

papuć *m* (-*cia*; -*cie*) F slipper

papug|a *f* (-*i*; *G* -) *zo.* parrot; ~żka *f* (-*i G* -*żek*): ~żka falista *zo.* budgie, budgerigar

par *m* (-*a*; -*owie*) *Brt.* peer

para[1] *f* (-*y*; *0*) steam, vapo(u)r; (na szybie) mist

par|a[2] *f* (-*y*; *G* -) pair; couple; ~a zakochanych (pair of) lovers; ~a małżonków married couple; w ~y, ~ami in pairs; nie do ~y odd; iść w parze go hand in hand

parad|a *f* (-*y*; *G* -) parade; piłka nożna: save; wejść komuś w ~ę get in s.o.'s way

paradoksalny paradoxical

parafia *f* (*GDL* -*ii*; -*e*) *rel.* parish; ~lny parish, parochial; ~nin *m* (-*a*; -*anie*,-), ~nka *f* (-*i*; *G* -*nek*) parishioner

parafinowy paraffin

para|gon *m* (-*u*; -*y*) sales slip, receipt; ~graf *m* (-*u*; -*y*) clause

paraliż *m* (-*u*; -*y*) *med.* paralysis; ~ dziecięcy polio; ~ować ⟨*s*-⟩ (-*uję*) paralyse (*też* fig.)

para|pet *m* (-*u*; -*y*) windowsill; ~sol *m* (-*a*; -*e*), ~solka *f* (-*i*; *G* -*lek*) umbrella; (od słońca) parasol; ~wan *m* (-*u*; -*y*) (folding)screen

parcela *f* (-*i*; -*e*) plot, lot

parciany sacking

parcie *n* (-*a*; *0*) pressure; *med.* pushing

pare (*GDL* -*ru*, *I* -*roma*; *m-os NA* -*ru*) (*G*) a couple (of), a few; ~ razy several times; ~set several hundred

P

park *m* (-*u*; -*i*) park
parkan *m* (-*u*; -*y*) fence
parkiet *m* (-*u*; -*y*) parquet
park|ing *m* (-*u*; -*i*) *Brt.* car park, *Am.*
parking lot; ~ometr *m* parking-meter
parkow|ać ⟨za-⟩ (-*uję*) park; ~anie *n*
(-*a*; *G* -*ań*) parking; ~y park
parlament *m* (-*u*; -*y*) parliament
parlamenta|rny parliamentary; ~rzys-
ta *m* (-*y*; -*ści*, -*tów*) *Brt.* Member of
Parliament, *Am.* Congressman
parn|o *adv.* close, sultry; ~y close, sultry
parodia *f* (*GDl* -*ii*; -*e*) parody
paro|godzinny of several hours; ~kon-
ny drawn by two horses; ~krotnie *adv.*
several times; repeatedly; ~krotny repeated, multiple
paroksyzm *m* (-*u*; -*y*) paroxysm, fit
paro|letni several years old; several
yearslong;~miesięcznyseveralmonths
long; ~statek *m* (-*tka*, -*tki*) → *parowiec*;~tygodniowy several weeks long
parować[1] (-*uję*) *cios* parry, ward off
paro|wać[2] (-*uję*) *v/i.* evaporate; vapor-
ize; *v/t.* steam; ~wiec *m* (-*wca*, -*wce*)
naut. steamship (*skrót:* SS); ~wóz *m*
(-*wozu*, -*wozy*) *rail.* steam engine;
~wy steam
parów *m* (-*rowu*, -*rowy*) ravine, gorge
parówka *f* (-*i*; *G* -*wek*) frankfurter, *Am.*
wiener
parsk|ać (-*am*) ⟨~nąć⟩ (-*nę*) snort;
~nąć śmiechem snort with laughter
parszywy *pies* mangy; *fig.* rotten
parta|cki botched, bungled; ~ctwo *n*
(-*a*; *G* -) botching, botched-up job;
~czyć ⟨s-⟩ (-*ę*) botch, bungle
parter *m* (-*u*; -*y*) *Brt.* ground floor, *Am.*
first floor; *teatr.* stalls *pl.*; ~owy *Brt.*
ground-floor, *Am.* first-floor; one-
stor(e)y
partia (*GDl* -*ii*; -*e*) *pol.* party; (*towaru
itp.*) shipment, lot; (*w sporcie*) game,
round; (*do małżeństwa*) match; *teatr
itp.* part
partner *m* (-*a*; -*rzy*), ~ka *f* (-*i*; *G* -*rek*)
partner; ~stwo *n* (-*a*; *G* -) partnership
partolić F ⟨s-⟩ (-*lę*) → *partaczyć*
party|jny party; ~kuła *f* (-*y*; *G* -) *gr.* par-
ticle; ~tura *f* (-*y*; *G* -) *mus.* score
partyza|ncki guerrilla; ~nt *m* (-*a*; -*nci*)
guerrilla; ~ntka *f* (*walka*) guerrilla war;
(*kobieta*) guerilla
paru(-) → *paro*(-)

paryski Paris
Paryż *m* (-*a*; *0*) Paris
parytet *m* (-*u*; -*y*) *econ.* parity
parzyć (-*ę*) *v/t.* ⟨zaparzać⟩ brew; *zwierzęta* mate; ⟨o-, po-, s-⟩ burn (*sobie
usta* one's lips); (*mocno*) scald; ~ się
burn (*też o.s.*), get burnt; *herbata*: draw;
zwierzęta: mate
parzysty even
pas *m* (-*a*; -*y*) band; (*do ubrania*) belt;
(*część ciała, sukni*) waist; ~ ratunkowy
life belt; ~ startowy runway; ~ ruchu
lane; w ~y striped; po ~ waist-high,
-deep; scald; → *klinowy*; ~ać (-*am*)
→ *paść*[2]
pasaż *m* (-*u*; -*e*) (*sklepowy*) shopping arcade; *mus. itp.* passage
pasażer *m* (-*a*; -*owie*), ~ka *f* (-*i*; *G* -*rek*)
passenger
pasek *m* (-*ska*, -*ski*) → *pas*; ~ do zegarka watchband
paser *m* fence, receiver of stolen goods;
~stwo *n* (-*a*; *0*) receiving (stolen goods)
pasieka *f* (-*i*; *G* -) apiary
pasierb *m* (-*a*; -*owie*) stepson; ~ica *f*
(-*y*; -*e*) stepdaughter
pas|ja *f* (-*i*; -*e*) passion; *wpaść w ~ję* get
furious; ~jonująco *adv.* excitingly;
~jonujący exciting
paska|rstwo *n* (-*a*; *0*) profiteering;~rka
f (-*i*; *G* -*rek*), ~rz *m* (-*a*; -*e*) profiteer
paskudny terrible, dreadful
pasmo *n* (-*a*; *G* -/-*sem*) strip, strand;
RTV: band; (*górskie*) range, chain;
(*ruchu*) lane, (*na autostradzie*) *Brt.*
carriageway
pasować[1] (-*uję*) *v/i.* be suitable, be appropriate (*do G* to); *v/t.* ⟨do-⟩ fit (*do
G* to); *kolory itp.*: match
pasować[2] (-*uję*) (*w grze w karty*) pass
pasożyt *m* (-*a*; -*y*) *biol., fig.* parasite; *fig.*
sponger; ~ować (-*uję*) parasitize (*na L*
on); *fig.* sponge
pasta *f* (-*y*; *G* -) paste; ~ do butów shoe
polish; ~ do zębów tooth paste; ~ do
podłogi floor polish
paster|ka *f* (-*i*; *G* -*rek*) → *pastuszka*;
rel. midnight mass (at Christmas); ~ski
shepherd; *rel.* pastoral
pasteryzowany pasteurized
pasterz *m* (-*a*; -*e*) → *pastuch*
pastewny fodder
pastor *m* (-*a*; -*orzy*/-*owie*) pastor, (*anglikański*) vicar

P

pastorał *m* (*-u*; *-y*) *rel.* crosier

pastować ⟨*na*-⟩ (*-uję*) *parkiet* polish

pastu|ch *m* (*-a*; *-y/-si/-owie*) shepherd; **~szka** *f* (*-i*; *G -szek*) shepherdess

past|wa: stać się, paść ~wą (*G*) fall prey (to); **~wisko** *n* (*-a*; *G -*) pasture

pastylka *f* (*-i*; *G -lek*) *med.* pill, dragée

pasywny passive

pasza *f* (*-y;-e*) *agr.* (**zielona** green) fodder

paszcza *f* (*-y*; *G -*) mouth, *fig.* jaws *pl.*

paszport *m* (*-u*; *-y*) passport; **~owy** passport; **biuro ~owe** passport office

paszte|cik *m* (*-a*; *-i*) *gastr.* pie, patty; **~t** *m* (*-u*; *-y*) *gastr.* pâté

paść¹ *pf.* fall (down) → **padać**

paść² *bydło* graze; (*karmić*) feed; **~ się** graze

patałach *m* (*-a*; *-y*) F botcher, bungler

patelnia *f* (*-i*; *G -e*) frying-pan

pa|tentowany patented; **~tetyczny** pathetic; **~tologiczny** pathological

patriot|a *m* (*-y*; *-ci*), **~ka** *f* (*-i*) patriot; **~yczny** patriotic

patrol *m* (*-u*; *-e*) patrol; **~ować** (*-uję*) patrol

patron *m* (*-a*; *-i*); **~ka** *f* (*-i*; *G -nek*) patron; *rel.* patron saint

patroszyć ⟨*wy*-⟩ (*-ę*) *gastr.* gut

patrz|eć, ~yć ⟨*po*-⟩ (*-ę*) look (**przez okno** out of the window; **na** *A* at); **jak się ~y** comme il faut, as it should be; **patrz** look

patyk *m* (*-a*; *-i*) stick

pauza *f* (*-y*; *G -*) break; (*przy mówieniu itp.*) pause; *mus.* rest

paw *m* (*-ia*; *-ie*) *zo.* peacock; **~i** peacock

pawian *m* (*-a*; *-y*) *zo.* baboon

pawilon *m* (*-u*; *-y*) (*sklep*) shop; *bud.* pavilion

pawlacz *m* (*-a*; *-e*) shallow mezzanine

pazerny greedy

paznok|ieć *m* (*-kcia*; *-kcie*) *anat.* nail; **do ~ci** nail

pazur *m* (*-a*; *-y*) claw, talon

październik *m* (*-a*; *-i*) October; **~owy** October

pączek *m* (*-czka*; *-czki*) *bot.* → **pąk**; *gastr.* doughnut

pąk *bot.* bud; **wypuszczać ~i** bud

pąsowy crimson

pchać (*-am*) push, (*mocno*) shove; thrust (**do** *G* into); **~ się** crowd, throng; (**przez** *A*) push one's way (through); → **pchnąć**

pch|ełka *f* (*-i*; *G -łek*) (*do gry*) tiddly-wink; **~ełki** *pl.* *gra*: tiddlywinks; **~ła** *f* (*-y*; *G pcheł*) *zo.* flea; **~li** flea; **~li targ** flea market

pchn|ąć *pf* (*-nę*) → **pchać**; (*nożem*) stab; **~ięcie** *n* (*-a*; *G -ęć*) thrust; (*w sporcie*) put; **~ięcie nożem** stab

PCK *skrót pisany:* **Polski Czerwony Krzyż** Polish Red Cross

pech *m* (*-a*; *0*) bad luck, misfortune; **mieć ~a** be unlucky; **~owiec** *m* (*-wca*; *-wcy*) unfortunate

pe|dagogiczny pedagogic(al); **~dał** *m* **1.** (*-u*; *-y*) pedal; **2.** (*-a*; *-y*) V (*homoseksualista*) queer; **~dantyczny** pedantic

pedi'kiur *m* (*-u*; *0*) pedicure

pejcz *m* (*-a*; *-e*) whip

pejzaż *m* (*-u*; *-e*) landscape

Pekin *m* (*-u*; *0*) Peking, Beiging

peklowany corned

pelargonia *f* (*-ii*; *-e*) geranium

peleryna *f* (*-y*; *G -*) cape

pelisa *f* (*-y*; *G -*) fur coat

peł|en → pełny; **~nia** *f* (*-i*; *-e*) full moon; (*szczyt*) heyday, peak; **~nia życia** the prime of life; **w ~ni lata** in high summer; **w całej ~ni** completely; **~nić** (*-ę*, *-ń/-nij!*) *obowiązki* fulfil; *wartę* keep; **~nić służbę** serve

pełno *adv.* (*G*) a lot (of); **~letni** of age; **~metrażowy** full-length

pełnomocn|ictwo *n* (*-a*; *G -*) proxy; *jur.* power of attorney; **~ik** *m* (*-a*; *-cy*) authorized representative; *jur.* proxy, plenipotentiary; **~y** plenipotentiary, authorized

pełno|morski *flota* deep-sea; *jacht* ocean-going; **~prawny** rightful; **~wartościowy** fully adequate

peł|ny full; complete; whole; **~ne mleko** full-cream milk; **na ~nym morzu** on the high seas; **~en nadziei** hopeful; **~en energii** vigorous; **do ~na** to the brim; **napełnić do ~na** fill up

pełz|ać (*-am*), **~nąć** (*-nę*) crawl

penicylina *f* (*-y*; *G -*) *med.* penicillin

pens *m* (*-a*; *-y*) penny, *pl.* pennies *lub* pence

pensja *f* (*-i*; *-e*) salary, (*robotnika, cotygodniowa*) wages *pl.*; (*dla panien*) boarding school

pensjonat *m* (*-u*; *-y*) guest-house

pepegi *pl.* (*-ów*) tennis-shoes *pl.*

pepitka *f* (*-i*; *G -tek*) shepherd's check

perfidny perfidious

perfum|eria f (GDL -ii; -e) perfumery; ~y pl. (-) perfume, scent

pergamin m (-u; -y) parchment; parchment paper

periody|czny periodic(al); ~k m (-u; -i) periodical

perkaty F: ~ nos snub nose

perku|sista m (-y; -śći) mus. drummer; percussionist; ~sja f (-i; 0) mus. drums; percussion

per|lić się (-lę) pearl; śmiech: ripple; ~listy beady, pearly; ~ła f (-y; G -reł) pearl; ~łowy pearly; kolor pearl-grey

peron m (-u; -y) rail. platform; ~ówka f (-i; G -wek) platform ticket

perski Persian; ~e oko wink

perso|nalny personal; (dotyczący pracowników) personnel; ~nel m (-u; 0) personnel, staff

perspektyw|a m (-y; G -) perspective; ~y pl. (szanse) prospects pl.

perswazja f (-i; -e) persuasion

pertrakt|acje pl. (-i) negotiations pl.; ~ować (-uję) negotiate

peruka f (-i; G -) wig

perwers|ja f (-i; -e) perversion; ~yjny perverse, perverted

peryferie f/pl. (GDL -ii) periphery; ~ miasta outskirts pl.

peryskop m (-u; -y) periscope

pestka f (-i; G -tek) stone, (mała) pit

pesymist|yczny pessimistic; ~a m (-y; -śći), ~ka f (-i; -tek) pessimist

peszyć ⟨s-⟩ (-ę) put out, disturb

petarda f (-y; G -) banger

petent m (-a; -ci), ~ka f (-i; G -tek) applicant

petycja f (-i; -e) petition

pew|ien[1] (-wna, -wne, m-os -wni) (niejaki) a certain; a, one; ~na ilość a certain amount; co ~ien czas from time to time; ~nego dnia one day; po ~nym czasie after some time

pew|ien[2] → pewny; ~nie adv. surely; reliably; stać firmly; ~nie! sure!; ~no adv.: na ~no for certain, sure; ~ność f (-śći; 0) certainty; (niezawodność) reliability; (zaufanie) confidence; ~ność siebie self-confidence; z całą ~nością surely; ~ny certain, sure; oparcie, krok firm; ręka, cięcie steady; (niezawodny) confident; nic ~nego nothing definite

pęcherz m (-a; -e) (z odparzenia) blis-

ter; anat. bladder; ~yk m (-a; -i) → pęcherz; anat. bladder

pęczak m (-u; 0) gastr. pearl barley

pęcz|ek m (-czka; -czki) bunch; (mały) wisp; ~nieć ⟨na-⟩ (-eję) swell

pęd rush; shoot, sprout; ~ do wiedzy thirst for knowledge; biec ~em dash

pędny tech. driving, propellent

pędzel m (-dzla; -dzle) brush

pędzić (-dzę) v/i. dash, hurry, race; v/t. drive; → spędzać, wypędzać

pędzlować (-uję) med. paint (D with)

pęk m (kluczy key) bunch; (chrustu) armful

pęk|ać (-am) ⟨-nąć⟩ (-nę) burst; lina itp.: break; szkło: crack; wargi: crack, chap; ~ać ze śmiechu laugh one's head off; ~aty squat; (wypchany) bulging; ~nięcie n (-a; G -ęć) (szczelina) crack; (rury pipe) burst; (kości) fracture

pęp|ek m (-pka; -pki) anat. navel; ~owina f (-y; G -) anat. umbilical cord

pęseta f (-y; G -) tweezers pl.

pęt|ak m F (-a; -i) sprog; ~elka f (-i; G -lek) loop; ~la f (-y; G -tel) loop; (na linie) noose; (tramwaju itp.) terminus

piach m (-u; -y) → piasek

piać ⟨za-⟩ (-eję) crow

piana f (-y; G -) foam; (z mydła) lather; (na napoju) froth

piani|no n (-a; G -) mus. (upright) piano; ~sta m (-y; -śći) pianist

pianka f (-i; G -nek) → piana

piano|guma f (-y; G -) foam rubber; ~wy: gaśnica ~wa foam extinguisher

pias|ek m (-ku; -ki) sand; ~kowiec m (-wca; -wce) sandstone; ~kownica f (-y; G -) Brt. sand-pit, Am. sand-box

piasta f (-y; G -) hub

piastować (-uję) hold

piaszczysty sandy, sand

piąć się (pnę, piął) climb

piąt. skrót pisany: piątek Fri. (Friday)

piąt|ek m (-tku; -tki) Friday; Wielki 2ek rel. Good Friday; ~ka f (-i; G -tek) five; (linia) number five; szkoła: jakby: A; w ~kę; in a group of five; ~kowy Friday; ~y fifth; o ~ej at five (o'clock)

pici|e n (-a; -) drinking; (napój) drink; do ~a to drink

pić (piję) drink; chce mi się ~ I am thirsty; → zdrowie

piec[1] m (-a; -e) stove; tech. furnace, kiln; ~ kuchenny range piec² ⟨na-, u-, wy-⟩ v/t. ciasto bake (się v/i.); mięso roast (się v/i.); v/t. impf. słońce beat down; oczy itp.: smart, sting

piechot|a f (-y; G -) mil. infantry; ~ą, na ~ę on foot

piecyk m (-a; -i) → piec²; (do wody itp.) heater

piecz|a f (-y; -e) care; on sprawuje ~ę nad he takes care of

piecza|ra f (-y; G -) cave; ~rka f (-i; G -rek) bot. meadow mushroom

pieczątka f (-i; G -tek) (rubber) stamp

pieczeń f (-eni; -nie) roast meat; ~ z sarny roast venison

pieczę|ć f (-ci; -cie) seal; stamp; ~tować ⟨o-⟩ (-uję) seal; stamp

pieczołowi|tość f (-ści; 0) care; ~cie adv. carefully; ~ty careful

piecz|ony roast; ~yste n (-go) roast meat; ~ywo n (-a; 0) bread, cakes, and pastries

piedestał m (-u; -y) pedestal; arch. plinth

pieg|i m/pl. (-ów) freckles pl.; ~owaty freckled

piek|arnia f (-i; -e) bakery; ~arnik m (-a; -i) oven; ~arz m (-a; -e) baker; ~ący ból stinging; ~ielny hellish; ~ło n (-a; G -kieł) hell

pielęgnacja f (-i; 0) care; (urządzenia) maintenance

pielęgnia|rka f (-i; G -rek) nurse; ~rz m (-a; -e) (male) nurse

pielęgnować (-uję) look after; ludzi care for; zęby take care of; ogródek look after

pielgrzym m (-a; -i) pilgrim; ~ka f (-i; G -mek) pilgrimage

pielić ⟨wy-⟩ (-lę) weed

pielu|chomajtki pl. nappy pants pl.; ~szka f (-i; G -szek) (do jednorazowego użytku disposable) Brt. nappy, Am. diaper

pieniądz m (-a; -e, -iędzy, I -iędzmi) coin; zbior. → pieniądze; ~e m/pl. money; przy ~ach in the money

pienić się (-ę, -ń!) foam, froth; mydło: lather

pieniężny money; kara ~a fine

pienisty foaming, frothing; → musujący

pień m (pnia; pnie, pni) trunk; (pniak) tree-stump

pie|prz m (-u; 0) bot., gastr. pepper;

~przny hot, peppery; kawał dirty; ~rnik m (-a; -i) gastr. ginger bread

pierogi pl. (-ów) dumplings pl.

pier|siowy chest; anat. pectoral; ~ś f (-si) (kobieca, też gastr.) breast; ~si pl. (klatka piersiowa) chest; pełną ~sią lustily

pierście|niowy ring (też fig.); ~ń m (-nia; -nie, -ni) ring

pier|ścionek m → pierścień; ~wiastek m (-stka; -stki) chem. element; math. root, radical; ~wiastek kwadratowy square root; ~wiosnek m (-snka; -snki) bot. primrose

pierwo|rodny first-born; ~tny (nieskażony) prim(a)eval; (prymitywny) primitive; (pierwszy) original; ~wzór m (-oru; -ory) prototype, archetype

pierwszeństwo n (-a; 0) priority; ~ przejazdu right of way; dać ~ (D) give precedence (to)

pierwszo|planowy foreground; ~rzędny first-class

pierwsz|y first; ~a godzina one o'clock; ~ego maja first of May; po ~e first(ly); po raz ~y for the first time

pierzch|ać (-am) ⟨~nąć¹⟩ (-nę) run away; ptaki: fly away; nastrój: disappear; ~nąć² (-nę) skóra: chap

pierze n (-a; 0) zbior. feathers pl.

pierzyna f (-y; G -) duvet, Brt. continental quilt, Am. stuffed quilt

pies m (psa, psu, L psie; psy) zo. dog; (myśliwski) hound; pod psem under the weather; ~ek m (-ska; -ski) → pies

pieszczot|a f (-y; G -) caress; ~y pl. petting; ~liwy gentle; ~liwe imię pet name

piesz|o on foot; ~y foot, pedestrian; ~a wycieczka hike; przejście dla ~ych pedestrian crossing

pieścić (-szczę) caress, pet

pieś|niarka f (-ki; G -rek), ~niarz m (-a; -e) singer

pieśń f (-ni) song; ~ ludowa folk song

pietruszka f (-i; G -szek) bot. parsley

pięcio|bok m pentagon; ~bój m (w sporcie) pentathlon; ~krotny fivefold; ~letni five-year-long, -old; ~linia f (-ii; -e) staff, stave; ~raczki pl. (-ów) quintuplets pl.; ~ro five → 666

pięć five; ~dziesiąt fifty; ~dziesiątka f (-i; G -tek) fifty; ~set five hundred; → 666

piękn|ie adv. prettily, beautifully; ~o n

(-a; 0), ~ość f (-ci) beauty; ~y beautiful

pięś|ciarstwo n (-a; 0) (w sporcie) boxing; ~ciarz m (-a; -e) (w sporcie) boxer

pięść f (-ci) anat. fist

pięta f (-y; G -) anat. heel

piętna|sto- w złoż. fifteen; ~stka f (-i; G -tek) (linia) number fifteen; ~ście fifteen; → 666

pięt|no n (-a, L -nie; G -tn) brand; mark, mole; fig. wyciskać swoje ~no (na l) take its toll (on); ~nować (-uję) brand; ~ro n (-a; G -ter) floor, storey; na drugim ~rze Brt. on the second floor, Am. on the third floor

piętrzyć się (-ę) be piled up

pigułka f (-i; G -łek) pill (też fig.)

pija|czka f (-i; G -czek), ~k m (-a; -i) drunk, drunkard; ~ny drunk; po ~nemu when drunk; ~ństwo n (-a; G -) alcoholism, drunkenness; ~tyka f (-i; G -) binge, spree

pijawka f (-i; G -wek) zo. leech (też fig.)

pik m (-a; -i) gra w karty: spade(s pl.); as ~ ace of spades; wyjść w ~i play spades

pikantny hot, piquant; fig. juicy

pikle m/pl. (-i) gastr. pickles pl.

pikling m (-a; -i) gastr. smoked herring

pilniczek m (-czka; -czki) file

pilno|ść f (-ści; 0) diligence; hard work; ~wać (-uję) (G) guard, keep watch (on); ~wać się take care, be careful; watch each other

pilny urgent, immediate; ktoś diligent, conscientious

pilot m (-a, -ci) aviat. pilot; (przewodnik, też fig.) guide; RTV: remote control; ~ować (-uję) navigate; aviat. pilot

pilśniow|y felt; płyta ~a bud. hardboard

piła f (-y; G -) saw; fig. pain in the neck

piłka[1] f (-i; G -łek) → piła

piłka[2] f (-i; G -łek) (w sporcie) ball; ~ nożna football, soccer; grać w piłkę play ball; ~rski football; ~rz m (-a; -e) (w sporcie) footballer, football player

piłować (-uję) saw

pinceta f (-y; G -) tweezers pl.

pineska (-i; G -sek), pinezka (-i; G -zek) Brt. drawing pin, Am. thumbtack

ping-pong m (-a; -i) table tennis

pingwin m (-a; -y) penguin

piołun m (-u; -y) bot. wormwood, mugwort

pion m (-u; -y) (narzędzie) plumb (line); (kierunek) perpendicular, verticality; fig. area of responsibility; ~ek m (-nka; -nki) (w grze w szachy) pawn; (w grze w warcaby) piece, counter

pi'onier m (-a; -rzy) pioneer

piono|wo adv. vertically; (w krzyżówce) down; ~wy vertical, perpendicular; ~wzlot m (-u; -y) aviat. VTOL

piorun m (-a; -y) lightning; huk ~a thunder; ~em like lightning; do ~a! damn it!

piorunochron m (-u; -y) lightning rod

piosenka f (-i; G -nek) song; ~rka f (-i; G -rek), ~rz m (-a; -e) singer

piórnik m (-a; -i) pen-case

pióro n (-a; G -) (ptaka) feather; (wieczne fountain) pen; ~ kulkowe rollerball (pen), ballpoint (pen)

pira|ckie wydanie n pirated edition; ~mida f (-y; G -) pyramid; ~t m (-a; -ci) pirate; (drogowy) F speeder

piro- w złoż. zwł. pyro-

pisa|ć ⟨na-⟩ (-szę) write; ~ć na maszynie type; ~nka f (-ki; G -nek) Easter egg; ~k m (-a; -i) felt-tip pen; ~rka f (-i; G -rek), ~rz m (-a; -e) writer, author

pisemn|ie adv. in writing; ~y written

pisk m (-u; -i) squeal; (człowieka) shriek; (opon) screech; ~lę n (-cia; -ta, G -ląt) nestling, fledgling; ~liwy shrill, squeaky

pism|o n (-a; G -) writing; (list) letter; → charakter; 2o Święte the Scriptures pl.; na piśmie in writing

pisnąć pf. → piszczeć; F nie ~ ani słówka not utter a single word

pisownia f (-i; 0) writing, spelling

pistolet m (-u; -y) pistol

piszcz|ałka f (-i; G -łek) mus. (w organach) pipe; (w orkiestrze) fife; ~eć ⟨-ę, -y⟩ mysz, urządzenie: squeal; koła: screech; ~el f (-i; -e) anat. tibia

piśmien|nictwo n (-a; G -) literature; ~ny writing; człowiek literate; artykuły pl. ~ne stationery, writing materials pl.

pitny drinking; miód ~ mead

piw|iarnia f (-i; -e) Brt. pub, Am. beer bar; ~nica f (-y; -e, G -) cellar; ~ny beer; oczy light brown, hazel; ~o n (-a; G -) (z beczki draught) beer; małe ~o fig. small beer

piwonia f (GDl -ii; -e) bot. peony

pizz|a f (-y ; G -) gastr. pizza; ~eria f (GDl -ii; -e) pizzeria piżama f (-y; G -) Brt. pyjamas pl., Am. pajamas pl.

piżmak m (-a; -i) zo. muskrat

piżmo n (-a; 0) musk

p-ko skrót pisany: **przeciwko** agst., ver. (against)

PKOl skrót pisany: **Polski Komitet Olimpijski** Polish Olympic Committee

PKP skrót pisany: **Polskie Koleje Państwowe** Polish State Railways

PKS skrót pisany: **Państwowa Komunikacja Samochodowa** Polish State Coach Company

pkt skrót pisany: **punkt** p. (point)

pl. skrót pisany: **plac** Sq. (Square)

plac m (-u; -e) square; ~ zabaw playground; ~ targowy market square; ~ budowy construction site

plac|ek m (-ka; -ki) (śliwkowy, z serem plum, cheese) cake; ~ki pl. kartoflane potato pancakes; ~ek nadziewany pie; ~ówka f (-i; G -wek) outpost, post

plaga f (-i; G -) plague (też fig.)

plagiat m (-u; -y) plagiarism

plajtować ⟨s-⟩ (-uję) go bankrupt, go bust

plakat m (-u; -y) poster

plakietka f (-i; G -tek) badge

plam|a f(-y; G-) stain, smudge; blot; ~ić ⟨po-, s-, za-⟩(-ię) stain, smudge; blot

plan m (-u; -y) plan; (zajęć itp.) schedule; (lekcji) timetable; (mapa) map; na pierwszym ~ie in the foreground

planeta f (-y; G -) planet

planow|ać ⟨za-⟩ (-uję) plan; ~anie n (-a; G -ań) planning; ~y planned, scheduled

plansza f (-y; -e, G -) (do gry) board

plantacja f (-i; -e) plantation

planty f/pl. (-) green space

plas|kać (-am) ⟨~nąć⟩ (-nę) slap

plaster m (-tra; -try) (przylepny sticking) plaster; ~ miodu honeycomb; ~ek m (-rka, -rki) slice

plastik(owy) → **plastyk²**, **plastikowy**

plastycz|ka f (-i; G -czek) artist; ~ny plastic; opis graphic, vivid; sztuki pl. ~ne fine arts pl.

plastyk¹ m (-a; -cy) artist

plastyk² m (-u; -i) plastic; ~owy plastic

platyna f (-y; 0) chem. platinum; ~owy platinum

plaża f (-y; G -) beach; na ~y on the beach; ~ować (-uję) sunbathe; ~owy beach

plądrować ⟨s-⟩ (-uję) loot, plunder

pląta|ć ⟨po-, s-, za-⟩ (-czę) tangle up, entangle; fig. confuse; ~ć ⟨po-, za-⟩ się get tangled; fig. get confused; (łazić) loaf around; ~nina f (-y; G -) tangle; fig. confusion

plebania f (GDL -ii; -e) (katolicka) presbytery, (protestancka) vicarage

plecak m (-a; -i) rucksack; (turystyczny) backpack

pleciony plaited, woven

plec|y pl. (-ców) back; za moimi ~ami behind my back; stać ~ami (do G) have one's back (to); szeroki w ~ach broad-shouldered

pleć ⟨wy-⟩ → **pielić**

plem|ię n (-ienia; -iona, G -ion) tribe; ~nik m (-a; -i) sperm

plenarny plenary

plene|r m (-u; -y) outdoors, open air; w ~rze on location

plenić się (-ę) reproduce, spread

plenum n (idkl.; -na; -nów) plenary session

pleść ⟨s-⟩ weave, plait; F ⟨na-⟩ natter

pleś|nieć ⟨s-⟩ (-eję) Brt. mould, Am. mold; ~ń f (-ni; -nie) Brt. mould, Am. mold

plewa f (-y; G -) husk

plik m (-u; -i) pile, stack; komp. file

plisowany pleated

pliszka f (-i; G -szek) zo. wagtail

PLN skrót pisany: **polski nowy złoty** new Polish zloty

plomb|a f (-y; G -) seal; med. filling; bud. infilling building; ~ować ⟨za-⟩ (-uję) seal; med. fill; ~owy: budownictwo ~owe infilling

plon m (-u; -y) harvest (też fig.); święto ~ów harvest festival

plotk|a f (-i; G -tek) rumo(u)r, gossip; ~i pl. gossip; ~ować (-uję) gossip

plucha f (-y; G -) wet weather

pluć (-uję) spit

plugaw|ić ⟨s-⟩ (-ię) defile; ~y foul, filthy → **obrzydliwy**

plunąć pf. → pluć

plus m (-a; -y) math. plus; ~ minus fig. give or take

pluskać (-am/-szczę) splash (o A against); ~ się splash about

pluskiewka m (-i; G -wek) → **pinezka**

P

pluskwa f (-y; G -kiew) zo. bedbug; F (urządzenie podsłuchowe) bug

plusnąć v/s. (-nę) → **pluskać**; ~ **do wody** plop into the water

plusz m (-u; -e) plush

pluton¹ m (-u; 0) chem. plutonium

pluton² m (-u; -y) mil. platoon; ~**owy** m (-ego; -wi) platoon leader

plwocina f (-y; G -) med. spit, spittle

płaca f (-y; -e, G -) payment, pay; ~ **za urlop** holiday pay

płachta f (-y; G -) tarpaulin; (papieru) sheet; ~ **ratownicza** safety blanket

płacić ⟨o-, za-⟩ (-cę) pay

płacowy pay, payment

płacz m (-u; -e) weeping, cry; ~**liwy** weepy, tearful; ~**czliwie** adv. tearfully; ~**kać** (-czę) cry, weep

płaski flat

płasko adv. flatly, flat; ~**rzeźba** f (-y; G -) bas-relief; ~**stopie** n (-a; 0) flat feet pl., med. platypodia; ~**wzgórze** n (-a; G -) plateau

płaszcz m (-a; -e) coat; biol. mantle

płaszczyć ⟨s-⟩ (-ę) flatten; ~ **się** fig. pej. crawl, grovel

płaszczyzna f (-y; G -) math. plane; fig. ground

płat m (-a; -y) (kawał) piece; (mięsa itp.) cut, slice; anat. lobe; ~**ek** m (-tka; -tki) flake; bot. petal; ~**ki** pl. **owsiane** oatmeal; ~**ki** pl. **kukurydziane** cornflakes pl.; F **jak z ~ka** without a hitch

płatn|iczy payment, of payment; ~**ik** m (-a; -nicy) payer; ~**ik podatku** taxpayer; ~**ość** f (-ści; 0) payment; **warunki** pl. ~**ości** terms pl. of payment; ~**y** paid

pława f (-y; G -) naut. beacon

płaz m **1.** (-a; -y) zo. reptile; **2.** (-u; -y) (klingi) flat; **puścić** ~**em** (A) let get away (with)

płciowy sexual

płd. skrót pisany: **południe** S (south); **południowy** S (southern)

płeć f (płci; płcie) sex, gender

płet|wa f (-y; G -) (ryby) fin; (nurka, foki itp.) flipper; ~**wonurek** m (-rka; -rkowie/-rki) diver; mil. frogman

płochliw|ie adv. shyly; ~**y** shy

płoć f (-ci; -cie) zo. roach

płodność f (-ści; 0) fertility

płodn|y fertile; ~**y** pl. → **płód**

płodzić ⟨s-⟩ (-dzę, płódź!) beget, engender

płomie|nny flaming; fig. fiery; ~**ń** m (-nia; -nie) flame

płomyk m (-a; -i) flame

płoną|cy burning; ~**ć** (-nę; -ń!) burn; twarz: glow

płonica f (-y; 0) med. scarlet fever

płonny vain, futile

płoszyć ⟨s-, wy-⟩ (-ę) shoo, scare; ~ **się**

płot m (-u; -y) fence; ~**ek** m (-tka; -tki) → **płot**; (w sporcie) hurdle; **bieg przez ~ki** hurdle race

płow|ieć ⟨s-, wy-⟩ (-eję) fade; ~**y** fawn

płoza f (-y; G płóz) runner

płócienny linen

płód m (-łodu; -łody) med. fo(e)tus; **płody ziemi** agricultural produce

płótno n (-a; G -cien) linen; mal. canvas

płuc|ny pulmonary; ~**o** n (-a; G -) anat. zw. ~**a** pl. lungs pl.; **zapalenie** ~ pneumonia

pług m (-a; -i) Brt. plough, Am. plow

płukać ⟨prze-, wy-⟩ (-czę) rinse; ~ **gardło** gargle

płycizna f (-y; G -) shallow

płyn m (-u; -y) liquid, fluid; **w ~ie** liquid; ~ **do włosów** hair lotion; ~**ąć** (-nę, -ń!) swim; statek: sail; patyk itp.: float; ~**ność** f (-ści; 0) fluidity, liquidity; ~**ność płatnicza** cash liquidity; ~**ny** liquid, fluid

płyt|a f (-y; G -) (kamienna) slab; (metalowa) plate; bud. tile; (dźwiękowa) record, (zwł. kompakt) disk; ~**a pamiątkowa** commemorative plaque; **muzyka z ~** canned music

płytk|i shallow; fig. superficial; ~**o** adv. shallowly; fig. superficially

pływa|czka f (-i; G -czek) swimmer; ~**ć** (-am) swim; (statkiem) sail; ~**k** m (-a; -cy) swimmer; (-a; -i) tech. float; ~**lnia** f (-i; -e) swimming pool; ~**nie** n (-a; 0) swimming; sailing

pływy m/pl. (-ów) tides pl.

p.n.e. skrót pisany: **przed naszą erą** BC (before Christ)

pneumatyczny pneumatic; inflatable

p.o. skrót pisany: **pełniący obowiązki** acting

po prp. (L) after; by, from; on; **odziedziczyć ~ ojcu** inherit after the father; ~ **wojnie** after the war; **pięć ~ piątej** five minutes past five (o'clock); ~ **ramieniu** on the shoulder; ~ **stole** on the table; ~ **pokoju** in the room; ~ **głosie** by the voice; **wędrować** ~ **kraju** wander all over the country; ~ **kolei** in succession; ~ **całych nocach** night after night; (A) to; for; per; ~ **co?** what for?; ~ ...*złotych za funta* ...zlotys per pound; *często nie tłumaczy się:* ~ **kolana** knee-deep; *puszka* ~ **konserwach** Am. can, *Brt.* tin; ~ **pierwsze** firstly; ~ **bohatersku** valiantly; ~ **niemiecku** (in) German

poba-, pobe- *pf.* → **ba-, be-**

pobi|cie *n* beating; *fig.* **nie do** ~**cia** unbeatable; ~**ć** *pf.* → **bić**

pobie|- → **bie-**; ~**lany** *rondel* tin; *fig.* whited; ~**rać** (-*am*) *pensję* draw; *lekcje, próbki* take; *podatki* levy; *opłaty* collect; ~**rać się** get married

pobieżny superficial, cursory

pobli|ski nearby; ~**że** *n*: **w** ~**żu** (G) nearby, in the vicinity (of)

pobłaż|ać (-*am*) (D) indulge, be lenient (towards); ~**liwie** *adv.* leniently; ~**liwy** lenient, permissive

po|bła-, ~błą-, ~bły- *pf.* → **bła-, błą-, bły-**; ~**bocze** *n* (-*a*; *G* -*y*) (*drogi*) *mot.* hard houlder; (*trawiaste*) verge; ~**boczny** collateral

pobo|jowisko *n* (-*a*; *G* -) battlefield; ~**rca** *m* (-*y*; *G* -*ców*): ~**rca podatków** tax collector; ~**rowy 1.** military; recruitment; **2.** *m* (-*ego*; -*wi*) recruit; ~**ry** *m/pl.* (-*ów*) → **pobór**; (*pensja*) pay, salary, wages *pl.*

po|bożność *f* (-*ści*; *0*) *rel.* piety; ~**bożny** pious; ~**bór** *m* (-*boru*; -*bory*) *mil. Brt.* conscription, *Am.* draft; *econ.* collection; (*wody*) consumption; ~**brać** *pf.* → **pobierać**

pobranie *n* (-*a*): **za** ~**m** cash on delivery

pobru- *pf.* → **bru-**

pobrzeże *n* (-*a*; -*y*) coast, riverside; (*skraj*) edge; **na** ~**u** on the edge

pobu|- → **bu-**; ~**dka** *f* (-*i*; *G* -*dek*) motive, impulse; *mil.* reveille; ~**dliwy** impetuous, impulsive

pobudz|ać (-*am*) ⟨~**ić**⟩ (-*ę*) stimulate (**do** *G* to); ~**ająco** *adv.* stimulatingly; ~**ający** stimulating; **środek** ~**ający** stimulant

poby|ć *pf.* stay; ~**t** *m* (-*u*; -*y*) stay; **miejsce stałego** ~**tu** place of residence, domicile

pocałunek *m* (-*nku*; -*nki*) kiss

pochleb|ca *m* (-*y*; *G* -*ców*), ~**czyni** *f* (-*yni*; *G* -*yń*) flatterer, sycophant; ~**czy** flattering, cajoling; ~**iać** (-*am*) flatter; ~**ny** flattering; ~**stwo** *n* (-*a*; *G* -) flattery; compliment

poch|łaniać (-*am*) ⟨~**onąć**⟩ → **chłonąć**; absorb; *ofiary* claim; ~**onięty** (*I*) absorbed (in)

pochmurny cloudy; *fig.* gloomy, dismal

pochodn|ia *f* (-*i*; -*e*) torch; ~**y** derivative; (*wtóry*) secondary

pochodz|enie *n* (-*a*; *0*) descent; origin(s *pl.*); ~**ić** (**z** *G*) come (from); be descended (**z** *G*, **od** *G* from); (*wynikać*) (**z** *G*) stem (from), result (from); date (**z** *G* from); → **chodzić**

po|chopny rash, impulsive; ~**chować** *pf.* → **chować**; ~**chód** *m* (-*chodu*; -*chody*) procession, parade; ~**chwa** *f* (-*y*; *G* -) (*kabura*) holster; (*na miecz itp.*) sheath; *anat.* vagina

pochwa|lać (-*am*)→**chwalić**; ~**lnie** *adv.* approvingly; ~**lny** commendatory, approving; ~**ła** *f* (-*y*; *G* -) praise (**za** *A* for)

pochwy- *pl.* → **chwy-**

pochy|lać (-*am*) ⟨~**lić**⟩ → **chylić**; ~**lony** sloping; bent (**nad** *I* over); ~**łość** *f* (-*ści*) inclination, slope; ~**ło** *adv.* at an angle, slopingly; ~**ły** sloping, slanted, oblique

pociąg *m* (-*u*; -*i*) *rail.* train; (*skłonność*) attraction (**do** *G* to); ~**drogowy** *mot.* road train; ~**iem** by rail; ~**ać** (-*am*) ⟨~**nąć**⟩ draw (**do** *G* to), pull (**za** *A* after); (*farbą itp.*) cover; (*nęcić*) attract; ~**ać za sobą** result in; ~**ająco** *adv.* attractively; ~**ający** attractive; ~**ły twarz** oval; ~**nięcie** *n* (-*a*; *G* -*ęć*) pull

po cichu *adv.* quietly, softly; *fig.* in silence, quietly

pocić *się* (-*cę*) sweat; *metal, szkło*: mist, steam up

pocie|cha *f* (-*y*; *G* -) comfort; (*dziecko*) offspring; ~**m-** *pf.* → **ciem-**

po ciemku *adv.* in dark

pocierać (-*am*) rub (**o** *A* on, *I* with)

pociesz|ać (-*am*) comfort, console; ~**ć się** take comfort (*I* in); ~**ający** comforting, consoling

pociesz|enie *n* (-*a*; *0*) comfort, consolation; **na** ~**enie** by way of consolation; ~**ny** funny; ~**yć** *pf.* → **pocieszać**

pocisk *m* (-*u*, -*i*) *karabinowy itp.* bullet; (*artyleryjski itp.*) shell; ~ **kierowany** guided missile

P

po co/cóż what for

pocu-, pocwa- pf. → **cu-, cwa-**

pocz|ąć pf. → **poczynać**

pocz|ątek m (-tku, -tki) start, beginning; (choroby itp.) onset; **~ki** pl. rudiments pl.; **na ~ek / ~ku** at the beginning; **od ~ku** from the start; ~kowo adv. initially, at first; ~kowy initial; ~kujący **1.** beginning; **2.** m (-ego; -y, G -ych) beginner; **dla ~kujących** for beginners

poczciw|ie adv. kindly; ~y kind; good

po|czekalnia f (-i; -e) waiting room; ~czesny hono(u)rable; ~częcie n (-a; G -ęć) conception; ~częstunek m (-nku; -nki) treat

po części adv. partly

pocz|ęty dziecko conceived; **życie ~ęte** unborn children pl.

poczt|a f (-y; G -) Brt. post, Am. mail; (placówka, instytucja) post office; **~a lotnicza** airmail; **~ą** by post/mail; **~a elektroniczny**; ~owy post; postal; ~ówka f (-i; G -wek) postcard

poczu|cie n (-a; 0) sense; **~cie czasu, honoru, winy, humoru** sense of time, hono(u)r, guilt, humo(u)r; ~ć pf. → **czuć**; ~wać się feel; **~wać się do winy** feel guilty

poczwarka f (-i; G -rek) zo. chrysalis

poczwórny fourfold; quadruple

poczyna|ć (-am) (-cznę) do; dziecko conceive; ~nia n/pl. (-ń) deeds pl., actions pl.

poczyt|ać pf. (-am) read; → **poczytywać**; ~alny sound of mind, responsible; ~ny best-selling, widely read; ~ywać (-uję) consider (**coś za dobre** s.th. good; **sobie za obowiązek** it one's duty)

pocłw- pf. → **ćw-**

pod prp. (A) kierunek under; below; **~ okno** under the window; czas towards; **~ wieczór** towards the evening; **~ sam(o)** ... up to; **~ dyskusję** for discussion; **~ światło** to the light; (I) miejsce under; below; beneath, underneath; **~ oknem** under the window; **~ warunkiem** under the condition; bliskość near, by; **~ Warszawą** near Warsaw; **~ ścianą** by the wall; **~ karą** G on the penalty (of); **~ postacią** (G) in the shape/form (of)

podać pf. → **podawać, dymisja**

podagra f (-y; 0) med. gout

podajnik m (-a; -i) tech. feeder

podanie n (-a; G -ań) (pismo) application; (legenda) legend; (w sporcie) pass; **~ do wiadomości** announcement; **~ ręki** handshake

podarować pf. → **darować**

podarty ragged

podat|ek m (-tku; -tki) (**dochodowy, obrotowy** income, sales) tax; **~ek od wartości dodanej** VAT; **wolny od ~ku** tax-free, exempt from taxation; ~kowy tax; **urząd ~kowy** Brt. Inland Revenue; ~nik m (-a; -cy) taxpayer; ~ny susceptible (**na A** to); **~ny grunt** fig. hotbed

podawać (wręczyć) pass; prośbę, skargę submit, hand in; adres give; obiad serve (up); lekarstwo administer; (w sporcie) piłkę pass; rękę hold out; **~ do sądu** sue; **~ do wiadomości** announce; **~ się** za (A) pass o.s. off (as); ~ **sobie ręce** shake hands

podaż f (-y; 0) econ. supply

podąż|ać (-am) (~yć) go; piłkę follow, go after; **~yć z pomocą** rush to s.o.'s aid

pod|bicie n (-a; G -ić) anat. instep; kraw. lining; ~bić pf. → **podbijać**; ~biegać (~biec, ~biegnąć) run up (**do G** to); ~biegunowy geogr. polar; ~bijać (-am) kraj conquer; piłkę flick (up), (wysoko) loft; oko black; cenę push up; buty sole; kraw. line; ~bój m (-boju; -boje) conquest (też fig.); ~bródek m (-a; -i) anat. chin; ~budowa f foundation, basis

pod|burzać (-am) (~burzyć) incite, stir up; ~chmielony F tipsy; ~chodzić approach (**do G**), come up (**do G** to); ~chorąży m mil. officer cadet

podchwy|tywać (-uję) (~cić) catch; melodie pick up

podciąć pf. → **podcinać**; ~gać (-am) (~gnąć) pull up (**się** o.s.); pull, draw up (**do G** towards)

podcinać (-am) cut; krzaki lop; (w baseballu) curve; (w tenisie) slice; ~śnienie n tech. low pressure; med. hypotension

podczas prp. (G) during; **~ gdy** while

podczerwony infrared

podda|ć pf. → **poddawać**; ~sze n (-a; G -y) attic (storey); ~wać (-ję) surrender (**się** v/i.); myśl suggest; **~wać próbie** try out; **~wać się** give up; (operacji) undergo; (żądaniom itp.) give way

poddostawca *m* subcontractor

pode → **pod**; ~ **mną** under me

podejmować (-*uję*) take, take up; (*wznosić*) lift up; *pieniądze* draw, withdraw; *decyzję* take; *walkę* take up; *podróż* make, undertake; *gości* receive, entertain; ~ **się** (*G*) undertake

podejrz|any 1. suspicious, suspect; **2.** *m* (-*ego*; -*ych*), ~**ana** *f* (-*ej*; -*e*) suspect; ~**enie** *n* (-*a*; *G* -*eń*) suspicion; ~**ewać** (-*am*) suspect (*o A* of); (*przypuszczać*) suspect, believe, suppose; ~**liwość** *f* (-*ści*; *0*) mistrust, distrust; ~**liwie** *adv.* suspiciously; ~**liwy** suspicious

podejś|cie *n* (-*a*; *G* -*jść*) approach (*też* fig. do *G* to); (*pod górę*) climb; fig. treatment; ~**ć** *pf.* (→ -*jść*) → **podchodzić**; fig. approach

podekscytowany excited

pode|przeć *pf.* → **podpierać**; ~**rwać** *pf.* → **podrywać**; ~**słać** *pf.* → **podścielić**; ~**szły** *wiek* advanced

podeszwa *f* (-*y*; *G* -*szew*) sole

pod|galać (-*am*) ⟨~**golić**⟩ shave

podgląda|cz *m* (-*a*, -*e*) peeper; voyeur; ~**ć** (-*am*) peep (*A* at)

pod|główek *m* (-*wka*; -*wki*) head-rest; ~**górze** *n* (-*a*) foothills *pl.*; ~**grzewać** (-*am*) ⟨~**grzać**⟩ warm up; ~**jazd** *m* (-*u*; -*y*) drive; ~**jąć** *pf.* → **podejmować**; ~**jeżdżać** (-*am*) ⟨~**jechać**⟩ drive up, draw up; ~**jęcie** *n* (-*a*; *0*) fig. start(ing); *por.* **podejmować**; ~**judzać** (-*am*) ⟨~**judzić**⟩ incite; ~**klejać** (-*am*) ⟨~**kleić**⟩ glue, paste

podkład *m* (-*u*; -*y*) (*o farbie*) undercoat; rail. *Brt.* sleeper, *Am.* tie; *med.* absorbent pad; ~**ać** (-*am*) put under; fig. plant; ~**ka** *f* (-*i*; *G* -*dek*) mat, pad; *tech.* washer

podkopywać (-*uję*) ⟨~**ać**⟩ dig in; fig. undermine, erode

podko|szulek *m* (-*lka*; -*lki*), ~**szulka** *f* (-*lki*; *G* -*lek*) *Brt.* vest, *Am.* undershirt; ~**wa** *f* (-*y*; *G* -*ków*) horse-shoe

podkra|dać się (-*am*) ⟨~**ść się**⟩ sneak up

podkreś|lać (-*am*) ⟨~**lić**⟩ underline; fig. *też* emphasize

pod|kusić *pf.* → **kusić**; ~**kuwać** (-*am*) ⟨~**kuć**⟩ shoe; ~**lać** *pf.* → **podlewać**; ~**latywać** (-*uję*) ⟨~**lecieć**⟩ (*w górę*) fly up; ~**le** *adv.* despicably, basely; ~**legać** (-*am*) ⟨~**lec**⟩ (→ **lec**) be subordinate (*D* to); *podatkowi* be subject (*D* to);

~**legły 1.** subordinate; subject; **2.** *m* (-*ego*; -*li*) subordinate

pod|lewać (-*am*) water; ~**liczać** (-*am*) ⟨~**liczyć**⟩ count up, add up; ~**lotek** *m* (-*tka*; -*tki*) teenager; ~**łączać** (-*am*) ⟨~**łączyć**⟩ (*do G*) connect (to), hook up (to); ~**łoga** *f* (-*i*; *G* -*łóg*) floor; ~**łość** *f* (-*ści*; *0*) meanness; nastiness; ~**łoże** *n* (-*a*; *G* -*ży*) foundation, base; ~**łożyć** *pf.* → **podkładać**

podłuż|nie *adv.* longitudinally; lengthways; ~**ny** longitudinal; oblong

podły mean; base, despicable

podma|kać (-*am*) get damp; ~**lowywać** (-*uję*) ⟨~**lować**⟩ paint

pod|miejski suburban; ~**miot** *m* (-*u*; -*y*) subject (*też* gr.); ~**moknąć** *pf.* → **podmakać**; ~**morski** submarine

podmuch *m* (-*u*; -*y*) gust

pod|mywać (-*am*) ⟨~**myć**⟩ *brzeg* undermine, underwash; ~**najemca** *m* (-*y*; *G* -*ców*) subtenant

podniebienie *n* (-*a*; *G* -*eń*) anat. palate

podnie|cać (-*am*) ⟨~**cić**⟩ excite; (*podsycać*) stimulate; ~**cać się** get excited; ~**cenie** *n* (-*a*; *G* -*eń*) excitement; stimulation; ~**ść** *pf.* → **podnosić**; ~**ta** *f* (-*y*; *G* -) incentive

pod|niosły lofty, elevated; ~**nosić** raise (*też* fig., math.); pick up; *flagę* hoist up, run up; *kotwicę* weigh; *kołnierz* turn up; *cenę też* put up; ~**nosić się** rise; get up, stand; (*w łóżku*) sit up; *mgła*: lift up; ~**nośnik** *m* (-*a*; -*i*) jack

podnóż|e *n* (-*a*; *G* -*y*) foot; *u* ~**a** (*G*) at the foot of (of); ~**ek** *m* (-*ka*; -*ki*) footstool

podob|ać się (-*am*) like, enjoy; **nie** ~**ać się** *też* dislike; **jak ci się to** ~**a?** how do you like it?; **ile ci się** ~**a** as much as you like it; ~**ieństwo** *n* (-*a*; *G*-*w*) similarity; ~**nie** *adv.* similarly (**jak** to), likewise; ~**no** *adv.* supposedly; **on** ~**no wyjechał** they say he has gone; ~**ny** like, similar (**do** *G* to); **i tym/temu** ~**ne** and the like

podoficer *m* (-*a*; -*owie*) non-commissioned officer

podokiennik *m* (-*a*; -*i*) → **parapet**

podołać *pf.* (*D*) cope (with), manage

podomka *f* (-*i*; *G* -*mek*) housecoat

podpa|dać (**pod** *A*) come under, fall into; (*D*) get into trouble (with); ~**lacz** *m* (-*a*; -*e*) arsonist; ~**lać** (-*am*) ⟨~**lić**⟩ (*A*) set fire (to); ~**ska** (-*i*; *G* -*sek*) *Brt.* san-

podpaść

itary towel, *Am.* sanitary napkin; ~**ść**
pf. → **podpadać**; ~**trywać** (-*uję*)
⟨~**trzyć**⟩ spy, peep

podpełz|**ać** (-*am*) ⟨~**nąć**⟩ crawl, creep
(*pod G* to)

pod|**piąć** *pf.* → **podpinać**; ~**pić**: ~**pić
sobie** get tipsy, get o.s. Dutch courage;
~**pierać** (-*am*) support, prop up; ~**pierać się** lean, support o.s.; ~**pinać** (-*am*)
(*do G*) pin up (to); *papier* attach (to)

podpis *m* (-*u*; -*y*) signature; (*pod rysunkiem*) caption; ~**ywać** (-*uję*) ⟨~**ać**⟩ (*też
się*) sign

pod|**pity** tipsy; ~**pływać** ⟨~**płynąć**⟩ (*do
G*) *pływak:* swim up (to); *wioślarz:* row
up (to); *statek:* sail up (to); ~**pora** *f*
(-*y*) support; ~**porucznik** *m* second
lieutenant

podpo|**rządkow**(**yw**)**ać** (-[-*w*]*uję*) sub-
ordinate; ~**rządkow**(**yw**)**ać się** con-
form to *s.th.*; comply with *s.th.*; defer
to *s.o.*; ~**wiadać** (-*am*) ⟨~**wiedzieć**⟩
prompt; suggest

podpórka *f* (-*i*; *G* -*rek*) support

podpułkownik *m* lieutenant colonel

podra|**biać** (-*am*) forge; *~pać pf.*
scratch; ~**stać** (-*am*) grow; ~**żać** (-*am*)
raise the cost of

podrażnienie *n* (-*a*) irritation (*też med.*)

podreperować *pf.* repair, mend; patch
up

podręczn|**ik** *m* manual; ~**ik szkolny**
textbook, handbook; ~**y** hand

pod|**robić** *pf.* → **podrabiać, drobić**;
~**rosnąć** *pf.* → **podrastać**; ~**rostek**
m (-*tka*; -*tki*) teenager; juvenile

podroż|**eć** *pfs.*, ~**yć** *pf.* (-*ę*) → **drożeć,
podrażać**

podróż *f* (-*y*; -*e*) (*krótka*) trip;
(*długa*) journey; voyage; *biuro ~y*
travel agency; ~**ny 1.** travel(l)ing,
travel(l)er's; **2.** *m* (-*ego*; -*i*), ~**na** *f*
(-*ej*; -*e*) travel(l)er; ~**ować** travel;
~**ować koleją** travel by train) (*po L* in)

podrumienić *pf.* roast/bake slightly
brown

podrywać (-*am*) raise; snatch; *fig.* undermine; F *dziewczynę* pick up; ~ **się**
start; jump to one's feet; *ptak:* take wing

podrzeć *pf.* tear up; tear *s.th.* to pieces;
ubranie też wear out

podrzędny inferior; (*mierny*) second-
-rate; *gr.* subordinate

podrzu|**cać** ⟨~**cić**⟩ toss/throw into the

air; *dziecko* expose; F (*dostarczyć*) deliver; let *s.o.* have *s.th.*; (*kogoś*) give *s.o.*
a lift; ~**tek** *m* (-*tka*; -*tki*) foundling

pod|**sadzać** ⟨~**sadzić**⟩ help up; ~**sąd-
ny** *m* (-*ego*; -*i*), ~**na** *f* (-*ej*; -*e*) defendant; ~**skakiwać** (-*uję*) jump up; *piłka:*
bounce; F *ceny:* shoot up; soar; ~**skakiwać z radości** jump for joy; ~**skok**
m jump; leap; ~**skórny** *med.* subcuta-
neous; *zastrzyk:* hypodermic

podsłuch *m* (-*u*) bug; tap; **założyć ~**
bug (s.o.'s room); tap (s.o.'s phone);
~**iwać** (-*uję*) ⟨~**ać**⟩ *v/i.* eavesdrop;
(*pod drzwiami*) overhear; ~**owy** tap-
ping; (*urządzenie*) device

podsmaż|**ać** (-*am*) ⟨~**yć**⟩ fry

podstarzały elderly

podstaw|**a** *f* (-*y*) base; basis; founda-
tion; *tech.* mount, pedestal; *mat.* base;
na ~ie czegoś on the ground of sth;
mieć ~ę (*do G*) to have good reason for
doing sth; **mieć ~ę** have good reason
for; **na ~ie** (*G*) on the basis of; ~**i**(**a**)**ć**
put *s.th.* under *s.th.*; substitute; *samochód* to bring round; ~**ka** *f* (-*i*; *G* -*wek*)
support; (*spodek*) saucer; ~**owy** basic;
fundamental; *szkoła* ~**owa** *Brt.* prim-
ary school, *Am.* elementary school

podstęp *m* (-*u*; -*y*) trick; ruse; ~**ny** de-
ceitful; scheming; tricky; *plan* insidious

pod|**strzygać** (-*am*) ⟨~**strzyc**⟩ trim;
~**sumow**(**yw**)**ać** (-[-*w*]*uję*) add up; *fig.*
sum up; ~**suwać** ⟨~**sunąć**⟩ push; shove;
draw; *myśl* suggest; ~**sycać** (-*am*) ⟨~**sycić**⟩ *nienawiść* hatred; ~**szeptywać**
(-*uję*) ⟨~**szepnąć**⟩ *fig.* prompt; hint;
insinuate; ~**szewka** *f* (-*i*; *G* -*wek*)
kraw. lining

podszy|**wać** (-*am*) ⟨~**ć**⟩ line; ~**ć się** im-
personate; pretend to be (*pod s.o.*)

pod|**ścielić** *pf.* (-*lę*) *koc* spread; ~**ściół-
ka** *f* (-*i*; *G* -*łek*) bed; (*słoma itp.*) litter;
~**śpiewywać** (-*uję*) hum; ~**świadomy**
subconscious; ~**tytuł** *m* (-*u*; -*y*) subtitle;
(*w gazecie*) subheading

podtrzym|**ywać** (-*uję*) ⟨~**ać**⟩ support;
hold up; *fig.* support; uphold; keep
up; *żądania, stosunki itp.* maintain;
~**ywać ogień** keep the fire burning

pod|**udzie** *n* (-*a*) shank; ~**upadać** ⟨~**u-
paść**⟩ (→**paść²**) deteriorate; fall into
decline; fall into poverty

poduszk|**a** *f* (-*i*; *G* -*szek*) pillow; cush-
ion; *tech.* cushion, pad; ~**owiec** *m*

(-wca; -wce) hovercraft

podwajać (-am) double

pod|walina f (-y) fig. foundations pl; ~ważać (-am) ⟨~ważyć⟩ lever up; prize upon; fig. undermine; challenge

podwiąz|ka f (-i; G -zek) garter; suspender; ~ywać (-uję) ⟨~zać⟩ tie; bind up; med. ligate

pod|wieczorek m (-rku; -rki) tea; ~wieźć pf → **podwozić**; ~wijać (-am) ⟨~winąć⟩ (-nę, -ń!) rękawy roll up; nogi draw up; z ~winiętym ogonem with the tail between the legs; ~władny subordinate; inferior; → **podległy**; ~wodny underwater; okręt ~ny submarine

podwo|lić pf. → **podwajać**; ~zić give s.o. a lift; ~zie n (-a; G -zi) mot. chassis; aviat. undercarriage

podwój|nie adv. double; doubly; (dwukrotnie) twice; ~ny double; gra ~na (w sporcie) doubles; fig. ~na gra double-dealing

podwór|ko n (-a; G -rek), ~rze n (-a) court, (back) yard

podwyż|ka f (-i; G -żek) rise, increase; ~ka płac Brt. rise, Am. raise; ~ka cen increase in prices; ~szać (-am) ⟨~szyć⟩ (-ę) raise, increase; ~szać się rise; ~szenie n (-a) rise; platform

podzelować [-dz-] pf. re-sole

po|dziać pf. → **podziewać**; ~dział m division; ~działka f scale; ~dzielić pf. → **dzielić**; ~dzielnik math. divisor

podziem|ie n [-dź-] n (-a; G -i) basement; fig. underground; ~ny underground

podziewać (-am) ⟨zgubić⟩ to get lost, to vanish; ⟨znaleźć schronienie⟩ ~ się to find shelter

podziękowanie n (-a) thanks

podziurawiony full of holes, in holes

podziw m (-u; 0) admiration; → **nad**; ~iać (-am) admire

podzwrotnikowy [-dz-] subtropical

podźwignąć pf. raise, lift; fig. restore; ~ się pull oneself up

podżegać [-dż-] (-am) incite (**przeciw** D against; **do** G to)

poe|mat m (-u; -y) poem; ~ta m (-y; -ci), ~tka f (-i; G -tek) poet; ~tycki (-ko), ~tyczny poetic; ~zja f (-i; 0) poetry; (pl. -e) poems

po|fa-, ~fi-, ~fo- pf. → **fa-, fi-, fo-**

poga|danka f (-i; G -nek) talk; ~niać drive; urge; ~nin m (-a; -anie, -), ~nka

f (-i; G -nek) pagan, heathen; ~ński pagan, heathen

pogar|da f (-y; 0) contempt; disdain; scorn; **godny ~dy** contemptible; despicable; **mieć w ~dzie** hold in contempt; ~dliwy (-wie) contemptuous; disdainful; scornful; ~dzać (-am) ⟨~dzić⟩ (I) despise; scorn; hold in contempt; (czymś też) renounce s.th.

pogarszać (-am) worsen; make s.th. worse; ~ **się** deteriorate

pogawędka f (-i; G -dek) chat

pogląd m (-u; -y) view; opinion; ~ **na świat** outlook; **wymiana ~ów** exchange of ideas; ~owy visual

po|głębiać (-am) ⟨~głębić⟩ deepen; fig. intensify; ~głębiarka f (-i) dredger; ~głos m (-u; 0) reverberation; ~głoska f rumo(u)r; hearsay; ~gmatwany entangled; intricate; ~gnać pf. → **poganiać** v/i. rush, speed off

pogod|a f (-y) weather; **będzie ~a** we're going to have fine weather; ~ny bright; fine; clear; fig. cheerful

pogodzeni|e n (-a) reconciliation; **niemożliwy do ~a** irreconcilable

pogo|nić pf. → **poganiać, pognać**; ~ń f (-ni; -nie) chase; pursuit

pogorsz|enie (się) n (-a) deterioration; ~yć pf. → **pogarszać**

pogorzelisko n (-a) site of a fire

pogotowi|e n (-a; 0) alert; (karetka) ambulance; ~e **górskie** mountain rescue team; ~e **awaryjne/techniczne** public utilities emergency service; ~e **górskie** mountain rescue service; **w ~u** in readiness; **on the alert**

pogranicz|e n (-a) borderland; **na ~u** on borderline; ~ny frontier; fig. borderline

pogrąż|ać (-am)⟨~yć⟩ (-ę) sink; plunge; fig. crash, destroy; ~yć **się** sink, become immersed

pogrom m (-u; -y) rout; hist. pogrom; ~ca m (-y; G -ów), ~czyni f (-i) conqueror; ~ca **zwierząt** tamer

pogróżka f (-i; G -żek) threat

pogru-, pogry- pf. → **gru-, gry-**

pogrzeb m (-u; -y) funeral; (kondukt) funeral procession; ~acz m (-a; -e) poker; ~ać pf. → **grzebać**; ciało bury (też fig.); ~owy funeral; **zakład ~owy** undertaker's; funeral parlour

pogu- pf. → **gu-**

pogwałc|ać (-am) ⟨**~ić**⟩ *uczucia* violate, transgress; *prawo* break

pogwizdywać (-uję) whistle

pohamowa|ć się *pf.* control o.s.; check o.s.; **~nie** *n* restraint, self-control

po|ić ⟨**~na-**⟩ (-ję, -isz, pój!) *v/t.*give *s.th.* to drink; *konie* water; F (*upijać*) ply *s.o.* with drink; **~ić** *m.* → *in-*; **~jawiać się** (-am) ⟨**~jawić się**⟩ appear; emerge; become visible; **~jazd** *m* (-u; -y) (*mechaniczny* motor) vehicle; **~jazd kosmiczny** spacecraft; **~jąć** *pf.* → **pojmować**; **~je-** *pf.* → **je-**

pojedna|nie *n* (-a) reconciliation; **~wczy** conciliatory

pojedyn|czy individual; (*nie podwójny*) single; **gra ~cza** (*w sporcie*) singles; **liczba ~cza** *gr.* singular; **~ek** *m* (-nku; -nki) duel (*też fig.*)

pojemn|ik *m* (-a; -i) container; **~ość** *f* (-ści; 0) capacity (*też phys.*); *mar.* tonnage; **~ość skokowa** cubic capacity; **~y** capacious; roomy

pojezierze *n* (-a; *G* -rzy) lake district

pojęcie *n* (-a) notion; F (*pl. 0*) idea; **nie do ~a** incomprehensible; **nie mam ~a** I have no idea

pojętny intelligent; clever

pojmować (-uję) understand; comprehend

pojutrze the day after tomorrow

po|ka- *pf.* → **ka-**

pokarm *m* (-u; -y) food; **~owy: przewód ~owy** alimentary canal

pokaz *m* (-u; -y) (*mody* fashion) show; demonstration; **na ~** for show; **~ywać** (-uję) ⟨**~ać**⟩ show; **~ywać się** turn up; show up

po|kaźny sizeable; considerable; **~kątny** illegal; *transakcja* under the table

poklask *m* (-u; 0) applause (*też fig.*)

poklep|ywać (-uję) ⟨**~ać**⟩ → **klepać**

pokła|d *m* (-u; -y) *mar.* deck; (*warstwa*) layer; stratum; (*w górnictwie*) seam; **na ~dzie** (*statku*) on board (a ship); **~dać** (-am) *nadzieję itp.* put (one's hopes) (**w** *L* in); **~dowy** deck

pokłosie *n* (-a; *G* -si) *fig.* aftermath

po|kłócić *pf.* turn *s.o.* against *s.o.*; **~kłócić się** quarrel (with); **~kochać** *pf.* *v/t.* fall in love (with); come to love

poko|jowy¹ peaceful; peace; **~jowy²** room; **~jówka** *f* (-i; *G* -wek) (chamber)maid

pokolenie *n* (-a) generation

poko|nywać ⟨**~nać**⟩ defeat; beat; *fig.* overcome; **~nany** beaten; conquered; **~ra** *f* (-y; 0) humility; **~rny** humble

pokost *m* (-u; -y) varnish

po|kój¹ *m* (-oju; 0) peace; **~kój²** *m* (-oju; -oje) (*hotelowy, stołowy* hotel, dining) room

pokra- *pf.* → **kra-**

pokrew|ieństwo *n* (-a) kinship; **~ny** related (*D* to)

pokro|- *pf.* → **kro-**; **~wiec** *m* (-wca; -wce) cover

pokrój *m* (-oju; 0) type; sort

pokrótce *adv.* briefly

pokry|cie *n* (-a) covering; *tech.* (roof) cover; *fin.*, *econ.* cover, backing; **wystawić czek bez ~cia** bounce a cheque; **słowa bez ~cia** empty words; **~ć** *pf.* → **pokrywać, kryć**

po kryjomu *adv.* secretly

pokryw|a *f* (-y) cover; *tech.* bonnet; **~ać** (-am) be covered (with); **~ać się z** (*I*) agree with; **~ka** *f* (-i; *G* -wek) lid

pokrzepi|ać (-am) ⟨**~ć**⟩ strengthen; fortify; **~ć na duchu** comfort; cheer; **~ający** strengthening; fortifying

pokrzywa *f* (-y) nettle

pokrzywdzony deprived, disadvantaged, harmed

pokrzywk|a *f* (-i; 0) *med.* rash, hives

pokupny *towar* sal(e)able; in demand

pokus|a *f* (-y) temptation; **~ić się** (*o* A) attempt to *inf.*

pokut|a *f* (-y) penance; **~ować** (-uję) *v/t.* do penance (**za** A for); *fig.* pay for *s.th.*

pokwa-, pokwę- *pf.* → **kwa-, kwę-**

pokwitowanie *f* (-a) receipt; **za ~m** against receipt

pola|- *pf.* → **la-**; **~ć** *pf.* → **polewać**

Polak *m* (-a; -cy) Pole

pola|na *f* (-y) clearing; **~no** *n* (-a) log

polarny polar; → **zorza**

pole *n* (-a; *G* pól) field (*też fig.*); *mat.* area; **wywieść w ~** hoodwink *s.o.*

pole|c *pf.* fall; be killed; **~c za ojczyznę** be killed for *one's* country; **~cać** (-am) ⟨**~cić**⟩ (-cę) command; (*powierzać*) entrust; (*doradzać*) recommend; **list ~cający** letter of recommendation; **list ~cony** registered letter; **~cenie** *n* (-a) (*zlecenie*) command, order; **z ~cenia** on *s.o.'s* recommendation;

~gać (-am) (na L) depend, rely (on); (zasadzać się) consist (in); ~gły killed; m (-ego; -li) casualty

polemiczny polemic

polepsz|ać (-am) ⟨~yć⟩ (-ę) improve (też się); ~enie n (-a) improvement

polerować ⟨wy-⟩ (-uję) polish

polew|a f (-y) glaze; (na cieście) icing; ~aczka f (-i; G -czek) → konewka; ~ać (-am) pour water on; tech. glaze; ~ka f (-i; G -wek) soup

poleżeć pf. lie (some time)

polędwica f (-y; -e) fillet, loin

polichlorek m (-rku; -rki); ~ winylu polyvinyl chloride

polic|ja f (-i; 0) (drogowa traffic) police; ~ja śledcza criminal investigation department, CID; ~jant m (-a, -ci) policeman; ~jantka f (-i; G -tek) policewoman; ~yjny police

policz|ek m (-czka; -czki) cheek; slap in the face; ~kować ⟨s-⟩ (-uję) slap s.o.'s face; ~yć pf. → liczyć

poli|etylenowy polythene; ~gon m (-u; -y) mil. military training ground; ~'grafia f (GDL -ii; 0) typography, printing

polisa f (-y) policy

politechnika f politechnic

politowanie n (-a; 0) pity, compassion; z ~m pitifully, with compassion

politur|a f (-y) French polish; ~ować (-uję) French-polish

polity|czny political; ~k m (-a; -cy) politician; ~ka ['li-] f (-i) politics; policy

polka f (-i; G -lek) (taniec) polka

Polka f (-i; G -lek) Pole; Polish girl lub woman

polny field; konik ~ grasshopper

polonez m (-a; -y) polonaise

polonijny: ośrodek ~ Polish community centre

polonistyka f (-i; 0) Polish studies

polot m (-u; 0) inspiration

polowa|ć (-uję) (na A) hunt; zwierzę: prey; ~nie n (-a) (na lisa fox) hunting; hunt

Polska f (-i; 0) Poland

pols|ki Polish; po ~ku Polish

polszczyzna f (-y; 0) Polish (language)

polub|ić pf. become fond (of); come to like; ~owny conciliatory; sąd ~owny court of conciliation

poła f (-y; G pół) tail

poła|- pf. → ła-; ~many broken

połącz|enie n (-a) combination; joint; kolej, tel. Brt. connection, Am. connexion; (firm itp.) merger; ~ony joint; fig. connected (z I with); ~yć pf. → łączyć

połknąć pf. (-nę) swallow

połow|a f (-y) (część) half; (środek) middle; do ~y half-…; w ~ie maja in the middle of May; w ~owie drogi halfway; podzielić na ~ę halve; ~iczny: środki ~iczne half measures

położ|enie n (-a) location; position, situation; ~na f (-ej; -e) midwife; ~nictwo n (-a; 0) obstetrics; ~yć pf. → kłaść

połóg m (-ogu; -ogi) med. puerperium

połów m (-owu; -owy) fishing; (złowione ryby) catch

połówka f (-i; G -wek) half

południ|e n (-a) noon; midday; geogr. south; po ~u in the afternoon; przed ~em in the morning; w ~e at noon, at midday; na ~e od (G) south of; ~k m (-a; -i) geogr. meridian

południo|wo-wschodni south-east-(ern); ~wo-zachodni south-west(ern); ~wy southern; south

połykać (-am) swallow

połysk m (-u; 0) polish; gloss; lustre/luster

połyskiwać (-uję) glitter; glisten

poma|- pf. → ma-; ~dka f (-i; G -dek): ~dka do ust lipstick; ~gać (-am) help; assist (przy, w L) with; ~gać na (A) kaszel itp. relieve; ~lo- pf. → malo-; ~łu adv. slowly; F fig. slow down!

pomarańcz|a f (-y; -e) orange; ~owy (-wo) orange

pomarszczony wrinkled

pomawiać (k-o o A) unjustly accuse (s.o. of s.th.)

po|mazać pf. smear; ~mą-, ~me-, ~mę- pf. → mą-, me-, mę-

pomiar m (-u; -y) measurement; ~owy measuring

pomi(ą)- pf. → mi(ą)-

pomidor m (-a; -y) tomato; ~owy tomato; kolor: tomato-red

pomie|- pf. → mie-; ~szanie n (-a; 0): ~szanie zmysłów insanity; ~szczenie n (-a) room; ~ścić pf. hold; find room for; ~ścić się find room

pomię|- pf. → mię-; ~ty crumpled

pomijać ⟨~nąć⟩ (opuścić) omit; (nie uwzględnić) pass over; ~jając (A) ex-

P

cepted;~mo *prp.* (G) in spite of, despite

pomnażać (-am) → **mnożyć**

pomniejsz|ać (-am) ⟨~yć⟩ (-ę) diminish; lessen; *fig.* diminish, belittle; ~y smaller; lesser

pomnik *m* (-a; -i) monument

pomoc *f* (-y; 0) help; assistance; aid; (*pl.* -e) help, aid; (*w sporcie*) midfield; ~e **naukowe** teaching aids; **przyjść z ~ą** come to s.o.'s help; **wzywać na ~** call for help; **przy ~y, za ~ą** by means of; ~nica *f* (-y; -e) helper; ~nictwo *n* (-a) *jur.* abetting; ~niczy auxiliary; ~nik *m* (-a; -cy) helper; assistant; ~ny helpful; **być ~nym** (w L) be helpful in

pomor|- *pf.* → **mor-**; ~ski Pomeranian

pomost *m* (-u; -y) pier; platform; *tech*; ~ **wieńcowy** bypass

pomóc *pf.* (-móż!) → **pomagać**

pomór *m* (-oru; 0) plague, pest

pomówić *pf.* → **pomawiać**

pomp|a¹ *f* (-y) pump; ~a² *f* (-y, 0) pomp; ~atyczny pompous; bombastic; ~ka *f* (-i) (*do roweru itp.*) pump; (*ćwiczenie*) *Brt.* press-up, *Am.* push-up; ~ować (-uję) ⟨na-⟩ pump (up); *powietrze* inflate

pomruk *m* (-u; -i) murmur; rumble

po|mstować (-uję)execrate;~mścić *pf.* (-mszczę) avenge; ~myje *pl.* (-) swill

pomy|lić *pf.* mistake; confuse; mix up; ~lić się → **mylić**; ~lony F crazy, loony; ~lka *f* (-i; G -lek) mistake, error; **przez ~lkę** by mistake; ~lka! wrong number

pomysł *m* (-u; -y) idea; ~odawca *m* (-y) originator; ~owy ingenious; inventive

pomyśleni|e: **nie do ~a** unthinkable, inconceivable

pomyśln|ość *f* (-ści) prosperity; success; **życzyć wszelkiej ~ości** wish *s.o.* the best of luck; ~y favo(u)rable

pona- *pf.* → **na-**

ponad *prp.* (A I) above, over; beyond; ~ **miarę** beyond measure, excessively; **to jest ~ moje siły** it is beyond me; ~dźwiękowy supersonic; ~to *adv.* besides; moreover

pona|glać (-am) rush, press; → **naglić**; ~glenie *n* (-a) (*pismo*) reminder; ~wiać (-am) renew; repeat

poncz *m* (-u; -e) punch

ponętny tempting

poniedział|ek *m* (-łku; -łki) Monday; ~kowy Monday

ponie|kąd *adv.* in a way; ~ść *pf.* → **ponosić**; ~waż *cj.* because; as; since; ~wczasie *adv.* too late; tardily

poniewierać (-am) (A, I) hold in contempt, treat *s.o.* badly; ~ **się** (*o rzeczach*) lie about

poniż|ać (-am) humiliate; ~ać **się** stoop, demean o.s.; ~ej *prp.* (G) below; beneath; *adv.* below; ~enie *n* (-a) humiliation; ~szy the following; ~yć *pf.* (-ę) → **poniżać**

ponosić (-szę) ⟨ponieść⟩ *v/t.* bear (*też fig.* koszty); *ryzyko* incur, *klęskę* suffer; *karę* undergo a punishment; *v/i.* bolt; ~ ⟨ponieść⟩ **winę** (za A) take blame for; **ponieść śmierć** meet one's death; **poniosło go** he got carried away

ponow|ić *pf.* (-ę) → **ponawiać**; ~nie *adv.* again ~ny renewed, repeated

ponton *m* (-u; -y) pontoon

pontyfikat *m* (-u; -y) *rel.* pontificate

ponu|- *pf.* → **nu-**; ~ry gloomy; bleak; dismal

pończocha *f* (-y) stocking

po|ob|- *pf.* → **ob-**; ~obiedni after-dinner; ~od- *pf.* → **od-**

po omacku *adv.* gropingly

po|op|- *pf.* → **op-**; ~operacyjny postoperative; ~os-, ~ot- *pf.* → **os-, ot-**; ~padać fall (into); ~pamiętać *pf.*: **popamiętasz mnie!** I'll show you!; ~parcie *n* (-a) support; ~parzenie *n* (-a) burn; ~paść → **popadać, paść²**; **brać co ~padnie** take whatever turns up; ~pchnąć *pf.* → **popychać**

popelinowy poplin

popełni|ać (-am) ⟨~ć⟩ commit; make

popę|d *m* (-u; -y) impulse, urge; inclination; ~dliwy impetuous; ~dzać (-am) ⟨~dzić⟩ rush; hurry; → **pędzić**; ~kany cracked

popić *pf.* → **popijać**

popiel|aty (-to) grey, *Am.* gray; 2ec *m* (-lca, -lce) Ash Wednesday; ~niczka *f* (-i; G -czek) ashtray

popierać (-am) support, back

popiersie *n* (-a; G -i) bust

popijać (-am) *v/t.* sip; *jedzenie* wash down

popiół *m* (-ołu, L -iele) -oły) ash

popis *m* (-u;-y) show; ~owy spectacular; ~ywać się (-uję) ~ać **się** (I) show off

po|pl|- *pf.* → **pl-**; ~plecznik *m* (-a; -cy) partisan, supporter; ~płacać (-am) pay; ~płatny well-paid; profitable; ~płoch *m* (*-u*; *0*) panic; **w ~płochu** in panic

popołudni|e *n* (*-a*) afternoon; → **po-południe**; **~owy** afternoon

popra- *pf.* → **pra-**

popraw|a *f* (*-y*) improvement; (*poprawienie*) correction; **~czy: zakład ~czy** Brt. borstal, Am. reformatory; **~iać** (*-am*) ⟨**~ić**⟩ correct; adjust; improve; **~i(a)ć się** correct o.s.; *v/i* improve; **~ka** *f* (*-i*; *G -wek*) correction; (*o sukni*) alteration; (*do ustawy*) amendment; F (*egzamin*) repeat an exam; **~ność** *f* (*-ści*; *0*) correctness; **~ny** correct

popro- *pf.* → **pro-**

po prostu *adv.* simply; → **prosty**

po|pró-, ~pru- *pf.* → **pró-, pru-**

poprzecz|ka *f* (*-i*; *G -czek*) cross-beam; (*w sporcie*) crossbar; **~ny** transversal

poprzeć *pf.* → **popierać**

poprzedni previous; **~ego dnia** the day before; **~czka** *f* (*-i*; *G -czek*), **~k** *m* (*-a*; *-cy*) predecessor; **~o** *adv.* previously

poprzedz|ać (*-am*) ⟨**~ić**⟩ (*-dzę*) *v/t.* precede

poprze|k: na *lub* **w ~k** crosswise; **~sta-(wa)ć** content o.s. (**na** *L* with s.th.)

poprzez *prp.* through; across

po|przy- *pf.* → **przy-**; **~psu-** *pf.* → **psu-**

popular|ność *f* (*-ści*; *0*) popularity; **~ny** popular; **~yzować** ⟨**s-**⟩ (*-uję*) popularize

popu|szczać ⟨**~ścić**⟩ *v/t.* loosen; slacken; *fig. v/i* relent

popycha|ć (*-am*) → **pchać**; *fig.* ill-treat; **~dło** *n* (*-a*; *G -deł*) *fig.* drudge

popyt *m* (*-u*; *0*) econ. demand

por *m* (*-u*; *-y*) anat. pore; (*-a*) (*warzywo*) leek

por. *skrót pisany:* **porównaj** cf. (compare); *skrót pisany:* **porucznik** Lt. (lieutenant)

po|ra *f* (*-y*; *G pór*) time; hour; **~ra roku** season; **w ~rę** at the right moment, in time; **nie w ~rę** ill-timed; **do tej ~ry** until now; so far; **o tej ~rze** at this time; **o każdej ~rze** at any time

porabia|ć (*-am*): **co ~sz?** what are you up to?; how are you getting on?

porachunki *m/pl. fig.* accounts

porad|a *f* advice; **za ~ą** (*G*) on s.o.'s advice; **~nia** *f* (*-i*; *-e*): **~nia lekarska** out-patient clinic; **~nik** *m* (*-a*; *-i*) guide

poran|ek *m* morning; (*impreza*) matinée; **~ny** morning

pora|stać (*-am*) *v/t* overgrow; *v/i* become overgrown; **~zać** (*-am*) ⟨**~zić**⟩ med., fig. Brt. paralyse, Am. paralyze; *agr.* attack; **~żenie** *n* (*-a*) paralysis; **~żenie słoneczne** sunstroke; **~żenie prądem** electric shock; **~żka** *f* (*-i*; *G -żek*) defeat

porcelana *f* (*-y*) china, porcelain

porcja *f* (*-i*; *-e*) portion, helping; **żelazna ~** emergency ration

pore- *pf.* → **re-**

poręcz *f* (*-y*; *-e*, *-y*) banister; handrail; (*oparcie*) arm; **~e** *pl.* (*w sporcie*) parallel bars; **~ać** (*-am*) ⟨**~yć**⟩; **~enie** *n* (*-a*) guarantee; **~ny** handy; **~yciel** *m* (*-a*; *-e*, *-i*), **~ycielka** *f* (*-i*; *G -lek*) guarantor

poręka *f* (*-i*; *0*) guarantee

porno F, **~graficzny** porno(graphic)

poro|- *pf.* → **ro-**; **~dowy: izba ~dowa** delivery room **~nienie** *n* (*-a*) miscarriage; abortion; **~niony** F *fig.* silly, foolish

poros|nąć *pf.* → **porastać**; **~t** *m* (*-u*; *0*) growth; **~ty** *pl. bot.* lichen(s)

porowaty porous

poroz- *pf.* → **roz-**

porozumie|nie *n* (*-a*) understanding, agreement; (*układ*) agreement; **dojść do ~nia** come to an agreement; **~wać się** (*-am*) ⟨**~ć się**⟩ communicate (**z** *I* with); (*dojść do zgody*) come to an agreement (**co do** *G* about s.th.); **~wawczy** knowing

poród *m* (*-odu*; *-ody*) (child)birth, delivery

porówn|anie *n* (*-a*) comparison; **~awczy** comparative; **~ywać** (*-uję*) ⟨**~ać**⟩ compare

poróżnić *pf.* set *s.o.* against *s.o.*; **~ się** fall out with *s.o.*

port *m* (*-u*; *-y*) port, harbo(u)r; *fig.* haven; **~ lotniczy** airport

portfel *m* (*-a*; *-e*) wallet

portier *m* (*-a*; *-rzy*) porter, doorman; **~a** *f* (*-y*) portière; **~nia** *f* (*-ni*; *-nie*) porter's lodge

portki F *pl.* (*-tek*) Brt. trousers, Am. pants

portmonetka *f* (*-i*) purse

porto *n* (*idkl./-a*; *0*) (*wino*) port; (*opłata*) postage

portowy port; dock

portret *m* (*-u*; *-y*) portrait

Portugalia *f* (*-ii*; *0*) Portugal

Portugal|czyk *m* (*-a*; *-cy*), ~ka *f* (*-i*; *G*
-lek) Portuguese; ~ski (**po -ku**) Portuguese

porucznik *m* (*-a*; *-cy*) lieutenant

porusz|ać ⟨~*yć*⟩ (*I*, *fig. A*) move; *tech.*
drive, propel; *temat itp.* touch (up)on;
~ać ⟨~*yć*⟩ się move; ~enie *n* (*-a*)
fig. agitation

porwa|ć *pf.* → **porywać, rwać**; ~nie *n*
(*-a*) kidnapping; (*samolotu*) hijacking

poryw *m* (*-u; -y*) gust; *fig.* outburst; ~acz
m (*-a*, *-e*) kidnapper; (*samolotu*)
hijacker; ~ać (*-am*) kidnap; *samolot*
hijack; (*unieść*) sweep away, carry
away; (*chwycić*) snatch, grab; *fig.* (*ogar-
nąć*) carry away; (*pociągać*) ravish,
enrapture; ~ać się (*z miejsca*) jump
to one's feet; (**na** *A*) fall (on s.o.); (*pod-
jąć się*) attempt *s.th.*; ~ać się z motyką na słońce attempt the impossible;
~ający ravishing; ~czy impetuous,
hot-tempered

porząd|ek *m* (*-dku; -dki*) order (*też
ciąg*); **w ~ku** in good order; **w ~ku!**
all right!, OK!; ~ek dzienny order of
the day; **robić ~ki** clean up; ~kować
⟨**u-**⟩ order; tidy; ~ny tidy; *fig.* respect-
able; proper

porzeczka *f* (*-i; G -czek*) currant

porzuc|ać ⟨~*ić*⟩ leave, abandon; →
rzucać

posa|- *pf.* → **sa-**; ~da *f* (*-y*) job; **bez ~dy**
out of work

posadzka *f* (*-i; G -dzek*) floor

posag *m* (*-u, -i*) dowry

posądz|ać (*-am*) ⟨~*ić*⟩ (**k-o o** *A*) sus-
pect (s.o. of s.th.)

posąg *m* (*-u; -i*) statue

posel|lski parliamentary; → **klub**; ~lstwo
n (*-a*) *pol.* legation; mission; ~ł *m* (*-sła;
-słowie*) envoy; *pol.* member of parliament

posesja *f* (*-i; -e*) estate; property

posępny gloomy, *Brt.* sombre, *Am.*
somber

posiadacz *m* (*-a; -e*), ~ka *f* (*-i; G -czek*)
owner

posiad|ać own; possess; **nie ~ać się
(z** *G*) be beside o.s. (with); ~łość *f*
(*-ci*) estate, property

po|siąść *pf.* acquire; ~siedzenie *n* sit-
ting, session; meeting

posi|lać się (*-am*) have a meal, take
some refreshment; ~łek *m* (*-łku; -łki*)

meal; *pl. mil.* reinforcements *pl.*; ~łko-
wy *gr.* auxiliary

po|sk- *pf.* → **sk-**; ~skramiać (*-am*)
⟨~**skromić**⟩ (*-ę*) tame; *fig.* restrain

posła|ć *pf.* → **słać, posyłać**; ~nie[1] *n*
(*-a*; *0*) message; ~niec[2] *n* (*-a*) (*do spania*)
bedding; ~niec *m* (*-ńca; -ńcy*) messen-
ger; ~nka *f* (*-i; G -nek*) *pol.* member of
parliament

posłowie *n* (*-a*) afterword; → **poseł**

posłuch *m* obedience, discipline; **dawać ~** (*D*) give s.o. a hearing; ~ać *pf.*
→ **słuchać**

posługacz *m* (*-a; -e*) attendant; ~ka *f*
(*-i; G -czek*) charwoman

posługiwać się (*-uję*) (*I*) use, employ

posłusz|eństwo *n* (*-a; 0*) obedience;
odmówić ~eństwa refuse obedience;
(*o przedmiocie*) **odmawia ~eństwa** it
won't work; ~ny obedient

po|służyć się *pf.* → **posługiwać się**;
~smak *m* aftertaste;~spa-*pf.*→**spa-**;
~spiech *m* → **pośpiech**; ~spolity
(*-cie*) common, ordinary; ~sprzeczać
się *pf.* quarrel; fall out

posrebrzany silver-plated

post *m* (*-u; -y*) fast; *rel. Wielki* ♀ Lent;
zachowywać ~ observe fast

posta|ć *f* (*-ci; -cie/-ci*) (*sylwetka*) figure;
(*w książce*) character; (*forma*) form,
shape; ~nawiać (*-am*) ⟨~**nowić**⟩ decide; ~nowienie *n* (*-a*) decision; (*u-
chwała*) resolution; ~rzać (*-am*) age;
~wa *f* (*-y*) bearing; posture; *fig.* attitude; ~wić *pf.* → **stawiać**; ~wny portly

postąpić *pf.* → **postępować**

posterunek *m* (*-nku; -nki*) post

postęp *m* (*-u; -y*) progress; ~ek *m* (*-pku;
-pki*) deed; (*zły*) misdeed; ~ować (*-uję*)
proceed; ~**ować za** (*I*) follow; *praca,
choroba:* progress; (*czynić*) act, behave;
~**ować z** (*I*) treat s.o.; ~owanie *n* (*-a*)
conduct, behavio(u)r; *jur.* legal action;
~owy progressive; ~ujący progressive

postny fast(-day); → **bezmięsny**

po|stojowy: **światła ~ stojowe**
mot. parking lights; ~stój *m* (*-oju; -oje,
-ojów/-oi*) (*odpoczynek*) halt, stop; *tech.*
stoppage; ~**stój taksówek** taxi rank

postrach *m* (*-u; 0*) terror

postradać *pf.* (*-am*) lose

postronny: ~ **widz** outsider, stranger

postrzał *m* gunshot wound; *med.* lumbago

postrze|gać (-*am*) ⟨~*c*⟩ perceive; ~**lić** *pf.* shoot; ~**lony** wounded; F *fig.* crazy, wacky; ~**żenie** *n* (-*a*) perception

postrzępiony *ubranie* ragged; *kontury* jagged, rugged

postu|lat *m* (-*u*; -*y*) postulate; ~**lować** (-*uję*) postulate, stipulate; ~**ment** *m* (-*u*; -*y*) pedestal

posucha *f* (-*y*) drought; *fig.* lack (**na** *A* of)

posu|nąć *pf.* → **posuwać, sunąć**; ~**nięcie** *n* (-*a*) (*w grze*) move (*też fig.*); ~**wać** *v/t.* move forward, advance; ~**wać się** move, advance, progress (*też fig.*); ~**wać się za daleko** go too far; → **suwać**

posy|łać (-*am*) *v/t.*send; *v/i.* (**po** *A*) send (for s.th.); ~**łka** *f* (-*i*; *G* -*łek*) errand; ~**pywać** (-*uję*) ⟨~**pać**⟩ sprinkle; → **sypać**

po|sza- → **sza-**; ~**nowanie** *n* (-*a*) respect; ~**szarpany** *ubranie* torn, ragged; *kontury* jagged, rugged; ~**szczególny** individual, particular

poszerz|ać (-*am*) ⟨~*yć*⟩ widen; broaden (*też* **się**); *ubranie* let out; ~**ać** ⟨~*yć*⟩ **się** *fig.* spread

poszewka *f* (-*i*; *G* -*wek*) pillow case

poszkodowany injured; *jur.* injured person; **być ~m** be injured, suffer damage

poszlak|a *f* (-*i*) circumstancial evidence; ~**owy** circumstancial

poszukiw|acz *m* (-*a*; -*e*),~**czka** *f* (-*i*; *G* -*czek*) searcher; ~**acz przygód** adventurer; ~**ać** (-*uję*) search (*G* for s.th.); ~**anie** *n* (-*a*) search; quest; hunt; *pl. też* investigation, inquiries; (*naukowe*) research; ~**any** sought after; *przestępca* wanted; ~**awczy** exploratory

poszwa *f* (-*y*) quilt cover

pościć (-*szczę*, *pość!*) fast

pościel *f* (-*i*; *0*) bedclothes, bedding; ~**ić** →**słać²**;~**owy**: *bielizna* ~**owa** bedlinen

pościg *m* (-*u*; -*i*) chase; pursuit

poślad|ek *m* (-*dka*; -*dki*) buttock; ~**ki** *pl. med.* nates; F bottom

pośledni mediocre, second-rate; *fig.* delay

poślizg *m* (-*u*) skid; **wpaść w ~** *mot.* go into a skid

pośliznąć się *pf.* (-*nę*) slip

po|ślubny: *podróż* ~*ślubna* honeymoon; ~*śmiertny* posthumous

pośmiewisko *n* (-*a*; *0*) laughing-stock

pośpie|ch *m* (-*u*; *0*) hurry, haste; ~**szać** (-*am*) ⟨~**szyć**⟩ hasten, hurry, be quick (**z** *I* in); ~**sznie** *adv.* hurriedly, in a hurry; ~**szny** hasty; **pociąg ~szny** fast train; → **pochopny**

pośredni indirect; (*stadium*) intermediate; ~**ctwo** *n* (-*a*) mediation; **za ~ctwem** (*G*) throgh the medium; *biuro ~ctwa pracy* employment agency; ~**czka** *f* (-*i*; *G* -*czek*) → **pośrednik**; ~**czyć** (-*ę*) mediate, be instrumental (**w** *L* in); ~**k** *m* (-*a*; -*cy*) intermediary; mediator; agent

po|środku *adv.* in the middle; ~**śród** *prp.* (*G*) among(st)

poświadcz|ać (-*am*) ⟨~*yć*⟩ certify; ~**enie** *n* (-*a*) certificate; certification

poświęc|ać (-*am*) ⟨~*ić*⟩ sacrifice, devote (**się** oneself); (*składać w ofierze*) sacrifice; *kościół* consecrate; ~**enie** *n* (-*a*) sacrifice; devotion; consecration; **z ~eniem** with devotion

poświst *m* (-*u*; -*y*) whistle; whizz

pot *m* (-*u*; -*y*) sweat, perspiration; *mokry od ~u, zlany ~em* in a sweat; **na ~y** sudorific

potajemny secret; clandestine; underhand

potakiwać (-*uję*) assent

potańcówka F *f* (-*i*; *G* -*wek*) dance

po|tar- *pf.* → **tar-**; ~**tas** *m* (-*u*; *0*) *chem.* potassium; ~**taż** *m* (-*u*; -*e*) potash

po|tąd up to here; ~**tem** then; afterwards, later; **na ~tem** for a future occasion

potencjał *m* (-*u*; -*y*) potential

potęg|a *f* (-*a*; *0*) might; force; power; *mat.* power; *druga* ~**a** square; *trzecia* ~**a** cube; ~**ować** ⟨*s*-⟩ (-*uję*) increase, intensify; *mat.* raise to a power; ~**ować** ⟨*s*-⟩ **się** be intensified

potępi|ać (-*am*) ⟨~*ć*⟩ damn; (*ganić*) condemn; disapprove (of); ~**enie** *n* (-*a*) condemnation; disapproval; *rel.* damnation; **godny ~enia** codemnable; blameworthy

potężny powerful; mighty

potkn|ąć się *pf.* (-*nę*) → **potykać się**; ~**ięcie** *n* (-*a*) stumble; *fig.* slip; lapse

potłuczenie *n* (-*a*) bruise

poto|czny everyday; common; ordinary; *język* ~**czny** colloquial speech; ~**czysty** fluent; well-turned; ~**czyście**

fluently; glibly; ~k *m* (-*u*; -*i*) stream, brook; (*nurt*) stream, torrent; ~**k słów** deluge of words; **lać się ~kiem** gush

potom|ek *m* (-*mka*; -*mkowie*), ~**kini** *f* (-*i*; -*e*, -*ń*) descendant; ~**ność** *f* (-*ci*; *0*) posterity; ~**stwo** *n* (-*a*; *0*) offspring; progeny; (*o zwierzętach*) breed, young

po|to- *pf.* → **to-**; ~**top** *m* (-*u*; *0*) deluge; flood; ~**tra** *pf.* → **tra-**; ~**trafić** *pf.* be able (to), be capable (of), manage (to); ~**trajać** → **troić**

potraw|a *f* (-*y*) dish; **spis potraw** menu; ~**ka** *f* (-*i*; *G* -*wek*) ragout; fricassee

potrąc|ać ⟨~**ić**⟩ jostle; push; (*autem*) run *s.o.* down; ~**enia** *n/pl.* (-*ń*) deduction

po|trójny threefold; triple; treble; ~**tru-**, ~**trw-** *pf.* → **tru-**, **trw-**; ~**trzask** *m* (-*u*; -*i*) trap (*też fig.*); ~**trzaskać** *pf.* smash, shatter, break (to pieces); *v/i.* crack; ~**trząsać** (-*am*) shake

potrzeb|a [-t.ʃ-] *f* (-*y*) need; ~**y** *pl.* needs; **bez ~y** needlessly; **w razie ~y** if necessary; *pred.* → **trzeba**; ~**ny** necessary, needed; **to jest mi ~ne** I need that; ~**ować** (-*uję*) (*G*) need; require; ~**ujący** (*G*) in need (of)

po|trzeć *pf.* → **pocierać**; ~**tulny** submissive; meek; ~**turbować** *pf.* beat; batter; ~**twarca** *m* (-*y*; *G* -*ów*) calumniator; slanderer; ~**twarz** *f* (-*y*; -*e*) (*ustna*) slander; (*na piśmie*) libel

potwierdz|ać (-*am*) ⟨~**ić**⟩ confirm; corroborate; ~**ać** ⟨~**ić**⟩ **się** be confirmed; ~**ająco** *adv.* affirmatively; ~**enie** *n* (-*a*) confirmation; ~**ony** confirmed

potworn|ość *f* (-*ści*) monstrosity; *pl.* (*postępki*) atrocities *pl.*; ~**y** monstrous; horrible

potwór *m* (-*a*; -*y*) monster

poty|czka *f* (-*i*) skirmish; ~**kać się** (-*am*) trip (up), stumble (**o** *A* against)

potylica *f* (-*y*; -*e*) occiput

poucz|ać (-*am*) ⟨~**yć**⟩ instruct; advise; (*strofować*) admonish; ~**ający** instructive; edifying; ~**enie** *n* (-*a*) instruction(s)

poufa|le *adv.* informally; ~**łość** *f* (-*ści*) familiarity; ~**ły** familiar; unceremonious

po|ufny confidential; secret; **informacja ~ufna** inside information; ~**uk-**, ~**um-**, ~**un-**, ~**us-**, ~**ut-** *pf.* → **uk-**, **um-**, **un-**, **us-**, **ut-**

powabny charming; attractive; alluring

powag|a *f* (-*i*; *0*) seriousness; dignity; authority; **cieszyć się ~ą** enjoy high reputation (**u** *G* among); **zachować ~ę** keep one's countenance, keep serious

powalać *pf.* (-*am*) strike down; → **walać**, **walić**

poważ|ać (-*am*) esteem; respect; ~**anie** *n* (-*a*; *0*) respect; regard; esteem; **z ~aniem** (*w listach*) yours sincerely *lub* faithfully; ~**nie** *adv.* seriously; in earnest; ~**ny** serious; grave; solemn; **wiek** old; (*wybitny*) respectable; (*znaczny*) considerable; **w ~nym stanie** in the family way; **muzyka ~na** classical music

powątpiewa|ć (-*am*) doubt (**o** *L* s.th.); be dubious (about s.th.); ~**nie** *n* (-*a*) doubt(s); **z ~niem** doubtfully; dubiously

powetować *pf.* (-*uję*): ~ **sobie** retrieve (**stratę** one's losses); ~ **sobie stracony czas** make up for the lost time

powia|ć *pf.* → **wiać**, **powiewać**; ~**damiać** (-*am*) ⟨~**domić**⟩ (-*ę*) inform, notify (**o** *L* of)

powiat *m* (-*u*; -*y*) administrative district; ~**owy** district

powiąza|ć *pf.* tie; bind; *fig.* connect; join; ~**nie** *n* *fig.* connection, connexion

powidła *n/pl.* (-*deł*) plum jam

powiedz|enie *n* (-*a*): **mieć dużo** (**nie mieć nic**) **do ~enia** have a lot (nothing) to say; ~**ieć** *pf.* say; tell; **że tak powiem** so to say; ~**onko** *n* (-*a*; *G* -*nek*) stock phrase

powieka *f* (-*i*) eyelid

powie|lacz *m* (-*a*; -*e*) duplicator; duplicating machine; ~**lać** (-*am*) ⟨~**lić**⟩ (-*ę*) copy; duplicate

powierni|ca *f* (-*y*; -*e*) confidante; ~**ctwo** *n* (-*a*) trusteeship; ~**czy: fundusz ~czy** trust fund; ~**k** *m* (-*a*; -*cy*) confidant

powierzać (-*am*) entrust (**komuś** *A* s.o. with s.th.)

powierzch|nia *f* (-*i*; -*e*) surface; (*obszar*) area; ~**niowy** surface ~**owność** *f* (-*ści*) (outward) appearance; *fig.* superficiality; ~**owny** superficial; shallow

powie|rzyć *pf.* → **powierzać**; ~**sić** *pf.* (-*szę*) → **wieszać**; ~**sić się** hang oneself

powieścio|pisarka *f*, ~**pisarz** *m* novelist; ~**wy** novel

powieść¹ *f* (-*ści*) novel

powieść² *pf.* → **wieść²**; ~ **się** succeed, be successful; **powiodło mi się** I made it; *nie powiodło mi się* I was unsuccessful *lub* I failed

powietrz|e [-t·ʃ-] *n* (*-a; 0*) air; *na wolnym ~u* outdoors; outside; in the open; *~ny* air; *trąba ~na* whirlwind; *poduszka ~na* mot. airbag

powiew *m* (*-u; -y*) puff of air, waft of air; *~ać* (*-am*) flutter; *~ać na wietrze* flutter in the wind; (*machać*) wave

powiększ|ać (*-am*) increase (*też się*); enlarge; *szkło ~ające* magnifying glass; *~alnik m* (*-a; -i*) phot. enlarger; *~enie n* (*-a*) phot. enlargement, F blow-up; *opt.* magnification; *~yć pf.* (*-ę*) → **powiększać**

powikłan|ie *n* (*-a*) complication (*też med.*); *~y* complicated

powinien (*m-os powinni*) *pred.* should, ought; *~em to zrobić* I should do it; *~em był to zrobić* I should have done it

powin|na (*pl. powinny*), *~no pred.* should, ought

powinność *f* (*-ści*) *lit.* duty, obligation

powinowaty related, akin

powinszowanie *n* (*-a*) congratulations

powita|lny welcoming; *~nie n* (*-a*) greeting, welcome; *na ~nie* by way of greeting; *~ć pf.* → **witać**

powk- *pf.* → **wk-**

powle-kać (*-am*) ⟨*~c*⟩ coat (*I* with); *~kać pościel* put on fresh bed-linen; *~kać się* become overcast

powło|czka *f* (*-czki; G -czek*) pillow-case; *~ka f* (*-i*) cover; (*warstwa*) coat; (*osłona*) shelter

powodować ⟨*s-*⟩ (*-uję*) cause; bring about; *impf.* *~ się* (*I*) be motivated, be prompted (by)

powodzeni|e *n* (*-a*) success; well-being; prosperity; (*popularność*) popularity; *cieszyć się ~em* be successful; prosper; *~a!* good luck

powodzi|ć: dobrze mu się ~i he is well off, he is thriving; *jak ci się ~i?* how are you?

powodziowy inundation, flood

po|wojenny post-war; *~woli adv.* slowly; (*stopniowo*) gradually; *~wolny* slow; leisurely

powoł|anie *n* appointment; *mil.* call-up; *~ywać* (*-uję*) ⟨*~ać*⟩ appoint (*na A* s.o. to); *~ać do życia* bring *s.th.* into being; *~ać do wojska* call up, conscript; *~ać się* refer, quote

powonienie *n* (*-a; 0*) (sense of) smell

powozić (*I*) drive

po|wód¹ *m* (*-odu; -ody*) (*G, do G*) reason or cause; *z ~wodu* due to; *bez żadnego ~wodu* for no reason

powó|d² *m* (*-oda; -owie*), *~dka f* (*-i; G -dek*) jur. plaintiff; *~dztwo n* (*-a*) complaint

powódź *f* (*-odzi; -odzie*) flood (*też fig.*); inundation

powóz *m* (*-ozu; -ozy*) carriage, coach

powr|acać ⟨*~ócić*⟩ → **wracać**; *~otny* return; *~ót m* (*-otu; -oty*) return; *~ót do domu* homecoming; *~ót do zdrowia* recovery; *z ~otem* back; *ponownie* again; *tam i z ~otem* to and fro, back and forth

powróz *m* (*-ozu; -ozy*) rope

powsta|ć *pf.* → (*po*)**wstawać**; *~nie n* (*-a*) rise; origin; *zbrojne* (up)rising; *~niec m* (*-ńca; -ńcy*) insurgent; *~ńczy* insurgent; *~wać* (*stać*) get up; rise; *fig.* revolt (*przeciw D* against); (*utworzyć się*) come into being; originate

powstrzym(yw)ać → **wstrzymywać**

powszechn|ie *adv.* universally; generally; *~y* (*-nie*) universal; general; public; widespread

powszedni everyday; commonplace; *chleb ~* daily bread, *fig.* everyday occurrence; *dzień ~* weekday

powściągliw|ość *f* (*-ści; 0*) moderation; restraint; *~y* moderate; reticent; reserved

powtarzać (*-am*) repeat; *~ się człowiek:* repeat o.s.; *zjawisko:* happen again, recur

powtór|ka *f* (*-i; G -rek*) repetition; *~kowy* repeat; *~nie adv.* once more; *~ny* second

po|wtórzyć *pf.* (*-ę*) → **powtarzać**; *~wyżej* *pf.* → **wy-**; *~wyżej prp.* (*G*) above, over; *adv.* above; *~wyższy* above-mentioned, the above; *~wziąć pf.* decyzję take, make; *podejrzenie* conceive

poza¹ *f* (*-y; G póz*) attitude

poza² *prp.* (*A, I*) behind, beyond; (*I*) outside, beside; *~ tym* besides; furthermore; *nikt ~ tym* nobody else

poza|- prp. → **za-**; *~czasowy* beyond the limits of time, eternal; *~grobowy* afterlife; *~małżeński* extramarital; *dziecko* illegitimate; *~ziemski* extraterrestrial

P

pozawałowy post-infractional

pozaziemski extraterrestrial

pozbawi|ać (*-am*) ⟨*~ć*⟩ deprive (*kogoś G* s.o. of s.th.); *~(a)ć się* (*G*) deprive o.s. (of); *~ony* (*G*) deprived (of); devoid (of)

po|zbierać *pf.* gather, collect; *~zby-(wa)ć się* (*G*) get rid (of)

pozdr|awiać (*-am*) ⟨*~owić*⟩ (*-ę, -rów!*) greet; *~awiać ~owić się* exchange greetings; *kazał cię ~owić* he sends his love *lub* regards; *~owienie* n (*-a*) greetings; regards

pozew m (*-zwu; -zwy*) *jur.* citation, summons; *wnieść ~* file a suit *lub* petition

pozie- *pf.* → *zie-*

poziom m (*-u; -y*) level; *fig.* standard; *~ morza* sea level; *na ~ie* up to the mark; *~ka* f (*-i; G -mek*) wild strawberry; *~o* adv. horizontally; (*w krzyżówce*) across; *~y* horizontal

pozł|acać (*-am*) → *złocić*; *~acany* gilt, gilded; *~ota* f (*-y*) gilding

pozna|ć *pf.* → *poznawać*; *~nie* n (*-a; 0*) knowledge; (*kogoś*) meeting; *filoz.* cognition; *nie do ~nia* unrecognizable; *~wać* (*-ję*) get to know; recognize (*po L* by); *~wać się* become acquainted; *~ć się* see the value (*na L* of)

pozor|ny apparent; seeming; *~ować* ⟨*u-*⟩ (*-uję*) simulate; feign

pozosta|ć *pf.* → *pozostawać*; *~łość* f (*-ści*) remainder, remains *pl.*; *fig.* relic; *~ły* remaining; *~ły przy życiu* surviving; *~wać* stay, remain; *~wać w tyle* lag behind; *nie ~je mi nic innego* nothing remains for me to do but; *~wi(a)ć* leave behind; *decyzję itp.* leave; → *zostawiać*

pozować (*-uję*) sit, pose; *fig.* show off; *~ na* (*A*) affect

poz|ór m (*-oru; -ory*) appearance; *na ~ór* seemingly; *pod ~orem* (*G*) under a pretence of s.th.; *pod żadnym ~orem* on no account; *zachowywać ~ory* keep up appearances; *~ory mylą* appearances are deceptive

pozwa|ć *pf.* (*-ę*) → *pozywać*; *~lać* (*-am*) permit, allow; *~lać sobie* (*na A*) be able to afford; *~lam sobie zauważyć ...* allow me to say that ...; → *pozwolić*; *~na* f (*-ej; -e*), *~ny* m (*-ego; -ni*) *jur.* defendant

pozwol|enie n (*-a*) permission; permit; → *zezwolenie*; *~ić* *pf.* (*-lę, -wól!*) →

pozwalać; *pan(i) ~i* let me ...

pozy|cja f (*-i; -e*) position (*też mil.*); (*w spisie*) item; *~sk(iw)ać* (*sobie*) gain, win (*do G* to); *~tyw* m (*-u; -y*) *fot.* positive; *~tywny odpowiedź* affirmative; *korzystny* favo(u)rable; *~wać* (*-am*) *jur.* sue

pożałowani|e n: *godny ~a* (*przykry*) regrettable, (*żałosny*) lamentable, pitiful

pożar m (*-u; -y*) fire; *~ny: straż ~na* *Brt.* fire brigade, *Am.* fire department; *~owy* fire

pożąd|ać (*G*) desire; *~anie* n (*-a*) desire; lust; *~any* (much-)desired; desirable; *gość itp.*: welcome; *~liwie* adv. greedily; lustfully; *~liwy* greedy; lustful; lewd

poże|- *pf.* → *że-*; *~gnalny* parting; farewell; *~gnanie* n (*-a*) farewell; goodbye; *ucałować na ~gnanie* kiss s.o. good-bye

pożerać (*-am*) devour

pożoga f (*-i; G -żóg*) conflagration

po|żółkły yellow(ed); *~żreć* *pf.* → *pożerać*

pożycie n life; *~ małżeńskie* married life; *~ seksualne* sexual relationship

pożycz|ać (*-am*) lend (*k-u A* s.s.th.); borrow (*od, u G* from); *~ka* f (*-i; G -czek*) loan; *~kobiorca* m borrower; *~yć* *pf.* → *pożyczać*

pożyt|eczny useful; *~ek* m (*-tku; -tki*) advantage, benefit; *z ~kiem* profitably; *z ~kiem dla kogoś* to s.o.'s advantage

pożyw|iać się (*-am*) ⟨*~ić się*⟩ have some food, have a bite; *~ienie* n (*-a; 0*) food, nourishment; *~ny* nutritious

pójść *pf.* → *iść*

póki *cj* till, until; as long as; → *póty*

pół (*idkl.*) half; *~ godziny* half an hour; *~ do drugiej* half past one; *~ na ~* half-and-half; *w ~ drogi* half-way; midway; *za ~ ceny* at half price; *~ na ~* fifty-fifty; *~automatyczny* semi-automatic; *~buty* m/pl. low shoes; *~etatowy* half-time, part-time; *~fabrykat* m semi-finished product; *~finał* m semifinal; *~głosem* adv. in an undertone; under one's breath; *~główek* m (*-wka; -wki*) halfwit; *~godziny* half-an-hour's, thirty minutes'

półka f (*-i; G -łek*) shelf; *~ na bagaż* rack

pół|kole n (-a; G -i) semicircle; ~kolisty semicircular; ~księżyc m half-moon; crescent; ~kula f hemisphere; ~litrów-ka f (-i; G -wek) half-litre bottle; ~me-tek m (-tka; -tki) halfway mark; fig. halfway; ~metrowy half-a-metre long; ~misek m (-ska; -ski) gastr. dish

północ f (-y; 0) midnight; geogr. north; o ~y at midnight; na ~y in the north; na ~ od (G) north of; ~ny northern, north

pół|okrągły semicircular; ~piętro n landing; ~przewodnik m semiconductor; ~rocze n (-a) half-year; ~słodki wino demi-sec; ~szlachetny: kamień ~szlachetny semi-precious stone; ~tora (m/n), ~torej (f) num. (idkl.) one and a half; ~wiecze n (-a) half-century; ~wysep m (-spu; -spy) peninsula; ~żartem adv. half-jokingly

póty: ~ ... aż, ~ ... póki till, until

późn|ić się (o zegarku) be slow; ~iej adv. comp. later; ~iejszy adj. comp. later; subsequent; ~o adv., ~y late

prababka f great-grandmother

prac|a f (-y; -e) work, labour; (zajęcie) occupation; (dzieło) work; ~a zawo-dowa employment; zwolnić z ~y dis-miss, fire; iść do ~y go to work

praco|biorca m (-y) worker, em-ployee; ~dawca m employer; ~holik m (-a; -cy) workaholic

pracow|ać <po-> (-uję) work (na A for; u G by; nad I on); ~icie adv. indus-triously; ~itość f (-ści; 0) diligence; ~ity hard-working; diligent; ~nia f(-i; -e) (artysty) studio; (fizyczna, chemicz-na) laboratory; (rzemieślnicza) work-shop; ~nica f (-y; -e) worker, em-ployee; →pracownik; ~niczy workers'; ~nik m (-a; -cy) worker, employee; ~nik fizyczny manual worker, labo(u)rer, blue-collar worker; ~nik naukowy re-search worker; ~nik umysłowy office worker, white-collar worker

prać <u-, wy-> wash, launder; (che-micznie) dry-clean

pra|dawny prim(a)eval; ~dziad(ek) m great-grandfather; ~dzieje pl. prim-(a)eval history

Praga f (-i; 0) Prague

pragn|ąć <za-> (-nę) (G) desire; long (for); be anxious (to do s.th.); ~ienie n (-a) thirst; fig. desire; longing

prakty|czny practical; ~ka ['pra-] f (-i)

Brt. practice, Am. practise; training; ~ki pl. practices pl.; ~kant m (-a; -ci), -tka f (-i; G -tek) trainee; apprentice; ~kować (-uję) Brt. practise, Am. prac-tice; carry on

pralinka f (-i; G -nek) chocolate cream

pral|ka f (-i; G -lek) washing machine; ~nia f (-i; -e) laundry; ~nia chemiczna (dry-)cleaner's

prałat m (-a; -ci) prelate

pranie n (-a) washing; (prana bielizna) laundry

pras|a f 1. (-y) tech. press; printing press; 2. (0) press; na łamach ~y, w ~ie in the press; ~ować <s-> press; <wy-> suknię iron; ~owy press

prastary prim(a)eval; ancient

prawd|a f (-y) truth; czy to ~a? is that true?

prawdo|mówny truthful; ~podobień-stwo n (-a) probability; likelihood; ~podobnie adv. probably

prawdziw|ie adv. truly; really; indeed; ~ość f (-ści; 0) truth; veracity; ~y (nie zmyślony) true; (realny, niefałszywy) real; genuine; authentic; (typowy) regular

prawi|ca f (-y; -e) right hand; pol. the right; ~cowy pol. right-wing; ~ć (-ę) talk; say; ~ć komplementy pay com-pliments

prawidło n (-a; G -deł) rule; (do butów) foot-tree; ~wo adv. properly; correctly; ~wy proper; correct; (regularny) regular

prawie adv. almost; nearly; ~ nie hardly; ~ nikt/nic hardly anybody/anything

prawnicz|ka f (-i; G -czek) lawyer; ~y legal

praw|nie adv. legally; legitimately; ~nik m (-a; -cy) lawyer

prawnu|czka f great-granddaughter; ~k m great-grandson

praw|ny legal; lawful; akt legislative; środki ~ne pl. legal measures pl.; oso-bowość ~na legal personality; ~o[1] n (-a) law; ~o autorskie copyright; ~o głosowania voting rights pl.; ~o kar-ne criminal law; ~o natury law of na-ture; ~a człowieka pl. human rights pl.; F ~o jazdy Brt. driving licence, Am. driver's license; mieć ~o be entitled (do G to); studiować ~o study law

prawo[2]: na ~, w ~ right, to the right

prawo|dawca m legislator; lawmaker;

~mocny legally valid; ~ręczny right-handed; ~rządność f (-ści; 0) law and order; ~rządny law-abiding; ~sławny Orthodox; ~stronny: **ruch ~stronny** right-hand traffic; ~wierny orthodox; ~wity legal; lawful; legitimate; ~znaw-stwo n (-a; 0) jurisprudence

praw|y right, right-handed; fig. hono(u)rable; honest; **po ~ej stronie** on the right side; **z ~a** on the right

prawzór m prototype

praży|ć (-ę) v/t. roast; v/i. słońce: beat down, scorch; ~nki f/pl. (-nek) Brt. crisps, Am. chips

prącie n (-a; G -i) anat. penis

prąd m (-u; -y) current (też elektryczny); stream; ~stały direct current; ~zmien-ny alternating current; **pod ~** up-stream; against the stream; **z ~em cza-su** with time; ~nica f (-y; -e) generator

prąż|ek m (-żka; -żki) line; stripe; **w ~ki** → ~kowany striped

precedens m (-u; -y) precedent; **bez ~u** unprecedented

precy|zować ⟨s-⟩ (-uję) specify; state precisely; ~zyjny precise; exact; tech. precision

precz adv. away; **~ z nim** down with him; ~ **stąd!** go away!, off with you

pre|destynowany predestined (**do** G, **na** A to); ~fabrykat m prefabricated element; ~fabrykowany prefabricated; ~ferencyjny preferential; ~historycz-ny prehistoric(al); ~kursor m (-a; -rzy), ~kursorka f (-i; G -rek) forerunner; ~legent m (-a; -ci), ~legentka f (-i; G -tek) lecturer; ~lekcja f lecture; talk

prelimin|arz m (-a; -e) budget estimate; ~ować (-uję) assign (**na** A for)

preludium n (idkl; -ia, -iów) prelude

premedytacj|a f (-i; 0) jur. premeditation; **z ~ą** with malice aforethought

premi|a f (GDL-ii; -e) bonus; ~er m (-a; -rzy) prime minister; ~era f (-y) premi-ère, first night; ~ować (-uję) award a bonus; ~owy bonus; premium

prenume|rata f (-y) subscription; ~ra-tor m (-a; -rzy), ~ratorka f (-i; G -rek) subscriber; ~rować ⟨za-⟩ (-uję) subscribe (to s.th.)

preparat m (-u; -y) chem. preparation; biol. specimen

preria f (-i; -e) prairie

prerogatywy f/pl. (-) prerogatives

presja f (-i; -e) pressure

prestiż m (-u; 0) prestige

pretekst m (-u; -y) pretext

preten|dent m (-a; -ci), ~dentka f (-i; G -tek) pretender; ~dować (-uję) (**do urzędu**) run for (an office); ~sja f (-i; -e) claim; (uraza) grudge; (żal) resentment; **nie mam do niej ~sji** I hold no grudge against her; ~sjonalny pretentious; affected

prewencyjny preventive

prezent m (-u; -y) present, gift; ~er m (-a; -rzy), ~erka f (-i; G -rek) RTV: presenter; ~ować ⟨za-⟩ (-uję) show; ~ować się look

prezerwatywa f (-y) condom, sheath, F French letter

prezes m (-a; -i) president; chairman, chairperson

prezy|dent m (-a; -nci) president; (mia-sta) mayor; ~dium n (idkl; -ia, -iów) presidium; ~dować (-uję) (D) preside

pręcik m (-a; -i) bot. stamen

pręd|ki fast, quick, swift; ~ko adv. quickly; → **rychło**; ~kościomierz m (-a; -e) speedometer; ~kość f (-ści) speed; velocity; ~kość dźwięku speed of sound; → **szybkość**; ~szy faster

prędzej adv. faster; (rychlej) sooner; **czym ~** as quickly as possible; **~ czy później** sooner or later

pręga f (-i) streak; ~ierz m (-a; -e) pil-lory

pręt m (-a; -y) rod; tech. bar, rod

pręż|ność f (-ści; 0) (działania) vigo(u)r; ~y ciało supple; krok springy; fig. resilient, buoyant, energetic

prima aprilis m (idkl) April Fool's Day

priorytetowy priority

probierczy: **urząd ~** assay office; **ka-mień ~** touchstone

problem m (-u; -y) problem, issue

problematyczny questionable

probo|stwo n (-a) (katolickie) presby-tery; (anglikańskie) rectory; ~szcz m (-a; -owie/-e) parish priest; rector

probówk|a f (-i; G -wek) test tube; F **dziecko z ~i** test-tube baby

proca f (-y) sling; hist. catapult

proce|der m (-u; 0) (underhand) deal-ings pl.; shady business; ~dura f (-y) procedure, practice

procent m (-u; -y) Brt. per cent, Am. percent; (odsetki) interest; **w stu ~ach** one hundred per cent; ~*owo adv.* in proportion; ~*owy* proportional; *stopa ~owa* interest rate

proces *m* (-*u*; -*y*) process (*też tech.*); *jur.* (law)suit, case, trial; ~**ja** *f* (-*i*; -*e*) procession; ~**or** *m* (-*a*; -*y*) *tech.* processor; ~*ować się* (-*uję*) take legal action (*z l* against), sue

proch *m* (-*u*; -*y*) gunpowder; (*pył*) dust; ~*y pl.* remains, (*popioły*) ashes; F dope; ~*owy* powder

producent *m* (-*a*; -*nci*) producer (*też filmowy*), manufacturer

produk|cja *f* (-*i*; *0*) production, manufacture; ~*cyjność* *f* (-*ści*; *0*) productivness, productivity; ~*ować* ⟨*wy*-⟩ (-*uję*) produce, manufacture, make; ~*t m* (-*u*; -*y*) product; produce; ~*tywny* productive

proekologiczny environmentally friendly, green

prof. *skrót pisany:* **profesor** Prof. (*Professor*)

profanacja *f* (-*i*; *0*) profanation, desecration

profes|jonalny professional; ~*or¹* *m* (-*a*; -*owie*/-*orzy*) professor; (*nauczyciel*) teacher; ~*or²* *f* (*idkl.*) professor; teacher; → ~*orka* F *f* (-*i*; *G* -*rek*) teacher

profil *m* (-*u*; -*e*) profile; (*zarys*) outline

profilaktyczny prophylactic, preventive

progi *pl.* → **próg**

prognoz|a *f* (-*y*) prognosis; ~*a pogody* weather forecast; ~*ować* (-*uję*) forecast

program *m* (-*u*; -*y*) *Brt.* programme, *Am.* program; (*wyborczy*) manifesto; ~ *nauczania* curriculum, syllabus; ~*ista m* (-*y*; -*ści*), ~*istka* *f* (-*i*; *G* -*tek*) programmer; ~*ować* ⟨*za*-⟩ (-*uję*) *Brt.* programme, *Am.* program; ~*owy* manifesto

pro|gresywny progressive; ~*jekcja f* (-*i*; -*e*) projection; ~*jekcyjny* projection

projekt *m* (-*u*; -*y*) plan; design; (*szkic*) draft; (*zamierzenie*) project; ~ *ustawy* bill; ~*ant m* (-*a*; -*ci*) designer; ~*or m* (-*a*; -*y*) projektor; ~*ować* ⟨*za*-⟩ (-*uję*) plan; *arch.*, *tech.* design; ~*owy* design(ing)

prokurator *m* (-*a*; -*rzy*), ~*ka* F *f* (-*i*; *G* -*rek*) prosecutor, prosecuting attorney

prokuratura *f* (-*y*) public prosecutor's office

proletariacki proletarian

proletariusz *m* (-*a*; -*e*), ~*ka* *f* (-*i*; *G* -*szek*) proletarian

prolong|ata *f* (-*y*) prolongation; extension; ~*ować* ⟨*s*-⟩ (-*uję*) prolong

prom *m* (-*u*; -*y*) ferry; ~ *kosmiczny* space shuttle

promienio|twórczy radioactive; ~*wać* (-*uję*) radiate; *fig.* (*l*) beam (with); ~*wanie* *n* (-*a*) radiation

promienny beaming, radiant

promie|ń *m* (-*nia*; -*nie*) ray; *mat.* radius; ~*ń słońca* sunbeam; *w* ~*niu* (*G*) within a radius (of)

promil *m* (-*a*; -*e*) per mil

prominentny prominent

promo|cja *f* (-*i*; -*e*) promotion (*też ucznia*); ~*cyjny:* *sprzedaż ~cyjna* promotion; ~*wać* (-*uję*) promote (*też ucznia*)

promyk *m* (-*a*; -*i*) ray

proniemiecki pro-German

propag|anda *f* (-*y*) propaganda; ~*ować* (-*uję*) popularize

proponować ⟨*za*-⟩ (-*uję*) suggest, propose; *towar, zakąskę* offer

proporc|ja *f* (-*i*; -*e*) proportion, ratio; ~*onalny* (*odwrotnie* inversely) proportional (*to*)

propo|rczyk *m* (-*a*; -*i*) banner; ~*rzec* *m* (-*rca*, -*rce*) banner

propozycj|a *f* (-*i*; -*e*) suggestion, proposal, offer; *zgodzić się na ~ę* accept a proposal

proro|ctwo *n* (-*a*) prophecy; ~*czy* prophetic; ~*k* *m* (-*a*; -*cy*), ~*kini* *f* (-*i*; -*e*) prophet(ess); ~*kować* (-*uję*) prophesy

pro|sić ⟨*po*-⟩ (-*szę*) ask (*o A* for; *na* A to); (*urzędowo, formalnie*) request; ~*szę!* come in!; ~*szę bardzo* (*odpowiedź na „dziękuję"*) you're welcome; ~*szę pana/pani,* ... sir/madam ...

prosię *n* (-*ięcia*; -*ięta*, *G* -*siąt*) piglet; ~ *pieczone* *gastr.* roast pig

proso *n* (-*a*) millet

prospekt *m* (-*u*; -*y*) brochure, prospectus

prosperować (-*uję*) prosper, thrive

prosta *f* (-*tej*; -*te*) straight line; ~*cki* coarse, boorish; ~*cko,* *po* ~*cku* coarsely, boorishly; ~*k* *m* (-*a*, -*cy*) boor

prosto *adv.* straight; (*niezawile*) clearly ~*duszny* simple-hearted, guileless; ~*kąt* *m* rectangle; ~*kątny* rectangular; ~*linijny* *fig.* straightforward; ~*liniowy* (-*wo*) rectilinear; ~*padłościan* *m* (-*u*; -*y*) cuboid; ~*padły* (-*le*) perpendicular;

(*liniowo*) square (to); ~ta f (*-y; 0*) simplicity; ~wać (*-uję*) ⟨**wy-**⟩ straighten; *prąd* rectify; ⟨**s-**⟩ *błąd itp.* rectify, correct; ~wnik m (*-a; -i*) *anat.* extensor; *electr.* rectifier

prost|y¹ *adj.* (*m-os -ści; comp. -tszy*) (*nie wygięty*) straight; (*zwykły*) simple; (*skromny*) plain; **kąt ~y** right angle; **po ~u** simply; (*bez ceremonii*) unceremoniously; ~y² m (*-ego; -e*) (*cios*) straight

prostytutka f (*-i; G -tek*) prostitute

prosz|ek m (*-szku; -szki*) (**do prania, do pieczenia** washing, baking) powder; **mleko w ~ku** powdered milk; *u-trzeć na ~ek* pulverize; ~kowy powder

prośb|a f (*-y; G próśb*) request; (*podanie*) application; **mam do ciebie ~ę** I have a favo(u)r to ask of you; → **prosić**

proś|ciej *comp.* → **prosto**; ~ciutki (*-ko*) perfectly straight; → **prosty**

protegować (*-uję*) pull strings for *s.o.*, open doors for *s.o.*

protek|cja f (*-i; -e*) favo(u)ritism; ~cjonalny patronizing, condescending; ~tor¹ m (*-a; -y*) (tyre) tread; ~tor² m (*-a; -rzy/-owie*), ~torka f (*-i; G -rek*) protector; ~torat m (*-u; 0*) patronage; *pol.* protectorate

protest m (*-u; -y*) protest; **na znak ~u** in protest; ~acyjny protest

protestan|cki Protestant; ~t m (*-a; -nci*), ~tka f (*-i; G -tek*) Protestant

protestować ⟨**za-**⟩ (*-uję*) protest (*against lub* about)

proteza f (*-y*) (*ortopedyczna*) artificial limb; (*dentystyczna*) dentures *pl.*

protoko|lant m (*-a; -nci*), ~lantka f (*-i; G -tek*) recorder; *jur.* clerk of the court; ~łować ⟨**za-**⟩ (*-uję*) record, (*zebranie*) keep the minutes

protokół m (*-ołu; -oły*) report; minutes; **sporządzić ~** take the minutes

prototyp m (*-u; -y*) prototype

prowadz|ąca f (*-ej; -e*), ~ący m (*-ego; -y*) *RTV:* host; ~enie n (*-a*) (*domu*) running; (*samochodu*) driving; **objąć ~enie** be in the lead; ~ić ⟨**po-**⟩(*-dzę*) *v/t.*lead; conduct; *pojazd* drive; *zakład* run; *rozmowę* carry on; *wojnę* wage; → **kierować**; *v/i.* lead; ⟨**do-, za-**⟩ lead (**do** *G* to); ~**ić się** conduct oneself, behave

prowiant m (*-u; -y*) provisions *pl.*, victuals *pl.*

prowi|ncja f (*-i; -e*) province; (*obszar*

poza stolicą) provinces; ~ncjonalny provincial; ~zja f (*-i; -e*) commission; ~zorka f (*-i; G -rek*) makeshift, improvisation; ~zoryczny makeshift, rough--and-ready

prowodyr m (*-a; -rzy/-owie*) ringleader

prowo|kacja f (*-i; -e*) provocation; instigation; ~kacyjny provocative; ~kować ⟨**s-**⟩ (*-uję*) provoke; ~kujący (*-co*) provocative; (*spojrzenie, uśmiech*) lascivious

proza f (*-y; 0*) prose; ~iczny prose; *fig.* prosaic; ~ik m (*-a; -cy*) prose writer

prób|a f (*-y*) test; (*w teatrze*) rehearsal; (*usiłowanie*) attempt; **na ~ę, dla ~y** on a trial basis; ~ka f (*-i; G -bek*) sample, specimen; ~ny: **lot ~ny** test flight; **zdjęcia ~ne** screen test; **okres ~ny** trial period; ~ować (*-uję*) try; attempt; ⟨**po-, s-**⟩ *potrawy* taste; ⟨**wy-**⟩ test, put *s.th.* to the test

próch|nica f (*-y; 0*) *med.* caries; *agr.* humus; ~nieć ⟨**s-**⟩ (*-eję*) rot; *ząb:* decay; ~no n (*-a; 0*) rotten wood

prócz *prp.* (*G*) apart from; beside(s); except; **~ tego** except

próg m (*-ogu; -ogi*) threshold (*też fig.*), doorstep; *zima u progu* winter is near; **u progu** *fig.* on the doorstep

prósz|yć (*-szę*): **śnieg ~y** it is snowing lightly

próżni|a f (*-i; -e*) void; *phys.* vacuum; ~ctwo n (*-a; 0*) idleness; ~k m (*-a; -cy*) idler

próżn|o: na ~o in vain; ~ość f (*-ści; 0*) vanity; ~ować (*-uję*) loaf; ~y empty; *fig.* vain; (*daremny*) futile

pruć ⟨**po-, s-**⟩ (*-ję*) *kraw.* undo, unravel; *suknię* unpick

pruderyjny prudish

prus|ak m (*-a; -i*) *zo.* cockroach; ~ki Prussian; **kwas ~ki** prussic acid

prych|ać (*-am*) ⟨~**nąć**⟩ (*-nę*) snort; → **parskać**

prycza f (*-y; -e*) bunk

pry|mas m (*-a; -i/-owie*) primate; ~mitywny primitive; ~muła f (*-i; -e*) primrose; ~mus m (*-a; -i/-y*), ~muska f (*-i; G -sek*) top student

prys|kać (*-am*) ⟨~**nąć**⟩ (*-nę*) splash; spray; *szkło:* burst; *fig.* vanish; F (*uciec*) scram, hop it

pryszcz m (*-a; -e*) spot, pimple; ~yca f (*-y; 0*) *vet.* foot-and-mouth disease

prysznic *m* (*-a*; *-e*) shower
prywat|ka *f* (*-i*; *G -tek*) party; **~nie** *adv.* privately; **~ność** *f* (*-ści*; *0*) privacy; **~ny** private; personal
prywatyz|acja *f* (*-i*; *0*) privatization; **~ować** ⟨*s-*⟩ (*-uję*) privatize
pryzmat *m* (*-u*; *-y*) prism
przaśny *chleb* unleavened
prząść ⟨*u-*⟩ spin
przebacz|ać (*-am*) ⟨*~yć*⟩ (*-ę*) forgive; **~enie** *n* (*-a*) forgiveness
przebi|cie *f electr.* breakdown; **~ć** *pf.* → **przebijać**
przebie|c *pf.* → **przebiegać**; **~g** *m* course; mil(e)age **~gać** run, rush, dash (*przez A* across); *droga:* go, run; *sprawa:* proceed; **~c wzrokiem** run one's eyes over *s.th.*; **~gły** cunning, shrewd
przebiera|ć (*-am*) be fussy; (*sortować*) sift; **~ się** disguise o.s. (*za A* as); (*zmienić ubranie*) change one's clothes; **~ć nogami** hop from one leg to the other; **~lnia** *f* (*-i*; *-e*) dressing-room
przebijać (*-am*) pierce; puncture; *tunel* dig up, drill; *barwa:* show through; (*w kartach*) beat
przebiśnieg *m* (*-u*; *-i*) snowdrop
przebitk|a *f* (*-i*; *G -tek*) copy, duplicate, carbon copy; **~owy: papier ~owy** copying paper
przebłysk *m* glimmer, flash
prze|boleć *pf.* (*-eję*) get over; **~bój** *m* hit
przebra|ć *pf.* → **przebierać**; **~ć miarę** go too far; **~nie** *n* (*-a*) disguise; **~ny** disguised
prze|brnąć *pf.* wade; struggle (*przez A* through *lub* across); →**brnąć**; **~brzmiały** out-of-date
przebudow|a *f* conversion; rebuilding; **~(yw)ać** (*-[w]uję*) convert; rebuild
przebudzenie *n (-a)* awakening
przeby(wa)ć *drogę* travel, cover; *granicę* cross; *chorobę itp.* suffer (from); (*zostawać*) stay
przecedzać (*-am*) ⟨*~ić*⟩ strain
przecen|a *f* (*-y*; *0*) repricing, sale; **~iać** (*-am*), ⟨*~ić*⟩ overestimate; *hdl.* reduce the price
przechadz|ać się (*-am*) stroll; **~ać się tam i z powrotem** walk up and down; **~ka** *f* (*-i*; *G -dzek*) stroll; **iść na ~kę** go for a walk
przecho|dni *gr.* transitive; **puchar ~dni** challenge cup; **pokój ~dni** passage-

-room; **~dzić**[1] *v/i.* go, get (**do** *G* to); (*przebyć*) go, come; *światło, kula:* go *lub* pass through; *droga itp.:* run; *zima, deszcz:* be over; *ból:* pass, ease; *czas:* pass; *v/t.* **biedę, chorobę** suffer; *wyobraźnię* be beyond; *oczekiwania* surpass; *samego siebie* excel o.s.; *kurs* go (through); **~dzić**[2] *pf.* pass (by), cross, go over; **~dzień** *m* (*-dnia; -dnie, -dniów*) passer-by
przechow|ać *pf.* → **przechowywać**; **~alnia** *f* (*-i; -e*) kolej: *Brt.* left-luggage office, *Am.* checkroom; **~anie** *n* (*-a; 0*) preservation, storage; **na ~anie** for safekeeping; **~ywać** (*-wuję*) keep; store; hold; *zbiega* hide
prze|chwalać się (*-am*) boast (*I* of *lub* about); **~chwytywać** (*-uję*) ⟨**~chwycić**⟩ intercept; **~chylać** (*-am*) ⟨**~chylić**⟩ tilt; **~chylać się** lean over; **~ciąć** *pf.* → **przeciąć**
przeciąg *m Brt.* draught, *Am.* draft; **w ~u tygodnia** in the course of a week; **~ać** (*-am*) ⟨**~nąć**⟩ *v/t.* pull; thread (*przez A* through); (*w czasie*) prolong, protract; *v/i.* **~ać ręką po** (*L*) run one's hand across *s.th.*; **~ać się** stretch out; drag on; *człowiek:* stretch o.s.; **~ły** *dźwięk* drawn-out; *spojrzenie* lingering
przeciąż|ać (*-am*) ⟨**~yć**⟩ overload; overburden
przecie|kać (*-am*) ⟨**~c, ~knąć**⟩ *beczka, łódź:* leak; *płyn:* leak through, (*też fig.*) leak out
przecier *m* (*-u; -y*) paste, purée; **~ać** (*-am*) sieve, *Am.* rice; **~ać się** *spodnie:* wear through
przecierpieć *pf.* suffer, endure; undergo *s.th.*
przecież *adv.* but, yet
przecię|cie *n* cut; intersection; **~tna** *f* (*-ej; -e*) average; **~tnie** *adv.* on (the) average; **~tny** average; mean; (*mierny*) mediocre
przecin|ać (*-am*) cut; *drogę, odwrót* block one's way; *rozmowę itp.* cut short; **~ać się** intersect; **~ek** *m* (*-a; -i*) cutter; **~ek** *m* (*-nka; -nki*) comma; *mat.* point
przecis|kać ⟨**~nąć**⟩ squeeze through, force through; **~kać** ⟨**~nąć**⟩ **się** squeeze o.s. (under *lub* through)
przeciw *prp.* (*D*) against; *w złoż.* anti-, counter-; **~bólowy** analgesic; **środek ~bólowy** painkiller; **~ciała** *n/pl.* anti-

bodies; ~deszczowy: *płaszcz ~de-szczowy* raincoat; ~działać (D) counteract

przeciwgrypowy against flu

przeciwieństw|o n (-a) contrast; contradiction; the opposite of; *w ~ie do* (G) in contrast to, unlike

przeciw|jad m counterpoison, antidote; ~ko → **przeciw**; ~kurczowy (-wo) antispasmodic; ~legły opposite; ~lotniczy anti-aircraft; *schron ~lotniczy* air-raid shelter; ~mgłowy: *reflektor ~mgłowy* fog-lamp; ~niczka f (-i; G -czek) adversary; opponent; ~nie adv. in reverse; on the contrary; ~nik m (-a; -cy) adversary; opponent; ~ność f (-ści) reverse (of fortune); pl. adversities; ~ny opposite; opposed to; (od-wrotny) contrary; *być ~nym* (D) oppose s.th., be against s.th.; *wiatr ~ny* headwind, opposing wind; *w ~nym razie* otherwise; or else

przeciw|odblaskowy anti-dazzle; ~pożarowy fire

przeciwsłoneczny: *okulary ~ne* sunglasses, F shades

przeciwstaw|i(a)ć (D) contrast (s.th. with s.th.); ~*ić się* oppose; ~ienie n (-a) contrast; → **przeciwieństwo**; ~ny opposing

przeciw|tężcowy antitetanic; ~waga f counterweight, counterbalance; ~wskazany med. contraindicated; ~zapalny med. antiphlogistic

przeczący negative

przeczekać pf. wait for the end (of)

przeczenie n (-a) negative

przecznica f (-y; -e) cross-street

przeczu|cie f intuition; *złe ~cie* premonition; ~*ć* pf. → **przeczuwać**; ~lenie n (-a; 0) oversensitiveness; ~wać sense; have an inkling of

przeczyć (-ę) deny

przeczyszcza|ć (-am) → **czyścić**; ~jący: *środek ~jący* laxative, purgative

przeć push (też med.)

przed prp. (I, A) (miejsce) in front of; (czas) before; (obrona) against; ~ *laty* years ago; *żalić się ~matką* open one's heart to one's mother, complain to one's mother

przedawkować pf. overdose

przedawni|enie n (-a) jur. limitation, prescription; ~ony prescribed

przeddzień m: *w ~* on the day before; on the eve of

przed|e → **przed**; ~*e wszystkim* first of all; ~emerytalny before retirement; *w wieku ~emerytalnym* heading for retirement; ~gwiazdkowy Christmas (sale itp.); ~imek m (-mka; -mki) gr. article; ~kładać (-am) ⟨wolеć⟩ prefer (s.th. to s.th.); ⟨~łożyć⟩ submit, present

przed|łuż|acz m (-a; -e) electr. Brt. extension lead, Am. extension cord; ~ać (-am) ⟨~yć⟩ extend; prolong; ~enie n (-a) extension

przed|małżeński premarital; ~miejski suburban; ~mieście n (-a) suburb(s); ~miot m (rzecz) object; (temat) topic, subject; ~miotowy topical; ~mowa f foreword, preface; ~mówca m, ~mówczyni f the preceding speaker

przedmuch|iwać (-uję) ⟨~ać⟩ blow; blow air (through)

przed|ni front; fig. exquisite, outstanding; ~nówek m time before the harvest; ~obiedni before the dinner; ~ostatni penultimate; Brt. last but one, Am. next to last

przedosta(wa)ć się get through

przed|płata f advance payment; ~pokój m hall; ~południe n morning; ~potopowy fig. obsolete; ~ramię n forearm; ~rostek m (-tka; -tki) gr. prefix

przedruk m reprint; ~ow(yw)ać (-[w]uję) reprint

przedrze|ć pf. → **przedzierać**; ~źniać (-am) mock

przedsię|biorca m (-y) entrepreneur; ~*biorca budowlany* building contractor; ~*biorca pogrzebowy* undertaker; ~biorczość f (-ści; 0) enterprise; ~biorczy enterprising; ~biorstwo n (-a) enterprise, company; ~brać ⟨~wziąć⟩ undertake; ~wzięcie n undertaking, venture

przed|sionek m (-nka; -nki) vestibule; ~smak m foretaste; ~sprzedaż f advance sale, pre-booking

przedstawiać introduce (s.o.); *sprawę*, *plan itp.* present; *wniosek* bring forward; *dowód* produce, submit; ⟨*zgłosić*⟩ put forward; (na scenie) act; ~ *się os.* introduce o.s., *widok*: present itself, *sprawa*: stand

przedstawi|ciel m (-a; -e, -i), ~cielka f (-i; G -lek) representative, agent; ~ciel-

stwo n (-a) agency; sales lub branch office; pol. diplomatic post; ~ć pf. → **przedstawiać**; ~enie n (-a) show; theatr. spectacle, performance; play

przedszkol|e f (-a) Brt. nursery school, Am. kindergarten; ~ny Brt. nursery school, Am. kindergarten

przed|śmiertny deathbed; ~świąteczny preceding a holiday; ~świt m (-u; -y) daybreak; dawn; fig. harbinger

przedtem adv. earlier; before

przed|terminowy early; executed ahead of time; ~wczesny premature, untimely; ~wcześnie adv. prematurely ~wczoraj the day before yesterday; ~wczorajszy of the day before yesterday; ~wieczorny (of) late afternoon; ~wiośnie n (-a) early spring; ~wojenny pre-war; ~wyborczy spotkanie election; pre-election

przedział m range; (kolejowy) compartment; ~ek m (-łka; -łki) parting

przedzie|lać (-am) ⟨~lić⟩ divide; ~rać (-am) tear (też się); ~rać się struggle (przez A through)

prze|dziurawiać (-am) → **dziurawić**; ~faksować pf. (-uję) fax; ~forsować pf.(postawić na swoim) carry; ~ganiać (-am) ⟨~gonić⟩ (przepędzić) chase away; (być szybszym) outrun; ~gapiać (-am) ⟨~gapić⟩ overlook; okazje miss; ~ginać (-am) ⟨~giąć⟩ bend; ~ginać ⟨~giąć⟩ się bend over

przegląd m (-u; -y) inspection; review; survey; ~ lekarski medical examination; ~ prasy review of the press; ~ać (-am) look through; (sprawdzać) check; ~ać się examine o.s. in the mirror; ~arka f (-i) komp. browser

przegłos m (-u; 0) gr. vowel change; ~ować pf. outvote; vote down; → **głosować**

przegotow(yw)ać (-[w]uję) boil; (za długo gotować) overboil; ~ się boil too much v/i.

prze|grać pf. → **przegrywać**; ~gradzać (-am) partition, divide; ~grana f (-ej; -e) loss; (porażka) defeat; ~groda f (-y) partition; division; (kojec, przedział) stall; ~grodzić pf. → **przegradzać**; ~gródka f (-i; G -dek) compartment; pigeon-hole

prze|grupow(yw)ać (-[w]uję) redeploy; ~grywać (-am) lose (też pie-

niądze); kasetę copy; ~gryzać (-am) ⟨~gryźć⟩ bite through; F rdza: eat; ~gryźć coś F have a bite to eat; ~grzewać (-am) ⟨~grzać⟩ overheat; ~grzewać ⟨~grzać⟩ się become overheated

przegub m (-u; -y) wrist; tech. joint

prze|holow(yw)ać (-[w]uję) F fig. go too far; ~inaczać (-am) ⟨~czyć⟩ (-czę) misrepresent; ~istoczenie n (-a) transformation; rel. transubstantiation; ~jadać spend on food; ~jaskrawiać (-am) ⟨~jaskrawić⟩ exaggerate

przejaśni|ać się (-am) ⟨~ć się⟩ clear up; ~enie n (-a): ~enia pl. sunny intervals pl.

przejaw m (-u; -y) manifestation; (choroby) symptom; (wyraz) expression, sign; ~iać (-am) ⟨~ić⟩ display; ~iać się manifest itself (in s.th.)

przejazd m (-u; -y) (samochodem) drive; (koleją) ride; ~ kolejowy Brt. level crossing, Am. grade crossing; ~em passing through

przejażdżka f (-i; G -dżek) ride

prze|jąć pf. (-jmę) → **przejmować**; ~jechać pf. → **przejeżdżać**; (rozjechać) run over; ~jechać się go for a ride; ~jeść pf. → **przejadać**; ~jeżdżić pf. czas, pieniądze spend on travel; ~jeżdżać (-am) (A, przez A) cross, pass; drive, ride (przez A through, po L in, koło G past, by)

przejęcie n (-a) taking over; (wzruszenie) excitement, emotion; z ~m with excitement

przejęzyczenie n (-a) slip of the tongue

przejm|ować (-uję) take over; adopt; strach itp.: seize; zimno itp.: penetrate; ~ować się (I) be concerned (about s.th.); ~ujący (-co) piercing; głos shrill; widok impressive, moving; smutek deep

przejrzały overripe

przejrz|eć pf. (-ę, -y, -yj!) v/t. → **przeglądać**; fig. see through; v/i. recover one's sight; fig. become conscious of; ~ysty transparent; fig. clear, lucid ~yście adv. clearly

przejści|e n (-a) passage; gangway; (w sporcie) transfer; (doznanie) ordeal; ~cie dla pieszych pedestrian crossing; ~cie podziemne Brt. subway, Am. underpass; ~ciowo adv. temporarily; ~ciowy passing, transitory, temporary;

(*pośredni*) transitional; ~ć *pf.* → **przechodzić**; ~ć się take a walk (**po** *L* in)

przekaz *m* (*-u*; *-y*) (**za** *pośrednictwem banku*) transfer; ~ **pocztowy** postal order; **środki** *m/pl.* ~**u** mass media; ~**anie** *n* (*-a*) (*paczki*) delivery; (*wiadomości*) transmission; (*własności*) transferrence; ~**ywać** (*-uję*) ⟨~**ać**⟩ pass; hand over; *prawo* transfer; ~**ywać komuś pozdrowienia** give one's regards to s.o.

przekąs *m*: **z** ~**em** sneeringly; ~**ić** *pf.* (*-szę*) have a bite to eat; ~**ka** *f* (*-i*; *G* *-sek*) snack

przekątna *f* (*-ej*; *-e*) diagonal

prze|kląć *pf.* → **przeklinać** *v/t.*; ~**kleństwo** *n* (*-a*) swear-word; ~**klęty** damned; ~**klinać** (*-am*) *v/t.* curse; *v/i.* swear

przekład *m* (*-u*; *-y*) translation; ~**ać** (*-am*) ⟨~**żyć**⟩ (*-ę*) rearrange; (*tłumaczyć*) translate; *termin* reschedule; ~**nia** *f* (*-i*; *-e*) *tech.* transmission (gear)

przekłamanie *n* (*-a*) distortion

przekłu|wać (*-am*) ⟨~**ć**⟩ *balon* prick; *uszy* pierce

przekon|anie *n* (*-a*) conviction, belief; **nie mieć** ~**ania do** (*G*) be wary of, be sceptical about; ~**ywać** (*-uję*) ⟨~**ać**⟩ convince (*s.o.* of *s.th.*); ~**ywać** ⟨~**ać**⟩ **się** become convinced; ~**ywujący** (*-co*) convincing

przekop *m* (*-u*; *-y*) ditch, excavation; ~**ywać** (*-uję*) ⟨~**ać**⟩ dig

przekor|a *f* (*-y*; *0*) perversity; ~**ny** perverse, contrary

przekór *m*: **na** ~ in defiance of

przekra|czać (*-am*) *v/t.* cross; exceed; *prawo* transgress; ~**czać stan konta** overdraw one's account; ~**dać się** (*-am*) ⟨~**ść się**⟩ slip through *lub* across; ~**wać** (*-am*) cut (**na pół** in two)

prze|kreślać (*-am*) ⟨~**kreślić**⟩ cross out; ~**kręcać** (*-am*) ⟨~**kręcić**⟩ turn; *fakty* twist; *sprężynę* overwind

przekro|czenie *n* (*-a*) transgression; (*przepisów*) infringement; *granicy* crossing; ~**czenie salda** overdraft; ~**czenie szybkości** speeding; ~**czyć** *pf.* → **przekraczać**; ~**ić** *pf.* → **przekrawać**

przekrój *m* (*-roju*; *-roje*) section; ~ **podłużny** longitudinal section; ~ **poprzeczny** cross section

przekrzywiony tilted, askew

przekształc|ać (*-am*) ⟨~**ić**⟩ convert; reshape; transform; ~**ać się** evolve; ~**enie** *n* conversion; transformation

przekup|ić *pf.* → **przekupywać**; ~**ka** *f* (*-i*; *G* *-pek*) tradeswoman, vendor; ~**ny** corruptible; ~**stwo** *n* (*-a*) bribery, corruption; ~**ywać** (*-uję*) bribe

prze|kwalifikować *pf.* retrain; ~**kwaterować** *pf.* change housing *lub* lodging; ~**kwitać** (*-am*) ⟨~**kwitnąć**⟩ wither; ~**kwitanie** *n* med. menopause; ~**lać** *pf.* → **przelewać**; ~**latywać** (*-uję*) ⟨~**lecieć**⟩ fly (**z** from **do/na** to, **nad** *I* over, **koło** *G* past); *czas* fly (by)

przelew *m* (*-u*; *-y*) fin., jur. transfer; ~ **krwi** bloodshed; ~**ać** (*-am*) *płyn* pour; *prawa* transfer; ~**ać krew** shed blood; ~**ać się** overflow

prze|lęknąć *pf.* → **przelazić**; ~**lęknąć się** *pf.* (*-nę*) take fright at

przelicz|ać (*-am*) ⟨~**yć**⟩ (*zliczać*) count; convert; ~**enie** *n* conversion; **w** ~**eniu** in conversion

przelot *m* flight; ~ **ptaków** passage; ~**nie** *adv.* fleetingly; ~**ny** fleeting, occasional; **deszcz** ~**ny** shower; **ptaki** ~**ne** birds of passage

przeludni|enie *n* (*-a*; *0*) overpopulation; ~**ony** overpopulated

przeład|ow(yw)ać (*-[w]uję*) reload; (*przeciążać*) overburden, overload; ~**unek** *m* reloading; ~**unkowy** reloading

przełaj *m*(*-u*; *-e*) cross; **bieg na** ~ cross-country race; **droga na** ~ short cut

przełam|ywać (*-uję*) ⟨~**ać**⟩ (*-ię*) break; *fig.* overcome

przełazić (**przez** *A*) get through *lub* over *lub* across

przełącz|ać (*-am*) ⟨~**yć**⟩ (*-ę*) switch (over); ~**nik** *m* (*-a*; *-i*) switch

przełęcz *f* (*-y*; *-e*) geogr. pass

przełknąć *pf.* (*-nę*) swallow, swallow down

przełom *m* fracture; geol. gorge; fig. breakthrough, turning point; **na** ~**ie wieków** on the turn of the centuries; ~**owy** crucial, critical

przełoż|ona *f* (*-ej*; *-e*), ~**ony** *m* (*-ego*; *-żeni*) superior; pl. też the people overhead *lub* in command; ~**yć** *pf.* → **przekładać**

przełyk *m* gullet, oesophagus; ~**ać** → **łykać**

prze|maczać ⟨**~moczyć**⟩ wet, drench; **~moczyć sobie nogi** get one's feet wet; **~magać** (-am) ⟨**~móc**⟩ v/t overcome; v/i prevail; **~móc się** conquer one's fears; **~makać** (-am) ⟨**~moknąć**⟩ get soaked, get drenched; **~marzać** [-r-z-] ⟨**~marznąć**⟩ freeze; **~maszerować** pf. v/i. march by; **~mawiać** give lub make a speech; speak (**do** G to; **za** I in s.o.'s favour)

przemądrzały bigheaded

przemeldow(yw)ać (-[w]uję) report s.o.'s change of address

przemęcz|ać (-am) ⟨**~yć**⟩ (over)strain; **~yć się** overexert o.s.; → **męczyć się; ~enie** n (-a; 0) exhaustion, fatigue; **~ony** (pracą) exhausted, fatigued

przemian: **na ~** alternately; **~a** f (-y) transformation; **~a materii** metabolism; **~owanie** n renaming

przemie|ni(a)ć transform, change; **~nić się** change (**w** A into); **~szać** pf. mix (thoroughly); **~szczać** (-am) move

przemi|jać ⟨**~nąć**⟩ pass, go by; come to an end; uroda: fade; **~lczać** (-am) ⟨**~lczeć**⟩ v/t. pass over (in silence); leave unsaid

przemknąć pf. → **przemykać**

przemoc f (-y; 0) violence; **akt ~y** act of violence; **~ą** through violence, forcibly

przemo|czyć pf. → **przemaczać**; **~knąć** pf. → **przemakać**; **~knięty** soaked, drenched

prze|mowa f → **przemówienie**; **~móc** pf. → **przemagać**; **~mówić** pf. → **przemawiać**; **~mówienie** n speech; **~mycać** (-am) ⟨**~mycić**⟩ smuggle; **~myć** pf. → **przemywać**; **~mykać** (-am) steal; myśli: flit; **~mykać się** steal

przemysł m (-u; -y) industry; F **własnym ~em** oneself, by one's own means

przemysłow|iec m (-wca; -wcy) industrialist; **~y** industrial

przemyśl|any well-thought-out, deliberate; **~eć** pf. think s.th. over; **~iwać** (-am) ponder (**o** L upon); **~ny** clever; urządzenie ingenious

prze|myt m (-u; 0) smuggling; **~mytniczka** f (-czek; -czki), **~mytnik** m (-a; -cy) smuggler; **~mywać** (-am) wash, bathe; **~nicować** pf. → **nicować**

przeniesieni|e n (-a) transfer (też służbowe); **z ~a** fin. brought forward

przenieść pf. → **przenosić**

przenik|ać (-am) penetrate (**do** G s.th. lub into s.th.) **~liwość** f (-ści; 0) fig. perspicacity; **~liwy** penetrating; fig. keen, searching; **~nąć** pf. → **przenikać**

przeno|cować pf. v/i. → **nocować**; v/t. put up; **~sić** move, carry; brwi hyphenate; **~sić na emeryturę** pension s.o.; **~sić się** move (**do** G to), ogień: spread **~śnia** f (-i; -e) metaphor; **~śnik** m (-a; -i) tech. conveyor; **~śny** portable; fig. figurative, metaphorical

przeobra|żać ⟨**~zić**⟩ transform; **~żać** ⟨**~zić**⟩ **się** be transformed, turn; **~żenie** n (-a) transformation, change

przeocz|ać (-am) ⟨**~yć**⟩ (-czę) overlook; **~enie** n oversight; **przez ~enie** by an oversight

przeor m (-a; -rzy/-owie) prior

prze|orać pf. plough; fig. furrow; **~organizować** pf. reorganize

przeorysza f (-y; -e) prioress

przepa|dać disappear; **~dać za** (I) be very fond of → **przepaść²**; **~dły** missing; **~jać** (-am) fill (I with); permeate; **~kow(yw)ać** (-[w]uję) repack; **~lać** (-am) ⟨**~lić**⟩ v/t. burn (through); **~lić dziurę** burn a hole; **~lić się** żarówka: blow; **~lony** blown

przepas|ka f (-i; G -sek) sweatband; (na oczy) blindfold; **~ywać** (-uję) ⟨**~ać**⟩ (się) tie s.th. around one's waist

przepa|ść¹ f (-ści; -ści/-ście) precipice; fig. gap, gulf; **~ść²** pf. → **przepadać**; (na egzaminie itp.) fail; **~ść bez wieści** he is missing; **~trywać** (-uję) ⟨**~trzyć, ~trzeć**⟩ examine, study

przepchnąć pf. → **przepychać**

przepełni|enie n (-a; 0) crowd; excess; **~ony** overcrowded; (wodą) overflowing

przepędz|ać (-am) ⟨**~ić**⟩ drive; ludzi drive away lub out of

prze|pić pf. → **przepijać**; **~pierać** (-am) launder; **~pierzenie** n partition; **~piękny** most beautiful, exquisite; **~pijać** (-am) v/t. spend on drink; v/i. (**do** G) drink to; **~piłow(yw)ać** (-[w]uję) saw through

przepiórka f (-i; G -rek) quail

przepis m (-u; -y) regulation; **~y bezpieczeństwa** safety code; **~ kucharski** recipe; **~y ruchu drogowego** highway code; **~y drogowe** traffic regulations, Highway Code; ~ać *pf.* → **prze-pisywać**; ~owy regulation; ~ywać (-*uje*) copy out; type out; *med.* pre-scribe

przepity *głos* hoarse from drinking; *człowiek* hung over

przeplatać (-*am*) interlace, inter-weave; ~ **się** alternate with *s.th.*

prze|płacać (-*am*) ⟨~**płacić**⟩ pay too much; ~płaszać (-*am*) ⟨~**płoszyć**⟩ frighten away; ~płukiwać (-*uje*) ⟨~**płu-kać**⟩ rinse; ~płukać ~płуwać ⟨~**pły-nąć**⟩ *v/t człowiek*: swim; *statek*: sail (**przez** *A* across); (*łodzią*) row; *wo-da*: flow; ~pocić *pf.* sweat; ~poić *pf.* → **przepajać**; ~pona *f* (-*y*) *anat.* dia-phragm; *tech.* diaphragm, membrane

przepowi|adać (-*am*) ⟨~**edzieć**⟩ pro-phesy; foretell; *pogodę* predict; ~ednia *f* (-*i*; -*e*) prophecy

prze|pracow(yw)ać (-[*w*]*uję*): ~**pra-cować trzy dni** work three days; (*na nowo*) do *s.th.* over again; ~**pracować się** overstrain o.s. ~prać *pf.* → **prze-pierać**; ~praszać (-*am*) apologize (**ko-goś za** *A* to s.o. for s.th.); ~**praszam!** (I'm) sorry!

przepraw|a *f* (-*y*) crossing; (*bród*) ford; ~iać (-*am*) ⟨~**ić**⟩ (-*ę*) ferry; ~**ić się na drugi brzeg** get to the other side; ~**ić się** (**przez** *A*) get across (*a river itp.*)

prze|prosić *pf.* → **przepraszać**; ~**prosić się** make friends again; ~szenie *n* (-*a*) apology

przeprowadz|ać (-*am*) ⟨~**ić**⟩ take (**przez** *A* across *lub* through); (*realizo-wać*) carry out; *szosę* build; ~**ić się** move; ~ka *f* (-*i*; *G* -*dzek*) move

przepuklina *f* (-*y*) *med.* hernia, rupture

przepu|st *m* (-*u*; -*y*) (*śluza*) sluice (-gate); ~stka *f* (-*i*; *G* -*dzek*) pass; ~szczać ⟨~**ścić**⟩ let through; F *zw. pf.* → **pominąć, przeoczyć**; ~szczal-ny penetrable, permeable

przepych *m* (-*u*; *0*) Brt. splendour, *Am.* splendor

przepychać (-*am*) *v/t.* shove (through); *rurę* unclog; ~ **się** elbow one's way

przera|biać (-*am*) alter; (*opracować na nowo*) rewrite; (*przetworzyć*) process; *lekcję* do; ~chow(yw)ać (-[*w*]*uję*) → **przeliczać**; ~dzać się (-*am*) turn into; ~stać (-*am*) *v/t.* outgrow; *fig.* surpass; ~zić *pf.* → **przerażać**; ~źliwy frightful;

krzyk: ear-piercing; ~żać (-*am*) terrify, horrify; ~**żać się** be terrified; ~żający terrifying, horrifying; ~żony terrified

prze|rdzewieć *pf.* be eaten up with rust; ~robić *pf.* → **przerabiać**; ~ro-dzić się *pf.* → **przeradzać się**; ~rosnąć *pf.* → **przerastać**; ~rób *m* (-*obu*; *0*) processing; ~róbka *f* (-*i*; *G* -*bek*) alteration; adaptation

przerw|a *f* (-*y*) break; *teatr.* interval; (*lu-ka*) gap; **bez** ~**y** without a break; ~ać *pf.* → **przerywać**; ~ać **się** break; ~anie *n* (-*a*) break; disconnection; ~**anie ciąży** abortion

przerywa|cz *m* (-*a*; -*e*) *tech.* interrupter, breaker; ~ć (-*am*) break, interrupt; dis-continue; (*nie skończyć*) break off; ~**ć ciążę** have an abortion; ~ny *oddech*, *głos* broken

przerzedz|ać (-*am*) ⟨~**ić**⟩ (-*dzę*) thin (*też agr.*)

przerzuc|ać ⟨~**ić**⟩ throw (**przez** *A* over); ~**ić most** bridge a river; ~**ić bieg** *Brt.* change gear, *Am.* shift gear; ~**ać kartki** (*G*) leaf through; → **przetrzą-sać**; ~**ić się** (**na** *A*) pass over (to)

prze|rynać (-*am*) ⟨~**rżnąć**⟩ cut; (*prze-piłować*) saw; F (*przegrać*) lose

przesa|da *f* (-*y*) exaggeration; ~dnie *adv.* excessively; ~dny exaggerated; ~dzać ⟨~**dzić**⟩ *ucznia* move (to an-other seat); *agr.* transplant; *v/i. fig.* ex-aggerate

przesalać (-*am*) → **przesolić**

przesącz|ać ⟨~**yć**⟩ filter, percolate

przesąd *m* superstition; (*uprzedzenie*) prejudice; ~dny superstitious; ~dzać (-*am*) ⟨~**dzić**⟩ determine; *niczego nie* ~**dzając** without prejudice

przesia|ć *pf.* → **przesiewać**; ~dać się move to another seat; (*w podróży*) change; ~dka *f* (-*i*; *G* -*dek*) change

przesią|kać (-*am*) ⟨~**knąć**⟩ (-*nę*) soak (through); *pf.* → **nasiąkać**; ~ść się *pf.* → **przesiadać się**

przesiedl|ać (-*am*) displace; rehouse; ~**ać się** migrate (**do** *G* to); *wenie n* (-*a*) displacement; rehousing; ~**enie się** migration; ~eniec *m* (-*ńca*; -*ńcy*) emigrant; displaced person; ~ić *pf.* (-*ę*) → **przesiedlać**

przesieka *f* (-*i*) cutting

przesiewać (-*am*) sift

przesilenie *n* (-*a*) turning point; *med.*

crisis; ~ **letnie** solstice

przesk|akiwać (-*uję*) ⟨*oczyć*⟩ v/t. jump (over), fig. skip (**przez** A over, **z** ... **na** ... from ... to ...); ~ok m jump

przeskrobać F pf. (zawinić) perpetrate; (*spsocić*) be up to (some mischief)

przesła|ć pf. → **przesyłać, prześcielać**; ~niać (-*am*) conceal; ~nie n (ka f -i, G -nek) circumstance; filoz. premise

przesło|dzić pf. make too sweet; ~na f (-*y*) screen; phot. aperture; ~nić pf. → **przesłaniać**

przesłuch|anie n (-*a*) jur. interrogation, questioning; (*świadków*) examination; ~iwać (-*uję*) ⟨*~ać*⟩ artystę audition; jur. interrogate, examine

prze|smyk m (-*u*; -*i*) pass; geogr. isthmus; ~solić put too much salt in; F fig. overdo; ~spać pf. → **przesypiać**

przestać[1] pf. (stać[1]) stand

przesta|ć[2] pf. (stać[2]) → **przestawać**; ~nkowy znaki m/pl. ~nkowe punctuation marks; ~rzały obsolete; ~wać (-*ję*): ~wać coś robić stop doing s.th.; ~wać z kimś associate with s.o.; ~wi(a)ć move, rearrange; ~wi(a)ć się na coś switch (over) to s.th.

przestąpić pf. → **przestępować**

przestęp|ca m (-*y*; G -*ów*) criminal; ~czość f (-*ści*; 0) crime; ~czy criminal; ~czyni f (-*i*; -*nie*, G -*ń*) criminal; ~ny jur. criminal, felonious; rok ~ny leap year; ~ować⟨-*ić*⟩ cross (**przez** A s.th.); ~stwo n (-*a*) crime; popełnić ~stwo commit a crime

przestój m (-*oju*; -*oje*) stoppage

przestra|ch m fright; ~szony frightened; ~szyć pf. frighten, scare; ~szyć się be frightened, take fright

przestroga f (-*i*; G -*óg*) admonition, (fore)warning

przestronny spacious

przestrzega|ć[1] (-*am*) (G) obey; abide by; observe; (o tajemnicach) keep; ~ać[2] ⟨*~c*⟩ (**przed** I) warn (of lub against)

przestrze|nny three-dimensional; spatial; ~ń f (-*ni*; -*nie*, -*ni*) (**życiowa** living) space; (*powierzchnia*) expanse; (*dystans*) distance; ~ń **kosmiczna** (outer) space

przestudiować pf. v/t. make a thorough study; examine

przesu|nięcie n (-*a*) shift; displacement; ~wać ⟨*~nąć*⟩ move, shift; ~wać ⟨*~nąć*⟩ się shift, człowiek: move over; ~nąć się do przodu move forward; ~wny mov(e)able, slidable

przesy|cać (-*am*) ⟨*~cić*⟩ saturate; ~cony permeated with s.th.; ~łać (-*am*) send; ~łać dalej forward; ~łka f (-i; G -łek) mail; (*przesyłanie*) sending, dispatch; ~pać pf. → **przesypywać**; ~piać (-*am*) sleep through; (*przepuścić*) fig. let slip; ~pywać (-*uję*) pour

przesyt m (-*u*; 0) surfeit

przeszczep m (-*u*; -*y*) med. transplant, graft; ~iać (-*am*)⟨*~ić*⟩ transplant, graft

przeszka|dzać (-*am*) disturb; interfere; **proszę sobie nie ~dzać** don't let me disturb you; → **przeszkodzić**; ~lać (-*am*) train, instruct

przeszko|da f (-*y*) obstruction; obstacle; **stać na ~dzie** stand in s.o.'s way; ~dzić pf. → **przeszkadzać**; ~lenie n training; ~lić pf. → **przeszkalać**

przesz|ło adv. more than, over; ~łość f (-*ści*; 0) past; ~ły past

przeszuk|iwać (-*uję*) ⟨*~ać*⟩ search; teren scour, comb

przeszy|wać (-*am*) ⟨*~ć*⟩ stitch; (*przebić*) pierce; fig. penetrate

przeście|łać (-*am*) łóżko rearrange; ~radło n (-*a*; G -*deł*) sheet; ~radło kąpielowe bath towel

prześcig|ać (-*am*) ⟨*~nąć*⟩ (-*nę*) outrun; fig. beat s.o. at s.th; ~ać się fig. try to outdo one another (**w** L at)

prześladow|ać (-*uję*) persecute; fig. haunt; (*dręczyć*) pester; ~anie n (-*a*) persecution; ~any persecuted, oppressed; ~ca m (-*y*) persecutor; ~czy **mania ~cza** persecution mania lub complex

prześliczny lovely

prześliz|giwać się (-*uję*) ⟨*~(g)nąć się*⟩ (-*nę*) steal through lub past; fig. skate (over s.th.)

prześmie|szny extremely funny

przeświadcz|enie n conviction; ~ony (o L) convinced (of)

prześwie|cać (-*am*) show (through); shine (**przez** A through); ~tlać (-*am*) ⟨*~tlić*⟩ (-*lę*) X-ray; pf. phot. overexpose; ~tlenie n (-*a*) X-ray

prześwit m (-*u*; -*y*) gap, clearance

przeta|czać (-*am*) roll; wagony strunt;

płyn decant; *krew* give a blood transfusion; **~czać się** roll by; **~piać** (*-am*) melt down; *gastr.* melt

przetarg *m* (*wybór ofert*) tender; (*licytacja*) auction

prze|tarty frayed; **~tasow(yw)ać** (*-[w]uję*) shuffle; **~terminowany** expired; **~tkać** *pf.* → **przetykać**

przeto *cj.* therefore; **niemniej ~** nevertheless; **~ka** *f* (*-i*) *med.* fistula; **~czyć** *pf.* → **przetaczać**; **~pić** *pf.* → **przetapiać**

przetraw|iać (*-am*) **⟨~ić⟩** digest; *fig.* mull over

prze|trącić F *pf.* break; have a snack; **~trenowany** stale; **~trwać** *pf.* survive

przetrzas|ać [-t·ʃ-] (*-am*) **⟨~nąć⟩** (*-nę*) (*szukać*) scour

przetrze|biać [-t·ʃe-] (*-am*) **⟨~bić⟩** (*-bię*) *fig.* thin, make thin; **~ć** *pf.* → **przecierać**

przetrzym|ywać [-t·ʃ-] (*-uję*) **⟨~ać⟩** keep; hold; detain; (*ukrywać*) conceal, hide; (*znieść*) endure

przetwarza|ć (*-am*) **⟨-rzyć⟩** process; *electr.* convert; *fig.* convert; **~nie** *n* (*-a; 0*): **~nie danych** data processing

przetwór *m* product; **przetwory** *pl.* preserves; **~czy** processing; **~nia** *f* (*-i; -e*) food processing plant

przetykać *v/t.* *rurę, fajkę* clear, clean out; *tkaninę* interweave, interlace

przewag|a *f* superiority; (*w tenisie*) advantage; **mieć ~ę nad kimś** have the upper hand over s.o.; **uzyskać ~ę** get the upper hand

przeważ|ać (*-am*) *v/i.* overweigh; *fig.* prevail, predominate; **~ający** *siła:* overwhelming; (*dominujący*) predominant, prevailing; **~nie** *adv.* mostly; **~yć** *pf.* → **przeważać**

przewąch|iwać (*-uję*) **⟨~ać⟩** F *v/t.* scent

przewiąz|ywać (*-uję*) **⟨~ać⟩** tie; *ranę* tie up

przewi|dujący foreseeing; far-sighted; **~dywać** (*-uję*) foresee, predict; *pogodę* forecast; (*planować*) anticipate

przewidywa|nie *n* (*-a*) expectation; **~nie pogody** weather forecast; **w ~niu** in anticipation (of); **według wszelkich ~ń** according to expectation; **~ny** expected

przewidz|enie *n*: **to było do ~enia** it was predictable *lub* foreseeable; **~iany**,

~ieć *pf.* → **przewidywany, przewidywać**

przewie|rcać (*-am*) **⟨~rcić⟩** drill through; *fig.* pierce; **~szać** **⟨~sić⟩** *v/t.* (**przez** *A*) hang, sling (over)

przewietrz|ać (*-am*) **⟨~yć⟩** air, ventilate

przewiew *m* (*-u; -y*) *Brt.* draught, *Am.* draft; **~ny** *ubiór* cool; *budynek* airy

prze|wieźć *pf.* → **przewozić**; **~wijać** (*-am*) **⟨~winąć⟩** (*-nę*) rewind; *dziecko* change; *ranę* put a new dressing on; **~winienie** *n* (*-a*) *Brt.* offence, *Am.* offense; (*w sporcie*) foul; **~wlekać** (*-am*) **⟨~wlec⟩** pass (*s.th.* through *s.th.*); *fig.* protract; **~wlekać się** drag on; **~wlekły** protracted; *med.* chronic

przewodni leading; **motyw ~** leitmotiv; **~ctwo** *n* (*-a; 0*) leadership; (*obrad*) chairmanship; *phys.* conduction, conductance (of); **~czący** *m* (*-ego; -y*), **~cząca** *f* (*-ej; -e*) chair, chairperson; **~czka** *f* (*-i; G -czek*) guide; **~czyć** (*-ę*) be in the chair; (*D*) chair (a meeting); **~k** *m* (*-a; -cy*) (*osoba*) guide; (*książka*) guidebook; *phys.* conductor

przewo|dowy wire; **~dzić** (*D*) lead; (*A*) *phys.* conduct; **~zić** *v/t.* transport; take; **~zowy** transport; *list* **~zowy** bill of lading, consignment note; **~źnik** *m* (*-a; -cy*) carrier; *Brt.* haulier, *Am.* hauler; (*na promie*) ferryman; **~źny** mobile

przewód *m* (*-odu; -ody*) (*gazowy*) pipe; *electr.* wire; **~ pokarmowy** alimentary canal; **~ słuchowy** accoustic duct; **~ sądowy** legal proceedings; *pod* **przewodem** under *s.o.'s* leadership

przewóz *m* transport; (*samochodowy*) haulage, trucking

przewracać ⟨po-⟩ *v/t.* overturn; knock over; *kartki* turn; (*obracać*) turn round; *v/i* (*szperać*) rummage; **~ się** fall over; turn over, roll over; **~ się do góry dnem** *łódź:* capsize

przewrażliwiony → **przeczulony**

przewrotny perverse

przewró|cić *pf.* → **przewracać**; **~t** *m* (*-otu; -oty*) revolution; *pol.* coup (d'état); (*w sporcie*) somersault

przewyższ|ać (*-am*) **⟨~yć⟩** outstrip, surpass; be better than; (*liczebnie*) outnumber

przez *prp.* (*A*) across; through; over; **~ radio** over *lub* on the radio; **~ przypadek** by accident; **~ telefon** over *lub* on the phone; ~ **cały rok** all year; ~ **sekundę** for a second; ~**e mnie** because of me

przeziębi|ać (-*am*) ⟨~**ć**⟩ catch (a) cold; ~enie *n* (-*a*) cold; ~ony: **jestem przeziębiony** have a cold

przeznacz|ać (-*am*) ⟨~**yć**⟩ intend, destine; assign (**na** *A*, **do** *G* for); ~enie *n* (-*a*) use, purpose; (*los*) destiny, fate; **miejsce ~enia** destination

przezorn|ie *adv.* providently, far-sightedly; ~y foreseeing, far-sighted; (*ostrożny*) circumspect

przezrocz|e *n* (-*a*) slide; ~ysty transparent; *material:* see-through; *płyn:* clear

prze|zwać *pf.* → **przezywać**; ~zwisko *n* (-*a*) nickname; → **wyzwisko**; ~zwyciężać ⟨~**zwyciężyć**⟩ overcome; ~**zwyciężyć się** control o.s., overcome a feeling; ~zywać (-*am*) *v/t.* nickname; (*ubliżać*) call *s.o.* names

prze|źrocz- → **przezrocz-**; ~żegnać się *pf.* cross o.s.; ~żerać (-*am*) ⟨~**żreć**⟩ eat away; ~żerać (-*am*) *krowa:* ruminate; ⟨~**żuć**⟩ chew

przeży|cie *n* survival; (*doznanie*) experience; ~tek *m* (-*u*; -*i*) anachronism; ~wać (-*am*) ⟨~**ć**⟩ experience, go **through**; ~**wać** ⟨~**ć**⟩ **się** become outdated

przędza *f* (-*y*) yarn; ~lnia *f* (-*i*; -*e*) spinning room; spinning mill

przęsło *n* (-*a*; *G* -*seł*) *arch.* span

przodek *m* (-*dka*; -*dki*) *górn.* coalface; (*pl.* -*dkowie*) ancestor, forefather

przodow|ać (-*uję*) (**w** *L*) excel (in *lub* at); ~nica *f* (-*y*; -*e*), ~nik *m* (-*a*; -*cy*) leader

przodujący leading

przód *m* (-*odu*; -*ody*) front; **w** ~, **do przodu** forward; **z przodu** in front; **przodem, na przedzie** in front

przy *prp* (*L*) by; at; ~ **stole** at the table; **mieć coś** ~ **sobie** have s.th. on *lub* about one; ~ **pracy** at work; ~ **czym** *lub* ~ **tym** at the same time; ~ **ulicy** on the street; ~**bić** *pf.* → **przybijać**; ~**biegać** ⟨~**biec**⟩ come running; ~**bierać** (-*am*) *v/t.* assume; (*zdobić*) decorate, *potrawę* garnish; *v/i. rzeka:* rise; ~**bierać na wadze** put on weight; ~**bijać** (-*am*) *v/t. gwóźdź* hammer, drive; *deskę* nail; *pieczęć* set; *v/i.* ~**bijać do brzegu** reach the shore, land

przybliż|ać ⟨~**yć**⟩ bring closer, bring nearer; *lornetka:* magnify; ~**ać** ⟨~**yć**⟩

się come closer, approach; ~enie *n* (-*a*) approximation; **w** ~**eniu** approximately, roughly; ~ony approximate

przy|błąkany *pies:* stray; ~boczny: **straż przyboczna** bodyguard; ~bój *m* surf; ~bory *m/pl.* (-*ów*) accessories *pl.*; gear; ~**bory do golenia** shaving gear; ~**bory toaletowe** toilet set; ~brać *pf.* → **przybierać**; ~brany → **przybierać**; ~**brane dziecko** foster child; ~**brane nazwisko** assumed name; ~**brani rodzice** *pl.* foster parents *pl.*; ~brudzony (slightly) soiled; ~brzeżny coastal

przybudówka *f* (-*i*; *G* -*wek*) *Brt.* annexe, *Am.* annex

przyby|cie *n* (-*a*) arrival; ~ć *pf.* → **przybywać**; ~sz *m* (-*a*; -*e*) newcomer; ~tek *m* (-*tku*; -*tki*) gain; (*świątynia*) shrine; ~wać arrive, come; ~**wa** (*G*): **dnia ~wa** the days are getting longer; ~**ło mu pięć lat** he is five years older

przycho|dnia *f* (-*i*; -*e*) out-patient clinic; ~dzić come; arrive; *fig.* ~**dzić do siebie** recover; ~**dzić na myśl** enter s.o.'s mind; ~**dzić po** (*A*) fetch, collect; **to ~dzi mu z trudem** he has difficulty in doing that

przychód *m* income; (*zysk*) profit

przychyl|ać (-*am*) ⟨~**ić**⟩ bend, incline; *fig.* ~**ić się do** (*G*) consent to; ~ność *f* (-*ści*; 0) *Brt.* favour, *Am.* favor; ~ny *Brt.* favourable, *Am.* favorable

przyciąć *pf.* → **przycinać**

przycią|gać (-*am*) ⟨~**nąć**⟩ pull closer; *zwł. impf. phys.* attract; *fig.* attract; ~**gać się** attract one another; ~anie *n* (-*a*; 0): ~**anie ziemskie** gravity

przyciemni|ać (-*am*) ⟨~**ć**⟩ (-*ę*) darken; *światło* dim

przycinać (-*am*) *v/t.* cut (to size); *włosy itp.* clip, trim; *v/i. fig.* gibe at s.o.

przyci|sk *m* (-*u*; -*i*) (*paper*-)weight; (*dzwonka itp.*) button; *fig.* emphasis; ~kać ⟨~**nąć**⟩ *v/t.* press (*też* *fig.*)

przycisz|ać (-*am*) ⟨~**yć**⟩ (-*ę*) *głos* subdue; *radio* turn down

przyczajony lurking, hidden

przyczep|a *f* (-*y*) *mot.* trailer; *motocyklowa* sidecar; ~i(a)ć attach, fasten; *fig.* ~**i(a)ć się** (**do** *G*) pick on s.o., find fault (with) → **czepiać się**; ~ka *f* (-*i*; *G* -*pek*) (*motocykla*) sidecar; ~ny adhesive; attachable

przyczołgać się *pf.* crawl up, creep up

przyczyn|a f (-y) reason, cause; **z tej ~y** for that reason; ~ek m (-nku; -nki) contribution; ~iać się (-am) ⟨~ić się⟩ (**do** G) contribute (to); ~owy causal

przyćm|iewać (-am) ⟨~ić⟩ niebo darken; światło, pamięć dim; fig. outshine; ~iony dim

przyda|ć pf. → przydawać; ~tność f (-ści; 0) usefulness, utility; ~tny useful, helpful; ~wać add; **~wać się (do** G, **na** A) come in useful, be of use (for s.o.); **~łby mi się ...** I could do with ...; **to na nic się nie ...** it's no use; ~wka f (-i; G -wek) gr. attribute

przydept|ywać (-uję) ⟨~ać⟩ v/t. tread, step (on s.th.)

przydługi F longish; lengthy

przydo|mek m (-mka; -mki) nickname; ~mowy adjacent (to the house)

przydrożny wayside

przydu|szać (-am) ⟨~sić⟩ v/t. smother; suppress; (ciężarem) press down

przyduży F somewhat too large

przydzi|ał m allowance; ration; (dokument) order of allocation; ~elać (-am) ⟨~elić⟩ allocate; assign

przyganiać (D) reprimand, rebuke

przygar|biony stooping; → garbić się; ~niać (-am) ⟨~nąć⟩ take in one's arms, (dać przytułek) take in, take under one's roof; **~nąć się do kogoś** nestle close to s.o.

przy|gasać (-am) ⟨~gasnąć⟩ ogień: going out; ~gaszać (-am) ⟨~gasić⟩ stifle; fig. dim, turn down; ~glądać się (-am) (D) watch, observe; ~gładzać (-am) ⟨~gładzić⟩ smooth

przygłu|chy hard of hearing; ~szać (-am) ⟨~szyć⟩ muffle; stifle, smother

przygnębi|ać (-am) ⟨~ić⟩ depress; ~ający depressing; ~enie n (-a; 0) depression; ~ony depressed

przy|gniatać (-am) ⟨~gnieść⟩ crush, squash; overwhelm; → **przyduszać, przytłaczać;** ~gniatający większość overwhelming; cisza oppressive

przygod|a f (-y) adventure; **~a miłosna** love affair; ~ny accidental, chance; ~owy adventure

przygotow|ać pf. → przygotowywać; ~anie n preparation; ~awczy preparatory; ~ywać (-wuję) prepare; **~ywać się (do** G) get ready (for); → **przyrządzać**

przy|graniczny border; ~gruby F thickish; człowiek stoutish; ~grywka f (-i; G -wek) prelude (też fig.); ~grzewać (-am) ⟨~grzać⟩ v/t. warm up; v/i. słońce: swelter

przyimek m (-mka; -mki) preposition

przyjaciel m (-a; -e, -ciół, -ciołom, -ciółmi, -ciołach) friend; ~ski friendly; **~sko, po ~sku** in a friendly manner

przyjaciółka f (-i; G -łek) (girl)friend

przyjazd m (-u; -y) arrival

przyja|zny friendly; ~źnić się (-ę, -nij!) be friends (**z** I with); ~źń f (-źni; -źnie) friendship

przy|jąć pf. (-jmę) → przyjmować; ~jechać pf. → przyjeżdżać

przyjemn|ie adv. pleasantly; ~ość f (-ści) pleasure; ~y pleasant; (miły) nice; **~ej zabawy!** have a good time!

przyje|zdny visiting; **dla ~zdnych** for visitors; ~żdżać (-am) arrive, come

przyję|cie n (-a) acceptance; reception; party; (gości) reception; (do szkoły itp.) admission; (do pracy) engagement; ~ty established

przyjmować (-uję) v/t. accept; admit; pokarm, lek take; pracownika engage; gościa, interesanta receive; **~ coś na siebie** undertake sth.; **~ do wiadomości** take note of; v/i. receive; **~ się moda:** catch on; roślina: take root; fig. take on, become generally accepted

przyj|rzeć się pf. (-ę, -rzyj!) → **przyglądać się;** ~ście n (-a) coming, arrival; **~ście do zdrowia** recovery; ~ść pf. → **przychodzić**

przykaz|anie n rel. commandment; ~ywać (-uję) ⟨~ać⟩ tell, enjoin

przyklas|kiwać (-uję) ⟨~nąć⟩ (D) applaud, praise

przykle|jać (-am) ⟨~ić⟩ stick

przyklęknąć pf. bend the knee

przykład m (-u; -y) example; **na ~** for example, for instance; **iść za ~em, brać ~** follow s.o.'s example; ~ać (-am) (**do** G) put s.th. (against); ~ny exemplary; ~owo for example, for instance; ~owy hypothetical, exemplary

przykręc|ać (-am) ⟨~ić⟩ screw in; screw; gaz itp. turn down

przykro adv.: **~ mi** I'm sorry; ~ść f (-ści) distress; unpleasantness; **sprawić ~ść** distress; annoy; **z ~ścią coś robić** regret to do s.th.

przykrótki F shortish

przykry unpleasant, nasty; *misja itp.* awkward; *wspomnienia itp.* bad; *człowiek* tiresome

przykry|cie n cover(ing); **~wać** ⟨-*am*⟩ ⟨**~ć**⟩ cover (up); **~wać** ⟨**~ć**⟩ **się** be covered; **~wka** f ⟨-i; G -wek⟩ lid, cover

przykrz|yć się ⟨-*ę*⟩: **~y mi się** (*bez G*) I'm longing (for)

przykuc|ać ⟨**~nąć**⟩ squat, crouch

przy|kuwać ⟨-*am*⟩ ⟨**~kuć**⟩ *fig.* rivet; catch; **~latywać** (-*uję*) fly in; *aviat.* arrive; F *fig.* come running; **~lądek** m ⟨-*dka; -dki*⟩ cape; **~lecieć** *pf.* → **przylatywać**

przyleg|ać ⟨-*am*⟩ (*do G*) stick (to *s.th.*); (*stykać się*) border (on *s.th.*); **~ać do siebie** lie close together, meet; **~ły** adjoining; adjacent

przylepi|ać ⟨-*am*⟩ ⟨**~ć**⟩ stick, glue; **~ć się** stick (*do G* to *s.th.*); **~ec** m ⟨-*pca, -pce*⟩ *Brt.* (sticking) plaster, *Am.* Band-Aid TM

przy|leźć *pf.* → **przyłazić**; **~lgnąć** *pf.* (*do G*) cling (to); **~lot** m zo. coming, return; *aviat.* arrival; **~łapywać** (-*uję*) ⟨**~łapać**⟩ catch; **~łapywać się na** (*L*) find o.s. doing s.th.; **~łazić** F come

przyłącz|ać ⟨-*am*⟩ ⟨**~yć**⟩ (*do G*) attach; *electr.* connect; **~yć się** join in; **~enie** n annexation; *electr.* connection; **~eniowy** additive

przyłbica f ⟨-*y; -e*⟩ *hist.* visor

przy|łożyć *pf.* → **przykładać**; **~marzać** [-rz-] ⟨-*am*⟩ ⟨**~marznąć**⟩ freeze; freeze on (*do s.th.*); **~mglony** hazy, misty; **~miarka** f F fitting

przymie|rać ⟨-*am*⟩: **~rać głodem** starve; **~rzać** ⟨-*am*⟩ ⟨**~rzyć**⟩ try on; **~rze** n ⟨-a⟩ alliance

przymilny cajoling, ingratiating

przymiot m attribute, quality; **~nik** m ⟨-*a; -i*⟩ *gr.* adjective

przy|mknąć *pf.* → **przymykać**; **~mocow(yw)ać** (-[*w*]*uję*) fasten; fix; **~mówka** f ⟨-i; G -wek⟩ gibe; (*aluzja*) hint; **~mrozek** m ⟨-*zka; -zki*⟩ ground frost

przymruż|ać ⟨-*am*⟩ ⟨**~yć**⟩ oczy screw up one's eyes; **z ~eniem oka** with tongue in cheek

przymus m ⟨-*u; 0*⟩ compulsion; **pod ~em, z ~u** under compulsion; *jur.* under duress; **~ić** (-*szę*) *pf.* → **przymu-**

~szać; **~owy** compulsory; **lądowanie ~owe** forced landing

przymuszać (-*am*) force *s.o.* (*do G* to)

przymykać (-*am*) cover up; *drzwi, okno* fasten, to set ajar; F *os.* arrest, lock *s.o.* up; **~ oko** *fig.* turn a blind eye (*na A* to *s.th.*)

przyna|glać ⟨-*am*⟩ ⟨**~glić**⟩ rush *s.o.*; **~jmniej** at least

przynależność f membership; **~ pań-stwowa** nationality

przy|nęcać (-*am*) → **nęcić**; **~nęta** f ⟨-*y*⟩ bait; *fig.* decoy; **~nosić** ⟨**~nieść**⟩ bring (*też fig.*); **~obiec(yw)ać** promise; **~padać** ⟨**~paść**⟩ fall (*do G* to); **~paść komuś do gustu** to take s.o.'s fancy

przypad|ek m ⟨-*dku; -dki*⟩ coincidence, chance; *med.* case; *gr.* ⟨-*dka*⟩ case; **~kiem** by chance, by accident; **~kowo** *adv.* accidentally; **~kowy** accidental

przypal|ać ⟨-*am*⟩ ⟨**~ić**⟩ singe; *pieczeń* burn; *papierosa* light; **~ić się** burn

przypas|ywać (-*uję*) ⟨**~ać**⟩ ⟨-*szę*⟩ buckle on; *fartuch* fasten on; **~ać się** fasten one's seat belt

przy|patrywać się (-*uję*) ⟨**~patrzyć się**⟩ → **przyglądać się**; **~pełzać** ⟨**~pełznąć**⟩ creep up, crawl up; **~pędzać** (-*am*) ⟨**~pędzić**⟩ v/t. drive; v/i. run up; **~piąć** *pf.* → **przypinać**; **~piec** *pf.* → **przypiekać**; **~pieczętować** *pf.* seal; *fig.* confirm; **~piekać** (-*am*) v/t. brown; v/i. *słońce*: beat down; **~pierać** (-*am*) press, push (*do G* against); **~pinać** pin, strap; *narty* put on

przypis m ⟨-*u; -y*⟩ note; (*u dołu strony*) footnote; (*na końcu tekstu*) endnote; **~ywać** (-*uję*) ⟨**~ać**⟩ ascribe; attribute

przypłac|ać (-*am*) ⟨**~ić**⟩ *fig.* pay for *s.th.* with *s.th.*

przypły|nąć *pf.* → **przypływać**; **~w** m ⟨-*u; -y*⟩ high tide; **w ~wie** (*G*) in a flash of; **~wać** (-*am*) swim up; *łódź, statek*: arrive, come in

przypo|minać (-*am*) ⟨**~mnieć**⟩ (*być podobnym*) resemble; **~minać** ⟨**~mnieć**⟩ **komuś o czymś** remind s.o. of s.th.; **~minać** ⟨**~mnieć**⟩ **sobie** (*A*) recall; **~minać** ⟨**~mnieć**⟩ **się** come back, (*o potrawie*) lie on s.o.'s stomach; **~mnienie** n ⟨-a⟩ reminder; **~wiastka** f ⟨-i; G -tek⟩ anecdote

przypraw|a f ⟨-*y*⟩ spice, seasoning; **~iać** (-*am*) ⟨**~ić**⟩ *gastr.* spice (up), season;

~iać ⟨~ić⟩ **kogoś o coś** give s.th. to s.o.

przyprostokątna f (-ej; -e) leg (of a right-angled triangle)

przyprowadz|ać (-am) ⟨~ić⟩ → **doprowadzać**

przyprzeć pf. → **przypierać**

przypuszcza|ć fig. suppose; ~ający: **tryb ~ający** conditional; ~alny presumable; ~enie n (-a) presumption, supposition

przy|puścić pf. → **przypuszczać;** ~rastać (-am) increase

przyro|da f (-y) nature; ~dni half-; ~dniczy nature; nauki natural; ~dnik m (-a; -cy) naturalist; ~dzony inborn, innate; ~rosnąć pf. → **przyrastać;** ~st m (-u; -y) increase, growth; ~st naturalny population growth, population rate, birth rate; ~stek m (-stka; -stki) suffix

przyrówn|ywać (-uję) ⟨~ać⟩ compare (**do** G to), equate

przyrzą|d m instrument, device, appliance; ~dzać (-am) ⟨~dzić⟩ prepare

przyrze|c pf. → **przyrzekać;** ~czenie n promise; ~kać (-am) promise

przysadzisty squat

przysądz|ać (-am) ⟨~ić⟩ jur. award

przysiad m knee bend; ~ać sit down; (kucnąć) crouch; ~ać się (**do** G) join s.o.

przy|siąc pf. (→ -siąc) → **przysięgać;** ~siąść pf. → **przysiadać**

przysięg|a f (-i; G -siąg) oath; **pod ~ą** under oath; **składać ~ę** take lub swear an oath; ~ać ⟨~nąć⟩ swear (**na** A by); ~ły sworn; **ława ~łych** zbior. jury

przy|skakiwać (-uję) ⟨~skoczyć⟩ jump up, spring up (**do** G to); ~stać → **przysłać;** ~słaniać (-am) cover up; obscure; lampę shade; ~słona f (-y) aperture; ~słonić pf. (-ę) → **przysłaniać;** ~słowie n (-a; G -słów) proverb; ~słowiowy proverbial; ~słówek m (-wka; -wki) adverb

przysłu|chiwać się (-uję) listen in (to); ~ga f (-i) favo(u)r; ~giwać (-uję): ~**guje mi ...** I am entitled to ...; ~żyć się pf. do s.o. a service

przysmak m delicacy

przysmaż|ać (-am) ⟨~yć⟩ fry, brown

przyspa|rzać (-am) (G) (o troskach itp.) cause s.o. trouble; ~wać pf. (-am) tech. weld on

przyspiesz|ać (-am) ⟨~yć⟩ speed up; accelerate; ~ony accelerated

przyspo|rzyć pf. (-ę) → **przysparzać;** ~sabiać (-am) ⟨~sobić⟩ (-ę) prepare; train; ~**sabiać się do czegoś** prepare o.s. for s.th.; dziecko adopt; ~sobienie n (-a) preparation, training; jur. adoption

przysta|ć pf. → **przystawać¹;** ~nąć pf. → **przystawać²;** ~nek m (-nku; -nki) stop; ~ń f (-ni; -nie, -ni) harbo(u)r, port; (jachtowa) marina; fig. haven; ~wać¹ (zgodzić się) (**na** A); → **przylegać;** (**na** A); **jak ~ło/jak przystoi** as befits s.o./s.th.; ~wać² stop, pause; ~wiać się (**do** G) put s.th. against s.th.; ~wka f (-wki; G -wek) gastr. Brt. starter, hors d'oeuvre; Am. appetizer

przystąpić pf. → **przystępować**

przystęp m (-u; -y) access, approach; ~ny approachable; wykład accessible, clear; cena affordable, moderate; ~ować (-uję) ⟨**do** G⟩ (zaczynać) begin, start; (przyłączyć się) join

przystoi → **przystawać²**

przystojny handsome

przystoso|wanie n adaptation; adjustment; ~w(yw)ać (-[w]uję) adapt s.th. to s.th.; ~**w(yw)ać się** adapt to s.th.

przy|strajać (-am) ⟨~stroić⟩ (I) adorn (with); ~strzygać (-am) ⟨~strzyc⟩ trim; ~suwać ⟨~sunąć⟩ (**do** G) bring s.th. nearer to s.th.; ~suwać ⟨~sunąć⟩ się move closer; ~swajać (-am) ⟨~swoić⟩ (-ję) sobie acquire; learn; metodę adopt; ~syłać (-am) send, send in; ~sypywać (-uję) ⟨~sypać⟩ (I) cover s.th. up (with); ~szkolny school

przyszł|ość f (-ści; 0) future; **w ~ości** in future; ~y future; next; prospective

przy|sztukować pf. tie on; stick on; sew on; nail on; ~szywać (-am) ⟨~szyć⟩ sew (on); ~śnić się pf.: ~**śniło mi się ...** I had a dream about ...; ~spie- → **przyspie-;** ~śrubowywać (-uję) ⟨~śrubować⟩ screw on; ~świecać (-am) słońce: shine; fig. (D) be s.o.'s guiding principle; ~taczać (-am) roll up; (wymienić) quote

przytak|iwać (-uję) ⟨~nąć⟩ (-nę) nod

przytę|piać (-am) ⟨~ić⟩ dull, deaden; ~i(a)ć się deaden, become dull; ~iony słuch, umysł dull; wzrok dim

przytknąć pf. → **przytykać**

przytłacza|ć (-am) ⟨~przytłoczyć⟩ overwhelm; (ciężarem) crush; ~jący fig. overwhelming

przytłumiony muffled;~toczyć pf. → przytaczać

przytomn|ie adv. consciously; (rozsądnie) sensibly;~ość f (-ści; 0) consciousness; ~ość umysłu presence of mind; ~y conscious; (bystry) astute

przy|trafi(a)ć się happen to s.o.; ~trzymywać (-uję) ⟨~trzymać⟩ support, hold; (zatrzymać) hold back

przytu|lać (-am) ⟨~lić⟩ hug, give a hug lub cuddle;~lny cosy, Am. cozy;~łek m (-łku; -łki) shelter

przytwierdz|ać (-am) ⟨~ić⟩ attach, affix; → przytakiwać

przytyk m (-u; -i) hint, allusion;~ać v/t. (do G) put s.th. (against s.th.); v/i. meet, abut

przyucz|ać (-am) ⟨~yć⟩ (kogoś do G) train (s.o. in s.th.)

przywa|lać (-am) ⟨~lić⟩ → przytłaczać

przywara f (-y) vice

przywiąz|anie n fig. attachment; ~ywać (-uję) ⟨~ać⟩ tie, attach; fig. wagę attach importance (to s.th.);~(yw)ać się (do G) become attached (to)

przy|widzieć się pf.: coś ci się przywidziało you must have been seeing things; ~wieść pf. → przywodzić; ~wieźć pf. → przywozić; ~więdnąć pf. wither

przywilej m (-u; -e) privilege

przywitanie n greeting, welcome

przywle|kać (-am) ⟨~c⟩ drag up

przywłaszcz|ać (-am) ⟨~yć⟩ (sobie) appropriate (G); władzę, tytuł usurp

przywo|dzić bring (do G to); → przyprowadzać;~ływać (-uję) ⟨~łać⟩ call; ~zić v/t. bring; (importować) import; ~zowy import

przywódca m (-y; G -ów) leader

przywóz m delivery; (z zagranicy) importation

przywr|acać ⟨~ócić⟩ restore

przywyk|ać (-am) ⟨~nąć⟩ (-ę) get used lub accustomed (do G to)

przyzna|nie n (-a) admission, recognition; ~nie się confession; ~wać (-ję) ⟨~ć⟩ admit, acknowledge; kredyt grant; nagrodę award; tytuł confer; (uznać) acknowledge; ~ć się do winy confess one's guilt, jur. plead guilty

przyzwoi|tość f (-ści; 0) decency; ~ty decent

przyzwycza|jać (-am) ⟨~ić⟩ (-ję) accustom; ~jać ⟨~ić⟩ się get accustomed lub used (do G to);~jenie n (-a) habit; ~jony accustomed (to), used (to)

psa (G) → pies

psalm m (-u; -y) psalm

pseudonim m (-u; -y) pseudonym; (literacki) pen name

psi canine, dog's; ~e życie dog's life; F za ~ grosz dog-cheap

psia|kość!, ~krew! F damnation!; ~rnia f (-i; -e) kennel; F zimno jak w ~rni it's icy cold

psikus (-a; -y) prank

psioczyć F (-czę) gripe (na A about lub at s.o./s.th.)

psisko n (-a) big dog

pso|cić (-cę) ⟨na-⟩ play tricks, be up to mischief;~ta f (-y) → psikus;~tnica f (-y; -e),~tnik m (-a; -cy) prankster

pstrąg m (-a; -i) trout

pstry (-o) gaudy

pstryk|ać (-am) ⟨~nąć⟩ click; ~ać palcami snap one's fingers

psu (DL) → pies; ~ć ⟨po-, ze-⟩ (-ję) break; ruin; nastrój itp. spoil; ~ć ⟨po-, ze-⟩ się break down; (gnić) go bad; pogoda itp.: get worse

psy pl. → pies

psychi|atra m (-y; -rzy, -ów) psychiatrist; ~czny mental; psychic; ~ka f (-i; 0) psyche

psycho|analiza f psychoanalysis; ~log m (-a; -dzy/-owie) psychologist; ~logiczny psychological; ~patyczny psychopathic; ~te'rapia f psychotherapy; ~za f (-y) psychosis

pszczela|rstwo n (-a; 0) bee-keeping; ~rz m (-a; -e) bee-keeper

pszczoła f (-y, G -czół) bee

pszen|ica f (-y; -e) wheat;~iczny, ~ny wheat

pta|ctwo n (-a; 0) zbior. birds, fowl; ~ctwo domowe domestic fowl, poultry;~k m (-a; -i) ptak; widok z lotu ~a bird's eye view; ~si bird('s); ~szek m (-szka; -szki) bird; F Brt. tick, Am. check

ptyś m (-ysia; -ysie) gastr. cream puff

publicz|ność f (-ści; 0) audience, public;~y public; dobro ~e common good; dom ~y brothel

publikować ⟨o-⟩ (-uję) publish
puch m (-u; -y) down; fluff
puchacz m (-a, -e) eagle owl
puchar m (-u; -y) cup
puch|lina f (-y): ~lina wodna med.
 dropsy, hydropsy; ~nąć ⟨s-⟩ swell;
 ~owy down, down-filled
pucołowaty chubby
pucybut m (-a; -ci/-y) shoeblack, boot-
 black
pucz m (-u; -e) coup (d'état)
pudełko n (-a; G -łek) box; ~ od zapałek matchbox
puder m (-dru; -dry) powder; ~niczka f
 (-i; G -czek) (powder) compact
pudło n (-a; G -deł) box; F fig. miss;
 (więzienie) pen; ~wać (-uję) ⟨s-⟩ miss
pudrować ⟨przy-⟩ (-uję) powder
puenta f (-y; G -) punchline
puka|ć (-am) knock; F (strzelać) pop;
 ~nina F f (-y) gun-fire
pukiel m (-kla; -kle) lock
puknięty F nuts, tonto, crazy
pula f (-i; -e) (w kartach) pool, kitty
pularda f (-y) poulard
pulchny ciasto spongy; ciało plump;
 grunt loose
pulower m (-u; -y) pullover, Brt.
 jumper
pulpet m (-a/-u; -y) meat ball
pulpit m (-u; -y) music stand; desk top;
 ~ sterowniczy console
puls m (-u; -y) pulse; ~ować (-uję) puls-
 ate (też fig.)
pulweryzator m (-a; -y) atomizer
pułap m (-u; -y) bud. ceiling (też aviat.,
 fig.)
pułapka f (-i; G -pek) trap (też fig.)
pułk m (-u; -i) regiment
pułkownik m (-a; -cy) colonel
pumeks m (-u; -y) pumice (stone)
punk|t m (-u; -y) point; (programu)
 item; ~t widzenia viewpoint, point of
 view; w dobrym ~cie well-situated; na
 ~cie (G) about; ~t zwrotny turning-
 point; ~towiec m (-wca; -wce) block
 of flats; ~tualny punctual
pupa F f (-y) bottom
pupil m (-a; -e) teacher's pet

purpurowy purplish red
Purym m (idkl.) rel. Purim
purytański puritan; fig. puritanical
pust|ak m (-a; -i) bud. hollow block;
 ~elnia f (-i; -e) hermitage; ~elnik m
 (-a; -cy) hermit; ~ka f (-i; G -tek) empti-
 ness; świecić ~kami be (half-)empty;
 ~kowie n (-a) waste
pusto adv.: było ~ na ulicach the streets
 were deserted; ~słowie n verbosity,
 empty talk; ~szyć ⟨s-⟩ (-ę) ravage
pusty fig. empty, hollow; ~nia f
 (-i; -e) desert; ~nny desert
puszcza f (-y; -e) (primeval) forest
puszczać (-am) v/t. release; let go; →
 w(y)puszczać; liście, korzenie send
 out; maszynę run; latawca fly; v/i. mróz:
 break; oczko: wink; farba: come off;
 ~ się (wyruszać) set out; F (o kobiecie)
 sleep around
pusz|czyk m (-a; -i) tawny owl; ~ek m
 (-szku; -szki) (na policzkach) down;
 (do pudru) powder puff; ~ka f (-i; G
 -szek) Brt. tin, Am. can
puszy|ć ⟨na-⟩ się (-ę) ptak: fluff the
 feathers; człowiek: swagger, give oneself
 airs ~sty fluffy; dywan: nappy; śnieg,
 ciasto: flaky; ogon: furry
puścić pf. (-szczę) → puszczać
puzon m (-u; -y) trombone
pycha f (-y; 0) pride; F ~! yum-yum!
py|kać (-am) puff; ~lić (-lę) dust; bot.
 pollen;
pył m (-u; -y) dust; ~ek m (-łku; -łki)
 speck of dust, mote; bot. pollen
pysk m (-a; -i) mouth, snout, muzzle;
 fig. F mug, gob; ~aty F cheeky; ~ować
 F (-uję) talk back
pyszałkowaty conceited, prancing
pyszn|ić się (-ię, -nij!) boast; ~y proud;
 (smaczny) delicious; (doskonały) excellent
pyta|ć(się) (-am) ask, inquire (o A
 about); ~jący questioning; gr. interrogative; ~jnik m (-a; -i) question mark;
 ~jny gr. interrogative; ~nie n (-a) question
pytlowy: chleb ~ whole meal bread
pyza f (-y) dumpling; ~ty chubby

R

r. *skrót pisany:* **rok** y. (*year*)

raban *m* (*-u; -y*) (*hałas*) din; (*protesty*) fuss

rabarbar *m* (*-u; -y*) *bot.* rhubarb

rabat *m* (*-u; -y*) *econ.* discount; *~a f* (*-y; G -*) flower-bed

rabin *m* (*-a; -i*) *rel.* rabbi

rabować ⟨*ob-, z-*⟩ (*-uję*) rob

rabun|ek *m* (*-nku; -nki*) robbery; *~ko-wy* predatory; *napad ~kowy* robbery

raca *f* (*-y; G -*) flare

rachmistrz *m* accountant

rachować *v/t.* ⟨*ob-*⟩ calculate; ⟨*po-*⟩ add up; *v/i.* (*na A*) count (on)

rachu|ba *f* (*-y; G -*) calculation; *brać w ~bę* take into account; *nie wcho-dzić w ~bę* be out of the question; *stracić ~bę* (*G*) lose count (of); *~nek m* (*-nku; -nki*) calculation; (*do zapła-cenia*) bill; (*konto*) account; *~nki pl. szkoła: Brt.* maths *sg., Am.* math

rachunkow|ość *f* (*-ści; 0*) account-ancy, bookkeeping; *~o adv.* by calcula-tion, mathematically; *~y* arithmetical; *wartość w figures*

racica *f* (*-y; -e, G -*) *zo.* hoof

racj|a *f* (*-i; -e*) reason; (*do jedzenia*) ra-tion; *~a stanu* reasons of state; *mieć ~ę* be right; *nie mieć ~i* be wrong; *nie bez ~i* not without reason; *z jakiej ~i* for what reason?; *z ~i* (*G*) by virtue (of), for reasons (of)

racjona|lizacja *f* (*-i; -e*) rationalization; *~lizować* ⟨*z-*⟩ rationalize; *~lny* rational

racjonować ⟨*z-*⟩ ration

raczej *adv.* rather, fairly

raczkować (*-uję*) *dziecko:* crawl

raczyć (*-ę*) condescend, deign; ⟨*u-*⟩ (*I*) treat o.s. to, help (to); *~* ⟨*u-*⟩ *się* (*I*) treat o.s. to, help o.s. to

rad[1] *m* (*-u; 0*) *chem.* radium

rad[2] *adj.* (*D, Z G*): *być ~* be glad (to); *~(a) bym* I would be glad (to); *~ nie-rad* willy-nilly, nolens volens

rada[1] *adj. f → rad*[2]

rad|a[2] *f* (*-y; G -*) a piece of advice; (*gru-pa ludzi*) council; (*nadzorcza* supervi-sory) board; *pójść za ~ą* (*G*) follow *s.o.'s* advice; *dać sobie ~ę* (*z I*) →

dzić sobie; dawać sobie ~ę bez (*G*) manage without, do without; *na to nie ma ~y* there is nothing one can do about it

radar *m* (*-u; -y*) radar; *~owy* radar

radca *m* (*-y; -y, G -ców*) *hist.* councillor; *~ prawny* legal advisor

radio *n* (*-a, L -w/-o, 0 lub -a*) radio; *~ak-tywność f* radioactivity; *~aktywny* ra-dioactive; *~amator m* radio ham; *~fo-nia f* (*GDL -ii; 0*) radio commun-ication; *~komunikacja f* radio com-munication; *~lokacja f* radio position--finding; *~magnetofon m* radio-cas-sette recorder *lub* player, *~odbiornik m* radio; *~pajęczarz m* (*-a; -e*) radio licence dodger

radio|słuchacz(ka *f*) *m* listener; *~sta-cja f* (*-i; -e*) radio station; *~telefon m* radiotelephone, radiophone; *~tele-gram m* radiotelegram, radiogram; *~terapia f med.* radiotherapy; *~wóz m* radio patrol car; *~wy* radio

radn|a *f* (*-nej; -e*), *~y m* (*-ego; -i*) coun-cillor; *~y miejski* city councillor

rado|sny joyful, happy, joyous; *~ść f* (*-ści; 0*) joy, happiness; *z ~ści* for *lub* with joy; *nie posiadać się z ~ści* be over-joyed; *~śnie adv.* joyfully, happily; *~wać* ⟨*po-, u-*⟩ (*-uję*) gladden, delight; *~wać się* rejoice

radykaln|ie *adv.* radically; *~y* radical

radzi *m-os → rad*[2]

radzić (*-dzę*) (*nad I*) discuss; ⟨*po-*⟩ ad-vise; ⟨*po-, za-*⟩ (*na A*) remedy; *~ so-bie* (*z I*) manage (with), cope (with); *~* ⟨*po-*⟩ *się* (*G*) consult, ask advice

radziecki *hist.* Soviet; *Związek ⚥ So-viet Union*

rafa *f* (*-y; G -*) reef

rafi'neria *f* (*GDL -ii; -e*) refinery

raj *m* (*-u; -e*) paradise; *rel.* Eden

rajd *m* (*-u; -y*) (*turystyczny*) trip, hike; *mot.* rally; *mil.* raid

rajski paradisiacal

rajstopy *f/pl. Brt.* tights *pl., Am.* panty-hose

rak *m* (*-a; -i*) *zo.* crayfish; *med.* cancer; *⚥ znak Zodiaku: Cancer; on(a) jest*

spod znaku ♌**a** he/she is (a) Cancer; **spiec** ~**a** flush, turn as red as a beet-root

rakarz *m* (*-a*; *-e*) dog-catcher

rakiet|a¹ *f* (*-y*; *G -*) (*w tenisie*) racket

rakiet|a² *f* (*-y*; *G -*) rocket; *mil.* missile; ~**a świetlna** flare; ~**ka** *f* (*-i*; *G -tek*) (*w sporcie*) bat; ~**nica** *f* (*- y*; *-e*, *G -*) flare pistol; ~**owy** rocket; missile

rakotwórczy carcinogenic

rakowy crayfish

ram|a *f* (*-y*; *G -*) frame; *fig. tylko* ~**y** *pl.* framework

ramiączko *n* (*-a*; *G -czek*) (shoulder) strap

ramię *n* (*-enia*; *-ona*) arm (*też fig.*, *tech.*); (*bark*) shoulder; ~**ę w ~ę** arm in arm, shoulder to shoulder; **z** ~**enia** (*G*) on behalf (of); **wzruszyć** ~**onami** shrug (one's shoulders)

ramka *f* (*-i*; *G -mek*) frame; (*w formularzu*) box

ramol F *m* (*-a*; *-e*) old geezer

ramowy framework

rampa *f* (*-y*; *G -*) loading platform; → **szlaban**

rana *f* (*-y*; *G -*) (*kłuta* stab) wound

randka F *f* (*-i*; *G -dek*) date

ran|ek *m* (*-nka*; *-nki*) morning; ~**kiem** in the morning

ranga *f* (*-i*; *G -*) rank, status

ran|ić (*-ę*) wound, injure (*też fig.*); *fig.* hurt; ~**iony** wounded; *fig.* hurt

ranking *m* (*-u*; *-i*) rating, ranking; (*lista*) ranking list

ran|ny¹ **1.** wounded; **2.** *m* (*-ego*; *-i*), ~**na** *f* (*-ej*; *-e*, *G -ych*) wounded person, casualty; ~**ni** *pl.* the wounded

ranny² morning

ran|o¹ *adv.* (early) in the morning; **dziś** ~**o** this morning

ran|o² *n* (*-a*; *G -*) morning; **nad** ~**em** in the morning; **od razu z** ~**a** first thing in the morning

raport *m* (*-u*; *-y*) report; ~**ować** ⟨*za-*⟩ (*-uję*) report

rap'sodia (*GDL -ii*; *-e*) rhapsody

rapt|em *adv.* all of a sudden; ~**owny** sudden, unexpected

ras|a *f* (*-y*; *G -*) race; (*psa*) breed; ~**istowski** racist; ~**owy** racial; *pies* pedigree

rat|a *f* (*-y*; *G -*) instal(l)ment; ~**ami**, **na** ~**y** by instal(l)ments; ~**alny**: **sprzedaż**

~**alna** *Brt.* hire purchase (*skrót:* HP), *Am.* instalment plan

ratow|ać ⟨*po-*, *u-*, *wy-*⟩ (*-uję*) save, rescue (*od G* from); *przedmioty* salvage; ~**ać się** escape; ~**niczy** rescue; ~**niczka** *f* (*-i*; *G -czek*), ~**nik** *m* (*-a*; *-cy*) rescuer; (*na plaży itp.*) life-guard

ratun|ek *m* (*-nku*; *0*) rescue, help; ~**ku!** help!; ~**kowy** rescue

ratusz *m* (*-a*; *-e*) town hall

ratyfikować (*-uję*) ratify

raut *m* (*-u*; *-y*) evening party

raz¹ *m* (*-u*; *-y*, *-ów*) blow; (*G/pl. -y*) time; **dwa** ~**y** twice, two times; **dwa** ~**y dwa** two times two; **ile** ~**y** how many times; **jeszcze** ~ once again; ~**po** ~, **za** ~**em** time and again; ~**na zawsze** once and for all; **za każdym** ~**em** every time; **pewnego** ~**u** once upon a time; **tym** ~**em** this time; **w obu** ~**ach** in both cases; **w** ~**ie** (*G*) in case (of); in the event (of); **w każdym** ~**ie** in any case; **w takim** ~**ie** in this case; **w przeciwnym** ~**ie** otherwise; **na przyszły** ~ next time; **na** ~**ie** for the time being; **od** ~**u** at once; *por.* **wypadek**

raz² **1.** *num.* (*idkl.*) one; **2.** *adv.* once; **3.** *cj.*, *part.* ~ ... ~ ... now ...now ...

razem *adv.* together; (*w sumie*) altogether

razić (*-żę*) annoy, make hostile; *światło*: dazzle; (*im*)*pf.* strike, hit; → **rażony**

razowy: chleb ~ *Brt.* wholemeal (*Am.* wholewheat) bread

raźn|ie *adv.* in a lively way; cheerfully; ~**y** lively

rażąc|o *adv.* dazzlingly; *fig.* glaringly; ~**y** *kolor* gaudy, garish; *światło* dazzling; *błąd* glaring

rażony (*I*) *chorobą itp.* stricken (with)

rąb|ać (*-ię*) ⟨*po-*, *na-*⟩ chop; ⟨*wy-*⟩ *las* fell, cut down; F → **rąbnąć**; ~**ek** *m* (*-bka*; *-bki*) hem; ~**nąć** F *v/s.* (*-nę*) *v/t.* clout *s.o.* one; ~**nąć się** F bum o.s., knock o.s.

rą|czka *f* (*-i*; *G -czek*) → **ręka**; (*uchwyt*) handle; → **rękojeść**; ~**k** *G pl.* → **ręka**

rdza *f* (*-y*; *0*) rust (*też bot.*); ~**wy** rusty, rust-colo(u)red

rdzen|iowy *anat.* spinal; *tech.* core; ~**ny** indigenous; *gr.* stem

rdzeń *m* (*-nia*; *-nie*) core (*też tech.*); *anat.* medulla; ~ **kręgowy** spinal cord

rdzewieć ⟨*za-*⟩ (*-wieję*) rust

rekonesans

reagować ⟨za-⟩ (-uję) react, respond (na A to)

reak|cja f (-i; -e) reaction, response; ~cjonista m (-y; -ści), ~cjonistka f (-i; G -tek) reactionary; ~cyjny reactionary; ~tor m (-a; -y) tech. reactor

reali|sta m (-y; -ści), ~stka f (-i; G -tek) realist; ~styczny realistic

realiza|cja f (-i; -e) realization; (projektu itp.) execution; econ. cashing; theat. staging, production; ~tor m (-a; -rzy), ~torka f (-i; G -rek) producer (filmu); ~torem projektu jest ... the project will be executed by ...

rea|lizm m (-u; 0) realism; ~lizować ⟨z-⟩ realize; econ. cash; ~lność f (-ści; 0) reality; ~lny real; genuine

reasekuracja f (-i; -e) reassurance, re-insurance

reasumować ⟨z-⟩ (-uję) summarize, recapitulate

rebus m (-u; -y) rebus

recenzja f (-i; -e) review

recep|cja f (-i; -e) reception; ~cjonista receptionist; ~cyjny reception; **sala ~cyjna** banqueting hall; ~ta f (-y; G -) remedy; med. prescription

recesja f (-i; -e) econ. recession

rechot m (-u; -y) croak; ~tać (-am) croak

recydyw|a f (-y; G -yw) relapse; ~ista m (-y; -ści), ~istka f (-i; -tek) habitual offender

recytować (-uję) recite

red. skrót pisany: **redaktor** ed. (editor); **redakcja** editorial office

redagować ⟨z-⟩ (-uję) edit

redak|cja f (-i; G -e) editing; (pomieszczenie) editorial department; (redaktorzy) editorial staff; ~cyjny editorial; ~tor m (-a; -rzy), ~torka f (-i; G -rek) editor

reduk|cja f (-i; -e) reduction (**personelu** in staff); cutback; ~cja płac wage cut; ~ować ⟨z-⟩ (-uję) reduce; **personel** make redundant

reedukacja f (-i; -e) re-education; (przestępcy) rehabilitation

refektarz m (-a; -e) refectory

refe|rat m (-u; -y) paper; ~rencja f (-i; -e) reference; ~rent m (-a; -ci), -tka f (-i; G -tek) speaker; (urzędnik) clerk; ~rować ⟨z-⟩ (-uję) give a paper (on v/i.)

refleks m (-u; -y) reflex; reflection, re-flexion

reflekt|ant m (-a; -ci), ~antka f (-i; -tek) customer; ~or m (-a; -y) flood light; mot. light; ~ować ⟨z-⟩ (-uję) v/i. (na A) be interested (in)

reform|a f (-y; G -) reform; ~acja f (-i; 0) rel. reformation; ~ować ⟨z-⟩ (-uję) reform

refren m (-u; -y) chorus, refrain

regał m (-u; -y) (set of) shelves pl.

regaty f/pl. (-) regatta

re|generować ⟨z-⟩ (-uję) regenerate (się v/i.); ~gion m (-u; -y) region; ~gionalny regional

reglament|acja f (-i; -e) rationing; ~ować (-uję) ration

regresowy math. regressive

regula|cja f (-i; -e) regulation; adjustment; (zapłacenie) settlement; ~min m (-u; -y) regulations pl.; ~minowy regulation; ~rnie adv. regularly; ~rny regular; ~tor m (-a; -ry) control

regu|lować (-uję) regulate; (na-) adjust, set; (u-) rachunek settle, pay; ~ła f (-y; G -) rule; z ~ły as a rule, usually

rehabilit|acja f (-i; -e) rehabilitation; ~ować ⟨z-⟩ (-uję) rehabilitate

rej: ~ wodzić ~ set the tone

reja f (-ei; -je) naut. yard

rejestr m (-u; -y) register

rejestrac|ja f (-i; -e) registration; (dźwięku itp.) recording; ~yjny: mot. **tablica ~yjna** number plate

rejestrow|ać ⟨za-⟩ (-uję) register (się v/i.); tech. też record; ~y register

rejon m (-u; -y) district, region; ~owy district, regional

rejs m (-u; -y) naut. cruise, voyage; aviat. flight

rekcja f (-i; -e) gr. rection, government

rekin m (-a; -y) zo. shark

reklam|a f (-y; G -) advertisement, F ad; RTV: commercial; ~acja f (-i; -e) complaint; ~ować ⟨za-⟩ (-uję) advertise; lodge a complaint about; ~owy advertising; ~ówka f (-i; G -wek) commercial; (torba) carrier-bag

rekolekcje f/pl. (-i) rel. spiritual exercises pl.

rekomendacja f (-i; -e) recommendation

rekompen|sata f (-y; G -) compensation; ~sować ⟨z-⟩ (-uję) (A) compensate (for)

rekonesans m (-u; -e) reconnaissance

rekonstruować ⟨z-⟩ (-*uję*) reconstruct, rebuild

rekord *m* (-*u*; -*y*) (**świata** world) record; *komp.* record; **bić** ~ beat a record; ~owy record

rekordzist|a *m* (-*y*; -*ści*), ~ka *f* (-*i*; *G* -*tek*) record holder; ~(k)a świata world-record holder

rekreacyjny recreational

rekrut *m* (-*a*; -*ci*) *mil.* recruit, conscript; ~ować (-*uję*) recruit; ~ować się come from

rektor *m* (-*a*; -*rzy*) rector, *Brt.* vice-chancellor, *Am.* president

rekultywacja *f* (-*i*; -*e*) *agr.* land reclamation

rekwiem *n* (*idkl*) *rel., mus.* requiem

rekwirować ⟨za-⟩ (-*uję*) requisition

rekwizyt *m* (-*u*; -*y*) prop

relacj|a *f* (-*i*; -*e*) relation; (**o** *L*) account (of), relation (about); **zdać** ~**ę** (**z** *G*) → relacjonować; ~onować ⟨z-⟩ (-*uję*) relate

relaks *m* (-*u*; *0*) relaxation; ~ować się (-*uję*) relax

relatywn|ie *adv.* relatively; ~y relative

relief *m* (-*u*; -*y*) relief

re'ligi|a *f* (*GDl* -*ii*; -*e*) religion; **nauka** ~**i** religious instruction

religijny religious

re'likwia *f* (*GDl* -*ii*; -*e*) relic

remanent *m* (-*u*; -*y*) stock-taking; (*stan*) stock; ~owy stock-taking

remis *m* (-*u*; -*y*) (*w sporcie*) draw, tie; ~ować (-*uję*) draw, tie; ~owo *adv.* in a draw *lub* tie; ~owy drawn

remiza *f* (-*y*; *G* -) depot; ~ strażacka fire station

remont *m* (-*u*; -*y*) renovation; repair; (re)decoration; ~ować ⟨od-, wy-⟩ (-*uję*) renovate; repair; (re)decorate; ~owy repairing

ren *m* (-*a*; -*y*) *zo.* → renifer

Ren *m* (-*u*; *0*) Rhine

rencist|a *m* (-*y*; -*ści*), ~ka *f* (-*i*; *G* -*tek*) (old-age) pensioner

renesans *m* (-*u*; -*y*) renaissance; **2** *hist.* the Renaissance

renifer *m* (-*a*; -*y*) *zo.* reindeer

renom|a *f* (-*y*) renown; ~owany renowned

renowacja *f* (-*i*; -*e*) renovation, redecoration

renta *f* (-*y*; *G* -) pension; ~ starcza old-age pension; ~ inwalidzka disability pension; być na rencie receive a pension

rentgen *m* (-*a*; -*y*) (*zdjęcie*) X-ray; (*urządzenie*) X-ray machine; **zrobić** ~ (*G*) X-ray

rentgeno|gram *m* (-*u*; -*y*) x-ray photograph; ~wski x-ray

rentowność *f* (-*ści*) profitability

rentowny profitable

reorganizować ⟨z-⟩ reorganize

repa|tri'acja *f* (-*i*; *0*) repatriation; ~triant *m* (-*a*; -*ci*), ~triantka *f* (-*i*; *G* -*tek*) repatriate

reperacja *f* (-*i*; -*e*) repair

reperować ⟨z-⟩ (-*uję*) repair

repertuar *m* (-*u*; -*y*) repertoire

repet|a *f* (-*y*; *G* -) second helping, F seconds; ~ować (-*uję*) (*w szkole*) repeat; *mil.* cock

replika *f* (-*i*; *G* -) replica; *theat.* cue

repor|taż *m* (-*u*; -*e*) report; ~tażysta *m* (-*y*; -*ści*), ~tażystka *f* (-*i*; *G* -*tek*) reporter, correspondent; ~ter *m* (-*a*; -*rzy*), ~terka *f* (-*i*; *G* -*rek*) reporter, journalist

repres|ja *f* (-*i*; -*e*) repression; ~yjny repressive

reprezent|acja *f* (-*i*; -*e*) representation; (*w sporcie*) selected team; ~acyjny representative; (*elegancki*) imposing; ~ować (-*uję*) represent

reproduk|cja *f* (-*i*; -*e*) reproduction; ~ować (-*uję*) reproduce, copy

reprywatyz|acja *f* (-*i*; -*e*) re-privatization; ~ować (-*uję*) re-privatize

re'publik|a *f* (-*i*; *G* -) republic; ~nin *m* (-*a*; -*nie*, -), ~nka *f* (-*i*; *G* -*nek*) republican; ~ński republican

reputacja *f* (-*i*; -*e*) reputation

resocjaliz|acja *f* (-*i*; *0*) rehabilitation; ~ować (-*uję*) rehabilitate

resor *m* (-*u*; -*y*) *tech.* spring

resort *m* (-*u*; -*y*) department

respekt *m* (-*u*; *0*) respect, deference; ~ować (-*uję*) respect

respirator *m* (-*a*; -*y*) respirator

respondent *m* (-*a*; -*ci*), ~ka *f* (-*i*; *G* -*tek*) respondent

restaura|cja *f* (-*i*; -*e*) restaurant; (*odnowienie*) restoration; ~cyjny restaurant; **wagon** ~cyjny *rail.* dining car; ~tor *m* (-*a*; -*rzy*), ~torka *f* (-*i*; *G* -*rek*) restaurateur

re|staurować ⟨od-⟩ (-*uję*) restore;

~**strukturyzować** (*-uję*) restructure; ~**strykcja** *f* (*-i*; *-e*) restriction

reszka *f* (*-i*): *orzeł czy* ~? heads or tails?

reszt|a *f* (*-y*; *G* -) rest; (*pieniądze*) change; *bez* ~*y* completely, totally; *do* ~*y* completely; ~**ka** *f* (*-i*; *G -tek*) rest; ~**ki** *pl.* remains *pl.*, (*jedzenia*) leftovers *pl.*

retoryczny rhetoric

retransmisja *f* (*-i*; *-e*) *RTV* broadcast, transmission

retuszować (*-uję*) retouch; *fig.* gloss over

reumaty|czny rheumatic; ~**zm** *m* (*-u*; *0*) *med.* rheumatism

rewaloryzacja *f* (*-i*; *-e*) revaluation

rewanż *m* (*-u*; *-e*) revenge; (*w sporcie*) return match *lub* game; ~**ować** ⟨*z-*⟩ *się* (*-uję*) settle accounts (*za A* for); ~**owy** (*w sporcie*) return

rewelacja *f* (*-i*; *-e*) revelation, sensation; ~**yjny** sensational

rewia *f* (*GDL -ii*; *-e*) revue

rewid|ent *m* (*-a*; *-ci*), ~**entka** *f* (*-i*; *-tek*) *econ.* auditor; ~**ować** ⟨*z-*⟩ (*-uję*) *tekst* revise; *bagaż* search; *econ.* audit

rewiowy revue

rewiz|ja *f* (*-i*; *-e*) (*tekstu*) review; ~**ja osobista** body search; *nakaz dokonania* ~**ji** search warrant; ~**jonistyczny** revisionist; ~**yjny** review; *komisja* ~**yjna** committee of auditors

rewizyta *f* (*-y*; *G* -) return visit

rewoluc|ja *f* (*-i*; *-e*) revolution; ~**jonista** *m* (*-y*; *-ści*), ~**jonistka** *f* (*-i*; *-tek*) revolutionary; ~**yjny** revolutionary

rewolwer *m* (*-u*; *-y*) revolver

rezerw|a *f* (*-y*; *G* -) reserve; *mil.*, (*w sporcie*) reserves *pl.*; *mieć/trzymać w* ~*ie* have in reserve; ~**acja** *f* (*-i*; *-e*) reservation, *Brt.* booking; ~**at** *m* (*-u*; *-y*) reserve; (*Indian*) reservation; ~**at przyrody** nature reserve; ~**ować** ⟨*za-*⟩ reserve, *Brt.* book; ~**owy** reserve

rezolu|cja *f* (*-i*; *-e*) resolution; ~**tność** *f* (*-ści*; *0*) resoluteness; ingenuity; ~**tny** resolute; ingenious

rezonans *m* (*-u*; *-e*) resonance; *fig.* response

rezultat *m* (*-u*; *-y*) result

rezurekc|ja *f* (*-i*; *-e*) *rel.* Resurrection service

rezy|dencja *f* (*-i*; *-e*) residence; ~**do-**

wać (*-uję*) reside; ~**gnacja** *f* (*-i*; *-e*) resignation; (*z A*) renunciation; ~**gno-wać** ⟨*z-*⟩ (*-uję*) (*z A*) give up; (*z jedzenia*) do without; (*z planu*) abandon; (*z pracy*) resign (from)

rezyst|ancja *f* (*-i*; *0*) *electr.* resistance; ~**or** *m* (*-a*; *-y*) *electr.* resistor

reż. *skrót pisany: reżyser dir.* (*director*)

reżim *m*, **reżym** *m* (*-u*; *-y*) regime

reżyser *m* (*-a*; *-rzy/-owie*) director; ~**ia** *f* (*GDL -ii*; *0*) direction; ~**ka** *f* (*-i*; *G -rek*) director; F direction; ~**ować** ⟨*wy-*⟩ (*-uję*) direct

rębacz *m* (*-a*; *-e*) *górnictwo*: face--worker

ręce *pl.* → **ręka**

ręczn|y *adv.* manually; by hand; *pisany* ~*ie* handwritten; ~**ik** *m* (*-a*; *-i*) towel; ~**ik kąpielowy** bath towel; ~**y** manual; *bagaż itp.* hand; hand-made; *hamulec* ~**y** *mot.* hand brake; emergency brake

ręczyć ⟨*po-, za-*⟩ (*-ę*) (*za A*) guarantee (for), vouch (for)

ręk|a *f* (*-i*, *L* ręce; *ręce, rąk, rękami/-ko-ma*, *L -kach/-ku*) hand; ~*a w* ~*ę* hand in hand; *za* ~*ę* by the hand; *przecho-dzić z rąk do rąk* change hands; *od* ~*i* on the spot; *pod* ~*ę* arm in arm, with linked arms; *być na* ~*ę* (*D*) be in convenient (for); *mieć pod* ~*ą* have s.th. at hand; *iść na* ~*ę* play ball; *dać/mieć wolną* ~*ę* have carte blanche; *na własną* ~*ę* on one's own initiative, F off one's own bat; *podać/wyciągnąć* ~*ę* stretch a hand; *uścisnąć* ~*ę* shake *s.o.'s* hand; *z pierwszej* (*drugiej*) ~*i* at first (second) hand

rękaw *m* (*-a*; *-y*) sleeve; ~**ica** *f* (*-y*; *-e*), ~**iczka** *f* (*-i*; *G -czek*) glove

rękoczyn *m* (*-u*; *-y*) manhandling; *po-sunąć się do* ~*u* start using one's fists

rękodzieł|o *n* (*-a*; *0*) handicraft; ~*a pl.* arts and crafts *pl.*

rękoj|eść *f* (*-ści*; *-e*) handle; (*łopaty*) stick; ~**mia** *f* (*-i*; *-e*) guarantee, security; ~**pis** *m* (*-u*; *-y*) manuscript

ring *m* (*-u*; *-i*) *sport*: ring; ~**owy** ring

r-k *skrót pisany: rachunek inv.* (*invoice*)

robactwo *n* (*-a*; *G* -) *zbior.* vermin

robacz|ek *m* (*-czka*; *-czki*) → **robak**; ~**ek świętojański** glow-worm; ~**kowy** *biol.* vermiform; *wyrostek* ~**kowy** *anat.* appendix; ~**ywy** worm-eaten

robak *m* (*-a*; *-i*) worm; F insect

rober *m* (-bra; -bry) rubber

robić ⟨z-⟩ (-ę, rób!) do, make; **co on robi?** what is he doing?; **co ~** (**z I**) what to do (with); **~ się** become, get; *nieos.* it is getting (**ciemno** dark; **gorąco** hot); **F już się robi!** will do!

robiony *fig.* artificial; forced

robocizna *f* (-y; *0*) labo(u)r; (*koszt pracy też*) wage costs *pl.*

roboczy labo(u)r; working; **siła ~a** labo(u)r force; **dzień ~y** work day

robot *m* (-a; -y) robot; **~ kuchenny** food-processor; **~a** *f* (-y; *G* robót) work, (*ciężka*) labo(u)r; **krecia ~a** *pej.* subversive activities *pl.*; *zw. pl.* **~y na drodze** men at work; *zw. pl.* **~y przymusowe** forced labo(u)r; **po robocie** after work; **własnej/swojej ~y** homemade; **nie mieć nic do ~y** have nothing to do; **~nica** *f* (-y; -e) worker; **~niczy** working; **~nik** *m* (-a; -cy) worker

robótka *f* (-i; *G* -tek) (**na drutach**) needlework

rockowy *mus.* rock

rocznica *f* (-y; *G* -) anniversary; **setna ~ca** centenary; **~ce** *adv.* annually; **~k** *m* (-a; -i) year; (*wina itp.*) vintage; (*czasopism*) volume; (*książka*) year-book

roczny annual, yearly

roda|czka *f* (-i; *G* -czek), **~k** *m* (-a; -cy) compatriot

rodo|wity indigenous, native; **~wity Polak** a Pole by birth; **~wód** *m* (-wodu; -wody) (*człowieka*) family tree; (*zwierzęcia*) pedigree; **~wy** pedigree; **szlachta ~wa** ancient nobility

rody *pl.* → **ród**

rodzaj *m* (-u; -e) type, kind; *biol.* species; *gr.* genus; *sztuka:* genre; **~ ludzki** humankind, mankind; **coś w ~u** (*G*) s.th. like; **jedyny w swoim ~u** unique; **~nik** *m* (-a; -i) *gr.* article; **~owy** generic; **malarstwo ~owe** genre painting

rodzeństwo *n* (-a; *G* -) brothers and sisters *pl.*; *biol.* siblings *pl.*

rodzi|c *m* (-a; -e) parent; **~ce** *pl.* (-ów) parents *pl.*; **~cielski** parent(al)

rodzić (-dzę, *też* ródź!) ⟨**na-, u-**⟩ give birth to, bear; ⟨**ob-, u-**⟩ *agr.* bear, produce; *fig.* produce, generate; ⟨**na-, u-**⟩ **się** be born

rodzi|my native, indigenous; **~na** *f* (-y; *G* -) family; **ojciec ~ny** paterfamilias; **bez ~ny** no family *lub* dependants;

~nny family; **dom ~nny** (parental) home

rodzony *dziecko, brat itp.* one's own

rodzyn|ek *m* (-nka, -nki), **~ka** *f* (-nki; -nek) raisin

roga|cz *m* (-a; -e) *zo.* deer; *iron.* cuckold; **~l** *m* (-a; -e), **~lik** *m* (-a; -i) croissant; **~tka** *f* (-i; *G* -tek) barrier; bar, toll-house **za ~tkami miasta** outside the city limits; **~ty** horned, antlered

rogi *pl.* → **róg**

rogow|acieć ⟨z-⟩ (-eję) become horny; **~aty** hornlike; **~y** horn

rogoża *f* (-y; -e) bast mat

rogówka *f* (-i; *G* -wek) *anat.* cornea

ro|ić (-ję; rój!) (**o L**) dream (of), fantasize (about); **~ić się** *muchy:* swarm, teem; **~i się** (**od** *G*) it is crawling (with); **~i mu się** (**A**) he fancies; **~i** *pl.* → **rój**

rojny busy, bustling; **na ulicach było ~o** the streets were crowded

rok *m* (-u; *lata*) year; **od ~u** for a year; **raz do ~u** once a year; **z ~u na ~** every year; **~ w ~** year in, year out; → **nowy, lata, przestępny**

rokowa|ć (-uję) *v/i.* negotiate (**o A** about; **z I** with); *v/t.* hope (**sobie** for); **~ć nadzieje** promise well; **~nie** *n* (-a; *G* -ań) *med.* prognosis; *t-ko pl.* **~nia** negotiations *pl.*

rokrocznie *adv.* annually, every year

rola¹ *f* (-i; -e, ról) soil; → **gleba**

rola² *f* (-i; -e, ról) *theat. fig.* role, part

rolada *f* (-y; *G* -) *gastr.* (*mięsna*) roulade

roleta *f* (-y; *G* -) (roller) shutter, (roller) blind

rolka *f* (-i; *G* -lek) roll, reel; **~ papieru** paper roll; **~ nici** thread reel

rolni|ctwo *n* (-a; *0*) agriculture; **~czka** *f* (-i; -czek), **~k** *m* (-a; -cy) farmer; **~czo** *adv.* agriculturally; **~czy** agricultural

rolny agricultural; **gospodarstwo ~e** farm; **produkty** *pl.* **~e** produce

roma|nistyka *f* (-i) (*studia*) French studies *pl.*; (*instytut*) French department **~ński** Romanesque

roman|s *m* (-u; -y) (*literatura, mus., fig.*) romance; (*miłostka*) love affair; **~sik** *m* (-u; -i) flirtation, casual affair; **~tyczny** romantic; *hist.* **~tyczka** *f* (-i; -czek), **~tyk** *m* (-a; -cy) romantic; **~tyzm** *m* (-u; -y) *hist.* Romanticism

romański Romanesque

romb *m* (-u; -y) *math.* diamond, rhombus

rondel *m* (-dla; -dle) pan

rond|o[1] n (-a; G -) (hat) brim; mus. rondo; lit. rondeau

rond|o[2] n (-a; G -) Brt. roundabout, Am. traffic circle

ronić (-ę) lit.: ~ **łzy** shed tears; ⟨**po-**⟩ med. miscarry

rop|a f (-y; 0) med. pus; (naftowa) oil; ~**ieć** (-eję) suppurate, fester; ~**ień** m (-pnia; -pnie) abscess; ~**ny** mot. Diesel; med. purulent

ropucha f (-y; G -) zo. toad

rosa f (-y; 0) dew

Rosja f (-i; 0) Russia; ~**nin** m (-a; -anie, -), ~**nka** f (-i; G -nek) Russian

ros|ły tall, big; ~**nąć** ⟨**u-, wy-**⟩ grow (też fig.); ciasto, ceny: rise

rosochaty forked, branching

ros|ołowy broth; ~**ół** m (-ołu; -oły) stock, broth, clear soup; ~**ół z kury** consommé

rostbef m (-u; -y) roast beef

rosyjs|ki Russian; **mówić po ~ku** speak Russian

roszczenie n (-a; G -eń) claim; **wysunąć ~ ⟨o A⟩** make a claim (for)

rościć (-szczę) claim; ~ **(sobie) prawo (do** G**) lay claim (to); ~ pretensje (do** G**) pretend (to)

roś|lejszy adj. comp. od → **rosły**; ~**lina** f (lekarska, ogrodowa, użytkowa) medicinal, garden, commercially useful) plant; ~**linność** f (-ści; 0) vegetation; flora; ~**linny** plant; ~**linożerny** herbivorous

rota f (-y; G -) **(przysięgi** oath) formula

rotacja f (-i; -e) rotation

rowek m (-wka; -wki) **(na płycie itp.)** groove; furrow; → **rów**

rowe|r m (-ru; -y) bicycle, F bike; **jeździć na ~rze** ride a bike, cycle; ~**rowy** bicycle, bike; ~**rzysta** m (-y; -ści), ~**rzystka** f (-i; -tek) cyclist

rowy pl. → **rów**

roz|bawiony amused; ~**bełtywać** (-uję) → **bełtać**; ~**bestwiony** (wściekły) raging, mad; (nieposłuszny) unruly, wild

rozbi|cie n (-a; G -ić) breaking, crashing, breakage; ~**cie okrętu** shipwreck; **ulec ~ciu** be broken; ~**ć** pf. → **rozbijać**

rozbie|g m (w sporcie) run-up; ~**gać się** ⟨**c się**⟩ tłum: scatter, disperse; take a run-up; ~**gany** oczy restless; ~**gać** (-am) undress **(się** v/i.); aparat take to pieces, dismantle; budynek demol-

ish, take down; ~**ralnia** f (-i; -e) changing-cubicle

rozbieżn|ość f (-ści) divergence, discrepancy; ~**y** divergent, different, differing

rozbijać (-am) break, smash **(się** v/i.; **o** A against); samochód itp. wreck; obóz, namiot set up, pitch; kolano itp. injure; kraj divide up **(na** A into); ~ **bank** break a bank; ~ **się** F move about the world

rozbiór m (-bioru; -biory) analysis; (państwa) partition; ~**ka** f (-i; G -rek) **(domu)** demolition; **(maszyny)** dismantling; ~**kowy** demolition

rozbit|ek m (-tka; -tkowie/-tki) castaway (też fig.); ~**y** broken, smashed

rozbój m robbery; ~**niczka** f (-i; G -czek), ~**nik** m (-a; -cy) robber; ~**nik morski** pirate

rozbraja|ć (-am) disarm (też fig.; **się** v/i.); ~**jąco** adv. disarmingly; ~**jący** disarming

rozbratel m (-tla; -tle) rump steak

rozbro|ić pf. → **rozbrajać**; ~**jenie** n (-a; 0) disarmament

roz|bryzgiwać (-uję) ⟨**~bryzgać, ~bryznąć**⟩ spray; ~**brzmiewać** (-am) ⟨**~brzmieć**⟩ resound, ring out; ~**budowa** f (-y; G -dów) extension; ~**budow(yw)ać** (-[w]uję) extend; ~**budow(yw)ać się** expand; ~**budzać** (-am) → **budzić**; ~**charakteryzow(yw)ać** (-[w]uję) remove make-up; ~**charakteryzow(yw)ać się** remove one's make-up; ~**chmurzać** **się** (-am) ⟨**~chmurzyć się**⟩ clear

roz|chodowy expenditure; ~**chodzić się** disperse; drogi: fork; fig. drift apart; wieść, ciepło: spread; wiadomość: get around; pieniądze: be spent; małżeństwo: break up, split up; ~**chorować się** pf. be taken ill, fall ill; ~**chód** m econ. expenditure; ~**chwiać** pf. set s.th. swinging, work s.th. loose

rozchwyt|ywać (-uję) ⟨**~ać**⟩ buy up; **być ~ywanym** be much sought-after; ~**ywany** in demand

rozchy|botany loose; krzesło itp. rickety, wobbly; ~**lać** (-am) ⟨**~lić**⟩ part **(się** v/i.); ~**lony** parted

rozciąc pf. → **rozcinać**

rozciąg|ać (-am) ⟨**~nąć**⟩ stretch **(się** v/i.); extend **(się** v/i.); sznury put up;

→ **rozpościerać**; ~liwy stretchy, stretch, elastic; ~łość *f* (-ści) extent, extension; **w całej ~łości** completely, to the full extent

rozcieńcz|ać (-*am*) ⟨~**yć**⟩ (-*ę*) dilute, thin, (*wodą*) water down; ~alnik *m* (-*a*; -*i*) thinner

roz|cierać (-*am*) rub; *maść* rub in; *żółtka* beat; crush (**na proch** to a powder); ~cięcie *n* (-*a*; *G* -*ęć*) slit; cut; ~cinać (-*am*) slit, cut

rozcza|pierzać (-*am*) ⟨~**pierzyć**⟩ (-*ę*) spread; ~rowanie *n* (-*a*; *0*) disappointment; ~row(yw)ać (-[*w*]*uję*) disappoint; ~row(yw)ać **się** become disappointed

rozcze|pi(a)ć separate; *tech.* uncouple; ~sywać (-*uję*) ⟨~**czesać**⟩ comb through

roz|członkow(yw)ać (-[*w*]*uję*) dismember; ~czochrany unkempt, dishevel(l)ed

rozczul|ać (-*am*) ⟨~**ić**⟩ (-*lę*) move (**do łez** to tears); ~**ić się nad** melt over; ~ająco *adv.* touchingly; ~ający touching; ~enie *n* (-*a*; *0*) emotion

rozczyn *m* (-*u*; -*y*) *chem.* solution; *gastr.* leaven; ~iać (-*am*) ⟨~**ić**⟩ (-*ę*) *ciasto* mix (**na** *A* for)

rozda|ć *pf.* → **rozdawać**; ~rcie *n* (-*a*; *G* -*rć*) tear; *fig.* inner turmoil; ~wać ⟨**po-**⟩ (*D*) give out (to), give away (to), distribute (to)

rozdąć *pf.* → **rozdymać**

rozdept|ywać (-*uję*) ⟨~**ać**⟩ stamp on, crush; *nowe buty* break in

rozdmuch|iwać (-*uję*) ⟨~**ać**⟩ *ogień* fan; *fig.* blow up, exaggerate

rozdrabniać (-*am*) break into small pieces, fritter; ~ **się** *fig.* try to do too many things at once

rozdrap|ywać (-*uję*) ⟨~**ać**⟩ scratch

rozdrażn|iać (-*am*) ⟨~**ić**⟩ annoy, irritate; ~ienie *n* (-*a*; *G* -*eń*) annoyance, irritation; ~iony annoyed, irritated

roz|drobnić *pf.* (-*ę*, *nij!*) → **rozdrabniać**; ~droże *n* (-*a*; *G* -*y*) crossroads *sg.*; **na ~drożu** *fig.* at the crossroads

rozdwaj|ać (-*am*) ⟨~**oić**⟩ split, divide; ~ajać ⟨~**oić**⟩ **się** split; *droga, konar*: fork; ~ojenie *n* (-*a*; *G* -*eń*) → **jaźń**

roz|dymać (-*am*) *żagiel, ubranie* billow (**się** *v/i.*); *fig.* blow up; ~dział *m* (-*u*; -*y*) (*funduszy itp.*) distribution, alloca-

tion; (*rozdzielenie*) separation (**od** *G* from); (*w książce*) chapter

rozdziawi|ać (-*am*) ⟨~**ć**⟩ (-*ę*) open wide

rozdziel|ać (-*am*) ⟨~**ić**⟩ distribute, allocate; separate; → **dzielić, rozdawać**; ~czy distributive; **tablica ~cza** *tech.* control panel; ~nia *f* (-*i*; -*e*) *electr.* switching station; ~nik *m* (-*a*; -*i*) distribution list; ~ny separate

rozdziera|ć (-*am*) tear, rip (**się** *v/i.*); ~jąco *adv.* piercingly; ~jący *krzyk* piercing; *ból* excruciating

rozdźwięk *m* dissonance, discord

roze|brać *pf.* → **rozbierać**; ~brany undressed; ~drzeć *pf.* → **rozdzierać**; ~gnać *pf.* → **rozganiać**; ~grać *pf.* → **rozgrywać**

rozejm *m* (-*u*; -*y*) truce, armistice

roze|jrzeć się *pf.* → **rozglądać się**; ~jść (-*dę*) *się* (→**-jść**) → **rozchodzić się**; ~pchać, ~pchnąć *pf.* → **rozpychać**

rozerwa|ć *pf.* → **rozrywać**; *fig.* entertain, amuse; ~**ć się** have fun; ~ny *torn*

roze|rżnąć *pf.* → **rozrżynąć**; ~słać *pf.* → **rozsyłać, rozścielać**; ~spany drowsy; ~śmiać się *pf.* laugh, burst into laughter; ~trzeć *pf.* → **rozcierać**; ~wrzeć *pf.* (→ **-wrzeć**) → **rozwierać**

rozezna|nie *n* (-*a*; *0*) knowledge, information; **mieć ~nie w sytuacji** be in the know; ~wać (-*ję*) ⟨~**ć**⟩ distinguish; ~(wa)ć **się** know what's what

rozgałęzi|ać się (-*am*) branch out; ~ęzienie *n* (-*a*; *G* -*eń*) branching; (*dróg*) crossroads *sg.*; ~niać disperse

roz'gar|diasz *m* (-*u*; *0*) mess, confusion; ~niać (-*am*) ⟨~**ać**⟩ move apart; *popiół* rake aside; ~'nięty brainy

roz|ginać (-*am*) ⟨~**giąć**⟩ unbend; bend apart; ~glądać się (-*am*) look around; (**za** *I*) *fig.* look for; ~głaszać (-*am*) publicize, make public

rozgłos *m* (-*u*; *0*) publicity; fame; **sprawa nabrała ~su** it has become public knowledge; **bez ~su** in quiet; ~sić *pf.* → **rozgłaszać**; ~śnia *f* (-*i*; -*e*) broadcasting station; ~śny loud

rozgni|atać (-*am*) ⟨~**eść**⟩ mash; *muchę* squash

rozgniewa|ć *pf.* → **gniewać**; ~ny angry, enraged

roz|gonić *pf.* → **rozganiać**; ~gorączkować się *pf.* become frantic; ~gorączkowany feverish, frantic (*też fig.*)

rozgoryczony embittered, bitter

rozgotować się *pf.* get overcooked

rozgra|biać (*-am*) ⟨*-bić*⟩ plunder; **~miać** (*-am*) crush, rout; **~niczać** (*-am*) ⟨*-niczyć*⟩ demarcate, delimit

rozgromić *pf.* → **rozgramiać**

rozgry|wać (*-am*) *mecz, partię* play; **~wać się** take place; **~wka** *f* (*-i; G -wek*) (*w sporcie*) game; **~wki** *pl.* games *pl.*, tournament; **~zać** ⟨*-źć*⟩ bit in two, crack; *fig.* solve

rozgrzać *pf.* → **rozgrzewać**

rozgrze|bywać (*-uję*)⟨*-bać*⟩rakeaside *lub* up; *fig.* rake up; **~szać** (*-ę*) ⟨*-szyć*⟩ *v/t. rel.* absolve; *fig.* (*z I*) forgive; **~szenie** *n* (*-a; G -eń*) *rel.* absolution; **~wać** (*-am*) (*też sport, mot.*) warm up (**się** *v/i.*), **~wka** *f* (*-i; G -wek*) warm-up

roz|gwiazda *f zo.* starfish; **~hermetyzowanie** *n* (*-a; G -ań*) depressurization; **~hukany** unruly, wild; **~huśtać** *pf.* → **rozkołysać**; **~jarzony** *pred.* ablaze; bright; **~jaśniacz** *m* (*-a; -e*) *chem.* bleach; **~jaśniać** (*-am*)⟨*-jaśnić*⟩ (*-ę; -nij!*) make lighter; lighten; *twarz* light up; *włosy, oczy* brighten (**się** *v/i.*); **~jazd** *m* (*-u; -y*) junction; **być w ~jazdach** travel much; **~jątrzać** *pf.* → **~jątrzyć**; **~jechać** *pf.* → **rozjeżdżać**

rozjem|ca *m* (*-y; G -ów*) arbitrator; **~czy** arbitration; **~czyni** *f* (*-; G -yń*) arbitrator

rozjeżdżać (*-am*) travel much; *coś* knock down; **~ się** part, go one's separate ways

rozjuszony enraged

rozkaz *m* (*-u; -y*) order, command; **być pod ~ami** (*G*) be under *s.o.'s* command; **~ać** *pf.* → **rozkazywać**; **~ująco** *adv.* commandingly; **~ujący** commanding; *tryb* **~ujący** *gr.* imperative; **~ywać** (*-uję*) *v/t.* command, order; *v/i.* be in command

rozkaźnik *m* (*-a; -i*) *gr.* imperative

roz|kiełznać *pf.* (*-am*) unbridle; **~klejać** (*-am*) ⟨*-kleić*⟩ *plakaty* stick up, post; *kopertę* undo, unstick; **~klejać się** come undone; **~kleić się** *fig.* go to pieces; **~klekotany** rickety; **~kloszowany** *suknia* (widely-)flared

rozkład *m* (*-u; -y*) arrangement; **~ jazdy** *Brt.* timetable, *Am.* schedule; **~ lekcji** schedule; *biol.* rot; *chem.* breakdown, disintegration; *fig.* decline, collapse;

math. distribution; **~ać** (*-am*) spread (out), unfold; *gazetę* open up; *łóżko* fold out; *pracę* assign; *maszynę* dismantle; *biol., chem.* decompose; *fig.* undermine; **~ać się** unfold; stretch (*o.s.*) up; (*z I*) spread out; *chem.* break down; *biol. też* decompose, decay; **~any** *łóżko* collapsible

rozkoch|iwać (*-uję*) ⟨*-ać*⟩ make enamo(u)red; inspire with love (**w sztuce** towards art); **~ać się** fall in love

rozkojarzony absent-minded

rozkołysać *pf. v/t.* (*-am*) sway (to and fro) (**się** *v/i.*)

rozkop|ywać (*-uję*) ⟨*-ać*⟩ dig over

rozkosz *f* (*-y; -e*) delight, joy; pleasure; **~e** *pl.* pleasures *pl.*, delights *pl.*; **~ny** delightful; sweet; **~ować się** (*-uję*) (*I*) delight (in), feast (on)

roz|kręcać (*-am*) ⟨*-kręcić*⟩ unscrew; *maszynę* take apart; *fig. gospodarkę itp.* boost up; **~kręcić się** bloom, burgeon; **~krok** *m* straddle; **~kruszać** (*-am*) ⟨*-kruszyć*⟩ **~krwawić** *pf.* make bleed; **~krzewiać** (*-am*) → **krzewić**; **~kupywać** (*-uję*) ⟨*-kupić*⟩ buy up; **~kurczać** (*-am*) ⟨*-kurczyć*⟩ *mięsień* relax; **~kurczowy** *med.* diastolic

rozkwit *m* (*-u; 0*) bloom, flowering, blossoming (*też fig.*); **w pełni ~u** in full bloom; **~ać** (*-am*) ⟨*-nąć*⟩ bloom, flower, blossom

roz|lać *pf.* → **rozlewać**; **~latywać się** (*-uję*) ⟨*-lecieć się*⟩ fall apart, go to pieces; → **rozbijać się**

rozleg|ać się (*-am*) ⟨*rozlec się*⟩ (→ **lec**) ring out; *echo:* resound, reverberate; *protest:* be vociferous; **~le** *adv.* extensively, widely; substantially; **~łość** *f* (*-ści; 0*) spaciousness; extensiveness; **~ły** extensive, wide; substantial; widespread

rozleniwi|ać (*-am*) ⟨*-ć*⟩ make lazy; **~(a)ć się** grow lazy

rozlepi|ać (*-am*) ⟨*-ć*⟩ → **rozklejać**

rozlew *m* (*-u; 0*) filling, (*do butelek itp.*) bottling; **~ krwi** bloodshed; **~ać** (*-am*) *v/t.* spill; *herbatę itp.* pour out; *krew* shed; fill (**do kieliszków** the glasses); **~ać do butelek** bottle; *v/i. rzeka:* overflow; **~ać się** spill

rozleźć się *pf.* → **rozłazić się**

rozlicz|ać (*-am*) ⟨*-yć*⟩ *wydatki* account for; *czek* clear; **~ać** ⟨*-yć*⟩ **się** (*z I*) settle (accounts) (with); ~enie n (-a; G -eń) settlement, clearing

rozlokow(yw)ać (-[w]uję) put up; mil. quarter; ~ się find accommodation

rozlosow(yw)ać (-[w]uję) raffle

rozluźni|ać (-am) ⟨~ć⟩ (-ę, -nij!) loosen; ~ać ⟨~ć⟩ się work o.s. loose; ~ony loosened

rozładow(yw)ać (-[w]uję) unload (się v/i.); ~ napięcie relax the tension

roz|ładunek m (-nku; -nki) unloading; ~łam m (-u; -y) split, division; ~łamywać (-uję) ⟨~łamać⟩ break (się v/i.). break (into pieces); fig. break up; ~łazić się F (po L) spread; ludzie: disperse; buty: fall apart

rozłą|czać (-am) disconnect, part; ~part (się v/i.); ~ka f (-i; G -) separation

rozłoży|ć pf. → rozkładać; ~sty spreading

rozłupywać (-uję) → łupać

rozmach m (-u; 0) swing; fig. drive, energy; ~iwać (-uję) (I) → machać

rozma|czać soak; ~gnesow(yw)ać (-[w]uję) demagnetize

rozmai|cie adv. variously; ~tość f (-ści; 0) diversity, variety; ~tości pl. sundries pl., bits and pieces pl.; ~ty diverse, various

rozmaryn m (-u; -y) bot. rosemary

roz|marzać [-r·z-] v/i. thaw; ~marzony dreamy; ~mawiać speak (o L about); talk (z I to, with); ~miar m (-u; -y) size; dimension

rozmie|niać (-am) ⟨~nić⟩ banknot change; ~szać (-am) pf. mix; ~szczać ⟨po-⟩ (-am) ⟨~ścić⟩ place, situate, position; → rozlokowywać; ~ścić się take place; ~szczenie n (-a; G -eń) placement, situation

rozmięka|ć (-am) v/i. get lub become soft; soften (up); ~czać (-am) ⟨~czyć⟩ v/i. soften; ~nąć pf → rozmiękać

rozmiłowany: być ~m (w L) be in love (with)

rozminąć się pf. → mijać się

rozmnaża|ć (-am) reproduce (się v/i. lub o.s.), bakterie itp. multiply; ~nie n (-a; 0) reproduction

roz|mnożyć się → rozmnażać; ~moczyć pf. → rozmaczać; ~moknąć pf. → rozmiękać; ~montow(yw)ać (-[w]uję) disassemble, take apart; ~mowa f (-y; G -mów) talk, conversation;

~mowy pl. pol. negotiations pl.; tel. call; ~mowny talkative

rozmów|ca m (-y; G -ów), ~czyni f (-i; -e) interlocutor; ~ić się pf. talk (na temat G on, about), come to an understanding; ~nica f (-y; -e) tel. (post office) telephone booth

roz|mrażać (-am) ⟨~mrozić⟩ defrost

rozmyć pf. → rozmywać

rozmy|sł m (-u; -y) deliberation; z ~słem intentionally, deliberately; ~ślać (-am) think, ponder (nad I on); ~ślić się pf. (-lę) change one's mind, think better of; ~ślny deliberate, intentional

rozmywać (-am) undermine and wash away

roznamiętni|ać (-am) ⟨~ć⟩ (-ę, -nij!) incense (się v/i.); ~ać się iron. become amorous; ~ony incensed, enflamed; amorous, passionate

roz|negliżowany undressed; ~niecać (-am) ⟨~niecić⟩ (-cę) kindle (też fig.); fig. provoke; ~nieść pf. → roznosić; ~nosiciel m (-a; -e), ~nosicielka f (-i; G -lek) delivery person; ~nosić (-szę) deliver, distribute; wieści, chorobę itp. spread (się v/i.; po L around); → rozbijać, rozrywać; ~ochocić się (-cę) pf. liven up; (do G) get excited (about); ~ogniony inflamed; fig. heated

rozpacz f (-y; 0) despair; doprowadzić do ~y drive to despair; szaleć z ~y be frantic; ~ać (-am) despair (nad I at, of); ~liwie adv. desperately; ~liwy desperate

rozpad m (-u; 0) disintegration, breakup; ~ać się (-am) disintegrate, break apart lub up, disunite; ~ało się it has begun to rain steadily; ~lina f (-y; G-) crack, crevice

rozpakow(yw)ać (-[w]uję) unpack

rozpal|ać (-am) ⟨~ić⟩ ogień kindle; kominek light; piec, kocioł fire up; fig. arouse, kindle; ~ić się start burning; catch fire

roz|paplać pf. let out, blab; ~parcelow(yw)ać (-[w]uję) divide into plots; ~pasany rampant, unbridled; ~paść się pf. → rozpadać się

rozpatrywać (-uję) ⟨rozpatrzyć⟩ examine, investigate; jur. hear; ~ ⟨rozpatrzyć⟩ się (w L) get acquainted (with)

rozpęd m (-u; 0) momentum, impetus;

nabierać *~u* gain momentum; *~owy*: **koło *~owe*** *tech.* flywheel

rozpędz|ać (*-am*) ⟨*~ić*⟩ *tłum, chmury* disperse, scatter; *pojazd* accelerate, speed up; *fig.* drive away; *~ać* ⟨*~ić*⟩ *się* speed up; (*w sporcie*) take a run-up; *fig.* gain momentum

rozpęt|ywać (*-uję*) ⟨*~ać*⟩ (*-am*) *fig.* foment, stir up; *~ać się* break off

rozpiąć *pf.* → **rozpinać**

rozpie|czętow(yw)ać (*-[w]uję*) unseal; *list* open; *~rać* (*-am*) distend, expand; *tech.* strut; *~rać się* lounge; *~rzchnąć się pf.* (*-nę*) scatter, disperse; *~szczać* (*-am*) ⟨*~ścić*⟩ spoil; *~szczony dziecko* spoiled

rozpiętość *f* (*-ści; 0*) span; *fig.* range, scope

rozpi|jaczony F boozy; *~łow(yw)ać* (*-[w]uję*) saw up; *~nać* (*-am*) undo, unbutton; *płótno itp.* stretch; *~nać się* come undone

rozpis|ywać (*-uję*) ⟨*~ać*⟩ *wybory* call, announce; *~ywać konkurs na coś* open s.th. to competition

rozplą|t|ywać (*-uję*) ⟨*~ać*⟩ disentangle, untangle

rozpleni|ać się (*-am*) ⟨*~ć się*⟩ (*-ę*) multiply

rozpłakać się *pf.* burst into tears

rozpła|szczać (*-am*) → **płaszczyć**; *~tać pf.* (*-am*) slit open, slash open

rozpłodowy foetal; *agr.* breeding

rozpły|wać się ⟨*~nąć się*⟩ melt away

rozpocz|ynać ⟨*~ąć*⟩ start, begin; *~ynać* ⟨*~ąć*⟩ *się* start

rozpo|gadzać (*-am*) ⟨*~godzić*⟩ brighten (*się v/i.*); *~godzenie n* (*-a; G -eń*) (*w pogodzie*) bright period

rozporek *m* (*-rka; -rki*) fly, flies *pl.*

rozporządz|ać (*-am*) ⟨*~ić*⟩ (*nakazywać*) order, decree; (*dysponować*) have at one's disposal; *~enie n* (*-a; G -eń*) order, decree

rozpo|ścierać (*-am*) *papier* spread (*się v/i.*); *~ścierać się* extend, stretch (out); *~wiadać* (*-am*) ⟨*~wiedzieć*⟩ tell; *pogłoski* spread

rozpowszechni|ać (*-am*) ⟨*~ć*⟩ (*-ę, -nij!*) spread (*się v/i.*); (*popularyzować*) popularize; *doktrynę* disseminate; *~enie n* (*-a; 0*) spreading; popularization; dissemination; *~ony* widespread

rozpozna|ć *pf.* → **rozpoznawać**; *~nie**

n (*-a; G -ań*) identification, recognition; *mil.* reconnaissance; *med.* diagnosis; *jur.* examination, cognizance; *~wać* recognize, identify (*się* o.s.); *med.* diagnose; *jur.* examine; *~wczy mil.* reconnaissance

rozpra|szać (*-am*) scatter, disperse (*się v/i.*); *kogoś, uwagę* distract; *~wa f* (*-y; G -*) debate; *jur.* hearing; (*traktat*) treatise, dissertation; (*walka*) fight, struggle; *~wa doktorska* doctoral *lub* PhD dissertation

rozpra|wiać[1] (*-am*) discourse, hold forth (*o L* on, about)

rozpra|wiać[2]Ё się (*-am*) ⟨*~wić się*⟩ (*z I*) settle matters (with); (*zabić*) dispose (of); **szybko się *~wić*** make short shrift (*z I* with)

rozpręż|ać (*-am*) ⟨*~yć*⟩ (*-ę*) *ramiona* strech out; *tech.* expand (*się v/i.*); *~yć się fig.* relax

rozpromieniony *fig.* beaming, radiant

rozpro|stow(yw)ać (*-am*) ⟨*-[w]uję*⟩ *drut itp.* straighten out; *ramiona* stretch out (*się v/i.*); *~szyć pf.* → **rozpraszać**; *~szony* scattered; *ktoś* distracted; *~wadzać* (*-am*) ⟨*~wadzić*⟩ distribute; *farbę* spread; (*rozcieńczać*) thin down, dilute; *posterunki* station

rozpru|wać (*-am*) → **pruć**; *brzuch* slash open; *kasę* rip open

rozprysk|iwać (*-uję*) ⟨*~ać*⟩ spray; **pryskać**

rozprząc (→ *-prząc*) → **rozprzęgać**

rozprzeda(wa)ć → **wyprzedawać**

rozprzestrzeni|ać (*-am*) ⟨*~ć*⟩ → **rozpowszechniać**; *~(a)ć się* spread

rozprzę|gać (*-am*) ⟨*~gnąć*⟩ (*-nę*) *konia* unharness, unhitch; *fig.* disarrange

rozprzężenie *n* (*-a; 0*) *fig.* disorder, confusion; anarchy; *~ obyczajów* dissoluteness

rozpust|a *f* (*-y; 0*) debauchery; *fig.* self-indulgence; *~ny* dissipated, dissolute; *fig.* self-indulgent

rozpuszcz|ać (*-am*) dissolve (*się v/i.*); (*topić*) melt (*się v/i.*); *załogę* dismiss; *plotkę* spread; *dziecko* spoil; *~alnik m* (*-a; -i*) solvent; (*łatwo*) *~alny* soluble; **kawa *~alna*** instant coffee

rozpuścić *pf.* → **rozpuszczać**

rozpy|chać (*-am*) *kieszeń* make baggy; push (*się* one's way); *~lacz m* (*-a; -e*) spray, atomizer; *~lać* (*-am*) ⟨*~lić*⟩ (*-lę*) spray; ~tywać (-uję) ⟨~tać⟩ question; enquire (się v/i.; o A about)

rozrabia|ctwo n (-a; 0) hooliganism, vandalism; ~cz m (-a; -e), ~czka (-i; G -czek) pej. stirrer; ~ć (-am) farbę mix; v/i. stir up trouble

rozrachun|ek m → rozliczenie; ~ek z przeszłością getting over the past; ~kowy econ. clearing

rozra|dowany overjoyed; ~dzać się (-am) multiply; ~rastać się (-am) increase, grow

roz|rąbać pf. chop up; ~regulow(yw)ać (-[w]uję) deregulate; adjust wrongly; ~regulow(yw)ać się go out of adjustment; ~robić pf. → rozrabiać; ~rodczy reproductive; ~rodzić się pf. → rozradzać się; ~rosnąć, ~róść się pf. → rozrastać się

rozróżni|ać (-am) ⟨~ć⟩ distinguish

rozruch m start(ing); mot. start-up; ~ próbny test run; t-ko pl. ~y riots pl.; ~owy electric, launching

rozrusz|ać pf. set in motion; cheer up (się v/i.); ~nik m (-a; -i) mot. starter

rozrywk|a (-am) tear (się v/i.); fig. break; → rozerwać; ~ka f (-i; G-wek) entertainment; ~kowy entertainment

rozrze|dzać (-am) ⟨~dzić⟩ (-dzę) thin (down) (się v/i.); ~wniająco adv. pathetically; ~wniający moving, pathetic; ~wnienie (-a; 0) emotion

rozrzu|cać ⟨~cić⟩ scatter; fig. waste

rozrzutn|ość f (-ści; 0) wastefulness, extravagance; ~y wasteful, extravagant

rozrzynać (-am) cut open, slit open

rozsa|da f (-y; G -) agr. seedling; ~dnik m (-a; -i) agr. seed-plot, nursery plot; ~dzać ⟨~dzić⟩ place, seat; uczniów separate; skałę itp. blow up; agr. plant; → sadzić

rozsą|dek m (-dku; 0) reason; zdrowy ~ek common sense; ~ny reasonable, sensible

rozsądz|ać (-am) ⟨~ić⟩ decide (on), arbitrate

rozsi|ewać (-am) ⟨~ać⟩ sow (też fig.); fig. scatter, spread; ~any też scattered over

rozsiodł|ywać (-uję) ⟨~ać⟩ unsaddle

roz|sławiać (-am) glorify, extol; ~smarow(yw)ać (-[w]uję) spread

rozsta|ć się pf. → rozstawać się; ~j m (-u/-a; -e, -ai/-ów) crossroads sg.; ~nie n

(-a; G -ań) parting; ~w m (-u; -y): rozstaw osi mot. wheelbase; ~wiać (-ję) ⟨z I⟩ part (with), part company (with); ~wi(a)ć place; mil. post, station; position (się o.s.); palce spread; ~wienie n (-a; G -eń) ⟨w sporcie⟩ line-up (też mil.); mil. deployment

roz|stępować się (się) ⟨~stąpić się⟩ part, divide; ziemia: open up, split; ~strajać (-am) ⟨~stroić⟩ mus. put out of tune; nerwy upset; ~strój m (-roju; -roje) shattering; ~strój żołądka stomach upset;

rozstrzel|iwać (-uję) ⟨~ać⟩ execute (by firing squad); ~ić print. space out

rozstrzyg|ać (-am) ⟨~nąć⟩ (-nę) decide (też v/i. się; o L on); turn the scales; ~ająco adv. conclusively; ~ający conclusive, final; ~nięcie n (-a; G -ęć) decision

rozsu|nąć pf. → rozsuwać; ~pływać (-uję) ⟨~płać⟩ (-am) untangle, undo, unravel; ~wać part; stół extend; ~wać się kurtyna: go up; → rozstępować się

rozsy|łać (-am) send out; ~pywać (-uję) ⟨~pać⟩ scatter (się v/i.)

rozszarp|ywać (-uję) ⟨~ać⟩ tear apart; ciało itp. tear limb from limb

rozszczep|iać (-am) ⟨~ić⟩ split up; światło disperse; atom split; ~ialny fissionable; ~ienie n (-a; 0) phys. fission

rozszerz|ać (-am) ⟨~yć⟩ (się) widen; extend (też fig.); źrenice itp. dilate; ~enie n (-a; G -eń) widening; extension

roz|sznurow(yw)ać (-[w]uję) undo, untie; ~szyfrow(yw)ać (-[w]uję) decipher, decode; ~ścielać (-am) spread (się v/i.); ~śmieszać (-am) ⟨~śmieszyć⟩ make s.o. laugh, amuse; ~świetlać (-am) ⟨~świetlić⟩ (-lę) light up; ~świetlać ⟨~świetlić⟩ się brighten

rozta|czać (-am) unfold; zapach give off; fig. display; ~czać opiekę (nad I) take care (of); ~czać się spread, extend; ~piać (-am) melt (się v/i.)

roztargni|enie n (-a; 0) absent-mindedness; przez ~enie absent-mindedly; w ~eniu → przez roztargnienie; ~ony absent-minded, distracted

rozter|ka f (-i; 0) dilemma; w ~ce in a dilemma

roztkliwi|ać (-am) ⟨~ć⟩ (-ę) move, touch; ~(a)ć się be moved; (nad sobą) feel sorry (for o.s.)

roztłuc smash, crush

rozto|cza *n/pl.* (*-y*) *zo.* mite; ~czyć *pf.* → roztaczać; ~pić *pf.* → roztapiać; ~py *m/pl.* (*-ów*) slush; okres ~pów thaw

roz|tratować *pf.* trample all over; ~trąbić *pf.* tell the whole world about; ~trącając ⟨~trącić⟩ push aside

roztropny reasonable, sound

roz|trwonić *pf.* → trwonić; ~trzaskać *pf.* smash, shatter; → rozbijać; ~trząsać (*-am*) *fig.* discuss

roztrzep|any *fig.* absent-minded, distracted; ~ywać (*-uję*) ⟨~ać⟩ włosy ruffle; *gastr.* beat

roz|trzęsiony rickety, wobbly; *fig.* worried, excited; ~twór *m* (*soli* salt) solution

rozum *m* (*-u; -y*) reason; odchodzić od ~u (z G) go out of one's mind (because of); brać na ~ consider; mieć swój ~ have a mind of one's own; ruszyć ~em think hard; uczyć ~u teach *s.o.* a lesson; ~ieć ⟨z-⟩ understand (*się* each other); co przez to ~iesz? what do you mean by that?; to się ~ie samo przez się that goes without saying; ma się ~ieć naturally, of course; ~ny reasonable; wise

rozumow|ać (*-uję*) consider, think; conclude; ~anie *n* (*-a; G -ań*) thinking; reasoning; tok ~ania train of thought; sposób ~ania way of thinking; mental attitude; ~o *adv.* rationally; ~y rational

roz|wadniać (*-am*) water down; ~waga *f* (*-i; 0*) caution, carefulness; brać pod ~wagę take into consideration

rozwal|ać ⟨~ić⟩ destroy, demolish; dom też pull down; ~ić się break down; fall apart; (*na krześle*) lounge

rozwalniający *med.* laxative

rozwałkow(yw)ać (*-[w]uję*) *ciasto* roll out; *fig.* go on about

rozwarty open; kąt ~ *math.* obtuse angle

rozważ|ać (*-am*) ⟨~yć⟩ *fig.* consider; weigh (up); ~ny considerate, thoughtful

rozwesel|ać (*-am*) ⟨~ić⟩ cheer up, brighten up; ~ać ⟨~ić⟩ się brighten; gaz ~ający laughing gas; ~ony cheerful, happy

rozwiać *pf.* → rozwiewać

rozwiąz|ać *pf.* → rozwiązywać; ~alny soluble; ~anie *n* (*-a; G -ań*) solution (*problemu, zadania, zagadki*) solution; (*umowy*) termination, cancellation; (*poród*) de-

livery; ~ły dissipated, licentious; ~ywać (*-uję*) *supeł* undo, untie; *problem* solve; zgromadzenie, firmę dissolve; *por.* rozwiązanie

rozwid|lać się (*-am*) ⟨~lić się⟩ (*-lę*) fork; ~lenie *n* (*-a; G -eń*) forking; ~niać się: ~nia się day is breaking

rozwie|dziony divorced; ~rać (*-am*) open (wide) (*się v/i.*); *ramiona* spread, stretch; ~szać (*-am*) ⟨~sić⟩ (*-szę*) hang up; ~ść *pf.* → rozwodzić; ~wać (*-am*) *v/t.* blow away; *włosy* ruffle; *obawy* dispel; *marzenia* dash; ~wać się mgła: clear, lift; *fig.* vanish, disappear; ~źć *pf.* → rozwozić

rozwi|jać (*-am*) unwind, unfold; *zwój* unroll; *sztandar, parasol* unfurl; *cechy, działalność, plany, kraj itp.* develop; *temat* expand on; ~jać się unfold; *fig.* develop, evolve; ~kływać (*-uję*) ⟨~kłać⟩ (*-am*) unravel (*się v/i.*); ~nąć *pf.* → rozwijać; ~nięty (*w pełni, słabo* fully, poorly) developed

rozwlek|le *adv.* in a lengthy way; ~ły long-winded, lengthy

rozwo|dnić *pf.* (*-ę*) → rozwadniać; ~dnik *m* (*-a; -cy*) divorcé; ~dowy divorce; ~dzić (*-dzę*) divorce; ~dzić się get divorced (*z k-ś* s.o.); dwell (*nad I* on); ~jowy developmental

rozwolnienie *n* (*-a*) *med.* diarrh(o)ea

roz|wozić *towar* deliver (*po domach* home); ~wód *m* (*-odu; -ody*) divorce; ~wódka *f* (*-i; G -dek*) divorcée; ~wój *m* (*-woju; 0*) development; *por.* rozwijać; ~wścieczony enraged; ~wydrzony impertinent; ~złoszczony furious, angry; *por.* złościć

rozzuchwa|lać się (*-am*) ⟨~lić się⟩ (*-lę*) grow insolent

rozża|lony embittered; morose, resentful; ~rzać (*-am*) ⟨~rzyć⟩ enflame; ~rzyć się heat until red-hot

roż|ek *m* (*-żka; -żki*) (*na lody*) cone; ~en *m* (*-żna; -żny*) spit; ~ny: rzut ~ny corner (kick)

ród *m* (*rodu, rody*) family, stock; ona jest rodem z ... she comes from...

róźdżkarz *m* (*-a; -e*) water diviner, water finder

róg *m* (*rogu; rogi*) *biol.* horn; (*kąt, zbieg ulic*) corner; *mus.* horn, zwł. French horn; w/na rogu on/at the corner; za rogiem round the corner

rój m (roju; roje) swarm

róść → **rosnąć**

rów m (rowu; rowy) ditch; (oceaniczny) trench

rówie|śnica f (-y; G -), **~śnik** m (-a; -cy) one's contemporary; **jest moim ~śnikiem** he is my age

rów|nać (-am) ⟨**wy-**⟩ level; (straighten (out)); ⟨**z-**⟩ (**z I**) make similar (to), bring into line (with); **~ać się** mil. dress ranks, line up; equal; match; math. **~a się** equals, is; **~anie** n (-a; G -ań) math. equation; **~ia** f (-i; -e, -i) tech. plane; **na ~i** (**z I**) on a par (with); **~ie** adv. equally; just as; exactly (the same); **~ież** adv. also, too, as well

równi|k m (-a; -i) equator; **~kowy** equatorial; **~na** f (-y; G -) plain, lowland

równo adv. evenly, equally; **~boczny** math. equilateral; **~brzmiący** identical; **~czesny** simultaneous, coincidental; **~legły** parallel; **~leżnik** m (-a; -i) parallel; **~mierny** even, regular; **~prawny** with equal rights; **~ramienny** math. isosceles; **~rzędny** of the same value; chem. equivalent; fig. equal

równość|ć f (-ści; 0) equality; **znak ~ci** equals sign

równo|uprawnienie n equality, equal rights pl.; **~waga** f balance (też fig.); **wyprowadzić z ~wagi** throw off balance; **~wartościowy** of the same value; **~ważyć** ⟨**z-**⟩ (-ę) balance (**się** out); equate, equalize; **~ważna** f (-i; -e) (w sporcie) balance beam; **~ważnik** m (-a; -i) equivalent; **~znaczny** synonymous

równy (gładki) even, smooth; (płaski) level, flat; (prosty) straight; oddech, krok regular, even; (spokojny) balanced; F kwota round; (jednakowy) (D, **z I**) equal (to); gr. **stopień ~** positive; **w ~m wieku** of the same age

rózga f (-i; G -z[e]g) rod, cane

róż m (-u; -e) rouge, pink

róża f (-y; G -) rose; **~niec** m (-ńca; -ńce) rel. rosary; **~ny** rosy, rose

różdżka f (-i; G -dżek) divining rod; **~ czarodziejska** magic wand

róż|nica f (-y; G -) difference (też math.); **~cować** (-uję) differentiate; **~czkowy:** math. **rachunek ~czkowy** differential calculus; **~ć** (-ę; -nij/) differ (**się** v/i.; I, **pod względem** G in; **od** G

from); **~e** adv. differently

różno|barwny multicolo(u)red; **~językowy** multilingual; **~raki → ~rodny** (-ko) adv. in a multifarious way; **~rodny** multifarious, diverse; **~ść** f (0) diversity; zwł. pl. (różne) all sorts

różny → rozmaity; (odmienny) different (**od** G from)

różow|ić ⟨**za-**⟩ (-ę) become pink lub rosy; **~ić** ⟨**za-**⟩ **się → ~ieć** ⟨**po-**⟩ (-eję) become pink lub rosy; **~o** adv. fig. in an optimistic way; **~y** pink; wino, fig. rosy

różyczka (-i; 0) med. German measles sg.

RP skrót pisany: **Rzeczpospolita Polska** Republic of Poland

RPA skrót pisany: **Republika Południowej Afryki** Republic of South Africa

rtęć f (-ci; 0) chem. mercury

rubaszny ribald, bawdy

rubin m (-u; -y) ruby; **~owy** ruby

rubryka f (-i; G -) column

ruch m (-u; -y) movement (też fig., pol.); (statku, ręki) motion; (drogowy) traffic; (w grach) move; (maszyny) operation; **bez ~u** motionless; **wprawić w ~** set in motion; **zażywać ~u** exercise

ruchliw|ość f (-ści; 0) mobility; **~ie** adv. busily; restlessly; **~y** busy; (bez przerwy) restless

rucho|mo adv. movably; movingly; **~mości** f/pl. jur. movables pl.; **~my** movable; moving

ruda f (-y; G -) (**żelaza** iron) ore

rudera f (-y; G -) hovel, dump

rudobrody with a red beard, red-bearded

rudowiec m (-wca; -wce) naut. ore carrier

rudy red

rudzik m (-a; -i) zo. robin

ruf|a f (-y; G -) naut. stern; **na ~ie** astern, aft

rugować ⟨**wy-**⟩ (-uję) drive out; oust

ru'ina f (-y; G -) ruin

rujnować ⟨**z-**⟩ (-uję) ruin (**się** o.s.)

rulet|a f (-y; G -), **~ka** f (-i; G -tek) roulette; **~ka** też tech. measuring tape

rulon m (-u; -y) roll

rum m (-u; -y) rum

rumian|ek m (-nku; -nki) bot. camomile, chamomile; **~y** ruddy

rumie|nić gastr. ⟨**ob-, przy-**⟩ brown; **~nić** ⟨**za-**⟩ **się** blush, flush; **~niec** m (-ńca; -ńce) blush, flush; **nabrać**

~ńców gain colo(u)r; *fig.* take shape

rumor *m* (*-u;* *-y*) racket, din

rumowisko *n* (*-a; G -*) debris

rumsztyk *m* (*-u; -i*) *gastr.* rump steak

Rumu|nia *f* (*-ii; 0*) Romania; **~n** *m* (*-a; -i*), **~nka** *f* (*-i; G -nek*) Romanian; **2ński** Romanian; **mówić po 2ńsku** speak Romanian

runąć *pf.* (*-nę, -ń!*) fall, collapse; *plany:* fail

runda *f* (*-y; G -*) (*w sporcie*) round, bout

rupieciarnia *f* (*-i; -e*) junk-room

rupiecie *m/pl.* (*-ci*) junk

rur|a *f* (*-y; G -*) pipe; **~ka** *f* (*-i; G -rek*) tube; **~ka do picia** straw

ruroc iąg *m* pipeline; **~ gazowy** gas pipe

rusałka *f* (*-i; G -łek*) nymph

ruski F Russian

rusy|cystyka *f* (*-i*) (*studia*) Russian studies *pl.*; (*instytut*) Russian department

ruszać (*-am*) *v/t.* move (**ręką** the hand; **się** *v/t.*); touch (*się v/t.*); **pojazd:** pull out; (*w podróż*) set off; *silnik:* start; **~ się** move; stir

ruszt *m* (*-u; -y*) (*pieca*) grate; (*do pieczenia*) grill

rusztowanie *n* (*-a; G -ań*) scaffolding

ruszyć *pf.* → **ruszać; nie ~ palcem** not lift a finger

rutynow|any experienced; **~y** routine

rwać (**~** (*się v/i.*); (**wy-**) tear out; **ząb** pull out; (*ze-*) **plakat** *itp.* tear off, tear down; *kwiaty itp.* pick; *v/i.* *impf.* (*t-ko 3. os.*) ache; **~** (*po-*) **się** break; *fig.* **~ się** (*do G*) be dying (to *bezok.*), be keen (on)

rwący *potok* raging; *ból* stabbing

rwetes *m* (*-u; 0*) hubbub, turmoil

ryb|a *f* (*-y; G -*) *zo.* fish; **gruba ~a** *fig.* big noise; **iść na ~y** go fishing; **2y** *pl.* *znak Zodiaku:* Pisces; **on/ona jest spod znaku 2** he/she is (a) Pisces

ryb|acki fishing; **~aczka** *m* (*-i; G -czek*), fisher; **~aczki** *pl.* (*spodnie*) dungarees *pl.*; **~ak** *m* (*-a; -cy*) fisher; **~ka** *f* (*-i; G -bek*) → **ryba; złota ~ka** goldfish; **~ny** fish

rybołówstwo *n* (*-a; 0*) fishery, fishing

ryc. *skrót pisany:* **rycina** fig. (*figure*)

rycerski knightly; (*też uprzejmy*) chivalrous

rycerz *m* (*-a; -e*) *hist.* knight

rychł|o *adv.* shortly; **~o patrzeć jak** at any moment; **~y** early

rycina *f* (*-y; G -*) figure

rycyna *f* (*-y; 0*) *med.* castor oil

ryczałt *m* (*-u; -y*) flat-rate payment; **~em** by flat-rate payment; **~owy** flat-rate, lump

ryczeć (*-ę, -y*) roar; *syrena:* wail

ry|ć (*-ję, ryj!; rył, ryty*) burrow; *napis* inscribe; **~del** *m* (*-dla; -dle*) spade

rydz *m* (*-a; -e*) *bot.* saffron milk cap

ryg|iel *m* (*-gla; -gle*) bolt; **~lować** (*za-*) (*-uję*) bolt

rygor *m* (*-u; -y*) discipline; *jur.* **pod ~em** (*G*) under the penalty (of); **~ystyczny** rigorous

ryj 1. *m* (*-a; -e*) snout; V mug; **2.** → **ryć**

ryk *m* (*-u; -i*) roar, bellow, yell; **~nąć** *v/s.* (*-nę*) → **ryczeć**

rym *m* (*-u; -y*) rhyme

rymarz *m* (*-a; -e*) leather-worker

rymować (*-uję*) rhyme (**się** *v/s.*)

rynek *m* (*-nku; -nki*) market(place); *econ.* (*krajowy* domestic) market; **wypuścić na ~** launch; **~ papierów wartościowych** stock exchange

rynkowy market

ryn|na *f* (*-y; G -nien*) gutter; drainpipe; **~sztok** *m* (*-u; -i*) gutter

rynsztunek *m* (*-nku; -nki*) gear; *hist.* suit of armo(u)r

rypsowy *włók.* rep

rys. *skrót pisany:* **rysunek** fig. (*figure*)

rys *m* (*-u; -y*) feature; **~ charakteru** trait; **~y twarzy** facial features; **~a** *f* (*-y; G -*) crack; scratch; *fig.* flaw; **~ik** *m* (*-a; -i*) lead

ryso|pis *m* (*-u; -y*) personal description; **~wać** (*na-*) (*-uję*) draw; (*po-*) scratch; **~wać** (*za-*) **się** begin to emerge; (*po-*) become scratched; **~wnica** *f* (*-y; G -*) drawing-board; **~wniczka** *f* (*-i; G -czek*) draughtswoman; **~wnik** *m* (*-a; -cy*) draughtsman

rysun|ek *m* (*-nku; -nki*) (*w ołówku, węglem* pencil, charcoal) drawing; **nauka ~ku** drawing lessons *pl.*; **~ki** *pl. szkoła:* drawing class; **~kowy** drawing; *film* **~kowy** (animated) cartoon

ryś *m* (*-sia; -sie*) *zo.* lynx

rytm *m* (*-u; -y*) rhythm; **~iczny** rhythmic(al)

rytować (*wy-*) engrave

rytualny ritual

rywal *m* (*-a; -e*) rival, competitor; **~izacja** *f* (*-i; -e*) rivalry; competition; **~izo-**

R

wać (-uję) compete (**z** *I* with; **o** *L* for); ~ka *f* (-*i*; *G* -lek) rival, competitor

ryzykancki risky; reckless

ryzyko *n* (-*a*; *0*) risk; ~wać (-uję) risk; ~wny risky

ryż *m* (-*u*; *0*) *bot.*, *gastr.* rice; ~owy rice

ryży → **rudy**

rzadk|i rare; uncommon; infrequent; *płyn, włosy itp.* thin; **z** ~**a** rarely, once in a while; ~**o** *adv.* rarely; uncommonly; thinly; sparsely; ~**o zaludniony** sparsely populated; ~**o kto** hardly anyone; ~ość *f* (-*ści*; *0*) rarity

rzadziej *adv. comp. od* → **rzadko**

rząd[1] *m* (*rzędu*; *rzędy*) line, row; *biol. math.* order; **z rzędu, pod** ~ in a row; in succession; **drugi z rzędu** next; **w pierwszym rzędzie** above all, in the first place; **wydatki rzędu ...** expenses in the order of ...

rząd[2] (-*u*; -*y*) government; ~**y** *pl.* rule, regime; **związek** ~**u** *gr.* agreement, concord; ~**ca** *m* (-*y*; *G* -ów) administrator, manager

rządek *m* (-*dka*; -*dki*) row, line

rzą|dowy government(al); ~**dzić** (-*dzę*) (*I*) govern (*też gr.*); *fig.* order about; ~**dzić się** give the orders

rzec say; **jak się rzekło** as I've said; ~ **można** one can say

rzecz *f* (-*y*) thing; (*sprawa*) matter; ~ **sama przez się zrozumiała** self-evident thing; **ogólnie** ~ **biorąc** in general; (*cała*) ~ **w tym, że** the matter is (that); **ściśle** ~ **biorąc** to be precise; **na** ~ (*G*) in favo(u)r (of); **od** ~**y** irrelevant(ly); **jak** ~**y stoją, jak się** ~ **ma** as things stand (at the moment); **mówić od** ~**y** wander; (**przystąpić**) **do** ~**y** come to the point; **co to ma do** ~**y?** what has that got to do with it?; **niestworzone** ~**y** nonsense

rzeczka *f* (-*i*; *G* -*czek*) → **rzeka**

rzeczni|czka *f* (-*i*; *G* -*czek*), ~**k** *m* (-*a*; -*cy*) (*rządu* government's) spokesperson; ~**k patentowy** patent agent; ~**k praw obywatelskich** ombudsman, ombudswoman

rzeczny river

rzeczo|wnik *m* (-*a*; -*i*) *gr.* noun; ~**wo** *adv.* to the point; ~**wość** *f* (-*ści*; *0*) matter-of-factness; ~**wy** matter-of-fact; businesslike; ~**znawca** *m* (-*y*; *G* -*ców*) expert

rzeczpospolita *f* [-'pOli-] (*rzecz[y]*... '*litej*, ...'*litą itp.*; '*lite*, -'*litych* -*itp.*) republic; **2 Polska** the Republic of Poland

rzeczywist|ość *f* (-*ści*; *0*) reality; **w** ~**ości** in reality; as a matter of fact; ~**y** real; ~**y członek** full member

rzeczywiście *adv.* really

rzednąć ⟨**z**-⟩ (-*nę*, -*nął*/-*dł!*) thin, become thin

rzek|a *f* (-*i*; *G* -) river; *fig.* stream; **w górę** ~**i** upstream

rzek|li, ~**ł**(*a*, -*o*) → **rzec**; ~**omo** *adv.* allegedly; ~**omy** alleged

rzekotka *f* (-*i*; *G* -*tek*) *zo.* tree frog

rzemie|nny leather; ~**ń** *m* (-*nia*; -*nie*) (leather) belt, (leather) strap

rzemieśln|czy craft guild; ~**k** *m* (-*a*; -*cy*) craftsman, tradesman

rzemiosło *n* (-*a*) craft, trade; ~ **artystyczne** arts and crafts *pl.*

rzemyk *m* (-*a*; -*i*) strap

rzep *m* (-*a*; -*y*) burr; (*zapięcie*) *TM* Velcro ; ~**a** *f* (-*y*; *G* -) *bot.* turnip; ~**ak** *m* (-*a*; -*i*) *bot.* rape

rzepka *f* (-*i*; *G* -*pek*) → **rzepa**; *anat.* kneecap

rzesz|a *f* (-*y*; *G* -*e*) throng, crowd; ~**e** *pl.* masses *pl.*; **2a** *hist.* Third Reich

rześk|i fresh; brisk; ~**o** *adv.* briskly

rzetelny upright; credible

rzewny sentimental, mawkish, maudlin

rzeź *f* (-*zi*; -*zie*) slaughter (*też fig.*); **bydło na** ~ animals for slaughter

rzeźba *f* (-*y*; *G* -) (**w brązie** bronze) sculpture; *geol.* relief

rzeźbi|arka *f* (-*i*; *G* -*rek*) sculptor; ~**arstwo** *n* (-*a*; *0*) sculpture; ~**arz** *m* (-*a*; -*e*) sculptor; ~**ć** ⟨**wy**-⟩ (-*bię*) sculpture, sculpt

rzeźni|a *f* (-*i*; -*e*) slaughterhouse, abattoir; ~**k** *m* (-*a*; -*cy*) butcher

rzeźwi|ąco *adv.*, ~**ć** (-*ę*) → **orzeźwiać**; ~**y** (-*wo adv.*) → **raźny, rześki**

rzeżączka *f* (-*i*; *0*) gonorrh(o)ea

rzęd|na *f* (-*nej*; -*ne*) *math.* ordinate; ~**owy: siew** ~**owy** drilling; **silnik** ~**owy** in-line engine; ~**y** *pl.* → **rząd**[1]

rzęsa *f* (-*y*; *G* -) eyelash

rzęsist|ek *m* (-*tka*; -*tki*) *med.* trichomonad; ~**y** *deszcz* heavy; *brawa* thunderous; ~**e łzy** a flood of tears

rzęsiście *adv.* heavily; thunderously

rzężenie *n* (-*a*; *G* -*eń*) *med.* death-rattle

rznąć → **rżnąć**

rzodkiew f (-kwi; -kwie), ~ka f (-i; G -wek) radish

rzuc|ać (-am) ⟨~**ić**⟩ (-cę) v/t. throw (też fig.); → **ciskać**; dom abandon; palenie give up; uwagę drop; kogoś walk out on; ~**ać** ⟨~**ić**⟩ **się** (**na** A) fall (on), pounce (on); (**do** G) rush (to bezok.); ~**ać się do ucieczki** take (to) flight; ~**ać się na szyję** fling one's arms around s.o.'s neck; ~**ać się w oczy** stand out

rzut m (-u; -y) throw (też sport); math., tech. projection; ~ **karny** penalty; **na pierwszy** ~ **oka** at first glance; (w piłce nożnej) ~ **rożny** corner (kick); ~ **wolny**

free kick; ~**ki** dynamic, go-ahead; enterprising; ~**kość** f (-ści; 0) spirit of enterprise; ~**nik** m (-a; -i) projector; ~**ować** (-uję) project

rzygać (-am) V puke

rzym. kat. skrót pisany: **rzymskokatolicki** RC (Roman Catholic)

Rzym m (-u; 0) Rome; **~ianin** m (-a; -anie, -), **~ianka** f (-i; G -nek) Roman; **2ski** Roman; **2skokatolicki** Roman Catholic

rżeć (-ę, -y) neigh

rżnąć (im)pf (-nę) saw; cut; bydło slaughter; (grać) blare out; V kogoś screw; ~ **w karty** play cards

rżysko n (-a) stubble

S

s skrót pisany: **strona** p. (page); **siostra** s. (sister); **sekunda** s (second)

sabot|aż m (-u; -e) sabotage, subversion; ~**ażysta** m (-y; -ści, -ów), ~**ka** f (-i; G -tek) saboteur; ~**ować** (-uję) sabotage

sacharyna f (-y; 0) saccharine

sad m (-u; -y) orchard

sadło n (-a; 0) fat

sadowić się ⟨**u- się**⟩ (-ę, -ów!) settle (o.s.)

sadownictwo n (-a; 0) fruit-growing

sadyst|a m (-y; -ści), ~**ka** f (-i; G -tek) sadist; ~**yczny** sadistic

sadza f (-y; -e) soot

sadz|ać (-am) seat, put; ~**awka** f (-i; G -wek) pond; ~**ić** ⟨**po-**⟩ (-dzę) agr. plant; ~**onka** f (-i; G -nek) seedling; ~**ony**: gastr. **jajko ~one** fried egg

sadź f (-dzi; 0) hoarfrost, white frost

sakiewka f (-i; G -wek) purse

sakrament m (-u; -y) rel. sacrament; **ostatnie ~y** extreme unction

saksofon m (-u; -y) mus. saxophone

saksoński Saxon

sala f (-i; -e) room, hall; (w szpitalu) ward; ~ **gimnastyczna** gym(nasium); ~ **operacyjna** Brt. operating theatre, Am. operating room

salaterka f (-i; G -rek) salad-bowl

salceson m (-u; -y) gastr. Brt. brawn, Am. head cheese

saldo n (-a) balance

saletra f (-y; G -) chem. Brt. saltpetre, Am. saltpeter

salomonowy Solomon's; **wyrok ~** a judgement of Solomon

salon m (-u; -y) drawing-room; (w hotelu) salon (też fryzjerski itp.); (ze sprzętem) showroom; ~**owy** drawing-room

salowa f (-ej; -e) ward maid

salutować ⟨**za-**⟩ (-uję) salute

salwa f (-y; G -) salvo, volley; (śmiechu) peal, burst

sałat|a f (-y; G -) bot., gastr. (**głowiasta** head) lettuce; ~**ka** f (-i; G -tek) (**śledziowa, jarzynowa** herring, vegetable) salad

sam 1. pron., oneself; m himself, ~**a** f herself; ~**o** n itself, ~**e** pl., ~**i** m-os themselves; (samotny) alone; (bez pomocy) by himself etc.; ~ **sobie** to himself etc.; ~ **w sobie** in itself; as such; ~**jeden** all alone; **do ~ej góry** to the very top; **nad ~ym brzegiem** just on the shore; ~**e fakty** only the facts; **z ~ego rana** first thing in the morning; **w ~ą porę** just in time; **ten ~, ta ~a, to ~o** the same; **tym ~ym** by the same token; ~ **na** ~ in private; n (idkl.) tête-à-tête; → **tak, tyle**, **2.** m (-u; -y) self-service shop

sami|ca f (-y; -e, G -), ~**czka** f (-i; G -czek) zo. female; w złoż. she-; ~**ec** m (-mca; -mce) zo. male; w złoż. hesamobój|ca *m* (*-y*; *G -ców*) suicide; ~czo *adv.* suicidally; ~czyni *f* (*-yń*; *-ynie*) suicide; ~czy suicidal; **gol ~czy** own goal; ~stwo *n* (*-a*; *G* -) suicide

samo|chodowy (motor)car, automobile; motoring; ~chód *m* (*-chodu*; *-chody*) *mot.* car, *zwł. Am.* automobile; **~chodem** by car; ~chwalstwo *n* (*-a*; *0*) self-praise; ~czynny automatic; ~dział *m* (*-u*; *-y*) homespun; ~dzielność *f* (*-ści*; *0*) independency; ~dzielny independent; ~głoska *f* *gr.* vowel; ~gon *m* (*-u*; *0*) *Brt.* poteen, *zwł. Am.* moonshine; ~istny spontaneous; ~krytyczny self-critical; ~krytyka *f* self-criticism; ~kształcenie *n* self-education

samolot *m* (*-u*; *-y*) *aviat. Brt.* (aero)plane, *Am.* (air)plane, aircraft; **~em** by plane; ~owy plane, aircraft

samo|lub *m* (*-a*; *-y/-i*) egoist; ~lubny egoistic, selfish; ~naprowadzający się *mil.* homing; ~obrona *f* self-defence; ~obsługa *f* self-service; ~obsługowy self-service; ~pał *m* (*-u*; *-y*) spring gun; *hist.* arquebus; ~poczucie *n* feeling; ~pomoc *f* self-help, mutual aid; ~przylepny self-adhesive; ~rodny self-generated; self-produced; autogenous

samorząd *m* self-government; local government; ~ny self-governing; independent; ~owy self-governing, local-government

samo|rzutny spontaneous; ~sąd *m* self-administered justice; ~spalenie *n* self-immolation by burning; ~stanowienie *n* (*-a*; *0*) *pol.* self-determination; ~tnica *f* (*-y*; *-e*) solitary, recluse; ~tnie *adv.* alone; ~tnik *m* (*-a*; *-cy*) solitary, recluse; ~tność *f* (*-ści*, *0*) loneliness; solitude; ~tny solitary, lonely; *rodzic* single

samo|uczek *m* (*-czka*; *-czki*) self-study textbook; ~uk *m* (*-a*; *-cy/-ki*) autodidact; **on jest ~ukiem** he is self-taught; ~wola *f* wil(l)fulness; arbitrariness; ~wolny wil(l)ful; arbitrary; ~wystarczalny self-sufficient; *pol.* autarkic; ~wyzwalacz *m* *phot.* delayed-action shutter release; self-timer; ~zachowawczy: **instynkt ~zachowawczy** survival instinct; ~zaparcie *n* self-denial; ~zapłon *m* *tech.* spontaneous ignition

samozwańczy self-assumed, self-styled

sanatorium *n* (*idkl.*; *-a*, *-iów*) sanatorium

sandacz *m* (*-a*; *-e*) *zo.* zander

sandał *m* (*-a*; *-y*) sandal; ~ek *m* (*-łka*; *-łki*) → **sandał**

sandałowy sandal

saneczk|i *pl.* (*-czek*) sledge

sanie *pl.* (*-sań*) sledge; (*konne*) sleigh

sanitar|iusz *m* (*-a*; *-e*) male nurse; *mil.* medical orderly; ~iuszka *f* (*-szki*; *-szek*) *mil.* nurse; ~ka F *f* (*-i*; *G -rek*) ambulance; ~ny sanitary

sankcj|a *f* (*-i*; *-e*) sanction; ~onować (*-uję*) sanction

san|ki *pl.* (*-nek*) sledge, *zwł. Am.* sled; *sport:* toboggan; ~na *f* (*-y*; *0*) sleigh ride

sapać (*-ię*) pant, gasp

saper *m* (*-a*; *-rzy*) *mil.* engineer

sardela *f* (*-i*; *-e*) *zo.* anchovy

sardynka *f* (*-i*; *-nek*) *zo.* sardine

sarkać (*-am*) grumble, complain

sarkastyczny sarcastic

sarn|a *f* (*-y*; *G -ren*) *zo.* deer; ~ina *f* (*-y*; *0*) venison; *gastr.* roast venison

sasanka *f* (*-i*; *G -nek*) *bot.* anemone

saski Saxon

saszetka *f* (*-i*; *G -tek*) sachet

sateli|ta *m* (*-y*; *G -tów*) satellite; ~tarny satellite; **antena ~tarna** satellite dish

satyna *f* (*-y*; *G -*) satin

satynow|any *papier* supercalendered; ~y satin; *fig.* satiny

satyr|a *f* (*-y*; *G -*) satire; ~yczny satirical

satysfakcj|a *f* (*-i*; *0*) satisfaction; gratification; ~onować (*-uję*) satisfy; ~onujący *też* rewarding

są 3. *os. pl. pres.* → **być**

sącz|ek *m* (*-czka*; *-czki*) filter; *tech.*, *med.* drain; ~yć (*-ę*) filter; *napój* sip; ~yć się seep, trickle

sąd *m* (*-u*; *-y*) *jur.* court; (*ocena*) judg(e)ment, verdict; **~ ostateczny** Last Judgement; **♀ Najwyższy** Supreme Court; **podawać do ~u** go to court, sue; **wyrobić sobie ~ (o** *L***)** form an opinion (about); ~ownictwo *n* (*-a*; *0*) jurisdiction; ~ownie *adv.* legally; ~owy judicial; *medycyna* forensic; **w drodze ~owej** through legal action

sądzić (*-dzę*) *v/i.* (*oceniać*) evaluate, judge; have an opinion (**o** *L* about); form an opinion (**po** *L*; **z** *G* by, from); *v/t. jur.* try (**za** *A* for); (*nie*) **sądzę, że** I (don't) think that sąg m (-a/-u; -i) cord

sąsiad m (-a; sąsiedzi, -adów); ~ka f (-i; G -dek) neighbo(u)r; ~ować (-uję) (z I) live next door (to); państwo: border (on)

sąsie|dni neighbo(u)ring; next door (to); ~dzki neighbo(u)rly; mieszkać po ~dzku live next door to; ~dztwo n (-a; 0) neighbo(u)rhood; vicinity

sążnisty very long

scalony obwód integrated

scen|a f (-y; G -) scene; theat., fig. stage; pol. arena; ~ariusz m (-a; -e) script, scenario (też fig.); ~arzysta m (-y; -ści) scriptwriter; ~eria f (GDL -rii; -e) scenery; setting; ~iczny stage

scenograf m (-a; -owie) set designer

sceptyczny sceptic

schab m (-u; -y) gastr. pork loin; ~owy: kotlet ~owy pork chop

schadzka f (-i; G -dzek) date, tryst

schemat m (-u; -y) pattern; (działania) routine; tech. circuit diagram; ~yczny działanie routine; wykres schematic

schlany F blind drunk

schlebiać (-am) flatter

schludn|ie adv. tidily, neatly; ~y tidy, neat

schnąć (-nę, -nął/sechł, schła) dry; roślina: wither; fig. pine away (z G for)

schod|ek m (-dka, -dki) stair, step; ~owy staircase; → klatka; ~y pl. (-ów) stairs pl.; ruchome ~y escalator; zejść po ~ach go down the stairs

schodzić (-dzę) go down, descend; move (na bok aside); get (z drogi out of one's way); farba, skóra: peel; plama: come out; ~ na ląd go ashore; ~ z konia dismount; → zejść; ~ się get together, meet; assemble

scho|rowany emaciated; ~rzenie n (-a; G -eń) disorder; (serca heart) condition

schow|ać pf. → chować; ~ek m (-wka, -wki) → skrytka

schron m (-u; -y) shelter

schroni|ć się pf. → chronić; ~enie n (-a; 0) shelter; ~sko n (-a; G -sk) youth hostel; mountain hut; ~sko dla zwierząt shelter

schrypnięty hoarse

schwy|cić pf. → chwytać; ~tać pf. grab, seize, grasp; catch (na L at)

schy|lać (-am) → chylić; ~łek m (-łku; 0) end(ing); u ~łku at the end; ~łek

życia autumn of one's life; ~łkowy decadent

scysja f (-i; -e) argument, row

scyzoryk m (-a; -i) pocket-knife

seans m (-u; -e) kino: show(ing); presentation; seance

secesyjny: styl ~ Art Nouveau

sedes m (-u; -y) toilet-seat

sedno n (-a; 0) heart (sprawy, rzeczy of the matter); trafić w ~ hit the nail on the head

segreg|ator m (-a; -y) file binder; ~ować ⟨po-⟩ (-uję) sort (out)

sejf m (-u; -y) safe

Sejm m (-u; 0) parl. the Sejm

sekc|iarski sectarian; ~ja f (-i; -e) section; ~ja zwłok med. post-mortem (examination), autopsy

sekr skrót pisany: sekretarz S(ec.) (secretary)

sekre|t m (-u; -y) secret; pod ~tem, w ~cie in secret, confidentially; ~tariat m (-u; -y) secretary's office; ~tarka f (-i; G -rek), secretary; automatyczna ~tarka answering machine; ~tarz m (-a; -e) secretary; ~tny secret

seks m (-u; 0) sex; ~owny sexy; ~ualny sexual

sekt|a f (-y; G -) sect; ~or m (-a; -y) sector

sekund|a f (-y; G -) second; chodzić co do ~y keep perfect time; ~nik m (-a; -i) second hand

Sekwana f (-y; 0) Seine

sekwencja f (-i; -e) sequence

seledyn m (-u; 0) celadon, greyish-green; ~owy celadon, greyish-green

selek|cja f (-i; -e) selection; ~tywność f (-ści; 0) RTV: selectivity

seler m (-a; -y) bot. celeriac; (nać) celery

se|mafor m (-a; -y) rail. semaphore

semestr m (-u; -y) semester, term

semi|narium n (idkl.; -a, -ów) seminar; rel. seminary

sen. skrót pisany: senator Sen. (Senator)

sen m (snu; sny) sleep; (marzenie) dream; kłaść się do snu go to sleep; ujrzeć we śnie see in a dream

sena|cki Senate; ~t m (-u; -y) parl. Senate

senior m (-a; -rzy/-owie), ~ka f (-i; G -rek) senior

sen|ność f (-ści; 0) sleepiness, drowsiness; ~ny sleepy, drowsy

sens m (-u; -y) sense; meaning; z ~em sensibly; co za ~ ... what point there is

...; **bez ~u** meaningless

sensac|ja f (-i; -e) sensation; **~yjny** sensational; **film ~yjny** thriller

sensowny sensible; meaningful

sentencja f (-i; -e) aphorism, maxim; jur. tenor

sentyment m (-u; -y) feeling; sentiment; liking; **~alny** sentimental

separ|acja f (-i; -e) jur. separation; **~atka** f (-i; G -tek) med. isolation room; **~ować** (-uję) separate

seplenić (-ę) lisp

ser m (-a; -y) cheese; **~ topiony** processed cheese; **biały ~** cottage cheese

Serb m (-a; -owie) Serb; **~ia** f (GDL -ii; 0) Serbia; **~ka** f (-i; G -bek) Serb; **2ski** Serbian; **mówić po 2sku** speak Serbian

serc|e n (-a; G -) heart (też fig.); (dzwonu) clapper; **chory na ~e** suffering from a heart condition; **brak ~a** heartlessness; **brać do ~a** take to heart; **przypaść do ~a** grow fond (of); **z całego ~a** whole-heartedly; **w głębi ~a** at heart; **~owy** med. cardiac; romantic

serdeczn|ość f (-ści; 0) kindness; warmth; **~y** kind; warm; **~y palec** ring finger; **~y przyjaciel** bosom friend

serdel|ek m (-lka; -lki) frankfurter; **~owy: kiełbasa ~owa** pork sausage

serduszko f n (-a; G -szek) → **serce**

seria f (GDL -ii; -e) series; (zastrzyków) set; (zastrzyków) course; mil. burst; **~** m (-a; -e) RTV: serial, series

serio: na ~ seriously, in earnest

sernik m (-a; -i) gastr. cheesecake

serwantka f (-i; G -tek) display cabinet

serwatka f (-i; G -tek) whey

serwet|a f (-y; G -) tablecloth; **~ka** f (-i; G -tek) (**bibułkowa** paper) napkin; → **serweta**

serwis m (-u; -y) (**do kawy** coffee) set; (obsługa) service; (w tenisie) serve

serwować (-uję) serve

seryjny serial; mass-produced

sesja f (-i; -e) session

set m (-a; -y) sport: set

seter m (-a; -y) zo. setter

set|ka f (-i; G -tek) hundred; F (w sporcie) hundred Brt. metres, Am. meters; F double vodka 100 Brt. gramme, Am. gram; F pure wool; **~ny** hundredth; **jedna ~na** one hundredth

Seul m (-u; 0) Seoul

sezon m (-u; -y) season

sędzia m (-i[ego], i[emu], -iego, -io!, -ią, i[m]; -owie, -iów) jur. judge; (w sporcie) judge, referee, umpire

sędziowski judicial

sędziwy aged, advanced in years

sęk m (-a; -i) knot; F **w tym ~; że** the snag is; **~aty** gnarled

sęp m (-a; -y) zo. vulture

sfał-, sfas- pf. → **fał-, fas-**

sfer|a f (-y; G -) sphere (też fig.); (w społeczeństwie) class; fig. area; **~yczny** spherical

sfi- pf. → **fi-**

sfor- pf. → **for-**; **~mułowanie** n (-a; G -ań) formulation, wording

sfru- pf. → **fru-**

siać ⟨**po-, za-**⟩ (-eję) sow (też fig.)

siad m (-u; -y) sport: seat, (kucnięcie) squat; **~ać** (-am) sit (down) (**do** G, **przy** I at); aviat. land

siano n (-a; 0) hay; **~kosy** pl. (-ów) hay harvest, haymaking

siarcz|an m (-u; -y) chem. Brt. sulphate, Am. sulfate; **~any** Brt. sulphurous, Am. sulfurous; **~yn** m (-u; -y) Brt. sulphite, Am. sulfite; **~ysty** (mocny) powerful; mróz biting

siark|a f (-i; 0) chem. Brt. sulphur, Am. sulfur; **~owodór** m chem. hydrogen Brt. sulphide, Am. sulfide; **~owy** Brt. sulphur, Am. sulfur

siatk|a f (-i; G -tek) net (też fig.); tech., el. grid; chem. lattice; **~a na zakupy** carrier bag, zwł. string bag; **~ówka** f (-i; G -wek) anat. retina; (w sporcie) volleyball

sią|pić (-ę): **siąpi** it is drizzling; **~ść** pf. → **siadać**

sidła n/pl. (-deł) snare, trap (też fig.)

siebie pron. (GDL **sobie**, A **siebie lub się**, I **sobą**) oneself; each other, one another; **dla/do/od ~** for/to/from oneself; **przy/w sobie** with/in oneself; **po sobie** after oneself; **z sobą** with oneself; **blisko ~** nearby, close at hand; **u ~** at home; **pewny ~** self-assured

siec v/t. chop, hack; deszcz: lash

sieciowy net, network

siecz|ka f (-i; G -czek) agr. chaff (też fig.); fig. jumble; **~na** f (-ej; -e) math. secant; **~ny broń** cutting

sieć f (-ci; -ci) net; (komputerowa itp.) network; (pająka) web

siedem seven; → *666;* ~**dziesiąt** seventy; ~**dziesiąty** seventieth; ~**dziesięcio-** *w złoż.* seventy; ~**nasto-** *w złoż.* seventeen; ~**nasty** seventeenth; ~**naście** seventeen

siedlisko *n (-a; G -)* seat; *fig.* breeding ground, hotbed; *biol.* habitat; ~ **choroby** site of the disease

siedmi|o- *w złoż.* seven; ~**okrotny** sevenfold; seven-times; ~**oletni** seven-year-old; ~**oro,** *u m-os* seven → *666*

siedz|enie *n (-a; G -dzeń)* seat; sitting; F (*pupa*) bottom, behind; ~**iba** *f (-y; G -)* seat; ~**ieć** (*-dzę, -i*) sit (*też fig.*); F (*w więzieniu*) do time

sieka|cz *m (-a; -e)* *anat.* incisor; chopper; ~**ć** ⟨*po-*⟩ (*-am*) chop, hack; → **siec**; **mięso** ~**ne** minced meat

siekiera *f (-y; G -)* ax(e)

sielank|a *f (-i; G -nek)* idyl(l); ~**owy** idyllic

siemię *n (-ienia; 0)* seed

sien|nik *m (-a; -i)* palliasse, *zwł. Am.* paillasse, pallet; ~**ny: katar** ~**ny** hay fever

sień *f (-ni; -nie)* hall-way, entrance-hall

siero|cy orphan; ~**ta** *f/m (-y; G -)* orphan

sierp *m (-a; -y)* sickle; (*cios*) hook; ~**ień** *m (-pnia; -pnie)* August; ~**niowy** August; ~**owy** *m (-ego; -e)* (*w sporcie*) hook

sierść *f (-ści; 0)* fur, coat

sierżant *m (-a; -ci)* *mil.* sergeant

siew *m (-u; -y)* sowing; ~**nik** *m (-a; -i)* *agr.* seeder, seed-drill; ~**ny** seed

się *pron.* oneself; *nieos.* one, *Brt.* you; **on ~ myje** he washes himself; *myj* ~ wash yourself; *jeśli ~ chce* if one *lub Brt.* you want it; *nigdy ~ nie wie* one never knows; → *czasowniki* + **się**

sięg|ać (*-am*) ⟨*-nąć*⟩ (*-nę*) reach (*po A* for; *do G* to); *impf.* reach, extend (*G,* [*aż*] *do G* as far as); *jak okiem* ~**nąć** as far as the eye can see

sik|ać F (*-am*) ⟨*-nąć*⟩ (*-nę*) squirt, spray; F *impf.* pee; ~**awka** *f (-i; G -wek*) fire hose

sikor|(k)a *f (-y; G-),* ~**ka** *f (-i; G -rek)* *zo.* tit

silić się (*-lę*) make an effort, exert o.s.; try (*na A* to be)

siln|ie *adv.* strongly; powerfully; ~**iej(szy)** *adv. (adj.). (comp. od → silnie, silny)* stronger; more powerful; ~**ik**

m (-a; -i) engine; ~**ikowy** engine; ~**y** strong; powerful

silos [s·i-] *m (-a; -y)* *agr., mil.* silo; storage bin; ~**ować** ⟨*za-*⟩ (*-uję*) ensile

siła *f (-y; G -)* (*fizyczna* physical) strength; power; force; violence; *mil. pl.* forces *pl.;* ~**ciężkości** gravity; ~ **dźwięku** volume; ~ **robocza** workforce; ~ **wyższa** act of God; **nabierać sił** recover; **czuć się na** ~**ch** feel up to; *co sił(y)* with all one's strength; *w sile wieku* in one's prime; *siłą* by force; *siłą rzeczy* inevitably; → *opadać, wola;* ~**cz** *m (-a; -e),* ~**czka** *f (-i; G -czek)* athlete

siłownia *f (-i; -e)* *electr.* power station; (*w sporcie*) fitness *Brt.* centre (*Am.* center)

singel *m (-gla; -gle) mus.* single

sini|ak *m (-a; -i),* ~**ec** *m (-ńca; -ńce)* bruise; ~**eć** ⟨*po-*⟩ (*-eję*) go *lub* turn blue

sin|o *w złoż.* blue-; ~**y** *adj. (comp. -ńszy)* blue; livid

siod|ełko *n (-a; G -łek) (roweru itp.)* saddle; ~**ło** *n (-a; G -deł)* saddle; ~**łać** ⟨*o-*⟩ (*-am*) saddle

siorbać (*-ię*) slurp

siost|ra *f (-y; G sióstr)* sister; (*zakonnica*) nun; (*pielęgniarka*) nurse; ~**rzenica** *f (-y; -e, G -)* niece; ~**rzeniec** *m (-ńca; -ńcy)* nephew

siód|emka *f (-i; G -mek)* seven; (*linia itp.*) number seven; *my* seventh; → *666*

sit|ko *n (-a; G -tek) (kuchenne)* strainer; → ~**o** *n (-a; G -)* sieve; ~**owie** *(a; 0) bot.* bulrush

siusiu F: ⟨*z*⟩*robić* ~ pee, wee

siw|ieć ⟨*o-,po-*⟩ (*-eję*) go *Brt.* grey, *Am.* gray; ~**izna** *f (-y; G -) Brt.* grey, *Am.* gray, hair; ~**owłosy** *Brt.* grey-haired, *Am.* gray-haired; ~**y** *Brt.* grey, *Am.* gray

ska, s-ka *skrót pisany:* **spółka** partnership

skafander *m (-dra; -dry)* parka; *Brt.* wind-cheater, *Am.* windbreaker; *astr.* spacesuit; *aviat.* pressure suit; *naut.* diving suit

skaka|ć (*-czę*) jump, leap; *ptak itp.:* hop; F (*do sklepu itp.*) pop; (*do wody*) dive; (*w sporcie*) hurdle; ~**nka** *f (-i; G -nek)* skipping rope; *skakać przez* ~**nkę** skip

skal|a *f (-i; -e, -i/-)* scale (*też fig.*); *w* ~**i 1:100** to a scale of 1:100; *na dużą/ wielką* ~**ę** on a large-scale

skalecz|enie n (-a; G -eń) injury; ~ony injured; ~yć pf. → **kaleczyć**

ska|listy rocky; ~lny rocky

skała f (-y; G -) rock

skamieniały petrified (też fig.)

skandal m (-u; -e) scandal, disgrace; ~iczny scandalous, disgraceful

Skandynaw m (-a; -owie) Scandinavian; ~ia f (GDl -ii) Scandinavia; 2is-tyka f (studia) Scandinavian studies pl.; (instytut) department of Scandinavian studies; ~ka f (-i; G -wek) Scandinavian; 2ski Scandinavian

skan|er m (-a; -y) komp. scanner; ~ować (-uję) scan

skansen m (-u; -y) outdoor museum; zwł. museum of traditional architecture

skap-, skar- pf. → **kap-, kar-**

skarb m (-u; -y) treasure; ~ państwa the Treasury, public purse; ~iec m (-bca; -bce) safe; (w banku) strong-room; hist. treasure-chamber; ~nica f (-y; -e, G -) fig. treasure; ~niczka f (-i; G -czek), ~nik m (-a; -cy) treasurer; ~onka f (-i; G -nek) money-box; (dziecka) piggy bank; ~owy fiscal; opłata ~owa stamp duty; urząd ~owy Brt. Inland Revenue, Am. Internal Revenue Service

skarga f (-i; G -) complaint (na A, przeciw D against)

skarpa f (-y; G -) bud. slope

skarpet|a f (-y; G -), ~ka f (-i; G -tek) sock

skarżyć (-ę) ⟨za-⟩ sue (o A for); ⟨na-⟩ inform (na A against); ~ się complain (na A about)

skas-, skat- pf. → **kas-, kat-**

skaut m (-a; -ci) scout; ~ka f (-i; G -tek) Brt. girl guide, Am. girl scout; ~owski scout

skaza f (-y; G -) flaw, defect

skaz|ać pf. → **skazywać**; ~anie n (-a; G -ań) jur. conviction; ~any 1. convicted; 2. m ~any (-ego; -ni), f ~ana (-ej; -e) convict; ~ić pf. → **skażać**; ~ywać (-uję) sentence (na A to)

skażać (-am) contaminate

skąd adv. from where; ~ jesteś? where are you from?; ~'inąd pron. from elsewhere; ~'kolwiek, ~ś pron. from anywhere

skąp|ić ⟨po-⟩ (-ę) (na L) be mean (with); (k-u G) skimp (s.o. sth.); ~o adv. sparingly; scantily; ~iec m (-pca;

-pcy) miser; ~stwo n (-a; 0) miserliness; ~y miserly, stingy

skierowa|ć pf. → **kierować**; ~ć się (do G, ku D) turn (to); ~nie n (-a; G -ań) pass, authorization

skin m (-a; -i/-owie) skinhead

skinąć pf. (-nę, -ń!) (na A) beckon (to); ~ głową nod

skinienie n (-a; G -eń) sign (with one's hand); (głową) nod

skisły sour, fermented; → **kisnąć**

skle|jać (-am) ⟨~ić⟩ cement (together), paste (together), glue (together)

sklejka f (-i; G -jek) plywood

sklep m (-u; -y) zwł. Brt. shop, zwł. Am. store

sklepienie n (-a; G -eń) vault

sklepika|rka f (-i; G -rek), ~rz m (-a; -e) Brt. shopkeeper, Am. storekeeper

sklep|iony vaulted; ~owy Brt. shop, Am. store

skleroza f (-y) sclerosis

skład m (-u; -y) composition (też chem.); (magazyn) store, warehouse; print. setting; (w sporcie) lineup; **wchodzić w ~** (G) be included (in), be a member (of); **w pełnym składzie** complete, in full strength

składać (-am) (zestawiać) put together, assemble; papier fold; jaja, wieniec lay; broń, obowiązki lay down, resign from; przysięgę swear; egzamin sit; podpis put, affix; wizytę pay; podanie submit; sprawozdanie present, submit; oświadczenie, ofiarę make; zeznanie, zastaw give; życzenia, dzięki express; wiersze write; pieniądze save; print. set; → **wkładać, złożyć**; ~ się (z G) be made up (of), be composed (of); (na A) form; (dać składkę) club together (for)

skład|ak m (-a; -i) (łódka) collapsible boat; (rower) folding bike; ~anka f (-i; G -nek) compilation; ~any collaps-ible; folding; ~ka f (-i; G -dek) collection; (członkowska) membership fee; ~nia f (-i; -e, -i) gr. syntax; ~nica f (-y; -e) warehouse; ~nik m (-a; -i) ingredient; component, element; math. summand; ~niowy gr. syntactical; ~ny mowa fluent; robota orderly

składow|ać (-uję) store; ~isko n (-a; G -) storage place lub yard; ~isko odpadów waste dump; ~y storage; component

skła|m- pf. → **kłam-**; ~niać (-am) persuade (*k-o do G* s.o. to *bezok.*); → **kło-nić**; **~niać się ⟨do G⟩** be inclined (to); (*ku D*) tend (towards)

skłon *m* (*-u; -y*) nod; (*w sporcie*) bend; (*góry*) slope; *~ić pf.* → **skłaniać**; ~ność *f* (*-ści*) inclination (*do G* to); susceptibility; *med.* predisposition; ~ny (*do G*) inclined (to); prone (to); susceptible (to)

skłóc|ać (*-am*) ⟨*~ić*⟩ → **pokłócić**

sknera *f/m* (*-y; G -/-ów*) skinflint

skobel *m* (*-bla; -ble, -bli*) staple

skocz|ek *m* (*-czka; -czkowie*) jumper; (*pl. -i*) (*w szachach*) knight; ~nia *f* (*-i; -e, -i*) ski jump; ~ny *rytm* lively; ~yć *pf.* v/s. (*-ę*) → **skakać**; ~yć na równe nogi jump up

skojarzenie *n* (*-a; G -eń*) association

skok *m* (*-u; -i*) (*w dal, wzwyż* long, high) jump; *~o tyczce* pole-vault; *mot.* (*tłoka* piston) stroke; *fig.* jump; ~owy *anat.* ankle; *mot.* cubic

skoligacony (*z I*) related (to)

skołatany confused; troubled; ~łowany confused

skom|en- *pf.* → **komen-**; ~leć (*-ę, -/-lij!*), ~lić (*-lę, -lij!*) whine, whimper; ~ple- *pf.* → **komple-**; ~plikowany complex, complicated; ~p(r)o-, ~u-*pf.* → **komp(r)o-, komu-**

skon|- *pf.* → **kon-**; ~ać (*-am*) *pf.* die; ~any *N* dead tired; ~sternowany dumbfounded

skończ|ony finished (*też fig.*); completed; ~yć *pf.* → **kończyć**; ~ywszy na (*L*) down to...

skoło-, ~p- *pf.* → **koło-, kop-**; ~ro *cj.* (*jak tylko*) as soon as; (*jeśli*) if; as ~ro-szyt *m* (*-u; -y*) loose-leaf binder; ~ro-widz *m* (*-u; -e*) index

skorpion *m* (*-a; -y*) *zo.* scorpion; ♏ *znak Zodiaku:* Scorpio; *on(a) jest spod znaku* ♏ he/she is (a) Scorpio

skorumpowany corrupt

skorup|a *f* (*-y; G -*) shell; (*raka*) carapace; (*gliniana*) potsherd; *~a ziemska* earth's crust; *~a ślimaka* snail shell; ~iak *m* (*-a; -i*) *zo.* crustacean; ~ka *f* (*-i*) shell; *~ka jajka* eggshell

sko|ry (*m-os skorzy*)→**chętny, skłonny**; ~ry- *pf.* → **kory-**; ~rzy- *pf.* → **korzy-**

skos *m:* na ~, *w* ~ obliquely, slantwise

skostniały numb

skośny oblique, slanting

skowronek *m* (*-nka; -nki*) *zo.* lark

skowyczeć (*-am*) howl

skór|a *f* (*-y; G -*) skin; (*wyprawiona*) leather; (*niewyprawiona*) hide (*też fig.*); *F dostać w ~ę* get a thrashing; ~ka *f* (*-i; G -rek*) → **skóra** (*przy paznokciu*) cuticle; (*sera*) rind; (*banana*) skin; *~ka chleba* crust; *~ka cytryny* lemon peel; *gęsia ~ka* goose flesh; *~kowy* leather; ~ny skin

skórzany leather

skra|cać (*-am*) shorten, abbreviate; *~cać się* be short; *~dać się* (*-am*) sneak (*do G* up to; *przez A* through)

skraj *m* (*-u; -e*) edge; (*przepaści, też fig.*) brink; *na ~u* (*G*) on the brink (of); ~ność *f* (*-ści*) extreme; ~ny extreme

skra|piać (*-am*) sprinkle; *~piać wodą* sprinkle with water; ~plać (*-am*) condense (*się* v/i.); *chem.* liquefy (*się* v/i.); *~ść pf.* → **kraść**; ~wać (*-am*) cut away; ~wek *m* (*-wka; -wki*) snippet; scrap

skreśl|ać (*-am*) ⟨*~ić*⟩→**kreślić;** *list* write

skrę|cać (*-am*) ⟨*~cić*⟩ v/t. *papierosa* roll; (*wygiąć, też linę*) twist; (*zwijać*) roll up (*się* v/i.); *nogę* sprain; *F ~cić kark* break one's neck; v/i. *os., pojazd:* turn; *rzeka, droga:* turn, bend; *~cać się* writhe (*z bólu* in pain); ~powanie *n* (*-a; 0*) discomfort, unease; ~powany *fig.* ← **krępować**

skręt *m* (*-u; -y*) twist; turning; (*zakręt*) turn; bend; *med.* torsion, twisting

skroba|czka *f* (*-i; G -czek*) scraper; ~ć (*-ię*) scrape (*się* o.s.); *~ć* ⟨*o-*⟩ scrape off *lub* clean; *ryb* ę scale; ~nka *f* (*-nki; -nek*) (*zabieg*) curettage; (*rezultat*) abortion

skrobi|a *f* (*GDL -bi; 0*) starch; ~owy starch

skroić *pf.* → **skrawać**

skromn|ie *adv.* modestly; ~ość *f* (*-ści; 0*) modesty; ~y modest

skroń *f* (*-ni; -nie*) *anat.* temple

skrop|ić *pf.* → **skrapiać**; ~lić *pf.* → **skraplać;** ~lina *f* (*-y; G -*) condensate

skró|cenie *n* (*-a; G -eń*) shortening; reduction; abbreviation; abridgement; ~cić *pf.* → **skracać**; ~cony shortened; abbreviated, abridged; ~t *m* (*-u; -y*) abbreviation; summary; (*drogi, też fig.*) shortcut; *w ~cie* in short *lub* brief; ~towiec *m* (*-wca; -wce*) *gr.* acronym; ~towo *adv.* in an abbreviated form; ~towy shortened; abbreviated

skruch|a f (-y; 0) rel. repentance; remorse; **okazywać ~ę** repent

skru|pić się pf.: **~pi(ło) się na mnie** I had to suffer the consequences (for it); **~pulatny** scrupulous, meticulous; **~puł** m (-u; -y) scruple(s pl.); **bez ~pułów** unscrupulous

skrusz|- pf. → **krusz-**; **~ony** repentant, penitent

skrutacyjn|y: komisja ~a tellers pl., Brt. scrutineers

skrwawiony bloody

skry|cie adv. in secret, secretly; **~ć** pf. → **skrywać**

skrypt m (-u; -y) (university) textbook; **~ dłużny** promissory note

skry|tka f (-i; G -tek) secret compartment; **~tka pocztowa** post-office box; **~tobójstwo** n (-a; G -stw) treacherous murder; **~tość** f (-ści; 0) reserve; secretiveness; **~ty** reserved; secretive; (tajemny) hidden; **~wać** (-am) hide (**się** v/i.), conceal; **uczucia** harbo(u)r

skrzat m (-a; -y) kobold, goblin; F nipper

skrze|czeć (-ę, -y) screech, squawk; **~k** m (-u; -i) screech, squawk; (jaja) spawn; **~kliwie** adv. in a rasping lub screeching way; **~kliwy** rasping, screeching

skrzel|e n/pl. (G -li) anat. gills pl.

skrzep m (-u; -y) med. clot; **~nięty** coagulated, clotted; **~owy** clot

skrzętny assiduous, diligent

skrzyć (się) (-ę) glitter, sparkle

skrzyd|laty winged; **~ło** n (-a; G -deł) anat., aviat. wing; mil. Brt. wing, Am. group

skrzyn|ia f (-i; -e) box, chest; **~ia biegów** gearbox; **~ka** f (-i; G -nek) → **skrzynia**; (piwa itp.) crate

skrzyp m (-u; -y) creak; bot. horsetail; **~aczka** f (-i; G -czek) violinist; **~ce** pl. (-piec) mus. violin; **~ek** m (-pka; -pkowie) violinist; **~ieć** (-ę, -i) ⟨~nąć⟩ (-nę) creak; śnieg: crunch

skrzyżowani|e n (-a; G -ań) crossing, crossroad(s sg.); **na ~u** at the crossroad(s sg.); **~e okrężne** Brt. roundabout, Am. traffic circle; **~e na autostradzie** interchange

skubać (-ę) jedzenie nibble; trawę browse, graze; drób pluck; ⟨o-⟩ kogoś fleece

sku|ć pf. → **skuwać**; **~lić** pf. → **kulić**

skup m (-u; -y) purchase, buying

skupi|ać (-am) ⟨~ć[1]⟩ **assemble, gather together**; focus; concentrate (**się** v/i.)

skupi|ć[2] pf. → **skupować**; **~enie** n (-a; G -eń) concentration; chem. **stan ~enia** state; **w ~eniu** with rapt attention, raptly; **~ony** concentrated; focused; **~sko** n (-a; G -) accumulation; cluster

skupować (-uję) buy up

skurcz m (-u; -e) cramp; med. contraction; **~ać** pf. → **kurczyć**

skurwysyn m (-a; -y) V son of a bitch, bastard

skuter m (-a; -y) motor scooter

sku|sić pf. → **kusić**; **~teczny** effective, efficient; **~tek** m (-tku; -tki) effect, result, consequence; **~tek prawny** legal effect; **~tek uboczny** side effect; **nie odnieść ~tku** have no effect; **~tkiem/na ~tek** (G) as a result (of)

skutkować ⟨po-⟩ (-uję) take effect, be effective

skwapliw|ie adv. eagerly; **~y** eager

skwar m (-u; -y) heat; **~ki** m/f/pl. (G - ków/-rek) cracklings (f), greaves pl.

skwaśnieć pf. → **kwaśnieć**

skwer m (-u; -y) green space

slajd m (-u; -y) phot. slide, transparency

slalomowy slalom

slipy m pl. (-ów) briefs, underpants; (kąpielówki) bathing trunks pl.

slogan m (-u; -y) slogan; (hasło) catchword

słab|iej adj. comp. od **słaby**; **~nąć** ⟨o-⟩ (-ę) get weaker; **~o** adv. weakly; **czuć się ~o** feel unwell; **~ostka** f (-i; G -tek) soft spot; **~ość** f (-ści; 0) weakness; **~owity** weak; (chorowity) sickly, feeble; **~y** weak; poor; **~y punkt** flaw

słać ⟨po-⟩ send, forward

słać[2] ⟨po-⟩: **~ łóżko** make the bed; → **rozścielać**; impf. **~ się** stretch, spread

słaniać się (-am) stagger, wobble

sław|a f (-y; 0) fame; **światowej ~y** world-famous; **cieszyć się złą ~ą** have a bad reputation; **~ić** (-ę) praise, exalt; **~ny** famous, eminent

słod|kawy sweetish; slightly sweet; **~ko** adv. sweetly; **~ki** sweet (też fig.); **~kowodny** freshwater; **~ycz** f (-y; 0) sweetness; **~ycze** pl. Brt. sweets pl., Am. candy

słodzi|ć ⟨o-⟩ (-dzę, też słódź!) sweeten; **~k** m (-a; -i) sweetener

słoik m (-a; -i) jar

słom|a f (-y; G -) straw; ~iany straw; ~ka f (-i; G -mek) straw; ~kowy straw

słoneczn|ik m (-a; -i) bot. sunflower; ~y sunny; sun; tech. solar; **udar ~y** sun stroke

słonica f (-y; G -) zo. she-elephant, cow

słonina f (-y; G -) pork fat

słoniowy elephant; → **kość**

słono adv. saltily; ~wodny salt-water

słony salty; **za ~** too salty

słoń m (-nia; -nie) zo. elephant

słońc|e n (-a; G -) sun; (światło) sunshine; **leżeć na ~u** lie in the sun; **jasne jak ~e** crystal clear; **mieć słońce prosto w oczy** have the sun in one's eyes

słot|a f (-y; G -) rainy weather; continuous rain; ~ny rainy

Sło|wacja f (-i; 0) Slovakia; Slovak Republic; ♀wacki Slovak; **mówić po** ♀wacku speak Slovak; ~waczka f (-i; G -czek), ~wak m (-a; -cy) Slovak

Sło|wenia f (GDL -ii;) Slovenia; ~weniec m (-ńca; -ńcy), ~wenka f (-i; G -nek) Slovene; ♀weński Slovenian; (język) Slovene; ~wianin m (-a; -anie, -), ~wianka f (-i; G -nek) Slav; ~wiański Slavonic, Slavic

słowik m (-a; -i) zo. nightingale

słow|nie adv. verbally; in words; ~nik m (-a; -i) dictionary; (zasób słów) vocabulary; ~ny verbal; **człowiek** reliable

słow|o n (-a; G -łów, 1 -wami/-wy) word; **~o w ~o** word for word, literally; **co do ~a** to the word; **dojść do ~a** get a word in; **w całym tego ~a znaczeniu** in the truest sense of the word; **ani ~a** not a word; **łapać za ~o, trzymać za ~o** take s.o. at one's word; **dać ~o** give s.o. one's word; **liczyć się ze ~ami** watch one's tongue; **swoimi ~ami** in one's own words; **innymi ~y** in other words; **w krótkich ~ach** briefly, in a few brief words; **~em** in a word; **brak mi słów** I'm lost for words; **być po ~ie** (z I) be engaged (to)

słowotwórczy word-building

słód m (-łodu;0) malt

słój m (-łoju; -oje, -oi/-ojów) → **słoik**; bot. annual ring

słówk|o n (-a; G -wek) word; zwł. pl. ~a vocabulary

słuch m (-u; 0) hearing; **zamienić się w ~** be all ears; **w zasięgu ~u** within hearing; **~ zaginął o nim** he was not

heard from any more; **~y** m/pl. (-ów) rumo(u)r; **chodzą ~y** there is a rumo(u)r; **~acz** m (-a; -e, -y/-ów), **~aczka** f (-i; G -czek) listener; **~ać ⟨po-⟩** (-am) (G) listen (to); follow (**rady** the advice); (też **się**) obey

słuchawk|a f (-i; G -wek) tel. receiver; med. stethoscope; **~i** pl. headphones pl.

słuchow|isko n (-a; G -) radio play; **~y** hearing

sługa m (-i; G -/-dzy, -) servant

słup m (-a; -y) pillar; (latarni) post; tel. pole; electr. pylon; **~ek** m (-pka; -pki) post; sport: goal-post; bot. pistil; **~ek drogowy** bollard; **~ek rtęci** column of mercury; **~ek startowy** starting-block

słuszn|ie adv. justly, deservedly; rightly; **~ość** f (-ści; 0) rightness; validity; correctness; **mieć ~ość** be right; **nie mieć ~ości** be wrong; **~y** right, correct; valid; → **sprawiedliwy**

służalcz|o in a servile manner; **~y** servile

służąc|a f (-ej; -e), **~y** (-ego; -) servant

służb|a f (-y; G -) service; **pełniący ~ę** (on) duty; **na ~ie** on duty; **po ~ie** off duty, in free time; **zdolny do ~y** fit for service; **~owo** adv. on business; **~owy** business; official

służ|yć ⟨po-⟩ (-żę) serve (**w** L, **u** G, D in; **do** G for; **za** A, **jako** as); **zdrowie mu ~y** he enjoys good health; **czym mogę pani ~yć?** can I help you, Madam?; **to mi nie ~y** it does not agree with me

słychać (t-ko bezok.) be heard; **co ~?** what's new?

słyn|ąć (-nę, -ń!) (**z** G, **jako**) be famous (for, as); **~ny** famous

słysz|alny audible; **~eć ⟨po-, u-⟩** (-ę, -y) hear

smaczn|y tasty; **~ego!** enjoy your meal!

smagać (-am) lash (też fig.)

smagły dark-skinned

smak m (-u; -i) taste (też fig.); (potrawy) flavo(u)r; **ze ~em** fig. tasteful; **bez ~u**, fig. **w złym ~u** tasteless; **przypaść do ~u** be to one's liking

smako|łyk m (-u; -i) delicacy; **~sz** m (-a; -e) gourmet; **~wać** (-uję) taste; **~wicie** adv. deliciously; **~wity** tasty, delicious

smalec m (-lca; 0) gastr. lard

smalić ⟨o-⟩ (-lę) singe off

smar m (-u; -y) grease, lubricant; **~ do nart** ski-wax

smark F m (-u; -i) snot; **~acz** m F (-a; -e) snotty brat; **~ać** F (-am) blow one's nose; **~aty** F fig. wet behind the ears; **~ula** F f (-i; -e) snotty brat

smarow|ać ⟨na-, po-⟩ (-uję) spread; (maść) apply; tech. grease, lubricate; **~idło** n (-a; G -deł) grease

smaż|ony fried; **~yć ⟨u-⟩** (-ę) fry (się v/i.); roast (**na słońcu** in the sun)

smętny gloomy

smoczek m (-czka; -czki) Brt. dummy, Am. pacifier

smok m (-a; -i) dragon

smoking m (-u; -i) Brt. dinner jacket, Am. tuxedo

smo|lić ⟨u-⟩ (-lę, smol/smól!) smear; **~listy**, **~lny** pitchy; **~ła** f (-y; -e) tar; **~łować** (-uję) tar

smro|dliwy stinky; **~dzić ⟨na-⟩** (-dzę) break wind

smród m (-rodu; -rody) stink, stench

smucić ⟨za-⟩ (-cę) sadden; **~ ⟨za-⟩ się** become sad

smuga f (-i; G -) streak; (brudu) smudge; (samolotu) trail

smukł|o adv. in a slim way; **~y** slender, slim

smut|ek m (-tku; -tki) sorrow; sadness; **~no** adv. sadly; with sorrow; **~ny** sad; sorrowful; **~no mi** I am sad

smycz f (-y; -e) leash; **~ek** m (-czka; -czki) mus. bow; **~kowy** instrument string

smyk m F (-a; -i) nipper

sna|ch, **~mi** → **sen**

snajper m (-a; -rzy) sniper

snem → **sen**

snop m (-u; -y) sheaf; **~ światła** beam of light; **~owiązałka** f (-i; G -łek) agr. sheaf-binder

snów, **snu** → **sen**

snuć (-ję) przędzę spin; **~ domysły** speculate; **~ marzenia** dream; **~ się** dym itp.: hang; myśli: buzz through (**po głowie** one's head)

sny → **sen**

snycerstwo n (-a; 0) wood-carving

sob. skrót pisany: **sobota** Sat. (Saturday)

sob|ą → **siebie**; **~ie** → **siebie**; **był ~ie** there was; **~kostwo** n (-a; G -) egoism

sobot|a f (-y; G -bót) Saturday; **w ~ę** on Saturday

sobowtór m (-a; -y) double

soból m (-bola; -bole) zo. sable

sobór m (-boru; -bory) rel. council; cathedral

sobótk|a f (-i; G -tek) Saint John's fire; też **~i** pl. Midsummer's night

socjal|demokratyczny social democratic; **~istyczny** socialist; **~ny** social

socjolog m (-a; -dzy) sociologist; **~ia** f (GDL -gii; 0) sociology

soczew|ica f (-y; G -) bot. lentil; **~ka** f (-i; G -wek) phot., phys. lens sg.

soczysty juicy; kolor, barwa itp. rich; język earthy; zieleń lush

sod|a f (-y; 0) chem. soda; **~a oczyszczona** bicarbonate of soda; F bicarb; **~a żrąca** caustic soda; **~owy: woda ~owa** soda (water)

sofa f (-y; G -) sofa

soj|a f (GDL soi; 0) agr. soy(a) bean; **~owy** soy(a)

sojusz m (-u; -e) alliance; **~niczy** allied; **~niczka** f (-i; G -czek), **~nik** m (-a; -cy) ally

sok m (-u; -i) juice

sokol|i falcon; **~nik** m (-a; -cy) falconer

sokół m (-koła; -koły) zo. falcon

sola f (-i; -e) zo. sole

sol|anka f (-i; G -nek) salt water, brine; (źródło) salt-water lub brine spring; **~ankowy** salt-water, brine

solarium n (idkl.; -a, -iów) solarium

sole pl. → **sól**

solenizant m (-a; -ci), **~ka** f (-i; G -tek) (person celebrating his/her name-day)

solenny solemn, festive

solić ⟨o-, po-; na-, za-⟩ salt

solidar|ność f (-ści; 0) solidarity; **~ny** cooperative; **być ~nym** show one's solidarity; **~yzować się** (-uję) show one's solidarity

solidny solid; fig. reliable, dependable

soli|sta m (-y; -ści), **~stka** f (-i; G -tek) soloist; **~ter** m (-a; -y) zo. tapeworm

sol|niczka f (-i; G -czek) salt sprinkler, Am. salt-shaker; **~ny** salt; chem., geol. saline; **kwas ~ny** chem. hydrochloric acid

solowy solo

sołtys m (-a; -i) president of the village council

sond|a f (-y; G -) probe; → **~aż** m (-a; -e) sounding out; (**opinii publicznej** public opinion) poll; **~ować** (-uję) sound out; *med.* probe; *naut.* sound, plumb

sopel *m* (*-pla*; *-ple*) icicle

sopran *m* (*-u*; *-y*) soprano; ~owy soprano

sortować {*-uję*} sort

sos *m* (*-u*; *-y*) sauce; gravy

sosn|a *f* (*-y*; *G -sen*) *bot.* pine; ~owy pine

sow|a *f* (*-y*; *G sów*) *zo.* owl; ~i owl

sowiecki *pej.* Soviet

sowi|cie *adv.* generously; ~ty generous

sód *m* (*sodu*; *0*) *chem.* sodium

sójka *f* (*-i*; *G -jek*) *zo.* jay

sól *f* (*soli*; *0*) (**kuchenna** common) salt; *chem.* (*pl. sole*) salt; **być solą w oku** be a thorn in s.o.'s side

spacer *m* (*-u*; *-y*) walk; **iść na ~** go for a walk; ~niak F *m* (*-a*; *-i*) prison yard; ~ować {*-uję*} walk, stroll (**po** L around)

spacz|enie *n* (*-a*; *G -eń*) warp(ing); ~ony warped

spać sleep (*też fig.*)

spad (*-y*; *-u*) slope, incline; ~y *pl.* (*owoce*) windfalls *pl.*; ~am (*-am*) fall, drop (**z** G from, off); *teren*: slope; *ceny*: go down, fall; (**na** A) *cios*: hit; *wina*: fall (**na** A on); *obowiązki*: fall (**na** A to)

spad|ek[1] *m* (*-dku*; *-dki*) decrease, fall; ~ek ciśnienia drop in pressure; → **spad**

spad|ek[2] *m* (*-dku*; *-dki*) heritage, legacy, inheritance (*też fig.*); **otrzymać w ~ku** (**po** L) inherit (from); **zostawić w ~ku** leave, bequeath

spadko|bierca *m* (*-y*; *G -ów*), ~bierczyni *f* (*-i*; *-ie*, *G -yń*) heir; ~dawca *m* (*-y*; *G -ców*), ~dawczyni *f* (*-i*; *-ie*, *G -yń*) *jur.* testator; ~wy decreasing, on the wane; *jur.* hereditary

spadochro|n *m* (*-u*; *-y*) parachute; ~niarka *f* (*-i*; *G -rek*), ~niarz *m* (*-a*; *-e*) parachutist; ~niarstwo *n* (*-a*; *0*) parachuting; ~nowy parachute

spadzi|sto *adv.* steeply; ~sty steep; ~ście *adv.* → **spadzisto**

spa|jać[1] (*-am*) join, connect; *fig.* unite

spa|jać[2] (*-am*) make drunk; ~kować *pf.* pack (**się** *v/i*); ~lać (*-am*) burn (**się** *v/i*); ~lanie *n* (*-a*; *G -ań*) burning; *tech.* combustion; ~lenie *n* (*-a*; *G -eń*) burning; ~larnia *f* (*-i*; *-e*) (*odpadków*) incinerating plant; ~lić *pf.* → **spalać**; ~linowy: **silnik ~linowy** internal-combustion engine; ~liny *f/pl.* *mot.* exhaust (fumes *pl.*); *tech.* waste gases *pl.*; ~lony

1. burnt; *fig.* uncovered, disclosed; **2.** *m* (*-ego*; *-e*) (**w** *sporcie*) offside

spani|e *n* (*-a*; *0*) sleeping; **miejsce do ~a** sleeping place

sparaliżowany paralysed (*też fig.*)

spa|r- *pf.* → **par-**; ~rz- *pf.* → **parz-**

spas|iony, ~ły obese, fat

spastyczny *med.* spastic

spaść[1] *pf.* → **spadać**

spawa|cz *m* (*-a*; *-e*) *tech.* welder; ~ć (*-am*) *tech.* weld; ~rka *f* (*-i*; *G -rek*) *tech.* welder, welding machine

spazm *m* (*-u*; *-y*) spasm

spec *m* F (*-a*; *-e*) expert

specjali|sta *m* (*- y*; *-ści*, *G -ów*), ~stka *f* (*-i*; *G -tek*) specialist; **lekarz ~sta** consultant, specialist; ~styczny specialist, specialized; ~zować się (**wy- się**) (*-uję*) specialize (**w** L in)

specjaln|ie *adv.* peculiarly, (e)specially; ~ość *f* (*-ści*) speciality (*też gastr.*); ~y special

specyficzny specific, peculiar

spedycyjny shipping, forwarding

spektrum *n* (*idkl.*; *-a*; *-ów*) spectrum; range

spektakl *m* (*-u*; *-e*) *theat.* performance

spekul|acja *f* (*-i*; *-e*) speculation; ~ant *m* (*-a*; *-ci*), ~antka *f* (*-i*; *G -tek*) speculator; ~ować {*-uję*} speculate

spełn|iać (*-am*) {~nić} *warunek itp.* meet; *prośbę itp.* grant; *postanowienia* fulfil(l); *funkcję* serve, perform; ~niać się *życzenie*: come true; ~nienie *n* (*-a*; *G -eń*) granting, meeting; performance; realization; ~zać (*-am*) {~znąć} fail, end in failure; *pf.* (*kolor*) → **płowieć**

sperma *f* (*-y*; *G -*) sperm, semen

speszony mixed-up, confused; → **peszyć**

spędz|ać (*-am*) {~ić} *bydło* round up, gather; *czas* spend; *płód* abort

spiąć *pf.* → **spinać**

spi|czasto *adv.* pointedly, sharply; ~czasty pointed, sharp; ~ć *pf.* → **spijać**

spie|kać (*-am*) {~c} bake, burn; *tech.* sinter; ~c się na słońcu sun-burn

spieniężać (*-am*) {~yć} {-ę} sell, cash in

spie|niony foamy, frothy, bubbly

spie|rać się[1] (*-am*) argue (**o** A about)

spie|rać[2] (*-am*) *plamę* wash up; ~rzchnięty parched; *wargi też* chapped

spiesz|ny, ~yć → **śpiesz-**

spięcie n (-a; G -ęć) electr. short-circuit; fig. clash

spiętrz|ać (-am) ⟨-yć⟩ tower up, pile up; wodę dam up

spijać (-am) drink off; F get drunk; spić się pf. get drunk

spiker m (-a; -rzy), ~ka f (-i; G -rek) announcer; newscaster

spilśniony → pilśniowy

spiłow(yw)ać (-[w]uję) saw off; (pilnikiem) file off

spin|acz m (-a; -e) paper-clip; ~ać(-am) staple together; ~ka f (-i; G -nek) cuff(-link); ~ka do włosów Brt. hair-grip, Am. bobby pin

spirala f (-i; -e) spiral; med. (domacicz-na) loop

spiry|tus m (-u; 0) spirit, ethyl alcohol; ~tusowy spirit; ~tystyczny spiritualist(ic)

spis m (-u; -y) list; ~ rzeczy table of contents; ~ ludności census; ~ potraw menu

spis|ać pf. → spisywać; ~ek m (-sku; -ski) plot; scheme; conspiracy; ~kować (-uję) plot, conspire; ~kowiec m (-wca; -wcy) conspirator; ~ywać (-uję) v/t. make a list of; list; ~ać na straty write off; ~ywać się behave (o.s.); ~ać się distinguish o.s., do well

spiżar|ka f (-i; G -rek), ~nia f (-i; -e) pantry, larder

spiżowy bronze

spla|- pf. → pla-; ~tać pf. (-am) → pleść

spleśniały mo(u)ldy

splot m (-u; -y) tangle, twist; włók. weave; anat. plexus; ~ okoliczności set of coincidences

splu|- pf. → plu-; ~nąć pf. → pluć, spluwać; ~wa f (-y; G -) F shooting-iron; ~waczka f (-i; G -czek) spittoon; ~wać (-am) spit

spłac|ać (-am) ⟨-ić⟩ pay off, pay back

spłakany tear-stained

spła|szczać (-am) → płaszczyć; ~ta f (-y; G -) payment; repayment; ~tać (-am): ~tać figla (D) play a trick (on)

spław m (-u; -0) rafting, floating; ~iać (-am) ⟨-ić⟩ float, raft; fig. get rid of; ~ny navigable

spłon|ąć pf. get burnt; ~ka f (-i; G -nek) detonator

spłowiały faded

spłu|czka f (-i; -czek) (w toalecie) flush;

~kiwać (-uję) ⟨-kać⟩ rinse (off); toaletę flush

spły|nąć pf. → spływać; ~w m (-u; -y) drain; outlet; ~w tratwą voyage by raft; ~wać (-am) drain away; flow off lub away; pot, łzy: run; tratwa: float downstream; ~wać krwią be stained with blood; F ~waj! get lost!

spocony sweaty

spocz|ąć pf. → spoczywać; ~ynek m (-nku; 0) rest; miejsce ostatniego ~ynku last resting-place; w stanie ~ynku retired; ~ywać (-am) rest; fig. lie

spod prp. (G) from under

spod|ek m (-dka; -dki) saucer; ~em adv. below, underneath; ~enki pl. (-nek) shorts pl.; ~ni bottom; ~nie pl. (-i) zwł. Brt. trousers pl., zwł. Am. pants pl.; ~nium n (-u; -y lub idkl.) Brt. trouser suit, Am. pant suit

spodoba|ć się pf.: to ci się ~ you will like it, you will enjoy it; → podobać się

spody pl. → spód

spodziewa|ć się (-am) (G) expect; hope; nie ~ł się niczego złego he was unsuspecting

spoglądać (-am) (na A) look (at), glance (at)

spo|ić pf. → spajać[1], spajać[2]; ~ina f (-y; G -) weld; joint; ~isty compact; fig. coherent; ~iwo n (-a; G -) binder, binding material

spojó|wka f (-i; G -wek) anat. conjunctiva; zapalenie ~wek conjunctivitis

spojrze|ć pf. → spoglądać; ~nie n (-a; G -eń) look, glance

spo|kojny calm, peaceful; ~kój m (-ko-ju) peace, calm; daj mi ~kój leave me alone

spokrewniony related (z I to)

spolszcz|ać (-am) ⟨-yć⟩ (-ę) translate into Polish; polonize

społecz|eństwo n (-a; G -) society, community; ~ność f (-ści) community; ~ny social; (dla społeczeństwa) community

społem adv. together

spo|między prp. (G) from among; ~nad prp. (G) from above

sponsorować (-uję) sponsor

spontaniczny spontaneous, impulsive

spo|pielały burnt to ashes; ~pu- pf. → popu-; ~radycznie adv. sporadically, occasionally; ~radyczny sporadic, occasional

spor|ny disputable, questionable; ~o adv. a lot of, plenty of

sport m (-u; -y) sport; ~y pl. zimowe winter sports pl.; ~owiec m (-wca; -wcy) sportsman; ~owo adv. in a sporty manner; ~owy sport, sporting, sports; ~smen m (-a; -i) sportsman; ~smenka f (-i; G -nek) sportswoman

spory 1. big, large; fair; 2. pl. → spór

sporysz m (-u; -e) bot. ergot

sporządz|ać (-am) ⟨~ić⟩ pismo, make; testament jur. draw up; → przyrządzać

sposobność f (-ści) opportunity

sposób m (-sobu; -soby) way, manner; means sg.; ~ użycia instructions pl. for use; w ten ~ (in) this way; w następujący ~ in the following way; jakimś sposobem in some way, somehow; w istotny ~ significantly; wszelkimi sposobami by hook or by crook; w żaden ~, żadnym sposobem by no means; nie ~ (jest) it is impossible

spostrze|gać (-am) ⟨~c⟩ perceive, sight; (też odczuwać) notice; ~żenie n (-a; G -eń) observation

spośród prp. (G) → spomiędzy

spotę|-pf. → potę-; ~kać pf. → spotykać; ~kanie n (-a; G -ań) meeting, encounter; sport: match; (umówione) appointment

spotnieć pf. → pocić się, potnieć

spotwarz|ać (-am) ⟨~yć⟩ (-ę) slander, libel

spotyka|ć (-am) v/t. meet, encounter; Nowy Rok greet; (t-ko 3. os.) bieda: happen to; kara, nieszczęście: befall to; ~ć się meet (z I v/i.); fig. (z I) meet (with); to się często ~ you can often see this

spowiadać ⟨wy-⟩ (-am) rel. hear s.o.'s confession; ~ ⟨wy-⟩ się go to confession; (z I) confess

spowiednik m (-a; -cy) rel. confessor

spowiedź f (-dzi) rel. confession

spo|winowacony related; ~wodowany caused (przez A by)

spowszedniały commonplace, ordinary

spoza prp. (G) from; from outside; from behind

spoży|cie n (-a; 0) consumption; use; ~wać (-am) ⟨~ć⟩ consume, use up; eat;

~wca m (-y; G -ców) consumer, user; ~wczy food; sklep ~wczy grocer('s), food shop

spód m (spodu; spody) bottom; (listy, strony) foot; (podeszwa) sole; na spodzie, u spodu at the bottom; pod spodem underneath; od spodu from below; ~nica f (-y; G -), ~niczka f (-i; G -czek) skirt

spój|nik m (-a; -i) gr. conjunction; ~ność f (-ści; 0) coherence, cohesion

spół|dzielczy cooperative; ~dzielnia f (-i; -e) cooperative; ~głoska f (-i; G -sek) gr. consonant; ~ka f (-i; G -łek) econ. partnership; company; do ~ki (z I) together (with); ~kować (-uję) copulate

spór m (sporu; spory) argument, quarrel (z powodu G about)

spóźni|ać się (-am) ⟨~ć się⟩ be late; impf. zegar: be slow; ~ć się na pociąg miss the train; ~enie n (-a; G -eń) delay, hold-up; ~ony late, delayed

spra|cowany worn out; ~ć pf. → spierać² F give s.o. a thrashing; ~gniony thirsty (też fig.)

spraw|a f (-y; G -) business, matter; question; cause; jur. case, proceedings pl.; gorsza ~a, że what is worse; na dobrą ~ę after all; zdać ~ę (z G) account (for); zdawać sobie ~ę (z G) realize, be aware (of); za jej ~ą at her instigation, because of her; pokpił ~ę F he botched it; ~ca m (-y; G -ców), ~czyni f (-i; -e, -yń) perpetrator; przeciw(ko) nieznanemu ~cy against person(s pl.) unknown

sprawdz|ać (-am) ⟨~ić⟩ (-dzę) check, verify; examine; (w słowniku) look up; ~ić się realize, come true; → spełniać się

sprawdzian m (-u; -y) szkoła: test; fig. lesson

spraw|iać (-am) ⟨~ić⟩ (-dzę) cause, give; → wywierać; ~ić sobie (A) buy, get o.s. s.th.

sprawiedliw|ie adv. fairly, justly; ~ość f (-ści) justice; → wymiar; Ministerstwo 2ości Ministry of Justice; ~y fair, just

spraw|ka f (-i; G -wek) doing; ~ność f (-ści; 0) ability, capability; skill; ~ny skil(l)ful, able, capable

sprawo|wać (-uję) władzę exercise;

urząd hold; **∼wać nadzór (nad** *I)* watch (over); **∼wać się** *urządzenie:* function; *ktoś:* behave; **∼wanie (się)** *n (-a; 0)* functioning; behavio(u)r

sprawozda|nie *n (-a; G -ań)* report; **∼wca** *m (-y; G -ców),* **∼wczyni** *f (-i; -e)* reporter; commentator; **∼wczy: referat ∼wczy** report

sprawun|ek *m (-nku; -nki)* purchase; **załatwić ∼ki** do the shopping

Sprewa *f (-y; 0)* Spree

spręż|arka *f (-i; G -rek)* compressor; **∼ony** compressed; *bud.* prestressed; *fig.* tense; **∼yna** *f (-y; G -)* spring; **∼ysty** springy; elastic; *fig. też* energetic; → **sprawny**

sprint *m (-u; -y) sport:* sprint; **∼er** *m (-a; -rzy),* **∼erka** *f (-i; G -rek) (w sporcie)* sprinter

spró|- *pf.* → **pro-;** **∼stać** *(-am) (D)* be equal (to), match

sprostowa|ć *pf.* → **prostować;** **∼nie** *n (-a; G -ań)* correction; denial

sproszkowany powdered

sprośny bawdy, ribald

sprowadza|ć *(-am) ⟨∼ić⟩ v/t.* bring, get; *Brt.* fetch; *lekarza itp.* send for; *towar* obtain; *fig.* lead **(na** *A* to); **(do** *G)* reduce (to); **(z** *I)* import (from), get (from); *v/i.* **co cię ∼a?** what brings you here?; **∼ać się (do** *G)* be reduced (to); **∼ić się (do** *G) (do miejscowości)* move in

spró|- *pf.* → **pró-;** **∼chniały** rotten; *ząb* decayed; *med.* carious

sprysk|iwać *(-uję) ⟨∼ać⟩* sprinkle

spryt *m (-u; 0)* cleverness; cunning; shrewdness; **∼ny** clever; cunning; shrewd

sprzą|c *pf.* (→ **-prząc**) → **sprzęgać;** **∼czka** *f (-i; G -czek)* buckle

sprzątaczka *f (-i; G -czek)* cleaner; *Brt.* char(lady); **∼ać ⟨po-⟩** *(-am) ⟨∼nąć⟩ (-nę)* clear up, tidy up *(też v/i.); (usunąć)* remove, get rid of; *zboże* gather in; *fig. (zabić)* eliminate; **∼nąć sprzed nosa** F snatch away from under *s.o.'s* nose; **∼nąć ze stołu** F clear; **∼anie** *n (-a; G -ań)* cleaning up, tidying up

sprzeciw *m (-u; -y)* protest; opposition; **bez ∼u** without objecting; **∼iać się** *(-am) ⟨∼ić się⟩ (-ę) (D)* oppose; be opposed (to)

sprzecz|ać się ⟨po- się⟩ *(-am)* argue, quarrel **(o** *A* about); **∼ka** *f (-i; G -czek)*

argument, quarrel; **∼ność** *f (-ści) (logiczna itp.)* contradiction; *(konflikt)* conflict; **∼ny** contradictory; **(z** *I)* incompatible (with); conflicting

sprzed *prp. (G)* (from) before

sprzeda|ć *pf.* → **sprzedawać;** **∼jący** *m (-ego; -y)* seller; **∼jny** mercenary; venal; **∼nie** *n (-a; 0)* selling; sale; **do ∼nia** for sale; **∼wać ⟨-ję⟩** sell; **∼wca** *m (-y; G -ów),* **∼wczyni** *f (-i; G -yń) econ.* assistant, salesperson; **∼ż** *f (-y; -e)* sale; **na ∼ż** for sale; **∼żny** sale(s)

sprzeniewierz|ać *(-am) ⟨∼yć⟩* embezzle; **∼yć się** *(D)* betray; **∼enie** *n (-a; G -eń)* embezzlement; **∼enie się** betrayal

sprzę|gać *(-am)* couple; interconnect; **∼gło** *n (-a; G -gieł) mot.* clutch; **włączyć ∼gło** clutch; **wyłączyć ∼gło** declutch; **∼t** *m (-u; -y)* equipment *(też RTV)*; gear; *agr.* harvest; **∼ty** *pl.* furniture; fittings *pl.;* **∼t komputerowy** hardware; **∼żony** *m* coupled

sprzyja|ć *(-am)* favo(u)r; encourage, further; **∼jący** favo(u)rable; auspicious

sprzykrzy|ć się *pf. (t-ko pret.)* **∼ł (a, -o, -y) mi się** I am tired of *lub* F fed up with it (him, her, them)

sprzymierz|eniec *m (-ńca; -ńcy)* ally; **∼ony** allied

sprzysi|ęgać się *(-am) ⟨∼ąc się⟩* conspire **(przeciwko** *D* against)

spuchnięty swollen

spulchni|ać *(-am) ⟨∼ć⟩ (-ę, -nij!) glebę itp.* break up, loosen

spust *m (-u; -y) tech. itp.* outlet; *phot.* shutter release; *(broni, też fig.)* trigger; F **mieć ∼** eat like a horse; **zamknąć na cztery ∼y** lock up

spustoszenie *n (-a; G -eń)* devastation

spuszcza|ć *(-am)* let down; *głowę, oczy, flagę* lower **(się** *v/i.)*; *płyn* let out; *psa* let go, **∼ na wodę** put out, launch; **∼ cenę** lower the price; **nie ∼ oczu z kogoś** not take one's eyes off s.o.; **∼ się** come down; F come, come off

spuści|ć *pf.* → **spuszczać;** **∼zna** *f (-y; G -)* legacy; *(pisarska)* output, work

spycha|cz *m (-a; -e)* bulldozer; **∼ć** *(-am)* push, shove **(w bok** aside); **∼rka** *f (-i; G -rek)* → **spychacz**

sp. z o.o. *skrót pisany:* **spółka z ograniczoną odpowiedzialnością** limited liability company; *(prywatna)* Ltd., plc *(publiczna)*

srać V *(-am)* shit

sreb|rnoszary silver-grey *n (-a; Am.* -gray; ~rny silver, silvery; ~ro *n (-a; 0) chem.* silver; *(naczynia) (pl. G -ber)* silver(ware); ~rzyć ⟨*po-*⟩ *(-ę)* silver-plate; ~rzysty silvery *(też fig.)*

sro|czy magpie; ~gi strict, severe; *mróz* severe,sharp;~go *adv.* strictly,severely; ~gość *f (-ści; 0)* strictness, severity

sroka *f (-i; G -)* zo. magpie; ~ty piebald

srom *m (-u; -y) anat.* vulva; ~otny shameful; ~owy vulval, vulvar; *wargi pl.* ~owe *anat.* labia *pl.*

sroż|ej, ~szy *adj. comp. od →* **srogo, srogi;** ~yć się *(-ę)* rage

ssa|ć suck; ~k *m (-a; -i) biol.* mammal; ~nie *n (-a; G -ań) tech.* suction; ~wka *f (-i; G -wek)* (suction) nozzle

st. *skrót pisany:* **stacja** railway station; **starszy** senior

stabil|izować ⟨*u-*⟩ *(-uję)* stabilize; ~izować ⟨*u-*⟩ **się** stabilize, become stabilized; ~ny stable

stacja *f (-i; -e)* station *(też mot.,* rail.); ~ **benzynowa** *Brt.* petrol station, filling station, *Am.* gas station; ~ **nadawcza** broadcasting station; *(urządzenie)* transmitter

stacyjka *f (-i; G -jek) →* **stacja;** *mot.* ignition (lock)

staczać *(-am)* roll down (**się** *v/i.*); ~ **się na dno** *fig.* sink low

stać¹ stand; *fabryka, maszyna:* be idle; ~!, *stój!* halt!; ~ **na straży** be on guard; *(nie)* ~ **go na to** he can(not) afford it

sta|ć ²E się *pf. (zajść)* become, get; **co się** ~ło? what has happened?; **co się z nim** ~ło? what has happened to him?; **dobrze się** ~ło, że it is good that; *→* **stawać się**

stadion *m (-u; -y) sport:* stadium

stad|ło *n (-a; G -deł)* (married) couple; ~nina *f (-y; G -)* stud-(farm); ~ny herd; ~o *n (-a; G -)* herd; *(wilków, psów)* pack; *(lwów)* pride; *(ptaków)* flock

sta|jać *pf. (-ję)* thaw, melt; ~je *→* **stawać**

stajnia *f (-i; -e, -i/-jen)* stable

stal *f (-i; -e)* steel

stal|e *adv.* steadily,constantly; ~i *→* **stały**

stalinowski Stalinist

stalo|wnia *f (-i; -e) tech.* steelworks; ~woszary steel-grey, *Am.* -gray; ~wy steel

stalówka *f (-i; G -wek)* nib

stał|a się, ~o się *→* **stawać się**

sta|łocieplny *zo.* warm-blooded; ~łość *f (-ści; 0)* constancy, permanence

stał|y **1.** *(m-os* stali) steady; regular; *phys., chem.* solid; *członek, korespondent* permanent; *komisja* standing; *math., koszty* constant; ~**y gość** regular (visitor); **na** ~**e** for ever; **2.** ~**a** *f (-ej; -e, G -ych) math.* constant

stamtąd *adv.* from there

stan *m (-u; -y)* condition; state; status; *(jednostka administracyjna)* state; ~ **dróg** road conditions *pl.;* ~ **wojny** state of war; ~ **zdrowia** state of health; ~ **pogody** weather situation; ~ **wody** water level; ~ **kasy** cash (at hand); ~ **rzeczy** state of affairs; ~ **wojenny** martial law; ~ **wyjątkowy** state of emergency; ⟨y **Zjednoczone (Ameryki)** the United States (of America); **w ...** ~**ie** in ... form, in ...state; **być w** ~**ie** be able to do, be capable of; **żyć ponad** ~ live beyond one's means; *→* **cywilny, liczebny, poważny**

stan|ąć *pf. (-nę, -ń!) →* **stawać;** *rzeka:* freeze over; *dom:* be erected; ~**ęło na tym** it was agreed that

stancja *f (-i; -e)* lodgings *pl.*

standaryzować *(-uję)* standardize

stanica *f (-u; -e, G -)* jakby: boat harbo(u)r *(with on-site facilities)*

stanieć *pf.* become cheaper

stanik *m (-a; -i)* bra

staniol *(-u; -e)* tin foil

stanow|czo *adv.* decidedly; decisively; ~czość *f (-ści; 0)* decisiveness; finality; ~czy decisive, definitive, final

stanowi|ć *(-ię, -nów!) v/i.* (**o** *L*) be decisive (in), determine; *v/t.* constitute; form; ~sko *n (-a; G-)* position *(też mil.);* *(wykopalisk itp.)* site; *(posada też)* post, appointment; *(pogląd)* viewpoint, stance; ~**sko pracy** work-place; **zająć** ~**sko** take a stand (**w sprawie** on)

stanowy *pol.* state

stapiać *(-am)* fuse; alloy

stara|ć się ⟨*po- się*⟩ *(-am)* (**o** *A*) try (to obtain); apply (for); *pf. też* gain; gain; ~nie *n (-a; G -ań):* zwł. *pl.* ~**nia** efforts *pl.;* **dołożyć** ~**ń (do** *G)* take pains (to do); **poczynić** ~**nia** *→* **starać się;** ~nność *f (-ści; 0)* care; ~nny careful

star|cie *n (-a; G -rć) mil.* engagement,

battle; *fig.* clash; (*w sporcie*) round; *med.* → **obtarcie**; ~cy *pl.* → **starzec**; ~cząć (*-am*) ⟨~czyć⟩ (*-ę*) be enough *lub* sufficient (**na** *A* for); ~czy *adj.* senile

staro *adv.* czuć się old; ~cie *n* (*-a; G -i*) jumble, junk; ~dawny ancient; ~miejski old town; ~modny old-fashioned; ~polski Old Polish; (*tradycja*) traditional; ~sta *m* (*-y; -towie, G -tów*), ~ścina *f* (*-y; G -*) szkoła: form captain; *hist.* starosta

starość *f* (*-ści; 0*) old age; **na** ~ for old age
staro|świecki old-fashioned; ~świecko *adv.* in an old-fashioned way; ~żytność *f* (*-ści, 0*) antiquity; → **antyk**; ~żytny ancient

star|si → **starszy**; ~szawy oldish
starszeństwo *n* (*-a; 0*) seniority
starszy 1. *adj.* (*comp. od* → **stary**; *m-os -rsi*); older, elder; (*w hierarchii*) senior; **2.** (*-rszego;-rsi*) adult; elder; ~zna *f* (*-y; G -*) elders *pl.*

start *m* (*-u; -y*) start; beginning; *aviat.* take-off; *astronautyka:* lift-off; ~er *m* **1.** (*-a; -rzy*) (*w sporcie*) starter; **2.** (*-u; -ry*) *mot.* starter; ~ować ⟨**wy-**⟩ (*-uję*) start, take part; *aviat.* take off; *astronautyka:* lift off; ~owy starting

starty *adj. gastr.* grated
starusz|ek *m* (*-ka; -kowie*) old man; ~ka *f* (*-i; G -szek*) old woman
star|y 1. (*m-os -rzy*) old; **2.** *m* (*-ego,-rzy*), ~a *f* (*-ej; -e*), ~e *n* (*-ego; -rzy*) the old, the past; **po** ~**emu** as before; as it was
starze|c *m* (*-rca; -rcy*) old man; ~ć ⟨**po-, ze-**⟩ się (*-ję*) grow old; ~j *adv.* (*comp. od* → **stary**) older
starzyzna *f* (*-y; 0*) junk
stateczny stable; *ktoś* sedate, staid
stat|ek *m* (*-tku; -tki*) (**handlowy, spacerowy, kosmiczny** merchant, excursion, space) ship; **na** ~**ku**/~**ek** on board; ~**kiem** by ship
statut *m* (*-u; -y*) statute(s *pl.*); ~owy statutory
statyczny static
statyst|a *m* (*-y; -ści, -ów*), ~ka *f* (*-i; G -tek*) extra; *fig.* bystander; ~yczny statistic(al); ~yka *f* (*-i; 0*) statistics *sg./pl.*
statyw *m* (*-u; -y*) tripod
staw *m* (*-u; -y*) pond; *med.* joint
stawać (*-ję*) stand (**na** *A, L* on; **za** *I* behind; **przed** *I* in front of); (*zatrzymać*

się) stop, halt; (*zgłaszać się*) report (**do** *G,* **przed** to); (*zaczynać*) go (**do** *G* to); → **dąb, stanąć**
stawać się (*-ję*) become; → **stać²**
staw|iać (*-am*) stand, put; *fig. zwł.* place; *pomnik* erect; *namiot* pitch; *płot* put up; *pytanie* ask; (*w grze*) bet; ~**iać opór** put up resistance; ~**iać się** appear; report (**do** *G* to); F get tough; ~ić (*-im*)*pf.* (*-ę*) → **czoło**; ~**ić się = stawiać się**; ~iennictwo *n* (*-a; 0*) appearance; ~ka *f* (*-i; G -wek*) (**dzienna, podatkowa** daily, tax) rate; (*w grze*) stake
staż *m* (*-u; -e*) (practical) training; ~ **pracy** seniority; **trzyletni** ~ **pracy** three years' service; ~ysta *m* (*-y; G -tów*), ~ystka *f* (*-i; G -tek*) trainee
stąd from here; (*dlatego*) therefore
stąp|ać (*-am*) ⟨~**nąć**⟩ (*-nę*) tread, stamp
stchórzyć *pf.* (*-ę*) back out, F chicken out
stek¹ *m* (*-u; -i*) (*wyzwisk itp.*) heap, pack
stek² *m* (*-u; -i*) *gastr.* steak
stek³ *m* (*-u; -i*) *biol.* cloaca; ~**owiec** *m* (*-wca; -wce*) *zo.* monotreme
stempel *m* (*-pla; -ple*) (rubber) stamp
stemplow|ać ⟨**o-**⟩ (*-uję*) stamp; ~y stamp; **znaczek** ~**y** postage mark
stenografi|a *f* (*GDL -ii; 0*) shorthand; ~ować (*-uję*) record in shorthand
step *m* (*-u; -y*) steppe; ~owy steppe
ster *m* (*-u; -y*) *naut.* rudder; *fig.* helm
sterburta *f* (*-y; G -*) starboard
stercz *m* (*-a; -e*) *anat.* prostate (gland); ~ący sticking out; ~eć (*-ę*) stick out, jut out, project; F stand around *lub* about
stereo (*idkl.*) stereo; stereophonic; ~foniczny stereophonic
stereotypow|o *adv.* in a stereotyped way; ~y stereotyped, stock
sternik *m* (*-a; -cy*) *naut.* helmsman, steersman; *sport:* cox(swain)
sterow|ać (*-uję*) steer; control; ~anie *n* (*-a; G -ań*) control; **zdalne** ~**anie** remote control; ~y steering
sterta *f* (*-y; G -*) heap, pile, stack
sterujący steering
sterydy *m/pl.* (*-ów*): *pharm.* → **anaboliczne** anabolic steroids *pl.*
steryl|izować (*-uję*) sterilize; ~ny sterile
steward *m* (*-da; -dzi*) *aviat.* flight attendant; *naut.* steward; ~essa *f* (*-y; G -*) *aviat.* air hostess, flight attendant; *naut.* stewardess

strach

stębnować (-uję) backstitch

stęch|lizna f (-y; 0) musty smell; ~ły musty

stękać (-am) ⟨~nąć⟩ (-nę) moan, groan

stępi|ać (-am) ⟨~ć⟩ blunt; ~ony blunted

stępka f (-i; G -pek) keel

stęskniony nostalgic; longing (za I for); ~ za ojczyzną homesick; → tęskny

stęż|ać (-am) ⟨~yć⟩ (-ę) chem. concentrate; bud. brace; ~enie n (-a; -eń) chem. concentration; bud. bracing; ~enie pośmiertne rigor mortis; ~ony concentrated; bud. braced

stłoczony crowded

stłu|c pf. → tłuc; ~czenie n (-a; G -eń) med. bruise, contusion; ~miony muted

sto (m-os stu) hundred; → 666

stocznia f (-i; -e) shipyard

sto|czyć pf. → staczać; ~doła f (-y; G -dół) barn; ~gi pl. → stóg

sto|i → stać¹; ~isko n (-a; G -) stand, stall; (w dużym sklepie: półki) gondola, shelves pl., (lada) counter; ~jak m (-a; -i) stand; (na płyty) rack; ~jący standing; miejsce ~jące standing place, standing room

stok m (-u; -i) slope

stokrot|ka f (-i; G -tek) bot. daisy; ~ny hundredfold

stola|rnia f (-i; -e) carpenter's/cabinet-maker's (workshop); ~rz m (-a; -e) carpenter; (meblowy) cabinet-maker

stol|ec m (-lca; -lce) med. stool; ~ica f (-y; G -) capital (city); (biskupstwa itp.) see; Ωica Apostolska Holy See; ~ik m (-a; -i) → stół; ~nica f (-y; -e, G -) (pastry) board

stol|eczny capital; ~ek m (-łka; -łki) stool; ~ować (-uję) cater for; ~ować się dine (u with)

stołowni|czka f (-i; G -czek), ~k m (-a; -cy) diner

sto|łowy table; ~łówka f (-i; G -wek) canteen; ~łówkowy canteen; ~ły pl. → stół

stomatologiczny dental, dentist's; fotel ~ dentist's chair

stonka f (-i; G-nek) zo. Colorado beetle

stonoga f (-i; G -nóg) zo. centipede

stop m (-u; -y) tech. alloy

stop|a f (-y; G stóp) foot (też fig.); (buta) sole; (jednostka miary) foot (= 0,30 m); econ. rate; ~a życiowa standard of living; u stóp (G) at the foot (of); od stóp

do głów from head to foot; → procentowy

stoper m (-a; -y) stopwatch

stop|ić pf. → stapiać; ~ień m (-pnia; -pnie) step (też fig.), stair; degree (też math., geogr., fig.); mil. rank; (w szkole) Brt. mark, Am. grade; ~ień wyższy, najwyższy gr. comparative, superlative degree; do tego ~nia, że to such an extent that; w mniejszym ~niu to a lesser extent; w wysokim ~niu to a high degree

stop-klatka f (-i) freeze-frame

stopniały melted

stopniow|ać (-uję) grade, change by degrees; gr. compare; ~o adv. gradually; ~y gradual, by degrees

stopować (-uję) stop, halt

storczyk m (-a; -i) bot. orchid

stornia f (-i; -e) zo. flounder

stornować ⟨wy-⟩ (-uję) econ. reverse

stos m (-u; -y) pile, stack; (dla czarownicy) stake; ułożyć w ~ stack, pile

stosow|ać ⟨za-⟩ (-uję) use, apply; ~ać się (do G) apply (to); conform (to); comply (with), be appropriate (for); → dostosowywać się; ~any nauka itp. applied; ~nie adv. appropriately (do G to); ~ny appropriate, suitable; w ~nej chwili in the appropriate moment; uważać za ~ne (A) think it fit (to)

stosun|ek m (-nku; -nki) math. ratio; (kontakt) relation, relationship; (płciowy) intercourse; w ~ku do (G) in relation (to); być w dobrych ~kach (z I) have good relations (with); ~kowo adv. relatively; ~kowy relative

stow. skrót pisany: stowarzyszenie association

stowarzysz|enie n (-a; G -eń) association; ~ony associated

stoż|ek m (-żka; -żki) cone (też math.); ~kowato adv. conically; ~kowaty conical

stóg m (stogu; stogi) haystack

stół m (stołu; stoły) table; (posiłki) board; przy stole at the table; nakryć ~ lay the table

stówka f (-i; G -wek) one hundred

str. skrót pisany: strona p. (page)

straceni|e n (-a; G -eń) (więźnia) execution; loss; nie mieć nic do ~a have nothing to lose

strach m (-u; -y) fear, fright, dread;

(zjawa) nightmare, *Brt.* spectre, *Am.* specter; **ze ~u (przed I)** for fear (of); **aż ~** awfully; **~ na wróble** scarecrow

strac|ić (-ę) *pf.* → **tracić**; *skazańca* execute; **~ony** executed; (*zgubiony*) lost

stragan m (-u; -y) stall; ~iarka f (-i; G -rek), ~iarz m (-a; -e) stall-holder

strajk m (-u; -i) (*powszechny, okupacyjny* general, sit-down/sit-in) strike; **~ować** (-uję) strike; go on strike; **~owy** striking; **~ujący 1.** striking; **2.** m (-ego; -y), **~ująca** f (-ej; -e) striker

strapi|enie n (-a; G -eń) trouble, problem, worry; **~ony** troubled, dejected

strasz|ak m (-a; -i) toy gun; → **straszydło**; **~liwie** adv. frightfully, horribly; **~liwy** frightful, horrible; **~ny** terrible; **~yć** *v/t.* ⟨na-, prze-⟩ frighten, scare; **~yć⟨wy-⟩ się** get a fright; *v/i.* haunt; **tu ~y** this place is haunted; **~ydło** n (-a; -deł) nightmare; *fig.* scarecrow, frump

strat|a f (-y; G -) loss (*też econ.*); **ze ~ą** at a loss; **narazić się na ~ę** suffer losses

strategiczny strategic

stratny: **być ~m** suffer a loss

straw|a f (-y; G -) food; **~ić** *pf.* → **trawić**; **~ny** digestible

straż f (-y; -e) (*przyboczna, przednia* body, advance) guard; **trzymać pod ~ą** keep under guard; **~ pożarny** → **~acki** fire; fireman's; **~ak** m (-a; -cy) fireman; **~nica** f (-y; -e) watchtower; **~niczka** f (-i; G -czek) guard, warder; **~nik** m (-a; -cy) watchman, guard, warder

strąc|ać ⟨~ić⟩ knock off; precipitate (*też ze szczytu itp.*)

strą|czek m (-czka; -czki), **~k** m (-a; -i) pod

stref|a f (-y; G -) zone, area, region; **~owy** zone, zonal

stremowany nervous

stres m (-u; -y) stress; **~owy** stressing

streszcz|ać ⟨-am⟩ ⟨**streścić**⟩ (-szczę) abbreviate, summarize; **~aćsię** be brief; **~enie** n (-a; G -eń) abbreviation, summary

stręczy|cielstwo n (-a; 0) procurement; **~ć** procure; → **nastręczać**

striptizerka f (-i; G -rek) striptease artist, stripper

strofa f (-y; G -) stanza

strofować (-uję) criticize, reprimand

stroić ⟨-ję, strój⟩ ⟨u-, wy-⟩ decorate; **~ ⟨wy-⟩ się** dress up ⟨na-⟩ *mus.*, *tech.*

tune; (*t-ko impf.*) figle play, make; *miny* make

stroj|e pl. → **strój**; **~ny** decorated, ornamented; *ktoś* dressed up

strom|o adv. steeply; **~y** steep, precipitous

stron|a f (-y; G -) side (*też fig.*); (*książki*) page; *jur.* party (**w** L to); **cztery ~y świata** the four points of the compass; **na ~ę** aside; **ze ~y** (G) *fig.* on the part of; **w ~ę** (G) in the direction (of); **z jednej ~y … z drugiej ~y …** on the one hand … on the other (hand) …; **~a tytułowa** title page

stronica f (-y; G -) page

stronić (-ę) (od G) avoid, escape (from)

stronni|ctwo n (-a; G -) *pol.* party; **~czka** f (-i; G -czek) supporter, adherent, follower; **~czo** adv. in a biased way; **~czy** biased, prejudiced; **~k** m (-a; -cy) supporter, adherent, follower

stront m (-u; 0) *chem.* strontium

strop m (-u; -y) ceiling, ceiling; *górnictwo:* roof

stroskany anxious, careworn

stroszyć ⟨na-⟩ (-ę) ruffle (up), bristle; **~ ⟨na-⟩ się** become ruffled, bristle

strój m (stroju; stroje, strojów) dress, costume; → **adamowy**

stróż m (-a; -e) watchman, caretaker; → **~ka** f (-i; G -żek) caretaker; → **anioł**

strul- *pf.* → **tru-**; **~dzony** weary, fatigued

strug m (-a; -i) *tech.* plane; **~a** f (-i; G -) stream, brook; (*wody*) gush, jet; **~ać** ⟨o-⟩ (-am) *figurkę* carve; *tech.* plane; F *fig.* play, act

struktura f (-y; G -) structure

strumie|ń m (-nia; -nie) stream; *fig. też* torrent; **padać ~niem, ~niami** pour with rain

strumyk m (-a; -i) → **strumień**; trickle

strun|a f (-y; G -) string; *anat.* chord; **~y** pl. **głosowe** vocal chords pl.; **~owy** string

strup m (-a; -y) *med.* scab

strusi ostrich

struś m (-sia; -sie) zo. ostrich

strwożony frightened

strych m (-u; -y) loft, attic

stryczek m (-czka; -czki) halter (*też fig.*)

stryj m (-a; -owie) uncle; **~eczny: brat ~eczny, siostra ~eczna** cousin; **~enka** f (-i; G -nek) aunt; **~ostwo** n

(-a; G -) uncle and aunt

strzał m (-u; -y) shot;~a f (-y; G-) arrow; ~ka f (-i; G -lek) arrow; (w sporcie) dart; anat. fibula; ~kowy anat. fibular

strząs|ać (-am) ⟨~nąć⟩ (-nę) shake down

strzec (G) guard, keep watch (over); ~ **się** be on one's guard; look out for

strzecha f (-y; G -) thatch

strzel|ać (-am) (**do** G) shoot (to) (też sport), fire (at); (trzaskać) snap, click; ~ać **bramkę** score; ~anina f (-y; G -) shooting; ~ba f (-y; G -) shotgun; ~ec m (-lca; G -lców) shot; ~**ec wyborowy** marksman; **Ɛec znak Zodiaku**: Sagittarius; **on(a) jest spod znaku Ɛca** he/she is (a) Sagittarius; ~**ić** (-a; 0) sport: shooting; ~**ić** pf. (-lę) → **strzelać**; ~**isty** slender, soaring; fig. lofty; ~**nica** f (-y; G -) shooting range

strzem|iączko n (-a; G -czek) strap; ~**ienny** m (-ego; 0) stirrup cup; ~**ię** n (-enia; -iona, G -ion) stirrup

strzep|ywać (-uję) ⟨~nąć⟩ (-nę) shake off, shake down

strzeżony guarded

strzęp m (-u; -y) shred, scrap; fig. bit, piece;~**ić** ⟨wy-⟩ (-ę) fringe; ~**ić się** fray

strzyc ⟨o-⟩ włosy cut, crop; trawę mow, cut; owce shear; ~ **się** have a haircut; impf. ~ **uszami** prick one's ears

strzyk|ać (-am) squirt, spurt; med. have a stabbing pain; ~**awka** f (-i; G -wek) syringe; ~**nąć** pf. → **strzykać**

strzyż|enie n (-a; G -eń) cutting, shearing; mowing; ~**ony** shorn

stu m-os → **sto**; → **666**

studen|cki student(s'); **dom ~cki** Brt. hall of residence, Am. dormitory;~**t** m (-a; -ci), ~**tka** f (-i; G -tek) student

studi|a pl. (**medyczne** medical) studies pl. (**na, w** L at); ~**ować** (-uję) study; ~**um** n (idkl.; -a; -iów) study; college

studnia f (-i; -e) well

studniówka f (-i; G -wek) graduation ball (in secondary schools, traditionally 100 days before the final exams)

studzić ⟨o-⟩ cool down

studzienny well

stuk m (-u; -i) knocking; ~**ać** ⟨~nąć⟩ knock (**do** G, **w** A on, at); serce: pound; silnik: knock, pink; ~**nięty** F loony, Brt. barmy

stu|lecie n (-a; G -eci) century; (roczni-

ca) centenary; ~**letni** a hundred years old; ~**metrówka** f (-i;G-wek) hundred metres sg.; ~**procentowy** (one-)hundred per cent

stwardni|ały hardened; ~**enie** n (-a; G -eń) hardening; ~**enie rozsiane** med. multiple sclerosis

stwarzać (-am) create

stwierdz|ać (-am) ⟨~**ić**⟩ find, establish, state; ~**enie** n (-a; G -eń) finding; statement

stworz|enie n (-a; 0) creation, rel. the Creation; (pl. -a) creature; ~**yć** pf. → **stwarzać**

stwórca m (-y; G -ców) creator

styczeń m (-cznia; -cznie) January

styczna f (-ej; G -ych) math. tangent

styczniowy January

styczn|ość f (-ści; 0) contact; **wejść w ~ość** (**z** I) get in touch lub contact (with); ~**y: punkt ~y** point of contact

stygnąć ⟨o-, wy-⟩ (-nę) cool (też fig.); ⟨za-⟩ set; krew: congeal

styk m (-u; -i) touch, contact; (miejsce) joint; **na ~** edge to edge; fig. by a narrow margin; ~**ać** (-am) bring into contact, bring together; ~**ać się** touch (**z** I to); ~**owy** contact; złącze butt

styl m (-u; -e) style; ~**istyczny** stylistic; ~**owo** adv. stylishly, elegantly; ~**owy** stylish, elegant

stymul|ator m (-a; -y): med. ~**ator serca** pace maker; ~**ować** (-uję) stimulate

stypa f (-y; G -) (funeral) wake

stypend|ium n (idkl.; -ia, -iów) scholarship, grant; ~**ysta** m (-y; -ści), ~**ystka** f (-i; -tek) scholar, grantee, scholarship holder

styropian m (-u; -y) polystyrene (foam)

subiektywn|ie adv. subjectively; ~**y** subjective

sub|lokator(ka f) m subtenant, lodger; ~**lokatorski: pokój ~lokatorski** subleased room; ~**ordynacja** f (-i; 0) obedience; ~**skrybować** (-uję) subscribe (A to), take out; ~**skrypcja** f (-i; -e) subscription (**na** A to); ~**stancja** f (-i; -e) substance

sub|sydiować (-uję)subsidize,support; ~**telny** subtle; ~**wencjonować** (-uję) subsidize

such|arek m (-rka; -rki) (**dla dzieci**) rusk, biscuit; ~**o** adv. dryly; ~**ość** f (-ści; 0) dryness

suchoty *hist. pl.* (-) consumption, tuberculosis

such|y (*m-os susi*) dry (*też fig.*); (*wyschnięty*) withered, dried up; *osoba* gaunt; **wytrzeć do ~a** wipe dry

Sudety *pl.* the Sudety *pl.*, the Sudeten *pl.*

sufit *m* (*-u; -y*) *bud.* ceiling

suflet *m* (*-u; -y*) *gastr.* soufflé

sufragan *m* (*-a; -i*) *rel.* suffragan (bishop)

suge|rować ⟨*za-*⟩ (*-uję*) suggest, propose; **~stia** *f* (*GDL -ii;-e*) suggestion

suita *f* (*-y; G -*) *mus.* suite

suka *f* (*-i; G -*) bitch (*też pej.*); she-dog

sukces *m* (*-y; -u*) success; **odnosić ~** succeed; **~ja** *f* (*-i; G -e*) succession; **~ywny** successive

sukien|ka *f* (*-i; G -nek*) dress; **~nice** *f/pl.* (*G -*) cloth hall; **~ny** cloth

sukinsyn *m* (*-a; -y*) ∨ son of a bitch

sukn|ia *f* (*-i; -e, -i/-ien*) (*zwł.* evening) dress; **~o** *n* (*-a; G sukien*) cloth

sułtan *m* (*-a; -i*) sultan; **~ka** *f* (*-i; G -nek*) *bot.* sultana

sum|a *f* (*-y; G -*) sum; (*kwota też*) amount; *rel.* high mass; **w ~ie** in all, *lub* altogether

sumien|ie *n* (*-a; G -eń*) conscience; **~ny** conscientious

sumow|ać (*-uję*) add up (**się** *v/i.*); **~anie** *n* (*-a; G -ań*) addition

sunąć (*-nę, -ń!*) glide; (*na kółkach, piłka*) roll

supeł *m* (*-pła; -pły*) knot

super super; *w złoż.* super-, ultra-; **~nowoczesny** ultra-modern; **~sam** *m* (*-u; -y*) (*zwł.* self-service) supermarket

surfing *m* (*-u; -i*) *sport:* surfing; **~owy** surfing; **deska ~owa** surf-board

surogat *m* (*-u; -y*) surrogate, substitute

surow|cowy raw material; **~ica** *f* (*-y; -e, G -*) serum; **~iec** *m* (*-wca; -wce*) raw material; **~ce** *pl.* **naturalne** natural resources *pl.*; **~o** *adv.* severely; harshly; **na ~o** raw; **~ość** *f* (*-ści; 0*) severity, harshness; **~y** raw; severe; harsh; **w stan ~y zakończony** *bud.* structurally complete

surówka *f* (*-i; G -wek*) (*zwł.* raw vegetable) salad; *tech.* pig-iron

sus *m* (*-a; -y*) jump, leap, bound

susi *m-os* → **suchy**

susza *f* (*-y; G -*) drought; **~rka** *f* (*-i; G* *-rek*) dryer; (*na naczynia*) *Brt.* draining rack, *Am.* (dish) drainer; **~rnia** *f* (*-i; -e*) drying room

susz|enie *n* (*-a; G -eń*) drying; **~ony** dried; **~yć** ⟨*wy-*⟩ (*-ę*) dry; **~yć sobie głowę** (*nad I*) rack one's brains over

sutanna *f* (*-y; G -*) *rel.* cassock

sutek *m* (*-tka, -tki*) *anat.* nipple

sutenerstwo *n* (*-a; 0*) pimping

suterena *f* (*-y; G -*) basement

suty generous; opulent

suw *m* (*-u; -y*) *tech., mot.* stroke; **~ać** (*-am*) *v/t.* slide; **~ać nogami** shuffle; **~ak** *m* (*-a; -i*) (**logarytmiczny** slide-)-rule; → **zamek błyskawiczny**

suwerenn|ość *f* (*-ści; 0*) sovereignty; **~y** sovereign

suwnica *f* (*-y; G -*) *tech.* (overhead) crane

swa (*ściągn. swoja*) → **swój**

swar|liwie *adv.* quarrelsomely; contentiously; **~liwy** quarrelsome, contentious; **~y** *m/pl.* (*-ów*) quarrels *pl.*, quarrelling

swastyka *f* (*-i; G -*) swastika

swat *m* (*-a; -owie/-ci*), **~ka** *f* (*-i; G -tek*) matchmaker; **~y** *m/pl.* (*G -ów*) matchmaking

swawol|a *f* (*-i; -e*) frolic, prank; **~ić** (*-ę*) frolic; **~ny** playful; → **figlarny**

swąd *m* (*swędu; 0*) smell of burning

swe (*ściągn. swoje*) → **swój**

sweter *m* (*-tra; -try*) sweater

swędz|enie *n* (*-a; 0*) itching; **~i(e)ć** (*-ę*) itch

swobod|a *f* (*-y; G -bód*) freedom; liberty; **~nie** *adv.* freely; **~ny** free

swoj|i *m-s* → **swój**; **~isty** specific; characteristic; **~iście** *adv.* specifically; characteristically; **~ja**, **~je 1.** → **swój**. **2. ~je** *n* (*-ego*; 0) one's own; **obstawać przy ~im** stand up to one's opinion; **postawić na ~im** get one's own way; **robić ~je** do one's job; → **czas, dopiąć**; **~jski** familiar; home-made

swój *poss.* (**swoja** *f,* **swoje** *n i pl.,* **swoi** *m-os*) my, your, his, her, our, your, their (*często + own*); **wziął swoje rzeczy** he took his things; **swoimi słowami** in your own words; **chodzić swoimi drogami** walk by oneself; **na ~ sposób** in one's own way; → **krewny, rodaczka, rodak, swoje**

Syberia *f* (*GDl -ii; 0*) Siberia

sycić ⟨na-⟩ (-cę) satiate; *fig.* satisfy

Sycylia *f* (*GDL -ii; 0*) Sicily

syczeć (-ę) hiss

syfon *m* (*-u; -y*) siphon

sygnalizator *m* (*-a; -y*) (**pożarowy** fire) alarm; **~ alarmowy** alarm system

sygnał *m* (*-u; -y*) signal; **~ świetlny** headlight flasher; **~ wzywania pomocy** *naut.* Mayday call

sygnatura *f* (*-y*) (*w bibliotece*) catalogue number

sygnet *m* (*-u; -y*) signet-ring

syjonistyczny Zionistic

syk *m* (*-u; -i*) hiss; **~ać** (*-am*), **~nąć** *v/s.* hiss

sylab|a *f* (*-y; G -*) syllable; **~izować** (*-uję*) read letter by letter

syl|wester *m* (*-a; -y*) New Year's Eve; **obchodzić ~westra** see the New Year in; **~westrowy** New Year's; **~wetka** *f* (*-i; G -tek*) silhouette; *fig.* portrait

symbol *m* (*-u; -e*) symbol; **~iczny** symbolic

symetr|ia *f* (*GDL -ii; -e*) symmetry; **~yczny** symmetric(al)

symfoni|a *f* (*GDL -ii; -e*) *mus.* symphony; **~czny** symphony; **poemat ~czny** symphonic poem

sympat|ia *f* (*GDL -ii; -e*) liking, affection; F (*dziewczyna*) girlfriend, (*chłopak*) boyfriend; **czuć ~ię** (**do** *G*) feel attracted (to); **~yczny** likeable; **~yk** *m* (*-a; -cy*) sympathizer

symptom *m* (*-u; -y*) symptom

symul|ować (-*uję*) simulate; *chorobę* fake; **~taniczny** simultaneous

syn *m* (*-a; -owie*) son

synagoga *f* (*-i; G -*) *rel.* synagogue

synchro|niczny synchronic; **~nizować** ⟨z-⟩ (-*uję*) synchronize

syndyk *m* (*-a; -cy/-owie*) receiver

synek *m* (*-nka; -nkowie*) son

syno|d *m* (*-u; -y*) synod; **~nim** *m* (*-u; -y*) synonym; **~nimiczny** synonymous

synoptyczny synoptic

synow|a *f* (-*ej; -e*) daughter-in-law; **~ski** filial; **po ~sku** like a son

syntetyczny synthetic; (*plastikowy*) plastic

sypać (-*ię*) *v/t.* mąkę *itp.* pour (**się** *v/i.*); sprinkle; *wał* build; *fig.* reel off; F *kogoś* split on; *v/i. śnieg:* snow; **~ się** *tynk itp.*: crumble off *lub* away (**z** *G* from); *wąsy:* sprout; *fig.* rain down; *iskry:* fly

sypial|nia *f* (*-i; -e*) bedroom; (*w internacie itp.*) dormitory; **~ny** bedroom

syp|ki loose; **~nąć** *pf.* → **sypać**

syrena *f* (*-y; G -*) *tech.* siren; *zo.* sea cow; (*w mitologii*) mermaid, siren

syrop (*-u; -y*) syrup

Syria *f* (*GDL -ii; 0*) Syria

syryj|ski Syrian; ♀czyk *m* (*-a; -cy*), ♀ka (*-i; G -jek*) Syrian

system *m* (*-u; -y*) system; **~atyczny** systematic

syt|ny filling; **~ość** *f* (*-ści; 0*) satiety, repleteness

sytuac|ja (*-i; -e*) situation; **~yjny** situational

sytuowa|ć ⟨u-⟩ (-*uję*) locate, situate; **dobrze ~ny** well-to-do

syty (*pred.* **do syta**) full-up

szabas *m* (*-u; -y*), szabat *m* (*-u; -y*) *rel.* Sabbath

szabl|a *f* (*-i; -e*) Brt. sabre, Am. saber; **~ista** *m* (*-y; -ści*) Brt. sabre (Am. saber) fencer

szablon *m m* pattern; (*językowy*) cliché; **~owo** *adv.* in a clichéd *lub* stereotyped manner; **~owy** clichéd, stereotyped

szach *m* (*-a; -owie*) shah; (*-u/-a; -y*) check (*też fig.*); **dać ~a** (give) check; **~ mat** checkmate; *t-ko pl.* **~y** (*-ów*) chess; **~ista** *m* (*-y; -ści, G -tów*), **~istka** *f* (*-i; G -tek*) chess-player; **~ownica** *f* (*-y; -e, G -*) chessboard; *fig.* patchwork

szachr|aj *m* (*-a; -e*), **~ajka** *f* (*-i; G -jek*) swindler; **~ajstwo** *n* (*-a; G -*) swindle; **~ować** (-*uję*) swindle

szachy *pl.* → **szach**

szacować ⟨o-⟩ (-*uję*) estimate

szacun|ek *m* (*-nku; 0*) esteem, respect; (*ocena*) estimate, estimation; → **wyraz**; **~kowo** *adv.* approximately

szafa *f* (*-y; G -*) wardrobe, cupboard; **~ grająca** jukebox

szafir *m* (*-u; -y*) sapphire; **~owy** sapphire

szafk|a *f* (*-i; G -fek*) cabinet; locker; **~a nocna** bedside table; **~owy** cabinet

szafować (-*uję*) (*I*) be wasteful (with)

szafran *m* (*-u; -y*) *bot.*, *gastr.* saffron

szajka *f* (*-i; G -jek*) gang

szal *m* (*-a; -e*) shawl, scarf

szala *f* (*-i; -e*) scale (pan)

szalbierstwo *n* (*-a; G -*) imposition

S

szale|ć (-eję) go wild, rage; be beside o.s. (**z** G with); be mad (**za** I about); ~niec m (-ńca; -ńcy) madman, maniac, lunatic; ~ńczo adv. madly, crazily; ~ńczy mad, crazy; lunatic; ~ństwo n (-a; G -) madness, craziness, craze

szalet m (-u; -y) public convenience

szalik m (-a; -i) scarf

szalony mad, crazy

szalować ⟨o-⟩ (-uję) board, shutter

szalunek m (-nku; -nki) boarding, shuttering

szalupa f (-y; G -) naut. launch; lifeboat

szał m (-u; 0) rage, frenzy; craze; **wpaść w ~** go mad; → **furia**

szałas m (-u; -e) shanty, shed, hut

szałowy great, fantastic

szałwia f (GDL -ii; -e) bot. sage

szamotać (-czę/-cę): ~ **się** struggle

szampa|n m (-a; -y) gastr. champagne; ~ński champagne; fig. wonderful

szampon m (-u; -y) shampoo

szaniec m (-ńca; -ńce) entrenchment

szanow|ać (-uję) respect, esteem; prawo respect, observe; ubranie treat with care; ~ny respected; (w listach) Dear

szansa f (-y; G -) chance, prospect

szantaż m (-u; -e) blackmail; ~ować (-uję) blackmail; ~ysta m (-y; G -stów), ~ystka f (-i; G -tek) blackmailer

szarak m (-a; -i) zo. hare

szarańcza f (-y; -e, -y) zo. locust

szarfa f (-y; G -) sash

szarlata|n m (-a; -i) charlatan; ~neria f (GDL -ii; 0) charlatanism

szarlotka f (-i; G -tek) apple-pie

szaro adv. w złoż. Brt. grey, Am. gray; ~tka f (-i; G -tek) bot. edelweiss; ~zielony grey-green

szarówka f (-i; G -wek) twilight, dusk

szarp|ać v/i. tug, yank (**za** A at); pojazd: jerk, jolt; ⟨po-, roz-⟩ v/t. tear up; ~ać się struggle; (na A) lash out (on); ~nąć v/s. (-nę) → szarpać; ~nięcie n (-a; G -ęć) jolt, jerk

szaruga f (-i; G -) rainy weather

szary (m-os -rzy) Brt. grey, Am. gray; fig. drab; **na ~m końcu** at the very end

szarz|eć ⟨po-⟩ (-eję) grow dusky; grow Brt. grey, Am. gray; ~eje it is getting dark; ~y pl. → szary; ~yzna f (-y; 0) fig. monotony, tediousness

szastać (-am) → szafować

szata f (-y; G -) dress, garment; print. layout

szata|n m (-a; -i/-y) satan; ~ński satanic

szatkować (-uję) gastr. shred

szatnia f (-i; -e) Brt. cloakroom, Am. checkroom; (do przebrania się) changing room; ~rka f (-i; G -rek), ~rz m (-a; -e) cloakroom attendant

szatyn m (-a; -i), ~ka f (-i; G -nek) dark-haired/brown-haired person

szczać V (-ę) piss

szczapa f (-y; G -) piece of wood

szczaw m (-wiu; -wie, -wi) bot. sorrel; ~iowy sorrel

szczą|tek m (-tka; -tki) fragment; przew. ~ki pl. remains pl.; (po katastrofie) debris; ~kowy residual

szczeb|el m (-bla; -ble) rung; fig. rank, level; pol. **na ... ~lu** at the ... level

szczebiot m (-u; -y) twittering; chirping; ~ać (-czę/-cę) twitter; chirp

szczecina f (-y; G -) bristle; (na brodzie) stubble

szczególn|ie adv. particularly, in particular; especially, specially; ~ość (-ści; 0): **w ~ości** in particular; ~y particular; especial, special

szczegół m (-u; -y) detail; ~owo adv. in detail; ~owy detailed

szczekać (-am) bark

szczel|ina f (-y; G -) split, crevice; ~ny air-tight, water-tight

szczeni|ak m (-a; -i) fig. pej. whippersnapper; → ~ę n (-cia; -nięta, G -niąt) puppy

szczep m (-u; -y) tribe; biol., med. strain; agr. scion, graft; ~ić (-ę) ⟨za-⟩ med. vaccinate; ⟨prze-⟩ med. graft; ~ienie n (-a; G -eń) med. vaccination; agr. grafting; ~ionka f (-i; G -nek) vaccine

szczerba f (-y; G -) chip, nick; (między zębami) gap (in one's teeth); ~ty gap-toothed; → **wyszczerbiony**

szcze|rość f (-ści; 0) frankness, openness, sincerity; ~ry frank, open, sincere; ~rze adv. frankly, openly, sincerely

szczerzyć ⟨wy-⟩ (-ę): ~ **zęby** bare one's teeth; fig. give a friendly smile (**do** G to)

szczędzić (-ę): **nie ~** (G) not spare, be generous

szczęk m (-u; -i) clank, clink; ~a f (-i; G -) anat. jaw; **sztuczna ~a** false teeth pl., denture; ~ać (-am) clink, clank szczęś|ciara f (-y; G -), ~ciarz m (-a; -e) lucky person; ~cić się: ~ci mu się he is lucky; ~cie n (-a; 0) (good) luck, fortune; ~ciem, na ~cie fortunately; luckily; ~liwie adv. fortunately; luckily; happily; ~liwy fortunate; lucky; happy

szczod|ry generous; ~rze adv. generously

szczot|eczka f (-i; G -czek) (do zębów tooth) brush; ~ka f (-i; G -tek) brush; ~ka do zamiatania broom; ~ka mechaniczna carpet sweeper; ~kować ⟨wy-⟩ (-uję) brush

szczuć ⟨po-⟩ (-ję) set the dog(s) on

szczudło n (-a; G -det) stilt; → kula²

szczupak m (-a; -i) zo. pike

szczup|leć ⟨ze-⟩ (-eje) slim down, get slimmer; ~ły slim, slender

szczu|r m (-a; -y) zo. rat (też fig.); ~rzy rat

szczwany shrewd, crafty

szczycić się (-cę) (I) boast, be proud (of)

szczygieł m (-gła, -gły) zo. goldfinch

szczy|pać (-pię) pinch; trawę nip; dym: sting, be stinging; ~pce pl. (-piec/ -pców) → kleszcze; ~piorek m (-rku; 0) chives pl.; ~pta f (-y; G -) pinch

szczyt m (-u; -y) top (też fig.); (góry) peak, summit; bud. gable; (łóżka, stołu) head; godziny pl. ~u rush hours pl.; spotkanie na szczycie summit meeting; ~ny noble; ~ować (-uję) climax; ~owanie n (-a; G -ań) climax; ~owy summit; climax; peak

szedł(em) 3. (1.) os. pret. sg. → iść

szef m (-a; -owie) boss, chief; (kuchni) chef; ~owa f (-ej; -e) boss, chief

szejk m (-a; -owie) sheikh

szele|st m (-u; -y) rustle; ~ścić (-ę) rustle

szelki pl. (G -lek) Brt. braces pl., Am. suspenders pl.

szelma f/m (-y; G -/ów) rogue

szemrać (-rzę) deszcz, drzewa: whisper; strumyk: babble; fig. grumble, murmur

szep|nąć v/s (-nę) whisper; ~t m (-u; -y) whisper; ~tać (-cze/-cę) whisper; ~tany whispered

szer. skrót pisany: szerokość w. (width); szeregowiec Pvt. (private)

szereg m (-u; -i) row; line; series; (wydarzeń) chain

szeregowa|ć ⟨u-⟩ (-uję) line up; ~iec m (-wca; -wcy) mil. private; ~y 1. ordinary; 2. m (-ego; -wi) mil. private; ~i pl. mil. the ranks; ~i członkowie pl. rank and file

szermie|rka f (-i; 0) sport: fencing; ~rz m (-a; -e) (w sporcie) fencer

szerok|i wide, broad; ~o adv. widely, broadly

szeroko|kątny phot. wide-angle; ~ść f (-ści) breadth, width; ~ść torów rail. gauge; ~torowy rail. broad-gauge

szerszeń m (-nia; -nie) zo. hornet

sze|rszy, ~rzej adj./adv. comp. od → szeroki, -ko

szerzyć (-ę) spread (się v/i.)

szesna|stka mus. Brt. semiquaver, Am. sixteenth note; ~sto- w złoż. sixteen; ~sty sixteenth; ~ście sixteen; → 666

sześć. skrót pisany: sześcienny c (cubic)

sześci|an m (-u; -y) math. cube; podnieść do ~anu cube; ~enny math. cubic; kształt cubical

sześ|cio- w złoż. six; ~ciokąt m (-a; -y) hexagon; ~ciokrotny sixfold; ~cioletni six-year-long, -old; ~ciu m-os, ~ć six → 666

sześ|cdziesiąt sixty; → 666; ~dziesiąty sixtieth; ~set six hundred; → 666; ~setny six hundredth

Szetlandy pl. (G -ów) Shetland Islands pl., Shetlands pl.

szew m (szwu; szwy) seam; med. suture; zdjąć szwy remove the stitches; bez szwu seamless

szew|c m (-a; -y) shoemaker; ~ski shoemaker's

szkalować ⟨o-⟩ (-uję) malign

szkapa f (-y; G -) nag, hack

szkaradny hideous

szkarlatyna f (-y; 0) med. scarlet fever

szkatułka f (-i; G -łek) box

szkic m (-u; -e) sketch; ~ować ⟨na-⟩ (-uję) sketch; ~owo adv. sketchily; in rough; ~owy sketchy

szkielet m (-u; -y) anat. skeleton (też fig.)

szkiełko n (-a; G -łek) glass; (zegarka) crystal

szkla|nka f (-i; G -nek) glass; ~ny glass; ~rnia f (-i; -e) greenhouse, Brt. glass-house; ~rski glazier's; ~rz m (-a; -e) glazier

szkli|ć ⟨o-⟩ (-lę; -lij!) glaze; ~sty glassy; ~ście adv. in a glassy manner; ~wo n (-a; G -) anat. enamel; tech. glaze

szkło n (-a; G szkieł) glass

Szko|cja f (-i; 0) Scotland; 2cki Scots, Scottish

szkod|a¹ f (-y; G szkód) damage, harm; mischief; **na ~ę, ze ~ą dla** (G) to the detriment (of)

szkod|a² adv. pity; **~a, że** a pity that; **jaka ~a!** what a pity!; ~liwość f (-ści; 0) harmfulness; ~liwie adv. harmfully; ~liwy harmful; (niezdrowy) unhealthy; ~nik m (-a; -i) pest

szkodz|ić (-dzę) damage, harm; **co to ~i?** what harm does it do?; **nie ~i** not at all

szkol|enie n (-a; G -eń) training; ~ić ⟨**wy-**⟩ (-lę) train; ~nictwo n (-a; G -) educational system; ~ny school

szkoła f (-y; G szkół) school (też fig.); **~ wyższa** higher education institution

szkopuł m (-u; -y) hitch, difficulty

Szkot m (-a; -ci), ~ka f (-i; G -tek) Scot

szkółka f (-i; G -lek) → szkoła; course for beginners; agr. nursery

szkuner m (-a; -y) schooner

szkwał m (-u; -y) squall

szlaban m (-u; -y) gate, barrier

szlach|cianka f (-i; G -nek) noblewoman; ~cic m (-a; -e) nobleman; ~ecki noble

szlachetn|ość f (-ści; 0) nobility; ~y noble

szlachta f (-y; G -) nobility

szlafrok m (-a; -i) dressing-gown, Am. bath robe

szlak m (-u; -i) route, track; (turystyczny) trail

szlam m (-u; 0) mire, sludge

szli 3. os. pret. pl. → iść

szlifować ⟨o-⟩ (-uję) grind

szlochać (-am) sob

szła(m) 3. (1.) os. pret. pl. → iść

szmacia|ny rag; **lalka ~na** rag doll; ~rz m (-a; -e) rag-and-bone man; fig. bum

szmaragd m (-u; -y) emerald; ~owy emerald

szmat m: **~ drogi** a long way; **~ czasu** a long time; ~a f (-y; G -) rag; → ~ka f (-i; G -tek) cloth; rag

szmelc m (-u; 0) junk, rubbish

szmer m (-u; -y) noise, sound

szminka f (-i; G -nek) (do ust) lipstick; (do charakteryzacji) make-up

szmira f (-y) trash, rubbish

szmuglować (-uję) smuggle

sznur m (-a; -y) string (też fig.); cord (też electr.); **~ do bielizny** clothes-line; ~ek m (-rka; -rki) string, line; ~owadło n (-a; G -del) lace

sznycel m (-cla; -cle) gastr. schnitzel

szofer m (-a; -rzy) driver; ~ka f (-i; G -rek) cab

szok m (-u; -i) shock; ~ować ⟨**za-**⟩ shock; ~owy shock

szop m (-a; -y) zo. racoon

szop|a f (-y; G szop) shed; ~ka f (-i; G -pek) rel. crib

szorować ⟨**wy-**⟩ (-uję) scrub, scour

szorstk|o adv. roughly; coarsely; ~i rough; ktoś coarse, abrupt

szorty pl. (G -tów) shorts pl.

szosa f (-y; G szos) high road, highway

szowinistyczny chauvinist

szóst|ka f (-i; G -tek) six; (linia itp.) number six; ~y sixth; → **666**

szpachl|a f (-i; -e) spatula; ~ować (-uję) stop, fill

szpa|da f (-y; G -) épée; ~del m (-dla; -dle) spade; ~dzista m (-y; G -tów), ~dzistka f (-i; G -tek) épéeist

szpa|gat m (-u; -y) splits pl.; (sznurek) string; ~k m (-a; -i) zo. starling; ~kowaty Brt. greying, Am. greying; koń roan; ~ler m (-u; -y) line; ~ra f (-y; G -) slit, cleft; crack

szparag m (-u; -y) bot.: zw. **~i** pl. asparagus

szpargał m (-u; -y) bit of paper; **~y** pl. useless papers

szpecić (-cę) mar; ⟨**o-, ze-**⟩ disfigure

szperać (-am) rummage about lub through

szpetny ugly, unsightly

szpic m (-a; -e) point, tip; zo. spitz; ~el m (-cla; -cle) pej. informer; ~ruta f (-y; G -) riding whip

szpieg m (-a; -dzy) spy

szpiego|stwo n (-a; G -) spying, espionage; ~wać (-uję) spy; ~wski spy

szpik m (-u; 0) anat. marrow; → **kość**

szpil|ka f (-i; G -lek) pin; (do włosów) hairpin; (obcas) stiletto; ~owy bot. coniferous

szpinak m (-u; -i) bot. spinach

szpital m (-a; -e) hospital; ~ny hospital

szpon m (-u; 0) claw, talon

szprotka f (-i; G -tek) zo. sprat

szprycha f (-y; G -) spoke

szpul|a *f* (*-i*; *-e*) reel, spool; **~ka** *f* (*-i*; *G -lek*) reel, spool

szrama *f* (*-y*; *G -*) scar

szreń *f* (*-ni*; *0*) firn, névé

szron *m* (*-u*; *0*) frost

szt. *skrót pisany:* **sztuk(a)** pc. (*piece*)

sztab *m* (*-u*; *-y*) staff; **~ główny** headquarters *pl.*

sztab|a *f* (*-y*; *G -*) bar; **~a złota** gold bar *lub* ingot

sztabowy staff

sztacheta *f* (*-y*; *G -*) pale

sztafet|a *f* (*-y*; *G -*) *sport.* relay; **~owy: bieg ~owy** relay race

sztalug|a *f* (*-i*; *G -*): *zw.* **~i** easel

sztandar *m* (*-u*; *-y*) flag, standard; **~owy** flag, standard

sztang|a *f* (*-i*; *G -*) (*w sporcie*) weight; **~ista** *m* (*-y*; *G -ów*) (*w sporcie*) weightlifter

sztolnia *f* (*-i*; *-e*) (*w górnictwie*) gallery

szton *m* (*-u*; *-y*) chip

sztorc: *na* **~** on end

sztorm *m* (*-u*; *-y*) storm; **~owy** storm

sztruks|owy corduroy; **~y** *pl.* cords *pl.*

sztucz|ka *f* (*-i*; *G -czek*) trick; **~ny** artificial, *biżuteria itp.* imitation

sztućce *m/pl.* (*-éćów*) cutlery

sztufada *f* (*-y*; *G -*) *gastr.* marinated roast beef

sztuk|a *f* (*-i*; *G -*) art; (*jednostka*) piece; *theat.* play; (*umiejętność*) artistry; (*robienia czegoś*) knack; **historia ~i** history of art; **~a mięsa** boiled beef; **~ować** ⟨*nad-*⟩ (*-uję*) piece together

szturch|ać ⟨**~nąć**⟩ nudge, elbow

szturm *m* (*-u*; *-y*) *mil.* assault, storm; **~ować** (*-uję*) *mil.* storm; **~owy** *mil.* assault

sztych *m* (*-u*; *-y*) stab; (*rycina*) engraving

sztygar *m* (*-a*; *-rzy*) (*w górnictwie*) pit foreman

sztylet *m* (*-u*; *-y*) dagger

sztywn|ieć ⟨**ze-**⟩ (*-eję*) stiffen; grow stiff; **~o** *adv.* stiffly; **~y** stiff

szubienica *f* (*-y*; *G -*) gallows

szubrawiec *m* (*-wca*, *-wcy*) *pej.* scoundrel

szuf|elka *f* (*-i*; *G -lek*) (*do zamiatania*) dustpan; **~la** *f* (*-i*; *-e*) shovel; **~lada** *f* (*-y*; *G -*) drawer; **~lować** (*-uję*) shovel

szukać (*-am*) ⟨**po-**⟩ look for, search

szuler *m* (*-a*; *-rzy*) card-sharper

szum *m* (*-u*; *-y*) noise; (*fal*) hum; (*wody*, *drzew*) rustle; F *fig.* fuss

szumieć[1] (*-ę*, *-i*) be noisy; rustle

szum|ieć[2] (*-ę*, *-i*) effervesce; **~i mu w głowie** his head is buzzing; **~ny** noisy; *fig.* high-flown; **~owiny** *f/pl.* (*-*) scum (*też fig.*)

szur|ać (*-am*)scrape(**nogami**one'sfeet)

szus *m* (*-u/-a*; *-y*) (*w sporcie*) schuss

szuter *m* (*-tru*; *0*) gravel

szuwary *m/pl.* (*-ów*) reeds *pl.*

szwaczka *f* (*-i*; *G -czek*) needlewoman, seamstress

szwagier *m* (*-gra*; *-growie*) brother-in-law; **~ka** *f* (*-i*; *G -rek*) sister-in-law

Szwajcar *m* (*-a*; *-rzy*) Swiss; **~ia** *f* (*GDL -ii*) Switzerland; **~ka** Swiss; **2ski** Swiss

szwalnia *f* (*-i*; *-e*) sewing workshop

szwank *m* (*-u*; *0*): **bez ~u** unscathed; **~ować** (*-uję*) go wrong, malfunction

Szwecja *f* (*-i*; *0*) Sweden

Szwed *m* (*-a*; *-dzi*), **~ka** *f* (*-i*; *G -dek*) Swede

szwedz|ki Swedish; **mówić po ~ku** speak Swedish

szwu, szwy → szew

szyb *m* (*-u*; *-y*) shaft; **~ naftowy** oil well; **~a** *f* (*-y*; *G -*) (*window*) pane

szyb|ciej *adv. comp. od* → **~ki** fast, quick, swift; **~ko** *adv.* fast, quickly, swiftly

szyberdach *m* *mot.* sunroof, sliding roof

szybko|strzelny *mil.* quick-fire, quick-firing; **~ściomierz** speedometer; **~ściowy** high-speed; **~ść** *f* (*-ści*) speed, rapidity; *tech.*, *phys.* velocity; **~war** *m* (*-u*, *-y*) *gastr.* pressure cooker

szybow|ać (*-uję*) glide; **~iec** *m* (*-wca*; *-wce*) glider; **~nictwo** *n* (*-a*; *0*) gliding; **~nik** *m* (*-a*; *-cy*) glider pilot; **~y** gliding

szybszy *adj.* (*m-os -bsi*) *comp. od* → **szybki**

szyci|e *n* (*-a*; *G -yć*) sewing; **do ~a** sewing

szyć ⟨**u-**⟩ (*szyję*) sew

szydełko *n* (*-a*; *G -lek*) crochet hook; **~wać** (*-uję*) crochet

szyder|czo *adv.* derisively; **~czy** derisive; **~stwo** *n* (*-a*; *G -*) derisiveness

szydło *n* (*-a*; *G -deł*) awl

szydzić (*-dzę*) (**z** *G*) ridicule, mock, deride

szyfr *m* (*-u*; *-y*) cipher, code; ~**ować** ⟨**za-**⟩ (*-uję*) cipher, code, encode

szyj|a *f* (*szyi*; *-e*, *szyj*) *anat.* neck; **po ~ę** up to one's neck; ~**ka** *f* (*-i*; *G* *-jek*) neck; *anat.* ~**ka macicy** cervix; ~**ny** neck

szyk[1] *m* (*-u*; *0*) chic, stylish

szyk[2] *m* (*-u*; *0*) order; formation; *gr.* (word) order; *t-ko pl.* ~**i** *pl.* (*-ów*) ranks *pl.*; *fig.* **pomieszać ~i** (*D*) thwart, frustrate

szykować ⟨**na-, przy-**⟩ (*-uję*) prepare;

~ ⟨**na-, przy-**⟩ **się** get prepared, get ready (**do** *G* for)

szyl|d *m* (*-u*; *-y*), ~**dzik** *m* (*-u*; *-i*) sign

szyling *m* (*-a*; *-i*) shilling

szympans *m* (*-a*; *-y*) *zo.* chimpanzee

szyna *f* (*-y*; *G* -) *rail.* rail; *med.* splint

szynel *m* (*-a*; *-e*) *mil.* overcoat

szynka *f* (*-i*; *G -nek*) ham

szynowy rail

szyper *m* (*-pra*; *-prowie*) skipper

szyszka *f* (*-i*; *G -szek*) cone

Ś

ścian|a *f* (*-y*; *G* -) wall; **mieszkać przez ~ę (z** *I*) live next door (to); ~**ka** *f* (*-i*; *G -nek*) wall (*też biol., anat.*)

ściąć *pf.* → **ścinać**

ściąg|a *f* (*-i*; *G* -) *szkoła*: F crib; ~**acz** *m* (*-a*; *-e*) (knitted) welt; ~**ać** (*-am*) ⟨~**nąć**⟩ *v/t.* pull down; *skórę* peel off; *pierścionek* pull off; *wino* bottle; *buty, ubranie* take off; *uwagę* draw (**na siebie** to o.s.); *podatki* levy; *wojska* move together; *brwi* knit; F (*w szkole*) copy, crib; *zw. pf.* (*ukraść*) pinch, swipe; *v/i. ludzie*: gather, congregate

ściec *pf.* → **ściekać**

ścieg *m* (*-u*; *-i*) stitch

ściek *m* (*-u*; *-i*) sewer; ~**i** *pl.* sewage, sewerage; ~**ać** (*-am*) ⟨~**nąć**⟩ flow off *lub* away

ściemni|ać (*-am*) ⟨~**ć**⟩ (*-ę*, *-nij!*) → **przyciemniać**; ~**a się** it is getting dark; ~**eć** *pf.* grow dark

ście|nny wall; ~**rać** (*-am*) *skórę* rub off (**się** *v/i.*) *gastr.* grate; (*gumką*) erase, rub out; (*gąbką, kurz*) wipe off; ~**rka** *f* (*-i*; *G -rek*) cloth; (*do wycierania naczyń*) *Brt.* drying-up cloth, *Am.* dish towel

ścier|nisko *f* (*-a*; *G* -) stubble field; ~**ny** *tech.* abrasive; ~**pieć** (*-ę*) *pf.* bear, tolerate; ~**pnąć** *pf.* → **cierpnąć**

ścieśni|ać (*-am*) ⟨~**ć**⟩ (*-ę*, *-nij!*) (**się**) narrow, become narrow; contract; crowd together; ~**ć szeregi** close ranks

ścieżka *f* (*-i*; *G -żek*) (foot)path; track ~ **dźwiękowa** sound track; ~ **zdrowia** keep-fit trail

ścięgno *n* (*-a*; *G -gien*) *anat.* tendon

ścięty cut off; *białko* stiff; **stożek ~**

truncated cone; ~ **skośnie** bevelled

ściga|cz *m* (*-a*; *-e*) speedboat; ~**ć** (*-am*) chase, pursue; *zbrodniarza* hunt; ~**ć się** race; *fig.* compete

ścinać (*-am*) cut (*też zakręt*); (*piłą*) saw off; (*w sporcie*) smash; *hist.* behead; ~ **się** coagulate, clot; *mleko*: curdle

ścis|k *m* (*-u*; *0*) crowd; ~**kać** *v/t.* (*w objęciach*) squeeze, hug; *rękę* press, squeeze; compress; clasp; *fig.* **coś ~ka mnie w gardle** I have a lump in my throat; ~ **uściskać; zaciskać;** ~**kać się** crowd, throng; move together

ścis|łość *f* (*-ści*; *0*) precision; **dla ~ło- ści** to be precise; ~**ły** (*m-os -śli*) precise; *więzi* close; *dieta* strict; *przepis* exact, strict; **nauki ~słe** the sciences; ~**snąć** *pf.* → **ściskać;** ~**szać** (*-am*) → **przyciszać;** ~**śle** *adv.*, ~**ślejszy** *adj.* (*comp. od* → **ścisły**); ~**śle biorąc** to be precise

ślad *m* (*-u*; *-y*) (*pojedynczy*) print; (*ciąg*) trail; (*pozostałość*) trace; **bez ~u** without trace; **ani ~u** (*G*) not a trace (of); **iść ~em, iść w ~y** (*G*) follow in s.o.'s footsteps

ślamazarny sluggish, slothful

ślaz *m* (*-u*; *-y*) *bot.* mallow

Śląs|k *m* (*-a*; *0*) Silesia; **2ski** Silesian; ~**zaczka** *f* (*-i*; *G -czek*) Silesian; ~**zak** *m* (*-a*; *-cy*) Silesian

śledczy *jur.* investigating

śledzić (*-dzę*) *v/t.* follow, trail; *por.* **tropić**

śledzio|na *f* (*-y*; *G* -) *anat.* spleen; ~**wy** herring

śledztwo *n* (*-a*; *G* -) investigation

śledź m (-dzia; -dzie) zo. herring; **~wę- dzony** bloater, smoked herring

ślep|ia n/pl. eyes pl.; **~iec** m (-pca, -cze!; -pcy, -pców) blind person; **~nąć** ⟨o-⟩ (-nę) go blind; lose one's sight; **~o** adv. blindly; **na ~o** blindly; **~ota** f (-y; 0) blindness; **~y 1.** blind (też fig.; **na** A to); → **uliczka, tor; 2.** m (-ego; -i), **~a** f (-ej; -e) blind person

ślęczeć (-ę, -y) ⟨nad I⟩ pore (over)

śliczny beautiful, lovely

ślima|czy sluggish; **~k** m (-a; -i) zo. (sko- rupkowy) snail, (nagi) slug; anat. coch- lea; tech. worm, screw; **~kowaty** hel- ical, helicoid

ślin|a f (-y; 0) saliva, (wypluta) spit; **~ić** (-ę) ⟨po-⟩ moisten; **~ić się** dribble, drool; ⟨za-⟩ slobber; **~ka** f (-i;G-nek) → **ślina; ~ka mi do ust idzie** my mouth waters

ślisk|i slippery; fig. tricky; **~o** adv.: **jest ~o** it is slippery

śliw|a f (-y; G -) bot. plum tree; **~ka** f (-i; G -wek) plum; **~ka suszona** prune; **~kowy** plum

ślizg m (-u; -i) chute; (łódka) → **~acz** m (-a; -e) hydroplane boat; **~ać się** (-am) slide, glide (**po** I on); **~ać się na łyż- wach** skate; **~awica** f (-y; G -) black ice; **~awka** f (-i; G -wek) ice-rink

ślub m (-u; -y) (cywilny, kościelny re- gistry office, church) wedding; **~ brać** be married; **dawać ~, udzielić ~u** marry; rel. **~y** pl. zakonne vows pl.; **~ny** wedding; marriage; **~ować** (im)pf. (-uję) vow, promise solemnly; **~owa- nie** n (-a; G -ań) vow

ślusa|rnia f (-i; -e) locksmith's work- shop; **~rz** m (-a; -e) locksmith

śluz m (-u; -y) med. mucus; biol. slime

śluz|a f (-y; G -) sluice(way), lock

śluz|owy¹ sluice, lock

śluz|owy² biol., med. mucous; **~ówka** f (-i; G -wek) mucous membrane

śmiać się ⟨za- się⟩ (-eję) laugh (**z** G at)

śmiał|ek m (-łka; -łkowie) daredevil; **~o** adv. bravely, boldly **~ość** f (-ści; 0) bravery, daring, boldness; **~y** brave, daring

śmiech m (-u; -y) laughter **pokładać się ze ~u** double up with laughter; **ze ~em** with laughter

śmie|ciarka f (-i; G -rek) Brt. dust-cart; Am. garbage truck; **~cić** ⟨na-⟩ (-cę)

dirty, soil; litter; **~ci(e)** pl. (-i) litter, re- fuse, Brt. rubbish; Am. garbage

śmie|ć 1. dare; **2.** m (-cia; -ci(e)) → **śmieci; ~lej** adv. comp. od → **śmiało; ~lszy** adj. comp. od → **śmiały**

śmier|ć f (-ci; 0) death; **ponieść ~ć** die; **na ~ć** to death; jur. **wyrok ~ci** death sentence

śmierdz|ący stinking; **~ieć** (-ę; -i) stink; fig. smell; **tu ~i** it stinks here

śmiertel|niczka f (-i; G -czek) **~ik** m (-a; -cy) mortal; **~ność** f (-ści; 0) mortal- ity; **~y człowiek** mortal **wypadek** fatal; dawka lethal

śmieszn|ie adv. funnily; **~ie niska ce- na** ridiculously low price; **~ość** f (-ści; 0) ridiculousness; ludicrousness; **~y** funny; ridiculous; ludicrous

śmietan|a f (-y; 0) cream; **~ka** f (-i; G -nek) cream (też fig.); **~kowy** cream

śmietni|czka f (-i; G -czek) dustpan; **~k** m (-a; -i) Brt. dustbin, Am. garbage can, trash can; fig. mess; **~sko** n (-a; G -) Brt. tip; rubbish dump

śmig|ać (-am) ⟨**~nąć**⟩ (-nę) v/i. flick, flit, dart; **~ło** n (-a; G -gieł) aviat. pro- peller; **~łowiec** m (-wca; -wce) aviat. he- licopter; **~łowy** aviat. propeller-driven

śniadani|e n (-a; G-ań) breakfast; **jeść ~e** have breakfast; **~owy** breakfast

śniady dark-skinned

śni|ć (-ę, -nij!) dream (**o** L about); **~ł(a) mu się** (A) he dreamt (about); **ani mi się ~!** I can't be bothered!

śniedź f (-dzi; 0) verdigris

śnieg m (-u; -i) snow; **biały jak ~** snow- -white; **~owce** m/pl. (-ów) overshoes pl.; **~owy** snow

śnież|ka f (-i; G -żek) snowball; **~ny** snow; **~yca** f (-y; G -) snowstorm; **~yczka** f (-i; -czek) bot. snowdrop

śp. skrót pisany: **świętej pamięci** the late

śpią|cy sleepy, drowsy; **~czka** f (-i; G -czek) coma

śpiesz|ny hurried; **~yć się** (-ę) hurry; zegar. be fast; (**z** I) hurry up (with)

śpiew m (-u; -y) mus. song, singing; **~aczka** f (-i; G -czek) mus. singer; **~aczy** singing; **~ać** (-am) sing; **~ak** m (-a; -cy) mus. singer; **~anie** n (-a; 0) singing; **~ka** f (-i; G -wek) → **śpiew**; **~nik** m (-a; -i) songbook; **~ny** melodi- ous; akcent singsong

śpio|ch *m* (*-a*; *-y*) late riser; → **~szki** *m/pl.* (*-ków*) playsuit, rompers *pl.*

śpiwór *m* (*-woru*; *-wory*) sleeping-bag

śr. *skrót pisany:* **średni(o)** on average; **środa** Wed.; **średnica** diameter

średni mean, average, mean, moderate; **~a** *f* (*-ej*; *-e*) mean (value); **~a roczna** annual average; **~ca** *f* (*-y*; *-e*) diameter; **~k** *m* (*-a*; *-i*) semicolon; **~o** *adv.* on (an) average; moderately

średnio|terminowy medium-term; **~wiecze** *n* (*-a*; *-i*) the Middle Ages *pl.*; **~wieczny** medi(a)eval

środ|a *f* (*-y*; *G środ*) Wednesday; **~ek** *m* (*-dka*; *-dki*) middle, *Brt.* centre, *Am.* center; inside; agent; *fig.* means *sg./pl.*, measures *pl.*; **~ek leczniczy** remedy; **~ek płatniczy** means of payment; *jur.* **~ek prawny** appeal; **~ki** *pl.* **trwałe** fixed assets *pl.*; → **ciężkość, przekaz** *itp.*; **do ~ka** inside; **od ~ka** from within; **bez ~ków** without means; **wszelkimi ~kami** by all means; **~kowy** central, middle

środowisk|o *n* (*-a*; *G* -) environment; surroundings *pl.*; **zanieczyszczenie ~a** environmental pollution; **~owy** environmental

środowy Wednesday

śród|mieście *n* (*-a*; *G -ść*) centre, *Am.* downtown; inner city; **~ziemnomorski** Mediterranean; **~ziemny: Morze Śziemne** the Mediterranean (Sea)

śruba *f* (*-y*; *G* -) screw; *naut.* propeller

śrubo|kręt *m* (*-u*; *-y*) screwdriver; **~wy** screw

śrut *m* (*-u*; *-y*) shot; **~a** *f* (*-y*; *G* -) crushed grain, groats *pl.*; **~owy** shot; *agr.* groats; **~ówka** *f* (*-i*; *G -wek*) shotgun

św. *skrót pisany:* **święty** St. (*saint*); **świadek** witness

świadcz|enie *n* (*-a*; *G -eń*), *zw. pl.* **~enia** benefits *pl.*; **~yć** (*-ę*) (**o** *L*) testify (to); testify (**w sądzie** in court); *usługi* provide, render

świad|ectwo *n* (*-a*; *G -ectw*) (*dokument*) certificate; (*stwierdzenie*) testimony; (*w szkole*) *Brt.* school report, *Am.* report card; **~ectwo urodzenia** birth certificate; **~ek** *m* (*-dka*; *-dkowie*) *jur.* (*naoczny* eye)witness

świadom|ość *f* (*-ści*; *0*) consciousness; **~y** (*nie nieprzytomny*) conscious; (*zamierzony*) deliberate, intentional; **być**

~ym (*G*) (*zdający sobie sprawę*) be aware (of)

świat *m* (*-a*; *-y*) world; *fig.* realm; **za nic w świecie** not for anything in the world

światł|o *n* (*-a*; *G -teł*) (**dzienne** daylight; *mot.* **~a** *pl.* **długie/drogowe** full beam; **~a** *pl.* **krótkie/mijania** *Brt.* dipped, *Am.* dimmed, beam; **pod ~o** to the light

światło|czuły photosensitive; **~mierz** *m* (*-a*; *-e*) *phot.* exposure meter; **~odporny** light-fast

świato|pogląd *m* (*-u*; *-y*) outlook, viewpoint; **~wy** *ktoś* worldly; (*na całym świecie*) worldwide

świąd *m* (*-u*; *0*) *med.* itch

świąt|eczny festive, holiday; *ubranie itp.* Sunday; **~ek** *m* (*-tka*; *-tki*) *rel.* holy figure; **Zielone Świątki** *pl.* Whitsuntide; **~ynia** *f* (*-i*; *-e*) temple; (*kościół*) church

świd|er *m* (*-dra*; *-dry*) *tech.* bit; *górnictwo*: drill, bore; **~rować** (*-uję*) drill; *fig.* bore; **~rujący** piercing

świec|a *f* (*-y*; *G* -) candle; *mot.* spark-plug; **~ący** shiny, luminous; **~ić** (*-cę*) (*też się*) shine, glow; **~ić pustkami** be deserted

świecki lay

świecz|ka *f* (*-i*; *G -czek*) → **świeca**; **~nik** *m* (*-a*; *-i*) candlestick, candle holder

świergot *m* (*-u*; *-y*) chirp, twitter; **~ać** (*-am*) chirp, twitter

świerk *m* (*-u*; *-i*) *bot.* spruce; **~owy** spruce

świerszcz *m* (*-a*; *-e*) *zo.* cricket

świerzb *m* (*-u*; *-y*) *med.* itch; **~ić, ~ieć** (*-ę*, *-i*) itch

świet|lany shining, luminous; *fig.* bright, rosy; **~lica** *f* (*-y*; *G* -) day-room; community-room; **~lik** *m* (*-a*; *-i*) *zo.* glow-worm; *bud.* skylight; *naut.* porthole; **~lny** light; **~lówka** *f* (*-i*;*G -wek*) fluorescent lamp

świetny splendid, magnificent

śwież|o *adv.* freshly; newly; **~lica** *f* (*-y*; *G* -) day-room... **~ość** *f* (*-ści*; *0*) freshness; newness; **~y** fresh; new

święc|ić (*-cę*) celebrate; ⟨*po-*⟩ *rel.* consecrate; *dzień* keep, observe; **~ie** *adv.* faithfully, solemnly; **~ony 1.** consecrated; sanctified; **2. ~one** *n* (*-ego*; *0*) Easter meal; (*food blessed in church at Easter*)

święto n (-a; G świąt) holiday; feast-day; special day; ♀ **Matki** Mother's Day; ~**jański** St. John's; ~**kradztwo** n (-a; G -) sacrilege, profanation, desecration; ~**szek** m (-szka; -szki/-szkowie) hypocrite, prude; ~**ść** f (-ści) holiness; sanctity, sacredness; ~**wać** (-uję) celebrate; keep, observe

święty holy, blessed; **Wszystkich** ♀**ch** All Saints' Day

świn|ia f (-i; -e) zo. pig; fig. swine; ~**ka** f (-i; G -nek) → **świnia**; ~**ka morska** zo. guinea pig; med. mumps sg.; ~**tuch** m (-a; -y) fig. pej. (bru-

das) slob, pig; (bezecny) dirty old man

świńs|ki piggish; fig. filthy; ~**two** n (-a; G -) (brud) mess; (jedzenie) nasty stuff; (postępek) dirty trick

świr m (-a; -y) F nut

świs|nąć v/s. (-nę) whistle; F pinch; ~**t** m (-u; -y) whistle; ~**tać** (-am) whistle; ~**tak** m (-a; -i) zo. marmot; ~**tek** m (-stka; -stki) slip of paper

świt m (-u; -y) dawn; **o świcie** at dawn; ~**a** f (-y; G -) entourage, retinue; ~**ać** (-am) dawn; fig. ⟨**za-**⟩ cross one's mind; ~**a** it dawns; the day breaks

T

ta pron. f → **ten**

t. skrót pisany: **tom** vol. (volume)

tabaka f (-i; G -) snuff

tabela f (-i; G -) table; chart; ~ **wygranych** list of winners; ~**ryczny** tabular

tabletka f (-i; G -tek) tablet

tablica f (-y; G -) plate; szkoła: blackboard; baseball: backboard; → **rejestracyjny, rozdzielczy**

tabliczka f (-i; G -czek) → **tablica**; (z numerem) number-plate, (z nazwiskiem) name-plate; ~ **czekolady** bar of chocolate; ~ **mnożenia** multiplication tables pl.

tabor m (-u; -y) transport fleet; rail. rolling stock; (cygański) Gypsy camp

taboret m (-u; -y) stool

taca f (-y; G -) plate (też rel.); tray

tacy pl. → **taki**

taczać (-am) roll (**się** v/i.)

taczk|a f (-i; -i f/pl. (G -czek) wheelbarrow

tafla f (-i; -e, -i/ -fel) sheet; expanse

taić ⟨**za-**⟩ (-ję) hide, conceal (**przed** I against); poglądy też keep secret, suppress

tajać (-ję) melt

tajemni|ca f (-y; -e, -) secret; **w ~cy** in secret; **trzymać w ~cy** keep secret; ~**czo** adv. secretly; ~**czy** secretive, enigmatic

taj|emny secret; underhand; ~**niak** F m (-a; -cy) secret agent; ~**nie** adv. secretly; underhand; ~**nik** m (-a; -i): zw. pl. ~**niki**

secrets pl.; ~**ność** f (-ści; 0) secrecy; ~**ny** secret; **ściśle ~ne** top secret

tak yes; (dla wzmocnienia znaczenia następującego wyrazu) so; ~ **jak on** like he (does itp.); ~ **że** so that; ~ **żeby** in such a way that; **i** ~ anyway; ~ **samo** just as, ~ **sobie** so-so, not too bad; ~ ... **jak i** ... ... as well as ...; ~ **czy owak/siak** one way or the other; mil. ~ **jest!** yes, sir!

tak|i pron. m (m-os tacy) such; so; → **jaki, jako, raz**[1]; ~**i sam** the same, identical; ~**i sobie** so-so; **nic ~iego** nothing special; ~**i czy owaki/siaki** it makes no odds; **coś ~iego** something like that, a thing like that; ~**iż** → **taki (sam)**; ~**o** → **jako**

tak|sa f (-y; G -): ~**sa klimatyczna** visitors' tax; ~**siarz** m (-a; -e) F → **taksówkarz**; ~**sować** ⟨**o-**⟩ (-uję) estimate; ~**sówka** f (-i; G -wek) taxi, cab; ~**sówkarz** m (-a; -e) taxi-driver, cab-driver

takt m (-u; -y) mus. bar; (poczucie) time, rhythm; fig. tact; ~**owny** tactful

taktyczny tactical

taktyka f (-i; G -) tactics sg.

także also

talarek m (-rka; -rki) gastr. slice

talent m (-u; -y) (**do** G) talent (to), gift (to)

talerz m (-a; -e), ~**yk** m (-a; -i) plate

tali|a f (GDL -ii; -e) waist; ~**a kart** pack, Am. deck; **wcięty w ~i** ubranie fit at the waist

talk m (-u; -0) talcum (powder)

talon m (-u; -y) coupon

tam (over) there; **kto ~?** who's there?; **tu i ~** here and there; **gdzie ~!** nothing of the kind!; **co mi ~!** what do I care!; **jakiś ~ ...** some ...; → **powrót**

tam|**a** f (-y; G -) dam; fig. **położyć ~ę** (D) check, stem

tamci pl. → **tamten**

Tamiza f (-y; 0) the Thames

tamować ⟨za-⟩ (-uję) stop; krwotok stanch

tam|**ta** f, **~te** f/pl. → **tamten**; **~tejszy** local; **~ten** that; **ani ten, ani ~ten** neither; **po ~tej stronie** on the other side; **na ~tym świecie** hereafter; **~tędy** that way; **~to** → **tamten**; **to i ~to** this and that; **~że** in the same place

tance|**rka** f (-i; G -rek), **~rz** m (-a; -e) dancer

tande|**ciarnia** f (-i; -e) junk shop; **~ta** f (-y; zw. 0) trashy goods pl., junk; **~tnie** adv. trashily, shoddily; **~tny** trashy, shoddy

taneczny dancing

tani cheap (też fig.); **za ~e pieniądze** dirt cheap

taniec m (-ńca; -ńce) dance

tanieć ⟨po-, s-⟩ get cheaper

tanio adv. cheaply; **~cha** F f (-y; G -) low price

tankow|**ać** ⟨za-⟩ (-uję) v/t. fill up; v/i. put Brt. petrol (Am. gas) in; **~iec** m (-wca; -wce) naut. tanker

tań|**ce** pl. → **taniec**; **~czyć** ⟨po-, za-⟩ (-ę) dance (też fig.)

tapczan m (-u; -y) divan

tapet|**a** f (-y; G -) wallpaper; **~ować** ⟨wy-⟩ (-uję) wallpaper, paper

tapicer m (-a; -rzy) upholsterer; **~ka** f (-i; G -rek) upholstery

tapirować ⟨u-⟩ (-uję) backcomb

tarapaty pl. (-ów) trouble; **wpaść w ~** get in trouble

taras m (-u; -y) terrace; **~ować** ⟨za-⟩ (-uję) block; drzwi barricade

tarci|**ca** f (-y; -e) cut timber; **~e** n (-a; G -rć) friction (też tech.); **~a** pl. friction

tarcz|**a** f (-y; -e, G -) shield; Brt., Am. disk; (do strzelania) target; tel. dial; **~a zegara** clock/watch face; **~owy** tech. disc/disk, circular; **piła ~owa** circular saw; **hamulce ~owe** disk brakes; **~yca** f (-y; -e) anat. thyroid (gland)

targ m (-u; -i) market; **~i** pl. econ. fair; **dobić ~u (z** I) come to an agreement (with); **po długich ~ach** after lengthy haggling

targ|**ać** (-am) ruffle one's hair; pull; → **szarpać**; **~nąć się** pf. (-nę) make an attempt (**na** A on); **~nąć się na życie** (attempt to) commit a suicide

targow|**ać** (-uję) (I) trade (with), deal (with); **~ać się** haggle (**o** A over); **~isko** n (-a; G -) market(-place); **~y** market, fair

tar|**ka** f (-i; G -rek) grater; **~lisko** n (-a; G -) spawning-ground; **~mosić** (-szę) → **targać, szarpać**; **~nik** m (-a; -i) tech. rasp; **~nina** f (-y; G -) bot. blackthorn

tart|**ak** m (-u; -i) sawmill; **~y** grated; **bułka ~a** breadcrumbs pl.

taryf|**a** f (-y; G -) (opłaty) rates pl.; (opłaty za przejazd) fares pl.; F (taksówka) cab; **~owy** tabela rate, fare

tarzać (-am) roll; **~ się** roll about

tasak m (-a; -i) chopper, cleaver

tasiem|**iec** m (-mca; -mce) zo. tapeworm; **~ka** f (-i; G -mek) tape

tasować ⟨prze-⟩ (-uję) karty shuffle

taśm|**a** f (-y; G -) tape; (montażowa) assembly line; **~a samoklejąca** adhesive tape, Brt. Sellotape; Am. Scotch tape; **~a maszynowa** typewriter ribbon; **~a filmowa** film; mil. cartridge-belt; **przy ~ie** tech. on the assembly line; **~owy** tape

tata m (-y; DL tacie; -owie, -ów) → **tatuś**

Tatar m **1.** (-a; -rzy) Tartar; **2.** 2 F (-a; -y) gastr. steak tartar(e); **2ak** m (-a; -i) bot. sweet flag, calamus; **2ski** Tartar; **sos 2ski** tartar(e) sauce

taterni|**czka** f (-i; G -czek), **~k** m (-a; -cy) mountaineer

tato m (-y; DL tacie; -owie, -ów) → **tatuś**

Tatry pl. (G Tatr) the Tatra Mountains pl.

tatrzański Tatra

tatuaż m (-u; -e) tattoo

tatuś m (-sia; -siowie) F dad

taż pron. f → **tenże**

tą pron. (I/sg, F A/sg. → **ta**) → **ten**

tch|**awica** f (-y; G -) anat. windpipe, trachea; **~em** → **dech**; **~nąć** (-nę) (im)pf. v/i smell (I of); v/t. pf. pf. breathe (into); **~nienie** n (-a; G -eń) breath

tchórz m (-a; -e) coward; **~liwie** adv. in a cowardly manner; **~liwy** cowardly;

~ostwo *n* (*-a*; *G -stw*) cowardliness;
~yć ⟨*s-*⟩ (*-ę*) back out

tchu → **dech**

te *pron. pl. f* → **ten**

teatr *m* (*-u*; *-y*) *Brt.* theatre, *Am.*
theater; ~alny theatrical

tech|niczny technical; ~nik *m* (*-a*; *-i*)
technician; ~nika *f* (*-i*; *G -*) technology;
(*sposób*) technique; ~nikum *n* (*idkl.*; *pl.
-ów*) technical secondary school; ~no-
kracja *f* (*-i*; *-e*) technocracy; ~nologia
f (*GDl -ii*; *-e*) technology

teczka *f* (*-i*; *G -czek*) briefcase; (*do akt*)
folder; ~ szkolna school-bag, satchel

teflonowy Teflon *TM*, non stick

tego *pron.* **GDL** → **ten** G; → **to**[1]; ~rocz-
ny this year('s)

tej *pron.* (*GDL/sg.* → **ta**) → **ten**

teka *f* (*-i*; *G -*) portfolio

tekowy teak

Teksas *m* (*-u*; *0*) Texas

tekst *m* (*-u*; *-y*) text

tekstylia *pl.* (*-ów*) textile goods *pl.*

tekściarz F *m* (*-a*; *-e*) songwriter; (*re-
klam*) copywriter

tektur|a *f* (*-y*; *G -*) cardboard; ~owy
cardboard

telefaks → **faks**

telefon *m* (*-u*; *-y*) (tele)phone; ~ **komórkowy** mobile (phone); **przez ~** on the
phone; ~iczny (tele)phone; **rozmowa
~iczna** phone call; **książka ~iczna**
(phone) directory; **karta ~iczna** phone-
card; ~ować ⟨*za-*⟩ (*do G*) call, phone

telegazeta *f* (*-y*; *G -*) *TV:* teletext

telegraf *m* (*-u*; *-y*) telegraph; ~iczny
telegraphic; **w stylu ~icznym** in tele-
graphese; ~ować ⟨*za-*⟩ (*-uję*) (*do G*)
cable, telegraph

tele|gram *m* (*-u*; *-y*) telegram, cable;
~komunikacja *f* telecommunications
sg.; ~ks *m* (*-u*; *-y*) telex; ~ksować
⟨*za-*⟩ (*-uję*) (*do G*) telex (to); ~ksowy
telex; ~obiektyw *m* (*-u*; *-y*) *phot.* tele-
photo lens; ~pajęczarz F *m* (*-a*; *-e*) licence dodger; ~patyczny telepathic;
~skop *m* (*-u*; *-y*) telescope; ~transmi-
sja *f* television broadcast; ~turniej *m*
quiz show; ~widz *m* viewer

telewiz|ja *f* (*-i*; *-e*) television; **oglądać
~ję** watch TV; ~or *m* (*-a*; *-y*) TV set;
~yjny television, TV

temat *m* (*-u*; *-y*) subject (matter); topic,
theme; *gr.* stem; ~ **do rozmowy** subject

of conversation; ~yczny thematic, topical

temblak *m* (*-a*; *-i*) *med.* sling; **na ~u** in a
sling

tempe|rament *m* (*-u*; *-y*) tempera-
ment; ~ratura *f* (*-y*; *G -*) temperature;
~rować ⟨*za-*⟩ (*-uję*) ołówek sharpen;
~rówka *f* (*-i*; *G -wek*) sharpener

temp|o *n* (*-a*; *G -*) speed; **dobrym ~em**
at a good speed

temu 1. *pron.* D → **ten**, **to**[1]; 2. *adv.*: **rok
~** a year ago; **dawno ~** a long time ago

ten *pron. m* (*f* **ta**, *n* **to**, *pl.* **te**, *ci*) this; →
chwila, czas, sam

tenden|cja *f* (*-i*; *-e*) trend, tendency;
~cyjny tendentious, biased

tenis *m* (*-a*; *0*): ~ **stołowy** table tennis;
~ówki *f/pl.* (*-wek*) tennis shoes, *Am.*
sneakers; ~ista *m* (*-y*; *-ści*), ~istka *f*
(*-i*; *G -tek*) tennis-player; ~owy tennis

tenor *m* (*-u/os. -a*; *-y/os. -rzy*) *mus.* tenor

tenże *pron. m* (**taż** *f*, **toż** *n*, *pl.* **też**, *ciż*)
the same; *por.* **ten**

teo|logiczny theological; ~retyczny
theoretical; ~ria *f* (*GDL -ii*; *-e*) theory

terapeu|ta *m* (*-y*; *-ci*) therapist; ~tycz-
ny therapeutic

te'rapia *f* (*GDL -ii*; *-e*) therapy

teraz now; **od ~** from now on

teraźniejsz|ość *f* (*-ści*; *0*) the present;
~y present; → **czas**

tercja *f* (*-i*; *-e*) *mus.* third; *szermierka:* tierce; (*w hokeju*) (*część meczu*)
period, (*część boiska*) zone

teren *m* (*-u*; *-y*) area; ground, terrain; ~y
pl. **zielone** green spaces *pl.*; **w ~ie** (*badania*) in the field; (*urzędowanie*) out
of the office; (*lokalny*) ~owy field;
local; **samochód ~owy** all-terrain car

terkotać (*-czę/-cę*) *maszyna:* clutter;
budzik: rattle; (*mówić*) jabber, chatter

termin *m* (*-u*; *-y*) time-limit; (*data*) date;
(*wyrażenie, też med.*) term; **przed ~em**
ahead of schedule; **po ~ie** behind schedule; **na ~** on time, to schedule; ~ **ostateczny** deadline; → **terminowy**

terminal *m* (*-u/-a*; *-e*) terminal

termin|arz *m* (*-a*; *-e*) schedule; (*kalen-
darz*) diary; ~ować (*-uję*) be appren-
ticed (**u** *G* to); ~owo *adv.* on time,
to schedule; ~owy with a deadline

termit *m* (*-u*; *-y*) *zo.* termite

termo|- *w złoż.* thermo-; ~jądrowy ther-
monuclear; ~metr *m* (*-u*; *-y*) thermo-

meter; ~s *m* (*-u*; *-y*) thermos *TM* flask, vacuum flask

terroryjsta *m* (*-y*; *-ści*), ~stka *f* (*-y*; *G -tek*) terrorist; ~styczny terrorist ~zm *m* (*-u*; *0*) terrorism; **akt ~zmu** act of terrorism; ~zować (*-uję*) terrorize

terytorium *n* (*idkl.*; *-a*) territory

test *m* (*-u*; *-y*) test

testament *m* (*-u*; *-y*) will; *rel.* testament; *fig.* legacy; ~owy testamentary

testowjać (*-uję*) test; ~y test

teściowa *f* (*-wej*; *-we*) mother-in-law; ~ć *m* (*-ścia*; *-ściowie*, *-ściów*) father-in-law

teza *f* (*-y*; *G -*) thesis

też[1] *adv.*, *part.* also

też[2] *pron.*: *f* → **tenże**

tę *pron.* (*A/sg.* → **ta**) → **ten**

tęcza|*a* *f* (*-y*; *G -*) rainbow; ~ówka *f* (*-i*; *G -wek*) *anat.* iris

tędy *adv.* this way

tęg|*i* stout; (*dobry*) efficient, good; (*mocny*) strong; ~o *adv.* strongly

tęp|*ić* ⟨*wy-*⟩ (*-ię*) eradicate, exterminate; ~*ić się* → ~*ieć* ⟨*s-*⟩ (*-eję*) blunt; *słuch:* deteriorate; ~y blunt; *fig.* dull; *człowiek* thick-headed; *wzrok* vacant; apathetic

tęsknj|*ić* ⟨*s- się*⟩ (*-ę*, *-nij!*) (*za I*) long (for); (*do I*) miss; ~*ić za krajem/domem* be homesick; ~*o adv.* nostalgically; *jest mu ~o do* he is longing for; ~*ota* *f* (*-y*; *G -*) longing; homesickness; ~y longing; homesick

tęt|*ent m* (*-u*; *0*) hoofbeats *pl.*, clatter; ~*nica* *f* (*-y*; *G -*) *anat.* artery (*też fig.*); ~*niczy* arterial; ~*nić* (*-ę*, *-nij!*) pulsate, throb; ~*no n* (*-a*; *G -*) pulse

tęż|*ec* *m* (*-żca*; *-żce*) *med.* tetanus; ~*eć* ⟨*s-*⟩ (*-ę*) set; *mróz itp.*: grow stronger; ~*yzna* *f* (*-y*; *0*) strength

tj. *skrót pisany:* **to jest** i.e. (*that is*)

tka|*ctwo n* (*-a*; *0*) weaving; ~*cz m* (*-a*; *-e*), ~*czka* *f* (*-i*; *G -czek*) weaver; ~*ć* ⟨*u-*⟩ (*-am*) weave

tkan|*ina* *f* (*-y*; *G -*) fabric; *fig.* tissue; ~*ka* *f* (*-i*; *G -nek*) *biol.* tissue (*też fig.*); ~*y* woven

tkliwjość *f* (*-ści*; *0*) tenderness; ~*ie adv.* tenderly; ~*y* tender

tknąć *pf.* (*-nę*) → (*do*)*tykać*

tkwić ⟨*u-*⟩ (*-ę*, *-wij!*) stick (*fig.* around)

tlejący *Brt.* smouldering, *Am.* smoldering; glowing; → **tlić**

tlen *m* (*-u*; *0*) *chem.* oxygen; ~*ek m* (*-nku*; *-nki*) *chem.* oxide; ~*ić* (*-ę*) → **u-tleniać**; ~*owy* oxygen

tlić się *Brt.* smoulder, *Am.* smolder; *fig.* glow

tłamsić ⟨*s-*⟩ (*-szę*) suppress

tło *n* (*-a*; *G teł*) background; *na białym* **tle** against a white background; *w tle* in the background

tłocz|*nia* *f* (*-i*; *-e*) *tech.* stamping press; ~*no adv.*: *jest ~no tu* it is overcrowded here; ~*ny* crowded; *ulica* busy; ~*yć* (*-ę*) ⟨*wy-*⟩ press out, squeeze out; *tech.* stamp; ⟨*prze-*⟩ *płyn* pump; ~*yć się* crowd, throng

tłok *m* (*-u*; *0*) crowd; (*-a*; *-i*) *tech.* piston

tłuc ⟨*po-*, *roz-*, *s-*⟩ smash, crush; ⟨*na-*, *u-*⟩ *ziemniaki* mash; *przyprawy* crush; ⟨*s-*, *wy-*⟩ *kogoś* beat up, clobber; ⟨*s-*⟩ bump (*o A* against); ~ *się szkło:* break; *fale itp.:* pound (*o A* on); *serce:* pound, thump; (*robić hałas*) make a noise; *F* travel a long distance

tłucz|*ek m* (*-czka*; *-czki*) pestle, (*do kartofli* potato) masher; ~*eń m* (*-nia*; *0*) broken stone

tłum *m* (*-u*; *-y*) crowd; ~*em* → **tłumnie**

tłumacz *m* (*-a*; *-e*) translator; (*ustny*) interpreter; ~*enie n* (*-a*; *G -eń*) translation; (*ustny*) interpreting; ~*ka* *f* (*-i*; *G -czek*) translator; (*ustny*) interpreter; ~*yć* (*-ę*) ⟨*wy-*⟩ explain; ~*yć się* excuse o.s.; ⟨*prze-*⟩ translate (*na polski* into Polish); ~*yć się jako* be translated as

tłum|*ić* ⟨*s-*⟩ (*-ę*) *płomienie* smother; *bunt*, *uczucie* suppress; *odgłos* muffle; ~*ik m* (*-a*; *-i*) *mot. Brt.* silence, *Am.* muffler; (*broni*) silencer; *mus.* mute

tłumn|*ie adv.* in huge numbers; ~*y* numerous

tłumok *m* (*-a*; *-i*) bundle, pack

tłust|*o adv.*: *jeść ~o* eat fatty things; ~*y ktoś* fat; *jedzenie* fatty; (*zatłuszczony*) greased

tłuszcz *m* (*-u*; *-e*) fat; ~*owy* *biol.* adipose, fatty

tłuśc|*ić* ⟨*na-*⟩ (*-szczę*) grease; (*kremem*) rub *cream* into; ~*eć* *F* ⟨*po-*⟩ (*-eję*) become fat; ~*och m* (*-a*; *-y*) *F* fatso, fatty

tną 3. *os. pl. pres.*, **tnę** *I*, *os. sg. pres.* → **ciąć**

tnący cutting

to[1] *pron. n* this, that; → **ten**; *do tego* moreover; *na tym*, *na ~* for it; *w tym* in it; **za** ~ behind it; **z tego** from that; **z tym, że** provided that; ~ **jest** that is

to² *part.* (*idkl.*) this, that, it; **kto ~?** who is there?; ~ **fakt** this is a fact; ~ ..., ~ ... now ... now ...; **no ~ co?** so what?; **a ~ ... !** what (a) ...!

toaleta *f* (*-y; G -*) toilet; ~**owy** toilet

toast *m* (*-u; -y*) toast

tobą (*I/sg.* → **ty**); **z** ~ with you

tobie (*DL/sg.* → **ty**); **o** ~ about you

tobół (*-bołu; -boły*) → **tłumok**

toczony *tech.* turned; ~**yć** (*-ę*) ⟨**po**-⟩ **kulę** *itp.* roll (**się** *v/i.*); ⟨**s**-⟩ **bój** fight out; ⟨**na**-⟩ *impf.* **płyn** fill in; ⟨**wy**-⟩ *tech.* turn; *impf.* **płyn**: draw off, tap; **spór** have; **drewno** live on; **rokowania** carry out; ~**yć się** roll; **łzy**: roll down, fine down; **czas, życie**: go, pass; **dyskusja, walka**: go on; **akcja**: take place; **rozmowa**: be (**o** *L* about); ~**ydło** *n* (*-a; G -deł*) grindstone

toga *f* (*-i; G tóg*) toga; *jur.* robe

tok *m* (*-u; 0*) course; process; **być w ~u** be under way; **w ~u** (*G*) in the course (of)

tokarka *f* (*-i; G -rek*) *tech.* (turning) lathe; ~**rz** *m* (*-a; -e*) *tech.* turner

tokować (*-uję*) *zo.* display (in courtship)

toksyczny toxic

tolerancyjny tolerant; ~**ować** (*-uję*) tolerate

tom *m* (*-u; -y*) volume

tomografia *f* (*GDL -ii; -e*) tomography; ~**komputerowa** *Brt.*computerized (*Am.* computer) tomography

ton *m* (*-u; -y*) tone

tona *f* (*-y; G ton*) ton; (**metryczna**) tonne, metric ton

tonacja *f* (*-i; -e*) *mus.* key; *fig.* tone

tonaż *m* (*-u; 0*) *naut.* tonnage

tonący *m* (*-ego, -cy*), ~**ca** *f* (*-ej; -e*) drowning person; ~**ć** (*-ę, toń!*) *fig.* be up to (**w** *L* in); ⟨**u**-⟩ drown; ⟨**za**-⟩ **statek**: sink, go down

tonować (*-uję*) tone down

toń *f*(*GDL -ni; -nie, -ni, -ńmi*) *lit.* depth

topić (*-ę*) ⟨**po**-, **u**-⟩ drown; ⟨**za**-⟩ sink; ⟨**roz**-⟩ melt (**się** *v/i.*); ~ **się** → **tonąć**

topiel *f* (*-i; -e*) whirlpool (*też fig.*); ~**ec** *m* (*-lca; -lcy*), ~**ica** *f* (*-cy; -ce*) drowned person

topik *m* (*-a; -i*) *electr.* fusible-element; ~**owy** fuse

topless(s) topless

topliwy fusible; ~**nieć** ⟨**s**-⟩ (*-eję*) melt; fuse *tech.*

topola *f* (*-i; -e*) *bot.* poplar

toporny ungainly, coarse; ~**rzysko** *n* (*-a; G -*) helve, handle

topór *m* (*-pora; -pory*) ax(e)

tor *m* (*-u; -y*) path; *rail.* track, line; (**w sporcie**) track, (**bobslejowy** *itp.*) run, (**koni**) course; ~ **wodny** *naut.* fairway; *fig.* **ślepy** ~ blind alley

Tora *f* (*-y; 0*) *rel.* the Torah

torba *f* (*-y; G -reb*) bag; *biol.* pouch; ~**ba na zakupy** shopping bag; → ~**ebka** *f* (*-i; G -bek*) bag; (**kobieca**) handbag

torf *m* (*-u; -y*) peat; ~**owisko** *n* (*-a; G -*) peat bog; ~**owy** peat

tornister *m* (*-tra; -try*) satchel

torowlać ⟨**u**-⟩⟨-**uję**⟩: ~**ać** (**sobie**) **drogę** clear a path; pave the way; ~**y** rail

torpedowlać ⟨**s**-⟩ (*-uję*) *mil.* torpedo (*też fig.*); ~**wiec** *m* (*-wca; -wce*) *mil.* torpedo boat

tors *m* (*-u; -y*) trunk, torso

torsje *pl.* (*-ji*) vomiting

tort *m* (*-u; -y*) layer cake, gateau *lub* gâteau; ~**owy** gateau *lub* gâteau

torturla *f* (*-y; G -*) torture (*też fig.*); **narzędzie** ~**r** instrument of torture; ~**rować** (*-uję*) torture

Toskania *f* (*-ii; 0*) Tuscany

tost *m* (*-u; -y*) toast

totalitarny totalitarian; ~**ny** total

toteż *cj.* that is why

totolotek *m* (*-tka; 0*) lottery

tow. *skrót pisany:* **towarzystwo** ass. (*association*)

towar *m* (*-u; -y*) article, commodity; goods *pl.*

towarowy commodity; trade; *rail.* *Brt.* goods, *Am.* freight; **dom** ~**wy** department store

towaryski (*m-os -scy*) sociable, social; **formy** *pl.* ~**kie** good manners *pl.*; (**w sporcie**) **spotkanie** ~**kie** friendly meeting; **agencja** ~**ka** escort agency; ~**two** *n* (*-a; G -tw*) company; (**stowarzyszenie**) association, society; *econ.* company

towarzysz *m* (*-a; -e*), ~**ka** *f* (*-i; G -szek*) companion; (**partyjny**) comrade; ~**(ka) niedoli** fellow-sufferer, ~**(ka) zabaw** playmate; ~**yć** (*-ę*) (*D*) accompany; (*czemuś*) go with

toż¹ *pron.* → **tenże**

toż² *part.* (*idkl.*) → **przecież**

tożsamość *f* (-ści; 0) identity

tracić ⟨**s-, u-**⟩ (-cę) lose (*też fig.*) miss; *pieniądze, czas* lose (**na** *L*) lose out (on); *prawo* forfeit

trady|cja *f* (-*i*; -*e*) tradition; ~**cyjny** traditional

traf *m* (-*u*; -*y*) chance; **szczęśliwym ~em** by a fluke; ~**iać** (-*am*) ⟨~**ić**⟩ (-*ę*) hit; find one's way (**do** *G* to); find o.s. (**do** *G* in); **nie ~ić** miss; ~**iać się** *okazja:* come up; ~**ienie** *n* (-*a*; *G* -*eń*) hit; **sześć ~ień** six right ones; ~**ność** *f* (-ści; 0) accuracy; (*uwagi*) relevance; ~**nie** *adv.* accurately; relevantly; aptly; ~**ny** accurate; relevant; apt

tragarz *m* (-*a*; -*e*) porter

tra'gedia *f* (*GDL* -*ii*; -*e*) tragedy (*też fig.*)

tragiczny tragic(al)

trajkotać ⟨-*cze-/-cę*⟩ → **terkotać**

trak|t *m* (-*u*; -*y*) country road; *bud.* section, wing; **w ~cie** (*G*) in the course (of)

traktat *m* (-*u*; -*y*) treatise, dissertation

trakto|r *m* (-*a*; -*y*) tractor; ~**rzysta** *m* (-*y*; -*ści*), -**tka** *f* (-*i*; *G* -*tek*) tractor-driver

traktowa|ć (-*uję*) treat (**się** each other); **źle ~ć** maltreat; *v/i.* (**o** *L*) treat (of), deal (with); ~**nie** *n* (-*a*; *G* -*ań*) treatment

trał *m* (-*u*; -*y*) *naut., mil.* sweep

trampki *m/pl.* (-*pek*) sports shoes *pl.*

trampolina *f* (-*y*; *G* -) (*w sporcie*) spring-board; (*przy basenie*) diving board

tramwaj *m* (-*u*; -*e*) *Brt.* tram(way), *Am.* streetcar; ~**owy** tramway, streetcar

tran *m* (-*u*; 0) cod-liver oil

trans *m* (-*u*; -*y*) trance

trans|akcja *f* (-*i*; -*e*) transaction; ~**akcje** *pl.* dealings *pl.*; ~**fer** *m* (-*u*; -*y*) *econ.*, (*też w sporcie*) transfer; ~**formator** *m* (-*a*; -*y*) transformer; ~**fuzja** *f* (-*i*; -*e*) *med.* transfusion; ~**kontynentalny** transcontinental; ~**misja** *f* (-*i*; -*e*) transmission; broadcast; ~**mitować** (-*uję*) transmit, broadcast; ~**parent** *m* (-*u*; -*y*) banner; ~**plantacja** *f* (-*i*; -*e*) transplantation

transport *m* (-*u*; -*y*) *Brt.* transport, *Am.* transportation; (*ładunek*) consignment; shipment; ~**ować** ⟨**od-, prze-**⟩ (-*uję*) transport, ship; ~**owy** transport

transwestyta *m* (-*y*; -*yci*) transvestite

tranzystor *m* (-*a*; -*y*) *electr.* transistor

tranzytowy transit

trapez *m* (-*u*; -*y*) *math. Brt.* trapezium, *Am.* trapezoid; (*w cyrku itp.*) trapeze

trapić (-*ę*) plague (with); → **martwić** (**się**)

trasa *f* (-*y*; *G* -) route; way

trasowany *econ. weksel* drawn

trata *f* (-*y*; *G* -) *econ.* bill of exchange

tratować ⟨**s-**⟩ (-*uję*) trample

tratwa *f* (-*y*; *G* -) raft

traumatyczny traumatic

trawa *f* (-*y*; *G* -) grass

trawestacja *f* (-*i*; -*e*) travesty

trawiasty grass(y)

trawi|ć ⟨**s-**⟩ (-*ę*) *biol.* digest; (*o ogniu itp.*) consume; *czas* waste (**na** *L* for); ⟨**wy-**⟩ *tech., chem.* etch; ~**enie** *n* (-*a*; *G* -*eń*) digestion; *chem., tech.* etching

trawler *m* (-*a*; -*y*) *naut.* trawler; ~**przetwórnia** *naut.* factory *lub* processing trawler

trawnik *m* (-*a*; -*i*) lawn

trąb|a *f* (-*y*; *G* -) *mus.* trumpet; *zo.* trunk; *meteo.* (*powietrzna*) whirlwind; (*wodna*) waterspout; F (*ktoś*) fool; ~**ić** (-*ę*) (**w** *A*) blow; *słoń:* trumpet; *mil.* sound (**na alarm** the alarm); *mot.* hoot, sound the horn; ~**ka** *f* (-*i*; *G* -*bek*) *mus.* trumpet; *mil.* bugle

trąc|ać (-*am*) ⟨~**ić**⟩ (-*cę*) knock (*A* against; (*łokciem itp.*) nudge, elbow; ~**ać się kieliszkami** clink glasses

trącić² (-*cę*; *nieos.*) (*I*) smell (of), smack (of)

trą|d *m* (-*u*; -0) *med.* leprosy; ~**dzik** *m* (-*a*; -*i*) *med.* acne

trefl *m* (-*a*; -*e*) (*w kartach*) club(*s pl.*); **as ~** ace of clubs; **wyjść w ~e** play clubs

trefny tref, not kosher

trema *f* (-*y*; *G* -) stage fright

tren¹ *m* (-*u*; -*y*) threnody

tren² *m* (-*u*; -*y*) train

tren|er *m* (-*a*; -*rzy*) trainer, coach; ~**ing** *m* (-*u*; -*i*) training; ~**ować** ⟨**wy-**⟩ (-*uję*) *v/t.* train, coach; *v/i. Brt.* practise, *Am.* practice; train

trep|ki *m/pl.*, ~**y** *m/pl.* (-*ów*) sandals

tresować ⟨**wy-**⟩ (-*uję*) train

treś|ciwie *adv.* succinctly; nutritiously; ~**ciwy** rich in substance; *jedzenie* nutritious, nourishing; *tekst* succinct; ~**ć** *f* (-ści; 0) content; meaning

trębacz *m* (-*a*; -*e*) trumpeter

trędowaty 1. leprous; **2.** *m* (-*ego*; -*ci*), ~**a** *f* (-*ej*; -*e*) leper

trik *m* (*-u*; *-i*) trick; play; **~owy** trick

triumf *m* (*-u*; *-y*) triumph; **~ować** ⟨**za-**⟩ (*-uję*) triumph (**nad** *I* over)

trochę a bit, a little; somewhat; **ani ~** not a bit; not at all

trociny *pl.* (*-*) wood shavings *pl.*

troć *f* (*-ci, -cie*) *zo.* brown trout

trofeum *n* (*idkl.; -ea, -eów*) trophy

tro|ić się (*-ję, trój!*) treble, triple; **~jaczki** *m/pl.* (*-ków*) triplets *pl.*; **~jaki** threefold; **~je** three; **we ~je** in three

trolejbus *m* (*-u; -y*) trolleybus

tron *m* (*-u, -y*) throne; **~owy** throne

trop *m* (*-y; G -ów*) trail, scent; **być na czyimś ~ie** be on s.o.'s trail; **~ić** (*-ę*) track, trail

tropikalny tropical

tro|ska *f* (*-i; G -*) care; **~skliwie** *adv.* carefully; **~skliwy** careful; **~szczyć się** ⟨**za- się**⟩ (*-ę*) (**o** *A*) look (after), take care (of); → **niepokoić się**

trosz|eczkę, ~kę → **trochę**

trój- *w złoż.* three-, tri-; **~ca** *f* (*-y; G -*): *rel.* **℞ca Święta** the Holy Trinity; **~drożny** *tech.* three-way; **~ka** *f* (*-i; G -jek*) three; (*linia*) number three; (*w szkole*) *jakby*: C; **we ~kę** in a group of three; **~kami** in threes

trójkąt *m* (*-a, -y*) *math.* triangle (*też fig.*); **~ny** triangular

trój|niak *m* (*-a; -i*) (*type of*) mead; **~nóg** *m* (*-noga; -nogi*) tripod; **~pasmowy** three-band; **~skok** *m* (*-u; 0*) triple jump; **~stronny** tripartite; **~wymiarowy** three-dimensional; **~ząb** *m* trident

truchle|ć (*-eję*) be terrified; **~ję na myśl o** (*I*) I tremble at the thought of

trucht *m* (*-u; 0*) trot; **~ać** (*-am*) trot

tru|cizna *f* (*-y; G -*) poison; **~ć** ⟨**o-**⟩ (*-ję*) poison (**się** o.s.)

trud *m* (*-u; -y*) trouble; **zadać sobie ~ z** (*I*) go to a lot of trouble over; **nie szczędzić ~ów** spare no efforts; **z ~em** with difficulty; **~nić się** (*-ę, -nij!*) (*I*) occupy o.s. (with); be engaged (in); **~no** *adv.* with difficulty; **~no mi powiedzieć** it is hard for me to say; **~no** (*A*) it is hard to get; (**no to**) **~no!** there's nothing I can do (about it)!; **~ność** *f* (*-ści; 0*) difficulty; **bez ~ności** without trouble; **~ny** difficult, hard; **~ny w pożyciu** difficult to get along with

trudzić (*-dzę*) trouble; **~ się** try; (**nad** *I*) struggle (with)

trujący poisonous

trumna *f* (*-y; G -mien*) coffin, *Am. też* casket

trun|ek *m* (*-nku; -nki*) (alcoholic) drink; **~kowy** F fond of drinking

trup *m* (*-a; -y*) corpse, (dead) body; **paść ~em** fall down dead; **iść po ~ach** stoop to anything, be ruthless; **~i** deathly; **~ia czaszka** skull and crossbones; **~io** *adv.* deathly; **~io blady** deathly pale

truskawk|a *f* (*-i; G -wek*) *bot.* raspberry; **~owy** raspberry

truteń *m* (*-tnia; -tnie*) *zo.* drone (*też Brt. fig.*); *fig.* parasite

trutka *f* (*-i; G -tek*) (**na szczury** rat) poison

trwa|ć (*-am*) last; (**długo**) take (long); (**w** *L*, **przy** *I*) persist (in); *rozmowa*: go on, continue; **~le** *adv.* long-lasting; **~łość** *f* (*-ści; 0*) durability; **~ły** long-lasting; *produkt* durable

trwog|a *f* (*-i; G trwóg*) fright, fear; horror; **bić na ~ę** sound the alarm

trwonić (*-ę*) waste; squander

trwoży|ć (*-ę*) frighten, worry; **~się** (**o** *A*) be frightened (about); be worried (about)

tryb *m* (*-u; -y*) course, mode; *tech.* cogwheel, gear; *gr.* mood; **iść swoim ~em** go on as usual; *jur.* **~ przyspieszony** summary proceedings *pl.*; **w ~ie przyspieszonym** *fig.* in a rush

trybun|a *f* (*-y; G -*) (grand)stand; **~ał** *m* (*-u; -y*) *jur.* tribunal

tryk *m* (*-a; -i*) *zo.* ram

trykot *m* (*-u; -y*) (*material*) cotton jersey; (*ubranie*) leotard; **~owy** cotton knitted

try|logia *f* (*GDL -ii; -e*) trilogy

trymestr *m* (*-u; -y*) trimester

trys|kać (*-am*) ⟨**~nąć**⟩ (*-nę*) spurt, squirt, gush; *iskry*: fly; *fig.* sparkle (*I* with); **~kać zdrowiem** be bursting with health

tryumf *m* → **triumf**

trzas|k *m* (*-u; -i*) crack, snap; *por.* **trzeszczeć**; **~kać** (*-am*) crack, snap; F *zdjęcia* snap; (*drzwiami*) slam; **~kający** *mróz* sharp; **~nąć** *pf.* → **trzaskać**

trząść ⟨**po-, za-**⟩ (*A*, *I*) shake; *pojazd*: jerk; **~ się** shake, shiver (**z zimna** with cold); quiver (**ze strachu** with fear)

trzcin|a *f* (*-y; G -*) *bot.* reed; **~a cukrowa** sugar cane; **~owy** reed, cane

trzeba (*nieos.*) one needs (**na to** to do it); it is necessary to; **~ to zrobić** it needs to be done; **ile ~** as much/many

as necessary; *jak* ~ if necessary; *nie* ~ it
is not necessary

trzebić ⟨*wy-*⟩ (*-ę*) *zwierzę* neuter; *fig.*
eradicate

trzech *m-os* three; *Święto 2 Króli* Epiphany; → *666*

trzeci third; *po ~e* thirdly; *jedna ~a, ~a
część* one third

trzeciorzędny third-class, third-rate

trzeć ⟨*po-*⟩ rub (*się* o.s.); *gastr.* grate

trzej *m-os* three; → *666*

trzep|aczka *f* (*-i; G -czek*) (*do dywanów*) carpet-beater; (*do piany itp.*)
whisk; ~*ać* (*-ię*) beat (*I* with) (*też dywan* ⟨*wy-*⟩); ~*ać językiem* blab,
babble; ~*nąć v/s.* (*-nę*) hit; ~*otać* (*-cze/
-cę*) flutter; flap (*na wietrze* in the
wind); ~*otać się* flutter; *ryba:* flounder

trzeszczeć (*-ę, -y*) *deski:* creak; (*w ogniu*) crackle; *lód:* crack; ~ *w szwach* be
bursting at the seams

trzewia *pl.* (*-i*) entrails *pl.*, insides *pl.*;
med. viscera; ~*owy* visceral

trzewik *m* (*-a; -i*) shoe

trzeźw|ić ⟨*o-*⟩ (*-ę, -wij!*) sober up; *fig.*
bring back to earth; ~*ieć* ⟨*o-, wy-*⟩
sober up; come to one's senses; ~*o
adv.* soberly; ~*y* sober

trzęsawisko *n* (*-a; G -*) bog, marsh

trzęsienie *n* (*-a; G -eń*) shaking; ~ *ziemi* earthquake

trzmiel *m* (*-a; -e*) *zo.* bumble bee

trzoda *f* (*-y; G trzód*) → *chlewny*

trzon *m* (*-u; -y*) core; nucleus; *tech.* shank,
stem, shaft; → ~*ek* *m* (*-nka; -nki*)
handle; ~*owy ząb ~owy* *anat.* molar

trzpień *m* (*-enia; -enie*) pin, bolt

trzustka *f* (*-i; G -tek*) *anat.* pancreas

trzy three; → *trój- i 666*; ~*cyfrowy*
three-figure; ~*częściowy* three-piece;
~*drzwiowy* three-door; ~*dziestka* *f*
(*-ki; G -tek*) thirty; ~*dziesty* thirtieth;
~*dzieści* thirty; → *666*; ~*krotnie adv.*
threefold; three times; ~*krotny* threefold; ~*letni* three-year-long, ~-old

trzyma|ć (*-am*) hold; keep; ~*ć się* hold
on (*za A, G* to); (*G*) keep (to); ~*ć się
razem* stick together; ~*ć się z dala* (*od
G*) keep away (from); ~*j się!* so long!,
take care!

trzyna|stka *f* (*-i; G -tek*) thirteen; ~*sto-
w złoż.* thirteen-; ~*stu* *m-os* thirteen;
~*sty* thirteenth; ~*ście*, ~*ścioro* *m-os*
thirteen; → *666*

trzy|osobowy for three persons; ~*po-
kojowy* three-room; ~*sta*, ~*stu* *m-os*
three hundred; → *666*

tu here; → *tam*

tub|a *f* (*-y; G -*) *mus.* tuba; *fig.* spokesperson, mouthpiece; → ~*ka* *f* (*-i; G
-bek*) tube

tubylczy native; indigenous; ~*ec* *m*
(*-ca; -cy*) native

tucz|nik *m* (*-a; -i*) fattening pig; ~*ny* fattening; ~*yć* ⟨*u-*⟩ (*-ę*) fatten

tulej|a *f* (*GDl -ei; -eje*), ~*ka* *f* (*-i; G -jek*)
tech. sleeve, bush

tulić ⟨*przy-*⟩ (*-lę*) hug, cuddle;
~ ⟨*przy-*⟩ *się* (*do G*) nestle close (to),
snuggle up (to)

tulipan *m* (*-a; -y*) *bot.* tulip

tułacz *m* (*-a; -e*) wanderer; ~*ka* *f* (*-i;
-czek*) wandering; ~*y* wandering

tułać *się* (*-am*) wander

tułów *m* (*-łowia; -łowie*) trunk

tuman *m* (*-u; -y*) cloud (*kurzu* of dust);
pej. (*-a; -i*) dunce, fool

tunel *m* (*-u; -e*) tunnel

Tunezj|a *f* (*-i; 0*) Tunisia; ~*yjczyk* *m*
(*-a; -cy*), ~*yjka* *f* (*-i; G -jek*) Tunisian;
2*yjski* Tunisian

tuńczyk *m* (*-a; -i*) *zo.* tuna

tupać (*-pię*) stamp

tupet *m* (*-u; -y*) nerve, cheek

tup|nąć *v/s.* (*-nę*) stamp; ~*ot* *m* (*-u; -y*)
patter, clatter

tura *f* (*-y; G -*) round

turbo|sprężarka *f* *tech.* turbocompressor; ~*śmigłowy* turbo-prop

Tur|cja *f* (*-i; 0*) Turkey; ~*czynka* *f* (*-i; G
-nek*) Turk; 2*ecki* Turkish; *mówić po
~ecku* speak Turkish; ~*ek* *m* (*-rka;
-rcy*) Turk

turkot *m* (*-u; -y*) rattle; ~*ać* (*-cę/-czę*)
rattle

turkus *m* (*-a; -y*) turquoise; ~*owy* turquoise

turniej *m* (*-u; -e*) tournament

turnus *m* (*-u; -y*) period

turyst|a *m* (*-y; G -tów*), ~*ka* *f* (*-i; G
-tek*) tourist; ~*yczny* tourist; *ruch
~yczny* tourism

tusz *m* (*-u; -e*) (*do pisania itp.*) India(n)
ink; (*prysznic*) shower; *mus.* flourish;
~ *do rzęs* mascara

tusza *f* (*-y; 0*) obesity; (*pl. -e*) (*zwierzęcia*) carcass

tut|aj → *tu*; ~*ejszy* local

tuzin m (-a; -y) dozen

tuż adv. immediately; ~ **przy** right to; ~ **za** right behind

twa pron f (ściągn. **twoja**) → **twój**

tward|nieć ⟨s-⟩ (-ję) harden; ~o adv. firmly; **jajko na** ~o hard-boiled egg; ~ość f (-ści; 0) hardness; ~y hard, firm; sen sound; mięso tough

twaróg m (-rogu; -rogi) cottage cheese

twarz f (-y; -e) face; **stać** ~**ą do** (G) face; **być do** ~**y** (D) suit; ~**ą w** ~ (z I) face to face (with); ~owy becoming, suitable; anat. facial

twe pron. f, n/pl. (ściągn. **twoje**) → **twój**

twierdz|a f (-y; -e) fortress; ~**ąco** adv. affirmatively; ~**ący** affirmative; ~enie n (-a; G -eń) claim; math. proposition; **bezpodstawne** ~enie allegation; ~ić (-ę) claim, maintain

twoj|i m-os pl., ~ja, ~je → **twój**

tworzy|ć (-ę, twórz!) ⟨s-⟩ create; całość constitute, make up; ⟨u-⟩ form (**się** v/i.); ~**ć się** też be formed, be created ~**wo** n (-a; G -) material, substance; **sztuczne** ~**wo** plastic

twój pron. m (f **twoja/twa**, n **twoje/ twe**; pl. **twoi/twoje/twe**) your, yours

twór m (tworu; twory) creation; ~**ca** m (-y; G -ów) creator; ~**czo** adv. creatively; ~**czość** f (-ści; 0) creativity; output; ~**czy** creative; ~**czyni** f (-yni; -ynie, -yń) creator

tw. szt. skrót pisany: **tworzywo sztuczne** plastic

ty pron. (GA **ciebie/cię**, D **tobie/ci**, I **tobą**, L **tobie**) you; **być na** ~ (z I) be on first name terms (with)

tych pron. GL/pl. → **ten, to**[1]

tyczka f (-i; G -czek) pole (też sport); ~**rz** m (-a; -e) (w sporcie) pole-vaulter

tycz|yć się (-ę, t-ko 3. os. lub bezok.) relate to, concern; **co się** ~**y** (G) as to

tyć ⟨u-⟩ (-ję) grow fat, put on weight

tydzień m (tygodnia; tygodnie) week; **za** ~ in a week; ~ **temu** a week ago; **całymi tygodniami** for weeks on end

tyfus m (-a; -y) med. typhoid fever; → **dur**[1]

tygodni|e pl. → **tydzień**; ~**k** m (-a; -i) weekly; ~**owo** adv. weekly; **dwu** ~**owo** two a/every week; ~**owy** weekly

tygrys m (-a; -y) zo. tiger; ~**ica** f (-y; -e) zo. tigress (też fig.)

tyka f (-i; G -) pole, stick

tykać[1] (-am) zegar: tick

tykać[2] (-am) touch; (zwracać się) be on first-name terms

tyle[1] (m-os GAL **tylu**, I **tyloma**) so much, so many; → **ile**; ~ **czasu** so much time; ~ ... **co** ... as much/many ... as ...; **drugie** ~ twice as much/many; **nie** ~ ..., **ile** ... not so much, ... as ...; ~ **samo**, ~**ż** just as much/many

tyle[2] → **tył**

tylko adv. only; merely; **jak** ~ as soon as

tyln|y back; tech. rear; zo. hind; ~**e światło** rear-light

tylu → **tyle**[1]

tył m (-u; -y) back; rear; ~**em, do** ~**u, w** ~ backwards; **w tyle** behind; **z** ~**u** in the back; **obrócić się** ~**em** turn back backwards (**do** G to); mil. pl. ~**y** rear; ~ **na przód** back to front; **pozostawać w tyle** drop behind; ~**ek** F m (-łka; -łki) behind, bottom

tym 1. DIL/pl. → **ten, to**[1]; **2.** part. (+ comp.) the; → **im, bardziej**

tymczas|em adv. (in the) meanwhile; ~**owość** f (-ści; 0) temporariness; ~**owo** adv. temporarily; provisionally; ~**owy** temporary; provisional

tymi → **ten, to**[1]

tymianek m (-nku; -nki) bot. thyme

tynk m (-u; -y) plaster; ~**ować** ⟨o-⟩ (-uję) plaster

typ m (-u; -y) type, sort; (-a; -y) pej. character

typow|ać (-uję) tip; (w loterii) do the lottery; ⟨**wy-**⟩ select, pick; ~**o** adv. typically; ~**y** typical

tyranizować bully, tyrannize

tys. skrót pisany: **tysiąc(e)** thou. (thousand)

tysiąc (G/pl. **tysięcy**) thousand; → **666**; ~**ami** by the thousands; ~**krotny** thousandfold; ~**lecie** n (-a; G -ci) millennium; ~**letni** thousand-year-long, -old

tysięczn|y thousandth; **jedna** ~**a** one thousandth; → **666**

tyto|niowy tobacco; ~**ń** m (-niu; -nie) bot. tobacco; (**fajkowy**) pipe) tobacco

tytuł m (-u; -y) title; ~**em** (G) as, by way (of)

tytułow|ać (-uję) address; ~**ać się** (I) use the title; ⟨**za-**⟩ **książkę** entitle; ~**y** title

tzn. skrót pisany: **to znaczy** i.e. (that is)

tzw. skrót pisany: **tak zwany** so-called

U

u *prp.* (*G*) at; with; **~ ciebie** with you, at your place; **~ brzegu** on the shore; *często nie tłumaczy się:* **klamka ~ drzwi** door handle; → **dół, góra**

uak|tualniać (*-am*) ⟨**~tualnić**⟩ (*-ę, -nij!*) update, bring up to date; **~tywniać** (*-am*) ⟨**~tywnić**⟩ (*-ę, -nij!*) activate, make active; **~tywniać** ⟨**~tywnić**⟩ **się** become active

ub. *skrót pisany:* **ubiegły** last

ubarwienie *n* (*-a; G -eń*) coloration; → **barwa**

ubezpiecz|ać (*-am*) insure (**się** o.s.; **od** *G* against); *mil.,* (*w sporcie*) cover; **~alnia** *f* (*-i; -e*) insurance company; **~enie** *n* (*-a; G -eń*) insurance, cover; **~enie od odpowiedzialności cywilnej** *mot.* third-party insurance; **~enie na życie** life insurance; **~eniowy** insurance; **~ony** *m* (*-ego; -eni*), **~ona** *f* (*-nej; -ne*) insured person; **~yciel** *m* (*-a; -e*) insurer; **~yć** *pf.* → **ubezpieczać**

ubić *pf.* → **ubijać**; *hunt.* shoot; **~ interes** strike a bargain

ubie|c *pf. v/t.* (*przebiec*) cover; *kogoś* beat *s.o.* to *s.th.*; *v/i.* → **~gać** (*-am*) *czas:* pass, go by; **~gać się** (**o** *A*) apply (for), try to obtain; **~gły** last, previous; **~gnąć** *pf.* → **ubiec**; **~rać** (*-am*) dress (**k-o w** *A* s.o. in); *choinkę itp.* decorate; **~rać się** dress, get dressed; **~rać się w** (*A*) put on

ubija|ć (*-am*) *ziemię* stamp; *gastr.* beat, whip; **~k** *m* (*-a; -i*) tamper, pestle

ubikacja *f* (*-i; -e*) toilet

ubiór *m* (*-bioru; -biory*) dress; costume

ubliż|ać (*-am*) ⟨**~yć**⟩ (*-ę*) insult; **~ająco** *adv.* insultingly; **~ający** insulting

uboczn|y *n:* **na ~u** out of the way; **~ie** *adv.* incidentally; **~ny** incidental; *działanie* **~ne** side effect

ubog|i 1. poor; **2.** *m* (*-ego; -odzy*), **~a** *f* (*-iej; -ie*) poor man/woman, pauper; **ubodzy** *pl.* the poor *pl.*; **~o** *adv.* poorly

ubolewa|ć (*-am*) (**nad** *I*) regret, deplore; **~nie** *n* (*-a; -ań*) regret; *godny* **~nia** regrettable

uboż|eć ⟨*z-*⟩ (*-eję*) become impoverished; **~ej** *adv. comp. od* → **ubogo**;

~szy *adj. comp. od* → **ubogi**

ubój *m* (*-boju; -boje*) slaughter

ubóstwiać (*-am*) adore

ubóstwo *n* (*-a; 0*) poverty

ubra|ć *pf.* → **ubierać**; **~nie** *n* (*-a; G -ań*) dress; **~nie ochronne** protective clothing; **~ny** dressed; **być ~nym w** be dressed in ..., wear ...

uby|ć *pf.* → **ubywać**; **~tek** *m* (*-tku; -tki*) loss; *med.* cavity; **~wać** (*-am*) (*D*) decrease, be on the decrease; *księżyc:* wane; *dnia* **~wa** the days are getting shorter

ucałowa|ć *pf.* kiss; **~nie** *n* (*-a; G -ań*) kiss

uchlany F blind drunk

ucho *n* **1.** (*-a; uszy, uszu, uszom, uszami, uszach*) *anat.* ear; **2.** (*pl. -a, uch*) handle; eye; *na własne uszy* with one's own ears; *obijać się o uszy* (*D*) come to one's ears; *szepnąć na* **~** whisper in s.o.'s ears; *po uszy* up to one's ears

uchodz|ić escape (*cało* unhurt), fly; *gaz, woda:* leak, escape; **~ić za** (*A*) pass (as); *to nie* **~i** it is not done; → **ujść**

uchodź|ca *m* (*-y, G -ców*) refugee; **~stwo** *n* (*-a; 0*) emigration

uchowa|ć *pf.* protect, preserve (*przed I* against); **~ się** survive

uchronić *pf.* protect (**od** *G* against)

uchwa|lać (*-am*) ⟨**~lić**⟩ *ustawę* pass; *wniosek* adopt; **~ła** *f* (*-y; G -*) resolution, decision

uchwy|cić *pf.* → **chwytać**; **~t** *m* grip, grasp, hold; (*rączka*) handle; **~tny** tangible, concrete; *ktoś* available

uchybi|(a)ć (*D*) insult; **~enie** *n* (*-a; G -eń*) insult

uchyl|ać (*-am*) ⟨**~ić**⟩ *drzwi* open slightly (**się** *v/i.*); *kotarę* draw aside; *decyzję itp.* cancel, annul; **~ić kapelusza** raise the hat; **~ić rąbka tajemnicy** reveal a secret; **~ać** ⟨**~ić**⟩ **się** (**od** *G*) shirk, evade, F dodge

uciąć *pf.* → **ucinać**

uciążliw|ie *adv.* arduously; **~y** arduous; burdensome, troublesome; **~y dla środowiska naturalnego** ecologically undesirable

ucichnąć pf. → **cichnąć**
ucie|c pf. (uciekną, -kniesz, -kł) → **uciekać**; ~**cha** f (-y; G -) fun, enjoyment; ~**czka** f (-i; G -czek) flight, escape; (zwł. z więzienia) break-out; **zmusić do ~czki** put to flight; ~**kać** (-am) (od G) escape (from), run away (from), flee; gaz: escape; (z więzienia) break out; ~**kać się** (do G) (-am) resort (to); ~**kać po wypadku** mot. fail to stop after an accident; commit a hit-and-run offence; ~**kinier** m (-a; -rzy), ~**kinierka** f (-i; G -rek) fugitive, runaway
ucieleśni|ać (-am) <~**ć**> (-ę, -nij!) embody; ~**a/a) się** be realized
ucier|ać (-am) gastr. grate; (rozmieszać) stir; ziarno grind; ~**pieć** pf. suffer
uciesz|ny comical, amusing; ~**yć** pf. → **cieszyć**
ucinać (-am) cut (off); cut short, curtail; → **ciąć**
ucisk m (-u; -i) pressure; fig. oppression, suppression; ~**ać** (-am) press; fig. oppress, suppress
ucisz|ać (-am) <~**yć**> (-ę) calm (down) (**się** v/i.)
uciśniony suppressed
ucywilizować pf. (-uję) civilize
uczci|ć pf. → **czcić**; rocznicę celebrate; ~**wość** f (-ści; 0) honesty, integrity; ~**wie** adv. honestly; ~**wy** honest
uczelnia f (-i; -e) college; ~ **wyższa** university
ucze|nie się¹ n (-a; 0) learning, study
ucze|nie² adv. learnedly, eruditely; ~**nnica** f (-y; G -), ~**ń** m (ucznia; uczniowie) pupil, student
ucze|pić się pf. → **czepiać się**; ~**rnić** pf. (-ę, ń/-nij!) blacken (też fig.); ~**sać** pf. → **czesać**; ~**sanie** n (-a; G -ań) hairdo, hairstyle
uczestni|ctwo n (-a; 0), ~**czenie** n (-a; 0) participation; ~**czka** f (-i; G -czek), ~**k** m (-a; -cy) participant (G in); ~**k wypadku** person involved in an accident; ~**czyć** (-ę) participate, take part (**w** L in)
uczęszcza|ć (-am) (**do** G, **na** A) attend, take part (in); ~**ny** well-attended, much-frequented
uczniowski student, pupil
uczon|ość f (-ści; 0) erudition; scholarship; ~**y 1.** scholarly, scientific; learned, erudite; **2.** m (-ego, uczeni), ~**a** f (-ej; -e) scholar; (przyrodnik) scientist

uczt|a f (-y; G -) feast; ~**ować** (-uję) feast
uczuci|e n (-a; G -) feeling; emotion; ~**owość** f (-ści; 0) sensitivity; ~**owo** adv. with feeling; sentimentally; affectionately; ~**owy** affectionate; emotional
uczu|ć pf. → **uczuwać, czuć**; ~**lać** (-am) <~**lić**> (-ę) make sensitive (**na** A to); chem., biol. make allergic (**na** A to); ~**lić się** (**na** A) become allergic (to); fig. be susceptible (to); ~**lenie** n (-a) med. allergy
uczyć <**na-**> (-ę) (**k-o** G) teach (s.o. s.th., przed.); ~ **się** (G) learn, study
uczyn|ek m (-nku; -nki) act, deed; **na gorący**; ~**ny** helpful, accommodating
uda|ć (się) pf. → **udawać (się)**; ~**ny** successful; dzieci fine; (nieszczery) pretended; simulated
udar m (-u; -y) med. (**cieplny** heat-)-stroke; ~ **słoneczny** sunstroke
udaremni|ać (-am) <~**ć**> (-ę, -nij!) upset, thwart, frustrate
uda|(wa)ć (-ję) v/t. chorobę feign; pretend (**głuchego** to be deaf), pose (**głuchego** as a deaf person); v/i. pretend, pose; ~**(wa)ć się** succeed, be successful; (**do** G, **na** A) doktora, miejsce go (to); miejsce make one's way to (to)
uderz|ać (-am) v/t. hit, strike; fig. strike, fascinate; v/i. (**o** A) (też **się**) knock (against, on), hit; bump (against, on); ~**ająco** adv. strikingly; ~**ający** striking; ~**enie** n (-a; G -eń) hit, knock, bang; strike (też mil.); ~**eniowy** mil. assault; med. shock; ~**yć** pf. (-ę) → **uderzać, bić**
udławić się pf. choke (**I** on)
udo n (-a; G ud) anat. thigh
udobruchać pf. (-am) placate, pacify, mollify
udogodni|ć pf. (-ę, -nij!) make (more) convenient; make easier; ~**enie** n (-a; G -eń) convenience
udoskonal|ać (-am) <~**ić**> perfect, improve; ~**enie** n (-a; G -eń) improvement, refinement
udostępni|ać (-am) <~**ć**> (-ę, -nij!) make accessible lub available
udowadni|ać (-am) <~**odnić**> (-ę, -nij!) prove; substantiate
udowy thigh; med. femoral
udrę|czenie n (-a; G -eń); ~**ka** f (-i; G -) agony, torment
udu|sić pf. choke, strangle; ~**sić się** (I)

U

choke (on); *por.* **dusić**; ~szenie *n* (*-a*, *G -eń*) strangling; choking; **śmierć od ~szenia** death by strangling

udział *m* (*-u*, *-y*) participation; (*wkład, też econ.*) share; **~ w zbrodni** participation in a crime; **brać ~ → uczestniczyć**; **~owiec** *m* (*-wca*, *-wcy*) *econ.* shareholder; **~owy** share

udziec *m* (*udźca*; *udźce*) *gastr.* leg

udziel|ać (*-am*) (*G*) offer; *pomocy, pożyczki* grant; *rady, słowa* give; **~ać się** *choroba itp.*: spread; *komuś* rub off (*D* on); ~enie *n* (*-a*; *0*) granting, giving; **~enie pomocy** assistance; **~ić** *pf.* **→ udzielać**

udziesięciokrotni|ać (*-am*) (*~ć*) (*-ę, -nij!*) increase tenfold (**się** *v/i.*)

udźwiękowi|ać (*-am*) (*~ć*) (*-ę, -wij!*) add sound to; *film*: add sound-track to

UE *skrót pisany*: **Unia Europejska** EC (*European Community*)

uf|ać (*-am*) (*za-*) (*-am*) trust (*D*; *impf. że* that); hope (*impf. że* that); **nie ~ać** distrust, mistrust; ~ność *f* (*-ści*; *0*) trust; ~ny trusting; (**w** *A*) confident (in)

uga|niać się → **ganiać**; ~nić *pf.* → **gasić**; ~szczać (*-am*) (*D*) give; entertain

ugi|nać się (*-am*) (*~ąć się*) bend, bow; sag (under the weight)

ugłaskać *pf. fig.* mollify, appease

ugni|atać (*-am*) *v/i. but*: pinch; *v/t.* (*~eść*) *ciasto* knead

ugo|da *f* (*-y*; *G ugód*) agreement, settlement; **~dowy** conciliatory; willing to compromise; **~dzić** *pf.* hit; *F* (*do pracy*) sign on; ~ścić *pf.* → **ugaszczać**

ugór *m* (*ugoru*; *ugory*) wasteland; fallow land; **leżeć ugorem** lie fallow

ugruntow|(yw)ać (*-[w]uję*) substantiate, ground

ugrupowanie *n* (*-a*; *G -ań*) group

ugryźć *pf.* bite; *komar.* sting

ugrząźć *pf.* → **grzęznąć**

ui|szczać (*-am*) (*~ścić*) (*-szczę*) pay (*z góry* in advance)

UJ *skrót pisany*: **Uniwersytet Jagielloński** Jagiellonian University

ujadać bark (**na** *A* at)

ujarzmi|ać (*-am*) (*~ć*) (*-ę, -mij!*) subjugate, enslave; *rzekę* master, control

ujawni|ać (*-am*) (*~ć*) (*-ę, -nij!*) reveal, expose; **~(a)ć się** manifest o.s.; *usterka itp.*: develop; *pol.* reveal o.s.

ująć *pf.* → **ujmować**

ujednolic|ać (*-am*) (*~ić*) (*-cę*) make uniform, standardize

ujemny negative

ujeżdża|ć (*-am*) (*ujeździć*) *konia* break in; ~lnia *f* (*-i, -e, -i*) riding school

ujęcie *n* (*-a*; *G -jęć*) capture; seizure; *fig.* point of view; *phot.* shot; (*wody itp.*) intake

ujm|a *f* (*-y*; *G ujm*) disgrace, discredit; **przynosić ~ę** (*D*) bring discredit (on); **~ować** (*-uję*) grab, seize (**za** *A* at); (*w słowa*) phrase, formulate; *fig. kogoś* enchant; (*odejmować, G*) take away; **~ować się** (**za** *I*) support; **~ujący** enchanting

ujrzeć *pf.* (*-ę, -yj!*) catch sight of, see

ujś|cie *n* (*-a*; *G ujść*) mouth; *fig.* outlet; **→ wylot**; ~ć (*-jść*) → **uchodzić**

ukartowany pre-arranged

ukatrupić F *pf.* (*-ę*) do in, bump off

ukaz|ywać (*-uję*) (*~ać*) reveal (**się** o.s.); **~(yw)ać się** appear

uką|sić *pf.* (*-szę*) → **kąsać**; ~szenie *n* (*-a*; *G -eń*) bite; (*skorpiona*) sting

UKF *skrót pisany*: **ultrakrótkie fale** VHF (*ultrashort waves*)

układ *m* (*-u, -y*) arrangement; system; (*kontrakt*) contract, agreement; *pol.* treaty; **zbiorowy ~ pracy** framework collective agreement; ♀ **Słoneczny** solar system; *t-ko pl.* **~y** negotiations *pl.*; *F* connections; **~ać** (*-am*) arrange, lay out; *tekst* compose; *plan* work out; *listę* make out; *sprawozdanie* compile; *melodię* compose; **~ać się** lie down (**do snu** to sleep); *stosunki*: turn out (**dobrze** all right); **~ać się wygodnie** snuggle, cuddle; **~ać się w fałdy** fall into folds; **~anka** *f* (*-i; G -nek*) jigsaw puzzle; **~ny** kind, charming; **~owy** system; contractual

ukłon *m* (*-u; -y*) bow; **~y** *pl. też* greetings; regards (**dla** *G* to); **~ić się** *pf.* bow; *por.* **kłaniać się**

ukłucie *n* (*-a; G -luć*) prick (*też fig.*); sting

ukochan|a *f* (*-ej; -e*), **~y 1.** *m* (*-ego; -ani*) darling; **2.** beloved, loved

ukon- *pf.* → **kon-**

ukończ|enie *n* (*-a; G -eń*) ending, conclusion; (*budowy itp.*) completion; (*szkoły* school-leaving) qualification; **~yć** *pf.* → **kończyć**

ukoronowanie *n* (*-a; G -ań*) crowning (*też fig.*)

ukorzeni|ać się (*-am*) ⟨*~ć się*⟩ take root; *~ony* rooted

ukos *m* (*-a; -y*) slant; *tech.* bevel; **na ~, z ~a, ~em** at a slant; obliquely; **patrzeć z ~a** look askance (**na** *A* at)

ukośny slanting; oblique

ukradkiem *adv.* stealthily, furtively

Ukra'i|na *f* (*-y; 0*) (the) Ukraine; **~niec** *m* (*-ńca; -ńcy*), **~nka** *f* (*-i; G -nek*) Ukrainian; **ⁿński** Ukrainian; **mówić po ~ńsku** speak Ukrainian

u|krajać (*-am*) cut off; **~kręcić** *pf. powróz* twist; (*oderwać*) twist off; *gastr.* mix; **~kroić** *pf.* → **ukrajać**

ukrop *m* (*-u; 0*) boiling water

ukry|cie *n* (*-a; G -yć*) hiding place; *fig.* concealment; → **kryjówka; z ~cia** from hiding; **~ty** concealed, hidden; *choroba* latent; **~wać** (*-am*) → **kryć**; *plany itp.* conceal, hide

ukrzyżowanie *n* (*-a; G -ań*) crucifixion; *rel.* the Crucifixion

ukształtowanie *n* (*-a; G -ań*) shape, shaping

ukuć *pf.* forge; *fig.* hatch

ukwiecony flower-bedecked, flowery

ul. *skrót pisany:* **ulica** St. (*street*)

ul *m* (*-a; -e*) beehive

ula|ć *pf.* → **ulewać**; **jak ~ł** fit like a glove; **~tniać się** (*-am*) evaporate; *zapach, nastrój:* disappear; *F fig.* clear off; **~tywać** (*-uję*) fly away/off; *woń:* disappear; → **uchodzić**

ule|c *pf.* → **ulegać**; **~ciec** *pf.* → **ulatywać**; **~czalny** curable; **~gać** (*-am*) (*D*) yield, submit; lose, give in; agree to (**prośbie** a request); **~gać woli** (*G*) bow to the will (of); **~gać wpływom** come under influence; **~c zmianie** undergo a change; **~c wypadkowi** have an accident; **~c zapomnieniu** fall into oblivion; *jur.* **~c przedawnieniu** be subject to prescription; → **wątpliwość**; **~gający zepsuciu** highly perishable

uleg|le *adv.* submissively; **~łość** *f* (*-ści; 0*) submission; **~ły** submissive, meek

ulepsz|ać (*-am*) ⟨*~yć*⟩ (*-ę*) improve; **~enie** *n* (*-a; G -eń*) improvement

ulewa *f* (*-y; G -*) downpour, heavy rain; **~ć** (*-am*) pour away; *niemowlę:* spit; **~ny** *deszcz* heavy

uleżeć *pf.:* **~ się** mellow, mature

ulg|a *f* (*-i; G -*) relief; (*zniżka*) discount, reduction; **~a podatkowa** *Brt.* tax al-

lowance, *Am.* tax deduction; **~owo** *adv.* traktować preferentially; **~owy** with a discount, reduced; *traktowanie* preferential

uli|ca *f* (*-y; G -*) street; **na/przy ~cy** *Brt.* in (*Am.* on) the street; **~czka** *f* (*-czki; G -czek*) street; **ślepa ~czka** blind alley (*też fig.*); **~cznik** *m* (*-a; -cy*) waif, street urchin; **~czny** street

ulokowa|ć *pf.* → **lokować**; **~nie** *n* (*-a; G -ań*) accommodation; location

ulot|ka *f* (*-i; G -tek*) leaflet; *reklamowa* prospectus, advertising brochure; **~ka z instrukcją** instruction leaflet; **~nić się** *pf.* (*-ę, -nij!*) → **ulatniać się**

ultra|dźwiękowy ultrasonic, ultrasound; **~fioletowy** ultraviolet; **~krótkofalowy** very high frequency; VHF; **~nowoczesny** ultramodern; **~sonograf** *m* (*-u; -y*) *med.* ultrasound scanner; **~sonograficzny** *med.* ultrasound

ulubi|enica *f* (*-y; G -*), **~eniec** *m* (*-ńca; -ńcy*) darling, pet; favo(u)rite; **~ony** favo(u)rite, pet

ulży|ć (*-ę*) *pf.* (*D*, **k-u w** *L*) relieve (s.o. of), make easier (s.o. with); **~ć sobie** (*w toalecie*) relieve o.s.; *fig.* get *s.th.* off one's chest; **~ło mi** (**na sercu**) that came as a relief to me

ułam|ać *pf.* → **ułamywać**; **~ek** *m* (*-mka; -mki*) *math.* fraction; piece; **w ~ku sekundy** in a split second; **~kowy** fraction; **~ywać** (*-uję*) break (off) (**się** *v/i.*)

ułaskawi|ać (*-am*) ⟨*~ć*⟩ (*-ę*) *jur.* pardon; **~enie** *n* (*-a; G -eń*) *jur.* pardon

ułatwi|ać (*-am*) ⟨*~ć*⟩ (*-ę*) simplify, make easier; facilitate; **~enie** *n* (*-a; G -eń*) simplification

ułom|ek *m* (*-mka; -mki*) fragment, piece; **~ność** *f* (*-ści; 0*) → **kalectwo**; **~ny** disabled, physically handicapped

ułoż|enie *n* (*-a; G -eń*) arrangement; **~yć** *pf.* → **układać**; **~yć się** *fig.* come to an agreement

ułuda *f* (*-y; G -*) illusion, hallucination

umacniać (*-am*) strengthen; *mil.* fortify; *fig.* consolidate; **~ się** become stronger; **~ się w** (*L*) make one's intentions stronger

umarł|y 1. dead; **2.** *m* (*-ego, -rli*), **~a** *f* (*-ej; -e*) dead person; **umarli** *pl.* the dead *pl.*

umarzać (*-am*) *econ. środek* amortize;

dług write off; *jur.* *rozprawę* abandon; *dochodzenie* stop

umawiać arrange (*też* **się** *v/i.*); agree; **~ się (co do** *G*) agree (on), reach an agreement (about); (**z** *I*) make an appointment (with)

umeblowanie *f* (*-a*; *0*) furniture

umiar *m* (*-u*; *0*) moderation; **z ~em** moderately, in moderation; **zacho- wać ~** be moderate; **~kowanie** *n* (*-a*; *0*) temperance (*też* **w** *piciu*), restraint → **~kowany** temperate; *poglądy, kie- runek* moderate

umie|ć (*-em*) be able to, can; **czy ~sz ...?** can you...?; **on ~ sobie poradzić** he can manage (it) on his own; **~jętność** *f* (*-ści*) skill; ability, capability; **~jętny** skilful

umiejs|cawiać (*-am*) ⟨**~cowić**⟩ (*-ę, -ców!*) locate; (*w klasyfikacji*) classify

umiera|ć (*-am*) die **~ć na raka** die of cancer, *fig.* **~ć ze strachu** die of fear; **~jący** dying

umie|szczać (*-am*) ⟨**~ścić**⟩ put, locate; place (*w* o.s.); (*publikować*) publish; *pieniądze* deposit

umięśniony muscular

umi|lać (*-am*) ⟨**~lić**⟩ (*-ę*) make more agreeable; brighten up; **~lknąć** (*-nę*) *pf.* fall silent; *muzyka, rozmowa:* stop; **~lowanie** *n* (*-a*) fondness (*G* for)

umizg|ać się (*-am*) (**do** *G*) flirt (with), make passes (to); (**o** *A*) woo, curry fa- vo(u)r (with); **~i** *pl.* flirting; wooing

umknąć *pf.* → **umykać**

umniejsz|ać (*-am*) ⟨**~yć**⟩ (*-ę*) decrease, diminish

umocn|ić *pp* → **umacniać**; **~ienie** *n* (*-a*; *G -eń*) fortification; *fig.* strengthen- ing, consolidation

umo|cow(yw)ać (*-[w]uję*) (*I*) fix (with), fasten (with); **~czyć** *pf.* → **maczać**; **~ru- sać** *pf.* (*-am*) smear; **~rusać się** get dirty; **~rzyć** *pf.* → **umarzać**; **~tywo- wanie** *n* (*-a*; *G -eń*) reason, grounds *pl.*

umow|a *f* (*-y*; *G umów*) agreement; contract; **~a kupna** contract of sale; **~a o pracę** contract of employment; **zgodnie z ~ą** as stipulated in the con- tract; **~ny** contractual; *econ.* **kara ~na** liquidated damages *pl.*

umożliwi|ać (*-am*) ⟨**~ć**⟩ (*-ę*) make pos- sible, enable

umówi|ć *pf.* → **umawiać**; **~ony** *spotka- nie* appointed

umrzeć *pf.* → **umierać**

umundurowa|ć *pf.* (*-uję*) uniform; **~nie** *n* (*-a*; *G -ań*) uniform

umy|ć *pf.* → **umywać, myć**; **~kać** (*-am*) escape, run away/off

umy|sł *m* (*-u*; *-y*) mind; intellect; **zdro- wy na ~śle** of sound mind; → **przy- tomność**; **~słowo** *adv.* mentally; intel- lectually; → *chory*; **~słowość** *f* (*-ści*) mentality; **~słowy** mental; intellectual; → **pracownik**

umyślny intentional, on purpose, delib- erate

umywa|ć (*-am*) wash (**się** o.s./*v/i.*); *na- czynia* wash up; **~lka** *f* (*-i*; *G -lek*) wash- basin; **~lnia** *f* (*-i*; *-e*) washing-room

unaoczni|ać (*-am*) ⟨**~ć**⟩ (*-ę, -nij!*) re- veal, show

unia *f* (*GDl -ii*; *-e*) union

uncja *f* (*-i*; *-e*) ounce

unicestwi|ać (*-am*) ⟨**~ć**⟩ (*-ę*) destroy, exterminate; *plany* wreck; *nadzieje* dash

uniemożliwi|ać (*-am*) ⟨**~ć**⟩ (*-ę*) pre- vent, frustrate; make impossible

unieru|chamiać (*-am*) ⟨**~chomić**⟩ (*-ę*) immobilize; *aviat.* ground; *tech.* lock; *kapitał* tie; *med.* set

uniesieni|e *n* (*-a*; *G -eń*) rapture, ela- tion; **w ~u** (*w zachwycie*) in rapture(s); (*w gniewie*) in anger

unieszkodliwi|ać (*-am*) ⟨**~ć**⟩ (*-ę*) neutralize; *śmieci* dispose of

unieść *pf.* → **unosić**

unieważni|ać (*-am*) ⟨**~ć**⟩ (*-ę, -nij!*) *legi- tymację, kontrakt* invalidate; *jur.* void, nullify, annul; **~enie** *n* (*-a*; *G -eń*) void- ance, nullification, annulment, inva- lidation

uniewinni|ać (*-am*) ⟨**~ć**⟩ (*-ę*) (**z** *G*) ex- onerate (from); *jur.* acquit (of); **~enie** *n* (*-a*; *G -eń*) exoneration; *jur.* acquittal

uniezależni|ać (*-am*) ⟨**~ć**⟩ (*-ę, -nij!*) make independent; **~(a)ć się** become independent (**od** *G* from)

unik *m* (*-u*; *-i*) dodge, duck; **zrobić ~** dodge, duck; **~ać** (*-am*) (*G*) avoid

unika|lny, **~towy** unique, only

uniknąć *pf.* → **unikać**; (*G*) escape, avoid

uniknięci|e *n* (*-a*; *G -ęć*) avoidance, es- cape; **nie do ~a** unavoidable

uniwer|salny universal; **~sytecki** uni- versity; academic; **~sytet** *m* (*-u*; *-y*) university

uniżony humble, servile

unosić raise; *rzeka*: carry away; **unie-siony** (*D*) in a fit (of); **~ się** rise; *w powietrzu, na wodzie* float; *na falach* drift

unowocześni|ać (*-am*) ⟨*~ć*⟩ (*-ę, -nij!*) modernize

uodporni|ać (*-am*) ⟨*~ć*⟩ (*-ę, -nij!*) immunize (**na** *A* against); **~ć się** (**na** *A*) become immune (to)

u|ogólniać (*-am*) ⟨*~ogólnić*⟩ (*-ę, -nij!*) generalize; **~osabiać** (*-am*) ⟨*~osobić*⟩ (*-ę, -nij!*) personify; **~osobienie** *n* (*-a*; *G -eń*) personification

upad|ać fall; *fig.* (*niszczeć*) decline, deteriorate; *pol.* fall, collapse; *econ.* go bankrupt; **~ać na duchu** lose heart; **~ek** *m* (*-dku; -dki*) fall; *fig.* decline, deterioration; *pol.* collapse; **~łość** *f* (*-ści; 0*) *econ.* bankruptcy, insolvency; **~ły** fallen; *fig.* sunk (low); **do ~łego** to the point of exhaustion

upa|jać (*-am*) (*alkoholem*) intoxicate, inebriate; *fig.* make euphoric, exhilarate; **~jać się** become intoxicated; become euphoric; **~lny** hot; **~ł** *m* (*-u; -y*) heat

upamiętni|ać (*-am*) ⟨*~ć*⟩ (*-ę, -nij!*) memorialize, commemorate; **~(a)ć się** be remembered, remain in memory

upaństw|awiać (*-am*) ⟨*~owić*⟩ (*-ę, -wów!*) nationalize

upar|cie *adv.* stubbornly, obstinately; **~ty** stubborn, obstinate

upaść[1] *pf.* (*paść*[1]) → (**u**)**padać**

upaść[2] *pf.* (*paść*[2]) fatten; **~trywać** (*-uję*) ⟨*~trzyć*⟩ → **wypatrywać, wypatrzyć**; **~trywać stosownej chwili** wait for the suitable time

upch|ać *pf.*, **~nąć** *pf.* → **upychać**

upełnomocni|ać (*-am*) ⟨*~ć*⟩ (*-ę, -nij!*) authorize (**do** *G* to)

uperfumowany scented, perfumed

upewni|ać (*-am*) assure (**k-o o** s.o. of); **~ć się** make sure (**co do** of)

upi|jać *pf.* → **upinać**; **~ć** *pf.* → **upijać**

upie|c *pf.* bake; *mięso* roast; **świeżo ~czony** *fig.* new, newly-qualified

upierać się (*-am*) insist (**przy** *L* on), persist (**przy** *L* in)

upierzenie *n* (*-a*; *G -eń*) plumage

upiększ|ać (*-am*) ⟨*~yć*⟩ (*-ę*) decorate, deck out; *fig.* embellish

upi|jać (*-am*) (*G*) make drunk, inebriate, intoxicate; **~jać się** get drunk; **~nać** (*-am*) *włosy* pin up

u|piorny ghastly; **~piór** *m* (*-piora,*

-piory) ghost

upły|nąć *pf.* → **upływać**; **~w** *m* (*-u; 0*) (*czasu*) passage, passing; **z ~wem lat** with years; **~w krwi** loss of blood; **~wać** *czas*: go by, fly; *termin*: expire, lapse

upodoba|ć (*-am*): **~ć sobie** (*A*) take a liking (to); **~nie** *n* (*-a; G -ań*) liking, fondness (**do** *G* for); **z ~niem** with pleasure; **według ~nia** to one's liking

upo|ić *pf.* → **upajać**; **~jenie** *n* (*-a; G -eń*) inebriation, intoxication (*też fig.*); **~karzać** (*-am*) ⟨*~korzyć*⟩ (*-ę, -kórz!*) humble (**się** o.s.)

upomin|ać (*-am*) admonish, rebuke; **~ać się** (**o** *A*) demand, insist (on); **~ek** *m* (*-nka; -nki*) souvenir, keepsake

upomnie|ć *pf.* → **upominać**; **~nie** *n* (*-a; G -eń*) (*na piśmie*) reminder; reprimand, rebuke

upor|ać się *pf.* (*-am*) (**z** *I*) get ready (with); clear (up); **~czywy** unrelenting; tenacious; *wzrok* insistent; *ból* persistent

uporządkow(yw)ać (*-[w]uję*) tidy up; *fig.* straighten out, sort out

uposaże|nie *n* (*-a; G -eń*) pay, salary; **~owy** pay, salary

upośledz|ać (*-am*) ⟨*~ić*⟩ handicap, impair; **~enie** *n* (*-a; G -eń*) disability; handicap; **~ony** disabled; underprivileged

upoważni|ać (*-am*) ⟨*~ć*⟩ (*-ę*) authorize, empower (**do** *G* to); **~enie** *n* (*-a; G -eń*) authorization, authority; *jur.* power of attorney; **z ~enia** by proxy

upowszechni|ać (*-am*) ⟨*~ć*⟩ (*-ę, -nij!*) spread, disseminate

upozorowanie *n* (*-a; G -ań*) simulation, feigning

upór *m* (*uporu; 0*) stubbornness, obstinacy

upragnienie *n*: **z ~m** longingly

upragniony longed for

uprasz|ać (*-am*) request; **~a się o ciszę!** silence, please!; **~czać** (*-am*) simplify; *ułamek* cancel

upraw|a *f* (*-y; G -*) *agr.* tillage, cultivation; growing; crop; *~iać* (*-am*) ⟨*~ić*⟩ *ziemię* cultivate; *t-ko impf. rośliny* grow; *sport itp.* go in for, *Brt.* practise, *Am.* practice; **~niać** (*-am*) ⟨*~nić*⟩ (*-ę, -nij!*) (**do** *G*) entitle (to); **~nienie** *n* (*-a; G -eń*) entitlement, right; **~niony** entitled (**do głosowania** to vote); eligible (**do** *G* for); **~ny** *agr.* arable

U

uprawomocnić się *pf.* (-ę, -nij!) come into force

upro|sić *pf.* → **upraszać**; ~**szczenie** *n* (-a; G -eń) simplification; ~**ścić** *pf.* → **upraszczać**; ~**wadzać** (-am) ⟨~**wadzić**⟩ (-ę) hijack; *samolot* skyjack; ~**wadzenie** *n* (-a; G -eń) hijacking; (*samolotu*) skyjacking

u|prząż *f* (*uprzęży; uprzęże*) harness; ~**przeć się** *pf.* → **upierać się**; ~**przednio** *adv.* previously, before

uprzedz|ać (-am) *v/t.* forestall, anticipate; (*przestrzegać*) (**o** L) forewarn, warn (of); ~**ać się** (**do** G) become prejudiced (against); ~**ająco** *adv.* obligingly; ~**ający** obliging; ~**enie** *n* (-a; G -eń) prejudice, bias; *bez* ~**enia** unbiased, open-minded; (*nagle*) without warning; ~**ić** (-am) *v/t. pf.* → **uprze-dzać**; ~**ony** prejudiced, biased

uprzejm|ość *f* (-ści; 0) kindness, politeness; ~**ie** *adv.*: *dziękuję* ~**ie** thank you very much; ~**y** (*dla* G, *wobec* A) polite (for), kind (for); *bądź tak* ~**y** (*i*) be so kind as to

uprzemysło|wienie *n* (-a; 0) industrialization; ~**wiony** industrialized

uprzyjemni|ać (-am) ⟨~**ć**⟩ (-ę, -nij!) make nicer, make enjoyable

uprzykrz|ać (-am) ⟨~**yć**⟩ spoil; make miserable; ~**yć sobie** (A) grow tired (of); ~**ać się** be a nuisance; ~**ony** tiresome

uprzy|stępniać (-am) ⟨~**stępnić**⟩ (-ę, -nij!) → **udostępniać**; ~**tamniać**, ~**tomniać** (-am) ⟨~**tomnić**⟩ (-ę, -nij!) (*też sobie*) realize; ~**wilejowany** privileged

upu|st *m* (-u; -y) *tech.* bleed(ing); (*śluza*) sluice; *dać* ~**st** (D) *fig.* give vent (to); ~**szczać** (-am) ⟨~**ścić**⟩ drop; ~**szczać krew** bleed, draw blood

upychać (-am) stuff

ura|biać (-am) form (*się v/i.*); (*w górnictwie*) mine, *kamień* quarry; F *kogoś* work on; ~**czać** (-am) → **raczyć**; ~**dowany** delighted, joyful; *por.* **radować**; ~**dzać** (-am) ⟨~**dzić**⟩ agree on; conclude

uran *m* (-u; 0) *chem.* uranium

Uran *m* (-a; 0) *astr.* Uranus

uranowy uranium

ura|stać (-am) grow, increase; (**do** G) take on the proportions (of); ~**tować** *pf.* save

uraz *m* (-u; -y) trauma, injury; ~**a** *f* (-y; G -) resentment, offence; grudge; *mieć* ~**ę** *Brt.* bear (*Am.* hold) a grudge (**do** G against); ~**ić** *pf.* → **urażać**; ~**owy** traumatic

urażać (-am) hurt, wound (*też fig.*)

urąg|ać (-am) defy; *lit. komuś* insult; → **wymyślać**; ~**owisko** *n* (-a; 0) laughingstock

urbanistyczny urbanistic, town-planning

uregulowanie *n* (-a; G -ań) regulation

urlop *m* (-u; -y) (*macierzyński* maternity) leave, (*wypoczynkowy*) holiday, *zwł. Am.* vacation; *być na* ~**ie**, *korzystać z* ~**u** be on *Brt.* holidays (*Am.* vacation); ~**ować** (*im*)*pf.* (-uję) give *s.o.* leave (of absence); ~**owy** holiday, vacation

urna *f* (-y; G *urn*) (*wyborcza*) ballot-box

uro|bić *pf.* → **urabiać**; ~**czo** *adv.* charmingly; ~**czy** charming, lovely; ~**czystość** *f* (-ści) ceremony; festivity, celebration; ~**czysty** solemn, ceremonial; ~**czyście** *adv.* solemnly; ceremonially; ~**da** *f* (-y; 0) beauty; looks *pl.*

urodz|aj *m* (-u; -e) good harvest/crop; ~**aj na owoce** a good year for fruit; ~**ajny** fertile; ~**enie** *n* (-a; G -eń) birth; *miejsce* ~**enia** birthplace; *rok* ~**enia** year of birth; *Polak z* ~**enia** a Pole by birth; ~**ić** *pf.* → **rodzić**; ~**inowy** birthday; ~**iny** *pl.* (-) birthday (party)

uro|jenie *n* (-a; -eń) illusion, hallucination; ~**jony** imaginary

urok *m* (-u; -i) charm; *pełen* ~**u** charming; *na psa* ~**!** touch wood!

urosnąć *pf.* → **urastać**

urozmaic|ać (-am) ⟨~**ić**⟩ (-ę) vary, diversify; ~**enie** *n* (-a; G -eń) variety, diversity; ~**ony** varied, diversified

uruch|amiać (-am) ⟨~**omić**⟩ (-ę) set in motion; turn on; *silnik* start up

urwać *pf.* → **urywać, rwać**

urwis *m* (-a; -y) young rascal

urwis|ko *n* (-a; G -) precipice, bluff; ~**ty** → **stromy**

uryw|ać (-am) *v/t.* cut short; tear off; *v/i.* ~**ać się** come off; break off; F *ktoś*: slip away; ~**any** interrupted; ~**ek** *m* (-wka; -wki) bit, snatch, snippet; ~**kowy** fragmentary, incomplete

urząd *m* (-rzędu; -rzędy) (*pocztowy, stanu cywilnego* post, registry) office;

authorities *pl.*; **z urzędu** because of one's profession; *jur.* assigned (by court)

urządz|ać (*-am*) arrange; *mieszkanie* furnish; *przyjęcie* give; **~ać się** furnish, make o.s. at home; **~enie** *n* (*-a*; *G -eń*) appliance, device; facility; **~enie sanitarne** sanitary facilities *pl.*; **~ić** *pf.* → **urządzać**

urze|c *pf.* → **urzekać**; **~czony** bewitched; **jak ~czony** like one bewitched

urzeczywistni|ać (*-am*) ⟨**~ć**⟩ (*-ę, -nij!*) realize, put into practice; **~ać** ⟨**~ć**⟩ **się** be realized, be fulfilled

urzeka|ć (*-am*) enchant, bewitch; *fig.* (*I*) win, captivate; **~jąco** *adv.* enchantingly; captivatingly; **~jący** enchanting; captivating

urzędni|czka *f* (*-i; G -czek*), **~k** *m* (*-a; -cy*) clerk, official

urzędow|ać (*-uję*) work (in an office); **~anie** *n* (*-a; 0*) discharge of one's duties; **godziny** *pl.* **~ania** office hours *pl.*; **~o** *adv.* officially; **~y** official

urznąć (*-am*) ⟨**urznąć, urżnąć**⟩ cut off; F **~** ⟨**urżnąć**⟩ **się** get drunk

usamodzielni|ać się (*-am*) ⟨**~ć się**⟩ (*-ę, -nij!*) become independent

USC *skrót pisany:* **Urząd Stanu Cywilnego** registry office

uschnąć *pf.* → **usychać**

USG *n skrót: med.* **ultrasonografia** F ultrasound scan; **zrobił sobie ~** he was given an ultrasound scan

usiany studded

usi|ąść *pf.* → **siadać**; **~edzieć** *pf.*: **nie móc ~edzieć** be on edge

usil|ny *prośba* insistent, urgent; *praca, starania* concentrated; **~łować** (*-uję*) (+ *bezok.*) try (to *bezok.*), endeavo(u)r (to *bezok.*); (*bardzo*) struggle (to *bezok.*); **~łowanie** *n* (*-a; G -ań*) endeavo(u)r; attempt

uskakiwać (*-uję*) jump aside

uskarżać się (*-am*) complain (**na** *A* about)

u|składać *pf.* (*-am*) save (**na** *A* for); **~skoczyć** *pf.* → **uskakiwać**; **~słany** (*I*) covered (with); **~słuchać** *pf.* (*G*) respond (to); (*być posłusznym*) listen (to)

usłu|ga *f* (*-i; G -*) service; (*grzeczność*) favo(u)r; → **przysługa**; **~giwać** (*-uję*) serve (**gościom** the guests; **przy stole** at table); **~gowy** service; **~żność** *f*

(*-ści; 0*) willingness to help; **~żny** → **uczynny**; **~żyć** *pf.* → **usługiwać**

usłyszeć *pf.* → **słyszeć**

usnąć *pf.* (*-nę*) fall asleep; *lit.* **~ na wieki** die

uspo|kajać (*-am*) ⟨**~koić**⟩ (*-ję*) calm down (**się** *v/i.*); **~koić się** *wiatr, burza*: die down; *morze:* become calm; **~kajająco** *adv.* soothingly; **~kajający** soothing; *med.* sedative

uspołeczni|ać (*-am*) ⟨**~ć**⟩ socialize; *econ.* nationalize

uspos|abiać (*-am*) ⟨**~obić**⟩ (*-ę, -sób!*) set (**przeciw** against); (**do** *G*) dispose (toward(s)); **nie być ~obionym** not feel like (**do czegoś** doing s.th.); **~obienie** *n* (*-a; G -eń*) nature, character

usprawiedliwi|ać (*-am*) ⟨**~ć**⟩ (*-ę*) excuse (**się** o.s.); (*wytłumaczyć*) justify; **~enie** *n* (*-a; G -eń*) excuse; (*wytłumaczenie*) justification

usprawni|ać (*-am*) ⟨**~ć**⟩ (*-ę, -nij!*) improve (on), make more efficient

ust. *skrót pisany:* **ustawa** act; **ustęp** paragraph, passage

usta *pl.* (*ust*) mouth, lips *pl.*

usta|ć¹ *pf.* (*stać²*) stop, end

usta|ć² *pf.* (*stać¹*) stand, keep standing; **~ć się** *płyn:* clear; **~lać** (*-am*) ⟨**~lić**⟩ (*-ę*) stabilize (**się** *v/i.*); *warunki, termin itp.* fix, determine; *fakt* establish; **~nawiać** (*-am*) ⟨**~nowić**⟩ *zwyczaj itp.* introduce; *rekord* establish; *spadkobiercę* appoint; name; **~wa** *f* (*-y; G -*) rule, law; **~wać** (*-ję*) stop, end

ustawi|(a)ć się put up, set up; **~(a)ć się** place o.s.; (*w szeregu itp.*) line up; **~czny** continual, incessant

ustawodaw|ca *m* (*-y; G -ców*) lawmaker, legislator; **~czy** legislative; **władza ~cza** legislative power; **~stwo** *n* (*-a; G -*) legislation

ustawow|o *adv.* by law *lub* statute; **~y** legal, statutory

ustąpi|ć *pf.* (*-ę*) → **ustępować**; **~enie** *n* (*-a; G -eń*) withdrawal, resignation

uster|ka *f* (*-i; G -rek*) defect, fault; **bez ~ek** faultless

ustęp *m* (*-u; -y*) excerpt; passage; → **klozet**; **~liwie** *adv.* yieldingly; compliantly; **~liwy** yielding; compliant; **~ować** (*-uję*) *v/i.* (*przed siłą itp.*) yield; give in; (*pod naciskiem*) give; (*z funkcji*) step down, resign; *pierwszeństwa itp.*,

U

też fig. give way; (**k-uw** *L*) be inferior (to s.o. in); *wróg*: retreat (**wobec** *A* against); *ból itp.*: subside, die away; **~ować z ceny** lower the price; *v/t.* let have, leave; **~stwo** *n* (*-a*; *G* -) concession

ustn|ie *adv.* orally; **~ik** *m* (*-a*; *-i*) mouthpiece; **~y** oral

ustokrotni|ać 〈**~ć**〉 (*-ę*, *-nij!*) increase a hundredfold (**się** *v/i.*)

ustosunkow(yw)ać się ~[-w]uję〉 (**do** *G*) react (to), respond (to); take a position (to)

ustrojowy *biol.* body, organic; *pol.* political, constitutional

ustronny remote, out-of-the-way

ustrój *m* (*-roju*; *-roje*) system; *biol.* organism; **~ państwowy** state system

ustrzec *pf.* preserve (**przed** *I*, **od** *G* from); **~ się** (**przed** *I*) avoid

usu|nąć *pf.* → **usuwać**; **~nięcie** *n* (*-a*; *G* -ęć) removal; elimination; **~wać** (*-am*) remove; (**z grupy** *itp.*) get rid of, eliminate; *med.* take out (**z** *G* from); **~wać się** withdraw (**od** *G* from); move (**na bok** aside)

usychać (*-am*) dry

usynowienie *n* (*-a*; *G* -eń) adoption

usy|pać *pf.* → **usypywać**; **~piać** (*-am*) fall asleep, doze off; **~piająco** adv. soporifically; **~piający** soporific

usy|pisko *n* (*-a*; *G* -) (*śmieci*) dump, *Brt.* tip; (*piasku itp.*) pile; **~pywać** (*-uję*) pile (up)

usytuowanie *n* (*-a*; *G* -ań) localization, location

uszanowani|e *n* (*-a*; *G* -ań) → **poszanowanie, szacunek**; **brak ~a** lack of respect

uszczel|ka *f* (*-i*; *G* -lek) seal, washer; **~niać** (*-am*) 〈**~nić**〉 (*-ę*, *-nij!*) make tight; seal, stop

uszczerb|ek *m* (*-bku*; *0*) damage; **z ~kiem** (**dla**) **zdrowia** to the detriment of health

uszczęśliwi|ać (*-am*) 〈**~ć**〉 (*-ę*) make happy

uszczupl|ać (*-am*) 〈**~ić**〉 (*-lę*, *-lij!*) reduce, deplete

uszczyp|liwie *adv.* caustically, stingingly; **~liwy** caustic, stinging; **~nąć** *v/s.* (*-ę*) pinch

uszkadzać (*-am*) damage

uszko *n* (*-a*; *G* -szek) → **ucho**; (*igły*) ear; (*filiżanki*) handle

uszkodz|enie *n* (*-a*; *G* -eń) damage; injury; **~enie ciała** bodily harm; **~ony** damaged; broken-down; **~ić** *pf.* → **uszkadzać**

uszlachetni|ać (*-am*) 〈**~ć**〉 (*-ę*, *-nij!*) ennoble; *tech.* enrich, refine

usz|ny ear; *med.* aural; **~y** *pl.* → **ucho**

uszy|ć *pf.* → **szyć**; **~kować** (*-uję*) prepare, make ready

uścis|k *m* (*-u*; *-i*) (*ramionami*) embrace; hug; (*ręką*) grip; **~k dłoni** handshake; **~kać** 〈**~nąć**〉 embrace, hug; grip; *dłoń* shake

uśmiać się laugh (**do łez, serdecznie** to tears, heartily; **z** *G* at)

uśmiech *m* (*-u*; *-y*) smile; **szyderczy ~** smirk, grin; **~ać się** (*-am*) 〈**~nąć się**〉 (*-nę*) smile; (**z** *G*) grin (at), smirk (at); (**do** *G*) give a smile (to), smile (at); **~nięty** smiling

uśmierc|ać (*-am*) 〈**~ić**〉 (*-cę*) kill; *zwł. zwierzę* put to death

uśmierz|ać (*-am*) 〈**~yć**〉 (*-ę*) *ból* alleviate, soothe; *bunt* suppress

u|śmieszek *m* (*-szka*; *-szki*) grin; **~śpić** *pf.* → **usypiać**

uświad|amiać (*-am*) 〈**~omić**〉 (*-ę*) educate; tell, inform (**co do** *G* about); **~omić sobie** realize; **~omienie** *n* (*-a*; *0*) education; realization

uświęcony sanctified; traditional

uta|jniony secret; classified; **~jony** secret; latent, dormant; **~lentowany** talented, gifted

utarczka *f* (*-i*; *G* -czek) *mil.* skirmish; **~ słowna** battle of words, clash

utarg *m* (*-u*; *-i*) (*dzienny* daily) proceeds *pl.*; **~ować** *pf.* take, earn, make

utarty *fig.* commonplace, stock; **~m zwyczajem** traditionally; **~ zwrot** platitude

utęsknienie *n*: **z ~m** longingly; yearningly

utknąć (*-nę*) get stuck

utkwić *pf.* *v/s.* fix; stick; stick; **~ w pamięci** stick in the memory

utleni|ać (*-am*) 〈**~ć**〉 (*-ę*) oxydize (**się** *v/i.*); *włosy* bleach; **~ony** oxydized; **woda ~ona** hydrogen peroxide

utonąć *pf.* drown; *por.* **tonąć**

utopić *pf.* sink; drown; **~ się** be drowned

utopijny utopian

utożsami|ać (*-am*) 〈**~ć**〉 (*-ę*) identify (**się** *v/i.*; **z** *I* with)

utra|cać (*-am*) → **tracić**; **~pienie** *n* (*-a*;

G -eń) sorrow, grief; **~ta** *f* (*-y; G -*) loss

utracić *pf.* knock off; *fig.* kill

utrudni|ać (*-am*) ⟨**~ć**⟩ (*-ę*) make difficult; impede; **~enie** *n* (*-a; G -eń*) impediment, handicap

utrwal|acz *m* (*-a; -e*) *phot.* fixer, F hypo; (*do włosów*) setting lotion; **~ać** (*-am*) ⟨**~ić**⟩ (*-lę*) strengthen; *fig.* cement, consolidate; record (*na taśmie filmowej* on film); preserve (*w pamięci* in memory); *phot.* fix; **~ać** ⟨**~ić**⟩ **się** become stronger

utrzeć *pf.* → **ucierać**

utrzyma|ć *pf.* → **utrzymywać**; **~nie** *n* (*-a; 0*) keep, living; (*maszyny*) maintenance; **nie do ~nia** not to be supported; **mieć na ~niu** (*A*) support; **całodzienne ~nie** full board

utrzymywać (*-uję*) *v/t.* support, bear; *rodzinę* support, provide for; *kochankę, spokój* keep; **~ przy życiu** keep alive; *v/i.* claim; **~ się** (*z G*) support o.s. (by), earn one's living (by)

utwardz|acz *m* (*-a; -e*) *chem.* hardener; **~ać** (*-am*) ⟨**~ić**⟩ (*-dzę*) harden; *fig.* *związki* strengthen, consolidate; *postawę* toughen

utwierdz|ać (*-am*) ⟨**~ić**⟩ (*-ę*) *fig.* confirm; **~ić się w przekonaniu, że** become convinced that

utwór *m* (*-woru; -wory*) piece, work; composition

utycie *n* (*-a; 0*) increase in weight

utykać (*-am*) limp, walk with a limp; → **utknąć**

utylizacja *f* (*-i; 0*) *tech.* utilization

utyskiwać (*-uję*) complain (*na A* about)

uwag|a *f* (*-i; 0*) attention; (*pl. -i*) remark, comment; **~a!** look out!; **brać pod ~ę** take into attention; **skupić ~ę** (*na L*) concentrate (on); **zwrócić ~ę k-u** (*na A*) draw s.o.'s attention (to); **zwrócić ~ę** (*na A*) pay attention (to); **zwrócić na siebie ~ę** catch s.o.'s attention; **nie zwracać ~i** not pay attention (*na A* to); **z ~i na** (*A*) because (of), considering; **mieć na uwadze** take into consideration

uwalniać (*-am*) free (*od G* from, of)

uwarunkow(yw)ać (-[w]*uję*) condition

uważ|ać (*-am*) *v/i.* look out; take care (*na siebie* of o.s.); (*z I*) be careful (with); (*za A*) consider (to be), regard (as); **~am, że ...** I think that ...; *jak pan*

~a as you wish; **~nie** *adv.* carefully, cautiously; **~ny** careful, cautious

uwertura *f* (*-y; G -*) *mus.* overture (*też fig.*)

uwiąz(yw)ać *pf.* → **przywiązywać**

uwidaczniać (*-am*) ⟨**uwidocznić**⟩ (*-ę, -nij!*) show; **~ się** manifest, be manifested

uwielbi|ać (*-am*) adore, worship; **~enie** *n* (*-a; 0*) adoration, worship

uwielokrotni|ać (*-am*) ⟨**~ć**⟩ (*-ę, -nij!*) multiply

uwieńczać *pf.* → **wieńczyć**

uwierać (*-am*) press, pinch

uwierz|enie *n*: **nie do ~enia** unbelievable, beyond belief; **~yć** *pf.* believe; *por.* **wierzyć**

uwierzytelni|ać (*-am*) ⟨**~ć**⟩ (*-ę, -nij!*) authenticate; **~enie** *n* (*-a*) authentication

uwie|sić *pf.* (*-szę*) hang; **~ść** *pf.* → **uwodzić**; **~źć** *pf.* → **uwozić**

uwięz|ić *pf.* (*-żę*) imprison; **~nąć** *pf.* (*-nę*) get stuck

uwię|ź *f* (*-zi; -zie, -zi*): **na ~zi** *balon* tethered; *fig.* tied down

uwijać się (*-am*) bustle (*koło G* about)

uwikłać *pf.* *v/t.* involve; *v/i.* **~ się** be involved, be entangled

uwłaczający derogatory

uwłosienie *n* (*-a; 0*) hair, hair cover

uwodziciel *m* (*-a, -e*), **~ka** *f* (*-i; G -lek*) seducer; **~sko** *adv.* seductively; **~ski** seductive

uwo|dzić (*-dzę*) seduce; **~lnić** *pf.* (*-ę, -nij!*) → **uwalniać**; **~lnienie** *n* (*-a; G -eń*) freeing, liberation; **~zić** carry away

uwspółcześniony modernized, updated

uwsteczniony *fig.* retarded, degenerated

uwydatni|ać (*-am*) ⟨**~ć**⟩ (*-ę, -nij!*) emphasize, enhance; **~(a)ć się** be prominent, stand out

uwypukl|ać (*-am*) ⟨**~ić**⟩ (*-lę, -lij!*) *fig.* emphasize; → **uwydatniać**

uwzględni|ać (*-am*) ⟨**~ć**⟩ (*-ę, -nij!*) *v/t.* take into consideration *lub* account; **nie ~ć** (*G*) ignore; **~enie** *n* (*-a; 0*) taking into account *lub* consideration

uwziąć się → **zawziąć się**

uzależni|ać (*-am*) ⟨**~ć**⟩ (*-ę, -nij!*) (*od G*) make dependent (on); **~ć się** become dependent (on); (*od narkotyków*)

U

become addicted (to); ~enie n (-a; G -eń) addiction; ~ony (od papierosów itp.) addicted; być ~onym be addicted (od G to)

uzasadni|ać (-am) ⟨~ć⟩ (-ę, -nij!) justify, give reasons for; ~enie n (-a; G -eń) justification; ~ony justified

uzbierać pf. (-am) gather (się v/i.; też together)

uzbr|ajać (-am) ⟨~oić⟩ arm (fig. się o.s.; w A with); tech. (w A) equip (with), fit (with); bud. develop; → zbroić; ~ojenie n (-a; G -eń) armament; tech. armo(u)r; bud. ~ojenie terenu territorial development

uzda f (-y; G -) bridle

u|zdatniać (-am) ⟨~zdatnić⟩ (-ę, -nij!) tech. treat, condition; ~zdolnienie n (-a; -eń) talent, gift; ~zdolniony talented, gifted

uzdrawia|ć (-am) heal, cure; fig. improve, repair; ~jąco adv. in a healing way; ~jący healing

uzdrowi|ciel m (-a; -e), ~cielka f (-i; G -lek) healer; ~ć (-ę; -ów!) pf. → uzdrawiać; ~enie n (-a; G -eń) healing; ~sko n (-a; G -) spa, health resort

uzewnętrzni|ać się (-am) ⟨~ć się⟩ (-ę, -nij!) manifest o.s., be expressed

uzębienie n (-a; 0) (set of) teeth pl.

uzgadniać (-am) ⟨uzgodnić⟩ (-ę, -nij!) agree on

uziemienie n (-a; G -eń) electr. Brt. earth, Am. ground

uzmysł|awiać (-am)⟨~owić⟩(-ę,-łów!) make s.o. realize; ~owić sobie realize

uzna|ć pf. → uznawać; ~nie n (-a; G -ań) acknowledge(e)ment; (szacunek) respect; zależeć od ~nia be at s.o.'s

discretion; według ... ~nia at s.o.'s discretion; spotkać się z ~niem be appreciated;~wać (-ję)recognize;błąd,winę admit, dług acknowledge; (za A) accept (as), regard (as), consider (się o.s. tobe); ~czas zmarłego pronounce dead; ~ć kogoś winnym admit one's guilt

uzupeł|niać (-am) ⟨~nić⟩ (-ę, -nij!) complete; supplement; ~niać się be complementary; ~niający supplementary; pol. wybory pl. ~niające by(e)-election

uzwojenie n (-a; -eń) electr. winding

uzysk|anie n (-a; 0) attainment; ~(iw)ać (-uję) obtain, get; attain

użal|ać się (-am) ⟨~ić się⟩ (na A) complain (about); (nad I) feel sorry for, pity

użądlić pf. (-ę) sting

uży|cie n (-a; G -yć) use; sposób ~cia instructions pl. for use; gotowy do ~cia ready for use; ~ć pf. → używać

użyteczn|ość f (-ści; 0) usefulness; przedsiębiorstwo ~ości publicznej public utility; ~y useful

użyt|ek m (-tku; -tki) use, application; do ~ku domowego for home use; ~ki pl. rolne agr. arable land

użytkowa|ć (-uję) use; ⟨z-⟩ use up; ~nie n (-a; G -ań) use

użytkow|niczka f (-i; G -czek), ~nik m (-a; -cy) user; (języka) speaker; ~y utilitarian; lokal for commercial purposes; powierzchnia ~a usable (floor) area

używ|ać (-am) use, make use of, employ; swobody enjoy; med. take; ~any used; ~ka f (-i; G -wek) stimulant

użyźni|ać (-am) ⟨~ć⟩ (-ę, -nij!) fertilize

W

w prp. (L) pozycja, stan, czas: in; ~ lesie in the forest; (A) ruch, kierunek: in(to); ~ pole to the field; ~e wszystkie strony in all directions; ~ czasie rozmowy during the talk; ~ dzień (G) on the day (of); ~ odwiedziny for a visit dzień ~ dzień day after day; ~ paski striped; tłumaczony też bez przyimka: ~ poprzek crosswise; → odnośne

rzeczowniki i czasowniki

w. skrót pisany: wyspa isl. (island); wiek c. (century); wieś v., vil. (village)

wabi|ć (-ę) ⟨z-⟩ lure; fig. attract; ~ć się pies: be called; ~k m (-a; -i) hunt. decoy; fig. enticement

wach|larz m (-a; -e) fan; fig. range, spectrum; ~lować (-uję) fan

wach|ta f (-y; G -) watch; ~towy watch

wada f (-y; G-) shortcoming, disadvantage, fault, defect

wadium n (-idkl.; -ia, -iów) econ. deposit

wadliw|ie adv. defectively; **~y** defective, faulty

wafel m (-fla; -fle) wafer; (do lodów) cone

wag|a f (-i; G -) weight (też sport); (przyrząd) scales pl.; (aptekarska itp.) balance; (ważność) importance; **na ~ę** by weight; **zrzucić ~ę** lose weight; **najwyższej ~i** of the utmost importance; **2a znak Zodiaku**: Libra; **on(a) jest spod znaku** 2i he/she is (a) Libra

wagarować (-uję) play Brt. truant (Am. hookey)

wagon m (-u; -y) rail. Brt. carriage, Am. car; **~ sypialny** sleeping car; **~ restauracyjny** dining car

waha|ć się (-am) swing; temperatura, ceny: fluctuate, vary; (za-) hesitate; **~dło** n (-a; G -deł) pendulum; **~dłowiec** m (-wca; -wce) space shuttle; **~dłowo** adv. as a shuttle; **~dłowy** zegar pendulum; drzwi swing; autobus itp. shuttle; **~nie** n (-a; G -ań) fig. hesitation, indecision; **bez ~nia** without hesitation

wakacj|e pl. (-i) Brt. holidays pl., Am. vacation; **~yjny** Brt. holiday, Am. vacation

wakować (-uję) be vacant

walać ⟨po-, u-, za-⟩ (-am) → **brudzić**; **~ się** F impf. be scattered about

walc m (-a; -e) mus. waltz

walcow|ać (-uję) roll; (tańczyć) waltz; **~nia** f (-i; -e, -i) rolling mill; **~y** cylindrical

walczyć (-ę) struggle (**o** A for), fight (**z** I with); **o** A for)

walec m (-lca; -lce, -lców) roller; math. cylinder

waleczn|ość f (-ści;0) courage, bravery; **~y** brave, courageous; valiant

walentynka f (-i; G -nek) Valentine

walerianow|y: krople pl. ~e valerian drops pl.

walet m (-a; -y) gra **w karty**: knave, jack

Wali|a f (GDL -ii; 0) Wales; **~jczyk** m (-a; -cy), **~jka** f (-i; G -jek) Welsh; **Walijczycy** pl. the Welsh pl.; **2jski** Welsh; **mówić po** 2**jsku** speak Welsh

walić (-lę) v/i. (uderzać) bang, pound;

lit. dym, ludzie: stream; v/t. ⟨z-⟩ mur pull down; **~** ⟨po-, z-⟩ **z nóg knock** over lub down; **~** ⟨za-⟩ **się** come down, collapse (też fig.); (bić się) fight; **~ się z nóg** be dead tired

waliz|a f (-y; G-), **~ka** f (-i; G -zek) suitcase; **~kowy** suitcase

walka f (-i; G -) fight (też sport, mil.); fig. struggle

walnąć v/s. (-nę) strike, hit

walny general, plenary

walor m (-u; -y) value; **~y** pl. też assets pl., holdings pl.

walut|a f (-y; G -) currency; (dewizy) foreign currency; **~owy** currency, foreign currency

wał m (-u; -y) (rzeczny) embankment, bank; tech. shaft; **~ek** m roll; (-łka; -łki) (do włosów itp.) roller; (maszyny do pisania, drukarki) platen; **~ek do ciasta** rolling-pin; **zwinąć w ~ek** roll up

wałęsać się (-am) hang around, loiter

wałkoń m (-nia; -nie, -ni[ów]) lazy-bones sg.

wam (D → **wy**) you; **z ~i** with you

wampir m (-a; -y) vampire

wanienka f (-i; G -nek) chem., phot. dish, tray

waniliowy vanilla

wanna f (-y; G wanien) (bath)tub, Brt. bath

wap|ienny lime; limy; chem. calcareous; **~ień** m (-enia; -enie) limestone; **~no** n (-a; 0) lime; **~ń** m (-nia; 0) chem. calcium

warcaby pl. (-ów) Brt. draughts pl., Am. checkers pl. **grać w ~** play draughts lub checkers

warchoł m (-a; -y) troublemaker

warczeć ⟨za-⟩ (-ę, -y) growl, gnarl; **~ na siebie** growl at each other; → **warkotać**

warga f (-i; G -) (**górna, dolna** upper, lower) lip; **zajęcza ~** med. harelip

wariack|i crazy; **po ~u** like crazy

wariant m (-u; -y) variant

wariat m (-a; -ci) madman, loony, lunatic; **~ka** f (-i; G -tek) madwoman, loony, lunatic

wariować ⟨z-⟩ (-uję) go mad lub mad; fig. ktoś: act crazy; coś: play up

warknąć v/s. (-nę) → **warczeć**

warkocz m (-a; -e) plait, braid

warkot m (-u; -y) whirr; **~ać** (-am) whirr

warown|ia f (-i-; -e) stronghold; ~y fortified

warstwa f (-y; G -) layer, stratum; (*społeczna*) class

Warszaw|a f (-y; 0) Warsaw; 2**ski** Warsaw; ~**wiak** m (-a; -cy) → ~**wianin** m (-a; -anie), ~**wianka** f (-i; G -nek) Varsovian

warsztat m (-u; -y) workshop; shop; ~**owy** workshop

wart (-**ta** f, -**te** n, pl. m-os **warci**) worth; **to nic nie** ~ it is worth nothing *lub* worthless; **śmiechu** ~**e** ridiculous, laughable

war|ta f (-y; G -) guard (duty); **stać na** ~**cie** keep guard; **zmiana** ~**y** changing of the guard

warto (*nieos.*): ~ **by było** it would be worth it

wartościow|o adv. valuably; ~**y** valuable

wartoś|ć f (-ści) value; **podanie** ~**ci** declaration of value; **bez** ~**ci** worthless; ~**ć dodatkowa** econ. value added

wartowni|a f (-i-; -e) guardroom, guardhouse; ~**k** m (-a; -cy) guard, sentry

warun|ek m (-nku; -nki) condition; ~**ki** (*umowy*) pl. też terms pl.; **pod żadnym** ~**kiem** on no account; ~**kowo** adv. conditionally; ~**kowy** conditional

warzyw|niczy, ~**ny** vegetable; ~**o** n (-a; G -) vegetable

was (*AL* → **wy**) you

wasz 1. (m-os **wasi**) your(s); **2. wasi** pl. też your people

Waszyngton m (-u; 0) Washington

waśń f (-śni; -śnie, -śni) feud

wat|a f (-y; G -) vaseline TM, petrolatum; ~**niarstwo** n (-a; 0) soft-soap

Watyka|n m (-u; 0) Vatican (City); 2**ński** Vatican

wawrzyn m (-u; -y) laurel

waza f (-y; G -) tureen

wazeli|na f (-y; G -) vaseline TM, petrolatum; ~**niarstwo** n (-a; 0) soft-soap

wazon m (-u; -y) vase

ważka f (-i; G -żek) zo. dragonfly

waż|ki important, significant; ~**niactwo** n (-a; 0) self-importance; pomposity; ~**niejszy** adj. (comp. od → **ważny**) more important; ~**ność** f (-ści; 0) importance, significance; **stracić** ~**ność** expire; **data** ~**ności** expiry date; ~**ny** important, significant; ~**ny do ...** valid

until ...; ~**yć** (-ę) v/t. ⟨**z-**⟩ weigh (*też* fig.); v/i. weigh; v/i. ~**yć się** weigh o.s.; (**na** A) dare, risk

wąchać ⟨**po-**⟩ (-am) smell; pies: scent

wąg|ier m (-gra; -gry) blackhead; biol., med. cysticercus

wąs m (-a; -y): zw. ~**y** pl. m(o)ustache, m(o)ustaches pl.; ~**aty** moustached, mustached

wąsk|o adv. narrowly; tightly; ~**i** narrow; tight

wąskotorow|y: kolejka ~**a** narrow--gauge railway

wątek m (-tku; -tki) włók. weft, woof; bud. bond; fig. thread; (*sztuki*) plot

wątł|o adv. delicately; fraily; ~**y** delicate; frail

wątp|ić ⟨**z-**⟩ (-ę) doubt (**w** A, **o** L in); ~**ienie** n: **bez** ~**ienia** no doubt; doubtless; ~**liwie** adv. doubtfully, dubiously; ~**liwość** f (-ści) doubt; **nie ulega** ~**liwości, że** there is no doubt that; ~**liwy** doubtful, dubious

wątrob|a f (-y; G -rób) anat., gastr. liver; ~**ianka** f (-i; G -nek) liver sausage; ~**owy** liver

wąwóz m (-wozu; -wozy) ravine, gorge

wąż m (węża; węże) zo. snake; (**gumowy** rubber) hose

wbić pf. → **wbijać**

wbie|gać ⟨~**c**, ~**gnąć**⟩ run in; run (**do pokoju** into the room; **na piętro** upstairs)

wbijać (-am) gwóźdź itp. hammer in; pal ram into; igłę, nóż plunge in; gola shoot; klin drive into

wbrew prp. (D) against, contrary to

w bród → **bród**

wbudow(yw)ać (-[w]uję) build in, fit; tech. install

wcale adv.: ~ **nie** not at all, not a bit

wchłaniać (-am) ⟨~**onąć**⟩ (-nę) absorb; zapach breathe in

wchodzić (**do** G, **w** A) come (in), get (in), enter; get on (**do wagonu** the carriage); (**na** A) trawnik itp. walk (on), step (on); drzewo itp. climb, go (up); (**do** G) (być w składzie) be included (in); ~ **na górę** go up (**w domu** the stairs); ~ **w położenie** (G) put o.s. in s.o.'s position; ~ **na ekrany** film: go on release; → **wejść**

wcią|ć pf. → **wcinać**; ~**gać** (-am) ⟨~**gnąć**⟩ (**do** G) draw (in, into), pull (in, into); (*na A*) pull (up); ~**gnąć się** (*do G*) *fig.* get used (to), get accustomed (to)

wciąż *adv.* ever, always

wciel|**ać** (*-am*)⟨~*ić*⟩(*-lę*)(*do G*) incorporate (into), integrate (into); ~*ać w życie* bring into effect, put into practice; ~*ić w czyn* put into action *lub* effect; ~enie *n* (*-a*; *G -eń*) integration; incorporation; ~**ony** incarnate, embodied

wcierać (*-am*) rub in

wcięcie *n* (*-a*; *G -ęć*) notch, indentation; (*linii*) indentation, indention

wcinać (*-am*) make a cut; F (*jeść*) tuck in; ~ **się** cut into

wcis|**kać** ⟨~**nąć**⟩ press into; ~**nąć się** (*do G*) push one's way into

wczasowicz *m* (*-a*; *-e*), ~**ka** *f* (*-i*; *G -czek*) holiday-maker

wczas|**owy** holiday; ~**y** *pl. Brt.* holiday, *Am.* vacation); ~**y lecznicze** rest cure

wczepi(**a**)**ć się** (*-am*) (*do G*) cling (to)

wcze|**sno-** *w złoż.* early; ~**sny** early; ~**śnie** *adv.* early; ~**śniejszy** *adj.* (*comp. od* → **wczesny**) earlier

wczoraj yesterday; ~**szy** yesterday

wczu(**wa**)**ć się** identify with

wda(**wa**)**ć:** ~ **się w coś** get involved in; F ~ **się w kogoś** take after

wdech *m* (*-u*; *-y*) inspiration; ~**owy** → **kapitalny**

wdow|**a** *f* (*-y*; *G wdów*) widow; ~**i** widow's; ~**iec** *m* (*-wca*; *-wcy*) widower; **słomiany** ~**iec** grass widower

wdrażać (*-am*) ⟨**wdrożyć**⟩ (*-ę*) implement, introduce; ~ *kogoś do* (*G*) bring s.o. up to; ~ **się do pracy** be training for the job

wdychać (*-am*) breathe in

wdzia|**ć** *pf.* → **wdziewać**; ~**nko** *n* (*-a*; *G -nek*) jacket

wdzierać się (*-am*) (*do G*) *ktoś*: burst (into); *coś*: penetrate; climb (*na szczyt* the peak)

wdziewać (*-am*) put on

wdzięczn|**ość** *f* (*-ści*; *0*) gratitude, thankfulness; **dług** ~**ości** indebtedness; ~**y** (*za A*) grateful (for), thankful (for); (*zgrabny*) graceful

we *prp.* → **w**

według *prp.* (*G*) according to

wedrzeć się *pf.* → **wdzierać się**

wegetaria|**nin** *m* (*-a*; *-e*), ~**nka** *f* (*-i*; *G -nek*) vegetarian; ~**ński** vegetarian

wegetować (*-uję*) vegetate

wejrze|**ć** *pf.* → **wglądać**; ~**nie** *n* (*-a*; *G -eń*): *od pierwszego* ~**nia** at first glance *lub* sight

wejś|**cie** *n* (*-a*; *G -jść*) entrance; entry; ~**ciowy** entrance; ~**ć** *pf.* → **wchodzić**

wek *m* (*-u*; *-i*) food preserve; ~**ować** ⟨**za-**⟩ (*-uję*) preserve

weksel *m* (*-sla*; *-sle*) bill of exchange

welon *m* (*-u*; *-y*) veil

welurowy suede

wełn|**a** *f* (*-y*; *G -łen*) wool; ~**iany** wool(en)

Wene|**cja** *f* (*-i*; *0*) Venice; Ձcki Venetian

weneryczn|**y**: *med. choroba* ~**a** venereal disease

wentyl *m* (*-a*; *-e*) *tech.* valve; *fig.* outlet

wentyla|**cyjny** ventilation; ~**ny** ventilation; ~**tor** *m* (*-a*; *-y*) fan; (*w murze*) ventilator

wepchnąć (**się**) *pf.* → **wpychać**

werbel *m* (*-bla*; *-ble*) *mus.* drum; (*dźwięk*) drum-roll

werb|**ować** ⟨**z-**⟩ (*-uję*) recruit (*też mil.*); ~**unek** *m* (*-nku*; *-nki*) recruitment

wersalka *f* (*-i*; *G -lek*) bed-settee

wersja *f* (*-i*; *-e*) version

wertować (*-uję*) leaf through, look through

werwa *f* (*-y*; *0*) enthusiasm, verve

weryfikować ⟨**z-**⟩ (*-uję*) verify

werżnąć się *pf.* → **wrzynać się**

wesel|**e** *n* (*-a*; *G -*) wedding; (*przyjęcie*) wedding party; ~**ny** wedding; ~**ej** *com. adv.*, ~**szy** *com. adj.* → **wesoło, wesoły**

wesoł|**o** *adv.* (*pred. wesół*) cheerfully; merrily; ~**ość** *f* (*-ści*; *0*) cheerfulness; mirth, merriment; ~**y** cheerful; merry

wes|**przeć** *pf.* → **wspierać**; ~**sać** *pf.* → **wsysać**; ~**tchnąć** *pf.* → **wzdychać**; ~**tchnienie** *n* (*-a*; *G -eń*) sigh

wesz *f* (*wszy*; *N*, *G wszy*) *zo.* louse

wetery|**'naria** *f* (*GDL -ii*; *0*) veterinary medicine; ~**narz** *m* (*-a*; *-e*) *Brt.* vet(erinary surgeon), *Am.* veterinarian

wetknąć *pf.* → **wtykać**

wetować ⟨**za-**⟩ (*-uję*) veto

we|**trzeć** *pf.* → **wcierać**; ~**wnątrz** *adv.* inside; *do* ~**wnątrz** inward; *od* ~**wnątrz** from the inside; ~**wnątrz-** *w złoż.* inside; ~**wnętrzny** inner; *kieszeń* inside; *med.*, *psych.*, *struktura itp.* internal; inward; *rynek itp.* home, domestic; *nu-*

W

mer ~**wnętrzny** *tel.* extension; ~**zbrać**
pf. → **wzbierać;** ~**zgłowie** *n* (-*a; G -wi*)
head end; (*podgłówek*) headrest
wezwa|ć *pf.* → **wzywać;** ~**nie** *n* (-*a; G
-añ*) summons *sg.;* (*monit*) demand;
(*apel*) call, appeal; **kościół pod ~niem
św. Piotra** St. Peter's Church
węch *m* (-*u; 0*) smell; *fig.* nose
wędka *f* (-*i; G -dek*) angling rod; ~**rski**
fishing; ~**rstwo** *n* (-*a; 0*) fishing, angling; ~**rz** *m* (-*a; -e*) angler
wędlin|a *f* (-*y; G -*): *zw. pl.* ~**y** cured
meat products *pl.;* ~**iarnia** *f* (-*i; -e*) retailer of sausages
wędrow|ać(-uję) wander(**po** L around);
~**iec** *m* (-*wca; -wcy*) wanderer; ~**ny**
wandering; *biol.* migrating, migratory;
ptak ~ny migrating bird, bird of passage
wędrówka *f* (-*i; G -wek*) wandering;
travel; *biol.* migration
wędz|ić〈u-〉 (-*ę*) smoke, cure; ~**onka** *f*
(-*i; G -nek*) *gastr.* smoked bacon; ~**ony**
smoked, cured
węgiel *m* (-*gla; -gle*) *chem.* coal; ~ **brunatny** lignite, brown coal; ~ **kamienny**
anthracite, hard coal; ~ **drzewny** char-
coal; ~**ny** → **kamień**
węgieł *m* (-*gła; -gły*) corner
Węg|ier *m* (-*gra; -grzy*), ~**ierka** *f* (-*i; G
-rek*) Hungarian; **2ierka** *bot.* garden
plum; **2ierski** Hungarian; **mówić po
2iersku** speak Hungarian
węg|lan *m* (-*u; -y*) *chem.* carbonate;
~**lowodór** *m chem.* hydrocarbon; ~**lowy** coal; carbon
węgorz *m* (-*a; -e*) *zo.* eel
Węgry *pl.* (*G -gier*) Hungary
węszyć〈z-〉 sniff; *fig.* sniff about
węz|eł *m* (-*zła; -zły*) knot; (*transporto-
wy*) hub; *med., anat.* node; ~**łowato**
adv.: **krótko i ~łowato** in brief, in a
nutshell; ~**łowaty** knobbly; ~**łowy** hub;
fig. central, crucial
węże *pl.* → **wąż**
wężow|nica *f* (-*y; G -*) *tech.* coil; ~**y** ser-
pentine
węższy *adj. comp. od* → **wąski**
wf. *skrót pisany:* **wychowanie fizyczne**
PE (*physical education*)
wg *skrót pisany:* **według** according to
wgięcie *n* (-*a; G -ęć*) dent
wgląd *m* (-*u; 0*) view; insight; **do ~u** for
inspection
wgłębienie *n* (-*a; G -eñ*) indentation

wgniatać (-*am*) 〈**wgnieść**〉 dent, de-
press
wgry|zać się (-*am*) 〈~**źć się**〉 bite into;
fig. get stuck into; (*weżreć się*) eat into
wiać (-*eję*) *v/i.* 〈**po-**〉 blow; F 〈**z-**〉 take
o.s. off; **wieje tu** there is a draught here
wiadomo *nieos.* it is known; **nigdy nie ~**
you never know; **jak ~** as is known; **o ile
mi ~** as far as I know; ~**ść** *f* (-*ści*) information; **do twojej ~ści** for your
knowledge
wiadomy known
wiadro *n* (-*a; G -der*) bucket, pail
wiadukt *m* (-*u; -y*) *mot.* Brt. flyover,
Am. overpass
wianek *m* (-*nka; -nki*) wreath, garland;
fig. hymen
wiar|a *f* (-*y; G -*) belief (**w** A in); faith
(*też rel.*); (**w siebie** self-)confidence;
nie do ~y unbelievable; **w dobrej wierze** in good faith
wiarołomny unfaithful
wiarygodny reliable, dependable,
credible
wiat|r *m* (-*u, L wietrze; -y*) wind; **pod ~r**
against the wind; **na ~** to the wind;
~**rak** *m* (-*a; -i*) windmill; ~**rówka** *f* (-*i;
G -wek*) (*ubranie*) Brt. wind-cheater,
Am. wind-breaker; (*broń*) airgun
wiąz *m* (-*u; -y*) *bot.* elm
wiąz|ać (-*żę*) bind (*też fig., chem.*); *jeńca
itp.* tie (up); *fig.* relate (**z** I to); ~**ać się**
(**z** I) be associated (with); ~**anie** *n* (-*a;
G -añ*) *sport.* binding; *chem.* bond;
~**anka** *f* (-*i; G -nek*) bunch, bouquet;
mus. potpourri, medley; ~**ka** *f* (-*i; G
-zek*) bundle; (*światła itp.*) beam
wiążąc|o *adv.* definitely; ~**y** binding;
definite
wice-|- *w złoż.* vice-, deputy; ~**dyrektor**
deputy director *lub* manager; ~**mistrz**
sport. runner-up
wicher *m* (-*chru; -chry*) gale
wichrzy|ciel *m* (-*a; -e*), ~**cielka** *f* (-*i; G
-lek*) trouble-maker; ~**ć** (-*ę*) *v/t.* 〈**z-**〉 **włosy** ruffle, tousle; *v/i.* make trouble; stir up
wić¹ *f* (-*ci; NG -ci*) *biol.* tendril; *zo.* fla-
gellum
wić² (-*ję*) 〈**u-**〉 **wianek** wreathe; **gniazdo**
build; *t-ko impf.* ~ **się** wind, meander
widać (*t-ko bezok.*) can be seen; **jak ~** as
can be seen; **to ~ po nim** he shows it
wide|lec *m* (-*lca; -lce*) fork; ~**łki** *pl.*
(-*łek*) *tech.* fork

wideo video; *film* ~ video (film); *wy-pożyczalnia* ~ video hire (shop); ~ka-seta f (-y; G -) video (cassette)

widły pl. (-deł) pitchfork, fork

widmo n (-a; G -) Brt. spectre, Am. specter; *phys.* spectrum; ~wy spectral

wid|nieć (-eję) appear, be visible; ~no adv.: *robi się* ~no it is getting light; ~nokrąg m horizon; *na* ~nokręgu on the horizon; ~ny *pokój* light

widoczn|ie adv. apparently, clearly; visibly; ~ość f (-ści; 0) visibility; ~y visible

wido|k m (-u; -i) (*na G*) view (of) (*też fig.*); (*wygląd*) appearance; (*co widać*) scene; *fig.* prospect, chance; *na* ~k (G) by the appearance (of), outwardly; *po-kój z* ~kiem *na morze* a room over-looking the sea; *na* ~ku at sight; *mieć na* ~ku have in prospect; ~kówka f (-i; G -wek) picture postcard; ~wisko n (-a; G -) show, spectacle; *fig.* exhibition; ~wnia f (-i; -e) (*ludzie*) audience, spectators pl.; (*pomieszczenie*) auditorium; house

widywać (-uję) see

widz m (-a; -owie) spectator, viewer; (*ki-nowy* Brt. cinema-, Am. movie-)goer

widzeni|e n (-a; G -eń) sight, seeing; (*więźnia*) visit; *z* ~a by sight; *do* ~a goodbye; *zezwolenie na* ~e visiting permit; → *punkt*

widzia|dło n (-a; G -deł) → **widmo**; ~lność f (-ści; 0) visibility; ~lny visible

widzieć (-dzę, -i) see; (*się* o.s., each other); ~ *się z kimś* → *zobaczyć*

wiec m (-u; -e) rally

wiech|a f (-y; G -) bud. wreath (*used in the topping-out ceremony*); *uroczys-tość zawieszenia* ~y topping-out ce-remony

wiecowy rally

wieczerza f (-y; -e) lit. supper

wieczn|ość f (-ści; 0) eternity; ~y eternal

wieczor|ek m (-rku; -rki): ~ek tanecz-ny dancing party; ~em in the evening; at night; *jutro* ~em tomorrow evening; ~ny evening, night; ~owy: *suknia* ~owa evening dress

wieczór m (-u; -czory) evening, night; *dobry* ~ good evening

Wiedeń m (-dnia; 0) Vienna; 2ński Viennese

wiedz|a f (-y; 0) knowledge; (*uczoność*) learning, scholarship; (*wyspecjalizo-wana*) know-how; *bez jego* ~y without his knowledge; ~ieć know (*o L* about); *o ile wiem* as far as I know

wiedźma f (-y; G -) witch

wiejski rural; country; village

wiek m (-u; 0) age; *dzie-cięcy* ~ childhood; (*pl. -i*) century; *fig.* age; ~i pl. *średnie* the Middle Ages pl.

wieko n (-a; G -) lid; cover

wiekowy centuries-old

wiekuisty eternal

wielbiciel m (-a; -e), ~ka f (-i; G -lek) admirer; worshipper; enthusiast, buff

wielbić (-ę, -bij!) → **uwielbiać**

wielbłą|d m (-a; -y) zo. camel; ~dzi camel

wiel|ce adv. much; ~cy m-os → **wielki**; ~e a lot of; many, much; *o* ~e (by) far; *o* ~e *za dużo* far too much

Wielkanoc f (-y/Wielkiejnocy, I -ą/Wiel-kąnocą; -e) rel. Easter; *na* ~ at Easter

wielkanocny easter

wielki big, large; *fig.* great; *już* ~ *czas* it is high time; *Kazimierz* 2 Casimir the Great; *nic* ~ego nothing much

wielko|duszny magnanimous; ~lud m (-a; -y) giant; ~miejski metropolitan; ~ść f (-ści) size; (*problemu itp.*) magni-tude; (*znaczenie*) greatness; *math.*, *phys.* quantity; ~ści grochu pea-sized; the size of a pea; *jednakowej* ~ści the same in size

wielo|barwny multicolo(u)red; ~bój m (*w sporcie*) multi-discipline event; ~dniowy lasting several days; ~dziet-ny with many children; *rodzina* large

wielokropek m (-pka; -pki) suspension points pl.

wielokrotn|ie adv. repeatedly; ~y re-peated, multiple

wielo|milionowy million; ~narodo-wy multinational; ~piętrowy multi-stor(e)y; ~raki multiple; ~rako adv. in many different ways

wieloryb m (-a; -y) zo. whale

wielo|stopniowy multistage; ~stron-ny multilateral; ~znaczny ambiguous; ~żeństwo n (-a; G -stw) polygamy

wielu m-os → **wiele**

wieniec m (-ńca; -ńce) garland; wreath (*też na pogrzeb*)

wień|cowy med. coronary; ~czyć ⟨*u-*⟩ crown

W

wieprz *m* (*-a*; *-e*) hog; **~owina** *f* (*-y*) pork; **~owy** pork

wiercić ⟨*-cę*⟩ drill; **~ się** fidget

wiern|ość *f* (*-ści*; *0*) fidelity, faithfulness; **~y 1.** faithful, **2. ~i** *m/pl.* the faithful

wiersz *m* (*-a*; *-e*) (*utwór*) poem; (*linijka*) line; **~owy** line

wiertarka *f* (*-i*; *G -rek*) drill

wiertło *n* (*-a*; *G -teł*) drill, bit

wierzba *f* (*-y*; *G -*) *bot.*: **~ płacząca** weeping willow

wierzch *m* (*-u*; *-y*) top; upper side; outside; (*buta*) upper; **na ~** on top; **do ~u, po ~u** to the top; **~em** on horseback; **~ni** outer, top; **~ołek** *m* (*-łka; -łki*) summit (*też fig.*), peak; *math.* apex, vertex; **~owiec** *m* (*-wca; -wce*) saddle-horse; **~owy** saddle

wierzy|ciel *m* (*-a*; *-e*), **~cielka** *f* (*-i*; *G -lek*) *econ.* creditor; **~ć** ⟨*-ę*⟩ (*w A*) believe (in); (*ufać*) trust, have faith (in); **~telność** *f* (*-ści*) *econ.* liability, claim

wiesza|ć ⟨*-am*⟩ hang (**na** *A* on; **się** o.s.); **~k** *m* (*-a*; *-i*) hanger

wieś *f* (*wsi*; *wsie, wsi*) village; (*region*) country; **na ~** to the country; **na wsi** in the country

wieść¹ *f* (*-ści*) news *sg.*, information; → **przepaść²**

wieść² lead; → **prowadzić**

wieśnia|czka *f* (*-i*; *G -czek*) countrywoman; peasant; **~k** *m* (*-a*; *-cy*) countryman; peasant

wietrze|ć ⟨*-eję*⟩ ⟨*wy-*⟩ *zapach*: fade, disappear; *geol.* erode; ⟨*z-*⟩ *wino*: become stale; **~nie** *adv.*: **jest ~nie** it is windy; **~ny** windy; **~yć** ⟨*-ę*⟩ *air*; ⟨*z-*⟩ scent, get wind of

wiewiórka *f* (*-i*; *G -rek*) *zo.* squirrel

wieźć ⟨*po-*⟩ carry, transport; *kogoś* drive

wieża *f* (*-y*; *-e*) tower; (*w szachach*) castle, rook; *mil.* turret; **~owiec** *m* (*-wca; -wce*) high-rise

więc so; **a ~** well; **tak ~** thus

więcej *adv.* (*comp. od* → **dużo, wiele**); **co ~** moreover; → **mniej**

więdnąć ⟨*z-*⟩ (*-nę, też zwiądł*) fade, wither

większ|ość *f* (*-ści*; *0*) majority; **~ością głosów** by the majority; **stanowić ~ość** be in the majority; **~y** *adj.* (*comp. od* → **duży, wielki**) larger, bigger

więzić (*-żę*) keep in prison

więzie|nie *n* (*-a*, *G -eń*) prison; **~nny** prison; **~ń** *m* (*-nia; -niowie*) prisoner

więź *f* (*-zi; -zie*) bond; **~niarka** *f* (*-rki; G -rek*) → **więzień**

wi'gilia *f* (*GDL -ii; -e*) eve; 2 Christmas Eve

wigor *m* (*-u; 0*) vigo(u)r

wiklina *f* (*-y*; *G -*) *bot.* oasier

wikłać ⟨*po-*⟩ (*-am*) *fig.* complicate; **~ się** become complicated; → **plątać**

wikt *m* (*-u*; *0*) fare

wilczur *m* (*-a, -y*) *zo.* Alsatian; **~y** wolfish

wilgo|ć *f* (*-ci*; *0*) humidity; damp(ness); moisture; **~tno** *adv.*, **~tny** *ściana, ubranie* damp; *klimat* humid; *wargi* moist

wilia *f* (*GDL -ii; -e*) → **wigilia**

wilk *m* (*-a*; *-i*) *zo.* wolf; **~ morski** sea dog

will|a *f* (*GDL -ii*) F (semi-)detached house; villa; **~owy** residential

win|a *f* (*-y*; *G -*) fault; blame; *jur.* guilt; **ponosić ~ę** (*za A*) be to blame (for); **z ~y** (*G*) because of; **z własnej ~y** because of one's own fault; (*nie*) **przyznawać się do ~y** plead (not) guilty

winda *f* (*-y*; *G -*) *Brt.* lift, *Am.* elevator

winiak *m* (*-a, -i*) brandy; **~rnia** *f* (*-i; -e*) wine bar

wini|ć ⟨*-ę*⟩ (*k-o o A*) blame (s.o. for); **~en** (*f -nna, n -nno, ż-rzecz. -nne, m-os -nni*) *pred.* guilty; **kto temu ~en?** who is to blame for it?; **jestem mu ~en ...** I owe him; → **powinien, powinna**

winni|ca *f* (*-y; G -*) vineyard; **~czek** *m* (*-czka; -czki*) *zo.* European edible snail

winno → **winien, powinno**

winny¹ wine; (*kwaśny*) tart; **~ krzew** grapevine

winny² guilty; **uznać za ~ego** consider guilty; → **winien**

wino *n* (*-a*; *G -*) wine; **~branie** *n* (*-a; G -ań*) grape picking; **~grono** *n* (*-a; G -*) grape; **~rośl** *f* (*-i; -e*) vine

winowaj|ca *m* (*-y; G -ców*), **~czyni** *f* (*-i; -e*) culprit

winszować (*-uję*) ⟨*k-u G*⟩ congratulate (s.o. on)

wiod|ą, ~ę → **wieść²**; **~ący** leading

wiolonczela *f* (*-i; -e*) *mus.* cello

wiosenny spring

wiosło *n* (*-a, L -śle; G -seł*) oar; paddle; **~wać** (*-uję*) row, paddle

wiosn|a *f* (*-y; G -sen*) spring; **~ą, na ~ę** in spring

wioślar|ka f (-i; G -rek) rower; oars-woman; ~**stwo** n (-a; 0) rowing

wioślarz m (-a; -e) rower; oarsman

wiotki limp; frail; (szczupły) thin

wioz|ą, ~**ę** → **wieźć**

wiór m (-u; -y) shaving; (metalu) swarf

wir m (-u; -y) whirl; (wody) eddy, whirl-pool

wiraż m (-u; -e) sharp bend, curve

wirnik m (-a; -i) tech., aviat. rotor

wirować (-uję) spin, whirl; (przed oczy-ma) swim; ⟨**od-**⟩ pranie spin-dry

wirówka f (-i; G -wek) spin-drier; tech. centrifuge

wirus m (-a; -y) biol. virus; ~**owy** virus; viral

wi|sieć (-szę) hang (**na** L on; **nad** I over); owad itp.: hover (**nad** I over, above); ~**sielec** m (-lca; -lcy, -lców) hanged person; ~**siorek** m (-rka; -rki, -rków) pendant; ~**szący** hanging

Wisła f (-y; 0) the Vistula

wiśni|a f (-i; -e) bot. sour cherry; ~**owy** (sour) cherry

witać (-am) ⟨**po-**⟩ greet; fig. welcome; ~ ⟨**przy-**⟩ **się** (**z** I) greet, exchange greetings (with)

witamina f (-y; G -) vitamin

witraż m (-a; -e) stained-glass window

witryna f (-y; G -) shop-window; komp. web site; ~**internetowa** komp. web site

wiwat: ~ ...! long live ...!; ~**ować** (-uję) cheer (**na cześć k-o** s.o.)

wiza f (-y; G -) visa

wizerunek m (-nku; -nki, -nki) picture

wiz|ja f (-i; -e) vision (też RTV); jur. in-spection; ~**jer** m (-a; -y) peephole; ~**owy** visa

wizyt|a f (-y; G -) visit; **składać** ~**ę** → ~**ować** (-uję) pay a visit; visit; ~**ówka** f (-i; G -wek) visiting card

wjazd m (-u; -y) entry; entrance; ~ **na autostradę** Brt. slip road, Am. ramp; ~**owy** entry

wje|żdżać (-am) ⟨~**chać**⟩ (**do** G) come (in), mot. drive (in); (**do** G, **na** A) rail. pull (in(to)); (najeżdżać) (**w** A) drive (into)

wkle|jać (-am) ⟨~**ić**⟩ paste

wklęsł|o adv. concavely; ~**y** concave

wkład m (-u; -y) (pieniężny itp.) contri-bution; fig. input; econ. deposit; tech. inset, cartridge; ~ **do długopisu** refill; ~**ać** (-am) put (**do** G into); insert; ubra-

nie itp. put on; nabój itp. load; kapitał, czas invest; ~**ka** f (-i; G -dek) inset; tech. cartridge; med. intrauterine de-vice (skrót: **IUD**)

wkoło prp. (a)round

wkop|ywać (-uję) ⟨~**ać**⟩ (**do** G; **w** A) dig (into); tyczkę sink (into); ~**ywać się** bury o.s.

wkra|czać (-am) (**do** G) enter, step (in); (**na czyjś teren**) encroach; (**z interwen-cją**) step (in); mil. invade; ~**czać niele-galnie** trespass; ~**dać się** (-am) sneak in; fig. creep in; ~**plać** (-am) put drops (in one's eyes); ~**ść się** pf. → **wkradać się**

wkręc|ać (-am) ⟨~**cić**⟩ screw in

wkręt m (-u; -y) screw

wkro|czyć pf. → **wkraczać**; ~**plić** pf. (-lę) → **wkraplać**

wkrótce soon

wkurzony f annoyed, peeved

wkuwać (-am) cram, Brt. swot (up)

wlać pf. → **wlewać**; ~ **się** F get com-pletely canned; **wlany** F canned, pissed

wlatywać ⟨**wlecieć**⟩ (-uję) → **wpadać**

wle|c drag (**się** o.s.); ~**c się** czas: wear on; draw out, drag out; ~**cieć** pf. → **wlatywać**; ~**piać** (-am) ⟨~**pić**⟩ stick in(to); F fig. (klepnąć) slap, (wcisnąć) give; ~**pić oczy** (**w** A) stare at

wlew m (-u; -y) med. infusion; ~**ać** (-am) pour (in); ~**ać się** flow in (**do** G to)

wleźć pf. → **włazić**

wlicz|ać (-am) ⟨~**yć**⟩ (**do** G) include (in); **kogoś** involve

wlotowy tech. inlet

wład|ać (-am) (I) rule; (językiem) speak; (bronią) wield; (nogą itp.) be able to move; ~**ca** m (-y; G -ców) ruler; ~**czo** adv. imperiously; ~**czy** imperious; overbearing; ~**czyni** f (-i; -e) ruler

władz|a f (-y; 0) power; rule, control; (pl. -e) authority; **dojść do** ~**y** come to power; **stracić** ~**ę nad** (I) lose control (over); **stracić** ~**ę w** (I) lose the use (of)

włam|ać się pf. → **włamywać się**; ~**anie** n (-a; G -ań) burglary; ~**ywacz** m (-a; -e) burglar; ~**ywać się** (-uję) break (**do** G into); Brt. burglarize, Am. burgle

własno|ręczny personal; ~**ściowy** mieszkanie Brt. owner-occupied, Am. condominium, co-op; ~**ść** f (-ści; 0) property; **mieć na** ~**ść** own

W

własn|y (one's) own; **z ~ej woli** of one's own free will; → **ręka**

właści|ciel *m* (*-a, -e*), **~cielka** *f* (*-i; G -lek*) owner; proprietor; holder; **~wie** *adv.* actually, in (actual) fact; **~wość** *f* (*-ści*) property, peculiarity; (*odpowiedniość*) appropriateness; **~wy** proper; correct; appropriate

właśnie *part.* just; (*akurat*) exactly, precisely; **no ~** quite

właz *m* (*-u; -y*) *mil.* hatch; (*do kanału itp.*) manhole; **~ić** (*-żę*) climb, get

włącz|ać (*-am*) ⟨**~yć**⟩ include; *electr.* turn on, switch on; **~ać** ⟨**~yć**⟩ **się** *electr.* go on; *któś:* join; (*do ruchu*) pull out; → **przyłączać**; **~nie** *adv.* inclusive

Włoch *m* (*-a; -si*) Italian

włochaty hairy; shaggy

Włochy *pl.* (*G Włoch*) Italy

włos *m* (*-a; -y*) hair; **~y** *pl.* hair; **nie odstąpić ani na ~ od** (*G*) not to budge an inch from; **o** (*mały*) **~** by a hair's breadth; **do ~ów** hair; **~ek** *m* (*-ska; -ski*) ~ **włos**; **~ie n** *n* (*-a; 0*) horsehair; **~ień** *m* (*-nia/-śnia; -nie/-śnie*) *zo., med.* trichina

włoski Italian; **mówić po ~u** speak Italian; → **kapusta**

włoszczyzna *f* (*-y; G* -) mixed vegetables (*for soup*)

Włoszka *f* (*-i; G -szek*) Italian

włożyć *pf.* → **wkładać**

włóczęga[1] *f* (*-i; G* -) wandering

włóczęga[2] *m* (*-i; -dzy/-i, -ów/-*) tramp, vagrant

włóczka *f* (*-i; G -czek*) yarn

włóczyć się (*-ę*) wander, roam

włókiennictwo *n* (*-a; G* -) textile industry

włókn|isty stringy; **~no** *n* (*-a; G -kien*) *Brt.* fibre, *Am.* fiber

w|mawiać (*-am*) persuade (**komuś** s.o.); **~mieszać** *pf.* → **mieszać**; **~montow(yw)ać** (*-[w]uję*) fit in, equip; **~mówić** *pf.* → **wmawiać**

wmurow(yw)ać (*-[w]uję*) set into the wall, build into

wnet soon

wnęka *f* (*-i; G* -) bay, recess, niche

wnętrz|e *n* (*-a; G* -) interior, inside; *bud.* interior; **do/od ~a** within, inward/from within; **~ności** *pl.* (*-ci*) entrails *pl.*; *gastr.* offal

Wniebo|wstąpienie *n rel.* the Ascension; **~wzięcie** *n rel.* the Assumption

wnieść *pf.* → **wnosić**

wnik|ać (*-am*) ⟨**~nąć**⟩ penetrate; inquire; **~liwie** *adv.* penetratingly; in depth; **~liwy** penetrating; → **dociekliwy**

wnios|ek *m* (*-sku; -ski*) conclusion; (*propozycja*) motion, proposition; **dojść do ~ku** come to the conclusion; **wystąpić z ~kiem, żeby** move that; **~kodawca** *m* (*-y; G -ców*), **~kodawczyni** *f* (*-i; -ie, G -yń*) mover; **~kować** ⟨**wy-**⟩ **~uję** conclude (**z** *G* from)

wnosić *v/t.* carry in, bring (into), get (into); **wkład** make; *skargę, protest* lodge, make; *prośbę* make; *sprawę jur.* bring; *v/i.* conclude; (**z** *G*) deduce (from), infer (from); *jur.* (**o** *A*) propose

wnu|czka *f* (*-i; G -czek*) granddaughter; **~k** *m* (*-a; -i*) grandson

woalka *f* (*-i; G -lek*) veil

wobec *prp.* (*G*) in the face (of), in view (of); **~ czego** consequently; **~ tego, że** in view of the fact that

wod|a *f* (*-y; G wód*) water; **z ~y** *gastr.* boiled

w oddali in the distance

wod|niak *m* (*-a; -cy*) water-sports enthusiast; **2nik** *m* (*-a; 0*) *znak Zodiaku:* Aquarius; **on(a) jest spod znaku 2nika** he/she is (an) Aquarius; **~nisty** watery; **~nosamolot** *m* seaplane; **~ny** water

wodociąg *m* water-pipe, (*główny*) water-main; **~i** *pl.* waterworks *sg.*; **~owy** *woda* tap

wodo|lecznictwo *n med.* hydrotherapy; **~lot** *m naut.* hydrofoil; **~pój** *m* (*-oju; -oje*) watering-place; **~rost** *m* (*-u; -y*) *bot.* seaweed; **~rowy** hydrogen; **~spad** *m* waterfall, falls *pl.*; **~szczelny** water-tight; **~trysk** *m* (*-u; -i*) fountain; F *figl.* frill(s *pl.*); **~wać** (*-uję*) *v/t. naut.* launch; *v/i.* (*wastronautyce*) splashdown

wodór *m* (*-doru*) *chem.* hydrogen

wodz|a *f* (*-y; -e*) *zw. pl.* rein; **trzymać (się) na ~y** restrain o.s., control o.s.; **puszczać ~e** (*D*) *fig.* give rein (to); **pod ~ą** (*G*) under s.o.'s command

wodz|ić (*-dzę, wódź!*) lead; *fig.* **~ić za nos** *fig.* lead by the nose; **~owie** *pl.* → **wódz**

woj. *skrót pisany:* **województwo** province; **wojewódzki** provincial

wojaż *m* (*-u; -e*) *żart., iron.* journey, voyage, trip

wojenn|y war; military; *jur.* martial; **być na stopie ~ej (z I)** be on a war footing (with)

woje|woda *m* (-y; G -dów) (*chief officer in the province*); **~wódzki** provincial; **~wództwo** *n* (-a; G -) province

wojłok *m* (-u; -i) felt

wojn|a *f* (-y; G -jen) (**domowa** civil) war; **iść na ~ę** go to war; **na ~ie** at war

wojow|ać (-uję) fight (**z** I with; **o** A for); wage war; **~niczo** *adv.* militantly, belligerently; **~niczy** militant, belligerent; **~nik** *m* (-a; -cy) warrior

wojsk|o *n* (-a; G -) army; troops *pl.*; **zaciągnąć się do ~a**, **iść do ~a** join up; **on po ~u** he was in the army; **~owy 1.** military; **służba ~owa** military service; **odmowa służby ~owej** conscientious objection; **po ~owemu** in a military way; (*ubrany*) in uniform; **2.** *m* (-ego; -i) military man, soldier

wokalist|a *m*, **~ka** *f* vocalist

wokalny vocal

wokanda *f* (-y; G -) *jur.* (court) calendar

wokoło, wokół *prp.* (a)round

wol|a *f* (-i; 0) will; **do ~i** at will; **mimo ~i** involuntarily; **dobra ~a** goodwill; **z własnej ~i** of one's own accord

wole *n* (-a; G -i) *med.* goitre; *zo.* crop

wol|eć (-ę, -i) prefer; **wolę ... niż/od ...** I prefer ... to ...; **~ał(a)bym** I would rather; **~ne** *n* (-ego; -e): **mieć ~ne** have a day off; **~nego!** just a minute!; **~niutki** very slow; **~niutko** *adv.* very slowly

wolno¹ *prp.* one can, it is allowed; **czy ~ zapytać** may I ask; **nie ~ mi** I must not; **nikomu nie ~** nobody is allowed to

wolno² *adv.* slowly; (*swobodnie*) freely; **~cłowy** duty-free; **~mularstwo** *n* (-a; 0) Freemasonry; **~myśliciel** *m* free thinker; **~rynkowy**: **cena ~rynkowa** free-market price

wolnoś|ciowy liberation; **~ć** *f* (-ści; 0) freedom, liberty; **~ć słowa** freedom of speech; **na ~ci** at liberty; free; **wypuścić na ~ć** set free

wolny free (**od** G from); (*powolny*) slow; **~ od opłaty** free (of charge); **dzień ~ od pracy** day off, holiday; **na ~m powietrzu** in the open; **na ~m ogniu** at a simmer; **wstęp ~** admission free

woltomierz *m* (-a; -e) *electr.* voltmeter

woła|cz *m* (-a; -e) *gr.* the Vocative; **~ć (za-)** (-am) call; **~nie** *n* (-a; G -ań)** call (**o pomoc** for help)

Wołga *f* (-i; 0) the Volga

woło|wina *f* (-y; G -) beef; **~wy** *gastr.* beef

woły *pl.* → **wół**

wonny fragrant, aromatic

woń *f* (woni, wonie, woni) smell; **przykra ~** odo(u)r; **przyjemna ~** fragrance, aroma

woreczek *m* → **worek**; *anat.* bladder; **~ żółciowy** *anat.* gall bladder

wor|ek *m* (-rka; -rki) bag; (*duży*) sac; **~ki pod oczami** bags under the eyes; **~y** *pl.* → **wór**

wosk *m* (-u; -i) wax; **~owy** wax

wotum *n* (*idkl.*; -a; -ów) vote (**zaufania, nieufności** of confidence, of no confidence); *rel.* votive offering

woz|ić (-żę, woź/wóź!) carry; transport; **kogoś** drive; **~y** *pl.* → **wóz**

woźn|a *f* (-ej; -e) *Brt.* janitor, *Am.* caretaker; **~ica** *m* (-y) coachman; **~y** *m* (-ego; -i) *Brt.* janitor, *Am.* caretaker; *jur.* court usher

wódka *f* (-i; G -dek) vodka

wódz *m* (wodza; wodzowie) leader; chief; **~ naczelny** commander-in--chief; → **dowódca, przywódca**

wójt *m* (-a; -owie) chairman of the village council

wół *m* (wołu; woły) ox

wór *m* (wora; wory) sack, bag

wówczas *lit. adv.* then, at that time

wóz *m* (wozu; wozy) cart; *mot.* car; **~ek** *m* (-zka; -zki) cart; (*dziecięcy*) *Brt.* pram, *Am.* baby carriage, (*spacerowy*) *Brt.* pushchair; *Am.* stroller; **~ek inwalidzki** wheelchair

W.P. *skrót pisany*: **Wielmożny Pan** Esq.

WP *skrót pisany*: **Wojsko Polskie** Polish Army

wpada|ć (-am) fall; *rzeka*: flow into; *po-liczki*: sink; (*wbiec*) rush into; (**na** A, **w** A) collide (with), bang (into); **~ w oczy** catch s.o.'s eye; (*zajść*) drop in (**do** G on); **~ w objęcia** fall into s.o.'s arms; **~ na pomysł** hit on an idea; **~ w złość** fly into a rage; **~ do rąk/w ręce** fall into s.o.'s hands; **~ w kłopoty** get into trouble; → **wpaść**

wpajać (-am) instil

wpakow(yw)ać (-[w]uję) pack, cram; **~ się** (*na przyjęcie*) gate crash; **~ się w kłopoty** get into trouble

wpaść → **wpadać**; (**na** A) bump into

wpatrywać się (*-uję*) (**w** A) stare (at)

wpędz|**ać** (*-am*) ⟨*~ić*⟩ (**w** A) drive into

wpić *pf.* → **wpijać**

wpierw *adv.* first

wpijać (*-am*) *paznokcie* dig; ~ **się** (*cisnąć*) cut (**w** A into); *kleszcz itp.*: attach o.s.; ~ (**się**) *zębami* sink o.s. teeth (**w** A into)

wpis *m* (*-u; -y*) entry; (*opłata*) fee; *~owy* admission; *~ywać* (*-uję*) ⟨*~ać*⟩ enrol(l) (**się** *v/i.*; **do** A in, for); write in

wpląt|**ywać** (*-uję*) ⟨*~ać*⟩ entangle, involve; *~ywać* ⟨*~ać*⟩ **się** get involved *lub* entangled (**w** L in)

wpła|**cać** (*-am*) ⟨*~cić*⟩ pay in, deposit; *~ta* *f* (*-y; G -*) payment, deposit

wpław *adv.* by swimming

wpły|**nąć** *pf.* → **wpływać**; *~w* *m* (*-u; -y*) influence; *tech.* inflow; *~wy* *pl. econ.* receipts *pl.*, revenue; *mieć ~wy* have connections; *~wać* (*-am*) *okręt*: come in, make port (**do** G to); *zapach itp.*: waft in; *kwota, listy*: come in; *rzeka*: flow in (to); (**na** A) have an influence (on); *~wowy* influential

wpoić *pf.* → **wpajać**

wpół *adv.* half; ~ **do drugiej** half past one; **na** ~ half-; *w złoż.* → **pół-**; *~darmo* *adv.* dirt cheap; *~żywy* dead tired

wpraw|**a** *f* (*-y; 0*) *Brt.* practice, skill, mastery; *wyjść z ~y* be out of practice

wprawdzie *part.* though

wprawi|**ać** (*-am*) ⟨*~ić*⟩ *szybę* fit, put in; *obraz* frame; make (**w** *podziw* astonished); *~ać* ⟨*~ić*⟩ **w** *ruch* set in motion; *~ać* ⟨*~ić*⟩ **się** get practice (**w** I in)

wpraw|**nie** *adv.* skil(l)fully, skilled; *~ny* skil(l)ful, skilled

wprost *adv.* straight; *fig.* directly

wprowadz|**ać** (*-am*) ⟨*~ić*⟩ (**do** G) show (into); (*przedstawić, zaprowadzić*) introduce (to, into); *~ać* **w** *zakłopotanie* embarrass; *~ić* **się** move in (**do** G to); *~enie* *n* (*-a; G -eń*) introduction; *~enie* **się** move

wprzęg|**ać** (*-am*) ⟨*~nąć*⟩ (*-nę*) harness

wprzód *adv. lit.* first

wpust *m* (*-u; -y*) *tech.* inlet; (*w drewnie*) groove; *~ ściekowy* drain

wpu|**szczać** ⟨*~ścić*⟩ let in

wpychać (*-am*) cram in, pack in; shove in; *fig.* palm off; *~ się* (**do** G) push in (to)

wracać (*-am*) return, come back (**do** G

to); *~ z drogi* turn back; *~ do zdrowia* recover; → **zwracać**

wrak *m* (*-a/-u; -i*) wreck

wrastać (*-am*) grow in

wraz (**z** I) *adv.* (together) with

wrażenie *n* (*-a; G -eń*) impression; feeling; *odnieść* ~ get an impression

wrażliw|**ość** *f* (*-ści; 0*) sensibility; (*też tech.*) sensitivity; *~y* sensitive (**na** A to)

wre → **wrzeć**

wreszcie *adv.* at last

wręcz *adv.* straight, directly; *walka* ~ *mil.* close combat; *~ać* (*-am*) ⟨*~yć*⟩ (*-ę*) hand in, hand over; present

wrodzony inborn; *med.* congenital

wrog|**i** hostile; *~o* *adv.* in a hostile manner; *~ość* *f* (*-ści; 0*) hostility, enmity; *~owie* *pl.* → **wróg**

wrona *f* (*-y; G -*) *zo.* crow

wrosnąć *pf.* → **wrastać**

wrota *pl.* (*wrót*) gate, door (*też fig.* **do** G to)

wrotka *f* (*-i; G -tek*) (*w sporcie*) roller skate

wróbel *m* (*-bla; -ble*) *zo.* sparrow

wrócić *pf.* (*-cę*) → **wracać, zwracać**

wróg *m* (*wroga; wrogowie*) enemy

wrós|**ć** *pf.* → **wrastać**; *~t* G → **wrota**

wróż|**ba** *f* (*-y; G -*) omen; prediction; *~biarstwo* (*-a; 0*) fortune-telling; *~bita* *m* (*-y; -ci*) fortune-teller; *~ka* *f* (*-i; G -ek*) fortune-teller; (*w baśni*) fairy; *~yć* ⟨*po-*⟩ (*-ę*) *v/i.* tell fortunes; read fortune (**z** *kart*, **z** *ręki* from the cards, from the hand); *v/t.* predict

wryć *pf.*: *fig.* ~ **w** *pamięć* be imprinted on one's memory

wrza|**sk** *m* (*-u; -i*) shout, shriek, scream; *~kliwy* noisy, tumultuous; *~nąć* *pf.* → **wrzeszczeć**

wrzawa *f* (*-y; G -*) uproar, clamo(u)r

wrzą|**cy** boiling; *~tek* *m* (*-tku*) boiling water (milk *etc.*)

wrzeciono *n* (*-a; G -*) spindle

wrze|**ć** boil; *fig.* seethe; *pol.* ferment; *praca wre* the work is in full swing; *~nie* *n* (*-a; 0*) boiling; ferment

wrzesień *m* (*-śnia; -śnie*) September

wrzeszczeć (*-ę*) yell, shriek

wrześniowy September

wrzodow|**y**: *choroba* *~a* *med.* chronic peptic ulcer disease

wrzos *m* (*-u; -y*) *bot.* heather; *~owisko* *n* (*-a; G -*) heath

wrzód *m* (*-rzodu; -rzody*) *med.* ulcer;

(*czyrak*) abscess, boil

wrzu|cać (*-am*) ⟨**~cić**⟩ throw in (**do** *G* to); *mot. bieg* engage; **~t** *m* (*-u*; *-y*) *sport*: throw(-in)

wrzynać się (*-am*) cut into

wsadz|ać (*-am*) ⟨**~ić**⟩ put (**do auta, do kieszeni,** into the car, into the pocket); *ubranie, okulary* put on; **~ać za kraty** lock up

wsch. *skrót pisany:* **wschód** E (*East*); **wschodni** E (*Eastern*)

wschodni Eastern

wschodzić (*-dzę*) rise, get up

wschód *m* (*-chodu*; *0*) east; (*pl. -chody*) **~ słońca** sunrise, sunup; **ze wschodu** from the east; **na ~ od** (*G*) east of

wsi → **wieś**

wsiadać (*-am*) get in (**do** *G*); get on, board (**na** *A*); **~ na statek** embark

wsiąkać (*-am*) seep in, soak up

wsiąść *pf.* → **wsiadać**

wsie *pl.* → **wieś**

wskakiwać (*-uję*) jump (on); (**do** *G*) jump (into), plunge (into)

wskaz|ać *pf.* → **wskazywać**; **~any** shown; (*zalecany*) advisable; **~ówka** *m* (*-i*; *G -wek*) (*zegara*) hand; (*wskaźnik*) pointer; (*sugestia*) hint; → **oznaka**; **~ujący** pointing; *anat.* index; **~ywać** (*-uję*) point (**na** *A* at, *fig.* to)

wskaźnik *m* (*-a*; *-i*) *tech.* indicator, gauge; pointer; (**cen** price) index; **~ benzyny** *mot.* fuel gauge

wskoczyć *pf.* → **wskakiwać**

wskórać *pf.* (*~am*) accomplish, achieve

wskroś: **na ~** through (and through)

wskrze|szać (*-am*) ⟨**~sić**⟩ (*-szę*) raise *s.o.* from the dead

wskutek *prp.* because of

wsławi|ać się (*-am*) ⟨**~ć się**⟩ become famous (**jako** as)

wsłuch|iwać się (*-uję*) ⟨**~ać się**⟩ listen; (**w** *A*) listen (to)

wspak: **na ~** *adv.* backwards

wspaniale *adv.* magnificently

wspaniał|omyślny magnanimous; generous; **~y** magnificent; splendid, grand

wsparcie *n* (*-a*; *G -rć*) support, backing

wspiąć się *pf.* → **wspinać się**

wspierać (*-am*) support; *fig.* back

wspina|czka *f* (*-i*; *G -czek*) mountaineering; **~ć się** (*-am*) climb

wspomag|ać help, assist; **~anie** *n* (*-a*; *0*):

~anie kierownicy *mot.* power steering

wspom|inać (*-am*) ⟨**~nieć**⟩ (*-nę*, *-nij!*) (*A*) recall, remember; (**o** *L*) mention; **~nienie** *n* (*-a*; *G -eń*) remembrance, memory; **~nienie pośmiertne** obituary; **na samo ~nienie** at the very thought; **~óc** *pf.* → **wspomagać**

wspól|niczka *f* (*-i*; *G -czek*), **~ik** *m* (*-a*; *-cy*) partner; *jur.* (**w** *zbrodni*) accomplice; **~ota** *f* (*-y*; *G-*) community; ℚ**ota Narodów** the Commonwealth of Nations; ℚ**ota Niepodległych Państw** Commonwealth of Independent States; **~y** common; mutual; **~ymi siłami** with combined efforts; **~a mogiła** mass grave; **nie mieć nic ~ego** (**z** *I*) have nothing in common (with)

współczes|ność *f* (*-ści*; *0*) presence; contemporaneity; **~ny** contemporary; *historia* **~na** contemporary history

współczu|cie *n* (*-a*; *0*) compassion; sympathy; **złożyć wyrazy ~cia** (*D*) offer one's condolences (to); **~ć** (*-uję*) (*D*) sympathize (with), pity; feel sorry (for); **~jąco** *adv.* with sympathy

współ|czynnik *m* (*-a*; *-i*) factor, coefficient; **~decydować** (*-uję*) have a say (**przy** *L* in); **~działać** (*-am*) cooperate, collaborate, work together (**przy** *L* with); **~istnienie** *n* (*-a*; *G -eń*) coexistence; **~małżonek** *m* spouse, marriage partner; **~mierny** (**do** *G*) appropriate (to); adequate (to); **~mieszkaniec** *m* (*-ńca*, *-ńcy*), **~mieszkanka** *f* (*-i*; *G-nek*) fellow occupant; (*pokoju*) roommate **~obywatel**(ka *f*) *m* fellow citizen; **~oskarżony** *m*, **~oskarżona** *f* co-defendant

współprac|a *f* cooperation, collaboration; **~ować** (**przy** *L*, **w** *L*) work together (on), collaborate (on), cooperate (on); **~owniczka** *f*, **~ownik** *m* co-worker, collaborator

współ|rządzić to control jointly; **~rzędna** *f* (*-ej*; *-e*) *math.* coordinate

współspraw|ca *m*, **~czyni** *f* *jur.* accomplice, accessory

współuczestni|ctwo *n* participation; **~czyć** (*-ę*) participate (**w** *L* in); *jur.* aid and abet; **~czka** *f*, **~k** *m* participant

współ|udział *m* participation; involvement; *jur.* complicity; **~więzień** *m*, **~więźniarka** *f* fellow prisoner; **~właściciel**(ka *f*) *m* co-owner, joint owner; **~wyznawca** *m* *rel.* fellow-believer

W

współzawodni|ctwo n (-a; 0) competition, rivalry; **~czka** f (w sporcie) competitor, contestant; **~czyć** (-ę) compete (**z** I with); **~k** m competitor, contestant

współży|cie n living together; zwł. married life; **trudny we ~ciu** difficult to get along with; **~ć** live together; biol. live in symbiosis

wsta|wać ⟨**wstać**⟩ (stać²) get up, rise; stand; **~wi(a)ć** put in, insert; **~wi(a)ć się (za** I) intercede (on s.o.'s behalf), put in a good word (for); **~wiennictwo** n (-a; 0) intercession; **~wka** f (-i; G -wek) insertion; theat. interlude

wstąpi|ć (-ę) → **wstępować**

wstąpienie n (-a) entry, joining; **~ na tron** ascension to the throne

wstążka f (-i; G -żek) ribbon

wstecz adv. back(wards); **~nictwo** n (-a; 0) backwardness; **~ny** jur. retrospective; fig. reactionary, retrograde; **bieg ~ny** mot. reverse (gear); **lusterko ~ne** mot. rear-view mirror

wstęga f (-i; G -) band, ribbon

wstęp m (-u; -y) entry, entrance; (do książki) introduction (też fig.); **na ~ie** at the beginning; to begin with; **~nie** adv. initially; **~ny** introductory; preliminary; initial; **słowo ~ne** foreword; → **egzamin**; **~ować** (-uję) ⟨**do G**⟩ enter, join; (zajść) drop in (at); (**na** A) enter; (**na tron**) ascend (to)

wstręt m (-u; -y) disgust, repulsion, revulsion; **~ny** disgusting, repulsive

wstrząs m (-u; -y) (pojazdu itp.) jolt; fig. shock (też med.); geol. tremor; **~ać** (-am) ⟨I⟩ shake (też fig.); pojazd itp.: jolt; **~ać się (z** G) shake (with), convulse (with); **~ająco** adv. shockingly; **~ający** shocking; **~nąć** pf. → **wstrząsać**; **~owy** shock

wstrzemięźliw|ie adv. temperately, abstemiously, abstinently; **~y** temperate, abstemious, abstinent

wstrzy|kiwać (-uję) ⟨**~knąć**⟩ med. inject; **~mywać** (-uję) ⟨**~mać**⟩ stop, hold up; fig. impede, inhibit; **~mać się** suppress, hold back (**od łez** tears); **~mać się od głosu** abstain; (**z** I) put off, delay

wstyd m (-u; 0) shame; (zakłopotanie) embarrassment; **~ mi** (G) I am ashamed (of); **ze ~u** with shame lub embarrassment; **~liwie** adv. timidly; with shame;

~liwy timid, embarrassed; → **nieśmiały, żenujący**

wsty|dzić ⟨**za-**⟩ (-dzę) put to shame; **~dzić** ⟨**za-**⟩ **się** (G; bezok.) be ashamed (of; to bezok.); **~dź się** shame on you

wsu|wać (-am) ⟨**~nąć**⟩ insert, slide in(to); (jeść) tuck in; **~nąć się (do** G, **pod** A) slip (into, under); **~wka** f (-i; G -wek) (do włosów) hairgrip

wsyp|ywać (-uję) **~ać**⟩ pour (**do** G into); **~ać się** fig. F get caught

wsysać (-am) suck into

wszakże lit. however, anyhow

wszcząć pf. → **wszczynać**

wszczepi|ać (-am) ⟨**~ć**⟩ med. implant; fig. instil(l)

wszczynać (-am) instigate; śledztwo, negocjacje open; **~ kłótnię** brawl

wszech|mocny almighty; **~obecny** omnipresent; **~stronny** versatile; **~świat** m (-a; -y) universe; **~światowy** world-wide; **~władny** omnipotent

wszelk|i every, any; **za ~ą cenę** at any price; **na ~i wypadek** just in case

wszerz adv. across; → **wzdłuż**

wszędzie adv. everywhere

wszy pl. → **wesz**; **~ć** pf. → **wszywać**

wszys|cy m-os everybody, all; **~tek** m (f **~tka**, n **~tko**, pl. **~tkie**) all; **~tko jedno** all the same; **nade ~tko** above all; **~tkiego najlepszego!** all the best!

wszywać (-am) sew in(to)

wścibski snooping; F nosy

wściec się pf. (o psie, fig.) go mad; → **wściekać się**

wściek|ać się (-am) fig. F rage, fume, seethe; **~le** adv. furiously, madly; **~lizna** f (-y; 0) med. rabies sg.; **~łość** f (-ści; 0) rage, madness; fury; **~ły** med. rabid; fig. mad, furious

wśliz|giwać się (-uję) ⟨**~(g)nąć się**⟩ (-nę) (**do** G) slip in(to)

wśród prp. (G) among, between

wt. skrót pisany: **wtorek** Tue(s). (Tuesday)

wtaczać roll (**się** v/i.; **do** G into)

wtajemnicz|ać (-am) ⟨**~yć**⟩ let s.o. in (**w** A on); **~ony** initiated

wtargnąć pf. (**do** G) invade; fig. burst in (on)

wte|dy adv. then; at that time; **~m** adv. suddenly; abruptly; **~nczas** adv. → **wtedy**

wtłaczać (-am) ⟨**wtłoczyć**⟩ stuff, cram;

~ **się** push (one's way) (**do** G into)

wtoczyć pf. → **wtaczać**

wtor|ek m (-rku; -rki) Tuesday; ~**kowy** Tuesday

wtór|nik m (-a; -i) duplicate, copy; ~**ny** secondary; ~**ować** mus., fig. (D) accompany; ~**y: po** ~**e** secondly

wtrąc|ać ⟨~**ić**⟩ v/t. uwagę throw in; ~**ić do więzienia** put in prison; v/i. interject, remark; ~**ać** ⟨~**ić**⟩ **się** interfere (**w** A, **do** A in), fig. butt in

wtrys|kiwać ⟨-uję⟩ ⟨~**nąć**⟩ inject

wtyczk|a f (-i; G -czek) electr. plug; F informer, plug; ~**owy** electr.: **gniazd-(k)o ~owe** power point, socket outlet

wtykać ⟨-am⟩ insert, put into

wuj m (-a; -owie, -ów), ~**ek** m (-ka; -kowie) uncle; ~**enka** f (-i; G -nek) aunt

wulgarny vulgar; gross

wulkan m (-u; -y) volcano; (czynny volcanic; ~**izować** ⟨-uję⟩ vulcanize

ww. skrót pisany: **wyżej wymieniony** above-mentioned

Wwa, W-wa skrót pisany: **Warszawa** Warsaw

wwozić ⟨**wwieźć**⟩ bring in; import (**do** G into)

wy pron. (GAL was, D wam, I wami) you

wybacz|ać ⟨-am⟩ forgive; ~**alny** forgivable, excusable; ~**enie** n (-a; G -eń) forgiveness; **nie do ~enia** unforgivable, inexcusable; ~**yć** pf. → **wybaczać**

wybaw|ca m (-y; G -ców), ~**czyni** f (-i; -e) rescuer; savio(u)r (też rel.); ~**iać** ⟨-am⟩ ⟨~**ić**⟩ rescue, save (**z** G from)

wybić pf. → **wybijać**; (wygubić) eradicate; drób itp. kill off; (zbić) beat up; ~ **sobie z głowy** get s.th. out of one's head; ~ **się ze snu** be unable to fall asleep again

wybie|g m (-u; -i) (drobiu) run; (koni) paddock; (dla modelek) Brt. catwalk, Am. runway; fig. device, trick; ~**gać** ⟨~**c, ~gnąć**⟩ run out (**z** G of); ~**lać** ⟨-am⟩ ⟨~**lić**⟩ make white, whiten; fig. clear; → **bielić**

wybierać ⟨-am⟩ (dokonywać wyboru) choose, select; (w wyborach) elect; numer dial; (wyjmować) take out; ~ **się** (**do** G) be going (to); ~ **się do teatru** gototheBrt. theatre (Am. theater);~ **się w podróż** get ready for the journey

wybijać ⟨-am⟩ dno, ząb, oko knock out; szybę break, smash; medal strike, mint;

(obić ścianę itp.) line (I with); takt beat; godzinę strike; ~**jać się** distinguish o.s.; excel (**w** L in); → **wybić**; ~**tnie** adv. eminently; ~**tny** eminent, distinguished

wyblakły faded

wyboisty uneven, bumpy

wybor|ca m (-y; G -ów) voter; ~**czy** electoral, election; ~**ny** excellent; → **wyśmienity**; ~**owy** elite; **strzelec ~owy** marksman; ~**y** pl. → **wybór**

wybój m (-boju; -boje, G -boi/-bojów) pothole

wybór m (-boru; -bory) selection, choice; (mianowanie) appointment (**na** A to); pol. **wybory** pl. elections pl. (**do parlamentu** to Parliament); **do wyboru** to choose from

wybra|ć pf. → **wybierać**; ~**kow(yw)ać** ⟨-[w]uję⟩ sort out; ~**kowany towar** rejects pl.; ~**ny** elected; chosen

wybredny fastidious, choosy

wybrnąć pf. (**z** G) work one's way out (of) (też fig.); fig. get out (**z długów** of one's debt)

wybro- pf., **wybru-** pf. → **bro-, bru-**

wybryk m (-u; -i) trick, prank; ~ **natury** freak of nature

wybrzeż|e n (-a; G -y) coast; (morza) seaside; **na ~e** to the coast; **na ~u** on the coast

wybrzuszenie n (-a; G -eń) bulge

wy|brzydzać f ⟨-am⟩ (**na** A) fuss (about); ~**bu-** pf. → **bu-**

wybuch m (-u; -y) explosion; (wulkanu) eruption (też fig.); (wojny, epidemii) outbreak; (gniewu) outburst; ~**ać** ⟨-am⟩ ⟨~**nąć**⟩ explode; wulkan: erupt; wojna, panika: break out; burst out (**śmie- chem, płaczem** laughing, crying); (gniewem) blow up; ~**owy** explosive; fig. bad-tempered

wybujały → **bujny**; tall

wyca-, wyce- pf. → **ca-, ce-**

wycena f (-y; G -) estimate, valuation

wych|adzać ⟨-am⟩ ⟨~**odzić**⟩ cool down; → **ochładzać, oziębiać**

wychodn|e n (-ego; 0) day off; F **być na ~ym** be just about to leave

wychodzić (**z** G) go out (of), leave; (**na** A) look out on (to); (**na** L) profit (from); książka, zdjęcie itp.: come out, appear; praca itp.: work; ~ **na pierw- sze miejsce** take the lead; ~ **na wol- ność** be released; ~ **z mody** go out of fashion; **~ w morze** put to sea; **nie ~ z głowy** haunt; **~ dobrze na** (L) profit (from); **~ na swoje** break even; → **iść, wyjść**

wychodź|ca m (-y; G -ów) emigrant; **~stwo** n (-a; 0) emigration

wychowa|ć (-am) → **wychowywać**; **~nek** m (-nka; -nkowie) foster-child; (był)y uczeń) graduate; **~nie** n (-a; 0) upbringing, education; **dobre ~nie** good manners pl.; **~nka** f (-i; G -nek) → **wychowanek**; **~wca** m (-cy; G -ców), **~wczyni** f (-ni; -ie, -yń) caregiver; **~wczo** adv. educationally; **~wczy** educational

wychowywać (-uję) dziecko bring up; ucznia educate; **~ się** grow up (u G with); be brought up

wychudły emaciated, drawn

wychwalać (-am) praise

wychyl|ać (-am) ⟨**~ić**⟩ kieliszek empty, drain; **~ać głowę z okna** put one's head out of the window; **~ać się** wskazówka: swing; look out (**zza** G from behind); **~ić się do przodu** bend lub lean forward

wyciąć pf. → **wycinać**

wyciąg m (-u; -i) med. itp. extract; (kuchenny, tech.) hood; tech. hoist; (winda) Brt. lift, Am. elevator; (narciarski) (ski)lift

wyciąg|ać (-am) ⟨**~nąć**⟩ pull out; gumę, rękę itp. stretch; ręce, nogi extend, stretch out; fig. wnioski, draw; math. pierwiastek extract; **~nąć się** stretch out

wycie n (-a; G wyć) howl

wyciec pf. → **wyciekać**

wycieczk|a f (-i; G -czek) outing, (zorganizowana, też fig.) excursion; trip; **~owy** excursion

wyciekać (-am) leak out

wycieńcz|ać (-am) ⟨**~yć**⟩ (-ę) weaken, exhaust

wyciera|czka f (-i; G -czek) (przy drzwiach) doormat; mot. screen wiper; **~ć** (-am) wipe; (osuszyć) dry; **~ć gumką** erase, rub out; **~ć się** dry o.s.; (ręcznikiem) towel o.s.; ubranie wear (out)

wycięcie n (-a; -ęć) opening; (ubrania) neckline

wycin|ać (-am) cut (out); drzewa fell; **~anka** f (-i; G -nek) silhouette, cutout; **~ek** m (-nka; -nki) clipping; med. specimen; math. segment

wycis|kać ⟨**~nąć**⟩ sok press out,

squeeze out; ubranie wring (out); pieczęć impress

wycisz|ać (-am) ⟨**~yć**⟩ (-ę) silence

wycof|ywać (-uję) ⟨**~ać**⟩ withdraw, pull out (**się** v/i.; **z** G from); → **cofać**

wyczek|ać pf. (G, A), **~iwać** (-uję) (**na** A) wait (for)

wyczerp|ać pf. → **wyczerpywać**; **~any** exhausted; towar out of stock; **~ujący** exhaustive; **~ywać** (-ać) exhaust; kogoś wear out; zapasy deplete; **~ywać się** get tired; zasoby: become depleted

wyczu|cie n (-a; 0) sensation; (G); feeling (of); **~(wa)ć** (-[w]am) sense; feel; zapach smell; **~walny** perceptible

wyczyn m outstanding performance; **~owy** (w sporcie) competitive

wyć (wyję) howl

wyćwiczony practised, mastered

wyda|ć pf. → **wydawać**; **~jność** f (-ści; 0) efficiency, effectiveness; productivity; agr. fertility; **~jny** efficient, effective; productive; **~lać** (-am) ⟨**~lić**⟩ (-lę) (z kraju) exile; (z pracy) dismiss; (ze szkoły) expel; biol. secrete; **~lenie** n (-a; G -leń) exile; dismissal; expulsion; **~nie** n (-a; G -ań) issuing; print. edition; jur. handing over, extradition; (zdrada) betrayal

wydarz|enie n (-a; G -eń) event; **~yć się** (t-ko 3. os.) occur, happen

wydat|ek m (-tku; -tki) expenditure; expense; **~kować** (imp)pf. (-uję) expend, pay; **~ny** prominent, protuberant; fig. considerable, significant

wydaw|ać pieniądze spend; rzeczy give out; dokument, dekret issue; książkę publish; woń give off; dźwięk make; przyjęcie, rozkaz give; zbiega give over; sekret reveal; córkę marry (**za** A to); jur. wyrok pronounce; **~ać się** seem, appear; sekret: be revealed, come out; get married (**za** A to); **~ca** m (-y; G -ców), **~czyni** f (-ni; -ie) publisher; **~nictwo** n (-a; G -ctw) publishing house

wy|dąć pf. → **wydymać**; **~dech** m (-u; -y) exhalation; **~dechowy: rura ~dechowa** mot. exhaust pipe

wydekoltowany suknia low-cut

wydept|ywać (-uję) ⟨**~ać**⟩ trawnik stamp on, tread; ścieżkę tread out

wydęty usta pouted

wydłub|ywać (-uję) ⟨**~ać**⟩ pick out

wydłuż|ać (-am) ⟨**~yć**⟩ extend, leng-

then; *okres* prolong; ~ony elongated
wydma *f* (*-y; G -*) dune
wydmuch|iwać (*-uję*) ⟨~**ać**⟩ blow out
wydoby|wać ⟨~**ć**⟩ get (**z** *A* out of);
rudę extract, mine; *informacje* elicit;
~(**wa**)**ć się** escape; → **wydostawać**
(**się**); ~**wczy** *przemysł* mining
wydolny efficient
wydoskonalać (*-am*) → **doskonalić**
wydosta(wa)ć get (**z** *A* out of); (*uzys-
kać*) receive, get; ~ **się** come out, get
out
wydra *f* (*-y; G -der/-*) *zo.* otter
wydrap|ywać (*-uję*) ⟨~**ać**⟩ (*usuwać*)
scrape out; *słowa* scratch
wydrążony hollow
wydruk *m* (*-u; -i*) *komp.* printout;
~**ować** (*-uję*) *komp.* print out
wydrwigrosz *m* (*-a; -e*) con man
wy|drzeć *pf.* → **wydzierać**; ~**dusić** *fig.*
squeeze out, wring out; ~**dychać**
(*-am*) breathe out; ~**dymać** (*-am*) *policzki* puff out; *brzuch* distend; ~**dział**
m (*-u; -y*) uniwersytet: faculty; department, section
wydziedzicz|ać (*-am*) ⟨~**yć**⟩ disinherit
wydziel|ać (*-am*) *biol.* excrete; *promie-
niowanie* radiate; *chem., med. itp.* emit,
release; *zapach* give off; *biol.* be ex-
creted; *chem.* be emitted; ⟨*też ~ić*⟩ ration, divide, distribute; destine, intend
(**na, pod** *A* for); ~**ina** *f* (*-y; G -*) secre-
tion; ~**ony**: *miasto ~one* (*a town that is
an administrative district in its own right*)
wydzierać (*-am*) tear out/away; *fig.* rescue, save; F ~ **się** roar, shout; → **wyrywać**
wydzierżawi|ać (*-am*) ⟨~**ć**⟩ rent;
(*wziąć w dzierżawę*) lease
wydźwięk *m* implication(s)
wy|egz-, ~eks-, ~el-, ~em-, ~fro- *pf.*
→ **egz-, eks-, el-, em-, fro-**
wyga|dać F *pf.* spill the beans; ~**dany** F
glib; ~**dywać** F (*-uję*) blab; find fault
(**na** *A* with); ~**lać** (*-am*) shave off; ~**niać**
→ **wypędzać**; ~**niać** (*-am*) ⟨~**rnąć**⟩
popiół remove; F *fig.* make *s.th.* clear
lub plain; ~**sać** (*-am*) ⟨~**snąć**⟩ go out
wy|giąć *pf.* → **wyginać**; ~**gięcie** *n* (*-a;
G -ęć*) curvature, curve; bend; ~**ginać**
(*-am*) bend, bow; *w łuk* arch; ~**ginać**
pf. die out; *zwł. biol.* become extinct
wygląd *m* (*-u; 0*) appearance, look; ~**ać**
(*-am*) look (**oknem** out of the window;

młodo young; *na artystę* like an artist;
na szczęśliwego happy); *sprawy*:
stand; (*spod, zza* *G*) appear (from behind, beneath); (*G*) look forward (to)
wygładz|ać (*-am*) ⟨~**ić**⟩ smooth out
wygłodzony famished, starving
wygł|aszać (*-am*) ⟨~**osić**⟩ *mowę* give,
deliver
wygłupia|ć się (*-am*) fool about; *nie ~j
się!* stop messing about!, (*bądź poważny*) stop joking!
wygna|ć *pf.* → **wypędzać**; ~**nie** *n* (*-a;
G -ań*) exile; *na ~niu* in exile; ~**niec**
m (*-ńca; -ńcy*) exile
wygni|atać (*-am*) ⟨~**eść**⟩ *ciasto* knead;
pf. crease, rumple; → **miąć**
wygod|a *f* (*-y; G -gód*) comfort, con-
venience; *z ~ami mieszkanie* with all
modern conveniences *pl.*; ~**ny** comfortable; convenient; → **dogodny**
wygo|lić *pf.* → **wygalać**; ~**nić** *pf.* →
wypędzać; ~**spodarować** *pf.* obtain
through careful management; ~**to-
w(yw)ać** (*-[w]uję*) boil out
wygórowany exorbitant, extravagant
wygra|ć *pf.* → **wygrywać**; ~**na** *f* (*-ej; -e*)
win, victory; *dać za ~ną* give up; *łatwa
~na* walk-over; ~**ny** won
wygr|ywać (*-am*) (*A, w*) win; ~**ać na
loterii** win (on) the lottery; *fig.* have
good luck; ~**yzać** (*-am*) ⟨~**źć**⟩ *dziurę*
eat through
wygrzeb|ywać (*-uję*) ⟨~**ać**⟩ dig out;
fig. dig up, unearth
wygrzewać się (*-am*) warm o.s., sun
wygwizd|ywać (*-uję*) ⟨~**ać**⟩ *melodię*
whistle; *zwł. pf. aktora* hiss
wy|ha-, ~ho- *pf.* → **ha-, ho-**; ~**imagi-
nowany** imaginary
wyja|dać eat up; ~**ławiać** (*-am*) ⟨~**ło-
wić**⟩ (*-ę*) exhaust, drain; *med.* sterilize;
~**śniać** (*-am*) ⟨~**śnić**⟩ (*-ę, -nij/-*) explain; ~**śniać** ⟨~**śnić**⟩ **się** be explained,
make clear; ~**śnienie** *n* (*-a; G -eń*) explanation; ~**wiać** (*-am*) ⟨~**wić**⟩ reveal;
skandal expose
wyjazd *m* (*-u; -y*) exit, departure; (*podróż*) journey, travel
wyjąć *pf.* → **wyjmować**
wyjąt|ek *m* (*-tku; -tki*) exception; *bez
~ku* without exception; *z ~kiem* (*G*)
with the exception (of); *w drodze ~ku*
→ ~**kowo** *adv.* exceptionally, by way
of exception; ~**kowy** exceptional

wyje|chać pf. → **wyjeżdżać**;~dnać pf.
obtain; ~ść pf. → **wyjadać**

wyjezdn|e : **na ~ym** just before leaving

wyjeżdżać (-am) leave, go away/out;
drive (**z** G out of, from; **po zakupy** to
do the shopping); ~ **na urlop** go on a
holiday (**do** A to); ~ **za granicę** go
abroad; → **odjeżdżać**

wyj|mować (-uję) get out, take out;
~rzeć pf. (-ę; -y) → **wyglądać**

wyjś|cie n (-a; G -jść) leaving, depar-
ture; (drzwi itp.) exit, way out; (na lot-
nisku) gate; fig. solution; tech. output;
~cie za mąż marriage; **położenie
bez ~cia** deadlock, stalemate; ~ciowy
drzwi itp. exit; (początkowy) starting;
tech. output; ~ć pf. → **wychodzić**; F
nie wyszło it did not work out

wy|kałaczka f (-i; G -czek) toothpick;
~kantować F pf. swindle; ~kańczać
(-am) finish off F fig. finish off

wykapan|y : ~y **ojciec** the spitting im-
age of the father

wykarmi|ać (-am) ⟨~ć⟩ feed

wykaz m (-u; -y) list; ~ywać ⟨~ać⟩
(udowodnić) prove; (przejawić) show;
(ujawnić) reveal; ~ać się prove o.s.

wykidajło F m (-u; -ów) bouncer,
chucker-out

wy|kipieć pf. boil out; ~kitować F
(-uję) pop off, snuff it; ~kiwać F(-am)
fool, con; ~knąć pf. → **wyklinać**; ~kle-
jać (-am) ⟨~kleić⟩ (I) line (with); ~kli-
nać (-am) dziecko curse; grzesznika
excommunicate

wyklucz|ać (-am) ⟨~yć⟩ (-ę) exclude,
rule out; ~ać się be mutually exclus-
ive; ~ony excluded; **to jest ~one** it's
out of the question

wyklu|wać (-am) ⟨~ć⟩ (-ję) się → **kluć**

wykład m (-u; -y) lecture, talk

wykładać¹ (-am) v/t. lecture (uczyć)
teach, zwł. Brt. read

wykład|ać² (-am) lay out; kołnierz turn
down; (płytami itp.) pave; myśl elucid-
ate; ~any mebel inlaid; ~nik m (-a;
-i) math. exponent; ~owca m (-y; G
-ców) lecturer, reader; ~owy lecture

wykładzina f (-y; G -) lining, coating;
(na podłogę) linoleum, Brt. lino; ~ dy-
wanowa fitted carpet

wykłu|wać (-am) ⟨~ć⟩ put out, gouge
out

wykole|jać się (-am) ⟨~ić się⟩ (-ję) po-

ciąg: derail; fig. go astray; ~jeniec m
(-ńca; -ńcy) social misfit

wykomb- pf. → **komb-**

wykona|ć pf. → **wykonywać** ~lny
practicable, feasible, workable; ~nie n
(-a; G -ań) execution; production; performance; playing; por. **wykonywać**
~wca m (-y; G -ców), ~wczyni f (-i;
-e) performer; jur. executor; econ. contractor; por. **wykonywać** ~wczy ex-
ecutive

wykonywać (-uję) pracę do, execute;
rzecz make, produce; zamiar, zadanie,
wyrok carry out; piosenkę, sztukę perform; rolę play; zawód work

wykończyć pf. → **wykańczać, kończyć**

wykop m (-u; -y) excavation; trench;
~ywać (-uję) ⟨~ać⟩ dół itp. dig (out)

wykorzyst|ywać (-uję) ⟨~ać⟩ use; em-
ploy; → **wyzyskiwać**

wykpi|wać (-am) ⟨~ć⟩ v/t. make fun of,
mock

wykra|czać (-am) (**poza** A) go beyond;
(**przeciw** D) infringe, contravene;~dać
(-am) steal; kogoś kidnap, abduct; ~dać
się steal out lub away; ~jać (-am) cut
out; ~ść pf. → **wykradać**;~wać (-am)
pf. → **wykrajać**

wykre|s m (-u; -y) diagram; chart;~ślać
(-am) ⟨~ślić⟩ cross lub strike out; tech.
plot, draw; ~ślny graphical; diagram-
matic

wykrę|cać (-am) ⟨~cić⟩ żarówkę screw
out, unscrew; bieliznę wring; szyję crick;
rękę twist; F numer dial; ~cać się turn;
fig. wriggle out (**od** G of); ~t m (-u; -y)
(ustny) excuse; dodge; ~tny evasive

wykro|czenie n (-a; G -eń) jur. Brt. of-
fence, Am. offense; ~czyć pf. → **wykraczać**; ~ić pf. → **wykrajać**

wykrój m (-kroju; -kroje) pattern

wykrusz|ać się (-am) ⟨~yć się⟩
crumble away (**z** G from); fig. decrease

wykrwawić się pf. bleed to death

wykry|cie n (-a; G -yć) detection;
uncovering, exposure; ~ć pf. → **wykrywać**;~wacz m detector; ~wacz kłamstw lie detector; ~wać (-am) detect;
zbrodnię find; (odkryć) discover

wykrzyk|iwać (-uję) shout, cry out;
~nąć v/s. call out, exclaim; ~nik m
(-a; -i) print. exclamation mark; gr. in-
terjection

wykrzywi|ać (-am) ⟨~ć⟩ contort, distort; bend; *usta* screw out; **z twarzą ~oną bólem** with the face twisted with pain

wykształceni|e n (-a; 0) education; (**zawodowe** vocational) training; **wyższe ~e** higher education; **z ~a** ... ... by profession

wykształcony educated

wyku|ć pf. → **wykuwać**; ~**pywać** (-uję) ⟨~**pić**⟩ buy up; *zastaw, jeńca* redeem; *zastaw itp.* buy back; ~**rzać** (-am) ⟨~**rzyć**⟩ smoke out

wykusz m (-a; -e) bay window

wykuwać (-am) forge; *posąg* carve, chisel; F (*w szkole*) cram

wykwalifikowany qualified, skilled

wykwintny elegant

wyla|ć pf. → **wylewać**; ~**nie** n F (*z pracy*) boot; throw-out; ~**tywać** (-uję) *samolot, ptak:* fly off; *samolot kursowy:* leave; (*jako pasażer*) leave (by plane); F (*z pracy*) get the boot; *dym itp.:* go up; → **wyskakiwać, wylecieć, wypadać**

wylądować pf. *aviat.* touch down; *astr.* (*na morzu*) splash down; (*na księżycu*) land

wyle|cieć pf. → **wylatywać**; ~**cieć w powietrze** blow up; ~**czyć** pf. cure; heal; ~**czyć się** recover (**z G** from); ~**giwać się** (-uję) lie around; loll; (*w łóżku*) lie in; ~**w** m (-u; -y) (*rzeki*) flood, overflow; *med.* h(a)emorrhage; ~**w krwi do mózgu** apoplexy, stroke; ~**wać** (-am) *v/t.* pour out; F *kogoś z pracy* give the boot; *v/i. rzeka:* overflow; ~**wać się** spill; ~**źć** pf. → **wyłazić**

wylęga|ć się (-am) → **lęgnąć się**; ~**nie** n (-a; 0) incubation; hatching; ~**rnia** f (-i; -e) *agr.* hatchery; *fig.* hotbed

wylęk|ły, ~niony frightened, scared

wylicz|ać (-am) ⟨~**yć**⟩ enumerate, list; (*obliczyć*) calculate, count; *sport.* count out; ~**yć się** (**z G**) account (for)

wylosow(yw)ać (-[w]uję) draw out

wylot m (-u; -y) (*otwór*) outlet, vent; (*rury*) nozzle; (*lufy*) muzzle; (*ulicy itp.*) end, exit; (*odlot*) departure; **na ~** through and through

wyludniony desolate, depopulated

wyład|ow(yw)ać (-[w]uję) unload; *naut.* land; *fig. złość* vent (**na L** on); ~**ow(yw)ać się** *electr.* run down; *fig.* take it out (**na L** on); ~**owanie** n (-a;

G -*ań*) *electr.* discharge; ~**unek** m (-*nku*; -*nki*) unloading

wyłam|ywać (-uję) ⟨~**ać**⟩ break (**się** *v/i.*); *zamek* force; ~**ywać** ⟨~**ać**⟩ **się** (**z G**) *fig.* break away (from)

wyłani|ać (-am) *komisję* form; ~ **się** emerge, appear

wyłazić (-żę) (**z G**) climb out (of), get out (of)

wyłącz|ać (-am) switch off, turn off (**się** *v/i.*); (*pomijać*) exclude; *tech.* disengage, disconnect; ~**ać się** go off; ~**enie** n (-a; *G* -*eń*) switching off; (*pominięcie*) exclusion; ~**nie** *adv.* exclusively; ~**nik** m (-a; -i) switch; ~**ny** exclusive, sole

wyłogi *m/pl.* (-ów) lapels *pl.*

wyło|m m (-u; -y) breach, break; ~**nić** pf. (-ę) → **wyłaniać**; ~**żyć** pf. → **wykładać**; ~**żyć się** (**na L**) trip up (on, over)

wyłudz|ać (-am) ⟨~**ić**⟩ swindle (**coś od k-o** s.o. out of s.th.)

wyłusk|iwać (-uję) ⟨~**ać**⟩ → **łuskać**

wyłuszcz|ać (-am) ⟨~**yć**⟩ → **łuszczyć**; *fig.* explain, set forth

wyłysiały bald

wymaga|ć (-am) (**G**) require; (*potrzebować też*) need, necessitate; ~**jący** *adj. szef* demanding, exacting; ~**nie** n (-a; *G* -*ań*) *zw. pl.* demands *pl.*, requirements *pl.*; ~**ny** required, needed

wymar|cie n (-a; 0): **być na ~ciu** be threatened with extinction; ~**ły** extinct

wymarsz m (-u; -e) departure, marching off

wymarzony ideal

wymawiać *słowa* pronounce; *umowę* terminate; ~ **sobie** reproach o.s.; ~ **się** be pronounced; → **wykręcać się, wytykać**

wymaz|ywać (-uję) ⟨~**ać**⟩ (*farbą*) smear, daub; (*usuwać*) rub out

wymeldow(yw)ać się (-[w]uję) report moving away (**się** *v/i.*); (*w hotelu*) check out (**się** *v/i.*)

wymian|a f (-y; *G* -) exchange (*też waluty*); (*kogoś, rury*) replacement; → **wymieniać**

wymiar m (-u; -y) dimension (*też math., phys.*); size; ~ **kary** sentence; ~ **sprawiedliwości** administration of justice; ~**podatku** assessment; ~ **godzin** teaching load

wy|miatać (-am) sweep out; ~**mie-**

ni(a)ć (-am) exchange; część itp. replace; pieniądze change; (wspominać) mention, name; ~mienialny waluta convertible; ~mieniony mentioned, named; ~mienny replaceable; interchangeable

wymie|rać (-am) die out; ~rny measurable; math. rational; ~rzać (-am) ⟨~rzyć⟩ measure; karę (D) mete out (to); podatek assess; sprawiedliwość administer; (skierować) direct, aim (przeciwko D at); → mierzyć; ~ść pf. → wymiatać

wymię n (-ienia; -iona) udder

wymi|jać (-am) ⟨~nąć⟩ pass, go past; ~jać się meet and pass, cross; → (o)mijać; ~jająco adv. evasively; ~jający evasive

wymiot|ować (-uję) ⟨z-⟩ vomit; ~y pl. (-ów) vomiting

wymknąć się pf. → wymykać się

wymogi m/pl. (-ogów) requirements pl.

wymontow(yw)ać (-[w]uję) remove, dismount

wymow|a f (-y; 0) pronunciation; ~ny eloquent, outspoken

wymóc pf. (na L) wrest (from), extort (from)

wymów|ić pf. → wymawiać; ~ienie n (-a) → wymawianie; ~ka f (-i; G -wek) excuse; (wyrzut) reproach

wymrzeć pf. → wymierać

wymu|szać (-am) ⟨~sić⟩ (-szę) (z G) force (from, out of), extract (from); (na L) extort (from); ~szenie n (-a; G -eń) extortion; extraction; ~szony fig. half-hearted

wymykać się (-am) slip away; fig. slip out

wymy|sł m (-u; -y) invention; (przekleństwa) zw. pl. insults pl; ~słać ⟨~ślić⟩ (-lę) invent, make up; t-ko impf. (D) insult; ~ślny intricate, fancy

wynagr|adzać (-am) ⟨~odzić⟩ (-ę) reward, award; krzywdy itp. compensate, recompense

wynagrodzenie n (-a; G -eń) payment, pay; compensation

wyna|jąć pf. → (wy)najmować; ~jdywać (-uję) find; → wynaleźć; ~jem m (-jmu; 0), ~jęcie renting; ~jem samochodu car rental lub Brt. hire; biuro ~jmu samochodów car rental lub Brt. hire car rental (firm); ~jmować

(-uję) rent, hire; mieszkanie let; (oddać w najem) rent out, let out; ~lazca m (-y; G -ców) inventor; ~lazek m (-zku;-zki) invention; ~leźć invent; → wyszukać

wynaturzenie n (-a; G -eń) degeneration

wynegocjować pf. (-uję) negotiate

wynieść pf. → wynosić

wynik m (-u; -i) result (też med.); finding; (w sporcie) score; ~i pl. też achievements pl.; w ~u (G) as a result (of); ~ać (-am) ⟨~nąć⟩ (z G) result (from); zw. impf. follow, ensue

wynio|sły haughty, proud; ~śle adv. haughtily, proudly

wyniszcz|ać (-am) ⟨~yć⟩ destroy; kogoś emaciate, weaken

wynos: na ~ Brt. take-away, Am. take-out; ~ić take lub carry away (z G from); carry up (na A to); sumę, ilość amount to; ~ić się F leave; (z dumą) turn one's nose up; wynoś się! get away!

wynurz|ać (-am) ⟨~yć⟩ put lub stick out (z wody of the water); ~yć się emerge, appear

wyobcowany alienated (z G from)

wyobra|źnia f (-i; 0) imagination; ~żać ⟨~zić⟩ represent; ~żać sobie imagine; ~ź sobie(, że) just imagine (that); ~żenie n (-a; G -eń) idea, notion; representation, picture

wyodrębni|ać (-am) ⟨~ć⟩ (-ę, -nij!) isolate, detach (się o.s.); ~(a)ć się (I) differ (from), stand out (from)

wyolbrzymi|ać (-am)⟨~ć⟩(-ę) exaggerate, overestimate

wypacz|ać (-am) ⟨~yć⟩ fig. distort

wypad m (-u; -y) trip; (w szermierce) lunge; (w piłce nożnej) attack; mil. foray; ~ać fall out; (wybiec) rush out; fall (w niedzielę on Sunday); do, turn out (dobrze, źle well, badly); (nagle zaistnieć) pop up; ~a(ło) it is (was) proper, it is (was) in order; (nie) ~a one should not, it is not fitting; fig. ~ać na kogoś be s.o.'s turn; ~ać z pamięci escape s.o.'s mind; ~ek m (-dku; -dki) event, case; (drogowy, przy pracy, road, industrial) accident; na ~ek (G) in case (of); w najlepszym ~ku at best; w żadnym ~ku in no case, on no account; ~kowy accident

wypal|ać (-am) ⟨~ić⟩ burn out; cegły itp. fire; ~ić się burn out

wypuszczać

wypa|row(yw)ać (-[w]uję) evaporate; *fig.* vanish ~siony well-fed; ~ść *pf.* → **wypadać**; ~trywać (-uję) (*G*) look out (for); ~trzyć *pf.* catch sight of; *fig.* spot

wypch|ać, ~nąć *pf.* → **wypychać**

wypeł|niać (-am) ⟨~nić⟩ → **spełniać**; fill (**się** *v/i.*); *blankiet* fill in, complete; *zadanie* carry out; ~niony full; *formularz* completed; ~zać ⟨~znąć⟩ (**z** *G*) crawl out (of)

wypędz|ać (-am) ⟨~ić⟩ drive (**na pastwisko** to the pasture); drive out; (*z kraju itp.*) expel; ~ony expelled

wypi|ąć *pf.* → **wypinać**; ~ć *pf.* → **wypijać**

wypiek *m* (-u; -i) baking; (*pieczywo*) baked product; ~i *pl.* flush, blush; ~ać (-am) → **piec²**

wypierać (-am) *konkurenta* oust; (*z miejsca*) dislodge; *phys.* displace; ~ **się** (*G*) deny; *kogoś* disown

wypi|jać (-am) drink up; ~nać (-am) push out; *tyłek itp.* stick out

wypis *m* (-u; -y) extract; ~y *pl.* anthology; ~ywać (-uję) ⟨~ać⟩ *czek, receptę* write *lub* make out; take notes (**sobie** for o.s.); (*ze szkoły itp.*) strike off the list; (*ze szpitala*) discharge; ~ać **się** (**z** *G*) withdraw (from); *pióro itp.*: run out

wypitka *f* (-i; *G* -tek) drink

wypląt|ywać (-uję) ⟨~ać⟩ disentangle (**się** *v/i.*); ~ywać ⟨~ać⟩ **się** *fig.* free o.s. (**z** *G* from)

wypleni|ać (-am) ⟨~ć⟩ eradicate

wyplu|wać (-am) ⟨~(ną)ć⟩ spit out

wypła|cać (-am) ⟨~cić⟩ pay; ~calny solvent; ~szać *pf.* → **płoszyć**; ~ta *f* (-y; *G* -) payment, pay; **dzień** ~**ty** payday

wypłoszyć *pf.* → **płoszyć**

wypłowiały faded

wypłuk|iwać (-uję) ⟨~ać⟩ wash out *lub* away

wypły|wać ⟨~nąć⟩ swim out; (*łódką*) sail out; *płyn*: flow out; → **wynurzać się, wynikać**

wypocz|ąć *pf.* → **wypoczywać**; ~ęty rested; ~ynek *m* (-nku; -nki) rest; ~ynkowy holiday; **meble** *pl.* ~ynkowe suite; ~ywać (-am) rest (**po** *L* after)

wypo|gadzać się (-am) ⟨~godzić się⟩ clear up, brighten up; ~minać (-am) ⟨~mnieć⟩ (-nę, -nij!) reproach (**k-u** *A* s.o. for); ~mpow(yw)ać (-[w]uję) pump out

wyporność *f* (-ści; 0) *naut.* draught

wyposaż|ać (-am) ⟨~yć⟩ (-ę) fit (**w** *A* with); equip; ~enie *n* (-a; *G* -eń) furnishing *pl.*; (*urządzenia*) fittings *pl.*; equipment

wypowi|adać (-am) utter; *pracę, mieszkanie* give notice; *wojnę* declare; *posłuszeństwo* renounce; ~**adać się** (**za** *I*, **przeciwko** *D*) declare *lub* pronounce o.s. (for, against); ~edzenie *n* (-a; *G* -eń) utterance; notice; declaration; ~edzieć *pf.* → **wypowiadać**; ~edź *f* (-dzi) statement; utterance

wypoży|czalnia *f* (-i; -e) (*sprzętu itp.*) hire firm; (*książek, płyt*) (lending) library; ~yć *pf.* *komuś* lend, *od kogoś* borrow; → **pożyczać**

wypracow|anie *n* (-a; *G* -ań) essay, composition; ~(yw)ać (-[w]uję) work-out, develop

wypra|ć *pf.* → **prać**; ~szać (-am) beg for; *natręta* show the door

wyprawa *f* (-y; *G* -) expedition; ~ **krzyżowa** crusade; (*ślubna*) trousseau; → **wycieczka**

wypraw|iać (-am) ⟨~ić⟩ send (**do** *G*, **na** *A* to; **po** *A* for); (*robić*) do; *wesele* make; *skóry* dress; ~ka *f* (-i; *G* -wek) layette

wypręż|ać (-am) ⟨~yć⟩ (-ę) stretch (**się** *v/i.*); tense; ~ony tight, taut

wypro|sić *pf.* → **wypraszać**; ~stowywać (-wuję) → **prostować**

wyprowadz|ać (-am) ⟨~ić⟩ lead out; *auto itp.* drive out; *fig. wniosek* draw; *math. wzór* derive; *psa* walk, take out; ~ić **z równowagi** unnerve; ~ić **się** move out

wy|próbowany tested; ~próbow(yw)ać (-[w]uję) test, try out; ~próżni(a)ć → **opróżniać**; ~prysk *m* (-u; -i) *med.* eczema; ~prysnąć *pf.* dash; ~prząc *pf.* → **wyprzęgać**; ~przeć *pf.* → **wypierać**

wyprzedany sold out

wyprzeda|wać (-ję) ⟨~ć⟩ (-am) sell off, clear; ~ż *f* (-y; -e) sale(s *pl.*)

wyprzedz|ać (-am) ⟨~ić⟩ (-dzę) *mot. Brt.* overtake, *Am.* pass; *math.* ~ać **epokę** *fig.* be ahead of one's times

wyprzęgać (-am) unharness

wypukł|ość *f* (-ści; 0) bulge; *tech.* convexity; ~o *adv.* convexly; ~y convex

wypu|szczać (-am) ⟨~ścić⟩ set free; *film, więźnia,* release; (*upuszczać*)

drop, let drop; *znaczek itp.* issue; *econ.*
put on the market; *tech.* discharge
wypychać *(-am)* pack (up), fill (up);
zwierzę stuff
wypyt|ywać *(-uję)* ⟨**~ać**⟩ question
wyrabiać *(-am)* make, produce; *sąd*
form; *paszport* obtain; *język itp.* develop; **~ się** develop, evolve
wyrachowan|ie *n (-a; 0)* deliberation,
calculation; **~y** calculating, mercenary
wyra|dzać się *(-am)* degenerate; **~fi-
nowany** sophisticated; **~stać** *(-am)*
grow; → **rosnąć**
wyraz *m (-u; -y)* expression; *(słowo)*
word; **dać ~** *(D)* voice; *bez* **~u** expres-
sionless, bland; *nad* **~** decidedly; *z* **~ami
szacunku** yours faithfully; **~ić** *pf.* →
wyrażać; **~isty** expressive; distinct;
~iście *adv.* expressively; distinct
wyra|źny distinct; clear; **~żać** *(-am)* ex-
press **(się** o.s.); **~żać się** też be ex-
pressed **(w** *L* by); **~żenie** *n (-a)* expression; **~żenie zgody** consent, approval
wy|rąbywać *(-uję)* ⟨**~rąbać**⟩ *drzewa*
fell; *polanę* clear (of trees); *otwór* hack;
~re- *pf.* → **re-**
wyręcz|ać *(-am)* ⟨**~yć**⟩ *(kogoś w* *L)*
stand in (for s.o. in); **(on) w tych spra-
wach ~a się synem** these things are
done by his son
wyrob|ić *(-ę) pf.* → **wyrabiać**; **~ienie** *n*
(-a; 0) skill; expertness; **~ienie życio-
we** experience of life; **~y** *pl.* → **wyrób**
wyrocznia *f (-i; G -e)* oracle
wyro|dek *m (-dka, -dki)* monster;
~dnieć ⟨**z-**⟩ *-eję)* degenerate; **~dny**
prodigal, profligate; **~dna matka** un-
caring mother; **~dzić się** *pf.* → **wyra-
dzać się**
wyrok *m (-u; -i)* jur. judg(e)ment, sentence, verdict; **~ skazujący** conviction;
~ować ⟨za-⟩ *-uję)* decide
wyros|nąć *pf.* → **wyrastać**; **~t: na ~t** a
size larger; **~tek** *m (-tka, -tki)* adoles-
cent, teenager; *anat.* **~tek robaczkowy** (vermiform) appendix
wyrozumia|le *adv.* forbearingly; under-
standingly; **~ły** forbearing; under-
standing
wyrób *m (-robu; -roby)* production,
manufacture; **wyroby** *pl. econ.* goods
pl., products *pl.*
wyrówn|ać *pf.* → **wyrównywać**; **~anie**
n (-a; G -ań) evening out; *(płaca)* ad-

ditional payment; *(zadośćuczynienie)*
compensation; *(w sporcie)* equalizer;
~any balanced; *pogoda* equable; **~aw-
czy** compensation; **~ywać** *(-uję)* wyni-
ki bring into line; *wynik, powierzchnię*
level; *dług* settle; *zaległości* make up
for; *(w sporcie)* level, equalize; **~ywać
się** balance out; level out; → **równać**
wyróżni|ać *(-am)* ⟨**~ć**⟩ favo(u)r; *(A)*
give preferential treatment (to); *(wy-
odrębniać)* distinguish; **~ać się** distinguish o.s.; **~enie** *n (-a; G -eń)* distinction; award; *z* **~eniem** with merit *lub*
distinction
wyru|gować *(-uję) pf.* drive out, oust;
~szać ⟨**~szyć**⟩ set off, start out; **~szyć
w podróż** set out on a journey
wyrwa *f (-y; G -)* gap; **~ć** *pf.* → **wyrywać**; **~ć się** blurt out *(z czymś* s.th.)
wyrywać *(-am)* snatch; *ząb, korzenie*
pull out; *fig.* **(z** *G)* arouse (from); **~ć
się** blurt out *(z czymś* s.th.); → **wyrwać**;
~kowo *adv.* randomly; **~kowy** random
wyrządz|ać *(-am)* ⟨**~ić**⟩ *szkody* cause;
krzywdę do
wyrze|c *pf.* → **wyrzekać**; **~czenie** *n (-a;
G -eń)* sacrifice; **~czenie się** renunciation; **~kać** *(-am)* complain **(na** *A*
about); **~kać się** *(G)* give up, renounce
wyrznąć *pf.* → **wyrzynać**
wyrzu|cać *(-am)* ⟨**~cić**⟩ throw out *lub*
away; *(z pracy)* F give the boot, fire; **~t**
m (-u; -y) reproach; **~y** *pl.* **sumienia** re-
morses *pl.*; **~tnia** *f (-i; -e)* astr., mil.
launch(ing) pad; launcher
wyrzynać *(-am)* ⟨**~nąć**⟩ cut out **(się**
jemu) **~ją się ząbki** he is teething
wys. *skrót pisany:* **wysokość**
wysadz|ać *(-am)* ⟨**~ić**⟩ blow up; *(z au-
tobusu)* put down; *(z auta)* drop off;
~ić na ląd disembark, put ashore;
~ić w powietrze blow up
wyschnąć *pf.* → **wysychać**
wysepka *f (-pki; G -pek)* → **wyspa**; is-
let; **~ na jezdni** traffic island
wysia|ć *pf.* → **wysiewać**; **~dać** *(wy-
siąść)* get off; disembark
wysiedl|ać *(-am)* ⟨**~ić**⟩ *(-lę)* evacuate
wysiedlenie *n (-a; G -eń)* evacuation;
displacement; **~c** *m (-a; -y)* displaced
person
wy|siewać *(-am)* sow; **~silać** *(-am)*
⟨**~silić**⟩ *oczy itp.* strain; **~silać się** exert o.s.; **~siłek** *m (-łku, -łki)* effort;

~skakiwać ⟨~skoczyć⟩ jump *lub* leap out; ~skok *m* excess; → *wypaść*; ~skokowy alcoholic; ~skrobywać (-uję) ⟨~skrobać⟩ scrape out; ~skubywać (-uję) → *skubać*; ~słać *pf.* → *wysyłać*, **wyściełać**

wysłanni|czka *f* (-*i*; *G* -czek), ~k *m* (-*a*; -*cy*) messenger

wysławiać¹ (-*am*) extol(l)

wysł|awiać² (-*am*) ⟨~owić⟩ (się) express (o.s.) (in words)

wysłuch|iwać (-*uję*) ⟨~ać⟩ (*G*, *A*) listen (to)

wysłu|giwać się (-*uję*) (*D*) *pej.* grovel (to); (*I*) use; ~żyć się *pf.*: ~żył się it has seen service, it has worn out

wy|sma- *pf.* → *sma-*; ~smukły slender

wysnu|wać (-*am*) ⟨~ć⟩ wniosek draw

wyso|ce *adv.* highly; ~ki high; człowiek tall; *electr.* ~kie napięcie high-voltage current; ~ki na 10 m 10 Brt. metres high (Am. meters)

wysoko *adv.* highly; ~gatunkowy high-quality; ~górski alpine

wysoko|ciomierz *m* (-*a*; -*e*) altimeter; ~ciowiec *m* (-*wca*; -*wce*) high-rise; ~ć *f* (-*ści*) height; altitude; (*na poziomem morza*) elevation; na dużej ~ci at a high altitude; o ~ci ... ... high; kwota itp.: w ~ci ... in the amount (of) ...; ~nabierać ~ci gain height

wysoko|wartościowy high-quality; ~wydajny highly efficient; drukarka itp. heavy-duty

wysp|a *f* (-*y*; *G* -) island (*też fig.*), isle; ⁹y Brytyjskie *pl.* British Isles *pl.*; ⁹y Normandzkie *pl.* Channel Islands *pl.*

wyspać się *pf.* get enough sleep

wyspia|rka *f* (-*i*; *G* -rek), ~rz *m* (-*a*; -*e*) islander

wysportowany athletic

wy|ssać *pf.* (-*ę*) → *wysysać*; ~stający protruding, projecting; ~starać się (o *A*) arrange, get

wystarcz|ać (-*am*) ⟨~yć⟩ be sufficient; ~yło ... it was enough ...; ~ająco *adv.* sufficiently; ~ający sufficient

wystaw|a *f* (-*y*; *G* -) exhibition, display, show; (*witryna*) shop-window; ~ać (-*ję*) protrude, jut out, stick out; (*stać*) stand (for a long time); ~ca *m* (-*y*; *G* -ców) exhibitor

wystawi(a)ć put out; obraz, towar display; czek make out; produkty itp. offer

(na *A* for); wartę post; kandydata put up; *theat.* stage; pomnik erect; dom build; (*narażać*) expose; (na *A* to); ~ na próbę test; ~ się (na *A* to) be exposed (to), risk

wystaw|ny sumptuous; ~owy exhibition, display

wystąpi|ć *pf.* → *występować*; ~enie *n* (-*a*; *G* -eń) appearance; presentation; speech

występ *m* (-*u*; -*y*) (muru) projection; *theat. itp.* appearance; ~ek *m* (-*pku*; -*pki*) vice; *jur.* felony; ~ny criminal; punishable; ~ować (-*uję*) come out; (*istnieć*) occur; (*ukazać się*) appear, make an appearance (w, na *L* in, at); act (*jako*); give (z mową a speech; z koncertem a concert); come out (w obronie *G* in support of); be (przeciwko *D* against); put forward (z wnioskiem a proposition); make (z prośbą a request); (*opuścić*) (z *A*) leave; rzeka: burst (z brzegów the banks)

wy|stosować *pf.* address; ~straszyć *pf.* → (prze)straszyć; ~strojony decked out; ~strzał *m* shot

wystrze|gać się (-*am*) (*G*) be wary (of); avoid, shun; ~lać *pf.* shoot dead; amunicję use up; ~lić *pf.* (z *G*) fire; *astr.* launch

wystrzępiony frayed

wystu-, wysty- *pf.* → stu-, sty-

wysu|wać ⟨~nąć⟩ pull out (się *v/i.*); nogę stick out; żądanie make, put forward; (*proponować*) suggest, propose; → **wymykać się**

wyswo|badzać (-*am*) ⟨~bodzić⟩ (-*dzę*, -*bódź*) free (się o.s.)

wysy|chać (-*am*) dry up; ~łać (-*am*) send; ~łka *f* (-*i*; *G* -łek) dispatch; (*czynność*) shipping; ~pać *f* → wysypywać; ~pisko *n* (-*a*; *G* -) (*śmieci* refuse) dump (Brt. tip); ~pka *f* (-*i*; *G* -pek) *med.* rash; ~pywać (-*uję*) tip out; scatter (piaskiem sand); ~pywać się spill; ~sać (-*am*) suck out

wyszarp|ywać (-*uję*) ⟨~ać, ~nąć⟩ → **wydzierać**, **wyrywać**

wyszczególni|ać (-*am*) ⟨~ć⟩ (-*ę*, -*nij!*) list, cite

wyszcze|rbiony jagged; talerz chipped ~rzać *pf.* → **szczerzyć**

wysz|czo-, ~czu-, ~k-, ~l-, ~o- *pf.* → szczo-, szczu-, szk-, szl-, szo-

W

wyszpiegować *pf.* spy out

wyszuka|ć *pf.* find; choose, pick; **~ny** → **wykwintny, wytworny**

wyszukiwarka *f (-i) komp.* search engine

wyszy|ć *pf.* → **wyszywać**; **~dzać** *(-am)* ⟨**~dzić**⟩ mock, deride, ridicule

wyszynk *m (-u; 0)* liquor *Brt.* licence, *Am.* license; **z ~iem** selling liquor

wyszywać *(-am)* sew; *zwł.* embroider

wyście|łać *(-am)*, **~łać** *kurtkę* pad; *meble* upholster

wyścig *m (-u; -i)* race *(też fig.)*; **~ zbrojeń** arms race; **~i** *pl. też* racing; **na ~i** racing one another; *fig.* vying with one another; **~owiec** *m (-wca; -wcy)* racehorse; **~owy** racing, race; **~ówka** *f (-i; G -wek) (rower)* racing bike; *(łyżwa)* speed skate

wyśledzić *pf.* spy out

wyśliz|giwać się *(-uję)* ⟨**~(g)nąć się**⟩ *(-nę)* slip *(z ręki* out of the hand; *z sukienki* out of the dress)

wyś|miać *pf.* → **wyśmiewać**; **~mienicie** *adv.* exquisitely; **~mienity** exquisite; **~piewywać** *(-uję)* sing

wyświadczać *(-am)* ⟨**~yć**⟩ do

wyświechtany well-worn, threadbare

wyświetl|ać *(-am)* ⟨**~ić**⟩ *(-lę) film* show; *sprawę* clear up; *tv. (na ekranie)* display; **~acz** *m (-a; -e) komp.* display

wyświę|cać *(-am)* ⟨**~cić**⟩ *(-ę) rel.* ordain

wyta|czać *pf.* → **(wy)toczyć**; **~rty** threadbare; → **wyświechtany**

wytchnieni|e *n (-a; 0)* rest; respite; **bez ~a** without intermission *lub* rest; **chwila ~a** a breather

wytę|- *pf.* → **tę-; **~pienie** *n (-a; 0)* extermination; eradication; **~żać** *(-am)* ⟨**~żyć**⟩ *(-ę)* strain; **~żać się** exert *o.s.*; **~żony** intense, concentrated

wy|tknąć *pf.* → **wytykać**; **~tłaczać** *(-am)* ⟨**~tłoczyć**⟩ press *lub* squeeze out; → **tłoczyć**

wytłumaczenie *n (-a; G -eń)* explanation

wy|tnę, ~tnie(sz) → **wycinać**; **~toczyć** *pf. proces* institute; → **toczyć**; **~topić** *pf.* → **wytapiać**; **~tra-** *pf.* → **tra-**; **~trawny** *podróżnik* seasoned; *wino* dry; **~trącać** *(-am)* ⟨**~trącić**⟩ knock out *(z ręki* of the hand); wake *(ze snu s.o.* from the sleep); **~trącić z równo-**

wagi upset *(też fig.)*; *chem.* precipitate; **~tropić** *pf.* track down

wytrwa|ć *pf.* stand, withstand; persevere *(w swoim zamiarze* in one's intention); **~łość** *f (-ści; 0) (duchowa)* perseverance; *(fizyczna)* stamina; **~le** *adv.* persistently; **~ły** persistent

wytrych *m (-u; -y)* passkey

wytrys|k *m (-u; -i)* jet; *(nasienia)* ejaculation; **~kiwać** *(-uję)* ⟨**~kać, ~nąć**⟩ *(nasieniem)* ejaculate; → **tryskać**

wytrzą|sać *(-am)* ⟨**~snąć, ~ść**⟩ shake out; **~ść się** be shaken

wytrze|ć *pf.* → **wycierać**; **~pywać** *(-uję)* → **trzepać**

wytrzeszcza|ć *(-am)* ⟨**wytrzeszczyć**⟩: **~ oczy** goggle *(na A* at)

wytrzeźwieć *pf.* sober up

wytrzyma|ć *pf.* → **wytrzymywać**; **~łość** *f (-ści; 0)* strength, resistance *(też tech.)*; *(kogoś)* endurance, stamina; *tech.* durability; **~ły** strong; durable; *(na A)* resistant (to); **~nie** *n:* **nie do ~nia** unbearable, unendurable

wytrzymywać *(-uję)* stand, bear, endure; *atak* withstand; *próbę* pass; *kryty-* kę stand up to

wytwarzać *(-am)* produce, manufacture; *fig.* create; **~ się** be formed; be produced

wytwo|rny refined, classy; **~rzyć** *pf.* → **wytwarzać**

wytwór *m (-woru; -wory)* product; **~ca** *m (-y; G -ców)* producer; **~czość** *f (-ści; 0)* production; **~czy** productive; **~nia** *f (-i; -e)* factory; **~nia filmowa** film company; *(miejsce)* film studios *pl.*

wytycz|ać *(-am) trasę* mark out; *fig.* lay down; **~na** *f (-ej; -e)* directive, guideline; **~yć** *pf.* → **wytyczać**

wyty|kać reproach *(komuś coś* s.o. for s.th.); F *głowę* stick out; **~po-** *pf.* → **typo-**

wyucz|ać *(-am)* ⟨**~yć**⟩ *(k-o G)* teach *(s.th.* to s.o.), educate *(s.o.* in s.th.)

wyuzdany unrestrained, unbridled

wywa|biacz *m (-a; -e) (plam* stain) remover; **~biać** *(-am)* ⟨**~bić**⟩ *plamę* remove; **~lać** *(-am)* throw out *(z pracy)* fire; *drzwi* force; **~lczyć** *pf.* win; **~lić** *pf.* → **wywalać**; **~lić się** F fall (down)

wywar *m (-u; -y):* **~ z mięsa** meat stock

wywa|żać *(-am)* ⟨**~yć**⟩ *(-ę) drzwi* force; *wieko* pry open; *tech.* balance; **~ony** balanced

wywąch|iwać (*-uję*) ⟨*~ać*, **wywęszyć**⟩ scent; *fig.* sense

wywiad *m* (*-u*; *-y*) interview; *med.* case history, anamnesis; *mil.*, *pol.* intelligence; *~***owca** *m* (*-y*; *G -ców*) secret agent; (*w policji itp.*) detective; *~***ówka** *f* (*-i*; *G -wek*) parents' meeting; *~***ywać się** (*-uję*) enquire (**o** *A* about)

wywią|zywać się (*-uję*) ⟨*~ać się*⟩ (*z* *G*) result (from), ensue (from); discharge, perform (*z zadań* one's duties)

wy|wichnąć (*-nę*) → **zwichnąć**; *~***wiedzieć się** *pf.* → **wywiadywać się**; *~***wierać** (*-am*) nacisk, wpływ exert; *wrażenie* make; *skutek* produce

wywie|rcać (*-am*) ⟨*~rcić*⟩ bore (out), drill (out); *szkło* ⟨*~sić*⟩ hang out; *~***szka** *f* (*-i*; *G -szek*) sign; notice; *~***ść** *pf.* → **wywodzić**; *~***trzeć** *pf.* → **wietrzeć**; *~***trznik** *m* (*-a*; *-i*) ventilator; *~***źć** *pf.* → **wywozić**

wywij|ać (*-am*) ⟨*~nąć*⟩ (*-nę*) rękaw roll up; (*l*) brandish (with), flourish (with); *~***nąć się** (*z*, *fig.* **od** *G*) evade, wriggle (out of); *~***kłać (się)** (*-am*) *pf.* → **wyplątywać (się)**

wy|wlekać (*-am*) ⟨*~wlec*⟩ pull out; drag out; *fig.* draw up; *~***właszczać** (*-am*) ⟨*~właszczyć*⟩ (*-szczę*) expropriate; *~***wnętrzać się** (*-am*) (*przed l*) pour out one's heart (to); *~***wnio-** *pf.* → **wnioskować**

wywo|dy *pl.* → **wywód**; *~***dzić** (*-dzę*) lead out (*z* *G* of); *fig.* derive (*z* *G* from); set forth; *~***dzić się** (*z* *G*) be descended (from), come (from); *~***łać** *pf.* → **wywoływać**

wywoły|wacz *m* (*-a*; *-e*) *phot.* developer; *~***wać** (*-uję*) call out (**do** *G* to); call (up)on (**do odpowiedzi** for an answer); *uczucie* evoke; *panikę itp.* cause; *dyskusję* provoke; *phot.* develop; → **powodować**

wy|wozić take away; F (*za granicę*) take abroad; (*eksportować*) export; *~***wód** *m* (*-odu*; *-ody*) argument; exposition; deduction; *~***wóz** *m* (*-ozu*; *0*) export; transport; → *~***wózka** *f* (*-i*; *G -zek*) deportation; *~***wracać** (*-am*) knock over; (*do góry nogami*) overturn; *łódź* capsize (**się** *v/i.*); *kieszeń* turn inside out; *~***wracać się** fall down; *coś*: overturn; *~***wrotny** unbalanced; *naut.* crank(y), tender; *~***wrotowy** subversive; **działalność** *~***wrotowa** subversion; *~***wrócić**

pf. → **wywracać**; *~***wróżyć** *pf.* → **wróżyć**; *~***wrzeć** *pf.* (→ *-wrzeć*) → **wywierać**; *~***zbyć się** (*G*) dispose (of), get rid (of); *nawyku* give up

wyzdrowie|ć *pf.* (*-eję*) recover; *~***nie** *n* (*-a*; *G -eń*) recovery

wyziewy *m/pl.* (*-ów*) fumes *pl.*

wyziębi|ać (*-am*) ⟨*~ć*⟩ chill

wyzna|ć *pf.* → **wyznawać**; *~***czać** (*-am*) ⟨*~czyć*⟩ mark; *fig.* (*określać*) name; *cenę* fix; appoint (**kogoś na kierownika** s.o. manager); *~***nie** *n* (*-a*; *G -ań*) confession (*też rel.*); *~***nie miłosne** declaration of love; **wolność** *~***nia** freedom of worship; *~***niowy** confessional; *~***wać** (*-ję*) grzech, winę confess; winę też own up to; *rel. impf.* declare one's faith

wyznaw|ca *m* (*-y*; *G -ców*), *~***czyni** *f* (*-i*; *-e*) believer (**buddyzmu, chrześcijaństwa** of Buddhism, Christianity); worshipper; → **zwolennik** (*-iczka*)

wyzwa|ć *pf.* → **wyzywać**; *~***lacz** *m* (*-a*; *-e*) *phot.* shutter release; *~***lać** (*-am*) free (**się** o.s.; **od, z** *G* from, of), kraj itp. liberate; *energię* release; *~***lać się** też release o.s.; *~***nie** *n* (*-a*; *G -ań*) challenge

wyzwisko *n* (*-a*; *G -*) insult, abuse

wyzwol|enie *n* (*-a*; *G -eń*) liberation; *~***eńczy** liberating; *~***ić** *pf.* (*-lę*, *-wól!*) → **wyzwalać**

wyzysk *m* (*-u*; *0*) exploitation; *~*(iw)ać exploit

wyzywa|ć (*-am*) challenge (**na** *A*, **do** *G* to); F abuse, insult; *~***jąco** *adv.* provocatively *~***jący** provocative

wyż *m* (*-u*; *-e*) *meteor.* high (pressure); *~* **demograficzny** population boom

wy|żąć *pf.* (*-żmę/-żnę*) → **wyżymać**, **wyżynać** (*-żrać*) *~***żebrać** *pf.* get by begging; *~***żej** *adv.* (*comp. od* → **wysoki**) higher

wy|żerać (*-am*) wszystko eat up; dziurę itp. eat away; *~***żłabiać** *pf.* → **żłobić**; *~***żłobienie** *n* (*-a*; *G -eń*) groove; *~***żowy** *meteor.* high-pressure *~***żreć** *pf.* → **wyżerać**

wyższ|ość *f* (*-ści*; *0*) superiority; **z** *~***ością** in a patronizing manner, condescendingly; *~***y** *adj.* (*comp. od* → **wysoki**) higher; **siła** *~***a** *act* of God

wyży|ć *pf.* survive; (**na** *L*) live (on); *~***mać** (*-am*) wring; *~***na** *f* (*-y*) plateau; *~***ny** *pl.* uplands *pl.*; *fig.* height; *~***nać** *pf.* → *~***żąć**; *~***nny** highland

wyżywi|ać (-am) ⟨~ć⟩ feed; *rodzinę* keep

wyżywienie (-a; 0) food; *całodzienne ~* full board; *pokój z ~m* board and lodging

wz. *skrót pisany:* **w zastępstwie** pp. (*by delegation to*)

wzajemn|ie *adv.* mutually, reciprocally; each other; (*dziękując*) the same to you; ~ość *f* (-ści; 0) mutuality; *miłość bez ~ości* unrequited love; ~y mutual, reciprocal

wzbi|erać (-am) swell up; *rzeka:* rise; ~jać się (-am) ⟨~ć się⟩ climb; rise

wzbogac|ać (-am) ⟨~ić⟩ enrich; ~ać ⟨~ić⟩ się get rich; ~enie n (-a; G -eń) enrichment

wzbr|aniać (-am) ⟨~onić⟩ prohibit, forbid; ~aniać się (*przed I*) shrink (from)

wzbudz|ać (-am) ⟨~ić⟩ *uczucie* wake, arouse; *tech.* induce; → **wywoływać**; ~enie n (-a; 0) excitement; *tech.* induction

wzburz|ać (-am) ⟨~yć⟩ annoy, irritate; ~ać ⟨~yć⟩ się get annoyed; → **burzyć**; ~enie n (-a; G -eń) annoyance, irritation; ~ony annoyed; *morze* choppy

wzdąć *pf.* → **wzdymać**

wzdęcie n (-a) *med.* flatulence

wzdłuż 1. *prp.* (G) along; 2. *adv.* lengthways; ~ *i wszerz* all over

wzdryg|ać się (-am) ⟨~nąć się⟩ (-nę) shudder, start

wzdy|chać (-am) sigh; ~mać (-am) distend; *policzki* puff out; *żagiel* billow (*się v/i.*)

wzejść (-jść) *pf.* → **wschodzić**

wzgard|a f (-y; 0) disdain, contempt; ~liwie *adv.* disdainfully; ~liwy disdainful

wzgardzić *pf.* (I) spurn

wzgl. *skrót pisany:* **względnie** or

wzgl|ąd m (-lędu; -lędy) respect; consideration; *mieć na ~ędzie* take into consideration; *ze ~ędu (na A)* in view (of); *pod tym ~ędem* in this respect; ~ędy pl. favo(u)rs pl.; grounds pl., reasons pl.; → **względem**

względ|em *prp.* (G) in relation (to); ~em siebie to one another; ~nie *adv.* relatively; or; ~ny relative

wzgórek m (-rka; -rki) hill, hillock

wziąć *pf.* → **brać**

wzię|cie n (-a; 0) taking; popularity;

~cie do niewoli capture; *do ~cia* to be taken; ~ty popular, in demand

wzlatywać (-uję) ⟨wzlecieć⟩ fly up, soar (*też fig.*)

wzma|cniacz m (-a; -e) *tech.* amplifier; ~cniać (-am) strengthen; *tech.* amplify; ~cniać się get stronger; ~gać (-am) intensify, strengthen, increase (*się v/i.*)

wzmianka f (-i; G -nek) mention (*o L* of)

wzmo|cnić *pf.* → **wzmacniać**; ~cnienie n (-a; G -eń) strengthening, intensification; *tech.* increase; ~żony increased

wzmóc (się) *pf.* → **wzmagać (się)**

wznak m: *na ~* on one's back, supine

wznawiać (-am) *pracę* renew; *książkę* republish; *sztukę* revive; *film* rerun

wznie|cać (-am) ⟨~cić⟩ (-cę) *fig.* provoke, start, incite; ~sienie n (-a; G -eń) hill; ~ść *pf.* → **wznosić**

wzniosły lofty; ~śle *adv.* loftily

wzno|sić raise; *toast* propose; *dom, pomnik* build, erect; ~sić się rise; ~wić *pf.* → **wznawiać**; ~wienie n (-a; G -eń) renewal; *theat.* revival; *print.* new impression

wzor|cowy model; ~ować się (-uję) (*na L*) model (on); copy (after); ~owo *adv.* perfectly; exemplarily; in a model manner; ~owy exemplary; perfect; model; ~y pl. → **wzór**

wzorz|ec m (-rca; -rce) model; pattern; ~ysty colo(u)red, colo(u)rful

wzór m (-oru; -ory) model; pattern; (*na tapecie*) design; *math.*, *chem.* formula

wzrastać (-am) grow, increase

wzrok m (-u; 0) sight; eye(s pl.), look; ~owo *adv.* visually; ~owy visual; *anat.* optic

wzros|nąć *pf.* → **wzrastać**; ~t m (-u; -y) (*rośliny itp.*) growth; (*człowieka*) height; *fig.* increase; *wysokiego ~tu* tall; *mieć ... ~tu* be ... tall

wzróść *pf.* → **wzrastać**

wzrusz|ać (-am) ⟨~yć⟩ *fig.* move, stir, touch; ~ająco *adv.* movingly, touchingly; ~ający moving, touching; ~enie n (-a; G -eń) *fig.* emotion; ~ony moved, touched

wzwód m (-wodu; -wody) *anat.* erection

wzwyż *adv.* up(wards); *sport:* **skok ~** high-jump

wzywać (-am) (*do G*) call; *jur.* summon; (*kogoś do G*) call (on s.o. to *bezok.*)

Z

z 1. *prp.* (*G*) from; of; at; out of; (*I*) with; of; **~ domu** from home; (*o nazwisku panieńskim*) née; **każdy ~ nas** each of us; **~e srebra** of silver; **drżeć ~ zimna** shake with cold; **~ ciekawości** out of curiosity; **~e śmiechem** with laughter; **cieszyć się ~ prezentu** be pleased with the present; **razem ~ nami** with us; **~ początkiem roku** at the beginning of the year; **dobry ~** good at; **~ nazwiska** by name; *często nie tłumaczy się:* **~e śpiewem** singing; **~ nagła** suddenly; **zegar ~ kukułką** cuckoo clock; **2.** *adv.* about, around, approximately; **~ pięć** around five

z. *skrót pisany:* **zobacz** see

za 1. *prp.* (*A*) *miejsce, następowanie:* behind, after; *cel:* for; with; *czas:* in; by; *funkcja:* as; (*I*) *miejsce:* behind, at; **~ drzewo/drzewem** behind the tree; **walczyć ~ wolność** fight for freedom; **~ rok** in a year; **trzymać ~ rękę** hold by the hand; **~ stołem** at the table; **jeden ~ drugim** one behind *lub* after the other; **~ rogiem** round the corner; **~ gotówkę** for cash; **~ pomocą** with the help; **~ panowania Stuartów** under the Stuarts; **~ moich czasów** in my day; **przebrać się ~ ...** dress as ...; **służyć ~ ...** serve as ...; **mieć ~ ...** consider to be ..., regard as ...; **2.** *adv.* (+ *adv.*, *adj.*) too; **~ ciężki** too heavy; **~ dużo** too much; **~ co**

za|a- *pf.* → **a-**; **~aferowany** preoccupied, absorbed; **~awansowany** advanced; **~ba-** *pf.* → **ba-**; **~barwienie** *n* (*-a; G -eń*) coloration; *fig.* slant

zabawa *f* (*-y; G -*) play; festival; party; **~a taneczna** dance; **przyjemnej/wesołej ~y!** enjoy yourself (-selves *pl.*); **dla ~y** for fun; **~iać** (*-am*) → **bawić**; **~ka** *f* (*-i; G -wek*) toy; *fig.* plaything; **~ny** funny, amusing

zabe- *pf.* → **be-**

zabezpiecz|ać (*-am*) **~yć** (*-ę*) protect, safeguard (**się** o.s.; **od** *G* against); (*łańcuchem itp., jur.*) secure (**od** *G,* **przed** *I* against); **~enie** *n* (*-a; G -eń*) protection; *econ.* security, cover; **~enie**

---

na starość provision for one's old age; **~ony** protected

zabi|cie *n* (*-a; 0*) killing; **~ć** *pf.* → **zabijać**

zabie|c *pf.* → **zabiegać**; **~g** *m* (*-u; -i*) *med.* procedure, operation; **~gi** *pl.* endeavo(u)rs *pl.*, attempts *pl.*; **~gać** ⟨**~c**⟩: **~gać drogę** block the way; *t-ko impf.* (**o** *A*) strive for, solicit; → **starać się**; **~gany** F busy

zabierać (*-am*) take, bring; (**z** *I*) take (with); *czas* take; (*na kolację*) take out; (*samochodem*) pick up; **~ głos** take the floor; **~ się** get away; (**do** *G*) get down (to), be about (to); F (**z** *I, z* **z** *I*) come (with)

zabi|jać (*-am*) kill (**się** o.s.; *też fig. czas*); *bydło* slaughter; (*gwoździami*) nail up; → **wbijać**; F **~jać się** work o.s. to death

zabliźni|ać (*-am*) ⟨**~ć się**⟩ (*-ę, -nij!*) (form a) scar, *med.* cicatrize

zabłą|dzić (*-ę*) *pf.*, **~kać się** *pf.* lose one's way, get lost

zabłocony F soiled; *por.* **błocić**

zabobon *m* (*-u; -y*) superstition; **~ny** superstitious

zabor|ca *m* (*-y; G -ców*) occupant, partitioning country; **~czo** *adv.* possessively; **~czy** possessive

zabój|ca *m* (*-y; G -ców*), **~czyni** *f* (*-i; -e*) killer; **~czo** *adv.* fatally; *fig.* irresistibly; **~czy** lethal, deadly; fatal; *uśmiech itp.* irresistible; **~stwo** *n* (*-a; G -*) killing

zabór *m* (*-boru; -bory*) (*mienia itp.*) seizure; *hist.* partition, annexation

zabra|ć *pf.* → **zabierać**; **~knąć** *pf.* → **brakować¹**; **~kło nam pieniędzy** we are short of money; **~niać** (*-am*) (*G*) prohibit, forbid; **~nia się ...** it is prohibited to (*bezok.*), ... is not allowed

zabroni|ć *pf.* → **zabraniać**, **bronić**; **~ony** forbidden, prohibited

za|brudzony dirty; **~bryzgać** *pf.* splash

zabudow|a *f* (*-y; G -dów*) development; buildings *pl.*; **~ania** *pl.* buildings *pl.*; **~(yw)ać** (*-[w]uję*) build up; develop

zaburz|ać (*-am*) disturb; **~enie** *n* (*-a; G -eń*) disturbance

zabyt|ek *m* (*-tku; -tki*) (*architektonicz-*

ny) historic monument; (*przedmiot*) period piece; ~kowy historic; period

zace- *pf.* → ce-

zach. *skrót pisany*: zachód W (*west*); zachodni W (*western*)

za|chcianka *f* (*-i*; *G* -*nek*) whim, caprice; → chętka; ~chęcać (*-am*) ⟨~chęcić⟩ (*-cę*) (do *G*) encourage (to); ~chęta *f* (*-y*; *G* -) incentive, encouragement; ~chlany F blind drunk; ~chłanność *f* (*-ści*; *0*) greed(iness); ~chłanny greedy; ~chłysnąć się (*-nę*) choke

zachmurz|ać się (*-am*) → chmurzyć się; ~enie *n* (*-a*; *0*) cloud; ~ony cloudy, overcast; *fig.* gloomy, dismal

zachodni western, west

zachodnioeuropejski West European

zachodzić *v/i.* reach ([aż] do as far as); (*wstępować*) drop in (do *G* on); *słońce*: set; *okoliczności*: arise; *pomyłka*: occur; *wypadek*: take place, happen; *zmiany*: take place; *oczy*: fill (łzami with tears); ~ parą mist *lub* steam up; → ciąża, głowa

zacho|rować *pf.* fall ill; be taken ill (na *A* with); ~wać *pf.* → zachowywać; ~wanie *n* (*-a*; *G* -*ań*) behavio(u)r, conduct; *phys.* conservation; keeping; ~wywać (*-wuję*) keep, retain; *dietę* keep to; *zwyczaj, miarę* preserve; *ostrożność* exercise; *pozory* keep up; ~wać przy sobie keep to o.s.; ~wywać się behave; (*trwać*) survive; act

zachód *m* (*-chodu*; *0*) west; na ~ to the west; na ~ od west of; ~ słońca sunset; F (*pl.* -*ody*) → fatyga, trud

za|chrypły, ~chrypnięty husky, hoarse; ~chwalać (*-am*) praise; ~chwaszczony weedy; ~chwiać (*I*) sway, upset; *fig.* shake

zachwy|cać (*-am*) ⟨~cić⟩ delight; ~cać się (*I*) go into raptures (over); ~cająco *adv.* delightfully; ~cający delightful; ~cenie *n* (*-a*; *G* -*eń*) → zachwyt; w ~ceniu in rapture, enraptured; ~t *m* (*-u*; -*y*) delight, fascination

zaciąć *pf.* → zacinać

zaciąg *m* (*-u*; -*i*) recruitment; ~ać (*-am*) ⟨~nąć⟩ drag, haul (do *G* to); *zasłonę* draw; *pas* pull tight; *pożyczkę* raise, take out; (*mówiąc*) drawl; ~ać ⟨~nąć⟩ się papierosem take a drag; (*do wojska itp.*) get enlisted (do *G* to); *niebo*: overcast

zacie|c *pf.* → zaciekać; ~k *m* (*-u*; -*i*) water stain; ~kać (*-am*) leak through; (*o deszczu*) come in

zaciekawi|ać *pf.* → ciekawić; ~enie *n* (*-a*; *0*) curiosity

zaciek|le *adv.* ferociously; fiercely; ~ły ferocious; fierce

zacie|knąć *pf.* → zaciekać; ~mniać (*-am*) ⟨~mnić⟩ (*-ę*, -*nij!*) arken, black out

zacier *m* (*-u*; -*y*) mash; ~ać (*-am*) smudge; *ślady, też fig.* cover up; *ręce* rub; ~ać się *pamięć*: fade away; *tech.* seize up; ~ki *pl.* (*-rek*) type of noodles

zacieśni|ać (*-am*) ⟨~ć⟩ (*-ę*, -*nij!*) *fig.* tighten (się *v/i.*)

zacietrzewi|ać się (*-am*) ⟨~ć się⟩ (*-ę*) get worked up

zacięcie[1] *n* (*-a*; *G* -*ęć*) cut; *fig.* verve; (*w drewnie*) notch

zacię|cie[2] *adv.* determinedly; doggedly; ~ty determined; dogged

zacinać (*-am*) *v/t.* cut; *drewno* notch; *zęby* clench together; *v/i. deszcz*: lash; ~ się cut o.s.; *tech.* jam; → jąkać się

zacis|k *m* (*-u*; -*i*) clamp; clip; *electr.* terminal; ~kać ⟨~nąć⟩ press; clench; *pętlę* pull tight; ~kać się get tight; ~nąć pasa tighten one's belt

zacisz|e *n* (*-a*; *G* -*szy*) privacy; retreat; ~ny secluded

zacny good

zacofan|ie *n* (*-a*; *0*) backwardness; ~y backward, old-fashioned

zaczadzieć *pf.* (*-eję*) get poisoned with carbon monoxide

zacza|jać się (*-am*) ⟨~ić się⟩ lie in wait; ~rowany bewitched; magic

zacząć *pf.* (*-nę*) → zaczynać

zacze|kać *pf.* → czekać; ~pi(a)ć catch, hook; F *fig.* accost; ~pić się (o *L*) catch (on); get stuck; ~pka *f* (*-i*; *G* -*pek*) provocation; *szukać* ~pki look for trouble; ~pny aggressive; *mil.* offensive

zaczerwieniony reddened; *por.* czerwienić się

zaczyn *m* (*-u*; -*y*) *gastr.* leaven; ~ać (*-am*) *v/t.* start, begin (się *v/i.*); *paczkę, butelkę* open; F ~a się it's starting

zaćmi|enie *n* (*-a*; *G* -*eń*) *astr.* eclipse; ~ewać (*-am*) ⟨~ć⟩ darken (się *v/i.*); *astr.* obscure; *fig.* (*I*) overshadow, outshine

zad *m* (*-u*; -*y*) *zo.* rump (*też kogoś*)

zada|ć *pf.* → zadawać; ~nie *n* (*-a*; *G*

-*ań*) problem; (*w szkole*) exercise; ~**rty** snub, upturned; ~**tek** *m* (*-tku*; *-tki*) down payment, deposit; **mieć ~tki na** have the makings of; ~**tkować** (*-uję*) deposit; ~**wać** *pytanie* ask; *zadanie domowe Brt.* set, *Am.* assign; *zagadkę* give; *cios* deliver; *ból* inflict; ~**wać klęskę** defeat; → **trud**; ~**wać się** (**z** *I*) go round (with)

za|dawniony *choroba* inveterate; ~**dbany** tidy; neat; ~**de-** *pf.* → **de-zadek** *m* (*-dka*, *-dki*) bottom; → **zad**

zadłuż|enie *n* (*-a*; *G -eń*) debt; ~**ony** in debt

zado|kumentować *pf. fig.* show; ~**mowić się** *pf.* (*-ę*, *-ów!*) make o.s. at home; get settled

zadośćuczyni|ć *pf.* (*D*) satisfy; ~**enie** *n* (*-a*; *G -eń*) satisfaction

zadowala|ć (*-am*) satisfy; ~**ć się** (*I*) be satisfied (with); ~**jąco** *adv.* satisfactorily; ~**jący** satisfactory

zadowol|enie *n* (*-a*; *0*) satisfaction; ~**ić** *pf.* (*-lę*, *-wól!*) → **zadowalać**; ~**ony** satisfied, pleased (**z** *G* with); ~**ony z siebie** complacent

zadra|pać ⟨~**pnąć**⟩ scratch; → **drasnąć**; ~**żnienia** *n/pl.* (*-ń*) frictions *pl.*; ~**żniony** *stosunki* strained, tense

zadrzeć *pf.* → **zadzierać**

zadrzewi|ać (*-am*) ⟨~**ć**⟩ (*-ę*) afforest; ~**ony** wooded

zaduch *m* (*-u*; *0*) stale air, *Brt. zwł.* fug

zadufany overconfident

zaduma *f* (*-y*; *0*) deep thought; ~**ny** thoughtful

zadurzony infatuated

zadusić *pf.* → (**u**)**dusić**

Zaduszki *pf.* (*-szek*) *rel.* All Souls' Day

zadym|a *f* F row, racket; ~**iać** (*-am*) ⟨~**ić**⟩ fill with smoke; ~**ka** *f* (*-i*; *G -mek*) driving snow, snowstorm

zadysz|any breathless, short-winded; ~**ka** *f* (*-i*; *G -szek*) breathlessness, shortness of breath

zadzierać (*-am*) *v/t.* *głowę* throw back; *spódnicę* pull up; *naskórek* tear; *ogon* raise; ~ **nosa** look down one's nose (at), put on airs; *v/i.* (**z** *I*) get in trouble (with); ~ **się** pull up

zadzierzysty defiant

zadziwi|ać (*-am*) ⟨~**ć**⟩ astonish, amaze; ~**ająco** *adv.* amazingly; ~**ający** amazing

za|dzwo- pf. → **dzwo-**; ~**dźgać** (*-am*)

---

stab (to death); ~**fascynowany** fascinated; ~**frapować** *pf.* (*-uję*) strike; ~**frasowany** worried

zagad|ka *f* (*-i*; *G -dek*) riddle, puzzle (*też fig.*); ~**kowo** *adv.* enigmatically; ~**kowy** enigmatic, puzzling; ~**nąć** *pf.* (*-nę*) speak (**kogoś o** *A* to s.o. about); ~**nienie** *n* (*-a*; *G -eń*) problem, question

zaga|jać (*-am*) ⟨~**ić**⟩ (*-ję*) open; ~**jenie** *n* (*-a*; *G -eń*) opening

zagajnik *m* (*-a*; *-i*) copse, wood

zagalopować się *pf.* go too far

zaganiać (*-am*) drive (**do** *G* to)

zagarn|iać (*-am*) ⟨~**ąć**⟩ *fig.* seize, grab

zagazować *pf.* (*-uję*) gas

zagę|szczać (*-am*) ⟨~**ścić**⟩ (*-szczę*) thicken; ~**ścić się** become thicker

zagi|ęcie *n* (*-a*; *G -ęć*) bend; ~**nać** (*-am*) ⟨~**ąć**⟩ bend (**się** *v/i.*); fold; ~**nąć** *pf.* → **ginąć**; ~**niony** missing

zaglądać (*-am*) (**do** *G*) look (into); (*z wizytą*) drop in (on); consult (**do książki** a book)

zagłada *f* (*-y*; *0*) extermination

zagłębi|ać (*-am*) ⟨~**ć**⟩ (*-ę*) immerse (**się** o.s.); *rękę* sink; ~**ć się** *fig.* (**w** *L*) become absorbed (in); ~**e** *n* (*-a*; *G -i*) *górnictwo*: coalfields *pl.*; ~**enie** *n* (*-a*; *G -eń*) hollow

za|głodzić *pf.* (*-ę*) starve; ~**główek** *m* (*-wka*, *-wki*) headrest; ~**głuszać** (*-am*) → **głuszyć**; ~**gmatwany** tangled, complicated; ~**gnać** *pf.* → **zaganiać**; ~**gniewany** angry; ~**gnieżdżać się** (*-am*) ⟨~**gnieździć się**⟩ nest; *med.* be implanted

zagon *m* (*-u*; *-y*) field; *hist.* incursion; ~**ić** *pf.* → **zaganiać**; ~**iony** exhausted

zagorzały fanatic, fervent

zagospodarow(yw)ać (*-[w]uję*) *teren* develop; ~**się** furnish, make o.s. at home

zagotować *pf.* boil

zagra|ć *pf.* → **grać**; ~**bić** *pf.* plunder; ~**dzać** (*-am*) (*płotem*) fence off; *ulicę* bar; block (**k-u drogę** s.o.'s path)

zagrani|ca *f* (*-y*; *0*) foreign countries *pl.*; ~**czny** foreign

zagraż|ać (*-am*) threaten; jeopardize, endanger ~**ać zdrowiu** be a threat to one's health; ~**a głód** hunger is threatening

zagroda *f* (*-y*; *G -ód*) farmstead

zagro|dzić *pf.* → **zagradzać**; ~**zić** *pf.* → **grozić, zagrażać**; ~**żenie** *n* (*-a*; *G*

-eń threat (*G* to); **stan ~żenia** state of emergency; **~żony** threatened

zagry|piony F down with flu; **~wka** *f* (*w sporcie*) serve; **~zać** (*-am*) ⟨**~źć**⟩ (*I*) have a snack; *pf.* bite to death; **~źć usta do krwi** bite one's lips till they bleed; **~zka** *f* (*-i; G -zek*) snack

za|grzać *pf.* → **zagrzewać**

Zagrzeb *m* (*-bia; 0*) Zagreb

za|grzebywać (*-uję*) ⟨**~grzebać**⟩ bury (**się** o.s.; *też fig.*); **~grzewać** (*-am*) *gastr.* heat, warm up; *fig.* (**do** *G*) spur on (to); **~grzać się** warm up, heat up

zagubion|y lost; *rzeczy pl.* **~e** lost property

zahacz|ać (*-am*) ⟨**~yć**⟩ (*-ę*) hook up (**się** *v/i.*); get *s.th.* caught (**o** *A* on); F ask (**kogoś o** *A* to s.o. about)

zahamowa|nie *n* (*-a; G -ań*) braking; *psych.* inhibition; **~ć** *pf.* → **hamować**

zahar|owany overworked; **~towany** hardened; seasoned; → **hartować**

zahipnotyzowany under hypnosis; **~hukany** meek, intimidated

zaimek *m* (*-mka; -mki*) *gr.* pronoun

za|improwizowany improvised; impromptu; **~ini-**, **~ink-**, **~ins-** *pf.* → *in-*

zainteresowan|ie *n* (*-a; G -ań*) interest; **~y** (**w** *L* in) interested

zaiste *przest.* indeed

zaistnieć *pf.* come into being; appear

zajad|ać (*-am*) F eat heartily, *zwł. Brt.* tuck in; **~le** *adv.* fiercely; **~ły** fierce; *zwolennik* staunch, stout

zajazd *m* (*-u; -y*) inn

zając *m* (*-a; -e*) *zo.* hare

zają|ć *pf.* (*-jmę*) → **zajmować**; **~knąć się** (*-nę*) stammer; **nie ~knąć się** (**o** *L*) not say a word (about)

zaje|chać *pf.* → **zajeżdżać**; **~zdnia** *f* (*-i; -e*) terminus, *Brt.* depot; **~żdżać** (*-am*) ⟨**do** *G*⟩ arrive (to); stop (at); (**przed** *A*) drive up (outside, in front of); **~żdżać drogę** *mot.* cut in

zajęcie *n* (*-a; G -ęć*) taking; (*siłą itp.*) capture; *jur.* seizure; (*praca*) occupation, job; (*w szkole zw. pl.*) classes *pl.*; lectures *pl.*; **z ~m** interested

zajęczy hare('s),*biol.* leporine; →**warga**

zajęty busy (*też Am. tel.*), *tel. Brt.* engaged; *stół* occupied

zajmować (*-uję*) *postawę* take; *miasto* capture; *przestrzeń, miejsce, kraj* occupy; *jur.* seize; (*zużyć czas*) take up;

pokój live in; *stanowisko* take, adopt; occupy (**się** o.s.; *I* with); (*budzić ciekawość*) interest

zajmując|o *adv.* interestingly; fascinatingly; **~y** interesting; fascinating

zajrzeć *pf.* (*-ę, -y*) → **zaglądać**

zajś|cie *n* (*-a; G -jść*) incident, occurrence; → **zatarg**; **~ć** *pf.* (*-dę*) → **zachodzić**

zakamarek *m* (*-rka;-rki*)*fig.* corner,spot

za|kamuflowany disguised; **~kańczać** *pf.* →**kończyć**; **~kasywać** (*-uję*) ⟨**~kasać** (*-szę*)⟩ roll up; **~katarzony** suffering from a cold; **~kaszleć** *pf.* (*-ę*) do in

zaka|z *m* (*-u; -y*) ban, prohibition; **~zać** *pf.* → **zakazywać**; **~zany** prohibited, forbidden; **~zić** *pf.* (*-żę*) → **zakażać**; **~zywać** (*-uję*) forbid, prohibit; **~kaźny** infectious; contagious;**~żać** (*-am*) *med.* infect; **~żenie** *n* (*-a; G -eń*) infection

zakąs|ić *pf.* (*-szę*) → **przekąsić**; **~ka** *f* (*-i; G -sek*) hors d'oeuvre, appetizer; **na ~kę** for a starter

zakątek *m* (*-tku; -tki*) → **zakamarek**

za|ki-, **~kla-** *pf.* → **ki-**, **kla-**; **~kląć** *pf.* → **kląć**; **zaklinać**; **~kler** *pf.* → **kle-**; **~klęcie** *n* (*-a;G-ęć*)spell; *fig.* magic formula

zaklinać (*-am*) bewitch; *fig.* beg, beseech; **~ się** swear (**na** *A* by)

zakład *m* (*-u; -y*) firm, business; (*fabryka*) works *sg.*; (*instytucja*) institution; (*założenie się*) bet; **~ pracy** place of work; **iść o ~** bet; **~ać** (*-am*) *rodzinę* start; *firmę* set up, establish; *miasto* found; *okulary* put on; (*w ubraniu*) tuck; *opatrunek* apply, put on; *gaz, prąd* lay; **~ać nogę na nogę** cross legs; **~ać, że ...** assume that ...; *v/i.* **~ać się** (**o** *A*) bet (on); **~ka** *f* (*-i; G -dek*) (*w książce*) bookmark; (*ubrania*) tuck

zakład|niczka *f* (*-i; G -czek*), **~nik** *m* (*-a; -cy*) hostage; **wzięcie ~ników** taking of hostages; **~owy** company; staff

zakłaman|ie *n* (*-a; 0*) hypocrisy; **~y** hypocritical

zakłopotan|ie *n* (*-a; 0*) embarrassment; **~y** embarrassed, perplexed

zakłóc|ać (*-am*) ⟨**~ić**⟩ disturb; **~enie** *n* (*-a; G -eń*) disturbance; *RTV:* static

zakoch|iwać się (*-uję*) ⟨**~ać się**⟩ fall in love (**w** *L* with); **~any 1.** in love (**w** *L* with), infatuated; **2.** *m* (*-ego; -ni*), **~ana** *f* (*-ej; -e*) lover

zako|do- *pf.*→**kodo-~mu-** *pf.*→**komu-**

zakon m (-u; -y) rel. order; ~nica f (-y; G -) nun; ~nik m (-a; -cy) monk; brother; ~ny monastic

za|kons- pf. → kons-; ~kończenie n (-a; G -eń) ending, conclusion; (palce itp.) tip; ~kończyć pf. → końćzyć; ~kopać pf. → zakopywać; ~kopcony covered in soot; ~kopywać (-uję) bury; ~korkowany corked; F blocked; ~korzenić się (-ę) take root; ~kotwiczać (-am) ⟨~kotwiczyć⟩ (-ę) v/t. naut. anchor; v/i. drop anchor

zakra|dać się (-am) ⟨~ść się⟩ steal in, sneak in; ~plać (-am) put drops in one's eye(s pl); ~towany barred; ~wać (-am) **(na** A) look (like)

zakres m (-u; -y) range, scope; **we własnym ~ie** on one's own

zakreśl|ać (-am) ⟨~ić⟩ (-ę) (w tekście) highlight, mark; koło describe

zakręc|ać (-am) ⟨~ić⟩ włosy curl; kran turn off; zawór screw shut; t-ko pf. turn (I; **się** v/i.); v/i. turn round; **~ić się (koło** G) busy o.s. (about)

zakręt m (-u; -y) bend, curve; ~as m (-a; -y) flourish; ~ka f (-i; G -tek) cap, lid

za|kroplić pf. → zakraplać; ~krwawić bleed; ~kryć pf. → zakrywać

za'krystia f (GDL -ii; -e) rel. vestry, sacristy

za|krywać (-am) hide, conceal; widok block; ~krzątnąć się pf. (-nę) → krzątać się

zakrzep m (-u; -y) med. thrombus; ~ica f (-y; 0) med. thrombosis; ~ły clotted; set

za|krzt- pf. → krzt-; ~krzywiony bent, crooked; ~księ- pf. → księ-

zaktualizowany updated, modernized

zakulisowy fig. behind the scenes

zakup m (-u; -y) purchase, buy; **na ~y** shopping; **iść po ~y** go shopping

zakurzony dusty, covered in dust

zakuty F fig.: ~**ty łeb** blockhead; ~wać (-am): ~**wać w kajdany** put in chains

za|kwaterow(yw)ać (-[w]uję) mil. quarter, billet; ~kwitnąć (-nę) blossom, bloom; ~lać pf. → zalewać; ~lany flooded; V fig. pissed; ~lążek m (-żka; -żki) bot. bud; fig. bud, germ

zale|c pf. → zalegać; ~cać (-am) ⟨~cić⟩ (-cę) recommend; ~cać się (do G) woo, court; ~cenie n (-a; G -eń) recommendation; med. order

zaledwie part., cj. hardly, scarcely

zalega|ć (-am) v/i. geol. occur, be found; milczenie: descend; ciemność: set in; (z I) be behind (with), (z opłatą) be in arrears (with); ~łość f (-ści; 0) zw. pl. (płatnicze) arrears pl.; (w pracy) backlog; ~ły outstanding, due

zale|piać (-am) ⟨~pić⟩ (-ę) stick down; dziurę seal up; ~siać (-am) ⟨~sić⟩ (-ę) afforest

zaleta f (-y; G -) advantage, value

zalew m (-u; -y) flooding; geogr. bay; ~ać (-am) v/t. flood; fig. swamp; (uszczelniać) seal; v/i. F tell stories; **~ać robaka** drown one's sorrows (in drink)

zależ|eć **(od** G) depend (on); be dependent (on); **~y mi na tym** it matters much to me; **to ~y** it depends; **~nie** adv.: **~nie od** (G) depending on; ~ność f (-ści) relationship; ~ny dependent; gr. indirect

zalicz|ać (-am) **(do** G) include (to); **~ać się** be included (with); (w szkole) pass; ~enie n (-a; G -eń) (w szkole) pass, (podpis) credit; **za ~eniem (pocztowym)** cash on delivery; ~ka f (-i; G -ek) advance payment; ~kowo adv. as an advance payment

zalot|ny flirtatious; coy; ~y pl. courtship; → umizgi

zaludni|ać (-am) ⟨~ć⟩ (-ę, -nij!) populate; ~**(a)ć się** fill in

zał. skrót pisany: **załącznik** enc. (enclosure)

zała|dowczy loading; ~dow(yw)ać (-uję) load; ~dunek m (-nku; -nki) loading; ~dunkowy loading; ~godzić pf. soothe; karę mitigate; spór settle

zała|mać pf. → załamywać; ~many desolate; crestfallen; ~nie n (-a; G -ań) phys. refraction; fig. breakdown, collapse

załamywać (-uję) bend; papier fold; ręce wring; phys. refract; **~ się** break; sufit, fig.: collapse; phys. be refracted; głos: fail

załatwi|ać (-am) ⟨~ć⟩ (-ę) deal with, settle; klienta serve; komuś fix up; F ~**ć się (z** I) finish (with); (w toalecie) relieve o.s.; ~enie n (-a; G -eń) completion, settling

załącz|ać (-am) enclose; ukłony send; ~enie n: **w ~eniu** enclosed; ~nik m (-a; -i) enclosure

załoga f (-i; G -łóg) crew; (fabryki) staff, workforce

załom m (-u; -y) fold, crease

założeni|e n (-a; G -eń) establishment, foundation; (teza) assumption; **~a** pl. basic conceptions; **wychodzić z ~a** start from the assumption

założyciel m (-a; -e), **~ka** f (-i; G -lek) founder; **~ski** founding

założyć pf. → **zakładać**

załzawiony runny, watery

zamach m (-u; -y) (**na życie** assassination) attempt; (ruch) stroke, swing; **~ stanu** coup d'état; (**wojskowy** military) putsch; **za jednym ~em** at one stroke; **~nąć się** (-nę) take a swing (**na** A at); **~owiec** m (-wca; -wcy) assassin; **~owy:** **koło ~owe** flywheel

zama|czać pf. → **moczyć**; **~low(yw)ać** (-[w]uję) paint over

za|martwiać się (-am) → **martwić się**; **~marzać** (-am) → **morzyć**; **~marzać** [-r-z-] (-am) jezioro itp.: freeze solid; → **marznąć**; **~maskowany** masked, disguised

zamaszy|sty sweeping; pismo bold; **~ście** adv. sweepingly

zama|wiać (-am) order; symfonię itp. commission; tel., miejsce book; **~zywać** (-uję) **~zać** smear, daub

zamącić wodę make cloudy, cloud; fig. → **zakłócić**

zamążpójście n (-q) marriage

zamczysko n (-a; G -) → **zamek**

zamek m (-mku; -mki) lock; (obronny) castle; **~ błyskawiczny** zip (fastener); **~ centralny** central locking

zameldowa|ć pf. → **meldować**; **~nie** n (-a; G -ań) registration

zamę|czać (-am) → **męczyć**; **~t** m (-u; 0) muddle, confusion

zamężna married

zamgl|enie n (-a; G -eń) fog, mist; **~ony** foggy, misty

zamian: w ~ (**za** A) in exchange (for); **~a** f (-y; G -) exchange (**mieszkania** of flats, Am. apartments); swap; (**jednostek**) conversion

zamiar m (-u; -y) intention; **nosić się z ~em, mieć ~** intend, plan

zamiast 1. prp. (G) instead (of); **2.** adv. instead of

zamiata|ć (-am) sweep; **~rka** f (-i; G -rek) Brt. road-sweeper, Am. street-sweeper

zamieć f (-ci; -cie) blizzard

zamiejscow|y non-local; visiting; **rozmowa ~a** long-distance call

zamien|iać (-am) **⟨~ić⟩** v/t. exchange (**na** A for); miejsca change, swap; (przeobrażać) convert; **~i(a)ć się** turn, change (**w** A into); (**na** A) change, swap; **~ny** interchangeable; **część ~na** spare part

zamierać (-am) die; fig. głos itp.: die away; śmiech, ktoś: freeze; be paralyzed (**ze strachu** with fear)

zamierzać (-am) intend, plan; **~ się** raise one's hand (**na** A against)

zamie|rzchły ancient; czasy remote; **~rzenie** n (-a; G -eń) intention; **~rzony** intended; **~rzać** pf. → **mieszać**; **~szanie** n (-a; 0) confusion; **~zamęt**; **~szany** fig. involved (**w** A in); **~szczać** (-am) → **umieszczać**

zamieszka|ć pf. inhabit; occupy; settle; **~ły** occupied, inhabited; (**w** L) resident (in); **~nie** n (-a; G -ań) living; **miejsce ~nia** residence, jur. abode

zamieszki pl. (-szek) riot, disturbance

zamieszkiwać (-uję) live, inhabit

zami|eścić pf. → **umieścić**; **~mieść** → **zamiatać**; **~milczeć** pf. pass over in silence; **~milknąć** pf. → **milknąć**

zamiłowani|e n (-a; G -ań) (**do** G) passion (for), enthusiasm (for); **z ~em** with passion; **~y** keen

zaminowany mined; → **minować**

zamkn|ąć pf. → **zamykać**; **~ięcie** n (-a; G -ęć) closure; closing; locking; (zamek) lock; (ksiąg) balancing; **w ~ięciu** under lock and key; **~ięty** closed; fig. withdrawn

zamkowy castle

za|mocow(yw)ać → **przymocowywać, mocować**; **~moczyć** pf. → **moczyć**; **~montowywać** (-uję) → **montować**

zamordowan|ie n (-a; G -ań) assassination, murdering; **~y** assassinated, murdered; → **mordować**

zamorski overseas

zamożny affluent, prosperous

zamówi|ć pf. → **zamawiać**; **~enie** n (-a; G -eń) order, commission

zamraczać (-am) daze

zamraża|ć (-am) freeze; **~lnik** m (-a; -i) freezing compartment; **~rka** f (-i; G -rek) freezer, deep freeze

zamrocz|enie n (-a; G -eń) daze; **stan**

~enia (*alkoholowego*) state of drunk-enness; **~ony** dazed; (*alkoholem*) in-toxicated; **~yć** (*-ę*) → **zamraczać**

zamrozić *pf.* → **zamrażać**

zamrzeć *pf.* → **zamierać**

zamsz *m* (*-u; -e*) suede

zamulony muddy

zamurow(yw)ać (*-[w]uję*) wall up

zamykać (*-am*) close, shut (**się** *v/i.*); *ko-goś w pokoju itp.* lock in (**się** *v/i.*); *mieszkanie* lock up; *ulicę* close, block; *fabrykę* close down; *komp.* quit, exit; *econ.* balance; **~ gaz** turn off the gas; **~ na klucz** lock; **~ pochód** bring up the rear; **~ się w sobie** clam up; **zamknij się!** shut up!

zamyś|lać (*-am*) ⟨**~lić**⟩ (*-lę*) plan, in-tend; **~lić się** fall into thought; (*nad I*) reflect (about), muse (on, about); **~lony** thoughtful, pensive

zanadto *adv.* too, exceedingly

zaniecha|ć *pf.* (*-am*) give up, abandon; **~nie** *n* (*-a; 0*) *jur.* omission

zanieczy|szczać (*-am*) ⟨**~ścić**⟩ (*-ę*) make dirty; *środowisko* pollute; *wodę* contaminate; **~szczenie** *n* (*-a; G -eń*) soiling; (*środowiska* environmental) pollution; **~szczenia** *pl.* impurities *pl.*

zaniedba|ć (*-am*) → **zaniedbywać**; **~nie** *n* (*-a; G -ań*) neglect, negligence; **~ny** neglected; (*brudny*) untidy; (*podniszczony*) run-down

zaniedbywać (*-uję*) neglect; **~ się** be negligent (**w** *L* in); become untidy, let o.s. go

zanie|móc *pf.* fall ill; **~mówić** *pf.* be-come dumb (**z** *G* with); **~pokojenie** *n* (*-a; G -eń*) concern, worry; → **niepokój, niepokoić**; **~pokojony** worried, anxious; alarmed

zanie|ść → **zanosić**; **~widzieć** *pf.* be-come blind

zanik *m* (*-u; -i*) decrease; (*zainteresowania*) waning; *med.* atrophy; **~ać** (*-am*) ⟨**~nąć**⟩ disappear, vanish; fade, die out; *zw. impf.* decrease

zanim *cj.* before

zaniż|ać (*-am*) ⟨**~yć**⟩ (*-ę*) lower; *liczbę* understate

zano|- *pf.* → **no-**; **~sić** *v/t.* take; carry; cover (*śniegiem* with snow); **~sić się** look like (**na deszcz** rain); **~sić od płaczu** cry uncontrollably; **~sić się od śmiechu** be in hysterics

zanu|dzać (*-am*) (*I*) bore (with); → **nu-dzić**; **~rzać** (*-am*) ⟨**~rzyć**⟩ (*-ę*) im-merse (**w** *I* in; **po szyję** to the neck; **się** *v/i.*); *pędzel itp.* dip; **~rzenie** *n* (*-a; G -eń*) immersion

zaoczn|ie *adv.* in one's absence; *jur.* in default; **~y: studia ~e** extramural studies

za|of- *pf.* → **of-**; **~ogniać** (*-am*) ⟨**~og-nić**⟩ (*-ę, -nij!*) (**się**) inflame (*też fig.*); *fig.* aggravate

zaokrągl|ać (*-am*) ⟨**~ić**⟩ (*-lę, -lij!*) round (**w górę, w dół** up, down); *rogi* round off

zaokrętować *pf.* (*-uję*) embark (**się** *v/i.*)

zaopatrywać (*-uję*) (**w** *A*) supply (with), provide (with); (*wyposażać*) equip (with); **~ się** (**w** *A*) provide o.s. (with)

zaopatrz|enie *n* (*-a; 0*) supply; *econ.* provision; (*na ekspedycję*) provisions *pl.*; (*dostarczenie*) delivery; **~yć** *pf.* (*-ę*) → **zaopatrywać**

za|opi- *pf.* → **opi-**; **~orywać** (*-uję*) ⟨**~orać**⟩ **~ostrzać** (*-am*) *fig.* aggravate; → **ostrzyć**; **~oszczę-** *pf.* → **oszczę-**

zapach *m* (*-u; -y*) smell

zapad|ać (*-am*) *kurtyna, cisza, ciem-ność:* fall; *oczy:* sink in; *policzki:* sag; *wyrok:* be pronounced; **~ać na zdro-wiu** be in poor health; **~ać w sen** sink into a sleep; **~ać się** cave in, sink; **~ły** sunken, sagged; **~ły kąt, ~ła dziura** godforsaken place

zapako- *pf.* → **pako-**

zapala|ć (*-am*) light; *światło* turn on; *ogień* kindle; *zapałkę* strike; *silnik* start; **~ć się** light; catch fire; *światło, silnik:* go on; *oczy:* light up; (**do** *G*) become en-thusiastic (over); **~jący** *mil.* incendiary

zapalcz|wie *adv.* impetuously; impulsively; **~ość** *f* (*-ści; 0*) impetuous-ness; **~y** impetuous, impulsive

zapal|enie *n* (*-a; G -eń*) *med.* inflam-mation; **~eniec** *m* (*-ńca; -ńcy*) enthu-siast; **~ić** *pf.* → **zapalać ~niczka** *f* (*-i; G -czek*) lighter; **~nik** *m* (*-a; -i*) *mil.* fuse; **~ny** inflammable (*też fig.*); *med.* inflammatory; **punkt ~ny** hot-spot; **~ony** enthusiastic, avid

zapał *m* (*-u; 0*) fervo(u)r; zeal; enthu-siasm; **~czany** match; **~ka** *f* (*-i; G -ek*) match

zapamięt|ać *pf.* remember; *komp.* save; **~ać się** (**w** *I*) become engrossed (in); ~ały obsessive; → **zagorzały, zapalony**; ~anie *n* (*-a*; *0*) obsessiveness; **łatwy do ~ania** easy to remember; ~ywać (*-uję*) → **zapamiętać**

zapanowa|ć *pf.* → **panować**; *fig.* prevail

zapar|- *pf.* → **par**-; ~cie *n* (*-a*; *G -rć*) *med.* constipation; ~ty: **z ~tym tchem** with bated breath

zaparz|**ać** (*-am*) ⟨~**yć**⟩ brew

zapas *m* (*-u*; *-y*) supply, stock; **w ~ie** in reserve; ~**y** *pl.* provisions *pl.*; *t-ko pl.* (*w sporcie*) wrestling; ~**owy** reserve; replacement; *część* spare; **wyjście ~owe** emergency exit

zapa|**ść** *pf.* → **zapadać**

zapa|**ść²** *f* (*-ści*; *0*) *med. fig.* collapse; ~**niczy** (*w sporcie*) wrestling; ~**nik** *m* (*-a*; *-cy*) *sport*: wrestler

zapatrywa|**ć się** (*-uję*) (**na** *A*) regard (as), view (as) **jak się na to zapatrujesz?** what is your opinion about it?; ~**nie** *n* (*-a*; *G -ań*) view, opinion

zapatrzyć się *pf.* → **wpatrywać się**

zapchać *pf.* → **zapychać**

zapełni|**ać** (*-am*) ⟨~**ć**⟩ fill (**się** *v/i.*)

zaperzony irritable, touchy

zapewn|**iać** *adv.* surely; ~**iać** (*-am*) ⟨~**ić**⟩ (*-ę, -nij!*) assure (**kogoś o** *L* s.o. of); (*gwarantować*) ensure, guarantee; ~**ienie** *n* (*-a*; *G -eń*) assurance

zapę|**dy** *m/pl.* (*-ów*) efforts *pl.*, attempts *pl.*; ~**dzać** (*-am*) ⟨~**dzić**⟩ drive (**do** *G* to); ~**dzić się** *fig.* go too far

zapiąć *pf.* → **zapinać**

zapie|**czętować** *pf.* seal (*też fig.*); ~**kać** (*-am*) ⟨~**c**⟩ *gastr.* bake (*zwł.* in a casserole); ~**kanka** *f* (*-i*; *G -nek*) casserole; ~**rać** (*-am*) *dech* take away; → **zaparty**; ~**rać się** (*G*) deny, disown

za|**pięcie** *n* (*-a*; *G -ęć*) (*zamek*) fastener; ~**pinać** (*-am*) *guzik, bluzkę* do up; *pasy* fasten; *zamek błysk.* zip up

zapis *m* (*-u*; *-y*) (*wpis*) entry; record; (**na taśmie** tape) recording; *jur.* bequest; → **dźwięk**; ~**ek** *m* (*-sku; -ski*) *zw. pl.* note; ~**ywać** (*-uję*) ⟨~**ać**⟩ take down, note down; *stronę* fill with writing; *dźwięk* record; *econ.* (**na** *A*) credit; *lek.* prescribe; *komp.* save; leave, bequeath (**w testamencie** in one's last will); → **wpisywać**

zapity besotted; *głos* boozy

zapla|**nowany** planned; → **planować**; ~**tać** (*-am*) weave

zapląt|**ywać** (*-uję*) ⟨~**ać**⟩ → **plątać**; ~**ać się** get involved (**w** *A* in)

zaplecze *n* (*-a*; *G -y*) *mil.* back area

za|**pleść** *pf.* → **zaplatać**; ~**pleśniały** mo(u)ldy; ~**plombowany** sealed; → **plombować**

zapła|**cenie** *n* (*-a*; *0*) payment; ~**cić** *pf.* → **płacić**; *dług, rachunek* settle; ~**dniać** (*-am*) *kobietę, samicę* impregnate; *jajko* fertilize; ~**kany** weeping; tear-stained; ~**ta** *f* (*-y*; *G -*) payment

zapłodni|**ć** *pf.* → **zapładniać**; ~**enie** *n* (*-a*; *G -eń*) fertilisation; **sztuczne ~enie** artificial insemination

zapłon *m* (*-u*; *-y*) *mot.* ignition; detonation; **włącznik ~u** ignition lock; ~**ać** *pf.* kindle (*też fig.*); ~**owy** ignition

zapobieg|**ać** (*-am*) ⟨**zapobiec**⟩ (*D*) prevent; ~**anie** *n* (*-a*; *0*) prevention; ~**awczo** *adv.* preventively; ~**awczy** preventive; ~**liwie** *adv.* providently; ~**liwy** provident; → **przezorny, przewidujący**

zapo|**cony** sweated; *szyba* misted-up, fogged-up; → **pocić się**; ~**czątkow**(**yw**)**ać** (*-[w]uję*) start; ~**dziać** (**się**) *pf.* → **podziewać**; ~**minać** (*-am*) ⟨~**mnieć**⟩ (*A, o* *L*) forget (about); ~**mnienie** *n* (*-a*; *0*) oblivion; forgetfulness; **pójść w ~mnienie** fall into oblivion; ~**moga** *f* (*-i*; *G -móg*) benefit

zapor|**a** *f* (*-y*; *G -pór*) barrier (*też rail.*); ~**a wodna** dam; ~**owy** *mil.* barrage

zapotrzebowa|**ć** *pf.* order; ~**nie** *n* (*-a*; *G -ań*) *econ.* demand (**na** *A* for)

zapowi|**adać** (*-am*) ⟨~**edzieć**⟩ announce; *występ* introduce; ~**adać się** (**z wizytą**) say one is coming; ~**adać się** (**na** *A*) promise (to be); ~**edź** *f* (*-dzi; -e*) announcement; (*oznaka*) sign, prognostic; **dać na ~edzi** put up the banns

zapozna|**ny** misunderstood, disregarded; ~**(wa)ć** (**z** *L*) acquaint (**z** *I* with; **się** o.s.); ~**(wa)ć się** get to know

zapożycz|**ać** (*-am*) ⟨~**yć**⟩ (*-ę*) (**od, z** *G*) borrow (from); ~**enie** *n* (*-a*; *G -eń*) borrowing

zapra|**cowany** *ktoś* overworked; *pieniądz* earned; ~**cow**(**yw**)**ać** (*-[w]uję*) earn, make; ~**cow**(**yw**)**ać się** overwork; ~**gn**- *pf.* → **pragn**-; ~**szać** (*-am*) (**na** *A*, **do** *G*) invite (to); ~**wa** *f* (*-y*; *G -*) training, exercise; *bud.* mortar; → **przyprawa**; ~**wiać** (*-am*) ⟨~**wić**⟩ train (**się** *v/i.*)

do *G* for); ~wiać się practise (for)

za|pre-, ~pro- *pf.* → **pre-**, **pro-**

zapro|sić *pf.* → **zapraszać**; ~szenie *n* (-a; *G* -eń) invitation; ~wadzać (-am) ⟨~wadzić⟩ lead; *zwyczaj, modę* introduce; → **zakładać**

zaprzą|c *pf.* → **zaprzęgać**; ~tać (-am) ⟨~tnąć, -nę, -nij!⟩ *czas* take up; *kogoś czymś* busy (with)

zaprzecz|ać (-am) ⟨~yć⟩ (*D*) deny; *doświadczeniu, komuś* contradict; → **przeczyć**; ~enie *n* (-a; *G* -eń) denial, contradiction

zaprze|ć *pf.* → **zapierać**; ~da(wa)ć betray; ~paszczać (-am) ⟨~paścić⟩ (-szczę) ruin; *szansę* squander; ~stawać (-ję) ⟨~stać⟩ (*G*) stop, cease; *produkcję* discontinue

zaprzęg *m* (-u; -i) team; ~ać (-am) ⟨~nąć⟩ (-nę) harness

zaprzyjaź|niać się (-am) ⟨~nić się⟩ (*z I*) make friends (with); ~niony friendly

zaprzy|sięgać (-am) ⟨~sięgnąć, ~siąc⟩ *jur.* swear in; swear (**komuś/ sobie** to s.o./o.s.); ~siężenie *n* (-a; *G* -eń) swearing in

zapuchnięty swollen

zapu|sty *pl.* (-tów) Shrovetide, *w szer. zn.* carnival; ~puszczać (-am) ⟨~ścić⟩ *włosy* grow; *korzenie* take; F *silnik* start; *ogród itp.* neglect; ~szczony neglected, run-down

zapychać (-am) block (**się** *v/i.*)

zapylony dusty

zapyt|anie *n* (-a; *G* -ań) question, inquiry; **znak ~ania** question mark; ~ywać (-uję) → **pytać**

zarabiać (-am) earn (**na** *L* for)

zara|dczy: **środki** *m/pl.* ~**dcze** remedies *pl.*; ~dny resourceful; ~dzać (-am) ⟨~dzić⟩ (*D*) remedy

zarastać (-am) overgrow

zaraz *adv.* at once, immediately

zaraz|a *f* (-y; *G* -) plague, *fig.* plague, pest; ~ek *m* (-zka; -zki) germ

zarazem *adv.* at the same time

zara|zić *pf.* → **zarażać**; ~źliwy infectious, contagious; ~żać (-am) infect; ~żać się become infected

zardzewiały rusty; → **rdzewieć**

zare- *pf.* → **re-**

zaręcz|ać (-am) ⟨~yć⟩ (-ę) → **ręczyć**, **zapewniać**; ~yć się become engaged (**z** *I* to); ~yny *pl.* (-) engagement

zarob|ek *m* (-bku; -bki) earnings *pl.*, wages *pl.*; ~ić (-ę) → **zarabiać**; ~kowy working; **pracować** ~**kowo** work for payment; have a job

zarod|ek *m* (-dka; -dki) germ; embryo; ~nik *m* (-a; -i) spore

zaro|snąć *pf.* → **zarastać**; ~st *m* (-u; 0) growth of hair; ~śla *n/pl.* thicket; ~śnięty overgrown; (*zarośnięty*) unshaven, unshaved

zarozumia|lec *m* (-lca; -lcy) show-off, boaster; ~łość *f* (-ści; 0) conceit; vanity; ~ły conceited, vain

zarówno: ~ ... **jak** ... both ... and ...

zaróżowiony rosy

zarumieniony flushed; → **rumiany, rumienić**

zaryglowany bolted; → **ryglować**

zarys *m* (-u; -y) outline; **w głównych** ~**ach** in broad outline

zarysow(yw)ać (-[w]uję) *arkusz* cover with drawings; *lakier* scratch; *fig.* outline; ~ się get scratched; *fig.* stand out

zarz. *skrót pisany:* **zarząd** board

zarzą|d *m* (-u; -y) board; (*dyrekcja*) management, administration; ~dzać (-am) (*I*) manage, administer; (*krajem*) govern; (*hotelem*) run; ⟨~dzić⟩ order; decree; ~dzenie *n* (-a; *G* -eń) order, decree; instruction

zarzu|cać (-am) ⟨~cić⟩ *v/t.* szal *itp.* throw on; *sieć* cast; *dół* fill up; *rynek* flood (*I* with); (*obwiniać*) accuse (*A* of), reproach (*A* with); *palenie itp.* give up; *v/i. pojazd:* skid; ~t *m* (-u; -y) reproach; accusation; **bez** ~**tu** faultless

za|rzynać (-am) ⟨~rżnąć⟩ slaughter

zasad|a *f* (-y; *G* -) principle; rule; basis; *chem.* base; **z** ~**y** on principle; ~niczo *adv.* essentially; ~niczy principal; *ustawa* ~**nicza** constitution; ~owy *chem.* basic, alkaline

zasa|dzać (-am) ⟨~dzić⟩ plant; ~dzić ⟨~dzić⟩ się (**na** *L*) be based on; (*w zasadzce*) lie in wait; ~dzka *f* (-i; *G* -dzek) ambush; ~lać → **zasolić**; ~pać się *pf.* lose one's breath

zasądz|ać(-am)⟨~ić⟩*jur. odszkodowanie* award; (*skazać*) sentence (**na** *A* for)

zaschnięty dried (up); withered

zasępiony gloomy

zasia|ć *pf.* → **zasiewać**; ~dać (-am) ⟨**zasiąść**⟩ sit down (**do** *G*, **za** *I* to); (*w komisji itp.*) sit (**w** *L* on)

z

zasiedl|ać (-*am*) ⟨~*ić*⟩ (-*lę*) settle

zasięg *m* (-*u*; *0*) range, scope; **~ widzenia** visibility; **dalekiego ~u** long-range; **w ~u** within reach; **~ać** ⟨~*nąć*⟩ *rady* seek, take; *informacji* get, gather

zasil|ać (-*am*) ⟨~*lić*⟩ supply (**w** *A* with); (*prądem*) power; (*wzmagać*) boost

zasiłek *m* (-*łku*; -*łki*) benefit, allowance; **~ chorobowy** sickness benefit; **~ rodzinny** family allowance; **~ dla bezrobotnych** unemployment benefit, F dole

zaska|kiwać (-*uję*) *v/t.* surprise; *v/i.* click to; **~kująco** *adv.* surprisingly; **~kujący** surprising; **~rżać** (-*am*) ⟨~*rżyć*⟩ *v/t. kogoś* sue; *wyrok* sue against, challenge; **~rżać do sądu** prosecute

zasko|czenie *n* (-*a*; *G* -*eń*) surprise; **~czony** surprised; **~czyć** *pf.* → **zaskakiwać**

zaskórny *geol.* → **podskórny**

zasła|bnąć *pf.* faint; **~ć** (*słać*) → **zaściełać**; **~niać** (**się** *v/i.*) *widok* obstruct; *twarz, okno* cover

zasłon|a *f* (-*y*; *G* -) curtain; (*osłona*) screen; *szermierka:* parry; **~ić** *pf.* (-*ę*) → **zasłaniać**

zasłu|ga *f* (-*i*; *G* -) merit, credit; **położyć ~gi** (**dla** *G*) make contribution (to); **~giwać** (-*uję*) deserve, merit; be worthy (**na uwagę** of attention); **~żenie** *adv.* deservedly; **~żony** of outstanding merit; well-deserved; **~żyć** *pf.* → **zasługiwać**; **~żyć się** (*D*) render outstanding services (to)

za|słynąć *pf.* (**z** *G*) become famous (for); **~smakować** *pf.* (**w** *L*) take a liking (to); **~smarkany** snotty; **~smarow(yw)ać** (-[*w*]*uję*) smear; **~smucony** sad; → **smucić**

zasnąć *pf.* (-*nę*) → **zasypiać**

zasobn|ik *m* (-*a*; -*i*) container; holder; **~y** prosperous; (*obfitujący*) (**w** *A*) abundant (in), rich (in)

zasolić *pf.* salt

za|sób *m* (-*sobu*; -*soby*) stock, reserve; **~soby** *pl.* resources *pl.*; **~sób wyrazów** vocabulary

zaspa *f* (-*y*; *G* -) snowdrift; **~ć** *pf.* oversleep; **~ny** half-asleep; (*gnuśny*) sad; → **smucić**

zaspok|ajać (-*am*) ⟨~*oić*⟩ (-*ję*) *głód, ciekawość itp.* satisfy; *potrzeby* meet

zasrany V *fig. Brt.* shitty, crap(py)

zastać *pf.* (*stać²*) → **zastawać**

zastanawiać (-*am*) *v/t.* puzzle; **~ się** (**nad** *I*) think (about), consider

zastanowi|ć (**się**) *pf.* → **zastanawiać**; **~enie** *n* (-*a*; *0*) thought, reflection

zastarzały old; *med.* inveterate

zastaw *m* (-*u*; -*y*) deposit; *econ.* security, collateral; **dać w ~** pawn; **~a** *f* (-*y*; *G* -) (**stołowa** dinner) service; **~ać** (**przy** *L*) meet (at); **~i(a)ć** block, obstruct; *pułapkę* set; (*dać w zastaw*) pawn; (*zagracać*) (*I*) clutter (with); **~ka** *f* (-*i*; *G* -*wek*) *anat.* valve

zastąpi|ć *pf.* (-*ę*) → **zastępować**; **~ć drogę** bar s.o.'s way; **~enie** *n*: **nie do ~enia** irreplaceable

zastęp *m* (-*u*; -*y*) (*harcerzy*) patrol; **~y** *pl.* (*aniołów*) hosts *pl.*

zastęp|ca *m* (-*y*; *G* -*ów*), **~czyni** *f* (-*i*; -*e*) deputy, assistant; **~ca dyrektora** deputy manager; **~czo** *adv. ktoś* as a deputy; *coś* as a substitute; **~czy** substitute; **~cza matka** *med.* surrogate mother; **~ować** (-*uję*) *coś* substitute, replace; *kogoś* deputize (*A* for); (*czasowo*) stand in (*A* for); **~stwo** *n* (-*a*; *G* -) substitution

zastopować (-*uję*) stop

zastosowanie *n* (-*a*; *G* -*ań*) use, application; → **stosować**

zastój *m* (-*toju*; -*toje*) stagnation

zastrasz|ający intimidating; **~yć** *pf.* intimidate, overawe

zastrze|gać (-*am*) ⟨~*c*⟩ *sobie prawo* reserve, *jur.* stipulate; **~c się** specify one's position; **~żenie** *n* (-*a*; *G* -*eń*) reservation; **~żony** reserved; *tel. Brt.* ex-directory, *Am.* unlisted

zastrzyk *m* (-*u*; -*i*) *med.* injection; *fig.* boost; **dawać ~** inject

zastyg|ać (-*am*) ⟨~*nąć*⟩ set; *fig.* be paralysed

zasu|- *pf.* → **su-**; **~nąć** *pf.* → **zasuwać**; **~szać** (-*am*) ⟨~*szyć*⟩ *liść* dry; **~wa** *f* (-*y*; *G* -) bolt; **~wać** *zasuwę* bolt; *firankę* draw; (*pracować*) *fig.* be on the go

zasy|chać (-*am*) → **schnąć**; **~łać** (-*am*) send; **~pać** *pf.* → **zasypywać**; **~piać** (-*am*) fall asleep; **~pka** *f* (-*i*; *G* -*pek*) *med.* dusting powder; **~pywać** (-*uję*) *dół* fill in; *ludzi* bury (alive); *fig.* shower (*I* with); → **obsypywać**

zaszczepiać (-*am*) → **szczepić**

zaszczy|cać (-*am*) ⟨~*cić*⟩ (*I*) hono(u)r (with); **~t** *m* (-*u*; -*y*) hono(u)r; **~ty** *pl.* hono(u)rs *pl.*; **~tny** hono(u)rable

za|szeregow(yw)ać (-[w]*uję*) classify; *pracownika* put (**do wyższej kategorii** in a higher income bracket); ~szkodzić *pf.* damage, harm; → **szkodzić**;~szo- *pf.* → **szo-**;~sztyletować (-*uję*) stab to death; ~szywać (-*am*) ⟨~**szyć**⟩ sew up; → **szyć**

zaś **1.** *cj.* whereas; **2.** *part.* however, yet

zaściankowy parochial

zaściełać → słać²

zaścielać (-*am*) *łóżko* make; → **słać²**

zaślepi|ać (-*am*) ⟨~**ć**⟩ (-*ę*) *fig.* blind; ~enie *n* (-*a*; *G* -*eń*) blindness

zaśmiec|ać (-*am*) ⟨~**ić**⟩ litter

zaśnieżony snow-covered, covered with snow

zaświadcz|ać (-*am*) ⟨~**yć**⟩ certify; ~enie *n* (-*a*; *G* -*eń*) certificate

zaświecić *pf. v/t.* light; *lampę* turn on; ~ **się** *v/i.* *fig.* light up

zata|czać (-*am*) *krąg* describe; ~**czać się** stagger, reel; ~**jać** *pf.* → **taić**; ~**m-**, ~**n-**, ~**ń-** *pf.* → **tam-, tan-, tań-**; ~**piać** (-*am*) sink; *pola* flood; ~**topić**, ~**rasowywać** (-*wuję*) → **tarasować**

zatarg *m* (-*u*; -*i*) conflict, friction

za|tel-, ~tem- *pf.* → **tel-, tem-**; ~tem (*też a* ~**tém**) *cj.* as a result; so; that is; ~**tęchły** musty; ~**tkać** *pf.*, ~**tknąć** *pf.* → **zatykać**; ~**tłoczony** crowded; ~**tłuc** *pf.* beat to death; ~**tłuszczony** greasy;~**tłuścić** *pf.* (-*szczę*) make greasy

zato|**ka** *f* (-*i*; *G* -) bay, *anat.* (**czołowa** frontal) sinus; *meteo.* ~**ka wyżowa** ridge; ~**nąć** *pf.* → **tonąć**; ~**nięcie** *n* (-*a*; *G* -*ęć*) drowning; *naut.* sinking; ~**pić** *pf.* → **zatapiać, topić**

zator *m* (-*u*; -*y*) traffic jam, *Brt.* tailback, *Am.* backup; *med.* embolism

zatrac|**ać** (-*am*) ⟨~**ić**⟩ *fig.* lose; ~**ony** F damned

za|**trącać** (-*am*) → **trącić²**; ~**troskany** worried, concerned, anxious; ~**trucie** *n* (-*a*; *G* -*uć*) poisoning; ~**truć** *pf.* → **zatruwać**

zatrudni|ać (-*am*) ⟨~**ć**⟩ employ; ~enie *n* (-*a*; *G* -*eń*) employment;~ony (**w** *L*) employed (by)

zatru|**ty** poisoned; ~**wać** (-*am*) poison

zatrważa|ć (-*am*) → **trwożyć**; ~**jąco** *adv.* frighteningly; ~**jący** frightening

zatrzask *m* (-*u*; -*i*) spring lock; (*do zapinania*) *Brt.* press-stud, snap-fastener; ~**iwać** (-*uję*) shut, close (**się** *v/i.*)

za|**trząść** *pf.* → **trząść**; ~**trzeć** *pf.* → **zacierać**

zatrzym|ywać (-*uję*) ⟨~**ać**⟩ *v/t.* stop (**się** *v/i.*); (*nie puszczać*) halt, check; *ciepło* retain, keep; *złodziej* arrest; (*zachować*) keep (**dla siebie** for o.s.); ~**ać się** come to a stop; stay (**w hotelu** at a hotel); *mot.* pull up

zatuszow(yw)ać (-[w]*uję*) hush up

zatwardz|enie *n* (-*a*; *G* -*eń*) *med.* constipation; ~**iały** inveterate

zatwierdz|ać (-*am*) ⟨~**ić**⟩ confirm, endorse; *plan itp.* approve

za|ty|czka *f* (-*i*; *G* -*czek*) plug; ~**kać** (-*am*) *zlew* block; *butelkę* cork; *uszy, dziurę* plug; ~**kać się** get blocked; → **wtykać**

zaufani|e *n* (-*a*; *0*) trust; confidence (**do** *G* in); **brak** ~**a** mistrust; **w** ~**u** confidentially

zaufany trusted

zaułek *m* (-*łka*; -*łki*) lane

zautomatyzowany automated; *też fig.* mechanized

zauważ|ać ⟨~**yć**⟩ (-*ę*) notice; (*mówić*) mention

zawadia|cki spirited, flamboyant; ~**ka** *m* (-*a*; *G* -*ów*) daredevil

zawadz|ać (-*am*) ⟨~**ić**⟩ (**o** *A*) knock, bump (against, on); get caught (on); *t-ko impf.* be in the way

zawa|hać się *pf.* → **wahać**

zawalać¹ *pf.* → **walać**

zawa|la**ć²** ⟨~**lić**⟩ *pokój* clutter (up); *drogę* block, obstruct; F mess up; ~**lić się** collapse;~**lony** F (*pracą*) snowed under

zawał *m* (-*u*; -*y*) (**serca** heart) attack, *med.* cardiac infarction

zawart|ość *f* (-*ści*; *0*) (*paczki*) contents *pl.*; (*książki*) content(s *pl.*); ~**y** *umowa* concluded

za|ważyć *pf.* (**na** *L*) weigh (on); ~**wczasu** *adv.* in good time; ~**wdzięczać** (-*am*) *owe*; ~**wezwać** *pf.* → **wzywać**; ~**wiać** *pf.* → **zawiewać**

zawiad|amiać ⟨~**omić**⟩ (**o** *L*) inform (about), notify (about); ~**omienie** *n* (-*a*; *G* -*eń*) notice, notification; announcement

zawiadowca *m* (-*y*; *G* -*ców*): ~ **stacji** *rail.* station master

zawiany F tipsy

zawias *m* (-*u*; -*y*) hinge

zawiąz|ywać ⟨~**ać**⟩ tie; *supeł też* knot;

Z

chustę itp. put on; *oczy* blindfold; *fig.*
spółkę establish, form; ~**(yw)ać się** *bot.*
owoc form; *fig.* become established

zawiedziony (*m-os.* -*dzeni*) disappointed

zawie|ja *f* (-*ei*; -*e*, -*ei*) blizzard; ~**rać**
(-*am*) contain; include; *kontrakt* conclude; *znajomość* make; ~**rucha** *f* (-*y*;
G -) gale; *fig.* turmoil; ~**ruszyć się** *I*
pf. (-*ę*) get lost; ~**sić** *pf.* (-*szę*) → **za-**
wieszać; ~**sisty** thick

zawiesz|ać (-*am*) *v/t.* hang (*też ściany*
itp. I with); *fig. obrady* suspend; *karę*
jur. defer; ~**ać w czynnościach** suspend from one's post; ~**enie** *n* (-*a*; *G*
-*eń*) suspension (*też mot.*); deferment;
~**enie broni** cease-fire; **z ~eniem** *jur.*
on probation

zawie|ść *pf. v/t.* disappoint; *nadzieje*
deceive; *v/i. głos:* fail; ~**ść się (na,**
w *L*) become disappointed (with)

zawietrzn|y: strona ~a lee

zawiewać (-*am*) *drogę* cover

zawieźć *pf.* → **zawozić**

zawi|jać (-*am*) *v/t.* fold; wrap (up); *ręka-*
wy roll up; ~**jać do portu** put in at a
port; ~**kłany** → **zawiły;** ~**le** *adv.* in a
complex way; intricately; ~**lgnąć** *pf.*
(-*nę*, *też* -*l*) become damp; ~**ły** complex,
complicated; intricate; ~**nąć** *pf.* → **za-**
wijać; ~**niątko** *n* (-*a*; *G* -*tek*) bundle;
parcel; ~**nić** *pf.* be guilty, be at fault
(*I* for); **w czym on ci ~nił?** what did
he do to you?; ~**niony: nie ~niony**
through no fault of one's own

zawis|ać (-*am*) *v/i.* hang; hover; ~**ać**
w powietrzu hover in the air; ~**ły** be
dependent; ~**nąć** *pf.* (-*nę*) → **zawisać**

zawi|stny envious, jealous; ~**ść** *f* (-*ści*;
0) envy, jealousy

za|witać *pf.* (**do** *G*) come (to), pay a
visit (to); ~**wlec** *pf.* drag (**się** o.s.); *cho-*
robę bring in; ~**władnąć** *pf.* (-*nę*) (*I*)
possess, seize

zawod|niczka *f* (-*i*; *G* -*czek*), ~**nik** *m*
(-*a*; -*cy*) (*w sporcie*) contestant; competitor; player; ~**ny** unreliable; *nadzieje*
deceptive; ~**owiec** *m* (-*wca*; -*wcy*) professional, F pro; (*sport*) professional
sportsman; ~**owo** *adv.* professionally;
~**owy** professional; ~**ówka** *f* (-*i*; *G*
-*wek*) F trade school; ~**y** *m/pl.* (-*dów*)
competition, contest; ~**y międzynaro-**
dowe international competition

zawodzić wail; → **zawieść**

zawojow(yw)ać (-[*w*]*uję*) win, conquer

zawołanie *n* call; *jak na* ~ on cue; **na**
każde ~ at s.o.'s beck and call

zawozić drive, carry

zawód *m* (-*wodu*; -*wody*) profession,
occupation; (*rozczarowanie*) disappointment; **z zawodu** by profession;
spotkał go ~ it was a disappointment
to him; **sprawić** ~ disappoint

zawór *m* (-*woru*, -*wory*) *tech.* valve
~ **bezpieczeństwa** safety valve

zawracać *v/i.* turn back; *mot.* make a
U-turn; ~ **komuś w głowie** turn s.o.'s
head; *v/t.* ~ **głowę** (*D*) bother, hassle

za|wrotny vertiginous, dizzying; ~**wró-**
cić *pf.* → **zawracać;** ~**wrót** *m* (-*otu*,
-*oty*): ~**wrót głowy** dizziness, vertigo;
~**wrzeć** *pf.* → **zawierać, wrzeć;**
~**wstydzić** (-*am*) → **wstydzić;** ~**wsty-**
dzony ashamed

zawsze 1. *adv.* ever; **na** ~ for ever; **2.**
part. yet, after all

zawy|- *pf.* → **wy-;** ~**żać** (-*am*) ⟨~**żyć**⟩
(-*ę*) *poziom* make too high

za|wziąć się *pf.* be determined (**że** to
bezok.); (**na** *A*) harass; ~**wzięty** fierce

zazdro|sny jealous, envious (**o** *A* of);
~**ścić ⟨po-⟩** (-*szczę*) (**k-u** *G*) envy (s.o.
s.th.); ~**ść** *f* (-*ści*; *0*) envy; jealousy;
~**śnie** *adv.* jealously, enviously

zazębi|ać się (-*am*) ⟨~**ć się**⟩ (-*ę*) mesh,
engage; ~**ony** meshed together

zazieleni|ać (-*am*) ⟨~**ć**⟩ make green;
~**ać się** become green

zazię|bia(a)ć się *pf.* → **przezię**bi(a)ć się

zaznacz|ać (-*am*) ⟨~**yć**⟩ (-*ę*) mark,
highlight; (*występować*) emphasize; ~**ać**
się be marked; (*pojawiać się*) appear

zazna|ć *pf.* → **zaznawać;** ~**jamiać**
(-*am*) ⟨~**jomić**⟩ (-*ę*) → **zapoznawać;**
~**wać** (-*ję*) → **doświadczać; nie ~ć**
spokoju have no peace

zazwyczaj *adv.* usually

zażalenie *n* (-*a*; *G* -*eń*) complaint,
grievance

za|żarcie *adv.* vehemently; fiercely;
~**żarty** vehement; fierce; ~**żą-** *pf.* →
żą-; ~**żegnywać** (-*uję*) ⟨~**żegnać**⟩
(*zapobiec*) prevent, forestall; *kłótni, re-*
belii head off

zażenowan|ie *n* (-*a*; *0*) embarrassment; ~**y** embarrassed, ashamed

zaży|ć *pf.* → **zażywać;** ~**łość** *f* (-*ści*; *0*)

closeness, intimacy; ~ły close, intimate; ~wać (-am) lek take; *spokoju itp.* enjoy; ~wny corpulent

ząb *m* (*zęba; zęby*) (**mądrości, mleczny** wisdom, milk) tooth; (*jadowy* poison) fang; **do zębów** dental, tooth; ~ek *m* (*-bka; -bki*) → **ząb; ~ek czosnku** clove of garlic; ~kować (-*uję*) teethe, cut teeth; ~kowany serrated

zba- *pf.* → **ba-**

zbaczać (-*am*) turn off (**z głównej drogi** the main road); *fig.* deviate

zbankrutowany bankrupt

zbaw|ca *m* (-*y*; *G -ców*), ~czyni *f* (-*i*; -*e*) savio(u)r; ~iać (-*am*) ⟨~ić⟩ (-*ę*) save; ₂iciel *m* (-*a*; -*e*) *rel.* Savio(u)r

zbawien|ie *n* (-*a*; *0*) salvation, redemption; ~ny salutary, beneficial

zbe- *pf.* → **be-**

zbędny needless; → **niepotrzebny**

zbić *pf.* beat up; *szybę* break; → **zbijać**

zbiec *pf.* (→ **biegnąć**) (**z** *G*) flee, run away (from); → **zbiegać**

zbieg *m* **1.** (-*a; -owie*) fugitive, runaway; **2.** (-*u; -i*): ~ **ulic** junction of the streets; ~ **okoliczności** coincidence; ~ać (-*am*) run down (**po schodach** the stairs); ~ać **się** *ludzie*: gather; *materiał*: shrink; (**w** *czasie*) coincide; ~owisko *n* (-*a; G* -) mixed lot

zbiera|cz *m* (-*a*; -*e*), ~czka *f* (-*i*; *G* -*czek*) collector; ~ć (-*am*) *fig.* summon; ~ć **się** *coś*: accumulate; *ktoś*: gather, assemble; ~ **mi się na** (*A*) I am going to …; ~ć **obfite żniwo** *fig.* take one's toll; ⟨**na-, po-**⟩ (**do kolekcji**) collect; *agr. kwiaty* pick, (**z pola**) harvest; ~nina *f* (-*y*; *G* -) jumble, hotchpotch; (*ludzi*) ill-assorted group

zbież|ność *f* (-*ści*; *0*) convergence; (*opinii itp.*) concurrence; ~ość **kół** *mot.* toe-in; ~y convergent; concurrent

zbija|ć (-*am*) *skrzynię* make; *deski* nail together; *argumenty* disprove; ~ **z tropu** disconcert, put off; → **zbić, bąk**

zbiorni|ca *f* (-*y*; *G* -) collecting point; ~k *m* (-*a*; -*i*) tank; container; (*jezioro*) reservoir; ~kowiec *m* (-*wca*; -*wce*) *naut.* tanker

zbiorow|isko *n* (-*a; G* -) collection; (*ludzi*) crowd; ~o *adv.* collectively; ~y collective; → **układ**

zbiór *m* (*zbioru, zbiory*) collection; *math.* set; *zw. agr.* harvest, crop; ~ka *f*

(-*i*; *G* -*rek*) *mil.* roll-call, muster; (*pieniędzy*) collection

zbity beaten; ~ **z tropu** baffled; *por.* **zbić**

zbla|- *pf.* → **bla-**; ~zowany blasé

zbliż|ać (-*am*) bring nearer *lub* closer, move closer (**do** *G* to); (**do siebie**) bring (closer) together; ~ać **się** get closer, approach; *data też*: be forthcoming; *ludzie*: be drawn together; ~enie *n* (-*a*; *G* -*eń*) approach; *phot.* close-up; (*stosunek*) intimacy; ~ony close (**do** *G* to); ~yć *pf.* (-*ę*) → **zbliżać**

zbłąkany lost, stray; → **błądzić**

zbocz|e *n* (-*a*; -*y*) slope; ~enie *n* (-*a*; *G* -*eń*) deviation, perversion; ~eniec *m* (-*ńca*; -*ńcy*) pervert; ~yć *pf.* → **zbaczać**

zbolały hurt, painful (*też fig.*)

zboż|e *n* (-*a*; *G* zbóż) *bot.* cereal, grain, *Brt.* corn; ~owy grain, cereal; **kawa** ~owa coffee substitute (*from barley*)

zbór *m* (*zboru, zbory*) (Protestant) church; (Protestant church) community

zbroczony: ~ **krwią** bloodstained

zbrodni|a *f* (-*i*; -*e*) crime; ~arka *f* (-*i*; *G* -*rek*), ~arz *m* (-*a*; -*e*) criminal; ~czy criminal

zbro|ić¹ ⟨**u-**⟩ (-*ę*, *zbrój!*) arm (**się** o.s.); supply with new weapons; *beton itp.* reinforce; *teren* develop

zbro|ić² *pf.* → **broić**; ~ja *f* (-*oi*; -*e*, -*oi/-ój*) *hist.* (suit of) armo(u)r; ~jenia *n/pl.* (-*ń*) armament; (*betonu itp.*) reinforcement; ~ **wyścig** ~jeniowy arms; ~jnie *adv.* militarily; ~jny armed; militarily; **siły** *f/pl.* ~jne armed forces *pl.*; ~jo-ny: *beton* ~jony reinforced concrete

zbrzy|dnąć *pf.* → **brzydnąć**; ~ło **mi** …I am sick of …

zbudzić *pf.* → **budzić**

zbulwersowany indignant

zbutwiały rotten, decayed

zby|cie *n* (-*a*; *0*) sale; ~ć *pf.* → **zbywać**

zbyt¹ *adv.* too, over…

zbyt² *m* (-*u*; *0*) sale; **cena** ~u selling price, retail price

zby|teczny superfluous; excessive; ~tek *m* (-*tku*; *0*) excess; (-*tku*; -*tki*) luxury; opulence; ~tki *pl.* → **figiel**

zbyt|kowny luxurious, sumptuous; ~ni excessive, exceeding; ~nio *adv.* excessively, exceedingly

zbywać (-*am*) sell; *fig. kogoś* put off, get rid of; **nie zbywa mu na** (*L*) he has enough of everything

zca, z-ca *skrót pisany:* **zastępca** Dep. (*deputy*)

z.d. *skrót pisany:* **z domu** née

zda|ć *pf.* → **zdawać**; *egzamin* pass; *szkoła:* (*do wyższej klasy*) be promoted; **nie ~ć** fail; F **~ć się** → **przydawać się**; **być ~nym** (**na** *A*) be at the mercy (of); depend (on); **~lny**: **~lnie kierowany** remote-controlled; *mil.* guided

zdanie *n* (-*a*; *G* -*ań*) sentence; (**podrzędne, główne** subordinate, main) clause; (*pogląd*) view, opinion; *moim ~m* in my view

zdarz|ać się (-*am*) ⟨**~yć się**⟩ happen, occur; **~enie** *n* (-*a*; *G* -*eń*) event; occurrence

zdatny fit (**do** *G* to)

zdawać (*przekazywać*) transfer, make over; *raport* hand over; ~ **bagaż** *aviat.* check in; *rail.* deposit; ~ **egzamin** take (*Brt.* sit) an exam(ination); ~ **się** (**na** *A*) rely (on), depend (on); **zdaje się, że** it seems/appears that; → **przydawać się**

zdawkowy trivial, insignificant

zdąż|ać (-*am*) ⟨**~yć**⟩ → **dążyć, nadążać; nie ~yć** be late, miss *s.th.*

zdech|ły dead; **~nąć** *pf.* → **zdychać**

zdecydowani[1] *n* (-*a*; *0*) determination; decisiveness

zdecydowan|ie[2] *adv.* decisively; **~y** determined, decisive; *por.* **decydować**

zdegustowany displeased,

zdejmować (-*uję*) remove (*też za stanowiska*); *ubranie* take off; *słuchawkę* pick up; (*z porządku dnia*) delete

zde|ma-, ~me-, ~mo- *pf.* → **ma-, me-, mo-;** ~**nerwowany** upset, irritated; ~**po-** *pf.* → **po-;** ~**prymowany** depressed, dejected

zderz|ać się (-*am*) (**z** *I*) collide (with), crash (into); **~ak** *m* (-*a*; -*i*) *mot.* bumper; *rail.* buffer; **~enie** *n* (-*a*; *G* -*eń*) collision, crash; **~yć się** *pf.* (-*ę*) → **zderzać się**

zde|terminowany determined; intent (**co do** *G* on); ~**tonowany** confused, bewildered; ~**wastowany** damaged; ravaged; ~**ze-,** ~**zo-** *pf.* → **deze-, dezo-**

zdjąć *pf.* → **zdejmować**

zdjęcie *n* (-*a*; *G* -*ęć*) removal; *phot.* photograph, F *snap*(*shot*); *też* picture

zdła|- *pf.* → **dła-;** ~**wiony** muted, choked

zdmuch|iwać (-*uję*) ⟨**~nąć**⟩ blow away

zdob|ić ⟨**o-**⟩ (-*ę*, -*ób!*) decorate; ~**niczy** decorative

zdoby|cie *n* (-*a*; *G* -*yć*) conquest; ~**ć** *pf.* → **zdobywać;** ~**cz** *f* (-*y*) haul, loot; capture; ~**czny** captured; ~**wać** (-*am*) get, obtain; *kraj* conquer; *wiedzę* gain; *bramkę* score; *rezultat* achieve; capture; ~**wca** *m* (-*y*; *G* -*ców*), ~**wczyni** *f* (-*i*; -*nie*, *G* -*yń*) conqueror; (*medalu* medal) winner

zdoln|ość *f* (-*ści*) ability; *zw. pl.* ~**ości** (**do** *G*) talent, gift; ~**y** talented, gifted; (**do** *G*) fit (for); ~**y do pracy** fit for work

zdołać *pf.* (-*am*) be able to

zdra|da *f* (-*y*; *G* -) betrayal, treachery; (*państwa* treason); ~**da małżeńska** infidelity; ~**dliwy** (-*wie*) treacherous; ~**dzać** (-*am*) ⟨**~dzić**⟩ (-*ę*) betray (*się* o.s.); be unfaithful (**żonę** to the wife); ~**dziecki** treacherous; ~**dziecko** *adv.* treacherously; ~**jca** *m* (-*y*; *G* -*ców*), ~**jczyni** *f* (-*i*; -*nie*, *G* -*yń*) traitor

zdrap|ywać (-*uję*) ⟨**~ać**⟩ scrape off

zdrętwiały numb; → **drętwieć**

zdrobnienie *n* (-*a*; *G* -*eń*) pet-name; *gr.* diminutive

zdro|je *pl.* → **zdrój; ~jowisko** *n* (-*a*; *G* -) spa; ~**jowy** spa

zdrow|ie *n* (-*a*; *0*) health; *on zapadł na ~iu* his health deteriorated; (*za*) ~**ie twoje!** your health!; *na ~ie!* bless you!; ~**o** *adv.* healthily; ~**otny** sanitary; healthy; ~**y** healthy (*też fig.*); ~**y rozsądek** common sense

zdrój *m* (-*oju*; -*oje*) spring; *lit.* fount

zdrów *pred.* → **zdrowy; bądź ~!** farewell!, good-bye!; *cały i ~* safe and well

zdruzgotany shattered (*też fig.*)

zdrzemnąć się *pf.* (-*nę*) drowse; nod off

zdumi|enie *n* (-*a*; *0*) astonishment; ~**ewać się** (-*am*) ⟨**~eć się**⟩ (-*eję*) (*I*) be astonished *lub* amazed (at); ~**ewająco** *adv.* amazingly; ~**ewający** astonishing, amazing; ~**ony** astonished

zdun *m* (-*a*; -*i*) stove-builder

zduszony choked; → **dusić**

zdwajać (-*am*) double; → **podwajać**

zdy|- *pf.* → **dy-;** ~**chać** (-*am*) die; ~**szany** out of breath;

zdziecinniały infantile

zdzier|ać (-*am*) tear off *lub* down; *odzież* wear out; ~**ać skórę** (*zwierzęcia*) skin; (*na kolanach itp.*) chafe the skin; F rip off; ~stwo n (-a; G -) F rip-off

zdzira f (-y; G -) pej. bitch

zdziwi|ć pf. → dziwić; ~enie n (-a; 0) astonishment

ze prp. → z

zebra m (-y; G -) zo. zebra; mot. Brt. zebra (crossing), Am. crosswalk

zebra|ć pf. → zbierać; ~nie n (-a; G -ań) (wyborcze election) meeting

zecernia f (-i; -e) print. composing room

zédrzeć pf. → zdzierać

zegar m (-a; -y) clock; ~ek m (-rka; -rki) watch; ~mistrz m watchmaker; ~ynka f (-i; G -nek) tel. speaking clock

ze|gnać pf. → zganiać; ~jście n (-a; G -jść) way down, descent; ~jść pf. (-jść) → schodzić

zelować ⟨pod-⟩ (-uję) sole

zelówka f (-i; G -wek) sole

ze|lżeć pf. (-eję) let up; ból, wiatr: ease; burza, gniew: die down; gorączka: go down; ~mdlenie n (-a; G -eń) faint; ~mdlony fainted; ~mknąć → zmykać

zemsta f (-y; 0) revenge

zepchnąć pf. → spychać

zepsu|cie n (-a; 0) decay; fig. corruptness, depravity; ulegać ~ciu decay; → psuć(się); ~ty broken; mięso off, bad;

zerk|ać (-am) ⟨~nąć⟩ (-nę) take a glance (na A at)

zer|o n (-a; G -) zero; nought; poniżej/ powyżej ~a below/above zero; dwa ~o two to nil

ze|rwać pf. → zrywać; ~rznąć, ~rżnąć pf. → zrznać; ~schnąć się pf. → zsychać się; ~skakiwać (-uję) ⟨~skoczyć⟩ (z G) jump (down); (z roweru) jump (off); ~skrobywać (-uję) ⟨~skrobać⟩ scrape off; ~słać pf. ⟨stać⟩ → zsyłać; ~słanie n (-a; G -ań) deportation

ze|spalać (-am) unite (się v/i.); ~spawać pf. tech. weld together; ~spolić pf. (-lę, -ól!) → zespalać; ~społowy group, collective; ~spół m (-połu; -poły) group (też mus.); team; tech. unit, set; med. syndrome

zestaw m (-u; -y) set; kit; ~ stereo stereo; ~iać ⟨~ić⟩ put together (z I with); ~ienie n (-a; G -eń) combination, comparison; compilation (danych); w ~ieniu z (I) in comparison with

zestrzelić pf. shoot down

zeszlifow(yw)ać (-[w]uję) grind down lub off

zesz|łoroczny of the previous year; ~ły last; w ~łym roku last lub previous year

zeszpecony disfigured; → szpecić

zeszyt m (-u; -y) exercise-book; (czasopisma) issue

ześliz|giwać się (-uję) ⟨~(g)nąć się⟩ (-nę) slide off; slip off lub down

ze|śrubow(yw)ać (-[w]uję) screw together; ~tknąć pf. → stykać; ~trzeć pf. → ścierać

zewnątrz: adv. na ~ outside; z ~ from the outside

ze|wnętrzny outside; external; outer; ~wrzeć pf. (-wrzeć) → zwierać; ~wsząd adv. from everywhere

zez m (-a; 0) squint; mieć ~a squint, have a squint

zezna|nie n (-a; G -ań) jur. statement; ~wać (-ję) ⟨~ć⟩ state, testify

zezowa|ć (-uję) squint, have a squint; ~ty cross-eyed

zezw|alać (-am) ⟨~olić⟩ (-ę, -ól!) (na A) allow (to bezok.), permit; ~olenie n (-a; G -eń) permission

zeżreć pf. → zżerać

zęb|aty toothed; tech. cog; ~owy dental, tooth; ~y pl. → ząb

ZG skrót pisany: Zarząd Główny head office

zgad|ywać (-uję) ⟨~nąć⟩ (-nę) guess; zagadkę solve; ~nij (have a) guess; ~ywanka f (-i; G -nek) guessing game

zgadzać się (-am) (na A, z I) agree (to, with); rachunek: be correct

zgaga f (-i; G -) med. heartburn

zga|lać (-am) shave off; ~niać herd together; → odganiać; ~rniać (-am) ⟨~nąć⟩ sweep; rake together; → zgrabiać, odgarniać; ~sły ogień extinguished; extinct

zgęszczać (-am) → zagęszczać

zgiąć pf. → zginać, giąć

zgiełk m (-u; 0) noise; din; ~liwy noisy

zgię|cie n (-a; G -ęć) bend; crook; ~ty bent

zgin|ać (-am) (się) bend; ~ać się double up; ~ać pf. → ginąć

zgliszcza pl. (-) smouldering ruins pl.

zgładzić pf. slay

zgłaszać (-am) kradzież itp. report; wniosek put forward, submit; protest lodge; akces, do oclenia declare; ~ się

(*u, do G*) report (to); (*do G*) enter
zgłębiać (*-am*) fathom, penetrate
zgłodniały hungry, famished
zgło|sić *pf.* → **zgłaszać**; ~**ska** *f* (*-i; G -sek*) syllable; ~**szenie** *n* (*-a; G -eń*) report; declaration; application; entry
z|głu- *pf.* → **głu-**; ~**gnębiony** harassed
zgniat|ać (*-am*) ⟨**zgnieść**⟩ squash; mash; ~**anie** *n* (*-a; G -eń*): **strefa** ~**ania** → **zgniot**
zgni|ć *pf.* → **gnić**; ~**lizna** (*-y; 0*) *fig.* decadence, decay; ~**ły** rotten, decayed
zgniot *m* (*-u; -y*): **strefa** ~**u** *mot.* crumple zone
zgod|a *f* (*-y; 0*) agreement, consent; **wyrazić** ~**ę** (**na** *A*) agree (to); **dojść do** ~**y** come to an agreement; ~**a!** OK!, (*przy kupowaniu*) done; → ~**ność**; ~**nie** *adv.* in harmony; ~**nie z** according to; ~**ność** *f* (*-ści*) agreement; unanimity; ~**ny** agreeable; *decyzja* unanimous; (**z** *I*) compatible (with); consistent (with); ~**ny z prawem** lawful
zgo|dzić się *pf.* → **zgadzać się**; ~**lić** *pf.* → **zgalać**; ~**la** *adv.* quite, completely
zgon *m* (*-u; -y*) death; ~**ić** *pf.* → **zganiać**
zgorsz|enie *n* (*-a; G -eń*) scandal, outrage; **wywołać** ~**enie** cause offence; ~**ony** offended, shocked
zgorzel *f* (*-i; 0*) *med.* gangrene
zgorzkniały embittered, bitter
zgotować *pf.* → **gotować, przygotowywać**
zgrabi|ać (*-am*) ⟨~**ć**⟩ rake together
zgrabiały numb (with cold)
zgrabny deft, adroit; (*kształtny*) shapely; (*zręczny*) nimble
zgraja *f* (*-ai; -e*) (*wilków*) pack; *fig.* gang
zgrany harmonious
zgromadz|ać *pf.* → **gromadzić**; ~**enie** *n* (*-a; G -eń*) assembly, gathering
zgroza *f* (*-y; 0*) horror
zgru|biały thickened, swollen; ~**bienie** *n* (*-a; G -eń*) thickening; swelling; *gr.* augmentative; ~**bny** rough; ~**cho-** *pf.* → **grucho-**
zgrupowanie *n* (*-a; G -ań*) group(ing)
zgry|wać (*-am*) harmonize; ~**wać się** overact; (**na** *A*) play; ~**zać** (*-am*) bite; ~**ziony** sorrowful; ~**zota** *f* (*-y; G -*) worry, anxiety; ~**źć** *pf.* → **zgryzać**; ~**źliwie** *adv.* caustically, bitingly; ~**źliwy** caustic, biting

zgrza|ć (*-eję*) *pf.* → **zgrzewać**; ~**łem się** I am hot
zgrzebło *n* (*-a; G -beł*) curry-comb
zgrzewa|ć (*-am*) *folię* seal; *tech.* weld (together); ~**rka** *f* (*-i; G -rek*) (*do folii*) (bag) sealer
zgrzybiały decrepit
zgrzyt *m* (*-u; -y*) screech, jar; *fig.* hitch; ~**ać** (*-am*) screech, grate; jar; (*zębami*) grind
zgub|a *f* (*-y; G -*) loss; (*-y; 0*) undoing; doom; ~**ić** *pf.* → **gubić**; ~**iony** lost; *fig.* doomed; ~**ny** pernicious
zgwałcenie *n* (*-a; G -eń*) raping, rape
zhań- *pf.* → **hań-**
ZHP *skrót pisany:* **Związek Harcerstwa Polskiego** Polish Scouts Organization
ziać (*zieję*) yawn; *otchłań:* gape; ~**stęchlizną** have a musty smell; ~ **ogniem** belch fire
ziar|(e)nko *n* (*-a; G -nek*) → **ziarno**; (*kawy itp.*) bean; *fig.* germ, seed; ~**nisty** grainy; **kawa** ~**nista** whole-bean coffee; ~**no** *n* (*-a; G -ren*) grain; (*nasienie*) seed
ziele *n* (*-a; zioła, G ziół*) herb; ~**niak** *m* (*-a; -i*) *F* greengrocer('s); ~**nić** ⟨**za-**⟩ **się** (*-ę*) turn green; ~**niec** *m* (*-ńca; -ńce*) green space; ~**nieć** (*-eję*) look green; ~**nina** *f* (*-y; G -*) greens *pl.*; ~**ń** *f* (*-ni; -nie*) green
zielon|o- *w złoż.* green-; ~**y** green
zielsko *n* (*-a; G -*) weed
ziem|ia *f* (*-i; 0*) earth; soil, ground; land; **Ziа** *astr.* (*pl. 0*) Earth; **nad Ziа** above ground; ~**iopłody** *m/pl.* (*-dów*) agricultural products *pl.*; produce; ~**niaczny** potato; ~**niak** (*-a; -i*) potato; ~**ny** ground; **orzeszek** ~**ny** peanut; ~**ski** earthly, worldly; Earth('s); *posiadłość* landed
ziew|ać (*-am*) ⟨~**nąć**⟩ (*-nę*) yawn
zięb|a *f* (*-y; G -*) *zo.* chaffinch; ~**ić** (*-ę*) chill, cool; ~**nąć** (*-nę, też ziąbł*) be *lub* feel cold
zięć *m* (*-cia; -ciowie*) son-in-law
zim|a *f* (*-y; G -*) winter; ~**ą** in winter; ~**niej(szy)** *adv.* (*adj.*) (*comp. od* → **cold**) colder
zimno[1] *n* (*-a; 0*) cold, chill
zim|no[2] *adv.* cold; *fig.* coldly; ~**no mi** I am cold; ~**ny** cold chilly; ~**orodek** *m* (*-dka; -dki*) *zo.* kingfisher; ~**ować** ⟨**prze-**⟩ (*-uję*) winter; ~**owy** winter

zioł|a *pl.* → **ziele**; **~olecznictwo** *n* phytotherapy; **~owy** herbal

ziomek *m* (*-mka; -mkowie*) fellow-countryman

zionąć (*im*)*pf.* (*-nę, -ń!*) → **ziać**

ziółk|o *n* (*-a; G -łek*) *fig.* good-for-nothing; **~a** *pl.* herb tea; → **ziele**

zirytowany irritated, annoyed

ziszczać (*-am*) ⟨**ziścić**⟩ (*-szczę*) realize, fulfill; **~ się** come true

zjad|ać (*-am*) eat up; **~liwie** *adv.* viciously; **~liwy** vicious, scathing; *med.* virulent

zjaw|a *f* (*-y; G -*) apparition; phantom; **~iać się** (*-am*) ⟨**~ić się**⟩ appear; **~isko** *n* (*-a; G -*) phenomenon

zjazd *m* (*-u; -y*) (*samochodem*) downhill drive; (*spotkanie*) assembly, meeting; *sport*: downhill racing; *mot.* exit; **~owy** *narty*: downhill

zje|chać *pf.* → **zjeżdżać**; **~d-** *pf.* → **jed-**

zjednocz|enie *n* (*-a; G -eń*) unification; union; **~ony** united, united; **Zone Królestwo** United Kingdom; **~yć** *pf.* → **jednoczyć**

zje|dnywać *pf.* → **jednać**; **~łczały** rancid; **~ść** *pf.* → **zjadać**; **~żdżać** (*-am*) drive down; (*na nartach*) go down; turn off (**z drogi** the road); slip down; **~żdżaj!** hop it!; **~żdżać się** come together; arrive; **~żdżalnia** *f* (*-i; -e*) slide

zla|ć *pf.* → **zlewać**; **~tywać** (*-uję*) fly down; (*spadać*) fall down; **~tywać się** come flying up; come together

zląc się *pf.* → **zlęknąć się**

zlec|ać (*-am*) (*k-u A*) commission (s.o. to do s.th.); **~enie** *n* (*-a; G -eń*) order, commission; (*wypłaty* payment) order; → **polecenie**; **~eniodawca** *m* client, customer; **~ić** *pf.* (*-cę*) → **zlecać**

zleciec *pf.* → **zlatywać**

zlep|ek *m* (*-pku, -pki*) conglomeration, aggregate; **~iać** (*-am*) ⟨**~ić**⟩ glue (**się** together)

zlew *m* (*-u; -y*) (*kuchenny* kitchen) sink; **~ać** (*-am*) pour away; **~ać się** run together; *dźwięki*: blend together; **~isko** *n* (*-a*) *geogr.* basin; **~ki** *m/pl.* swill, slops *pl.*; **~ozmywak** *m* (*-a; -i*) sink

zleźć *pf.* → **złazić**

zlęknąć się become frightened

zli|czać ⟨**~czyć**⟩ total, add up; **~kwi-**, **~to-** *pf.* → **likwi-**, **lito-**; **~zywać** (*-uję*) ⟨**~ać**⟩ lick off

zlodowaciały iced up; (*też fig.*) icy

zlot *m* (*-u; -y*) meeting, reunion

ZLP *skrót pisany*: **Związek Literatów Polskich** Polish Writers' Association

zlustr-, zluz- *pf.* → **lustr-, luz-**

zł *skrót pisany*: **złoty** zloty

zła → **zło**, **zły**; **~go-** *pf.* → **łago-**; **~godzenie** *n* (*-a; G -eń*) alleviation; moderation; *jur.* mitigation

zła|mać *pf.* → **łamać**; **~manie** *n* (*-a; G -ań*) breaking; break; *med.* fracture; **~many** broken; **~zić** (*-żę*) (**z G**) climb (down); *farba*: flake off

złącz|ać *pf.* → **łączyć**; **~e** *n* (*-a; G -y*) *tech.* joint, connection; **~ka** *f* (*-i; G -czek*) *tech.* coupling

zł|e → **zły**; **~o** *n* (*-a; DL złu; 0*) (**mniejsze** lesser) evil; → **zły**

złoci *m-os* → **złoty**; **~ć** ⟨**po-**⟩ (*-ę*) gild; **~sty** golden

złoczyńca *m* (*-y; G -ców*) lawbreaker, criminal

złodziej *m* (*-a; -e*), **~ka** *f* (*-i; G jek*) thief; (*w sklepie*) shop-lifter; **~ka** F *electr.* adapter; **~ski** thievish; **~stwo** *n* (*-a; G -*) thieving

złom *m* (*-u; 0*) scrap metal; **~ować** (*-uję*) scrap

złorzeczyć (*-ę*) (*D*) curse

złoś|cić ⟨**roz-**⟩ (*-szczę*) make angry; irritate; **~cić się** get angry (**na A** at; **z powodu** G, o A about); get cross (**na A** with); **~ć** *f* (*-ści; 0*) anger; irritation; **na ~ć** (*G*) in defiance (of); **~liwie** *adv.* maliciously; **~liwość** *f* (*-ści; 0*) malice; maliciousness; **~liwy** malicious

złot|(aw)o **obrażowy** golden brown; **~nictwo** *n* (*-a; 0*) goldsmithery; **~nik** *m* (*-a; -cy*) goldsmith; **~o** *n* (*-a; 0*) *chem.* gold; **~ówka** *f* (*-i; G -wek*) one zloty coin; **~y 1.** gold; golden; **2.** *m* (*-ego; -e*) zloty

zło|wieszczo *adv.* ominously; **~wieszczy** ominous; **~wrogi** sinister; **~wrogo** *adv.* in a sinister manner

złoż|en- *n* (*-a; G złóż*) *geol.* deposit; **~enie** *n* submission; resignation; laying; saving; *gr.* compound; *por.* **składać**; **~ony** composed (**z G** of); complicated; **~yć** *pf.* → **składać**

złu|dny illusory; deceptive; **~dzenie** *n* (*-a; G -eń*) illusion, delusion; deception; **być ~dzenia podobnym do kogoś** be s.o.'s spit(ting) image

zły 1. (*comp.* **gorszy**) bad; evil; *odpowiedź też* wrong; *uczony* poor; **2. złe** *n* (*-ego*; *0*) evil; **brać/mieć za złe** take amiss; → **zło**

zm. *skrót pisany:* **zmarł(a)** died

zmal|- pf. → **ma-;** **~gać się** (*-am*) (**z** *I*) struggle (with); **~gania** *n/pl.* (*-ań*) struggle

zmar|ły dead, deceased; **~n-** *pf.* → **marn-**

zmarszcz|ka *f* (*-i*; *G -szczek*) wrinkle; **~ony** wrinkled

zmartwi|enie *n* (*-a*; *G -eń*) worry; **~ony** worried

zmartwychwsta|(wa)ć rise from the dead; **~nie** *n* (*-a*; *G -ań*) resurrection

zmarznięty [-r-z-] cold

zmaz|ywać (*-uję*) ⟨**~ać**⟩ wipe away *lub* off; *fig.* **winę** expiate

zmą-, zme-, zmę- *pf.* → **mą-, me-, mę-**

zmęcz|enie *n* (*-a*; *0*) exhaustion; weariness; **~ony** tired, weary, exhausted

zmia|- pf. → **mia-;** **~na** *f* (*-y*; *G -*) change; transformation; shift; (*nocna* night) duty; **na ~nę** interchangeably; **bez ~n** unchanged; *med.* no abnormality detected (*skrót:* **NAD**); **~tać** (*-am*) sweep away

zmiażdżenie *n* (*-a*; *G -eń*) *med.* crush

zmien|iać (*-am*) ⟨**~ić**⟩ change, alter (**się** *v/i.*); **~iać się** vary; (*przy pracy*) take turns; (**w** *A*) change over (to); **~ny 1.** changing; *tech.* alternating → **prąd; 2. ~na** *f* (*-ej*; *-e*) *math.* variable

zmierz|- pf. → **mierz-;** **~ać** (*-am*) (**ku** *D*, **do** *G*) head (for); *fig.* be driving (**do** *G* at); → **podążać**

zmierzch *m* (*-u*; *-y*) twilight, dusk; **~ać** (**się**) (*-am*) ⟨**~nąć (się)**⟩ (*-nę*, *-ł*) grow dark

zmierzwiony ruffled; matted

zmiesza|ć *pf.* → **mieszać, peszyć;** **~ć się** get confused; **~nie** *n* (*-a*; *0*) confusion

zmieść *pf.* → **zmiatać**

zmiękcz|acz *m* (*-a*; *-e*) softener; *chem.* plasticizer; **~ać** (*-am*) → **miękczyć**

zmiłowa|ć się *pf.* (**nad** *I*) have mercy (on); **~nie** *n* (*-a*; *0*) mercy

zmizerowany → **mizerny**

zmniejsz|ać (*-am*) decrease, diminish (**się** *v/i.*); reduce; *ból też* alleviate; **~enie** *n* (*-a*; *G -eń*) decrease; reduction

zmo|- pf. → **mo-;** **~gą, ~gę**

zmora *f* (*-y*; *G zmór*) nightmare (*też fig.*)

zmordowany dead tired

zmotoryzowany *mil.* motorized; with a car

zmowa *f* (*-y*; *G zmów*) conspiracy; *jur.* collusion

zmó|c *pf. sen:* overcome; *choroba:* lay low; **~wić** *pf.* **pacierz** say; **~wić się** → **umawiać**

zmrok *m* (*-u*; *0*) darkness; → **mrok, zmierzch**

zmurszały rotten, decayed

zmu|szać (*-am*) ⟨**~szę**⟩ force (**do** *G* to); **~szać się** force o.s. (**do** *G*); **~szony** forced; **być ~szonym** be forced (**do** *G* to)

zmy|ć *pf.* → **zmywać;** **~kać** (*-am*) → **umykać;** **~lić** *pf.* → **mylić**

zmysł *m* (*-u*; *-y*) sense, faculty; (**do** *G*) instinct (for); **postradać ~y** be out of one's mind; **~owo** *adv.* sensuously; **~owość** *f* (*-ści*; *0*) sensuousness, sensuality; **~owy** sensual, sensuous

zmyśl|ać (*-am*) ⟨**~ić**⟩ (*-ę*) make up, fib; **~ony** made-up; fictional

zmywa|ć (*-am*) wash up; **~lny** washable; **~rka** *f* (*-i*; *G -rek*) dishwasher

znachor *m* (*-a*; *-rzy*), **~ka** *f* (*-i*; *G -rek*) quack

znacz|ąco *adv.* significantly; **~ący** significant; meaningful; **~ek** *m* (*-czka*; *-czki*) (**stemplowy, pocztowy** fiscal, postage) stamp; (*oznaka*) badge; **~enie** *n* (*-a*; *G -eń*) meaning; significance, importance; **mieć ~enie dla** mean for; **~ny** considerable, substantial; significant; **~ony** marked; **~yć** (*-ę*) mean; **to ~y** that means *lub* is (*skrót:* i.e.); → **oznaczać**

znać (*-am*) know; **dać ~** (*D*) let know; **~ po niej, że ...** one can see that she...; **~ się** be acquainted; (*nawzajem*) know each other; **~ się (na** *L*) know (about); be familiar (with)

znad *prep.* (*G*) from above; **~ morza** from the seaside

znajdować (*-uję*) find; **~ się** be; *dom, wieś:* be situated *lub* located; (*po zgubieniu*) be found; (*zjawiać się*) turn up

znajom|ość *f* (*-ści*) acquaintance; (*przedmiotu*) (*G*) familiarity (with); **po ~ości** through connections *pl.*; **~y** *m* (*-ego*; *-i*), **~a** *f* (*-ej*; *-e*) acquaintance

znak *m* (*-u*; *-i*) (**drogowy** road) sign; (*oznaka*) symbol; (*przestankowy*) mark; **~ firmowy** logo; trademark; **~ życia**

sign of life; **na ~** (G) as a sign that; **~i** pl.
szczególne distinguishing features
pl.; **dawać się we ~i** (D) plague; (*wy-darzenie*) be a heavy blow (for)
znakomi|cie *adv.* eminently, outstand-ingly; **~tość** f (*-ści*) (*ktoś*) celebrity;
~ty eminent, outstanding
znakować ⟨*o-*⟩ (*-uję*) mark
znalaz|ca m (*-y*; G *-ców*), **~czyni** f (*-ni*;
-nie, *-yń*) founder
znale|ziony found; biuro rzeczy ~zio-nych Brt. lost property office, Am. lost
and found office; **~zisko** n (*-a*; G *-*)
finding; **~źć** pf. → **znajdować**; **~źne** n
(*-ego*; *-e*) reward
zna|mienity outstanding; **~mienny**
symptomatic (**dla** G of); **~mię** n (*-mie-nia*; *-miona*) birthmark; (*cecha*) charac-teristic
znany known (**z tego, że** from)
znaw|ca m (*-y*; G *-ców*), **~czyni** f (*-ni*;
-nie, *-yń*) expert; **okiem ~cy** with an
expert eye
znę|cać się (*-am*) (**nad** I) abuse, mal-treat; **~cić** pf. → **nęcić**; **~kany** (I) ex-hausted (with)
znicz m (*-a*; *-e*) grave-light; (*w kościele*)
sanctuary lamp; **~ olimpijski** the Olym-pic torch
zniechęc|ać (*-am*) ⟨*~ić*⟩ (*-cę*) (**do** G)
discourage (from); **~ić się** (**do** G) be-come discouraged; **~ający** discour-aging; **~enie** n (*-a*; *0*) discouragement
zniecierpliwi|enie n (*-a*; *0*) impatience;
~ony impatient; → **niecierpliwić**
znieczu|lać (*-am*) ⟨*~ić*⟩ (*-lę*) med.
an(a)esthetize; (*miejscowo*) give a local
an(a)esthetic; **~lający** an(a)esthetic;
~lenie n (*-a*; G *-eń*) med. an(a)esthesia
zniedołężniały infirm, frail
zniekształc|ać (*-am*) ⟨*~ić*⟩ (*-cę*) *informa-cje* distort; *palce itp.* deform, disfigure
znie|nacka *adv.* suddenly; out of the
blue; **~nawidzony** hated; → **nienawi-dzić**; **~sienie** n (*-a*; *0*) jur. abolition;
nie do ~sienia unbearable
zniesławi|ać (*-am*) ⟨*~ć*⟩ (*-ę*) slander;
libel; **~enie** n (*-a*; G *-eń*) slander; libel;
znieść pf. → **znosić¹**
zniewaga f (*-i*; G *-*) insult; **~żać** (*-am*)
⟨*~żyć*⟩ insult
zniewieściały effeminate
znikać (*-am*) → **niknąć**
znikąd *adv.* from nowhere

znik|nąć pf. → **znikać**; **~nięcie** n (*-a*; G
-ęć) disappearance; **~omy** slight, small,
trivial; **~omo krótki/mało** very short/
little
zniszcz|ały dilapidated; → **niszczeć**;
~enie n (*-a*; G *-eń*) damage; **~ony**
broken, damaged
zni|we- pf. → **niwe-**; **~żać** (*-am*) lower;
let down, take down; **~żać się** go down;
teren: drop away, slope
zniżk|a f (*-i*; G *-żek*) reduction; dis-count; **~ować** (*-uję*) econ. go down,
sink; **~owy** reduced; *trend* downhill;
po cenie ~owej at a discount price;
zno|- pf. → **no-**
znosić¹ carry; *prawo* abolish, repeal; *jaj-ka* lay; *dom* demolish; *most* wash away;
łódź drift (**z kursu** off the course); *za-kaz* lift; *przykrość, ból* bear, endure;
klimat tolerate; *kogoś* stand; **~ się** (**z** I)
get on *lub* along (with);
zno|sić² pf. *ubranie* wear out; **~śny**
bearable, passable, Brt. not (so) bad
znowu, ~ż, znów 1. *adv.* again; once
again; **2.** *part.* so
znudz|enie n (*-a*; *0*) boredom, dullness,
tedium; **do ~enia** ad nauseam; **ze
~eniem** bored; **~ić** pf. bore; pall on;
~ić się (I) be bored (with); **~ony** bored
znuż|enie n (*-a*; *0*) exhaustion; weari-ness; **~yć się** (I) become exhausted;
→ **nużyć**
zob. *skrót pisany:* **zobacz** see
zobacz|enie n: **do ~enia!** good-bye!;
~yć pf. (*-ę*) see; **~yć się** meet, meet each
other; **~ymy** we'll see
zobo|- pf. → **obo-**; **~jętniały** indifferent
zobowiąz|ać pf. → **zobowiązywać**;
~anie n (*-a*; G *-ań*) obligation, commit-ment; *econ.* liability; **~ywać** (*-uję*) ob-lige (**do** G to); **~ywać się** commit o.s.
(**do** G to)
zodiak m (*-u*; *0*) zodiac
zohydz|ać (*-am*) ⟨*~ić*⟩ make *s.o.*
loathe *s.th.*
zoolog m (*-a*; *-dzy*) zoologist; **~iczny**
zoological
zop-, zor- pf. → **op-, or-**
zorza f (*-y*; *-e*, G *zórz*) dawn; **~ polarna**
aurora, polar lights pl.
zosta|(wa)ć stay; remain, be (**przy**
I with); *t-ko* pf. become (**uszkodzonym**
damaged; **ojcem** a father); **~wi(a)ć** →
pozostawiać

ZOZ *skrót pisany:* **Zespół Opieki Zdrowotnej** health-care centre

zra|- *pf.* → **ra-**; **~stać się** (*-am*) *kości:* knit together; **~szać** (*-am*) spray; water

zraz *m* (*-u; -y*) *gastr.* steak

zrażać (*-am*) ⟨**zrazić**⟩: **~ do siebie**, **~ sobie** (*A*) set s.o. against; prejudice against; **nie ~ się** (*I*) not be put off

zrąb *m* (*zrębu; zręby*) log framing; *pl. fig.* foundations *pl.;* **~ać** *pf.* drzewo fell; hew down

zre|- *pf.* → **re-**; **~formowany** reformed; **~organizowany** re-organized

zresztą *adv.* incidentally

zrezygnowany resigned

zręby *pl.* → **zrąb**

zręczn|ość *f* (*-ści; 0*) dexterity, deftness; **~y** deft, dexterous, skil(l)ful

zro|dzić (*-ę*) → **rodzić**; **~gowacenie** *n* (*-a; G -eń*) callosity; **~sić** *pf.* → **zraszać**; **~snąć się** *pf.* → **zrastać się**; **~st** *m* (*-u; -y*) *med.* adhesion; **~śnięty** grown together; knitted together

zrozpaczony despairing

zrozumi|ale *adv.* understandably; comprehensibly; **~ały** understandable; comprehensible; **~ały sam przez się** natural; self-evident; **~enie** *n* (*-a; G -eń*) understanding; comprehension; **nie do ~enia** beyond comprehension; **dać do ~enia** give to understand; hint; **~eć** *pf.* → **rozumieć**

zróść się *pf.* → **zrastać się**

zrówn|ać *pf.* → **równać, zrównywać**; **~anie** *n* (*-a; G -ań*) equalization; parity; *astr.* equinox

zrównoważony balanced

zrówny|wać (*-uję*) *teren* level, even out; (*z I*) equate (with); **~ z ziemią** raze to the ground

zróżnicowany varied, differentiated

zrujnowany ruined; → **rujnować**

zryć *pf.* → **ryć**

zryw *m* (*-u; -y*) spurt; *mot.* acceleration; → **poryw**; **~ać** (*-am*) *v/t.* tear off *lub* down; *agr.* pick; *stosunki, zaręczyny* break off; *umowę* cancel, terminate; *głos* strain; *v/i.* (*z I*) break up (with); part (with); (*ukochanym*) walk out (on); **~ać się** break; (*ruszyć*) rush off; *ptak:* fly up; *wiatr:* spring up; → **rwać**

zrządz|ać (*-am*) ⟨**~ić**⟩ bring about

zrze|czenie (się) *n* (*-a; G -eń*) renunciation; relinquishment; **~kać się**(*-am*)

⟨**~c się**⟩ renounce, relinquish; *tronu, funkcji* abdicate; **~szać** (*-am*) ⟨**~szyć**⟩ bring together; unite; **~szać się** be associated; organize; **~szenie** *n* (*-a; G -eń*) association; **~szony** unionized (*w L* in)

zrzę|da *m/f* (*-y; G -*) grumbler, fault-finder; **~dzić** (*-ę*) (*na A*) grumble (at), find fault (with)

zrzu|cać (*-am*) ⟨**~cić**⟩ *v/t.* drop; *rogi, liście* shed; *ubranie, maskę* throw off; *winę* shift; **~t** *m* (*-u; -y*) *aviat.* (air)drop; **~tka** *f* (*-i; G -tek*) collection, *Brt.* F whip-round

zrzynać (*-am*) F copy (*od G* from)

zsadz|ać (*-am*) ⟨**~ić**⟩ help down; get down

zsiad|ać (*-am*) ⟨**zsiąść**⟩ (*z G*) get off; → **wysiadać**; **~ać się** curdle, set; **~łe mleko** sour milk

zstąpić *pf.* → **zstępować**

zstęp|ny *jur.* descending; **~ować** (*-uję*) descend (**po schodach** down the stairs); come down

zsu|wać (*-am*) ⟨**~nąć**⟩ (*z G*) slide (down); *stoły* push together; **~nąć się** (*z G*) slide (off), slip (off)

zsy|chać się (*-am*) dry up; wither; **~łać** (*-am*) deport, expel; **~p** *m* (*-u; -y*): **~p do śmieci** (*Brt.* garbage, *Am.* rubbish) chute; **~pywać** (*-uję*) ⟨**~pać**⟩ (*do G*) tip, pour off

zszy|wacz *m* (*-a; -e*) stapler; **~wać** (*-am*) ⟨**~ć**⟩ sew together; **~wka** *f* (*-i; G -wek*) staple

zubożały impoverished

zuch *m* (*-a; -y*) Cub; **~!** nice show!; **~owaty** daring, bold

zuchwa|le *adv.* audaciously; **~lstwo** *n* (*-a; G -*) impudence, impertinence; nerve; audacity; **~ły** bold; impudent, impertinent; audacious

zupa *f* (*-y; G -*) soup; **~ w proszku** instant soup

zupełn|ie *adv.* completely, entirely, wholly; **~y** complete, entire, whole; *por.* **całkowity**

Zurych *m* (*-u; 0*) Zurich

ZUS *skrót pisany:* **Zakład Ubezpieczeń Społecznych** state social insurance company

zuży|cie *n* use; (*paliwa itp.*) consumption; **~ć** *pf.* → **zużywać**; *też* → **~tkow(yw)ać**(*-[w]uję*)exploit, utilize, make use of; ~ty used; ~wać use up; use (*na* A for); ~wać się wear out, become used

zw. *skrót pisany*: zwany called; zwyczajny ordinary

zwać call (się o.s.)

zwal|ać pile up, heap up; (*z G*) unload (off, from); *winę, obowiązek* shift; *drzewo* fell; ~ać *z nóg* knock out; ~ać się fall down; → walić; ~czać (-*am*) ⟨~czyć⟩ combat; fight (*się* each other); *pf. fig.* overcome, get over; ~ić *pf.* → zwalać, walić; ~niać (-*am*) *bieg*, *tempo* reduce, slow down; (*z lekcji*) dismiss, send out; *hamulec* release; *pokój* vacate; *przejście* clear; (*z wojska*) discharge; *kogoś z pracy* lay off, dismiss; *kogoś* set free; liberate (*od G* from; *się* o.s.); *v/i.* slow down; ~niać się (*z pracy*) give notice; → zwolnić

zwał *m* (-*u*; -*y*) *górnictwo*: slag-heap; ~y *pl. fig.* heap, pile; mountains *pl.*

zwany → zwać; tak ~ so-called

zwapnienie *n* (-*a*; *G* -*eń*) calcification

zwarcie[1] *n* (-*a*; *G* -*rć*) *electr.* short circuit; *sport*: clinch; *gr.* stop

zwarcie[2] *adv.* densely, tightly

zwariowany crazy; → wariować

zwarty compact; *tłum* thick; dense, tight; *gr.* stop

zwarzyć się *pf.* (-*ę*) curdle; go sour

zważ|ać (-*am*) ⟨~yć⟩ (*na A*) pay attention (to), allow (for); *nie ~ając na* notwithstanding, despite; ~ywszy, *że* in view of the fact that; → ważyć

zwątpi|ć *pf.* (*w A*) doubt (in); ~enie *n* (-*a*; *G* -*eń*) doubt

z|we- *pf.* → we-; ~wędzić F *pf.* pinch

zwę|glony charred; ~szyć *pf.* scent, get wind of; ~żać (-*am*) ⟨~zić⟩ (-*żę*) narrow (się *v/i.*); *źrenice itp.* constrict; *suknię* take in; ~żenie *n* (-*a*; *G* -*eń*) narrowing; constriction

zwia|ć *pf.* → zwiewać; ~d *m* (-*u*; -*y*) *mil.* reconnaissance; (*patrol*) scouting patrol; ~dowca *m* (-*y*; *G* -*ców*) *mil.* scout

zwiastowa|ć (-*uję*) announce; *fig.* herald; 2nie *n* (-*a*; *G* -*ań*) *rel.* the Annunciation

zwiastun *m* (-*a*; -*i*/-*owie*) harbinger; *med.* symptom; (-*a*; -*y*) trailer (*filmu*)

związ|ać *pf.* → związywać; ~ek *m* (-*zku*; -*zki*) connection; relation; relationship; ~ek zawodowy trade union; *wstąpić w* ~ki małżeńskie enter into

the bond of marriage; *w* ~ku *z* in relation to; ~kowiec *m* (-*wca*; -*wcy*) (trade) unionist; ~kowy trade-union; ~ywać (-*uję*) tie together, tie up; associate; ~ywać się (*z I*) associate (with), be joined together (with)

zwichnąć (-*nę*) sprain, wrench, dislocate; ~ięcie *n* (-*a*; *G* -*ęć*) *med.* dislocation

zwiedz|ać (-*am*) visit; *miasto* see the sights, see; ~ający *m* (-*ego*; *G* -*ych*), ~ająca *f* (-*ej*; -*e*) visitor; ~anie *n* (-*a*; *G* -*ań*) (*G*) visit (to); sightseeing; ~ić *pf.* → zwiedzać

zwierać (-*am*) *electr.* short-circuit; ~ się clinch

zwierciadło *n* (-*a*; *G* -*deł*) looking-glass

zwierz|ać (-*am*) confide; ~ się (*k-o*) unburden o.s. (to s.o.), confide (in s.o.)

zwierzątko *n* (-*a*; *G* -*tek*) (small) animal

zwierzchni superior; ~czka *f* (-*i*; *G* -*czek*), ~k *m* (-*a*; -*cy*) superior

zwierzenie *n* (-*a*; *G* -*eń*) confession

zwierzę *n* (-*ęcia*; -*ęta*, *G* -*rząt*) animal; ~cy animal

zwie|rzyna *f* (-*y*; *G* -) *zbior.* animals; *hunt.* (*gruba* big) game; (*płowa* red) deer; ~szać (-*am*) ⟨~sić⟩ droop; ~ść *pf.* → zwodzić; ~trzały stale, flat; *geol.* eroded; ~wać (-*am*) *v/t.* blow away; *v/i.* F clear off; ~wny flimsy, gossamer

zwieźć *pf.* → zwozić

zwiędnięty wilted; → więdnąć

zwiększ|ać (-*am*) ⟨~yć⟩ (-*ę*) increase (się *v/i.*) → mnożyć

zwięzły concise; ~źle *adv.* concisely

zwijać (-*am*) wind up; roll up (się *v/i.*); *obóz* break, strike; *interes* wind up; F ~ się *fig.* → uwijać się

zwil|gotnieć *pf.* (-*eję*) become damp; ~żać (-*am*) ⟨~żyć⟩ (-*ę*) dampen, wet; *wargi* moisten

zwin|ąć *pf.* → zwijać; ~ny nimble, agile

zwiotczały flaccid, flabby

zwis|ać (-*am*) ⟨~snąć⟩ (-*nę*, -*ł*) droop, sag; ~tek *m* (-*tka*; -*tki*) roll (*papieru* of paper)

zwlekać (-*am*) *v/i.* (*z*) linger (with)

zwłaszcza *adv.* especially

zwłok|a *f* (-*i*; *G* -) delay; *kara za* ~ę *econ.* interest for late payment; *nie cierpiący* ~*i* imperative, urgent

zwłoki *pl.* (-) corpse, dead body

Z

zwodniczy misleading

zwodz|lić (-ę) mislead, deceive; **~ony → most**

zwolenni|czka f (-i; G -czek), **~k** m (-a; -cy) supporter; adherent

zwolni|ć pf. → **zwalniać**; **~ć się** lokal: become vacant; (z pracy) give notice, leave; **~enie** n (-a; G -eń) reduction, slow-down; dismissal, redundancy; release; vacating; clearing; discharge; liberation; (z obowiązku, podatku itp.) exemption; por. **zwalniać**; **~enie lekarskie** sick leave; szkoła: Brt. doctor's note, Am. doctor's excuse; **~ony** (z pracy) redundant, dismissed; (z obowiązku, płacenia) exempt; (z lekcji) excused

zwoł|ywać (-uję) ⟨**~ać**⟩ call together; zebranie call for, convene

zwozić (-żę) deliver, bring

zwój m (zwoju, zwoje) (drutu itp.) coil; (papieru) roll; (pergaminu) scroll

zwracać return, take back, give back; pieniądze repay; (kierować) direct (**do** G to); twarz, wzrok turn (**do** G to); (wymiotować) vomit, bring up; **~ koszty** reimburse; → **uwaga**; **~** turn (**do** G to, **ku** D towards); (być opłacalnym) pay

zwrot m (-u; -y) turn; (zwrócenie) return; repayment; (wyrażenie) expression; **~ w tył** mil. Brt. about-turn, Am. about-face; **~** reimbursement; **~ka** f (-i; G -tek) stanza; **~nica** f (-y; -e, G -) rail. Brt. points, Am. switch; **~nik** m (-a; -i) geogr. tropic; **~nikowy** tropical; **~ność** f (-ści; 0) mot. Brt. manoeuvrability, Am. maneuverability; **~ny** mot. Brt. manoeuvrable, Am. maneuverable; econ. repayable; gr. reflexive

zwrócić pf. → **zwracać**

zwycię|ski victorious; **~sko** adv. victoriously; **~stwo** n (-a; G -) victory; **~zca** m (-y; G -ców) victor, (w konkursie itp.) winner **~żać** (-am) ⟨**~żyć**⟩ (-ę) v/i. win; v/t. defeat; fig. overcome; **~żony** defeated; overcome

zwyczaj m (-u; -e) habit; (ludowy popular) custom; **starym ~em** in the traditional way; **wejść w ~** become a habit; **~ny** ordinary, normal; profesor, członek full; **~owo** adv. customarily; **~owy** customary

zwyk|le adv. usually; **jak ~le** as usual; **~ły** usual; regular; normal

zwymyślać (-am) pf. insult, abuse

zwyrodniały degenerate

zwyżk|a f (-i; G -żek) increase; rise; **~ować** (-uję) be on the increase; rise

zygzak m (-a; -i) zigzag; **~owaty** zigzag

zysk m (-u; -i) profit; fig. gain, benefit; **~iwać** (-uję) ⟨**~ać**⟩ (-am) (**na** L) profit (by, from); gain (**na czasie** time; **na wartości** in value); sławę acquire; **~owny** profitable

z.z. skrót pisany: **za zgodność** (G) for the correctness of

zza prp. (G) from behind, from beyond

zziajany out of breath; pies panting

zzielenieć pf. become green; turn green

zziębnięty chilled, cold

zżerać (-am) eat; rdza też: corrode

zżół|kły, ~nięty yellow; (ze starości) discolo(u)red

zży|ć się pf. → **zżywać się**; **~mać się** (-am) wince (**na** A at); **~mał się na myśl** (**o** L) he was annoyed at the thought (of); **~wać się** (-am) (z I) get accustomed (to), get familiar (with); (z kimś) get close (to)

Ź

ździebko F a little bit

ździebło n (-a, L ździeble; G ździeł) blade

źl|e adv. (comp. gorzej) badly, poorly; (ze złym wynikiem) wrongly; **~e, że ...** it's bad that; **~e się czuć** feel bad; **~i** m-os pl. → **zły**

źreb|lak m (-a; -i) zo. colt; **~ić** ⟨**o-**⟩ się (-ę) foal; **~ię** n (-ęcia; -ęta) foal

źrenic|a f (-y; G -) anat. pupil; **pilnować jak ~y oka** cherish s.th. like life itself

źródlan|y: woda ~a spring water

źródł|o n (-a; G -deł) (**mineralne, gorące** mineral, thermal) spring (też fig.); lit., fig. fount; **~wy** source

-ż *part.* → **-że**

żab|a *f* (*-y*; *G* -) *zo.* frog; **~i** frog('s); *fig.* froggy; **~ka** *f* (*-i*; *G* -*bek*) → **żaba**; (*drzewna*) arboreal frog, *zwł.* tree frog; *tech.* pipe wrench; *sport:* breaststroke; **~karka** *f* (*-i*; *G* -*rek*) *naut.* sailing ship; **~karz** *m* (*-a*; *-e*) F *sport:* breaststroke swimmer

żad|en (*f* **~na**, *n/pl.* **~ne**) no, none; no one, nobody; (*z przeczeniem*) any, anybody; **w ~en sposób** in no way; → **wypadek**

żag|iel *m* (*-gla*; *-gle*) *naut.* sail; **~lowiec** *m* (*-wca*; -*wce*) *naut.* sailing ship; **~lowy** sailing; **~lówka** *f* (*-i*; *G* -*wek*) *naut.* Brt. sailing boat, Am. sailboat

żakie|cik *m* (*-a*; *-i*) → **~t** *m* (*-u*; *-y*) jacket

żal[1] *m* (*-u*; *-e*) sorrow, regret; (*uraza*) grudge; (*skrucha*) remorse; *rel.* penitence; **~e** *pl.* complaints *pl.*

żal[2] *pred.:* **~(,** *że*) it is a pity (that); **~ mi go** I am sorry for him; **było jej ~** (*G*) she felt sorry (for); **czuć ~** (*do G*) bear a grudge (against); **~ić się** (*-lę*) complain (**na** *A* about)

żaluzja *f* (*-i*; *-e*) (*listwowa*) venetian blind; (*roleta*) Brt. roller blind, Am. roller window shade

żałob|a *f* (*-y*; *0*) mourning; **nosić ~ę,** **chodzić w ~ie** be in mourning; **~ny** mourning; **msza ~na** requiem (mass)

żało|sny pitiful; pathetic; **~śnie** *adv.* pitifully; pathetically; **~wać** ⟨*po-*⟩ (*G*) feel sorry (for); pity (*skąpić*) begrudge, deny; **nie ~wać sobie** (*G*) not deny o.s., allow o.s.; **nie ~wać** (*G*) not spare; **bardzo żałuję** I am very sorry

żar *m* (*-u*; *0*) heat; glow; *fig.* fervo(u)r

żarcie *f* (*-a*; *0*) F grub

żargon *m* (*-u*; *-y*) jargon, slang

żarliw|ie *adv.* fervently, ardently; **~y** fervent, *miłość* ardent; → **gorliwy**

żarłoczn|ość *f* (*-ści*; *0*) gluttony (*też rel.*), greed; **~ie** *adv.* greedily; **~y** greedy

żarłok *m* (*-a*; *-i*) glutton, overeater

żaroodporny heat-resistant

żarówka *f* (*-i*; *G* -*wek*) *electr.* bulb

żart *m* (*-u*; *-y*) joke; prank, trick; **~em,** **dla ~u** for fun; **z nim nie ma ~ów ...** he is not to be trifled with

żarto|bliwie *adv.* jokingly; **~bliwy** joking; **~wać** ⟨*za-*⟩ (*-uję*) joke

żartowni|sia *f* (*-i*; *-e*), **~ś** *m* (*-sia*; *-sie*) joker; prankster

żarzyć się (*-ę*) glow (*też fig.*)

żąć ⟨*z-*⟩ (*żnę*) reap

żąda|ć ⟨*za-*⟩ (*-am*) demand; **~nie** *n* (*-a*; *G* -*ań*) demand; **na ~nie** on demand

żądło *n* (*-a*; *G* -*deł*) sting

żą|dny (*G*) craving (for); avid (for, of); **~dny wiedzy** thirsty for knowledge; **~dza** *f* (*-y*; *-e*) (*G*) desire (for); (*pożądanie*) lust (for); **~dza wiedzy** thirst for knowledge

że 1. *cj.* that; **2.** *part.:* **ledwo ~** hardly, scarcely; **tyle ~** only; → **dlatego, mimo, omal**

-że *part.* (*wzmacniająca*) **siadajże!** do sit down!

żeberka *m/pl.* *gastr.* spare ribs *pl.*

żebra|czka *f* (*-i*; *G* -*czek*) beggar; **~ć** (*-am*) beg (**o** *A* for); **~k** *m* (*-a*; *-cy*) beggar; **~nina** *f* (*-y*; *0*) begging

żebro *n* (*-a*; *G* -*ber*) *anat.* rib

żeby 1. *cj.* (in order) to, in order that; **nie ~** not that; **2.** → **oby, chyba**

żegla|rka *f* (*-o*; *G* -*rek*) *naut.* yachtswoman; sailor; **~rski** sailing; **~rstwo** *n* (*-a*; *0*) *naut.* sailing; **~rz** *m* (*-a*; *-e*) *naut.* yachtsman; sailor

żeglow|ać (*-uję*) sail; **~lowny** navigable; **~luga** *f* (*-i*; *G* -) navigation

żegnać (*-am*) *v/t.* say goodbye (*się v/i.*; **z** *I* to); **~j!** farewell!; **~** ⟨*prze-*⟩ cross (*się* o.s.)

żel *m* (*-u*; *-e*) gel (*też chem.*)

żelatyna *f* (*-y*; *G* -) gelatine

żela|zisty *geol.* ferruginous; *woda* tasting of iron; **~zko** *n* (*-a*; *G* -*zek*) iron; **~zny** iron; **~zo** *n* (*-a*; *0*) *chem.* iron

żelbet *m* (*-u*; *-y*) reinforced concrete, ferroconcrete

żeliw|ny cast-iron; **~o** *n* (*-a*; *0*) cast iron

żeni|aczka *f* (*-i*; *G* -*czek*) marriage; **~ć** ⟨*o-*⟩ (*-ę*) marry; **~ć** ⟨*o-*⟩ **się** (*z I*) get married (to)

żen|ować (się) ⟨*za-*⟩ (*-uję*) → **krępować;** **~ująco** *adv.* embarrassingly, awkwardly; **~ujący** embarrassing, awkward

żeński female; *gr.* feminine

żeń-szeń *m* (*-nia*; *-nie*) *bot.* ginseng

żer *m* (*-u*; *0*) prey

żerdź *f* (*-dzi*; *-dzie*) pole

żerować (*-uję*) (*też fig.*) prey (**na** *L* on)

żeton *m* (*-u*; *-y*) token; chip; → **szton**

żgać (*-am*) ⟨**~nąć**⟩ (*-nę*) stab, prick

żleb *m* (*-u*; *-y*) gully

żłob|ek *m* (*-bka*; *-bki*) day nursery; *Brt.* crèche; (*rowek*) groove; **~ić** ⟨**wy-**⟩ (*-ę*) groove; **~kowy** day nursery

żłopać (*-ię*) guzzle, swill

żłób *m* (*-łobu*; *-łoby*) manger

żmija *f* (*GDL - ii*; *-e*) viper; **~ zygzakowata** adder

żmudny strenuous

żniw|a *n/pl.* (*-*) → **żniwo**; **~iarka** *f* (*-i*; *G -rek*) (*też maszyna*), **~iarz** *m* (*-a*; *-e*) reaper; **~ny** harvesting; **~o** *n* (*-a*; *G -*) harvest

żołąd|ek *m* (*-dka*; *-dki*) *anat.* stomach; **~kowy** stomach

żołądź *f* (F *m*) (*-ędzi*; *-ędzie*) *bot.* acorn; *anat.* glans penis

żołd *m* (*-u*; *zw. 0*) pay; **~dak** *m* (*-a*; *-cy*) *pej.* mercenary, soldier; **~nierski** soldier('s), military; **po ~niersku** like a soldier; **~nierz** *m* (*-a*; *-e*) *mil.* soldier

żona *f* (*-y*; *G -*) wife; **~ty** married

żonglować (*-uję*) (*I*) juggle (with)

żół|cić ⟨**po-**⟩ make yellow; **~ciowy** bilious; **~ć** *f anat.* bile; (*kolor*) yellow; **~knąć** ⟨**po-**, **z-**⟩ (*-nę*, *-ł*) turn yellow; (*ze starości*) discolo(u)r; **~taczka** *f* (*-i*; *G -czek*) *med.* jaundice; (*wirusowa*) hepatitis; **~tawo** *adv.* sallowly; **~tawy** yellowish; *skóra* sallow; **~tko** *n* (*-a*; *G -tek*) yolk

żółto *adv.* (*comp. żółciej*) yellow; **~ść** *f* (*-ści*; *0*) yellow; **~zielony** yellowish-green

żółty yellow; (*niezdrowa skóra*) sallow; (*w sygnalizacji*) amber; (*z zazdrości*) green

żółw *m* (*-wia*; *-wie*, *-wi*) *zo.* turtle; tortoise; **~i** turtle; **~im krokiem** at a snail's pace

żrący corrosive; **~o** *adv.* corrosively

żreć ⟨**po-**, **ze-**⟩ F devour; eat, corrode

żubr *m* (*-a*; *-y*) *zo.* wisent, European bison

żu|chwa *f* (*-y*; *G -*) *anat.* mandible, lower jaw; **~ć** (*-ję*) chew; → **przeżuwać**

żuk *m* (*-a*; *-i*) *zo.* beetle

żuławy *f/pl.* (*G -*) marshland

żur *m* (*-u*; *-y*) type of Polish soup

żuraw *m* (*-wia*; *-wie*) *zo.*, *tech.* crane; **~i** crane; **~ina** *f* (*-y*; *G -*) *bot.* cranberry

żurnal *m* (*-a/-u*; *-e*) fashion magazine, glossy

żuż|el *m* (*-żla*; *-żle*) cinders *pl.*, (*większy*) clinker; *sport:* **wyścigi** *m/pl.* **na ~lu** speedway; **~lowy** cinder; *sport:* speedway

żwaw|o *adv.* briskly; **~y** brisk

żwir *m* (*-u*; *-y*) gravel; **~ownia** *f* (*-i*; *-e*) gravel pit; **~owy** gravel

życi|e *n* (*-a*; *0*) life; *przy* **~u** living; *bez* **~a** lifeless; *za mego* **~a** in my lifetime; *powołać do* **~a** bring into life; *wejść w* **~e** *ustawa*: come into force; *zarabiać na* **~e** earn one's living

życio|rys *m* (*-u*; *-y*) c.v., curriculum vitae; *Am.* résumé; **~wo** *adv.* practically, realistically; **~wy** vital; F practical, realistic

życz|enie *n* (*-a*; *G -eń*) wish, desire; **~enia** *pl.* (*świąteczne itp.*) greetings *pl.*; *pozostawiać wiele do* **~enia** leave much to be desired; *na* **~enie** on request; **~liwie** *adv.* kindly; **~liwość** *f* (*-ści*; *0*) kindness, friendliness; **~liwy** kind, friendly; **~yć** (*-ę*) wish (*szczęścia* (*dobrze*) *k-u* s.o. good luck (well)); (*sobie*) desire

żyć (*-ję*) live (*z I* with; *z G* on, by); *niech żyje ...!* long live ...!

Żyd *m* (*-a*; *-dzi*) Jew; **ʒowski** Jewish; *po* **ʒowsku** like a Jew; **~ówka** *f* (*-i*; *G -wek*) Jewess

żyją|cy living, alive; **~tko** *n* (*-a*; *G -tek*) living being, creature

żyła|k *m* (*-a*; *-i*) *med.* varicose vein; **~sty** *mięso* stringy, wiry; *ramiona* sinewy

żyletka *f* (*-i*; *G -tek*) razor-blade

żył|ny venous; **~ła** *f* (*-y*; *G -*) *anat.* vein; **~łka** *f* (*-i*; *G -łek*) *anat.*, *bot.* → **żyła**; (*wędki*) fishing-line; *fig.* **mieć ~łkę** (*do G*) have a flair (to); **~łowaty** *mięso* → **żylasty**

żyrafa *f* (*-y*; *G -*) giraffe

żyrandol *m* (*-a*; *-e*) chandelier

żyro *n* (*-a*); *econ.* endorsement **~kompas** *m* gyro compass; **~wać** (*-uję*) endorse

żyt|ni rye; **~o** *n* (*-a*; *G -*) *bot.* rye

żywcem *adv.* → **żywiec**

żywica *f* (-y; -e) resin (*też chem.*)

żywiciel *m* (-a; -e) *biol.* host; ~ka *f* (-i; G -lek) breadwinner

żywiczny resinous

żyw|ić (-ę) feed; nourish; *rodzinę* keep; *fig.* cherish; **~ić się** *ktoś*: live on, *zwierzę*: feed on; **~iec** *m* **1.** (-wca; -wce) *wędkowanie*: live-bait; **2.** (-wca; 0) livestock on the hoof; **~cem** alive, living

żywienie *n* (-a; 0) nourishment; feeding

żywioł *m* (-u; -y) element; ~owo *adv.*

vigorously; spontaneously; ~owy vigorous; spontaneous; *klęska* natural

żywnoś|ciowy food; ~ć *f* (-ści; 0) food

żywo *adv.* vividly; **na ~** live; ~płot *m* hedge; ~t *m* (-a; -y) life; ~tność *f* (-ści; 0) vitality; (*urządzenia*) life; ~tny vital

żywy living; *pred.* alive; (*ruchliwy*) lively, vivacious; *światło, barwa* vivid; **handel ~m towarem** trade in human beings; *jak* ~ lifelike

żyzny fertile

Ż

Wskazówki dla użytkownika
Guide to Using the Dictionary

Porządek alfabetyczny i dobór haseł
Wszystkie wyrazy hasłowe podane są
w porządku alfabetycznym. Do ich opisu
stosowane są odpowiednie kwalifikatory
gramatyczne – ilustrujące kategorię gra-
matyczną, do której należą, kwalifikatory działowe – przedstawiające ich przynależność do poszczególnych dziedzin
oraz kwalifikatory stylistyczne – wskazujące na różne style danego wyrazu.
W liście haseł podane są także nieregularne formy stopniowania przymiotników i przysłówków.

Alphabetical order and the choice of entries
The entries are given in a strictly alphabetical order. Special labels are used to
help to describe them. Grammatical labels indicate their grammatical catego-
ry. Stylistic labels show the register to
which the entry belongs. There are also
labels for words that are restricted to
specific fields of usage.
Irregular forms of adjectives and ad-
verbs are also listed as entries.

Użycie tyldy (~) i dywizu
Tylda zastępuje cały wyraz hasłowy lub
jego część, znajdującą się po lewej stronie kreski pionowej.

The use of the swung dash (~) and the hyphen The swung dash replaces
the headword or the part of it that ap-
pears to the left of the vertical bar.

a·lone [ə'ləun] **1.** *adj.* sam; **2.** *adv.* samotnie; *let* ~ zostawiać ⟨-wić⟩ w spoko-
ju; *let* ~ ... nie mówiąc już o (*L*)

a·lone [ə'ləun] **1.** *adj.* sam; **2.** *adv.* samotnie; *let* ~ zostawiać ⟨-wić⟩ w spoko-
ju; *let* ~ ... nie mówiąc już o (*L*)

W formach gramatycznych, podawanych w nawiasach okrągłych lub w nawiasach
trójkątnych wyrazy hasłowe lub ekwiwalenty wyrazów hasłowych zastąpiono
dywizem.

In grammatical forms given in round or
angle brackets the entries or their equivalents are replaced with a hyphen.

gor·y ['gɔːrɪ] F (*-ier, -iest*) zakrwawio-
ny; *fig.* krwawy

gor·y ['gɔːrɪ] F (*-ier, -iest*) zakrwawio-
ny; *fig.* krwawy

gorge [gɔːdʒ] **1.** wąwóz *m*; gardziel *f*; **2.** pochłaniać ⟨-łonąć⟩ napychać
⟨-pchać⟩ (się)

gorge [gɔːdʒ] **1.** wąwóz *m*; gardziel *f*; **2.** pochłaniać ⟨-łonąć⟩ napychać
⟨-pchać⟩ (się)

Hasła mające kilka odpowiedników
Odpowiedniki bliskoznaczne wyrazu hasłowego podano obok siebie oddzielając je przecinkami.

Entries with more than one meaning
Translations of the headword which are
used synonymously are given next to
each other and are separated by commas.

chip [tʃɪp] **1.** wiór *m*, drzazga *f*

chip [tʃɪp] **1.** wiór *m*, drzazga *f*

Jeżeli wyraz hasłowy ma kilka odpowiedników dalekoznacznych, w takim
przypadku na pierwszym miejscu podano znaczenie bliższe lub pierwotne,
a potem kolejno znaczenia dalsze lub
pochodne, oddzielone średnikiem.

If the English headword has more than
one Polish equivalent, it is the basic
or original meaning that is presented
first. Further or derivative meanings
come later and are separated by a semicolons.

a·buse 1. [ə'bjuːs] znęcanie *n* się; nadużywanie *n*; nadużycie *n*; wymysły *pl.*

a·buse 1. [ə'bjuːs] znęcanie *n* się; nadużywanie *n*; nadużycie *n*; wymysły *pl.*

Jeżeli wyraz hasłowy występuje w chara-

If the English headword is used as more

kterze różnych części mowy, identycznych pod względem formy, to w takim przypadku podano go w jednym artykule hasłowym z jego odpowiednikami w języku polskim, uszeregowanymi według ustalonej w gramatyce kolejności. Poszczególne znaczenia zostały wyróżnione cyframi arabskimi i oddzielone średnikiem.

than one part of speech, then it appears under one entry together with its Polish equivalents arranged according to the accepted grammar order. Separate meanings have been marked with Arabic numerals and separated by semicolons.

ab·stract 1. ['æbstrækt] abstrakcyjny; **2.** ['æbstrækt] abstrakt *m*; **3.** [æb'strækt] abstrahować

ab·stract 1. ['æbstrækt] abstrakcyjny; **2.** ['æbstrækt] abstrakt *m*; **3.** [æb'strækt] abstrahować

Homonimy podano w osobnych hasłach oznaczonych kolejnymi cyframi arabskimi, podanymi w górnym indeksie.

Homonyms are presented under separate entries marked with exponent numerals.

air¹ [eə] powietrze *n*
air² [eə] *mus.* aria *f*

air¹ [eə] powietrze *n*
air² [eə] *mus.* aria *f*

Hasła rzeczownikowe
Przy polskich odpowiednikach angielskich haseł rzeczownikowych podano za pomocą skrótów *m*, *f*, *n* ich rodzaj gramatyczny.
Regularne formy liczby mnogiej zostały pominięte, natomiast formy nieregularne lub nasuwające wątpliwości podano w nawiasach okrągłych.

Nouns
Polish equivalents are always accompanied by an abbreviation of the grammatical gender: *m*, *f* or *n*.

Plurals formed regularly have been omitted. Irregular or problematic forms are given in round brackets.

leaf [li:f] (*pl.* **leaves** [li:vz]) liść *m*; *drzwi itp.*: skrzydło *n*

leaf [li:f] (*pl.* **leaves** [li:vz]) liść *m*; *drzwi itp.*: skrzydło *n*

Hasła przymiotnikowe
Przy przymiotnikach stopniowanych nieregularnie podano w nawiasach okrągłych formy stopnia wyższego i najwyższego. Dodatkowo formy te zostały także ujęte w liście haseł.

Adjectives
When the comparative and superlative forms of an adjective are irregular, these have been given in round brackets. Additionally, these forms have been included in the list of entries.

good [gʊd] **1.** (*better*, *best*) dobry; grzeczny

good [gʊd] **1.** (*better*, *best*) dobry; grzeczny

Hasła czasownikowe
W słowniku nie uwzględniono form podstawowych czasowników regularnych, tworzonych za pomocą końcówki -*ed*. Przy hasłach podano natomiast w nawiasach okrągłych formy czasowników nieregularnych. Jako odpowiedniki podano polskie czasowniki niedokonane. W nawiasy trójkątne ujęto przedrostki lub przyrostki, za pomocą których tworzone są ich formy dokonane.

Verbs
The endings of regular verbs have been omitted, while those of irregular verbs have been included in round brackets. For their equivalents imperfect Polish verbs have been supplied. Prefixes and suffixes which are used to make perfect forms of verbs are given in angle brackets.

come [kʌm] (*came*, *come*) przychodzić ⟨przyjść⟩ przyjeżdżać ⟨przyjechać⟩
re·sign [rɪ'zaɪn] *v/i.* ⟨z⟩rezygnować

come [kʌm] (*came*, *come*) przychodzić ⟨przyjść⟩ przyjeżdżać ⟨przyjechać⟩
re·sign [rɪ'zaɪn] *v/i.* ⟨z⟩rezygnować

Różnice w rekcji angielskich i polskich czasowników zaznaczane są za pomocą

The differences in grammar governing usage are marked by means of special odpowiednich zaimków i skrótów przypadków, podawanych w nawiasach okrągłych, zaraz po polskim odpowiedniku.

ag·i·tate ['ædʒɪteɪt] v/t. poruszać ⟨-ruszyć⟩; *płyn* wstrząsać ⟨-snąć⟩; v/i. agitować (**for** za *I*, **against** przeciw *D*)

Transkrypcja
Przy wyrazach hasłowych podano w nawiasach kwadratowych transkrypcję fonetyczną. W słowniku zastosowano międzynarodową transkrypcję fonetyczną.

Fałszywi przyjaciele
Symbol △ ostrzega przed fałszywymi przyjaciółmi tłumacza

ru·mo(u)r ['ruːmə] **1.** pogłoska *f*, plotka *f*; **~ has it that** wieść niesie że; **he is ~ed to be** mówi się że on; △ *nie* **rumor**

pronouns and shortened forms of cases given in round brackets following their Polish equivalent.

ag·i·tate ['ædʒɪteɪt] v/t. poruszać ⟨-ruszyć⟩; *płyn* wstrząsać ⟨-snąć⟩; v/i. agitować (**for** za *I*, **against** przeciw *D*)

Phonetic transcription
Dictionary entries are accompanied by phonetic transcriptions. The symbols used are those of the International Phonetic Association.

False friends
The sign △ warns of false friends.

ru·mo(u)r ['ruːmə] **1.** pogłoska *f*, plotka *f*; **~ has it that** wieść niesie że; **he is ~ed to be** mówi się że on; △ *nie* **rumor**

English – Polish

A

A, a [eɪ] A, a; *from A to B* od A do B

A [eɪ] *ocena:* celujący; bardzo dobry

a [ə, *akcentowane:* eɪ], *przed samogłoską:* **an** [ən, *akcentowane:* æn] *rodzajnik nieokreślony:* jeden; na; za; *a horse* koń; *not a(n)* żaden, ani jeden; *all of a size* wszyscy (wszystkie) tego samego rozmiaru; *£10 a year* dziesięć funtów na rok; *twice a week* dwa razy na tydzień

a·back [ə'bæk]: *taken ~* zaskoczony

a·ban·don [ə'bændən] opuszczać ⟨-ścić⟩; porzucać ⟨-cić⟩; poniechać; *~ed be found ~ed samochód itp.:* zostać znalezionym po porzuceniu

a·base [ə'beɪs] poniżać ⟨-yć⟩; upokarzać ⟨-orzyć⟩; *~ment* poniżenie *n*, upokorzenie *n*

a·bashed [ə'bæʃt] speszony

ab·at·toir ['æbætwɑː] rzeźnia *f*

ab·bess ['æbɪs] przeorysza *f*

ab·bey ['æbɪ] opactwo *n*

ab·bot ['æbət] przeor *m*, opat *m*

ab·bre·vi·ate [ə'briːvɪeɪt] skracać ⟨-rócić⟩; *~ation* [əbriːvɪ'eɪʃn] skrót *m*

ABC[1] [eɪ biː 'siː] abecadło *n*, alfabet *m*

ABC[2] [eɪ biː 'siː] *skrót:* **American Broadcasting Company** *(amerykańska firma telewizyjna i radiowa)*

ab·di·cate ['æbdɪkeɪt] *prawo, władza itp.:* zrzekać ⟨-ec⟩ się; *~cate from (the) throne* abdykować; *~ca·tion* [æbdɪ'keɪʃn] zrzeczenie się *n*, abdykacja *f*

ab·do·men ['æbdəmən] *anat.* brzuch *m*; **ab·dom·i·nal** [æb'dɒmɪnl] *anat.* brzuszny

ab·duct [əb'dʌkt] *kogoś* porywać ⟨-rwać⟩

a·bet [ə'bet] → *aid*

ab·hor [əb'hɔː] odczuwać ⟨-czuć⟩ wstręt; *~rence* [əb'hɒrəns] wstręt *m (of* do *D); ~rent* [əb'hɒrənt] odrażający *(to* dla *D);* wstrętny

a·bide [ə'baɪd] *v/i.:* **~ *by the law itp.* przestrzegać prawa *itp.*; *v/t.* **I can't ~ him** nie mogę go znieść

a·bil·i·ty [ə'bɪlətɪ] umiejętność *f*, zdolność *f*

ab·ject ['æbdʒekt] uniżony; *in ~ poverty* w skrajnej nędzy

ab·jure [əb'dʒʊə] odwoływać ⟨-łać⟩ publicznie

a·blaze [ə'bleɪz] w płomieniach; rozjarzony, rozświetlony *(with* L)

a·ble ['eɪbl] zdolny; *be ~ to* móc, potrafić; *~'bod·ied fizycznie* krzepki, zdrowy

ab·nor·mal [æb'nɔːml] nienormalny

a·board [ə'bɔːd] na pokładzie; *all ~! naut.* wszyscy na pokład!, *rail.* proszę wsiadać!; *~ a bus* w autobusie; *go ~ a train* wsiadać ⟨wsiąść⟩ do pociągu

a·bode [ə'bəʊd] *też place of ~* miejsce zamieszkania; *of lub with no fixed ~* bez stałego miejsca zamieszkania

ab·ol·ish [ə'bɒlɪʃ] obalać ⟨-lić⟩

ab·o·li·tion [æbə'lɪʃn] obalenie *n*

A-bomb ['eɪbɒm] → *atom(ic) bomb*

a·bom·i·na·ble [ə'bɒmɪnəbl] odrażający, wstrętny; *~nate* [ə'bɒmɪneɪt] czuć wstręt; *~na·tion* [əbɒmɪ'neɪʃn] wstręt *m*, odraza *f*

a·bo·rig·i·nal [æbə'rɪdʒənl] **1.** pierwotny; **2.** aborygen(ka *f*) *m*

a·bo·rig·i·ne [æbə'rɪdʒəniː] aborygen(ka *f*) *m (zwł. w Australii)*

a·bort [ə'bɔːt] *med.* ciążę przerwać *(A); płód* usunąć *(A); dziecka* pozbyć się *(G);* przerwać *(też komp.); v/i.* dokonać aborcji; *fig.* nie powieść się; **a·bor·tion** [ə'bɔːʃn] *med.* aborcja *f;* poronienie *n*, przerwanie *n* ciąży; *have an ~* przerwać ciążę, dokonać aborcji; **a·bor·tive** [ə'bɔːtɪv] nieudany

a·bound [ə'baʊnd] mnożyć się; obfitować *(in* w *A);* być wypełnionym

a·bout [ə'baʊt] **1.** *prp.* o *(L);* po *(L);* przy *(L); I had no money ~ me* nie miałem pieniędzy przy sobie; *what ~ going to the cinema?* może byśmy poszli do kina?; **2.** *adv.* około *(G);* w przybliżeniu, dookoła *(G)*

a·bove [ə'bʌv] **1.** *prp.* nad *(I);* ponad *(I); fig.* ponad; *~ all* ponad wszystko; **2.** *adv.* (po)wyżej *(I);* **3.** *adj.* powyższy, (wy)żej) wspomniany

a·breast [ə'brest] obok siebie; *keep ~*

of, be ~ of *fig.* być na bieżąco z (*I*)
a·bridge [ə'brɪdʒ] skracać ⟨-rócić⟩; **a'bridg(e)·ment** skrót *m*
a·broad [ə'brɔːd] za granicę, za granicą; wszędzie; **the news soon spread ~** wieści szybko się rozniosły
a·brupt [ə'brʌpt] nagły; stromy
ab·scess ['æbsɪs] ropień *m*
ab·sence ['æbsəns] nieobecność *f*; brak *m*
ab·sent 1. ['æbsənt] nieobecny; **be ~** być nieobecnym (**from school** w szkole); **2.** [æb'sent]: **~ o.s. from school** być nieobecnym w szkole; **~·mind·ed** [æbsənt'maɪndɪd] roztargniony
ab·so·lute ['æbsəluːt] absolutny; *chem.* czysty
ab·so·lu·tion [æbsə'luːʃn] rozgrzeszenie *n*
ab·solve [əb'zɒlv] grzechy odpuszczać; oczyszczać (*z winy*)
ab·sorb [əb'sɔːb] absorbować; wchłaniać (*też fig.*); **~·ing** absorbujący
ab·stain [əb'steɪn] powstrzymywać ⟨-mać⟩ się (**from** od *A*)
ab·ste·mi·ous [æb'stiːmɪəs] wstrzemięźliwy
ab·sten·tion [əb'stenʃn] powstrzymanie *n* się; *pol.* głos wstrzymujący
ab·sti|·nence ['æbstɪnəns] abstynencja *f*; wstrzemięźliwość *f*
ab·stract 1. ['æbstrækt] abstrakcyjny; **2.** ['æbstrækt] abstrakt *m*; **3.** [æb'strækt] abstrahować; *najważniejsze punkty z artykułu* streszczać ⟨streścić⟩; **ab·stract·ed** [əb'stræktɪd] zatopiony w myślach; **ab·strac·tion** [əb'strækʃn] abstrakcja *f*; pojęcie *n* abstrakcyjne
ab·surd [əb'sɜːd] absurdalny; groteskowy
a·bun|·dance [ə'bʌndəns] obfitość *f*; nadmiar *m*; mnóstwo *n*; **~·dant** obfity
a·buse 1. [ə'bjuːs] znęcanie *n* się; nadużywanie *n*; nadużycie *n*; wymysły *pl.*; **~ of drugs** nadużywanie narkotyków; **~ of power** nadużycie *n* władzy; **2.** [ə'bjuːz] znęcać się; nadużywać; **a·bu·sive** [ə'bjuːsɪv] obelżywy; obraźliwy
a·but [ə'bʌt] (**-tt-**) graniczyć (**on** z *L*)
a·byss [ə'bɪs] otchłań *f* (*też fig.*)
a/c, A/C [eɪ 'siː] *skrót:* **account** konto *m* bankowe
AC [eɪ 'siː] *skrót:* **alternating current** prąd *m* zmienny

ac·a·dem·ic [ækə'demɪk] **1.** nauczyciel(ka *f*) *m* akademicki (-ka); **2.** (**~·ally**) akademicki; uniwersytecki; **a·cad·e·mi·cian** [əkædə'mɪʃn] członek *m* akademii (*nauk*)
a·cad·e·my [ə'kædəmɪ] akademia *f*; **~ of music** wyższa szkoła muzyczna, akademia muzyczna
ac·cede [æk'siːd]: **~ to** zgadzać ⟨-dzić⟩ się na (*A*); *urząd* obejmować ⟨-jąć⟩; *wstępować* ⟨wstąpić⟩ na (*L*) (*tron*)
ac·cel·e|·rate [ək'seləreɪt] przyspieszać ⟨-szyć⟩; **~·ra·tion** [əksele'reɪʃn] przyspieszenie *n*; **~·ra·tor** [ək'seləreɪtə] pedał *m* gazu, gaz *m* F
ac·cent ['æksənt] akcent *m*; **ac·cen·tu·ate** [æk'sentjʊeɪt] ⟨za⟩akcentować, podkreślać
ac·cept [ək'sept] przyjmować ⟨-jąć⟩; ⟨za⟩akceptować; **ac·cep·ta·ble** (*możliwy*) do przyjęcia; **ac'cept·ance** przyjęcie *n*; akceptacja *f*
ac·cess ['ækses] dojście *n* (**to** do *G*); dostęp (*też komp.*); **~ code** *komp.* kod *m* dostępu; **~ road** droga *f* dojazdowa; **~ time** *komp.*, (*odtwarzacz CD*) czas *m* dostępu
ac·ces·sa·ry [ək'sesərɪ] → **accessory**
ac·ces·si·ble [ək'sesəbl] łatwo dostępny; **~·sion** [ək'seʃn] objęcie *n* (*urzędu*); **~·sion to power** przejęcie *n* władzy; **~·sion to the throne** objęcie *n* tronu
ac·ces·so·ry [ək'sesərɪ] *jur.* współsprawca *m* (*-wczyni f*) przestępstwa; *zw.* **accessories** *pl.* dodatki *pl.*, *tech.* akcesoria *pl.*
ac·ci·dent ['æksɪdənt] przypadek *m*; *samochodowy* wypadek *m*; **by ~dent** przypadkiem; **~·den·tal** [æksɪ'dentl] przypadkowy
ac·claim [ə'kleɪm] zdobyć uznanie (**as** jako)
ac·cla·ma·tion [æklə'meɪʃn] aklamacja *f*, aplauz *m*
ac·cli·ma·tize [ə'klaɪmətaɪz] ⟨za⟩aklimatyzować się; przyzwyczaić ⟨-jać się⟩
ac·com·mo|·date [ə'kɒmədeɪt] (*w domu*) przyjmować ⟨-jąć⟩; (*w hotelu*) ⟨po⟩mieścić; wyświadczać ⟨-czyć⟩ przysługę; dostosowywać ⟨-ować⟩ się (**to** do *G*); **~·da·tion** [əkɒmə'deɪʃn] (*Am. zw. pl.*) miejsce *n*; zakwaterowanie *n*

ac·com·pa|·ni·ment [ə'kʌmpənɪmənt] akompaniament *m*; **~·ny** [ə'kʌmpənɪ] towarzyszyć (*też muz.*)

ac·com·plice [ə'kʌmplɪs] współsprawca *m*, współsprawczyni *f*

ac·com·plish [ə'kʌmplɪʃ] osiągać ⟨-gnąć⟩; **~ed** znakomity; **~·ment** osiągnięcie *n*; (*w pracy*) osiągnięcia *pl.*

ac·cord [ə'kɔːd] **1.** uznanie *n*; *of one's own* ~ z własnej woli; *with one* ~ jednogłośnie; △ *nie akord*; **2.** przyznawać ⟨-nać⟩; **~·ance:** *in ~ance with* zgodnie z (*L*); **~·ing:** *~ing to* według (*G*); zgodnie z (*L*); **~·ing·ly** stosownie, odpowiednio

ac·cost [ə'kɒst] *kogoś na ulicy* zaczepiać ⟨-pić⟩

ac·count [ə'kaʊnt] **1.** *econ.* rachunek *m*; *econ.* konto *n*; sprawozdanie *n*; *by all* ~ podobno; *of no* ~ bez znaczenia; *on no* ~ w żadnym wypadku; *on* ~ *of* w przypadku (*G*); *take into* ~, *take* ~ *of* brać ⟨wziąć⟩ (*A*) pod uwagę; *turn s.th. to* (*good*) ~ coś dobrze wykorzystywać ⟨-stać⟩; *keep* ~s prowadzić księgi *pl.* rachunkowe; *call to* ~ pociągać ⟨-gnąć⟩ do odpowiedzialności; *give* (*an*) ~ *of s.th.* wyjaśniać ⟨-nić⟩; *give an* ~ *of s.th* składać ⟨złożyć⟩ sprawozdanie z czegoś, opisywać ⟨-sać⟩ coś; **2.** *v/i.* ~ *for* wyjaśniać ⟨-nić⟩; (*w liczbie*) stanowić; **ac·coun·ta·ble** odpowiedzialny; **ac·coun·tant** księgowy *m* (-wa *f*); **ac·count·ing** księgowość *f*

acct *skrót pisany: account* konto *n*

ac·cu·mu|·late [ə'kjuːmjʊleɪt] ⟨na-, z⟩gromadzić (się); **~·la·tion** [əkjuːmjʊ'leɪʃn] nagromadzenie *n*; **~·la·tor** *electr.* [ə'kjuːmjʊleɪtə] akumulator *m*

ac·cu|·ra·cy ['ækjʊrəsɪ] dokładność *f*, precyzja *f*; **~·rate** ['ækjʊrət] dokładny

ac·cu·sa·tion [ækjuː'zeɪʃn] oskarżenie *n*

ac·cu·sa·tive [ə'kjuːzətɪv] *też* ~ *case* biernik *m*

ac·cuse [ə'kjuːz] oskarżać ⟨-żyć⟩; *the* ~*d* oskarżony *m* (-na *f*); **ac·cus·er** oskarżyciel(ka *f*) *m*; **ac·cus·ing** oskarżycielski

ac·cus·tom [ə'kʌstəm] przyzwyczajać (*to* do *G*); **~ed** przyzwyczajony (*to* do *G*), przywykły

AC/DC [eɪ siː 'diː siː] → *bisexual*

ace [eɪs] as *m* (*też fig.*); *have an* ~ *up*
one's sleeve, Am. *have an* ~ *in the hole fig.* mieć asa w rękawie; *within an* ~ o włosek

ache [eɪk] **1.** czuć ból; *my stomach* ~s brzuch mnie boli; **2.** ciągły ból *m*

a·chieve [ə'tʃiːv] osiągać ⟨-gnąć⟩; **~·ment** osiągnięcie *n*

ac·id ['æsɪd] **1.** kwaśny (*też fig.*); skwaśniały (*też fig.*); **2.** *chem.* kwas *m*; ~ *rain* kwaśny deszcz *m*; **a·cid·i·ty** [ə'sɪdətɪ] kwasowość *f*

ac·knowl·edge [ək'nɒlɪdʒ] potwierdzać ⟨-dzić⟩ (*przyjęcie*); przyznawać ⟨-znać⟩; **ac·knowl·edg(e)·ment** potwierdzenie *n* (*przyjęcia*); przyznanie *n*

a·corn ['eɪkɔːn] żołądź *f*

a·cous·tics [ə'kuːstɪks] *pl.* akustyka *f* (*pomieszczenia*)

ac·quaint [ə'kweɪnt] zaznajamiać ⟨-jomić⟩; ~ *s.o. with s.th.* zaznajamiać ⟨-jomić⟩ kogoś z czymś; *be* ~ed *with* znać (*A*); **~·ance** znajomość *f*; znajomy *m* (-ma *f*)

ac·quire [ə'kwaɪə] nabywać ⟨-yć⟩ (*też umiejętność*)

ac·qui·si·tion [ækwɪ'zɪʃn] nabycie *n*; nabytek *m*; *umiejętność:* przyswojenie *n*

ac·quit [ə'kwɪt] (*-tt-*) *jur.* uniewinniać ⟨-nić⟩ (*of z G*); ~ *o.s. well* dobrze się spisać; **~·tal** [ə'kwɪtl] *jur.* uniewinnienie *n*

a·cre ['eɪkə] akr *m* (4047 *m²*)

ac·rid ['ækrɪd] ostry, gryzący

ac·ro·bat ['ækrəbæt] akrobata *m* (-tka *f*); **~·ic** [ækrə'bætɪk] akrobatyczny

a·cross [ə'krɒs] **1.** *adv.* na szerokość, o szerokości; na krzyż; (*w krzyżówce*) poziomo; **2.** *prp.* w poprzek (*G*); na drugą stronę (*G*), po drugiej stronie (*G*); przez (*A*); *come* ~, *run* ~ przebiegać ⟨-biec⟩

act [ækt] **1.** *v/i.* działać; funkcjonować; zachowywać ⟨-ować⟩ się; (za)grać; *theat.* (za)grać (*też fig.*); *sztukę* wystawiać ⟨-wić⟩; ~ *as* funkcjonować jako; **2.** czyn *m*; uczynek *m*; postępek *m*; *jur.* ustawa *f*; *theat.* akt *m*; '~·ing **1.** *theat.* gra *f*; aktorstwo *n*; **2.** pełniący obowiązki (*dyrektora*)

ac·tion ['ækʃn] akcja *f* (*też mil., theat.*); działanie *n*; funkcjonowanie *n*; uczynek *m*, czyn *m*; *jur.* powództwo *n*, sprawa *f* sądowa; *mil.* działania *pl.*; *take* ~ podejmować ⟨-jąć⟩ działanie

ac·tive ['æktɪv] aktywny; czynny; ożywiony (*też* econ.); rzutki

ac·tiv·ist ['æktɪvɪst] *zwł. pol.* działacz(ka f) m

ac·tiv·i·ty [æk'tɪvɪtɪ] działalność f; działanie n; zajęcie n; ~ hol·i·day czynny urlop m; czynne wakacje *pl.*

ac·tor ['æktə] aktor m; actress ['æktrɪs] aktorka f

ac·tu·al ['æktʃʊəl] faktyczny, rzeczywisty; sam; △ *nie* aktualny

ac·u·punc·ture ['ækjʊpʌŋktʃə] akupunktura f

a·cute [ə'kjuːt] (~r, ~est) ostry (*też* med.); przenikliwy; silny; *trudności:* zaostrzony

ad [æd] → *advertisement*

ad·a·mant ['ædəmənt] *fig.* nieugięty

a·dapt [ə'dæpt] *v/i.* ⟨za⟩adaptować się (*to* do G); dostosowywać ⟨-ować⟩ się; *v/t.* ⟨za⟩adaptować; *tekst* dostosowywać ⟨-ować⟩; *tech.* przystosowywać ⟨-ować⟩; a·dapt·a·ble [ə'dæptəbl] *ktoś* łatwo się przystosowujący; *coś* dające się dostosować; ad·ap·ta·tion [ædæp'teɪʃn] adaptacja f; przystosowanie n; a·dapt·er, a·dapt·or *electr.* [ə'dæptə] rozgałęziacz m; △ *nie* adapter

add [æd] *v/t.* dodawać ⟨-dać⟩; ~ up ⟨z⟩sumować, podliczać ⟨-czyć⟩; *v/i.* ~ to powiększać ⟨-szyć⟩; ~ up *fig.* F mieć sens, zgadzać się

ad·der ['ædə] *zo.* żmija f

ad·dict ['ædɪkt] osoba f uzależniona; *alcohol* ~ alkoholik m (-iczka f); *drug* ~ narkoman(ka f) m; entuzjasta m (-tka f) (*sportu, filmu itp.*), fanatyk m (-yczka f); ad·dict·ed [ə'dɪktɪd] uzależniony (*to* od); *be* ~ *to alcohol lub drugs* być uzależnionym od alkoholu *lub* narkotyków; ad·dic·tion [ə'dɪkʃn] uzależnienie n; *alcohol* ~ alkoholizm m; *drug* ~ narkomania f

ad·di·tion [ə'dɪʃn] dodanie n; dodatek m; *math.* dodawanie n; sumowanie n; *in* ~ w dodatku; *in* ~ *to* oprócz (G); ~·al [ə'dɪʃənl] dodatkowy

ad·dress [ə'dres] 1. *słowa* kierować; (*do kogoś*) zwracać ⟨-rócić⟩ się do (G); przemawiać ⟨-mówić⟩ do (G); *przesyłkę* ⟨za⟩adresować (A); 2. adres m; przemowa f; ~·ee [ædre'siː] adresat(ka f) m

ad·ept ['ædept] biegły (*at, in* w L)

ad·e·qua·cy ['ædɪkwəsɪ] adekwatność f; dostateczność f; ~·quate ['ædɪkwət] odpowiedni; dostateczny

ad·here [əd'hɪə] (*to*) przylegać ⟨-lgnąć⟩ do (G); ⟨za⟩stosować się do (G); *fig.* obstawać (przy L); ad·her·ence [əd'hɪərəns] przyleganie n (*to* do G); *prawa* stosowanie n się (*to* do G); *fig.* obstawanie n (*to* przy L); ad·her·ent [əd'hɪərənt] stronnik m (-niczka f)

ad·he·sive [əd'hiːsɪv] 1. klejący (się); 2. klej m; ~ *plas·ter* plaster m, przylepiec m; ~ *tape* taśma f klejąca; *Am.* plaster m, przylepiec m

ad·ja·cent [ə'dʒeɪsnt] przyległy (*to* do G); sąsiadujący (*to* z I)

ad·jec·tive ['ædʒɪktɪv] *gr.* przymiotnik m

ad·join [ə'dʒɔɪn] przylegać do (G)

ad·journ [ə'dʒɜːn] *v/t.* odraczać ⟨-roczyć⟩; *v/i.* zostawać ⟨-stać⟩ odroczonym; ~·ment odroczenie n; zawieszenie n (*obrad*)

ad·just [ə'dʒʌst] poprawiać ⟨-wić⟩; *tech.* ⟨wy⟩regulować; nastawiać ⟨-wić⟩; ~·a·ble [ə'dʒʌstəbl] *tech.* nastawny; regulowany; ~·ment regulacja f; nastawienie n

ad·min·is·ter [əd'mɪnɪstə] zarządzać, administrować; *lekarstwo* podawać ⟨-dać⟩; ~·*ter justice* wymierzać ⟨-rzyć⟩ sprawiedliwość; ~·tra·tion [ədmɪnɪ'streɪʃn] administracja f; *zwł. Am. pol.* rząd m; *zwł. Am.* kadencja f (*prezydenta*); ~·tra·tive [əd'mɪnɪstrətɪv] administracyjny; ~·tra·tor [əd'mɪnɪstreɪtə] administrator(ka f) m

ad·mi·ra·ble ['ædmərəbl] wspaniały, godny podziwu

ad·mi·ral ['ædmərəl] admirał m

ad·mi·ra·tion [ædmə'reɪʃn] podziw m

ad·mire [əd'maɪə] podziwiać; ad·mir·er [əd'maɪərə] wielbiciel(ka f) m

ad·mis·si·ble [əd'mɪsəbl] dopuszczalny; ~·sion [əd'mɪʃn] wstęp m; opłata f za wstęp; przyjęcie n; ~·*sion free* wstęp wolny

ad·mit [əd'mɪt] (*-tt-*) *v/t.* przyznawać ⟨-nać⟩ się do (G); wpuszczać ⟨-uścić⟩ (*to, into* do G); przyjmować ⟨-jąć⟩ (*to* do G); dopuszczać ⟨-uścić⟩; ~·tance [əd'mɪtəns] wstęp m; przyjęcie n; dopuszczenie n; *no* ~*tance* wstęp wzbroniony

ad·mon·ish [əd'mɒnıʃ] upominać ⟨-nieć⟩; przestrzegać ⟨-rzec⟩ (**of**, **against** przed I)

a·do [ə'duː] (pl. **-dos**) zamieszanie n; **without more** lub **further** ~ bez dalszych ceregieli

ad·o·les·cence [ædə'lesns] okres m dojrzewania; **~cent** [æd'lesnt] **1.** nastoletni; młodociany; **2.** nastolatek m (-tka f); jur. młodociany m (-na f)

a·dopt [ə'dɒpt] ⟨za⟩adoptować; przyjmować ⟨przyjąć⟩; **~ed child** przybrane dziecko n; **a·dop·tion** [ə'dɒpʃn] adopcja f; **a'dop·tive**: ~ **child** przybrane dziecko n; ~ **par·ents** pl. przybrani rodzice pl.

a·dor·a·ble [ə'dɔːrəbl] F cudowny, wspaniały; **ad·o·ra·tion** [ædə'reıʃn] uwielbienie n, adoracja f; **a·dore** [ə'dɔː] uwielbiać ⟨-bić⟩; adorować

a·dorn [ə'dɔːn] ozdabiać ⟨ozdobić⟩; upiększać ⟨-szyć⟩; **~ment** ozdobienie n; upiększenie n

A·dri·at·ic Sea Adriatyk m

a·droit [ə'drɔıt] zręczny

ad·ult [ˈædʌlt] **1.** dorosły; **2.** dorosły m (-sła f); **~s only** tylko dla dorosłych; ~ **ed·u·ca·tion** kształcenie n dorosłych

a·dul·ter·ate [ə'dʌltəreıt] ⟨s⟩fałszować; **wino** rozcieńczać ⟨-czyć⟩, ⟨o⟩chrzcić; **~er** [ə'dʌltərə] cudzołożnik m; **~ess** [ə'dʌltəris] cudzołożnica f; **~ous** [ə'dʌltərəs] cudzołożny; **~y** [ə'dʌltərı] cudzołóstwo n

ad·vance [əd'vɑːns] **1.** v/i. posuwać ⟨-unąć⟩ się (do przodu), iść ⟨pójść⟩ do przodu (też o czasie); ⟨po⟩czynić postępy pl.; nadchodzić ⟨-dejść⟩; v/t. **pieniądze** wypłacać ⟨-cić⟩ z góry; **cenę** zwiększać ⟨-szyć⟩; **argument** przedstawiać ⟨-wić⟩; **wzrost** przyspieszać ⟨-szyć⟩; **pracownika** awansować; **2.** posuwanie n się; postęp m; zwiększenie n; zaliczka f; **in** ~ z góry; **~d** zaawansowany; **kraj** rozwinięty; **~d for one's years** dobrze rozwinięty jak na swój wiek; **~ment** postęp m; awans m

ad·van·tage [əd'vɑːntıdʒ] korzyść f; zaleta f; (w sporcie) przewaga f; **~tage rule** reguła f przewagi; **take ~tage of** wykorzystywać ⟨-tać⟩; **~ta·geous** [ædvən'teıdʒəs] korzystny

ad·ven·ture [əd'ventʃə] przygoda f; ryzykowne przedsięwzięcie n; **~tur·er** [əd'ventʃərə] poszukiwacz m przygód; spekulant m; **~tur·ess** [əd'ventʃɒrıs] poszukiwaczka f przygód; spekulantka f; **~tur·ous** [əd'ventʃɒrəs] śmiały; ryzykowny; **życie**: pełen przygód

ad·verb [ˈædvɜːb] przysłówek m

ad·ver·sa·ry [ˈædvəsərı] przeciwnik m (-niczka f)

ad·ver·tise [ˈædvətaız] ⟨za⟩reklamować (się); ogłaszać ⟨-łosić⟩ (się); **~tise·ment** [əd'vɜːtısmənt] ogłoszenie n; reklama f; **~tis·ing** [ˈædvətaızıŋ] **1.** reklama f; reklamowanie n; **2.** reklamowy; **~tising agency** agencja f reklamowa

ad·vice [əd'vaıs] rada f; porada f; econ. zawiadomienie n; **a piece of** ~ rada f; **take medical** ~ zasięgać ⟨-gnąć⟩ porady lekarskiej; **take my** ~ proszę mnie posłuchać; **~ cen·tre** Brt. poradnia f

ad·vi·sab·le [əd'vaızəbl] wskazany, celowy; **ad·vise** [əd'vaız] v/t. komuś ⟨po⟩radzić; zwł. econ. zawiadamiać ⟨-domić⟩, awizować; v/i. radzić się; **ad·vis·er** zwł. Brt., **ad·vis·or** Am. [əd'vaızə] doradca m; **ad·vi·so·ry** [əd'vaızərı] doradczy

aer·i·al [ˈeərıəl] **1.** powietrzny; lotniczy; **2.** antena f; ~ **'pho·to·graph** zdjęcie n z lotu ptaka lub lotnicze; ~ **'view** widok m z lotu ptaka

ae·ro... [ˈeərəʊ] aero...

aer·o·bics [eə'rəʊbıks] (sg. w sporcie) aerobik m; **~drome** [ˈeərədrəʊm] zwł. Brt. lotnisko n; **~dy·nam·ic** [eərəʊdaı'næmık] (**~ally**) aerodynamiczny; **~dy·nam·ics** sg. aerodynamika f; **~nau·tics** [eərə'nɔːtıks] sg. aeronautyka f; **~plane** Brt. [ˈeərəpleın] samolot m; **~sol** [ˈeərəsɒl] aerozol m

aes·thet·ic [iːs'θetık] estetyczny; **~s** sg. estetyka f

a·far [ə'fɑː]: **from** ~ z oddali

af·fair [ə'feə] sprawa f; F rzecz f, urządzenie n; romans m

af·fect [ə'fekt] mieć wpływ na (A), wpływać ⟨-łynąć⟩ na; med. ⟨za⟩atakować; oddziaływać na (A); mieć oddziaływanie na (A); wzruszać ⟨-szyć⟩, poruszać ⟨-szyć⟩

af·fec·tion [ə'fekʃn] uczucie n; **~ate** [ə'fekʃnət] czuły; uczuciowy

af·fil·i·ate [ə'fılıeıt] stowarzyszać ⟨-szyć⟩ (jako członek); zrzeszać ⟨-szyć⟩;

af·fin·i·ty [ə'fɪnətɪ] podobieństwo *n*; *duchowe* pokrewieństwo *n*; sympatia *f* (*for*, *to* do *G*)

af·firm [ə'fɜːm] potwierdzać ⟨-dzić⟩; zapewniać ⟨-nić⟩; ⟨s⟩twierdzić, stwierdzać ⟨-dzić⟩; **af·fir·ma·tion** [æfə'meɪʃn] potwierdzenie *n*; zapewnienie *n*; stwierdzenie *n*; **af·fir·ma·tive** [ə'fɜːmətɪv] **1.** twierdzący; **2.** *answer in the* ~ odpowiadać ⟨-wiedzieć⟩ twierdząco; potwierdzać ⟨-dzić⟩

af·fix [ə'fɪks] (*to*) przyklejać ⟨-leić⟩ (do *A*); przytwierdzać ⟨-dzić⟩ (do *A*)

af·flict [ə'flɪkt] dotykać ⟨-tknąć⟩; *~ed with* dotknięty (*I*), cierpiący na (*A*); **af·flic·tion** [ə'flɪkʃn] przypadłość *f*; nieszczęście *n*

af·flu|·ence ['æfluəns] dostatek *m*; bogactwo *n*; *~·ent* dostatni; zamożny; *~·ent so·ci·e·ty* społeczeństwo *n* dobrobytu

af·ford [ə'fɔːd] pozwalać sobie na (*A*); *czas* mieć; *I cannot ~ it* nie stać mnie na to

af·front [ə'frʌnt] **1.** znieważać ⟨-żyć⟩; **2.** zniewaga *f*

a·float [ə'fləʊt] unosząc(y) się na wodzie, pływając(y); *set ~ naut.* puszczać ⟨puścić⟩ na wodę; puszczać ⟨puścić⟩ w obieg (*plotkę*)

a·fraid [ə'freɪd] *be ~ of* bać się, obawiać się; *I'm ~ she won't be coming* obawiam się, że nie przyjdzie; *I'm ~ I have to go now* niestety muszę już iść

a·fresh [ə'freʃ] od nowa

Af·ric·a ['æfrɪkə] Afryka *f*; **Af·ri·can** ['æfrɪkən] **1.** afrykański; **2.** Afrykańczyk *m*, Afrykanka *f*; Murzyn(ka *f*) *m*

af·ter ['ɑːftə] **1.** *adv.* potem; później; **2.** *prp.* po (*L*); za (*I*); *~ all* przecież; mimo wszystko; ostatecznie; **3.** *cj.* gdy; po (*tym*, *jak*); **4.** *adj.* późniejszy; tylny; *~·ef·fect med.* następstwo *n*; efekt *m*; *~·glow* zorza *f* (*wieczorna*); *~·math* ['ɑːftəmæθ] pokłosie *n*; następstwa *pl.*; *~·noon* popołudnie *n*; *this ~noon* dzisiaj po południu; *good ~noon!* dzień dobry!; *~·taste* posmak *m*; *~·thought* zastanowienie się; refleksja *f*; *~·ward Am.*, *~·wards Brt.* ['ɑːftəwəd(z)] później, następnie

a·gain [ə'gen] znowu, znów, ponownie; jeszcze raz; *~ and ~*, *time and ~* ciągle;

as much ~ drugie tyle; *never ~* nigdy więcej

a·gainst [ə'genst] przeciw(ko) (*D*); o (*A*); *as ~* w porównaniu z (*I*); *she was ~ it* była temu przeciwna

age [eɪdʒ] **1.** wiek *m*; *old ~* zaawansowany wiek *m*, starość *f*; *at the ~ of* w wieku (*G*); *your ~* w twoim wieku; *come of ~* stać się pełnoletnim, osiągnąć pełnoletniość; *be over ~* przekroczyć (*właściwy*) wiek; *be under ~* być niepełnoletnim; *wait for ~s* F czekać wieki całe; **2.** postarzeć się; *~d* ['eɪdʒd] stary, w podeszłym wieku; [eɪdʒd]: *~d 20* w wieku 20 lat; '*~·less* wieczny; wiecznie młody

a·gen·cy ['eɪdʒənsɪ] agencja *f*; urząd *m*, biuro *n*

a·gen·da [ə'dʒendə] porządek *m* dnia; *be on the ~* być w programie; △ *nie agenda*

a·gent ['eɪdʒənt] agent(ka *f*) *m* (*też pol.*); przedstawiciel(ka *f*) *m*; ajent(ka *f*) *m*; makler *m*; środek *m*, czynnik *m*

ag·glom·er·ate [ə'glɒməreɪt] skupiać ⟨-pić⟩ się

ag·gra·vate ['ægrəveɪt] pogarszać ⟨-szyć⟩; zaostrzać ⟨-rzyć⟩; F ⟨z⟩irytować

ag·gre·gate 1. ['ægrɪgeɪt] skupiać ⟨skupić⟩ (się); ⟨po⟩łączyć (się) (*to* z); wynosić ⟨-nieść⟩ łącznie **2.** ['ægrɪgət] łączny; globalny; **3.** ['ægrɪgət] całość *f*; suma *f* ogólna

ag·gres|·sion [ə'greʃn] agresja *f*; *~·sive* [ə'gresɪv] agresywny; *fig.* intensywny, energiczny; *~·sor* [ə'gresə] agresor *m*

ag·grieved [ə'griːvd] dotknięty; pokrzywdzony

a·ghast [ə'gɑːst] wstrząśnięty; przerażony

ag·ile ['ædʒaɪl] zwinny, zręczny; **a·gil·i·ty** [ə'dʒɪlətɪ] zwinność *f*, zręczność *f*

ag·i|·tate ['ædʒɪteɪt] *v/t.* poruszać ⟨-ruszyć⟩; *płyn* wstrząsać ⟨-snąć⟩; *v/i.* agitować (*for* za *I*, *against* przeciw *D*); *~·ta·tion* [ædʒɪ'teɪʃn] poruszenie *n*; agitacja *f*; *~·ta·tor* ['ædʒɪteɪtə] agitator(ka *f*) *m*

a·glow [ə'gləʊ]: *be ~* jarzyć się (*with* od *G*)

a·go [ə'gəʊ]: *a year/month ~* rok/miesiąc temu

ag·o·ny ['ægənɪ] *wielki* ból *m*; męczarnia *f*

a·gree [ə'griː] *v/i.* zgadzać ⟨-godzić⟩ się; uzgadniać ⟨-godnić⟩; porozumiewać ⟨-mieć⟩ się; **~ to** przystawać ⟨-rzystać⟩ na (*A*); być zgodnym (**with** z *I*); **~ with** *jedzenie:* ⟨po⟩służyć (*D*); **~·a·ble** [ə'grɪəbl] zgodny; chętny; **be ~able to** zgadzać ⟨-godzić⟩ się na (*A*); **~·ment** [ə'griːmənt] zgoda *f*; porozumienie *n*; umowa *f*

ag·ri·cul·tur|·al [ægrɪ'kʌltʃərəl] rolniczy; **~e** ['ægrɪkʌltʃə] rolnictwo *n*

a·ground [ə'graʊnd] *naut.* na mieliźnie; **run ~** osiadać ⟨osiąść⟩ na mieliźnie

a·head [ə'hed] z przodu; na przedzie; naprzód; do przodu; **~ of** przed (*I*); **go ~!** proszę bardzo!; **straight ~** prosto

aid [eɪd] **1.** wspierać ⟨wesprzeć⟩; *komuś* pomagać ⟨pomóc⟩ (**in** przy *L*); **he was accused of ~ing and abetting** *jur.* oskarżony został o pomoc w dokonaniu przestępstwa; **2.** pomoc *f*; wsparcie *n*

AIDS, Aids [eɪdz] AIDS *m*; **person with ~** chory na AIDS

ail [eɪl] niedomagać; **~·ment** dolegliwość *f*

aim [eɪm] **1.** *v/i.* ⟨wy⟩celować (**at** do *G*); **~ at** *fig.* dążyć do (*G*), mieć na celu; **be ~ing to** do s.th. mieć zamiar coś zrobić; *v/t.* **~ at** *broń itp.:* celować do (*G*); kierować w stronę (*G*); **2.** cel *m* (*też fig.*); **take ~ at** mierzyć do (*G*); **~·less** bezcelowy

air¹ [eə] powietrze *n*; *fig.* atmosfera *f*; wygląd *m*; **by ~** powietrzem, samolotem; **in the open ~** na powietrzu, na dworze; **on the ~** na wizji *lub* fonii; **be on the ~** *program:* być na antenie; *stacja:* nadawać; **go off the ~** ⟨s⟩kończyć *program; stacja:* przestawać ⟨-stać⟩ nadawać; **give o.s. ~s, put on ~s** zadzierać ⟨-drzeć⟩ nosa; **2.** ⟨wy⟩wietrzyć; przewietrzać ⟨-wietrzyć⟩; *fig.* przedstawiać ⟨-wić⟩; wygłaszać ⟨-głosić⟩

air² [eə] *mus.* aria *f*; melodia *f*

'air|·bag poduszka *f* powietrzna; **'~·base** baza *f* powietrzna; **'~·bed** materac *m* dmuchany; **'~·borne** *samolot:* lecący, w powietrzu; *mil.* powietrzno-desantowy; **'~·brake** *mot.* hamulec *m* pneumatyczny; **'~·bus** *aviat.* aerobus *m*, airbus *m*; **'~·con·di·tioned** klimatyzowany; **'~·con·di·tion·ing** klimatyza-

cja *f*; **'~·craft car·ri·er** *mil.* lotniskowiec *m*; **'~·field** lotnisko *n*; **'~·force** *mil.* siły *pl.* powietrzne; **'~·host·ess** *aviat.* stewardessa *f*; **'~·jack·et** kamizelka *f* ratunkowa; **'~·lift** *aviat.* most *m* powietrzny; **'~·line** *aviat.* linia *f* lotnicza; **'~·lin·er** *aviat.* samolot *m* pasażerski; **'~·mail** poczta *f* lotnicza; **by ~mail** pocztą lotniczą; **'~·man** (*pl.* **-men**) wojskowy lotnik *m*; **'~·plane** *Am.* samolot *m*; **'~·pock·et** *aviat.* dziura *f* powietrzna; **'~·pol·lu·tion** zanieczyszczenia *pl.* powietrza; **'~·port** port *m* lotniczy, lotnisko *n*; **~ raid** nalot *m*; **~·raid pre'cau·tions** *pl.* obrona *f* przeciwlotnicza; **~·raid·shel·ter** schron *m* przeciwlotniczy; **'~·route** *aviat.* trasa *f* przelotu; **'~·sick: be ~sick** mieć mdłości, czuć się niedobrze; **'~·space** przestrzeń *f* powietrzna; **'~·strip** *aviat.* pas startowy *lub* lądowania; **'~·ter·mi·nal** *aviat.* terminal *m* lotów; **'~·tight** hermetyczny, szczelny; **'~·traf·fic** *aviat.* ruch *m* lotniczy; **~·traf·fic con'trol** *aviat.* kontrola *f* ruchu lotniczego; **~·traf·fic con·trol·ler** *aviat.* kontroler *m* ruchu lotniczego; **'~·way** *aviat.* trasa *f* lotnicza; **'~·wor·thy** zdatny do lotu

air·y ['eərɪ] (**-ier, -iest**) przewiewny, przestronny

aisle [aɪl] *arch.* nawa *f* boczna; przejście *n*

a·jar [ə'dʒɑː] uchylony

a·kin [ə'kɪn] pokrewny (**to** *D*)

a·lac·ri·ty [ə'lækrətɪ] ochota *f*; ochoczość *f*

a·larm [ə'lɑːm] **1.** alarm *m*; sygnał *m* alarmowy; urządzenie *n* alarmowe; budzik *m*; niepokój *m*; **2.** ⟨za⟩alarmować; ⟨za⟩niepokoić; **~ clock** budzik *m*

Al·ba·ni·a Albania *f*

al·bum ['ælbəm] album *m* (*też płytowy*)

al·bu·mi·nous [æl'bjuːmɪnəs] białkowy; zawierający białko

al·co·hol ['ælkəhɒl] alkohol *m*; **~·ic** [ælkə'hɒlɪk] **1.** alkoholowy; **2.** alkoholik *m* (**-liczka** *f*)

ale [eɪl] ale *m* (*piwo jasne, mocno chmielone*)

a·lert [ə'lɜːt] **1.** czujny; **2.** stan *m* pogotowia; pogotowie *n*; **on the ~** w stanie gotowości; w pogotowiu; **3.** ⟨za⟩alarmować; ostrzegać ⟨-rzec⟩ (**to** przed *I*)

alga ['ælgə] (*pl. algae* ['ældʒiː]) glon *m*, alga *f*

al·ge·bra ['ældʒɪbrə] *math.* algebra *f*

al·i·bi ['ælɪbaɪ] alibi *n*

a·li·en ['eɪljən] **1.** obcy, odmienny; cudzoziemski; **2.** cudzoziemiec *m* (-mka *f*); **~ate** ['eɪljəneɪt] odpychać ⟨odepchnąć⟩; zrażać ⟨zrazić⟩

a·light [ə'laɪt] **1.** płonący; **2.** (*alighted lub alit*) *ptak:* siadać ⟨usiąść⟩; wysiadać ⟨-siąść⟩

a·lign [ə'laɪn] wyrównywać ⟨-nać⟩ (*with* w stosunku do *G*)

a·like [ə'laɪk] **1.** *adj.* podobny; **2.** *adv.* podobnie, jednakowo

al·i·men·ta·ry [ælɪ'mentərɪ] pokarmowy; odżywczy; **~ ca·nal** przewód *m* pokarmowy

al·i·mo·ny ['ælɪmənɪ] *jur.* alimenty *pl.*

alive [ə'laɪv] żywy, żyjący; pełen życia; **~ and kicking** w świetnym stanie; *be ~ with* pełen (*G*), wypełniony (*I*)

all [ɔːl] **1.** *adj.* wszyscy *pl.* wszystkie *pl.*; cały; wszystek; **2.** *pron.* wszystko; wszystkie *pl.*, wszyscy *pl.*; **3.** *adv.* zupełnie, całkowicie; **~ at once** nagle; **~ the better** tym lepiej; **~ but** prawie, nieomalże; **~ in** *Am.* F wykończony; **~ in ~** ogółem; **~ right** w porządku; dobrze; *for ~ that* mimo tego; *for ~ I know* na ile wiadomo; *at ~* wcale, w ogóle; *not at ~* bynajmniej; ani trochę; nie ma za co; *the score was two ~* wynik był dwa dwa

all-A·mer·i·can [ɔːlə'merɪkən] ogólnoamerykański; typowo amerykański

al·lay [ə'leɪ] rozpraszać ⟨-szyć⟩; zmniejszać ⟨-szyć⟩

al·le·ga·tion [ælɪ'geɪʃn] *bezpodstawne* twierdzenie *n*

al·lege [ə'ledʒ] ⟨s⟩twierdzić; **~d** rzekomy; domniemany

al·le·giance [ə'liːdʒəns] lojalność *f*; wierność *f*

al·ler|·gic [ə'lɜːdʒɪk] alergiczny (*to* na *A*); **~·gy** ['ælədʒɪ] alergia *f*

al·le·vi·ate [ə'liːvɪeɪt] zmniejszać ⟨-szyć⟩; ⟨z⟩łagodzić

al·ley ['ælɪ] aleja *f*; (*w parku, ogrodzie*) alejka *f*, dróżka *f*, ścieżka *f*; tor (*do gry w kręgle*) *m*

al·li|·ance [ə'laɪəns] przymierze *n*, sojusz *m*; **~ed** [ə'laɪd] sprzymierzony

al·li·ga·tor ['ælɪgeɪtə] *zo.* aligator *m*

al·lo|·cate ['æləkeɪt] przydzielać ⟨-lić⟩; ⟨wy⟩asygnować; **~·ca·tion** [ælə'keɪʃn] przydział *m*

al·lot [ə'lɒt] (*-tt-*) przeznaczać ⟨-czyć⟩; przydzielać ⟨-lić⟩; rozdzielać ⟨-lić⟩; **~·ment** przydział *m*; działka *f*

al·low [ə'laʊ] pozwalać ⟨-wolić⟩; dopuszczać ⟨-puścić⟩; dawać ⟨dać⟩; udzielać ⟨udzielić⟩; **~ for** uwzględniać ⟨-nić⟩ (*A*); **~·a·ble** dopuszczalny; **~·ance** (*w delegacji*) dieta *f*; zasiłek *m*; stypendium *m*; odpis *m* podatkowy; *fig.* uwzględnienie; *make ~ance(s) for s.th.* uwzględniać ⟨-nić⟩ coś

al·loy 1. ['ælɔɪ] stop *m*; **2.** [ə'lɔɪ] ⟨s⟩tworzyć stop

all-round ['ɔːlraʊnd] wszechstronny; **~·er** [ɔːl'raʊndə] osoba *f* wszechstronna; wszechstronny sportowiec *m*

al·lude [ə'luːd] ⟨z⟩robić aluzje *pl.* (*to* do *G*)

al·lure [ə'ljʊə] ⟨z-, przy⟩nęcić; **~·ment** atrakcja *f*, przynęta *f*

al·lu·sion [ə'luːʒn] aluzja *f*

all-wheel 'drive *mot.* napęd *m* na wszystkie koła

al·ly 1. [ə'laɪ] sprzymierzać ⟨-rzyć⟩ się (*to, with* z *I*); ['ælaɪ] sojusznik *m*; sprzymierzeniec *m*; *the Allies pl.* państwa sprzymierzone *pl.*, alianci *pl.*

al·might·y [ɔːl'maɪtɪ] wszechmocny; *the* ♀ Bóg *m* Wszechmogący

al·mond ['ɑːmənd] *bot.* migdał *m*; *attr.* migdałowy

al·most ['ɔːlməʊst] prawie, niemal

alms [ɑːmz] *pl.* jałmużna *f*

a·loft [ə'lɒft] w górę, w górze

a·lone [ə'ləʊn] **1.** *adj.* sam; **2.** *adv.* samotnie; *let ~* zostawiać ⟨-wić⟩ w spokoju; *let ~ ...* nie mówiąc już o (*L*)

a·long [ə'lɒŋ] **1.** *adv.* naprzód, w przód; *all ~* (przez) cały czas; *come ~ with s.o.* iść ⟨pójść⟩ z kimś; *get ~* dawać ⟨dać⟩ sobie radę; ⟨po⟩radzić sobie; być w dobrych stosunkach (*with* z *I*); dobrze się porozumiewać ⟨-mieć⟩; *take ~* brać ⟨wziąć⟩ z (*I*); **2.** *prp.* wzdłuż(*G*); **~·sideobok**(*G*);wzdłuż(*G*)

a·loof [ə'luːf] powściągliwy; pełen rezerwy

a·loud [ə'laʊd] na głos, głośno

al·pha·bet ['ælfəbet] alfabet *m*

al·pine ['ælpaɪn] alpejski, wysokogórski

Alps *pl.* Alpy *pl.*

al·read·y [ɔːl'redɪ] już

al right [ɔːl'raɪt] → *all right*

Al·sa·tian [æl'seɪʃən] *zwł. Brt.* owczarek *m* alzacki *lub* niemiecki, F wilczur *m*

al·so ['ɔːlsəʊ] też, także

al·tar ['ɔːltə] ołtarz *m*

al·ter ['ɔːltə] zmieniać ⟨-nić⟩ (się); *ubranie* przerabiać ⟨-robić⟩; **~·a·tion** [ɔːltə'reɪʃn] zmiana *f* (*to* na A); przemiana *f*; przeróbka *f* (*ubrania*)

al·ter·nate 1. ['ɔːltəneɪt] następować ⟨-tąpić⟩ na zmianę; **2.** [ɔːl'tɜːnət] naprzemienny; **~·nat·ing cur·rent** ['ɔːltəneɪtɪŋ -] prąd *m* zmienny; **~·na·tion** [ɔːltə'neɪʃn] zmiana *f*; przemiana *f*; **~·na·tive** [ɔːl'tɜːnətɪv] **1.** alternatywny; **2.** alternatywa *f*; wybór *m*

al·though [ɔːl'ðəʊ] choć, chociaż

al·ti·tude ['æltɪtjuːd] wysokość *f*; *at an ~ of* na wysokości (G)

al·to·geth·er [ɔːltə'geðə] ogólnie; ogółem; zupełnie, całkowicie

al·u·min·i·um [ælju'mɪnjəm] *Brt.*, **a·lu·mi·num** [ə'luːmɪnəm] *Am. chem.* aluminium *n*, glin *m*; *attr.* aluminiowy

al·ways ['ɔːlweɪz] zawsze

am [æm; *we frazie* əm] *1. os. poj. ter. od* **be** jestem

am, AM [eɪ 'em] *skrót: before noon* (*łacińskie ante meridiem*) przed południem

a·mal·gam·ate [ə'mælgəmeɪt] *też econ.* ⟨po-, z⟩łączyć się; *econ.* dokonywać ⟨-nać⟩ fuzji

a·mass [ə'mæs] ⟨na-, z⟩gromadzić

am·a·teur ['æmətə] **1.** amator(ka *f*); **2.** amatorski

a·maze [ə'meɪz] zdumiewać ⟨-mieć⟩; **a'maze·ment** zdumienie *n*; **a'maz·ing** zdumiewający

am·bas·sa·dor [æm'bæsədə] ambasador *m* (*to* w L); *fig.* przedstawiciel(ka *f*) *m*; **~·dress** [æm'bæsədrɪs] kobieta *f* ambasador; *fig.* przestawicielka *f*

am·ber ['æmbə] bursztyn *m*; bursztynowy

am·bi·gu·i·ty [æmbɪ'gjuːɪtɪ] dwuznaczność *f*; wieloznaczność *f*; niejasność *f*; **am·big·u·ous** [æm'bɪgjʊəs] dwuznaczny; wieloznaczny; niejasny

am·bi·tion [æm'bɪʃn] ambicja *f*; **~·tious** [æm'bɪʃəs] ambitny

am·ble ['æmbl] **1.** przechadzka *f*; spo-

kojny chód *m*; **2.** przechadzać ⟨przejść⟩ się; spokojnie iść ⟨pójść⟩;

am·bu·lance ['æmbjʊləns] karetka *f* (*pogotowia*)

am·bush ['æmbʊʃ] **1.** zasadzka *f*; *be lub lie in ~ for s.o.* czekać w zasadzce na kogoś; czatować na kogoś; **2.** wciągać ⟨-gnąć⟩ w zasadzkę

a·men [ɑː'men] *int.* amen; niech tak będzie

a·mend [ə'mend] poprawiać ⟨-wić⟩; ⟨z⟩modyfikować; *prawo* wnosić ⟨wnieść⟩ poprawki; **~·ment** poprawka *f* (*też parl.*, *Am. do konstytucji*); modyfikacja *f*; zmiana *f*; **~s** *pl.* rekompensata *f*; *make ~s* ⟨z⟩rekompensować; naprawiać ⟨-wić⟩ szkody; *make ~s to s.o. for s.th.* wynagradzać coś komuś, rekompensować coś komuś

a·men·i·ty [ə'miːnətɪ] *często* **amenities** *pl.* wygody *pl.*; urządzenia *pl.* ułatwiające życie

A·mer·i·ca [ə'merɪkə] Ameryka *f*; **A·mer·i·can** [ə'merɪkən] **1.** amerykański; **~' plan** pełne utrzymanie *n*; **2.** Amerykanin *m* (-nka *f*)

A·mer·i·can·is·m [ə'merɪkənɪzəm] amerykanizm *m*; **~·ize** [ə'merɪkənaɪz] ⟨z⟩amerykanizować (się)

a·mi·a·ble ['eɪmjəbl] przyjazny; miły

am·i·ca·ble ['æmɪkəbl] przyjacielski; *jur.* polubowny, ugodowy

a·mid(st) [ə'mɪd(st)] wśród (G); (po)między (I)

a·miss [ə'mɪs] źle, błędnie; *take ~* ⟨poczuć się urażonym

am·mo·ni·a [ə'məʊnjə] amoniak *m*

am·mu·ni·tion [æmjʊ'nɪʃn] amunicja *f*

am·nes·ty ['æmnɪstɪ] **1.** amnestia *f*; **2.** ułaskawiać ⟨-wić⟩

a·mok [ə'mɒk] amok *m*; *run ~* dostawać ⟨-tać⟩ amoku

a·mong(st) [ə'mʌŋ(st)] (po)między (I)

am·o·rous ['æmərəs] rozkochany (*of* w L)

a·mount [ə'maʊnt] **1.** (*to*) wynosić ⟨-nieść⟩ (A); stanowić (A); sprowadzać ⟨-dzić⟩ się do (G); **2.** kwota *f*; liczba *f*; suma *f*

am·ple ['æmpl] (*~r, ~st*) obfity; pokaźny; dostateczny

am·pli·fi·ca·tion [æmplɪfɪ'keɪʃn] zwiększenie *n*; *electr.* wzmocnienie *n*; **~·fi·er** *electr.* ['æmplɪfaɪə] wzmacniacz *m*; ~·fy ['æmplıfaı] zwiększać ⟨-szyć⟩; *electr.* wzmacniać ⟨-nić⟩; ~·tude ['æmplıtjuːd] zasięg; amplituda

a·muck [ə'mʌk] → *amok*

a·muse [ə'mjuːz] (*o.s.* się) ⟨roz⟩bawić, zabawiać ⟨-wić⟩; ~·ment rozrywka *f*; zabawa *f*; radość *f*; ~·ment arcade salon *m* gier automatycznych *lub* komputerowych; ~·ment park wesołe miasteczko *n*; a'mus·ing zabawny

an [æn, ən] → *a*

an·a·bol·ic ster·oid [ænəbɒlık 'stıərɔıd] *pharm.* steryd *m* anaboliczny

a·nae·mi·a [ə'niːmjə] anemia *f*

an·aes·thet·ic [ænıs'θetık] *med.* 1. (~*ally*) znieczulający; 2. środek *m* znieczulający

a·nal ['eınl] *anat.* odbytniczy; analny

a·nal·o·|·gous [ə'næləgəs] analogiczny, podobny; ~·gy [ə'nælədʒı] analogia *f*

an·a·lyse *zwł. Brt.,* an·a·lyze *Am.* ['ænəlaız] ⟨prze-, z⟩analizować; przeprowadzać ⟨-dzić⟩ analizę; a·nal·y·sis [ə'næləsıs] (*pl. -ses* [-siːz]) analiza *f*

an·arch·y ['ænəkı] anarchia *f*

a·nat·o·|·mize [ə'nætəmaız] *med.* przeprowadzać ⟨-dzić⟩ sekcję; *fig.* ⟨prze-, z⟩analizować; ~·my [ə'nætəmı] anatomia *f*; analiza *f*

an·ces·|·tor ['ænsestə] przodek *m*; protoplasta *m*; ~·tress ['ænsestrıs] protoplastka *f*

an·chor ['æŋkə] 1. kotwica *f*; *at* ~ na kotwicy; 2. zakotwiczać ⟨-czyć⟩

an·chor·|·man ['æŋkəmæn] *Am. TV* (*pl. -men*) prowadzący *m* (*wiadomości*); '~·wom·an *Am. TV* (*pl. -women*) prowadząca *f* (*wiadomości*)

an·cho·vy ['æntʃəvı] sardela *f*

an·cient ['eınʃənt] 1. starożytny; prastary; 2. *the* ~*s pl. hist.* starożytni *pl.*

and [ænd, ənd] i; a

an·ec·dote ['ænıkdəʊt] anegdota *f*

a·ne·mi·a [ə'niːmjə] *Am.* → *anaemia*

an·es·thet·ic [ænıs'θetık] *Am.* → *anesthetic*

an·gel ['eındʒəl] anioł *m*

an·ger ['æŋgə] 1. gniew *m* (*at* z powodu *G*); 2. rozgniewać

an·gi·na (pec·to·ris) [ænˈdʒaınə('pektərıs)] *med.* dusznica *f* bolesna, angina *f* pectoris; △ *nie* **angina**

an·gle¹ ['æŋgl] kąt *m*; róg *m*

an·gle² ['æŋgl] ⟨z⟩łowić; '~r wędkarz *m*

An·gli·can ['æŋglıkən] 1. anglikański; 2. anglikanin *m* , anglikanka *f*

An·glo-Sax·on [æŋgləʊ'sæksən] 1. anglosaski; 2. Anglosas *m*

an·gry ['æŋgrı] (*-ier, -iest*) zły, rozgniewany (*at, with* na *A*)

an·guish ['æŋgwıʃ] cierpienie *n*

an·gu·lar ['æŋgjʊlə] kanciasty

an·i·mal ['ænıml] 1. zwierzę *n*; 2. zwierzęcy; '~ lov·er miłośnik *m* ⟨-niczka *f*⟩ zwierząt

an·i·|·mate ['ænımeıt] ożywiać ⟨-wić⟩; pobudzać ⟨-dzić⟩; '~·ma·ted ożywiony; pobudzony; ~·ma·ted car'toon film *m* animowany; ~·ma·tion [ænı'meıʃn] ożywienie *n*; pobudzenie *n*; animacja *f*; *komp.* grafika *f* animowana

an·i·mos·i·ty [ænı'mɒsətı] wrogość *f*; wrogie nastawienie *n*

an·kle ['æŋkl] *anat.* kostka

an·nals ['ænlz] *pl.* roczniki *pl.*; annały *pl.*

an·nex 1. [ə'neks] dołączać ⟨-czyć⟩; ⟨za⟩anektować; 2. ['æneks] aneks *m*, dodatek *m*; przybudówka *f*

an·ni·ver·sa·ry [ænı'vɜːsərı] rocznica *f*

an·no·tate ['ænəʊteıt] zaopatrywać ⟨-trzyć⟩ w adnotacje *lub* przypisy

an·nounce [ə'naʊns] ogłaszać ⟨ogłosić⟩; oświadczać ⟨-czyć⟩; *radio, TV*: zapowiadać ⟨-wiedzieć⟩; △ *nie* anonsować; ~·ment zapowiedź *f* (*też radio, TV*); ogłoszenie *n*; komunikat *m*; an'nounc·er spiker(ka *f*) *m*

an·noy [ə'nɔı] ⟨z⟩irytować; ~·ance irytacja *f*; poirytowanie *n*; ~·ing irytujący

an·nu·al ['ænjʊəl] 1. roczny; coroczny; doroczny; 2. *bot.* roślina *f* jednoroczna; rocznik *m*

an·nu·i·ty [ə'njuːıtı] renta *f* (roczna)

an·nul [ə'nʌl] (*-ll-*) anulować; unieważniać ⟨-nić⟩; ~·ment anulowanie *n*; unieważnienie *n*

an·o·dyne ['ænəʊdaın] *med.* 1. uśmierzający bóle; 2. środek *m* uśmierzający bóle

a·noint [ə'nɔınt] namaszczać ⟨-maścić⟩

a·nom·a·lous [ə'nɒmələs] nieprawidłowy; nieregularny

a·non·y·mous [ə'nɒnıməs] anonimowy

A

an·o·rak ['ænəræk] skafander *m* (*z kapturem*); kurtka *f*

an·oth·er [ə'nʌðə] inny; jeszcze jeden

ANSI ['ænsɪ] *skrót: American National Standards Institute* Amerykański Urząd Norm

an·swer ['ɑːnsə] **1.** *v/t.* odpowiadać ⟨-wiedzieć⟩; *cel* spełniać ⟨-nić⟩; *problem* rozwiązywać ⟨-zać⟩; *opis* odpowiadać; **~ the bell** *lub* **door** otworzyć drzwi; **~ the telephone** odbierać ⟨-debrać⟩ telefon; *v/i.* odpowiadać ⟨-wiedzieć⟩; podnosić ⟨-nieść⟩ słuchawkę; **~ back** odpyskowywać ⟨-ować⟩, odcinać ⟨-ciąć⟩ się; **~ for** ponosić ⟨-nieść⟩ odpowiedzialność za (*G*); **2.** odpowiedź *f* (*to* na *A*); ~·**a·ble** ['ɑːnsərəbl] odpowiedzialny (*for* za *A*); ~·**ing machine** *tel.* ['ɑːnsərɪŋ -] automatyczna sekretarka *f*

ant [ænt] *zo.* mrówka *f*

an·tag·o·nis·m [æn'tæɡənɪzəm] antagonizm *m*; wrogość *f*; ~·**nist** [æn'tæɡənɪst] przeciwnik *m* (-niczka *f*); ~·**nize** [æn'tæɡənaɪz] zrażać ⟨zrazić⟩, wzbudzać ⟨-dzić⟩ wrogość

Ant·arc·tic [æn'tɑːktɪk] antarktyczny

Ant·arc·tica [æn'tɑːktɪkə] Antarktyda *f*

an·te·ced·ent [æntɪ'siːdənt] poprzedni, uprzedni

an·te·lope ['æntɪləʊp] *zo.* (*pl. -lopes, -lope*) antylopa *f*

an·ten·na[1] [æn'tenə] *zo.* (*pl. -nae* [-niː]) czułek *m*

an·ten·na[2] [æn'tenə] *Am.* antena *f*

an·te·ri·or[æn'tɪərɪə] poprzedni; wcześniejszy (*to* niż)

an·them ['ænθəm] hymn *m*

an·ti... ['æntɪ] anty..., przeciw...; ~·**aircraft** mil. przeciwlotniczy; ~·**bi·ot·ic** [æntɪbaɪ'ɒtɪk] *pharm.* antybiotyk *m*; '~·**body** *biol.* przeciwciało *n*

an·tic·i·pate [æn'tɪsɪpeɪt] przewidywać ⟨-widzieć⟩; oczekiwać, wyczekiwać; ~·**pa·tion** [æntɪsɪ'peɪʃn] oczekiwanie *n*; przewidywanie *n*; *in ~pation* z góry, naprzód

an·ti·clock·wise [æntɪ'klɒkwaɪz] *Brt.* w kierunku odwrotnym do ruchu wskazówek zegara

an·tics ['æntɪks] *pl.* błazeństwa *pl.*, wygłupy *pl.*; △ *nie antyk*

an·ti·dote ['æntɪdəʊt] antidotum *n*,

odtrutka *f*; '~·**freeze** płyn *m* nie zamarzający; ~·**lock braking sys·tem** *mot.* (system) ABS *m* (*przeciwdziałający blokadzie hamulców*); ~·**mis·sile** przeciwrakietowy; ~·**nu·cle·ar ac·tiv·ist** działacz(ka *f*) *m* ruchu przeciw broni nuklearnej

an·tip·a·thy [æn'tɪpəθɪ] antypatia

an·ti·quat·ed ['æntɪkweɪtɪd] przestarzały, staroświecki; △ *nie antykwaryczny*

an·tique [æn'tiːk] **1.** antyczny; starożytny; **2.** antyk *m*, zabytek *m*; **~ deal·er** antykwariusz *m*; **~ shop** zwł. *Brt.*, **~ store** *Am.* sklep *m* z antykami

an·tiq·ui·ty [æn'tɪkwətɪ] starożytność *f*

an·ti·sep·tic [æntɪ'septɪk] **1.** antyseptyczny, odkażający; **2.** środek antyseptyczny *lub* odkażający

ant·lers ['æntləz] *pl.* rogi *pl.*, poroże *n*

a·nus ['eɪnəs] *anat.* odbyt *m*

an·vil ['ænvɪl] kowadło *n*

anx·i·e·ty [æŋ'zaɪətɪ] lęk *m*; niepokój *m*, obawa *f*; troska *f*

anx·ious ['æŋkʃəs] zatroskany; zaniepokojony; wyczekujący; *he is ~ about you* niepokoi się o ciebie; *he is ~ to do s.th.* zależy mu, by coś zrobić

an·y ['enɪ] **1.** *adj.* i *pron.* jakiś, trochę; jakikolwiek; którykolwiek; każdy; *z przeczeniem:* żaden; *not ~* w ogóle; żaden; **2.** trochę, nieco; '~·**bod·y** ktokolwiek; każdy; *z przeczeniem:* nikt; '~·**how** jakkolwiek; byle jak; '~·**one** → *anybody*; '~·**thing** cokolwiek; coś; cokolwiek; *z przeczeniem:* nic; ~·**thing but** w ogóle; wcale; ani trochę; ~·**thing else?** czy coś jeszcze?; '~·**way** → *anyhow*; '~·**where** gdziekolwiek; gdzieś; *z przeczeniem:* nigdzie

AP [eɪ 'piː] *skrót: Associated Press* (*amerykańska agencja prasowa*)

a·part [ə'pɑːt] osobno, na boku; od siebie; **~ from** oprócz

a·part·heid [ə'pɑːtheɪt] apartheid *m*, polityka *f* segregacji rasowej

a·part·ment [ə'pɑːtmənt] *Am.* mieszkanie *n*; △ *nie apartament*; **~ build·ing** zwł. *Brt.*, **~ house** *Am.* blok *m* mieszkaniowy, kamienica *f*

ap·a·thet·ic [æpə'θetɪk] (*-ally*) apatyczny, obojętny, zobojętniały; ~·**thy** ['æpəθɪ] apatia *f*, obojętność *f*, zobojętnienie *n*

ape [eɪp] *zo.* małpa *f* człekokształtna

ap·er·ture ['æpətjuə] otwór *m*; szczelina *f*

a·pi·a·ry ['eɪpjərɪ] pasieka *f*

a·piece [ə'piːs] za sztukę; na głowę, na osobę

a·pol·o·gize [ə'pɒlədʒaɪz] przepraszać ⟨-prosić⟩; **~·gy** [ə'pɒlədʒɪ] przeprosiny *pl.*; **make an ~gy (for s.th.)** przepraszać ⟨-prosić⟩ (za coś)

ap·o·plex·y ['æpəpleksɪ] apopleksja *f*, udar *m*

a·pos·tle [ə'pɒsl] *rel.* apostoł *m* (*też fig.*)

a·pos·tro·phe [ə'pɒstrəfɪ] apostrof *m*

ap·pal(l) [ə'pɔːl] (*-ll-*) przerażać ⟨-razić⟩; trwożyć ⟨zatrważać⟩

Ap·pa·la·chians *pl.* Appalachy *pl.*

ap'pal·ling przerażający; zatrważający

ap·pa·ra·tus [æpə'reɪtəs] aparat *m*; aparatura *f*; urządzenie *n*; przyrząd *m*

ap·par·ent [ə'pærənt] pozorny; widoczny

ap·pa·ri·tion [æpə'rɪʃn] widmo *n*, zjawa *f*

ap·peal [ə'piːl] **1.** *jur.* składać ⟨złożyć⟩ odwołanie, odwoływać ⟨odwołać⟩ się; ⟨za⟩apelować (*for* do *G*); wzywać ⟨wezwać⟩ (*to* do *G*); **~ to** odwoływać ⟨odwołać⟩ się do (*G*), przemawiać ⟨-mówić⟩ do (*G*); kogoś pociągać (*to* A), ⟨s⟩podobać się; **2.** *jur.* apelacja *f*, odwołanie *n* się; urok *m*, powab *m*; prośba *f* (*to* do *G*, *for* o A), apel *m*; **~ for mercy** *jur.* prośba *f* o łaskę; **sex ~** seksapil *m*, atrakcyjność *f*; **~·ing** pociągający; błagalny

ap·pear [ə'pɪə] ukazywać ⟨-zać⟩ się; pojawiać ⟨-wić⟩ się; *publicznie* występować ⟨-stąpić⟩; wydawać się; **~·ance** [ə'pɪərəns] pojawienie *n* się; wygląd *m*; wystąpienie *n*; **keep up ~ances** zachowywać ⟨-chować⟩ pozory; **~ to** lub **by all ~ances** pozornie, na pozór

ap·pease [ə'piːz] uspokajać ⟨-koić⟩; *pragnienie itp.* zaspokajać ⟨-koić⟩

ap·pend [ə'pend] dołączać ⟨-czyć⟩, przyłączać ⟨-łączyć⟩; **~·age** [ə'pendɪdʒ] dodatek *m*; uzupełnienie *n*

ap·pen·di·ci·tis [əpendɪ'saɪtɪs] *med.* zapalenie *n* wyrostka robaczkowego; **~·dix** [ə'pendɪks] (*pl.* **-dixes, -dices** [-dɪsiːz]) dodatek *m*, suplement *m*;

też **vermiform ~·dix** *anat.* wyrostek *m* robaczkowy, ślepa kiszka *f*

ap·pe·tite ['æpɪtaɪt] apetyt *m*; *fig.* chęć *f*, chętka *f* (*for* na *L*); **~·tiz·er** ['æpɪtaɪzə] przystawka *f*, zakąska *f*; aperitif *m*; **~·tiz·ing** ['æpɪtaɪzɪŋ] apetyczny, smakowity

ap·plaud [ə'plɔːd] *v/t.* oklaskiwać; *v/i.* ⟨za⟩klaskać; **ap·plause** [ə'plɔːz] aplauz *m*, brawa *pl.*

ap·ple ['æpl] jabłko *n*; '**~ cart: upset s.o.'s ~cart** F ⟨po⟩psuć komuś szyki; **~ 'pie** szarlotka *f*; **in ~pie order** F w porządku, jak z pudełka; **~ 'sauce** przecier *m* jabłkowy; *Am. sl.* bzdury *pl.*, banialuki *pl.*; **~ 'tree** *bot.* jabłoń *f*

ap·pli·ance [ə'plaɪəns] urządzenie *n*; przyrząd *m*

ap·plic·a·ble ['æplɪkəbl] mający zastosowanie (*to* do *G*)

ap·pli·cant ['æplɪkənt] kandydat(ka *f*) *m* (*for* do *G*), aplikant(ka *f*) *m*; **~·ca·tion** [æplɪ'keɪʃn] zastosowanie *n*; podanie *n* (*to* do *G*); ubieganie *n* się (*for* o A); nałożenie *n* (*kremu*)

ap·ply [ə'plaɪ] *v/t.* ⟨na⟩ (*to*) ⟨za⟩stosować (do *G*); nakładać ⟨nałożyć⟩ (na *L*); **~ o.s. to** przykładać ⟨-łożyć⟩ się (do *G*); *v/i.* (*to*) stosować się (do *G*), mieć zastosowanie (do *G*); zgłaszać ⟨zgłosić⟩ się (*for* do *G*), składać ⟨złożyć⟩ podanie (*for* na A)

ap·point [ə'pɔɪnt] wyznaczać ⟨-czyć⟩; mianować (*s.o. director* kogoś *I*); mianować (*s.o. director* kogoś na A); **~·ment** mianowanie *n*, nominacja *f*; stanowisko *n*; (*z lekarzem itp.*) umówione spotkanie *n*; termin *m* (*wizyty*); **by ~ment** po uzgodnieniu terminu; **~ment book** terminarz *m*

ap·por·tion [ə'pɔːʃn] przydzielać ⟨-dzielić⟩

ap·prais·al [ə'preɪzl] oszacowanie *n*, ocena *f*; **~e** [ə'preɪz] oszacowywać ⟨-wać⟩, oceniać ⟨-nić⟩

ap·pre·cia·ble [ə'priːʃəbl] znaczny, dostrzegalny; **~·ci·ate** [ə'priːʃɪeɪt] *v/t.* doceniać ⟨-nić⟩; cenić sobie; uznać ⟨-wać⟩; *v/i.* wzrastać ⟨wzrosnąć⟩ na wartości; **~·ci·a·tion** [əpriːʃɪ'eɪʃn] uznanie *n*; wzrost *m* wartości *lub* ceny; uznanie *n*, wdzięczność *f*

ap·pre·hend [æprɪ'hend] pojmować ⟨-jąć⟩, ⟨z⟩rozumieć; ⟨za⟩aresztować;

obawiać się; **~·hen·sion** [æprɪˈhenʃn]
obawa f; aresztowanie n; pojmowanie n, zrozumienie n; **~·hen·sive**
[æprɪˈhensɪv] pełen obaw (**for** o A,
that że); bojaźliwy

ap·pren·tice [əˈprentɪs] **1.** prakty-
kant(ka f) m; terminator m; **2.** ⟨od⟩da-
wać w termin; **~·ship** praktyka f; termin m

ap·proach [əˈprəʊtʃ] **1.** v/i. zbliżać
⟨zbliżyć⟩ się, przybliżać ⟨przybliżyć⟩
się, nadchodzić ⟨nadejść⟩; v/t. zbliżać
⟨zbliżyć⟩ się do (G), przybliżać ⟨przy-
bliżyć⟩ się do (G); podchodzić ⟨po-
dejść⟩ do (G); zwracać ⟨zwrócić⟩ się
do (G); **2.** nadejście n; podejście n; dostęp m; zbliżanie n się

ap·pro·ba·tion [æprəˈbeɪʃn] aprobata f; akceptacja f

ap·pro·pri·ate [əˈprəʊprɪeɪt] przywłaszczać ⟨-łaścić⟩ sobie; ⟨wy⟩asygno-
wać, przeznaczać ⟨-czyć⟩; **2.** [əˈprəʊ-
prɪɪt] (**for, to**) właściwy (do G); odpowiedni (do G)

ap·prov·al [əˈpruːvl] aprobata f; zgoda f; **~e** [əˈpruːv] ⟨za⟩aprobować; uznawać ⟨-nać⟩; zatwierdzać ⟨-dzić⟩; **~ed**
zatwierdzony, zaaprobowany

ap·prox·i·mate [əˈprɒksɪmət] przybliżony

Apr skrót pisany: **April** kw., kwiecień m
a·pri·cot [ˈeɪprɪkɒt] morela f
A·pril [ˈeɪprəl] (skrót: **Apr**) kwiecień m;
attr. kwietniowy

a·pron [ˈeɪprən] fartuch m; **~ strings**
pl. tasiemki pl. fartucha; **be tied to
one's mother's ~ strings** trzymać
się maminego fartucha

apt [æpt] trafny, celny; zdatny, nadający
się; zdolny; **be ~ to do s.th.** mieć skłonności do robienia czegoś; **ap·ti·tude**
[ˈæptɪtjuːd] (**for**) zdatność f (do G); talent m; **~ test** test m zdolności

aq·ua·plan·ing [ˈækwəpleɪnɪŋ] Brt.
mot. akwaplanacja f; tech. poślizg hydro-
dynamiczny m

a·quar·i·um [əˈkweərɪəm] (pl. **-iums**,
-ia [-ɪə]) akwarium n

A·quar·i·us [əˈkweərɪəs] znak Zodiaku: Wodnik m; **he/she is (an)** ~ on(a)
jest spod znaku Wodnika

a·quat·ic [əˈkwætɪk] wodny; **~ plant**
bot. roślina f wodna; **~s** sg.: **~ sports**
pl. sporty pl. wodne

aq·ue·duct [ˈækwɪdʌkt] akwedukt m
aq·ui·line [ˈækwɪlaɪn] nos: orli; **~ nose**
orli lub rzymski nos m

Ar·ab [ˈærəb] **1.** Arab(ka f) m; **2.** kraj
arabski; **A·ra·bi·a** [əˈreɪbjə] Arabia f;
Ar·a·bic [ˈærəbɪk] **1.** arabski; **2.** język
m arabski

ar·a·ble [ˈærəbl] orny; uprawny

ar·bi·tra·ry [ˈɑːbɪtrərɪ] arbitralny;
przypadkowy; **~trate** [ˈɑːbɪtreɪt] rozstrzygać ⟨-gnąć⟩ w arbitrażu; ˈos⟩pełnić
rolę arbitra; **~tra·tion** [ɑːbɪˈtreɪʃn] arbitraż m; **~tra·tor** [ˈɑːbɪtreɪtə] arbi-
ter m, rozjemca m (-czyni f)

ar·bo(u)r [ˈɑːbə] altana f

arc [ɑːk] łuk m (electr. elektryczny);
ar·cade [ɑːˈkeɪd] arkada f; pasaż m

ARC [eɪ ɑː ˈsiː] skrót: **American Red
Cross** Amerykański Czerwony Krzyż

arch¹ [ɑːtʃ] **1.** łuk m; sklepienie n; przęsło n (mostu); **2.** wyginać ⟨-giąć⟩ (się)
w łuk

arch² [ɑːtʃ] arcy...; arch...

arch³ [ɑːtʃ] psotny, figlarny

ar·cha·ic [ɑːˈkeɪɪk] (**~ally**) archaiczny
arch|·an·gel [ˈɑːkeɪndʒəl] archanioł m;
~·bish·op [ˈɑːtʃbɪʃəp] arcybiskup m

ar·cher [ˈɑːtʃə] łucznik m, (-niczka f);
~·y [ˈɑːtʃərɪ] łucznictwo n

ar·chi|·tect [ˈɑːkɪtekt] architekt m;
~·tec·ture [ˈɑːkɪtektʃə] architektura f

ar·chives [ˈɑːkaɪvz] pl. archiwum n, ar-
chiwa pl.

'arch·way pasaż m, sklepione przejście n

arc·tic [ˈɑːktɪk] arktyczny

ar·dent [ˈɑːdənt] płonący, rozżarzony;
fig. gorliwy, ożywiony

ar·do(u)r [ˈɑːdə] żar m; gorliwość f

are [ɑː] 2. os. ter. poj. i 1., 2., 3. mn. od **be**;
ty jesteś, my jesteśmy, wy jesteście, oni,
one są

ar·e·a [ˈeərɪə] powierzchnia f; obszar m;
miejsce n; dziedzina f; rejon m, strefa f;
~ code Am. tel. numer m kierunkowy

Ar·gen|·ti·na [ɑːdʒənˈtiːnə] Argenty-
na f; **~·tine** [ˈɑːdʒəntaɪn] **1.** argentyń-
ski; **2.** Argentyńczyk m, Argentynka f

a·re·na [əˈriːnə] arena f; miejsce n

ar·gue [ˈɑːgjuː] spierać się, ⟨po⟩sprze-
czać się; argumentować, wysuwać
⟨-nąć⟩ argumenty; utrzymywać (**that**
że)

ar·gu·ment [ˈɑːgjʊmənt] sprzeczka f,

spór *m*; argument *m*; dyskusja *f*

ar·id ['ærɪd] suchy, jałowy

Ar·ies ['eəri:z] *znak Zodiaku:* Baran *m*; he/she is (an) ~ on(a) jest spod znaku Barana

a·rise [ə'raɪz] (**arose, arisen**) powstawać ⟨-stać⟩, pojawiać ⟨-wić⟩ się; wynikać ⟨-knąć⟩; **a·ris·en** [ə'rɪzn] *p.p. od* **arise**

ar·is|·toc·ra·cy [ærɪ'stɒkrəsɪ] arystokracja *f*; ~·to·crat ['ærɪstəkræt] arystokrata *m* (-tka *f*)

a·rith·me·tic[1] [ə'rɪθmətɪk] *math.* arytmetyka *f*; obliczenia *pl.*, wyliczenia *pl.*

ar·ith·met·ic[2] [ærɪθ'metɪk] arytmetyczny, rachunkowy; ~ 'u·nit *komp.* arytmometr *m*, jednostka *f* arytmetyczno-logiczna

ark [ɑːk] arka *f*

arm[1] [ɑːm] ramię *n*; ręka *f*; poręcz *f*; **keep s.o. at ~'s length** trzymać kogoś na dystans

arm[2] [ɑːm] ⟨u⟩zbroić (się)

ar·ma·ment ['ɑːməmənt] zbrojenie *n* się; zbrojenia *pl.*

'arm·chair fotel *m*

ar·mi·stice ['ɑːmɪstɪs] zawieszenie *n* broni

ar·mo(u)r ['ɑːmə] **1.** *mil.* pancerz *m* (*też fig., zo.*); opancerzenie *n*; wojska *pl.* pancerne; zbroja *f*; **2.** opancerzać ⟨-rzyć⟩; **~ed 'car** wóz *m* opancerzony, samochód *m* pancerny

'arm·pit pacha *f*

arms [ɑːmz] *pl.* broń *f*, uzbrojenie; '~ con·trol kontrola *f* zbrojeń; '~ race wyścig *m* zbrojeń

ar·my ['ɑːmɪ] wojsko *n*, armia *f*

a·ro·ma [ə'rəumə] aromat *m*, woń *f*; ar·o·mat·ic [ærə'mætɪk] aromatyczny, wonny

a·rose [ə'rəuz] *pret. od* **arise**

a·round [ə'raund] **1.** *adv.* dookoła, wokoło; w pobliżu; **2.** *prp.* wokół (*G*), dokoła (*G*), koło (*G*); około (*G*)

a·rouse [ə'rauz] ⟨z⟩budzić; *fig.* pobudzać ⟨-dzić⟩; rozbudzać ⟨-dzić⟩

ar·range [ə'reɪndʒ] układać ⟨ułożyć⟩, ustawiać ⟨-wić⟩, rozmieszczać ⟨-ścić⟩, ⟨z⟩organizować, załatwiać ⟨-wić⟩; *muz.* aranżować, opracowywać ⟨-ować⟩ (*też theat.*); ~·ment ułożenie *n*, ustawienie *n*, rozłożenie *n*; załatwienie *n*; zorganizowanie *n*; *muz.* aranżacja *f*, opra-

cowanie *n* (*też theat.*)

ar·rears [ə'rɪəz] *pl.* zaległości *pl.*; **be in ~ with** zalegać z (*I*)

ar·rest [ə'rest] **1.** *jur.* aresztowanie *n*, zatrzymanie *n*; **2.** *jur.* ⟨za⟩aresztować, zatrzymywać ⟨-ymać⟩

ar·riv·al [ə'raɪvl] przybycie *n*, przyjazd *m*, przylot *m*; *fig.* przybycie *n*, nadejście *n*; ~**s** *pl.* przyjazdy (*przyloty itp. - informacja*); ar·rive [ə'raɪv] przybywać ⟨-być⟩, przyjeżdżać ⟨-jechać⟩, przylatywać ⟨-lecieć⟩; *fig.* nadchodzić ⟨-dejść⟩; ~ **at** przybywać ⟨-być⟩ do (*G*), *fig.* dochodzić ⟨dojść⟩ do (*G*)

ar·ro|·gance ['ærəgəns] arogancja *f*; '~·gant arogancki

ar·row ['ærəu] strzała *f*, strzałka *f*; '~·head grot *m* (*strzały*)

ar·se·nic ['ɑːsnɪk] *chem.* arsen *m*; arszenik *m*

ar·son ['ɑːsn] *jur.* podpalenie *n*

art [ɑːt] sztuka *f*

ar·ter·i·al [ɑː'tɪərɪəl] *anat.* tętniczy; ~ **road** droga *f* przelotowa; ar·te·ry ['ɑːtərɪ] *anat.* tętnica *f*, arteria *f*; arteria *f* komunikacyjna

ar·te·ri·o·scle·ro·sis [ɑːtɪərɪəu-sklə'rəusɪs] *med.* stwardnienie *n* tętnic

'art·ful chytry, przemyślny

'art gal·le·ry galeria *f* sztuki

ar·thri·tis [ɑː'θraɪtɪs] *med.* artretyzm *m*

ar·ti·choke ['ɑːtɪtʃəuk] *bot.* karczoch *m*

ar·ti·cle ['ɑːtɪkl] artykuł *m*; *gr.* rodzajnik *m*, przedimek *m*

ar·tic·u|·late **1.** [ɑː'tɪkjuleɪt] wyraźnie mówiący; wyraźny; **2.** [ɑː'tɪkjulət] wymawiać ⟨-mówić⟩, ⟨wy⟩artykułować; ~·lat·ed [ɑː'tɪkjuleɪtɪd] przegubowy; ~**lated lorry** *Brt. mot.* ciągnik *m* lub ciężarówka *f* z naczepą; ~·la·tion [ɑːtɪkju'leɪʃn] wyraźna wymowa *f*; przegub *m*

ar·ti·fi·cial [ɑːtɪ'fɪʃl] sztuczny; ~ **person** *jur.* osoba *f* prawna

ar·til·le·ry [ɑː'tɪlərɪ] *mil.* artyleria *f*

ar·ti·san [ɑːtɪ'zæn] rzemieślnik *m*

art·ist ['ɑːtɪst] artysta *m* (-tka *f*); ar·tis·tic [ɑː'tɪstɪk] (~**ally**) artystyczny

'art·less naturalny, bezpretensjonalny

arts [ɑːts] *pl.* nauki *pl.* humanistyczne; **Faculty of** ≳, *Am.* ≳ **Department** wydział *m* nauk humanistycznych

as [æz] **1.** *adv.* (tak) jak, równie, tak samo jak; **2.** *cj.* gdy, kiedy; ponieważ, jako że; jako; **~ ... ~ ...** tak ... jak ...; **~ for, ~ to** co do, co się tyczy; **~ from** począwszy od; **~ it were** jak gdyby; **~ Hamlet** jako Hamlet; **~ usual** jak zwykle

as·bes·tos [æs'bestəs] azbest *m*

as·cend [ə'send] iść ⟨pójść⟩ do góry; wspinać ⟨wspiąć⟩ się (na *L*); (*na tron*) wstępować (*L*)

as·cen·dan·cy, ~·den·cy [ə'sendənsı] przewaga *f*, dominacja *f*; **~·sion** [ə'senʃn] wznoszenie *n* się (*balonu itp.*); wschodzenie *n* (*zwł. astr.*); **2·sion (Day)** *rel.* Wniebowstąpienie *n*; **~t** [ə'sent] wznoszenie *n* się; wspinanie *n* się; wzlot *m*

as·cet·ic [ə'setık] (**~ally**) ascetyczny

ASCII ['æskı] *skrót: komp.* **American Standard Code for Information Interchange** (kod *m*) ASCII (*standardowy kod do reprezentacji znaków alfanumerycznych*)

a·sep·tic [æ'septık] **1.** aseptyczny; **2.** środek *m* aseptyczny

ash¹ [æʃ] *bot.* jesion *m*; drewno *n* jesionowe

ash² [æʃ] *też* **~es** *pl.* popiół *m*; prochy *pl.*

a·shamed [ə'ʃeımd] zawstydzony; **be ~ of s.th.** wstydzić się (*G*)

'ash·can *Am.* → **dustbin**

ash·en ['æʃn] popielaty, zszarzały

a·shore [ə'ʃɔː] na brzeg *lub* brzegu

'ash|·tray popielniczka *f*; **2 'Wednes·day** *rel.* Popielec *m*, środa *f* popielcowa

A·sia ['eıʃə] Azja *f*; **A·sian** ['eıʃn, 'eıʒn]; **A·si·at·ic** [eıʃı'ætık] **1.** azjatycki; **2.** Azjata *m*, Azjatka *f*

a·side [ə'saıd] **1.** *adv.* na bok; na stronę; **~ from** *Am.* oprócz, z wyjątkiem; **2.** uwaga *f* na stronie *lub* marginesie

ask [ɑːsk] *v/t.* pytać (**s.th.** o *A*, **s.o. about** kogoś o *A*); prosić (**of, from s.o.** kogoś, **s.o. (for)** kogoś o coś, **that** o *A*); **~ s.o. a question** zadawać komuś pytanie; *v/i.* **~ for** prosić o (*A*); **he ~ed for it** lub **for trouble** sam się o to prosił; **to be had for the ~ing** do otrzymania za darmo

a·skance [ə'skæns]: **look~ at s.o.** krzywo na kogoś ⟨po⟩patrzeć

a·skew [ə'skjuː] krzywy, przekrzywiony

a·sleep [ə'sliːp] śpiący; **be (fast,** *sound*) **~** spać (twardo); **fall ~** zasnąć

as·par·a·gus [ə'spærəgəs] *bot.* szparag *m*; asparagus *m*

as·pect ['æspekt] aspekt *m*; strona *f*; wygląd *m*; widok *m*

as·phalt ['æsfælt] **1.** asfalt *m*; **2.** ⟨wy⟩asfaltować

as·pic ['æspık] galareta *f* (*np. z nóżek*)

as·pi·rant ['æspaıərənt] kandydat(ka *f*) *m*, reflektant *m*; **~·ra·tion** [æspə'reıʃn] ambicja *f*, aspiracje *pl.*

as·pire [ə'spaıə] mieć ambicję, aspirować (**to, for** do *G*)

ass [æs] *zo.* osioł *m*

as·sail [ə'seıl] napadać ⟨-paść⟩; **be ~ed with doubts** być owładniętym wątpliwościami; **as·sai·lant** [ə'seılənt] napastnik *m* (-iczka *f*)

as·sas·sin [ə'sæsın] morderca *m*, (-czyni *f*) (*zwł. z przyczyn politycznych*), zamachowiec *m*; **~·ate** *zwł. pol.* [ə'sæsıneıt] ⟨za⟩mordować, dokonywać ⟨-nać⟩ zamachu; **~·a·tion** [əsæsı'neıʃn] (*zwł. polityczne*) morderstwo *n*, zamach *m*

as·sault [ə'sɔːlt] **1.** napad *m*; napaść *f*; **2.** napadać ⟨-paść⟩

as·sem|·blage [ə'semblıdʒ] zgromadzenie *n*; zbiór *m*; *tech.* montaż; **~·ble** [ə'sembl] zbierać (się); ⟨z⟩montować; **~·bler** [ə'semblə] *komp.* (*język programowania; program tłumaczący na kod maszynowy*) asembler *m*; **~·bly** [ə'semblı] zgromadzenie *n*, zebranie *n*; *tech.* montaż *m*; **~·bly line** *tech.* linia *f* montażowa

as·sent [ə'sent] **1.** zgoda *f*; **2.** zgadzać ⟨-odzić⟩ się (**to** na *A*)

as·sert [ə'sɜːt] ⟨s⟩twierdzić; zapewniać ⟨-nić⟩; *autorytet* utwierdzać ⟨-dzić⟩; **~ o.s.** przebijać ⟨-bić⟩ się; **as·ser·tion** [ə'sɜːʃn] stwierdzenie *n*; zapewnienie *n*

as·sess [ə'ses] *koszty* ⟨o⟩szacować (*też fig.*); *podatku* ustalić ⟨-lać⟩ wysokość (**at** na *A*); **~·ment** oszacowanie *n* (*też fig.*); ustalenie *n* wysokości (*podatku*)

as·set ['æset] *econ.* rzecz *f* wartościowa; *fig.* zaleta *f*, plus *m*; **~s** *pl. jur.* majątek *m*; stan *m* posiadania; *econ.* aktywa *pl.*, środki *pl.* finansowe

as·sid·u·ous [ə'sıdjuəs] skrzętny, pracowity

as·sign [ə'saın] wyznaczać ⟨-czyć⟩; przydzielać ⟨-lić⟩; przeznaczać ⟨-czyć⟩;

~·ment wyznaczenie *n*; przydział *m*; zadanie *n* (*do wykonania*); *jur.* cesja *f*, przeniesienie *n* (*własności*)

as·sim·i·late [ə'sɪmɪleɪt] przyswajać <-woić>; <z>asymilować (się) (*to, with* z *I*); ~·la·tion [əsɪmɪ'leɪʃn] asymilacja *f*; przyswojenie *n*

as·sist [ə'sɪst] pomagać <-móc>; wspierać <wesprzeć>; ~·ance pomoc *f*; wsparcie *n*; as·sis·tant 1. zastępca *m*, (-czyni *f*); asystent(ka *f*) *m*; pomocnik *m*, (-ica *f*); *Brt.* (*shop*) ~ ekspedient-(ka *f*) *m*; 2. pomocny; zastępujący

as·so·ci·ate 1. [ə'səʊʃɪeɪt] zrzeszać <-szyć> (się), stowarzyszać <-szyć>(się); <z>łączyć (się); ~ate with obcować z (*I*), przestawać z (*I*); 2. [ə'səʊʃɪət] partner(ka *f*) *m*; ~·a·tion [əsəʊsɪ'eɪʃn] stowarzyszenie *n*, towarzystwo *n*; asocjacja *f*

as·sort [ə'sɔːt] <po>segregować, <po>sortować; ~·ment *econ.* (*of*) asortyment *m* (*G*), wybór *m* (*G*)

as·sume [ə'sjuːm] przyjmować <-jąć>, zakładać <założyć>; *władzę* przejmować <-jąć>; as·sump·tion [ə'sʌmpʃn] założenie *n*, przypuszczenie *n*; przejęcie *n* (*władzy*); *the* 2 *rel.* Wniebowzięcie *n* (*Matki Boskiej*)

as·sur·|ance [ə'ʃɔːrəns] pewność *f*; zapewnienie *n*; *zwł. Brt.* ubezpieczenie *n* (*na życie*); ~e [ə'ʃɔː] upewniać <-nić>, zapewniać <-nić>; *zwł. Brt.* czyjeś życie ubezpieczać <-czyć>; ~ed 1. pewny; 2. *zwł. Brt.* ubezpieczony *m* (-na *f*); ~·ed·ly [ə'ʃɔːrɪdlɪ] z całkowitą pewnością

as·te·risk [ˈæstərɪsk] gwiazdka *f*

asth·ma [ˈæsmə] *med.* astma *f*, dychawica *f*

as·ton·ish [ə'stɒnɪʃ] zadziwiać <-wić>, zdumiewać <-mieć>; *be ~ed* zdumiewać <-mieć> się; ~·ing zadziwiający, zdumiewający; ~·ment zdumienie *n*

as·tound [ə'staʊnd]zdumiewać <-mieć>

a·stray [ə'streɪ]: *go ~* schodzić <zejść> z drogi; *fig.* schodzić <zejść> na manowce; *lead ~* <po>prowadzić na manowce

a·stride [ə'straɪd] okrakiem (*of* na *L*)

as·trin·gent [ə'strɪndʒənt] *med.* 1. ściągający; 2. środek *m* ściągający

as·trol·o·gy [ə'strɒlədʒɪ] astrologia *f*

as·tro·naut [ˈæstrənɔːt] astronauta *m*

(-tka *f*), kosmonauta *m* (-tka *f*)

as·tron·o·my [ə'strɒnəmɪ] astronomia *f*

as·tute [ə'stjuːt] bystry, sprytny

a·sun·der [ə'sʌndə] na kawałki

a·sy·lum [ə'saɪləm] azyl *m*; *right of ~* prawo *n* azylu; ~ *seek·er* azylant-(ka *f*) *m*

at [æt] *prp. miejsce:* przy (*L*), na (*L*), w (*L*); *kierunek:* na (*L*), w (*A*), do (*G*); *zajęcie:* przy (*L*); *czas:* o; *okres:* w; *cena:* po; ~ *the baker's* u piekarza, w piekarni; ~ *the door* przy drzwiach; ~ *school* w szkole, na zajęciach; ~ *10 pounds* po 10 funtów; ~ *the age of* w wieku (*G*); ~ *8 o'clock* o ósmej

ate [et] *pret. od eat*

Ath·ens *pl.* Ateny *pl.*

a·the·is·m [ˈeɪθɪɪzəm] ateizm *m*

ath·lete [ˈæθliːt] (*zwł.* lekko)atleta *m*; ~·let·ic [æθˈletɪk] (*-ally*) atletyczny; ~·let·ics *sg. lub pl.* (*zwł.* lekka) atletyka *f*

At·lan·tic [ətˈlæntɪk] 1. *też ~ Ocean* Ocean *m* Atlantycki, Atlantyk *m*; 2. atlantycki

ATM [eɪ tiː 'em] *Am. skrót: automatic teller machine → cash dispenser*

at·mo·|sphere [ˈætməsfɪə] atmosfera *f* (*też fig.*); ~·spher·ic [ætməsˈferɪk] (*-ally*) atmosferyczny

a·toll [ˈætɒl] atol *m*

at·om [ˈætəm] atom *m* (*też fig.*); ~ *bomb* bomba *f* atomowa

a·tom·ic [ə'tɒmɪk] (*-ally*) atomowy, jądrowy, nuklearny; ~ *'age* era *f* nuklearna, okres *m* panowania atomu; ~ *'bomb* bomba *f* atomowa; ~ *'en·er·gy* energia *f* nuklearna *lub* jądrowa; ~ *'pile* reaktor *m* atomowy, stos *m* atomowy; ~ *'pow·er* energia *f* atomowa; ~·*'pow·ered* zasilany energią nuklearną *lub* jądrową; ~ *'waste* odpady *pl.* radioaktywne

at·om·|ize [ˈætəmaɪz] rozbijać <-bić> w drobne cząstki; *płyn, proszek* rozpylać <-lić>; ~·*iz·er* rozpylacz *m*, atomizer *m*

a·tone [ə'təʊn]: ~ *for* odpokutowywać <-wać> za *A*; ~·ment odpokutowanie *n*, zadośćuczynienie *n*

a·tro·|cious [ə'trəʊʃəs] okropny, odrażający; ~·*ci·ty* [ə'trɒsətɪ] okrucieństwo *n*, czyn *m* nieludzki

at·tach [ə'tætʃ] *v/t.* **(to)** przytwierdzać ⟨-dzić⟩ (do *G*), przyklejać ⟨-leić⟩ (do *G*), przymocowywać ⟨-wać⟩ (do *G*); *znaczenie* przywiązywać ⟨-zać⟩ (do *G*); **be ~ed to** *fig.* być przywiązanym do (*G*); **~ment** przytwierdzenie *n* (do *G*), przywiązanie *n* (do *G*)

at·tack [ə'tæk] **1.** ⟨za⟩atakować, napadać ⟨-paść⟩; **2.** *też med.* atak *m*, napad *m*

at·tempt [ə'tempt] **1.** usiłować, ⟨s⟩próbować; **2.** próba *f*; **an ~ on s.o.'s life** zamach *m* na kogoś

at·tend [ə'tend] *v/t. chorego* doglądać ⟨-dnąć⟩, pielęgnować; *lekarz:* zajmować ⟨zająć⟩ się; *(do szkoły itp.)* uczęszczać (*G*), chodzić ⟨pójść⟩ (*G*); *(na zajęcia)* uczęszczać (*A*); *fig.* towarzyszyć; *v/i.* być obecnym; **~ to** (*w sklepie*) obsługiwać ⟨obsłużyć⟩ (*A*), **are you being ~ed to?** czy jest pan(i) obsługiwany ⟨-na⟩?; **~ to** załatwiać ⟨-wić⟩ (*A*); **~ance** opieka *f*, pielęgnacja *f*; obecność *f*; obecni *pl.*, publiczność *f*; liczba *f* obecnych, frekwencja *f*; **~ant** pomocnik *m* (-ica *f*); osoba *f* dozorująca; pracownik *m* stacji benzynowej

at·ten·tion [ə'tenʃn] uwaga (*też fig.*); troska *f*; **~tion!** *mil.* baczność!; **~tive** [ə'tentɪv] uważny, gorliwy, troskliwy

at·tic ['ætɪk] strych *m*, poddasze *n*

at·ti·tude ['ætɪtjuːd] postawa *f*

at·tor·ney [ə'tɜːnɪ] *jur.* pełnomocnik *m*; *Am. jur.* adwokat *m*, obrońca *m*; **power of ~** pełnomocnictwo *n*; ♀ **'Gen·e·ral** *Brt. jur.* Prokurator *m* Generalny; *Am. jur.* Minister *m* Sprawiedliwości

at·tract [ə'trækt] przyciągać ⟨przyciągnąć⟩; *uwagę* skupiać ⟨-pić⟩; *fig.* pociągać, ⟨z⟩nęcić; **at·trac·tion** [ə'trækʃn] urok *m*, atrakcyjność *f*; atrakcja *f*; przyciąganie *n*; **at·trac·tive** [ə'træktɪv] atrakcyjny

at·trib·ute[1] [ə'trɪbjuːt] przypisywać ⟨-sać⟩

at·tri·bute[2] ['ætrɪbjuːt] cecha *f*; atrybut *m*

at·tune [ə'tjuːn]: **~ to** *fig.* dostrajać ⟨-troić⟩ się do (*G*), dostosowywać ⟨-sować⟩ się do (*G*)

au·ber·gine ['əʊbəʒiːn] *bot.* bakłażan *m*

au·burn ['ɔːbən] *włosy:* kasztanowy

auc·tion ['ɔːkʃn] **1.** aukcja *f*, przetarg *m*; **2.** *zw.* **~tion off** licytować, wystawiać na aukcji *lub* przetargu; **~tio·neer** [ɔːkʃə'nɪə] licytator(ka *f*) *m*

au·da·cious [ɔː'deɪʃəs] śmiały, zuchwały; **~c·i·ty** [ɔː'dæsətɪ] śmiałość *f*, zuchwałość *f*

au·di·ble ['ɔːdəbl] słyszalny

au·di·ence ['ɔːdjəns] publiczność *f*, widownia *f*; widzowie *pl.*, słuchacze *pl.*; audiencja *f*

au·di·o... ['ɔːdɪəʊ] audio...'; **~ cassette** kaseta *f* audio *lub* magnetofonowa; **~vis·u·al** '~visual 'aids *pl.* pomoce *pl.* audiowizualne

au·dit ['ɔːdɪt] *econ.* **1.** rewizja *f* ksiąg; **2.** dokonywać ⟨-nać⟩ rewizji ksiąg

au·di·tion [ɔː'dɪʃn] *mus., theat.* przesłuchanie *n*; △ *nie* **audycja**

au·di·tor ['ɔːdɪtə] *econ.* rewident *m*, audytor *m*

au·di·to·ri·um [ɔːdɪ'tɔːrɪəm] widownia *f*; *Am.* sala *f* zebrań *lub* koncertowa

Aug *skrót pisany:* **August** sierp., sierpień *m*

au·ger ['ɔːgə] *tech.* wiertło *n* kręte; świder *m* ziemny

Au·gust ['ɔːgəst] *(skrót:* **Aug)** sierpień *m*; *attr.* sierpniowy

aunt [ɑːnt] ciotka *f*; **~ie**, **~y** ['ɑːntɪ] ciocia *f*

au pair (girl) [əʊ 'peə gɜːl] *Brt. (młoda cudzoziemka poznająca angielski zamieszkując z rodziną angielską w zamian za swą pomoc)*

aus·pic·es ['ɔːspɪsɪz] *pl.:* **under the ~ of** pod auspicjami (*G*)

aus·tere [ɒ'stɪə] oschły, surowy

Aus·tra·li·a [ɒ'streɪljə] Australia *f*; **Aus·tra·li·an** [ɒ'streɪljən] **1.** australijski; **2.** Australijczyk *m* (-jka *f*)

Aus·tri·a ['ɒstrɪə] Austria *f*; **Aus·tri·an** ['ɒstrɪən] **1.** austriacki; **2.** Austriak *m* (-aczka *f*)

au·then·tic [ɔː'θentɪk] (**~ally**) autentyczny; prawdziwy

au·thor ['ɔːθə] autor(ka *f*) *m*; pisarz *m*, pisarka *f*; **~ess** ['ɔːθərɪs] autorka *f*; pisarka *f*

au·thor·i·ta·tive [ɔː'θɒrɪtətɪv] autorytatywny, władczy, apodyktyczny; miarodajny; **~ty** [ɔː'θɒrətɪ] autorytet *m*; znaczenie *n*; zaświadczenie *n*, pozwo-

lenie *n*; wpływ *m* (**over** na *A*); zw.
authorities *pl.* władze *pl.*, urząd *m*
au·thor·ize ['ɔːθəraɪz] autoryzować,
upoważniać ⟨-nić⟩
'**au·thor·ship** autorstwo *n*
au·to ['ɔːtəʊ] *Am.* (*pl.* **-tos**) auto *n*, samochód *m*
au·to ... ['ɔːtəʊ] auto..., samo...
au·to·bi·og·ra·phy [ɔːtəbaɪˈɒɡrəfɪ]
autobiografia *f*
au·to·graph ['ɔːtəɡrɑːf] autograf *m*
au·to·mat ['ɔːtəmæt] *TM Am.* zautomatyzowana restauracja *f*
au·to·mate ['ɔːtəmeɪt] ⟨z⟩automatyzować
au·to·mat·ic [ɔːtəˈmætɪk] **1.** (**~ally**) automatyczny; **2.** (*broń itp.*) automat *m*;
~ **tel·ler ma·chine** *Am.* (*skrót:* **ATM**)
→ **cash dispenser**
au·to·ma·tion [ɔːtəˈmeɪʃn] automatyzacja *f*
au·tom·a·ton [ɔːˈtɒmətən] *fig.* (*pl.* **-ta**
[-tə], **-tons**) automat *m*, robot *m*
au·to·mo·bile ['ɔːtəməbiːl] *zwł. Am.*
auto *n*, samochód *m*
au·ton·o·my [ɔːˈtɒnəmɪ] autonomia *f*
'**au·to·tel·ler** *Am.* → **cash dispenser**
au·tumn ['ɔːtəm] jesień *f*; **au·tum·nal**
[ɔːˈtʌmnəl] jesienny
aux·il·i·a·ry [ɔːɡˈzɪljərɪ] pomocniczy
a·vail [əˈveɪl]: **to no** ~ bezskutecznie,
daremnie; **a·vai·la·ble** dostępny, osiągalny; wolny; *econ.* do nabycia
av·a·lanche ['ævəlɑːnʃ] lawina *f*
av·a·rice ['ævərɪs] skąpstwo *n*; **~·ri·cious** [ævəˈrɪʃəs] skąpy
Ave *skrót pisany:* **Avenue** aleja
a·venge [əˈvendʒ] ⟨ze-, po⟩mścić;
a·veng·er mściciel
av·e·nue ['ævənjuː] aleja *f*; bulwar *m*
av·e·rage ['ævərɪdʒ] **1.** przeciętna *f*,
średnia *f*; **2.** przeciętny, średni
a·verse [əˈvɜːs] niechętny; **a·ver·sion**
[əˈvɜːʃn] niechęć *f*, awersja *f*
a·vert [əˈvɜːt] *nieszczęściu* zapobiegać
⟨-biec⟩, *oczy* odwracać ⟨-wrócić⟩
a·vi·a·ry ['eɪvɪərɪ] ptaszarnia *f*
a·vi·a·tion [eɪvɪˈeɪʃn] *aviat.* lotnictwo
n; **~·tor** ['eɪvɪeɪtə] lotnik *m*
av·id ['ævɪd] entuzjastyczny; żądny

av·o·ca·do [ævəˈkɑːdəʊ] *bot.* awokado *n*
a·void [əˈvɔɪd] unikać ⟨-knąć⟩ (*G*); wymijać; **~·ance** unikanie *n*
a·vow·al [əˈvaʊəl] przyznanie *n* się
AWACS ['eɪwæks] *skrót:* **Airborne
Warning and Control System** (system *m*) AWACS (*lotniczy system kontroli radarowej*)
a·wait [əˈweɪt] oczekiwać na (*A*)
a·wake [əˈweɪk] **1.** nie śpiący; **be** ~ nie
spać; **2.** *też* **a·wak·en** [əˈweɪkən]
(**awoke** *lub* **awoken, awoken** *lub*
awaked) *v/t.* ⟨z⟩budzić; *v/i.* ⟨z⟩budzić
się; **a·wak·en·ing** [əˈweɪkənɪŋ] *też fig.*
obudzenie *n*, przebudzenie *n*
a·ward [əˈwɔːd] **1.** nagroda *f*; odznaczenie *n*, wyróżnienie *n*; **2.** nagradzać
⟨-grodzić⟩, *odznaczenie itp.* przyznawać ⟨-znać⟩
a·ware [əˈweə]: **be** ~ **of s.th.** zdawać sobie sprawę z czegoś, uświadamiać sobie coś; **become** ~ **of s.th.** zdać sobie
sprawę z czegoś, uświadomić sobie coś
a·way [əˈweɪ] **1.** *adv.* z dala, w oddaleniu; nieobecny; **far** ~ daleko; **5 kilo·metres** ~ w odległości 5 km; **2.** *adj.*
(*w sporcie*) na wyjeździe; ~ **match**
mecz *m* na wyjeździe
awe [ɔː] **1.** cześć *f*, głębokie poważanie *n*; **2.** wzbudzać ⟨-dzić⟩ głębokie poważanie *lub* cześć
aw·ful ['ɔːfl] (**~ly**) straszny, okropny
awk·ward ['ɔːkwəd] niezręczny, niezdarny; niewygodny, nieporęczny; niedogodny
awn·ing ['ɔːnɪŋ] (*nad sklepem*) markiza *f*, daszek *m*
a·woke [əˈwəʊk] *pret. od* **awake** 2; *też*
a·wok·en [əˈwəʊkən] *p.p. od* **awake** 2
A.W.O.L. [eɪ dʌbljuː əʊ 'el, 'eɪwɒl]
skrót: **absent without leave** nieobecny nieusprawiedliwiony
a·wry [əˈraɪ] krzywy, skośny; **be** ~ leżeć
krzywo
ax(e) [æks] topór *m*, siekiera *f*
ax·is ['æksɪs] (*pl.* **-es** [-siːz]) oś *f*
ax·le ['æksl] *tech.* oś *f*
ay(e) [aɪ] *parl.* głos *m* za
A–Z [eɪ tə 'zed] *Brt.* plan *m* miasta
az·ure ['æʒə] lazurowy

B

B, b [bi:] b *n*; *mus.* H, h
b *skrót pisany*: **born** ur., urodzony
BA [bi: 'eɪ] **1.** *skrót*: **Bachelor of Arts**
(*niższy stopień naukowy*) licencjat *m*,
bakalaureat *m*; **2. British Airways**
(*brytyjskie linie lotnicze*)
bab·ble ['bæbl] **1.** ⟨za⟩bełkotać; ⟨po⟩-
paplać; *dziecko*: ⟨za⟩gaworzyć; *potok*:
⟨za⟩szemrać; **2.** bełkot *m*; paplanina *f*; gaworzenie *n*; szemranie *n*
babe [beɪb] dziecinka *f*, dziecko *n*; *Am.*
F dziewczyna *f*
ba·boon [bə'bu:n] *zo.* pawian *m*
ba·by ['beɪbɪ] **1.** niemowlę *n*, dziecko *n*;
osesek *m*; *Am.* F dziewczyna *f*; **2.** dziecięcy, dla dzieci; mały; **~ boom** wyż *m*
demograficzny; **~ bug·gy** *Am.*, **~ car-**
riage *Am.* wózek *m* dla dziecka;
~hood ['beɪbɪhʊd] dzieciństwo *n*;
~ish ['beɪbɪʃ] *pej.* dziecinny;
~mind·er ['beɪbɪmaɪndə] *Brt.* opie-
kun(ka *f*) *m* (do) dzieci (*zwykle do po-*
łudnia); **~sit** (-*tt, -sat*) opiekować się
dzieckiem; **~sit·ter** opiekun(ka *f*) *m*
(do) dzieci (*zwykle po południu*)
bach·e·lor ['bætʃələ] kawaler *m*; *univ.*
bakałarz *m*, licencjat *m* (*posiadacz niż-*
szego stopnia naukowego)
back [bæk] **1.** plecy *pl.*, grzbiet *m*; tył *m*;
tylna *lub* odwrotna strona *f*; oparcie *n*;
sport: obrońca *m*; **2.** *adj.* tylny; grzbietowy; *opłata*: zaległy; *podwórko*: za domem; *czasopismo*: nieaktualny; **be ~**
wrócić; **3.** *adv.* do tyłu, w tył; **4.** *v/t.*
⟨wy⟩cofać; wspierać ⟨wesprzeć⟩; *też*
~ up popierać ⟨poprzeć⟩; **~ up** *komp.*
⟨z⟩robić kopię bezpieczeństwa z (*G*);
v/i. często **~ up** cofać ⟨wycofywać⟩
się; *mot.* cofać się; **~ in(to a parking**
space) ⟨za⟩parkować tyłem; **~ up**
komp. ⟨z⟩robić kopię bezpieczeństwa;
~ache ból(e *pl.*) *m* pleców; **~bite**
(-*bit, bitten*) obgadywać ⟨-gadać⟩ (*za*
plecami); **~bone** kręgosłup *m*; *fig.*
kościec *m*; **~break·ing** *praca*: morderczy, wykańczający **~chat** *Brt.* pyskowanie *n*; **~comb** włosy ⟨na⟩tapiro-
wać; **~door** tylne drzwi *pl.*, *fig.* ukryty,
nieoficjalny; **~er** sponsor(ka *f*) *m*, in-

westor(ka *f*) *m*; **~fire** *mot.* zapłon *m*
przedwczesny; **~ground** tło *n*; *fig.* sytuacja *f*; **~hand** *sport*: bekhend *m*;
~ing wsparcie *n*, pomoc *f*; **~ num-**
ber stary numer (*czasopisma*) *m*;
~pack duży plecak *m*; **~pack·er** turysta *m* (-tka *f*) pieszy (-sza) (*z pleca-*
kiem); **~pack·ing** turystyka *f* piesza
(*z plecakiem*); **~ seat** siedzenie *n lub*
miejsce *n* z tyłu; **~side** tyłek *m*;
~space (key) *komp. itp.*: klawisz *m*
Backspace (*cofania lub kasowania*);
~ stairs *pl.* tylne schody *pl.*; **~ street**
boczna uliczka *f*; **~stroke** *sport*: styl
m grzbietowy; **~ talk** *Am.* pyskowanie
n; **~track** *fig.* wycofywać ⟨-fać⟩ się;
~up wsparcie *n*, pomoc *f*; *komp.*
itp.: kopia *f* zapasowa *lub* bezpieczeństwa; *Am. mot.* nagromadzenie *n*, zatkanie n się; **~ward** ['bækwəd] **1.** *adj.*
wsteczny; zmierzający do tyłu; zacofa-
ny; **2.** *adv.* (*też* **~wards**) do tyłu, w tył;
~yard *Brt.* (*z tyłu domu*) podwórko *n*;
Am. (*z tyłu domu*) ogród *m*
ba·con ['beɪkən] boczek *m*, bekon *m*
bac·te·ri·a [bæk'tɪərɪə] *biol. pl.* bakte-
rie *pl.*
bad [bæd] (**worse, worst**) zły, niedobry;
niewłaściwy, niepoprawny; niegrzeczny; **go ~** ⟨ze⟩psuć się; **he is in a ~**
way źle mu idzie, niedobrze z nim;
(*-ly*) **he is ~ly off** źle mu się powodzi;
~ly wounded ciężko ranny; **want ~ly**
F bardzo chcieć
bade [beɪd] *pret. od* **bid** 1
badge [bædʒ] odznaka *f*, plakietka *f*
bad·ger ['bædʒə] **1.** *zo.* borsuk *m*; **2.**
⟨u⟩dręczyć
bad·min·ton ['bædmɪntən] badminton
m, kometka *f*
bad-'tempered o przykrym usposobieniu
baf·fle ['bæfl] zdumiewać ⟨-mieć⟩;
plan itp. ⟨po⟩krzyżować, udaremniać
⟨-nić⟩
bag [bæg] **1.** worek *m*; torba *f*; torebka *f*
(*damska, z cukrem*); **~ and baggage**
ze wszystkimi rzeczami, z całym dobyt-
kiem; **2.** (-*gg-*) ⟨za⟩pakować do worka

B

lub worków; *hunt.* upolować; *też* **~ out** wybrzuszać ⟨-szyć⟩ się

bag·gage ['bægɪdʒ] *zwł. Am.* bagaż *m*; '**~ car** *Am. rail.* wagon *m* bagażowy; '**~ check** *Am.* kwit *m* na bagaż; '**~ claim** *aviat.* odbiór *m* bagażu; '**~ room** *Am.* przechowalnia *f* bagażu

bag·gy ['bægɪ] F (*-ier, -iest*) wypchany; *spodnie*: workowaty

'**bag·pipes** *pl.* dudy *pl.*, F kobza *m*

bail [beɪl] *jur.* **1.** kaucja *f*; **be out on ~** być zwolnionym za kaucją; **go** *lub* **stand ~ for s.o.** (za)płacić kaucję za kogoś; **2. ~ out** zwalniać ⟨zwolnić⟩ za kaucją; *Am. aviat.* → **bale²**

bai·liff ['beɪlɪf] *Brt. zwł. Am.* urzędnik *m* sądowy (*rodzaj komornika*)

bait [beɪt] **1.** przynęta *f* (*też fig.*); **2.** zakładać przynętę na (*A*); *fig.* ⟨z⟩nęcić (*A*)

bake [beɪk] ⟨u⟩piec; wypiekać ⟨-piec⟩; *cegły* wypalać ⟨-lić⟩; suszyć (*w piecu*); **~d 'beans** *pl.* puszkowana fasolka *f* po bretońsku; **~d po·ta·toes** *pl.* pieczone ziemniaki *pl.* (*w piekarniku*); '**bak·er** piekarz *m*; **bak·er·y** ['beɪkərɪ] piekarnia *f*; '**bak·ing-pow·der** proszek *m* do pieczenia

bal·ance ['bæləns] **1.** waga *f*; równowaga *f* (*też econ.*); *econ.* bilans *m*; *econ.* saldo *n*, stan *m* konta; *econ.* reszta *f*, pozostałość *f*; **keep one's ~** utrzymywać ⟨-mać⟩ równowagę; **lose one's ~** ⟨s⟩tracić równowagę (*też fig.*); **~ of payments** *econ.* bilans *m* płatniczy; **~ of power** *pol.* równowaga *f* sił; **~ of trade** *econ.* bilans *m* handlowy; **2.** *v/t.* utrzymywać ⟨-mać⟩ w równowadze, ⟨z⟩balansować; *konta itp.* utrzymywać ⟨-mać⟩ w równowadze, uzgadniać; *v/i.* utrzymywać ⟨-mać⟩ się w równowadze; '**~ sheet** *econ.* zestawienie *n* bilansowe, bilans *m*

bal·co·ny ['bælkənɪ] balkon *m* (*też theat.*)

bald [bɔːld] łysy

bale¹ [beɪl] *econ.* bela *f*

bale² [beɪl] *Brt. aviat.*: **~ out** wyskakiwać ⟨-skoczyć⟩ (*ze spadochronem*)

bale·ful ['beɪlfl] złowrogi, złowieszczy

balk [bɔːk] **1.** belka *f*; **2.** wzdragać się, lękać się

Bal·kans *pl.* Bałkany *pl.*

ball¹ [bɔːl] **1.** kula *f*; piłka *f*; *anat.* kłąb *m*;

kłębek *m*; bryła *f*; **keep the ~ rolling** podtrzymywać ⟨-trzymać⟩ rozmowę; **play ~** F iść na rękę

ball² [bɔːl] bal *m*

bal·lad ['bæləd] ballada *f*

bal·last ['bæləst] **1.** balast *m*; **2.** obciążać ⟨-żyć⟩ balastem

ball 'bear·ing *tech.* łożysko *n* kulkowe

bal·let ['bæleɪ] balet *m*

bal·lis·tics [bə'lɪstɪks] *mil., phys., sg.* balistyka *f*

bal·loon [bə'luːn] **1.** balon *m*; dymek *m* (*w komiksie*); **2.** wydymać ⟨-dąć⟩ się (*jak balon*)

bal·lot ['bælət] **1.** głos *m*, kartka *f* z głosem; głosowanie *n* (*zwł. tajne*); **2.** ⟨za⟩głosować (**for** na *A*), wybierać ⟨-brać⟩ (*A*) (*zwł. w tajnym głosowaniu*); '**~ box** urna *f* wyborcza; '**~ pa·per** kartka *f* z głosem

'**ball·point**, **~ 'pen** długopis *m*

'**ball·room** sala *f* balowa

balls [bɔːlz] V *pl.* jaja *pl.*(*jądra*)

balm [bɑːm] balsam *m* (*też fig.*)

balm·y ['bɑːmɪ] (*-ier, -iest*) łagodny

ba·lo·ney [bə'ləʊnɪ] *Am. sl.* bzdury *pl.*, brednie *pl.*

Bal·tic Sea Bałtyk *m*

bal·us·trade [bælə'streɪd] balustrada *f*

bam·boo [bæm'buː] *bot.* (*pl. -oos*) bambus *m*; pęd *m* bambusa; *attr.* bambusowy

bam·boo·zle [bæm'buːzl] F oszukiwać ⟨-szukać⟩, ⟨o-, wy⟩kantować

ban [bæn] **1.** oficjalny zakaz *m*; *rel.* klątwa *f*, interdykt *m*; **2.** (*-nn-*) zakazywać ⟨-zać⟩

ba·nal [bə'nɑːl] banalny; nieistotny

ba·na·na [bə'nɑːnə] *bot.* banan *m*; *attr.* bananowy

band [bænd] **1.** taśma *f*, wstęga *f*; opaska *f*; *kryminalna* banda *f*; kapela *f* *muzyczna*, grupa *f*, orkiestra *f* (*do tańca*); pasmo *n* (*częstotliwości*); **2.** **~ together** skupiać ⟨-pić⟩ się, zbierać ⟨zebrać⟩ się razem

ban·dage ['bændɪdʒ] **1.** bandaż *m*; opatrunek *m*; opaska *f*; *Am.* przylepiec *m*, plaster *m*; **2.** ⟨za-, o⟩bandażować

'**Band-Aid** *TM Am.* przylepiec *m*, plaster *m*

b & b, B & B [biː ənd 'biː] *skrót:* **bed and breakfast** nocleg ze śniadaniem

ban·dit ['bændɪt] bandyta *m*

'band|**·lead·er** *mus.* kierownik *m* orkiestry (*zwł. jazzowej*), bandleader *m*; **'~·mas·ter** dyrygent *m*

ban·dy ['bændɪ] (*-ier, -iest*) krzywy; **~·'legged** krzywonogi

bang [bæŋ] **1.** *silne* uderzenie *n*, walnięcie *n*; wrzawa *f*; *zw.* **~s** *pl.* grzywka; **2.** uderzać ⟨-rzyć⟩, walić ⟨walnąć⟩; V **⟨po-, wy⟩dupczyć**; **~** (*away*) walić ⟨walnąć⟩

ban·gle ['bæŋgl] bransoletka *f* (*na ramię, nogę*)

ban·ish ['bænɪʃ] wypędzać ⟨-pędzić⟩ z kraju, skazywać ⟨-zać⟩ na banicję; **'~·ment** banicja *f*, wygnanie *n*

ban·is·ter ['bænɪstə] *też* **~s** *pl.* poręcz *f*, bariera *f*

ban·jo ['bændʒəʊ] *mus.* (*pl. -jos, joes*) bandżo *n*

bank[1] [bæŋk] **1.** *econ.* bank *m* (*też krwi itp.*); **2.** *v/t.* pieniądze wpłacać ⟨-cić⟩ do banku; *v/i.* mieć konto bankowe (*with* w L)

bank[2] [bæŋk] brzeg *m*; *ziemna* skarpa *f*, nasyp *m*; nagromadzenie *n* (*chmur, piasku*)

'bank| **ac·count** konto *n* bankowe; **'~·bill** *Am.* → **bank note**; **'~·book** książeczka *f* oszczędnościowa; **'~ code** *też* **~ sorting code** *econ.* numer *m* banku; **'~·er** bankier *m*, bankowiec *m*; **'~·er's card** karta *f* bankowa; **'~·hol·i·day** *Brt.* święto *n* państwowe (*gdy banki są nieczynne*); **'~·ing** bankowość *f*, bankowy; **'~ note** banknot *m*; **'~ rate** bankowa stopa *f*

bank·rupt ['bæŋkrʌpt] *jur.* **1.** dłużnik *m* niewypłacalny, bankrut *m*; **2.** ⟨z⟩bankrutować; *kogoś* doprowadzać ⟨-dzić⟩ do bankructwa; **~·cy** ['bæŋkrʌptsɪ] upadłość *f*, bankructwo *n*

ban·ner ['bænə] transparent *m*

banns [bænz] *pl.* zapowiedzi *pl.*

ban·quet ['bæŋkwɪt] bankiet *m*

ban·ter ['bæntə] przekomarzać się

bap|**·tis·m** ['bæptɪzəm] chrzest *m*; **~·tize** [bæp'taɪz] ⟨o⟩chrzcić

bar [bɑː] **1.** sztaba *f*; zasuwa *f*, rygiel *m*; poprzeczka *f*; zapora *f*, bariera *f*; *fig.* przeszkoda *f*; bar *m*, lokal *m*; kontuar *m*; gruba kreska *f*; *jur.* sąd *m*; *jur.* ława *f* oskarżonych; *jur.* adwokatura *f*; *mus.* kreska *f* taktowa, takt *m*; **a ~ of choc·olate** tabliczka *f* czekolady, baton *m* czeko-

koladowy; **a ~ of soap** kostka *f* mydła; **~s** *pl.* kraty *pl.*; **2.** zamykać ⟨-knąć⟩ na zasuwę, ⟨za⟩ryglować; ⟨za⟩tarasować, zagradzać ⟨-dzić⟩; zabraniać ⟨-bronić⟩

barb [bɑːb] kolec *m*, zadzior *m*

bar·bar·i·an [bɑː'beərɪən] **1.** barbarzyński; **2.** barbarzyńca *m*

bar·be·cue ['bɑːbɪkjuː] **1.** grill *m*; barbecue *n*; przyjęcie *n z* grillem; **2.** ⟨u⟩piec na grillu

barbed wire [bɑːbd 'waɪə] drut *m* kolczasty

bar·ber ['bɑːbə] fryzjer *m* (*męski*)

'bar code kod *m* paskowy

bare [beə] **1.** (**~r, ~st**) goły, nagi; bosy; nieosłonięty; **2.** obnażać ⟨-żyć⟩; odsłaniać ⟨-słonić⟩; **'~·faced** bezwstydny, bezczelny; **'~·foot, '~·footed** bosą stopą, na bosaka; **~'head·ed** z gołą głową; **'~·ly** ledwie, ledwo

bar·gain ['bɑːgɪn] **1.** interes *m*, transakcja *f*; okazja *f* (*kupna*); **a** (**dead**) **~** świetna okazja *f*; **make a ~** dochodzić ⟨dojść⟩ do porozumienia; **it's a ~!** zgoda!; **into the ~** w dodatku; **2.** ⟨wy-, u⟩targować się; **~ sale** wyprzedaż *f* po obniżonych cenach

barge [bɑːdʒ] **1.** barka *f*; **2.** ~ **in** wpychać ⟨wepchnąć⟩ się, wtrącać ⟨wtrącić⟩ się

bark[1] [bɑːk] kora *f*

bark[2] [bɑːk] **1.** ⟨za⟩szczekać; ~ **up the wrong tree** F kierować *coś* pod niewłaściwym adresem; **2.** szczekanie *n*

bar·ley ['bɑːlɪ] *bot.* jęczmień *m*

barn [bɑːn] stodoła *f*, obora *f*

ba·rom·e·ter [bə'rɒmɪtə] barometr *m*

bar·on ['bærən] baron *m*; **~·ess** ['bærə-nɪs] baronowa *f*

bar·racks ['bærəks] *sg., mil.* koszary *pl.*, *pej.* kamienica *f*; △ *nie* **baraki**

bar·rage ['bærɑːʒ] zapora *f*; *mil.* ogień *m* zaporowy; potok *m* (*słów*)

bar·rel ['bærəl] beczka *f*, baryłka *f*; lufa *f*; *tech.* bęben *m*, tuleja *f*; **'~ or·gan** *mus.* katarynka *f*

bar·ren ['bærən] jałowy, niepłodny

bar·ri·cade [bærɪ'keɪd] **1.** barykada *f*; **2.** ⟨za⟩barykadować (się)

bar·ri·er ['bærɪə] bariera *f*, przegroda *f* (*też fig.*); ogrodzenie *n*

bar·ris·ter ['bærɪstə] *Brt. jur.* adwokat *m* (*-ka f*) (*uprawniony do występowania przed sądami wyższej instancji*)

bar·row ['bærəʊ] taczka *f*; wózek *m*

bar·ter ['bɑːtə] **1.** handel *m* wymienny; *econ. attr.* barterowy; **2.** prowadzić handel wymienny, wymieniać ⟨-nić⟩ się (**for** na *A*)

base[1] [beɪs] (**~r, -est**) podły, nikczemny

base[2] [beɪs] **1.** podstawa *f*; baza *f*; fundament *m*; *mil.* stanowisko *n*, pozycja *f*; *mil.* baza; **2.** opierać ⟨-przeć⟩ się (**on** na *L*), bazować

base[3] [beɪs] *chem.* zasada *f*

'**base·ball** (*w sporcie*) baseball *m*; '**~board** *Am.* listwa przypodłogowa; '**~less** bezpodstawny; '**~line** (*w tenisie itp*) linia *f* główna; (*w tenisie itp*) linia *f* główna; '**~ment** suterena *f*, przyziemie *n*

bash·ful ['bæʃfl] wstydliwy, płochliwy

ba·sic[1] ['beɪsɪk] **1.** podstawowy, zasadniczy; **2.** **~s** *pl.* podstawy *pl.*

ba·sic[2] ['beɪsɪk] *chem.* zasadowy, alkaliczny

BA·SIC ['beɪsɪk] *komp.* (język programowania) BASIC *m*

ba·sic·al·ly ['beɪsɪkəlɪ] zasadniczo

ba·sin ['beɪsn] misa *f*, miska *f*; miednica *f*; zbiornik *m*; *sportowy* basen *m*; *geogr.* dorzecze *n*, zlewisko *n*;

ba·sis ['beɪsɪs] (*pl.* **-ses** [-siːz]) podstawa *f*, baza *f*, zasada *f*

bask [bɑːsk] grzać ⟨pogrzać⟩ się; *fig.* pławić się

bas·ket ['bɑːskɪt] kosz(yk) *m*; '**~ball** *sport:* koszykówka *f*

Basle Bazylea *f*

bass[1] [beɪs] *mus.* bas *m*; *attr.* basowy

bass[2] [bæs] *zo.* (*pl.* **bass, basses**) okoń *m*

bas·tard ['bɑːstəd] bękart *m*, bastard *m*; F świnia *f*, gnój *m*

baste[1] [beɪst] *pieczeń* polewać ⟨-lać⟩ tłuszczem

baste[2] [beɪst] ⟨przy⟩fastrygować

bat[1] [bæt] *zo.* nietoperz *m*; **as blind as a ~** ślepy jak kret; **be lub have ~s in the belfry** F mieć nierówno pod sufitem

bat[2] [bæt] (*w baseballu, krykiecie*) kij *m*; *Brt.* (*w ping-pongu*) rakietka *f*

batch [bætʃ] partia *f*; grupa *f*; wsad *m*; **~ 'file** *komp.* plik *m* typu batch, plik *m* wsadowy

bate [beɪt]: **with ~d breath** z zapartym tchem

bath [bɑːθ] **1.** (*pl.* **baths** [bɑːðz]) wanna *f*; kąpiel *f* (*w wannie*); **have a ~** *Brt.*, **take a ~** *Am.* ⟨wy⟩kąpać się; brać

⟨wziąć⟩ kąpiel; **~s** *pl.* kąpielisko *n*, pływalnia *f*; uzdrowisko *n*; **2.** *Brt. v/t. dziecko itp.* ⟨wy⟩kąpać; *v/i.* ⟨wy⟩kąpać się, brać ⟨wziąć⟩ kąpiel

bathe [beɪð] *v/t. dziecko, zwł. Am.* ⟨wy⟩kąpać; *ranę* obmywać ⟨-myć⟩; *v/i.* ⟨wy⟩kąpać się, ⟨po⟩pływać; *zwł. Am.* ⟨wy⟩kąpać się, brać ⟨wziąć⟩ kąpiel

bath·ing ['beɪðɪŋ] kąpiel *f*; *attr.* kąpielowy, do kąpieli; '**~ cos·tume**, '**~ suit → swimsuit**

'**bath|·robe** płaszcz *m* kąpielowy; *Am.* szlafrok *m*; '**~·room** łazienka *f*; '**~·tub** wanna *f*

bat·on ['bætən] pałeczka *f*; *mus.* batuta *f*; pałka *f* (policyjna); △ *nie* **baton**

bat·tal·i·on [bə'tæljən] *mil.* batalion *m*

bat·ten ['bætn] listwa *f*; łata *f*

bat·ter[1] ['bætə] walić, ⟨po⟩bić; *żonę, dziecko* ⟨z⟩maltretować; ⟨po⟩giąć; **~ down**, **~ in** *drzwi* wyłamywać ⟨-mać⟩

bat·ter[2] ['bætə] *gastr.* ciasto *n* (*na naleśniki*); panier *m*, panierka *f*

bat·ter[3] ['bætə] (*w baseballu, krykiecie*) gracz *m* przy piłce

bat·ter·y ['bætərɪ] *mil.* bateria *f*; *electr.* bateria *f*, akumulator *m*; *jur.* pobicie *n*, naruszenie *n* nietykalności cielesnej; **assault and ~** *jur.* napad z pobiciem; '**~ charg·er** *electr.* ładowarka *f* do baterii *lub* akumulatorów; '**~·op·e·rat·ed** na baterie

bat·tle ['bætl] **1.** bitwa *f* (**of** pod *I*), *fig.* walka *f* (**for** o *A*); **2.** walczyć; '**~·field**, '**~·ground** pole *n* bitwy; **~·ments** ['bætlmənts] *pl.* blanki *pl.*; '**~·ship** *mil.* pancernik *m*

baulk [bɔːk] → **balk**

Ba·va·ri·a [bə'veərɪə] Bawaria *f*; **Ba·var·i·an** [bə'veərɪən] **1.** bawarski; **2.** Bawarczyk *m*, Bawarka *f*

bawd·y ['bɔːdɪ] (**-ier, -iest**) sprośny

bawl [bɔːl] ryczeć ⟨ryknąć⟩, wrzeszczeć ⟨wrzasnąć⟩

bay[1] [beɪ] zatoka *f*; *arch.* wykusz

bay[2] [beɪ] *bot. też* **~ tree** laur *m*, drzewo *n* laurowe, wawrzyn *m*

bay[3] [beɪ] **1.** ryczeć ⟨ryknąć⟩; *psy:* ujadać; **2. hold lub keep at ~** trzymać w szachu, trzymać na dystans

bay[4] [beɪ] **1.** gniady, kasztanowaty; **2.** kasztanek *m*, gniady *m*

bay·o·net ['beɪənɪt] *mil.* bagnet *m*

bay·ou ['baɪuː] *Am.* leniwy dopływ *m*

bay 'win·dow wykusz *m*

ba·zaar [bə'zɑ:] bazar *m*, targ *m*

BBC [bi: bi: 'si:] *skrót:* **British Broad-casting Corporation** BBC *n* (*brytyj-ska radiofonia*)

BC [bi: 'si:] *skrót:* **before Christ** p.n.e., przed naszą erą, przed narodzeniem Chrystusa

be [bi:] (*was lub were, been*) być; istnieć; znajdować się; stawać się; *he wants to ~ ...* chce zostać ...; *how much are the shoes?* ile kosztują te buty?; *that's five pounds* (kosztuje) pięć funtów; *she is reading* właśnie czyta; *there is* jest; *there are* są; *there isn't* nie ma

B/E *skrót pisany:* **bill of exchange** *econ.* weksel *m*

beach [bi:tʃ] plaża *f*; '*~ ball* piłka *f* plażowa; '*~ bug·gy* buggy *m* (*pojazd do jazdy po wydmach dla przyjem-ności*); '*~wear* strój *m* plażowy

bea·con ['bi:kən] światło *n* sygnalne; *naut.* latarnia *n* kierunkowa

bead [bi:d] paciorek *m*, koralik *m*, kul-ka *f* (*naszyjnika*); *~s pl. rel.* różaniec *m*; korale *pl.*; '*~·y* (*-ier, -iest*) oczy jak koraliki *lub* paciorki

beak [bi:k] dziób *m*; dzióbek *m* (*dzban-ka*)

bea·ker ['bi:kə] kubek *m*, kubeczek *m*

beam [bi:m] **1.** belka *f*, dźwigar *m*; pro-mień *m*; wiązka *f* (*światła, promieni*); **2.** promieniować, wysyłać wiązkę (*światła, promieni*); promienieć, roz-promienić się

bean [bi:n] *bot.* fasolka *f*; ziarno (*fasoli*) *n*; *be full of ~s* F być pełnym wigoru

bear¹ [beə] *zo.* niedźwiedź *m*

bear² [beə] (*bore, borne lub w str. bier-nej urodzić się: born*) dźwigać, nieść; wydawać (-dać) na świat, (u)rodzić; *zwłaszcza z przeczeniem:* znosić (znieść), wytrzymywać (-mać); *~ out* potwierdzać (-dzić); *~·a·ble* ['beərəbl] do zniesienia, znośny

beard [bɪəd] broda *f*; *bot.* wąs *m* kłosa; '*~ed* brodaty

bear·er ['beərə] okaziciel(ka *f*) *m* (*do-kumentu*); *econ.* posiadacz(ka *f*) *m*; do-ręczyciel(ka *f*) *m*

bear·ing ['beərɪŋ] podpora *f*; postawa *f*; *fig.* związek *m*, odniesienie *n*; namiar *m*; sytuacja *f*, położenie *n*; *take one's*

~s brać 〈wziąć〉 namiar; *lose one's ~s* stracić kierunek

beast [bi:st] *dzikie zwierzę n*; bestia *f*; *~ of 'prey* drapieżnik *m*; '*~·ly* obrzyd-liwy, wstrętny

beat [bi:t] **1.** (*beat, beaten lub beat*) 〈po〉bić; uderzać 〈-rzyć〉; ubijać〈-bić〉; pokonywać 〈-nać〉; przewyższać 〈-szyć〉; *~ it!* F wynocha!; *that ~s all!* to już szczyty!; *that ~s me* to za trudne dla mnie; *~ about the bush* obwijać w bawełnę; *~ down econ.* cenę zniżać 〈-niżyć〉; *~ up kogoś* pobić doszczętnie; **2.** uderzenie *n*; *mus.* rytm *m*, takt *m*; (*w jazzie*): beat *m*, rytmika *f*; runda *f*; obchód *m*; **3.** (*dead*) ~ F cał-kiem wykończony; *~·en* ['bi:tn] *p.p. od beat* 1; *off the ~en track* niezwykły

beau·ti·cian [bju:'tɪʃn] (*zawód*) kos-metyczka *f*

beau·ti·ful ['bju:təfl] piękny; *the ~ people pl.* wyższe warstwy *pl.*

beaut·y ['bju:tɪ] piękno *n*; *Sleeping ♀ Śpiąca Królewna f*; '*~ par·lo(u)r*, '*~ sal·on m* kosmetyczny

bea·ver ['bi:və] *zo.* bóbr

be·came [bɪ'keɪm] *pret. od become*

be·cause [bɪ'kɒz] ponieważ; *~ of* z po-wodu (*G*)

beck·on ['bekən] przywoływać 〈-łać〉, skinąć na (*A*); △ *nie* bekon

be·come [bɪ'kʌm] (*-came, -come*) *v/i.* stawać się; *v/t. komuś* pasować, być do twarzy; **be·com·ing** pasujący, twarzo-wy; stosowny

bed [bed] **1.** łóżko *n*, tapczan *m*; legowi-sko *n* (*zwierzęcia*); *agr.* grzęda *f*, klomb *m*; dno *n*, (*rzeki*) koryto *n*; ściółka *f* (*zwierzęcia*); *~ and breakfast* pokój *m* ze śniada-niem; **2.** (*-dd-*): *~ down* 〈przy〉szyko-wać sobie spanie; '*~·clothes pl.* bielizna *f* pościelowa; '*~·ding* posłanie *n*, pościel *f*

bed·lam ['bedləm] *fig.* dom *m* wariatów

'bed|·rid·den przykuty do łóżka; '*~·room* sypialnia *f*; '*~·side: at the ~side* przy łóżku (*chorego*); '*~·side 'lamp* lampka *f* na stoliczku nocnym; '*~·sit* F, '*~·sit·ter*, '*~·sit·ting room Brt.* kawalerka *f*; '*~·spread* narzuta *f* na łóżko; '*~·stead* łóżko *n* (*bez mate-racy*); '*~·time* czas zaśnięcia *lub* zasy-piania

bee [bi:] **1.** *zo.* pszczoła *f*; *have a ~ in*

B

one's **bonnet** F mieć bzika; *attr.* pszczeli

beech [biːtʃ] *bot.* buk *m*; *attr.* bukowy; '**~·nut** bukiew *f* (*orzeszek buka*)

beef [biːf] wołowina *f*; '**~·bur·ger** *gastr. zwł. Brt.* hamburger *m* (*z wołowiny*); **~ 'tea** bulion *m*; '**~·y** (**-ier, -iest**) F muskularny

'**bee·hive** ul *m*; '**~·keep·er** pszczelarz *m*, pasiecznik *m*; '**~·line: make a ~line for** F iść ⟨pójść⟩ jak po sznurku *lub* prosto do (*G*)

been [biːn, bɪn] *p.p. od* **be**

beep·er ['biːpə] *Am.* → **bleeper**

beer [bɪə] piwo *n*

beet [biːt] *bot.* burak *m*; *Am.* burak *m* ćwikłowy

bee·tle ['biːtl] *zo.* żuk *m*, chrząszcz *m*

'**beet·root** *bot. Brt.* burak *m* ćwikłowy

be·fore [bɪ'fɔː] **1.** *adv.* (*w czasie*) przedtem, poprzednio, wcześniej; (*w przestrzeni*) przed, z przodu, na przedzie; **2.** *cj.* zanim, nim; **3.** *prp.* przed (*I*); **~·hand** wcześniej, uprzednio

be·friend [bɪ'frend] okazywać ⟨-zać⟩ przyjaźń, ⟨po⟩traktować jak przyjaciela

beg [beg] (**-gg-**) *v/t.* wypraszać ⟨-rosić⟩ (*from s.o.* kogoś); upraszać ⟨uprosić⟩; wyżebrać; *v/i.* żebrać

be·gan [bɪ'gæn] *pret. od* **begin**

be·get [bɪ'get] (**-tt-**; **-got**, **-gotten**) ⟨s⟩płodzić

beg·gar ['begə] **1.** żebrak *m*, (-aczka *f*); F facet *m*, chłop *m*; **2.** *it ~s all description* nie da się opisać

be·gin [bɪ'gɪn] (**-nn-**; **began, begun**) zaczynać ⟨-cząć⟩ (się), rozpoczynać ⟨-cząć⟩ (się); **~·ner** początkujący *m* (-ca *f*); **~·ning** początek *m*, rozpoczęcie *n*

be·got [bɪ'gɒt] *pret. od* **beget**; **~·ten** [bɪ'gɒtn] *p.p. od* **beget**

be·grudge [bɪ'grʌdʒ] ⟨po⟩żałować, ⟨po⟩skąpić

be·guile [bɪ'gaɪl] łudzić, zwodzić ⟨zwieść⟩, ⟨o⟩mamić

be·gun [bɪ'gʌn] *p.p. od* **begin**

be·half [bɪ'hɑːf]: *on* (*Am. in*) ~ *of* w imieniu (*G*), na rzecz (*G*)

be·have [bɪ'heɪv] zachowywać ⟨-wać⟩ się

be·hav·io(u)r [bɪ'heɪvjə] zachowanie *n*, postępowanie *n*; **~·al** [bɪ'heɪvjərəl]

psych. behawioralny

be·head [bɪ'hed] ścinać ⟨ściąć⟩ ⟨głowę⟩

be·hind [bɪ'haɪnd] **1.** *adv.* z tyłu, w tyle; *be ~ with* zalegać z (*I*), opóźniać się (*I*); **2.** *prp.* za (*I*), z tyłu (*G*), poza (*I*); **3.** F tyłek *m*, pupa *f*

beige [beɪʒ] beż *m*; *attr.* beżowy

be·ing ['biːɪŋ] byt *m*, bycie *n*; istnienie *n*, stworzenie *n*; istota *f*, natura *f*

Be·la·rus Białoruś *f*

be·lat·ed [bɪ'leɪtɪd] opóźniony

belch [beltʃ] **1.** F bekać ⟨beknąć⟩; *she ~ed* odbiło jej się, F beknęła; *też* ~ *out* buchać ⟨-chnąć⟩ ⟨dymem itp.⟩, zionąć; **2.** odbicie *n* się, F beknięcie *n*

bel·fry ['belfrɪ] dzwonnica *f*

Bel·gium ['beldʒəm] Belgia *f*; **Bel·gian** ['beldʒən] **1.** belgijski; **2.** Belg(ijka *f*) *m*

Bel·grade Belgrad *m*

be·lief [bɪ'liːf] przekonanie *n*, wiara *f* (*in* w *A*)

be·lie·va·ble [bɪ'liːvəbl] możliwy do uwierzenia, wiarygodny

be·lieve [bɪ'liːv] ⟨u⟩wierzyć (*in* w *A*); sądzić (*that* że), uważać; *I couldn't ~ my eyes* (*ears*) nie mogłem uwierzyć własnym oczom (uszom); **be'liev·er** *rel.* wierzący *m* (-ca *f*), wyznawca *m* (-czyni *f*)

be·lit·tle [bɪ'lɪtl] *fig.* pomniejszać ⟨-szyć⟩

bell [bel] dzwon *m*; dzwonek *m* (*do drzwi*); '**~·boy**, '**~·hop** *Am.* hotelowy boy *m*, goniec *m* hotelowy

-bel·lied [belɪd] (*o dużym itp.* brzuchu)

bel·lig·er·ent [bɪ'lɪdʒərənt] wojowniczy, bojowy, napastliwy

bel·low ['beləʊ] **1.** ⟨za⟩ryczeć; **2.** ryk *m*

bel·lows ['beləʊz] *pl.*, *sg.* miech *m*, *zw. pl.*

bel·ly ['belɪ] **1.** brzuch *m*; **2.** ~ *out* wybrzuszać ⟨-szyć⟩ (się); '**~·ache** ból *m* brzucha

be·long [bɪ'lɒŋ] należeć; ~ *to* należeć do (*G*); być na właściwym miejscu; **~·ings** *pl.* mienie *n*, rzeczy *pl.*

be·loved [bɪ'lʌvd] **1.** ukochany, umiłowany; **2.** ukochany *m* (-na *f*)

be·low [bɪ'ləʊ] **1.** *adv.* poniżej (*G*); **2.** pod (*I*), poniżej (*G*)

belt [belt] **1.** pas *m*; pasek *m*; strefa *f*, pas *m*; *tech.* taśma *f*; **2.** *też* ~ *up mot.* zapinać ⟨zapiąć⟩ pasek; ~ *up mot.* zapinać ⟨zapiąć⟩ pas(y *pl.*) bezpieczeństwa; '**~·ed**

z paskiem, na pasek; '~·way *Am.* obwodnica *f*

be·moan [bɪˈməʊn] opłakiwać

bench [bentʃ] ławka *f*, ława *f*; warsztat *m*, stół *m* roboczy; ława *f* sędziowska, sąd *m*

bend [bend] **1.** zakręt *m*; zgięcie *n*, zagięcie *n*; **drive s.o. round the ~** F doprowadzać ⟨-dzić⟩ *kogoś* do obłędu; **2.** (*bent*) zginać ⟨zgiąć⟩ (się), wyginać ⟨wygiąć⟩ (się); *wysiłki* zwracać ⟨-cić⟩ (*to, on* na *A*)

be·neath [bɪˈniːθ] → *below*

ben·e·dic·tion [benɪˈdɪkʃn] błogosławieństwo *n*

ben·e·fac·tor ['benɪfæktə] dobroczyńca *m*

be·nef·i·cent [bɪˈnefɪsnt] dobroczynny, zbawienny

ben·e·fi·cial [benɪˈfɪʃl] korzystny, pożyteczny

ben·e·fit ['benɪfɪt] **1.** korzyść *f*; zysk *m*; pożytek *m*; impreza *f* dobroczynna; *socjalne* świadczenie *n*, zapomoga *f*; *chorobowy* zasiłek; **2.** przynosić ⟨-nieść⟩ korzyść; **~ by, ~ from** odnosić ⟨odnieść⟩ korzyść z (*G*)

be·nev·o·lence [bɪˈnevələns] życzliwość *f*, dobrodziejstwo *n*; **~·lent** życzliwy, dobroczynny

be·nign [bɪˈnaɪn] *med.* łagodny, niezłośliwy

bent [bent] **1.** *pret. i p.p. od* **bend** 2; **2.** *fig.* skłonność *f*, upodobanie *n*, predyspozycja *f*

ben·zene ['benziːn] *chem.* benzen *m*

be·queath [bɪˈkwiːð] *jur.* pozostawiać ⟨-wić⟩ w spadku

be·quest [bɪˈkwest] *jur.* spadek *m*, spuścizna *f*

be·reave [bɪˈriːv] (*bereaved lub bereft*) pozbawiać ⟨-wić⟩, osierocać ⟨cić⟩

be·reft [bɪˈreft] *pret. i p.p. od* **bereave**

be·ret ['bereɪ] beret *m*

Ber·lin Berlin *m*

Bern Berno *n*

ber·ry ['berɪ] *bot.* jagoda *f*

berth [bɜːθ] **1.** *naut.* miejsce *n* cumowania; *naut.* koja *f*; *rail.* miejsce *n* leżące, kuszetka *f*; **2.** ⟨przy⟩cumować, ⟨przy⟩bijać

be·seech [bɪˈsiːtʃ] (*besought lub beseeched*) błagać

be·set [bɪˈset] (*-tt-; beset*) dotykać

⟨dotknąć⟩, prześladować; **~ with difficulties** prześladowany przez trudności

be·side [bɪˈsaɪd] *prp.* obok; przy; **be ~ o.s.** nie posiadać się (**with** z *G*); **be ~ the point, ~ the question** nie mieć nic do rzeczy; **~s** [bɪˈsaɪdz] **1.** *adv.* oprócz tego, poza tym; **2.** *prp.* poza (*I*), oprócz (*G*)

be·siege [bɪˈsiːdʒ] oblegać ⟨oblec⟩

be·smear [bɪˈsmɪə] obsmarowywać ⟨-ować⟩

be·sought [bɪˈsɔːt] *pret. i p.p. od* **beseech**

be·spat·ter [bɪˈspætə] opryskiwać ⟨-kać⟩

best [best] **1.** *adj.* (*sup. od* **good** 1) najlepszy; **~ before ...** należy spożyć (zużyć) do ...; (*sup. od* **well**[1]) najlepiej; **3.** najlepszy *m*; **all the ~!** wszystkiego najlepszego!; **to the ~ of...** jak najlepiej jak...; **make the ~ of** wykorzystywać ⟨-stać⟩ (*A*) jak najlepiej; **at ~** w najlepszym wypadku; **be at one's ~** być w najlepszej formie; **~ be'fore date, ~ 'by date** okres *m* przydatności do spożycia

bes·ti·al ['bestjəl] zwierzęcy, bestialski

best 'man (*pl. -men*) drużba *m*

be·stow [bɪˈstəʊ] obdarzać ⟨-rzyć⟩, nadawać ⟨nadać⟩

bet [bet] **1.** zakład *m*; **make a ~** założyć się; **2.** (*-tt-; bet lub betted*) zakładać ⟨założyć⟩ się; **you ~!** F no pewnie!, jesże jak!

Beth·le·hem Betlejem *m*

be·tray [bɪˈtreɪ] zdradzać ⟨-dzić⟩ (*też fig.*); zawodzić ⟨-wieść⟩; **~·al** [bɪˈtreɪəl] zdrada *f*; **~·er** zdrajca *m* (-czyni *f*)

bet·ter ['betə] **1.** *adj.* (*comp. od* **good** 1) lepszy; **he is ~** lepiej mu; **2. get the ~ of** brać ⟨wziąć⟩ górę nad (*I*); **3.** *adv.* (*comp. od* **well**[1]) lepiej; bardziej; **so much the ~** tym lepiej; **you had ~** (*Am.* F **you ~**) **go** lepiej już idź; **4.** *v/t.* polepszać ⟨-szyć⟩; *v/i.* polepszać ⟨-szyć⟩ się

be·tween [bɪˈtwiːn] **1.** *adv.* pośrodku; **few and far ~** F co jakiś czas, sporadyczny; **2.** *prp.* pomiędzy (*I*), między (*I*); spośród (*G*); **~ you and me** tylko między nami

bev·el ['bevl] ukos *m*, skośna krawędź *f*

bev·er·age ['bevərɪdʒ] napój *m*

bev·y ['bevɪ] *zo.* stadko *n* (*przepiórek*);

gromadka f (dziewcząt)

be·ware [bɪ'weə] **(of)** wystrzegać się (G); strzec się (G); **~ of the dog!** uwaga zły pies!

be·wil·der [bɪ'wɪldə] oszałamiać ⟨-łomić⟩; zbijać ⟨zbić⟩ z tropu; **~·ment** konsternacja f

be·witch [bɪ'wɪtʃ] oczarowywać ⟨-ować⟩, urzekać ⟨urzec⟩

be·yond [bɪ'jɒnd] **1.** adv. dalej; więcej; powyżej; **2.** prp. poza (I), za (I); **~ remedy** nie do naprawienia

bi... [baɪ] bi..., dwu...

bi·as ['baɪəs] uprzedzenie n; skłonność f, przychylność f; **'~(s)ed** uprzedzony; jur. stronniczy

bi·ath·lete [baɪ'æθliːt] (w sporcie) biatlonista m (-tka f); **~·lon** [baɪ'æθlən] (w sporcie) biatlon m

bib [bɪb] śliniaczek m; góra f (fartucha)

Bi·ble ['baɪbl] Biblia f (też fig.)

bib·li·cal ['bɪblɪkl] biblijny

bib·li·og·ra·phy [bɪblɪ'ɒgrəfɪ] bibliografia f

bi·car·bon·ate [baɪ'kɑːbənɪt] też **~ of soda** soda f oczyszczona, tech. wodorowęglan m sodu

bi·cen·te·na·ry [baɪsen'tiːnərɪ], **~·ten·ni·al** [baɪsen'tenɪəl] Am. dwustulecie n

bi·ceps ['baɪseps] anat. biceps m, mięsień m dwugłowy

bick·er ['bɪkə] ⟨po⟩kłócić się, ⟨po⟩żreć się

bi·cy·cle ['baɪsɪkl] rower m

bid [bɪd] **1.** (-dd-; **bid** lub **bade, bid** lub **bidden**) (na licytacji) zgłaszać ⟨zgłosić⟩ ofertę lub cenę; (w kartach) ⟨za⟩licytować; **2.** econ. oferta f, cena f; (w kartach) (odzywka) f; **~·den** ['bɪdn] p.p. od **bid** 1

bi·en·ni·al [baɪ'enɪəl] roślina: dwuletni; (odbywający się) co dwa lata; **~·ly** co dwa lata

bier [bɪə] mary pl.

big [bɪg] (**-gg-**) duży, wielki; gruby; **talk ~** przechwalać się, chełpić się

big·a·my ['bɪgəmɪ] bigamia f

big'busi·ness wielki interes m; **'~·head** F mądrala m/f; **~ 'shot** osoba: gruba ryba f

bike [baɪk] F rower m; motorower m; motor m; **'bik·er** rowerzysta m; motorowerzysta m; motocyklista m

bi·lat·er·al [baɪ'lætərəl] dwustronny

bile [baɪl] anat. żółć (też fig.)

bi·lin·gual [baɪ'lɪŋgwəl] dwujęzyczny; **~ 'sec·re·ta·ry** sekretarka f władająca obcym językiem

bill[1] [bɪl] dziób m

bill[2] [bɪl] faktura f; rachunek m; econ. weksel; pol. projekt m ustawy; jur. powództwo; afisz m, plakat m; Am. banknot m; **~ of de'liv·er·y** econ. pokwitowanie n dostawy; **~ of ex'change** econ. weksel m; **~ of 'sale** jur. akt m kupna-sprzedaży; **'~·board** Am. tablica f reklamowa, billboard m; **'~·fold** Am. portfel m

bil·li·ards ['bɪljədz] sg. bilard m

bil·li·on ['bɪljən] miliard m

bil·low ['bɪləʊ] **1.** kłąb m; **2.** też **~ out** wybrzuszać ⟨-szyć⟩ się; kłębić się

bil·ly goat ['bɪlɪgəʊt] zo. kozioł m

bin [bɪn] (duży) pojemnik m na śmieci

bi·na·ry ['baɪnərɪ] math., phys. itp. binarny, dwójkowy; **~'code** komp. kod m binarny; **~ 'num·ber** liczba f w zapisie dwójkowym

bind [baɪnd] (**bound**) v/t. ⟨za-, przy-, ob-, z⟩wiązywać ⟨-zać⟩; zobowiązywać ⟨-zać⟩; książkę oprawiać ⟨-wić⟩; v/i. wiązać; **~·er** introligator m; segregator m, skoroszyt m; **'~·ing 1.** wiążący; zobowiązujący; **2.** oprawa f

bin·go ['bɪŋgəʊ] (gra) bingo n

bi·noc·u·lars[bɪ'nɒkjʊləz]pl.lornetka f

bi·o·chem·is·try [baɪəʊ'kemɪstrɪ] biochemia f

bi·o·de·gra·da·ble [baɪəʊdɪ'greɪdəbl] podlegający biodegradacji

bi·og·ra·pher [baɪ'ɒgrəfə] biograf m; **~·phy** biografia f

bi·o·log·i·cal [baɪə'lɒdʒɪkl] biologiczny; **bi·ol·o·gist** [baɪ'ɒlədʒɪst] biolog m; **bi·ol·o·gy** [baɪ'ɒlədʒɪ] biologia f

bi·o·rhyth·m ['baɪəʊrɪðəm] biorytm m

bi·o·tope ['baɪəʊtəʊp] biotop m

bi·ped ['baɪped] zo. dwunóg m, zwierzę n dwunożne

birch [bɜːtʃ] bot. brzoza f; attr. brzozowy

bird [bɜːd] ptak m; attr. ptasi; **'~·cage** klatka f na ptaki; **~ of 'pas·sage** ptak m przelotny lub wędrowny; **~ of 'prey** ptak m drapieżny; **~ 'sanc·tu·a·ry** rezerwat m ptaków; **'~·seed** pokarm m dla ptaków

bird's-eye 'view widok *m* z lotu ptaka

bi·ro ['baɪrəʊ] *TM Brt.* (*pl.* **-ros**) długopis *m*

birth [bɜːθ] urodziny *pl.*; narodziny *pl.*; '**~·cer·ti·fi·i·cate** metryka *f* (*urodzenia*); '**~con·trol** antykoncepcja *f*; ~ **con·trol** '**pill** pigułka *f* antykoncepcyjna; '**~·day** urodziny *pl.*; *attr.* urodzinowy; '**~·mark** znamię *n* wrodzone; '**~·place** miejsce *n* urodzenia; '**~·rate** przyrost *m* naturalny

bis·cuit ['bɪskɪt] ciastko *n*, herbatnik *m*

bi·sex·u·al [baɪ'sekʃʊəl] obupłciowy, dwupłciowy; biseksualny

bish·op ['bɪʃəp] biskup *m*; (*w szachach*) goniec *m*, laufer *m*; **~·ric** ['bɪʃəprɪk] biskupstwo *n*

bi·son ['baɪsn] *zo.* bizon *m*; żubr *m*

bit [bɪt] **1.** kawałek *m*, odrobina *f*; wiertło *n*, świder *m*; wędzidło *n*; łopatka *f*, bródka *f* (*klucza*); *komp.* bit *m*; **a ~** trochę; **a little ~** odrobina; **2.** *pret. od* **bite** 2

bitch [bɪtʃ] *zo.* suka *f*, *pej.* dziwka *f*

'**bit den·si·ty** *komp.* gęstość *f* zapisu cyfrowego

bite [baɪt] **1.** ugryzienie *n*, ukąszenie *n*; kęs *m*, kąsek *m*; *tech.* chwyt *m*, zaciśnięcie *n* (*śruby itp.*); **have a ~** przekąsić coś; **2.** (**bit**, **bitten**) ⟨u⟩gryźć; kąsać ⟨ukąsić⟩ (*też o owadach, zimnie*); paznokcie gryźć ⟨obgryzać⟩; *pieprz:* ⟨za⟩piec; *dym:* ⟨za⟩szczypać; *tech.* chwytać ⟨chwycić⟩; *śrubę* zaciskać ⟨się⟩

bit·ten ['bɪtn] *p.p. od* **bite** 2

bit·ter ['bɪtə] gorzki; *fig.* zgorzkniały

bit·ters ['bɪtəz] *pl.* (*lecznicza*) nalewka *f* gorzka

biz [bɪz] F → **business**

black [blæk] **1.** czarny; ciemny; mroczny; **have s.th. in ~ and white** mieć coś czarno na białym; **be ~ and blue** być posiniaczonym; **beat s.o. ~ and blue** posiniaczyć kogoś; **2.** ⟨po⟩czernić; **~ out** chwilowo ⟨u⟩tracić przytomność; *okna* zaciemniać ⟨-nić⟩; **3.** czerń *f*, czarny kolor *m*; *człowiek:* czarnoskóry *m*, czarny *m*; '**~·ber·ry** *bot.* jeżyna *f*; '**~·bird** *zo.* kos *m*; '**~·board** tablica *f* (*szkolna*); '**~·box** *aviat.* czarna skrzynka *f*; **~·cur·rant** *bot.* czarna porzeczka *f*; '**~·en** *v/t.* ⟨za⟩czernić; *fig.* oczerniać ⟨-nić⟩; *v/i.* ⟨s⟩czernieć; ~ '**eye** podbite oko *n*; '**~·head** *med.* zaskórnik *m*, wągier *m*; ~ '**ice** gołoledź *f*; '**~·ing** czar-

na pasta *f* do butów, czernidło *n*; '**~·leg** *Brt.* łamistrajk *m*; '**~·mail 1.** szantaż *m*; **2.** ⟨za⟩szantażować; '**~·mail·er** szantażysta *m* (-tka *f*); ~ '**mar·ket** czarny rynek *m*; '**~·ness** czerń *f*; '**~·out** zaciemnienie *n*; brak *m* energii (*prądu itp.*); ~ '**pud·ding** *gastr.* kaszanka *f*; ~ ' **Sea** Morze Czarne; ~ '**sheep** (*pl.* -**sheep**) *fig.* czarna owca *f*; '**~·smith** kowal *m*

blad·der ['blædə] *anat.* pęcherz *m* moczowy

blade [bleɪd] *bot.* źdźbło; łopatka *f* (*ramienia*); ostrze *n*, brzeszczot *m*; klinga *f*; łopata *f* (*śmigła*)

blame [bleɪm] **1.** wina *f*; odpowiedzialność *f*; **2.** obwiniać ⟨-nić⟩; **be to ~ for** ponosić ⟨-nieść⟩ winę za (*A*); '**~·less** bez winy, niewinny

blanch [blɑːntʃ] ⟨wy⟩bielić; *gastr.* ⟨za⟩blanszować; ⟨z⟩blednąć

blanc·mange [blə'mɒnʒ] *gastr.* budyń *m*

blank [blæŋk] **1.** pusty, czysty; nie zapełniony, nie wypełniony, nie zapisany; *econ.* in blanko, na okaziciela; **2.** puste miejsce *n*; luka *f*; formularz *m*, blankiet *m*, druk *m*; *los na loterii:* pusty; ~ '**car·tridge** ślepy nabój *m*; ~ '**cheque** (*Am.* '**check**) *econ.* czek *m* na okaziciela

blan·ket ['blæŋkɪt] **1.** koc *m*; **2.** przykrywać ⟨-ryć⟩

blare [bleə] *radio:* ⟨za⟩ryczeć; *trąba:* ⟨za⟩grzmieć

blas·pheme [blæs'fiːm] ⟨z⟩bluźnić; **~·phe·my** ['blæsfəmɪ] bluźnierstwo *n*

blast [blɑːst] **1.** (*wiatru*) podmuch *m*; wybuch *m*; fala *f* wybuchu; dźwięk *m* (*instrumentu dętego*); **2.** wysadzać ⟨-dzić⟩; *fig.* ⟨z⟩niszczyć, ⟨z⟩niweczyć; ~ **off** (*into space*) wystrzelić w przestrzeń kosmiczną; *rakieta:* ⟨wy⟩startować; ~*!* cholera!; ~ **you!** szlag by cię trafił!; **~·ed** cholerny; '**~·fur·nace** *tech.* wielki piec *m*; '**~-off** start *m* (*rakiety*)

bla·tant ['bleɪtənt] rażący; bezczelny

blaze [bleɪz] **1.** płomień *m*, ogień *m*; jaskrawe światło *n*, blask *m*; *fig.* wybuch *m*; **2.** ⟨s⟩płonąć, ⟨s⟩palić (się); błyszczeć ⟨błysnąć⟩; wybuchać ⟨-nąć⟩ płomieniami

blaz·er ['bleɪzə] blezer *m*

bla·zon ['bleɪzn] herb *m*

B

bleach [bliːtʃ] ⟨wy⟩bielić

bleak [bliːk] odludny, ogołocony, srogi; *fig.* ponury, posępny

blear·y ['blɪərɪ] (*-ier, iest*) mglisty, niewyraźny

bleat [bliːt] **1.** ⟨za⟩beczeć; **2.** beczenie *n*, bek *m*

bled [bled] *pret. i p.p. od* **bleed**

bleed [bliːd] (*bled*) *v/i.* krwawić; *v/t.* *krew* puszczać ⟨puścić⟩; *fig.* F wyzyskiwać ⟨-skać⟩, ⟨wy⟩żyłować; '~**ing 1.** *med.* krwawienie *n*, *med.* puszczanie *n* krwi; **2.** *sl.* cholerny, pieprzny

bleep [bliːp] **1.** krótki sygnał *m* (*jak w telefonie*), brzęk *n*; **2.** wzywać ⟨wezwać⟩ sygnałem (*pagera itp.*); '~**er** *Brt.* F brzęczyk *m* (*w urządzeniu przyzywającym*)

blem·ish ['blemɪʃ] **1.** skaza *f* (*na urodzie*); brak *m*, skaza *f*; **2.** ⟨o⟩szpecić

blend [blend] **1.** ⟨z⟩mieszać (się); *wina* kupażować; **2.** mieszanka *f*; '~**er** mikser *m*, malakser *m*

bless [bles] (*blessed lub blest*) ⟨po⟩błogosławić; *be ~ed with* być obdarzonym (*I*); (*God*) ~ *you!* na zdrowie!; ~ *me*, ~ *my heart*, ~*my soul* F Boże mój!; '~**ed** błogosławiony, szczęśliwy; F przeklęty, cholerny; '~**ing** błogosławieństwo *n*

blest [blest] *pret. i p.p. od* **bless**

blew [bluː] *pret. od* **blow**

blight [blaɪt] *bot.* rdza *f* zbożowa

blind [blaɪnd] **1.** niewidomy, ślepy (*fig. to* na *A*); *zakręt:* niewidoczny; **2.** żaluzja *f*, roleta *f*; *the ~ pl.* niewidomi *pl.*, ślepi *pl.*; **3.** oślepiać ⟨-pić⟩; *fig.* zaślepiać ⟨-pić⟩, ⟨u⟩czynić ślepym (*to* na *I*, wobec *G*); '~'al·ley ślepa ulica *f*; '~**ers** *pl. Am.* klapki *pl.* na oczy; '~**fold 1.** z zawiązanymi oczyma; **2.** zawiązywać ⟨-zać⟩ oczy; **3.** przepaska *f* na oczy; '~**ly** *fig.* ślepo, na ślepo; '~**worm** *zo.* padalec *m*

blink [blɪŋk] **1.** mrugnięcie *n*; **2.** ⟨za⟩mrugać; ⟨za⟩migać; '~**ers** *pl.* klapki *pl.* na oczy

bliss [blɪs] szczęśliwość *f*, rozkosz *f*

blis·ter ['blɪstə] **1.** *med.*, *tech.* pęcherz *m*; bąbel *m*; **2.** wywoływać ⟨-łać⟩ pęcherze; pokrywać ⟨-ryć⟩ (się) pęcherzami

blitz [blɪts] silny nalot *m* lotniczy; bombardowanie *n*; **2.** mocno ⟨z⟩bombardować

bliz·zard ['blɪzəd] zamieć *f* śnieżna

bloat|·ed ['bləʊtɪd] nadmuchany, wydęty; *fig.* nadęty, odęty; '~**er** *gastr.* wędzony śledź *m lub* makrela *f*

blob [blɒb] kleks *m*

block [blɒk] **1.** blok *m*; klocek *m*; kloc *m*; blok, (pod)zespół; *tech.* blok budowlany, cegła *f*; *zwł. Am.* kwartał *m* (*domów*), działka *f*; korek; zator; *tech.* zatkanie *n* się; ~ *(of flats) Brt.* mieszkaniowy blok *m*; **2.** *też* ~ *up* zatykać ⟨-kać⟩, zapychać ⟨-chać⟩; ⟨za⟩blokować

block·ade [blɒ'keɪd] **1.** blokada *f*, **2.** ⟨za⟩blokować

block|·bust·er ['blɒkbʌstə] F szlagier *m*, hit *m*; '~**head** F dureń *m*; ~ **'letters** *pl.* drukowane litery *pl. lub* pismo *n*

bloke [bləʊk] *Brt.* F facet *m*

blond [blɒnd] **1.** blondyn *m*; **2.** *adj.* blond; ~**e** [blɒnd] **1.** blondynka *f*; **2.** *adj.* blond

blood [blʌd] krew *f*; *in cold ~* z zimną krwią; '~ **bank** *med.* bank *m* krwi; '~·**cur·dling** ['blʌdkɜːdlɪŋ] mrożący krew w żyłach; '~ **do·nor** *med.* dawca *m* krwi; '~ **group** *med.* grupa *f* krwi; '~**hound** *zo.* ogar *m*; '~ **pres·sure** *med.* ciśnienie *n* krwi; '~**shed** rozlew *m* krwi; '~**shot** nabiegły krwią; '~**thirst·y** żądny krwi, krwiożerczy; '~ **ves·sel** *anat.* naczynie *n* krwionośne; '~·**y** (*-ier, -iest*) krwawy; *Brt.* F cholerny, pieprzny

bloom [bluːm] **1.** *poet.* kwiat *m*, kwiecie *n*; *fig.* rozkwit *m*; **2.** kwitnąć ⟨rozkwitać⟩; *fig.* kwitnąć, promienować

blos·som ['blɒsəm] **1.** kwiat *m*; **2.** kwitnąć ⟨rozkwitać⟩

blot [blɒt] **1.** kleks *m*; *fig.* skaza *f*, plama *f*; **2.** (*-tt-*) ⟨s-, po⟩plamić (się); osuszać ⟨-szyć⟩ (bibułą)

blotch [blɒtʃ] kleks *m*; plama *f lub* przebarwienie *n* na skórze; '~**y** (*-ier, -iest*) *skóra:* plamisty

blot|·ter ['blɒtə] suszka *f*; '~·**ting pa·per** bibuła *f*

blouse [blaʊz] bluzka *f*

blow[1] [bləʊ] uderzenie *n*, cios *m*

blow[2] [bləʊ] (*blew, blown*) *v/i.* ⟨po⟩wiać, ⟨za⟩dąć; dmuchać ⟨-chnąć⟩; ⟨za⟩sapać; *przedziurawiać* ⟨-wić⟩ dętkę; *electr. bezpiecznik:* przepalać ⟨-lić⟩ się;

~ *up* wylatywać ⟨-lecieć⟩ w powietrze; *v/t.* ~ *one's nose* wydmuchiwać ⟨-chać⟩ nos; ~ *one's top* F dostawać ⟨dostać⟩ szału; ~ *out* zdmuchiwać ⟨-chnąć⟩; ~ *up* wysadzać ⟨-dzić⟩; *fotografię* powiększać ⟨-szyć⟩; '~-dry *włosy* ⟨wy⟩suszyć; '~-fly *zo.* (*mucha*) plujka *f*; ,~n [bləʊn] *p.p. od* blow²; '~-pipe *tech.* palnik *m*, dmuchawka *f*; '~-up *phot.* powiększenie *n*

blud·geon ['blʌdʒən] pałka *f*

blue [bluː] **1.** niebieski, błękitny; melancholijny; **2.** *blight m, kolor:* niebieski *m*; *out of the* ~ jak grom z jasnego nieba, nagle; '~-ber·ry *bot.* borówka *f* wysoka *lub* amerykańska; '~-bot·tle *zo.* (*mucha*) plujka *f*; ~'col·lar work·er pracownik *m* fizyczny

blues [bluːz] *pl. lub sg. mus.* blues *m* (*też fig.*); *have the* ~ F mieć chandrę

bluff¹ [blʌf] urwisko *n*, stromy brzeg *m*

bluff² [blʌf] **1.** blef *m*; **2.** ⟨za⟩blefować

blu·ish ['bluːɪʃ] niebieskawy

blun·der ['blʌndə] **1.** błąd *m*, F byk *m*; **2.** F strzelić byka, zrobić (*duży*) błąd; ⟨s⟩fuszerować, ⟨s⟩partaczyć

blunt [blʌnt] tępy; *fig.* bezceremonialny; '~-ly *bez ceregieli lub* ceremonii

blur [blɜː] (-*rr*-) *v/t.* zamazywać ⟨-zać⟩; *phot. TV* zniekształcać ⟨-cić⟩; *znaczenie* zamazywać ⟨-zać⟩; *v/i.* zamazywać ⟨-zać⟩ się; *wspomnienia* zacierać ⟨zatrzeć⟩ się

blurt [blɜːt]: ~ *out* wyrzucać ⟨-cić⟩ z siebie

blush [blʌʃ] **1.** rumieniec *m*; zaczerwienienie *n* się; **2.** ⟨za⟩czerwienić się, ⟨za⟩rumienić się

blus·ter ['blʌstə] *wiatr:* ⟨za⟩huczeć; *fig.* wydzierać ⟨wydrzeć⟩ się; wychwalać się

Blvd *skrót pisany:* **Boulevard** bulwar

BMI [biː em 'waɪ] *skrót:* **Body Mass Index** wskaźnik masy ciała

BMX [biː em 'eks] *skrót:* **bicycle motocross** kros *m* rowerowy; rower *m* BMX; ~ **bike** rower *m* BMX

BO[biː 'əʊ] *skrót* → **body odo(u)r**

boar [bɔː] *zo.* dzik *m*; knur *m*

board [bɔːd] **1.** deska *f*; tablica *f*; tektura *f*, karton *m*; plansza *f* (*do gry*); stół *m* konferencyjny; utrzymanie *n*, wyżywienie *n*; komisja *f*, zarząd *m*, dyrekcja *f*; (*w sporcie*) deska *f* (*surfingowa*); *naut.*

burta *f*; **2.** *v/t.* wykładać ⟨wyłożyć⟩ deskami, ⟨o⟩szalować, ⟨o⟩deskować; wchodzić ⟨wejść⟩ na pokład (*G*); ⟨za⟩kwaterować, utrzymywać ⟨-mać⟩; ~ *a train* wsiadać ⟨wsiąść⟩ do pociągu; *v/i.* stołować się, mieszkać; '~-er gość *m* (*w pensjonacie itp.*), stołownik *m*; mieszkaniec *m* (-nka *f*) internatu; '~ **game** gra *f* planszowa; '~-ing card *aviat.* karta *f* wstępu (*do samolotu*); '~-ing house pensjonat *m*; '~-ing school internat *m*; ~ of 'di·rec·tors *econ.* dyrekcja *f*, rada *f* nadzorcza; ⸙ of 'Trade *Brt.* Ministerstwo *n* Handlu, *Am.* Izba *f* Handlowa; '~-walk *zwł. Am.* promenada *f* nad brzegiem

boast [bəʊst] **1.** przechwałki *pl.*, chełpliwość *f*; **2.** *v/i.* (*of, about*) chwalić się (*I*), przechwalać się (*I*); *v/t.* szczycić się, być dumnym z (*G*)

boat [bəʊt] łódź *f*, łódka *f*; szalupa *f*; statek *m*

bob [bɒb] **1.** dygnięcie *n*, dyg *m*; krótka fryzura *f*; *Brt. hist.* F szyling *m*; **2.** (-*bb-*) *v/t. włosy:* krótko obcinać ⟨obciąć⟩; *v/i.* dygać ⟨-gnąć⟩

bob·bin ['bɒbɪn] szpula *f*, szpulka *f*; *electr.* cewka *f*

bob·by ['bɒbɪ] *Brt.* F *policjant:* bobby *m*

bob·sleigh ['bɒbsleɪ] *sport:* bobslej *m*

bode [bəʊd] *pret. od* **bide**

bod·ice ['bɒdɪs] stanik *m*; góra *f* (*sukni*)

bod·i·ly ['bɒdɪlɪ] cieleśnie

bod·y ['bɒdɪ] ciało *n*; zwłoki *pl.*; korpus *m*; organizacja *f*, stowarzyszenie *n*; gromada *f*, grupa *f*, ciało *n*; główna część *f*; *wodny* zbiornik *m*; *mot.* karoseria *f*, nadwozie *n*; '~-guard ochrona *f*, F ochroniarz *m*; '~-o·do(u)r (*skrót:* **BO**) nieprzyjemny zapach *m* ciała; '~ stock·ing *ubiór:* body *m*; '~-work *mot.* karoseria *f*, nadwozie *n*

Boer [bɔː] Bur *m*; *attr.* burski

bog [bɒg] bagno *n*, mokradło *n*

bo·gus ['bəʊgəs] fałszywy, podrabiany

boil¹ [bɔɪl] *med.* czyrak *m*, ropień *m*

boil² [bɔɪl] **1.** *v/t.* ⟨za-, u⟩gotować; *v/i.* ⟨za-, u⟩gotować się; ⟨za⟩wrzeć, ⟨za⟩kipieć; **2.** gotowanie *n* się, wrzenie *n*; '~-er bojler *m*, kocioł *m*; '~-er suit kombinezon *m*; '~-ing point punkt *m* *lub* temperatura *f* wrzenia; *fig.* punkt *m* krytyczny

bois·ter·ous ['bɔɪstərəs] hałaśliwy, ło-

B

buzerski, wrzaskliwy

bold [bəʊld] dzielny, śmiały; bezczelny; *kolory*: krzykliwy, rażący; *print.* wytłuszczony, pogrubiony; *as ~ as brass* F bezczelny na całego

bol·ster ['bəʊlstə] **1.** wałek *m* (*na tapczanie*); **2.** ~ *up* podtrzymywać ⟨-mać⟩

bolt [bəʊlt] **1.** śruba *f*, sworzeń *m*; rygiel *m*; uderzenie *n* błyskawicy, błyskawica *f*; *make a ~ for* rzucić się do (*G*); **2.** *adv.* sztywno wyprostowany; **3.** ⟨za⟩ryglować, zamykać ⟨-knąć⟩; F *jedzenie* pochłaniać ⟨-łonąć⟩; *v/i.* uciekać ⟨uciec⟩, ⟨s⟩płoszyć się; *koń:* ponosić ⟨ponieść⟩

bomb [bɒm] **1.** bomba *f*; *the ~* bomba *f* atomowa; **2.** ⟨z⟩bombardować; **'~·er** *aviat.* bombowiec *m*

bom·bard [bɒm'bɑːd] ⟨z⟩bombardować

bomb|·proof ['bɒmpruːf] zabezpieczony przed bombami *lub* bombardowaniem; **'~·shell** bomba *f*; *fig.* zupełne zaskoczenie *n*

bond [bɒnd] wiązanie *n* (*też chem.*), więź *f*; *econ.* obligacja *f*, zobowiązanie *n* zapłaty; *in ~* w składzie wolnocłowym, pod zamknięciem celnym; **~·age** ['bɒndɪdʒ] niewola *f*, poddaństwo *n*

bonds [bɒndz] *pl.* więzy *pl.* (*przyjaźni*)

bone [bəʊn] kość *f*, ość *f*; *bones pl.* kości *pl.*, szczątki *pl.*; ~ *of contention* kość *f* niezgody; *have a ~ to pick with s.o.* mieć z kimś do pomówienia; *make no ~ about s.th.* nie obwijać czegoś w bawełnę, nie robić tajemnicy z czegoś; **2.** usuwać ⟨-nąć⟩ kości *lub* ości

bon·fire ['bɒnfaɪə] ognisko *n*

bonk [bɒŋk] *Brt. sl.* (*mieć stosunek płciowy*) pieprzyć (się)

bon·net ['bɒnɪt] czepek *m*; *mot.* maska

bon·ny ['bɒnɪ] *zwł. Szkoc.* (*-ier, -iest*) śliczny, urodziwy; *dziecko*: zdrowe

bo·nus ['bəʊnəs] *econ.* premia *f*, gratyfikacja *f*

bon·y ['bəʊnɪ] (*-ier, -iest*) kościsty, ościsty

boo [buː] *int.* uu!; *theat.* ~ *off the stage*, (*w piłce nożnej*) ~ *off the park* kogoś wygwizdać

boobs [buːbz] F *pl.* cycki *pl.*, cyce *pl.*

boo·by ['buːbɪ] F przygłup

book [bʊk] **1.** książka *f*, księga *f*; zeszyt *m*; wykaz *m*, lista *f*; ⟨za⟩rejestrować, ⟨za⟩księgować; *bilet* ⟨za⟩rezerwować;

(*w sporcie*) dawać ⟨dać⟩ ostrzeżenie; ~ *in zwł. Brt.* ⟨za⟩meldować się; ~ *in at* zatrzymywać ⟨-mać⟩ się w (*L*); **~·ed up** zarezerwowany, zajęty, wykupiony; **'~·case** biblioteczka *f*; **'~·ing** rezerwacja *f*; *sport:* ostrzeżenie *n*; **'~·ing clerk** pracownik *m* (-nica *f*) działu rezerwacji; **'~·ing of·fice** (*dział firmy*) rezerwacja *f*; kasa *f* (*biletowa*); **'~·keep·er** księgowy *m* (-wa *f*); **'~·keep·ing** księgowość *f*; **~·let** ['bʊklɪt] broszura *f*; **'~·mark**(·er)zakładka*f*; **'~·sell·er**księgarz *m*; **'~·shelf** (*pl. -shelves*) regał *m lub* półka *f* na książki; **'~·shop**, *zwł. Brt.,* **'~·store** *Am.* księgarnia *f*

boom¹ [buːm] **1.** *econ.* boom *m*, prosperity *f*, świetność *f* gospodarcza, dobra koniunktura *f*; **2.** osiągać ⟨-gnąć⟩ okres boomu

boom² [buːm] *naut.* bom *m*; wysięgnik *m* (*też mikrofonowy itp.*)

boom³ [buːm] ⟨za⟩huczeć, ⟨za⟩buczeć

boor [bʊə] cham(ka *f*) *m*, chamidło *n*; **~·ish** ['bʊərɪʃ] chamowaty, chamski

boost [buːst] **1.** zwiększać ⟨-szyć⟩, wzmagać ⟨wzmóc⟩; *napięcie prądu* wzmacniać ⟨-mocnić⟩; *fig.* pokrzepiać ⟨-pić⟩, dodawać ⟨dodać⟩ odwagi; **2.** pokrzepienie *n*, wzmocnienie *n*, zwiększenie *n*

boot¹ [buːt] but *m* (*wysoki*); *Brt. mot.* bagażnik *m*; **~·ee** ['buːtiː] but *m* (*zakrywający kostkę*); △ *nie but*

boot² [buːt]: ~ (*up*) *komp.* uruchamiać ⟨-chomić⟩ system

boot³ [buːt]: *to~* w dodatku, na dodatek

booth [buːð] budka *f*; stragan *m*; kabina *f*

'boot·lace sznurowadło *n*

boot·y ['buːtɪ] łup *m*

booze [buːz] F **1.** popijać ⟨popić⟩; **2.** popijawa *f*, pijatyka *f*; alkohol *m*, F wóda *f*

bor·der ['bɔːdə] **1.** obramowanie *n*, ramka *f*; lamówka *f*; granica *f*; rabat(k)a *f*; **2.** ogradzać ⟨ogrodzić⟩, opasywać ⟨-sać⟩, obramowywać ⟨-mować⟩; graniczyć (*on z I*)

bore¹ [bɔː] **1.** średnica *f* otworu; *tech.* kaliber *m*; *mil.* przewód *m* lufy; **2.** wiercić, rozwiercać

bore² [bɔː] **1.** nudziarz *m* (-ara *f*); *zwł. Brt.* nudziarstwo *n*; **2.** nudzić, zanudzać ⟨-dzić⟩; *be ~d* nudzić się

bore³ [bɔː] *pret. od bear*

B

bore·dom ['bɔːdəm] nuda *f*

bor·ing ['bɔːrɪŋ] nudny

born [bɔːn] *p.p. od bear²* urodzony

borne [bɔːn] *p.p. od bear²* znosić

bo·rough ['bʌrə] dzielnica *f (miejska)*; okręg *m* miejski (*Brt. wyborczy*)

bor·row ['brəu] *od kogoś* pożyczać ⟨-czyć⟩, wypożyczać ⟨-czyć⟩

Bos·ni·a and Hercegovina Bośnia i Hercegowina

bos·om ['buzəm] piersi *pl.*; *fig.* łono *m*

boss [bɒs] F **1.** boss *m*, szef(owa *f*) *m*; **2.** *v/t.* rozkazywać ⟨-zać⟩; *v/i.* ~ *about*, ~ *around* szarogęsić się, panoszyć się; '~·y F ⟨-ier, -iest⟩ apodyktyczny, despotyczny

bo·tan·i·cal [bə'tænɪkl] botaniczny; **bot·a·ny** ['bɒtənɪ] botanika *f*

botch [bɒtʃ] F **1.** *też* ~*-up* knot *m*; chałtura *f*; **2.** ⟨s⟩knocić, ⟨s⟩paprać

both [bəuθ] oba, obie, obaj, oboje; ~ *...* *and* *...* zarówno ..., jak i ..., tak ..., jak ...

both·er ['bɒðə] **1.** kłopot *m*, przykrość *f*; nieprzyjemność *f*; **2.** *v/t.* kłopotać; niepokoić; przeszkadzać; *v/i.* naprzykrzać ⟨-rzyć⟩ się, sprawiać ⟨-wić⟩ kłopot; *don't* ~*!* nie sprawiaj sobie kłopotu!, nie zawracaj sobie głowy!

bot·tle ['bɒtl] **1.** butelka *f*, flaszka *f*; **2.** ⟨za⟩butelkować; '~ bank *Brt.* pojemnik *m* na szkło; '~·neck *fig.* wąskie gardło *n*

bot·tom ['bɒtəm] dno *n*; spód *m*; dół *m*; F siedzenie *n*, pupa *f*; *be at the* ~ *of* znajdować się na *lub* w dole (*G*); *get to the* ~ *of s.th.* docierać ⟨-trzeć⟩ do sedna sprawy

bough [bau] konar *m*, gałąź *f*

bought [bɔːt] *pret. i p.p. od buy*

boul·der ['bəuldə] głaz *m*, otoczak *m*

bounce [bauns] **1.** odbijać ⟨-bić⟩ (się); podskakiwać ⟨-koczyć⟩, skakać ⟨skoczyć⟩; odskakiwać ⟨-koczyć⟩; F *czek:* nie mieć pokrycia, wrócić; **2.** odbicie się; podskok *m*, odskok *m*, skok *m*; '**bounc·ing** energiczny, *dziecko:* dziarski

bound¹ [baund] **1.** *pret. i p.p. od bind;* **2.** w drodze (*for* do *G*), do (*G*)

bound² [baund] *zw.* ~*s* granica *f*, limit *m*

bound³ [baund] **1.** skok *m*, podskok *m*; **2.** odbijać ⟨-bić⟩ (się); podskakiwać ⟨-koczyć⟩, skakać ⟨-koczyć⟩

bound·a·ry ['baundərɪ] granica *f*

'bound·less bezgraniczny

boun|·te·ous ['bauntɪəs], ~*·ti·ful* ['bauntɪfl] szczodrobliwy, hojny, szczodry

boun·ty ['bauntɪ] szczodrobliwość *f*, hojność *f*, szczodrość *f*; premia *f*, nagroda *f*

bou·quet [bu'keɪ] bukiet *m* (*też wina*)

bout [baut] *boks:* starcie *n*, walka *f*

bou·tique [buː'tiːk] butik *m*, boutique *m*

bow¹ [bau] **1.** ukłon *m*, skłon *m*; **2.** *v/i.* kłaniać ⟨ukłonić⟩ się, skłaniać ⟨-łonić⟩ się (*to* przed *I*); *fig.* chylić się, skłaniać się (*to* przed *I*); *v/t.* wyginać ⟨-giąć⟩, ⟨wy⟩giąć

bow² [bau] *naut.* dziób *m*

bow³ [bəu] łuk *m*; *muz.* smyczek *m*; kokarda *f*

bow·els ['bauəlz] *anat. pl.* jelita *pl.*, kiszki *pl.*

bowl¹ [bəul] miska *f* (*też klozetowa*), miseczka *f*; donica *f*; cukiernica *f*; miednica *f*; główka *f* (*fajki*); czarka *f* (*łyżki*)

bowl² [bəul] **1.** (*w grze w kręgle*) kula *f*, (*w grze w krykieta*) piłka *f*; **2.** rzucać ⟨-cić⟩ kulą *lub* piłką

bow-leg·ged ['bəulegd] krzywonogi, o kabłąkowatych nogach

'bowl·er gracz *m* w kręgle, kręglarz *m*; (*w grze w krykieta*) (*gracz rzucający piłkę*); ~ '*hat* melonik *m*

'bowl·ing (gra w) kręgle *pl.*

box¹ [bɒks] pudełko *n*, pudło *n*; karton *m*; kaseta *f*, szkatułka *f*; puszka *f*; skrzynka *f* (*pocztowa*); obudowa *f* (*maszynowa*); (*dla konia*) boks *m*; *Brt.* budka *f* (*telefoniczna*); *theat.* loża *f*; *jur.* ława *f* (*przysięgłych, oskarżonych*); (*dla samochodów*) koperta *f*

box² [bɒks] **1.** *sport.* boks; F ~ *s.o.'s ears* natrzeć komuś uszu; **2.** F *a* ~ *on the ear* palnięcie *n* w ucho; '~·*er* bokser *m*; '~·ing boks *m*, boksowanie *n*; '2·ing Day *Brt.* drugi dzień Bożego Narodzenia

box³ [bɒks] *bot.* bukszpan *m*; *attr.* bukszpanowy

'box| num·ber numer *m* oferty (*w gazecie*); numer *m* skrzynki pocztowej; '~ **of·fice** kasa *f* teatralna

boy [bɔɪ] chłopiec *m*

boy·cott ['bɔɪkɒt] **1.** ⟨z⟩bojkotować; **2.** bojkot *m*

'boy|·friend chłopiec *m*, sympatia *f*, przyjaciel *m*; ~·**hood** ['bɔɪhʊd] chłopięctwo *n*; ~·**ish** chłopięcy; ~ **scout** skaut *m*, harcerz *m*

BPhil [biː 'fɪl] *skrót:* **Bachelor of Philosophy** (*niższy stopień naukowy*) licencjat *m*

BR [biː 'ɑː] *skrót:* **British Rail** (*brytyjskie koleje*)

bra [brɑː] stanik *m*, biustonosz *m*

brace [breɪs] **1.** *tech.* wspornik *m*, podpora *f*; aparat *m* korekcyjny (*na zęby*); nawias *m* kwadratowy; **2.** *tech.* usztywniać ⟨-nić⟩, wzmacniać ⟨wzmocnić⟩

brace·let ['breɪslɪt] bransoletka *f*

brac·es ['breɪsɪz] *pl. Brt.* szelki *pl.*

brack·et ['brækɪt] *tech.* wspornik *m*, podpora *f*; nawias *m*; *podatkowy* przedział *m*; **lower income** ~ grupa *f* w przedziale o niższych dochodach

brack·ish ['brækɪʃ] słonawy

brag [bræg] (*-gg-*) chwalić się, przechwalać się (**about,** *of* o *L*); ~·**gart** ['brægət] samochwał *m*, pyszałek *m*

braid [breɪd] **1.** *zwł. Am.* warkocz *m*; galon *m*; **2.** *zwł. Am.* ⟨za⟩pleść, zaplatać ⟨zapleść⟩; obszywać ⟨-szyć⟩ galonem

brain [breɪn] *anat.* mózg *m*; często ~**s** *fig.* umysł *m*, głowa *f*; '~**s trust** *Brt.*, '~ **trust** *Am.* grupa *f* ekspertów; '~·**wash** ⟨z⟩robić pranie mózgu; '~·**wash·ing** pranie *n* mózgu; '~·**wave** olśnienie *n*, oświecenie *f*; ~·**y** (*-ier, -iest*) *F* niegłupi, rozgarnięty

brake [breɪk] **1.** *tech.* hamulec *m*; **2.** ⟨za⟩hamować; '~·**light** *mot.* światło *n* hamowania

bram·ble ['bræmbl] *bot.* jeżyna *f*

bran [bræn] otręby *pl.*

branch [brɑːntʃ] **1.** gałąź *f*, konar *m*; dziedzina *f*; specjalizacja *f*; filia *f*, oddział *m*; **2.** rozgałęziać ⟨-zić⟩ się

brand [brænd] **1.** *econ.* marka *f*, gatunek *m*, rodzaj *m*; znak *m* towarowy; piętno *n*; **2.** ⟨na⟩piętnować ⟨o⟩znakować

bran·dish ['brændɪʃ] wymachiwać, wywijać

'brand| name *econ.* znak *m* towarowy; nazwa *f* firmowa; ~'**new** nowy jak spod igły

bran·dy ['brændɪ] brandy *n*, winiak *m*, koniak *m*

brass [brɑːs] mosiądz *m*; *mus.* instrumenty *pl.* dęte blaszane, *F* blacha *f*; *F*

bezczelność *f*; ~ **'band** orkiestra *f* dęta

bras·sière ['bræsɪə] biustonosz *m*, stanik *m*

brat [bræt] *pej.* bachor *m*

Bratislava Bratysława *f*

brave [breɪv] **1.** (*-er, -est*) odważny, dzielny, nieustraszony; **2.** stawić czoło, przeciwstawiać się odważnie; **brav·er·y** ['breɪvərɪ] odwaga *f*, śmiałość *f*, nieustraszoność *f*

brawl [brɔːl] **1.** bijatyka *f*; bójka *f*; **2.** wszczynać ⟨-cząć⟩ bójkę

brawn·y ['brɔːnɪ] (*-ier, -iest*) muskularny, atletyczny

bray [breɪ] **1.** ryk *m* (*osła*); **2.** ⟨za⟩ryczeć; *samochody:* hałasować

bra·zen ['breɪzn] bezwstydny, bezczelny

Bra·zil [brə'zɪl] Brazylia *f*; **Bra·zil·ian** [brə'zɪljən] **1.** brazylijski; **2.** Brazylijczyk *m* (*-jka f*)

breach [briːtʃ] **1.** wyłom *m*, luka *f*; *fig.* naruszenie *n*, zerwanie *n*; pauza *f*; *mil.* przerwanie *n* (*frontu*); **2.** przerywać ⟨-rwać⟩ (front), dokonywać ⟨-nać⟩ wyłomu

bread [bred] chleb *m*; **brown** ~ razowiec *m*; **know which side one's ~ is buttered** *F* wiedzieć, z czego można wyciągnąć korzyść

breadth [bredθ] szerokość *f*

break [breɪk] **1.** złamanie *n*; luka *f*; przerwa *f* (*Brt. też w szkole*), pauza *f*; zmiana *f*, przemiana *f*; świt *m*; **bad** ~ *F* pech *m*; **lucky** ~ *F* szczęście *n*, pomyślność *f*; **give s.o. a** ~ *F* dawać ⟨dać⟩ komuś szansę; **take a** ~ ⟨z⟩robić przerwę; **without a** ~ bez przerwy; **2.** (**broke, broken**) *v/t.* ⟨z-, po-, ob-, wy⟩łamać ⟨s-, po⟩tłuc; ⟨z⟩niszczyć, ⟨ze⟩psuć; *zwierzę* oswoić, obłaskawiać ⟨-wić⟩, *konia* ujeżdżać ⟨ujeździć⟩ (*też* ~ **in**); *prawo* naruszać ⟨-szyć⟩, *przepisy, szyfr itp.* ⟨z⟩łamać; *złą wiadomość* przekazywać ⟨-zać⟩; *v/i.* ⟨z-, po-, ob-, wy⟩łamać się; ⟨s-, po⟩tłuc się; ⟨z⟩niszczyć się, ⟨ze⟩psuć się; *pogoda:* zmieniać ⟨-nić⟩ się nagle; zalewać ⟨-lać⟩ się; ~ **away** uciekać ⟨uciec⟩; odrywać ⟨oderwać⟩ się; ~ **down** załamywać ⟨-mać⟩ (się); *drzwi* wyważać ⟨-żyć⟩; (*do domu*) włamywać ⟨-mać⟩ się; ⟨ze⟩psuć (się); *mot.* mieć awarię; *chemikalia* rozkładać ⟨rozłożyć⟩; ~ **in** (*do domu*) włamywać ⟨-mać⟩ się; wtrącać ⟨wtrącić⟩ się; przyuczać ⟨-czyć⟩; ~ **off** zrywać ⟨zerwać⟩;

przerywać ⟨-rwać⟩; odłamywać ⟨-mać⟩ (się); **~ out** wybuchać ⟨-chnąć⟩; *skóra:* pokrywać ⟨-kryć⟩ się; uciekać ⟨uciec⟩ (*of z G*); **~ through** przebijać ⟨-bić⟩ się; dokonywać ⟨-nać⟩ wyłomu; **~ up** rozbijać ⟨-bić⟩ (się); zakańczać ⟨-kończyć⟩; *małżeństwo itp.:* rozstawać ⟨-stać⟩ się; *Brt.* zaczynać ⟨-cząć⟩ wakacje; '**~·a·ble** łamliwy, kruchy; **~age** ['breɪkɪdʒ] stłuczenie *n*, szkoda *f*, zniszczenie *n*; '**~·a·way** rozdzielenie *n*, separacja *f*, odłączenie *n*; *attr.* frakcyjny

'**break·down** załamanie *n* się (*też fig.*); *tech.* awaria *f*, uszkodzenie *n*, defekt *m*; **nervous ~** załamanie *n* nerwowe; '**~ lor·ry** *Brt. mot.* pojazd *m* pomocy drogowej; '**~ ser·vice** *mot.* pomoc *f* drogowa; '**~ truck** *Brt. mot.* pojazd *m* pomocy drogowej

break·fast ['brekfəst] śniadanie *f*; **have ~** → **have**; ⟨z⟩jeść śniadanie

'**break·through** *fig.* przełom *m*, wyłom *m*; '**~·up** rozpad *m*, dezintegracja *f*

breast [brest] pierś *f*; *fig.* serce *n*; **make a clean ~ of s.th.** wyznawać ⟨-nać⟩ coś; '**~·stroke** (*w sporcie*) styl *m* klasyczny

breath [breθ] oddech *m*, dech *m*; **be out of ~** być bez tchu; **waste one's ~** mówić na próżno

breath·a·lyse *Brt.*, **~lyse** *Am.* ['breθə-laɪz] F dmuchać ⟨dmuchnąć⟩ w balonik; '**~·lys·er** *Brt.*; '**²-lyz·er** *Am.* TM miernik *m* zawartości alkoholu we krwi, alkomat *m*, F balonik *m*

breathe [briːð] oddychać ⟨odetchnąć⟩; '**breath·less** bez tchu, zadyszany; '**~·tak·ing** zapierający dech

bred [bred] *pret. i p.p. od* **breed**

breech·es ['brɪtʃɪz] *pl.* bryczesy *pl.*

breed [briːd] **1.** rasa *f*, odmiana *f*; **2.** (**bred**) *v/t.* rośliny, zwierzęta hodować; *v/i.* rozmnażać ⟨-nożyć⟩ się; '**~·er** hodowca *m*; zwierzę *n* hodowlane; *phys.* reaktor *m* powielający; '**~·ing** rozmnażanie *n*; hodowla *f*; chów *m*

breeze [briːz] wietrzyk *m*, bryza *f*

breth·ren ['breðrən] *zwł. rel., pl.* bracia *pl., przest.* bracia *f*

brew [bruː] piwo warzyć (się); *herbatę* parzyć (się), zaparzać (się); '**~·er** piwowar *m*; '**~·er·y** ['brʊərɪ] browar *m*

bri·ar ['braɪə] → **brier**

bribe [braɪb] **1.** łapówka *f*; **2.** dawać

⟨dać⟩ łapówkę, przekupywać ⟨-pić⟩; **brib·er·y** ['braɪbərɪ] przekupstwo *n*, łapownictwo *n*

brick [brɪk] **1.** cegła *f*; *Brt.* klocek *m*; '**~·lay·er** murarz *m*; '**~·yard** cegielnia *f*

brid·al ['braɪdl] ślubny, małżeński, zaślubiony

bride [braɪd] panna *f* młoda; **~·groom** ['braɪdɡrʊm] pan *m* młody; **~s·maid** ['braɪdzmeɪd] druhna *f*

bridge [brɪdʒ] **1.** most *m*, pomost *m*; *naut., med.* mostek *m*; brydż *m*; **2.** kłaść ⟨położyć⟩ most nad (*I*); *fig.* pokonywać ⟨-nać⟩, przerzucić pomost nad (*I*)

bri·dle ['braɪdl] **1.** uzda *f*; **2.** zakładać ⟨założyć⟩ uzdę; *fig.* ⟨o⟩kiełznać; '**~ path** ścieżka *f* do jazdy konnej

brief [briːf] **1.** zwięzły, krótki; **2.** ⟨po⟩instruować, ⟨po⟩informować; '**~·case** aktówka *f*

briefs [briːfs] *pl.* majtki *pl., męskie slipy pl., damskie figi pl.*

bri·er ['braɪə] *bot.* dzika róża *f*, szypszyna *f*

bri·gade [brɪ'ɡeɪd] *mil.* brygada

bright [braɪt] jasny, jaskrawy, błyszczący; żywy, pogodny; bystry; **~·en** ['braɪtn] *v/t. też* **~en up** rozjaśniać ⟨-śnić⟩; ożywiać ⟨-wić⟩; *v/i. też* **~en up** rozpogadzać ⟨-godzić⟩ się, rozjaśniać ⟨-śnić⟩ się; '**~·ness** jasność *f*, jaskrawość *f*; żywość *f*; pogoda *f*, bystrość *f*

bril·liance, ~·lian·cy ['brɪljəns, -jənsɪ] blask *m*, połysk *m*; *fig.* błyskotliwość *f*, lotność *f*; '**~·liant 1.** błyszczący; połyskujący; błyskotliwy, lotny; **2.** brylant *m*

brim [brɪm] **1.** brzeg *f*, krawędź *f*; rondo *n*; **2.** (**-mm-**) napełniać ⟨-nić⟩ po brzegi *lub* do pełna; **~·ful(l)** ['brɪmfʊl] pełny, napełniony po brzegi

brine [braɪn] solanka *f*

bring [brɪŋ] (**brought**) przyprowadzać ⟨-dzić⟩, przynosić ⟨-nieść⟩, przywozić ⟨-wieźć⟩; *kogoś* skłaniać ⟨skłonić⟩ (**to do s.th.** aby coś zrobił); *coś* doprowadzać ⟨to do G⟩; **~ about** ⟨s⟩powodować, wywoływać ⟨-łać⟩; **~ back** zwracać ⟨zwrócić⟩; oddawać ⟨oddać⟩; **~ forth** wydawać ⟨wydać⟩; *fig.* błyskotliwość *f*; **~ off** wykonywać ⟨-nać⟩; **~ on** ⟨s⟩powodować; **~ out** *produkt* wypuszczać ⟨-uścić⟩; *cechy* wywoływać ⟨-łać⟩, wyzwalać ⟨-wolić⟩; **~ round** ⟨o⟩cucić; przekonywać ⟨-nać⟩; **~ up** wychowywać ⟨-wać⟩; dawać dobre wyniki; wspominać ⟨wspomnieć⟩; *zwł. Brt. jedzenie* zwracać ⟨zwrócić⟩

brink [brɪŋk] brzeg *f*; krawędź (*też fig.*)

brisk [brɪsk] energiczny, dynamiczny; *powietrze*: świeży

bris·tle [ˈbrɪsl] **1.** szczecina *f*; szczeciniasty zarost *m*; **2.** *też ~ up* ⟨z-, na⟩jeżyć się, ⟨na⟩stroszyć się; być najeżonym; tętnić; '**bris·tly** (*-er, -iest*) szczeciniasty

Brit [brɪt] F Angol *m*

Brit·ain [ˈbrɪtn] Brytania *f*

Brit·ish [ˈbrɪtɪʃ] brytyjski; *the ~ pl.* Brytyjczycy *pl.*; '*~ Isles pl.* Wyspy Brytyjskie *pl.*

Brit·on [ˈbrɪtn] Brytyjczyk *m* (*-jka f*)

brit·tle [ˈbrɪtl] kruchy, łamliwy, delikatny

broach [brəʊtʃ] *temat* poruszać ⟨-szyć⟩, omawiać ⟨-mówić⟩

broad [brɔːd] szeroki; *dzień*: biały; *mrugnięcie itp.*: wyraźny; *dowcip*: rubaszny; ogólny; rozległy, szeroki; liberalny; '*~·cast* **1.** (*-cast lub -casted*) nadawać ⟨-dać⟩, ⟨wy⟩emitować, przekazywać ⟨-zać⟩; **2.** (*w telewizji, radiu*) program *m*, audycja *f*; '*~·cast·er* spiker(ka *f*) *m*; *~·en* [ˈbrɔːdn] rozszerzać ⟨-rzyć⟩ (się), poszerzać ⟨-rzyć⟩ (się); '*~ jump Am.* (*w sporcie*) skok *m* w dal; *~'mind·ed* tolerancyjny, liberalny

bro·cade [brəˈkeɪd] brokat *m*

bro·chure [ˈbrəʊʃə] broszura *f*, prospekt *m*, folder *m*

brogue [brəʊg] *mocny skórzany but m*; dialekt *m* (*zwł. irlandzki*)

broil [brɔɪl] *zwł. Am.* → *grill* 1

broke [brəʊk] **1.** *pret. od break*; **2.** F bez grosza *przy duszy*, goły; **bro·ken** [ˈbrəʊkən] **1.** *p.p. od break*; **2.** złamany, stłuczony; zepsuty; rozbity (*też fig.*); *angielski itp.*: łamany; **brok·en·'heart·ed**: *be ~* mieć złamane serce

bro·ker [ˈbrəʊkə] *econ.* makler *m*, broker *m*, agent *m*

bron·chi·tis [brɒŋˈkaɪtɪs] *med.* zapalenie *n* oskrzeli, bronchit *m*

bronze [brɒnz] **1.** (*metal*) brąz *m*; **2.** z brązu; w kolorze brązu, brązowy

brooch [brəʊtʃ] broszka *f*

brood [bruːd] **1.** wyląg *m*, lęg *m*; *attr.* lęgowy; **2.** wysiadywać (*jaja*) (*też fig.*)

brook [brʊk] strumień *m*

broom [bruːm, brʊm] miotła *f*; '*~·stick* kij *m* do miotły

Bros. [brɒs] *skrót*: **brothers** bracia *pl.* (*w nazwach firm*)

broth [brɒθ] bulion *m*, rosół *m*

broth·el [ˈbrɒθl] burdel *m*, dom *m* publiczny

broth·er [ˈbrʌðə] brat *m*; *~(s) and sister(s)* rodzeństwo *n*; *~·hood rel.* [ˈbrʌðəhʊd] braterstwo *n*; *~·in-law* [ˈbrʌðərɪnlɔː] (*pl. brothers-in-law*) szwagier *m*; '*~·ly* **1.** *adj.* braterski; **2.** *adv.* po bratersku

brought [brɔːt] *pret. i p.p. od bring*

brow [braʊ] brew *f*; czoło *n*; grzbiet *m* (*wzgórza*); '*~·beat* (**browbeat, browbeaten**) zastraszać ⟨-szyć⟩, onieśmielać ⟨-lić⟩

brown [braʊn] **1.** brązowy; **2.** *kolor*: brąz *m*; **3.** ⟨z⟩brązowieć; ⟨pod-, przy⟩rumienić

browse [braʊz] przeglądać ⟨-dnąć⟩, ⟨po⟩szperać; *zwierzę*: ⟨po⟩skubać (*trawę*), paść się

bruise [bruːz] **1.** siniak *m*; obicie *n*; **2.** ⟨po⟩siniaczyć; *owoce* ⟨po⟩obijać

brunch [brʌntʃ] (*późne obfite śniadanie*)

brush [brʌʃ] **1.** szczotka *f*, szczoteczka *f*; pędzel *m*; *lisia* kita *f*, ogon *m*; scysja *f*, zwada *f*; otarcie *n* się; zarośla *pl.*; **2.** ⟨wy⟩szczotkować; zamiatać ⟨-mieść⟩; ocierać ⟨otrzeć⟩ się; *~ against* ocierać ⟨otrzeć⟩ się o (*A*); *~ away, ~ off* odrzucać ⟨-cić⟩; odsuwać ⟨-sunąć⟩ na bok; *~ aside, ~ away* ⟨z⟩ignorować; *~ up* znajomość języka ⟨pod⟩szlifować, odświeżać ⟨-żyć⟩; *give one's English a ~ up* podszlifować swój angielski; '*~·wood* chrust *m*, zarośla *pl.*

brusque [bruːsk] szorstki, opryskliwy

Brus·sels Bruksela *f*

Brus·sels sprouts [brʌslˈspraʊts] *bot. pl.* brukselka *f*

bru·tal [ˈbruːtl] brutalny; *~·i·ty* [bruːˈtælətɪ] brutalność *f*

brute [bruːt] **1.** brutalny; **2.** zwierzę *n*, zwierz *m*, *fig.* F bydlę *n*, bydlak *m*

BS [biː ˈes] *Brt. skrót*: **British Standard** Norma *f* Brytyjska; *Am.* → *BSc*

BSc [biː es ˈsiː] *Brt. skrót*: **Bachelor of Science** licencjat *m* (*nauk przyrodniczych*)

BST [biː es ˈtiː] *Brt. skrót*: **British**

Summer Time czas letni w Wielkiej Brytanii

BT [bi: 'ti:] *skrót:* **British Telecom** Brytyjski Telecom (*brytyjska firma telekomunikacyjna*)

BTA [bi: ti: 'eɪ] *skrót:* **British Tourist Authority** (*brytyjski urząd ds. turystyki*)

bub·ble ['bʌbl] **1.** bańka *f*, pęcherzyk *m*; **2.** musować; ⟨za⟩kipieć; ⟨za⟩wrzeć, ⟨za⟩kipieć (*też fig.*)

buck¹ [bʌk] **1.** (*pl.* **buck, bucks**) kozioł *m* (*antylopy, jelenia*); **2.** *v/i.* brykać ⟨bryknąć⟩, podskakiwać ⟨-koczyć⟩

buck² [bʌk] *Am.* (*dolar*) F dolec *m*, zielony *m*

buck·et ['bʌkɪt] kubeł *m*, wiadro *n*, ceber *m*; *tech.* czerpak *m*

buck·le ['bʌkl] **1.** klamra *f*; sprzączka *f*, zapinka *f*; **2.** *też* ~ **up** zapinać ⟨-piąć⟩ (*na klamrę lub sprzączkę*); ~ **on** przypinać ⟨-piąć⟩ (się)

'buck·skin zamsz *m*, ircha *f*

bud [bʌd] **1.** *bot.* pączek *m*, pąk *m*; *fig.* pączek *m*, zarodek *m*; **2.** (**-dd-**) puszczać ⟨puścić⟩ pączki

Bu·da·pest Budapeszt *m*

bud·dy ['bʌdɪ] *Am.* F koleś *m*, facet *m*

budge [bʌdʒ] *v/i.* ruszać ⟨ruszyć⟩ się (*z miejsca*); *v/t.* ruszać ⟨ruszyć⟩ (*z miejsca*)

bud·ger·i·gar ['bʌdʒərɪgɑ:] *zo.* papużka *f* falista

bud·get ['bʌdʒɪt] budżet *m*, *parl.* plan *m* budżetowy

bud·gie ['bʌdʒɪ] *zo.* F → *budgerigar*

buff [bʌf] *F w złożeniach*: entuzjasta *m* (-tka *f*) (*G*), znawca *m* (-czyni *f*) (*G*)

buf·fa·lo ['bʌfələʊ] (*pl.* **-loes, -los**) bawół *m*; (*w USA*) bizon *m*

buff·er ['bʌfə] *tech.* bufor *m*; zderzak *m*

buf·fet¹ ['bʌfɪt] uderzać ⟨-rzyć⟩ o (*A*) *lub* w (*A*); ~ **about** obijać ⟨obić⟩ (się)

buf·fet² ['bʌfɪt] bufet *m*; kredens *m*

bug [bʌg] **1.** *zo.* pluskwa *f*; *Am. zo.* owad *m*, robak *m*; F (*ukryty mikrofon*) pluskwa *f*; *komp.* F (*błąd w programie*) pluskwa *f*; **2.** (**-gg-**) F zakładać ⟨-łożyć⟩ pluskwę (*podsłuch*); F wnerwiać ⟨-wić⟩; '~**ging de·vice** F pluskwa *f*; urządzenie *n* podsłuchowe; '~**ging op·e·ration** akcja *f* założenia podsłuchu

bug·gy ['bʌgɪ] *mot.* buggy *m* (*pojazd do jazdy po wydmach dla rozrywki*); *Am.* wózek *m* dziecięcy

bu·gle ['bju:gl] trąbka *f* sygnałowa, sygnałówka *f*

build [bɪld] **1.** (**built**) ⟨z⟩budować; **2.** budowa *f* (*ciała*), figura *f*; '~**er** budowniczy *m*, F budowlaniec *m*

build·ing ['bɪldɪŋ] budowa *f*, budowanie *n*; budynek *m*; *attr.* budowlany, ... budowy; '~ **site** plac *m* budowy

built [bɪlt] *pret. i p.p. od* **build** 1; ~**'in** wbudowany; ~**'up:** ~**-up area** teren *m* *lub* obszar *m* zabudowany

bulb [bʌlb] *bot.* cebulka *f*, bulwa *f*; *electr.* żarówka *f*

Bul·gar·i·a Bułgaria *f*

bulge [bʌldʒ] **1.** wybrzuszenie *n*, wypukłość *f*; **2.** wybrzuszać ⟨-szyć⟩ (się); wypychać ⟨-pchać⟩

bulk [bʌlk] duża ilość *f*, masa *f*; większość *f*; *econ.* towar *m* masowy; *in* ~ *econ.* luzem, w całości; '~**y** (*-ier, -iest*) zajmujący wiele miejsca; mało poręczny

bull [bʊl] *zo.* byk *m*, samiec *m* (*słonia*); '~**dog** *zo.* buldog *m*

bull·doze ['bʊldəʊz] ⟨z⟩niwelować; *fig.* ⟨z⟩równać; '~**doz·er** *tech.* buldożer *m*, spycharka *f*

bul·let ['bʊlɪt] nabój *m*, kula *f*

bul·le·tin ['bʊlɪtɪn] biuletyn *m*; '~ **board** tablica *f* ogłoszeń

'bul·let-proof kuloodporny

bul·lion ['bʊljən] sztaby *pl.* kruszcu (*złota, srebra*)

bul·lock ['bʊlək] *zo.* wół *m*

'bull's-eye *hit the* ~ trafić w dziesiątkę

bul·ly ['bʊlɪ] **1.** (*osoba znęcająca się nad słabszymi*); **2.** ⟨s⟩tyranizować

bul·wark ['bʊlwək] przedmurze *n* (*też fig.*); szaniec *m*; *naut.* nadburcie *n*

bum¹ [bʌm] *Am.* F **1.** włóczęga *m*, tramp *m*; nierób *m*, obibok *m*; **2.** włóczyć się; obijać się

bum² [bʌm] *Brt.* F zadek *m*, tyłek *m*

'bum·ble·bee *zo.* trzmiel *m*

bump [bʌmp] **1.** uderzenie *n*, stuknięcie *n*; guz *m* (*na kolanie itp.*); nierówność *f*, wybój *m*; **2.** *v/t.* uderzać, stuknąć; *v/i.* podskakiwać; ~ *into* natykać ⟨-knąć⟩ się na (*A*)

'bump·er zderzak *m*; '~**-to-'~** zderzak do zderzaka, zderzak w zderzak

'bump·y (*-ier, -est*) wyboisty

bun [bʌn] słodka bułka *f*; kok *m* (*na głowie*)

bunch [bʌntʃ] wiązka *f*, pęk *m*; wiązanka *f*, bukiet *m*; F paczka *f*, grupa *f*; **a ~ of grapes** kiść *f* winogron; **~ of keys** pęk *m* kluczy

bun·dle ['bʌndl] **1.** tłumok *m*, tobół *m*; wiązka *f* (*drew*); pakunek *m*; **2.** *v/t.* tłub **~ up** ⟨z⟩wiązać razem

bun·ga·low ['bʌŋgələu] bungalow *m*, domek *m* parterowy

bun·gee [bən'dʒiː] lin(k)a *f* elastyczna; **~ jumping** (*skoki z bardzo dużej wysokości na elastycznej linie*)

bun·gle ['bʌŋgl] **1.** partanina *f*; **2.** ⟨s⟩partaczyć, ⟨s⟩paprać

bunk [bʌŋk] koja *f*; **~ bed** łóżko *n* piętrowe

bun·ny ['bʌnɪ] króliczek *m*

buoy [bɔɪ] *naut.* **1.** boja *f*; **2. ~ up** *fig.* wspierać ⟨wesprzeć⟩ duchowo

bur·den ['bɜːdn] **1.** ciężar *m*; obciążenie *n*; **2.** obciążać ⟨-żyć⟩, obarczać ⟨-czyć⟩ brzemieniem

bu·reau ['bjuərəu] (*pl.* **-reaux** [-rəuz], **-reaus**) *Brt.* sekretarzyk *m*, biurko *n*; *Am.* komoda *f*, komódka *f* (*zwł. z lustrem*); biuro *n*, urząd *m*

bu·reauc·ra·cy [bjuə'rɒkrəsɪ] biurokracja *f*

burg·er ['bɜːgə] *gastr.* hamburger *m*

bur·glar ['bɜːglə] włamywacz *m* (-ka *f*); **~·glar·ize** ['bɜːgləraɪz] *Am.* → **burgle**; **~·glar·y** ['bɜːglərɪ] włamanie *n*; **~·gle** ['bɜːgl] włamywać ⟨-mać⟩ się do (*G*)

bur·i·al ['berɪəl] pogrzeb *m*, pochówek *m*

bur·ly ['bɜːlɪ] (**-ier, -iest**) krzepki, zwalisty

burn [bɜːn] **1.** *med.* oparzenie *n*; przypalenie *n*; **2.** (**burnt** *lub* **burned**) ⟨po-, s⟩parzyć; **~ down** spalić (się); **~ up** spalić (się); rozpalać ⟨-lić⟩ (się); '**~·ing** płonący (*też fig.*)

burnt [bɜːnt] *pret. i p.p. od* **burn** 2

burp [bɜːp] F beknąć; **she ~ed** odbiło jej się, beknęła; **he ~ed the baby** sprawił, że dziecku odbiło się

bur·row ['bʌrəu] **1.** nora *f*; **2.** ⟨wy-, za⟩grzebać (się)

burst [bɜːst] **1.** pękanie *n*; pęknięcie *n*; rozrywanie *n* się; *fig.* wybuch *m*; **2.** (**burst**) *v/i.* pękać ⟨-knąć⟩; rozrywać ⟨-zerwać⟩ się; eksplodować; **~ in on** *lub*

upon wpadać ⟨wpaść⟩ na (*A*); **~ into tears** wybuchać ⟨-nąć⟩ płaczem; **~ out of** *fig.* wypadać ⟨-paść⟩ z (*G*); *v/t.* przebijać ⟨-bić⟩

bur·y ['berɪ] *kogoś* ⟨po⟩grzebać, pochować; *coś* zakopywać ⟨-pać⟩

bus [bʌs] (*pl.* **-es, -ses**) autobus *m*; '**~ driv·er** kierowca *m* autobusu

bush [buʃ] krzak *m*, krzew *m*

bush·el ['buʃl] buszel *m* (*Brt. 36,37 l, Am. 35,24 l*)

'**bush·y** (**-ier, -iest**) krzaczasty

busi·ness ['bɪznɪs] sprawa *f*; zadanie *n*; interes *m*, biznes *m*; działalność *f*; transakcja *f* handlowa; interesy *pl.*; przedsiębiorstwo *n*, firma *f*; branża *f*; *attr.* służbowy, handlowy, gospodarczy; **~ of the day** porządek *m* dnia; **on ~** służbowo; **you have no ~ doing** (*lub* **to do**) **that** nie masz żadnego prawa tak robić; **that's none of your ~** to nie twoja sprawa; → **mind** 2; '**~ hours** *pl.* godziny *pl.* pracy; '**~·like** rzeczowy; '**~·man** (*pl.* **-men**) biznesmen *m*; '**~ trip** podróż *f* służbowa; '**~·wom·an** (*pl.* **-women**) kobieta *f* interesu, bizneswoman *f*

'**bus stop** przystanek *m* autobusowy

bust[1] [bʌst] biust *m*

bust[2] [bʌst] F: **go ~** ⟨s⟩plajtować

bus·tle ['bʌsl] **1.** ożywienie *n*, krzątanina *f*; **2. ~ about** krzątać się, uwijać się

bus·y ['bɪzɪ] **1.** (**-ier, -iest**) zajęty (*też at I*); *ulica:* ruchliwy; *dzień:* pracowity *Am. tel.* zajęty; **2. ~ o.s. with** zajmować się (*I*); '**~·bod·y** wścibski *m* (-ka *f*); '**~ sig·nal** *Am. tel.* sygnał *m* zajęty

but [bʌt, bət] **1.** *cj.* ale, lecz; ależ, jednak; **~ then** z drugiej strony; **he could not ~ laugh** musiał się wówczas roześmiać; **2.** *prp.* oprócz, prócz, poza; **all ~ him** wszyscy oprócz niego; **the last ~ one** przedostatni; **nothing ~** wyłącznie, jedynie; **~ for** gdyby nie; **3.** *adv.* tylko, dopiero; **all ~** prawie

butch·er ['butʃə] **1.** rzeźnik *m*; **2.** ⟨za⟩szlachtować, zarzynać ⟨zarżnąć⟩ (*też fig.*)

but·ler ['bʌtlə] kamerdyner *m*

butt[1] [bʌt] **1.** kolba *f* (*broni*); uchwyt *m*; niedopałek *m*, F pet *m*; uderzenie *n* głową; **2.** uderzać ⟨-rzyć⟩ głową; **~ in** F ⟨w⟩mieszać się (**on do** *G*)

butt[2] [bʌt] beczka *f*, baryłka *f*

but·ter ['bʌtə] **1.** masło *n*; **2.** ⟨po⟩sma-

rować masłem; '~·cup *bot.* jaskier *m*;
'~·fly *zo.* motyl *m*
but·tocks ['bʌtəks] *pl.* pośladki *pl.*, F
lub zo. zad *m*
but·ton ['bʌtn] **1.** guzik *m*; przycisk *m*;
plakietka *f*, znaczek *m* (*z nazwiskiem*);
2. *zw.* ~ **up** zapinać ⟨-piąć⟩ na guziki;
'~·hole dziurka *f* (*od guzika*)
but·tress ['bʌtrɪs] *arch.* przypora *f*; **fly-**
ing ~ łuk *m* przyporowy
bux·om ['bʌksəm] dorodny, postawny
buy [baɪ] **1.** kupno *n*, nabytek *m*; **2.**
(**bought**) *v/t.* kupować ⟨kupić⟩ (**of,**
from od *G*, *z G*, **at** u *G*), nabywać ⟨na-
być⟩; ~ **out** *lub* **up** wykupywać ⟨wy-
kupić⟩; '~·er nabywca *m*, kupujący *m*
(-ca *f*)
buzz [bʌz] **1.** brzęczenie *n*; szmer *m*
(*głosów*); **2.** *v/i.* ⟨za⟩brzęczeć, ⟨za⟩-
szemrać; ~ **off!** *Brt.* F odwal się!
buz·zard ['bʌzəd] *zo.* myszołów *m*
buzz·er ['bʌzə] *electr.* brzęczyk *m*
by [baɪ] **1.** *prp. przestrzeń:* przy (*L*),
u (*G*), obok (*G*); *czas:* do (*G*), aż do
(*G*) (**be back by 9.30** wróć do 9.30);
pora dnia: za (*G*), w ciągu (*G*) (~ **day**
w ciągu dnia); *przyczyna:* przez (*A*)
(**done ~ Mary** zrobione przez Mary);
środek transportu: ~ **bus** autobusem;
~ **rail** koleją; ~ **letter** listownie; na (*A*)

(~ **the dozen** na tuziny); na (*L*), według (*G*) (~ **my watch** na moim zegarku *lub* według mojego zegarka);
z (~ **nature** z natury); *autor:* (napisane) przez (*G*) (**a play ~ Osborne**
sztuka Osborne'a); *porównania wiel-*
kości: o (*A*) (~ **an inch** o cal); *math.*
(pomnożone) przez (*A*), razy (**2 ~ 4** 2
razy 4); *math.* (podzielone) przez (*A*)
(**2 ~ 4** 2 przez 4); **2.** *adv.* obok (*G*),
w pobliżu (*G*) (**go ~** przechodzić obok
(*G*), *czas:* przelatywać); na bok (**put ~**
odłożyć na bok); ~ **and large** ogólnie,
generalnie
by... [baɪ] uboczny, boczny
bye [baɪ] *int.* F: ~'**bye** do widzenia!,
cześć!
'**by**|·**e·lec·tion** wybory *pl.* uzupełnia-
jące; '~·**gone 1.** miniony, były; **2.** *let*
~**gones be ~gones** co było, to było;
'~·**pass 1.** obwodnica *f*; *med.* bypass
m, połączenie *n* omijające; **2.** omijać
⟨ominąć⟩; unikać ⟨-knąć⟩; '~·**prod·uct**
produkt *m* uboczny; '~·**road** boczna
droga *f*; '~·**stand·er** przechodzień *m*,
świadek *m*
byte [baɪt] *komp.* bajt *m*
'**by**|·**way** boczna droga *f*; '~·**word** sym-
bol *m*, uosobienie *n*; **be a ~word for**
uosabiać (*A*)

C

C *skrót pisany:* **Celsius** C, Celsjusza;
centigrade w skali stustopniowej *lub*
Celsjusza
c *skrót pisany:* **cent(s)** cent *m lub pl.*;
century w., wiek(u); **circa** ok., ok.,
około; **cubic** sześcienny
cab [kæb] taksówka *f*, kabina *f* (*cięża-*
rówki, dźwigu); *rail.* przedział *m* maszynisty, budka *f* maszynisty; dorożka *f*
cab·a·ret ['kæbəreɪ] kabaret *m*
cab·bage ['kæbɪdʒ] *bot.* kapusta *f*
cab·in ['kæbɪn] *naut., aviat.* kabina *f*;
naut. kajuta *f*; chata *f*
cab·i·net ['kæbɪnɪt] szafka *f*, witryna *f*,
gablota *f*; *pol.* gabinet *m*; '~·**mak·er**
stolarz *m*; '~ **meet·ing** spotkanie *n* ga-
binetu
ca·ble ['keɪbl] **1.** *electr.* kabel *m*, prze-

wód *m*; **2.** ⟨za-, prze⟩telegrafować; *pie-*
niądze przesyłać ⟨-słać⟩ telegraficznie;
TV połączyć kablem; '~ **car** wagon (*ko-*
lejki linowej) *m*; '~·**gram** telegram *m*
(*zagraniczny*); '~·**rail·way** kolej *m* linowa; ~ '**tel·e·vi·sion**, ~ **TV** [- tiː 'viː] telewizja *f* kablowa
'**cab**|**rank**, '~·**stand** postój *m* taksówek
lub dorożek
cack·le ['kækl] **1.** gdakanie *n*; *ludzki* rechot *m*; **2.** ⟨za⟩gdakać; ⟨za⟩rechotać
cac·tus ['kæktəs] *bot.* (*pl.* **-tuses, -ti**
['kæktaɪ]) kaktus *m*
CAD [siː eɪ 'diː, kæd] *skrót:* **com-**
puter-aided design CAD (*projekto-*
wanie wspomagane komputerowo)
ca·dence ['keɪdəns] *mus.* kadencja *f*;
rytm *m* (*mowy*)

ca·det [kə'det] *mil.* kadet *m*

caf·é, caf·e ['kæfeɪ] kawiarnia *f*, kafejka *f*

caf·e·te·ri·a [kæfɪ'tɪərɪə] bar *m* samoobsługowy; bufet *m*; stołówka *f*

cage [keɪdʒ] **1.** klatka *f*, kabina *f* (*windy*); **2.** zamykać ⟨-knąć⟩ w klatce

Cai·ro Kair *m*

cake [keɪk] **1.** ciasto *n*, ciastko *n*, tort *m*; tabliczka *f* (*czekolady*), kostka *f* (*mydła*); **2.** *~d with mud* oblepiony błotem

CAL [kæl] *skrót:* ***computer-aided lub -assisted learning*** CAL (*nauczanie wspomagane komputerowo*)

ca·lam·i·ty [kə'læmɪtɪ] katastrofa *f*, klęska *f*, zguba *f*

cal·cu·late ['kælkjuleɪt] *v/t.* liczyć, ⟨ob-, wy⟩liczyć, kalkulować; *Am.* F przypuszczać ⟨-puścić⟩, sądzić; *v/i.* *~late on* liczyć na (*A*); *~·la·tion* [kælkju'leɪʃn] obliczenie *n*, wyliczenie *n*, kalkulacja *f* (*też fig., econ.*); namysł *m*; *~·la·tor* ['kælkjuleɪtə] kalkulator *m*

cal·en·dar ['kælɪndə] kalendarz *m*

calf¹ [kɑːf] (*pl.* **calves** [kɑːvz]) łydka *f*

calf² [kɑːf] (*pl.* **calves** [kɑːvz]) cielę *n*; *'~·skin* skóra *f* cielęca

cal·i·bre *zwł. Brt.,* **cal·i·ber** *Am.* ['kælɪbə] kaliber *m*

Cal·i·for·nia Kalifornia *f*

call [kɔːl] **1.** wołanie *n*; *tel.* rozmowa *f*; głos *m*; wezwanie *n* (*to* do *G*); powołanie *n* (*for* na *A*); krótka wizyta *f* (*on s.o.* u kogoś); *econ.* popyt *m*, zapotrzebowanie *n* (*for* na *A*); potrzeba *f*; *on ~* na żądanie; *be on ~ lekarz:* być dostępnym na wezwanie; *make a ~* ⟨za⟩dzwonić; składać ⟨złożyć⟩ wizytę (*on s.o.* komuś); **2.** *v/t.* ⟨za⟩wołać, wzywać ⟨wezwać⟩; *tel.* ⟨za⟩dzwonić do (*G*); nazywać ⟨nazwać⟩; powoływać ⟨-łać⟩ (*to* na *A*); *uwagę* ⟨s⟩kierować; *be called* nazywać się; *~ s.o. names* przezywać ⟨-zwać⟩ kogoś; *v/i.* wołać, wzywać ⟨wezwać⟩; *tel.* ⟨za⟩dzwonić; przybywać ⟨-być⟩ w odwiedziny (*on s.o.* do kogoś, *at s.o.'s* [*house*] do czyjegoś domu); *~ at a port* zawijać ⟨zawinąć⟩ do portu; *~ collect Am. tel.* ⟨za⟩dzwonić na koszt odbiorcy; *~ for* wymagać, domagać się; *pomoc* wzywać ⟨wezwać⟩; *paczkę* zgłaszać ⟨zgłosić⟩ się po (*A*); *~ on* zwracać się do *kogoś* (*for* o *A*), wzywać *kogoś* (*to do s.th.* aby coś zro-

bił); *~ on s.o.* odwiedzać ⟨-wiedzić⟩ kogoś; *'~ box Brt.* budka *f* telefoniczna; *'~·er* telefonujący *m* (-ca *f*), rozmówca *m* (-czyni *f*); gość *m*; *'~ girl* (*prostytutka wzywana telefonicznie*) call girl *f*; *'~-in Am.* → *phone-in*; *'~·ing* powołanie *n*; zawód *m*

cal·lous ['kæləs] *skóra:* zgrubiały; *fig.* gruboskórny

calm [kɑːm] **1.** spokojny; **2.** spokój *m*; cisza *f*; **3.** *często ~ down* uspokajać ⟨-koić⟩ się

cal·o·rie ['kælərɪ] kaloria *f*; *rich lub high in ~s pred.* wysokokaloryczny; *low in ~s pred.* niskokaloryczny; → *high-calorie, low-calorie*; *'~-con·scious* zwracający uwagę na ilość kalorii

calve [kɑːv] ⟨o⟩cielić się

calves [kɑːvz] *pl. od calf²*

CAM [siː eɪ 'em, kæm] *skrót:* ***computer-aided manufacture*** (*produkcja wspomagana komputerowo*)

cam·cor·der ['kæmkɔːdə] (*kamera wideo zintegrowana z urządzeniem nagrywającym*) kamkorder *m*

came [keɪm] *pret. od come*

cam·el ['kæml] *zo.* wielbłąd *m*

cam·e·o ['kæmɪəʊ] (*pl. -os*) kamea *f*; *theat., film:* krótka scenka *f* (*dla znanego aktora*)

cam·e·ra ['kæmərə] kamera *f*; aparat *m* fotograficzny

cam·o·mile ['kæməmaɪl] *bot.* rumianek *m*; *attr.* rumiankowy

cam·ou·flage ['kæməflɑːʒ] **1.** kamuflaż *m*; **2.** ⟨za⟩maskować

camp [kæmp] **1.** obóz *m*; **2.** obozować; *~ out* biwakować

cam·paign [kæm'peɪn] **1.** *mil., fig.* kampania *f*; *pol.* walka *f* wyborcza; **2.** *fig.* prowadzić ⟨przeprowadzić⟩ kampanię (*for* za *I*, *against* przeciw *D*)

camp 'bed *Brt.,* ~ 'cot *Am.* łóżko *n* składane *lub* polowe; *'~·er* (*van*) samochód *m* kempingowy; *'~·ground*, *'~-site* kemping *m*, pole *n* namiotowe

cam·pus ['kæmpəs] campus *m*, miasteczko *n* uniwersyckie

can¹ [kæn, kən] *v/aux.* (*pret. could*; *z przeczeniem: cannot, can't*) móc; potrafić, umieć

can² [kæn, kən] **1.** puszka *f*; konserwa *f* (*w puszce*); kanister *m*; blaszanka *f*; **2.**

(**-nn-**) ⟨za⟩puszkować, ⟨za⟩konserwować

Can·a·da ['kænədə] Kanada *f*; **Ca·na·di·an** [kə'neɪdjən] **1.** kanadyjski; **2.** Kanadyjczyk *m* (-jka *f*)

ca·nal [kə'næl] kanał *m* (*też* anat.)

ca·nar·y [kə'neərɪ] zo. kanarek *m*

can·cel ['kænsl] (*zwł. Brt. -ll-, Am. -l-*) odwoływać ⟨-łać⟩; anulować; unieważniać ⟨-nić⟩; odmawiać ⟨odmówić⟩; ⟨s⟩kasować; *be ~(l)ed* nie odbywać ⟨odbyć⟩ się

can·cer ['kænsə] med. rak *m*; **2** znak Zodiaku: Rak *m*; *he/she is (a)* **2** on(a) jest spod znaku Raka; **~·ous** ['kænsərəs] rakowaty, rakowy

can·did ['kændɪd] szczery, otwarty

can·di·date ['kændɪdət] kandydat *m* (-ka *f*) (*for* u A), ubiegający *m* się (-ca *f*) (*for* o A)

can·died ['kændɪd] kandyzowany

can·dle ['kændl] świeca *f*, świeczka *f*; *burn the ~ at both ends* łapać wiele srok za ogon na raz; **'~·stick** lichtarz *m*, świecznik *m*

can·do(u)r ['kændə] szczerość *f*, otwartość *f*

C&W [si: ənd 'dʌblju:] skrót: *country and western* (muzyka) country

can·dy ['kændɪ] **1.** cukier *m* grubokrystaliczny; *Am.* słodycze pl.; **2.** kandyzować; **'~·floss** Brt. wata *f* cukrowa; **'~ store** sklep *m* ze słodyczami

cane [keɪn] bot. trzcina *f*

ca·nine ['keɪnaɪn] psi

canned [kænd] puszkowy, puszkowany; konserwowy, konserwowany; **~ 'fruit** konserwowane owoce pl.

can·ne·ry ['kænərɪ] zwł. Am. fabryka *f* konserw

can·ni·bal ['kænɪbl] kanibal *m*

can·non ['kænən] armata *f*, działo *n*; mil. lotnicze działko *f* szybkostrzelne

can·not ['kænɒt] → *can¹*

can·ny ['kænɪ] (-*ier*, -*iest*) przebiegły, sprytny

ca·noe [kə'nu:] **1.** kanoe *n*, canoe *n*, kajak *m*; **2.** pływać w kajaku *lub* kanoe

can·on ['kænən] kanon *m*

'can o·pen·er Am. otwieracz *m* do konserw

can·o·py ['kænəpɪ] baldachim *m*

cant [kænt] żargon *m*; frazesy pl.

can't [kɑːnt] zamiast *cannot* → *can¹*

can·tan·ker·ous [kæn'tæŋkərəs] zrzędliwy, gderliwy

can·teen [kæn'ti:n] zwł. Brt. stołówka; mil. kantyna *f*; mil. manierka; zestaw pl. sztućców

can·ter ['kæntə] **1.** kłus *m*; **2.** kłusować, iść kłusem

can·vas ['kænvəs] brezent *m*, płótno *n* żeglarskie; płótno *n*, obraz *m* na płótnie; naut. żagle pl.

can·vass ['kænvəs] **1.** pol. kampania *f* wyborcza; econ. akcja *f* reklamowa; akwizycja *f*; werbowanie *n*; **2.** v/t. opinię ⟨z⟩badać; ⟨z⟩werbować; pol. głosy zdobywać ⟨-być⟩; v/i. pol. ⟨prze⟩prowadzić kampanię wyborczą

can·yon ['kænjən] kanion *m*

cap [kæp] **1.** czapka *f*; kąpielowy, pielęgniarski czepek *m*; kapsel *m*, kapsla *f*; nakrętka *f*; **2.** (*-pp-*) nakrywać ⟨-ryć⟩, przykrywać ⟨-ryć⟩; fig. ⟨u⟩koronować; przewyższać ⟨-szyć⟩, przebijać ⟨-bić⟩

ca·pa·bil·i·ty [keɪpə'bɪlətɪ] zdolność *f*; **~·ble** ['keɪpəbl] zdolny (*of* do G); *be ~·ble of doing s.th.* móc *lub* potrafić coś zrobić

ca·pac·i·ty [kə'pæsətɪ] pojemność *f*, możliwość *f*, zdolność *f*, zdatność *f*; tech. wydajność *f*, przepustowość *f*; *in my ~ as* w ramach moich obowiązków jako, jako

cape¹ [keɪp] przylądek *m*, cypel *m*

cape² [keɪp] peleryna *f*

Cape Town Kapsztad *m*

ca·per ['keɪpə] **1.** bot. kapar *m*; psota *f*, figlarny podskok *m* **2.** podskakiwać (*z radości*)

ca·pil·la·ry [kə'pɪlərɪ] anat. naczynie *n* włosowate

cap·i·tal ['kæpɪtl] **1.** stolica *f*; wersalik *m*, wielka litera *f*; **2.** główny, podstawowy, zasadniczy; econ. kapitałowy, inwestycyjny; jur. przestępstwo: karany śmiercią; **~ 'crime** przestępstwo *n* zagrożone karą śmierci

cap·i·tal|·is·m ['kæpɪtəlɪzəm] kapitalizm *m*; **~·ist** ['kæpɪtəlɪst] kapitalistyczny; **~·ize** ['kæpɪtəlaɪz] econ. ⟨z⟩kapitalizować, ⟨z⟩gromadzić kapitał; zaopatrywać ⟨-trzyć⟩ w kapitał; **~·ize on** odcinać ⟨-ciąć⟩ kupony od (G)

cap·i·tal|·let·ter print. wielka litera *f*,

wersalik *m*; ~ '**pun·ish·ment** *jur.* kara *f* śmierci

ca·pit·u·late [kə'pɪtjuleɪt] ⟨s⟩kapitulować (**to** przed *I*)

ca·pri·cious [kə'prɪʃəs] kapryśny

Cap·ri·corn ['kæprɪkɔːn] *znak Zodiaku*: Koziorożec *m*; *he/she is (a)* ~ on(a) jest spod znaku Koziorożca

cap·size [kæp'saɪz] przewracać ⟨-wrócić⟩ (się) do góry dnem

cap·sule ['kæpsjuːl] *pharm.* kapsułka *f*; *astr.* kapsuła *f*, kabina *f* (*statku kosmicznego*)

cap·tain ['kæptɪn] kapitan *m*; dowódca *m*

cap·tion ['kæpʃn] podpis *m* (*pod rysunkiem, zdjęciem*); napis *m* (*na filmie*)

cap|·ti·vate ['kæptɪveɪt] *fig.* porywać ⟨porwać⟩, urzekać ⟨urzec⟩; ~**tive** ['kæptɪv] 1. pojmany, schwytany; zniewolony; *balon*: na uwięzi; *hold* ~**tive** pojmować ⟨pojmać⟩ do niewoli; 2. jeniec *m*; ~**tiv·i·ty** [kæp'tɪvətɪ] niewola *f*

cap·ture ['kæptʃə] 1. pojmanie *n*, schwytanie *n*, ujęcie *n*; 2. pojmować ⟨-jąć⟩, schwytać, pojmować ⟨pojąć⟩; *naut.* ⟨s⟩kaperować

car [kɑː] samochód *m*, auto *n*; *tramwajowy, kolejowy* wagon *m*; gondola *f*, kosz *m*; kabina *f* (*windy*); *by* ~ samochodem

car·a·mel ['kærəmel] (*cukier*) karmel *m*, cukier *m* palony; (*cukierek*) karmelek *m*

car·a·van ['kærəvæn] karawana *f*; *Brt.* przyczepa *f* kempingowa; ⚠ *nie* ***karawan***; '~ *site* pole *n* kempingowe (*dla przyczep*)

car·a·way ['kærəweɪ] *bot.* kminek *m*

car·bine ['kɑːbaɪn] *mil.* karabin *m*

car·bo·hy·drate [kɑːbəʊ'haɪdreɪt] *chem.* węglowodan *m*

'**car bomb** bomba *f* w samochodzie

car·bon ['kɑːbən] *chem.* węgiel *m*; ~ '**cop·y** kopia *f*, przebitka *f*; '~ (*paper*) kalka *f* (*maszynowa*)

car·bu·ret·(**t**)**or** [kɑːbə'retə] *tech.* gaźnik *m*

car·case *Brt.*, **car·cass** ['kɑːkəs] tusza *f* (*zwierzęcia*); resztki *pl.*

car·cin·o·genic [kɑːsɪnə'dʒenɪk] *med.* rakotwórczy

card [kɑːd] karta *f*; *pocztowa* kartka *f*; *play* ~*s* grać w karty; *have a* ~ *up one's*

---

sleeve *fig.* trzymać asa w rękawie; '~**board** tektura *f*, karton *m*; '~**board box** pudełko *n* z tektury

car·di·ac ['kɑːdɪæk] *med.* sercowy; ~ '**pace·mak·er** *med.* stymulator *m* serca

car·di·gan ['kɑːdɪgən] *rozpinany* sweter *m*

car·di·nal ['kɑːdɪnl] 1. główny; zasadniczy; kardynalny; szkarłatny; 2. *rel.* kardynał *m*; ~ '**num·ber** *math.* liczba *f* kardynalna; liczebnik *m* główny

'**card|·in·dex** kartoteka *f*; '~ **phone** automat *m* telefoniczny na karty; '~**sharp·er** szuler *m*, kanciarz *m*

'**car dump** złomowisko *n* samochodów, *F* szrot *m*

care [keə] 1. troska *f*; ostrożność *f*; opieka *f*, nadzór *m*; *medical* ~ opieka *f* medyczna; *take* ~ *of* ⟨za⟩troszczyć się o (*A*); uważać na (*A*); *with* ~*!* ostrożnie!; 2. mieć ochotę; ~ *about* ⟨za⟩troszczyć się o (*A*); ~ *for* lubić; pokochać się; mieć ochotę; *I don't* ~ F nie obchodzi mnie to; *I couldn't* ~ *less* wszystko mi jedno

ca·reer [kə'rɪə] 1. kariera *f*; działalność *f* zawodowa; 2. zawodowy; 3. ⟨po⟩gnać, ⟨po⟩mknąć

ca'reers| **ad·vice** *Brt.* poradnictwo *n* zawodowe; ~ **ad·vi·sor** *Brt.* doradca *m* w sprawach zawodu; ~ **guid·ance** *Brt.* poradnictwo *n* zawodowe; ~ **of·fice** *Brt.* biuro *m* porad zawodowych; ~ **of·fic·er** *Brt.* doradca *m* w sprawach zawodu

'**care|·free** beztroski; '~**ful** staranny; troskliwy, uważny; dokładny, skrupulatny; *be* ~*ful!* uważaj!; '~**less** niedbały, niestaranny; nieostrożny, lekkomyślny

ca·ress [kə'res] 1. pieszczota *f*; 2. ⟨po⟩pieścić

'**care|·tak·er** dozorca *m* (-czyni *f*); '~**worn** zatroskany, udręczony

'**car|·fare** *Am.* opłata *f* za przejazd (*autobusem*); '~ **fer·ry** prom *m* samochodowy

car·go ['kɑːgəʊ] (*pl.* -**goes**, *Am. też* -**gos**) ładunek *m*, *econ.* fracht *m*

'**car hire** *Brt.* wynajem *m* samochodów

Car·ib·be·an Sea Morze Karaibskie *n*

car·i·ca|·ture ['kærɪkətjʊə] 1. karykatura *f*; 2. ⟨s⟩karykaturować; ~**tur·ist**

['kærɪkətjuərɪst] karykaturzysta *m*
(-tka *f*)

car·ies ['keərɪːz] *med. też* **dental ~**
próchnica *m*

'car me·chan·ic mechanik *m* samochodowy

car·mine ['kɑːmaɪn] **1.** karminowy; **2.**
karmin *m*

car·na·tion [kɑː'neɪʃn] *bot.* goździk *m*;
△ *nie* **karnacja**

car·ni·val ['kɑːnɪvl] karnawał *m*

car·niv·o·rous [kɑː'nɪvərəs] mięsożerny

car·ol ['kærəl] kolęda *f*

carp [kɑːp] *zo.* (*pl.* **carp** *lub* **-s**) karp *m*

'car park *zwł. Brt.* parking *m* samochodowy

car·pen·ter ['kɑːpɪntə] cieśla *m*, stolarz *m*

car·pet ['kɑːpɪt] **1.** dywan *m*; wykładzina *f*; **sweep s.th. under the ~** tuszować coś, kryć coś w tajemnicy; **2.** wykładać ⟨wyłożyć⟩ dywanem

'car| phone telefon *m* w samochodzie;
'~ pool (*grupa ludzi korzystająca przy
dojazdach do pracy z jednego prywatnego samochodu*); '~ pool(·ing)
ser·vice bank *m* przewozów; '~·port
wiata *f* na samochód (*w funkcji garażu*); '~ rent·al *Am.* wynajem *m* samochodów; '~ re·pair shop warsztat
m naprawy samochodów

car·riage ['kærɪdʒ] transport *m*, przewóz *m*; koszt *m* transportu; powóz *m*;
Brt. rail. wagon *m* osobowy; postawa *f*;
'~·way *Brt. mot.* jezdnia *f* (*o jednym
kierunku ruchu*); pas *m* ruchu

car·ri·er ['kærɪə] przewoźnik *m*, spedytor *m*; bagażnik *m* rowerowy; *mil.* lotniskowiec *m*; '~ bag *Brt.* torba *f* (*na zakupy*)

car·ri·on ['kærɪən] padlina *f*, ścierwo *n*

car·rot ['kærət] *bot.* marchew *f*, marchewka *f*

car·ry ['kærɪ] *v/t.* nosić ⟨zanieść⟩; ciężar dźwigać; przewozić ⟨przewieźć⟩,
⟨prze⟩transportować; mieć *lub* nosić (*przy sobie*); chorobę przenosić
⟨-nieść⟩; wniosek przyjmować ⟨-jąć⟩,
uchwalać ⟨-lić⟩; korzyść przynosić
⟨-nieść⟩; artykuł zamieszczać ⟨-mieścić⟩; *v/i.* głos: nieść się; *działo:* nieść;
be carried zostawać ⟨-stać⟩ przyjętym
lub uchwalonym; **~ the day** wygrywać

⟨-grać⟩; **~ s.th. too far** przesadzać
⟨-dzić⟩ z czymś; **get carried away** *fig.*
dawać ⟨dać⟩ się ponieść; **~ forward,
over** *econ.* sumę na następną stronę
przenieść; **~ on** kontynuować; *biznes
itp.* prowadzić; **~ out, ~ through** wykonywać ⟨-nać⟩, przeprowadzać ⟨-dzić⟩;
'~·cot *Brt.* (*torba do noszenia dziecka*)
nosidło *n*

cart [kɑːt] **1.** wózek *m*; wóz *m*; *Am.* wózek *m* na zakupy; **put the ~ before the
horse** odwracać kota ogonem; **2.** przewozić ⟨-wieźć⟩ (*wozem, wózkiem*)

car·ti·lage ['kɑːtɪlɪdʒ] *anat.* chrząstka *f*

car·ton ['kɑːtən] karton *m*

car·toon [kɑː'tuːn] karykatura *f*; film *m*
rysunkowy; **~·ist** [kɑː'tuːnɪst] karykaturzysta *m* (-tka *f*)

car·tridge ['kɑːtrɪdʒ] *mil.* nabój *m* (*też
do pióra*); *phot.* kaseta; pojemnik *m*
(*z tonerem lub tuszem*); wkładka *f* gramofonowa

'cart·wheel: **turn ~s** ⟨z⟩robić gwiazdę

carve [kɑːv] *mięso* ⟨po⟩kroić; ⟨wy⟩rzeźbić; wycinać ⟨-ciąć⟩; 'carv·er snycerz *m*; rzeźbiarz *m*; nóż *m* do krojenia;
'carv·ing snycerka *f*, rzeźbiarstwo *n*

'car wash myjnia *f* samochodów

cas·cade [kæ'skeɪd] kaskada *f*

case¹ [keɪs] **1.** pudełko *n*, pudło *n*; skrzynia *f*; futerał *m*, pokrowiec *m*; kaseta *f*;
gablota *f*, witryna *f*; skrzynka *f* (*wina*);
powłoczka *f*; *tech.* obudowa *f*; **2.** wkładać ⟨włożyć⟩ do pokrowca; *tech.* obudowywać ⟨-wać⟩, umieszczać ⟨umieścić⟩ w osłonie

case² [keɪs] przypadek (*też med., gr.*);
jur. sprawa *f* (*sądowa*); stan *m*, sytuacja
f; **in ~ of** w przypadku (*G*), w razie (*G*)

case·ment ['keɪsmənt] skrzydło *n*
okienne; '~·win·dow okno *n* skrzynkowe

cash [kæʃ] **1.** gotówka *f*; zapłata *f* gotówką; **~ on delivery** płatne gotówką
przy odbiorze; **2.** *czek itp.* ⟨z⟩realizować; '~·book księga *f* kasowa; '~ desk
(*w domu towarowym itp.*) kasa *f*;
'~ di·spens·er *zwł. Brt.* bankomat *m*;
'~·ier [kæ'ʃɪə] kasjer(ka *f*) *m*; '~·less
bezgotówkowy; '~ ma·chine, '~·point
Brt. → **~ dispenser**; '~ re·gis·ter kasa
f rejestrująca

cas·ing ['keɪsɪŋ] obudowa *f*, osłona *f*;
powłoka *f* (*kabla*)

C

cask [kɑːsk] beczka *f*, baryłka *f*

cas·ket ['kɑːskɪt] pudełko *n*, kasetka *f*; *Am.* trumna *f*

cas·se·role ['kæsərəʊl] naczynie *n* do zapiekanek; zapiekanka *f*

cas·sette [kə'set] kaseta *f*; **~ deck** magnetofon *m* kasetowy (*bez wzmacniacza*); **~ play·er** odtwarzacz *m* kasetowy; **~ ra·di·o**, **~ re·cord·er** magnetofon *m* kasetowy

cas·sock ['kæsək] *rel.* sutanna *f*

cast [kɑːst] **1.** rzut *m*; *tech.* odlew *m*; *theat.* obsada *f*; (*w wędkarstwie*) rzut *m*; *med.* opatrunek *m* gipsowy, gips *m*; typ *m*, rodzaj *m*; odcień *m*; **2.** (*cast*) *v/t.* zarzucać ⟨-cić⟩, rzucać ⟨-cić⟩; *zo.* skórę *itp.* zrzucać ⟨-cić⟩; *zęby itp.* gubić; *pol.* rzucać ⟨-cić⟩ oddawać ⟨-dać⟩; ⟨u⟩kształtować; *tech.* odlewać ⟨-lać⟩; *też* **~ up** podliczać ⟨-czyć⟩, dodawać ⟨-dać⟩; *theat.* obsadzać ⟨-dzić⟩ w (*L*) (*sztuce itp.*); obsadzać w roli (*G*); **~ lots** rzucać ⟨rzucić⟩ losy (**for** o *A*); **~ away** odrzucać ⟨-cić⟩; **~ down** przygnębiać ⟨-bić⟩; **~ off** *ubrania* pozbywać ⟨-być⟩ się; *przyjaciela itp.* odrzucać ⟨-cić⟩; *oczko* spuszczać ⟨spuścić⟩; *v/i.* **~ about for**, **~ around for** szukać (*A*); *fig.* rozglądać się za (*I*)

cas·ta·net [kæstə'net] *mus.* kastaniet *m*

cast·a·way ['kɑːstəweɪ] *naut.* rozbitek *m*

caste [kɑːst] kasta *f* (*też fig.*)

cast·er ['kɑːstə] kółko *n* jezdne (*pod meblem*); *Brt.* dozownik *m* do cukru; *Brt.* solniczka *f*

cast·i·gate ['kæstɪgeɪt] surowo ⟨u⟩karać; ⟨s⟩krytykować

cast 'i·ron żeliwo *n*, lane żelazo *n*; **~·'i·ron** żeliwny; *fig.* żelazny

cas·tle ['kɑːsl] (*rycerski*) zamek *m*; (*w szachach*) wieża *f*

cast·or ['kɑːstə] → **caster**

cast·or oil [kɑːstə 'ɔɪl] olej *m* rycynowy

cas·trate [kæ'streɪt] ⟨wy⟩kastrować

cas·u·al ['kæʒʊəl] przypadkowy, niezamierzony; dorywczy; *ubranie, etc.*: swobodny, nieformalny; **~ 'wear** ubranie *n* codzienne

cas·u·al·ty ['kæʒʊəltɪ] nieszczęście *n*; ofiara *f*; **casualties** *pl.* ofiary *pl.*, *mil.* straty *pl.* w ludziach; **~ (department)** (*w szpitalu*) oddział *m* urazowy; **~·ward**

(*w szpitalu*) stacja *f* pogotowia ratunkowego

cat [kæt] *zo.* kot *m*

cat·a·logue *zwł. Brt.*, **cat·a·log** *Am.* ['kætəlɒg] **1.** katalog *m*, spis *m*; **2.** ⟨s⟩katalogować

cat·a·lyt·ic con·ver·ter [kætəlɪtɪc kən'vɜːtə] *mot.* katalizator *m*

cat·a·pult ['kætəpʌlt] katapulta *f*; *Brt.* proca *f*

cat·a·ract ['kætərækt] katarakta *f*; *med.* katarakta *f*, zaćma *f*

ca·tarrh [kə'tɑː] *med.* katar *m*

ca·tas·tro·phe [kə'tæstrəfɪ] katastrofa *f*

catch [kætʃ] **1.** złapanie *n*, schwytanie *n*, pojmanie *n*; połów *m*, zdobycz *f*; zaczep *m*; zatrzask *m*; zaparcie *n* (*tchu*); *fig.* haczyk *m*; pułapka *f*; **2.** (*caught*) *v/t.* ⟨s⟩chwytać, ⟨z⟩łapać; pojmować ⟨-jąć⟩, ujmować ⟨-jąć⟩; zaskakiwać ⟨-koczyć⟩, ⟨z⟩łapać; *pociąg itp.* ⟨z⟩łapać, zdążyć na (*A*); pojmować ⟨-jąć⟩, ⟨z⟩łapać; *zarazać* ⟨-razić⟩ się, *chorobę itp.* ⟨z⟩łapać; *atmosferę itp.* chwytać ⟨uchwycić⟩; **~ a cold** przeziębiać ⟨-bić⟩ się; **~ the eye** wpadać ⟨wpaść⟩ w oko; **~ s.o.'s eye** przyciągać ⟨-gnąć⟩ czyjeś oko; **~ s.o. up** doganiać ⟨dogonić⟩ kogoś; **be caught up in** być zaplątanym w (*A*); *v/i.* złapać się, zaczepiać ⟨-pić⟩ się; ⟨za⟩łapać, sczepiać ⟨-pić⟩ się; *zamek itp.*: zatrzaskiwać ⟨-snąć⟩ się; **~ up with** doganiać ⟨dogonić⟩; **'~·er** osoba *f* łapiąca (*zwł. w sporcie*); **'~·ing** zaraźliwy; **'~·word** hasło *n*, hasło *n* słownikowe; **'~·y** (**-ier, -iest**) *melodia*: chwytliwy

cat·e·chis·m ['kætɪkɪzəm] *rel.* katechizm *m*

cat·e·go·ry ['kætɪgərɪ] kategoria *f*

ca·ter ['keɪtə] zaopatrywać (**for** w); *fig.* ⟨za⟩troszczyć się o (*A*)

cat·er·pil·lar ['kætəpɪlə] *zo.* gąsienica *f* (*też tech.*); *TM* pojazd *m* gąsienicowy; **~ 'trac·tor** *TM* ciągnik *m* gąsienicowy

cat·gut ['kætgʌt] *med.* katgut *m*, nić *f* chirurgiczna

ca·the·dral [kə'θiːdrəl] katedra *f*

Cath·o·lic ['kæθəlɪk] *rel.* **1.** katolicki; **2.** katolik *m* (*-iczka f*)

cat·kin ['kætkɪn] *bot.* bazia *f* (*wierzby*)

cat·tle ['kætl] bydło *n*

Cau·ca·sus Kaukaz *m*

ceremony

caught [kɔːt] *pret. i p.p. od* **catch** 2
ca(u)l·dron [ˈkɔːldrən] kocioł *m*
cau·li·flow·er [ˈkɒlɪflaʊə] *bot.* kalafior *m*
cause [kɔːz] **1.** przyczyna *f*, powód *m*; sprawa *f*; **2.** ⟨s⟩powodować, być przyczyną; sprawiać ⟨-wić⟩; '**~·less** bezpodstawny
cau·tion [ˈkɔːʃn] **1.** ostrożność *f*, przezorność *f*; ostrzeżenie *n*; △ *nie* **kaucja**; **2.** ostrzegać ⟨ostrzec⟩; udzielać ⟨-ić⟩ ostrzeżenia; *jur.* pouczać ⟨-czyć⟩
cau·tious [ˈkɔːʃəs] ostrożny, przezorny
cav·al·ry [ˈkævlrɪ] *mil.* kawaleria *f*
cave [keɪv] **1.** jaskinia *f*; **2.** *v/i.:* **~ in** zapadać ⟨-paść⟩ się
cav·ern [ˈkævən] jaskinia *f*, jama *f*
cav·i·ty [ˈkævətɪ] dziura *f*; *med.* ubytek *m* (*w zębie*), F dziura *f*
caw [kɔː] **1.** krakać; **2.** krakanie *n*
CB [siː ˈbiː] *skrót:* **Citizens' Band** radio *n* CB, CB *n*
CBS [siː biː ˈes] *skrót:* **Columbia Broadcasting System** (*amerykańska firma fonograficzna, radiowa i TV*)
CD [siː ˈdiː] *skrót:* **compact disc** płyta *f* kompaktowa, kompakt *m*, CD *n*; **CD 'play·er** odtwarzacz *m* płyt kompaktowych; **CD-ROM** [siː diː ˈrɒm] *skrót:* **compact disc read-only memory** CD-ROM *m*
cease [siːs] (za)przestawać, przerywać ⟨-rwać⟩; spłaty *itp.* zawieszać ⟨zawiesić⟩; '**~·fire** zawieszenie *n* broni, zaprzestanie *n* ognia; '**~·less** nieustanny
cei·ling [ˈsiːlɪŋ] sufit *m*, strop *m*; *econ., techn.* pułap *m*; *econ.* górna granica *f*
cel·e·|brate [ˈselɪbreɪt] celebrować, świętować ⟨święcić⟩, czcić; '**~·brat·ed** znany, sławny (**for** *z G*); **~·bra·tion** [selɪˈbreɪʃn] świętowanie *n*, obchody *pl.*
ce·leb·ri·ty [sɪˈlebrətɪ] (*osoba*) sława *f*
cel·e·riac [səˈlerɪæk] *bot.* seler *m* korzeniowy
cel·e·ry [ˈselərɪ] *bot.* seler *m* naciowy
ce·les·ti·al [sɪˈlestjəl] niebiański, niebieski
cel·i·ba·cy [ˈselɪbəsɪ] celibat *m*
cell [sel] komórka *f*; *electr. też* ogniwo *n*
cel·lar [ˈselər] piwnica *f*
cel·|list [ˈtʃelɪst] *mus.* wiolonczelista *m* (-tka *f*); **~·lo** [ˈtʃeləʊ] *mus.* (*pl. -los*) wiolonczela *f*
cel·lo·phane [ˈseləʊfeɪn] *TM* celofan *m*

cel·lu·lar [ˈseljʊlə] komórkowy; **~ 'phone** telefon *m* komórkowy
Cel·tic [ˈkeltɪk] celtycki
ce·ment [sɪˈment] **1.** cement *m*; klej *m*, kit *m*; **2.** ⟨s⟩cementować (*też fig.*); ⟨s⟩kleić
cem·e·tery [ˈsemɪtrɪ] cmentarz *m*
cen·sor [ˈsensə] **1.** cenzor *m* (-ka *f*); **2.** ⟨o⟩cenzurować; '**~·ship** cenzura *f*
cen·sure [ˈsenʃə] **1.** krytyka *f*, nagana *f*; △ *nie* **cenzura, cenzurka**; **2.** ⟨s⟩krytykować; ⟨z⟩ganić
cen·sus [ˈsensəs] spis *m* ludności; △ *nie* **cenzus**
cent [sent] cent *m* (*1/100 jednostki pieniężnej USA, etc.*); **per ~** procent *n*
cen·te·na·ry [senˈtiːnərɪ] stulecie *n*, setna rocznica *f*
cen·ten·ni·al [senˈtenjəl] **1.** stuletni; **2.** *Am.* → **centenary**
cen·ti·|grade [ˈsentɪɡreɪd]: **10 degrees ~grade** 10 stopni Celsjusza; '**~·me·tre**, *Brt.;* '**~·me·ter** *Am.* centymetr; **~pede** [ˈsentɪpiːd] *zo.* stonoga *f*
cen·tral [ˈsentrəl] centralny; główny; środkowy; △ *nie* **centrala**; **~ 'heating** ogrzewanie *n* centralne; **~·ize** [ˈsentrəlaɪz] ⟨s⟩centralizować; **~ 'locking** *mot.* zamek *m* centralny; **~ res·er·va·tion** *Brt.* pas *m* dzielący (*jezdnie na autostradzie*)
cen·tre *Brt.;* **cen·ter** *Am.* [ˈsentə] **1.** centrum *n*; środek *m*; ośrodek *m*; (*w piłce nożnej*) centra *f*, dośrodkowanie *n*; **2.** skupiać ⟨-pić⟩ (się); centrować, dośrodkowywać ⟨dośrodkować⟩; **~ 'back** (*w piłce nożnej*) stoper *m*; **~ 'for·ward** (*w piłce nożnej*) środkowy napastnik *m*; **~ of 'grav·i·ty** *phys.* punkt *m* ciężkości
cen·tu·ry [ˈsentʃʊrɪ] wiek *m*, stulecie *n*
ce·ram·ics [sɪˈræmɪks] *pl.* ceramika *f*, wyroby *pl.* ceramiczne
ce·re·al [ˈsɪərɪəl] **1.** zbożowy; **2.** zboże *n*, roślina *f* zbożowa; płatki *pl.* zbożowe; produkty *pl.* zbożowe (*na śniadanie*)
cer·e·bral [ˈserɪbrəl] *anat.* mózgowy
cer·e·mo·|ni·al [serɪˈməʊnjəl] **1.** ceremonialny, uroczysty; **2.** ceremonia *f*, uroczystość *f*; **~·ni·ous** [serɪˈməʊnjəs] ceremonialny, sztywny; **~·ny** [ˈserɪmənɪ] ceremonia *f*, uroczystość *f*; ceremoniał *m*

cer·tain ['sɜːtn] pewien, pewny; pewny, niejaki; niezawodny, pewny; '~·ly z pewnością, na pewno, niewątpliwie; (*w odpowiedzi*) oczywiście, naturalnie; '~·ty pewność *f*, przeświadczenie *n*; fakt *m* pewny

cer·tif·i·cate [sə'tɪfɪkət] świadectwo *n*; zaświadczenie *n*, metryka *f*; ~ *of* (*good*) *conduct* zaświadczenie *n* moralności; *General ♀ of Education advanced level* (*A level*) *Brt. szkoła:* jakby: matura *f*, świadectwo *n* dojrzałości; *General ♀ of Education ordinary level* (*O level*) *Brt. hist.* jakby: mała matura *f*, *medical* ~ świadectwo *n* lekarskie

cer·ti·fy ['sɜːtɪfaɪ] zaświadczać ⟨-czyć⟩; poświadczać ⟨-czyć⟩

cer·ti·tude ['sɜːtɪtjuːd] pewność *f*

CET [siː iː 'tiː] *skrót: Central European Time* czas *m* środkowoeuropejski

cf (*łacińskie confer*) *skrót pisany: compare* por., porównaj

chafe [tʃeɪf] *v/t.* ocierać ⟨otrzeć⟩; *v/i.* trzeć; ocierać

chaff [tʃɑːf] sieczka *f*, plewy *pl.*

chaf·finch ['tʃæfɪntʃ] *zo.* zięba *f*

chag·rin ['ʃæɡrɪn] **1.** rozgoryczenie *n*, żal *m*, frustracja *f*; **2.** rozgoryczać ⟨-czyć⟩, ⟨s⟩frustrować

chain [tʃeɪn] **1.** łańcuch *m*; *fig.* okowy *pl.*, pęta *pl.*; sieć *f* (*sklepów itp.*); **2.** przykuwać ⟨-kuć⟩ łańcuchem; wziąć na łańcuch; ~ re'ac·tion reakcja *f* łańcuchowa; '~·smok·er: *she/he is a ~·smoker* pali jednego (*papierosa*) za drugim; '~·smok·ing palenie *n* jednego (*papierosa*) za drugim; '~ *store* sklep *m* firmowy

chair [tʃeə] krzesło *n*, fotel *m*; katedra *f*; przewodniczenie *n*; przewodniczący *m* (*-ca f*); *be in the* ~ przewodniczyć; '~ *lift* wyciąg *m* krzesełkowy; '~·man (*pl. -men*) przewodniczący *m*; kierujący *m* dyskusją; '~·man·ship przewodniczenie *n*; '~·wom·an (*pl. -women*) przewodnicząca *f*, kierująca *f* dyskusją

chal·ice ['tʃælɪs] *mszalny* kielich *m*

chalk [tʃɔːk] **1.** kreda *f*; **2.** ⟨na⟩pisać kredą; zaznaczać ⟨-czyć⟩ kredą

chal·lenge ['tʃælɪndʒ] **1.** wyzwanie *n*; kwestionowanie *n*; **2.** wyzywać⟨-zwać⟩, rzucać ⟨-cić⟩ wyzwanie; ⟨za⟩kwestionować; '~·len·ger (*w sporcie*) pretendent *m*; ubiegający *m* (*-ca f*) się o tytuł

cham·ber ['tʃeɪmbə] *tech.* komora *f*; *parl.* izba *f*; *hist.* komnata *f*, sala *f*; '~·maid pokojówka *f*; ~ *of* '*com·merce* izba *f* handlowa

cham·ois ['ʃæmwɑː] *zo.* kozica *f*

cham·ois (*leath·er*) ['ʃæmɪ ⟨leðə⟩] zamsz *m*

champ [tʃæmp] F → *champion* (*sport*)

cham·pagne [ʃæm'peɪn] szampan *m*

cham·pi·on ['tʃæmpjən] bojownik *m* (-iczka *f*) (*of*), orędownik *m* (-iczka *f*); (*w sporcie*) mistrz(yni *f*) *m*; '~·ship mistrzostwa *pl.*

chance [tʃɑːns] **1.** przypadek *m*; okazja *f*, (korzystna) sposobność *f*; perspektywa *f*, możliwość *f*; ryzyko *n*; *by* ~ przypadkiem; *take a* ~ podejmować ⟨-djąć⟩ ryzyko; *take no* ~*s* nie ⟨za⟩ryzykować; **2.** przypadkowy; **2.** F ⟨za⟩ryzykować

chan·cel·lor ['tʃɑːnsələ] kanclerz *m*; *Brt.* rektor *m* (*honorowy uczelni*)

chan·de·lier [ʃændə'lɪə] kandelabr *m*, żyrandol *m*

change [tʃeɪndʒ] **1.** zmiana *f*, przemiana *f*, wymiana *f*, zamiana *f*; drobne *pl.* (*pieniądze*); reszta *f* (*z zapłaty*); *for a* ~ dla odmiany; ~ *for the better* (*worse*) *zmiana* na lepsze (gorsze); **2.** *v/t.* zmieniać ⟨-nić⟩, wymieniać ⟨-nić⟩ (*for* na *A*); zamieniać ⟨-nić⟩; *tech. mot.* zmieniać ⟨-nić⟩ (*biegi*); ~ *over* zmieniać ⟨-nić⟩, przechodzić ⟨przejść⟩ (*to* na *A*); ~ *trains* przesiadać się; *v/i.* zmieniać ⟨-nić⟩ się; ulegać ⟨ulec⟩ zmianie; zamieniać ⟨-nić⟩ się; '~·a·ble zmienny; '~ ma·chine automat *m* rozmieniający pieniądze; '~·o·ver zmiana *f*, przejście *n*

'**chang·ing room** (*w sporcie*) przebieralnia *f*, szatnia *f*

chan·nel ['tʃænl] **1.** kanał *m* (*też fig.*); *TV itp.* kanał *m*, program *m*; kanał *m*, sposób *m*, droga *f*; **2.** (*zwł. Brt. -ll-, Am. -l-*) *fig.* ⟨s⟩kierować; ♀ '**Is·lands** *pl.* Wyspy Normandzkie *pl.*; ♀ '**Tun·nel** tunel *m* pod kanałem La Manche

chant [tʃɑːnt] **1.** (*gregoriański itp.*) śpiew *m*; zaśpiew *m*; zawodzenie *n*, skandowanie *n*; **2.** ⟨za⟩śpiewać; *tłum itp.:* zawodzić, skandować

cha·os ['keɪɒs] chaos *m*

chap¹ [tʃæp] pęknięcie *n*

chap² [tʃæp] F facet *m*, gość *m*

chap·el ['tʃæpl] kaplica *f*

C

chap·lain ['tʃæplɪn] kapelan *m*

chap·ter ['tʃæptə] rozdział; *rel.* kapituła *f*

char [tʃɑː] (*-rr-*) zwęglać ⟨-lić⟩

char·ac·ter ['kærəktə] charakter *m*; reputacja *f*; (*drukarski, pisma itp.*) znak *m*, litera *f*; postać (*literacka itp.*) *f*; *theat.* rola *f*; **~·is·tic** [kærəktə'rɪstɪk] **1.** (*-ally*) charakterystyczny (*of* dla *G*); **2.** cecha *f* charakterystyczna; **~·ize** ['kærəktəraɪz] ⟨s⟩charakteryzować

char·coal ['tʃɑːkəʊl] węgiel *m* drzewny

charge [tʃɑːdʒ] **1.** *v/t.* akumulator, *broń itp.* ⟨na⟩ładować; zlecać ⟨-cić⟩; obciążać ⟨-żyć⟩; obwiniać ⟨-nić⟩, zarzucać ⟨-cić⟩ (*też jur.*); pobierać ⟨pobrać⟩, naliczać ⟨-czyć⟩ (*for* za *A*); *mil.* ⟨za⟩atakować, szturmować; **~ s.o. with s.th.** *econ.* zapisywać ⟨-sać⟩ coś na czyjś rachunek; *v/i.* **~ at s.o.** ⟨za⟩atakować kogoś, rzucać ⟨-cić⟩ się na kogoś; **2.** (*baterii, palny*) ładunek *m*; zlecenie *n*; odpowiedzialność *f*; zarzut *m* (*też jur.*), oskarżenie *n*; opłata *f*; atak *m*, szturm *m*; **~s** *pl.* koszty *pl.*, opłaty *pl.*, wydatki *pl.*; podopieczny *m* (-na *f*); **free of ~** bezpłatny; **be in ~ of** ponosić ⟨-nieść⟩ odpowiedzialność za (*A*), kierować; **take~ of** przejmować ⟨-jąć⟩ kierownictwo (*G*)

char·i·ot ['tʃærɪət] *poet. lub hist.* rydwan *m*

cha·ris·ma [kə'rɪzmə] charyzmat *m*

char·i·ta·ble ['tʃærɪtəbl] dobroczynny

char·i·ty ['tʃærətɪ] dobroczynność *f*; pobłażliwość *f*, wyrozumiałość; instytucja *f* dobroczynna

char·la·tan ['ʃɑːlətən] szarlatan(ka *f*) *m*; znachor *m*

charm [tʃɑːm] **1.** czar *m*, urok *m*; wdzięk *m*, urok *m*; talizman *m*, amulet *m*; **2.** ⟨o⟩czarować; **~·ing** czarujący

chart [tʃɑːt] mapa *f* (*morza, nieba, pogody*); diagram *m*, wykres *m*; **~s** *pl.* lista *f* przebojów

char·ter ['tʃɑːtə] **1.** statut *m*; *hist.* karta *f*, edykt *m*; czarter *m*; **2.** ⟨wy⟩czarterować, wynajmować ⟨-jąć⟩; **'~ flight** lot *m* czarterowy

char·wom·an ['tʃɑːwʊmən] (*pl. -wom·en*) sprzątaczka *f*

chase [tʃeɪs] **1.** pościg *m*, pogoń *f*; **2.** ścigać, gonić; ⟨po⟩pędzić, ⟨po⟩gnać

chas·m ['kæzəm] otchłań *f*, czeluść *f*, przepaść *f*

chaste [tʃeɪst] czysty, cnotliwy

chas·tise [tʃæ'staɪz] ⟨u⟩karać (*bijąc*)

chas·ti·ty ['tʃæstətɪ] płciowa czystość *f*; cnotliwość *f*

chat [tʃæt] **1.** pogawędka *f*, pogaduszka *f*; gadanina *f*; **2.** ⟨po⟩gawędzić (*sobie*); **'~ show** *Brt. TV* talk-show *m*; **~-show 'host** prezenter(ka *f*) *m* talk-show

chat·tels ['tʃætlz] *pl. zw.:* **goods and ~** dobytek *m*, majątek *m* ruchomy

chat·ter ['tʃætə] **1.** paplać; *małpa, ptak itp.:* ⟨za⟩skrzeczeć; *zęby itp.:* ⟨za⟩szczękać; **2.** paplanina *f*; skrzeczenie *n*; szczękanie *n*; '**~·box** F gaduła *m*, *f*, papla *m*, *f*

chat·ty ['tʃætɪ] (*-ier, -iest*) gadatliwy

chauf·feur ['ʃəʊfə] szofer *m*, kierowca *m*

chau·vinism ['ʃəʊvɪnɪzm] szowinizm *m*

chau·vin·ist ['ʃəʊvɪnɪst] szowinista *m* (*-tka f*); F **male ~ pig** męska szowinistyczna świnia *f*, męski szowinista *m*

cheap [tʃiːp] tani (*też fig.*); *fig.* podły; '**~·en** spadać ⟨spaść⟩ w cenie, zmniejszać ⟨-szyć⟩ wartość; *fig.* poniżać ⟨-żyć⟩ się

cheat [tʃiːt] **1.** oszust(ka *f*) *m*; szalbierz *m*; oszustwo *n*; **2.** oszukać ⟨-kać⟩

check [tʃek] **1.** sprawdzanie *n*, kontrola *f*; ograniczenie *n*, powstrzymanie *n*; odcinek *m* kontrolny, pokwitowanie *n*, kwit *m*; *Am.* żeton *m* (*do szatni, etc.*), numerek *m*; *Am.* czek *m*; *Am.* ptaszek *m*, znaczek *m* (*na pozycji listy*); *Am.* paragon *m*, wydruk *m* kasowy; (*w szachach*) szach *m*; kratka *f* (*na materiale*), materiał *m* w kratkę; **keep s.th. in ~** powstrzymywać ⟨-mać⟩ coś; **2.** *v/i.* zatrzymywać ⟨-mać⟩ się (*nagle*); **~ in** ⟨za⟩meldować się (*w hotelu itp.*) (*at* w *L*); *aviat.* zgłaszać ⟨zgłosić⟩ się do odprawy; **~ out** ⟨wy⟩meldować się (*z hotelu itp.*); **~ up (on)** F sprawdzać ⟨-dzić⟩, ⟨z⟩weryfikować; *v/t.* sprawdzać ⟨-dzić⟩, ⟨s⟩kontrolować; zatrzymywać ⟨-mać⟩, wstrzymywać ⟨-mać⟩, ⟨za⟩hamować; *Am.* zaznaczać ⟨-czyć⟩ (*na liście*); *Am.* zostawiać ⟨-wić⟩ (*w szatni itp.*); (*w szachach*⟨za⟩szachować; '**~·card** *Am.* gwarancyjna karta *f* czekowa (*określająca wysokość pokrycia czeku*); **~ed** [tʃekt]

kratkowany, w kratkę; **~·ers** *Am.*
['tʃekəz] *sg.* warcaby *pl.*; **'~·in** zamel-
dowanie *n* się; *aviat.* odprawa *f*; **'~·in**
coun·ter *aviat.*, **'~·in desk** *aviat.* miejsce *n* odpraw; **'~·ing ac·count** *Am.*
econ. rachunek czekowy *m*, *jakby:* rachunek *m* oszczędnościowo-rozlicze-
niowy; **'~·ist** lista *f* kontrolna; **'~·mate**
1. (*w szachach*) szach-mat *m*; **2.** dawać
⟨dać⟩ mata; **'~·out** wymeldowanie *n*
się (*z hotelu*); **'~·out coun·ter** kasa *f*
(*zwł.* **w** *supermarkecie*); **'~·point** punkt
m kontrolny; **'~·room** *Am.* garderoba *f*,
szatnia *f*; przechowalnia *f* bagażu;
'~·up sprawdzenie *n*, kontrola *f*; *med.*
kontrola *f* lekarska

cheek [tʃiːk] policzek *m*; F czelność *f*;
bezczelność; **'~·y** F (*-ier, -iest*) bezczelny

cheer [tʃɪə] **1.** wiwat *m*, aplauz *m*; otucha *f*, pociecha *f*; **three ~s!** trzy razy
hura!; **~s!** na zdrowie!; **2.** *v/t.* wiwatować na cześć; *też* **~ on** kibicować; *też*
~ up pocieszać ⟨-szyć⟩ dodawać ⟨do-
dać⟩ otuchy; *v/i.* wiwatować; cieszyć się;
też **~ up** rozchmurzać ⟨-rzyć⟩ się; **~ up!**
głowa do góry!; **'~·ful** wesoły, radosny,
pogodny

cheer·i·o [tʃɪərɪ'əʊ] *int.* Brt. cześć!

'cheer·lead·er organizator *m* wiwa-
tów (*zwykle dziewczyna*); **'~·less** ponury; **~·y** ['tʃɪərɪ] (*-ier, -iest*) radosny

cheese [tʃiːz] ser *m*

chee·tah ['tʃiːtə] gepard *m*

chef [ʃef] szef *m* kuchni; ⚠ *nie szef*

chem·i·cal ['kemɪkl] **1.** chemiczny; **2.**
chemikalia *pl.*, środek *m* chemiczny

chem|·ist ['kemɪst] chemik *m* (-micz-
ka *f*); aptekarz *m* (-arka *f*); pracownik *m* (-ica *f*) lub właściciel(ka *f*) *m*
drogerii; **~·is·try** ['kemɪstrɪ] chemia *f*;
'~·ist's shop apteka *f*; drogeria *f*

chem·o·ther·a·py [kiːməʊ'θerəpɪ]
med. chemioterapia *f*

cheque [tʃek] Brt. econ. (*Am.* **check**)
czek *m*; **crossed ~** czek *m* zakreślony;
'~ ac·count konto *n* czekowe; **'~ card**
Brt. karta *f* czekowa (*określająca wysokość pokrycia czeku*)

cher·ry ['tʃerɪ] *bot.* wiśnia *f*; czereśnia *f*

chess [tʃes] szachy *pl.*; **a game of ~** partia *f* szachów; **'~·board** szachownica *f*;
'~·man (*pl.* **-men**) bierka *f* szachowa;
'~ piece figura *f*

chest [tʃest] *anat.* klatka *f* piersiowa,
piersi *pl.*; skrzynia *f*, kufer *m*; **get s.th.**
off one's ~ zrzucić ten ciężar *z* serca

chest·nut ['tʃesnʌt] **1.** *bot.* kasztan *m*,
kasztanowiec *m*; **2.** kasztanowy

chest of drawers [tʃest əv 'drɔːz] komoda *f*

chew [tʃuː] żuć, przeżuć ⟨-żuwać⟩;
'~·ing gum guma *f* do żucia

chick [tʃɪk] pisklę *n*; F (*dziewczyna*) laska *f*

chick·en ['tʃɪkɪn] kurczę *n*, kur-
czak *m*; **~'heart·ed** tchórzliwy, strachliwy; **~ pox** ['tʃɪkɪnpɒks] *med.* ospa *f*
wietrzna

chic·o·ry ['tʃɪkərɪ] *bot.* cykoria *f*

chief [tʃiːf] **1.** główny, naczelny, najważniejszy; **2.** kierownik *m* (-iczka *f*),
szef(owa *f*) *m*; naczelnik *m*; wódz *m*;
'~·ly głównie

chil·blain ['tʃɪlbleɪn] odmrożenie *n*

child [tʃaɪld] (*pl.* **children**) dziecko *n*;
from a ~ od dziecka, od okresu dzieciń-
stwa; **with ~** ciężarny; **~ a·buse** znęcanie *n* się nad dziećmi; **~ 'ben·e·fit**
Brt. zasiłek *f* rodzinny; **'~·birth** poród
m; **~·hood** ['tʃaɪldhʊd] dzieciństwo *n*;
'~·ish *fig.* dziecinny; **'~·like** dziecinny;
dziecięcy; **'~·mind·er** opiekun *m* *f*
do dzieci (*zwykle do południa, we własnym domu*)

chil·dren ['tʃɪldrən] *pl. od* **child**

chill [tʃɪl] **1.** chłodny (*też fig.*); **2.** chłód
m (*też fig.*); przeziębienie *n*; **3.** ⟨s⟩chło-
dzić, schładzać ⟨-dzić⟩; ⟨o⟩ziębić się;
'~·y (*-ier, -iest*) chłodny (*też fig.*)

chime [tʃaɪm] **1.** kurant *m*; dźwięk *m* lub
bicie *n* dzwonu; **2.** ⟨za⟩dzwonić

chim·ney ['tʃɪmnɪ] komin *m*; **'~·sweep**
kominiarz *m*

chimp [tʃɪmp], **chim·pan·zee** [tʃɪm-
pən'ziː] *zo.* szympans *m*

chin [tʃɪn] broda *f*, podbródek *m*; **~ up!**
głowa do góry!

chi·na ['tʃaɪnə] porcelana *f*

Chi·na ['tʃaɪnə] Chiny *pl.*; **Chi·nese**
[tʃaɪ'niːz] **1.** chiński; **2.** Chińczyk *m*,
Chinka *f*; język *m* chiński; **the ~** Chiń-
czycy

chink [tʃɪŋk] szczelina *f*; *fig.* słaby punkt
m; brzęczenie *n*

chip [tʃɪp] **1.** wiór *m*, drzazga *f*; okruch
m, odłamek *m*, szczerba *f*, wyszczerbienie *n*; żeton *m*, szton *m*; *komp.* płytka *f*

półprzewodnika, F kość f; 2. (**-pp-**) v/t.
wyszczerbiać ⟨-bić⟩; ⟨wy⟩strugać; v/i.
wyszczerbiać ⟨-bić⟩ się

chips [tʃɪps] pl. Brt. frytki pl.; Am. chipsy pl., chrupki pl.

chi·rop·o·dist [kɪ'rɒpədɪst] specjalista m (-tka f) od chorób stóp; pedikurzysta m (-ka f)

chirp [tʃɜːp] ćwierkać; owady: cykać, brzęczeć

chis·el ['tʃɪzl] 1. dłuto n; 2. (zwł. Brt. **-ll-**, Am. **-l-**) ⟨wy⟩dłutować

chit-chat ['tʃɪttʃæt] pogaduszki pl.

chiv·al·rous ['ʃɪvlrəs] rycerski

chive [tʃaɪv(z)] (**-s** pl.) bot. szczypior m,
F szczypiorek m

chlo·ri·nate ['klɔːrɪneɪt] chlorować;
chlo·rine ['klɔːriːn] chem. chlor m

chlor·o·form ['klɔrəfɔːm] chem., med.
1. chloroform m; 2. ⟨za⟩stosować chloroform

choc·o·late ['tʃɒkələt] czekolada f, czekoladka f, pralinka f; **'~s** pl. czekoladki pl.

choice [tʃɔɪs] 1. wybór m; rzecz f wybrana, osoba f wybrana; 2. pierwszej jakości; najlepszy; dobrany

choir ['kwaɪə] chór m

choke [tʃəʊk] 1. ⟨za⟩dławić (się), dusić (się); **~ back** gniew itp. ⟨z⟩dusić, łzy itp.
⟨po⟩wstrzymywać; **~ down** słowa ⟨po⟩wstrzymywać; też **~ up** zatykać (się);
2. mot. zasysacz m, F ssanie n

choose [tʃuːz] (**chose**, **chosen**) wybierać ⟨wybrać⟩; postanawiać ⟨postanowić⟩ (**to do s.th.** coś zrobić)

chop [tʃɒp] 1. cios m; gastr. kotlet m;
2. (**-pp-**) v/t. ⟨po⟩rąbać, ⟨po⟩siekać;
~ down ⟨z⟩rąbać; v/i. rąbać; '~**per** tasak m; F helikopter m; '~**py** wzburzony; '~**stick** pałeczka f (do jedzenia)

cho·ral ['kɔːrəl] chóralny

cho·rale [kɒ'rɑːl] chorał m

chord [kɔːd] mus. akord m

chore [tʃɔː] nieprzyjemna lub ciężka praca f; **~s** praca f domowa

cho·rus ['kɔːrəs] chór m; refren m; zespół m (tancerzy lub śpiewaków), zespół m towarzyszący

chose [tʃəʊz] pret. od **choose**;
cho·sen ['tʃəʊzn] p.p. od **choose**

Christ [kraɪst] Chrystus m

chris·ten ['krɪsn] ⟨o⟩chrzcić; '~**ing** chrzest m; attr. chrzestny

Chris·tian ['krɪstʃən] 1. chrześcijański;
2. chrześcijanin m (-anka f); **Chris·ti·an·i·ty** [krɪstɪ'ænətɪ] chrześcijaństwo n

'**Christian name** imię n

Christ·mas ['krɪsməs] Boże Narodzenie n; **at ~** na Boże Narodzenie, w ciągu Bożego Narodzenia; attr. bożonarodzeniowy; **~ 'Day** pierwszy dzień m Bożego Narodzenia; **~ 'Eve** wigilia f Bożego Narodzenia

chrome [krəʊm] chem. (pierwiastek)
chrom m; **chro·mi·um** ['krəʊmjəm]
(pierwiastek) chrom m

chron·ic ['krɒnɪk] (**~ally**) chroniczny,
przewlekły

chron·i·cle ['krɒnɪkl] kronika f

chron·o·log·i·cal [krɒnə'lɒdʒɪkl]
(**~ally**) chronologiczny; **chro·nol·o·gy** [krə'nɒlədʒɪ] chronologia f

chub·by ['tʃʌbɪ] F (**-ier, -est**) pyzaty,
pucołowaty

chuck [tʃʌk] F 1. rzucać ⟨-cić⟩; **~ out** wyrzucać ⟨-cić⟩; **~ up** pracę itp. rzucać ⟨-cić⟩; 2. uchwyt m (wiertła itp.)

chuck·le ['tʃʌkl] 1. ⟨za⟩chichotać; 2. chichot m

chum [tʃʌm] kumpel F m (-ka f), przyjaciel m (-ciółka f); '~**my** F (**-ier, -iest**) zaprzyjaźniony

chump [tʃʌmp] głuptas m

chunk [tʃʌnk] kawał m, bryła f

Chun·nel ['tʃʌnl] F → **Channel Tunnel**

church [tʃɜːtʃ] kościół m; attr. kościelny; '~ **ser·vice** nabożeństwo n; '~**yard** cmentarz m (przy kościele)

churl·ish ['tʃɜːlɪʃ] arogancki, grubiański

churn [tʃɜːn] 1. maselnica f; Brt. bańka f lub kanka f na mleko; 2. ⟨z⟩robić masło (w maselnicy); fig. wzburzać ⟨-rzyć⟩ się

chute [ʃuːt] zjeżdżalnia f; zsyp m (na śmieci); tech. rynna f zsypowa; F spadochron m; próg m wodny

CIA [si: aɪ 'eɪ] skrót: **Central Intelligence Agency** CIA, Centralna Agencja f Wywiadowcza (w USA)

CID [si: aɪ 'di:] skrót: **Criminal Investigation Department** (wydział policji kryminalnej w Wielkiej Brytanii)

ci·der ['saɪdə] (Am. **hard ~**) jabłecznik m, wino n jabłkowe; (Am. **sweet ~**) sok m jabłkowy

cif [si: aɪ 'ef] *skrót:* **cost, insurance, freight** koszt, ubezpieczenie i fracht

ci·gar [sɪ'gɑː] cygaro *n*

cig·a·rette, cig·a·ret [sɪgə'ret] *Am.* papieros *m*

cinch [sɪntʃ] F (*łatwa rzecz*) małe piwo *n*, pestka *f*

cin·der ['sɪndə] żużel *m*; **~s** *pl.* popiół *m*

Cin·de·rel·la [sɪndə'relə] Kopciuszek *m*

cin·der track (*w sporcie*) tor *m* żużlowy; żużel *m*

cin·e|·cam·e·ra ['sɪnɪkæmərə] kamera *f* filmowa (*na wąski film*); **'~·film** (wąska) taśma *f* filmowa

cin·e·ma ['sɪnəmə] *Brt.* kino *n*; kino *n*, film *m*, sztuka *f* filmowa

cin·na·mon ['sɪnəmən] cynamon *m*

ci·pher ['saɪfə] szyfr *m*, zero *n* (*też fig.*)

cir·cle ['sɜːkl] **1.** krąg *m*, koło *n*; *theat.* balkon *m*; *fig.* krąg *m*

cir·cuit ['sɜːkɪt] obieg *m*, okrążenie *n*; *electr.* obwód *m*, układ *m*; objazd *m*; *sport:* runda *f* spotkań; **short ~** *electr.* zwarcie *n*

cir·cu·i·tous [sə'kjuːɪtəs] okrężny

cir·cu·lar ['sɜːkjʊlə] **1.** kołowy, kolisty; okrężny; **2.** okólnik *m*, nota *f*; druk *m* reklamowy

cir·cu|·late ['sɜːkjʊleɪt] *v/i.* krążyć, wchodzić ⟨wejść⟩ w obieg; *v/t.* wprowadzać ⟨-dzić⟩ w obieg, rozprowadzać⟨-dzić⟩; **'~·lat·ing li·bra·ry** wypożyczalnia *f*; **~·la·tion** [sɜːkjʊ'leɪʃn] obieg *m*, krążenie *n* (*też anat.*); cyrkulacja *f*; *econ.* krążenie *n*; nakład *m* (*czasopisma*)

cir·cum·fer·ence [sə'kʌmfərəns] obwód *m*

cir·cum·nav·i·gate [sɜːkəm'nævɪgeɪt] okrążać ⟨-żyć⟩

cir·cum·scribe ['sɜːkəmskraɪb] *math.* opisywać ⟨-sać⟩; *fig.* ograniczać ⟨-czyć⟩

cir·cum·spect ['sɜːkəmspekt] ostrożny, przezorny

cir·cum·stance ['sɜːkəmstəns] okoliczność *f*; warunek *m*; **~s** *pl.* okoliczności *pl.*; *in lub under no ~s* w żadnym wypadku; *in lub under the ~s* w tej sytuacji

cir·cum·stan·tial [sɜːkəm'stænʃl] pośredni; szczegółowy; **~ evidence** dowody *pl.* poszlakowe

cir·cus ['sɜːkəs] cyrk *m*; *Brt.* plac *m*

CIS [si: aɪ 'es] *skrót:* **Commonwealth of Independent States** WNP, Wspólnota Niepodległych Państw

cis·tern ['sɪstən] cysterna *f*, zbiornik *m*; spłuczka *f*

ci·ta·tion [saɪ'teɪʃn] *jur.* wezwanie *n*; cytat *m*; **cite** [saɪt] *jur.* wzywać ⟨wezwać⟩, pozywać ⟨pozwać⟩; ⟨za⟩cytować

cit·i·zen ['sɪtɪzn] obywatel(ka *f*) *m*; **'~·ship** obywatelstwo *n*

cit·y ['sɪtɪ] **1.** (duże) miasto *n*; *the* ♀ City *n*; **2.** miejski; **~ 'cen·tre** *Brt.* centrum *n* miasta; **~ 'coun·cil·(l)or** *Am.* rajca *m* (-jczyni *f*); **~ 'hall** ratusz *m* *zwł. Am.* zarząd *m* miasta; **~ 'slick·er** *często pej.* mieszczuch *m*; **~ 'va·grant** włóczęga *m*, tramp *m*

civ·ic ['sɪvɪk] obywatelski; miejski; **'~s** wychowanie *n* obywatelskie

civ·il ['sɪvl] cywilny (*też jur.*); obywatelski; społeczny; uprzejmy; △ *nie cywil*; **ci·vil·i·an** [sɪ'vɪljən] cywil *m*

ci·vil·i·ty [sɪ'vɪlətɪ] uprzejmość *f*

civ·i·li|·za·tion [sɪvɪlaɪ'zeɪʃn] cywilizacja *f*; **~·ze** ['sɪvɪlaɪz] ⟨u⟩cywilizować

civ·il 'rights *pl.* prawa *pl.* obywatelskie; **~ rights 'ac·tiv·ist** działacz(ka *f*) *m* ruchu obywatelskiego; **~ rights 'move·ment** ruch *m* obywatelski

civ·il| 'ser·vant urzędnik *m* (-iczka *f*) państwowy (-a); **~ 'ser·vice** administracja *f* państwowa; **~ 'war** wojna *f* domowa

CJD [si: dʒeɪ di:] *skrót:* **Creutzfeld(t)-Jakob disease** choroba *f* Creutzfelda-Jakoba

clad [klæd] **1.** *pret. i p.p. od* **clothe**; **2.** odziany, przyodziany

claim [kleɪm] **1.** żądanie *n*, roszczenie *n*; pretensja *f*; reklamacja *f*, zażalenie *n*; prawo *n*; *Am.* działka *f* górnicza; twierdzenie *n*; **2.** ⟨za⟩żądać, domagać się; twierdzić

clair·voy·ant [kleə'vɔɪənt] jasnowidz *m*

clam·ber ['klæmbə] ⟨wy⟩gramolić się, ⟨wy⟩leźć

clam·my ['klæmɪ] (**-ier, -iest**) lepki, kleisty

clam·o(u)r ['klæmə] **1.** wrzawa *f*, zgiełk *m*, larum *n*; **2.** domagać się (**for** o G)

clamp [klæmp] *tech.* zacisk *m*, klamra *f*; *mot.* (*klamra blokująca*) klema *f*

clan [klæn] klan *m*

clan·des·tine [klæn'destɪn] potajemny, tajny

clang [klæŋ] ⟨za⟩dźwięczeć, ⟨za⟩brzęczeć

clank [klæŋk] **1.** brzęczenie *n*, łoskot *m*; **2.** ⟨za⟩brzęczeć, ⟨za⟩łoskotać

clap [klæp] **1.** łoskot *m*, grzmot *m*; aplauz *m*; klepnięcie *n*; **2.** (**-pp-**) ⟨za⟩klaskać; klepnąć

clar·et ['klærət] czerwone wino *z*

clar·i·fy ['klærɪfaɪ] *v/t.* wyjaśniać ⟨-śnić⟩, ⟨wy⟩tłumaczyć; *v/i.* tłumaczyć się; *tłuszcz itp.:* ⟨wy⟩klarować się

clar·i·net [klærɪ'net] *muz.* klarnet *m*

clar·i·ty ['klærətɪ] jasność *f*

clash [klæʃ] **1.** zderzenie *n*, konflikt *m*; starcie *n*, szczęk *m*; **2.** zderzyć się; ścierać się; kolidować; nie pasować (**with** do *G*)

clasp [klɑːsp] **1.** objema *f*, klamra *f*; zatrzask *m*, zapięcie *n*; **2.** obejmować ⟨objąć⟩, ściskać ⟨ścisnąć⟩; zamykać ⟨zamknąć⟩; '~knife (*pl.* **-knives**) nóż *m* składany

class [klɑːs] **1.** klasa *f*, kurs *m*, zajęcia *pl.* (**in** z *G*); *Am.* rocznik *m* (*absolwentów*); **2.** ⟨s-, za⟩klasyfikować

clas·sic ['klæsɪk] **1.** klasyk *m*; **2.** (**-ally**) klasyczny; '~si·cal klasyczny

clas·si·fi·ca·tion [klæsɪfɪ'keɪʃn] klasyfikacja *f*; ~fied ['klæsɪfaɪd] sklasyfikowany; *mil.*, *pol.* poufny; ~fied 'ad drobne ogłoszenie *n*; ~fy ['klæsɪfaɪ] ⟨za⟩klasyfikować, ⟨po⟩grupować

'**class|·mate** kolega *m* (-żanka *f*) z klasy; '~room klasa *f*, pomieszczenie *n* szkolne

clat·ter ['klætə] **1.** stukot *m*, stukanie *n*; łomot *m*; **2.** ⟨za⟩stukać; ⟨za⟩łomotać

clause [klɔːz] *jur.* klauzula *f*, paragraf *m*; *gr.* zdanie *n* (składowe)

claw [klɔː] **1.** szpon *m*, pazur *m*; kleszcz *m* (*raka*); **2.** ⟨za-, po⟩drapać

clay [kleɪ] glina *f*, ił *m*

clean [kliːn] **1.** *adj.* czysty; porządny, równy; (*bez narkotyków*) *sl.* czysty; **2.** zupełnie, całkowicie, całkiem; **3.** ⟨wy⟩czyścić, oczyszczać, ⟨wy⟩sprzątać; ~out ⟨wy⟩czyścić; ~ up gruntownie ⟨wy⟩czyścić; ⟨u⟩porządkować; '~er sprzątaczka *f*; osoba *f* myjąca (*okna itp.*); środek *m* czyszczący; ~s *pl.* pralnia *f* (*chemiczna*); **take to the ~ers** zanosić ⟨-nieść⟩ do pralni; F oskubać (*z pienię-*

dzy); '~ing: **do the ~ing** sprzątać; → **spring-cleaning**; ~li·ness ['klenlɪnɪs] czystość *f*, porządek *m*; ~ly **1.** ['kliːnlɪ] *adv.* porządnie; **2.** ['klenlɪ] *adj.* (**-ier, -iest**) czysty, porządny

cleanse [klenz] ⟨o⟩czyścić, oczyszczać ⟨oczyścić⟩; '**cleans·er** środek *m* czyszczący

clear [klɪə] **1.** jasny; czysty; klarowny, przezroczysty; wyraźny; wolny (**of** od *G*); *econ.* netto; **2.** *v/t.* oczyszczać ⟨oczyścić⟩; ⟨z⟩robić jasnym; usuwać ⟨usunąć⟩, sprzątać ⟨-tnąć⟩ (*też* ~ **away**); *las* ⟨wy⟩karczować; zaaprobować, udzielać ⟨-lić⟩ zezwolenia na (*A*); *przeszkodę itp.* pokonywać ⟨-nać⟩; *econ.* dokonywać ⟨-nać⟩ odprawy celnej; *dług* ⟨u⟩regulować; (*w sporcie*) wybijać ⟨-bić⟩ (*piłkę itp.*); *jur.* uniewinniać ⟨-nnić⟩; *v/i.* oczyszczać ⟨oczyścić⟩ się; *niebo itp.:* przejaśniać ⟨-śnić⟩ się; *fig.* rozchmurzać ⟨-rzyć⟩ się; przerzedzać ⟨-dzić⟩ się; ~ **out** ⟨u-, s⟩przątnąć; F zmywać się; ~ **up** ⟨z⟩robić porządek; uporać się; *zagadkę* rozwiązywać ⟨-zać⟩; *pogoda:* przejaśniać ⟨-śnić⟩ się; ~ance ['klɪərəns] oczyszczenie *n*; usunięcie *n*; *tech.* prześwit *m*, odstęp *m*; zwolnienie *n*; odprawa *f*; '~ance sale wyprzedaż *f* (*likwidacyjna*); ~ing ['klɪərɪŋ] polana *f*

cleave [kliːv] (**cleaved** *lub* **cleft** *lub* **clove, cleaved** *lub* **cleft** *lub* **cloven**) rozszczepiać ⟨-pić⟩; '**cleav·er** tasak *m*

clef [klef] *mus.* klucz *m*

cleft [kleft] **1.** rozszczepienie *n*, szczelina *f*, szpara *f*; **2.** *pret.* i *p.p. od* **cleave**

clem·en·cy ['klemənsɪ] łaska *f*; pobłażliwość *f*, wyrozumiałość *f*; '~ent łagodny

clench [klentʃ] *wargi, pięść itp.* zaciskać ⟨-snąć⟩

cler·gy ['klɜːdʒɪ] kler *m*, duchowieństwo *n*; ~man (*pl.* -**men**) duchowny *m*

clerk [klɑːk] urzędnik *m* (-iczka *f*); *Am.* sprzedawca *m* (-czyni *f*)

clev·er ['klevə] roztropny, mądry; sprytny

click [klɪk] **1.** pstryknięcie *n*, szczęknięcie *n*, stuknięcie *n*; *komp.* kliknięcie *n*; mlaśnięcie *n* (*językiem*); **2.** *v/i.:* ~ **shut** zamknąć się ze szczękiem; *v/t.* pstrykać ⟨-knąć⟩, szczękać ⟨szczęknąć⟩, stukać ⟨-knąć⟩; *komp.* kliknąć na (*A*)

cli·ent ['klaɪənt] klient(ka f) m

cliff [klɪf] klif m

cli·mate ['klaɪmɪt] klimat m (też fig.)

cli·max ['klaɪmæks] punkt m kulminacyjny; klimaks m; szczytowanie n, orgazm m

climb [klaɪm] v/i. wspinać ⟨wspiąć⟩ się; iść ⟨pójść⟩ w górę; wchodzić ⟨wejść⟩, ⟨po⟩leźć; **go ~ing** uprawiać wspinaczkę; v/t. wspinać ⟨wspiąć⟩ się po (I); wchodzić ⟨wejść⟩ na (A) lub po (I); '**~·er** alpinista m (-tka f); bot. roślina f pnąca

clinch [klɪntʃ] **1.** tech. zaciskać ⟨-snąć⟩ (w boksie) wchodzić ⟨wejść⟩ w zwarcie, klinczować; rozstrzygać ⟨-gnąć⟩; **that ~ed** to było rozstrzygające; **2.** tech. zaciśnięcie; (w boksie) zwarcie n, klincz m

cling [klɪŋ] (clung) (to) przylegać ⟨-lec⟩ (do G); przytulać ⟨-lić⟩ się, przywrzeć ⟨-wierać⟩ (do G); '**~·film** samoprzylegająca folia f (do żywności)

clin·ic ['klɪnɪk] klinika f; '**~·i·cal** kliniczny

clink [klɪŋk] **1.** brzęk m; **2.** ⟨za⟩brzęczeć, ⟨za⟩dzwonić (łańcuchem)

clip¹ [klɪp] **1.** (-pp-) przycinać ⟨-ciąć⟩, owcę itp. ⟨o⟩strzyc; **2.** cięcie n, nacięcie n; wideo itp.: klip m lub clip m; urywek m (filmu)

clip² [klɪp] **1.** klamra f, spinacz m; zacisk m; klips m; magazynek m (do broni); **2.** (-pp-) spinać ⟨spiąć⟩; zaciskać ⟨zacisnąć⟩

clip·per ['klɪpə]: (a pair of) **~·pers** pl. nożyce pl., sekator m; cążki pl., obcinarka f; maszynka f do włosów; '**~·pings** pl. wycinki pl.; skrawki pl., obcinki pl.

clit·o·ris ['klɪtərɪs] anat. łechtaczka f

cloak [kləʊk] **1.** peleryna f; **2.** fig. okrywać ⟨-ryć⟩; '**~·room** garderoba f; Brt. toaleta f

clock [klɒk] **1.** ścienny, wieżowy zegar m; **9 o'** 9 godzina; licznik m; **2.** (w sporcie) ⟨z⟩mierzyć (czas); **~ in**, **~ on** podbijać ⟨-bić⟩ kartę (przychodząc); **~ out**, **~ off** podbijać ⟨-bić⟩ kartę (wychodząc); '**~·wise** [ˈklɒkwaɪz] zgodnie z ruchem wskazówek zegara; '**~·work** werk m, mechanizm m zegarowy; **like ~·work** jak w zegarku

clod [klɒd] gruda f, bryła f

clog [klɒg] **1.** chodak m, drewniak m;

kłoda f (też fig.); **2.** (-gg-) też **~ up** zatykać ⟨zatkać⟩

clois·ter ['klɔɪstə] krużganek m; klasztor m

close 1. [kləʊs] adj. zamknięty; bliski; tłumaczenie itp.: dokładny; gęsty, ścisły, zwarty; dzień itp.: duszny; przyjaciel itp.: serdeczny, bliski; **keep a ~ watch on** dobrze pilnować (A); **2.** [kləʊs] adv. ściśle; dokładnie; blisko; gęsto; **~ by** tuż obok, w pobliżu; **3.** [kləʊz] koniec m, zakończenie n; zamknięcie n; **come lub draw to a ~** zbliżać się do końca; [kləʊs] Brt. mała zamknięta uliczka; **4.** [kləʊz] v/t. zamykać ⟨-knąć⟩; ⟨s-, za⟩kończyć; v/i. zamykać ⟨-knąć⟩ się; ⟨s-, za⟩kończyć się; **~ down** program TV itp. ⟨s-, za⟩kończyć ⟨się⟩; fabrykę itp. zamykać ⟨-knąć⟩ ⟨się⟩; **~ in** okrążać ⟨-żyć⟩; fig. nadchodzić ⟨nadejść⟩; **~ up** zamykać ⟨-knąć⟩ ⟨się⟩; szeregi zwierać ⟨zewrzeć⟩; **~d** zamknięty

clos·et ['klɒzɪt] szafa f ścienna; △ nie klozet

close-up ['kləʊsʌp] phot., film. powiększenie n

clos·ing date ['kləʊzɪŋdeɪt] termin m ostateczny, ostatni dzień m; '**~ time** godzina f zamknięcia;

clot [klɒt] **1.** bryła f, grudka f; **~ of blood** med. skrzep m; **2.** (-tt-) ⟨s⟩krzepnąć

cloth [klɒθ] (pl. **cloths** [klɒðs, klɒðz]) tkanina f, sukno n; ścierka f, ściereczka f; szmatka f; '**~·bound** oprawny w płótno

clothe [kləʊð] (clothed lub clad) ubierać ⟨ubrać⟩

clothes [kləʊðz] pl. ubranie n, ubrania pl., odzież f; (uprana bielizna) pranie n; '**~ bas·ket** kosz m na pranie; '**~ horse** suszarka f do rozwieszania bielizny; '**~ line** sznur m na bieliznę; '**~ peg** Brt., '**~·pin** Am. klamerka f (do bielizny)

cloth·ing ['kləʊðɪŋ] ubranie n, odzież f

cloud [klaʊd] **1.** chmura f, obłok m; zachmurzenie n; fig. cień m; **2.** ⟨za⟩chmurzyć (się) (też fig.); '**~·burst** oberwanie n chmury; '**~·less** bezchmurny; '**~·y** (-ier, -iest) zachmurzony

clout [klaʊt] F cios m, F walnięcie n; fig. siła f przebicia, wpływ m;

clove¹ [kləʊv] bot., gastr. goździk m; **a ~ of garlic** ząbek m czosnku

clove[2] [kləuv] *pret. od* **cleave**; clo·ven
['kləuvn] *pret. od* **cleave**; clo·ven
'hoof (*pl.* **- hoofs, - hooves**) *zo.* racica *f*

clo·ver ['kləuvə] *bot.* koniczyna *f*

clown [klaun] klown *m, klaun m*

club [klʌb] **1.** pałka *f,* kij *m; sport:* kij *m;*
klub *m;* **~s** *pl.* trefle *pl.;* **2.** (**-bb-**) obijać
〈obić〉 pałką; '**~·foot** (*pl.* **-feet**) zdefor-
mowana stopa *f*

cluck [klʌk] **1.** 〈za〉gdakać; **2.** gdakanie *n*

clue [kluː] wskazówka *f,* klucz *m;*
(*w krzyżówce*) określenie *n*

clump [klʌmp] **1.** grupa *f,* kępa *f;* bryła *f,* grud(k)a *f;* **2.** ciężko chodzić 〈iść〉

clum·sy ['klʌmzɪ] (**-ier, -iest**) niezgrabny, niezręczny

clung [klʌŋ] *pret. i p.p. od* **cling**

clus·ter ['klʌstə] **1.** skupisko *n,* grupa *f;*
bot. grono *n,* kiść *f;* **2.** skupiać 〈-pić〉 się

clutch [klʌtʃ] **1.** uścisk *m; tech.* sprzęgło *n; fig.* szpon *m;* **2.** ściskać 〈ścisnąć〉
(*mocno*)

CNN [siː en 'en] *skrót:* **Cable News Network** (*amerykańska telewizja kablowa,
nadająca wiadomości ze świata*)

c/o [siː 'əu] *skrót:* **care of** na adres, pod
adresem

Co[1] [kəu] *skrót:* **company** *econ.* spółka *f*

Co[2] *skrót pisany:* **County** *Brt.* hrabstwo
n; Am. okręg *m* (*wyborczy*)

coach [kəutʃ] **1.** autobus *m* (*turystyczny*), autokar *m; Brt. rail.* wagon *m* osobowy; powóz *m; sport:* trener(ka *f*) *m;*
korepetytor(ka *f*) *m;* **2.** *sport:* trenować; dawać 〈dać〉 korepetycje; '**~·man**
(*pl.* **-men**) trener *m*

co·ag·u·late [kəu'ægjuleɪt] 〈s〉koagu-
lować, 〈s〉krzepnąć

coal [kəul] węgiel *m;* **carry ~s to New-
castle** wozić drewno do lasu

co·a·li·tion [kəuə'lɪʃn] *pol.* koalicja *f;*
przymierze *n*

'coal·mine, '**~·pit** kopalnia *f*

coarse [kɔːs] (**-r, -st**) gruby, chropowaty; surowy; grubiański

coast [kəust] **1.** brzeg *m;* **2.** *naut.* płynąć
wzdłuż wybrzeża; jechać rozpędem
(*samochodem, rowerem itp.*); *Am.* ślizgać się; '**~·guard** straż *f* przybrzeżna;
'**~·line** linia *f* brzegowa

coat [kəut] **1.** płaszcz *m; zo.* sierść *f;*
warstwa *f,* powłoka *f* (*farby itp.*); **2.** po-

wlekać 〈powlec〉, pokrywać 〈po-
kryć〉, nakładać 〈nałożyć〉 powłokę;
'**~ hang·er** → **hanger**; '**~·ing** powłoka
f; tkanina *f* płaszczowa

coat of 'arms herb *m*

coax [kəuks] namawiać 〈namówić〉
(*into* do *G*), przekonywać 〈-nać〉

cob [kɒb] kolba *f* (*kukurydzy*)

cob·bled ['kɒbld] wybrukowany

cob·bler ['kɒblə] szewc *m*

cob·web ['kɒbweb] pajęczyna *f*

co·caine [kə'keɪn] kokaina *f*

cock [kɒk] **1.** *zo.* kogut *m;* V kutas *m;* zawór *m,* kurek *m;* **2.** naciągać
〈naciągnąć〉; **~ one's ears** nastawiać
〈-wić〉 uszu

cock·a·too [kɒkə'tuː] *zo.* kakadu *n*

cock·chaf·er ['kɒktʃeɪfə] *zo.* chrabąszcz *m*

cock'eyed F stuknięty; zezowaty

Cock·ney ['kɒknɪ] (*rodowity londyń-
czyk; dialekt Londynu*) cockney *m*

'cock·pit kokpit *m*

cock·roach ['kɒkrəutʃ] *zo.* karaluch *m*

cock'sure F pewny swego, arogancki

'cock·tail koktajl *m* alkoholowy

cock·y ['kɒkɪ] F (**-ier, -iest**) zarozumiały, zadufany

co·co ['kəukəu] *bot.* (*pl.* **-cos**) palma *f*
kokosowa

co·coa ['kəukəu] *gastr.* kakao *n*

co·co·nut ['kəukənʌt] *bot.* kokos *m*

co·coon [kə'kuːn] kokon *m*

cod [kɒd] *zo.* dorsz *m,* wątłusz *m*

COD [siː əu 'diː] *skrót:* **cash** (*Am.* **collect**) **on delivery** za zaliczeniem
pocztowym

cod·dle ['kɒdl] rozpieszczać 〈rozpieś-
cić〉

code [kəud] **1.** kod *m;* **2.** 〈za〉szyfrować,
〈za〉kodować

'cod·fish *zo.* → **cod**

cod·ing ['kəudɪŋ] kodowanie *n*

cod-liv·er 'oil tran *m* (*z wątroby dor-
sza*)

co·ed·u·ca·tion [kəuedjuː'keɪʃn] koe-
dukacja *f*

co·ex·ist [kəuɪg'zɪst] koegzystować,
współżyć, współistnieć; **~·ence** koeg-
zystencja *f,* współżycie *n,* współistnie-
nie *n*

C of E [siː əu 'iː] *skrót:* **Church of England** Kościół *lub* kościół anglikański

cof·fee ['kɒfɪ] kawa *f;* '**~ bar** *Brt.* kawiarnia *f*, bar *m* kawowy; '~ **bean** ziar-no *n* kawy; '~ **pot** dzbanek *m* do kawy; '~ **set** serwis *m* do kawy; '~ **shop** *zwł.* *Am.* → **coffee bar**; '~ **ta·ble** ława *f*, stolik *a*

cof·fin ['kɒfɪn] trumna *f*

cog [kɒg] *tech.* ząb *m* (zębatki); '~**wheel** *tech.* zębatka *f*, koło *n* zębate

co·her|·ence, **~·en·cy** [kəʊ'hɪərəns, -rənsɪ] spójność *f*, koherencja *f*; **~·ent** spójny, koherentny

co·he|·sion [kəʊ'hiːʒn] zwartość *f*, spójność *f*; **~·sive** [kəʊ'hiːsɪv] zwarty, spójny

coif·fure [kwɑː'fjʊə] fryzura *f*

coil [kɔɪl] **1.** *też* ~ **up** zwijać ⟨zwinąć⟩ (się); **2.** *tech.* zwój *m*, krąg *m*; spirala *f*

coin [kɔɪn] **1.** moneta *f*; **2.** ⟨u⟩kuć

co·in·cide [kəʊɪn'saɪd] nakładać ⟨-łożyć⟩ się, zbiegać ⟨zbiec⟩ się; **~·ci·dence** [kəʊ'ɪnsɪdəns] zbieg *m* okoliczności, przypadek *m*

'**coin-op·e·rat·ed:** ~ (**petrol,** *Am.* **gas**) **pump** automatyczny dystrybutor paliwa *m* na monety

coke [kəʊk] koks *m* (*też sl.* kokaina)

Coke *TM* [kəʊk] coca-cola *f*, koka-kola *f*

cold [kəʊld] **1.** zimny, chłodny; oziębły *m*; **2.** chłód *m*, zimno *n*; przeziębienie *n*; **catch (a)** ~ przeziębić się; **have a** ~ być przeziębionym; **~·'blood·ed** zimnokrwisty; **~·'heart·ed** o twardym sercu; '**~·ness** zimno *n*; ~ '**war** *pol.* zimna wojna *f*

cole·slaw ['kəʊlslɔː] *gastr.* surówka *f* z kapusty

col·ic ['kɒlɪk] *med.* kolka *f*

col·lab·o·|rate [kə'læbəreɪt] współpracować; **~·ra·tion** [kəlæbə'reɪʃn] współpraca *f*; *in* ~*ration with* wraz *z* (*I*)

col·|lapse [kə'læps] **1.** zawalać ⟨-lić⟩ się; rozpadać ⟨-paść⟩ się; załamać ⟨-mywać⟩ się; runąć; składać ⟨złożyć⟩ się; *fig.* rozpadać ⟨-paść⟩ się; załamać ⟨-mywać⟩ się; **2.** zawalenie *n* się, rozpad *m*, upadek *m*; '**~·lap·si·ble** składany, rozkładany

col·lar ['kɒlə] **1.** kołnierz *m*; obroża *f*; *rel.* koloratka *f*; **2.** ⟨z⟩łapać, ⟨s⟩chwytać *F* capnąć; '**~·bone** *anat.* obojczyk *m*

col·league ['kɒliːg] kolega *m*, koleżanka *f*

col·|lect [kə'lekt] *v/t.* zbierać ⟨zebrać⟩;

kolekcjonować; odbierać ⟨odebrać⟩; *pieniądze itp.* pobierać ⟨pobrać⟩; *v/i.* zbierać ⟨zebrać⟩ się; **~·lect·ed** zebrany; *fig.* opanowany; **~·lec·tion** zbieranie *n*; zbiór *m*; kolekcja *f*, *econ.* inkaso *n*; *rel.* kolekta *f*; odbiór *m*; '**~·lec·tive** zbiorowy, wspólny; **~·lec·tive·ly** zbiorowo, wspólnie; **~·lec·tor** kolekcjoner-(ka *f*) *m*; inkasent(ka *f*) *m*; *rail.* kontroler(ka *f*) *m*; *electr.* kolektor *m*

col·lege ['kɒlɪdʒ] koledż *m*; wyższa szkoła *f*; szkoła *f* pomaturalna

col·lide [kə'laɪd] zderzać ⟨-rzyć⟩ się

col·lie·ry ['kɒljərɪ] kopalnia *f* węgla

col·li·sion [kə'lɪʒn] zderzenie *n*, kolizja *f*; → **head-on** ~, **rear-end** ~

col·lo·qui·al [kə'ləʊkwɪəl] potoczny

co·lon ['kəʊlən] dwukropek *m*; *anat.* okrężnica *f*

colo·nel ['kɜːnl] *mil.* pułkownik *m*

co·lo·ni·al·is·m [kə'ləʊnjəlɪzəm] kolonializm *m*

col·o·|nize ['kɒlənaɪz] ⟨s⟩kolonizować, zasiedlać ⟨-dlić⟩; **~·ny** ['kɒlənɪ] kolonia *f*

co·los·sal [kə'lɒsl] kolosalny

col·o·u(r) ['kʌlə] **1.** kolor *m*, barwa *f*; ~**s** *pl. mil.* sztandar *m*, barwy *pl.*; *naut.* bandera *m*; *what* ~ *is ...?* jakiego koloru jest ...?; *with flying* ~**s** triumfalnie, z wielkim sukcesem; **2.** *v/t.* ⟨za⟩barwić; ⟨za⟩farbować; *fig.* kolorować; *v/i.* ⟨za⟩barwić się; ⟨za⟩czerwienić się; '~ **bar** segregacja *f* rasowa; '**~·blind** ślepy na kolory; '**~·ed** kolorowy; '**~·fast** o trwałych kolorach; '~ **film** *phot.* film *m* kolorowy; '**~·ful** kolorowy; *fig.* barwny; '**~·ing** ['kʌlərɪŋ] barwnik *m*; cera *f*, karnacja *f*; '**~·less** bezbarwny; '~ **line** segregacja *f* rasowa; '~ **set** telewizor *m* kolorowy; '~ **tel·e·vi·sion** telewizja *f* kolorowa

colt [kəʊlt] źrebię *n*, źrebak *m*

col·umn ['kɒləm] kolumna *f* (*też mil.*); *print.* szpalta *f*; felieton *m*; **~·ist** ['kɒləmnɪst] felietonista *m* (-tka *f*)

comb [kəʊm] **1.** grzebień *m*; **2.** *v/t.* ⟨wy-, roz⟩czesać

com·|bat ['kɒmbæt] **1.** walka *f*; *single* ~*bat* pojedynek *m*; *attr.* bojowy; **2.** (*-tt-*, *Am. też* *-t-*) zwalczać ⟨-czyć⟩; '**~·ba·tant** ['kɒmbətənt] walczący *m* (-ca *f*), żołnierz *m*; △ *nie* **kombatant**

com·bi·na·tion [kɔmbɪˈneɪʃn] połączenie n, kombinacja f; ~·bine [kəmˈbaɪn] 1. łączyć (się), ⟨z⟩wiązać (się); zespalać ⟨zespolić⟩ (się); 2. econ. koncern m; agr. też ~bine harvester kombajn m

com·bus·ti·ble [kəmˈbʌstəbl] 1. łatwopalny; 2. materiał m łatwopalny; ~·tion [kəmˈbʌstʃən] spalanie n

come [kʌm] (came, come) przychodzić ⟨przyjść⟩, przyjeżdżać ⟨przyjechać⟩; to ~ nadchodzący, w przyszłości; ~ and go przychodzić i odchodzić; ~ to see odwiedzać ⟨-dzić⟩; ~ about stać się, wydarzyć się; ~ across natrafiać ⟨-fić⟩ na (A); ~ along iść; nadchodzić ⟨-dejść⟩; ~ apart rozpadać ⟨-paść⟩ się; ~ away odchodzić ⟨-dejść⟩; ~ back wracać ⟨wrócić⟩, powracać ⟨-wrócić⟩; ~ by natrafiać ⟨-fić⟩ na (A); ~ down schodzić ⟨zejść⟩; cena: spadać ⟨spaść⟩; runąć; ~ down with F zachorować na (A); ~ for przychodzić ⟨przyjść⟩ po (A); ⟨za⟩atakować (A); ~ forwards zgłaszać ⟨zgłosić⟩ się; ~ from pochodzić z (G); ~ home przychodzić lub przyjeżdżać do domu; ~ in wchodzić ⟨wejść⟩ do (G); informacja: nadchodzić ⟨nadejść⟩; pociąg: nadjeżdżać ⟨nadjechać⟩; ~ in! proszę wejść!; ~ loose obluzować się, poluzować się; ~ off odpadać ⟨odpaść⟩, odrywać ⟨oderwać⟩ się; przechodzić ⟨przejść⟩; wypadać ⟨wypaść⟩; ~ on! daj spokój!; dalej!; no już!; ~ out książka, sumowanie itp.: wychodzić; plama: schodzić ⟨zejść⟩; ujawniać ⟨ujawnić⟩ się; ~ over przyjeżdżać ⟨-jechać⟩, przychodzić ⟨przyjść⟩, przybywać ⟨przybyć⟩; ~ round przyjeżdżać ⟨-jechać⟩, przychodzić ⟨przyjść⟩, przybywać ⟨przybyć⟩; przychodzić ⟨przyjść⟩ do siebie; ~ through przechodzić ⟨przejść⟩; docierać ⟨dotrzeć⟩, wiadomość itp.: zostać ujawnionym; ~ to wynosić ⟨-nieść⟩; odchodzić ⟨dojść⟩ do siebie; ~ up to być równym, dorównywać ⟨-wnać⟩, odpowiadać; '~·back powrót m, comeback m

co·me·di·an [kəˈmiːdjən] komik m
com·e·dy [ˈkɔmədɪ] komedia f
come·ly [ˈkʌmlɪ] (-ier, -iest) atrakcyjny, dobrze wyglądający
com·fort [ˈkʌmfət] 1. wygoda f, komfort m; pociecha f, otucha f; 2. pocie

szać ⟨-szyć⟩, dodawać ⟨-dać⟩ otuchy; 'com·for·ta·ble wygodny; spokojny; nieskrępowany; dobrze sytuowany; be ~able być spokojnym; czuć się wygodnie; chory itp.: być w dobrym stanie; '~·er pocieszyciel(ka f) m; zwł. Brt. smoczek m; Am. kołdra f (pikowana); szalik m wełniany; '~·less niepocieszony, nieukojony; '~ sta·tion Am. toaleta f publiczna

com·ic [ˈkɔmɪk] (~ally) komiczny
com·i·cal [ˈkɔmɪkl] komiczny
com·ics [ˈkɔmɪks] pl. komiks m
com·ma [ˈkɔmə] przecinek m
com·mand [kəˈmɑːnd] 1. rozkaz m, komenda f; kierownictwo n; mil. dowództwo n, komenda f; 2. rozkazywać ⟨-zać⟩; mil. dowodzić, komenderować; poparcie itp. uzyskiwać ⟨-skać⟩; panować nad (I) (terenem itp.); dysponować (zasobami itp.); ~·er mil. dowódca m, dowódczyni m ⟨-ca f⟩; ~·er in chief mil. [kəmaˈndɑːntʃiːf] (pl. commanders in chief) głównodowodzący m, wódz m naczelny; ~·ment przykazanie n; ~ mod·ule (w astronautyce) człon m dowodzenia, kabina f załogi

com·man·do [kəˈmɑːndəu] mil. (pl. -dos, -does) jednostka f do zadań specjalnych; żołnierz m jednostki do zadań specjalnych, F komandos m
com·mem·o·rate [kəˈmeməreɪt] upamiętniać ⟨upamiętnić⟩, ⟨u⟩czcić (pamięć); ~·ra·tion [kəmeməˈreɪʃn] uczczenie n (pamięci); in ~ration of dla uczczenia pamięci (G); ~·ra·tive [kəˈmemərətɪv] upamiętniający, pamiątkowy

com·ment [ˈkɔment] 1. komentarz m (on o L), uwaga f (o L); no ~ment! bez komentarza!; 2. v/i. ~ment on ⟨s⟩komentować (A); v/t. zauważać ⟨-żyć⟩ (that że); ~·men·ta·ry [ˈkɔməntərɪ] komentarz m (on o L); ~·men·ta·tor [ˈkɔməntetə] komentator m (-ka f); radio, TV: sprawozdawca m, reporter(ka f) m

com·merce [ˈkɔmɜːs] handel m
com·mer·cial [kəˈmɜːʃl] 1. handlowy, komercyjny; 2. radio, TV: reklama f; ~ art sztuka f użytkowa; ~ art·ist grafik m użytkowy; ~·ize [kəˈmɜːʃəlaɪz] ⟨s⟩komercjalizować; ~ tel·e·vi·sion

telewizja *f* komercyjna *lub* prywatna;
~ 'trav·el·ler → *sales representative*

com·mis·e·rate [kə'mɪzəreɪt]: *~rate with* współczuć (*D*); *~ra·tion* [kəmɪzə'reɪʃn] współczucie *n* (*for* dla *G*), wyrazy *pl.* współczucia

com·mis·sion [kə'mɪʃn] **1.** zlecenie *n*, zamówienie *n*; *econ.* prowizja *f*; komisja *f*; *jur.* popełnienie *n* (*wykroczenia itp.*); **2.** zlecać 〈-cić〉, zamawiać 〈-mówić〉; *~·er* pełnomocnik *m*; komisarz *m*

com·mit [kə'mɪt] (*-tt-*) wykroczenie *itp.* popełniać 〈-nić〉; powierzać 〈-rzyć〉, przeznaczać 〈-czyć〉; angażować (się); *kogoś* umieszczać; *~ o.s.* zobowiązywać się (*to* do *G*); *~·ment* zobowiązanie *n*; zaangażowanie *n*, poświęcenie *n*; *~·tal* [kə'mɪtl] *jur.* uwięzienie *n*, przekazanie *n*; *~·tee* [kə'mɪtɪ] komitet *m*

com·mod·i·ty [kə'mɒdətɪ] *econ.* artykuł *m* handlowy; produkt *m*

com·mon ['kɒmən] **1.** wspólny; zwykły, zwyczajny; pospolity; powszechny; ogólny; *zwł. Brt.* pospolity, gminny; **2.** wspólna ziemia *f*; *in ~* wspólnie, razem (*with* z *I*); *'~·er* człowiek *m* z gminu, F pospolitak *m*; *~ 'law* (*niepisane*) prawo *n* zwyczajowe; ♀ '**Mar·ket** *econ.* pol. Wspólny Rynek *m*; '*~·place* **1.** banał *m*; **2.** zwykły, pospolity, powszedni; '*~s: the* ♀*s, lub the House of* ♀*s* Brt. parl. Izba *f* Gmin; ~ '**sense** zdrowy rozsądek *m*; '*~·wealth: the* ♀*wealth (of Nations)* Wspólnota *f* Narodów; *the* ♀*wealth of Independent States* Wspólnota *f* Niepodległych Państw

com·mo·tion [kə'məʊʃn] zamieszanie *n*

com·mu·nal ['kɒmjunl] komuna*f*; wspólnodostępny

com·mune['kɒmju:n]komuna*f*;wspólnota *f*; gmina *f*

com·mu·ni|·cate [kə'mju:nɪkeɪt] *v/t.* przekazywać 〈-zać〉, komunikować; *v/i.* porozumiewać 〈-mieć〉 się (*with* z *I*), komunikować się; *pokoje itp.*: być połączonym; *~·ca·tion* [kəmju:nɪ'keɪʃn] porozumiewanie *n*, komunikowanie *n* się; komunikacja *f*; przekazanie *n*

com·mu·ni·ca·tions [kəmju:nɪ'keɪʃnz] *pl.* połączenia *pl.*; komunikacja *f*, telekomunikacja *f*; *attr.* (tele)komunikacyjny; ~ sat·el·lite satelita *m* telekomunikacyjny

com·mu·ni·ca·tive [kə'mju:nɪkətɪv] komunikatywny, rozmowny

Com·mu·nion [kə'mju:njən] *rel. też* **Holy ~** Komunia *f* (*Święta*)

com·mu|·nis·m ['kɒmjunɪzəm] komunizm *m*; '*~·nist* **1.** komunista *m* (*-tka f*); **2.** komunistyczny

com·mu·ni·ty [kə'mju:nətɪ] wspólnota *f*; społeczność *f*, społeczeństwo *n*

com|·mute [kə'mju:t] *rail.* dojeżdżać 〈-jechać〉 (*do pracy*); *jur.* 〈z〉łagodzić karę; *~'mut·er* dojeżdżający *m* (*-ca f*) do pracy; *~'mut·er train* pociąg *m* dla dojeżdżających do pracy

com·pact **1.** ['kɒmpækt] puderniczka *f*; *Am.* niewielki samochód *m*, compact *m*; **2.** [kəm'pækt] *adj.* zwarty; niewielki; lapidarny; *~ car* [kɒmpækt'kɑ:] *Am.* niewielki samochód *m*, compact *m*; *~ disc*, *~ disk* [kɒmpækt 'dɪsk] (*skrót: CD*) kompakt *m*, płyta *f* kompaktowa, CD *n*; *~ 'disk play·er* odtwarzacz *m* kompaktowy

com·pan·ion [kəm'pænjən] towarzysz(ka *f*) *m*; dama *f* do towarzystwa; encyklopedia *f*, podręcznik *m*; *~·ship* towarzystwo *n*

com·pa·ny ['kʌmpənɪ] towarzystwo *n*; *econ.* firma *f*, spółka *f*; mil. kompania *f*; *theat.* zespół; *keep s.o. ~* dotrzymywać komuś towarzystwa

com|·pa·ra·ble ['kɒmpərəbl] porównywalny,zbliżony;*~·par·a·tive*[kəm'pærətɪv] **1.** porównawczy; względny; **2.** *też* *~parative degree* gr. stopień *m* wyższy; *~·pare* [kəm'peə] **1.** *v/t.* porównywać 〈-wnać〉; *v/i.* wypadać (*z I*); *v/i.* wypadać 〈-paść〉 w porównaniu; **2.** *beyond ~pare, without ~pare* nie do opisania; *~·pa·ri·son* [kəm'pærɪsn] porównanie *n*

com·part·ment [kəm'pɑ:tmənt] przegródka *f*; rail. przedział *m*; komora *f*; schowek *m*

com·pass ['kʌmpəs] kompas *m*; *a pair of ~es pl.* cyrkiel *m*

com·pas·sion [kəm'pæʃn] współczucie *n*; *~·ate* [kəm'pæʃənət] współczujący; *urlop itp.*: okolicznościowy

com·pat·i·ble [kəm'pætəbl] zgodny; *be ~(with)* odpowiadać (*D*), *komp.*, *radio*: być kompatybilnym (*z I*)

compress

com·pat·ri·ot [kəm'pætrɪət] rodak *m* (-aczka *f*)

com·pel [kəm'pel] (*-ll-*) nakłaniać ⟨-łonić⟩, zmuszać ⟨-sić⟩; **~·ling** nieodparty, ważny

com·pen|·sate ['kɒmpenseɪt] wynagradzać ⟨-grodzić⟩, rekompensować; stanowić kompensatę; wypłacać⟨-cić⟩ rekompensatę; **~·sa·tion** [kɒmpen'seɪʃn] rekompensata *f*; kompensata *f*, *jur.* wynagrodzenie *n*, odszkodowanie *n*

com·pere ['kɒmpeə] *Brt.* konferansjer *m*, prezenter(ka *f*) *m*

com·pete [kəm'piːt] współzawodniczyć (*for* o A), konkurować (*for* o A); (*w sporcie*) brać ⟨wziąć⟩ udział

com·pe|·tence ['kɒmpɪtəns] fachowość *f*, kompetencje *pl.*, kwalifikacje *pl.*; znajomość *f* (*języka obcego itp.*); **'~·tent** fachowy, kompetentny

com·pe·ti·tion [kɒmpɪ'tɪʃn] zawody *pl.*, konkurs *m*; rywalizacja *f*, współzawodnictwo *n*; konkurencja *f*

com·pet·i|·tive [kəm'petɪtɪv] konkurencyjny; **~·tor** [kəm'petɪtə] współzawodniczący *m* (-ca *f*), konkurent(ka *f*) *m*

com·pile [kəm'paɪl] ⟨s⟩kompilować, opracowywać ⟨-wać⟩, zbierać ⟨zebrać⟩

com·pla|·cence, **~·cen·cy** [kəm'pleɪsns, -snsɪ] samozadowolenie *n*; **~·cent** [kəm'pleɪsnt] zadowolony z siebie, pełen samozadowolenia

com·plain [kəm'pleɪn] ⟨po⟩skarżyć się (*about* o L, *to* D), składać ⟨złożyć⟩ skargę *lub* zażalenie (*of* na A); **~t** skarga *f*; zażalenie *n*; *med.* dolegliwość *f*

com·ple|·ment 1. ['kɒmplɪmənt] uzupełnienie *n*, dopełnienie *n*; △ *nie* **komplement**; **2.** ['kɒmplɪment] uzupełniać ⟨-nić⟩; **~·men·ta·ry** [kɒmplɪ'mentərɪ] uzupełniający, dopełniający; wzajemnie się dopełniający

com|·plete [kəm'pliːt] **1.** całkowity, kompletny; cały, zupełny; skończony; **2.** ⟨u-, za⟩kończyć; uzupełniać ⟨-nić⟩; *formularz itp.* wypełniać ⟨-nić⟩; **~·ple·tion** [kəm'pliːʃn] zakończenie *n*, uzupełnienie *n*

com·plex ['kɒmpleks] **1.** złożony, skomplikowany; **2.** kompleks *m* (*też psych.*)

com·plex·ion [kəm'plekʃn] cera *f*, karnacja *f*; *fig.* odmiana *f*

com·plex·i·ty [kəm'pleksətɪ] złożoność *f*, skomplikowanie *n*

com·pli|·ance [kəm'plaɪəns] zgodność *f*; stosowność *f*; uległość *f*; *in* **~ance with** zgodnie z (*I*); **~ant** uległy, ustępliwy

com·pli|·cate ['kɒmplɪkeɪt] ⟨s⟩komplikować; **'~·cat·ed** skomplikowany; **~·ca·tion** [kɒmplɪ'keɪʃn] komplikacja *f*, problem *m*; *med.* powikłanie *n*

com·plic·i·ty [kəm'plɪsətɪ] *jur.* współudział (*in* w L)

com·pli|·ment 1. ['kɒmplɪmənt] komplement *m*; **~ments** *pl.* pozdrowienia *pl.*; **2.** ['kɒmplɪment] *v/t.* prawić komplementy; ⟨po⟩gratulować; **~·men·ta·ry** [kɒmplɪ'mentərɪ] gratisowy, bezpłatny, okazowy

com·ply [kəm'plaɪ] zgadzać ⟨-zgodzić⟩ się (*with* z I); ⟨za⟩stosować się (do *G*) (*umowy itp.*)

com·po·nent [kəm'pəʊnənt] składnik *m*, część *f* składowa; *tech. electr.* podzespół *m*

com|·pose [kəm'pəʊz] składać ⟨złożyć⟩; *mus.* ⟨s⟩komponować; *be* **~posed of** składać się z (*G*); **~·pose o.s.** uspokajać ⟨-koić⟩ się; **~'posed** spokojny, opanowany; **~'pos·er** *mus.* kompozytor(ka *f*) *m*; **~·po·si·tion** [kɒmpə'zɪʃn] skład *m*; *mus.* kompozycja *f*, utwór *m*; *ped.* wypracowanie *n*; **~·po·sure** [kəm'pəʊʒə] opanowanie *n*, samokontrola *f*

com·pound[1] ['kɒmpaʊnd] *ogrodzony* teren *m*; obóz *m* dla jeńców *lub* więźniów; (*w zoo*) wybieg *m*

com·pound[2] **1.** ['kɒmpaʊnd] *chem.* związek *m*; *gr.* złożenie *n*; **2.** ['kɒmpaʊnd] złożony; **~ interest** *econ.* procent *m* składany; **3.** [kəm'paʊnd] *v/t.* składać ⟨złożyć⟩; zwiększać ⟨-szyć⟩, *zwł.* pogarszać ⟨pogorszyć⟩

com·pre·hend [kɒmprɪ'hend] ⟨z⟩rozumieć, pojmować ⟨pojąć⟩

com·pre·hen|·si·ble [kɒmprɪ'hensəbl] zrozumiały; **~·sion** [kɒmprɪ'henʃn] zrozumienie *n*, pojmowanie *n*; *past* **~sion** nie do zrozumienia; **~·sive** [kɒmprɪ'hensɪv] **1.** ogólny; wszechstronny; zupełny; **2.** *też Brt.* średnia szkoła *f* ogólnokształcąca (*nie stosująca selekcji*)

com|·press [kəm'pres] ściskać ⟨ścisnąć⟩, sprężać ⟨-żyć⟩; **~pressed air**

sprężone powietrze *n*; **~·pres·sion** [kəm'preʃn] *phys.* ściskanie *n*; *tech.* sprężanie *n*

com·prise [kəm'praɪz] zawierać ⟨zawrzeć⟩, obejmować ⟨objąć⟩; **be ~d of** składać się z (G)

com·pro·mise ['kɒmprəmaɪz] **1.** kompromis *m*; **2.** *v/t.* dochodzić ⟨dojść⟩ do porozumienia; ⟨s⟩kompromitować; *zasady itp.* zdradzać ⟨-dzić⟩; *v/i.* zawierać ⟨zawrzeć⟩ kompromis

com·pul·sion [kəm'pʌlʃn] przymus *m*; *psych.* natręctwo *n*; **~·sive** [kəm'pʌlsɪv] przymusowy; *psych.* nałogowy, poddany natręctwu; **~·so·ry** [kəm'pʌlsərɪ] obowiązkowy, obligatoryjny

com·punc·tion [kəm'pʌŋkʃn] skrupuły *pl.*, obiekcje *pl.*

com·pute [kəm'pjuːt] ⟨wy-, po⟩liczyć

com·put·er [kəm'pjuːtə] komputer *m*; **~·aid·ed** wspomagany komputerowo; **~·con·trolled** sterowany komputerowo; **~ game** gra *f* komputerowa; **~ 'graph·ics** *pl.* grafika *f* komputerowa; **~·ize** [kəm'pjuːtəraɪz] ⟨s⟩komputeryzować (się); **~ pre'dic·tion** prognoza *f* komputerowa *lub* przewidywanie *n* komputerowe; **~ 'sci·ence** informatyka *f*; **~ 'sci·en·tist** informatyk *m*; **~ 'vi·rus** wirus *m* komputerowy

com·rade ['kɒmreɪd] towarzysz(ka *f*) *m*

con[1] [kɒn] *skrót:* → **contra**

con[2] [kɒn] F (**-nn-**) oszwabiać ⟨-bić⟩, nabierać ⟨nabrać⟩

con·ceal [kən'siːl] ukrywać ⟨ukryć⟩, skrywać ⟨skryć⟩

con·cede [kən'siːd] przyznawać ⟨-znać⟩; przyznawać ⟨-znać⟩ rację; uznawać ⟨uznać⟩; ustępować ⟨ustąpić⟩

con·ceit [kən'siːt] zarozumiałość *f*; **~ed** zarozumiały

con·ceiv·a·ble [kən'siːvəbl] wyobrażalny; *do pomyślenia*; **~ve** [kən'siːv] *v/i.* zachodzić ⟨zajść⟩ w ciążę; *v/t. dziecko* począć; obmyślać ⟨-lić⟩

con·cen·trate ['kɒnsəntreɪt] ⟨s⟩koncentrować (się)

con·cept ['kɒnsept] pojęcie *n*

con·cep·tion [kən'sepʃn] pojęcie *n*, koncepcja *f*; *biol.* poczęcie *n*

con·cern [kən'sɜːn] **1.** sprawa *f*, rzecz *f*; zagadnienie *n*; zmartwienie *n*, niepokój *m*, troska *f*; *econ.* przedsiębiorstwo *n*, biznes *m*; **2.** dotyczyć (G); ⟨z⟩martwić, ⟨za⟩niepokoić; **~ed** zaniepokojony, zatroskany; zamieszany (*in* w L); **~·ing** *prp.* odnośnie (G), dotyczący (G)

con·cert ['kɒnsət] *mus.* koncert *m*; koncertowy; **~ hall** sala *f* koncertowa

con·ces·sion [kən'seʃn] ustępstwo *n*; koncesja *f*; ulga *f*, zwolnienie *n*

con·cil·i·a·to·ry [kən'sɪliətərɪ] pojednawczy, ugodowy

con·cise [kən'saɪs] zwięzły, krótki; **~·ness** zwięzłość *f*

con·clude [kən'kluːd] ⟨s-, za⟩kończyć, ⟨s⟩finalizować; *umowę itp.* zawierać ⟨zawrzeć⟩; wnioskować, dochodzić ⟨dojść⟩ do wniosku; **to be ~d** ciąg dalszy nastąpi

con·clu·sion [kən'kluːʒn] wniosek *m*, konkluzja *f*; zakończenie *n*; podsumowanie *n*; zawarcie *n*; **~·sive** [kən'kluːsɪv] ostateczny, nieodparty

con|·coct [kən'kɒkt] ⟨s⟩preparować (*też* fig.); przygotowywać ⟨-tować⟩; **~·coc·tion** [kən'kɒkʃn] mikstura *f*; *fig.* mieszanina *f*

con·crete[1] ['kɒŋkriːt] konkretny

con·crete[2] ['kɒŋkriːt] **1.** beton *m*; *attr.* betonowy; **2.** ⟨za⟩betonować

con·cur [kən'kɜː] (**-rr-**) zgadzać ⟨zgodzić⟩ się; współdziałać; zbiegać ⟨zbiec⟩ się; **~·rence** [kən'kʌrəns] zgodność *f*; zbieżność *f*; współdziałanie *n*; △ *nie* **konkurencja**

con·cus·sion [kən'kʌʃn] *med.* wstrząs *m* (*zwł.* mózgu)

con|·demn [kən'dem] potępiać ⟨-pić⟩; *jur.* skazywać ⟨-zać⟩; *budynek itp.* uznawać ⟨uznać⟩ za zagrożony; **~·demn to death** skazywać na śmierć; **~·dem·na·tion** [kɒndem'neɪʃn] potępienie *n*; skazanie *n*

con|·den·sa·tion [kɒndən'seɪʃn] kondensacja *f*, skraplanie *n*; skroplona para *f*; zaparowanie *n*; **~·dense** [kən'dens] ⟨s⟩kondensować, skraplać ⟨-kroplić⟩; **~·densed 'milk** słodzone mleko *n* skondensowane; **~·dens·er** *tech.* kondensator *m*; skraplacz *m*

con·de·scend [kɒndɪ'send] zniżać ⟨zniżyć⟩ się; **~·ing** łaskawy, protekcjonalny

con·di·ment ['kɒndɪmənt] przyprawa *f*

con·di·tion [kən'dɪʃn] **1.** warunek *m*; stan *m*; kondycja *f*, forma *f*; *med.* dolegliwość *f*, schorzenie *n*; **~s** *pl.* warunki *pl.*, okoliczności *pl.*, sytuacja *f*; **on ~ that** pod warunkiem że; **be out of ~** nie mieć kondycji; **2.** ⟨u⟩warunkować; ⟨na⟩uczyć; utrzymywać ⟨-mać⟩ w dobrej formie; **~al** [kən'dɪʃənl] **1.** warunkowy; **be ~al on** *lub* **upon** być uzależnionym od (*G*); **2.** *też* **~al clause** gr. zdanie *n* warunkowe; *też* **~al mood** gr. tryb *m* warunkowy

con·do ['kɒndəʊ] *Am.* → **condominium**

con|·dole [kən'dəʊl] **~dole with** składać kondolencje (*D*); **~'do·lence** zw. *pl.* kondolencje *pl.*

con·dom ['kɒndəm] kondom *m*, prezerwatywa *f*

con·do·min·i·um [kɒndə'mɪnɪəm] *Am. jakby*: mieszkanie *m* własnościowe; *jakby*: budynek *m* z mieszkaniami własnościowymi

con·done [kən'dəʊn] wybaczać ⟨-czyć⟩, godzić się na (*A*)

con·du·cive [kən'djuːsɪv] sprzyjający (**to** *D*), prowadzący (**to** do *G*)

con|·duct **1.** ['kɒndʌkt] prowadzenie *n*; zachowanie *n* (się) **2.** [kən'dʌkt] prowadzić; kierować; zachowywać się; *phys.* przewodzić; *mus.* dyrygować; **~ducted tour** wycieczka *f* z przewodnikiem; **~·duc·tor** [kən'dʌktə] przewodnik *m*; (*w autobusie, tramwaju, Am. też pociągu*) konduktor(ka *f*) *m*; *mus.* dyrygent *m*; *phys.* przewodnik *m*; *electr.* piorunochron *m*, odgromnik *m*

cone [kəʊn] stożek *m*; wafel *m* (*na lody*), rożek *m*; *bot.* szyszka *f*

con·fec·tion [kən'fekʃn] wyrób *m* cukierniczy; △ *nie* **konfekcja**; **~·er** [kən'fekʃnə] cukiernik *m*; **~·e·ry** [kən'fekʃnərɪ] słodycze *pl.*, wyroby *pl.* cukiernicze; cukiernia *f*; △ *nie* **konfekcyjny**

con·fed·e·ra·cy [kən'fedərəsɪ] konfederacja *f*; **the 2·ra·cy** *Am. hist.* Konfederacja Południa; **~·rate 1.** [kən'fedərət] skonfederowany, konfederacyjny; **2.** [kən'fedərət] konfederat *m*; **3.** [kən'fedəreɪt] konfederować (się); **~·ra·tion** [kənfedə'reɪʃn] konfederacja *f*

con·fer [kən'fɜː] (*-tt-*) *v/t.* tytuł *itp.* nadawać ⟨-dać⟩; *v/i.* naradzać ⟨-dzić⟩ się

con·fe·rence ['kɒnfərəns] konferencja *f*

con|·fess [kən'fes] wyznawać ⟨-znać⟩; przyznawać się; spowiadać się; **~·fes-**

sion [kən'feʃən] wyznanie *n*; przyznanie *n* się; *rel.* spowiedź *f*; **~·fes·sion·al** [kən'feʃənl] *rel.* konfesjonał *m*; **~·fes·sor** [kən'fesə] *rel.* spowiednik *m*

con·fide [kən'faɪd] **~ s.th. to s.o.** wyznawać coś komuś; **~ in s.o.** ufać komuś, zawierzyć komuś

con·fi·dence ['kɒnfɪdəns] zaufanie *n*; przekonanie *n*, wiara *f* (w siebie); **'~ man** (*pl. -men*) → **conman**; **'~ trick** szwindel *m*, oszustwo *n*

con·fi·dent ['kɒnfɪdənt] ufny; pełen ufności; przekonany, pewny; **be ~dent of** być pewnym (*G*); **~·den·tial** [kɒnfɪ'denʃl] poufny, zaufany

con·fine [kən'faɪn] ograniczać ⟨-czyć⟩; ⟨u⟩więzić, odosobniać ⟨-nić⟩; **be ~d to** być odosobnionym w (*L*), być przykutym do (*G*; *łóżka itp.*); **~·ment** zamknięcie *n*; odosobnienie *n*; poród *m*

con|·firm [kən'fɜːm] potwierdzać ⟨-dzić⟩, zatwierdzać; **be ~firmed** *rel.* być bierzmowanym; *rel.* otrzymywać ⟨-mać⟩ konfirmację; **~·fir·ma·tion** [kɒnfə'meɪʃn] potwierdzenie *n*, zatwierdzenie *n*; *rel.* bierzmowanie *n*; *rel.* konfirmacja *f*

con·fis·cate ['kɒnfɪskeɪt] ⟨s⟩konfiskować; **~·ca·tion** [kɒnfɪ'skeɪʃn] konfiskata *f*

con·flict **1.** ['kɒnflɪkt] konflikt *m*; **2.** [kən'flɪkt] wchodzić ⟨wejść⟩ w konflikt; kolidować; **~·ing** [kən'flɪktɪŋ] kolidujący, sprzeczny

con·form [kən'fɔːm] dostosowywać ⟨-wać⟩ się; być zgodnym (**to** *z I*), zachowywać ⟨-wać⟩ się konformistycznie

con·found [kən'faʊnd] zmieszać, wprawiać ⟨-wić⟩ w zakłopotanie

con|·front [kən'frʌnt] stawać ⟨stanąć⟩ przed (*I*); natykać się na (*A*); stawiać czoło (*D*); ⟨s⟩konfrontować; **~·front·a·tion** [kɒnfrʌn'teɪʃn] konfrontacja *f*

con|·fuse [kən'fjuːz] zmieszać, wprawiać ⟨-wić⟩ w zakłopotanie; pomieszać, pomylić; **~·fused** zmieszany; pomieszany, zmieszanie *n*; pomieszanie *n*; **~·fu·sion** [kən'fjuːʒn] zmieszanie *n*, zamieszanie *n*; pomieszanie *n*

con·geal [kən'dʒiːl] ⟨s⟩krzepnąć; ⟨z⟩gęstnieć

con|·gest·ed [kən'dʒestɪd] zatłoczony; zapchany; **~·ges·tion** [kən'dʒestʃən] *med.* przekrwienie *n*; *też* **traffic ~gestion** zator *m* drogowy

con·grat·u|·late [kənˈgrætjuleɪt] ⟨po⟩-
gratulować; **~·la·tion** [kəngrætjuˈleɪʃn]
gratulacje *pl.*; **~lations!** moje gratulacje!

con·gre|·gate [ˈkɒŋgrɪgeɪt] zbierać
(się); **~·ga·tion** [kɒŋgrɪˈgeɪʃn] *rel.* zebranie *n*; wierni *pl.*; kongregacja *f*

con·gress [ˈkɒŋgres] kongres *m*; 2 *Am.
parl.* Kongres *m*; '2·**man** (*pl.* **-men**)
Am. parl. kongresman *m*; '2·**wom·an**
(*pl.* **-women**) *Am. parl.* kobieta *f* kongresman

con|·ic [ˈkɒnɪk] *zwł. tech.*, '**~·i·cal** stoż-
kowy

co·ni·fer [ˈkɒnɪfə] *bot.* drzewo *n* szpil-
kowe *lub* iglaste

con·jec·ture [kənˈdʒektʃə] **1.** przypuszczenie *n*, domysł *m*; **2.** przypuszczać,
wysuwać ⟨-sunąć⟩ przypuszczenie

con·ju·gal [ˈkɒndʒʊgl] małżeński

con·ju|·gate [ˈkɒndʒʊgeɪt] *gr.* odmie-
niać ⟨-nić⟩, koniugować; **~·ga·tion**
[kɒndʒʊˈgeɪʃn] *gr.* koniugacja *f*

con·junc·tion [kənˈdʒʌŋkʃn] związek;
gr. spójnik *m*; *in* **~** *with* wraz z (*I*)

con·junc·ti·vi·tis [kɒndʒʌŋktɪˈvaɪtɪs]
med. zapalenie *n* spojówek

con|·jure [ˈkʌndʒə] wyczarowywać
⟨-ować⟩; *diabła itp.* wywoływać ⟨-łać⟩;
robić sztuczki magiczne; ~*jure up* wy-
czarowywać ⟨-ować⟩, wywoływać⟨-łać⟩
(*też fig.*); [kənˈdʒuə] *przest.* błagać;
~·jur·er [ˈkʌndʒərə] *zwł. Brt.* sztuk-
mistrz *m*, iluzjonista *m*; **~·jur·ing
trick** [ˈkʌndʒərɪŋ -] sztuczka *f* magicz-
na; **~·jur·or** [ˈkʌndʒərə] → *conjurer*

con·man [ˈkɒnmæn] (*pl.* **-men**) hoch-
sztapler *m*, oszust *m*

con|·nect [kəˈnekt] ⟨po⟩łączyć; *electr.*
przyłączać ⟨-czyć⟩, podłączać ⟨-czyć⟩;
rail., aviat itp. mieć połączenie (*with*
z *I*); '**~·nect·ed** połączony; spójny;
~·nec·tion, **~·nex·ion** *Brt.* [kəˈnekʃn]
połączenie *n* (*też aviat.*, *rail.*); przyłą-
czenie *n*, podłączenie *n* (*też electr.*, *tel.*);
spójność *f*; *zwł.* **~nections** *pl.* stosunki
pl., związki *pl.*; krewni *pl.*

con·quer [ˈkɒŋkə]zdobywać ⟨-być⟩, pokonywać ⟨-nać⟩; **~·or** [ˈkɒŋkərə] zdobywca *m* ⟨-wczyni *f*⟩

con·quest [ˈkɒŋkwest] podbój *m* (*też
fig.*)

con·science [ˈkɒnʃəns] sumienie *n*

con·sci·en·tious [kɒnʃɪˈenʃəs] su-

mienny, staranny; **~·ness** sumienność *f*,
staranność *f*; **~ ob'jec·tor** (*odmawiają-
cy pełnienia służby wojskowej ze względu na przekonania*)

con·scious [ˈkɒnʃəs] świadomy; przy-
tomny; *be* **~** *of* zdawać sobie sprawę
z (*I*); '**~·ness** świadomość *f*

con|·script 1. *mil.* [kənˈskrɪpt] powo-
ływać ⟨-łać⟩; **2.** [ˈkɒnskrɪpt] poborowy *m*; **~·scrip·tion** [kənˈskrɪpʃn] *mil.*
pobór *m*

con·se|·crate [ˈkɒnsɪkreɪt] *rel.* poświę-
cać; **~·cra·tion** [kɒnsɪˈkreɪʃn] *rel.* poświęcenie *n*

con·sec·u·tive [kənˈsekjʊtɪv] kolejny

con·sent [kənˈsent] **1.** zgoda *f*; **2.** zgadzać się (*to* na *A*)

con·se|·quence [ˈkɒnsɪkwəns] skutek
m, konsekwencja *f*; znaczenie *n*; *in
~quence of* wskutek (*G*); '**~·quent·ly**
w rezultacie, wreszcie; △ *nie* **konsek-
wentnie**

con·ser·va|·tion [kɒnsəˈveɪʃn] konser-
wacja *f*; ochrona *f*; ochrona *f* przyrody; **~tion area** rezerwat *m* przyrody;
~·tion·ist [kɒnsəˈveɪʃnɪst] ekolog *m*;
~·tive [kənˈsɜːvətɪv] **1.** konserwatyw-
ny, zachowawczy; **2.** 2*tive* konserwa-
tysta *m* (-stka *f*); **~·to·ry** [kɒnˈsɜːvətrɪ]
szklarnia *f*, cieplarnia *f*; **con·serve**
[kənˈsɜːv] zachowywać ⟨-wać⟩, oszczędzać; utrzymywać ⟨-mać⟩, *owoce itp.*
⟨za⟩konserwować

con·sid|·er [kənˈsɪdə] *v/t.* rozważać
⟨-żyć⟩; rozpatrywać ⟨-trzyć⟩; zastanawiać ⟨-nowić⟩ się; uważać; brać ⟨wziąć⟩
pod uwagę; *v/i.* zastanawiać ⟨-nowić⟩
się'; **~·e·ra·ble** [kənˈsɪdərəbl] znaczny; **~·e·ra·bly** [kənˈsɪdərəblɪ] znacznie; **~·er·ate** [kənˈsɪdərət] taktowny,
grzeczny; **~·e·ra·tion** [kənsɪdəˈreɪʃn]
wzgląd *m*; rozwaga *f*, rozważanie *n*;
zapłata *f*, rekompensata *f*; *take into
~eration* brać ⟨wziąć⟩ pod uwagę;
under ~eration rozważany; **~·er·ing**
[kənˈsɪdərɪŋ] zważywszy (*że*)

con·sign [kənˈsaɪn] *econ.* przesyłać
⟨-słać⟩; **~·ment** *econ.* przesyłka *f*, partia *f*

con·sist [kənˈsɪst]: **~ in** polegać na (*L*);
~ of składać się z (*G*)

con·sis|·tence, **~·ten·cy** [kənˈsɪstəns,
-tənsɪ] konsystencja *f*, spoistość *f*; konsekwencja *f*, spójność *f*; **~·tent** [kənˈsɪs-

tənt] konsekwentny, spójny; zgodny (**with** z *I*); stały

con·so·la·tion [kɒnsəˈleɪʃn] pociecha *f*; **~·sole** [kənˈsəʊl] pocieszać ⟨-szyć⟩

con·sol·i·date [kənˈsɒlɪdeɪt] ⟨s⟩konsolidować; wzmacniać ⟨wzmocnić⟩

con·so·nant [ˈkɒnsənənt] *gr.* spółgłoska *f*

con·spic·u·ous [kənˈspɪkjʊəs] *dobrze* widoczny, rzucający się w oczy

con·spi·ra·cy [kənˈspɪrəsɪ] konspiracja *f*; spisek *m*, zmowa *f*; **~·spi·ra·tor** [kənˈspɪrətə] konspirator(ka *f*) *m*; spiskowiec *m*; **~·spire** [kənˈspaɪə] zmawiać ⟨zmówić⟩ się, spiskować, konspirować

con·sta·ble [ˈkʌnstəbl] *Brt.* posterunkowy *m*

con·stant [ˈkɒnstənt] stały; niezmienny

con·ster·na·tion [kɒnstəˈneɪʃn] konsternacja *f*, zakłopotanie *n*

con·sti·pat·ed [ˈkɒnstɪpeɪtɪd] *med.*: **be ~·pated** cierpieć na zatwardzenie; **~·pa·tion** [kɒnstɪˈpeɪʃn] *med.* zatwardzenie *n*

con·sti·tu·en·cy [kənˈstɪtjʊənsɪ] okręg *m* wyborczy; **~·ent** część *f* składowa, składnik *m*; wyborca *m*

con·sti·tute [ˈkɒnstɪtjuːt] (u)stanowić; ⟨u⟩konstytuować; (u)stanowić,⟨u⟩tworzyć

con·sti·tu·tion [kɒnstɪˈtjuːʃn] *pol.* konstytucja *f*; statut *m*; ustanowienie *n*, ukonstytuowanie *n*; skład *m*; kondycja *f* (*fizyczna*); **~·al** [kɒnstɪˈtjuːʃənl] konstytucyjny; *prawo itp.*: statutowy

con·strained [kənˈstreɪnd] wymuszony, nienaturalny

con·strict [kənˈstrɪkt] zaciskać⟨-snąć⟩, ściskać ⟨-snąć⟩; **~·stric·tion** [kənˈstrɪkʃn] zaciśnięcie *n*, ściśnięcie *n*

con·struct [kənˈstrʌkt] ⟨z⟩budować; ⟨s⟩konstruować; **~·struc·tion** [kənˈstrʌkʃn] konstrukcja *f*; budowa *f*; (*w przemyśle*) budownictwo *n*; **under ~struction** w trakcie budowy; **~·struc·tion site** plac *m* budowy; **~·struc·tive** [kənˈstrʌktɪv] konstruktywny; **~·struc·tor** [kənˈstrʌktə] konstruktor *m*, budowniczy *m*

con·sul [ˈkɒnsəl] konsul *m*; **con·su·late** [ˈkɒnsjʊlət] konsulat *m*; **con·su·late 'gen·e·ral** (*pl.* **~s general**) konsulat *m* generalny; **con·sul 'gen·e·ral** (*pl.* **-s general**) konsul *m* generalny

con·sult [kənˈsʌlt] *v/t.* coś ⟨s⟩konsultować, zasięgnąć porady; ⟨po⟩radzić się; (*w książce*) sprawdzać ⟨-dzić⟩; *v/i.* udzielać ⟨-lić⟩ konsultacji; konsultować się (**with** z *I*)

con·sul·tant [kənˈsʌltənt] konsultant(ka *f*) *m*; *Brt.* specjalista (*lekarz*) *m* (-tka *f*); **~·ta·tion** [kɒnslˈteɪʃn] konsultacja *f*; porada *f*; narada *f*

con·sult·ing [kənˈsʌltɪŋ] udzielający konsultacji; *lekarz, adwokat itp.* z praktyką (*prywatną*); **~ hours** *pl.* godziny *pl.* przyjęć; **~ room** gabinet *m*

con·sume [kənˈsjuːm] *v/t.* ⟨s⟩konsumować, spożywać ⟨-żyć⟩; *paliwo itp.* zużywać ⟨-żyć⟩, *prąd itp.* pobierać ⟨pobrać⟩; ⟨s⟩trawić (*przez pożar, też fig.*); **~'sum·er** *econ.* konsument(ka *f*) *m*; **~'sum·er so·ci·e·ty** społeczeństwo *n* konsumpcyjne

con·sum·mate 1. [kənˈsʌmɪt] doskonały, wyśmienity; **2.** [ˈkɒnsəmeɪt] wysiłki ukoronować, zakończyć; *małżeństwo* skonsumować

con·sump·tion [kənˈsʌmpʃn] zużycie *n* (*paliwa*), pobór *m* (*prądu*); *przest. med.* suchoty *pl.*, gruźlica *f*

cont *skrót pisany:* **continued** cd., ciąg dalszy

con·tact [ˈkɒntækt] **1.** kontakt *m*; styczność *m*, zetknięcie *n* się; osoba *f* kontaktowa; *med.* osoba *f* stykająca się z chorym; **make ~s** nawiązywać ⟨-zać⟩ kontakty; **2.** ⟨s⟩kontaktować się z (*I*); **'~ lens** szkło *f* kontaktowe

con·ta·gious [kənˈteɪdʒəs] *med.* zakaźny; zaraźliwy (*też fig.*)

con·tain [kənˈteɪn] zawierać; *fig.* powstrzymywać ⟨-mać⟩, trzymać na wodzy; **~·er** pojemnik *m*; *econ.* kontener *m*; **~·er·ize** [kənˈteɪnəraɪz] *econ.* ⟨s⟩konteneryzować

con·tam·i·nate [kənˈtæmɪneɪt] zanieczyszczać ⟨-czyścić⟩; skażać ⟨skazić⟩; **~·na·tion** [kəntæmɪˈneɪʃn] skażenie *n*; zanieczyszczenie *n*

contd *skrót pisany:* **continued** cd., ciąg dalszy

con·tem·plate [ˈkɒntempleɪt] rozważać ⟨-żyć⟩; rozmyślać o (*L*); kontemplować; **~·pla·tion** [kɒntemˈpleɪʃn] rozmyślanie *n*; kontemplacja *f*; **~·pla·tive** [kənˈtemplətɪv, ˈkɒntempleɪtɪv] kontemplacyjny, medytacyjny con·tem·po·ra·ry [kən'tempərərı] **1.** współczesny; **2.** współczesny m (-na f)

con|·tempt [kən'tempt] pogarda f, wzgarda f; ~·temp·ti·ble [kən'temptəbl] zasługujący na pogardę; ~·temp·tu·ous [kən'temptʃʊəs] pogardliwy, lekceważący

con·tend [kən'tend] v/t. ⟨s⟩twierdzić, u-trzymywać (*that* że); v/i. walczyć (*for* o A, *with* z I); rywalizować (*for* o A); ~·er *zwł. sport:* zawodnik m (-iczka f); rywal(ka f) m

con·tent¹ ['kɒntent] zawartość f; *książ-ki itp.:* treść f; ~s zawartość f; (*table of*) ~s spis m treści

con·tent² [kən'tent] **1.** zadowolony; **2.** zadowalać ⟨-wolić⟩; ~·o.s. zadowalać się, poprzestawać na (I); ~·ed zadowolony; ~·ment zadowolenie n

con|·test **1.** ['kɒntest] współzawodnictwo n, rywalizacja f; konkurs m; **2.** [kən'test] rywalizować o (A), ubiegać się o (A); *też jur.* ⟨za⟩kwestionować, podawać ⟨-dać⟩ w wątpliwość; ~·test·ant [kən'testənt] rywal(ka f) m, konkurent(ka f) m; *jur.* strona f w sporze

con·text ['kɒntekst] kontekst m

con·ti|·nent ['kɒntınənt] kontynent m; *the* 2ent *Br.* Europa f (*bez Wlk. Brytanii*); ~·nen·tal [kɒntı'nentl] kontynentalny

con·tin·gen|·cy [kən'tındʒənsı] ewentualność f, możliwość f; ~·t **1.** *be* ~t *on* zależeć od (G); **2.** kontyngent m

con·tin·u|·al [kən'tınjʊəl] bezustanny, nieustający; ~·u·a·tion [kəntınjʊ'eıʃn] kontynuacja f; przedłużenie n; ciąg m dalszy; ~·ue [kən'tınjuː] v/t. ciągnąć *coś* dalej, kontynuować; *to be* ~ued ciąg dalszy nastąpi; v/i. ciągnąć się dalej, trwać dalej; trwać nadal, utrzymywać się; con·ti·nu·i·ty [kɒntı'njuːətı] ciągłość f; ~·u·ous [kən'tınjʊəs] nieprzerwany; ~·u·ous 'form *gr.* forma f czasu ciągłego

con|·tort [kən'tɔːt] wykręcać (się), wy-krzywiać (się), wyginać (się); ~·tor·tion [kən'tɔːʃn] wygięcie n się, wykręcenie n się

con·tour ['kɒntʊə] kontur m; ~s *pl.* za-rys m; con·tra ['kɒntrə] przeciw, prze-ciwko

con·tra·band ['kɒntrəbænd] *econ.* kontrabanda f

con·tra·cep|·tion [kɒntrə'sepʃn] *med.* antykoncepcja f; zapobieganie n ciąży; ~·tive [kɒntrə'septıv] *med.* środek m antykoncepcyjny

con|·tract **1.** ['kɒntrækt] kontrakt m, umowa f; **2.** [kən'trækt] ściągać (się), kurczyć (się); ~·trac·tion [kən'trækʃn] skurcz m, skurczenie n; zwężenie n; ~·trac·tor [kən'træktə]: *building* ~*tractor* przedsiębiorca m budowlany

con·tra|·dict [kɒntrə'dıkt] zaprzeczać ⟨-czyć⟩ (D), zadawać ⟨zadać⟩ kłam; ~·dic·tion [kɒntrə'dıkʃn] sprzeczność f, zaprzeczenie n; ~·dic·to·ry [kɒntrə'dıktərı] sprzeczny

con·tra·ry ['kɒntrərı] **1.** przeciwstawny; ~ *to* niezgodnie z (I), wbrew (D); **2.** przeciwieństwo n; *on the* ~ przeciwnie

con·trast **1.** ['kɒntrɑːst] kontrast m, przeciwstawienie n; **2.** [kən'trɑːst] v/t. przeciwstawiać ⟨-wić⟩, porównywać ⟨-nać⟩; v/i. odróżniać się (*with* od G), stać w sprzeczności (*with* z I)

con|·trib·ute [kən'trıbjuːt] wnosić ⟨wnieść⟩ udział (*to* do G), wpłacać ⟨-cić⟩; przyczyniać ⟨-nić⟩ się; pisywać ⟨pisać⟩; ~·tri·bu·tion [kɒntrı'bjuːʃn] wkład m, udział m; przyczynek m; ~·trib·u·tor [kən'trıbjʊtə] ofiarodaw-ca m (-czyni f); (*w czasopiśmie*) współ-pracownik m (-iczka f); ~·trib·u·to·ry [kən'trıbjʊtərı] przyczyniający się; ~*tributory cause* przyczyna f sprawcza

con·trite ['kɒntraıt] skruszony

con·trive [kən'traıv] wymyślać ⟨-lić⟩; zdołać (zrobić), doprowadzić do (G)

con·trol [kən'trəʊl] **1.** panowanie n, wła-dza f; kontrola f, sprawdzanie n; *tech.* regulator m, przełącznik m; ~s *tech.* urządzenia *pl.* sterujące; *bring* (*get*) ~ opanować, wziąć pod kontrolę; *have* (*keep*) *under* ~ kontrolować; *get out of*~ wymykać ⟨wymknąć⟩ się spod kon-troli; *lose* ~ *of* stracić kontrolę nad (I); **2.** (-*ll*-) kontrolować; sprawdzać ⟨-dzić⟩; opanowywać ⟨-wać⟩; panować nad (I), sprawować władzę nad (I); *econ.* regu-lować, kontrolować; *tech.* regulować, sterować; ~ *desk electr.* pulpit m ste-rowniczy; ~ *pan·el electr.* tablica f sterownicza; ~ *tow·er aviat.* wieża f kontroli lotów

con·tro·ver|·sial [kɒntrə'vɜːʃl] kontro-wersyjny; ~·sy ['kɒntrəvɜːsı] kontrowersja *f*; zatarg *m*

con·tuse [kən'tjuːz] *med.* kontuzjować, stłuc

con·va·lesce [kɒnvə'les] odzyskiwać ⟨-skać⟩ zdrowie, powracać ⟨-rócić⟩ do zdrowia; **~·les·cence** [kɒnvə'lesns] rekonwalescencja *f*, zdrowienie *n*; **~·les·cent 1.** zdrowiejący; zdrowotny; **2.** rekonwalescent(ka *f*) *m*

con·vene [kən'viːn] *zebranie itp.* zwoływać ⟨-łać⟩; zbierać ⟨zebrać⟩ się

con·ve·ni·ence [kən'viːnjəns] wygoda *f*, dogodność *f*; *Brt.* toaleta *f* (*publiczna*); **~ences** z wszelkimi wygodami; **at your earliest ~ence** możliwie jak najszybciej; **~ent** wygodny, dogodny

con·vent ['kɒnvənt] klasztor *m* (*żeński*)

con·ven·tion [kən'venʃn] zebranie *n*; zjazd *m*; umowa *f*; **~al** [kən'venʃənl] konwencjonalny, umowny

con·verge [kən'vɜːdʒ] zbiegać ⟨zbiec⟩ się

con·ver·sa·tion [kɒnvə'seɪʃn] rozmowa *f*, konwersacja *f*; **~al** [kɒnvə'seɪʃənl] potoczny; konwersacyjny; **~al English** potoczny angielski

con·verse [kən'vɜːs] rozmawiać, rozprawiać

con·ver·sion [kən'vɜːʃn] konwersja *f*, przeliczenie *n*; przekształcenie *n*; przebudowa *f*; *rel.* nawrócenie *n*; *econ.* przeliczenie *n*, wymiana *f*; **~ ta·ble** tabela *f* przeliczeniowa

con|·vert [kən'vɜːt] przeliczać ⟨-czyć⟩, wymieniać ⟨-nić⟩; przekształcać ⟨-cić⟩ (*into* w *A*); *rel.* nawracać ⟨-wrócić⟩ (się); *math.* przeliczać ⟨-czyć⟩; **~'vert·er** *electr.* przetwornica *f*, przetwornik *m*; **~'ver·ti·ble 1.** zamienny; *econ.* wymienialny; **2.** *mot.* kabriolet *m*

con·vey [kən'veɪ] przewozić ⟨przewieźć⟩, ⟨prze⟩transportować; przekazywać ⟨-zać⟩; **~ance** transport *m*, przewóz *m*; środek *m* transportu; przekazanie *n*; **~er belt** przenośnik *m* transportowy

con|·vict 1. ['kɒnvɪkt] skazaniec *m*; więzień *m*, więźniarka *f*; **2.** [kən'vɪkt] *jur.* (*of*) uznawać ⟨-znać⟩ winnym (*G*), skazywać (na *A*); **~'vic·tion** [kən'vɪkʃn] *jur.* skazanie *n*; przekonanie *n*

con·vince [kən'vɪns] przekonywać ⟨-nać⟩

con·voy ['kɒnvɔɪ] **1.** konwój *m* (*też naut.*), eskorta *f*; **2.** konwojować, eskortować

con·vul|·sion [kən'vʌlʃn] *med. zw. pl.* konwulsje *pl.*, drgawki *pl.*; **~·sive** [kən'vʌlsɪv] konwulsyjny

coo [kuː] ⟨za⟩gruchać

cook [kʊk] **1.** kucharz *m* (*-arka f*); **2.** ⟨u⟩gotować (się); *F sprawozdanie itp.* ⟨s⟩fałszować; **~ up** *F* wymyślać ⟨-lić⟩; **'~·book** *Am.* książka *f* kucharska; **'~·er** *Brt.* kuchenka *f*; **'~·e·ry** ['kʊkərɪ] kucharstwo *n*; **'~·e·ry book** *Brt.* książka *f* kucharska; **~·ie** ['kʊkɪ] *Am.* ciastko *n*, herbatnik *m*; **'~·ing** gotowanie (*umiejętność*) *n*; **'~·y** ['kʊkɪ] *Am.* → **cookie**

cool [kuːl] **1.** chłodny; *fig.* zimny, opanowany; obojętny; *F* świetny, kapitalny; **2.** chłód *m*, zimno *n*; *F* opanowanie *n*, spokój *m*; **3.** ⟨o⟩chłodzić (się); studzić (się); **~ down**, **~ off** uspokajać ⟨-koić⟩ się

coon [kuːn] *zo. F* szop pracz *m*

coop [kuːp] **1.** klatka *f* (*dla królików itp.*); **2.** **~ up**, **~ in** włączać ⟨-łoczyć⟩

co-op ['kəʊɒp] *F* spółdzielnia *f*, sklep *m* spółdzielczy

co·op·e·rate [kəʊ'ɒpəreɪt] współpracować; kooperować; pomagać ⟨pomóc⟩; **~·ra·tion** [kəʊɒpə'reɪʃn] współpraca *f*; pomoc *f*; kooperacja *f*; **~·ra·tive** [kəʊ'ɒpərətɪv] **1.** wspólny; pomocny; *econ.* spółdzielczy; **2.** *też* **~rative society** spółdzielnia *f*; *też* **~rative store** sklep *m* spółdzielczy

co·or·di|·nate 1. [kəʊ'ɔːdɪneɪt] ⟨s⟩koordynować; **2.** [kəʊ'ɔːdɪnət] równorzędny; **~·na·tion** [kəʊɔːdɪ'neɪʃn] koordynacja *f*

cop [kɒp] *F* (*policjant*) glina *m F*

cope [kəʊp]: **~ with** dawać sobie radę z (*I*), radzić sobie z (*I*)

Co·pen·ha·gen Kopenhaga *f*

cop·i·er ['kɒpɪə] kopiarka *f*

co·pi·ous ['kəʊpjəs] obfity, duży

cop·per¹ ['kɒpə] **1.** *min.* miedź *f*; **2.** miedziany

cop·per² ['kɒpə] *F* (*policjant*) gliniarz *m*

cop·pice ['kɒpɪs], **copse** [kɒps] zagajnik *m*

cop·y ['kɒpɪ] **1.** kopia *f*; odpis *m*; reprodukcja *f*; egzemplarz *m* (*książki*); numer *m* (*czasopisma*); *print.* materiał *m*

do druku; *fair* ~ czystopis *m*; **2.** ⟨s⟩ko-
piować; przepisywać ⟨-sać⟩, sporządzać
⟨-dzić⟩ odpis; naśladować; '~·**book** notatnik *m*; '~·**ing** kopiujący; '~·**right**
prawo n autorskie, copyright *m*

cor·al ['kɒrəl] *zo.* koral *m*; *attr.* koralowy

cord [kɔːd] **1.** sznur *m* (*też electr.*), linka *f*; sztruks; (*a pair of*) ~*s* sztruksy
pl.; **2.** zawiązywać ⟨-wiązać⟩ sznurem

cor·di·al[1] ['kɔːdjəl] sok *m* (skoncentrowany); *med.* lek wzmacniający

cor·di·al[2] ['kɔːdjəl] kordialny; ~·**i·ty**
[kɔːdi'ælətɪ] kordialność *f*

'**cord·less** bezprzewodowy; '~ **phone**
telefon bezprzewodowy

cor·don ['kɔːdn] **1.** kordon *m*; **2.** ~ **off**
odgradzać ⟨-rodzić⟩ kordonem

cor·du·roy ['kɔːdərɔɪ] sztruks *m*; (*a pair
of*) ~*s* (*spodnie*) sztruksy *pl.*

core [kɔː] **1.** rdzeń *m*; jądro *n*; ogryzek
m; *fig.* sedno *n*; '~ **time** *Brt.* (*okres, gdy
większość pracujących w nienormowa-
nym czasie pracy znajduje się w miejscu
pracy*)

cork [kɔːk] **1.** korek *m*; **2.** *też* ~ **up** ⟨za⟩-
korkować; '~·**screw** korkociąg *m*

corn[1] [kɔːn] **1.** zboże *n*; ziarno *n*; *też Indian* ~ *Am.* kukurydza *f*; **2.** ⟨za⟩pe-
klować

corn[2] [kɔːn] *med.* odcisk *m*

cor·ner ['kɔːnə] **1.** róg *m*; kąt *m*; *zwł.
mot.* zakręt *m*; (*w piłce nożnej*) rzut
m rożny, róg *m* F; *fig.* ciężka sytuacja
f; **2.** rożny; **2.** przypierać ⟨-przeć⟩ do
muru; '~·**ed** ...rożny; '~ **kick** (*w piłce
nożnej*) rzut *m* rożny, róg *m* F; '~ **shop**
Brt. sklep *m* na rogu

cor·net ['kɔːnɪt] *mus.* kornet *m*; *Brt.*
rożek *m* (*na lody*)

'**corn·flakes** *pl.* płatki *pl.* kukurydziane

cor·nice ['kɔːnɪs] *arch.* gzyms *m*

cor·o·na·ry ['kɒrənərɪ] **1.** *anat.* wieńcowy; **2.** *med.* zakrzepica *f* tętnicy wień-
cowej; F zawał *m* serca

cor·o·na·tion [kɒrə'neɪʃn] koronacja *f*

cor·o·ner ['kɒrənə] *jur.* koroner *m*
(*urzędnik badający przyczynę nagłego zgonu nie z przyczyn naturalnych*);
~'**s 'in·quest** śledztwo *n* (*przeprowa-
dzone przez koronera*)

cor·o·net ['kɒrənɪt] (*mała*) korona *f*

cor·po·ral ['kɔːpərəl] *mil.* kapral *m*

cor·po·ral 'pun·ish·ment kara *f* cie-
lesna

cor·po|·**rate** ['kɔːpərət] zbiorowy; kor-
poracyjny; dotyczący firmy; ~·**ra·tion**
[kɔːpə'reɪʃn] *jur.* korporacja *f*; władze
pl. miasta; osoba *f* prawna; spółka *f*,
Am. też spółka *f* akcyjna

corps [kɔː] (*pl. corps* [kɔːz]) korpus *m*

corpse [kɔːps] zwłoki *pl.*

cor·pu·lent ['kɔːpjʊlənt] korpulentny

cor·ral [kəˈrɑːl, *Am.* kəˈræl] **1.** korral *m*,
zagroda; **2.** *bydło* zaganiać ⟨-gonić⟩ do
korralu

cor|·**rect** [kəˈrekt] **1.** poprawny, prawi-
dłowy; *też czas:* dokładny; **2.** poprawiać ⟨-wić⟩, ⟨s⟩korygować; ~·**rec·tion**
[kəˈrekʃn] poprawa *f*, poprawka *f*

cor·re|·**spond** [kɒrɪˈspɒnd] (*with, to*)
odpowiadać (*D*); zgadzać się (z *I*); korespondować (*with z I*); ~·**spon·dence**
odpowiedniość *f*; korespondencja *f*;
~·**spon·dence course** kurs *m* kores-
pondencyjny; ~·**spon·dent 1.** odpowiadający; **2.** korespondent(ka *f*) *m*;
~·**spon·ding** odpowiadający

cor·ri·dor ['kɒrɪdɔː] korytarz *m*.

cor·rob·o·rate [kəˈrɒbəreɪt] potwierdzać ⟨-dzić⟩, podtrzymywać ⟨-mać⟩

cor·rode [kəˈrəʊd] *chem., tech.* ⟨s⟩ko-
rodować, ⟨za⟩rdzewieć; ~·**ro·sion**
[kəˈrəʊʒn] *chem., tech.* korozja *f*, rdza *f*;
~·**ro·sive** [kəˈrəʊsɪv] korodujący, ko-
rozyjny; *fig.* niszczący

cor·ru·gated ['kɒrʊgeɪtɪd] falisty;
'~ **i·ron** blacha *f* falista

cor|·**rupt** [kəˈrʌpt] **1.** skorumpowa-
ny; przekupny; *moralnie* zepsuty; **2.**
⟨s⟩korumpować; przekupić; *moralnie* ⟨ze⟩psuć, ⟨z⟩demoralizować;
~·**rupt·i·ble** przekupny, sprzedajny;
~·**ruption** [kəˈrʌpʃn] korupcja *f*; sprze-
dajność *f*; *moralne* zepsucie *n*

cor·set ['kɔːsɪt] gorset *m*

cos|·**met·ic** [kɒzˈmetɪk] **1.** (*-ally*) kosme-
tyczny; **2.** kosmetyk *m*; ~·**me·t**-
i·cian [kɒzməˈtɪʃn] kosmetyczka *f*

cos·mo·naut ['kɒzmənɔːt] *astr.* kosmonauta *m*

cos·mo·pol·i·tan [kɒzməˈpɒlɪtən] **1.**
kosmopolityczny; **2.** kosmopolita *m*,
obywatel *m* świata

cost [kɒst] **1.** koszt *m*, koszty *pl.*; cena *f*;
2. (*cost*) kosztować; '~·**ly** (*-ier, -iest*)
drogi, kosztowny; ~ **of 'liv·ing** koszty
pl. utrzymania

cos·tume ['kɒstjuːm] ubiór *m*, strój *m*;

'~ **jew·el**(·**le**)**ry** sztuczna biżuteria *f*

co·sy ['kəʊzɪ] **1.** (*-ier, -iest*) przytulny; **2.** → **egg cosy, tea cosy**

cot [kɒt] łóżko *n* polowe; *Brt.* łóżeczko *n* dziecięce

cot·tage ['kɒtɪdʒ] chata *f*, chałupa *f*; *Am.* dom *m* letniskowy, dacza *f* F; ~ **'cheese** biały ser *m*

cot·ton ['kɒtn] **1.** bawełna *f*; przędza *f* bawełniana; *Am.* wata *f*; **2.** bawełniany; '~**wood** *bot.* topola *f* kanadyjska; ~ **'wool** *Brt.* wata *f*

couch [kaʊtʃ] sofa *f*, leżanka *f*

cou·chette [ku:'ʃet] *rail.* kuszetka *f*, miejsce *n* do leżenia; *też* ~ **coach** wagon *m* z miejscami do leżenia

cou·gar ['ku:gə] *zo.* (*pl.* *-gars, -gar*) kuguar *m*, puma *f*

cough [kɒf] **1.** kaszel *m*; **2.** ⟨za⟩kaszleć

could [kʊd] *pret. od* **can**[1]

coun·cil ['kaʊnsl] rada *f*; '~ **house** *Brt.* jakby: mieszkanie *n* kwaterunkowe

coun·cil·(**l**)**or** ['kaʊnsələ] radny *m* (-na *f*), członek *m* (-kini *f*) rady

coun·sel ['kaʊnsl] **1.** rada *f*, porada *f*; *Brt. jur.* adwokat *m*, obrońca *m*; ~**sel for the defense** (*Am.* **for the defence**) obrońca *m*; ~**sel for the prosecution** oskarżyciel *m*; **2.** (*zwł. Brt.* *-ll-*, *Am.* *-l-*) doradzać ⟨-dzić⟩, ⟨po⟩radzić; udzielać ⟨-lić⟩ rady; ~**se**(**l**)**ing centre** poradnia *f*; ~**sel·**(**l**)**or** ['kaʊnsələ] doradca *m*; *zwł. Am. jur.* adwokat *m*, obrońca *m*

count[1] [kaʊnt] hrabia *m* (*nie brytyjski*)

count[2] [kaʊnt] **1.** liczenie *n*, przeliczanie *n*; *jur.* punkt *m* (*oskarżenia*), zarzut *m*; **2.** *v/t.* ⟨po⟩liczyć, wyliczać ⟨-czyć⟩, obliczać ⟨-czyć⟩; ⟨po⟩rachować; liczyć do (*G*) (~ **ten** do dziesięciu); *fig.* uważać za (*A*); *v/i.* ⟨po⟩liczyć; liczyć się, mieć znaczenie; ~ **down** pieniądze podliczać ⟨-czyć⟩, odliczać wstecz (*przed startem rakiety*), wyczekiwać; ~ **on** liczyć na (*A*); spodziewać się; '~**down** odliczanie *n* wstecz (*przed startem rakiety*); wyczekiwanie *n*

coun·te·nance ['kaʊntɪnəns] wyraz *m* twarzy, oblicze *n*; poparcie *n*

count·er[1] ['kaʊntə] *tech.* licznik *m*; pionek *m*

coun·ter[2] ['kaʊntə] lada *f*, kontuar *m*; okienko *n*

coun·ter[3] ['kaʊntə] **1.** przeciw, wbrew,

na przekór; **2.** przeciwstawiać się, odparowywać ⟨-ować⟩, ⟨za⟩reagować

coun·ter·act [kaʊntər'ækt] przeciwdziałać; ⟨z⟩neutralizować

coun·ter·bal·ance 1. ['kaʊntəbæləns] przeciwwaga *f*; **2.** [kaʊntə'bæləns] ⟨z⟩równoważyć

coun·ter·clock·wise [kaʊntə'klɒkwaɪz] *Am.* → **anticlockwise**

coun·ter·es·pi·o·nage ['kaʊntər'espɪənɑ:ʒ] kontrwywiad *m*

coun·ter·feit ['kaʊntəfɪt] **1.** fałszywy, sfałszowany; **2.** fałszerstwo *n*; **3.** pieniądze, podpis itp. ⟨s⟩fałszować; ~ '**mon·ey** fałszywe pieniądze *pl.*

coun·ter·foil ['kaʊntəfɔɪl] odcinek *m* (*kontrolny*), talon *m*

coun·ter·mand [kaʊntə'mɑ:nd] *rozkaz, zamówienie itp.* odwoływać ⟨-łać⟩, ⟨z⟩anulować

coun·ter·pane ['kaʊntəpeɪn] narzuta *f*; → **bedspread**

coun·ter·part ['kaʊntəpɑ:t] odpowiednik *m*; kopia *f*, duplikat *m*

coun·ter·sign ['kaʊntəsaɪn] kontrasygnować

coun·tess ['kaʊntɪs] hrabina *f*

'**count·less** niezliczony

coun·try ['kʌntrɪ] **1.** kraj *m*, państwo *n*; wieś *f*; **in the** ~ na wsi; **2.** wiejski; '~**man** (*pl.* *-men*) wieśniak *m*; *też* **fellow** ~**man** rodak *m*; '~ **road** droga *f* wiejska; '~**side** wieś *f*; tereny *pl.* wiejskie; '~**wom·an** (*pl.* *-women*) wieśniaczka *f*; *też* **fellow** ~**woman** rodaczka *f*

coun·ty ['kaʊntɪ] hrabstwo *n*; ~ '**seat** *Am.* siedziba *f* władz hrabstwa; ~ '**town** *Brt.* siedziba *f* władz hrabstwa

coup [ku:] znakomite posunięcie *n*; zamach *m* stanu, pucz *m*

cou·ple ['kʌpl] **1.** para *f*; **a** ~ **of** F trochę, kilka; **2.** ⟨z-, po⟩łączyć; *tech.* sprzęgać ⟨-gnąć⟩; *zo.* parzyć się

coup·ling ['kʌplɪŋ] *tech.* sprzęg *m*; łącznik *m*

cou·pon ['ku:pɒn] odcinek *m*, kupon *m*; talon *m*

cour·age ['kʌrɪdʒ] odwaga *f*; **cou·ra·ge·ous** [kə'reɪdʒəs] odważny, śmiały

cou·ri·er ['kʊrɪə] kurier *m*; pilot *m* (*wycieczki*); *attr.* kurierski

course [kɔ:s] *naut., aviat., fig.* kurs *m*; (*w sporcie*) tor *m* wyścigowy, bieżnia f, pole n golfowe; bieg m, przebieg m; ciąg m; seria f, cykl m; kurs m, zajęcia pl.; **of ~** oczywiście; **in the ~ of events** normalnym biegiem rzeczy; **in due ~** we właściwym czasie *lub* trybie;

court [kɔːt] **1.** dwór m (*króla itp.*); dziedziniec m; (*w nazwach*) plac m; (*w sporcie*) kort m tenisowy; *jur.* sąd m, trybunał m; **2.** zalecać się do (*G*); starać się o (*A*)

cour·te|·ous ['kɜːtjəs] uprzejmy; **~·sy** ['kɜːtɪsɪ] uprzejmość f; **by ~sy of** przez grzeczność (*G*), dzięki uprzejmości (*G*)

'court|·house *jur.* gmach m sądu; **~·ier** ['kɔːtjə] dworzanin m; '**~·ly** dworski; '**~·mar·tial** (*pl.* **courts martial, court martials**) *jur.* sąd m wojenny; **~'mar·tial** (*zwł. Brt.* **-ll-** , *Am.* **-l-**) oddawać ⟨-dać⟩ pod sąd wojenny; '**~·room** *jur.* sala f rozpraw; '**~·ship** zalecanie się; '**~·yard** podwórze n

cous·in ['kʌzn] kuzyn(ka f) m

cove [kəʊv] zatoczka f

cov·er ['kʌvə] **1.** pokrywa f, wieko n; pokrowiec m; okładka f, obwoluta f; powłoczka f, kapa f; schronienie n; *fig.* maska f, przykrywka f; nakrycie n stołowe; ubezpieczenie n; *take~* schronić się; *under plain ~* jako zwykła przesyłka; *under separate ~* jako osobna przesyłka; **2.** przykrywać ⟨-ryć⟩, zakrywać ⟨-ryć⟩, pokrywać ⟨-ryć⟩; przebywać ⟨-być⟩, pokonywać ⟨-nać⟩; *obszar* zajmować ⟨-jąć⟩; rozciągać się na (*L*); *tematem* zajmować się (*I*); *przepis* ujmować ⟨ująć⟩; *econ.* pokrywać ⟨-ryć⟩; *econ.* ubezpieczać ⟨-czyć⟩; *TV, radio, prasa:* ⟨z⟩relacjonować, omawiać ⟨-mówić⟩; (*w sporcie*) przeciwnika kryć; **~ up** zakrywać ⟨-ryć⟩; okrywać ⟨-ryć⟩ się; *fig.* ⟨za⟩tuszować; **~ up for s.o.** kryć kogoś; **~·age** ['kʌvərɪdʒ] relacja f (*of z G*), sprawozdanie n; '**~ girl** cover girl f (*zdjęcie atrakcyjnej dziewczyny na okładce czasopisma*); **~·ing** ['kʌvərɪŋ] pokrywa f, przykrywa f; warstwa f; '**~ sto·ry** relacja f tytułowa

cow¹ [kaʊ] *zo.* krowa f (*też fig.*)

cow² [kaʊ] zastraszać ⟨-szyć⟩

cow·ard ['kaʊəd] tchórz m; *attr.* tchórzliwy; **~·ice** ['kaʊədɪs] tchórzostwo n; '**~·ly** tchórzliwy

cow·boy ['kaʊbɔɪ] kowboj m

cow·er ['kaʊə] ⟨s⟩kulić się

'cow|·herd pastuch m; '**~·hide** skóra f bydlęca; '**~·house** obora f

cowl [kaʊl] habit m (*z kapturem*); kaptur m; *tech.* nasada f kominowa

'cow|·shed obora f; '**~·slip** *bot.* pierwiosnek m; *Am.* knieć f błotna

cox [kɒks], **~·swain** ['kɒksən, 'kɒkswein] sternik m

coy [kɔɪ] płochliwy, nieśmiały

coy·ote ['kɔɪəʊt] *zo.* kojot m

co·zy ['kəʊzɪ] *Am.* (**-ier, -iest**) → **cosy**

CPU su pi: 'juː] skrót: **central processing unit** *komp.* jednostka f centralna

crab [kræb] *zo.* krab m

crack [kræk] **1.** szczelina f, pęknięcie n; rysa f, zarysowanie n; trzask m, huk m; uderzenie n; **2.** *v/i.* pękać ⟨-knąć⟩, ⟨za⟩rysować się; *głos:* ⟨za⟩łamać się; *też* **~ ing** *fig.* załamywać ⟨-mać⟩ się; *get* **~ing** F brać ⟨wziąć⟩ się ostro do roboty; *v/t.* trzaskać ⟨-snąć⟩ (*batem, palcami*); ⟨s⟩tłuc, rozbijać ⟨-bić⟩, ⟨z⟩łamać; *orzech* łupać; *szyfr* F ⟨z⟩łamać; **~ a joke** F opowiadać kawał; '**~·er** krakers m; (*papierowy rulon z małą petardą w środku*); **~·le** ['krækl] trzaskać

Cracow Kraków m

cra·dle ['kreidl] **1.** kołyska f; **2.** kołysać, ⟨u⟩tulić

craft¹ [krɑːft] (*pl.* **craft**) *naut.* statek m; *aviat.* samolot m; *astr.* pojazd m kosmiczny

craft² [krɑːft] rzemiosło n; umiejętność f, biegłość f; *fig.* sztuka f; podstęp m; '**~·s·man** (*pl.* **-men**) rzemieślnik m; '**~·y** (**-ier, -iest**) przebiegły, podstępny

crag [kræg] grań f, ostry występ m skalny

cram [kræm] (**-mm-**) wpychać ⟨wepchnąć⟩, wtykać ⟨wetknąć⟩; F wkuwać ⟨wkuć⟩, kuć (*for do G*)

cramp [kræmp] **1.** *med.* kurcz m; *tech.* klamra f, zwora f; *fig.* więzy pl.; **2.** ⟨za⟩hamować, wstrzymywać ⟨-mać⟩

cran·ber·ry ['krænbərɪ] *bot.* żurawina f

crane¹ [krein] *tech.* żuraw m, dźwig m

crane² [krein] **1.** *zo.* żuraw m; **2. ~ forward, ~ out one's neck** wyciągać ⟨-gnąć⟩ szyję

crank [kræŋk] **1.** *tech.* korba f; *tech.* wahacz m; F szajbus m; **2.** obracać ⟨-rócić⟩ korbą; '**~·shaft** wał m korbowy; '**~·y** (**-ier, -iest**) F szajbnięty; *Am.* marudny

cran·ny ['krænɪ] szczelina f

crap ['kræp] gówno n, bzdury fpl
crape [kreɪp] krepa f
crap·py ['kræpɪ] sl. (-ier, -iest) gówniany
craps [kræps] Am. pl. (rodzaj gry w kości)
crash [kræʃ] **1.** trzask m, grzmot m; mot. zderzenie n, katastrofa f; aviat. katastrofa f, runięcie n; econ. krach m (na giełdzie), załamanie n; **2.** v/t. rozbijać ⟨-bić⟩ (mot. into o A); aviat. rozbijać ⟨-bić⟩ przy lądowaniu; v/i. zwł. mot. rozbijać ⟨-bić⟩ się, zderzać ⟨-rzyć⟩ się; zwł. econ. załamywać ⟨-mać⟩ się; wjeżdżać ⟨wjechać⟩, wpadać ⟨wpaść⟩ (**against**, **into** w A); mot., aviat. ulegać ⟨ulec⟩ katastrofie; **3.** intensywny, przyspieszony; '~ bar·ri·er bariera f ochronna; '~ course kurs m przyspieszony lub intensywny; '~ di·et intensywna dieta f (odchudzająca); '~ hel·met kask m; '~·land aviat. ⟨wy⟩lądować awaryjnie; '~land·ing aviat. awaryjne lądowanie n
crate [kreɪt] skrzynka f, kontener m
cra·ter ['kreɪtə] krater m; lej m
crave [kreɪv] mieć wielką ochotę (**for**, **after** na A), mieć zachcianki; 'crav·ing wielka ochota f, zachcianka f
craw·fish ['krɔːfɪʃ] zo. (pl. -fish, -fishes) → crayfish
crawl [krɔːl] **1.** pełzanie n; dziecko: raczkowanie n; (w sporcie) kraul m; **2.** ⟨po⟩pełznąć, ⟨po⟩czołgać się, dziecko: raczkować; pływać kraulem; roić się (**with** od G); **it makes one's flesh ~** dostaje się gęsiej skórki od tego
cray·fish ['kreɪfɪʃ] zo. (pl. -fish, -fishes) rak m, langusta f
cray·on ['kreɪən] kredka f (do rysowania)
craze [kreɪz] też fig. szał m, szaleństwo n; **be the ~** być w modzie; 'cra·zy (-ier, -iest) zwariowany (**about** na punkcie G)
creak [kriːk] ⟨za⟩skrzypieć
cream [kriːm] **1.** śmietan(k)a f; krem m; elita f, śmietanka f; **2.** kremowy, koloru kremowego; ~·e·ry (-ier, -iest) mleczarnia f; '~·y (-ier, -iest) kremowy; śmietankowy; ze śmietanką
crease [kriːs] **1.** fałda f, zmarszczka f; (w spodniach) kant m; **2.** miąć (się), ⟨z-, po⟩gnieść (się); fałdować się, marszczyć się

cre·ate [kriː'eɪt] ⟨s⟩tworzyć; ~·a·tion [kriː'eɪʃn] tworzenie n; stworzenie n (też świata); ~·a·tive twórczy; ~·a·tor twórca m; stwórca m
crea·ture ['kriːtʃə] stworzenie n
crèche [kreɪʃ] żłobek m; Am. żłobek lub żłóbek m, szopka f (bożonarodzeniowa)
cre·dence ['kriːdns]: **give ~ to** dawać wiarę w (A)
cre·den·tials [krɪ'denʃlz] pl. referencje pl.; listy pl. uwierzytelniające; dokumenty pl. tożsamości
cred·i·ble ['kredəbl] wiarygodny
cred·it ['kredɪt] **1.** wiara f, zaufanie n; uznanie n; (w szkole) zaliczenie n; econ. kredyt m; ~·it (**side**) econ. strona „ma"; **on ~it** econ. na kredyt; attr. kredytowy; **2.** ⟨u⟩wierzyć, ⟨za⟩ufać; econ. zapisywać ⟨-sać⟩ (**to** na dobro G); ~·it **s.o. with s.th.** przypisywać ⟨-sać⟩ coś komuś; '~·i·ta·ble chlubny (**to** dla G); '~it **card** econ. karta f kredytowa; '~·i·tor econ. wierzyciel m; '~·u·lous ['kredjʊləs] łatwowierny
creed [kriːd] wiara f, wyznanie n
creek [kriːk] Brt. zatoczka f; Am. strumień m, potok m
creep [kriːp] (**crept**) pełzać, ⟨po⟩pełznąć; skradać się; roślina: piąć się; ~ **in** wkradać ⟨-raść⟩ się, zakradać ⟨-raść⟩ się; **it makes my flesh ~** dostaje gęsiej skórki od tego; '~·er bot. roślina f rozłogowa; ~s pl.: F **the sight gave me the ~s** ten widok przyprawił mnie o gęsią skórkę
cre·mate [krɪ'meɪt] ⟨s⟩kremować, poddawać ⟨-dać⟩ kremacji
crept [krept] pret. i p.p. od creep
cres·cent ['kresnt] półksiężyc m
cress [kres] bot. rzeżucha f
crest [krest] zo. grzebień m, czub m; szczyt m (górski); wierzchołek m; pęk m piór, kita f; **family ~** herb m rodzinny; '~·fal·len przybity
cre·vasse [krɪ'væs] szczelina f (lodowcowa)
crev·ice ['krevɪs] szczelina f, pęknięcie n
crew[1] [kruː] obsada f, załoga f
crew[2] [kruː] pret. od crow 2
crib [krɪb] **1.** żłób m; Am. łóżeczko n dla dziecka; zwł. Brt. żłóbek m, Boże Narodzenie: szopka f; F (w szkole) ściąga f; **2.** (-bb-) F odpisywać ⟨-sać⟩, ściągać ⟨-gnąć⟩

crick [krɪk]: *a ~ in one's back* (*neck*) strzyknięcie *n* w plecach (*karku*)

crick·et¹ ['krɪkɪt] *zo.* świerszcz *m*

crick·et² ['krɪkɪt] (*w sporcie*) krykiet *m*

crime [kraɪm] *jur.* przestępstwo *n*, zbrodnia *f*, występek *m*; *~ nov·el* (*powieść*) kryminał *m*

crim·i·nal ['krɪmɪnl] **1.** kryminalny, przestępczy, zbrodniczy; **2.** przestępca *m* (*-czyni f*), zbrodniarz *m* (*-arka f*), kryminalista *m* (*-ka f*)

crimp [krɪmp] *zwł.* włosy podkręcać ⟨-ręcić⟩

crim·son ['krɪmzn] karmazynowy

cringe [krɪndʒ] ⟨s⟩kulić się

crin·kle ['krɪŋkl] **1.** zagiecie *n*; zmarszczka *f*; **2.** ⟨po⟩miąć (się); ⟨z⟩marszczyć (się)

crip·ple ['krɪpl] **1.** kulawy *m* (*-wa f*), kaleka *m/f*; **2.** okulawiać ⟨-wić⟩; okaleczać ⟨-czyć⟩ (*też fig.*)

cri·sis ['kraɪsɪs] (*pl. -ses* [-siːz]) kryzys *m*

crisp [krɪsp] *chleb:* chrupiący; *warzywo:* kruchy, świeży; *powietrze:* świeży, ostry; *włosy:* kędzierzawy; *'~bread* chleb *m* chrupki

crisps [krɪsps] *pl.*, też *potato ~ Brt.* chrupki *pl.* (*ziemniaczane*)

criss·cross ['krɪskrɒs] **1.** kratkowany wzór *m*; **2.** krzyżować (się)

cri·te·ri·on [kraɪˈtɪərɪən] (*pl. -ria* [-rɪə], *-rions*) kryterium *n*

crit·ic ['krɪtɪk] krytyk *m*; *~·i·cal* ['krɪtɪkl] krytyczny; *~·i·cis·m* ['krɪtɪsɪzəm] krytyka *f*; *~·i·cize* ['krɪtɪsaɪz] ⟨s⟩krytykować

cri·tique [krɪˈtiːk] krytyka *f*, omówienie *n*

croak [krəʊk] ⟨za⟩rechotać; ⟨za⟩skrzeczeć; ⟨za⟩chrypieć

Cro·a·tia Chorwacja *f*

cro·chet ['krəʊʃeɪ] **1.** szydełkowanie *n*; **2.** szydełkować

crock·e·ry ['krɒkərɪ] *niemetalowe* naczynia *pl.* stołowe

croc·o·dile ['krɒkədaɪl] *zo.* krokodyl *m*

cro·ny ['krəʊnɪ] F kumpel(ka *f*) *m*

crook [krʊk] **1.** zagięcie *n*, zgięcie *n*, zakrzywienie *n*; F oszust *m*; **2.** zakrzywiać ⟨-wić⟩(się), zaginać ⟨-giąć⟩ (się); *~·ed* ['krʊkɪd] zagięty, krzywy; F nieuczciwy, oszukańczy

croon [kruːn] ⟨za⟩nucić; śpiewać ckl   wie; *'~·er* śpiewak *m* (-waczka *f*) (*ckliwych utworów*)

crop [krɒp] **1.** zbiór *m*, plon *m*; *zo.* wole *n*; krótka fryzura *f*; **2.** (*-pp-*) trawę *itp.* skubać; *włosy* przycinać ⟨-ciąć⟩ (*krótko*)

cross [krɒs] **1.** krzyż *m* (*też fig. ciężar*), krzyżyk *m*; skrzyżowanie *n*; *biol.* krzyżówka *f*; (*w piłce nożnej*) podanie *n* w poprzek; **2.** zły, rozzłoszczony; **3.** ⟨s⟩krzyżować (się); *ulice* przecinać ⟨-ciąć⟩, przechodzić ⟨przejść⟩; *plan* ⟨po⟩krzyżować; *biol.* ⟨s⟩krzyżować; *~ off, ~ out* przekreślać ⟨-lić⟩, skreślać ⟨-lić⟩; *~ o.s.* ⟨prze⟩żegnać się; *~ one's arms* ⟨s⟩krzyżować ramiona; *~ one's legs* zakładać ⟨założyć⟩ nogę na nogę; *keep one's fingers ~ed* trzymać kciuki; *'~·bar* (*w sporcie*) poprzeczka *f*; *'~·breed* mieszaniec *m*; *~·'coun·try* przełajowy; *~·country skiing* narciarstwo *n* biegowe; *~·ex·am·i·na·tion* przesłuchiwanie *n* w formie pytań krzyżowych; *~·ex·am·ine* zadawać ⟨-dać⟩ pytania krzyżowe; *'~·eyed: be ~-eyed* zezować, mieć zeza; *'~·ing* skrzyżowanie *n*; przejazd *m* (*przez tory itp.*); *Brt.* przejście *n* dla pieszych; *naut.* przeprawa *f*; *'~·road Am.* droga *f* poprzeczna; *'~·roads pl. lub sg.* skrzyżowanie *n*; *fig.* rozstaje *pl.*, punkt *m* przełomowy; *'~·sec·tion* przekrój *m* poprzeczny; *'~·walk Am.* przejście *n* dla pieszych; *'~·wise* poprzecznie, w poprzek; *'~·word* (*puz·zle*) krzyżówka *f*

crotch [krɒtʃ] *anat.* krocze *n* (*też spodni*)

crouch [kraʊtʃ] **1.** kucać ⟨kucnąć⟩, przykucać ⟨-kucnąć⟩; **2.** przysiad *m*, kucnięcie *n*

crow [krəʊ] **1.** *zo.* wrona *f*; **2.** (*crowed lub crew, crowed*) ⟨za⟩krakać

'crow·bar łom *m*

crowd [kraʊd] **1.** tłum *m*; masa *f*; **2.** tłoczyć się; *ulice* zatłaczać ⟨-tłoczyć⟩; *'~·ed* zatłoczony, przepełniony

crown [kraʊn] **1.** korona *f*; *med.* korona *f*; **2.** ⟨u⟩koronować; nakładać ⟨nałożyć⟩ koronkę (*na ząb*); *fig.* ⟨s⟩koronować, ⟨u⟩wieńczyć

cru·cial ['kruːʃl] krytyczny, decydujący

cru·ci·fix ['kruːsɪfɪks] krucyfiks *m*; *~·fix·ion* [kruːsɪˈfɪkʃn] ukrzyżowanie *n*; *~·fy* ['kruːsɪfaɪ] ⟨u⟩krzyżować

crude [kru:d] surowy, nieprzetworzony; *fig.* prymitywny; ~ **('oil)** ropa *f* naftowa

cru·el [krʊəl] **(-ll-)** okrutny; '**~·ty** okrucieństwo *n*; **~ty to animals (children)** okrucieństwo *n* wobec zwierząt (dzieci); **society for the prevention of ~ty to animals** towarzystwo *n* zapobiegania okrucieństwu wobec zwierząt

cru·et ['kru:ɪt] komplet *m* do przypraw; pojemnik *m* na ocet *lub* oliwę

cruise [kru:z] **1.** rejs *m*; wycieczka *f* morska; **2.** krążyć; odbywać ⟨-być⟩ rejs; *aviat.*, *mot.* lecieć *lub* jechać z prędkością podróżną; ~ **'mis·sile** *mil.* rakietowy pocisk *m* manewrujący, F rakieta *f* cruise; **'cruis·er** *mil. naut.* krążownik *m*; jacht *m* motorowy; *Am.* policyjny wóz *m* patrolowy

crumb [krʌm] okruch *m*, okruszek *m*

crum·ble ['krʌmbl] *v/t.* ⟨po⟩kruszyć; *v/i.* rozpadać ⟨-paść⟩ się

crum·ple ['krʌmpl] zgniatać ⟨zgnieść⟩, ⟨z⟩miąć (się); załamywać ⟨-mać⟩ (się); '~ **zone** *mot.* strefa *f* zgniecenia

crunch [krʌntʃ] ⟨za⟩chrzęścić; ⟨s⟩chrupać

cru·sade [kru:'seɪd] wyprawa *f* krzyżowa

crush [krʌʃ] **1.** tłok *m*, ścisk *m*; *have a ~ on s.o.* ⟨s⟩tracić głowę dla kogoś; **2.** *Brt.* sok *m* (ze *świeżych owoców*); *orange ~* sok ze świeżych pomarańczy; **3.** *v/t.* rozgniatać ⟨-nieść⟩, ⟨z⟩miażdżyć (*też fig.*); *tech.* rozdrabniać ⟨-drobnić⟩, ⟨s⟩kruszyć; *fig.* ⟨z⟩miażdżyć, ⟨z⟩dławić; *v/i.* tłoczyć się; '~ **bar·ri·er** bariera *f* ochronna

crust [krʌst] skórka *f* (*chleba*); skorupa *f*

crus·ta·cean [krʌ'steɪʃn] *zo.* skorupiak *m*

crust·y ['krʌstɪ] **(-ier, -iest)** chrupiący

crutch [krʌtʃ] kula *f*, szczudło *n*

cry [kraɪ] **1.** krzyk *m*, okrzyk *m*; głos *m* (*ptaka itp.*); płacz *m*; **2.** ⟨za⟩płakać; krzyczeć ⟨krzyknąć⟩; ⟨za⟩wołać (*for* o *A*); wydawać ⟨-dać⟩ głos

crypt [krɪpt] krypta *f*

crys·tal ['krɪstl] kryształ *m*; *Am.* szkiełko *n* zegarka; *attr.* kryształowy; ~·**line** ['krɪstəlaɪn] krystaliczny; ~·**lize** ['krɪstəlaɪz] ⟨s⟩krystalizować

CST [si: es 'ti:] *skrót: Central Standard Time* (*amerykański czas standardowy*)

ct(s) *skrót pisany: cent(s) pl.* cent *m*

cu *skrót pisany: cubic* sześcienny

cub [kʌb] młode *n* (*drapieżnika*); *jakby:* zuch *m*

cube [kju:b] kostka *f*; *math.* sześcian *m*; *math.* sześcian *m*, trzecia potęga *f*; *phot.* kostka *f* lampy błyskowej; ~ '**root** *math.* pierwiastek *m* sześcienny *lub* trzeciego stopnia; '**cu·bic** (~**ally**), '**cu·bi·cal** sześcienny; trzeciego stopnia

cu·bi·cle ['kju:bɪkl] kabina *f*

cuck·oo ['kʊku:] *zo.* (*pl.* **-oos**) kukułka *f*

cu·cum·ber ['kju:kʌmbə] ogórek *m*; **(as) cool as ~** F niezwykle spokojny

cud [kʌd] (*u przeżuwaczy*) miazga *f* pokarmowa; **chew the ~** rozmyślać, dumać

cud·dle ['kʌdl] *v/t.* przytulać ⟨-tulić⟩ do siebie, tulić; *v/i.* ~ **up** przytulać ⟨-tulić⟩ się (*to* do *G*)

cud·gel ['kʌdʒəl] **1.** pałka *f*; **2.** (*zwł. Brt. -ll-*, *Am. -l-*) ⟨po⟩bić

cue¹ [kju:] *theat.* replika *f*; *fig.* sygnał *m*, hasło *n*; rada *f*, wskazówka *f*

cue² [kju:] *bilard:* kij *m* bilardowy

cuff¹ [kʌf] mankiet *m* (*Am. też u spodni*)

cuff² [kʌf] **1.** klaps *m*; **2.** dawać ⟨dać⟩ klapsa

'cuff link spinka *f* do mankietów

cui·sine [kwi:'zi:n] (*sztuka gotowania*) kuchnia *f*

cul·mi·nate ['kʌlmɪneɪt] ⟨za⟩kończyć się

cu·lottes [kju:'lɒts] *pl.* spódnica *f*, *damskie* spodnie *pl.*

cul·prit ['kʌlprɪt] winowajca *m* (*-jczyni f*)

cul·ti·vate ['kʌltɪveɪt] *agr.* uprawiać ⟨-wić⟩; kultywować, pielęgnować; '~·**vat·ed** *agr.* uprawny; *fig.* kulturalny; ~·**va·tion** [kʌltɪ'veɪʃn] *agr.* uprawa *f*, uprawianie *n*; *fig.* kultywowanie *n*

cul·tu·ral ['kʌltʃərəl] kulturalny

cul·ture ['kʌltʃə] kultura *f*; hodowla *f*; '~·**d** kulturalny

cum·ber·some ['kʌmbəsəm] niezręczny, nieporęczny

cu·mu·la·tive ['kju:mjʊlətɪv] kumulujący się; kumulacyjny

cun·ning ['kʌnɪŋ] **1.** przebiegły, sprytny; **2.** przebiegłość *f*, spryt *m*

cup [kʌp] **1.** filiżanka *f*; *sport:* puchar *m*;

kielich *m*; miseczka *f*; **2. (-pp-)** dłoń składać ⟨złożyć⟩; ujmować ⟨ująć⟩; **she ~ped her chin in her hand** objęła dłonią brodę; **~·board** ['kʌbəd] kredens *m*, szafka *f*; **~·board bed** łóżko *n* składane; **'~ fi·nal** *sport*: finał *m* rozgrywek pucharowych

cu·po·la ['kju:pələ] kopuła *f*

'cup| tie (*w sporcie*) rozgrywka *f* eliminacyjna (*w zawodach pucharowych*); **'~ win·ner** (*w sporcie*) zwycięzca *m* w zawodach pucharowych

cur [kɜː] ostry kundel *m*; *fig.* łotr *m*

cu·ra·ble ['kjʊərəbl] uleczalny

cu·rate ['kjʊərət] wikary *m* (*w kościele anglikańskim*)

curb [kɜːb] **1.** wędzidło *n* (*też fig.*); *zwł. Am.* → **kerb(stone)**; **2.** okiełznywać ⟨-znać⟩

curd [kɜːd] *też* **~s** *pl.* zsiadłe mleko *n*; twaróg *m*

cur·dle ['kɜːdl] *v/t.* mleko ⟨s⟩powodować zsiadanie się; *v/i.* zsiadać ⟨zsiąść⟩ się; **the sight made my blood ~** na ten widok krew zastygła mi w żyłach

cure [kjʊə] **1.** *med.* lekarstwo *n* (**for** na A), środek *m*; kuracja *f*; **2.** *med.* ⟨wy⟩leczyć; ⟨za⟩konserwować; ⟨u⟩wędzić; ⟨wy⟩suszyć

cur·few ['kɜːfjuː] *mil.* godzina *f* policyjna

cu·ri·o ['kjʊərɪəʊ] (*pl.* **-os**) kuriozum *n*, osobliwość *f*

cu·ri·os·i·ty [kjʊərɪ'ɒsɪtɪ] ciekawość *f*; osobliwość *f*; **~ous** ['kjʊərɪəs] ciekawy, ciekawski; żądny wiedzy; dziwny, osobliwy

curl [kɜːl] **1.** lok *m*; **2.** *v/t.* włosy podkręcać ⟨-ręcić⟩; *v/i.* kręcić się; zwijać się; **'~·er** lokówka *f*; **'~·y** (**-ier, -iest**) kręcony; skręcony; zakręcany

cur·rant ['kʌrənt] *bot.* czarna *lub* czerwona porzeczka *f*; rodzynka *f*

cur·ren| ·cy ['kʌrənsɪ] *econ.* waluta *f*; **foreign~cy** dewizy *pl.*; **~t 1.** miesiąc *itp.*: bieżący; obecny, aktualny; pogląd: powszechny; **~t events** bieżące wydarzenia *pl.*; **2.** prąd *m*, nurt *m* (*oba też fig.*); *electr.* prąd *m* (elektryczny); **~t ac·count** *Brt. econ.* rachunek *m* bieżący

cur·ric·u·lum [kə'rɪkjʊləm] (*pl.* **-la** [-lə], **-lums**) program *m* zajęć; **~ vi·tae** [- 'vaːtiː] życiorys *m*

cur·ry¹ ['kʌrɪ] curry *n*

cur·ry² ['kʌrɪ] czesać *konia* zgrzebłem

curse [kɜːs] **1.** klątwa *f*; przekleństwo *n*; **2.** wyklinać ⟨-kląć⟩; kląć, przeklinać ⟨-kląć⟩; **curs·ed** ['kɜːsɪd] przeklęty

cur·sor ['kɜːsə] *komp.* kursor *m*

cur·so·ry ['kɜːsərɪ] pobieżny, powierzchowny

curt [kɜːt] zwięzły; zdawkowy

cur·tail [kɜː'teɪl] skracać ⟨-rócić⟩; *prawa* ograniczać ⟨-czyć⟩

cur·tain ['kɜːtn] **1.** zasłona *f*, firanka *f*, kurtyna *n*; **draw the ~s** zasuwać *lub* odsuwać zasłony; **2. ~ off** oddzielać ⟨-lić⟩ zasłoną

curt·s(e)y ['kɜːtsɪ] **1.** dygnięcie *n*; **2.** dygać ⟨dygnąć⟩ (**to** przed *I*)

cur·va·ture ['kɜːvətʃə] krzywizna *f*, zakrzywienie *n*

curve [kɜːv] **1.** krzywa *f*; zagięcie *n*; łuk *m*, zakręt *m*; **2.** wyginać ⟨-giąć⟩ się (*w łuk*)

cush·ion ['kʊʃn] **1.** poduszka *f*; **2.** ⟨z⟩amortyzować; *uderzenie* osłabiać ⟨-bić⟩

cuss [kʌs] *sl.* **1.** przekleństwo *n*; **2.** przeklinać ⟨-kląć⟩

cus·tard ['kʌstəd] *zwł. Brt.* sos *m* waniliowy (*do deserów*)

cus·to·dy ['kʌstədɪ] *jur.* opieka *f*, nadzór *m*; areszt *m*

cus·tom ['kʌstəm] zwyczaj *m*, obyczaj *m*; '**~·a·ry** zwyczajowy, tradycyjny; zwykły, zwyczajny; **~·'built** zrobiony na życzenie *lub* zamówienie; '**~·er** klient(ka *f*) *m*; '**~ house** urząd *m* celny; **~·'made** zrobiony na życzenie *lub* zamówienie

cus·toms ['kʌstəmz] *pl.* cło *n*; '**~ clearance** odprawa *f* celna; '**~ of·fi·cer**, '**~ of·fi·cial** celnik *m* (-iczka *f*)

cut [kʌt] (**cut**) **1.** *v/t.* ⟨po⟩kroić, obcinać ⟨-ciąć⟩, przycinać ⟨-ciąć⟩; *cenę* obniżać ⟨-niżyć⟩; *karty* przełożyć; *v/i.* ciąć; **~ one's finger** skaleczyć się w palec; **~ s.o. dead** umyślnie kogoś nie dostrzegać; **2.** skaleczenie *n*; cięcie *n*; '**~·back** *rośliny* przycinać ⟨-ciąć⟩; *wydatki* ograniczyć

cute [kjuːt] F (**~r, ~st**) sprytny, zmyślny; *Am.* fajny

cu·ti·cle ['kjuːtɪkl] skórka *f* (*paznokcia*)

cut·le·ry ['kʌtlərɪ] sztućce *pl.*

cut·let ['kʌtlɪt] *gastr.* kotlet *m*; sznycel *m*

cut|·'price, **~·'rate** *econ.* obniżony,

przeceniony; '**~·ter** krajarka *f*, przeci-
narka *f*; szlifierz *m* (*diamentów, szkła*);
tech. frez *m*, nóż *m*; *film*: ; *naut.* kuter
m; '**~·throat 1.** morderca *m* (*-czyni f*);
2. morderczy, bezlitosny; '**~·ting 1.**
tnący; *tech.* skrawający; **2.** cięcie *n*, wy-
cinanie *n*; *bot.* sadzonka *f*; *zwł. Brt.*
wycinek *m*; '**~·tings** *pl.* wycinki *pl.*;
wióry *pl.*
Cy·ber·space ['saɪbəspeɪs] → *virtual
reality*
cy·cle¹ ['saɪkl] cykl *m*; obieg *m*
cy·cle² ['saɪkl] rower *m*; *attr.* rowerowy; **~ path** ścieżka *f* dla rowerów;
'**cy·cling** cyklistyka *f*, jazda *m* na ro-

werze; kolarstwo *n*; '**cy·clist** rowerzysta *m* (*-stka f*), cyklista *m*; kolarz *m*
cy·clone ['saɪkləʊn] cyklon *m*; obszar
m niskiego ciśnienia
cyl·in·der ['sɪlɪndə] cylinder *m*, *tech.* też
walec *m*
cyn·ic ['sɪnɪk] cynik *m*; '**~·i·cal** cyniczny
cy·press ['saɪprɪs] *bot.* cyprys *m*
Cy·prus Cypr *m*
cyst [sɪst] *med.* cysta *f*
czar [zɑː] → *tsar*
Czech [tʃek] **1.** czeski; **~ Republic** Cze-
chy *pl.*, Republika *f* Czeska; **2.** Czech
m; Czeszka *f*; *ling.* język *m* czeski

D

D, d [diː] D, d *n*
d *skrót pisany*: *died* zm., zmarł(a)
DA [diː 'eɪ] *skrót*: *District Attorney Am.*
prokurator *m* okręgowy
dab [dæb] **1.** pacnięcie *n*, pryśnięcie *n*,
maźnięcie *n*; odrobina *f*; **2.** (*-bb-*) wycierać ⟨wytrzeć⟩; *krem itp.* nakładać
⟨-łożyć⟩
dab·ble ['dæbl] opryskiwać⟨-skać⟩; **~ at,
~ in** imać się (*po amatorsku*) (*G*)
dachs·hund ['dækshʊnd] *zo.* jamnik *m*
dad [dæd] F, **~·dy** ['dædɪ] tatuś *m*
dad·dy long·legs [dædɪ 'lɒŋlegz] (*pl.
daddy longlegs*) koziułka *f*, komarni-
ca *f*; *Am.* kosarz *m*
daf·fo·dil ['dæfədɪl] *bot.* żonkil *m*
daft [dɑːft] F głupi
dag·ger ['dægə] sztylet *m*; *be at ~s
drawn with s.o.* *fig.* być z kimś na
noże
dai·ly ['deɪlɪ] **1.** dzienny, codzienny; *the
~ grind lub rut* codzienny mozół *m*; **2.**
dziennik *m*; pomoc *f* domowa
dain·ty ['deɪntɪ] **1.** (*-ier, -iest*) delikatny, filigranowy; **2.** przysmak *m*
dair·y ['deərɪ] mleczarnia *f*; *attr.* mle-
czarski, mleczny
dai·sy ['deɪzɪ] *bot.* stokrotka *f*
dale [deɪl] *dial. lub poet.* dolina *f*, kotlina *f*
dal·ly ['dælɪ]: **~ about** guzdrać się
Dal·ma·tian [dæl'meɪʃn] *zo.* dalmatyń-
czyk *m*

dam [dæm] **1.** tama *f*, zapora *f*; **2.** (*-mm-*)
też **~ up** ⟨za⟩tamować, stawiać ⟨posta-
wić⟩ tamę
dam·age ['dæmɪdʒ] **1.** szkoda *f*, uszkodzenie *n*; **~s** *pl. jur.* odszkodowanie; **2.**
uszkadzać ⟨-kodzić⟩
dam·ask ['dæməsk] adamaszek *m*
damn [dæm] **1.** potępiać ⟨-tępić⟩; **~** (*it*)!
F cholera!, niech to szlag (trafi)!; **2.** *adj
i adv.* F → *damned*; **3.** *I don't care a ~*
F mało mnie to obchodzi; '**~·a·tion**
[dæm'neɪʃn] *rel.* potępienie *n*; **~ed** F
[dæmd] cholerny; '**~·ing** potępiający,
obciążający
damp [dæmp] **1.** wilgotny; **2.** wilgoć *f*; **3.**
też; '**~·en** nawilżać ⟨-lżyć⟩; ⟨z⟩dławić;
wygaszać ⟨-gasić⟩; '**~·ness** wilgotność
f; wilgoć *f*
dance [dɑːns] **1.** taniec *m*; **2.** ⟨za⟩tań-
czyć; '**danc·er** tancerz *m* (*-rka f*);
'**danc·ing** tańczenie *n*; taniec *m*; *attr.*
taneczny
dan·de·li·on ['dændɪlaɪən] *bot.* mniszek *m* lekarski; F mlecz *m*, dmucha-
wiec *m*
dan·druff ['dændrʌf] łupież *m*
Dane [deɪn] Duńczyk *m*; Dunka *f*
dan·ger ['deɪndʒə] niebezpieczeństwo
n; *be out of ~* być poza zasięgiem zagrożenia; '**~ ar·e·a** strefa *f* zagrożenia;
'**~·ous** ['deɪndʒərəs] niebezpieczny;
'**~ zone** strefa *f* zagrożenia
dan·gle ['dæŋgl] ⟨po⟩majtać

Da·nish ['deɪnɪʃ] **1.** duński; **2.** *ling.* język *m* duński

dank [dæŋk] wilgotny

Dan·ube Dunaj *m*

dare [deə] *v/i.* mieć śmiałość, ważyć się; *I ~ say* sądzę, że; wprawdzie; *how ~ you!* jak śmiesz! *v/t.* czemuś stawić czoło; *kogoś* ⟨s⟩prowokować (*to do s.th.* aby coś zrobił); **'~dev·il** śmiałek *m*, chojrak *m*; *attr.* wyzywająco śmiały; **dar·ing** ['deərɪŋ] **1.** śmiały, wyzywający; **2.** śmiałość *f*

dark [dɑːk] **1.** ciemny; mroczny; ciemnoskóry; *fig.* ponury; tajemniczy; **2.** ciemność *f*; zmrok *m*; *before* (*after*) *~* przed zmrokiem (po zmroku); *nie wyjawiać* ⟨-wić⟩ *czegoś komuś*; '*2* **Ag·es** *pl.* Średniowiecze *n*; '*~·en* ściemniać (się); '*~·ness* ciemność *f*, zmrok *m*; '*~·room phot.* ciemnia *f*

dar·ling ['dɑːlɪŋ] **1.** kochanie *n*; **2.** kochany, ukochany

darn [dɑːn] ⟨za⟩cerować

dart [dɑːt] **1.** strzałka *f*, skok *m*; *~s sg.* (*gra*) strzałki *pl.*; **2.** *v/t.* rzucać ⟨-cić⟩ *v/i.* rzucać ⟨-cić⟩ się; '*~·board* tarcza *f* (*do gry w strzałki*)

dash [dæʃ] **1.** uderzenie *n*; łoskot *m* (*fal*); odrobina *f*, szczypta *f* (*soli*), domieszka *m* (*koloru*); *print.* myślnik *m*, pauza *f*; (*w sporcie*) sprint *m*; *fig.* szyk *m*; *make a ~ for* rzucać ⟨-cić⟩ się do (*G*); **2.** *v/t.* rzucać, ciskać; *nadzieje* unicestwiać ⟨-wić⟩; *v/i.* uderzać ⟨-rzyć⟩ (*against* o *A*); *~ off list* naskrobać; '*~·board mot.* deska *f* rozdzielcza; '*~·ing* pełen fantazji

da·ta ['deɪtə] *pl.*, *sg.* dane *pl.* (*też komp.*); △ *nie data*; '*~ bank*, '*~·base* baza *f* danych; '*~ 'cap·ture* pozyskiwanie *n* danych; *~ 'car·ri·er* nośnik *m* danych; *~ 'in·put* wprowadzanie *n* danych; *~ 'me·di·um* nośnik *m* danych; *~ 'mem·o·ry* pamięć *f* danych; *~ 'out·put* wyprowadzanie *n* danych; *~ 'pro·cess·ing* przetwarzanie *n* danych; *~ pro'tec·tion* zabezpieczanie *n* danych; *~ 'stor·age* przechowywanie *n* danych; *~ 'trans·fer* transfer *m* lub przesyłanie *n* danych; *~ 'typ·ist* osoba *f* wprowadzająca dane

date¹ [deɪt] *bot.* daktyl *m*

date² [deɪt] data *f*; dzień *m*; termin *m*;

randka *f*; *Am.* F dziewczyna *f*, chłopak *m*; *out of ~* przeterminowany; *up to ~* nowoczesny, aktualny; **2.** datować; ustalać ⟨-lić⟩ datę; ⟨po⟩starzeć; *Am.* F iść ⟨pójść⟩ na randkę z (*I*), chodzić z (*I*); '*dat·ed* przestarzały

da·tive ['deɪtɪv] *gr. też ~ case* celownik *m*

daub [dɔːb] ⟨za⟩smarować

daugh·ter ['dɔːtə] córka; *~-in-law* ['dɔːtərɪnlɔː] (*pl.* *daughters-in-law*) synowa *f*

daunt [dɔːnt] onieśmielać ⟨-lić⟩; zniechęcać ⟨-cić⟩

daw [dɔː] *zo.* → *jackdaw*

daw·dle ['dɔːdl] mitrężyć, guzdrać się

dawn [dɔːn] **1.** świt *m* (*też fig.*); *at ~* o świcie; **2.** ⟨za⟩świtać; *~ on fig. komuś* ⟨za⟩świtać

day [deɪ] dzień *m*; doba *f*; *często ~s pl.* czas *m* życia; *any ~* kiedykolwiek; *these ~s* obecnie; *the other ~* niedawno; *the ~ after tomorrow* pojutrze; *open all ~* otwarty całą dobę; *let's call it a ~!* koniec na dzisiaj!; '*~·break* świt *m*; '*~ care cen·tre* (*Am.* cen·ter) → *day nursery*; '*~·dream* **1.** marzenie *n*, mrzonka *f*; **2.** (*dreamed lub dreamt*) marzyć, śnić na jawie; '*~·dream·er* marzyciel(ka *f*) *m*; '*~·light* światło *n* dzienne; *in broad ~light* w biały dzień; *~ nur·se·ry* żłobek *m*; *~ 'off* (*pl.* *days off*) dzień *m* wolnego, wolny dzień *m*; *~ re'turn Brt.* bilet *m* powrotny na jeden dzień; '*~·time: in the ~time* w ciągu dnia, za dnia

daze [deɪz] **1.** oszałamiać ⟨oszołomić⟩; **2.** *in a ~* oszołomiony, w stanie oszołomienia

DC [diː 'siː] *skrót: direct current* prąd *m* stały; *District of Columbia* Dystrykt *m* Kolumbii

DD [diː 'diː] *skrót: double density* podwójna gęstość *f* (*zapisu dyskietek komp.*)

dead [ded] **1.** martwy, nieżywy; *zwierzę:* zdechły, *ryba:* śnięty, *roślina:* zwiędły; obojętny (*to* na *A*); *ręka:* zdrętwiały, bez czucia; *bateria:* wyładowany; nieczynny; *farba itp.:* matowy, bez połysku; *econ.* bez obrotów; *econ.* martwy, nie procentujący; **2.** *adv.* całkiem, zupełnie; od razu, bezpośrednio; *~ slow mot.* krok za krokiem; *~ tired* śmiertelnie zmęczony; **3. the ~** pl. martwi pl., zmarli pl.; **in the ~ of winter (night)** w samym środku zimy (nocy); **~ 'bar·g·ain** niebywała okazja m, gratka; **~ 'centre,** (Am. '**cen·ter**) sam środek m; '**~·en** ⟨z⟩amortyzować, osłabiać ⟨-bić⟩; ⟨wy⟩tłumić; '**~'end** ślepa ulica f (też fig.); **~ 'heat** sport: nierozstrzygnięty bieg m; '**~·line** termin ostateczny m; '**~·lock** fig. pat m, impas m; '**~·locked** w impasie; '**~·loss** econ. czysta strata f; '**~·ly** (**-ier, -iest**) śmiertelny

deaf [def] **1.** głuchy; **~·mute, pej. ~·and dumb** głuchoniemy; **2. the ~** pl. głusi pl.; '**~·en** osłabiać ⟨-bić⟩, zagłuszyć

deal [diːl] **1.** F interes m, transakcja f; postępowanie n; **it's a** ~! zgoda!; **a good ~** dużo, wiele; **a great ~** bardzo dużo, bardzo wiele; **2.** (**dealt**) v/t. rozdawać ⟨-dać⟩ (też karty); uderzenie wymierzać ⟨-rzyć⟩; v/i. handlować; sl. handlować narkotykami; karty: rozdawać ⟨-dać⟩; **~ with** zajmować się; poradzić sobie z (I); econ. mieć interesy z (I); '**~·er** econ. dealer m (też narkotyków), handlarz m (-rka f); '**~·ing** postępowanie n; econ. transakcja; '**~·ings** pl. stosunki pl. handlowe; interesy pl.; **~t** [delt] pret. i p.p. od **deal** 2

dean [diːn] dziekan m

dear [dɪə] **1.** coś drogi, kosztowny; ktoś drogi, szanowny; **2 Sir,** (w listach) Szanowny Panie; **2.** kochany m (-na f); kochanie n; **my dear** mój drogi m, moja droga f; **3.** (**oh**), **~!, ~!, ~ me!** F o Boże!; '**~·ly** gorąco, całym sercem; drogo

death [deθ] śmierć f; wypadek m śmiertelny, zgon m; '**~·bed** łoże n śmierci; '**~ cer·tif·i·cate** świadectwo n zgonu; '**~·ly** (**-ier, -iest**) śmiertelny; '**~ war·rant** jur. wyrok m śmierci

de·bar [dɪ'bɑː] (**-rr-**): **~ from doing s.th.** kogoś powstrzymywać ⟨-mać⟩ przed zrobieniem czegoś

de·base [dɪ'beɪs] ⟨z⟩degradować; ⟨z⟩dewaluować; ⟨z⟩deprecjonować

de·ba·ta·ble [dɪ'beɪtəbl] dyskusyjny; **de·bate** [dɪ'beɪt] **1.** dyskusja f, debata f; **2.** debatować (nad I), dyskutować

deb·it econ. [debɪt] **1.** debet m; strona "winien" ~ **and credit** przychód f i rozchód; **2.** kogoś, konto obciążać ⟨-żyć⟩

deb·ris ['debriː] szczątki pl., pozostałości pl.

debt [det] dług m; wierzytelność f; **be in** ~ mieć dług; **be out of** ~ nie mieć długu; '~·**or** dłużnik m (-iczka f), wierzyciel(ka f) m

de·bug [diː'bʌɡ] tech. (**-gg-**) usuwać ⟨usunąć⟩ usterki (zwł. programu)

de·but [deɪbjuː] debiut m

Dec skrót pisany: **December** grudz., grudzień m

dec·ade ['dekeɪd] dekada f, dziesięciolecie n

dec·a·dent ['dekədənt] dekadencki

de·caf·fein·at·ed [diː'kæfɪneɪtɪd] bezkofeinowy

de·camp [dɪ'kæmp] F nawiewać ⟨-wiać⟩

de·cant [dɪ'kænt] przelewać ⟨-lać⟩; ~·**er** karafka f

de·cath·l·ete [dɪ'kæθliːt] (w sporcie) dziesięciobista m; ~·**lon** [dɪ'kæθlɒn] (w sporcie) dziesięciobój m

de·cay [dɪ'keɪ] **1.** v/i. ⟨ze⟩psuć się, ⟨z⟩gnić; rozkładać ⟨-łożyć⟩ się; upadać ⟨upaść⟩; v/t. rozkładać ⟨-łożyć⟩; **2.** rozkład m, rozpad m; upadek m

de·cease [dɪ'siːs] zwł. jur. śmierć f, zgon m; ~·**d** zwł. jur. **1. the** ~**d** zmarły m (-ła f), zmarli pl.; **2.** zmarły

de·ceit [dɪ'siːt] oszustwo n; fałsz m; ~·**ful** oszukańczy; fałszywy

de·ceive [dɪ'siːv] oszukiwać ⟨-kać⟩; **de'ceiv·er** oszust(ka f) m

De·cem·ber [dɪ'sembə] (skrót: **Dec**) grudzień m

de·cen|·cy ['diːsnsɪ] przyzwoitość f; uczciwość f; '~·**t** przyzwoity; uczciwy

de·cep|·tion [dɪ'sepʃn] oszustwo n; ~·**tive: be** ~**tive** być podstępnym lub zwodniczym

de·cide [dɪ'saɪd] ⟨z⟩decydować się; ⟨za⟩decydować; rozstrzygać ⟨-gnąć⟩; **de'cid·ed** zdecydowany; wyraźny

dec·i·mal ['desɪml] **1.** dziesiętny; **2.** też ~ **fraction** ułamek m dziesiętny

de·ci·pher [dɪ'saɪfə] odcyfrować; odszyfrować

de·ci|·sion [dɪ'sɪʒn] decyzja f; postanowienie n; stanowczość f; **make (reach, come to) a** ~**sion** podejmować ⟨-djąć⟩ decyzję; ~·**sive** [dɪ'saɪsɪv] decydujący; zdecydowany

deck [dek] **1.** naut. pokład m; piętro n (autobusu itp.); Am. talia f; tech. deck m; **2.** ~ **out** ⟨wy⟩stroić (się); '~·**chair** leżak m

dec·la·ra·tion [deklə'reɪʃn] deklaracja *f*; oświadczenie *n*; wypowiedzenie *n*; deklaracja *f* celna

de·clare [dɪ'kleə] zadeklarować, ogłaszać ⟨ogłosić⟩; zgłaszać ⟨zgłosić⟩ do oclenia; *wojnę* wypowiadać ⟨-wiedzieć⟩

de·clen·sion [dɪ'klenʃn] deklinacja *f*

de·cline [dɪ'klaɪn] **1.** odmawiać ⟨-mówić⟩, odmawiać ⟨-mówić⟩ przyjęcia; zmniejszać ⟨-szyć⟩ (się); chylić się do upadku; *ceny* spadać ⟨spaść⟩; *gr.* deklinować; **2.** upadek *m*; spadek *m*

de·cliv·i·ty [dɪ'klɪvətɪ] stok *m*, zbocze *n*

de·clutch [di:'klʌtʃ] *mot.* wyłączać ⟨-czyć⟩ sprzęgło

de·code [di:'kəʊd] dekodować

de·com·pose [di:kəm'pəʊz] rozkładać ⟨-łożyć⟩ (się)

de·con·tam·i·nate [di:kən'tæmɪneɪt] odkażać ⟨odkazić⟩; **~·na·tion** odkażenie *n*; dekontaminacja *f*

dec·o·rate ['dekəreɪt] ⟨u⟩dekorować, ozdabiać ⟨-dobić⟩; odnawiać ⟨-nowić⟩, ⟨od-, wy⟩malować; ⟨wy⟩tapetować; nadawać ⟨-dać⟩ odznaczenie; **~·ra·tion** [dekə'reɪʃn] dekoracja *f*; odnowienie *n*, wymalowanie *n*, wytapetowanie *n*; odznaczenie *n*; **~·ra·tive** ['dekərətɪv] dekoracyjny, ozdobny; **~·ra·tor** ['dekəreɪtə] dekorator *m*; malarz *m*, tapeciarz *m*

dec·o·rous ['dekərəs] przywoity; **de·co·rum** [dɪ'kɔ:rəm] przywoitość *f*

de·coy 1. ['di:kɔɪ] przynęta *f*; **2.** [dɪ'kɔɪ] ⟨z⟩wabić (*into* do *G*)

de·crease 1. ['di:kri:s] spadek *m*, zmniejszenie n się; **2.** [di:'kri:s] spadać ⟨spaść⟩, zmniejszać ⟨-szyć⟩ się

de·cree [dɪ'kri:] **1.** dekret *m*, rozporządzenie *n*; *zwł. Am.* jur. decyzja *f*, wyrok *m*; **2.** nakazywać ⟨-zać⟩

ded·i·cate ['dedɪkeɪt] ⟨za⟩dedykować; **~·cat·ed** wyspecjalizowany; **~·ca·tion** [dedr'keɪʃn] dedykacja *f*

de·duce [dɪ'dju:s] ⟨wy⟩dedukować; ⟨wy⟩wnioskować

de·duct [dɪ'dʌkt] odejmować ⟨-jąć⟩; *kwotę itp.* potrącać ⟨-cić⟩ (*from* z *G*), odliczać ⟨-czyć⟩; **~·i·ble**: **~·ible from tax** podlegający odpisaniu od podatku; **de·duc·tion** [dɪ'dʌkʃn] potrącenie *n* (*kwoty itp.*); odliczenie *n*, odpis *m*; wniosek *m*

deed [di:d] czyn *m*, uczynek *m*; wy-

czyn *m* (*bohaterski*); *jur.* dokument *m* (*prawny*)

deep [di:p] **1.** głęboki (*też fig.*); **2.** głębokość *f*; **~·en** pogłębiać ⟨-bić⟩ (się) (*też fig.*); **~'freeze 1.** (*-froze, -frozen*) zamrażać ⟨-mrozić⟩; **2.** zamrażarka *f*; **~'fro·zen** zamrożony; **~'fry** ⟨u⟩smażyć (*jak we frytkownicy*); **'~·ness** głębia *f*, głębokość *f*

deer [dɪə] *zo.* (*pl. deer*) jeleń *m*, sarna *f*; zwierzyna *f* płowa

de·face [dɪ'feɪs] ⟨o⟩szpecić; zacierać ⟨zatrzeć⟩

def·a·ma·tion [defə'meɪʃn] zniesławienie *n*

de·fault [dɪ'fɔ:lt] **1.** *jur.* niestawienie się (*przed sądem*); (*w sporcie*) niestawiennictwo *n*; *econ.* zwłoka; *komp.* domyślna wartość *f lub* nastawienie *n* domyślne; *attr., komp.* domyślny, standardowy; **2.** *econ.* nie wywiązywać ⟨-wiązać⟩ się ze zobowiązania; *jur.* nie stawiać ⟨-wić⟩ się (*przed sądem*); (*w sporcie*) nie stawić się

de·feat [dɪ'fi:t] **1.** porażka *f*, klęska *f*; **2.** pobić; pokonywać ⟨-nać⟩; ⟨z⟩niweczyć

de·fect [dɪ'fekt] defekt *m*, wada *f*; **de·fec·tive** wadliwy

de·fence *Brt.*, **de·fense** *Am.* [dɪ'fens] obrona *f*; **witness for the ~** świadek *m* obrony; **~·less** bezbronny

de·fend [dɪ'fend] (*from, against*) bronić (się) (przed *I*); (*w sporcie*) ⟨o⟩bronić; **de'fen·dant** *jur.* pozwany *m* (-na *f*); oskarżony *m* (-na *f*); **de'fend·er** obrońca *m*

de·fen·sive [dɪ'fensɪv] **1.** defensywa *f*; **on the ~** w defensywie; **2.** defensywny, obronny

de·fer [dɪ'fɜ:] (*-rr-*) odkładać ⟨-łożyć⟩, odraczać ⟨-roczyć⟩

de·fi·ance [dɪ'faɪəns] wyzwanie *n*, bunt *m*; **in ~ance of** wbrew (*D*); **~·ant** wyzywający, buntowniczy

de·fi·cien·cy [dɪ'fɪʃnsɪ] brak *m*, niedostatek *m*; niedobór *m*; **~t** brakujący, niedostateczny; **~t in** ubogi w (*A*), o niewystarczającej ilości (*G*)

def·i·cit ['defɪsɪt] *econ.* deficyt *m*, niedobór *m*

de·file[1] ['di:faɪl] wąwóz *m*, przesmyk *m*

de·file[2] [dɪ'faɪl] ⟨z⟩bezcześcić, ⟨s⟩kalać

de·fine [dɪ'faɪn] ⟨z⟩definiować, określać ⟨-lić⟩; wyjaśniać ⟨-nić⟩; **def·i·nite**

['definit] określony; jasny, sprecyzowany; **def·i·ni·tion** [defi'niʃn] definicja *f*; (*w TV, filmie*) rozdzielczość *f*; **de·fin·itive** [di'finitiv] ostateczny, rozstrzygający; wzorcowy
de·flect [di'flekt] *v/t.* odbijać ⟨-bić⟩; *v/i.* zbaczać ⟨zboczyć⟩, zmieniać ⟨-nić⟩ kierunek
de·form [di'fɔːm] ⟨z⟩deformować, zniekształcać ⟨-cić⟩; **~ed** zdeformowany, zniekształcony; **de·for·mi·ty** [di'fɔːməti] deformacja *f*, zniekształcenie *n*
de·fraud [di'frɔːd] ⟨z⟩defraudować (*of* na A), sprzeniewierzać ⟨-rzyć⟩
de·frost [diː'frɒst] rozmrażać ⟨-rozić⟩ (się)
deft [deft] zręczny, zgrabny, zdolny
de·fy [di'fai] wyzywać ⟨-zwać⟩; przeciwstawiać ⟨-wić⟩ się (*D*); wzywać ⟨wezwać⟩
de·gen·e·rate 1. [di'dʒenəreit] ⟨z⟩degenerować się, ⟨z⟩wyrodnieć; **2.** [di'dʒenərət] zdegenerowany, zwyrodniały; **3.** degenerat *m*
deg·ra·da·tion [degrə'deiʃn] poniżenie *n*; **de·grade** [di'greid] *v/t.* poniżać ⟨-żyć⟩
de·gree [di'griː] stopień *m* (*też naukowy*); **by ~s** stopniowo; **take one's ~** otrzymywać ⟨-mać⟩ stopień naukowy (*in* w zakresie *G*)
de·hy·drat·ed [diː'haidreitid] odwodniony, suszony
de·i·fy ['diːifai] ubóstwiać ⟨-wić⟩, deifikować
deign [dein] być łaskawym, raczyć
de·i·ty ['diːiti] bóstwo *n*
de·jec·ted [di'dʒektid] przygnębiony, przygaszony; **~tion** [di'dʒekʃn] przygnębienie *n*
de·lay [di'lei] **1.** zwłoka *f*; *rail itp.* opóźnienie *n*; okres *m* opóźnienia; **2.** zwlekać ⟨-wlec⟩; opóźniać ⟨-nić⟩; odłożyć ⟨odkładać⟩
del·e·gate 1. ['deligeit] *kogoś* ⟨od⟩delegować; *uprawnienia itp.* przekazywać ⟨-zać⟩, delegować; **2.** ['deligət] delegat *m*, wysłannik *m* (-iczka *f*); **~·ga·tion** [deli'geiʃn] delegacja *f*; przekazanie *n*
de·lete [di'liːt] wymazywać ⟨-zać⟩; *komp.* ⟨s⟩kasować
de·lib·e·rate [di'libərət] umyślny; rozważny; **~·ra·tion** [dilibə'reiʃn] zasta-

nowienie *n*, rozwaga *f*; **with ~·ra·tion** z namaszczeniem
del·i·ca·cy ['delikəsi] delikatność *f*; subtelność *f*; smakołyk *m*, przysmak *m*; **~·cate** ['delikət] delikatny; subtelny; **~·ca·tes·sen** [delikə'tesn] delikatesy *pl.*
de·li·cious [di'liʃəs] smakowity
de·light [di'lait] **1.** zachwyt *m*, przyjemność *f*; **2.** *v/t.* zabawiać; *v/i.* znajdować wielką przyjemność (*in* w *L*); **~·ful** zachwycający
de·lin·quen·cy [di'liŋkwənsi] przestępczość *f*; **~·t 1.** winny przewinienia; **2.** przestępca *m* → *juvenile delinquent*
de·lir·i·ous [di'liriəs] *med.* majaczący; **~·um** [di'liriəm] majaczenie *n*; delirium *n*
de·liv·er [di'livə] dostarczać ⟨-czyć⟩; *listy itp.* doręczać ⟨-czyć⟩; *cios itp.* wymierzać ⟨-czyć⟩; *wykład itp.* wygłaszać ⟨-głosić⟩; uwalniać ⟨-wolnić⟩; *med. dziecko itp.* odbierać ⟨odebrać⟩; **~·ance** [di'livərəns] oswobodzenie *n*; **~·er** [di'livərə] oswobodziciel(ka *f*) *m*; **~·y** [di'livəri] dostarczenie *n*; doręczenie *n* (*poczty itp.*); wygłoszenie *n* (*mowy itp.*); odczyt *m*, referat *m*; *med.* poród *m*; **~·y van** furgonetka *f* dostawcza
dell [del] dolina *f*
de·lude [di'luːd] łudzić
del·uge ['deljuːdʒ] potop *m, fig.* zalew *m*
de·lu·sion [di'luːʒn] ułuda *f*, złudzenie *n*
de·mand [di'mɑːnd] **1.** żądanie *n*; zapotrzebowanie *n*, popyt *m* (*for* na *A*); obciążenie *n*; *in ~* na żądanie, w razie potrzeby; **2.** ⟨za⟩żądać, domagać się; wymagać; **~·ing** wymagający
de·men·ted [di'mentid] obłąkany; *med.* otępiały
demi... ['demi] pół..., demi...
de·mil·i·ta·rize [diː'militəraiz] ⟨z⟩demilitaryzować
dem·o ['deməu] F (*pl.* **-os**) demo *n* (*wersja demonstracyjna*), demonstracja *f* (*uliczna*)
de·mo·bi·lize [diː'məubilaiz] ⟨z⟩demobilizować
de·moc·ra·cy [di'mɒkrəsi] demokracja *f*
dem·o·crat ['deməkræt] demokrata *m*

(-tka f); ~·ic [demə'krætɪk] demokratyczny

de·mol·ish [dɪ'mɒlɪʃ] ⟨z⟩burzyć; ⟨z⟩niszczyć, obalać ⟨-lić⟩; F *jedzenie* pochłaniać ⟨-łonąć⟩; dem·o·li·tion [demə'lɪʃn] (z)burzenie n; zniszczenie n, obalenie n

de·mon ['diːmən] demon m; czart m

dem·on|·strate ['demənstreɪt] ⟨za⟩monstrować; wykazywać ⟨-zać⟩; dowodzić ⟨-wieść⟩; ~·stra·tion [demən'streɪʃn] demonstracja f; dowód m; pokaz m; manifestacja f; ~·stra·tive [dɪ'mɒnstrətɪv] gr. wskazujący; *be* ~*strative* być wylewnym; ~·stra·tor ['demənstreɪtə] demonstrator(ka f) m

de·mor·al·ize [dɪ'mɒrəlaɪz] ⟨z⟩demoralizować; zniechęcać ⟨-cić⟩

de·mote [diː'məʊt] ⟨z⟩degradować

de·mure [dɪ'mjʊə] potulny, nieśmiały

den [den] jaskinia f, legowisko n; fig. własny kąt m

de·ni·al [dɪ'naɪəl] zaprzeczenie n; odmowa f; wyparcie n się; *official* ~ dementi n

den·ims ['denɪmz] pl. dżinsy pl.

Den·mark ['denmɑːk] Dania f

de·nom·i·na·tion [dɪnɒmɪ'neɪʃn] rel. wyznanie n

de·note [dɪ'nəʊt] oznaczać, znaczyć

de·nounce [dɪ'naʊns] *kogoś* ⟨za⟩denuncjować; *coś* potępiać ⟨-pić⟩

dense [dens] (*-r, -st*) gęsty; fig. ciemny, przygłupi; den·si·ty ['densətɪ] gęstość f

dent [dent] 1. wgniecenie n; 2. wgniatać ⟨wgnieść⟩

den·tal ['dentl] zębny, nazębny; ~ 'plaque osad m nazębny; ~ 'plate proteza f; ~ 'sur·geon dentysta m (-tka f), stomatolog m

den·tist ['dentɪst] dentysta m (-tka f), stomatolog m

den·tures ['dentʃəz] med. pl. proteza f dentystyczna

de·nun·ci·a·tion [dɪnʌnsɪ'eɪʃn] potępienie n; denuncjacja f; ~·tor [dɪ'nʌnsɪeɪtə] denuncjator(ka f) m

de·ny [dɪ'naɪ] zaprzeczać ⟨-czyć⟩; ⟨z⟩dementować; odmawiać ⟨-mówić⟩; wypierać ⟨-przeć⟩ się

de·o·do·rant [diː'əʊdərənt] dezodorant m

dep *skrót pisany*: **depart** odjeżdżać; *departure* odj., odjazd m

de·part [dɪ'pɑːt] odjeżdżać ⟨-jechać⟩; odejść ⟨odchodzić⟩ (*from* od G), odstępować ⟨-stąpić⟩

de·part·ment [dɪ'pɑːtmənt] dział m; wydział m; *univ. też* zakład m, instytut m; *pol.* ministerstwo n; 2 of De'fense, *też* **Defence** *Am.* Ministerstwo n Obrony; 2 of the En'vi·ron·ment *Brt.* Ministerstwo n Ochrony Środowiska; 2 of the In·te·ri·or *Am.* Ministerstwo n Spraw Wewnętrznych; 2 of 'State, *też* **State** 2 *Am. pol.* Departament m Stanu, Ministerstwo n Spraw Zagranicznych; ~ store dom m towarowy

de·par·ture [dɪ'pɑːtʃə] *też rail.* odjazd m, *aviat.* odlot m; odejście n (od tematu); ~*s pl.* odjazdy pl. (*w rozkładzie jazdy*); ~ gate *aviat.* przejście n do samolotu; ~ lounge *aviat.* hala f odlotów

de·pend [dɪ'pend]: ~ *on* polegać na (L); liczyć na (A); zależeć od (G); *that ~s* to zależy

de·pen·da·ble [dɪ'pendəbl] godny zaufania; ~·dant osoba f na czyimś utrzymaniu; ~·dence zależność f; zaufanie n; ~·dent 1. zależny (*on* od G); 2. → *dependant*

de·plor·a·ble [dɪ'plɔːrəbl] godny pożałowania; ~e [dɪ'plɔː] ubolewać nad (I)

de·pop·u·late [diː'pɒpjʊleɪt] wyludniać ⟨-nić⟩

de·port [dɪ'pɔːt] deportować, wywozić ⟨-wieźć⟩; usuwać ⟨usunąć⟩

de·pose [dɪ'pəʊz] usuwać ⟨-nąć⟩ z urzędu; jur. zaświadczać ⟨-czyć⟩

de·pos·it [dɪ'pɒzɪt] 1. składać ⟨złożyć⟩; ⟨z⟩deponować; geol., chem. osadzać ⟨-dzić⟩ (się); econ. zaliczkę uiszczać ⟨uiścić⟩; 2. chem. osad m; geol. też złoże n; depozyt m; econ. wpłata f; kaucja f; *make a ~it* wpłacać ⟨-cić⟩ zaliczkę lub zadatek; ~it ac·count zwł. Brt. rachunek m lokat okresowych; ~·i·tor deponent(ka f) m

dep·ot ['depəʊ] skład m, magazyn m; Am. ['diːpəʊ] dworzec m

de·prave [dɪ'preɪv] etycznie ⟨z⟩deprawować

de·pre·ci·ate [dɪ'priːʃɪeɪt] ⟨z⟩deprecjonować, obniżać ⟨-żyć⟩ wartość

de·press [dɪ'pres] naciskać ⟨-cisnąć⟩; przygnębiać ⟨-bić⟩; ⟨z⟩tłumić, przygłuszać ⟨-szyć⟩; **~ed** w depresji; przygnębiony; *econ. rynek*: osłabiony; **~ed ar·e·a** obszar dotknięty depresją; **~ing** deprymujący, przygnębiający; **de·pression** [dɪ'preʃn] depresja *f* (*też econ.*); przygnębienie *n*; obniżenie *n*; *meteor.* niskie ciśnienie *n*, obszar *m* niskiego ciśnienia

de·prive [dɪ'praɪv]: **~ s.o. of s.th.** pozbawiać ⟨-wić⟩ kogoś czegoś; **~d** nieuprzywilejowany

dept, Dept *skrót pisany:* **Department** dział, wydział

depth [depθ] głębokość *f*, głębia *f*

dep·u·ta·tion [depjʊ'teɪʃn] delegacja *f*; **~tize** ['depjʊtaɪz]: **~tize for s.o.** zastępować ⟨-stąpić⟩ kogoś; **~ty** ['depjʊtɪ] zastępca *m* (-czyni *f*); *pol.* poseł *m* (-słanka *f*); *też* **~ty sheriff** zastępca *m* (-czyni *f*) szeryfa

de·rail [dɪ'reɪl] wykolejać; **be ~ed** wykoleić się

de·ranged [dɪ'reɪndʒd] obłąkany

der·e·lict ['derəlɪkt] opuszczony

de·ride [dɪ'raɪd] ⟨wy⟩szydzić; **de·ri·sion** [dɪ'rɪʒn] szyderstwo *n*; **de·ri·sive** [dɪ'raɪsɪv] szyderczy

de·rive [dɪ'raɪv] pochodzić (**from** z *A*); wywodzić się (**from** z *A*); **~ pleasure from** znajdować ⟨znaleźć⟩ przyjemność w (*L*)

der·ma·tol·o·gist [dɜːmə'tɒlədʒɪst] *med.* dermatolog *m*

de·rog·a·to·ry [dɪ'rɒgətərɪ] poniżający, uwłaczający, przynoszący ujmę

der·rick ['derɪk] *tech.* żuraw *m* masztowy; *naut.* żuraw *m* ładunkowy; wieża *f* wiertnicza

de·scend [dɪ'send] obniżać ⟨-żyć⟩ się, zniżać ⟨-żyć⟩ się; schodzić ⟨zejść⟩; *aviat.* wytracać ⟨-cić⟩ wysokość, schodzić ⟨zejść⟩ w dół; pochodzić, wywodzić się (**from** z *G*); **~ on** zwalać ⟨-lić⟩ się na (*A*), ⟨za⟩atakować, napadać ⟨-paść⟩; **de·scen·dant** potomek *m*

de·scent [dɪ'sent] obniżanie *n* się; zniżanie *n* się; schodzenie *n*; *aviat.* wytracanie *n* wysokości; pochodzenie *n*; najście *n*, desant *m*

de·scribe [dɪ'skraɪb] opisywać ⟨-sać⟩

de·scrip·tion [dɪ'skrɪpʃn] opis *m*; rodzaj *m*; **~tive** [dɪ'skrɪptɪv] opisowy; obrazowy

des·e·crate ['desɪkreɪt] ⟨z⟩bezcześcić, ⟨s⟩profanować

de·seg·re·gate [diː'segrɪgeɪt] znosić ⟨-nieść⟩ segregację rasową; **~ga·tion** [diːsegrɪ'geɪʃn] znoszenie *n* segregacji rasowej

des·ert¹ ['dezət] pustynia *f*; *attr.* pustynny

de·sert² [dɪ'zɜːt] *v/t.* opuszczać ⟨opuścić⟩, porzucać ⟨-cić⟩; *v/i.* ⟨z⟩dezerterować; **~er** *mil.* dezerter *m*; **de·ser·tion** [dɪ'zɜːʃn] (*jur. też złośliwe*) porzucenie *n*; dezercja *f*

de·serve [dɪ'zɜːv] zasługiwać ⟨-służyć⟩ na (*A*); **de·serv·ed·ly** [dɪ'zɜːvɪdlɪ] zasłużenie; **de·serv·ing** zasłużony

de·sign [dɪ'zaɪn] **1.** projekt *m*, plan *m*; *tech.* projekt *m*, rysunek *m* techniczny; wzór *m*, deseń *m*; zamiar *m*; **2.** ⟨za⟩projektować, ⟨za⟩planować; zamyślać ⟨-ślić⟩

des·ig·nate ['dezɪgneɪt] wyznaczać ⟨-czyć⟩

de·sign·er [dɪ'zaɪnə] konstruktor(ka *f*) *m*; projektant(ka *f*) *m*

de·sir·a·ble [dɪ'zaɪərəbl] pożądany; **~e** [dɪ'zaɪə] **1.** chęć *f*, zamiar *m*; pożądanie *n* (**for** *G*), chętka *f*; **2.** ⟨za⟩pragnąć, ⟨za⟩życzyć sobie; pożądać, mieć chęć

de·sist [dɪ'zɪst] zaprzestawać ⟨-tać⟩

desk [desk] biurko *n*; ławka *f*; recepcja *f*; punkt *m* informacyjny; **~·top com'put·er** komputer *m* biurkowy; **~·top 'pub·lish·ing** (*skrót:* **DTP**) *komp.* DTP *n*, mała poligrafia *f*

des·o·late ['desələt] wyludniony, opuszczony

de·spair [dɪ'speə] **1.** rozpacz *f*; **2.** ⟨s⟩tracić nadzieję (**of** na *A*); **~·ing** [dɪ'speərɪŋ] zrozpaczony

de·spatch [dɪ'spætʃ] → **dispatch**

des·per·ate ['despərət] zdesperowany; desperacki; F rozpaczliwy, beznadziejny; **~·a·tion** [despə'reɪʃn] desperacja *f*

des·pic·a·ble [dɪ'spɪkəbl] zasługujący na pogardę, nikczemny

de·spise [dɪ'spaɪz] ⟨po⟩gardzić, ⟨z⟩lekceważyć

de·spite [dɪ'spaɪt] (po)mimo (*G*)

de·spon·dent [dɪ'spɒndənt] pozbawiony nadziei, przygnębiony

des·pot 'despɒt] despota *m* (-tka *f*)

des·sert [dɪ'zɜːt] deser *m*

des‧ti‧na‧tion [destɪˈneɪʃn] przeznaczenie *n*, miejsce *n* przeznaczenia;
~tined [ˈdestɪnd] przeznaczony; zdążający (*for* do *G*); **~ti‧ny** [ˈdestɪnɪ]
przeznaczenie *n*

des‧ti‧tute [ˈdestɪtjuːt] bez środków do
życia

de‧stroy [dɪˈstrɔɪ] ⟨z⟩niszczyć; *zwierzęta* uśmiercać ⟨-cić⟩; **~er** niszczy-
ciel(ka *f*) *m*; *mil. naut.* niszczyciel *m*

de‧struc‧tion [dɪˈstrʌkʃn] zniszczenie *n*; **~tive** [dɪˈstrʌktɪv] niszczyciel-
ski, destruktywny

de‧tach [dɪˈtætʃ] odczepiać ⟨-pić⟩, odłączać ⟨-czyć⟩; **~ed** oddzielny, osobny;
ktoś: pełen dystansu; **~ed house** do-
m(ek) *m* wolnostojący; **~ment** dystans *m*; *mil.* oddział *m* (*wydzielony*)

de‧tail [ˈdiːteɪl] **1.** szczegół *m*, detal *m*; *mil.* oddział *m* (*wydzielony*);
in ~ szczegółowo; **2.** wyszczególniać
⟨-nić⟩; *mil.* odkomenderować; **~ed**
szczegółowy

de‧tain [dɪˈteɪn] zatrzymywać ⟨-mać⟩;
jur. ⟨za⟩aresztować

de‧tect [dɪˈtekt] wykrywać ⟨-ryć⟩, wyczuwać ⟨-czuć⟩; **de‧tec‧tion** [dɪˈtekʃn]
wykrycie *n*; **de‧tec‧tive** [dɪˈtektɪv] detektyw *m*, wywiadowca *m*; **de‧tec‧tive
nov‧el**, **de‧tec‧tive sto‧ry** powieść *f*
detektywistyczna

de‧ten‧tion [dɪˈtenʃn] zatrzymanie *n*;
areszt *m*

de‧ter [dɪˈtɜː] (*-rr-*) odstraszać ⟨-szyć⟩
(*from* od *G*)

de‧ter‧gent [dɪˈtɜːdʒənt] detergent *m*;
proszek *m* do prania; środek *m* do prania; *attr.* detergentowy

de‧te‧ri‧o‧rate [dɪˈtɪərɪəreɪt] podupa-
dać ⟨-paść⟩; pogarszać ⟨-gorszyć⟩ się

de‧ter‧mi‧na‧tion [dɪtɜːmɪˈneɪʃn] zdecydowanie *n*, stanowczość *f*; determinacja *f*; stwierdzenie *n*, ustalenie *n*;
~mine [dɪˈtɜːmɪn] postanawiać ⟨-no-
wić⟩, ⟨z⟩decydować się na (*A*); stwierdzać ⟨-dzić⟩, określać ⟨-lić⟩, ustalać
⟨-lić⟩; **~mined** zdeterminowany, zdecydowany

de‧ter‧rence [dɪˈterəns] odstrasza-
nie *n*; **~rent 1.** odstraszający; **2.** środek
m odstraszający

de‧test [dɪˈtest] nie cierpieć

de‧throne [dɪˈθrəʊn] ⟨z⟩detronizować

de‧to‧nate [ˈdetəneɪt] *v/t.* ⟨z⟩detono-

wać; **2.** wybuchać ⟨-chnąć⟩, eksplodować

de‧tour [ˈdiːtʊə] objazd *m*

de‧tract [dɪˈtrækt]: **~ from** zmniejszać
⟨-szyć⟩ (*A*)

de‧tri‧ment [ˈdetrɪmənt] szkoda *f*, u-
szczerbek *m*

deuce [djuːs] (*w kartach*) dwa, dwójka *f*; (*w tenisie*) równowaga *f*

de‧val‧u‧a‧tion [diːvæljuˈeɪʃn] dewaluacja *f*; **~e** [diːˈ] ⟨z⟩dewaluować

dev‧a‧state [ˈdevəsteɪt] ⟨z⟩dewasto-
wać, ⟨z⟩niszczyć; **~stat‧ing** niszczy-
cielski

de‧vel‧op [dɪˈveləp] rozwijać (się); *phot.*
wywoływać ⟨-łać⟩; *teren budowlany* za-
gospodarowywać ⟨-ować⟩, rozbudowy-
wać ⟨-ować⟩; *stare miasto*: dokonywać
⟨-konać⟩ sanacji; **~er** *phot.* wywoły-
wacz *m*; przedsiębiorca *m* budowlany; **~ing** rozwijający (się); **~ing
'coun‧try**, **~ing 'na‧tion** kraj *m* rozwijający się; **~ment** rozwój *m*; zagos-
podarowanie *n*, sanacja *f*

de‧vi‧ate [ˈdiːvɪeɪt] zbaczać ⟨zboczyć⟩
(*from* z *G*), odchodzić (*from* od *G*);
~a‧tion [diːvɪˈeɪʃn] zboczenie *n*; de-
wiacja *f*

de‧vice [dɪˈvaɪs] urządzenie *n*, przyrząd *m*; plan *m*, pomysł *m*; *literacki*
chwyt *m*; **leave s.o. to his own ~s** po-
zostawić kogoś samego

dev‧il [ˈdevl] czart *m*, diabeł *m*; **~ish**
diabelski

de‧vi‧ous [ˈdiːvjəs] *coś*: kręty; *ktoś*: po-
krętny; **~ route** droga *f* okrężna

de‧vise [dɪˈvaɪz] wymyślić

de‧void [dɪˈvɔɪd]: **~ of** pozbawiony (*G*)

de‧vote [dɪˈvəʊt] poświęcać ⟨-cić⟩;
de‧vot‧ed poświęcony; oddany; **de-
vo‧tee** [devəʊˈtiː] wielbiciel(ka *f*) *m*;
wyznawca *m* (-czyni *f*); **de‧vo‧tion**
[dɪˈvəʊʃn] poświęcenie *n*; ofiarność *f*;
oddanie *n*

de‧vour [dɪˈvaʊə] pożerać ⟨-żreć⟩

de‧vout [dɪˈvaʊt] pobożny; *nadzieja*:
gorący

dew [djuː] rosa *f*; **~drop** kropla *f* rosy;
~y (*-ier, -iest*) wilgotny

dex‧ter‧i‧ty [dekˈsterətɪ] zręczność *f*,
sprawność *f*; **~ter‧ous**, **~trous** [ˈdeks-
trəs] zręczny, sprawny

di‧ag‧nose [ˈdaɪəɡnəʊz] ⟨z⟩diagno-
zować, stawiać ⟨postawić⟩ diagno-

zę; **~·no·sis** [daɪəg'nəʊsɪs] (*pl. -ses* [-siːz]) diagnoza *f*

di·ag·o·nal [daɪ'ægənl] **1.** przekątny, ukośny; **2.** przekątna *f*

di·a·gram ['daɪəgræm] diagram *m*, wykres *m*

di·al ['daɪəl] **1.** cyferblat *m*; *tel.* tarcza *f* (*telefonu*); *tech.* skala *f*; **2.** (*zwł. Brt. -ll-, Am. -l-*) *tel.* nakręcać ⟨-cić⟩, wybierać ⟨-brać⟩; **~ direct** wybierać bezpośredni numer (*to* do *G*); **direct ~(l)ing** bezpośrednie połączenie *n*

di·a·lect ['daɪəlekt] dialekt *m*

'di·al·ling code *Brt. tel.* numer *m* kierunkowy

di·a·logue *Brt.*, **di·a·log** *Am.* ['daɪəlɒg] dialog *m*, rozmowa *f*

di·am·e·ter [daɪ'æmɪtə] średnica *f*; **in ~** średnicy

di·a·mond ['daɪəmənd] diament *m*, brylant *m*; romb *m*; (*w kartach*) karo *n*

di·a·per ['daɪəpə] *Am.* pielucha *f*, pieluszka *f*

di·a·phragm ['daɪəfræm] *anat.* przepona *f*; *opt.* przesłona *f*; *tel.* membrana *f*

di·ar·rh(o)e·a [daɪə'rɪə] *med.* biegunka *f*

di·a·ry ['daɪərɪ] pamiętnik *m*; kalendarzyk *m* kieszonkowy

dice [daɪs] **1.** *pl. od* **die**[2]; kostka *f* do gry; kości (*gra*) *pl.*; **2.** *gastr.* ⟨po⟩kroić w kostkę; ⟨za-, po⟩grać w kości

dick [dɪk] *Am. sl.* (*prywatny detektyw*) glina *m*

dick·y·bird ['dɪkɪbɜːd] F ptaszek *m*; słówko *n*

dic·tate [dɪk'teɪt] ⟨po⟩dyktować (*też fig.*); **~·ta·tion** [dɪk'teɪʃn] dyktowanie *n*; (*w szkole*) dyktando *n*

dic·ta·tor [dɪk'teɪtə] dyktator(ka *f*) *m*; **~·ship** dyktatura *f*

dic·tion ['dɪkʃn] wymowa *f*; styl *m*

dic·tion·a·ry ['dɪkʃnrɪ] słownik *m*

did [dɪd] *pret. od* → **do**

die[1] [daɪ] umierać ⟨umrzeć⟩, ⟨z⟩ginąć; *zwierzęta*: zdychać ⟨zdechnąć⟩; ⟨u⟩schnąć; zamierać ⟨-mrzeć⟩, przestawać ⟨-stać⟩ pracować; **~ of hunger** (*thirst*) umierać ⟨umrzeć⟩ z głodu *lub* pragnienia; **~ away** wiatr, dźwięk: zanikać ⟨-niknąć⟩; **~ down** zamierać ⟨-mrzeć⟩; niknąć; **~ out** wymierać ⟨-mrzeć⟩ (*też fig.*)

die[2] [daɪ] *Am.* (*pl. dice*) kostka *f*

di·et ['daɪət] **1.** dieta *f*; odżywianie *n* się; **be on a ~** być na diecie; **2.** być na diecie

dif·fer ['dɪfə] różnić się; być odmiennego zdania (**with, from** od *G*);

dif·fe|·rence ['dɪfrəns] różnica *f*; różnica *f* zdań; **'~·rent** różny, odmienny (**from** od *G*); różniący się; **~·ren·ti·ate** [dɪfə'renʃɪeɪt] rozróżniać, odróżniać

dif·fi|·cult ['dɪfɪkəlt] trudny; **'~·cul·ty** trudność *f*

dif·fi|·dence ['dɪfɪdəns] nieśmiałość *f*, rezerwa *f*; **'~·dent** nieśmiały, pełen rezerwy

dif|·fuse 1. *fig.* [dɪ'fjuːz] rozpraszać ⟨-proszyć⟩; promieniować; **2.** [dɪ'fjuːs] rozproszony; *fig.* chaotyczny; **~·fu·sion** [dɪ'fjuːʒn] *chem., phys.* rozproszenie *n*

dig [dɪg] **1.** (*-gg-; dug*) kopać; **~ (up)** wykopywać ⟨-pać⟩; **~ (up lub out)** wykopywać ⟨-pać⟩; wygrzebywać ⟨-grzebać⟩ (*też fig.*); **~ s.o. in the ribs** szturchać ⟨-chnąć⟩ kogoś (*łokciem*); **2.** F szturchaniec *n*; **~s** *pl. Brt.* F (*wynajęte mieszkanie*) chata *f*

di·gest 1. [dɪ'dʒest] ⟨s⟩trawić; **~ well** być lekkostrawnym; **2.** ['daɪdʒest] wyciąg *m*, przegląd *m*; **~·i·ble** [dɪ'dʒestəbl] strawny; **di·ges·tion** [dɪ'dʒestʃən] trawienie *n*; **di·ges·tive** [dɪ'dʒestɪv] trawienny

dig·ger ['dɪgə] poszukiwacz(ka *f*) *m* złota

di·git ['dɪdʒɪt] cyfra *f*; palec *m*; **three-~ number** liczba trzycyfrowa

di·gi·tal ['dɪdʒɪtl] cyfrowy; **~ 'clock**, **~ 'watch** zegar(ek) *m* cyfrowy

dig·ni|·fied ['dɪgnɪfaɪd] dystyngowany; pełen godności *lub* dostojeństwa; **~·ta·ry** ['dɪgnɪtərɪ] dygnitarz *m*; **'~·ty** ['dɪgnɪtɪ] godność *f*; dostojeństwo *n*

di·gress [daɪ'gres] ⟨z⟩robić dygresję

dike[1] [daɪk] grobla *f*, wał *m*; rów *m*

dike[2] [daɪk] *sl.* lesbijka *f*

di·lap·i·dat·ed [dɪ'læpɪdeɪtɪd] zrujnowany, zdemolowany

di·late [daɪ'leɪt] rozszerzać ⟨-rzyć⟩ (się); **di·a·to·ry** ['dɪlətərɪ] opieszały

dil·i|·gence ['dɪlɪdʒəns] pilność *f*; **'~·gent** pilny

di·lute [daɪ'ljuːt] **1.** rozcieńczać ⟨-czyć⟩, rozrzedzać ⟨-dzić⟩; **2.** rozcieńczony, rozrzedzony

dim [dɪm] **1.** (*-mm-*) ciemny; niewyraźny; *wzrok:* słaby; *światło:* nikły; *Brt.* tępy; **2.** przyciemniać ⟨-mnić⟩ (się); stawać ⟨stać⟩ się niewyraźnym; **~ one's headlights** *Am. mot.* włączać ⟨-czyć⟩ światła mijania

dime [daɪm] *Am.* dziesięciocentówka *f*

di·men·sion [dɪ'menʃn] wymiar *m*; aspekt *m*; **~s** *pl.* też wymiary *pl.*; **~·al** [dɪ'menʃənl]: **three·~al** trójwymiarowy

di·min·ish [dɪ'mɪnɪʃ] zmniejszać ⟨-szyć⟩ (się)

di·min·u·tive [dɪ'mɪnjʊtɪv] malutki, maluśki

dim·ple ['dɪmpl] dołek *m*

din [dɪn] hałas *m*, wrzawa *f*

dine [daɪn] ⟨z⟩jeść (*obiad*); **~ in** *lub* **out** jeść w domu *lub* na mieście; **'din·er** (*w restauracji*) gość *m*; *Am. rail.* wagon *m* restauracyjny; *Am.* restauracja *f*

din·ghy ['dɪŋgɪ] *naut.* ponton *m*

din·gy ['dɪndʒɪ] (*-ier, -iest*) brudny

'din·ing *car rail.* wagon *m* restauracyjny; **'~ room** jadalnia *f*; restauracja *f*

din·ner ['dɪnə] obiad *m*; *obfita* kolacja *f*; przyjęcie *n*; **'~ jack·et** smoking *m*; **'~ par·ty** przyjęcie *n*; **'~ ser·vice**, **'~ set** serwis *m* stołowy; **'~·time** obiad *m*

di·no ['daɪnəʊ] *zo. skrót:* **di·no·saur** ['daɪnəʊsɔː] dinozaur *m*

dip [dɪp] **1.** *v/t.* (*-pp-*) zanurzać ⟨-rzyć⟩; **~ one's headlights** *Brt. mot.* włączać ⟨-czyć⟩ światła mijania; *v/i.* zanurzyć ⟨-rzać⟩ się; opadać ⟨opaść⟩, spadać ⟨spaść⟩; **2.** zanurzenie *n*; nachylenie *n*, pochylenie *n*; *F krótka* kąpiel *f*; sos *m*, dip *m*

diph·ther·i·a [dɪf'θɪərɪə] *med.* dyfteryt *m*, błonica *f*

di·plo·ma [dɪ'pləʊmə] dyplom *m*, zaświadczenie *n* ukończenia

di·plo·ma·cy [dɪ'pləʊməsɪ] dyplomacja *f*

dip·lo·mat ['dɪpləmæt] dyplomata *m*; **~·ic** [dɪplə'mætɪk] (*-ally*) dyplomatyczny

dip·per ['dɪpə] chochla *f*, czerpak *m*

dire ['daɪə] (*-r, -st*) okropny, skrajny

di·rect [dɪ'rekt] **1.** *adj.* bezpośredni; szczery; **2.** *adv.* bezpośrednio; szczerze; **3.** ⟨s⟩kierować; ⟨po⟩kierować; nakazywać ⟨-zać⟩; ⟨wy⟩reżyserować; *list* ⟨za⟩-

adresować; **~ 'cur·rent** *electr.* prąd *m* stały; **~ 'train** pociąg *m* bezpośredni

di·rec·tion [dɪ'rekʃn] kierunek *m*; kierownictwo *n*; reżyseria *f*; **~s** *pl.* wskazówki *pl.*; **~s for use** instrukcja *f* obsługi; △ *nie* **dyrekcja**; **~ find·er** namiernik *m*; **~ in·di·ca·tor** kierunkowskaz *m*, migacz *m*

di·rec·tive [dɪ'rektɪv] dyrektywa *f*, zarządzenie *n*

di·rect·ly [dɪ'rektlɪ] **1.** *adv.* bezpośrednio; **2.** *cj.* od razu, natychmiast

di·rec·tor [dɪ'rektə] dyrektor(ka *f*) *m*; reżyser *m* (*filmowy itp.*)

di·rec·to·ry [dɪ'rektərɪ] książka *f* z adresami; **telephone ~** książka *f* telefoniczna; *komp.* katalog *m*

dirt [dɜːt] brud *m*; *zbita* ziemia *f*; **~ 'cheap** F tani jak barszcz; **'~·y 1.** (*-ier, -iest*) brudny (*też fig.*), zabrudzony; **2.** ⟨za-, u⟩brudzić

dis·a·bil·i·ty [dɪsə'bɪlətɪ] kalectwo *n*; inwalidztwo *n*, niezdolność *f* do pracy

dis·a·bled [dɪs'eɪbld] **1.** niezdolny do pracy; *mil.* będący inwalidą w wyniku działań wojennych; kaleki, upośledzony; **2.** *the* **~** *pl.* inwalidzi *pl.*

dis·ad·van·tage [dɪsəd'vɑːntɪdʒ] wada *f*; strona *f* ujemna; **~·ta·geous** [dɪsædvɑːn'teɪdʒəs] ujemny, niekorzystny, niepomyślny

dis·a·gree [dɪsə'griː] nie zgadzać się, różnić się; *jedzenie:* szkodzić; **~·a·ble** nieprzyjemny, przykry; **~·ment** niezgoda *f*; rozbieżność *f*, niezgodność *f*; różnica *f* poglądów

dis·ap·pear [dɪsə'pɪə] znikać ⟨-knąć⟩; **~·ance** [dɪsə'pɪərəns] zniknięcie *n*

dis·ap·point [dɪsə'pɔɪnt] *kogoś* rozczarowywać ⟨-ować⟩; *plan itp.* ⟨po⟩krzyżować; **~·ing** rozczarowujący; **~·ment** rozczarowanie *n*

dis·ap·prov·al [dɪsə'pruːvl] dezaprobata *f*; **~e** [dɪsə'pruːv] nie ⟨za⟩aprobować, nie pochwalać ⟨-lić⟩

dis·arm [dɪs'ɑːm] rozbrajać ⟨-broić⟩ (się) (*też fig., mil., pol.*); **~·ar·ma·ment** [dɪs'ɑːməmənt] *mil., pol.* rozbrojenie *n*

dis·ar·range [dɪsə'reɪndʒ] ⟨z⟩robić bałagan, ⟨po⟩rozpraszać, ⟨po⟩rozstawiać

dis·ar·ray [dɪsə'reɪ] nieporządek *m*

di·sas·ter [dɪ'zɑːstə] katastrofa *f* (*też fig.*); klęska *f* (*żywiołowa*); **~ ar·e·a** obszar *m* klęski żywiołowej

di·sas·trous [dɪˈzɑːstrəs] katastrofalny

dis·be|·lief [dɪsbɪˈliːf] niedowierzanie *n*, niewiara *f*; wątpliwość (**in** względem *G*); **~·lieve** [dɪsbɪˈliːv] nie wierzyć, nie dowierzać, wątpić w (*A*)

disc [dɪsk] *Brt.* tarcza *f*, krążek *m*; dysk *m*; płyta *f* (*gramofonowa*); (*okrągły wskaźnik czasu parkowania*); *anat.* chrząstka *f* międzykręgowa, F dysk *m*; *komp.* → **disk**; **slipped ~** wypadnięcie *n* dysku

dis·card [dɪˈskɑːd] odrzucać ⟨-cić⟩; pozbywać ⟨-zbyć⟩ się; *karty* dokładać

di·scern [dɪˈsɜːn] dostrzegać ⟨-rzec⟩; rozróżniać ⟨-nić⟩; **~·ing** wybredny, wyrobiony; **~·ment** wybredność *f*, znawstwo *n*

dis·charge [dɪsˈtʃɑːdʒ] **1.** *v/t.* zwalniać ⟨zwolnić⟩; rozładowywać ⟨-ować⟩; *baterię itp.* wyładowywać ⟨-ować⟩; ⟨wy⟩strzelić z (*G*) (*broni itp.*); wypływać ⟨-łynąć⟩, wylewać ⟨-lać⟩; ⟨wy⟩emitować; *obowiązek* spełniać ⟨-nić⟩; *gniew itp.* wyładowywać ⟨-ować⟩ (**on** na *I*); *dług itp.* spłacać ⟨-cić⟩; *med.* wydzielać ⟨-lić⟩; *v/i. electr.* wyładowywać ⟨-ować⟩ się; *rzeka itp.*: wpływać, wpadać; *med.* ropieć; **2.** zwolnienie *n*; rozładunek *m* (*statku*); wystrzał *m* (*z broni*); *med.* wydzielina *f*, wydalina *f*; emisja *f*; *electr.* wyładowanie *n*; spełnienie *n* (*obowiązku*)

di·sci·ple [dɪˈsaɪpl] uczeń *m* (-ennica *f*); *rel.* apostoł *m*

dis·ci·pline [ˈdɪsɪplɪn] **1.** dyscyplina *f*; **2.** wprowadzać ⟨-dzić⟩ dyscyplinę; **well ~d** zdyscyplinowany; **badly ~d** niezdyscyplinowany

'disc jock·ey dyskdżokej *m*

dis·claim [dɪsˈkleɪm] zrzekać ⟨zrzec⟩ się; *jur.* wypierać ⟨-przeć⟩ się

dis|·close [dɪsˈkləʊz] odsłaniać ⟨-łonić⟩, ujawniać ⟨-nić⟩; **~·clo·sure** [dɪsˈkləʊʒə] odsłonięcie *n*, ujawnienie *n*

dis·co [ˈdɪskəʊ] *f* (*pl.* **-cos**) disco *n*

dis·col·o(u)r [dɪsˈkʌlə] zmieniać ⟨-nić⟩ barwę, odbarwiać ⟨-wić⟩ się

dis·com·fort [dɪsˈkʌmfət] **1.** niewygoda *f*; dyskomfort *m*; zażenowanie *n*

dis·con·cert [dɪskənˈsɜːt] zbijać ⟨-bić⟩ z tropu, ⟨z⟩deprymować

dis·con·nect [dɪskəˈnekt] rozłączać ⟨-czyć⟩, odłączać ⟨-czyć⟩ (*też electr., tech.*); *prąd, gaz, telefon* wyłączać

⟨-czyć⟩; *tel. rozmowę* przerywać ⟨-rwać⟩; **~·ed** rozłączony

dis·con·so·late [dɪsˈkɒnsələt] niepocieszony

dis·con·tent [dɪskənˈtent] niezadowolenie *n*; **~·ed** niezadowolony

dis·con·tin·ue [dɪskənˈtɪnjuː] przerywać ⟨-rwać⟩, zaprzestawać ⟨-stać⟩

dis·cord [ˈdɪskɔːd] niezgoda *f*; *mus.* dysonans *m*; **~·ant** [dɪˈskɔːdənt] niezgodny; *mus.* dysonansowy, nieharmonijny

dis·co·theque [ˈdɪskətek] dyskoteka *f*

dis·count [ˈdɪskaʊnt] *econ.* dyskonto *n*; *econ.* rabat *m*, bonifikata *f*

dis·cour·age [dɪˈskʌrɪdʒ] zniechęcać ⟨-cić⟩, odradzać ⟨-dzić⟩; **~·ment** zniechęcanie *n*, odradzanie *n*

dis·course 1. [ˈdɪskɔːs] dyskusja *f*, dysputa *f*; wykład *m*, wywód *m*; dyskurs *m*; **2.** [dɪˈskɔːs] rozprawiać (**on** o *L*)

dis·cour·te|·ous [dɪsˈkɜːtjəs] niegrzeczny; **~·sy** [dɪsˈkɜːtəsɪ] niegrzeczność *f*

dis·cov|·er [dɪˈskʌvə] odkrywać ⟨-ryć⟩, odnajdować ⟨-naleźć⟩; **~·e·ry** [dɪˈskʌvərɪ] odkrycie *n*

'disc park·ing *mot.* (*miejsce parkowania dla kierowców z wykupionym specjalnym krążkiem*)

dis·cred·it [dɪsˈkredɪt] **1.** kompromitacja *f*, niesława *f*, hańba *f*; **2.** poddawać ⟨-dać⟩ w wątpliwość; ⟨z⟩dyskredytować; podważać ⟨-żyć⟩

di·screet [dɪˈskriːt] dyskretny; ostrożny, rozważny

dis·crep·an·cy [dɪˈskrepənsɪ] rozbieżność *f*, rozdźwięk *m*

di·scre·tion [dɪˈskreʃn] dyskrecja *f*; (*własne*) uznanie *n*

di·scrim·i|·nate [dɪˈskrɪmɪneɪt] rozróżniać ⟨-nić⟩, odróżniać ⟨-nić⟩; **~nate against** ⟨z⟩dyskryminować (*A*); **~·nat·ing** wyrobiony; **~·na·tion** [dɪskrɪmɪˈneɪʃn] dyskryminacja *f*

dis·cus [ˈdɪskəs] (*w sporcie*) dysk *m*

di·scuss [dɪˈskʌs] ⟨prze⟩dyskutować, omawiać ⟨omówić⟩; **di·scus·sion** [dɪˈskʌʃn] dyskusja *f*; omówienie *n*

'dis·cus| throw *sport:* rzut *m* dyskiem; **'~ throw·er** dyskobol *m*

dis·ease [dɪˈziːz] choroba *f*; **~d** chory

dis·em·bark [dɪsɪmˈbɑːk] *v/i.* wysiadać ⟨-siąść⟩; *v/t.* wysadzać ⟨-dzić⟩, wyładowywać ⟨-ować⟩

dis·en·chant·ed [dɪsɪn'tʃɑːntɪd] rozczarowany; **be ~ with** nie łudzić się więcej (*I*)

dis·en·gage [dɪsɪn'ɡeɪdʒ] rozłączać ⟨-czyć⟩; *sprzęgło* zwalniać ⟨zwolnić⟩

dis·en·tan·gle [dɪsɪn'tæŋɡl] rozplątywać ⟨-tać⟩; wyplątywać ⟨-tać⟩ (się)

dis·fa·vo(u)r [dɪs'feɪvə] niechęć *f*; niełaska *f*

dis·fig·ure [dɪs'fɪɡə] ⟨o⟩szpecić, zeszpecać ⟨-cić⟩

dis·grace [dɪs'ɡreɪs] **1.** hańba *f*; niełaska *f*; **2.** sprowadzać ⟨-dzić⟩ hańbę na (*A*), przynosić *komuś* hańbę; **~·ful** haniebny

dis·guise [dɪs'ɡaɪz] **1.** przebierać ⟨-brać⟩ się (*as* za *A*); *głos* zmieniać ⟨-nić⟩; *coś* ukrywać ⟨ukryć⟩; **2.** przebranie *n*; przemiana *f*, zmiana *f*; ukrycie *n*; *in* ~ w przebraniu (*też fig.*); *in the* ~ *of* w przebraniu (*G*)

dis·gust [dɪs'ɡʌst] **1.** obrzydzenie *n*, wstręt *m*; **~·ing** obrzydliwy

dish [dɪʃ] **1.** talerz *m*; półmisek *m*; potrawa *f*, danie *n*; *the* **~es** *pl.* brudne naczynia *pl.*; **wash** *lub* **do the ~es** ⟨z⟩myć naczynia; **2.** ~ **out** F nakładać ⟨-łożyć⟩; *często* ~ **up** *potrawy* nakładać ⟨-łożyć⟩; F *fakty*: podpicować; **'~·cloth** ścierka *f* do naczyń

dis·heart·en [dɪs'hɑːtn] zniechęcać ⟨-cić⟩

di·shev·el·(l)ed [dɪ'ʃevld] rozczochrany, potargany

dis·hon·est [dɪs'ɒnɪst] nieuczciwy; **~·y** nieuczciwość *f*

dis·hon·o(u)r [dɪs'ɒnə] **1.** hańba *f*; zhańbić; *econ. weksla* nie honorować; **~·o(u)·ra·ble** [dɪs'ɒnərəbl] niehonorowy; haniebny

'dish·wash·er zmywarka *f* do naczyń; **'~·wa·ter** pomyje *pl.*

dis·il·lu·sion [dɪsɪ'luːʒn] **1.** rozczarowanie *n*, zawód *m*; **2.** rozczarowywać ⟨-ować⟩, pozbawiać ⟨-wić⟩ złudzeń

dis·in·clined [dɪsɪn'klaɪnd] oporny, niechętny

dis·in|·fect [dɪsɪn'fekt] ⟨z⟩dezynfekować; **~'fec·tant** środek *m* dezynfekujący

dis·in·her·it [dɪsɪn'herɪt] wydziedziczać ⟨-czyć⟩

dis·in·te·grate [dɪs'ɪntɪɡreɪt] rozpadać ⟨-aść⟩ (się)

dis·in·terest·ed [dɪs'ɪntrəstɪd] obiektywny, bezstronny; obojętny, niezainteresowany

disk [dɪsk] *zwł. Am.* → *Brt.* **disc**; *komp.* dysk *m*, dyskietka *f*; **'~ drive** *komp.* napęd *m lub* stacja *f* dyskietek

disk·ette [dɪ'sket, 'dɪsket] *komp.* dyskietka *f*

dis·like [dɪs'laɪk] **1.** niechęć *f*, awersja *f*; (*of, for* do *G*); **take a ~ to** odczuwać ⟨-czuć⟩ niechęć do (*G*); **2.** nie lubić; **he ~s this** nie podoba mu się to

dis·lo·cate ['dɪsləkeɪt] *med.* zwichnąć

dis·loy·al [dɪs'lɔɪəl] nielojalny

dis·mal ['dɪzməl] ponury, przygnębiający

dis·man·tle [dɪs'mæntl] *tech.* rozbierać ⟨rozebrać⟩, ⟨z⟩demontować, rozmontowywać ⟨-ować⟩

dis·may [dɪs'meɪ] **1.** niepokój *m*, zaniepokojenie *n*, konsternacja *f*; **in ~, with** ~ z przerażenia; **to my** ~ ku mojej konsternacji; **2.** *v/t.* przestraszyć się

dis·miss [dɪs'mɪs] *v/t.* odprawiać ⟨-wić⟩, zwalniać ⟨zwolnić⟩; odrzucać ⟨-cić⟩; odstępować ⟨-tąpić⟩ (*od tematu*); *jur. skargę* oddalać ⟨-lić⟩; **~·al** [dɪs'mɪsl] zwolnienie *n*; *jur.* oddalenie *n*

dis·mount [dɪs'maʊnt] *v/t.* zsiadać ⟨zsiąść⟩ (*from* z *konia, roweru itp.*); *v/t.* ⟨z⟩demontować; rozbierać ⟨zebrać⟩

dis·o·be·di|·ence [dɪsə'biːdjəns] nieposłuszeństwo *n*; **~·ent** nieposłuszny

dis·o·bey [dɪsə'beɪ] nie ⟨po⟩słuchać, być nieposłusznym

dis·or·der [dɪs'ɔːdə] nieporządek *m*, bałagan *m*; wzburzenie *n*, zamieszki *pl.*; *med.* dolegliwość *f*; **~·ly** nieporządny; niespokojny; buntowniczy

dis·or·gan·ize [dɪs'ɔːɡənaɪz] ⟨z⟩deorganizować

dis·own [dɪs'əʊn] nie uznawać; wypierać się

di·spar·age [dɪ'spærɪdʒ] ⟨z⟩dyskredytować, poniżać ⟨-żyć⟩

di·spar·i·ty [dɪ'spærətɪ] nierówność *f*; ~ *of lub in age* różnica *f* wieku

dis·pas·sion·ate [dɪ'spæʃnət] beznamiętny; obiektywny

di·spatch [dɪ'spætʃ] **1.** wysyłka *f*, przesyłka *f*; sprawność *f*, szybkość *f*; depesza *f*, doniesienie *n*; **2.** wysyłać ⟨-słać⟩, nadawać ⟨-dać⟩, ⟨wy⟩ekspediować

distaste

di·spel [dɪ'spel] (*-ll-*) rozwiewać ⟨-zwiać⟩, rozpraszać ⟨-proszyć⟩ (*też fig*)
di·spen·sa|·ble [dɪ'spensəbl] zbyteczny, zbędny; ~ry [dɪ'spensərɪ] szkolna, szpitalna apteka f
dis·pen·sa·tion [dɪspen'seɪʃn] dyspensa f, zwolnienie n; *jur.* wymierzanie n
di·spense [dɪ'spens] wydawać ⟨-dać⟩; sprawiedliwość wymierzać ⟨-rzyć⟩; ~ with obywać się bez (G); stawać się zbytecznym; di'spens·er automat m, maszyna f (*do znaczków itp.*); rolka f (*do taśmy samoprzylepnej*)
di·sperse [dɪ'spɜːs] rozpraszać (się)
di·spir·it·ed [dɪ'spɪrɪtɪd] przygnębiony, przybity
dis·place [dɪs'pleɪs] przemieszczać ⟨-eścić⟩; *kogoś* wysiedlać ⟨-dlić⟩, wypierać ⟨-przeć⟩
di·splay [dɪ'spleɪ] 1. pokaz m; demonstracja f; *komp.* monitor m; *econ.* wystawa f, ekspozycja f; *be on* ~ być wystawionym; 2. pokazywać ⟨-zać⟩, ⟨za⟩demonstrować; wystawiać ⟨-wić⟩; wyświetlać ⟨-lić⟩
dis|·please [dɪs'pliːz] ⟨z⟩denerwować, ⟨z⟩irytować; ~'pleased zdenerwowany, zirytowany; niezadowolony; ~·plea·sure [dɪs'pleʒə] zdenerwowanie n, zirytowanie n; niezadowolenie n
dis|·po·sa·ble [dɪ'spəʊzəbl] *pojemnik itp.*: jednorazowy; ~·pos·al [dɪ'spəʊzl] oczyszczanie n, wywóz m (*śmieci*); usuwanie n; rozmieszczenie n (*wojsk*); *at s.o.'s ~posal* do czyjejś dyspozycji; ~·pose [dɪ'spəʊz] *v/t.* rozmieszczać ⟨-mieścić⟩, ⟨u⟩lokować; usposabiać ⟨-bić⟩; ~*pose of* pozbywać ⟨-być⟩ się, usuwać ⟨-unąć⟩; dawać ⟨dać⟩ sobie radę; *econ.* odstępować ⟨-tąpić⟩; ~posed skłonny, chętny; ~·po·si·tion [dɪspə'zɪʃn] usposobienie n; △ *nie* dyspozycja
dis·pos·sess [dɪspə'zes] pozbawiać ⟨-wić⟩; wywłaszczać ⟨-czyć⟩
dis·pro·por·tion·ate [dɪsprə'pɔːʃnət] nieproporcjonalny
dis·prove [dɪs'pruːv] obalać ⟨-lić⟩
di·spute [dɪ'spjuːt] 1. kontrowersja f; polemika f, dysputa f; spór m; 2. spierać się (o A); ⟨za⟩kwestionować
dis·qual·i·fy [dɪs'kwɒlɪfaɪ] ⟨z⟩dyskwalifikować; uznawać ⟨-nać⟩ za niezdolnego (*from* do G)

dis·re·gard [dɪsrɪ'gɑːd] 1. ignorowanie n, lekceważenie n; 2. ⟨z⟩ignorować, ⟨z⟩lekceważyć
dis|·rep·u·ta·ble [dɪs'repjʊtəbl] naganny, o złej reputacji; ~·re·pute [dɪsrɪ'pjuːt] zła reputacja f
dis·re·spect [dɪsrɪ'spekt] nieuprzejmość f, brak m respektu; ~·ful nieuprzejmy
dis·rupt [dɪs'rʌpt] przerywać ⟨-rwać⟩
dis·sat·is|·fac·tion [dɪssætɪs'fækʃn] niezadowolenie n; ~·fied [dɪs'sætɪsfaɪd] niezadowolony (*with* z G)
dis·sect [dɪ'sekt] rozcinać ⟨-ciąć⟩, ⟨wy-, s⟩preparować; ⟨z⟩analizować
dis·sen·sion [dɪ'senʃn] niezgoda f, różnica f zdań; niejednomyślność f; ~t [dɪ'sent] 1. różnica f zdań; rozbieżność f poglądów; protest m; 2. nie zgadzać się, być innego zdania (*from* od G); ~·ter *rel.* dysydent m, odszczepieniec m; osoba f o odmiennych poglądach
dis·si·dent [dɪsɪdənt] osoba f o odmiennych poglądach; *pol.* dysydent m
dis·sim·i·lar [dɪ'sɪmɪlə] niepodobny (*to* do G), odmienny (*to* od G)
dis·sim·u·la·tion [dɪsɪmjʊ'leɪʃn] obłuda f, udawanie n
dis·si|·pate [dɪsɪpeɪt] rozpraszać ⟨-roszyć⟩; ⟨s⟩trwonić; ~·pat·ed hulaszczy, rozwiązły
dis·so·ci·ate [dɪ'səʊʃɪeɪt] rozdzielać ⟨-lić⟩; ~ *o.s.* odseparowywać ⟨-ować⟩ się, odcinać ⟨odciąć⟩ się
dis·so|·lute [dɪsəluːt] → dissipated; ~·lu·tion [dɪsə'luːʃn] rozkład m, rozpad m
dis·solve [dɪ'zɒlv] rozpuszczać ⟨-uścić⟩ (się)
dis·suade [dɪ'sweɪd] wyperswadować (*s.o. from* komuś A); odwodzić ⟨-wieść⟩ (*s.o. from* kogoś od G)
dis·tance ['dɪstəns] 1. odległość f; oddalenie n; dystans m; *fig.* odstęp m; *at a* ~ z odległości; *keep s.o. at a* ~ trzymać kogoś na dystans; 2. odseparowywać ⟨-ować⟩ się, trzymać się na dystans; '~ race (*w sporcie*) bieg m długodystansowy; '~ run·ner biegacz m na długie dystanse
dis·tant [dɪstənt] dległy; chłodny, dystansujący się
dis·taste [dɪs'teɪst] niesmak m, niechęć

f, awersja *f*; ~·ful nieprzyjemny, antypatyczny; **be ~ful to s.o.** być przykrym dla kogoś

dis·tem·per [dɪ'stempə] *zo.* nosówka *f*

dis·tend [dɪ'stend] rozszerzać (się); nadymać ⟨-dąć⟩ (się)

dis·til(l) [dɪ'stɪl] (*-ll-*) ⟨wy⟩destylować

dis·tinct [dɪ'stɪŋkt] wyraźny; różny, odmienny; ~·tinc·tion [dɪ'stɪŋkʃn] różnica *f*; odróżnienie *n*, wyróżnienie *n*; rozróżnienie *n*; ~·tinc·tive [dɪ'stɪŋktɪv] wyróżniający się; odrębny

dis·tin·guish [dɪ'stɪŋgwɪʃ] rozróżniać ⟨-nić⟩; ~ **o.s.** wyróżniać ⟨-nić⟩ się; ~ed wyróżniający się; wybitny; znakomity

dis·tort [dɪ'stɔːt] zniekształcać ⟨-cić⟩, wykrzywiać ⟨-wić⟩

dis·tract [dɪ'strækt] rozpraszać ⟨-roszyć⟩; *uwagę* odrywać ⟨oderwać⟩; ~·ed roztargniony, przejęty (**by, with** *I*), zaniepokojony; **dis·trac·tion** [dɪ'strækʃn] rozproszenie *n*; zaniepokojenie *n*

dis·traught [dɪ'strɔːt] → *distracted*

dis·tress [dɪ'stres] **1.** cierpienie *n*; troska *f*; trudna sytuacja *f*; niebezpieczeństwo *n*, stan *m* zagrożenia; **2.** ⟨s⟩powodować cierpienie; ⟨za⟩niepokoić; ~ed dotknięty nieszczęściem; bez środków do życia; ~ed ar·e·a obszar *m* dotknięty klęską; ~·ing niepokojący

dis·trib·ute [dɪ'strɪbjuːt] rozprowadzać ⟨-dzić⟩, rozdzielać ⟨-lić⟩; *econ.* dystrybuować; *filmy* rozpowszechniać ⟨-nić⟩; ~·tri·bu·tion [dɪstrɪ'bjuːʃn] rozdział *m*, rozprowadzenie *n*; dystrybucja *f*; rozpowszechnianie *n*

dis·trict ['dɪstrɪkt] dystrykt *m*, okręg *m*; dzielnica *f*

dis·trust [dɪs'trʌst] **1.** nieufność *f*, niedowierzanie *n*; **2.** nie ufać, nie mieć zaufania; niedowierzać; ~·ful nieufny, niedowierzający

dis·turb [dɪ'stɜːb] zakłócać ⟨-cić⟩; niepokoić; przeszkadzać ⟨-skodzić⟩; poruszać ⟨-szyć⟩; ~·ance [dɪ'stɜːbəns] zakłócenie *n*, naruszenie *n*; niepokój *m*; ~·ances *pl.* zamieszki *pl.*, rozruchy *pl.*; ~·ance of the peace *jur.* naruszenie *n* spokoju; **cause a ~ance** spowodować naruszenie spokoju; ~·ed [dɪ'stɜːbd] niespokojny; niezrównoważony

dis·used [dɪs'juːzd] *maszyna*: nie będą-

cy w użyciu, *kopalnia*: nie eksploatowany

ditch [dɪtʃ] rów *m*

Div *skrót pisany*: **division** *sportowa* liga *f*

di·van [dɪ'væn, 'daɪvæn] kanapa *f*, sofa *f*; △ *nie* **dywan**; ~ **bed** sofa *f*

dive [daɪv] **1.** (*dived lub Am. też* **dove, dived**) ⟨za⟩nurkować (*też aviat.*); (*z trampoliny*) skakać ⟨skoczyć⟩; skakać ⟨skoczyć⟩ do wody (*na głowę*); rzucać ⟨-cić⟩ się po (*A*); **2.** skok *m* (*do wody*); zanurkowanie *n*; (*w piłce nożnej*) (*upadek mający wymusić rzut karny*); *aviat.* lot *m* nurkowy; F knajpa *f*, speluna *f*; **div·er** nurek *m*; (*w sporcie*) skoczek *m* (*do wody*)

di·verge [daɪ'vɜːdʒ] rozchodzić się; **di·ver·gence** [daɪ'vɜːdʒəns] rozbieżność *f*; **di·ver·gent** rozbieżny

di·verse [daɪ'vɜːs] różny; różnoraki, różnorodny; **di·ver·si·fy** [daɪ'vɜːsɪfaɪ] ⟨z⟩różnicować; **di·ver·sion** [daɪ'vɜːʃn] rozrywka *f*; objazd *m*; **di·ver·si·ty** [daɪ'vɜːsətɪ] różnorodność *f*, zróżnicowanie *f*

di·vert [daɪ'vɜːt] *uwagę* odwracać ⟨-rócić⟩; *kogoś* zabawiać ⟨-wić⟩; *w ruchu ulicznym* zmieniać ⟨-nić⟩ kierunek

di·vide [dɪ'vaɪd] **1.** *v/t.* ⟨po⟩dzielić (*też math.*), rozdzielać ⟨-lić⟩, oddzielać ⟨-lić⟩ (**by** przez *A*); *v/i.* ⟨po⟩dzielić się; *math.* dzielić się (**by** przez *A*); **2.** *geogr.* wododział *m*; **di·vid·ed** podzielony; ~ **highway** *Am.* autostrada *f*

div·i·dend ['dɪvɪdend] *econ.* dywidenda *f*

di·vid·ers [dɪ'vaɪdəz] *pl.*: **a pair of ~** (*jeden*) cyrkiel *m* traserski, przenośnik *m*

di·vine [dɪ'vaɪn] (*-r, -st*) boski; ~ 'ser·vice nabożeństwo *n*

div·ing ['daɪvɪŋ] nurkowanie *n*; (*w sporcie*) skoki *pl.* do wody; ~·board trampolina *f*; ~·suit skafander *m* do nurkowania

di·vin·i·ty [dɪ'vɪnətɪ] boskość *f*; bóstwo *n*; teologia *f*

di·vis·i·ble [dɪ'vɪzəbl] podzielny; **di·vi·sion** [dɪ'vɪʒn] podział *m*; dział *m*; *mil.* dywizja *f*; *math.* dzielenie *n*; *sport:* liga *f*

di·vorce [dɪ'vɔːs] **1.** rozwód *m*; **get a ~** rozwodzić ⟨-wieść⟩ się (**from** z); **2.** *jur.* brać ⟨wziąć⟩ rozwód z (*I*); **get ~d** rozwodzić ⟨-wieść⟩ się; **di·vor·cee** [dɪvɔː'siː] rozwodnik *m* (-wódka *f*)

done

DIY *zwł. Brt.* [diː aɪ 'waɪ] → **do-it-your-self**; ~ **store** sklep *m* z materiałami dla majsterkowiczów

diz·zy ['dɪzɪ] (**-ier, -iest**) cierpiący na zawroty głowy; zawrotny

DJ [diː 'dʒeɪ] *skrót:* **disc jockey** dyskdżokej *m*

do [duː] (**did, done**) *v/t.* ⟨z⟩robić; ⟨u⟩czynić; przygotowywać ⟨-ować⟩; *pokój* ⟨wy⟩sprzątać; *naczynia* ⟨wy⟩myć; *odcinek drogi* przebywać ⟨-być⟩; ~ **you know him** ~? **no, I don't** znasz go? nie; **what can I** ~ **for you?** czym mogę służyć?; ~ **London** F zaliczać ⟨-czyć⟩ Londyn; **have one's hair done** zrobić sobie fryzurę; **have done reading** skończyć czytać; *v/i.* ⟨z⟩robić; ⟨po⟩radzić sobie, dawać ⟨dać⟩ sobie radę; wystarczać ⟨-czyć⟩; dziać się; **that will** ~ wystarczy; **how** ~ **you** ~? dzień dobry (*przy przedstawianiu*); ~ **be quick** pospiesz się w miarę możności; ~ **you like Guildford? I** ~ czy podoba się Panu (Pani) Guildford? owszem; **she works hard, doesn't she?** ciężko pracuje, nieprawda?; ~ **well** dobrze sobie ⟨po⟩radzić; ~ **away with** *Am.* ⟨z⟩likwidować, usuwać ⟨-unąć⟩; **I'm done in** F jestem wykończony (-na); ~ **up** *ubranie itp.* zapinać ⟨-piąć⟩; *dom itp.* ⟨wy⟩remontować; *paczkę itp.* ⟨za⟩pakować; ~ **o.s. up** ⟨wy⟩stroić się; **I could** ~ **with ...** przydałby się ...; ~ **without** obywać ⟨obyć⟩ się bez (*G*)

doc¹ [dɒk] F → (*lekarz*) **doctor**

doc² [dɒk] *skrót:* **document** dokument *m*

do·cile ['dəʊsaɪl] potulny, uległy

dock¹ [dɒk] przycinać ⟨-ciąć⟩; *pensję* ⟨z⟩redukować, *pieniądze* potrącać ⟨-cić⟩

dock² [dɒk] **1.** *naut.* dok *m*; nabrzeże *n*; *jur.* ława *f* oskarżonych; **2.** *v/t. naut.* ⟨za⟩dokować, *statek* wprowadzać ⟨-dzić⟩ do doku; ⟨po⟩łączyć na orbicie; '~**·er** doker *m*; robotnik *m* portowy; '~**·ing** dokowanie *n*; połączenie *n*; '~**·yard** *naut.* stocznia *f*

doc·tor ['dɒktə] doktor *m*; lekarz *m* (*-rka f*); ~**·al** ['dɒktərəl] doktorski

doc·trine ['dɒktrɪn] doktryna *f*, nauka *f*

doc·u·ment 1. ['dɒkjʊmənt] dokument *m*; **2.** ['dɒkjʊment] ⟨u⟩dokumentować

doc·u·men·ta·ry [dɒkjʊ'mentrɪ] **1.** do-kumentalny; dokumentowy; **2.** film *m* dokumentalny

dodge [dɒdʒ] unikać ⟨-knąć⟩, uskakiwać ⟨uskoczyć⟩ przed (*I*); F uchylać ⟨-lić⟩ się przed (*I*); '**dodg·er: tax dodger** osoba *f* uchylająca się od płacenia podatków; **draft dodger** *Am.* osoba *f* odmawiająca przyjęcia karty poborowej; → **fare dodger**

doe [dəʊ] *zo.* łania *f*; królica *f*; zajęczyca *f*

dog [dɒg] **1.** *zo.* pies *m*; **2.** (**-gg-**) chodzić krok w krok; prześladować; '~**-eared** ['dɒg·] uparty, zaparty

dog·ma ['dɒgmə] dogmat *m*; prawda *f* wiary; ~**·mat·ic** [dɒg'mætɪk] (**-ally**) dogmatyczny

dog-'tired F skonany, wykończony

do-it-your·self [duːɪtjɔː'self] **1.** majsterkowanie *n*; **2.** *attr.* dla majsterkowiczów; ~**·er** majsterkowicz *m*

dole [dəʊl] **1.** datek *m*; *Brt.* F zasiłek *m* (*dla bezrobotnych*); **go** *lub* **be on the** ~ *Brt.* F być na zasiłku; **2.** ~ **out** wydzielać ⟨-lić⟩ skąpo

dole·ful ['dəʊlfl] żałosny

doll [dɒl] lalka *f*

dol·lar ['dɒlə] dolar *m*

dol·phin ['dɒlfɪn] *zo.* delfin *m*

dome [dəʊm] kopuła *f*

do·mes·tic [də'mestɪk] **1.** (**~ally**) do-mowy; rodzinny; krajowy, rodzimy; *polityka itp.*: wewnętrzny; **2.** członek *m* rodziny; ~ **'an·i·mal** zwierzę *n* domowe *lub* udomowione; **do·mes·ti·cate** [də'mestɪkeɪt] udomawiać ⟨-mowić⟩; ~ **'flight** *aviat.* lot *m* krajowy; ~ **'mar·ket** rynek *m* wewnętrzny *lub* krajowy; ~ **'trade** handel *m* wewnętrzny; ~ **'vio·lence** przemoc *f* w obrębie rodziny (*wobec żony i dzieci*)

dom·i·cile ['dɒmɪsaɪl] miejsce *n* zamieszkania

dom·i·|·nant ['dɒmɪnənt] dominujący, panujący; ~**·nate** ['dɒmɪnent] ⟨z⟩dominować; ~**·na·tion** [dɒmɪ'neɪʃn] dominacja *f*; ~**·neer·ing** [dɒmɪ'nɪərɪŋ] apodyktyczny

do·nate [dəʊ'neɪt] ofiarowywać ⟨-ować⟩, przekazywać ⟨-zać⟩ (w darze); **do·na·tion** [dəʊ'neɪʃn] darowizna *f*, donacja *f*

done [dʌn] **1.** *p.p. od* **do**; **2.** *adj.* zrobio-

D

ny, wykonany; gotowy; *gastr.* przyrządzony → **well-done**

don·key ['dɒŋkɪ] *zo.* osioł *m*

do·nor ['dəʊnə] *med.* dawca *m* (*zwł. krwi, organu*)

don't [dəʊnt] *zamiast:* **do not** → **do**; *zamiast: Am.* F *does not* (*she don't*) → **do**

doom [du:m] **1.** przeznaczenie *n*, zły los *m*; **2.** skazywać 〈-zać〉 (*na zgubę*); **~s-day** ['du:mzdeɪ]: *till* **~sday** po wieczność, na zawsze

door [dɔ:] drzwi *pl.*; drzwiczki *pl.*; brama *f*, furtka *f*; *next* **~** obok, w sąsiedztwie; '**~·bell** dzwonek *m* do drzwi; '**~ han·dle** klamka *f*; '**~·keep·er** odźwierny *m*; '**~·knob** gałka *f* (*do drzwi*); '**~·mat** wycieraczka *f*; '**~·step** próg *m*; '**~·way** wejście *n*, drzwi *pl.*

dope [dəʊp] **1.** F narkotyk *m*; środek *m* odurzający; (*w sporcie*) środek *m* dopingujący; *sl.* dureń *m*; **2.** F 〈z〉narkotyzować; (*w sporcie*) podawać 〈-dać〉 środek dopingujący; '**~ test** kontrola *f* antydopingowa

dor·mant ['dɔ:mənt] *zw. fig.* uśpiony, nieaktywny; *wulkan:* drzemiący

dor·mer (win·dow) ['dɔ:mə (-)] okno *n* mansardowe

dor·mi·to·ry ['dɔ:mətrɪ] sypialnia *f*; *zwł. Am.* akademik *m*, dom *m* akademicki

dor·mo·bile ['dɔ:məbi:l] *TM* wóz *m* kempingowy

dor·mouse ['dɔ:maʊs] *zo.* (*pl. -mice*) suseł *m*

DOS [dɒs] *skrót:* **disk operating system** DOS *m*, dyskowy system *m* operacyjny

dose [dəʊs] **1.** dawka *f*; doza *f*; **2.** dawkować; *lekarstwo* podawać 〈-dać〉 (*w dużych ilościach*)

dot [dɒt] **1.** punkt *m*, kropka *f*; plama *f*; *on the* **~** F (*punktualnie*) co do sekundy; **2.** (*-tt-*) 〈wy-, za〉kropkować; rozrzucić 〈-cać〉; *czymś* zarzucać 〈-cić〉; **~ted line** kropkowana linia *f*

dote [dəʊt]: **~ on** bezgranicznie uwielbiać (*A*), świata nie widzieć poza (*I*); **dot·ing** ['dəʊtɪŋ] rozkochany

dou·ble ['dʌbl] **1.** podwójny; dwu...; **2.** *adv.* podwójnie; **3.** sobowtór *m*; (*w filmie itp.*) dubler *m*; **4.** podwajać 〈-woić〉 (się); (*w filmie itp.*) dublować; *też* **~ up** składać się na dwoje; składać 〈złożyć〉

~ back zawracać 〈-rócić〉; **~ up with** zwijać 〈-zwinąć〉 się z (*J*), skręcać 〈-ręcić〉 się (*G*); **~'breast·ed** *marynarka:* dwurzędowy; **~'check** dokładnie sprawdzać 〈-dzić〉; **~'chin** podbródek *m*; **~'cross** *v/t.* oszukiwać 〈-kać〉; **~'deal·ing** oszukańczy, krętacki; **2.** krętacz *m*, oszust(ka *f*) *m*; **~'deck·er** autobus *m* dwupoziomowy; F piętrowy *m*; **~ Dutch** *Brt.* F nierozumiałe słowa *pl.*, chińszczyzna *f*; **~'edged** dwusieczny, obosieczny; **~'en·try** *econ.* podwójny zapis *m*; **~ 'fea·ture** *filmowy* seans *m* z dwoma filmami pełnometrażowymi; **~'park** *mot.* 〈za〉parkować w drugim rzędzie; **~'quick** F w przyspieszonym tempie; *sl.* **in** **~ *quick*** (*zwł. w tenisie*) debel *m*; **~'sid·ed** dwustronny

doubt [daʊt] **1.** *v/i.* wątpić w (*A*); *v/t.* 〈z〉wątpić w *A* (*A*); mieć wątpliwości co do (*G*); nie wierzyć (*D*); **2.** wątpliwość *f*, zwątpienie *n*; **~·ful** wątpliwy, niepewny; **~·less** niewątpliwie, bez wątpliwości

douche [du:ʃ] **1.** irygacja *f*; przemywanie *n*; tusz *m*, irygator *m*; **2.** *v/t.* przemywać 〈-myć〉; *v/i.* 〈za〉stosować irygację

dough [dəʊ] ciasto *n*; **~·nut** *jakby:* pączek *m* (*do jedzenia*)

dove[1] [dʌv] *zo.* gołąb *m* (*mały, o długim ogonie*)

dove[2] [dəʊv] *Am. pret. od* **dive** 1

dow·dy ['daʊdɪ] nieelegancki, niegustowny

dow·el ['daʊəl] *tech.* kołek *m*

down[1] [daʊn] puch *m*, meszek *m*

down[2] [daʊn] **1.** *adv.* w dół, do dołu, na dół; **2.** *prp.* w dół (*G*); **~ the river** w dół rzeki; **3.** *adj.* przygnębiony, przybity; skierowany w dół; **~ platform** peron *m* dla odjeżdżających (*np. z Londynu*); **~ train** pociąg *m* (*odjeżdżający z Londynu*); **4.** *v/t.* kogoś powalić, obalać 〈-lić〉; *samolot* zestrzelać 〈-lić〉; F *napój* wychylać 〈-lić〉 duszkiem; **~ tools** przerywać 〈-rwać〉 pracę (*przy strajku*); **~·cast** przybity, przygnębiony; '**~·fall** ulewa *f*; *fig.* upadek *m*; '**~·heart·ed** przybity, przygnębiony; '**~·hill 1.** *adv.* w dół (*zbocza*); **2.** *adj.* biegnący w dół zbocza; (*w narciarstwie*) zjazdowy; stok *m*, zbocze *n*; (*w narciarstwie*) zjazd *m*; **~'pay·ment** *econ.* zapłata *f* z góry; '**~·pour** ulewa *f*; '**~·right 1.** *adv.* zupełnie, całkowicie; **2.** całkowity, zupełny; bezpośredni

downs [daʊnz] *pl.* pogórze *n* (*trawiaste, z wapieni*)

down'stairs na dół; na dole; na parterze; **~'stream** w dole (*rzeki*); w dół (*rzeki*); **~-to-'earth** realistyczny, chodzący po ziemi; **~'town** *Am.* **1.** *adv.* w centrum; do centrum; **2.** *adj.* w centrum; '**~town** *Am.* centrum *n*, śródmieście *n*; **~'ward(s)** ['daʊnwəd(z)] w dół, do dołu

down·y ['daʊnɪ] (*-ier, -iest*) puchaty, pokryty meszkiem

dow·ry ['daʊərɪ] posag *m*

doz. *skrót pisany:* **dozen** tuzin *m*

doze [dəʊz] **1.** ⟨po⟩drzemać; **2.** drzemka *f*

doz·en ['dʌzn] tuzin *m*

Dr *skrót pisany:* **Doctor** dr, doktor

drab [dræb] szary; ponury

draft [drɑːft] **1.** szkic *m*; projekt *m*; *econ.* trata *f*; *econ.* przekaz *m* bankowy; *Am. mil.* pobór *m*; **2.** ⟨na⟩szkicować; *list itp.* sporządzać ⟨-dzić⟩ pierwszą wersję; *Am. mil.* przeprowadzać ⟨-dzić⟩ pobór; **~·ee** [drɑːfˈtiː] *Am. mil.* poborowy *m*; '**~s·man** *Am.* (*pl. -men*), '**~s·wom·an** (*pl. -women*) → **draughtsman, draughtswoman**; '**~·y** *Am.* (*-ier, -iest*) → **draughty**

drag [dræg] **1.** ciągnięcie *n*, wleczenie *n*; *fig.* przeszkoda *f*; F nudziarstwo *n*, nuda *f*; **2.** (*-gg-*) *v/t.* ⟨za⟩ciągnąć, ⟨za-, po⟩wlec; *v/i.* ciągnąć się, wlec się; *też* **~ behind** wlec się z tyłu, zostawać ⟨-tać⟩ z tyłu; **~ on** wlec się, ciągnąć się; '**~ lift** wyciąg *m* (*narciarski*)

drag·on ['drægən] smok *m*; '**~·fly** *zo.* ważka *f*

drain [dreɪn] **1.** ściek *m*, kratka *f* ściekowa; dren *m*; **2.** *v/t.* odprowadzać ⟨-dzić⟩ ścieki; ⟨z⟩drenować; odwadniać ⟨-wodnić⟩; opróżniać ⟨-nić⟩; odcedzać ⟨-dzić⟩; *fig. energię* wyczerpywać ⟨-pać⟩; *v/i.* **~ away** odprowadzać ⟨-dzić⟩; odpływać ⟨-łynąć⟩; **~ off** odcedzać ⟨-dzić⟩; ociec; **~·age** ['dreɪnɪdʒ] drenaż *m*; odwadnianie *n*; odprowadzanie *n*; system *m* odwadniający; '**~·pipe** rura *f* spustowa *lub* odpływowa

drake [dreɪk] *zo.* kaczor *m*

dram [dræm] F łyczek *m*, kieliszeczek *m* (*alkoholu*)

dra·ma ['drɑːmə] dramat *m*; **dra·mat·ic** [drəˈmætɪk] dramatyczny; **dram·a·tist** ['dræmətɪst] dramaturg *m*; **dram·a·t·ize** ['dræmətaɪz] ⟨u⟩dramatyzować

drank [dræŋk] *pret. od* **drink** 2.

drape [dreɪp] **1.** ⟨u⟩drapować; **2.** *zw.* **~s** *pl. Am.* zasłony *pl.*; **drap·er·y** *Brt.* ['dreɪpərɪ] artykuły *pl.* tekstylne

dras·tic ['dræstɪk] (*~ally*) drastyczny

draught [drɑːft] (*Am.* **draft**) przeciąg *m*, przeciew *m*; ciąg *m*; zanurzenie *n* (*statku*); *beer on* **~, ~ beer** piwo *n* beczkowe, piwo *n* z beczki; **~s** *sg. Brt.* warcaby *pl.*; '**~s·man** (*pl. -men*) *Brt. tech.* kreślarz *m*; '**~s·wom·an** (*pl. -women*) *Brt. tech.* kreślarka *f*; '**~·y** (*-ier, -iest*) *Brt.* pełen przeciągów

draw [drɔː] **1.** (*drew, drawn*) *v/t.* ⟨po-, za⟩ciągnąć, wyciągać ⟨-gnąć⟩; *zasłonę itp.* zaciągać ⟨-gnąć⟩; *oddech* wciągać ⟨-gnąć⟩; *fig. tłumy* przyciągać ⟨-gnąć⟩; ⟨na⟩rysować; *gotówkę* podejmować ⟨-djąć⟩; *czek* wystawiać ⟨-wić⟩; *v/i.* rysować; *komin:* ciągnąć; *herbata:* naciągać ⟨-gnąć⟩; (*w sporcie*) ⟨z⟩remisować; **~ back** cofać ⟨-fnąć⟩ się; **~ near** przysuwać ⟨-sunąć⟩ się; **~ out** *pieniądze* podejmować ⟨-djąć⟩; *fig.* ciągnąć się, przeciągać ⟨-gnąć⟩ się; **~ up** *tekst, listę itp.* przygotowywać ⟨-ować⟩; *pensję* pobierać ⟨-brać⟩; *samochód* zatrzymywać ⟨-mać⟩ się; podjeżdżać ⟨-jechać⟩; **2.** ciągnięcie *n*; (*na loterii*) losowanie *n*, ciągnienie *n*; (*w sporcie*) remis *m*; atrakcja *f*; '**~·back** wada *f*; '**~·bridge** most *m* zwodzony

draw·er¹ [drɔː] szuflada *f*

draw·er² ['drɔːə] rysownik *m*; *econ.* wystawca *m* (*czeku itp.*)

'**draw·ing** rysunek *m*; ciągnienie *n*, losowanie *n*; '**~ board** deska *f* kreślarska; rajzbret *m*; '**~ pin** *Brt.* pinezka *f*; pluskiewka *f*; '**~ room** → **living room**; salon *m*

drawl [drɔːl] **1.** zaciągać (*przy mówieniu*); **2.** zaciąganie *n*

drawn [drɔːn] **1.** *p.p. od* **draw** 1; **2.** *adj.* (*w sporcie*) remisowy, nierozstrzygnięty; *twarz:* wyciągnięty

dread [dred] **1.** przerażenie *n*, strach *m*; **2.** bać się; '**~·ful** straszliwy, przerażający

dream [driːm] **1.** sen *m*, marzenie *n*; **2.** (*dreamed lub dreamt*) śnić, marzyć;

'~·er marzyciel(ka f) m; ~t [dremt] pret. i p.p. od **dream** 2; ~·y (-ier, -iest) marzycielski, rozmarzony

drear·y ['drɪərɪ] (-ier, -iest) ponury; nudny

dredge [dredʒ] 1. pogłębiarka f; 2. pogłębiać ⟨-bić⟩; 'dredg·er pogłębiarka f

dregs [dregz] pl. fusy pl.; fig. męty pl.

drench [drentʃ] przemoczyć

dress [dres] 1. ubranie n; suknia f, sukienka f; △ nie **dres**; 2. ubierać ⟨ubrać⟩ (się); ozdabiać ⟨-dobić⟩, przystrajać ⟨-roić⟩; poprawiać ⟨-wić⟩; sałatkę przybierać ⟨-brać⟩, sałatę przyprawiać ⟨-wić⟩; drób sprawiać ⟨-wić⟩; ranę opatrywać ⟨-trzyć⟩; włosy ⟨u⟩czesać; **get** ~**ed** ubrać się; ~ **down** kogoś ⟨z⟩łajać; ~ **up** ubierać ⟨-ubrać⟩ się (ładnie); przebierać ⟨-brać⟩ się; '~ **cir·cle** theat. pierwszy balkon m; '~ **de·sign·er** projektant(ka f) m mody; '~·er toaletka f; kredens m

'dress·ing ubieranie n (się); med. opatrunek m; sos m sałatkowy; Am. nadzienie n; ~ '**down** łajanie n; ~ **gown** szlafrok m; płaszcz m kąpielowy; '~ **room** garderoba f, szatnia f; '~ **ta·ble** toaletka f

'dress·mak·er krawiec m (-cowa f) (dla kobiet)

drew [druː] pret. od **draw** 1

drib·ble ['drɪbl] sączyć się; ⟨po⟩ciec kroplami; ślinić się; (w piłce nożnej) dryblować

dried [draɪd] suszony, wysuszony

dri·er ['draɪə] → **dryer**

drift [drɪft] 1. prąd m, dryf m; zaspa f; sterta f, kupa f; fig. przesuwanie n się; 2. ⟨z⟩dryfować, przesuwać ⟨-sunąć⟩ się; znosić ⟨znieść⟩, nanosić ⟨nanieść⟩; gromadzić (się)

drill [drɪl] 1. tech. wiertarka f, wiertło n, świder m; mil. dryl m (też fig.), musztra f; 2. ⟨na⟩wiercić; mil., fig. musztrować; '~·ing site tech. teren m wiertniczy

drink [drɪŋk] 1. napój m; 2. (**drank, drunk**) ⟨wy⟩pić; ~ **to s.o.** pić za kogoś; ~·'**driv·ing** Brt. prowadzenie n samochodu w stanie nietrzeźwym; '~·er pijąca osoba f; '~s ma·**chine** automat m z napojami

drip [drɪp] 1. kapanie n; med. kroplówka f; 2. (-**pp**-) ⟨na⟩kapać; ociekać

⟨-ciec⟩; ~·'**dry** nie wymagający prasowania; '~·**ping** tłuszcz m z pieczeni

drive [draɪv] 1. jazda f; przejażdżka f; droga f dojazdowa; prywatna droga f tech. napęd m; komp. napęd m, stacja f; psych. popęd m; fig. kampania f, akcja f; fig. energia f, wigor m; mot. **left-hand ~e** lewostronny układ m kierowniczy; 2. (**drove, driven**) v/t. ⟨po⟩jechać (autem), auto itp. prowadzić, ⟨po⟩kierować; ⟨po⟩jechać, ⟨za⟩wieźć (samochodem); doprowadzać ⟨-wić⟩ (do szału itp.); bydło itp. pędzić; tech. napędzać ⟨-dzić⟩; wbijać ⟨wbić⟩; ~**e off** odjeżdżać ⟨-jechać⟩; **what are you ~ing at?** F o co ci chodzi?

'drive-in 1. auto...; dla zmotoryzowanych (nie wysiadających z samochodu); ~ **cinema**, Am. ~ **motion-picture theater** kino n dla zmotoryzowanych; 2. kino n dla zmotoryzowanych; restauracja f dla zmotoryzowanych; bankowy itp. punkt m obsługi dla zmotoryzowanych

driv·el ['drɪvl] 1. (zwł. Brt. -**ll**-, Am. -**l**-) brednie pl., banialuki pl.; 2. pleść brednie

driv·en ['drɪvn] p.p. od **drive** 2

driv·er ['draɪvə] mot. kierowca m; maszynista m (lokomotywy); komp. drajwer m, sterownik m; '~'s li·**cense** Am. prawo n jazdy

driv·ing ['draɪvɪŋ] tech. napędowy, napędzający; mot. ~ **school** nauka f nauki jazdy; '~ li·**cence** Brt. prawo n jazdy; '~ **test** egzamin m na prawo jazdy

driz·zle ['drɪzl] 1. mżawka f, kapuśniak m; 2. mżyć

drone [drəʊn] 1. zo. truteń m (też fig.); 2. ⟨za⟩brzęczeć, byczeć ⟨bzykać⟩

droop [druːp] opadać ⟨-paść⟩

drop [drɒp] 1. kropla f; spadek m, upadek m; zmniejszanie n się; cukierek m; **fruit ~s** pl. drops m, zw. pl.; 2. (-**pp**-) v/t. kapać; upuszczać⟨-uścić⟩, spuszczać ⟨-uścić⟩; temat itp. zarzucać ⟨-cić⟩, zaniechać; ~ **s.o. a postcard** F naskrobać kartkę do kogoś; pasażera itp. wysadzać ⟨-dzić⟩; v/i. kapać; spadać ⟨-aść⟩; opadać ⟨-aść⟩; ~ **in** wpadać ⟨-aść⟩ (z wizytą); ~ **off** spadać ⟨-aść⟩; F zdrzemnąć się; ~ **out** wypadać ⟨-aść⟩; wysiadać ⟨-siąść⟩ (of z G); też ~ **out of school** (**university**) rzucać

⟨-cić⟩ szkołę (uniwersytet); '~-out odszczepieniec *m*, outsider *m*; *(osoba,
która porzuciła szkołę)*

drought [draut] susza *f*

drove [drəuv] *pret. od* **drive** 2

drown [draun] *v/t.* ⟨u⟩topić; zatapiać
⟨-topić⟩; *fig.* zagłuszać ⟨-szyć⟩; *v/i.* ⟨u⟩-
tonąć, ⟨u⟩topić się

drow·sy ['drauzi] (*-ier, -iest*) senny

drudge [drʌdʒ] harować; drudg·e·ry
['drʌdʒəri] harówka *f*

drug [drʌg] **1.** lekarstwo *n*, środek *m* far-
maceutyczny; narkotyk *m*; **be on ~s**
brać narkotyki; **be off ~s** nie brać narkotyków; **2.** (*-gg-*) podawać ⟨-dać⟩ lekarstwo *lub* narkotyk; dodawać ⟨-dać⟩
narkotyk *lub* środek odurzający do
(*G*); *fig.* znieczulać ⟨-lić⟩, zobojętniać
⟨-nić⟩; '~ a·buse nadużywanie *n* narkotyków; '~ ad·dict narkoman(ka *f*)
m; **be a ~ addict** brać narkotyki; ~·gist
['drʌgist] *Am.* aptekarz *m* (-arka *f*);
właściciel(ka *f*) (*drugstore'u*); '~·store
Am. drugstore *m*, *jakby:* apteka *f*, drogeria *f*; '~ vic·tim ofiara *f* zażywania
narkotyków

drum [drʌm] **1.** *mus.* bęben(ek) *m*; *anat.*
bębenek *m*; ~s *pl.* perkusja *f*; **2.** (*-mm-*)
⟨za-, po⟩bębnić; '~·mer *mus.* perkusis-
ta *m* (-tka *f*)

drunk [drʌŋk] **1.** *p.p. od* **drink** 2; **2.** *adj.*
pijany; *get~* upijać ⟨upić⟩ się; **3.** pijany
m; pijak *m* (-aczka *f*); ~·ard ['drʌŋkəd]
pijak *m* (-aczka *f*); '~·en pijany; ~·en
'driv·ing (*Am. też* **drunk driving**) jazda po pijanemu (*samochodem*)

dry [drai] **1.** (*-ier, -iest*) suchy; wys-
chnięty; *wino:* wytrawny; bezdeszczo-
wy; **2.** ⟨wy⟩suszyć; *też* ~ **up** wysychać
⟨-schnąć⟩; ~ **'clean** ⟨wy⟩czyścić che-
micznie; ~ '**clean·er** pralnia *f* chemiczna; '~·er (*też* **drier**) suszarka *f*;
'~ **goods** *pl. Am.* pasmanteria *f*

DTP [di: ti: 'pi:] *skrót:* **desktop publishing** *komp.* DTP *n*, mała poligrafia *f*

du·al ['djuəl] podwójny; ~ '**car·riage-
way** *Brt.* droga *f* szybkiego ruchu

dub [dʌb] (*-bb-*) (*w filmie*) podkładać
⟨-dłożyć⟩ dubbing

du·bi·ous ['djuːbjəs] wątpliwy

duch·ess ['dʌtʃis] księżna *f*

duck [dʌk] **1.** *zo.* kaczka *f*; **my ~s** F *Brt.*
mój skarbie; **2.** uchylić (się); skrywać

⟨-ryć⟩ (się); '~·ling *zo.* kaczątko *n*

due [djuː] **1.** planowy, oczekiwany, spo-
dziewany; należny; *econ.* przypadający
do zapłaty; ~ **to** z powodu (*G*); **be ~ to**
być spowodowanym (*I*); **2.** *adv.* bezpośrednio, prosto; dokładnie; ~ **north** dokładnie na północ

du·el ['djuːəl] pojedynek *m*

dues [djuːz] *pl.* należności *pl.*, opłaty *pl.*

du·et [djuː'et] *mus.* duet *m*

dug [dʌg] *pret. i p.p. od* **dig** 1

duke [djuːk] książę *m*

dull [dʌl] **1.** *kolor:* matowy; *dźwięk:* głuchy; *słuch:* przytępiony; *wzrok:* przygu-
szony; zachmurzony; nudny; tępy (*też
fig.*); *econ.* mało aktywny, martwy; **2.**
przytępić ⟨-tępiać⟩, osłabiać ⟨-bić⟩; stę-
piać ⟨-pić⟩

du·ly ['djuːlɪ] *adv.* należycie, właściwie;
punktualnie, na czas

dumb [dʌm] niemy; *zwł. Am.* F durny;
dum(b)'found·ed oniemiały

dum·my ['dʌmɪ] atrapa *f*, makieta *f*; manekin *m* (*też do testów*); *Brt.* smoczek
m; (*w brydżu*) dziadek *m*

dump [dʌmp] **1.** *v/t.* rzucać ⟨-cić⟩, ⟨z-,
wy⟩rzucać ⟨-cić⟩; porzucać ⟨-cić⟩; *śmieci* wysypywać ⟨-pać⟩; *nieczystości* pozbywać się, zrzucać; *econ. cenę* obniżać
dumpingowo; **2.** wysypisko *n*, hałda *f*,
zwał *m*; usypisko *n*; skład *m*; '~·ing
econ. dumping *m*

dune [djuːn] wydma *f*

dung [dʌŋ] **1.** obornik *m*, gnój *f*; **2.** nawozić ⟨-wieźć⟩ (*obornikiem*)

dun·ga·rees [dʌŋgə'riːz] *pl. Brt.* (**a pair
of ~**) spodnie *pl.* robocze, kombinezon
m; (*spodnie*) rybaczki *pl.*

dun·geon ['dʌndʒən] loch *m*

dupe [djuːp] oszukiwać ⟨-kać⟩

du·plex ['djuːpleks] podwójny; '~ (a-
part·ment) *Am.* mieszkanie *n* dwu-
poziomowe; '~ (**house**) *Am.* dom bliźniak

du·pli·cate 1. ['djuːplɪkət] podwójny; ~ **key** drugi klucz *m*, duplikat *m*;
2. ['djuːplɪkət] duplikat *m*, kopia *f*, odpis *m*; **3.** ['djuːplɪkeɪt] ⟨z⟩duplikio-
wać, ⟨s⟩kopiować, wykonywać ⟨-nać⟩
odpis

du·plic·i·ty [djuː'plɪsɪtɪ] dwulicowość *f*,
obłuda *f*

dur·a·ble ['djuərəbl] wytrzymały, trwały; do trwałego użytku; **du·ra·tion** [djuə'reɪʃn] okres *m*, czas *m* trwania

du·ress [djuə'res] przymus *m*

dur·ing ['djuərɪŋ] *prp.* podczas (*G*)

dusk [dʌsk] zmierzch *m*; '**~·y** (*-ier, -iest*) mroczny (*też fig.*)

dust [dʌst] **1.** kurz *m*; pył *m*; **2.** *v/t.* odkurzać ⟨-rzyć⟩; posypywać ⟨-pać⟩; ⟨przy⟩pudrować; *tech.* opylać ⟨-lić⟩; *v/i.* ścierać ⟨zetrzeć⟩ kurz; ⟨przy⟩pudrować się; '**~·bin** *Brt.* kubeł *m* na kosz *m* na śmieci; '**~·bin lin·er** jednorazowy worek *m* (*do kubła na śmieci*); '**~·cart** *Brt.* śmieciarka *f*; '**~·er** ścierka *f* (*do kurzu*); (*w szkole*) gąbka *f* do tablicy; '**~ cov·er**, '**~ jack·et** obwoluta *f*; '**~·man** (*pl. -men*) *Brt.* śmieciarz *m*; '**~·pan** śmietniczka *f*; '**~·y** (*-ier, -iest*) zakurzony, zapylony

Dutch [dʌtʃ] **1.** *adj.* holenderski; **2.** *adv.* **go ~** ⟨za⟩płacić składkowo; **2.** *ling.* holenderski; **the ~** *pl.* Holendrzy *pl.*; '**~·man** (*pl. -men*) Holender *m*; '**~·wo·m·an** (*pl. -women*) Holenderka *f*

du·ty ['dju:tɪ] obowiązek *m*, powinność *f*; *econ.* cło *n*; podatek *m*; **on ~**

dyżurny; **be on ~** mieć dyżur *lub* służbę; **be off ~** być po dyżurze *lub* służbie; **~·'free** bezcłowy

dwarf [dwɔ:f] **1.** (*pl. dwarfs* [dwɔ:fs], **dwarves** [dwɔ:vz]) karzeł *m*; krasnal *m*, krasnoludek *m*; **2.** pomniejszać ⟨-szyć⟩, ⟨z⟩robić małym

dwell [dwel] (*dwelt lub dwelled*) mieszkać; *fig.* rozpamiętywać; '**~·ing** mieszkanie *n*

dwelt [dwelt] *pret. i p.p. od dwell*

dwin·dle ['dwɪndl] ⟨s⟩kurczyć się

dye [daɪ] **1.** farba *f*; barwnik *m*; **of the deepest ~** najgorszego rodzaju; **2.** ⟨za⟩farbować

dy·ing ['daɪɪŋ] **1.** umierający; **2.** umieranie *n*

dyke [daɪk] → **dike**[1, 2]

dy·nam·ic [daɪ'næmɪk] dynamiczny; **~s** *zw. sg.* dynamika *f*

dy·na·mite ['daɪnəmaɪt] **1.** dynamit *m*; **2.** wysadzać ⟨-dzić⟩ dynamitem

dys·en·te·ry ['dɪsntrɪ] *med.* czerwonka *f*, dyzenteria *f*

dys·pep·si·a [dɪs'pepsɪə] *med.* niestrawność *f*

E

E, e [i:] E, e *n*

E *skrót pisany:* **east**; wschodni; **east(ern)** wschodni

each [i:tʃ] każdy; **~ other** siebie *lub* się nawzajem, wzajemnie; na osobę, na sztukę

ea·ger ['i:gə] chętny; gorliwy; '**~·ness** gorliwość *f*

ea·gle ['i:gl] *zo.* orzeł *m*; **~·'eyed** o ostrym wzroku, sokolooki

ear [ɪə] *anat.* ucho *n* (*też igielne, naczynia*); kłos *m*; **keep an ~ to the ground** słuchać co piszczy w trawie, mieć uszy otwarte; '**~·ache** ból *m* ucha; '**~·drum** *ant.* bębenek *m* uszny; **~ed: pink-eared** o różowych uszach

earl [ɜ:l] *angielski* hrabia *m*

'**ear·lobe** płatek *m* ucha

ear·ly ['ɜ:lɪ] wczesny; początkowy; **as ~ as May** już w maju; **as ~ as possible** najszybciej *lub* najwcześniej jak można; **~ 'bird** ranny ptaszek *m*; **~ 'warn·ing**

sys·tem system *m* wczesnego ostrzegania

'**ear·mark 1.** oznaczenie *n*, cecha *f*; **2.** oznaczać ⟨-czyć⟩; ⟨wy⟩asygnować (**for** na *A*), alokować

earn [ɜ:n] zarabiać ⟨-robić⟩; przynosić ⟨-nieść⟩

ear·nest ['ɜ:nɪst] **1.** poważny, zasadniczy; **2.** zadatek *m*; **in ~** na serio, na poważnie

earn·ings ['ɜ:nɪŋz] *pl.* wpływy *pl.*

'**ear|·phones** *pl.* słuchawki *pl.*; '**~·piece** *tel.* słuchawka *f*; '**~·ring** kolczyk *m*; '**~·shot: within (out of) ~shot** w zasięgu (poza zasięgiem) słuchu

earth [ɜ:θ] **1.** ziemia *f*; Ziemia *f*; ląd *m*; **2.** *v/t. electr.* uziemiać ⟨-mić⟩; **~·en** ['ɜ:θn] gliniany; '**~·en·ware** wyroby *pl.* gliniane; '**~·ly** ziemski, doczesny; F możliwy; '**~·quake** trzęsienie *n* ziemi; '**~·worm** *zo.* dżdżownica *f*

ease [i:z] **1.** łatwość *f*; spokój *m*; beztroska *f*; lekkość *f*; *at (one's)* ~ spokojny, w spokoju; swobodny; *be lub feel ill at* ~ nie czuć się swobodnie; **2.** *v/t.* ⟨z⟩łagodzić; ⟨o⟩słabnąć; *v/i. zw.* ~ *off*, ~ *up* ⟨z⟩łagodnieć, ⟨ze⟩lżeć; ⟨o⟩słabnąć

ea·sel ['i:zl] sztalugi *pl.*

east [i:st] **1.** wschód *m*; **2.** *adj.* wschodni; **3.** *adv.* na wschód

Eas·ter ['i:stə] Wielkanoc *f*; *attr.* wielkanocny; ~ '**bun·ny** króliczek *m* wielkanocny; '~ **egg** jajko *n* wielkanocne, pisanka *f*

eas·ter·ly ['i:stəlı] wschodni; **eastern** ['i:stən] wschodni; **east·ward(s)** ['i:stwəd(z)] wschodni; na wschód

eas·y ['i:zı] (*-ier*, *-iest*) łatwy; beztroski; *go ~, take it* ~ nie kłopotać się; *take it* ~*!* nie przejmuj się!; ~ '**chair** fotel *m*; ~'**go·ing** swobodny, nieskrępowany

eat [i:t] (*ate*, *eaten*) ⟨z⟩jeść; *rdza itp.*: zżerać ⟨zeżreć⟩; ~ *out* jeść na mieście *lub* poza domem; ~ *up* zjeść; '~·**a·ble** jadalny; ~**en** ['i:tn] *p.p. od eat* 1; '~·**er**: *he is a slow* ~**er** wolno je

eaves [i:vz] *pl.* okap *m*; '~·**drop** (*-pp-*) podsłuchiwać ⟨-chać⟩

ebb [eb] **1.** odpływ *m*; **2.** cofać ⟨-fnąć⟩ się; odpływać ⟨-łynąć⟩; ~ *away* uchodzić ⟨ujść⟩, uciekać ⟨uciec⟩; ~ '*tide* odpływ *m*

eb·o·ny ['ebənı] heban *m*

ec *skrót pisany*: *Eurocheque* Brt. euroczek *m*

EC [i: 'si:] *skrót*: *European Community* Wspólnota *f* Europejska

ec·cen·tric [ık'sentrık] **1.** (*~ally*) ekscentryczny; **2.** ekscentryk *m* (-yczka *f*), oryginał *m*

ec·cle·si·as·tic [ıklı:zı'æstık] (*-ally*), ~**ti·cal** kościelny

echo ['ekəu] **1.** (*pl.-oes*) echo *n*; **2.** *v/t.* powtarzać ⟨-tórzyć⟩; *fig. v/i.* odbijać ⟨-bić⟩ się, powtarzać⟨-tórzyć⟩ jak echo

e·clipse *astr.* [ı'klıps] zaćmienie *n* (*księżyca, słońca*)

e·co·cide ['i:kəsaıd] niszczenie *n* przyrody

e·co·lo·gi·cal [i:kə'lɒdʒıkl] ekologiczny

e·col·o·gist [i:'kɒlədʒıst] ekolog *m*; ~·**gy** [i:'kɒlədʒı] ekologia *f*

ec·o·nom·ic [i:kə'nɒmık] (*-ally*) eko-

nomiczny; gospodarczy; ~**ic growth** rozwój *m* gospodarczy; ~·**i·cal** ekonomiczny, gospodarczy; oszczędny; ~**ics** *sg.* ekonomia *f*, ekonomika *f*; gospodarka *f*

e·con·o·mist [ı'kɒnəmıst] ekonomista *m* (-tka *f*); ~**mize** [ı'kɒnəmaız] oszczędzać ⟨-dzić⟩; ~**my** [ı'kɒnəmı] **1.** gospodarka *f*; ekonomia *f*, ekonomika *f*; oszczędność *f*; **2.** dający oszczędności

e·co·sys·tem ['i:kəusıstəm] ekosystem *m*

ec·sta·sy ['ekstəsı] ekstaza *f*; ~**t·ic** [ık'stætık] ekstatyczny

ECU ['ekju:, eı'ku:] *skrót*: *European Currency Unit* ecu *n*

ed. [ed] *skrót*: *edited* red., redakcja *f*, redagował; *edition* wyd., wydanie *f*; *editor* red., redaktor *m*

ed·dy ['edı] **1.** wir *m*, zamęt *m*; **2.** ⟨za⟩wirować

edge [edʒ] **1.** brzeg *m*, skraj *m*; krawędź *f*, ostrze *n*; *be on* ~ być poirytowanym; *have the* ~ *over* mieć przewagę nad (*I*); **2.** obszywać ⟨-szyć⟩; ⟨za-, na⟩ostrzyć; przysuwać się; ~**ways** ['edʒweız], ~**wise** ['edʒwaız] bokiem, na boku

edg·ing ['edʒıŋ] obramowanie *n*; obszycie *n*

edg·y ['edʒı] (*-ier*, *-iest*) ostry; F zirytowany

ed·i·ble ['edıbl] jadalny

e·dict ['i:dıkt] edykt *m*

ed·i·fice ['edıfıs] budynek *m*

Ed·in·burgh Edynburg *m*

ed·it ['edıt] *tekst* ⟨z⟩redagować; *komp.* ⟨wy⟩edytować; ⟨na⟩pisać; *czasopismo* być wydawcą, wydawać; *film* ⟨z⟩montować; **e·di·tion** [ı'dıʃn] wydanie *n*; **ed·i·tor** ['edıtə] wydawca *m*; redaktor(ka *f*) *m*; **ed·i·to·ri·al** [edı'tɔ:rıəl] **1.** artykuł *m* wstępny; **2.** redakcyjny

EDP [i: di: 'pi:] *skrót*: *electronic data processing* elektroniczne przetwarzanie *n* danych

ed·u·cate ['edʒukeıt] ⟨wy⟩kształcić; ⟨wy⟩edukować; ~**cat·ed** wykształcony; ~·**ca·tion** [edʒu'keıʃn] wykształcenie *n*, edukacja *f*; kształcenie *n*, wychowanie *n*; *Ministry of* 2**cation** Ministerstwo *n* Oświaty; ~·**ca·tion·al** [edʒu'keıʃənl] edukacyjny; oświatowy

eel [i:l] *zo.* węgorz *m*

ef·fect [ɪ'fekt] rezultat *m*; skutek *m*; wynik *m*; wpływ *m*; efekt *m*; wrażenie *n*; **~s** *pl.*, *econ.* walory *pl.*; majątek *m* ruchomy; **be in ~** być w mocy; **in ~** faktycznie; **take ~** wchodzić ⟨wejść⟩ w życie; **ef'fec·tive** efektywny, skuteczny; faktyczny, realny; działający

ef·fem·i·nate [ɪ'femɪnət] zniewieściały

ef·fer·|·vesce [efə'ves] musować;**~·ves·cent** [efə'vesnt] musujący

ef·fi·cien|·cy [ɪ'fɪʃənsɪ] skuteczność *f*; sprawność *f*; wydajność; **~cy measure** *econ.* środek *m* zwiększenia wydajności; **~t** skuteczny, sprawny; wydajny

ef·flu·ent ['efluənt] wyciek *m*; ścieki *pl.*

ef·fort ['efət] wysiłek *m*; staranie *n* (**at** o *A*); **without ~** → '**~·less** bez wysiłku

ef·fron·te·ry [ɪ'frʌntərɪ] zuchwałość *f*, bezczelność *f*

ef·fu·sive [ɪ'fjuːsɪv] wylewny

EFTA ['eftə]*skrót:* **European Free Trade Association** EFTA, Europejskie Stowarzyszenie *n* Wolnego Handlu

e.g. [iː 'dʒiː] *skrót:* **for example** (*łacińskie exempli gratia*) np., na przykład

egg[1] [eg] jajko; **put all one's ~s in one basket** postawić wszystko na jedną kartę

egg[2] [eg]: **~ on** podpuszczać ⟨-puścić⟩, podbechtywać ⟨-bechtać⟩

'**egg**| **co·sy** osłona *f* dla jaj; '**~·cup** kieliszek *m* dla jaj; '**~·head** (*intelektualista*) jajogłowy *m* (-wa *f*); '**~·plant** *bot.*, *zwł. Am.* bakłażan *m*; '**~·shell** skorupka *f* jajka; '**~ tim·er** minutnik *m*

e·go·is·m ['egəʊɪzəm] egoizm *m*, samolubstwo *n*; **~t** ['egəʊɪst] egoista *m* (-tka *f*), samolub *m*

E·gypt ['iːdʒɪpt] Egipt *m*; **E·gyp·tian** [ɪ'dʒɪpʃn] **1.** egipski; **2.** Egipcjanin *m* (-anka *f*)

ei·der·down ['aɪdədaʊn] puch *m* (*edredona*); kołdra *f* puchowa

eight [eɪt] **1.** osiem; **2.** ósemka *f*; **eigh·teen** [eɪ'tiːn] osiemnaście; **eigh·teenth** [eɪ'tiːnθ] osiemnasty; '**~·fold** ośmiokrotny; **eighth** [eɪtθ] **1.** ósmy; **2.** jedna ósma; '**eighth·ly** po ósme; **eigh·ti·eth** ['eɪtɪɪθ] osiemdziesiąty; '**eigh·ty 1.** osiemdziesiąt; **2.** osiemdziesiątka *f*

Ei·re ['eərə] (*irlandzka nazwa Irlandii*)

ei·ther ['aɪðə, 'iːðə] którykolwiek, jakikolwiek (z dwóch); jeden (z dwóch);

oba, obydwa; **~ ... or ...** albo ... albo ...; **not ~** też nie (*po zdaniu przeczącym*)

e·jac·u·late [ɪ'dʒækjʊleɪt] *v/t.* *physiol.* tryskać ⟨-snąć⟩ (*nasieniem*); wykrzyknąć; *v/i.* wytrysnąć, mieć wytrysk

e·ject [ɪ'dʒekt] ⟨wy⟩eksmitować; *tech.* wyrzucać ⟨-cić⟩, wypychać ⟨-pchnąć⟩

eke [iːk]: **~ out** *dochody* uzupełniać ⟨-nić⟩; *pieniądze* oszczędzać ⟨-dzić⟩; **~ out a living** ledwo zarabiać na życie

e·lab·o·rate 1. [ɪ'læbərət] skomplikowany, złożony; **2.** [ɪ'læbəreɪt] opracowywać ⟨-wać⟩, uzupełniać ⟨-nić⟩, ⟨s⟩konkretyzować

e·lapse [ɪ'læps] upływać ⟨-łynąć⟩, przechodzić ⟨przejść⟩

e·las|·tic [ɪ'læstɪk] **1.** (**-ally**) elastyczny, rozciągliwy; **2.** guma *f*, gumka *f*; **~·ti·ci·ty** [elæ'stɪsətɪ] elastyczność *f*

e·lat·ed [ɪ'leɪtɪd] zachwycony

Elbe Łaba *f*

el·bow ['elbəʊ] **1.** łokieć *m*; ostry zakręt *m*; *tech.* kolanko *n*; **at one's ~** pod ręką; **2.** *drogę* ⟨u⟩torować łokciami; **~ one's way through** przepychać ⟨-pchnąć⟩ się przez (*A*)

el·der[1] ['eldə] **1.** starszy; **2.** starszy *m*; **~s** starszyzna *f*; '**~·ly** starszy

el·der[2] *bot.* ['eldə] czarny bez *m*

el·dest ['eldɪst] najstarszy

e·lect [ɪ'lekt] **1.** elekt, wybrany; **2.** wybierać ⟨-brać⟩

e·lec|·tion [ɪ'lekʃn] **1.** wybory *pl.*; **2.** *pol.* wyborczy; **~·tor** [ɪ'lektə] wyborca *m*, *Am. pol.*, *hist.* elektor *m*; **~·to·ral** [ɪ'lektərəl] wyborczy; **~·toral college** *Am. pol.* kolegium elektorskie; **~·to·rate** [ɪ'lektərət] *pol.* elektorat *m*

e·lec·tric [ɪ'lektrɪk] (**~ally**) elektryczny, elektro...

e·lec·tri·cal [ɪ'lektrɪkl] elektryczny, elektro...;**~ en·gi·neer** inżynier *m* elektryk; elektrotechnik *m*; **~ en·gi·neer·ing** elektrotechnika *f*

e·lec·tric 'chair krzesło *n* elektryczne

e·lec·tri·cian [ɪlek'trɪʃn] elektryk *m*

e·lec·tri·ci·ty [ɪlek'trɪsətɪ] elektryczność *f*

e·lec·tric 'ra·zor elektryczna maszynka *f* do golenia

e·lec·tri·fy [ɪ'lektrɪfaɪ] ⟨z⟩elektryzować (*też fig.*); ⟨z⟩elektryfikować

e·lec·tro·cute [ɪ'lektrəkjuːt] porażać

⟨-razić⟩ *kogoś* śmiertelnie prądem; wykonywać ⟨-nać⟩ *na kimś* wyrok śmierci na krześle elektrycznym

e·lec·tron [ɪ'lektrɒn] elektron *m*

el·ec·tron·ic [ɪlek'trɒnɪk] (**~ally**) elektroniczny; **~ 'da·ta pro·ces·sing** elektroniczne przetwarzanie *n* danych

el·ec·tron·ics [ɪlek'trɒnɪks] *sg.* elektronika *f*

el·e|·gance ['elɪɡəns] elegancja *f*; **'~·gant** elegancki, wytworny

el·e|·ment ['elɪmənt] element *m*; składnik *m*; *chem.* pierwiastek *m*; **~ments** *pl.* elementy *pl.*, podstawy *pl.*; żywioły *pl.*; **~·men·tal** [elɪ'mentl] elementarny; istotny

el·e·men·ta·ry [elɪ'mentərɪ] elementarny, początkowy; **~ school** *Am.* szkoła *f* podstawowa

el·e·phant ['elɪfənt] *zo.* słoń

el·e|·vate ['elɪveɪt] podnosić ⟨-nieść⟩, podwyższać ⟨-szyć⟩; dawać ⟨dać⟩ awans; '**~·vat·ed** podniesiony, podwyższony; *fig.* wyniosły; **~·va·tion** [elɪ'veɪʃn] podniesienie *n*, podwyższenie *n*; wyniosłość *f*; awans *m*; wysokość *f*, wzniesienie *n*; **~·va·tor** *tech.* ['elɪveɪtə] *Am.* winda *f*; dźwig *m*

el·ev·en [ɪ'levn] **1.** jedenaście; **2.** jedenastka *f*; **~th** [ɪ'levnθ] **1.** jedenasty; **2.** jedna jedenasta

elf [elf] (*pl.* **elves**) elf *m*

e·li·cit [ɪ'lɪsɪt] wydobywać ⟨-być⟩ (**from** od *G*); wydostawać ⟨-tać⟩

el·i·gi·ble ['elɪdʒəbl] nadający się do (*G*) *lub* na (*A*); uprawniony (**for** do *G*); wolny

e·lim·i|·nate [ɪ'lɪmɪneɪt] ⟨wy⟩eliminować; usuwać ⟨usunąć⟩; **~·na·tion** [ɪlɪmɪ'neɪʃn] eliminacja *f*; wyeliminowanie *n*; usunięcie *n*

é·lite [eɪ'liːt] elita *f*

elk [elk] *zo.* łoś *m*; *Am.* wapiti *n*

el·lipse [ɪ'lɪps] *math.* elipsa *f*

elm [elm] *bot.* wiąz *m*

e·lon·gate ['iːlɒŋɡeɪt] wydłużać ⟨-żyć⟩

e·lope [ɪ'ləʊp] uciekać ⟨-ciec⟩ (*z ukochanym lub ukochaną*)

e·lo|·quence ['eləkwəns] elokwencja *f*, łatwość *f* wysławiania się; '**~·quent** elokwentny

else [els] jeszcze; inny; **~'where** gdzie indziej

e·lude [ɪ'luːd] umykać ⟨-knąć⟩ (*prze-*

biegle) (*D*), unikać ⟨-knąć⟩ (*przebiegle*); nie przychodzić do głowy, umykać

e·lu·sive [ɪ'luːsɪv] nieuchwytny

elves [elvz] *pl. od* **elf**

e·ma·ci·ated [ɪ'meɪʃɪeɪtɪd] wychudzony, wymizerowany

em·a|·nate ['eməneɪt] wydobywać się, pochodzić (**from** z *G*); promieniować, emanować; **~·na·tion** [emə'neɪʃn] emanacja *f*; wydzielanie *n* się

e·man·ci|·pate [ɪ'mænsɪpeɪt] ⟨wy⟩emancypować; **~·pa·tion** [ɪmænsɪ'peɪʃn] emancypacja *f*

em·balm [ɪm'bɑːm] ⟨za⟩balsamować

em·bank·ment [ɪm'bæŋkmənt] nasyp *m*, wał *m*; nabrzeże *n*

em·bar·go [em'bɑːɡəʊ] (*pl. -goes*) embargo *n*, ograniczenie *n*

em·bark [ɪm'bɑːk] *nat.*, *aviat.* ⟨za⟩ładować; przyjmować ⟨-jąć⟩ na pokład; *naut.* (*na statek*) wsiadać ⟨wsiąść⟩; **~ on** przedsiębrać ⟨-sięwziąć⟩ (*A*), podejmować ⟨-djąć⟩ (*A*)

em·bar·rass [ɪm'bærəs] ⟨za⟩kłopotać, wprawiać ⟨-wić⟩ w zakłopotanie; **~·ing** kłopotliwy, kłopoczący; **~·ment** zakłopotanie *n*, konsternacja *f*

em·bas·sy ['embəsɪ] *pol.* ambasada *f*

em·bed [ɪm'bed] (*-dd-*) osadzać ⟨-dzić⟩, zakleszczać ⟨-czyć⟩

em·bel·lish [ɪm'belɪʃ] upiększać ⟨-szyć⟩ (*też fig.*)

em·bers ['embəz] *pl.* żar *m*

em·bez·zle [ɪm'bezl] sprzeniewierzać ⟨-rzyć⟩, ⟨z⟩defraudować; **~·ment** sprzeniewierzenie *n*, defraudacja *f*

em·bit·ter [ɪm'bɪtə]: *be* **~ed** być zgorzkniałym *lub* rozgoryczonym

em·blem ['embləm] emblemat *m*

em·bod·y [ɪm'bɒdɪ] ucieleśniać ⟨-nić⟩; zawierać ⟨-wrzeć⟩; włączać ⟨-czyć⟩

em·bo·lis·m ['embəlɪzəm] *med.* embolia *f*, zator *m*

em·brace [ɪm'breɪs] **1.** obejmować ⟨objąć⟩ (się), ⟨przy⟩tulić (się); uścisk *m*, obejmowanie *n* się

em·broi·der [ɪm'brɔɪdə] ⟨wy⟩haftować; *fig.* upiększać ⟨-szyć⟩, ubarwiać ⟨-wić⟩; **~·y** [ɪm'brɔɪdərɪ] haft *m*; *fig.* upiększanie *n*

em·broil [ɪm'brɔɪl] wciągać ⟨-gnąć⟩ (*w kłopoty itp.*), wplątywać ⟨-tać⟩

e·mend [ɪ'mend] poprawiać ⟨-wić⟩, wnosić ⟨wnieść⟩ poprawki

em·e·rald ['emərəld] **1.** szmaragd *m*; **2.** szmaragdowy

e·merge [ɪ'mɜːdʒ] wyłaniać ⟨-łonić⟩ się; ukazywać ⟨-zać⟩ się; wychodzić ⟨wyjść⟩ na jaw

e·mer·gen·cy [ɪ'mɜːdʒənsɪ] stan *m* wyjątkowy; wypadek *m*; awaria *f*; *pol.* **state of ~** stan *m* wyjątkowy; **~ brake** ręczny hamulec *m*; hamulec *m* bezpieczeństwa; **~ call** wezwanie *n* w razie nagłego wypadku; **~ exit** wyjście *n* bezpieczeństwa; **~ land·ing** lądowanie *n* awaryjne; **~ num·ber** numer *m* pogotowia (*ratunkowego, policji itp.*); **~·room** *Am.* izba *m* przyjęć (*na ostrym dyżurze*)

em·i|·grant ['emɪgrənt] emigrant(ka *f*) *m*; **~·grate** ['emɪgreɪt] ⟨wy⟩emigrować; **~·gra·tion** [emɪ'greɪʃn] emigracja *f*

em·i|·nence ['emɪnəns] sława *f*; **♀nence** *rel.* Eminencja *f*; **'~·nent** sławny; wybitny; **'~·nent·ly** wybitnie; bardzo

e·mis·sion [ɪ'mɪʃn] emisja *f*, promieniowanie *n*; **~·'free** nie wydzielający spalin

e·mit [ɪ'mɪt] ⟨wy⟩emitować, ⟨wy⟩promieniować; wydzielać ⟨-lić⟩

e·mo·tion [ɪ'məʊʃn] uczucie *n*, emocja *f*; **~·al** [ɪ'məʊʃənl] uczuciowy, emocjonalny; wzruszony; wzruszający; **~·al·ly** [ɪ'məʊʃnəlɪ] uczuciowo, emocjonalnie; wzruszająco; **~·ally disturbed** mający zaburzenia emocjonalne; **~·less** nieczuły

em·pe·ror ['empərə] cesarz *m*, imperator *m*

em·pha|·sis ['emfəsɪs] (*pl.* **-ses** [-siːz]) nacisk *m*; **~·size** ['emfəsaɪz] podkreślać ⟨-lić⟩, ⟨za⟩akcentować; **~t·ic** [ɪm'fætɪk] (**-ally**) stanowczy, dobitny; wyraźny

em·pire ['empaɪə] cesarstwo *n*, imperium *n*

em·pir·i·cal [em'pɪrɪkl] empiryczny

em·ploy [ɪm'plɔɪ] **1.** zatrudniać ⟨-nić⟩; ⟨za⟩stosować, używać ⟨-żyć⟩; **2.** zatrudnienie *n*; **in the ~ of** zatrudniony u (*G*); **~·ee** [emplɔɪ'iː] pracownik *m* (-ica *f*); **~·er** [ɪm'plɔɪə] pracodawca *m*; **~·ment** [ɪm'plɔɪmənt] zatrudnienie *n*, praca *f*, użycie *n*; **~·ment ad** ogłoszenie *n* o możliwości zatrudnienia; **~·ment of·fice** urząd *m* zatrudnienia

em·pow·er [ɪm'paʊə] upoważniać ⟨-nić⟩, uprawniać ⟨-nić⟩

em·press ['emprɪs] cesarzowa *f*

emp|·ti·ness ['emptɪnɪs] pustka *f* (*też fig.*); **'~·ty 1.** (**-ier, -iest**) pusty (*też fig.*); **2.** opróżniać ⟨-nić⟩ (się); wysypywać ⟨-pać⟩; *rzeka:* uchodzić (**into** do *G*)

em·u·late ['emjuleɪt] naśladować; *komp.* emulować

e·mul·sion [ɪ'mʌlʃn] emulsja *f*

en·a·ble [ɪ'neɪbl] umożliwiać ⟨-wić⟩, dawać ⟨dać⟩ możność

en·act [ɪ'nækt] *prawo* ustanawiać ⟨-nowić⟩; nadawać ⟨-dać⟩ moc prawną

e·nam·el [ɪ'næml] **1.** emalia *f*; *anat.* szkliwo *n*; lakier *m*; lakier *m* do paznokci; **2.** (*zwł. Brt. -ll-, Am. -l-*) ⟨po⟩emaliować; ⟨po⟩lakierować; szklić

en·am·o·u·red [ɪ'næməd]: **~ of** rozkochany w (*L*)

en·camp·ment [ɪn'kæmpmənt] *zwł. mil.* obóz *m*

en·cased [ɪn'keɪst]: **~ in** oprawny w (*A*), osadzony w (*A*), pokryty (*I*)

en·chant [ɪn'tʃɑːnt] oczarowywać ⟨-ować⟩; **~·ing** czarujący; **~·ment** oczarowanie *n*, czar *m*

en·cir·cle [ɪn'sɜːkl] okrążać ⟨-żyć⟩; otaczać ⟨otoczyć⟩; obejmować ⟨objąć⟩

encl *skrót pisany:* **enclosed, enclosure** zał., załącznik(i *pl*) *m*

en·close [ɪn'kləʊz] otaczać ⟨otoczyć⟩; załączać ⟨-czyć⟩ (*do listu*); **en·clo·sure** [ɪn'kləʊʒə] zagroda *f*, ogrodzone miejsce *n*; załącznik *m*

en·code [en'kəʊd] ⟨za⟩kodować

en·com·pass [ɪn'kʌmpəs] obejmować bjąć

en·coun·ter [ɪn'kaʊntə] **1.** spotkanie *n*; potyczka *f*; **2.** spotykać ⟨-tkać⟩, napotykać ⟨-tkać⟩; natrafiać ⟨-fić⟩ na (*A*), napotykać ⟨-tkać⟩ na (*A*)

en·cour·age [ɪn'kʌrɪdʒ] zachęcać ⟨-cić⟩; popierać ⟨-przeć⟩; **~·ment** zachęta *f*; poparcie *n*

en·cour·ag·ing [ɪn'kʌrɪdʒɪŋ] zachęcający

en·croach [ɪn'krəʊtʃ] (**on**) *prawo, teren* naruszać; wkraczać ⟨-roczyć⟩ (na *teren*) wdzierać ⟨wedrzeć⟩ się; *czas* zabierać ⟨-brać⟩; **~·ment** naruszenie *n*; wkroczenie *n*, wtargnięcie *n*

en·cum·ber [ɪn'kʌmbə] obarczać ⟨-czyć⟩, obciążać ⟨-żyć⟩; ⟨za⟩hamować; **~·brance** [ɪn'kʌmbrəns] obciążenie *n*; przeszkoda *f*

en·cy·clo·p(a)e·di·a [ensaɪklə'piːdjə] encyklopedia *f*

end [end] **1.** koniec *m*, zakończenie *n*; cel *m*; *no ~ of* bez liku; *at the ~ of May* pod koniec maja; *in the ~* w końcu, wreszcie; *on ~* bez przerwy; *stand on ~* włosy: stawać ⟨-nąć⟩ dęba; *to no ~* na próżno; *go off the deep ~* ⟨s⟩tracić cierpliwość; *make (both) ~s meet* ⟨z⟩wiązać koniec z końcem; **2.** ⟨s⟩kończyć (się), ⟨za⟩kończyć (się)

en·dan·ger [ɪn'deɪndʒə] narażać ⟨-razić⟩, zagrażać ⟨-rozić⟩

en·dear [ɪn'dɪə] zdobywać ⟨-być⟩ popularność (*to s.o.* wśród kogoś), przysparzać ⟨-porzyć⟩ popularności; **~ing** [ɪn'dɪərɪŋ] ujmujący, urzekający; **~·ment: words** *pl.* *of ~ment*, **~ments** *pl.* czułe słówka *pl.*, czułości *pl.*

en·deav·o(u)r [ɪn'devə] **1.** staranie *n*, usiłowanie *n*; **2.** ⟨po⟩starać się, dokładać ⟨-łożyć⟩ starań

end·ing ['endɪŋ] zakończenie *n*, koniec *m*; *gr.* końcówka *f*

en·dive ['endɪv, 'endaɪv] *pot.* cykoria *f*, endywia *f*

'end·less nie kończący się, nieskończony, niezmierzony; *tech.* bez końca

en·dorse [ɪn'dɔːs] *econ.* czek ⟨za⟩indosować, żyrować; umieszczać ⟨-eścić⟩ adnotację (*on* na *odwrocie*); ⟨za⟩akceptować; **~·ment** adnotacja *f*, uwaga *f*; *econ.* indosowanie *n*

en·dow [ɪn'dau] *fig.* wyposażać ⟨-żyć⟩, obdarowywać ⟨-ować⟩; dotować; **~ s.o. with s.th.** obdarzać ⟨-rzyć⟩ kogoś czymś; **~·ment** dotacja *f*; **~ments** *pl.* talenty *pl.*, możliwości *pl.*

en·dur|·ance [ɪn'djuərəns] wytrzymałość *f*; *beyond ~ance, past ~ance* nie do zniesienia; **~e** [ɪn'djuə] wytrzymywać ⟨-mać⟩, znosić ⟨znieść⟩

'end us·er użytkownik *m* końcowy, odbiorca *m*

en·e·my ['enəmɪ] **1.** wróg *m*, nieprzyjaciel *m*; **2.** wrogi, nieprzyjacielski

en·er·get·ic [enə'dʒetɪk] (**~ally**) energiczny

en·er·gy ['enədʒɪ] energia *f* (*też elektryczna*); **~ cri·sis** kryzys *m* energetyczny; **~·sav·ing** oszczędność *f* energii; **~ sup·ply** dostawa *f* energii

en·fold [ɪn'fəuld] otaczać ⟨-toczyć⟩ ramieniem; zawierać ⟨-wrzeć⟩

en·force [ɪn'fɔːs] wymuszać ⟨-musić⟩, ⟨wy⟩egzekwować; *prawo* wprowadzać ⟨-dzić⟩ w życie, nadawać ⟨-dać⟩ moc; **~·ment** *econ., jur.* narzucenie *n*; wprowadzenie *n* w życie

en·fran·chise [ɪn'fræntʃaɪz] *komuś* nadawać ⟨-dać⟩ prawo wyborcze

en·gage [ɪn'geɪdʒ] *v/t.* ⟨za⟩angażować, zatrudniać ⟨-nić⟩; *uwagę* przyciągać ⟨-gnąć⟩; *tech.* zaczepiać ⟨-pić⟩, sprzęgać ⟨-gnąć⟩; *mot.* włączać ⟨-czyć⟩ sprzęgło; *v/i. tech.* scepiać ⟨-pić⟩ (się); *~ in* ⟨za⟩angażować się w (*L*); zajmować ⟨-jąć⟩ się (*I*); **~d** zaręczony (*to* z *I*); *toaleta:* Brt. zajęta; **~d tone** lub **signal** Brt. tel. zajęty sygnał *m*; **~·ment** zaręczyny *pl.*; umowa *f*, zobowiązanie *n*; *mil.* potyczka *f*, starcie *n*; *tech.* włączenie *n*, zaczepienie *n*

en·gag·ing [ɪn'geɪdʒɪŋ] zajmujący; *uśmiech:* uroczy

en·gine ['endʒɪn] silnik *m*; *rail.* lokomotywa *f*; **~·driv·er** Brt. rail. maszynista *m*

en·gi·neer [endʒɪ'nɪə] **1.** inżynier *m*, technik *m*, mechanik *m*; Am. rail. maszynista *m*; *mil.* saper *m*; **2.** ⟨wy⟩budować, ⟨za⟩projektować; *fig.* ukartować, ⟨u⟩knuć; **~·ing** [endʒɪ'nɪərɪŋ] inżynieria *f*; technika *f*

Eng·land Anglia *f*

En·glish ['ɪŋglɪʃ] **1.** angielski; **2.** *ling.* angielski (*język*); *the ~ pl.* Anglicy *pl.*; *in plain ~* prosto; '~ **Chan·nel** Kanał La Manche; '~·**man** (*pl. -men*) Anglik *m*; '~·**wom·an** (*pl. -women*) Angielka *f*

en·grave [ɪn'greɪv] ⟨wy⟩grawerować, rytować; *fig.* wyryć, zapadać ⟨-paść⟩; **en·grav·er** grawer *m*; rytownik *m*; **en·grav·ing** rycina *f*, sztych *m*; drzeworyt *m*

en·grossed [ɪn'grəust]: **~ in** pochłonięty (*I*)

en·hance [ɪn'hɑːns] wzmacniać ⟨-mocnić⟩, zwiększać ⟨-szyć⟩

e·nig·ma [ɪ'nɪgmə] zagadka *f*; **e·nigmat·ic** [enɪg'mætɪk] (**~ally**) enigmatyczny, zagadkowy

en·joy [ɪn'dʒɔɪ] cieszyć się (*I*); lubić; *did you ~ it?* podobało ci się to?; *~ o.s.* bawić się; *~ yourself!* baw się dobrze!;

E

I ~ my dinner obiad mi odpowiada; ~·a·ble miły, przyjemny; ~·ment przyjemność *f*

en·large [ɪn'lɑːdʒ] powiększać ⟨-szyć⟩ (się); *phot.* powiększać ⟨-szyć⟩; ~ *on* uszczegóławiać ⟨-łowić⟩ (*A*); rozprawiać nad (*I*); ~·ment powiększenie *n* (*też phot.*)

en·light·en [ɪn'laɪtn] oświecać ⟨-cić⟩; ~·ment oświecenie *n*

en·list [ɪn'lɪst] *mil. v/t.* ⟨z⟩werbować; *v/i.* wstępować ⟨wstąpić⟩ do wojska

en·liv·en [ɪn'laɪvn] ożywiać ⟨-wić⟩

en·mi·ty ['enmətɪ] wrogość *f*

en·no·ble [ɪ'nəubl] nobilitować

e·nor|·mi·ty [ɪ'nɔːmətɪ] ogrom *m*; potworność *f*, ~·mous [ɪ'nɔːməs] ogromny

e·nough [ɪ'nʌf] wystarczający

en·quire [ɪn'kwaɪə], en·qui·ry [ɪn'kwaɪərɪ] → *inquire, inquiry*

en·rage [ɪn'reɪdʒ] rozwścieczać ⟨-czyć⟩; ~d rozwścieczony

en·rap·ture [ɪn'ræptʃə] wprawiać ⟨-wić⟩ w zachwyt; ~d zachwycony

en·rich [ɪn'rɪtʃ] wzbogacać ⟨-cić⟩

en·rol(l) [ɪn'rəul] (*-ll-*) zapisywać ⟨-sać⟩ (się) (*for, in* na *A*); (*na uniwersytet*) wstępować ⟨-tąpić⟩ (*at* na *A*)

en·sign ['ensaɪn] *naut. zwł.* flaga *f*, bandera *f*; ['ensn] *Am.* podporucznik *m* marynarki

en·sue [ɪn'sjuː] następować ⟨-tąpić⟩

en·sure [ɪn'ʃuə] zapewniać ⟨-nić⟩

en·tail [ɪn'teɪl] pociągać za sobą, wymagać

en·tan·gle [ɪn'tæŋgl] wplątywać ⟨-tać⟩

en·ter ['entə] *v/t.* wchodzić ⟨wejść⟩ do (*G*); wjeżdżać ⟨wjechać⟩ do (*G*); *naut.,* wpływać ⟨-łynąć⟩; wstępować ⟨-tąpić⟩ do (*G*); nazywiać, *dane* wprowadzać ⟨-dzić⟩; (*w sporcie*) przystępować ⟨-tąpić⟩ (*for* do *G*); *v/i.* wchodzić ⟨wejść⟩; wjeżdżać ⟨wjechać⟩; *naut.,* wpływać ⟨-łynąć⟩ do portu; *theat.* wchodzić; zgłaszać ⟨-łosić⟩ się (*for* do *G*) (*też w sporcie*); ~ *key* klawisz *m* Enter

en·ter|·prise ['entəpraɪz] przedsięwzięcie *n*; *econ.* przedsiębiorstwo *n*; przedsiębiorczość *f*; ~·pris·ing przedsiębiorczy

en·ter·tain [entə'teɪn] zabawiać ⟨-wić⟩; przyjmować ⟨-jąć⟩ (*gości*); ~·er artysta *m* (*-tka f*) estradowy (*-wa*); ~·ment

rozrywka *f*; widowisko *n*; przyjmowanie *n* gości

en·thral(l) [ɪn'θrɔːl] *fig.* (*-ll-*) oczarowywać ⟨-wać⟩; ⟨za⟩fascynować

en·throne [ɪn'θrəun] intronizować

en·thu·si·as·m [ɪn'θjuːzɪæzəm] entuzjazm *m*; ~t [ɪn'θjuːzɪæst] entuzjasta *m* (*-tka f*); ~·tic [ɪnθjuːzɪ'æstɪk] (*-ally*) entuzjastyczny

en·tice [ɪn'taɪs] ⟨z⟩nęcić, ⟨z⟩wabić; ~·ment atrakcja *f*, powab *m*

en·tire [ɪn'taɪə] cały; niepodzielny, całkowity; ~·ly całkowicie; w zupełności

en·ti·tle [ɪn'taɪtl] uprawniać ⟨-nić⟩ (*to* do *G*)

en·ti·ty ['entətɪ] jednostka *f*

en·trails ['entreɪlz] *anat. pl.* wnętrzności *pl.*

en·trance ['entrəns] wejście *n*; pojawienie *n* się; wstęp *m*; *make an ~* zjawiać się; '~ ex·am·(i·na·tion) egzamin *m* wstępny; '~ fee opłata *f* za wejście; opłata *f* za wstęp

en·treat [ɪn'triːt] błagać; en·trea·ty błaganie *n*

en·trench [ɪn'trentʃ] *mil.* okopywać ⟨-pać⟩ się

en·trust [ɪn'trʌst] powierzać ⟨-rzyć⟩ (*s.th. to s.o.* coś komuś)

en·try ['entrɪ] wejście *n*; wjazd *m*; wstęp *m* (*to* do *G*); wjazd *m*, wlot *m*; (*w słowniku*) hasło *n*; (*w spisie*) pozycja *f*; (*w sporcie*) udział *m*; *bookeeping by double* (*single*) ~ *econ.* podwójna (*pojedyncza*) księgowość *f*; *no ~!* wstęp wzbroniony; *mot.* brak wjazdu!; '~ per·mit pozwolenie *n* na wjazd; '~·phone domofon *m*; '~ vi·sa wiza *f* wjazdowa

en·twine [ɪn'twaɪn] oplatać ⟨-pleść⟩, splatać ⟨-pleść⟩

e·nu·me·rate [ɪ'njuːməreɪt] wyliczać ⟨-czyć⟩

en·vel·op [ɪn'veləp] owijać ⟨owinąć⟩, otaczać ⟨otoczyć⟩

en·ve·lope ['envələup] koperta *f*

en·vi·a·ble ['envɪəbl] godny zazdrości; '~·ous zazdrosny

en·vi·ron·ment [ɪn'vaɪərənmənt] otoczenie *n*; środowisko *n*; środowisko *n* naturalne

en·vi·ron·men·tal [ɪnvaɪərən'mentl] środowiskowy; ~·ist [ɪnvaɪərən'mentəlɪst] ekolog *m*; ~ *law* prawo *n* ochrony środowiska; ~ pol·lu·tion zanieczyszczanie *n* środowiska

en·vi·ron·ment **'friend·ly** przyjazny dla środowiska

en·vi·rons ['envırənz] *pl.* okolice *pl.*

en·vis·age [ın'vızıdʒ] przewidywać ⟨-idzieć⟩

en·voy ['envoı] wysłannik *m* (-niczka *f*)

en·vy ['envı] **1.** zazdrość *f*; **2.** ⟨po⟩zazdrościć

ep·ic ['epık] **1.** epicki; **2.** epos *m*, epopeja *f*

ep·i·dem·ic [epı'demık] **1.** (**~ally**) epidemiczny; **~** *disease* → *disease*; **2.** epidemia *f*, zaraza *f*

ep·i·der·mis [epı'dɜːmıs] naskórek *m*

ep·i·lep·sy ['epılepsı] epilepsja *f*

ep·i·logue *zwł. Brt.*, **ep·i·log** *Am.* ['epılɒg] epilog *m*, posłowie *n*

e·pis·co·pal [ı'pıskəpl] *rel.* biskupi

ep·i·sode ['epısəud] epizod *m*

ep·i·taph ['epıtɑːf] epitafium *n*

e·poch ['iːpɒk] epoka *f*

eq·ua·ble ['ekwəbl] łagodny (*też* klimat)

e·qual ['iːkwəl] **1.** równy; jednakowy; *be ~ to* fig. móc podołać (*D*); *~ rights pl. for women* równe prawa *pl.* dla kobiet; **2.** równy *m*; **3.** (*zwł. Brt. -ll-, Am. -l-*) równać się *z* (*I*); **~·i·ty** [iː'kwɒlətı] równość *f*; **~·i·za·tion** [iːkwəlaı'zeıʃn] wyrównywanie *n*; **~·ize** ['iːkwəlaız] wyrównywać ⟨-nać⟩, zrównywać ⟨-nać⟩; *'~·iz·er* gol *m* wyrównujący; *tech.* urządzenie *n* wyrównawcze

eq·ua·nim·i·ty [iːkwə'nımətı] równowaga *f*, opanowanie *n*

e·qua·tion [ı'kweıʒn] *math.* równanie *n*

e·qua·tor [ı'kweıtə] równik *m*

e·qui·lib·ri·um [iːkwı'lıbrıəm] równowaga *f*

e·quip [ı'kwıp] (*-pp-*) wyposażać ⟨-żyć⟩; *~·ment* sprzęt *m*, wyposażenie *n*

e·quiv·a·lent [ı'kwıvələnt] **1.** ekwiwalentny, równoważny; **2.** ekwiwalent *m*, odpowiednik *m*

e·ra ['ıərə] epoka *f*

e·rad·i·cate [ı'rædıkeıt] wykorzeniać ⟨-nić⟩

e·rase [ı'reız] wymazywać ⟨-zać⟩; ⟨s⟩kasować (*też zapis magnetyczny*); *fig.* zmazywać ⟨-zać⟩; **e'ras·er** gumka *f*

e·rect [ı'rekt] **1.** wyprostowany; **2.** stawiać ⟨postawić⟩; *budynek* wznosić ⟨wznieść⟩; *maszynę itp.* ⟨z⟩montować;

e·rec·tion [ı'rekʃn] wznoszenie *n*; *physiol.* erekcja *f*, wzwód *m*

er·mine ['ɜːmın] *zo.* gronostaj *m*; *ubiór*: gronostaje *pl.*

e·rode [ı'rəud] *geol.* ⟨z⟩erodować; **e·ro·sion** [ı'rəuʒn] *geol.* erozja *f*

e·rot·ic [ı'rɒtık] (**~ally**) erotyczny

err [ɜː] ⟨po⟩mylić (się)

er·rand ['erənd] zlecenie *n*, polecenie *n*; *go on an~, run an~* załatwiać sprawy; *'~ boy* chłopiec *m* na posyłki

er·rat·ic [ı'rætık] zmienny; *ruchy*: nieskoordynowany

er·ro·ne·ous [ı'rəunjəs] błędny

er·ror ['erə] błąd *m* (*też komp.*); *~s excepted* z zastrzeżeniem błędów; *'~ mes·sage komp.* komunikat *m* o błędzie

e·rupt [ı'rʌpt] *wulkan itp.*: wybuchać ⟨-chnąć⟩; *ząb*: wyrzynać ⟨-rżnąć⟩ się; **e·rup·tion** [ı'rʌpʃn] wybuch *m* (*wulkanu*); *med.* wyrzynanie *n* się (*zęba*)

ESA [iː es 'eı] *skrót:* ***European Space Agency*** Europejska Agencja *f* Przestrzeni Kosmicznej

es·ca|·late ['eskəleıt] nasilać ⟨-lić⟩ (się); doprowadzać ⟨-dzić⟩ do eskalacji; *~·la·tion* [eskə'leıʃn] eskalacja *f*

es·ca·la·tor ['eskəleıtə] schody *pl.* ruchome

es·ca·lope ['eskələup] *gastr.* kotlet *m*, eskalopek *m* (*zwł. cielęcy*)

es·cape [ı'skeıp] **1.** uciekać ⟨uciec⟩; zbiec; *gaz*: ulatniać ⟨-lotnić⟩ się; *woda itp.*: przeciekać ⟨-ciec⟩; unikać ⟨-knąć⟩; *komuś* umykać ⟨umknąć⟩; **2.** ucieczka *f*; ulatnianie *n* się; przeciek *m*; *have a narrow ~* ledwie ujść cało; *~ chute aviat.* ślizg *m* ratunkowy; *~ key komp.* klawisz *m* Escape

es·cort 1. ['eskɔːt] *mil.* eskorta *f*; obstawa *f*; konwój *m*; osoba *f* towarzysząca; **2.** [ı'skɔːt] *mil.* eskortować; *aviat., naut.* konwojować; towarzyszyć

es·cutch·eon [ı'skʌtʃən] tarcza *f* herbowa

esp. *skrót pisany:* ***especially*** zwł., zwłaszcza

es·pe·cial [ı'speʃl] szczególny; *~·ly* szczególnie

es·pi·o·nage [espıə'nɑːʒ] szpiegostwo *n*

es·pla·nade [esplə'neıd] promenada *f* (*zwł. nad brzegiem*)

es·say ['eseɪ] esej *m*; wypracowanie *n*

es·sence ['esns] istota *f*; esencja *f*

es·sen·tial [ɪ'senʃl] **1.** istotny; niezbędny; **2.** *zw.* **~s** *pl.* najistotniejsze rzeczy *pl.*; **~ly** zasadniczo, właściwie

es·tab·lish [ɪ'stæblɪʃ] ustanawiać ⟨-nowić⟩; zakładać ⟨założyć⟩; **~ o.s.** osiedlać ⟨-lić⟩ się; obejmować ⟨objąć⟩ stanowisko; ustalać ⟨-lić⟩; **~ment** założenie *n*, ustanowienie *n*; *econ.* przedsiębiorstwo *n*, firma *f*; **the ℒment** establishment *m*, warstwa *f* panująca

es·tate [ɪ'steɪt] posiadłość *f*, majątek *m* (ziemski); *jur.* majątek *m*, mienie *n*; **housing ~** *Brt.* osiedle *n* mieszkaniowe; **industrial ~** dzielnica *f* przemysłowa; **real ~** nieruchomość *pl.*; **~ a·gent** *Brt.* pośrednik *m* w handlu nieruchomościami; **~ car** *Brt. mot.* kombi *n*

es·teem [ɪ'stiːm] **1.** szacunek *m*, poważanie *n* (**with** wśród *G*); **2.** poważać, darzyć szacunkiem

es·thet·ic(s) [es'θetɪk(s)] *Am.* → **aesthetic(s)**

es·ti|·mate 1. ['estɪmeɪt] oceniać ⟨-nić⟩, ⟨o⟩szacować; **2.** ['estɪmɪt] oszacowanie *n*; kosztorys *m*; **~·ma·tion** [estɪ'meɪʃn] zdanie *n*; oszacowanie *n*

Es·to·ni·a Estonia *f*

es·trange [ɪ'streɪndʒ] zrażać ⟨zrazić⟩

es·tu·a·ry ['estjʊərɪ] ujście *n*

etch [etʃ] rytować; wytrawiać ⟨-wić⟩; *fig.* ⟨wy⟩ryć; **~·ing** rycina *f*; miedzioryt *m*

e·ter|·nal [ɪ'tɜːnl] wieczny; **~·ni·ty** [ɪ'tɜːnətɪ] wieczność *f*

e·ther ['iːθə] eter *m*; **e·the·re·al** [iː'θɪərɪəl] eteryczny (też *fig.*)

eth|·i·cal ['eθɪkl] etyczny; **~·ics** ['eθɪks] *sg.* etyka *f*

EU [iː 'juː] *skrót:* **European Union** Unia *f* Europejska

Eu·ro... ['jʊərəʊ] Euro..., europejski; **~·cheque** *Brt.* euroczek *m*

Eu·rope ['jʊərəp] Europa *f*; **Eu·ro·pe·an** [jʊərə'piːən] europejski *m*; **Eu·ro·pe·an Com·mu·ni·ty** (*skrót:* **EC**) Wspólnota *f* Europejska

e·vac·u·ate [ɪ'vækjʊeɪt] ewakuować, dokonywać ⟨-nać⟩ ewakuacji

e·vade [ɪ'veɪd] unikać ⟨-knąć⟩; uchylać ⟨-lić⟩ się od (*G*); uchodzić ⟨ujść⟩ przed (*I*)

e·val·u·ate [ɪ'væljʊeɪt] oceniać ⟨-nić⟩; ⟨o⟩szacować

e·vap·o·rate [ɪ'væpəreɪt] parować; odparowywać ⟨-ować⟩; znikać ⟨-knąć⟩; **~rated milk** mleko *n* skondensowane (niesłodzone); **~·ra·tion** [ɪvæpə'reɪʃn] parowanie *n*; odparowanie *n*

e·va|·sion [ɪ'veɪʒn] unikanie *n*, uchylanie się *n*; wymówka *f*; **~·sive** [ɪ'veɪsɪv] wymijający; **be ~sive** unikać ⟨-knąć⟩

eve [iːv] przeddzień *m*; wigilia *f*; **on the ~ of** w przededniu (*G*)

e·ven ['iːvn] **1.** *adj.* równy; gładki; *liczba:* parzysty; regularny, równomierny; **get ~ with s.o.** odpłacać się komuś; **2.** *adv.* nawet; **not ~** nawet nie; **~ though**, **~ if** nawet jeśli; **3.** **~ out** zrównywać ⟨-wnać⟩, wyrównywać ⟨-wnać⟩ (się)

eve·ning ['iːvnɪŋ] wieczór *m*; **in the ~** wieczorem; **'~ class·es** *pl.* kurs *m* wieczorowy; **'~ dress** strój *m* wieczorowy; smoking *m*, frak *m*, suknia *f* wieczorowa

e·ven·song ['iːvnsɒŋ] nabożeństwo *n* wieczorne (w kościele anglikańskim)

e·vent [ɪ'vent] zdarzenie *n*, wydarzenie *n*; (w sporcie) konkurencja *f*, dyscyplina *f*; **at all ~s** w każdym razie; **in the ~ of** w przypadku (*G*); **~·ful** obfitujący w wydarzenia

e·ven·tu·al [ɪ'ventʃʊəl] ostateczny; ⚠ *nie* **ewentualny**; **~·ly** ostatecznie

ev·er ['evə] zawsze; kiedykolwiek; **~ after**, **~ since** od tego czasu; **~ so** *F* bardzo; **for ~** na zawsze; **Yours ~, ..., ℒ yours ...** (w liście) Pozdrawiam, Twój; Pański; **have you ~ been to Poland?** czy byłeś kiedyś w Polsce?; **'~·green 1.** wiecznozielony; zimozielony; nie do zdarcia, *zwł.* zawsze przyjemny do słuchania; **2.** roślina *f* zimozielona; **'~·last·ing** wieczny; **~'more** (**for**) **~** na zawsze

ev·ery ['evrɪ] każdy; wszyscy *pl.*, wszystkie *pl.*; **~ now and then** od czasu do czasu; **~ one of them** każdy z nich; **~ other day** co drugi dzień; **'~·bod·y** każdy; **'~·day** codziennie; **'~·one** każdy, wszyscy *pl.*; **'~·thing** wszystko; **'~·where** wszędzie

e·vict [ɪ'vɪkt] *jur.* ⟨wy⟩eksmitować; *majątek* odzyskiwać ⟨-kać⟩

ev·i|·dence ['evɪdəns] dowód *m*, dowody *pl.*; zeznania *pl.*; **give ~ence** świadczyć; **'~·dent** oczywisty e·vil ['iːvl] 1. (zwł. Brt. -ll-, Am. -l-) zły, niedobry; paskudny; 2. zło n; ~'mind·ed złośliwy

e·voke [ɪ'vəʊk] wywoływać ⟨-łać⟩

ev·o·lu·tion [iːvə'luːʃn] ewolucja f, rozwój m

e·volve [ɪ'vɒlv] rozwijać ⟨-winąć⟩ się

ewe [juː] zo. (samica) owca f

ex [eks] prp. econ. loco, loko; ~ works loco fabryka

ex... [eks] eks..., były ...

ex·act [ɪg'zækt] 1. dokładny, ścisły; 2. wymuszać ⟨-musić⟩, ⟨wy⟩egzekwować; ~·ing wymagający; uciążliwy; ~·ly dokładnie; (w odpowiedzi) właśnie (tak); ~·ness dokładność f

ex·ag·ge·rate [ɪg'zædʒəreɪt] przesadzać ⟨-dzić⟩; ~·ra·tion [ɪgzædʒə'reɪʃn] przesada f

ex·am [ɪg'zæm] F egzamin m

ex·am|·i·na·tion [ɪgzæmɪ'neɪʃn] egzamin m; badanie n; jur. przesłuchanie n, śledztwo n; ~·ine [ɪg'zæmɪn] badać; sprawdzać ⟨-dzić⟩; szkoła itp.: ⟨prze⟩egzaminować (in, on w zakresie G); jur. przesłuchiwać ⟨-chać⟩, przeprowadzać ⟨-dzić⟩ śledztwo;

ex·am·ple [ɪg'zɑːmpl] przykład m; wzorzec m, wzór m; for ~ dla przykładu, na przykład

ex·as·pe|·rate [ɪg'zæspəreɪt] doprowadzać ⟨-dzić⟩ do rozpaczy; ~·rat·ing doprowadzający do rozpaczy

ex·ca·vate ['ekskəveɪt] v/t. wykopywać ⟨-pać⟩; v/i. prowadzić wykopaliska

ex·ceed [ɪk'siːd] przekraczać ⟨-roczyć⟩; przewyższać ⟨-szyć⟩; ~·ing nadmierny; ~·ing·ly nadmiernie

ex·cel [ɪk'sel] v/t. przewyższać ⟨-szyć⟩; wyobrażenie itp. przechodzić ⟨-ejść⟩; v/i. wyróżniać ⟨-nić⟩ się, celować; ~·lence ['eksələns] doskonałość f, świetność f; Ex·cel·lency ['eksələnsɪ] ekscelencja f/m; ex·cel·lent ['eksələnt] doskonały, świetny

ex·cept [ɪk'sept] 1. wykluczać ⟨-czyć⟩, wyłączyć ⟨-czać⟩; 2. prp. oprócz, poza; ~ for z wyjątkiem (G); ~·ing z wyjątkiem, wyłączając

ex·cep·tion [ɪk'sepʃn] wyjątek m; uraza f (to do G); make an ~ robić wyjątek; take ~ to obruszać ⟨-szyć⟩ się na (A); without ~ bez wyjątku; ~·al [ɪk'sepʃənl] wyjątkowy; ~·al·ly

[ɪk'sepʃnəlɪ] wyjątkowo

ex·cerpt ['eksɜːpt] wyjątek m; urywek m

ex·cess [ɪk'ses] nadmiar m, nadwyżka f; dopłata f; ~ 'bag·gage aviat. bagaż m dodatkowy; ~ 'fare dopłata f za przejazd; ex·ces·sive nadmierny; ~ 'lug·gage → excess baggage; ~ 'post·age dopłata f

ex·change [ɪks'tʃeɪndʒ] 1. wymieniać ⟨-nić⟩ (for za); 2. wymiana f (też pieniędzy); bill of ~ weksel m; giełda f; kantor m wymiany walut; centrala f telefoniczna; foreign ~(s pl.) dewizy pl.; rate of ~ → exchange rate; ~ of·fice kantor m wymiany walut; ~ pu·pil uczeń m (uczennica f) w ramach programu wymiany; ~ rate kurs m wymiany; ~ stu·dent student m (studentka f) w ramach programu wymiany; Am. uczeń m (uczennica f) w ramach programu wymiany

Ex·cheq·uer [ɪks'tʃekə]: Chancellor of the ~ Brt. Minister Skarbu

ex·cise [ek'saɪz] akcyza f, opłata f akcyzowa

ex·ci·ta·ble [ɪk'saɪtəbl] łatwo się irytujący lub ekscytujący

ex·cite [ɪk'saɪt] ⟨pod⟩ekscytować; podniecać ⟨-cić⟩; pobudzać ⟨-dzić⟩; ex·cit·ed podekscytowany; podniecony; ex'citement ekscytacja f; podniecenie n; ex'cit·ing ekscytujący; podniecający

ex·claim [ɪk'skleɪm] wykrzykiwać ⟨-nąć⟩

ex·cla·ma·tion [eksklə'meɪʃn] wykrzyknięcie n, okrzyk m; ~ mark Brt., ~ point Am. wykrzyknik m

ex·clude [ɪk'skluːd] wyłączać ⟨-czyć⟩; wykluczać ⟨-czyć⟩

ex·clu|·sion [ɪk'skluːʒn] wyłączenie n, wykluczenie n; ~·sive [ɪk'skluːsɪv] wyłączny; ekskluzywny; ~·sive of z wyłączeniem (G)

ex·com·mu·ni|·cate [ekskə'mjuːnɪkeɪt] rel. ekskomunikować; ~·ca·tion [ekskəmjuːnɪ'keɪʃn] rel. ekskomunika f

ex·cre·ment ['ekskrɪmənt] physiol. ekskrementy pl., odchody pl.

ex·crete [ek'skriːt] physiol. wydzielać ⟨-lić⟩

ex·cur·sion [ɪk'skɜːʃn] wycieczka f, wyprawa f

ex·cu·sa·ble [ɪk'skju:zəbl] wybaczalny, do wybaczenia; **ex·cuse 1.** [ɪk'skju:z] ⟨wy⟩tłumaczyć; usprawiedliwiać ⟨-wić⟩; wybaczać ⟨-czyć⟩; przepraszać ⟨-rosić⟩; zwalniać ⟨zwolnić⟩ *(from z I)*; *~ me* przepraszam; **2.** [ɪk'skju:s] usprawiedliwienie *n*, wytłumaczenie *n*; wymówka *f*

ex·di·rec·to·ry num·ber [eksdɪ'rektərɪ -] *Brt. tel.* numer *m* zastrzeżony

ex·e|·cute ['eksɪkju:t] wykonywać ⟨-nać⟩; *skazańca* ⟨s⟩tracić; przeprowadzać ⟨-dzić⟩; **~·cu·tion** [eksɪ'kju:ʃn] wykonanie *n*; egzekucja *f*, stracenie *n*; *jur.* egzekucja *f* sądowa; *put lub carry a plan into ~cution* realizować *lub* wprowadzać w życie plan; **~·cu·tion·er** [eksɪ'kju:ʃnə] kat *m*

ex·ec·u·tive [ɪg'zekjutɪv] **1.** wykonawczy; *econ.* kierowniczy, dyrektorski; **2.** *pol.* egzekutywa *f*, organ *m* wykonawczy; *econ.* dyrektor *m*, kierownik *m*

ex·em·pla·ry [ɪg'zemplərɪ] przykładowy, wzorcowy

ex·em·pli·fy [ɪg'zemplɪfaɪ] służyć jako przykład, stanowić przykład; egzemplifikować

ex·empt [ɪg'zempt] **1.** wolny, zwolniony; **2.** uwalniać ⟨uwolnić⟩, zwalniać ⟨zwolnić⟩

ex·er·cise ['eksəsaɪz] **1.** ćwiczenie *n (też w szkole)*; ćwiczenia *pl.* fizyczne, ruch *m*; *mil.* manewry *pl.*, ćwiczenia *pl.*; *do one's ~s* gimnastykować się; *take ~* zażywać ruchu, ruszać się; **2.** ćwiczyć; ruszać się; ⟨s⟩korzystać z *(G)*; *mil.* przeprowadzać ⟨-dzić⟩ manewry; *'~ book* zeszyt *m*

ex·ert [ɪg'zɜ:t] *wpływ itp.* wywierać ⟨wywrzeć⟩; *~ o.s.* wysilać ⟨-lić⟩ się; **ex·er·tion** [ɪg'zɜ:ʃn] wywieranie *n (wpływu)*; wysiłek *m*, trud *m*

ex·hale [eks'heɪl] wydychać; *dym* wydmuchiwać ⟨-chać⟩, wypuszczać ⟨-puścić⟩

ex·haust [ɪg'zɔ:st] **1.** wyczerpywać ⟨-pać⟩; **2.** *tech.* rura *f* wydechowa; *też ~ fumes pl.* spaliny *pl.*; **~·ed** wyczerpany; zmęczony; **ex·haus·tion** [ɪg'zɔ:stʃən] wyczerpanie *n*; **ex·haus·tive** wyczerpujący; *~ pipe* rura *f* wydechowa

ex·hib·it [ɪg'zɪbɪt] **1.** wystawiać ⟨-wić⟩; *fig.* ukazywać ⟨-zać⟩; ⟨za⟩demonstro-

wać; **2.** eksponat *m*; *jur.* dowód *m* rzeczowy; **ex·hi·bi·tion** [eksɪ'bɪʃn] wystawa *f*; demonstracja *f*

ex·hil·a·rat·ing [ɪg'zɪləreɪtɪŋ] radosny; *wiatr itp.*: odświeżający

ex·hort [ɪg'zɔ:t] nawoływać

ex·ile ['eksaɪl] **1.** wygnanie *n*; emigracja *f*; emigrant(ka *f*) *m*, wygnaniec *m*; *in ~* na emigracji *lub* wygnaniu; **2.** skazywać ⟨-zać⟩ na wygnanie

ex·ist [ɪg'zɪst] istnieć; egzystować, żyć; **~·ence** istnienie *n*; egzystencja *f*; **~·ent** istniejący

ex·it ['eksɪt] **1.** wyjście *n*; zjazd *m (z drogi)*; **2.** *theat.* wychodzić

ex·o·dus ['eksədəs] exodus *m*; *general ~* ogólna ucieczka *f*

ex·on·e·rate [ɪg'zɒnəreɪt] uwalniać ⟨uwolnić⟩, zwalniać ⟨zwolnić⟩

ex·or·bi·tant [ɪg'zɔ:bɪtənt] wygórowany, nadmierny

ex·or·cize ['eksɔ:saɪz] wypędzać ⟨-dzić⟩ *(from z G)*; egzorcyzmować; uwalniać ⟨-wolnić⟩ *(of od G)*

ex·ot·ic [ɪg'zɒtɪk] (*~ally*) egzotyczny

ex·pand [ɪk'spænd] rozszerzać ⟨-rzyć⟩ (się); omawiać ⟨-mówić⟩ szczegółowo; *econ.* powiększać ⟨-szyć⟩ (się), rozszerzać ⟨-rzyć⟩ (się); **ex·panse** [ɪk'spæns] przestrzeń *f*, przestwór *m*; **ex·pan·sion** [ɪk'spænʃn] ekspansja *f*; rozszerzanie *n* się; **ex·pan·sive** [ɪk'spænsɪv] ekspansywny

ex·pat·ri·ate [eks'pætrɪeɪt] **1.** emigrant(ka *f*) *m*; **2.** *kogoś* skazywać ⟨-zać⟩ na wygnanie; *kogoś* pozbawiać ⟨-wić⟩ obywatelstwa

ex·pect [ɪk'spekt] spodziewać się; oczekiwać, przypuszczać; *be ~ing (a baby)* spodziewać się dziecka; **ex·pec·tant** pełen oczekiwania; *~ mother* przyszła matka *f*; **ex·pec·ta·tion** [ekspek'teɪʃn] oczekiwanie *n*; nadzieja *f*

ex·pe·dient [ɪk'spi:dɪənt] **1.** celowy; **2.** sposób *m*, środek *m (zwł. doraźny)*

ex·pe·di|·tion [ekspɪ'dɪʃn] ekspedycja *f*, wyprawa *f*; **~·tious** [ekspɪ'dɪʃəs] szybki

ex·pel [ɪk'spel] (*-ll-*) *(from)* usuwać ⟨-sunąć⟩ (z *G*); wydalać ⟨-lić⟩ (z *G*); wyrzucać ⟨-cić⟩ (z *G*)

ex·pen·di·ture [ɪk'spendɪtʃə] wydatek *m*; *econ.* koszty *pl.*, wydatki *pl.*

ex·pense [ɪk'spens] wydatek *m*; *at the ~ of* na koszt *(G)*; **ex·pen·ses** koszty *pl.*, wydatki *pl.*; **ex·pen·sive** drogi

ex·pe·ri·ence [ɪk'spɪərɪəns] **1.** doświadczenie *n*; przeżycie *n*; **2.** doświadczać ⟨-czyć⟩, przeżywać ⟨-żyć⟩; **~d** doświadczony

ex·per·i·ment 1. [ɪk'sperɪmənt] doświadczenie *n*; **2.** [ɪk'sperɪment] eksperymentować; **~·men·tal** [eksperɪ'mentl] eksperymentalny

ex·pert ['ekspɜːt] **1.** specjalistyczny; doświadczony; *komp.* ekspercki; **2.** ekspert *m*; specjalista *m* (-tka *f*)

ex·pi·ra·tion [ekspɪ'reɪʃn] upłynięcie *n*, koniec *m*; wygaśnięcie *n*; **ex·pire** [ɪk'spaɪə] upływać ⟨-łynąć⟩, ⟨s⟩kończyć się; wygasać ⟨-snąć⟩

ex·plain [ɪk'spleɪn] wyjaśniać ⟨-nić⟩; **ex·pla·na·tion** [eksplə'neɪʃn] wyjaśnienie *n*

ex·pli·cit [ɪk'splɪsɪt] jasny; wyraźny; **(*sexually*)** **~** *film itp.*: *(pokazujący seks bez ogródek)*

ex·plode [ɪk'spləʊd] wybuchać ⟨-chnąć⟩, eksplodować; *bombę itp.* ⟨z⟩detonować; *fig.* wybuchać ⟨-chnąć⟩; *fig. teorię itp.* obalać ⟨-lić⟩; *fig.* rozwijać ⟨-winąć⟩ się gwałtownie

ex·ploit 1. ['eksplɔɪt] wyczyn *m* (*bohaterski*); **2.** [ɪk'splɔɪt] ⟨wy⟩eksploatować; **ex·ploi·ta·tion** [eksplɔɪ'teɪʃn] eksploatacja *f*, wykorzystywanie *n*

ex·plo·ra·tion [eksplə'reɪʃn] badanie *n*, eksploracja *f*; **ex·plore** [ɪk'splɔː] ⟨z⟩badać, eksplorować; **ex·plor·er** [ɪk'splɔːrə] eksplorator *m*, badacz(ka *f*) *m*

ex·plo·sion [ɪk'spləʊʒn] eksplozja *f*, wybuch *m*; *fig.* wybuch *m*; *fig.* gwałtowny rozwój *m*; **~·sive** [ɪk'spləʊsɪv] **1.** wybuchowy (*też fig.*); rozwijający się gwałtownie; **2.** środek *m* wybuchowy

ex·po·nent [ek'spəʊnənt] *math.* wykładnik *m*, eksponent *m*

ex·port 1. [ɪk'spɔːt] ⟨wy⟩eksportować; **2.** ['ekspɔːt] eksport *m*; artykuł *m* eksportowy; **ex·por·ta·tion** [ekspɔː'teɪʃn] eksport *m*; **ex·port·er** [ɪk'spɔːtə] eksporter *m*

ex·pose [ɪk'spəʊz] odsłaniać ⟨-łonić⟩; wystawiać ⟨-wić⟩; *phot.* naświetlać ⟨-lić⟩; *towary* ⟨wy⟩eksponować; *kogoś* ⟨z⟩demaskować; *coś* wyjawiać ⟨-wić⟩; **ex·po·si·tion** [ekspə'zɪʃn] ekspozycja *f*; przedstawienie *n*

ex·po·sure [ɪk'spəʊʒə] odsłonięcie *n*; wystawienie *n* (*na czynniki zewnętrzne*) (**to** na *A*); *phot.* naświetlanie *n*; *phot.* klatka *f*; **die of ~** umrzeć z zimna; **~ me·ter** *phot.* światłomierz *m*

ex·press [ɪk'spres] **1.** jawny, wyraźny; ekspresowy; **2.** ekspres *m*; **go by ~** jechać ekspresem **3.** *adv.* ekspresem; **4.** wyrażać ⟨-razić⟩; **ex·pres·sion** [ɪk'spreʃn] wyrażenie *n*; **ex·pres·sion·less** bez wyrazu; **ex·pres·sive** [ɪk'spresɪv] wyrazisty; **be ~ of** *coś* wyrażać ⟨-razić⟩; **ex·press 'let·ter** *Brt.* przesyłka *f* ekspresowa; **ex·press·ly** wyraźnie, jawnie; ekspres *m*; **ex·press·way** *zwł. Am.* droga *f* szybkiego ruchu

ex·pro·pri·ate *jur.* [eks'prəʊprɪeɪt] wywłaszczać ⟨-czyć⟩, ⟨s⟩konfiskować

ex·pul·sion [ɪk'spʌlʃn] (**from**) wypędzenie (z *G*), wydalenie (z *G*)

ex·pur·gate ['ekspɜːgeɪt] ⟨o⟩czyścić, usuwać ⟨usunąć⟩

ex·qui·site ['ekskwɪzɪt] wyborny; znakomity; wspaniały

ex·tant [ek'stænt] wciąż istniejący *lub* żyjący

ex·tend [ɪk'stend] *v/i.* rozciągać ⟨-nąć⟩ się; ciągnąć się; *v/t.* przedłużać ⟨-żyć⟩; *fabrykę* powiększać ⟨-szyć⟩; rozciągać ⟨-gnąć⟩; *rękę itp.* wyciągać ⟨-gnąć⟩; *podziękowania itp.* ⟨s⟩kierować; **~·ed 'fam·i·ly** wielopokoleniowa rodzina *f*

ex·ten·sion [ɪk'stenʃn] przedłużenie *n*; powiększenie *n*; rozszerzenie *n*; *arch.* przybudówka *f*, rozbudowa *f*; *tel.* wewnętrzny (*numer*) *m*; telefon *m* wewnętrzny; *też* **~·sion lead** (*Am. cord*) *electr.* przedłużacz *m*; **~·sive** rozległy, obszerny

ex·tent [ɪk'stent] rozciągłość *f*; rozmiar *m*; zakres *m*; stopień *m*; **to some ~, to a certain ~** w pewnym stopniu; **to such an ~ that** do tego stopnia, że

ex·ten·u·ate [ek'stenjʊeɪt] ⟨z⟩łagodzić, zmniejszać ⟨-szyć⟩; **extenuating circumstances** *pl. jur.* okoliczności *pl.* łagodzące

ex·te·ri·or [ek'stɪərɪə] **1.** zewnętrzny; **2.** strona *f* zewnętrzna; powierzchowność *f*

ex·ter·mi·nate [ek'stɜːmɪneɪt] eksterminować; ⟨wy⟩tępić, ⟨wy⟩niszczyć

ex·ter·nal [ek'stɜːnl] zewnętrzny

ex·tinct [ɪk'stɪŋkt] wymarły; wygasły;

ex·tinc·tion [ɪk'stɪŋkʃn] wymarcie n; wyginięcie n; wygaśnięcie n

ex·tin·guish [ɪk'stɪŋgwɪʃ] ⟨u⟩gasić/ fig. zagasić; ⟨wy⟩niszczyć; **~er** gaśnica f

ex·tort [ɪk'stɔːt] wymuszać ⟨-sić⟩

ex·tra ['ekstrə] **1.** adj. dodatkowy, ekstra; **be ~** być osobno liczonym; **2.** adv. ekstra, osobno; **charge~ for** liczyć dodatkowo za (A); **3.** dopłata f; coś n ekstra; zwł. mot. dodatek m; theat., (w filmie) statysta m (-tka f)

ex·tract 1. ['ekstrækt] ekstrakt m, wyciąg m; wyciąg m, wypis m; fragment m; **2.** [ɪk'strækt] wyciągać ⟨-gnąć⟩; zgb itp. usuwać ⟨-unąć⟩; uzyskiwać ⟨-skać⟩; fig. wydobywać ⟨-być⟩; chem. ekstrahować; **ex·trac·tion** [ɪk'strækʃn] wyciąganie n; ekstrakcja f, usuwanie n; ekstrahowanie n; wydobywanie n; pochodzenie n

ex·tra·dite ['ekstrədaɪt] dokonywać ⟨-nać⟩ ekstradycji, wydalać ⟨-lić⟩; **~di·tion** [ekstrə'dɪʃn] ekstradycja f, wydalenie n

extra·or·di·na·ry [ɪk'strɔːdnrɪ] nadzwyczajny; niezwykły

ex·tra 'pay dodatek m (pieniężny)

ex·tra·ter·res·tri·al [ekstrətə'restrɪəl] pozaziemski

ex·tra 'time sport: dogrywka f

ex·trav·a·gance [ɪk'strævəgəns] rozrzutność f, marnotrawstwo n; ekstrawagancja f, ekscentryczność f; **~gant** rozrzutny, marnotrawny; ekstrawagancki, ekscentryczny

ex·treme [ɪk'striːm] **1.** skrajny; ekstremalny; najdalszy; największy; **~ right** skrajnie prawicowy; **~ right wing** skraj-

ne skrzydło n prawicowe; **2.** skrajność f, krańcowość f; ostateczność f; **~·ly** skrajnie, ekstremalnie; krańcowo

ex·trem·is·m [ɪk'striːmɪzm] zwł. pol. ekstremizm m; **~·ist** [ɪk'striːmɪst] ekstremista m (-tka f)

ex·trem·i·ties [ɪk'str04tɪz] pl. skrajności pl.; kończyny pl.

ex·trem·i·ty [ɪk'stremətɪ] skrajność f; ostateczność f; sytuacja f krytyczna

ex·tri·cate ['ekstrɪkeɪt] wyplątywać ⟨-tać⟩; oswobadzać ⟨-bodzić⟩

ex·tro·vert ['ekstrəʊvɜːt] ekstrawertyk m (-yczka f)

ex·u·be·rance [ɪg'zjuːbərəns] euforia f; bujność f; **~·rant** euforyczny, pełen euforii; bujny

ex·ult [ɪg'zʌlt] radować się (**at** I)

eye [aɪ] okon; oczkon (na ziemniaku itp.); ucho n (igły); uszko n (w igle); **see ~ to ~ with s.o.** zgadzać się z kimś całkowicie; **be up to the ~s in work** mieć roboty po uszy; **with an ~ to s.th.** ze względu na coś; **2.** ⟨z⟩mierzyć wzrokiem; przypatrywać się (D); '**~·ball** gałka f oczna; '**~·brow** brew f; '**~·catch·ing** chwytający oko; **~·d** ...oczny; '**~·doc·tor** F okulista m (-tka f); '**~·glass·es** pl., też **a pair of ~glasses** okulary pl.; '**~·lash** rzęsa f; '**~·lid** powieka f; '**~·lin·er** ołówek m do brwi; '**~·o·pen·er**: **that was an ~opener to me** to mi całkowicie oczy otworzyło; '**~ shad·ow** cień m do powiek; '**~·sight** wzrok m; '**~·sore** F okropieństwo n; **be an ~sore** kłuć w oczy; '**~ spe·cial·ist** okulista m (-tka f); '**~·strain** zmęczenie n oczu; '**~·wit·ness** naoczny świadek m

F

F, [ef] F, f n pl

F skrót pisany: **Fahrenheit** F, Fahrenheita (skala termometru)

FA [ef 'eɪ] Brt. skrót: **Football Association** Związek m Piłki Nożnej

fa·ble ['feɪbl] bajka f; legenda f

fab·ric ['fæbrɪk] materiał m, tkanina f; struktura f; materia f; △ nie **fabryka**; **~·ri·cate** ['fæbrɪkeɪt] ⟨s⟩fabrykować (też fig.)

fab·u·lous ['fæbjʊləs] kapitalny; bajeczny; bajkowy

fa·cade, fa·çade [fə'sɑːd] arch. fasada f

face [feɪs] **1.** twarz f; mina f; powierzchnia f; cyferblat m, tarcza f; front m, strona f lub ściana f przednia; **~ to ~ with** oko w oko z (I); **save** lub **lose one's ~** zachować lub stracić twarz; **on the ~ of it** na pierwszy rzut oka;

pull a long ~ zrobić cierpką minę; *have the* ~ *to do s.th.* mieć czelność coś zrobić; **2.** *v/t.* zwracać ⟨-rócić⟩ się przodem do (G); wychodzić na (A); stawiać ⟨-wić⟩ czoło (D); stawać ⟨stanąć⟩ wobec (G); *arch.* licować, okładać; *v/i.* ~ *about* obracać ⟨-rócić⟩ się (*w tył*); '~**cloth** ściereczka *f* do mycia twarzy; ~**d: stony~d** o kamiennej twarzy; '~ **flan·nel** *Brt.* → **facecloth**; ~**lift** lifting *m*, face lifting *m*; *fig.* renowacja *f*, odnowienie *n*

fa·ce·tious [fəˈsiːʃəs] zabawny; dowcipny

fa·cial [ˈfeɪʃl] **1.** *wyraz, rysy itp.*: twarzy; do twarzy; **2.** zabieg *m* kosmetyczny twarzy

fa·cile [ˈfæsaɪl] płytki; pusty

fa·cil·i·tate [fəˈsɪlɪteɪt] ułatwiać ⟨-wić⟩

fa·cil·i·ty [fəˈsɪlətɪ] łatwość *f*; łatwość *f* uczenia się; prostota *f*; opcja *f*, funkcja *f*; **facilities** *pl.* udogodnienia *pl.*, urządzenia *pl.*

fac·ing [ˈfeɪsɪŋ] *tech.* okładzina *f*; lamówka *f* (*przy ubraniu*)

fact [fækt] fakt *m*; rzeczywistość *f*; *in* ~ faktycznie, w rzeczywistości; ~*s pl.*, *jur.* okoliczności *pl.*

fac·tion [ˈfækʃn] *zwł. pol.* frakcja *f*, odłam *m*

fac·ti·tious [fækˈtɪʃəs] sztuczny

fac·tor [ˈfæktə] czynnik *m*; element *m*; *math.* współczynnik *m*

fac·to·ry [ˈfæktrɪ] fabryka *f*

fac·ul·ty [ˈfækəltɪ] zdolność *f*, umiejętność *f*; *fig.* dar *m*; *univ.* wydział *m*; *Am.* grono *n* nauczycielskie

fad [fæd] przelotna moda *f*

fade [feɪd] ⟨z⟩blaknąć; ⟨s⟩płowieć; ⟨z⟩więdnąć; niknąć, znikać; ~ *in film itp.* rozjaśniać ⟨-nić⟩, wzmacniać ⟨-mocnić⟩; ~ *out* ściemniać ⟨-nić⟩, wygaszać ⟨-gasić⟩; ~*d jeans pl.* sprane dżinsy *pl.*

fag¹ [fæg] F męczarnia *f*, mordęga *f*; *Brt.* kot *m* (*uczeń, którym wysługują się starsi*)

fag² [fæg] *sl.*, *Brt.* (*papieros*) fajka *f*; *Am.* pedał *m*; '~ *end Brt.* F (*niedopałek*) pet *m*

fail [feɪl] **1.** *v/i.* zawodzić ⟨-wieść⟩; nie powodzić się; nie udać się; nie zdać (*egzaminu*); *biznes itp.*: załamywać się; pogarszać się; *he* ~*ed* nie udało mu się; ~ *to do s.th.* nie zrobić czegoś, zanied-

bać zrobienie czegoś; *v/t. kogoś* zawodzić ⟨-wieść⟩; (*na egzaminie*) *kogoś* oblewać ⟨-blać⟩; **2.** *without* ~ na pewno, z pewnością; ~*·ure* [ˈfeɪljə] niepowodzenie *n*; fiasko *n*, porażka *f*; niedomoga *f*; nieurodzaj *m*; *be a ~ure* ktoś: nie mieć szczęścia

faint [feɪnt] **1.** słaby, nikły; **2.** ⟨ze⟩mdleć, ⟨za⟩słabnąć (*with* od G); **3.** omdlenie *n*, zasłabnięcie *n*; ~ˈheart·ed małego serca; strachliwy

fair¹ [feə] uczciwy; szczery; sprawiedliwy; prawidłowy; niezły; spory; *skóra, włosy*: jasny; *pogoda*: ładny; *wiatr*: sprzyjający; *play* ~ grać fair; *fig.* postępować ⟨-tąpić⟩ fair

fair² [feə] jarmark *m*, targ *m*; święto *n* ludowe; targi *pl.*

fair 'game gra *f* fair

'fair·ground wesołe miasteczko *n*

'fair|·ly sprawiedliwie; dość, prawie; '~**ness** sprawiedliwość *f*; ~ ˈplay fair play *f*

fai·ry [ˈfeərɪ] wróżka *f*; elf *m*; *sl. Brt.* pedał *m*; '~**land** kraina *f* czarów; '~ ˈsto·ry, '~ ˈtale baśń *f*, bajka *f*

faith [feɪθ] wiara *f*; zaufanie *n*; '~**ful** wierny; *Yours ~ly* (*w liście*) Z poważaniem; '~**less** niewierny

fake [feɪk] **1.** falsyfikat *m*; oszust(ka *f*) *m*; **2.** ⟨s⟩fałszować; podrabiać ⟨-robić⟩; symulować; **3.** podrabiany, sfałszowany

fal·con [ˈfɔːlkən] sokół *m*

fall [fɔːl] **1.** upadek *m* (*też fig.*); spadek *m*, zmniejszenie *n* się; opad *m*, opady *pl.*; *Am.* jesień *f*; *zw.* ~*s pl.* wodospad *m*; **2.** (*fell, fallen*) upaść ⟨upaść⟩; spadać ⟨spaść⟩; *deszcz itp.*: padać, spadać ⟨spaść⟩; *wiatr, teren itp.*: opadać ⟨opaść⟩; *noc itp.*: zapadać ⟨zapaść⟩; *miasto itp.*: padać ⟨paść⟩; ~ *ill*, ~ *sick* zachorować; ~ *in love with* zakochać się w (L); ~ *short of* oczekiwań nie spełniać ⟨-nić⟩; ~ *back* cofać ⟨-fnąć⟩ się; ~ *back on* uciekać się do (G); ~ *for* łapać się na (A); F zakochiwać ⟨-chać⟩ się w (L); ~ *off popyt itp.*: spadać ⟨spaść⟩; zmniejszać ⟨-szyć⟩ się; ~ *on* rzucać ⟨-cić⟩ się; ~ *out* ⟨po⟩sprzeczać się (*with* z *I*); ~ *through* nie dochodzić ⟨dojść⟩ do skutku; ~ *to* zabrać się do (G); brać ⟨wziąć⟩ się do jedzenia

fal·la·cious [fəˈleɪʃəs] błędny

fal·la·cy [ˈfæləsɪ] błąd *m*

fall·en ['fɔːlən] *p.p. od* **fall** 2

'fall guy *Am.* F kozioł *m* ofiarny

fal·li·ble ['fæləbl] omylny

fal·ling 'star gwiazda *f* spadająca

'fall-out opad *m* radioaktywny

fal·low ['fæləʊ] *zo.* jałowy; *agr.* jałowy, wyjałowiony

false [fɔːls] fałszywy; sztuczny; **∼·hood** ['fɔːlshʊd], **'∼·ness** fałsz *m*; **∼ 'start** falstart *m*

fal·si·fi·ca·tion [fɔːlsɪfɪ'keɪʃn] fałszerstwo *n*; **∼·fy** ['fɔːlsɪfaɪ] ⟨s⟩fałszować, podrobić ⟨-rabiać⟩; **∼·ty** ['fɔːlsɪtɪ] fałsz *m*

fal·ter ['fɔːltə] *v/i.* ⟨za⟩chwiać się; *głos* załamywać ⟨-mać⟩ się; ⟨za⟩wahać się; załamywać ⟨-mać⟩ się; *v/t. słowa* ⟨wy⟩bąkać

fame [feɪm] rozgłos *m*, sława *f*; **∼d** słynny (**for** ze względu na *A*)

fa·mil·i·ar [fə'mɪljə] znany; znajomy, bliski; poufały; **∼·i·ty** [fəmɪlɪ'ærətɪ] znajomość *f*; obeznanie *n*; poufałość *f*; **∼·ize** [fə'mɪljəraɪz] zaznajamiać ⟨-jomić⟩ się

fam·i·ly ['fæməlɪ] **1.** rodzina *f*; **2.** rodzinny; domowy; **be in the ∼ way** F być w odmiennym stanie; **∼ al'low·ance** → **child allowance**; '**∼ name** nazwisko *n* (*rodowe*); **∼ 'plan·ning** planowanie *n* rodziny; **∼ 'tree** drzewo *n* genealogiczne

fam|·ine ['fæmɪn] głód *m*; brak *m*; **'∼·ished** wygłodzony; **I'm ∼ished** F strasznie głodny jestem

fa·mous ['feɪməs] słynny, znany

fan¹ [fæn] **1.** wentylator *m*; wachlarz *m*; **2.** (**-nn-**) wachlować (się); *fig.* podsycać ⟨-cić⟩

fan² [fæn] kibic *m*, fan(ka *f*) *m*

fa·nat·ic [fə'nætɪk] fanatyk *m* (-yczka *f*); **∼·i·cal** [fə'nætɪkl] fanatyczny

'fan belt *tech.* pas klinowy

fan·ci·er ['fænsɪə] miłośnik *m* (-niczka *f*) (*zwierząt itp.*)

fan·ci·ful ['fænsɪfl] wymyślny; fantastyczny

fan·cy ['fænsɪ] **1.** fantazja *f*; upodobanie *n*, pociąg *m*; **2.** wymyślny; *cena itp.*: fantastyczny; **3.** mieć ochotę na (*A*); ⟨wy⟩obrażać ⟨-razić⟩ sobie; **I really ∼ her** naprawdę mi się podoba; **∼ that!** no po myśl tylko!; **∼ 'ball** bal *m* kostiumowy; **∼ 'dress** kostium *m*, przebranie

n; **∼'free** całkiem wolny; **∼ 'goods** *pl.* upominki *pl.*; **'∼·work** haft *m*; wyszywanie *n*

fang [fæŋ] kieł *m*

'fan mail listy *pl.* od fanów

fan|·tas·tic [fæn'tæstɪk] (**-ally**) fantastyczny; **∼·ta·sy** ['fæntəsɪ] fantazja *f*; wyobraźnia *f*; (literatura) fantasy *f*

far [fɑː] (**farther, further, farthest, furthest**) **1.** *adj.* daleki, odległy; oddalony; **2.** *adv.* daleko; znacznie; **as ∼ as** (aż) do; na ile; **in so ∼ as** na ile; **so ∼** dotąd; **∼·a·way** ['fɑːrəweɪ] oddalony; odległy

fare [feə] **1.** opłata *f* za przejazd; pasażer(ka *f*) *m*; wyżywienie *n*, strawa *f*; **2.** radzić sobie; **she ∼d well** dobrze jej poszło; '**∼ dodg·er** pasażer(ka *f*) *m* na gapę; **∼'well 1.** *int.* żegnaj!; **2.** pożegnanie *n*

far'fetched *fig.* przesadny, naciągany

farm [fɑːm] **1.** gospodarstwo *n* (*rolne*); ferma *f*; **chicken ∼** ferma *f* kurza; **2.** uprawiać; '**∼·er** rolnik *m*, gospodarz *m*; farmer *m*; '**∼·hand** robotnik *m* rolny; '**∼·house** budynek *m* wiejski; dom *m* (*w gospodarstwie*); '**∼·ing 1.** rolny; wiejski; **2.** rolnictwo *n*; gospodarka *f* rolna; hodowla *f*; '**∼·stead** budynek *m* wiejski; zabudowania *pl.* gospodarcze; '**∼·yard** podwórze *n* (*w gospodarstwie rolnym*)

far|·off [fɑːr'ɒf] daleki, odległy; **∼ 'right** *pol.* skrajnie prawicowy; **∼'sight·ed** *zwł. Am.* dalekowzroczny

far|·ther ['fɑːðə] *comp. od* **far**, **∼·thest** ['fɑːðɪst] *sup. od far*

fas·ci|·nate ['fæsɪneɪt] ⟨za⟩fascynować; '**∼·nat·ing** fascynujący; **∼·na·tion** [fæsɪ'neɪʃn] fascynacja *f*, zafascynowanie *n*

fas·cis|·m ['fæʃɪzəm] *pol.* faszyzm *m*; **∼t** ['fæʃɪst] *pol.* faszysta *m* (-tka *f*)

fash·ion ['fæʃn] **1.** moda *f*; sposób *m*; **be in ∼** być modnym; **out of ∼** niemodny; **2.** ⟨u⟩kształtować; ⟨u⟩formować; **∼·a·ble** ['fæʃnəbl] modny; '**∼ pa·rade**, '**∼ show** pokaz *m* mody

fast¹ [fɑːst] **1.** post *m*; **2.** pościć

fast² [fɑːst] szybki; trwały; mocno przymocowany; **be ∼** *zegar.*: spieszyć się; '**∼·back** coupé *n*, fastback *m*; **∼ breed·er**, **∼ breed·er re'ac·tor** *phys.* reaktor *m* powielający prędki

421

fas·ten ['fɑːsn] zapinać ⟨-piąć⟩ (się); umocowywać ⟨-wać⟩, przymocowywać ⟨-wać⟩; *spojrzenie itp.* ⟨s⟩kierować (**on** na *A*); '~·er zamknięcie *n*

'fast| food dania *pl.* na szybko; ~·**food** 'res·tau·rant bar *m lub* restauracja *f* szybkiej obsługi

fas·tid·i·ous [fə'stɪdɪəs] wybredny

'fast lane *mot.* pas *m* szybkiego ruchu

fat [fæt] **1.** (*-tt-*) tłusty; otyły; gruby; **2.** tłuszcz *m*; **low in** ~ o niskiej zawartości tłuszczu

fa·tal ['feɪtl] śmiertelny; zgubny (**to** dla *G*); △ *nie* **fatalny**; ~·i·**ty** [fə'tælətɪ] wypadek *m* śmiertelny; ofiara *f*

fate [feɪt] los *m*; przeznaczenie *n*

fa·ther ['fɑːðə] ojciec *m*; ♀ **'Christ·mas** *zwł. Brt. jakby:* Św. Mikołaj; '~·**hood** ojcostwo *n*; ~·**in-law** ['fɑːðərɪnlɔː] (*pl.* **fathers-in-law**) teść *m*; '~·**less** bez ojca; '~·**ly** ojcowski

fath·om ['fæðəm] **1.** *naut.* sążeń *m*; **2.** *naut.* sondować; *fig.* zgłębiać ⟨-bić⟩; '~·**less** bezdenny

fa·tigue [fə'tiːg] **1.** zmęczenie *n*; **2.** ⟨z⟩męczyć

fat|·ten ['fætn] ⟨u⟩tuczyć; '~·**ty** (*-ier, -iest*) tłusty; otłuszczony

fau·cet ['fɔːsɪt] *Am.* kurek *m*, kran *m*

fault [fɔːlt] błąd *m*; wina *f*; skaza *f*; wada *f*; **find~with** ⟨s⟩krytykować (*A*); **be at** ~ ponosić winę; '~·**less** bezbłędny; '~·**y** (*-ier, -iest*) wadliwy, błędny

fa·vo(u)r ['feɪvə] **1.** uznanie *n*; przychylność *f*; faworyzowanie *n*; przysługa *f*; **be in** ~ **of** popierać (*A*); **in** ~ **of** na korzyść (*G*); **do s.o. a** ~ wyświadczyć komuś przysługę; **2.** popierać ⟨-przeć⟩; faworyzować; sprzyjać; wyróżniać ⟨-nić⟩; **fa·vo(u)·ra·ble** ['feɪvərəbl] przychylny; sprzyjający; **fa·vo(u)·rite** ['feɪvərɪt] **1.** faworyt(ka *f*) *m*, ulubieniec *m* (-ica *f*); **2.** ulubiony

fawn¹ [fɔːn] **1.** *zo.* jelonek *m*; **2.** płowy

fawn² [fɔːn]: ~ **on** *pies:* łasić się do (*G*); schlebiać ⟨-bić⟩ (*D*)

fax [fæks] **1.** faks *m*; **2.** ⟨prze⟩faksować; ~ **s.th.** (**through**) **to s.o.** przefaksować coś do kogoś; '~ (**ma·chine**) faks *m*, telefaks *m*

FBI [ef biː 'aɪ] *skrót:* **Federal Bureau of Investigation** FBI *n* (*federalny urząd śledczy w USA*)

---

feed

fear [fɪə] **1.** strach *m* (**of** przed *I*); lęk *m*; obawa *f*; **2.** bać się; lękać się; obawiać się (**for** o *A*); '~·**ful** lękliwy; bojaźliwy; '~·**less** nieustraszony

fea·si·ble ['fiːzəbl] możliwy do wykonania, wykonalny

feast [fiːst] **1.** *rel.* święto *n*, dzień *m* świąteczny; uczta *f* (*też fig.*); **2.** *v/t.* podejmować ⟨-djąć⟩ uroczyście; *v/i.* cieszyć się

feat [fiːt] wyczyn *m* (*bohaterski*)

fea·ther ['feðə] **1.** pióro *n*; *też* ~**s** upierzenie *n*; **birds of a** ~ **flock together** swój ciągnie do swego; **that is a** ~ **in his cap** to dla niego powód do dumy; **2.** wyściełać ⟨-ścielić⟩ piórami, przystrajać ⟨-roić⟩ w pióra; ~ **'bed** materac *m* puchowy, piernat *m*; '~·**bed** (*-dd-*) ⟨po⟩traktować ulgowo; '~·**brained** *F* o ptasim móżdżku; '~·**ed** upierzony; '~·**weight** (*w sporcie*) waga *f* piórkowa; zawodnik *m* (-niczka *f*) wagi piórkowej; ~·**y** ['feðərɪ] upierzony; lekki jak piórko

fea·ture ['fiːtʃə] **1.** rysa *f* (*twarzy*); *charakterystyczna* cecha *f*; gazeta, *TV:* reportaż *m* specjalny; film *m* pełnometrażowy; **2.** przedstawiać ⟨-wić⟩, pokazywać ⟨-zać⟩; pokazywać w głównej roli; '~ **film** film *m* fabularny; '~**s** *pl.* rysy *pl.* twarzy

Feb *skrót pisany:* **February** luty *m*

Feb·ru·a·ry ['februərɪ] (*skrót:* **Feb**) luty *m*

fed [fed] *pret i p.p. od* **feed** 2

fed·e·ral ['fedərəl] *pol.* federalny; ♀ **Bu·reau of In·ves·ti·ga·tion** (*skrót:* **FBI**) FBI *n*, federalny urząd *m* śledczy (*w USA*); ♀ **Re·pub·lic of 'Ger·man·y** Federalna Republika Niemiec (*skrót:* **RFN**)

fed·e·ra·tion [fedə'reɪʃn] *pol.* federacja *f*; stowarzyszenie *n*, związek *m*; *sport:* zrzeszenie *n*

fee [fiː] opłata *f*; honorarium *n*; składka *f* (*członkowska*); opłata *f* za wstęp

fee·ble ['fiːbl] (*-r, -st*) wątły, mizerny

feed [fiːd] **1.** pokarm *m*; karma *f*, pasza *f*; *tech.* zasilanie *n*, podawanie *n*; **2.** (**fed**) *v/t.* ⟨na⟩karmić; żywić; *tech.* zasilać ⟨-lić⟩; podawać ⟨-dać⟩; *komp.* wprowadzać ⟨-dzić⟩, podawać ⟨-dać⟩; **be fed up with s.th.** mieć serdecznie dość czegoś; **well fed** dobrze odżywiony; *v/i.* żywić się, odżywiać się; jeść; '**~•back** *electr.*, (*w cybernetyce*) feedback *m*, sprzężenie *n* zwrotne; reakcja *f* (**to** na *A*); '**~•er** *tech.* zasilacz *m*, podajnik *m*; *be a noisy ~er* jeść głośno; '**~•er road** droga *f* łącząca; '**~•ing bot•tle**butelka*f z*pokarmem(*dla dzieci*)

feel [fi:l] **1.** (*felt*) czuć (się); odczuwać ⟨-czuć⟩; dotykać ⟨-tknąć⟩, macać; sądzić; *he feels sorry for you* żal mu ciebie; *I ~ hot* gorąco mi; *~ like s.th.* mieć ochotę na coś; **2.** uczucie *n* (*przy dotyku*); dotyk *m*; '**~•er** *zo.* czułek *m*; '**~•ing** uczucie *n*, odczucie *n*

feet [fi:t] *pl.* od **foot** 1

feign [fein] *chorobę, zainteresowanie itp.* udawać ⟨udać⟩

feint [feint] zwód *m*

fell [fel] **1.** *pret. od **fall** 2*; **2.** zwalać ⟨-lić⟩; ścinać ⟨ściąć⟩

fel•low ['feləʊ] **1.** towarzysz(ka*f*) *m*, kolega *m*; F facet *m*, gość *m*; drugi *m* z pary; *old ~* stary *m*; **2.** wspól...; *~* being bliźni *m*; *~* '**cit•i•zen** współobywatel(ka *f*) *m*; *~* '**coun•try•man** (*pl. -men*) rodak *m*), '**~•ship** koleżeństwo *n*; związek *m*; *~* '**trav•el•(l)er** współtowarzysz(ka *f*) *m*

fel•o•ny ['feləni] *jur.* przestępstwo *n*, zbrodnia *f*

felt[1] [felt] *pret. i p.p. od **feel** 1*

felt[2] [felt] filc *m*; '*~* **pen**, '*~* **tip**, *~***•tip-** (**ped**) '**pen** mazak *m*, flamaster *m*

fe•male [fi:meil] **1.** żeński; **2.** *pej.* kobieta *f*; *zo.* samica *f*

fem•i•nine ['feminin] kobiecy; żeński; *~***•nis•m** ['feminizəm] feminizm *m*; *~***•nist** ['feminist] feminista *m* (-tka *f*)

fen [fen] tereny *pl.* podmokłe

fence [fens] **1.** płot *m*; *sl.* paser *m*; **2.** *v/t.* *~ in* ogradzać ⟨-rodzić⟩; *~ off* odgradzać ⟨-rodzić⟩; *v/i.* fechtować; (*w sporcie*) uprawiać szermierkę; '**fenc•er** (*w sporcie*) szermierz *m*; '**fenc•ing** ogrodzenie *n*; *sport:* szermierka *f*; *attr.* szermierczy

fend [fend]: *~ off* odparowywać ⟨-ować⟩; *~ for o.s.* radzić sobie samemu; '**~•er** ochraniacz *m*; *Am. mot.* błotnik *m*; osłona *f* (*przy kominku*)

fen•nel ['fenl] *bot.* koper *m* włoski

fer•ment 1. ['fɜ:ment] ferment *m*, wzburzenie *n*; **2.** [fə'ment] ⟨s⟩fermentować; *~***•men•ta•tion** [fɜ:men'teɪʃn] fermentacja *f*

fern [fɜ:n] *bot.* paproć *f*

fe•ro•cious [fə'rəʊʃəs] zaciękły; dziki; *fig.* wielki; *~***•ci•ty** [fə'rɒsəti] zaciekłość *f*; dzikość *f*

fer•ret ['ferit] **1.** *zo.* fretka *f*; *fig.* szperacz *m*; **2.** węszyć, myszkować; *~ out* wywęszyć, wymyszkować

fer•ry ['feri] **1.** prom *m*; **2.** przewozić ⟨-wieźć⟩; '**~•boat** prom *m*; '**~•man** (*pl. -men*) przewoźnik *m*

fer•tile ['fɜ:tail] żyzny; płodny; *~***•til-i•ty** [fə'tɪlətɪ] żyzność *f*; płodność *f*; *~***•ti•lize** ['fɜ:tɪlaɪz] zapładniać ⟨-łodnić⟩; nawozić ⟨-wieźć⟩; '**~•ti•liz•er** nawóz *m* (*zwł. sztuczny*)

fer•vent ['fɜ:vənt] żarliwy

fer•vo(u)r ['fɜ:və] zapał *m*

fes•ter ['festə] jątrzyć się, zaogniać ⟨-nić⟩ się

fes•ti•val ['festəvl] festiwal *m*; święto *n*; *~***•tive** ['festɪv] świąteczny; *~***•tiv-i•ties** [fe'stɪvətɪ] pl. uroczystości *pl.*

fes•toon [fe'stu:n] girlanda *f*

fetch [fetʃ] przynosić ⟨-nieść⟩; *ceny* osiągać ⟨-gnąć⟩; '**~•ing** F niebrzydki

fete, fête [feit] festyn *m*; *village ~* odpust *m*

fet•id ['fetid] cuchnący

fet•ter ['fetə] **1.** *też ~s pl.* okowy *pl.*, pęta *pl.*; **2.** ⟨s⟩pętać

feud [fju:d] zwada *f*; *~•al* ['fju:dl] feudalny; *•dal•is•m* ['fju:dəlɪzəm] feudalizm *m*

fe•ver ['fi:və] gorączka *f*; *~•ish* ['fi:vərɪʃ] rozpalony; *fig.* rozgorączkowany, gorączkowy

few [fju:] niewiele, niewielu; *a ~* kilka, kilku; *no ~er than* nie mniej niż; *quite a ~, a good ~* dość dużo

fi•an•cé [fɪ'ɑ̃ŋseɪ] narzeczony *m*; *~e* [fɪ'ɑ̃ŋseɪ] narzeczona *f*

fib [fib] **1.** kłamstewko *n*, bujda *f*; **2.** (*-bb-*) bujać

fi•bre *Brt.*, **fi•ber** *Am.* ['faɪbə] włókno *n*; '**~•glass** włókno *n* szklane; **fi•brous** ['faɪbrəs] włóknisty

fick•le ['fɪkl] zmienny, niestały; '**~•ness** zmienność *f*, niestałość *f*

fic•tion ['fɪkʃn] fikcja *f*; (*proza*) literatura *f* piękna, beletrystyka *f*; *~•al* ['fɪkʃnl] fikcyjny; beletrystyczny

fic•ti•tious [fɪk'tɪʃəs] fikcyjny, nieprawdziwy

fid•dle ['fɪdl] **1.** skrzypki *pl.*; *play first*

(*second*) ~ *fig.* grać pierwsze (drugie) skrzypce; *as fit as a* ~ zdrów jak ryba; **2.** *mus.* ⟨za⟩grać na skrzypcach; *też* ~ *about lub around* (*with*) zabawiać się (*I*); '~*r* skrzypek *m* (-paczka *f*); '~*·sticks int.* bzdury!

fi·del·i·ty [fɪ'delətɪ] wierność *f*

fid·get ['fɪdʒɪt] F wiercić się; bawić się; '~·y nerwowy, wiercący się

field [fiːld] pole *n*; *sport:* boisko *n*; obszar *m* (*zainteresowań*); dziedzina *f*; '~ e·vents *pl.* (*w sporcie*) lekka atletyka *f*; '~ glass·es *pl.*, *też a pair of ~glasses* lornetka *f* polowa; '~ mar·shal *mil.* feldmarszałek *m*; '~ sports *pl.* sport *m* na powietrzu; '~·work praca *f* terenowa, zajęcia *pl.* terenowe; badania *pl.* terenowe

fiend [fiːnd] szatan *m*, diabeł *m*; F fanatyk *m* (-tyczka *f*); '~·ish szatański, diabelski

fierce [fɪəs] (*-r, -st*) zażarty; zaciekły; dziki; '~·ness zażartość *f*; zaciekłość *f*; dzikość *f*

fi·er·y ['faɪərɪ] (*-ier, -iest*) ognisty; zapalczywy

fif|·teen [fɪf'tiːn] **1.** piętnaście; **2.** piętnastka *f*; ~·**teenth** [fɪf'tiːnθ] piętnasty; ~th [fɪfθ] **1.** piąty; **2.** jedna *f* piąta; '~·th·ly po piąte; ~·ti·eth ['fɪftɪɪθ] pięćdziesiąty; ~·ty ['fɪftɪ] **1.** pięćdziesiąt; **2.** pięćdziesiątka *f*; ~·ty-'fif·ty F fifty-fifty, po pół

fig [fɪg] *bot.* figa *f*

fight [faɪt] **1.** walka *f* (*też mil., sport*); starcie *n*; kłótnia *f*, awantura *f*; **2.** (*fought*) *v/t.* bić się *z* (*I*) *lub* przeciw (*D*); walczyć *z* (*I*) *lub* przeciw (*D*); *walkę, pojedynek itp.*⟨s⟩toczyć, brać ⟨wziąć⟩ udział w (*L*) walce, pojedynku *itp.*; *grypę itp.* zwalczać ⟨-czyć⟩; *v/i.* bić się, walczyć; '~·er walczący *f* (-ca *f*); bojownik *m* (-iczka *f*); (*w sporcie*) bokser *m*; *też* ~*er plane mil.* myśliwski samolot *m*; '~·ing walka *f*

fig·u·ra·tive ['fɪgjʊrətɪv] przenośny

fig·ure ['fɪgə] **1.** figura *f*, kształt *m*; postać *f*; cyfra *f*; liczba *f*; cena *f*; rycina *f*, rysunek *m*; *be good at ~s* dobrze liczyć; **2.** *v/t.* wyobrażać ⟨-razić⟩ (sobie); przedstawiać ⟨-wić⟩; *Am.* F sądzić; ~ *out problem* rozwiązywać ⟨-zać⟩; pojmować ⟨-jąć⟩; ~ *up* podliczać ⟨-czyć⟩; *v/i.* figurować, pojawiać ⟨-wić⟩ się; ~ *on*

zwł. Am. liczyć się z (*I*); '~ skat·er *sport:* łyżwiarz *m* (-wiarka *f*) figurowy (-a); '~ skat·ing (*w sporcie*) łyżwiarstwo *n* figurowe

fil·a·ment ['fɪləmənt] *electr.* włókno *n*

filch [fɪltʃ] F podwędzić, zwinąć

file[1] [faɪl] **1.** kartoteka *f*; akta *pl.*; teczka *f*; *komp.* plik *m*, zbiór *m*; rząd *m*; *mil.* szereg *m*; *on* ~ w aktach; **2.** *v/t.* listy *itp.* wciągać ⟨-nąć⟩ do akt; wciągać ⟨-gnąć⟩ do ewidencji; *podanie, powództwo* wnosić ⟨wnieść⟩; *v/i.* iść ⟨pójść⟩ jeden za drugim

file[2] [faɪl] **1.** pilnik *m*; **2.** ⟨s⟩piłować (*pilnikiem*)

'**file**| **man·age·ment** *komp.* zarządzanie *n* plikami; '~ pro·tec·tion *komp.* ochrona *f* plików

fi·li·al ['fɪljəl]: ~ *love* miłość *f* dzieci

fil·ing ['faɪlɪŋ] wprowadzanie *n* do ewidencji; '~ cab·i·net szafka *f* na akta

fill [fɪl] **1.** napełniać ⟨-nić⟩ (się), zapełniać ⟨-nić⟩ (się), wypełniać ⟨-nić⟩(się); *ząb* wypełniać ⟨-nić⟩, ⟨za⟩plombować; ~ *in* zastępować ⟨-stąpić⟩; *formularz* wypełniać ⟨-nić⟩ (*Am. też* ~ *out*); ~ *up* napełniać ⟨-nić⟩ (się), wypełniać ⟨-nić⟩ (się); ~ *her up!* F *mot.* proszę do pełna!; **2.** wypełnienie *n*, napełnienie *n*; *eat one's* ~ najeść się do syta

fil·let *Brt.*, **fil·et** *Am.* ['fɪlɪt] filet *m*

fill·ing ['fɪlɪŋ] wypełnienie *n*; *med.* wypełnienie *n*, plomba *f*; '~ sta·tion stacja *f* benzynowa

fil·ly ['fɪlɪ] *zo.* młoda klacz *f*

film [fɪlm] **1.** warstwa *f*; błona *f*; *phot. zwł. Brt.* film *m* kinowy; folia *f*; zmętnienie *n* (*oka*); mgiełka *f*; *make lub shoot a* ~ ⟨na⟩kręcić film; **2.** ⟨s⟩filmować; '~ star *zwł. Brt.* gwiazda *f* filmowa

fil·ter ['fɪltə] **1.** filtr *m*; **2.** ⟨prze⟩filtrować; '~ tip filtr *m* (*papierosa*); ~·'tipped: ~*tipped cigarette* papieros *m* z filtrem

filth [fɪlθ] brud *m*; '~·y (*-ier, -iest*) brudny; *fig.* plugawy

fin [fɪn] *zo.* płetwa *f* (*Am. też* płetwonur·ka)

fi·nal ['faɪnl] **1.** końcowy; finałowy; ostateczny; **2.** (*w sporcie*) finał *m*; *zw.* ~*s pl.* egzaminy *pl.* końcowe; ~·**dis'pos·al** ostateczne usuwanie *n* (*odpadów radioaktywnych*); ~·**ist** ['faɪnəlɪst] (*w spor-*

cie) finalista *m* (-tka *f);* '~·ly ostatecznie; w końcu; ~ 'whis·tle *sport:* gwizdek *m* końcowy

fi·nance [faɪˈnæns] **1.** nauka *f* o finansach; ~**s** *pl.* finanse *pl.;* **2.** ⟨s⟩finansować; **fi·nan·cial** [faɪˈnænʃl] finansowy; **fi·nan·cier** [faɪˈnænsɪə] finansista *m*

finch [fɪntʃ] *zo.* zięba *f*

find [faɪnd] **1. (found)** znajdować ⟨znaleźć⟩; odnajdować ⟨odnaleźć⟩; *pieniądze itp.* zdobywać ⟨-być⟩; stwierdzać ⟨-dzić⟩; *jur.* uznawać *(kogoś za (nie)winnego);* **be found** występować; ~ **out** stwierdzać ⟨-dzić⟩; odkrywać ⟨-ryć⟩; dowiadywać ⟨-wiedzieć⟩ się; **2.** znalezisko *n;* odkrycie *n;* '~·ings *pl.* znalezisko *n; jur.* wnioski *pl.*

fine¹ [faɪn] **1.** *adj.* **(-r, -st)** świetny; wspaniały, znakomity; delikatny; cienki; drobny; subtelny; *I'm ~* świetnie się czuję; **2.** *adv.* F świetnie, znakomicie; drobno

fine² [faɪn] **1.** grzywna *f,* kara *f* pieniężna; **2.** nakładać ⟨-łożyć⟩ grzywnę

fin·ger [ˈfɪŋgə] **1.** palec *m* (*u ręki*); → *cross* 2; **2.** dotykać ⟨-tknąć⟩ palcami, obmacywać ⟨-cać⟩; '~·nail paznokieć *m;* '~·print odcisk *m* palca; '~·tip koniec *m* palca

fin·i·cky [ˈfɪnɪkɪ] pedantyczny; wybredny

fin·ish [ˈfɪnɪʃ] **1.** ⟨za-, s⟩kończyć (się); wykańczać ⟨-kończyć⟩; *też ~ off* dokończyć, skończyć; *też ~ off, ~ up* skończyć (*jeść, pić*); **2.** koniec *m,* zakończenie *n;* końcówka *f;* (*w sporcie*) finisz *m,* meta *f;* wykończenie *n;* '~·ing line meta *f*

Fin·land [ˈfɪnlənd] Finlandia *f;* **Finn** [fɪn] Fin(ka *f*) *m;* '**Finn·ish 1.** fiński; **2.** *ling.* język *m* fiński

fir [fɜː] *też ~ tree* jodła *f;* '~ cone szyszka *f* jodły

fire [ˈfaɪə] **1.** ogień *m* (*też mil.*); pożar *m;* **be on ~** palić się; **catch ~** zapalić się, zająć się ogniem; **set on ~, set ~ to** podpalać ⟨-lić⟩; **2.** *v/t.* podpalać ⟨-lić⟩; *fig.* rozpalać ⟨-lić⟩; *cegły itp.* wypalać ⟨-lić⟩; wystrzeliwać ⟨-lić⟩; strzelać ⟨-lić⟩ z (*I*); F *pracownika itp.* wylewać ⟨-lać⟩; *v/i.* strzelać ⟨-lić⟩; ~ **a·larm** [ˈfaɪərəlɑːm] alarm *m* pożarowy; ~·arms [ˈfaɪərɑːmz] *pl.* broń *f* palna; '~ bri·gade *Brt.* straż *f* pożarna; '~·bug

F podpalacz(ka *f*) *m;* '~·crack·er petarda *f;* '~ de·part·ment *Am.* straż *f* pożarna; ~ en·gine [ˈfaɪərendʒɪn] wóz *m* strażacki; ~ es·cape [ˈfaɪərɪskeɪp] wyjście *n* pożarowe, schody *pl.* pożarowe; ~ ex·tin·guish·er [ˈfaɪərɪkstɪŋgwɪʃə] gaśnica *f;* '~ fight·er strażak *m;* '~·guard osłona *f* przy kominku; '~ hy·drant *Brt.* hydrant *m* przeciwpożarowy; '~·man (*pl. -men*) strażak *m;* '~·place kominek *m;* '~·plug *Am.* hydrant *m* przeciwpożarowy; '~·proof ognioodporny, ogniotrwały; '~·rais·ing *Brt.* podpalenie *n;* '~·screen *Am.* osłona *f* przy kominku; '~·side kominek *m;* '~ sta·tion remiza *f* straży pożarnej; '~ truck *Am.* wóz *m* strażacki; '~·wood drewno *n* na podpałkę; '~·works *pl.* fajerwerk *n*

fir·ing squad [ˈfaɪərɪŋskwɒd] *mil.* pluton *m* egzekucyjny

firm¹ [fɜːm] twardy; mocny; *podstawa itp.:* solidny; *przekonanie:* niewzruszony; *oferta itp.:* wiążący; *głos itp.:* stanowczy

firm² [fɜːm] firma *f*

first [fɜːst] **1.** *adj.* pierwszy; najlepszy; **2.** *adv.* po pierwsze; najpierw; ~ *of all* przede wszystkim; **3.** pierwszy *m* (-sza *f*); *mot.* jedynka *f,* pierwszy bieg *m;* **at ~** najpierw; **from the ~** od początku; ~ 'aid pierwsza pomoc *f;* ~ 'aid box, ~ 'aid kit apteczka *f;* '~·born pierworodny; ~ 'class (*w pociągu itp.*) pierwsza klasa; ~'class znakomity, pierwszorzędny; '~ floor *Brt.* pierwsze piętro *n, Am.* parter *m;* → **second hand;** '~ hand z pierwszej ręki; ~ 'leg (*w sporcie*) pierwszy mecz *m;* '~·ly po pierwsze; '~ name imię *n;* ~'rate pierwszorzędny

firth [fɜːθ] odnoga *f* morska, fiord *m*

fish [fɪʃ] **1.** (*pl. fish, fishes*) ryba *f;* **2.** łowić ryby; wędkować; '~·bone ość *f*

fish·er·man [ˈfɪʃəmən] (*pl. -men*) rybak *m;* ~·e·ry [ˈfɪʃərɪ] rybołówstwo *n;* łowisko *n*

fish| '**fin·ger** *zw. Brt.* paluszek *m* rybny; '~·hook haczyk *m*

'**fish·ing** rybołówstwo *n,* wędkowanie *n;* '~ line linka *f* wędkarska, żyłka *f;* '~ rod wędka *f;* '~ tack·le sprzęt *m* wędkarski

'**fish·|mon·ger** *zw. Brt.* handlarz *m* ryb;

~ 'stick zwł. Am. paluszek m rybny; '~·y (-ier, -iest) śliski, podejrzany

fis·sion ['fɪʃn] rozszczepienie n

fis·sure ['fɪʃə] szczelina f, pęknięcie n

fist [fɪst] pięść f

fit¹ [fɪt] 1. (-tt-) odpowiedni; zdatny; przydatny; stosowny; (w sporcie) w dobrej kondycji; keep ~ utrzymywać dobrą kondycję; 2. (-tt-; fitted, Am. też fit) v/t. pasować na (G); pasować do (G); odpowiadać; dopasowywać <-wać>; tech. <za>montować; przytwierdzać <-dzić>; czynić zdatnym (for, to do G); ~ in kogoś przyjmować <-jąć>; robić miejsce (dla kogoś, na coś); też ~ on przymierzać <-rzyć>; też ~ out wyposażać <-żyć> (with w A), <za>montować; też ~ up załadować <załóżyć>, <za>montować; przerabiać <-robić>; v/i. pasować; ubranie: leżeć; 3. be a beautiful ~ pięknie leżeć

fit² [fɪt] atak m, napad m

'fit|·ful niespokojny, sen itp. przerywany; '~·ness zdatność f; (w sporcie) dobra kondycja f; '~·ness cen·tre (Am. cen·ter) siłownia f; '~·ted wyposażony; wbudowany; ~ted carpet wykładzina f dywanowa; ~ted kitchen zabudowana kuchnia f; '~·ter monter m; '~·ting 1. stosowny, właściwy; 2. montaż m, instalacja f; ~tings pl. wyposażenie n; armatura f

five [faɪv] 1. pięć; 2. piątka f

fix [fɪks] 1. przymocowywać <-ować>, przytwierdzać <-dzić> (to do G); cenę ustalać <-lić>, wyznaczać <-czyć>; oczy wlepiać (on w A); bilety itp. załatwiać <-wić>; zdjęcie utrwalać <-lić>; naprawiać <-wić>; zwł. Am. jedzenie robić; rezultaty <s>preparować; 2. F trudna sytuacja f; ~ed przytwierdzony, przymocowany; niewzruszony; '~·ings pl. Am. gastr. dodatki pl. (do głównego dania); ~·ture ['fɪkstʃə] element m osprzętu; lighting ~ture oprawa f świetlna

fizz [fɪz] musować; perkotać, syczeć

fl skrót pisany: floor piętro

flab·ber·gast ['flæbəgɑːst] F zdumiewać <-mieć>; be ~ed osłupieć

flab·by ['flæbɪ] (-ier, -iest) zwiotczały

flac·cid ['flæksɪd] sflaczały, zwiotczały

flag¹ [flæg] 1. flaga f, sztandar m; 2. (-gg-) oflagowywać <-ować>; ~ down zatrzymywać <-mać> (taksówkę)

flag² [flæg] 1. płyta f (kamienna lub

chodnikowa); 2. wykładać (płytami)

flag³ [flæg] <o>słabnąć

'flag|·pole, '~·staff maszt m flagowy; '~·stone płyta f (chodnikowa)

flake [fleɪk] 1. płatek m; 2. też ~ off łuszczyć się, złuszczać <-czyć> się; 'flak·y (-ier, -iest) łuszczący się; ~ 'pas·try ciasto n francuskie

flame [fleɪm] 1. płomień m (też fig.); be in ~s stanąć w płomieniach; 2. płonąć, rozpłomieniać <-nić> się

flam·ma·ble ['flæməbl] Am. i tech. → inflammable

flan [flæn] tarta f

flank [flæŋk] 1. bok m; mil. flanka f; 2. otaczać <otoczyć>

flan·nel ['flænl] flanela f, myjka f; ~s pl. spodnie pl. flanelowe

flap [flæp] 1. klapa f; (w ubraniu) patka f; płachta f (namiotu); uderzenie n (skrzydeł); 2. (-pp-) <za>łopotać (skrzydłami)

flare [fleə] 1. <za>migotać; nozdrza: rozszerzać się; ~ up wybuchać <-chnąć>; 2. sygnał m świetlny; rakieta f świetlna

flash [flæʃ] 1. błysk m, rozbłysk m; wiadomość f z ostatniej chwili; phot. flesz m; zwł. Am. F latarka f; like a ~ jak błyskawica; in a ~ migiem; a ~ of lightning rozbłysk m błyskawicy; 2. błyskać <-snąć>, rozbłyskać <-snąć>; przesyłać <-słać>; <po>mknąć; '~·back (w filmie) retrospekcja f; ~ 'freeze Am. (-froze, frozen) → quick-freeze; '~·light phot. lampa f błyskowa, flesz m; zwł. Am. latarka f; '~·y (-ier, -iest) krzykliwy, jaskrawy

flask [flɑːsk] piersiówka f; termos m

flat¹ [flæt] 1. (-tt-) płaski, równy; mot. dętka: bez powietrza; bateria: wyładowany; zwietrzały, bez gazu; econ. apatyczny; econ. jednolity; 2. adv. fall ~ zawodzić <-wieść>; sing ~ <za>śpiewać za nisko; 3. płaska powierzchnia; płask m; zwł. Am. mot. F (dętka bez powietrza) guma f

flat² [flæt] zwł. Brt. mieszkanie n

flat|·'foot·ed z płaskostopiem; '~·mate Brt. współmieszkaniec m; ~·ten ['flætn] spłaszczać <-czyć>; przywierać <-wrzeć>; też ~ten out wyrównywać <-wnać> (nad ziemią)

flat·ter ['flætə] pochlebiać <-bić> (D);

~·er ['flætərə] pochlebca *m*; **~·y** ['flætərı] pochlebstwo *n*

fla·vo(u)r ['fleɪvə] **1.** smak *m*, aromat *m*; *wina* bukiet *m*; przyprawa *f*; **2.** przyprawiać ⟨-wić⟩; **~·ing** ['fleɪvərɪŋ] przyprawa *f*, aromat *m*

flaw [flɔː] skaza *f*; wada *f*; *tech. też* defekt *m*; **'~·less** nieskazitelny, nienaganny

flax [flæks] *bot. roślina*: len *m*

flea [fliː] *zo.* pchła *f*; **'~ mar·ket** pchli targ *m*

fleck [flek] plama *f*, plamka *f*

fled [fled] *pret. i p.p. od* **flee**

fledg|ed [fledʒd] opierzony; **~(e)·ling** ['fledʒlɪŋ] pisklę *n*; *fig.* żółtodziób *m*

flee [fliː] uciekać

fleece [fliːs] runo *n*, wełna *f*

fleet [fliːt] *naut.* flota *f*

'Fleet Street *fig.* prasa *f* brytyjska (*zwł. londyńska*)

flesh [fleʃ] ciało *n*; mięso *n* (*zwierzęcia*); miąższ *m* (*owocu*); **'~·y** (*-ier, -iest*) korpulentny

flew [fluː] *pret. od* **fly⁸**

flex¹ [fleks] *zwł. anat.* zginać ⟨zgiąć⟩

flex² [fleks] *zwł. Brt. electr.* przedłużacz *m*, sznur *m*

flex·i·ble ['fleksəbl] elastyczny; giętki (*też fig.*); **~ working hours** ruchomy czas *m* pracy

flex·i·time *Brt.* ['fleksɪtaɪm]; **flex·time** *Am.* ['flekstaɪm] ruchomy czas *m* pracy

flick [flɪk] **1.** strzepywać ⟨-pnąć⟩; machać ⟨-chnąć⟩; trzepać ⟨-pnąć⟩; **2.** strzepnięcie *n*; machnięcie *n*; trzepnięcie *n*

flick·er ['flɪkə] **1.** ⟨za⟩migotać; **2.** migotanie *n*

fli·er ['flaɪə] *aviat.* lotnik *m*; *reklamowy* folder *m*, ulotka *f*

flight [flaɪt] lot *m*; ucieczka *f*; stado *n* (*ptaków*); **put to ~** zmusić ⟨-sić⟩ do ucieczki; **take (to) ~** rzucać ⟨-cić⟩ się do ucieczki; **'~ at·tend·ant** steward(essa *f*) *m*; **'~·less** nielotny; **'~ re·cord·er** *aviat.* rejestrator *m* przebiegu lotu, F czarna skrzynka *f*; **'~·y** (*-ier, -iest*) niestały, chimeryczny

flim·sy ['flɪmzɪ] (*-ier, -iest*) wątły, mizerny; cienki; *fig.* kiepski

flinch [flɪntʃ] wzdrygać ⟨-gnąć⟩ się; cofać ⟨-fnąć⟩ się (*from* przed *I*)

fling [flɪŋ] **1.** (*flung*) rzucać, cisnąć

⟨-skać⟩; **~ o.s.** rzucać ⟨-cić⟩ się; **~ open** *lub to* okno *itp.* otwierać ⟨-worzyć⟩ *lub* zamykać ⟨-mknąć⟩ z rozmachem; **2. have a ~** ⟨za⟩bawić się; **have a ~ at** flirtować z

flint [flɪnt] krzemień *m*; kamień *m* (*do zapalniczki*)

flip [flɪp] (*-pp-*) przerzucać ⟨-cić⟩, przewracać ⟨-rócić⟩; *monetę* rzucać ⟨-cić⟩

flip·pant ['flɪpənt] bezceremonialny, niepoważny

flip·per ['flɪpə] *zo.* płetwa *f* (*foki itp., też pływaka*)

flirt [flɜːt] **1.** ⟨po⟩flirtować; **2. be a ~** chętnie flirtować; **flir·ta·tion** [flɜː'teɪʃn] flirt *m*

flit [flɪt] (*-tt-*) przelatywać ⟨-lecieć⟩, przemykać ⟨-mknąć⟩

float [fləʊt] **1.** *v/i.* pływać, unosić się; *też econ.* być w obiegu; *v/t.* spływać; przepływać; spławiać ⟨-wić⟩; *naut.* ⟨z⟩wodować; *econ.* puszczać w obieg; *econ.* upłynniać ⟨-nić⟩*kurs walut*; **2.** pływak *m*; spławik *m*; **'~·ing** **1.** pływający, unoszący się (*na wodzie*); *econ. pieniądz itp.*: w obiegu; *kurs*: płynny, zmienny; *kapitał*: obrotowy; **2.** kurs *m* zmienny; **~·ing 'vot·er** *pol.* niestały wyborca

flock [flɒk] **1.** stado *n* (*zwł. owiec i kóz*); trzoda *f* (*też rel.*); tłum *m*; *fig.* pchać się

floe [fləʊ] kra *f*

flog [flɒg] (*-gg-*) biczować, chłostać; **'~·ging** biczowanie *n*, chłosta *f*

flood [flʌd] **1.** *też* **~·tide** zalew (*też fig.*); powódź *f*, wylew *m*; **2.** wylewać ⟨-lać⟩, zalewać ⟨lać⟩; **'~·gate** śluza *f*; **'~·lights** *pl. electr.* reflektor *m*

floor [flɔː] **1.** podłoga *f*; strop *m*; piętro *n*, kondygnacja *f*; parkiet (*do tańczenia*); dno *n*; → **first floor, second floor; take the ~** zabierać ⟨-brać⟩ głos; **2.** kłaść podłogę; powalić na podłogę; F pokonać; **'~·board** deska *f* (*na podłodze*); **'~ cloth** ścierka *f* do podłogi; **~·ing** ['flɔːrɪŋ] materiał *m* na podłogę; **'~ lamp** *Am.* lampa *f* stojąca; **'~ lead·er** *Am.* przewodniczący *m* klubu partyjnego; **'~ show** występ *m* w klubie nocnym; **'~·walk·er** *zwł. Am.* → **shopwalker**

flop [flɒp] **1.** (*-pp-*) padać ⟨paść⟩, upadać ⟨upaść⟩; F ⟨z⟩robić klapę *lub* plajtę; **2.** F klapa *f*; plajta *f*; klapnięcie *n*;

'~·py, ~·py '**disk** *komp.* dyskietka *f*

Flor·ence Florencja *f*

flor·id ['florɪd] czerwony, rumiany

Flor·i·da Floryda *f*

flor·ist ['florɪst] kwiaciarz *m* (-arka *f*)

floun·der¹ ['flaʊndə] *zo.* (*pl. flounder, flounders*) flądra *f*, płastuga *f*

floun·der² ['flaʊndə] rzucać ⟨-cić⟩ się, trzepotać się; *fig.* plątać się

flour ['flaʊə] mąka *f*

flour·ish ['flʌrɪʃ] **1.** ozdobny gest *m*; ozdobnik *m*; *mus.* tusz *m*; **2.** *v/i.* rozwijać ⟨-winąć⟩ się, rozkwitać ⟨-tnąć⟩; *v/t.* wymachiwać

flow [fləʊ] **1.** ⟨po⟩płynąć, ⟨po-, wy⟩ciec; ⟨po⟩toczyć się; wzbierać ⟨wezbrać⟩; **2.** strumień *m*; wypływ *m*, wyciek *m*; przypływ *m*

flow·er ['flaʊə] **1.** kwiat *m* (*też fig*); **2.** kwitnąć, rozkwitać ⟨-tnąć⟩; '~·**bed** klomb *m*; '~·**pot** doniczka *f*

flown [fləʊn] *p.p. od fly³*

fl. oz. *skrót pisany: fluid ounce (jednostka objętości: Brt. 28,4 cm³, Am. 29,57 cm³)*

fluc·tu·ate ['flʌktʃʊeɪt] podlegać fluktuacji, zmieniać ⟨-nić⟩ się; ~·**a·tion** [flʌktʃʊ'eɪʃn] fluktuacja *f*

flu [fluː] F grypa *f*

flue [fluː] przewód *m* kominowy

flu·en·cy ['fluːənsɪ] biegłość *f*; płynność *f*; potoczystość *f*; '~·t biegły; płynny; potoczysty; *mówca:* wymowny

fluff [flʌf] **1.** puch *m*; włoski *pl.*, meszek *m*; **2.** pióra ⟨na⟩stroszyć; '~·y (-*ier, -iest*) puszysty

flu·id ['fluːɪd] **1.** płynny; ciekły; **2.** płyn *m*; ciecz *f*

flung [flʌŋ] *pret. i p.p. od fling 1*

flunk [flʌŋk] *Am.* F *egzamin* oblewać ⟨-lać⟩

flu·o·res·cent [flʊə'resnt] fluorescencyjny; jarzeniowy

flu·o·ride ['flɔːraɪd] *chem.* fluorek *m*

flu·o·rine ['flɔːriːn] *chem.* fluor *m*

flur·ry ['flʌrɪ] zawieja *f*; *fig.* poruszenie *n*, niepokój *m*

flush [flʌʃ] **1.** spłukanie *n* (*wodą*); zaczerwienienie *n*, wypieki *pl.*; **2.** *v/t. też* ~ *out* przepłukiwać ⟨-kać⟩; ~ *down* spłukiwać ⟨-kać⟩; ~ *the toilet* spuszczać ⟨spuścić⟩ wodę; *v/i.* zaczerwienić ⟨-nić⟩ się; spuszczać ⟨spuścić⟩ wodę

flus·ter ['flʌstə] **1.** denerwować (się);

2. zdenerwowanie *n*

flute [fluːt] *mus.* **1.** flet *m*; **2.** ⟨za⟩grać na flecie

flut·ter ['flʌtə] **1.** ⟨za⟩trzepotać; **2.** trzepot *m*; *fig.* podniecenie *n*

flux [flʌks] *fig.* zmiana *f*, zmienianie *n* się

fly¹ [flaɪ] *zo.* mucha *f*

fly² [flaɪ] rozporek *m*;

fly³ [flaɪ] (*flew, flown*) *v/i.* latać; lecieć; fruwać; uciekać ⟨-ciec⟩; *czas:* płynąć; ~ *at* rzucać się na (*A*); ~ *into a passion lub rage* wpadać ⟨-paść⟩ w pasję *lub* szał; *v/t.* pilotować; ⟨prze⟩transportować; *latawca* puszczać; '~·**er** → *flier*

'fly·ing latający; ~ **'sau·cer** latający spodek *m*; ~ **squad** lotna brygada *f* (*policji*)

'fly·o·ver *Brt.* estakada *f* (*dróg, kolejowa*); '~·**weight** *boks:* waga *f* musza; '~·**wheel** koło *n* zamachowe

FM [ef 'em] *skrót: frequency modulation* FM, UKF *m*, fale *pl.* ultrakrótkie

foal [fəʊl] *zo.* źrebak *m*

foam [fəʊm] **1.** piana *f*; **2.** pienić się; ~ **'rub·ber** guma *f* piankowa, F pianka *f*; '~·**y** pienisty; spieniony

fo·cus ['fəʊkəs] **1.** (*pl. -cuses, -ci* [-saɪ]) ognisko *n* (*opt., też fig.*); centrum *n*; *phot.* ostrość *f*; **2.** *opt., phot.* nastawiać ⟨-wić⟩ ostrość; *fig.* skupiać ⟨-pić⟩ się (*on* na *L*)

fod·der ['fɒdə] karma *f*, pasza *f*

foe [fəʊ] *poet.* wróg *m*, nieprzyjaciel *m*

fog [fɒg] mgła *f*; '~·**gy** (-*ier, -iest*) zamglony; *figt.* mglisty

foi·ble ['fɔɪbl] *fig.* słabość *f*

foil¹ [fɔɪl] folia *f*; *fig.* tło *n*

foil² [fɔɪl] ⟨po⟩krzyżować, udaremniać ⟨-nić⟩

foil³ [fɔɪl] (*w szermierce*) floret *m*

fold¹ [fəʊld] **1.** fałda *f*; zagięcie *n*; **2.** składać ⟨złożyć⟩, zaginać ⟨-giąć⟩; *ramiona itp.* zakładać ⟨założyć⟩; zawijać ⟨-winąć⟩; *często ~ up* składać ⟨złożyć⟩ się; ⟨za⟩kończyć się

fold² [fəʊld] okólnik *m*, zagroda *f*; *rel.* trzoda *f*, owczarnia *f*

'fold·er skoroszyt *m*, teczka *f*; folder *m*; broszura *f*

'fold·ing składany; '~ **bed** łóżko *n* składane *lub* polowe; '~ **bi·cy·cle** rower *m* składany, F składak *m*; '~ **boat** łódź *f* składana; '~ **chair** krzesło *n* składane;

'~ door(s pl.) drzwi pl. składane

fo·li·age ['fəulɪɪdʒ] liście pl., listowie f

folk [fəuk] pl. ludzie pl.; ~s pl. F ludziska pl.; attr. ludowy; '~·lore folklor m; '~ mu·sic muzyka f ludowa; '~ song pieśń f ludowa

fol·low ['fɒləu] podążać ⟨-żyć⟩ za (D); iść ⟨pójść⟩ za (I); następować ⟨-tąpić⟩ po (D); śledzić; ~ **through** plan itp. przeprowadzać ⟨-dzić⟩ do końca; ~ **up** (za)stosować się do (G), sugestię itp. rozwijać ⟨-winąć⟩; as ~s jak następuje; '~·er zwolennik m ⟨-iczka f⟩; '~·ing 1. uznanie n; zwolennicy pl.; **the ~ing** osoby: następujący pl., coś: co następuje; 2. następujący; następny; 3. bezpośrednio po (L)

fol·ly ['fɒlɪ] szaleństwo n

fond [fɒnd] czuły; naiwny; be ~ of lubić (A)

fon·dle ['fɒndl] pieścić

'fond·ness czułość f

font [fɒnt] chrzcielnica f; komp. czcionka f

food [fuːd] jedzenie n; pożywienie n; żywność f

fool [fuːl] 1. głupiec m, dureń m; make a ~ of s.o. robić z kogoś durnia; make a ~ of o.s. robić z siebie durnia; 2. oszukiwać ⟨-kać⟩; wyłudzać ⟨-dzić⟩; też ~ around, ~ around wygłupiać się; '~·har·dy ryzykowny, brawurowy; '~·ish głupi, durny; '~·ish·ness głupota f; '~·proof bezpieczny, nie do zepsucia

foot [fut] 1. (pl. feet) stopa f; (pl. F też foot, skrót: ft) stopa f (=30,48 cm); podstawa f; podnóże n; on ~ pieszo; 2. F rachunek pokrywać ⟨-ryć⟩; ~ it iść ⟨pójść⟩ piechotą

'foot·ball piłka f nożna (też gra); Am. futbol m; 'foot·bal·ler piłkarz m; Am. futbolista m; ~ hoo·li·gan pseudokibic m; '~ play·er piłkarz m (-arka f)

'foot·bridge kładka f dla pieszych; '~·fall (odgłos) krok m; '~·hold mocne oparcie n (dla stóp)

'foot·ing oparcie n, podstawa f; be on a friendly ~ with s.o. mieć dobre stosunki z kimś; lose one's ~ ⟨s⟩tracić oparcie lub równowagę

'foot·lights pl. theat. światła pl. rampy; '~·loose nieskrępowany; ~loose

and fancy-free swobodny jak ptak; '~·path ścieżka f; '~·print odcisk m (stopy); ~prints ślady pl.; '~·sore otarcie n; '~·step krok m; '~·wear obuwie n

fop [fɒp] strojniś m, elegancik m

for [fɔː, fə] 1. prp. dla (G); wymiana, przyczyna, cena, cel: za (I); tęsknić itp.: za (I); cel, przeznaczenie, kierunek: do (G); czekać, mieć nadzieję itp.: na (A); posyłać itp. po (A); popierać: za (I); okres czasu: ~ three days przez trzy dni, od trzech dni; ~ tomorrow na jutro; odległość: I walked ~ a mile przeszedłem milę; I ~ one ja na przykład; ~ sure na pewno, z pewnością; it is hard ~ him to do it ciężko jest mu to zrobić; 2. cj. ponieważ

for·age ['fɒrɪdʒ] ⟨po⟩szukiwać; też ~ about szperać (in w L)

for·ay ['fɒreɪ] mil. wypad m; fig. wycieczka; ~ into politics w dziedzinę polityki

for·bad(e) [fə'bæd] pret. od forbid

for·bear [fɔː'beə] → forebear

for·bid [fə'bɪd] (-dd-; -bade lub -bad [-bæd], -bidden lub -bid) zabraniać ⟨-ronić⟩; zakazywać ⟨-zać⟩; ~·ding odpychający, przerażający

force [fɔːs] 1. siła f; przemoc f; the (police) ~ policja f; (armed) ~s siły pl. zbrojne; by ~ siłą, przemocą; come lub put into ~ wchodzić lub wprowadzać w życie; 2. kogoś zmuszać ⟨-musić⟩; coś wymuszać ⟨-musić⟩; wpychać ⟨wepchnąć⟩ (na siłę); włamywać ⟨-mać⟩, wyłamywać ⟨-mać⟩; ~ s.th. on s.o. wmuszać ⟨-sić⟩ coś komuś; ~ o.s. on s.o. narzucać ⟨-cić⟩ się komuś; ~ open otwierać ⟨-worzyć⟩ siłą; ~d wymuszony; przymusowy; ~d 'land·ing aviat. lądowanie n awaryjne; '~·ful energiczny, silny; mocny, dobitny

for·ceps ['fɔːseps] med. kleszcze pl., szczypce pl.

for·ci·ble ['fɔːsəbl] dokonany siłą lub przemocą; potężny, dobitny

ford [fɔːd] 1. bród m; 2. przeprawiać ⟨-wić⟩ się w bród

fore [fɔː] 1. przedni; dziobowy; 2. przednia część f; come to the ~ wyróżniać ⟨-nić⟩ się; ~·arm ['fɔːrɑːm] przedramię n; '~·bear: zw. ~bears przodkowie pl.; ~·bod·ing [fɔː'bəudɪŋ] (złe) przeczucie *n*; '**∼·cast 1.** (*-cast lub -casted*) przewidywać ⟨-widzieć⟩; prognozować; **2.** prognoza *f*; '**∼·fa·ther** przodek *m*; '**∼·fin·ger** palec *m* wskazujący; '**∼·foot** (*pl. feet*) zo. przednia łapa *f*; **∼·gone** con'clu·sion sprawa *f* z góry przesądzona; '**∼·ground** pierwszy plan *m*; '**∼·hand 1.** (*w sporcie*) forhend *m*; **2.** (*w sporcie*) z forhendu; '**∼·head** ['fɒrɪd] czoło *n*

for·eign ['fɒrən] zagraniczny; cudzoziemski; obcy; **∼** af'fairs *pl.* sprawy *pl.* zagraniczne; **∼** 'aid pomoc *f* z zagranicy; '**∼·er** cudzoziemiec *m* (-mka *f*); **∼** 'lan·guage język *m* obcy; **∼** 'min·is·ter *pol.* minister *m* spraw zagranicznych; '2 Of·fice *Brt. pol.* Ministerstwo *m* Spraw Zagranicznych; **∼** 'pol·i·cy polityka *f* zagraniczna; 2 'Se·cre·ta·ry *Brt. pol.* minister *m* spraw zagranicznych; **∼** 'trade *econ.* handel *m* zagraniczny; **∼** 'work·er pracownik *m* cudzoziemski, gastarbeiter *m*

fore|'knowl·edge uprzednia wiedza *f*; '**∼·leg** zo. noga *f* przednia; '**∼·man** (*pl. -men*) brygadzista *m*; *jur.* przewodniczący *m* (*ławy przysięgłych*); '**∼·most** naczelny, najważniejszy; '**∼·name** imię *n*

fo·ren·sic [fə'rensɪk] sądowy; **∼** 'medi·cine medycyna *f* sądowa

'**fore|·run·ner** prekursor *m*, poprzednik *m*; **∼·'see** (*-saw, -seen*) przewidywać ⟨-widzieć⟩; **∼·'shad·ow** zapowiadać ⟨-wiedzieć⟩; '**∼·sight** fig. przenikliwość *f*, dalekowzroczność *f*

for·est ['fɒrɪst] las *m* (*też fig.*)

fore·stall [fɔː'stɔːl] uprzedzać ⟨-dzić⟩, ubiegać ⟨ubiec⟩

for·est|·er ['fɒrɪstə] leśniczy *m*; **∼·ry** ['fɒrɪstrɪ] leśnictwo *n*

'**fore|·taste** przedsmak *m*; **∼·'tell** (*-told*) przepowiadać ⟨-wiedzieć⟩; '**∼·thought** przezorność *f*, roztropność *f*

for·ev·er, for ev·er [fə'revə] na zawsze

'**fore|·wom·an** (*pl. -women*) brygadzistka *f*; '**∼·word** przedmowa *f*

for·feit ['fɔːfɪt] ⟨u-, s⟩tracić; być ⟨zostać⟩ pozbawionym

forge [fɔːdʒ] **1.** kuźnia *f*; **2.** ⟨s⟩fałszować; '**forg·er** fałszerz *m*; ·**ge·ry** ['fɔːdʒərɪ] fałszerstwo *n*, falsyfikat *m*; '**forge·ry-proof** trudny do sfałszowania

for·get [fə'get] (*-got, gotten*) zapominać ⟨-mnieć⟩; **∼·ful** zapominalski;

∼·me-not *bot.* niezapominajka *f*

for·give [fə'gɪv] (*-gave, -given*) wybaczać ⟨-czyć⟩, przebaczać ⟨-czyć⟩; **∼·ness** wybaczenie *n*, przebaczenie *n*; **for·'giv·ing** wyrozumiały

fork [fɔːk] **1.** widelec *m*; widły *pl.*; rozwidlenie *n*; **2.** rozwidlać ⟨-lić⟩ (się); **∼ed** rozwidlony; **∼·lift** 'truck wózek *m* widłowy

form [fɔːm] **1.** forma *f*, kształt *m*; formularz *m*; *zwł. Brt.* klasa *f*; formalności *pl.*; kondycja *f*; **in great ∼** w wielkiej formie; **2.** ⟨u⟩kształtować (się); ⟨u⟩formować (się); ⟨u⟩tworzyć (się); ustawiać ⟨-wić⟩ (się)

for|m·al ['fɔːml] formalny; oficjalny; uroczysty; **∼·mal·i·ty** [fɔː'mælətɪ] formalność *f*, oficjalność *f*; uroczystość *f*

for·mat ['fɔːmæt] **1.** format *m*; forma *f*; **2.** (*-tt-*) *komp.* ⟨z⟩formatować

for·ma·tion [fɔː'meɪʃn] tworzenie *n*, utworzenie *n*; formacja *f*, szyk *m*; **∼·tive** ['fɔːmətɪv] tworzący, kształtujący; **∼tive years** *pl.* okres *m* rozwoju osobowości

'**for·mat·ting** *komp.* formatowanie *n*

for·mer ['fɔːmə] **1.** były; wcześniejszy; **2.** **the ∼** pierwszy (*z wymienionych*); '**∼·ly** uprzednio, wcześniej

for·mi·da·ble ['fɔːmɪdəbl] straszny; wzbudzający respekt; *pytanie itp.*: trudny

'**form|· mas·ter** wychowawca *m* (*klasy*); '**∼· mis·tress** wychowawczyni *f* (*klasy*); '**∼· teach·er** wychowawca *m* (-czyni *f*) (*klasy*)

for·mu·la ['fɔːmjʊlə] *chem.*, *math.* wzór *m*; formuła *f*; recepta *f*; **∼·late** ['fɔːmjʊleɪt] ⟨s⟩formułować

for|·sake [fə'seɪk] (*-sook, -saken*) porzucać ⟨-cić⟩, opuszczać ⟨-uścić⟩; **∼·sak·en** [fə'seɪkən] *p.p. od* **forsake**; **∼·sook** [fə'sʊk] *pret. od* **forsake**; **∼·swear** [fɔː'sweə] (*-swore, -sworn*) wyrzekać ⟨-rzec⟩ się pod przysięgą

fort [fɔːt] *mil.* fort *m*, twierdza *f*

forth [fɔːθ] naprzód; dalej; **and so∼** i tak dalej; **∼·'com·ing** nadchodzący; przychylny; *książka*: mający się ukazać; **be ∼coming** pojawiać się

for·ti·eth ['fɔːtɪɪθ] czterdziesty

for·ti|·fi·ca·tion [fɔːrtɪfɪ'keɪʃn] *mil.* fortyfikacja *f*; **∼·fy** ['fɔːtɪfaɪ] *mil.* ⟨u⟩ fortyfikować; *fig.* wzmacniać ⟨-mocnić); **~tude** ['fɔːtɪtjuːd] hart *m* (ducha), męstwo *n*

fort·night ['fɔːtnaɪt] czternaście dni *pl.*, dwa tygodnie *pl.*

for·tress ['fɔːtrɪs] *mil.* forteca *f*

for·tu·i·tous [fɔːˈtjuːɪtəs] nieprzewidziany, przypadkowy

for·tu·nate ['fɔːtʃnət] szczęśliwy; pomyślny; *be ~* mieć szczęście; **'~·ly** na szczęście

for·tune ['fɔːtʃn] fortuna *f*, majątek *m*; szczęście *n*; los *m*, pomyślność *f*; **'~·tell·er** wróżbita *m*, wróżka *f*

for·ty ['fɔːtɪ] **1.** czterdzieści; *have ~ winks* F uciąć ⟨-ciąć⟩ sobie drzemkę; **2.** czterdziestka *f*

for·ward ['fɔːwəd] **1.** *adv.* naprzód, wprzód; **2.** *adj.* przedni; zdążający do przodu; zaawansowany; obcesowy; **3.** (*w piłce nożnej*) napastnik *m*; **4.** przesyłać ⟨-słać⟩, wysyłać ⟨-słać⟩; ⟨wy⟩ekspediować; wspierać⟨wesprzeć⟩,popierać⟨-przeć⟩; **'~·ing a·gent** spedytor *m*

fos·sil ['fɒsl] **1.** *geol.* skamielina *f*; *fig.* żywy relikt *m*; **2.** *adj.* kopalny; *paliwo:* z surowców kopalnych

fos·ter|-child ['fɒstətʃaɪld] (*pl. -chil-dren*) wychowanek *m*; przybrane dziecko *n*; **'~-par·ents** *pl.* przybrani rodzice *pl.*

fought [fɔːt] *pret. i p.p. od* **fight** 2

foul [faʊl] **1.** okropny; *jedzenie:* cuchnący; *powietrze, jedzenie:* nieświeży; zanieczyszczony; *język:* plugawy; (*w sporcie*) nieprawidłowy; **2.** (*w sporcie*) faul *m*; *vicious ~* złośliwy faul *m*; **3.** (*w sporcie*) ⟨s⟩faulować; ⟨s⟩plugawić, ⟨za⟩brudzić

found¹ [faʊnd] *pret. i p.p. od* **find** 1

found² [faʊnd] zakładać ⟨założyć⟩; ⟨u⟩fundować

found³ [faʊnd] *tech.* odlewać ⟨odlać⟩

foun·da·tion [faʊnˈdeɪʃn] *arch.* fundament *m*, podłoże *n*; założenie *n*; fundacja *f*; podstawa *f*

found·er¹ ['faʊndə] założyciel(ka *f*) *m*; fundator(ka *f*) *m*

foun·der² ['faʊndə] *naut.* ⟨za⟩tonąć

found·ling ['faʊndlɪŋ] podrzutek *m*

foun·dry ['faʊndrɪ] odlewnia *f*

foun·tain ['faʊntɪn] fontanna *f*; **'~ pen** pióro *n* wieczne

four [fɔː] **1.** cztery; **2.** czwórka *f* (*też w łodzi*); *on all ~s* na czworakach

'four|star *Brt.* F (*benzyna*) super; **~-star** **'pet·rol** *Brt.* benzyna F super; **~-stroke** **'en·gine** silnik *m* czterosuwowy

four|·teen [fɔːˈtiːn] **1.** czternaście; **2.** czternastka *f*; **~·teenth** [fɔːˈtiːnθ] czternasty; **~th** [fɔːθ] **1.** czwarty; **2.** jedna *f* czwarta; **'~th·ly** po czwarte

four-wheel 'drive *mot.* napęd *m* na cztery koła

fowl [faʊl] ptak *m*; drób *m*, ptactwo *n* (*domowe*)

fox [fɒks] *zo.* lis *m*; **'~·glove** *bot.* naparstnica *f*; **'~·y** (*-ier, -iest*) przebiegły, chytry

frac·tion ['frækʃn] ułamek *m* (*też math.*)

frac·ture ['fræktʃə] **1.** złamanie *n* (*zwł. kości*), pęknięcie; **2.** łamać (się); pękać

fra·gile ['frædʒaɪl] kruchy, łamliwy

frag·ment ['frægmənt] fragment *m*, kawałek *m*; urywek *m*

fra|·grance ['freɪgrəns] woń *f*, zapach *m*; **'~·grant** wonny, pachnący

frail [freɪl] kruchy; delikatny; *fig.* słaby; **'~·ty** kruchość *f*, delikatność *f*; słabość *f*

frame [freɪm] **1.** rama *f*, ramka *f*; oprawka *f* (*do okularów*); budowa *f* (*ciała*); *film:* kadr *m*; *~ of mind* usposobienie *n*, nastrój *m*; **2.** oprawiać ⟨-wić⟩; obramowywać ⟨-wać⟩; ⟨s⟩formułować; *też* *~ up* F kogoś wplątywać ⟨-tać⟩; **'~-up** F ukartowana gra *f*; intryga *f*; **'~·work** *tech.* szkielet *m* konstrukcji; *fig.* struktura *f*, system *m*, ramy *pl.*

franc [fræŋk] frank *m*

France [frɑːns] Francja *f*

fran·chise ['fræntʃaɪz] *pol.* prawo *n* wyborcze; koncesja *f*

frank [fræŋk] **1.** szczery, otwarty; **2.** *Brt.* ⟨o⟩frankować (*maszynowo*)

frank·fur·ter ['fræŋkfɜːtə] parówka *f*

'frank·ness szczerość *f*, otwartość *f*

fran·tic ['fræntɪk] (*~ally*) gorączkowy, rozgorączkowany; hektyczny

fra·ter|·nal [frəˈtɜːnl] braterski; **~·ni·ty** [frəˈtɜːnətɪ] braterstwo *n*; bractwo *n*; *Am. univ.* związek *m*

fraud [frɔːd] oszustwo *n*; F oszust(ka *f*) *m*; **~·u·lent** ['frɔːdjʊlənt] oszukańczy

fray [freɪ] ⟨po-, wy⟩strzępić (się)

freak [friːk] *też ~ of nature* wybryk *m* (natury); dziwoląg *m*; potworek *m*; fanatyk *m* (-tyczka *f*); *attr.* dziwaczny; *film ~* maniak *m* (-aczka *f*) na punkcie filmów

freck·le ['frekl] pieg *m*; '~d piegowaty

free [fri:] **1.** (*-r, -st*) wolny, swobodny; darmowy, bezpłatny; ~ *and easy* beztroski; *set* ~ uwalniać ⟨uwolnić⟩; **2.** (*freed*) uwalniać ⟨uwolnić⟩, oswobadzać ⟨-bodzić⟩; ~**dom** ['fri:dəm] wolność *f*, swoboda *f*; ~'**fares** *pl.* przejazd *m* bezpłatny; ~**lance** ['fri:lɑːns] *pisarz*: niezależny; '⒉**·ma·son** mason *m*; ~ 'skat·ing (*w łyżwiarstwie*) jazda *f* dowolna; '~**style** (*w sporcie*) styl *m* dowolny; ~ 'time czas *m* wolny; ~ 'trade wolny handel *m*; ~ trade 'ar·e·a strefa *f* wolnego handlu; '~·way *Am.* droga *f* szybkiego ruchu; ~'wheel jechać na wolnym biegu

freeze [fri:z] **1.** (*froze, frozen*) *v/i.* zamarzać ⟨-marznąć⟩; ⟨za⟩krzepnąć; *v/t.* zamrażać ⟨-mrozić⟩ (*też ceny itp.*); **2.** mróz *m*; *econ., pol.* zamrożenie *n*; *wage* ~, ~ *on wages* zamrożenie *n* płac; ~'dried liofilizowany; ~'dry liofilizować

'**freez·er** zamrażalnik *m*; (*też deep freeze*) zamrażarka *f*

freeze-frame stop-klatka *f*

'**freez·ing** lodowaty; '~ com·part·ment zamrażalnik *m*; '~ point punkt *m* zamarzania

freight [freit] **1.** fracht *m*; ładunek *m*; *Am. attr.* towarowy; **2.** przesyłać ⟨-słać⟩ frachtem; ⟨za⟩frachtować; '~·car *Am. rail* wagon *m* towarowy; '~·er frachtowiec *m*; samolot *m* frachtowy; '~ train *Am.* pociąg *m* towarowy

French [frentʃ] **1.** francuski; **2.** *ling.* język *m* francuski; *the* ~ *pl.* Francuzi *pl.*; ~ 'doors *pl. Am.* → *French windows*; ~ 'fries *pl. zwł. Am.* frytki *pl.*; '~·man (*pl. -men*) Francuz *m*; ~ 'win·dow(s *pl.*) drzwi *pl.* balkonowe *lub* przeszklone; '~·wom·an (*pl. -women*) Francuzka *f*

fren·zied ['frenzid] rozgorączkowany; szalony; rozszalały; ~·zy ['frenzi] podniecenie *n*; rozgorączkowanie *n*; szaleństwo *n*

fre·quen·cy ['fri:kwənsi] częstotliwość *f* (*też electr.*); ~**t 1.** ['fri:kwənt] częsty; **2.** [fri'kwent] uczęszczać, odwiedzać ⟨-dzić⟩

fresh [freʃ] świeży; rześki; nowy; F obcesowy, chamski; ~·en ['freʃn] *wiatr.* przybierać ⟨-brać⟩ na sile; ~**en** (*o.s.*)

up odświeżać ⟨-żyć⟩ się; '~·man (*pl. -men*) *univ.* student(ka *f*) *m* pierwszego roku; '~·ness świeżość *f*; ~ 'wa·ter słodka woda *f*; '~·wa·ter słodkowodny

fret [fret] zamartwiać się; '~·ful kapryśny, płaczliwy, przykry

FRG [ef ɑː 'dʒiː] *skrót: Federal Republic of Germany* RFN *f*

Fri *skrót pisany: Friday* piątek *m*

fri·ar ['fraiə] mnich *m*

fric·tion ['frikʃn] tarcie *n* (*też fig.*)

Fri·day ['fraidi] (*skrót: Fri*) piątek *m*; *on* ~ w piątek; *on* ~*s* co piątek

fridge [fridʒ] F lodówka *f*

friend [frend] przyjaciel *m* (*przyjaciółka f*); znajomy *m* (-ma *f*); *make* ~*s with* ⟨za⟩przyjaźnić się z (*I*), zawierać ⟨-wrzeć⟩ przyjaźń z (*I*); '~·ly **1.** przyjacielski; przyjazny; **2.** *zwł. Brt.* (*w sporcie*) spotkanie *n* towarzyskie; '~·ship przyjaźń *f*

fries [fraiz] *zwł. Am. pl.* F frytki *pl.*

frig·ate ['frigit] *naut.* fregata *f*

fright [frait] przerażenie *n*; *look a* ~ F okropnie wyglądać; ~·en ['fraitn] wystraszyć ⟨-szać⟩; *be* ~**ened** wystraszyć się; '~·ful przerażający, straszliwy

fri·gid ['fridʒid] *psych.* oziębły; zimny

frill [fril] falbanka *f*; dodatek *m*

fringe [frindʒ] **1.** frędzle *pl.*; brzeg *m*, skraj *m*; grzywka *f*; **2.** otaczać ⟨otoczyć⟩, obramowywać ⟨-mować⟩; '~ ben·e·fits *pl.* świadczenia *pl.* dodatkowe; '~ e·vent impreza *f* dodatkowa; '~ group grupa *f* marginesowa

frisk [frisk] skakać, brykać; F *kogoś* przeszukiwać ⟨-kać⟩; '~·y (*-ier, -iest*) żywotny, dziarski

frit·ter ['fritə]: ~ *away* ⟨z⟩marnować

fri·vol·i·ty [fri'vɒləti] brak *m* powagi; lekkomyślność *f*; **friv·o·lous** ['frivələs] niepoważny; lekkomyślny

friz·zle ['frizl] *gastr.* F przypalać się; ⟨za⟩skwierczeć

frizz·y ['frizi] (*-ier, -iest*) *włosy*: kręcony

fro [frəu]: *to and* ~ tam i z powrotem

frock [frɒk] sukienka *f*; habit *m*

frog [frɒg] żaba *f*; '~·man (*pl. -men*) płetwonurek *m*

frol·ic ['frɒlik] **1.** zabawa *f*; figle *pl.*; **2.** (*-ck-*) brykać, ⟨po⟩skakać; '~·some rozbrykany, figlarny

from [frɒm, frəm] z; od (*G*); *from ... to*

... od *lub* z ... do ...; *where are you ~?* skąd jesteś?

front [frʌnt] **1.** przód *m*; front *m* (*też mil.*); fasada *f*; *at the ~*, *in ~* z przodu, na przedzie; *in ~ of* w przestrzeni: przed (*I*); *be in ~* być na przedzie; **2.** przedni; **3.** *też ~ on, to(wards)* wychodzić przodem na (*A*); **~·age** ['frʌntɪdʒ] elewacja *f*, fronton *m*; '*~ cov·er* strona *f* tytułowa; '*~ door* przednie drzwi *pl.*; *~ 'en·trance* przednie wejście *n*

fron·tier ['frʌntɪə] granica *f* (*państwowa*); *Am. hist.* pogranicze *n* (*Dzikiego Zachodu*); *attr.* graniczny, przygraniczny

'**front|-page** F *wiadomości*: najnowszy; *~-wheel 'drive mot.* napęd *m* na przednie koła

frost [frɒst] **1.** mróz *m*; *też hoar ~*, *white ~* szron *m*; **2.** oszraniać ⟨-ronić⟩, pokrywać ⟨pokryć⟩ szronem; *szkło* ⟨za⟩matować; *gastr.*, *zwł. Am.* ⟨po⟩lukrować, posypywać ⟨-pać⟩ cukrem pudrem; *~ed glass* matowe *lub* mleczne szkło *n*; '*~·bite* odmrożenie *n*; '*~·bit·ten* odmrożony; '*~·y (-ier, -iest)* mroźny (*też fig.*); zaszroniony, oszroniony

froth [frɒθ] **1.** piana *f*; **2.** ⟨s⟩pienić (się); ⟨po⟩toczyć pianę; '*~·y (-ier, -iest)* spieniony, pienisty

frown [fraʊn] **1.** zmarszczenie *n* brwi; *with a ~* ze zmarszczonymi brwiami; **2.** ⟨z⟩marszczyć brew; *~ (up)on s.th.* ⟨s⟩krzywić się na coś

froze [frəʊz] *pret. od* **freeze** 1; **fro·zen** ['frəʊzn] **1.** *p.p. od* **freeze** 1; **2.** *adj.* zamarznięty; zamrożony; mrożony; **fro·zen 'foods** *pl.* mrożonki *pl.*

fru·gal ['fru:gl] oszczędny; skromny

fruit [fru:t] owoc *m*; owoce *pl.*; *~·er·er* ['fru:tərə] sklep *m* z owocami; handlarz *m* owocami; '*~·ful* owocny; '*~·less* bezowocny; '*~ juice* sok *m* owocowy; '*~·y (-ier, -iest)* owocowy; *głos*: donośny

frus|·trate ['frʌstreɪt] ⟨s⟩frustrować; udaremniać ⟨-mnić⟩, uniemożliwiać ⟨-wić⟩; *~·tra·tion* [frʌ'streɪʃn] frustracja *f*; uniemożliwienie *n*, udaremnienie *n*

fry [fraɪ] ⟨u⟩smażyć; *fried eggs pl.* jajka *pl.* sadzone; *fried potatoes pl.* smażone ziemniaki *pl.*; *~·ing pan* ['fraɪɪŋ -] patelnia *f*

ft *skrót pisany:* **foot** stopa *f lub pl.* (*30,48 cm*)

fuch·sia ['fju:ʃə] *bot.* fuksja *f*

fuck [fʌk] V pierdolić (się), jebać; *~ off!* odpierdol się!; '*~·ing* V pierdolony; *~ing hell!* kurwa (jego) mać!

fudge [fʌdʒ] (*cukierek*) krówka *f*

fu·el ['fjʊəl] **1.** paliwo *n*; opał *m*; **2.** (*zwł. Brt. -ll-, Am. -l-*) *mot.*, *aviat.* ⟨za⟩tankować; '*~ in·jec·tion mot.* wtrysk *m* paliwa

fu·gi·tive ['fju:dʒɪtɪv] **1.** przelotny, ulotny; **2.** uciekinier(ka *f*) *m*

ful·fil *Brt.*, **ful·fill** *Am.* [fʊl'fɪl] (*-ll-*) wypełniać ⟨-nić⟩, spełniać ⟨-nić⟩; wykonywać ⟨-nać⟩; **ful'fil(l)·ment** spełnienie *n*, wypełnienie *n*; wykonanie *n*

full [fʊl] **1.** pełny; *~ of* pełen (*G*); *~ (up)* wypełniony; F najedzony, napchany; *house ~!* *theat.* wolnych miejsc brak; *~ of o.s.* zarozumiały; **2.** *adv.* całkiem, zupełnie; **3.** *in ~* cały, w całości; *write out in ~* *zdanie itp.* zapisać całe; *~ 'board* pełne wyżywienie *n*; *~ 'dress* strój *m* wieczorowy; *attr.* wyjściowy; *~·'fledged Am.* → **fully-fledged**; *~·'grown* dorosły; *~·'length* w całej postaci; *suknia*: długi; *film*: pełnometrażowy; *~ 'moon* pełnia *f*; *~ 'stop ling.* kropka *f*; *~ 'time* (*w sporcie*) koniec *m* gry; *~·'time* w pełnym wymiarze; *~·time 'job* praca *f* na pełen etat

ful·ly ['fʊlɪ] w pełni; całkowicie; *~·'fledged* opierzony; *fig.* samodzielny, wykwalifikowany; *~·'grown Brt.* → **full-grown**

fum·ble ['fʌmbl] ⟨po⟩szukać po omacku; zabawiać ⟨-wić⟩ się (*I*); nieczysto zatrzymywać ⟨-mać⟩ piłkę

fume [fju:m] być wściekłym; wściekać się

fumes [fju:mz] *pl.* wyziewy *pl.*; spaliny *pl.*; opary *pl.*

fun [fʌn] radość *f*, zabawa *f*; *for ~* dla zabawy; *make ~ of* śmiać się z (*G*); *have ~!* baw(cie) się dobrze!

func·tion ['fʌŋkʃn] **1.** funkcja *f* (*też math.*); funkcjonowanie *n*; zadanie *n*; uroczystość *f*; **2.** funkcjonować; działać; *~·a·ry* ['fʌŋkʃnərɪ] funkcjonariusz(ka *f*) *m*; '*~ key komp.* klawisz *m* funkcyjny

fund [fʌnd] fundusz *m*; kapitał *m*; rezerwa *f*

fun·da·men·tal [fʌndə'mentl] **1.** fundamentalny; podstawowy; **2.** ~**s** pl. podstawy pl.; podstawowe zasady pl.; ~**ist** [fʌndə'mentəlist] fundamentalista m

fu·ne·ral ['fju:nərəl] pogrzeb m; attr. pogrzebowy

'fun·fair ['fʌnfeə] wesołe miasteczko n

fun·gus ['fʌŋgəs] bot. (pl. **-gi** [-gaɪ], **-guses**) grzyb m

fu·nic·u·lar [fju:'nɪkjʊlə] też ~ **railway** kolejka f linowa

funk·y ['fʌŋkɪ] zwł. Am. F super (o używanym przedmiocie); muz. muzyka f funky

fun·nel ['fʌnl] lejek m; naut., rail. komin m (metalowy)

fun·nies ['fʌnɪz] Am. F pl. komiks m

fun·ny ['fʌnɪ] (**-ier, -iest**) śmieszny, komiczny, zabawny; dziwny

fur [fɜː] futro n, sierść f; (na języku) nalot m; (w czajniku) kamień m

fu·ri·ous ['fjʊərɪəs] wściekły

furl [fɜːl] zwijać ⟨-winąć⟩; parasol składać ⟨złożyć⟩

fur·nace ['fɜːnɪs] piec m

fur·nish ['fɜːnɪʃ] ⟨u⟩meblować; zaopatrywać ⟨-trzyć⟩ (**with** w A); dostarczać ⟨-czyć⟩

fur·ni·ture ['fɜːnɪtʃə] meble pl.; **a piece of** ~ mebel m; **sectional** ~ meble pl. w segmentach

furred [fɜːd] obłożony nalotem

fur·ri·er ['fʌrɪə] kuśnierz m

fur·row ['fʌrəʊ] **1.** bruzda f; rowek m; **2.** ⟨z⟩marszczyć; pomarszczyć

fur·ry ['fɜːrɪ] futrzany; puszysty

fur·ther ['fɜːðə] **1.** comp. od **far**; **2.** fig. dalej; **3.** wspierać ⟨wesprzeć⟩; ~ **ed·u·'ca·tion** Brt. edukacja f dla dorosłych; ~**'more** fig. dodatkowo, poza tym; '~·**most** najdalszy

fur·thest ['fɜːðɪst] sup. od **far**

fur·tive ['fɜːtɪv] skryty

fu·ry ['fjʊərɪ] wściekłość f, furia f

fuse [fjuːz] **1.** electr. bezpiecznik m; lont m; **2.** electr. przepalać (się); ⟨s⟩topić (się); '~ **box** electr. skrzynka f bezpiecznikowa

fu·se·lage aviat. ['fju:zɪlɑːʒ] kadłub n

fu·sion ['fju:ʒn] fuzja f, połączenie n; **nuclear** ~ synteza f jądrowa

fuss [fʌs] **1.** zamieszanie n; histeria f; **2.** ⟨z⟩robić zamieszanie; niepotrzebnie się podniecać; '~·**y** (**-ier, -iest**) wybredny; przeładowany, przepełniony; rozgorączkowany, rozemocjonowany

fus·ty ['fʌstɪ] (**-ier, -iest**) zatęchły, zastały; fig. zaśniedziały

fu·tile ['fju:taɪl] daremny, nadaremny

fu·ture ['fju:tʃə] **1.** przyszły; **2.** przyszłość f; gr. czas m przyszły; **in (the)** ~ w przyszłości

fuzz¹ [fʌz] puszek m, meszek m

fuzz² [fʌz]: **the** ~ sg., pl. (policja) gliny pl.

fuzz·y ['fʌzɪ] F (**-ier, -iest**) niestry, rozmyty; kędzierzawy; pokryty meszkiem

G

G, g [dʒiː] G, g n

gab [gæb] F gadanina f, trajkotanie n; **have the gift of the** ~ mieć dar wymowy

gab·ar·dine ['gæbədiːn] gabardyna f

gab·ble ['gæbl] **1.** gadanina f, trajkotanie n; **2.** gadać, ⟨po⟩trajkotać

gab·er·dine ['gæbədiːn] hist. chałat m (Żydów); → **gabardine**

ga·ble ['geɪbl] arch. szczyt m

gad [gæd] F (**-dd-**): ~ **about** włóczyć się

gad·fly ['gædflaɪ] zo. giez m

gad·get ['gædʒɪt] tech. urządzenie n,

aparat m; często pej. zabawka f mechaniczna, gadżet m

gag [gæg] **1.** knebel (też fig.); F gag m; **2.** (**-gg-**) ⟨za⟩kneblować; fig. zamykać ⟨-mknąć⟩ usta

gage [geɪdʒ] Am. → **gauge**

gai·e·ty ['geɪətɪ] wesołość f, radość f

gai·ly ['geɪlɪ] adv. od **gay** 1

gain [geɪn] **1.** zyskiwać ⟨-skać⟩; odnosić ⟨-nieść⟩ korzyść; wagę, szybkość zwiększać; doganiać ⟨-gonić⟩; zegarek: spieszyć się; ~ **5 pounds** przybierać ⟨-brać⟩ pięć funtów; ~ **in** zdobywać (A); **2.** zysk m, korzyść f; wzrost m, zwiększenie n

gait [geɪt] chód *m*; krok *m*

gai·ter ['geɪtə] kamasz *m*

gal [gæl] F dziewczyna *f*

ga·la ['gɑːlə] gala *f*; pokaz *m*, zawody *pl.*; *attr.* galowy

gal·ax·y ['gæləksɪ] *astr.* galaktyka *f*; **the 2** Droga *f* Mleczna

gale [geɪl] burza *f*, sztorm *m*

gall¹ [ɡɔːl] bezczelność *f*, czelność *f*

gall² [ɡɔːl] otarcie *n*, nadżerka *f*

gall³ [ɡɔːl] ⟨roz⟩drażnić

gall·lant ['gælənt] uprzejmy, grzeczny; odważny;~·**lan·try** ['gæləntrɪ] galanteria *f*, kultura *f*; odwaga *f*

'gall blad·der *anat.* woreczek *m* żółciowy

gal·le·ry ['gælərɪ] galeria *f*, empora *f*, balkon *m*

gall·ley ['gælɪ] *naut.* kambuz *m*; *naut.* galera *f* (*też ~ proof print.* odbitka *f* szczotkowa

gal·lon ['gælən] galon *m* (*Brt.* 4,55 *l, Am.* 3,79 *l*)

gal·lop ['gæləp] **1.** galop *m*; **2.** ⟨po⟩galopować; puścić galopem

gal·lows ['gæləʊz] *sg.* szubienica *f*; '~ **hu·mo(u)r** wisielczy humor *m*

ga·lore [gə'lɔː] w bród

gam·ble ['gæmbl] **1.** ⟨za⟩grać hazardowo; stawiać ⟨postawić⟩, ⟨za⟩ryzykować; **2.** gra *f* hazardowa; '~**r** hazardzista *m* (-tka *f*)

gam·bol ['gæmbl] **1.** skok *m*; **2.** (*zwł. Brt.* -**ll-**, *Am.* -**l-**) brykać, hasać

game [geɪm] gra *f*; mecz *m*; *hunt.* dzika zwierzyna *f*; dziczyzna *f*; ~**s** *pl.* igrzyska *pl.*; *szkolne* zajęcia *pl.* sportowe; '~**keep·er** leśniczy *m*; '~ **park** rezerwat *m* zwierząt; '~ **re·serve** rezerwat *m* zwierząt

gam·mon ['gæmən] *zwł. Brt.* szynka *f* wędzona

gan·der ['gændə] *zo.* gąsior *m*

gang [gæŋ] **1.** brygada *f* robocza, ekipa *f*; gang *m*, banda *f*; grupa *f*; **2.** ~ **up** F współdziałać; spiskować

gang·ster ['gæŋstə] gangster *m*

'gang| war, ~ war·fare [gæŋ'wɔːfeə] wojna *f* między gangami

gang·way ['gæŋweɪ] *naut.* trap *m*; *aviat.* przejście *n*

gaol [dʒeɪl], '~·**bird**, '~·**er** → *jail itp.*

gap [gæp] przerwa *f*, luka *f*, dziura *f*; przełęcz *f*

gape [geɪp] ziać; otwierać się; gapić się

gar·age ['gærɑːʒ] **1.** garaż *m*; warsztat *m* samochodowy; **2.** trzymać w garażu; wprowadzać ⟨-dzić⟩ do garażu

gar·bage ['gɑːbɪdʒ] *zwł. Am.* śmieci *pl.*; '~ **bag** *Am.* worek *m* na śmieci; '~ **can** *Am.* pojemnik *m* na śmieci, kubeł *m* na śmieci; '~ **truck** *Am.* śmieciarka *f*

gar·den ['gɑːdn] ogród *m*; '~·**er** ogrodnik *m*; '~·**ing** ogrodnictwo *n*

gar·gle ['gɑːgl] ⟨wy⟩płukać gardło

gar·ish ['geərɪʃ] jaskrawy, rażący

gar·land ['gɑːlənd] wieniec *m*, girlanda *f*

gar·lic ['gɑːlɪk] *bot.* czosnek *m*

gar·ment ['gɑːmənt] ubranie *n*

gar·nish ['gɑːnɪʃ] *gastr.* ⟨u⟩garnirować, przybierać ⟨-brać⟩

gar·ret ['gærət] pokój *m* na poddaszu

gar·ri·son ['gærɪsn] *mil.* garnizon *m*

gar·ter ['gɑːtə] podwiązka *f*

gas [gæs] gaz; *Am.* F benzyna *f*;~**·e·ous** ['gæsjəs] gazowy

gash [gæʃ] głębokie cięcie *n*, nacięcie *n*

gas·ket ['gæskɪt] *tech.* uszczelnienie *n*, uszczelka *f*

'gas me·ter licznik *m* gazu

gas·o·lene, gas·o·line ['gæsəliːn] *Am.* benzyna *f*, etylina *f*; '~ **pump** dystrybutor *m* benzyny

gasp [gɑːsp] **1.** westchnięcie *n*, dyszenie *n*; **2.** ⟨z⟩łapać powietrze; ~ **for breath** łapać powietrze (*z trudem*)

'gas| sta·tion *Am.* stacja *f* benzynowa; '~ **stove** kuchnia *f* gazowa; '~·**works** *sg.* gazownia *f*

gate [geɪt] brama *f*, bramka *f*; furtka *f*; szlaban *m*; *aviat.* przejście *n* do samolotu; '~·**crash** F wchodzić ⟨wejść⟩ bez zaproszenia; '~·**post** słupek *m*; '~·**way** przejście *m*, przejazd *m*; wjazd *m*; '~·**way drug**

gath·er ['gæðə] *v/t.* zbierać ⟨zebrać⟩; ⟨z⟩gromadzić (*zwł. informacje*); *materiał itp.* zbierać ⟨zebrać⟩, ⟨z⟩marszczyć; *fig.* ⟨wy⟩wnioskować, sądzić (*from* z *I*); ~ **speed** nabierać ⟨-brać⟩ prędkości; *v/i.* zbierać ⟨zebrać⟩ się; ⟨z⟩gromadzić się;~·**ing** ['gæðərɪŋ] zebranie *n*, zgromadzenie *n*

GATT [gæt] *skrót:* ***General Agreement on Tariffs and Trade*** GATT *m*, Układ Ogólny w Sprawie Ceł i Handlu

gau·dy ['gɔ:dı] (*-ier, -iest*) krzykliwy, krzyczący

gauge [geıdʒ] **1.** miara *f*, skala *f*; *tech.* przyrząd *m* pomiarowy, wskaźnik *m*; *tech.* grubość *f* (*blachy lub drutu*); *rail.* szerokość *f* toru; **2.** *tech.* ⟨z⟩mierzyć, dokonywać ⟨-nać⟩ pomiaru

gaunt [gɔ:nt] wynędzniały; ponury

gaunt·let ['gɔ:ntlıt] rękawica *f* ochronna

gauze [gɔ:z] gaza *f*; *Am.* bandaż *m*

gave [geıv] *pret. od* **give**

gav·el ['gævl] młotek *m* (*licytatora, sędziego itp.*)

gaw·ky ['gɔ:kı] (*-ier, -iest*) niezgrabny

gay [geı] **1.** wesoły; *kolor itp.*:. żywy; radosny; F homoseksualny, dla homoseksualistów; **2.** F homoseksualista *m*, gej *m*

gaze [geız] **1.** uporczywy wzrok *m*, spojrzenie *n*; △ *nie* **gaza**; **2.** wpatrywać się (*at* w *A*)

ga·zette [gə'zet] dziennik *m* urzędowy

ga·zelle [gə'zel] *zo.* (*pl.* *-zelles, -zelle*) gazela *f*

GB [dʒi: 'bi:] *skrót:* **Great Britain** Wielka Brytania *f*

gear [gıə] *tech.* koło *n* zębate, tryb *m*; *mot.* bieg *m*; *zwł.* w *złożeniach* sprzęt *m*, urządzenie *n*; F strój *m*, ubranie *n*; **change** (*zwł. Am.* **shift**) ~(**s**) zmieniać bieg(*i*); **change** (*zwł. Am.* **shift**) **into second** ~ wrzucić ⟨-cać⟩ drugi bieg; '~**box** *mot.* skrzynia *f* biegów; '~ **lever** *Brt. mot.*,'~ **shift** *Am.*,'~ **stick** *Brt. mot.* drążek *m* zmiany biegów

geese [gi:s] *pl. od* **goose**

Gei·ger count·er ['gaıgə -] *phys.* licznik *m* Geigera-Müllera

geld·ing ['geldıŋ] *zo.* wałach *m*

gem [dʒem] klejnot *m*, kamień *m* szlachetny

Gem·i·ni [dʒemınaı] *astr.* Bliźnięta *pl.*; **he/she is** (**a**) ~ on(a) jest spod znaku Bliźniąt

gen·der ['dʒendə] *gr.* rodzaj *m*

gene [dʒi:n] *biol.* gen *m*

gen·e·ral ['dʒenərəl] **1.** ogólny; generalny; **2.** generał *m*; **in** ~ ogólnie rzecz biorąc; ~ **de·liv·er·y**: (**in care of**) ~ **de·livery** *Am.* poste restante *n*; ~ **e'lec·tion** *Brt.* wybory *pl.* do parlamentu; ~**ize** [dʒenərəlaız] uogólniać ⟨-nić⟩; '~·**ly** ogólnie, w ogólności; ~ **prac·ti·**

tion·er (*skrót:* **GP**) lekarz *m* ogólny

gen·e·rate ['dʒenəreıt] wytwarzać ⟨-worzyć⟩; ⟨s⟩powodować; ⟨wy⟩generować; ~·**ra·tion** [dʒenə'reıʃn] wytwarzanie *n*; generowanie *n*; generacja *f*, pokolenie *n*; ~·**ra·tor** ['dʒenəreıtə] generator *m*; *Am. mot.* prądnica *f*

gen·e·ros·i·ty [dʒenə'rɒsətı] hojność *f*, szczodrobliwość *f*; ~·**rous** ['dʒenərəs] hojny, szczodrobliwy

ge·net·ic [dʒı'netık] (*~ally*) genetyczny; ~ '**code** kod *m* genetyczny; ~ **en·gin'eer·ing** inżynieria *f* genetyczna; ~**s** *sg.* genetyka *f*

ge·ni·al ['dʒi:njəl] przyjazny; △ *nie* **genialny**

gen·i·tive ['dʒenıtıv] *gr. też* ~ **case** dopełniacz *m*

ge·ni·us ['dʒi:njəs] geniusz *m*

gent [dʒent] F dżentelmen *m*; ~**s** *sg. Brt.* F (*ubikacja*) dla panów

gen·tle ['dʒentl] (*-r, -st*) delikatny; łagodny; '~·**man** (*pl.* **-men**) dżentelmen *m*; '~·**man·ly** po dżentelmeńsku; '~·**ness** delikatność *f*; łagodność *f*

gen·try ['dʒentrı] *Brt.* wyższa warstwa *f*; *jakby*: ziemiaństwo *n*

gen·u·ine ['dʒenjuın] prawdziwy

ge·og·ra·phy [dʒı'ɒgrəfı] geografia *f*

ge·ol·o·gy [dʒı'ɒlədʒı] geologia *f*

ge·om·e·try [dʒı'ɒmətrı] geometria *f*

Geor·gia Gruzja *f*

germ [dʒɜ:m] *biol.* zarodek *m*, zalążek *m*; *bot.* kiełek *m*; *med.* zarazek *m*, bakteria *f*

Ger·man ['dʒɜ:mən] **1.** niemiecki; **2.** Niemiec *m* (-mka *f*); *ling.* język *m* niemiecki; ~ '**shep·herd** *zwł. Am.* owczarek *m* niemiecki, wilczur *m*; '**German·y** Niemcy *pl.*

ger·mi·nate ['dʒɜ:mıneıt] ⟨za⟩kiełkować

ger·und ['dʒerənd] *gr.* rzeczownik *m* odsłowny

ges·tic·u·late [dʒe'stıkjuleıt] gestykulować

ges·ture ['dʒestʃə] gest *m*

get [get] (*-tt-; got, got lub gotten*) *v/t.* otrzymywać ⟨-mać⟩; dostawać ⟨-tać⟩; zdobywać ⟨-być⟩; uzyskiwać ⟨-kać⟩; przynosić ⟨-nieść⟩, sprowadzać ⟨-dzić⟩; załatwiać ⟨-wić⟩; F ⟨z⟩łapać; F ⟨z⟩rozumieć; ⟨s⟩chwytać; wydostawać ⟨-tać⟩; *kogoś* nakłaniać (**to do**

do zrobienia); *tel.* połączyć się z (*I*); ~ **one's hair cut** obcinać ⟨-ciąć⟩ sobie włosy; ~ **going** uruchamiać ⟨-chomić⟩, *fig.* nabierać ⟨-brać⟩ rozpędu; ~ **s.th. by heart** nauczyć się czegoś na pamięć; ~ **s.th. ready** przygotować coś; **have got** mieć; **have got to** musieć; *v/i.* docierać, dostawać się, przyjeżdżać; *z p.p. lub adj.* stawać się; ~ **tired** zmęczyć się; ~ **going** uruchamiać ⟨-chomić⟩ się, działać; ~ **home** jechać do domu; ~ **ready** przygotowywać ⟨-wać⟩ się; ~ **to know s.th.** poznawać ⟨-nać⟩ coś; ~ **about** ruszać się (*z miejsca na miejsce*); *pogłoska itp.*: rozchodzić ⟨-zejść⟩ się; ~ **ahead of** wyprzedzać ⟨-dzić⟩ (*A*); ~ **along** iść naprzód; dawać sobie radę (**with** *z I*); być w dobrych stosunkach (**with** *z I*); ~ **at** zbliżać się do (*G*), dosięgnąć ⟨-gać⟩; **what is she getting at?** o co jej chodzi?; ~ **away** uciekać ⟨-ciec⟩; odchodzić ⟨odejść⟩; ~ **away with** wychodzić ⟨wyjść⟩ obronną ręką z (*G*); ~ **back** wracać ⟨wrócić⟩; *coś* odzyskiwać ⟨-kać⟩; ~ **in** wchodzić ⟨wejść⟩, dostawać się (do *G*); wsiadać ⟨wsiąść⟩ do (*G*); ~ **off** wysiadać ⟨-siąść⟩ z (*G*); wychodzić ⟨wyjść⟩ obronną ręką (**with** *z I*); *coś* zdejmować ⟨zdjąć⟩; ~ **on** wsiadać ⟨wsiąść⟩; → **get along**; ~ **out** wychodzić ⟨wyjść⟩ (**of** *z G*); wysiadać ⟨-siąść⟩ (**of** *z G*); wydostawać ⟨-tać⟩ się; ~ **over s.th.** dochodzić ⟨dojść⟩ do siebie po (*L*); ~ **to** dochodzić ⟨dojść⟩ do (*G*); ~ **together** zbierać ⟨zebrać⟩ się; ~ **up** wstawać ⟨-tać⟩; '~·a·way u-cieczka *f*, zbiegnięcie *n*; ~ **car** samochód *m* dla uciekających; '~·up *dziwaczne ubranie n*

gey·ser ['gaɪzə] gejzer *m*; ['giːzə] *Brt.* przepływowy grzejnik *m* wody

ghast·ly ['gɑːstlɪ] (**-ier, -iest**) okropny, straszny; *wygląd itp.*: upiorny

gher·kin ['gɜːkɪn] ogórek *m* konserwowy, korniszon *m*

ghost [ɡəʊst] duch *m*; '~·ly (**-ier, -iest**) upiorny

GI [dʒiː 'aɪ] (*żołnierz amerykański*)

gi·ant ['dʒaɪənt] **1.** gigant *m*; olbrzym *m*; **2.** gigantyczny

gib·ber·ish ['dʒɪbərɪʃ] bełkot *m*

gib·bet ['dʒɪbɪt] szubienica *f*

gibe [dʒaɪb] **1.** szydzić, drwić (**at** *z G*); **2.** szyderstwo *n*

gib·lets ['dʒɪblɪts] *pl.* podroby *pl.* drobiowe

gid·di·ness ['gɪdɪnɪs] *med.* zawroty *pl.* głowy; ~·dy ['gɪdɪ] (**-ier, -iest**) wysokość *itp.*: przyprawiający o zawrót głowy; **I feel ~dy** w głowie mi się kręci

gift [gɪft] dar *m*; talent *m*; '~·ed utalentowany

gig [gɪg] *mus.* F występ *m*, koncert *m*

gi·gan·tic [dʒaɪˈɡæntɪk] (**~ally**) gigantyczny, olbrzymi

gig·gle ['gɪgl] **1.** ⟨za⟩chichotać; **2.** chichot *m*

gild [gɪld] pozłacać, złocić

gill [gɪl] *zo.* skrzele *n*; *bot.* blaszka *f*

gim·mick ['gɪmɪk] F sztuczka *f*, trik *m*

gin [dʒɪn] dżin *m*, jałowcówka *f*

gin·ger ['dʒɪndʒə] **1.** imbir *m*; **2.** rudy, czerwony; '~·bread piernik *m*; '~·ly ostrożnie

gip·sy ['dʒɪpsɪ] Cygan(ka *f*) *m*

gi·raffe [dʒɪˈrɑːf] *zo.* (*pl.* **-raffes, -raffe**) żyrafa *f*

gir·der ['ɡɜːdə] *tech.* dźwigar *m*

gir·dle ['ɡɜːdl] pas *m* elastyczny

girl [ɡɜːl] dziewczyna *f*, dziewczynka *f*; '~·friend dziewczyna *f*, sympatia *f*; ~ **'guide** *Brt.* harcerka *f*; ~·hood ['ɡɜːlhʊd] lata *pl.* dziewczęce; młodość *f*; '~·ish dziewczęcy; ~ **'scout** *Am.* harcerka *f*

gi·ro ['dʒaɪrəʊ] *Brt.* pocztowy system *m* przelewowy; '~ **ac·count** *Brt.* pocztowy rachunek *m* rozliczeniowy; '~ **cheque** *Brt.* czek *m* przelewowy

girth [ɡɜːθ] obwód *m*; popręg *m*

gist [dʒɪst] sedno *n*, jądro *n*

give [ɡɪv] (**gave, given**) dawać ⟨dać⟩; *jako podarek* ⟨po⟩darować; *tytuł, prawo itp.* nadawać ⟨-dać⟩; *życie, pomoc* ofiarowywać ⟨-ować⟩; *pracę domową* zadawać ⟨-dać⟩; *pomoc, odpowiedź itp.* udzielać ⟨-lić⟩; *dotację itp.* przyznawać ⟨-nać⟩; *wykład* wygłaszać ⟨-łosić⟩; *radość* przysparzać ⟨-porzyć⟩; *sztukę* wystawiać ⟨-wić⟩; *pozdrowienia* przekazywać ⟨-zać⟩; ~ **her my love** przekaż jej moje serdeczne pozdrowienia; ~ **birth to** wydawać ⟨-dać⟩ (*A*) na świat; ~ **s.o. to understand that** dać komuś do zrozumienia, że; ~ **way** ustępować ⟨-tąpić⟩, *Brt. mot.* ustąpić pierwszeństwa przejazdu; ~ **away** oddawać ⟨-dać⟩; rozdawać ⟨-dać⟩; *kogoś* zdradzać ⟨-dzić⟩; **~ back** zwracać ⟨zwrócić⟩; **~ in** *podanie itp.* składać ⟨złożyć⟩; **pracę**, *itp.* oddawać ⟨-dać⟩; poddawać ⟨-dać⟩ się; ustępować ⟨-tąpić⟩; **~ off** *zapach itp.* wydzielać ⟨-lić⟩; wydobywać ⟨-być⟩ się; **~ on(to)** wychodzić na (A); **~ out** rozdawać ⟨-dać⟩; wydawać ⟨-dać⟩; kończyć się; wyczerpywać ⟨-pać⟩ się; *zwł. Brt.* ogłaszać ⟨-łosić⟩; *silnik itp.*: F nawalać ⟨-lić⟩; **~ up** ⟨z⟩rezygnować, rzucać ⟨-cić⟩; poddawać ⟨-dać⟩ się; przestawać ⟨-tać⟩; *kogoś* wydawać ⟨-dać⟩; **~ o.s. up** oddawać się (**to the police** w ręce policji); **~-and-take** [ɡɪvənˈteɪk] wzajemne ustępstwa *pl.*, kompromis *m*; **giv·en** [ˈɡɪvn] **1.** *p.p. od* **give**; **2. be ~ to** mieć skłonności do (G); **~-en name** *zwł. Am.* imię *n*

gla·cial [ˈɡleɪsjəl] lodowcowy; *fig.* lodowaty

gla·ci·er [ˈɡlæsjə] lodowiec *m*

glad [ɡlæd] (**-dd-**) szczęśliwy, zadowolony; **be ~ of** być wdzięcznym za (A); **~·ly** za radością, z przyjemnością

glam·o(u)r [ˈɡlæmə] urok *m*, splendor *m*, świetność *f*; **~ous** [ˈɡlæmərəs] świetny, urokliwy, czarujący

glance [ɡlɑːns] **1.** spojrzenie *n*, rzut *m* okiem (**at** na A); **at a ~** od razu; **2.** rzucać ⟨-cić⟩ okiem, spojrzeć (**at** na A)

gland [ɡlænd] *anat.* gruczoł *m*

glare [ɡleə] **1.** ⟨za⟩świecić jaskrawo, oślepiać ⟨-pić⟩; być bardzo widocznym; **~ at s.o.** wpatrywać się ze wściekłością w kogoś; **2.** jaskrawe światło *n*; wściekłe spojrzenie *n*

glass [ɡlɑːs] **1.** szkło *n*; szklanka *f*; kieliszek *m*; lornetka *f*; *Brt.* F lustro *n*; *Brt.* barometr *m*; (**a pair of**) **~es** *pl.* okulary *pl.*; **2.** szklany, ze szkład; **3.** **~ in** *lub* **up** ⟨o⟩szklić; **~ case** witryna *f*, gablota *f*; **~·ful** szklanka *f*, kieliszek *m* (*miara*); **~·house** szklarnia *f*; **~·ware** wyroby *pl.* ze szkła; **~·y** (**-ier, -iest**) szklany, zamglisty

glaz|e [ɡleɪz] **1.** *v/t.* ⟨o⟩szklić; glazurować; *v/i. też* **~e over** oczy: szklić się; **2.** glazura *f*, szkliwo *n*; **~ier** [ˈɡleɪzjə] szklarz *m*

gleam [ɡliːm] **1.** blask *m*, odblask *m*; **2.** błyszczeć ⟨błysnąć⟩

glean [ɡliːn] *v/t.* ⟨z⟩gromadzić; *v/i.* zbierać ⟨zebrać⟩ kłosy

glee [ɡliː] radość *f*; **~·ful** radosny, szczęśliwy

glen [ɡlen] (głęboka)dolina *f*

glib [ɡlɪb] (**-bb-**) wymowny, wygadany; natychmiastowy

glide [ɡlaɪd] **1.** ⟨po⟩szybować; sunąć, ślizgać się; **2.** *aviat.* szybowanie *n*, lot *m* ślizgowy; ślizg *m*; **'glid·er** *aviat.* szybowiec *m*; **'glid·ing** *aviat.* szybownictwo *n*

glim·mer [ˈɡlɪmə] **1.** ⟨za⟩migotać; **2.** migotanie *n*

glimpse [ɡlɪmps] **1.** ujrzeć na chwilę; **2.** przelotne spojrzenie *n*

glint [ɡlɪnt] **1.** ⟨za⟩skrzyć się; **2.** skrzenie *n* się; iskierka *f*

glis·ten [ˈɡlɪsn] ⟨za⟩skrzyć się

glit·ter [ˈɡlɪtə] **1.** ⟨za⟩skrzyć się; ⟨za⟩migotać; **2.** skrzenie *n* się; migotanie *n*

gloat [ɡləʊt]: **~ over** cieszyć się, cieszyć się (*złośliwie lub ukradkiem*) (A); **'~·ing** cieszący się, zadowolony

glo·bal [ˈɡləʊbl] globalny, światowy, ogólnoświatowy; **~ 'warm·ing** ogrzewanie *n* atmosfery ziemskiej

globe [ɡləʊb] kula *f*; kula *f* ziemska; globus *m*

gloom [ɡluːm] mrok *m*; ciemność *f*; ponurość *f*, przygnębienie *n*; **'~·y** (**-ier, -iest**) mroczny; ponury, przygnębiający

glo|·ri·fy [ˈɡlɔːrɪfaɪ] gloryfikować, sławić; **~·ri·ous** [ˈɡlɔːrɪəs] wspaniały, znakomity; **~·ry** [ˈɡlɔːrɪ] chwała *f*, świetność *f*

gloss [ɡlɒs] **1.** połysk *m*; *ling.* glosa *f*; **2.** **~ over** przymykać się nad (*I*)

glos·sa·ry [ˈɡlɒsərɪ] słowniczek *m*

gloss·y [ˈɡlɒsɪ] (**-ier, -iest**) połyskliwy, błyszczący

glove [ɡlʌv] rękawiczka *f*; **it fits like a ~** leży jak ulał; **'~ com·part·ment** *mot.* schowek *m*

glow [ɡləʊ] **1.** żarzyć się; *fig.* promieniować, płonąć; **2.** żar *m*; promieniowanie *n*, płonięcie *n*

glow·er [ˈɡlaʊə] patrzeć się ze złością

'glow-worm *zo.* świetlik *m*

glu·cose [ˈɡluːkəʊs] glukoza *f*

glue [ɡluː] **1.** klej *m*; **2.** ⟨s⟩kleić

glum [ɡlʌm] (**-mm-**) przygnębiony

glut·ton [ˈɡlʌtn]: *fig.* **be a ~ for s.th.** strasznie coś lubić; **'~·ous** żarłoczny

GMT [dʒiː em ˈtiː] *skrót:* **Greenwich**

Mean Time ['grenɪdʒ -] czas *m* Greenwich

gnarled [nɑːld] sękaty; powykrzywiany

gnash [næʃ] zgrzytać (*I*)

gnat [næt] *zo.* komar *m*

gnaw [nɔː] gryźć, wygryzać ⟨-ryźć⟩; *fig.* trapić

gnome [nəʊm] gnom *m*; krasnal *m* ogrodowy

go [gəʊ] 1. (***went, gone***) iść ⟨pójść⟩, ⟨po⟩jechać (**to** do *G*); odchodzić ⟨odejść⟩, odjeżdżać ⟨-jechać⟩; *ulica:* ⟨po⟩prowadzić (**to** do *G*), rozciągać się; *autobus:* kursować, jeździć; *tech.* poruszać się, funkcjonować; *czas itp.:* przechodzić ⟨przejść⟩, upływać ⟨-łynąć⟩; *kapelusz:* pasować (**with** do *G*); wchodzić ⟨wejść⟩; *żarówka itp.:* zepsuć się, nie działać; (*do szkoły*) uczęszczać; *praca itp.:* iść ⟨pójść⟩, wypadać; stawać się (**~ *mad***, **~ *blind***); **be ~ing to do s.th.** zabierać się do zrobienia czegoś, mieć coś zrobić; **~ *shares*** ⟨po⟩dzielić się; **~ *swimming*** iść popływać; **it is ~ing to rain** będzie padało; **I must be ~ing** muszę już iść; **~ *for a walk*** iść na spacer; **~ *to bed*** iść do łóżka; **~ *to school*** chodzić do szkoły; **~ *to see*** iść z wizytą; **let ~** puszczać ⟨puścić⟩; **~ *after*** iść za (*I*); starać się o (*A*); **~ *ahead*** udawać ⟨udać⟩ się naprzód; iść ⟨pójść⟩ naprzód; **~ *ahead with*** zaczynać ⟨-cząć⟩ (*A*), przystępować ⟨-tąpić⟩ do (*G*); **~ *at*** zabierać ⟨-brać⟩ się do (*G*); **~ *away*** odchodzić ⟨odejść⟩, odjeżdżać ⟨-jechać⟩; **~ *between*** pośredniczyć między (*I*); **~ *by*** przejeżdżać ⟨-jechać⟩, przechodzić ⟨-ejść⟩; upływać ⟨-łynąć⟩; *fig.* kierować się, powodować się; **~ *down*** spadać ⟨-paść⟩ zachodzić ⟨zajść⟩; **~ *for*** udawać ⟨udać⟩ się po (*A*); stosować się do (*G*); **~ *in*** wchodzić ⟨wejść⟩; **~ *in for an examination*** przystępować ⟨-tąpić⟩ do egzaminu; **~ *off*** wybuchać ⟨-chnąć⟩; uruchamiać ⟨-chomić⟩ się; **~ *on*** kontynuować (***doing*** robienie); nadal robić; mieć miejsce, dziać się; **~ *out*** wychodzić ⟨wyjść⟩; chodzić (**with** z *I*); *światło:* ⟨z⟩gasnąć; **~ *through*** przechodzić (przez *A*), doświadczać; zużyć, wyczerpać; **~ *up*** wznosić ⟨-nieść⟩ się; iść ⟨pójść⟩ do góry; **~ *without*** obywać ⟨-być⟩ się; 2. (*pl.* ***goes***) F witalność *f*, dynamizm *m*; *zwł.*

Brt. F próba *f*; **it's my ~** *zwł. Brt.* F teraz moja kolej; **on the ~** w ruchu; **in one ~** za jednym razem; **have a ~ at** *Brt.* F spróbować (*G*)

goad [gəʊd] *fig.* podjudzać ⟨-dzić⟩

'go-a·head[1]: **get the ~** otrzymywać ⟨-mać⟩ zielone światło; **give s.o. the ~** zapalać ⟨-lić⟩ komuś zielone światło

'go-a·head[2] F postępowy, przodujący

goal [gəʊl] cel *m* (*też fig.*); (*w sporcie*) bramka *f*; **score a ~** zdobywać ⟨-być⟩ bramkę; **consolation ~** bramka *f* honorowa; **own ~** bramka *f* samobójcza; **'~·area** *sport:* pole *n* bramkowe; **~ie** F ['gəʊlɪ], **'~·keep·er** *sport:* bramkarz *m*; **~ kick** (*w piłce nożnej*) wybicie *n* piłki od bramki; **~ line** (*w sporcie*) linia *f* bramkowa; **'~·post** (*w sporcie*) słupek *m*

goat [gəʊt] *zo.* koza *f*; kozioł *m*

gob·ble ['gɒbl]: *zw.* **~ up** pochłaniać ⟨-łonąć⟩

'go-be·tween pośrednik *m* (-iczka *f*)

gob·lin ['gɒblɪn] chochlik *m*, diablik *m*

god [gɒd], *rel.* 2 Bóg *m*; *fig.* bożek *m*; **'~·child** (*pl.* **-children**) chrześniak *m*; **~·dess** ['gɒdɪs] bogini *f*; **'~·fa·ther** ojciec *m* chrzestny (*też fig.*); **'~·for·sak·en** *pej.* zapomniany, porzucony; **'~·less** bezbożny; **'~·like** podobny bogom; **'~·moth·er** matka *f* chrzestna; **'~·pa·rent** rodzic *m* chrzestny; **'~·send** dar *m* niebios

gog·gle ['gɒgl] gapić się; **'~ box** *Brt.* F *TV* telewizja *f*; **'~s** *pl.* gogle *pl.*

go·ings-on [gəʊɪŋz'ɒn] F *pl.* wydarzenia *pl.*

gold [gəʊld] 1. złoto *n*; 2. złoty; **'~·en** *zw. fig.* ['gəʊldən] złoty, złocisty; **'~·finch** *zo.* szczygieł *m*; **'~·fish** *zo.* złota rybka *f*; **'~·smith** złotnik *m*

golf [gɒlf] 1. golf *m*; *attr.* golfowy; 2. ⟨za-, po⟩grać w golfa; **'~ club** kij *m* golfowy; klub *m* golfowy; **'~ course**, **'~ links** *pl. lub sg.* pole *n* golfowe

gon·do·la ['gɒndələ] gondola *f*

gone [gɒn] 1. *p.p. od* **go** 1; 2. *adj.* miniony; zużyty; F martwy; F upity

good [gʊd] 1. (***better, best***) dobry; grzeczny; **~ at** dobry w (*L*); **real ~** F naprawdę dobry; 2. dobro *n*; dobroć *f*; **for ~** na dobre; **~·bye** [gʊd'baɪ] 1. **wish s.o. ~bye**, **say ~bye to s.o.** mówić ⟨powiedzieć⟩ komuś do widzenia; 2. *int.* do widzenia!; 2 **'Fri·day** Wielki

Piątek *m*; ~'**hu·mo(u)red** dobrze u-
sposobiony; dobroduszny; ~'**look·ing**
przystojny, atrakcyjny; ~'**natured**
o dobrym usposobieniu; '~**ness** dobro; *thank* ~*ness!* dzięki Bogu!; (*my*)
~*ness!*, ~*ness gracious!* Boże mój!;
for ~*ness' sake* na litość Boską!;
~*ness knows* Bóg jeden wie

goods [gʊdz] *econ.*, *pl.* towary *pl.*

good'will dobra wola *f*; *econ.* wartość *f*
przedsiębiorstwa

good·y ['gʊdɪ] F cukierek *m*

goose [guːs] *zo.* (*pl.* **geese**) gęś *f*

goose·ber·ry ['gʊzbərɪ] *bot.* agrest *m*

goose|·flesh ['guːsfleʃ], '~**pim·ples** *pl.*
gęsia skórka *f*

GOP [dʒiː əʊ 'piː] *skrót:* **Grand Old
Party** Partia Republikańska (*w USA*)

go·pher ['gəʊfə] *zo.* suseł *m* amerykański; wiewiórka *f ziemna*

gore [gɔː] brać na rogi

gorge [gɔːdʒ] **1.** wąwóz *m*; gardziel *f*;
2. pochłaniać ⟨-łonąć⟩, napychać
⟨-pchać⟩ (się)

gor·geous ['gɔːdʒəs] wspaniały

go·ril·la [gə'rɪlə] *zo.* goryl *m*

gor·y ['gɔːrɪ] F (*-ier, -iest*) zakrwawio-
ny; *fig.* krwawy

gosh [gɒʃ] *int.* F *by* ~ o Boże!

gos·ling ['gɒzlɪŋ] *zo.* gąsiątko *n*

go-slow [gəʊ'sləʊ] *Brt. econ.* strajk *m*
włoski (*w którym pracownicy pracują
bardzo mało wydajnie*)

Gos·pel ['gɒspəl] *rel.* ewangelia *f*

gos·sa·mer ['gɒsəmə] nić *f* pajęcza,
pajęczyna *f*; *attr.* bardzo cienki

gos·sip ['gɒsɪp] **1.** plotka *f*; plotkarz *m*
(-arka *f*); **2.** ⟨po⟩plotkować; '~·**y** plot-
karski; *ktoś* rozplotkowany

got [gɒt] *pret. i p.p. od* **get**

Goth·ic ['gɒθɪk] **1.** gotyk *m*; **2.** *adj.* go-
tycki; ~ *novel* powieść *f* gotycka

got·ten ['gɒtn] *Am. p.p. od* **get**

gourd [gʊəd] *bot.* tykwa *f*

gout [gaʊt] *med.* gościec *m*

gov·ern ['gʌvn] *v/t.* rządzić; kierować;
v/i. sprawować władzę; '~·**ess** guwer-
nantka *f*; '~·**ment** rząd *m*; rządze-
nie *n*; *attr.* rządowy; ~·**or** ['gʌvənə] gu-
bernator *m*; zarządca *m*; F *ojciec*, *szef*:
stary *m*

gown [gaʊn] suknia *f*; toga *f*; szlafrok *m*

GP [dʒiː 'piː] *skrót:* **general practi-
tioner** *jakby:* lekarz *m* (-arka *f*) ogólny

(-a), internista *m* (-tka *f*)

GPO [dʒiː piː 'əʊ] *skrót:* **General
Post Office** poczta *f* główna

grab [græb] **1.** (*-bb-*) ⟨s⟩chwytać, ⟨z⟩ła-
pać; **2.** złapanie *n*, schwytanie *n*; *tech.*
chwytak *m*

grace [greɪs] **1.** gracja *f*, wdzięk *m*; przy-
zwoitość *f*; *econ.* ulga *f*, prolongata *f*;
rel. łaska *f*; *rel.* modlitwa *f* (*przy stole*);
2. zaszczycać ⟨-cić⟩; '~·**ful** wdzięczny;
pełen wdzięku; '~·**less** niedzięczny

gra·cious ['greɪʃəs] łaskawy; miło-
sierny

gra·da·tion [grə'deɪʃn] stopniowanie *n*

grade [greɪd] **1.** ranga *f*; jakość *f*; gatunek *m*; → **gradient**; *Am.* klasa (*w sys-
temie edukacyjnym*) *f*; *zwł. Am.* stopień
m, ocena *f*; **2.** ⟨po⟩sortować; oceniać
⟨-nić⟩; ~ **cross·ing** *Am.* jednopoziomowy przejazd *m* kolejowy; ~ **school**
Am. szkoła *f* podstawowa

gra·di·ent ['greɪdjənt] *rail. itp.* nachylenie *n*, pochylenie *n*

grad·u|·al ['grædjʊəl] stopniowy;
'~·**al·ly** stopniowo; ~·**ate 1.** ['grædjʊət]
univ. absolwent(ka *f*) *m* (*szkoły
wyższej*); *Am.* absolwent(ka *f*) *m*;
2. ['grædjʊeɪt] skalować; stopniować;
univ. studiować (*from* na L); otrzymywać ⟨-mać⟩ dyplom uniwersytecki
(*from* na L); *Am.* ⟨s⟩kończyć; ~·**a·tion**
[grædʒʊ'eɪʃn] podziałka *f*, skala *f*; *univ.*
nadawanie *n* stopnia naukowego; *Am.*
zakończenie *n*

graf·fi·ti [grə'fiːtɪ] *pl.* graffiti *pl.*, ~ba-
zgroły *pl.* na ścianach

graft [grɑːft] **1.** *med.* przeszczep *m*;
agr. szczep *m*; **2.** *med.* przeszczepiać
⟨-pić⟩, ⟨prze⟩transplantować; *agr.* ⟨za⟩-
szczepić

grain [greɪn] ziarno *n*; zboże *n*; ziarenko
n; (*w drewnie*) włókno *n*; rysunek *m*
słojów; *go against the* ~ *fig.* postępować ⟨-tąpić⟩ niezgodnie z zasadami

gram [græm] gram *m*

gram·mar ['græmə] gramatyka *f*;
'~ **school** *Brt. jakby:* liceum *n* (*ogól-
nokształcące*); *Am. jakby:* szkoła *f* podstawowa

gram·mat·i·cal [grə'mætɪkl] gramatyczny

gramme [græm] gram *m*

gra·na·ry ['grænərɪ] spichlerz *m*

grand [grænd] **1.** *fig.* wspaniały, znakomity; wyniosły; dostojny; ♀ *Old Party* Partia *f* Republikańska (*USA*), (*pl. grand*) F (*tysiąc dolarów lub funtów*) patyk *m*

grand·child ['grændʃaild] (*pl. -children*) wnuk *m*; ~·daugh·ter ['grændɔ:tə] wnuczka *f*

gran·deur ['grændʒə] wzniosłość *f*, dostojeństwo *n*; wielkość *f*

grand·fa·ther ['grændfɑ:ðə] dziadek *m*

gran·di·ose ['grændiəus] wspaniały

grand·moth·er ['grænmʌðə] babcia *f*; ~·par·ents ['grænpeərənts] *pl.* dziadkowie *pl.*; ~·son ['grænsʌn] wnuk *m*

grand·stand ['grændstænd] (*w sporcie*) trybuna *f* (*główna*)

gran·ny ['grænı] F babcia *f*

grant [grɑ:nt] 1. przyznawać ⟨-znać⟩; uznawać ⟨-nać⟩; *pozwolenia* udzielać ⟨-lić⟩; nadawać ⟨-dać⟩; *prośbę* spełniać ⟨-nić⟩; *take s.th. for ~ed* uznawać coś za oczywiste; 2. stypendium *n*; grant *m*; dotacja *f*

gran|u·lat·ed ['grænjuleitid] granulowany; *~ulated sugar* cukier *m* kryształ; ~·ule ['grænju:l] granulka *f*, ziarno *n*

grape [greip] winogrono *n*; winorośl *f*; '~·fruit grapefruit *lub* grejpfrut *m*; '~·vine winorośl *f*

graph [græf] graf *m*, wykres *m*; ~·ic ['græfik] (*-ally*) graficzny; *opis* plastyczny; ~·ic arts *pl.* grafika *f*; ~·ic artist artysta *m* grafik; '·ics *pl.* grafika *f*

grap·ple ['græpl]: ~ with walczyć z (*I*), *fig.* borykać się z (*I*)

grasp [grɑ:sp] 1. ⟨s⟩chwytać, ⟨z⟩łapać; *fig.* ⟨z⟩rozumieć,⟨z⟩łapać; ⟨z⟩łapać; zasięg *m*; *fig.* pojmowanie *n*

grass [grɑ:s] trawa *f*; *sl.* (*marihuana*) trawka *f*; ~·hop·per ['grɑ:shɒpə] *zo.* pasikonik *m*; ~ 'wid·ow słomiana wdowa *f*; ~ 'wid·ow·er słomiany wdowiec *m*; 'gras·sy (*-ier, -iest*) trawiasty

grate [greit] 1. krata *f*; *kominowy* ruszt *m*; 2. ⟨u⟩trzeć; ⟨za⟩zgrzytać, ⟨za⟩skrzypieć; ~ on s.o.'s nerves działać komuś na nerwy

grate·ful ['greitfl] wdzięczny

grat·er ['greitə] tarka *f*

grat·i|·fi·ca·tion [grætıfı'keıʃn] wynagrodzenie *n*, gratyfikacja *f*; satysfakcja *f*; ~·fy ['grætıfaı] dawać ⟨dać⟩ satysfakcję; ⟨u⟩cieszyć

grat·ing[1] ['greitın] zgrzytający, zgrzytliwy

grat·ing[2] ['greitın] krata *f*, okratowanie *n*

grat·i·tude ['grætıtju:d] wdzięczność *f*

gra·tu·i|·tous [grə'tju:ıtəs] zbędny, niepotrzebny; dobrowolny; ~·ty [grə'tju:ətı] napiwek *m*

grave[1] [greiv] (*-r, -st*) poważny; stateczny

grave[2] [greiv] grób *m*; '~·dig·ger grabarz *m*

grav·el ['grævl] 1. żwir *m*; 2. (*zwł. Brt. -ll-*) ⟨po⟩żwirować

'grave|·stone nagrobek *m*, kamień *m* nagrobny; '~·yard cmentarz *m*

grav·i·ta·tion [grævı'teıʃn] *phys.* grawitacja *f*, siła *f* ciężkości

grav·i·ty ['grævətı] siła *f* ciężkości; powaga *f*

gra·vy ['greıvı] sos *m* (*z pieczeni*)

gray [greı] *zwł. Am.* → **grey**

graze[1] [greız] *v/t.* pasać ⟨paść⟩; *v/i.* paść się

graze[2] [greız] 1. ocierać ⟨otrzeć⟩ (się); 2. otarcie *n*

grease 1. [gri:s] tłuszcz *m*; *tech.* smar *m*; 2. [gri:z] natłuszczać ⟨-łuścić⟩; *tech.* ⟨na⟩smarować

greas·y ['gri:zı] (*-ier, -iest*) tłusty, zatłuszczony; zabrudzony smarem

great [greit] wielki; F wspaniały, super; pra...

Great Brit·ain [greit'britn] Wielka Brytania *f*

Great 'Dane *zo.* dog *m*

great·-'grand·child prawnuk *m*; ~·'grand·par·ents *pl.* pradziadkowie *pl.*

'great|·ly wielce, bardzo; '~·ness wielkość *f*

Greece [gri:s] Grecja *f*

greed [gri:d] chciwość *f*, zachłanność *f*; '~·y (*-ier, -iest*) chciwy; zachłanny (*for* na *A*)

Greek [gri:k] 1. grecki; 2. Grek *m*, Greczynka *f*; *ling.* język *m* grecki

green [gri:n] 1. zielony; *fig.* zielony, niedojrzały; 2. zieleń *f*; teren *m* zielony; ~s *pl.* warzywa *pl.* (*zielone*); ~ belt *zwł. Brt.* pas *m* zieleni; ~ 'card *Am.* zielona karta *f* (*pozwalająca pracować*); '~·gro·cer *zwł. Brt.* sprzedawca *m*

(-czyni *f*) warzyw i owoców; sklep *m* warzywny; '**~·horn** żółtodziób *m*; '**~·house** cieplarnia *f*, szklarnia *f*; '**~·house ef·fect** efekt *m* cieplarniany; '**~·ish** zielonawy, zielonkawy

Green·land Grenlandia *f*

greet [griːt] ⟨po⟩witać; '**~·ing** powitanie *n*; pozdrowienie *n*; **~ings** *pl.* pozdrowienia *pl.*

gre·nade *mil.* [grɪˈneɪd] granat *m*

grew [gruː] *pret. od* **grow**

grey [greɪ] **1.** szary; popielaty; *włosy:* siwy; szpakowaty; **2.** szarość *f*; szary *lub* popielaty kolor *m*; **3.** ⟨z⟩szarzeć; ⟨po⟩siwieć; '**~·hound** *zo.* chart *m*

grid [grɪd] krata *f*; *electr. itp.* sieć *f*; *kartograficzna* siatka *f*; '**~·i·ron** ruszt *m*

grief [griːf] zmartwienie *n*

griev|**·ance** [ˈgriːvns] skarga *f*; zażalenie *n*; **~e** [griːv] *v/t.* martwić; *v/i.* ⟨z⟩martwić się; **~e for** żałować (*G*); **~·ous** [ˈgriːvəs] poważny

grill [grɪl] **1.** ⟨u⟩piec na grillu; **2.** grill *m*; ruszt *m*; pieczeń *f* z grilla

grim [grɪm] (**-mm-**) ponury; zacięty; F okropny

gri·mace [grɪˈmeɪs] **1.** grymas *m*; **2.** ⟨z⟩robić grymas

grime [graɪm] brud *m*; '**grim·y** (**-ier, -iest**) zabrudzony

grin [grɪn] **1.** uśmiech *m* (*szyderczy*); **2.** (**-nn-**) uśmiechać ⟨-chnąć⟩ się (*szyderczo*)

grind [graɪnd] **1.** (**ground**) *v/t.* ⟨ze⟩mleć *lub* ⟨z⟩mielić; rozdrabniać ⟨-drobnić⟩; *noże itp.* ⟨na⟩ostrzyć; *soczewkę* ⟨o⟩szlifować; **~ one's teeth** ⟨za⟩zgrzytać zębami; *v/i.* harować; wkuwać ⟨-kuć⟩; **2.** harówka *f*; **the daily ~** codzienny znój *m*; '**~·er** szlifierz *m*; *tech.* szlifierka *f*; młynek *m*; '**~·stone** kamień *m* do ostrzenia

grip [grɪp] **1.** (**-pp-**) ⟨s⟩chwytać, ⟨z⟩łapać (*też fig.*); **2.** uścisk *m*; uchwyt *m*; rękojeść *f*; torba *f* podróżna; *fig.* władza *f*, moc *f*; **come to ~s (with s.th.)** zmierzyć się (z *I*)

gripes [graɪps] *pl.* kolka *f* (*jelitowa*)

gris·ly [ˈgrɪzlɪ] (**-ier, -iest**) koszmarny, makabryczny

gris·tle [ˈgrɪsl] chrząstka *f*

grit [grɪt] **1.** grys *m*, żwir *m*; *fig.* determinacja *f*; **2.** (**-tt-**): **~ one's teeth** zaciskać ⟨-snąć⟩ zęby

griz·zly (bear) *zo.* [ˈgrɪzlɪ (-)] *niedźwiedź:* grizzly *m*

groan [grəʊn] **1.** jęczeć ⟨jęknąć⟩; **2.** jęk *m*

gro·cer [ˈgrəʊsə] handlarz *m* (-rka *f*) artykułami spożywczymi; **~·ies** [ˈgrəʊsə-rɪz] *pl.* artykuły *pl.* spożywcze; **~·y** [ˈgrəʊsərɪ] sklep *m* z artykułami spożywczymi

grog·gy [ˈgrɒgɪ] F (**-ier, -iest**) zamroczony, oszołomiony

groin *anat.* [grɔɪn] pachwina *f*

groom [grʊm] **1.** pan *m* młody; stajenny *m*; koniuszy *m*; **2.** *konie* oporządzać ⟨-dzić⟩, doglądać; **well-groomed** wypielęgnowany, zadbany

groove [gruːv] rowek *m*; żłobek *m*; bruzda *f*; '**groov·y** *sl.* (**-ier, -iest**) *przest.* bombowy, fajowy

grope [grəʊp] ⟨po⟩szukać (po omacku); *sl. dziewczynę* obmacywać ⟨-cać⟩

gross [grəʊs] **1.** *econ.* brutto; gruby, zwalisty; toporny; rażący; ordynarny; **2.** (*12 tuzinów*) gros *m*

gro·tesque [grəʊˈtesk] groteskowy

ground[1] [graʊnd] **1.** *pret. i p.p. od* **grind** 1; **2.** mielony; **~ meat** mięso *n* mielone

ground[2] [graʊnd] **1.** ziemia *f*; ląd *m*; teren *m*, miejsce *n*; (*w sporcie*) boisko *n*; tło *n*; *Am. electr.* uziemienie *n*; *fig.* motyw *m*, powód *m*; **~s** *pl.* osad *m*, fusy *pl.*; działka *f* (*gruntu*), teren *m*, park *m*; **on the ~(s)** of na podstawie (*G*); **hold** *lub* **stand one's ~** dotrzymywać ⟨-mać⟩ pola; **2.** *naut.* osiadać ⟨osiąść⟩ na mieliźnie; *Am. electr.* uziemiać ⟨-mić⟩; *fig.* opierać ⟨oprzeć⟩ się, polegać ⟨-lec⟩; '**~ crew** *aviat.* personel *m* naziemny; '**~ floor** *zwł. Brt.* parter *m*; '**~ forc·es** *pl. mil.* siły *pl.* lądowe; '**~·hog** *zo.* świstak *m* amerykański; '**~·ing** *Am. electr.* uziemienie *n*, podstawy *pl.*; '**~·less** bezpodstawny; '**~·nut** *Brt. bot.* orzeszek *m* ziemny; '**~·s·man** (*pl.* **-men**) (*w sporcie*) dozorca *m* obiektu sportowego; '**~ staff** *Brt. aviat.* personel *m* naziemny; '**~ sta·tion** (*w astronautyce*) stacja *f* naziemna; '**~·work** *fig.* fundament *m*

group [gruːp] **1.** grupa *f*; **2.** ⟨z⟩grupować (się)

group·ie [ˈgruːpɪ] F *natrętna* fanka *f*

group·ing [ˈgruːpɪŋ] zgrupowanie *n*

grove [grəʊv] gaj *m*, zagajnik *m*

grov·el ['grɒvl] (*zwł. Brt.* **-ll-** , *Am.* **-l-**) płaszczyć się, upokarzać ⟨-korzyć⟩ się

grow [grəʊ] (**grew, grown**) *v/i.* ⟨wy-, u⟩rosnąć; wzrastać ⟨-rosnąć⟩; **~ up** dorastać ⟨-rosnąć⟩; *v/t. bot.* ⟨wy⟩hodować; uprawiać; **~ a beard** zapuszczać ⟨-puścić⟩ brodę; **'~·er** hodowca *m*

growl [graʊl] ⟨za⟩warczeć

grown [grəʊn] **1.** *p.p. od* **grow**; **2.** *adj.* dorosły; **~-up 1.** [grəʊn'ʌp] dorosły; **2.** ['grəʊnʌp] F dorosły *m* (-ła *f*)

growth [grəʊθ] wzrost *m*, rozrost *m*; *fig.* przyrost *m*; *med.* narośl *f*

grub [grʌb] **1.** *zo.* larwa *f*; F żarcie *n*; **2.** (**-bb-**) ⟨wy⟩ryć, ⟨wy⟩grzebać; **'~·by** (**-ier, -iest**) zabrudzony

grudge [grʌdʒ] **1.** ⟨po⟩żałować (**s.o. s.th.** komuś czegoś); **2.** żal *m*, uraza *f*; **'grudg·ing·ly** niechętnie

gru·el [grʊəl] kleik *m*, papka *f* (*z owsa*)

gruff [grʌf] szorstki, opryskliwy

grum·ble ['grʌmbl] **1.** marudzić, narzekać; **2.** marudzenie *n*, narzekanie *n*; **'~·r** *fig.* maruda *m lub f*

grump·y ['grʌmpɪ] F (**-ier, -iest**) marudny

grun·gy ['grʌndʒɪ] *Am. sl.* (**-ier, -iest**) zaniedbany; cuchnący; paskudny

grunt [grʌnt] **1.** chrząkać ⟨-knąć⟩; zrzędzić; **2.** chrząkanie *n*; zrzędzenie *n*

Gt *skrót pisany:* **Great** (*Gt Britain*)

guar·an|·tee [gærən'tiː] **1.** gwarancja *f*; *fig.* pewność *f*; **2.** ⟨za⟩gwarantować; ⟨po⟩ręczyć za (*A*); **~·tor** [gærən'tɔː] gwarant *m*, poręczyciel *m*; **~·ty** ['gærəntɪ] *jur.* gwarancja *f*, poręka *f*

guard [gɑːd] **1.** strażnik *m*, wartownik *m*; straż *f*, warta *f*; *Brt. rail.* konduktor(ka *f*) *m*; osłona *f*; garda *f*; **be on ~** trzymać straż; **be on (off) one's ~** nie mieć się na baczności; **2.** *v/t.* ⟨o⟩chronić, ⟨u⟩strzec (**from** przed *I*); *v/i.* ⟨u⟩chronić się, wystrzegać się; **'~·ed** ostrożny; **~·i·an** ['gɑːdjən] *jur.* kurator(ka *f*) *m*, opiekun(ka *f*) *m*; **'~·i·an·ship** *jur.* kuratela *f*, ochrona *f*

gue(r)·ril·la [gə'rɪlə] *mil.* partyzant(ka *f*) *m*; **~ 'war·fare** partyzantka *f*

guess [ges] **1.** zgadywać ⟨-dnąć⟩, odgadywać ⟨-dnąć⟩; *Am.* sądzić, mniemać; **2.** odgadnięcie *n*; **'~·work** zgadywanka *f*, domysły *pl.*

guest [gest] gość *m*; **'~·house** pensjonat *m*; **'~·room** pokój *m* gościnny

guf·faw [gʌ'fɔː] **1.** głośny, nieprzyjemny śmiech *m*; **2.** głośno, nieprzyjemnie roześmiać (się)

guid·ance ['gaɪdns] prowadzenie *n*, kierowanie *n*

guide [gaɪd] **1.** przewodnik *m* (-niczka *f*); (*książka*) przewodnik *m* (**to** po *L*); → **girl guide**; **2.** ⟨po⟩prowadzić; oprowadzać ⟨-dzić⟩; kierować (się); **~ book** (*książka*) przewodnik *m*; **~d 'tour** wycieczka *f* z przewodnikiem, oprowadzanie *n*; **'~·lines** pl. wytyczne *pl.* (**on** w sprawie *G*)

guild [gɪld] *hist.* cech *m*

guile·less ['gaɪllɪs] prostoduszny, ufny

guilt [gɪlt] wina *f*; **'~·less** niewinny; **'~·y** (**-ier, -iest**) winny; czujący się winnym

guin·ea pig ['gɪnɪ -] *zo.* świnka *f* morska

guise [gaɪz] *fig.* przebranie *n*, płaszczyk *m*

gui·tar [gɪ'tɑː] *mus.* gitara *f*

gulch [gʌlʃ] *zwł. Am.* głęboki wąwóz *m*

gulf [gʌlf] zatoka *f*; *fig.* przepaść *f*

gull [gʌl] *zo.* mewa *f*

gul·let [gʌlɪt] *anat.* przełyk *m*; gardło *n*

gulp [gʌlp] **1.** duży łyk *m*; **2.** często **~ down** łykać ⟨połknąć⟩

gum¹ [gʌm] *anat.:* zw. **~s** *pl.* dziąsła *pl.*

gum² [gʌm] **1.** guma *f*; klej *m*; guma *f* do żucia; żelatynka *f*; **2.** (**-mm-**) ⟨s⟩kleić

gun [gʌn] **1.** karabin *m*, strzelba *f*; działo *n*; pistolet *m*, rewolwer *m*; **2.** (**-nn-**): **~ down** zastrzelić; **'~·fight** *zwł. Am.* strzelanina *f*; **'~·fire** ogień *m* (*z broni palnej*); **~ li·cence** (*Am.:* **li·cense**) zezwolenie *n* na broń; **'~·man** (*pl.* **-men**) rewolwerowiec *m*; **'~·point: at ~ point** pod groźbą użycia broni; **'~·pow·der** proch *m* strzelniczy; **'~·run·ner** przemytnik *m* broni; **'~·run·ning** przemyt *m* broni; **'~·shot** strzał *m*; **within (out of) ~shot** w zasięgu (poza zasięgiem) strzału

gur·gle ['gɜːgl] **1.** gaworzyć; ⟨za⟩gulgotać; **2.** gaworzenie *n*; gulgotanie *n*

gush [gʌʃ] **1.** tryskać ⟨trysnąć⟩ (**from** z *G*); **2.** nagły wypływ *m*; wytrysk *m* (*też fig.*)

gust [gʌst] poryw *m* (*wiatru*), podmuch *m*

guts [gʌts] F pl. wnętrzności *pl.*; *fig.* odwaga *f*

gut·ter ['gʌtə] rynsztok *m* (*też fig.*); rynna *f*

guy [gaɪ] F facet *m*, gość *m*

guz·zle ['gʌzl] ⟨po⟩żreć; pochłaniać ⟨łonąć⟩

gym [dʒɪm] F ośrodek *m* odnowy biologicznej; fitness center *m*; → *gymnasium*; → *gymnastics*; ~·na·sium [dʒɪm'neɪzjəm] hala *f* sportowa; △ *nie*

gimnazjum; ~·nast ['dʒɪmnæst] gimnastyk *m* (-tyczka *f*); ~·nas·tics [dʒɪm'næstɪks] gimnastyka *f*

gy·n(a)e·col·o·gist [gaɪnɪ'kɒlədʒɪst] ginekolog *m*; ~·gy [gaɪnɪ'kɒlədʒɪ] ginekologia *f*

gyp·sy ['dʒɪpsɪ] *zwł. Am.* → *gipsy*

gy·rate [dʒaɪə'reɪt] ⟨za⟩kręcić się, ⟨za⟩wirować

H

H, h [eɪtʃ] H, h *n*

hab·er·dash·er ['hæbədæʃə] *Brt.* sprzedawca *m* artykułów pasmanteryjnych; *Am.* sprzedawca *m* odzieży męskiej; ~·y [hæbədæʃərɪ] *Brt.* pasmanteria *f*, *Am.* odzież *f* męska; *Am.* sklep *m* z odzieżą męską

hab·it ['hæbɪt] przyzwyczajenie *n*, zwyczaj *m*; habit *m*; *drink has become a* ~ *with him* uzależnił się od alkoholu

ha·bit·u·al [hə'bɪtjuəl] zwyczajowy; nałogowy

hack¹ [hæk] ⟨po⟩rąbać

hack² [hæk] pismak *m*

hack³ [hæk] szkapa *f*

hack·er ['hækə] *komp.* haker *m*, maniak *m* komputerowy

hack·neyed ['hæknɪd] wytarty, wyświechtany

had [hæd] *pret. i p.p. od* **have**

had·dock ['hædək] *zo.* (*pl. -dock*) *ryba:* łupacz *m*

h(a)e·mor·rhage ['heməridʒ] *med.* krwawienie *n*, krwotok *m*

hag [hæg] *fig.* jędza *f*, sekutnica *f*

hag·gard ['hægəd] wymizerowany, wynędzniały

hag·gle ['hægl] targować się

Hague: *the* ~ Haga *f*

hail [heɪl] 1. grad *m*; 2. *grad:* padać; '~·stone (*kulka*) grad *m*; '~·storm burza *f* gradowa

hair [heə] *pojedynczy* włos *m*; *zbior.* włosy *pl.*; '~·breadth = *hair's breadth*; '~·brush szczotka *f* do włosów; '~·cut strzyżenie *n*, obcięcie *n* włosów; ~·do (*pl. -dos*) F fryzura *f*; '~·dress·er fryzjer(ka *f*) *m*; '~·dri·er, '~·dry·er suszarka *f* do włosów; '~·grip *Brt.* klamra *f* do

włosów; '~·less bezwłosy; '~·pin spinka *f* do włosów; ~·pin 'bend ostry zakręt *m*; ~·rais·ing ['heəreɪzɪŋ] podnoszący włosy na głowie; '~'s breadth; *by a* ~'s *breadth* o włos; '~·slide spinka *f* do włosów; '~·split·ting rozszczepianie *n* włosa; '~·spray lakier *m* do włosów; '~·style fryzura *f*; '~·styl·ist fryzjer(ka *f*) *m* damski (-a); '~·y (-*ier, -iest*) włochaty, owłosiony

half [hɑːf] (*pl. halves* [hɑːvz]) połowa *f*; *go halves* ⟨po⟩dzielić się po połowie; 2. pół; ~ *an hour* pół godziny; ~ *a pound* pół funta; ~ *past ten* (w)pół do jedenastej; ~ *way up* w połowie wysokości; '~·breed mieszaniec *m*; '~·broth·er brat *m* przyrodni; '~·caste mieszaniec *m*; ~·'heart·ed bez przekonania; ~ *time sport:* przerwa *f*; ~ *time 'score* (*w sporcie*) rezultat *m* do przerwy; ~'way w pół, w połowie; ~'way 'line linia *f* środkowa; ~'wit·ted niedorozwinięty

hal·i·but ['hælɪbət] *zo.* (*pl. -buts, but*) halibut *m*

hall [hɔːl] sala *f*, hala *f*; dwór *m*; przedpokój *m*, korytarz *m*; *univ.* ~ *of residence* dom *m* akademicki

Hal·low·e'en [hæləʊ'iːn] dzień *m* przed dniem Wszystkich Świętych

hal·lu·ci·na·tion [həluːsɪ'neɪʃn] halucynacja *f*

'**hall·way** *zwł. Am.* przedpokój *m*, korytarz *m*

ha·lo ['heɪləʊ] (*pl. -loes, los*) aureola *f* (*też astr.*)

halt [hɔːlt] 1. zatrzymanie *n* się; 2. zatrzymywać (-mać) (się)

hal·ter ['hɔːltə] stryczek *m*

halve [hɑːv] przepoławiać ⟨-łowić⟩; ~s [hɑːvz] *pl. od* **half** 1

ham [hæm] szynka *f*; *~ and eggs* jajecznica *f* na szynce

ham·burg·er ['hæmbɜːgə] *gastr.* hamburger *m*; *Am.* mięso *n* mielone

ham·let ['hæmlɪt] *mała wioska f*

ham·mer ['hæmə] 1. młotek *m*, młot *m*; 2. walić (*młotkiem*); wbijać ⟨-bić⟩

ham·mock ['hæmək] hamak *m*

ham·per[1] ['hæmpə] kosz(yk) *m* z przykrywą

ham·per[2] ['hæmpə] przeszkadzać ⟨-kodzić⟩

ham·ster ['hæmstə] *zo.* chomik *m*

hand [hænd] 1. ręka *f* (*też fig.*); pismo *n*; wskazówka *f* (*zegara*); *często* w złoż. pracownik *m*, robotnik *m*; ręka *f* (*karty trzymane przez gracza w jednym rozdaniu*); *~ in glove* w zmowie, ręka w rękę; *change ~s* przechodzić ⟨przejść⟩ z rąk do rąk; *give lub lend a ~* pomóc *komuś* (*with* w *L*); *shake ~s with s.o.* ⟨u⟩ścisnąć komuś rękę; *at ~* pod ręką; *at first ~* z pierwszej ręki; *by ~* ręcznie; *on the one ~* z jednej strony; *on the other ~* z drugiej strony; *on the right ~* z prawej strony; *~s off!* ręce przy sobie!; 2. wręczać ⟨-czyć⟩, dawać ⟨dać⟩, podawać ⟨-dać⟩; *~ around* rozdawać ⟨-dać⟩; *~ down* przekazywać ⟨-zać⟩; *~ in test itp.* oddawać ⟨-dać⟩; *sprawozdanie* składać ⟨złożyć⟩; *~ on* przekazywać ⟨-zać⟩; *~ out* rozdzielać ⟨-lić⟩, rozdawać ⟨-dać⟩; *~ over* przekazywać ⟨-zać⟩; *~ up* przekazywać ⟨-zać⟩; '*~·bag* torebka *f*; '*~·ball* piłka *f* ręczna; (*w piłce nożnej*) zagranie *n* ręką; '*~·bill* ulotka *f*; '*~·brake* *tech.* hamulec *m* ręczny; '*~·cuffs* *pl.* kajdanki *pl.*; '*~·ful* garść *f*, garstka *f*; F żywe srebro *n*

hand·i·cap ['hændɪkæp] 1. ułomność *f*, *med. też* upośledzenie *n*; przeszkoda *f*; *sport*: handicap *m*, wyrównanie *n*; → *mental*; → *physical*; 2. (*-pp-*) utrudniać ⟨-nić⟩; '*~·ped* 1. upośledzony; niepełnosprawny; → *mental*; → *physical*; 2. *the ~ped pl. med.* niepełnosprawni *pl.*

hand·ker·chief ['hæŋkətʃɪf] (*pl. -chiefs*) chusteczka *f*, chustka *f*

han·dle ['hændl] 1. uchwyt *m*, rączka *f*; rękojeść *f*; klamka *f*; *fly off the ~* F

wściec się; 2. dotykać ⟨-tknąć⟩ (*G*); obchodzić się z (*I*); ⟨po⟩radzić sobie z (*I*); prowadzić; handlować; '*~·bar(s pl.)* kierownica *f* (*roweru*)

'**hand**| **lug·gage** bagaż *m* ręczny; *~·made* ręcznie zrobione; '*~·out* datek *m*, darowizna *f*; konspekt *m*, tekst *m*; '*~·rail* poręcz *f*; '*~·shake* uściśnięcie *n* dłoni

hand·some ['hænsəm] (*-er, -est*) przystojny; *suma*: pokaźny

'**hand**| **writ·ing** pismo *n*; *~'writ·ten* napisany ręcznie; '*~·y* (*-ier, -iest*) poręczny; przydatny; dogodnie położony; *come in ~y* przydawać ⟨-dać⟩ się

hang [hæŋ] (*hung*) *v/i.* wisieć; zwisać; *v/t.* wieszać, zawieszać ⟨-sić⟩; zwieszać ⟨-sić⟩; *tapetę* przyklejać ⟨-leić⟩; (*pret. i p.p.* **hanged**) *kogoś* wieszać ⟨powiesić⟩; *~ o.s.* powiesić się; *~ about, ~ around* kręcić się, snuć się; *~ on* uczepiać ⟨-pić⟩ się; *tel.* nie odkładać słuchawki; *~ up tel.* rozłączać ⟨-czyć⟩ się; *she hung up on me* rozłączyła się ze mną

han·gar ['hæŋə] *aviat.* hangar *m*

hang·er ['hæŋə] wieszak *m*

hang| **glid·er** ['hæŋglaɪdə] lotnia *f*; '*~ glid·ing* lotniarstwo *n*

hang·ing ['hæŋɪŋ] 1. wiszący; 2. wieszanie *n*; '*~s pl.* draperia *f*

'**hang·man** (*pl. -men*) kat *m*

'**hang·o·ver** kociokwik *m*, kac *m*

han·ker ['hæŋkə] F tęsknić (*after, for* do *G*)

han| **kie, ~·ky** ['hæŋkɪ] F chustka *f*

hap·haz·ard [hæp'hæzəd] przypadkowy

hap·pen ['hæpən] zdarzać ⟨-rzyć⟩ się, wydarzać ⟨-rzyć⟩ się; *~ to* stać się (*D*), przytrafiać (*D*) się; *he ~ed to be at home* akurat był w domu; *~·ing* ['hæpnɪŋ] wydarzenie *n*; happening *m*

hap·pi·ly ['hæpɪlɪ] szczęśliwie; '*~·ness* szczęście *n*

hap·py ['hæpɪ] (*-ier, -iest*) szczęśliwy; zadowolony; *~·go·'luck·y* beztroski

ha·rangue [hə'ræŋ] 1. pouczenie *n*, kazanie *n*; 2. pouczać ⟨-czyć⟩

har·ass ['hærəs] nękać, dręczyć; szykanować; '*~·ment* nękanie *n*; dręczenie *n*; szykany *pl.*; → *sexual harassment*

har·bo(u)r ['hɑːbə] 1. port *m*; przystań *f*; schronienie *n*; 2. ofiarowywać

⟨-ować⟩ schronienie; *urazę itp.* żywić

hard [hɑːd] **1.** *adj.* twardy; *zadanie itp.:* trudny; silny; *życie:* ciężki; *zima, osoba itp.:* surowy; *pracodawca:* stanowczy; *dowód:* niezbity; *trunek:* mocny; *narkotyk:* niebezpieczny; **~ of hearing** niedosłyszący; **be ~ up** F być w ciężkiej sytuacji finansowej, odczuwać brak; **2.** *adv.* mocno; ciężko; ostro; '**~·back** książka *f* w twardej oprawie; **~'boiled** ugotowany na twardo; *fig.* twardy, mało sentymentalny; **~ 'cash** gotówka *f*; **~ 'core** trzon *m*; *mus.* hardcore *m*; **~·'core** hard core; *pornografia:* ostry; '**~·cov·er** *print.* **1.** oprawny, oprawiony; **2.** twarda oprawa *f*; dzieło *n* oprawne; **~ 'disk** *komp.* twardy dysk *m*; **~·en** ['hɑːdn] ⟨s⟩twardnieć; utwardzać ⟨-dzić⟩; hartować; '**~** hat kask *m*; **~·'head·ed** wyrachowany *zwł. Am.* twardogłowy; **~·'heart·ed** o twardym sercu, bezwzględny; **~ 'la·bo(u)r** *jur.* ciężkie roboty *pl.*; **~ 'line** *zwł. pol.* twardy kurs *m*; **~·'line** *zwł. pol.* twardy, dogmatyczny; **~·ly** prawie (nie); ledwo, ledwie; '**~·ness** twardość *f*; **~·ship** trudność *f*; **~ 'shoul·der** *Brt. mot.* pobocze *n* utwardzone; '**~·top** *mot.* dach *m* sztywny (*czasem zdejmowany; też typ samochodu*); '**~·ware** *komp.* sprzęt *m* komputerowy; wyroby *pl.* metalowe; towary *pl.* żelazne

har·dy ['hɑːdɪ] **(-ier, -iest)** mocny, wytrzymały; *roślina:* zimotrwały

hare [heə] *zo.* zając *m*; '**~·bell** *bot.* dzwonek *m*; '**~·brained** *osoba, plan:* zbzikowany; **~·lip** *anat.* warga *f* zajęcza

harm [hɑːm] **1.** szkoda *f*, krzywda *f*; **2.** ⟨s⟩krzywdzić, wyrządzać krzywdę; ⟨z⟩ranić; '**~·ful** szkodliwy; '**~·less** nieszkodliwy

har·mo|·ni·ous [hɑː'məʊnjəs] harmonijny; **~·nize** ['hɑːmənaɪz] harmonizować; współbrzmieć; **~·ny** ['hɑːmənɪ] harmonia *f*

har·ness ['hɑːnɪs] **1.** uprząż *f*; **die in ~** *fig.* umrzeć w kieracie; **2.** zaprzęgać ⟨-rząc⟩ (*też fig.*); wykorzystywać ⟨-tać⟩ (**to** do *G*)

harp [hɑːp] **1.** *mus.* harfa *f*; **2.** *mus.* ⟨za⟩grać na harfie; **~ on (about)** *fig.* ględzić o (*L*)

har·poon [hɑː'puːn] **1.** harpun *m*; **2.** wbijać ⟨wbić⟩ harpun

har·row ['hærəʊ] *agr.* **1.** brona *f*; **2.** ⟨po⟩bronować

har·row·ing ['hærəʊɪŋ] wstrząsający, przygniatający

harsh [hɑːʃ] ostry; surowy

hart [hɑːt] *zo.* (*pl.* **harts, hart**) jeleń *m*

har·vest ['hɑːvɪst] **1.** żniwo *n*, *zw.* żniwa *pl.*; plon *m*, zbiory *pl.*; **2.** zbierać ⟨zebrać⟩; '**~·er** kombajn *m* żniwny

has [hæz] *on, ona, ono* ma

hash¹ [hæʃ] *gastr.* (*mięso krojone z warzywami w sosie*); **make a ~ of s.th.** *fig.* spartaczyć coś

hash² [hæʃ] F haszysz *m*

hash 'browns *pl. Am.* przysmażane kartofle *pl.*

hash·ish ['hæʃiːʃ] haszysz *m*

hasp [hɑːsp] klamra *f* zamka

haste [heɪst] pośpiech *m*; **has·ten** ['heɪsn] *kogoś* popędzać ⟨-dzić⟩; spieszyć się; *coś* przyspieszać ⟨-szyć⟩; '**hast·y (-ier, -iest)** pospieszny; pochopny

hat [hæt] kapelusz *m*

hatch¹ [hætʃ] *też* **~ out** wykluwać ⟨-luć⟩ się, wylęgać ⟨-lęgnąć⟩ się

hatch² [hætʃ] właz *m*; okienko *n*; '**~·back** (*typ samochodu i nadwozia*) hatchback *m*

hatch·et ['hætʃɪt] topór *m*; **bury the ~** zakopać topór wojenny

'**hatch·way** właz *m*, luk *m*

hate [heɪt] **1.** nienawiść *f*; **2.** ⟨z⟩nienawidzić; '**~·ful** okropny; pełen nienawiści; **ha·tred** ['heɪtrəd] nienawiść *f*

haugh·ty ['hɔːtɪ] wyniosły

haul [hɔːl] **1.** ciągnąć ⟨-gnąć⟩; ⟨za⟩wlec; ⟨za⟩holować; ⟨prze⟩transportować, ⟨prze⟩wozić; **2.** ciągnienie *n*; połów *m*; łup *m*; transport *m*, przewóz *m*; **~·age** ['hɔːlɪdʒ] transport *m*, przewóz *m*; **~·er** ['hɔːlə] *Am.*, **~·i·er** ['hɔːljə] *Brt.* przewoźnik *m*

haunch [hɔːntʃ] pośladek *m*, biodro *n*; udo *n*

haunt [hɔːnt] **1.** nawiedzać ⟨-dzić⟩; często odwiedzać; prześladować; **2.** często odwiedzane miejsce *n*; kryjówka *f*; '**~·ing** dojmujący, dotkliwy

have [hæv] **(had)** *v/t.* mieć, posiadać; otrzymywać ⟨-mać⟩, dostawać ⟨-tać⟩; ⟨z⟩jeść, pić; **~ breakfast** ⟨z⟩jeść śniadanie; **~ a cup of tea** wypić filiżankę herbaty; *przed bezok.:* musieć; **I ~ to**

go now muszę już iść; *z dopełnieniem i p.p.*: *kazać komuś coś* (*sobie*) *zrobić*; *I had my hair cut* obciąłem sobie włosy; ~ **back** dostawać ⟨-tać⟩ *z* powrotem; *ubranie*: ~ **on** mieć na sobie; *v/aux*. *I* ~ **not finished yet** jeszcze nie skończyłem; ~ **you had your breakfast yet?** czy już zjadłeś śniadanie?; *I* ~ **come** przyszedłem

ha·ven ['heɪvn] przystań *m* (*zwł. fig.*)

hav·oc ['hævək] zniszczenie *n*, spustoszenie *n*; *play* ~ *with* ⟨z⟩niszczenie, ⟨s⟩pustoszyć, *fig.* wprowadzać ⟨-dzić⟩ zamęt

Ha·wai·i [hə'waɪiː] Hawaje *pl.*; ~an [hə'waɪən] **1.** hawajski; **2.** Hawajczyk *m* (-jka *f*); *ling.* język *m* hawajski

hawk¹ [hɔːk] *zo.* jastrząb *m* (*też fig.*)

hawk² [hɔːk] prowadzić sprzedaż domokrążną *lub* uliczną; ~er domokrążca *m*; sprzedawca *m* uliczny; kolporter *m* (*subskrypcji prasy*)

haw·thorn ['hɔːθɔːn] *bot.* głóg *m*

hay [heɪ] siano *n*; ~ **fe·ver** katar *m* sienny; ~**loft** stryszek *m* na siano; ~**rick**, ~**stack** stóg *m* siana

haz·ard ['hæzəd] zagrożenie *n*, niebezpieczeństwo *n*; ~**ous** niebezpieczny, zagrażający życiu; ~**ous 'waste** niebezpieczne odpady *pl.*

haze [heɪz] mgła *f*

ha·zel ['heɪzl] **1.** *bot.* leszczyna *f*; **2.** orzechowy, brązowy; ~**nut** orzech *m* laskowy

haz·y ['heɪzɪ] (*-ier, -iest*) mglisty (*też fig.*); zamglony

H-bomb ['eɪtʃbɒm] bomba *f* wodorowa

HD *skrót*: *Hard Disk*

he [hiː] **1.** *pron.* on; **2.** *zo.* samiec *m*; **3.** *adj.*: *w złoż.* *he-goat* kozioł *m*

head [hed] **1.** głowa *f*; kierownik *m* (-niczka *f*), dyrektor(ka *f*) *m*; prowadzący *m* (-ca *f*); góra *f*, część *f* górna; reszka *f*; nagłówek *m*; głowica *f* (*w magnetofonie itp.*); łeb *m* (*śruby itp.*); główka *f* (*młotka, gwoździa itp.*); *20 pounds a* ~ *lub per* ~ po 20 funtów na głowę *lub* na osobę; *40* ~ *pl.* (*of cattle*) 40 sztuk *pl.* (bydła); ~*s or tails* orzeł czy reszka?; *at the* ~ *of* na przedzie (*G*); ~ *over heels* bez opamiętania; po uszy; *bury one's* ~ *in the sand* ⟨s⟩chować głowę w piasek; *get it into one's* ~ *that...* wbić sobie do głowy, że...; *lose one's* ~ ⟨s⟩tracić głowę *lub* nerwy; **2.** główny;

naczelny; najważniejszy; **3.** *v/t.* stać na czele; prowadzić; kierować; (*w piłce nożnej*) odbijać ⟨-bić⟩ głową; *v/i.* (*for*) kierować się (do *G*); *fig.* zmierzać (do *G*); trzymać kurs (na *A*); ~**ache** ból *m* głowy; ~**band** opaska *f* na głowę; ~**dress** przybranie *n* głowy; ~**er** odbicie *n* głową, *f* głowka *f*; ~**first** głową wprzód; *fig.* bez opamiętania; ~**gear** nakrycie *n* głowy; ~**ing** nagłówek *m*, tytuł *m*; ~**land** [hedlənd] przylądek *m*; ~**light** *mot.* reflektor *m*; ~**line** nagłówek *m*; *news* ~*lines pl. TV, radio*: skrót *m* najważniejszych wiadomości; ~**long** głową naprzód; na łeb na szyję; ~**mas·ter** dyrektor *m* szkoły; ~**mis·tress** dyrektorka *f* szkoły; ~**on** frontalny; czołowy; ~**on collision** zderzenie czołowe; ~**phones** *pl.* słuchawki *pl.*; ~**quar·ters** *pl.* (*skrót*: *HQ*) kwatera *f* główna; centrala *f*; ~**rest** *Am.*, ~ **re·straint** *Brt.* *mot.* zagłówek *m*; ~**set** słuchawki *pl.*; ~**start** (*w sporcie*) przewaga *f*, fory *pl.*; ~**strong** zawzięty, uparty; ~'**teach·er** → *headmaster*, → *headmistress* → *Am. principal*; ~**wa·ters** dopływy *pl.* w górnym biegu rzeki; ~**way** *fig.* postęp (*y pl.*) *m*; *make* ~**way** iść ⟨pójść⟩ naprzód; ~**word** (*w słowniku*) hasło *n*; ~**y** (*-ier, -iest*) uderzający do głowy

heal [hiːl] ⟨wy⟩leczyć; ~ *over*, ~ *up* ⟨za⟩goić się

health [helθ] zdrowie *n*; ~ **cer·tif·i·cate** świadectwo *n* zdrowia; ~ **club** ośrodek *m* odnowy biologicznej; '~ **food** zdrowa żywność *f*; '~ **food shop** *Brt.*, '~ **food store** *zwł. Am.* sklep *m* ze zdrową żywnością; ~**ful** zdrowy; dobrze wpływający na zdrowie; '~ **in·su·rance** ubezpieczenie *f* na wypadek choroby; '~ **re·sort** kurort *m*; '~ **ser·vice** służba *f* zdrowia; '~**y** (*-ier, -iest*) zdrowy

heap [hiːp] **1.** kupa *f*, sterta *f*; stos *m*; **2.** *też* ~*up* składać ⟨złożyć⟩ na stos *lub* stertę; *fig. też* nagromadzać ⟨gromadzić⟩

hear [hɪə] (*heard*) ⟨u⟩słyszeć; ⟨wy⟩słuchać (*G*); ⟨po⟩słuchać; *świadka* przesłuchiwać ⟨-chać⟩; *jur.* sądzić; ~**d** [hɜːd] *pret. i p.p. od hear*, ~**er** ['hɪərə] słuchacz(ka *f*) *m*; ~**ing** ['hɪərɪŋ] słuch *m*; słyszalność *f*; *jur.* przesłuchanie *n*, rozprawa *f*; *within* (*out of*) ~*ing* w zasięgu

(poza zasięgiem) słuchu; '~·ing aid
aparat m słuchowy; '~·say pogłoska f;
by ~say według pogłosek

hearse [hɜːs] karawan m

heart [hɑːt] anat. serce n (też fig.); centrum n, środek m; gry w karty: kier(y
pl.) m; lose ~ ⟨s⟩tracić serce; take ~ nabierać ⟨-brać⟩ otuchy; take s.th. to ~
brać ⟨wziąć⟩ coś do serca; with a
heavy ~ z ciężkim sercem; by ~ na pamięć; '~·ache ból m serca; '~ at·tack
atak m serca, zawał m; '~·beat bicie
n serca; '~·break zawód m sercowy;
rozczarowanie n; '~·break·ing rozdzierający serce; '~·brok·en: be
~broken mieć złamane serce; '~·burn
zgaga f; ~en ['hɑːtn] dodawać ⟨-dać⟩
otuchy; ~ failure med. niewydolność
f serca; '~·felt z głębi serca, z wnętrza

hearth [hɑːθ] palenisko n, fig. ognisko n
domowe

'heart·less bez serca; '~·rend·ing rozdzierający serce; '~ trans·plant przeszczep m lub transplantacja f serca;
'~·y (-ier, -iest) serdeczny; zdrowy

heat [hiːt] 1. ciepło n (też tech.); upał m,
gorąco n; zapał m; zo. ruja f; (w sporcie) bieg m; preliminary ~ bieg m eliminacyjny; 2. v/t. ogrzewać ⟨-rzać⟩; też
~ up ⟨o⟩grzać, podgrzewać ⟨-rzać⟩; v/i.
ogrzewać ⟨-rzać⟩ się (też fig.); '~·ed
ogrzewany; podgrzewany; rozmowa:
roznamiętniony, gorący; '~·er grzejnik
m, grzałka f; podgrzewacz m, bojler m

heath [hiːθ] wrzosowisko n

hea·then ['hiːðn] 1. poganin m (-anka
f); 2. pogański

heath·er ['heðə] bot. wrzosiec m,
wrzos m

'heat·ing ogrzewanie n; attr. grzejny,
grzewczy; '~·proof, '~·re·sis·tant,
'~·re·sist·ing żaroodporny; '~ shield
(w astronautykce) osłona f termiczna;
'~·stroke med. porażenie n słoneczne;
'~ wave fala f gorąca

heave [hiːv] (heaved, zwł. naut. hove)
v/t. dźwigać ⟨-gnąć⟩; miotać ⟨-tnąć⟩;
kotwicę podnosić ⟨-nieść⟩; westchnienie wydawać ⟨-dać⟩; v/i. podnosić
⟨-nieść⟩ się; dźwigać ⟨-gnąć⟩ się

heav·en ['hevn] niebo n; '~·ly niebiański

heav·y ['hevɪ] (-ier, -iest) ciężki;
deszcz, opady, ruch: silny; palacz itp.:

nałogowy; narzut, podatek itp.: wysoki; jedzenie: ciężkostrawny; ~ 'cur·rent
electr. prąd m o dużym natężeniu;
~'du·ty tech. przewidziany do pracy
o dużym obciążeniu; wytrzymały;
~'hand·ed surowy; mało taktowny;
grubo ciosany; '~·weight (w boksie) waga f ciężka, zawodnik m wagi ciężkiej

He·brew ['hiːbruː] 1. hebrajski; 2. Hebrajczyk m (-jka f); ling. język m hebrajski

Heb·ri·des pl. Hebrydy pl.

heck·le ['hekl] mówcy przeszkadzać
⟨-kodzić⟩ (uwagami)

hec·tic ['hektɪk] (~ally) rozgorączkowany, gorączkowy

hedge [hedʒ] 1. żywopłot m; 2. v/t. też
~ in ogradzać ⟨-rodzić⟩; v/i. fig. odpowiadać ⟨-wiedzieć⟩ wymijająco; '~·hog
zo. jeż m; Am. jeżozwierz m; '~·row
żywopłot m

heed [hiːd] 1. brać ⟨wziąć⟩ pod uwagę;
2. give lub pay ~ to, take ~ of zważać
na; '~·less: be ~less of nie zważać na
(A), nie mieć względu na (A)

heel [hiːl] 1. anat. pięta f (też w skarpecie
itp.); obcas m; down at ~ wytarty, starty; fig. niechlujny, zaniedbany; 2. dorabiać ⟨-robić⟩ obcasy do (G)

hef·ty ['heftɪ] (-ier, -iest) zwalisty; mocny, uderzenie: silny; cena itp.: wielki

heif·er ['hefə] zo. jałówka f

height [haɪt] wysokość f; fig. szczyt m,
maksimum n; ~en ['haɪtn] podwyższać ⟨-szyć⟩; zwiększać ⟨-szyć⟩; wzmacniać ⟨-mocnić⟩

heir [eə] spadkobierca m, dziedzic m,
następca m; ~ to the throne następca
m tronu; ~·ess ['eərɪs] spadkobierczyni f, następczyni f; ~·loom ['eəluːm]
pamiątka f rodzinna

held [held] pret. i p.p. od hold 1

hel·i·cop·ter aviat. ['helɪkɒptə] helikopter m, śmigłowiec m; '~·port aviat.
lądowisko n helikopterów

hell [hel] 1. piekło n; attr. piekielny;
what the ~...? co u diabła ...?; raise ~
F ⟨z⟩robić karczemną awanturę; 2. int.
F cholera!, szlag by to!; ~'bent: he is
~bent on s.th. strasznie mu zależy na
czymś; '~·ish piekielny

hel·lo [həˈləʊ] int. cześć!

helm [helm] naut. ster m; △ nie helm

hel·met ['helmɪt] hełm m; kask m

helms·man ['helmzmən] *naut. (pl. -men)* sternik *m*

help [help] **1.** pomoc *f*; pomoc *f* domowa; *a call lub cry for ~* wołanie *n* o pomoc; **2.** pomagać ‹-móc›; *~ o.s.* obsługiwać ‹-łużyć› się, poczęstować się; *I cannot ~ it* nie mogę nic na to poradzić; *I could not ~ laughing* nie mogłem się powstrzymać od śmiechu; '*~·er* pomocnik *m* (-ica *f*); '*~·ful* pomocny; użyteczny; '*~·ing* porcja *f*; '*~·less* bezradny; '*~·less·ness* bezradność *f*; '*~ men·u komp.* menu *n* pomocy

hel·ter-skel·ter [heltə'skeltə] **1.** *adv.* na łeb na szyję; **2.** *adj.* pospiesznie; **3.** *Brt.* zjeżdżalnia *f*

helve [helv] stylisko *n* (*topora*)

Hel·ve·tian [hel'vi:ʃjən] szwajcarski

hem [hem] **1.** obręb *m*, obwódka *f*; **2.** (*-mm-*) obrębiać ‹-bić›; *~ in* zamykać ‹-mknąć›

hem·i·sphere ['hemɪsfɪə] półkula *f*

'**hem·line** brzeg *m*

hem·lock ['hemlɒk] *bot.* cykuta *f*

hemp [hemp] *bot.* konopie *pl.*

'**hem·stitch** mereżka *f*

hen [hen] *zo.* kura *f* (*też samica różnych ptaków*); kwoka *f*

hence [hens] stąd, dlatego; *a week ~* za tydzień; *~'forth, ~'for·ward* od teraz, odtąd

'**hen|house** kurnik *m*; '*~ pecked husband* mąż *m* pod pantoflem

her [hɜː, hə] jej, niej; nią; niej

her·ald ['herəld] **1.** *hist.* herold *m*; **2.** zapowiadać ‹-wiedzieć›, zwiastować; *~ry* ['herəldrɪ] heraldyka *f*

herb [hɜːb] *bot.* ziele *n*; *~·a·ceous bot.* [hɜː'beɪʃəs] ziołowy, zielny; *~·al* ['hɜːbəl] ziołowy; roślinny

her·bi·vore ['hɜːbɪvɔː] *zo.* roślinożerca

herd [hɜːd] **1.** stado *n* (*też fig.*); **2.** *v/t. bydło* spędzać ‹-dzić›; *v/i. też ~ together* skupiać ‹-pić› się; *~s·man* ['hɜːdzmən] (*pl. -men*) pastuch *m*

here [hɪə] tu, tutaj; *~ you are* proszę (*przy dawaniu czegoś*); *~'s to you!* za pana (panią)!

here|·a·bout(s) ['hɪərəbaut(s)] gdzieś tu(taj), w pobliżu; *~·af·ter* [hɪər'ɑːftə] **1.** odtąd; **2.** zaświaty *pl.*; *~·by* niniejszym; przez to

he·red·i·ta·ry [hɪ'redɪtərɪ] dziedziczny; *~·ty* [hɪ'redɪtɪ] dziedziczność *f*

here|·in [hɪər'ɪn] tu, tutaj, w niniejszym; *~·of* [hɪər'ɒv] niniejszego, tego

her·e·sy ['herəsɪ] herezja *f*; *~·tic* ['herətɪk] heretyk *m* (-yczka *f*)

here|·up·on [hɪərə'pɒn] wówczas, wobec tego; *~·with* w załączeniu, z niniejszym

her·i·tage ['herɪtɪdʒ] dziedzictwo *n*

her·mit ['hɜːmɪt] *rel.* pustelnik (-ica *f*) *m*

he·ro ['hɪərəu] (*pl. -roes*) bohater *m*; *~·ic* [hɪ'rəuɪk] (*-ally*) bohaterski

her·o·in ['herəuɪn] heroina *f*

her·o|·ine ['herəuɪn] bohaterka *f*; *~·is·m* ['herəuɪzəm] bohaterstwo *n*

her·on ['herən] *zo.* (*pl. -ons, -on*) czapla *f*

her·ring ['herɪŋ] *zo.* (*pl. -rings, -ring*) śledź *m*

hers [hɜːz] jej

her·self [hɜː'self] się, sobie, siebie; sama; *by ~* przez siebie, bez pomocy

hes·i|·tant ['hezɪtənt] niezdecydowany, niepewny; *~·tate* ['hezɪteɪt] wahać się, zastanawiać się; *~·ta·tion* [hezɪ'teɪʃn] wahanie *n*, niepewność *f*, brak *m* zdecydowania; *without ~tation* bez zawahania

hew [hju:] (*hewed, hewed lub hewn*) ‹po›rąbać, ‹po›ciosać; *~ down* zrąbywać ‹-bać›; *~n* [hju:n] *p.p. od hew*

hey [heɪ] *int.* F hej!, halo!

hey·day ['heɪdeɪ] szczyt *m*, okres *m* rozkwitu

hi [haɪ] *int.* F halo! cześć!

hi·ber·nate ['haɪbəneɪt] *zo.* zapadać ‹-paść› w sen zimowy

hic·cup, ~·cough ['hɪkʌp] **1.** czkawka *f*; **2.** czkać

hid [hɪd] *pret. od hide*[1]; *~·den* ['hɪdn] *p.p. od hide*[1]

hide[1] [haɪd] (*hid, hidden*) ‹s›chować się, ‹s›kryć się; *coś* ukrywać ‹-ryć›

hide[2] [haɪd] skóra *f* (*zwierzęca*)

hide-and-seek [haɪdn'siːk] zabawa *f* w chowanego; '*~·a·way* F kryjówka *f*

hid·e·ous ['hɪdɪəs] okropny; ohydny, obrzydliwy

'**hide·out** kryjówka *f*

hid·ing[1] ['haɪdɪŋ] F lanie *n*, baty *pl.*

hid·ing[2] ['haɪdɪŋ]: *be in ~* ukrywać się; *go into ~* skryć się; '*~ place* kryjówka *f*

hi-fi ['haɪfaɪ] hi-fi *n*; sprzęt *m* hi-fi

high [haɪ] **1.** wysoki; *nadzieja*: duży; *mięso*: skruszały; F (*pijany*) zalany; F na haju (*narkotycznym*); **be in ~ spirits** być w świetnym humorze; **2.** *meteor.* wysokie ciśnienie n, wysoki poziom m; *Am.* F szkoła f średnia; '**~·brow** F **1.** intelektualista m (-tka f); **2.** intelektualny, przeintelektualizowany; **~·cal·o·rie** o dużej kaloryczności; **~·class** pierwszej klasy; **~·er ed·u·ca·tion** wyższe wykształcenie n; **~·fi·del·i·ty** hi-fi n, audiofilska jakość f (*dźwięku*); **~·grade** wysokiej jakości; **~·hand·ed** władczy, despotyczny; **~·heeled** na wysokich obcasach; '**~ jump** (*w sporcie*) skok m wzwyż; '**~ jump·er** (*w sporcie*) skoczek m wzwyż; **~·land** ['haɪlənd] wyżyna f, pogórze n; '**~·light 1.** główna atrakcja f; punkt m kulminacyjny; **2.** podkreślać ‹-lić›, uwypuklać ‹-lić›; '**~·ly** wysoko; *fig.* dodatnio, pochlebnie; *think ~ly of* myśleć dobrze o (*L*); **~·ly-'strung** napięty, nerwowy; '**~·ness** *zw. fig.* wysokość f; ⁀**ness** (*tytuł*) Wysokość f; **~·'pitched** *ton*: ostry; *dach*: stromy; **~·'pow·ered** *tech.* o dużej mocy; *fig.* dynamiczny; **~·'pres·sure** *meteor.*, *tech.* wysokie ciśnienie n; '**~ road** *zw.* wysokościowiec m; '**~ road** *Brt.* droga f główna; **~ school** *Am.* szkoła f średnia; '**~ sea·son** szczyt m sezonu; **~ so·ci·e·ty** socjeta f, elita f; '**~ street** *Brt.* droga f główna; **~·'strung** → **highly-strung;** '**~ tea** *Brt.* wczesna kolacja f; **~ tech** [haɪ 'tek] *też* **hi-tech;** **~ tech'nol·o·gy** najnowocześniejsza technologia f; *attr.* najnowocześniejszy; **~·'ten·sion** *electr.* wysokie napięcie n; **~·'tide** przypływ m; **~ 'time:** *it is ~time* najwyższy czas; **~ 'wa·ter** wysoka woda f (*pływu*); '**~·way** *zw. Am.* droga f główna, autostrada f; ⁀·way 'Code *Brt.* kodeks drogowy

hi·jack ['haɪdʒæk] **1.** *samolot*, *kogoś* porywać ‹-rwać›; *transport* napadać ‹-paść›; **2.** porwanie n; napad m; '**~·er** porywacz(ka f) m; rabuś m

hike [haɪk] **1.** wędrować; **2.** wędrówka f; '**hik·er** turysta m (-tka f); '**hik·ing** wycieczki pl

hi·lar·i·ous [hɪ'leərɪəs] przekomiczny, prześmieszny; **~·ty** [hɪ'lærətɪ] ogromna wesołość f

hill [hɪl] wzgórze n; **~·bil·ly** *Am.* ['hɪlbɪ-

lɪ] nieokrzesany wieśniak m (*z górskich rejonów USA*); **~ music** (*odmiana muzyki country*); '**~·ock** ['hɪlək] pagórek m; '**~·side** zbocze n, stok m; '**~·top** szczyt m wzgórza; '**~·y** (*-ier, -iest*) pagórkowaty

hilt [hɪlt] rękojeść f

him [hɪm] mu, jemu; go, jego; niego; nim; **~·self** [hɜː'self] się, sobie, siebie; sam; *by ~self* samodzielnie, bez pomocy

Hi·ma·la·ya Himalaje *pl.*

hind¹ [haɪnd] *zo.* (*pl.* **hinds, hind**) łania f

hind² [haɪnd] tylny, zadni

hin·der ['hɪndə] przeszkadzać ‹-kodzić› (*from* w *L*); utrudniać ‹-nić›

hind·most ['haɪndməʊst] ostatni; najdalszy

hin·drance ['hɪndrəns] przeszkoda f, utrudnienie n

Hin·du [hɪn'duː] **1.** Hindus m; **2.** *adj.* hinduski; **~·is·m** ['hɪnduːɪzəm] hinduizm

hinge [hɪndʒ] **1.** zawias m; **2.** ~ *on fig.* zależeć od (*G*)

hint [hɪnt] **1.** aluzja f; sugestia f; wskazówka f, rada f; *take a ~* ‹z›rozumieć sugestię; **2.** ‹za›sugerować, ‹z›robić aluzję; dawać ‹dać› do zrozumienia

hip [hɪp] *anat.* biodro n

hip·po ['hɪpəʊ] *zo.* F (*pl.* **-pos**) hipcio m; **~·pot·a·mus** ['hɪpə'pɒtəməs] *zo.* (*pl.* **-muses, -mi** [-maɪ]) hipopotam m

hire ['haɪə] **1.** *Brt.* auto itp. wynajmować ‹-jąć›, *samolot*: ‹wy›czarterować; *kogoś* zatrudniać ‹-nić›, ‹za›angażować, najmować ‹-jąć›; ~ *out Brt.* wynajmować ‹-jąć›; **2.** wynajęcie n; najem m; *for ~* do wynajęcia; *taksówka*: wolny; ~ *car* wynajęty samochód m; **~·'pur·chase: on ~purchase** *Brt. econ.* na raty

his [hɪz] jego

hiss [hɪs] **1.** syczeć ‹syknąć›; *kot*: prychać ‹-chnąć›; wysyczeć; **2.** syk m; prychnięcie n

his·to·ri·an [hɪ'stɔːrɪən] historyk m (-yczka f); **~·tor·ic** [hɪ'stɒrɪk] (*-ally*) historyczny, epokowy; **~·tor·i·cal** historyczny, odnoszący się do historii; **~torical novel** powieść historyczna; **~·to·ry** ['hɪstərɪ] historia f, **~tory of civilization** historia kultury *lub* cywilizacji; *contemporary ~tory* historia *f* najnowsza

hit [hɪt] **1.** (*-tt-*; *hit*) uderzać ⟨-rzyć⟩; trafiać ⟨-fić⟩ (*też fig.*); *mot. itp. kogoś* potrącać ⟨-cić⟩, *coś* wjeżdżać ⟨-jechać⟩ w (*A*); *~ it off with* zaskarbić sobie sympatię (*G*); *~ on* natrafiać ⟨-fić⟩ na (*A*); **2.** uderzenie *n*; *fig.* trafienie *n*; (*piosenka, książka itp.*) hit *m*

hit-and-'run *kierowca:* zbiegły z miejsca wypadku; *~ offence* (*Am. offense*) zbiegnięcie z miejsca wypadku

hitch [hɪtʃ] **1.** przytwierdzać ⟨-dzić⟩, przyczepiać ⟨-pić⟩, zaczepiać ⟨-pić⟩ (*to* do *G*); *~ up* podciągać ⟨-gnąć⟩; *~ a ride lub lift* ⟨z⟩łapać okazję, F → *hitch-hike*; **2.** pociągnięcie *n*; trudność *f*, problem *m*; *without a ~* bez problemów; *'~·hike* ⟨po⟩jechać (auto)stopem; *'~·hik·er* autostopowicz(ka *f*) *m*

hi-tech [haɪ'tek] → *high tech*

HIV [eɪtʃ aɪ 'viː]: *~ carrier* nosiciel(ka *f*) *m* wirusa HIV; *~ negative* (*positive*) o ujemnym (dodatnim) wyniku testu na nosicielstwo HIV

hive [haɪv] ul *m*, rój *m*

HM [eɪtʃ 'em] *skrót:* *His/Her Majesty* Jego/Jej Królewska Mość

HMS [eɪtʃ em es] *skrót:* *His/Her Majesty's Ship* okręt Jego/Jej Królewskiej Mości

hoard [hɔːd] **1.** skarb *m*; **2.** *też ~ up* ⟨na-, z⟩gromadzić

hoard·ing ['hɔːdɪŋ] ogrodzenie *n* (*na budowie*); *Brt.* billboard *m*

hoar·frost ['hɔːfrɒst] szron *m*

hoarse [hɔːs] (*-r*, *-st*) ochrypły, zachrypnięty

hoax [həʊks] **1.** fałszywy alarm *m*; głupi kawał *m*; **2.** *kogoś* nabierać ⟨-brać⟩

hob·ble ['hɒbl] ⟨po⟩kuśtykać

hob·by ['hɒbɪ] hobby *n*, konik *m*, zainteresowania *pl.*; *'~·horse* konik *m*

hob·gob·lin ['hɒbɡɒblɪn] kobold *m*, gnom *m*

ho·bo ['həʊbəʊ] *Am.* F (*pl. -boes, -bos*) włóczęga *m*

hock[1] [hɒk] (*białe wino reńskie*) riesling *m*

hock[2] [hɒk] staw *m* skokowy (*konia*)

hock·ey ['hɒkɪ] *zwł. Brt.* hokej *m* (*na trawie*); *zwł. Am.* hokej *m* (*na lodzie*)

hoe [həʊ] *agr.* **1.** motyka *f*, graca *f*; **2.**

okopywać ⟨-pać⟩ motyką, ⟨wy⟩gracować

hog [hɒg] świnia *f*

hoist [hɔɪst] **1.** podnosić ⟨-nieść⟩, wciągać ⟨-gnąć⟩; **2.** wyciąg *m*; podnośnik *m*

hold [həʊld] **1.** (*held*) trzymać; podtrzymywać ⟨-mać⟩, podpierać ⟨-deprzeć⟩; *ciężar* dźwigać; powstrzymywać ⟨-mać⟩, wstrzymywać ⟨-mać⟩ (*from* przed *I*); *wybory, spotkanie* odbywać ⟨-być⟩; *pozycję, stanowisko* mieć, posiadać; *urząd* piastować; *miejsce* zajmować; (*w sporcie*) *mistrzostwo* utrzymywać ⟨-mać⟩; *rekord świata* utrzymywać, być zdobywcą; zawierać; utrzymywać, być zdania (*that* że); mieć *kogoś* za (*A*); *uwagę* przykuwać ⟨-kuć⟩; być aktualnym, mieć ważność; obowiązywać; *pogoda, szczęście:* utrzymywać ⟨-mać⟩ się; *~ one's ground*, *~ one's own* nie ulegać ⟨-lec⟩, nie poddawać ⟨-dać⟩ się; *~ the line tel.* nie rozłączać ⟨-czyć⟩ się; *~ responsible* czynić odpowiedzialnym; *~ still* nie ruszać się; *~ s.th. against s.o.* mieć coś przeciwko komuś; *~ back* powstrzymywać ⟨-mać⟩ (się), *fig.* nie wyjawiać; *~ on* trzymać się (*to G*) mocno; zatrzymywać ⟨-mać⟩; *tel.* pozostawać ⟨-tać⟩ przy aparacie; *~ out* wyciągać ⟨-gnąć⟩; wytrzymywać ⟨-mać⟩; *zapasy:* wystarczać ⟨-czyć⟩; *~ up* unosić ⟨unieść⟩; wstrzymywać ⟨-mać⟩; *bank, kogoś* napadać ⟨-paść⟩ na (*A*); przedstawiać ⟨-wić⟩ (*as* jako *przykład*); wspierać ⟨wesprzeć⟩, podtrzymywać ⟨-mać⟩; **2.** chwyt *m*; uchwyt *m*; władanie *n*, władza *f*; *naut.* ładownia *f*; *catch* (*get*, *take*) *~ of s.th.* chwycić ⟨się⟩, złapać za (*A*); *'~·er* oprawka *f*, uchwyt *m*; posiadacz *m*, okaziciel *m* (*zwł. econ.*); *'~·ing* udziały *m*, własność *f*; *'~ com·pa·ny* holding *m*, przedsiębiorstwo *n* holdingowe; *'~·up* zator *m*, korek *m*; napad *m* rabunkowy

hole [həʊl] **1.** dziura *f* (*też fig.*), otwór *m*; **2.** ⟨po⟩dziurawić, przedziurawiać ⟨-wić⟩

hol·i·day ['hɒlɪdɪ] święto *n*; dzień *m* wolny; *zwł. Brt. zw. ~s* wakacje *pl.*, urlop *m*; *be on ~* być na wakacjach *lub* urlopie; *'~ home* dom *m* wczasowy; *'~·mak·er* urlopowicz(ka *f*) *m*

hol·i·ness ['həʊlɪnɪs] świętość *f*; *His ♀*

(*papież*) Jego Świątobliwość
Hol·land Holandia *f*
hol·ler ['hɒlə] *Am.* F wrzeszczeć ⟨wrzasnąć⟩
hol·low ['hɒləʊ] **1.** pusty, wydrążony; zapadnięty; głuchy; **2.** zagłębienie *n*, dziura *f*; **3.** ~ *out* wydrążać ⟨-żyć⟩
hol·ly ['hɒlɪ] *bot.* ostrokrzew *m*
hol·o·caust ['hɒləkɔ:st] zagłada *f*, eksterminacja *f*; *hist.* **the** ♀ holocaust *m*
hol·ster ['həʊlstə] kabura *f*
ho·ly ['həʊlɪ] (*-ier, -iest*) święty; ~ 'water woda *f* święcona; '♀ Week Wielki Tydzień *m*
home [həʊm] **1.** dom *m*; mieszkanie *n*; kraj *m* ojczysty, ojczyzna *f*; *at* ~ w domu; w kraju; *make oneself at* ~ czuć się jak u siebie w domu; *at* ~ *and abroad* w kraju i za granicą; **2.** domowy; krajowy; ojczysty; (*w sporcie*) miejscowy; **3.** *adv.* w domu; do domu; *fig.* w celu *lub* dziesiątce; *strike* ~ trafiać ⟨-fić⟩ w sedno; ~ *sick* cierpiący na nostalgię; '~com·put·er komputer *m* domowy; '~·less bezdomny; '~·ly (*-ier, -iest*) zwykły, prosty; *Am.* nieatrakcyjny; ~·made domowego wyrobu; '~·market rynek *m* wewnętrzny *lub* krajowy; '♀ Of·fice *Brt. pol.* Ministerstwo *n* Spraw Wewnętrznych; ♀ 'Sec·ret·a·ry Minister *n* Spraw Wewnętrznych; '~·sick; *be* ~*sick* cierpieć na nostalgię; '~·sick·ness nostalgia *f*; ~'team (*w sporcie*) drużyna *f* miejscowa; ~·ward ['həʊmwəd] **1.** *adj.* powrotny (*w stronę domu*); **2.** *adv. Am.* w stronę domu; do domu; '~·wards w stronę domu; do domu; '~·work zadanie *n* domowe; *do one's* ~*work* ⟨z⟩robić zadanie domowe (*też fig.*)
hom·i·cide ['hɒmɪsaɪd] *jur.* zabójstwo *n*; zabójca *m* (*-czyni f*); '~ squad wydział *m* zabójstw
ho·mo·ge·ne·ous [hɒmə'dʒi:njəs] homogeniczny, jednolity
ho·mo·sex·u·al [hɒməʊ'seksʃʊəl] **1.** homoseksualny; **2.** homoseksualista *m* (*-tka f*)
hone [həʊn] *tech.* ⟨na-, wy⟩ostrzyć
hon·est ['ɒnɪst] uczciwy; szczery; '~·es·ty uczciwość *f*; szczerość *f*
hon·ey ['hʌnɪ] miód *m*; *Am.* kochanie *n*, skarb *m*; ~·comb ['hʌnɪkəʊm] plaster *m* miodu; ~ed ['hʌnɪd] słodki (*jak*

miód); '~·moon **1.** miesiąc *m* miodowy; podróż *f* poślubna; **2.** *be* ~*moon·ing* być w podróży poślubnej
honk [hɒŋk] *mot.* ⟨za⟩trąbić
hon·ky-tonk ['hɒŋkɪtɒŋk] *Am.* speluna *f*
hon·or·ar·y ['ɒnərərɪ] honorowy
hon·o(u)r ['ɒnə] **1.** honor *m*; zaszczyt *m*; ~*s pl.* wyróżnienie *n*; *Your* ♀ Wysoki Sądzie; zaszczycać ⟨-cić⟩; *econ.* czek *itp.* honorować, uznawać ⟨-nać⟩; ~·a·ble ['ɒnərəbl] honorowy; szanowany; szanowny
hood [hʊd] kaptur *m*; *mot.* dach *m* opuszczany; *mot. Am.* maska *f*; *tech.* pokrywa *f*, osłona *f*
hood·lum ['hu:dləm] *sl.* chuligan *m*, zbir *m*
hood·wink ['hʊdwɪŋk] kogoś nabierać ⟨-brać⟩
hoof [hu:f] (*pl. hoofs* [hu:fs], *hooves* [hu:vz]) kopyto *m*
hook [hʊk] **1.** hak *m*; haczyk *m*; *by* ~ *or by crook* F nie przebierając w środkach; **2.** przyczepiać ⟨-pić⟩ na haczyk, zahaczać ⟨-czyć⟩; ⟨z⟩łapać na haczyk (*też fig.*); ~ed [hʊkt] haczykowaty; zakrzywiony; F uzależniony (*on* od *G*) (*też fig.*); '~·y: *play* ~*y zwł. Am.* F wagarować
hoo·li·gan ['hu:lɪgən] chuligan *m*; ~·is·m ['hu:lɪgənɪzəm] chuligaństwo *n*
hoop [hu:p] obręcz *f*, opaska *f*
hoot [hu:t] **1.** pohukiwanie *n* (*sowy*); *mot.* klakson *m*, sygnał *m* dźwiękowy; drwiący okrzyk *m*; **2.** *v/i.* ⟨za⟩wyć; *mot.* ⟨za⟩trąbić; *sowa:* ⟨za⟩huczeć; *v/t.* ⟨za⟩trąbić (*I*)
Hoo·ver ['hu:və] *Brt. TM* **1.** odkurzacz *m*; **2.** *zw.* ♀ odkurzać ⟨-rzyć⟩
hooves [hu:vz] *pl. od* **hoof**
hop¹ [hɒp] **1.** (*-pp-*) skakać ⟨skoczyć⟩, podskakiwać ⟨-skoczyć⟩; przeskakiwać przez (*A*); *be* ~*ping mad* F być w furii; **2.** podskok *m*
hop² [hɒp] *bot.* chmiel *m*; ~*s* chmiel *m* (*szyszki*)
hope [həʊp] **1.** nadzieja *f*; **2.** mieć nadzieję; spodziewać się, wyczekiwać; ~ *for the best* mieć dobrej myśli; *I* ~ *so, let's* ~ *so* odpowiadając mam nadzieję; *I* (*sincerely*) ~ *so* mam nadzieję; '~·ful: *be* ~*ful that* mieć nadzieję, że; '~·ful·ly z nadzieją, wyczekująco; ma-

m(y) nadzieję (że); '~·less beznadziejny; rozpaczliwy

hop·scotch ['hɒpskɒtʃ] gra f w klasy

ho·ri·zon [hə'raɪzn] horyzont m

hor·i·zon·tal [hɒrɪ'zɒntl] horyzontalny, poziomy

hor·mone ['hɔːməʊn] biol. hormon m

horn [hɔːn] róg m; mot. klakson m; ~s pl. poroże n

hor·net ['hɔːnɪt] zo. szerszeń m

horn·y ['hɔːnɪ] (-ier, -iest) rogaty; V mężczyzna: podniecony, rozochocony

hor·o·scope ['hɒrəskəʊp] horoskop m

hor·ri·ble ['hɒrəbl] straszny, przerażający, okropny; ~·rid ['hɒrɪd] zwł. Brt. straszny, okropny; ~·rif·ic [hɒ'rɪfɪk] (-ally) okropny, przerażający; ~·ri·fy ['hɒrɪfaɪ] przerażać ⟨-razić⟩; ~·ror ['hɒrə] przerażanie n; potworność f; F postrach m; '~·ror film horror m

horse [hɔːs] zo. koń m; (w sporcie) kozioł m, koń m; **wild ~s couldn't drag me there** szóstką wołów by mnie tam nie zaciągnęli; ~ 'back: on ~back wierzchem, konno; ~ 'chest·nut bot. kasztanowiec m; '~·hair końskie włosie n; '~·man (pl. -men) jeździec m; '~·pow·er phys. koń m mechaniczny; (jednostka anglosaska) koń parowy (1,0139 KM); ~ 'race gonitwa f konna; ~ 'rac·ing wyścigi pl. konne; '~·rad·ish bot. chrzan m; '~·shoe podkowa f; '~·wom·an (pl. -women) f, amazonka f

hor·ti·cul·ture ['hɔːtɪkʌltʃə] ogrodnictwo n

hose¹ [həʊz] wąż m; szlauch m

hose² [həʊz] rajstopy pl.

ho·sier·y ['həʊʒərɪ] wyroby pl. pończosznicze

hos·pice ['hɒspɪs] hospicjum n

hos·pi·ta·ble ['hɒspɪtəbl] gościnny

hos·pi·tal ['hɒspɪtl] szpital m; in (Am. in the) ~ w szpitalu

hos·pi·tal·i·ty [hɒspɪ'tælətɪ] gościnność f

hos·pi·tal·ize ['hɒspɪtəlaɪz] hospitalizować, umieszczać ⟨umieścić⟩ w szpitalu

host¹ [həʊst] 1. gospodarz m; biol. żywiciel m; radio, TV: gospodarz m programu. prowadzący m program; **your ~ was...** audycję prowadził...; 2. radio, TV: F audycję ⟨po⟩prowadzić

host² [həʊst] zastęp m, rzesza f

host³ [həʊst] rel. często 2 hostia f

hos·tage ['hɒstɪdʒ] zakładnik m (-niczka f); **take s.o. ~** brać ⟨wziąć⟩ kogoś jako zakładnika

hos·tel ['hɒstl] zwł. Brt. dom m (studencki); zw. **youth ~** schronisko n młodzieżowe

host·ess ['həʊstɪs] gospodyni f; aviat. stewardessa f; hostessa f

hos·tile ['hɒstaɪl] wrogi; nieprzyjazny (**to** wobec G); ~·til·i·ty [hɒ'stɪlətɪ] wrogość f (**to** wobec G)

hot [hɒt] (-tt-) gorący; przyprawa: ostry; temperament: zapalczywy; wiadomości: najnowszy; **she is ~** gorąco jej; **it's ~** gorąco (jest); '~·bed rozsadnik m (też fig.), fig. siedlisko n

hotch·potch ['hɒtʃpɒtʃ] miszmasz m

hot 'dog hot dog m (bułka z parówką na gorąco)

ho·tel [həʊ'tel] hotel m

'hot|·head zapalczywy człowiek m; '~·house inspekt m; '~ line pol. gorąca linia f; '~ spot zwł. pol. punkt m zapalny; ~·'wa·ter bot·tle termofor m

hound [haʊnd] zo. pies m myśliwski

hour ['aʊə] godzina f; ~s pl. godziny pl. (pracy); '~·ly adj. cogodzinny; godzinny; 2. adv. co godzinę, na godzinę

house 1. [haʊs] dom m; budynek m; theat. widownia f, publika f; 2. [haʊz] ⟨z⟩mieścić, pomieścić; dawać ⟨dać⟩ mieszkanie; '~·bound fig. nie mogący wyjść z domu; '~·break·ing włamanie n; '~·hold gospodarstwo n domowe; dom m; rodzina f; ~ 'hus·band domator m; mężczyzna m prowadzący dom; '~·keep·er gosposia f; '~·keep·ing gospodarstwo n, gospodarowanie n; '~·maid pokojówka f; służąca f; '~·man (pl. -men) lekarz m stażysta; '~·warm·ing (par·ty) parapetówa f, oblewanie n nowego domu; '~·wife (pl. -wives) gospodyni f domowa; '~·work prace pl. domowe

hous·ing ['haʊzɪŋ] budownictwo n mieszkaniowe; gospodarka f mieszkaniowa; attr. mieszkaniowy; '~ de·vel·op·ment, Am.; '~ es·tate Brt. dzielnica f mieszkaniowa

hove [həʊv] pret. i p.p. od **heave** 2

hov·er ['hɒvə] unosić się (w powietrzu); zawisnąć (w powietrzu); kręcić się; fig.

być zawieszonym; '~·craft (pl. -craft, -crafts) poduszkowiec m

how [haʊ] jak; ~ **are you?** jak się masz?; ~ **about...?** a co z ...?; ~ **do you do?** przy przedstawianiu dzień dobry!; ~ **much water?** ile wody?; ~ **many spoons?** ile łyżeczek?

how·dy ['haʊdɪ] Am. int. F cześć!, siemanko!

how·ev·er [haʊ'evə] 1. adv. jakkolwiek; 2. jednak(że)

howl [haʊl] 1. ⟨za⟩wyć; wiatr, dziecko: zawodzić; 2. wycie n; zawodzenie n; '~·er F błąd m, byk m

HP [eɪtʃ 'piː] skrót: **horsepower** KM, koń m mechaniczny; skrót: **hire purchase** Brt. kupno n na raty

HQ [eɪtʃ 'kjuː] skrót: **headquarters** kwatera f główna

hr (pl. **hrs**) skrót pisany: **hour** godz., godzina f

HRH [eɪtʃ ɑː(r) 'eɪtʃ] skrót: **His/Her Royal Highness** Jego/Jej Królewska Wysokość

hub [hʌb] piasta f; fig. ośrodek m, centrum n

hub·bub ['hʌbʌb] tumult m, rwetes m

hub·by ['hʌbɪ] F mężuś m

huck·le·ber·ry ['hʌklberɪ] bot. jagoda f amerykańska

huck·ster ['hʌkstə] domokrążca m, kramarz m

hud·dle ['hʌdl] ~ **together** tulić (się); ~**d up** pozwijany

hue[1] [hjuː] barwa f, kolor m; odcień m

hue[2] [hjuː]: ~ **and cry** fig. wrzawa f protestów

huff [hʌf]: **in a** ~ rozsierdzony

hug [hʌg] 1. (-**gg**-) obejmować ⟨-bjąć⟩ (się); przytulać ⟨-lić⟩ się; 2. objęcie n, uścisk m

huge [hjuːdʒ] wielki, ogromny

hulk [hʌlk] zawalidroga m/f; moloch m; kolos m

hull [hʌl] 1. bot. łuska f, łupina f, szypułka f; naut. kadłub m; 2. ⟨ob⟩łuskać, truskawki obierać ⟨-brać⟩

hul·la·ba·loo ['hʌləbə'luː] (pl. -**loos**) wrzawa f, zgiełk m

hul·lo [hə'ləʊ] int. halo!, hej!

hum [hʌm] (-**mm**-) ⟨za⟩mruczeć, ⟨za⟩nucić

hu·man ['hjuːmən] 1. ludzki; 2. też ~ **being** człowiek m; ~**e** [hjuː'meɪn]

ludzki, humanitarny; ~·i·tar·i·an [hjuːmænɪ'teərɪən] humanitarny; ~·i·ty [hjuː'mænətɪ] ludzkość f; humanitaryzm m; **humanities** pl. nauki pl. humanistyczne; '~·ly **as** **ly possible** w ludzkiej mocy; ~ **'rights** pl. prawa pl. człowieka

hum·ble ['hʌmbl] 1. (-**r, -st**) pokorny; skromny; uniżony; 2. poniżać ⟨-żyć⟩; '~·ness uniżoność f; pokora f; skromność f

hum·drum ['hʌmdrʌm] monotonny, jednostajny

hu·mid ['hjuːmɪd] wilgotny; ~·i·ty [hjuː'mɪdətɪ] wilgotność f

hu·mil·i·ate [hjuː'mɪlɪeɪt] poniżać ⟨-żyć⟩, upokarzać ⟨-korzyć⟩; ~·a·tion [hjuːmɪlɪ'eɪʃn] poniżenie n, upokorzenie n; ~·ty [hjuː'mɪlətɪ] pokora f

hum·ming·bird ['hʌmɪŋbɜːd] zo. koliber m

hu·mor·ous ['hjuːmərəs] humorystyczny, zabawny

hu·mo(u)r ['hjuːmə] 1. humor m; komizm m; 2. udobruchać; spełniać ⟨-nić⟩ (zachcianki)

hump [hʌmp] wybrzuszenie n; garb m; '~·back(ed) → **hunchbacked**

hunch [hʌntʃ] 1. → **hump**; kawał m; przeczucie n; 2. też ~ **up** krzywić się; ~ **one's shoulders** ⟨z⟩garbić się; '~·back garbus m; '~·backed garbaty

hun·dred ['hʌndrəd] 1. sto; 2. setka f; ~**th** ['hʌndrədθ] 1. setny; 2. jedna f setna; '~·weight jakby: cetnar (=50,8 kg)

hung [hʌŋ] pret. i pp. od **hang**[1]

Hun·ga·ri·an [hʌŋ'geərɪən] 1. węgierski; 2. Węgier(ka f) m; ling. język m węgierski; **Hun·ga·ry** ['hʌŋgərɪ] Węgry pl.

hun·ger ['hʌŋgə] 1. głód, łaknienie n; 2. fig. łaknąć; ~ **strike** strajk m głodowy

hun·gry ['hʌŋgrɪ] (-**ier, -iest**) głodny

hunk [hʌŋk] kawał m

hunt [hʌnt] 1. polować na (A); poszukiwać ⟨-kać⟩, ⟨wy⟩tropić; ~ **out, ~ up** wy-tropić (A); 2. polowanie n (też fig.); tropienie n, poszukiwanie n; '~·er myśliwy m; '~·ing myślistwo n; '~·ing ground teren m łowiecki

hur·dle ['hɜːdl] sport: płotek m (też fig.); przeszkoda f (też fig.); '~·r (w sporcie) płotkarz m (-rka f); '~ **race** (w sporcie) bieg m przez płotki

hurl

hurl [hɜːl] miotać ⟨-tnąć⟩; **~ abuse at s.o.** obrzucać ⟨-cić⟩ kogoś wyzwiskami

hur·rah [hʊˈrɑː] *int.*, **~·ray** *int.* [hʊˈreɪ] hurra!

hur·ri·cane ['hʌrɪkən] huragan *m*, orkan *m*

hur·ried ['hʌrɪd] pospieszny

hur·ry ['hʌrɪ] **1.** *v/t.* przyspieszać ⟨-szyć⟩; *często* **~ up** kogoś poganiać ⟨-gonić⟩, popędzać ⟨-dzić⟩; zwiększać ⟨-szać⟩ tempo; *v/i.* ⟨po⟩śpieszyć się; **~ (up)** śpieszyć się; **~ up!** pośpiesz się!; **2.** pośpiech *m*; **be in a ~** śpieszyć się

hurt [hɜːt] (**hurt**) ⟨z⟩ranić (*też fig.*); boleć; ⟨s⟩krzywdzić; **'~·ful** bolesny

hus·band ['hʌzbənd] mąż *m*

hush [hʌʃ] **1.** *int.* cicho!; **2.** cisza *f*; **3.** uciszać ⟨-szyć⟩; **~ up** ⟨za⟩tuszować; **'~ mon·ey** pieniądze *pl.* (*na zatuszowanie czegoś*)

husk [hʌsk] *bot.* **1.** łuska *f*, plewa *f*, łupina *f*; **2.** ⟨ob⟩łuskać

'hus·ky (*-ier, -iest*) ochrypły; F silny, mocarny

hus·sy ['hʌsɪ] dziwka *f*

hus·tle ['hʌsl] **1.** *kogoś* poganiać ⟨-gonić⟩, popędzać ⟨-dzić⟩; wypychać ⟨-pchnąć⟩; nakłaniać ⟨-łonić⟩; śpieszyć się; **2. ~ and bustle** wrzawa *f*, zamęt *m*, ruch *m*

hut [hʌt] chata *f*

hutch [hʌtʃ] klatka *f* (*zwł. dla królików*)

hy·a·cinth ['haɪəsɪnθ] *bot.* hiacynt *m*

hy·ae·na [haɪˈiːnə] *zo.* hiena *f*

hy·brid ['haɪbrɪd] *biol.* hybryda *f*, mieszaniec *m*

hy·drant ['haɪdrənt] hydrant *m*

hy·drau·lic [haɪˈdrɔːlɪk] (**~ally**) hydrauliczny; **~s** *sg.* hydraulika *f*

hy·dro... ['haɪdrə] hydro..., wodno...; **~'car·bon** węglowodór *m*; **~·chlor·ic ac·id** [haɪdrəklɒrɪk ˈæsɪd] kwas *m* solny; **'~·foil** *naut.* wodolot *m*; **~·gen** ['haɪdrədʒən] wodór *m*; **'~·gen bomb** bomba *f* wodorowa; **'~·plane** *aviat.* hydroplan *m*; *naut.* ślizgacz *m*; **'~·plan·ing** *Am. mot.* akwaplaning *n*

hy·e·na [haɪˈiːnə] *zo.* hiena *f*

hy·giene ['haɪdʒiːn] higiena *f*; **hy·gien·ic** [haɪˈdʒiːnɪk] (**~ally**) higieniczny

hymn [hɪm] kościelny hymn *m*

hype [haɪp] F **1.** *też* **~ up** nakręcać ⟨-cić⟩ reklamę; **2.** *nadmierna* reklama *f*; **me·dia ~** wrzawa *f* (*w gazetach*)

hy·per... ['haɪpə] hiper..., ponad..., nad...; **'~·mar·ket** *Brt.* (*duży supersam*) hipermarket *m*; **~'sen·si·tive** nadpobudliwy (**to** na A)

hy·phen ['haɪfn] łącznik *m*, tiret *n*; **~·ate** ['haɪfəneɪt] wstawiać ⟨-wić⟩ łączniki

hyp·no·tize ['hɪpnətaɪz] ⟨za⟩hipnotyzować

hy·po·chon·dri·ac [haɪpəˈkɒndrɪæk] hipochondryk *m*

hy·poc·ri·sy [hɪˈpɒkrəsɪ] hipokryzja *f*, obłuda *f*; **hyp·o·crite** ['hɪpəkrɪt] hipokryta *m* (*-tka f*), obłudnik *m* (*-ica f*); **hyp·o·crit·i·cal** [hɪpəˈkrɪtɪkl] obłudny

hy·poth·e·sis [haɪˈpɒθɪsɪs] (*pl.* **-ses** [-siːz]) hipoteza *f*

hys·te·ri·a [hɪˈstɪərɪə] *med.* histeria *f*; **~·ter·i·cal** [hɪˈsterɪkl] histeryczny, rozhisteryzowany; **~·ter·ics** [hɪˈsterɪks] *pl.* histeria *f*; **go into ~terics** dostawać ⟨-tać⟩ histerii; pękać ze śmiechu

---

I

I, i [aɪ] I, i *n*

I [aɪ] ja

IC [aɪ ˈsiː] *skrót:* **integrated circuit** obwód *m* zintegrowany

ice [aɪs] **1.** lód *m*; **2.** napoje *itp.* ⟨s⟩chłodzić w lodzie; *gastr.* ⟨po⟩lukrować; **~d over** *jezioro itp.*: zamarznięty; **~d up** *ulica itp.*: oblodzony; **'~ age** epoka *f* lodowcowa; **~·berg** ['aɪsbɜːg] góra *f* lodowa; **'~·bound** przymarznięty; **~ cream** lody *pl.*; **~·cream 'par·lo(u)r** lodziarnia *f*; **'~ cube** kostka *f* lodu; **'~ floe** kra *f*, **~d** mrożony; schłodzony; **'~ hock·ey** (*w sporcie*) hokej *m* na lodzie; **'~ lol·ly** *Brt.* lody *pl.* na patyku; **'~ rink** *sztuczne* lodowisko *n*; **'~ skate** łyżwa *f*; **'~·skate** jeździć ⟨jechać⟩ na łyżwach; **'~ show** rewia *f* na lodzie

i·ci·cle ['aɪsɪkl] sopel *m* (*lodu*)

ic·ing ['aɪsɪŋ] lukier *m*

i·con ['aɪkɒn] ikona *f* (*też komp.*)

i·cy ['aɪsɪ] (*-ier, -iest*) lodowaty; oblodzony

ID [aɪ 'di:] *skrót*: **identity** tożsamość *f*; **ID card** dowód *m* tożsamości

i·dea [aɪ'dɪə] pomysł *m*; pojęcie *n*; idea *f*, pogląd *m*; zamiar *m*; **have no ~** nie mieć pojęcia

i·deal [aɪ'dɪəl] **1.** idealny; **2.** ideał *m*; **~·is·m** [aɪ'dɪəlɪzəm] idealizm *m*; **~·ize** [aɪ'dɪəlaɪz] ⟨wy⟩idealizować

i·den·ti·cal [aɪ'dentɪkl] identyczny (**to, with** z I); **~ 'twins** *pl.* bliźnięta *pl.* jednojajowe

i·den·ti·fi·ca·tion [aɪdentɪfɪ'keɪʃn] identyfikacja *f*; **~** (**pa·pers** *pl.*) dowód *m* tożsamości

i·den·ti·fy [aɪ'dentɪfaɪ] ⟨z⟩identyfikować; **~ o.s.** zidentyfikować się

i·den·ti·kit pic·ture [aɪ'dentɪkɪt -] portret *m* pamięciowy (*przestępcy*)

i·den·ti·ty [aɪ'dentətɪ] tożsamość *f*; **~ card** dowód *m* tożsamości

i·de·o·log·i·cal [aɪdɪə'lɒdʒɪkl] ideologiczny; **~·ol·o·gy** [aɪdɪ'ɒlədʒɪ] ideologia *f*

id·i·om ['ɪdɪət] idiom *m*, idiomatyzm *m*; **~·o·mat·ic** [ɪdɪə'mætɪk] idiomatyczny

id·i·ot ['ɪdɪət] idiota *m* (*-tka f*) (*też med.*); **~·ic** [ɪdɪ'ɒtɪk] idiotyczny

i·dle ['aɪdl] **1.** (*-r, -st*) bezczynny; bezproduktywny; próżniaczy; czczy, bezzasadny; *econ.* pieniądze: nieprodukcyjny, *wydajność*: niewykorzystany; *tech.* jałowy, nieobciążony; **2.** spędzać ⟨-dzić⟩ nieproduktywnie czas; chodzić ⟨iść⟩ na jałowym biegu; **~ away** czas ⟨z⟩marnować

i·dol ['aɪdl] idol *m*; bożek *m*; **~·ize** ['aɪdəlaɪz] ubóstwiać ⟨-wić⟩

i·dyl·lic [aɪ'dɪlɪk] (**~ally**) idylliczny

i.e. [aɪ 'iː] *skrót*: **that is to say** (*łacińskie* **id est**) tj., to jest

if [ɪf] jeżeli, jeśli; gdyby; czy; **~ I were you** gdybym był na twoim miejscu

ig·loo ['ɪgluː] (*pl. -loos*) iglo *n*

ig·nite [ɪg'naɪt] zapalać ⟨-lić⟩ (się); *mot.* zapalać ⟨-lić⟩; **ig·ni·tion** [ɪg'nɪʃən] *tech.* zapłon; **~ key** kluczyk *m* zapłonu

ig·no·min·i·ous [ɪgnə'mɪnɪəs] haniebny, nikczemny

ig·no·rance ['ɪgnərəns] niewiedza *f*, ignorancja *f*; **ig·no·rant**: **be ~ of s.th.** nie wiedzieć o czymś, nie mieć pojęcia o czymś; **ig·nore** [ɪg'nɔː] ⟨z⟩ignorować; pomijać ⟨-minąć⟩

ill [ɪl] **1.** (*worse, worst*) chory; zły, niedobry; **fall ~**, **be taken ~** zachorować; **2. ~s** *pl.* problemy *pl.*; zło *n*; **~·ad'vised** nierozważny; **~'bred** niewychowany

il·le·gal [ɪ'liːgl] nielegalny, bezprawny; **~ parking** niewłaściwe parkowanie *n*

il·le·gi·ble [ɪ'ledʒəbl] nieczytelny

il·le·git·i·mate [ɪlɪ'dʒɪtɪmət] nieślubny; bezprawny

ill·**'fat·ed** fatalny; nieszczęśliwy; **~'hu·mo(u)red** w złym humorze

il·li·cit [ɪ'lɪsɪt] zakazany, nielegalny

il·lit·e·rate [ɪ'lɪtərət] niepiśmienny

ill·**'man·nered** niewychowany; **~'na·tured** złośliwy

'ill·ness choroba *f*

ill·**'tem·pered** w złym humorze; **~'timed** w złą porę; **~'treat** źle traktować; maltretować

il·lu·mi·**nate** [ɪ'ljuːmɪneɪt] oświetlać ⟨-lić⟩, iluminować; oświecać ⟨-cić⟩; **~·nat·ing** pouczający; **~·na·tion** [ɪljuːmɪ'neɪʃn] oświetlenie *n*; **~·nations** *pl.* iluminacja *f*

il·lu·sion [ɪ'luːʒn] iluzja *f*, złudzenie *n*; **~·sive** [ɪ'luːsɪv], **~·so·ry** [ɪ'luːsərɪ] złudny, iluzoryczny

il·lus·trate ['ɪləstreɪt] ⟨z⟩ilustrować; ⟨z⟩obrazować; **~·tra·tion** [ɪlə'streɪʃn] ilustracja *f*; obrazowanie *n*; **~·tra·tive** ['ɪləstrətɪv] ilustracyjny; obrazujący

il·lus·tri·ous [ɪ'lʌstrɪəs] znamienity

ill 'will wrogość *f*, nieprzyjazne uczucie *n*

im·age ['ɪmɪdʒ] wizerunek *m*, obraz *m*; odbicie *n*; metafora *f*, porównanie *n*; **im·ag·e·ry** ['ɪmɪdʒərɪ] symbolika *f*

i·ma·gi·na·**ble** [ɪ'mædʒɪnəbl] wyobrażalny; **~·ry** [ɪ'mædʒɪnərɪ] urojony, zmyślony; **~·tion** [ɪmædʒɪ'neɪʃn] wyobraźnia *f*; **~·tive** [ɪ'mædʒɪnətɪv] o dużej wyobraźni, pełen fantazji, pomysłowy; **i·ma·gine** [ɪ'mædʒɪn] wyobrażać ⟨-razić⟩ sobie; sądzić

im·bal·ance [ɪm'bæləns] brak *m* równowagi

im·be·cile ['ɪmbɪsiːl] imbecyl *m*, kretyn(ka *f*) *m*

IMF [aɪ em 'ef] *skrót*: **International Monetary Fund** MFW, Międzynarodowy Fundusz *m* Walutowy

im·i·tate ['ɪmɪteɪt] naśladować, imitować; **~·ta·tion** [ɪmɪ'teɪʃn] **1.** imitacja *f*, naśladownictwo *n*; naśladowanie *n*; **2.** sztuczny; **~*tation leather** imitacja *f* skóry

im·mac·u·late [ɪ'mækjʊlət] *rel.* niepokalany; nieskazitelny

im·ma·te·ri·al [ɪmə'tɪərɪəl] nieistotny, bez znaczenia (**to** dla *G*)

im·ma·ture [ɪmə'tjʊə] niedojrzały

im·mea·su·ra·ble [ɪ'meʒərəbl] niezmierzony, nieprzejrzany

im·me·di·ate [ɪ'miːdjət] bezpośredni; natychmiastowy, bezzwłoczny; *przyszłość*, *rodzina*: najbliższy; **~·ly** bezpośrednio; natychmiastowo, bezzwłocznie

im·mense [ɪ'mens] ogromny

im·merse [ɪ'mɜːs] zanurzać ⟨-rzyć⟩ **~ o.s.** in zagłębiać ⟨-bić⟩ się w (*L*); im·mer·sion [ɪ'mɜːʃn] zanurzenie *n*; im'mer·sion heat·er grzałka *f* (*nurkowa*)

im·mi·grant ['ɪmɪgrənt] imigrant(ka *f*) *m*; **~·grate** ['ɪmɪgreɪt] imigrować (**into** do *G*); **~·gra·tion** [ɪmɪ'greɪʃn] imigracja *f*

im·mi·nent ['ɪmɪnənt] zagrażający, nadchodzący; **~ danger** bezpośrednie zagrożenie

im·mo·bile [ɪ'məʊbaɪl] nieruchomy

im·mod·e·rate [ɪ'mɒdərət] nieumiarkowany

im·mod·est [ɪ'mɒdɪst] nieskromny

im·mor·al [ɪ'mɒrəl] niemoralny

im·mor·tal [ɪ'mɔːtl] **1.** nieśmiertelny; **2.** człowiek *m* nieśmiertelny; **~·i·ty** [ɪmɔː'tælətɪ] nieśmiertelność

im·mo·va·ble [ɪ'muːvəbl] nieruchomy, *fig.* niewzruszony

im·mune [ɪ'mjuːn] odporny (**to** na *A*); nie podlegający; im·mu·ni·ty [ɪ'mjuːnətɪ] odporność *f*; niepodleganie *n*; immunitet *m*; im·mu·nize ['ɪmjuːnaɪz] immunizować, ⟨u⟩czynić odpornym (**against** na *A*)

imp [ɪmp] chochlik *m*, diabełek *m*

im·pact ['ɪmpækt] zderzenie *n*, uderzenie *n*; *fig.* wpływ *m* (**on** na *A*)

im·pair [ɪm'peə] osłabiać ⟨-bić⟩, pogarszać ⟨-gorszyć⟩

im·part [ɪm'pɑːt] (**to**) przekazywać ⟨-zać⟩ (*D*); nadawać (*D*)

im·par·tial [ɪm'pɑːʃl] obiektywny, bezstronny; **~·ti·al·i·ty** [ɪmpɑːʃɪ'ælətɪ] obiektywność *f*, bezstronność *f*

im·pass·a·ble [ɪm'pɑːsəbl] nieprzejezdny, nie do przejścia

im·passe [æm'pɑːs] *fig.* impas *m*, ślepa uliczka *f*

im·pas·sioned [ɪm'pæʃnd] namiętny, żarliwy

im·pas·sive [ɪm'pæsɪv] beznamiętny, obojętny, bierny

im·pa·tience [ɪm'peɪʃns] niecierpliwość *f*; **~·tient** niecierpliwy

im·peach [ɪm'piːtʃ] *jur.* pociągać ⟨-gnąć⟩ do odpowiedzialności (**for, of, with** za *A*), oskarżać ⟨-rżyć⟩ (**for, of, with** o *A*); ⟨za⟩kwestionować

im·pec·ca·ble [ɪm'pekəbl] nienaganny, bez zarzutu

im·pede [ɪm'piːd] przeszkadzać ⟨-kodzić⟩, utrudniać ⟨-nić⟩

im·ped·i·ment [ɪm'pedɪmənt] przeszkoda *f*; trudność *f* (**to** przy *L*)

im·pel [ɪm'pel] (**-ll-**) nakłaniać ⟨-łonić⟩

im·pend·ing [ɪm'pendɪŋ] zagrażający, bliski

im·pen·e·tra·ble [ɪm'penɪtrəbl] niedostępny, nieprzenikniony (*też fig.*)

im·per·a·tive [ɪm'perətɪv] **1.** imperatywny; nakazujący; *gr.* rozkazujący; **2.** *też* **~ mood** *gr.* tryb *m* rozkazujący

im·per·cep·ti·ble [ɪmpə'septəbl] niedostrzegalny, niezauważalny

im·per·fect [ɪm'pɜːfɪkt] **1.** niedoskonały, nienajlepszy; **2.** *też* **~ tense** *gr.* czas przeszły niedokonany

im·pe·ri·al·is·m [ɪm'pɪərɪəlɪzəm] *pol.* imperializm *m*; **~t** [ɪm'pɪərɪəlɪst] *pol.* imperialista *m*

im·per·il [ɪm'perəl] (*zwł. Brt.* **-ll-** , *Am.* **-l-**) narażać ⟨-razić⟩

im·pe·ri·ous [ɪm'pɪərɪəs] władczy

im·per·me·a·ble [ɪm'pɜːmjəbl] nieprzepuszczalny

im·per·son·al [ɪm'pɜːsnl] bezosobowy

im·per·so·nate [ɪm'pɜːsəneɪt] podawać ⟨-dać⟩ się za (*A*); naśladować; *theat. itp.* odgrywać ⟨-degrać⟩

im·per·ti·nence [ɪm'pɜːtɪnəns] bezczelność *f*, tupet *m*; **~·nent** imperty-nencki, bezczelny

im·per·tur·ba·ble [ˌɪmpəˈtɜːbəbl] nie-wzruszony

im·per·vi·ous [ɪmˈpɜːvjəs] nieprze-puszczalny; *fig.* niepodatny (**to** na *A*)

im·pe·tu·ous [ɪmˈpetjuəs] porywczy, impulsywny

im·pe·tus [ˈɪmpɪtəs] rozpęd *m*, impet *m*

im·pi·e·ty [ɪmˈpaɪətɪ] bezbożność *f*; nie-poszanowanie

im·pinge [ɪmˈpɪndʒ]: **~ on** wpływać na (*A*), mieć wpływ na (*A*)

im·pi·ous [ˈɪmpɪəs] bezbożny; nie sza-nujący

im·plac·a·ble [ɪmˈplækəbl] nieubłaga-ny, nieustępliwy

im·plant [ɪmˈplɑːnt] *med.* wszczepiać ⟨-pić⟩; *fig.* zaszczepiać ⟨-pić⟩

im·ple·ment 1. [ˈɪmplɪmənt] narzędzie *n*; **2.** [ˈɪmplɪment] wprowadzać ⟨-dzić⟩ do użytku

im·pli·cate [ˈɪmplɪkeɪt] wplątywać ⟨-tać⟩ (**in** do *G*), ⟨u⟩wikłać; **~·ca·tion** [ɪmplɪˈkeɪʃn] wplątanie *n*, uwikłanie *n*, wmieszanie *n*

im·pli·cit [ɪmˈplɪsɪt] domniemany, nie powiedziany otwarcie

im·plore [ɪmˈplɔː] ⟨u⟩błagać

im·ply [ɪmˈplaɪ] ⟨za⟩sugerować, dawać ⟨dać⟩ do zrozumienia; oznaczać; impli-kować

im·po·lite [ɪmpəˈlaɪt] nieuprzejmy

im·pol·i·tic [ɪmˈpɒlɪtɪk] niezręczny; nierozsądny

im·port 1. [ɪmˈpɔːt] importować, wwo-zić ⟨wwieźć⟩; **2.** [ˈɪmpɔːt] import *m*; **~s** *pl.* towary *pl.* importowane

im·por|·tance [ɪmˈpɔːtəns] ważność *f*, duże znaczenie *n*; **~·tant** ważny, du-żo znaczący

im·por|·ta·tion [ɪmpɔːˈteɪʃn] → **import** 2; **~·ter** [ɪmˈpɔːtə] importer *m*

im·pose [ɪmˈpəʊz] nakładać ⟨nałożyć⟩, narzucać ⟨-cić⟩ (**on s.o.** na kogoś); **~ o.s. on s.o.** narzucać ⟨-cić⟩ się ko-muś; **im'pos·ing** imponujący, robiący duże wrażenie

im·pos·si|·bil·i·ty [ɪmpɒsəˈbɪlətɪ] nie-możliwość *f*; **~·ble** [ɪmˈpɒsəbl] niemoż-liwy

im·pos·tor *Brt.*, **im·pos·ter** *Am.* [ɪmˈpɒstə] oszust(ka *f*) *m*, szalbierz *m*

im·po|·tence [ˈɪmpətəns] niemożność

f, niemoc *f*; nieudolność *f*; *med.* impo-tencja *f*; **~·tent** bezsilny, bezradny;

im·pov·e·rish [ɪmˈpɒvərɪʃ] zubażać ⟨-bożyć⟩

im·prac·ti·ca·ble [ɪmˈpræktɪkəbl] nie-wykonalny

im·prac·ti·cal [ɪmˈpræktɪkl] nieprak-tyczny, mało praktyczny

im·preg·na·ble [ɪmˈpregnəbl] *zamek itp.*: nie do zdobycia; niezbity

im·preg·nate [ˈɪmpregneɪt] ⟨za⟩im-pregnować; zapładniać ⟨-łodnić⟩

im·press [ɪmˈpres] *komuś* ⟨za⟩impono-wać; wywierać ⟨-wrzeć⟩ wrażenie; za-zmysławiać ⟨-łowić⟩; *coś* odciskać ⟨-ci-snąć⟩; **im·pres·sion** [ɪmˈpreʃn] wraże-nie *n*; odcisk *m*; **be under the ~** that mieć wrażenie, że; **im·pres·sive** [ɪmˈpresɪv] imponujący

im·print 1. [ɪmˈprɪnt] odciskać ⟨-snąć⟩; **~ s.th. on s.o.'s memory** utrwalić coś w czyjejś pamięci; **2.** [ˈɪmprɪnt] od-cisk *m*; *print.* nazwa *f* (*wydawnictwa*), metryczka *f*

im·pris·on [ɪmˈprɪzn] ⟨u⟩więzić; **~·ment** uwięzienie *n*

im·prob·a·ble [ɪmˈprɒbəbl] nieprawdo-podobny

im·prop·er [ɪmˈprɒpə] niewłaściwy, nie-stosowny

im·pro·pri·e·ty [ɪmprəˈpraɪətɪ] niewła-ściwość *f*, niestosowność *f*

im·prove [ɪmˈpruːv] polepszać ⟨-szyć⟩ (się), ulepszać ⟨-szyć⟩ (się); *wartość itp.* zwiększać ⟨-szyć⟩ (się); **~ on** osiągać lepszy wynik od (*G*); poprawić wynik (*G*); **~·ment** polepszenie *n*, ulepszenie *n*; postęp *m* (**on** ze względu na *D*)

im·pro·vise [ˈɪmprəvaɪz] ⟨za⟩improwi-zować

im·pru·dent [ɪmˈpruːdənt] nieroztrop-ny, nierozważny

im·pu|·dence [ˈɪmpjʊdəns] czelność *f*, zuchwałość *f*; **~·dent** zuchwały

im·pulse [ˈɪmpʌls] impuls *m* (*też fig.*); bodziec *m*; **im·pul·sive** [ɪmˈpʌlsɪv] impulsywny, zapalczywy

im·pu·ni·ty [ɪmˈpjuːnətɪ]: **with ~** bez-karnie

im·pure [ɪmˈpjʊə] nieczysty (*też rel.*, *fig.*); zanieczyszczony

im·pute [ɪmˈpjuːt]: **~ s.th. to s.o.** przy-pisywać ⟨-sać⟩ coś komuś

in¹ [ɪn] **1.** *prp. przestrzeń*: (*miejsce*) w (*L*),

na (L); ~ **London** w Londynie, ~ **the street** na ulicy; *ruch:* do (G); **put it ~ your pocket** włóż to do kieszeni; *czas:* w (L), w ciągu (G), w czasie (G), za (G); ~ **1999** w 1999 roku; ~ **two hours** za dwie godziny; ~ **the morning** rano; *stan, sposób:* po (D); na (D): ~ **pencil** ołówkiem; ~ **writing** na piśmie; ~ **Polish** po polsku; *stan, okoliczności:* przy (L), podczas (G); ~ **crossing the street** przechodząc przez ulicę; *materiał:* w (A), na; *dressed ~ jeans (blue)* ubrany w dżinsy (na niebiesko); *liczba, proporcja:* na (A), z (G); **one ~ ten** jeden na dziesięciu; **three ~ all** łącznie trzech; **have confidence ~** ufać (D); **~ defence of** w obronie (G);**~ my opinion** w moim przekonaniu; **2.** *adv.* wewnątrz (G), do wewnątrz (G); w domu; w pracy; w modzie; **3.** *adj.* F modny
in² *skrót pisany: inch(es)* cal *m (2,54 cm)*
in·a·bil·i·ty [ɪnə'bɪlətɪ] niezdolność *f*
in·ac·ces·si·ble [ɪnæk'sesəbl] niedostępny (**to** dla *G*)
in·ac·cu·rate [ɪn'ækjʊrət] niedokładny
in·ac|·tive [ɪn'æktɪv] nieaktywny, bierny; **~·tiv·i·ty** [ɪnæk'tɪvətɪ] bierność *f*, nieaktywność *f*
in·ad·e·quate [ɪn'ædɪkwət] niedostateczny; nieodpowiedni; nieadekwatny
in·ad·mis·si·ble [ɪnəd'mɪsəbl] niedopuszczalny, nie do przyjęcia
in·ad·ver·tent [ɪnəd'vɜːtənt] (**~·ly**) nieumyślny, nierozmyślny
in·an·i·mate [ɪn'ænɪmət] nieożywiony
in·ap·pro·pri·ate [ɪnə'prəʊprɪət] nieodpowiedni, niestosowny; niezdatny (**for** dla *G*, **to** do *G*)
in·apt [ɪn'æpt] nieodpowiedni, niestosowny
in·ar·tic·u·late [ɪnɑː'tɪkjʊlət] niewyraźny, niezrozumiały; nie potrafiący się wysłowić
in·at·ten·tive [ɪnə'tentɪv] nieuważny
in·au·di·ble [ɪn'ɔːdəbl] niesłyszalny
in·au·gu|·ral [ɪ'nɔːgjʊrəl] inauguracyjny; **~·rate** [ɪ'nɔːgjʊreɪt] kogoś (*na stanowisko*) wprowadzać ⟨-dzić⟩ uroczyście; ⟨za⟩inaugurować, otwierać ⟨-worzyć⟩; rozpoczynać ⟨-cząć⟩; **~·ra·tion** [ɪnɔːgjʊ'reɪʃn] inauguracja *f*; wprowadzenie *n*; otwarcie *n*; rozpoczęcie *n*; **2ration Day** *Am.* dzień wprowadzenia

prezydenta USA na urząd (*20 stycznia*)
in·born [ɪn'bɔːn] wrodzony
Inc [ɪŋk] *skrót: Incorporated* posiadający osobowość prawną
in·cal·cu·la·ble [ɪn'kælkjʊləbl] nieobliczalny
in·can·des·cent [ɪnkæn'desnt] żarzący się; **~ lamp** lampa *f* żarowa
in·ca·pa·ble [ɪn'keɪpəbl] niezdolny (**of** do *G*), nie będący w stanie (**of doing s.th.** zrobić czegoś)
in·ca·pa·ci·tate [ɪnkə'pæsɪteɪt] ⟨u⟩czynić niezdatnym *lub* niezdolnym; **~·ty** [ɪnkə'pæsətɪ] niezdolność *f*, niezdatność *f*
in·car·nate [ɪn'kɑːnət] wcielony, ucieleśniony
in·cau·tious [ɪn'kɔːʃəs] nieostrożny
in·cen·di·a·ry [ɪn'sendjərɪ] zapalający, *fig.* zapalczywy
in·cense¹ ['ɪnsens] kadzidło *n*
in·cense² [ɪn'sens] rozwścieczać ⟨-czyć⟩
in·cen·tive [ɪn'sentɪv] bodziec *m*, podnieta *f*, zachęta *f*
in·ces·sant [ɪn'sesnt] nieprzerwany, ustawiczny
in·cest ['ɪnsest] kazirodztwo *n*
inch [ɪntʃ] **1.** cal *m* (=*2,54 cm*) (*też fig.*); **by ~es, ~ by ~** stopniowa, krok za krokiem; **every ~** w każdym calu; **2.** posuwać się krok po kroku
in·ci·dence ['ɪnsɪdəns] rozmiar *m*, zasięg *m*, zakres *m* (*występowania*); **'~·dent** incydent *m*, zajście *n*; **~·den·tal** [ɪnsɪ'dentl] uboczny, marginesowy; **~·den·tal·ly** na marginesie, nawiasem mówiąc
in·cin·e|·rate [ɪn'sɪnəreɪt] spalać ⟨-lić⟩ (*na popiół*); **~·ra·tor** piec *m* do spalania śmieci
in·cise [ɪn'saɪz] nacinać ⟨-ciąć⟩, ⟨wy⟩ryć; **in·ci·sion** [ɪn'sɪʒn] nacięcie *n*; **in·ci·sive** [ɪn'saɪsɪv] ostry, cięty; **in·ci·sor** [ɪn'saɪzə] *anat.* siekacz *m*
in·cite [ɪn'saɪt] podżegać, podburzać ⟨-rzyć⟩; **~·ment** podżeganie *n*, podburzanie *n*
incl *skrót pisany: including, inclusive* wł., włącznie
in·clem·ent [ɪn'klemənt] zły, *pogoda:* burzliwy
in·cli·na·tion [ɪnklɪ'neɪʃn] pochyłość *f*,

spadek *m*; *fig.* inklinacja *f*, skłonność *f*, upodobanie *n*; **in·cline** [ɪn'klaɪn] **1.** *v/i.* pochylać ⟨-lić⟩ się, nachylać ⟨-lić⟩ się (*to, towards* w stronę *G*); *fig.* skłaniać ⟨-łonić⟩ się (*to, towards* do *G*); *v/t.* nachylać; *fig.* nakłaniać ⟨-łonić⟩; **2.** zbocze *n*

in·close [ɪn'kləʊz], **in·clos·ure** [ɪn'kləʊʒə] → **enclose, enclosure**

in·clude [ɪn'klu:d] włączać ⟨-czyć⟩; zawierać ⟨-wrzeć⟩, obejmować ⟨objąć⟩; *tax* ~ *d* włączenie za podatkiem; **in'clud·ing** łącznie z (*I*); **in·clu·sion** [ɪn'klu:ʒn] włączenie *n*; wliczenie *n*; **in·clu·sive** [ɪn'klu:sɪv] łączny, obejmujący (*wszystko*); włącznie (*of* z *I*); ryczałtowy; *be* ~ *of* obejmować łącznie (*A*)

in·co·her·ent [ɪnkəʊ'hɪərənt] niespójny, niejasny

in·come ['ɪnkʌm] *econ.* dochód *m*, przychód *m*; '~ *tax econ.* podatek *m* dochodowy

in·com·ing ['ɪnkʌmɪŋ] nadchodzący; nowy, następujący; przybywający; ~ *mail* poczta przychodząca

in·com·mu·ni·ca·tive [ɪnkə'mju:nɪkətɪv] niekomunikatywny, mało rozmowny

in·com·pa·ra·ble [ɪn'kɒmpərəbl] nieporównany; nie do porównania

in·com·pat·i·ble [ɪnkəm'pætəbl] niedobrany, nieprzystający; niekompatybilny

in·com·pe·tence [ɪn'kɒmpɪtəns] niekompetencja *f*, niefachowość *f*; ~·tent niekompetentny, niefachowy

in·com·plete [ɪnkəm'pli:t] niekompletny; niedokończony

in·com·pre·hen·si·ble [ɪnkɒmprɪ'hensəbl] niezrozumiały, niejasny; ~·sion [ɪnkɒmprɪ'henʃn] niezrozumienie *n*

in·con·cei·va·ble [ɪnkən'si:vəbl] nie do pomyślenia, nie do pojęcia

in·con·clu·sive [ɪnkən'klu:sɪv] nieprzekonujący; bezwocny; nie zakończony pomyślnie; nie rozstrzygający

in·con·gru·ous [ɪn'kɒŋgrʊəs] nie na miejscu; nie pasujący (*to, with* do *G*); niespójny

in·con·se·quen·tial [ɪnkɒnsɪ'kwenʃl] mało znaczący, nieważny

in·con·sid·|e·ra·ble [ɪnkən'sɪdərəbl] nieznaczny; ~·er·ate [ɪnkən'sɪdərət] nieczuły; bezwzględny

in·con·sis·tent [ɪnkən'sɪstənt] niespójny, niekonsekwentny

in·con·so·la·ble [ɪnkən'səʊləbl] niepocieszony

in·con·spic·u·ous [ɪnkən'spɪkjʊəs] niepozorny

in·con·stant [ɪn'kɒnstənt] niestały, zmienny

in·con·ti·nent [ɪn'kɒntɪnənt] *med.* nie mogący utrzymać odchodów

in·con·ve·ni·ence [ɪnkən'vi:njəns] **1.** niedogodność *f*; niewygoda *f*, kłopot *m*; **2.** sprawiać *komuś* kłopot; przysparzać kłopotów; ~·ent niewygodny; niedogodny

in·cor·po·|rate [ɪn'kɔ:pəreɪt] ⟨po-, z⟩łączyć się; włączać ⟨-czyć⟩, obejmować ⟨objąć⟩; uwzględniać ⟨-nić⟩; *econ., jur.* ⟨za⟩rejestrować; nadawać ⟨-dać⟩ osobowość prawną; ~·rat·ed 'com·pa·ny *Am.* spółka *f* o osobowości prawnej; ~·ra·tion [ɪnkɔ:pə'reɪʃn] złączenie *n* (się); objęcie *n*; włączenie *n*; uwzględnienie *n*; rejestracja *f* (*firmy*); *Am.* nadanie *n* osobowości prawnej

in·cor·rect [ɪnkə'rekt] nieprawidłowy, niewłaściwy

in·cor·ri·gi·ble [ɪn'kɒrɪdʒəbl] niepoprawny

in·cor·rup·ti·ble [ɪnkə'rʌptəbl] nieprzekupny

in·crease 1. [ɪn'kri:s] wzrastać ⟨-rosnąć⟩; zwiększać ⟨-szyć⟩ (się); powiększać ⟨-szyć⟩ (się); **2.** ['ɪnkri:s] wzrost *m*; zwiększenie *n*; powiększenie *n*; podwyżka *f*; **in·creas·ing·ly** [ɪn'kri:sɪŋlɪ] wzrastająco, w coraz większym stopniu; ~ *difficult* coraz trudniejszy

in·cred·i·ble [ɪn'kredəbl] niewiarygodny

in·cre·du·li·ty [ɪnkrɪ'dju:lətɪ] niedowierzanie *n*; **in·cred·u·lous** [ɪn'kredjʊləs] niedowierzający, sceptyczny

in·crim·i·nate [ɪn'krɪmɪneɪt] obwiniać ⟨-nić⟩

in·cu|·bate ['ɪnkjʊbeɪt] wysiadywać; wylęgać się; '~·ba·tor inkubator *m*; *agr.* wylęgarka *f*

in·cur [ɪn'kɜ:] (*-rr-*) wywoływać ⟨-łać⟩; *koszty, szkody* ponosić ⟨-nieść⟩

in·cu·ra·ble [ɪn'kjʊərəbl] nieuleczalny

in·cu·ri·ous [ɪn'kjʊərɪəs] mało dociekliwy, mało ciekawy

in·cur·sion [ɪnˈkɜːʃn] wtargnięcie *n*, najście *n*

in·debt·ed [ɪnˈdetɪd] zobowiązany; wdzięczny

in·de·cent [ɪnˈdiːsnt] nieprzyzwoity; *jur.* lubieżny; niemoralny; **~ assault** *jur.* czyn *m* lubieżny

in·de·ci·sion [ɪndɪˈsɪʒn] niezdecydowanie *n*; **~·sive** [ɪndɪˈsaɪsɪv] niezdecydowany; nie rozstrzygnięty, nie rozstrzygający

in·deed [ɪnˈdiːd] **1.** *adv.* rzeczywiście, faktycznie, naprawdę; **thank you very much ~!** serdecznie dziękuję; **2.** *int.* doprawdy?, naprawdę?

in·de·fat·i·ga·ble [ɪndɪˈfætɪɡəbl] niestrudzony, niezmordowany

in·de·fen·si·ble [ɪndɪˈfensəbl] niewybaczalny

in·de·fi·na·ble [ɪndɪˈfaɪnəbl] nieokreślony, nie ustalony

in·def·i·nite [ɪnˈdefɪnət] nieograniczony; niejasny; **~·ly** nieograniczenie *n*

in·del·i·ble [ɪnˈdelɪbl] nie do usunięcia, nie do zmazania (*też fig.*)

in·del·i·cate [ɪnˈdelɪkət] mało taktowny, nietaktowny; niedelikatny

in·dem·ni·fy [ɪnˈdemnɪfaɪ] wynagradzać ⟨-rodzić⟩ straty **(for, against** za A); zabezpieczać ⟨-czyć⟩ **(for,** za A); **~·ty** [ɪnˈdemnətɪ] wynagrodzenie *n* strat; zabezpieczenie *n*

in·dent [ɪnˈdent] wgniatać ⟨-gnieść⟩; *print. wiersz* wcinać ⟨wciąć⟩

in·de·pen·dence [ɪndɪˈpendəns] niepodległość *f*, niezależność *f*; **2·dence Day** *Am.* Dzień Niepodległości (*4 lipca*); **~·dent** niepodległy; niezależny

in·de·scri·ba·ble [ɪndɪˈskraɪbəbl] nieopisany, nie do opisania

in·de·struc·ti·ble [ɪndɪˈstrʌktəbl] niezniszczalny; niespożyty

in·de·ter·mi·nate [ɪndɪˈtɜːmɪnət] nieokreślony; niejasny

in·dex [ˈɪndeks] (*pl.* **-dexes, -dices** [-dɪsiːz]) indeks *m*, skorowidz *m*, wykaz *m*; wskaźnik *m*; **cost of living ~** wskaźnik *m* kosztów utrzymania; **'~ card** karta *f* kartotekowa; **'~ fin·ger** palec *m* wskazujący

In·di·a [ˈɪndjə] Indie *pl.*; **In·di·an** [ˈɪndjən] **1.** indyjski, hinduski; indiański; **2.** Hindus(ka *f*) *m*; *też* **American ~** Indianin *m* (-anka *f*)

In·di·an| **'corn** *bot.* kukurydza *f*; **'~ file:** **in ~ file** gęsiego; **~ 'sum·mer** babie lato *n*

in·di·a 'rub·ber kauczuk *m* (*naturalny*)

in·di·cate [ˈɪndɪkeɪt] wskazywać ⟨-zać⟩ (*też tech.*); *mot.* wskazywać ⟨-zać⟩ (*kierunek ruchu*); *fig.* ⟨za⟩sygnalizować; **~·ca·tion** [ɪndɪˈkeɪʃn] wskazywanie *n*; wskazanie *n*; zasygnalizowanie *n*; **in·dic·a·tive** [ɪnˈdɪkətɪv] *też* **~cative mood** *gr.* tryb *m* oznajmujący; **~·ca·tor** [ˈɪndɪkeɪtə] *tech.* wskaźnik *m*; *mot.* kierunkowskaz *m*, migacz *m*

in·di·ces [ˈɪndɪsiːz] *pl. od* **index**

in·dict [ɪnˈdaɪt] *jur.* oskarżać ⟨-żyć⟩ **(for** o A); **~·ment** oskarżenie *n*, stan *m* oskarżenia

in·dif·fer|·ence [ɪnˈdɪfrəns] obojętność *f*; **~·ent** obojętny **(to** wobec G)

in·di·gent [ˈɪndɪdʒənt] ubogi

in·di·ges|·ti·ble [ɪndɪˈdʒestəbl] niestrawny; **~·tion** [ɪndɪˈdʒestʃən] niestrawność *f*

in·dig|·nant [ɪnˈdɪɡnənt] oburzony **(about, at, over** na A); **~·na·tion** [ɪndɪɡˈneɪʃn] oburzenie *n* **(about, at, over** na A); **~·ni·ty** [ɪnˈdɪɡnətɪ] upokorzenie *n*

in·di·rect [ɪndɪˈrekt] pośredni; okrężny; **by ~ means** *fig.* pośrednimi środkami

in·dis|·creet [ɪndɪˈskriːt] niedyskretny; nierozważny; **~·cre·tion** [ɪndɪˈskreʃn] niedyskrecja *f*; nierozwaga *f*

in·dis·crim·i·nate [ɪndɪˈskrɪmɪnət] niewybredny, bezkrytyczny; jak popadnie, na oślep

in·dis·pen·sa·ble [ɪndɪˈspensəbl] nieodzowny

in·dis|·posed [ɪndɪˈspəʊzd] niedysponowany; **~·po·si·tion** [ɪndɪspəˈzɪʃn] niedyspozycja *f*; niechęć *f* **(to** do G)

in·dis·pu·ta·ble [ɪndɪˈspjuːtəbl] bezsporny

in·dis·tinct [ɪndɪˈstɪŋkt] niewyraźny

in·dis·tin·guish·a·ble [ɪndɪˈstɪŋɡwɪʃəbl] nie do odróżnienia **(from** od G)

in·di·vid·u·al [ɪndɪˈvɪdjʊəl] **1.** indywidualny; jednostkowy; poszczególny; pojedynczy; **2.** jednostka *f*; osoba *f*; osobnik *m*; **~·is·m** [ɪndɪˈvɪdjʊəlɪzəm] indywidualizm *m*; **~·ist** [ɪndɪˈvɪdjʊəlɪst] indywidualista *m* (-tka *f*); **~·i·ty** [ɪndɪvɪdjʊˈælətɪ] indywidualność *f*; **~·ly**

[indi·vid·u·al·ly] indywidualnie; pojedynczo

in·di·vis·i·ble [ɪndɪˈvɪzəbl] niepodzielny

in·dom·i·ta·ble [ɪnˈdɒmɪtəbl] nieposkromiony

In·do·ne·sia Indonezja f

in·door [ˈɪndɔː] wewnętrzny; domowy; *basen*: kryty; *sport*: halowy; **~s** [ɪnˈdɔːz] wewnątrz; w domu; (*w sporcie*) w hali; do wnętrza, do środka

in·dorse [ɪnˈdɔːs] → endorse

in·duce [ɪnˈdjuːs] *kogoś* namawiać ⟨-mówić⟩, nakłaniać ⟨-łonić⟩; *coś* wywoływać⟨-łać⟩, ⟨s⟩powodować; **~·ment** bodziec *m*, zachęta *f*

in·duct [ɪnˈdʌkt] wprowadzać ⟨-dzić⟩ (na stanowisko); **in·duc·tion** [ɪnˈdʌkʃn] wprowadzenie *n* na stanowisko; *electr.* indukcja *f*

in·dulge [ɪnˈdʌldʒ] *komuś, sobie* pobłażać; spełniać ⟨-nić⟩ zachcianki; zaspokajać ⟨-koić⟩; **~ in s.th.** pozwalać sobie na (*A*), oddawać się (*D*); in·dulgence [ɪnˈdʌldʒəns] pobłażanie *n* (sobie); pobłażliwość *f*; słabość *f*; ekstrawagancja *f*, luksus *m*; in·dul·gent pobłażliwy, wyrozumiały

in·dus·tri·al [ɪnˈdʌstrɪəl] przemysłowy; industrialny; **~ 'ar·e·a** region *m* przemysłowy, zagłębie *n* przemysłowe; **~·ist** [ɪnˈdʌstrɪəlɪst] *econ.* przemysłowiec *m*; **~·ize** [ɪnˈdʌstrɪəlaɪz] *econ.* uprzemysławiać ⟨-łowić⟩, ⟨z⟩industrializować

in·dus·tri·ous [ɪnˈdʌstrɪəs] pracowity, skrzętny

in·dus·try [ˈɪndəstrɪ] *econ.* przemysł *m*; gałąź *f* przemysłu; pracowitość *f*

in·ed·i·ble [ɪnˈedɪbl] niejadalny

in·ef·fec·tive [ɪnɪˈfektɪv], **~·tu·al** [ɪnɪˈfektʃuəl] bezskuteczny, nieskuteczny; nieefektywny

in·ef·fi·cient[ɪnɪˈfɪʃnt]niesprawny,nieskuteczny; nieudolny

in·el·e·gant [ɪnˈelɪgənt] mało elegancki

in·eli·gi·ble [ɪnˈelɪdʒəbl] niezdatny, nieodpowiedni; nie spełniający warunków

in·ept [ɪˈnept] niezręczny; niedorzeczny, nierozsądny

in·e·qual·i·ty [ɪnɪˈkwɒlətɪ] nierówność *f*

in·ert [ɪˈnɜːt] *phys.* bezwładny; inercyjny, nieaktywny; in·er·tia [ɪˈnɜːʃjə] inercja *f*, bezwład *m* (*też fig.*)

in·es·ca·pa·ble [ɪnɪˈskeɪpəbl] nieunikniony

in·es·sen·tial [ɪnɪˈsenʃl] niepotrzebny, zbyteczny

in·es·ti·ma·ble [ɪnˈestɪməbl] nieoszacowany, bezcenny

in·ev·i·ta·ble [ɪnˈevɪtəbl] nieunikniony, nieuchronny

in·ex·act [ɪnɪgˈzækt] niedokładny

in·ex·cu·sa·ble [ɪnɪˈskjuːzəbl] niewybaczalny

in·ex·haus·ti·ble [ɪnɪgˈzɔːstəbl] niewyczerpany

in·ex·o·ra·ble [ɪnˈeksərəbl] nieubłagany, nieprzejednany

in·ex·pe·di·ent [ɪnɪkˈspiːdjənt] niecelowy, niepraktyczny

in·ex·pen·sive [ɪnɪkˈspensɪv] niedrogi

in·ex·pe·ri·ence [ɪnɪkˈspɪərɪəns] niedoświadczenie *n*, brak *m* doświadczenia; **~d** niedoświadczony

in·ex·pert [ɪnˈekspɜːt] nieudolny; niedoświadczony

in·ex·plic·a·ble [ɪnɪkˈsplɪkəbl] niepojęty, niewytłumaczalny

in·ex·pres·si·ble [ɪnɪkˈspresəbl] niewyrażalny, niewysłowiony, nieopisany; **~·sive** [ɪnɪkˈspresɪv] beznamiętny, bez emocji

in·ex·tri·ca·ble [ɪnˈekstrɪkəbl] nieunikniony; zaplątany, zawiły

in·fal·li·ble [ɪnˈfæləbl] nieomylny

in·fa·mous [ˈɪnfəməs] haniebny; niesławny; **~·my** hańba *f*; niesława *f*, zła sława *f*

in·fan·cy [ˈɪnfənsɪ] wczesne dzieciństwo *n*; **in its ~·cy** *fig.* w powijakach; **~t** dziecko *n*, niemowlę *n*

in·fan·tile [ˈɪnfəntaɪl] dziecinny; dziecięcy, niemowlęcy

in·fan·try [ˈɪnfəntrɪ] *mil.* piechota *f*

in·fat·u·at·ed [ɪnˈfætʃueɪtɪd] zakochany, zadurzony (**with** w *L*)

in·fect [ɪnˈfekt] *med. kogoś* zarażać ⟨-razić⟩ (*też fig.*); *coś* zakażać ⟨-kazić⟩; in·fec·tion [ɪnˈfekʃn] *med.* zakażenie *n*; zarażenie *n*; in·fec·tious [ɪnˈfekʃəs] *med.* zakaźny; zaraźliwy (*też fig.*)

in·fer [ɪnˈfɜː] (**-rr-**) ⟨wy⟩wnioskować (**from** z *G*); wyciągać ⟨-gnąć⟩ wnioski;

~·ence ['ɪnfərəns] wniosek *m*; wnioskowanie *n*

in·fe·ri·or [ɪn'fɪərɪə] **1.** podległy (**to** D), niższy (**to** wobec G); pośledniejszy, gorszy (**to** w stosunku do G); mniej wart (**to** od G); **be ~ to s.o.** podlegać komuś (*służbowo*); **2.** podwładny *m* (-na *f*); ~·i·ty [ɪnfɪərɪ'ɒrətɪ] niższość *f*; podrzędność *f*; ~·i·ty com·plex kompleks *m* niższości

in·fer|·nal [ɪn'fɜːnl] piekielny; ~·no [ɪn'fɜːnəʊ] (*pl. -nos*) piekło *n*

in·fer·tile [ɪn'fɜːtaɪl] niepłodny

in·fest [ɪn'fest] zakażać ⟨-kazić⟩; **be ~ed with** być zaatakowanym przez (A)

in·fi·del·i·ty [ɪnfɪ'delətɪ] niewierność *f*, zdrada *f*

in·fil·trate ['ɪnfɪltreɪt] przesączać ⟨-czyć⟩ się przez (A); przenikać przez (A); *pol.* infiltrować

in·fi·nite ['ɪnfɪnət] nieskończony

in·fin·i·tive [ɪn'fɪnətɪv] *gr.* bezokolicznik *m*

in·fin·i·ty [ɪn'fɪnətɪ] nieskończoność *f*

in·firm [ɪn'fɜːm] słaby, niesprawny, wątły; in·fir·ma·ry [ɪn'fɜːmərɪ] szpital *m*; (*w szkole*) izolatka *f*; in·fir·mi·ty [ɪn'fɜːmətɪ] słabość *f*, niesprawność *f*, wątłość *f*

in·flame [ɪn'fleɪm] rozpalać ⟨-lić⟩ (*zw. fig.*) zapalać ⟨-lić⟩; ⟨s⟩powodować stan zapalny; **become ~d** *med.* zaognić się

in·flam·ma|·ble [ɪn'flæməbl] palny; zapalny; łatwopalny; ~·tion [ɪnflə'meɪʃn] *med.* zapalenie *n*; ~·to·ry [ɪn'flæmətərɪ] *med.* zapalny; *fig.* wzburzający

in·flate [ɪn'fleɪt] nadmuchiwać ⟨-chać⟩, nadymać ⟨-dąć⟩ (*też fig.*); ⟨na⟩pompować (*powietrze*); *econ.* cenę zawyżać ⟨-żyć⟩; in·fla·tion *econ.* [ɪn'fleɪʃn] inflacja *f*

in·flect [ɪn'flekt] *gr.* odmieniać ⟨-nić⟩; in·flec·tion [ɪn'flekʃn] *gr.* fleksja *f*, odmiana *f*

in·flex|·i·ble [ɪn'fleksəbl] sztywny (*też fig.*); nieelastyczny; ~·ion *Brt. gr.* [ɪn'flekʃn] → **inflection**

in·flict [ɪn'flɪkt] (**on**) *krzywdę* wyrządzać ⟨-dzić⟩; *rany* zadawać ⟨-dać⟩; *cierpienie* ⟨s⟩powodować; *karę* wymierzać ⟨-rzyć⟩; **~ s.th. on s.o.** narzucać coś komuś; in·flic·tion [ɪn'flɪkʃn] narzucenie *n*, nałożenie *n*

in·flu|·ence ['ɪnfluəns] **1.** wpływ *m*; **2.**

wpływać ⟨-łynąć⟩ na (A); ~·en·tial [ɪnflu'enʃl] wpływowy

in·flux ['ɪnflʌks] napływ *m*, przypływ *m*, dopływ *m*

in·form [ɪn'fɔːm] ⟨po⟩informować, zawiadamiać ⟨-domić⟩ (**of** *o* L); **~ against** *lub* **on s.o.** donosić ⟨-nieść⟩ na kogoś, ⟨za⟩denuncjować kogoś

in·for·mal [ɪn'fɔːml] nieoficjalny; nieformalny; ~·i·ty [ɪnfɔː'mælətɪ] nieoficjalność *f*; nieformalność *f*;

in·for·ma|·tion [ɪnfə'meɪʃn] informacja *f*; ~·tion (su·per·)'high·way *komp.* autostrada *f* informatyczna; ~·tive [ɪn'fɔːmətɪv] informacyjny, pouczający, kształcący

in·form·er [ɪn'fɔːmə] donosiciel(ka *f*) *m*; informator(ka *f*) *m*

in·fra·struc·ture ['ɪnfrəstrʌktʃə] infrastruktura *f*

in·fre·quent [ɪn'friːkwənt] rzadki, nieczęsty

in·fringe [ɪn'frɪndʒ] *też* **~ on** *prawa*, *porozumienia* naruszać ⟨-szyć⟩ (A), ⟨z⟩łamać (A)

in·fu·ri·ate [ɪn'fjʊərɪeɪt] rozwścieczać ⟨-czyć⟩

in·fuse [ɪn'fjuːz] *herbatę* zaparzać ⟨-rzyć⟩; in·fu·sion [ɪn'fjuːʒn] napar *m*; *med.* wlew *m*, infuzja *f*

in·ge|·ni·ous [ɪn'dʒiːnjəs] zmyślny, sprytny, pomysłowy; ~·nu·i·ty [ɪndʒɪ'njuːətɪ] zmyślność *f*, sprytność *f*, pomysłowość *f*

in·gen·u·ous [ɪn'dʒenjʊəs] prostoduszny

in·got ['ɪŋgət] sztabka *f* (*złota itp.*), sztaba *f*

in·gra·ti·ate [ɪn'greɪʃɪeɪt]: **~ o.s. with s.o.** łasić się do kogoś, nadskakiwać komuś

in·grat·i·tude [ɪn'grætɪtjuːd] niewdzięczność *f*

in·gre·di·ent [ɪn'griːdjənt] składnik *m*

in·grow·ing ['ɪngrəʊɪŋ] wrastający

in·hab·it [ɪn'hæbɪt] zamieszkiwać ⟨-szkać⟩; ~·it·a·ble zdatny do zamieszkania; ~·i·tant mieszkaniec *m*

in·hale [ɪn'heɪl] wdychać; zaciągać ⟨-gnąć⟩ się (D); *med.* wziewać

in·her·ent [ɪn'hɪərənt] (**in**) wrodzony; swoisty dla (G), właściwy dla (G); nieodłączny (od G)

in·her|·it [ɪn'herɪt] ⟨o⟩dziedziczyć

(*from po L*); ~·i·tance dziedzictwo *n*, spadek *m*

in·hib·it [ɪn'hɪbɪt] ⟨za⟩hamować (*też psych.*), wstrzymywać ⟨-mać⟩ (*from przed I*); ~ed *psych.* zahamowany; in·hi·bi·tion [ɪnhɪ'bɪʃn] zahamowanie *n*

in·hos·pi·ta·ble [ɪn'hɒspɪtəbl] niegościnny; nieprzyjazny

in·hu·man [ɪn'hjuːmən] nieludzki; ~e [ɪnhjuː'meɪn] niehumanitarny, nieludzki

in·im·i·cal [ɪ'nɪmɪkl] wrogi, nieprzyjazny (*to D*)

in·im·i·ta·ble [ɪ'nɪmɪtəbl] nie do podrobienia

i·ni·tial [ɪ'nɪʃl] **1.** początkowy, wstępny; **2.** inicjał *m*; ~·tial·ly [ɪ'nɪʃəlɪ] początkowo; ~·ti·ate [ɪ'nɪʃɪeɪt] zaczynać ⟨-cząć⟩, zapoczątkowywać ⟨-wać⟩, ⟨za⟩inicjować; wprowadzać ⟨-dzić⟩ (*into do G*); ~·ti·a·tion [ɪnɪʃɪ'eɪʃn] zapoczątkowanie *n*; wprowadzenie *n*; ~·tiative [ɪ'nɪʃɪətɪv] inicjatywa *f*; *take the ~tiative* podejmować ⟨-djąć⟩ inicjatywę; *on one's own ~tiative* z własnej inicjatywy

in·ject [ɪn'dʒekt] *med.* wstrzykiwać ⟨-knąć⟩; in·jec·tion [ɪn'dʒekʃn] *med.* wstrzyknięcie *n*, iniekcja *f*, zastrzyk *m*

in·ju·di·cious [ɪndʒuː'dɪʃəs] nierozsądny

in·junc·tion [ɪn'dʒʌŋkʃn] *jur.* nakaz *m* sądowy

in·jure ['ɪndʒə] ⟨z⟩ranić; wyrządzać ⟨-dzić⟩ krzywdę (*D*); szkodzić (*D*); ~d zraniony, ranny; skrzywdzony, urażony; in·ju·ri·ous [ɪn'dʒʊərɪəs] szkodliwy; *be ~ to* ⟨za⟩szkodzić (*D*); *be ~ to health* szkodzić zdrowiu; in·ju·ry ['ɪndʒərɪ] *med.* zranienie *n*, obrażenie *n*; szkoda *f*; *'in·ju·ry time Brt.* (*zwł. w piłce nożnej*) doliczony czas *m* (*gry*)

in·jus·tice [ɪn'dʒʌstɪs] niesprawiedliwość *f*

ink [ɪŋk] **1.** tusz *m*, atrament *m*; **2.** ~jet ['ɪŋkdʒet] drukarka: atramentowy

ink·ling ['ɪŋklɪŋ] pojęcie *n*

'ink·pad poduszka *f* do tuszu; '~·y (*-ier, -iest*) atramentowy; poplamiony atramentem

in·laid ['ɪnleɪd] inkrustowany; ~ *work* inkrustacja *f*

in·land **1.** *adj.* ['ɪnlənd] lądowy, śródlądowy; krajowy; **2.** *adv.* [ɪn'lænd] w głąb kraju *lub* lądu; ♀ 'Rev·e·nue *Brt.* urząd *m* skarbowy, fiskus *m*

in·lay ['ɪnleɪ] inkrustacja *f*; *med.* wypełnienie *n*, plomba

in·let ['ɪnlet] zatoczka *f*; *tech.* wlot *m*

in·mate ['ɪnmeɪt] współwięzień *m*; pacjent *m*

in·most ['ɪnməʊst] wewnętrzny, najgłębszy

inn [ɪn] gospoda *f*, zajazd *m*; *hist.* karczma *f*

in·nate ['ɪneɪt] wrodzony

in·ner ['ɪnə] wewnętrzny; skryty; '~·most → *inmost*

in·nings ['ɪnɪŋz] (*pl. innings*) (*w krykiecie, baseballu*) runda *f*

'inn·keep·er właściciel(ka *f*) gospody *lub* zajazdu; *hist.* karczmarz *m*

in·no·cence ['ɪnəsns] niewinność *f*; naiwność *f*; '~·cent niewinny; naiwny

in·noc·u·ous [ɪ'nɒkjuəs] nieszkodliwy

in·no·va·tion [ɪnəʊ'veɪʃn] innowacja *f*, nowatorski pomysł *m*

in·nu·en·do [ɪnju:'endəʊ] (*pl. -does, -dos*) aluzja *f*, insynuacja *f*

in·nu·me·ra·ble [ɪ'nju:mərəbl] niezliczony

i·noc·u·late [ɪ'nɒkjuleɪt] *med.* ⟨za⟩szczepić; ~·la·tion [ɪnɒkjʊ'leɪʃn] *med.* szczepienie *n*, zaszczepienie *n*

in·of·fen·sive [ɪnə'fensɪv] nieszkodliwy

in·op·e·ra·ble [ɪn'ɒpərəbl] *med.* nieoperacyjny, nie nadający się do operowania; *plan:* nie dający się przeprowadzić

in·op·por·tune [ɪn'ɒpətju:n] niefortunny, nie na miejscu, niestosowny

in·or·di·nate [ɪ'nɔ:dɪnət] nieumiarkowany, niepohamowany; nadmierny, przesadny

'in·pa·tient *med.* pacjent(ka *f*) *m* hospitalizowany (-na)

in·put ['ɪnpʊt] wejście *n* (*też komp.*); wkład *m* (*pracy*); *komp.* dane *pl.* wejściowe, wprowadzanie *n* (*danych*)

in·quest ['ɪnkwest] *jur.* dochodzenie *n* sądowe; → *coroner's inquest*

in·quire [ɪn'kwaɪə] ⟨za-, s⟩pytać (*o A*); ~ *into* ⟨z⟩badać; in·quir·ing [ɪn'kwaɪrɪŋ] dociekliwy, badawczy; in·quir·y [ɪn'kwaɪrɪ] dowiadywanie *n* się; badanie *n*, dochodzenie *n*

in·qui·si·tion [ɪnkwɪ'zɪʃn] przesłucha-

nie n, śledztwo n; **2** rel. hist. Inkwizycja;
in·quis·i·tive [ɪn'kwɪzɪtɪv] badawczy,
dociekliwy
in·roads['ɪnrəʊdz] (*in, into, on*) najazd
m (na *A*); **make ~ into one's savings**
naruszać ⟨-szyć⟩ oszczędności
in·sane [ɪn'seɪn] szalony, pomylony
in·san·i·ta·ry [ɪn'sænɪtərɪ] niehigieniczny
in·san·i·ty [ɪn'sænətɪ] szaleństwo n,
wariactwo n
in·sa·tia·ble [ɪn'seɪʃjəbl] nizaspoko-
jony, nienasycony
in·scrip·tion [ɪn'skrɪpʃn] napis m; dedykacja f
in·scru·ta·ble [ɪn'skruːtəbl] niezbada-
ny, nieprzeniknony
in·sect ['ɪnsekt] zo. owad m; **in-
sec·ti·cide** [ɪn'sektɪsaɪd] środek m
owadobójczy, insektycyd m
in·se·cure[ɪnsɪ'kjʊə] niepewny, niesta-
bilny
in·sen·si·ble[ɪn'sensəbl] nieczuły, niewrażliwy (*to* na *A*); nieprzytomny; nieświadomy
in·sen·si·tive [ɪn'sensətɪv] nieczuły,
niewrażliwy
in·sep·a·ra·ble [ɪn'sepərəbl] nieodłączny, nierozłączny
in·ser|**t 1.** [ɪn'sɜːt] wstawiać ⟨-wić⟩,
wkładać ⟨włożyć⟩; umieszczać ⟨-eścić⟩;
2. ['ɪnsɜːt] wkładka f (*do gazety*);
~tion [ɪn'sɜːʃn] wstawienie n, zamie-
szczenie n; umieszczenie n; wkładka
f, dopisek m; ogłoszenie n; **'~t key**
komp. klawisz m "Insert" (*wstawiania*)
in·shore [ɪn'ʃɔː] przy *lub* do brzegu;
przybrzeżny
in·side 1. [ɪn'saɪd] wnętrze n, **turn ~ out**
wywrócić do góry nogami, przenico-
wać; **2.** ['ɪnsaɪd] adj. wewnętrzny; poufny; **3.** [ɪn'saɪd] adv. do wewnątrz *lub*
środka; w środku, wewnątrz; **~ of** wewnątrz, w środku (*czegoś*) **4.** [ɪn'saɪd]
prp. w ciągu (*G*); wewnątrz (*G*); **in-
sid·er** [ɪn'saɪdə] osoba zaangażowana
(*przy czymś*)
in·sid·i·ous [ɪn'sɪdɪəs] podstępny,
skrycie działający
in·sight ['ɪnsaɪt] wgląd m, intuicja f
in·sig·ni·a [ɪn'sɪgnɪə] pl. insygnia pl.;
atrybuty pl., oznaki pl.
in·sig·nif·i·cant [ɪnsɪg'nɪfɪkənt] nieważki, nieważny, bez znaczenia

in·sin·cere [ɪnsɪn'sɪə] nieszczery
in·sin·u|**·ate** [ɪn'sɪnjʊeɪt] insynuować,
imputować; **~a·tion** [ɪnsɪnju'eɪʃn] insynuacja f
in·sip·id [ɪn'sɪpɪd] bez smaku *lub* zapachu, mdły
in·sist [ɪn'sɪst] nalegać, upierać się (**on**
przy *D*); **in·sis·tence** [ɪn'sɪstəns] na-
tarczywość f, uporczywość f; **in·sis-
tent** uporczywy, natarczywy
in·sole ['ɪnsəʊl] podeszwa f wewnętrzna, brandzel m
in·so·lent ['ɪnsələnt] bezczelny
in·sol·u·ble [ɪn'sɒljʊbl] nierozpuszs-
czalny
in·sol·vent [ɪn'sɒlvənt] niewypłacalny;
w stanie upadłości, zbankrutowany
in·som·ni·a [ɪn'sɒmnɪə] bezsenność f
in·spect [ɪn'spekt] sprawdzać ⟨-dzić⟩,
⟨s⟩kontrolować; ⟨z⟩robić przegląd; **in-
spec·tion** [ɪn'spekʃn] sprawdzenie n;
kontrola f; przegląd m; inspekcja f;
in·spec·tor kontroler(ka f) m; inspek-
tor m; Brt. wizytator(ka f) m
in·spi·ra·tion [ɪnspə'reɪʃn] inspira-
cja f, natchnienie n; **in·spire** [ɪn'spaɪə]
⟨za⟩inspirować, natchnąć; otuchy dodawać
in·stall [ɪn'stɔːl] tech. ⟨za⟩instalować,
zakładać ⟨założyć⟩; (*na urząd*) wprowadzać ⟨-dzić⟩; **in·stal·la·tion** [ɪnstə-
'leɪʃn] tech. instalacja f, założenie n;
wprowadzenie n (*na urząd*)
in·stal·ment Brt., **in·stall·ment** Am.
[ɪn'stɔːlmənt] econ. rata f, spłata f czę-
ściowa; kolejna część f (*książki*); odcinek
m (*audycji radiowej lub telewizyjnej*)
in·stall·ment Am.: **buy on the ~**
kupować ⟨-pić⟩ na raty
in·stance ['ɪnstəns] przykład m; przypadek m; jur. instancja f; **for ~** na przykład
in·stant ['ɪnstənt] **1.** moment m, chwila
f; **2.** natychmiastowy; *kawa itp.*: rozpuszczalny; **~a·ne·ous** [ɪnstən'teɪnjəs]
natychmiastowy; **~ cam·er·a** phot. po-
laroid m TM; **~ 'cof·fee** kawa f roz-
puszczalna, neska f; **'~·ly** natychmiastowo, od razu
in·stead [ɪn'sted] zamiast tego; **~ of** zamiast (*G*)
'in·step podbicie n
in·sti|**·gate** ['ɪnstɪgeɪt] wszczynać
⟨-cząć⟩, ⟨za⟩inicjować; podburzać

‹-rzyć›, podżegać; '**~·ga·tor** podżegacz(ka f) m

in·stil Brt., **in·still** Am. [ɪn'stɪl] (**-ll-**) przekonania wpajać ‹wpoić›; strach wzbudzać ‹-dzić›

in·stinct ['ɪnstɪŋkt] instynkt m; **in·stinc·tive** [ɪn'stɪŋktɪv] instynktowny

in·sti|·tute ['ɪnstɪtjuːt] instytut m; **~·tu·tion** [ɪnstɪ'tjuːʃn] instytucja f, organizacja f; zakład m

in·struct [ɪn'strʌkt] nauczać ‹-czyć›; ‹wy›szkolić; ‹po›instruować; ‹po›informować; pouczać ‹-czyć›; **in·struc·tion** [ɪn'strʌkʃn] nauczanie n, szkolenie n; instruktaż n; komp. rozkaz m; **~s** pl. for use instrukcja f użytkowania; **operating ~s** pl. instrukcja f obsługi; **in·struc·tive** [ɪn'strʌktɪv] pouczający, kształcący; **in'struc·tor** instruktor m; **in'struc·tress** instruktorka f

in·stru|·ment ['ɪnstrʊmənt] instrument m; narzędzie n (też fig.); **~·men·tal** [ɪnstrʊ'mentl] mus. instrumentalny; (bardzo) pomocny; **be ~·mental in** przyczyniać ‹-nić› się znacząco do (G)

in·sub·or·di|·nate [ɪnsə'bɔːdənət] niesubordynowany, niezdyscyplinowany; **~·na·tion** [ɪnsəbɔːdɪ'neɪʃn] niesubordynacja f, brak m dyscypliny

in·suf·fe·ra·ble [ɪn'sʌfərəbl] nie do wytrzymania

in·suf·fi·cient [ɪnsə'fɪʃnt] niewystarczający, niedostateczny

in·su·lar ['ɪnsjʊlə] wyspiarski; fig. odizolowany

in·su|·late ['ɪnsjʊleɪt] ‹za›izolować; **~·la·tion** [ɪnsjʊ'leɪʃn] izolacja f

in·sult 1. ['ɪnsʌlt] obelga f, zniewaga f; 2. [ɪn'sʌlt] ‹ze›lżyć, znieważać ‹-żyć›

in·sur|·ance [ɪn'ʃɔːrəns] ubezpieczenie n; **~·ance com·pa·ny** firma f ubezpieczeniowa; **~·ance pol·i·cy** polisa f ubezpieczeniowa; **~·e** [ɪn'ʃɔː] ubezpieczać ‹-czyć› (**against** przeciw D); **~·ed: the ~·ed** ubezpieczony m (-na f)

in·sur·gent [ɪn'sɜːdʒənt] 1. powstańczy; 2. powstaniec m

in·sur·moun·ta·ble [ɪnsə'maʊntəbl] niepokonany

in·sur·rec·tion [ɪnsə'rekʃn] powstanie n

in·tact [ɪn'tækt] nietknięty; nienaruszony

'in·take tech. wlot m; miejsce n poboru; pobór m; spożycie n, zużycie n; nabór m

in·te·gral ['ɪntɪgrəl] integralny, cały

in·te|·grate ['ɪntɪgreɪt] ‹z›integrować (się); scalać ‹-lić›; ‹z-, po›łączyć w całość; **~·grated circuit** układ m scalony; **~·gra·tion** [ɪntɪ'greɪʃn] integracja f; scalenie n

in·teg·ri·ty [ɪn'tegrəti] integralność f; prawość f

in·tel·lect ['ɪntəlekt] intelekt m, inteligencja f; **~·lec·tual** [ɪntə'lektjʊəl] 1. intelektualny; 2. intelektualista m (-tka f)

in·tel·li|·gence [ɪn'telɪdʒəns] inteligencja f; mil. wywiad m; **~·gent** inteligentny

in·tel·li·gi·ble [ɪn'telɪdʒəbl] zrozumiały (**to** dla G)

in·tem·per·ate [ɪn'tempərət] nieumiarkowany

in·tend [ɪn'tend] zamierzać, planować, mieć zamiar; **~ed for** przeznaczony dla (D)

in·tense [ɪn'tens] intensywny, silny

in·ten·si|·fy [ɪn'tensɪfaɪ] ‹z›intensyfikować; stawać się silniejszym; **~·ty** [ɪn'tensəti] intensywność f

in·ten·sive [ɪn'tensɪv] intensywny; **~ care u·nit** oddział m intensywnej terapii

in·tent [ɪn'tent] 1. zdeterminowany; **~ on doing s.th.** zdecydowany na zrobienie czegoś; skoncentrowany; 2. intencja f; **in·ten·tion** [ɪn'tenʃn] zamiar m; jur. intencja f, cel m; **in·ten·tion·al** [ɪn'tenʃənl] celowy, intencjonalny

in·ter [ɪn'tɜː] (**-rr-**) ‹po›chować, ‹po›grzebać

in·ter... ['ɪntə] inter..., między...

in·ter·act [ɪntər'ækt] współdziałać, wzajemnie oddziaływać; wchodzić ‹wejść› w interakcje

in·ter·cede [ɪntə'siːd] wstawiać ‹-wić› się (**with** u G, **for** za A)

in·ter|·cept [ɪntə'sept] przechwytywać ‹-wycić›; **~·cep·tion** [ɪntə'sepʃn] przechwycenie n

in·ter·ces·sion [ɪntə'seʃn] wstawiennictwo n

in·ter·change 1. [ɪntə'tʃeɪndʒ] wymieniać ‹-nić› (się); 2. ['ɪntətʃeɪndʒ] wymiana *f*; *mot.* (*na autostradzie*) skrzyżowanie *n*

in·ter·com ['ɪntəkɒm] interkom *m*; domofon *m*

in·ter·course ['ɪntəkɔːs] stosunek *m*; **sexual ~** stosunek *m* płciowy

in·terest ['ɪntrɪst] **1.** zainteresowanie *n*; interes *m*; korzyść *f*; znaczenie *n*, ważność *f*; *econ.* udział *m*; *econ.* odsetki *pl.*, procent *m*; **take an ~ in** zainteresować się (*D*); **2.** ⟨za⟩interesować się; **'~ed** zainteresowany; **be ~ed in** interesować się (*I*); **'~ing** interesujący; **' ~ rate** *econ.* stopa *f* procentowa

in·ter·face ['ɪntəfeɪs] *komp.* interface *m lub* interfejs *m*

in·ter|·fere [ɪntə'fɪə] ⟨w⟩mieszać się, wtrącać ⟨-cić⟩ się (**with do** *G*); ingerować; przeszkadzać; **~·fer·ence** [ɪntə'fɪərəns] wtrącanie *n* się; przeszkadzanie *n*; ingerencja *f*; *tech.* interferencja *f*

in·te·ri·or [ɪn'tɪərɪə] **1.** wewnętrzny; **2.** wnętrze *n*; wnętrze kraju; *pol.* sprawy *pl.* wewnętrzne; → **Department of the ☉;** **~ 'dec·o·ra·tor** architekt *m* wnętrz

in·ter|·ject [ɪntə'dʒekt] wykrzyknąć ⟨-rzyczeć⟩; **~·jec·tion** [ɪntə'dʒekʃn] wykrzyknięcie *n*; wtrącenie *n*; *ling.* wykrzyknik *m*

in·ter·lace [ɪntə'leɪs] przeplatać ⟨-leść⟩ (się)

in·ter·lock [ɪntə'lɒk] sczepiać ⟨-pić⟩ (się), łączyć (się)

in·ter·lop·er ['ɪntələʊpə] intruz *m*, natręt *m*

in·ter·lude ['ɪntəluːd] interludium *n*, intermedium *n*; przerwa *f* (*też fig.*), antrakt *m*

in·ter·me·di|·a·ry [ɪntə'miːdjərɪ] pośrednik *m* (-niczka *f*); **~ate** [ɪntə'miːdjət] pośredni

in·ter·ment [ɪn'tɜːmənt] pochówek *m*, pogrzebanie *n*

in·ter·mi·na·ble [ɪn'tɜːmɪnəbl] niekończący się

in·ter·mis·sion [ɪntə'mɪʃn] przerwa *f* (*też Am. theat.*)

in·ter·mit·tent [ɪntə'mɪtənt] przerywany, periodyczny; **~ fever** *med.* gorączka *f* przerywana

in·tern¹ [ɪn'tɜːn] internować

in·tern² ['ɪntɜːn] *Am.* lekarz *m* (-arka *f*) stażysta (-tka)

in·ter·nal [ɪn'tɜːnl] wewnętrzny; krajowy; **~·com'bus·tion en·gine** silnik *m* spalinowy

in·ter·na·tion·al [ɪntə'næʃənl] **1.** międzynarodowy; **2.** (*w sporcie*) spotkanie *n* międzypaństwowe; **~ 'call** *tel.* rozmowa *f* międzynarodowa; **~ 'law** *jur.* prawo *n* międzynarodowe

in·ter|·pret [ɪn'tɜːprɪt] ⟨z⟩interpretować; wyjaśniać ⟨-nić⟩, ⟨wy⟩tłumaczyć; ⟨prze⟩tłumaczyć (*ustnie*); **~·pre·ta·tion** [ɪntɜːprɪ'teɪʃn] interpretacja *f*; wytłumaczenie *n*; **~·pret·er** [ɪn'tɜːprɪtə] tłumacz *m* (*tekstów ustnych*)

in·ter·ro|·gate [ɪn'terəgeɪt] przesłuchiwać ⟨-chać⟩, indagować; **~·ga·tion** [ɪnterə'geɪʃn] przesłuchanie *n*; wypytywanie *n* się; **~·ga·tion mark →** **question mark**

in·ter·rog·a·tive [ɪntə'rɒgətɪv] *gr.* pytajny

in·ter|·rupt [ɪntə'rʌpt] przerywać ⟨-rwać⟩; **~·rup·tion** [ɪntə'rʌpʃn] przerwanie *n*

in·ter|·sect [ɪntə'sekt] przecinać ⟨-ciąć⟩ się; **~·sec·tion** [ɪntə'sekʃn] przecięcie *n*; miejsce *n* przecięcia; skrzyżowanie *n*

in·ter·sperse [ɪntə'spɜːs] rozsiewać ⟨-siać⟩, rozrzucić ⟨-cać⟩ (**among** pomiędzy *A*); przeplatać się (*o okresach pogody*)

in·ter·state [ɪntə'steɪt] *Am.* międzystanowy; **~ 'highway** autostrada *f* (*łącząca kilka stanów*)

in·ter·twine [ɪntə'twaɪn] ⟨s⟩platać (się)

in·ter·val ['ɪntəvl] przerwa *f*; odstęp *m* (*czasu*); interwał *m* (*też mus.*); *Brt.* antrakt *m*; **at ~s of 5 inches,** **at 5-inch ~s** co 5 cali; **sunny ~** przejaśnienie *n*

in·ter·vene [ɪntə'viːn] ⟨za⟩interweniować; ⟨za⟩ingerować; stawać ⟨stanąć⟩ na przeszkodzie; **~·ven·tion** [ɪntə'venʃn] interwencja *f*, ingerencja *f*

in·ter·view ['ɪntəvjuː] **1.** wywiad *m*; rozmowa *f* (*zwł. kwalifikacyjna*); **2.** przeprowadzać ⟨-dzić⟩ wywiad *lub* rozmowę; **~·ee** [ɪntəvjuː'iː] osoba *f*, z którą przeprowadza się wywiad *lub* rozmowę; **~·er** ['ɪntəvjuːə] osoba *f* przeprowadzająca wywiad *lub* rozmowę

in·ter·weave [ɪntə'wiːv] (**-wove,** **-woven**) przeplatać ⟨-leść⟩ (się)

in·tes·tate [ɪn'testeɪt] *jur.:* **die ~** umrzeć bez pozostawienia testamentu

in·tes·tine [ɪnˈtestɪn] *anat.* jelito *n*; **~s**
pl. wnętrzności *pl.*; *large* ~ jelito *n* grube; *small* ~ jelito *n* cienkie

in·ti·ma·cy [ˈɪntɪməsɪ] poufałość *f*, bliskość *f*; stosunek *m* intymny

in·ti·mate [ˈɪntɪmət] **1.** intymny; *przyjaciel*: bliski; kameralny; *wiedza*: gruntowny; **2.** powiernik *m* (-nica *f*), zausz-
nik *m* (-iczka *f*)

in·tim·i·date [ɪnˈtɪmɪdeɪt] zastraszać
⟨-szyć⟩; **~·da·tion** [ɪntɪmɪˈdeɪʃn] za-
straszenie *n*

in·to [ˈɪntʊ, ˈɪntə] do (*G*); w (*L*); *rozbić
itp.* na (*A*); *three ~ six is two* sześć
(*dzielone*) przez trzy to dwa

in·tol·e·ra·ble [ɪnˈtɒlərəbl] nie do wytrzymania, nie do zniesienia

in·tol·e·rance [ɪnˈtɒlərəns] nietole-
rancja *f*, brak *m* tolerancji (*of* na *A*);
~·rant nietolerancyjny, nie tolerujący

in·to·na·tion [ɪntəʊˈneɪʃn] *mus.*, *gr.* intonacja *f*

in·tox·i·cat·ed [ɪnˈtɒksɪkeɪtɪd] nie-
trzeźwy; *be ~cated* być w stanie upojenia alkoholowego; **~·ca·tion** [ɪn-
tɒksɪˈkeɪʃn] nietrzeźwość *f*, rausz *m*;
stan *m* upojenia alkoholowego; oszoło-
mienie *n*, podniecenie *n* (*też fig.*)

in·trac·ta·ble [ɪnˈtræktəbl] nie do rozwiązania; nieustępliwy

in·tran·si·tive [ɪnˈtrænsətɪv] *gr.* nie-
przechodni

in·tra·ve·nous [ɪntrəˈviːnəs] *med.* dożylny

'in tray: *in the* ~ w poczcie przychodzą-
cej

in·trep·id [ɪnˈtrepɪd] nieustraszony,
nieulękły

in·tri·cate [ˈɪntrɪkət] zawiły, skomplikowany

in·trigue [ɪnˈtriːg] **1.** intryga *f*; **2.** ⟨za⟩-
intrygować, ⟨z⟩fascynować

in·tro·duce [ɪntrəˈdjuːs] wprowadzać
⟨-dzić⟩ (*to* do *G*); *kogoś* przedstawiać; **~·duc·tion** [ɪntrəˈdʌkʃn] wprowadzenie *n*, przedstawienie *n*; *letter
of ~duction* list *m* polecający;
~·duc·to·ry [ɪntrəˈdʌktərɪ] wstępny

in·tro·spec·tion [ɪntrəʊˈspekʃn] in-
trospekcja *f*, samoobserwacja *f*; **~·tive**
[ɪntrəʊˈspektɪv] introspekcyjny

in·tro·vert [ˈɪntrəʊvɜːt] *psych.* intro-
wertyk *m* (-yczka *f*); **'~·ed** intro-

wertyczny, introwersyjny, zamknięty
w sobie

in·trude [ɪnˈtruːd] wtrącać ⟨-cić⟩ (się),
przeszkadzać ⟨-kodzić⟩ (*on s.o.* komuś); *am I intruding?* czy przeszka-
dzam?; in'trud·er intruz *m*, natręt *m*;
in·tru·sion [ɪnˈtruːʒn] najście *n*, wtargnięcie *n*; in·tru·sive [ɪnˈtruːsɪv] natrętny, niepożądany

in·tu·i·tion [ɪntjuːˈɪʃn] intuicja *f*;
~·tive [ɪnˈtjuːɪtɪv] intuicyjny

in·un·date [ˈɪnʌndeɪt] zalewać ⟨-lać⟩,
zatapiać ⟨-topić⟩

in·vade [ɪnˈveɪd] naruszać ⟨-szyć⟩, zakłócać ⟨-cić⟩; *mil.* najeżdżać ⟨-jechać⟩
na (*A*), dokonywać ⟨-nać⟩ inwazji (*G*);
fig. nachodzić ⟨najść⟩, nękać; **~r** na-
jeźdźca *m*

in·va·lid¹ [ˈɪnvəlɪd] **1.** niesprawny,
ułomny; **2.** inwalida *m* (-dka *f*); kaleka
m/f

in·val·id² [ɪnˈvælɪd] *jur.* nieprawomoc-
ny, nie posiadający mocy prawnej

in·val·u·a·ble [ɪnˈvæljʊəbl] nieoceni-
ony

in·var·i·a·ble [ɪnˈveərɪəbl] niezmienny; **~·bly** niezmiennie; zawsze

in·va·sion [ɪnˈveɪʒn] inwazja *f* (*też mil.*),
wtargnięcie *n*, najazd *m*

in·vec·tive [ɪnˈvektɪv] inwektywa *f*,
obelga *f*

in·vent [ɪnˈvent] wynajdywać ⟨-naleźć⟩;
zmyślać ⟨-lić⟩; in·ven·tion [ɪnˈvenʃn]
wynalazek *m*; in·ven·tive [ɪnˈventɪv]
pomysłowy, pełen inwencji; in·ven·tor
[ɪnˈventə] wynalazca *m*; in·ven·tory
[ˈɪnvəntrɪ] spis *m*, inwentarz *m*

in·verse [ɪnˈvɜːs] **1.** odwrotny; **2.** odwrotność *f*, in·ver·sion [ɪnˈvɜːʃn] odwrócenie *n*, inwersja *f*

in·vert [ɪnˈvɜːt] odwracać ⟨-rócić⟩; **~·ed**
'com·mas *pl.* cudzysłów *m*

in·ver·te·brate [ɪnˈvɜːtɪbrət] *zo.* **1.** bez-
kręgowy; **2.** bezkręgowiec *m*

in·vest [ɪnˈvest] ⟨za⟩inwestować

in·ves·ti·gate [ɪnˈvestɪgeɪt] ⟨z⟩ba-
dać; ⟨po⟩prowadzić dochodzenie (*into*
w sprawie *G*); **~·ga·tion** [ɪnvestɪ-
geɪʃn] dochodzenie *n*; **~·ga·tor** [ɪnˈves-
tɪgeɪtə]: *private ~gator* prywatny detektyw *m*

in·vest·ment [ɪnˈvestmənt] *econ.* in-
westycja *f*; inwestowanie *n*; lokata *f*, nakład *m*; in'ves·tor *econ.* investor *m*

in·vet·e·rate [ɪnˈvetərət] niepoprawny; uporczywy; zagorzały

in·vid·i·ous [ɪnˈvɪdɪəs] krzywdzący; *zadanie*: niedzięczny

in·vig·o·rate [ɪnˈvɪgəreɪt] ożywiać ⟨-wić⟩, orzeźwiać ⟨-wić⟩

in·vin·ci·ble [ɪnˈvɪnsəbl] niepokonany, niezwyciężony

in·vis·i·ble [ɪnˈvɪzəbl] niewidzialny

in·vi·ta·tion [ɪnvɪˈteɪʃn] zaproszenie *n*; wezwanie *n*; **in·vite** [ɪnˈvaɪt] zapraszać ⟨-rosić⟩; poprosić o (*A*); zachęcać do (*G*); **in·vit·ing** wabiący, kuszący

in·voice [ˈɪnvɔɪs] *econ.* **1.** faktura *f*; **2.** wystawiać ⟨-wić⟩ fakturę; ⟨za⟩fakturować

in·voke [ɪnˈvəʊk] wzywać; powoływać się na (*A*); przywoływać ⟨-łać⟩; błagać o (*A*)

in·vol·un·ta·ry [ɪnˈvɒləntərɪ] mimowolny

in·volve [ɪnˈvɒlv] *kogoś* uwikływać ⟨-kłać⟩, wplątywać ⟨-tać⟩ (*in* w *L*); dotyczyć (*G*), tyczyć się (*G*); obejmować ⟨objąć⟩; odnosić się do (*G*); **~d** zawiły; *be* **~d** *with s.o.* być związanym z kimś; **~·ment** wplątanie *n*, uwikłanie *n*; wmieszanie *n*; zaangażowanie *n*

in·vul·ne·ra·ble [ɪnˈvʌlnərəbl] nie do zranienia; *fig* odporny

in·ward [ˈɪnwəd] **1.** wewnętrzny, intymny; **2.** *adv.*: *zw.* **~s** do środka, do wewnątrz

I/O [aɪ ˈəʊ] *skrót*: *input/output* komp. wejście/wyjście (*danych*)

IOC [aɪ əʊ ˈsiː] *skrót*: *International Olympic Committee* MKOl, Międzynarodowy Komitet *m* Olimpijski

i·o·dine [ˈaɪədiːn] *chem.* jod *m*; jodyna *f*

i·on [ˈaɪən] *phys.* jon *m*

IOU [aɪ əʊ ˈjuː] *skrót*: *I owe you* skrypt *m* dłużny

IQ [aɪ ˈkjuː] *skrót*: *intelligence quotient* IQ, iloraz *m* inteligencji

IRA [aɪ ɑːr ˈeɪ] *skrót*: *Irish Republican Army* IRA, Irlandzka Armia *f* Republikańska

I·ran [ɪˈrɑːn] Iran *m*; **I·ra·ni·an** [ɪˈreɪnjən] **1.** irański; **2.** Irańczyk *m* (*Iranka f*); *ling.* język *m* irański

I·raq [ɪˈrɑːk] Irak *m*; **I·ra·qi** [ɪˈrɑːkɪ] **1.** iracki; **2.** Irakijczyk *m* (-jka *f*)

i·ras·ci·ble [ɪˈræsəbl] drażliwy, porywczy

i·rate [aɪˈreɪt] rozjątrzony

Ire·land [ˈaɪələnd] Irlandia *f*

ir·i·des·cent [ɪrɪˈdesnt] opalizujący

i·ris [ˈaɪərɪs] *anat.* tęczówka *f*; *bot.* irys *m*, kosaciec *m*

I·rish [ˈaɪərɪʃ] irlandzki; *the* **~** *pl.* Irlandczycy *pl.*; **~·man** (*pl.* **-men**) Irlandczyk *m*; **~·wom·an** (*pl.* **-women**) Irlandka *f*

irk·some [ˈɜːksəm] drażniący

i·ron [ˈaɪən] **1.** żelazo *ni*; żelazko *n*; *strike while the* **~** *is hot* kuć żelazo, póki gorące; **2.** żelazny; **3.** ⟨u-, wy⟩prasować; **~** *out* rozprasowywać ⟨-ować⟩; *fig.* rozwiązywać ⟨-zać⟩; **2** *'Cur·tain pol. hist.* żelazna kurtyna *f*

i·ron·ic [aɪˈrɒnɪk] (**~ally**), **i·ron·i·cal** [aɪˈrɒnɪkl] ironiczny

i·ron·ing board deska *f* do prasowania

i·ron'lung *med.* sztuczne płuca *pl.*; **~·mon·ger** *Brt.* [ˈaɪənmʌŋgə] handlarz *m* (-arka *f*) towarami żelaznymi, właściciel(ka *f*) *m* sklepu z towarami żelaznymi; **~·works** *sg.* huta *f* żelaza

i·ron·y [ˈaɪərənɪ] ironia *f*

ir·ra·tion·al [ɪˈræʃənl] irracjonalny, mało racjonalny

ir·rec·on·ci·la·ble [ɪˈrekənsaɪləbl] nie do pogodzenia; nieprzejednany

ir·re·cov·e·ra·ble [ɪrɪˈkʌvərəbl] nie do odzyskania; niepowetowany

ir·reg·u·lar [ɪˈregjʊlə] nieprawidłowy; nieregularny

ir·rel·e·vant [ɪˈreləvənt] nieistotny (*to* dla *G*)

ir·rep·a·ra·ble [ɪˈrepərəbl] nie do naprawienia; niepowetowany

ir·re·place·a·ble [ɪrɪˈpleɪsəbl] niezastąpiony

ir·re·pres·si·ble [ɪrɪˈpresəbl] niepowstrzymany, niepohamowany, niekontrolowany

ir·re·proa·cha·ble [ɪrɪˈprəʊtʃəbl] nienaganny, bez zarzutu

ir·re·sis·ti·ble [ɪrɪˈzɪstəbl] nieodparty; fascynujący

ir·res·o·lute [ɪˈrezəluːt] niezdecydowany, niepewny

ir·re·spec·tive [ɪrɪˈspektɪv]: **~ of** niezależnie od (*G*), bez względu na (*A*)

ir·re·spon·si·ble [ɪrɪˈspɒnsəbl] nieodpowiedzialny; lekkomyślny

ir·re·trie·va·ble [ɪrɪˈtriːvəbl] nie do odzyskania

ir·rev·e·rent [ɪ'revərənt] bez szacunku, lekceważący

ir·rev·o·ca·ble [ɪ'revəkəbl] nie do odwołania, nieodwołalny

ir·ri|·gate ['ɪrɪgeɪt] nawadniać ⟨-wodnić⟩, ⟨z⟩irygować; ~·ga·tion [ɪrɪ'geɪʃn] nawodnienie *n*, irygacja *f* (*też med.*)

ir·ri|·ta·ble ['ɪrɪtəbl] drażliwy; ~·tant ['ɪrɪtənt] środek *m* drażniący; ~·tate ['ɪrɪteɪt] ⟨roz⟩drażnić; *med.* ⟨po⟩drażnić; ~·tat·ing drażniący; irytujący; ~·ta·tion [ɪrɪ'teɪʃn] irytacja *f*, rozdrażnienie *n*; podrażnienie *n*; gniew *m* (*at* na *A*)

is [ɪz] *on, ona, ono* jest

ISBN [aɪ es bi: 'en] *skrót:* **International Standard Book Number** ISBN, Międzynarodowy Standardowy Numer *m* Książki

Is·lam ['ɪzlɑːm] islam *m*

is·land ['aɪlənd] wyspa *f; też* **traffic ~** (*na ulicy*) wysepka *f;* '~·er wyspiarz *m*

isle [aɪl] *poet.* wyspa *f,* ostrów *m*

i·so·late ['aɪsəleɪt] izolować; *kogoś* odizolowywać ⟨-wać⟩; *coś* wyizolowywać ⟨-wać⟩; ~·lat·ed osamotniony, odosobniony; △ *nie* **izolowany**; ~·lation [aɪsə'leɪʃn] izolacja *f*, odseparowanie *n*; ~'la·tion·ward *med.* izolatka *f*

Is·rael ['ɪzreɪəl] Izrael *m;* Is·rae·li [ɪz'reɪlɪ] **1.** izraelski; *hist.* izraelicki; **2.** Izraelczyk (-ka *f*), *hist.* Izraelita *m* (-tka *f*)

is·sue ['ɪʃuː] **1.** zagadnienie *n;* sporna kwestia *f;* numer *m* (*czasopisma*); wydanie *n* (*czasopisma*); *jur.* spór *m*, zagadnienie *n;* potomstwo *n;* **be at ~** być przedmiotem sporu; **point at ~** kwestia *f* sporna; **die without ~** umrzeć bez potomstwa; **2.** *v/t. czasopismo, dokument* wydawać ⟨-dać⟩; *banknoty* ⟨wy⟩emitować; *v/i.* wynikać ⟨-knąć⟩; wypływać ⟨-nąć⟩

it [ɪt] to; ono, jego, jemu

I·tal·i·an [ɪ'tæljən] **1.** włoski; **2.** Włoch *m*, Włoszka *f; ling.* język *m* włoski

I·tal·ics [ɪ'tælɪks] *print.* kursywa *f*

It·a·ly ['ɪtəlɪ] Włochy *pl.*

itch [ɪtʃ] **1.** swędzenie *f;* **2.** ⟨za⟩swędzieć; *I ~ all over* wszędzie mnie swędzi; **be~ing for s.th.** strasznie czegoś chcieć; **be ~ing to do s.th.** F mieć chęć coś zrobić; '~·y swędzący

i·tem ['aɪtəm] punkt *m* (*porządku dziennego*), (*na liście*) pozycja *f;* przedmiot *m*, rzecz *f;* wiadomość *f; prasowa* informacja *f; jur.* klauzula *f*, paragraf *m;* ~·ize ['aɪtəmaɪz] wyszczególniać ⟨-nić⟩, wyliczać ⟨-czyć⟩

i·tin·e·ra·ry [aɪ'tɪnərəri] trasa *f* podróży, marszruta *f*, droga *f*

its [ɪts] jego

it's [ɪts] *skrót:* **it is; it has**

it·self [ɪt'self] się, sobie, siebie; **by ~** sam, bez pomocy; **in ~** samo w sobie

ITV [aɪ tiː 'viː] *skrót:* **Independent Television** ITV (*niezależna brytyjska komercyjna stacja TV*)

I've [aɪv] *skrót:* **I have**

i·vo·ry ['aɪvərɪ] kość *f* słoniowa

i·vy ['aɪvɪ] *bot.* bluszcz *m*

J

J, j [dʒeɪ] J, j *n*

J *skrót pisany:* **joule(s)** J, dżul *m lub* joule *m*

jab [dʒæb] **1.** (*-bb-*) żgać ⟨żgnąć⟩, dźgać ⟨dźgnąć⟩; **2.** dźgnięcie *n*, żgnięcie *n*, pchnięcie *n*

jab·ber ['dʒæbə] paplać, trajkotać

jack [dʒæk] **1.** *tech.* podnośnik *m;* walet *m* (*w kartach*)

jack·al ['dʒækɔːl] *zo.* szakal *m*

jack|·ass ['dʒækæs] *zo.* osioł *m* (*też fig.*); '~·boots *pl.* wysokie buty *pl.* wojskowe; '~·daw *zo.* kawka *f*

jack·et ['dʒækɪt] marynarka *f;* kurtka *f;* żakiet *m; tech.* płaszcz *m*, osłona *f;* obwoluta *f; Am.* koperta *f* (*płyty*); **~ potatoes** *pl.*, **potatoes (boiled) in their ~s** *pl.* Brt. ziemniaki *pl.* w mundurkach

jack| knife ['dʒæknaɪf] **1.** (*pl.* **-knives**) scyzoryk *m;* **2.** składać ⟨złożyć⟩ się (*jak scyzoryk*); '~·of-'all-trades majster-klepka *m;* '~·pot główna wygrana *f;* **hit the ~pot** wygrać główną wygraną; *fig.* wygrać główny los na loterii, zgarnąć pulę

jag [dʒæg] szczerba *f*, wyszczerbienie *f*; **~·ged** ['dʒægɪd] wyszczerbiony; poszarpany

jag·u·ar ['dʒægjuə] *zo.* jaguar *m*

jail [dʒeɪl] **1.** więzienie *n*; **2.** ⟨u⟩więzić; '**~·bird** F wyrokowiec *m*, kryminalista *m* (-tka *f*); '**~·er** strażnik *m* (-niczka *f*) więzienny (-a); '**~·house** *Am.* więzienie *n*

jam[1] [dʒæm] dżem *m*

jam[2] [dʒæm] **1.** (*-mm-*) *v/t.* ściskać ⟨-snąć⟩, wciskać ⟨-snąć⟩, wtłaczać ⟨-łoczyć⟩; *też ludzi* wpychać ⟨wepchnąć⟩; *też* **~ up** ⟨za⟩blokować, zatykać ⟨-tkać⟩; *radio* zagłuszać ⟨-szyć⟩; **~ on the brakes** *mot.* nagle zahamować; *v/i.* wtłaczać ⟨-łoczyć⟩ się, wpychać ⟨wepchać⟩ się; *tech.* zakleszczać ⟨-czyć⟩ się, ⟨za⟩blokować się; **2.** tłok *m*, ścisk *m*; *tech.* blokada *f*, zakleszczenie *n*; zator *m*; **traffic ~** korek *m*; **be in a ~** F mieć kłopoty

Ja·mai·ca [dʒə'meɪkə] Jamajka *f*; **Ja·mai·can** [dʒə'meɪkən] **1.** *adj.* jamajski; **2.** Jamajczyk *m* (-jka *f*)

jamb [dʒæm] ościeże *n*

jam·bo·ree [dʒæmbə'riː] *mus.* jamboree *n*; mityng *m*

Jan *skrót pisany:* **January** stycz., styczeń *m*

jan·gle ['dʒæŋgl] ⟨za⟩brzęczeć; *fig.* zgrzytać ⟨-tnąć⟩

jan·i·tor ['dʒænɪtə] *Am.* dozorca *m* (-czyni *f*); (*w szkole*) woźny *m* (-na *f*)

Jan·u·a·ry ['dʒænjuərɪ] (*skrót:* **Jan**) styczeń *m*; *attr.* styczniowy

Ja·pan [dʒə'pæn] Japonia *f*; **Jap·a·nese** [dʒæpə'niːz] **1.** Japoński, -a, -e; **2.** Japończyk *m* (-onka *f*); *ling.* język *m* japoński; **the ~** *pl.* Japończycy *pl.*

jar[1] [dʒɑː] słój *m*, słoik *m*;

jar[2] [dʒɑː] (*-rr-*): **~ on** barwa: być krzykliwym; *zapach:* drażnić

jar·gon ['dʒɑːgən] żargon *m*, odmiana *f* środowiskowa

jaun·dice ['dʒɔːndɪs] *med.* żółtaczka *f*

jaunt [dʒɔːnt] **1.** wycieczka *f*, eskapada *f*; **2.** wyjeżdżać ⟨-jechać⟩ na wycieczkę

jaun·ty ['dʒɔːntɪ] (*-ier, -iest*) rzutki, żwawy

jav·e·lin ['dʒævlɪn] (*w sporcie*) oszczep *m*; **~ (throw), throwing the ~** rzut *m* o-

szczepem; **~ thrower** oszczepnik *m* (-niczka *f*)

jaw [dʒɔː] *anat., tech.* szczęka *f*, **lower** (**upper**) **~** dolna (górna) szczęka *f*; **~s** *pl. zo.* pysk *m*, zęby *pl.*; '**~·bone** *anat.* kość *f* szczękowa

jay [dʒeɪ] *zo.* sójka *f*; '**~·walk** nieprawidłowo przechodzić ⟨przejść⟩ przez jezdnię; '**~·walk·er** osoba *f* nieprawidłowo przechodząca przez jezdnię

jazz [dʒæz] *mus.* jazz *m*

jeal·ous ['dʒeləs] zawistny (*of* o *A*); zazdrosny; '**~·y** zawiść *f*; zazdrość *f*

jeans [dʒiːnz] *pl.* dżinsy *pl.*

jeep [dʒiːp] *TM* dżip *m*, jeep *m*

jeer [dʒɪə] **1.** (*at*) wyśmiewać ⟨-miać⟩ się (z *A*); drwić (z *A*); szydzić (z *A*); **2.** szyderstwo *n*; drwina *f*

jel·lied ['dʒelɪd] w galarecie

jel·ly ['dʒelɪ] galareta *f*; galaretka *f*; '**~ ba·by** *Brt.* F cukierek *m* z żelatyny, żelatynka *f*; '**~ bean** cukierek *m* z żelatyny, żelatynka *f*; '**~·fish** *zo.* (*pl.* **-fish, -fishes**) meduza *f*

jeop·ar·dize ['dʒepədaɪz] zagrażać ⟨-rozić⟩; narażać ⟨-razić⟩ na niebezpieczeństwo; '**~·dy** niebezpieczeństwo *n*, zagrożenie *n*

jerk [dʒɜːk] **1.** szarpać ⟨-pnąć⟩ (się); wzdrygnąć się; **2.** szarpnięcie *n*; *med.* odruch *m*; '**~·y** (*-ier, -iest*) szarpany; nierówny; trzęsący

Je·rusa·lem [dʒə'ruːsələm] Jerozolima *f*

jer·sey ['dʒɜːzɪ] pulower *m*

jest [dʒest] **1.** żart *m*; **2.** ⟨za⟩żartować; '**~·er** *hist.* trefniś *m*, wesołek *m*

jet [dʒet] **1.** strumień *m*, struga *f*; *tech.* dysza *f*, rozpylacz *m*; *aviat.* odrzutowiec *m*; **2.** (*-tt-*) wytryskać ⟨-snąć⟩, tryskać ⟨-snąć⟩ strumieniem (*from* z *G*); *aviat.* F latać odrzutowcami; **~ 'en·gine** silnik *m* odrzutowy; '**~ lag** (*zaburzenia organizmu spowodowane nagłą zmianą rytmu dobowego po długiej podróży samolotem*); '**~ plane** odrzutowiec *m*; **~·pro'pelled** odrzutowy; napędzany silnikiem odrzutowym; **~·pro'pul·sion** napęd *m* odrzutowy; '**~ set** elita *f* towarzyska, high life *m*; '**~·set·ter** członek *m* elity towarzyskiej

jet·ty ['dʒetɪ] *naut.* nabrzeże *n*; pomost *m*, pirs *m*

Jew [dʒuː] Żyd *m*

jew·el ['dʒuːəl] klejnot *m*, kamień *m*

szlachetny; 'jew·eler *Am.*, 'jew·el·ler *Brt.* jubiler *m*; jew·el·lery *Brt.*, jew·elry *Am.* ['dʒu:əlrɪ] biżuteria *f*

Jew|·ess ['dʒu:ɪs] Żydówka *f*; '~·ish żydowski

jif·fy ['dʒɪfɪ]: *in a* ~ za chwileczkę

jig·saw ['dʒɪgsɔ:] *tech.* wyrzynarka *f*, F piła *f* włosowa, laubzega *f*; → *saw*; '~ puz·zle puzzle *m*, układanka *f*

jilt [dʒɪlt] porzucać ⟨-cić⟩

jin·gle ['dʒɪŋgl] 1. podzwaniać, dzwonić; 2. podzwanianie *n*, pobrzękiwanie *n*; melodyjka *f*

jit·ters ['dʒɪtəz] F *pl.*: *the* ~ zdenerwowanie *n*, trema *f*

Jnr *skrót pisany*: *Junior* jr., junior; młodszy

job [dʒɒb] 1. praca *f*; zajęcie *n*; miejsce *n* pracy; trudne zadanie *n*; *komp.* zadanie *n*; *też* ~ *work* praca *f* na akord; *by the* ~ na akord; *out of a* ~ bez pracy; 2. ~ *around* szukać pracy; '~ ad, ~ad'ver·tise·ment ogłoszenie *o* pracy; '~·ber *Brt.* makler *m*; spekulant *m* giełdowy; '~ cen·tre *Brt.* urząd *m* zatrudnienia; '~ hop·ping *Am.* częste zmiany *pl.* miejsca pracy; '~·hunt·ing poszukiwanie *n* pracy; '~·less bez pracy, bezrobotny; '~·shar·ing dzielenie się etatem, podział *m* etatu (*między pracowników niepełnoetatowych*)

jock·ey ['dʒɒkɪ] dżokej *m*

jog [dʒɒg] 1. potrącać ⟨-cić⟩; ~ *along*, ~ *on* ⟨po⟩truchtać; biegać, biec; (*w sporcie*) uprawiać jogging; 2. potrącenie *n*; bieg *m*; przebieżka *f*; '~·ger (*w sporcie*) osoba *f* uprawiająca jogging; '~·ging jogging *m*

join [dʒɔɪn] 1. *v/t.* ⟨z-, po⟩łączyć; dołączać ⟨-czyć⟩, przyłączać ⟨-czyć⟩; dołączać ⟨-czyć⟩ się do (*G*), przyłączać ⟨-czyć⟩ się do (*G*); wstępować ⟨-tąpić⟩ do (*G*); łączyć się z (*I*); *v/i.* dołączać ⟨-czyć⟩, przyłączać ⟨-czyć⟩; łączyć się; ~ *in* brać ⟨wziąć⟩ udział, przyłączać ⟨-czyć⟩; 2. miejsce *n* złączenia; złączenie *n*; '~·er stolarz *m*

joint [dʒɔɪnt] 1. miejsce *n* złączenia, połączenie *n*, spoina *f*; *anat.* staw *m*; *tech.* złącze *n*; *bot.* kolanko *n*; *Brt. gastr.* pieczeń *f*; *sl.* knajpa *f*, spelunа *f*; *sl.* skręt *m* (*marihuany itp.*); *out of* ~ zwichnięty; *fig.* wypaść z kolein; 2. połączony; łączny; wspólny; współ...;

'~·ed przegubowy; ruchomy; ~'stock com·pa·ny *Brt.* spółka *f* akcyjna; ~ 'ven·ture *econ.* joint venture

joke [dʒəʊk] 1. dowcip *m*, kawał *m*; żart *m*; *practical* ~ kawał *m*, figiel *m*; *play a* ~ *on s.o.* zrobić komuś kawał; 2. ⟨za⟩żartować; dowcipkować; 'jok·er dowcipniś *m*, kawalarz *m*; (*w kartach*) dżoker *m*, joker *m*

jol·ly ['dʒɒlɪ] 1. *adj.* (*-ier, -iest*) wesoły, radosny; 2. *adv. Brt.* F okropnie, bardzo; ~ *good* znakomicie

jolt [dʒəʊlt] 1. potrząsnąć; trząść; *fig.* wstrząsnąć; 2. trzęsienie *n*, wstrząsanie *n*; *fig.* szok *m*

jos·tle ['dʒɒsl] popychać ⟨-chnąć⟩, szarpać ⟨-pnąć⟩

jot [dʒɒt] 1. *not a* ~ ani krztyny; 2. (*-tt-*): ~ *down* ⟨za⟩notować

joule [dʒu:l] *phys.* dżul *m*

jour·nal ['dʒɜːnl] dziennik *m*; czasopismo *n*; ~·is·m ['dʒɜːnəlɪzəm] dziennikarstwo *n*; ~·ist ['dʒɜːnəlɪst] dziennikarz *m* (-arka *f*)

jour·ney ['dʒɜːnɪ] 1. podróż *f*; 2. podróżować; '~·man (*pl. -men*) towarzysz(ka *f*) *m* podróży

joy [dʒɔɪ] radość *f*; *for* ~ dla przyjemności; '~·ful radosny; rozradowany; '~·less ponury, smutny; '~·ride (*-rode, -ridden*) jeździć ⟨jechać⟩ skradzionym po to samochodem; '~·stick *aviat.* drążek sterowy; *komp.* joystick *m*, dżojstik *m*

Jr → *Jnr*

jub·i·lant ['dʒu:bɪlənt] rozradowany, radosny

ju·bi·lee ['dʒu:bɪli:] jubileusz *m*

Ju·da·ism ['dʒu:deɪɪzəm] *rel.* judaizm *m*

judge [dʒʌdʒ] 1. *jur.* sędzia *m* (-ina *f*) (*też fig.*); juror *m* (-ka *f*); znawca *m* (-czyni *f*); 2. *jur.* orzekać ⟨orzec⟩; wydawać ⟨-dać⟩ sąd

judg(e)·ment ['dʒʌdʒmənt] *jur.* orzeczenie *n*, wyrok *m*; sąd *m*, pogląd *m*; *rel.* dzień *m* sądu, sąd *m*; *the Last* 2 Sąd *m* Ostateczny; '2 Day, *lub Day of* 2 dzień *m* Sądu Ostatecznego

ju·di·cial [dʒu:'dɪʃl] *jur.* sądowy; sędziowski

ju·di·cia·ry [dʒu:'dɪʃɪərɪ] *jur.* sądownictwo *n*; sędziowie *pl.*

ju·di·cious [dʒu:'dɪʃəs] rozumny, rozsądny

ju·do ['dʒu:dəʊ] judo *n lub* dżudo *n*

J

jug [dʒʌg] dzbanek *m*, dzban *m*

jug·gle ['dʒʌgl] żonglować (*I*); dopasować, dostosować; '*~r* żongler *m* (-ka *f*)

juice [dʒuːs] sok *m*; *sl. mot.* benzyna *f*; **juic·y** ['dʒuːsɪ] (*-ier*, *-iest*) soczysty; *F* pikantny

juke·box ['dʒuːkbɒks] szafa *f* grająca

Jul *skrót pisany:* **July** lipiec *m*

Ju·ly [dʒuːˈlaɪ] (*skrót:* **Jul**) lipiec *m*

jum·ble ['dʒʌmbl] **1.** *też* **~ together**, **~ up** ⟨z-, po⟩mieszać; ⟨po⟩rozrzucać; **2.** mieszanina *f*, mieszanka *f*; '**~ sale** *Brt.* wyprzedaż *f* (*rzeczy używanych*)

jum·bo ['dʒʌmbəʊ] **1.** ogromny, potężny; **2.** (*pl. -bos*) F → **colossal**; '**~ jet** jumbo jet *m* (*wielki odrzutowiec pasażerski*); '**~-sized** ogromny

jump [dʒʌmp] **1.** *v/i.* skakać ⟨skoczyć⟩; podskakiwać ⟨-koczyć⟩; **~ at** rzucać się na (*A*); **~ at the chance** korzystać skwapliwie z okazji; **~ to conclusions** przedwcześnie wyciągać ⟨-gnąć⟩ wnioski; *v/t.* przeskakiwać ⟨-koczyć⟩; **~ the queue** *Brt.* wpychać ⟨wepchnąć⟩ się do kolejki; **~ the lights** przejeżdżać ⟨-jechać⟩ przez skrzyżowanie na czerwonym świetle; **2.** skok *m*; **high** (**long**) **~** (*w sporcie*) skok *m* wzwyż (w dal)

'**jump·er¹** (*w sporcie*) skoczek *m*

'**jump·er²** *Brt.* pulower *m*; *Am.* fartuch *m*

'**jump·ing jack** pajac *m*; '**~·y** (*-ier*, *-iest*) nerwowy

Jun *skrót pisany:* **June** czerwiec *m*; → **Jnr**

junc·tion ['dʒʌŋkʃn] skrzyżowanie *n*; *rail.* punkt *m* węzłowy; **~·ture** ['dʒʌŋktʃə]: **at this ~ture** w tym momencie

June [dʒuːn] (*skrót:* **Jun**) czerwiec *m*

jun·gle ['dʒʌŋgl] dżungla *f*

ju·ni·or ['dʒuːnjə] **1.** junior; młodszy; podwładny; (*w sporcie*) w kategorii juniorów; **2.** junior *m*; młodszy *m*; pod-

władny *m*; **~ high (school)** *Am.* (*ostatnie klasy szkoły średniej*); '**~ school** *Brt.* szkoła *f* podstawowa (*dla dzieci od 7 do 11 roku życia*)

junk¹ [dʒʌŋk] *naut.* dżonka *f*

junk² [dʒʌŋk] F rupiecie *pl.*, graty *pl.*; odpadki *pl.*; *sl.* heroina *f*; '**~ food** złe jedzenie *n* (*wysokokaloryczne o niskiej wartości odżywczej*); **~·ie**, **~·y** ['dʒʌŋkɪ] *sl.* narkoman(ka *f*) *m*, ćpun(ka *f*) *m*; '**~·yard** *Am.* złomowisko *n*; **auto~yard** złomowisko *n* samochodów, F szrot *m*

jur·is·dic·tion ['dʒʊərɪs'dɪkʃn] jurysdykcja *f*; kompetencja *f lub* właściwość *f* sądu

ju·ris·pru·dence ['dʒʊərɪs'pruːdəns] prawoznawstwo *f*

ju·ror ['dʒʊərə] *jur.* członek *m* sądu przysięgłych

ju·ry ['dʒʊərɪ] *jur.* sąd *m* przysięgłych; jury *n*; '**~·man** (*pl. -men*) *jur.* członek *m* sądu przysięgłych; '**~·wom·an** (*pl. -wo·men*) *jur.* członkini *f* sądu przysięgłych

just [dʒʌst] **1.** *adj.* sprawiedliwy, słuszny; zasłużony; **2.** *adv.* właśnie; zaledwie; tylko, jedynie; po prostu; **~ about** w przybliżeniu, prawie; **~ like that** po prostu tak; **~ now** właśnie teraz; dopiero co

jus·tice ['dʒʌstɪs] sprawiedliwość *f*; *jur.* sędzia *m*; **2 of the Peace** sędzia *m* pokoju; **court of ~** (*budynek*) sąd *m*

jus·ti·fi·ca·tion [dʒʌstɪfɪ'keɪʃn] usprawiedliwienie *n*; uzasadnienie *n*; **~·fy** ['dʒʌstɪfaɪ] usprawiedliwiać ⟨-wić⟩

just·ly ['dʒʌstlɪ] słusznie; sprawiedliwie

jut [dʒʌt] (*-tt-*): **~ out** wystawać, sterczeć

ju·ve·nile ['dʒuːvənaɪl] **1.** młodociany; nieletni; **2.** młodociany *m* (*-na f*); nieletni *m* (*-nia f*); **~ 'court** *jur.* sąd *m* dla nieletnich; **~ de·lin·quen·cy** *jur.* przestępczość *f* nieletnich; **~ de·lin·quent** młodociany przestępca *m*

K

K, k [keɪ] K, k *n*

kan·ga·roo [kæŋgə'ruː] *zo.* kangur *m*

ka·ra·te [kə'rɑːtɪ] karate *n*

KB [keɪ 'biː] *skrót:* **kilobyte** KB, kilobajt *m*

keel [kiːl] **1.** kil *m*, stępka *f*; **2.** **~ over**

przewracać ⟨-rócić⟩ się

keen [kiːn] ostry (*też fig.*); *zimno:* przenikliwy; zapalony, gorliwy; **be~ on s.th.** bardzo się czymś interesować; palić się do czegoś

keep [kiːp] **1.** (*kept*) trzymać; mieć;

zatrzymywać ⟨-mać⟩; przechowywać ⟨-wać⟩; *obietnicę, słowa* dotrzymywać ⟨-mać⟩; *porządek, pracę, rodzinę* u-trzymywać; *dziennik, sklep* prowa-dzić; *zwierzęta* hodować; dochowywać ⟨-wać⟩ (*sekretu*); powstrzymywać ⟨-ymać⟩ (*from* przed *D*); ~ *early hours* wcześnie chodzić spać; ~ *s.o.* panować nad sobą; ~ *s.o. company* dotrzymywać ⟨-mać⟩ komuś towarzy-stwa; ~ *s.th. from s.o.* trzymać coś w sekrecie przed kimś; ~ *time* dobrze pokazywać czas; trzymać rytm *lub* takt; *v/i.* trzymać się; *z ger.* wciąż, ciągle; ~ *going* idź dalej; ~ *smiling* zawsze się uśmiechaj!; ~ (*on*) *talking* nadal mówić; ~ (*on*) *trying* próbuj dalej; ~ *s.o. waiting* kazać komuś czekać; ~ *away* trzymać się z daleka (*from* od *G*); ~ *back* wstrzymywać ⟨-mać⟩ się (*też fig.*); ~ *from doing s.th.* nie robić cze-goś; ~ *in* ucznia zatrzymywać ⟨-mać⟩; ~ *off* trzymać się z daleka; ~ *off!* wstęp wzbroniony!; ~ *on* ubranie nadal nosić; *światło* zostawiać ⟨-wić⟩ zapalo-ne; nadal (*doing s.th.*) robić coś; ~ *out* trzymać z daleka; ~ *out!* Wstęp wzbro-niony!; ~ *to* trzymać się (*G*); ~ *up* za-chowywać ⟨-wać⟩, utrzymywać ⟨-mać⟩; ~ *it up* tylko tak dalej; ~ *up with* do-trzymywać kroku (*D*); ~ *up with the Joneses* nie odstawać od sąsiadów; **2.** utrzymanie *n*, koszty *pl.* utrzymania; *for* ~*s* F na zawsze

'**keep|·er** dozorca *m*; opiekun(ka *f*) *m*; *zwł. w złożeniach* właściciel(ka *f*) *m*; '~·**ing** nadzór *m*, dozór *m*; *be in* (*out of*) ~*ing with ...* (nie) pasować do (*G*); ~·**sake** ['ki:pseɪk] pamiątka *f*

keg [keg] beczułka *f*

ken·nel ['kenl] buda *f*; ~*s sg.* schroni-sko *n* dla psów

kept [kept] *pret. i p.p. od* **keep** 1

kerb [kɜ:b], '~·**stone** krawężnik *m*

ker·chief ['kɜ:tʃɪf] chustka *f* (*na głowę itp.*)

ker·nel ['kɜ:nl] jądro *n* (*też fig.*)

ket·tle ['ketl] czajnik *m*; '~·**drum** *mus.* kocioł *m*

key [ki:] **1.** klucz *m* (*też fig.*); klawisz *m*; *mus.* tonacja *f*; *attr.* kluczowy; **2.** dosto-sowywać ⟨-wać⟩ (*to* do *G*); *komp.* wpi-sywać ⟨-sać⟩, wprowadzać ⟨-dzić⟩; ~*ed up* spięty; '~·**board** klawiatura *f*;

'~·**hole** dziurka *f* od klucza; '~·**man** (*pl.* -**men**) kluczowa figura *f*; ~·**note** *mus.* tonika *f*, dźwięk centralny; *fig.* za-sadnicza myśl *f*; '~ **ring** kółko *n* na klu-cze; '~·**stone** *arch.* zwornik *m*; *fig.* fi-lar *m*; '~ **word** wyraz *m* kluczowy

kick [kɪk] **1.** kopać ⟨-pnąć⟩; (*w sporcie*) strzelać ⟨-lić⟩; *koń*: wierzgać ⟨-gnąć⟩; ~ *off* rozpoczynać ⟨-cząć⟩ grę; ~ *out* F wyrzucić, wykopać; ~ *up* wybijać ⟨-bić⟩ kopnięciem; ~ *up a fuss lub row* F wszcząć awanturę; **2.** kopnięcie *n*, kopniak *m*; wierzgnięcie *n*; (*w piłce nożnej*) rzut *m*, strzał *m*; *free* ~ rzut *m* wolny; *for* ~*s* F dla draki; *they get a* ~ *out of it* strasznie ich to bawi; '~·**off** (*w piłce nożnej*) początek *m* gry

kid¹ [kɪd] koźlę *n*; skóra *f* koźlęcia; F dzieciak *m*; ~ **brother** F młodszy brat *m*

kid² [kɪd] (-**dd**-) *v/t.* kogoś naciągać ⟨-gnąć⟩; ~ *s.o.* oszukiwać ⟨-kać⟩ kogoś; *v/i.* ⟨za⟩żartować, robić żarty; *he is only* ~*ding* on tylko żartuje; *no* ~*ding!* słowo honoru!

kid 'gloves *pl.* rękawiczki *pl.* z koźlej skóry (*też fig.*)

kid·nap ['kɪdnæp] (-**pp**-, *Am. też* -**p**-) porywać ⟨-rwać⟩; '**kid·nap·(p)er** pory-wacz *m* (-ka *f*); '**kid·nap·(p)ing** por-wanie *m*, kidnaperstwo *n*

kid·ney ['kɪdnɪ] *anat.* nerka *f*; '~ **bean** fasola *f*; '~ **ma·chine** *med.* sztuczna nerka *f*

Kiev Kijów *m*

kill [kɪl] zabijać ⟨-bić⟩, uśmiercać ⟨-cić⟩ (*też fig.*); *humor, nastrój* zwarzyć; *szan-se* unicestwiać ⟨-wić⟩; *be* ~*ed in an accident* zostać zabitym w wypadku; ~ *time* zabijać ⟨-bić⟩ czas; '~·**er** zabój-ca *m* (-czyni *n*); '~·**ing** morderczy

kiln [kɪln] piec *m* (*do wypalania*)

ki·lo ['ki:ləʊ] F (*pl.* -*los*) kilo *n*

kil·o|·gram ['kɪləgræm] kilogram *m*; '~·**me·tre** *Brt.*, '~·**me·ter** *Am.* kilo-metr *m*

kilt [kɪlt] kilt *m*, spódniczka *f* szkocka

kin [kɪn] krewny

kind¹ [kaɪnd] uprzejmy, miły; grzeczny, życzliwy; serdeczny

kind² [kaɪnd] rodzaj *m*, typ *m*; gatunek *m*; odmiana *f*; *all* ~*s of* wszyscy, wszyst-kie; *nothing of the* ~ nic w tym rodza-ju; ~ *of* jakby; *in* ~ w naturze; *this* ~ *of* tego rodzaju

K

kin·der·gar·ten ['kɪndəgɑːtn] przedszkole *n*

kind-'heart·ed dobry, o dobrym sercu

kin·dle ['kɪndl] rozpalać ⟨-lić⟩, zapalać ⟨-lić⟩ (się); *fig. zainteresowanie itp.* rozbudzać ⟨-dzić⟩

kind·ly ['kaɪndlɪ] **1.** *adj.* (**-ier, -iest**) przyjazny, przyjacielski; **2.** *adv.* uprzejmie; przyjaźnie, przyjacielsko; '**~ness** uprzejmość *f*, serdeczność *f*, życzliwość *f*

kin·dred ['kɪndrɪd] pokrewny; **~ spirits** *pl.* pokrewne dusze *pl.*

king [kɪŋ] król *m* (*też fig. w szachach, grach*); **~dom** ['kɪŋdəm] królestwo *n* (*też rel.*); **animal** (**vegetable**) **~dom** królestwo *n* zwierząt (roślin); '**~ly** (**-ier, -iest**) królewski; '**~size(d)** ogromny

kink [kɪŋk] zapętlenie *n*, załamanie *n*; *fig.* dziwactwo *n*, perwersja *f*; '**~y** (**-ier, -iest**) dziwaczny, osobliwy; perwersyjny

ki·osk ['kiːɒsk] kiosk *m*; *Brt.* budka *f* telefoniczna

kip·per ['kɪpə] śledź *m* wędzony

kiss [kɪs] **1.** pocałunek *m*, całus *m*; **2.** ⟨po⟩całować

kit [kɪt] ekwipunek *m*; *Brt.* wyposażenie *n*, zestaw *m* (*przyborów*), komplet *m*; zestaw *m* (*do sklejenia*); → **first-aid kit**; '**~ bag** worek *m* na wyposażenie

kitch·en ['kɪtʃɪn] kuchnia *f*; *attr.* kuchenny; **~ette** [kɪtʃɪ'net] kuchenka *f*, wnęka *f* kuchenna; **~'gar·den** ogród *m* warzywny

kite [kaɪt] latawiec *m*; *zo.* kania *f*; *fly a* **~** puszczać latawiec

kit·ten ['kɪtn] kociak *m*, kocię *n*

knack [næk] umiejętność *f*, zdolność *f*, talent *m*

knave [neɪv] łotr *m*, niegodziwiec *m*; (*w kartach*) *Brt.* walet *m*

knead [niːd] miesić; rozrabiać ⟨-robić⟩, gnieść

knee [niː] kolano *n*; *tech.* kolanko *n*; '**~·cap** *anat.* rzepka *f* (kolana); **~'deep** po kolana; na głębokość kolan; '**~ joint** *anat.* połączenie *n* kolankowo-stawowe

kneel [niːl] (**knelt**, *Am. też* **kneeled**) klękać ⟨-nąć⟩; uklęknąć (**to** *przed I*)

'**knee-length** sukienka do kolan

knell [nel] dzwon *m* żałobny

knelt [nelt] *pret. i p.p. od* **kneel**

knew [njuː] *pret. od* **know**

knick·er·bock·ers ['nɪkəbɒkəz] *pl.* pludry *pl.*, pumpy *pl.*

knick·ers ['nɪkəz] *Brt. F pl.* figi *pl.*

knick-knack ['nɪknæk] drobiazg *m*, błahostka *f*, bibelot *m*

knife [naɪf] **1.** (*pl.* **knives** [naɪvz]) nóż *m*; **2.** dźgać ⟨-gnąć⟩ *nożem*

knight [naɪt] **1.** rycerz *m*; (*w szachach*) skoczek *m*, konik *m*; **2.** pasować na rycerza; nadawać ⟨-dać⟩ tytuł rycerski; **~·hood** ['naɪthud] tytuł *m lub* stan *m* rycerski

knit [nɪt] (**-tt-**; **knit** *lub* **knitted**) *v/t.* ⟨z⟩robić na drutach; *też* **~ together** związywać ⟨-zać⟩, zespalać ⟨-polić⟩ (się); **~ one's brows** ⟨z⟩marszczyć brwi; *v/i.* ⟨z⟩robić na drutach; zespalać ⟨-polić⟩ się; *kości:* zrastać się; '**~ting** robótka *f* na drutach; robienie *n* na drutach; '**~ting nee·dle** drut *m* (*do robót dzianych*); '**~wear** dzianina *f*, wyroby *pl.* z dzianiny

knives [naɪvz] *pl. od* **knife** 1

knob [nɒb] pokrętło *n*, gałka *f*; kulka *f* (*masła itp.*)

knock [nɒk] **1.** stukać ⟨-knąć⟩, pukać ⟨-knąć⟩; uderzać ⟨-rzyć⟩; **~ at the door** pukać do drzwi; **~ about, ~ around** obijać ⟨-bić⟩, ⟨s⟩tłuc; F włóczyć się, wędrować; F walać się; **~ down** budynek itp. ⟨z⟩burzyć; *przechodnia* potrącić, przejechać; *cenę* zbijać ⟨zbić⟩, obniżać ⟨-żyć⟩ *be* **~ed down** zostać przejechanym; **~ off** *cenę* spuszczać ⟨-puścić⟩; F dawać sobie spokój (z *I*); F wyprodukować, wypuścić ⟨-puszczać⟩; F (*ukraść, zabić*) rąbnąć; *v/i.* skończyć pracę; **~ out** powalić; pozbawić ⟨-wić⟩ przytomności; *fajkę* wytrząsać ⟨-snąć⟩; (*w boksie*) ⟨z⟩nokautować; ⟨wy⟩eliminować; *fig.* F zwalać ⟨-lić⟩ z nóg; **~ over** przewracać ⟨-rócić⟩, powalić; *be* **~ed over** zostać przejechanym; **2.** uderzenie *n*; pukanie *n*, stukanie *n*; *there is a* **~** (*at* [*Am.* **on**] *the door*) ktoś stuka; '**~·er** kołatka *f*; **~'kneed** o krzywych nogach; z krzywymi nogami; '**~-out** *boks:* nokaut *m*

knoll [nəʊl] pagórek *m*

knot [nɒt] **1.** węzeł *m*, supeł *m*; sęk *m*; *naut.* węzeł *m*; **2.** (**-tt-**) wiązać, zawiązywać ⟨-zać⟩; '**~·ty** (**-ier, -iest**) węzłowaty, węźlasty; *fig.* skomplikowany

know [nəʊ] (*knew, known*) wiedzieć; znać; poznać; umieć **~ how to do s.th.** umieć coś zrobić; rozpoznawać ⟨-nać⟩; zapoznawać się (z *I*); **~ French** umieć po francusku; **~ one's way around** orientować się w (*L*); **~ all about it** dobrze się znać na czymś; **get to ~** poznawać ⟨-nać⟩; zapoznać się z (*I*); **~ one's business, ~ the ropes, ~ a thing or two, ~ what's what** F orientować się w czymś; **you ~** no wiesz; '**~-how** know-how *m*, wiedza *f* wyspecjalizowana, technologia *f*; '**~·ing** zorientowany, znający się na rzeczy; porozumiewawczy; '**~·ing·ly** świadomie, u-myślnie; porozumiewawczo

knowl·edge ['nɒlɪdʒ] wiedza *f*, znajomość *f*; **to my ~** o ile wiem; **have a good ~ of** dobrze znać (*A*), dobrze się znać na (*L*); '**~·a·ble: be very ~able about** dobrze się znać na (*L*)

known [nəʊn] *p.p. od* **know**

knuck·le ['nʌkl] **1.** kostka *f* (ręki); **2. ~ down to work** zabierać ⟨-brać⟩ się ostro do pracy

KO [keɪ'əʊ] *skrót:* **knockout** F nokaut *m*

Ko·re·a Korea *f*

Krem·lin ['kremlɪn]: **the ~** Kreml *m*

L

L, l [el] L, l *n*

L [el] *skrót:* **learner** (**driver**) *Brt. mot.* nauka *f* jazdy; **large** (**size**) duży

l *skrót pisany:* **left** lewy, lewo; **line** linia *f*; **litre(s)** l, litr *m*

£ *skrót pisany:* **pound(s) sterling** GBP, funt *m* szterling

lab [læb] F laboratorium *n*

la·bel ['leɪbl] **1.** etykieta *f*, etykietka *f*; metka *f*; nalepka *f*; znak *m* wytwórni; **on the X ~** na płytach wytwórni X; **2.** (*zwł. Brt.* **-ll-,** *Am.* **-l-**) etykietować, metkować; oznaczać ⟨-czyć⟩ etykietką *lub* metką; *fig.* określać ⟨-lić⟩, nadawać ⟨-dać⟩ miano

la·bor·a·to·ry [lə'bɒrətərɪ] laboratorium *n*; **~ as'sis·tant** laborant(ka *f*) *m*

la·bo·ri·ous [lə'bɔːrɪəs] żmudny, ciężki

la·bor u·ni·on ['leɪbə -] *Am.* związek *m* zawodowy

la·bo(u)r ['leɪbə] **1.** ciężka praca *f*; trud *m*, wysiłek *m*; robocizna *f*; pracownicy *pl.* najemni, siła *f* robocza; *med.* poród *m*; **Labour** *pol.* Partia *f* Pracy; *attr.* laburzystowski; **2.** ciężko pracować; trudzić się; męczyć się, mozolić się; rozwodzić się (nad *I*); '**~ed** wysilony; **~·er** ['leɪbərə] robotnik *m* (-nica*f*); '**labour ex·change** → **job centre**; '**La·bour Par·ty** *pol.* Partia *f* Pracy

lace [leɪs] **1.** koronka *f*; sznurowadło *n*; **2. ~ up** ⟨za⟩sznurować; '**~d with brandy** z dodatkiem brandy

la·ce·rate ['læsəreɪt] poszarpać, rozdzierać ⟨-zedrzeć⟩; *fig.* ⟨z⟩ranić

lack [læk] **1.** (**of**) brak *m*; niedostatek *m*; △ *nie* **lak** ; **2.** *v/t.* nie mieć; **he ~s money** brak mu pieniędzy; *v/i.* **be ~ing** brakować; **he is ~ing in courage** brakuje mu odwagi; **~·lus·tre** *Brt.,* **~·lus·ter** *Am.* ['læklʌstə] bezbarwny, bez wyrazu

la·con·ic [lə'kɒnɪk] (**~ally**) lakoniczny

lac·quer ['lækə] **1.** lakier *m* (*też do włosów*); **2.** ⟨po⟩lakierować

lad [læd] chłopiec *m*, chłopak *m*

lad·der ['lædə] drabina *f*; *Brt.* oczko *n* (*w rajstopach*); '**~-proof** z nielecącymi oczkami

la·den ['leɪdn] obładowany, objuczony

la·dle ['leɪdl] chochla *f*

la·dy ['leɪdɪ] pani *f*; dama *f*; ♀ lady *f*; **~ doctor** lekarka *f*, kobieta *f* lekarz; **Ladies(')**, *Am.* **Ladies' room** toaleta damska; '**~·bird** *Brt.,* '**~·bug** *Am.* biedronka *f*; '**~·like** wytworny; jak dama

lag [læg] **1.** (**-gg-**): *zw.* **~ behind** zostawać ⟨-tać⟩ w tyle; **2.** → **time lag**

la·ger ['lɑːgə] piwo *n* jasne pełne

la·goon [lə'guːn] laguna *f*

laid [leɪd] *pret. i p.p. od* **lay³**

lain [leɪn] *p.p. od* **lie²**

lair [leə] legowisko *n*, łoże *n*; kryjówka *f*

la·i·ty ['leɪɪtɪ] laikat *m*

lake [leɪk] jezioro *n*

lamb [læm] **1.** jagnię *n*; *rel.* baranek *m*;

attr. mięso *n* z jagnięcia; **2.** *owca*: ⟨o⟩- kocić się

lame [leɪm] **1.** kulawy; *fig.* kulejący; **2.** kuleć, utykać

la·ment [ləˈment] **1.** lamentować, rozpaczać; biadać; **2.** lament *m*, biadanie *n*; **lam·en·ta·ble** [ˈlæməntəbl] opłakany, tragiczny; żałosny; **lam·en·ta·tion** [læmənˈteɪʃn] opłakiwanie *n*, biadanie *n*

lam·i·nat·ed [ˈlæmɪneɪtɪd] laminowany; (wielo)warstwowy, laminatowy; **~ 'glass** szkło *n* wielowarstwowe

lamp [læmp] lampa *f*; latarnia *f* (* uliczna*); **~·post** słup *m* latarni (*ulicznej*); **~·shade** abażur *m*, klosz *m*

lance [lɑːns] lanca *f*

land [lænd] **1.** ziemia *f*; ląd *m*; *agr.* ziemia *f*, grunt *m*; ląd *m*, strona *f* świata; **by ~** lądem; **2.** ⟨wy⟩lądować; *ładunek* wyładowywać ⟨-ować⟩; *ludzi* wysadzać ⟨-dzić⟩ na ląd; **'~ a·gent** *Brt.* zarządca *m* majątku; **~·ed** wyładowany; posiadający ziemię; **~ed gentry** ziemiaństwo *n*

land·ing [ˈlændɪŋ] lądowanie *n*; wyładunek *m*; podest *m*, podest *m*; **'~ field** *aviat.* lądowisko *n*; **'~ gear** *aviat.* podwozie *n* samolotu; **'~ stage** przystań *f*, miejsce *n* cumowania; **'~ strip** *aviat.* lądowisko *n*

land·**la·dy** [ˈlænleɪdɪ] właścicielka *f*; gospodyni *f*; **~·lord** [ˈlænlɔːd] właściciel *m*; gospodarz *m*; **~·lub·ber** [ˈlændlʌbə] *naut. pej.* szczur *m* lądowy; **~·mark** [ˈlændmɑːk] punkt *m* charakterystyczny *lub* orientacyjny; *fig.* kamień *m* milowy; **~·own·er** [ˈlændəʊnə] właściciel(ka *f*) *m* ziemski (*-a*); **~ scape** [ˈlænskeɪp] krajobraz *m*; **~·slide** [ˈlændslaɪd] obsunięcie *n* się ziemi; osuwisko *n*; **a ~slide victory** *pol.* przygniatające zwycięstwo *n*; **~·slip** [ˈlændslɪp] osuwisko *n*

lane [leɪn] dróżka *f* (*polna*); uliczka *f*, alejka *f*; *aviat.* droga *f* powietrzna, trasa *f* lotnicza; (*w sporcie*) tor *m*; *mot.* pas *m* (*ruchu*); **change ~s** zmieniać ⟨-nić⟩ pas ruchu; **get in ~** *mot.* włączać ⟨-czyć⟩ się do ruchu

lan·guage [ˈlæŋgwɪdʒ] język *m*; **'~ lab·or·a·to·ry** laboratorium *n* językowe

lan·guid [ˈlæŋgwɪd] rozleniwiony; anemiczny, wątły

lank [læŋk] *włosy*: jak strąki, w strąkach; **'~·y** (*-ier, -iest*) tyczkowaty; szczudłowaty

lan·tern [ˈlæntən] latarnia *f*

lap¹ [læp] łono *n* (*też fig.*), podołek *m*, kolana *pl.*

lap² [læp] **1.** (*w sporcie*) okrążenie *n*, etap *m*; **~·of hono(u)r** runda *f* honorowa; **2.** (*-pp-*) (*w sporcie*) wykonać okrążenie; *przeciwnika* zdublować

lap³ [læp] (*-pp-*): *v/t.* ~ **up** wychłeptywać ⟨-tać⟩; *v/i.* chlupać ⟨-pnąć⟩, pluskać

la·pel [ləˈpel] klapa *f* (*marynarki itp.*)

Lapland Laponia *f*

lapse [læps] **1.** upłynięcie *n* (*terminu, praw itp.*); błąd *m*, lapsus *m*; *jur.* wygaśnięcie *n*; **he had a ~ of memory** zawiodła go pamięć; **2.** upływać ⟨-łynąć⟩, wygasać ⟨-snąć⟩; *jur.* ulegać ⟨ulec⟩ przedawnieniu

lar·ce·ny [ˈlɑːsənɪ] *jur.* kradzież *f*, zabór *f* (*mienia*)

larch [lɑːtʃ] *bot.* modrzew *m*

lard [lɑːd] **1.** smalec *m*; **2.** *mięso* ⟨na⟩szpikować; **lar·der** [ˈlɑːdə] spiżarnia *f*

large [lɑːdʒ] (*-r, -st*) duży, wielki; znaczny; **at ~** na wolności; ogół, wszyscy; **~·ly** w dużej mierze; **~·'mind·ed** tolerancyjny, wielkoduszny; **~·ness** wielkość *f*; znaczenie *n*

lar·i·at [ˈlærɪət] *zwł. Am.* lasso *n*

lark¹ [lɑːk] *zo.* skowronek *m*

lark² [lɑːk] F kawał *m*, szpas *m*

lar·va [ˈlɑːvə] *zo.* (*pl. -vae* [-viː]) larwa *f*

lar·yn·gi·tis [lærɪnˈdʒaɪtɪs] *med.* zapalenie *n* krtani

lar·ynx [ˈlærɪŋks] *anat.* (*pl. -ynges* [ləˈrɪndʒiːz], **-ynxes**) krtań *f*

las·civ·i·ous [ləˈsɪvɪəs] lubieżny, rozpustny

la·ser [ˈleɪzə] *phys.* laser *m*; **'~ beam** wiązka *f* lasera; **'~ print·er** drukarka *f* laserowa; **'~ tech·nol·o·gy** technika *f* laserowa

lash [læʃ] **1.** bicz *m*; uderzenie *n* (*biczem*); rzęsa *f*; **2.** biczować, chłostać (*też o wietrze*); **~ out** ⟨wy⟩smagać

lass [læs], **~·ie** [ˈlæsɪ] dziewczyna *f*, dziewczę *n*

las·so [læˈsuː] (*pl. -sos, -soes*) lasso *n*

last¹ [lɑːst] **1.** *adj.* ostatni; **~ but one** przedostatni; **~ night** ostatniej *lub* poprzedniej nocy; **2.** *adv.* ostatnio, ostatnim razem; **~ but not least** wreszcie;

należy wspomnieć; **3**. ostatni *m*, końcowy *m*; **at ~** wreszcie; **to the ~** do końca

last² [lɑːst] trwać; wystarczać ⟨-czyć⟩

last³ [lɑːst] kopyto *n* szewskie

'last·ing trwały, stały

'last·ly wreszcie, w końcu

latch [lætʃ] **1**. zatrzask *m*; (*przy drzwiach*) haczyk *m*, zasuwa *f*; **2**. zatrzaskiwać ⟨-snąć⟩; **'~·key** klucz *m* do zamka

late [leɪt] **(-r, -st) 1**. *adj*. późny; spóźniony; niedawny, były; zmarły; **2**. *adv*. późno; do późna; **be ~** spóźniać się; *pociąg itp*.: mieć opóźnienie; **~r on** później; **3**. *of ~* ostatnio; **'~·ly** ostatnio, niedawno

lath [lɑːθ] listwa *f*

lathe [leɪð] *tech.* tokarka *f*

la·ther ['lɑːðə] **1**. piana *f*; **2**. *v/t.* namydlać ⟨-lić⟩; *v/i.* ⟨s⟩pienić się

Lat·in ['lætɪn] **1**. *ling.* łaciński; latynoski; **2**. *ling.* łacina *f*; **~ A'mer·i·ca** Ameryka *f* Łacińska; **~ A'mer·i·can 1**. latynoamerykański; **2**. Latynos *m*

lat·i·tude ['lætɪtjuːd] *geogr.* szerokość *f* (*geograficzna*)

lat·ter ['lætə] drugi, ostatni (*z dwóch*)

lat·tice ['lætɪs] kratownica *f*; krata *f*

Lat·via Łotwa *f*

lau·da·ble ['lɔːdəbl] chwalebny, godny pochwały; przynoszący zaszczyt

laugh [lɑːf] **1**. śmiać się (*at* z *G*); **~ at s.o.** śmiać się z kogoś, wyśmiewać kogoś; **2**. śmiech *m*; dowcip *m*; **'~·a·ble** śmieszny; **~·ter** ['lɑːftə] śmiech *m*

launch¹ [lɔːntʃ] **1**. statek ⟨z⟩wodować; *pocisk* wyrzucać ⟨-cić⟩; *rakietę* wystrzeliwać ⟨-lić⟩; *projekt itp.* zaczynać ⟨-cząć⟩, rozpoczynać ⟨-cząć⟩; **2**. *naut.* szalupa *f*; start *m*, wystrzelenie *n*; zaczęcie *n*

launch² [lɔːntʃ] *naut.* barkas *m*

'launch·ing → launch¹; **'~ pad** *też* **launch pad** płyta *f* wyrzutni; **'~ site** płyta *f* startowa

laun·der ['lɔːndə] ⟨wy⟩prać; F *pieniądze* prać

laun·d(e)rette [lɔːn'dret] *Brt.*, **~·dromat** ['lɔːndrəmæt] *TM zwł. Am.* pralnia *f* samoobsługowa; **~·dry** ['lɔːndrɪ] (*rzeczy prane*) pranie *n*

laur·el ['lɔrəl] *bot.* laur *m*, drzewo *n* laurowe, wawrzyn *m*; *attr.* laurowy

la·va ['lɑːvə] lawa *f*

lav·a·to·ry ['lævətərɪ] toaleta *f*, ubikacja *f*; **public ~** toaleta *f* publiczna

lav·en·der ['lævəndə] *bot.* lawenda *f*; *attr.* lawendowy

lav·ish ['lævɪʃ] **1**. szczodrobliwy; *nadmiernie* hojny, **be ~ with s.th.** nie żałować czegoś; **2. ~ s.th. on s.o.** nie szczędzić komuś czegoś, obsypywać kogoś czymś

law [lɔː] prawo *n*; ustawa *f*; przepis(y *pl.*) *m*; reguła *f*; F gliniarze *pl.*, glina *m*; **~ and order** prawo i porządek; **~·a·bid·ing** ['lɔːəbaɪdɪŋ] praworządny; **'~·court** sąd *m*; **'~·ful** legalny, zgodny z prawem; **'~·less** nielegalny, niezgodny z prawem

lawn [lɔːn] trawnik *m*; **'~·mow·er** kosiarka *f* (*do trawników*)

'law·suit proces *m* sądowy

law·yer ['lɔːjə] *jur.* prawnik *m* (-iczka *f*), adwokat *m*

lax [læks] rozluźniony; nie rygorystyczny, mało skrupulatny

lax·a·tive ['læksətɪv] *med.* **1**. rozwalniający; **2**. środek *m* rozwalniający

lay¹ [leɪ] *pret. od* **lie²**

lay² [leɪ] *rel.* świecki, laicki

lay³ [leɪ] **(laid)** *v/t.* kłaść ⟨położyć⟩; wykładać ⟨wyłożyć⟩ **(with s.th.** czymś); *stół* nakrywać ⟨-ryć⟩; *jaja* składać ⟨złożyć⟩; *przedkładać* ⟨-łożyć⟩ **(before** przed *A*); *winę* składać ⟨złożyć⟩; *v/i. kura:* nieść się; **~ aside** odkładać ⟨-łożyć⟩; **~ off** *econ. pracowników* zwalniać ⟨zwolnić⟩ (*zwł. okresowo*); przestawać ⟨-stać⟩; F odczepić się, zostawić w spokoju; **~ s.th. open** coś otwierać ⟨-worzyć⟩; **~ out** rozkładać ⟨-łożyć⟩; *ogród itp.* ⟨za⟩projektować; *print.* ⟨z⟩robić skład; **~ up** odkładać ⟨-łożyć⟩; **be laid up** być przykutym do łóżka; **'~·by** (*pl. -bys*) *Brt. mot.* zatoka *f* (*do parkowania lub zatrzymywania się*); **'~·er** warstwa *f*; *bot.* odkład *m*

'lay·man (*pl. -men*) laik *m*

'lay·off *econ.* zwolnienie *n* (*zwł. przejściowe*); **'~·out** układ *m*; rozkład *m*; *print.* projekt *m* graficzny

la·zy ['leɪzɪ] **(-ier, -iest)** leniwy

lb *skrót pisany:* **pound** (*łacińskie* **libra**) funt (*453,59 g*)

LCD [el siː 'diː] *skrót:* **liquid crystal display** wyświetlacz *m* ciekłokrystaliczny

lead¹ [liːd] **1**. **(led)** *v/t.* ⟨za-, po⟩prowadzić; ⟨po⟩kierować; skłaniać ⟨skłonić⟩ (*to do* do zrobienia); *v/i.* prowadzić (*też w sporcie*); **~ off** rozpoczynać ⟨-cząć⟩; **~ on** *kogoś* nabierać ⟨-brać⟩; **~ to** *fig.* ⟨do⟩prowadzić do (*G*); **~ up to** *fig.* ⟨do⟩prowadzić do (*G*); **2.** prowadzenie *n* (*też w sporcie i fig*), kierownictwo *n*; przewodnictwo *n*; czołowa pozycja *f*; przykład *m*, wzór *m*; przewaga *f*; *theat.* czołowa rola *f*; smycz *f*; sugestia *f*, trop *m*; **be in the ~** prowadzić; *take the* **~** wychodzić ⟨wyjść⟩ na prowadzenie, obejmować ⟨objąć⟩ prowadzenie

lead² [led] *chem.* ołów *m*; *naut.* sonda *f*, ołowianka *f*; **~ed** ['ledɪd] *okno:* gomółkowy; *benzyna:* ołowiowy, etylizowany; **~en** [ˈledn] ołowiany (*też fig.*)

lead·er [ˈliːdə] przywódca *m* (*-dczyni f*); lider *m*; *Brt.* artykuł *m* wiodący; **'~ship** przewodnictwo *m*, prowadzenie *n*

lead-free [ˈledfriː] bezołowiowy

lead·ing [ˈliːdɪŋ] prowadzący; główny, przewodni

leaf [liːf] (*pl.* **leaves** [liːvz]) liść *m*; skrzydło *n* (*drzwi itp*); (*składana część blatu*); **2. ~ through** kartkować, przekartkowywać ⟨-ować⟩; **~·let** [ˈliːflɪt] ulotka *f*, folder *m*, prospekt *m*

league [liːg] liga *f*, związek *m*

leak [liːk] **1.** *woda:* przeciekać ⟨-ciec⟩; wyciekać ⟨-ciec⟩; *gaz:* ulatniać ⟨-lotnić⟩ się; *zbiornik:* przepuszczać ⟨-uścić⟩ *ciecz, gaz*; **~ out** wyciekać ⟨-ciec⟩; *fig.* przedostawać ⟨-stać⟩ się; **2.** przeciek *m* (*też fig*), wyciek *m*, ulatnianie *n*; **~·age** [ˈliːkɪdʒ] wyciek *m*; **'~·y** (*-ier, -iest*) nieszczelny, przeciekający

lean¹ [liːn] (*leant lub leaned*) wychylać ⟨-lić⟩ się; pochylać ⟨-lić⟩ się; **~ on** opierać ⟨oprzeć⟩ się (na *L*)

lean² [liːn] **1.** chudy (*też fig.*), szczupły; **2.** chude mięso *n*

leant [lent] *pret. i p.p. od* **lean¹**

leap [liːp] **1.** (*leapt lub leaped*) skakać ⟨skoczyć⟩; **~ at** *fig.* rzucać się na (*A*); **2.** skok *m*; **'~·frog** *play* **~·frog** skakać jeden przez drugiego; **~t** [lept] *pret. i p.p. od* **leap** 1; **'~ year** rok *m* przestępny

'**~·ing** wiedza *f*, uczoność *f*; **~t** [lɜːnt] *pret. i p.p. od* **learn**

lease [liːs] **1.** wynajem *m*, najem *m*, dzierżawa *f*; umowa *f* dzierżawy; **2.** najmować ⟨-jąć⟩, wynajmować ⟨-jąć⟩; ⟨wy⟩dzierżawić; brać ⟨wziąć⟩ w leasing; udzielać ⟨-lić⟩ leasingu; **~ out** wydzierżawiać ⟨-wić⟩

leash [liːʃ] smycz *f*

least [liːst] **1.** *adj.* (*sup. od* **little** 1) najmniejszy; **2.** *adv.* (*sup. od* **little** 2) najmniej; **~ of all** szczególnie zaś; **3.** *at ~* przynajmniej; *to say the ~* mówiąc oględnie

leath·er [ˈleðə] **1.** skóra *f*; **2.** skórzany, ze skóry

leave [liːv] **1.** (*left*) *v/t.* ⟨po⟩zostawiać ⟨-wić⟩; porzucać ⟨-cić⟩; odjeżdżać ⟨-jechać⟩, odejść ⟨odchodzić⟩; wyjeżdżać ⟨-jechać⟩ (*for* do *G*); wychodzić (z *G*); zwalniać się z (*G*); *be left* by zostawionym *lub* porzuconym; *v/i.* odchodzić ⟨odejść⟩; wyjeżdżać ⟨-jechać⟩; **~ alone** zostawiać ⟨-wić⟩ w spokoju; **~ behind** zostawiać ⟨-wić⟩; **~ on** pozostawiać ⟨-wić⟩; **~ out** pomijać ⟨-minąć⟩; wykluczać ⟨-czyć⟩ ⟨do⟩izolować; **2.** urlop *m*; przepustka *f*, zwolnienie *n*; *on ~* w czasie urlopu *lub* przepustki; pozwolenie *n*, zgoda *f*

leav·en [ˈlevn] zakwas *m*, zaczyn *m*

leaves [liːvz] *pl. od* **leaf** 1; listowie *n*

leav·ings [ˈliːvɪŋz] *pl.* pozostałości *pl.*, resztki *pl.*

lech·er·ous [ˈletʃərəs] lubieżny

lec·ture [ˈlektʃə] **1.** *univ.* wykład *m*; referat *m*; *fig.* kazanie *n*; △ *nie* **lektura**; **2.** *v/i. univ.* wykładać; wygłaszać wykłady; *v/t. komuś* prawić kazanie; **~·tur·er** [ˈlektʃərə] wykładowca *m*; *univ.* docent *m*; mówca *m*

led [led] *pret. i p.p. od* **lead¹**

ledge [ledʒ] parapet *m*, półka *f*

leech [liːtʃ] *zo.* pijawka *f*

leek [liːk] *bot.* por *m*

leer [lɪə] **1.** lubieżne spojrzenie *n*, lubieżny uśmiech *m*; **2.** lubieżnie się uśmiechać *lub* patrzeć (*at* na *A*)

left¹ [left] *pret. i p.p. od* **leave** 1

left² [left] **1.** *adj.* lewy; lewostronny; **2.** *adv.* na lewo, w lewo; *turn ~* iść na lewo; **3.** lewa strona *f*; lewica *f* (*też pol.*); (*w boksie*) lewa *f*; *on the ~* z/po lewej; *to the ~* na lewo, w lewo; *keep to the ~*

trzymać się lewej; jechać po lewej; **~'hand** lewostronny; **~hand 'drive** *mot.* z lewostronnym układem kierowniczym; **~'hand·ed** leworęczny; dla leworęcznych

left'lug·gage of·fice *Brt. rail.* przechowalnia bagażu; **~·o·vers** *pl.* resztki *pl.*; **~'wing** *pol.* lewicowy, na lewicy

leg [leg] noga *f*; *barani* udziec *m*; *math.* ramię *n* (*cyrkla*); **pull s.o.'s ~** F naciągać kogoś; **stretch one's ~s** rozprostowywać ⟨-ować⟩ nogi

leg·a·cy ['legəsɪ] spadek *m*, dziedzictwo *n*

le·gal ['li:gl] legalny, prawny, zgodny z prawem

le·ga·tion [lɪ'geɪʃn] misja *f* poselska, legacja *f*

le·gend ['ledʒənd] legenda *f* (*też fig.*); **le·gen·da·ry** ['ledʒəndərɪ] legendarny

le·gi·ble ['ledʒəbl] czytelny

le·gis·la·tion [ledʒɪs'leɪʃn] legislacja *f*, ustawodawstwo *n*, prawodawstwo *n*; **~tive** ['ledʒɪslətɪv] *pol.* **1.** legislacyjny, ustawodawczy; **2.** legislatywa *f*, władza *f* ustawodawcza; **~tor** ['ledʒɪsleɪtə] ustawodawca *m*

le·git·i·mate [lɪ'dʒɪtɪmət] prawowity, legalny

lei·sure ['leʒə] czas *m* wolny; odpoczynek *m*; **at ~** bez pośpiechu; **~ cen·tre** *Am.* ośrodek *m* rekreacyjny; *Brt.* ośrodek *m* sportowy; **~·ly** niespieszny; **~ time** czas *m* wolny; **~time ac'tiv·i·ties** *pl.* rekreacja *f*; **~'wear** ubranie *n* nieformalne

lem·on ['lemən] *bot.* cytryna *f*; *attr.* cytrynowy; **~·ade** [lemə'neɪd] lemoniada *f*

lend [lend] *komuś* pożyczać ⟨-czyć⟩

length [leŋθ] długość *f*; odcinek *m*; czas *m* trwania; **at ~** wreszcie; **~·en** ['leŋθən] wydłużać ⟨-żyć⟩ (się); przedłużać ⟨-żyć⟩ (się); **~·ways**, **~·wise** na długość; wzdłuż; **~·y** (*-ier, -iest*) zbyt długi

le·ni·ent ['li:njənt] wyrozumiały, łagodny; pobłażliwy

lens [lenz] *anat.*, *phot.*, *phys.* soczewka *f*; *phot.* obiektyw *m*

lent [lent] *pret. i p.p. od* **lend**

Lent [lent] *rel.* wielki post *m*

len·til ['lentɪl] *bot.* soczewica *f*

Le·o ['li:əʊ] *znak Zodiaku:* Lew *m*; **he/ she is** (**a**) **~** on(a) jest spod znaku Lwa

leop·ard ['lepəd] *zo.* leopard *m*; **~·ess** ['lepədes] *zo.* leopard *m* samica

le·o·tard ['li:əʊtɑ:d] *gimnastyczny* trykot *m*

lep·ro·sy ['leprəsɪ] *med.* trąd *m*

les·bi·an ['lezbɪən] **1.** lesbijski; **2.** lesbijka *f*

less [les] **1.** *adj. i adv.* (*comp. od* **little** 1, 2) mniejszy; **2.** *prp.* mniej o (*A*), odjąć (*A*), minus (*A*)

less·en ['lesn] zmniejszać (się)

less·er ['lesə] mniejszy, pomniejszy

les·son ['lesn] lekcja *f*; *fig.* nauka *f*; **~s** *pl.* zajęcia *pl.*

let [let] (**let**) dawać, pozwalać; *zwł. Brt.* wynajmować ⟨-jąć⟩; **~ alone** zostawiać ⟨-wić⟩ w spokoju; **~ down** obniżać ⟨-żyć⟩, spuszczać ⟨-uścić⟩; *Am. ubrania* przedłużać ⟨-żyć⟩; zawodzić ⟨-wieść⟩; **~ go** puszczać ⟨puścić⟩; **~ o.s. go** zaniedbywać ⟨-bać⟩ się; F odpuszczać ⟨-uścić⟩ sobie; **~'s go!** chodźmy!; **~ in** wpuszczać ⟨-uścić⟩; **~ s.o. in for s.th.** dopuścić kogoś do czegoś

le·thal ['li:θl] śmiertelny, zabójczy, śmiercionośny

leth·ar·gy ['leθədʒɪ] letarg *m*

let·ter ['letə] litera *f*; *print.* czcionka *f*; list *m*, pismo *n*; **~·box** *zwł. Brt.* skrzynka *f* na listy; **~ car·ri·er** *Am.* listonosz(ka *f*) *m*, pocztowy (-a) doręczyciel(ka *f*) *m*

let·tuce ['letɪs] *bot.* sałata *f*

leu·k(a)e·mia [lu:'ki:mɪə] *med.* białaczka *f*

lev·el ['levl] **1.** *adj.* poziomy; równy; **be ~ with** być na równej wysokości z (*N*); **do one's ~ best** F robić, co w czyjejś mocy; **2.** poziom *m* (*też fig.*); poziomica *f*; warstwa *f*; **sea ~** poziom *m* w morza; **on the ~** F na poziomie; **3.** (*zwł. Brt. -ll-, Am. -l-*) równać, zrównywać ⟨-nać⟩; **~ at** *broń* ⟨s⟩kierować na (*A*); *oskarżenie* wymierzyć; **4.** *adv.:* **~ with** na wysokości (*G*); **~'cross·ing** *Brt.* jednopoziomowy przejazd *m* kolejowy; **~'head·ed** zrównoważony

le·ver ['li:və] dźwignia *f*

lev·y ['levɪ] **1.** podatek *m*, pobór *m* podatku; **2.** *podatki* nakładać ⟨-łożyć⟩, pobierać ⟨-brać⟩

lewd [lju:d] obleśny, lubieżny

L

li·a·bil·i·ty [laɪə'bɪlətɪ] *econ., jur.* odpowiedzialność *f*, zobowiązanie *n*; *econ.* **liabilities** *pl.* pasywa *pl.*, należności *pl.*; obciążenie *n* (**to** dla *G*), ciężar *m* (**to** dla *G*)

li·a·ble [laɪəbl] *econ., jur.* odpowiedzialny; **be ~ for** odpowiadać za (*A*); **be ~ to** być podatnym na (*A*)

li·ar [laɪə] kłamca *m*

li·bel [laɪbl] *jur.* **1.** (*na piśmie*) zniesławienie *n*, oszczerstwo *n*, potwarz *f*; **2.** (*zwł. Brt. -ll-*, *Am. -l-*) (*na piśmie*) zniesławiać ⟨-wić⟩

lib·e·ral [lɪbərəl] **1.** liberalny (*też pol.*); tolerancyjny; szczodry, hojny; **2.** *pol.* liberał *m*

lib·e·rate [lɪbəreɪt] oswobadzać ⟨-bodzić⟩; **~ra·tion** [lɪbə'reɪʃn] oswobodzenie *n*; **~ra·tor** [lɪbəreɪtə] oswobodziciel *m*

lib·er·ty [lɪbətɪ] wolność *f*; **take liberties with s.o.** pozwalać sobie za dużo z kimś; **take the ~ of** pozwolić sobie na (*A*); **at ~** na wolności

Li·bra [laɪbrə] *znak Zodiaku:* Waga *f*; **he/she is (a) ~** on(a) jest spod znaku Wagi

li·brar·i·an [laɪ'breərɪən] bibliotekarz *m* (-arka *f*); **li·bra·ry** [laɪbrərɪ] biblioteka *f*

lice [laɪs] *pl. od* **louse**

li·cence *Brt.*, **li·cense** *Am.* [laɪsəns] koncesja *f*, licencja *f*; zezwolenie *n*, pozwolenie *n*; **'li·cense plate** *Am. mot.* tablica *f* rejestracyjna

li·cense *Brt.*, **li·cence** *Am.* [laɪsəns] udzielać ⟨-lić⟩ licencji *lub* koncesji; *urzędowo* zezwalać ⟨-wolić⟩

li·chen [laɪkən] *bot.* porost *m*

lick [lɪk] **1.** liźnięcie *n*, poliżanie *lub* lizawka *f* (*solna*); **2.** ⟨po⟩lizać, oblizywać ⟨-zać⟩; wylizywać ⟨-zać⟩; F pokonywać ⟨-nać⟩, przezwyciężać ⟨-żyć⟩

lic·o·rice [lɪkərɪs] → **liquorice**

lid [lɪd] **1.** pokrywka *f*; wieczko *n*; powieka *f*

lie¹ [laɪ] **1.** ⟨s⟩kłamać, okłamywać ⟨-mać⟩; **~ to s.o.** okłamywać ⟨-mać⟩ kogoś; **2.** kłamstwo *n*; **tell a ~, tell ~s** mówić kłamstwa; **give the ~ to s.o.** zadawać kłam komuś

lie² [laɪ] **1.** (*lay, lain*) leżeć; **let sleeping dogs ~** nie budzić licha; **~ behind** *fig.* leżeć u podstaw; **~ down** kłaść ⟨położyć⟩ się; **2.** położenie *n*, miejsce *n*; **'~-down** *Brt.* F drzemka; **go for a ~-down** *fig.* iść przyłożyć głowę do poduszki; **'~-in** *zwł.: Brt.* F **have a ~-in** długo nie wstawać z łóżka

lieu [ljuː]: **in ~ of** w miejsce (*G*)

lieu·ten·ant [lef'tenənt, *Am.* luː'tenənt] porucznik *m*

life [laɪf] (*pl. lives* [laɪvz]) życie *n*; *jur.* dożywocie *n*; **all her ~** przez jej całe życie; **for ~** na całe życie; *zwł. jur.* dożywotnio; **'~ as·sur·ance** ubezpieczenie *n* na życie; **'~ belt** pas *m* ratunkowy; koło *n* ratunkowe; **'~·boat** łódź *f* ratunkowa; **'~·buoy** koło *n* ratunkowe; **'~·guard** (*na basenie*) ratownik *m*; **~ im·pris·on·ment** *jur.* kara *f* dożywotniego więzienia; **~ in·sur·ance** ubezpieczenie *n* na życie; **'~·jack·et** kamizelka *f* ratunkowa; **'~·less** bez życia; niemrawy; martwy; **'~·like** realistyczny; jak żywy; **'~·long** na całe życie; **'~ pre·serv·er** *zwł. Am.* kamizelka *f* ratunkowa; koło *n* ratunkowe; **~ 'sen·tence** *jur.* wyrok *m* dożywotniego więzienia; **'~·time** okres *m* życia; życie *n*

lift [lɪft] **1.** *v/t.* podnosić ⟨-nieść⟩; unosić ⟨unieść⟩; zakaz *itp.* znosić ⟨znieść⟩; *wzrok* unieść; F podprowadzić, zwędzić; *v/i.* unosić ⟨unieść⟩ się, podnosić ⟨unieść⟩ się (*też o mgle*); **~ off** *rakieta:* ⟨wy⟩startować; *samolot:* unosić ⟨-nieść⟩ się w powietrze; **2.** podniesienie *n*; *aviat.* siła *f* nośna; *phys.* wypór *m*, siła *f* wyporu; *Brt.* winda *f*, dźwig *m*; **give s.o. a ~** podrzucać ⟨-cić⟩ kogoś (*samochodem*); F podwieźć kogoś na duchu; **'~-off** start *m*; wzniesienie *n* się (*rakiety, samolotu*)

lig·a·ment [lɪgəmənt] *anat.* wiązadło *n*

light¹ [laɪt] **1.** światło *n* (*też fig.*); oświetlenie *n*; blask *m* (*świecy*); ogień *m* (*dla papierosa*); *Brt. zw.* **~s** *pl.* drogowe światła *pl.*; **have you got a ~, can you give me a ~?** czy ma pan ogień?; **2.** (*lit lub lighted*) *v/t.* oświetlać ⟨-lić⟩; *też* **~ up** zapalać ⟨-lić⟩; *v/i.* zapalać ⟨-lić⟩ się; **~ up** *oczy itp.:* rozjarzać ⟨-rzyć⟩ się; **3.** jasny

light² [laɪt] lekki (*też fig.*); **make ~ of** coś lekko ⟨po⟩traktować (*A*), umniejszać ⟨-szyć⟩ (*A*)

light·en [laɪtn] rozjaśniać ⟨-nić⟩ (się), przejaśniać ⟨-nić⟩ (się)

light·en² ['laɪtn] zmniejszać ⟨-szyć⟩ (się)

'light·er zapalniczka *f*

light·'**head·ed** lekkomyślny, niefrasobliwy; oszołomiony; **~·'heart·ed** beztroski; **~·'heart·ed** bez *m* troski; **'~·ing** oświetlenie *n*; **'~·ness** lekkość *f*

light·ning ['laɪtnɪŋ] błyskawica *f*; **like ~** jak błyskawica; **'~ con·duc·tor** *Brt.*, **'~ rod** *Am. electr* piorunochron *m*, odgromnik *m*

'light·weight *sport*: waga *f* lekka

like¹ [laɪk] **1.** *v/t.* ⟨po⟩lubić; *I ~ it* podoba mi się to; *I ~ her* lubię ją; *how do you ~ it?* jak ci się to podoba?; *I should lub would ~ to know* chciałbym wiedzieć; *v/i.* chcieć; *(just) as you ~* (tak) jak chcesz; *if you ~* jeżeli chcesz; **2.** **~s** *pl.* **and dislikes** *pl.* sympatie *pl.* i antypatie *pl.*

like² [laɪk] **1.** jak; **~ that** tak; **feel ~** mieć ochotę; **what does it look ~?** jak to wygląda?; **what is he ~?** jaki on jest?; **that is just ~ him!** to podobne do niego!; **2.** podobny; **the ~ of him** ktoś podobny do niego; **the ~s of you** ludzie podobni do was

like·li·hood ['laɪklɪhʊd] prawdopodobieństwo *n*; **'~·ly 1.** *adj.* (**-ier, -iest**) prawdopodobny; **2.** *adv.* prawdopodobnie; **not ~ly!** z pewnością nie!

like·ness ['laɪknɪs] podobieństwo *n*; **'~·wise** podobnie

lik·ing ['laɪkɪŋ] sympatia *f*

li·lac ['laɪlək] **1.** lila; **2.** *bot.* bez *m*

lil·y ['lɪlɪ] *bot.* lilia *f*; **~ of the valley** konwalia *f*

limb [lɪm] kończyna *f*, członek *m*; konar *m*

lime¹ [laɪm] wapno *n*

lime² [laɪm] *bot.* limona *f*

'lime·light światła *pl.* rampy; *fig.* centrum *n* uwagi

lim·it ['lɪmɪt] **1.** granica *f*; *within* **~s** w pewnych granicach; *off* **~s** *Am.* wstęp wzbroniony (*to* do *G*); *that is the* **~!** F to już szczyty!

lim·i·ta·tion [lɪmɪ'teɪʃn] ograniczenie *n*; *fig.* granica *f*

'lim·it·ed ograniczony; **~ed liability company** *Brt.* spółka z ograniczoną odpowiedzialnością; **'~·less** nieograniczony; bezgraniczny

limp¹ [lɪmp] **1.** utykać, kuśtykać; **2.** utykanie *n*, kuśtykanie *n*

limp² [lɪmp] wiotki, zwiotczały

line¹ [laɪn] **1.** linia *f* (*też fig.*); kreska *f*; zmarszczka *f*; sznur *m*, linka *f*, żyłka *f* (*przy wędce, etc.*); kabel *m*, przewód *m*; *zwł. Am.* kolejka *f*, ogonek *m*; *autobusowa, telefoniczna itp.* linia *f*; rząd *m*, szereg *m*; branża *f*, dziedzina *f*, specjalność *f*; wiersz *m* (*tekstu*); itp. połączenie *n*; *fig.* granica *f*, *fig.* kurs *m*; **~s** *pl. theat.* rola *f*, kwestia *f*; *the ~* równik *m*; *draw the ~* ustalać ⟨-lić⟩ granice (*at s.th.* czegoś); *the ~ is busy lub engaged tel.* linia jest zajęta; *hold the ~ tel.* proszę nie odkładać słuchawki; *stand in ~ Am.* stać w kolejce (*for* za *I*); **2.** ⟨po⟩liniować; *twarz* ⟨z⟩marszczyć; *drzewa*: ⟨u⟩tworzyć szpaler, *ludzie*: stanąć (*szeregami*); **~ up** ustawiać (się) w szeregu; (*w sporcie*) ustawiać ⟨-wić⟩ się; *zwł. Am.* stawać ⟨stanąć⟩ w kolejce (*for* za *I*)

line² [laɪn] *ubranie* podbijać ⟨-bić⟩; wykładać (*wyłożyć*), wyściełać ⟨-lić⟩

lin·e·ar ['lɪnɪə] linearny, liniowy

lin·en ['lɪnɪn] **1.** *materiał*: len *m*; *pościelowa itp.* bielizna *f*; **2.** lniany; **'~·clos·et** *Am.*, **'~·cup·board** (*szafka*) bieliźniarka *f*

lin·er ['laɪnə] liniowiec *m*; samolot *m* kursowy; → *eyeliner*

lines·man ['laɪnzmən] (*pl.* **-men**) (*w sporcie*) sędzia *m* liniowy; **'~·wom·an** (*pl.* **-women**) (*w sporcie*) kobieta-sędzia *m* liniowy

'line-up (*w sporcie*) skład *m*; *zwł. Am.* rząd *m* ludzi

lin·ger ['lɪŋgə] zatrzymywać ⟨-mać⟩ się, zwlekać; **~ on** utrzymywać się, trwać; *fig.* wegetować

lin·ge·rie ['lɛ̃ːʒəriː] bielizna *f* damska

lin·i·ment ['lɪnɪmənt] *pharm.* środek *m* do nacierania, mazidło *n*

lin·ing ['laɪnɪŋ] wyściółka *f*; podszewka *f*, podpinka *f*; *tech.* okładzina *f*

link [lɪŋk] **1.** ogniwo *n* (*łańcucha też fig.*); spinka *f* (*do mankietów*); połączenie *n*; zależność *f*; **2.** *też* **~ up** ⟨po⟩łączyć się

links [lɪŋks] → *golf links*

'link-up połączenie *n*

lin·seed ['lɪnsiːd] *bot.* siemię *n* lniane; **~ 'oil** olej *m* lniany

li·on ['laɪən] *zo.* lew *m*; **~·ess** *zo.* ['laɪənes] lwica *f*

lip [lɪp] *anat.* warga *f*; brzeg *m* (*filiżanki*

itp.); *sl.* czelność *f*; '**~·stick** szminka *f* (*do ust*)

liq·ue·fy ['lıkwıfaı] skraplać ⟨-roplić⟩ (się)

liq·uid ['lıkwıd] **1.** ciecz *f*; **2.** ciekły

liq·ui·date ['lıkwıdeıt] ⟨z⟩likwidować; *dług* spłacać ⟨-cić⟩

liq·uid·ize ['lıkwıdaız] ⟨z⟩miksować; rozdrabniać ⟨-robnić⟩; '**~·iz·er** mikser *m*

liq·uor ['lıkə] *zwł. Am.* silny napój alkoholowy; *Brt.* napój *m* alkoholowy, alkohol *m*; △ *nie* **likier**

liq·uo·rice ['lıkərıs] lukrecja *f*

Lis·bon Lizbona *f*

lisp [lısp] **1.** ⟨za⟩seplenić; **2.** seplenienie *n*

list [lıst] **1.** lista *f*, spis *m*; **2.** umieszczać ⟨umieścić⟩ na liście; wpisywać ⟨-sać⟩

lis·ten ['lısn] słuchać; **~** *in* ⟨wy⟩słuchać w radio (*to s.th.* czegoś); **~** *in* rozmowę telefoniczną podsłuchiwać ⟨-chać⟩; **~** *to* ⟨po-, wy⟩słuchać (*G*); '**~·er** słuchacz(ka *f*) *m*

'**list·less** bierny, apatyczny

lit [lıt] *pret. i p.p. od* **light¹**

lit·e·ral ['lıtərəl] dosłowny, literalny

lit·e·ra·ry ['lıtərərı] literacki; **~·ture** ['lıtərətʃə] literatura *f*

lithe [laıð] gibki, sprężysty

Lith·u·a·nia Litwa *f*

li·tre *Brt.*, **li·ter** *Am.* ['liːtə] litr *m*

lit·ter ['lıtə] **1.** (*zwł. papier*) śmieci *pl.*; podściółka *f*; *zo.* miot *m*; lektyka *f*; **2.** zaśmiecać ⟨-cić⟩; **be ~ed with** być zaśmieconym (*I*); '**~ bas·ket**, '**~ bin** kosz *m* na śmieci

lit·tle ['lıtl] **1.** *adj.* (**less, least**) mały; **the ~ ones** *pl.* mali *pl.*; **2.** *adv.* (**less, least**) mało, niewiele; **3.** (za) mało; **a ~** trochę, nieco; **~ by ~** po trochę, stopniowo;

live¹ [lıv] żyć (*też* **with** z *I*); mieszkać; **~ to see** dożyć; **~ on** trwać; utrzymywać się z (*I*); **~ up to** spełniać ⟨-nić⟩, *reputację* sprostać

live² [laıv] **1.** *adj.* żywy, żyjący; *electr.* pod napięciem; *amunicja:* uzbrojony; *transmisja:* na żywo; **2.** *adv.* na żywo, bezpośrednio

live·li·hood ['laıvlıhud] środki *pl.* utrzymania; '**~·li·ness** żywość *f*, dynamizm *m*; '**~·ly** (**-ier, -iest**) żywy, żwawy, dynamiczny

liv·er ['lıvə] *anat.* wątroba *f*; *gastr.* wątróbka *f*

liv·e·ry ['lıvərı] liberia *n*

lives [laıvz] *pl. od* **life**

'**live·stock** inwentarz *m* żywy

liv·id ['lıvıd] siny; F rozwścieczony

liv·ing ['lıvıŋ] **1.** żywy, żyjący; **the ~ image of** dokładna podobizna *f* (*G*); **2.** środki *pl.* utrzymania; **the ~** *pl.* żywi *pl.*; **standard of ~** stopa *f* życiowa; **earn** *lub* **make a ~** zarabiać ⟨-robić⟩ na utrzymanie; '**~ room** salon *m*, pokój *m* dzienny

liz·ard ['lızəd] *zo.* jaszczurka *f*

load [ləud] **1.** ładunek *m*, obciążenie *n*; *fig.* ciężar *m*; ⟨za⟩ładować; **~** *broń* ⟨za⟩ładować; **~ a camera** włożyć film do aparatu; *też* **~ up** załadowywać ⟨-ować⟩

loaf¹ [ləuf] (*pl.* **loaves** [ləuvz]) bochenek *m*

loaf² [ləuf] *też* **~ about, ~ around** F próżnować; '**~·er** próżniak *m*

loam [ləum] glina *f*, ił *m*; '**~·y** (**-ier, -iest**) gliniasty, ilasty

loan [ləun] **1.** pożyczka *f*; *bankowy* kredyt *m*; wypożyczenie *n*; **on ~** wypożyczony; **2.** *zwł. Am.* komuś pożyczać ⟨-czyć⟩, wypożyczać ⟨-czyć⟩; udzielać ⟨-lić⟩ pożyczki; '**~ shark** *econ.* lichwiarz *m* (-arka *f*)

loath [ləuθ]: **be ~ to do s.th.** nie chcieć zrobić czegoś

loathe [ləuð] nienawidzić (*G*), nie cierpieć (*G*); '**loath·ing** obrzydzenie *n*, awersja *f*

loaves [ləuvz] *pl. od* **loaf¹**

lob [lɒb] *zwł.* (*w tenisie*) lob *m*

lob·by ['lɒbı] **1.** przedsionek *m*, westybul *m*; *theat.* foyer *n*; kuluary *pl.; pol.* lobby *n*, grupa *f* nacisku; **2.** *pol.* wywierać ⟨-rzeć⟩ nacisk

lobe [ləub] *anat., bot.* płat *m*, płatek *m*; → **earlobe**

lob·ster ['lɒbstə] *zo.* homar *m*

lo·cal ['ləukl] **1.** lokalny, miejscowy; **2.** miejscowy *m* (-wa *f*); *Brt.* F stała knajpa *f* (*do której stale się chodzi*); △ *nie* **lokal**; '**~ call** *tel.* rozmowa *f* miejscowa; **~ e'lec·tions** *pl.* wybory *pl.* komunalne *lub* do władz miejscowych; '**~ 'gov·ern·ment** samorząd *m* terytorialny; '**~ time** czas *m* miejscowy; '**~ 'traf·fic** ruch *m* (*uliczny*) miejscowy

lo·cate [ləu'keıt] ⟨z⟩lokalizować, umiejscawiać ⟨-owić⟩; **be ~d** być położonym, znajdować się; **lo·ca·tion** [ləʊ'keɪʃn] lokalizacja *f*, umiejscowienie *n*; miejsce (**for** na *A*); *filmowy:* plener *m*; **on ~** w plenerze, poza studiem

loch [lɒk] jezioro *n*

lock¹ [lɒk] **1.** zamek *m* (*do drzwi, broni*); śluza *f*, komora *f* śluzowa; zamknięcie *n*; **2.** *v/t.* zamykać ⟨-mknąć⟩ (*na klucz*) (*też ~ up*); trzymać *kogoś* w uścisku; *tech.* unieruchamiać ⟨-chomić⟩, ⟨za⟩blokować; *v/i.* zamykać ⟨-knąć⟩ się (na klucz); *mot.* kierownica: ⟨za⟩blokować się; **~ away** zamykać ⟨-mknąć⟩; **~ in** zamykać ⟨-mknąć⟩ (*w środku*); **~ out** ⟨za⟩stosować lokaut; **~ up** zamykać ⟨-mknąć⟩; ⟨u⟩więzić

lock² [lɒk] lok *m*

lock·er ['lɒkə] szafka *f* (*w szatni*); schowek *m* bagażu; '**~ room** *zwł.* (*w sporcie*) szatnia *f*, kabina *f* w szatni

lock·et ['lɒkɪt] medalion *m*

'lock|·out lokaut *m*; '**~·smith** ślusarz *m*; '**~·up** cela *f* w areszcie

lo·co·mo·tion [ləʊkə'məʊʃn] zdolność *f* poruszania się, lokomocja *f*; **~·tive** ['ləʊkəməʊtɪv] lokomocyjny

lo·cust ['ləʊkəst] *zo.* szarańcza *f*

lodge [lɒdʒ] **1.** budka *f* stróża, stróżówka *f*; domek *m* (*myśliwski, narciarski*); altanka *f*; loża *f* (*masońska*); **2.** *v/i.* przebywać, ⟨za⟩mieszkać; *kul itp.:* utkwić; *v/t.* ⟨prze⟩nocować; *zażalenie itp.* składać ⟨złożyć⟩; '**lodg·er** lokator(ka *f*) *m*; '**lodg·ing** zamieszkanie *n*, mieszkanie *n*; **~s** *pl. zwł.* pokój *m* umeblowany

loft [lɒft] strych *m*, poddasze *n*; empora *f*; *Am.* piętro *n* w budynku niemieszkalnym; '**~·y** (*-ier, -iest*) wysoki; wzniosły; wyniosły

log [lɒg] kłoda *f*, pień *m*; *sleep like a ~* spać jak kamień; '**~·book** *naut., aviat.* dziennik *m* okrętowy; *aviat.* dziennik *m* pokładowy; *mot.* książka *f* jazd; **~ 'cab·in** chata *f* z okrąglaków

log·ger·heads ['lɒgəhedz]: *be at ~* nie zgadzać się (*with z I*)

lo·gic ['lɒdʒɪk] logika *f*; '**~·al** logiczny

loin [lɔɪn] *gastr.* polędwica *f*; **~s** *pl. anat.* lędźwie *pl.*

loi·ter ['lɔɪtə] pętać się, pałętać się; kręcić się

loll [lɒl] rozwalać ⟨-lić⟩ się, uwalić się; **~ out** zwieszać ⟨-sić⟩ się

lol·li·pop ['lɒlɪpɒp] lizak *m*; *zwł. Brt.*

lody *pl.* na patyku; **~ man**, **~ woman**, **~ lady** *Brt.* (osoba, pomagająca dzieciom przechodzić przez ulicę)

Lon·don Londyn *m*

lone|·li·ness ['ləʊnlɪnɪs] samotność *f*; '**~·ly** (*-ier, -iest*), '**~·some** samotny

long¹ [lɒŋ] **1.** *adj.* długi; *odległość:* duży; **2.** *adv.* długo; *as lub so ~ as* jeżeli tylko; **~ ago** dawno temu; *so ~!* F cześć!; **3.** *for ~* na długo; *take ~* długo trwać *lub* wymagać dużo czasu

long² [lɒŋ] ⟨za⟩tęsknić (**for** za *I*)

long-'dis·tance długodystansowy; zamiejscowy; ~ **'call** rozmowa *f* zamiejscowa; '**~·run·ner** długodystansowiec

lon·gev·i·ty [lɒn'dʒevətɪ] długowieczność *f*

'**long·hand** pismo *n* ręczne

long·ing ['lɒŋɪŋ] **1.** tęskniący; **2.** tęsknota *f*

lon·gi·tude ['lɒndʒɪtjuːd] *geogr.* długość *f*

'**long| jump** (*w sporcie*) skok *m* w dal; **~-life 'milk** *zwł. Brt.* mleko *n* o przedłużonej trwałości; **~-'play·er**, **~-play·ing 'rec·ord** płyta *f* długogrająca; **~-'range** *mil., aviat.* o dalekim zasięgu; *długofalowy*; **~-shore·man** ['lɒŋʃɔːmən] *zwł. Am.* (*pl. -men*) doker *m*; **~-'sight·ed** *zwł. Brt. fig.* dalekowzroczny; *be ~sighted* być dalekowidzem; **~-'stand·ing** dawny; **~-'term** długoterminowy; **~ 'wave** *radiowe* długie fale *pl.*; **~-'wind·ed** rozwlekły, nużący

loo [luː] *Brt.* F ubikacja *f*

look [lʊk] **1.** ⟨po⟩patrzeć (*at* na *A*); wyglądać (*happy* na szczęśliwego; *good* dobrze); *okno:* wychodzić (*onto a street* na ulicę); *dom:* być skierowanym (*west* na zachód); ~ *here!* posłuchaj!; ~ *like* wyglądać jak; *it ~s as if* wygląda, jakby; ~ *after* ⟨za⟩troszczyć się o (*A*), zajmować ⟨-jąć⟩ się (*I*); ~ *ahead* patrzeć naprzód, *fig.* spoglądać w przyszłość; ~ *around* rozglądać ⟨-zejrzeć⟩ się; ~ *at* ⟨po⟩patrzeć na (*A*); ~ *back* oglądać ⟨obejrzeć⟩ się; *fig.* spoglądać ⟨spojrzeć⟩ za siebie; ~ *down on* patrzeć z góry na (*A*); ~ *for* ⟨po⟩szukać (*G*); ~ *forward to* wyczekiwać (*A*); ~ *in* F wpadać ⟨wpaść⟩ z wizytą (*on s.o.* do kogoś); ~ *onto* wychodzić na (*A*); ~ *out* wyglądać (*of* z *G*); uważać; wypatrywać, wyszukiwać ⟨-kać⟩;

L

~ *over* coś przeglądać ⟨przejrzeć⟩; *ko-goś* ⟨z⟩lustrować; ~ *round* rozglądać ⟨-zejrzeć⟩ się; ~ *through* coś przeglądać ⟨przejrzeć⟩; ~ *up* podnosić ⟨-ieść⟩ wzrok na (*A*); *coś* ⟨po⟩szukać (*G*); *ko-goś* odwiedzać ⟨-dzić⟩; **2.** spojrzenie *n*; wygląd *m*; (*good*) ~*s pl.* uroda *f*; *have a* ~ *at s.th.* popatrzeć na coś; *I don't like the* ~ *of it* nie podoba mi się to; '~*-ing glass* lustro *n*; '~*-out* punkt *m* obserwacyjny; *naut.* wachta *f*; obserwator(ka *f*) *m*; *fig.* F perspektywa *f*; *be on the* ~*out for* rozglądać się za (*I*); *that's his* ~*out Brt.* F to jego sprawa

loom¹ [lu:m] krosno *n*

loom² [lu:m] *też* ~ *up* wyłaniać ⟨-łonić⟩ się

loop [lu:p] **1.** pętla *f* (*też naut., komp.*); *med.* domaciczna spirala *f*; **2.** owijać ⟨-winąć⟩ (się) dookoła, obwiązywać ⟨-zać⟩ dookoła; '~*-hole* otwór *m*; *mil.* otwór *m* strzelniczy; *fig.* furtka *f*; *a* ~*hole in the law* luka *f* prawna

loose [lu:s] **1.** (*-r, -st*) luźny; ruszający się; *włosy:* rozpuszczony; wolny; *let* ~ puszczać wolno; *be on the* ~ znajdować się na wolności; **loos-en** ['lu:sn] rozluźnić ⟨-nić⟩ (się) (*też fig.*); ~ *up* (*w sporcie*) rozgrzewać ⟨-rzać⟩ się

loot [lu:t] **1.** łup *m*; **2.** ⟨z⟩łupić, ⟨s⟩plądrować

lop [lɒp] (*-pp-*) obcinać ⟨-ciąć⟩; ~ *off* obciosywać ⟨-sać⟩; ~'*sid-ed* krzywy

loq-ua-cious [ləʊ'kweɪʃəs] gadatliwy

lord [lɔːd] pan *m*; władca *m*; *Brt.* lord *m*, par *m*; *the* ♫ *Pan* ♫ Bóg; *the* ♫*'s Supper* Wieczerza *f* Pańska; *House of* ♫*s Brt.* Izba *f* Parów *lub* Lordów; ♫ '*Mayor Brt.* lord *m* burmistrz

lor-ry ['lɒrɪ] *Brt.* ciężarówka *f*

lose [lu:z] (*lost*) ⟨s-, u⟩tracić; ⟨z⟩gubić; przegrywać ⟨-rać⟩; *zegarek:* późnić ⟨spóźniać⟩ się; ~ *o.s.* ⟨z⟩gubić się; '*los-er* przegrywający *m* (-ca *f*); nieudacznik *m*, ofiara *f*

loss [lɒs] strata *f*, utrata *f*; zguba *f*; *at a* ~ *econ.* ze stratą; *be at a* ~ nie umieć znaleźć

lost [lɒst] **1.** *pret. i p.p. od lose;* **2.** *adj.* zagubiony; zaginiony; *be* ~ zgubić się, pogubić się; *be* ~ *in thought* zatopić się w myślach; *get* ~ ⟨z⟩gubić się; *get* ~! *sl.* spadaj!; ~*-and-'found (of-*

fice) Am., ~ '*prop-er-ty of-fice Brt.* biuro *n* rzeczy znalezionych

lot [lɒt] los *m*; parcela *f*, działka *f*; *econ.* partia *f*; zestaw *m*, grupa *f*; △ *nie lot; the* ~ wszystko; *a* ~ *of* F, ~*s of* F dużo; *a bad* ~ F niegodziwiec *m*; *cast lub draw* ~*s* rzucać ⟨-cić⟩ *lub* '0⟨po⟩ciągnąć losy

loth [ləʊθ] → **loath**

lo-tion ['ləʊʃn] płyn *m* (*kosmetyczny*)

lot-te-ry ['lɒtərɪ] loteria *f*

loud [laʊd] **1.** *adj.* głośny; *fig.* barwy krzykliwy; **2.** *adv.* głośno; ~'*speak-er* głośnik *m*

lounge [laʊndʒ] **1.** pokój *m* dzienny; salon *m*; (*w hotelu*) hall *m*; *aviat.* hala przylotów *lub* odlotów; **2.** ~ *about,* ~ *around* leniuchować; '~ *suit Brt.* garnitur *m*

louse [laʊs] *zo.* (*pl. lice* [laɪs]) wesz *f*; **lou-sy** ['laʊzɪ] (*-ier, -iest*) zawszony (*też fig.*); F podły, nędzny

lout [laʊt] ordynus *m*

lov-a-ble ['lʌvəbl] uroczy

love [lʌv] **1.** miłość *f* (*of, for, to, to-wards* do *G*); kochany *m* (-na *f*), skarb *m*; zamiłowanie *n*, pasja *f*; (*w tenisie*) zero *n*; *be in* ~ *with s.o.* kochać kogoś; *fall in* ~ *with s.o.* zakochać się w kimś; *make* ~ *with s.o.* kochać się z kimś; *give my* ~ *to her* proszę ją serdecznie pozdrowić ode mnie; *send one's* ~ *to* kogoś przekazać ⟨-zywać⟩ pozdrowienia; ~ *from* serdeczne pozdrowienia od (*G*); **2.** ⟨po⟩kochać; ~ *af-fair* romans *m*; '~*-ly* (*-ier, -iest*) uroczy; wspaniały; '*lov-er* kochanek *m*; ukochany *m* (-na *f*); miłośnik *m* (-iczka *f*); ~*s pl.* zakochani *pl.*

lov-ing ['lʌvɪŋ] kochający, pełen miłości

low [ləʊ] **1.** *adj.* niski (*też fig.*); głęboki (*też fig.*); cichy; przygnębiony; **2.** *adv.* nisko; cicho; **3.** *meteor.* niż *m*, obszar *m* niskiego ciśnienia; *fig.* niski poziom *m*; '~*-brow* F 1. osoba *f* o niewyszukanych gustach; **2.** o niewyszukanym guście; ~'*cal-o-rie* niskokaloryczny; ~*-e'mis-sion* o niskiej zawartości szkodliwych związków

low-er ['ləʊə] **1.** niższy; głębszy; dolny; **2.** obniżać ⟨-żyć⟩; opuszczać ⟨-puścić⟩; *oczy itp.* spuszczać ⟨-puścić⟩; *fig.* zniżać ⟨-żyć⟩

low-|-'fat o niskiej zawartości tłuszczu;

~·land ['ləʊlənd] nizina f; '~·ly (-ier, -iest) niski; ~'necked suknia: głęboko wycięty; ~·'pitched mus. głęboki, niski; ~'pres·sure meteor. niskie ciśnienie n; '~·rise zwł. Am. niski (budynek); ~'spir·it·ed przygnębiony

loy·al ['lɔɪəl] lojalny; '~·ty lojalność f

loz·enge ['lɒzɪndʒ] romb m; pastylka f (do ssania)

LP [el'piː]skrót: long-player, long-playing record LP n, płyta f długogrająca

Ltd skrót pisany: limited z o.o., z ograniczoną odpowiedzialnością

lu·bri·cant ['luːbrɪkənt] środek do smarowania; smar m; ~·cate ['luːbrɪkeɪt] ⟨na⟩smarować; ~·ca·tion [luːbrɪ'keɪʃn] smarowanie n

lu·cid ['luːsɪd] klarowny

luck [lʌk] szczęście n; pomyślny los m; bad ~, hard ~, ill ~ pech m; good ~ szczęście n; good ~ ! powodzenia!; be in ~ mieć szczęście, be out of ~ nie mieć szczęścia; ~·i·ly ['lʌkɪlɪ] na szczęście; '~·y (-ier, -iest) szczęśliwy, pomyślny; be ~y mieć szczęście; ~y day szczęśliwy lub pomyślny dzień m; ~y fellow szczęściarz m

lu·cra·tive ['luːkrətɪv] lukratywny, intratny

lu·di·crous ['luːdɪkrəs] śmieszny

lug [lʌg] (-gg-) ⟨za⟩taszczyć, ⟨za⟩tachać

luge [luːʒ] (w sporcie) sanki pl. sportowe; saneczkarstwo n

lug·gage ['lʌgɪdʒ] zwł. Brt. bagaż m; '~ car·ri·er bagażowy m; '~ rack zwł. Brt. półka m na bagaż; '~ van Brt. wagon m bagażowy

luke·warm ['luːkwɔːm] letni (też fig.)

lull [lʌl] 1. uciszać ⟨-szyć⟩; burza: uspokajać ⟨-koić⟩ się; zw. ~ to sleep ⟨u⟩kołysać do snu; 2. okres m uspokojenia się (też fig)

lul·la·by ['lʌləbaɪ] kołysanka f

lum·ba·go [lʌm'beɪgəʊ] med. postrzał m, lumbago n

lum·ber[1] ['lʌmbə] ⟨po⟩wlec się (z wysiłkiem lub głośno); ⟨po⟩telepać się

lum·ber[2] ['lʌmbə] 1. zwł. Am. drewno n budowlane; tarcica f; zwł. Brt. rupiecie pl.; 2. v/t.: ~ s.o. with s.th. Brt. F obładować kogoś czymś; '~·jack Am. drwal m; '~ mill Am. tartak m; '~·room zwł. Brt. graciarnia f; '~·yard Am. skład m drzewny

lu·mi·na·ry fig. ['luːmɪnərɪ] luminarz m, koryfeusz m

lu·mi·nous ['luːmɪnəs] świecący; ~'dis·play tarcza f świecąca; ~'paint fosforyzująca farba f

lump [lʌmp] 1. gruda f, bryła f; kawał m; med. guz m; kostka f, kawałek m (cukru); Δ nie lump; in the ~ ryczałtem (też econ.); 2. v/t. ~ together fig. połączyć; v/i. Am. zbijać ⟨zbić⟩ się w grudy; ~ 'sug·ar cukier m w kostkach; ~ 'sum suma f ryczałtowa; '~·y (-ier, -iest) grudowaty, bryłowaty

lu·na·cy ['luːnəsɪ] szaleństwo n

lu·nar ['luːnə] księżycowy, lunarny; ~ 'mod·ule (w astronautyce) lądownik m księżycowy

lu·na·tic ['luːnətɪk] 1. szalony; fig. szaleńczy, wariacki; 2. wariat(ka f) m, szaleniec m (też fig.); Δ nie lunatyk

lunch [lʌntʃ], dawniej lun·cheon ['lʌntʃən] 1. lunch m; 2. ⟨z⟩jeść lunch; 'lunch hour, 'lunch time pora f lunchu lub obiadowa

lung [lʌŋ] anat. płuco n; the ~s pl. płuca pl.

lunge [lʌndʒ] rzucać ⟨-cić⟩ się (at na A)

lurch [lɜːtʃ] 1. zataczać się; samochód: szarpać ⟨-pnąć⟩ się; 2. leave in the ~ zostawiać ⟨-wić⟩ na łasce losu

lure [lʊə] 1. przynęta f; fig. pokusa f; 2. ⟨z⟩nęcić, ⟨z⟩wabić

lu·rid ['lʊərɪd] kolor: krzykliwy; odrażający, koszmarny

lurk [lɜːk] ⟨za⟩czaić się; ~ about, ~ around czatować

lus·cious ['lʌʃəs] apetyczny (też dziewczyna)

lush [lʌʃ] bujny; fig. pełen przepychu

lust [lʌst] 1. żądza f; 2. ~ after, ~ for pożądać (G)

lus·|tre Brt., ~·ter Am. ['lʌstə] połysk m, blask m; ~·trous ['lʌstrəs] błyszczący, połyskliwy

lust·y ['lʌstɪ] (-ier, -iest) dziarski, witalny

lute [luːt] mus. lutnia f

Lu·ther·an ['luːθərən] 1. adj. luterański; 2. luteranin m (-anka f)

lux·u·|ri·ant [lʌg'ʒʊərɪənt] bujny; ~·ri·ate [lʌg'ʒʊərɪeɪt] upajać się; ~·ri·ous [lʌg'ʒʊərɪəs] luksusowy; ~·ry ['lʌkʃərɪ] luksus m; komfort m; attr. luksusowy

L

LV [el 'vi:] *Brt. skrót*: *lunch(eon)* **voucher** bon *m* obiadowy

lye [laɪ] *chem.* ług *m*

ly·ing ['laɪɪŋ] **1.** *pret. i p.p. od lie¹ i lie²*; **2.** *adj.* kłamliwy, oszczerczy

lymph [lɪmf] *med.* limfa *f*

lynch [lɪntʃ] ⟨z⟩linczować; '~ **law** prawo *n* linczu

lynx [lɪŋks] *zo.* ryś *m*

lyr·ic ['lɪrɪk] **1.** *adj.* liryczny; **2.** liryka *f*; ~**ics** *pl.* słowa *pl.* (*piosenki*); '~·i·cal* liryczny, nastrojowy

M

M, m [em] M, m *n*

M [em] *skrót*: *Brt.* autostrada *f*; *medium* (*size*) o średnich rozmiarach

m *skrót pisany*: *metre* m, metr *m*; *mile* mila (*1,6 km*); *married* zam., zamężny; żon., żonaty; *male, masculine* męski

ma [mɑ:] F mamusia *f*

MA [em 'eɪ] *skrót*: *Master of Arts* magister *m* nauk humanistycznych

ma'am [mæm] → *madam*

mac [mæk] *Brt.* F → *mackintosh*

ma·cad·am [məˈkædəm] *Am.* → *tarmac*

mac·a·ro·ni [mækəˈrəʊnɪ] *sg.* makaron *m* rurki

ma·chine [məˈʃiːn] **1.** maszyna *f*; **2.** obrabiać ⟨-robić⟩ maszynowo; ⟨u⟩szyć na maszynie; ~**gun** karabin *m* maszynowy; ~**-made** wytworzony maszynowo; ~**'read·a·ble** *komp.* mogący być przetwarzany komputerowo

ma·chin·e·ry [məˈʃiːnərɪ] maszyneria *f*; maszyny *pl.*; ~**ist** [məˈʃiːnɪst] maszynista *m*; operator *m* obrabiarek

mach·o ['mætʃəʊ] *pej.* (*pl.* **-os**) macho *m*, stuprocentowy mężczyzna *m*

mack [mæk] *Brt.* F → *mackintosh*

mack·e·rel ['mækrəl] *zo.* (*pl. mackerel lub mackerels*) makrela *f*

mack·in·tosh ['mækɪntɒʃ] *zwł. Brt.* płaszcz *m* przeciwdeszczowy

mac·ro... ['mækrəʊ] makro...

mad [mæd] szalony, zwariowany; *vet.* wściekły, chory na wściekliznę; *zwł. Am.* rozwścieczony; *be ~ about s.th.* mieć bzika na punkcie czegoś, szaleć za czymś; *drive s.o.* ~ doprowadzać ⟨-dzić⟩ kogoś do szaleństwa; *go ~* oszaleć; *like ~* jak szalony

mad·am ['mædəm] pani *f*

'mad·cap szalony; ~**den** ['mædn] rozwścieczać ⟨-czyć⟩; ~**den·ing** ['mædnɪŋ] rozwścieczający

made [meɪd] *pret. i p.p. od make* 1; ~ *of gold* zrobione ze złota

'mad·house *fig.* F dom *m* wariatów; '~·ly* jak szalony; F nieprawdopodobnie, szalenie; '~·man* (*pl.* -*men*) szaleniec *m*, wariat *m*; '~·ness* szaleństwo *n*, wariactwo *n*; '~·wom·an* (*pl.* -*women*) wariatka *f*

Ma·drid Madryt *m*

mag·a·zine [mægəˈziːn] magazyn *m*, pismo *n*; magazynek *m* (*broni, aparatu itp.*); magazyn *m*, skład *m*

mag·got ['mægət] *zo.* czerw *m*, robak *m*

Ma·gi ['meɪdʒaɪ] *pl.*: *the* (*three*) ~ Trzej Królowie *pl.*

ma·gic ['mædʒɪk] **1.** magia *f*, czary *pl.*; czar *m*; sztuczka *f* (*iluzjonisty*); **2.** (~*ally*) *też* ~*al* magiczny, czarodziejski; **magi·cian** [məˈdʒɪʃn] czarodziej *m*; magik *m*, iluzjonista *m*

ma·gis·trate ['mædʒɪstreɪt] sędzia *m* pokoju, sędzia *m* policyjny; △ *nie magistrat*

mag·na·nim·i·ty [mægnəˈnɪmətɪ] wspaniałomyślność *f*; ~**nan·i·mous** [mægˈnænɪməs] wspaniałomyślny

mag·net ['mægnɪt] magnes *m*; ~**ic** [mægˈnetɪk] (~*ally*) magnetyczny

mag·nif·i·cent [mægˈnɪfɪsnt] wspaniały

mag·ni·fy ['mægnɪfaɪ] powiększać ⟨-szyć⟩; '~**ing glass** szkło *n* powiększające, lupa *f*

mag·ni·tude ['mægnɪtjuːd] wielkość *f*, rozmiar *m*

mag·pie ['mægpaɪ] *zo.* sroka *f*

ma·hog·a·ny [məˈhɒgənɪ] mahoń *m*; *attr.* mahoniowy

maid [meɪd] pokojówka *f*; pomoc *f* domowa; *old* ~ *przest.* stara panna *f*; ~ *of*

all work *zwł. fig.* dziewczyna *f* do wszystkiego; **~ of hono(u)r** dama *f* dworu; *zwł. Am.* druhna *f*

maid·en ['meɪdn] panna *f*; dziewica *f*; *attr.* panieński; dziewiczy; **'~ name** nazwisko *n* panieńskie

mail [meɪl] **1.** poczta *f*; **by ~** *zwł. Am.* pocztą; **2.** *zwł. Am.* wysyłać ⟨-słać⟩ pocztą; *list* wrzucać ⟨-cić⟩; **'~·bag** torba *f* pocztowa; **'~·box** *Am.* skrzynka *f* pocztowa; **'~·car·ri·er** *Am.*, **'~·man** (*pl. -men*) *Am.* listonosz(ka *f*) *m*, doręczyciel(ka *f*) *m* poczty; **~ 'or·der** zamówienie *n* pocztowe; **~·or·der 'firm**, **~·or·der 'house** dom *m* sprzedaży wysyłkowej

maim [meɪm] okaleczać ⟨-czyć⟩

Main Men *m*

main [meɪn] **1.** główny, najważniejszy; **2.** *zw.* **~s** *gazowa, elektryczna itp.* sieć *f*; *gazowa, elektryczna itp.* magistrala *f*; **in the ~** przeważnie, na ogół; **'~·frame** *komp.* duży system *m* komputerowy, duży komputer *m* o wielkiej mocy; **~·land** ['meɪnlənd] ląd *m* stały; **'~·ly** głównie; **~ 'mem·o·ry** *komp.* pamięć *f* główna *lub* operacyjna; **~ 'men·u** *komp.* menu *n* główne; **~ 'road** droga *f* główna; **'~·spring** sprężyna *f* napędowa; *fig.* spiritus movens *m*; **'~·stay** *fig.* podstawa *f*; podpora *f*; **'~ street** *Am.* ulica *f* główna

main·tain [meɪn'teɪn] utrzymywać; ⟨s⟩twierdzić; zapewniać ⟨-nić⟩; ⟨za⟩konserwować; *życie* podtrzymywać ⟨-mać⟩

main·te·nance ['meɪntənəns] utrzymanie *n*; utrzymywanie *n* w dobrym stanie; konserwacja *f*; *jur.* alimenty *pl.*

maize [meɪz] *zwł. Brt.* kukurydza *f*

ma·jes·tic [mə'dʒestɪk] (**-ally**) majestatyczny; **~·ty** ['mædʒəstɪ] majestat *m*

ma·jor ['meɪdʒə] **1.** większy; *fig.* ważny; *jur.* pełnoletni; **C ~** *mus.* C-dur; **2.** *mil.* major *m*; *jur.* osoba *f* pełnoletnia; *Am. univ.* główna specjalizacja *f*; *mus.* dur; **~ 'gen·e·ral** *mil.* generał *m* dywizji; **~·i·ty** [mə'dʒɒrətɪ] większość *f*; *jur.* pełnoletność *f*; *attr.* większościowy; większością; **be in the ~ity** stanowić większość; **~ 'league** *Am.* (*w baseballu*) pierwsza liga *f*; **~ 'road** droga *f* główna

make [meɪk] **1.** (*made*) ⟨z⟩robić; ⟨u⟩czynić; wytwarzać ⟨-worzyć⟩; wyra-

biać ⟨-robić⟩, ⟨wy⟩produkować; *obiad* przyrządzić ⟨-dzać⟩; *pieniądze* zarabiać ⟨-robić⟩; *zysk, rezultat* osiągać ⟨-gnąć⟩; *mowę* wygłaszać ⟨-łosić⟩, *odległość* pokonywać ⟨-nać⟩; *sumę* stanowić; *podróż* odbywać ⟨-być⟩; *czas* ustalać ⟨-lić⟩; mianować, ustanawiać ⟨-nowić⟩; **~ s.o. do s.th.** nakłaniać ⟨-łonić⟩ *lub* zmuszać ⟨-sić⟩ kogoś do zrobienia czegoś; **~ it** zdążyć; mieć szczęście; **~ do with s.th.** zadowalać ⟨-wolić⟩ się czymś; **what do you ~ of it?** co o tym sądzisz?; **will you ~ one of the party?** dołączysz się do imprezy?; **~ the bed** ⟨po⟩ścielić łóżko; **~ believe** udawać; **~ friends with s.o.** zaprzyjaźnić się z kimś; **~ good** naprawiać ⟨-wić⟩, wyrównywać ⟨-nać⟩; dobrze ⟨z⟩robić; **~ haste** ⟨po⟩spieszyć się; **~ way** robić miejsce; **~ for** ⟨s⟩kierować się do (*G*); ułatwiać ⟨-wić⟩ (*A*); **~ into** przerabiać ⟨-robić⟩ w (*A*); **~ off** ulatniać ⟨ulotnić⟩ się; **~ out** *czek* wypisywać ⟨-sać⟩, *rachunek, dokument* sporządzać ⟨-dzić⟩, *formularz* wypełniać ⟨-nić⟩ ⟨z⟩rozumieć, pojmować ⟨-jąć⟩; udawać; **~ over** przekazywać ⟨-zać⟩; przerabiać ⟨-robić⟩; **~ up** sporządzać ⟨-dzić⟩, wykonywać ⟨-nać⟩; zestawiać ⟨-wić⟩; składać się; wynagradzać ⟨-rodzić⟩, ⟨z⟩rekompensować; zmyślać ⟨-lić⟩; nakładać ⟨-łożyć⟩ makijaż, ⟨u⟩malować się; **~ it up** ⟨po⟩godzić się (*with z I*); **~ up one's mind** zdecydować się; **be made up of** być zrobionym z (*I*); **~ up for** nadrabiać ⟨-robić⟩ braki; **2.** marka *f*; **'~·be·lieve** iluzja *f*, pozory *pl.*; **'~r** wytwórca *m*; **2r** *Bóg:* Twórca *m*; **'~·shift 1.** prowizorka *f.* **2.** prowizoryczny, improwizowany; **'~·up** makijaż *m*; charakteryzacja *f*; szminka *f*, kosmetyki *pl.*; skład *m*, struktura *f*

mak·ing ['meɪkɪŋ] produkcja *f*; powstawanie *n*, tworzenie *n* się; **in the ~** w trakcie powstawania; **have the ~s of** mieć zadatki (*G*)

mal·ad·just·ed [mælə'dʒʌstɪd] źle przystosowany, niedostosowany

mal·ad·min·i·stra·tion [mælədmɪnɪ'streɪʃn] złe zarządzanie *n*, *pol.* niegospodarność *f*

mal·con·tent ['mælkəntent] **1.** niezadowolony; **2.** malkontent *m*

male [meɪl] **1.** męski; samczy; płci męskiej; **2.** mężczyzna *m*; *zo.* samiec *m*;

M

~ 'nurse pielęgniarz m

mal·for·ma·tion [mælfɔːˈmeɪʃn] deformacja f (*zwł.* wrodzona)

mal·ice [ˈmælɪs] złośliwość f; *jur.* zła wola f

ma·li·cious [məˈlɪʃəs] złośliwy; *jur.* uczyniony w złej woli

ma·lign [məˈlaɪn] **1.** *adj.* szkodliwy; **2.** ⟨o⟩szkalować; **ma·lig·nant** [məˈlɪgnənt] złośliwy (*też med.*)

mall [mɔːl, mæl] *Am.* centrum n handlowe

mal·le·a·ble [ˈmælɪəbl] *tech.* kowalny, ciągliwy; *fig.* plastyczny, podatny na wpływy

mal·let [ˈmælɪt] pobijak m; młotek m drewniany; (w grze w polo itp.) młotek m

mal·nu·tri·tion [mælnjuːˈtrɪʃn] złe odżywianie n, niedożywienie n

mal·o·dor·ous [mælˈəʊdərəs] o nieprzyjemnym zapachu

mal·prac·tice [mælˈpræktɪs] zaniedbanie n; *med.* błąd m w sztuce lekarskiej

malt [mɔːlt] słód m; *attr.* słodowy

mal·treat [mælˈtriːt] maltretować, znęcać się nad (*I*)

mam·mal [ˈmæml] *zo.* ssak m

mam·moth [ˈmæməθ] **1.** *zo.* mamut m; **2.** olbrzymi, kolosalny

mam·my [ˈmæmɪ] F mamusia f

man [mæn, *w złożeniach wymowa* -mən] (*pl.* **men** [men]) mężczyzna m; człowiek m; ludzkość f; F mąż m; F ukochany m, facet m; (*w szachach*) figura f; (*w grze w warcaby*) pionek m; **the ~ in** (*Am. też* **on**) **the street** szary człowiek m; **2.** [mæn] (**-nn-**) statek itp. obsadzać ⟨-dzić⟩ załogą

man·age [ˈmænɪdʒ] *v/t.* firmą ⟨po⟩kierować (*I*); zarządzać (*I*); dawać sobie radę z (*I*); zdołać, podołać (**to do** zrobić); umieć się obchodzić z (*I*); *v/i.* ⟨po⟩radzić sobie (**with** z *I*, **without** bez *G*); dawać ⟨dać⟩ sobie radę; '**~·a·ble** możliwy do wykonania; '**~·ment** zarządzanie n, kierowanie n; *econ.* kierownictwo n, dyrekcja f

man·ag·er [ˈmænɪdʒə] kierownik m (-czka f), dyrektor(ka f) m; menedżer m; *sport:* trener m; **~·ess** [mænɪdʒəˈres] kierowniczka f, dyrektorka f; kobieta menedżer f; (*w sporcie*) trenerka f

man·a·ge·ri·al [mænəˈdʒɪərɪəl] *econ.* kierowniczy; **~ position** kierownicze stanowisko; **~ staff** kadra f kierownicza

man·ag·ing [ˈmænɪdʒɪŋ] *econ.* zarządzający, kierujący; **~ di·rec·tor** naczelny dyrektor m

man·date [ˈmændeɪt] *pol.* mandat m; zadanie n, zlecenie n; **~·da·to·ry** [ˈmændətərɪ] obowiązkowy, obligatoryjny

mane [meɪn] grzywa f

ma·neu·ver [məˈnuːvə] *Am.* → **manoeuvre**

man·ful [ˈmænfʊl] męski, mężny

mange [meɪndʒ] *vet.* świerzb m

manger [ˈmeɪndʒə] żłób m

man·gle [ˈmæŋgl] **1.** magiel m; **2.** ⟨wy⟩maglować; ⟨z⟩deformować

mang·y [ˈmeɪndʒɪ] (**-ier, -iest**) *vet.* chory na świerzb; *fig.* wyliniały

'**man·hood** wiek m męski, męskość n

ma·ni·a [ˈmeɪnjə] mania f; **have a ~ for** być maniakiem na punkcie (*G*); **~·c** [ˈmeɪnæk] maniak m, szaleniec m; *fig.* fanatyk m

man·i·cure [ˈmænɪkjʊə] manicure n

man·i·fest [ˈmænɪfest] **1.** oczywisty, jawny; **2.** *v/t.* ⟨za⟩manifestować

man·i·fold [ˈmænɪfəʊld] różnorodny, różnoraki

ma·nip·u·late [məˈnɪpjʊleɪt] manipulować(*I*); **~·la·tion** [mənɪpjuˈleɪʃn] manipulacja f

man·'jack F: **every ~ jack** każdy z osobna; **~·kind** ludzkość f; '**~·ly** (**-ier, -iest**) męski; '**~·made** sztuczny, wytworzony przez człowieka; **~·made fibre** (*Am.* **fiber**) sztuczne włókno n

man·ner [ˈmænə] sposób m; styl m; postawa f; sposób m zachowania; (**good**) **~s** *pl.* dobre maniery *pl.*; zwyczaje *pl.*

ma·noeu·vre *Brt.*, **ma·neu·ver** *Am.* [məˈnuːvə] **1.** manewr m (*też fig.*); **2.** manewrować (*też fig.*)

man·or [ˈmænə] posiadłość f ziemska; '**~ house** dwór m

'**man·pow·er** siła f robocza; personel m, kadra f

man·sion [ˈmænʃn] rezydencja f

'**man·slaugh·ter** *jur.* nieumyślne zabójstwo n

man·tel·|piece [ˈmæntlpiːs], '**~·shelf** (*pl.* **-shelves**) gzyms m kominka

man·u·al ['mænjʊəl] **1.** ręczny; fizyczny; **2.** podręcznik *m*

man·u·fac·ture [mænju'fæktʃə] **1.** wytwarzać ⟨-worzyć⟩, ⟨wy⟩produkować; **2.** produkcja *f*, wytwórstwo *n*, wytwarzanie *n*; **~tures** *pl.* produkty *pl.*; **~tur·er** [mænju'fæktʃərə] wytwórca *m*, producent *m*; **~tur·ing** [mænju'-fæktʃərɪŋ] przemysł *m* (*wytwórczy*); wytwarzanie *n*; *attr.* wytwórczy

ma·nure [mə'njʊə] **1.** obornik *m*, gnój *m*, mierzwa *f*; **2.** nawozić ⟨-wieźć⟩

man·u·script ['mænjʊskrɪpt] rękopis *m*; manuskrypt *m*

man·y ['menɪ] **1.** (**more**, **most**) wiele, wielu; **~ a** niejeden; **~ times** często; **as ~** równie często; **2.** wiele; **a good ~** dużo; **a great ~** bardzo dużo

map [mæp] **1.** mapa *f*, plan *m* (*miasta*); **2.** (**-pp-**) sporządzać ⟨-dzić⟩ mapę *lub* plan, nanosić ⟨-nieść⟩ na mapę *lub* plan; **~ out** *fig.* ⟨za⟩planować

ma·ple ['meɪpl] *bot.* klon *m*

mar [mɑː] (**-rr-**) ⟨ze⟩szpecić; ⟨ze⟩psuć, ⟨z⟩niszczyć

Mar *skrót pisany:* **March** marzec *m*

mar·a·thon ['mærəθən] **1.** *też* **~ race** maraton *m*, wyścig maratoński; **2.** maratoński; *fig.* forsowny

ma·raud [mə'rɔːd] ⟨s⟩plądrować

mar·ble ['mɑːbl] **1.** marmur *m*; kulka *f* (do gry); **2.** marmurowy

march [mɑːtʃ] **1.** ⟨po⟩maszerować; *fig.* iść ⟨pójść⟩ naprzód; ⟨wy⟩prowadzić; **2.** marsz *m*; *fig.* postęp *m*; (*demonstracja*) pochód *m*; **the ~ of time** bieg *m* czasu

March [mɑːtʃ] (*skrót:* **Mar**) marzec *m*

'march·ing or·ders *pl.:* **give s.o. his/ her ~** *Brt.* F posłać kogoś na zieloną trawkę

mare [meə] *zo.* klacz *f*, kobyła *f*

mar·ga·rine [mɑːdʒə'riːn], **marge** *Brt.* [mɑːdʒ] F margaryna *f*

mar·gin ['mɑːdʒɪn] margines *m* (*też fig.*); brzeg *m*, krawędź *f*; *fig.* dopuszczalny zakres *m*; rozpiętość *f*; *econ.* marża *f*; **by a wide ~** dużą przewagą; **'~·al** marginesowy; **'~·al note** notatka *f* na marginesie

mar·i·hua·na, **mar·i·jua·na** [mærjʊ'ɑːnə] marihuana *f*

ma·ri·na [mə'riːnə] przystań *f* jachtowa

ma·rine [mə'riːn] **1.** *mil.* żołnierz *m* pie-

choty morskiej; **merchant ~** marynarka *f* handlowa; **2.** *adj.* morski

mar·i·ner ['mærɪnə] marynarz *m*

mar·i·tal ['mærɪtl] małżeński; **~ 'status** stan *m* cywilny

mar·i·time ['mærɪtaɪm] morski; żeglugowy

mark¹ [mɑːk] *econ.* marka *f*

mark² [mɑːk] **1.** znak *m*; plama *f*; ślad *m*; oznaka *f*; znamię *n*; cel *m*; cecha *f*, oznaczenie *n*; (*w szkole*) ocena *f*, stopień *m*; (*w sporcie*) linia startowa; *fig.* poziom *m*, jakość *f*, norma; *tech.* oznaczenie *n*; **be up to the ~** być na (odpowiednim) poziomie; *zdrowotnie* czuć się dobrze; **be wide of the ~** chybić celu, być chybionym; *fig.* nie być trafnym; **hit the ~** trafić (*do celu*); *fig.* trafić w dziesiątkę; **miss the ~** nie trafić (*do celu*), spudłować (*też fig.*); △ *nie* **marka**; **2.** zostawiać ⟨-wić⟩ ślady; ⟨po⟩plamić; oznaczać ⟨-czyć⟩; zaznaczać ⟨-czyć⟩; cechować; oznaczać ⟨-czyć⟩ upamiętnić ⟨-nić⟩; *towar* ⟨o⟩znakować; *cenę* ustalać ⟨-lić⟩; (*w szkole*) sprawdzać ⟨-dzić⟩, oceniać ⟨-nić⟩; (*w sporcie*) *zawodnika* kryć; **~ my words** zważaj na moje słowa; **to ~ the occasion** w celu uświetnienia tej okazji; **~ time** iść w miejscu; *fig.* dreptać w miejscu; **~ down** odnotowywać ⟨-ować⟩ *cenę* obniżać ⟨-żyć⟩; **~ out** *linią* oznaczać ⟨-czyć⟩ (*I*); *kogoś* wyróżniać ⟨-nić⟩, wyznaczać ⟨-czyć⟩ (*for* do *G*); **~ up** *cenę* podwyższać ⟨-szyć⟩; **~ed** wyraźny, dobitny; **'~·er** marker *m*, pisak *m*; zakładka *f*; znacznik *m*

mar·ket ['mɑːkɪt] **1.** rynek *m*; targ *m*; hala *f* targowa; *econ.* zbyt *m*; *econ.* popyt *m* (**for** na *A*); **on the ~** na rynku, w handlu; **put on the ~** wprowadzać ⟨-dzić⟩ na rynek *lub* do handlu; *attr.* rynkowy; **2.** *v/t.* wprowadzać ⟨-dzić⟩ na rynek *lub* do handlu; zbywać ⟨-być⟩, sprzedawać ⟨-dać⟩; **~·a·ble** *econ.* nadający się do sprzedaży rynkowej; łatwo zbywalny; **'~gar·den** *Brt.* zakład *m* ogrodniczy; **'~·ing** *econ.* marketing *m*

'mark·ing znak *m*, plama *f*; oznaczanie *n*, *zo.* cechowanie *n*; (*w sporcie*) krycie *n*

'marks·man (*pl.* **-men**) dobry strzelec *m*; **'~·ship** umiejętność *f* strzelania

mar·ma·lade ['mɑːməleɪd] marmolada *f* (*zwł. z cytrusów*)

mar·mot ['mɑ:mət] *zo.* świstak *m*

ma·roon [mə'ru:n] **1.** *adj.* bordo (*idkl.*);
2. wyrzucać na ląd (*na wyspę*)

mar·quee [mɑ:'ki:] duży namiot *m*
(*używany na festynach itp.*)

mar·quis ['mɑ:kwɪs] markiz *m*

mar·riage ['mærɪdʒ] małżeństwo (**to**
z I); ślub *m*; **civil ~** ślub *m* cywilny;
'mar·ria·gea·ble zdolny do zawarcia
małżeństwa; **'~ cer·tif·i·cate** akt *m*
ślubu

mar·ried ['mærɪd] *ktoś*: mężczyzna: żonaty, *kobieta*: zamężna; *coś*: ślubny,
małżeński; **~ couple** małżeństwo *n*;
~ life życie *n* małżeńskie

mar·row ['mærəʊ] *anat.* szpik *m* (*też*
fig.); *fig.* sedno *n*; *też* **vegetable ~** *Brt.*
bot. kabaczek *m*

mar·ry ['mærɪ] *v/t. para*: brać ⟨wziąć⟩
ślub; *mężczyzna*: ⟨o⟩żenić się *z* (*I*), *ko-*
bieta: wychodzić ⟨wyjść⟩ za mąż za (*A*);
be married mieć ślub (**to** *z I*); **get**
married *mężczyzna*: ⟨o⟩żenić się (**to**
z I), *kobieta*: wychodzić ⟨wyjść⟩ za
mąż (**to** za *A*); *v/i.* dawać ⟨dać⟩ ślub

marsh [mɑ:ʃ] mokradło *n*, moczary *pl.*

mar·shal ['mɑ:ʃl] **1.** *mil.* marszałek *m*;
Am. naczelnik *m* (*okręgu policyjnego*);
2. (*zwł. Brt. -ll- , Am. -l-*) ⟨z⟩organizo-
wać, układać ⟨ułożyć⟩; ⟨za⟩prowadzić,
⟨po⟩kierować

marsh·y ['mɑ:ʃɪ] podmokły, bagnisty

mar·ten ['mɑ:tɪn] *zo.* kuna *f*

mar·tial ['mɑ:ʃl] wojskowy, wojenny;
~ 'arts *pl.* wschodnie sztuki walki *pl.*;
~ 'law prawo *n* wojenne; stan *m* wyjątkowy, stan *m* wojenny

mar·tyr ['mɑ:tə] męczennik *m* (*-ica f*)

mar·vel ['mɑ:vl] **1.** cud *m*; **2.** zadziwiać
⟨-wić⟩się; **~·(l)ous** ['mɑ:vələs] cudowny

mar·zi·pan [mɑ:zɪ'pæn] marcepan *m*

mas·ca·ra [mæ'skɑ:rə] tusz *m* do rzęs

mas·cot ['mæskət] maskotka *f*

mas·cu·line ['mæskjʊlɪn] męski; rodzaju męskiego

mash [mæʃ] **1.** ugniatać ⟨-nieść⟩; **2.** *Brt.*
F purée *n* ziemniaczane; mieszanka *f*
pastewna; **~ed po'ta·toes** *pl.* purée *n*
ziemniaczane

mask [mɑ:sk] **1.** maska *f*; **2.** ⟨za⟩masko-
wać; *fig.* zakryć ⟨-ywać⟩; *~ed* zamasko-
wany; **~ed ball** bal *m* maskowy

ma·son ['meɪsn] murarz *m*; kamie-

niarz *m*; *zw.* ♀ wolnomularz *m*, mason
m (*-ka f*); **~·ry** ['meɪsnrɪ] murarka *f*;
kamieniarka *f*

masque [mɑ:sk] *theat. hist.*: maska *f*

mas·que·rade [mæskə'reɪd] **1.** maska-
rada *f* (*też fig.*); przebranie *n*; **2.** *fig.*
przebierać się (**as** jako)

mass [mæs] **1.** masa *f* (*też fiz.*); kawał *m*;
ogrom *m*; wielka ilość *f*; **the ~es** *pl.*
szerokie masy *pl.*; **2.** zbierać ⟨zebrać⟩
się, ⟨z⟩gromadzić się; **3.** masowy

Mass [mæs] msza *f*

mas·sa·cre ['mæsəkə] **1.** masakra *f*; **2.**
⟨z⟩masakrować

mas·sage ['mæsɑ:ʒ] **1.** masaż *m*; **2.**
⟨roz-, po⟩masować

mas·seur [mæ'sɜ:] masażysta *m*;
~·seuse [mæ'sɜ:z] masażystka *f*

mas·sif ['mæsi:f] masyw *m* (*górski*)

mas·sive ['mæsɪv] masywny; rozległy

mass·'me·di·a *pl.* mass media *pl.*;
~·pro'duce ⟨wy⟩produkować masowo;
~ pro'duc·tion produkcja *f* masowa

mast [mɑ:st] *naut.* maszt *m*

mas·ter ['mɑ:stə] **1.** mistrz *m*; pan *m*;
zwł. Brt. nauczyciel *m*; oryginał *m*; kapitan *m*; *univ.* magister *m*; ♀ **of Arts**
(*skrót:* **MA**) magister *m* nauk humanistycznych; **~ of ceremonies** konferansjer *m*; **2.** mistrzowski, główny; **~ copy**
oryginał *m*; **~ tape** *tech.* kopia-matka *f*;
3. opanowywać ⟨-wać⟩; **'~ key** klucz *m*
uniwersalny; **'~·ly** mistrzowski; **'~·pie-**
ce arcydzieło *n*; **~·y** ['mɑ:stərɪ] opanowanie *n*, panowanie *n*

mas·tur·bate ['mæstəbeɪt] masturbo-
wać (się), onanizować (się)

Masuria Mazury *pl.*

mat[1] [mæt] **1.** mata *f*, podstawka *f*; **2.**
(*-tt-*) sklejać ⟨-leić⟩ się; ⟨s⟩filcować się

mat[2] [mæt] matowy

match[1] [mætʃ] zapałka *f*

match[2] [mætʃ] **1.** para *f*, odpowiednik
m; *w sporcie* mecz *m*, walka *f* (*bokser-*
ska); *ktoś*: dobra partia *f*; ożenek *m*; **be**
a ~ for s.o. dorównywać komuś; **be no**
~ for s.o. nie móc się równać z kimś;
find *lub* **meet one's ~** spotkać sobie
równego; **2.** *v/t.* dorównywać ⟨-nać⟩
(*D*); zestawiać ⟨-wić⟩, przeciwstawiać
⟨-wić⟩; dopasowywać ⟨-ować⟩, dobierać ⟨-brać⟩; *v/i.* pasować (*do siebie*), odpowiadać sobie; **gloves to ~** pasujące
rękawiczki

'**match·box** pudełko *n* od zapałek
'**match|·less** nie do pary, niedopasowany; '**~·mak·er** swat(ka *f*) *m*; **~'point** (*w tenisie*) meczbol *m*
mate¹ [meɪt] → *checkmate*
mate² [meɪt] **1.** towarzysz *m* (*pracy*); kolega *m*; partner *m* (*w parze zwierząt*); *naut.* oficer *m* pokładowy; **2.** parzyć (się), kojarzyć (się) (*w pary*)
ma·te·ri·al [məˈtɪərɪəl] **1.** materiał *m*; tworzywo *n*; *writing* **~s** *pl.* materiały *pl.* piśmienne; **2.** materialny; materiałowy; znaczny, poważny
ma·ter·nal [məˈtɜːnl] matczyny, macierzyński; ze strony matki
ma·ter·ni·ty [məˈtɜːnəti] **1.** macierzyństwo *n*; **2.** położniczy; **~** *dress* sukienka *f* ciążowa; **~** *leave* urlop *m* macierzyński; **~** *ward* oddział *m* położniczy
math [mæθ] *Am.* F matematyka *f*
math·e|·ma·ti·cian [mæθəməˈtɪʃn] matematyk *m* (-yczka *f*); **~·mat·ics** [mæθəˈmætɪks] *zw. sg.* matematyka *f*
maths [mæθs] *Brt.* F matematyka *f*
mat·i·née [ˈmætɪneɪ] *theat. itp.* przedstawienie *n* popołudniowe
ma·tric·u·late [məˈtrɪkjuleɪt] immatrykulować (się)
mat·ri·mo|·ni·al [mætrɪˈməʊnjəl] małżeński; matrymonialny; **~·ny** [ˈmætrɪmənɪ] małżeństwo *n*, stan *m* małżeński
ma·trix *tech.* [ˈmeɪtrɪks] (*pl.* **-trices** [-trɪsɪːz], **-trixes**) matryca *f*
ma·tron [ˈmeɪtrən] *Brt.* siostra *f* przełożona; *Brt. jakby:* pielęgniarka *f* szkolna (*zajmująca się też opieką nad dziećmi*)
mat·ter [ˈmætə] **1.** materia *f* (*też phys.*), substancja *f*; sprawa *f*, kwestia *f*; przedmiot *m*; *med.* ropa *f*; *printed* **~** pocztowy druk *m*; *what's the* **~** (*with you*)? co się z tobą dzieje?; *no* **~** *who* nieważne kto; *for that* **~** jeśli o to chodzi; *a* **~** *of course* rzecz *f* oczywista; *a* **~** *of fact* fakt *m*; *as a* **~** *of fact* właściwie; *a* **~** *of form* zagadnienie *n* formalne; *a* **~** *of time* kwestia *f* czasu; **2.** mieć znaczenie (*to* dla *G*); *it doesn't* **~** nie szkodzi; **~·of-'fact** rzeczowy, praktyczny
mat·tress [ˈmætrɪs] materac *m*
ma·ture [məˈtjʊə] **1.** (*-r, -st*) dojrzały (*też fig.*); **2.** dojrzewać ⟨-rzeć⟩; **ma·tu·ri·ty** [məˈtjʊərətɪ] dojrzałość *f* (*też fig.*)
maud·lin [ˈmɔːdlɪn] ckliwy, rzewny

maul [mɔːl] ⟨po⟩kiereszować; *fig.* dobierać się do (*G*)
Maun·dy Thurs·day [ˈmɔːndɪ -] Wielki Czwartek *m*
mauve [məʊv] wrzosowy, jasnoliliowy
mawk·ish [ˈmɔːkɪʃ] czułostkowy, sentymentalny
max·i... [ˈmæksɪ] maksi...
max·im [ˈmæksɪm] maksyma *f*
max·i·mum [ˈmæksɪməm] **1.** (*pl.* **-ma** [-mə]) maksimum *n*; **2.** maksymalny, największy
May [meɪ] maj *m*
may [meɪ] *v/aux.* (*pret.* *might*) móc
may·be [ˈmeɪbɪ] może
'**May|·bee·tle** *zo.*, '**~·bug** *zo.* chrabąszcz *m* majowy
'**May Day** 1 Maja; **mayday** (*międzynarodowe wołanie o pomoc, słowny odpowiednik SOS*)
may·on·naise [meɪəˈneɪz] majonez *m*
mayor [meə] burmistrz *m*; △ *nie major*
'**may·pole** (*gałązka*) gaik *m*
maze [meɪz] labirynt *m* (*też fig.*)
Mazovia Mazowsze *n*
MB [em ˈbiː] *skrót:* **megabyte** MB, megabajt *m*
MCA [em siː ˈeɪ] *Skrót:* **maximum credible accident**
MD [em ˈdiː] *skrót:* **Doctor of Medicine** (*łacińskie* **medicinae doctor**) dr n. med., doktor *m* nauk medycznych
me [miː] mnie, mi; F ja
mead·ow [ˈmedəʊ] łąka *f*
mea·gre *Brt.*, **mea·ger** *Am.* [ˈmiːgə] skąpy, niewielki
meal¹ [miːl] posiłek *m*; danie *n*
meal² [miːl] mąka *f* (*zwł. na paszę*)
mean¹ [miːn] skąpy, chytry; podły; nędzny
mean² [miːn] (*meant*) znaczyć; oznaczać; mieć na myśli; przywiązywać wagę; zamierzać; mieć zamiar (*to do s.th.* zrobić coś); *be* **~t for** być przeznaczonym dla (*G*); **~** *well* (*ill*) mieć dobre (złe) intencje
mean³ [miːn] **1.** średnia *f*, przeciętna *f*; środek *m*; **2.** średni, przeciętny
'**mean·ing** **1.** znaczenie *n*, sens *m*; **2.** znaczący; '**~·ful** znaczący, sensowny; '**~·less** bez znaczenia, bezsensowny
means [miːnz] (*pl.* **means**) środek *m*, środki *pl.*; środki *pl.* pieniężne; środki *pl.* do życia; *by all* **~** ależ oczywiście; *by*

no ~ w żaden sposób; **by** ~ **of** za pomocą (G)

meant [ment] *pret. i p.p. od* **mean²**

'**mean**|**·time** *też* **in the ~time** tymczasem; '**.~while** tymczasem

mea·sles ['mi:zlz] *med.* odra *f*; **German** ~ różyczka *f*

mea·su·ra·ble ['meʒərəbl] mierzalny, wymierny

mea·sure ['meʒə] **1.** miara *f* (*też fig.*); rozmiar *m*, wymiar *m*; *mus.* takt *m*; krok *m*, środek *m*; **beyond** ~ ponad miarę; **in a great** ~ w dużej mierze; **take ~s** przedsięwziąć ⟨-sięwziąć⟩ kroki; **2.** ⟨z-, po⟩mierzyć, dokonywać ⟨-nać⟩ pomiaru; ~ **up to** znaleźć się na wysokości (G), spełniać oczekiwania (G); **~d** wymierzony; miarowy; ostrożny; '~**ment** wymiar *m*; pomiar *m*; **leg ~ment** długość *f* nogawki

meas·ur·ing ['meʒərɪŋ] pomiarowy; '~ **tape** → **tape measure**

meat [mi:t] mięso *n*; **cold ~s** *pl.* wędliny *pl.*; ' ~**·ball** klops *m*

me·chan|**·ic** [mɪ'kænɪk] mechanik *m*; ~**·i·cal** mechaniczny; ~**·ics** *phys. zw. sg.* mechanika *f*

mech·a|**·nis·m** ['mekənɪzəm] mechanizm *m*; ~**·nize** ['mekənaɪz] ⟨z⟩mechanizować

med·al ['medl] medal *m*; order *m*; ~**·(l)ist** ['medlɪst] (*w sporcie*) medalista *m* (-tka *f*)

med·dle ['medl] ⟨w⟩mieszać się (**with**, **in** do *A*); '~**·some** ciekawski

me·di·a ['mi:djə] *sg., pl.* media *pl.*, środki *pl.* masowego przekazu

med·i·ae·val ['medɪ'i:vl] → **medieval**

me·di·an ['mi:djn] *też* ~ **strip** *Am.* (*na autostradzie*) pas *m* zieleni

me·di|**·ate** ['mi:dɪeɪt] pośredniczyć, być mediatorem; ~**·a·tion** [mi:dɪ'eɪʃn] pośredniczenie *n*, mediacja *f*; ~**·a·tor** ['mi:dɪeɪtə] mediator *m* (-ka *f*), rozjemca *m*

med·i·cal ['medɪkl] **1.** medyczny; **2.** badanie *n* lekarskie; ~ **cer·tif·i·cate** zaświadczenie *n* lekarskie

med·i·cated ['medɪkeɪtɪd] leczniczy; ~ **soap** mydło *n* lecznicze

me·di·cine ['medsɪn] medycyna *f*; lekarstwo *n*

med·i·e·val [medɪ'i:vl] średniowieczny

me·di·o·cre [mi:dɪ'əʊkə] przeciętny

med·i|**·tate** ['medɪteɪt] *v/i.* medytować (**on** nad *I*); rozmyślać (**on** o *I*); ~**·ta·tion** [medɪ'teɪʃn] medytacja *f*; rozmyślanie *n*; ~**·ta·tive** ['medɪtətɪv] medytacyjny

Med·i·ter·ra·ne·an [medɪtə'reɪnjən] śródziemnomorski; ~ **Sea** Morze Śródziemne

me·di·um ['mi:djəm] **1.** (*pl.* **-dia** [-djə], **-diums**) środek *m*; środek *m* przekazu; środowisko *n*, ośrodek *m*; medium *n*; **2.** średni; pośredni; *gastr.* nie wysmażony

med·ley ['medlɪ] mieszanka; *mus.* potpourri *n*, wiązanka *f*, składanka *f*

meek [mi:k] potulny, uległy; '~**·ness** potulność *f*, uległość *f*

meet [mi:t] *v/t.* spotykać ⟨-tkać⟩, spotkać ⟨-tykać⟩ się z (*I*); poznawać ⟨-nać⟩; wychodzić na spotkanie (G), wyjeżdżać na spotkanie (G); *oczekiwania, życzenia itp.* spełniać ⟨-nić⟩; *potrzeby itp.* zaspokajać ⟨-koić⟩; *spłacać* ⟨-cić⟩, pokrywać ⟨-ryć⟩; *terminu* dotrzymywać; *v/i.* spotykać ⟨-tkać⟩ się; poznawać się; zbierać ⟨zebrać⟩ się; schodzić ⟨zejść⟩ się; ~ **with** napotykać ⟨-tkać⟩; spotykać ⟨-tkać⟩ się z (*I*); '~**·ing** spotkanie *n*; zebranie *n*, konferencja *f*; '~**·ing place** miejsce *n* spotkania, miejsce *n* zebrania

mel·an·chol·y ['melənkəlɪ] **1.** melancholia *f*; **2.** melancholijny

mel·low ['meləʊ] **1.** łagodny; dojrzały (*też fig.*); *światło, kolor itp.*: ciepły

me·lo·di·ous [mɪ'ləʊdjəs] melodyjny

mel·o·dra·mat·ic [meləʊdrə'mætɪk] melodramatyczny

mel·o·dy ['melədɪ] melodia *f*

mel·on ['melən] *bot.* melon *m*

melt [melt] ⟨s⟩topnieć; ⟨s⟩topić (się); roztapiać ⟨-topić⟩ (się); ~ **down** przetapiać ⟨-topić⟩

mem·ber ['membə] członek *m*; *anat.* członek *m* (*ciała*); **☿ of Parliament** *Brt. parl.* poseł *m* (-słanka *f*) do parlamentu; '~**·ship** członkostwo *n*

mem·brane ['membreɪn] błona *f*; membrana *f*

mem·o ['meməʊ] (*pl.* **-os**) notka *f* służbowa, okólnik *m*

mem·oirs ['memwa:z] *pl.* pamiętniki *pl.*

M

mem·o·ra·ble ['memərəbl] pamiętny

me·mo·ri·al [mɪ'mɔːrɪəl] pomnik *m*, statua *f*; *attr.* pamiątkowy, upamiętniający

mem·o·rize ['meməraɪz] ⟨wy-, na⟩uczyć się na pamięć

mem·o·ry ['me* memorə ri] pamięć *f* (*też* komp.); **in~ of** ku pamięci (*G*); wspomnienie *n*; ~ **ca'pac·i·ty** komp. pojemność *f* pamięci

men [men] *pl. od* **man** 1

men·ace ['menəs] 1. zagrażać ⟨-rozić⟩; grozić; 2. zagrożenie *n*; groźba *f*

mend [mend] 1. *v/t.* naprawiać ⟨-wić⟩; ⟨z⟩reperować; ⟨za⟩cerować, zaszyć ⟨-ywać⟩; ~ **one's ways** poprawiać ⟨-wić⟩ się; *v/i.* poprawiać ⟨-wić⟩ się; 2. cera *f*, zaszyte miejsce *n*; **on the ~** dochodzący do siebie

men·di·cant ['mendɪkənt] 1. żebrzący; 2. zakonnik *m* żebrzący

me·ni·al ['miːnjəl] *praca*: podrzędny

men·in·gi·tis [menɪn'dʒaɪtɪs] *med.* zapalenie *n* opon mózgowych

men·o·pause ['menəupɔːz] menopauza *f*

men·stru|·ate ['menstrʊeɪt] miesiączkować, mieć miesiączkę; ~**a·tion** [menstrʊ'eɪʃn] menstruacja *f*, miesiączka *f*

men·tal ['mentl] umysłowy, mentalny; psychiczny; ~ **a'rith·me·tic** rachunek *m* pamięciowy; ~ **'hand·i·cap** upośledzenie *n* umysłowe; ~ **'hos·pi·tal** szpital *m* psychiatryczny; ~**·i·ty** [men'tælətɪ] mentalność *f*; ~**·ly** ['mentəlɪ] umysłowo; ~**ly handicapped** upośledzony umysłowo; ~**ly ill** chory umysłowo

men·tion ['menʃn] 1. wspominać ⟨-mnieć⟩; **don't ~ it!** nie ma za co!, proszę bardzo!; 2. wspomnienie *n*

men·u ['menjuː] menu *n* (*też* komp.), karta *f*

MEP [em iː 'piː] *skrót:* **Member of the European Parliament** poseł do Parlamentu Europejskiego

mer·can·tile ['mɜːkəntaɪl] handlowy, kupiecki; merkantylny

mer·ce·na·ry ['mɜːsɪnərɪ] 1. najemnik *m*; 2. najemniczy

mer·chan·dise ['mɜːtʃəndaɪz] towar(y *pl.*) *m*

mer·chant ['mɜːtʃənt] 1. kupiec *m*; 2. handlowy

mer·ci|·ful ['mɜːsɪfl] litościwy, miłosierny; '~·less bezlitosny, niemiłosierny

mer·cu·ry ['mɜːkjʊrɪ] *chem.* rtęć *f*

mer·cy ['mɜːsɪ] litość *f*, miłosierdzie *n*

mere [mɪə] (**-r, -st**), '~·ly tylko, jedynie

merge [mɜːdʒ] ⟨po⟩łączyć (**into, with** z *I*) (się); *econ.* dokonywać fuzji; 'merg·er *econ.* fuzja *f*

me·rid·i·an [mə'rɪdɪən] *geogr.* południk *m*; *fig.* szczyt *m*

mer·it ['merɪt] 1. zasługa *f*; wartość *f*; zaleta *f*; 2. zasługiwać ⟨-służyć⟩

mer·maid ['mɜːmeɪd] syrena *f*

mer·ri·ment ['merɪmənt] wesołość *f*

mer·ry ['merɪ] (**-ier, -iest**) wesoły; **♀ Christmas!** Wesołych Świąt!; '~·go-round karuzela *f*

mesh [meʃ] 1. oko *n*, oczko *f*; *fig.* często ~**es** sieć *f*; siatka *f*; **in ~** tech. zazębiać ⟨-bić⟩ się; 2. zazębiać ⟨-bić⟩ się; *fig.* pasować (**with** do *G*)

mess [mes] 1. bałagan *m*, nieporządek *m* (*też fig.*); brud *m*; paskudztwo *m*; łajno *n*; *mil.* kantyna *f*, kasyno *n*; (*na statku*) mesa *f*; **make a ~ of** F ⟨s⟩knocić (*A*); *plany* pokręcić (*A*); 2. ~ **about**, ~ **around** F obijać się; wygłupiać się (**with** z *I*); ~ **up** zrobić bałagan; F ⟨s⟩knocić; *plany* pokręcić

mes·sage ['mesɪdʒ] wiadomość *f*; informacja *f* (*filmu itp.*) przesłanie *n*; **can I take a ~?** czy może coś powtórzyć? **get the ~** F ⟨po⟩kapować się

mes·sen·ger ['mesɪndʒə] posłaniec *m*

mess·y ['mesɪ] (**-ier, -iest**) pobrudzony, zapaskudzony; *fig.* pogmatwany

met [met] *pret. i pp. od* **meet**

me·tab·o·lis·m [me'tæbəlɪzəm] *physiol.* metabolizm *m*

met·al ['metl] metal *m*; **me·tal·lic** [mɪ'tælɪk] (~**ally**) metaliczny; metalowy

met·a·mor·pho·sis [metə'mɔːfəsɪs] metamorfoza *f*, przekształcenie *n*

met·a·phor ['metəfə] metafora *f*

me·tas·ta·sis [mɪ'tæstəsɪs] *med.* (*pl.* **-ses** [-siːz]) metastaza *f*, przerzut *m*

me·te·or ['miːtɪɔː] meteor *m*

me·te·o·ro·log·i·cal [miːtjərə'lɒdʒɪkl] meteorologiczny; pogodowy, synoptyczny; ~ **'of·fice** *lub* F **met office** stacja *f* meteorologiczna

me·te·o·rol·o·gy [miːtjə'rɒlədʒɪ] meteorologia *f*

M

meter 494

me·ter ['mi:tə] *tech.* miernik *m*, przyrząd *m* pomiarowy; △ *Brt. nie* **metr**
meth·od ['meθəd] metoda *f*; me·thod-
i·cal [mɪ'θɒdɪkl] metodyczny
me·tic·u·lous [mɪ'tɪkjʊləs] drobiazgowy, skrupulatny
me·tre *Brt.,* me·ter *Am.* ['mi:tə] metr *m*
met·ric ['metrɪk] (~ally) metryczny;
'~ sys·tem system *m* metryczny
met·ro·pol·i·tan [metrə'pɒlɪtən] wielkomiejski, metropolitalny, stołeczny
met·tle ['metl]: *show one's ~* wykazać
się owagę; *try s.o.'s ~* podawać ⟨-dać⟩
kogoś próbie
Mex·i·can ['meksɪkən] 1. meksykański;
2. Meksykanin *m* (-anka *f*)
Mex·i·co ['meksɪkəʊ] Meksyk *m*
mi·aow [mi:'aʊ] ⟨za⟩miauczeć
mice [maɪs] *pl. od* **mouse**
mi·cro... ['maɪkrəʊ] mikro...
mi·cro|·chip ['maɪkrəʊtʃɪp] układ *m*
scalony; ~com'put·er mikrokompu-
ter *m*
mi·cro·phone ['maɪkrəfəʊn] mikrofon *m*
mi·cro·pro·ces·sor [maɪkrəʊ'prəʊse-
sə] mikroprocesor *m*
mi·cro·scope ['maɪkrəskəʊp] mikro-
skop *m*
mi·cro·wave ['maɪkrəweɪv] mikrofala *f*;
attr. mikrofalowy; → ~ 'ov·en kuchenka *f* mikrofalowa
mid [mɪd] środkowy; ~'air: *in* ~*air* powietrzu; '~·day 1. południe *n*; 2. południowy
mid·dle ['mɪdl] 1. środkowy; 2. środek
m; ~·'aged w średnim wieku; 2 'Ag·es
średniowiecze *n*; ~ 'class(·es *pl.*) klasa *f* średnia; '~·man (*pl.* -men) *econ.*
pośrednik *m*; ~ 'name drugie imię *n*;
~·'sized o średnim rozmiarze;
'~·weight (*w boksie*) waga *f* średnia
mid·dling ['mɪdlɪŋ] F średni, przeciętny
'mid·field *zwł.* (*w piłce nożnej*) środek
boiska *m*; '~·er, ~ 'play·er (*w piłce nożnej*) pomocnik *m*
midge [mɪdʒ] *zo.* komar *m*
midg·et ['mɪdʒɪt] karzeł *m* (-rlica *f*), liliput *m*
'mid|·night północ *f*; *at* ~*night* o północ-
cy; ~st [mɪdst]: *in the* ~*st of* w środku
(*G*); '~·sum·mer środek *m* lata; *astr.*
przesilenie *n* letnie; '~·way w połowie
drogi; '~·wife (*pl.* -wives) położna *f*;

~·'win·ter środek *m* zimy; *astr.* przesilenie *n* zimowe
might [maɪt] **1.** *pret. od* **may; 2.** moc *f*,
siła *f*; potęga *f*; '~·y (-ier, -iest) potężny
mi·grate [maɪ'greɪt] migrować (*też zo.*);
⟨wy⟩wędrować; mi·gra·tion [maɪ-
'greɪʃn] migracja *f*, wędrówka *f*; mi-
gra·to·ry ['maɪgrətərɪ] wędrowny (*też
zo.*); migracyjny
mike [maɪk] F mikrofon *m*
Mi·lan Mediolan *m*
mild [maɪld] łagodny
mil·dew ['mɪldju:] *bot.* pleśń *f*
'mild·ness łagodność *f*
mile [maɪl] mila *f (1,6 km)*
mile·age ['maɪlɪdʒ] odległość *f lub* długość *f* w milach; *też* ~ **allowance** zwrot
m kosztów podróży
'mile·stone kamień *m* milowy (*też fig.*)
mil·i·tant ['mɪlɪtənt] bojowy, wojowniczy
mil·i·ta·ry ['mɪlɪtərɪ] 1. militarny; wojskowy; 2. *the* ~ wojsko *n*; ~ 'gov·ern-
ment rząd *m* wojskowy; ~ po'lice
(*skrót:* **MP**) żandarmeria *f lub* policja *f*
wojskowa
mi·li·tia [mɪ'lɪʃə] straż *f* miejska
milk [mɪlk] 1. mleko; *attr.* mleczny, z mleka; *it's no use crying over spilt* ~
co się stało, to się nie odstanie; 2. *v/t.*
⟨wy⟩doić; *v/i.* dawać ⟨dać⟩ mleko;
~·man (*pl.* -men) mleczarz *m*); ~·'powder mleko *n* w proszku; ~ 'shake koktajl *m* mleczny; '~·sop maminsynek *m*;
'~ tooth (*pl.* - teeth) ząb *m* mleczny;
'~·y (-ier, -iest) mleczny; 2·y 'Way *astr.*
Droga *f* Mleczna
mill [mɪl] 1. młyn *m*; młynek *m*; fabryka *f*, wytwórnia *f*; 2. ⟨z⟩mielić *lub*
⟨ze⟩mleć; *metal* frezować; *monety*
⟨wy⟩tłoczyć; ~ *about,* ~ *around* kotło-
wać się
mil·le·pede ['mɪlɪpi:d] *zo.* → *millipede*
'mill·er młynarz *m*
'mil·let ['mɪlɪt] *bot.* proso *n*
mil·li·ner ['mɪlɪnə] modystka *f*
mil·lion ['mɪljən] milion *m*; ~·aire
[mɪljə'neə] milioner *m*; ~th ['mɪljənθ]
1. milionowy; 2. jedna *f* milionowa
mil·li·pede ['mɪlɪpi:d] *zo.* stonoga *f*
'mill·stone kamień *m* młyński
milt [mɪlt] mlecz *m*
mime [maɪm] 1. pantomima *f*; mim *m*;

M

migi *pl.*; **2.** pokazywać ⟨-zać⟩ na migi

mim·ic ['mɪmɪk] **1.** mimiczny; **2.** mimik *m*; imitator *m*; **3.** (**-ck-**) imitować, naśladować; ~·**ry** ['mɪmɪkrɪ] mimikra *f*

mince [mɪns] **1.** *v/t.* ⟨po⟩siekać, ⟨z⟩mielić *lub* ⟨ze⟩mleć; *he doesn't ~ matters lub his words* mówi prosto z mostu; *v/i.* ⟨po⟩dreptać; **2.** *też ~d meat* mięso *n* siekane; '~**·meat** *słodkie* nadzienie *n* do ciasta; ~'**pie** ciasto *n* nadziewane bakaliami; '**minc·er** maszynka *f* do mięsa

mind [maɪnd] **1.** umysł *m*; rozum *m*; myśli *pl.*, głowa *f*; duch *m*; zdanie *n*; *be out of one's ~* nie być przy zdrowych zmysłach; *bear lub keep in ~* ⟨za⟩pamiętać, nie zapominać ⟨-mnieć⟩; *change one's ~* zmieniać ⟨-nić⟩ zdanie; *come into sb's ~* przychodzić ⟨-yjść⟩ komuś do głowy; *give s.o. a piece of one's ~* wygarnąć komuś; *have a ~* nie mieć chęci zrobić (*A*); *have a half ~ to* nie mieć zbytnio chęci zrobić (*A*); *lose one's ~* postradać zmysły; *make up one's ~* zdecydować się; *to my ~* według mnie; **2.** uważać (na *A*); mieć coś przeciwko (*D*), sprzeciwiać ⟨-wić⟩ się; ⟨za⟩troszczyć się o (*A*); *~ the step!* uwaga, stopień!; *~ your own business!* zajmij się swoimi sprawami!; *do you ~ if I smoke?, do you ~ my smoking?* czy będzie panu przeszkadzało, jak zapalę?; *would you ~ opening the window?* czy mógłby pan otworzyć okno?; *would you ~ coming* czy mógłby pan przyjechać?; ~ (*you*) proszę zauważyć; *never ~!* nie szkodzi!; *I don't ~* wszystko mi jedno; '~**·less** bezmyślny; *~·less of s.th.* nie zważając na coś

mine¹ [maɪn] mój, moje; *that's ~* to moje

mine² [maɪn] **1.** kopalnia *f* (*też fig.*); *mil.* mina *f*; **2.** wydobywać ⟨-być⟩ (*for A*) ⟨wy⟩eksploatować; *mil.* zaminowywać ⟨-ować⟩; '**min·er** górnik *m*

min·e·ral ['mɪnərəl] minerał *m*; *attr.* mineralny; ~**s** *pl. Brt. słodkie* napoje *pl. gazowane*; *~ oil* olej *m* mineralny; '~ **wa·ter** woda *f* mineralna

min·gle ['mɪŋgl] ⟨wy⟩mieszać (się); wmieszać się (*with* do *G*)

min·i... ['mɪnɪ] mini...; → *miniskirt*

min·i·a·ture ['mɪnətʃə] **1.** miniatura *f*; **2.** miniaturowy; ~ '**cam·e·ra** fotograficzny aparat *m* miniaturowy

min·i|·mize ['mɪnɪmaɪz] ⟨z⟩minimalizować; zmniejszać ⟨-szyć⟩, pomniejszać ⟨-szyć⟩, ⟨z⟩bagatelizować; ~·**mum** ['mɪnɪməm] (*pl. -ma* [-mə], *-mums*) **1.** minimum *n*; **2.** minimalny

min·ing ['maɪnɪŋ] górnictwo *n*; górniczy

min·i·on ['mɪnjən] *pej. fig.* sługus *m*, fagas *m*

'**min·i·skirt** minispódniczka *f*

min·is·ter ['mɪnɪstə] minister *m*; *rel.* duchowny *m*

min·is·try ['mɪnɪstrɪ] ministerstwo *n*; *rel.* urząd *m* duchowny

mink [mɪŋk] *zo.* (*pl. mink*) norka *f*

mi·nor ['maɪnə] **1.** mniejszy, *fig.* nieznaczny, drobny; *jur.* niepełnoletni; *A ~* mus. a-moll *n*; ~ *key* mus. tonacja *f* molowa; **2.** *jur.* niepełnoletni *m* (*-nia f*); *Am. univ.* specjalizacja *f* dodatkowa; *mus.* moll; ~·**i·ty** [maɪ'nɒrətɪ] mniejszość *f*; *jur.* niepełnoletniość *f*

min·ster ['mɪnstə] kościół *m* opacki

mint¹ [mɪnt] **1.** mennica *f*; **2.** bić

mint² [mɪnt] *bot.* mięta *f*

min·u·et [mɪnjʊ'et] *mus.* menuet *m*

mi·nus ['maɪnəs] **1.** *prp.* odjąć; poniżej; F bez (*G*); **2.** *adj.* minusowy, ujemny; **3.** minus *m* (*też fig.*)

min·ute¹ ['mɪnɪt] minuta *f*; *in a ~* za chwilę; *just a ~!* chwileczkę!; *~s pl.* protokół *m*

mi·nute² [maɪ'njuːt] mały, maleńki; drobiazgowy

mir·a·cle ['mɪrəkl] cud *m*

mi·rac·u·lous [mɪ'rækjʊləs] cudowny; ~·**ly** cudownie

mi·rage ['mɪrɑːʒ] miraż *m*, fatamorgana *f*

mire ['maɪə] szlam *m*; *drag through the ~ fig.* obsmarowywać

mir·ror ['mɪrə] **1.** lustro *n*, zwierciadło *n*; **2.** odzwierciedlać ⟨-lić⟩

mirth [mɜːθ] wesołość *f*

mis... [mɪs] niewłaściwie ..., źle ...

mis·ad·ven·ture niepowodzenie *n*; *jur. Brt.* nieszczęśliwy wypadek *m*

mis·an·thrope ['mɪzənθrəʊp], ~·**thro·pist** [mɪ'zænθrəpɪst] mizantrop *m*

mis·ap·ply źle ⟨za⟩stosować

mis·ap·pre·hend źle ⟨z⟩rozumieć

M

mis·ap'pro·pri·ate sprzeniewierzać ⟨-rzyć⟩

mis·be'have niewłaściwie się zachowywać ⟨-wać⟩

mis·cal·cu·late przeliczyć się; źle obliczyć

mis·car|·riage *med.* poronienie *n*; błąd *m*, pomyłka *f*; **~riage of justice** *jur.* błąd *m* sądowy; **~·ry** *med.* poronić; popełniać ⟨-nić⟩ błąd

mis·cel·la|·ne·ous [mɪsɪ'leɪnjəs] różnoraki, różnorodny; **~·ny** [mɪ'selənɪ] różnorodność *f*; różnorakość *f*; zbiór *m*

mis·chief ['mɪstʃɪf] figlowanie *n*, dokazywanie *n*; figlarność *f*, psotliwość *f*; szkoda *f*; '**~·mak·er** figlarz *m*, psotnik *m* (-nica *f*)

mis·chie·vous ['mɪstʃɪvəs] figlarny, psotliwy; szelmowski

mis·con·ceive źle ⟨z⟩rozumieć, źle pojmować ⟨-jąć⟩

mis·con·duct 1. [mɪs'kɒndʌkt] złe zachowanie *n*; niewłaściwe prowadzenie się; **2.** [mɪskən'dʌkt] źle prowadzić; **~ o.s.** źle się prowadzić

mis·con·strue [mɪskən'struː] źle ⟨z⟩interpretować

mis'deed zły czyn *m*, nieprawość *f*

mis·de·mea·no(u)r [mɪsdɪ'miːnə] *jur.* wykroczenie *n*, występek *m*

mis·di·rect źle ⟨s⟩kierować; *list itp.* źle ⟨za⟩adresować

mise-en-scène [miːzãːn'seɪn] *theat.* inscenizacja *f*

mi·ser ['maɪzə] skąpiec *m*

mis·e·ra·ble ['mɪzərəbl] żałosny, nieszczęsny; nędzny

'**mi·ser·ly** skąpy; *fig.* nędzny

mis·e·ry ['mɪzərɪ] niedola *f*, nieszczęście *n*; ubóstwo *n*

mis'fire broń zawodzić ⟨-wieść⟩; *mot.* nie zapalać ⟨-lić⟩; *fig.* nawalać ⟨-lić⟩

'**mis·fit** człowiek *m* niedostosowany

mis'for·tune nieszczęście *n*

mis'giv·ing obawa *f*, niepokój *m*

mis'guid·ed mylny, opaczny

mis·hap ['mɪshæp] nieszczęście *n*; **without ~** bez wypadku

mis·in'form źle ⟨po⟩informować

mis·in'ter·pret źle ⟨z⟩interpretować, mylnie ⟨wy⟩tłumaczyć

mis'lay (-*laid*) zagubić, podziać

mis'lead zwodzić ⟨zwieść⟩

mis'man·age źle zarządzać

mis'place kłaść ⟨położyć⟩ na niewłaściwym miejscu; **~d** *fig.* nie na miejscu, niestosowny

mis'print 1. [mɪs'prɪnt] źle ⟨wy⟩drukować; **2.** ['mɪsprɪnt] omyłka *f* w druku

mis'read (-*read* [-red]) źle odczytywać ⟨-tać⟩

mis·rep·re'sent błędnie przedstawiać ⟨-wić⟩, przekręcać ⟨-cić⟩

miss¹ [mɪs] **1.** *v/t.* chybiać ⟨-bić⟩ (*G*), nie trafiać ⟨-fić⟩ do (*G*); opuszczać ⟨opuścić⟩; spóźniać ⟨-nić⟩ się na (*A*); tęsknić za (*I*); *też* **~ out** pomijać ⟨-minąć⟩; *v/i.* chybiać ⟨-bić⟩, spóźniać ⟨-nić⟩ się; **~ out on** ⟨s⟩tracić na (*L*); **2.** chybienie *n*, niecelny strzał *m*

miss² [mɪs] (*z następującym nazwiskiem* 2) panna *f*

mis·shap·en zniekształcony

mis·sile ['mɪsaɪl, *Am.* 'mɪsəl] pocisk *m*; *mil.* pocisk *m* rakietowy, rakieta *f*; *attr.* rakietowy

'**miss·ing** brakujący; **be ~** brakować; (*mil. też* **~ in action**) zaginiony; **be ~** *mil.* zaginąć

mis·sion ['mɪʃn] misja *f* (*też pol., rel.*); *mil.* zadanie *n*; *aviat., mil.* lot *m*; posłannictwo *n*; **~·a·ry** ['mɪʃənrɪ] **1.** misjonarz *m* (-rka *f*); **2.** *adj.* misyjny

Mis·sis·sip·pi Missisipi *f*

mis'spell (-*spelt lub* -*spelled*) źle (na)pisać

mis'spend (-*spent*) rozrzutnie wydawać ⟨-dać⟩

mist [mɪst] **1.** (*lekka lub drobna*) mgła *f*; **2.** **~ over** zaparowywać ⟨-ować⟩; zachodzić ⟨zajść⟩ mgłą; **~ up** zaparowywać ⟨-ować⟩

mis'take 1. (-*took*, -*taken*) wziąć (*kogoś* **for** za *A*); ⟨po⟩mylić (się); źle ⟨z⟩rozumieć; **2.** pomyłka *f*, błąd *m*; **by ~take** przez pomyłkę, pomyłkowo; **~'tak·en** pomyłkowy, błędny

mis·ter ['mɪstə] (*używa się jedynie jako skrótu przed nazwiskiem*) → **Mr**

mis·tle·toe ['mɪsltəʊ] *bot.* jemioła *f*

mis·tress ['mɪstrɪs] pani *f*; *zwł. Brt.* nauczycielka *f*; ukochana *f*, kochanka *f*

mis'trust 1. nie ufać (*D*), nie wierzyć (*D*); **2.** nieufność *f* (*of* wobec *G*); **~·ful** nieufny

mist·y ['mɪstɪ] (-*ier*, -*iest*) zamglony

mis·un·der'stand (-*stood*) źle ⟨z⟩rozumieć; **~·ing** nieporozumienie *n*;

niezrozumienie *n*

mis·use 1. [mɪs'juːz] niewłaściwie używać ⟨-żyć⟩; nadużywać ⟨-żyć⟩; **2.** [mɪs'juːs] niewłaściwe użycie *n*; nadużycie

mite [maɪt] *zo.* roztocz *m*; *Brt.* F berbeć *m*; **a ~** F trochę, nieco

mi·tre *Brt.*, **mi·ter** *Am.* ['maɪtə] mitra *f*, infuła *f*

mitt [mɪt] (*w baseballu*) rękawica *f* (*do łapania piłki*); *sl.* łapa *f*; → **mitten**

mit·ten ['mɪtn] rękawiczka *f* (*z jednym palcem*)

mix [mɪks] **1.** ⟨z-, wy⟩mieszać (się); ⟨z⟩miksować (się); *drink itp.* ⟨z⟩robić; zadawać się (**with** z *I*); **~ well** mieć łatwość nawiązywania kontaktów; **~ up** ⟨z⟩mieszać; ⟨po⟩mieszać; *kogoś* pomylić (**with** z *I*); **be ~ed up** być wmieszanym (**in** w *L*); być zmieszanym; **2.** mieszanka *f*; **~ed** wymieszany; zmieszany; pomieszany; '**~·er** mikser *m*; *tech.* mieszarka *f*, mieszadło *n*; **concrete ~er** betoniarka *f*; **be a bad ~er** źle nawiązywać kontakty towarzyskie; **~·ture** ['mɪkstʃə] mieszanka *f*

MO [em 'əʊ] *skrót*: **money order** przekaz *m* pieniężny, polecenie *n* wypłaty

moan [məʊn] **1.** jęczenie *n*, jęk *m*; **2.** ⟨za⟩jęczeć

moat [məʊt] fosa *f*

mob [mɒb] **1.** motłoch *m*, tłum *m*; zgraja *f*; **2.** (**-bb-**) otaczać ⟨otoczyć⟩, osaczać ⟨-czyć⟩

mo·bile ['məʊbaɪl] **1.** ruchomy, mobilny; przewoźny; *mil.* zmotoryzowany; **2.** → **mobile telephone; ~** mieszkalna; **~ 'tel·e·phone**, **~ 'phone** telefon *m* komórkowy, F komórka *f*

mo·bil·ize ['məʊbɪlaɪz] ⟨z⟩mobilizować; *mil.* przeprowadzać ⟨-dzić⟩ mobilizację

moc·ca·sin ['mɒkəsɪn] mokasyn *m*

mock [mɒk] **1.** *v/t.* naśmiewać się z (*A*); przedrzeźniać (*G*); *v/i.* **~ at** naśmiewać się, z (*A*); **2.** niby-, quasi-; pseudo-; **~·e·ry** ['mɒkərɪ] kpina *f*, kpiny *pl.*; '**~·ing·bird** *zo.* przedrzeźniacz *m*

mod cons [mɒd 'kɒnz] *Brt.* F *pl.*: **with all ~** ze wszelkimi wygodami

mode [məʊd] tryb *m* (*pracy, życia*); sposób *m*; *tech.* mod *m*

mod·el ['mɒdl] **1.** model *m*; wzór *m*, wzorzec *m*; model(ka *f*) *m*; **2.** modelowy; wzorcowy; idealny; **3.** *v/t.* (*zwł. Brt.* **-ll-**, *Am.* **-l-**) ⟨wy⟩modelować, ⟨u⟩formować; budować model (*G*); *ubranie itp.* ⟨za⟩prezentować; *v/i.* pracować jako model(ka); pozować

mo·dem ['məʊdem] *komp.* modem *m*

mod·e·rate 1. ['mɒdərət] umiarkowany; *rozmiar, zdolności:* przeciętny; **2.** ['mɒdəreɪt] ⟨z⟩łagodzić; ⟨ze⟩lżeć; **~·ra·tion** [mɒdə'reɪʃn] umiarkowanie *n*, złagodzenie *n*

mod·ern ['mɒdən] współczesny, nowy; nowoczesny; **~·ize** ['mɒdənaɪz] ⟨z⟩modernizować

mod·est ['mɒdɪst] skromny; '**~·es·ty** skromność *f*

mod·i·fi·ca·tion [mɒdɪfɪ'keɪʃn] modyfikacja *f*; **~·fy** ['mɒdɪfaɪ] ⟨z⟩modyfikować

mod·u·late ['mɒdjʊleɪt] ⟨z⟩modulować

mod·ule ['mɒdjuːl] *tech.* moduł *m*; (*w astronautyce*) człon *m*

moist [mɔɪst] wilgotny; **~·en** ['mɔɪsn] *v/t.* zwilżać ⟨-żyć⟩; *v/i.* ⟨z⟩wilgotnieć; **mois·ture** ['mɔɪstʃə] wilgoć *m*

mo·lar ['məʊlə] *anat.* ząb *m* trzonowy

mo·las·ses [mə'læsɪz] *Am. sg.* melasa *m*, syrop *m*

mole[1] [məʊl] *zo.* kret *m*

mole[2] [məʊl] pieprzyk *m*; myszka *f*

mole[3] [məʊl] molo *n*

mol·e·cule ['mɒlɪkjuːl] molekuła *f*

'**mole·hill** kretowisko *n*; **make a mountain out of a ~** robić z igły widły

mo·lest [məʊ'lest] napastować

mol·li·fy ['mɒlɪfaɪ] ⟨u⟩łagodzić, uspokajać ⟨-koić⟩ się

mol·ly·cod·dle ['mɒlɪkɒdl] F *dziecko* rozpuszczać ⟨-puścić⟩

mol·ten ['məʊltən] stopiony, roztopiony

mom [mɒm] F mamusia *f*

mo·ment ['məʊmənt] moment *m*, chwila *f*; znaczenie *n*; *phys.* moment *m*; **mo·men·ta·ry** ['məʊməntərɪ] chwilowy; **mo·men·tous** [məʊ'mentəs] znaczący, doniosły; **mo·men·tum** [məʊ'mentəm] (*pl.* **-ta** [-tə], **-tums**) *phys.* moment *m*; rozmach *m*, impet *m*

Mon *skrót pisany*: **Monday** pon., poniedziałek *m*

mon·arch ['mɒnək] monarcha *m*; '**~·ar·chy** monarchia *f*

M

mon·as·tery ['mɒnəstrɪ] klasztor *m*

Mon·day ['mʌndɪ] poniedziałek *m*

mon·e·ta·ry ['mʌnɪtərɪ] monetarny; pieniężny; walutowy

mon·ey ['mʌnɪ] pieniądze *pl.*; *attr.* pieniężny; '~·box *Brt.* skarbonka *f*; '~·chang·er właściciel(ka *f*) *m* kantoru wymiany pieniędzy; *zwł. Am.* automat *m* do rozmieniania pieniędzy; '~ or·der przekaz *m* pieniężny

mon·ger ['mʌŋgə] *w złożeniach* handlarz *m*, kupiec *m*

mon·grel ['mʌŋgrəl] kundel *m*

mon·i·tor ['mɒnɪtə] **1.** monitor *m*; wskaźnik *m* kontrolny, ekran *m* kontrolny; **2.** monitorować; nadzorować; wsłuchiwać się w (*A*)

monk [mʌŋk] mnich *m*

mon·key ['mʌŋkɪ] **1.** *ogoniasta* małpa *f*; F psotnik *m*; **make a ~ (out) of s.o.** ⟨z⟩robić sobie żarty z kogoś; **2.** **~ about**, **~ around** F wydurniać się; '~ wrench klucz *m* nastawny; **throw a ~ wrench into s.th.** *Am.* wsadzać kij w szprychy; '~ busi·ness ciemne interesy *pl.*

mon·o ['mɒnəʊ] **1.** (*pl. -os*) dźwięk *m* mono *n*; **2.** mono...

mon·o... ['mɒnəʊ]..., pojedynczy

mon·o·logue *zwł. Brt.*, mon·o·log *Am.* ['mɒnəlɒg] monolog *m*

mo·nop·o·lize [mə'nɒpəlaɪz] ⟨z⟩monopolizować; ⟨z⟩dominować; ~·ly monopol *m* (*of* na *A*)

mo·not·o·nous [mə'nɒtənəs] monotonny; ~·ny monotonia *f*

mon·soon [mɒn'suːn] monsun *m*

mon·ster ['mɒnstə] monstrum *n*, potwór *m*; *attr.* monstrualny

mon·stros·i·ty [mɒn'strɒsətɪ] monstrualność *f*; monstrum *n*; ~·strous ['mɒnstrəs] potworny, monstrualny

Montenegro Czarnogóra *f*

month [mʌnθ] miesiąc *m*; '~·ly **1.** miesięczny; **2.** miesięcznik *m*; F *zwł. Am.* miesiączka *f*

mon·u·ment ['mɒnjʊmənt] pomnik *m*, monument *m*; ~·al [mɒnjʊ'mentl] monumentalny

moo [muː] ⟨za⟩ryczeć

mood [muːd] nastrój *m*, humor *m*; **be in a good (bad) ~** być w dobrym (złym) nastroju; '~·y (*-ier, -iest*) humorzasty

moon [muːn] **1.** księżyc *m*; **once in a blue ~** F od wielkiego dzwonu; **2.** **~ about**, **~ around** F pętać się; F dumać; '~·light światło *n* księżycowe; '~·lit oświetlony księżycem; '~·shine *sl.* samogon *m*; '~·struck F trzepnięty

moor¹ [mʊə] wrzosowisko *n*

moor² [mʊə] *naut.* ⟨za-, przy⟩cumować; ~·ing ['mʊərɪŋz] *naut.* cumowisko *n*; ~·ings *pl.* cumy *pl.*, liny *pl.* cumownicze

moose [muːs] (*pl.* **moose**) północnoamerykański łoś *m*

mop [mɒp] **1.** zmywak *m*, myjka *f*; grzywa *f*, kudły *pl.*; **2.** (*-pp-*) *też* **~ up** ścierać ⟨zetrzeć⟩, zmywać ⟨zmyć⟩

mope [məʊp] mieć chandrę, być w depresji

mo·ped ['məʊped] *Brt.* moped *m*

mor·al ['mɒrəl] **1.** moralny, prawy; **2.** morał *m*, nauka *f*; **~s** *pl.* moralność *f*; mo·rale [mɒ'rɑːl] morale *n*; mor·al·ize ['mɒrəlaɪz] moralizować (*about*, *on* na temat *G*)

mor·bid ['mɔːbɪd] chorobliwy

more [mɔː] **1.** *adj.* więcej; jeszcze (*więcej*); **some ~ tea** jeszcze trochę herbaty; **2.** *adv.* bardziej; jeszcze (*troche*); **~ and ~** coraz bardziej; **~ or less** mniej lub bardziej; **once ~** jeszcze raz; **the ~ so because** tym bardziej, że; *przy tworzeniu comp.* **~ important** ważniejszy; **~ often** częściej; **3.** więcej (*of G*, *than* niż); **a little ~** trochę więcej *lub* bardziej

mo·rel [mɒ'rel] *bot.* smardz *m*

more·o·ver [mɔː'rəʊvə] ponadto, poza tym

morgue [mɔːg] kostnica *f*

morn·ing ['mɔːnɪŋ] rano *n*, poranek *m*; **good ~!** dzień dobry!; **in the ~** rano, ranem; przed południem; **tomorrow ~** jutro rano

mo·rose [mə'rəʊs] ponury

mor·phi·a ['mɔːfjə], ~·phine ['mɔːfiːn] morfina *f*

mor·sel ['mɔːsl] kąsek *m*; **a ~ of** odrobina (*G*)

mor·tal ['mɔːtl] **1.** śmiertelny; **2.** śmiertelnik *m*; ~·i·ty [mɔː'tælətɪ] śmiertelność *f*

mor·tar¹ ['mɔːtə] zaprawa *f* murarska

mor·tar² ['mɔːtə] moździerz *m*

mort·gage ['mɔːgɪdʒ] hipoteka *f*; dług *m* hipoteczny; wpis *m* hipoteczny; **2.** obciążać ⟨-żyć⟩ hipotekę

mor·ti·cian [mɔː'tɪʃn] *Am.* przedsiębiorca *m* pogrzebowy

mor·ti|·fi·ca·tion [mɔːtɪfɪ'keɪʃn] wstyd *n*; umartwianie *n* się; **~·fy** ['mɔːtɪfaɪ] zawstydzać 〈-dzić〉; umartwiać 〈-twić〉 się

mor·tu·a·ry ['mɔːtjʊərɪ] kostnica *f*

mo·sa·ic [mə'zeɪɪk] mozaika *f*; *attr.* mozaikowy

Mos·cow Moskwa *f*

Mos·lem ['mɒzləm] → **Muslim**

mosque [mɒsk] meczet *m*

mos·qui·to [mə'skiːtəʊ] *zo.* (*pl.* **-to(e)s**) moskit *m*

moss [mɒs] *bot.* mech *m*; **'~·y** *bot.* (**-ier, -iest**) omszały

most [məʊst] **1.** *adj.* najwięcej; większość; **~ people** *pl.* większość ludzi *pl.*; **2.** *adv.* najwięcej; **~ of all** najwięcej; *przed adj.* najbardziej; *też przy tworzeniu sup.* **the ~ important** najważniejszy; **3.** *at (the)* ~ co najwyżej; *make the ~ of s.th.* wykorzystać 〈-tać〉 coś do maksimum; **'~·ly** przeważnie, głównie

MOT [em əʊ 'tiː] *Brt.* F *też* **~ test** *jakby*: kontrola *f* sprawności pojazdu

mo·tel [məʊ'tel] motel *m*

moth [mɒθ] *zo.* ćma *f*; mól *m*; **'~·eat·en** zżarty przez mole

moth·er ['mʌðə] **1.** matka *f*; *attr.* ojczysty, rodzimy; krajowy; **2.** matkować (*D*); **'~·coun·try** ojczyzna *f*; **'~·hood** macierzyństwo *n*; **~·in-law** ['mʌðərɪnlɔː] (*pl.* **mothers-in-law**) teściowa *f*; **'~·ly** matczyny; macierzyński; **~·of-pearl** [mʌðərəv'pɜːl] macica *f* perłowa; **~·tongue** język *m* ojczysty

mo·tif [məʊ'tiːf] (*w sztuce, muzyce*) motyw *m*; deseń *m*

mo·tion ['məʊʃn] **1.** ruch *m*; *parl.* wniosek *m*; *put lub set in* ~ wprawić w ruch; *fig.* nadawać *czemuś* bieg; **2.** *v/t.* skinąć na (*A*); wzywać 〈wezwać〉 gestem (*G*); *v/i.* skinąć, kiwnąć; **'~·less** nieruchomy; **~ 'pic·ture** *Am.* film *m*

mo·ti|·vate ['məʊtɪveɪt] nakłaniać 〈-łonić〉, zachęcać 〈-cić〉; 〈s〉powodować; **~·va·tion** [məʊtɪ'veɪʃn] motywacja *f*, pobudka *f*

mo·tive ['məʊtɪv] **1.** motyw *m*, pobudka *f*; **2.** napędowy (*też fig.*)

mot·ley ['mɒtlɪ] pstrokaty, różnoraki

mo·to·cross ['məʊtəʊkrɒs] (*w sporcie*) motokros *m*

mo·tor ['məʊtə] motor *m*, silnik *m*; siła *f* napędowa; *attr.* motoryzacyjny; **'~·bike** *Brt.* F motorower *m*; **'~·boat** motorówka *f*; **'~·cade** ['məʊtəkeɪd] kolumna *f* samochodów; **'~·car** *Brt.* samochód *m*; **'~·car·a·van** *Brt.* samochód *m* mieszkalny; **'~·cy·cle** motocykl *m*; **'~·cyc·list** motocyklista *m*; **'~ home** *Am.* samochód *m* mieszkalny; **~·ing** ['məʊtərɪŋ] jazda *f* samochodem; *school of ~ing* szkoła *f* nauki jazdy; *attr.* samochodowy; **~·ist** ['məʊtərɪst] kierowca *m*; **~·ize** ['məʊtəraɪz] 〈z〉motoryzować; **'~ launch** motorówka *f*; **'~·way** *Brt.* autostrada *f*

mot·tled ['mɒtld] cętkowany

mo(u)ld[1] [məʊld] pleśń *f*; próchnica *f*

mo(u)ld[2] [məʊld] **1.** *tech.* forma *f* odlewnicza; **2.** *tech.* odlewać 〈-lać〉

mo(u)l·der ['məʊldə] *też* **~ away** rozkładać 〈-łożyć〉 się

mo(u)ld·y ['məʊldɪ] (**-ier, -iest**) zapleśniały, spleśniały; stęchły, zatęchły

mo(u)lt [məʊlt] pierzyć się; *włosy* 〈s〉tracić

mound [maʊnd] wzgórek *m*; kopiec *m*

mount [maʊnt] **1.** *v/t.* dosiadać 〈-siąść〉 (*G*), *konia* wsiąść na (*A*); 〈z〉montować (*też fig.*); zamontowywać 〈-ować〉; wspinać 〈-piąć〉 się; *obraz itp.* oprawiać 〈-wić〉; *kamień szlachetny* oprawiać 〈-wić〉; **~ed police** policja *f* konna; *v/i.* dosiadać 〈-siąść〉 konia; wzrastać 〈-rosnąć〉; **~ up** 〈na〉gromadzić się; **2.** zawieszenie *n*, podstawa *f*; oprawa *f*; wierzchowiec *m*; (*w nazwach*) góra *f*

moun·tain ['maʊntɪn] **1.** góra *f*; **2.** górski; **'~ bike** rower *m* górski

moun·tain·eer [maʊntɪ'nɪə] alpinista *m* (-tka *f*); **~·eer·ing** [maʊntɪ'nɪərɪŋ] alpinistyka *f*

moun·tain·ous ['maʊntɪnəs] górzysty

mourn [mɔːn] opłakiwać 〈-kać〉 (*for, over A*), żałować; **'~·er** żałobnik *m* (-nica *f*); **'~·ful** żałobny; **'~·ing** żałoba *f*

mouse [maʊs] (*pl. mice* [maɪs]) mysz *f*, (*pl. też mouses*) *komp.* mysz *f*

mous·tache [mə'stɑːʃ] *też* **mustache** wąsy *pl.*

mouth [maʊθ] (*pl. mouths* [maʊðz]) usta *pl.*; pysk *m* (*zwierzęcia*); ujście *n* (*rzeki*); otwór *m* (*pojemnika*); **'~·ful** kęs *m*; **'~·or·gan** *ustna* harmonijka *f*, F organki *pl.*; **'~·piece** ustnik *m*; *fig.*

M

rzecznik *m* (-czka *f*); '~·wash płyn *m*
do ust

mo·va·ble ['mu:vəbl] ruchomy

move [mu:v] **1.** *v*/*t*. ruszać (-szyć); poruszać (-szyć); przesuwać (-unąć); (*w szachach*) ⟨z⟩robić ruch (*D*); *parl.* stawiać ⟨postawić⟩ wniosek; wzruszać (-szyć); ~ **house** przeprowadzać (-dzić) się; ~ **heaven and earth** poruszać niebo i ziemię; *v*/*i*. ruszać (-szyć) się; poruszać (-szyć) się; przesuwać (-unąć) się; przeprowadzać (-dzić) się, przenosić (-nieść) się (**to** do *G*); (*w szachach*) robić ruch; ~ **away** wyprowadzać (-dzić) się; ~ **in** wprowadzać (-dzić) się; ~ **on** iść ⟨pójść⟩ dalej; ~ **out** wyprowadzać (-dzić) się; **2.** ruch *m*; *fig.* posunięcie *n*, krok *m*; (*w szachach*) ruch *m*, posunięcie *n*; przeprowadzka *f*; **on the** ~ w ruchu; **get a** ~ **on!** F ruszaj się!; '~·a·ble → **movable**; '~·ment ruch (*też fig.*); *mus.* część *f*; *tech.* mechanizm *m*

mov·ie ['mu:vɪ] *zwł. Am.* film *m*; kino *n*; *attr.* filmowy, kinowy; '~ cam·e·ra kamera *f* filmowa; '~ star *Am.* gwiazda *f* filmowa; '~ thea·ter *Am.* kino *n*

mov·ing ['mu:vɪŋ] ruszający się, ruchomy; *fig.* wzruszający; ~ 'stair·case ruchome schody *pl.*; '~ van *Am.* samochód *m* do przeprowadzek

mow [məʊ] (**mowed, mowed** *lub* **mown**) ⟨s⟩kosić; '~·er kosiarka *f*; ~n [məʊn] *p.p. od* **mow**

MP [em 'pi:] *skrót*: **Member of Parliament** *Brt.* poseł *m* (-słanka *f*); **military police** żandarmeria *f* wojskowa

mph *skrót pisany*: **miles per hour** mile na godzinę

Mr ['mɪstə] *skrót*: **Mister** pan *m*

Mrs ['mɪsɪz] *skrót*: **Mistress** pani *f*

MS *pl.* **MSS** *skrót pisany*: **manuscript** rękopis *m*

Ms [mɪz, məz] pani *f* (*neutralnie*)

Mt *skrót pisany*: **Mount** góra *f*

much [mʌtʃ] **1.** *adj.* (**more, most**) dużo; **2.** *adv.* bardzo; w złożeniach dużo; *przed comp.* znacznie; **very** ~ bardzo; **I thought as** ~ tak właśnie myślałem; **3.** *nothing* ~ nic szczególnego; **make** ~ **of** wiele sobie robić o (*G*); **think** ~ **of** mieć dobrą opinię o (*L*); **I am not** ~ **of a dancer** F nie tańczę najlepiej

muck [mʌk] F łajno *n*, gnój *m*; paskudztwo *n*, brud *m*

mu·cus ['mju:kəs] śluz *m*

mud [mʌd] błoto *n*; brud *m* (*też fig.*)

mud·dle ['mʌdl] **1.** rozgardiasz *m*; **be in a** ~ być skołowanym; **2.** *też* ~ **up** kogoś skołować; *coś* namieszać; ~ **through** F przebrnąć przez (*A*)

mud·dy ['mʌdɪ] (**-ier, -iest**) zabłocony; błotnisty, bagnisty; '~·guard błotnik *m*

mues·li ['mju:zlɪ] muesli *n* (*śniadaniowa mieszanka zbożowa*)

muff [mʌf] mufka *f*

muf·fin ['mʌfɪn] bułeczka *f* (*jedzona na gorąco*)

muf·fle ['mʌfl] *dźwięk* ⟨s⟩tłumić; *często* ~ **up** obwijać (-inąć), otulać (-lić); '~r (*gruby*) szalik *m*; *mot.* tłumik *m*

mug¹ [mʌg] kubek *m*, kufel *m*; *sl.* ryj *m*, morda *f*

mug² [mʌg] (**-gg-**) (*zwł. na ulicy*) napadać (-paść), ⟨z⟩rabować; ~·**ger** F rabuś *m*, napastnik *m*; '~·ging F rabunek *m*, napaść *m*

mug·gy ['mʌgɪ] parny, duszny

mul·ber·ry ['mʌlbərɪ] *bot.* morwa *f*

mule [mju:l] *zo.* muł *m*

mulled [mʌld]: ~ **wine** wino *n* grzane

mul·li·on ['mʌljən] *arch.* słupek *m* okienny

mul·ti... ['mʌltɪ] multi..., wielo...

mul·ti|·far·i·ous [mʌltɪ'feərɪəs] różnoraki, różnorodny; ~·lat·e·ral [mʌltɪ'lætərəl] wielostronny

mul·ti·ple ['mʌltɪpl] **1.** wielokrotny; **2.** *math.* wielokrotność *f*; ~'store *też* F **multiple** *zwł. Brt.* sklep *m* firmowy

mul·ti·pli·ca·tion [mʌltɪplɪ'keɪʃn] powielanie *n*; *math.* mnożenie *n*; ~ **table** tabliczka *f* mnożenia

mul·ti·pli·ci·ty [mʌltɪ'plɪsətɪ] wielokrotność *f*; wielość *f*

mul·ti·ply ['mʌltɪplaɪ] powielać (-lić); rozmnażać (-nożyć) (się); *math.* ⟨po⟩mnożyć (**by** przez *A*)

mul·ti|'pur·pose wielofunkcyjny; ~'sto·rey *Brt.* wielopiętrowy; ~·sto·rey 'car park *Brt.* parking *m* wielopiętrowy

mul·ti·tude ['mʌltɪtju:d] wielość *f*, mnogość *f*; ~·tu·di·nous [mʌltɪ'tju:dɪnəs] mnogi, liczny

mum¹ [mʌm] *Brt.* F mamusia *f*

mum² [mʌm] **1.** *int.*: ~'s **the word** ani słowa o tym!; buzia na kłódkę; **2.** *adj.*: **keep** ~ trzymać język za zębami

mum·ble ['mʌmbl] ⟨za-, wy⟩mamrotać
mum·mi·fy ['mʌmɪfaɪ] ⟨z⟩mumifikować
mum·my[1] ['mʌmɪ] mumia f
mum·my[2] ['mʌmɪ] Brt. F mamusia f
mumps [mʌmps] med. świnka f, naigminne zapalenie n przyusznicy
munch [mʌntʃ] ⟨z⟩żuć z chrzęstem, ⟨s⟩chrupać
mun·dane [mʌn'deɪn] przyziemny
Mu·nich Monachium n
mu·ni·ci·pal [mju:'nɪsɪpl] miejski; komunalny; **~ council** rada f miejska; **~·i·ty** [mju:nɪsɪ'pælətɪ] gmina f miejska
mu·ral ['mjʊərəl] 1. malowidło n ścienne; 2. ścienny
mur·der ['mɜːdə] 1. morderstwo n; 2. ⟨za⟩mordować; fig. wykończyć ⟨-kańczać⟩; **~·er** ['mɜːdərə] morderca m (-czyni f); **~·ess** ['mɜːdərɪs] morderczyni f; **~·ous** ['mɜːdərəs] morderczy
murk·y ['mɜːkɪ] (-ier, -iest) mroczny, nieprzejrzysty
mur·mur ['mɜːmə] 1. szmer m; szemranie n; 2. szemrać, ⟨wy⟩mamrotać
mus|·cle ['mʌsl] mięsień m, muskuł m; **'~·cle-bound:** be ~cle-bound być nadmiernie umięśnionym; **~·cu·lar** ['mʌskjʊlə] muskularny, umięśniony
muse[1] [mju:z] ⟨za⟩dumać (się), ⟨po⟩medytować (**on, over** nad I)
muse[2] [mju:z] też ♀ muza f
mu·se·um [mju:'zɪəm] muzeum n
mush [mʌʃ] bryja f, breja f; Am. zupa f z kukurydzy
mush·room ['mʌʃrom] 1. bot. grzyb m, zwł. pieczarka f; attr. grzybowy, pieczarkowy; 2. fig. wyrastać ⟨-rosnąć⟩jak grzyby po deszczu
mu·sic ['mju:zɪk] muzyka f; nuty pl.; **it was put** lub **set to ~** napisano do niego muzykę
'mu·si·cal 1. muzyczny; muzykalny; melodyjny; **2.** musical m; **'~ box** zwł. Brt. pozytywka f; **~ 'in·stru·ment** instrument m muzyczny
'mu·sic| box zwł. Am. pozytywka f; **'~·cen·tre** (Am.;**cen·ter**) sprzęt m stereo, wieża f stereo; **'~ hall** Brt. teatr m rewiowy, music-hall m
mu·si·cian [mju:'zɪʃn] muzyk m
'mu·sic stand pulpit m
musk [mʌsk] piżmo n; **'~ ox** (pl. **-oxen**) wół m piżmowy, piżmowół m; **'~·rat** szczur m piżmowy, piżmak m

Mus·lim ['mʊslɪm] 1. muzułmanin m (-anka f); 2. muzułmański
mus·quash ['mʌskwɒʃ] szczur m piżmowy, piżmak m; futro n z piżmaków
mus·sel ['mʌsl] małż m, zwł. omułek m
must[1] [mʌst] 1. v/aux. musieć; **you must not** (F **mustn't**) nie wolno ci; 2. konieczność f
must[2] [mʌst] moszcz m
mus·tache [mə'staːʃ] Am. wąsy pl.
mus·tard ['mʌstəd] musztarda f; bot. gorczyca f
mus·ter ['mʌstə] 1. ~ **up** siłę itp. zbierać ⟨zebrać⟩; zdobywać ⟨-być⟩ się na (A) odwagę; 2. **pass ~** fig. ⟨u⟩czynić zadość wymogom
must·y ['mʌstɪ] (-ier, -iest) zatęchły; stęchły
mu·ta·tion [mju:'teɪʃn] mutacja f (też bot.)
mute [mju:t] 1. niemy; 2. niemy m; niema f; mus. tłumik m
mu·ti·late ['mju:tɪleɪt] okaleczać ⟨-czyć⟩, zniekształcać ⟨-cić⟩
mu·ti·neer [mju:tɪ'nɪə] rebeliant m, buntownik m; **~·nous** ['mju:tɪnəs] rebeliancki, buntowniczy; **~·ny** ['mju:tɪnɪ] rebelia f, bunt m
mut·ter ['mʌtə] 1. ~ ⟨wy⟩mamrotać; 2. mamrotanie n, szemranie n
mut·ton ['mʌtn] gastr. baranina f; **leg of ~** udziec m barani; **~ 'chop** kotlet m barani
mu·tu·al ['mju:tʃʊəl] wzajemny, obopólny; wspólny
muz·zle ['mʌzl] 1. zo. pysk m, morda f; wylot m (lufy); kaganiec m; 2. zakładać ⟨założyć⟩ kaganiec (D); fig. zamykać ⟨-mknąć⟩ usta
my [maɪ] mój
myrrh [mɜː] bot. mirra f, mira f
myr·tle ['mɜːtl] bot. mirt m
my·self [maɪ'self] ja, mnie; się, sobie; ja sam; **by ~** samotnie
mys·te|·ri·ous [mɪ'stɪərɪəs] tajemniczy, zagadkowy; **~·ry** ['mɪstərɪ] tajemnica f; zagadka f; rel. misterium n; **~ry tour** podróż f w nieznane
mys|·tic ['mɪstɪk] 1. mistyk m (-yczka f); 2. adj. mistyczny; **~·tic·al** mistyczny; **~·ti·fy** ['mɪstɪfaɪ] zwodzić ⟨zwieść⟩; oszałamiać ⟨oszołomić⟩
myth [mɪθ] mit m
my·thol·o·gy [mɪ'θɒlədʒɪ] mitologia f

M

N

N, n [en] N, n *n*

N *skrót pisany*: **north** płn., północny; **northern** północny

nab [næb] F (**-bb-**) ⟨z⟩łapać, ⟨s⟩chwytać

na·dir ['neıdıə] *astr.* nadir *m*, *fig.* najniższy poziom *m*

nag¹ [næg] **1.** (**-gg-**) ⟨za-, u⟩dręczyć; zrzędzić (**at** na *A*); **2.** F zrzęda *m/f*

nag² [næg] F szkapa *f*, chabeta *f*

nail [neıl] **1.** *tech.* gwóźdź *m*; paznokieć *m*; **2.** przybijać ⟨-bić⟩ gwoździami (**to** do *G*); '~**pol·ish** lakier *m* do paznokci; '~ **scis·sors** *pl.* nożyczki *pl.* do paznokci; ~**var·nish** lakier *m* do paznokci

na·ive, na·ïve [naı'i:v] naiwny; na·ive·té, na·ïve·té [naı'i:vətı], na·ive·ty [naı'i:vıtı] naiwność *f*

na·ked ['neıkıd] nagi; odsłonięty; *fig.* nieosłonięty; '~·ness nagość *f*

name [neım] **1.** nazwa *f*; imię *n*; nazwisko *n*; **by** ~ z imienia; **by the** ~ **of** ... imieniem ...; **what's your** ~? jak się pan(i) nazywa?; **call s.o.** ~**s** przezywać ⟨-zwać⟩ kogoś; **2.** nazywać ⟨-zwać⟩; dawać ⟨dać⟩ imię; dawać ⟨dać⟩ na imię; wymieniać ⟨-nić⟩ z imienia; '~·less bezimienny; nieznany; '~·ly mianowicie; '~·plate tabliczka *f* z nazwiskiem *lub* nazwą; '~·sake imiennik *m* (-iczka *f*); '~·tag (*na ubraniu*) naszywka *f* z nazwiskiem

nan·ny ['nænı] niania *f*; ~ **goat** *zo.* koza *f*

nap [næp] **1.** drzemka *f*; **have** *lub* **take a** ~ ucinać ⟨uciąć⟩ sobie drzemkę **2.** (**-pp-**) ucinać ⟨uciąć⟩ sobie drzemkę

nape [neıp] *zw.* ~ **of the neck** kark *m*

nap·kin ['næpkın] serwetka *f*; *Brt.* → **nappy**

Na·ples Neapol *m*

nap·py *Brt.* F pielucha *f*

nar·co·sis [nɑr'kəʊsıs] *med.* (*pl.* **-ses** [-si:z]) narkoza *f*

nar·cot·ic [nɑr'kɒtık] **1.** (**~ally**) narkotyczny *m*; ~ **addiction** uzależnienie *n* narkotyczne; **2.** narkotyk *m*; środek *m* odurzający; ~**s** *pl.* narkotyki *pl.*; ~**s squad** wydział służb *pl.* antynarkotykowych

nar·|·rate [nə'reıt] opowiadać ⟨-wiedzieć⟩; ⟨po⟩informować; ~**·ra·tion** [nə'reıʃn] narracja *f*; ~**·ra·tive** ['nærətıv] **1.** narracja *f*; relacja *f* (**of** z *G*); **2.** narracyjny; ~**·ra·tor** [nə'reıtə] narrator(ka *f*) *m*

nar·row ['nærəʊ] **1.** wąski, nieznaczny; dokładny; *fig.* ograniczony; **2.** zwężać ⟨zwęzić⟩ (się); zmniejszać ⟨-szyć⟩ ;(się); ograniczać ⟨-czyć⟩; '~·ly ledwo; ~**·'mind·ed** ograniczony; o wąskich horyzontach; '~·ness ograniczenie *n*

NASA ['næsə] *skrót*: **National Aeronautics and Space Administration** NASA *f*

na·sal ['neızl] nosowy

nas·ty ['nɑːstı] (**-ier, -iest**) paskudny; *charakter itp.*: okropny; złośliwy, niedobry; *człowiek, zachowanie*: agresywny; *umysł*: plugawy

na·tal ['neıtl] urodzeniowy

na·tion ['neıʃn] naród *m*; państwo *n*

na·tion·al ['næʃənl] **1.** narodowy; państwowy; **2.** obywatel(ka *f*) *m* (*danego państwa*); ~ **'an·them** hymn *m* państwowy

na·tion·al·|·i·ty [næʃə'nælətı] narodowość *f*; obywatelstwo *f*; ~**·ize** ['næʃnəlaız] ⟨z⟩nacjonalizować, upaństwawiać ⟨-wowić⟩

na·tion·al| 'park park *m* narodowy; ~ 'team (*w sporcie*) reprezentacja *f* kraju

'na·tion-wide ogólnokrajowy

na·tive ['neıtıv] **1.** rodzimy, ojczysty; krajowy, miejscowy; wrodzony; **2.** krajowiec *m*, tubylec *m*; ~ 'lan·guage język *m* rodzimy *lub* ojczysty; ~ 'speak·er rodzimy użytkownik (*języka*) *m*

Na·tiv·i·ty [nə'tıvətı] narodzenie *n* Chrystusa; opowieść *f* o narodzeniu Chrystusa; jasełka *pl.*

NATO ['neıtəʊ] *skrót*: **North Atlantic Treaty Organization** NATO *n*, Pakt *m* Północnoatlantycki

nat·u·ral ['nætʃrəl] naturalny, przyrodzony; urodzony, zawołany; przyrodniczy; ~ 'gas gaz *m* ziemny; ~·ize ['nætʃrəlaız] naturalizować (się); nadawać ⟨-dać⟩ obywatelstwo; '~·ly natural-nie; z natury; ~ re'sourc·es pl. bogactwa pl. naturalne; ~ 'sci·ence nauka f przyrodnicza

na·ture ['neɪtʃə] przyroda f, natura f; '~ con·ser·va·tion ochrona f przyrody; '~ re·serve rezerwat m przyrodniczy; '~ trail szlak m przyrodoznawczy

naugh·ty ['nɔːtɪ] (-ier, -iest) niegrzeczny; dowcip: nieprzystojny

nau·se·a [ˈnɔːsjə] nudności pl., mdłości pl.; ~·ate ['nɔːsɪeɪt]: ~ate s.o. doprowadzać ⟨-dzić⟩ kogoś do mdłości, przyprawiać ⟨-wić⟩ kogoś o mdłości; '~·ating przyprawiający o mdłości

nau·ti·cal ['nɔːtɪkl] morski, żeglarski

na·val ['neɪvl] morski; okrętowy; '~·base baza f morska; '~ of·fi·cer oficer m marynarki wojennej; '~ pow·er potęga f morska

nave [neɪv] arch. nawa f główna

na·vel ['neɪvl] anat. pępek m

nav·i·ga·ble ['nævɪɡəbl] żeglowny; ~·gate ['nævɪɡeɪt] naut. ⟨po⟩żeglować, pływać; nawigować; fig. pilotować; ~·ga·tion [nævɪˈɡeɪʃn] naut., aviat. nawigacja f; pływanie n; fig. pilotowanie n; ~·ga·tor ['nævɪɡeɪtə] naut., aviat. nawigator m

na·vy ['neɪvɪ] marynarka f wojenna; ~ 'blue kolor: granat m

nay [neɪ] parl. głos m przeciw

NBC [en biː 'siː] skrót: National Broadcasting Company (amerykańska firma radiowa i TV)

NE skrót pisany: northeast płn.-wsch., północny wschód; northeast(ern) płn.--wsch., północno-wschodni

near [nɪə] 1. adj. bliski, niedaleki; brzeg: bliższy; it was a ~ miss ledwie brakowało (do zderzenia itp.); 2. adv. blisko, niedaleko (też ~ at hand); prawie, nieomal; 3. prp. w pobliżu (G); 4. zbliżać ⟨-żyć⟩ się; ~·by 1. adj. ['nɪəbaɪ] bliski, pobliski; 2. [nɪəˈbaɪ] w pobliżu, blisko; '~·ly prawie, blisko; ~ 'sight·ed zwł. Am. krótkowzroczny

neat [niːt] porządny; schludny; rozwiązanie: zgrabny; wódka itp.: czysty

neb·u·lous ['nebjʊləs] mglisty, mętny

ne·ces·sar·i·ly ['nesəsərəlɪ] nieodzownie, koniecznie; not ~ sarily niekoniecznie; ~·sa·ry ['nesəsərɪ] nieodzowny, konieczny

ne·ces·si·tate [nɪˈsesɪteɪt] wymagać (G), stwarzać ⟨stworzyć⟩ konieczność (G); ~·ty [nɪˈsesətɪ] konieczność f, potrzeba f

neck [nek] 1. szyja f; szyjka f; kołnierzyk m; → neckline: ~ and ~ F łeb w łeb; be up to one's ~ in debt F być po uszy w długach; 2. F pieścić się

neck·er·chief ['nekətʃɪf] (pl. -chiefs, -chieves) apaszka f

neck·lace ['neklɪs] naszyjnik m; ~·let ['neklɪt] naszyjnik m; '~·line wycięcie n (ubrania); '~·tie zwł. Am. krawat m

née [neɪ]: ~ Smith z domu Smith

need [niːd] 1. potrzeba f; brak m; bieda f; be in ~ of s.th. potrzebować czegoś; in ~ w potrzebie; be in ~ of help potrzebować pomocy; 2. v/t. potrzebować (G); v/aux. potrzebować (G), musieć; it ~s to be done trzeba to zrobić

nee·dle ['niːdl] 1. igła f (też świerka itp.); 2. F komuś dawać się we znaki

'need·less niepotrzebny, zbyteczny

'nee·dle·wom·an (pl. -women) szwaczka f; '~·work robótki pl. ręczne

'need·y (-ier, -iest) potrzebujący, ubogi

ne·ga·tion [nɪˈɡeɪʃn] przeczenie n, negacja f; neg·a·tive ['neɡətɪv] 1. negatywny; odmowny; przeczący; 2. przeczenie n; phot. negatyw m; answer in the ~ odpowiadać odmownie

ne·glect [nɪˈɡlekt] 1. zaniedbywać ⟨-dbać⟩; zapominać ⟨-mnieć⟩ (doing, to do zrobić); 2. zaniedbanie n, niedbalstwo n

neg·li·gence ['neɡlɪdʒəns] zaniedbanie n, nieuwaga f; neg·li·gent ['neɡlɪdʒənt] niedbały

neg·li·gi·ble ['neɡlɪdʒəbl] bez znaczenia

ne·go·ti·ate [nɪˈɡəʊʃɪeɪt] ⟨wy⟩negocjować; ⟨po⟩prowadzić rozmowy, rokować; F przeszkodę pokonywać ⟨-nać⟩; czek ⟨z⟩realizować; ~·a·tion [nɪɡəʊʃɪˈeɪʃn] negocjacje pl.; rokowania pl.; ~·a·tor [nɪˈɡəʊʃɪeɪtə] negocjator m (-ka f)

neigh [neɪ] 1. ⟨za⟩rżeć; 2. rżenie n

neigh·bo(u)r ['neɪbə] sąsiad(ka f); rel. bliźni m; '~·hood sąsiedztwo n; najbliższa okolica f; ~·ing ['neɪbərɪŋ] sąsiedni, sąsiadujący; '~·ly życzliwy, przychylny

nei·ther ['naɪðə, 'niːðə] 1. adj., pron. żaden (z dwóch); 2. ~ ...nor... ani ... ani ...

N

ne·on ['ni:ən] *chem.* neon *m*; '~ lamp lampa *f* neonowa; '~ sign neon *m*

neph·ew ['nevju:] siostrzeniec *m*, bratanek *m*

nerd [nɜːd] F ćwok *m*, żłób *m*

nerve [nɜːv] nerw *m*; odwaga *f*, śmiałość *f*; F czelność *f*; **get on s.o.'s ~s** działać komuś na nerwy; **he lost his ~** nerwy go poniosły; **you've got a ~!** ty to masz tupet!; '~·less mało odważny

ner·vous ['nɜːvəs] nerwowy; '~·ness nerwowość *f*

nest [nest] **1.** gniazdo *n*; **2.** gnieździć się

nes·tle ['nesl] ⟨przy⟩tulić się (**against, on** do *G*); *też* **~ down** ⟨u⟩mościć się (**in** w *L*)

net¹ [net] **1.** sieć *f*, siatka *f*; **~ curtain** firanka *f*; **2.** (**-tt-**) ⟨z⟩łowić *lub* ⟨s⟩chwytać siecią

net² [net] **1.** netto; na czysto; **2.** (**-tt-**) przynosić ⟨-nieść⟩ na czysto *lub* netto

Neth·er·lands ['neðələndz] *pl.* Holandia *pl.*

net·tle ['netl] *bot.* **1.** pokrzywa *f*; **2.** ⟨po⟩kłócić się

'net·work sieć *f* (*połączeń, komputerowa itp.*)

neu·ro·sis [njuə'rəusɪs] *med.* (*pl.* **-ses** [-siːz]) neuroza *f*, nerwica *f*; **~·rot·ic** [njuə'rɒtɪk] neurotyk *m* (-yczka *f*)

neu·ter ['njuːtə] **1.** *gr.* nijaki; bezpłciowy; **2.** *gr.* rodzaj *m* nijaki; **3.** ⟨wy⟩trzebić, ⟨wy⟩kastrować

neu·tral ['njuːtrəl] **1.** neutralny; obojętny; *electr.* zerowy; *mot.* jałowy; **2.** osoba *f* neutralna; państwo neutralne; **~ gear** bieg *m* jałowy; '~·i·ty [nju:'trælətɪ] neutralność *f*; ~·ize ['nju:trəlaɪz] ⟨z⟩neutralizować

neu·tron ['njuːtrɒn] *phys.* neutron *m*

nev·er ['nevə] nigdy; '~'end·ing nie kończący się; ~·the'less pomimo to

new [njuː] nowy; *ziemniaki itp.*: młody; **it's ~ to me** to dla mnie nowy; '~·born nowo narodzony; '~·com·er przybysz *m*; nowy *m* (-wa *f*); nowy pracownik *m*; '~·ly nowo

New Or·leans Nowy Orlean *m*

news [njuːz] *sg.* wiadomości *pl.*, informacje *pl.*; '~·a·gent sprzedawca *m* (-czyni *f*) czasopism; '~·boy roznosiciel *m* gazet; '~·bul·le·tin skrót *m* wiadomości; '~·cast (*w radio, TV*) wiadomości *pl.*, dziennik *m*; '~·cast·er (*w ra-*

dio, TV) spiker(ka *f*) *m* (*prezentujący wiadomości w radio i w TV*); '~·deal·er → *Am.* **newsagent**; '~·flash *TV*, (*w radio*) wiadomości *pl.* z ostatniej chwili; '~·let·ter biuletyn *m*; ~·mon·ger ['njuːzmʌŋgə] '~·pa·per ['njuːspeɪpə] gazeta *f*, dziennik *m*; *attr.* gazetowy; '~·print papier *m* gazetowy; '~·read·er *zwł. Brt.* → **newscaster**, '~·reel kronika *f* filmowa; '~·room redakcja *f* dziennika; '~·stand kiosk *m*, stoisko *n* z gazetami; '~·ven·dor *zwł. Brt.* sprzedawca (-czyni *f*) gazet

new year nowy rok; **New Year's Day** Nowy Rok *m*; **New Year's Eve** Sylwester *m*

New York Nowy Jork *m*

New Zea·land Nowa Zelandia *f*

next [nekst] **1.** *adj.* następny; sąsiedni; (**the**) ~ **day** następnego dnia; ~ **door** sąsiedni; ~ **but one** przedostatni; ~ **to nothing** tyle co nic; ~ **to nothing** tyle co nic; **2.** *adv.* następnie; później; sąsiedni *m*; ~·'door obok (*G*); ~ **of kin** najbliższy krewny

NHS [en eɪtʃ 'es] *Brt. skrót:* **National Health Service** Państwowa Służba *f* Zdrowia

nib·ble ['nɪbl] skubać ⟨-bnąć⟩ (**at** *A*), ⟨wy⟩skubać

nice [naɪs] (**-r, -st**) miły; przyjacielski; przyjemny; subtelny; '~·ly miło; przyjemnie; ni·ce·ty ['naɪsətɪ] subtelność *f*

niche [nɪtʃ] nisza *f*

nick [nɪk] **1.** zadraśnięcie *n*, zadrapanie *n*; **in the ~ of time** w ostatnim momencie; **2.** zadrasnąć (się); *Brt.* F (*ukraść*) gwizdnąć; *Brt.* F przymykać ⟨-mknąć⟩

nick·el ['nɪkl] **1.** *chem.* nikiel *m*; *Am.* moneta *m* pięciocentowa; **2.** (*zwł. Brt.* **-ll-**, *Am.* **-l-**) ⟨po⟩niklować; '~·plate ⟨po⟩niklować

'nick·nack ['nɪknæk] → **knick-knack**

nick·name ['nɪkneɪm] **1.** przezwisko *n*, przydomek *m*; **2.** przezywać ⟨-zwać⟩, nadawać ⟨-dać⟩ przydomek

niece [niːs] siostrzenica *f*, bratanica *f*

nig·gard ['nɪgəd] skąpiec *m*; '~·ly skąpy, mało szczodry

night [naɪt] noc *f*; *późny* wieczór *m*; *attr.* nocny; **at ~, by ~, in the ~** nocą, w nocy; '~·cap kieliszek *m* przed zaśnięciem; '~·club klub *m* nocny; '~·dress koszula *f* nocna; '~·fall: **at**

~fall o zmroku; **~ie** F ['naɪtɪ] koszula f nocna

nigh·tin·gale ['naɪtɪŋgeɪl] zo. słowik m

'night|·ly nocny, wieczorny; co noc, co wieczór; **~mare** ['naɪtmeə] koszmar m (też fig.); **'~ school** szkoła f wieczorowa; **'~ shift** zmiana f nocna; **'~·shirt** (męska) koszula f nocna; **'~·time: in the ~time, at ~time** nocą; **~ 'watch·man** (pl. **-men**) stróż m nocny; '**~·y** F → **nightdress**

nil [nɪl] nic n, zero n; **our team won two to ~ lub by two goals to ~** (2-0) nasz zespół wygrał dwa do zera (2-0)

nim·ble ['nɪmbl] (**-r, -st**) gibki; lotny

nine [naɪn] **1.** dziewięć; **~ to five** zwykłe godziny pracy (od 9 do 17); **a ~-to-five job** etat m o unormowanym czasie pracy; **2.** dziewiątka f; '**~·pins** kręgle pl.; **~·teen** [naɪn'tiːn] **1.** dziewiętnaście; **2.** dziewiętnastka f; **~·teenth** [naɪn'tiːnθ] dziewiętnasty; **~·ti·eth** ['naɪntɪɪθ] dziewięćdziesiąty; **~·ty** ['naɪntɪ] **1.** dziewięćdziesiąt; **2.** dziewięćdziesiątka f

nin·ny ['nɪnɪ] F głupiec m

ninth [naɪnθ] **1.** dziewiąty; **2.** jedna dziewiąta; '**~·ly** po dziewiąte

nip[1] [nɪp] **1.** (**-pp-**) szczypać ⟨-pnąć⟩; rośliny ścinać (mróz); F wyskakiwać ⟨-koczyć⟩; **~ in the bud** fig. ⟨z⟩niszczyć w zarodku; **2.** uszczypnięcie n; **there's a ~ in the air today** zimno już dzisiaj

nip[2] [nɪp] łyk m (whisky itp.)

nip·per ['nɪpə]: (**a pair of**) **~s** pl. szczypce pl.

nip·ple ['nɪpl] anat. sutek m; Am. smoczek m (na butelkę)

ni·tre Brt., **ni·ter** Am. ['naɪtə] chem. saletra f

ni·tro·gen ['naɪtrədʒən] chem. azot m

no [nəʊ] **1.** adv. nie; **2.** adj. żaden; **~ one** nikt, żaden; **in ~ time** błyskawicznie

No., no. skrót pisany: **number** (łacińskie numero) nr, numer

no·bil·i·ty [nəʊ'bɪlətɪ] szlachta f; szlachetność f

no·ble ['nəʊbl] (**-r, -st**) szlachetny; szlachecki; budynek: wyniosły; '**~·man** (pl. **-men**) szlachcic m; '**~·wom·an** (pl. **-women**) szlachcianka f

no·bod·y ['nəʊbədɪ] **1.** nikt; **2.** fig. nikt m

no·'cal·o·rie di·et dieta f niskokaloryczna

noc·tur·nal [nɒk'tɜːnl] nocny

nod [nɒd] **1.** (**-dd-**) kiwać (wnąć); kłaniać ⟨ukłonić⟩ się; **~ off** odkładać ⟨-łonić⟩ się; **have a ~ding acquaintance** znać kogoś z widzenia; **2.** skinięcie n głową; ukłon m

node [nəʊd] węzeł m (też med.)

noise [nɔɪz] **1.** hałas m; dźwięk m; **2.** **~ about** (**abroad, around**) nagłaśniać ⟨-łośnić⟩; '**~·less** bezdźwięczny

nois·y ['nɔɪzɪ] (**-ier, -iest**) głośny

no·mad ['nəʊmæd] nomada m

nom·i|·nal ['nɒmɪnl] nominalny; **~nal value** econ. wartość f nominalna; **~·nate** ['nɒmɪneɪt] nominować, wyznaczać ⟨-czyć⟩; **~·na·tion** [nɒmɪ'neɪʃn] nominacja f

nom·i·na·tive ['nɒmɪnətɪv] gr. też **~ case** mianownik m

nom·i·nee [nɒmɪ'niː] kandydat(ka f) m

non... [nɒn] nie...

non·al·co·hol·ic bezalkoholowy

non·a·ligned pol. neutralny

non·com·mis·sioned 'of·fi·cer mil. podoficer m

non·com·mit·tal [nɒnkə'mɪtl] wymijający

non·con·duc·tor electr. nieprzewodnik m

non·de·script ['nɒndɪskrɪpt] nijaki, bez wyrazu

none [nʌn] **1.** pron. żaden (zw. jako pl.); nikt; nic; **~ but** tylko; **2.** adv. **~ the...** wcale nie...; **I'm ~ the wiser** nie jestem ani trochę mądrzejszy

non·en·ti·ty [nɒ'nentətɪ] osoba f bez znaczenia, miernota f

none·the·less mimo to

non·ex·ist·ence brak m istnienia, nieistnienie n; **~ent** nieistniejący

non'fic·tion książki pl. popularnonaukowe

non'flam·ma·ble, non·in'flam·ma·ble niepalny, ogniotrwały

non·in·ter·fer·ence, non·in·ter'ven·tion pol. nieinterweniowanie n

non·'i·ron non-iron, nie wymagający prasowania

no·'non·sense rzeczowy, realistyczny

non·par·ti·san [nɒnpɑːtɪ'zæn] pol. niezależny

non'pay·ment niezapłacenie n

non'plus (**-ss-**) ⟨s⟩konsternować

non·pol'lut·ing nie zanieczyszczający

N

non·prof·it *Am.*, non-'prof·it-making *Brt.* nie obliczony na zysk

non·res·i·dent 1. zamiejscowy; *pacjent:* ambulatoryjny; 2. osoba *f* zamiejscowa

non-re'turn-a·ble bezzwrotny; ~ bot·tle butelka *f* bez kaucji

non·sense ['nɒnsəns] nonsens *m*, bzdura *f*

non-'skid przeciwślizgowy

non'smok·er osoba *f* niepaląca, niepalący *m* (-ca *f*); *Brt. rail.* wagon *m* dla niepalących; ~·ing dla niepalących

non'stick *jakby:* teflonowy

non'stop bez zatrzymania; nie zatrzymujący się; bezpośredni; ~ flight przelot *m* bezpośredni

non'u·ni·on niezrzeszony, nie należący do związków zawodowych

non·vi·o·lence postawa *f* powstrzymania się od przemocy; ~·lent powstrzymujący się od przemocy

noo·dles ['nu:dl] *pl.* makaron *m*

nook [nʊk] zakątek *m*, zakamarek *m*

noon [nu:n] południe *n*; *at* ~ w południe

noose [nu:s] pętla *f*

nope F [nəʊp] nie

nor [nɔ:] → *neither*, też nie

norm [nɔ:m] norma *f*; nor·mal ['nɔ:ml] normalny; nor·mal·ize ['nɔ:məlaɪz] ⟨z⟩normalizować (się)

north [nɔ:θ] 1. północ *f*; 2. *adj.* północny; 3. *adv.* na północ; ~'east 1. północny wschód; 2. *adj.* północno-wschodni; 3. *adv.* na północny wschód; ~'east·ern północno-wschodni

nor·ther·ly ['nɔ:ðəlɪ], nor·thern ['nɔ:ðn] północny

North 'Pole biegun *m* północny

north·ward(s) ['nɔ:θwəd(z)] *adv.* północny, na północ; ~'west 1. północny zachód; 2. *adj.* północno-zachodni; 3. *adv.* na północny zachód; ~'west·ern północno-zachodni

Nor·way ['nɔ:weɪ] Norwegia *f*

Nor·we·gian [nɔ:'wi:dʒən] 1. norweski; 2. Norweg *m* (-weżka *f*); *ling.* język *m* norweski

nos. *skrót pisany:* **numbers** liczby *pl.*, numery *pl.*

nose [nəʊz] 1. *anat.* nos *m*; *aviat.* nos *m*, dziób *m*; 2. jechać ostrożnie (*samochodem*); *też* ~ **about,** ~ **around** *fig.* F węszyć, myszkować; ~·bleed krwotok *m* z nosa; '~·cone stożek *m* ochronny ra-

kiety; '~·dive *aviat.* nurkowanie *n*

nose·gay ['nəʊzgeɪ] bukiecik *m* (*przy ubraniu*)

nos·ey ['nəʊzɪ] → *nosy*

nos·tal·gia [nɒ'stældʒɪə] nostalgia *f*

nos·tril ['nɒstrəl] dziurka *f* od nosa, nozdrze *n*

nos·y ['nəʊzɪ] F (-ier, -iest) wścibski; ~ 'park·er *Brt.* F wścibska osoba *f*

not [nɒt] nie; ~ a żaden

no·ta·ble ['nəʊtəbl] godny uwagi

no·ta·ry ['nəʊtərɪ]: *zw.* ~ **public** notariusz *m*

notch [nɒtʃ] 1. nacięcie *n*, karb *m*; *Am. geol.* przełęcz *f*; 2. nacinać ⟨-ciąć⟩, wycinać ⟨-ciąć⟩

note [nəʊt] (*zw.* ~s *pl.*) notatka *f*, uwaga *f*; przypis *m*; nota *f* dyplomatyczna; list *m*; banknot *m*, weksel *m*; *mus.* nuta *f*; *fig.* ton *m*; **take** ~ **(of)** zanotowywać ⟨-ować⟩ (*A*); '~·book notes *m*; *komp.* notebook *m*, komputer *m* przenośny

not·ed ['nəʊtɪd] znany, notowany (**for** z *G*)

'note·pa·per papier *m* listowy; '~·wor·thy znaczący

noth·ing ['nʌθɪŋ] nic; ~ **but** nic prócz; ~ **much** F nic wielkiego; **for** ~ za nic; na nic; **to say** ~ **of** nie mówiąc już o (*L*); **there is** ~ **like** nie ma to jak

no·tice ['nəʊtɪs] 1. zawiadomienie *n*; obwieszczenie *n*; ogłoszenie *n*, informacja *f*; wymówienie *n*, wypowiedzenie *n*; uwaga *f*, recenzja *f*; **give lub hand in one's** ~ składać ⟨złożyć⟩ wymówienie; **give s.o.** ~ dawać ⟨dać⟩ komuś wypowiedzenie; **give s.o.** (*his, etc.*) ~ wypowiedzieć komuś (*np. pokój*); **at six months'** ~ za sześciomiesięcznym wypowiedzeniem; **take (no)** ~ **of** zwracać uwagę (nie zwracać uwagi) na (*A*); **at short** ~ na krótki termin; **until further** ~ do odwołania; **without** ~ bezzwłocznie; 2. zauważać ⟨-żyć⟩, spostrzegać ⟨-rzec⟩; zwracać uwagę na (*A*); △ *nie* **notować**; '~·a·ble zauważalny; godny uwagi; '~ **board** tablica *f* ogłoszeń

no·ti·fy ['nəʊtɪfaɪ] zawiadamiać ⟨-domić⟩, podawać ⟨-dać⟩ do wiadomości; ogłaszać ⟨-łosić⟩

no·tion ['nəʊʃn] pojęcie *n*; idea *f*

no·tions ['nəʊʃnz] *pl. zwł. Am.* pasmanteria *f*

no·to·ri·ous [nəʊˈtɔːrɪəs] notoryczny, o złej sławie (**for** z powodu *G*)

not·with·stand·ing [nɒtwɪθˈstændɪŋ] jednak; pomimo

nought [nɔːt] *Brt.:* **0.4 (~ point four)** 0,4 (zero przecinek cztery)

noun [naʊn] rzeczownik *m*

nour·ish [ˈnʌrɪʃ] żywić; karmić; odżywiać ⟨-wić⟩; **~·ing** pożywny; **~·ment** pokarm *m*

Nov *skrót pisany:* **November** listopad *m*

nov·el [ˈnɒvl] **1.** powieść *f*; △ *nie no-wela* ; **2.** nowatorski; **~·ist** [ˈnɒvəlɪst] powieściopisarz *m* (-arka *f*); **no·vel·la** [nəʊˈvelə] (*pl.* **-las**, **-le** [-liː]) nowela *f*; **~·ty** [ˈnɒvltɪ] nowatorstwo *n*; nowość *f*

No·vem·ber [nəʊˈvembə] (*skrót:* **Nov**) listopad *m*

nov·ice [ˈnɒvɪs] nowicjusz(ka *f*) *m* (*też rel.*)

now [naʊ] **1.** *adv.* teraz, obecnie; **~ and again**, (**every**) **~ and then** od czasu do czasu; **by ~** teraz; **from ~** (**on**) od dzisiaj; **just ~** właśnie w tej chwili; przed chwilą; **2.** *cj. też* **~ that** teraz, gdy

now·a·days [ˈnaʊədeɪz] obecnie

no·where [ˈnəʊweə] nigdzie

nox·ious [ˈnɒkʃəs] szkodliwy

noz·zle [ˈnɒzl] *tech.* wylot *m*; dysza *f*

NSPCC *Brt.* [en es pi: si: ˈsiː] *skrót:* **National Society for the Prevention of Cruelty to Children** (*stowarzyszenie ochrony dzieci przed okrucieństwem*)

nu·ance [ˈnjuːɑːns] niuans *m*

nub [nʌb] sedno *n*

nu·cle·ar [ˈnjuːklɪə] nuklearny, jądrowy; atomowy; **~ˈen·er·gy** energia *f* nuklearna; **~ˈfam·i·ly** (*rodzina złożona tylko z rodziców i dzieci*); **~ˈfis·sion** rozszczepienie *n* jądra; **~ˈfree** pozbawiony broni nuklearnej; **~ˈfu·sion** synteza *f* jądrowa; **~ˈphys·ics** fizyka *f* nuklearna; **~ˈpow·er** potęga *f* atomowa; **~ˈpow·ered** o napędzie atomowym; **~ˈpow·er plant** elektrownia *f* jądrowa; **~ˈre·ac·tor** reaktor *m* atomowy; **~ˈwar** wojna *f* nuklearna; **~ˈwar·head** głowica *f* jądrowa; **~ˈwaste** odpady *pl.* radioaktywne; **~ˈweap·ons** *pl.* broń *f* jądrowa

nu·cle·us [ˈnjuːklɪəs] (*pl.* **-clei** [-klaɪ]) jądro *n* (*też fig.*)

nude [njuːd] **1.** nagi; **2.** akt *m* (*sztuki*)

nudge [nʌdʒ] **1.** *kogoś* trącać ⟨-cić⟩, *ko-*

goś szturchnąć ⟨-chać⟩; **2.** szturchnięcie *n*

nug·get [ˈnʌgɪt] bryłka *f* (*zwł. złota*)

nui·sance [ˈnjuːsns] przykrość *f*; rzecz *f lub* osoba *f* dokuczliwa; **what a ~!** co za utrapienie!; **be a ~ to s.o.** naprzykrzać się komuś; **make a ~ of o.s.** działać komuś na nerwy

nukes [njuːks] *F* broń *f* jądrowa

null [nʌl] *zwł. jur.:* **~ and void** nieważny, bez mocy prawnej

numb [nʌm] **1.** odrętwiały, zdrętwiały; skostniały (**with** z *I*); *fig.* odrętwiały (**with** pod wpływem *G*); **2.** ⟨s⟩powodować zdrętwienie

num·ber [ˈnʌmbə] **1.** liczba *f*; ilość *f*; cyfra *f*; numer *m*; *ling.* liczba *f*; **a ~ of** kilka; **sorry, wrong ~** *tel.* pomyłka; **2.** ⟨po⟩numerować; wynosić ⟨-nieść⟩, liczyć; wyliczać ⟨-czyć⟩; policzyć; **~·less** niezliczony; **~·plate** *zwł. Brt. mot.* tablica *f* rejestracyjna

nu·me·ral [ˈnjuːmərəl] cyfra *f*; *ling.* liczebnik *m*

nu·me·rous [ˈnjuːmərəs] liczny

nun [nʌn] zakonnica *f*; **~·ne·ry** [ˈnʌnərɪ] klasztor *m* żeński

nurse [nɜːs] **1.** siostra *f*; pielęgniarka *f*, → **male nurse**; **wet ~** mamka *f*; opiekunka *f* do dzieci; **2.** pielęgnować; piastować, niańczyć; karmić piersią; pracować jako pielęgniarka; **~ s.o. back to health** otaczać ⟨otoczyć⟩ kogoś opieką do powrotu do zdrowia

nur·se·ry [ˈnɜːsərɪ] żłobek *m*; *przest.* pokój *m* dziecięcy; *agr.* szkółka *f*; **~ˈrhyme** piosenka *f* dziecięca, wierszyk *m* dziecięcy; **~ˈschool** przedszkole *n*; **~ˈslope** ośla łączka *f* (*dla narciarzy*)

nurs·ing [ˈnɜːsɪŋ] pielęgniarstwo *n*; opiekowanie *n* się; **~ˈbot·tle** butelka *f* dla niemowląt; **~ˈhome** dom *m* opieki (*dla starszych*); *Brt.* prywatna klinika *f*

nut [nʌt] *bot.* orzech *m*; *tech.* nakrętka *f*; *F* dureń *m*; *F* łeb *m*; **be off one's ~** *F* dostać świra; **~·crack·er(s** *pl.*) dziadek *m* do orzechów; **~·meg** [ˈnʌtmeg] *bot.* gałka *f* muszkatołowa

nu·tri·ent [ˈnjuːtrɪənt] **1.** substancja *f* odżywcza; **2.** odżywczy

nu·tri·tion [njuːˈtrɪʃn] odżywianie *n* się; **~·tious** [njuːˈtrɪʃəs] odżywczy; **~·tive** [ˈnjuːtrɪtɪv] odżywczy

N

'nut|·shell skorupka f orzecha; (to put
it) in a ~shell F w skrócie, jednym słowem; ~·ty ['nʌti] (-ier, -iest) orzechowy; sl. kopnięty

NW skrót pisany: northwest płn.-zach.,
północny-zachód; northwest(ern)
płn.-zach., północno-zachodni

NY skrót pisany: New York Nowy
Jork

NYC skrót pisany: New York City (miasto) Nowy Jork

ny·lon ['nailən] nylon m; attr. nylonowy;
~s pl. pończochy pl. nylonowe

nymph [nimf] nimfa f

O

O, o [əʊ] O, o n

o [əʊ] (cyfra, też przy czytaniu numerów)
zero n

oaf [əʊf] gamoń m; fajtłapa m

oak [əʊk] dąb m

oar [ɔː] wiosło n; ~s·man ['ɔːzmən] (pl.
-men) (w sporcie) wioślarz m; '~s-
wom·an (pl. -women) (w sporcie)
wioślarka f

OAS [əʊ eɪ 'es] skrót: Organization
of American States Organizacja f
Państw Ameryki

o·a·sis [əʊ'eɪsɪs] (pl. -ses [-siːz]) oaza f
(też fig.)

oath [əʊθ] (pl. oaths [əʊðz]) przysięga f;
przekleństwo n; be on lub under~ być
pod przysięgą; take the ~ składać
⟨złożyć⟩ przysięgę

oat·meal ['əʊtmiːl] płatki pl. owsiane

oats [əʊts] pl. bot. owies m; sow one's
wild ~ wyszumieć się za młodu

o·be·di|·ence [ə'biːdjəns] posłuszeń-
stwo n; ~ent posłuszny

o·bese [əʊ'biːs] otyły; o·bes·i·ty
[əʊ'biːsəti] otyłość f

o·bey [ə'beɪ] być posłusznym (D), słuchać (G); rozkazowi podporządkowywać ⟨- wać⟩ się

o·bit·u·a·ry [ə'bɪtjʊərɪ] też ~ notice nekrolog m; wspomnienie n pośmiertne

ob·ject 1. ['ɒbdʒɪkt] obiekt m, przedmiot m; cel m; gr. dopełnienie n; 2.
[əb'dʒekt] sprzeciwiać ⟨-wić⟩ się; mieć
obiekcje; ⟨za⟩protestować

ob·jec|·tion [əb'dʒekʃn] sprzeciw m
(to wobec G); sprzeciw m (też jur.);
~·tio·na·ble niewłaściwy, naganny

ob·jec·tive [əb'dʒektɪv] 1. obiektywny; 2. cel m; (w mikroskopie) obiektyw m

ob·li·ga·tion [ɒblɪ'geɪʃn] zobowiąza-

nie n; be under an ~ to s.o. (to do
s.th.) być zobowiązanym wobec kogoś
(coś zrobić); ob·lig·a·to·ry [ə'blɪgə-
təri] obowiązkowy, obligatoryjny

o·blige [ə'blaɪdʒ] zobowiązywać ⟨-zać⟩
(się); ~ s.o. wyświadczać ⟨-czyć⟩ komuś przysługę (D); much ~d wielce
zobowiązany; o'blig·ing uczynny

o·blique [ə'bliːk] skośny, ukośny; fig.
pośredni

o·blit·er·ate [ə'blɪtəreɪt] unicestwiać
⟨-wić⟩; przesłaniać ⟨-łonić⟩, zasłaniać
⟨-łonić⟩

o·bliv·i|·on [ə'blɪvɪən] zapomnienie n;
stan m nieświadomości; ~ous [ə'blɪ-
vɪəs]: be ~ous of lub to s.th. być nie-
świadomym czegoś

ob·long ['ɒblɒŋ] prostokątny

ob·nox·ious [əb'nɒkʃəs] obmierzły,
okropny

ob·scene [əb'siːn] obsceniczny, nieprzyzwoity (też fig.)

ob·scure [əb'skjʊə] 1. ciemny; niewyraźny, słabo widoczny; fig. ciemny,
niejasny; ponury; nieznany; △ nie ob-
skurny; 2. zaciemniać ⟨-nić⟩; zasłaniać
⟨-łonić⟩; ob·scu·ri·ty [əb'skjʊərəti]
niejasność f; zapomnienie n

ob·se·quies ['ɒbsɪkwɪz] pl. uroczystości pl. żałobne

ob·ser·va·ble [əb'zɜːvəbl] zauważalny, dostrzegalny; ~·vance [əb'zɜːvns]
przestrzeganie n; ~·vant [əb'zɜːvnt]
spostrzegawczy; ~·va·tion [ɒbzə'veɪʃn]
obserwacja f; uwaga f (on w sprawie
G); ~·va·to·ry [əb'zɜːvətri] obserwa-
torium n

ob·serve [əb'zɜːv] ⟨za⟩obserwować;
zauważyć, spostrzec; przestrzegać, stosować się do (G); ob'serv·er obserwa-
tor(ka f) m

offender

ob·sess [əb'ses]: *be ~ed by lub with* mieć obsesję na punkcie czegoś; **ob·ses·sion** [əb'seʃn] obsesja *f*; idée fixe *f*; **ob·ses·sive** [əb'sesɪv] obsesyjny

ob·so·lete ['ɒbsəliːt] przestarzały

ob·sta·cle ['ɒbstəkl] przeszkoda *f*

ob·sti·nate ['ɒbstɪnət] uparty

ob·struct [əb'strʌkt] przeszkadzać ⟨-kodzić⟩; utrudniać ⟨-nić⟩; ⟨za⟩blokować, ⟨za⟩tarasować; **ob·struc·tion** [əb'strʌkʃn] przeszkoda *f*; zablokowanie *n*, zatarasowanie *n*; △ *nie* **obstrukcja** (*w znaczeniu: zatwardzenie*); **ob·struc·tive** [əb'strʌktɪv] przeszkadzający, stwarzający trudności

ob·tain [əb'teɪn] uzyskiwać ⟨-kać⟩, otrzymywać ⟨-mać⟩; stosować się, obowiązywać; **~·a·ble** osiągalny

ob·tru·sive [əb'truːsɪv] natrętny, nieznośny

ob·tuse [əb'tjuːs] *kąt:* rozwarty

ob·vi·ous ['ɒbvɪəs] oczywisty, niewątpliwy

oc·ca·sion [ə'keɪʒn] okazja *f*, sposobność *f*; sytuacja *f*; powód *m*; *on the ~ of* przy okazji (*G*); **~·al** [ə'keɪʒənl] okazjonalny, okolicznościowy, przypadkowy

Oc·ci·dent ['ɒksɪdənt] Zachód *m*; ♀**·den·tal** [ɒksɪ'dentl] okcydentalny, zachodni

oc·cu·pant ['ɒkjʊpənt] lokator(ka *f*) *m*, mieszkaniec *m* (-nka *f*); pasażer(ka *f*) *m*; **~·pa·tion** [ɒkjʊ'peɪʃn] zawód *m*; zajęcie *n*; *mil., pol.* okupacja *f*, zajęcie *n*; **~·py** ['ɒkjʊpaɪ] zajmować ⟨-jąć⟩; *mil., pol.* okupować; *be occupied* być zajętym, być zamieszkanym

oc·cur [ə'kɜː] ⟨-*rr*-⟩ zdarzać ⟨-rzyć⟩ się, wydarzać ⟨-rzyć⟩ się; występować; *it ~red to me that* przyszło mi do głowy, że; **~·rence** [ə'kʌrəns] występowanie *n*, pojawienie się *n*; wydarzenie *n*

o·cean ['əʊʃn] ocean *m*

o'clock [ə'klɒk] godzina (*przy podawaniu czasu*); (*at*) *five ~* o piątej (*godzinie*)

Oct *skrót pisany:* **October** październik *m*

Oc·to·ber [ɒk'təʊbə] (*skrót:* **Oct**) październik *m*

oc·u·lar ['ɒkjʊlə] oczny; **~·list** ['ɒkjʊlɪst] okulista *m* (-tka *f*)

OD [əʊ'diː] F *v/i.:* **~** *on heroin* przedawkować heroinę

odd [ɒd] dziwny, osobliwy; nieparzysty; *rękawiczka itp.:* nie do pary, pojedynczy; dodatkowy; doraźny; *30* **~** ponad 30, trzydzieści kilka; **~** *jobs pl.* doraźne zajęcia *pl.*

odds [ɒdz] *pl.* szanse *pl.*; *the* **~** *are 10 to 1* szanse są jak jeden do dziesięciu; *the* **~** *are that* bardzo prawdopodobne, że; *against all* **~** wbrew oczekiwaniom; *be at* **~** kłócić się (*with* z *I*); **~** *and ends* różności *pl.*, różne różności *pl.*; **~**'*on* najprawdopodobniejszy

ode [əʊd] oda *f*

Oder Odra *f*

o·do(u)r ['əʊdə] nieprzyjemny zapach *m*

of [ɒv, əv] *prp.* odpowiada dopełniaczowi *the leg* **~** *the table* noga stołu; *the works* **~** *Swift* dzieła Swifta; z (*G*); **~** *wood* z drewna; *proud* **~** dumny z; *your letter* **~**... pański list z...; na (*A*); *die* **~** umrzeć na; o (*L*); *speak* **~** mówić o; *think* **~** myśleć o; ze strony (*G*); *how kind* **~** *you* jak miło z twojej strony; *five minutes* **~** *twelve Am.* za pięć dwunasta

off [ɒf] **1.** *adv.* z, od, w; z dala; od strony; spoza; w odległości; *3 miles* **~** trzy mile od; *I must be* **~** muszę już iść; **~** *with you!* zabieraj się!; *be* **~** być odwołanym; *10%* **~** *econ.* 10% rabatu; **~** *and on* czasami, od czasu do czasu; *take a day* **~** wziąć dzień wolnego; *s.o. is well* (*badly*) **~** komuś się dobrze (źle) powodzi; **2.** *prp.* od (*G*); z (*G*); *naut.* tuż przy (*L*) (brzegu); *be* **~** *duty* nie być na służbie, nie mieć dyżuru; *be* **~** *smoking* przestać palić; **3.** *adj. światło:* wyłączony, zgaszony; *pokrętło:* zakręcony; *jedzenie:* nieświeży; wolny (*od pracy*); poza sezonem; *dzień:* niedobry

of·fal ['ɒfl] *Brt. gastr.* podroby *pl.*, podróbki *pl.*

of·fence *Brt.*, **of·fense** *Am.* [ə'fens] obraza *f* zniewaga *f*; *jur.* wykroczenie *n*, przestępstwo *n*; *take* **~** obrażać ⟨-razić⟩ się (*at* na *A*)

of·fend [ə'fend] obrażać ⟨-razić⟩, znieważać ⟨-żyć⟩; wykraczać ⟨-roczyć⟩ (*against* przeciw(ko) *D*), naruszać ⟨-szyć⟩; **~·er** przestępca *m* (-czyni *f*); *first* **~er**

jur. przestępca *m* (-czyni *f*) dotychczas nie karany (-a)

of·fen·sive [ə'fensɪv] **1.** obraźliwy; *zapach*: okropny; *działania*: ofensywny, zaczepny; **2.** ofensywa *f*

of·fer ['ɒfə] **1.** *v/t.* ⟨za⟩proponować, ⟨za⟩oferować (*też econ.*); *modlitwę* ⟨za⟩ofiarować; *opór* stawiać; ⟨za⟩proponować (**to do s.th.** zrobienie czegoś); **2.** oferta *f*, propozycja *f*

off·hand [ɒf'hænd] bezceremonialny; bez przygotowania, improwizowany

of·fice ['ɒfɪs] biuro *n*; urząd *m*; kancelaria *f*; *zw.* 2 *zwł. Brt.* ministerstwo *n*; stanowisko *n*, urząd *m*; '~ **hours** *pl.* godziny *pl.* urzędowania

of·fi·cer ['ɒfɪsə] oficer *m*; urzędnik *m* (-iczka *f*), funkcjonariusz *m*

of·fi·cial [ə'fɪʃl] **1.** urzędnik *m* (-iczka *f*), funkcjonariusz *m*; **2.** oficjalny, urzędowy, służbowy

of·fi·ci·ate [ə'fɪʃɪeɪt] urzędować

of·fi·cious [ə'fɪʃəs] nadgorliwy, namolny

'off|·licence *Brt.* sklep *m* z alkoholem; '~·line *komp.* autonomiczny, rozłączny; ~·'peak *electr.* pozaszczytowy; ~·**peak hours** *pl.* okres *m* poza godzinami szczytu; '~ **sea·son 1.** *adj.* okres poza szczytem; **2.** okres *m* poza szczytem; '~·**set** ⟨z⟩rekompensować, kompensować; ~·**shoot** *bot.* pęd *m* boczny, odrośl *m*; ~·**shore** przybrzeżny; ~·**side** (*w sporcie*) ofsajd, spalony; ~**side position** spalony; ~**side trap** pułapka *f* ofsajdowa; '~·**spring** potomek *m*, potomstwo *n*; ~·**the-'rec·ord** nieoficjalny

of·ten ['ɒfn] często

oh [əʊ] *int.* och, ach

oil [ɔɪl] **1.** oliwa *f*, olej *m*; ropa *f* naftowa; **2.** ⟨na⟩smarować; ⟨na⟩oleić; ⟨na⟩oliwić; '~ **change** *mot.* zmiana *f* oleju; '~·**cloth** cerata *f*; '~·**field** pole *n* naftowe; '~ **paint·ing** obraz *m* olejny; *olejne* malarstwo *n*; '~ **plat·form** → **oil rig**; '~·**pol·lu·tion** zanieczyszczenie *n* wody olejami *lub* ropą naftową; '~·**pro·duc·ing coun·try** kraj-producent *m* ropy naftowej; '~ **re·fin·e·ry** rafineria *f* ropy naftowej; '~ **rig** platforma *f* wiertnicza; '~·**skin** tkanina *f* nieprzemakalna; ~·**skins** *pl.* ubranie *n* sztormowe; '~ **slick** plama *f* ropy naftowej; '~ **well**

szyb *m* naftowy; '~·**y** (**-ier, -iest**) oleisty, tłusty; *fig.* brudny, nieczysty

oint·ment ['ɔɪntmənt] maść *f*

OK, o·kay [əʊ'keɪ] **1.** *adj. i int.* OK, okay; w porządku; dobra; **2.** wyrażać ⟨-razić⟩ zgodę; **3.** zgoda *f*

old [əʊld] **1.** stary; **2.** **the ~** *pl.* starzy *pl.*; '~ **age** wiek *m* podeszły, starość *f*; ~ **age** '**pen·sion** renta *f*, emerytura *f*; ~ **age** '**pen·sion·er** rencista *m* (-tka *f*), emeryt(ka *f*) *m*; '~·**fash·ioned** przestarzały; '~·**ish** starawy; ~ '**peo·ple's home** dom *m* starości

ol·ive ['ɒlɪv] *bot.* oliwka *f*; zieleń *f* oliwkowa

O·lym·pic Games [əlɪmpɪk 'geɪmz] *pl.* Igrzyska *pl.* Olimpijskie

om·i·nous ['ɒmɪnəs] złowieszczy

o·mis·sion [əʊ'mɪʃn] pominięcie *n*, opuszczenie *n*; zaniechanie *n*

o·mit [ə'mɪt] (**-tt-**) pomijać ⟨-minąć⟩, opuszczać ⟨-puścić⟩; ~ **to do s.th.** nie zrobić czegoś

om·nip·o·tent [ɒm'nɪpətənt] wszechmocny

om·nis·ci·ent [ɒm'nɪsɪənt] wszechwiedzący

on [ɒn] **1.** *prp.* na (*A lub L*); ~ **the table** na stole; w (*L*); ~ **TV** w telewizji; *okres czasu*: w (*A*); ~ **Sunday** w niedzielę; *leżący, znajdujący się*: w (*L*); ~ **the committee** w komisji; według (*G*); ~ **this model** według tego modelu; z (*G*); *live* ~ **s.th.** żyć z czegoś; ~ **his arrival** (zaraz) po jego przybyciu; ~ **duty** na służbie; ~ **the street** *Am.* na ulicy; ~ **the train** *Am.* w pociągu; ~ **hearing it** po usłyszeniu tego; **have you any money** ~ **you?** masz przy sobie jakieś pieniądze?; **2.** *adj. i adv.* *światło, urządzenie*: włączony; *pokrętło*: otwarty; **have a coat** ~ mieć na sobie płaszcz; **keep one's hat** ~ być w nakryciu głowy; **and so** ~ i tak dalej; **from this day** ~ od dzisiaj; **be** ~ *theat., TV* być granym, być w repertuarze; być transmitowanym (*w radio*); **what's** ~? co się dzieje?

once [wʌns] **1.** raz; jednokrotnie; ~ **again**, ~ **more** jeszcze raz; ~ **in a while** od czasu do czasu; ~ **and for all** raz na zawsze; **not** ~ ani razu; **at** ~ od razu, natychmiast; jednocześnie; **all at** ~ nagle; **for** ~ choć raz; **this** ~ ten jeden raz; **2.** skoro tylko

one [wʌn] **1.** *adj.* jeden; pewien; **~ day** pewnego dnia; **~ Smith** jakiś Smith; **2.** *pron.* jeden *m*; ten *m*; **which ~?** który?, która?, które?; **~'s** swój *m*; **~ should do ~'s duty** należy wykonywać swoje obowiązki; **~ another** siebie, sobie; **3. ~ by ~,** **~ after ~,** **~ after another** jeden za drugim; **I for ~** ja na przykład; **the little ~s** *pl.* mali *pl.*; **~'self** się; siebie; sobie; **(all) by ~self** całkiem sam; **to ~self** dla siebie; **~'sid·ed** jednostronny; **'~-time** były; **~-track 'mind: have a one-track mind** mieć w głowie tylko jedno; **~-'two** (*w płdze nożnej*) podwójne podanie *n*; **~'way** jednokierunkowy; w jedną stronę; **~-way 'street** ulica *f* jednokierunkowa; **~-way 'tick·et** bilet *m* w jedną stronę; **~-way 'traf·fic** ruch *m* jednokierunkowy

on·ion ['ʌnjən] *bot.* cebula *f*

'on·line *komp.* bezpośredni; '**~-look·er** widz *m*, przechodzień *m*

on·ly ['əʊnlɪ] **1.** *adj.* jedyny; **2.** *adv.* tylko, jedynie; **~ yesterday** dopiero wczoraj; **3.** *cj.* F tylko, jedynie

'on·rush naplyw *m*, przypływ *m*; napór *m*; '**~-set** zimy początek *m*; wybuch *m* (*choroby*); **~-slaught** ['ɒnslɔːt] szturm *m*

on·to ['ɒntu, 'ɒntə] na (*L*)

on·ward(s) ['ɒnwəd(z)] naprzód, wprzód; **from now ~** od dzisiaj

ooze [uːz] *v/i.* sączyć się; przesączać ⟨-czyć⟩ się; **~ away** *fig.* zanikać ⟨-knąć⟩; *v/t.* wydzielać; *fig.* promieniować

o·paque [əʊ'peɪk] (**-r, -st**) nieprzezroczysty; *fig.* niejasny

OPEC ['əʊpek] *skrót:* **Organization of Petroleum Exporting Countries** OPEC *f/m*, Organizacja *f* Krajów Eksportujących Ropę Naftową

o·pen ['əʊpən] **1.** otwarty (*też fig.*); dostępny, wolny; *fig.* dostępny, przystępny (*to* dla *G*); **~ all day** otwarty całą dobę; **in the ~ air** na dworze; **2.** (*w golfie, tenisie*) zawody *pl.* open; **in the ~** na dworze; **come out into the ~** *fig.* wychodzić ⟨wyjść⟩ na jaw; **3.** *v/t.* otwierać ⟨-worzyć⟩ (się); rozpoczynać ⟨-cząć⟩ (się); **~ into** wychodzić na (*A*); **~ onto** wychodzić na (*A*); **~ air** na wolnym powietrzu; *basen:* otwarty; **~-'end·ed** *dyskusja:* płynny; **~-er** ['əʊpnə] otwieracz

m; **~ -'eyed** zadziwiony; **~ -'hand·ed** szczodry, hojny; **~ -'ing** ['əʊpnɪŋ] otwarcie *n*; *econ.* wakat *m*, wolne miejsce *n* (*pracy*); możliwość *f*; **~ -'mind·ed** otwarty, przystępny; bez uprzedzeń

op·e·ra ['ɒpərə] opera *f*; '**~ glass·es** *pl.* lornetka *f* operowa; '**~ house** opera *f*, budynek *m* operowy

op·e·rate ['ɒpəreɪt] *v/i.* działać; *tech. maszyna, urządzenie:* pracować, chodzić; *med.* operować (**on s.o.** kogoś); *v/t. tech. urządzenie* obsługiwać; posługiwać się (*I*); *firmę* prowadzić

'op·e·rat·ing room *Am.* sala *f* operacyjna; '**~ sys·tem** system *m* operacyjny; '**~ thea·tre** *Brt.* sala *f* operacyjna

op·e·ra·tion [ɒpə'reɪʃn] operacja *f*; funkcjonowanie *n*, działanie *n* (*maszyny, firmy*); *tech.* obsługa *f*; **in ~tion** w działaniu; działający; **~·tive** ['ɒpərətɪv] skuteczny, operatywny; czynny, działający; *med.* operacyjny, chirurgiczny; **~·tor** ['ɒpəreɪtə] *tech.* operator *m*; *tel.* telefonista *m* (-tka *f*)

o·pin·ion [ə'pɪnjən] opinia *f*, zdanie *n*; mniemanie *n* (**on o** *L*); **in my ~** moim zdaniem

op·po·nent [ə'pəʊnənt] przeciwnik *m* (-iczka *f*)

op·por·tune ['ɒpətjuːn] dogodny; na czasie, we właściwym czasie; **~·tu·ni·ty** [ɒpə'tjuːnətɪ] sposobność *f*

op·pose [ə'pəʊz] przeciwstawiać ⟨-wić⟩ się (*D*), sprzeciwiać ⟨-wić⟩ się (*D*); **op·posed** przeciwny; **be ~ to** sprzeciwiać się (*D*); **op·po·site** ['ɒpəzɪt] **1.** przeciwieństwo *n*; **2.** *adj.* przeciwny; naprzeciwko; przeciwległy; **3.** *adv.* naprzeciwko; **4.** *prp.* naprzeciw; **op·po·si·tion** [ɒpə'zɪʃn] opozycja *f* (*też parl.*); opór *m*; przeciwstawianie *n* się

op·press [ə'pres] uciskać, ciemiężyć; **op·pres·sion** [ə'preʃn] ucisk *m*, ciemiężenie *n*; **op·pres·sive** [ə'presɪv] uciskający; uciążliwy; przygnębiający

op·tic ['ɒptɪk] optyczny; wzrokowy; '**~·ti·cal** optyczny; **op·ti·cian** [ɒp'tɪʃn] optyk *m* (-yczka *f*)

op·ti·|mis·m ['ɒptɪmɪzəm] optymizm *m*; **~·mist** ['ɒptɪmɪst] optymista *m* (-tka *f*); **~·mist·ic (-ally)** optymistyczny

op·tion ['ɒpʃn] wybór *m*; *econ.* opcja *f*, prawo *n* zakupu; *mot.* wyposażenie *n*

dodatkowe; ~·al ['ɒpʃnl] nie obowiązkowy, wariantowy; *tech.* opcjonalny
or [ɔː] lub, albo; ~ **else** bo inaczej
o·ral ['ɔːrəl] ustny; oralny
or·ange ['ɒrɪndʒ] **1.** *bot.* pomarańcza *f*;
2. pomarańczowy; ~·**ade** [ɒrɪndʒ'eɪd]
oranżada *f*
o·ra·tion [ɔː'reɪʃn] przemowa *f*, oracja
f; **or·a·tor** ['ɒrətə] mówca *m* (-czyni *f*),
orator *m*
or·bit ['ɔːbɪt] **1.** orbita *f*; **get** *lub* **put
into** ~ umieszczać ⟨umieścić⟩ na orbi-
cie; **2.** *v/t.* Ziemię *itp.* okrążać ⟨-żyć⟩;
v/i. orbitować, krążyć po orbicie
or·chard ['ɔːtʃəd] sad *m*
or·ches·tra ['ɔːkɪstrə] *mus.* orkiestra *f*;
Am. theat. parter *m*
or·chid ['ɔːkɪd] *bot.* orchidea *f*, storczyk *m*
or·dain [ɔː'deɪn] ~ **s.o. (priest)** wy-
święcać ⟨-cić⟩ kogoś na księdza
or·deal [ɔː'diːl] udręka *f*, ciężkie przejście *n*
or·der ['ɔːdə] **1.** porządek *m* (*też parl.*);
rząd *m* (*też biol.*); rozkaz *m*; *econ.* zamówienie *n*; *rel. itp.* zakon *m*; kolejność *f*; ~ **to pay** *econ.* polecenie *n* zapłaty; **in** ~ **to** aby; **out of** ~ nie w porządku; zepsuty; **make to** ~ ⟨z⟩robić
na zamówienie; **2.** *v/t.* komuś rozkazywać ⟨-zać⟩ (**to do s.th.** coś zrobić); *coś*
polecać ⟨-cić⟩; *med.* komuś coś zalecać ⟨-cić⟩; *econ.* zamawiać ⟨-mówić⟩
(*też w restauracji*); *fig.* ⟨u⟩porządko-
wać; *v/i.* (*w restauracji*) zamawiać ⟨-mó-
wić⟩; ~·**ly 1.** uporządkowany; *fig.* spokojny; **2.** *med.* sanitariusz(ka *f*) *m*
or·di·nal ['ɔːdɪnl] *math. też* ~ **number**
math. liczba *f* porządkowa
or·di·na·ry ['ɔːdnrɪ] zwyczajny, zwykły;
△ *nie* **ordynarny**
ore [ɔː] ruda *f*
or·gan ['ɔːgən] *anat.* organ *m*, narząd *m*
(*też fig.*); *mus.* organy *pl.*; '~ **grind·er**
kataryniarz *m*; ~·**ic** [ɔː'gænɪk] (*-ally*)
organiczny; ~·**is·m** ['ɔːgənɪzəm] organ
nizm *m*; ~·**i·za·tion** [ɔːgənaɪ'zeɪʃn]
organizacja *f*; ~·**ize** ['ɔːgənaɪz] ⟨z⟩orga-
nizować; *zwł. Am.* utworzyć się;
'~·**iz·er** organizator(ka *f*) *m*
or·gas·m ['ɔːgæzəm] orgazm *m*, szczytowanie *m*
o·ri·ent ['ɔːrɪənt] **1.** ♀ Wschód *m*,
Orient *m*; **2.** orientować; zapoznawać

⟨-nać⟩; ~·**en·tal** [ɔːrɪ'entl] **1.** oriental-
ny, wschodni; **2.** ♀ człowiek *m* Wschodu; ~·**en·tate** ['ɔːrɪentet] → **orient**
or·i·gin ['ɒrɪdʒɪn] pochodzenie *n*; początek *m*
o·rig·i·nal [ə'rɪdʒənl] **1.** oryginalny, początkowy; **2.** oryginał *m*; ~·**i·ty** [ərɪdʒə-
'nælətɪ] oryginalność *f*; ~·**ly** [ə'rɪdʒənə-
lɪ] pierwotnie; oryginalnie
o·rig·i·nate [ə'rɪdʒəneɪt] *v/t.* dawać
⟨dać⟩ początek, zapoczątkowywać
⟨-ować⟩; *v/i.* brać ⟨wziąć⟩ początek, pochodzić
Ork·neys *pl.* Orkady *pl.*
or·na·ment 1. ['ɔːnəmənt] ornament *m*
(*też fig.*), ozdoba *f*; **2.** ['ɔːnəment] ozdabiać ⟨-dobić⟩; ~·**men·tal** [ɔːnə'mentl]
ozdobny, ornamentalny
or·nate [ɔː'neɪt] *fig.* styl *itp.* przeładowany, ciężki
or·phan ['ɔːfn] **1.** sierota *m/f*; **2.** **be** ~**ed**
być osieroconym; ~·**age** ['ɔːfənɪdʒ] sie-
rociniec *m*
or·tho·dox ['ɔːθədɒks] ortodoksyjny
os·cil·late ['ɒsɪleɪt] *phys.* oscylować;
fig. wahać się (**between** między *I*)
os·ten·si·ble [ɒ'stensəbl] pozorny, rzekomy
os·ten·ta·tion [ɒsten'teɪʃn] ostentacja
f, demonstracja *f*; ~·**tious** [ɒsten'teɪ-
ʃəs] ostentacyjny, demonstracyjny
os·tra·cize ['ɒstrəsaɪz] ostracyzować
os·trich ['ɒstrɪtʃ] *zo.* struś *m*
oth·er ['ʌðə] *zo.* inny; **the** ~ **day** niedawno;
every ~ **day** co drugi dzień; '~·**wise**
inaczej; poza tym; w przeciwnym ra-
zie
ot·ter ['ɒtə] *zo.* wydra *f*
ought [ɔːt] *v/aux. ja*: powinienem, *ty*:
powinieneś *itp.* (**to do** zrobić); **she** ~
to have done it powinna była to zrobić
ounce [aʊns] uncja *f* (*28,35 g*)
our ['aʊə] nasz; ~**s** ['aʊəz] nasz;
~·**selves** [aʊə'selvz] się, sobie, siebie; my sami; **by** ~ przez siebie, bez pomocy
oust [aʊst] wysiedlać ⟨-lić⟩, usuwać
⟨-sunąć⟩
out [aʊt] **1.** *adv. adj.* na zewnątrz, poza;
na powietrzu, na powietrze; (*w sporcie*)
na aut, na aucie; F niemodny; wygasły;
rozkwitły; **way** ~ wyjście *n*; ~ **of** *z* (*G*);
poza (*zasięgiem*); bez (*oddechu*); (*zrobiony*) z (*G*); **be** ~ **of ...** już ... nie mieć ...

in nine ~ of ten cases na dziewięć przypadków z dziesięciu; **2.** *prp.* F przez (*A*); **3.** F wydawać ⟨-dać⟩

out'bal·ance przeważać ⟨-żyć⟩; ~**'bid** (*-dd-*; *-bid*) przelicytowywać ⟨-ować⟩; ~**'board 'mo·tor** silnik *m* burtowy; '~**break** wybuch *m* (*choroby itp.*); '~**build·ing** dobudówka *f*; '~**burst** wybuch *m* (*uczuc*); '~**cast 1.** odrzucać ⟨-cić⟩; **2.** wyrzutek *m*; '~**come** wynik *m*, rezultat *m*; '~**cry** protest *m*, dezaprobata *f*; ~**'dat·ed** przestarzały; ~**'dis·tance** prześcigać ⟨-gnąć⟩, zdystansować; ~**'do** (*-did, -done*) przewyższać ⟨-szyć⟩, wyprzedzać ⟨-dzić⟩; '~**door** *adj.* na dworze, na świeżym powietrzu; '~**doors** *adv.* na dwór

out·er ['autə] zewnętrzny; '~**most** najdalszy; ~ **'space** kosmos *m*, przestrzeń *f* kosmiczna

'out·fit ubiór *m*, strój *m*; ekwipunek *m*; F zespół *m*, grupa *f*; '~**fit·ter** dostawca *m*; *sports ~fitters* artykuły *pl.* sportowe; '~**go·ing** wychodzący; '~**go·ings** *pl. zwł. Brt.* wydatki *pl.*; ~**'grow** (*-grew, -grown*) wyrastać ⟨-rosnąć⟩ z (*G*) *ubrania*); przerastać ⟨-rosnąć⟩; '~**house** przybudówka *f*

out·ing ['autɪŋ] wycieczka *f*

out'land·ish dziwaczny; ~**'last** przetrwać; przeżyć; '~**law** *hist.* banita *m*; '~**lay** *pl.* wydatki *pl.*; '~**let** ujście *n*, wylot *m*; sklep *m*; *fig.* wentyl *m*; '~**line 1.** zarys *m*; kontur *m*; szkic *m*; **2.** zarysowywać ⟨-ować⟩, ⟨za-, na⟩szkicować; ~**'live** przeżywać ⟨-żyć⟩; '~**look** widok *m*, perspektywa *f*; punkt *m* widzenia; ~**'ly·ing** oddalony, odległy; ~**'num·ber** *kogoś* liczebnie przewyższać ⟨-szyć⟩; ~**of-'date** przestarzały; ~**of-the-'way** niedostępny; odległy; ~**'pa·tient** *ambulatoryjny* (*-a*) pacjent(ka *f*) *m*; '~**post** placówka *f*; '~**pour·ing** ulewa *f*; '~**put** *econ.* wydajność *f*; moc *f* wyjściowa; produkcja *f*; *komp.* dane *pl.* wyjściowe; '~**rage 1.** pogwałcenie *n*; gwałt *m*; przestępstwo *n*; zamach *m*; oburzenie *n*; **2.** zadawać ⟨-dać⟩ gwałt; wzburzać ⟨-rzyć⟩; ~**ra·geous** [aut'reɪdʒəs] skandaliczny, oburzający; horrendalny; ~**'right 1.** *adj.* ['autraɪt] całkowity; wyraźny, jawny; **2.** [aut'raɪt] *adv.* całkowicie; wyraźnie; jawnie; wprost; ~**'run** (*-nn-; -ran, -run*)

prześcigać ⟨-gnąć⟩; *fig.* przekraczać ⟨-roczyć⟩; ~**'set** początek *m*; ~**'shine** (*-shone*) przewyższać ⟨-szyć⟩; przyćmiewać ⟨-mić⟩; ~**'side 1.** zewnętrzna strona *f*; (*w sporcie*) napastnik *m* na skrzydle; *at the* (*very*) *~side* najdalej; najwyżej; *left* (*right*) *~* lewo-(prawo-)-skrzydłowy *m*; **2.** *adj.* zewnętrzny; **3.** *adv.* na zewnątrz; **4.** poza (*I*); za (*I*); pod (*I*); ~**'sid·er** outsider *m*, autsajder *m*; osoba *f* postronna; '~**size 1.** duży rozmiar *m*; **2.** o dużych rozmiarach; '~**skirts** *pl.* przedmieścia *pl.*, peryferie *pl.*; ~**'smart** → *outwit*; ~**'spo·ken** szczery, otwarty; ~**'spread** rozciągnięty; ~**'stand** wybitny; *econ. rachunek*: zaległy; *sprawa*: nie załatwiony; '~**stay** przebywać dłużej niż; → *welcome* 4; ~**'stretched** rozpostarty; '~**strip** (*-pp-*) prześcigać ⟨-gnąć⟩; *fig.* zostawić w tyle; '~**tray**: *in the ~tray* w poczcie wychodzącej; ~**'vote** przegłosowywać ⟨-ować⟩

out·ward ['autwəd] **1.** zewnętrzny; **2.** *adv.*: *zw.* ~**s** na zewnątrz; '~**ly** zewnętrznie, na zewnątrz

out'weigh *fig.* przeważać ⟨-żyć⟩; ~**'wit** (*-tt-*) przechytrzać ⟨-rzyć⟩; ~**'worn** zużyty, przestarzały

o·val ['əuvl] **1.** owalny; **2.** owal *m*

o·va·tion [əu'veɪʃn] owacja *f*; *give s.o. a standing ~* oklaskiwać kogoś na stojąco

ov·en ['ʌvn] piec *m*; piekarnik *m*; ~**'read·y** gotowy do pieczenia

o·ver ['əuvə] **1.** *prp.* nad (*I*), ponad (*I*); na (*L*); przez (*A*); po drugiej stronie (*G*); podczas (*G*); **2.** *adv.* na drugą stronę (*G*); więcej; zbytnio; ~ *here* tutaj; (*all*) ~ *again* jeszcze raz; *all* ~ od nowa, od początku; ~ *and above* oprócz (*G*); *and* ~ (*again*) ciągle, nieustannie

o·ver·act [əuvər'ækt] przesadzać ⟨-dzić⟩ (*w grze*); ~**age** [əuvər'eɪdʒ] ponad wymagany wiek; ~**all 1.** [əuvər'ɔːl] całkowity, ogólny; **2.** ['əuvərɔːl] *Brt.* fartuch *m*, kitel *m*; *Am.* kombinezon *m* roboczy; ~**s** *pl. Brt.* kombinezon *m* roboczy; *Am.* spodnie *m* robocze; ~**awe** [əuvər'ɔː] onieśmielać ⟨-lić⟩; ~**'bal·ance** ⟨s⟩tracić równowagę; ~**'bear·ing** despotyczny; ~**'board** *naut.* za burtą, za burtę; ~**'cast** zachmurzony;

~'charge przeciążać ⟨-żyć⟩ (*też electr.*); za dużo (po)liczyć; '~coat płaszcz *m*; ~come (*-came, -come*) przezwyciężać ⟨-żyć⟩; *be ~come with emotion* być ogarniętym uczuciem; ~'crowd·ed zatłoczony; ~'do (*-did, -done*) przesadzać ⟨-dzić⟩; *gastr.* smażyć *lub* gotować za długo; *overdone też* zbytnio wysmażony; ~'dose przedawkowanie *n*, nadmierna dawka *f*; '~·draft *econ.* przekroczenie *n* (*w konta*); ~'draw *econ. konto* przekraczać ⟨-roczyć⟩ (*by* o *A*); ~'dress ubierać ⟨ubrać⟩ się nadmiernie oficjalnie; *~dressed* ubrany oficjalnie; '~·drive *mot.* overdrive *n*, nadbieg *m*; ~'due zaległy, przeterminowany; spóźniony; ~eat [əʊvərˈiːt] (*-ate, -eaten*) ⟨prze⟩jeść się; ~·es·ti·mate [əʊvərˈestɪmeɪt] przeceniać ⟨-nić⟩, zbyt wysoko ⟨o⟩szacować; ~·ex·pose *phot.* [əʊvərɪkˈspəʊz] prześwietlać ⟨-lić⟩; ~flow 1. [əʊvəˈfləʊ] *v/t.* przepełniać ⟨-nić⟩; *v/i.* przelewać ⟨-lać⟩ się; 2. [ˈəʊvəfləʊ] przelew *m*; przelewanie *n* się; ~grown zarosły, zarośnięty; ~hang (*-hung*) *v/t.* nawisać nad; *v/i.* wystawać; ~haul przeglądać, poddawać generalnemu remontowi; ~head 1. *adv.* na górze; 2. *adj.* górny; *econ.* ogólny; (*w sporcie*) (po)nad głową; *~head kick* strzał *m* przewrotką; '~·head(s *pl. Brt.*) *Am. econ.* koszty *pl.* bieżące; ~hear (*-heard*) podsłuchiwać ⟨-chać⟩; ~·heat·ed przegrzany; ~joyed nadzwyczaj zadowolony; '~kill *mil.* możliwość *f* wielokrotnego unicestwienia; *fig.* przesada *f* (*of z I*); ~lap (*-pp-*) nakładać ⟨-łożyć⟩ się; zachodzić na siebie; ~leaf na odwrocie strony; ~load przeciążać ⟨-żyć⟩ (*też electr.*); ~look wychodzić na (*A*); przeoczyć; nie dostrzegać ⟨-rzec⟩; ~night 1. przez noc; *stay ~night* ⟨za⟩nocować ⟨-tać⟩ na noc; 2. podróżny; na noc; *~night bag* torba *f* podróżna; '~·pass *zwł. Am.* kładka *f* (*nad ulicą*); ~'pay (*-paid*) przepłacać ⟨-cić⟩; ~·pop·u·lat·ed przeludniony; ~'pow·er pokonywać, obezwładniać ⟨-nić⟩ (*też fig.*); ~'rate przeceniać ⟨-nić⟩, oceniać ⟨-nić⟩ zbyt wysoko; ~reach: *~reach o.s.* przeliczyć się, przerachować się; ~re'act przesadnie ⟨za⟩reagować; ~re'ac·tion przesadna reakcja *f*; ~ride (*-rode, -rid-*

den) odsuwać ⟨-unąć⟩ na bok, anulować; ~'rule unieważniać ⟨-nić⟩, uchylać ⟨-lić⟩; ~'run (*-nn-; -ran, -run*) ogarniać ⟨-nąć⟩; przekraczać ⟨-roczyć⟩ (*ustalony czas*); *sygnał* przejeżdżać ⟨-jechać⟩; *be ~run with* być ogarniętym (*D*); ~seas 1. *adj.* zagraniczny; zamorski; 2. *adv.* za granicę; za granicą; ~'see (*-saw, -seen*) nadzorować; '~·seer nadzorca *m*; ~'shad·ow przyćmiewać ⟨-mić⟩; rzucać ⟨-cić⟩ cień na (*A*); ~'sight niedopatrzenie *n*; ~'size(d) dużego rozmiaru; ~'sleep (*-slept*) zaspać; ~'staffed o nadmiernym zatrudnieniu; ~'state wyolbrzymiać ⟨-mić⟩; przesadzać ⟨-dzić⟩; ~'state·ment przesada *f*; wyolbrzymienie *n*; ~'stay przebywać dłużej niż; → *welcome* 4; '~·step *fig.* przekraczać ⟨-roczyć⟩; ~'take (*-took, -taken*) mijać (*mot.*) wyprzedzać ⟨-dzić⟩; *fig.* zaskakiwać ⟨-skoczyć⟩; ~'tax nakładać ⟨nałożyć⟩ zbyt wysoki podatek; *fig.* naruszać ⟨-szyć⟩; ~throw 1. [əʊvəˈθrəʊ] (*-threw, -thrown*) *rząd itp.* obalać ⟨-lić⟩; 2. [ˈəʊvəθrəʊ] obalenie *f*, przewrót *m*; '~·time *econ.* praca *f* nadliczbowa, F nadgodziny *pl.*; *Am.* (*w sporcie*) dogrywka *f*; *be on ~time, do ~time, work ~time* pracować w nadgodzinach

o·ver·ture [ˈəʊvətjʊə] *mus.* uwertura *f*

o·ver'turn przewracać ⟨-rócić⟩; *rząd* obalać ⟨-lić⟩; *naut.* wywracać ⟨-rócić⟩ się; *jur.* anulować; '~·view *fig.* zarys *m*; ~weight 1. [ˈəʊvəweɪt] nadwaga *f*; 2. [əʊvəˈweɪt] z nadwagą; zbyt ciężki (*by* o *A*); *be five pounds ~weight* mieć pięć funtów nadwagi; ~whelm przytłaczać ⟨-łoczyć⟩; zakrywać ⟨-ryć⟩; ~whelm·ing przytłaczający; ~work nadmiernie pracować, przepracowywać ⟨-ować⟩ się; ~wrought przewrażliwiony

owe [əʊ] *komuś coś* być winnym, być dłużnym; *coś* zawdzięczać

ow·ing [ˈəʊɪŋ]: ~ *to* dzięki (*D*), na skutek (*G*)

owl [aʊl] *zo.* sowa *f*

own [əʊn] 1. własny; *my ~* mój (*własny*); (*all*) *on one's ~* sam; 2. posiadać; przyznawać się (*to* do *G*)

own·er [ˈəʊnə] właściciel(ka *f*) *m*; posiadacz(ka *f*) *m*; ~'oc·cu·pied *zwł. Brt.* zajmowany przez właściciela;

'~·ship własność *f*, posiadanie *n*
ox [ɒks] *zo.* (*pl.* **oxen** ['ɒksn]) wół *m*
Ox·ford Oksford *m*
ox·ide ['ɒksaɪd] *chem.* tlenek *m*;
ox·i·dize *chem.* ['ɒksɪdaɪz] utleniać
⟨-nić⟩ (się)
ox·y·gen ['ɒksɪdʒən] *chem.* tlen *m*
oy·ster ['ɔɪstə] *zo.* ostryga *f*

oz *skrót pisany:* **ounce(s** *pl.*) uncja *f*
(uncje *pl.*) (28,35 *g*)
o·zone ['əʊzəʊn] *chem.* ozon *m*;
'~-friend·ly nie niszczący warstwy ozonu; '~ hole dziura *f* ozonowa; '~ lay·er
warstwa *f* ozonu; '~ lev·els *pl.* poziom
m zawartości ozonu; '~ shield osłona *f*
ozonowa

P

P, p [pi:] P, p *n*
p¹ *Brt.* [pi:] *skrót:* **penny (pence** *pl.*)
pens(y *pl.*) *m*
p² (*pl.* **pp**) *skrót pisany:* **page** s., str.,
strona *f*
pace [peɪs] **1.** tempo *n*, szybkość *f*; krok
m; chód *m* (*konia*); **2.** *v/t.* chodzić po
(*L*) (*pokoju itp.*); *też* ~ **out** ⟨z-, wy⟩mie-
rzyć (*krokami*); *v/i.* kroczyć, chodzić;
~ **up and down** chodzić tam i z powrotem; '~·mak·er *med.* stymulator *m*;
→ '~·set·ter *Am.* (*w sporcie*) zając *m*
(*zawodnik nadający tempo*)
Pa·cif·ic [pə'sɪfɪk] *też* ~ **Ocean** Pacyfik *m*, Ocean *m* Spokojny
pac·i·fi·er ['pæsɪfaɪə] *Am.* smoczek *m*;
~·fist ['pæsɪfɪst] pacyfista *m* (-tka *f*);
~·fy ['pæsɪfaɪ] uspokajać ⟨-koić⟩
pack [pæk] **1.** paczka *f*, pakunek *m*; *Am.*
paczka *f* (*papierosów*); stado *n*, wata-
ha *f* (*wilków*); sfora *f*, zgraja *f* (*psów*);
grupa *f*; *med.* kosmetyczny okład *m*;
med. tampon *m*; talia *f* (*kart*); **a** ~ **of
lies** stek *m* kłamstw; **2.** *v/t. też* ~ **up**
⟨s-, za⟩pakować; upychać ⟨upchać⟩;
opakowywać ⟨-ować⟩; ~ **off** F odsyłać
⟨odesłać⟩; *v/i.* ⟨s-, za⟩pakować się; wpychać ⟨wepchnąć⟩ się (**into** do *G*); ~ **up**
zapakować się; **send s.o.** ~**ing** odsyłać
⟨odesłać⟩ kogoś
pack·age ['pækɪdʒ] paczka *f*, pakiet *m*;
software ~ *komp.* pakiet *m* oprogramowania; '~ **deal** F transakcja *f* wiązana; '~·hol·i·day wczasy *pl.* zorganizowa-
ne; '~ **tour** wycieczka *f* zorganizowana *f*
'**pack·er** pakowacz(ka *f*) *m*; *Am.* producent *m* konserw
pack·et ['pækɪt] paczka *f*, pakiet *m*
'**pack·ing** opakowanie *n*; opakowanie *n*

pact [pækt] pakt *m*, układ *m*
pad [pæd] **1.** poduszka *f* (*do ubrania,
pieczątek*); (*w sporcie*) ochraniacz *m*;
blok *m* (*papieru*); *zo.* poduszeczka *f*;
płyta *f* (*wyrzutni*); tampon *m*; *Am.*
podpaska *f*; **2.** (**-dd-**) wyściełać ⟨-elić⟩,
watować; '~·ding wyściółka *f*, obicie *n*,
watowanie *n*
pad·dle ['pædl] **1.** wiosło *n*; *naut.* łopatka *f*; **2.** wiosłować; brodzić; '~ **wheel**
naut. koło *n* łopatkowe
pad·dock ['pædək] padok *m*, wybieg *m*
pad·lock ['pædlɒk] kłódka *f*
pa·gan ['peɪgən] **1.** poganin *m* (-anka *f*);
2. pogański
page¹ [peɪdʒ] **1.** strona *f*; **2.** numerować
strony
page² [peɪdʒ] **1.** boy *m* hotelowy; **2.**
wzywać ⟨wezwać⟩
pag·eant ['pædʒənt] widowisko *n* histo-
ryczne
pa·gin·ate ['pædʒɪneɪt] numerować
strony
paid [peɪd] *pret. i p.p. od* **pay** 1
pail [peɪl] wiadro *n*, kubeł *m*
pain [peɪn] **1.** ból *m*; problem *m*; ~**s** *pl.*
starania *pl.*, fatyga *f*; **be in (great)** ~
mieć silne bóle; **be a** ~ **(in the neck)**
F strasznie się naprzykrzać; **take** ~**s**
trudzić się; **2.** *zwł. fig.* czuć ból; boleć;
'~·ful bolesny; '~·kill·er środek *m* u-
śmierzający ból; '~·less bezbolesny;
~**s·tak·ing** ['peɪnzteɪkɪŋ] drobiazgowy
paint [peɪnt] **1.** farba *f*; **2.** ⟨po⟩malować;
samochód itp. ⟨po⟩lakierować; '~·box
pudełko *n* na farby; '~·brush pędzel
m malarski; '~·er malarz *m* (-arka *f*);
'~·ing malowanie *n*; obraz *m*, malowidło *n*
pair [peə] **1.** para *f*; **a** ~ **of** para (*G*); **a** ~ **of**

scissors nożyczki, para nożyc; **2.** v/i. zo. parzyć się; *też* ~ **off**, ~ **up** ⟨u⟩tworzyć parę; v/t. ~ **off**, ~ **up** dobierać ⟨brać⟩ parami; ~ **off** tworzyć parę z (G)

pa·ja·ma(s) [pəˈdʒɑːmə(z)] *Am.* → **pyjama(s)**

pal [pæl] kolega *m*, koleżanka *f*, F kumpel *m*, kumpelka *f*

pal·ace [ˈpælɪs] pałac *m*

pal·a·ta·ble [ˈpælətəbl] do przełknięcia (*też fig.*)

pal·ate [ˈpælɪt] *anat.* podniebienie; *fig.* smak *m*

pale[1] [peɪl] **1.** (**-r, -st**) blady; *kolor:* jasny; **2.** ⟨z⟩blednąć; rozjaśniać ⟨-nić⟩ (się)

pale[2] [peɪl] pal *m*; *fig.* granica *f*

'pale·ness bladość *f*

Pal·es·tine Palestyna *f*

Pal·e·stin·i·an [pælɪˈstɪnɪən] **1.** palestyński; **2.** Palestyńczyk (-tynka *f*)

pal·ings [ˈpeɪlɪŋz] częstokół *m*; pale *pl.*

pal·i·sade [pælɪˈseɪd] palisada *f*; *zwł. Am.* strome skały *pl.*

pal·let [ˈpælɪt] *tech.* paleta *f*

pall·lid [ˈpælɪd] blady; '~**lor** bladość *f*

palm[1] [pɑːm] *bot. też* ~ **tree** palma *f*

palm[2] [pɑːm] **1.** dłoń *f*; **2.** ⟨s⟩chować w dłoni; ~ **s.th. off on s.o.** opychać ⟨-chnąć⟩ coś komuś

pal·pa·ble [ˈpælpəbl] wyczuwalny, namacalny

pal·pi·tate [ˈpælpɪteɪt] *med. serce:* kołatać; ~**ta·tions** [pælpɪˈteɪʃnz] *pl.* palpitacje *pl.*, kołatanie *n*

pal·sy [ˈpɔːlzɪ] *med.* porażenie *n*

pal·try [ˈpɔːltrɪ] (**-ier, -iest**) marny, nędzny

pam·per [ˈpæmpə] dogadzać ⟨-godzić⟩; *dziecko itp.* rozpieszczać ⟨-pieścić⟩

pam·phlet [ˈpæmflɪt] broszura *f*; △ *nie* **pamflet**

pan [pæn] patelnia *f*

pan·a·ce·a [pænəˈsɪə] panaceum *n*

pan·cake [ˈpænkeɪk] naleśnik *m*

pan·da [ˈpændə] *zo.* panda *f*; '~ **car** *Brt.* samochód *m* policyjny

pan·de·mo·ni·um [pændɪˈməʊnjəm] pandemonium *n*, zamieszanie *n*, chaos *m*

pan·der [ˈpændə] schlebiać (*gustom*)

pane [peɪn] szyba *f*

pan·el [ˈpænl] **1.** tafla *f*, płyta *f*, płycina *f*; *electr.*, *tech.* tablica *f* (*rozdzielcza*); *jur.* lista *f* sędziów przysięgłych; panel *m*,

grupa *f* (*ekspertów*); **2.** (*zwł. Brt.* **-ll-**, *Am.* **-l-**) wykładać ⟨-łożyć⟩ boazerią

pang [pæŋ] ukłucie *n* (*bólu*); ~**s** *pl. of hunger* skurcze *pl.* głodowe; ~**s** *pl. of conscience* wyrzuty *pl.* sumienia

'pan·han·dle *Am.* żebrać; '~**dler** żebrak *m* (-aczka *f*)

pan·ic [ˈpænɪk] **1.** paniczny; **2.** panika *f*; **3.** (**-ck-**) panikować; wpadać ⟨wpaść⟩ w panikę

pan·sy [ˈpænzɪ] *bot.* bratek *m*, fiołek *m* trójbarwny; F pedał *m*

pant [pænt] dyszeć; ziajać

pan·ther [ˈpænθə] *zo.* (*pl.* **-thers, -ther**) pantera *f*; *Am.* puma *f*; *Am.* jaguar *m*

pan·ties [ˈpæntɪz] *pl.* majtki *pl.*, *kobiece* figi *pl.*

pan·to·mime [ˈpæntəmaɪm] *Brt.* F jasełka *pl.*; *theat.* pantomima *f*

pan·try [ˈpæntrɪ] spiżarnia *f*; *naut.* pentra *f*

pants [pænts] *pl. Brt.* majtki *pl.*; *zwł. Am.* spodnie *pl.*

'pant·suit *Am.* spodnium *m*

pan·ty hose [ˈpæntɪhəʊz] *zwł. Am.* rajstopy *pl.*

pap [pæp] bryja *f*, ciapka *f*

pa·pal [ˈpeɪpl] papieski

pa·per [ˈpeɪpə] **1.** papier *m*; gazeta *f*, czasopismo *n*; praca *f* (pisemna *lub* semestralna); referat *m*; tapeta *f*; ~**s** *pl.* papiery *pl.*, dowody *pl.* tożsamości; **2.** ⟨wy⟩tapetować; '~**back** książka *f* w miękkich okładkach; '~ **bag** torba *f* papierowa; '~**boy** gazeciarz *m*; '~ **clip** wycinek *m* prasowy; '~ **cup** kubek *m* papierowy; '~**girl** gazeciarka *f*; '~**hang·er** tapeciarz *m*; '~ **knife** (*pl. knives*) *Brt.* nóż *m* do papieru; '~ **mon·ey** pieniądz *m* papierowy; '~**weight** przycisk *m* do papieru

par [pɑː] *econ.* wartość *f* nominalna, nominał *m*; parytet *m* kurs *m* wymian; *at* ~ na równi; według parytetu; *on a* ~ *with* na równi z (I)

par·a·ble [ˈpærəbl] przypowieść *f*

par·a|·chute [ˈpærəʃuːt] spadochron *m*; '~**chut·ist** spadochroniarz *m* (-arka *f*)

pa·rade [pəˈreɪd] **1.** parada *f*; pochód *m*; *fig.* pokaz *m*; *make a* ~ *of fig.* robić pokaz z (G); **2.** iść w pochodzie (*through* przez A); *mil.* ⟨prze⟩defilować; ⟨po⟩prowadzić w paradzie; *fig.* ⟨za⟩prezentować (się)

P

par·a·dise ['pærədaɪs] raj *m*

par·a·glid·er ['pærəglaɪdə] paralotnia *m*; lotniarz *m*; '~·ing lotniarstwo *n*

par·a·gon ['pærəgən] wzór *m*, wzorzec *m*

par·a·graph ['pærəgrɑːf] akapit *m*; paragraf *m*; notka *f* (*prasowa*)

par·al·lel ['pærəlel] 1. równoległy (*to*, *with* do *G*, *z I*); 2. *math.* prosta *f* równoległa, równoległa *f* (*też fig.*); *without* ~ bez analogii; *geogr.* równoleżnik *m*; 3. (*zwł. Brt. -ll-* , *Am. -l-*) odpowiadać (*D*), być podobnym do (*G*)

par·a·lyse *Brt.*, par·a·lyze *Am.* ['pærəlaɪz] *med.* ⟨s⟩paraliżować (*też fig.*); pa·ral·y·sis [pə'rælɪsɪs] (*pl. -ses* [-siːz]) *med.* paraliż *m* (*też fig.*)

par·a·mount ['pærəmaʊnt] nadrzędny, najważniejszy; *of ~ importance* najwyższego znaczenia

par·a·pet ['pærəpɪt] bariera *f*, balustrada *f*

par·a·pher·na·li·a [pærəfə'neɪljə] *pl.* parafernalia *pl.*, rzeczy *pl.* osobiste; *Brt.* zabiegi *pl.*, zachody *pl.*

par·a·site ['pærəsaɪt] pasożyt *m*

par·a·troop·er ['pærətruːpə] *mil.* spadochroniarz *m*; '~s *pl.* wojska *pl.* spadochronowe

par·boil ['pɑːbɔɪl] obgotowywać ⟨-ować⟩

par·cel ['pɑːsl] 1. paczka *f*, parcela *f*, działka *f*; 2. (*zwł. Brt. -ll-* , *Am. -l-*): ~ *out* rozdzielać ⟨-lić⟩, rozparcelowywać ⟨-ować⟩; ~ *up* zapakowywać ⟨-ować⟩ (*jako paczkę*)

parch [pɑːtʃ] wysychać ⟨-schnąć⟩; wysuszać ⟨-szyć⟩

parch·ment ['pɑːtʃmənt] pergamin *m*

par·don ['pɑːdn] 1. *jur.* ułaskawienie *n*, darowanie *n* kary; *I beg your* ~! przepraszam!; *też* ~? F słucham?; 2. wybaczać ⟨-czyć⟩; darować; *jur.* ułaskawiać ⟨-wić⟩; ~ *me* → *I beg your* ~; *Am.* F słucham?; '~·a·ble wybaczalny

pare [peə] *paznokcie* obcinać ⟨-ciąć⟩; *jabłko* obierać ⟨-brać⟩

par·ent ['peərənt] rodzic *m*; matka *f*, ojciec *m*; ~s *pl.* rodzice *pl.*; ~·age ['peərəntɪdʒ] rodzicielstwo *n*; pa·rental [pə'rentl] rodzicielski

pa·ren·the·ses [pə'renθɪsiːz] *pl.* nawiasy *pl.* (*zwł. okrągłe*)

'par·ents-in-law *pl.* teściowie *pl.*

par·ent-'teach·er meet·ing wywiadówka *f*

par·ings ['peərɪŋz] *pl.* obierki *pl.*

Pa·ris Paryż *m*

par·ish ['pærɪʃ] parafia *f*; pa·rish·io·ner [pə'rɪʃənə] *rel.* parafianin *m* (-anka *f*)

park [pɑːk] 1. park *m*; 2. *mot.* ⟨za⟩parkować

par·ka ['pɑːkə] skafander *m*

'park·ing *mot.* parkowanie *n*; *no* ~ zakaz *m* parkowania; '~ *disc* tarcza *f* czasu parkowania; '~ *fee* opłata *f* za parkowanie; '~ *ga·rage Am.* (*w budynku*) parking *m*; '~ *lot Am.* parking *m*; '~ *me·ter* parkometr *m*; '~ *space* miejsce *n* do ⟨za⟩parkowania; '~ *tick·et* mandat *m* za nieprawidłowe parkowanie

par·ley ['pɑːlɪ] *zwł. mil. pokojowe* rokowania *pl.*

par·lia·ment ['pɑːləmənt] parlament *m*; ~·men·tar·i·an [pɑːləmən'teərɪən] parlamentarzysta *m*; ~·men·ta·ry [pɑːlə'mentərɪ] parlamentarny

par·lo(u)r ['pɑːlə]: *zw. w złożeniach beauty* ~ gabinet *m* kosmetyczny

pa·ro·chi·al [pə'rəʊkjəl] parafialny; ziaściankowy

pa·role [pə'rəʊl] 1. zwolnienie *n* warunkowe; *he is out on* ~ jest na zwolnieniu warunkowym; 2. ~ *s.o.* zwolnić kogoś warunkowo

par·quet ['pɑːkeɪ] parkiet *m*; *Am. theat.* parter *m*; '~ *floor* parkiet *m*

par·rot ['pærət] 1. *zo.* papuga *f* (*też fig.*); 2. powtarzać (*jak papuga*)

par·ry ['pærɪ] ⟨od⟩parować, odbijać ⟨-bić⟩

par·si·mo·ni·ous [pɑːsɪ'məʊnjəs] skąpy

pars·ley ['pɑːslɪ] *bot.* pietruszka *f*

par·son ['pɑːsn] proboszcz *m*; ~·age ['pɑːsnɪdʒ] probostwo *n*

part [pɑːt] 1. część *f*; *tech.* element *m*, część *f*; udział *m*; strona *f*; *theat.*, *fig.* rola *f*; *mus.* głos *m*, partia *f*; odcinek *m* (*filmu*); *Am.* przedziałek *m*; *for my* ~ z mojej strony; *for the most* ~ w większości, przeważnie; *in* ~ częściowo; *on the* ~ *of* ze strony (*G*); *on my* ~ z mojej strony; *take* ~ *in s.th.* brać ⟨wziąć⟩ w czymś udział; *take s.th. in good* ~ przyjmować ⟨-jąć⟩ coś w dobrej wierze;

2. v/t. ⟨po-, roz⟩dzielić; *włosy* ⟨u⟩czesać z przedziałkiem; **~ company** rozstawać ⟨-tać⟩ się (**with** z *I*); v/i. rozstawać ⟨-tać⟩ się (**with** z *I*); **3.** *adj.* częściowy; **4.** *adv.* **~ ... ~ ...** częściowo ... a częściowo ...

par·tial ['pɑːʃl] częściowy; stronniczy, tendencyjny (**to** wobec *G*); **~·ti·al·i·ty** [pɑːʃɪ'ælətɪ] stronniczość *f*, tendencyjność *f* (**for** wobec *G*); **~·tial·ly** ['pɑːʃəlɪ] stronniczo, tendencyjnie

par·tic·i·pant [pɑː'tɪsɪpənt] uczestnik *m* (-iczka *f*); **~·pate** [pɑː'tɪsɪpeɪt] uczestniczyć, brać ⟨wziąć⟩ udział (**in** w *L*); **~·pa·tion** [pɑːtɪsɪ'peɪʃn] uczestnictwo *n*

par·ti·ci·ple ['pɑːtɪsɪpl] *gr.* imiesłów *m*

par·ti·cle ['pɑːtɪkl] cząstka *f*

par·tic·u·lar [pə'tɪkjʊlə] **1.** szczególny; indywidualny; wybredny, wymagający; dokładny, drobiazgowy; **2.** szczegół *m*, detal *m*; **~s** *pl.* dane *pl.* szczegółowe; dane *pl.* osobiste; **in ~** w szczególności; **~·ly** szczególnie

'part·ing 1. rozstanie *n*, pożegnanie *n*; *zwł. Brt.* przedziałek *m*; **2.** pożegnalny

par·ti·san [pɑːtɪ'zæn] **1.** stronnik *m* (-iczka *f*); *mil.* partyzant *m*; **2.** stronniczy

par·ti·tion [pɑː'tɪʃn] **1.** podział *m*; rozbiór *m*; ścianka *f* działowa; przepierzenie *n*; **2. ~ off** oddzielać ⟨-lić⟩

'part·ly częściowo

part·ner ['pɑːtnə] partner(ka *f*) *m*; *econ.* wspólnik *m* (-iczka *f*); **~·ship** partnerstwo *n*; *econ.* spółka *f*

part-'own·er współwłaściciel(ka *f*) *m*

par·tridge ['pɑːtrɪdʒ] *zo.* kuropatwa *f*

part|-'time 1. *adj.* niepełnoetatowy; **~ worker → part-timer; 2.** *adv.* na niepełny etat; na pół etatu; **~·'tim·er** pracownik *m* niepełnoetatowy *lub* na pół etatu

par·ty ['pɑːtɪ] partia *f*, stronnictwo *n*; grupa *f*, ekipa *f*; strona *f* (*umowy itp.*); *mil.* oddział *m*; uczestnik *m* (-iczka *f*); przyjęcie *n*, F impreza *f*; **'~ line** *pol.* linia *f* partyjna; **~ 'pol·i·tics** *sg. lub pl.* polityka *f* partyjna

pass [pɑːs] **1.** v/i. przechodzić ⟨-ejść⟩, przejeżdżać ⟨-jechać⟩ (**by** koło *G*); przechodzić ⟨-ejść⟩ (**to** do *G*); *ból, czas itp.*: przechodzić ⟨-ejść⟩, mijać ⟨minąć⟩; *egzamin itp.* zdawać ⟨-dać⟩ (*A*); (*w spor-*

cie) podawać ⟨-dać⟩ piłkę (**to** do *G*); *parl.* uchwalać ⟨-lić⟩ ustawę; być uważanym (**as, for** jako *A*); **let s.o. ~** przepuszczać ⟨-puścić⟩ kogoś; **let s.th. ~** puszczać ⟨puścić⟩ coś mimochodem; v/t. mijać ⟨minąć⟩; *czas* spędzać ⟨-dzić⟩; *egzamin itp.* zdawać ⟨-dać⟩; *pieprz, piłkę* podawać ⟨-dać⟩ (**to** do *G*); sięgać ⟨-gnąć⟩ (**over** do *G*); *parl.* uchwalać ⟨-lić⟩; *jur. wyrok* wydawać ⟨-dać⟩ (**on** na *A*); *sąd* wydawać ⟨-łosić⟩; *fig.* przewyższać; **~ away** umrzeć; **~ off** zakończyć się (*dobrze itp.*); uchodzić (**as** za *A*); **~ out** ⟨ze⟩mdleć; **2.** przepustka *f*; zdanie *n* (*egzaminu*); (*w sporcie*) podanie *n*; przełęcz *f*; **free~** bilet *m* bezpłatny; **make a ~ at** F dobierać się do (*G*); **'~·a·ble** znośny; *droga*: przejezdny

pas·sage ['pæsɪdʒ] korytarz *m*, przejście *n*; przejazd *m*, rejs *m*; pasaż *m* (*też mus.*); passus *m*; **bird of ~** ptak *m* wędrowny

'pass·book *zwł. Am.* książeczka *f* oszczędnościowa

pas·sen·ger ['pæsɪndʒə] pasażer-(ka *f*) *m*

pass·er·by [pɑːsə'baɪ] (*pl.* **passersby**) przechodzień *m*

pas·sion ['pæʃn] pasja *f*; namiętność *f*; zamiłowanie *n*; uczucie *n*; ♀ *rel.* pasja; **~·ate** ['pæʃənət] namiętny

pas·sive ['pæsɪv] bierny (*też gr.*), pasywny

pass·port ['pɑːspɔːt] paszport *m*

pass·word ['pɑːswɜːd] hasło *n*

past [pɑːst] **1.** *adj.* przeszły; wcześniejszy; *pred.* miniony, ubiegły; **for some time ~** od jakiegoś czasu; **~ tense** *gr.* czas przeszły; **2.** *adv.* obok (*G*), mimo (*G*); **3.** *prp. czas:* po (*D*); *miejsce:* obok (*G*), mimo (*G*); za (*D*); **half ~ two** (w)pół do trzeciej; **~ hope** beznadziejny

pas·ta ['pæstə] *gastr.* makaron *m*; △ *nie* **pasta**

paste [peɪst] **1.** ciasto *n*; pasta *f*; klej *m*; klajster *m*; **2.** ⟨przy⟩kleić (**to** do *G*, **on** na *A*); **~ up** naklejać ⟨-leić⟩, przylepiać ⟨-pić⟩; **'~·board** karton *m*, tektura *f*

pas·tel [pæ'stel] **1.** pastel *m*; **2.** pastelowy

pas·teur·ize ['pɑːstʃəraɪz] pasteryzować

pas·time ['pɑːstaɪm] zajęcie *n* (*w wolnych chwilach*)

pas·tor ['pɑːstə] pastor *m*; **~·al** ['pɑːstərəl] *rel.* duszpasterski; idylliczny, bukoliczny

pas·try ['peɪstrɪ] ciasto *n*; ciastko *n*; **'~ cook** cukiernik *m*

pas·ture ['pɑːstʃə] **1.** pastwisko *n*; **2.** paść (się); wypasać

pas·ty¹ ['pæstɪ] *zwł. Brt.* pasztecik *m*

past·y² ['peɪstɪ] kredowobiały, blady

pat [pæt] **1.** klaps *m*, klepnięcie *n*; porcja *f* (*zwł. masła*); **2.** (**-tt-**) klepać ⟨-pnąć⟩, poklepywać ⟨-pać⟩

patch [pætʃ] **1.** plama *f*; miejsce *n*; łata *f*; działka *f*; przepaska *f* na oko; **~es** miejscami; **2.** ⟨za-, po⟩łatać; **'~·work** patchwork *m*

pa·tent ['peɪtənt] **1.** patentowy; opatentowany; oczywisty, ewidentny; **2.** patent *m*; **3.** coś ⟨o⟩patentować; **~·ee** [peɪtən'tiː] posiadacz(ka *f*) *m* patentu; **~ 'leath·er** skóra *f* lakierowana

pa·ter·nal [pə'tɜːnl] ojcowski; **~·ni·ty** [pə'tɜːnətɪ] ojcostwo *n*

path [pɑːθ] (*pl.* **paths** [pɑːðz]) ścieżka *f*; trajektoria *f*, tor *m*

pa·thet·ic [pə'θetɪk] (**~ally**) patetyczny; żałosny, pożałowania godny

pa·thos ['peɪθɒs] żałosność *f*, współczucie *n*

pa·tience ['peɪʃns] cierpliwość *f*; *zwł. Brt.* pasjans *m*

pa·tient¹ ['peɪʃnt] cierpliwy

pa·tient² ['peɪʃnt] pacjent(ka *f*) *m*

pat·i·o ['pætɪəʊ] (*pl.* **-os**) patio *n*, dziedziniec *m*

pat·ri·ot ['pætrɪət] patriota *m* (-tka *f*); **~·ic** [pætrɪ'ɒtɪk] (**~ally**) patriotyczny

pa·trol [pə'trəʊl] **1.** patrol *m*; **on ~** na patrolu; **2.** (**-ll-**) patrolować; **~ car** wóz *m* patrolowy; **~·man** (*pl.* **-men**) *zwł. Am.* policjant(ka *f*) *m* na służbie patrolowej; *Brt.* (*osoba pomagająca zmotoryzowanym w razie awarii*)

pa·tron ['peɪtrən] mecenas *m*, sponsor *m*; patron(ka *f*) *m*; *stały klient m, stała klientka f* **pat·ron·age** ['pætrənɪdʒ] patronaż *m*; **pat·ron·ess** ['peɪtrənɪs] patronka *f*; *stała klientka f*; **pat·ron·ize** ['pætrənaɪz] ⟨po⟩traktować protekcjonalnie; być gościem ⟨G⟩; być patronem ⟨G⟩; **~ saint** [peɪtrən 'seɪnt] *rel.* patron(ka *f*) *m*

pat·ter ['pætə] *deszcz:* ⟨za⟩stukać; ⟨za⟩tupać

pat·tern ['pætən] **1.** wzór *m* (*też fig.*); **2.** wzorować się

paunch ['pɔːnʃ] brzuszysko *n*

pau·per ['pɔːpə] nędzarz *m* (-arka *f*)

pause [pɔːz] **1.** przerwa *f*; pauza *f*; **2.** zatrzymywać się; ⟨z⟩robić przerwę

pave [peɪv] ⟨wy⟩brukować; **~ the way for** *fig.* ⟨u⟩torować drogę do ⟨G⟩; **'~·ment** *Brt.* bruk *m*; *Am.* chodnik *m*

paw [pɔː] **1.** łapa *f* (*też fig.*); **2.** *v/t.* grzebać w (*ziemi itp*); ⟨za⟩skrobać do (*drzwi*); F macać, obmacywać ⟨-cać⟩; *v/i.* skrobać (**at** po *L*)

pawn¹ [pɔːn] *szachy:*pionek *m* (*też fig.*)

pawn² [pɔːn] **1.** zastawiać ⟨-wić⟩; **2. be in ~** znajdować się w zastawie; **'~·broker** właściciel *m* lombardu; **'~·shop** lombard *m*

pay [peɪ] **1.** (**paid**) *v/t.* coś ⟨za⟩płacić (*też* za *A*); komuś ⟨za⟩płacić; *uwagę* poświęcać ⟨-cić⟩; *wizytę* składać ⟨złożyć⟩; *komplement* mówić ⟨powiedzieć⟩; **~ attention** zwracać ⟨-rócić⟩ uwagę (**to** na *A*); **~ cash** ⟨za⟩płacić gotówką; *v/i.* ⟨za⟩płacić; *fig.* opłacać ⟨-cić⟩ się; **~ for** ⟨za⟩płacić za (*A*) (*też fig.*); **~ in** wpłacać ⟨-cić⟩; **~ into** wpłacać ⟨-cić⟩ na (*A*); **~ off** coś spłacać ⟨-cić⟩; ⟨za⟩płacić się; wypłacać ⟨-cić⟩ odprawę; **2.** zapłata *f*, wypłata *f*; płaca *f*, pobory *pl.*; **'~·a·ble** wypłacalny; **'~·day** dzień *m* wypłaty; **~·ee** [peɪ'iː] odbiorca *m* (*pieniędzy*); beneficjent *m*; **'~ en·ve·lope** *Am.* koperta *f* z wypłatą; **'~·ing** płatność *f*; wypłata *f*; **~·ing 'guest** gość *m* (*na kwaterze turystycznej*); podnajemca *m*, sublokator(ka *f*) *m*; **'~·ment** wypłata *f*; **'~ pack·et** *Brt.* koperta *f* z wypłatą; **'~ phone** *Brt.* automat *m* telefoniczny; **'~·roll** lista *f* płac; **'~·slip** odcinek *m* wypłaty

PC [piː 'siː] *skrót:* **personal computer** komputer osobisty *m*, F pecet *m*; **~ user** użytkownik *m* komputera osobistego

P.C., PC [piː 'siː] *Brt. skrót:* **police constable** policjant *m*

pd *skrót pisany:* **paid** zapł., zapłacony

pea [piː] *bot.* groszek *m*, groch *m*

peace [piːs] pokój *m jur.* spokój *m*; cisza *f*; **at ~** w spokoju; **'~·a·ble** pokojowy; **'~·ful** pokojowy; **'~·lov·ing** miłujący pokój; **'~ move·ment** ruch *m* obrony pokoju; **'~·time** pokój *m*

peach [piːtʃ] *bot.* brzoskwinia *f*

pea|**·cock** ['pi:kɒk] *zo.* paw *m*; '~**·hen** *zo.* pawica *f*

peak [pi:k] szczyt *m* (*też fig.*); wierzchołek *m*; daszek *m* (*czapki*); ~**ed cap** [pi:kt 'kæp] czapka *f* z daszkiem; '~ **hours** *pl.* godziny *pl.* szczytu; *electr.* okres *m* szczytowego obciążenia; '~ **time** *też* **peak viewing hours** *pl. Brt. TV* okres *m* największej oglądalności

peal [pi:l] **1.** bicie *n* (*dzwonu lub dzwonów*); kurant *m*; grzmot *m* (*pioruna*); ~ **of laughter** gromki śmiech *m*; **2.** *też* ~ **out** rozbrzmiewać

pea·nut ['pi:nʌt] *bot.* orzeszek *m* ziemny, fistaszek *m*; ~**s** *pl.* F śmieszna suma *f*

pear [peə] *bot.* gruszka *f*; grusza *f*

pearl [pɜ:l] perła *f*; *attr.* perłowy; '~**·y** (*-ier, -iest*) perłowy

peas·ant ['peznt] chłop *m*, wieśniak *m*

peat [pi:t] torf *m*; *attr.* torfowy

peb·ble ['pebl] kamień *m*, kamyk *m*, otoczak *m*

peck [pek] dziobać ⟨-bnąć⟩; cmokać ⟨-knąć⟩; ~ **at one's food** przebierać ⟨-brać⟩ w jedzeniu

pe·cu·li·ar [pɪ'kju:ljə] szczególny, charakterystyczny; dziwny, osobliwy; ~**·i·ty** [pɪkju:lɪ'ærətɪ] szczególność *f*; osobliwość *f*

pe·cu·ni·a·ry [pɪ'kju:njərɪ] pieniężny, finansowy

ped·a·go·gic [pedə'gɒdʒɪk] pedagogiczny

ped·al ['pedl] **1.** pedał *m*; **2.** (*zwł. Brt. -ll-, Am. -l-*) ⟨po⟩pedałować; ⟨po⟩jechać (*na rowerze*)

pe·dan·tic [pɪ'dæntɪk] (*~ally*) pedantyczny

ped·dle ['pedl] handlować (*I*); ~ **drugs** handlować narkotykami; '~**r** → *Am.* **pedlar**

ped·es·tal ['pedɪstl] piedestał *m* (*też fig.*)

pe·des·tri·an [pɪ'destrɪən] **1.** pieszy *m* (*-sza f*); **2.** pieszy; ~ **'cross·ing** przejście *n* dla pieszych; ~ **'mall** *Am.*, ~ **'pre·cinct** *zwł. Brt.* strefa *f* ruchu pieszego

ped·i·cure ['pedɪkjʊə] pedicure *m*

ped·i·gree ['pedɪgri:] rodowód *m*; *attr.* rodowodowy

ped·lar ['pedlə] handlarz *m* (*-arka f*)

pee [pi:] F **1.** siusiać; **2.** **have** (*lub* **go for**) **a** ~ wysiusiać się

peek [pi:k] **1.** zerkać ⟨-knąć⟩ (*at* na *A*); **2.** **have** *lub* **take a** ~ **at** zerkać ⟨-knąć⟩ na (*A*)

peel [pi:l] **1.** *v/t.* obierać ⟨-brać⟩; *też* ~ **off** tapetę, *ubranie itp.* zdzierać ⟨zedrzeć⟩; *v/i. też* ~ **off** tapeta: odchodzić ⟨odejść⟩, *skóra, farba:* schodzić ⟨zejść⟩; **2.** skórka *f*

peep[1] [pi:p] **1.** zerkać ⟨-knąć⟩ (*at* na *A*); **2.** **take a** ~ **at** zerkać ⟨-knąć⟩ na (*A*)

peep[2] [pi:p] **1.** pisk *m*, zabrzęczenie; **2.** ⟨za⟩piszczeć, ⟨za⟩brzęczeć

'peep·hole wizjer *m*, judasz *m*

peer [pɪə] **1.** przyglądać ⟨przyjrzeć⟩ się (*at D*); **2.** równy *m* (*-na f*); *Brt.* par *m*, arystokrata *m*; '~**·less** niezrównany

peev·ish ['pi:vɪʃ] drażliwy, pobudliwy

peg [peg] **1.** kołek *m*; palik *m*; wieszak *m*; *Brt.* klamerka *f* do bielizny; śledź *m* (*do namiotu*)

Pe·king Pekin *m*

pel·i·can ['pelɪkən] *zo.* (*pl. -can, -cans*) pelikan *m*; ~ **'cross·ing** *Brt.* przejście *n* dla pieszych (*na światłach*)

pel·let ['pelɪt] kulka *f* (*też śrutu*), grudka *f*

pelt[1] [pelt] *v/t.* obrzucać ⟨-cić⟩; *v/i.* **it's ~ing (down)**, *zwł. Brt.* **it's ~ing with rain** leje jak z cebra

pelt[2] [pelt] skóra *f* (surowa)

pel·vis ['pelvɪs] *anat.* (*pl. -vises, -ves* [-vi:z]) miednica *f*

pen[1] [pen] pióro *n*, długopis *m*, pisak *m*

pen[2] [pen] **1.** zagroda *f*; **2.** (*-nn-*): ~**in**, ~**up** *zwierzęta, ludzi* zamykać ⟨-knąć⟩

pe·nal ['pi:nl] karny, karalny; '~ **code** kodeks *m* karny; ~**·ize** ['pi:nəlaɪz] penalizować; ⟨u⟩karać

pen·al·ty ['penltɪ] kara *f*, grzywna *f*; (*w sporcie*) kara *f*, punkt *m* karny; (*w piłce nożnej*) rzut *m* karny; '~ **ar·e·a**, '~ **box** (*w piłce nożnej*) pole *n* karne; '~ **goal** (*w piłce nożnej*) bramka *f* z rzutu karnego; '~ **kick** (*w piłce nożnej*) rzut *m* karny; ~ **'shoot-out** (*w piłce nożnej*) strzały *pl.* z pola karnego (*dla rozstrzygnięcia meczu*); '~ **spot** (*w piłce nożnej*) punkt

pen·ance ['penəns] *rel.* pokuta *f*

pence [pens] (*skrót:* **p**) *pl. od* **penny**

pen·cil ['pensl] **1.** ołówek *m*; **2.** (*zwł. Brt. -ll-, Am. -l-*) zaznaczać ⟨-czyć⟩, zapisywać ⟨-sać⟩ (*ołówkiem*); '~ **case** piórnik *m*; '~ **sharp·en·er** temperówka *f*

pen·dant, pen·dent ['pendənt] wisiorek *m*

pend·ing ['pendɪŋ] **1.** *prp.* w trakcie (*G*); **2.** *adj.* zwł. *jur.* będący w toku

pen·du·lum ['pendjʊləm] wahadło *n*

pen·e|·trate ['penɪtreɪt] przenikać ⟨-knąć⟩ do (*G*) *lub* przez (*A*), przenikać ⟨-knąć⟩ (*into* do *G*, *through* przez *A*); '**~·trat·ing** przenikliwy; bystry; **~·tra·tion** [penɪ'treɪʃn] przeniknięcie *n*, wniknięcie *n*; bystrość *f*

'**pen friend** (*osoba, z którą się koresponduje*)

pen·guin ['peŋgwɪn] *zo.* pingwin *m*

pe·nin·su·la [pə'nɪnsjʊlə] półwysep *m*

pe·nis ['piːnɪs] *anat.* penis *m*, członek *m*

pen·i·tence ['penɪtəns] skrucha *f*, żal *m* za grzechy; '**~·tent 1.** skruszony, żałujący za grzechy; **2.** *rel.* penitent *m*; **~·ten·tia·ry** [penɪ'tenʃərɪ] *Am.* zakład *m* karny

'**pen|·knife** (*pl.* **-knives**) scyzoryk *m*; '**~ name** pseudonim *m* literacki

pen·nant ['penənt] wimpel *m*, proporczyk *m*

pen·ni·less ['penɪlɪs] bez pieniędzy

pen·ny ['penɪ] (*skrót:* **p**) (*pl.* **-nies**, *coll.* **pence**) *też* **new ~** *Brt.* pens *m*

'**pen pal** *zwł. Am.* → **pen friend**

pen·sion ['penʃn] **1.** renta *f*, emerytura *f*; △ *nie* **pensja**; **2.** **~ off** przenosić ⟨-nieść⟩ w stan spoczynku; **~·er** ['penʃənə] rencista *m* (-tka *f*), emeryt(ka *f*) *m*

pen·sive ['pensɪv] zadumany, zamyślony

pen·tath|·lete [pen'tæθliːt] (*w sporcie*) pięcioboista *m*; **~·lon** [pen'tæθlɒn] (*w sporcie*) pięciobój *m*

Pen·te·cost ['pentɪkɒst] Zielone Świątki *pl.* Szawuot *m* (*w judaizmie*)

pent·house ['penthaʊs] penthouse *m* (*apartament na ostatnim piętrze wieżowca*)

pent-up [pent'ʌp] *uczucie itp.:* powstrzymywany

pe·o·ny ['pɪənɪ] *bot.* piwonia *f*

peo·ple ['piːpl] **1.** *pl.* ludzie *pl.*; **the ~** naród *m*; (*pl.* **peoples**) lud *m*; **2.** zasiedlać ⟨-lić⟩; **~'s re·pub·lic** republika *f* ludowa

pep [pep] F **1.** ikra *f*, werwa *f*; **2.** (**-pp-**) uatrakcyjniać ⟨-nić⟩, pobudzać ⟨-dzić⟩

pep·per ['pepə] **1.** pieprz *m*; (*strąk*) papryka *f*; **2.** ⟨po⟩pieprzyć; '**~·mint** *bot.*

mięta *f* (pieprzowa); miętus *m*; **~·y** ['pepərɪ] pieprzny; *fig.* drażliwy

'**pep pill** F środek *m* stymulujący

per [pɜː] na (*A*); za (*A*); od (*A*); według (*A*)

per·am·bu·la·tor [pə'ræmbjʊleɪtə] *zwł. Brt.* wózek *m* dziecięcy

per·ceive [pə'siːv] spostrzegać ⟨-ec⟩, dostrzegać ⟨-ec⟩

per cent, per·cent [pə'sent] procent *m*

per·cen·tage [pə'sentɪdʒ] procent *m*; F zysk *m*, procenty *pl.*

per·cep|·ti·ble [pə'septəbl] dostrzegalny, zauważalny; **~·tion** [pə'sepʃn] percepcja *f*, dostrzeganie *n*

perch[1] [pɜːtʃ] **1.** grzęda *f*; **2.** ~ *o.s.* (*on*) ⟨u⟩sadowić się (na *L*)

perch[2] [pɜːtʃ] *zo.* (*pl.* **perch, perches**) okoń *m*

per·co|·late ['pɜːkəleɪt] kawę *itp.* zaparzać ⟨-rzyć⟩ (się); '**~·la·tor** ekspres *m* do kawy

per·cus·sion [pə'kʌʃn] uderzenie *n*; *mus.* instrumenty *pl.* perkusyjne; **~ in·stru·ment** *mus.* instrument *m* perkusyjny

pe·remp·to·ry [pə'remptərɪ] władczy, kategoryczny

pe·ren·ni·al [pə'renjəl] wieczny; *bot.* wieloletni, trwały

per|·fect 1. ['pɜːfɪkt] doskonały, perfekcyjny; zupełny, całkowity; wykończony; **2.** [pə'fekt] udoskonalać ⟨-lić⟩, ulepszać ⟨-szyć⟩; **3.** ['pɜːfɪkt] *też* **~·fect tense** *gr.* czas *m* dokonany; **~·fec·tion** [pə'fekʃn] doskonałość *f*; perfekcja *f*; udoskonalenie *n*

per·fo·rate ['pɜːfəreɪt] ⟨prze⟩dziurawić, ⟨prze⟩dziurkować; perforować

per·form [pə'fɔːm] *v/t.* wykonywać ⟨-nać⟩ (*też mus., theat.*); dokonywać ⟨-ać⟩; *theat., mus.* grać; *v/i. theat. itp.* dawać ⟨dać⟩ przedstawienie, grać; *samochód:* sprawiać ⟨-wić⟩ się; **~·ance** wykonanie *n*; działanie *n*; osiągi *pl.*; *mus, theat.* występ *m*, przedstawienie *n*; **~·er** wykonawca *m* (-czyni *f*)

per·fume 1. ['pɜːfjuːm] perfumy *pl.*; **2.** [pə'fjuːm] ⟨u⟩perfumować

per·haps [pə'hæps, præps] (być) może

per·il ['perəl] niebezpieczeństwo *n*; '**~·ous** niebezpieczny

pe·ri·od ['pɪərɪəd] okres *m*; lekcja *f*; *physiol.* okres *m* (*kobiety*); *gr.* zwł. *Am.*

P

kropka *f; attr.* stylowy, zabytkowy; **~ic** [pɪərɪ'ɒdɪk] periodyczny, okresowy; **~·i·cal** [pɪərɪ'ɒdɪkl] **1.** periodyczny, okresowy; **2.** periodyk *m*

pe·riph·e·ral [pə'rɪfərəl] **1.** peryferyjny; **2.** *komp.* urządzenie *n* peryferyjne; **~ e'quip·ment** *komp.* urządzenia *pl.* peryferyjne

pe·riph·e·ry [pə'rɪfərɪ] obrzeże *n*, peryferia *pl.*

per·ish ['perɪʃ] ⟨z⟩ginąć; *Brt.* gumę rozłożyć; **~·a·ble** *jedzenie itp.*: nietrwały; **~·ing** *zwł. Brt.* F przenikliwy, przejmująco zimny

per·jure ['pɜːdʒə] **~jure o.s.** krzywoprzysięgać ⟨-gnąć⟩; **~·ju·ry** ['pɜːdʒərɪ] krzywoprzysięstwo *n; commit ~jury* popełniać ⟨-nić⟩ krzywoprzysięstwo *n*

perk [pɜːk]: **~ up** *v/i.* ożywiać ⟨-wić⟩ się; *v/t.* pobudzać ⟨-dzić⟩

perk·y ['pɜːkɪ] F (*-ier, -iest*) żywotny, rozradowany

perm [pɜːm] **1.** trwała *f;* **2.** *get one's hair ~ed* zrobić sobie trwałą

per·ma·nent ['pɜːmənənt] **1.** trwały; stały; **2.** *Am.* ~ **wave** trwała *f*

per·me·a·ble ['pɜːmjəbl] przepuszczalny (*to* dla *G*); **~ate** ['pɜːmɪeɪt] przenikać ⟨-knąć⟩ (*into* do *A*, *through* przez *A*)

per·mis·si·ble [pə'mɪsəbl] dozwolony, dopuszczalny; **~·sion** [pə'mɪʃn] pozwolenie *n*, zezwolenie *n;* **~·sive** [pə'mɪsɪv] przyzwalający, pobłażliwy; **~·sive so'ci·e·ty** społeczeństwo *n* przyzwalające

per·mit 1. [pə'mɪt] (*-tt-*) zezwalać ⟨-lić⟩, pozwalać ⟨-wolić⟩; **2.** ['pɜːmɪt] zezwolenie *n;* przepustka *f*

per·pen·dic·u·lar [pɜːpən'dɪkjulə] prostopadły

per·pet·u·al [pə'petʃuəl] wieczny, trwały; dożywotni

per·plex [pə'pleks] ⟨za⟩kłopotać, ⟨z⟩mieszać, stropić; **~·i·ty** [pə'pleksətɪ] zakłopotanie *n*, stropienie *n*

per·se|·cute ['pɜːsɪkjuːt] prześladować, szykanować; ⟨u⟩karać; **~·cu·tion** [pɜːsɪ'kjuːʃn] prześladowanie *n*, szykanowanie *n;* **~·cu·tor** ['pɜːsɪkjuːtə] prześladowca *m*

per·se|·ver·ance [pɜːsɪ'vɪərəns] wytrwałość *f;* **~·vere** [pɜːsɪ'vɪə] wytrwać, nie poddawać się

per·sist [pə'sɪst] trwać, utrzymywać się; **~sist in doing s.th.** nie zaprzestawać czegoś robić; **~'sis·tence** wytrzymałość *f*, uporczywość *f;* **~'sis·tent** uporczywy

per·son ['pɜːsn] osoba *f* (*też gr.*)

per·son·al ['pɜːsnl] osobisty, osobowy (*też gr.*); prywatny; **~ col·umn** ogłoszenia *pl.* drobne; **~ com'pu·ter** (*skrót:* **PC**) komputer *m* osobisty, F pecet *m;* **~ 'da·ta** *pl.* dane *pl.* osobiste

per·son·al·i·ty [pɜːsə'nælətɪ] osobowość *f; personalities pl.* uwagi *pl.* osobiste

per·son·al| 'or·ga·ni·zer (*notes, spis adresów*) kalendarz *m* biznesmena; **~ 'ster·e·o** walkman *m* (*TM*)

per·son·i·fy [pɜː'sɒnɪfaɪ] uosabiać ⟨-sobić⟩

per·son·nel [pɜːsə'nel] kadra *f*, personel *m*, załoga *f;* (*dział*) kadry *pl.;* **~ depart·ment** kadry *pl.;* **~ man·ag·er** dyrektor *m* do spraw osobowych

per·spec·tive [pə'spektɪv] perspektywa *f;* widok *m;* punkt *m* widzenia

per·spi·ra·tion [pɜːspə'reɪʃn] pot *m*, pocenie *n* się; **~·spire** [pə'spaɪə] ⟨s⟩pocić się

per·suade [pə'sweɪd] przekonywać ⟨-nać⟩; **~·sua·sion** [pə'sweɪʒn] przekonanie *n;* przekonywanie *n*, perswazja *f;* **~·sua·sive** [pə'sweɪsɪv] przekonujący

pert [pɜːt] *kapelusz:* szykowny; *dziewczyna:* czupurny

per·tain [pɜː'teɪn]: **~ to s.th.** odnosić się do czegoś

per·ti·nent ['pɜːtɪnənt] stosowny, właściwy

per·turb [pə'tɜːb] ⟨za⟩niepokoić

pe·ruse [pə'ruːz] przeglądać ⟨-dnąć⟩, ⟨z⟩badać

per·vade [pə'veɪd] przenikać ⟨-knąć⟩, wypełniać ⟨-nić⟩

per|·verse [pə'vɜːs] perwersyjny, zboczony; **~·ver·sion** [pə'vɜːʃn] perwersja *f*, zboczenie *n;* wypaczenie *n*, przekręcenie *n;* **~·ver·si·ty** [pə'vɜːsətɪ] perwersja *f*

per·vert 1. [pə'vɜːt] ⟨z⟩deprawować; przekręcać ⟨-cić⟩; **2.** ['pɜːvɜːt] zboczeniec *m*

pes·sa·ry ['pesərɪ] *med.* pesarium *n*, krążek *m* domaciczny

pes·si|·mis·m ['pesɪmɪzəm] pesymizm *m*; ~**mist** ['pesɪmɪst] pesymista *m* (-tka *f*); ~'**mist·ic** (-*ally*) pesymistyczny

pest [pest] szkodnik *m*; utrapienie *n*

pes·ter ['pestə] F ⟨z⟩nękać, dręczyć

pes·ti·cide ['pestɪsaɪd] pestycyd *m*

pet [pet] **1.** zwierzę *n* domowe; *często pej.* ulubieniec *m*; kochanie *n*; **2.** ulubiony, ukochany; pieszczotliwy; dla zwierząt domowych; **3.** (-*tt*-) pieścić (się)

pet·al ['petl] *bot.* płatek *m*

'**pet food** pokarm *m* dla zwierząt domowych

pe·ti·tion [pɪ'tɪʃn] **1.** petycja *f*, prośba *f*; skarga *f*; **2.** składać ⟨złożyć⟩ petycję (*for* o *A*); ⟨po⟩prosić (*for* o *A*)

'**pet name** pieszczotliwe przezwisko *n*

pet·ri·fy ['petrɪfaɪ] petryfikować, zmieniać w kamień; *fig.* ⟨s⟩paraliżować

pet·rol ['petrəl] etylina *f*, benzyna *f*

pe·tro·le·um [pə'trəʊljəm] ropa *f* naftowa

'**pet·rol| pump** dystrybutor *m* paliwa; pompa *f* paliwowa; ~ **sta·tion** stacja *f* benzynowa

'**pet| shop** sklep *m* zoologiczny; ~ '**sub·ject** konik *m*

pet·ti·coat ['petɪkəʊt] półhalka *f*; halka *f*

pet·ting ['petɪŋ] F petting *m*

pet·tish ['petɪʃ] rozdrażniony, rozhisteryzowany

pet·ty ['petɪ] (-*ier, -iest*) drobny, mały; nieznaczny; małostkowy; ~ '**cash** drobne *pl.*, podręczna gotówka *f*; ~ '**lar·ce·ny** *jur.* drobna kradzież *f*

pet·u·lant ['petjʊlənt] uprzykrzony

pew [pjuː] ławka *f* (*w kościele*)

pew·ter ['pjuːtə] cyna *f*; *też* ~ **ware** naczynia *pl.* cynowe

phan·tom ['fæntəm] fantom *m*, zjawa *f*

phar·ma·cist ['fɑːməsɪst] aptekarz *m* (-arka *f*); ~**cy** ['fɑːməsɪ] apteka *f*

phase [feɪz] faza *f*

PhD [piː eɪtʃ 'diː] *skrót:* **Doctor of Philosophy** (*łacińskie* **philosophiae doctor**) dr, doktor *m*; ~ '**the·sis** rozprawa *f* doktorska

pheas·ant ['feznt] *zo.* bażant *m*

phe·nom·e·non [fɪ'nɒmɪnən] (*pl.* -*na* [-nə]) zjawisko *n*

Phi·la·del·phia Filadelfia *f*

phi·lan·thro·pist [fɪ'lænθrəpɪst] filantrop *m*

Phil·ip·pines *pl.* Filipiny *pl.*

phi·lol·o|·gist [fɪ'lɒlədʒɪst] filolog *m*; ~**gy** [fɪ'lɒlədʒɪ] filologia *f*

phi·los·o|·pher [fɪ'lɒsəfə] filozof *m*; ~**phy** [fɪ'lɒsəfɪ] filozofia *f*

phlegm [flem] *med.* flegma *f* (*też fig.*); opanowanie *n*

phone [fəʊn] **1.** telefon *m*; **answer the** ~ odbierać ⟨odebrać⟩ telefon; **by** ~ telefonicznie, przez telefon; **on the** ~ przy telefonie; **be on the** ~ rozmawiać przez telefon; być przy telefonie; **2.** ⟨za⟩telefonować, ⟨za⟩dzwonić; ~ **book** książka telefoniczna *f*; ~ **booth** *Am.*, ~ **box** *Brt.* budka *f* telefoniczna; ~ **call** rozmowa *f* telefoniczna; ~ '**card** karta *f* telefoniczna; '~**in** *Brt.*: audycja (*radiowa lub telewizyjna*) *f* z telefonicznym udziałem odbiorców; ~ **num·ber** numer *m* telefoniczny

pho·net·ics [fə'netɪks] *sg.* fonetyka *f*

pho·n(e)y ['fəʊnɪ] F **1.** krętactwo *n*; krętacz *m*; **2.** (-*ier, -iest*) fałszywy, udawany

phos·pho·rus ['fɒsfərəs] *chem.* fosfor *m*

pho·to ['fəʊtəʊ] F (*pl.* -*tos*) fotografia *f*, zdjęcie *n*; **in the** ~ na fotografii; **take a** ~ zrobić zdjęcie; '~**cop·i·er** fotokopiarka *f*; '~**cop·y** fotokopia *f*

pho|·to·graph ['fəʊtəɡrɑːf] **1.** fotografia *f*, zdjęcie *n*; △ *nie* **fotograf**; **2.** ⟨s⟩fotografować; ~**tog·ra·pher** [fə'tɒɡrəfə] fotograf *m*; ~**tog·ra·phy** [fə'tɒɡrəfɪ] fotografia *f*

phras·al verb [freɪzl 'vɜːb] czasownik *m* złożony

phrase [freɪz] zwrot *m*, wyrażenie *n*, idiom *m*; fraza *f*; **2.** wyrażać ⟨-razić⟩; '~**book** rozmówki *pl.*

phys·i·cal ['fɪzɪkl] **1.** fizyczny; materialny; fizykalny; ~*ly* **handicapped** upośledzony fizycznie; **2.** badanie *n* lekarskie; ~ **ed·u·ca·tion** wychowanie *n* fizyczne; ~ **ex·am·i·na·tion** badanie *n* lekarskie; ~ '**hand·i·cap** upośledzenie *n* fizyczne; ~ '**train·ing** wychowanie *n* fizyczne

phy·si·cian [fɪ'zɪʃn] lekarz *m* (-arka *f*); △ *nie* **fizyk**

phys|·i·cist ['fɪzɪsɪst] fizyk *m*; ~**ics** ['fɪzɪks] *sg.* fizyka *f*

phy·sique [fɪ'ziːk] budowa *f* ciała

P

pi·a·nist ['pɪənɪst] pianista f (-tka f)

pi·an·o [pɪ'ænəʊ] (pl. -os) fortepian m, pianino n; attr. fortepianowy, na fortepian

pick [pɪk] 1. wybierać ⟨-brać⟩; odrywać ⟨oderwać⟩, zrywać ⟨zerwać⟩; zbierać ⟨zebrać⟩; ⟨po⟩grzebać, ⟨po⟩dłubać; *zamek itp.* otwierać ⟨-worzyć⟩ wytrychem; *kłótnię itp.* ⟨s⟩prowokować; **~ one's nose** *(teeth)* 'Opo⟩dłubać w nosie (zębach); **~ s.o.'s pocket** okradać ⟨-raść⟩ kogoś; **have a bone to ~ with s.o.** mieć coś komuś do powiedzenia; **~ out** wybrać ⟨-brać⟩, dostrzegać ⟨-rzec⟩, odróżniać ⟨-nić⟩; **~ up** podnosić ⟨-nieść⟩ (się); zbierać ⟨zebrać⟩ (się); podejmować ⟨-jąć⟩; *kogoś, rzeczy itp.* odbierać ⟨-debrać⟩; *autostopowicza itp.* zabierać ⟨-brać⟩; F *dziewczynę itp.* poderwać ⟨-drywać⟩; *policja:* zatrzymywać ⟨-mać⟩; *sygnał itp.* odbierać ⟨-debrać⟩; *też* **~ up speed** *mot.* zwiększać ⟨-szyć⟩ (prędkość); *choremu* pomagać ⟨-móc⟩; 2. kilof *m*, oskard *m*; wybór *m*; *take your* **~** proszę sobie wybrać; **~-a-back** ['pɪkbæk] na barana; '**~-axe** *Brt.*, **~ax** *Am.* kilof *m*, oskard *m*

pick·et ['pɪkɪt] 1. pikieta f; 2. pikietować; '**~-fence** płot *m* ze sztachet; '**~ line** linia f pikietujących

pick·le ['pɪkl] 1. zalewa f octowa; marynata f; *Am.* ogórki *pl.* konserwowe; *zw.* **~s** *pl. zwł. Brt.* pikle *pl.*; **be in a** *(pretty)* **~** F fig. narobić sobie bigosu; 2. *gastr.* przyrządzać ⟨-dzić⟩ marynatę, ⟨za⟩marynować

'pick·lock 1. włamywacz(ka f) m; '**~-pock·et** kieszonkowiec *m*; '**~-up** *mot.* pickup m, pikap m; F zdobycz f (poderwanie)

pic·nic ['pɪknɪk] 1. piknik *m*; 2. (-ck-) ⟨z⟩robić piknik, piknikować

pic·ture ['pɪktʃə] 1. obraz *m*, obrazek *m*; *phot.* zdjęcie *n*; film *m*; **~s** *pl. zwł. Brt.* kino *n*; 2. przedstawiać ⟨-wić⟩ (sobie); wyobrażać sobie; '**~ book** książka f z obrazkami; **~ 'post·card** widokówka f

pic·tur·esque [pɪktʃə'resk] malowniczy

pie [paɪ] pasztecik *m*; ciasto *n*

piece [piːs] 1. sztuka f; kawałek *m*; część f *(maszyny, serwisu itp.)*; figura f *(sza-*chowa; pionek *m (do gry)*; *(w gazecie)* artykuł *m*, notatka f; **by the ~** na sztuki; **a ~ of advice** *(news)* rada f; **a ~ of news** informacja f, wiadomość f; **give s.o. a ~ of one's mind** nagadać komuś; **go to ~s** F załamywać ⟨-mać⟩ się; **take to ~s** rozbierać ⟨-zebrać⟩ na części; 2. **~ together** zestawiać ⟨-wić⟩ razem; ⟨po⟩składać; '**~-meal** kawałkami, po kawałku; '**~-work** praca f na akord; **do ~work** pracować na akord

pier [pɪə] pirs *m*, molo *n*

pierce [pɪəs] przedziurawić ⟨-wiać⟩, przebijać ⟨-bić⟩

pierc·ing ['pɪəsɪŋ] *zimno, ból, spojrzenie:* przenikliwy; *krzyk:* rozdzierający

pi·e·ty ['paɪətɪ] pobożność f

pig [pɪg] *zo.* świnia; *sl. pej.* gliniarz *m*

pi·geon ['pɪdʒɪn] (pl. -geons, -geon) gołąb *m*; '**~-hole** 1. przegródka f 2. odkładać ⟨odłożyć⟩; ⟨za⟩szufladkować

pig·gy ['pɪgɪ] F świnka f *(w języku dzieci)*; '**~-back** na barana

pig'head·ed durny; '**~-let** ['pɪglɪt] prosiak *m*; '**~-sty** chlew *m (też fig.)*; '**~-tail** warkoczyk *m*

pike[1] [paɪk] *zo.* (pl. **pikes, pike**) szczupak *m*

pike[2] [paɪk] → **turnpike**

pile[1] [paɪl] 1. stos *m*, sterta f; F forsa f; 2. **~ up** układać ⟨ułożyć⟩ w stertę; ⟨na⟩gromadzić się; *mot.* F wpadać na siebie

pile[2] [paɪl] włos *n (dywanu)*

pile[3] [paɪl] pal *m*

piles [paɪlz] *med.* F *pl.* hemoroidy *pl.*

'pile-up *mot.* F masowy karambol *m*

pil·fer ['pɪlfə] ⟨u⟩kraść, F podwędzić

pil·grim ['pɪlgrɪm] pielgrzym *m*; **~-age** ['pɪlgrɪmɪdʒ] pielgrzymka f

pill [pɪl] pigułka f, tabletka f; **the ~** pigułka f antykoncepcyjna; **be on the ~** brać pigułkę antykoncepcyjną

pil·lar ['pɪlə] filar *m*, słup *m*; '**~ box** *Brt.* skrzynka f pocztowa

pil·li·on [ˈpɪljən] *mot.* siodełko *n* pasażera

pil·lo·ry ['pɪlərɪ] 1. *hist.* pręgierz *m*; 2. *fig.* stawiać pod pręgierzem

pil·low ['pɪləʊ] poduszka f; '**~-case**, '**~ slip** powłoczka f na poduszkę

pi·lot ['paɪlət] 1. *aviat., naut.* pilot *m*; *attr.* pilotażowy; 2. pilotować; sterować; '**~ film** *TV* zapowiedź f filmu *(serialu itp.)*; '**~ scheme** projekt *m* pilotażowy

P

pimp [pɪmp] alfons *m*, sutener *m*

pim·ple ['pɪmpl] krosta *f*, pryszcz *m*

pin [pɪn] **1.** szpilka *f*; spinka *f* *(do krawata, włosów)*; *Am.* broszka *f*; *tech.* bolec *m*, sworzeń *m*, kołek *m*; kręgiel *m*; *Am.* klamerka *f (do bielizny)*; *Brt.* pinezka *f*; **2. (-nn-)** przyszpilać ⟨-lić⟩, przypinać ⟨-piąć⟩ *(to* do *G)*; unieruchamiać ⟨-chomić⟩ *(against, to* do *G)*

PIN [pɪn] *też* ~ **number** *skrót:* **personal identification number** PIN, numer *m* PIN, osobisty numer *m* użytkownika

pin·a·fore ['pɪnəfɔː] bezrękawnik *m*, kamizelka *f*

'**pin·ball** *(automat)* bilard *m*; '~ **machine** automat *m* do gry w bilard; F fliper *m*

pin·cers ['pɪnsəz] *pl. (też* **a pair of)** ~ szczypce *pl.*

pinch [pɪntʃ] **1.** *v/t.* szczypać ⟨-pnąć⟩; ściskać ⟨-snąć⟩ *(boleśnie)*; zaciskać ⟨-snąć⟩; F *(ukraść)* zwinąć; *v/i.* buty itp.: cisnąć, uciskać; **2.** szczypta *f*; uszczypnięcie *n*; F trudne położenie *n*

'**pin·cush·ion** poduszka *f* do szpilek

pine¹ [paɪn] *bot. też* ~ **tree** sosna *f*

pine² [paɪn] (bardzo) tęsknić *(for* za *D)*

'**pine·ap·ple** *bot.* ananas *m*; '~ **cone** *bot.* szyszka *f* sosny

pin·ion ['pɪnjən] *zo.* koło *n* zębate trzpieniowe

pink [pɪŋk] **1.** różowy; **2.** róż *m*; *bot.* goździk *m*

pint [paɪnt] pół kwarty *m (Brt. 0,57 l, Am. 0,47 l)*; *Brt.* F duże piwo *n*

pi·o·neer [paɪə'nɪə] **1.** pionier *m* (-ka *f)*; **2.** przecierać ⟨-trzeć⟩ szlak

pi·ous ['paɪəs] pobożny, nabożny

pip¹ [pɪp] pestka *f (jabłka, pomarańczy)*

pip³ [pɪp] *(w grze w karty)* oczko *n*; *(w grze w kości)* punkt *m*; *zwł. Brt. mil. (oznaka stopnia)* gwiazdka *f*

pipe [paɪp] **1.** rura *f*, przewód *m*; fajka *f*; *organowa* piszczałka *f*; fujarka *f*; ~**s** *pl. Brt.* F dudy *pl.*; **2.** dostarczać ⟨-czyć⟩ przewodowo; *⟨za⟩*grać na piszczałce; '~**line** rurociąg *m*; '~**r** dudziarz *m*

pip·ing ['paɪpɪŋ] **1.** instalacja *f* rurowa *lub* przewodowa; **2.** ~ **hot** wrzący, kipiący

pi·quant ['piːkənt] pikantny

pique [piːk] **1.** **in a fit of** ~ w przypływie urazy; **2.** urażać ⟨urazić⟩; **be** ~**d** *też* ⟨po⟩czuć się urażonym

pi·rate ['paɪərət] **1.** pirat *m*; **2.** ⟨s⟩kopiować po piracku; ~ **ra·di·o** radio *n* pirackie

Pis·ces ['paɪsiːz] *sg.* Ryby *pl.*; **he/she is (a)** ~ on/ona jest spod znaku Ryb

piss [pɪs] V szczać; ~ **off!** odpieprz się!

pis·tol ['pɪstl] pistolet *m*

pis·ton ['pɪstən] *tech.* tłok *m*; '~ **rod** drążek *m* tłoka; '~ **stroke** skok *m* tłoka

pit¹ [pɪt] **1.** dół *m*, zagłębienie *n*, wżer *m*; wgłębienie *n*; jama *f (też anat.)*; kopalnia *f*; *zwł. Brt. theat.* parter *m*; *też* **orchestra** ~ *theat.* kanał *m*; **2. (-tt-)** ⟨z⟩robić zagłębienia

pit² [pɪt] *Am.* **1.** *bot.* pestka *f*; **2. (-tt-)** usuwać ⟨-unąć⟩ pestki

pitch¹ [pɪtʃ] **1.** *v/t.* namiot, obóz itp. rozbijać ⟨-bić⟩; rzucać ⟨-cić⟩, miotać ⟨-tnąć⟩; *mus.* ustawiać ⟨-wić⟩ wysokość *(dźwięku)*; *v/i.* przewracać ⟨-rócić⟩ się; *naut. statek:* kołysać się; *dach itp.*: opadać; ~ **in** F zabierać się do roboty *lub* jedzenia; **2.** *zwł. Brt.* boisko *n*; *mus.* strój *m*; *fig.* poziom *m*, stopień *m*; *zwł. Brt. miejsce n* na ulicy *(np. handlu)*; *naut.* kołysanie *n*, kiwanie *n*; pochylenie *n (dachu itp.)*; *mot.* kanał *m (sprawdzania pojazdów)*

pitch² [pɪtʃ] smoła *f*; ~'**black**, ~'**dark** czarny jak smoła, kruczoczarny

pitch·er¹ ['pɪtʃə] dzbanek *m*

pitch·er² ['pɪtʃə] *(w baseballu)* zawodnik *m* rzucający piłkę

'**pitch·fork** widły *pl.*

pit·e·ous ['pɪtɪəs] żałosny

'**pit·fall** pułapka *f*, zasadzka *f*

pith [pɪθ] *bot.* rdzeń *m*; biała część skórki *(pomarańczy itp.)*; *fig.* sedno *n*, jądro *n*; '~**y** **(-ier, -iest)** treściwy, zwięzły

pit·i·a·ble ['pɪtɪəbl] → **pity**; '~**ful** żałosny; '~**less** bezlitosny

pits [pɪts] *pl. (w sportach motorowych)* miejsce *n* kontroli pojazdów

'**pit stop** *(w sportach motorowych)* kontrola *f* pojazdu

pit·tance ['pɪtəns] psi pieniądz *m*

pit·y ['pɪtɪ] **1.** litość *f*; współczucie *n (on* do *G)*; żal *m*; **it is a (great)** ~ wielka szkoda; **what a** ~**!** jaka szkoda!; **2.** współczuć, czuć litość

piv·ot ['pɪvət] **1.** *tech.* oś *f (przegubu)*, czop *m*; *fig.* oś *f*, sedno *n*; **2.** obracać się; ~ **on** *fig.* zależeć od *(G)*

pix·el ['pɪksəl] *komp.* piksel *m*

P

piz·za ['pi:tsə] pizza f

plac·ard ['plæka:d] **1.** plakat m; transparent m; **2.** ⟨o⟩plakatować

place [pleɪs] **1.** miejsce n; mieszkanie n, dom m; (w pracy itp.) pozycja f; posada f; okazja f; **in the first ~** przede wszystkim; **in third ~** (w sporcie) na trzecim miejscu; **in~ of** na miejscu (G); zamiast (G); **out of ~** nie na swoim miejscu; **take ~** odbywać ⟨-być⟩ się; mieć miejsce; △ **nie zajmować miejsce**; **take s.o.'s ~** zajmować ⟨-jąć⟩ czyjeś miejsce; **2.** umieszczać ⟨umieścić⟩; zamówienie itp. składać ⟨złożyć⟩ (**with** u G); stawiać ⟨-wić⟩ (w sytuacji); **be ~ed** (w sporcie) znaleźć się (**second** na drugim miejscu)

pla·ce·bo [plə'si:bəʊ] med. (pl. **-bos, -boes**) placebo n

'place|·ment test podkładka f pod naczynia; **'~·ment** test egzamin m wstępny; **'~ name** nazwa f miejscowości

plac·id ['plæsɪd] spokojny, cichy

pla·gia·rize ['pleɪdʒjəraɪz] popełnić ⟨-nić⟩ plagiat

plague [pleɪg] **1.** dżuma f; zaraza f; fig. plaga f; **2.** dręczyć

plaice [pleɪs] zo. (pl. **plaice**) flądra f, płastuga f

plaid [plæd] pled m, koc m

plain [pleɪn] **1.** adj. zwykły; zwyczajny; nieozdobny, prosty; oczywisty, wyraźny; bezpośredni; szczery; **2.** adv. F po prostu; **3.** równina f; **~'choc·olate** czekolada f gorzka; **~'clothes** w ubraniu cywilnym

plain|·tiff ['pleɪntɪf] powód m, strona f skarżąca; **~·tive** [pleɪntɪv] żałosny

plait [plæt] zwł. Brt. **1.** warkocz m; **2.** zaplatać ⟨-leść⟩

plan [plæn] **1.** plan m; **2.** (**-nn-**) ⟨za⟩planować

plane¹ [pleɪn] samolot m; **by ~** samolotem; **go by ~** ⟨po⟩lecieć

plane² [pleɪn] **1.** równy, płaski; **2.** math. płaszczyzna f; fig. poziom m

plane³ [pleɪn] **1.** strug m, hebel m; **2.** ⟨ze⟩strugać, ⟨z⟩heblować

plan·et ['plænɪt] astr. planeta f

plank [plæŋk] deska f; listwa f; **'~·ing** deskowanie n, odeskowanie n; deski pl., listwy pl.

plant [plɑ:nt] **1.** bot. roślina f; zakład m, fabryka f; elektrownia f; urządzenia pl.

techniczne; attr. roślinny; **2.** ⟨ob-, po-, za⟩sadzić; ogród zakładać ⟨założyć⟩; umieszczać ⟨-mieścić⟩; wtykać ⟨we-tknąć⟩; **~ s.th. on s.o.** F podkładać ⟨-dłożyć⟩ coś komuś;

plan·ta·tion [plæn'teɪʃn] plantacja f

plant·er ['plɑ:ntə] plantator m; sadzarka f

plaque [plɑ:k] tablica f pamiątkowa, epitafium n; med. kamień m nazębny

plas·ter ['plɑ:stə] **1.** zaprawa f tynkowa; tynk m; med. plaster; med. opatrunek m gipsowy; **~ of Paris** gips m; **have one's leg in ~** mieć nogę w gipsie; **2.** ⟨za-, o⟩tynkować; oklejać ⟨-eić⟩; **'~ cast** odlew m gipsowy; med. opatrunek m gipsowy

plas·tic ['plæstɪk] **1.** (**~ally**) plastyczny; plastikowy; **2.** plastik m, tworzywo n sztuczne; **~ 'mon·ey** F karty pl. kredytowe; **~ 'wrap** Am. samoprzylegająca folia f (do żywności)

plate [pleɪt] **1.** talerz m; płyta f; płytka f (np. protezy); tabliczka f (z nazwiskiem); tablica f (rejestracyjna); rycina f; (gruba) blacha f; (w kościele) taca f; print. klisza f; plater m; **2.** **~d with gold, gold·~ed** platerowany złotem

plat·form ['plætfɔ:m] platforma f; rail. peron m; trybuna f, podium n (mówcy); pol. platforma f; **party ~** pol. program m partyjny; **election ~** pol. program m wyborczy

plat·i·num ['plætɪnəm] chem. platyna f

pla·toon [plə'tu:n] mil. pluton m

plat·ter ['plætə] taca f

plau·si·ble ['plɔ:zəbl] wiarygodny, prawdopodobny

play [pleɪ] **1.** gra f; zabawa f; przedstawienie n, sztuka f; tech. luz m; fig. swoboda f działania; **at ~** przy zabawie; **in ~** żartem; w grze (piłka); **out of ~** na aucie; **2.** v/i. ⟨za⟩grać; ⟨po⟩bawić się; v/t. sztukę itp. ⟨za⟩grać; rolę, itp. odgrywać ⟨odegrać⟩; w karty itp. grać w (A); (w sporcie) piłkę ⟨s⟩kierować; **~ s.o.** (w sporcie) grać przeciwko komuś; **~ the guitar** ⟨za⟩grać na gitarze; **~ a trick on s.o.** ⟨z⟩robić komuś kawał; piłkę itp. ⟨s⟩kierować z powrotem (**to** do G); kasetę odtwarzać ⟨-worzyć⟩; **~ off** fig. wygrywać (**s.o. against s.o.** kogoś przeciwko D); **~ on** fig. wykorzystywać ⟨-stać⟩; **'~·back** playback m; powtórka *f*; '~·**boy** playboy *m*; '~·**er** (*w sporcie*) gracz *m*; *theat.* aktor(ka *f*) *m*; *mus.* instrumentalista *m* (-tka *f*); '~·**fel·low** *Brt.* → **playmate**; '~·**ful** rozbawiony; żartobliwy; '~·**go·er** bywalec *m* teatralny; '~·**ground** plac *m* zabaw; podwórko *n* szkolne; '~·**group** *zwł.* *Brt.* (*rodzaj przedszkola*); '~·**house** *theat.* teatr *m*; domek *m* do zabawy

'**play·ing**| **card** karta *f* do gry; '~ **field** boisko *n*

'**play**|·**mate** towarzysz(ka *f*) *m* zabaw; '~·**pen** kojec *m* (*dla małych dzieci*); '~·**thing** zabawka *f* (*też fig.*); '~·**wright** dramaturg *m*

plc, PLC [pi: el 'si:] *Brt. skrót*: *public limited company* S.A., spółka *f* akcyjna

plea [pli:] *jur.*: **enter a ~ of** (**not**) **guilty** (nie) przyznawać ‹-nać› się do winy

plead [pli:d] (**-ed, *zwł. Szkoc., Am.* pled**) *v/i.* błagać (**for** o A); ~ (**not**) **guilty** *jur.* (nie) przyznawać ‹-nać› się do winy; *v/t. jur. i ogóln.* odpowiadać ‹-wiedzieć› na zarzuty; ~ *s.o.'s case* bronić czyjejś sprawy (*też jur.*)

pleas·ant ['pleznt] przyjemny; przyjazny

please [pli:z] **1.** zadowalać ‹-wolić›; sprawiać ‹-wić› przyjemność; ‹ze›chcieć (*coś robić*); *only to ~ you* tylko by ci sprawić przyjemność; ~ *o.s.* robić co się chce; ~ *yourself!* wolna wola!; **2.** *int.* proszę; (**yes,** ~) proszę (tak), z przyjemnością; ~ *come in!* proszę wejść!; ~**d** zadowolony; *be ~d about* cieszyć się z (G); *be ~d with* być zadowolonym z (G); *I am ~d with it* to mi się podoba; *be ~d to do s.th.* z przyjemnością coś ‹z›robić; ~**d to meet you!** bardzo mi miło

pleas·ing ['pli:zɪŋ] przyjemny

plea·sure ['pleʒə] przyjemność *f*; *at* (*one's*) ~ według czyjejś woli

pleat [pli:t] fałda *f*; '~·**ed skirt** spódnica *f* plisowana

pled [pled] *pret. i p.p. od* **plead**

pledge [pledʒ] **1.** przyrzeczenie *n*; zastaw *m*; *fig.* oznaka *f*; **2.** przyrzekać ‹-rzec›; zastawiać ‹-wić›

plen·ti·ful ['plentɪfl] obfity

plen·ty ['plentɪ] **1.** obfitość *f*; *in* ~ w obfitości; ~ *of* dużo; **2.** F zupełnie, całkowicie

pleu·ri·sy ['pluərəsɪ] *med.* zapalenie *n* opłucnej, pleuritis *f*

pli·a·ble ['plaɪəbl], ~·**ant** ['plaɪənt] plastyczny, giętki; *fig.* podatny; ugodowy

pli·ers ['plaɪəz] *pl.* (*a pair of* ~) szczypce *pl.*, kombinerki *pl.*

plight [plaɪt] ciężkie położenie *n*, opresja *f*

plim·soll ['plɪmsəl] *Brt.* tenisówka *f*

plod [plɒd] (**-dd-**) *też* ~ **along** wlec się; ~ **away** ‹po›pracować

plop [plɒp] F **1.** plusk *m*; pluśnięcie *n*; **2.** (**-pp-**) plusnąć

plot [plɒt] **1.** działka *f*, parcela *f*; akcja *f*, fabuła *f* (*filmu itp.*); spisek *m*; intryga *f*; *tech.* wykres *m*; **2.** (**-tt-**) *v/i.* spiskować, ‹u›knuć intrygę (**against** przeciw D); *v/t.* ‹za›planować; wykreślać ‹-lić›; '~·**ter** ploter *m*

plough *Brt.*, **plow** *Am.* [plaʊ] **1.** pług *m*; **2.** ‹za›orać; '~·**share** lemiesz *m*

pluck [plʌk] **1.** *v/t.* zbierać ‹zebrać›; *mus.* **strunę** szarpać ‹-pnąć›, uderzać ‹-rzyć› w (A); *ptaka* oskubywać ‹-bać›; *zw.* ~ **out** wyskubywać ‹-bać›; ~ **up** (*one's*) *courage* zebrać odwagę; *v/i.* szarpać ‹szarpnąć› (**at** za A); **2.** F odwaga *f*; '~·**y** F (**-ier, -iest**) odważny

plug [plʌg] **1.** korek *m*, zatyczka *f*; *electr.* wtyczka *f*; *electr.* wtyczka *f*; F *mot.* świeca *f* zapłonowa; **2.** (**-gg-**) *też* ~ **up** zatykać ‹-tknąć›; ~ **in** *electr.* włączać ‹-czyć›

plum [plʌm] *bot.* śliwka *f*; śliwa *f*

plum·age ['pluːmɪdʒ] upierzenie *n*

plumb [plʌm] **1.** ołowianka *f*, ciężarek *m* pionu; **2.** ‹z›mierzyć głębokość; *fig.* zgłębiać ‹-bić›; ~ **in** *zwł. Brt.* pralkę podłączać ‹-czyć› do odpływu; **3.** *adj.* pionowy; **4.** *adv.* F prosto; '~·**er** hydraulik *m*; '~·**ing** instalacja *f* wodociągowa

plume [pluːm] pióro *n*; pióropusz *m* (*też fig.*)

plump [plʌmp] **1.** pulchny, krągły; **2.** ~ **down** zwalić się

plum 'pud·ding pudding *m* śliwkowy

plun·der ['plʌndə] **1.** ‹z›łupić, ‹s›plądrować; **2.** łup *m*; łupienie *n*

plunge [plʌndʒ] **1.** zanurzać ‹-rzyć› (się), pogrążać ‹-żyć› (się) (**into** w L); *ceny itp.*: spadać ‹spaść›; **2.** (za)nurkowanie *n*; spadek *m* (*cen itp.*); *take the ~ fig.* podejmować ‹-djąć› decydujący krok

plu·per·fect [pluːˈpɜːfɪkt] *gr. też*
~ *tense* czas *m* zaprzeszły
plu·ral [ˈplʊərəl] *gr.* liczba *f* mnoga
plus [plʌs] **1.** *prp.* plus (*N*), i, oraz; *econ.*
z dodatkiem (*G*); **2.** *adj.* plusowy, dodatni; ~ *sign* znak *m* plusa; **3.** plus *m*,
znak *m* plusa; *fig.* F plus *m*, zaleta *f*
plush [plʌʃ] plusz *m*
ply¹ [plaɪ] kursować (*between* między *I*)
ply² [plaɪ] *zw. w złoż.* warstwa *f*; *three~*
trójwarstwowy; *~-wood* sklejka *f*
pm, PM [piː ˈem] *skrót:* **after noon** (*ła-cińskie* **post meridiem**) po poł., po
południu
PM [piː ˈem] *zwł. Brt.* F *skrót:* **Prime
Minister** premier *m*
pneu·mat·ic [njuːˈmætɪk] (*~ally*)
pneumatyczny; ~ *drill* młot *m* pneu-matyczny
pneu·mo·ni·a [njuːˈməʊnjə] *med.* za-palenie *n* płuc
PO [piː ˈəʊ] *skrót:* **post office** urząd *m*
pocztowy; **postal order** przekaz *m*
pocztowy
poach¹ [pəʊtʃ] ⟨u⟩gotować *jajko* bez
skorupki; *~ed eggs pl.* jajka *pl.* w ko-szulkach (*gotowane bez skorupki*)
poach² [pəʊtʃ] kłusować; *~er* kłusow-nik *m* (-iczka *f*)
POB [piː əʊ ˈbiː] *skrót:* **post office box**
(**number**) skr. pocz., skrytka *f* poczto-wa
PO Box [piː əʊ ˈbɒks] skrytka *f* poczto-wa
pock [pɒk] *med.* krosta *f*
pock·et [ˈpɒkɪt] **1.** kieszeń *f*; *aviat.* → *air
pocket*; **2.** *adj.* kieszonkowy; **3.** wkła-dać ⟨włożyć⟩ do kieszeni; *fig.* przywła-szczać ⟨-czyć⟩ sobie; *~·book* notes *m*;
Am. teczka *f*; ~ *'cal·cu·la·tor* kalku-lator *m* kieszonkowy; *~·knife* (*pl.
-knives*) scyzoryk *m*; ~ *mon·ey* drob-ne *pl.*
pod [pɒd] *bot.* strączek *m*
po·em [ˈpəʊɪm] wiersz *m*
po·et [ˈpəʊɪt] poeta *m*; ~·ic [pəʊˈetɪk]
(*-ally*) poetyczny; *~·i·cal* poetyczny;
~·ic 'jus·tice fig. symbol *m* sprawiedli-wości; *~·ry* [ˈpəʊɪtrɪ] poezja *f*
poi·gnant [ˈpɔɪnjənt] *wspomnienie:* bolesny; przejmujący
point [pɔɪnt] **1.** punkt *m* (*też sport,
math., phys.*); szpic *m*, koniuszek *m*;
math. przecinek *m*; miejsce *n*; stopień

m (*skali, kompasu itp.*); cel *m*; kwestia
f; sens *m*; sprawa *f*; *geogr.* przylądek *m*;
electr. gniazdko *n*; **two ~ five** (**2.5**) dwa
przecinek pięć (2,5); ~ *of view* punkt *m*
widzenia; **be on the** ~ *of doing s.th.*
(mieć) właśnie coś zrobić; *be to the* ~
należeć do rzeczy; *be beside the* ~ nie
należeć do rzeczy; *come to the* ~ przy-stępować ⟨-tąpić⟩ do rzeczy; *that's not
the* ~ to nie należy do rzeczy; *what's
the* ~? jaki w tym sens?; *win on ~s* wy-grywać ⟨-rać⟩ na punkty; *winner on ~s*
zwycięzca *m* na punkty; **2.** wskazywać
⟨-zać⟩; *broń itp.* ⟨s⟩kierować (*at* w stro-nę *G*); ~ *one's finger at s.o.* wska-zywać ⟨-zać⟩ (palcem) na kogoś; ~ *out*
wskazywać ⟨-zać⟩; *fig.* wykazywać
⟨-zać⟩; ~ *to* wskazywać ⟨-zać⟩; *fig.* wska-zywać ⟨-zać⟩ na (*A*); *~·ed* zaostrzony;
spiczasty; *fig.* uszczypliwy; *fig.* znaczą-cy; *~·er* wskaźnik *m*, wskazówka *f*; *zo.*
pointer *m*; *~·less* bezcelowy
points [pɔɪnts] *Brt. pl. rail.* zwrotnica *f*;
electr. styki *pl.*
poise [pɔɪz] **1.** postawa *f*; *fig.* równowa-ga *f*; opanowanie *n*; **2.** stawiać ⟨posta-wić⟩ w równowadze; *be ~d* być w za-wieszeniu; być gotowym
poi·son [ˈpɔɪzn] **1.** trucizna *f*; **2.** ⟨o⟩-truć; *~·ous* [ˈpɔɪznəs] trujący (*też fig.*)
poke [pəʊk] **1.** *v/t.* szturchać ⟨-chnąć⟩;
wtykać ⟨wetknąć⟩; *palenisko* przegar-niać ⟨-nąć⟩; *v/i.* ~ *about*, ~ *around* F
⟨po⟩szperać (*in* w *L*); **2.** szturchaniec
m; ˈpok·er pogrzebacz *m*
pok·y [ˈpəʊkɪ] F (*-ier, -iest*) przyciasny
Po·land [ˈpəʊlənd] Polska *f*
po·lar [ˈpəʊlə] polarny; ~ *'bear zo.* nie-dźwiedź *m* polarny
pole¹ [pəʊl] biegun *m*
pole² [pəʊl] drąg *m*, żerdź *f*; słup *m*;
maszt *m*; (*w sporcie*) tyczka *f*
Pole [pəʊl] Polak *m* (-lka *f*)
'pole·cat *zo.* tchórz *m*; *Am.* skunks *m*
po·lem·ic [pəˈlemɪk], *~·i·cal* pole-miczny
'pole star *astr.* gwiazda *f* polarna
'pole vault (*w sporcie*) skok *m* o tyczce
'pole-vault (*w sporcie*) skakać o tyczce;
~·er (*w sporcie*) tyczkarz *m*
po·lice [pəˈliːs] **1.** policja *f*; **2.** patrolo-wać, dozorować; ~ *car* wóz *m* policyj-ny; *~·man* (*pl. -men*) policjant *m*; ~ *of-fi·cer* policjant *m*; ~ *sta·tion* komisa-

riat *m*; **~·wom·an** (*pl.* **-women**) policjantka *f*

pol·i·cy ['pɒləsɪ] polityka *f*; taktyka *f*; polisa *f* ubezpieczeniowa

po·li·o ['pəʊlɪəʊ] *med.* polio *n*, paraliż *m* dziecięcy, choroba *f* Heinego-Medina

pol·ish ['pɒlɪʃ] **1.** ⟨wy⟩polerować, ⟨wy⟩glansować, ⟨wy⟩froterować; *buty* czyścić; **~ up** *fig.* podciągać ⟨-gnąć⟩; **2.** połysk *m*; środek *m* do nadawania połysku; pasta *f* (*do butów*, *podłogi*); *fig.* polor *m*

Pol·ish ['pəʊlɪʃ] **1.** polski; **2.** *ling.* język *m* polski

po·lite [pə'laɪt] (*-r, -st*) uprzejmy; **~·ness** uprzejmość

po·lit·i·cal [pə'lɪtɪkl] polityczny; **pol·i·ti·cian** [pɒlɪ'tɪʃn] polityk *m*; **pol·i·tics** ['pɒlɪtɪks] *zw. sg.* polityka *f*

pol·ka ['pɒlkə] *mus.* polka *f*; **'~-dot** *materiał:* nakrapiany, cętkowany

poll [pəʊl] **1.** sondaż *m* opinii publicznej; głosowanie *n*; liczba *f* głosów; *też* **~s** *pl.* wybory *pl.*; **2.** przeprowadzać ⟨-dzić⟩ sondaż; otrzymywać ⟨-mać⟩ liczbę głosów

pol·len ['pɒlən] *bot.* pyłek *m* kwiatowy

poll·ing ['pəʊlɪŋ] wybory *pl.*, głosowanie *n*; **'~ booth** *zwł. Brt.* kabina *f* dla głosujących; **'~ day** dzień *m* wyborów; **'~ place** *Am.*, **'~ sta·tion** *Brt.* lokal *m* wyborczy

polls [pəʊlz] *pl.* wybory *pl.*; *Am.* lokal *m* wyborczy

poll·ster ['pəʊlstə] ankieter(ka *f*) *m* opinii publicznej

pol·lut·ant [pə'luːtənt] polutant *m*, środek *m* zanieczyszczający środowisko; **~·lute** [pə'luːt] zanieczyszczać ⟨-czyścić⟩ środowisko; **~·lut·er** [pə'luːtə] *też* **environmental ~luter** zakład *m* zanieczyszczający środowisko; **~·lu·tion** [pə'luːʃn] zanieczyszczenie *n* środowiska

po·lo ['pəʊləʊ] (*w sporcie*) polo *n*; **'~ neck** *zwł. Brt.* (*odzież*) golf *m*

pol·yp ['pɒlɪp] *zo.*, *med.* polip *m*

pol·y·sty·rene [pɒlɪ'staɪriːn] polistyren *m*; *attr.* polistyrenowy

pom·mel ['pʌml] łęk *m* (*siodła*)

pomp [pɒmp] pompa *f*, przepych *m*; △ *nie* **pompa** (*do pompowania*)

pom·pous ['pɒmpəs] pompatyczny

pond [pɒnd] staw *m*

pon·der ['pɒndə] *v/i.* medytować, rozmyślać (*on, over* o *L*); *v/t.* roztrząsać; **~·ous** ['pɒndərəs] ociężały

pon·toon [pɒn'tuːn] ponton *m*; **~ bridge** most *m* pontonowy

po·ny ['pəʊnɪ] kucyk *m*; **'~-tail** *fryzura:* kucyk *m*

poo·dle ['puːdl] *zo.* pudel *m*

pool¹ [puːl] staw *m*, sadzawka *f*; kałuża *f*; basen *m*;

pool² [puːl] **1.** grupa *f*, zespół *m*; park *m* samochodowy; wspólny *m* fundusz; *zwł. Am. econ.* kartel *m*; (*w kartach*) pula *f*; *Am.* bilard *m*; **2.** pieniądze, siły *itp.* zbierać ⟨zebrać⟩; **'~ hall** *Am.*, **'~·room** sala *f* bilardowa; **~s** *pl. Brt też* **foot·ball ~** *jakby:* totalizator *m* piłkarski

poor [pʊə] **1.** biedny, ubogi; marny, lichy, słaby; **2.** *the ~ pl.* biedni *pl.*; **'~·ly 1.** *adj. zwł. Brt.* F niezdrowy; **2.** *adv.* biednie, ubogo; marnie, licho, słabo

pop¹ [pɒp] **1.** (*-pp-*) *v/t.* otwierać ⟨-worzyć⟩ z hukiem; wtykać ⟨wetknąć⟩; *v/i.* strzelić ⟨-lać⟩; **~ in** wpadać ⟨wpaść⟩ na chwilę; **~ off** F wykorkować; **~ up** (*pojawiać się*) wyskoczyć; **2.** *dźwięk:* wystrzał *m*, trzask *m*; F oranżada *f*

pop² [pɒp] *mus.* pop *m*

pop³ [pɒp] *zwł. Am.* tatuś *m*

pop⁴ *skrót pisany:* **population** ludn., ludność *f*

'pop con·cert koncert *m* muzyki pop

'pop·corn popcorn *m*

pope [pəʊp] *rel.: zw.* 2 papież *m*

pop-'eyed o wybałuszonych oczach

'pop group grupa *f* muzyki pop

pop·lar ['pɒplə] topola *f*

pop·py ['pɒpɪ] *bot.* mak *m*; *attr.* makowy; **'~·cock** F bzdury *pl.*

pop·u·lar ['pɒpjʊlə] popularny, ulubiony; powszechny; **~·i·ty** [pɒpjʊ'lærətɪ] popularność *f*, powszechność *f*

pop·u·late ['pɒpjʊleɪt] zasiedlać ⟨-lić⟩, zaludniać ⟨-nić⟩; **~·la·tion** [pɒpjʊ'leɪʃn] ludność *f*, populacja *f*; **~·lous** ['pɒpjʊləs] ludny

porce·lain ['pɔːslɪn] porcelana *f*; *attr.* porcelanowy

porch [pɔːtʃ] ganek *m*; *Am.* weranda *f*

por·cu·pine ['pɔːkjʊpaɪn] *zo.* jeżozwierz *m*

pore¹ [pɔː] *anat.* por *f*

pore² [pɔː]: **~ over** ślęczeć nad (*I*)

P

pork [pɔːk] wieprzowina *f*

porn [pɔːn] F → **porno** F; **por·no** ['pɔː-nəʊ] (*pl. -nos*) porno *n*; pornos *m*; **por·nog·ra·phy** [pɔː'nɒɡrəfɪ] pornografia *f*

po·rous ['pɔːrəs] porowaty

por·poise ['pɔːpəs] *zo.* morświn *m*

por·ridge ['pɒrɪdʒ] owsianka *f*

port¹ [pɔːt] port *m*; miasto *n* portowe

port² [pɔːt] *naut., aviat.* lewa burta *f*

port³ [pɔːt] *komp.* port *m*

port⁴ [pɔːt] portwajn *m*

por·ta·ble ['pɔːtəbl] przenośny

por·ter ['pɔːtə] bagażowy *m*; *zwł. Brt.* portier *m*; *Am. rail.* konduktor *m* wagonu sypialnego

'port·hole iluminator *m*

por·tion ['pɔːʃn] **1.** porcja *f*; część *f*; **2.** **~ out** (po)dzielić (*among, between* pomiędzy *A*)

port·ly ['pɔːtlɪ] (*-ier, -iest*) korpulentny

por·trait ['pɔːtrɪt] portret *m*

por·tray [pɔː'treɪ] ⟨s⟩portretować; przedstawiać ⟨-wić⟩; **~·al** [pɔː'treɪəl] sportretowanie *n*, przedstawienie *n*

Por·tu·gal ['pɔːtʃʊɡl] Portugalia *f*; **Por·tu·guese** [pɔːtʃʊ'ɡiːz] **1.** portugalski; **2.** Portugalczyk *m* (-lka *f*); język *m* portugalski; **the ~** *pl.* Portugalczycy *pl.*

pose [pəʊz] **1.** *problem* przedstawiać ⟨-wić⟩; *pytanie* stawiać ⟨postawić⟩; pozować (*też jako model*); **~ as s.o.** udawać kogoś; **2.** poza *f*

posh [pɒʃ] *zwł. Brt.* F wyszukany, wytworny

po·si·tion [pə'zɪʃn] **1.** pozycja *f*, miejsce *n* (*też fig.*); właściwe miejsce *n*; miejsce *n* pracy, etat *m*; opinia *f*; **2.** ustawiać ⟨-wić⟩, umieszczać ⟨-eścić⟩

pos·i·tive ['pɒzətɪv] **1.** pozytywny; dodatni (*też math., electr.*); przekonany, pewny; konkretny; **2.** *phot.* pozytyw *m*; *gr.* stopień *m* równy

pos|·sess [pə'zes] posiadać; *fig. uczucie, itp.:* owładnąć, opętać; **~·sessed** [pə'zest] opętany; **~·ses·sion** [pə'zeʃn] posiadanie *n*; *fig.* opętanie *n*; **~·ses·sive** [pə'zesɪv] zachłanny; *gr.* dzierżawczy

pos·si|·bil·i·ty [pɒsə'bɪlətɪ] możliwość *f*; **~·ble** ['pɒsəbl] możliwy; **~·bly** ['pɒsəblɪ] możliwie; *if I ~bly can* jeżeli tylko mogę; *I can't ~bly do this* zupełnie nie mogę tego zrobić

post¹ [pəʊst] **1.** słupek *m*, kołek *m*; **2.** *też* **~ up** *plakat itp.* przyklejać ⟨-leić⟩, wywieszać ⟨-esić⟩; *be ~ed missing naut., aviat.* zostać ogłoszonym za zaginionego

post² [pəʊst] *zwł. Brt.* **1.** poczta *f*; *by ~* pocztą; **2.** przesyłać ⟨-słać⟩ pocztą; *list* wrzucać ⟨-cić⟩

post³ [pəʊst] **1.** miejsce *n*; praca *f*; placówka *f*, posterunek *m*; **2.** *posterunek itp.* wystawiać ⟨-wić⟩; *zwł. Brt.* ⟨od⟩delegować (*to* do *G*); *mil.* odkomenderowywać ⟨-wać⟩

post... [pəʊst] po..., post...

post·age ['pəʊstɪdʒ] opłata *f* pocztowa, porto *n*; **'~ stamp** znaczek *m* pocztowy

post·al ['pəʊstl] pocztowy; **'~ or·der** *Brt.* przekaz *m* pocztowy; **'~ vote** *pol.* głos *m* oddany drogą pocztową

'post|·bag *zwł. Brt.* torba *f* listonosza; **'~·box** skrzynka *f* pocztowa; **'~·card** kartka *f* pocztowa; *też picture ~card* widokówka *f*; **'~·code** *Brt.* kod *m* pocztowy

post·er ['pəʊstə] plakat *m*

poste res·tante [pəʊst'restɑːnt] *Brt.* poste restante *n*

pos·te·ri·or [pɒ'stɪərɪə] *hum.* tyłek *m*, sempiterna *f*

pos·ter·i·ty [pɒ'sterɪtɪ] potomność *f*

post-'free *zwł. Brt.* wolny od opłaty pocztowej

post·grad·u·ate [pəʊst'ɡrædjʊət] podyplomowy (*po licencjacie lub magisterium*)

post·hu·mous ['pɒstjʊməs] pośmiertny

'post|·man (*pl. -men*) *zwł. Brt.* listonosz *m*; **'~·mark 1.** stempel *m* pocztowy; **2.** ⟨o⟩stemplować (*pieczęcią pocztową*); **'~·mas·ter** naczelnik *m* urzędu pocztowego; ♀*master General* jakby: Minister *m* Poczty; **'~ of·fice** urząd *m* pocztowy; **'~ of·fice box → PO Box**; **~'paid** *zwł. Am.* wolny od opłaty pocztowej

post·pone [pəʊst'pəʊn] odkładać ⟨odłożyć⟩; przekładać ⟨przełożyć⟩; **~·ment** odłożenie *n*

post·script ['pəʊsskrɪpt] dopisek *m*, postscriptum *n*, PS *n*

pos·ture ['pɒstʃə] **1.** postura *f*, postawa *f*; **2.** *fig.* pozować

post'war powojenny

'post·wom·an (*pl.* **-women**) listonoszka *f*

po·sy ['pəuzɪ] bukiecik *m*

pot [pɒt] **1.** garnek *m*; dzbanek *m*; słoik *m* (*dżemu*); doniczka *f*; nocnik *m*; *sport*. F puchar *m*; *sl.* (*marihuana*) trawka *f*; **2.** (**-tt-**) *rośliny* przesadzać ⟨-dzić⟩

po·ta·to [pə'teɪtəʊ] (*pl.* **-toes**) ziemniak *m*, kartofel *m*; *attr.* ziemniaczany, kartoflany; → **chips, crisps**

'pot·bel·ly duży brzuch *m*

po·ten|·cy ['pəutənsɪ] siła *f*, moc *f*; *physiol.* potencja *f*; ∼t ['pəutənt] silny, mocny; przekonujący; zdolny do życia płciowego; ∼·tial [pə'tenʃl] **1.** potencjalny; **2.** potencjał *m*, możliwości *pl.*

'pot·hole *mot.* wybój *m*

po·tion ['pəuʃn] napój *m* (*leczniczy, trujący, magiczny*)

pot·ter¹ ['pɒtə]: ∼ **about** plątać się

pot·ter² ['pɒtə] garncarz *m*; ∼·y ['pɒtərɪ] garncarstwo *n*; wyroby *pl.* garncarskie

pouch [paʊtʃ] torba *f* (*też zo.*); *zo.* kieszeń *f*

poul·tice ['pəultɪs] *med.* kataplazm *m*

poul·try ['pəultrɪ] drób *m*, ptactwo *n*

pounce [paʊns] **1.** rzucać ⟨-cić⟩ się (**on** na *A*); **2.** skok *m*

pound¹ [paʊnd] funt *m* (*453,59 g*); ∼ (**sterling**) funt *m* szterling

pound² [paʊnd] schronisko *n* dla zwierząt; (*miejsce odholowywania nieprawidłowo zaparkowanych samochodów*)

pound³ [paʊnd] *v/t.* ⟨u⟩tłuc; walić *o* (*A*); walić *w* (*A*); *v/i. serce:* walić; ⟨po⟩biec ciężko

pour [pɔː] *v/t.* nasypywać ⟨-pać⟩; nalewać ⟨-lać⟩; ∼ **out** rozlewać ⟨-lać⟩; *v/i.* lać się; wylewać ⟨-lać⟩ się; *deszcz:* lać

pout [paʊt] **1.** *v/t. usta* odymać ⟨-dąć⟩; *v/i.* wydymać usta; **2.** odęte usta *pl.*

pov·er·ty ['pɒvətɪ] ubóstwo *n*

POW [pi: əʊ 'dʌblju:] *skrót:* **prisoner of war** jeniec *m* wojenny

pow·der ['paʊdə] **1.** proszek *m*; puder *m*; **2.** ⟨s⟩proszkować; pudrować (się); '∼ puff puszek *m* do pudru; '∼ room toaleta *f* damska

pow·er ['paʊə] **1.** moc *f*, siła *f*, potęga *f*; władza *f*; zdolność *f*; *jur.* pełnomocnictwo *n*, uprawnienie *n*; *jur.* moc *f* prawna; *math.* potęga *f*, wykładnik *m* potęgi; *electr.* energia *f*, prąd *m*; **in** ∼ przy władzy; **2.** *tech.* zasilać ⟨-lić⟩; '∼ **cut** *electr.* przerwa *f* w dostawie energii elektrycznej; '∼ **fail·ure** *electr.* przerwa *f* w dostawie energii elektrycznej; '∼·**ful** mocny, silny; potężny; '∼·**less** bezsilny; '∼ **plant** *zwł. Am.* → **power station**; '∼ **pol·i·tics** *często sg.* polityka *f* siły; '∼ **sta·tion** elektrownia *f*

pp *skrót pisany:* **pages** str., strony *pl.*

PR [pi: 'ɑː] *skrót:* **public relations** służba *f* informacyjna

prac·ti|·ca·ble ['præktɪkəbl] możliwy do wykonania; ∼·**cal** ['præktɪkl] praktyczny; ∼·**cal** '**joke** psota *f*, psikus *m*; '∼·**cal·ly** praktycznie

prac·tice ['præktɪs] **1.** praktyka *f*, ćwiczenie *n*; doświadczenie *n*, wprawa *f*; zwyczaj *m*; **it's common** ∼ w powszechnym zwyczaju jest; **put into** ∼ wprowadzić w życie; **2.** *Am.* → **practise**

prac·tise, *Brt.*, prac·tice *Am.* ['præktɪs] *v/t.* ćwiczyć; praktykować; (*w sporcie*) trenować; *zawód* praktykować; ∼ **law** (**medicine**) prowadzić praktykę prawniczą (lekarską); *v/i.* ćwiczyć; praktykować; '∼d wyćwiczony (**in** w *L*)

prac·ti·tion·er [præk'tɪʃnə]: **general** ∼ lekarz *m* rejonowy, lekarz *m* domowy

Prague Praga *f*

prai·rie ['preərɪ] preria *f*; *attr.* prepriowy

praise [preɪz] **1.** chwalić, wychwalać; **2.** pochwała *f*; '∼·**wor·thy** godny pochwały

pram [præm] *zwł. Brt.* F wózek *m* dziecięcy

prance [prɑːns] *koń:* tańczyć; *ludzie:* paradować, pysznić się

prank [præŋk] psikus *m*, figiel *m*

prat·tle ['prætl] F paplać

prawn [prɔːn] *zo.* krewetka *f*

pray [preɪ] modlić się (**to** do *G*, **for** o *A*)

prayer [preə] modlitwa *f*; '∼ **book** modlitewnik *m*

preach [priːtʃ] wygłaszać ⟨wygłosić⟩ (*kazanie*) (*też fig.*); głosić (*też fig.*); '∼·**er** kaznodzieja *m*

pre·am·ble [priː'æmbl] preambuła *f*

pre·ar·range [priːə'reɪndʒ] ustalać ⟨-lić⟩ wcześniej

pre·car·i·ous [prɪ'keərɪəs] niebezpieczny, ryzykowny; niepewny

pre·cau·tion [prɪ'kɔːʃn] środek *n* ostrożności; ∼·**a·ry** [prɪ'kɔːʃnərɪ] zapo biegawczy, zabezpieczający

pre·cede [pri:'si:d] poprzedzać ⟨-dzić⟩

pre·ce|·dence ['presidəns] pierwszeń-stwo *n*; **~dent** precedens *m*

pre·cept ['pri:sept] zasada *f*

pre·cinct ['pri:sıŋkt] *zwł. Brt.* handlo-wa dzielnica *f*, rejon *m* (*ruchu piesze-go*); *Am.* okręg *m* (*wyborczy*); *Am.* okręg *m* (*policyjny*); **~s** *pl.* teren *m*

pre·cious ['preʃəs] **1.** *adj.* cenny; dro-gocenny; *kamień:* szlachetny; **2.** *adv.:* **~ little** F bardzo mało

pre·ci·pice ['presıpıs] urwisko *n*

pre·cip·i|·tate 1. [prı'sıpıteıt] *v/t.* przyspieszać ⟨-szyć⟩; wywracać się; *chem.* wytrącać ⟨-cić⟩; *fig.* popychać ⟨-pchnąć⟩ (*into* do *G*); *v/i. chem.* wy-trącać ⟨-cić⟩ się; **2.** [prı'sıpıtət] *adj.* pochopny; **3.** [prı'sıpıteıt] *chem.* osad *m* wytrącony; **~ta·tion** [prısıpı'teıʃn] *chem.* wytrącenie *n* (się); strącenie *n* (się); *meteor.* opad *m* atmosferyczny; *fig.* pośpiech *m*; **~tous** [prı'sıpıtəs] stromy; *fig.* pochopny

pré·cis ['preısi:] (*pl.* **-cis** [-si:z]) stre-szczenie *n*

pre|·cise [prı'saıs] dokładny; precyzyj-ny; **~·ci·sion** [prı'sıʒn] dokładność *f*; precyzja *f*

pre·clude [prı'klu:d] wykluczać ⟨-czyć⟩

pre·co·cious [prı'kəʊʃəs] nad wiek rozwinięty, wcześnie dojrzały

pre·con|·ceived [pri:kən'si:vd] u-przednio powzięty, z góry powzięty; **~·cep·tion** [pri:kən'sepʃn] uprzedze-nie *n*; pogląd *m* przyjęty z góry

pre·cur·sor [pri:'kɜ:sə] prekursor *m*, zwiastun *m*

pred·a·to·ry ['predətərı] drapieżny

pre·de·ces·sor ['pri:dısesə] poprzed-nik *m* (*-iczka f*)

pre·des|·ti·na·tion [pri:destı'neıʃn] predestynacja *f*, przeznaczenie *n*; **~·tined** [pri:'destınd] przeznaczony, skazany (*to* na *A*)

pre·de·ter·mine [pri:dı'tɜ:mın] ustalać ⟨-lić⟩ z góry

pre·dic·a·ment [prı'dıkəmənt] opre-sja *f*, trudne położenie *f*

pred·i·cate ['predıkət] *gr.* predykat *m*, orzeczenie *n*; **pre·dic·a·tive** *gr.* [prı'dıkətıv] predykatywny

pre|·dict [prı'dıkt] przewidywać ⟨-wi-dzieć⟩, prognozować; **~·dic·tion** [prı'-dıkʃn] prognoza *f*, przewidywanie *n*

pre·dis|·pose [pri:dı'spəʊz] usposa-biać ⟨-sobić⟩; (*in favo(u)r of* pozytyw-nie wobec *G*), sprzyjać; *med.* predyspo-nować (*to* do *G*); **~·po·si·tion** [pri:-dıspə'zıʃn]: **~position to** skłonność *f* do (*G*), dyspozycja *f* (*G*), predyspozy-cja *f* do (*G*)

pre·dom·i|·nant [prı'dɒmınənt] domi-nujący; **~nate** [prı'dɒmıneıt] domi-nować

pre·em·i·nent [pri:'emınənt] wyróżnia-jący się

pre·emp·tive [pri:'emptıv] uprzedzają-cy; *mil.* wyprzedzający

preen [pri:n] czyścić (*pióra*) (*ptaki*); *fig.* stroić się

pre·fab ['pri:fæb] F budynek *m* z pre-fabrykatów; **~·ri·cate** [pri:'fæbrıkeıt] prefabrykować; **~ricated house** budy-nek *m* z prefabrykatów

pref·ace ['prefıs] **1.** przedmowa *f* (*to* do *G*); **2.** książkę itp. poprzedzać ⟨-dzić⟩

pre·fect ['pri:fekt] *Brt.* (*starszy uczeń odpowiedzialny za młodszych chłop-ców*)

pre·fer [prı'fɜ:] (*-rr-*) (*to*) woleć od (*G*), przedkładać nad (*A*), preferować

pref·e|·ra·ble ['prefərəbl]: **be ~rable** (*to*) być lepszym (niż *N*); **'~·ra·bly** naj-lepiej, możliwie; **~·rence** ['prefərəns] preferencja *f*

pre·fix ['pri:fıks] *gr.* przedrostek *m*, pre-fiks *m*

preg·nan|·cy ['pregnənsı] ciąża *f*; **~t** ['pregnənt] ciężarna, w ciąży

pre·heat [pri:'hi:t] *piekarnik itp.* wstęp-nie nagrzewać ⟨-rzać⟩

pre·judge [pri:'dʒʌdʒ] osądzać ⟨-dzić⟩ z góry

prej·u·dice ['predʒudıs] **1.** uprzedze-nie *n*; *pozytywne* nastawienie *n*; **to the ~ of** ze szkodą dla (*G*); **2.** uprzedzać; **'~d** uprzedzony; **~d in favo(u)r** z góry przychylnie nastawiony

pre·lim·i·na·ry [prı'lımınərı] **1.** wstęp-ny; **2. preliminaries** *pl.* wstęp *m*, wprowadzenie *n*

prel·ude ['prelju:d] *mus.* preludium *n*; *fig.* wstęp *m*, zapowiedź *f*

pre·mar·i·tal [pri:'mærıtl] przedmał-żeński

pre·ma·ture ['premətjʊə] przedwczes-ny

pre·med·i·l·tat·ed [pri:'mediteitid] rozmyślny, z premedytacją; **~·ta·tion** [pri:medi'teiʃn] premedytacja **f**: *with* **~tation** z premedytacją

prem·i·er ['premjə] głowa **f** państwa

prem·i·ere, prem·i·ère ['premieə] premiera **f**, prawykonanie **n**

prem·is·es ['premisiz] *pl.* teren **m**, siedziba **f**; lokal **m**; *on the ~* na miejscu

pre·mi·um ['pri:mjəm] premia **f**; składka **f** ubezpieczeniowa; '**~** (**gas·o·line**) *Am. mot.* (benzyna **f**) super

pre·mo·ni·tion [pri:mə'niʃn] złe przeczucie **n**

pre·oc·cu·l·pa·tion [pri:ɒkjʊ'peiʃn] zajęcie **n**, zaaferowanie **n**; **~·pied** [pri:'ɒkjupaid] zajęty, zaaferowany; **~·py** [pri:'ɒkjupai] *bardzo* zajmować ⟨-jąć⟩

prep [prep] *Brt.* F zadanie **n** domowe

pre·packed [pri:'pækt], **pre·pack·aged** [pri:'pækidʒd] *pożywienie:* zapakowany

pre·paid [pri:'peid] *poczta:* opłacony z góry; **~ envelope** ofrankowana koperta **f**, koperta **f** z opłaconym doręczeniem

prep·a·ra·tion [prepə'reiʃn] przygotowanie (*for* do G); *chem., med.* preparat **m**

pre·par·a·to·ry [pri'pærətəri] przygotowawczy, przygotowujący; **~ school** prywatna szkoła podstawowa

pre·pare [pri'peə] *v/t.* przygotowywać ⟨-ować⟩; *jedzenie, etc.* przyrządzać ⟨-dzić⟩; *v/i.* **~ for** przygotowywać ⟨-ować⟩ się do (G) *lub* na (A), czynić przygotowania do (G); **~d** przygotowywany

prep·o·si·tion [prepə'ziʃn] *gr.* przyimek **m**

pre·pos·sess·ing [pri:pə'zesiŋ] pociągający, miły

pre·pos·ter·ous [pri'pɒstərəs] śmieszny, groteskowy

pre·pro·gram(me) [pri:'prəugræm] wstępnie zaprogramowywać ⟨-ować⟩

'**prep school** F → **preparatory school**

pre·req·ui·site [pri:'rekwizit] warunek **m** wstępny

pre·rog·a·tive [pri'rɒgətiv] prerogatywa **f**, przywilej **m**

pre·scribe [pri'skraib] *med.* przepisywać ⟨-sać⟩; zalecać

pre·scrip·tion [pri'skripʃn] *med.* re-cepta **f**; zalecenie **n**; zarządzenie **n**

pres·ence ['prezns] obecność **f**; postawa **f**; **~ of 'mind** przytomność **f** umysłu

pres·ent¹ ['preznt] prezent **m**, podarunek **m**

pre·sent² [pri'zent] przedstawiać ⟨-wić⟩ (*też theat.*); ⟨za⟩prezentować; ⟨po⟩darować; wręczać ⟨-czyć⟩; *program* ⟨po⟩prowadzić

pres·ent³ ['preznt] **1.** obecny; aktualny; *rok, etc.*: bieżący; teraźniejszy; **~ tense** czas **m** teraźniejszy; **2.** teraźniejszość **f**; *gr.* czas **m** teraźniejszy; *at* **~** obecnie; *for the* **~** na razie

pre·sen·ta·tion [prezən'teiʃn] prezentacja **f**; wręczenie **n**; podarowanie **n**; przedstawienie **n**; wystąpienie **n**; prowadzenie **n** (*programu radiowego lub telewizyjnego*)

pres·ent-'day obecny, współczesny

pre·sent·er [pri'zentə] *radio, TV itp.*: prezenter(ka **f**) **m**

pre·sen·ti·ment [pri'zentimənt] (złe) przeczucie **n**

pres·ent·ly ['prezntli] wkrótce; *zwł. Am.* obecnie

pres·er·va·tion [prezə'veiʃn] zachowanie **n**; konserwacja **f**; zabezpieczenie **n**; ochrona **f**

pre·ser·va·tive [pri'zɜ:vətiv] środek **m** konserwujący; △ *nie* **prezerwatywa**

pre·serve [pri'zɜ:v] **1.** zachowywać ⟨-ować⟩; ⟨o⟩chronić; ⟨za⟩konserwować; **2.** rezerwat **m**; teren **m** myśliwski; *fig.* dziedzina **f**; *zw.* **~s** *pl.* przetwory *pl.*

pre·side [pri'zaid] przewodniczyć

pres·i·l·den·cy ['prezidənsi] *pol.* prezydentura **f**; **~·dent** ['prezidənt] prezydent **m**; przewodniczący **m** (-ca **f**)

press [pres] **1.** *v/t.* naciskać ⟨-snąć⟩; przyciskać ⟨-snąć⟩; wciskać ⟨-snąć⟩; ściskać ⟨-snąć⟩; *owoce* wyciskać ⟨-snąć⟩; ⟨u⟩prasować; naciskać na (A); wywierać ⟨wywrzeć⟩ presję na (A); *v/i.* naciskać ⟨-nąć⟩; *czas:* naglić; wywierać ⟨wywrzeć⟩ presję; **~ for** nalegać na (A); **~ on** dalej podążać ⟨-żyć⟩; **2.** nacisk **m** (*też fig.*); prasa **f** (*gazety itp.*); prasa **f** (*drukarska, do wina*); *printing* ~ prasa **f** drukarska; '**~ a·gen·cy** agencja **f** prasowa; '**~ box** trybuna **f** dla prasy; '**~·ing**pilny, naglący; '**~·stud** *Brt.* (*zapięcie*) zatrzask **m**; '**~-up** *zwł. Brt.* pompka **f**; *do ten* **~-ups** zrobić dziesięć pompek

pres·sure ['preʃə] *phys.*, *tech. itp.* ciśnienie *n* ⟨*też fig.*⟩; nacisk *m*; presja *f*; napięcie *n*; '~ **cook·er** szybkowar *m*

pres·tige [pre'sti:ʒ] prestiż *m*, powaga *f*

pre·su·ma·bly [prɪ'zju:məblɪ] przypuszczalnie; **~·sume** [prɪ'zju:m] *v/t.* mniemać, przypuszczać; *niewinność* domniemywać ⟨-mać⟩; *v/i.* ośmielać ⟨-lić⟩ się (**to do s.th.** robić coś); **~·sume on** wykorzystywać ⟨-tać⟩ niewłaściwie

pre·sump·tion [prɪ'zʌmpʃn] przypuszczenie *n*, mniemanie *n*; domniemanie *n*; czelność *f*, arogancja *f*; **~·tu·ous** [prɪ'zʌmptʃʊəs] czelny, arogancki

pre·sup·pose [pri:sə'pəʊz] zakładać; **~·po·si·tion** [pri:sʌpə'zɪʃn] założenie *n*

pre·tence *Brt.*, **pre·tense** *Am.* ['prɪ'tens] pozór *m*, pretekst *m*; pretensja *f* (**to** do *G*)

pre·tend [prɪ'tend] udawać ⟨udać⟩; rościć pretensje (**to** do do *G*); **~·ed** udawany

pre·ten·sion [prɪ'tenʃn] pretensja *f* (**to** do *G*); pretensjonalność *f*

pre·ter·it(e) ['pretərɪt] *gr.* czas *m* przeszły

pre·text ['pri:tekst] pretekst *m*

pret·ty [prɪtɪ] **1.** (*-ier, -iest*) ładny; **2.** *adv.* F całkiem, dość

pret·zel ['pretsl] precel *m*

pre·vail [prɪ'veɪl] zwyciężać ⟨-żyć⟩ (**over, against** nad *D*); zapanować ⟨-ować⟩; przeważać; **~·ing** przeważający

pre·|vent [prɪ'vent] zapobiegać ⟨-biec⟩; uniemożliwiać ⟨-wić⟩; nie dawać możności; **~·ven·tion** [prɪ'venʃn] zapobieganie *n*; uniemożliwienie *n*; **~·ven·tive** [prɪ'ventɪv] zapobiegawczy; prewencyjny

pre·view ['pri:vju:] *film, TV*: pokaz *m* przedpremierowy

pre·vi·ous ['pri:vjəs] poprzedni; uprzedni; **~ to** przed (*I*); '~·ly uprzednio

pre·war [pri:'wɔ:] przedwojenny

prey [preɪ] **1.** zdobycz *f*, łup *m*; ofiara *f*; **of ~** drapieżny; **be easy ~ for** lub **to** stanowić łatwy łup dla (*G*); **2. ~ on** *zo.* polować na (*A*); *fig.* dręczyć (*A*)

price [praɪs] **1.** cena *f*; **2.** ustalać ⟨-lić⟩ cenę (*G*), wyceniać ⟨-nić⟩ (**at** na *L*); '~·less bezcenny; '~·tag metka *f* (*z ceną*)

prick [prɪk] **1.** ukłucie *n*; V kutas *m*; **~s pl. of conscience** wyrzuty *pl.* sumienia; **2.** *v/t.* ⟨po-, na-, u⟩kłuć; *her conscience ~ed her* ⟨po⟩czuła wyrzuty sumienia; **~ up one's ears** nadstawiać ⟨-wić⟩ uszu

prick·le ['prɪkl] kolec *m*; uczucie *n* kłucia; '~·ly (*-ier, -iest*) kolczasty, kłujący

pride [praɪd] **1.** duma *f*; pycha *f*; *take (a) ~ in* szczycić się (*I*); **2. ~ o.s. on** szczycić się (*I*)

priest [pri:st] ksiądz *m*, duchowny *m*

prig [prɪg] bigot *m*, świętoszek *m*; pedant *m*; '~·gish świętoszkowaty

prim [prɪm] (*-mm-*) pruderyjny, sztywny

pri·mae·val *zwł. Brt.* [praɪ'mi:vl] → *primeval*

pri·ma·ri·ly ['praɪmərəlɪ] przede wszystkim

pri·ma·ry ['praɪmərɪ] **1.** podstawowy; główny; pierwotny; **2.** *Am. pol.* wybory *pl.* wstępne; '~ **school** *Brt.* szkoła *f* podstawowa

prime [praɪm] **1.** *math.* liczba *f* pierwsza; *fig.* rozkwit *m*; **in the ~ of life** w kwiecie wieku; **be past one's ~** mieć już za sobą najlepsze lata; **2.** *adj.* pierwszy, początkowy; najważniejszy; główny; wyborowy, pierwszorzędny; **3.** *v/t.* *ścianę* ⟨za⟩gruntować; ⟨po⟩instruować, przygotowywać ⟨-ować⟩; **~ 'min·is·ter** premier *m*; **~ 'num·ber** *math.* liczba *f* pierwsza

prim·er ['praɪmə] elementarz *m*; środek *m* do gruntowania

'prime time *zwł. Am.* okres *m* największej oglądalności

pri·me·val [praɪ'mi:vl] odwieczny; pierwotny; pradawny

prim·i·tive ['prɪmɪtɪv] prymitywny; pierwotny

prim·rose ['prɪmrəʊz] *bot.* pierwiosnek *m*, prymula *f*

prince [prɪns] książę *m*; **prin·cess** [prɪn'ses], (*przed nazwiskiem*) ['prɪnses] księżniczka *f*; księżna *f*

prin·ci·pal ['prɪnsəpl] **1.** główny; zasadniczy; △ *nie* **pryncypialny**; **2.** *Am. szkoła:* dyrektor(ka *f*) *m*, kierownik *m* (-iczka *f*); *theat.* odtwórca *m* (-czyni *f*) głównej roli; *mus.* solista *m* (-tka *f*); *econ.* suma *f* nominalna

prin·ci·pal·i·ty [prɪnsɪ'pælətɪ] księstwo *n*

prin·ci·ple ['prɪnsəpl] zasada *f*; **on ~** z zasady

print [prɪnt] **1.** *print.* druk *m*; odcisk *m* (*palca*); *phot.* odbitka *f*; rycina *f*; tkanina *f* drukowana; *in ~* w druku; *out of ~* wyczerpany; **2.** *v/i.* drukować; *v/t.* ⟨wy-, za⟩drukować; odciskać ⟨-snąć⟩; ⟨na⟩pisać drukowanymi literami; *fig.* zapadać (*on* w *A*); *też ~ off phot.* odbijać ⟨-bić⟩; *~ out komp.* wydrukowywać ⟨-ować⟩; *'~ed mat·ter* druki *pl.* (*przesyłane pocztą*)

'print·er drukarz *m*; drukarka *f*; *~'s error* błąd *m* drukarski; *~'s ink* farba *f* drukarska

print·ing ['prɪntɪŋ] *print.* drukowanie *n*; *'~ ink* farba *f* drukarska; *'~ press* prasa *f* drukarska

'print·out *komp.* wydruk *m*

pri·or ['praɪə] wcześniejszy; uprzedni; priorytetowy; *~·i·ty* [praɪ'ɒrɪtɪ] priorytet *f*; *mot.* pierwszeństwo *n*

prise [praɪz] *zwł. Brt.* → *prize²*

pris·m ['prɪzəm] pryzmat *m*; graniastosłup *m*

pris·on ['prɪzn] więzienie *n*; *'~·er* więzień *m* (-*eźniarka f*); *hold ~er*, *keep ~er* więzić (*G*); *take ~er* uwięzić (*G*)

priv·a·cy ['prɪvəsɪ] prywatność *f*; sfera *f* osobista; odosobnienie *n*

pri·vate ['praɪvɪt] **1.** prywatny; odosobniony; *życie itp.*: osobisty; skryty, ukryty; *~ parts pl.* przyrodzenie *n*; **2.** *med.* szeregowy; *in ~* w cztery oczy, na osobności

pri·va·tion [praɪ'veɪʃn] prywacja *f*, wyrzeczenie *n*

priv·i·lege ['prɪvɪlɪdʒ] przywilej *m*; zaszczyt *m*; *'~d* uprzywilejowany

priv·y ['prɪvɪ] (*-ier, -iest*): *be ~ to* być wtajemniczonym w (*A*)

prize¹ [praɪz] **1.** nagroda *f*; premia *f*; wygrana *f*; **2.** nagrodzony; pierwszej jakości; **3.** wysoko cenić

prize² [praɪz]: *~ open* wyważać ⟨-żyć⟩

'prize-win·ner zdobywca *m* (-czyni *f*) pierwszej nagrody

pro¹ [prəʊ] F (*pl. -s*) profesjonalista *m* (-tka *f*)

pro² [prəʊ] (*pl. -s*): *the ~s and cons pl.* za i przeciw

prob|·a·bil·i·ty [prɒbə'bɪlətɪ] prawdopodobieństwo *n*; *in all ~ability* według wszelkiego prawdopodobieństwa; *~·a·ble* ['prɒbəbl] prawdopodobny; *'~·a·bly* prawdopodobnie

pro·ba·tion [prə'beɪʃn] próba *f*, okres *m* próbny, staż *m*; *jur.* dozór *m* kuratora sądowego; *~ of·fi·cer jur.* kurator *m* sądowy

probe [prəʊb] **1.** *med.*, *tech.* sonda *f*; *fig.* dochodzenie *n* (*into* w *A*); △ *nie próba*; **2.** sondować; ⟨z⟩badać (*dokładnie*); △ *nie próbować*

prob·lem ['prɒbləm] problem *m*, zagadnienie *n*; *math. itp.* zadanie *n*; *~·at·ic* [prɒblə'mætɪk] (*-ally*); *~·at·i·cal* problematyczny

pro·ce·dure [prə'si:dʒə] procedura *f*

pro·ceed [prə'si:d] iść ⟨pójść⟩ dalej; podążać; postępować; przystępować ⟨-tąpić⟩ (*to* do *G*); *fig.* kontynuować; *~ from* wynikać ⟨-knąć⟩, wypływać ⟨-łynąć⟩; *~ to s.th.* przystępować ⟨-tąpić⟩ do robienia czegoś; *~·ing jur.* postępowanie *n* sądowe; *~·ings pl.* obrady *pl.*; sprawozdanie *n*; *jur.* proces *m* sądowy; *start lub take (legal) ~ings against jur.* wszczynać ⟨-cząć⟩ postępowanie sądowe

pro·ceeds ['prəʊsi:dz] *pl.* wpływy *pl.*, przychód *m*

pro·cess ['prəʊses] **1.** proces *m*; tok *m*; *jur.* postępowanie *n* sądowe; *in the ~* w toku, w trakcie; *be in ~* toczyć się, zachodzić; *in the ~ of construction* w trakcie budowy, w budowie; **2.** *tech.* przetwarzać ⟨-worzyć⟩; *film* wywoływać ⟨-łać⟩

pro·ces·sion [prə'seʃn] procesja *f*; pochód *m*

pro·ces·sor ['prəʊsesə] *komp.* procesor *m*; procesor *m* tekstu; robot *m* kuchenny

pro·claim [prə'kleɪm] proklamować, ogłaszać ⟨-łosić⟩

proc·la·ma·tion [prɒklə'meɪʃn] proklamacja *f*, obwieszczenie *n*

pro·cure [prə'kjʊə] uzyskiwać ⟨-kać⟩, zdobywać⟨-być⟩; stręczyć (*do nierządu*)

prod [prɒd] **1.** (*-dd-*) szturchać ⟨-chnąć⟩; dźgać ⟨-gnąć⟩, ⟨u⟩kłuć; pobudzać ⟨-dzić⟩ (*into* do *G*); **2.** szturchnięcie *n*; dźgnięcie *n*

prod·i·gal ['prɒdɪgl] **1.** marnotrawny; **2.** F hulaka *m*

pro·di·gious [prə'dɪdʒəs] znakomity; monumentalny

prod·i·gy ['prɒdɪdʒɪ] cud *m*; *child ~* cudowne dziecko *n*

P

pro·duce¹ [prə'dju:s] tworzyć; *econ.* ⟨wy⟩produkować; wytwarzać ⟨-worzyć⟩; przedstawiać ⟨-wić⟩, okazywać ⟨-zać⟩ **(from** z G); *econ.* zysk *itp.* przynosić ⟨-nieść⟩; być producentem *(filmu)*; *sztukę* wystawiać ⟨-wić⟩; *fig.* dawać ⟨dać⟩

prod·uce² ['prɒdju:s] *zwł. rolne* produkty *pl.*, płody *pl.*, wyroby *pl.*

pro·duc·er[prə'dju:sə]producent(ka *f*) *m*, wytwórca *m*; *film, TV:* producent *m*; *theat.* reżyser *m*

prod·uct ['prɒdʌkt] produkt *m*, wyrób *m*; iloczyn *m*

pro·duc·tion [prə'dʌkʃn] *econ.* produkcja *f*; wytwórstwo *n*, wytwarzanie *n*; okazanie *n*; *theat.* wystawianie *n*, inscenizacja *f*; **~·tive** [prə'dʌktɪv] produktywny *(też fig.)*; produkcyjny; owocny; *fig.* twórczy; **~·tiv·i·ty** [prɒdʌk'tɪvətɪ] produktywność *f*

prof [prɒf] F profesor *m*

pro|·fa·na·tion [prɒfə'neɪʃn] profanacja *f*, zbezczeszczenie *n*; **~·fane** [prə'feɪn] **1.** świecki; bluźnierczy; **2.** ⟨s⟩profanować; **~·fan·i·ty** [prə'fænətɪ]: *profanities pl.* bluźnierstwa *pl.*

pro·fess [prə'fes] wyrażać ⟨-razić⟩; utrzymywać; podawać się **(to be** za); wyznawać; **~ed** [prə'fest] zdeklarowany, otwarty

pro·fes|·sion [prə'feʃn] zawód *m (zwł. lekarza, prawnika itp.)*; **the ~sions** *pl.* wolne zawody *pl.*; **~·sion·al** [prə'feʃənl] **1.** profesjonalny, fachowy; zawodowy; **2.** profesjonalista *m* (-tka *f*); zawodowiec *m*; zawodowy sportowiec *m*; **~·sor** [prə'fesə] profesor *m*

pro·fi·cien|·cy [prə'fɪʃnsɪ] biegłość *f*; wprawa *f*; **~t** [prə'fɪʃnt] biegły; wprawny

pro·file ['prəʊfaɪl] profil *m*; zarys *m*; notka *f*, opis *m*

prof|·it ['prɒfɪt] **1.** zysk *m*, profit *m*; korzyść *f*; **2. ~it by, ~it from** odnosić ⟨-nieść⟩ korzyść; **~·i·ta·ble** zyskowny, dochodowy; korzystny, pożyteczny; **~·i·teer** *pej.* [prɒfɪ'tɪə] spekulant *m*, paskarz *m*; **'~·it shar·ing** udział *m* w zyskach

prof·li·gate ['prɒflɪgət] marnotrawny, rozrzutny

pro·found [prə'faʊnd] głęboki

pro|·fuse [prə'fju:s] obfity; *fig.* wylew-ny; **~·fu·sion** [prə'fju:ʒn] obfitość *f*; wylewność *f*; **in ~fusion** w obfitości

prog·e·ny ['prɒdʒənɪ] potomstwo *n*

prog·no·sis [prɒg'nəʊsɪs] *med.* (*pl.* **-ses** [-si:z]) prognoza *f*

pro·gram ['prəʊgræm] **1.** *komp.* program *m*; *Am.* → **programme**; **2.** (**-mm-**) *komp.* ⟨za⟩programować; *Am.* → **programme 2**; '**~·er** → **programmer**

pro·gramme *Brt.*; **pro·gram** *Am.* ['prəʊgræm] **1.** program *m*; transmisja *f (radiowa lub telewizyjna)*; **2.** ⟨za⟩programować; ⟨za⟩planować; '**pro·gram·mer** *komp.* programista *m*

pro|·gress 1. ['prəʊgres] postęp *m*; **make slow ~gress** wolno się rozwijać; **be in ~gress** być w toku; **2.** [prəʊ'gres] iść ⟨pójść⟩ dalej; ⟨z⟩robić postępy; **~·gres·sive** [prəʊ'gresɪv] postępowy, progresywny

pro|·hib·it [prə'hɪbɪt] zabraniać ⟨-ronić⟩, zakazywać ⟨-zać⟩; **~·hi·bi·tion** [prəʊɪ'bɪʃn] zakaz *m*; prohibicja *f*; **~·hib·i·tive** [prə'hɪbɪtɪv] nadmierny, przesadny

pro|·ject¹ ['prɒdʒekt] projekt *m*, plan *m*; przedsięwzięcie *n*

pro·ject² [prə'dʒekt] *v/i.* wystawać, sterczeć; *v/t.* ⟨za⟩projektować, ⟨za⟩planować, prognozować; wyrzucać ⟨-cić⟩, wysuwać ⟨-sunąć⟩; wyświetlać ⟨-lić⟩

pro·jec·tile [prə'dʒektaɪl] pocisk *m*

pro·jec|·tion [prə'dʒekʃn] prognoza *f*, szacowanie *n*; projekcja *f*; występ *m (skalny, budowlany)*; **~·tor** [prə'dʒektə] projektor *m*

pro·le·tar·i·an [prəʊlɪ'teərɪən] **1.** proletariacki, robotniczy; **2.** proletariusz (ka *f*) *m*

pro·lif·ic [prə'lɪfɪk] (**~ally**) płodny

pro·logue *zwł. Brt.*, **pro·log** *Am.* ['prəʊlɒg] prolog *m*

pro·long [prəʊ'lɒŋ] przedłużać ⟨-żyć⟩

prom·e·nade [prɒmə'nɑ:d] **1.** *nadmorska* promenada *f*; **2.** przechadzać się

prom·i·nent ['prɒmɪnənt] wybitny, znakomity; prominentny

pro·mis·cu·ous [prə'mɪskjʊəs] rozwiązły

prom|·ise ['prɒmɪs] **1.** obietnica *f*, przyrzeczenie *n*; *fig.* zapowiedź *f*; **2.** obiecywać ⟨-cać⟩; '**~·is·ing** obiecujący

prom·on·to·ry [ˈprɒməntrɪ] przylądek *m*, cypel *m*

pro|·mote [prəˈməʊt] *też* (*w wojsku, szkole*) promować, awansować; *produkt itp.* 'sprzedawać; ~·mot·er [prəˈməʊtə] sponsor *m*; rzecznik *m* (*-niczka f*); ~·motion [prəˈməʊʃn] promocja *f*; awans *m*

prompt [prɒmpt] **1.** wywoływać ⟨-łać⟩, prowadzić do (*G*); zachęcać ⟨-cić⟩ (**to do** do zrobienia *G*); *theat.* podpowiadać ⟨-wiedzieć⟩, suflerować; **2.** bezzwłoczny, niezwłoczny; punktualny, terminowy; '~·er sufler(ka *f*) *m*

prone [prəʊn] (**-r, -st**) leżący na brzuchu *lub* twarzą w dół; **be ~ to** *fig.* być skłonnym do (*G*), być podatnym na (*A*)

prong [prɒŋ] ząb *m* (*widelca, wideł*)

pro·noun [ˈprəʊnaʊn] *gr.* zaimek *m*

pro·nounce [prəˈnaʊns] wymawiać ⟨-mówić⟩; wypowiadać ⟨-wiedzieć⟩ się (**on** *o L*); *jur.* wyrok *itp.* ogłaszać ⟨-łosić⟩

pron·to [ˈprɒntəʊ] F szybko, rączo

pro·nun·ci·a·tion [prənʌnsɪˈeɪʃn] wymowa *f*

proof [pruːf] **1.** dowód *m*, dowody *pl.*; próba *f*, sprawdzenie *n*; *print.* korekta *f*; *print., phot.* odbitka *f* próbna; stopień *m* zawartości alkoholu; **2.** *adj. w złoż.* odporny; → **heatproof, soundproof, waterproof, be ~ against** być zabezpieczonym przed (*I*); **3.** ⟨za⟩impregnować; ~·read [ˈpruːfriːd] (*-read* [-red]) ⟨z⟩robić korektę; '~·read·er korektor(ka *f*) *m*

prop [prɒp] **1.** podpora *f* (*też fig.*); **2.** (*-pp-*) *też* ~ **up** podpierać ⟨-deprzeć⟩; *się lub* coś opierać (**against** *o A*)

prop·a·gate [ˈprɒpəgeɪt] *biol.* rozmnażać ⟨-nożyć⟩ (się); propagować, rozprzestrzeniać ⟨-nić⟩; ~·ga·tion [prɒpəˈgeɪʃn] rozmnażanie *n*, propagacja *f*, propagowanie *n*

pro·pel [prəˈpel] (*-ll-*) napędzać ⟨-dzić⟩, wprawiać ⟨-wić⟩ w ruch; ~·lant, ~·lent gaz *m* pędny (*w aerozolu itp.*); paliwo *n* silnikowe, materiał *m* napędowy; ~·ler *aviat.* śmigło *n*; *naut.* śruba *f* napędowa; ~·ling 'pen·cil ołówek *m* automatyczny

pro·pen·si·ty [prəˈpensətɪ] *fig.* skłonność *f*

prop·er [ˈprɒpə] właściwy, odpowiedni; stosowny; *zwł. Brt.* F straszny, całkowity; ~ 'name imię *n* własne; ~ 'noun rzeczownik *m* własny

prop·er·ty [ˈprɒpətɪ] własność *f*; nieruchomość *f*, posiadłość *f*; właściwość *f*, cecha *f*

proph·e·cy [ˈprɒfɪsɪ] proroctwo *n*; ~·e·sy [ˈprɒfɪsaɪ] ⟨wy⟩prorokować; ~et [ˈprɒfɪt] prorok *m*

pro·por·tion [prəˈpɔːʃn] **1.** proporcja *f* (*też math.*); stosunek *m*; ~s wielkość *f*, rozmiary *pl.*; udział *m*, część *f*, odsetek *m*; proporcjonalność *f*; **in ~ to** w proporcji do (*G*); **2.** (**to**) nadawać ⟨-dać⟩ właściwe proporcje (*D*); ⟨po⟩dzielić właściwie; ~·al [prəˈpɔːʃnl] stosunkowy; → ~·ate [prəˈpɔːʃnət] proporcjonalny (**to** do *G*)

pro·pos·al [prəˈpəʊzl] propozycja *f*; oświadczyny *pl.*; ~e [prəˈpəʊz] *v/t.* ⟨za⟩proponować; przedstawiać ⟨-wić⟩; zamierzać (**to do s.th.** coś zrobić); *toast itp.* wznosić ⟨-nieść⟩ (**to** do *G*); ~**e s.o.'s health** ⟨wy⟩pić za czyjeś zdrowie; *v/i.* ~**e to** oświadczać ⟨-czyć⟩ się (*D*); **pro·p·o·si·tion** [prɒpəˈzɪʃn] propozycja *f*; projekt *m*; *math.* twierdzenie *n*

pro·pri·e|·ta·ry [prəˈpraɪətərɪ] *econ.* prawnie zastrzeżony; opatentowany; *fig.* władczy; ~·tor [prəˈpraɪətə] posiadacz *m*, właściciel *m*; ~·tress [prəˈpraɪətrɪs] posiadaczka *f*, właścicielka *f*

pro·pri·e·ty [prəˈpraɪətɪ] stosowność *f*; właściwość *f*

pro·pul·sion [prəˈpʌlʃn] *tech.* napęd *m*

pro·sa·ic [prəʊˈzeɪɪk] (*~ally*) prozaiczny; przyziemny

prose [prəʊz] proza *f*

pros·e|·cute [ˈprɒsɪkjuːt] *jur.* ścigać sądownie (**for** za *A*), zaskarżać ⟨-żyć⟩; ~·cu·tion *jur.* [prɒsɪˈkjuːʃn] dochodzenie *n* sądowe; **the ~cution** oskarżenie *n*, strona *f* oskarżająca; ~·cu·tor *jur.* [ˈprɒsɪkjuːtə] *też* **public ~cutor** oskarżyciel *m* (*publiczny*)

pros·pect 1. [ˈprɒspekt] widok *m* (*też fig.*), perspektywa *f* (*też fig.*); *econ.* potencjalny klient *m*; △ *nie* **prospekt**; **2.** [prəˈspekt]: ~ **for** (*w górnictwie*) prowadzić poszukiwania

pro·spec·tive [prəˈspektɪv] potencjalny, ewentualny

pro·spec·tus [prəˈspektəs] (*pl. -tuses*)

prospekt *m*, informator *m* (*o uczelni itp.*)

pros·per ['prɒspə] prosperować, pomyślnie się rozwijać; **~·i·ty** [prɒ'sperɪtɪ] dobra passa *f*, rozkwit *m*; dobra koniunktura *f*; **~·ous** ['prɒspərəs] rozkwitający, dobrze prosperujący

pros·ti·tute ['prɒstɪtjuːt] prostytutka *f*; **male ~** męska prostytutka *f*

pros|·trate 1. ['prɒstreɪt] leżący (*twarzą w dół*); *fig.* złamany; **~trate with grief** pogrążony w smutku; **2.** [prɒ'streɪt] padać ⟨paść⟩ na twarz (**before** przed *I*); *fig.* złamywać ⟨-mać⟩się; **~·tra·tion** [prɒ'streɪʃn] padnięcie *n* na twarz; *fig.* załamanie *n* się

pros·y ['prəʊzɪ] (**-ier, -iest**) przegadany

pro·tag·o·nist [prəʊ'tægənɪst] bojownik *m* (**of** o *A*); *theat.* bohater(ka *f*) *m*

pro·tect [prə'tekt] ochraniać ⟨ochronić⟩, chronić (**from**, **against** przed *I*)

pro·tec·tion [prə'tekʃn] ochrona *f*; F opłata *f* za ochronę; △ *nie* **protekcja**; **~ mon·ey** opłata *f* za ochronę; **~ racket** F wyłudzanie *n* pieniędzy za ochronę

pro·tec·tive [prə'tektɪv] ochronny; dbały, troskliwy; **~ 'cloth·ing** ubranie *n* ochronne; **~ 'cus·to·dy** *jur.* areszt *m* zapobiegawczy; **~'du·ty, ~'tar·iff** *econ.* cła *pl.* ochronne

pro·tec·tor [prə'tektə] obrońca *m*; ochraniacz *m*; **~·ate** [prə'tektərət] protektorat *m*

pro·test 1. ['prəʊtest] protest *m*; sprzeciw *m*; **2.** [prə'test] *v/i.* ⟨za⟩protestować (**against** przeciw *D*); *v/t. Am.* protestować przeciw (*D*); zapewniać o (*L*)

Prot·es·tant ['prɒtɪstənt] **1.** protestancki; **2.** protestant(ka *f*) *m*

prot·es·ta·tion [prɒte'steɪʃn] zapewnienie *n*; protest *m* (**against** przeciw *D*)

pro·to·col ['prəʊtəkɒl] protokół *m*

pro·to·type ['prəʊtətaɪp] prototyp *m*

pro·tract [prə'trækt] przedłużać się, przewlekać się

pro|·trude [prə'truːd] wystawać, sterczeć (**from** z *G*); **~'trud·ing** wystający, sterczący

proud [praʊd] dumny (**of** z *G*)

prove [pruːv] (**proved, proved** lub *zwł. Am.* **proven**) *v/t.* udowodniać ⟨-wodnić⟩, wykazywać ⟨-zać⟩; *v/i.* **~ (to be)**

okazywać ⟨-zać⟩ się (*I*); **prov·en** ['pruːvən] **1.** *zwł. Am. p.p. od* **prove**; **2.** udowodniony

prov·erb ['prɒvɜːb] przysłowie *n*

pro·vide [prə'vaɪd] *v/t.* dostarczać ⟨-czyć⟩ (**with** *A*), zaopatrywać ⟨-trzyć⟩ (**with** w *A*); postanawiać ⟨-nowić⟩ (**that** że); *v/i.* **~ against** zabezpieczać ⟨-czyć⟩ się przeciwko (*I*); *prawo* zakazywać ⟨-zać⟩; **~ for** utrzymywać ⟨-mać⟩; przewidywać; uwzględniać ⟨-nić⟩; **pro·vid·ed**: **~ed (that)** pod warunkiem(, że), z zastrzeżeniem(, że)

prov·i·dent ['prɒvɪdənt] zapobiegliwy

pro·vid·er [prə'vaɪdə] dostawca *m*

prov·ince ['prɒvɪns] prowincja *f*; *fig.* kompetencja *f*; **pro·vin·cial** [prə'vɪnʃl] **1.** prowincjonalny; **2.** *pej.* prowincjusz-(ka *f*) *m*

pro·vi·sion [prə'vɪʒn] zaopatrzenie *n* (**of** w *A*); zabezpieczenie *n* się (**for** na wypadek *G*, **against** przeciwko *D*); postanowienie *n*, klauzula *f*; **with the ~ that** pod warunkiem, że; **~s** *pl.* prowiant *m*, żywność *f*; △ *nie* **prowizja**; **~·al** [prə'vɪʒənl] tymczasowy, prowizoryczny

pro·vi·so [prə'vaɪzəʊ] (*pl.* **-soes**) zastrzeżenie *n*, warunek *m*; **with the ~ that** pod warunkiem, że

prov·o·ca·tion [prɒvə'keɪʃn] prowokacja *f*; **pro·voc·a·tive** [prə'vɒkətɪv] prowokacyjny; wyzywający

pro·voke [prə'vəʊk] ⟨s⟩prowokować; wywoływać ⟨-łać⟩, ⟨s⟩powodować

prov·ost ['prɒvəst] rektor *m* (*w niektórych uczelniach*); *Szkoc.* burmistrz *m*

prowl [praʊl] **1.** *v/i. też* **~ about**, **~ around** *banda:* grasować, buszować; *v/t.* grasować po (*L*), buszować po (*L*); **2.** grasowanie *n*, buszowanie *n*; **~ car** *Am.* radiowóz *m*, wóz *m* patrolowy

prox·im·i·ty [prɒk'sɪmɪtɪ] bliskość *f*

prox·y ['prɒksɪ] pełnomocnictwo *n*, zastępstwo *n*; pełnomocnik *m*, zastępca *m*; **by ~** przez pełnomocnika

prude [pruːd]: **be a ~** być pruderyjnym

pru|·dence ['pruːdns] roztropność *f*, rozsądek *m*; **~·dent** roztropny, rozsądny

'prud·ish pruderyjny

prune¹ [pruːn] *drzewa itp.* przycinać ⟨-ciąć⟩

prune² [pruːn] suszona śliwka *f*

pry¹ [praɪ] myszkować, wtrącać się; ~ **about** węszyć wkoło; ~ **into** wtykać nos w (A)

pry² [praɪ] zwł. Am. → **prize²**

PS [piː 'es] skrót: **postscript** PS, postscriptum n, dopisek m

psalm [sɑːm] psalm m

pseu·do·nym ['sjuːdənɪm] pseudonim m, przydomek m

psy·chi·a·trist [saɪ'kaɪətrɪst] psychiatra m; ~·try [saɪ'kaɪətrɪ] psychiatria f

psy·cho·log·i·cal [saɪkə'lɒdʒɪkl] psychologiczny; ~·chol·o·gist [saɪ'kɒlədʒɪst] psycholog m; ~·chol·o·gy [saɪ'kɒlədʒɪ] psychologia f; ~·cho·so·mat·ic [saɪkəʊsəʊ'mætɪk] psychosomatyczny

pt skrót pisany: **part** cz., część f; **pint** kwarta f (ok. 1/2 l); zw. **Pt**, skrót: **port** port m

PT [piː 'tiː] zwł. Brt. skrót: **physical training** wf., wychowanie n fizyczne

PTO, pto [piː tiː 'əʊ] skrót: **please turn over** verte

pub [pʌb] pub m

pu·ber·ty ['pjuːbətɪ] okres m dojrzewania, pokwitanie n

pu·bic ['pjuːbɪk] anat. łonowy; ~ **'bone** kość f łonowa; ~ **'hair** owłosienie n łonowe

pub·lic ['pʌblɪk] **1.** publiczny, ogólny, powszechny; skandal: jawny; **2.** ogół m; społeczeństwo n; publiczność f; **in** ~ publicznie

pub·li·ca·tion [pʌblɪ'keɪʃn] publikacja f, wydanie n; opublikowanie n

pub·lic| con've·ni·ence Brt. toaleta f publiczna; ~ **'health** zdrowie n społeczeństwa; ~ **'hol·i·day** święto n państwowe; ~ **'house** Brt. → **pub**

pub·lic·i·ty [pʌb'lɪsətɪ] reklama f; rozgłos m

pub·lic| 'li·bra·ry biblioteka f publiczna; ~ **re'la·tions** (skrót: **PR**) służba f informacyjna; ~ **'school** Brt. prywatna szkoła f (dla zamożnych); Am. szkoła f państwowa; ~ **'trans·port** zwł. Brt. sg., ~ **trans·por'ta·tion** Am. sg. komunikacja f publiczna

pub·lish ['pʌblɪʃ] ⟨o⟩publikować, wydawać ⟨-dać⟩; ogłaszać ⟨ogłosić⟩, ujawniać ⟨-nić⟩; ~·**er** wydawca m; wydawnictwo n; '~·**er's**, '~·**ers** pl., '~·**ing house** wydawnictwo n

puck·er ['pʌkə] też ~ **up** twarz, usta krzywić, wykrzywiać ⟨-wić⟩; czoło ⟨z⟩marszczyć

pud·ding ['pʊdɪŋ] pudding m; Brt. deser m; Am. budyń m; **black** ~ Brt. kaszanka f

pud·dle ['pʌdl] kałuża f

pu·er·ile ['pjʊəraɪl] dziecięcy, infantylny

puff [pʌf] **1.** v/i. sapać; też ~ **away** papieros itp. pociągać (**at** z G); fajkę pykać (**at** z G); ~ **up** nadymać (się), obrzęknąć ⟨-kać⟩; v/t. dym wydmuchiwać ⟨-chać⟩; ~ **out** świecę zdmuchiwać ⟨-chnąć⟩; policzki wydymać ⟨-dąć⟩, pierś wypinać ⟨-piąć⟩; **2.** ~ pociągnięcie n, zaciągnięcie się (przy paleniu); podmuch m, powiew m (powietrza); puszek m (do pudru); F dech m; ~ed 'sleeve rękaw m z bufką; ~ 'pas·try ciasto n francuskie; '~ sleeve rękaw m z bufką; '~·**y** (-**ier**, -**iest**) zasapany; obrzmiały

pug [pʌg] zo. też ~ **dog** mops m

pug·na·cious [pʌg'neɪʃəs] bojowy, wojowniczy

puke [pjuːk] sl. rzygać ⟨-gnąć⟩, puszczać ⟨puścić⟩ pawia

pull [pʊl] **1.** ciągnięcie n, pociągnięcie n; przyciąganie n; podejście n; F wpływ m; **2.** ⟨po⟩ciągnąć; przyciągać ⟨-gnąć⟩ (też fig.); naciągać ⟨-gnąć⟩, wyciągać ⟨-gnąć⟩; rozciągać ⟨-gnąć⟩; Brt. piwo natoczyć, nalewać ⟨-lać⟩; ~ **ahead of** wyprzedzać ⟨-dzić⟩; ~ **away** odjeżdżać ⟨-jechać⟩, oddalać ⟨-lić⟩ się; ~ **down** budynek ⟨z⟩burzyć; ~ **in** pociąg: wjeżdżać ⟨-jechać⟩; podjeżdżać ⟨-jechać⟩; ~ **off** F dokonywać ⟨-nać⟩; ~ **out** wycofywać ⟨-fać⟩ się (**of** z G); odjeżdżać ⟨-jechać⟩; oddalać ⟨-lić⟩ się; stół wyciągać ⟨-gnąć⟩; ~ **over** zjeżdżać ⟨zjechać⟩ na bok; ~ **round** ⟨wy⟩zdrowieć; ~ **through** ⟨wy⟩zdrowieć; pokonywać ⟨-nać⟩ trudności; ~ **o.s. together** brać ⟨wziąć⟩ się w garść; ~ **up** zatrzymywać ⟨-mać⟩ się; wstrzymywać ⟨-mać⟩, ~ **up to**, ~ **up with** (w sporcie) doganiać ⟨-gonić⟩ (G)

pul·ley ['pʊlɪ] tech. koło n pasowe

'pull|-in Brt. bar m przy szosie; '~·o·ver pulower m; '~·up Brt. (na drążku) podciągnięcie n; **do a ~-up** podciągać ⟨-gnąć⟩ się na drążku

pulp [pʌlp] miąższ *m* (*owocu*); miazga *f* (*też anat.*); lichota *f*; ~ **novel** brukowa literatura *f*

pul·pit ['pulpɪt] ambona *f*

pulp·y ['pʌlpɪ] (*-ier, -iest*) miazgowaty

pul·sate [pʌl'seɪt] pulsować, tętnić

pulse [pʌls] puls *m*, tętno *n*

pul·ver·ize ['pʌlvəraɪz] rozdrabniać ⟨-drobnić⟩, ⟨s⟩proszkować

pu·ma ['pjuːmə] *zo.* puma *f*

pum·mel ['pʌml] (*zwł. Brt. -ll-, Am. -l-*) okładać kułakami

pump [pʌmp] **1.** pompa *f*, pompka *f*; dystrybutor *m* (*paliwa*); ⟨na⟩pompować; tłoczyć; *pieniądze itp.* wtłaczać ⟨-tłoczyć⟩; tryskać; F ciągnąć za język; '~ **at·tend·ant** operator *m* dystrybutora paliwa

pump·kin ['pʌmpkɪn] *bot.* dynia *f*

pun [pʌn] **1.** gra *f* słów; kalambur *m*; **2.** (*-nn-*) ⟨u⟩tworzyć kalambury

punch¹ [pʌntʃ] **1.** uderzać ⟨-rzyć⟩ (*pięścią*); **2.** uderzenie *n* (*pięścią*)

punch² [pʌntʃ] **1.** ⟨prze⟩dziurkować; *dziurkę* ⟨z⟩robić; *bilet* ⟨s⟩kasować; ~ **in** *zwł. Am.* podbijać ⟨-bić⟩ kartę przy przyjściu do pracy; ~ **out** *zwł. Am.* podbijać ⟨-bić⟩ kartę przy wychodzeniu z pracy; **2.** dziurkarka *f*, dziurkacz *m*; *tech.* przebijak *m*; stempel *m*

punch³ [pʌntʃ] poncz *m*

Punch [pʌntʃ] Punch *m* (*okrutna postać teatru kukiełkowego*); **be as pleased lub proud as** ~ cieszyć się jak dziecko; ~ **and Ju·dy show** [pʌntʃ ən 'dʒuːdɪ ʃəʊ] Punch i Judy (*postacie teatru kukiełkowego*)

'punch card, punched 'card karta *f* perforowana

punc·tu·al ['pʌŋktʃʊəl] punktualny

punc·tu·ate ['pʌŋktʃʊeɪt] wstawiać ⟨-wić⟩ znaki przestankowe; ~**a·tion** [pʌŋktʃʊ'eɪʃn] interpunkcja *f*; ~**a·tion mark** znak *m* przestankowy

punc·ture ['pʌŋktʃə] **1.** dziura *f*, przedziurawienie *n*; *mot.* przebicie *n* dętki, F guma *f*; **2.** ⟨prze⟩dziurawić; ⟨prze⟩dziurawić dętkę; F ⟨z⟩łapać gumę

pun·gent ['pʌndʒənt] ostry (*też fig.*); dotkliwy

pun·ish ['pʌnɪʃ] ⟨u⟩karać; '~**a·ble** karalny, podlegający karze; '~**ment** kara *f*; ukaranie *n*

punk [pʌŋk] punk *m*; *attr.* punkowy; ~ '**rock** punk-rock *m*

pu·ny ['pjuːnɪ] (*-ier, -iest*) wątły

pup [pʌp] *zo.* szczeniak *m*, szczenię *n*

pu·pa ['pjuːpə] *zo.* (*pl. -pae* [-piː], *-pas*) poczwarka *f*; △ *nie* **pupa**

pu·pil¹ ['pjuːpl] uczeń *m* (uczennica); △ *nie* **pupil**

pu·pil² ['pjuːpl] *anat.* źrenica *f*

pup·pet ['pʌpɪt] lalka *f*; *fig.* marionetka *f*; *attr.* marionetkowy; '~ **show** teatr *m* lalek; **pup·pe·teer** [pʌpɪ'tɪə] lalkarz *m*

pup·py ['pʌpɪ] *zo.* szczeniak *m*, szczenię *n*

pur·chase ['pɜːtʃəs] **1.** kupować⟨-pić⟩, nabywać ⟨-być⟩; **2.** nabytek *m*; **make ~chases** kupować; '~**chas·er** kupujący *m* (-ca *f*), nabywca

pure [pjʊə] (*-r, -st*) czysty; '~**bred** czystej krwi

pur·ga·tive ['pɜːɡətɪv] *med.* **1.** przeczyszczający; **2.** środek *m* przeczyszczający

pur·ga·to·ry ['pɜːɡətərɪ] *rel.* czyściec *m*

purge [pɜːdʒ] **1.** *w partii itp.* ⟨z⟩robić czystkę; oczyszczać ⟨-yścić⟩ (*of* z *G*); **2.** czystka *f*

pu·ri·fy ['pjʊərɪfaɪ] oczyszczać ⟨-yścić⟩

pu·ri·tan ['pjʊərɪtən] **1.** purytanin *m* (-anka *f*); **2.** purytański

pu·ri·ty ['pjʊərətɪ] czystość *f*

purl [pɜːl] **1.** lewe oczko *n*; **2.** wyrabiać ⟨-robić⟩ lewe oczko

pur·loin [pɜː'lɔɪn] przywłaszczać ⟨-czyć⟩ sobie

pur·ple ['pɜːpl] fioletowy; purpurowy

pur·pose ['pɜːpəs] **1.** cel *m*; zdecydowanie *n*; **on** ~ celowo; **to no** ~ bezskutecznie, daremnie; **2.** zamierzać, mieć zamiar; '~**ful** celowy, rozmyślny; '~**less** bezcelowo, daremnie; '~**ly** celowo

purr [pɜː] *kot, silnik*; ⟨za⟩mruczeć

purse¹ [pɜːs] portmonetka *f*; *Am.* torebka *f* (*damska*); pieniądze pl., fundusz *m*

purse² [pɜːs]: ~ (**up**) **one's lips** zaciskać ⟨-snąć⟩ usta

pur·su·ance [pə'sjuːəns]: **in** (**the**) ~ **of his duty** w trakcie wykonywania swoich obowiązków

pur|·sue [pə'sjuː] ścigać; *studia itp.* kontynuować; *zawód* wykonywać; dążyć do (*G*) (*celu*); *fig.* prześladować;

~'**su·er** prześladowca *m* ścigający *m* (-ca *f*); ~**suit** [pə'sjuːt] pościg *m*; zajęcie *n*

pur·vey [pəˈveɪ] *żywność* dostarczać ⟨-czyć⟩; ~**or** dostawca *m*

pus [pʌs] *med.* ropa *m*

push [puʃ] **1.** pchać, popychać ⟨-pchnąć⟩; *guzik itp.* naciskać ⟨-snąć⟩; ⟨za-, roz⟩reklamować; *narkotykami itp.* handlować; *fig.* naciskać ⟨-snąć⟩ (*to do* *s.th.* aby coś zrobić); ~**one's way** przepychać ⟨-pchnąć⟩ się (*through* przez *A*); ~ **ahead with** zamierzenie kontynuować; ~ **along** F jechać, iść; *around* F pomiatać (*I*); ~ *for* domagać się (*G*); ~ **forward with** → **push ahead with**; ~ *o.s. forward fig.* pchać się do przodu; ~ *in* F wpychać ⟨wepchnąć⟩ się; ~ *off!* F spływaj!; ~ *on with* → **push** *ahead with*; ~ *out fig.* wyrzucać ⟨-cić⟩; ~ *through fig.* przepychać ⟨-pchnąć⟩; ~ *up cenę* ⟨wy⟩windować; **2.** *pchnięcie n*; popchnięcie *n*; naciśnięcie *n*; *akcja f* reklamowa; F energia *f*, zapał *m*; '~ *but·ton* guzik *m*, przycisk *m*, klawisz *m*; '~*but·ton tech.* na guziki, na klawisze; ~*button* (*tele*)*phone* telefon *m* na klawisze; '~*chair Brt.* wózek *m* spacerowy; '~*er pej.* handlarz *m* narkotykami; '~·*o·ver* F dziecinna zabawka *f*, łatwizna *f*; '~*up Am.* → *press-up*

puss [pus] F kicia *f*

'**pus·sy** *też* ~ *cat* kiciuś *m*; V cipa *f*; '~·*foot* F: ~*foot about/around* postępować ⟨-tąpić⟩ ostrożnie

put [put] (*-tt-*; *put*) kłaść ⟨położyć⟩, umieszczać ⟨-mieścić⟩; odkładać ⟨odłożyć⟩; stosować; *na rynek, do obrotu itp.* wprowadzać ⟨-dzić⟩; *na miejsce* stawiać ⟨-wić⟩, kłaść ⟨położyć⟩; *porządek* zaprowadzać ⟨-dzić⟩; *uczucia* wkładać ⟨włożyć⟩; (*w sporcie*) *kulę* pchać; *słowami* wyrażać ⟨-razić⟩; *kłopoty* przysparzać ⟨-porzyć⟩; *pytania* przedstawiać ⟨-wić⟩; przekładać ⟨przełożyć⟩ (*into* *Polish* na polski); *winę* składać ⟨złożyć⟩; ~ *right* ⟨u⟩porządkować; ~ *s.th.* *before s.o. fig.* przedstawiać ⟨-wić⟩ coś komuś; ~ *to bed* kłaść ⟨położyć⟩ do łóżka; ~ *about plotki* rozgłaszać; ~ *across* przekazywać ⟨-zać⟩, ⟨u⟩czynić zrozumiałym; ~ *ahead* wychodzić na prowadzenie; ~ *aside* odkładać

⟨odłożyć⟩; nie zwracać uwagi na (*A*); ~ *away* odkładać ⟨odłożyć⟩ (*z powrotem*); ~ *back* (*na miejsce*) odkładać ⟨odłożyć⟩; przekładać ⟨przełożyć⟩; *wskazówki zegara* cofać ⟨-fnąć⟩ (*by* o *A*); ~ *by pieniądze* odkładać ⟨odłożyć⟩; ~ *down v/t.* odkładać ⟨odłożyć⟩; kłaść ⟨położyć⟩ *poniżad* ⟨-żyć⟩; (*z samochodu*) wysadzać ⟨-dzić⟩; *bunt* ⟨s⟩tłumić, zdusić; *zapisywać* ⟨-sać⟩; *zwierzę* usypiać ⟨uśpić⟩; (*też v/i.*) *aviat.* ⟨wy⟩lądować; ~ *down to* przypisywać ⟨-sać⟩; ~ *forward plan itp.* przedstawiać ⟨-wić⟩; *wskazówki zegara* przesuwać ⟨-sunąć⟩ do przodu (*by* o *A*); przesuwać ⟨-sunąć⟩ (*two days* o dwa dni; *to* na *A*); ~ *in v/t.* wkładać ⟨włożyć⟩, umieszczać ⟨-mieścić⟩ w (*L*); *rośliny* ⟨po⟩sadzić; *sprzęt* ⟨za⟩instalować; *żądanie, dokument, rachunek itp.* przedstawiać ⟨-wić⟩; *pieniądze* wpłacać ⟨-cić⟩; ⟨za⟩inwestować; *czas, pracę* wkładać ⟨włożyć⟩ (*on* przy *L*); *v/i.* *naut.* wchodzić ⟨wejść⟩ do portu (*to* do *G*); ~ *off* odkładać ⟨odłożyć⟩ (*until* do *G*); *kogoś* zwodzić ⟨zwieść⟩ ⟨z⟩deprymować; rozpraszać ⟨-roszyć⟩; ~ *on ubranie, czapkę itp.* wkładać ⟨włożyć⟩ (*na siebie*), nakładać ⟨nałożyć⟩; *światło, radio* włączać ⟨-czyć⟩; *dodatkowy pociąg* podstawiać ⟨-wić⟩; *theat. sztukę* przedstawiać ⟨-wić⟩; F nabierać ⟨-brać⟩; *cenę* zwiększać ⟨-szyć⟩; ~ *on airs* wywyższać się ⟨-szyć⟩; ~ *on weight* przybierać ⟨-brać⟩ na wadze; ~ *out v/t.* wyjmować ⟨-jąć⟩; ⟨z⟩gasić; *przed dom* wystawiać ⟨-wić⟩; *kota* wypuszczać ⟨-puścić⟩; *rękę* wyciągać ⟨-gnąć⟩; *język* wystawiać ⟨-wić⟩; nadawać ⟨-dać⟩ (*program*); oświadczenie wydawać ⟨-dać⟩; *kogoś* ⟨z⟩denerwować; *komuś* sprawiać kłopot; *ramię* zwichnąć, naciągnąć; *v/i.* *naut.* wypływać ⟨-łynąć⟩; ~ *over* → *put* *across*; ~ *through tel.* ⟨po⟩łączyć (*to* z *I*); przeprowadzać ⟨-dzić⟩; ~ *together* składać ⟨złożyć⟩; zestawiać ⟨-wić⟩; ~ *up* *v/t.* *rękę, cenę* podnosić ⟨-nieść⟩; *namiot* stawiać ⟨postawić⟩; *budynek* wznosić ⟨wznieść⟩; *obraz* zawieszać ⟨-wiesić⟩; *plakat* wywieszać ⟨-wiesić⟩; *parasol* rozkładać ⟨-złożyć⟩; *na noc* ⟨u⟩lokować; *na sprzedaż* wystawiać ⟨-wić⟩; *pieniądze* zbierać ⟨zebrać⟩; *opór* stawiać ⟨-wić⟩; *obóz* rozkładać ⟨-złożyć⟩;

P

~ **up with** znosić ⟨znieść⟩

pu·tre·fy ['pju:trɪfaɪ] powodować gnicie

pu·trid ['pju:trɪd] gnijący; F okropny

put·ty ['pʌtɪ] **1.** kit m; **2.** ⟨za⟩kitować

'put-up job F ukartowana gra f

puz·zle ['pʌzl] **1.** zagadka f, łamigłówka f; → **jigsaw (puzzle)**; **2.** v/t. stanowić zagadkę; **be** ~**d** być zaskoczonym; ~ **out** rozwiązanie wymyślić, znaleźć; v/i. łamać sobie głowę (**about, over** nad I)

PX [pi: 'eks] TM (pl. -**s** [- 'eksɪz]) skrót:

post exchange (kasyno dla członków sił zbrojnych USA)

pyg·my ['pɪgmɪ] Pigmej(ka f) m; karzeł m; attr. karłowaty

py·ja·mas [pə'dʒɑːməz] Brt. pl. (**a pair of** ~) piżama f

py·lon ['paɪlən] pylon m; słup m wysokiego napięcia

pyr·a·mid ['pɪrəmɪd] piramida f

pyre ['paɪə] stos m pogrzebowy

py·thon ['paɪθn] zo. (pl. -**thons, -thon**) pyton m

pyx [pɪks] rel. puszka f na komunikanty

Q

Q, q [kju:] Q, q n

qt skrót pisany: **quart** kwarta f (Brt. 1,14 l, Am. 0,95 l)

quack¹ [kwæk] **1.** ⟨za⟩kwakać, kwaknąć; **2.** kwaknięcie n

quack² [kwæk] też ~ **doctor** szarlatan m; Brt. konował m; ~**er·y** ['kwækərɪ] szarlataństwo n

quad·ran·gle ['kwɒdræŋgl] czworokąt m; ~**gu·lar** [kwɒ'dræŋgjʊlə] czworokątny

quad·ra·phon·ic [kwɒdrə'fɒnɪk] (~**ally**) kwadrofoniczny

quad·ri·lat·er·al [kwɒdrɪ'lætərəl] **1.** czworobok m; **2.** czworoboczny

quad·ro·phon·ic [kwɒdrə'fɒnɪk] kwadrofoniczny

quad·ru·ped ['kwɒdruped] zo. czworonóg m

quad·ru·ple ['kwɒdrupl] **1.** poczwórny; czterokrotny; **2.** zwiększać (się) czterokrotnie lub poczwórnie; ~**plets** ['kwɒdruplɪts] pl. czworaczki pl.

quads [kwɒdz] F pl. czworaczki pl.

quag·mire ['kwægmaɪə] bagno n, trzęsawisko n (też fig.)

quail [kweɪl] zo. (pl. **quail, quails**) przepiórka f

quaint [kweɪnt] osobliwy, niespotykany

quake [kweɪk] **1.** trząść się (**with, for** z D, **at** na A); **2.** F trzęsienie n ziemi

Quak·er ['kweɪkə] rel. kwakier(ka f) m

qual·i·fi·ca·tion [kwɒlɪfɪ'keɪʃn] kwalifikacje pl., predyspozycje pl. (**for** do G); zastrzeżenie n; ~**fied** ['kwɒlɪfaɪd]

wykwalifikowany; dyplomowany; **be** ~**fied to** mieć kwalifikacje do (G); z zastrzeżeniami; ~**fy** ['kwɒlɪfaɪ] v/t. ⟨za⟩kwalifikować (**for** do G); nadawać ⟨-dać⟩ kwalifikacje (**to do** do wykonywania); ⟨z⟩modyfikować; v/i. kwalifikować się (**for** do G); nabywać ⟨-być⟩ kwalifikacji; nabywać prawa (**for** do G); sport: ⟨za⟩kwalifikować się (**for** do G); ~**ty** ['kwɒlətɪ] jakość f; właściwość f, cecha f

qualms [kwɑːmz] pl. skrupuły pl., obiekcje pl.

quan·da·ry ['kwɒndərɪ]: **be in a** ~ **about what to do** nie wiedzieć, co robić

quan·ti·ty ['kwɒntətɪ] ilość f

quan·tum ['kwɒntəm] phys. (pl. -**ta** [-tə]) kwant m; attr. kwantowy

quar·an·tine ['kwɒrəntiːn] **1.** kwarantanna f; **2.** poddawać ⟨-dać⟩ kwarantannie

quar·rel ['kwɒrəl] **1.** kłótnia f, sprzeczka f; spór m; **2.** (zwł. Brt. -**ll-**, Am. -**l-**) kłócić się; ⟨s⟩kłócić; ~**some** kłótliwy

quar·ry¹ ['kwɒrɪ] kamieniołom m

quar·ry² ['kwɒrɪ] hunt. zdobycz f; fig. ofiara f

quart [kwɔːt] kwarta f (skrót: **qt**) (Brt. 1,14 l, Am. 0,95 l)

quar·ter ['kwɔːtə] **1.** ćwierć f, ćwiartka f; kwartał m; kwadrans m; ćwierć f funta; ćwierć f dolara; (w sporcie) kwarta f; (księżyca) kwadra f; dzielnica f, strona f (świata); ćwierćtusza f; ~**s** pl. zakwaterowanie *n*; *mil.* kwatera *f*; **a ~ of an hour** kwadrans *m*; **a ~ to** (*Am. of*) **five** za kwadrans piąta; **a ~ past** (*Am. after*) **five** piętnaście po piątej; **at close ~s** z bliska; **from official ~s** ze strony urzędu; **2.** ⟨po⟩ćwiartować; *zwł. mil.* zakwaterować (**on** u *A*); '**~·deck** achterdek *m*, pokład *m* rufowy; '**~·fi·nals** *pl.* ćwierćfinały *pl.*; '**~·ly 1.** kwartalnie; **2.** kwartalnik *m*

quar·tet(te) [kwɔːˈtet] *mus.* kwartet *m*

quartz [kwɔːts] *mins.* kwarc *m*; *attr.* kwarcowy; **~ clock** zegar *m* kwarcowy; '**~ watch** naręczny zegarek *m* kwarcowy

qua·ver [ˈkweɪvə] **1.** *głos:* ⟨za⟩drżeć; mówić ⟨powiedzieć⟩ drżącym głosem; **2.** drżenie *n*; *mus.* ósemka *f*

quay [kiː] *naut.* nabrzeże *n*, keja *f*

quea·sy [ˈkwiːzɪ] (*-ier*, *-iest*): **I feel ~** niedobrze mi, mdli mnie

queen [kwiːn] królowa *f*; (*w kartach*) dama *f*; (*w grze w warcaby*) damka *f*; (*w szachach*) królowa *f*, hetman *m*; *sl.* pedał *m*, homo *m*; **~ 'bee** (*w ulu*) matka *f*; '**~·ly** królewski, jak królowa

queer [kwɪə] **1.** dziwaczny; F pedałowaty, pedalski; **2.** F pedał *m*

quench [kwentʃ] *pragnienie* ugasić

quer·u·lous [ˈkwerʊləs] marudny

que·ry [ˈkwɪərɪ] **1.** pytanie *n*, zapytanie *n*; wątpliwość *f*; **2.** zapytywać ⟨-tać⟩, dowiadywać się

quest [kwest] **1.** poszukiwanie *n*; **in ~ of** w poszukiwaniu (*G*); **2.** poszukiwać

ques·tion [ˈkwestʃən] **1.** pytanie *n*; problem *m*, zagadnienie *n*; kwestia *f*; wątpliwość *f*; **only a ~ of time** tylko kwestia czasu; **this is not the point in ~** to nie o to chodzi; **there is no ~ that, it is beyond ~ that** nie ulega kwestii, że; **there is no ~ about this** co do tego nie ma żadnych wątpliwości; **be out of the ~** być wykluczonym; **2.** ⟨za⟩pytać (**about** o *A*); *jur.* pytać (**about** o *A*); ⟨za⟩kwestionować; '**~·a·ble** wątpliwy, sporny; '**~·er** osoba *f* zadająca pytanie; '**~ mark** znak *m* zapytania; '**~ mas·ter** *zwł. Brt.* osoba *f* prowadząca kwiz

ques·tion·naire [kwestʃəˈneə] kwestionariusz *m*

queue *zwł. Brt.* [kjuː] **1.** ogonek *m*, kolejka *f*; **2.** *zw.* **~ up** stawać ⟨stanąć⟩ do kolejki, ustawiać ⟨-wić⟩ się w kolejce

quib·ble [ˈkwɪbl] ⟨po⟩sprzeczać się (**with** z *I*, **about, over** o *A*)

quick [kwɪk] **1.** *adj.* szybki, prędki; zapalczywy; **be ~!** pospiesz się!; **2.** *adv.* szybko, prędko; **3.** **cut s.o. to the ~** dotknąć kogoś do żywego; '**~en** przyspieszać ⟨-szyć⟩; '**~-freeze** (*-froze, -frozen*) żywność szybko zamrażać ⟨-rozić⟩; **~ie** [ˈkwɪkɪ] F (*coś krótkiego, naprędce, np.*) krótkie pytanie *n*; '**~·ly** szybko, prędko; '**~-sand** lotne piaski *pl.*, kurzawka *f*; **~·tem·pered** zapalczywy; **~·wit·ted** lotny

quid *Brt. sl.* [kwɪd] (*pl.* **quid**) pieniądze: funt *m*

qui·et [ˈkwaɪət] **1.** cichy; spokojny; **~, please** proszę o ciszę; **be ~!** siedź cicho!; **2.** cisza *f*, spokój *m*; **on the ~** F cichaczem; **3.** *zwł. Am.* → **~·en** *zwł. Brt.* [ˈkwaɪətn] *też* **~en down** uciszać ⟨-szyć⟩; uspokajać ⟨-koić⟩ (się); '**~·ness** cisza *f* spokój *m*

quill [kwɪl] *zo.* długie pióro *n*; kolec *m*; **~** (*'pen*) gęsie pióro *n* (*do pisania*)

quilt [kwɪlt] kołdra *f*; narzuta *f*, kapa *f*; '**~·ed** pikowany

quince [kwɪns] *bot.* pigwa *f*

quin·ine [kwɪˈniːn] *pharm.* chinina *f*

quins [kwɪnz] *Brt.* F *pl.* pięcioraczki *pl.*

quin·tes·sence [kwɪnˈtesns] kwintesencja *f*, esencja *f*

quin·tet(te) [kwɪnˈtet] *mus.* kwintet *m*

quints [kwɪnts] *Am.* F *pl.* pięcioraczki *pl.*

quin·tu·ple [ˈkwɪntjupl] **1.** pięciokrotny; **2.** zwiększać (się) pięciokrotnie; **~·plets** [ˈkwɪntjuplts] pięcioraczki *pl.*

quip [kwɪp] **1.** dowcipna uwaga *f*; **2.** (*-pp-*) zrobić dowcipną uwagę

quirk [kwɜːk] osobliwość *f*; **by some ~ of fate** jakimś zrządzeniem losu

quit [kwɪt] F (*-tt-*; *Brt.* **~** *lub* **~ted,** *Am. zwł.* **~**) *v/t.* opuszczać; przestawać ⟨-tać⟩; **~ one's job** porzucić ⟨-cić⟩ pracę; *v/i.* odchodzić ⟨odejść⟩

quite [kwaɪt] całkiem, zupełnie; dość; **~ a few** dość dużo; **~ nice** całkiem przyjemny; **~** (*so*)! *zwł. Brt.* ano właśnie!; **be ~ right** mieć zupełnie rację; **she's a ~ beauty** z niej jest całkiem piękna dziewczyna

quits [kwɪts] F kwita (**with** z *I*); **call it ~** to kwita

quit·ter ['kwɪtə] F: *be a ~* łatwo się poddawać ⟨-ddać⟩

quiv·er¹ ['kwɪvə] ⟨za⟩drżeć (*with* z G;
at na A)

quiv·er² ['kwɪvə] kołczan m

quiz [kwɪz] **1.** (*pl.* **quizzes**) kwiz m, quiz
m; *zwł. Am.* test m, sprawdzian m; **2.**
(**-zz-**) wypytywać ⟨-tać⟩, rozpytywać
⟨-tać⟩ (*about* o L); *'~-mas·ter zwł.
Am.* prowadzący m ⟨-ca f⟩ kwiz; *~-zi-
cal* ['kwɪzɪkl] *spojrzenie*: zagadkowy

quo·ta ['kwəʊtə] limit m, dopuszczalna
ilość f; kontyngent m

quo·ta·tion [kwəʊ'teɪʃn] cytat m; *econ.*
oferta f; *econ.* stawka f, *econ.* giełdo-
we notowanie n; *~ marks pl.* cudzysłów m

quote [kwəʊt] ⟨za⟩cytować, *przykład*
przytaczać ⟨-toczyć⟩; *econ.* cenę podawać ⟨-dać⟩; *be ~d at econ.* być noto-
wanym na (L); → *unquote*

quo·tient ['kwəʊʃnt] *math.* iloraz m

R

R, r [ɑː] R, r n

rab·bi ['ræbaɪ] *rel.* rabin m; *tytuł:* rabbi m

rab·bit ['ræbɪt] *zo.* królik m

rab·ble ['ræbl] hołota f, motłoch m;
~-rous·ing ['ræblraʊzɪŋ] podżegający,
judzący

rab·id ['ræbɪd] *vet.* wściekły; *fig.* fanatyczny

ra·bies ['reɪbiːz] *vet.* wścieklizna f

rac·coon [rə'kuːn] *zo.* szop m pracz

race¹ [reɪs] rasa f

race² [reɪs] **1.** wyścig m; **2.** *v/i.* ścigać się;
brać ⟨wziąć⟩ udział w wyścigu; ⟨po⟩-
pędzić, ⟨po⟩mknąć; *serce:* walić; *v/t.*
ścigać się z (I); *konia* wystawiać ⟨-wić⟩
w wyścigach; *silnik:* pracować na przy-
spieszonych obrotach; *'~ car zwł. Am.*
samochód m wyścigowy; *'~-course
sport konny:* tor m wyścigowy; hipo-
drom m; *'~-horse* koń m wyścigowy; *'rac·er* koń m wyścigowy; rower
m wyścigowy; samochód m wyścigowy;
'~-track (*w sporcie*) tor m wyścigowy;
bieżnia f

ra·cial ['reɪʃl] rasowy

rac·ing ['reɪsɪŋ] wyścigowy; *~ car zwł.
Brt.* samochód m wyścigowy

ra|·cis·m ['reɪsɪzəm] rasizm m; *~·cist*
['reɪsɪst] **1.** rasista m ⟨-tka f⟩; **2.** rasis-
towski

rack [ræk] **1.** stojak m; suszarka f (*na naczynia*); stelaż m (*na gazety*); *rail.* półka f; *mot.* bagażnik m (*dachowy*); **2.** *be
~ed by lub with* być dręczonym (I);
~ one's brains łamać sobie głowę

rack·et¹ ['rækɪt] *tenisowa* rakieta f

rack|·et² ['rækɪt] harmider m, rejwach
m; oszustwo n; wymuszenie n, szantaż
m; *~·e·teer* [rækə'tɪə] szantażysta m
(-tka f)

ra·coon [rə'kuːn] *zo.* → *raccoon*

rac·y ['reɪsɪ] (*-ier, -iest*) *opowiadanie:*
pikantny

ra·dar ['reɪdə] radar m; *attr.* radarowy;
'~ screen ekran m radaru; *~ 'speed
check* kontrola f radarowa; *'~ sta·tion*
stacja f radarowa; *'~ trap mot.* kontrola f radarowa

ra·di·al ['reɪdjəl] **1.** radialny; promienio-
wy; **2.** opona f radialna; *~ 'tire Am.*,
~ 'tyre Brt. → *radial* 2

ra·di·ant ['reɪdjənt] promienisty; *fig.*
promienny, rozpromieniony (*with* z powodu G)

ra·di|·ate ['reɪdɪeɪt] promieniować; roz-
chodzić się promieniowo (*from* z G);
~·a·tion [reɪdɪ'eɪʃn] radiacja f, promieniowanie n; *~·a·tor* ['reɪdɪeɪtə] grzejnik m, kaloryfer m; *mot.* chłodnica f

rad·i·cal ['rædɪkl] **1.** radykalny (*też
pol.*); *math.* pierwiastkowy; **2.** radykał
m; *math.* pierwiastek m, znak m pier-
wiastka

ra·di·o ['reɪdɪəʊ] **1.** (*pl. -os*) radio m; ra-
dioodbiornik m; *attr.* radiowy; *by ~* ra-
diem, drogą radiową; *on the ~* w radiu;
2. przekazywać ⟨-zać⟩ drogą radiową;
~·ac·tive radioaktywny, promienio-
twórczy; *~active waste* odpady *pl.*
promieniotwórcze; *~·ac·tiv·i·ty* radio-
aktywność f, promieniotwórczość f;
'~ ham radioamator m; *'~ play* słucho-
wisko n; *'~ set* odbiornik m radiowy;

'~ sta·tion stacja *f* radiowa; **~'ther·a·py** *med.* radioterapia *f*; **~ 'tow·er** wieża *f* radiowa

rad·ish ['rædɪʃ] *bot.* rzodkiew(ka) *f*

ra·di·us ['reɪdjəs] (*pl. -dii* [-dɪaɪ]) promień *m*

RAF [ɑːr eɪ 'ef, ræf] *skrót: Royal Air Force* RAF *m*

raf·fle ['ræfl] **1.** loteria *f* fantowa, tombola *f*; **2.** *też* **~ off** dawać ⟨dać⟩ w nagrodę

raft [rɑːft] tratwa *f*

raf·ter ['rɑːftə] krokiew *f*

rag [ræg] szmata *f*; ścierka *f*; łach *m*; *in* **~s** w łachmanach; **~-and-'bone man** (*pl. -men*) *zwł. Brt.* szmaciarz *m* (-ciarka *f*), handlarz *m* (-arka *f*) starzyzną

rage [reɪdʒ] **1.** wściekłość *f*, szał *m*; *fly into a ~* wpaść we wściekłość *f*; *the latest ~* f najnowsza moda *f*; *be all the ~* być ostatnim krzykiem *m* mody; **2.** wściekać się (*against, at* na *A*); *choroba*: szaleć

rag·ged ['rægɪd] obszarpany; obdarty; *broda, linia:* nierówny

raid [reɪd] **1.** (*on*) napad (na *A*); *mil. też* nalot *m* (na *A*), wypad *m* (na *A*); obława *f* (na *A*); **2.** napadać ⟨-paść⟩, najeżdżać ⟨-jechać⟩; ⟨z⟩robić obławę

rail [reɪl] **1.** poręcz *f*; barierka *f*; wieszak *m* (*na ręczniki*); szyna *f*; *rail.* kolej *f*; **~s** *pl. też* tory *pl.*; *by* **~** koleją, pociągiem; **2.** **~ off** odgradzać ⟨-rodzić⟩; **'~·ing**, *często* **~s** *pl.* balustrada *f*, ogrodzenie *n*

'rail·road *Am. →* **railway**

'rail·way *zwł. Brt.* kolej *f*; **'~ line** *Brt.* linia *f* kolejowa; **'~·man** (*pl. -men*) kolejarz *m*; **'~ sta·tion** *Brt.* dworzec *m*, stacja *f* kolejowa

rain [reɪn] **1.** deszcz *m*; **~s** *pl.* opady *pl.* deszczu; *the* **~s** pora *f* deszczowa; (*come*) *or shine* bez względu na pogodę; **2.** *deszcz:* padać; *it is ~ing* (deszcz) pada; *it is ~ing cats and dogs* F leje jak z cebra; *it never ~s but pours* nieszczęścia chodzą parami; **'~·bow** tęcza *f*; **'~·coat** płaszcz *m* przeciwdeszczowy; **'~·fall** opady *pl.* deszczu; **'~ for·est** *bot.* wilgotny las równikowy, selwa *f*; **'~·proof** wodoodporny; **'~·y** (*-ier, -iest*) deszczowy; *save s.th. for a ~y day* odkładać ⟨odłożyć⟩ coś na czarną godzinę

raise [reɪz] **1.** podnosić ⟨-nieść⟩; *budy-*

nek wznosić ⟨-nieść⟩; unosić ⟨unieść⟩; uprawiać, hodować; wychowywać ⟨-wać⟩; *pieniądze* zdobywać ⟨-być⟩; zbierać ⟨zebrać⟩; *zagadnienie* poruszać ⟨-szyć⟩; *blokadę, zakaz* znosić ⟨znieść⟩; **2.** *Am.* podwyżka *f* (*płacy*)

rai·sin ['reɪzn] rodzynka *f*, rodzynek *m*

rake [reɪk] **1.** grabie *pl.*; **2.** *v/t.:* **~** (*up*) grabić, zagrabiać ⟨-bić⟩, zgrabiać ⟨-bić⟩; *v/i.* **~ about, ~ around** przetrząsnąć

rak·ish ['reɪkɪʃ] hulaszczy; zawadiacki

ral·ly ['rælɪ] **1.** zbierać ⟨zebrać⟩ się; poprawiać ⟨-wić⟩ się, ożywiać ⟨-wić⟩ się (*też econ.*); **~ round** skupiać ⟨-pić⟩ się wokół (*G*); **2.** wiec *m*, zgromadzenie *n*; *mot.* rajd *m*; (*w tenisie itp.*) wymiana *f* piłek

ram [ræm] **1.** *zo.* baran *m*, tryk *m*; *tech.* kafar *m*; bijak *m*; **2.** (*-mm-*) ⟨s⟩taranować; ubijać ⟨ubić⟩; wbijać ⟨wbić⟩, zasuwać ⟨-unąć⟩; **~ s.th. down s.o.'s throat** wciskać coś komuś na siłę

RAM [ræm] *skrót: random access memory komp.* RAM *m*, pamięć *f* o swobodnym dostępie

ram·ble ['ræmbl] **1.** wędrować, włóczyć się; ględzić (chaotycznie); płozić się, rozrastać ⟨-rosnąć⟩ się; **2.** wędrówka *f*; **'~·bler** wędrowiec *m*; *bot.* pnącze *n*; **'~·bling** chaotyczny, bez ładu i składu; chaotycznie zbudowany; *bot.* pnący

ram·i·fy ['ræmɪfaɪ] rozwidlać ⟨-lić⟩ się

ramp [ræmp] rampa *f*, pochylnia *f*; *Am. → slip road*

ram·page [ræm'peɪdʒ] **1.** **~ through** przejść tratując przez (*A*); **2.** *go on the ~ through* przejść niszcząc przez (*A*)

ram·pant ['ræmpənt]: *be ~* szerzyć się; rozrastać się

ram·shack·le ['ræmʃækl] rozklekotany; rozwalający się

ran [ræn] *pret. od* **run**

ranch [rɑːntʃ, *Am.* ræntʃ] ranczo *n*, rancho *n*; *Am.* ferma *f* (*drobiu itp.*); **'~·er** ranczer *m*; farmer *m*, hodowca *m*

ran·cid ['rænsɪd] zjełczały

ran·co(u)r ['ræŋkə] nienawiść *f*, wrogość *f*

ran·dom ['rændəm] **1.** *adj.* przypadkowy; losowy; *~ sample* próba *f* losowa; **2.** *at ~* przypadkowo, na oślep

rang [ræŋ] *pret. od* **ring**[2]

range [reɪndʒ] **1.** zakres *m*; przedział *m* (cenowy), rozpiętość *f*; zasięg *m*; donośność *f*; *econ.* asortyment *m*, wybór *m*; łańcuch *m* (*górski*); strzelnica *f*, poligon *m*; *Am.* kuchenka *f*; piec *m* (*kuchenny*); pastwisko *n*; *at close ~* z bliska; *within ~ of vision* w zasięgu wzroku; *a wide ~ of* ...szeroki asortyment (*G*); **2.** *v/i. ~ ... to ...*, *~ between ...and ...* *cena:* wahać się od ... do ...; *v/t.* ⟨u⟩szeregować; '*~ find·er* *phot.* dalmierz *m*; '*rang·er* leśniczy *m*, strażnik *m* leśny; *Am.* komandos *m*

rank¹ [ræŋk] **1.** ranga *f* (*też mil.*), stanowisko *n*; *mil.* stopień *m*; pozycja *f*; rząd *m*, szereg *m*; postój *m* taksówek; *of the first ~* *fig.* pierwszorzędny; *the ~ and file* szeregowi członkowie *pl.*; doły *pl.* (*partyjne*); *the ~s pl.* *fig.* szeregi *pl.*, masy *pl.*; **2.** zaliczać (się) (*among* pomiędzy *A*); zajmować miejsce (*G*); ⟨za⟩klasyfikować (się) (*as* jako)

rank² [ræŋk] *trawa:* rozrosły; cuchnący, obrzydliwy; *nowicjusz:* zupełny, całkowity

ran·kle ['ræŋkl] *fig.* napełniać ⟨-nić⟩ goryczą, rozgoryczać

ran·sack ['rænsæk] przewrócić wszystko do góry nogami; ⟨s⟩plądrować

ran·som ['rænsəm] **1.** okup *m*; **2.** ⟨za⟩płacić okup

rant [rænt]: *~ (on) about*, *~ and rave about* rozprawiać o (*L*), perorować o (*L*)

rap [ræp] **1.** uderzenie *n*, stukanie *n*; *mus.* rap *m*; **2.** (*-pp-*) uderzać ⟨-rzyć⟩, stukać ⟨-knąć⟩

ra·pa·cious [rə'peɪʃəs] łapczywy, zachłanny

rape¹ [reɪp] **1.** ⟨z⟩gwałcić; **2.** gwałt *m*

rape² [reɪp] *bot.* rzepak *m*; *attr.* rzepakowy

rap·id ['ræpɪd] prędki, bystry; **ra·pid·i·ty** [rə'pɪdətɪ] prędkość *f*; **rap·ids** ['ræpɪdz] *pl.* progi *pl.* rzeczne

rapt [ræpt]: *with ~ attention* z niesłabnącą uwagą; **rap·ture** ['ræptʃə] zachwyt *m*; *go into ~s* unosić się z zachwytu

rare¹ [reə] (*-r*, *-st*) rzadki; *światło:* wątły, niedosmażony

rare² [reə] *gastr.* (*-r*, *-st*) befsztyk: krwisty, niedosmażony

rare·bit ['reəbɪt] *gastr.* → *Welsh rarebit*

rar·e·fied ['reərɪfaɪd] rozrzedzony

rar·i·ty ['reərətɪ] rzadkość *f*

ras·cal ['rɑːskəl] łajdak *m*; *hum.* łobuziak *m*

rash¹ [ræʃ] pochopny, nieprzemyślany

rash² [ræʃ] *med.* wysypka *f*

rash·er ['ræʃə] (cienki) plasterek *m* (*bekonu itp.*)

rasp [rɑːsp] **1.** ⟨wy⟩chrypieć; ⟨o⟩trzeć; **2.** tarnik *m*, raszpla *f*; chrypienie *n*, zgrzyt *m*, zgrzytanie *n*

rasp·ber·ry ['rɑːzbərɪ] *bot.* malina *m*; *attr.* malinowy

rat [ræt] *zo.* szczur *m* (*też pej.*); *smell a ~* *fig.* ⟨wy⟩czuć coś (*niedobrego*); *~s!* F cholera!

rate [reɪt] **1.** stopa *f*, stawka *f*; *econ.* cena *f*, kurs *m* (*walut itp.*); tempo *n*, szybkość *f*, △ *nie rata (instal[l]ment)*; *at any ~* w każdym bądź razie; **2.** ⟨o⟩szacować (*as* jako *A*), oceniać ⟨-nić⟩; *na pochwałę* zasłużyć; *be ~d as* być uważanym za (*A*); *~ of ex'change* kurs *m* wymiany; *~ of 'in·ter·est* stopa *f* procentowa

ra·ther ['rɑːðə] raczej; dosyć, dość; *I would lub had ~ go* chciał(a)bym już pójść

rat·i·fy ['rætɪfaɪ] *pol.* ratyfikować

rat·ing ['reɪtɪŋ] oszacowanie *n*, ocena *f*; klasyfikacja filmu (*dla dzieci, dorosłych itp.*); *~s pl.* radio, *TV*: klasyfikacja *f*, lista *f* (*oglądalności*)

ra·ti·o ['reɪʃɪəʊ] *math.* (*pl.* *-os*) stosunek *m*, proporcja *f*

ra·tion ['ræʃn] **1.** racja *f* (*żywności itp.*); **2.** racjonować; *~ out* wydzielać ⟨-lić⟩

ra·tion·al ['ræʃənl] racjonalny, rozsądny; *~·i·ty* [ræʃə'nælətɪ] racjonalność *f*, rozsądek *m*; *~·ize* ['ræʃnəlaɪz] ⟨z⟩racjonalizować; *econ. zwł. Brt.* usprawniać ⟨-nić⟩

'rat race F wyścig *m* szczurów (*niekończące się konkurowanie*)

rat·tle ['rætl] **1.** stukać (*I*); ⟨za⟩grzechotać (*I*); ⟨za⟩terkotać; ⟨za⟩turkotać; *pociąg:* łoskotać, stukotać; F zdeprymować (*się*), speszyć (się); *~ at ~ off* F odklepywać ⟨-pać⟩; *~ on* F trajkotać (*about* o *L*); *~ through* F odbębnić (*A*); **2.** stukot *m*, grzechot *m*, terkotanie; grzechotka *f*; '*~·snake* *zo.* grzechotnik *m*

rau·cous ['rɔːkəs] jazgotliwy

rav·age ['rævɪdʒ] ⟨z⟩dewastować, ⟨s⟩pustoszyć; '*~s pl.* spustoszenia *pl.*

rave [reɪv] majaczyć, bredzić (*about* o *L*); pomstować (*against* przeciw *D*);

piać z zachwytu (*about* nad *I*)

rav·el ['rævl] (*zwł. Brt. -ll-*, *Am. -l-*) rozplątywać ⟨-tać⟩ (się); plątać (się); → **unravel**

ra·ven ['reɪvn] *zo.* kruk *m*

rav·e·nous ['rævənəs] wygłodniały; nienasycony

ra·vine [rə'viːn] wąwóz *m*

rav·ings ['reɪvɪŋz] *pl.* majaczenia *pl.*

rav·ish ['rævɪʃ] zniewalać ⟨-wolić⟩; '**~·ing** zniewalający

raw [rɔː] surowy (*też fig.*); *econ., tech. też* nieprzetworzony; *skóra:* zaczerwieniony; *wiatr:* lodowaty; niedoświadczony; **~ vegetables and fruit** *pl.* surówka *f*; **~ materials** *pl.* surowce *pl.*; '**~·hide** skóra *f* surowa

ray [reɪ] promień *m*, *fig.* promyk *m*

ray·on ['reɪɒn] sztuczny jedwab *m*

ra·zor ['reɪzə] brzytwa *f*; maszynka *f* do golenia; golarka *f*; **electric:** ~ elektryczna maszynka *f* do golenia; '**~ blade** żyletka *f*; **~('s) edge:** *be on a* **~ edge** *fig.* wisieć na włosku, stać na skraju przepaści

RC [ɑː 'siː] *skrót:* **Roman Catholic** rzym.-kat., rzymsko-katolicki

Rd *skrót pisany:* **Road** ul., ulica *f*

re [riː]: **~ your letter of ...** odnośnie Pańskiego listu z dnia ...

re... [riː] re..., ponownie, powtórnie

reach [riːtʃ] **1.** *v/t.* sięgać ⟨-gnąć⟩ (*G*); dosięgać ⟨-gnąć⟩ (*G*); osiągać ⟨-gnąć⟩; docierać ⟨dotrzeć⟩ do (*G*); dochodzić ⟨dojść⟩ do (*G*); **~ down to** dochodzić do (*G*); **~ out** sięgać ⟨-gnąć⟩ (**for** po *A*); *ramię* wyciągać ⟨-gnąć⟩; **2.** zasięg *m*; zakres *m*; **within ~** w zasięgu, **out of ~** poza zasięgiem; **within easy ~** w pobliżu

re·act [rɪ'ækt] ⟨za⟩reagować (**to** na *A*, **chem. with** *z I*); **~ against** występować przeciwko (*D*); **re·ac·tion** [rɪ'ækʃn] reakcja *f* (*też chem., pol.*)

re·ac·tor [rɪ'æktə] *phys.* reaktor *m*

read 1. [riːd] (*read* [red]) ⟨prze⟩czytać; *termometr itp.:* odczytywać ⟨-tać⟩; *univ.* studiować (*też* **for** *A*); ⟨z⟩rozumieć (*as* jako); czytać się dobrze; przekaż; **~ (s.th.) to s.o.** komuś coś ⟨prze⟩czytać; **~ medicine** studiować medycynę; **2.** [red] *pret. i p.p. od* **read 1;** '**rea·da·ble** do czytania (*nadający się*); '**read·er** czytelnik *m* (-iczka *f*); lektor

m (-ka *f*), starszy *m* wykładowca; czytanka *f*

read·i·ly ['redɪlɪ] łatwo; bez przeszkód; '**~·ness** gotowość *f*

read·ing ['riːdɪŋ] czytanie *n* (*też parl.*); *tech.* wskazanie *n*; odczyt (*termometru*) *m*; rozumienie *n*

re·ad·just [riːə'dʒʌst] *tech.* dostrajać ⟨-roić⟩; ⟨s⟩korygować; ~ (**o.s.**) **to** przystosowywać ⟨-ować⟩ się do (*G*)

read·y ['redɪ] (*-ier, -iest*) gotowy, gotów; zakończony; **be ~ to do** być bliskim zrobienia czegoś; **~ for use** gotowy do użycia; **get ~** przygotowywać ⟨-wać⟩ (się); '**~ cash** → **ready money**; **~'made** konfekcyjny; **~·made clothes** *pl.* konfekcja *f*; **~'meal** wyrób *m* garmażeryjny; **~ 'mon·ey** F gotówka *f*

real [rɪəl] prawdziwy; rzeczywisty; **for ~** *zwł. Am.* F naprawdę; '**~ es·tate** nieruchomość *f*; '**~ es·tate a·gent** pośrednik *m* handlu nieruchomościami

re·a·lis|·m ['rɪəlɪzəm] realizm *m*; **~t** ['rɪəlɪst] realista *m* (-tka *f*); **~·tic** [rɪə'lɪstɪk] (*-ally*) realistyczny

re·al·i·ty [rɪ'ælɪtɪ] rzeczywistość *f*; **~ show**, **~ TV** F reality show

re·a·li·za·tion [rɪəlaɪ'zeɪʃn] realizacja *f*, urzeczywistnienie *n*; uprzytomnienie *n* sobie, zrozumienie *n*; *econ.* sprzedaż *f*; **~·lize** ['rɪəlaɪz] ⟨z⟩realizować; urzeczywistnić; zdawać ⟨zdać⟩ sobie sprawę, uświadamiać ⟨-domić⟩ sobie; sprzedawać ⟨-dać⟩, spieniężać ⟨-żyć⟩

real·ly ['rɪəlɪ] naprawdę, faktycznie, rzeczywiście

realm [relm] królestwo *n*; *fig.* domena *f*

real·tor ['rɪəltə] *Am.* pośrednik *m* handlu nieruchomościami

reap [riːp] *zboże* żąć, zżynać ⟨zżąć⟩; *plony* zbierać ⟨zebrać⟩ (*też fig*)

re·ap·pear [riːə'pɪə] ponownie się pojawiać ⟨-wić⟩

rear [rɪə] **1.** *v/t. dziecko* wychowywać ⟨-wać⟩, *zwierzę* ⟨wy⟩hodować; *głowę* podnosić ⟨-nieść⟩; *v/i. koń:* stawać ⟨stanąć⟩ dęba; **2.** tył *m*; tyłek *m*; **at** (*Am. in the*) **~** z tyłu, w tyle; **bring up the ~** zamykać ⟨-mknąć⟩ pochód; **3.** tylny; '**~·guard** *mil.* ariergarda *f*, straż *f* tylna; '**~ light** *mot.* światło *n* tylne

re·arm [riː'ɑːm] *mil.* ponownie uzbrajać ⟨-roić⟩; **re·ar·ma·ment** [riː'ɑːməmənt] ponowne uzbrajanie *n* (się)

R

'rear·|most położony najdalej z tyłu; ~·view 'mir·ror lusterko *n* wsteczne; ~·ward ['rɪəwəd] **1.** *adj.* tylny; **2.** *adv.* też **~wards** do tyłu, w tył; ~wheel 'drive *mot.* napęd *m* na tylne koła; '~ win·dow *mot.* szyba *f* tylna

rea·son ['riːzn] **1.** powód *m*, przyczyna *f*; rozsądek *m*; rozum *m*; **by ~ of** z powodu (*G*); **for this ~** z tego powodu; **listen to ~** słuchać głosu rozsądku; **it stands to ~** jest to oczywiste, że; **2.** *v/i.* rozumować; przemawiać ⟨-mówić⟩ do rozsądku; *v/t.* ⟨wy⟩wnioskować (**that** że); **~ s.o. into/out of s.th.** namówić kogoś, by coś zrobił, wyperswadować komuś, by czegoś nie robił; 'rea·so·na·ble rozsądny; należyty; *ce·na itp.*: umiarkowany

re·as·sure [riːə'ʃɔː] uspokajać ⟨-koić⟩

re·bate ['riːbeɪt] *econ.* rabat *m*, bonifikata *f*; zapłata *f* zwrotna

reb·el[1] ['rebl] **1.** buntownik *m* (-iczka *f*), rebeliant *m*;**2.**rebeliancki,buntowniczy

re·bel[2] [rɪ'bel] ⟨z⟩buntować się, powstawać ⟨-tać⟩ (**against** przeciwko *D*); ~·lion [rɪ'beljən] bunt *m*, rebelia *f*; ~·lious [rɪ'beljəs] buntowniczy, rebeliancki

re·birth [riː'bɜːθ] ponowne narodziny *pl.*

re·bound **1.** [rɪ'baund] odbijać ⟨-bić⟩ się (**from** z/od *G*); *fig.* opadać ⟨-paść⟩ z powrotem; **2.** ['riːbaund] (*w sporcie*) odbicie *n* się

re·buff [rɪ'bʌf] **1.** (ostra) odmowa *f*, odprawa *f*; **2.** odtrącać ⟨-cić⟩

re·build [riː'bɪld] (*-built*) odbudowywać ⟨-ować⟩ (*też fig.*)

re·buke [rɪ'bjuːk] **1.** upominać ⟨-mnieć⟩, strofować; **2.** upomnienie *n*, strofowanie *n*

re·call [rɪ'kɔːl] **1.** odwoływać ⟨-łać⟩, wycofywać ⟨-fać⟩; przypominać ⟨-mnieć⟩ (sobie); **2.** odwołanie *n*, wycofanie *n*; przypomnienie *n*

re·ca·pit·u·late [riːkə'pɪtjʊleɪt] ⟨z⟩rekapitulować, podsumowywać ⟨-ować⟩

re·cap·ture [riː'kæptʃə] ponownie ⟨s⟩chwytać; *mil.* odbijać ⟨-bić⟩; *fig.* oddawać ⟨oddać⟩, uchwycić

re·cast [riː'kɑːst] (*-cast*) *tech.* przetapiać ⟨-topić⟩; przerabiać ⟨-robić⟩; *theat.* obsadzać ⟨-dzić⟩ na nowo

re·cede [rɪ'siːd] cofać się, wycofywać ⟨-fać⟩ się; *fig.* zamierać ⟨zamrzeć⟩; **re·**ceding *broda, czoło*: cofnięty

re·ceipt [rɪ'siːt] *zwł. econ.* przyjęcie *n*, odebranie *n*; rachunek *m*, pokwitowanie *n*; **~s** *pl.* wpływy *pl.*; △ *nie* **recepta**

re·ceive [rɪ'siːv] otrzymywać ⟨-mać⟩; przyjmować ⟨-jąć⟩ (*też* **into** do *G*); odbierać ⟨odebrać⟩ (*TV itp.*); **re·**ceiv·er odbiornik *m*; *tel.* słuchawka *f*; *też* **official ~** *Brt.* syndyk *m* masy upadłościowej

re·cent ['riːsnt] niedawny, ostatni; '~·ly niedawno, ostatnio

re·cep·tion [rɪ'sepʃn] odbiór *m* (*też* radiowy lub telewizyjny); przyjęcie *n* (**into** do *G*); *też* **~ desk** (*hotelu*) recepcja *f*; **~·ist** [rɪ'sepʃənɪst] recepcjonista *m* (-tka *f*); *med.* rejestrator(ka *f*) *m*

re·cep·tive [rɪ'septɪv] *umysł*: chłonny; otwarty (**to** na *A*)

re·cess [rɪ'ses] przerwa *f* (*Am. też między lekcjami*); *parl.* przerwa *f*; nisza *f*, wnęka *f*

re·ces·sion [rɪ'seʃn] *econ.* recesja *f*

re·ci·pe ['resɪpɪ] przepis *m* (*kulinarny*)

re·cip·i·ent [rɪ'sɪpɪənt] odbiorca *m* (-czyni *f*)

re·cip·ro·cal [rɪ'sɪprəkl] wzajemny; ~·cate [rɪ'sɪprəkeɪt] *v/i.* poruszać się ruchem postępowo-zwrotnym; odwzajemniać ⟨-nić⟩ się; *v/t.* zaproszenie od wzajemniać ⟨-nić⟩

re·cit·al [rɪ'saɪtl] recital *m*; re·ci·ta·tion [resɪ'teɪʃn] recytacja *f*; re·cite [rɪ'saɪt] ⟨za-, wy⟩recytować; wyliczać ⟨-czyć⟩, wymieniać ⟨-nić⟩

reck·less ['rekls] nieostrożny; lekkomyślny

reck·on ['rekən] *v/t.* obliczać ⟨-czyć⟩ ⟨o⟩szacować; sądzić; zaliczać (**among** do *G*, **as** jako); *też* **~ up** wyliczać ⟨-czyć⟩; *v/i.* **~ on** liczyć na (*A*); **~ with** liczyć się z (*I*); **~ without** nie przewidywać ⟨-widzieć⟩ (*G*); **~·ing** ['reknɪŋ] obliczenie *n*, rachunek *m*; **be out in one's ~ing** pomylić się w liczeniu

re·claim [rɪ'kleɪm] odbierać ⟨odebrać⟩; ⟨z⟩rekultywować, ⟨z⟩meliorować; *tech.* odzyskiwać ⟨-skać⟩; *przestępcę* nawracać ⟨-wrócić⟩; △ *nie* **reklamować**

re·cline [rɪ'klaɪn] leżeć; w pół leżeć

re·cluse [rɪ'kluːs] odludek *m*

rec·og|·ni·tion [rekəg'nɪʃn] rozpoznanie *n*; uznanie *n*; ~·nize ['rekəgnaɪz] rozpoznawać ⟨-nać⟩; uznawać ⟨-nać⟩

re·coil 1. [rɪˈkɔɪl] odskakiwać ⟨-koczyć⟩ (*z przestrachu*) (**from** przed *I*); *fig.* uchylać ⟨-lić⟩ się (**from** od *G*); **2.** [ˈriːkɔɪl] odrzut *m*, odskok *m*

rec·ol·lect [rekəˈlekt] przypominać ⟨-mnieć⟩ (sobie); **~·lec·tion** [rekəˈlekʃn] przypomnienie *n* sobie (**of** *G*), wspomnienie *n*

rec·om·mend [rekəˈmend] ⟨za⟩rekomendować, polecać ⟨-cić⟩ (**as** jako, **for** na *A*); **~·men·da·tion** [rekəmenˈdeɪʃn] rekomendacja *f*

rec·om·pense [ˈrekəmpens] **1.** ⟨z⟩rekompensować, wynagradzać ⟨-rodzić⟩ (**for** za *A*); **2.** rekompensata *f*, wynagrodzenie *n*

rec·on·cile [ˈrekənsaɪl] ⟨po⟩godzić; doprowadzać ⟨-dzić⟩ do zgody (**with** z *I*); **~·cil·i·a·tion** [rekənsɪlɪˈeɪʃn] pogodzenie *n*; pojednanie *n* (**between** pomiędzy *I*, **with** z *I*)

re·con·di·tion [riːkənˈdɪʃn] przeprowadzać ⟨-dzić⟩ generalny remont, przywracać ⟨-rócić⟩ do stanu użytkowego

re·con·nais·sance [rɪˈkɒnɪsəns] *mil.* rekonesans *m*, rozpoznanie *n*, zwiad *m*; **~·noi·tre** *Brt.*, **~·noi·ter** [rekəˈnɔɪtə] *Am. mil.* przeprowadzać ⟨-dzić⟩ rekonesans

re·con·sid·er [riːkənˈsɪdə] ponownie rozważyć

re·con·struct [riːkənˈstrʌkt] ⟨z⟩rekonstruować, odbudowywać ⟨-ować⟩ (*też fig.*); **~·struc·tion** [riːkənˈstrʌkʃn] rekonstrukcja *f*, odbudowa *f*

rec·ord¹ [ˈrekɔːd] zapis *m*; *jur.* protokół *m*; rejestr *m*; akta *pl.*; płyta *f* (*winylowa*); *sport, komp.* rekord *m*; **off the ~** F nie do protokołu, nieoficjalnie; **have a criminal ~** mieć kryminalną przeszłość; *attr.* rekordowy

re·cord² [rɪˈkɔːd] zapisywać ⟨-sać⟩; ⟨za⟩rejestrować; *jur.* ⟨za⟩protokołować; *na taśmie itp.* zapisywać ⟨-sać⟩, nagrywać ⟨-rać⟩; **~·er** magnetofon *m*; *mus.* flet *m* prosty; **~·ing** nagranie *n*

rec·ord play·er [ˈrekɔːd-] gramofon *m* (*do płyt winylowych*)

re·count [rɪˈkaʊnt] przeliczać ⟨-czyć⟩

re·cov·er [rɪˈkʌvə] *v/t.* odzyskiwać ⟨-kać⟩; **~ o.s.** odzyskiwać ⟨-kać⟩ równowagę (*też fig.*); ⟨z⟩rekompensować; wyciągać ⟨-gnąć⟩; *v/i.* dochodzić ⟨dojść⟩ do siebie (**from** po *L*); **~·y** [rɪˈ-

kʌvərɪ] wyzdrowienie *n*; powrót *m* do normy; odzyskanie *n*; rekompensata *f*

rec·re·a·tion [rekrɪˈeɪʃn] odpoczynek *m*; rekreacja *f*

re·cruit [rɪˈkruːt] **1.** *mil.* rekrut *m*; nowy członek *m*, nowy *m* (nowa *f*); **2.** *też mil.* rekrutować, ⟨z⟩werbować; zatrudniać ⟨-nić⟩

rec·tan·gle [ˈrektæŋgl] *math.* prostokąt *m*; **~·gu·lar** [rekˈtæŋgjʊlə] prostokątny

rec·ti·fy [ˈrektɪfaɪ] prostować (*też prąd*)

rec·tor [ˈrektə] proboszcz *m*; (*na uniwersytecie*) rektor *m*; **~·to·ry** [ˈrektərɪ] probostwo *n*

re·cu·pe·rate [rɪˈkjuːpəreɪt] odzyskiwać ⟨-kać⟩ (*zdrowie*), *econ.* wyrównywać ⟨-nać⟩

re·cur [rɪˈkɜː] (**-rr-**) powracać ⟨-rócić⟩; wracać ⟨wrócić⟩; powtarzać ⟨-tórzyć⟩ się; **~·rence** [rɪˈkʌrəns] powrót *m*, nawrót *m* (*choroby*); powtarzanie *n* się; **~·rent** [rɪˈkʌrənt] powracający, nawracający

re·cy·cle [riːˈsaɪkl] *odpadki* ⟨z⟩utylizować, przetwarzać ⟨-worzyć⟩; **~cled paper** papier z surowców wtórnych; **~·cla·ble** [riːˈsaɪkləbəl] nadający się do utylizacji; **~·cling** [riːˈsaɪklɪŋ] recykling *m*, utylizacja *f*

red [red] **1.** czerwony; **2.** czerwień *f*; **be in the ~** *econ.* mieć debet *m* lub deficyt *m*; **'~·breast** *zo.* → **robin**; ♀ **'Crescent** Czerwony Półksiężyc *m*; ♀ **'Cross** Czerwony Krzyż *m*; **'~·cur·rant** *bot.* czerwona porzeczka *f*; **~·den** [ˈredn] ⟨za⟩czerwienić (się), poczerwienieć; **~·dish** [ˈredʃ] czerwonawy

re·dec·o·rate [riːˈdekəreɪt] *pokój* ⟨wy⟩remontować, odmalowywać ⟨-ować⟩

re·deem [rɪˈdiːm] *zastaw itp.* wykupywać ⟨-kupić⟩; *rel.* odkupywać ⟨-pić⟩; ♀·**er** *rel.* Odkupiciel *m*

re·demp·tion [rɪˈdempʃn] wykupienie *n*; *rel.* odkupienie *n*

re·de·vel·op [riːdɪˈveləp] ⟨z⟩modernizować

red·-'faced poczerwieniony, spąsowiały; **~·'hand·ed: catch s.o. ~-handed** ⟨s⟩chwytać kogoś na gorącym uczynku; **'~·head** F rudzielec *m*; **~·'head·ed** rudy; **~ 'her·ring** *fig.* fałszywy trop *m*; **~·'hot** rozgrzany do czerwoności; *fig.* rozpłomieniony; ♀ **'In·di·an** V czerwonoskóry *m*; **~-'let·ter day** święto *n*; **'~-ness** czerwień *f*

re·dou·ble [riː'dʌbl] *zwł. aktywność* zdwajać ⟨-woić⟩

red 'tape biurokratyzm *f*, formalizm *m*

re·duce [rɪ'djuːs] zmniejszać ⟨-szyć⟩ ⟨z⟩redukować; *cenę itp.* obniżać ⟨-żyć⟩; zmniejszyć ⟨-szać⟩ ilość; doprowadzać ⟨-dzić⟩ **(to** do *G*), zmieniać ⟨-nić⟩ **(to** w *A*), nakłaniać ⟨-łonić⟩; **re·duc·tion** [rɪ'dʌkʃn] zmniejszenie *n*; redukcja *f*; obniżka *f*

re·dun·dant [rɪ'dʌndənt] nadmierny; zbyteczny

reed [riːd] *bot.* trzcina *f*

re·ed·u·|·cate [riː'edʒukeɪt] reedukować; **~·ca·tion** ['riːedʒu'keɪʃn] reedukacja *f*

reef [riːf] rafa *f*

reek [riːk] **1.** smród *m*, odór *m*; **2.** cuchnąć

reel[1] [riːl] **1.** szpula *f*, szpulka *f*, rolka *f*; *(skoczny taniec szkocki)*; **2. ~ off** odwijać ⟨-winąć⟩ ze szpul(k)i; *fig.* ⟨wy⟩recytować

reel[2] [riːl] zataczać ⟨-toczyć⟩ się; ⟨za⟩wirować; *my head ~ed* w głowie mi się kręciło

re·e·lect [riːɪ'lekt] ponownie wybierać ⟨-brać⟩

re·en·|·ter [riː'entə] ponownie wchodzić ⟨wejść⟩; *(w astronautyce)* wchodzić ⟨wejść⟩ *(w atmosferę)*; **~·try** [riː'entrɪ] ponowne wejście *n*; *(w astronautyce)* wejście *n* w atmosferę

ref[1] [ref] F *(w sporcie)* sędzia *f*

ref.[2] *skrót pisany:* **reference** odesłanie *n*

re·fer [rɪ'fɜː]: **~ to** odnosić się do *(G)*; powoływać się na *(A)*, wspominać ⟨-mnieć⟩ o *(L)*; odsyłać ⟨odesłać⟩ do *(G)*; ⟨s⟩kierować do *(G)*; ⟨s⟩korzystać *(z notatek)*

ref·er·ee [refə'riː] *(w sporcie)* sędzia *m*; osoba *f* polecająca

ref·er·ence ['refrəns] odniesienie *n* **(to** do *G*); odesłanie *n* **(to** do *G*); powołanie *n* się **(to** na *A*), wzmianka *f* **(to** o *L*); referencje *pl.*; *list of ~s* bibliografia *f*; *with ~ to* w odniesieniu do *(G)*; **'~ book** poradnik *m*, encyklopedia *f*, słownik *m*; **'~ li·bra·ry** biblioteka *f* podręczna; **'~ num·ber** numer *m* akt

ref·e·ren·dum [refə'rendəm] *(pl. -da [-də], -dums)* referendum *n*

re·fill 1. [riː'fɪl] ponownie napełniać ⟨-nić⟩; **2.** ['riːfɪl] wkład *m (do długopisu)*, nabój *m (do pióra)*; dolewka *f*

re·fine [rɪ'faɪn] *tech.* rafinować, oczyszczać ⟨oczyścić⟩; *fig.* udoskonalać ⟨-lić⟩; **~d** rafinowany, oczyszczony; *fig.* wyrafinowany; **~·ment** *tech.* rafinacja *f*; wyrafinowanie *n*; **re·fin·e·ry** [rɪ'faɪnərɪ] *tech.* rafineria *f*

re·flect [rɪ'flekt] *v/t.* odbijać ⟨-bić⟩; odzwierciedlać ⟨-lić⟩; *be ~ed in* odbijać się w *(L)*; *v/i.* przemyśleć; **~ (badly) on** rzucać (złe) światło na *(A)*; **re·flec·tion** [rɪ'flekʃn] odbicie *n*; odzwierciedlenie *n (też fig.)*; refleksja *f*, namysł *m*; **re·flec·tive** [rɪ'flektɪv] refleksyjny; odblaskowy

re·flex ['riːfleks] refleks *m*; odruch *m*; **'~ ac·tion** odruch *m* bezwarunkowy; **'~ cam·e·ra** *phot.* lustrzanka *f*

re·flex·ive [rɪ'fleksɪv] *gr.* zwrotny

re·form [rɪ'fɔːm] **1.** ⟨z⟩reformować, ulepszać ⟨-szyć⟩; poprawiać ⟨-wić⟩ się; **2.** reforma *f*; poprawa *f*; **ref·or·ma·tion** [refə'meɪʃn] poprawa *f*; *the ♎ Reformacja f*; **~·er** [rɪ'fɔːmə] reformator *m*

re·fract [rɪ'frækt] *światło* załamywać ⟨-mać⟩ (się); **re·frac·tion** [rɪ'frækʃn] załamanie *n*, refrakcja *f*

re·frain[1] [rɪ'freɪn]: **~ from** powstrzymywać ⟨-mać⟩ się od *(G)*

re·frain[2] [rɪ'freɪn] refren *m*

re·fresh [rɪ'freʃ] *(o.s.* się) odświeżać ⟨-żyć⟩ *(też pamięć)*; **~·ing** orzeźwiający *(też fig.)*; **~·ment** odświeżenie *n*, napój *m* odświeżający

re·fri·ge·|·rate [rɪ'frɪdʒəreɪt] ⟨s⟩chłodzić; **~·ra·tor** lodówka *f*

re·fu·el [riː'fjuːəl] *(zwł. Brt. -ll-, Am. -l-)* ⟨za⟩tankować

ref·uge ['refjuːdʒ] schronienie *n*; *Brt. (na jezdni)* wysepka *f*

ref·u·gee [refjʊ'dʒiː] uchodźca; **~ camp** obóz *m* dla uchodźców

re·fund 1. ['riːfʌnd] spłata *f*, zwrot *m*; **2.** [riː'fʌnd] spłacać ⟨-cić⟩, zwracać ⟨zwrócić⟩

re·fur·bish [riː'fɜːbɪʃ] przeprowadzać ⟨-dzić⟩ renowację *(G)*, *fig.* odświeżać ⟨-żyć⟩

re·fus·al [rɪ'fjuːzl] odmowa *f*

re·fuse[1] [rɪ'fjuːz] *v/t.* odmawiać ⟨-mówić⟩ *(też to do s.th.* zrobienia czegoś);

ofertę itp. odrzucać ⟨-cić⟩; *v/i.* odmawiać ⟨-mówić⟩

ref·use² ['refju:s] odpadki *pl.*, śmieci *pl.*; '~ **dump** wysypisko *n* śmieci

re·fute [rɪ'fju:t] obalać ⟨-lić⟩

re·gain [rɪ'geɪn] odzyskiwać ⟨-kać⟩

re·gale [rɪ'geɪl]: ~ *s.o.* **with** *s.th.* zabawiać ⟨-wić⟩ kogoś czymś

re·gard [rɪ'gɑːd] **1.** szacunek *m*, poważanie *n*; wzgląd *m*; **in this** ~ w tym względzie; **with** ~ **to** w odniesieniu do (*G*); ~*s pl.* (*w listach*) pozdrowienia *pl.*; **2.** uważać; patrzeć na (*A*); ~ **as** uważać za (*A*); **as** ~**s** co się tyczy (*G*); ~·**ing** odnośnie (*G*); ~·**less** = *less of* niezależnie od (*G*), bez względu na (*A*)

regd *skrót pisany:* **registered** *econ.* zarejestrowany; *przesyłka:* polecony

re·gen·e·rate [rɪ'dʒenəreɪt] ⟨z⟩regenerować (się); odradzać ⟨-rodzić⟩ (się)

re·gent ['riːdʒənt] regent(ka *f*) *m*

re·gi·ment 1. ['redʒɪmənt] *mil.* pułk *m*; *fig.* zastępy *pl.*; **2.** ['redʒɪment] sprawować ścisłą kontrolę nad (*I*)

re·gion ['riːdʒən] region *m*; rejon *m*; obszar *m*; ~·**al** regionalny

re·gis·ter ['redʒɪstə] **1.** rejestr *m*; spis *m*, lista *f*; dziennik *m* lekcyjny; **2.** *v/t.* ⟨za⟩rejestrować, zapisywać ⟨-sać⟩; *uczucia, wartość* pokazywać ⟨-zać⟩; *list itp.* nadawać ⟨-dać⟩ (*jako polecony*); *v/i.* wpisywać ⟨-sać⟩ się; ~**ed** '**let·ter** list *m* polecony

re·gis·tra·tion [redʒɪ'streɪʃn] rejestracja *f*, zarejestrowanie *n*; wpis *m*; ~ **fee** opłata *f* rejestracyjna; wpisowe *n*; ~ **num·ber** *mot.* numer *m* rejestracyjny

re·gis·try ['redʒɪstrɪ] miejsce *n* przechowywania akt stanu cywilnego; '~ **of·fice** *zwł.* *Brt.* urząd *m* stanu cywilnego

re·gret [rɪ'gret] **1.** (**-tt-**) żałować; ⟨po⟩informować z przykrością; **2.** żal *m*; ubolewanie *n*; ~·**ful·ly** z żalem, z ubolewaniem; ~·**ta·ble** godny ubolewania

reg·u·lar ['regjʊlə] **1.** regularny; miarowy; stały; prawidłowy; *zwł. Am.* zwykły, normalny; *mil.* zawodowy; **2.** F stały (-a) klient(ka *f*), *m* stały bywalec; gość *m*; *mil.* żołnierz *m* zawodowy; *Am. mot.* zwykła benzyna *f*; ~·**i·ty** [regjʊ'lærətɪ] regularność *f*

reg·u·late ['regjʊleɪt] regulować, kontrolować; *tech.* ⟨wy-, na-, u⟩regulować;

~·**la·tion** [regjʊ'leɪʃn] przepis *m*, zarządzenie *n*; kontrola *f*; regulacja *f*; ~·**la·tor** ['regjʊleɪtə] *tech.* regulator *m*, stabilizator *m*

re·hears·al [rɪ'hɜːsl] *mus., theat.* próba *f*; ~**e** [rɪ'hɜːs] *mus., theat.* ⟨z⟩robić próbę

reign [reɪn] **1.** panowanie *n*, władanie *n* (*też fig.*); **2.** panować, władać

re·im·burse [riːɪm'bɜːs] *wydatki* zwracać ⟨-rócić⟩

rein [reɪn] **1.** *zwł. pl.* cugle *pl.*; **2.** ~ **in** *konia itp.* wziąć ⟨brać⟩ w cugle (*też fig.*)

rein·deer ['reɪndɪə] *zo.* (*pl.* **reindeer**) renifer *m*

re·in·force [riːɪn'fɔːs] wzmacniać ⟨-mocnić⟩; ~·**ment** wzmocnienie *n*; ~**ments** *pl. mil.* posiłki *pl.*

re·in·state [riːɪn'steɪt] przywracać ⟨-rócić⟩ (**as** jako, in na *A*)

re·in·sure [riːɪn'ʃɔː] reasekurować

re·it·e·rate [riː'ɪtəreɪt] powtarzać

re·ject [rɪ'dʒekt] odrzucać ⟨-cić⟩; nie przyjmować ⟨-jąć⟩; **re·jec·tion** [rɪ'dʒekʃn] odrzucenie *n*

re·joice [rɪ'dʒɔɪs] radować się (**at**, **over** *I lub z G*); **re**'**joic·ing**(**s** *pl.*) radowanie *n* się

re·join¹ [riː'dʒɔɪn] wstąpić ⟨wstępować⟩ powtórnie

re·join² [rɪ'dʒɔɪn] odpowiadać ⟨-wiedzieć⟩

re·ju·ve·nate [rɪ'dʒuːvɪneɪt] ożywiać ⟨-wić⟩

re·kin·dle [riː'kɪndl] *ogień* rozpalać ⟨-lić⟩ ponownie

re·lapse [rɪ'læps] **1.** popaść ponownie (**into** w *A*); *med.* mieć nawrót; **2.** nawrót *m*

re·late [rɪ'leɪt] *v/t.* ⟨z⟩relacjonować, zdawać ⟨zdać⟩ sprawę; ⟨po⟩wiązać, ⟨po⟩łączyć (**to** *z G*); *v/i.* ~ **to** odnosić się do (*G*); **re·lat·ed** powiązany (**to** *z G*)

re·la·tion [rɪ'leɪʃn] krewny *m* (-na *f*); związek *m*, relacja *f* (**between** (po)między *I*, **to** do *G*); **in** *lub* **with** ~ **to** w odniesieniu do (*G*); ~**s** *pl.* dyplomatyczne *itp.* stosunki *pl.*; ~·**ship** związek *m*; stosunek *m*; relacja *f*

rel·a·tive¹ ['relətɪv] krewny *m* (-na *f*)

rel·a·tive² ['relətɪv] relatywny, stosunkowy; odnoszący się (**to** do *G*); *gr.* względny; ~ '**pro·noun** *gr.* zaimek *m* względny

re·lax [rɪ'læks] *v*/*t*. rozluźniać ⟨-nić⟩; *fig.* ⟨z⟩łagodzić; *v*/*i.* rozluźniać ⟨-nić⟩ się; odprężać ⟨-żyć⟩ się; ulegać ⟨-lec⟩ złagodzeniu; **~·a·tion** [riːlæk'seɪʃn] rozluźnienie *n*; odprężenie *n*; złagodzenie *n*; **~ed** rozluźniony; odprężony;

re·lay¹ 1. ['riːleɪ] zmiana *f*; (*w sporcie*) sztafeta *f*; przekaźnik *m* (*radiowy lub telewizyjny*); [tezriːˈleɪ] **2.** [riːˈleɪ] przekazywać ⟨-zać⟩, ⟨prze⟩transmitować

re·lay² [riːˈleɪ] (**-laid**) *kabel, dywan* kłaść ⟨położyć⟩ na nowo

re·lay race ['riːleɪreɪs] (*w sporcie*) bieg *m* sztafetowy, sztafeta *f*

re·lease [rɪ'liːs] **1.** *ptaka, płytę, gaz itp.* wypuszczać ⟨-puścić⟩; *gaz* spuszczać ⟨spuścić⟩; *więźnia, hamulec* zwalniać ⟨zwolnić⟩; ⟨o⟩publikować; **2.** wypuszczenie *n*; spuszczenie *n*; zwolnienie *n*; *tech.*, zwalniacz *m*; *phot.* wyzwalacz *m*; udostępnienie *n*; wydanie *n*; film *m*

rel·e·gate ['relɪgeɪt] przenosić ⟨-nieść⟩ (*na gorsze miejsce*); (*w sporcie*) przesuwać ⟨-nąć⟩ (**to** do *G*)

re·lent [rɪ'lent] okazywać ⟨-zać⟩ litość; *fig.*⟨z⟩łagodnieć; **~·less** bezlitosny, nieustępliwy

rel·e·vant ['reləvənt] istotny (**to** dla *G*), ważny; właściwy; **be ~ to** mieć znaczenie dla (*G*)

re·li·a·bil·i·ty [rɪlaɪə'bɪlətɪ] wiarygodność *f*; niezawodność *f*; **~·a·ble** [rɪ'laɪəbl] wiarygodny; niezawodny; **~·ance** [rɪ'laɪəns] zaufanie *n*; uzależnienie *n*, zależność *f* (**on** od *G*)

rel·ic ['relɪk] relikt *m*; *rel.* relikwia *f*; *attr.* reliktowy

re·lief [rɪ'liːf] ulga *f*; ulżenie *n*; pomoc *f* (*materialna*); *Am.* zapomoga *f*; relief *m*; płaskorzeźba *f*

re·lieve [rɪ'liːv] *ból itp.* ⟨z⟩łagodzić; *wartownika itp.* zmieniać ⟨-nić⟩; *nudę itp.* zmniejszać ⟨-szyć⟩; **~ s.o. of s.th.** odejmować ⟨odjąć⟩ komuś czegoś

re·li·gion [rɪ'lɪdʒən] religia *f*; **~·gious** religijny

rel·ish ['relɪʃ] **1.** *fig.* smak *m*, upodobanie *n* (**for** do *G*); *gastr.* przyprawa *f*; **with ~** z przyjemnością; **2.** delektować się (*I*), unosić się nad (*I*); znajdować ⟨znaleźć⟩ upodobanie w (*L*)

re·luc·tance [rɪ'lʌktəns] niechęć *f*; **with ~tance** niechętnie; **~·tant** niechętny;

be ~tant to do s.th. nie mieć chęci czegoś zrobić

re·ly [rɪ'laɪ]: **~ on** polegać na (*L*); zależeć od (*G*)

re·main [rɪ'meɪn] **1.** pozostawać ⟨-tać⟩, zostawać ⟨-tać⟩; **2.** **~s** pl. resztki *pl.*, pozostałości *pl.*; **~·der** [rɪ'meɪndə] pozostałość *f*, reszta *f*

re·make 1. [riːˈmeɪk] (**-made**) ⟨z⟩robić powtórnie *lub* ponownie; **2.** ['riːmeɪk] nowa wersja *f* filmu, remake *m*

re·mand [rɪ'mɑːnd] *jur.* **1.** **be ~ed in custody** być odesłanym do aresztu śledczego; **2.** **be on ~** pozostawać w areszcie śledczym

re·mark [rɪ'mɑːk] **1.** *v*/*t.* zauważać ⟨-żyć⟩; *v*/*i.* **~ on** ⟨s⟩komentować (*A*); **2.** uwaga *f*; **re·mar·ka·ble** godny uwagi

rem·e·dy ['remədɪ] **1.** środek *m* (*leczniczy, zapobiegawczy*); **2.** *szkodę* naprawiać ⟨-wić⟩; *złu* zaradzać ⟨-dzić⟩ (*D*)

re·mem·ber [rɪ'membə] ⟨za⟩pamiętać; przypominać ⟨-mnieć⟩ sobie; **please ~ber me to her** proszę przekazać jej moje pozdrowienia; **~·brance** [rɪ'membrəns] pamiętanie *n*; pamięć *f*; **in ~brance of** ku pamięci (*G*)

re·mind [rɪ'maɪnd] przypominać ⟨-mnieć⟩ (**of** o *L*); **~·er** przypomnienie *n*; upomnienie *n*

rem·i·nis·cences [remɪ'nɪsnsɪz] *pl.* wspomnienia *pl.* (**of** o *L*); **~·cent: be ~·cent of** przypominać o (*L*)

re·mit [rɪ'mɪt] (**-tt-**) *grzechy* odpuszczać ⟨-puścić⟩, przebaczać ⟨-czyć⟩; *winy* darować; *pieniądze* przekazywać ⟨-zać⟩, przesyłać ⟨-słać⟩; **~·tance** przekaz *m* (*pieniężny*) (**to** dla *G*)

rem·nant ['remnənt] pozostałość *f*

re·mod·el [riː'mɒdl] (*zwł. Brt.* **-ll-**, *Am.* **-l-**) przemodelować, przekształcać ⟨-cić⟩

re·mon·strance [rɪ'mɒnstrəns] protest *m*; upomnienie *n*; **re·mon·strate** ['remənstreɪt] ⟨za⟩protestować (**against** przeciw *D*); czynić zarzuty (**with** *D*, **about** w sprawie *G*)

re·morse [rɪ'mɔːs] wyrzuty *pl.* sumienia; **~·less** niemiłosierny

re·mote [rɪ'məʊt] (**-r, -st**) odległy, oddalony; *ktoś* pełen rezerwy; *szansa:* niewielki; **~ con'trol** *tech.* zdalne sterowanie *n*; *radio, TV:* pilot *m*

re·mov·al [rɪ'muːvl] usuwanie *n*; usu-

report

nięcie *n*; przeprowadzka *f*; ~ **van** wóz *m* meblowy

re·move [rɪ'muːv] *v/t.* usuwać ⟨usunąć⟩; zdejmować ⟨zdjąć⟩: *z drogi itp.* zabierać ⟨zabrać⟩; *v/i.* przenosić ⟨-nieść⟩ się (*from ... to ...* z *G ...* do *G ...*); **re'-mov·er** środek *m* do usuwania (plam)

Re·nais·sance [rə'neɪsəns] renesans *m lub* Renesans *m*

ren·der ['rendə] *możliwym, trudnym itp.* ⟨u⟩czynić; *przysługę* oddawać ⟨-dać⟩; *sprawozdanie* zdawać ⟨zdać⟩; *mus.* ⟨z⟩interpretować; przekładać ⟨-łożyć⟩ (*into* na *A*); ~**ing** *zwł.* Brt. ['rendərɪŋ] → *rendition*

ren·di·tion [ren'dɪʃn] interpretacja *f*; tłumaczenie *n*

re·new [rɪ'njuː] odnawiać ⟨-nowić⟩; *rozmowę itp.* wznawiać ⟨-nowić⟩; *atak* ponawiać ⟨-nowić⟩; *przedłużać* ⟨-żyć⟩; *siły* ⟨z⟩regenerować; ~**al** odnowienie *n*; wznowienie *n*; ponowienie *n*; przedłużenie *n*

re·nounce [rɪ'naʊns] wyrzekać ⟨-rzec⟩ się; zrzekać ⟨zrzec⟩ się (*G*); wypierać ⟨-przeć⟩ się

ren·o·vate ['renəveɪt] odnawiać ⟨-nowić⟩, ⟨wy⟩remontować

re·nown [rɪ'naʊn] sława *f*; ~**ed** sławny, słynny (*as* jako, *for* z *G*)

rent[1] [rent] **1.** czynsz *m*, komorne *n*; *zwł.* Am. opłata *f* za wypożyczenie; *for* ~ *zwł.* Am. do wynajęcia; ⚠ *nie renta*; **2.** wynajmować ⟨-jąć⟩ (*from* od *G*, *to* D); ~ *out zwł.* Am. wynajmować ⟨-jąć⟩

rent[2] [rent] rozdarcie *n*

'Rent-a-... wynajem (*G*)

rent·al [rentl] czynsz *m*; *zwł.* Am. opłata *f* za wynajęcie; *zwł.* Am. → ~**ed 'car** wynajęty samochód *m*

re·nun·ci·a·tion [rɪnʌnsɪ'eɪʃn] wyrzeczenie *n* się, zrzeczenie *n* się

re·pair [rɪ'peə] **1.** naprawiać ⟨-wić⟩, ⟨z⟩reperować, ⟨wy⟩remontować; *fig.* naprawiać ⟨-wić⟩, ⟨s⟩korygować; **2.** naprawianie *n*, reperowanie *n*, remontowanie *n*; ~*s pl.* naprawa *f*, reperacja *f*, remont *m*; *beyond* ~ nie do naprawiania; *in good/bad* ~ w dobrym/ złym stanie; *be under* ~ być w naprawie

rep·a·ra·tion [repə'reɪʃn] odszkodowanie *n*; ~*s pl.* odszkodowania *pl.* wojenne, reparacje *pl.*

rep·ar·tee [repɑ'tiː] cięta odpowiedź *f*; błyskotliwość *f*

re·pay [riː'peɪ] (*-paid*) zapłacić (*to* D), spłacać ⟨-cić⟩; odpłacać ⟨-cić⟩ za (*A*); ~**ment** spłata *f*

re·peal [rɪ'piːl] uchylać ⟨-lić⟩, unieważniać ⟨-nić⟩

re·peat [rɪ'piːt] **1.** *v/t.* powtarzać ⟨-tórzyć⟩; *zamówienie* ponawiać ⟨-nowić⟩; ~ *o.s.* powtarzać ⟨-tórzyć⟩ się; *v/i.* F *potrawa:* przypominać się, odbijać się (*on* D); **2.** powtórka *f* (*programu*); *mus.* znak *m* powtórzenia; ~**ed** powtórzony, powtórny

re·pel [rɪ'pel] (*-ll-*) odpierać ⟨odeprzeć⟩; odpychać ⟨odepchnąć⟩ (*też fig*); ~**lent** [rɪ'pelənt] **1.** *adj.* odpychający, odstręczający; **2.** środek *m* odstraszający owady

re·pent [rɪ'pent] żałować; **re'pent·ance** żal *m*, skrucha *f*; **re'pen·tant** żałujący; skruszony

re·per·cus·sion [riːpə'kʌʃn]: *zw.* ~*s pl.* reperkusje *pl.*

rep·er·toire ['repətwɑː] *theat.* repertuar *m*

rep·er·to·ry thea·tre ['repətəri -] (*teatr, w którym grane są różne sztuki*)

rep·e·ti·tion [repɪ'tɪʃn] powtórzenie *n*

re·place [rɪ'pleɪs] zastępować ⟨-tąpić⟩; wymieniać ⟨-nić⟩ (*na miejsce*) odkładać ⟨odłożyć⟩; ~**ment** zastępstwo *n*; wymiana *f*; odłożenie *n* na miejsce

re·plant [riː'plɑːnt] przesadzać ⟨-dzić⟩

re·play 1. [riː'pleɪ] (*w sporcie*) *mecz* powtarzać ⟨-tórzyć⟩; *kasetę* odtwarzać ⟨-wtórzyć⟩; **2.** ['riːpleɪ] powtórny mecz *m*, Brt. *action* ~, Am. *instant* ~ replay *m*

re·plen·ish [rɪ'plenɪʃ] dopełniać ⟨-nić⟩; uzupełniać ⟨-nić⟩

re·plete [rɪ'pliːt] nasycony; pełny; całkowicie wyposażony (*with* w *A*)

rep·li·ca ['replɪkə] replika *f*; kopia *f*

re·ply [rɪ'plaɪ] **1.** odpowiadać ⟨-wiedzieć⟩ (*to* na *A*); **2.** odpowiedź *f* (*to* na *A*); replika *f*; *in* ~ *to* w odpowiedzi na (*A*); ~ *'cou·pon* (*kupon pokrywający koszt znaczka na odpowiedź*); ~**paid 'en·ve·lope** koperta *f* z opłaconą odpowiedzią

re·port [rɪ'pɔːt] **1.** sprawozdanie *n*; relacja *f*; raport *m*; meldunek *m*; Brt. (Am. ~ *card*) świadectwo *n* szkolne; pogłos *m* (*strzału*); **2.** składać ⟨złożyć⟩ spra-

R

wozdanie; ⟨z⟩relacjonować, ⟨po⟩informować; donosić⟨-nieść⟩;zgłaszać⟨zgłosić⟩ (się), ⟨za⟩meldować ⟨się⟩; donosić ⟨-nieść⟩; na (A); **it is ~ed that** mówi się, że; **~ed speech** gr. mowa f zależna; **~·er** reporter(ka f) m, korespondent(ka f) m

re·pose [rɪ'pəʊz] spokój m; spoczynek m

re·pos·i·to·ry [rɪ'pɒzɪtərɪ] skład m, magazyn m; fig. źródło n, skarbnica f

rep·re·sent [reprɪ'zent] reprezentować; przedstawiać ⟨-wić⟩ (też **as, to be** jako); stanowić; **~·sen·ta·tion** [reprɪzen'teɪʃn] reprezentacja f; przedstawienie n; jur. zastępstwo n prawne; **~·sen·ta·tive** [reprɪ'zentətɪv] 1. reprezentatywny, typowy (**of** dla G); 2. przedstawiciel(ka f) m (też handl.,pol.); parl. deputowany m (-na f); **House of** **Representative** Am. Izba f Reprezentantów

re·press [rɪ'pres] ⟨s⟩tłumić, zdusząć ⟨zdusić⟩; psych. hamować; **re·pres·sion** [rɪ'preʃn] (s)tłumienie n; psych. (za)hamowanie n

re·prieve [rɪ'priːv] 1. **he was ~d** odroczono lub zawieszono mu wykonywanie kary; 2. (kary) odroczenie n; zawieszenie n

rep·ri·mand ['reprɪmɑːnd] 1. udzielać ⟨-lić⟩ nagany (**for** za A); 2. nagana f, upomnienie n, reprymenda f

re·print 1. [riː'prɪnt] przedrukowywać ⟨-ować⟩; książkę wznawiać ⟨wznowić⟩; 2. ['riːprɪnt] przedruk m, wznowienie n; reprint m

re·pri·sal [rɪ'praɪzl] odwet m, środek odwetowy; jur. retorsja f

re·proach [rɪ'prəʊtʃ] 1. wyrzut m; zarzut m; 2. zarzucać ⟨-cić⟩ (**s.o. with** **s.th.** coś komuś); ⟨z⟩robić wyrzuty (**for** za A); **~·ful** pełny wyrzutu

rep·ro·bate ['reprəbeɪt] ladaco m; rozpustnik m (-nica f)

re·pro·cess [riː'prəʊses] paliwo nuklearne przetwarzać ⟨-worzyć⟩; **~·ing** **plant** zakład m przetwarzania paliwa nuklearnego

re·pro·duce [riːprə'djuːs] ⟨od⟩tworzyć; ⟨z⟩reprodukować; ⟨s⟩kopiować; **~duce o.s.** v/i. biol. rozmnażać ⟨-no-żyć⟩ się; **~·duc·tion** [riːprə'dʌkʃn] biol. rozmnażanie m (się); reprodukcja f, reprodukowanie n; kopia f; **~·duc·tive** biol. [riːprə'dʌktɪv] rozrodczy

re·proof [rɪ'pruːf] wyrzut m, zarzut m

re·prove [rɪ'pruːv] zarzucać ⟨-cić⟩

rep·tile ['reptaɪl] zo. gad m

re·pub·lic [rɪ'pʌblɪk] republika f; **~·li·can** [rɪ'pʌblɪkən] 1. republikański; 2. republikanin m

re·pu·di·ate [rɪ'pjuːdɪeɪt] odrzucać ⟨-cić⟩; econ. zapłaty odmawiać ⟨-mówić⟩

re·pug·nance [rɪ'pʌgnəns]: **in ~nance,** **with ~nance** z odrazą, ze wstrętem; **~·nant** odrażający, wstrętny

re·pulse [rɪ'pʌls] 1. odpychać ⟨odepchnąć⟩; ⟨z⟩mierzić; mil. atak odpierać ⟨odeprzeć⟩; 2. odepchnięcie n; odparcie n

re·pul·sion [rɪ'pʌlʃn] wstręt m; niechęć f; phys. odpychanie n; **~·sive** [rɪ'pʌlsɪv] wstrętny; phys. odpychający

rep·u·ta·ble ['repjʊtəbl] szanowany, szanowny; **~·tion** [repjʊ'teɪʃn] reputacja f

re·pute [rɪ'pjuːt] renoma f; **re·put·ed** renomowany

re·quest [rɪ'kwest] 1. (**for**) prośba f (o A), życzenie n; **at the ~ of s.o.**, **at** **s.o.'s ~** na czyjeś życzenie; **on ~** na życzenie; 2. prosić o (A); **be ~ed to** **do s.th.** być proszonym o zrobienie czegoś; **~ stop** Brt. przystanek m na żądanie

re·quire [rɪ'kwaɪə] wymagać, potrzebować (G); **~·ment** wymóg m, potrzeba f; żądanie n

req·ui·site ['rekwɪzɪt] 1. niezbędny, wymagany; 2. zw. **~s** pl. artykuły pl., przybory pl.; **toilet ~s** pl. przybory pl. toaletowe; △ nie **rekwizyt**

req·ui·si·tion [rekwɪ'zɪʃn] 1. zapotrzebowanie n, zamówienie n; mil. rekwizycja f; **make a ~** coś zgłaszać ⟨zgłosić⟩ zapotrzebowanie na (A); 2. zgłaszać ⟨zgłosić⟩ zapotrzebowanie na (A); mil. ⟨za⟩rekwirować

re·sale ['riːseɪl] odprzedaż f, odsprzedaż f

re·scind jur. [rɪ'sɪnd] unieważniać ⟨-nić⟩; anulować; odwoływać ⟨-łać⟩

res·cue ['reskjuː] 1. ⟨wy-, u⟩ratować (**from** z G, od G); 2. ratunek m; pomoc f

re·search [rɪ'sɜːtʃ] 1. badanie n naukowe; 2. v/i. prowadzić badania naukowe;

v/t. ⟨z⟩badać; **~·er** naukowiec *m*, badacz(ka *f*) *m*

re·sem|·blance [rɪ'zembləns] podobieństwo *n* (**to** do *G*, **among** między *I*); **~·ble** [rɪ'zembl] przypominać; być podobnym do (*G*)

re·sent [rɪ'zent] nie cierpieć (*G*), nie znosić (*G*); czuć urazę do (*G*); **~·ful** urażony, dotknięty; **~·ment** uraza *f* (**against, at** wobec *G*); niechęć *f*

res·er·va·tion [rezə'veɪʃn] rezerwacja *f*; zastrzeżenie *n*; rezerwat *m* (*dla Indian, Am. przyrodniczy*); → **central reservation**

re·serve [rɪ'zɜːv] 1. przeznaczać ⟨-czyć⟩ (**for** na *A*); zastrzegać ⟨-rzec⟩; ⟨za⟩rezerwować; 2. rezerwa *f* (*też mil., fig*); zapas *m*; powściągliwość *f*; rezerwat *m* (*przyrody*); (*w sporcie*) gracz *m* rezerwowy; **~d** zarezerwowany

res·er·voir ['rezəvwɑː] rezerwuar *m*, zbiornik *m*; *fig.* źródło *n*

re·set [riː'set] (**-tt-; -set**) zegar, *miernik* przestawiać ⟨-wić⟩; *med.* kość zestawiać ⟨-wić⟩ na nowo; *komp.* ⟨z⟩resetować

re·set·tle [riː'setl] przesiedlać ⟨-lić⟩ się

re·side [rɪ'zaɪd] mieszkać, rezydować

res·i·dence ['rezɪdəns] miejsce *n* zamieszkania; zamieszkanie *n*; rezydencja *f*; siedziba *f*; **'~ per·mit** zezwolenie *n* na zamieszkanie

res·i·dent ['rezɪdənt] 1. zamieszkały (na stałe); miejscowy; 2. mieszkaniec *m* (-nka *f*); *hotelowy* gość *m*

res·i·den·tial [rezɪ'denʃl] *dzielnica:* mieszkaniowy; *konferencja:* poza miejscem zamieszkania; **~ 'ar·e·a** dzielnica *f* mieszkaniowa

re·sid·u·al [rɪ'zɪdjʊəl] szczątkowy; resztkowy; **~ pol'lu·tion** zanieczyszczenia *pl*; **res·i·due** ['rezɪdjuː] pozostałość *f*; *chem.* residuum *n*

re·sign [rɪ'zaɪn] *v/i.* ⟨z⟩rezygnować (**from** z *G*); ustępować ⟨-tąpić⟩; *v/t.* ustępować ⟨-tąpić⟩ się *z* (*G*) (*stanowiska*); zrzekać ⟨-rzec⟩ się (*G*); **~ o.s. to** pogodzić się *z* (*I*); **res·ig·na·tion** [rezɪg'neɪʃn] rezygnacja *f*; ustąpienie *n*; zrzeczenie się *n*; pogodzenie się *n*; **~ed** [rɪ'zaɪnd] zrezygnowany

re·sil·i·ence [rɪ'zɪliəns] elastyczność *f*, sprężystość *f*; *fig.* odporność *f*; **~·ent** sprężysty, elastyczny; *fig.* odporny

res·in ['rezɪn] żywica *f*

re·sist [rɪ'zɪst] opierać ⟨oprzeć⟩ się (*D*); przeciwstawiać ⟨-wić⟩ się; **~·ance** opór *m*; odporność *f*; *electr.* rezystancja *f*; **line of least ~ance** droga *f* najmniejszego oporu; **re·sis·tant** oporny (**to** na *A*)

res·o·lute ['rezəluːt] zdecydowany, zdeterminowany; **~·lu·tion** [rezə'luːʃn] *pol.* rezolucja *f*; uchwała *f*, postanowienie *n*; zdecydowanie *n*; *komp.* rozdzielczość *f*

re·solve [rɪ'zɒlv] 1. *problem itp.* rozwiązywać ⟨-zać⟩; postanawiać ⟨-nowić⟩; **~ on doing s.th.** ⟨z⟩decydować się coś zrobić; 2. postanowienie *n*; zdecydowanie *n*

res·o|·nance ['rezənəns] pogłos *m*, rezonans *m*; **'~·nant** *pokój itp.:* o dużym pogłosie; *głos:* głęboki, dźwięczny

re·sort [rɪ'zɔːt] 1. uzdrowisko *n*, kurort *m*, miejscowość *f* wypoczynkowa; **~ health** (**seaside, summer**) **resort**; 2. **~ to** uciekać ⟨-ciec⟩ się do (*G*)

re·sound [rɪ'zaʊnd] rozbrzmiewać ⟨-mieć⟩

re·source [rɪ'sɔːs] zasób *m*; rozwiązanie *n*; pociecha *f*, schronienie *n*; pomysłowość *f*; **~s** *pl.* środki *pl.*; zasoby *pl.*, bogactwa *pl.* naturalne; **~·ful** pomysłowy

re·spect [rɪ'spekt] 1. szacunek *m*, poważanie *n*; respekt *m* (**for** dla *G*); wzgląd (**for** dla *G*); **with~ to** odnośnie (*G*); **in this ~** pod tym względem; **give my ~s to** proszę przekazać pozdrowienia (*D*); 2. *v/t.* szanować, poważać; respektować, przestrzegać (*G*); **re'spec·ta·ble** szanowny, szacowny; **~·ful** pełen szacunku

re·spect·ive [rɪ'spektɪv] odnośny, właściwy; **we went to our ~ places** każdy udał się na swoje miejsce; **~·ly** właściwie, odpowiednio

res·pi·ra·tion [respə'reɪʃn] oddychanie *n*; **~·tor** ['respəreɪtə] respirator *m*

re·spite ['respaɪt] wytchnienie *n*, spoczynek *m*; **without ~** bez wytchnienia

re·splen·dent [rɪ'splendənt] olśniewający

re·spond [rɪ'spɒnd] odpowiadać ⟨-wiedzieć⟩ (**to** na *A*, **that** że); ⟨za⟩reagować (**to** na *A*)

re·sponse [rɪ'spɒns] odpowiedź *f*; odzew *m*, reakcja *f* (**to** na *A*)

re·spon|·si·bil·i·ty [rɪspɒnsə'bɪlətɪ] odpowiedzialność *f*; **on one's own ~sibility** na własną odpowiedzialność; **sense of ~sibility** poczucie *n* odpowiedzialności; **take** (**full**) **~ sibility for** przyjmować ⟨-jąć⟩ pełną odpowiedzialność za (*A*); **~·si·ble** [rɪ'spɒnsəbl] odpowiedzialny

rest[1] [rest] **1.** odpoczynek *m*, spoczynek *m*; *tech.* oparcie *n*; *tel.* widełki *pl.*; **have** *lub* **take a ~** odpoczywać ⟨-cząć⟩; **set s.o.'s mind at ~** uspokoić kogoś; **2.** *v/i.* odpoczywać ⟨-cząć⟩; spoczywać ⟨-cząć⟩; opierać ⟨oprzeć⟩ się (**against**, **on** o *A*); **let s.th. ~** zostawiać ⟨-wić⟩ coś w spokoju; **~ on** spoczywać ⟨-cząć⟩ na (*L*) (*też fig.* spojrzenie); *v/t.* opierać ⟨-przeć⟩ (**against, on** o *A*); dawać ⟨dać⟩ odpoczać

rest[2] [rest] reszta *f*; **all the ~ of them** wszyscy pozostali; **for the ~** co do reszty

res·tau·rant ['restərɒnt, 'restərənt, 're-stərɔːŋ] restauracja *f*

'rest·ful spokojny; uspokajający; **'~ home** *jakby*: dom *m* spokojnej starości

res·ti·tu·tion [restɪ'tjuːʃn] przywrócenie *n*, restytucja *f*

res·tive ['restɪv] niespokojny, zaniepokojony

'rest·less niespokojny

res·to·ra·tion [restə'reɪʃn] przywrócenie *n*, zwrot *m*, restytucja *f*; odbudowa *f*, restauracja *f*

re·store [rɪ'stɔː] przywracać ⟨-rócić⟩; zwracać ⟨-rócić⟩; ⟨od⟩restaurować, odbudowywać ⟨-ować⟩; **be ~d to health** wrócić do zdrowia

re·strain [rɪ'streɪn] (**from**) powstrzymywać ⟨-mać⟩ przed (*I*); **I had to ~ myself** musiałem się powstrzymywać (**from doing s.th.** przed zrobieniem czegoś); **~ed** [rɪ'streɪnd] powściągliwy, opanowany; *kolor itp.*: stonowany; **~t** [rɪ'streɪnt] opanowanie *n*, powściągliwość *f*

re·strict [rɪ'strɪkt] ograniczać ⟨-czyć⟩ (**to** do *G*); **re·stric·tion** [rɪ'strɪkʃn] ograniczenie *n*; **without ~s** bez ograniczeń

'rest room *Am.* (*w hotelu itp.*) toaleta *f*

re·sult [rɪ'zʌlt] **1.** wynik *m*, rezultat *m*; skutek *m*, efekt *m*; **as a ~ of** na skutek *G*, w wyniku *G*; **without ~** bez wyniku, bezskutecznie; **2.** wynikać ⟨-knąć⟩ (**from** z *G*); **~ in** dawać ⟨dać⟩ w wyniku (*A*)

re·sume [rɪ'zjuːm] podejmować ⟨-djąć⟩, wznawiać ⟨wznowić⟩; *miejsce* zajmować ⟨-jąć⟩ ponownie; **re·sump·tion** [rɪ'zʌmpʃn] podjęcie *n* (*na nowo*); wznowienie *n*

Res·ur·rec·tion [rezə'rekʃn] Zmartwychwstanie *n*

re·sus·ci·tate [rɪ'sʌsɪteɪt] *med.* reanimować; ocucić; **~·ta·tion** *med.* [rɪsʌ-sɪ'teɪʃn] reanimacja *f*

re·tail **1.** ['riːteɪl] handel *m* detaliczny; detal *m*; **by ~** detalicznie; **2.** ['riːteɪl] *adv.* detalicznie; **3.** [riː'teɪl] *v/t.* sprzedawać ⟨-dać⟩ detalicznie (**at, for** za *A*); *v/i.* być sprzedawanym detalicznie (**at, for** za *A*); **~·er** [riː'teɪlə] detalista *m*

re·tain [rɪ'teɪn] zatrzymywać ⟨-mać⟩; zachowywać ⟨-ować⟩

re·tal·i·ate [rɪ'tælɪeɪt] odwzajemniać ⟨-mnić⟩ się; ⟨za⟩stosować odwet; **~·a·tion** [rɪtælɪ'eɪʃn] odwet *m*, retorsja *f*

re·tard [rɪ'tɑːd] opóźniać ⟨-nić⟩; wstrzymywać ⟨-mać⟩; (**mentally**) **~ed** opóźniony umysłowo

retch [retʃ] *med.* mieć odruchy wymiotne

re·tell [riː'tel] (**-told**) opowiadać ⟨-wiedzieć⟩ na nowo

re·think [riː'θɪŋk] (**-thought**) przemyśleć

re·ti·cent ['retɪsənt] milczący, milkliwy

re·tire [rɪ'taɪə] *v/i.* przechodzić ⟨przejść⟩ na rentę *lub* emeryturę; wycofywać ⟨-fać⟩ się; *v/t.* przenosić ⟨przenieść⟩ na rentę *lub* emeryturę; **~d** emerytowany, w stanie spoczynku; **be ~d** być na rencie *lub* emeryturze; **~·ment** emerytura *f*, stan *m* spoczynku; **re·tir·ing** [rɪ'taɪərɪŋ] płochliwy

re·tort [rɪ'tɔːt] **1.** odpowiadać ⟨-wiedzieć⟩ ostro; **2.** ostra odpowiedź *f*

re·touch [riː'tʌtʃ] *phot.* ⟨wy⟩retuszować

re·trace [rɪ'treɪs] ⟨z⟩rekonstruować; **~ one's steps** wracać ⟨-rócić⟩ po własnych śladach

R (left margin)

re·tract [rɪ'trækt] *v/t.* wycofywać ⟨-fać⟩, odwoływać ⟨-łać⟩; wciągać ⟨-gnąć⟩, ⟨s⟩chować

re·train [riː'treɪn] przeszkalać ⟨-kolić⟩; zmieniać ⟨-nić⟩ kwalifikacje

re·tread 1. [riː'tred] *oponę* bieżnikować; **2.** ['riːtred] bieżnikowana opona *f*

re·treat [rɪ'triːt] **1.** odwrót *m*; wycofanie n się; *beat a* (*hasty*) ~ pospiesznie się wycofywać ⟨-fać⟩; **2.** wycofywać ⟨-fać⟩ się (*from* z *G*)

ret·ri·bu·tion [retrɪ'bjuːʃn] odpłata *f*, odwet *m*

re·trieve [rɪ'triːv] odzyskiwać ⟨-skać⟩; *błąd* naprawiać ⟨-wić⟩; *komp.* uzyskiwać dostęp; *hunt.* aportować

ret·ro|·ac·tive [retrəʊ'æktɪv] *jur.* działający wstecz; ~·grade ['retrəʊɡreɪd] wsteczny, regresywny; ~·spect ['retrəʊspekt]: *in ~spect z* perspektywy (*lat lub czasu*); ~·spec·tive [retrəʊ'spektɪv] retrospektywny; *jur.* działający wstecz

re·try [riː'traɪ] *jur. przypadek* ponownie sądzić

re·turn [rɪ'tɜːn] **1.** *v/i.* wracać ⟨wrócić⟩, powracać ⟨-rócić⟩; ~ *to* powracać ⟨-rócić⟩ do (*G*); *v/t.* oddawać ⟨-dać⟩ zwracać ⟨-rócić⟩; odsyłać ⟨odesłać⟩; *zysk* przynosić ⟨-nieść⟩, dawać ⟨dać⟩; odwzajemniać ⟨-nić⟩; (*w sprawozdaniu*) zgłaszać ⟨-łosić⟩; → *verdict*; **2.** powrót *m*; zwrot *m*, zwrócenie *n*; odesłanie *n*; sprawozdanie *n*; *podatkowa* deklaracja *n*; (*w tenisie*) odbicie *n*; *też* ~s zysk *m*, dochód *m*, wpływy *pl.*; *many happy* ~s (*of the day*) wszystkiego najlepszego z okazji urodzin; *by* ~ (*of post*) *Brt.* odwrotną pocztą; *in* ~ *for* (*w zamian*) za (*A*); **3.** *adj.* powrotny; zwrotny; **re·tur·na·ble** do zwrotu; ~ *bottle* butelka *f* z kaucją

re·turn| 'key *komp.* klawisz *m* powrotu karetki; klawisz *m* Enter; ~ 'game, ~ 'match *sport:* mecz *m* rewanżowy; ~ 'tick·et *Brt.* bilet *m* powrotny

re·u·ni·fi·ca·tion [riːjuːnɪfɪ'keɪʃn] *pol.* zjednoczenie *n*

re·u·nion [riː'juːnjən] zjazd *m*; zejście n się

re·us·a·ble [riː'juːzəbl] zdatny do ponownego użytku

rev [rev] F *mot.* **1.** obroty *pl.*; ~ *counter*

obrotomierz *m*; **2.** (*-vv-*) *też.* ~ *up* zwiększać ⟨-szyć⟩ obroty (*silnika*)

Rev *skrót pisany: Reverend rel.* wielebny (*tytuł i zwrot*)

re·val·ue [riː'væljuː] *econ.* przeszacowywać ⟨-wywać⟩

re·veal [rɪ'viːl] odsłaniać ⟨-łonić⟩; ujawniać ⟨-nić⟩; ~·ing *sukienka itp.:* mało osłaniający; *fig. uwaga itp.:* dużo odkrywający

rev·el ['revl] (*zwł. Brt. -ll-* , *Am. -l-*): ~ *in* lubować się (w *L*), rozkoszować się (*I*)

rev·e·la·tion [revə'leɪʃn] rewelacja *f*; ujawnienie *n*; *rel.* objawienie *n*

re·venge [rɪ'vendʒ] **1.** zemsta *f*; rewanż *m*; *in* ~ *for* z zemsty za (*A*); **2.** ⟨po⟩mścić; ~ *o.s. on* mścić się na (*L*); ~·*ful* mściwy

rev·e·nue ['revənjuː] *rel.* dochody *pl.*, wpływy *pl.*

re·ver·be·rate [rɪ'vɜːbəreɪt] rozlegać ⟨-lec⟩ się; rozbrzmiewać ⟨-mieć⟩

re·vere [rɪ'vɪə] czcić

rev·e|·rence ['revərəns] cześć *f*, szacunek *m* (*for* dla *G*); 2·rend ['revərənd] *rel.* wielebny; ~·rent ['revərənt] pełen atencji

rev·er·ie ['revərɪ] marzenia *pl.*

re·vers·al [rɪ'vɜːsl] odwrócenie *n*; anulowanie *n*, uchylenie *n*

re·verse [rɪ'vɜːs] **1.** *adj.* odwrotny, przeciwny; *bieg:* wsteczny; *in* ~ *order* w odwrotnym kierunku; **2.** *samochód:* cofać ⟨-fnąć⟩ (się); wycofywać ⟨-fać⟩; *porządek* odwracać ⟨-rócić⟩; *decyzję* uchylać ⟨-lić⟩; ~ *the charges Brt. tel.* ⟨za⟩dzwonić na koszt odbiorcy; **3.** odwrotność *f*; odwrócenie *n*; *mot.* cofanie *n*; strona *f* odwrotna; rewers *m* (*monety*); ~ 'gear *mot.* bieg *m* wsteczny; ~ 'side lewa strona *f* (*materiału itp.*)

re·vers·i·ble [rɪ'vɜːsəbl] odwracalny; odwołalny

re·vert [rɪ'vɜːt]: ~ *to* powracać ⟨-rócić⟩ do (*G*); cofać ⟨-nąć⟩ się (*w rozwoju*)

re·view [rɪ'vjuː] **1.** przegląd *m*; rewizja *f*, badanie *n*; krytyka *f*, recenzja *f*; omówienie *n*; *mil.* defilada *f*; *Am. ped.* powtórka *f* (*materiału*) (*for* do *G*); **2.** dokonywać ⟨-nać⟩ przeglądu; poddawać ⟨-dać⟩ rewizji; ⟨z⟩badać; omawiać ⟨o-mówić⟩; ⟨z⟩recenzować; *Am. ped.* po-

R

wtarzać ⟨-tórzyć⟩ (*materiał*) (*for* do *G*);
~er recenzent(ka *f*) *m*, krytyk *m*

re·vise [rɪ'vaɪz] ⟨z⟩rewidować; *opinię* ⟨s⟩korygować; *książkę* poprawiać ⟨-wić⟩, ⟨s⟩korygować; *Brt. ped.* powtarzać ⟨-tórzyć⟩ (*materiał*) (*for* do *G*); **re·vi·sion** [rɪ'vɪʒn] rewizja *f*; korekta *f*; zmiana *f*; *Brt. ped.* powtórka *f* (*materiału*) (*for* do *G*)

re·viv·al [rɪ'vaɪvl] odrodzenie *n*; ożywienie *n*; wznowienie *n* (*sztuki*); **re·vive** [rɪ'vaɪv] odradzać ⟨-rodzić⟩; ożywiać ⟨-wić⟩; wznawiać ⟨-nowić⟩

re·voke [rɪ'vəʊk] cofać ⟨-fnąć⟩; odwoływać ⟨-łać⟩; anulować

re·volt [rɪ'vəʊlt] **1.** *v/i.* ⟨z⟩buntować się, burzyć się (*against* przeciwko *D*); wzbudzać ⟨-dzić⟩ odrazę (*against, at, from* przeciwko *D*); *v/t.* napełniać ⟨-nić⟩ odrazą; **2.** bunt *m*, rewolta *f*; ~ing wzbudzający odrazę

rev·o·lu·tion [revə'luːʃn] rewolucja (*też pol.*), przewrót *m*; *astr., tech.* obrót *m*; **number of ~s** *tech.* liczba *f* obrotów; ~ **counter** *mot.* obrotomierz *m*; ~·ar·y [revə'luːʃnərɪ] **1.** rewolucyjny; **2.** *pol.* rewolucjonista *m* (-tka *f*); ~·ize *fig.* [revə'luːʃnaɪz] ⟨z⟩rewolucjonizować

re·volve [rɪ'vɒlv] obracać się (*on, round* wokół *G*); ~ *around fig.* obracać się wokół (*G*); **re'volv·er** rewolwer *m*; **re'volv·ing** obrotowy; ~ *door(s pl.)* drzwi *pl.* obrotowe, turnikiet *m*

re·vue [rɪ'vjuː] *theat.* rewia *f*

re·vul·sion [rɪ'vʌlʃn] wstręt *m*, odraza *f*

re·ward [rɪ'wɔːd] **1.** nagroda *f*; **2.** nagradzać ⟨-rodzić⟩; ~·ing zyskowny; dający satysfakcję, satysfakcjonujący

re·write [riː'raɪt] (*-wrote, -written*) tekst przerabiać ⟨-robić⟩; ⟨na⟩pisać na nowo

rhap·so·dy [ræpsədɪ] *mus.* rapsodia *f*

rhe·to·ric [ˈretərɪk] retoryka *f*

rheu·ma·tism *med.* [ˈruːmətɪzəm] reumatyzm *m*

Rhine Ren *m*

rhi·no [ˈraɪnəʊ] *zo.* F (*pl. -nos*), rhi·no·ce·ros [raɪ'nɒsərəs] *zo.* (*pl. -ros* [-sɪz], **-roses**) nosorożec *m*

rhu·barb [ˈruːbɑːb] *bot.* rabarbar *m*; *attr.* rabarbarowy

rhyme [raɪm] **1.** rym *m*; wiersz *m*; **without ~ or reason** bez ładu i składu; **2.** rymować (się)

rhyth·m [ˈrɪðəm] rytm *m*; ~·mic [ˈrɪðmɪk] (*-ally*), ~·mi·cal rytmiczny

rib [rɪb] *anat.* żebro *n*

rib·bon [ˈrɪbən] wstążka *f*; taśma *f* (*maszyny do pisania*)

'rib cage *anat.* klatka *f* piersiowa

rice [raɪs] *bot.* ryż *m*; *attr.* ryżowy; ~ **pud·ding** pudding *m* ryżowy

rich [rɪtʃ] **1.** bogaty (*też* in w *A*); kosztowny, wystawny; *jedzenie*: ciężki, tłusty; *ziemia*: tłusty, żyzny; *ton*: pełny; *ton*: głęboki; ~ (*in calories*) wysokokaloryczny; **2.** *the* ~ *pl.* bogaci *pl.*

rick [rɪk] stóg *m*

rick·ets [ˈrɪkɪts] *med.* krzywica *f*

rick·et·y [ˈrɪkətɪ] F chwiejny, kiwający się

rid [rɪd] (*-dd-; rid*) uwalniać ⟨uwolnić⟩ (*of* od *G*); **get ~ of** pozbywać ⟨-być⟩ się (*G*)

rid·dance [ˈrɪdəns]: **good ~!** krzyżyk na drogę!

rid·den [ˈrɪdn] **1.** *p.p. od ride* 1; **2.** *w złoż.* nękany

rid·dle¹ [ˈrɪdl] zagadka *f*

rid·dle² [ˈrɪdl] **1.** rzeszoto *n*; **2.** ⟨po⟩dziurawić (*with l*) (*jak rzeszoto*)

ride [raɪd] **1.** (*rode, ridden*) *v/i.* ⟨po⟩jechać (*on* na rowerze, *in* lub *Am. on* w *autobusie itp.*); ⟨po⟩jechać (*konno*); *v/t.* jeździć na (*L*) (*koniu, rowerze*); ⟨po⟩jechać (*L*) (*samochodem itp.*); **2.** jazda *f*; przejażdżka *f*; **'rid·er** jeździec *m*; rowerzysta *m* (-tka *f*); motocyklista *m* (-tka *f*)

ridge [rɪdʒ] (*górski*) grzebień *m*; (*dachu*) kalenica *f*

rid·i·cule [ˈrɪdɪkjuːl] **1.** szyderstwo *n*, drwina *f*; **2.** drwić z (*G*); szydzić z (*G*), kpić z (*G*); **ri·dic·u·lous** [rɪ'dɪkjʊləs] śmieszny, groteskowy

rid·ing [ˈraɪdɪŋ] jeździecki

riff-raff [ˈrɪfræf] *pej.* motłoch *m*, hołota *f*

ri·fle¹ [ˈraɪfl] karabin *m*, strzelba *f*

ri·fle² [ˈraɪfl] ⟨s⟩plądrować

rift [rɪft] szczelina *f* (*też fig.*); pęknięcie *n*

rig [rɪg] **1.** (*-gg-*) *statek* ⟨o⟩taklować; ~ **out** kogoś ⟨wy⟩stroić; ~ **up** F ⟨s⟩klecić, ⟨z⟩montować (*from do*); **2.** *naut.* takielunek *m*; *tech.* urządzenie wiertnicze; F ciuchy *pl.*; '~·ging *naut.* takielunek *m*

right [raɪt] **1.** *adj.* prawy; dobry, popraw-

rival

ny; właściwy, prawidłowy; *pol.* prawicowy; *all ~!* w porządku!, dobrze!; *that's all ~!* nie ma za co!, proszę!; *that's ~!* dobrze!, zgoda!; *be ~* mieć rację; *put ~*, *set ~* ⟨u⟩porządkować, naprawiać ⟨-wić⟩; **2.** *adv.* na prawo, w prawo; dobrze, poprawnie, właściwie, prawidłowo; bezpośrednio, wprost; *~ away* od razu; *~ now* obecnie; *~ on* prosto; *turn ~* skręcić w prawo; **3.** prawa strona *f*; *pol.* prawica *f*; *on the ~* z prawej; *to the ~* na prawo; *keep to the ~* trzymać się prawej; jechać z prawej strony; **4.** ⟨wy⟩prostować; *coś* ⟨s⟩prostować; ⟨s⟩korygować; *~* **an·gle** kąt *m* prosty; *~·an·gled* *math.* pod kątem prostym; *~·eous* ['raɪtʃəs] człowiek: prawy; *oburzenie:* słuszny; *~·ful* legalny; słuszny; *~·hand* prawostronny; *~·hand* 'drive z prawostronnym układem kierowniczym; *~·hand·ed* praworęczny; *~·ly* słusznie; *~ of 'way* *mot.* pierwszeństwo przejazdu *n*; *~·wing* *pol.* prawicowy

rig·id ['rɪdʒɪd] sztywny; *fig.* nieugięty

rig·ma·role ['rɪgmərəʊl] F ceregiele *pl.*

rig·or·ous ['rɪgərəs] rygorystyczny; surowy

rig·o(u)r ['rɪgə] surowość *f*; ostrość *f*; rygor *m*

rile [raɪl] F ⟨z⟩denerwować, ⟨z⟩irytować

rim [rɪm] brzeg *m*, krawędź *f*; obrzeże *n*; obwódka *f*; *tech.* obręcz *f*; *~·less* *okulary:* bezobwódkowy; *~·med* z obwódką

rind [raɪnd] skórka *f* (*cytryny, sera itp.*)

ring[1] [rɪŋ] **1.** pierścień *m*; kółko *n*; obrączka *f*; pierścionek *m*; krążek *m*; (*w boksie*) ring *m*; arena *f*; *przestępcza* siatka *f*; **2.** otaczać ⟨-toczyć⟩; okrążać ⟨-żyć⟩; *ptaki* ⟨za⟩obrączkować

ring[2] [rɪŋ] **1.** (*rang, rung*) ⟨za⟩dzwonić; ⟨za⟩brzmieć, rozbrzmiewać ⟨-mieć⟩; *zwł. Brt. tel.* ⟨za⟩telefonować, ⟨za⟩dzwonić; *the bell is ~ing* dzwoni; *~ the bell* zadzwonić; *~ back* oddzwaniać ⟨-wonić⟩; *~ for* ⟨za⟩dzwonić po (*A*); *~ off* *zwł. Brt. tel.* odkładać ⟨odłożyć⟩ słuchawkę; *~ s.o. (up)* ⟨za⟩dzwonić do kogoś; **2.** dzwonienie *n*; dzwonek *m*; dźwięk *m*; brzmienie *n*; *give s.o. a ~* ⟨za⟩dzwonić do kogoś

'**ring**| **bind·er** kołonotatnik *m*;

~·lead·er przywódca *m* (*szajki itp.*); *~·mas·ter* dyrektor *m* cyrku; *~ road* *Brt.* obwodnica *f*; *~·side*: *at the ~side boks* przy ringu

rink [rɪŋk] *sztuczne* lodowisko *n*; tor *m* wrotkarski

rinse [rɪns] *też ~ out* ⟨wy⟩płukać

ri·ot ['raɪət] **1.** zamieszki *pl.*, rozruchy *pl.*; *run ~* rozszaleć się; *~ police* oddziały *pl.* prewencji. **2.** wszczynać ⟨-cząć⟩ rozruchy; *~·er* uczestnik *m* zamieszek; *~·ous* rozszalały, wzburzony

rip [rɪp] **1.** (*-pp-*) *też ~ up* ⟨po⟩drzeć; *~ open* rozdzierać ⟨-zedrzeć⟩; **2.** rozdarcie *n*

ripe [raɪp] dojrzały; **rip·en** ['raɪpən] dojrzewać ⟨-jrzeć⟩

rip·ple ['rɪpl] **1.** ⟨z⟩marszczyć się; rozchodzić ⟨-zejść⟩ się falą; **2.** zmarszczka *f*; fala *f*

rise [raɪz] **1.** (*rose, risen*) wstawać ⟨-tać⟩ (*też rano*); podnosić ⟨-nieść⟩ się; *dym:* unosić ⟨unieść⟩ się; *ciasto:* ⟨u⟩rosnąć; *nastrój:* poprawiać ⟨-wić⟩ się; *temperatura itp.:* wzrastać ⟨-rosnąć⟩; *wiatr:* wzmagać ⟨wzmóc⟩ się; wschodzić ⟨wzejść⟩; *drzewa, góry itp.:* wznosić się; *fig.* ⟨z⟩rodzić się (*from, out of* z *D*); *też ~ up* powstawać ⟨-tać⟩ (*against* przeciw *D*); *~ to the occasion* stawać ⟨stanąć⟩ na wysokości zadania; **2.** wzrost *m*; podniesienie *n* się; zwyżka *f*, podwyżka *f* (*Brt. też płacy*); rośnięcie *n*; *astr.* wschód *m*; wzniesienie *n* się; *fig.* rozrost *m*; *give ~ to* prowadzić do (*G*); **ris·en** ['rɪzn] *p.p. od* **rise** 1; **ris·er** ['raɪzə]: *be an early riser* wcześnie wstawać (*z łóżka*); **ris·ing** ['raɪzɪŋ] **1.** powstanie *n*; **2.** *fig.* wschodzący

risk [rɪsk] **1.** ryzyko *n*; *at one's own ~* na własną odpowiedzialność; *at the ~ of* (*ger.*) ryzykując, że; *be at ~* być zagrożonym; *run the ~ of doing s.th.* narażać ⟨-razić⟩ się na zrobienie czegoś; *run a ~*, *take a ~* podejmować ⟨-djąć⟩ ryzyko; **2.** ⟨za⟩ryzykować; *~·y* (*-ier, -iest*) ryzykowny, niebezpieczny

rite [raɪt] obrządek *m*, obrzęd *m*, ceremoniał *m*; **rit·u·al** ['rɪtʃʊəl] **1.** rytualny; **2.** ryt *m*, rytuał *m*

ri·val ['raɪvl] **1.** rywal(ka *f*) *m*; konkurent(ka *f*) *m*; **2.** rywalizujący, konkurencyjny; **3.** (*zwł. Brt. -ll-, Am. -l-*) rywalizować z (*I*), konkurować z (*I*), współzawodniczyć z (*I*); **~·ry** ['raɪvlrɪ] rywalizacja *f*, współzawodnictwo *n*

riv·er ['rɪvə] rzeka *f*; *attr.* rzeczny; **'~·side** brzeg *m*; **by the ~side** nad rzeką

riv·et ['rɪvɪt] **1.** *tech.* nit *m*; **2.** *tech.* (przy)nitować; spojrzenie utkwić ⟨-kuć⟩ (**on** w *A*); *uwagę* przykuwać ⟨-kuć⟩ (**to** do *G*)

RN [ɑːr 'en] *skrót:* ***Royal Navy*** *Brt.* Marynarka *f* Królewska

road [rəʊd] droga *f* (*też fig.*); szosa *f*; **on the ~** w drodze; na drodze (**to** do *G*); **na tour(e)**; *attr.* drogowy; **'~ ac·ci·dent** wypadek *m* drogowy; **'~·block** korek *m* uliczny; **'~ map** mapa *f* drogowa; **~ 'safe·ty** bezpieczeństwo *n* drogowe; **'~·side** pobocze *n*; **~ toll** myto *n*, opłata *f* za korzystanie z drogi; **'~·way** jezdnia *f*; **'~ works** *pl.* prace *f* na drodze; **'~·wor·thy** nadający się do poruszania po drogach

roam [rəʊm] *v/i.* błąkać się, wędrować; *v/t.* błąkać się po (*L*), wędrować po (*L*)

roar [rɔː] **1.** ryk *m*; **~s** *pl.* **of laughter** ryk *pl.* śmiechu; **2.** ryczeć ⟨ryknąć⟩, zaryczeć

roast [rəʊst] **1.** *v/t. mięso* ⟨u⟩piec; *kawę itp.* palić; **2.** pieczeń *f*; **3.** *adj.* pieczony; **~ 'beef** rostbef *m*, pieczeń *f* wołowa

rob [rɒb] (**-bb-**) okraść ⟨okraść⟩, obrabowywać ⟨-ować⟩; **~·ber** ['rɒbə] rabuś *m*; **~·ber·y** ['rɒbərɪ] rabunek *m*, obrabowanie *n*

robe [rəʊb] *też* **~s** *pl.* toga *f*; *zwł. Am.* szlafrok *m*

rob·in ['rɒbɪn] *zo.* (*w Europie*) rudzik *m*; (*w Ameryce*) drozd *m* wędrowny

ro·bot ['rəʊbɒt] robot *m*

ro·bust [rə'bʌst] czerstwy, kwitnący

rock¹ [rɒk] **1.** kołysać (się); ⟨za-, po⟩kiwać, ⟨po⟩bujać; wstrząsać ⟨-snąć⟩ (*I*) (*też fig.*)

rock² [rɒk] skała *f*; głaz *m*; *Am.* kamień *m*; *Brt.* długi, twardy, jaskrawy cukierek *m*; **~s** *pl.* rafy *pl.*; **on the ~s** *firma* w opałach; *małżeństwo:* w rozpadzie; *whisky:* z lodem

rock³ [rɒk] *też* **~ music** rock *m*; → **rock'n'roll**

'rock·er fotel *m* bujany; płoza *f*; **off one's ~** F zbzikowany

rock·et ['rɒkɪt] **1.** rakieta *f*; **2.** *też* **~ up** wystrzelić w górę; pędzić, przemykać ⟨-mknąć⟩

'rock·ing| chair fotel *m* bujany; **~ horse** koń *m* na biegunach

rock 'n' roll [rɒkən'rəʊl] rock and roll *m*

'rock·y (**-ier, -iest**) skalisty, kamienisty; twardy jak kamień

Rock·y Moun·tains *pl.* Góry Skaliste *pl.*

rod [rɒd] *tech.* pręt *m*, drąg *m*

rode [rəʊd] *pret. od* **ride** 1

ro·dent ['rəʊdənt] *zo.* gryzoń *m*

ro·de·o [rəʊ'deɪəʊ, 'rəʊdɪəʊ] (*pl.* **-os**) rodeo *n*

roe [rəʊ] *zo. też* **hard ~** ikra *f*; **soft ~** mlecz *m*

roe|·buck ['rəʊbʌk] *zo.* (*pl.* **-bucks, -buck**) kozioł *m* (*sarny*); **~ deer** sarna *f*

rogue [rəʊg] łobuz *m*; drań *m*; **ro·guish** ['rəʊgɪʃ] łobuzerski

role [rəʊl] *theat. itp.* rola *f* (*też fig.*)

roll [rəʊl] **1.** *v/i.* ⟨po⟩toczyć się; *naut.* przechylać ⟨-lić⟩ się; ⟨za⟩kołysać się; *grzmot:* przetaczać ⟨-toczyć⟩ się; *v/t.* ⟨po⟩toczyć; przetaczać ⟨-toczyć⟩; *papierosa* zwijać ⟨zwinąć⟩; **~ down** *rękaw* odwijać ⟨-winąć⟩; *mot. okno* otwierać ⟨-worzyć⟩ (*korbką*); **~ out** rozwijać ⟨-winąć⟩; **~ up** podwijać ⟨-winąć⟩; zwijać ⟨-zwinąć⟩; *mot. okno* zamykać ⟨-mknąć⟩ (*korbką*); **2.** rolka *f*; wałek *m*; zwój *m*, zwitek *m*; bułka *f*; lista *f* (*nazwisk*); pomruk *m* (*grzmotu*); werbel *m*; *naut.* kołysanie *n*; **~ call** odczytanie *n* listy obecności

'roll·er *tech.* wałek *m*; krążek *m*; rolka *f*; walec *m*; lokówka *f*; **'~·blades** *pl.* łyżworolki *pl.*; **~ coast·er** kolejka *f* górska (*w wesołym miasteczku*); **~ skate** wrotka *f*; **'~·skate** jeździć na wrotkach; **'~·skat·ing** jazda *f* na wrotkach; **~ tow·el** ręcznik *m* na wałku

'roll·ing pin wałek *m* (*do ciasta*)

'roll-on dezodorant *m* z kulką

ROM [rɒm] *skrót:* ***read only memory*** ROM *m*

Ro·man ['rəʊmən] **1.** rzymski; romański; **2.** Rzymianin *m* (*-anka f*)

ro·mance [rəʊ'mæns] romans *m*; przygoda *f*

Ro·mance [rəʊ'mæns] język romański

Ro·ma·ni·a [ruː'meɪnjə] Rumunia *f*;

Ro·ma·ni·an [ruːˈmeɪnjən] **1.** rumuński; **2.** Rumun(ka f) m; ling. język m rumuński

ro·man|·tic [rəʊˈmæntɪk] **1.** romantyczny; **2.** romantyk m (-yczka f); **~·ti·cism** [rəʊˈmæntɪsɪzəm] romantyzm m

Rome Rzym m

romp [rɒmp] też **~ about, ~ around** dokazywać; **'~·ers** pl. śpiochy pl.

roof [ruːf] **1.** dach m; **2.** przykrywać ⟨-ryć⟩ dachem; **~ in, ~ over** zadaszać ⟨-szyć⟩; **'~·ing felt** papa f; **'~ rack** bagażnik m dachowy

rook¹ [rʊk] zo. gawron m

rook² [rʊk] (w szachach) wieża f

rook³ [rʊk] F oszwabić ⟨-bić⟩

room¹ [ruːm, w złoż.rʊm] **1.** pokój m; pomieszczenie n, izba f; sala f; miejsce n; wolne miejsce n; **2.** Am. mieszkać; **'~·er** zwł. Am. sublokator(ka f) m; **'~·ing-house** Am. mieszkalny blok m; **'~·mate** współlokator(ka f) m; **'~ ser·vice** dostarczanie n posiłków do pokoju; **'~·y** (-ier, -iest) przestronny

roost [ruːst] **1.** grzęda f; **2.** siedzieć lub spać na grzędzie; **'~·er** zwł. Am. zo. kogut m

root [ruːt] **1.** korzeń m; fig. źródło n, przyczyna f; math. pierwiastek m; **2.** v/i. zakorzeniać ⟨-nić⟩ się; ryć (for w poszukiwaniu G); **~ about** grzebać (among wśród G); v/t. **~ out** fig. wykorzeniać ⟨-nić⟩; **~ up** wyrywać ⟨-rwać⟩ z korzeniami; **'~·ed: deeply ~ed** fig. głęboko zakorzeniony; **stand ~ed to the spot** stać jak wryty w miejscu

rope [rəʊp] **1.** lina f, powróz m; naut. cuma f; sznur m (pereł itp.); **give s.o. plenty of ~** dawać ⟨dać⟩ komuś dużo swobody; **know the ~s** F dobrze się orientować; **show s.o. the ~s** F wprowadzać ⟨-dzić⟩ kogoś; **2.** przywiązywać ⟨-zać⟩ (to do G); **~ off** odgradzać ⟨-grodzić⟩ (linami); **'~ lad·der** drabinka f sznurowa

ro·sa·ry [ˈrəʊzərɪ] rel. różaniec m

rose¹ [rəʊz] pret. od **rise** 1

rose² [rəʊz] **1.** bot. róża f; (w konewce itp.) sitko n; **2.** różowy

ros·trum [ˈrɒstrəm] (pl. -tra [-trə], -trums) podium n

ros·y [ˈrəʊzɪ] (-ier, -iest) różowy (też fig.)

rot [rɒt] **1.** (-tt-) ⟨ze⟩psuć (też fig.); v/i. też **~ away** ⟨ze⟩psuć się, ⟨z⟩gnić;

⟨s⟩próchnieć, ⟨z⟩murszeć,⟨z⟩butwieć;

2. gnicie n, butwienie n

ro·ta·ry [ˈrəʊtərɪ] obrotowy, rotacyjny

ro·tate [rəʊˈteɪt] obracać (się); wirować; **ro·ta·tion** [rəʊˈteɪʃn] ruch m obrotowy, obrót m; rotacja f

ro·tor [ˈrəʊtə] tech., aviat. wirnik m

rot·ten [ˈrɒtn] zgniły, zepsuty; drewno: zmurszały, spróchniały; zbutwiały; kiepski, podły; **feel ~** F czuć się okropnie

ro·tund [rəʊˈtʌnd] okrągły, korpulentny

rough [rʌf] **1.** adj. szorstki; chropowaty; ulica itp.: nierówny; morze: wzburzony; pogoda: burzliwy; obcesowy, grubiański; pomiar: niedokładny, przybliżony; warunki, przejścia: ciężki, męczący; jedzenie: prosty; warunki: prymitywny; **2.** adv. **sleep ~** spać pod gołym niebem; **play ~** (w sporcie) ⟨za⟩grać brutalnie; **3.** (w golfie) zarośla pl., krzaki pl.; **write it out in ~ first** napisać najpierw na brudno; **4. ~ it** F żyć w prymitywnych warunkach; **~ out** ⟨na⟩szkicować; **~·age** [ˈrʌfɪdʒ] biol. nietrawiona część f pożywienia; **~·cast** arch. tynk m kamyczkowy; **~ 'cop·y** brudnopis m; **~ 'draft** brudnopis m, szkic m; **~·en** [ˈrʌfn] czynić szorstkim; skóra: ⟨z⟩grubieć; **'~·ly** szorstko; fig. w przybliżeniu, orientacyjnie; **~·neck** naftowiec m; Am. F grubianin m; **~·shod: ride ~shod over** ⟨z⟩ranić, dotykać ⟨-tknąć⟩

round [raʊnd] **1.** adj. okrągły; **a ~ dozen** okrągły tuzin; **in ~ figures** w zaokrągleniu; **2.** adv. wokoło, dookoła; **turn ~** obracać ⟨-rócić⟩ się dookoła; **invite s.o. ~** zapraszać ⟨-rosić⟩ kogoś do siebie; **~ about** F coś koło; **all (the) year ~** okrągły rok; **the other way ~** na odwrót; **3.** prp. wokół (G), dookoła (G); po (L); za (I); **trip ~ the world** podróż dookoła świata; **4.** runda f (też sportowa); tura f; obchód m (też med.); kolejka f (piwa itp.); ładunek m, nabój m; (w sporcie) partia f (golfa); mus. kanon m; **5.** okrążać ⟨-żyć⟩; zaokrąglać ⟨-lić⟩; zakręt brać ⟨wziąć⟩; **~ down** liczbę zaokrąglać ⟨-lić⟩ (to do G); **~ off** posiłek zakończyć, ukoronować; liczbę zaokrąglać ⟨-lić⟩ (to do G); **~ up** bydło zaganiać ⟨-gonić⟩; ludzi spędzać ⟨-dzić⟩; liczbę zaokrąglać ⟨-lić⟩ (to do

R

G); '~·a·bout **1.** *Brt.* skrzyżowanie *n* okrężne, rondo *n*; *Brt.* karuzela *f*; **2. take a ~about route** ⟨po⟩jechać okrężną drogą; **in a ~about way** *fig.* w zawoalowany sposób; ~ **'trip** podróż *f* tam i z powrotem; ~**trip 'tick·et** bilet *m* tam i z powrotem

rouse [raʊz] *kogoś* ⟨o⟩budzić; *fig. kogoś* pobudzać ⟨-dzić⟩

route [ruːt] droga *f*, trasa *f*; *autobusowa* linia *f*; szlak *m*

rou·tine [ruːˈtiːn] **1.** procedura *f*, tok *m*; **the same old (daily)** ~ codzienne obowiązki *pl.*; rutyna *f*; **2.** rutynowy, utarty

rove [rəʊv] wędrować (*też po L*)

row[1] [raʊ] rząd *m*, szereg *m*

row[2] [rəʊ] **1.** wiosłować; **2.** przejażdżka *f* (*łodzią*)

row[3] [raʊ] *Brt.* F **1.** awantura *f*; rejwach *m*; **2.** kłócić się

row·boat ['rəʊbəʊt] *Am.* łódź *f* wiosłowa; '~·er wioślarz *m* (-arka *f*)

row house ['rəʊhaʊs] *Am.* domek *m* szeregowy

row·ing boat ['rəʊɪŋ bəʊt] *zwł. Brt.* łódź *f* wiosłowa

roy·al ['rɔɪəl] królewski; ~·ty ['rɔɪəltɪ] rodzina *f* królewska; tantiemy *pl.* (**on** od *G*)

RSPCA [ɑːr es piː siː 'eɪ] *skrót:* **Royal Society for the Prevention of Cruelty to Animals** (*towarzystwo opieki nad zwierzętami*)

RSVP [ɑːr es viː 'piː] *skrót:* **please reply** (*francuskie répondez s'il vous plaît*) proszę o odpowiedź

rub [rʌb] **1.** (**-bb-**) *v/t.* trzeć, nacierać ⟨natrzeć⟩; wcierać ⟨wetrzeć⟩; pocierać ⟨potrzeć⟩; ~ **dry** wycierać ⟨wytrzeć⟩ do sucha; ~ **it in** *fig.* F wytykać ⟨-tknąć⟩ coś, odgrzebywać bez przerwy coś; ~ **shoulders with** F zadawać się z (*I*), stykać się z (*I*); *v/i.* trzeć; ocierać ⟨o-trzeć⟩ (**against, on** o *A*); ~ **down** wycierać ⟨wytrzeć⟩; wygładzać ⟨-ładzić⟩; ~ **off** ścierać ⟨zetrzeć⟩ się; *farba:* od-chodzić ⟨odejść⟩; ~ **off on(to)** *fig.* przenosić ⟨-nieść⟩ się na (*A*); ~ **out** *Brt.* wycierać ⟨wytrzeć⟩ (*gumką*); **2. give s.o. a** ~ natrzeć coś, wytrzeć coś

rub·ber ['rʌbə] guma *f*; *zwł. Brt.* gumka *f* (*do wycierania*); gąbka *f* (*do tablicy*); F (*prezerwatywa*) kondom *m*; ~ **'band** gumka *f* (*aptekarska*), recepturka *f*;

~ **'din·ghy** dingi *n*; '~·neck *Am.* F **1.** gapić się; **2.** *też* **rubbernecker** ciekawski *m* (-ka *f*); ~·y ['rʌbərɪ] gumowy; *mięso:* gumowaty, jak guma

rub·bish ['rʌbɪʃ] śmieci *pl.*, odpadki *pl.*; *fig.* bzdury *pl.*; barachło *n*; '~ **bin** *Brt.* kubeł *m* na śmieci; '~ **chute** zsyp *m* na śmieci

rub·ble ['rʌbl] gruz *m*, rumowisko *n*, gruzy *pl.*

ru·by ['ruːbɪ] rubin *m*; *attr.* rubinowy

ruck·sack ['rʌksæk] plecak *m*

rud·der ['rʌdə] *naut., aviat.* ster *m*

rud·dy ['rʌdɪ] (**-ier, -iest**) czerstwy, rumiany; rdzawy

rude [ruːd] (**-r, -st**) niegrzeczny, nietaktowny; *dowcip:* brzydki; *szok:* silny

ru·di·men·ta·ry [ruːdɪˈmentərɪ] rudymentarny, elementarny; ~·ments ['ruː-dɪmənts] *pl.* podstawy *pl.*

rue·ful ['ruːfʊl] zafrasowany

ruff [rʌf] kreza *f*; *zo.* pióra *pl.* (*wokół szyi*)

ruf·fle ['rʌfl] **1.** ⟨z⟩wichrzyć; *włosy* ⟨po⟩czochrać; ~ **s.o.'s composure** zirytować kogoś; **2.** falbanka *f*

rug [rʌg] dywanik *m*; *zwł. Brt.* pled *m*

rug·by ['rʌgbɪ] *też* ~ **football** (*w sporcie*) rugby *n*

rug·ged ['rʌgɪd] wytrzymały; *okolica:* surowy; *rysy:* gruby

ru·in ['ruːɪn] **1.** ruina *f*; *zw.* ~**s** *pl.* ruiny *pl.*; **2.** ⟨z⟩rujnować, ⟨z⟩niszczyć; '~·ous zrujnowany

rule [ruːl] **1.** reguła *f*; zasada *f*; przepis *m*; panowanie *n*, rządy *pl.*; linijka *f*, przymiar *m*; **against the** ~**s** wbrew przepisom, niezgodnie z regułami; **as a** ~ z reguły; **as a** ~ **of thumb** jako praktyczna zasada; **work to** ~ pracować zgodnie z przepisami; **2.** *v/t.* panować (*I*), rządzić (*I*); *zwł. jur.* orzekać; *papier* ⟨po⟩liniować; *linię* ⟨po⟩ciągnąć; **be ~d by** *fig.* rządzić się (*I*); ~ **out** coś wykluczać ⟨-czyć⟩; *v/i.* panować (**over** nad *I*); *zwł. jur.* postanawiać ⟨-nowić⟩; 'rul·er władca *m*; linijka *f*, przymiar *m*

rum [rʌm] rum *m*

rum·ble ['rʌmbl] ⟨za⟩łoskotać, ⟨za⟩-dudnić; *żołądek:* ⟨za⟩burczeć

ru·mi·nant ['ruːmɪnənt] *zo.* przeżuwacz *m*; ~·nate ['ruːmɪneɪt] przeżuwać ⟨-żuć⟩

rum·mage ['rʌmɪdʒ] F **1.** *też* ~ *about* ⟨po⟩grzebać, ⟨po⟩gmerać (*among, in, through* w L); **2.** *zwł. Am.* rzeczy *pl.* używane; '~ **sale** *Am.* wyprzedaż *f* rzeczy używanych

ru·mo(u)r ['ruːmə] **1.** pogłoska *f*, plotka *f*; ~ **has it that** wieść niesie, że; **he is** ~**ed to be** mówi się, że on; △ *nie* **rumor**

rump [rʌmp] zad *m*; *fig.* pozostałości *pl.*, niedobitki *pl.*

rum·ple ['rʌmpl] ⟨po⟩gnieść, ⟨z⟩gnieść

run [rʌn] **1.** (*-nn-; ran, run*) *v/i.* ⟨po⟩biec, ⟨po⟩biegnąć, (*w sporcie*) biegać; *pojazd:* ⟨po⟩jechać; *autobus, pociąg:* kursować; spływać ⟨-łynąć⟩; *kolory:* puszczać ⟨puścić⟩; *tech.* silnik: chodzić, pracować; być w ruchu; *ulica:* biec; *zwł. jur.* obowiązywać (*for one year* przez jeden rok); *theat.* sztuka: iść; *tekst, melodia:* brzmieć; *zwł. Am. pol.* kandydować; ~ **dry** wysychać ⟨-schnąć⟩; ~ **low** wyczerpywać ⟨-pać⟩ się; ~ **short** wyczerpywać ⟨-pać⟩ się; ~ **short of petrol** nie mieć już benzyny; *v/t.* odległość ⟨prze⟩biec, przebiegać ⟨-biec⟩; *pociągiem, autobusem* ⟨po⟩kierować; *tech. maszynę* uruchamiać ⟨-chomić⟩; *wodę* puszczać ⟨puścić⟩; *firmę, hotel* ⟨po⟩prowadzić; *artykuł* ⟨o⟩publikować, zamieszczać ⟨-mieścić⟩; ~ **s.o. home** F zawozić ⟨-wieźć⟩ kogoś do domu; **be ~ning a temperature** mieć temperaturę; → **errands**; ~ **across** kogoś spotykać ⟨-tkać⟩ przypadkiem; ~ **after** pogonić ⟨-gnać⟩ za (*I*); narzucać się (*D*); ~ **along!** F uciekaj!; ~ **away** uciekać ⟨uciec⟩; ~ **away with** uciekać ⟨uciec⟩ z (*I*); dawać ⟨dać⟩ się ponieść (*D*); ~ **down** *mot.* potrącać ⟨-ącić⟩; F obmawiać ⟨-mówić⟩; wyszukiwać ⟨-kać⟩; *czas:* upływać ⟨-łynąć⟩; *bateria:* wyczerpywać ⟨-pać⟩ się; ~ **in** samochód *itp.* docierać ⟨dotrzeć⟩; F ⟨s⟩chwytać; ~ **into** zderzać ⟨zderzyć⟩ się (*I*); *kogoś* spotykać ⟨-tkać⟩ przypadkiem; *fig.* wpadać ⟨wpaść⟩ w (*A*) (*kłopoty*); *fig.* wynosić ⟨-nieść⟩ (*A*); ~ **off with** → **run away with**; ~ **on** przeciągać ⟨-gnąć⟩ się (*until* do G); F ględzić (*about* o L); ~ **out** *jedzenie:* wyczerpywać ⟨-pać⟩ się; *czas:* uciekać; ~ **out of sugar** nie mieć już cukru; ~ **over** *mot.* przejechać; przelewać ⟨-lać⟩ się; ~ **through** powtarzać

⟨-tórzyć⟩; przelatywać ⟨-lecieć⟩ (*wzrokiem*); zużywać ⟨-żyć⟩; ~ **up** *flagę* podnosić ⟨-nieść⟩; *dług* zaciągnąć ⟨-gać⟩; ~ **up against** napotykać ⟨-tkać⟩; **2.** bieg *m*; kurs *m*; przejazd *m*, wycieczka *f*; tok *m*, przebieg *m*; okres *m*; *econ.* run *m*, popyt *m* (*on* na *A*); *theat. itp.* okres *m* wystawiania; *Am.* oczko *n* (*w rajstopach itp.*); zagroda *f*, kojec *m*; wybieg *m*; (*w sporcie*) tor *m*; ~ **of good** (**bad**) **luck** pasmo *n* (nie)powodzeń; **in the long** ~ na dłuższą metę; **in the short** ~ na krótszą metę; **on the** ~ uciekający

'run·a·bout F *mot.* mały samochód *m*, samochód *m* miejski; '~·**a·way** zbieg *m*

rung[1] [rʌŋ] *p.p. od* **ring**[2]

rung[2] [rʌŋ] szczebel *m*

run·ner ['rʌnə] (*w sporcie*) biegacz(ka *f*) *m*; koń *m* wyścigowy; *zw. w złoż.* szmugler *m*; płoza *f*, prowadnica *f*; *bot.* pęd *m* rozłogowy; ~ '**bean** *Brt. bot.* fasolka *f* szparagowa; '~·**up** [rʌnər'ʌp] (*pl.* **runners-up**) (*w sporcie*) drugi *m* (-ga *f*), zdobywca *m* (-czyni *f*) drugiego miejsca

run·ning ['rʌnɪŋ] **1.** bieganie *n*; prowadzenie *n*, kierowanie *n*; bieg *m*, praca *f*; **2.** *woda* bieżący; ciągły; (*w sporcie*) *buty:* do biegania; **two days** ~ dwa dni pod rząd; '~ **costs** *pl.* koszty *pl.* bieżące

run·ny ['rʌnɪ] F *nos* cieknący; *oczy* łzawiący

'run·way *aviat.* pas *m* startowy

rup·ture ['rʌptʃə] **1.** pęknięcie *n*, rozerwanie *n*; *med.* przepuklina *f*; **2.** pękać ⟨-knąć⟩, rozrywać ⟨-zerwać⟩; ~ **o.s.** dostawać ⟨-tać⟩ przepukliny

ru·ral ['ruərəl] wiejski

ruse [ruːz] trik *m*, sztuczka *f*

rush[1] [rʌʃ] *v/i.* ⟨po⟩pędzić, ⟨po⟩gnać, ⟨po⟩biec, ⟨prze-, po⟩mknąć (*to* do G, *towards* w stronę G); spieszyć się; ~ **into** spieszyć się do (G); *v/t.* szybko przewozić ⟨-wieźć⟩; szybko przesyłać ⟨-słać⟩; spieszyć się z (*I*); popędzać, poganiać; **don't** ~ **it** nie spiesz się z tym; ⟨s⟩forsować; **2.** pośpiech *m*; gonitwa *f*, pogoń *f*; pęd *m*; gorączka *f* (*złota*); *econ.* ogromny popyt *m*; **what's all the** ~? po co ten pośpiech?

rush[2] [rʌʃ] *bot.* sit *m*

'rush| **hour** godzina *f* szczytu; **~·hour**

'traf·fic ruch *m* uliczny w godzinie szczytu

rusk [rʌsk] *zwł. Brt.* sucharek *m*

Rus·sia ['rʌʃə] Rosja *f*; Rus·sian ['rʌʃn] **1.** rosyjski; **2.** Rosjanin *m* (-anka *f*); *ling.* język *m* rosyjski

rust [rʌst] **1.** rdza *f*, korozja *f*; **2.** ⟨za⟩rdzewieć, ⟨s⟩korodować

rus·tic ['rʌstɪk] (**~ally**) chłopski, wieśniaczy; rustykalny

rus·tle ['rʌsl] **1.** szeleścić; *Am.* bydło

⟨u⟩kraść; **2.** szelest *m*

'rust|·proof nierdzewny; '**~·y** (**-ier, -iest**) zardzewiały (*też fig.*), *fig.* mało używany

rut[1] [rʌt] **1.** koleina *f*; *fig.* sztampa *f*, rutyna *f*; **the daily ~** codzienna rutyna *f*

rut[2] *zo.* [rʌt] ruja *f*, okres *m* godowy

ruth·less ['ruːθlɪs] bezlitosny, nielitościwy, bez skrupułów

rye [raɪ] *bot.* żyto *n*; *attr.* żytni

S

S, s [es] S, s *n*

S *skrót pisany:* **South** płd., południe *n*, południowy; **south(ern)** południowy; **small** (**size**) mały, eska *f*

$ *skrót pisany:* **dollar(s** *pl.*) USD, $, dolar(y *pl.*)

sa·ble ['seɪbl] *zo.* soból *m*; *futro:* sobole *pl.*

sab·o·tage ['sæbətɑːʒ] **1.** sabotaż *m*; **2.** ⟨za⟩sabotować

sa·bre *Brt.*, sa·ber *Am.* ['seɪbə] szabla *f*

sack [sæk] **1.** worek *m*; **get the ~** F (*być zwolnionym*) dostawać ⟨-tać⟩ kopa; **give s.o. the ~** F wywalić kogoś; **hit the ~** F walnąć się do wyra; **2.** ⟨za⟩pakować do worka; F wywalać ⟨-lić⟩ kogoś; '**~·cloth**, '**~·ing** tkanina *f* workowa

sac·ra·ment ['sækrəmənt] *rel.* sakrament *m*

sa·cred ['seɪkrɪd] sakralny; święty

sac·ri·fice ['sækrɪfaɪs] **1.** ofiara *f*; poświęcenie *n*; **2.** ofiarować; poświęcać ⟨-cić⟩

sac·ri·lege ['sækrɪlɪdʒ] świętokradztwo *n*

sad [sæd] smutny

sad·dle ['sædl] siodło *n*

sa·dis·m ['seɪdɪzəm] sadyzm *m*; **~t** ['seɪdɪst] sadysta *m* (-tka *f*); **~·tic** [sə'dɪstɪk] sadystyczny

'sad·ness smutek *m*

sa·fa·ri [sə'fɑːrɪ] safari *n*; **~ park** park *m* safari

safe [seɪf] **1.** (**-r, -st**) bezpieczny; **2.** sejf *m*; skarbiec *m*; '**~·con·duct** gwarancja *f* bezpieczeństwa, glejt *m*; '**~·guard 1.** zabezpieczenie *n* (**against** przeciw

D); **2.** zabezpieczać ⟨-czyć⟩ (**against** przeciw *D*); '**~·keep·ing** ochrona *f*, bezpieczne przechowywanie *n*

safe·ty ['seɪftɪ] bezpieczeństwo *n*; *attr.* zabezpieczający; '**~ belt** → **seat belt**; '**~ catch** bezpiecznik *m*; '**~ is·land** *Am.* (*na jezdni*) wysepka *f*; '**~ mea·sure** środek *m* bezpieczeństwa; '**~ pin** agrafka *f*; '**~ ra·zor** *nieelektryczna* maszynka *f* do golenia

sag [sæg] (**-gg-**) obwisać ⟨-snąć⟩; *policzki:* zapadać ⟨-paść⟩ się; *wartość:* spadać ⟨spaść⟩; *popyt:* zmniejszać ⟨-szyć⟩ się; *książka:* nużyć

sa·ga·cious [sə'ɡeɪʃəs] bystry, roztropny; **~·ci·ty** [sə'ɡæsətɪ] bystrość *f*, roztropność *f*

sage [seɪdʒ] *bot.* szałwia *f*

Sa·git·tar·i·us [sædʒɪ'teərɪəs] *znak Zodiaku:* Strzelec *m*; **he/she is** (**a**) **~** on(a) jest spod znaku Strzelca

said [sed] *pret. i p.p. od* **say**

sail [seɪl] **1.** żagiel *m*; przejażdżka *f* łodzią; śmigło *n* (*wiatraka*); **set ~** wypływać (**for** do *G*); **go for a ~** iść ⟨pójść⟩ popływać łodzią; *attr.* żaglowy; **2.** *v/i. naut.* ⟨po⟩żeglować, pływać; przepłynąć przez (*A*); *naut.* wypływać ⟨-łynąć⟩ (**for** do *G*); *ktoś:* wpływać ⟨-łynąć⟩, *coś:* szybować; **go ~·ing** iść ⟨pójść⟩ na żagle; *v/t. naut.* przepływać ⟨-łynąć⟩; *łódką* żeglować; *statek* ⟨po⟩prowadzić; '**~·board** deska *f* surfingowa; '**~·boat** *Am.* żaglówka *f*, łódź *f* żaglowa

'sail·ing żeglarstwo *n*, rejs *m*; **when is the next ~ to ?** kiedy będzie następny

sank

rejs do (G)?; '~ boat *zwł. Brt.* żaglówka *f;* łódź *f* żaglowa; '~ ship żaglo-
wiec *m*

'**sail·or** żeglarz *m;* **be a good** (**bad**) ~
dobrze (źle) czuć się na morzu

saint [seɪnt] święty *m; przed imionami* 2
[snt] (*skrót:* **St**): **St George** święty Je-
rzy; '**~·ly** święty

sake [seɪk]: **for the** ~ **of** ze względu na
(*A*); **for my** ~ ze względu na mnie; **for
God's** ~ F na litość boską

sa·la·ble ['seɪləbl] pokupny; sprzedaż-
ny

sal·ad ['sæləd] sałatka *f;* △ *nie* **sałata**
(*zielona*); '~ **dress·ing** przybranie *n*
do sałatki, sos *m*

sal·a·ried ['sælərɪd]: ~ **employee** (*pracownik m* (*-nica f*) *otrzymujący* (*-a*)
pensję co miesiąc)

sal·a·ry ['sælərɪ] pensja *f*

sale [seɪl] sprzedaż *f;* wyprzedaż *f;* aukcja *f;* **for** ~ na sprzedaż; **not for** ~ nie
na sprzedaż; **be on** ~ być na sprzedaż; **~s**
pl. obroty *pl* **sale·a·ble** ['seɪləbl] →
salable

sales|·clerk ['seɪlzklɑːk] *Am.* sprze-
dawca *m* (*-czyni f*); '**~·girl** sprzedawczyni *f;* '**~·man** (*pl.* **-men**) sprzedawca *m;* akwizytor *m;* '**~· rep·re·sen·ta·t-
ive** przedstawiciel(ka *f*) *m* handlowy (*-wa f*); '**~·wom·an** (*pl.* **-women**)
sprzedawczyni *f;* akwizytorka *f*

sa·line ['seɪlaɪn] słony, zasolony

sa·li·va [sə'laɪvə] ślina *f*

sal·low ['sæləʊ] *skóra:* zżółkły, żółtawy

salm·on ['sæmən] *zo.* (*pl.* **-on, -ons**)
łosoś *m*

sal·on ['sæləʊ̃, 'sælɒn] *kosmetyczny itp.*
salon *m*

sa·loon [sə'luːn] *Brt. mot.* sedan *m; Am.
hist.* saloon *m,* bar *m; naut.* salon *m;*
→ ~ **bar** *Brt.* (*elegancka część pubu*);
~ **car** *Brt. mot.* sedan *m*

salt [sɔːlt] sól *f;* 2. ⟨po⟩solić; zasalać
⟨-solić⟩ (*też* ~ **down**); *ulicę* posypywać
⟨-pać⟩ solą; 3. słony; solny; solony;
'~·**cel·lar** solniczka *f;* ~·**pe·tre** *zwł.
Brt.,* ~·**pe·ter** *Am.* [sɔːlt'piːtə] *chem.* saletra *f* potasowa; '~·**wa·ter** solanka *f;*
'~·**y** (**-ier, -iest**) słony

sa·lu·ta·tion [sæljuː'teɪʃn] pozdrowienie *n;* początek *m* (*listu*)

sa·lute [sə'luːt] 1. *mil.* ⟨za⟩salutować;
oddawać ⟨-dać⟩ honory (*D*); pozdra-

wiać ⟨-rowić⟩; 2. *mil.* oddanie *n* hono-
rów; honory *pl.;* salut *m* (*armatni*); pozdrowienie *n*

sal·vage ['sælvɪdʒ] 1. ratowanie *n* mienia; akcja *f* ratownicza; uratowane mienie *n;* 2. ⟨u⟩ratować (**from** od *G*)

sal·va·tion [sæl'veɪʃn] *rel.* zbawienie *n;*
wybawienie *n;* 2 **Army** Armia *f* Zbawienia

salve [sælv] maść *f*

same [seɪm]: **the** ~ ten sam, ta sama, to
samo; **all the** ~ mimo wszystko; **it is all
the** ~ **to me** wszystko mi jedno

sam·ple ['sɑːmpl] 1. próbka *f;* 2. pobierać ⟨-brać⟩ próbkę; ⟨s⟩próbować

san·a·to·ri·um [sænə'tɔːrɪəm] (*pl.
-riums, -ria* [-rɪə]) sanatorium *n*

sanc·ti·fy ['sæŋktɪfaɪ] uświęcać ⟨-cić⟩

sanc·tion ['sæŋkʃn] 1. aprobata *f;* zw.
~s *pl.* sankcje *pl.;* 2. ⟨za⟩aprobować,
⟨u⟩sankcjonować

sanc·ti·ty ['sæŋktətɪ] świętość *f*

sanc·tu·a·ry ['sæŋktʃʊərɪ] rezerwat *m;*
azyl *m,* schronienie *n*

sand [sænd] 1. piasek *m;* **~s** *pl.* piaski
pl.; 2. ⟨prze⟩szlifować papierem ścier-
nym; posypywać ⟨-pać⟩ piaskiem

san·dal ['sændl] sandał *m*

'**sand|·bag** worek *m* z piaskiem;
'~·**bank** piaszczysty brzeg *m;* '~·**box**
Am. piaskownica *f;* '~·**cas·tle** zamek
m z piasku; '~·**pa·per** papier *m* ścierny;
'~·**pip·er** *zo.* siewka *f,* biegus *m;* '~·**pit**
Brt. piaskownica *f;* '~·**stone** *geol.* pias-
kowiec *m;* '~·**storm** burza *f* piaskowa

sand·wich ['sænwɪdʒ] 1. kanapka *f;* 2.
be ~ed between być wciśniętym pomiędzy (*A*); ~ **s.th. in between** wciskać ⟨-snąć⟩ coś pomiędzy (*A*)

sand·y ['sændɪ] (**-ier, -iest**) piaszczysty;
rudoblond

sane [seɪn] (**-r, -st**) zdrowy na umyśle;
rozsądny, sensowny

sang [sæŋ] *pret. od* **sing**

san·i·tar·i·um [sænɪ'teərɪəm] *Am.* →
sanatorium

san·i·ta·ry ['sænɪtərɪ] higieniczny;
'~ **nap·kin** *Am.,* '~ **tow·el** *Brt.* podpaska *f*

san·i·ta·tion [sænɪ'teɪʃn] urządzenia
pl. sanitarne; kanalizacja *f*

san·i·ty ['sænətɪ] zdrowie psychiczne;
rozsądek *m*

sank [sæŋk] *pret. od* **sink** 1

S

San·ta Claus ['sæntəklɔːz] Święty Mikołaj

sap¹ [sæp] *bot.* sok *m (np. brzozy)*

sap² [sæp] **(-pp-)** zdrowie nadwątlać ⟨-lić⟩

sap·phire ['sæfaɪə] szafir *m*; szafirowy

sar·cas·m ['sɑːkæzm] sarkazm *m*; ~**tic** [sɑːˈkæstɪk] sarkastyczny

sar·dine [sɑːˈdiːn] *zo.* sardynka *f*

SASE [es eɪ es 'iː] *Am. skrót:* **self-addressed, stamped envelope** koperta *f* zwrotna ze znaczkiem

sash¹ [sæʃ] szarfa *f*

sash² [sæʃ] skrzydło *n* okienne; rama *f* okienna; ~ **win·dow** okno *n* otwierane pionowo (*z przesuwanymi do góry skrzydłami*)

sat [sæt] *pret. i p.p. od* **sit**

Sat *skrót pisany:* **Saturday** sob., sobota *f*

Sa·tan ['seɪtn] *rel.* szatan *m*

satch·el ['sætʃəl] tornister *m*

sat·el·lite ['sætəlaɪt] satelita *m*; *attr.* satelitarny

sat·in ['sætɪn] satyna *f*; atłas *m*; *attr.* satynowy

sat·ire ['sætaɪə] satyra *f*; ~**ir·ist** ['sætərɪst] satyryk *m*; ~**ir·ize** ['sætəraɪz] satyryzować, przedstawiać ⟨-wić⟩ satyrycznie

sat·is·fac·tion [sætɪsˈfækʃn] satysfakcja *f*, zadowolenie *n*; spełnienie *n*; zadośćuczynienie *n*; ~**to·ry** [sætɪsˈfæktərɪ] zadowalający; dostateczny

sat·is·fy ['sætɪsfaɪ] zadowalać ⟨-lić⟩; zaspokajać ⟨-koić⟩, zadośćuczynić; **be satisfied that** być przekonanym, że

sat·u·rate ['sætʃəreɪt] nasycać ⟨-cić⟩; *chem.* wysycać ⟨-cić⟩

Sat·ur·day ['sætədɪ] sobota *f*; **on** ~ w sobotę; **on** ~**s** sobotami, co sobotę

sauce [sɔːs] sos *m*; ~**pan** rondel *m*

sau·cer ['sɔːsə] spodek *m*

sauc·y ['sɔːsɪ] F **(-ier, -iest)** zadziorny, z tupetem

saun·ter ['sɔːntə] kroczyć, przechadzać się

saus·age ['sɒsɪdʒ] kiełbasa *f*; *też* **small** ~ parówka *f*

sav·age ['sævɪdʒ] **1.** dziki; niecywilizowany; bestialski; **2.** dzikus *m*; ~**ag·e·ry** ['sævɪdʒərɪ] bestialstwo *n*, okrucieństwo *n*

save [seɪv] **1.** ⟨u⟩ratować *(from* z *G)*; życie ocalać ⟨-lić⟩; *pieniądze itp.* oszczę-

dzać ⟨-dzić⟩, zaoszczędzać ⟨-dzić⟩; *coś* zachowywać ⟨-wać⟩ *(for* na *A)*; *komp.* zapisywać ⟨-sać⟩; *(w sporcie)* strzał ⟨o⟩bronić; **2.** *(w sporcie)* parada *f*, obrona *f*

sav·er ['seɪvə] ratownik *m (-niczka f)*; *Brt.* oszczędzający *m (-ca f)*; **it is a time~** to bardzo oszczędza czas

sav·ings ['seɪvɪŋz] *pl.* oszczędności *pl.*; '~ **ac·count** konto *n* oszczędności; '~ **bank** kasa *f* oszczędności; '~ **de·pos·it** wkład *m* oszczędnościowy

sa·vio(u)r ['seɪvjə] zbawca *m*; **the** 2 *rel.* Zbawiciel *m*

sa·vo(u)r ['seɪvə] ⟨z⟩jeść *lub* ⟨wy⟩pić ze smakiem, rozkoszować się; ~ **of** *fig.* smakować *(I)*; ~**y** ['seɪvərɪ] smakowity; pikantny, nie słodki

saw¹ [sɔː] *pret. od* **see¹**

saw² [sɔː] **1.** piła *f*; **2.** **(~ed, ~n** *lub zwł. Am.* ~**ed)** ⟨s-, o⟩piłować; '~**dust** trociny *pl.*; '~**mill** tartak *m*; ~**n** [sɔːn] *p.p. od* **saw²**

Sax·on ['sæksn] **1.** Anglosas *m*; **2.** (anglo)saski

say [seɪ] **1.** **(said)** mówić ⟨powiedzieć⟩; *pacierz* odmawiać⟨-mówić⟩; **what does your watch ~?** która godzina na twoim zegarku?; **he is said to be ...** podobno jest...; **it ~s** napisane jest; **it ~s here** tu jest napisane; **it goes without ~ing** to rozumie się samo przez siebie; **no sooner said than done** zostało wykonane od razu; **that is to ~** to znaczy; **(and) that's ~ing s.th.** a to coś mówi; **you said it** to ty tak powiedziałeś; **you can ~ that again!** szczera prawda!; **you don't ~ (so)!** niemożliwe!; nie mów!; *I ~ Brt.* przepraszam; **not to ~ no to** nie odmawiać *(G)*; **2.** prawo *n* głosu; głos *m (in* w *L)*; **have one's ~** wypowiadać ⟨-wiedzieć⟩ się; **he always has to have his ~** on zawsze musi coś powiedzieć; '~**ing** po- rzekadło *n*, powiedzenie *n*; **as the ~ing goes** jak to mówią

scab [skæb] *med.* strup *m*; *vet.* świerzb *m*; *sl.* łamistrajk *m*

scaf·fold ['skæfəld] rusztowanie *n*; szafot *m*; '~**ing** rusztowanie *n*

scald [skɔːld] **1.** oparzać ⟨-rzyć⟩, sparzyć; **2.** ~**ing hot** gorący jak ukrop; **2.** sparzenie *n*; poparzenie *n*

scale [skeɪl] **1.** *tech., math., też fig.* skala *f*; podziałka *f (math., też mapy)*; *zwł.*

Am. waga *f*; *mus.* gama *f*; **to ~** w skali; **2.** sporządzać ⟨-dzić⟩ w skali; **~ down** *fig.* ⟨z⟩redukować; **~ up** *fig.* zwiększać ⟨-szyć⟩; wspinać ⟨-piąć⟩ się

scale² [skeɪl] szala *f* wagi; **(a pair of) ~s** *pl.* waga *f*

scale³ [skeɪl] **1.** łuska *f*; kamień *m* (*w czajniku*); **the ~s fell from my eyes** łuski mi spadły z oczu; **2.** *rybę* ⟨o⟩skrobać

scal·lop [ˈskɒləp] *zo.* (*małż*) przegrzebek *m*

scalp [skælp] **1.** skóra *f* głowy; skalp *m*; **2.** ⟨o⟩skalpować

scal·y [ˈskeɪlɪ] (**-ier, -iest**) łuskowaty

scamp [skæmp] F urwis *m*, huncwot *m*

scam·per [ˈskæmpə] pierzchać ⟨-chnąć⟩; smyknąć

scan [skæn] **1.** (**-nn-**) przeszukiwać ⟨-kać⟩; *gazetę* przeglądać ⟨-dnąć⟩; *komp.* ⟨ze⟩skanować; przeszukiwać zakres *radio*; *telewizyjny obraz* ⟨prze-, z⟩analizować, składać ⟨złożyć⟩; **2.** *med. itp.* skaning *m*

scan·dal [ˈskændl] skandal *m*; słuchy *pl.*; **~ize** [ˈskændəlaɪz]: **be ~ized at s.th.** ⟨z⟩gorszyć się czymś; **~ous** [ˈskændələs] skandaliczny; **it's ~ous that** to skandal, że

Scan·di·na·vi·a [skændɪˈneɪvjə] Skandynawia *f*; **Scan·di·na·vi·an** [skændɪˈneɪvjən] skandynawski

scan·ner [ˈskænə] *tech.* skaner *m*

scant [skænt] skąpy, niewielki, mały; **~·y** (**-ier, -iest**) skąpy, niewielki, mały

scape·goat [ˈskeɪpgəʊt] kozioł *m* ofiarny

scar [skɑː] **1.** blizna *f*; **2.** (**-rr-**) pokrywać ⟨-ryć⟩ bliznami; pozostawiać ⟨-wić⟩ uraz; **~ over** zabliźniać ⟨-nić⟩ się

scarce [skeəs] (**-r, -st**) rzadki, mało dostępny; **~·ly** ledwo, ledwie; **scar·ci·ty** [ˈskeəsəti] skąpość *f*, mała dostępność *f*

scare [skeə] **1.** ⟨wy⟩straszyć; **be ~d** bać się; **~ away, ~ off** odstraszać ⟨-szyć⟩; **2.** strach *m*; panika *f*; **bomb ~** alarm *m* bombowy; **~·crow** strach *m* na wróble

scarf [skɑːf] (*pl.* **scarfs**, **scarves** [skɑːvz]) szal *m*, szalik *m*; chusta *f* (*na głowę, ramię itp.*)

scar·let [ˈskɑːlət] pąsowy; **~·fe·ver** *med.* szkarlatyna *f*, płonica *f*; **~·run·ner** *bot.* fasola *f* wielokwiatowa

scarred [skɑːd] pokryty bliznami, zbliznowaciały

scarves [skɑːvz] *pl. od* **scarf**

scath·ing [ˈskeɪðɪŋ] *krytyka*: niszczący, zjadliwy

scat·ter [ˈskætə] rozpraszać ⟨-roszyć⟩ (się); rozbiegać ⟨-biec⟩ się; rozrzucać ⟨-cić⟩; **~·brained** F roztrzepany, roztargniony; **~ed** rozproszony

scav·enge [ˈskævɪndʒ]: **~ on** *zo.* żerować na (*L*); **~ for** wyszukiwać ⟨-kać⟩

sce·na·ri·o [sɪˈnɑːrɪəʊ] (*pl.* **-os**) scenariusz *m* (*filmowy, telewizyjny, też fig.*)

scene [siːn] scena *f*; **behind the ~s** za kulisami; **sce·ne·ry** [ˈsiːnərɪ] sceneria *f*; krajobraz *m*

scent [sent] **1.** zapach *m*, aromat *m*; *zwł. Brt.* perfumy *pl.*; *hunt.* wiatr *m*, zapach *m*; trop *m*, ślad *m*; **2.** ⟨z⟩wietrzyć, wyczuwać ⟨-czuć⟩ (*też fig.*); *zwł. Brt.* ⟨u⟩perfumować; napełniać ⟨-nić⟩ aromatem; **~·less** bezwonny, bezzapachowy

scep·tic [ˈskeptɪk] *Brt.* sceptyk *m*; **~·ti·cal** *Brt.* sceptyczny

scep·tre *Brt.*, **scep·ter** *Am.* [ˈseptə] berło *n*

sched·ule [ˈʃedjuːl, *Am.* ˈskedʒʊl] **1.** harmonogram *m*, plan *m*; wykaz *m*, spis *m*; taryfa *f*; *zwł. Am.* rozkład *m* jazdy; **ahead of ~** przed terminem; **be behind ~** mieć opóźnienie, z opóźnieniem; **on ~** w terminie, zgodnie z planem; **2.** ⟨za⟩planować; wstawiać do rozkładu; **the meeting is ~d for Monday** spotkanie zostało zaplanowane na poniedziałek; **it is ~d to take place tomorrow** zostało zaplanowane na jutro; **~d de·par·ture** planowy odjazd *m*; **~d 'flight** rejsowy lot *m*

scheme [skiːm] **1.** *zwł. Brt.* program *m*, projekt *m*; schemat *m*; intryga *f*, spisek *m*; **2.** ⟨u⟩knuć intrygę; ⟨u⟩knuć

schnit·zel [ˈʃnɪtsl] *gastr.* sznycel *m*

schol·ar [ˈskɒlə] uczony *m* (*-a f*); *univ.* stypendysta *m* (*-tka f*); **~·ly** uczony; naukowy; **~·ship** uczoność *f* (*duża*) wiedza *f*; *univ.* stypendium

school¹ [skuːl] **1.** szkoła (*też fig.*); *univ.* fakultet *m*; *Am.* uczelnia *f*, szkoła *f* wyższa; **at ~** w szkole; **go to ~** chodzić ⟨pójść⟩ do szkoły; *attr.* szkolny; **2.** ⟨wy⟩szkolić; *zwierzę* ⟨wy⟩tresować

school² [skuːl] *zo.* ławica *f* (*ryb*); stado *n* (*wielorybów*)

S

'**school**|·**bag** torba *f*; '**~·boy** uczeń *m*; '**~·child** (*pl.* **-children**) uczeń *m*; '**~·fel·low** → **schoolmate**; '**~·girl** uczennica *f*; '**~·ing** szkolenie *n*, nauka *f* szkolna; '**~·mate** kolega *m* (-leżanka *f*) szkolny (-na); '**~·teach·er** nauczyciel(ka *f*) *m*; '**~·yard** podwórko *n* szkolne

schoo·ner ['sku:nə] *naut.* skuner *m*

sci·ence ['saɪəns] *przyrodnicza* nauka *f*; **natural ~s** *pl.* przyrodnicze nauki *pl.*; '**~·fic·tion** (*skrót:* **SF**) science-fiction *n*

sci·en·tif·ic [saɪən'tɪfɪk] (**~ally**) naukowy

sci·en·tist ['saɪəntɪst] naukowiec *m*, uczony *m* (-na *f*)

sci-fi ['saɪ'faɪ] F science-fiction *n*

scin·til·lat·ing ['sɪntɪleɪtɪŋ] błyskotliwy, efektowny

scis·sors ['sɪzəz] *pl.* (**a pair of ~**) nożyce *pl.*, nożyczki *pl.*

scoff [skɒf] **1.** natrząsać się (**at** z G); **2.** szyderstwo *n*, kpina *f*

scold [skəʊld] strofować

scol·lop ['skɒləp] *zo.* → **scallop**

scone [skɒn] *zwł. Brt.* bułka *f* słodka (*jedzona z masłem*)

scoop [sku:p] **1.** szufla *f*, szufelka *f*; łopatka *f*; łyżka *f* (*koparki, do lodów*); gałka *f* (*lodów*); sensacyjna wiadomość *f*, scoop *m*; **2.** nabierać (-brać), czerpać (zaczerpnąć); **~ down** wybierać (-brać); **~ up** podnosić (-nieść)

scoot·er ['sku:tə] hulajnoga *f*; skuter *m*

scope [skəʊp] zakres *m*, zasięg *m*; pole *n* widzenia; pole *n* działania;

scorch [skɔːtʃ] *v/t.* przypalać (-lić), przypiekać (-piec); *v/i. Brt.* (*jechać*) *mot.* grzać

score [skɔː] **1.** wynik *m* (*gry*); punkt *m*; *mus.* partytura *f*; muzyka *f* filmowa; dwudziestka *n*; *też* **~ mark** karb *m*, nacięcie *n*; **what is the ~?** jaki wynik?; **the ~ stood at** *lub* **was 3-2** w grze było 3-2; **keep (the) ~** zapisywać (-sać) punkty; **~s pl. of** dziesiątki *pl.* (G); **four ~ and ten** dziewięćdziesiąt; **on that ~** pod tym względem; **have a ~ to settle with s.o.** mieć z kimś porachunki do załatwienia; **2.** *v/t.* (*w sporcie*) *punkty* zdobywać (-być), *bramkę* strzelać (-lić); *zwycięstwo* odnosić (-nieść); *mus.* (z)instrumentować (na)pisać muzykę do (G); (wy)kar-

bować, nacinać (-ciąć); *v/i.* (*w sporcie*) zdobywać (-być) punkty, strzelać (-lić) bramkę; odnosić (-nieść) sukces; '**~·board** *v/i.* (*w sporcie*) tablica *f* wyników; **scor·er** ['skɔːrə] *v/i.* (*w sporcie*) strzelec *m*, zdobywca *m* (-czyni *f*) punktu; *v/i.* (*w sporcie*) (*osoba zapisująca punktację, wyniki*)

scorn [skɔːn] pogarda *f*; '**~·ful** pogardliwy

Scor·pi·o ['skɔːpɪəʊ] *znak Zodiaku:* Skorpion *m*; **he/she is (a) ~** on(a) jest spod znaku Skorpiona

Scot [skɒt] Szkot(ka *f*) *m*

Scotch [skɒtʃ] **1.** *whisky itp.* szkocki; **2.** *whisky:* szkocka *f*

scot-free [skɒt'friː] F: **he got off ~** uszło mu na sucho

Scot·land ['skɒtlənd] Szkocja *f*

Scots [skɒts] szkocki (*o osobach*); '**~·man** (*pl.* **-men**) Szkot *m*; '**~·wom·an** (*pl.* **-women**) Szkotka *f*

Scot·tish ['skɒtɪʃ] szkocki

scoun·drel ['skaʊndrəl] łajdak *m*

scour[1] ['skaʊə] (wy)szorować, (o)skrobać

scour[2] ['skaʊə] przeszukiwać (-kać)

scourge [skɜːdʒ] **1.** plaga *f*; bicz *m* (*też fig.*); **2.** biczować; (z)nękać

scout [skaʊt] **1.** *zwł. mil.* zwiadowca *m*; *Brt.* (*osoba pomagająca zmotoryzowanym w razie awarii*); *też boy* ~ skaut *m*; *też girl* ~ skautka *f*; *też talent* ~ poszukiwacz(ka *f*) *m* talentów; **2.** ~ **about**, ~ **around** rozglądać się (**for** za *I*); *też* ~ **out** *mil.* wynajdywać (-naleźć)

scowl [skaʊl] **1.** ponura mina *f*; **2.** (s)krzywić się (*też* **at** na *A*)

scram·ble ['skræmbl] **1.** wdrapywać (-pać) się; pchać się (**for** do G); *tech.* (za)kodować; **2.** wdrapywanie *n* się; przepychanka *f*, szarpanina *f*; **~d 'eggs** *gastr. pl.* jajecznica *f*

scrap[1] [skræp] **1.** strzęp *m*, skrawek *m*; złom *m*; **~s** *pl.* odpadki *pl.*, resztki *pl.* (*jedzenia*); **2.** (**-pp-**) *plan itp.* porzucać (-cić), odrzucać (-cić); (ze)złomować

scrap[2] F [skræp] **1.** scysja *f*, zatarg *m*; **2.** (po)kłócić się, wszczynać (-cząć) sprzeczkę

'**scrap**·**book** album *m* z wycinkami

scrape [skreɪp] **1.** skrobać, zeskrobywać (-bać); *kolano itp.* ocierać (otrzeć); *samochód* zarysowywać (-ować); trzeć, pocierać ⟨potrzeć⟩ (*against* o *A*); **2.** otarcie *n*, zarysowanie *n*

'**scrap**| **heap** kupa *f* złomu; '~ **met·al** złom *m*; '~ **pa·per** *zwł. Brt.* makulatura *f*; '~ **val·ue** wartość *f* złomowa; '~ **yard** złomowisko *n*

scratch [skrætʃ] **1.** ⟨po-, za-, wy⟩drapać; *plan* pokreslić ⟨-cić⟩; ⟨po⟩drapać (się); **2.** zadrapanie *n*, rysa *f*; podrapanie *n*, zadraśnięcie *n*; *from* ~ F od zera; **3.** prowizoryczny, zrobiony na łapu capu; '~**pad** *zwł. Am.* notatnik *m*; '~ **pa·per** *Am.* papier *m* do pisania na brudno

scrawl [skrɔːl] **1.** ⟨na⟩bazgrać; **2.** bazgroły *pl.*

scraw·ny ['skrɔːnɪ] (*-ier, -iest*) kościsty

scream [skriːm] **1.** krzyczeć ⟨-yknąć⟩ (*with* z *G*); *też* ~ *out* wrzasnąć; ~ *with laughter* zanosić się ze śmiechu; **2.** krzyk *m*; ~**s** *pl. of laughter* rozgłośny śmiech *m*; *he is a* ~ F przy nim można pęknąć ze śmiechu

screech [skriːtʃ] **1.** wydzierać ⟨-drzeć⟩ się (*piszcząco*); ⟨za⟩piszczeć; **2.** pisk *m*

screen [skriːn] **1.** ekran *m*; parawan *m*; zasłona *f*, szpaler *m* (*drzew*); **2.** osłaniać ⟨-łonić⟩ (*też fig.*), zasłaniać ⟨-łonić⟩; *kandydatów* przesiewać ⟨-siać⟩; odsiewać ⟨-siać⟩ (*G*); *film* wyświetlać ⟨-lić⟩, pokazywać ⟨-zać⟩; ~ *off* przedzielać⟨-lić⟩ (*parawanem*); '~**play** scenariusz *m*; '~ **sav·er** *komp.* (*program oszczędzający ekran komputerowy*)

screw [skruː] **1.** *tech.* wkręt *m*, śruba *f*; *he has a loose* ~ F szajba mu odbiła; **2.** wkręcać ⟨-cić⟩, przyśrubowywać ⟨-wać⟩; V ⟨wy⟩dupczyć; ~ *up twarz* wykrzywiać ⟨-wić⟩; *oczy* ⟨z⟩mrużyć; ~ *up one's courage* zdobyć się na odwagę; '~**ball** *zwł. Am.* F szajbus *m*; '~**driv·er** śrubokręt *m*, wkrętak *m*; ~ '**top** nakrętka *f*

scrib·ble ['skrɪbl] **1.** ⟨na⟩bazgrać, ⟨na⟩gryzmolić; ; **2.** bazgroły *pl.*, gryzmoły *pl.*

scrimp [skrɪmp]: ~ *and save* liczyć każdy grosik

script [skrɪpt] manuskrypt *m*; tekst *m* (*też theat.*); scenariusz *m* (*filmowy lub telewizyjny*); pismo *n*; *Brt. univ.* test *m*

Scrip·ture ['skrɪptʃə] *też the* ~**s** *pl.* Pismo *n* Święte

scroll [skrəʊl] **1.** zwój *m*, rulon *m* (*per-*

gaminu itp.); **2.** ~ *down/up obraz na ekranie* przewijać ⟨-winąć⟩, przesuwać ⟨-sunąć⟩

scro·tum *anat.* ['skrəʊtəm] (*pl. -ta* [-tə], *-tums*) moszna *f*

scrub[1] [skrʌb] **1.** (*-bb-*) ⟨wy⟩szorować; **2.** (wy)szorowanie *n*

scrub[2] [skrʌb] skrub *m*, busz *m* australijski

scru·ple ['skruːpl] **1.** skrupuł *m*; wątpliwość *f*; **2.** mieć skrupuły; ~**pu·lous** ['skruːpjʊləs] skrupulatny

scru·ti·nize ['skruːtɪnaɪz] dokładnie ⟨z⟩badać; ~**ny** ['skruːtɪnɪ] dokładne badanie *f*, analiza *f*

scu·ba ['skuːbə] akwalung *m*; '~ *div·ing* nurkowanie *n* swobodne

scud [skʌd] (*-dd-*) sunąć szybko, ⟨po⟩szybować

scuf·fle ['skʌfl] **1.** bójka *f*; **2.** wszczynać ⟨-szcząć⟩ bójkę

scull [skʌl] **1.** *jednopiórowe* krótkie wiosło *n*; skul *m*, jedynka *f*; **2.** wiosłować

scul·le·ry ['skʌlərɪ] zmywalnia *f*, pomywalnia *f*

sculp·tor ['skʌlptə] rzeźbiarz *m* (*-arka f*); ~**ture** ['skʌlptʃə] **1.** rzeźba *f*; **2.** ⟨wy⟩rzeźbić; ⟨u⟩kształtować

scum [skʌm] piana *f*; szumowiny *pl.* (*też fig.*)

scurf [skɜːf] łupież *m*

scur·ri·lous ['skʌrɪləs] obelżywy, nie przebierający w słowach

scur·ry ['skʌrɪ] przemykać ⟨-mknąć⟩; ⟨po⟩tuptać

scur·vy ['skɜːvɪ] *med.* szkorbut *m*, gnilec *m*

scut·tle ['skʌtl]: ~ *away*, ~ *off* uciekać ⟨-ciec⟩ drobnymi kroczkami

scythe [saɪð] kosa *f*

SE *skrót pisany: southeast* płd.-wsch., południowy wschód *m*; *southeast(ern)* płd.-wsch., południowo-wschodni

sea [siː] morze *n* (*też fig.*); *at* ~ na morzu; *be all lub completely at* ~ *fig.* F pogubić się; *by* ~ morzem, drogą morską; *by the* ~ nad morzem; *attr.* morski; nadmorski; '~**food** owoce *pl.* morza; '~**gull** *zo.* mewa *f*

seal[1] [siːl] *zo.* (*pl. seals, seal*) foka *f*

seal[2] [siːl] **1.** pieczęć *f*; *tech.* uszczelka *f*; **2.** ⟨o-, za⟩pieczętować; zamykać

⟨-mknąć⟩, zaklejać ⟨-leić⟩; *tech.* uszczelniać ⟨-nić⟩; *fig.* przypieczętowywać ⟨-ować⟩; **~ed envelope** zamknięta koperta *f*; **~ off** *dostęp* zamykać ⟨-mknąć⟩
'**sea lev·el: above ~** nad poziomem morza; *below* ~ poniżej poziomu morza
'**seal·ing wax** lak *m* (*do pieczętowania*)
seam [si:m] szew *m*; połączenie *n*; *geol.* pokład *m*
'**sea·man** (*pl.* **-men**) żeglarz *m*
seam·stress ['semstrɪs] krawcowa *f*
'**sea|·plane** wodnosamolot *m*, hydroplan *m*, wodnopłat *m*; '**~·port** port *m* morski; miasto *n* portowe; '**~·pow·er** potęga *f* morska
sear [sɪə] wypalać ⟨-lić⟩ (*też fig.*); palić, piec (w *A*); *mięso* obsmażać ⟨-żyć⟩
search [sɜːtʃ] **1.** *v/i.* szukać (*for G*), poszukiwać ⟨-kać⟩ (*for A*); **~ through** przeszukiwać ⟨-kać⟩; *v/t.* szukać; przeszukiwać ⟨-kać⟩; ⟨z⟩rewidować; **~ me!** F nie mam pojęcia!; **~·ing** *n* (*for G*); szukanie *n*; rewizja *f*; '**~·ing** spojrzenie: badawczy; *przegląd*: wnikliwy; '**~·light** (*reflektor*) szperacz *m*; '**~·par·ty** wyprawa *f* poszukiwawcza; '**~ war·rant** nakaz *m* rewizji
'**sea|·shore** brzeg *m* morza; '**~·sick: be ~sick** cierpieć na chorobę morską; '**~·side: at** *lub* **by the ~side** nad morzem; **go to the ~side** ⟨po⟩jechać nad morze; **~side re'sort** uzdrowisko *n* nadmorskie
sea·son¹ ['si:zn] pora *f* roku, sezon *m* (*też theat.*); myśliwski, urlopowy okres *m*; *in* ~ w sezonie, *out of* ~ poza sezonem; *cherries are now in* ~ teraz jest sezon na czereśnie; *2!* Wesołych Świąt (*Bożego Narodzenia*)!; *with the compliments of the ~* najlepsze życzenia z okazji świąt
sea·son² ['si:zn] przyprawiać ⟨-wić⟩, doprawiać ⟨-wić⟩; *drewno* sezonować
sea·son·al ['si:zənl] sezonowy; okresowy
sea·son·ing ['si:znɪŋ] przyprawa *f*
'**sea·son tick·et** *rail.* bilet *m* okresowy; *theat.* abonament *m*
seat [si:t] **1.** miejsce *n*; siedzenie *n*; siedziba *f*; *take one's/a* ~ zajmować ⟨-jąć⟩ miejsce; ⟨po⟩sadzić ⟨posadzić⟩; *sala*: ⟨po⟩mieścić; *uszczelkę* osadzać ⟨-dzić⟩; *be* ~ed siedzieć; *please be*

~ed proszę usiąść; *remain* ~ed pozostawać na swoim miejscu; '~ belt *aviat.*, *mot.* pas *m* bezpieczeństwa; *fasten one's* ~ *belt* zapinać ⟨-piąć⟩ pas bezpieczeństwa; '...~·seat·er: *forty-seater* o 40 miejscach
sea| ur·chin ['si:ɜːtʃɪn] *zo.* jeżowiec *m*; ~·**ward(s)** ['si:wəd(z)] w stronę morza; '~·**weed** *bot.* wodorost *m* morski; '~·**wor·thy** zdatny do żeglugi
sec [sek] zwł. *Brt.* F *fig.* chwileczka *f*, sekunda *f*; *just a* ~ sekundeczka *f*
se·cede [sɪ'si:d] odłączać ⟨-czyć⟩ się (*from* od *G*); **se·ces·sion** [sɪ'seʃn] secesja *f*, odłączenie *n* się
se·clud·ed [sɪ'klu:dɪd] *dom*: odosobniony; *życie*: samotniczy; **se·clu·sion** [sɪ'klu:ʒn] odosobnienie *n*; samotnictwo *n*
sec·ond¹ ['sekənd] **1.** *adj.* drugi; *every ~ day* co drugi dzień; **~ to none** nie ustępujący nikomu; *but on* ~ *thoughts* (*Am.* **thought**) jednak po namyśle; **2.** *adv.* jako drugi; **3.** drugi *m*, druga *f*, drugie *n*; *mot.* drugi bieg *m*; sekundant *m*; ~**s** *pl.* F *econ.* drugi wybór *m*, resztki *pl.*; **4.** *wniosek itp.* popierać ⟨poprzeć⟩
sec·ond² ['sekənd] sekunda *f*; *fig.* sekunda *f*, chwila *f*; *just a* ~ (za) chwilkę
sec·ond·a·ry ['sekəndərɪ] drugorzędny, wtórny, uboczny; *ped. szkoła itp.* średni
sec·ond-'best drugiej jakości; na drugim miejscu; ~ **'class** *rail.* druga klasa *f*; ~**'class** drugiej klasy; ~ **'floor** *Brt.* drugie piętro; *Am.* pierwsze piętro; ~**'hand** używany; antykwaryczny; ~**'hand** sekundnik *m*; '~**·ly** po drugie; ~**'rate** drugiego gatunku
se·cre·cy ['si:krɪsɪ] tajemnica *f*; dyskrecja *f*
se·cret ['si:krɪt] **1.** tajny, poufny; sekretny; **2.** sekret *m*; tajemnica *f*; *in* ~ w skrytości, w tajemnicy; *keep s.th. a* ~ zachowywać ⟨-ować⟩ coś w sekrecie; *can you keep a* ~**?** umiesz dotrzymywać tajemnicy?; '~·a·gent tajny ⟨-a⟩ agent(-ka *f*) *m*
sec·re·ta·ry ['sekrɪtrɪ] sekretarz *m* (-arka *f*); **2 of 'State** *Brt.* Minister *m*; *Am.* Sekretarz *m* Stanu
se·crete [sɪ'kri:t] *physiol.* wydzielać ⟨-lić⟩; **se·cre·tion** [sɪ'kri:ʃn] *physiol.* wydzielina *f*

se·cre·tive ['si:krətɪv] skryty
se·cret·ly ['si:krɪtlɪ] potajemnie, w tajemnicy
se·cret 'ser·vice tajna służba f
sec·tion ['sekʃn] część f; sekcja f; jur. paragraf m; część f; tech. przekrój m; math. odcinek m
sec·u·lar ['sekjulə] świecki
se·cure [sɪ'kjuə] 1. bezpieczny; zabezpieczony (**against, from** przed I); 2. drzwi itp. umocowywać ⟨-ować⟩; zabezpieczać ⟨-czyć⟩ (**against, from** przed I)
se·cu·ri·ty [sɪ'kjuərətɪ] bezpieczeństwo n, zabezpieczenie n; **securities** pl. papiery pl. wartościowe; ~ check kontrola f bezpieczeństwa; ~ mea·sure środek m bezpieczeństwa; ~ risk zagrożenie n bezpieczeństwa
se·dan [sɪ'dæn] Am. mot. sedan m
se·date [sɪ'deɪt] 1. stateczny; 2. podawać ⟨-dać⟩ środki uspokajające
sed·a·tive ['sedətɪv] środek m uspokajający
sed·i·ment ['sedɪmənt] osad m
se·duce [sɪ'dju:s] uwodzić ⟨uwieść⟩; se·duc·er [sɪ'dju:sə] uwodziciel(ka f) m; se·duc·tion [sɪ'dʌkʃn] uwiedzenie n; se·duc·tive [sɪ'dʌktɪv] uwodzicielski
see¹ [si:] (**saw, seen**) v/i. widzieć; zobaczyć; ⟨z⟩rozumieć; **I ~!** rozumiem!; ach tak!; **you ~** widzisz; **let me ~** pozwól mi się zastanowić; **we'll ~** zobaczymy; v/t. widzieć; ⟨z⟩rozumieć; ⟨u⟩żyć; wybierać się ⟨-brać się⟩ do (G), ⟨s⟩konsultować się z (I); ~ **s.o. home** odprowadzać ⟨-dzić⟩ kogoś do domu; ~ **you!** cześć!; na razie!; ~ **about** zajmować ⟨-jąć⟩ się; zobaczyć; ~ **off** odprowadzać ⟨-dzić⟩ (**at** na L); ~ **out** towarzyszyć; odprowadzać ⟨-dzić⟩; ~ **through** przejrzeć kogoś na wskroś; pomagać ⟨-móc⟩ komuś przetrwać; ~ **to it that** dopilnować, że
see² [si:] biskupstwo n, diecezja f; **Holy** 2 Stolica f Święta
seed [si:d] 1. bot. nasienie n; ziarno n (też fig.); Am. (jabłka itp.) pestka f; (w sporcie) rozstawiony (-a) zawodnik m (-niczka f); **go lub run to ~** wydawać ⟨-dać⟩ nasiona; fig. F ⟨s⟩kapcanieć; 2. v/t. wysiewać ⟨-siać⟩; siać, obsiewać ⟨-siać⟩; ⟨wy⟩drylować; (w sporcie) rozstawiać ⟨-wić⟩; v/i. bot. wysiewać ⟨-siać⟩ się; '~·less bezpłodny; '~·y F (-ier,

-iest) zapuszczony, zaniedbany
seek [si:k] (**sought**) szukać, poszukiwać ⟨-kać⟩
seem [si:m] wydawać ⟨-dać⟩ się, zdawać ⟨zdać⟩ się; '~·ing pozorny
seen [si:n] p.p. od **see¹**
seep [si:p] przeciekać ⟨-ciec⟩, przesączać ⟨-czyć⟩ się
see·saw ['si:sɔ:] huśtawka f
seethe [si:ð] gotować się, kipieć (też fig.)
'see-through przezroczysty, przeświecający
seg·ment ['segmənt] math. odcinek m; segment m, cząstka f; przekrój m
seg·re|·gate ['segrɪgeɪt] ⟨po⟩segregować; rozdzielać ⟨-lić⟩; ~·ga·tion [segrɪ'geɪʃn] segregacja f; rozdział m
Seine Sekwana f
seize [si:z] ⟨s⟩chwytać, ⟨z⟩łapać; władzę itp. przechwytywać ⟨-wycić⟩; uczucia: owładnąć; sei·zure ['si:ʒə] przechwycenie n władzy; zajęcie n (majątku); med. atak m, napad m
sel·dom ['seldəm] adv. rzadko
se·lect [sɪ'lekt] 1. wybierać ⟨-brać⟩; ⟨wy⟩selekcjonować; 2. wyselekcjonowany; ekskluzywny; se·lec·tion [sɪ'lekʃn] wybór m; dobór m
self [self] (pl. **selves** [selvz]) ja m, ego n; ~·as'sured pewny siebie; ~·'cen·tred Brt., ~·'cen·tered Am. egocentryczny; ~·'col·o(u)red jednobarwny, jednokolorowy; ~·'con·fi·dence pewność f siebie; ~·'con·fi·dent pewny siebie; ~·'con·scious niepewny (siebie), skrępowany, odrębny; zamknięty w sobie; ~·'con·trol samoopanowanie n; ~·de'fence Brt., ~·de'fense Am. samoobrona f; **in ~-defence/-defense** w obronie własnej; ~·de·ter·mi'na·tion pol. samostanowienie n; ~·em'ployed na własnym rozrachunku; ~·es'teem poczucie n własnej wartości; ~·'ev·i·dent oczywisty; ~·'gov·ern·ment samorząd m; ~·'help samopomoc f; ~·im'por·tant zarozumiały; ~·in'dul·gent folgujący swoim zachciankom; ~·'in·ter·est własny interes m; '~·ish egoistyczny, sobkowski; ~·made 'man (pl. **-men**) self-made man m (człowiek wszystko zawdzięczający tylko sobie); ~·'pit·y roztkliwianie n się nad sobą; ~·pos'sessed

opanowany; ~·pos'ses·sion opanowanie n; ~·re·li·ant [selfrɪ'laɪənt] niezależny, samodzielny; ~'re·spect poważanie m dla siebie samego;
~'right·eous, faryzeuski, świętoszkowaty; ~'sat·is·fied zadowolony z siebie; ~'serv·ice 1. samoobsługowy; 2.
samoobsługa f; ~·suf'ficient samowy-
starczalny; ~·sup'porting niezależny
materialnie; ~'willed krnąbrny

sell [sel] (**sold**) sprzedawać ⟨-dać⟩;
sprzedawać ⟨-dać⟩ się (**at, for** za A);
iść (dobrze); ~ **by ...** okres przydatności
do ...; ~ **off** wyprzedawać ⟨-dać⟩ (zw.
tanio); ~ **out** wyprzedać; **be sold out**
zostać wyprzedanym; ~ **up** zw. Brt.
rozprzedawać ⟨-dać⟩ (swój majątek);
'~·by date data f przydatności do spożycia; '~·er sprzedawca m (-czyni f);
zbywający m (-ca f); **good ~er** artykuł
dobrze się sprzedający

selves [selvz] pl. od **self**

sem·blance ['sembləns] pozór m

se·men ['si:men] physiol. nasienie n,
sperma f

se·mes·ter [sɪ'mestə] univ. semestr m

sem·i... ['semɪ] pół..., semi...

'**sem·i·cir·cle** półkrąg m; ~'co·lon
średnik m; ~·de'tached (house) (dom)
bliźniak m; ~'fi·nals pl. (w sporcie)
półfinały pl.

sem·i·nar·y ['semɪnərɪ] seminarium n

Sen → Snr

sen·ate ['sent] senat m; ~·a·tor ['sen-
ətə] senator m

send [send] (**sent**) wysyłać ⟨-słać⟩,
posyłać (**to** do G); pomoc nadsyłać ⟨-de-
słać⟩ (**to** do G); pozdrowienia, towary
itp. przesyłać ⟨-słać⟩ (**to** do G); list, program itp. nadawać ⟨-nadać⟩; z adj. i
p.pr. czynić; ~ **s.o. mad** Brt. doprowadzać kogoś do szaleństwa; ~ **word to
s.o.** przesyłać ⟨-łać⟩ komuś wiadomości; ~ **away** odsyłać ⟨odesłać⟩; odprawiać ⟨-wić⟩; ~ **down** Brt. relegować
z uczelni; fig. cenę obniżać⟨-żyć⟩; ~ **for**
posyłać ⟨-słać⟩ po (A); wzywać ⟨wez-
wać⟩(G); zamawiać ⟨-mówić⟩; ~ **in** nadsyłać ⟨-desłać⟩; ~ **off** odsyłać ⟨odesłać⟩;
wysyłać ⟨-słać⟩; (w sporcie) usunąć
z boiska; ~ **on** przesyłać ⟨-słać⟩ (**to** na
nowy adres); bagaże przesyłać ⟨-słać⟩
wcześniej; ~ **out** rozsyłać ⟨-zesłać⟩; wysyłać ⟨-słać⟩; ~ **up** fig. cenę itp. podwyż-

szać ⟨-szyć⟩; '~·er nadawca m

se·nile ['si:naɪl] zniedołężniały (ze starości); se·nil·i·ty [sɪ'nɪlətɪ] zniedołęż-
nienie m (starcze)

se·ni·or ['si:njə] 1. senior (po nazwisku); starszy (**to** od G); starszy rangą;
2. starszy m (-sza f); Am. student-
(ka f) m ostatniego roku; **he is my ~
by a year** jest ode mnie starszy o rok;
~ **cit·i·zens** pl. emeryci pl.; ~·i·ty [si:
nɪ'ɒrətɪ] starszeństwo n; wysługa f lat,
staż m pracy; ~ **part·ner** econ. główny
wspólnik m

sen·sa·tion [sen'seɪʃn] odczucie n; u-
czucie n; czucie n; sensacja f; ~·al
[sen'seɪʃənl] F sensacyjny; rewelacyjny

sense [sens] 1. sens m; znaczenie n; rozsądek m; zmysł m; poczucie n, uczucie
n; **bring s.o. to his ~s** przywrócić komuś poczucie rzeczywistości; **come to
one's ~s** opamiętać się; **in a ~** w pewnym stopniu; **make ~** mieć sens; ~ **of
duty** poczucie n obowiązku; ~ **of security** poczucie n bezpieczeństwa. 2.
odczuwać ⟨-czuć⟩; wyczuwać ⟨-czuć⟩;
'~·less bezsensowny

sen·si·bil·i·ty [sensɪ'bɪlətɪ] wrażliwość
f; też **sensibilities** uczucia pl.

sen·si·ble ['sensəbl] rozsądny; praktyczny;

sen·si·tive ['sensɪtɪv] wrażliwy; aparat:
czuły

sen·sor ['sensə] tech. czujnik m; sen-
sor m

sen·su·al ['sensjuəl] zmysłowy

sen·su·ous ['sensjuəs] zmysłowy

sent [sent] pret. i p.p. od **send**

sen·tence ['sentəns] 1. gr. zdanie n; jur.
wyrok m; **pass** lub **pronounce ~** ogłaszać ⟨-łosić⟩ wyrok, skazywać ⟨-zać⟩; 2.
jur. skazywać ⟨-zać⟩ (**to** na A)

sen·ti·ment ['sentɪmənt] uczucie n;
nastrój m; sentyment m; ~·ment·al
[sentɪ'mentl] sentymentalny; ~·men-
tal·i·ty [sentɪmen'tælətɪ] sentymental-
ność f, sentymentalizm m

sen·try ['sentrɪ] mil. wartownik m; warta f

Seoul Seul m

sep·a·ra·ble ['sepərəbl] rozdzielny,
rozłączny; ~·rate 1. ['sepəreɪt] rozdzielać ⟨-lić⟩ (się); oddzielać ⟨-lić⟩ (się);
⟨po⟩dzielić (się) (**into** na A); 2. ['se-
prət] oddzielny; odrębny; osobny; ~·ra-

tion [sepə'reɪʃn] oddzielenie *n*; rozłąka *f*; separacja *f*; rozdzielanie *n*

Sept *skrót pisany:* ***September*** wrzes., wrzesień *m*

Sep·tem·ber [sep'tembə] wrzesień *m*

sep·tic ['septɪk] *med.* (*~ally*) septyczny, zakaźny

se·quel ['si:kwəl] ciąg *m* dalszy; następstwo *n*

se·quence ['si:kwəns] kolejność *f*; następstwo *n*; ciąg *m*; sekwencja *f* (*w filmie, TV*); *~ of tenses* gr. następstwo *n* czasów

Ser·bi·a Serbia *f*

ser·e·nade [serə'neɪd] *mus.* **1.** serenada *f*; **2.** ⟨*za*⟩grać *lub* ⟨*za*⟩śpiewać serenadę

se·rene [sɪ'ri:n] spokojny; jasny, bezchmurny

ser·geant ['sɑːdʒənt] sierżant *m*

se·ri·al ['sɪərɪəl] **1.** serial *m*; powieść *f* w odcinkach; **2.** seryjny; w odcinkach; *komp.* szeregowy

se·ries ['sɪəriːz] (*pl.* *-ries*) seria *f*, szereg *m*; seria *f* (*wydawnicza*); ciąg *m*

se·ri·ous ['sɪərɪəs] poważny; *be ~* zachowywać się poważnie; '*~ness* powaga

ser·mon ['sɜːmən] *rel.* kazanie *n* (*też fig.*)

ser·pen·tine ['sɜːpəntaɪn] powykręcany; *droga*: serpentynowy

se·rum ['sɪərəm] (*pl.* *-rums, -ra* [-rə]) serum *n*, surowica *f*

ser·vant ['sɜːvənt] służący *m* (*-ca f*) (*też fig.*); *fig.* sługa *m*; → *civil servant*

serve [sɜːv] **1.** *v/t.* komuś, krajowi, celowi *itp.* służyć (*D*); praktyki *itp.* odbywać ⟨*-być*⟩; ⟨*s*⟩pełnić obowiązki; pracować dla (*G*); zaopatrywać ⟨*-trzyć*⟩ (*with* w *A*); *jedzenie* podawać ⟨*-dać*⟩; *kogoś* obsługiwać ⟨*-łużyć*⟩; *jur.* karę odbywać ⟨*-być*⟩; *jur.* wezwanie doręczać ⟨*-czyć*⟩ (*on s.o.* komuś); (*w tenisie*) ⟨*za*⟩serwować; *are you being ~d?* czy jest już Pan obsługiwany?; (*it*) *~s him right* F dobrze mu tak; *v/i.* *zwł. mil.* odbywać ⟨*-być*⟩ służbę; służyć (*as, for* jako); ⟨*s*⟩pełnić funkcję; (*w tenisie*) ⟨*za*⟩serwować; podawać ⟨*-dać*⟩; *XY to ~* (*w tenisie*) serw XY; *~ on a committee* być członkiem komitetu; **2.** (*w tenisie itp.*) serw *m*, serwis *m*; 'serv·er (*w tenisie itp.*) serwujący *m* (*-ca f*); łyżka *f* (*do nakładania*); *komp.* serwer *m*

ser·i·vice ['sɜːvɪs] **1.** służba *f* (*to* dla *G*) (*też fig.*); służba *f* publiczna; *pocztowa, transportowe itp.* usługi *pl.*; połączenie *n*, *kolejowa itp.* komunikacja *f*; serwis *m*; obsługa *f*; *rel.* nabożeństwo *n*; usługa *f*, przysługa *f*; *jur.* doręczenie *n* (*wezwania*); (*w tenisie itp.*) serw *m*, serwis *m*; *~vices mil. pl.* siły *pl.* zbrojne; **2.** *tech.* obsługiwać ⟨*-łużyć*⟩; *~·vi·cea·ble* ['sɜːvɪsəbl] zdatny do użytku; przydatny; '*~vice ar·e·a Brt.* usługi *pl.* dla zmotoryzowanych (*przy autostradzie*); '*~vice charge* dodatek *m* za obsługę; '*~vice sta·tion* stacja *f* benzynowa; warsztat *m* naprawy samochodowy

ser·vi·ette [sɜːvɪ'et] *zwł. Brt.* serwetka *f*

ser·vile ['sɜːvaɪl] służalczy; niewolniczy

serv·ing ['sɜːvɪŋ] porcja *f*

ser·vi·tude ['sɜːvɪtjuːd] służalczość *f*

ses·sion ['seʃn] sesja *f*, zebranie *n*; posiedzenie *n* (*sądu itp.*); *be in ~ jur., parl.* odbywać ⟨*-być*⟩ sesję

set [set] **1.** (*-tt-; set*) *v/t.* ustawiać ⟨*-wić*⟩, stawiać ⟨*postawić*⟩; umieszczać ⟨*-mieścić*⟩; przykładać ⟨*-łożyć*⟩; *zegar, urządzenie, kość itp.* nastawiać ⟨*-wić*⟩; *stół* nakrywać ⟨*-ryć*⟩; *cenę, termin* ustalać ⟨*-lić*⟩; *rekord* ustanawiać ⟨*-nowić*⟩; *klejnot* oprawiać ⟨*-wić*⟩ (*in w A lub L*), osadzać ⟨*-dzić*⟩; *galaretę* zestalać ⟨*-lić*⟩; *włosy* układać ⟨*ułożyć*⟩; *mus. print.* składać ⟨*złożyć*⟩; *pytanie, zadanie* zadawać ⟨*-dać*⟩; *hunt.* wystawiać ⟨*-wić*⟩; *~ s.o. at ease* uspokajać ⟨*-koić*⟩ kogoś; *~ an example* ustanawiać ⟨*-nowić*⟩ przykład; *~ s.o. free* uwalniać ⟨*-wolnić*⟩ kogoś; *~ s.th. going* uruchamiać ⟨*-mić*⟩ coś; *~ s.o. thinking* dawać ⟨*dać*⟩ komuś do myślenia; *~ one's hopes on s.th.* wiązać z czymś nadzieję; *~ s.o.'s mind at rest* uspokajać ⟨*-koić*⟩ kogoś; *~ s.th. to music* napisać muzykę do czegoś; *~ great (little) store by* przykładać wielką (małą) wagę do czegoś; *the novel is ~ in* akcja powieści dzieje się w (*L*); *v/i. słońce:* zachodzić ⟨*zajść*⟩; *galareta:* ⟨*za*⟩stygnąć, zestalać ⟨*-lić*⟩ się; *hunt.* wystawiać ⟨*-wić*⟩ zwierzynę; *~ about doing s.th.* zabrać się do czegoś; *~ about s.o.* F rzucać ⟨*-cić*⟩ się na kogoś; *~ aside* odkładać ⟨*odłożyć*⟩; *jur. wyrok* uchylać ⟨*-lić*⟩; *~ back* opóźniać ⟨*-nić*⟩ (*by two months* o dwa miesiące); *be set back* być cofniętym (*from* od *G*); ~ *in pogo-da*: nastawać ⟨-tać⟩; ~ *off* wyruszać ⟨-szyć⟩; ⟨z⟩detonować, odpalać ⟨-lić⟩; wywoływać ⟨-łać⟩; uwydatniać ⟨-nić⟩; podkreślać ⟨-lić⟩; ~ *out* ustawiać ⟨-wić⟩; wyruszać ⟨-szyć⟩; wyjaśniać ⟨-nić⟩; ~ *out to do s.th.* zabierać ⟨-brać⟩ się do zrobienia czegoś, podejmować ⟨-djąć⟩ się zrobienia czegoś; ~ *up* wznosić ⟨-nieść⟩; *urządzenie itp.* ⟨z⟩montować; *komitet, firmę itp.* ⟨z⟩organizować; zaopatrywać (*with* w *A*); *problemy itp.* stwarzać ⟨-worzyć⟩; ~ *o.s. up* urządzać ⟨-dzić⟩ się (*as* w charakterze *G*); **2.** *adj.* położony; osadzony; *godziny*: ustalony; *lektura*: obowiązkowy; *miód*: zestalony; ~ *lunch Brt.* obiad *m* firmowy; ~ *phrase* utarty zwrot *m*, fraza *f*; *be* ~ *on doing s.th.* być zdecydowanym coś zrobić; *be* ~ *against s.th.* być nastawionym przeciw czemuś; *be all* ~ F być gotowym; **3.** zestaw *m* (*narzędzi itp.*); komplet *m* (*narzędzi, mebli itp.*); aparat *m*, *telewizyjny, radiowy* odbiornik *m*; *theat.* scenografia *f*; plan *m* filmowy; (*w tenisie*) set *m*; grupa *f* (*ludzi*); modelowanie *n* (*włosów*); *math.* zbiór *m*; *poet.* zachód *m*; *have a shampoo and* ~ umyć i ułożyć sobie włosy; '~*back* porażka *f*, zahamowanie *n*; '~*square Brt.* ekierka *f*

set·tee [se'tiː] sofa *f*

'set the·o·ry *math.* teoria *f* zbiorów

set·ting ['setŋ] zachód *m* (*słońca itp.*); *tech.* nastawienie *n*; oprawa *f* (*klejnotu*); usytuowanie *n* (*budynku*), miejsce *n*; '~ lo·tion lakier *m* do włosów

set·tle ['setl] *v/i.* osiadać ⟨osiąść⟩ (*on* na *L*); osiadać, osiedlać ⟨-lić⟩ się (*in* w *mieście*); usadawiać ⟨-dowić⟩ się; *płyn*: ⟨wy⟩klarować się; uspokajać ⟨-koić⟩ się; zabierać ⟨-brać⟩ się (*to* do *G*) (*też* ~*down*); układać ⟨ułożyć⟩ się; *v/t.* *problem* załatwiać ⟨-wić⟩; *sprawy* ⟨u⟩regulować; *spór* rozstrzygać ⟨-gnąć⟩; *rachunek* ⟨u⟩regulować; *kogoś* usadawiać ⟨-dowić⟩; *teren* zasiedlać ⟨-lić⟩; ~ *o.s.* usadowić się (*on* na *L*); *that ~s it* to przesądza sprawę; *that's ~d then* wszystko więc jasne; ~ *down* → *v/i.*; ~ *for* ugodzić się do (*D*); ~ *in* przywyknąć (do *G*), wrosnąć w (*A*); ~ *on* ugodzić się co do (*G*); ~ *up* roz-

liczać ⟨-czyć⟩ się (*with* z *I*); '~*d* ustalony (*też pogoda*); *życie* uregulowany; '~*ment* osiedle *n*; uregulowanie *n*; ustalenie *n*; ułożenie *n* się; rozstrzygnięcie *n*; porozumienie *n*, ugoda *f*; zapłata *f*; rozliczenie *n*; *reach a ~ment* dochodzić ⟨dojść⟩ do porozumienia; '~*r* osadnik *m* (-iczka *f*)

sev·en ['sevn] **1.** siedem; **2.** siódemka *f*; ~*teen* [sevn'tiːn] **1.** siedemnaście; **2.** siedemnastka *f*; ~*teenth* [sevn'tiːnθ] **1.** siedemnasty; **2.** siedemnasta część *f*; ~*th* ['sevnθ] **1.** siódmy; **2.** siódma część *f*; '~*th·ly* po siódme; ~*ti·eth* ['sevntiːəθ] siedemdziesiąty; ~*ty* ['sevntiː] **1.** siedemdziesiąt; **2.** siedemdziesiątka *f*

sev·er ['sevə] przerywać ⟨-rwać⟩; *znajomość itp.* zrywać ⟨zerwać⟩

sev·e·ral ['sevrəl] kilka; kilku; '~*·ly* osobno, pojedynczo

se·vere [sɪ'vɪə] (*-r, -st*) *zima, człowiek*: surowy; *choroba itp.*: poważny; *ból*: silny; *krytyka*: ostry; ~*·ly* surowo; ~*·i·ty* [sɪ'verətɪ] surowość *f*; ostrość *f*; powaga *f*; duża siła *f*

sew [səʊ] (*sewed, sewn lub sewed*) szyć

sew·age ['suːɪdʒ] ścieki *pl.*; '~ *works* *sg.* oczyszczalnia *f* ścieków

sew·er [suə] ściek *m*; ~*·age* ['suərɪdʒ] kanalizacja *f*

sew·ing ['səʊɪŋ] szycie *n*; '~ *ma·chine* maszyna *f* do szycia

sewn [səʊn] *p.p.* od *sew*

sex [seks] płeć *f*; seksualność *f*; seks *m*; stosunek *m* płciowy

sex·i·s·m ['seksɪzəm] seksizm *m*; '~*·ist* **1.** seksistowski; **2.** seksista *m*

sex·ton ['sekstən] zakrystian *m*, kościelny *m*

sex·u·al ['sekʃʊəl] płciowy; seksualny; ~ *har·ass·ment* prześladowanie *n* na tle seksualnym; ~ *in·ter·course* stosunek *m* płciowy; ~*·i·ty* [sekʃʊ'ælətɪ] płciowość *f*

sex·y ['seksɪ] F sexy, seksowny

SF [es 'ef] *skrót*: *science fiction* science fiction *n*

shab·by ['ʃæbɪ] (*-ier, -iest*) niechlujny, zaniedbany

shack [ʃæk] buda *f*, szopa *f*

shack·les ['ʃæklz] *pl.* okowy *pl.* (*też fig.*), kajdany *pl.*

shade [ʃeɪd] **1.** cień *m* (*też fig.*); osłona *f*;

odcień *m* (*koloru, znaczenia*); *Am.* żaluzja *f*, roleta *f*; **a ~** *fig.* trochę, nieco; **2.** osłaniać ⟨-łonić⟩ (*from* przed *I*); ocieniać ⟨-nić⟩; *kolory:* przechodzić ⟨przejść⟩ (*off/into* w *A*); **~s** *pl.* F okulary *pl.* przeciwsłoneczne

shad·ow ['ʃædəʊ] **1.** cień *m* (*też fig.*); **there's not a lub the ~ of a doubt** nie ma nawet cienia wątpliwości; **2.** *kogoś* ocieniać ⟨-nić⟩; '**~·y** (**-ier, -iest**) zacieniony, ciemny; nieokreślony

shad·y ['ʃeɪdɪ] (**-ier, -iest**) zacieniony, ciemny; F ciemny, podejrzany

shaft [ʃɑːft] trzonek *m*; drzewce *n* (*strzały*); wał *m* (*samochodu*); szyb *m* (*kopalni*); promień *m* (*słońca*); dyszel *m*

shag·gy ['ʃægɪ] (**-ier, -iest**) *pies:* kosmaty; *broda:* nastroszony; *płaszcz:* kosmaty

shake [ʃeɪk] **1.** (**shook, shaken**) *v/t.* trząść (*I*), potrząsać ⟨-nąć⟩ (*I*); otrząsać ⟨-snąć⟩; *koktajl* ⟨z⟩robić (*mieszając*); **~ hands** uścisnąć ⟨ścisnąć⟩ czyjąś dłoń; *v/i.* trząść się (*with* z *G*); otrząsać ⟨-snąć⟩ się; **~ down** *Brt.* przespać się; *Brt.* przywykać ⟨-knąć⟩; **~ off** strząsać ⟨-snąć⟩; *choroby* pozbywać ⟨-być⟩ się; **~ up** poduszki wzruszać ⟨-szyć⟩; *napój* wymieszać; *fig.* wstrząsać ⟨-snąć⟩; **2.** potrząśnięcie *n*, wstrząśnięcie *n*; otrząśnięcie *n* (się); *Am.* F koktajl *m* mleczny; '**~·down** F **1.** *Am.* szantaż *m*, wymuszenie *n*; *Am.* rewizja *f*, przeszukanie *n*; *tymczasowe* miejsce *n* noclegu; ostateczny test *m*; **2.** *adj. lot, podróż:* testowy; **shak·en** ['ʃeɪkən] **1.** *p.p. od* **shake** 1; **2.** *adj. też* **~ up** wstrząśnięty

shak·y ['ʃeɪkɪ] (**-ier, -iest**) trzęsący się; *fig.* słaby

shall *v/aux.* [ʃæl] (*pret.* **should**) **I ~ be** będę; **we ~ be** będziemy; **you ~ do it** masz to zrobić, powinieneś to zrobić; *w pytaniach:* **~ we go?** może byśmy poszli?

shal·low ['ʃæləʊ] płytki (*też fig.*); *fig.* powierzchowny; '**~s** *pl.* mielizna *f*, płycizna *f*

sham [ʃæm] **1.** fikcja *f*; pozór *m*; **2.** fikcyjny, pozorny; fałszywy, udawany; **3.** (**-mm-**) *v/t.* współczucie pozorować; *chorobę* symulować; *v/i.* udawać ⟨-dać⟩, symulować

sham·bles ['ʃæmblz] *sg.* F bałagan *m*, chaos *m*

shame [ʃeɪm] **1.** wstyd *m*; hańba *f*; **~ !** hańba!; **~ on you!** ale wstyd!; **put to ~** *kogoś* zawstydzać ⟨-dzić⟩ **2.** zawstydzać ⟨-dzić⟩; przynosić ⟨-nieść⟩ *komuś* wstyd; przewyższać ⟨-szyć⟩; **~·faced** zawstydzony; '**~·ful** haniebny; '**~·less** bezwstydny

sham·poo [ʃæm'puː] **1.** (*pl.* **-poos**) szampon *m*; → **set** 3; **2.** *włosy* ⟨u⟩myć; *dywan* ⟨wy⟩prać

sham·rock ['ʃæmrɒk] koniczyna *f* drobnogłówkowa

shank [ʃæŋk] *tech.* trzon(ek) *m*; goleń *f*

shan't [ʃɑːnt] = **shall not**

shan·ty¹ ['ʃæntɪ] buda *f*, szopa *f*

shan·ty² ['ʃæntɪ] szanta *f*

shape [ʃeɪp] **1.** kształt *m*; forma *f*; stan *m* (*budynku itp.*); **2.** *v/t.* ⟨u⟩kształtować; ⟨u⟩formować; *v/i.* **~ up** dawać ⟨dać⟩ sobie radę; brać ⟨wziąć⟩ się w garść; *zwł. Am.* ⟨u⟩formować się; **~d** uformowany; '**~·less** bezkształtny, bezforemny; '**~·ly** (**-ier, -iest**) kształtny

share [ʃeə] **1.** udział *m* (*in* w *L*, *of* w *G*); część *f*; *zwł. Brt. econ.* akcja *f*; **go ~** ⟨po⟩dzielić się (*kosztami itp.*); **have a ~ in** mieć w (*L*) udział; **have no ~ in** nie mieć w (*L*) udziału; **2.** *v/t.* ⟨po⟩dzielić się (*with* z *I*); dzielić; *też* **~ out** rozdzielać ⟨-lić⟩ (*among, between* (po)między *A*); *v/i.* dzielić się; **in** brać ⟨wziąć⟩ udział w (*L*); '**~·hold·er** *zwł. Brt.* udziałowiec *m*, akcjonariusz *m*

shark [ʃɑːk] (*pl.* **shark, sharks**) *zo.* rekin *m*; F *finansowy* rekin *m*

sharp [ʃɑːp] **1.** *adj.* ostry (*też fig.*); *umysł:* lotny; *mus.* (*o pół tonu*) podwyższony; **C ~** *mus.* Cis lub cis; **2.** *adv.* ostro; nagle; *mus.* za wysoko; punktualnie, dokładnie; **at eight o'clock ~** punkt o ósmej; **look ~** F ⟨po⟩spieszyć się; **look ~!** F tempo!; uwaga!; '**~·en** ['ʃɑːpən] ⟨na-, za⟩ostrzyć; *ołówek też* ⟨za⟩temperować; '**~·en·er** ['ʃɑːpnə] ostrzałka *f*, przyrząd *m* do ostrzenia; temperówka *f*; '**~·ness** ostrość *f* (*też fig.*); '**~·shoot·er** snajper *m*, strzelec *m* wyborowy; **~·'sight·ed** o ostrym wzroku

shat·ter ['ʃætə] *v/t.* ⟨s⟩trzaskać; rozbijać ⟨-bić⟩; *nadzieje* rozwiewać ⟨-wiać⟩; *v/i.* roztrzaskać się, rozbijać ⟨-bić⟩ się

shave [ʃeɪv] **1.** ⟨o⟩golić (się); ⟨o⟩golić; zeskrobywać ⟨-bać⟩; **2.** ogolenie *n*, ostrzyżenie *n*; **have a ~** ⟨o⟩golić się; **that**

***was a close* ~** niewiele brakowało; **shav·en** ['ʃeɪvn] ogolony; **shav·er** ['ʃeɪvə] *elektryczna* golarka *f*, maszynka *f* do golenia; **shav·ing** ['ʃeɪvɪŋ] 1. golenie *n*; **~s** *pl.* wióry *pl.*; 2. do golenia

shawl [ʃɔːl] chusta *m* (*na głowę itp.*)

she [ʃiː] 1. *pron.* ona; 2. *zo.* samica *m*; 3. *adj. w złoż.* **she-bear** niedźwiedzica *f*

sheaf [ʃiːf] (*pl.* **sheaves**) *agr.* snop *m*; plik *m* (*papierów*)

shear [ʃɪə] 1. (**sheared, sheared** *lub* **shorn**) ⟨o⟩strzyc; 2. (**a pair of**) **~s** *pl.* nożyce *pl.*

sheath [ʃiːθ] (*pl.* **sheaths** [ʃiːðz]) pochwa *f* (*na miecz itp.*); *Brt.* prezerwatywa *f*; *tech.* osłona *f*, pokrowiec *m*; **~e** [ʃiːð] ⟨s⟩chować do pochwy; *tech.* osłaniać ⟨-nić⟩

sheaves [ʃiːvz] *pl. od* **sheaf**

shed[1] [ʃed] szopa *f*

shed[2] [ʃed] (**-dd-**; **shed**) łzy wylewać ⟨-lać⟩; *liście, skórę* zrzucać ⟨-cić⟩; *krew* przelewać ⟨-lać⟩; *fig.* pozbywać ⟨-być⟩ się; **~ *a few pounds*** zrzucać ⟨-cić⟩ kilka funtów

sheen [ʃiːn] połysk *m*

sheep [ʃiːp] *zo.* (*pl.* **sheep**) owca *f*; '**~·dog** owczarek *m*; '**~ farm·ing** owczarstwo *n*; '**~·fold** okólnik *m*, zagroda *f* dla owiec; '**~·ish** zbaraniały; głupkowaty; **~·skin** kożuch *m*

sheer [ʃɪə] czysty, sam; *brzeg*: pionowy; *materiał*: przejrzysty

sheet [ʃiːt] prześcieradło *n*; arkusz *m* (*papieru, blachy*); kartka *f*; płyta *f* (*szkła*); tafla *f* (*szkła, lodu itp.*); **the rain was coming down in ~s** lało strumieniami; **~ light·ning** błyskawica *f* (*rozświetlająca całe niebo*)

shelf [ʃelf] (*pl.* **shelves**) półka *f* (*też skalna*); **shelves** *pl.* regał *m*

shell [ʃel] 1. skorup(k)a *f* (*jaja, orzecha, ślimaka itp.*); łupina *f*; muszla *f*; *zo.* pancerz *m*; *mil.* pocisk *m* artyleryjski; szkielet *m* (*budynku, też fig.*); 2. łuskać; obierać ⟨obrać⟩; *mil.* ostrzeliwać ⟨-lać⟩; '**~·fire** ostrzał *m* artyleryjski; '**~·fish** *zo.* (*pl.* **-fish**) skorupiak *m*

shel·ter ['ʃeltə] 1. schronienie *n*; *mil.* schron *m*, bunkier *m*; (*na przystanku*) wiata *f*; osłona *f*; **run for~** ⟨po⟩szukać schronienia; **take ~** ⟨s⟩chronić się (**under** *pod I*); 2. *v/t.* osłaniać ⟨-łonić⟩ (**from** *przed I*); *v/i.* ⟨s⟩chronić się

shelve [ʃelv] *v/t.* *książki* ustawiać ⟨-wić⟩; *fig. plan* odkładać ⟨odłożyć⟩ na półkę, zaniechać; *v/i.* opadać ⟨opaść⟩

shelves [ʃelvz] *pl. od* **shelf**

she·nan·i·gans [ʃɪ'nænɪɡənz] F *pl.* nonsens *m*; manipulacje *pl.*

shep·herd ['ʃepəd] 1. pasterz *m*; 2. ⟨po⟩prowadzić

sher·iff ['ʃerɪf] *Am.* szeryf *m*

Shet·land Is·lands *pl.* Szetlandy *pl.*

shield [ʃiːld] 1. tarcza *f*; osłona *f*; *tech.* ekran *m*; 2. osłaniać ⟨-łonić⟩ (**from** *przed I*); ekranować

shift [ʃɪft] 1. *v/t.* coś przesuwać ⟨-sunąć⟩, przemieszczać ⟨-mieścić⟩; *winę itp.* przerzucać ⟨-cić⟩ (**on**(**to**) *na A*); *koszt itp.* przenosić ⟨-nieść⟩; *plamy* usuwać ⟨usunąć⟩; **~ *gear*(*s*)** *zwł. Am. mot.* zmieniać ⟨-nić⟩ bieg(i); *v/i.* przesuwać ⟨-sunąć⟩ się; *wiatr*: zmieniać ⟨-nić⟩ się; *Am.* zmieniać ⟨-nić⟩ bieg(i) ((**in**)**to** *na A*); **~ *from one foot to another*** przestępować z nogi na nogę; **~ *on one's chair*** kręcić się na krześle; *fig.* przesunięcie *n*, zmiana *f*; *econ.* zmiana *f* (*pracowników, czasu*); '**~ key** klawisz *m* "shift" (*zmieniający małe litery na duże*); '**~ work·er** pracownik *m* (**-nica** *f*) zmianowy (**-wa**); **~·y** (**-ier, -iest**) F *oczy*: rozbiegany; kombinatorski

shil·ling ['ʃɪlɪŋ] *Brt. hist.* szyling *m*

shim·mer ['ʃɪmə] ⟨za⟩migotać; *powietrze*: drgać

shin [ʃɪn] 1. *też* **~bone** *anat.* goleń *f*; 2. (**-nn-**): **~ up** wspinać ⟨-piąć⟩ się na (*A*) (*drzewo*)

shine [ʃaɪn] 1. *v/i.* (**shone**) błyszczeć ⟨błysnąć⟩; świecić (się); *v/t.* (**shined**) *buty* ⟨wy⟩polerować, ⟨wy⟩glansować; 2. połysk *m*

shin·gle[1] ['ʃɪŋɡl] otoczak *m*, kamień *m*

shin·gle[2] ['ʃɪŋɡl] gont *m* (*na dachu*)

shin·gles ['ʃɪŋɡlz] *med. sg.* półpasiec *m*

shin·y ['ʃaɪnɪ] (**-ier, -iest**) błyszczący, wyglansowany

ship [ʃɪp] 1. statek *m*, okręt *m*; 2. (**-pp-**) przewozić ⟨-wieźć⟩ drogą morską; przesyłać ⟨-słać⟩; ⟨prze⟩transportować; '**~·board: on ~board** na pokładzie; '**~·ment** przesyłka *f*; '**~·own·er** właściciel(ka *f*) statku; '**~·ping** handlowa żegluga *f*; flota *f* (*danego kraju*); przesyłka *f*, ekspedycja *f*; '**~·wreck** rozbicie *n* statku; wrak *m* statku; '**~·wrecked** 1.

be **~wrecked** przejść rozbicie statku; **2.** ocalały z katastrofy morskiej; '**~·yard** stocznia *f*

shire ['ʃaɪə, ʃə] *w złoż., przest.* hrabstwo *n*

shirk [ʃɜːk] uchylać ⟨-lić⟩ się przed (*I*); '**~·er** dekownik *m*, lawirant *m*

shirt [ʃɜːt] koszula *f*; '**~·sleeve 1.** rękaw *m* (*koszuli*); **in** (*one's*) **~s** w samej koszuli; **2.** w (*samej*) koszuli

shit [ʃɪt] V **1.** gówno *n* (*też fig.*); **2.** (*-tt-*, *shit lub shat*) srać

shiv·er ['ʃɪvə] **1.** ⟨za⟩drżeć (*with* z *G*); **2.** drżenie *n*; **~s** *pl.* F dreszcze *pl.*

shoal¹ [ʃəʊl] mielizna *f*, płycizna *f*
shoal² [ʃəʊl] ławica *f*

shock¹ [ʃɒk] **1.** szok *m*; wstrząs *m*; uderzenie *n*; porażenie *n* (*prądem*); **2.** wstrząsać ⟨-snąć⟩; ⟨za⟩szokować; porażać ⟨-razić⟩ (*prądem*)

shock² [ʃɒk] (*~ of hair*) czupryna *f*, szopa *f* (*włosów*)

'**shock**| **ab·sorb·er** *tech.* amortyzator *m*; '**~·ing** szokujący

shod [ʃɒd] *pret. i p.p. od* **shoe** 2

shod·dy ['ʃɒdɪ] (*-ier*, *-iest*) niskiej jakości; podły

shoe [ʃuː] **1.** but *m*; podkowa *f*; **2.** (*shod*) *konia* podkuwać ⟨-kuć⟩; '**~·horn** łyżka *f* do butów; '**~·lace** sznurowadło *n*; '**~·mak·er** szewc *m*; '**~·shine boy** czyścibut *m*; '**~·shine boy** czyścibut *m*; '**~·string** sznurowadło *n*

shone [ʃɒn, *Am.* ʃəʊn] *pret. i p.p. od* **shine** 1

shook [ʃʊk] *pret. od* **shake** 1

shoot [ʃuːt] **1.** (*shot*) *v/t.* zastrzelić; zabijać ⟨-bić⟩ (*strzelając*); rozstrzelać; postrzelić; wystrzelić; strzelać ⟨-lić⟩ z (*G*); *hunt.* polować na (*A*); *kogoś* ⟨s⟩fotografować; *film* ⟨na⟩kręcić; *pytanie*, *spojrzenie* miotać; *narkotyk* wstrzykiwać ⟨-knąć⟩; **~ the lights** przejechać na czerwonym świetle; *v/i.* strzelać ⟨-lić⟩ (*at* do *G*); polować; przemykać ⟨-mknąć⟩; ⟨s⟩fotografować; *bot.* ⟨za-, wy⟩kiełkować; wyrastać ⟨-rosnąć⟩; **2.** *bot.* kiełek *m*; pęd *m*; polowanie *n*; teren *m* myśliwski; '**~·er** *zwł. Brt. sl.* (*broń*) gnat *m*

'**shoot·ing 1.** strzelanie *n*, strzelanina *f*; postrzelenie *n*; zastrzelenie *n*; polowanie *n*; kręcenie *n* (*filmu*, *programu*), filmowanie *n*; **2.** ból rwący; '**~ gal·le·ry**

(*pomieszczenie*) strzelnica *f*; '**~ range** (*teren*) strzelnica *f*; '**~ star** spadająca gwiazda *f*

shop [ʃɒp] **1.** sklep *m*; zakład *m*; warsztat *m*; **talk** ~ rozmawiać na tematy zawodowe; **2.** (*-pp-*): *zw.* **go ~ping** chodzić ⟨iść⟩ na zakupy; **~ as·sis·tant** ekspedient(ka *f*) *m*; '**~·keep·er** sklepikarz *m* (*-rka f*); '**~·lift·er** *sklepowy* (*-a*) złodziej(ka *f*) *m*; '**~·lift·ing** kradzież *f* w sklepie; '**~·per** klient(ka *f*) *m*, kupujący *m* (*-ca f*)

'**shop·ping** ['ʃɒpɪŋ] **1.** kupowanie *n*; zakupy *pl.*; **do one's** ~ robić zakupy; **2.** handlowy; na zakupy; '**~ bag** torba *f* na zakupy; '**~ cart** (*w sklepie*) wózek *m*; '**~ cen·tre** *Brt.*, (*Am. center*) centrum *f* handlowe; '**~ list** lista *f* zakupów; '**~ mall** *Am.* centrum *f* handlowe; '**~ street** ulica *f* handlowa

shop| '**stew·ard** mąż *m* zaufania; '**~·walk·er** *Brt.* osoba *f* oglądająca towary; '**~ win·dow** witryna *f*, wystawa *f*, okno *n* wystawowe

shore¹ [ʃɔː] brzeg *m*; wybrzeże *n*; **on** ~ na lądzie; *attr.* brzegowy, przybrzeżny

shore² [ʃɔː]: **~ up** podeprzeć ⟨-dpierać⟩

shorn [ʃɔːn] *p.p. od* **shear** 1

short [ʃɔːt] **1.** *adj.* krótki; *ktoś*: niski; skrócony; opryskliwy (*with* wobec *G*); *ciasto*: kruchy; **be~for** być skrótem (*G*); **be~of** ... nie mieć wystarczająco ...; **2.** *adv.* nagle; **~of** z wyjątkiem (*G*); **cut** ~ przerywać ⟨-rwać⟩ nagle; **fall~of** nie osiągać ⟨-gnąć⟩ (*G*); **stop~** przerywać ⟨-rwać⟩ nagle; **stop~of** powstrzymywać się przed (*I*); **~run 1.; 3.** F krótkometrażówka *f*; *electr.* spięcie *n*; **for~** w skrócie; **in~** w skrócie; '**~·age** ['ʃɔːtɪdʒ] niedostatek *m*, niedobór *m*, brak *m*; '**~·com·ings** *pl.* niedostatki *pl.*, braki *pl.*; '**~ cut** skrót *m*; **take a~cut** iść ⟨pójść⟩ na skróty; '**~·en** ['ʃɔːtn] *v/t.* skracać ⟨skrócić⟩; *v/i.* ⟨s⟩kurczyć się

short·en·ing ['ʃɔːtnɪŋ] tłuszcz *m* do pieczenia

'**short**| **hand** stenografia *f*; **~·hand 'typ·ist** stenografista *m* (*-tka f*); '**~·ly** niebawem, wkrótce; opryskliwie; lakonicznie; **~s** *pl.* też **a pair of ~s** szorty *pl.*; *zwł. Am.* krótkie kalesony; '**~·sight·ed** krótkowzroczny; '**~·sto·ry** opowiadanie *n*, nowela *f*; **~'term** *econ.* krótkoterminowy; **~ 'time** *econ.* niepeł-

S

ny wymiar *m* (*pracy*); ~ **'wave** *zw.* fale *pl.* krótkie; ~**'wind·ed** łatwo tracący oddech

shot [ʃɒt] **1.** *pret. i p.p. od* **shoot** 1; **2.** strzał *m*, wystrzał *m*; śrut *m*; śrucina *f*; kula *f*; strzelec *m*; (*w tenisie, golfie*) uderzenie *n*; (*w fotografii, filmie, TV*) F zdjęcie *n*, ujęcie *n*; *med.* F zastrzyk *m*; *fig.* F próba *f*; ~ **in the dark** strzał *m* na oślep; **I'll have a ~ at it** spróbuję jednak; **not by a long ~** *zwł. Am.* F nic takie nie; → **big shot**; ~**'·gun** strzelba *f*; ~**·gun 'wed·ding** F przyspieszone małżeństwo *n*; ~ **put** *sport*: pchnięcie *n* kulą; '~ **put·ter** *sport*: miotacz *m* kulą

should [ʃʊd] *pret. od* **shall**

shoul·der ['ʃəʊldə] **1.** ramię *n* (*też fig.*), bark *m*; *Am. mot.* pobocze *n* utwardzone; **2.** brać (*wziąć*) na ramię; *koszty itp.* brać (*wziąć*) na *swoje* barki; '~ **bag** torba *f* na ramię; '~ **blade** *anat.* łopatka *f*; '~ **strap** ramiączko *n*; pasek *m* (*torby*)

shout [ʃaʊt] **1.** *v/i.* krzyczeć (**to** do *G*, **at** na *A*); wołać (**for** o *A*); **2.** *v/t.* krzyczeć, wykrzykiwać ⟨-rzyczeć⟩; **2.** krzyk *m*; wołanie *n*

shove [ʃʌv] **1.** pchać ⟨pchnąć⟩; *coś* wpychać ⟨wepchnąć⟩; **2.** pchnięcie *n*, popchnięcie *n*; wepchnięcie *n*

shov·el ['ʃʌvl] **1.** łopata *f*, szufla *f*; **2.** (*zwł. Brt. -ll-, Am. -l-*) zgarniać ⟨-nąć⟩; ⟨s⟩kopać

show [ʃəʊ] **1.** (**showed, shown** *lub* **showed**) *v/t.* pokazywać ⟨-zać⟩; ukazywać ⟨-zać⟩; okazywać ⟨-zać⟩; (*w galerii*) wystawiać ⟨-wić⟩; ⟨za⟩prowadzić (**to** do *G*); *v/i.* być widocznym; **be ~ing**: iść; być wyświetlanym; ~ **around** oprowadzać ⟨-dzić⟩; ~ **in** wprowadzać ⟨-dzić⟩; ~ **off** popisywać ⟨-sać⟩ się (*I*); ⟨po⟩chwalić się (*I*); ~ **out** wyprowadzać ⟨-dzić⟩; ~ **round** oprowadzać ⟨-dzić⟩; ~ **up** *v/t.* wykazywać ⟨-zać⟩; *odsłaniać* ⟨-łonić⟩; kłopotać, przynosić ⟨-nieść⟩ *komuś* wstyd; **2.** być widocznym; F zjawiać ⟨-wić⟩ się; **2.** *theat.* przedstawienie *n*, spektakl *m*; show *m*; seans *m*; pokaz *m*; wystawa *f*; pozór *m*, pretekst *m*; **be on ~** być pokazywanym; **steal the ~** przyćmić wszystkich; **make a ~ of** ⟨za⟩demonstrować (*A*); **put up a poor ~** F nie popisać się; **be in charge of the ~** F kierować interesem; **3.** wzorcowy; ~ **flat** mieszkanie *n* wzorcowe;

'~**·biz** F, '~ **busi·ness** show-biznes *m*; '~**·case** witryna *f*, okno *n* wystawowe; '~**·down** ostateczna rozgrywka *f*

show·er ['ʃaʊə] **1.** przelotny opad *m*; *fig.* grad *m*, deszcz *m*; prysznic *m*, natrysk *m*; **have** *lub* **take a ~** brać ⟨wziąć⟩ prysznic; **2.** *v/t.* *kogoś* zasypywać ⟨-pać⟩ (*I*); opryskiwać ⟨-kać⟩ (*I*); *v/i.* brać⟨wziąć⟩ prysznic; padać; ~**·down** opadać ⟨opaść⟩

'show jump·er (*w sporcie*) jeździec *m*; '~ **jump·ing** (*w sporcie*) konkurs *m* hippiczny; ~**n** [ʃəʊn] *p.p. od* **show** 1; '~**·off** F pokaz *m*; popis *m*; ~-room salon *f* wystawowy; '~**·y** (**-ier, -iest**) krzykliwy, wyzywający

shrank [ʃræŋk] *pret. od* **shrink**

shred [ʃred] **1.** strzęp *m*; *fig.* odrobina *f*; **2.** (**-dd-**) ⟨po⟩drzeć (*na strzępy*); *gastr.* ⟨po⟩szatkować; *dokumenty* ⟨z⟩niszczyć; '~**·der** niszczarka *f*; szatkownica *f*

shrew [ʃruː] *zo.* ryjówka *f*; sekutnica *f*, jędza *f*

shrewd [ʃruːd] chytry, sprytny

shriek [ʃriːk] **1.** wykrzykiwać ⟨-knąć⟩, zakrzyczeć ⟨-knąć⟩; ~ **with laughter** ⟨za⟩rechotać ze śmiechu; **2.** przenikliwy krzyk *m*

shrill [ʃrɪl] ostry (*też fig.*)

shrimp [ʃrɪmp] *zo.* krewetka *f*; F karzełek *m*

shrine [ʃraɪn] sanktuarium *n*, przybytek *m* świąty

shrink [ʃrɪŋk] **1.** (**shrank, shrunk**) ⟨s⟩kurczyć się; *tkanina itp.* zbiegać ⟨zbiec⟩ się; zmniejszać ⟨-szyć⟩ się; **2.** F (*psychiatra*) lekarz *m* od czubków; ~**·age** ['ʃrɪŋkɪdʒ] (s)kurczenie *n* się, zbiegnięcie *n* się, zmniejszenie *n* się; ubytek *m*; '~**·wrap** (**-pp-**) pakować w folię

shriv·el ['ʃrɪvl] (*zwł. Brt. -ll-, Am. -l-*) wysuszać ⟨-suszyć⟩; zsychać ⟨zeschnąć⟩ (się)

shroud [ʃraʊd] **1.** całun *m*; **2.** *fig.* okrywać ⟨-ryć⟩

Shrove Tues·day [ʃrəʊv 'tjuːzdɪ] ostatki *pl.*

shrub [ʃrʌb] krzew *m*; ~**·be·ry** ['ʃrʌbərɪ] krzewy *pl.*

shrug [ʃrʌg] **1.** (**-gg-**) *też* ~ **one's shoulders** wzruszać ⟨-szyć⟩ ramionami; **2.** wzruszenie *n* (*ramion*)

shrunk [ʃrʌŋk] *p.p. od* **shrink** 1

shuck *zwł. Am.* [ʃʌk] **1.** łuska *f*, łupina *f*; **2.** łuskać, obierać ⟨-brać⟩

shud·der ['ʃʌdə] **1.** *v/i.* wzdrygać ⟨-gnąć⟩ się, ⟨za⟩drżeć; **2.** wzdrygnięcie *n*, dreszcz *m*

shuf·fle ['ʃʌfl] **1.** *v/t.* karty ⟨po⟩tasować; *papiery* przekładać ⟨-łożyć⟩; ~ **one's feet** powłóczyć nogami; *v/i.* przekładać ⟨-łożyć⟩; **2.** tasowanie *n* (*kart*)

shun [ʃʌn] (*-nn-*) odrzucać ⟨-cić⟩, unikać ⟨-knąć⟩

shunt [ʃʌnt] *pociąg itp.* przetaczać ⟨-toczyć⟩, manewrować; *też* ~ **off** F *kogoś* odstawiać ⟨-wić⟩ na bok

shut [ʃʌt] (*-tt-*; **shut**) zamykać ⟨-mknąć⟩; ~ **down** zamykać ⟨-mknąć⟩ *fabrykę itp.*; ~ **off** *wodę, gaz itp.* odcinać ⟨-ciąć⟩; *maszynę* wyłączać ⟨-czyć⟩; ~ **up** zamykać ⟨-mknąć⟩ się; zamykać ⟨-mknąć⟩ (*w pokoju, itp., zakład*); ~ **up!** zamknij się!; '**~·ter** okiennica *f*; *phot.* migawka *f*; '**~·ter speed** *phot.* czas *m* naświetlania

shut·tle ['ʃʌtl] **1.** samolot *m*, autobus *m itp.*, wahadłowy; *prom m* kosmiczny, wahadłowiec *m*; *tech.* czółenko *n*; **2.** kursować tam i z powrotem; '**~·cock** (*w sporcie*) lotka *f*; ~ **di·plo·ma·cy** *pol.* dyplomacja *f* wahadłowa; ~ **ser·vice** połączenie *n* wahadłowe

shy [ʃaɪ] **1.** nieśmiały; lękliwy, płochliwy; **2.** ⟨s⟩płoszyć się (*zwł. koń*); ~ **away from** *fig.* wycofywać ⟨-fać⟩ się; '**~·ness** nieśmiałość *f*, płochliwość *f*

Si·be·ri·a Syberia *f*

Sic·i·ly Sycylia *f*

sick [sɪk] **1.** chory; *be* ~ *zwł. Brt.* ⟨z⟩wymiotować; *she was lub felt* ~ ⟨po⟩czuła się źle; *fall* ~ zachorować; *be off* ~ być na zwolnieniu, F być na chorobowym; *report* ~ zgłaszać, że się jest chorym; *be* ~ *of s.th.* F mieć czegoś serdecznie dość; *it makes me* ~ F niedobrze mi się od tego robi; **2.** *the* ~ *pl.* chorzy *pl.*; ~*en* *v/t.* napełniać ⟨-nić⟩ obrzydzeniem, przyprawiać ⟨-wić⟩ *kogoś* o mdłości; *v/i.* ⟨za⟩chorować

sick·le ['sɪkl] sierp *m*

'**sick| leave**: *be on* ~ *leave* być na zwolnieniu, F być na chorobowym; '**~·ly** (*-ier, -iest*) chorobliwy; chorowity; *zapach*: mdlący; '**~·ness** choroba *f*;

mdłości *pl.*; '**~·ness ben·e·fit** *Brt.* zasiłek *m* chorobowy

side [saɪd] **1.** strona *f*; bok *m*; *zwł. Brt.* zespół *m*; stok *m*; ~ **by** ~ obok siebie; *take* ~ **s with s.o.** stawać ⟨stanąć⟩ po czyjejś stronie; **2.** *boczny*; *efekt*: uboczny; **3.** ~ **with s.o.** stawać ⟨stanąć⟩ po czyjejś stronie; '**~·board** (*kredens*) pomocnik *m*; '**~·car** *mot.* boczny wózek *m* (*motocykla*); ~ **dish** *gastr.* przystawka *f*; '**~·long** z boku, boczny; '~ **street** ulica *f* boczna; '**~·stroke** (*w sporcie*) pływanie *n* na boku; '**~·track** zbaczać ⟨zboczyć⟩ z tematu; *Am. pociąg* przetaczać ⟨-toczyć⟩, manewrować; '**~·walk** *zwł. Am.* chodnik *m*; '**~·ways** z boku; bokiem; na bok

sid·ing ['saɪdɪŋ] *rail.* bocznica *f*

si·dle ['saɪdl]: ~ **up to s.o.** przysuwać ⟨-unąć⟩ się do kogoś

siege [siːdʒ] oblężenie *n*; *lay* ~ *to* oblegać ⟨-ec⟩ (*A*)

sieve [sɪv] **1.** sito *n*; **2.** ⟨prze⟩siewać ⟨-siać⟩

sift [sɪft] ⟨prze⟩siewać ⟨-siać⟩; *też* ~ **through** *fig.* ⟨prze⟩studiować, przeszukiwać ⟨-kać⟩

sigh [saɪ] **1.** wzdychać ⟨westchnąć⟩; **2.** westchnięcie *n*

sight [saɪt] **1.** wzrok *m*; widok *m*; ~*s pl.* przyrząd *m* celowniczy; wizjer *m*; osobliwość *f*, turystyczna atrakcja *f*; *at* ~, *on* ~ natychmiast; *at* ~ *econ.* za okazaniem; *at the* ~ *of* na widok (*G*); *at first* ~ na pierwszy rzut oka; *catch* ~ *of* ujrzeć (*A*); *know by* ~ znać *kogoś* z widzenia; *lose* ~ *of* ⟨s⟩tracić *kogoś* z oczu; *be (with)in* ~ być w zasięgu wzroku (*też fig.*); **2.** dojrzeć, spostrzegać ⟨-rzec⟩; '**~·ed** widzący; '**~·read** *mus.* czytać a (*prima*) *vista* (*nuty*); '**~·see·ing** zwiedzanie *n*; *go* ~*·seeing* iść ⟨pójść⟩ na zwiedzanie; '**~·see·ing tour** wycieczka *f* (*na zwiedzanie*); '**~·se·er** turysta *m* (*-tka f*)

sign [saɪn] **1.** znak *m*; gest *m*; napis *m*, wywieszka *f*; *fig.* oznaka *f*, objaw *m*; **2.** podpisywać ⟨-sać⟩; ~ **in** wpisywać ⟨-sać⟩ się; ~ **out** wypisywać ⟨-sać⟩ się

sig·nal ['sɪgnl] **1.** sygnał *m* (*też fig.*); sygnalizator *m*; znak *m* (*też fig.*); **2.** (*zwł. Brt. -ll-, Am. -l-*) ⟨za⟩sygnalizować; dawać ⟨-dać⟩ sygnał(y) (*D*)

sig·na·to·ry ['sɪgnətərɪ] sygnatariusz *m*

S

sig·na·ture ['sɪgnətʃə] podpis *m*; '~ **tune** *radio*, *TV*: sygnał (*muzyczny*) *m* audycji (*radiowej lub telewizyjnej*)

'**sign|·board** szyld *m*; '~·**er** niżej podpisany *m* (-na *f*)

sig·net ring ['sɪgnɪt] sygnet *m*

sig·nif·i|·cance [sɪg'nɪfɪkəns] znaczenie *n*; doniosłość *f*; ~·**cant** znaczący, ważny, doniosły

sig·ni·fy ['sɪgnɪfaɪ] oznaczać, znaczyć

'**sign·post** drogowskaz *m*

si·lence ['saɪləns] **1.** cisza *f*; spokój *m*; ~! spokój!; *in* ~ w milczeniu; *reduce to* ~ kogoś uciszać ⟨-szyć⟩ **2.** uciszać ⟨-szyć⟩; '**si·lenc·er** *tech.* tłumik *m*

si·lent ['saɪlənt] cichy; milczący; bezgłośny; *film*: niemy; ~ *partner* cichy (-a) wspólnik *m* (-iczka *f*)

Si·le·sia Śląsk *m*

sil·i|·con ['sɪlɪkən] *chem.* krzem *m*; *attr.* krzemowy; ~·**cone** ['sɪlɪkəʊn] *chem.* silikon *m*; *attr.* silikonowy

silk [sɪlk] jedwab *m*; *attr.* jedwabny; '~·**worm** *zo.* jedwabnik *m*; '~·**y** (*-ier*, *-iest*) jedwabny; jedwabisty

sill [sɪl] parapet *m* (*okienny*)

sil·ly ['sɪlɪ] (*-ier*, *-iest*) głupi; **2.** głuptas *m*

sil·ver ['sɪlvə] **1.** *chem.* srebro; **2.** srebrny; **3.** ⟨po⟩srebrzyć; '~·**plat·ed** posrebrzany; '~·**ware** naczynia *pl.* ze srebra; ~·**y** ['sɪlvərɪ] *fig.* srebrzysty

sim·i·lar ['sɪmɪlə] podobny (*to* do *G*); ~·**i·ty** [sɪmɪ'lærətɪ] podobieństwo *n*

sim·i·le ['sɪmɪlɪ] porównanie *n*

sim·mer ['sɪmə] ⟨u⟩gotować (się) na wolnym ogniu; ~ *with fig.* kipieć z (*złości itp.*); ~ *down* F ochłonąć

sim·per ['sɪmpə] uśmiechać ⟨-chnąć⟩ się głupawo

sim·ple ['sɪmpl] (*-r*, *-st*) prosty, nieskomplikowany; naiwny; ~·'**mind·ed** naiwny

sim·pli|·ci·ty [sɪm'plɪsətɪ] prostota *f*; naiwność *f*; ~·**fi·ca·tion** [sɪmplɪfɪ'keɪʃn] uproszczenie *n*; ~·**fy** ['sɪmplɪfaɪ] upraszczać ⟨-rościć⟩

sim·ply ['sɪmplɪ] po prostu; prosto

sim·u·late ['sɪmjoleɪt] naśladować; *mil.*, *tech.* przeprowadzać ⟨-dzić⟩ symulację

sim·ul·ta·ne·ous [sɪməl'teɪnjəs] równoczesny, jednoczesny

sin [sɪn] **1.** grzech *m*; **2.** (*-nn-*) ⟨z⟩grzeszyć

since [sɪns] **1.** *adv.* też *ever* ~ od tego czasu; **2.** *prp.* od (*G*); **3.** *cj.* ponieważ; odkąd

sin·cere [sɪn'sɪə] szczery; *Yours* ~*ly*, ♀ *yours* Z poważaniem (*w zakończeniu listu*); **sin·cer·i·ty** [sɪn'serətɪ] szczerość *f*

sin·ew ['sɪnjuː] *anat.* ścięgno *n*; '~·*y* mięso: żylasty; *fig.* muskularny

'**sin·ful** grzeszny

sing [sɪŋ] (*sang, sung*) ⟨za⟩śpiewać; ~ *s.th. to s.o.* zaśpiewać coś komuś

singe [sɪndʒ] przypalać ⟨-lić⟩ (się)

sing|·er ['sɪŋə] śpiewak *m* (-aczka *f*); pieśniarz *m* (-arka *f*); ~·**ing** ['sɪŋɪŋ] śpiewanie *n*

sin·gle ['sɪŋgl] **1.** pojedynczy; jeden; *in file* gęsiego; **2.** *Brt.* bilet *m* w jedną stronę (*też* ~ *ticket*); (*płyta*) singel *m*; osoba *f* stanu wolnego; **3.** ~ *out* wyróżniać ⟨-nić⟩, wybierać ⟨-brać⟩; ~·'**breast·ed** *marynarka*: jednorzędowy; ~·'**en·gined** *aviat.* jednosilnikowy; ~ *entry econ.* pojedynczy zapis *m*; ~ *fam·i·ly* '*home* dom *m* jednorodzinny; ~·'*fa·ther* samotny ojciec *m*; ~·'**hand·ed** samotnie, samodzielnie; ~·'**lane** *mot.* jednopasmowy; ~·'**mind·ed** silnie zdeterminowany; ~ '*moth·er* samotna matka *f*; ~·'*pa·rent* samotny rodzic *m*; ~ '*room* pojedynczy pokój *m*; '~·*s sg.* (*zwł. w tenisie*) gra *f* pojedyncza, gra *f* singlowa

sin·glet ['sɪŋglɪt] *Brt.* podkoszulek *m*

'**sin·gle-track** jednotorowy, jednopasmowy

sin·gu·lar ['sɪŋgjolə] **1.** wyjątkowy, jedyny; **2.** *gr.* liczba *f* pojedyncza

sin·is·ter ['sɪnɪstə] złowieszczy; złowrogi

sink [sɪŋk] **1.** (*sank, sunk*) *v/i.* ⟨za-, u⟩tonąć; opadać ⟨-paść⟩; *wartość*: spadać ⟨spaść⟩; pogrążać ⟨-żyć⟩ się; ~ *in* docierać ⟨dotrzeć⟩ do (*G*); *v/t.* ⟨za⟩topić; *studnię* ⟨wy⟩wiercić, ⟨wy⟩kopać; *obniżać* ⟨-żyć⟩; *pieniądze* ⟨w⟩pakować; *zęby* zatapiać ⟨-topić⟩ (*into* w *A*); **2.** zlew *m*, zlewozmywak *m*; *Am.* umywalka *f*

sin·ner ['sɪnə] grzesznik *m* (-ica *f*)

Sioux [suː] (*pl. Sioux* [suːz]) Siuks *m*

sip [sɪp] **1.** łyk *m*; **2.** (*-pp-*) *napój itp.* sączyć, popijać

sir [sɜː] pan (*przy zwracaniu się*); (*w li-*

ście) Dear ♀ Szanowny Panie; ♀ *Brt. (tytuł szlachecki)* sir *m*

sire ['saɪə] ojciec

si·ren ['saɪərən] syrena *f*

sir·loin ['sɜːlɔɪn] *gastr.*: ~ '**steak** pieczeń *f* z polędwicy

sis·sy ['sɪsɪ] F baba *f*, maminsynek *m*

sis·ter ['sɪstə] siostra *f* (*też rel.*); *Brt. med.* siostra *f*, pielęgniarka *f*; ~**-in-law** ['sɪstərɪnlɔː] (*pl. sisters-in-law*) szwagierka *f*; '~·**ly** siostrzany

sit [sɪt] (*-tt-*; sat) *v/i.* siedzieć ⟨siąść⟩; siadać ⟨usiąść⟩; *komisja itp.*: obradować ⟨książka, wioska, garnitur itp.*: leżeć; *v/t. kogoś* sadzać ⟨posadzić⟩; *zwł. Brt. egzamin* zdawać; ~ *down* siadać ⟨usiąść⟩; ~ *for Brt.* pozować do (*G*); *egzamin* zdawać; ~ *in for* zastępować ⟨-tąpić⟩; ~ *in on* uczestniczyć w (*L*); ~ *on w komisji* zasiadać⟨-siąść⟩; ~ *out taniec* przesiedzieć; dotrwać do końca; *kryzys* przeczekiwać ⟨-kać⟩; ~ *up* prosto siadać ⟨siąść⟩; (*w łóżku itp.*) sadzać ⟨posadzić⟩; nie kłaść się spać

sit·com ['sɪtkɒm] → *situation comedy*

'**sit-down** *też* ~ *strike* strajk *m* okupacyjny; ~ *demonstration* blokada *f* (*przez siedzących ludzi*)

site [saɪt] miejsce *n*; teren *m* (*wykopalisk itp.*); plac *m* budowy

'**sit-in** strajk *m* okupacyjny

sit·ting ['sɪtɪŋ] sesja *f*; tura *f* (*przy stole*); *in a single* ~ nie wstając; '~ *room zwł. Brt.* pokój *m* dzienny

sit·u·at·ed ['sɪtjʊeɪtɪd]: *be* ~ być położonym

sit·u·a·tion [sɪtjʊ'eɪʃn] sytuacja *f*; położenie *n*; posada *f*, praca *f*; ~ '**com·e·dy** komedia *f* sytuacyjna, sitcom *m* (*seria odcinków komediowych o tych samych postaciach*)

six [sɪks] **1.** sześć; **2.** szóstka *f*; ~·**teen** [sɪks'tiːn] **1.** szesnaście; **2.** szesnastka *f*; ~·**teenth** [sɪks'tiːnθ] szesnasty; ~·**th** [sɪksθ] **1.** szósty; **2.** jedna *f* szósta; '~·**th·ly** po szóste; ~·**ti·eth** ['sɪkstɪɪθ] sześćdziesiąty; ~·**ty** ['sɪkstɪ] **1.** sześćdziesiąt; **2.** sześćdziesiątka *f*

size [saɪz] **1.** rozmiar *m*; wielkość *f*; wymiar *m*, format *m*; **2.** ~ *up* F oceniać ⟨-nić⟩, ⟨z⟩mierzyć (*wzrokiem*)

siz(e)·a·ble ['saɪzəbl] duży

siz·zle ['sɪzl] ⟨za⟩skwierczeć

skate[1] [skeɪt] **1.** łyżwa *f*; łyżworolka *f*;

wrotka *f*; **2.** ślizgać się (*na łyżwach*); jeździć na wrotkach; '~·**board** skateboard *m*; '**skat·er** łyżwiarz *m* (-arka *f*), wrotkarz *m* (-arka *f*)

skate[2] [skeɪt] *zo.* płaszczka *f*, raja *f*

skat·ing ['skeɪtɪŋ] łyżwiarstwo *n*; wrotkarstwo *n*; *free* ~ jazda *f* dowolna na łyżwach; '~ *rink* lodowisko *n*; tor *m* wrotkarski

skel·e·ton ['skelɪtn] szkielet *m* (*też konstrukcji*); szkic *m*, plan *m*; '~**key** klucz *m* główny (*do wszystkich drzwi budynku*)

skep·tic ['skeptɪk] *itp. zwł. Am.* → *sceptic*

sketch [sketʃ] **1.** szkic *m*; *theat. itp.* skecz *m*; **2.** ⟨na⟩szkicować

ski [skiː] **1.** narta *f*; *attr.* narciarski; **2.** jeździć na nartach

skid [skɪd] **1.** (*-dd-*) *mot.* wpadać ⟨wpaść⟩ w poślizg; **2.** *mot.* poślizg *m*; *aviat.* płoza *f*; '~ *mark(s pl.)* *mot.* ślady *pl.* poślizgu

ski·er ['skiːə] narciarz *m* (-arka *f*); '~·**ing** narciarstwo *n*; '~ *jump* skocznia *f*; '~ *jump·er* (*w sporcie*) skoczek *m*; '~ *jump·ing* (*w sporcie*) skoki *pl.* narciarskie

skil·ful ['skɪlfl] zręczny, wprawny

'**ski lift** wyciąg *m* narciarski

skill [skɪl] umiejętność *f*, wprawa *f*, zręczność *f*; ~**ed** wprawny; wykwalifikowany (*at, in* w *L*); ~**ed** '**work·er** pracownik *m* wykwalifikowany

'**skill·ful** *Am.* → *skilful*

skim [skɪm] (*-mm-*) *tłuszcz itp.* zbierać ⟨zebrać⟩ (*też* ~ *off*); *mleko* odtłuszczać ⟨-łuścić⟩; *też* ~ *over*, ~ *through* przebiegać ⟨-biec⟩ wzrokiem; ślizgać się nad (*I*); ~(med) '**milk** mleko *n* odtłuszczone

skimp [skɪmp] *też* ~ *on* skąpić (*G*); '~·**y** (*-ier, -iest*) skąpy

skin [skɪn] **1.** skóra *f*; łupina *f* (*owocu*); kożuch *m* (*na mleku itp.*); **2.** (*-nn-*) *zwierzę* oskórować, obdzierać ⟨obedrzeć⟩ ze skóry; *łupinę* zdejmować ⟨zdjąć⟩, obierać ⟨obrać⟩; *kolano itp.* otrzeć; '~·**deep** powierzchowny; '~·**dive** nurkować swobodnie; '~ *div·ing swobodne* nurkowanie *n*; '~·**flint** sknera *f/m*; '~·**ny** (*-ier, -iest*) kościsty, chudy; '~·**ny-dip** F ⟨wy⟩kąpać się nago

skip [skɪp] **1.** (*-pp-*) *v/i.* podskakiwać; skakać, przeskakiwać; uciekać ⟨-ciec⟩; skakać przez skakankę; *v/t.* opuszczać

⟨-uścić⟩, pomijać ⟨-minąć⟩; **2.** podskok *n*; '**~p·ing rope** *Brt.* skakanka *f*

skip·per ['skɪpə] *naut.*, kapitan *m* (*drużyny sportowej*)

skir·mish ['skɜːmɪʃ] potyczka *f*; scysja *f*

skirt [skɜːt] **1.** spódnica *f*, spódniczka *f*; **2.** *też* **~ (a)round** obchodzić ⟨-bejść⟩; *fig. problem itp.*: unikać; '**~·ing board** *Brt.* listwa *f* przypodłogowa

'**ski| run** nartostrada *f*; '**~ tow** wyciąg *m* orczykowy

skit·tle ['skɪtl] kręgiel *m*

skulk [skʌlk] ⟨s⟩kryć się

skull [skʌl] *anat.* czaszka *f*

skul(l)·dug·ge·ry [skʌl'dʌgərɪ] F kombinatorstwo *n*

skunk [skʌŋk] *zo.* skunks *m*

sky [skaɪ] *też* **skies** *pl.* niebo *n*; '**~·jack** *samolot* porywać ⟨-rwać⟩; '**~·jack·er** porywacz(ka *f*) *m*; '**~·lark** *zo.* skowronek *m*; '**~·light** (*okno*) świetlik *m*; '**~·line** sylwetka *f*; linia *f* (*horyzontu*); '**~·rock·et** F (*ceny itp.*) strzelać ⟨-lić⟩ w górę; '**~·scrap·er** drapacz *m* chmur

slab [slæb] *kamienna itp.* płyta *f*; kawał *m* (*ciasta itp.*)

slack [slæk] **1.** zwisający, obwisły; *dyscyplina*: luźny; *econ. popyt*: słaby; *sezon*: martwy; niestaranny; **2.** *też* **~ off** obijać się; '**~·en** *v/t.* zmniejszać ⟨-szyć⟩ (się); ⟨o⟩słabnąć; ⟨po⟩luzować; **~s** *pl. zwł. Am.* F spodnie *pl.*

slag [slæg] żużel *m*

slain [sleɪn] *p.p. od* **slay**

sla·lom ['slɑːləm] (*w sporcie*) slalom *m*

slam [slæm] **1.** (**-mm-**) *też* **~ shut** zatrzaskiwać ⟨-snąć⟩; *też* **~ down** F zwalać ⟨-lić⟩; **~ on the brakes** *mot.* gwałtownie zahamować; **2.** trzaśnięcie *n*; zatrzaśnięcie *n*

slan·der ['slɑːndə] **1.** zniesławienie *n*; potwarz *f*; **2.** zniesławiać ⟨-wić⟩; spotwarzać ⟨-rzyć⟩; **~·ous** ['slɑːndərəs] oszczerczy, zniesławiający

slang [slæŋ] **1.** slang *m*; *gr.* gwara *f* środowiskowa; **2.** *zwł. Brt.* F przeklinać, kląć

slant [slɑːnt] **1.** nachylać ⟨-lić⟩ (się), pochylać ⟨-lić⟩ (się); być stronniczym; **2.** pochyłość *f*; nachylenie *n*; *fig.* perspektywa *f*; **at** *lub* **on a ~** pod kątem, nachylony; '**~·ing** pochyły

slap [slæp] **1.** klaps *m*; **2.** (**-pp-**) klepać ⟨-nąć⟩; dawać ⟨dać⟩ klapsa; zwalić

(***down on*** na *A*); pacnąć; **~·stick** *theat.* slapstick *m*, farsa *f*; '**~·stick com·e·dy** komedia *f* slapstickowa

slash [slæʃ] **1.** ciąć; przecinać ⟨-ciąć⟩; rozcinać ⟨-ciąć⟩; *deszcz*: zacinać (***against*** o *A*); *wydatki* obcinać ⟨-ciąć⟩; **2.** cięcie *n*; nacięcie *n*, rozcięcie *n*

slate [sleɪt] **1.** łupek *m*, *zw.* łupki *pl.*; łupek *m* dachówkowy; *Am. pol.* lista *f* kandydatów; **2.** ⟨po⟩kryć łupkiem; *Am.* wybierać ⟨-brać⟩; *Am.* ⟨za⟩planować

slaugh·ter ['slɔːtə] **1.** rzeź *f* (*też fig.*); masakra *f*; ubój *m*; **2.** ⟨za⟩szlachtować, ubić; urządzać ⟨-dzić⟩ masakrę *lub* rzeź; '**~·house** rzeźnia *f*

Slav [slɑːv] **1.** Słowianin *m* (**-anka** *f*); **2.** słowiański

slave [sleɪv] **1.** niewolnik *m* (**-nica** *f*) (*też fig.*); **2.** *też* **~ away** zaharowywać ⟨-ować⟩ się

slav·er ['slævə] ślinić się

sla·ve·ry ['sleɪvərɪ] niewolnictwo *n* (*też fig.*)

Slavic ['slævɪk] słowiański

slav·ish ['sleɪvɪʃ] niewolniczy

Sla·von·ic [slə'vɒnɪk] słowiański

slay [sleɪ] (**slew**, **slain**) ⟨za⟩mordować, zabijać ⟨-bić⟩

sleaze [sliːz] flejtuch *m*; plugawość *f*; **slea·zy** ['sliːzɪ] odrażający; flejtuchowaty

sled [sled] *Am.* → **sledge**

sledge [sledʒ] **1.** sanie *pl.*, sanki *pl.*; **2.** jeździć saniami, ⟨po⟩jechać saniami

'**sledge·ham·mer** młot *m* dwuręczny

sleek [sliːk] **1.** lśniący, błyszczący; *samochód itp.*: wytworny; **2.** nabłyszczać ⟨-czyć⟩

sleep [sliːp] **1.** sen *m*; **I couldn't get to ~** nie mogłem zasnąć; **go to ~** iść ⟨pójść⟩ spać; *ramię*: ⟨z⟩drętwieć; **put to ~** zwierzę usypiać ⟨uśpić⟩; **2.** (**slept**) *v/i.* spać; **~ late** spać do późna; **~ on** *podjęcie decyzji* przeczekać przez noc; **~ with s.o.** spać z kimś; *v/t.* przenocowywać ⟨-ować⟩; '**~·er** śpiący *m* (**-ca** *f*); *Brt. rail.* podkład *m*; *rail.* wagon *m* sypialny

'**sleep·ing| bag** śpiwór *m*; ♀ '**Beau·ty** Śpiąca Królewna *f*; '**~ car** *rail.* wagon *m* sypialny; '**~·part·ner** *Brt. econ.* cichy (**-a**) wspólnik *m* (**-iczka** *f*)

'**sleep|·less** bezsenny; '**~·walk·er** luna-

tyk *m* (-yczka *f*); '**~∙y** (*-ier, -iest*) śpią-cy; senny

sleet [sli:t] **1.** śnieg *m* z deszczem, chla-pawica *f*, **2.** *it's ~ing* pada deszcz ze śniegiem

sleeve [sli:v] rękaw *m*; *tech.* tuleja *f*; *zwł. Brt.* okładka *f* (*płyty*)

sleigh [sleɪ] sanie *pl.* (*zwł. konne*)

sleight of hand [slaɪt əv 'hænd] zręcz-ny gest *m*; *fig.* trik *m*

slen∙der ['slendə] smukły, wysmukły; szczupły; *fig.* niewielki, znikomy

slept [slept] *pret. i p.p. od* **sleep** 2

sleuth F [slu:θ] detektyw *m*

slew [slu:] *pret. od* **slay**

slice [slaɪs] **1.** plasterek *m*; kromka *f*; kawałek *m* (*tortu*); łopatka *f* (*do nabie-rania*); *fig.* część *f*; **2.** *też ~ up* ⟨po⟩kroić na plasterki *lub* kromki; **~ off** odcinać ⟨-ciąć⟩

slick [slɪk] **1.** gładki; *człowiek:* ulizany; dobrze zrobiony; *droga:* śliski; **2.** F pla-ma *f* ropy naftowej; **3.** *~down* włosy nabłyszczać ⟨-czyć⟩; '**~∙er** *Am.* płaszcz *m* przeciwdeszczowy; F cwaniak *m*

slid [slɪd] *pret. i p.p. od* **slide** 1

slide [slaɪd] **1.** (*slid*) ślizgać się; prześliz-giwać ⟨-gnąć⟩ się; przesuwać ⟨-sunąć⟩; wysuwać ⟨-sunąć⟩ się; spadać ⟨spaść⟩; *let things ~* machnąć na wszystko rę-ką; **2.** zsunięcie *n* się; poślizg *m*; ześlizg *m*; zjazd *m*; spadek *m*; zjeżdżalnia *f*; *phot.* przezrocze *n*, slajd *m*, diapozy-tyw *m*; preparat *m* mikroskopowy; *Brt.* spinka *f* (*do włosów*); *tech.* suwak *m*; '**~ rule** suwak *m* logarytmiczny; '**~∙tack∙le** *piłka nożna:* wślizg *m*

slid∙ing door [slaɪdɪŋ 'dɔ:] przesuwane drzwi *pl.*

slight [slaɪt] **1.** lekki; nieznaczny; drob-ny; **2.** ubliżać ⟨-żyć⟩, znieważać ⟨-żyć⟩; **2.** zniewaga *f*; ubliżenie *n*

slim [slɪm] (*-mm-*) **1.** szczupły; *fig.* mały, niewielki; **2.** *też be ~ming, be on a ~ming diet* odchudzać się

slime [slaɪm] śluz *m*

slim∙y ['slaɪmɪ] (*-ier, -iest*) ośliz(g)ły, śliski (*też fig.*)

sling [slɪŋ] **1.** (*slung*) zawieszać ⟨-sić⟩; F rzucać ⟨-cić⟩, ciskać ⟨-snąć⟩; **2.** tem-blak *m*; proca *f*; pętla *f*; nosidełko *n* (*dla dziecka*)

slink [slɪŋk] (*slunk*) wycofywać ⟨-wać⟩ się

slip¹ [slɪp] **1.** (*-pp-*) *v/i.* pośliz(g)nąć się; wślizgiwać ⟨-z(g)nąć⟩ się, wyślizgiwać ⟨-z(g)nąć⟩ się, pomylić się; spadać ⟨spaść⟩; *v/t.* wsuwać ⟨wsunąć⟩; wysu-wać ⟨-sunąć⟩ się z (*G*); **~ s.th. into s.o.'s hand** wsuwać ⟨wsunąć⟩ coś do czyjejś ręki; **~ s.o.'s attention** umykać ⟨-knąć⟩ czyjejś uwadze; **~ s.o.'s mind** nie przychodzić ⟨-yjść⟩ do głowy; *she has ~ped a disc med.* dysk jej wypadł; **~ by, ~ past** *czas:* przelatywać; **~ off** *ubranie* zrzucać ⟨-cić⟩; **~ on** *ubranie* narzucać ⟨-cić⟩; **2.** poślizgnięcie *n*; po-myłka *f*, błąd *m*; halka *f*; poszewka *f*; **~ of the tongue** lapsus *m*; *give s.o. the ~* F nawiać komuś

slip² [slɪp] *też ~ of paper* kawałek *m* papieru

'**slip**∙**case** pudełko *n* (*na książkę*); '**~∙on 1.** *adj.:* **~-on shoe** nieznurowa-ny but **2.** but *m* niesznurowany; **~ped** '**disc** *med.* wypadnięty dysk *m*; '**~∙per** pantofel *m*, kapeć *m*; **~∙per∙y** ['slɪpərɪ] (*-ier, -iest*) śliski; '**~ road** *Brt.* wjazd *m* (*na autostradę*), zjazd *m* (*z autostrady*); '**~∙shod** byle jaki

slit [slɪt] **1.** nacięcie *n*, rozcięcie *n*; szcze-lina *f*, szpara *f*; **2.** (*-tt-*; *slit*) nacinać ⟨-ciąć⟩; **~ open** rozcinać ⟨-ciąć⟩

slith∙er ['slɪðə] wić się, pełznąć; ślizgać się

sliv∙er ['slɪvə] odłamek *m* (*szkła itp.*); drzazga *f*

slob∙ber ['slɒbə] ślinić się

slo∙gan ['sləʊgən] slogan *m*

sloop [slu:p] *naut.* szalupa *f*

slop [slɒp] **1.** (*-pp-*) *v/t.* rozlewać ⟨-lać⟩; *v/i.* wylewać ⟨-lać⟩ się, przelewać ⟨-lać⟩ się (*over* nad *A*); **2.** *też ~s pl.* pomy-je *pl.*; fusy *pl.*, resztki *pl.*; *Brt.* F lura *f*, siki *pl.*

slope [sləʊp] **1.** zbocze *n*, stok *m*; nachy-lenie *n*, pochylenie *n*; **2.** opadać ⟨opaść⟩

slop∙py ['slɒpɪ] (*-ier, -iest*) niechlujny; F *ubranie:* znoszony; F ckliwy

slot [slɒt] szczelina *f*, szpara *f*, otwór *m* (*podłużny*); *komp.* miejsce *n* (*na kartę itp.*); czas *m* emisji (*programu radiowe-go lub telewizyjnego*)

sloth [sləʊθ] *zo.* leniwiec *m*

'**slot ma∙chine** automat *m* wrzutowy (*do biletów itp.*)

slouch [slaʊtʃ] **1.** przygarbienie *n*; sku-lona postawa *f*; F leniuch *m*; **2.** ⟨z⟩gar-

S

bić się, ⟨s⟩kulić się; **~ around** łazić

slough¹ [slʌf]: **~ off** *skórę* zrzucać ⟨-cić⟩

slough² [slaʊ] bagno *n*, trzęsawisko *n*

Slo·vak ['sləʊvæk] **1.** słowacki; **2.** Słowak *m* (-aczka *f*); *ling.* język *m* słowacki; **Slo·va·ki·a** [sləʊ'vækɪə] Słowacja *f*

Slo·ve·ni·a Słowenia *f*

slov·en·ly ['slʌvnlɪ] niechlujny, niestaranny

slow [sləʊ] **1.** *adj.* wolny, powolny; leniwy; opieszały (*też* econ.); **be (ten) minutes ~** spóźniać się (10) minut; **2.** wolno, powoli; **3.** *v/t.* często **~ down, ~ up** spowalniać ⟨-wolnić⟩, zwalniać ⟨zwolnić⟩; *v/i.* często **~ down, ~ up** zwalniać ⟨zwolnić⟩; '**~coach** *Brt.* guzdrała *f/m*; '**~·down** *Am.* econ. strajk *m* włoski; '**~·lane** *mot.* pasmo *n* wolnego ruchu; '**~·mo·tion** *phot.* zwolnione tempo *n*; '**~·mov·ing** *samochód*: wolno poruszający się; '**~·poke** *Am.* → **slowcoach**; '**~·worm** zo. padalec *m*

sludge [slʌdʒ] szlam *m*; osad *m* kanalizacyjny

slug¹ [slʌg] zo. ślimak *m* nagi

slug² [slʌg] zwł. *Am.* F kula *f*, pocisk *m*; łyczek *m* (*wódki itp.*)

slug³ [slʌg] zwł. *Am.* F (-gg-) komuś przywalić

slug·gish ['slʌgɪʃ] leniwy, powolny; econ. w stanie zastoju

sluice [sluːs] tech. śluza *f*, upust *m*

slum [slʌm] *też* **~s** slumsy *pl.*

slum·ber ['slʌmbə] *lit.* **1.** spać; **2.** sen *m*

slump [slʌmp] **1.** econ. załamywać ⟨-mać⟩ się (*gwałtownie*); **sit ~ed over** siedzieć bezwładnie nad (*I*); **~ into a chair** opadać ⟨-paść⟩ na krzesło; **2.** econ. załamanie *n* się

slung [slʌŋ] *pret. i p.p. od* **sling** 1

slunk [slʌŋk] *pret. i p.p. od* **slink**

slur¹ [slɜː] (-rr-) *mus.* ⟨za⟩grać legato; **~ one's speech** ⟨za⟩bełkotać; **2.** bełkot *m*

slur² [slɜː] (-rr-) oczerniać ⟨-nić⟩; **2.** potwarz *f*

slurp [slɜːp] F siorbać ⟨-bnąć⟩

slush [slʌʃ] błoto *n* (*ze śniegu*)

slut [slʌt] V dziwka *f*

sly [slaɪ] (-er, -est) skryty; przebiegły, chytry; **on the ~** skrycie, po kryjomu

smack¹ [smæk] **1.** klepać ⟨-pnąć⟩; dawać ⟨dać⟩ klapsa; **~ one's lips** cmokać

⟨-knąć⟩; **~ down** plaskać ⟨-snąć⟩ (*I*); **2.** klepnięcie *n*; (*calus*) cmoknięcie *n*; klaps *m*

smack² [smæk]: **~ of** *fig.* trącić *lub* pachnieć (*I*), przypominać (*A*)

small [smɔːl] **1.** *adj.* mały, niewielki; drobny; **~ wonder (that)** nic dziwnego(, że); **feel ~** czuć się nieważnym; **2.** *adv.* mało; **3.** **~ of the back** anat. krzyż *m*; '**~ ad** ogłoszenie drobne *n*; '**~ arms** *pl.* broń *f* palna ręczna; '**~ change** *monety*: reszta *f*, drobne *pl.*; '**~ hours** *pl.*: **in the ~ hours** nad ranem; '**~·mind·ed** o ciasnym horyzontach; małostkowy; '**~·pox** ['smɔːlpɒks] med. ospa *f*; '**~ print** *fig.* informacje *pl.* szczegółowe; '**~ talk** zdawkowa rozmowa *f*, rozmowa *f* towarzyska; '**~-'time** F nieznaczący; '**~ town** małe miasto *n*

smart [smɑːt] **1.** elegancki; zwł. *Brt.* wytworny; zwł. *Am.* bystry; szybki; *wzrok*: ostry; **2.** ⟨za⟩boleć, ⟨za⟩piec; cierpieć (**from, over** z powodu *G*); **3.** piekący ból *m*; **~ aleck** ['smɑːt ælɪk] F spryciarz *m*; '**~·ness** elegancja *f*; wytworność *f*

smash [smæʃ] **1.** *v/t.* rozbijać ⟨-bić⟩ (*też* **~ up**); pięścią *itp.* walić ⟨-lnąć⟩; *rekord* pobić; (*w tenisie*) ścinać ⟨ściąć⟩; *v/i.* roztrzaskiwać ⟨-kać⟩ się; **~ into** zderzać ⟨-rzyć⟩ się z (*I*); **2.** cios *m*; trzask *m*; (*w tenisie*) smecz *m*, ścięcie *n*; → **~ hit, ~ up**; '**~ hit hit** *m*; '**~·ing** zwł. *Brt.* F niesamowity, kapitalny; '**~-up** *mot.*, kraksa *f*; rail. katastrofa *f*

smat·ter·ing ['smætərɪŋ]: **a ~ of English** bardzo ograniczona znajomość *f* angielskiego

smear [smɪə] **1.** plama *f* (*też* fig.); med. wymaz *m*; **2.** ⟨po⟩mazać (się); ⟨za⟩smarować (się); *wydruk itp.*: zamazywać ⟨-zać⟩ (się); *fig.* obsmarować

smell [smel] **1.** (*smelt lub smelled*) *v/i.* czuć zapach; pachnieć, zwł. śmierdzieć; *v/t.* ⟨po⟩wąchać; ⟨po⟩czuć; *fig.* wyczuwać, przeczuwać; **2.** zapach *m*; woń *f*; smród *m*; węch *m*; '**~·y** (-ier, -iest) śmierdzący, cuchnący

smelt¹ [smelt] *pret. i p.p. od* **smell** 1

smelt² [smelt] *metal* wytapiać ⟨-topić⟩

smile [smaɪl] **1.** uśmiech *m*; **2.** uśmiechać ⟨-chnąć⟩ się; **~ at** wyśmiewać się z (*G*)

smirk [smɜːk] uśmieszek *m*

smith [smɪθ] kowal *m*

smith·e·reens [smɪðəˈriːnz] F pl.: **smash s.th.** (in)to ~ rozbić ⟨-bijać⟩ coś w drobny mak

smith·y [ˈsmɪðɪ] kuźnia f

smit·ten [ˈsmɪtn] zwł. humor. rozmiłowany, rozkochany (with, by w L)

smock [smɒk] bluzka f (tunika, ciążowa); fartuch m, kitel m

smog [smɒg] smog m

smoke [sməʊk] **1.** dym m; **have a ~** zapalić papierosa; **2.** dymić ⟨się⟩; ⟨za-, wy⟩palić; '**smok·er** palacz(ka f) m; rail. wagon m dla palących; '**smoke·stack** komin m

smok·ing [ˈsməʊkɪŋ] palenie n; **no ~** palenie n wzbronione; ⚠ nie **smoking**; ~ **com'part·ment** rail. przedział m dla palących

smok·y [ˈsməʊkɪ] (**-ier, -iest**) zadymiony; przydymiony; koloru dymu

smooth [smuːð] **1.** gładki (też fig.); ciasto itp.: jednolity; ruch, smak itp.: łagodny; uprzejmie grzeczny; **2.** też ~ **out** wygładzać ⟨-dzić⟩; ~ **away** wygładzać; trudności usuwać ⟨usunąć⟩; ~ **down** włosy przygładzać ⟨-dzić⟩

smoth·er [ˈsmʌðə] ⟨s⟩tłumić; ⟨u⟩dusić

smo(u)l·der [ˈsməʊldə] żarzyć się, tlić się

smudge [smʌdʒ] **1.** plama f (też fig.); **2.** ⟨za⟩plamić; rozmazywać ⟨-zać⟩ ⟨się⟩

smug [smʌg] (**-gg-**) zadowolony z siebie

smug·gle [ˈsmʌgl] ⟨prze⟩szmuglować, przemycać ⟨-cić⟩ (**into** do G); '**~r** szmugler m, przemytnik m (-niczka f)

smut [smʌt] płatek m sadzy; brud m; fig. plugastwo n; '**~·ty** (**-ier, -iest**) fig. plugawy

snack [snæk] przekąska f; **have a ~** ⟨z⟩jeść coś; '**~ bar** snack-bar m

snag [snæg] **1.** fig. problem m; zadzior m; **2.** (**-gg-**) czymś zaczepiać ⟨-pić⟩ (o coś), coś zadzierać ⟨-drzeć⟩

snail [sneɪl] zo. skorupkowy ślimak m

snake [sneɪk] zo. wąż m

snap [snæp] **1.** (**-pp-**) v/i. ⟨z⟩łamać się, trzasnąć; też ~ **shut** zatrzaskiwać ⟨-snąć⟩ się; ~ **at** warczeć ⟨-rknąć⟩ na (A), ⟨chcieć⟩ ⟨u⟩kąsić; pies: kłapać zębami na (A); ~ **out of it!** F głowa do góry!; ~ **to it!** F pospiesz się! v/t. ⟨z⟩łamać; phot. F zdjęcie pstrykać ⟨-knąć⟩; ~ **one's fingers** strzelać ⟨-lić⟩ palcami; ~ **one's fingers at** fig. lekceważyć (A);

~ **off** odłamywać ⟨-mać⟩; ~ **up** coś kupować ⟨-pić⟩; **2.** phot. zdjęcie n; Am. zatrzask m; fig. F (energia) ikra f; **cold~** krótkotrwałe nagłe ochłodzenie n; '**~ fas·ten·er** Am. zatrzask m; '**~·pish** fig. wściekły; '**~·py** (**-ier, -iest**) szykowny; **make it ~py!** Brt. też **look ~py!** pospiesz się!; '**~·shot** phot. zdjęcie n

snare [sneə] **1.** sidła pl.; fig. pułapka f; **2.** ⟨s⟩chwytać w sidła; F ⟨s⟩chwytać w pułapkę

snarl [snɑːl] **1.** warczeć ⟨-rknąć⟩; ⟨za⟩burczeć (**at** na A); **2.** warknięcie n, burknięcie n

snatch [snætʃ] **1.** v/t. coś ⟨s⟩chwytać, ⟨z⟩łapać (też ~ **at**); kogoś, coś porywać ⟨-rwać⟩; ze sposobności ⟨s⟩korzystać (też ~ **at**); ~ **s.o.'s handbag** wyrywać ⟨-rwać⟩ komuś torebkę; ~ **an hour's sleep** zdołać przespać się godzinę; **2.** **make a ~** ⟨s⟩chwytać (A); ~ **of conversation** urywek m rozmowy

sneak [sniːk] **1.** v/i. przekradać ⟨-raść⟩ się, wkradać ⟨-raść⟩ się (**into** do G); Brt. F donosić ⟨-nieść⟩; v/t. F podkradać ⟨-raść⟩; ~ **a look** ukradkiem rzucić spojrzenie; **2.** Brt. F donosiciel(ka f) m; '**~·er** Am. adidas m, tenisówka f

sneer [snɪə] **1.** uśmiechać ⟨-chnąć⟩ się drwiąco; ⟨za⟩drwić (**at** z G); **2.** drwiący uśmieszek m; drwiąca uwaga f, drwina f

sneeze [sniːz] **1.** kichać ⟨-chnąć⟩; **2.** kichnięcie n

snick·er [ˈsnɪkə] zwł. Am. → **snigger**

sniff [snɪf] **1.** v/i. pociągać ⟨-gnąć⟩ nosem; ⟨po⟩wąchać; ~ **at** fig. krzywić nos na (A); v/t. narkotyk wdychać; **2.** pociągnięcie n nosem

snif·fle [ˈsnɪfl] **1.** pociągać ⟨-gnąć⟩ nosem; **2.** pociągnięcie n nosem; **she's got the ~s** F ona ma zatkany nos

snig·ger zwł. Brt. [ˈsnɪgə] podśmiewać się (**at** z G)

snip [snɪp] **1.** cięcie n; **2.** (**-pp-**) przecinać ⟨-ciąć⟩; ~ **off** odcinać ⟨-ciąć⟩

snipe[1] [snaɪp] zo. kszyk m

snipe[2] [snaɪp] strzelać ⟨-lić⟩ z ukrycia (**at** do G); '**snip·er** snajper m, strzelec m wyborowy

sniv·el [ˈsnɪvl] (zwł. Brt. **-ll-**, Am. **-l-**) chlipać, labeldzić

snob [snɒb] snob m; '**~·bish** snobistyczny

snoop [snu:p]: ~ *about*, ~ *around* F myszkować, węszyć; '~·er wścibski m (-ka f)

snooze [snu:z] F **1.** drzemka f; **2.** drzemać

snore [snɔ:] **1.** chrapać; **2.** chrapanie n

snor·kel ['snɔ:kl] **1.** fajka f (*do nurkowanie*); *naut.* chrapy pl. (*okrętu podwodnego*); **2.** nurkować z fajką

snort [snɔ:t] **1.** parskać ⟨-knąć⟩; *narkotyk* wdychać; **2.** parsknięcie n

snout [snaut] pysk m

snow [snəu] **1.** śnieg m; F (*kokaina*) koka f; **2.** śnieżyć; *śnieg*: padać ⟨spaść⟩; *be ~ed in lub up* być przysypanym śniegiem; '~·ball kula f śniegowa; ~·ball 'fight bitwa na kule śniegowe; '~·bound zaśnieżony, pokryty śniegiem; '~·drift zaspa f (*śniegu*); '~·drop *bot.* przebiśnieg m; '~·fall opady pl. śniegu; '~·flake płatek m śniegu; '~·man (pl. -men) bałwan m śniegowy; '~·plough *Brt.*, '~·plow *Am.* pług m śnieżny; '~·storm burza f śniegowa, śnieżyca f; ~·'white śnieżnobiały; '² White Królewna f'Śnieżka; ~·y (-ier, -iest) zaśnieżony; śnieżny; ośnieżony

Snr *skrót pisany: Senior* sen., senior m

snub [snʌb] **1.** (-bb-) ⟨po⟩traktować lekceważąco; **2.** lekceważenie n; '~ nose zadarty nos m; ~·'nosed z zadartym nosem

snuff¹ [snʌf] tabaka f

snuff² [snʌf] *świecę* ⟨z⟩gasić; ~ *out* życie przerwać

snuf·fle ['snʌfl] obwąchiwać ⟨-chać⟩

snug [snʌg] (-gg-) przytulny, zaciszny; *ubranie*: dobrze leżący; przyciasny

snug·gle ['snʌgl]: ~ *up to s.o.* przytulać ⟨-lić⟩ się do kogoś; ~ *down in bed* wtulać ⟨-lić⟩ się do łóżka

so [səu] **1.** *adv.* tak, w ten sposób; także; → *hope* 2, *think*, *is that* ~? naprawdę?; *an hour or* ~ coś koło godziny; *she is tired* – ~ *am I* ona jest zmęczona – ja też; ~ *far* dotąd, dotychczas; **2.** *cj.* tak więc, więc; aby

soak [səuk] *v/t.* ⟨za⟩moczyć (*in* w L); ~ *up* gąbką, gałgan: wchłaniać ⟨wchłonąć⟩; *v/i.* przemoczyć; *leave the dirty clothes to* ~ namocz brudne rzeczy

soap [səup] **1.** mydło n; F → *soap opera*; **2.** namydlać ⟨-lić⟩ (się); '~ op·e·ra opera f mydlana (*radiowa lub te-*

lewizyjna) '~·y (-ier, -iest) mydlany; *fig.* F wazeliniarski

soar [sɔ:] ⟨po⟩szybować; wzbijać ⟨-bić⟩ się, wznosić ⟨-nieść⟩ się; iść ⟨pójść⟩ w górę

sob [sɒb] **1.** (-bb-) szlochać; **2.** szloch m

so·ber ['səubə] **1.** trzeźwy (*też fig.*); **2.** ⟨wy⟩trzeźwieć; ~ *up* otrzeźwiać ⟨-wić⟩

so-'called tak zwany

soc·cer ['sɒkə] piłka f nożna; '~ hoo·li·gan pseudokibic m

so·cia·ble ['səuʃəbl] towarzyski

so·cial ['səuʃl] społeczny; socjalny; towarzyski; ~ 'dem·o·crat socjaldemokrata m (-tka f); ~ in'sur·ance ubezpieczenie n społeczne

so·cial·is·m ['səuʃəlɪzəm] socjalizm m; '~·ist **1.** socjalista m (-tka f); **2.** socjalistyczny

so·cial·ize ['səuʃəlaɪz] utrzymywać kontakty towarzyskie (*with* z I)

so·cial 'sci·ence nauka f społeczna; ~ se'cu·ri·ty *Brt.* pomoc f społeczna; *be on* ~ *security* otrzymywać zasiłek z pomocy społecznej; ~ 'serv·i·ces pl. zwł. *Brt.* opieka f społeczna; '~ work praca f społeczna; '~ work·er pracownik m (-nica f) opieki społecznej

so·ci·e·ty [sə'saɪətɪ] społeczeństwo n; towarzystwo n

so·ci·ol·o·gy [səusɪ'ɒlədʒɪ] socjologia f

sock [sɒk] skarpetka f

sock·et ['sɒkɪt] *electr.* gniazdko n; *electr.* oprawka f (*żarówki*); *anat.* oczodół m

sod [sɒd] *Brt.* V kutas m, ciul m

so·da ['səudə] woda f sodowa; *zwł. Am.* napój m gazowany f

sod·den ['sɒdn] przemoczony, nasiąknięty wodą

so·fa ['səufə] sofa f, kanapa f

soft [sɒft] miękki; delikatny; *głos*: cichy; *światło*: łagodny; *napój*: bezalkoholowy; *narkotyk*: nie powodujący uzależnienia; *też* ~ *in the head* F przygłupiasty; *a* ~ *job* F łatwa (prosta, spokojna) praca; ~ *drink* napój m bezalkoholowy

soft·en ['sɒfn] *v/t.* zmiękczać ⟨-czyć⟩; *ton, światło* ⟨z⟩łagodzić; ~ *up* F kogoś zmiękczać ⟨-czyć⟩; *v/i.* ⟨z⟩mięknąć; ⟨z⟩łagodnieć

soft·|**·head·ed** przygłupi; ~·**'heart·ed** dobroduszny, o miękkim sercu; ~ **'land-**

ing (*w astronautyce*) miękkie lądowanie *f*; **'~ware** *komp.* software *n*, oprogramowanie *n*; **~ware 'pack·age** *komp.* pakiet *m* oprogramowania; **'~·y** F (*osoba*) mięczak *m*

sog·gy ['sɒgi] (*-ier, -iest*) namiękły, rozmokły

soil[1] [sɔɪl] gleba *f*, ziemia *f*

soil[2] [sɔɪl] ⟨u-, za⟩brudzić

sol·ace ['sɒləs] pociecha *f*, pocieszenie *n*

so·lar ['səʊlə] słoneczny; **~ 'en·er·gy** energia *f* słoneczna; **~ 'pan·el** bateria *f* słoneczna; **'~ sys·tem** układ *m* słoneczny

sold [səʊld] *pret. i p.p. od* **sell**

sol·der ['sɒldə] ⟨z-, przy⟩lutować

sol·dier ['səʊldʒə] żołnierz *m*

sole[1] [səʊl] **1.** podeszwa *f*; **2.** ⟨pod⟩zelować

sole[2] [səʊl] *zo.* (*pl.* **sole, soles**) sola *f*

sole[3] [səʊl] jedyny; wyłączny; **'~·ly** jedynie; wyłącznie

sol·emn ['sɒləm] poważny; uroczysty

so·li·cit [sə'lɪsɪt] ⟨po⟩prosić

so·lic·i·tor [sə'lɪsɪtə] *Brt. jur.* adwokat *m* (*uprawniony do występowania w sądach niższej instancji*); doradca *m* prawny

so·lic·i·tous [sə'lɪsɪtəs] troskliwy; uczynny

sol·id ['sɒlɪd] **1.** stały; pełny; lity; solidny; *ściana itp.*: masywny; *math. geometria*: przestrzenny; *Brt. protest*: solidarny; *okres czasu*: bity; **2.** *math.* bryła; *phys.* ciało *n* stałe

sol·i·dar·i·ty [sɒlɪ'dærətɪ] solidarność *f*

so·lid·i·fy [sə'lɪdɪfaɪ] zestalać się; zastygać ⟨-gnąć⟩; ⟨s⟩krzepnąć

so·lil·o·quy [sə'lɪləkwɪ] *theat.* monolog *m*

sol·i·taire [sɒlɪ'teə] *Am.* pasjans *m*; (*gra*) samotnik *m*

sol·i·ta·ry ['sɒlɪtərɪ] samotny, pojedynczy; odludny, odosobniony; **~ con'fine·ment** *jur.* kara *f* izolatki

so·lo ['səʊləʊ] (*pl.* **-los**) *mus.* solo *n*; *aviat.* samotny lot *m*; *attr.* solowy; samotny; **'~·ist** *mus.* solista *m* (*-tka f*)

sol·u·ble ['sɒljʊbl] rozpuszczalny; *fig.* do rozwiązania; **so·lu·tion** [sə'luːʃn] roztwór *m*; rozwiązanie *n*

solve [sɒlv] rozwiązywać ⟨-zać⟩; **sol·vent** ['sɒlvənt] **1.** *econ.* wypłacalny; **2.** *chem.* rozpuszczalnik *m*

som·bre *Brt.,* **som·ber** *Am.* ['sɒmbə]

poważny, smutny; *fig.* ponury

some [sʌm] jakiś; *przed pl.*: trochę (*G*); kilka (*G*); nieco (*G*); niektórzy; **~ 20 miles** jakieś 20 mil; **~ more cake** jeszcze trochę ciasta; **to ~ extent** w pewnej mierze; **~·bod·y** ['sʌmbədɪ] ktoś; **'~·day** kiedyś; **'~·how** jakoś; **'~·one** ktoś; **'~·place** *zwł. Am.* → **somewhere**

som·er·sault ['sʌməsɔːlt] **1.** salto *n*; przewrót *m* w przód; **turn a ~** ⟨z⟩robić przewrót *m* w przód; **2.** ⟨z⟩robić salto; wykonać przewrót w przód

'some|·thing coś; **~thing like** coś jakby; **'~·time** kiedyś; **'~·times** czasami; **'~·what** trochę (*G*), nieco (*G*); **'~·where** gdzieś

son [sʌn] syn *m*; **~ of a bitch** *zwł. Am.* V sukinsyn *m*

song [sɒŋ] pieśń *f*, piosenka *f*; **for a ~** F za Bóg zapłać; **'~·bird** ptak *m* śpiewający

son·ic ['sɒnɪk] dźwiękowy; **~ 'bang** *Brt.,* **~ 'boom** *aviat.* uderzenie *n* dźwiękowe (*przy przekraczaniu prędkości dźwięku*)

son-in-law ['sʌnɪnlɔː] (*pl.* **sons-in-law**) zięć *m*

son·net ['sɒnɪt] sonet *m*

so·nor·ous [sə'nɔːrəs] donośny, dźwięczny

soon [suːn] wkrótce, niebawem; **as ~ as** skoro tylko; **as ~ as possible** jak najszybciej można; **'~·er** prędzej, wcześniej; **~er or later** wcześniej lub później; **the ~er the better** im szybciej, tym lepiej; **no ~er... than** nie szybciej niż ...; **no ~er said than done** od razu zrobione

soot [sʊt] sadza *f*

soothe [suːð] ⟨u⟩koić, uspokajać ⟨-koić⟩ (*też down*); ⟨za-, u⟩łagodzić; *ból itp.* uśmierzać ⟨-rzyć⟩; **sooth·ing** ['suːðɪŋ] kojący, uśmierzający

soot·y ['sʊtɪ] (*-ier, -iest*) czarny (*od sadzy*)

sop[1] [sɒp] (*rzecz dana lub zrobiona na odczepnego*)

sop[2] [sɒp] (*-pp-*): **~ up** ścierka, gałgan: wchłaniać ⟨wchłonąć⟩ (*płyn*)

so·phis·ti·cat·ed [sə'fɪstɪkeɪtɪd] wyrafinowany; obyty; *tech.* wysoko rozwinięty

soph·o·more ['sɒfəmɔː] *Am.* student(ka *f*) *m* drugiego roku

S

sop·o·rif·ic [sɒpəˈrɪfɪk] (*-ally*) usypiający; nasenny

sop·ping [ˈsɒpɪŋ]: **~ wet** F ociekający wodą

sor·cer·er [ˈsɔːsərə] czarownik *m*, czarodziej *m*, czarnoksiężnik *m*; **~·ess** [ˈsɔːsərɪs] czarownica *f*, czarodziejka *f*; **~·y** [ˈsɔːsərɪ] czarodziejstwo *n*

sor·did [ˈsɔːdɪd] nędzny, brudny; nikczemny

sore [sɔː] 1. (*-r, -st*) obolały; bolący; *fig.* bolesny; punkt czuły; *zwł. Am.* F *fig.* wściekły (*at* na *A*); **I'm ~ all over** wszystko mnie boli; **~ throat** zapalenie *n* gardła; **I have a ~ finger** palec mnie boli; 2. rana *f*, owrzodzenie *n*

sor·rel[1] [ˈsɒrəl] *bot.* szczaw *m*; *attr.* szczawiowy

sor·rel[2] [ˈsɒrəl] *koń* kasztanowy

sor·row [ˈsɒrəʊ] smutek *m*, żal *m*; **~·ful** smutny, przygnębiony

sor·ry [ˈsɒrɪ] 1. *adj.* (*-ier, -iest*) smutny; przygnębiony; *be* **lub** *feel* **~ for s.o.** współczuć komuś; **I'm ~ for her** żal mi jej; **I am ~ to say** z przykrością muszę powiedzieć 2. *int.* przepraszam!; **~?** *zwł. Brt.* słucham?

sort [sɔːt] 1. rodzaj *m*, gatunek *m*; **~ of** jakby, jakoś; **of a ~, of ~s** F coś w rodzaju; **all ~s of things** najróżniejsze rzeczy; **nothing of the ~** nic podobnego; **what ~ of(a) man is he?** jaki on jest?; **be out of ~s** F być nie w sosie; **be completely out of ~s** (*w sporcie*) kompletnie nie mieć formy; 2. ⟨po⟩sortować, ⟨po⟩układać; **~ out** oddzielać ⟨-lić⟩; *problem itp.* rozwiązywać ⟨-zać⟩; **~·er** sortownik *m*; klasyfikator(ka *f*) *m*

SOS [es əʊ ˈes] SOS *n*; **send an ~** wysyłać ⟨-słać⟩ sygnał SOS; **~ call lub message** wezwanie *n* SOS

sought [sɔːt] *pret. i p.p. od* **seek**

soul [səʊl] dusza *f* (*też fig.*); *mus.* soul *m*

sound[1] [saʊnd] 1. dźwięk *m*; odgłos *m*; (*w głośniku radiowym lub telewizyjnym*) głos *m*, fonia *f*; *gr.* głoska *f*; *med.* szmer *m*, ton *m*; *attr.* dźwiękowy; 2. *v/i.* ⟨za⟩brzmieć; ⟨za⟩dźwięczeć; *v/t.* alarm włączać ⟨-czyć⟩; **~ the bell** bić w dzwon; *ling.* wypowiadać ⟨-wiedzieć⟩; *naut.* sondować; **~ one's horn** *mot.* dawać ⟨dać⟩ sygnał (*klaksonem*), ⟨za⟩trąbić

sound[2] [saʊnd] zdrowy; w dobrym stanie; rozsądny; *przeszkolenie:* dogłębny; solidny; *sen:* głęboki

'sound| bar·ri·er bariera *f* dźwiękowa; **~ film** film *m* dźwiękowy; **~·less** bezgłosny; **~·proof** dźwiękoszczelny; **~·track** ścieżka *f* dźwiękowa; **~ wave** fala *f* dźwiękowa

soup [suːp] 1. zupa *f*; 2. **~ up** *mot.* F *silnik* podrasowywać ⟨-ować⟩

sour [ˈsaʊə] 1. kwaśny; skwaśniały; *mleko:* zsiadły; *fig.* cierpki; 2. ⟨s⟩kwaśnieć, zsiadać ⟨zsiąść⟩ się

source [sɔːs] źródło *n* (*też fig.*)

south [saʊθ] 1. południe *n*; 2. *adj.* południowy; 3. *adv.* na południe

South Af·ri·ca Republika *f* Południowej Afryki

south east [saʊθ ˈiːst] 1. południowy wschód *m*; 2. *adj.* południowo-wschodni; 3. *adv.* na południowy wschód; **~·east·ern** południowo-wschodni

south·er·ly [ˈsʌðəlɪ], **~·ern** [ˈsʌðən] południowy; **~·ern·most** wysunięty najbardziej na południe

South Pole biegun *m* południowy

south|·ward(s) [ˈsaʊθwəd(z)] na południe; **~·west** 1. południowy zachód *m*; 2. *adj.* południowo-zachodni; 3. *adv.* na południowy zachód; **~·west·ern** południowo-zachodni

sou·ve·nir [suːvəˈnɪə] pamiątka *f*

sove·reign [ˈsɒvrɪn] 1. monarcha *m*, władca *m*; 2. *państwo itp.:* suwerenny; **~·ty** [ˈsɒvrəntɪ] suwerenność *f*

So·vi·et [ˈsəʊvɪət] *hist.* radziecki, sowiecki

sow[1] [səʊ] (*sowed, sown lub sowed*) ⟨za⟩siać

sow[2] [saʊ] *zo.* maciora *f*

sown [səʊn] *p.p. od* **sow**[1]

spa [spɑː] uzdrowisko *n*, kurort *m*

space [speɪs] 1. miejsce *n*; obszar *m*; przestrzeń *f*; kosmos *m*; 2. *też* **~ out** rozstawiać ⟨-wić⟩; *print.* rozstrzeliwać ⟨-lać⟩; **~ age** era *f* kosmiczna; **~ bar** klawisz *m* spacji; **~·cap·sule** kapsuła *f*, kabina *f* (*statku kosmicznego*); **~ cen·tre** centrum *n* lotów kosmicznych; **~·craft** (*pl. -craft*) statek *m* kosmiczny; **~ flight** lot *m* kosmiczny; **~·lab** laboratorium *n* kosmiczne; **~·man** (*pl. -men*) F astronauta *m*, kosmonauta *m*; **~ probe** sonda *f* kosmiczna; **~ research** badanie *n* przestrzeni

kosmicznej; '**~·ship** statek *m* kosmiczny; '**~ shut·tle** prom *m* kosmiczny; '**~ sta·tion** stacja *f* kosmiczna; '**~·suit** skafander *m* kosmiczny; **~ walk** spacer *m* w przestrzeni kosmicznej; '**~·wom·an** (*pl.* **-women**) astronautka *f*, kosmonautka *f*

spa·cious ['speɪʃəs] przestrzenny

spade [speɪd] szpadel *m*; (*w kartach*) pik *m*; **king of ~s** król *m* pik; **call a ~** nazywać rzeczy po imieniu

Spain [speɪn] Hiszpania *f*

span [spæn] **1.** rozpiętość *f*; okres *m* czasu; **2.** (**-nn-**) spinać 〈spiąć〉 brzegi; obejmować 〈objąć〉

span·gle ['spæŋgl] **1.** cekin *m*; **2.** naszywać 〈-szyć〉 cekiny

Span·iard ['spænjəd] Hiszpan *m* (-nka *f*)

span·iel ['spænjəl] *zo.* spaniel *m*

Span·ish ['spænɪʃ] **1.** hiszpański; **2.** *ling.* język *m* hiszpański; **the ~** *pl.* Hiszpanie *pl.*

spank [spæŋk] dawać 〈dać〉 klapsa (*D*); '**~·ing 1.** *adj.* szybki; prędki; **2.** *adv.* **~·ing clean** czyściutki; **~ing new** nowiutki; **1.** lanie *n*

span·ner ['spænə] *zwł. Brt.* klucz *m* (maszynowy); **put** *lub* **throw a ~ in the works** F wsadzać kij między szprychy

spar [spɑː] (**-rr-**) (*w boksie*) odbywać 〈-być〉 sparing (**with** *z I*); przeprowadzać 〈-dzić〉 pojedynek na słowa (**with** *z I*)

spare [speə] **1.** przeznaczać 〈-czyć〉, *ko-goś* wyznaczać 〈-czyć〉; *pieniądze, czas itp.* oszczędzać 〈-dzić〉; **~ no expenses** nie szczędzić wydatków; **~ s.o. s.th.** oszczędzać coś komuś; **can you ~ me a minute?** czy może mi pan poświęcić minutę?; **to ~** do dyspozycji; **2.** zapasowy; *czas:* wolny; **3.** część *f* zapasowa; opona *f* zapasowa; **~ 'part** *mot.* część *f* zapasowa; **~ 'room** pokój *m* gościnny; **~ 'time** wolny czas *m*

spar·ing ['speərɪŋ] oszczędny

spark [spɑːk] **1.** iskra *f* (*też fig.*); **2.** 〈za〉iskrzyć; '**~·ing plug** *Brt. mot.* → **spark plug**

spar·kle ['spɑːkl] **1.** skrzyć się; błyszczeć 〈błysnąć〉 (**with** od *G*); *napój:* musować; **2.** migotanie *n*; połysk *m*; **spark·ling** ['spɑːklɪŋ] migocący; *fig.* błyskotliwy; **~ wine** wino *n* musujące

'**spark plug** *mot.* świeca *f* zapłonowa

spar·row ['spærəʊ] *zo.* wróbel *m*; '**~·hawk** krogulec *m*

sparse [spɑːs] rzadki, przerzedzony

spas·m ['spæzəm] *med.* skurcz *m*, spazm *m*; *med.* atak *m*; **spas·mod·ic** [spæz'mɒdɪk] (**~ally**) *med.* spazmodyczny, spazmatyczny; *fig.* sporadyczny

spas·tic ['spæstɪk] *med.* **1.** (**~ally**) spastyczny, kurczowy; **2.** osoba *f* z porażeniem spastycznym

spat [spæt] *pret. i p.p. od* **spit¹**

spa·tial ['speɪʃl] przestrzenny

spat·ter ['spætə] obryzgiwać 〈-gać〉; opryskiwać 〈-kać〉; posypywać 〈-pać〉

spawn [spɔːn] **1.** *zo.* składać 〈złożyć〉 skrzek *lub* ikrę; *fig.* 〈s〉płodzić, 〈z〉rodzić; **2.** *zo.* skrzek *m*; ikra *f*

speak [spiːk] (**spoke, spoken**) *v/i.* mówić 〈powiedzieć〉 〈po〉rozmawiać (**to, with** do *G*, **about** o *L*); **so to ~** że tak powiem; '**~ing!** *teleph.* przy aparacie!; **~ up** mówić głośniej; *v/t.* mówić; **~ Polish** mówić po polsku; '**~·er** mówca *m* (-czyni *f*); ♀ *parl. Brt., Am.* speaker *m* (*w niższej izbie parlamentu*)

spear [spɪə] **1.** oszczep *m*; włócznia *f*; **2.** nabijać 〈-bić〉, przeszywać 〈-szyć〉 oszczepem; '**~·head** grot *m*; *mil.* szpica *f*, czołówka *f* (*też fig.*); '**~·mint** *bot.* mięta *f* zielona

spe·cial ['speʃl] **1.** specjalny; szczególny; nadzwyczajny; dodatkowy; **2.** pociąg *m* *lub* autobus *m* specjalny *lub* dodatkowy; audycja *f* specjalna (*radiowa lub telewizyjna*); *Am. econ.* okazja *f*; **be on ~** *Am. econ.* F być dostępnym po obniżonej cenie; **spe·cial·ist** ['speʃəl-ɪst] specjalista *m* (-tka *f*); *med.* lekarz *m* specjalista *m* (**in** w zakresie *G*); *attr.* specjalistyczny; **spe·ci·al·i·ty** [speʃ-ɪ'ælətɪ] specjalność *f*; **spe·cial·ize** ['speʃəlaɪz] 〈wy〉specjalizować się; **spe·cial·ty** *Am.* ['speʃltɪ] → **speciality**

spe·cies ['spiːʃiːz] (*pl.* **-cies**) gatunek *m*

spe|·cif·ic [spɪ'sɪfɪk] (**-ally**) konkretny; szczegółowy; właściwy; specyficzny, swoisty (**to** dla *G*); **~·ci·fy** ['spesɪfaɪ] określać 〈-lić〉; wyszczególniać 〈-nić〉

spe·ci·men ['spesɪmən] okaz *m*; próbka *f*

speck [spek] plamka *f*; cętka *f*; *fig.* kropka *f*

speck·led ['spekld] plamiasty

spec·ta·cle ['spektəkl] przedstawienie

n (*też fig.*); spektakl *m*; (*a pair of*) ~**s** *pl.* okulary *pl.*

spec·tac·u·lar [spek'tækjulə] **1.** spektakularny; widowiskowy; **2.** uroczystość *f*, gala *f*

spec·ta·tor [spek'teɪtə] widz *m*

spec·|·tral ['spektrəl] widmowy (*też phys.*); *phys.* spektralny; ~**tre** *Brt.*, ~**ter** *Am.* ['spektə] widmo *n*, zjawa *f*; ~**trum** ['spektrəm] *phys.* widmo *n*, spektrum *n*

spec·u·|·late ['spekjuleɪt] rozważać ⟨-żyć⟩ (*about, on* A), spekulować (*about, on* nad A); *econ.* spekulować, dokonywać ⟨-nać⟩ spekulacji; ~**la·tion** [spekju'leɪʃn] domysł *m*; *econ.* spekulacja *f*; ~**la·tive** ['spekjulətɪv] spekulatywny; *econ.* spekulacyjny; ~**la·tor** ['spekjuleɪtə] *econ.* spekulator *m*

sped [sped] *pret. i p.p. od* **speed** 2

speech [spiːtʃ] mowa *f*; przemówienie *n*, przemowa *f*; **make a ~** przemawiać ⟨-mówić⟩; '~ **day** *Brt.* (*w szkole*) *m* rozdania nagród; '~**less** oniemiały; **be ~less with** oniemieć od (*G*)

speed [spiːd] **1.** prędkość *f*, szybkość *f*; *phot.* czułość *f*; *sl.* (*narkotyk amfetamina*) speed *m*; bieg *m* (*roweru itp.*); **five-~ gearbox** pięciobiegowa skrzynia *f* biegów; **at a ~ of** z prędkością (*G*); **at full** lub **top ~** z pełną prędkością; **2.** (**sped**) *v/i.* ⟨po⟩pędzić, ⟨po⟩mknąć; **be ~ing** *mot.* przekraczać ⟨-roczyć⟩ dozwoloną prędkość; **~ up** (*pret. i p.p.* **speeded**) przyspieszać ⟨-szyć⟩; '~**boat** *naut.* ślizgacz *m*; '~**ing** *mot.* przekraczanie *n* właściwej prędkości; '~ **lim·it** *mot.* ograniczenie *n* prędkości

spee·do ['spiːdəu] *Brt. mot.* F licznik *m*, prędkościomierz *m*

speed·om·e·ter [spɪ'dɒmɪtə] *mot.* licznik *m*, prędkościomierz *m*

'**speed trap** pułapka *f* radarowa (*miejsce kontroli prędkości*)

'**speed·y** (*-ier, -iest*) prędki

spell[1] [spel] (**spelt** lub *zwł. Am.* **spelled**) *też* ~ **out** ⟨prze⟩literować; ⟨na⟩pisać ortograficznie

spell[2] [spel] okres *m*; atak *m*; **a ~ of fine weather** okres *m* pięknej pogody; **hot ~** fala *f* upałów

spell[3] [spel] czar *m*, urok *m*; '~**bound** zauroczony

'**spell·|·er** *komp.* program *m* sprawdzania pisowni; **be a good** (**bad**) ~**er**

umieć (nie umieć) pisać ortograficznie; '~**ing** pisownia *f*; '~**ing mis·take** błąd *m* ortograficzny

spelt [spelt] *pret. i p.p. od* **spell**[1]

spend [spend] (**spent**) pieniądze wydawać ⟨-dać⟩; *urlop itp.* spędzać ⟨-dzić⟩; '~**ing** wydatki *pl.*; '~**thrift** marnotrawca *m*

spent [spent] **1.** *pret. i p.p. od* **spend**; **2.** *adj.* wyczerpany

sperm [spɜːm] sperma *f*, nasienie *n*; plemnik *m*

SPF [es piː 'ef] *skrót:* **Sun Protection Factor** faktor ochronny IP (*przed słońcem*)

sphere [sfɪə] kula *f*; *fig.* sfera *f*; **spher·i·cal** ['sferɪkl] kulisty, sferyczny

spice [spaɪs] **1.** przyprawa *f*; *fig.* pikanteria *f*; **2.** doprawiać ⟨-wić⟩, przyprawiać ⟨-wić⟩

spick-and-span [spɪkən'spæn] lśniący od czystości

spic·y ['spaɪsɪ] (*-ier, -iest*) doprawiony, przyprawiony; *fig.* pikantny

spi·der ['spaɪdə] *zo.* pająk *m*

spike [spaɪk] **1.** ostrze *n*; kolec *m*; szpic *m*; ~**s** *pl.* (*w sporcie*) kolce *pl.*; **2.** wbijać ⟨wbić⟩ kolce

spill [spɪl] **1.** (**spilt** lub *zwł. Am.* **spilled**) *v/t.* rozlewać ⟨-lać⟩; ~ **the beans** F wyśpiewać wszystko; → **milk** 1; *v/i.* rozlewać ⟨-lać⟩ się; *fig.* ogarniać ⟨-nąć⟩; **2.** F upadek *m*

spilt [spɪlt] *pret. i p.p. od* **spill** 1

spin [spɪn] **1.** (**-nn-**; **spun**) *v/t.* obracać ⟨-rócić⟩; *pranie* odwirowywać ⟨-ować⟩; *monetą* rzucać ⟨-cić⟩; *przędzę itp.* ⟨u⟩prząść; ~ **out** *pracę* przeciągać ⟨-gnąć⟩; *pieniądze* oszczędzać ⟨-dzić⟩; *v/i.* obracać ⟨-rócić⟩ się; wirować; ⟨u⟩prząść; **my head was ~ning** kręciło mi się w głowie; ~ **along** *mot.* F ⟨po⟩mknąć; ~ **round** obracać ⟨-rócić⟩ się; **2.** wirowanie *n*; obrót *m*; (*w sporcie*) podkręcenie *n*; odwirowanie *n* (*prania*); *aviat.* korkociąg *m*; *mot.* F przejażdżka *f*; **be in a** (**flat**) ~ *zwł. Brt.* F wpadać ⟨wpaść⟩ w popłoch; **go for a ~** *mot.* F wyruszyć na przejażdżkę

spin·ach ['spɪnɪdʒ] *bot.* szpinak *m*; *attr.* szpinakowy

spin·al ['spaɪnl] *anat.* kręgowy; '~ **col·umn** *anat.* kręgosłup *m*; ~ '**cord**, '**mar·row** *anat.* rdzeń *m* kręgowy

spin·dle ['spɪndl] wrzeciono n

spin|-'dri·er wirówka f; **~-'dry** *pranie* ⟨od⟩wirować; **~-'dry·er** wirówka f

spine [spaɪn] *anat.* kręgosłup m; *zo., bot.* kolec m; grzbiet m (*książki*)

'spin·ning| mill przędzalnia f; **'~ top** (*zabawka*) bąk m; **'~ wheel** kołowrotek m

spin·ster ['spɪnstə] stara panna f

spin·y ['spaɪnɪ] (**-ier, -iest**) *zo., bot.* kolczasty

spi·ral ['spaɪərəl] **1.** spiralny; **2.** spirala f; **~ 'stair·case** schody *pl.* kręte

spire [spaɪə] iglica f, stromy hełm m (*na wieży*)

spir·it ['spɪrɪt] dusza f; duch m; nastrój m, humor m; zaangażowanie n, determinacja f; *chem.* spirytus m; *zw.* **~s** *pl.* napoje *pl.* alkoholowe; *Holy* 2 Duch m Święty; '**~ed** energiczny; zaangażowany; dynamiczny; *koń* ognisty; '**~·less** bez temperamentu

spir·its ['spɪrɪts] *pl.* nastrój m; *be in high* (*low*) *~* być w znakomitym (podłym) nastroju

spir·i·tu·al ['spɪrɪtʃʊəl] **1.** duchowy; **2.** *mus.* spirituals *pl.*

spit¹ [spɪt] **1.** (**-tt-;** *spat lub zwł. Am.* **spit**) pluć; spluwać ⟨-lunąć⟩; *ogień:* trzaskać ⟨-snąć⟩; *tłuszcz itp.:* ⟨za⟩skwierczeć; *też ~ out* opluwać ⟨-luć⟩; *~ at s.o.* opluwać ⟨-luć⟩ kogoś; *it is ~ting* (*with rain*) siąpi; **2.** plwocina f

spit² [spɪt] rożen m; *geogr.* cypel m

spite [spaɪt] **1.** złośliwość f; *out of ~ lub from pure ~* z czystej złośliwości; *in ~ of* mimo, pomimo (G); **2.** komuś ⟨z⟩robić na złość; '**~·ful** złośliwy

spit·ting 'im·age: *be the ~ of s.o.* być kubek w kubek jak ktoś

spit·tle ['spɪtl] plwocina f, ślina f

splash [splæʃ] **1.** opryskiwać ⟨-kać⟩, ochlapywać ⟨-pać⟩; *dywan* zachlapać ⟨-pywać⟩; *wodę* rozbryzgiwać ⟨-gać⟩; chlapać się; *~ down statek kosmiczny* wodować; **2.** pochlapanie n, chlapnięcie n; plusk m, pluśnięcie n; plama f; rozbryzg m (*koloru*); *zwł. Brt.* dodatek m (*wody sodowej*); '**~·down** wodowanie n (*statku kosmicznego*)

splay [spleɪ] *też ~ out* palce itp. rozpościerać ⟨-postrzeć⟩

spleen [spliːn] *anat.* śledziona f

splen|·did ['splendɪd] znakomity, wspa-

niały; doskonały; '**~·do(u)r** przepych m, świetność f

splice [splaɪs] *sznur* ⟨z-, po⟩łączyć, *taśmę fot. itp.* ⟨s⟩kleić

splint [splɪnt] *med.* szyna f, *zw.* łubki *pl.*; *put in a ~, put in ~* zakładać ⟨założyć⟩ szynę

splin·ter ['splɪntə] **1.** drzazga f, odprysk m, odłamek m; **2.** rozszczepiać ⟨-pić⟩; rozłupywać ⟨-pać⟩; *~ off* odseparowywać ⟨-ować⟩ się (*from od G*)

split [splɪt] **1.** (**-tt-;** *split*) *v/t.* rozszczepiać ⟨-pić⟩ (*też phys.*), rozłupywać ⟨-pać⟩; *też ~ up* ⟨po⟩dzielić (*into* na A); *~ hairs* dzielić włos na czworo; *~ one's sides* F zrywać boki ze śmiechu; *v/i.* pękać ⟨-knąć⟩; rozszczepiać ⟨-pić⟩ się; *też ~ up* ⟨po⟩dzielić się (*into* na A); *też ~ up* (*with*) rozstawać ⟨-tać⟩ się z (I); **2.** pęknięcie n, szczelina f; podział m; *fig.* rozłam m; '**~·ting** *ból:* rozsadzający

splut·ter ['splʌtə] krztusić się (*też mot.*); *płomień:* syczeć

spoil [spɔɪl] **1.** (**spoilt** *lub* **spoiled**) *v/t.* ⟨ze-, po⟩psuć; ⟨z⟩niszczyć; *ze* ⟨ze⟩psuć, rozpieszczać ⟨-pieścić⟩ (*też dziecko*); *v/i.* ⟨ze-, po⟩psuć się; ⟨z⟩niszczyć się; **2.** *zw.* **~s** *pl.* łupy *pl.*

'spoil·er *mot.* spoiler m

'spoil·sport F (*osoba psująca innym zabawę*)

spoilt [spɔɪlt] *pret. i p.p. od* **spoil** 1

spoke¹ [spəʊk] *pret. od* **speak**

spoke² [spəʊk] szprycha f

spok·en ['spəʊkən] *p.p. od* **speak**

spokes|·man ['spəʊksmən] (*pl.* **-men**) rzecznik m; '**~·per·son** rzecznik m (**-niczka** f); '**~·wom·an** (*pl.* **-women**) rzeczniczka f

sponge [spʌndʒ] **1.** gąbka f (*też zo.*); *fig.* pasożyt m; *Brt.* → *sponge cake*; **2.** *v/t.* *też ~ down*, obmywać ⟨-myć⟩ (*gąbką*); *~ off, ~ down* zmywać ⟨-myć⟩; *~up* płyn zbierać ⟨zebrać⟩; *fig.* F ciągnąć (*from, off, on z G*) (*zyski itp.*); '*~ cake* biszkopt m; '*sponge·er fig.* pasożyt m; '*spong·y* (**-ier, -iest**) gąbczasty

spon·sor ['spɒnsə] **1.** sponsor m; projektodawca m (**-czyni** f), inicjator(ka f) m (*ustawy itp.*); **2.** ⟨za⟩sponsorować, wspierać ⟨wesprzeć⟩ finansowo; *projekt itp.* ⟨za⟩inicjować

spon·ta·ne·ous [spɒn'teɪnjəs] spontaniczny; samoistny; samorzutny

spook [spuːk] F duch *m*, widmo *n*; **'~y** (*-ier, -iest*) F niesamowity, widmowy

spool [spuːl] szpula *f*, rolka *f*

spoon [spuːn] **1.** łyżka *f*, łyżeczka *f*; **2.** nabierać ⟨-brać⟩ łyżką; **'~-feed** *dziecko* ⟨na⟩karmić łyżką *lub* łyżeczką; **'~ful** (*ilość*) łyżka *f*, łyżeczka *f*

spo·rad·ic [spəˈrædɪk] (*-ally*) sporadyczny, jednostkowy

spore [spɔː] *bot.* spora *f*, zarodnik *m*

sport [spɔːt] **1.** sport *m*; F kumpel(ka *f*) *m*; **~s** pl. sport(y *pl.*) *m*; **2.** ⟨za⟩demonstrować, ⟨za⟩prezentować

sports [spɔːts] sportowy; **~ car** samochód *m* sportowy; **~ cen·tre** (*Am. center*) centrum *n* sportowe; **'~-man** (*pl. -men*) sportowiec *m*, zawodnik *m*; **'~-wear** odzież *f* sportowa; **'~-wom·an** (*pl. -women*) sportsmenka *f*; zawodniczka *f*

spot [spɒt] **1.** punkt *m*; plamka *f*, plama *f* (*też med., anat.*); cętka *f*, kropka *f*; skaza *f*, znamię *n*; miejsce *n*; spot *m* reklamowy; F reflektor *m* punktowy; **a ~ of** *Brt.* F trochę, nieco; **on the ~** na miejscu; od razu; w miejscu (*biec*); **be in a ~** F być w tarapatach; **soft ~** słabość *f* (**for** *dla G*); **tender ~** czułe miejsce *n*; **weak ~** słabe miejsce *n*; **2.** (*-tt-*) dostrzegać ⟨-rzec⟩, zauważać ⟨-żyć⟩; ⟨po-, s⟩plamić; **~ 'check** próba *f* losowa, kontrola *f* losowa; **'~·less** nieskazitelny (*też fig.*); **'~·light** reflektor *m* punktowy; **'~·ted** cętkowany, nakrapiany; plamiasty, nakrapiany; **'~·ter** obserwator *m*; **'~·ty** (*-ier, -iest*) krostowaty

spouse [spaʊz] małżonek *m*

spout [spaʊt] **1.** tryskać ⟨-snąć⟩ (**from** z *G*); *fig.* F chlustać ⟨-snąć⟩; **2.** dziobek *m*; struga *f* (*płynu*)

sprain [spreɪn] *med.* **1.** *nogę itp.* skręcić; **2.** skręcenie *n*

sprang [spræŋ] *pret. od* **spring** 1

sprat [spræt] *zo.* szprot *m*

sprawl [sprɔːl] rozciągać ⟨-gnąć⟩ się; (*też ~ out*) rozwalać ⟨-lić⟩ się

spray [spreɪ] **1.** rozpylać ⟨-lić⟩, rozpryskiwać ⟨-kać⟩; opryskiwać ⟨-kać⟩; *włosy* ⟨s⟩pryskać (*lakierem*); **2.** pył *m* wodny; spray *m*; rozpylacz *m*; → **sprayer**; **'~ can** → **'~er** pojemnik *m* ciśnieniowy, spray *m*, aerozol *m*

spread [spred] **1.** (**spread**) *v/t.* rozkładać ⟨-złożyć⟩; *ramiona itp.* rozpościerać ⟨-postrzeć⟩; *masło itp.* rozsmarowywać ⟨-ować⟩; *chleb itp.* ⟨po⟩smarować; *chorobę itp.* roznosić ⟨-nieść⟩; *wiadomość itp.* rozpowszechniać ⟨-nić⟩; *v/i.* rozciągać ⟨-gnąć⟩ się (*też ~ out*); rozchodzić ⟨-zejść⟩ się; *wiadomość itp.* roznosić ⟨-nieść⟩ się; **2.** rozszerzanie *n* się; rozpiętość *f*; zasięg *m*; rozprzestrzenianie *n* się; pasta *f* (*do chleba*); *w gazecie* rozkładówka *f*; **'~-sheet** *komputer:* arkusz *m* kalkulacyjny

spree [spriː] F: **go (out) on a ~** wypuszczać ⟨-puścić⟩ się na balangę; **go on a buying** (*lub* **shopping, spending**) **~** kupować bez opamiętania

Spree Sprewa *f*

sprig [sprɪg] *bot.* gałązka *f*

spright·ly [ˈspraɪtlɪ] (*-ier, -iest*) *taniec:* skoczny; *starsza osoba:* żwawy, dziarski

spring [sprɪŋ] **1.** (**sprang** *lub Am.* **sprung, sprung**) *v/i.* skakać ⟨skoczyć⟩; **~ from** wynikać ⟨-knąć⟩ z (*G*); pojawiać ⟨-wić⟩ się; **~ up** *wiatr.* zrywać ⟨zerwać⟩ się; wyrastać ⟨-rosnąć⟩, zjawiać ⟨-wić⟩ się (*też fig*); *v/t.* **~ a leak** zaczynać ⟨-cząć⟩ przeciekać; **~ a surprise on s.o.** zaskakiwać ⟨-skoczyć⟩ kogoś; **2.** wiosna *f*; źródło *n*; sprężyna *f*; sprężystość *f*; żwawość *f*; skok *m*; **in (the) ~** na wiosnę, wiosną; **'~·board** trampolina *f*; odskocznia *f* (*też fig.*); **~'clean** przeprowadzać ⟨-dzić⟩ gruntowne *lub* wiosenne porządki (w *L*); **'~-clean** *Brt.*, **'~-clean·ing** *Am.* gruntowne *lub* wiosenne porządki *pl.*; **~ 'tide**; **'~·time** wiosna *f*; **~·y** [ˈsprɪŋɪ] (*-ier, -iest*) elastyczny, sprężysty

sprin·kle [ˈsprɪŋkl] **1.** *wodą* ⟨po⟩kropić, skrapiać ⟨-ropić⟩; *solą itp.* posypywać ⟨-pać⟩; **it is sprinkling** (*deszcz*) kropi; **2.** (*deszcz*) kapuśniaczek *m*; posypanie *n*; pokropienie *n*; **'~·kler** zraszacz *m*; przeciwpożarowe urządzenie *n* tryskaczowe; **'~·kling: a ~kling of** trochę (*G*), nieco (*G*)

sprint [sprɪnt] (*w sporcie*) **1.** ⟨po⟩biec sprintem; **2.** sprint *m*; **'~·er** (*w sporcie*) sprinter(ka *f*) *m*

sprite [spraɪt] duszek *m*; *fig.* chochlik *m*

sprout [spraʊt] **1.** ⟨wy⟩kiełkować; ⟨wy⟩rosnąć; **~ a beard** zapuszczać ⟨-puścić⟩ brodę; **2.** *bot.* kiełek *m*, pęd *m*; odrost *m*; (**Brussels**) **~s** *pl. bot.* brukselka *f*

spruce¹ [spruːs] *bot.* świerk *m*

spruce² [spru:s] wytworny

sprung [sprʌŋ] *pret. i p.p. od* **spring** 1

spry [spraɪ] *starsza osoba:* żwawy, dziarski

spun [spʌn] *pret. i p.p. od* **spin** 1

spur [spɜ:] **1.** ostroga *f; fig.* bodziec *m; on the ~ of the moment* pod wpływem chwili; **2.** (*-rr-*) *konia* spinać ⟨spiąć⟩ ostrogami; *często ~ on fig.* zachęcać ⟨-cić⟩

spurt¹ [spɜ:t] **1.** ⟨po⟩mknąć; **2.** zryw *m*, przypływ *m* energii

spurt² [spɜ:t] **1.** tryskać ⟨-snąć⟩ (*from* z *G*); **2.** struga *f*, strumień *m* (*pary*)

sput·ter ['spʌtə] krztusić się (*też mot.*); *płomień:* syczeć

spy [spaɪ] **1.** szpieg *m*; **2.** szpiegować; *~ into fig.* wnikać ⟨-knąć⟩ w (*A*); '*~hole* judasz *m*, wizjer *m*

Sq *skrót pisany:* **Square** pl., plac *m*

sq *skrót pisany:* **square** kw., kwadratowy

squab·ble ['skwɒbl] ⟨po⟩sperać się

squad [skwɒd] grupa *f;* ekipa *f;* oddział *m* (*policji itp.*); '*~ car zwł. Am.* radiowóz *m*

squad·ron ['skwɒdrən] *mil.* szwadron *m; naut.* eskadra *f; aviat.* dywizjon *m*

squal·id ['skwɒlɪd] zapuszczony, zaniedbany; nędzny

squall [skwɔ:l] szkwał *m*

squan·der ['skwɒndə] *pieniądze* ⟨z⟩marnotrawić; *szansę* zaprzepaszczać ⟨-paścić⟩

square [skweə] **1.** kwadrat *m;* czworokąt *m;* plac *m,* skwer *m; math.* kwadrat *m* (*liczby*); pole *n* (*szachownicy*); (*w krzyżówce*) kratka *f; tech.* kątownik *m;* **2.** kwadratowy; czworokątny; prostopadły; *math.* kwadratowy, do kwadratu; rzetelny; rozliczony; *be (all) ~* być kwita; **3.** nadawać ⟨-dać⟩ kwadratowy kształt; ustawiać ⟨-wić⟩ pod kątem prostym (*też ~ off, up*); ⟨wy⟩kalkować (*też ~ off*); *math.* podnosić ⟨-nieść⟩ do kwadratu; *należności* uregulowywać ⟨-ować⟩, wyrównywać ⟨-nać⟩; *rachunki* uzgadniać ⟨-godnić⟩; *~ with fig.* pasować do (*G*), dopasowywać ⟨-ować⟩ do (*G*); wyjaśniać ⟨-nić⟩; *~ up v/i.* F rozliczać ⟨-czyć⟩ się; *~ up to* stawiać ⟨-wić⟩ czoło (*D*); *~d 'pa·per* kratkowany papier *m; ~ 'root math.* pierwiastek *m* kwadratowy

squash¹ [skwɒʃ] **1.** ⟨z⟩miażdżyć, zgniatać ⟨zgnieść⟩; wtłaczać ⟨-łoczyć⟩ (się) (*into* do *G*); *~ flat* zgniatać ⟨zgnieść⟩ na miazgę; **2.** ścisk *m;* (*w sporcie*) squash *m; lemon lub orange ~* sok *m* pitny cytrynowy *lub* pomarańczowy

squash² [skwɒʃ] *zwł. Am. bot.* kabaczek *m*

squat [skwɒt] **1.** (*-tt-*) kucać ⟨-cnąć⟩, przykucać ⟨-cnąć⟩ (*też ~ down*); *mieszkanie* zamieszkiwać ⟨-kać⟩ nielegalnie; **2.** krępy; '*~ter* dziki lokator(ka *f*) *m*

squaw [skwɔ:] squaw *f*

squawk [skwɔ:k] **1.** ⟨za⟩skrzeczeć; F ⟨za⟩protestować (*about* w sprawie *G*)

squeak [skwi:k] **1.** *mysz itp.:* ⟨za⟩piszczeć; *drzwi:* ⟨za⟩skrzypieć; **2.** pisk *m;* skrzypienie *n;* '*~·y* (*-ier, -iest*) *głos:* piskliwy; *drzwi:* skrzypiący

squeal [skwi:l] **1.** ⟨za⟩piszczeć (*with* z *G*); *~ on s.o. sl.* donosić ⟨-nieść⟩ na kogoś; **2.** pisk *m*

squeam·ish ['skwi:mɪʃ] drażliwy, czuły

squeeze [skwi:z] **1.** ściskać ⟨-snąć⟩; wyciskać ⟨-snąć⟩; zgniatać ⟨-nieść⟩; wciskać ⟨-snąć⟩ (się) (*into* do *G*); przepychać ⟨-pchnąć⟩ się; **2.** uścisk *m,* ściśnięcie *n;* odrobina *f* (*soku itp.*); ścisk *m,* tłok *m;* '*squeez·er* wyciskarka *f* do soku

squid [skwɪd] *zo.* (*pl.* **squids, squid**) mątwa *f,* kałamarnica *f,* kalmar *m*

squint [skwɪnt] **1.** zezować; ⟨po⟩patrzeć przez zmrużone oczy; **2.** zez *m*

squirm [skwɜ:m] wiercić się; wić się

squir·rel ['skwɪrəl] *zo.* wiewiórka *f*

squirt [skwɜ:t] **1.** strzykać ⟨-knąć⟩; tryskać ⟨-snąć⟩; **2.** strzyknięcie *n;* tryśnięcie *n*

Sr → **Snr**

SS ['es es] *skrót:* **steamship** SS, statek *m* parowy

St *skrót pisany:* **Saint** ... św. ..., święty ... *m* (-ta *f*); **Street** ul., ulica *f*

st *skrót pisany:* **stone** Brt. (*jednostka masy = 6,35 kg*)

Sta *skrót pisany:* **Station** st., stacja *f* (*zwł. na mapach*)

stab [stæb] **1.** (*-bb-*) *v/t.* pchnąć (*nożem itp.*); dźgać ⟨dźgnąć⟩; *be ~bed in the arm* otrzymać pchnięcie w ramię; *v/i.* dźgać ⟨dźgnąć⟩; **2.** pchnięcie *n;* dźgnięcie *n*

sta·bil·i·ty [stə'bɪlətɪ] stabilizacja *f;*

ustabilizowanie *n*; **~ize** ['steɪbəlaɪz] ⟨u⟩stabilizować (się)

sta·ble¹ ['steɪbl] ustabilizowany; stały

sta·ble² ['steɪbl] stajnia *f*

stack [stæk] **1.** stos *m*, sterta *f*; **~s of, a ~ of** F kupa (*roboty itp.*); → **haystack**; **2.** układać ⟨ułożyć⟩ w stos; zastawiać ⟨-wić⟩; **~ up** zwł. *Am.* porównywać

sta·di·um ['steɪdjəm] (*w sporcie*) stadion *m*

staff [stɑːf] **1.** personel *m*, pracownicy *pl.*; (*w szkole*) grono *n* pedagogiczne, nauczyciele *pl.*; *mil.* sztab *m*; kij *m*, laska *f*; **2.** obsadzać ⟨-dzić⟩ (*personelem*); **'~ room** pokój *m* nauczycielski

stag [stæg] zo. (*pl.* **stags, stag**) jeleń *m*

stage [steɪdʒ] **1.** *theat.* scena *f* (*też fig.*); podium *n*; stadium *n*; etap *m* (*też fig.*); odcinek *m* (*podróży*); *Brt.* biletowa strefa *f*; *tech.* człon *m* (*rakiety*); **2.** *theat.* ⟨za⟩inscenizować, wystawiać ⟨-wić⟩; ⟨z⟩organizować; **'~·coach** *hist.* dyliżans *m*; **'~ di·rec·tion**; **'~ fright** trema *f*; **'~ man·ag·er** inspicjent *m*

stag·ger ['stægə] **1.** *v/i.* zataczać ⟨-toczyć⟩ się (**towards** w stronę *G*); iść ⟨pójść⟩ zataczając się; *v/t.* wstrząsać ⟨-snąć⟩; zamykać ⟨-mknąć⟩ usta; **~ imagination** przerastać ⟨-rosnąć⟩ wyobraźnię; *czas pracy* układać ⟨ułożyć⟩ przemiennie

stag·nant ['stægnənt] *woda*: stojący; *zwł. econ.* (*będący*) w zastoju; **~·nate** *zwł. econ.* [stæg'neɪt] trwać w stagnacji

stain [steɪn] **1.** *v/t.* ⟨po⟩plamić; ⟨za⟩barwić, ⟨za⟩farbować; *drewno itp.* ⟨za⟩bejcować; *v/i.* ulegać ⟨-lec⟩ zaplamieniu; **2.** plama *f* (*też fig.*); zabarwienie *n*, zafarbowanie *n*; bejca *f*; **~ed 'glass** szkło *n* witrażowe; **~ed glass 'window** witraż *m*; **'~·less** nierdzewny

stair [steə] stopień *m*; **~s** *pl.* schody *pl.*; **'~·case**, **'~·way** klatka *f* schodowa

stake¹ [steɪk] **1.** pal *m*, słup *m*; *hist.* stos *m*, słup męczeński; **2.** **~ off, ~ out** ogradzać ⟨-rodzić⟩

stake² [steɪk] **1.** udział *m* (**in** w *L*) (*też econ.*); stawka *f*; **be at ~** *fig.* wchodzić w grę; **2.** *pieniądze itp.* stawiać ⟨postawić⟩ (**on** na *A*); *pieniądze, reputację itp.* ⟨za⟩ryzykować

stale [steɪl] (**-r, -st**) *chleb*: czerstwy; *jedzenie*: nieświeży; *piwo*: zwietrzały; *powietrze*: stęchły

stalk¹ [stɔːk] *bot.* łodyga *f*

stalk² [stɔːk] *v/t.* ⟨wy⟩tropić, ⟨wy⟩śledzić; *v/i.* kroczyć, stąpać

stall¹ [stɔːl] **1.** stragan *m*, stoisko *n*; (*w stajni*) boks *m*; **~s** *rel. pl.* stalle *pl.*; *Brt. theat.* parter *m*; **2.** *v/t.* ⟨s⟩powodować zgaśnięcie; *v/i.* zgasnąć

stall² [stɔːl] *v/i.* zwlekać ⟨-lec⟩; *v/t.* *kogoś* wstrzymywać ⟨-mać⟩; zwodzić ⟨zwieść⟩

stal·li·on ['stæljən] *zo.* ogier *m*

stal·wart ['stɔːlwət] wierny, oddany

stam·i·na ['stæmɪnə] wytrwałość *f*, hart *m*

stam·mer ['stæmə] **1.** jąkać się; **2.** jąkanie *n* się

stamp [stæmp] **1.** *v/i.* tupać; nadeptywać ⟨-pnąć⟩; *v/t.* ⟨o⟩stemplować, ⟨przy-, o⟩pieczętować; naklejać ⟨-leić⟩ znaczek na (*A*) (*list*); *fig. kogoś* określać ⟨-lić⟩ (**as** jako); **~·out** *ogień* ⟨s⟩tłumić; *tech.* ⟨wy⟩tłoczyć; **2.** znaczek *m* (*na list*); stempel *m*, pieczątka *f*; **~ed (addressed) envelope** zaadresowana koperta z naklejonym znaczkiem

stam·pede [stæm'piːd] **1.** popłoch *m*, panika *f*; paniczna ucieczka *f* (*zwierząt*); gonitwa *f*, pogoń *f* (**for** za *I*); **2.** ⟨s⟩płoszyć (się)

stanch [stɑːntʃ] *Am.* → **staunch**

stand [stænd] **1.** (**stood**) *v/i.* stać; wstawać ⟨wstać⟩; *wartość*: utrzymywać się; *fig.* pozostawać ⟨-stać⟩; *być w mocy lub* ważnym; **~ still** stać bez ruchu; *v/t.* stawiać ⟨postawić⟩ (**on** na *L*); znosić ⟨znieść⟩; *test* wytrzymywać ⟨-mać⟩; *szanse itp.* mieć; *drinka itp.* stawiać ⟨postawić⟩ (*D*); *sprawy*: wyglądać, przedstawiać się; **I can't ~** him nie mogę go znieść; **~ aside** odchodzić ⟨odejść⟩ na bok; **~ back** cofać ⟨-fnąć⟩ się; **~ by** stać bezczynnie; *fig.* stać przy *kimś*; dotrzymywać ⟨-mać⟩ (*obietnicy itp.*); stać w pogotowiu; **~ down** ustępować ⟨-tąpić⟩ (*ze stanowiska*); **~ for** oznaczać; znosić ⟨znieść⟩; reprezentować; *zwł. Brt.* kandydować na (*A*); **~ in** zastępować ⟨-tąpić⟩; **~·out** rzucać się w oczy, odznaczać się; wyróżniać się (**against** wśród *G*); **~ over** stać nad (*I*); **~ together** trzymać się razem; **~·up** stawać ⟨-tać⟩, powstawać ⟨-tać⟩; **~·up for** ⟨o⟩bronić, popierać ⟨poprzeć⟩; **~·up to** przeciwstawiać ⟨-wić⟩ się; stawiać *komuś* czoło; **2.** stoisko *n*, stragan *m*; stojak *m*, podstawka *f*; (*w sporcie*) trybuna *f*; postój *m* (*taksówek*); *Am. jur.* miejsce *n* dla świadka; **take a ~** *fig.* zajmować ‹-jąć› stanowisko

stan·dard¹ ['stændəd] **1.** standard *m*; norma *f*; miara *f*; **~ of living, living ~** poziom *m* życia, stopa *f* życiowa; **2.** standardowy. normalny; typowy

stan·dard² ['stændəd] sztandar *m*

stan·dard·ize ['stændədaɪz] standaryzować, ujednolicać ‹-cić›

'stan·dard lamp *Brt.* lampa *f* stojąca

'stand·by 1. (*pl.* **-bys**) rezerwa *f*; *aviat.* stand-by (*tańszy bilet tuż przed wyjazdem*); **be on ~** być w pogotowiu; **2.** rezerwowy; awaryjny; *aviat.* stand-by; **'~-in** (*w filmie, telewizji*) dubler(ka *f*) *m*; zastępca *m* (-czyni *f*)

stand·ing ['stændɪŋ] **1.** stojący; *fig.* stały; → *ovation*; **2.** pozycja *f*, ranga *f*; **of long ~** znany od dawna; długotrwały; **~ 'or·der** *econ.* zamówienie *n* stałe; **'~ room: ~ room only** brak miejsc siedzących

stand·off·ish [stænd'ɒfɪʃ] *F* oficjalny, sztywny; **'~·point** *fig.* punkt *m* widzenia; **'~·still** bezruch *m*; **be at a ~still** nie ruszać się; *produkcja*: być w zastoju; **bring to a ~still** *auto* zatrzymywać; doprowadzać produkcję do zastoju; **'~-up** *posiłek*: na stojąco

stank [stæŋk] *pret. of* **stink**

stan·za ['stænzə] strofa *f*, zwrotka *f*

sta·ple¹ ['steɪpl] **1.** główny typ pożywienia; główny produkt *m*; **2.** główny

sta·ple² ['steɪpl] **1.** zszywka *f*; **2.** zszywać ‹zszyć›; **'~r** zszywacz *m* (*do papieru*)

star [stɑː] **1.** gwiazda *f*; *print.* gwiazdka *f*; (*w filmie, telewizji, sporcie*) gwiazda *f*; **2.** (**-rr-**) *v/t.* oznaczać ‹-czyć› gwiazdką; **~ring ...** w roli głównej występuje ...; **a film ~ring ...** film z ... w roli głównej; *v/i.* grać rolę główną (**in** w *L*)

star·board ['stɑːbəd] *naut.* (*prawa strona*) sterburta *f*

starch [stɑːtʃ] **1.** krochmal *m*; skrobia *f*; **2.** *pranie:* ‹na›krochmalić

stare [steə] **1.** wpatrywać ‹-trzyć› się (**at** w *A*); gapić się (**at** w *A*); **2.** uporczywe spojrzenie *n*

stark [stɑːk] **1.** *adj.* surowy; ponury; **be in ~ contrast to** różnić się krańcowo od (*G*); **2.** *adv.* F **~ naked** całkiem goły; **~ raving mad** zupełnie stuknięty

'star·light światło *n* gwiazd

star·ling ['stɑːlɪŋ] *zo.* szpak *m*

star·lit ['stɑːlɪt] rozświetlony gwiazdami

star·ry ['stɑːrɪ] (**-ier, -iest**) gwiaździsty, rozgwieżdżony; **~-eyed** *F* naiwny

Stars and 'Stripes *flaga USA*

Star-Span·gled Ban·ner [stɑː-spæŋgld 'bænə] (*hymn narodowy USA*)

start [stɑːt] **1.** *v/i.* zaczynać ‹-cząć› (*też* **~ off**); rozpoczynać ‹-cząć›; wyruszać ‹-szyć› (**for** do *G*) (*też* **~ off, ~ out**); *autobus itp.*: odjeżdżać ‹-jechać›, *statek:* odpływać ‹-łynąć›; *aviat.* ‹wy›startować; *silnik:* zaskoczyć; *maszynę* uruchamiać ‹-chomić się› (*w sporcie*) ‹wy›startować; wzdrygać ‹-gnąć› się (**at** z powodu *G*); **to ~ with** na początek; najpierw; **~ from scratch** zaczynać ‹-cząć› od zera; *v/t.* zaczynać ‹-cząć› (*też* **~ off**); rozpoczynać ‹-cząć›; *silnik, maszynę* uruchamiać ‹-chomić›; *firmę* zakładać ‹-założyć›; *produkcję* uruchamiać ‹-chomić›; **2.** początek *m* (*zwł. sport, aviat.*) start *m*; odjazd *m*, odpłynięcie *n*; wzdrygnięcie *n* się; przewaga *f* (**on, over** nad *I*); **at the ~** na początku; *sport:* na starcie; **for a ~** na początek, najpierw; **from ~ to finish** od początku do końca; **'~er** (*w sporcie*) starter *m*; *mot.* rozrusznik *m*, starter *m*; zawodnik *m* (-niczka *f*); *zwł. Brt.* przystawka *f* (*do posiłku*); **for ~s** F na dobry początek

star·tle ['stɑːtl] *kogoś* zaskakiwać ‹-koczyć›, wystraszać ‹-szyć›

starv·a·tion [stɑː'veɪʃn] głód *n*; **die of ~ation** umrzeć z głodu; **~ation diet** F dieta *f* zerowa; **~e** [stɑːv] *v/i.* głodować; **~e** (**to death**) zagłodzić się; **I'm starving!** *Brt.*, **I'm ~ed!** umieram z głodu!; *v/t.* ‹za›głodzić

state [steɪt] **1.** stan *m* (*też pol.*); państwo *n*; **be in a ~** być zdenerwowanym; **2.** państwowy; stanowy; **3.** określać ‹-lić›; stwierdzać ‹-dzić›; **'2 De·part·ment** *Am. pol.* Departament *m* Stanu, Ministerstwo *n* Spraw Zagranicznych; **'~·ly** (**-ier, -iest**) uroczysty; majestatyczny, wyniosły; **'~·ment** stwierdzenie *n*; określenie *n*; *jur.* oświadczenie *n*; *econ.* wyciąg *m* (*z konta*); **make a ~ment** oświadczać ‹-czyć›; **~-of-the-'art** *adj.* nowoczesny; **'~·room** *naut.* luksusowa kabina *f* jednoosobowa;

S

'~·side *Am.* F w Stanach, do Stanów; **~s·man** *pol.* ['steɪtsmən] (*pl.* **-men**) mąż *m* stanu

stat·ic ['stætɪk] (**~ally**) statyczny

sta·tion ['steɪʃn] **1.** *badawcza, benzynowa* stacja *f*; *autobusowy* dworzec *m*; remiza *f* (*straży pożarnej*); komisariat *m*; *pol.* lokal *m* wyborczy; **2.** *wojsko:* stacjonować; *posterunek* ustawiać ⟨-wić⟩

sta·tion·a·ry ['steɪʃnərɪ] stacjonarny

sta·tion·er ['steɪʃnə] sprzedawca *m* (-czyni *f*) artykułów piśmiennych; **'~'s** (**shop**) sklep *m* z artykułami piśmiennymi; **~·y** ['steɪʃnərɪ] artykuły *pl.* piśmienne

'sta·tion|·mas·ter *rail.* naczelnik *m* stacji; **'~ wag·on** *Am. mot.* kombi *n*

sta·tis|ti·cal [stə'tɪstɪkəl] statystyczny; **~·tics** [stə'tɪstɪks] *pl. i sg.* statystyka *f*

stat·ue ['stætʃuː] pomnik *m*, posąg *m*

sta·tus ['steɪtəs] status *m*; pozycja *f*; stan *m*; stan *m* cywilny; **'~ line** *komp.* wiersz *m* stanu

stat·ute ['stætjuːt] ustawa *f*; **~s** *pl.* statut *m*

staunch[1] [stɔːntʃ] lojalny, oddany

staunch[2] [stɔːntʃ] *krwotok* ⟨za⟩tamować

stay [steɪ] **1.** pozostawać ⟨-tać⟩; przebywać (**at** w *L*, **with** u *G*); **~ away** trzymać się z daleka (**from** od *G*); **~ put** F pozostawać na miejscu; **~ up** nie kłaść się (*spać*); **2.** pobyt *m*; *jur.* odroczenie *n*

stead·fast ['stedfɑːst] *przyjaciel:* oddany; *wzrok:* nieruchomy

stead·y ['stedɪ] **1.** *adj.* (**-ier, -iest**) stały; niezmienny; regularny; solidny; *ręka:* pewny; *nerwy:* dobry; **2.** ⟨u⟩stabilizować (się); wyrównywać ⟨-nać⟩; *nerwy* uspokajać ⟨-koić⟩; **3.** *int. też* **~ on!** *Brt.* F uważaj!; **4.** *adv. Am.:* **go ~ with s.o.** chodzić z kimś na poważnie; **5.** *Am.* stały chłopak *m*, stała dziewczyna *f*

steak [steɪk] stek *m*, zraz *m*; filet *m*

steal [stiːl] (**stole, stolen**) ⟨u⟩kraść (*też fig.*); skradać się; wymykać ⟨-mknąć⟩ się (**out of** z *G*)

stealth [stelθ]: **by ~** ukradkiem; **'~·y** (**-ier, -iest**) ukradkowy

steam [stiːm] **1.** para *f* (*wodna*); *attr.* parowy; **let off ~** spuszczać ⟨spuścić⟩ parę; *fig.* ulżyć sobie; **2.** *v/i.* parować; **~ up** *szkło:* zaparować się; *v/t. gastr.* ⟨u⟩gotować na parze; **'~·boat** *naut.* łódź *m*

parowa; **'~·er** *naut.* parowiec *m*; szybkowar *m*; **'~·ship** *naut.* parowiec *m*

steel [stiːl] **1.** stal *f*; *attr.* stalowy; **2. ~ o.s. for** przygotować się na (*A*); **'~·works** *sg.* stalownia *f*

steep[1] [stiːp] stromy; *wzrost:* ostry, gwałtowny; F *cena:* nadmierny

steep[2] [stiːp] *pranie* namaczać ⟨-moczyć⟩ (**in** w *L*); zanurzać⟨-rzyć⟩ (**in** w *L*)

stee·ple ['stiːpl] wieża *f* kościelna; **'~·chase** (*w sportach konnych*) steeplechase *m* (*wyścig z przeszkodami*); (*w lekkiej atletyce*) steeplechase *m* (*bieg z przeszkodami*)

steer[1] [stɪə] *zo.* młody wół *m*

steer[2] [stɪə] ⟨po⟩sterować, ⟨po⟩kierować; **~·ing col·umn** *mot.* ['stɪərɪŋkɒləm] kolumna *f* kierownicy; **~·ing wheel** ['stɪərɪŋwiːl] *mot.* koło *n* kierownicy; *naut. też* koło *n* sterowe

stein [staɪn] kufel *m*

stem [stem] **1.** *bot.* łodyga *f*; ogonek *m*; nóżka *f* (*kieliszka*); *ling.* rdzeń *m*; **2.** (**-mm-**): **~ from** wynikać ⟨-knąć⟩ z (*G*)

stench [stentʃ] odór *m*, smród *m*

sten·cil ['stensl] szablon *m*; *print.* matryca *f*

ste·nog·ra·pher [ste'nɒɡrəfə] *Am.* stenograf(ka *f*) *m*

step [step] **1.** krok *m* (*też fig.*); stopień *m*; (**a pair of**) **~s** *pl.* składana drabina *f*; **mind the ~!** uwaga na stopień!; **~ by ~** krok za krokiem; **take ~s** podejmować ⟨-djąć⟩ kroki; **2.** (**-pp-**) iść ⟨pójść⟩; następować ⟨-tąpić⟩ (**on** na *A*); wdeptywać ⟨-pnąć⟩ (**in** w *A*); **~ on it, ~ on the gas** *mot.* F dodaj gazu!; **~ aside** odstępować ⟨-tąpić⟩; *fig.* ustępować ⟨-tąpić⟩ miejsca; **~ down** schodzić ⟨zejść⟩; *fig.* ustępować ⟨-tąpić⟩ miejsca; **~ up** *produkcję* zwiększać ⟨-szyć⟩

'step·broth·er brat *m* przyrodni

step-by-'step *fig.* stopniowo

'step·daugh·ter pasierbica *f*

'step·fa·ther ojczym *m*

'step·lad·der składana drabina *f*

'step·moth·er macocha *f*

'step·sis·ter siostra *f* przyrodnia

'step·son pasierb *m*

steppe [steps] *geogr.* step *m*

step·ping-stone *fig.* ['stepɪŋstəʊn] odskocznia *f*

ster·e·o ['sterɪəʊ] (*pl.* **-os**) stereo *n*; zestaw *m* stereo; sprzęt *m* elektroniczny; *attr.* stereo; '~ **sys·tem** *Am. mus.* zestaw *m* stereo

ster·ile ['sterail] sterylny (*też fig.*); wyjałowiony; niepłodny, bezpłodny; *fig.* jałowy; **ste·ril·i·ty** [ste'rɪlətɪ] sterylność *f*; jałowość *f*; bezpłodność *f*; **ster·il·ize** ['sterəlaɪz] ⟨wy⟩sterylizować

ster·ling ['stɜːlɪŋ] funt *m* szterling

stern¹ [stɜːn] surowy

stern² [stɜːn] *naut.* rufa *f*

stew [stjuː] *gastr.* **1.** mięso *itp.* ⟨u⟩dusić, *owoce* ⟨u⟩gotować; **~ed apples** kompot *m* z jabłek; **2.** potrawka *f*; *be in a ~* być w tarapatach

stew·ard [stjuəd] *naut., aviat.* steward *m*; gospodarz *m* (*imprezy*); **~·ess** ['stjuədɪs] *naut., aviat.* stewardesa *f*

stick¹ [stɪk] patyk *m*; kij *m* (*też do hokeja itp.*); laska *f*; *aviat.* drążek *m* sterowy; laska *f* (*warzywa, dynamitu itp.*); kredka *f* (*do ust*)

stick² [stɪk] (**stuck**) *v/t.* wbijać ⟨wbić⟩ (*into* w *A*); przebijać ⟨-bić⟩; przyklejać ⟨-kleić⟩ (*on* do *G*); sklejać ⟨skleić⟩ (*with* z *I*); F wtykać ⟨wetknąć⟩; *I can't ~ him zwł. Brt.* F nie mogę go znieść; *v/i.* przywierać ⟨-wrzeć⟩ (*to* do *G*); przyklejać ⟨-leić⟩ się (*to* do *G*); utykać ⟨utknąć⟩, ⟨u⟩więznąć; *~ at nothing* nie cofać ⟨-fnąć⟩ się przed niczym; *~ by* trwać przy (*L*); stosować się do (*G*); *~ out* wystawiać; *język itp.* wysuwać ⟨-nąć⟩; przetrwać *coś*; *~ to* trwać przy (*L*); '*~·er* naklejka *f*; *~·ing plas·ter Brt.* przylepiec *m*; '*~·y* (*-ier, -iest*) lepki; kleisty (*with* od *G*); F *położenie itp.*: niezręczny

stiff [stɪf] **1.** *adj.* sztywny; F *alkohol, lekarstwo:* mocny; *zadanie:* trudny, ciężki; *konkurencja:* silny; *wyrok:* surowy; *opór:* twardy; F *cena:* wygórowany; *keep a ~ upper lip fig.* nie okazywać ⟨-zać⟩ emocji; **2.** *adv.* bardzo; *be bored ~* F być śmiertelnie znudzonym; *frozen ~* zamarznięty na kość; **3.** *sl.* truposz *m*; *~·en* ['stɪfn] *coś* usztywniać ⟨-nić⟩; ⟨ze⟩sztywnieć; *fig.* wzmacniać ⟨-mocnić⟩ (się)

sti·fle ['staɪfl] dusić (się); *fig.* ⟨s⟩tłumić

stile [staɪl] przełaz *m*

sti·let·to [stɪ'letəʊ] (*pl. -tos*) sztylet *m*; *~ 'heels pl.* szpilki *pl.* (*buty, też obcasy*)

still¹ [stɪl] **1.** *adv.* wciąż, jeszcze; *~ higher* jeszcze wyższy; **2.** *cj.* jednak, mimo to

still² [stɪl] **1.** *adj.* spokojny; nieruchomy; cichy; *napój:* niegazowany; **2.** fotos *m*; '*~·born* płód *n:* martwo urodzony; *~ 'life* (*pl. - lifes*) martwa natura *f*

stilt [stɪlt] szczudło *n*; pal *m*; '*~·ed styl:* zmanierowany

stim·u·lant ['stɪmjʊlənt] *med.* środek *m* stymulujący *lub* pobudzający; używka *f*; impuls *m*, bodziec *m* (*to* do *G*); *~·late* ['stɪmjʊleɪt] *med.* stymulować (*też fig.*); pobudzać ⟨-dzić⟩; *~·lus* ['stɪmjʊləs] (*pl. -li* [-laɪ]) bodziec *m* (*też fig.*); *fig.* zachęta *f* (*for* do *G*)

sting [stɪŋ] **1.** (**stung**) *v/t.* ⟨u⟩ciąć, ⟨u⟩kłuć, ⟨u⟩kąsić; *pszczoła itp.:* ⟨u⟩żądlić; *piec* w (*A*); F oszukać, naciągnąć; *fig.* dotykać ⟨-tknąć⟩; *v/i.* ⟨za⟩piec, szczypać; *roślina itp.:* parzyć; **2.** żądło *n*; włosek *m* parzący (*rośliny*); oparzenie *n*; użądlenie *n*; ukąszenie *n*; pieczenie *n*, szczypanie *n*

stin·gy ['stɪndʒɪ] F (*-ier, -iest*) *osoba:* chciwy; *posiłek:* lichy, nędzny

stink [stɪŋk] **1.** (**stank** *lub* **stunk**, **stunk**) śmierdzieć, cuchnąć; **2.** smród *m*

stint [stɪnt]: *~ o.s.* (*of s.th.*) odmawiać sobie (*G*); *~ (on) s.th.* skąpić (*G*)

stip·u·late ['stɪpjʊleɪt] postanawiać ⟨-nowić⟩; przewidywać ⟨-dzieć⟩; *~·la·tion* [stɪpjʊ'leɪʃn] postanowienie *n*; warunek *m*

stir [stɜː] **1.** (*-rr-*) *v/t.* ⟨po-, za⟩mieszać; poruszać ⟨-szyć⟩ (*też fig.*); *fig.* wywoływać ⟨-łać⟩; *~ up* kłopoty *itp.* wywoływać ⟨-łać⟩; *kogoś* poruszać ⟨-szyć⟩; *v/i.* ruszać się (*z domu itp.*); ⟨po⟩ruszać się (*we śnie*); **2.** *give s.th. a ~* zamieszać *coś*; *cause a ~*, *create a ~* wywoływać ⟨-łać⟩ poruszenie

stir·rup ['stɪrəp] strzemię *n*

stitch [stɪtʃ] **1.** *szycie:* ścieg *m*; *wydziergane* oczko *n*; *med.* szew *m*; kolka *f* (*w boku*); **2.** zszywać ⟨-szyć⟩, przyszywać ⟨-szyć⟩ (*on* do *G*); *~ up fig.* dopinać na ostatni guzik

stock [stɒk] **1.** zapas *m*; zasób *m*; *gastr.* bulion *m*, wywar *m*; *też* **live ~** inwentarz *m* żywy; kolba *f* (*karabinu*); *fig.* ród *m*; *zwł. Am. econ.* akcja *f*; *~s pl. econ.* papiery *pl.* wartościowe; *have s.th. in ~ econ.* mieć coś na stanie; *take ~ econ.* przeprowadzać ⟨-dzić⟩ spis *lub* inwentaryzację; *take ~ of fig.* oceniać ⟨-nić⟩ (*G*); **2.** *econ.* *towar* mieć

S

na składzie, prowadzić; **~ up** zaopatrywać ⟨-trzyć⟩ się (**on, with** w *A*); **3.** *wyrażenie itp.*: oklepany, wyświechtany; seryjny; *rozmiar itp.*: standardowy; '**~·breed·er** hodowca *m* bydła; '**~·brok·er** *econ.* broker *m*, makler *m*; '**~ ex·change** *econ.* giełda *f* pieniężna; '**~·hold·er** *zwł. Am. econ.* akcjonariusz(ka *f*) *m*
Stock·holm Sztokholm *m*
stock·ing ['stɒkɪŋ] pończocha *f*
'**stock·mar·ket** *econ.* giełda *f* walorów; '**~·pile 1.** zapas *m*; **2.** ⟨z⟩gromadzić zapasy (*G*); **~·still** bez ruchu; '**~·tak·ing** *econ.* inwentaryzacja *f*, spis *m*; *fig.* ocena *f*
stock·y ['stɒkɪ] (**-ier, -iest**) przysadzisty
stole [stəʊl] *pret. od* **steal**; **sto·len** ['stəʊlən] *p.p. od* **steal**
stol·id ['stɒlɪd] bezwolny, bierny
stom·ach ['stʌmək] **1.** żołądek *m*; *fig.* apetyt *m* (**for** na *A*); **2.** ⟨s⟩trawić (*też fig.*); '**~·ache** ból *m* brzucha; '**~ up·set** rozstrój *m* żołądkowy
stone [stəʊn] **1.** kamień *m* (*też med.*); *bot.* pestka *f*; kulka *f* (*gradu*); (*pl.* **stone(s)**; skrót: **st**) *Brt.* jednostka wagi (= 6,35 *kg*); **2.** ⟨u⟩kamienować; ⟨ob⟩rzucać kamieniami; usuwać ⟨usunąć⟩ pestki z (*G*); **~·'dead** martwy na amen; **~·'deaf** głuchy jak pień; '**~·ma·son** kamieniarz *m*; '**~·ware** naczynia *pl.* z kamionki
ston·y ['stəʊnɪ] (**-ier, -iest**) kamienny (*też fig.*); *fig.* spojrzenie *itp.*: niewzruszony
stood [stʊd] *pret. i p.p. od* **stand** 1
stool [stuːl] stołek *m*, taboret *m*; *med.* stolec *m*; '**~·pi·geon** F szpicel *m*
stoop [stuːp] **1.** *v/i.* schylać ⟨-lić⟩ się (*też* **~ down**); ⟨z⟩garbić się; **~** *to fig.* posuwać ⟨-sunąć⟩ się do (*G*), nie cofać ⟨-fnąć⟩ się przed (*I*); **2.** garbienie *n* się
stop [stɒp] **1.** (**-pp-**) *v/t.* zatrzymywać ⟨-mać⟩ się; stawać ⟨stanąć⟩ (*też zegar*); przerywać ⟨-rwać⟩; *Brt.* pozostawać ⟨-tać⟩; **~ dead** zatrzymywać ⟨-mać⟩ się jak wryty; **~ at nothing** nie cofać ⟨-fnąć⟩ się przed niczym; **~ short of doing, ~ short to s.th.** powstrzymywać ⟨-mać⟩ się przed (*I*); *v/t.* zatrzymywać ⟨-mać⟩; powstrzymywać ⟨-mać⟩ (**from** przed *I*); przerywać ⟨-rwać⟩;

krwawienie ⟨za⟩tamować; *rurę* zatykać ⟨-tknąć⟩ (*też* **~ up**); *dziurę* wypełniać ⟨-nić⟩; *wypłatę itp.* wstrzymywać ⟨-mać⟩; **~ by** wpadać ⟨wpaść⟩ (*z wizytą*); **~ in** wpadać ⟨wpaść⟩ (**at** do *G*) (*z wizytą*); **~ off** F zatrzymywać ⟨-mać⟩ się; **~ over** przerywać ⟨-rwać⟩ podróż; **2.** postój *m*; przystanek *m* (*autobusu*); *phot.* otwór *m* przesłony; *zw.* **full ~** kropka *f*; '**~·gap** rozwiązanie *n* tymczasowe; *attr.* tymczasowy, prowizoryczny; '**~·light** *mot.* światło *n* stop; *zwł. Am. zw.* **~·lights** *pl.* światła *pl.* sygnalizacyjne; '**~·o·ver** przerwa *f* w podróży; *aviat.* lądowanie *n* pośrednie; **~·page** ['stɒpɪdʒ] zatrzymanie *n* (*pracy itp.*), wstrzymanie *n*; przerwa *f*, postój *m*; *zwł. Brt.* potrącenie *n* (*z pensji*); blokada *f*, zatkanie *n*; '**~·per** zatyczka *f*, korek *m*; '**~ sign** *mot.* znak *m* zatrzymania się; '**~·watch** stoper *m*
stor·age ['stɔːrɪdʒ] składowanie *n*, magazynowanie *n*; skład *m*; *komp.* pamięć *f*
store [stɔː] **1.** ⟨z⟩gromadzić (*też dane*); ⟨z⟩magazynować; *też* **~ up** *fig.* zachowywać ⟨-ować⟩; **2.** zapas *m*, zasób *m*; magazyn *m*, skład *m*; *zwł. Brt.* dom *m* towarowy; *zwł. Am.* sklep *m*; △ *nie* **stora**; '**~·house** magazyn *m*, skład *m*; *fig.* kopalnia *f*, skarbnica *f*; '**~·keep·er** *zwł. Am.* sklepikarz *m* (-arka *f*), właściciel(ka *f*) *m* sklepu; '**~·room** schowek *m*
sto·rey *Brt.*, **sto·ry** *Am.* ['stɔːrɪ] piętro *n* ...**sto·reyed** *Brt.*, ...**sto·ried** *Am.* ['stɔːrɪd] ...piętrowy, o ... piętrach
stork [stɔːk] *zo.* bocian *m*
storm [stɔːm] **1.** burza *f* (*też fig.*), sztorm *m*; **2.** *v/t. mil.* szturmować; *v/i.* wypadać ⟨-paść⟩ jak burza; '**~·y** (**-ier, -iest**) burzliwy
sto·ry¹ ['stɔːrɪ] opowiadanie *n*; historia *f*; fabuła *f*; *gazeta itp.* artykuł *m*, relacja *f* (**on** z *G*)
sto·ry² *Am.* ['stɔːrɪ] → **storey**
stout [staʊt] **1.** korpulentny, otyły; *fig.* zagorzały, zapalony; **2.** porter *m*
stove [stəʊv] piec *m*; kuchenka *f*
stow [stəʊ] *też* **~ away** umieszczać ⟨-mieścić⟩, składać ⟨złożyć⟩; '**~·a·way** pasażer(ka *f*) *m* na gapę
strad·dle ['strædl] siedzieć ⟨usiąść⟩ okrakiem na (*I*)

strag|·gle ['strægl] słać się; *domy*: być rozrzuconym; *ludzie*: ⟨po⟩dzielić się na grupki; **'~·gler** maruder *m*; **'~·gly** (*-ier, -iest*) *włosy*: nastroszony; *bot.* płożący się

straight [streɪt] **1.** *adj.* prosty; *whisky*: czysty; porządny, uporządkowany; szczery; prosty; jasny; *koncert*: bez przerwy; *sl.* (*nie homoseksualny*) normalny; (*nie narkoman*) czysty; *put* ~ uporządkowywać ⟨-ować⟩; **2.** *adv.* prosto; natychmiast, od razu; szczerze; porządnie; wyraźnie (*myśleć, widzieć*); ~ *ahead* prosto; ~ *off* F od razu; ~ *on* prosto; ~ *out* F wyraźnie; **3.** (*w sporcie*) prosta *f*; **'~·en** *v/t.* ⟨wy⟩prostować (się)) poprawiać ⟨-wić⟩; **~en out** doprowadzać ⟨-dzić⟩ do porządku, uporządkowywać ⟨-ować⟩; *v/i. też* **~en out** *ulicę itp.* ⟨wy⟩prostować; **~en up** wyprostowywać ⟨-ować⟩ się; **'~'for·ward** prosty; nieskomplikowany

strain [streɪn] **1.** *v/t.* linę *itp.* naprężać ⟨-żyć⟩; *oczy itp.* wytężać ⟨-żyć⟩; wytężać ⟨-żyć⟩ się; *mięsień* nadwerężać ⟨-żyć⟩; *herbatę itp.* cedzić, przecedzać ⟨-dzić⟩; *v/i.* wytężać ⟨-żyć⟩ się; ~ *at* napinać ⟨-piąć⟩ (*A*); **2.** napięcie *n* (*też fig.*); nadwerężenie *n*; przeciążenie *m*; odmiana *f* (*zwierzęcia, rośliny*); **~ed** przeciążony; *śmiech*: wysilony; *relacje*: napięty; *look* **~ed** wyglądać na spiętego; **'~·er** sitko *n*, sito *n*

strait [streɪt] (*w nazwach własnych* **2s** *pl.*) cieśnina *f*; **~s** *pl.* tarapaty *pl.*; **2 of Dover** Cieśnina *f* Kaletańska

strait|·ened ['streɪtnd]: *live in* **~ened circumstances** żyć w trudnych warunkach (*finansowych*); **'~·jack·et**med. kaftan *m* bezpieczeństwa

strand [strænd] pasmo *n* (*włóczki, włosów; też fig.*); żyła *f* (*kabla*); plaża *f*, brzeg *m*

strand·ed ['strændɪd]: *be* ~ *naut.* osiadać ⟨-siąść⟩ na mieliźnie; *be* (*left*) ~ *fig.* zostać osamotnionym (*w kłopotach*)

strange [streɪndʒ] (*-r, -st*) dziwny; obcy; nieznajomy; **'strang·er** obcy *m* (*-ca f*); nieznajomy (*-ma f*)

stran·gle ['stræŋgl] ⟨u⟩dusić; *fig.* zdusząć ⟨zdusić⟩

strap [stræp] **1.** pasek *m*; ramiączko *n*; **2.** (*-pp-*) przypinać ⟨-piąć⟩

stra·te·gic [strə'tiːdʒɪk] (*-ally*) strate-

giczny; **strat·e·gy** ['strætɪdʒɪ] strategia *f*

stra·tum ['strɑːtəm] *geol.* (*pl.* **-ta** [-tə]) warstwa *f*

straw [strɔː] słoma *f*; słomka *f* (*do picia*); **~·ber·ry** ['strɔːbəri] *bot.* truskawka *f*

stray [streɪ] **1.** odchodzić ⟨odejść⟩; zabłądzić, zabłąkać się; *fig.* odbiegać ⟨-biec⟩ (*from* od *G*); **2.** zabłąkane zwierzę *n*; **3.** zabłąkany; *przykład*: przypadkowy

streak [striːk] **1.** pasmo *n*; smuga *f* (*światła*); cecha *f*; *a* ~ *of lightning* błyskawica *f*; *lucky* ~ dobra passa *f*; **2.** przemykać ⟨-mknąć⟩; pokrywać ⟨-ryć⟩ pasmami; **'~·y** (*-ier, -iest*) w pasmach; *bekon*: tłusty

stream [striːm] **1.** strumień *m*; potok *m*; *fig. prąd m*; **2.** ⟨po⟩płynąć strumieniami; wypływać ⟨-łynąć⟩; **'~·er** serpentyna *f*; proporzec *m*; *komp.* streamer *m*

street [striːt] **1.** ulica *f*; *attr.* uliczny; in (*zwł. Am.* **on**) *the* ~ na ulicy; **'~·car** *Am.* tramwaj *m*

strength [streŋθ] **1.** siła *f* (*też fig.*); silny punkt *m*; *tech.* wytrzymałość *f*; **'~·en** *v/t.* wzmacniać ⟨-mocnić⟩; *v/i.* umacniać ⟨-mocnić⟩ się

stren·u·ous ['strenjʊəs] wyczerpujący, forsowny

stress [stres] **1.** *fig.* stres *m*; *phys., tech.* naprężenie *n*, nacisk *m*; *ling.* przycisk *m*, akcent *m*; *fig.* nacisk *m*; **2.** ⟨za⟩akcentować; **'~·ful** stresujący

stretch [stretʃ] **1.** *v/t.* rozciągać ⟨-gnąć⟩; ~ *out* wyciągać ⟨-gnąć⟩; *fig. fakty* naciągać; *v/i.* rozciągać ⟨-gnąć⟩ się; wyciągać ⟨-gnąć⟩ się; ciągnąć się; ~ *out* ktoś: przeciągać ⟨-gnąć⟩ się; **2.** rozciągnięcie *n*; naprężenie *n*; elastyczność *f*; odcinek *m* (*też czasu*); okres *m*; *have a* ~ przeciągnąć się; **'~·er** nosze *pl.*

strick·en ['strɪkən] udręczony, umęczony; ~ *with* dotknięty (*I*)

strict [strɪkt] ścisły; surowy; srogi; **~·ly speaking** dokładnie rzecz biorąc

strid·den ['strɪdn] *p.p.* **stride** 1

stride [straɪd] **1.** (*strode, stridden*) kroczyć (*dużymi krokami*); **2.** duży krok *m*

strife [straɪf] walka *f*

strike [straɪk] **1.** (*struck*) *v/t.* uderzać ⟨-rzyć⟩; ⟨z⟩bić; ⟨za⟩atakować; *zapałkę* pocierać ⟨potrzeć⟩; natrafiać ⟨-fić⟩ na (ropę, złoto); *godzinę wybijać* ⟨-bić⟩; *monety* bić; *obóz* rozbijać ⟨-bić⟩; *flagę, żagiel* zwijać ⟨zwinąć⟩; *równowagę itp.* osiągać ⟨-gnąć⟩; *transakcję* zawierać ⟨-wrzeć⟩; wykreślać ⟨-lić⟩ *(from, off z listy)*; **~ out** przekreślać ⟨-lić⟩; **~ up** *melodię* rozpoczynać ⟨-cząć⟩; *przyjaźń itp.* zawierać ⟨-wrzeć⟩; *v/i. econ.* ⟨za⟩strajkować; wydarzać się; wybijać ⟨-bić⟩ *godzinę*; ⟨za⟩atakować; uderzać ⟨-rzyć⟩; **~ (out) at s.o.** ⟨za⟩atakować kogoś; uderzać ⟨-rzyć⟩ na kogoś; **2.** *econ.* strajk *m*; odkrycie *n* (*ropy, złota*); *mil.* uderzenie *n*; **be on ~** strajkować; **go on ~** zastrajkować; **a lucky ~** szczęśliwe odkrycie; '**strik·er** *econ.* strajkujący *m* (*-ca f*); (*w piłce nożnej*) napastnik *m* (*-niczka f*); '**strik·ing** uderzający; zachwycający

string [strɪŋ] **1.** sznurek *m*; sznur *m* (*też fig.*); nić *f*, drut *m* (*do marionetki*); struna *f* (*skrzypiec, rakiety tenisowej itp.*); cięciwa *f* (*łuku*); włókno *n*, łyko *n* (*fasoli itp.*); *komp.* ciąg *m*; **the ~s** *pl. mus.* smyczki *pl.*, instrumenty *pl.* smyczkowe; **pull ~s** *fig.* pociągać za sznurki; **with no ~s attached** *fig.* bez dodatkowych warunków; **2.** (*strung*) *paciorki itp.* ⟨na⟩nizać na (*sznur*); zakładać ⟨założyć⟩ strunę; usuwać ⟨-sunąć⟩ łyko z (*fasoli itp.*); **3.** *mus.* smyczkowy; **~ 'bean** *zwł. Am.* fasolka *f* szparagowa
strin·gent ['strɪndʒənt] ostry
string·y ['strɪŋɪ] (*-ier, -iest*) łykowaty
strip [strɪp] **1.** (*-pp-*) *v/i. też* **~ off** rozbierać ⟨-zebrać⟩ się *(to do G)*; *v/t. ubranie, farbę itp.*. ściągać ⟨-gnąć⟩; rozbierać ⟨-zebrać⟩; *tapetę* zrywać ⟨zerwać⟩ *(from, off z G)*; *też* **~ down** *tech.* ⟨z⟩demontować, rozmontowywać ⟨-tować⟩; **~ s.o. of s.th.** pozbawiać ⟨-wić⟩ kogoś czegoś; **2.** pasek *m*; pas *m* (*wody itp.*); striptiz *m*
stripe [straɪp] pasek *m*; prążek *m*; ~d prążkowany
strode [strəʊd] *pret. od* stride 1
stroke [strəʊk] **1.** ⟨po⟩głaskać ⟨po⟩gładzić; **2.** uderzenie *n* (*zegara, batem, w grze itp.*); pociągnięcie *n* (*pędzlem*); *med.* udar *m*, porażenie *n*; (*w pływaniu*) ruch *m*; *tech.* suw *m*, skok *m*; **four-~ engine** silnik *m* czterosuwowy; **~ of luck** *fig.* szczęśliwy traf *m*

stroll [strəʊl] **1.** przechadzać się; spacerować; **2.** przechadzka *f*; spacer *m*; '**~·er** (*f* ['strəʊlə] spacerowicz(ka *f*) *m*; *Am.* wózek *m* spacerowy
strong [strɒŋ] silny, mocny; *kraj:* potężny; *wyrażenie:* dosadny; **70 ~** w liczbie 70; '**~·box** sejf *m*, kasa *f*; '**~·hold** twierdza *f*, warownia *f*; *fig.* bastion *m*; ~'**mind·ed** przekonany; '**~ room** skarbiec *m*
struck [strʌk] *pret. i p.p. od* **strike** 1
struc·ture ['strʌktʃə] struktura *f*; budowa *f*; budowla *f*; konstrukcja *f*
strug·gle ['strʌgl] **1.** walczyć, zmagać się (*with z I, for za A*); **2.** walka *f*, zmaganie *n* się
strum [strʌm] (*-mm-*) uderzać w (*struny*), brzdąkać ⟨-knąć⟩ na (*instrumencie*)
strung [strʌŋ] *pret. i p.p. od* **string** 2
strut¹ [strʌt] (*-tt-*) dumnie kroczyć
strut² [strʌt] *tech.* rozpórka *f*; zastrzał *m*
stub [stʌb] **1.** ogryzek *m* (*ołówka*); niedopałek *m* (*papierosa*); odcinek *m* kontrolny; **2.** (*-bb-*) uderzyć się w (*palec stopy*); **~ out** *papierosa* ⟨z⟩gasić
stub·ble ['stʌbl] ściernisko *n*; (*broda*) szczecina *f*
stub·born ['stʌbən] uparty; zawzięty; *plama:* oporny
stuck [stʌk] *pret. i p.p. od* **stick** 2; ~'**up** F wynoszący się, nadęty
stud¹ [stʌd] **1.** nit *m* (*na ubraniu*); zatrzask *m*; spinka *f* (*do kołnierzyka itp.*); korek *m* (*na bucie*); **~s** *pl. mot.* kolce *pl.*; **2.** **be ~ed with** być nabijanym (*I*); być usianym (*I*); **~ed tyres** (*Am. tires*) *pl.* opony *pl.* z kolcami
stud² [stʌd] stadnina *f*
stu·dent ['stjuːdnt] student(ka *f*) *m*; *zwł. Am.* ogólnie uczeń *m*; uczennica *f*
'**stud| farm** stadnina *f*; '**~ horse** ogier *m* rozpłodowy
stud·ied ['stʌdɪd] wystudiowany
stu·di·o ['stjuːdɪəʊ] (*pl. -os*) studio *n*, atelier *n*; *też* **~ flat** *Brt.*, **~ apartment** *zwł. Am.* kawalerka *f*
stu·di·ous ['stjuːdjəs] staranny, obowiązkowy
stud·y ['stʌdɪ] **1.** studium *n*; nauka *f*; gabinet *m*; **studies** *pl.* studia *pl.*; **2.** studiować (*for do G*); uczyć się (*G*)
stuff [stʌf] **1.** rzecz *f*; rzeczy *pl.*; coś; **2.** wypychać ⟨-pchać⟩; wpychać ⟨wep

chnąć (**into** do G); gastr. nadziewać ⟨-dziać⟩, ⟨na⟩faszerować; **~ o.s.** F napychać ⟨-pchać⟩ się; '**~ing** gastr. nadzienie n, farsz m; (*pierze itp.*) wypełnienie n; '**~y** (**-ier, -iest**) duszny; staromodny

stum·ble ['stʌmbl] **1.** potykać ⟨-tknąć⟩ się (**on, over, fig. at, over** o A); **~ across, ~ on** natykać ⟨-tknąć⟩ się na (A); **2.** potknięcie n się

stump [stʌmp] **1.** kikut m; pieniek m; **2.** chodzić ⟨iść⟩ ciężkim krokiem; wprawiać w zakłopotanie; '**~y** (**-ier, -iest**) F kikutowaty

stun [stʌn] (**-nn-**) ogłuszać⟨-szyć⟩; oszałamiać ⟨-szołomić⟩

stung [stʌŋ] *pret. i p.p. od* **sting** 1

stunk [stʌŋk] *pret. i p.p. od* **stink** 1

stun·ning ['stʌnɪŋ] fantastyczny; oszałamiający

stunt[1] [stʌnt] ⟨za⟩hamować; **~ed** skarlały

stunt[2] [stʌnt] wyczyn m (*akrobatyczny*); wyczyn m kaskaderski; *reklamowa* akcja f; '**~ man** (*pl.* **-men**) kaskader m; '**~ wom·an** (*pl.* **-women**) kaskaderka f

stu·pid ['stjuːpɪd] głupi, durny; **~·i·ty** [stjuː'pɪdətɪ] głupota f, durnota f

stu·por ['stjuːpə] stupor m; osłupienie n; **in a drunken ~** w otępieniu pijackim

stur·dy ['stɜːdɪ] (**-ier, -iest**) krzepki; wytrzymały; *fig.* zacięty

stut·ter ['stʌtə] **1.** ⟨za⟩krztusić się; jąkać się; **2.** jąkanie n się

sty[1] [staɪ] → **pigsty**

sty[2]**, stye** [staɪ] *med.* jęczmień m

style [staɪl] **1.** styl m; rodzaj m; moda f; *bot.* słupek m; **2.** stylizować; ⟨u⟩kształtować

styl·ish ['staɪlɪʃ] elegancki; pełen stylu; '**~·ist** fryzjer(ka f) m; stylista m

sty·lus ['staɪləs] *gramofonowa* igła f

sty·ro·foam ['staɪrəfəʊm] *TM zwł. Am.* styropian m

suave [swɑːv] naskakujący

sub·di·vi·sion ['sʌbdɪvɪʒn] podział m wtórny

sub·due [səb'djuː] opanowywać ⟨-nować⟩; **~d** ktoś, coś: przygaszony; *głos*: przytłumiony

sub|·ject 1. ['sʌbdʒɪkt] temat m; *ped., univ.* przedmiot m; *gr.* podmiot m; poddany m (**-na** f); **2.** ['sʌbdʒɪkt] *adj.* **~ject to** podlegający (D), za zastrzeżeniem

(G); **be ~·ject to** podlegać (D); być podatnym na (A); **prices ~ject to change** ceny mogą ulec zmianie; **3.** [səb'dʒekt] poddawać ⟨-ddać⟩ (D); **~·jec·tion** [səb'dʒekʃn] poddanie n, podporządkowanie n

sub·ju·gate ['sʌbdʒʊgeɪt] podporządkowywać ⟨-ować⟩

sub·junc·tive [səb'dʒʌŋktɪv] *gr. też* **~ mood** tryb m łączący, koniunktyw m

sub|·lease [sʌb'liːs], **~·let** (**-tt-, -let**) podwynajmować ⟨-jąć⟩

sub·lime wzniosły

sub·ma·chine gun [sʌbmə'ʃiːn -] pistolet m maszynowy

sub·ma·rine [sʌbmə'riːn] **1.** podwodny; **2.** okręt m podwodny

sub·merge [səb'mɜːdʒ] zanurzać ⟨-rzyć⟩ się (**in** w I)

sub·mis·sion [səb'mɪʃn] poddanie n się, podporządkowanie n się; składanie n, złożenie n; zgłoszenie n; **~·sive** [səb'mɪsɪv] uległy, podporządkowany

sub·mit [səb'mɪt] (**-tt-**) przedstawiać ⟨-wić⟩; poddawać ⟨-ddać⟩ się; (D)

sub·or·di·nate 1. [sə'bɔːdnət] podporządkowany, podległy; **2.** [sə'bɔːdnət] podwładny m (**-na** f); **3.** [sə'bɔːdɪneɪt]: **~ to** podporządkowywać ⟨-ować⟩ (D); **~ 'clause** *gr.* zdanie n podrzędne

sub|·scribe [səb'skraɪb] *v/t.* pieniądze ofiarowywać ⟨-ować⟩; *v/i.* **~·scribe to** prenumerować (A); składać ⟨złożyć⟩ pieniądze na (A); *idee itp.* popierać ⟨-przeć⟩ (A); **~'scrib·er** prenumerator(ka f) m; *tel.* abonent m

sub·scrip·tion [səb'skrɪpʃn] prenumerata f, subskrypcja f; abonament m

sub·se·quent ['sʌbsɪkwənt] następujący, późniejszy

sub·side [səb'saɪd] *ulica, budynek*: zapadać ⟨-paść⟩ się; *wiatr itp.*: uspokajać ⟨-koić⟩ się

sub·sid·i·a·ry [səb'sɪdjərɪ] **1.** pomocniczy; **~ question** pytanie n dodatkowe; **2.** *econ.* przedsiębiorstwo n zależne, filia f

sub·si·dize ['sʌbsɪdaɪz] subsydiować; **~·dy** ['sʌbsɪdɪ] subsydium n, subwencja f

sub·sist [səb'sɪst] utrzymywać się, żyć (**on** z G); **~'sis·tence** egzystencja f

sub·stance ['sʌbstəns] substancja f (*też fig.*); *fig.* istota f

sub·stan·dard [sʌb'stændəd] gorszego gatunku

sub·stan·tial [səb'stænʃl] *mebel*: solidny; *ilość*: znaczny; *zmiany*: poważny

sub·stan·ti·ate [səb'stænʃɪeɪt] popierać ⟨poprzeć⟩, udowadniać ⟨-wodnić⟩

sub·stan·tive [sʌbstəntɪv] *gr.* rzeczownik *m*

sub·sti·tute [sʌbstɪtjuːt] **1.** substytut *m*; surogat *m*, namiastka *f*; zastępca *m* (-czyni *f*); (*w sporcie*) zmiennik *m* (-niczka *f*); *attr.* zastępczy; rezerwowy; **2.** *~tute s.th. for s.th.* zastępować ⟨-tąpić⟩ coś czymś; *~·tu·tion* [sʌbstɪ'tjuːʃn] zamiana *f*; (*w sporcie*) zmiana *f*

sub·ter·fuge [sʌbtəfjuːdʒ] podstęp *m*, wybieg *m*

sub·ter·ra·ne·an [sʌbtə'reɪnjən] podziemny

sub·ti·tle [sʌbtaɪtl] (*na filmie*) napis *m*

sub·tle [sʌtl] (*-r, -st*) subtelny; delikatny; zmysłowy

sub|·tract [səb'trækt] *math.* odejmować ⟨-djąć⟩ (*from* od *G*); *~·trac·tion* [səb'trækʃn] *math.* odejmowanie *n*

sub·trop·i·cal [sʌb'trɒpɪkl] subtropikalny, podzwrotnikowy

sub|·urb [sʌbɜːb] przedmieście *n*; *~·ur·ban* [sə'bɜːbən] podmiejski

sub·ver·sive [səb'vɜːsɪv] wywrotowy

sub·way [sʌbweɪ] *Brt.* przejście *n* podziemne; *Am.* metro *n*

suc·ceed [sək'siːd] *v/i.* odnosić ⟨-nieść⟩ sukces (*in w L*); powodzić ⟨-wieść⟩ się; *~ to* urząd *itp.* przejmować ⟨-jąć⟩; *~ to the throne* ⟨o⟩dziedziczyć tron; *v/t. ~ s.o. as* być czyimś następcą *w* (*L*)

suc·cess [sək'ses] sukces *m*, powodzenie *n*; *~·ful* udany, pomyślny

suc·ces·sion [sək'seʃn] następstwo *n*; szereg *m*; dziedziczenie *n*, sukcesja *f*; *five times in ~sion* pięć razy pod rząd; *in quick ~sion* szybko jeden za drugim; *~·sive* [sək'sesɪv] sukcesywny, kolejny, stopniowy; *~·sor* [sək'sesə] następca *f* (-czyni *f*)

suc·cu·lent [sʌkjʊlənt] *mięso itp.*: soczysty

such [sʌtʃ] taki *m*, taka *m*

suck [sʌk] **1.** ssać ⟨(*at*) *s.th.* coś⟩; wysać ⟨wessać⟩, zasysać ⟨zassać⟩; **2.** *have lub take a ~ at* possać (*A*); *~·er m zo.* ssawka *f*; *tech.*, *zo.* przyssawka *f*; *bot.*

odrost *m*; F frajer *m*, jeleń *m*; *Am.* lizak *m*; *~·le* [sʌkl] pierś ssać; karmić piersią

suc·tion [sʌkʃn] ssanie *n*, zasysanie *n*; *'~ pump tech.* pompa *f* ssąca

sud·den [sʌdn] nagły; *all of a ~* F nagle, znienacka; *'~·ly* nagle

suds [sʌdz] *pl.* mydliny *pl.*

sue [suː] *jur.* kogoś pozywać ⟨-zwać⟩, zaskarżać ⟨-żyć⟩ (*do sądu*) (*for* za *A*); wnosić (*for* o *A*)

suede, suède [sweɪd] zamsz *m*; *attr.* zamszowy

su·et [sʊɪt] sadło *n*

suf·fer [sʌfə] *v/i.* ⟨u-, wy⟩cierpieć (*for* za *A*); doznawać ⟨-nać⟩ uszczerbku; *~ from* cierpieć na (*A*); *v/t.* konsekwencje, straty ponosić ⟨-nieść⟩; doznawać ⟨-nać⟩; doświadczać ⟨-czyć⟩ (*upokorzenia*); *~·er* [sʌfərə] cierpiący *m* (-ca *f*); poszkodowany *m* (-na *f*); *~·ing* [sʌfərɪŋ] cierpienie *n*

suf·fice [sə'faɪs] wystarczać ⟨-czyć⟩ (*for* na *A*)

suf·fi·cient [sə'fɪʃnt] wystarczający, dostateczny; *be ~* wystarczać ⟨-czyć⟩

suf·fix [sʌfɪks] *gr.* przyrostek *m*, sufiks *m*

suf·fo·cate [sʌfəkeɪt] ⟨u⟩dusić się

suf·frage [sʌfrɪdʒ] *pol.* prawo *n* głosowania

suf·fuse [sə'fjuːz] zalewać ⟨-lać⟩ (*światłem*)

sug·ar [ʃʊgə] **1.** cukier *m*; *attr.* cukrowy; **2.** ⟨po⟩słodzić; *'~ bowl* cukiernica *f*; *'~·cane* trzcina *f* cukrowa; *'~·y* [ʃʊgərɪ] cukrowy; słodki; *fig.* przesłodzony, cukiwy

sug|·gest [sə'dʒest] ⟨za⟩proponować; ⟨za⟩sugerować; wskazywać; podsuwać ⟨-sunąć⟩ (*myśl*); *~·ges·tion* [sə'dʒestʃən] sugestia *f*; wskazówka *f*; propozycja *f*; *~·ges·tive* [sə'dʒestɪv] niedwuznaczny; *spojrzenie itp.*: wiele mówiący

su·i·cide [sjʊɪsaɪd] samobójstwo *n*; *commit ~* popełnić samobójstwo

suit [suːt] **1.** garnitur *m*; *kąpielowy* kostium *m*; (*w kartach*) kolor *m*; *jur.* proces *m*; *follow ~ fig.* iść ⟨pójść⟩ za przykładem; **2.** *v/t.* komuś odpowiadać (*termin itp.*); pasować do (*G*); *~ s.th., be ~ed to s.th.* pasować do czegoś, nadawać się do czegoś; *~ yourself!* rób jak chcesz!; *'sui·ta·ble* odpowiedni, właściwy, stosowny (*for, to* do *G*); '~·**case** walizka *f*

suite [swi:t] komplet *m* (*mebli*); zestaw *m*; apartament *m*; świta *f*; *mus.* suita *f*

sul·fur ['sʌlfə] *Am.* → *sulphur*

sulk [sʌlk] ⟨na⟩dąsać się, boczyć się; ~s *pl.*: **have the ~s** dąsać się

sulk·y[1] ['sʌlkɪ] (*-ier, -iest*) dąsający się; nadąsany

sulk·y[2] ['sʌlkɪ] (*w wyścigach konnych*) sulki *pl.*

sul·len ['sʌlən] ponury

sul|·phur ['sʌlfə] *chem.* siarka *f*; ~**phu·ric ac·id** [sʌlfjuərɪk 'æsɪd] *chem.* kwas *m* siarkowy

sul·try ['sʌltrɪ] (*-ier, -iest*) duszny; *glos, spojrzenie:* zmysłowy

sum [sʌm] **1.** suma *f*; kwota *f*; **do ~s** ⟨wy⟩liczyć; **2.** (*-mm-*): ~ **up** podsumowywać ⟨-mować⟩; dokonywać ⟨-nać⟩ podsumowania; *fig.* oceniać ⟨-nić⟩

sum·mar·ize ['sʌmərɑɪz] streszczać ⟨-reścić⟩; ~**ma·ry** ['sʌmərɪ] streszczenie *n*

sum·mer ['sʌmə] lato *n*; *in* (*the*) ~ latem, w lecie; '~ **camp** kolonia *f* (*dla dzieci*); ~ '**hol·i·days** *pl.* wakacje *pl.* letnie; ~ **re'sort** (*miejscowość*) letnisko *n*; '~ **school** szkoła *f* letnia; '~**time** lato *n*; *in* (*the*) ~**time** latem, w lecie; '~ **time** *zwł. Brt.* czas *m* letni; ~ **va'ca·tion** *zwł. Am.* wakacje *pl.* letnie; ~·**y** ['sʌmərɪ] letni

sum·mit ['sʌmɪt] wierzchołek *m*; szczyt *m* (*też econ., pol., fig.*); '~ (**con-fe·rence**) konferencja *f* na szczycie; '~ (**meet·ing**) spotkanie *n* na szczycie

sum·mon ['sʌmən] wzywać ⟨wezwać⟩, zwoływać ⟨-łać⟩; *jur.* pozywać ⟨-zwać⟩; ~ **up** siłę, męstwo *itp.* zbierać ⟨zebrać⟩; ~**s** ['sʌmənz] *jur.* wezwanie *n*

sump·tu·ous ['sʌmptʃuəs] wystawny, okazały

sun [sʌn] **1.** słońce *n*; *attr.* słoneczny; **2.** (*-nn-*): ~ **o.s.** opalać się

Sun *skrót pisany:* **Sunday** niedz., niedziela *f*

'**sun|·bathe** brać ⟨wziąć⟩ kąpiele słoneczne; '~**beam** promień *m* słońca; '~**bed** (*urządzenie*) solarium*n*; '~**burn** oparzenie *n* słoneczne

sun·dae ['sʌndeɪ] puchar *m* lodowy

Sun·day ['sʌndɪ] (*skrót:* **Sun**) niedziela *f*; **on** ~ w niedzielę; **on ~s** co niedzielę

'**sun|·dial** ['sʌndaɪəl] zegar *m* słoneczny; '~·**down** → *sunset*

sun|·dries ['sʌndrɪz] *pl.* różności *pl.*; ~**dry** ['sʌndrɪ] różny, rozmaity

sung [sʌŋ] *p.p.* od *sing*

'**sun·glass·es** (*a pair of ~*) *pl.* okulary *pl.* słoneczne

sunk [sʌŋk] *pret. i p.p.* od *sink* 1

sunk·en ['sʌŋkən] *policzki:* zapadnięty; *statek itp.:* zatopiony; *ogród itp.:* wgłębiony

'**sun|·light** światło *n* słoneczne; '~·**lit** oświetlony słońcem

sun·ny ['sʌnɪ] (*-ier, -iest*) słoneczny

'**sun|·rise** wschód *m* słońca; '~·**roof** taras *m*; *mot.* (*dachowe okno uchylne*) szyberdach *m*; '~·**set** zachód *m* słońca; '~·**shade** parasol *m* przeciwsłoneczny; parasolka *f* przeciwsłoneczna; osłona *f* od słońca; '~·**shine** światło *n* słońca; '~·**stroke** porażenie *n* słoneczne; '~·**tan** opalenizna *f*

su·per ['su:pə] F super

su·per... ['su:pə] nad...

su·per|·a·bun·dance [su:pərə'bʌndəns] nadmiar *m*; ~·**an·nu·at·ed** [su:pə'rænjueɪtɪd] emerytowany, w stanie spoczynku

su·perb [su:'pɜ:b] znakomity

'**su·per|·charg·er** *mot.* sprężarka *f* doładowująca; ~·**cil·i·ous** [su:pə'sɪlɪəs] wyniosły; ~·**fi·cial** [su:pə'fɪʃl] powierzchowny; ~·**flu·ous** [su:'pɜ:fluəs] nadmierny; zbyteczny; ~·**hu·man** nadludzki; ~·**im·pose** [su:pərɪm'pəuz] nakładać ⟨nałożyć⟩; ~·**in·tend** [su:pərɪn'tend] nadzorować; ⟨s⟩kontrolować; ~·**in·tend·ent** [su:pərɪn'tendənt] nadzorca *m* (*-rczyni f*); *Brt.* inspektor *m*

su·pe·ri·or [su:'pɪərɪə] **1.** zwierzchni, przełożony; *starszy* (*rangą*); lepszy; *Father 2* Ojciec Przełożony; *Mother 2* Matka Przełożona; **2.** zwierzchnik *m* (*-niczka f*), przełożony *m* (*-na f*); ~·**i·ty** [su:pɪərɪ'ɒrɪtɪ] starszeństwo *n*, wyższość *f*, przewaga *f* (*over* nad *I*)

su·per·la·tive [su:'pɜ:lətɪv] **1.** doskonały, znakomity; **2.** *też* ~ **degree** *gr.* stopień *m* najwyższy

'**su·per|·mar·ket** supermarket *m*; ~·'**nat·u·ral** nadprzyrodzony; ~·**nu-me·ra·ry**[su:pə'nju:mərərɪ]nadliczbowy; ~·**sede** [su:pə'si:d] zastępować ⟨-tąpić⟩; ~·'**son·ic** *aviat., phys.* nad-

S

dźwiękowy; **~·sti·tion** [su:pə'stɪʃn] zabobon *m*; **~·sti·tious** [su:pə'stɪʃəs] zabobonny; **'~·store** megasam *m*; **~·vene** [su:pə'vi:n] zachodzić ‹-zajść›; **~·vise** ['su:pəvaɪz] nadzorować; **~·vi·sion** [su:pə'vɪʒn] nadzór *m*, dozór *m*; **under s.o.'s ~vision** pod czyimś nadzorem *lub* kierownictwem; **~·vi·sor** ['su:pəvaɪzə] nadzorca *m* ‹-czyni *f*›, kontroler(ka *f*) *m*

sup·per ['sʌpə] kolacja *f*; **have~** ‹z›jeść kolację; → **lord**

sup·plant [sə'plɑːnt] zastępować ‹-tąpić›; wypierać ‹-przeć›

sup·ple ['sʌpl] (**-er, -est**) giętki, elastyczny

sup·ple|·ment 1. ['sʌplɪmənt] dodatek *m*; uzupełnienie *n*; suplement *m*; **2.** ['sʌplɪment] dodawać ‹-dać›, uzupełniać ‹-nić›; **~·men·ta·ry** [sʌplɪ'mentərɪ] uzupełniający, dodatkowy

sup·pli·er [sə'plaɪə] dostawca *m*; *też* **~s** *pl.* firma *f* dostawcza, dostawcy *pl.*

sup·ply [sə'plaɪ] **1.** dostarczać ‹-czyć›; *econ.* zaopatrywać ‹-trzyć› (**with** *w A*); *potrzebę* zaspokajać ‹-koić›; **2.** dostawa *f*; dostarczenie *n*; *econ.* zaopatrzenie *n*; *zw.* **supplies** *pl.* rezerwy *pl.*, zapasy *pl.*; prowiant *m*, **school ~** *pl.* materiały *pl.* szkolne; **~ and demand** podaż *i* popyt

sup·port [sə'pɔːt] **1.** podpierać ‹-deprzeć›; podtrzymywać ‹-mać›; *ciężar* wytrzymywać ‹-mać›; wspierać ‹wesprzeć› (*finansowo*); *żądania itp.* popierać ‹-przeć›; *rodzinę itp.* utrzymywać ‹-mać›; **2.** podpora *f* (*też fig.*); oparcie *n*; wsparcie *n*; utrzymanie *n*; **~·er** poplecznik *m*, stronnik *m*; *sportowy* kibic *m*

sup|·pose [sə'pəʊz] **1.** sądzić; przypuszczać; **be~posed to** mieć *inf.*; **what is that ~posed to mean?** co to ma znaczyć?; **I~pose so** tak mi się wydaje; **2.** *cj.* przypuśćmy że; jeżeli; a może; **~'posed** domniemany; **~'pos·ing** *→* **suppose** 2; **~·po·si·tion** [sʌpə'zɪʃn] przypuszczenie *n*

sup|·press [sə'pres] ‹s›tłumić; ‹po›hamować; skrywać ‹-ryć›; zakazywać ‹-zać› publikacji (*G*); **~·pres·sion** [sə'preʃn] stłumienie *n*; pohamowanie *n*; skrycie *n*; zakaz *m* publikacji

sup·pu·rate ['sʌpjʊəreɪt] *med.* ‹z›ropieć

su·prem·a·cy [sʊ'preməsɪ] wyższość *f*; supremacja *f*; dominacja *f*

su·preme [suː'priːm] naczelny; najwyższy; krańcowy

sur·charge 1. [sɜː'tʃɑːdʒ] obciążać ‹-żyć› dodatkową opłatą; **2.** ['sɜːtʃɑːdʒ] dopłata *f*

sure [ʃɔː] **1.** *adj.* (**-r, -st**) pewny; **~ of s.o.** pewny czegoś; **~ of winning** przekonany o swej wygranej; **~ thing!** *zwł. Am.* F oczywiście!; **be** *lub* **feel ~** czuć się pewnie; **be ~ to ....** nie zapomnieć ...; **for ~** na pewno, z pewnością; **make ~ that** upewniać ‹-nić› się, że; **to be ~** dla pewności; **2.** *adv.* F z pewnością, na pewno; **~ enough** oczywiście; faktycznie; **'~·ly** z pewnością; pewnie; zapewne; **sure·ty** ['ʃɔːrətɪ] przekonanie *n*, pewność *f*; poręka *f*; **stand ~ for s.o.** poręczyć za kogoś

surf [sɜːf] **1.** przybój *m*; **2.** uprawiać surfing

sur·face ['sɜːfɪs] **1.** powierzchnia *f*; nawierzchnia *f* (*ulicy itp.*); tafla *f* (*jeziora itp.*); **2.** wychodzić ‹wyjść› na powierzchnię; wynurzać ‹-rzyć› się; *ulicę* pokrywać ‹-ryć› nawierzchnią; **3.** powierzchniowy; **'~ mail** poczta *f* naziemna

'surf·board *sport*: deska *f* surfingowa; **'~·er** (*osoba uprawiająca surfing*); **'~·ing** surfing *m*

surge [sɜːdʒ] **1.** *fig.* fala *f*, napływ *m* (*uczuć*); przypływ *m*; **2.** napływać ‹-łynąć›; przepływać ‹-łynąć›; *też* **~ up** wzbierać ‹wezbrać›

sur·geon ['sɜːdʒən] *med.* chirurg *m*

sur·ge·ry ['sɜːdʒərɪ] *med.* chirurgia *f*; operacja *f*; *Brt.* gabinet *m* lekarski; *Brt.* godziny *pl.* przyjęć; *też* **doctor's ~** praktyka *f* lekarska; **'~ hours** *pl. Brt.* godziny *pl.* przyjęć

sur·gi·cal ['sɜːdʒɪkl] *med.* chirurgiczny

sur·ly ['sɜːlɪ] (**-ier, -iest**) gburowaty, mrukliwy

sur·name ['sɜːneɪm] nazwisko *n*

sur·pass [sə'pɑːs] *oczekiwania itp.* przewyższać ‹-szyć›

sur·plus ['sɜːpləs] **1.** nadwyżka *f*; **2.** dodatkowy

sur·prise [sə'praɪz] **1.** niespodzianka *f*; **take s.o. by ~** brać ‹wziąć› kogoś przez zaskoczenie; **2.** zaskakiwać ‹-koczyć⟩; **be ~d at** *lub* **by** być zaskoczonym (*I*)

sur·ren·der [sə'rendə] **1.** ~ **to** *mil.*, *też fig.* poddawać ⟨-dać⟩ (się) (*D*), kapitulować przed (*I*); ~ (**o.s.**) **to the police** oddawać ⟨-dać⟩ się w ręce policji; zrzekać ⟨zrzec⟩ się (*G*); **2.** *mil.* kapitulacja *f* (*też fig.*); poddanie *n* się; zrzeczenie *n* się

sur·ro·gate ['sʌrəgeɪt] surogat *m*, substytut *m*; ~ '**moth·er** zastępcza matka *f*

sur·round [sə'raʊnd] otaczać ⟨otoczyć⟩; ~**·ing** otaczający; ~**·ings** *pl.* otoczenie *n*

sur·vey 1. [sə'veɪ] oglądać ⟨-dnąć⟩, poddawać ⟨-dać⟩ oględzinom; dokonywać ⟨-nać⟩ przeglądu (*budynku*); zmierzę ⟨z⟩mierzyć; opinię ⟨z⟩badać; **2.** ['sɜːveɪ] badanie *n* (*opinii itp.*); przegląd *m*; zbadanie *n*, oględziny *pl.*; ~**·or** [sə'veɪə] geodeta *m*, mierniczy *m*

sur·viv·al [sə'vaɪvl] przeżycie *n*; przetrwanie *n*; ~ **kit** zestaw *m* ratunkowy; ~ **train·ing** szkoła *f* przetrwania

sur|·vive [sə'vaɪv] przetrwać; przeżyć; ~'**vi·vor** ocalały *m* (-ła *f*) (**from**, *od* z *G*)

sus·cep·ti·ble [sə'septəbl] podatny (**to** na *A*)

sus·pect 1. [sə'spekt] podejrzewać (**of** o *A*); nie dowierzać (*D*); obawiać się; **2.** ['sʌspekt] podejrzany *m* (-na *f*); **3.** ['sʌspekt] podejrzany; niepewny

sus·pend [sə'spend] zawieszać ⟨-wiesić⟩; *coś* wstrzymywać ⟨-mać⟩; wykluczać ⟨-czyć⟩ (**from** z *G*); ~·**er** *Brt.* podwiązka *f*; (*też* **a pair of**) ~**ers** *pl. Am.* szelki *pl.*

sus·pense [sə'spens] napięcie *n*

sus·pen·sion [sə'spenʃn] zawieszenie *n* (*też mot.*); wykluczenie *n*; wstrzymanie *n*; zawiesina *f*; ~ **bridge** most *m* wiszący

sus·pi|·cion [sə'spɪʃn] podejrzenie *n*; podejrzliwość *f*; ~**·cious** podejrzliwy; podejrzany

sus·tain [sə'steɪn] utrzymywać ⟨-mać⟩; utrzymywać *kogoś* na siłach; *zainteresowanie itp.* podtrzymywać ⟨-mać⟩; *obrażenia itp.* ponosić ⟨-nieść⟩; *uszkodzenia itp.* doznawać ⟨-nać⟩

SW *skrót pisany:* **southwest** płd.--zach.; **południowy zachód** *m*; **southwest(ern)** południowo-zachodni

swab *med.* [swɒb] **1.** wacik *m*, gazik *m*; wymaz *m*; **2.** (**-bb-**) oczyszczać ⟨-yścić⟩ wacikiem

swad·dle ['swɒdl] *niemowlę* opatulać ⟨-lić⟩

swag·ger ['swægə] chodzić ⟨iść⟩ kołyszącym się krokiem

swal·low[1] ['swɒləʊ] **1.** łykać; połykać ⟨-łknąć⟩ (*też fig.*); przełykać ⟨-łknąć⟩; *fig.* pochłonąć; ~ **one's pride** ⟨s⟩chować dumę do kieszeni; **2.** łyk *m*

swal·low[2] ['swɒləʊ] *zo.* jaskółka *f*

swam [swæm] *pret. od* **swim** 1

swamp [swɒmp] **1.** bagnisko *n*; **2.** zalewać ⟨-lać⟩ (*też fig.*); **be ~ed with** *fig.* być zasypanym (*I*); '~**·y** (**-ier, -iest**) bagnisty

swan [swɒn] *zo.* łabędź *m*

swank [swæŋk] F *zwł. Brt.* **1.** przechwalać się; **2.** przechwałki *pl.*; chełpienie się; '~**·y** (**-ier, -iest**) F chełpliwy

swap [swɒp] F **1.** (**-pp-**) wymieniać ⟨-nić⟩ (się), zamieniać ⟨-nić⟩ (się); **2.** wymiana *f*, zamiana *f*

swarm [swɔːm] **1.** chmara *f* (*owadów, turystów*); rój *m* (*pszczół*); **2.** pszczoły, ludzie: ⟨wy⟩roić się

swar·thy ['swɔːðɪ] (**-ier, -iest**) *cera*: śniady, smagły

swat [swɒt] (**-tt-**) *muchę* pacnąć

sway [sweɪ] **1.** *v/i.* kołysać się, chwiać się; ~ **between** *fig.* wahać się między (*I*); *v/t.* kołysać; wpływać ⟨-łynąć⟩ (*A*); **2.** kołysanie *n*, kiwanie *n*

swear [sweə] (**swore, sworn**) przysięgać ⟨-siąc⟩; przeklinać ⟨-ląć⟩; ⟨za⟩kląć; ~ **at s.o.** kląć na kogoś; ~ **by** *fig.* F kląć się na (*A*); ~ **s.o. in** zaprzysięgać ⟨-siąc⟩ kogoś

sweat [swet] **1.** (**sweated**, *Am. też* **sweat**) ⟨s⟩pocić się (**with** *od* G *lub* z *G*); *v/t.* ~ **out** wypacać ⟨-pocić⟩ (*w chorobie*); ~ **blood** F naharować się jak wół; **2.** pot *m*; **get into a ~ about** F podniecać ⟨-cić⟩ się (*I*); '~**·er** sweter *m*; '~**·shirt** bluza *f*; '~**·y** (**-ier, -iest**) spocony; przepocony

Swede [swiːd] Szwed(ka *f*) *m*; **Sweden** ['swiːdn] Szwecja *f*; **Swe·dish** ['swiːdɪʃ] **1.** szwedzki; **2.** *ling.* język *m* szwedzki

sweep [swiːp] **1.** (**swept**) zamiatać ⟨-mieść⟩; zmiatać ⟨-mieść⟩; *horyzont* omiatać ⟨-mieść⟩ (**for** w poszukiwaniu

G); *v/i.* przelatywać ⟨-lecieć⟩; przemykać ⟨-mknąć⟩; rozciągać ⟨-gnąć⟩ się; **2.** zamiecenie *n*; półkolisty ruch *m*; półkolista linia *f*; cios *m*; *give the floor a good* ~ zamieść dobrze podłogę; *make a clean* ~ dokonać daleko idących zmian *f*; (*w sporcie*) osiągnąć całkowite zwycięstwo; '~**er** zamiatacz *m*; (*maszyna*) zamiatarka *f*; (*w sporcie*) libero *m*; '~**ing** zamaszysty; daleko idący; '~**ings** *pl.* zmiotki *pl.*

sweet [swiːt] **1.** słodki (*też fig.*); ~ *nothings pl.* czułości *pl.*; *have a* ~ *tooth* lubić słodycze; **2.** *Brt.* słodycze *pl.*, cukierek *m*; *Brt.* deser *m*; '~ *corn zwł. Brt. bot.* kukurydza *f* cukrowa; '~**en** ⟨po⟩słodzić; '~**heart** (*ktoś*) skarb *m*; ~ *pea bot.* groszek *m* pachnący; '~ *shop zwł. Brt.* sklep *m* ze słodyczami

swell [swel] **1.** (**swelled, swollen** *lub* **swelled**) *v/i.* też ~ *up med.* ⟨s⟩puchnąć; *też* ~ *out* wydymać ⟨-dąć⟩ się, nadymać ⟨-dąć⟩ się; *v/t. fig. liczba itp.*: rozdymać ⟨-dąć⟩; *też* ~ *out* żagiel wydymać ⟨-dąć⟩; **2.** *naut.* fala *f* martwa; '~**ing** swędnięcie *n*

swel·ter ['sweltə] człowiek: prażyć się

swept [swept] *pret. i p.p. od* **sweep** 1

swerve [swɜːv] **1.** skręcać ⟨-cić⟩ ostro (*to the left* na lewo); *fig.* odchodzić ⟨odejść⟩ (*from* od G); **2.** skręcenie *n*, skręt *m*; odchylenie *n* się

swift [swift] **1.** szybki, prędki; **2.** *zo.* jerzyk *m*

swim [swim] **1.** (**-mm-; swam, swum**) *v/i.* pływać ⟨płynąć⟩; *fig.* kręcić się; *my head was ~ming* kręciło mi się w głowie; *v/t.* przepływać ⟨-łynąć⟩; *kraulem* pływać; **2.** kąpiel *f*; '~**mer** pływak *m* (-waczka *f*)

'**swim·ming** pływanie *n*; '~ *bath(s pl.) Brt.* pływalnia *f*; '~ *cap* czepek *m* kąpielowy; '~**cos·tume** kostium *m* kąpielowy; '~ *pool* basen *m* kąpielowy; '~ *trunks pl.* kąpielówki *pl.*

'**swim·suit** kostium *m* kąpielowy

swin·dle ['swindl] **1.** wyłudzać ⟨-dzić⟩ (*s.o. out of s.th.* coś od kogoś); **2.** wyłudzenie *n*

swine [swain] (*pl. zo.* **swine**, *sl. pej. też* **swines**) świnia *f*

swing [swiŋ] **1.** (**swung**) *v/i.* ⟨po-, za⟩huśtać się; ⟨za⟩kołysać się; wjeżdżać

⟨wjechać⟩ łukiem (*into* do G); *mus.* swingować; ~ *round* obrócić się; ~ *shut* zatrzasnąć się; *v/t.* machać (*ramionami itp.*); **2.** huśtawka *f* (*też fig.*); zamachnięcie *n*; zmiana *f*; *mus.* swing *m*; *in full* ~ w pełni, na cały gaz; ~ '*door* drzwi *pl.* wahadłowe

swin·ish ['swainiʃ] świński

swipe [swaip] **1.** uderzenie *n*; **2.** uderzać ⟨-rzyć⟩ (*at* w A)

swirl [swɜːl] **1.** ⟨za⟩wirować; **2.** wir *m*

swish¹ [swiʃ] **1.** *v/i. bat, ogon:* świstać ⟨-snąć⟩; *jedwab:* ⟨za⟩szeleścić; *v/t.* machać ⟨-chnąć⟩ ze świstem; **2.** świst *m*; szelest *m*; machnięcie *n*

swish² [swiʃ] F szykowny

Swiss [swis] **1.** szwajcarski; **2.** Szwajcar(ka *f*) *m*; *the* ~ *pl.* Szwajcarzy *pl.*

switch [switʃ] **1.** *electr., tech.* przełącznik *m*, wyłącznik *m*; *Am. rail.* zwrotnica *f*; gałązka *f*; *fig.* diametralna zmiana *f*; **2.** *electr., tech.* przełączać ⟨-czyć⟩ (*też* ~ *over*) (*to* na A); *Am. rail.* manewrować, przetaczać ⟨-toczyć⟩; zmieniać ⟨-nić⟩ (*to* na A); ~ *off* wyłączać ⟨-czyć⟩; ~ *on* włączać ⟨-czyć⟩; '~**board** *electr.* tablica *f* rozdzielcza; *tel.* centrala *f*

Swit·zer·land ['switsələnd] Szwajcaria *f*

swiv·el ['swivl] (*zwł. Brt. -ll-*, *Am. -l-*) obrócić (się); '~ *chair* krzesło *n* obrotowe

swol·len ['swəʊlən] *p.p. od* **swell** 1

swoon [swuːn] ⟨ze-, o⟩mdleć

swoop [swuːp] **1.** *fig.* F policja: ⟨z⟩robić nalot; *też* ~ *down ptak drapieżny:* spadać ⟨-paść⟩ (*on* na A); **2.** nalot *m*

swop [swɒp] F → *swap*

sword [sɔːd] miecz *m*

swore [swɔː] *pret. od* **swear**

sworn [swɔːn] *p.p. od* **swear**

swum [swʌm] *p.p. od* **swim**

swung [swʌŋ] *pret. i p.p. od* **swing** 1

syc·a·more ['sikəmɔː] *bot.* jawor *m*; *Am.* platan *m*; sykomora *f*

syl·la·ble ['siləbl] *gr.* sylaba *f*

syl·la·bus ['siləbəs] *pred. univ.* ['siləbəs] (*pl. -buses, -bi* [-bai]) program *m* nauczania

sym·bol ['simbl] symbol *m*; ~**ic** [sim'bɒlik] symboliczny; ~**ism** ['simbəlizəm] symbolizm *m*; ~**ize** ['simbəlaiz] symbolizować

sym|·met·ri·cal [sı'metrıkl] symetryczny; **~·me·try** ['sımıtrı] symetria *f*

sym·pa|·thet·ic [sımpə'θetık] (**-ally**) współczujący; rozumiejący; życzliwy; **~·thize** ['sımpəθaız] współczuć; **~·thy** ['sımpəθı] współczucie *n*

sym·pho·ny ['sımfənı] *mus.* symfonia *f*; *attr.* symfoniczny

symp·tom ['sımptəm] symptom *m*, oznaka *f*

syn·chro|·nize ['sıŋkrənaız] *v/t.* ⟨z⟩synchronizować; *zegarki itp.* uzgadniać ⟨-godnić⟩; *v/i.* być zsynchronizowanym

syn·o·nym ['sınənım] synonim *m*;

sy·non·y·mous [sı'nɒnıməs] synonimiczny

syn·tax ['sıntæks] *gr.* składnia *f*

syn·the·sis ['sınθəsıs] (*pl.* **-ses** [-si:z]) synteza *f*

syn·thet·ic [sın'θetık] (**~ally**) syntetyczny; **~ 'fi·bre** *Brt.*, (*Am.*; **fi·ber**) włókno *n* syntetyczne

sy·ringe ['sırındʒ] *med.* strzykawka *f*

syr·up ['sırəp] syrop *m*

sys·tem ['sıstəm] system *m*; *uliczna* sieć *f*; organizm *m*

sys·te·mat·ic [sıstə'mætık] (**~ally**) systematyczny

'sys·tem er·ror *komp.* błąd *m* systemu

T

T, t [ti:] T, t

t *skrót pisany:* **ton(s)** tona *f* (-ny *pl.*) (*Brt.* =1016 kg, *Am.* = 907,18 kg)

ta *Brt. int.* F [tɑ:] dzięki

tab [tæb] etykietka *f*; wieszak *m*; konik *m*, (*w kartotece*) nalepka *f*; F rachunek *m*

ta·ble ['teıbl] **1.** stół *m*, stolik *m*; tabela *f*; zestawienie *n*; *math.* tablica *f*; *attr.* stołowy; **at ~** przy stole; **be on the ~** *fig.* być na tapecie; **turn the ~s** (**on s.o.**) *fig.* odwracać ⟨-rócić⟩ role; **2.** *fig.* przedstawiać ⟨-wić⟩ (*do rozpatrzenia*); *zwł. Am. fig.* odkładać ⟨odłożyć⟩; **'~·cloth** obrus *m*; **'~·land** plateau *n*, płaskowyż *m*; **'~ lin·en** bielizna *f* stołowa; **'~·mat** podkładka *f* (*pod talerz*); **'~·spoon** duża łyżka *f* stołowa (*do nabierania potraw*)

tab·let ['tæblıt] tabletka *f*; *kamienna* tablica *f*; kostka *f* (*mydła*)

'table| ten·nis (*w sporcie*) tenis *m* stołowy; **'~·top** blat *m*; **'~·ware** naczynia *pl.* stołowe

tab·loid ['tæblɔıd] gazeta *f* bulwarowa; **'~ press** prasa *f* bulwarowa

ta·boo [tə'bu:] **1.** tabu; **2.** (*pl.* **-boos**) tabu *n*

tab·u|·lar ['tæbjʊlə] tabelaryczny; **~·late** ['tæbjʊleıt] układać ⟨ułożyć⟩ tabelarycznie; **'~·la·tor** tabulator *m*

tach·o·graph ['tækəʊgrɑ:f] *mot.* tachograf *m*, tachometr *m* piszący

ta·chom·e·ter [tæ'kɒmıtə] *mot.* obrotomierz *m*, tachometr *m*

ta·cit ['tæsıt] milczący; **ta·ci·turn** ['tæsıtɜ:n] małomówny

tack [tæk] **1.** gwóźdź *m* (*tapicerski*); pinezka *f*; fastryga *f*; *naut.* hals *m*; **2.** ⟨przy⟩fastrygować (**to do** *G*); **~ on** doklejać ⟨-kleić⟩, doczepiać ⟨-czepić⟩ (**to** do *G*)

tack·le ['tækl] **1.** *problem itp.* zabierać ⟨-brać⟩ się do (*G*); (*w piłce nożnej*) przeciwnika ⟨za⟩atakować; dawać ⟨dać⟩ znać (*D*); **2.** *tech.* wielokrążek *m*; sprzęt *m* (*wędkarski itp.*)

tack·y ['tækı] (**-ier, -iest**) kleisty, lepki; *zwł. Am.* F tandetny

tact [tækt] takt *m*; **'~·ful** taktowny

tac·tics ['tæktıks] *pl. i sg.* taktyka *f*

'tact·less nietaktowny

tad·pole ['tædpəʊl] *zo.* kijanka *f*

taf·fe·ta ['tæfıtə] tafta *m*

taf·fy ['tæfı] *Am.* → **toffee**

tag [tæg] **1.** etykieta *f*; metka *f*; plakietka *f* (*z nazwiskiem*); skuwka *f* (*na sznurowadł itp.*); *też* **question ~** pytanie *n* ucięte; **2.** (**-gg-**) etykietować, przyczepiać ⟨-pić⟩ etykietę do (*G*); **~ along** F przyklejać ⟨-leić⟩ się; **~ along behind s.o.** ciągnąć się za kimś

tail [teıl] **1.** ogon *m* (*też aviat.*); tylna część *f*; F (*osoba śledząca*) ogon *m*; **put a ~ on** śledzić (*A*); **turn ~** *fig.* dawać ⟨-dać⟩ nogę; **with one's ~ between**

one's legs fig. z podkulonym ogonem; ~*s* pl. odwrotna strona f *(monety)*; frak *m*; **2.** F *kogoś* śledzić; **~ back** *zwł. Brt. mot.* ciągnąć się **(to** do G); **~ off** zmniejszać ⟨-szyć⟩ się; '**~-back** *zwł. Brt. mot.* korek *m*; '**~coat** frak *m*; **~ 'end** koniec *m*, tył *m*; '**~-light** *mot.* światło *n* tylne

tai·lor ['teɪlə] **1.** krawiec *m* (męski); **2.** ⟨u⟩szyć, ⟨s⟩kroić; fig. dopasowywać ⟨-sować⟩; ~**'made** szyte na miarę

'**tail| pipe** *Am. tech.* rura f wydechowa; '**~-wind** tylny wiatr *m*

taint·ed ['teɪntɪd] *zwł. Am. mięso:* zepsuty; fig. splamiony

take [teɪk] **1.** *(took, taken)* v/t. brać ⟨wziąć⟩ *(też mil. itp.)*; przyjmować ⟨-jąć⟩; *(w szachach)* figurę zbijać ⟨zbić⟩; *egzamin* zdawać ⟨-dać⟩; *univ. specjalność* studiować; *nagrodę itp.* zdobywać ⟨-być⟩; *czek, odpowiedzialność itp.* przyjmować ⟨-jąć⟩; *miejsce itp.* zajmować ⟨-jąć⟩; *phot.* ⟨z⟩robić; *temperaturę itp.* ⟨z⟩mierzyć; *kąpiel* brać ⟨wziąć⟩; *autobusem itp.* jeździć, pojechać; *drogą itp.* ⟨po⟩jechać; *samolotem* polecieć; korzystać z (G) *(sposobności itp.)*; *odwagę* zbierać ⟨zebrać⟩; *czas* zabierać ⟨-brać⟩; *gazety* ⟨za⟩prenumerować; *kroki* podejmować ⟨-djąć⟩; *it took him four hours* zajęło mu to cztery godziny; *I ~ it* that sądzę, że; ~ *it or leave* F rób co chcesz; *be ~n* miejsce: być zajętym; *be ~n by lub with* zachwycony (D); *be ~n ill lub sick* zachorować; ~ *to bits lub pieces* rozbierać ⟨-zebrać⟩; ~ *the blame* przyjmować⟨-jąć⟩ winę; ~ *care* ⟨za⟩opiekować się, ⟨za⟩troszczyć się; ~ *care!* F trzymaj się!; → *care* 1; ~ *hold of* ⟨s⟩chwytać; ~ *part* brać ⟨wziąć⟩ udział; → *part* 1; ~ *pity on* żałować (G); ~ *a walk* iść ⟨pójść⟩ na spacer; ~ *my word for it* dajesz ci słowo; → *advice, bath, break, lead, message, oath, place, prisoner, risk, seat, step, trouble itp.*; v/i. *med.* ⟨po⟩działać; ~ *after* być podobnym do (G); ~ *along* brać ⟨wziąć⟩ ze sobą (A); ~ *apart* rozbierać ⟨-zebrać⟩ *(na części)*; ~ *away* umniejszać ⟨-szyć⟩; ~*...to ~ away Brt.* ...na wynos; ~ *back* odbierać ⟨-debrać⟩; *słowa* cofać ⟨-fnąć⟩; przywracać ⟨-rócić⟩ *(do łas itp.)*; ⟨o⟩budzić *czyjeś* wspomnienia;

~ *down* ⟨za⟩notować; rozbierać ⟨-zebrać⟩; *ubranie itp.* ściągać ⟨-gnąć⟩ do dołu; ~ *for* brać ⟨wziąć⟩ za (A); ~ *from* przejmować ⟨-jąć⟩ *coś* od *kogoś*; *math.* odejmować ⟨-djąć⟩ (od G); ~ *in* przyjmować ⟨-jąć⟩ *(u siebie)*; fig. obejmować ⟨-bjąć⟩; *ubranie* zwężać ⟨zwęzić⟩; *coś* ⟨z⟩rozumieć; *kogoś* oszukiwać ⟨-kać⟩; ~ *off* zdejmować ⟨zdjąć⟩; *aviat.* *(w sporcie)* ⟨wy⟩startować *(też fig.)*; F odjeżdżać ⟨odjechać⟩; ~ *a day off* brać ⟨wziąć⟩ dzień wolnego; ~ *on* przyjąć *kogoś* (do pracy); *odpowiedzialność* brać ⟨wziąć⟩; *kolor* przybierać ⟨-brać⟩; *podejmować* ⟨-jąć⟩ walkę *(pracy)*; przeciwstawiać ⟨-wić⟩ się; ~ *out* wyjmować ⟨-jąć⟩; wychodzić ⟨wyjść⟩ z (I) *(to do* *(kina itp.)*; *ząb* usuwać ⟨-sunąć⟩; *polisę itp.* uzyskiwać ⟨-kać⟩; ~ *out on* wyżywać ⟨-żyć⟩ się na (I); ~ *over* władzę *itp.* przejmować ⟨-jąć⟩; przyjmować ⟨-jąć⟩ *obowiązki*; ~ *to* polubić (od razu); ~ *to doing s.th.* zaczynać ⟨-cząć⟩ *coś* robić; ~ *up* zainteresować się (I); *kwestię* podejmować ⟨-djąć⟩; *zajmować* ⟨-jąć⟩; *opowieść* kontynuować; ~ *up doing s.th.* zabierać ⟨-brać⟩ się do (robienia) czegoś; podnosić; ~ *up with* zajmować się (I); **2.** *film, TV:* ujęcie *n*; F wpływ *m*

'**take·a·way** *Brt.* posiłki *pl.* na wynos; restauracja f z posiłkami na wynos

tak·en ['teɪkən] *p.p. od take* 1

'**take·off** start *m* *(samolotu)*

tak·ings ['teɪkɪŋz] *pl.* wpływy *pl.*, dochód *m*

tale [teɪl] opowieść f; baśń f; **tell** ~*s* puszczać ⟨puścić⟩ plotki

tal·ent ['tælənt] talent *m*; powołanie *n*; '**~-ed** utalentowany

tal·is·man ['tælɪzmən] talizman *m*

talk [tɔːk] **1.** v/i. mówić; rozmawiać (to, with do G, about o L); s.o. to ~ to osoba, z którą można porozmawiać; v/t. bzdury mówić, wygadywać; mówić (L) *(interesach itp.)*; ~ *s.o. into s.th.* namawiać ⟨-mówić⟩ kogoś do czegoś; ~ *s.o. out of s.th.* wyperswadować komuś coś; ~ *s.th. over problem itp.* omawiać ⟨-mówić⟩ *(with z I)*; ~ *round kogoś* namówić **(to do** do G); **2.** rozmowa f (with z I, about o L); pogadanka f, prelekcja f, mowa f *(dziecka itp.)*; gadanina f; *give a* ~ wygłaszać ⟨-łosić⟩ pogadan-

kę (**to** D, **about, on** o L); **be the ~ of
the town** być na językach wszystkich;
baby ~ mowa f dziecka; → **small talk**

talk|·a·tive ['tɔːkətɪv] gadatliwy; '**~·er:
be a good ~er** umieć dobrze mó-
wić; '**~·ing-to** (pl. **-tos**) F bura f; **give
s.o. a good ~ing-to** nagadać ko-
muś; '**~·show** zwł. Am. talkshow m;
~·show 'host zwł. Am. prowadzący
m (-ca f) talkshow

tall [tɔːl] wysoki; **be 5 feet ~** mieć 5 stóp
wzrostu

tal·low ['tæləʊ] łój m

tal·ly¹ ['tælɪ] econ., (w sporcie) wynik m;
liczenie n; **keep a ~ of** prowadzić rejestr (G)

tal·ly² ['tælɪ] zgadzać ⟨zgodzić⟩ się
(**with** z I); też **~ up** podliczać ⟨-czyć⟩

tal·on ['tælən] zo. szpon m

tame [teɪm] **1.** (**-r, -st**) zo. oswojony;
łagodny; **2.** zwierzę oswajać ⟨-woić⟩

tam·per ['tæmpə]: **~ with** manipulo-
wać (I), dokonywać manipulacji z (I)

tam·pon ['tæmpən] tampon m

tan [tæn] **1.** (**-nn-**) opalać ⟨-lić⟩ się; skórę
⟨wy⟩garbować; **2.** opalenizna f; jasny
brąz m; **3.** jasnobrązowy

tang [tæŋ] ostry smak m lub zapach m

tan·gent ['tændʒənt] math. tangens m;
fly lub **go off at a ~** zbaczać ⟨zboczyć⟩
z tematu

tan·ge·rine [tændʒəˈriːn] bot. mandarynka f

tan·gi·ble ['tændʒəbl] dotykalny; fig.
namacalny

tan·gle ['tæŋgl] **1.** ⟨za⟩plątać się; włosy
⟨z⟩mierzwić; **2.** plątanina f; bałagan m

tank [tæŋk] mot. itp. zbiornik m; mil.
czołg m

tank·ard ['tæŋkəd] kufel m (do piwa)

tank·er ['tæŋkə] naut. zbiornikowiec m;
aviat. samolot m cysterna; mot. (samochód) cysterna f

tan|·ner ['tænə] garbarz m; **~·ne·ry**
['tænərɪ] garbarnia f

tan·ta·lize ['tæntəlaɪz] dręczyć (I);
'**~·liz·ing** dręczący

tan·ta·mount ['tæntəmaʊnt]: **be ~ to**
być równoznacznym z (I)

tan·trum ['tæntrəm] fig. histeria f

tap¹ [tæp] **1.** kran m; tech. kurek m; zawór m; **beer on ~** piwo n z beczki; **2.**
(**-pp-**) zasoby wykorzystywać ⟨-tać⟩,
eksploatować; zakładać ⟨założyć⟩ pod-

słuch; podsłuchiwać ⟨-chać⟩; ⟨na⟩czer-
pać (z beczki)

tap² [tæp] **1.** (**-pp-**) palcami pukać, stukać (**on** o A); **~ s.o. on the shoulder**
⟨po⟩klepać kogoś po ramieniu; **~ on**
⟨za⟩stukać w (A); **2.** (lekkie) uderzenie
n; klaps m; '**~ dance** stepowanie n

tape [teɪp] **1.** taśma f; tasiemka f; taśma
f klejąca; TV, video, magnetofonowa
itp. kaseta f; → **red tape**; TV zapis
m; **2.** zapisywać ⟨-sać⟩ na taśmie; też
~ up zaklejać ⟨-leić⟩ taśmą; '**~ deck**
deck m magnetofonowy; '**~ meas·ure**
taśma f krawiecka, przymiar m

ta·per ['teɪpə] też **~ off** zwężać się (do
dołu); fig. zmniejszać ⟨-szyć⟩ się

'**tape| re·cord·er** magnetofon m; '**~ re-
cord·ing** nagranie n magnetofono-
we

ta·pes·try ['tæpɪstrɪ] gobelin m

'**tape·worm** zo. tasiemiec m

taps [tæps] zwł. Am. pl. (sygnał) capstrzyk m

'**tap water** woda f bieżąca

tar [tɑː] **1.** smoła f; (w papierosie) substancja f smolista; **2.** (**-rr-**) ⟨na⟩smo-
łować

tare [teə] econ. tara f

tar·get ['tɑːgɪt] cel m (też mil., fig.); mil.
zadanie n; tarcza f strzelnicza; attr.
docelowy; '**~ ar·e·a** mil. rejon m celu; '**~ group** reklamy: grupa f odbiorców; '**~ lan·guage** język m docelowy;
'**~ prac·tice** ćwiczenia pl. w strzelaniu
do tarczy

tar·iff ['tærɪf] taryfa f; taryfa f celna;
zwł. Brit. stawki pl.

tar·mac ['tɑːmæk] asfalt m; aviat. pas m
startowy

tar·nish ['tɑːnɪʃ] ⟨z⟩matowieć, ⟨s⟩tra-
cić połysk; fig. reputację ⟨s⟩plamić

tart¹ [tɑːt] zwł. Brit. placek m lub ciastko
n z owocami; F dziwka f, puszczalska f

tart² [tɑːt] ostry; cierpki (też fig.)

tar·tan ['tɑːtn] tartan m

tar·tar ['tɑːtə] osad m nazębny; chem.
kamień m winny

task [tɑːsk] zadanie n; **take s.o. to ~** fig.
udzielać ⟨-lić⟩ komuś reprymendy (**for**
za A); '**~ force** mil. oddział m specjalny
(wojska, policji)

tas·sel ['tæsl] frędzel m

taste [teɪst] **1.** smak m (też fig.); gust m;
posmak m; zamiłowanie (**for** do G);

2. v/i. ⟨s⟩próbować, ⟨s⟩kosztować; v/t. smakować (*of I*), mieć smak; '~·ful gustowny; '~·less niesmaczny (*też fig*); niegustowny

tast·y ['teɪstɪ] (*-ier, -iest*) smaczny

ta-ta [tæ'tɑː] *int.* Brt. F cześć!

Tatra Mountains *pl.* Tatry *pl.*

tat·tered ['tætəd] obszarpany

tat·tle ['tætl] plotkować

tat·too¹ [tə'tuː] **1.** (*pl. -toos*) tatuaż *m*; **2.** ⟨wy⟩tatuować

tat·too² [tə'tuː] *mil.* (*pl. -toos*) capstrzyk *m*

taught [tɔːt] *pret. i p.p. od* **teach**

taunt [tɔːnt] **1.** ⟨za⟩drwić z (*I*); **2.** drwina *f*

Tau·rus ['tɔːrəs] *znak Zodiaku*: Byk *m*; (*s*)**he is** (*a*)~ on(a) jest spod znaku Byka

taut [tɔːt] napięty (*też fig.*), naprężony

taw·dry ['tɔːdrɪ] (*-ier, -iest*) (tani i) tandetny

taw·ny ['tɔːnɪ] (*-ier, -iest*) płowy

tax [tæks] **1.** podatek *m* (*on* od *G*); **2.** opodatkowywać ⟨-ować⟩; *cierpliwość* wystawiać ⟨-wić⟩ na ciężką próbę; ~·a·tion [tæk'seɪʃn] opodatkowanie *n*

tax·i ['tæksɪ] **1.** taksówka *f*; **2.** *aviat.* kołować; '~·driv·er taksówkarz *m*; '~·rank, '~ stand postój *m* taksówek

'**tax·i·pay·er** podatnik *m*; '~ re·turn deklaracja *f* podatkowa

T-bar ['tiːbɑː] teownik *m*; *też* ~ **lift** wyciąg *m*

tea [tiː] herbata *f*; *have a cup of* ~ wypić filiżankę herbaty; *make some* ~ zaparzyć herbatę; → *high tea*; '~·bag herbata *f* ekspresowa

teach [tiːtʃ] (*taught*) uczyć, nauczać ⟨-czyć⟩ (*G*); '~·er nauczyciel(ka *f*) *m*

'**tea co·sy** kapturek *m* (*na naczynie z herbatą*); '~·cup filiżanka *f* do herbaty

team [tiːm] zespół *m*; (*w sporcie*) drużyna *f*; zespół *m*; ~·ster *Am.* ['tiːmstə] kierowca *m* ciężarówki; '~·work praca *f* zespołowa

'**tea·pot** czajniczek *m*

tear¹ [tɪə] łza *f*; *in* ~**s** we łzach;

tear² [teə] **1.** (*tore, torn*) v/t. rozdzierać ⟨-zedrzeć⟩; *też* ~ *up* ⟨po⟩drzeć (*into* na *A*); wydzierać ⟨-drzeć⟩; odrywać ⟨oderwać⟩ (*from* od *G*); *drzewo, kartkę itp.* wyrywać ⟨-rwać⟩ (*from, out of* z *G*);

dach itp. zrywać ⟨zerwać⟩; v/i. ⟨po⟩rwać się; F ⟨po⟩gnać, ⟨po⟩mknąć; ~ *down plakat itp.* zrywać ⟨zerwać⟩; *dom* ⟨z⟩burzyć; ~ *off ubranie* zrywać z siebie; **2.** rozdarcie *n*

'**tear·drop** łza *f*; '~·ful łzawy; zapłakany

'**tea·room** herbaciarnia *f*

tease [tiːz] dokuczać ⟨-czyć⟩; dręczyć

'**tea·spoon** łyżeczka *f* do herbaty

teat [tiːt] *zo.* cycek *m*, sutek *m*; Brt. smoczek *m* (*na butelkę*)

tech·ni·cal ['teknɪkl] techniczny; fachowy; *jur.* formalny; ~·i·ty [teknɪ'kælətɪ] szczegół *m* techniczny; *jur.* kwestia *f* formalna

tech·ni·cian [tek'nɪʃn] technik *m*

tech·nique [tek'niːk] technika *f* (*sposób wykonywania*); △ *nie* **technika** (*przemysłowa*)

tech·nol·o·gy [tek'nɒlədʒɪ] technologia *f*

'**ted·dy bear** ['tedɪ -] miś *m* pluszowy

te·di·ous ['tiːdjəs] nużący

teem [tiːm]: ~ *with* roić się od (*G*), mrowić się od (*G*)

teen·age(d) ['tiːneɪdʒ(d)] nastoletni; '~·ag·er nastolatek *m* (-tka *f*)

teens [tiːnz] *pl.*: *be in one's* ~ mieć kilkanaście lat

tee·ny ['tiːnɪ], ~·wee·ny [tiːnɪ'wiːnɪ] (*-ier, -iest*) malutki, maluśki

tee shirt ['tiːʃɜːt] → *T-shirt*

teeth [tiːθ] *pl. od* **tooth**

teethe [tiːð] ząbkować

tee·to·tal·(l)er [tiː'təʊtlə] abstynent(ka *f*) *m*

tel·e·cast ['telɪkɑːst] transmisja *f* telewizyjna

tel·e·com·mu·ni·ca·tions [telɪkəmjuːnɪ'keɪʃnz] *pl.* telekomunikacja *f*

tel·e·gram ['telɪɡræm] telegram *m*

tel·e·graph ['telɪɡrɑːf] **1.** telegraf *m*; *by*~ telegraficznie; **2.** ⟨za⟩telegrafować; ~·ic [telɪ'ɡræfɪk] (*-ally*) telegraficzny

te·leg·ra·phy [tɪ'leɡrəfɪ] telegrafia *f*

tel·e·phone ['telɪfəʊn] (*też phone* 1, 2) **1.** telefon *m*; **2.** ⟨za⟩telefonować; '~ *booth zwł. Am.,* '~ *box Brt.* budka *f* telefoniczna; '~ *call* rozmowa *f* telefoniczna; '~ *di·rec·to·ry* → *phone book*; '~ *ex·change* centrala *f* telefoniczna; '~ *num·ber* numer *m* telefoniczny

te·leph·o·nist [tɪ'lefənɪst] *zwł.* Brt. telefonista *m* (-tka *f*)

tel·e·pho·to lens [telɪfəutəu 'lenz] *phot.* teleobiektyw *m*

tel·e·print·er ['telɪprɪntə] dalekopis *m*

tel·e·scope ['telɪskəup] teleskop *m*

tel·e·text ['telɪtekst] teletekst *m*, telegazeta *f*

tel·e·type·writ·er [telɪ'taɪpraɪtə] *zwł.* Am. dalekopis *m*

tel·e·vise ['telɪvaɪz] *TV* transmitować

tel·e·vi·sion ['telɪvɪʒn] telewizja *f*; *attr.* telewizyjny; **on ~** w telewizji; **watch ~** oglądać telewizję; *też* **~ set** telewizor *m*

tel·ex ['teleks] **1.** teleks *m*, dalekopis *m*; **2.** ⟨za⟩teleksować **(to** do *G*)

tell [tel] **(told)** *v/t.* mówić ⟨powiedzieć⟩; opowiadać ⟨-wiedzieć⟩ **(about, of** o *L*); *wskaźnik*: wskazywać ⟨-zać⟩; polecać ⟨-cić⟩ **(to do** zrobić); odróżniać ⟨-nić⟩ **(from** od *G*); **I can't ~ them apart** nie mogę ich odróżnić; *v/i.* dawać znać **(on** po *L*); **who can ~?** kto wie?; **you can never ~, you never can ~** nigdy nie wiadomo; **~ against** świadczyć przeciwko (*D*); *v/t.* **~ off** F ⟨z⟩rugać (*A*); *v/i.* **~ on s.o.** ⟨na⟩skarżyć na kogoś; **'~·er** *zwł.* Am. (w banku) kasjer(ka *f*) *m*; **'~·ing** znaczący, wymowny; **'~·tale 1.** niedwuznaczny, wymowny; **2.** F skarżypyta *m, f*

tel·ly ['telɪ] Brt. F telewizor *m*

te·mer·i·ty [tɪ'merətɪ] czelność *f*

tem·per ['tempə] **1.** temperament *m*; humor *m*, nastrój *m*; *tech.* stopień *m* twardości (*stali*); **keep one's ~** nie dawać ⟨dać⟩ się ponieść; **lose one's ~** ⟨s⟩tracić panowanie nad sobą; **2.** *stal* ⟨za⟩hartować

tem·pe·ra·ment ['tempərəmənt] temperament *m*; usposobienie *n*; **~·ra·men·tal** [tempərə'mentl] porywczy, o żywym temperamencie; kapryśny

tem·pe·rate ['tempərət] *klimat itp.*: umiarkowany

tem·pe·ra·ture ['temprətʃə] temperatura *f*; **have** *lub* **be running a ~** mieć podwyższoną temperaturę

tem·pest ['tempɪst] *poet.* burza *f*

tem·ple[1] ['templ] świątynia *f*

tem·ple[2] ['templ] *anat.* skroń *f*

tem·po·ral ['tempərəl] doczesny; *gr.* (*dotyczący czasów*), czasowy; **~·ra·ry** ['tempərərɪ] prowizoryczny, tymczasowy

tempt [tempt] ⟨s⟩kusić (*też rel.*); ⟨z⟩wabić **(to** do *G*); **temp·ta·tion** [temp'teɪʃn] kuszenie *n* (*też rel.*); wabienie *n*; **'~·ing** kuszący

ten [ten] **1.** dziesięć; **2.** dziesiątka *f*

ten·a·ble ['tenəbl] (*argument dający się obronić*)

te·na·cious [tɪ'neɪʃəs] uporczywy, wytrwały

ten·ant ['tenənt] lokator(ka *f*) *m*

tend [tend] mieć tendencję **(to** do *G*); skłaniać się **(towards** w stronę *G*); **~ to do s.th.** zwykle coś robić; **~ upwards** mieć tendencje zwyżkowe; **ten·den·cy** ['tendənsɪ] tendencja *f*

ten·der[1] ['tendə] czuły; tkliwy, bolesny; *pieczeń itp.*: miękki

ten·der[2] ['tendə] *rail., naut.* tender *m*

ten·der[3] ['tendə] *econ.* **1.** oferta *f*; **legal ~** prawny środek *m* płatniczy; **2.** przedstawiać ⟨-wić⟩ ofertę **(for** na *A*)

'ten·der|·foot (*pl.* **-foots, -feet**) Am. F nowicjusz(ka *f*) *m*; **'~·loin** polędwica *f*; **'~·ness** czułość *f*; tkliwość *f*, obolałość *f*

ten·don ['tendən] *anat.* ścięgno *n*

ten·dril ['tendrɪl] *bot.* wąs *m* pnącza

ten·e·ment ['tenɪmənt] dom *m* czynszowy

ten·nis ['tenɪs] (*w sporcie*) tenis *m*; **'~ court** kort *m* tenisowy; **'~ play·er** tenisista *m* (-tka *f*)

ten·or ['tenə] *mus.* tenor *m*; wydźwięk *m*, brzmienie *p*

tense[1] [tens] *gr.* czas *m*

tense[2] [tens] **(-r, -st)** ktoś, coś napięty; *ktoś* spięty; *żagiel* naprężony; **ten·sion** ['tenʃn] napięcie *n*

tent [tent] namiot *m*

ten·ta·cle ['tentəkl] *zo.* macka *f*; czułek *m*

ten·ta·tive ['tentətɪv] próbny; nie ostateczny

ten·ter·hooks['tentəhuks]: **be on ~** siedzieć jak na szpilkach

tenth [tenθ] **1.** dziesiąty; **2.** dziesiątka *f*; **'~·ly** po dziesiąte

ten·u·ous ['tenjuəs] *fig.* nieznaczny, niepozorny

ten·ure ['tenjuə] posiadanie *n*; okres *m* posiadania; **~ of office** piastowanie *n* urzędu

tep·id ['tepɪd] letni

term [tɜːm] **1.** termin *m*, okres *m*; kadencja *f*; *zwł. Brt. ped., univ.* trymestr *m*, *Am.* semestr *m*; określenie *n*, wyrażenie *n*; **~ of office** kadencja *f*; **~s** *pl.* warunki *pl.*; **be on good (bad) ~ with** być z kimś w dobrych (złych) stosunkach; **they are not on speaking ~s** nie rozmawiają ze sobą; **come to ~s with** 〈po〉godzić się z (*I*); **2.** nazywać 〈-zwać〉, określać 〈-lić〉

ter·mi·nal ['tɜːmɪnl] **1.** końcowy; *med.* terminalny; krańcowy; **~ally ill** śmiertelnie chory; **2.** *rail. itp.* stacja *f* końcowa; terminal *m*; → *air terminal*; *electr.* zacisk *m*, przyłącze *n*; *komp.* terminal *m*; **~nate** ['tɜːmɪnert] *v/t.* 〈za〉kończyć; *umowę* rozwiązywać 〈-zać〉; *ciąg* przerywać 〈-rwać〉; *v/i.* 〈za〉kończyć się; wygasać 〈-snąć〉; **~na·tion** [tɜːmɪ'neɪʃn] zakończenie *n*; rozwiązanie *n*; przerwanie *n*; upłynięcie *n*

ter·mi·nus ['tɜːmɪnəs] (*pl. -ni* [-naɪ], *-nuses*) *rail. itp.* stacja *f* końcowa

ter·race ['terəs] taras *m*; szereg *m* domów; *zw.* **~s** *pl. zwł. Brt.* (*na trybunie sportowej*) miejsca *pl.* stojące; **~d 'house** dom *m* szeregowy

ter·res·tri·al [tə'restrɪəl] ziemski; *zwł. zo., bot.* lądowy

ter·ri·ble ['terəbl] straszny

ter·rif·ic [tə'rɪfɪk] (**~ally**) fantastyczny, wspaniały; *prędkość* straszny

ter·ri·fy ['terɪfaɪ] przerażać 〈-razić〉

ter·ri·to·ri·al [terə'tɔːrɪəl] terytorialny; **~ry** ['terətəri] terytorium *n*, obszar *m*

ter·ror ['terə] terror *m*; przerażenie *n*; **~is·m** ['terərɪzm] terroryzm *m*; **~ist** ['terərɪst] terrorysta *m* (*-tka f*); **~ize** ['terəraɪz] 〈s〉terroryzować

terse [tɜːs] (**-r, -st**) zwięzły

test [test] **1.** test *m*, sprawdzian *m*; egzamin *m*; badanie *n*; próba *f*; **2.** 〈prze〉testować; sprawdzać 〈-dzić〉; 〈z〉badać; próbować 〈-ddać〉 próbie

tes·ta·ment ['testəmənt] testament *m* (*też rel.*); *last will and* **~** ostatnia wola *f*

'test card *TV* obraz *m* kontrolny; **'~ drive** *mot.* jazda *f* próbna

tes·ti·cle ['testɪkl] *anat.* jądro *n*

tes·ti·fy ['testɪfaɪ] *jur.* świadczyć, zeznawać 〈-nać〉

tes·ti·mo·ni·al [testɪ'məʊnjəl] referencja *f*; **~ny** ['testɪmənɪ] *jur.* świadectwo *n*, zaświadczenie *n*

'test pi·lot *aviat.* oblatywacz *m*; **'~ tube** probówka *f*; **'~-tube ba·by** *med.* dziecko *n* z probówki

tes·ty ['testɪ] (**-ier, -iest**) drażliwy

tet·a·nus ['tetənəs] *med.* tężec *m*

teth·er ['teðə] **1.** *zw.* więzy *pl.*; *at the end of one's* **~** u kresu wytrzymałości; **2.** *zwierzę* przywiązywać 〈-zać〉

Texas Teksas *m*

text [tekst] tekst *m*; **'~·book** podręcznik *m*

tex·tile ['tekstaɪl] tekstylny; **~s** *pl.* artykuły *pl.* tekstylne

tex·ture ['tekstʃə] faktura *f*; budowa *f*, struktura *f*

Thames Tamiza *f*

than [ðæn, ðən] niż

thank [θæŋk] **1.** *komuś* 〈po〉dziękować (*for* za *A*); **~ you** (*very much*) dziękuję (*bardzo*); *no,* **~ you** nie, dziękuję; (*yes,*) **~ you** tak, proszę; **2.** **~s** *pl.* podziękowania *pl.*; **~s!** dzięki!; *no,* **~s** nie, dziękuję; **~s to** dzięki (*D*); **'~·ful** wdzięczny; **'~·less** niewdzięczny

'Thanks·giv·ing (Day) *Am.* Dzień *m* Dziękczynienia

that [ðæt, ðət] **1.** *pron. i adj.* (*pl. those* [ðəʊz]) ten *m*; tamten *m*; to, tamto; **2.** *relative pron.* (*pl. that*) kiedy; gdy; **3.** *cj.* że; **4.** *adv.* F tak; *it's* **~** *simple* to takie proste

thatch [θætʃ] **1.** 〈po〉kryć strzechą; **2.** strzecha *f*

thaw [θɔː] **1.** 〈od〉tajać; **2.** odwilż *f* (*też fig.*)

the [ðə, *przed samogłoskami* ðɪ, *akcentowane* ðiː] **1.** *rodzajnik określony:* (*najczęściej nie tłumaczony*); **~** *horse* koń *m*; **2.** *adv.* **~ ... ~ ...** im ..., tym ...; **~** *sooner* **~** *better* im szybciej, tym lepiej

the·a·tre *Brt.*, **the·a·ter** *Am.* ['θɪətə] teatr *m*; sala *f* wykładowa; *Brt. med.* sala *f* operacyjna; *mil.* teatr *m* działań wojennych; **'~·go·er** teatroman(ka *f*) *m*; **the·at·ri·cal** [θɪ'ætrɪkl] teatralny; *fig.* kabotyński

theft [θeft] kradzież *f*

their [ðeə] *pl.* ich; **~s** [ðeəz] ich

them [ðem, ðəm] ich (*G, A*) *pl.*; im (*D*) *pl.*

theme [θi:m] temat *m*

them·selves [ðəm'selvz] się; sobie; sami; **by ~** przez siebie, bez pomocy

then [ðen] **1.** *adv.* wtedy; wówczas; **by ~** do tego czasu; **from ~ on** od tego czasu; → *every, now* 1, *there*; **2.** *adj.* zwł. **the ~** ówczesny

the·o·lo·gian [θɪə'ləʊdʒən] teolog *m*; **the·ol·o·gy** [θɪ'ɒlədʒɪ] teologia *f*

the·o|·ret·i·cal [θɪə'retɪkl] teoretyczny; **~ry** ['θɪərɪ] teoria *f*

ther·a|·peu·tic [θerə'pju:tɪk] terapeutyczny; **~pist** ['θerəpɪst] terapeuta *m* (-tka *f*); **~py** ['θerəpɪ] terapia *f*

there [ðeə] **1.** tam; **~ is** jest; **~ are** *pl.* są; **~ isn't, aren't** nie ma; **~ and then** na miejscu; **~ you are** proszę; ano właśnie!; **2.** *int.* no; **~, ~** no już dobrze; **~·a·bout(s)** ['ðeərəbaut(s)] coś koło tego; **~·after** [ðeər'ɑ:ftə] następnie, później; **~·by** [ðeə'baɪ] poprzez to; **~·fore** ['ðeəfɔ:] dlatego; **~·up·on** [ðeərə'pɒn] następnie

ther·mal ['θɜ:ml] **1.** termiczny; cieplny; *odzież:* ocieplany; termo...; **2.** prąd *m* termiczny

ther·mom·e·ter [θə'mɒmɪtə] termometr *m*

ther·mos ['θɜ:mɒs] *TM* termos *m*

the·sis ['θi:sɪs] (*pl.* **-ses** [-si:z]) teza *f*; *univ.* rozprawa *f*, praca *f* doktorska

they [ðeɪ] oni *pl.*, one *pl.*

thick [θɪk] **1.** *adj.* gruby; *mgła, zupa itp.:* gęsty; F głupi; *akcent:* ciężki; *głos:* ochrypły; **be ~ with** roić się od (*G*); **that's a bit ~!** zwł. *Brt.* F tego już za dużo; **2.** *adv.* grubo; gęsto; **lay it on ~** F przesadzać (*about* z *I*); **3.** **in the ~ of** w środku (*G*); **through ~ and thin** na dobre i na złe; **~·en** zagęszczać ⟨-ęścić⟩; ⟨z⟩gęstnieć; **~·et** ['θɪkɪt] gąszcz *m*; **~·head·ed** F tępy; **~·ness** grubość *f*; **~'set** krępy; **~'skinned** *fig.* gruboskóry

thief [θi:f] (*pl.* **thieves** [θi:vz]) złodziej(ka *f*) *m*

thigh [θaɪ] *anat.* udo *m*

thim·ble ['θɪmbl] naparstek *m*

thin [θɪn] **1.** *adj.* (**-nn-**) cienki; chudy; rzadki; rozrzedzony; *głos, wymówka itp.:* słaby; **2.** *adv.* cienko; **3.** (**-nn-**) rozrzedzać ⟨-dzić⟩ (się); *rośliny:* przerzedzać ⟨-dzić⟩ rzednąć

thing [θɪŋ] rzecz *f*; przedmiot *m*, obiekt *m*; coś *n*; **I couldn't see a ~** nie widziałem niczego; **another ~** coś innego; **the right ~** właściwa rzecz *f*; **~s** *pl.* rzeczy *pl.*; sprawy *pl.*

thing·a·ma·jig F ['θɪŋəmɪdʒɪg] wihajster *m*, dings *m*

think [θɪŋk] *v/i.* (**thought**) ⟨po⟩myśleć (**about** o *L*); zastanawiać ⟨-nowić⟩ się (**of** nad *I*); rozważać ⟨-żyć⟩; sądzić, przypuszczać (**that** że); **I ~ so** tak sądzę; **I'll ~ about it** zastanowię się nad tym; **~ of** przypominać ⟨-mnieć⟩ sobie o (*L*); **~ of doing s.th.** zastanawiać się nad zrobieniem czegoś; **what do you ~ of... lub about...?** co myślisz o ...?; *v/t.* ⟨po⟩myśleć; rozważać ⟨-żyć⟩; uważać (się) za (*A*); **~ over** zastanowić się nad (*I*), przemyśleć; **~ up** wymyślać ⟨-lić⟩; **'~ tank** grupa *lub* komisja *f* ekspertów

third [θɜ:d] **1.** trzeci; **2.** trzecia część *f*; **'~·ly** po trzecie; **~'rate** trzeciorzędny; **2 'World** Trzeci Świat *m*

thirst [θɜ:st] pragnienie *n*; **'~·y** (**-ier, -iest**) spragniony; **he's ~y** pić mu się chce

thir|·teen [θɜ:'ti:n] **1.** trzynaście; **2.** trzynastka *f*; **~·teenth** [θɜ:'ti:nθ] trzynasty; **~·ti·eth** ['θɜ:tɪɪθ] trzydziesty; **~·ty** ['θɜ:tɪ] **1.** trzydzieści; **2.** trzydziestka *f*

this [ðɪs] (*pl.* **these** [ði:z]) to, ten; **~ morning** dzisiejszego ranka; **~ is John speaking** John przy telefonie

this·tle ['θɪsl] *bot.* oset *m*

thong [θɒŋ] rzemień *m*, rzemyk *m*

thorn [θɔ:n] cierń *m*, kolec *m*; **'~·y** (**-ier, -iest**) ciernisty, kolczasty; *fig.* trudny

thor·ough ['θʌrə] dokładny, gruntowny; całkowity; drobiazgowy; **'~·bred** *zo.* koń *m* pełnej krwi; **'~·fare** magistrala *f*, arteria *f*

those [ðəʊz] *pl. od* **that**

though [ðəʊ] **1.** *cj.* chociaż, choć; **as ~** jakby; **2.** *adv.* jednak

thought [θɔ:t] **1.** *pret. i p.p. od* **think**; **2.** myśl *f*; zastanowienie *n* się; **on second ~s** po zastanowieniu się; **'~·ful** zamyślony; troskliwy; **'~·less** bezmyślny

thou·sand ['θaʊznd] **1.** tysiąc; **2.** tysiąc *m*; **~th** ['θaʊzntθ] **1.** tysięczny; **2.** tysięczna część *f*

thrash [θræʃ] *kogoś* ⟨wy⟩młócić; (*w grze*) pobić; **~ about, ~ around** rzu-

T

cać ⟨-cić⟩ się; **~ out** *problem* przedyskutować; '**~·ing** młócka *f*; lanie *n*

thread [θred] **1.** nić *f* (*też fig.*); wątek *m* (*też fig.*); *tech.* gwint *m*; **2.** igłę nawlekać ⟨-lec⟩; ⟨na⟩gwintować; '**~·bare** wytarty; *fig.* oklepany

threat [θret] groźba *f*; zagrożenie *n* (**to** dla *G*); **~·en** [ˈθretn] zagrażać ⟨-rozić⟩; '**~·en·ing** zagrażający

three [θriː] **1.** trzy; **2.** trójka *f*; '**~·fold** trzykrotny, potrójny; '**~·ply → ply¹**; '**~·score** sześćdziesiąt; '**~·stage** trójstopniowy

thresh [θreʃ] *agr.* ⟨wy⟩młócić; '**~·ing ma·chine** młocarnia *f*

thresh·old [ˈθreʃhəʊld] próg *m* (*też fig.*)

threw [θruː] *pret. od* **throw** 1

thrift [θrɪft] oszczędność *f*; gospodarność *f*; '**~·y** (*-ier, -iest*) oszczędny; gospodarny

thrill [θrɪl] **1.** dreszcz *m* (*zwł. emocji*); przeżycie *n*; **2.** *v/t.* **be ~ed** być podekscytowanym (**at, about** *z* powodu *G*); '**~·er** dreszczowiec *m*, kryminał *m*; '**~·ing** ekscytujący

thrive [θraɪv] (**thrived** *lub* **throve**) dobrze się rozwijać; *fig.* rozkwitać ⟨-tnąć⟩

throat [θrəʊt] gardło *n*; *clear one's* ~ odchrząkiwać ⟨-knąć⟩; → *sore* 1

throb [θrɒb] **1.** (*-bb-*) *puls*: tętnić; *ból*: pulsować; *serce*: walić; *silnik*: dudnić; **2.** tętnienie *n*; pulsowanie *n*; walenie *n*

throm·bo·sis [θrɒmˈbəʊsɪs] *med.* (*pl. -ses* [-siːz]) zakrzepica *f*

throne [θrəʊn] tron *m* (*też fig.*)

throng [θrɒŋ] **1.** tłum *m*, ciżba *f*; **2.** tłoczyć się; cisnąć się; zatłaczać

throt·tle [ˈθrɒtl] **1.** ⟨z-, za⟩dusić; **~ down** ⟨z⟩dławiać; *mot.*, *tech.* ⟨z⟩dławić; **2.** *tech.* przepustnica *f*

through [θruː] **1.** *prp.* przez (*A*), poprzez (*A*); *Am.* do (*G*) (*włącznie*); *Monday ~ Friday Am.* od poniedziału do piątku (*włącznie*); **2.** *adv.* całkiem, zupełnie; prosto; **~ and ~** całkowicie; *put s.o. ~ to tel.* połączyć kogoś z (*I*); *wet ~* całkiem mokry; **3.** *adj.* *pociąg*: przelotowy; **~'out 1.** *prp.* przez (*A*); **~ the night** przez (całą) noc; **2.** *adv.* całkowicie; zupełnie; '**~ traf·fic** ruch *m* przelotowy; '**~·way** *Am.* → **thruway**

throve [θrəʊv] *pret. od* **thrive**

throw [θrəʊ] **1.** (**threw, thrown**) rzu-

cać ⟨-cić⟩, ciskać ⟨-snąć⟩; *przełącznik* przerzucać ⟨-cić⟩; F *imprezę* urządzać ⟨-dzić⟩; **~ a four** wyrzucić cztery punkty; **~ off** *ubranie* zrzucać ⟨-cić⟩; pozbywać ⟨-być⟩ się (*choroby, prześladowców*); **~ out** *kogoś* wyrzucać ⟨-cić⟩; **~ up** *v/t.* podrzucać ⟨-cić⟩; F *pracę* porzucać ⟨-cić⟩; F zwracać ⟨-rócić⟩; *v/i.* F ⟨z⟩wymiotować; **2.** rzucenie *n*; '**~·a·way** jednorazowy; *uwaga*: rzucony niedbale; '**~·a·way pack** opakowanie *n* jednorazowe; '**~·in** (*w piłce nożnej*) wrzut *m z* autu; **~n** [θrəʊn] *p.p. od* **throw** 1

thru [θruː] *Am.* → **through**; '**~·way** *Am.* droga *f* przelotowa

thrum [θrʌm] (*-mm-*) → **strum**

thrush [θrʌʃ] *zo.* drozd *m*

thrust [θrʌst] **1.** (**thrust**) wpychać ⟨wepchnąć⟩ (**into** w *A*), wbijać ⟨wbić⟩ (**into** w *A*); **~ at** pchnąć (*A*); **~ upon s.o.** narzucać ⟨-cić⟩ komuś; **2.** pchnięcie *n*; *tech.* ciąg *m*, siła *f* ciągu; *mil.* wypad *m*

thud [θʌd] **1.** głuche uderzenie *n*; **2.** (*-dd-*) uderzyć głucho

thug [θʌg] kryminalista *m*

thumb [θʌm] **1.** *anat.* kciuk *m*; **2.** **~ a lift** *lub* **ride** zatrzymywać ⟨-mać⟩ samochody na (auto)stopie (**to** w kierunku *G*); **~ through a book** przekartkowywać ⟨-wać⟩ książkę; *well-~ed* zaczytany; '**~·tack** *Am.* pinezka *f lub* pineska *f*

thump [θʌmp] *v/t.* *kogoś* palnąć, walnąć; **~ out** melodię ⟨wy⟩bębnić (**on the piano** na fortepianie); *v/i.* walić, łomotać; **2.** walnięcie *n*; walenie *n*, łomot *m*

thun·der [ˈθʌndə] **1.** grzmot *m*; piorun *m*; **2.** ⟨za⟩grzmieć (*też fig.*); '**~·bolt** błyskawica *f*; '**~·clap** uderzenie *n* pioruna; '**~·cloud** chmura *f* burzowa; **~·ous** [ˈθʌndərəs] *oklaski*: burzliwy; '**~·storm** burza *f z* piorunami; '**~·struck** (jak) rażony piorunem

Thur(s) *skrót pisany*: **Thursday** czw., czwartek *m*

Thurs·day [ˈθɜːzdɪ] (*skrót*: **Thur, Thurs**) czwartek *m*; **on ~** w czwartek; **on ~s** w czwartki

thus [ðʌs] tak; w ten sposób; **~ far** jak dotąd

thwart [θwɔːt] udaremniać ⟨-nić⟩, ⟨po⟩krzyżować

thyme [taɪm] *bot.* tymianek *m*
thy·roid (gland) ['θaɪrɔɪd (-)] *anat.* tarczyca *f*
tick¹ [tɪk] **1.** tykanie *n*; znaczek *m*, ptaszek *m*; **2.** *v/i.* tykać; *v/t. zw.* **~ off** odfajkowywać ⟨-ować⟩, odhaczać ⟨-czyć⟩
tick² [tɪk] *zo.* kleszcz *m*
tick³ [tɪk]: **on ~** *Brt.* F na kredyt
tick·er·tape ['tɪkəteɪp] taśma *f* perforowana; *jakby:* serpentyna *f*; **~ pa'rade** ceremonia *f* (*z rzucaniem serpentyn*)
tick·et ['tɪkɪt] **1.** bilet *m*; (*w sklepie*) metka *f*; mandat *m*; kwit *m* (*do przechowalni itp.*); etykietka *f*; paragon *m*; *Am. pol.* mandat *m*; '**~-can·cel·(l)ing ma·chine** kasownik *m*; '**~ col·lec·tor** konduktor(ka *f*) *m*; '**~ ma·chine** automat *m* do biletów; '**~ of·fice** *rail.* kasa *f* biletowa
tick·ing ['tɪkɪŋ] płótno *n* pościelowe
tick|·le ['tɪkl] ⟨po⟩łaskotać; **~·lish** ['tɪklɪʃ] łaskotliwy
tid·al ['taɪdl]: **~ wave** fala *f* pływu
tid·bit ['tɪdbɪt] *Am.* → **titbit**
tide [taɪd] **1.** pływ *m*, odpływ *m* morza; *fig.* napływ *m*; **high ~** przypływ *m*; **low ~** odpływ *m*; **2. ~ over** *fig.* pomagać ⟨-móc⟩ przetrwać
ti·dy ['taɪdɪ] **1.** (*-ier, -iest*) schludny; porządny (*też fig.*); F *suma:* niezły; **2.** *też* **~ up** uporządkowywać ⟨-ować⟩; doprowadzać ⟨-dzić⟩ do porządku; ⟨po⟩sprzątać; **~ away** uprzątać, ⟨-tnąć⟩
tie [taɪ] **1.** krawat *m*; sznur *m*; (*w sporcie*) remis *m*; (*w sporcie*) mecz *m* (*w rozgrywkach pucharowych*); *Am. rail.* podkład *m*; *zw.* **~s** *pl.* więzy *pl.*; **2.** *v/t.* ⟨za⟩wiązać, zawiązać ⟨-zywać⟩; powiązać (**to** z *I*); **the game was ~d** (*w sporcie*) mecz zakończył się wynikiem remisowym; *v/i.* **they ~d for second place** (*w sporcie*) zdobyli ex aequo drugie miejsce; **~ down** *fig.* 'Oz⟩wiązać ręce, wiązać ⟨związywać⟩ terminem (**to do** G); **~ in with** odpowiadać (D), zgadzać się z (I), korelować z (I); **~ up** *pieniądze* związywać ⟨-zać⟩, unieruchamiać ⟨-chomić⟩; powiązywać ⟨-zać⟩; *ruch* unieruchamiać ⟨-chomić⟩; '**~-break(·er)** (*w tenisie*) tie-break *m*; '**~-in** powiązanie *n*; *econ.* sprzedaż *f* wiązana; **a ~-in with his latest movie** *jakby:* książka *f* oparta na fabule jego najnowszego filmu; '**~-on** przywiązany

tier [tɪə] rząd *m*; poziom *m* (*też fig.*); warstwa *f*
'**tie-up** powiązanie *n*; związek *m*; *econ.* fuzja *f*
ti·ger ['taɪgə] *zo.* tygrys *m*
tight [taɪt] **1.** *adj.* szczelny; *żagiel itp.*: napięty; (*za*) ciasny, *ubranie itp.*: opięty; *econ. pieniądz:* ograniczony; F (*pijany*) wstawiony; *w złoż.* ...szczelny; **be in a ~ corner** F być w trudnej sytuacji; **2.** *adv.* mocno; F dobrze; **sleep ~!** F śpij dobrze; **~·en** ['taɪtn] zaciskać ⟨-snąć⟩; napinać ⟨-piąć⟩; **~ one's belt** *fig.* zaciskać ⟨-snąć⟩ pasa; **~·en up (on)** *prawo* zaostrzać ⟨-rzyć⟩; **~'fist·ed** F skąpy; **~s** *pl.* trykot *m*; *zwł. Brt.* rajstopy *pl.*
ti·gress ['taɪgrɪs] *zo.* tygrysica *f*
tile [taɪl] **1.** dachówka *f*; kafel(ek) *m*; **2.** pokrywać ⟨-ryć⟩ dachówką; wykładać (*wyłożyć*) kaflami; '**til·er** dekarz *m*; kafelkarz *m*
till¹ [tɪl] → **until**
till² [tɪl] kasa *f*
tilt [tɪlt] **1.** przechylać ⟨-lić⟩ (się); nachylać ⟨-lić⟩ się; **2.** nachylenie *n*; pochylenie *n*; **at a ~** przechylony; (*at*) **full ~** F na całego (*jechać itp.*)
tim·ber ['tɪmbə] *Brt.* drewno *n* budowlane; budulec *m*; belka *f*
time [taɪm] **1.** czas *m*; godzina *f*; pora *m*; raz *m*; *mus.* takt *m*; **~ after ~** i **~ and again** ciągle; **every ~ he** ...za każdym razem, gdy on; **how many ~s?** ile razy?; **next ~** następnym razem; **this ~** tym razem; **three ~s** trzy razy; **three ~s four equals** *lub* **is twelve** trzy razy cztery równa się dwanaście; **what's the ~?** która godzina?; **all the ~** cały czas; **at all ~s, at any ~** za każdym razem; **at the same ~** w tym samym czasie; **at ~s** czasami; **by the ~** do czasu gdy; **for a ~** na jakiś czas; **for the ~ being** w tej chwili; **from ~ to ~** od czasu do czasu; **have a good ~** dobrze się bawić; **in ~** punktualnie, na czas; **in no ~** (*at all*) szybko; wkrótce; **on ~** punktualnie; **some ~ ago** jakiś czas temu; **take one's ~** nie spieszyć się (**to do s.th.** ze zrobieniem czegoś); **2.** mierzyć czas (G) (*też w sporcie*); ustalać ⟨-lić⟩ czas (G); wyliczać ⟨-czać⟩ czas; '**~ card** *Am.* karta f kontrolna; '**~ clock** zegar *m* kontrolny; '**~ lag** różnica *f* czasowa; '**~·lapse:** **~ photography** (*w fil-*

T

mie) zdjęcia *pl.* poklatkowe; '**~·less** bezczasowy; wieczny; '**~·ly** (**-ier, -iest**) terminowy, planowy; **~ sheet** karta *f* kontrolna; '**~ sig·nal** radiowy sygnał *m* czasu; '**~·ta·ble** rozkład *m* jazdy *lub* lotów; program *m*; szkolny rozkład *m* zajęć

tim·id ['tɪmɪd] nieśmiały, płochliwy

tim·ing ['taɪmɪŋ] timing *m*; wybór *m* najwłaściwszego momentu

tin [tɪn] **1.** cyna *f*; *Brt.* blaszana, konserwowa puszka *f*; **2.** (**-nn-**) ⟨po⟩cynować; *Brt.* ⟨za⟩konserwować, ⟨za⟩puszkować

tinc·ture ['tɪŋktʃə] tynktura *f*

'**tin·foil** folia *f* aluminiowa, staniol *m*

tinge [tɪndʒ] **1.** nadawać odcień; **be ~d with** być zabarwionym (*I*); **2.** odcień *m*; *fig.* odrobina *f*

tin·gle ['tɪŋgl] mrowić, szczypać, kłuć

tink·er ['tɪŋkə] grzebać się (**with** przy *L*)

tin·kle ['tɪŋkl] ⟨za⟩dźwięczeć; ⟨za⟩dzwonić

tinned [tɪnd] *Brt.* puszkowany; konserwowy; **~ 'fruit** owoce *pl.* w puszkach

'**tin o·pen·er** *Brt.* otwieracz *m* do konserw

tin·sel ['tɪnsl] lameta *f*

tint [tɪnt] **1.** barwa *f*; zabarwienie *n*; **2.** zabarwiać ⟨-wić⟩

ti·ny ['taɪnɪ] (**-ier, -iest**) malutki, drobny

tip¹ [tɪp] **1.** szpic *m*, koniuszek *m*, wierzchołek *m*; filtr *m* (*papierosa*); **it's on the ~ of my tongue** mam to na końcu języka; **2.** (**-pp-**) zakańczać ⟨-kończyć⟩ szpicem

tip² [tɪp] **1.** (**-pp-**) *zwł. Brt.* wysypywać ⟨-pać⟩; przechylać ⟨-lić⟩; **~ over** przewracać ⟨-rócić⟩; **2.** *zwł. Brt.* wysypisko *n*; *Brt. fig.* F chlew *m*

tip³ [tɪp] **1.** napiwek *m*; **2.** (**-pp-**) dawać ⟨dać⟩ napiwek (*D*)

tip⁴ [tɪp] **1.** porada *f*, rada *f*; **2.** (**-pp-**) ⟨po⟩radzić; ⟨po⟩stawiać (**for** na *A*); typować (**as** jako *A*); **~ off** dawać ⟨dać⟩ znać (*D*)

tip·sy ['tɪpsɪ] (**-ier, -iest**) wstawiony, podpity

'**tip·toe 1. on ~** na palcach; **2.** iść na końcach palców

tire¹ ['taɪə] *Am.* → **tyre**

tire² ['taɪə] ⟨z⟩męczyć (się); '**~d** zmęczony; **be ~d of** być zmęczonym (*I*); '**~·less** niestrudzony, niezmordowany; '**~·some** męczący; uciążliwy

Ti·rol [tɪ'rəʊl, 'tɪrəl] Tyrol *m*

tis·sue ['tɪʃuː] *biol.* tkanka *f*; chusteczka *f* higieniczna; '**~ pa·per** bibułka *f*

tit¹ [tɪt] *sl.* cycek *m*

tit² [tɪt] *zo.* sikor(k)a *f*

tit·bit ['tɪtbɪt] *zwł. Brt.* smakołyk *m*

tit·il·late ['tɪtɪleɪt] kogoś (*seksualnie*) podniecać ⟨-cić⟩

ti·tle ['taɪtl] tytuł *m*; nagłówek *m*; *jur.* tytuł *m* prawny (**to** do *G*); '**~ page** strona *f* tytułowa

tit·mouse ['tɪtmaʊs] *zo.* (*pl.* **-mice**) sikor(k)a *f*

tit·ter ['tɪtə] **1.** ⟨za⟩chichotać; **2.** chichot *m*

TM *skrót pisany:* **trademark** znak *m* towarowy

tn *Am.* → **t**

to [tuː, tʊ, tə] **1.** *prp.* do (*G*); na (*A*); przy (*I*); dla (*G*); w relacji do, w stosunku do (*G*); ku (*D*) (*zdumieniu itp.*); *w określeniach czasu za* (*A*); **~ me** mnie *lub* mi *itp.*; **from Monday ~ Friday** od poniedziału do piątku; **a quarter to ~ one** za kwadrans pierwsza; **go ~ Poland** jechać do Polski; **go ~ school** chodzić do szkoły; **have you ever been ~ London?** czy byłeś kiedyś w Londynie?; **here's ~ you!** za twe zdrowie!; **~ the left** na lewo; **~ my regret** ku mojemu żalowi; **2.** *adv.* **pull ~** zamykać ⟨-mknąć⟩; **come ~** przyjść do siebie; **~ and fro** tam i z powrotem; **3.** *z bezokolicznikiem:* **~ go** iść ⟨pójść⟩; *cel:* w celu, żeby; **easy ~ learn** łatwy do nauczenia się; **... ~ earn money** ... aby zarabiać pieniądze

toad [təʊd] *zo.* ropucha *f*; **~·stool** *bot.* ['təʊdstuːl] muchomor *m*

toad·y ['təʊdɪ] **1.** pochlebca *m*; **2.** przypochlebiać się

toast¹ [təʊst] **1.** tost *m*, grzanka *f*; **2.** przypiekać ⟨-piec⟩; ⟨z⟩robić grzanki

toast² [təʊst] **1.** toast *m*; **2.** wznosić ⟨-nieść⟩ toast

toast·er ['təʊstə] opiekacz *m* do grzanek, toster *m*

to·bac·co [tə'bækəʊ] (*pl.* **-cos**) tytoń *m*; *attr.* tytoniowy; △ *nie tabaka*; **~·nist** [tə'bækənɪst] właściciel(ka *f*) *m* sklepu z wyrobami tytoniowymi

to·bog·gan [tə'bɒgən] **1.** sanki *pl.*; tobogan *m*; **2.** zjeżdżać ⟨zjechać⟩ na sankach

torpedo

to·day [təˈdeɪ] **1.** *adv.* dzisiaj; dziś; *a week ~, ~ week* od dzisiaj za tydzień; **2.** dzisiejszy; *of ~, ~'s* z dnia dzisiejszego, dzisiejszy

tod·dle [ˈtɒdl] ⟨po⟩dreptać (*zwł. małe dziecko*)

tod·dy [ˈtɒdɪ] grog *m* (*z whisky*)

to-do [təˈduː] F *fig.* (*pl.* **-dos**) zamieszanie *n*, rejwach *m*

toe [təʊ] *anat.* palec *m* nogi; czubek *m* (*buta*); *~-nail* paznokieć *m* palec u nogi

tof·fee, **~fy** [ˈtɒfɪ] toffi *n*

to·geth·er [təˈɡeðə] razem; wspólnie; *~ with* wraz z (*I*)

toi·let [ˈtɔɪlɪt] toaleta *f*; *'~ pa·per* papier *m* toaletowy; *'~ roll zwł. Brt.* rolka *f* papieru toaletowego

to·ken [ˈtəʊkən] **1.** znak *m*; żeton *m*; *as a ~, in ~ of* na znak (*G*); *by the same ~* tym samym; **2.** *adj.* zdawkowy; symboliczny

told [təʊld] *pret. i p.p. od* **tell**

tol·e·ra·ble [ˈtɒlərəbl] znośny; *~rance* [ˈtɒlərəns] tolerancja *f*; *~rant* [ˈtɒlərənt] tolerancyjny (*of, towards* względem *G*); *~rate* [ˈtɒləreɪt] tolerować, znosić ⟨-nieść⟩

toll¹ [təʊl] opłata *f* (*portowa, za przejazd itp.*); cło *n*; *heavy death ~* duża liczba ofiar śmiertelnych; *take its ~ (on) fig.* wyciskać swoje piętno (na *I*)

toll² [təʊl] dzwony: ⟨za⟩dzwonić

toll·'free *Am. tel.* wolny od opłaty drogowej; *~ road* droga *f* płatna

to·ma·to [təˈmɑːtəʊ, təˈmeɪtəʊ] *bot.* (*pl.* **-toes**) pomidor *m*

tomb [tuːm] grobowiec *m*

tom·boy [ˈtɒmbɔɪ] chłopczyca *f*

'tomb·stone nagrobek *m*, kamień *m* nagrobny

tom·cat [ˈtɒmkæt] *zo. też* F kocur *m*

tom·fool·e·ry [tɒmˈfuːlərɪ] błazenada *f*

to·mor·row [təˈmɒrəʊ] **1.** *adv.* jutro; *a week ~, ~ week* od jutra za tydzień; *~ morning* jutro rano; *~ night* jutro wieczorem; **2.** *the day after ~* pojutrze; *of ~, ~'s* jutrzejszy

ton [tʌn] (*skrót:* **t**, **tn**) (*waga*) tona; ∆ *nie* **ton**

tone [təʊn] **1.** ton *m*, dźwięk *m*; brzmienie *n*; *Am. mus.* nuta *f*; *med.* tonus *m*; *fig.* poziom *m*; **2.** *~ down* osłabiać ⟨-bić⟩; *~ up* wzmacniać ⟨-mocnić⟩

tongs [tɒŋz] *pl.* (*a pair of ~*) szczypce *pl.*

tongue [tʌŋ] *anat.* język *m* (*też w bucie*); ozór *m* (*zwierzęcia*); *gastr.* ozorek *m*; mowa *f*, język *m*; *hold one's ~* trzymać język za zębami

ton·ic [ˈtɒnɪk] tonik *m*; *med.* lek *m* tonizujący; *mus.* tonika *f*

to·night [təˈnaɪt] dzisiaj w nocy, dzisiejszej nocy

ton·sil [ˈtɒnsl] *anat.* migdał *m*; *~·li·tis med.* [tɒnsɪˈlaɪtɪs] zapalenie *n* migdałków; angina *f*

too [tuː] też, także; zbyt, zbytnio

took [tʊk] *pret. od* **take** 1

tool [tuːl] narzędzie *n*; *~ bag* torba *f* na narzędzia; *'~ box* skrzynka *f* na narzędzia; *'~ kit* zestaw *m* narzędzi; *'~·shed* szopa *f* na narzędzia

toot [tuːt] ⟨za⟩trąbić

tooth [tuːθ] (*pl.* **teeth**) ząb *m*; *'~·ache* ból *m* zęba; *'~·brush* szczotka *f* do zębów; *'~·less* bezzębny; *'~·paste* pasta *f* do zębów; *'~·pick* wykałaczka *f*

top¹ [tɒp] **1.** góra *f*; wierzch *m*; szczyt *m* (*góry*); wierzchołek *m*; czubek *m*; korona *f* (*drzewa*); zakrętka *f* (*butelki, tubki itp.*); *mot.* (*składany*) dach *m*; *mot.* najwyższy bieg *m*; *at the ~ of the page* na górze strony; *at the ~ of one's voice* na całe gardło; *on ~* na wierzchu; *on ~ of* na (*L*); **2.** górny; szczytowy; maksymalny; **3.** (*-pp-*) przykrywać ⟨-ryć⟩; *fig.* przewyższać ⟨-szyć⟩, przekraczać, ⟨-roczyć⟩; *~ up* zbiornik dopełniać ⟨-nić⟩; F uzupełniać ⟨-nić⟩

top² [tɒp] (*zabawka*) bąk *m*

top| 'hat cylinder *m*; *~·'heav·y* przeładowany u góry; *fig.* o zbyt dużej górze

top·ic [ˈtɒpɪk] temat *m*; *~·al* aktualny

top·ple [ˈtɒpl]: *zw. ~ over* przewracać ⟨-rócić⟩ się; *fig.* rząd itp. obalać ⟨-lić⟩

top·sy-tur·vy [tɒpsɪˈtɜːvɪ] postawiony do góry nogami

torch [tɔːtʃ] *Brt.* latarka *f*; pochodnia *f*; *'~·light* światło *n* pochodni

tore [tɔː] *pret. od* **tear²**

tor·ment 1. [ˈtɔːment] męczarnia *f*; **2.** [tɔːˈment] ⟨u⟩męczać się nad (*I*)

torn [tɔːn] *p.p. od* **tear²**

tor·na·do [tɔːˈneɪdəʊ] (*pl.* **-does**, **-dos**) tornado *n*

tor·pe·do [tɔːˈpiːdəʊ] (*pl.* **-does**) torpeda *f*

T

tor|·rent ['tɔrənt] *wartki* strumień *m*, potok *m* (*też fig.*); **~·ren·tial** [təˈrenʃl]: **~rential rain** ulewny deszcz *m*

tor·toise ['tɔːtəs] *zo.* żółw *m*

tor·tu·ous ['tɔːtʃʊəs] kręty; zawikłany

tor·ture ['tɔːtʃə] **1.** tortura (*też fig.*); **2.** torturować

toss [tɒs] **1.** *v/t.* rzucać ⟨-cić⟩ (*też monetą*); *naleśnik* przewracać ⟨-rócić⟩; *v/i. też* **~ about**, **~ and turn** rzucać się (*we śnie*); **~ for s.th.** rzucać ⟨-cić⟩ monetą o coś; **~ off** *drinka* strzelić sobie; *szkic itp.* machnąć; **2.** rzut *m* (*też monetą*); podrzucenie *n*; szarpnięcie *n* (*głową*)

tot [tɒt] F berbeć *m*

to·tal ['təʊtl] **1.** całkowity; ogólny; całkowity; totalny; **2.** suma *f* (*całkowita*); liczba *f* całkowita *lub* ogólna; **3.** (*zwł. Brt. -ll-, Am. -l-*) wynosić ⟨-nieść⟩ ogółem; **~ up** podsumowywać ⟨-ować⟩

tot·ter ['tɒtə] chwiać się; iść ⟨pójść⟩ chwiejnie

touch [tʌtʃ] **1.** dotykać ⟨-tknąć⟩ (się); zbliżać ⟨-żyć⟩ się do (*G*) (*standardu itp.*); wzruszać ⟨-szyć⟩ (się); **~ wood!** odpukaj w niemalowane!; **~ down** *aviat.* ⟨wy⟩lądować; **~ up** ulepszać ⟨-szyć⟩; *phot.* ⟨z⟩retuszować; **2.** dotyk *m*; dotknięcie *n*; ślad *m* (*pędzla itp.*); kontakt *m*; **a ~ of flu** lekka grypa *f*; **get in ~ with s.o.** wchodzić ⟨wejść⟩ z kimś w kontakt; **a personal ~** akcent *m* osobisty; **~-and-go** [tʌtʃənˈgəʊ] *sytuacja*: niepewny; **it was ~-and-go whether** wcale nie było pewne, czy; **'~·down** *aviat.* lądowanie *n*; **~ed** wzruszony; **'~·ing** wzruszający; **'~·line** (*w piłce nożnej*) linia *f* autowa; **'~·stone** probierz *m*; **'~·y** (*-ier, -iest*) drażliwy

tough [tʌf] wytrzymały; twardy; *negocjacje*: nieustępliwy; ciężki; *problem*: trudny; *okolica*: niebezpieczny; **~·en** ['tʌfn] *też* **~en up** ⟨s⟩twardnieć; utwardzać ⟨-dzić⟩

tour [tʊə] **1.** podróż *f* ((*a*)*round* wokół *G*); wycieczka *f*; zwiedzanie *n*; obchód *m*; *theat.* tourn(e)e *n* (*of* po *L*); → **conduct**; **2.** objeżdżać ⟨-jechać⟩; zwiedzać ⟨-dzić⟩

tour·is·m ['tʊərɪzəm] turystyka *f*, ruch *m* turystyczny

tour·ist ['tʊərɪst] turysta *m* (-tka *f*); *attr.* turystyczny; **'~ class** *aviat.*, *naut.* klasa *f* turystyczna; **'~ in·dus·try** przemysł *m* turystyczny; **'~ in·for·ma·tion of·fice**, **'~ of·fice** biuro *n* turystyczne; **'~ sea·son** sezon *m* turystyczny

tour·na·ment ['tʊənəmənt] turniej *m*

tou·sled ['taʊzld] *włosy*: zmierzwiony

tow [təʊ] **1.** *łódź, samochód* holować; **2.** hol *m*; **give s.o. a ~** poholować kogoś; **take in ~** brać ⟨wziąć⟩ na hol

to·ward *zwł. Am.*, **to·wards** *zwł. Brt.* [təˈwɔːd(z)] do (*G*), w stronę (*G*); w kierunku (*G*); *czas*: pod (*A*); w odniesieniu do (*G*); na (*A*)

tow·el ['taʊəl] **1.** ręcznik *m*; **2.** (*zwł. Brt. -ll-, Am. -l-*) wycierać ⟨wytrzeć⟩ (się) (*ręcznikiem*)

tow·er ['taʊə] **1.** wieża *f*; **2.** **~ above**, **~ over** górować nad (*I*); **'~ block** *Brt.* wieżowiec *m*; **~·ing** ['taʊərɪŋ] wyniosły; *fig.* niebotyczny

town [taʊn] miasto *n*; **~ 'cen·tre** *Brt.* centrum *n* miasta; **~ 'coun·cil** rada *f* miejska; **~ 'coun·ci(l)·lor** radny *m* (-dna *f*); **~ 'hall** ratusz *m*; **~s·peo·ple** ['taʊnzpiːpl] *pl.* mieszkańcy *pl.* miasta

'tow·rope *mot.* lina *f* holownicza

tox·ic ['tɒksɪk] (*~ally*) toksyczny; **~ 'waste** odpadki *pl.* toksyczne; **~waste 'dump** składowisko *n* odpadków toksycznych

tox·in ['tɒksɪn] *biol.* toksyna *f*

toy [tɔɪ] **1.** zabawka *f*; **~s** *pl.* zabawki *pl.*, *econ.* wyroby *pl.* zabawkarskie; **2.** zabawkowy; miniaturowy; mały; **3.** **~ with** bawić się (*I*); *fig.* igrać *z* (*I*)

trace [treɪs] **1.** ⟨prze-, wy⟩śledzić; odnajdować ⟨-naleźć⟩; *też* **~ back** wywodzić się (*to* od *G*); **~ s.th. to** odnajdować ⟨-naleźć⟩ źródło (*G*); odkalkowywać ⟨-kować⟩

track [træk] **1.** ślad *m* (*też fig.*); trop *m*; szlak *m*, droga *f*; tor *m*, bieżnia *f*; *rail.* tor *m*; dźwiękowa ścieżka *f*; *tech.* gąsienica *f*; **2.** ⟨wy⟩tropić; **~ down** ⟨wy⟩śledzić; **~ and 'field** *zwł. Am.* (*w sporcie*) lekkoatletyczny; **~ e·vent** (*w sporcie*) bieg *m* lekkoatletyczny; **'~·ing sta·tion** (*w astronautyce*) stacja *f* naziemna; **'~·suit** dres *m*

tract [trækt] przestrzeń *f*, obszar *m*; *anat.* przewód *m*; traktat *m*, rozprawa *f*

trac·tion ['trækʃn] trakcja *f*; **'~ en·gine** lokomobila *f*

trac·tor ['træktə] traktor *m*

trade[treɪd] **1.** handel *m*; branża *f*, gałąź *f*; zawód *m*, fach *m*; **2.** handlować (*I*), prowadzić handel (*I*); **~ on** żerować na (*L*); **'~·mark**(*skrót*: **TM**) znak *m* towarowy; **'~·name**nazwa *f* handlowa, marka *f*; **'~ price**cena *f* hurtowa; **'trad·er** hurtownik *m*; **~s·man**['treɪdzmən] (*pl.* **-men**) detalista *m*; właściciel(ka *f*) sklepu; **~(s)** **'un·i·on**związek *m* zawodowy; **~(s)** **'un·i·on·ist**działacz(ka *f*) *m* związkowy (-a)

tra·di·tion [trə'dɪʃn] tradycja *f*; **~·al** [trə'dɪʃənl] tradycyjny

traf·fic ['træfɪk] **1.** ruch *m*; (*zwł. nielegalny*) handel *m*; **2.** (**-ck-**) (*zwł. nielegalnie*) handlować; **'~ cir·cle** *Am.* rondo *n*; **'~ is·land** wysepka *f* drogowa; **'~ jam** zator *m lub* korek *m* drogowy; **'~ lights** *pl.* światła *pl.* drogowe; **'~ of·fence** (*Am.* **offense**) *jur.* wykroczenie *n* drogowe; **'~ of·fend·er** *jur.* osoba *f* popełniająca wykroczenie drogowe; **'~ reg·u·la·tions***pl.* przepisy *pl.* ruchu drogowego; **'~ sign** znak *m* drogowy; **'~ sig·nal → traffic lights**; **'~ war·den** *Brt.* (*kontroler prawidłowości parkowania pojazdów*)

tra|·ge·dy ['trædʒɪdɪ] tragedia *f*; **~·gic** ['trædʒɪk] (**-ally**) tragiczny

trail[treɪl] **1.** *v/t.* ⟨po⟩ciągnąć; ⟨po⟩wlec; (*w sporcie*) przegrywać ⟨rać⟩ z (*I*) (**by** *I*); *v/i. też* **~ along** (**behind**) ciągnąć się; wlec się; (*w sporcie*) przegrywać; **2.** trop *m*, ślad *m*; szlak *m*; smuga *f*; **~ of blood** ślad *m* krwi; **~ of dust** pióropusz *m* pyłu; **'~·er** *mot.* przyczepa *f*; *Am. mot.* przyczepa *f* kempingowa; *TV* zwiastun *m* (*filmu*); **'~·er park**parking *m* dla przyczep

train [treɪn] **1.** *rail.* pociąg *m*; kolumna *f*, szereg *m*; tren *m*; *fig.* ciąg *m*; **by ~** pociągiem, koleją; **~ of thought** bieg *m* myśli; **2.** *v/t.* kogoś ⟨wy⟩szkolić (**as** jako *G*); (*w sporcie*) ⟨wy⟩trenować; *zwierzę* ⟨wy⟩tresować; *kamerę* ⟨s⟩kierować (**on** na *A*); *v/i.* ⟨wy⟩szkolić się (**as** na *A*); *sport:* trenować (**for** do); **~·ee** [treɪ'niː] praktykant(ka *f*) *m*; **'~·er**trener(ka *f*) *m*; treser(ka *f*) *m*; **'~·ing** szkolenie *n*; *sport:* trening *m*; tresura *f*

trait [treɪ, treɪt] cecha *f* (*charakterystyczna*)

trai·tor ['treɪtə] zdrajca *m* (-czyni *f*)

tram [træm] *Brt.* tramwaj *m*; **'~·car**

Brt. wóz *m* tramwajowy

tramp [træmp] **1.** stąpać; ⟨z⟩deptać; **2.** włóczęga *m*, tramp *m*; wędrówka *f*; *zwł. Am.* dziwka *f*

tram·ple ['træmpl] ⟨z-, po⟩deptać

trance [trɑːns] trans *m*

tran·quil ['træŋkwɪl] spokojny, cichy; **~·(l)i·ty** [træŋ'kwɪlətɪ] spokój *m*, cisza *f*; **~·(l)ize** ['træŋkwɪlaɪz] uspokajać ⟨-koić⟩; **~·(l)iz·er** *med.* ['træŋkwɪlaɪzə] środek *m* uspokajający, trankwilizator *m*

trans|·act [træn'zækt] *interesy*, *handel* ⟨po⟩prowadzić; **~·ac·tion**[træn'zækʃn] transakcja *f*, interes *m*

trans·at·lan·tic [trænzət'læntɪk] transatlantycki

tran·scribe [træn'skraɪb] ⟨prze⟩transkrybować; *mus.* dokonywać ⟨-nać⟩ transkrypcji

tran|·script ['trænskrɪpt] zapis *m*; **~·scrip·tion** [træn'skrɪpʃn] transkrypcja *f*

trans·fer1. [træns'fɜː] (**-rr-**) *v/t.* (**to**) *pracownika, produkcję* przenosić ⟨-nieść⟩ (do *G*); (*w sporcie*) *zawodnika* dokonywać ⟨-nać⟩ transferu (do *G*); *pieniądze* przekazywać ⟨-zać⟩, przelewać ⟨-lać⟩ (na *A*); *jur. prawo* ⟨s⟩cedować (na *A*), odstępować ⟨-tąpić⟩ (*D*); *v/i.* (*w sporcie*) *zawodnik:* przechodzić ⟨-ejść⟩ (**to** do *G*); przesiadać ⟨-siąść⟩ się (**from ... to ...** z ... na ...); **2.** ['trænsfɜː] przeniesienie *n*; (*w sporcie*) transfer *m*; przelew *m*; przekazanie *n*; *jur.* cesja *f*; *zwł. Am.* bilet *m* na połączenie z przesiadkami; **~·a·ble**[træns'fɜːrəbl] dający się przekazać *lub* odstąpić innej osobie

trans·fixed [træns'fɪkst] *fig.* sparaliżowany

trans|·form [træns'fɔːm] przekształcać ⟨-cić⟩, ⟨prze⟩transformować; **~·for·ma·tion** [trænsfə'meɪʃn] przekształcenie *n*; transformacja *f*

trans·fu·sion [træns'fjuːʒn] *med.* transfuzja *f*, przetoczenie *n* krwi

trans·gress [træns'gres] *termin* przekraczać ⟨-roczyć⟩; *prawo* naruszać ⟨-szyć⟩

tran·sient ['trænzɪənt] ulotny, przelotny

tran·sis·tor [træn'sɪstə] tranzystor *m*

tran·sit['trænsɪt] tranzyt *m*; *econ.* przewóz *m*, transport *m*; *attr.* tranzytowy;

T

in ~ w trakcie tranzytu, w tranzycie
tran·si·tion [træn'sıʒn] przejście *n*
tran·si·tive ['trænsıtıv] *gr. czasownik*:
przechodni
tran·si·to·ry ['trænsıtərı] → *transient*
trans·late [træns'leıt] ⟨prze⟩tłuma-
czyć, przekładać ⟨-łożyć⟩ (*from English into Polish* z angielskiego na polski); **~·la·tion** [træns'leıʃn] tłumaczenie *n*, przekład *m*; **~·la·tor** [træns'leıtə]
tłumacz(ka *f*) *m*
trans·lu·cent [trænz'lu:snt] półprzez-
roczysty
trans·mis·sion [trænz'mıʃn] przeno-
szenie *n* (*choroby*); transmisja *f*; *mot.*
przekładnia *f*, napęd *m*
trans·mit [trænz'mıt] (*-tt-*) sygnał wysyłać ⟨-słać⟩; transmitować, nadawać
⟨-dać⟩; *chorobę* przenosić ⟨-nieść⟩;
światło przepuszczać ⟨-puścić⟩; **~·ter**
transmiter *m*, nadajnik *m*
trans·par·en·cy [træns'pærənsı]
przezroczystość *f* (*też fig.*); przezrocze
n, slajd *m*; folia *f* (*do wyświetlania*);
~·ent przezroczysty; *fig.* ewidentny
tran·spire [træn'spaıə] ⟨s⟩pocić się; *fig.*
okazywać ⟨-zać⟩ się; F zdarzać ⟨-rzyć⟩
się
trans·plant 1. [træns'plɑ:nt] przesadzać ⟨-dzić⟩; przenosić ⟨-nieść⟩; *med.*
przeszczepiać ⟨-pić⟩; **2.** ['trænsplɑ:nt]
med. przeszczep *m*
trans·port 1. ['trænspɔ:t] transport *m*,
przewóz *m*; środek *m* transportu; *mil.*
transportowiec *m*; **2.** [træns'pɔ:t] przewozić ⟨-wieźć⟩, ⟨prze⟩transportować;
~·por·ta·tion [trænspɔ:'teıʃn] transport *m*, przewóz *m*
trap [træp] **1.** pułapka *f* (*też fig.*); *set a* ~
for s.o. zastawiać ⟨-wić⟩ pułapkę na
kogoś; *shut one's* ~, *keep one's* ~
shut sl. zamknąć japę; **2.** (*-pp-*) ⟨z⟩ła-
pać w pułapkę (*też fig.*); *be* **~ped** być
uwięzionym (*jak w pułapce*); **~·door**
klapa *f* w podłodze; *theat.* zapadnia *f*
tra·peze [trə'pi:z] trapez *m* (*w cyrku*)
trap·per ['træpə] traper *m*
trap·pings ['træpıŋz] *pl.* atrybuty *pl.*,
fig. insygnia *pl.*
trash [træʃ] szmira *f*; bzdura *f*; *Am.*
śmieci *pl.*; *zwł. Am.* hołota *f*; **~·can**
Am. kosz *m* na śmieci; kubeł *m* na
śmieci; **~·y** (*-ier, -iest*) kiczowaty
trav·el ['trævl] **1.** (*zwł. Brt. -ll-, Am. -l-*)

v/i. jeździć, podróżować; *tech.* przesuwać ⟨-sunąć⟩ się; *światło itp.*: poruszać
się; *dźwięk*: rozchodzić ⟨-zejść⟩ się;
fig. ⟨po⟩wędrować; *v/t.* objeżdżać ⟨-je-
chać⟩; *drogę* przejeżdżać ⟨-jechać⟩; **2.**
podróż *f*; *attr.* podróżny; '~ **a·gen·cy**
biuro *n* podróży; '~ **a·gent** właści-
ciel(ka *f*) *m* biura podróży; '~ **a·gent's**,
'~ **bu·reau** (*pl. -reaux* [-rəuz], *-reaus*)
biuro *n* podróży; '~·(l)er podróż-
nik *m* (-niczka *f*), podróżny *m* (-na *f*);
'~·(l)er's cheque (*Am.* check) czek *m*
podróżny; '~·sick chory *m* (-na *f*) na
chorobę lokomocyjną; '~·sick·ness
choroba *f* lokomocyjna
trav·es·ty ['trævıstı] trawestacja *f*
trawl [trɔ:l] **1.** niewód *m*; **2.** ⟨z⟩łowić
niewodem, ⟨wy⟩trałować; **~·er** *naut.*
trawler *m*
tray [treı] taca *f*; *tech.* paleta *f*
treach·er·ous ['tretʃərəs] zdradziecki;
~·y ['tretʃərı] zdrada *f*
trea·cle ['tri:kl] *zwł. Brt.* syrop *m*
tread [tred] **1.** (*trod, trodden lub trod*)
deptać; nadeptywać ⟨-pnąć⟩ (*on* na *A*);
ścieżkę wydeptywać ⟨-ptać⟩; **2.** stąpa-
nie *n*; *mot.* bieżnik *m*; stopień *m* (*na
schodach*); '~·mill kierat *m* (*też fig.*)
trea·son ['tri:zn] zdrada *f* stanu
trea·sure ['treʒə] **1.** skarb *m*; **2.** cenić; **~·sur·er** ['treʒərə] skarbnik *m*
(-niczka *f*)
trea·sure trove [treʒə 'trəuv] ukryty
skarb *m*
Trea·su·ry ['treʒərı] *Brt.*, '~ **De·part-
ment** *Am.* Ministerstwo *n* Skarbu,
Skarb *m* Państwa
treat [tri:t] **1.** ⟨po⟩traktować (*as* jako
A); obchodzić się z (*I*); traktować; *med.*
⟨wy⟩leczyć (*for* z *G*), leczyć (*for* na *A*);
komuś ⟨za⟩fundować; **~ s.o. to s.th.**
też stawiać ⟨postawić⟩ komuś coś;
~ o.s. to s.th. ⟨po⟩częstować się czymś; *be* **~ed for** być leczonym na (*A*);
2. uczta *f*; poczęstunek *m*; *this is
my* ~ ja stawiam
trea·tise ['tri:tız] rozprawa *f*
treat·ment ['tri:tmənt] traktowanie *n*
treat·y ['tri:tı] układ *m*
tre·ble¹ ['trebl] **1.** potrójny; **2.** ⟨po⟩troić
(się)
tre·ble² ['trebl] *mus.* dyszkant *m*; wysokie dźwięki *pl.* (*radiowe*)
tree [tri:] drzewo *n*

tre·foil ['trefɔɪl] *bot.* koniczyna *f*

trel·lis ['trelɪs] ażurowa krata *f*, treliaż *m*

trem·ble ['trembl] trząść się (**with** od *G*)

tre·men·dous [trɪ'mendəs] ogromny; F wspaniały

trem·or ['tremə] drżenie *n*, dreszcz *m*

trench [trentʃ] rów *m*; *mil.* okop *m*

trend [trend] trend *m*, tendencja *f*; moda *f*; '**~·y** F 1. (**-ier, -iest**) modny; **be ~y** być szykownym; 2. *zwł. Brt. pej.* modniś *m* (-nisia *f*)

tres·pass ['trespəs] 1. **~ on** ląd wkraczać ⟨-roczyć⟩ *nielegalnie* na (*A*); *prawa* naruszać ⟨-szyć⟩ (*A*); *hojność* nadużywać ⟨-żyć⟩; **no ~ing** wstęp wzbroniony!; 2. przekroczenie *n*; naruszenie *n*; nadużycie *n*; '**~·er: ~ers will be prosecuted** Wstęp pod karą wzbroniony!

tres·tle ['tresl] stojak *m*, kozioł *m*

tri·al ['traɪəl] *jur.* rozprawa *f* sądowa, proces *m*; próba *f*; test *m*; *fig.* utrapienie *n*; *attr.* próbny; **on ~** na próbę, na okres próbny; wypróbowany; **be on ~, stand ~** *jur.* stawać ⟨stanąć⟩ przed sądem

tri·an·gle ['traɪæŋgl] trójkąt *m*; *Am.* ekierka *f*; *mus.* triangel *m*, trójkąt *m*; **~·gu·lar** [traɪ'æŋgjʊlə] trójkątny

tri·ath·lon [traɪ'æθlɒn] (*w sporcie*) trójbój *m*

trib·al ['traɪbl] szczepowy; **~e** [traɪb] szczep *m*

tri·bu·nal [traɪ'bjuːnl] *jur.* trybunał *m*, sąd *m*

trib·u·ta·ry ['trɪbjʊtərɪ] dopływ *m*

trib·ute ['trɪbjuːt] danina *f*; **be a ~ to** dawać ⟨dać⟩ dowód (*D*); **to pay ~ to** składać ⟨złożyć⟩ hołd (*D*)

trice [traɪs] *zwł. Brt.*: **in a ~** w mig

trick [trɪk] 1. sztuczka *f*; trick *m*; podstęp *m*; figiel *m*; (*w grze w karty*) lewa *f*; zwyczaj *m*; **play a ~ on s.o.** ⟨s⟩płatać komuś psikusa; 2. podstępny; **~ question** podstępne pytanie *n*; 3. *kogoś* podchodzić ⟨-dejść⟩, oszukiwać ⟨-kać⟩; **~·e·ry** ['trɪkərɪ] oszustwo *n*

trick·le ['trɪkl] 1. sączyć się, kapać; przeciekać ⟨-ciec⟩; 2. strużka *f*

trick·ster ['trɪkstə] oszust(ka *f*) *m*; **~·y** ['trɪkɪ] (**-ier, -iest**) podstępny, trudny, skomplikowany

tri·cy·cle ['traɪsɪkl] rowe(ek *m*) *m* trójkołowy

tri·dent ['traɪdənt] trójząb *m*

---

tri·fle ['traɪfl] 1. drobiazg *m*; błahostka *f*; **a ~fle** trochę, nieco; **~·fle with** *fig.* zabawiać ⟨-wić⟩ się; **he is not to be ~fled with** z nim nie ma żartów; '**~·fling** ['traɪflɪŋ] błahy, drobny

trig·ger ['trɪgə] 1. język *m* spustowy, cyngiel *m*; **pull the ~** pociągać za cyngiel; 2. **~ off** wywoływać ⟨-łać⟩; '**~·hap·py** z lubością sięgający po broń

trill [trɪl] 1. (*śpiew*) tryl *m*, trele *pl.* (*ptaków*); 2. używać ⟨-żyć⟩ trylu; *ptaki*: wywodzić ⟨-wieść⟩ trele

trim [trɪm] 1. (**-mm-**) przycinać ⟨-ciąć⟩; *ubranie* ozdabiać ⟨-dobić⟩; **~·med with fur** podbity futrem; **~ off** odcinać ⟨-ciąć⟩; 2. przycięcie *n*; **give s.th. a ~** przycinać ⟨-ciąć⟩ coś; **in ~** F w dobrej formie; 3. (**-mm-**) schludny; '**~·ming: ~s** *pl.* ścinki *pl.*; *gastr.* dodatki *pl.*

Trin·i·ty ['trɪnɪtɪ] *rel.* Trójca *f*

trin·ket ['trɪŋkɪt] ozdóbka *f* (*zwł. tania*)

trip [trɪp] 1. (**-pp-**) *v/i.* potykać ⟨-tknąć⟩ się (**over** *o A*); *v/t. też* **~ up** podstawiać ⟨-wić⟩ nogę (*D*); ⟨z⟩mieszać; 2. wycieczka *f*, krótka podróż *f*; potknięcie *n* się; *sl.* trip *m*, odlot *m*

tripe [traɪp] *gastr.* flaki *pl.*

trip·le ['trɪpl] potrójny; '**~ jump** (*w sporcie*) trójskok *m*

trip·lets ['trɪplɪts] *pl.* trojaczki *pl.*

trip·li·cate ['trɪplɪkɪt] 1. potrójny; 2. **in ~** w trzech egzemplarzach

tri·pod ['traɪpɒd] *phot.* statyw *m*

trip·per ['trɪpə] *zwł. Brt.* (*zwł. na jeden dzień*) podróżny *m* (**-na** *f*)

trite [traɪt] banalny, trywialny

tri·umph ['traɪəmf] 1. triumf *m*; *fig.* zwycięstwo *n* (**over** nad *I*); 2. ⟨za⟩triumfować (**over** nad *I*); **~·um·phal** [traɪ'ʌmfl] triumfalny; **~·um·phant** [traɪ'ʌmfənt] triumfujący

triv·i·al ['trɪvɪəl] trywialny; błahy

trod [trɒd] *pret.* i *p.p. od* **tread** 1; **~·den** ['trɒdn] *p.p. od* **tread** 1

trol·ley ['trɒlɪ] *zwł. Brt.* wózek *m* (*na zakupy itp.*); stolik *m* na kółkach; '**~·bus** trolejbus *m*

trom·bone [trɒm'bəʊn] *mus.* puzon *m*

troop [truːp] 1. gromada *f*; oddział *m*; **~s** *mil.* wojska *pl.*, oddziały *pl.*; 2. iść ⟨pójść⟩ gromadą; **~ out** wychodzić ⟨wyjść⟩ gromadą; '**~·er** *mil.* kawalerzysta *m*; (*w kawalerii*) szeregowy *m*; *Am.* federalny policjant *m*

T

tro·phy ['trəufɪ] trofeum *n*

trop·ic ['trɒpɪk] *astr., geogr.* zwrotnik *m*; **the ~ of Cancer** Zwrotnik *m* Raka; **the ~ of Capricorn** Zwrotnik *m* Koziorożca

trop·i·cal ['trɒpɪkl] tropikalny; (pod)zwrotnikowy

trop·ics ['trɒpɪks] *pl.* tropiki *pl.*

trot [trɒt] **1.** kłus *m* (*konia*); trucht *m*; ⟨po⟩kłusować; ⟨po⟩truchtać

trou·ble ['trʌbl] **1.** kłopot *m*, zmartwienie *n*; niedogodność *f*; zagrożenie *n*; *med.* dolegliwość *f*; **~s** *pl.* zamieszki *pl.*, niepokoje *pl.*; **be in ~** mieć kłopoty; **get into ~** napytać *sobie lub komuś* kłopotów; **get** *lub* **run into ~** mieć kłopoty *lub* problemy; **put s.o. to ~** narobić komuś kłopotów; **take the ~ to do s.th.** podejmować ⟨-djąć⟩ fatygę zrobienia czegoś; **2.** *v/t.* kłopotać; ⟨z⟩martwić; niepokoić; prosić (**for** *o A*, **to do s.th.** o zrobienie czegoś); **s.o. is ~d by s.th.** coś dokucza komuś; *v/i.* zadawać ⟨-dać⟩ sobie trud (**to do s.th.** zrobienia czegoś); **'~·mak·er** wichrzyciel(ka *f*) *m*; **'~·some** dokuczliwy

trough [trɒf] koryto *n*

trounce [trauns] (*w sporcie*) sprawić lanie (*D*)

troupe [tru:p] *theat.* trupa *f*, zespół *m* teatralny

trou·ser ['trauzə]: (**a pair of**) **~s** *pl.* spodnie *pl.*; **~ leg** nogawka *f* spodni; **'~ suit** *Brt.* spodnium *n*

trous·seau ['tru:səu] (*pl.* **-seaux** [-səuz], **-seaus**) ślubna wyprawa *f*

trout [traut] *zo.* (*pl.* **trout, trouts**) pstrąg *m*

trow·el ['trauəl] kielnia *f*

tru·ant ['tru:ənt] *Brt.* wagarowicz *m*; **play ~** iść na wagary

truce [tru:s] zawieszenie *n* broni

truck[1] [trʌk] **1.** *mot.* ciężarówka *f*; *Brt. rail.* towarowa platforma *f*; **2.** *zwł. Am.* ⟨prze⟩transportować samochodami ciężarowymi

truck[2] [trʌk] *Am.* warzywa *pl.*, owoce *pl.* (*na sprzedaż*)

'truck driv·er, '~·er *zwł. Am.* kierowca *m* ciężarówki

'truck farm *Am. econ.* gospodarstwo *n* warzywnicze *lub* owocowe

trudge [trʌdʒ] stąpać ciężko

true [tru:] (**-r, -st**) prawdziwy; rzeczy-

wisty; *przyjaciel*: wierny; wierny; **be ~** mieć rację; **come ~** spełniać ⟨-nić⟩ się; **~ to life** wiernie oddający rzeczywistość

tru·ly ['tru:lɪ] faktycznie; rzeczywiście; szczerze; **Yours ~** *zwł. Am.* Z poważaniem (*na zakończenie listu*)

trump [trʌmp] **1.** atut *m* (*też fig.*); karta *f* atutowa; **2.** bić atutem

trum·pet ['trʌmpɪt] **1.** *mus.* trąbka *f*; **2.** ⟨za⟩trąbić; *fig.* roztrąbiać ⟨-bić⟩

trun·cheon ['trʌntʃən] policyjna pałka *f*

trun·dle ['trʌndl] wózek popychać ⟨-pchać⟩

trunk [trʌŋk] pień *m*; *anat.* tułów *m*; waliza *f*, skrzynia *f*; *zo.* trąba *f* (*słonia*); *Am. mot.* bagażnik *m*; **'~ road** *Brt.* droga *f* główna, szosa *f*

trunks [trʌŋks] *pl.* (**a pair of ~**) kąpielówki *pl.*; szorty *pl.*, spodenki *pl.*

truss [trʌs] **1.** *też* **~ up** ⟨z⟩wiązać; *gastr.* kurczaka związywać ⟨-zać⟩; **2.** *med.* pas *m* przepuklinowy

trust [trʌst] **1.** zaufanie *n* (**in** *do G*); *jur.* powiernictwo *n*; *econ.* trust *m*; **hold s.th. in ~** mieć coś w zarządzie powierniczym (**for** *dla G*); **place s.th. in s.o.'s ~** powierzać ⟨-rzyć⟩ coś komuś; **2.** *v/t.* ⟨za⟩ufać (*D*); ⟨~⟩ee [trʌs'ti:] powiernik *m*; zarządca *m*; **'~·ful, '~·ing** ufny; **'~·wor·thy** godny zaufania, solidny

truth [tru:θ] (*pl.* **-s** [tru:ðz, tru:θs]) prawda *f*; **'~·ful** prawdziwy

try [traɪ] **1.** *v/t.* ⟨s⟩próbować; ⟨po⟩próbować; *jur.* sądzić; *jur.* ubiegać się (**for** *o A*); *cierpliwość* wystawiać ⟨-wić⟩ na próbę; **~ s.th. on** przymierzać ⟨-rzyć⟩; **~ s.th. out** wypróbowywać ⟨-ować⟩; **~ for** *Brt.,* **~ out for** *Am.* starać się *o* (*A*); **2.** próba *f*; **'~·ing** dokuczliwy, męczący

tsar [zɑː] *hist.* car *m*

T-shirt ['ti:ʃɜːt] koszulka *f lub* podkoszulek *m* (*z krótkim rękawem*), T-shirt *m*

TU [ti: 'ju:] *skrót:* **trade union** związek *m* zawodowy

tub [tʌb] kadź *f*; F wanna *f*

tube [tju:b] rura *f*, przewód *m*; tubka *f* (*pasty, etc*); *anat.* **bronchial ~s** *pl.* oskrzela *pl.*; *Brt.* T metro *n* (*w Londynie*); dętka *f*; *Am.* T telewizja *f*; **'~·less** bezdętkowy *m*

tu·ber ['tju:bə] *bot.* bulwa *f*

tu·ber·cu·lo·sis [tju:bɜːkjʊ'ləusɪs] *med.* gruźlica *f*

tu·bu·lar ['tju:bjʊlə] cylindryczny; rurowy

TUC [ti: ju: 'si:] *Brt. skrót:* ***Trades Union Congress*** TUC *m*, Kongres Związków Zawodowych (*w Wielkiej Brytanii*)

tuck [tʌk] **1.** zakładać ⟨założyć⟩; **~ away** F odkładać ⟨odłożyć⟩; **~ in** *zw. Brt.* F *jedzenie:* wcinać; **~ up** (*in bed*) *dziecko* otulać ⟨-lić⟩ (w łóżku); **2.** zakładka *f*, fałda *f*

Tue(s) *skrót pisany:* wt., wtorek *m*

Tues·day ['tju:zdɪ] (*skrót:* **Tue**) wtorek *m*; **on ~** we wtorek; **on ~s** we wtorki

tuft [tʌft] kępka *f* (*włosów, trawy*)

tug [tʌg] **1.** (*-gg-*) ⟨po⟩ciągnąć; szarpać ⟨-pnąć⟩ (*at za A*); **2.** *give s.th. a* **~** po-ciągnąć coś; **~-of-'war** przeciąganie *n* liny

tu·i·tion [tju:'ɪʃn] nauka *f*; nauczanie *n*; opłata *f* za naukę, czesne *n*

tu·lip ['tju:lɪp] *bot.* tulipan *m*

tum·ble ['tʌmbl] **1.** spadać ⟨spaść⟩ (*też ceny*); upadać ⟨upaść⟩; staczać ⟨stoczyć⟩ się; **2.** spadek *m*, upadek *m*; **'~-down** walący się

tum·bler ['tʌmblə] szklanka *f*

tu·mid ['tju:mɪd] *med.* obrzmiały

tum·my ['tʌmɪ] F brzuszek *m*, brzusio *n*

tu·mo(u)r ['tju:mə] *med.* nowotwór *m*

tu·mult ['tju:mʌlt] zgiełk *m*, hałas *m*; **tu·mul·tu·ous** [tju:'mʌltjʊəs] zgiełkliwy, hałaśliwy

tu·na ['tu:nə] *zo.* (*pl.* *-na, -nas*) tuńczyk *m*

tune [tju:n] **1.** melodia *f*; *be out of* **~** *mus.* fałszować; *fortepian itp.:* nie być nastrojonym; **2.** *v/t.:* *zw.* **~** *in radio* dostrajać ⟨-roić⟩ (*to do G*); *też* **~ up** *mus.* ⟨na⟩stroić; *mot. silnik* ⟨wy⟩regulować; *v/i.* **~** *in* dostrajać ⟨-roić⟩ *radio*; **~ up** brzmieć prawidłowo; **'~-ful** melodyjny; **'~-less** niemelodyjny

tun·er ['tju:nə] *TV* tuner *m*

tun·nel ['tʌnl] **1.** tunel *m*; **2.** (*zwł. Brt. -ll-, Am. -l-*) ⟨wy⟩drążyć tunel; *górę* przebijać ⟨-ebić⟩ tunelem

tun·ny ['tʌnɪ] *zo.* (*pl.* *-ny, -nies*) tuńczyk *m*

tur·ban ['tɜːbən] turban *m*

tur·bid ['tɜːbɪd] *płyn itp.:* mętny (*też fig.*); *dym itp.:* gęsty

tur·bine ['tɜːbaɪn] *tech.* turbina *f*

tur·bo ['tɜːbəʊ] F *mot.* (*pl.* *-bos*),

~·charg·er ['tɜːbəʊtʃɑːdʒə] turbosprężarka *f* doładowująca

tur·bot ['tɜːbət] *zo.* (*pl.* *-bot, -bots*) turbot *m*

tur·bu·lent ['tɜːbjʊlənt] wzburzony, burzliwy

tu·reen [tə'ri:n] waza *f*

turf [tɜːf] **1.** (*pl.* *turfs, turves* [tɜːvz]) darń *f*; bryła *f* (*ziemi*), gruda *f*; *the* **~** tor *m* wyścigów konnych; **2.** pokrywać ⟨-ryć⟩ darnią

tur·gid ['tɜːdʒɪd] *med.* obrzmiały, nabrzmiały

Turk [tɜːk] Turek *m* (*-rzynka f*)

Tur·key ['tɜːkɪ] Turcja *f*

tur·key ['tɜːkɪ] *zo.* indyk *m* (*-dyczka f*); *talk* **~** *zwł. Am.* F wykładać ⟨wyłożyć⟩ kawę na ławę

Turk·ish ['tɜːkɪʃ] **1.** turecki; **2.** *ling.* język *m* turecki

turn [tɜːn] **1.** *v/t.* obracać ⟨-rócić⟩; *klucz itp.* ⟨prze⟩kręcić; *stronę, naleśnik* przewracać ⟨-rócić⟩, ⟨s⟩kierować (*on* na *A*, *towards* w stronę *A*); zwracać ⟨-rócić⟩ się (*to do G*); zmieniać ⟨-nić⟩ (*into* w *A*); *liście* ⟨za⟩barwić; *mleko* ⟨z⟩warzyć; *tech.* ⟨wy⟩toczyć (*na obrabiarce itp.*); **~** *the corner* zakręcać ⟨-cić⟩ na rogu; **~** *loose* zwalniać ⟨-wolnić⟩, wypuszczać ⟨-puścić⟩; *s.th.* **~s** *s.o.'s stomach* od czegoś wywraca się komuś w żołądku; → *inside*, *upside down*, *somersault*; *v/i.* obracać ⟨-rócić⟩ się; ⟨prze⟩kręcić się, skręcać ⟨-cić⟩ (*into, onto* w *A*); odwracać ⟨-rócić⟩ się; *kwaśnym, siwym* stawać ⟨stać⟩ się, ⟨z⟩robić się; *fig.* zmieniać się (*into* w *A*); → *left²*, *right²*; **~** *against* zwracać ⟨-rócić⟩ się przeciw(ko) (*D*); **~** *away* odwracać ⟨-rócić⟩ się (*from* od *G*); *kogoś* odsyłać ⟨odesłać⟩ (*G*) z niczym; **~** *back* zawracać ⟨-rócić⟩; cofać ⟨-fnąć⟩; **~** *down radio* ściszać ⟨-szyć⟩; *gaz itp.* przykręcać ⟨-cić⟩; *ogrzewanie* zmniejszać ⟨-szyć⟩; *prośbę itp.* odrzucać ⟨-cić⟩; *kołdrę* zawijać ⟨-winąć⟩; *kołnierzyk itp.* odwijać ⟨-winąć⟩; **~** *in v/t.* zwracać ⟨-rócić⟩; *zyski* uzyskiwać ⟨-skać⟩; *zwł. Am.* pracę przedstawiać ⟨-wić⟩, oddawać ⟨-dać⟩; *w ręce policji* oddawać ⟨-dać⟩ (*o.s.* się); *v/t.* F iść ⟨pójść⟩ spać; **~** *off v/t. gas*, wodę *itp.*

zakręcać ⟨-cić⟩; *światło*, ⟨z⟩gasić; *silnik* wyłączać ⟨-czyć⟩; F wzbudzać ⟨-dzić⟩ obrzydzenie; *v/i.* skręcać ⟨-cić⟩; **~ on** odkręcać ⟨-cić⟩; włączać ⟨-czyć⟩; F podniecać ⟨-cić⟩; **~ out** *v/t. światło* ⟨z⟩gasić; *kogoś* wyrzucać ⟨-cić⟩ **(of** z *G*); *econ.* F ⟨wy⟩produkować; *kieszeń* wywracać ⟨-rócić⟩; opróżniać ⟨-nić⟩; *v/i.* przychodzić ⟨-yjść⟩ **(for** na *A*); okazywać ⟨-zać⟩ się; układać ⟨ułożyć⟩ się; **~ over** *v/i.* obracać ⟨-rócić⟩ się; odwracać ⟨-rócić⟩ się; *v/t.* przewracać ⟨-rócić⟩; odwracać ⟨-rócić⟩ na drugą stronę; rozważać, przemyśliwać; zwracać ⟨-rócić⟩; przekazywać ⟨-zać⟩; *econ.* mieć obroty (rzędu *G*); **~ round** obracać ⟨się⟩; odwracać ⟨się⟩; **~ one's car round** zawracać ⟨-rócić⟩; **~ to** zwracać ⟨-rócić⟩ się do *(G)*; przechodzić ⟨-ejść⟩ na (*strong itp.*); **~ up** *v/t.* podnosić ⟨-nieść⟩; *radio* ⟨z⟩robić głośniej; *natężenie* zwiększać ⟨-szyć⟩; podwijać ⟨-winąć⟩; odkrywać ⟨-ryć⟩; *v/i.* przybywać ⟨-być⟩; zjawiać ⟨-wić⟩ się; zdarzać ⟨-rzyć⟩ się; **2.** obrót *m*; zakręt *m*, skręt *m*; kolej *f*, kolejność *f*; skłonność *f*, zdolność *f*; *fig.* zwrot *m*, zmiana *f*; **at every ~** na każdym kroku; **by ~s** na zmianę; **in ~** kolejno; **out of ~** poza kolejnością; **it's my ~** to moja kolej; **make a left ~** skręcać ⟨-cić⟩ w lewo; **take ~s** zmieniać ⟨-nić⟩ się **(at** przy *L)*; **take a ~ for the better/worse** zmieniać ⟨-nić⟩ się na lepsze/gorsze; **do s.o. a good/bad ~** wyrządzać ⟨-dzić⟩ komuś dobrą/złą przysługę; **at the ~ of the 20th century** na przełomie XX i XXI wieku; **'~·coat** zdrajca *m* (-czyni *f*); **'~·er** tokarz *m*

'turn·ing *zwł. Brt.* zakręt *m*; **'~ cir·cle** *mot.* promień *m* skrętu; **'~ point** *fig.* punkt *m* zwrotny

tur·nip ['tɜːnɪp] *bot.* rzepa *f*

'turn·off zakręt *m*; **'~·out** frekwencja *f*; wydajność *f*; F ubiór *m*; **'~·o·ver** *econ.* obrót *m*; zmiana *f*; fluktuacja *f*; **'~·pike** *Am.*, **~·pike 'road** *Am.* płatna autostrada *f*; **'~·stile** kołowrót *m*; **'~·ta·ble** talerz *m* (*gramofonu itp.*); **'~·up** *Brt.* mankiet *m* (*spodni*)

tur·pen·tine ['tɜːpəntaɪn] *chem.* terpentyna

tur·quoise ['tɜːkwɔɪz] *min.* turkus *m*; *attr.* turkusowy

tur·ret ['tʌrɪt] *mil., arch.* wieżyczka *f*; *naut.* kiosk *m* (*okrętu podwodnego*)

tur·tle ['tɜːtl] *zo.* żółw *m*; *attr.* żółwiowy; **'~·dove** *zo.* sierpówka *f*, synogarlica *f*; **'~·neck** *zwł. Am.* golf *m*

Tus·ca·ny Toskania *f*

tusk [tʌsk] kieł *m* (*słonia, morsa*)

tus·sle ['tʌsl] F bójka *f*

tus·sock ['tʌsək] kępa *f* trawy

tu·te·lage ['tjuːtɪlɪdʒ] prowadzenie *n*, kierownictwo *n*; *jur.* kuratela *f*, opieka *f*

tu·tor ['tjuːtə] korepetytor(ka *f*) *m*; *Brt. univ.* tutor *m*, prowadzący *m* (-ca *f*) (*grupę studentów*)

tu·to·ri·al [tjuːˈtɔːrɪəl] *Brt. univ.* zajęcia *pl.* pod opieką tutora

tux·e·do [tʌkˈsiːdəʊ] *Am.* (*pl.* **-dos**) smoking *m*

TV [tiːˈviː] TV *f*, telewizja *f*; *attr.* telewizyjny; **on ~** w telewizji; **watch ~** oglądać telewizję

twang [twæŋ] **1.** brzęk *m*, brzęknięcie *n*; *zw.* **nasal ~** wymowa *f* nosowa; **2.** brzęczeć ⟨brzęknąć⟩

tweak [twiːk] F ⟨po⟩ciągnąć za (*A*)

tweet [twiːt] ⟨za⟩ćwierkać

tweez·ers ['twiːzəz] *pl.* (**a pair of ~**) pinceta *f*

twelfth [twelfθ] **1.** dwunasty; **2.** jedna *f* dwunasta

twelve [twelv] **1.** dwanaście; **2.** dwunastka *f*

twen·ti·eth ['twentɪɪθ] **1.** dwudziesty; **2.** jedna *f* dwudziesta; **~·ty** ['twentɪ] **1.** dwudziesty; **2.** dwudziestka *f*

twice [twaɪs] dwa razy

twid·dle ['twɪdl] bawić się; **~ one's thumbs** *fig.* marnować czas

twig [twɪg] gałązka *f*

twi·light ['twaɪlaɪt] zmrok *m*, zmierzch *m*; półmrok *m*

twin [twɪn] **1.** bliźniak *m* (-niaczka *f*); **~s** *pl.* bliźniaki *pl.*; **2.** bliźniaczy; podwójny; **3.** (-*nn*-): **be ~ned with** mieć partnerstwo z (*I*); **~·bed·ded 'room** pokój *m* z dwoma łóżkami; **~ 'beds** *pl.* dwa pojedyncze łóżka *pl.*; **~ 'broth·er** bliźniak *m*

twine [twaɪn] **1.** sznurek *m*, szpagat *m*; **2.** owijać ⟨owinąć⟩ (się) (**round** wokół *G*); *też* **~ together** splatać ⟨spleść⟩

twin·en·gined *aviat.* dwusilnikowy

twinge [twɪndʒ] ukłucie *n* (*bólu*); **a ~ of conscience** wyrzut *m* sumienia

twin·kle ['twɪŋkl] **1.** ⟨za⟩migotać; błyszczeć ⟨-łysnąć⟩ (**with** od *G*); **2.** migotanie *n*; błysk *m* (*też oka*)

twin¹ 'sis·ter bliźniaczka *f*; ~ 'town miasto *n* siostrzane

twirl [twɜːl] **1.** kręcić ⟨za⟩wirować; **2.** (za)kręcenie *n*; wirowanie *n*

twist [twɪst] **1.** *v/t.* skręcać ⟨-cić⟩; okręcać ⟨-cić⟩ (**round** wokół *G*); obracać ⟨-rócić⟩; *kostkę itp.* wykręcać ⟨-cić⟩; *pranie* wyżymać ⟨-żąć⟩; *słowa* przekręcać ⟨-cić⟩; ~ **off** odkręcać ⟨-cić⟩; ~ **on** zakręcać ⟨-cić⟩; *her face was* ~*ed with pain* twarz miała wykrzywioną z bólu; *v/i.* wić się; skręcać ⟨-cić⟩ się (*z bólu itp.*); **2.** skręt *m*; skręcenie *n*; zakręt *m*; wykręcenie *n*; *fig.* zwrot *m*; *mus.* twist *m*

twitch [twɪtʃ] **1.** *v/i.* drgać; ⟨s⟩krzywić się (**with** od *G*); *v/t.* szarpać ⟨-pnąć⟩; **2.** drgnięcie *n*; drganie *n*; szarpnięcie *n*, tik *m*

twit·ter ['twɪtə] **1.** ćwierkać ⟨-knąć⟩; **2.** ćwierkanie *n*; świergot *m*; *be all of a* ~ F być rozgorączkowanym

two [tuː] **1.** dwa; *the* ~ *cars* oba samochody; *the* ~ *of us* my obaj *m lub* obie *f lub* oboje; *in* ~*s* dwójkami; *cut in* ~ przecinać ⟨-ciąć⟩ na dwoje; *put* ~ *and* ~ *together* ⟨s⟩kojarzyć fakty; **2.** dwójka *f*; ~'edged obosieczny (*też fig.*); ~'faced dwulicowy; '~·fold dwojaki; ~·pence ['tʌpəns] *Brt.* dwa pensy *pl.*;

~·pen·ny ['tʌpnɪ] *Brt.* F za dwa pensy; ~'piece dwuczęściowy; ~'seat·er *mot.* samochód *m* dwumiejscowy; *aviat.* samolot *m* dwumiejscowy; '~·stroke *tech.* **1.** dwutaktowy; **2.** *też* ~**-stroke engine** silnik *m* dwutaktowy; ~'way dwustronny; ~-way 'traf·fic ruch *m* dwukierunkowy

ty·coon [taɪ'kuːn] *przemysłowy* magnat *m*

type [taɪp] **1.** typ *m*; rodzaj *m*; *print.* czcionka *f*; druk *m*, rodzaj *m* druku; **2.** *v/t. coś* ⟨na⟩pisać na maszynie, ⟨na⟩pisać (przy użyciu klawiatury); *v/i.* ⟨na⟩pisać na maszynie, ⟨na⟩pisać (*przy użyciu klawiatury*); '~·writ·er maszyna *f* do pisania; '~·writ·ten napisany na maszynie

ty·phoid ['taɪfɔɪd] *med.*, ~ 'fe·ver dur *m lub* tyfus *m* brzuszny

ty·phoon [taɪ'fuːn] tajfun *m*

ty·phus ['taɪfəs] *med.* dur *m lub* tyfus *m* plamisty

typ·i·cal ['tɪpɪkl] typowy (*of* dla *G*); ~·fy ['tɪpɪfaɪ] być typowym dla (*G*)

typ·ing 'er·ror ['taɪpɪŋ -] błąd *m* maszynowy; '~ pool hala *m* maszyn

typ·ist ['taɪpɪst] maszynistka *f*

ty·ran·ni·cal [tɪ'rænɪkl] tyrański

tyr·an·nize ['tɪrənaɪz] ⟨s⟩tyranizować; ~·ny ['tɪrənɪ] tyrania *f*

ty·rant ['taɪərənt] tyran *m*

tyre ['taɪə] *Brt.* opona *f*

tzar [zɑː] *hist.* → **tsar**

U

U, u [juː] U, u *n*

ud·der ['ʌdə] *zo.* wymię *n*

UEFA [juː'iːfə] *skrót:* **Union of European Football Associations** UEFA *n*

UFO ['juːfəʊ, juː ef 'əʊ] (*pl. -os*) *skrót:* **unidentified flying object** UFO *n*

ug·ly ['ʌglɪ] (*-ier, -iest*) brzydki (*też fig.*); *rana:* paskudny

UHF [juː eɪtʃ 'ef] *skrót:* **ultrahigh frequency** UHF *n*, fale *pl.* ultrakrótkie

UK [juː 'keɪ] *skrót:* **United Kingdom** Zjednoczone Królestwo *n* (*Wielkiej Brytanii i płn. Irlandii*)

U·kraine Ukraina *f*

ul·cer ['ʌlsə] *med.* wrzód *m*

ul·te·ri·or [ʌl'tɪərɪə]: ~ *motive* ukryty motyw *lub* pobudka *f*

ul·ti·mate ['ʌltɪmət] ostateczny; końcowy; krańcowy; '~·ly ostatecznie; w końcu

ul·ti·ma·tum [ʌltɪ'meɪtəm] (*pl. -tums, -ta* [-tə]) ultimatum *n*

ul·tra·high fre·quen·cy [ʌltrəhaɪ 'friːkwənsɪ] fale *pl.* ultrakrótkie; ~·ma·rine ultramaryna *f*; ~'son·ic ponaddźwiękowy; ~'sound ultradźwięk *m*; ~'vi·o·let ultrafioletowy, nadfioletowy

um·bil·i·cal cord [ʌmˈbɪlɪkl ˈkɔːd] *anat.* pępowina *f*

um·brel·la [ʌmˈbrelə] parasol *m* (*przeciwdeszczowy*); *fig.* osłona *f*

um·pire [ˈʌmpaɪə] (*w sporcie*) **1.** sędzia *m*; **2.** sędziować

UN [juː ˈen] *skrót: United Nations pl.* ONZ *m*, Narody *pl.* Zjednoczone

un·a·bashed [ʌnəˈbæʃt] nie zbity z tropu

un·a·bat·ed [ʌnəˈbeɪtɪd] nie zmniejszony, nie obniżony

un·a·ble [ʌnˈeɪbl]: *be ~ to do s.th.* nie być w stanie czegoś zrobić

un·ac·coun·ta·ble [ʌnəˈkaʊntəbl] niewytłumaczalny

un·ac·cus·tomed [ʌnəˈkʌstəmd] nieprzyzwyczajony

un·ac·quaint·ed [ʌnəˈkweɪntɪd]: *be ~ with s.th.* nie być zaznajomionym z czymś

un·ad·vised [ʌnədˈvaɪzd] nierozsądny; niecelowy

un·af·fect·ed [ʌnəˈfektɪd] naturalny, niewymuszony; *be ~ by s.th.* nie ulegać ⟨ulec⟩ wpływowi czegoś

un·aid·ed [ʌnˈeɪdɪd] samodzielnie, bez pomocy

un·al·ter·a·ble [ʌnˈɔːltərəbl] niezmienny

u·nan·i·mous [juːˈnænɪməs] jednogłośny

un·an·nounced [ʌnəˈnaʊnst] niezapowiedziany

un·an·swer·a·ble [ʌnˈɑːnsərəbl] niepodważalny, nie do obalenia

un·ap·proach·a·ble [ʌnəˈprəʊtʃəbl] niedostępny; nieprzystępny

un·armed [ʌnˈɑːmd] nieuzbrojony

un·asked [ʌnˈɑːskt] *ktoś:* nie pytany; *pytanie:* nie zadany

un·as·sist·ed [ʌnəˈsɪstɪd] bez pomocy, samodzielnie, nie wspomagany

un·as·sum·ing [ʌnəˈsjuːmɪŋ] bezpretensjonalny

un·at·tached [ʌnəˈtætʃt] niezwiązany, wolny

un·at·tend·ed [ʌnəˈtendɪd] działający *lub* pozostawiony bez opieki

un·at·trac·tive [ʌnəˈtræktɪv] nieatrakcyjny

un·au·thor·ized [ʌnˈɔːθəraɪzd] nieupoważniony; nie uprawniony; nie autoryzowany

un·a·void·a·ble [ʌnəˈvɔɪdəbl] nieunikniony

un·a·ware [ʌnəˈweə]: *be ~ of s.th.* nie zdawać ⟨-zdać⟩ sobie sprawy z czegoś; *~s* [ʌnəˈweəz] niespodzianie, niespodziewanie; *catch lub take s.o. ~* zaskoczyć kogoś

un·bal·ance [ʌnˈbæləns] wyprowadzać ⟨-dzić⟩ z równowagi; *~d* niezrównoważony

un·bar [ʌnˈbɑː] otwierać ⟨-worzyć⟩

un·bear·a·ble [ʌnˈbeərəbl] nie do zniesienia

un·beat·a·ble [ʌnˈbiːtəbl] bezkonkurencyjny; **un·beat·en** [ʌnˈbiːtn] niepokonany; nie przetarty

un·be·known(st) [ʌnbɪˈnəʊn(st)]: *~ to s.o.* bez czyjejś wiedzy

un·be·lie·va·ble [ʌnbɪˈliːvəbl] nie do uwierzenia

un·bend [ʌnˈbend] (*-bent*) rozluźniać ⟨-nić⟩ się; odprężać ⟨-żyć⟩ się, ⟨wy⟩prostować; *~ing* nieugięty

un·bi·as(s)ed [ʌnˈbaɪəst] nieuprzedzony, bezstronny

un·bind [ʌnˈbaɪnd] (*-bound*) rozwiązywać ⟨-zać⟩

un·blem·ished [ʌnˈblemɪʃt] niesplamiony, nieskalany

un·born [ʌnˈbɔːn] nienarodzony

un·break·a·ble [ʌnˈbreɪkəbl] nietłukący (się)

un·bri·dled [ʌnˈbraɪdld] nieokiełznany; rozpasany

un·bro·ken [ʌnˈbrəʊkən] nie zbity, nie uszkodzony; *rekord itp.:* nie pobity; *koń:* nieujeżdżony

un·buck·le [ʌnˈbʌkl] rozpinać ⟨-piąć⟩

un·bur·den [ʌnˈbɜːdn]: *~ o.s. to s.o.* zwierzać ⟨-rzyć⟩ się komuś

un·but·ton [ʌnˈbʌtn] *guziki* rozpinać ⟨-piąć⟩

un·called-for [ʌnˈkɔːldfɔː] nie na miejscu; niepożądany

un·can·ny [ʌnˈkænɪ] (*-ier, -iest*) niesamowity

un·cared-for [ʌnˈkeədfɔː] zaniedbany, zapuszczony

un·ceas·ing [ʌnˈsiːsɪŋ] nieustanny

un·ce·re·mo·ni·ous [ʌnserɪˈməʊnjəs] bezceremonialny

un·cer·tain [ʌnˈsɜːtn] niepewny; wątpliwy; *be ~ of* nie być pewnym (*G*); *~ty* [ʌnˈsɜːtntɪ] niepewność *f*; wątpliwość *f*

un·chain [ʌn'tʃeɪn] rozkuwać ‹-kuć›

un·changed [ʌn'tʃeɪndʒd] nie zmieniony; **un·chang·ing** [ʌn'tʃeɪndʒɪŋ] niezmienny, nie zmieniający się

un·char·i·ta·ble [ʌn'tʃærɪtəbl] nieżyczliwy

un·checked [ʌn'tʃekt] nie sprawdzony; nie kontrolowany

un·chris·tian [ʌn'krɪstʃən] niechrześcijański

un·civ·il [ʌn'sɪvl] niegrzeczny, nieuprzejmy; **un·civ·i·lized** [ʌn'sɪvlaɪzd] niecywilizowany; barbarzyński

un·cle ['ʌŋkl] wuj(ek) *m*, stryj(ek) *m*

un·com·for·ta·ble [ʌn'kʌmfətəbl] niewygodny; **feel ~** ‹po›czuć się niezręcznie

un·com·mon [ʌn'kɒmən] niepowszedni, rzadki

un·com·mu·ni·ca·tive [ʌnkə'mjuːnɪkətɪv] mało komunikatywny, niekomunikatywny

un·com·pro·mis·ing [ʌn'kɒmprəmaɪzɪŋ] bezkompromisowy

un·con·cerned [ʌnkən'sɜːnd]: **be ~ about** nie przejmować się (*I*); **be ~ with** nie być zainteresowanym (*I*)

un·con·di·tion·al [ʌnkən'dɪʃənl] bezwarunkowy

un·con·firmed [ʌnkən'fɜːmd] nie potwierdzony

un·con·scious [ʌn'kɒnʃəs] *med.* nieprzytomny; nieświadomy (*też of G*); **be ~ of s.th.** nie zdawać sobie sprawy z czegoś; **~·ness** nieprzytomność *f*; nieświadomość *f*

un·con·sti·tu·tion·al [ʌnkɒnstɪˈtjuːʃənl] niekonstytucyjny

un·con·trol·la·ble [ʌnkən'trəʊləbl] nie do opanowania; nieopanowany; rozjuszony; **un·con·trolled** [ʌnkən'trəʊld] niekontrolowany

un·con·ven·tion·al [ʌnkən'venʃənl] niekonwencjonalny

un·con·vinced [ʌnkən'vɪnst]: **be ~ about** nie być przekonanym o (*L*); **un·con'vinc·ing** nieprzekonujący

un·cooked [ʌn'kʊkt] nie gotowany, surowy

un·cork [ʌn'kɔːk] odkorkowywać ‹-ować›

un·count·a·ble [ʌn'kaʊntəbl] niepoliczalny

un·cou·ple [ʌn'kʌpl] *wagony* rozłączać ‹-czyć›

un·couth [ʌn'kuːθ] nieokrzesany

un·cov·er [ʌn'kʌvə] odsłaniać ‹-łonić›; odkrywać ‹-ryć›

un·crit·i·cal [ʌn'krɪtɪkl] bezkrytyczny; **be ~ of s.th.** nie być krytycznym względem czegoś

unc·tion ['ʌŋkʃn] *rel.* namaszczenie *n*; **~·tu·ous** ['ʌŋktjʊəs] obłudny

un·cut [ʌn'kʌt] *film, powieść:* nieokrojony; *diament:* nieoszlifowany

un·dam·aged [ʌn'dæmɪdʒd] nieuszkodzony

un·dat·ed [ʌn'deɪtɪd] nie datowany, bez daty

un·daunt·ed [ʌn'dɔːntɪd] nieustraszony

un·de·cid·ed [ʌndɪ'saɪdɪd] niezdecydowany

un·de·mon·stra·tive [ʌndɪ'mɒnstrətɪv] opanowany, powściągliwy

un·de·ni·a·ble [ʌndɪ'naɪəbl] niezaprzeczalny

un·der ['ʌndə] **1.** *prp.* pod (*I, A*); pod kierownictwem lub rozkazami (*G*); zgodnie z (*I*); **2.** *adv.* pod spodem; **~·age** [ʌndər'eɪdʒ] niepełnoletni; **~'bid** (*-dd-; -bid*) ‹za›oferować lepsze warunki; przelicytowywać ‹-ować›; '**~·brush** *zwł. Am.* → **undergrowth**; '**~·car·riage** *aviat.* podwozie *n*; **~'charge** ‹po›liczyć za mało; **~·clothes** ['ʌndəkləʊðz] *pl.*, **~·cloth·ing** ['ʌndəkləʊðɪŋ] → **underwear**; '**~·coat** podkład *m*; **~'cov·er: ~cover agent** tajny agent *m*; **~'cut** (*-tt-; -cut*) konkurować ceną z (*I*); **~·de'vel·oped** zacofany, nierozwinięty; '**~·dog** strona *f* słabsza; słabszy człowiek *m*; **~'done** niedosmażony, niedogotowany; **~·es·ti·mate** [ʌndər'estɪmeɪt] nie doceniać ‹-nić› (*też fig.*); **~·ex·pose** [ʌndərɪk'spəʊz] niedoświetlać ‹-lić›; **~'fed** niedożywiony; **~'go** (*-went, -gone*) przechodzić ‹przejść›; ulegać ‹-lec›; **~·grad·u·ate** [ʌndə'grædʒʊət] student(ka *f*) *m* (*niższych lat*); **~'ground 1.** *adv.* [ʌndə'graʊnd] pod ziemią; **2.** *adj.* ['ʌndəgraʊnd] podziemny; *fig.* undergroundowy, niekomercyjny; **3.** ['ʌndəgraʊnd] *zwł. Brt.* metro *n*; **by '~ground** metrem; '**~·growth** poszycie *n*; **~'hand, ~'hand·le** za-

U

kulisowy; **~·lie** (*-lay*, *-lain*) znajdować się u podstaw (*G*); **~·line** podkreślać ⟨-lić⟩; **'~·ling** *pej.* podwładny *m* (-na *f*); **~·ly·ing** leżący u podstaw; **~·mine** podminowywać ⟨-ować⟩; *fig.* podkopywać ⟨-pać⟩; **~·neath** [ʌndɪ'ni:θ] **1.** *prp.* pod (*I*); **2.** *adv.* pod spodem; **~'nour·ished** niedożywiony; **'~·pants** *pl.* kalesony *pl.*; **'~·pass** *Brt.* przejście *n* podziemne; przejazd *m* podziemny; **~'pay** (*-paid*) niedopłacać ⟨-cić⟩; **~'priv·i·leged** upośledzony (*pod względem statusu społecznego*); biedny; **~'rate** niedoceniać⟨-nić⟩; **~'sec·re·ta·ry** *pol.* podsekretarz *m*; **~'sell** (*-sold*) *econ.* sprzedawać⟨-dać⟩ poniżej wartości; **~·sell o.s.** *fig.* źle się sprzedać; **'~·shirt** *Am.* podkoszulek *m*; **'~·side** spód *m*; **'~·signed 1.** podpisany; **2. the ~signed** niżej podpisany *m* (-na *f*) *lub* podpisani *pl. m* (-ne *pl. f*); **~'size(d)** za mały; **~'staffed** o niedostateczną ilości personelu; **~'stand** (*-stood*) ⟨z⟩rozumieć; pojmować ⟨-jąć⟩; **make o.s. ~stood** dogadywać ⟨-dać⟩ się; **am I to ~stand that** czy mam to zrozumieć, że; **~'stand·a·ble** zrozumiały; **~'stand·ing 1.** rozumienie *n*; zrozumienie *n*; porozumienie *n*; **come to an ~standing** dochodzić ⟨dojść⟩ do porozumienia (**with** z *I*); **on the ~standing that** pod warunkiem, że; **2.** zrozumiały; **~'state** umniejszać ⟨-szyć⟩, pomniejszać ⟨-szyć⟩; **~'state·ment** pomniejszanie *n*, umniejszanie *n*; niedopowiedzenie *n*; **~'take** (*-took*, *-taken*) podejmować ⟨-djąć⟩ się (*G*) (**to do sth.** zrobienia); przedsiębrać ⟨-wziąć⟩; zobowiązywać ⟨-zać⟩ się; **'~·tak·er** przedsiębiorca *m* pogrzebowy; **~'tak·ing** przedsięwzięcie *n*; zobowiązanie *n*; **'~·tone** *fig.* zabarwienie *n* (*głosu*); **~'val·ue** nie doceniać⟨-nić⟩; **~'wa·ter 1.** *adj.* podwodny; **2.** *adv.* pod wodą; **'~·wear** bielizna *f*; **~'weight 1.** ['ʌndəweɪt] niedowaga *f*; **2.** [ʌndə'weɪt] z niedowagą; zbyt lekki (**by** o *G*); **be five pounds ~weight** mieć pięć funtów niedowagi; **'~·world** środowisko *n* przestępcze, świat *m* przestępczy

un·de·served [ʌndɪ'zɜːvd] niezasłużony

un·de·si·ra·ble [ʌndɪ'zaɪərəbl] niepożądany

un·de·vel·oped [ʌndɪ'veləpt] nierozwinięty

un·dies ['ʌndɪz] *F pl.* bielizna *f* damska

un·dig·ni·fied [ʌn'dɪgnɪfaɪd] mało dystyngowany

un·dis·ci·plined [ʌn'dɪsɪplɪnd] niezdyscyplinowany

un·dis·cov·ered [ʌndɪ'skʌvəd] nie odkryty

un·dis·put·ed [ʌndɪ'spjuːtɪd] bezdyskusyjny

un·dis·turbed [ʌndɪ'stɜːbd] niezakłócony

un·di·vid·ed [ʌndɪ'vaɪdɪd] niepodzielony

un·do [ʌn'duː] (*-did*, *-done*) rozpinać ⟨-piąć⟩; rozwiązywać ⟨-zać⟩; *fig.* ⟨z⟩niweczyć; **un'do·ing: be s.o.'s ~** stawać się czyjąś ruiną; **un'done** rozwiązany, rozpięty; **come ~** rozwiązywać ⟨-zać⟩ się, rozpinać ⟨-piąć⟩ się

un·doubt·ed [ʌn'daʊtɪd] niewątpliwy; **~·ly** niewątpliwie

un·dreamed-of [ʌn'driːmdɒv], **un·dreamt-of** [ʌn'dremtɒv] niesłychany

un·dress [ʌn'dres] rozbierać ⟨-zebrać⟩ (się)

un·due [ʌn'djuː] nadmierny, przesadny

un·du·lat·ing ['ʌndjuleɪtɪŋ] falujący

un·dy·ing [ʌn'daɪɪŋ] nieśmiertelny; dozgonny

un·earned [ʌn'ɜːnd] *fig.* niezasłużony

un·earth [ʌn'ɜːθ] wykopywać ⟨-pać⟩; *fig.* wygrzebywać ⟨-bać⟩, wydobywać ⟨-być⟩ na światło dzienne; **~·ly** niesamowity; **at an ~ly hour** o nieludzkiej porze

un·eas·i·ness [ʌn'iːzɪnɪs] niepokój *m*; zaniepokojenie *n*; **~·y** [ʌn'iːzɪ] (*-ier*, *-iest*) *sen:* niespokojny; niepewny; niepokojący; zaniepokojony; **feel ~y** czuć się nieswojo; **I'm ~y about** jestem niespokojny co do (*G*)

un·e·co·nom·ic ['ʌniːkə'nɒmɪk] nieekonomiczny, niepopłatny

un·ed·u·cat·ed [ʌn'edjukeɪtɪd] niewykształcony

un·e·mo·tion·al [ʌnɪ'məʊʃənl] beznamiętny, chłodny; racjonalny

un·em·ployed [ʌnɪm'plɔɪd] **1.** niezatrudniony, bezrobotny; **2. the ~** *pl.* bezrobotni *pl.*

un·em·ploy·ment [ʌnɪm'plɔɪmənt] bezrobocie *n*; **~ ben·e·fit** *Brt.*, **~ com-**

pen·sa·tion *Am.* zasiłek *m* dla bezrobotnych

un·end·ing [ʌnˈendɪŋ] niekończący się

un·en·dur·a·ble [ʌnɪnˈdjʊərəbl] nie do wytrzymania

un·en·vi·a·ble [ʌnˈenvɪəbl] nie do pozazdroszczenia

un·e·qual [ʌnˈiːkwəl] nierówny; *be ~ to* nie potrafić sprostać (*D*); ~(l)ed niezrównany

un·er·ring [ʌnˈɜːrɪŋ] nieomylny

UNESCO [juːˈneskəʊ] *skrót:* **United Nations Educational, Scientific and Cultural Organization** UNESCO *n*, Organizacja Narodów Zjednoczonych do Spraw Oświaty, Nauki i Kultury

un·e·ven [ʌnˈiːvn] nierówny; *liczba:* nieparzysty

un·e·vent·ful [ʌnɪˈventfl] bez zakłóceń, spokojny

un·ex·am·pled [ʌnɪɡˈzɑːmpld] bezprzykładny

un·ex·pec·ted [ʌnɪkˈspektɪd] niespodziewany

un·ex·posed [ʌnɪkˈspəʊzd] *phot.* niewywołany

un·fail·ing [ʌnˈfeɪlɪŋ] niezawodny, pewny

un·fair [ʌnˈfeə] nie fair, nieprzepisowy; niesprawidliwy, nieuczciwy

un·faith·ful [ʌnˈfeɪθfl] niewierny (*to* wobec *G*)

un·fa·mil·i·ar [ʌnfəˈmɪljə] nieznany; nie obeznany (*with* z *I*)

un·fas·ten [ʌnˈfɑːsn] rozpinać ⟨-piąć⟩, otwierać ⟨-worzyć⟩

un·fa·vo(u)·ra·ble [ʌnˈfeɪvərəbl] nieprzychylny (*to* wobec *G*); niesprzyjający; niepomyślny

un·feel·ing [ʌnˈfiːlɪŋ] nieczuły, nieludzki

un·fin·ished [ʌnˈfɪnɪʃt] niezakończony, nieukończony

un·fit [ʌnˈfɪt] nie w formie; nieodpowiedni, niezdatny; niezdolny (*for* do *G*, *to do* do zrobienia)

un·flag·ging [ʌnˈflæɡɪŋ] nie słabnący

un·flap·pa·ble [ʌnˈflæpəbl] F niewzruszony

un·fold [ʌnˈfəʊld] rozwijać ⟨-winąć⟩ (się)

un·fore·seen [ʌnfɔːˈsiːn] nieprzewidziany

un·for·get·ta·ble [ʌnfəˈɡetəbl] niezapomniany, pamiętny

un·for·got·ten [ʌnfəˈɡɒtn] nie zapomniany, pamiętny

un·for·mat·ted [ʌnˈfɔːmæɪd] *komp.* niesformatowany

un·for·tu·nate [ʌnˈfɔːtʃnət] nieszczęsny; niefortunny; pechowy; ~·ly niestety

un·found·ed [ʌnˈfaʊndɪd] nieuzasadniony, bezpodstawny

un·friend·ly [ʌnˈfrendlɪ] (*-ier, -iest*) nieprzyjazny (*to, towards* wobec *G*)

un·furl [ʌnˈfɜːl] *sztandar* rozpościerać ⟨-postrzeć⟩; *żagiel* rozwijać ⟨-winąć⟩

un·fur·nished [ʌnˈfɜːnɪʃt] nie umeblowany

un·gain·ly [ʌnˈɡeɪnlɪ] niezgrabny, niezdarny

un·god·ly [ʌnˈɡɒdlɪ] bezbożny; *at an ~ hour* o nieprzyzwoitej godzinie

un·gra·cious [ʌnˈɡreɪʃəs] niewdzięczny

un·grate·ful [ʌnˈɡreɪtfl] niewdzięczny

un·guard·ed [ʌnˈɡɑːdɪd] niebaczny, nieostrożny

un·hap·pi·ly [ʌnˈhæpɪlɪ] nieszczęśliwie, pechowo; **un·hap·py** [ʌnˈhæpɪ] (*-ier, -iest*) nieszczęśliwy, pechowy

un·harmed [ʌnˈhɑːmd] nietknięty, cały

un·health·y [ʌnˈhelθɪ] niezdrowy; *pej.* chorobliwy

un·heard [ʌnˈhɜːd]: *go ~* nie znajdować ⟨-naleźć⟩ posłuchu; ~-*of* [ʌnˈhɜːdɒv] niesłychany, bezprzykładny

un·hinge [ʌnˈhɪndʒ]: *~ s.o.('s mind)* pozbawiać ⟨-wić⟩ rozumu

un·ho·ly [ʌnˈhəʊlɪ] F (*-ier, -iest*) nieprawdopodobny, niesłychany

un·hoped-for [ʌnˈhəʊptfɔː] nieoczekiwany

un·hurt [ʌnˈhɜːt] cało, bez szwanku

UNICEF [ˈjuːnɪsef] *skrót:* **United Nations International Children's Fund** UNICEF *m*, Fundusz Narodów Zjednoczonych Pomocy Dzieciom

u·ni·corn [ˈjuːnɪkɔːn] jednorożec *m*

un·i·den·ti·fied [ʌnaɪˈdentɪfaɪd] niezidentyfikowany

u·ni·fi·ca·tion [juːnɪfɪˈkeɪʃn] zjednoczenie *n*

u·ni·form [ˈjuːnɪfɔːm] **1.** uniform *m*; mundur *m*; **2.** jednolity; jednaki; ~·i·ty [juːnɪˈfɔːmətɪ] jednorodność *f*, jednolitość *f*

u·ni·fy ['juːnɪfaɪ] ⟨z⟩jednoczyć; ⟨z⟩unifikować; ⟨s⟩konsolidować

u·ni·lat·e·ral [juːnɪ'lætərəl] *fig.* jednostronny

un·i·ma·gi·na·ble [ʌnɪ'mædʒɪnəbl] niewyobrażalny; **un·i·ma·gi·na·tive** [ʌnɪ'mædʒɪnətɪv] bez wyobraźni, pozbawiony wyobraźni

un·im·por·tant [ʌnɪm'pɔːtənt] nieważny

un·im·pressed [ʌnɪm'prest] nieporuszony (**by** przez *A*)

un·in·formed [ʌnɪn'fɔːmd] nie poinformowany, nieświadomy

un·in·hab·i·ta·ble [ʌnɪn'hæbɪtəbl] niezdatny do zamieszkania; **un·in·hab·it·ed** [ʌnɪn'hæbɪtɪd] niezamieszkały, bezludny

un·in·jured [ʌn'ɪndʒəd] cały, bez szwanku

un·in·tel·li·gi·ble [ʌnɪn'telɪdʒəbl] niezrozumiały

un·in·ten·tion·al [ʌnɪn'tenʃənl] nieumyślny

un·in·terest·ed [ʌn'ɪntrɪstɪd] nie zainteresowany; **be ~ in** też nie interesować się (*I*); **un·in·te·rest·ing** [ʌn'ɪntrɪstɪŋ] nieinteresujący

un·in·ter·rupt·ed ['ʌnɪntə'rʌptɪd] nieprzerwany

un·ion ['juːnjən] unia *f*; połączenie *n*; związek *m*; **~·ist** ['juːnjənɪst] związkowiec *m*; **~·ize** ['juːnjənaɪz] zrzeszać się (*w związek*), przyłączać ⟨-czyć⟩ się do związku; 2 **'Jack** (*brytyjska flaga narodowa*) Union Jack *m*

u·nique [juː'niːk] unikalny, unikatowy; wyjątkowy; niespotykany

u·ni·son ['juːnɪzn]: **in ~** zgodnie; *mus.* unisono

u·nit ['juːnɪt] jednostka *f*; *ped.* godzina *f* nauczania; *math.* jednostka *f*, jedność *f*; *tech.* element *m*, moduł *m*; **sink ~** szafka *f* pod zlewozmywak

u·nite [juː'naɪt] ⟨z⟩jednoczyć (się), ⟨z⟩łączyć (się); **u·nit·ed** zjednoczony

U·nit·ed 'King·dom (*skrót:* **UK**) Zjednoczone Królestwo *n* (*Anglia, Szkocja i płn. Irlandia*)

U·nit·ed 'Na·tions *pl.* (*skrót:* **UN**) Narody *pl.* Zjednoczone, ONZ *m*

U·nit·ed States of A'mer·i·ca *pl.* (*skrót:* **USA**) Stany *pl.* Zjednoczone Ameryki, USA *pl.*

u·ni·ty ['juːnətɪ] jedność *f*

u·ni·ver·sal [juːnɪ'vɜːsl] uniwersalny, powszechny; ogólny

u·ni·verse ['juːnɪvɜːs] wszechświat *m*

u·ni·ver·si·ty [juːnɪ'vɜːsətɪ] uniwersytet *m*, wyższa uczelnia *f*; **~ 'grad·u·ate** absolwent *m* szkoły wyższej

un·just [ʌn'dʒʌst] niesprawiedliwy

un·kempt [ʌn'kempt] *włosy*: rozczochrany; *ubranie*: zaniedbany

un·kind [ʌn'kaɪnd] nieprzyjazny, nieżyczliwy

un·known [ʌn'nəʊn] **1.** nieznany (**to** *D*); niewiadomy; **2.** niewiadoma *f* (*też math.*); **~ 'quan·ti·ty** wielkość *f* nieznana

un·law·ful [ʌn'lɔːfl] bezprawny, nielegalny

un·lead·ed [ʌn'ledɪd] *benzyna*: bezołowiowy

un·learn [ʌn'lɜːn] (**-ed** *lub* **-learnt**) oduczać ⟨-czyć⟩ się

un·less [ən'les] jeżeli nie, o ile nie

un·like [ʌn'laɪk] *prp.* niepodobny do (*G*), mało podobny do (*G*); **he is very ~ his father** jest bardzo niepodobny do swego ojca; **that is very ~ him** to do niego zupełnie niepodobne; **~·ly** mało prawdopodobny; **she's ~ly to be there** mało prawdopodobne, by tam była

un·lim·it·ed [ʌn'lɪmɪtɪd] nieograniczony

un·list·ed [ʌn'lɪstɪd] *Am. tel. numer:* zastrzeżony; **~ 'num·ber** numer *m* zastrzeżony

un·load [ʌn'ləʊd] wyładowywać ⟨-ować⟩, rozładowywać ⟨-ować⟩

un·lock [ʌn'lɒk] otwierać ⟨-worzyć⟩

un·loos·en [ʌn'luːsn] rozwiązywać ⟨-zać⟩; rozluźniać ⟨-nić⟩

un·loved [ʌn'lʌvd] niekochany

un·luck·y [ʌn'lʌkɪ] (**-ier, -iest**) nieszczęśliwy, pechowy; **be ~** mieć pecha

un·made [ʌn'meɪd] *łóżko*: nie posłielony

un·manned [ʌn'mænd] bezzałogowy

un·marked [ʌn'mɑːkt] nie oznaczony; bez skazy; *sport:* nie kryty

un·mar·ried [ʌn'mærɪd] *kobieta*: niezamężny; *mężczyzna*: nieżonaty

un·mask [ʌn'mɑːsk] *fig.* ⟨z⟩demaskować

un·matched [ʌn'mætʃt] niezrównany

un·men·tio·na·ble [ʌn'menʃnəbl] tabu; **be ~** być tabu

un·mis·ta·ka·ble [ˌʌnmɪˈsteɪkəbl] niewątpliwy, jednoznaczny

un·moved [ʌnˈmuːvd] nieporuszony; **she remained ~ by it** nie poruszyło jej to

un·mu·si·cal [ʌnˈmjuːzɪkl] mało muzykalny, niemuzykalny

un·named [ʌnˈneɪmd] nienazwany

un·nat·u·ral [ʌnˈnætʃrəl] nienaturalny, wbrew naturze

un·ne·ces·sa·ry [ʌnˈnesəsəri] niepotrzebny

un·nerve [ʌnˈnɜːv] wytrącać ⟨-cić⟩ z równowagi

un·no·ticed [ʌnˈnəʊtɪst] niezauważony

un·num·bered [ʌnˈnʌmbəd] nienumerowany

UNO [ˈjuːnəʊ] *skrót:* **United Nations Organization** ONZ *n*

un·ob·tru·sive [ˌʌnəbˈtruːsɪv] nie rzucający się w oczy

un·oc·cu·pied [ʌnˈɒkjʊpaɪd] nie zajęty; niezamieszkały

un·of·fi·cial [ˌʌnəˈfɪʃl] nieoficjalny

un·pack [ʌnˈpæk] rozpakowywać ⟨-ować⟩ (się)

un·paid [ʌnˈpeɪd] nie zapłacony; nie opłacany, nie wynagradzany

un·par·al·leled [ʌnˈpærəleld] niezrównany, bezprzykładny

un·par·don·a·ble [ʌnˈpɑːdnəbl] niewybaczalny

un·per·turbed [ˌʌnpəˈtɜːbd] niewzruszony

un·pick [ʌnˈpɪk] rozpruwać ⟨-ruć⟩

un·placed [ʌnˈpleɪst] **be ~** (*w sporcie*) nie zająć miejsca medalowego

un·play·a·ble [ʌnˈpleɪəbl] (*w sporcie*) nie nadający się do rozgrywek

un·pleas·ant [ʌnˈpleznt] nieprzyjemny, przykry

un·plug [ʌnˈplʌg] odłączać ⟨-czyć⟩ od sieci

un·pol·ished [ʌnˈpɒlɪʃt] nie oszlifowany; nie polerowany *fig.* bez polotu

un·pol·lut·ed [ˌʌnpəˈluːtɪd] nie zanieczyszczony

un·pop·u·lar [ʌnˈpɒpjʊlə] mało popularny, niepopularny; **~·i·ty** [ˌʌnpɒpjʊˈlærətɪ] niepopularność *f*

un·prac·ti·cal [ʌnˈpræktɪkl] niepraktyczny, mało praktyczny

un·prac·tised *Brt.*, **un·prac·ticed** *Am.* [ʌnˈpræktɪst] nie przećwiczony

un·pre·ce·dent·ed [ʌnˈpresɪdentɪd] bezprecedensowy

un·pre·dict·a·ble [ˌʌnprɪˈdɪktəbl] nieprzewidywalny; nie dający się przewidzieć

un·prej·u·diced [ʌnˈpredʒʊdɪst] nie uprzedzony, bezstronny

un·pre·med·i·tat·ed [ˌʌnpriːˈmedɪteɪtɪd] nieumyślny, nierozmyślny

un·pre·pared [ˌʌnprɪˈpeəd] nie przygotowany

un·pre·ten·tious [ˌʌnprɪˈtenʃəs] bezpretensjonalny

un·prin·ci·pled [ʌnˈprɪnsəpld] bez skrupułów, pozbawiony skrupułów

un·prin·ta·ble [ʌnˈprɪntəbl] nie nadający się do druku

un·pro·duc·tive [ˌʌnprəˈdʌktɪv] nieproduktywny, mało produktywny

un·pro·fes·sion·al [ˌʌnprəˈfeʃənl] nieprofesjonalny, mało profesjonalny

un·prof·i·ta·ble [ʌnˈprɒfɪtəbl] nierentowny

un·pro·nounce·a·ble [ˌʌnprəˈnaʊnsəbl] nie do wymówienia

un·pro·tect·ed [ˌʌnprəˈtektɪd] nieosłonięty

un·proved [ʌnˈpruːvd], **un·prov·en** [ʌnˈpruːvn] nie udowodniony

un·pro·voked [ˌʌnprəˈvəʊkt] nie sprowokowany

un·pun·ished [ʌnˈpʌnɪʃt] bezkarny, nie karany

un·qual·i·fied [ʌnˈkwɒlɪfaɪd] niewykwalifikowany, bez kwalifikacji; nie nadający się (**for** do *G*); *odmowa*: kategoryczny

un·ques·tio·na·ble [ʌnˈkwestʃənəbl] bezsporny, bezsprzeczny; **un·question·ing** [ʌnˈkwestʃənɪŋ] zupełny, absolutny

un·quote [ʌnˈkwəʊt]: **quote ... ~** cytuję ... koniec cytatu

un·rav·el [ʌnˈrævl] (*zwł. Brt.* **-ll-**, *Am.* **-l-**) rozplątywać ⟨-tać⟩; *sweter itp.*: ⟨s⟩pruć (się); *zagadkę* rozwiązać

un·rea·da·ble [ʌnˈriːdəbl] nieczytelny, nie do przeczytania

un·re·al [ʌnˈrɪəl] nierzeczywisty; **un·re·a·lis·tic** [ˌʌnrɪəˈlɪstɪk] (**~ally**) nierealistyczny

un·rea·so·na·ble [ʌnˈriːznəbl] nierozsądny; nadmierny; *cena*: wygórowany

U

un·rec·og·niz·a·ble [ʌnˈrekəgnaɪzəbl] nie do rozpoznania

un·re·lat·ed [ʌnrɪˈleɪtɪd]: **be ~ to** nie mieć odniesienia do (G)

un·re·lent·ing [ʌnrɪˈlentɪŋ] nie słabnący; bezlitosny

un·re·li·a·ble [ʌnrɪˈlaɪəbl] niepewny; nierzetelny

un·re·lieved [ʌnrɪˈliːvd] nieprzerwany, nieustający

un·re·mit·ting [ʌnrɪˈmɪtɪŋ] nieustanny

un·re·quit·ed [ʌnrɪˈkwaɪtɪd] nie wynagrodzony

un·re·served [ʌnrɪˈzɜːvd] bezwarunkowy; *miejsce:* nie zarezerwowany

un·rest [ʌnˈrest] *pol. itp.* niepokój *m*

un·re·strained [ʌnrɪˈstreɪnd] nieskrępowany

un·re·strict·ed [ʌnrɪˈstrɪktɪd] nieograniczony

un·ripe [ʌnˈraɪp] niedojrzały

un·ri·val(l)ed [ʌnˈraɪvld] niezrównany, niedościgniony

un·roll [ʌnˈrəʊl] rozwijać ⟨-winąć⟩

un·ruf·fled [ʌnˈrʌfld] spokojny; nieporuszony

un·ru·ly [ʌnˈruːlɪ] (**-ier, -iest**) niesforny, krnąbrny

un·sad·dle [ʌnˈsædl] *konia* rozsiodływać ⟨-łać⟩; zsiadać ⟨zsiąść⟩ z (G)

un·safe [ʌnˈseɪf] niebezpieczny; niepewny, ryzykowny

un·said [ʌnˈsed] niewypowiedziany

un·sal(e)·a·ble [ʌnˈseɪləbl] niepokupny

un·salt·ed [ʌnˈsɔːltɪd] nie solony, niesłony

un·san·i·tar·y [ʌnˈsænɪtərɪ] niehigieniczny

un·sat·is·fac·to·ry [ˈʌnsætɪsˈfæktərɪ] niezadowalający

un·sat·u·rat·ed [ʌnˈsætʃəreɪtɪd] *chem.* nienasycony

un·sa·vo(u)r·y [ʌnˈseɪvərɪ] podejrzany, mętny

un·scathed [ʌnˈskeɪðd] nietknięty

un·screw [ʌnˈskruː] odkręcać ⟨-cić⟩

un·scru·pu·lous [ʌnˈskruːpjʊləs] bez skrupułów

un·seat [ʌnˈsiːt] *jeźdźca* wysadzać ⟨-dzić⟩ z siodła; usuwać ⟨-nąć⟩ (*ze stanowiska*)

un·seem·ly [ʌnˈsiːmlɪ] niewłaściwy, niestosowny

un·self·ish [ʌnˈselfɪʃ] bezinteresowny; **~ness** bezinteresowność *f*

un·set·tle [ʌnˈsetl] zaburzać ⟨-rzyć⟩ spokój, pozbawiać ⟨-wić⟩ spokoju; **~d** niespokojny; nierozstrzygnięty; *pogoda:* zmienny

un·sha·k(e)a·ble [ʌnˈʃeɪkəbl] niewzruszony, niezachwiany

un·shav·en [ʌnˈʃeɪvn] nieogolony

un·shrink·a·ble [ʌnˈʃrɪŋkəbl] niekurczliwy

un·sight·ly [ʌnˈsaɪtlɪ] okropny, paskudny

un·skilled [ʌnˈskɪld] niewykwalifikowany

un·so·cia·ble [ʌnˈsəʊʃəbl] mało towarzyski, nietowarzyski

un·so·cial [ʌnˈsəʊʃl]: **work ~ hours** pracować poza normalnymi godzinami pracy

un·so·lic·it·ed [ʌnsəˈlɪsɪtɪd] nie zamawiany; nieproszony

un·solved [ʌnˈsɒlvd] nie rozwiązany

un·so·phis·ti·cat·ed [ʌnsəˈfɪstɪkeɪtɪd] mało wyrafinowany

un·sound [ʌnˈsaʊnd] niezdrowy; *budynek:* zagrożony; *towar:* wadliwy; *argument:* mało rozsądny; **of ~ mind** *jur.* o zaburzonych władzach umysłowych

un·spar·ing [ʌnˈspeərɪŋ] hojny, szczodry

un·spea·ka·ble [ʌnˈspiːkəbl] niewypowiedziany; okropny

un·spoiled [ʌnˈspɔɪld], un·spoilt [ʌnˈspɔɪlt] nie zepsuty; nietknięty

un·sta·ble [ʌnˈsteɪbl] chwiejny; niepewny; *człowiek:* niezrównoważony

un·stead·y [ʌnˈstedɪ] (**-ier, -iest**) niestały, chwiejny; niepewny

un·stop [ʌnˈstɒp] (**-pp-**) *butelkę* odkorkowywać ⟨-ować⟩; odblokowywać ⟨-kować⟩

un·stressed [ʌnˈstrest] *ling.* nieakcentowany

un·stuck [ʌnˈstʌk]: **come ~** odchodzić ⟨-dejść⟩, odklejać ⟨-kleić⟩ się; *fig.* zawodzić ⟨-wieść⟩

un·stud·ied [ʌnˈstʌdɪd] niewymuszony

un·suc·cess·ful [ʌnsəkˈsesfl] nieudany; nie mający szczęścia; nie mający powodzenia

un·suit·a·ble [ʌnˈsjuːtəbl] nieodpowiedni (**for** do G)

un·sure [ʌnˈʃɔː] (**-r, -st**) niepewny; **be ~**

of o.s. nie być pewnym siebie

un·sur·passed [ʌnsəˈpɑːst] nieprze-
ścigniony

un·sus·pect·ed[ʌnsəˈspektɪd] nie po-
dejrzewany; **~·ing** niczego nie podejrzewający

un·sus·pi·cious [ʌnsəˈspɪʃəs] niczego
nie podejrzewający

un·sweet·ened [ʌnˈswiːtnd] niesło-
dzony

un·swerv·ing [ʌnˈswɜːvɪŋ] niezachwiany

un·tan·gle [ʌnˈtæŋgl] rozplątywać
⟨-tać⟩ (*też fig.*)

un·tapped [ʌnˈtæpt] *surowce itp.*: nie
wykorzystany

un·teach·a·ble [ʌnˈtiːtʃəbl] niewyu-
czalny

un·ten·a·ble [ʌnˈtenəbl] *teoria itp.*: nie
do utrzymania

un·think|·a·ble [ʌnˈθɪŋkəbl] nie do po-
myślenia; **~·ing** bezmyślny

un·ti·dy [ʌnˈtaɪdɪ] (*-ier, -iest*) nieporządny

un·tie [ʌnˈtaɪ] rozwiązywać ⟨-zać⟩; od-
wiązywać ⟨-zać⟩

un·til [ənˈtɪl] *prp., cj.* aż do (*G*), do (*G*);
not ~ dopóki nie

un·time·ly [ʌnˈtaɪmlɪ] przedwczesny;
nie w porę; niewczesny

un·tir·ing [ʌnˈtaɪərɪŋ] niezmordowany

un·told [ʌnˈtəʊld] niewypowiedziany,
nieopisany; przemilczany

un·touched [ʌnˈtʌtʃt] nietknięty

un·true [ʌnˈtruː] nieprawdziwy

un·trust·wor·thy [ʌnˈtrʌstwɜːðɪ] niegodny zaufania; wątpliwy

un·used[1] [ʌnˈjuːzd] nie używany; nie
wykorzystany

un·used[2] [ʌnˈjuːst]: *be ~ to* (*doing*)
s.th. nie być przyzwyczajonym do (robienia) czegoś

un·u·su·al [ʌnˈjuːʒʊəl] niezwykły

un·var·nished [ʌnˈvɑːnɪʃt] nie ozdo-
biony; nie upiększony; *prawda*: nagi

un·var·y·ing [ʌnˈveərɪŋ] niezmienny

un·veil [ʌnˈveɪl] *pomnik itp.* odsłaniać
⟨-łonić⟩

un·versed [ʌnˈvɜːst] nie zaznajomiony
(*in* z *I*)

un·voiced [ʌnˈvɔɪst] niewypowiedziany

un·want·ed [ʌnˈwɒntɪd] niechciany

un·war·rant·ed [ʌnˈwɒrəntɪd] nie za-

gwarantowany; bezpodstawny

un·washed [ʌnˈwɒʃt] nie umyty

un·wel·come [ʌnˈwelkəm] niechciany

un·well [ʌnˈwel]: *be lub feel ~* źle się
czuć

un·whole·some [ʌnˈhəʊlsəm] niezdrowy; niedobry

un·wield·y [ʌnˈwiːldɪ] nieporęczny

un·will·ing [ʌnˈwɪlɪŋ] niechętny; *be ~
to do s.th.* nie chcieć czegoś robić

un·wind [ʌnˈwaɪnd] (*-wound*) odwijać
⟨-winąć⟩, rozwijać ⟨-winąć⟩

un·wise [ʌnˈwaɪz] niemądry

un·wit·ting [ʌnˈwɪtɪŋ] nieświadomy,
niezamierzony

un·wor·thy [ʌnˈwɜːðɪ] niegodny; *he is
~ of it* on nie jest godzien tego

un·wrap [ʌnˈræp] rozwijać ⟨-winąć⟩

un·writ·ten [ʌnˈrɪtn] niepisany; *~ 'law
jur* prawo *n* niepisane

un·yield·ing [ʌnˈjiːldɪŋ] nieugięty, nieustępliwy

un·zip [ʌnˈzɪp] rozpinać ⟨-piąć⟩ (*zamek
błyskawiczny*)

up [ʌp] *adv.* w górę, do góry; w górze;
~ there tam w górze; *jump ~ and down*
skakać w górę i w dół; *walk ~ and
down* chodzić tam i z powrotem; *~ to*
aż do (*G*); *be ~ to s.th.* F kombinować
coś; *not to be ~ to s.th.* nie spełniać
⟨-nić⟩ czegoś; *it's ~ to you* co zależy od
ciebie; **2.** *prp.* w górę (*G*); *~ the river*
w górę rzeki; **3.** *adj.* idący *lub* skierowany w górę; *okres czasu*: zakończony;
the ~ train pociąg do Londynu (*do sto-
licy itp.*); *be ~ and about* ruszać się
(już); *what's ~?* co się dzieje?; *road ~
mot.* roboty *pl.* drogowe; **4.** (*-pp-*) F *v/t.*
cenę itp. podwyższać ⟨-szyć⟩; **5.** *the ~s
and downs pl.* wzloty i upadki *pl.*

up-and-com·ing [ʌpənˈkʌmɪŋ] dobrze
się zapowiadający

up·bring·ing [ˈʌpbrɪŋɪŋ] wychowanie *n*

up·com·ing [ˈʌpkʌmɪŋ] nadchodzący

up·coun·try [ʌpˈkʌntrɪ] **1.** *adv.* w głąb
kraju; **2.** *adj.* w głębi kraju

up·date [ʌpˈdeɪt] ⟨z⟩aktualizować,
⟨z⟩modernizować

up·end [ʌpˈend] stawiać ⟨postawić⟩
pionowo

up·grade [ʌpˈgreɪd] **1.** przenosić
⟨-nieść⟩ do wyższej grupy; ulepszać
⟨-szać⟩; ⟨z⟩aktualizować; **2.** *komp.* nowa wersja *f* programu, upgrade *m*

U

up·heav·al *fig.* [ʌp'hi:vl] wstrząs *m*

up·hill [ʌp'hɪl] pod górę; *fig.* mozolny

up·hold [ʌp'həʊld] (**-held**) podtrzymywać ‹-ymać›; *jur.* utrzymywać ‹-mać› w mocy

up|·hol·ster [ʌp'həʊlstə] *meble* pokrywać ‹-ryć›; **~·hol·ster·er** [ʌp'həʊlstərə] tapicer *m*; **~·hol·ster·y** [ʌp'həʊlstərɪ] tapicerka *f*, obicie *n*

UPI [ju: pi: 'aɪ] *skrót:* **United Press International** UPI *n*

up·keep ['ʌpki:p] utrzymanie *n*

up·land ['ʌplənd] *zw.* **~s** *pl.* pogórze *n*

up·lift 1. [ʌp'lɪft] podnosić ‹-nieść› na duchu; **2.** ['ʌplɪft] podniesienie *n* na duchu

up·on [ə'pɒn] → **on**; **once ~ a time** pewnego razu

up·per ['ʌpə] górny; wierzchni; '**~·most 1.** *adj.* najwyższy; najważniejszy; **be ~most** być na górze; stać na pierwszym miejscu; **2.** *adv.* najwyżej

up·right ['ʌpraɪt] **1.** *adj.* pionowy, prosty; *fig.* uczciwy, prawy; **2.** *adv.* pionowo, prosto

up·ris·ing ['ʌpraɪzɪŋ] powstanie *n*, insurekcja *f*

up·roar ['ʌprɔ:] hałas *m*, zamieszanie *n*; **~·i·ous** [ʌp'rɔ:rɪəs] *śmiech:* grzmiący

up·root [ʌp'ru:t] wyrywać z korzeniami; *fig.* przenosić ‹-nieść›

UPS [ju: pi: 'es] *Am. skrót:* **United Parcel Service** (*firma przesyłająca paczki*)

up·set [ʌp'set] (**-set**) przewracać ‹-rócić›, wywracać ‹-rócić›; *fig. plany itp.* ‹po›krzyżować; *fig.* ‹z›denerwować, **the fish has ~ me lub my stomach** po tej rybie dostałem rozstroju żołądka; **be ~** być zdenerwowanym

up·shot ['ʌpʃɒt] rezultat *m*, wynik *m*

up·side down [ʌpsaɪd'daʊn] do góry nogami

up·stairs [ʌp'steəz] **1.** na górze (*domu itp.*); na górę; w górę; **2.** *adj.* górny, na górze

up·start ['ʌpstɑ:t] karierowicz(ka *f*) *m*

up·state [ʌp'steɪt] *Am.* na północy (*stanu*)

up·stream [ʌp'stri:m] pod prąd

up·take ['ʌpteɪk] F: **be quick on the ~** pojmować w lot, **be slow on the ~** mieć ciężki opóźnisz pomyślunek

up-to-date [ʌptə'deɪt] aktualny; nowoczesny

up·town [ʌp'taʊn] *Am.* w dzielnicach mieszkaniowych, do dzielnic mieszkaniowych (*poza centrum miasta*)

up·turn ['ʌptɜːn] poprawa *f*

up·ward(s) ['ʌpwəd(z)] w górę

u·ra·ni·um [jʊ'reɪnɪəm] *chem.* uran *m*

ur·ban ['ɜːbən] miejski

ur·chin ['ɜːtʃɪn] łobuz *m*

urge [ɜːdʒ] **1.** nastawać, nalegać (**to do s.th.** na zrobienie czegoś); też **~ on** zalecać ‹-cić›; popędzać ‹-dzić›; **2.** pragnienie *n*, chęć *f*; **ur·gen·cy** ['ɜːdʒənsɪ] nagła potrzeba *f*; **ur·gent** ['ɜːdʒənt] pilny, naglący

u·ri·|nal ['jʊərɪnl] pisuar *m*; **~·nate** ['jʊərɪneɪt] oddawać ‹-dać› mocz; **u·rine** ['jʊərɪn] mocz *m*, uryna *f*

urn [ɜːn] urna *f*; duży termos *m*

us [ʌs, əs] nas, nam, nami; **all of ~** my wszyscy; **both of ~** my obaj

US [ju: 'es] *skrót:* **United States** USA *pl.*, Stany *pl.* Zjednoczone

USA [ju: es 'eɪ] *skrót:* **United States of America** USA *pl.*, Stany *pl.* Zjednoczone Ameryki

USAF [ju: es eɪ 'ef] *skrót:* **United States Air Force** lotnictwo *n* USA

us·age ['ju:zɪdʒ] zwyczaj *m*; zwyczaj *m*; stosowana praktyka *f*; *gr.* uzus *m*, użycie *n* języka

use 1. [ju:z] *v/t.* używać ‹użyć›; ‹wy›korzystać; **~ up** zużywać ‹-żyć›; **2.** [ju:s] użycie *n*; wykorzystanie *n*; użytek *m*; korzyść *f*; pożytek *f*; **be of ~** być przydatnym (**to do** G); **it's no ~ ...** nie ma sensu ...; → **milk 1**

used¹ [ju:st]: **I ~ to live here** kiedyś tu mieszkałem; **be ~ to do (doing) s.th.** być przyzwyczajonym do (robienia) czegoś

used² [ju:zd] użyty, zużyty; używany; **~ 'car** używany samochód *m*; **~ 'deal·er** sprzedawca *m* (-wczyni *f*) używanych samochodów

use|·ful ['ju:sfl] użyteczny; '**~·less** bezużyteczny

us·er [ju:zə] użytkownik *m* (-niczka *f*); posługujący *m* (-ca *f*) się; **~·'friend·ly** przyjazny dla użytkownika; **~·'in·ter·face** *komp.* interfejs *m* użytkownika

ush·er ['ʌʃə] **1.** bileter *m*; *jur.* woźny *m* sądowy; **2.** wprowadzać ‹-dzić› (**into** do G), ‹za›prowadzić (**into** do G); **~·ette** [ʌʃə'ret] bileterka *f*

USN [juː es 'en] *skrót:* **United States Navy** marynarka *f* Stanów Zjednoczonych

USS [juː es 'es] *skrót:* **United States Ship** okręt Stanów Zjednoczonych

USSR [juː es es 'ɑː] *hist. skrót:* **Union of Socialist Soviet Republics** ZSRR *n*, Związek *m* Socjalistycznych Republik Radzieckich

u·su·al ['juːʒl] zwykły; **as ~** jak zwykle; **~·ly** ['juːʒəlɪ] zwykle

u·sur·er ['juːʒərə] lichwiarz *m* (-rka *f*)

u·su·ry ['juːʒʊrɪ] lichwiarstwo *n*

u·ten·sil [juː'tensl] przybór *m*, urządzenie *n*

u·te·rus ['juːtərəs] (*pl.* **-ri** [-raɪ],

-ruses) *anat.* macica *f*

u·til·i·ty [juː'tɪlɪtɪ] użyteczność *f*; **utilities** *pl.* usługi *pl.* komunalne

u·til·ize ['juːtɪlaɪz] używać ⟨-żyć⟩, ⟨s⟩pożytkować, wykorzystywać ⟨-tać⟩

ut·most ['ʌtməʊst] najwyższy

U·to·pi·an [juː'təʊpjən] utopijny

ut·ter¹ ['ʌtə] całkowity, zupełny

ut·ter² ['ʌtə] wypowiadać ⟨-wiedzieć⟩; *dźwięki* wydawać ⟨-dać⟩ (z siebie)

U·turn ['juːtɜːn] *mot.* zawrócenie *n*; *fig.* zwrot *m* o 180 stopni

UV [juː 'viː] *skrót:* **ultraviolet** nadfiolet *m*

u·vu·la ['juːvjʊlə] *anat.* (*pl.* **-las, -lae** [-liː]) języczek *m*

V

V, v [viː] V, v *n*

v. *Brt. skrót pisany:* **against** (*łacińskie* **versus**) *hud.* sport, jur.: przeciw

val·can·cy ['veɪkənsɪ] wolne miejsce *n*; wakat *m*; **vacancies** wolne miejsca; **no vacancies** brak wolnych miejsc; **'~·cant** próżny, pusty; wolny; *miejsce:* wakujący; *fig. wyraz twarzy:* nieobecny

va·cate [və'keɪt] *pokój, etat itp.* zwalniać ⟨zwolnić⟩; *miejsce* opuszczać ⟨opuścić⟩

va·ca·tion [və'keɪʃn] **1.** *zwł. Am.* wakacje *pl.*; urlop *m*; *zwł. Brt. univ.* ferie *pl.*; *jur.* wakacje *pl.* sądowe; **be on ~** *zwł. Am.* być na urlopie, mieć urlop; **2.** *zwł. Am.* urlopować; odbywać wakacje *lub* urlop; **~·er** [və'keɪʃnə], **~·ist** [və'keɪʃnɪst] *zwł. Am.* urlopowicz(ka *f*) *m*; wczasowicz(ka *f*) *m*

vac|·cin·ate ['væksɪneɪt] zaszczepiać ⟨-pić⟩; **~·cin·a·tion** [væksɪ'neɪʃn] szczepienie *n*; **~·cine** ['væksiːn] szczepionka *f*

vac·il·late ['væsɪleɪt] *fig.* wahać się

vac·u·um ['vækjʊəm] **1.** *phys.* próżnia *f*; **2.** F *dywan, pokój itp.* odkurzać ⟨-rzyć⟩; **'~ bot·tle** *Am.* termos *m*; **'~ clean·er** odkurzacz *m*; **'~ flask** *Brt.* termos *m*; **'~-packed** (za)pakowane próżniowo

vag·a·bond ['væɡəbɒnd] włóczęga *m*, wagabunda *m*

va·ga·ry ['veɪɡərɪ] *zw.* **vagaries** *pl.* fanaberie *pl.*

va·gi·na [və'dʒaɪnə] *anat.* pochwa *f*; **~·nal** [və'dʒaɪnl] *anat.* pochwowy; dopochwowy

va·grant ['veɪɡrənt] włóczęga *m*

vague [veɪɡ] (**-r, -st**) niewyraźny; *fig.* mglisty; *fig.* mętny

vain [veɪn] próżny; bezskuteczny; *pogróżka itp.:* czczy; **in ~** na próżno

vale [veɪl] *poet. lub w nazwach:* dolina *f*

val·en·tine ['væləntaɪn] walentynka *f*; (*osoba, do której wysyła się walentynkę*)

va·le·ri·an [və'lɪərɪən] *bot., pharm.* waleriana *f*

val·et ['vælɪt] kamerdyner *m*; '~ **ser·vice** (*w hotelu*) czyszczenie *n* odzieży

val·id ['vælɪd] ważny (**for two weeks** na dwa tygodnie); uzasadniony; przekonujący; **be ~** też być ważny; **va·lid·i·ty** [və'lɪdətɪ] ważność *f*; *jur.* legalność *f*

va·lise [və'liːz] walizka *f*

val·ley ['vælɪ] dolina *f*

val·u·a·ble ['væljʊəbl] **1.** wartościowy; **2. ~s** *pl.* przedmioty *pl.* wartościowe

val·u·a·tion [vælju'eɪʃn] ocena *f*, oszacowanie *n*

val·ue ['væljuː] **1.** wartość *f*; **be of ~** mieć wartość (**to** dla *G*); **get ~ for money** nie przepłacić; **2.** *dom itp.* ⟨o⟩szacować, wyceniać ‹-nić›; *radę itp.* doceniać ‹-nić›; **~·ad·ded 'tax** *Brt. econ.* (*skrót:* **VAT**) podatek *m* od wartości dodanej, VAT *m*; **'~·less** bezwartościowy

valve [vælv] *tech.* zawór *m; anat.* zastawka *f; mus.* wentyl *m*

vam·pire ['væmpaɪə] wampir *m*

van [væn] furgonetka *f; Brt. rail. zamknięty* wagon *m* towarowy

van·dal ['vændl] wandal *m;* ~·is·m ['vændəlɪzəm] wandalizm *m;* ~·ize ['vændəlaɪz] ‹z›demolować

vane [veɪn] łopata *f (śmigła);* chorągiewka *f* kierunkowa

van·guard ['vænɡaːd] *mil.* straż *f* przednia

va·nil·la [və'nɪlə] wanilia *f; attr.* waniliowy

van·ish ['vænɪʃ] znikać ‹-knąć›

van·i·ty ['vænɪtɪ] próżność *f;* **~ bag**, **'~ case** kosmetyczka *f*

van·tage·point ['vaːntɪdʒpɔɪnt] punkt *m* widzenia

va·por·ize ['veɪpəraɪz] odparowywać ‹-ować›; parować

va·po(u)r ['veɪpə] para *f (wodna);* **'~ trail** *aviat.* smuga *f* kondensacyjna

var·i·|·a·ble ['veərɪəbl] **1.** zmienny; *fig.* nierówny; **2.** *math., phys.* zmienna *f (też fig.);* **~·ance** ['veərɪəns]: **be at ~ance with** znajdować się w sprzeczności; **~·ant** ['veərɪənt] **1.** odmienny; zmienny; **2.** wariant *m;* **~·a·tion** [veərɪ'eɪʃn] zmiana *f;* zmienność *f,* wahania *pl.; mus.* wariacja *f*

var·i·cose veins [værɪkəʊs 'veɪnz] *med. pl.* żylaki *pl.*

var·ied ['veərɪd] zróżnicowany

va·ri·e·ty [və'raɪətɪ] różnorodność *f; bot.* odmiana *f; econ.* wybór *m;* **for a ~ of reasons** dla licznych powodów; **~ show** przedstawienie *n* teatru rozmaitości; vari(t)s *n;* **~ thea·tre** teatr *m* rozmaitości; vari(t)s *n*

var·i·ous ['veərɪəs] różny

var·nish ['vaːnɪʃ] **1.** lakier *m;* **2.** ‹po›lakierować

var·si·ty team ['vaːsətɪ -] *Am.* (*w sporcie*) drużyna *f* uniwersytecka *lub* szkolna

var·y ['veərɪ] *v/i.* różnić się; zmieniać ‹-nić› się; **~ in size** różnić się wielkością; *v/t.* zmieniać ‹-nić›; ‹z›różnicować

vase [vaːz, *Am.* veɪs, veɪz] wazon *m*

vast [vaːst] ogromny; rozległy; **'~·ly** niezmiernie

vat [væt] kadź *f*

VAT [viː eɪ 'tiː, væt] *skrót:* **value-added tax** VAT *m,* podatek *m* od wartości dodanej

Vat·i·can Cit·y Watykan *m*

vau·de·ville ['vɔːdəvɪl] *Am.* wodewil *m; attr.* wodewilowy

vault[1] [vɔːlt] *arch.* sklepienie *n; też* **~s** *pl.* skarbiec *m;* krypta *f;* piwnica *f (na wino)*

vault[2] [vɔːlt] **1. ~ (over)** przeskakiwać ‹-skoczyć› nad (*I*); **2.** *zwł.* (*w sporcie*) skok *m;* **'~·ing horse** koń *m (do skoków);* **'~·ing pole** tyczka *f (do skoku o tyczce)*

VCR [viː siː 'aː] *skrót:* **video cassette recorder** magnetowid *m*

VDU [viː diː 'juː] *skrót:* **visual display unit** *komp.* monitor *m,* wyświetlacz *m*

veal [viːl] cielęcina *f; attr.* cielęcy; **~ chop** kotlet *m* cielęcy; **roast ~** pieczona cielęcina *f*

veer [vɪə] skręcać ‹-cić› nagle

vege·ta·ble ['vedʒtəbl] **1.** *zw.* **~s** *pl.* warzywo *n,* jarzyna *f;* **2.** warzywny; jarzynowy; roślinny

ve·ge·tar·i·an [vedʒɪ'teərɪən] **1.** wegetarianin *m (-anka f),* jarosz *m;* **2.** wegetariański; jarski

ve·ge|·tate ['vedʒɪteɪt] wegetować; **~·ta·tion** [vedʒɪ'teɪʃn] wegetacja *f*

ve·he|·mence ['viːɪməns] zawziętość *f;* gwałtowność *f;* **'~·ment** zawzięty, gwałtowny

ve·hi·cle ['viːɪkl] pojazd *m; fig.* medium *n*

veil [veɪl] **1.** welon *m;* woalka *f; fig.* zasłona *f;* **2.** skrywać ‹-ryć›

vein [veɪn] *anat., geol.* żyła *f; bot.* żyłka *f; fig.* ton *m*

ve·loc·i·ty [vɪ'lɒsətɪ] prędkość *f,* szybkość *f*

ve·lour(s) [və'lʊə] welur *m*

vel·vet ['velvɪt] aksamit; **~·y** aksamitny

vend·|er ['vendə] → **vendor; '~·ing machine** automat *m (do sprzedaży);* **'~·or** sprzedawca *m (-czyni f)* uliczny (-na)

ve·neer [və'nɪə] **1.** fornir *m; fig.* fasada *f;* **2.** fornirować

ven·e|·ra·ble ['venərəbl] czcigodny; **~·rate** ['venəreɪt] poważać; **~·ra·tion** [venə'reɪʃn] cześć *f,* poważanie *n,* głęboki szacunek *m*

V

vexed question

ve·ne·re·al dis·ease [vɪnɪərɪəl dɪ'ziːz] *med.* choroba *f* weneryczna

Ve·ne·tian [vɪ'niːʃn] **1.** wenecjanin *m* (-janka *f*); **2.** wenecki; **2 'blind** żaluzja *f*

ven·geance ['vendʒəns] zemsta *f*; **take ~ on** ⟨ze⟩mścić się na (*L*); **with a ~** F zajadle

ve·ni·al ['viːnjəl] *grzech itp.*: lekki

Ven·ice Wenecja *f*

ven·i·son ['venɪzn] dziczyzna *f*

ven·om ['venəm] *zo.* jad *m* (*też fig.*); **'~·ous** *med.* (*też fig.*)

ve·nous *med.* ['viːnəs] żylny

vent [vent] **1.** *v/t. fig.* gniew *itp.* wyładowywać ⟨-ować⟩ (**on** na *L*); **2.** otwór *m* wentylacyjny; (*w ubraniu*) rozcięcie *n*; **give ~ to** gniew wyładowywać ⟨-ować⟩ (*A*)

ven·ti|·late ['ventɪleɪt] wentylować; przewietrzać ⟨-rzyć⟩; **~·la·tion** [ventɪ'leɪʃn] wentylacja *f*; **~·la·tor** ['ventɪleɪtə] wywietrznik *m*

ven·tri·cle ['ventrɪkl] *anat.* komora *f* serca

ven·tril·o·quist [ven'trɪləkwɪst] brzuchomówca *m*

ven·ture ['ventʃə] **1.** *zwł. econ.* przedsięwzięcie *n*; *econ.* ryzyko *n*; → **joint venture**; **2.** przedsiębrać ⟨-ewziąć⟩; ⟨za⟩ryzykować

verb [vɜːb] *gr.* czasownik *m*; **~·al** ['vɜːbl] czasownikowy; werbalny

ver·dict ['vɜːdɪkt] *jur.* werdykt *m*, wyrok *m*; *fig.* sąd *m*; **bring in** *lub* **return a ~ of (not) guilty** wydawać ⟨-dać⟩ werdykt o winie (niewinności)

ver·di·gris ['vɜːdɪgrɪs] grynszpan *m*

verge [vɜːdʒ] **1.** brzeg *m*, krawędź *f* (*też fig.*); **be on the ~ of** być prawie gotowym na (*A*); **be on the ~ of despair (tears)** być na krawędzi rozpaczy (łez); **2. ~ on** *fig.* graniczyć z (*I*)

ver·i·fy ['verɪfaɪ] ⟨z⟩weryfikować; sprawdzać ⟨-dzić⟩, ⟨s⟩kontrolować

ver·i·ta·ble ['verɪtəbl] *święto, triumf itp.*: prawdziwy

ver·mi·cel·li [vɜːmɪ'selɪ] makaron *m* nitki

ver·mi·form ap·pen·dix [vɜːmɪfɔːm ə'pendɪks] *anat.* wyrostek *m* robaczkowy

ver·mil·i·on [və'mɪljən] **1.** cynobrowy; **2.** cynober *m*

ver·min ['vɜːmɪn] robactwo *n*; szkodniki *pl.*; **'~·ous** rojący się od robactwa

ver·nac·u·lar [və'nækjulə] język *m* miejscowy

ver·sa·tile ['vɜːsətaɪl] wszechstronny; uniwersalny

verse [vɜːs] wiersz *m*; wers *m*; strofa *f*

versed [vɜːst]: **be (well) ~ in** być dobrze zaznajomionym z (*I*)

ver·sion ['vɜːʃn] wersja *f*

ver·sus ['vɜːsəs] (*skrót: v., vs.*) *sport, jur.:* (na)przeciw (*G*)

ver·te|·bra ['vɜːtɪbrə] *anat.* (*pl.* **-brae** [-riː]) kręg *m*; **~·brate** ['vɜːtɪbreɪt] *zo.* kręgowiec *m*

ver·ti·cal ['vɜːtɪkl] pionowy, wertykalny

ver·ti·go ['vɜːtɪgəʊ] *med.* zawroty *pl.* głowy; **suffer from ~** cierpieć na zawroty głowy

verve [vɜːv] werwa *f*

ver·y ['verɪ] **1.** *adv.* bardzo; **I ~ much hope that** mam wielką nadzieję, że; **the ~ best things** same najlepsze rzeczy; **2.** *adj.* **the ~** właśnie ten; sam; **the ~ opposite** dokładne przeciwieństwo; **the ~ thing** właśnie to; **the ~ thought of** sama myśl o (*L*)

ves·i·cle ['vesɪkl] *med.* pęcherzyk *m*

ves·sel ['vesl] *anat., bot.* naczynie *n*; statek *m*

vest [vest] *Brt.* podkoszulka *f*, podkoszulek *m*; kamizelka *f* kuloodporna; *Am.* kamizelka *f*

ves·ti·bule ['vestɪbjuːl] westybul *m*, kruchta *f*

ves·tige ['vestɪdʒ] *fig.* ślad *m*

vest·ment ['vestmənt] ornat *m*

ves·try ['vestrɪ] *rel.* zakrystia *f*

vet¹ [vet] F weterynarz *m*

vet² [vet] *zwł. Brt.* F ⟨z⟩badać

vet³ [vet] *Am. mil.* kombatant *m*

vet·e·ran ['vetərən] **1.** *mil.* kombatant(ka *f*) *m*; weteran(ka *f*) *m*; **2.** zaprawiony; doświadczony; **'~ car** *Brt. mot.* stary samochód *m* (*sprzed 1919 roku*)

vet·e·ri·nar·i·an [vetərɪ'neərɪən] *Am.* weterynarz *m*

vet·e·ri·na·ry ['vetərɪnərɪ] weterynaryjny; **~ 'sur·geon** *Brt.* weterynarz *m*

ve·to ['viːtəʊ] **1.** (*pl.* **-toes**) weto *n*; **2.** ⟨za⟩wetować

vexed ques·tion [vekst 'kwestʃən] pytanie *n* pozostające bez odpowiedzi

V

VHF [viː eɪtʃ 'ef] *skrót*: **very high frequency** UKF *m*, fale *pl.* ultrakrótkie

vi·a ['vaɪə] poprzez (*A*)

vi·a·duct ['vaɪədʌkt] wiadukt *m*

vi·al ['vaɪəl] próbówka *f*

vibes [vaɪbz] F *pl.* wibracje *pl.*, atmosfera *f* (*miejsca*)

vi·brant ['vaɪbrənt] *barwa*: żywy; energiczny; *głos*: donośny; rozedrgany (**with** od *G*)

vi·brate [vaɪ'breɪt] *v/i.* wibrować; *powietrze*: drżeć; *fig.* tętnić; *v/t.* wprawiać ⟨-wić⟩ w drganie; **vi·bra·tion** [vaɪ'breɪʃn] wibracja *f*; drganie *n*; **~s** *pl.* F atmosfera *f* (*miejsca*)

vic·ar ['vɪkə] *rel.* (*w kościele protestanckim*) pastor *m*; (*w kościele protestanckim*) wikariusz *m*; **~·age** ['vɪkərɪdʒ] plebania *f*

vice[1] [vaɪs] przywara *f*, wada *f*

vice[2] [vaɪs] *zwł. Brt. tech.* imadło *n*

vi·ce... [vaɪs] wice..., zastępca (*G*)

'vice squad wydział *m* obyczajowy (*policji*); wydział *m* służb antynarkotykowych

vi·ce ver·sa [vaɪsɪ'vɜːsə] **and ~** i vice versa; i na odwrót

vi·cin·i·ty [vɪ'sɪnətɪ] bliskość *f*; pobliże *n*

vi·cious ['vɪʃəs] brutalny; zły

vi·cis·si·tudes [vɪ'sɪsɪtjuːdz] *pl.* koleje *pl.* losu

vic·tim ['vɪktɪm] ofiara *f*; **~·ize** ['vɪktɪmaɪz] dyskryminować

vic·to|·ri·ous [vɪk'tɔːrɪəs] zwycięski; **~·ry** ['vɪktərɪ] zwycięstwo *n*

vid·e·o ['vɪdɪəʊ] **1.** (*pl. -os*) wideo *n*; kaseta *f* wideo; F taśma *f* wideo; *zwł. Brt.* wideo *n*, magnetowid *m*; **on ~** na wideo; **2.** *zwł. Brt.* nakręcać ⟨-cić⟩ na wideo; **'~ cam·er·a** kamera *f* wideo; **~ cas'sette** kaseta *f* wideo; **~ cas'sette re·cor·der → video recorder**; **'~ clip** wideoklip *m*, teledysk *m*; **~·disc** płyta *f* wizyjna; **'~ game** gra *f* wideo; **'~ li·bra·ry** wideoteka *f*; **'~ re·cord·er** magnetowid *m*, wideo *n*; **'~ re·cord·ing** nagranie *n* wideo; **'~ shop** *Brt.*; **'~ store** *Am.* sklep z kasetami wideo; **~·tape 1.** kaseta *f* wideo; taśma *f* wideo; **2.** nagrywać ⟨-rać⟩ na wideo; **'~·text** *Am.* teletekst *m*

vie [vaɪ] rywalizować (**with** z *I*)

Vi·en·na Wiedeń *m*

Vi·en·nese [vɪə'niːz] **1.** wiedeńczyk *m* (-denka *f*); **2.** wiedeński

view [vjuː] **1.** widok *m*; spojrzenie *n* (**of** na *A*); pogląd *m* (**about, on** w sprawie *G*); *fig.* orientacja *f*; **a room with a ~** pokój z (*dobrym*) widokiem; **be on ~** być wystawionym na pokaz; **be hidden from ~** nie być widocznym; **come into ~** stać się widocznym; **in full ~ of** *fig.* na oczach *G*; **in ~ of** *fig.* ze względu na (*A*); **in my ~** moim zdaniem; **keep in ~** coś mieć na uwadze; **with a ~ to** *fig.* z zamiarem (*G*); **2.** *v/t. dom itp.* oglądać ⟨obejrzeć⟩; *fig.* oceniać⟨-nić⟩ (**as** jako); zapatrywać się na (*A*) (**with** z *I*); *v/i.* oglądać telewizję; **'~ da·ta** *pl.* teletekst *m*, telegazeta *f*; **'~·er** widz *m*; **'~·find·er** dalmierz *m*; **'~·point** punkt *m* widzenia

vig|·il ['vɪdʒɪl] *nocne* czuwanie *n*; **~·i·lance** ['vɪdʒɪləns] czujność *f*; **'~·i·lant** czujny

vig|·or·ous ['vɪɡərəs] energiczny; pełen wigoru; **~·o(u)r** ['vɪɡə] wigor *m*; sprawność *f*

Vi·king ['vaɪkɪŋ] wiking *m*

vile [vaɪl] nikczemny, niegodziwy; F okropny

vil|·lage ['vɪlɪdʒ] wieś *m*, wioska *f*; *attr.* wiejski; **~·lage green** *Brt.* łąka *f* (*wspólna dla całej wioski*); **'~·lag·er** mieszkaniec *m* (-nka *f*) wsi

vil·lain ['vɪlən] łotr *m*, niegodziwiec *m*; czarny charakter *m*; *Brt.* F złoczyńca *m*

vin·di·cate ['vɪndɪkeɪt] ⟨z⟩rehabilitować

vin·dic·tive [vɪn'dɪktɪv] mściwy

vine [vaɪn] *bot.* winorośl *f*; △ *nie* **wino**

vin·e·gar ['vɪnɪɡə] ocet *m*

'vine|·grow·er hodowca *m* winorośli; **~·yard** ['vɪnjəd] winnica *f*

vin·tage ['vɪntɪdʒ] **1.** rocznik *m* (*wina*); winobranie *n*; **2.** *wino*: z dobrego rocznika; *film*: klasyczny; *okres*: znakomity; **a 1994 ~** rocznik 1994; **'~ car** *zwł. Brt. mot.* stary samochód *m* (*produkcja 1919-1930*)

vi·o·la [vɪ'əʊlə] *mus.* altówka *f*

vi·o|·late ['vaɪəleɪt] *umowę itp.* pogwałcić; ⟨z⟩łamać; *grób* ⟨z⟩bezcześcić; *ciszę* zakłócać ⟨-cić⟩; *granice itp.* naruszać ⟨-szyć⟩; **~·la·tion** [vaɪə'leɪʃn] naruszenie *n*; pogwałcenie *n*; zbezczeszczenie *n*

vi·o|·lence ['vaɪələns] gwałtowność *f*; przemoc *f*, gwałt *m*; '**~·lent** gwałtowny

vi·o·let ['vaɪələt] **1.** *bot.* fiołek *m*; **2.** fioletowy

vi·o·lin [vaɪə'lɪn] *mus.* skrzypce *pl.*; **~·ist** [vaɪə'lɪnɪst] *mus.* skrzypek *m* (-paczka *f*)

VIP [viː aɪ 'piː] *skrót:* ***very important person*** VIP *m*, ważna osobistość *f*; ~ **lounge** pomieszczenie *n* dla ważnych osobistości

vi·per ['vaɪpə] *zo.* żmija *f*

vir·gin ['vɜːdʒɪn] **1.** dziewica *f*; **2.** dziewiczy; **~·i·ty** [vəˈdʒɪnətɪ] dziewictwo *n*

Vir·go ['vɜːɡəʊ] (*pl.* **-gos**) znak Zodiaku: Panna *f*; *he/she is* (*a*) ~ on(a) jest spod znaku Panny

vir·ile ['vɪraɪl] męski; **vi·ril·i·ty** [vɪˈrɪlətɪ] męskość *f*

vir·tu·al ['vɜːtʃʊəl] faktyczny; *komp.* wirtualny; '**~·ly** faktycznie, praktycznie; ~ **re'al·i·ty** rzeczywistość *f* wirtualna

vir|·tue ['vɜːtʃuː] cnota *f*; zaleta; *by lub in ~tue of* z mocy (*G*), z tytułu (*G*); *make a ~tue of necessity* robić cnotę z konieczności; **~·tu·ous** ['vɜːtʃʊəs] cnotliwy

vir·u·lent ['vɪrʊlənt] *med.* zjadliwy (*też fig.*)

vi·rus ['vaɪərəs] wirus *m*; *attr.* wirusowy

vi·sa ['viːzə] wiza *f*; **~ed** ['viːzəd] opatrzony wizą

vis·cose ['vɪskəʊz, 'vɪskəʊs] wiskoza *f*; *attr.* wiskozowy

vis·cous ['vɪskəs] lepki

vise [vaɪs] *Am. tech.* imadło *n*

vis·i|·bil·i·ty [vɪzɪˈbɪlətɪ] widoczność *f*; **~·ble** ['vɪzəbl] widoczny; wyraźny

vi·sion ['vɪʒn] wizja *f*; wzrok *m*; widzenie *n*; **~·a·ry** ['vɪʒnrɪ] **1.** wizjonerski; **2.** wizjoner(ka *f*) *m*

vis·it ['vɪzɪt] **1.** *v/t.* odwiedzać ⟨-dzić⟩; *zabytek* zwiedzać ⟨-dzić⟩; wizytować; *v/i. be ~ing* być z wizytą (*Am.:* with u *G*); **~ with** *Am.* ucinać ⟨-ciąć⟩ pogawędkę; **2.** odwiedziny *pl.*, wizyta *f* (*to* w *L*); *Am.* pogawędka *f*; *for lub on a ~* z wizytą; *have a ~* from mieć wizytę ze strony (*G*); *pay a ~ to* składać ⟨złożyć⟩ wizytę (*D*); △ *nie odwiedziny w szpitalu*

vis·i·ta·tion [vɪzɪ'teɪʃn] wizytacja *f*; inspekcja *f*

'vis·it·ing hours *pl.* godziny *pl.* odwiedzin

'vis·it·or gość *m*, odwiedzający *m* (-ca *f*)

vi·sor ['vaɪzə] osłona *f* (*hełmu*); *mot.* osłona *f* przeciwsłoneczna; przyłbica *f*

vis·u·al ['vɪzjʊəl] wizualny; wzrokowy; ~ **'aids** *pl.*: wizualne pomoce *pl.* naukowe; ~ **dis'play u·nit** *komp.* monitor *m*; ~ **in'struc·tion** (*nauka f z wykorzystaniem wizualnych pomocy naukowych*); **~·ize** ['vɪzjʊəlaɪz] przedstawiać sobie, wyobrażać ⟨-zić⟩ sobie

vi·tal ['vaɪtl] istotny, zasadniczy; życiowy; *organ:* ważny dla życia; *ktoś:* żywotny, pełen życia; *of ~ importance* o zasadniczym znaczeniu; **~·i·ty** [vaɪ'tælətɪ] witalność *f*

vit·a·min ['vɪtəmɪn] witamina *f*; *attr.* witaminowy; ~ **de'fi·cien·cy** niedobór *m* witamin

vit·re·ous ['vɪtrɪəs] szklisty

vi·va·cious [vɪ'veɪʃəs] pełen temperamentu, żywiołowy

viv·id ['vɪvɪd] *światło, kolor:* jaskrawy; *opis:* żywy; *wyobraźnia:* bujny

vix·en ['vɪksn] *zo.* lisica *f*

viz. [vɪz] *skrót: namely* (*łacińskie videlicet*) mianowicie

V-neck ['viːnek] (*wycięcie ubrania*) szpic *m*; '**V-necked** wycięty w szpic

vo·cab·u·la·ry [vəˈkæbjʊlərɪ] słownictwo *n*

vo·cal ['vəʊkl] *mus.* wokalny; głosowy; *F* donośny; ~ **cords** *anat. pl.* struny *pl.* głosowe; **~·ist** ['vəʊkəlɪst] wokalista *m* (-tka *f*); '**~·s:** ~ *XY* śpiew XY

vo·ca·tion [vəʊ'keɪʃn] powołanie *n* (*for* do *G*)

vo·ca·tion·al [vəʊ'keɪʃənl] zawodowy; ~ **ed·u·ca·tion** wykształcenie *n* zawodowe; ~ **'guid·ance** poradnictwo *n* zawodowe; ~ **'train·ing** szkolenie *n* zawodowe

vogue [vəʊɡ] moda *f*; *be in* ~ być modnym, być w modzie

voice [vɔɪs] **1.** głos *m*; *active* ~ *gr.* strona *f* czynna; *passive* ~ *gr.* strona *f* bierna; **2.** wygłaszać ⟨-łosić⟩, wyrażać ⟨-razić⟩; **~d** *ling.* dźwięczny; '**~·less** *ling.* bezdźwięczny

void [vɔɪd] **1.** pusty; pozbawiony; *jur.* nieważny; **2.** pustka *f*

vol [vɒl] (*pl.* **vols**) *skrót: volume* vol., wolumin *m*, tom *m*

vol·a·tile ['vɒlətaɪl] pobudliwy, choleryczny; *chem.* ulotny

vol·ca·no [vɒl'keɪnəʊ] (*pl.* **-noes, -nos**) wulkan *n*

Vol·ga Wołga *f*

vol·ley ['vɒlɪ] **1.** salwa *f*; *fig.* (*wyzwisk*) grad *m*; (*w tenisie, piłce nożnej*) wolej *m*; **2.** *piłkę* odbijać ⟨-bić⟩ wolejem *lub* z woleja (*into the net* w siatkę); '~·**ball** (*w sporcie*) siatkówka *f*

volt [vəʊlt] *electr.* wolt *m*; ~·**age** ['vəʊltɪdʒ] *electr.* napięcie *n*

vol·u·ble ['vɒljʊbl] gadatliwy; *wymówka itp.*: przegadany

vol·ume ['vɒljuːm] objętość *f*; wolumen *m* (*handlu itp.*); wolumin *m*, tom *m*; głośność *f*, głos *m*; ~·**lu·mi·nous** [və'luːmɪnəs] *ubranie*: obszerny; *walizka*: pakowny; *pisarz*: płodny

vol·un·ta·ry ['vɒləntərɪ] ochotniczy

vol·un·teer [vɒlən'tɪə] **1.** *v/i.* zgłaszać ⟨-łosić⟩ się na ochotnika (*for* do *G*); *v/t. pomoc itp.* zgłaszać ⟨-łosić⟩ dobrowolnie; **2.** ochotnik *m* (-niczka *f*)

vo·lup·tu·ous [və'lʌptʃʊəs] *usta*: zmysłowy; *kształt*: pełny, krągły

vom·it ['vɒmɪt] **1.** ⟨z⟩wymiotować; **2.** wymiociny *pl.*

vo·ra·cious [və'reɪʃəs] *apetyt*: nienasycony

vote [vəʊt] **1.** głosowanie *n* (*about, on* na *A*); głos *m*; *też* ~**s** prawo *n* głosowania; ~ *of no confidence* wotum *n* nieufności; *take a ~ on s.th.* poddawać ⟨-ddać⟩ coś głosowaniu; **2.** *v/i.* głosować (*for* na *A*, *against* przeciw *D*); ~ *on* poddawać ⟨-ddać⟩ coś głosowaniu; *v/t.* wybierać ⟨-brać⟩; ~ *out of office* pozbawiać ⟨-wić⟩ urzędu przez głosowanie; '**vot·er** wyborca *m*; '**vot·ing booth** kabina *f* wyborcza

vouch [vaʊtʃ]: ~ *for* ⟨za⟩ręczyć za (*A*); '~·**er** kupon *m*, talon *m*; kwit *m*, rachunek *m*

vow [vaʊ] **1.** przyrzeczenie *n*; *take a ~*, *make a ~* przyrzekać ⟨-rzec⟩; **2.** przyrzekać ⟨-rzec⟩ (*to do s.th.* zrobić coś)

vow·el ['vaʊəl] *gr.* samogłoska *f*

voy·age ['vɔɪdʒ] podróż *f*, rejs *m*

vs. *Am. skrót pisany:* *against* (*łacińskie **versus**) zwł. sport, jur.:* przeciw(ko)

vul·gar ['vʌlgə] wulgarny; ordynarny; pospolity

vul·ne·ra·ble ['vʌlnərəbl] *fig.* łatwy do zranienia; wrażliwy; nieodporny (*to* na *A*)

vul·ture ['vʌltʃə] *zo.* sęp *m*

vy·ing ['vaɪɪŋ] → *vie*

W

W, w ['dʌblju:] W, w *n*

W *skrót pisany:* *west* zach., zachód *m*, zachodni; *west(ern)* zachodni; *watt(s)* W, wat(y *pl*) *m*

wad [wɒd] tampon *m* (*waty*); zwitek *m* (*banknotów*); zwój *m* (*papieru*); ~·**ding** ['wɒdɪŋ] wyściółka *f*; *med.* podściółka *f*

wad·dle ['wɒdl] człapać

wade [weɪd] *v/i.* brodzić; ~ *through* przechodzić ⟨-ejść⟩ w bród; F ⟨prze⟩brnąć; *v/t.* przechodzić ⟨-ejść⟩ w bród

wa·fer ['weɪfə] wafel *m* (*zwł. do lodów*); *rel.* opłatek *m*

waf·fle[1] ['wɒfl] wafel *m*

waf·fle[2] ['wɒfl] *Brt.* F nudzić

waft [wɑːft] *v/i.* unosić się; *v/t.* unosić ⟨unieść⟩

wag [wæg] **1.** (*-gg-*) ⟨po⟩machać; ⟨za⟩merdać; **2.** *with a ~ of its tail* machnięciem ogona

wage[1] [weɪdʒ] *zw.* ~**s** *pl.* pensja *f*, wypłata *f* (*zwł. robotnika*)

wage[2] [weɪdʒ]: ~ (*a*) *war against lub on mil.* toczyć wojnę przeciw (*D*) *lub* wobec (*G*) (*też fig.*)

'wage| earn·er żywiciel(ka *f*) rodziny; '~ *freeze* zamrożenie *n* płac; '~ *ne·go·ti·a·tions pl.* negocjacje *pl.* płacowe; '~ *pack·et* wypłata *f*; '~ *rise* podwyżka *f* pensji

wa·ger ['weɪdʒə] zakład *m*

wag·gle ['wægl] F ruszać (się)

wag·gon *Brt.*, **wag·on** *Am.* ['wægən] wóz *m*; *Brt. rail.* otwarty wagon *m* towarowy; *Am.* wózek *m* (*z napojami* *itp.*); ⚠ *nie* **wagon**

wag·tail ['wægteɪl] *zo.* pliszka *f*

wail [weɪl] **1.** *ktoś, wiatr:* zawodzić; *syrena:* ⟨za⟩wyć; **2.** zawodzenie *n;* wycie *n*

wain·scot ['weɪnskət] boazeria *f*

waist [weɪst] talia *f,* kibić *f;* ~·**coat** *zw. Brt.* ['weɪskəut] kamizelka *f;* '~·**line** talia *f*

wait [weɪt] **1.** *v/i.* ⟨po⟩czekać (*for* na A), oczekiwać (*for G lub* na A); *keep s.o.* ~*ing* kazać komuś czekać; ~ *and see!* tylko poczekaj!; ~ *at* (*Am. on*) *table* podawać ⟨-dać⟩ do stołu; ~ *on s.o.* obsługiwać ⟨-łużyć⟩ kogoś; ~ *up* F nie kłaść ⟨położyć⟩ się spać; *v/t.* ~ *one's chance* czekać na swoją szansę (*to do s.th.* zrobienia czegoś); ~ *one's turn* czekać na swoją kolej; **2.** oczekiwanie *n; have a long* ~ musieć długo czekać; *lie in* ~ *for s.o.* czekać w zasadzce na kogoś; '~·**er** kelner *m;* ~**er, the bill** (*Am. check*)! proszę o rachunek!

'**wait·ing** oczekiwanie *n; no* ~ (*na znaku*) zakaz postoju; '~ **list** lista *f* oczekujących; '~ **room** poczekalnia *f*

wait·ress ['weɪtrɪs] kelnerka *f;* ~**, the bill** (*Am. check*)! proszę o rachunek!

wake¹ [weɪk] (*woke lub waked, woken lub waked*) *v/i.* też ~ *up* ⟨o⟩budzić się; *v/t.* ~ *up* ⟨o⟩budzić

wake² [weɪk] *naut.* kilwater *m; follow in the* ~ *of fig.* podążać ⟨-żyć⟩ czymś śladem

wake·ful ['weɪkfl] bezsenny; mało śpiący

wak·en ['weɪkən] *v/i.* też ~ *up* ⟨o⟩budzić się; *v/t.* ~ *up* ⟨o⟩budzić

Wales Walia *f*

walk [wɔ:k] **1.** *v/i.* iść, chodzić ⟨pójść⟩; spacerować; *v/t.* chodzić po (*L*) (*ulicach*); przechodzić ⟨przejść⟩ pieszo, odprowadzać ⟨-dzić⟩ (*to do G, home* do domu); *psa* wyprowadzać ⟨-dzić⟩ (*na spacer*); ~ *away* → ~ *off*; ~ *off* odchodzić ⟨odejść⟩; ~ *off with* F buchnąć; F *nagrodę* łatwo zdobywać ⟨-być⟩; ~ *out* wychodzić ⟨wyjść⟩; opuszczać ⟨opuścić⟩ salę (*na znak protestu*); *econ.* ⟨za⟩strajkować; ~ *out on s.o.* F porzucać ⟨-cić⟩ kogoś; ~ *up* podchodzić ⟨-dejść⟩; **2.** chód *m;* spacer *m;* przechadzka *f;* trasa *f* spacerowa; ścieżka *f;* przejście *n; go for a* ~, *take a* ~ iść ⟨pójść⟩ na spacer; *it's half an hour's* ~ *from here* stąd jest pół godziny spa-

cerem; *from all* ~*s* (*lub every* ~) *of life* ludzie: z wszystkich grup społecznych; '~·**er** spacerowicz *m;* (*w sporcie*) chodziarz *m; be a good* ~**er** być dobrym piechurem

walk·ie-talk·ie [ˌwɔːkɪ'tɔːkɪ] walkie-talkie *n,* krótkofalówka *f*

'**walk·ing** chodzenie *n;* spacery *pl.;* wycieczki *pl.;* '~ **pa·pers** *pl.: give s.o. his/her* ~ *papers Am.* F posłać kogoś na zieloną trawkę; '~ **shoes** *pl.* buty *pl.* turystyczne; '~ **stick** laska *f;* '~ **tour** wycieczka *f* piesza

'**Walk·man** *TM* (*pl. -mans*) walkman *m TM*

'**walk·out** demonstracyjne opuszczenie *n* konferencji; *econ.* strajk *m;* '~·**over** *sport:* walkower *m;* F łatwe zwycięstwo *n;* '~·**up** *Am.* F budynek *m* bez windy

wall [wɔːl] **1.** ściana *f;* mur *m;* **2.** *też* ~ *in* otaczać ⟨-toczyć⟩ murem; ~ *up* zamurowywać ⟨-ować⟩; '~·**chart** plansza *f* ścienna

wal·let ['wɒlɪt] portfel *m*

'**wall·flow·er** *fig.* F osoba *f* nie uczestnicząca w tańcach

wal·lop ['wɒləp] F ⟨przy⟩lać; (*w sporcie*) położyć na obie łopatki, pobić (*at w L*)

wal·low ['wɒləu] ⟨wy⟩tarzać się; *fig.* pogrążać ⟨-żyć⟩ się (*in w L*)

'**wall**|·**pa·per 1.** tapeta *f;* **2.** ⟨wy⟩tapetować; ~·**to-**'~ ~**to-wall carpet(ing)** wykładzina *f* podłogowa

wal·nut ['wɔːlnʌt] *bot.* orzech *m* włoski

wal·rus ['wɔːlrəs] *zo.* (*pl. -ruses, -rus*) mors *m*

waltz [wɔːls] **1.** walc *m;* **2.** ⟨za⟩tańczyć walca, walcować

wand [wɒnd] pałeczka *f* czarodziejska, różdżka *f*

wan·der ['wɒndə] wędrować, ⟨za⟩błąkać się; zbaczać ⟨-boczyć⟩; *fig.* fantazjować

wane [weɪn] **1.** ⟨z⟩maleć, zmniejszać się; zanikać ⟨-knąć⟩; ubywać (*o księżycu*); **2.** *be on the* ~ maleć

wan·gle ['wæŋgl] F wydostawać ⟨-tać⟩; ~ *s.th. out of s.o.* wycisnąć coś z kogoś; ~ *one's way out of* wykręcać ⟨-cić⟩ się z (*G*)

want [wɒnt] **1.** *v/t.* chcieć (*G*); potrzebować; F wymagać; *be* ~*ed* być poszukiwanym (*for* za A) (*przez policję*); *v/i.*

W

he does not ~ for anything nie brak mu niczego; **2.** brak *m*; potrzeba *f*; niedostatek *m*; **be in ~ of** wymagać (*G*); *'~ ad* *zwł. Am.* drobne ogłoszenie *n*; *'~ed* poszukiwany

wan·ton ['wɒntən] lubieżny, rozpustny

war [wɔ:] wojna *f* (*też fig.*); *fig.* walka *f* (*against* przeciwko *D*)

war·ble ['wɔ:bl] (za)ćwierkać

ward [wɔ:d] **1.** *med.* oddział *m*; *Brt. pol.* okręg *m* policyjny; *jur.* podopieczny *m* (-na *f*) (*pod kuratelą*); **2.** *~ off* uderzenie odpierać (-deprzeć); *chorobie itp.* zapobiegać (-biec); *duchy itp.* odganiać (-gonić); **war·den** ['wɔ:dn] opiekun- (ka *f*) *m*; nadzorca *m*; kustosz *m*; kurator *m*; *Am.* naczelnik *m* więzienia; *~er Brt.* ['wɔ:də] strażnik *m* (-niczka *f*) więzienny (-na)

war·drobe ['wɔ:drəʊb] szafa *f*; garderoba *f*

ware [weə] *w złożeniach* naczynia *pl.*, wyroby *pl.*

'ware·house skład *m* (*hurtowy*)

war·|fare ['wɔ:feə] wojna *f*, działania *pl.* wojenne; *'~head mil.* głowica *f* bojowa; *'~like* bojowy

warm [wɔ:m] **1.** *adj.* ciepły (*też fig. barwy, głos, przyjęcie*); *I am ~, I feel ~* ciepło mi; **2.** *też ~ up* ogrzewać (-rzać) (się); **3.** *come into the ~! zwł. Brt.* chodź do ciepła!; *~th* [wɔ:mθ] ciepło *n*; *'~-up* (*w sporcie*) rozgrzewka *f*

warn [wɔ:n] ostrzegać (-rzec) (*against, of* przeciwko *D*); *~* przeciw ostrzeżenie *n* (*of* o *L*); *'~ing sig·nal* sygnał *m* ostrzegawczy

warp [wɔ:p] (wy-, s)paczyć się

war·rant ['wɒrənt] **1.** *jur.* sądowy nakaz *m* (*rewizji itp.*); → *death ~;* **2.** uzasadniać (-nić), usprawiedliwiać; *~ of ar'rest jur.* nakaz *m* aresztowania

war·ran·ty ['wɒrəntɪ] *econ.* gwarancja *f*; *it's still under ~* nadal jest na gwarancji

war·ri·or ['wɒrɪə] wojownik *m* (-niczka *f*)

War·saw Warszawa *f*

'war·ship okręt *m*

wart [wɔ:t] brodawka *f*

war·y ['weərɪ] (*-ier, -iest*) nieufny

was [wɒz, wəz] *ja* byłem, *ja* byłam, *on* był, *ona* była, *ono* było

wash [wɒʃ] **1.** *v/t.* (u)myć; (wy)prać;

v/i. (u)myć się; *~ up v/i. Brt.* zmywać (-myć) naczynia; *v/t.* wyrzucać (-cić) coś na brzeg; **2.** umycie *n*; pranie *n*; *be in the ~* być w praniu; *give s.th. a ~* wyprać coś, umyć coś; *have a ~* (u)myć się; *'~·a·ble* mogący być prany; zmywalny; *'~-and-'wear* nie wymagający prasowania; *'~·ba·sin, '~·bowl Am.* umywalka *f*; *'~·cloth Am.* myjka *f*; *'~·er Am.* pralka *f*; → *dishwasher, tech.* podkładka *f*; *tech.* uszczelka *f*; *'~ing* pranie *n*; mycie *n*; *'~ing ma·chine* pralka *f*; *'~ing pow·der* proszek *m* do prania

Wash·ing·ton Waszyngton *m*

wash·ing-'up *Brt.* zmywanie *n* naczyń; *do the ~* zmywać naczynia; *'~·rag Am.* ścierka *f* do zmywania; *'~·room Am.* toaleta *f*

wasp [wɒsp] *zo.* osa *f*

WASP [wɒsp] *skrót: White Anglo-Saxon Protestant* (*biały Amerykanin, protestant, pochodzenia anglosaskiego*)

waste [weɪst] **1.** marnotrawstwo *n*; marnowanie *n*; strata *f*; odpady *pl.*, odpadki *pl.*; *~ of time* strata *f* czasu; *hazardous ~* niebezpieczne odpady *pl.*; **2.** *v/t.* (z)marnować, (s)tracić; *ciało itp.* wyniszczać (-czyć); *v/i. ~ away* (z)marnieć; **3.** *produkt:* odpadowy; *ziemia:* jałowy, leżący odłogiem; *lay ~* (s)pustoszyć; *~ dis·pos·al* usuwanie *n* odpadków; *~ dis·pos·al 'site* składowisko *n* śmieci; *'~·ful* marnotrawny; rozrzutny; *'~ gas zo.* gazy *pl.* odlotowe; *~ 'pa·per* makulatura *f*; *~·'pa·per bas·ket* kosz *m* na śmieci; *'~ pipe* rura *f* ściekowa

watch [wɒtʃ] **1.** *v/i.* patrzeć, przyglądać się, obserwować; *~ for* oczekiwać (*G*); *~ out!* uwaga!; *~ out for* uważać na (*A*); wyglądać (*G*); *v/t.* oglądać (obejrzeć); przyglądać się → *television;* **2.** zegarek *m* (*naręczny*); wachta *f*; *be on the ~ for* mieć się na baczności przed (*I*); *keep (a) careful lub close ~ on* obserwować bacznie (*A*); *'~·dog* pies *m* podwórzowy; *'~·ful* baczny; *'~·ma·k·er* zegarmistrz *m*; *'~·man* (*pl. -men*) dozorca *m* (-czyni *f*)

wa·ter ['wɔ:tə] **1.** woda *f*; **2.** *v/t.* kwiaty podlewać (-lać); *bydło* (na)poić; *~ down* rozwadniać (-wodnić) (*też fig*); *make s.o.'s mouth ~* sprawiać, że komuś ślinka ciecknie; '~ **bird** *zo.* ptak *m* wodny; '~**col·o(u)r** akwarela *f*; '~**course** tor *m* wodny; '~**cress** *bot.* rzeżucha *f*; '~**fall** wodospad *m*; '~**front** nabrzeże *n*; '~**hole** wodopój *m*

wa·ter·ing can ['wɔːtərɪŋ -] konewka *f*

'**wa·ter| jump** (*w sporcie*) przeszkoda *f* wodna; '~ **lev·el** poziom *m* wody; '~ **lil·y** *bot.* lilia *f* wodna; '~**mark** znak *m* wodny; '~**mel·on** *bot.* arbuz *m*; '~ **pol·lu·tion** zanieczyszczenie *n* wody; '~ **po·lo** (*w sporcie*) piłka *f* wodna; '~**proof 1.** wodoszczelny; **2.** *Brt.* płaszcz *m* przeciwdeszczowy; **3.** ⟨za⟩impregnować; '~**s** *pl.* wody *pl.*; woda *f*; '~**shed** *geogr.* dział *m* wodny; *fig.* punkt *m* zwrotny; '~**side** nabrzeże *n*; '~ **ski·ing** *sport*: narciarstwo *n* wodne; '~**tight** wodoszczelny; *fig.* niepodważalny; '~**way** magistrala *f* wodna; '~**works** *często sg.* wodociąg *m*; ~**y** ['wɔːtərɪ] wodnisty, rozwodniony

watt [wɔt] *electr.* (*skrót:* **W**) wat *m*

wave [weɪv] **1.** *v/t.* ⟨po⟩machać (*I*); *flagą* powiewać (*I*); *włosy* ⟨za⟩kręcić; ~ **one's hand** pomachać ręką; ~ **s.o. goodbye** pomachać na pożegnanie; *v/i.* falować; *włosy*: kręcić się; ~ **at s.o.**, ~ **to s.o.** ⟨po⟩machać do kogoś; **2.** fala *f* (*też fig.*); pomachanie *n*; '~**length** *phys.* długość *f* fali

wa·ver ['weɪvə] ⟨za⟩wahać się; *płomień*: ⟨za⟩migotać; *głos*: ⟨za⟩drżeć

wav·y ['weɪvɪ] (*-ier, -iest*) falisty, pofalowany

wax¹ [wæks] **1.** wosk *m*; woskowina *f*; **2.** ⟨na⟩woskować; ⟨wy⟩pastować

wax² [wæks] *księżyc*: przybywać

wax·en ['wæksən] woskowy; nawoskowany; biały, blady; '~**works** *sg.* gabinet *m* figur woskowych; ~**y** ['wæksɪ] (*-ier, -iest*) blady, biały

way [weɪ] **1.** droga *f*; trasa *f*; kierunek *m*; przejście *n*; przejazd *m*; sposób *m*; zwyczaj *m*; ~**s and means** *pl.* środki *pl.*, sposoby *pl.*; **by ~ back** droga *f* powrotna; ~ **home** droga *f* do domu; ~ **in** wejście *n*; ~ **out** wyjście *n*; **be on the ~ to**, **be on one's ~ to** być w drodze do (*G*); **by ~ of** przez (*A*); *Brt.* zamiast (*G*); **by the ~** przy sposobności; **give ~** ustępować (*-tąpić*) drogi; **in a ~** w jakiś sposób; **in no ~** w żaden sposób; **lead the ~** prowadzić; **let s.o. have his/her**

(*own*) ~ dawać komuś postępować według jego woli; **lose one's ~** ⟨z⟩gubić się; **make ~** ustępować ⟨-tąpić⟩ miejsca; **no ~** F aleź skąd; w ogóle nie; **out of the ~** niezwykły, niespotykany; **this ~** tędy; **2.** *adv.* daleko; '~**bill** list *m* przewozowy; '~**lay** (*-laid*) zasadzać się ⟨-dzić⟩ się (*s.o.* na kogoś); ~**ward** ['weɪwəd] samowolny

we [wiː, wɪ] my *pl.*

weak [wiːk] słaby (*też at, in* w *L*); '~**en** *v/t.* osłabiać ⟨-bić⟩ (*też fig.*); *v/i.* ⟨o⟩słabnąć; ustępować ⟨-tąpić⟩; '~**ling** słabeusz *m*; '~**ness** słabość *f*

weal [wiːl] ślad *m* (*jak po uderzeniu batem*)

wealth [welθ] bogactwo *n*, majątek *m*; *fig.* obfitość *f*; '~**y** (*-ier, -iest*) bogaty, majętny

wean [wiːn] *dziecko* odstawiać ⟨-wić⟩ od piersi; ~ **s.o. from** *lub* **off s.th.** odzwyczajać ⟨-czaić⟩ kogoś od czegoś

weap·on ['wepən] broń *f*

wear [weə] **1.** (*wore, worn*) *v/t.* nosić; mieć na sobie; ubierać się w (*A*); wycierać ⟨wytrzeć⟩; ~ **the trousers** (*Am. pants*) F być głową rodziny; ~ **an angry expression** przybrać gniewny wyraz twarzy; *v/i.* wycierać ⟨wytrzeć⟩ się; zużywać ⟨zużyć⟩ się; trzymać się (*dobrze itp.*); **s.th.** to ~ coś do ubrania; ~ **away** wycierać ⟨wytrzeć⟩ się; ~ **down** ścierać ⟨zetrzeć⟩; *opór itp.* ⟨z⟩łamać; ~ **off** ⟨ze⟩lżeć; ~ **on** ciągnąć się (*all day* cały dzień); ~ **out** zużywać ⟨-żyć⟩ się; wyczerpywać ⟨-pać⟩; **2.** *często w złożeniach* ubranie *n*, strój *m*; ~ **and tear** zużycie *n*; **the worse for** ~ zużyty; F *osoba*: wyczerpany

wea·ri·some ['wɪərɪsəm] męczący; ~**y** ['wɪərɪ] (*-ier, -iest*) zmęczony, znużony; F męczący

wea·sel ['wiːzl] *zo.* łasica *f*

weath·er ['weðə] **1.** pogoda *f*; **2.** *v/t.* poddawać ⟨-ddać⟩ działaniu czynników atmosferycznych; *kryzys* przetrwać; *v/i.* ⟨z⟩wietrzeć; '~**beat·en** osmagany wiatrem, ogorzały; '~ **chart** mapa *f* pogody; '~ **fore·cast** prognoza *f* pogody; '~**man** (*pl. -men*) synoptyk *m* dyżurny (*radiowy lub telewizyjny*); '~**proof 1.** odporny na działanie czynników atmosferycznych; nieprzemakalny; **2.** ⟨za⟩impregnować; '~ **re·port** komunikat *m* meteorologiczny; '~ **sta·tion** stacja *f* meteorologiczna; '~ **vane** kurek *m* na dachu

weave [wiːv] (**wove, woven**) ⟨u⟩tkać; sieć pleść, zaplatać ⟨-pleść⟩; *kosz* wyplatać ⟨-pleść⟩; (*pret. i pp.* **weaved**); *~***one's way through** prześliz(g)nąć się przez (*A*); '**~er** tkacz/ka *f*) *m*

web [web] pajęczyna *f* (*też fig.*); sieć *f* (*też komp.*); *zo.* błona *f* pławna; '**~bing** gurt *m*, taśma *f* tapicerska

wed [wed] (**-dd-; wedded** *lub rzadko* **wed**) poślubiać ⟨-bić⟩

Wed(**s**) *skrót pisany:* **Wednesday** śr., środa *f*

wed·ding ['wedɪŋ] ślub *m*; wesele *f*; *attr.* weselny; *~* **ring** obrączka *f* ślubna

wedge [wedʒ] **1.** klin *m*; kawałek *m* (*klinowaty*); **2.** ⟨za⟩klinować

wed·lock ['wedlɒk]: **born in** (**out of**) *~* (nie)ślubny

Wednes·day ['wenzdɪ] środa *f*

wee[1] [wiː] F maluśki; *a ~ bit* malusieńki kawałek

wee[2] [wiː] F **1.** siusiać; **2.** *do lub* **have a** *~* wysiusiać się

weed [wiːd] **1.** chwast *m*; **2.** ⟨wy⟩pielić; *~ out fig.* wykluczać ⟨-czyć⟩ (**from** *z G*); '**~·kill·er** środek *m* chwastobójczy; '**~·y** (**-ier, -iest**) zachwaszczony; F słabowity; F słaby

week [wiːk] tydzień *m*; *~* **after** *~* tydzień za tygodniem; *a ~ today, today ~* od dzisiaj za tydzień; *every other ~* co drugi tydzień; *for ~s* przez całe tygodnie; *four times a ~* cztery razy na tydzień; *in a ~*(**'s time**) za tydzień; '**~·day** dzień *m* tygodnia; '**~·end** weekend *m*, koniec *m* tygodnia; weekend *m*; *at* (*Am.* **on**) *the ~end* w ciągu weekendu; '**~·end·er** (*osoba udająca się poza miasto na weekend*); '**~·ly 1.** tygodniowy; **2.** tygodnik *m*

weep [wiːp] (**wept**) płakać (**for** za *I*, **over** nad *I*); *the wound is ~ing* sączy się z rany; *~·ing* **'wil·low** *bot.* wierzba *f* płacząca; '**~·y** (**-ier, -iest**) F płaczliwy; rzewny, cklliwy

wee-wee ['wiːwiː] F → **wee**[2]

weigh [wei] *v/t.* ⟨z⟩ważyć; *fig.* rozważać ⟨-żyć⟩; *~* **anchor** *naut.* podnosić ⟨-nieść⟩ kotwicę; *be ~ed down with fig.* być przybitym (*I*); *~* **on** *fig.* ciążyć (*D*) **weight** [weit] **1.** waga *f* (*też fig.*); ciężar *m* (*tech., fig.*); *gain ~, put on ~* przybie-

rać ⟨-brać⟩ na wadze; *lose ~* ⟨s⟩tracić na wadze; **2.** obciążać ⟨-żyć⟩; '**~·less** nieważki; '**~·less·ness** nieważkość; '**~·lift·er** (*w sporcie*) ciężarowiec *m*; '**~ lift·ing** (*w sporcie*) podnoszenie *n* ciężarów; '**~·y** (**-ier, -iest**) ciężki; *fig.* doniosły, ważki

weir [wɪə] jaz *m*

weird [wɪəd] niesamowity; F nie z tej ziemi

wel·come ['welkəm] **1.** *int. ~ back!, ~ home!* witaj w domu!; *~ to England!* witamy w Anglii!; **2.** *v/t.* ⟨po⟩witać; ⟨za⟩akceptować; **3.** *adj.* mile widziany; *you are ~ to do it* oczywiście możesz to zrobić; *you're ~!* *Am.* nie ma za co!; **4.** powitanie *n*; *outstay lub* **overstay one's** *~* zbyt długo u kogoś gościć

weld *tech.* [weld] ⟨ze⟩spawać

wel·fare ['welfeə] dobro *n*, interes *m*; *Am.* opieka *f* społeczna; *be on ~* być na zasiłku z opieki społecznej; *~* **'state** państwo *n* opiekuńcze; *~* **'work** praca *f* w opiece społecznej; *~* **'work·er** pracownik *m* (-nica *f*) opieki społecznej

well[1] [wel] **1.** *adv.* (**better, best**) dobrze; *as ~* również, też; *... as ~ as ...* tak ... jak ..., zarówno ... jak i ...; *very ~* bardzo dobrze; *~ done!* → cłt I; **2.** *int.* no; więc; *~ !* no, no!; **3.** *adj.* zdrowy; *feel ~* dobrze się czuć

well[2] [wel] **1.** studnia *f*; szyb *m*; **2.** *też ~ out* tryskać ⟨trysnąć⟩; *tears ~ed* (**up**) *in their eyes* ich oczy wezbrały łzami **well-'bal·anced** zrównoważony; *~-be·ing* dobre samopoczucie *n*; *~-'done* dobrze wysmażony; *~-'earned* należny; *~-'found·ed* w pełni uzasadniony; *~-in'formed* dobrze poinformowany; *~-'known* dobrze znany; *~-'mean·ing* w dobrej wierze; mający dobre intencje; *~-'meant* w dobrej wierze; *~-'off* **1.** (**better-off, best-off**) zamożny; **2.** *the ~-off pl.* bogaci *pl.*, zamożni *pl.*; *~-'read* oczytany; *~-'timed* w porę (*zrobiony*); *~-to-'do* F → **well-odd**; *~-'worn* zużyty, wytarty

Welsh [welʃ] **1.** walijski; **2.** *ling.* język *m* walijski; *the ~ pl.* Walijczycy *pl.*; *~man* (**-men**) Walijczyk *m*; *~*'**rab·bit,** *~*'**rare·bit** *gastr. jakby:* grzanka *f* z serem

welt [welt] wypustka *f*, lamówka *f*

wel·ter ['weltə] stos *m*, góra *f*

went [went] *pret. od* **go** I

wept [wept] *pret. i p.p. od* **weep**

were [wɜː, wə] *ty* byłeś *lub* byłaś, *my* byliśmy *lub* byłyśmy, *oni* byli, *one* były, *wy* byliście *lub* byłyście

west [west] **1.** zachód *m*; **the 2** *pol.* Zachód *m*; *Am.* Zachód *m*; **2.** *adj.* zachodni; **3.** *adv.* na zachód, ku zachodowi; **~·er·ly** ['westəli] zachodni; **~·ern** ['westən] **1.** zachodni; **2.** western *m*; **~·ward(s)** ['westwəd(z)] na zachód, zachodni

wet [wet] **1.** mokry; wilgotny; **2.** wilgoć *f*; **3.** (*-tt-*; **wet** *lub* **wetted**) zwilżać ⟨-żyć⟩; ⟨z⟩moczyć (się)

weth·er ['weðə] *zo.* skop *m*, kastrowany baran *m*

'wet nurse mamka *f*

whack [wæk] głośne uderzenie *n*; F udział *m*, dola *f*; **have a ~ at** spróbować (*G*); **~ed** F wykończony; **'~·ing 1.** F kobylasty; **2.** lanie *n*

whale [weɪl] *zo.* wieloryb *m*

wharf [wɔːf] (*pl.* **-wharfs, wharves** [wɔːvz]) nabrzeże *n*

what [wɒt] **1.** *pron.* co; **~ about...?** a co z ...?; **~ for** po co?; **so ~?** no to co?; **know ~'s ~** F wiedzieć, co jest co; **2.** *adj.* jaki *m*, jaka *m*, jakie *n*; **~·cha·ma·call·it** F ['wɒtʃəməkɔːlɪt] **~whatsit**; **'~·ev·er 1.** *pron.* cokolwiek; jakikolwiek; cóż; **2.** *adj.* **no ... ~ever** w ogóle ...

whats·it ['wɒtsɪt] F wihajster *m*, dings *m*

what·so·ev·er → whatever

wheat [wiːt] *bot.* pszenica *f*; *attr.* pszeniczny, z pszenicy

whee·dle ['wiːdl] skłaniać; **~ s.o. out of s.th.** wyłudzać ⟨-dzić⟩ coś od kogoś

wheel [wiːl] **1.** koło *n*; *mot.* kierownica *f*; *naut.* koło *n* sterowe; **2.** wózek pchać; *ptaki:* krążyć; **~ about, (a)round** odwracać ⟨-rócić⟩ się; **'~·bar·row** taczka *f*; **'~·chair** wózek *m* inwalidzki; **'~ clamp** *mot.* blokada *f* koła; **~ed** kołowy

wheeze [wiːz] *ktoś:* sapać; *silnik:* rzęzić

whelp [welp] *zo.* szczeniak *m*, młode *n*

when [wen] kiedy; gdy; **since ~?** od kiedy?

when·ev·er kiedykolwiek

where [weə] gdzie; dokąd; **~ ... (from)?** skąd ...; **~ ... (to)?** dokąd?; **~·a·bouts 1.** *adv.* [weər'baʊts] gdzie; **2.** *sg., pl.* ['weərəbaʊts] miejsce *n* przebywania; **~·as** [weər'æz] podczas gdy; **~·by**

[weə'baɪ] dzięki któremu; **~·u·pon** [weərə'pɒn] na co; po czym

wher·ev·er [weər'evə] gdziekolwiek; skądże

whet [wet] (*-tt-*) noże itp. ⟨na⟩ostrzyć; *apetyt fig.* zaostrzać ⟨-rzyć⟩

wheth·er ['weðə] czy

whey [weɪ] serwatka *f*

which [wɪtʃ] który; *w odniesieniu do poprzedzającego zdania* co; **~ of you?** który z was?; **~·ev·er** którykolwiek; jakikolwiek

whiff [wɪf] zapaszek *m* (*też fig.* of *G*); haust *m* (*powietrza itp.*)

while [waɪl] **1.** chwila *f*; **for a ~** na chwilę; **2.** *cj.* podczas, w czasie; **3.** *zw.* **~ away** skracać ⟨-rócić⟩ *sobie* czas (**by doing s.th.** robiąc coś)

whim [wɪm] zachcianka *f*

whim·per ['wɪmpə] **1.** ⟨za⟩jęczeć, ⟨za⟩chlipać; *pies:* ⟨za⟩skomleć; **2.** jęczenie *n*, chlipanie *n*; skomlenie *n*

whim|·si·cal ['wɪmzɪkl] chimeryczny; kapryśny; **~·sy** ['wɪmzɪ] kaprys *m*

whine [waɪn] **1.** *pies:* ⟨za⟩skomleć; ⟨za⟩jęczeć; **2.** skomlenie *n*; jęczenie *n*

whin·ny ['wɪnɪ] **1.** ⟨za⟩rżeć; **2.** rżenie *n*

whip [wɪp] **1.** bicz *m*, pejcz *m*; *gastr.* krem *m*; **2.** (*-pp-*) *v/t.* ⟨wy⟩chłostać, ⟨o⟩bić; *jajka, śmietanę* ubijać ⟨-bić⟩; *v/i. wiatr:* zacinać; **~ s.th. out** wyciągać ⟨-gnąć⟩ coś (*nagle*); **'~ped cream** bita śmietana *f*; **'~ped eggs** *pl.* piana *f* z białek

whip·ping ['wɪpɪŋ] bicie *n*; chłosta *f*; **'~ boy** chłopiec *m* do bicia; **'~ cream** bita śmietana *f*

whir [wɜː] *zwł. Am.* → **whirr**

whirl [wɜːl] **1.** ⟨za⟩wirować; kręcić się; **my head is ~ing** w głowie mi wiruje; **2.** wirowanie *n* (*też fig.*); kręcenie się; **my head's in a ~** w głowie mi wiruje; **'~·pool** wir *m* (*w rzece itp.*); **'~·wind** trąba *f* powietrzna

whirr [wɜː] (*-rr-*) ⟨za⟩warczeć

whisk [wɪsk] **1.** machnięcie *n*; *gastr.* trzepaczka *f* do piany; **2.** *pianę* ubijać ⟨ubić⟩; **~ one's tail** *koń:* machnąć ogonem; **~ away** *muchy* odganiać ⟨-gonić⟩; szybko *kogoś* zabierać ⟨-brać⟩

whis·kers ['wɪskəz] baczki *pl.*; wąsy (*kota itp.*)

whis·key ['wɪskɪ] (*amerykańska lub irlandzka*) whisky *f*

whis·ky ['wɪskɪ] *zwł. szkocka*: whisky *f*

whis·per ['wɪspə] **1.** ⟨za⟩szeptać; **2.** szept *m*; **to say s.th. in a ~** wyszeptać coś

whis·tle ['wɪsl] **1.** gwizdek *m*; gwizd *m*; **2.** ⟨za⟩gwizdać

white [waɪt] **1.** (*-r, -st*) biały; **2.** biel *f*; biały kolor *m*; człowiek: biały *m* (-ła *f*); białko *n* (*jajka, oka*); ~ 'bread biały chleb *m*; ~ 'cof·fee kawa *f* z mlekiem, kawa *f* mleczna; ~·col·lar work·er pracownik *m* biurowy; ~ 'lie niewinne kłamstwo *n*, kłamstewko *n*; whit·en ['waɪtn] ⟨z⟩bieleć; pobielić; '~·wash **1.** wapno *n* (*do malowania*); *tech.* mleko *n* wapienne; **2.** ⟨po⟩bielić (*wapnem*)

whit·ish ['waɪtɪʃ] białawy

Whit·sun ['wɪtsn] Zielone Świątki *pl.*; Whit Sunday [wɪt 'sʌndɪ] niedziela *f* Zielonych Świątek; 'Whit·sun·tide okres *m* Zielonych Świątek

whit·tle ['wɪtl] ⟨po⟩rąbać; *też* ~ away, ~ down zmniejszać ⟨-szyć⟩

whiz(z) [wɪz] F **1.** (*-zz-*): ~ by *lub* past przelatywać ⟨-lecieć⟩ obok (*G*), przemykać ⟨-mknąć⟩ obok (*G*); **2.** wizg *m*; geniusz *m* (**at s.th.** w czymś); '~ kid F mały geniusz *m*

who [huː] kto; który

WHO [dʌbljuː eɪtʃ 'əʊ] *skrót:* **World Health Organization** WHO *n*, Światowa Organizacja *f* Zdrowia

who·dun·(n)it [huː'dʌnɪt] F (*książka*) kryminał *m*

who'ev·er ktokolwiek; którykolwiek

whole [həʊl] **1.** *adj.* cały; **2.** całość *f*; **the ~ of London** cały Londyn; **on the ~** w ogóle; ~·'heart·ed stuprocentowy, zupełny; ~·'heart·ed·ly stuprocentowo, całkowicie; '~·meal pełne ziarno *n*; **~·meal bread** chleb *m* z pełnego ziarna

'whole·sale *econ.* **1.** handel *m* hurtowy; **2.** hurtowy; '~ mar·ket *econ.* rynek *m* hurtowy; 'whole·sal·er *econ.* hurtownik *m*

'whole·some zdrowy; '~ wheat → wholemeal

whol·ly ['həʊllɪ] *adv.* całkowicie, zupełnie

whom [huːm] *formy zależne od* who

whoop [huːp] **1.** wrzeszczeć ⟨wrzasnąć⟩ (*z radości*); ~ it up F cieszyć się; **2.** okrzyk *m*

whoop·ing cough ['huːpɪŋkɒf] *med.* koklusz *m*

whore [hɔː] kurwa *f*

whose [huːz] G *od* who

why [waɪ] dlaczego; **that's ~** dlatego

wick [wɪk] knot *m*

wick·ed ['wɪkɪd] nikczemny; haniebny

wick·er ['wɪkə] wiklinowy; '~ bas·ket kosz *m* wiklinowy; '~·work wyroby *pl.* wiklinowe

wick·et ['wɪkɪt] (*w grze w krykieta*) bramka *f*

wide [waɪd] **1.** *adj.* szeroki; *oczy*: szeroko otwarty; *fig.* zainteresowania: rozległy; **2.** *adv.* szeroko; **go ~ (of the goal)** (*w sporcie*) przechodzić ⟨przejść⟩ (z daleka od celu); ~·'eyed o wielkich *lub* szeroko otwartych oczach; *fig.* naiwny

wid·en ['waɪdn] poszerzać ⟨-szyć⟩, rozszerzać ⟨-rzyć⟩

wide·'o·pen *oczy*: szeroko otwarty; '~·spread rozpowszechniony, powszechny

wid·ow ['wɪdəʊ] wdowa *f*; '~ed owdowiały; '~·er wdowiec *m*

width [wɪdθ] szerokość *f*

wield [wiːld] *władzę* dzierżyć; *głosy, wpływy* posiadać; władać (*mieczem*)

wife [waɪf] (*pl.* wives [waɪvz]) żona *f*

wig [wɪg] peruka *f*

wild [waɪld] **1.** *adj.* dziki; *aplauz, pogoda*: burzliwy; oszalały (**with** z *gniewu*); *pomysł*: szalony; **make a ~ guess** zgadywać w ciemno; **be ~ about** przepadać za (*I*); **2.** *adv.* **go ~** oszaleć; wściec się; **let one's children run ~** pozwolić dzieciom robić, co chcą; **3.** **in the ~** na wolności; **the ~s** *pl.* pustkowie *n*; '~·cat *zo.* żbik *m*; ~·cat 'strike dziki strajk *m*

wil·der·ness ['wɪldənɪs] pustkowie *n*

'wild·fire: **spread like a ~fire** rozchodzić się błyskawicznie; '~·life przyroda *f* w stanie naturalnym

wil·ful ['wɪlfl] krnąbrny, uparty, samowolny; *zwł. jur.* rozmyślny, z premedytacją

will[1] [wɪl] *v/aux.* (*pret.* **would**; *przeczenie* ~ **not, won't**): ~ **be** ja będę, ty będziesz, on, ona, ono będzie, my będziemy, wy będziecie, oni będą

will[2] [wɪl] wola *f*; testament *m*; **of one's own free ~** z własnej nieprzymuszonej woli

W

will³ [wɪl] ⟨ze⟩chcieć; *jur.* pozostawiać ⟨-wić⟩ w testamencie

'will·ful → **wilful**

'will·ing chętny (**to do s.th.** do zrobienia czegoś); chcący

will-o'-the-wisp [wɪləðəˈwɪsp] błędny ognik *m*

wil·low ['wɪləʊ] *bot.* wierzba *f*; '**~·y** *fig.* wysmukły

'will·pow·er siła *f* woli

wil·ly-nil·ly [wɪlɪˈnɪlɪ] chcąc niechcąc

wilt [wɪlt] usychać ⟨-schnąć⟩, ⟨z⟩więdnąć

wi·ly ['waɪlɪ] (**-ier, -iest**) zmyślny, przebiegły

win [wɪn] **1.** (**-nn-; won**) *v/t.* zwyciężać ⟨-żyć⟩, wygrywać ⟨-rać⟩; **~ s.o. over** lub **round to** zdobywać ⟨-być⟩ czyjeś poparcie co do (G); **OK, you ~** dobra, wygrałeś; **2.** (*zwł. w sporcie*) wygrana *f*, zwycięstwo *n*

wince [wɪns] ⟨s⟩krzywić się

winch [wɪntʃ] *tech.* wyciąg *m*, wciągarka *f*

wind¹ [wɪnd] **1.** wiatr *m*; dech *m*; *med.* wzdęcie, wiatry *pl.*; **the ~s** *sg.* lub *pl. mus.* instrumenty *pl.* dęte; **2.** pozbawiać ⟨-wić⟩ tchu

wind² [waɪnd] **1.** (**wound**) *v/t. zegarek itp.* nakręcać ⟨-cić⟩; nawijać ⟨-winąć⟩, zwijać ⟨zwinąć⟩; owijać ⟨owinąć⟩ (**round** wokół G); *v/i. ścieżka itp.:* wić się; **~ back** *film itp.* przewijać ⟨-winąć⟩ do tyłu; **~ down** okno *w samochodzie* otwierać ⟨-worzyć⟩; produkcję zwijać ⟨zwinąć⟩; **~ forward** *film itp.* przewijać ⟨-winąć⟩ do przodu; **~ up** *v/t. okno w samochodzie* zamykać ⟨-knąć⟩; *zegarek itp.* nakręcać ⟨-cić⟩; *zebranie* ⟨za⟩kończyć (*też* **with** I); *firmę* zamykać ⟨-knąć⟩; *v/i.* F ⟨za⟩kończyć (**by saying** mówiąc); **2.** obrót *m*

'wind·bag F gaduła *m/f*; '**~·fall** (*owoc*) spad *m*; szczęśliwa gratka *f*

wind·ing ['waɪndɪŋ] kręty, wijący się; '**~ stairs** *pl.* schody *pl.* kręte

wind in·stru·ment ['wɪnd ɪnstrʊmənt] *mus.* instrument *m* dęty

wind·lass ['wɪndləs] *tech.* kołowrót *m*

'wind·mill ['wɪnmɪl] wiatrak *m*

win·dow ['wɪndəʊ] okno *n*; okno *n* wystawowe; okienko *n* (*w instytucji itp.*); '**~ clean·er** osoba *f* myjąca okna; '**~ dres·ser** dekorator *m* wystaw;

'**~ dress·ing** dekoracja *f* wystawy; F mamienie *n* oczu; '**~·pane** szyba *f*; '**~ seat** siedzenie *n* przy oknie; '**~ shade** *Am.* roleta *f*; '**~·shop** (**-pp-**): **go ~·shopping** iść ⟨pójść⟩ pooglądać wystawy sklepowe; '**~·sill** parapet *m*

wind·pipe ['wɪndpaɪp] *anat.* tchawica *f*; '**~·screen** *Brt. mot.* szyba *f* przednia; '**~·screen wip·er** *mot.* wycieraczka *f*; '**~·shield** *Am.* → **windscreen**; '**~·shield wip·er** → **windscreen wiper**; '**~·surf·ing** windsurfing *m*

wind·y ['wɪndɪ] (**-ier, -iest**) wietrzny; *med.* wywołujący wzdęcia, cierpiący na wzdęcia

wine [waɪn] wino *n*

wing [wɪŋ] skrzydło *n*; *Brt. mot.* błotnik *m*; *theat.* **~s** *pl.* kulisy *pl.* (*też fig.*); '**~·er** (*w sporcie*) skrzydłowy *m* (-wa *f*)

wink [wɪŋk] **1.** mrugać ⟨-gnąć⟩ (**at** do G); **~ one's lights** *Brt. mot.* ⟨za⟩mrugać światłami; **2.** mrugnięcie *n*; **I didn't get a ~ of sleep last night** zeszłej nocy nawet nie zmrużyłem oka

win·ner ['wɪnə] zwycięzca *m* (-zczyni *f*); '**~·ning** **1.** zwycięski; **2.** **~·nings** *pl.* wygrana *f*

win·ter ['wɪntə] **1.** zima *f*; *in* (**the**) **~** w zimie, zimą; **2.** ⟨prze⟩zimować; **~ 'sports** *pl.* sporty *pl.* zimowe; '**~·time** zima *f*, okres *m* zimowy; *in* (**the**) **~time** w zimie, zimą

win·try ['wɪntrɪ] zimowy; *fig.* lodowaty

wipe [waɪp] wycierać ⟨wytrzeć⟩; **~ off** ścierać ⟨zetrzeć⟩; **~ out** wymazywać ⟨-zać⟩ z powierzchni ziemi; **~ up** wycierać ⟨wytrzeć⟩; '**wip·er** *mot.* wycieraczka *f* (*do szyby*)

wire ['waɪə] **1.** drut *m*; *electr.* przewód *m*; *Am.* telegram *m*; **2.** podłączać ⟨-czyć⟩ (*też* **~ up**); *Am.* ⟨za⟩telegrafować do (G); przesyłać ⟨-słać⟩ telegraficznie; '**~·less** bezprzewodowy; **~ net·ting** [waɪə ˈnetɪŋ] siatka *f* metalowa; '**~·tap** (**-pp-**) rozmowy telefoniczne podsłuchiwać ⟨-chać⟩

wir·y ['waɪərɪ] (**-ier, -iest**) postać: żylasty

wis·dom ['wɪzdəm] mądrość *f*; '**~ tooth** (*pl.* **teeth**) ząb *m* mądrości

wise¹ [waɪz] (**-r, -st**) mądry

wise² [waɪz] *przest.* sposób *m*

'wise·crack F **1.** wic *m*, dowcipna uwaga *f*; **2.** dowcipkować; '**~·guy** F mądrala *m*

W

wish [wɪʃ] **1.** życzyć (sobie), chcieć; **~ s.o. well** życzyć komuś wszystkiego dobrego; **if you ~ (to)** jeżeli sobie tak życzysz; **~ for s.th.** pragnąć czegoś; **2.** życzenie *n*, pragnienie *n*; **(with) best ~es** (*zakończenie listu*) serdeczne pozdrowienia; **~ful** 'think·ing pobożne życzenia *pl.*

wish·y-wash·y ['wɪʃɪwɒʃɪ] *zupa itp.:* rozwodniony; *osoba, poglądy:* bezbarwny

wisp [wɪsp] kosmyk *m* (*włosów itp.*)

wist·ful ['wɪstfl] nostalgiczny

wit [wɪt] dowcip *m*; inteligencja *f*; kpiarz *m*; *też* **~s** *pl.* rozsądek *m*; **be at one's ~s' end** nie wiedzieć, co ⟨z⟩robić; **keep one's ~s about one** zachowywać ⟨-ować⟩ rozsądek

witch [wɪtʃ] czarownica *f*; '**~·craft** czary *pl.*; '**~·hunt** *pol.* polowanie *n* na czarownice

with [wɪð] z (*I*); u (*G*) (**stay**); z (*G*)

with·draw [wɪð'drɔː] (**-drew, -drawn**) *v/t.* cofać ⟨-fnąć⟩; *pieniądze* podejmować ⟨-djąć⟩ (**from** z *G*); *mil. oddziały* wycofywać ⟨-fać⟩; *v/i.* cofać ⟨-fnąć⟩ się; wycofywać ⟨-fać⟩ się (**from** z *G*)

with·draw·al [wɪð'drɔːəl] wycofanie *n* (się) (*też mil.*); cofanie *n* (się); odwołanie *n*; *mil.* odwrót *m*; *med.* wycofanie *n* (leku); **make a ~** wycofać się (**from** z *G*); *~ cure med.* leczenie *n* objawów abstynencji; *~ symp·toms pl. med.* (*przykre objawy towarzyszące kuracji odwykowej*)

with·er ['wɪðə] usychać ⟨uschnąć⟩, ⟨z⟩więdnąć

with'hold (**-held**) wstrzymywać ⟨-mać⟩; **~ s.th. from s.o.** powstrzymywać ⟨-mać⟩ kogoś przed zrobieniem czegoś

with·in [wɪ'ðɪn] wewnątrz (*G*), w środku (*G*); w zakresie (*G*); w przedziale (*G*); w ciągu (*G*); **~·out** [wɪ'ðaʊt] bez (*G*)

with'stand (**-stood**) wytrzymywać ⟨-mać⟩; powstrzymywać ⟨-mać⟩

wit·ness ['wɪtnɪs] **1.** świadek *m*; **~ for the defence** (*Am.* **defense**) *jur.* świadek *m* obrony; **~ for the prosecution** *jur.* świadek *m* oskarżenia; **2.** być świadkiem (*G*); świadczyć o (*L*); '**~ box** *Brt.*, '**~ stand** *Am.* miejsce *n* dla świadka (*do składania zeznań w sądzie*)

wit·ti·cis·m ['wɪtɪsɪzəm] żart *m*, dowcipne powiedzenie *n*; **~·ty** ['wɪtɪ] (**-ier, -iest**) dowcipny

wives [waɪvz] *pl. od* **wife**

wiz·ard ['wɪzəd] czarodziej *m*, czarnoksiężnik *m*; *fig.* geniusz *m* (*at* w *L*)

wiz·ened ['wɪznd] pomarszczony

wob·ble ['wɒbl] *v/i.* stół: chwiać się; *głos:* drgać ⟨drżeć⟩; *galareta:* ⟨za⟩trząść się; *mot. koła:* bić; *v/t.* chwiać; trząść

woe [wəʊ] żal *m*, żałość *f*; '**~·ful** żałosny

woke [wəʊk] *pret. od* **wake¹**; **wok·en** ['wəʊkən] *p.p. od* **wake¹**

wold [wəʊld] pogórze *n*

wolf [wʊlf] **1.** *zo.* wilk *m*; **lone ~** *fig.* samotnik *m*; **2.** *też* **~ down** F *fig.* pochłaniać ⟨-chłonąć⟩

wolves [wʊlvz] *pl. od* **wolf** 1

wom·an ['wʊmən] (*pl.* **women** ['wɪmɪn]) kobieta *f*; **~ 'doc·tor** lekarka *f*; **~ 'driv·er** kobieta *f* kierowca; **~·ish** kobiecy; zniewieściały; '**~·ly** kobiecy

womb [wuːm] *anat.* macica *f*; *fig.* łono *m*

wom·en ['wɪmɪn] *pl. od* **woman**

women's 'lib [wɪmɪnz 'lɪb] F ruch *m* feministyczny; **~ 'lib·ber** F feministka *f*; '**~ move·ment** ruch *m* feministyczny; '**~ ref·uge** *Brt.*, '**~ shel·ter** *Am.* dom *m* kobiet

won [wʌn] *pret. i p.p. od* **win** 1

won·der ['wʌndə] **1.** dziwić się; zastanawiać się (**about** nad *I*, **if, whether** czy); **I ~ if you could help me** czy mógłbyś mi może pomóc?; **2.** podziw *m*, zadziwienie *n*; cud *m*; **do lub work·~s** czynić cuda; **no ~ that** nic dziwnego, że; **it's a ~ that** to zadziwiające, że; '**~·ful** cudowny

wont [wəʊnt] **1.** *s.o. is~ to do s.th.* ktoś zwykł coś robić; **2.** *as was his ~* jak to było w jego zwyczaju

won't [wəʊnt] *zamiast* **will not** → **will¹**

woo [wuː] zalecać się do (*G*); starać się o (*A*) (*też fig.*); ubiegać się o (*A*)

wood [wʊd] drewno *n*; *też* **~s** *pl.* las-(y *pl.*) *m*; **touch ~** odpukaj w niemalowane!; **he can't see the ~ for the trees** im dalej w las, tym więcej drzew; '**~·cut** drzeworyt *m*; '**~·cut·ter** drzeworytnik *m*; '**~·ed** zalesiony; '**~·en** drewniany (*też fig.*), z drewna; **~·peck·er** *zo.* ['wʊdpekə] dzięcioł *m*; **~·wind** *mus.* ['wʊdwɪnd] **1. the ~** *sg. lub pl.* instrumenty *m* dęte drewniane; **2.** *adj.* dęty drewniany; '~·work stolarka f; '~·y (-ier, -iest) lesisty

wool [wυl] wełna f; ~·(l)en ['wυlən] 1. wełniany; 2. ~(l)ens pl. odzież f wełniana; '~·(l)y 1. (-ier, -iest) wełniany; fig. mętny; 2. wool(l)ies pl. F odzież f wełniana

Worces·ter sauce [wυstə 'sɔːs] sos m Worcester

word [wɜːd] 1. wyraz m, słowo n; wieść f; też ~s pl. słówko n, rozmowa f; ~s pl. słowa f (piosenki itp.); have a ~ lub a few ~s with odbyć z kimś rozmowę; 2. wyrazić ⟨-razić⟩, ⟨s⟩formułować; '~·ing sformułowanie n; '~ or·der gr. szyk m wyrazów; '~ pro·cess·ing komp. przetwarzanie n tekstów; '~ pro·ces·sor komp. procesor m tekstów, edytor m

'word·y (-ier, -iest) przegadany, wielosłowny

wore [wɔː] pret. od wear 1

work [wɜːk] 1. praca f; dzieło n; ~s pl. tech. zakład m, fabryka f; at ~ przy pracy; be in ~ mieć pracę; be out of ~ nie mieć pracy; set to ~ wziąć się do pracy; 2. v/i. pracować (at, on nad I); działać, funkcjonować; ~ to rule pracować (wyłącznie) zgodnie z przepisami; v/t. obciążać ⟨-żyć⟩ pracą; maszynę itp. obsługiwać ⟨-łużyć⟩; materiał itp. obrabiać; kopalnię itp. eksploatować; cuda itp. sprawiać ⟨-wić⟩; przepracować, zapracować; sprawiać ⟨-wić⟩, ⟨s⟩powodować; ~ one's way ⟨u⟩torować sobie drogę; ~ off długi odpracowywać ⟨-ować⟩; gniew odreagowywać ⟨-ować⟩; ~ out v/t. wypracowywać ⟨-ować⟩; plan itp. opracowywać ⟨-ować⟩; wynik znajdować ⟨znaleźć⟩; stwierdzać ⟨-dzić⟩; problem rozwiązywać ⟨-ować⟩; v/i. układać ⟨ułożyć⟩ się; liczenie: wychodzić ⟨wyjść⟩; F (w sporcie) trenować; ~ up słuchaczy itp. pobudzać ⟨-dzić⟩; wprawiać ⟨-wić⟩ się (into w A); opracowywać ⟨-ować⟩; be ~ed up być podekscytowanym (about w sprawie G)

work|·a·ble ['wɜːkəbl] plastyczny; fig. wykonalny; ~·a·day ['wɜːkədeɪ] powszedni; ~·a·hol·ic [wɜːkə'hɒlɪk] pracoholik m (-liczka f); '~·bench tech. stół m warsztatowy; '~·book zeszyt m do ćwiczeń; '~·day dzień m roboczy; on ~days w dnie robocze; '~·er robot-

nik m (-nica f), pracownik m (-nica f); '~ ex·pe·ri·ence uprzednie doświadczenie n

'work·ing roboczy; praktyczny; pracujący; ~ knowledge znajomość f praktyczna; in ~ order działający; ~ 'class· (·es pl.) klasa f pracująca; ~ 'day → workday; ~ 'hours pl. godziny pl. pracy; reduced ~ hours pl. skrócony dzień m pracy; '~s pl. działanie n

'work·man (pl. -men) robotnik m; '~·like; '~·ship fachowość f

work| of 'art (pl. works of art) dzieło n sztuki; '~·out F (w sporcie) trening m; '~·place miejsce n pracy, stanowisko n robocze; '~s coun·cil zwł. Brt. rada f pracownicza lub zakładowa; '~·sheet arkusz m roboczy; '~·shop warsztat m; '~·shy stroniący od pracy; '~·sta·tion komp. stacja f robocza; ~·to-'rule Brt. praca f (wyłącznie) zgodnie z przepisami

world [wɜːld] 1. świat m; all over the ~ na całym świecie; bring into the ~ wydawać ⟨-dać⟩ na świat; do s.o. a lub the ~ of good bardzo dobrze komuś zrobić; mean all the ~ to s.o. wszystko znaczyć dla kogoś; they are ~s apart są diametralnie różni; think the ~ of s.o. mieć o kimś dobre mniemanie; what in the ~...? co u licha ...?; 2. światowy; ♔ 'Cup Puchar m Świata

'world·ly (-ier, -iest) światowy, bywały; doczesny, ziemski; ~·'wise światowo

world| 'pow·er pol. mocarstwo n światowe; ~·'wide ogólnoświatowy

worm [wɜːm] 1. zo. robak m; 2. psa itp. odrobaczać ⟨-czyć⟩; ~ one's way through przeciskać ⟨-cisnąć⟩ się przez (G); ~ o.s. into s.o.'s confidence wkradać ⟨-raść⟩ się w czyjeś zaufanie; ~ s.th. out of s.o. wyciągać ⟨-ciągnąć⟩ coś z czegoś; '~·eat·en zżarty prze korniki; '~'s-eye 'view perspektywa f żabia

worn [wɔːn] p.p. od wear 1; ~·'out zużyty; wyczerpany

wor·ried ['wʌrɪd] zmartwiony

wor·ry ['wʌrɪ] 1. v/t. ⟨z⟩martwić; ⟨za⟩niepokoić; v/i. ⟨z⟩martwić się, ⟨za⟩niepokoić się; don't ~! nie przejmuj się!; 2. zmartwienie n, niepokój m

worse [wɜːs] (comp. od bad) gorszy; ~ still co gorsze; to make matters ~ na domiar złego; wors·en ['wɜːsn] po-

W

garszać ⟨-gorszyć⟩ (się)

wor·ship ['wɜːʃɪp] **1.** cześć *f* (*religijna*); nabożeństwo *n*; **2.** (*zwł. Brt.* **-pp-**, *Am.* **-p-**) *v/t.* czcić; *v/i.* oddawać ⟨-dać⟩ cześć; uczęszczać na nabożeństwa; '~·(p)er czciciel(ka *f*) *m*, wyznawca (-wczyni *f*) *m*

worst [wɜːst] **1.** *adj.* (*sup. od bad*) najgorszy; **2.** *adv.* (*sup. od badly*) najgorzej; **3.** najgorsze *n*; *at* (*the*) ~ w najgorszym razie

wor·sted ['wʊstɪd] wełna *f* czesankowa

worth [wɜːθ] **1.** warty; ~ *reading* wart przeczytania; **2.** wartość *f*; *20 pounds' ~ of groceries* artykuły spożywcze o wartości 20 funtów; '~·less bezwartościowy; ~*while* opłacający się, wart zachodu; *be ~while* opłacać się; ~·y ['wɜːðɪ] (*-ier, -iest*) godny, godzien; szanowany

would [wʊd] *pret. od will*[1]; *would you like ... ?* czy chciał(a)byś ...?; '~·be niedoszły

wound[1] [waʊnd] *pret. i p.p. od wind*[2]

wound[2] [wuːnd] **1.** rana *f*; **2.** ⟨z⟩ranić

wove [wəʊv] *pret. od weave*; wov·en ['wəʊvən] *p.p. od weave*

wow [waʊ] *int.* F no, no!

WP [dʌbljuː 'piː] *skrót:* *word processing komp.* przetwarzanie *n* tekstów; *word processor komp.* procesor *m* tekstów, edytor *m*

wran·gle ['ræŋgl] **1.** kłócić się; **2.** kłótnia *f*

wrap [ræp] **1.** (*-pp-*) *v/t. też* ~ *up* ⟨za⟩pakować, opakowywać ⟨-ować⟩ (*in* w *A*); owijać ⟨owinąć⟩ ([*a*]*round* wokół *G*); *v/i.* ~ *up* ubierać ⟨-brać⟩ się ciepło; **2.** *zwł. Am.* szal *m*; '~·per obwoluta *f*; '~·ping opakowanie *n*; '~·ping paper papier *m* pakowy

wrath [rɒθ] *lit.* gniew *m*

wreath [riːθ] (*pl. wreaths* [riːðz]) wieniec *m*

wreck [rek] **1.** *naut.* wrak *m* (*też człowieka*); **2.** plany unicestwiać ⟨-wić⟩; *be ~ed naut.* rozbić się; ~·age ['rekɪdʒ] szczątki *pl.*; '~·er *Am.mot.* samochód *m* pomocy drogowej; '~·ing com·pa·ny *Am.* (*firma*) pomoc *f* drogowa; '~·ing ser·vice *Am. mot.* pomoc *f* drogowa

wren *zo.* [ren] strzyżyk *m*

wrench [rentʃ] **1.** *med.* ramię *itp.* skręcić; ~ *s.th. from lub out of s.o.'s*

hands wyrwać *lub* wyszarpnąć coś komuś z rąk; ~ *off* coś oderwać; ~ *open* szarpnięciem *coś* otworzyć; **2.** szarpnięcie *n*; *med.* skręcenie *n*; *Brt. tech.* klucz *m* nastawny *lub* francuski; *Am. tech.* nienastawny klucz *m*

wrest [rest]: ~ *s.th. from lub out of s.o.'s hands* wyszarpnąć coś komuś

wres·tle ['resl] *v/t.* mocować się (*with* z *I*); *fig.* zmagać się (*with* z *I*); *v/t.* (*w sporcie*) uprawiać zapasy; '~·tler (*w sporcie*) zapaśnik *m* (-niczka *f*); '~·tling (*w sporcie*) zapasy *pl.*

wretch [retʃ] *często humor.* szelma *m/f*; *też poor ~* biedak *m* (-aczka *f*), nieborak *m* (-aczka *f*); '~·ed [retʃɪd] *pogoda*, *ból:* paskudny; przeklęty

wrig·gle ['rɪgl] *v/i.* wiercić się; ~ *out of fig.* F wywinąć się z (*G*); *v/t.* ⟨po⟩machać (*I*)

wring [rɪŋ] (*wrung*) ukręcać ⟨-cić⟩; *rękę* ściskać ⟨-snąć⟩; ~ *hands* załamywać ręce (*ze smutku*); ~ *out pranie* wykręcać ⟨-cić⟩, wyżymać ⟨-żąć⟩; ~ *s.o.'s heart* złamać komuś serce

wrin·kle ['rɪŋkl] **1.** zmarszczka *f*; **2.** *v/i.* pomarszczyć się; *v/t. nos* zmarszczyć

wrist [rɪst] nadgarstek *m*, przegub *m*; '~·band pasek *m*, bransoleta *f* (*do zegarka itp.*); mankiet *m* (*koszuli*); '~·watch zegarek *m* (*naręczny*)

writ [rɪt] *jur.* pismo *n* urzędowe; nakaz *m*

write [raɪt] **1.** (*wrote, written*) ⟨na⟩pisać; ~ *down* zapisywać ⟨-sać⟩; ~ *off econ.* odpisywać ⟨-sać⟩; ~ *out nazwiska itp.* wypisywać ⟨-sać⟩; *rachunek itp.* wystawiać ⟨-wić⟩; '~ pro·tec·tion *komp.* zabezpieczenie *n* przed zapisaniem; 'writ·er pisarz *m* (-rka *f*); autor(ka *f*) *m*

writhe [raɪð] wić się

writ·ing ['raɪtɪŋ] pisanie *n*; pismo *n*; *attr.* pisemny, piśmienny; *in* ~ na piśmie; ~*s pl.* dzieła *pl.*; '~ case teczka *f*; '~ desk biurko *m*; '~ pad notes *m*, blok *m* papieru; '~ pa·per papier *m* listowy

writ·ten ['rɪtn] **1.** *p.p. od write*; **2.** *adj.* napisany

wrong [rɒŋ] **1.** *adj.* zły; nieprawidłowy; *be ~* nie mieć racji; *zegar:* źle chodzić; *be on the ~ side of forty* przekroczyć czterdziestkę; *is anything ~?* czy coś nie w porządku?; *what's ~ with her?* co się z nią dzieje?; **2.** *adv.* źle; niepra-

widłowo; **get** ~ źle zrozumieć; **go** ~ popełnić błąd; iść źle; zepsuć się; **3.** zło *n*;
be in the ~ nie mieć racji; **4.** ⟨s⟩krzyw-
dzić; ~'**do·er** sprawca *m* (-czyni *f*)
szkody; ~'**do·ing** przestępstwo *n*; bez-
prawie *n*; '~·**ful** zły; krzywdzący; bezprawny
wrote [rəʊt] *pret. od* write
wrought| 'l·**ron** kute żelazo *n*; ~·'**i·ron**
z kutego żelaza
wrung [rʌŋ] *pret. i p.p. od* wring
wry [raɪ] (**-ier, -iest**) uśmiech, *humor.*
cierpki

wt *skrót pisany:* **weight** waga *f*
WTO [dablju: ti: 'əʊ] *skrót:* **World Trade
Organization** WTO *n*/*f*, Światowa
Organizacja *f* Handlu
WWF [dablju: dablju: 'ef] *skrót:* **World
Wide Fund for Nature** (*towarzystwo
ochrony przyrody*)
wwoofer ['wu:fə]
WYSIWYG ['wɪzɪwɪg] *skrót:* **what you
see is what you get** WYSIWYG *m*,
to się ma, co się widzi (*identyczność
graficznej reprezentacji tekstu na ekranie i wydruku*)

X

X, x [eks] X, x *n*
xen·o·pho·bi·a [zenə'fəʊbjə] ksenofo-
bia *f*
XL [eks 'el] *skrót:* **extra large** (**size**) bardzo duży (*rozmiar*)
X·mas['krɪsməs,'eksməs]→ **Christmas**

X-ray ['eksreɪ] **1.** prześwietlać ⟨-lić⟩
(*aparatem rentgenowskim*); **2.** promień
m rentgenowski; zdjęcie *n* rentgenowskie; badanie *n* rentgenowskie
xy·lo·phone ['zaɪləfəʊn] *mus.* ksylofon *m*

Y

Y, y [waɪ] Y, y *n*
yacht [jɒt] **1.** (*w sporcie*) jacht *m*; **2.** ⟨po⟩-
żeglować; **go**~**ing** iść na żagle; '~ **club**
klub *m* jachtowy; '~·**ing** żeglarstwo *n*
Yan·kee ['jæŋkɪ] F **1.** Jankes *m*; **2.** jan-
keski
yap [jæp] (**-pp-**) ujadać
yard[^1] [jɑːd] (*skrót:* **yd**) jard *m*
(*=91,44 cm*)
yard[^2] [jɑːd] podwórko *n*; plac *m* (*budowy itp.*); *Am.* ogród *m*
'**yard·stick** *fig.* miara *f*
yarn [jɑːn] przędza *f*; **spin s.o. a** ~
about komuś sprzedawać dzikie opo-
wieści o (*I*)
yawn [jɔːn] **1.** ziewać ⟨-wnąć⟩; **2.** ziew-
nięcie *n*
yd *skrót pisany:* **yard**(**s**) jard(y *pl.*) *m*
yeah [jeə] F tak
year [jɪə, jɜː] rok *m*; **all the** ~ **round**
(*przez*) okrągły rok; ~ **after** ~ rok po
roku; ~ **in,** ~ **out** z roku na rok; **this**
~ tego roku, w tym roku; **this** ~'**s** tego-

roczny; '~·**ly** corocznie, doroczny
yearn [jɜːn] tęsknić (**for** za *I*), **to do**
tego, by coś zrobić; '~·**ing** tęsknota *f*
yeast [jiːst] drożdże *pl.*
yell [jel] **1.** wrzeszczeć (**with** od *G*, ~ **at**
na *A*); ~ (**out**) wykrzykiwać ⟨-knąć⟩; **2.**
wrzask *m*
yel·low ['jeləʊ] **1.** żółty; F tchórzliwy; **2.**
żółć *f*; **at** ~ *Am. mot.* na żółtym świetle;
3. ⟨z⟩żółknąć; ~ '**fe·ver** *med.* żółta febra *f*; '~·**ish** żółtawy; ♀ '**Pag·es** *pl. TM
tel.* (*spis instytucji*) żółte strony *pl.*;
~ '**press** prasa *f* brukowa
yelp [jelp] **1.** *pies:* skowyczeć ⟨zasko-
wytać⟩; ⟨wy⟩krzyknąć; **2.** skowyt *m*;
krzyk *m*
yes [jes] tak
yes·ter·day ['jestədɪ] wczoraj; ~ **after-
noon/morning** wczoraj wieczorem/ra-
no; **the day before** ~ przedwczoraj
yet [jet] **1.** *adv.* jeszcze; już; **as** ~ jak dotąd; **not** ~ jeszcze nie; **2.** *cj.* ale, mimo to

[^1]: yard
[^2]: yard

yew [ju:] *bot.* cis *m*

yield [ji:ld] **1.** *v/t. owoce, zysk* dawać ⟨dać⟩; *korzyści* przynosić ⟨-nieść⟩; *v/i.* ustępować ⟨-tąpić⟩; ⟨z⟩rezygnować; **~ to** *Am. mot.* ustępować ⟨-tąpić⟩ pierwszeństwa przejazdu; **2.** wydajność *f*; plon *m*; dochód *m*

yip·pee [jɪ'pi:] *int.* F hurra!

YMCA [waɪ em si: 'eɪ] *skrót:* **Young Men's Christian Association** YMCA *f*, Chrześcijańskie Stowarzyszenie *n* Młodzieży Męskiej

yo·del ['jəʊdl] **1.** (*zwł. Brt. -ll-*, *Am. -l-*) ⟨za⟩jodłować; **2.** jodlowanie *n*

yo·ga ['jəʊgə] joga *f*

yog·h(o)urt, yog·urt ['jɒgət] jogurt *m*

yoke [jəʊk] jarzmo *n* (*też fig.*)

yolk [jəʊk] żółtko *n*

you [ju:, ju] ty; wy; pan(i); (*G*) ciebie, was *pl.*; (*D*) tobie, ci, wam *pl.*; (*A*) ciebie, cię, was *pl.*; (*I*) tobą, wami *pl.*; (*L*) tobie, was *pl.*; **~ cannot buy it in Poland** tego nie da się kupić w Polsce

young [jʌŋ] **1.** młody; **2.** *zo.* młode *pl.*; **the ~** *pl.* młodzi *m*, młodzież *f*; **~ster** ['jʌŋstə] młodzieniec *m*; dziewczyna *f*, chłopak *m*

your [jɔ:] twój, wasz *pl.*; państwa *pl.*; **~s** [jɔ:z] twój, wasz *pl.*; państwa *pl.*; **a friend of ~s** twój przyjaciel; **2, Bill** (*zakończenie listu*) Twój Bill; **~self** [jɔ:'self] (*pl.* **yourselves** [jɔ:'selvz]) się, sobie, siebie; sam; **by ~self** samodzielnie, bez pomocy

youth [ju:θ] (*pl.* **-s** [ju:ðz]) młodość *f*; młodzieniec *m*; **'~ club** klub *m* młodzieżowy; **'~·ful** młodzieńczy; **'~ hostel** schronisko *n* młodzieżowe

yuck·y ['jʌkɪ] F *cont.* (*-ier, -iest*) paskudny

Yu·go·slav [ju:gəʊ'slɑ:v] **1.** jugosłowiański; **2.** Jugosłowianin *m* (*-anka*) *f*; **Yu·go·sla·vi·a** [ju:gəʊ'slɑ:vjə] Jugosławia *f*

yule·tide ['ju:ltaɪd] *zwł. poet.* Boże Narodzenie *n*

yup·pie, yup·py ['jʌpɪ] (*ze skrótu*) **young upwardly-mobile** *lub* **urban professional** (*młody wielkomiejski przedstawiciel wolnego zawodu*), yuppie *m*; F japiszon *m*

YWCA [waɪ dʌbljuː siː 'eɪ] *skrót:* **Young Women's Christian Association** YWCA *f*, Chrześcijańskie Stowarzyszenie *n* Młodzieży Żeńskiej

Z

Z, z [zed, *Am.* zi:] Z, z *n*

Zagreb Zagrzeb *m*

zap [zæp] F (*-pp-*) *zwł. komp.* wykańczać ⟨-kończyć⟩; usuwać ⟨-sunąć⟩; *samochód* rozpędzać ⟨-dzić⟩; przełączać ⟨-czyć⟩ (*kanały pilotem*); '**~·per** *Am.* F *TV* pilot *m*

zap·py ['zæpɪ] (*-ier, -iest*) energiczny

zeal [zi:l] zapał *m*; **~ot** ['zelət] fanatyk *m* (*-tyczka f*), gorliwiec *m*; **~·ous** ['zeləs] gorliwy, pełen zapału

ze·bra ['zebrə, 'zi:brə] *zo.* (*pl.* **-bra, -bras**) zebra *f*; **~ 'cross·ing** *Brt.* zebra *f lub* przejście *n* dla pieszych

zen·ith ['zenɪθ] zenit *m* (*też fig.*)

ze·ro ['zɪərəʊ] (*pl.* **-ros, -roes**) zero *n*; *attr.* zerowy; **20 degrees below ~** 20 stopni poniżej zera; **~ 'growth** wzrost *m* zerowy; **~ 'in·terest: have ~ inter-** **est in s.th.** wykazywać zero zainteresowania czymś; **~ 'op·tion** *pol.* opcja *f* zerowa

zest [zest] *fig.* zapał *m*, entuzjazm *m*; **~ for life** radość *f* z życia

zig·zag ['zɪgzæg] **1.** zygzak *m*; *attr.* zygzakowy; **2.** (*-gg-*) ⟨po⟩jechać zygzakiem; *droga:* iść zygzakami

zinc [zɪŋk] *chem.* cynk *m*; *attr.* cynkowy

zip[1] [zɪp] **1.** zamek *m* błyskawiczny; **2.** (*-pp-*): **~ the bag open/shut** otworzyć/zamknąć zamek błyskawiczny w torbie; **~ s.o. up** zapinać ⟨-piąć⟩ komuś zamek błyskawiczny (*w ubraniu*)

zip[2] [zɪp] **1.** świst *m*; F energia *f*; **2.** świsnąć; **~ by, ~ past** przemykać ⟨-knąć⟩ ze świstem obok (*G*)

'zip| code *Am.* kod *m* pocztowy;

~ 'fas·ten·er *Brt.* '~·per *Am.* zamek *m* błyskawiczny

zo·di·ac ['zəʊdɪæk] *astr.* zodiak *m*; **signs** *pl.* **of the** ~ znaki *pl.* zodiaku

zone [zəʊn] strefa *f*

zoo [zuː] (*pl.* **zoos**) zoo *n*; ogród *m* zoologiczny

zo·o·log·i·cal [zəʊə'lɒdʒɪkl] zoologiczny; ~ gar·dens [zʊlɒdʒɪkl 'gɑːdnz] *pl.* ogród *m* zoologiczny

zo·ol·o·gist [zəʊ'ɒlədʒɪst] zoolog *m*; ~·gy [zəʊ'ɒlədʒɪ] zoologia *f*

zoom [zuːm] **1.** przemykać ⟨-mknąć⟩; F ⟨po⟩szybować w górę; ~ **by,** ~ **past** przemykać ⟨-mknąć⟩ obok; ~ **in on** *phot.* najeżdżać na (*A*); **2.** warkot *m* (*samochodu itp.*); *też* ~ **lens** *phot.* obiektyw *m* z zoomem *lub* transfokatorem

Zu·rich Zurych *m*

Z

Summary of Polish Grammar

A. Declension

Declension is the inflection of nouns, adjectives, numerals, pronouns and adjectival participles by using endings that indicate case, number and gender. Note: nouns and substantival pronouns are not inflected according to gender. They appear in a specified gender: masculine, feminine or neuter.

The Declension of Nouns

The following declensions are distinguished according to the kind of noun: masculine, feminine or neuter.

The Masculine Declension

I. The table below shows the declension of masculine nouns whose stem ends in a hard consonant: *-b, -d, -f, -t, -m, -n, -p, -r, -s, -t, -w, -z*.

		N	G	D	A	I	L	V
sg.	anim.	syn-ɸ	syn-a	syn-owi	= G	syn-em	syn-u	= L
	inanim.	sen-ɸ	sn-u	sn-owi	= N	sn-em	śn(i)-e	= L
	inanim.	dom-ɸ	dom-u	dom-owi	= N	dom-em	dom-u	= L
pl.	anim.	syn-owie	syn-ów	syn-om	= G	syn-ami	syn-ach	= N
	inanim.	sn-y	sn-ów	sn-om	= N	sn-ami	sn-ach	= N
	inanim.	dom-y	dom-ów	dom-om	= N	dom-ami	dom-ach	= N

II. The table below shows the declension of masculine nouns whose stem ends in a soft consonant: *-ć, -dź, -j, -l, -ń, -ś*, or a functionally soft consonant: *-c, -cz, -dz, -dź, -rz, -sz, -ż* and *-g, -ch, -k*.

		N	G	D	A	I	L	V
sg.	anim.	harcerz-ɸ	harcerz-a	harcerz-owi	= G	harcerz-em	harcerz-u	= L
	anim.	dziadek-ɸ	dziadk-a	dziadk-owi	= G	dziadk-iem	dziadk-u	= L
	inanim.	ból-ɸ	ból-u	ból-owi	= N	ból-em	ból-u	= L
pl.	anim.	harcerz-e	harcerz-y	harcerz-om	= G	harcerz-ami	harcerz-ach	= N
	anim.	dziadk-owie	dziadk-ów	dziadk-om	= G	dziadk-ami	dziadk-ach	= N
	inanim.	ból-e	ból-ów	ból-om	= N	ból-ami	ból-ach	= N

III. List of endings of the masculine declension

	sg.	pl.
N	-ɸ, -o	-owie, -i, -y, -e
G	-a, -u	-ów, -i, -y
D	-a, -owi	-om
A	-a, -ɸ	-ów, -i, -y, -e
I	-em	-ami, -mi
L	-e, -u	-ach
V	-e, -u	-owie, -i, -y, -e

IV. Summary of noun inflectional endings: masculine declension

1. Nominative sg.: *-φ, syn-φ, ból-φ* (diminutive forms are exceptions, e.g. *Józi-o, dzia-dzi-o*, which end in *-o*).

2. Genetive sg.: *-a* for animate nouns, e.g. *harcerz-a, ps-a* and for nouns denoting the names of tools and parts of the body, e.g. *talerz-a, kolan-a; -u* for inanimate nouns, e.g. *ból-u, dom-u, sn-u*.

3. Locative sg.: *-e* for hard-stemmed nouns, e.g. *śni-e*, (exceptions: *dom-u, syn-u*); *-u* for soft-stemmed nouns and for those whose stem ends in *-k, -g, -ch*, np. *chłopc-u, ból-u*.

4. Vocative sg. has the same endings as locative sg. Exception: nouns that end in *-ec*, e.g. *chłopiec – chłopcz-e!*

5. Nominative pl.: *-e* for soft-stemmed and for functionally soft-stemmed nouns, e.g.: *harcerz-e, ból-e*; *-y, -i* for hard-stemmed nouns, but *-y* is characteristic of inanimate nouns: *dom-y, sn-y, -i* for animate nouns: *chłop-i*, (exception: nouns which end in *-k, -g, -ch*, and *-ec*, e.g.: *Polak – Polac-y, Norweg – Norwedz-y, chłopiec – chłopc-y*); *-owie* for words which denote the names of degrees of relationships; e.g.: *sędzi-owie, syn-owie*.

6. Genetive pl.: *-ów* for nouns ending in a hard stem, e.g.: *syn-ów, dom-ów; -i, -y* for soft-stemmed and for functionally soft nouns, e.g.: *harcerz-y; -φ* is rare, e.g. *mie-szczan-φ*.

7. Accusative pl. for animate nouns A = G pl., e.g. *harcerz-y, chłopc-ów*; for inanimate nouns A = N pl., e.g.: *sn-y, ból-e*.

The Feminine Declension

I. The table below shows the declension of feminine nouns whose stem ends in a hard consonant: *-ba, -cha, -da, -fa, -ła, -ta, -ma, -na, -pa, -ra, -sa, -ta, -wa, -za*.

	N	G	D	A	I	L	V
sg.	wdow-a	wdow-y	wdow(i)-e	wdow-ę	wdow-ą	wdow(i)-e	wdow-o!
	wizyt-a	wizyt-y	wizyc(i)-e	wizyt-ę	wizyt-ą	wizyc(i)-e	wizyt-o!
pl.	wdow-y	wdów-φ	wdow-om	= N	wdow-ami	wdow-ach	= N
	wizyt-y	wizyt-φ	wizyt-om	= N	wizyt-ami	wizyt-ach	= N

II. The table below shows the declension of feminine nouns whose stem ends in a soft consonant or a functionally soft consonant or *-k, -g, -ch*. They end as follows: *-ca, -cza, -dza, -dża, -rza, -sza, -ża, -la, -bia, -cia, -dzi1a, -fia, -gia, -ja, -kia, -lia, -mia, -nia, -pia, -ria, -sia, -tia, -wia, -zia*.

	N	G	D	A	I	L	V
sg.	niani- a	nian-i	nian-i	niani-ę	niani-ą	nian-i	niani-u!
	wież-a	wież-y	wież-y	wież-ę	wież-ą	wież-y	wież-o!
pl.	niani-e	niań-φ	niani-om	= N	niani-ami	niani-ach	= N
	wież-e	wież-φ	wież-om	= N	wież-ami	wież-ach	= N

III. The table below shows the declension of feminine nouns that end in a consonant in the nominative sg.

	N	G	D	A	I	L	V
sg.	brew-ϕ	brw-i	brw-i	= N	brwi-ą	brw-i	= G
	noc-ϕ	noc-y	noc-y	= N	noc-ą	noc-y	= G
pl.	brw-i	brw-i	brwi-om	= N	brwi-ami	brwi-ach	= N
	noc-e	noc-y	noc-om	= N	noc-ami	noc-ach	= N

IV. List of endings of the feminine declension

	sg.	*pl.*
N	-a, -i, -ϕ	-y, -i, -e
G	-y, -i	-ϕ, -i, -y
D	-e, -i, -y	-om
A	-ę, -ϕ	= N
I	-ą	-ami,-mi
L	= G	-ach
V	-o, -i, -y	= N

V. Summary of noun inflectional endings: feminine declension

1. Nominative sg.: **-a** for nouns with a hard stem, e.g.: *wdow-a*; **-i** for nouns with a soft stem, e.g.: *pan-i*; **-ϕ** for nouns ending in a consonant, e.g.: *noc-ϕ*.

2. Genitive sg.: **-y** for nouns with a hard stem, e.g.: *wizyt-y*; **-i** for nouns ending in *-k*, *-g*, e.g. *matk-i*, *nog-i*; and such nouns whose stem ends in a soft consonant: nominative sg. *dłoń-ϕ*, genitive sg. *dłon-i*.

3. Accusative sg.: **-ę**, e.g. *matk-ę*, apart from nouns ending in a consonant in the nominative sg., e.g.: *noc-ϕ* (A sg. = N sg.). Exception: **-ą**, *pani-ą*.

4. In the genitive pl. most nouns take the form of the stem, e.g.: *wdów-ϕ*, *niań-ϕ*. Nouns which end in: *-alnia*, *-arnia*, *-ernia*, *-ja* have the ending **-i**, e.g. *księgarnia* – *księgarn-i*, *cukiernia* – *cukiern-i*, *transmisja* – *transmisj-i*. Nouns that end in a consonant in the nominative sg. take the following endings: **-y**, **-i**, e.g. *noc – noc-y*, *dłoń – dłon-i*.

5. Instrumental pl.: **-ami**, e.g.: *wdow-ami*, *noc-ami*, with the exception of nouns with the suffix *-ość* which take the ending **-mi**, e.g.: *kość – kość-mi*.

The Neuter Declension

I. The table below shows the declension of neuter nouns with the ending *-o* in the nominative sg.

	N	G	D	A	I	L	V
sg.	okn-o	okn-a	okn-u	= N	okn-em	okni-e	= N
	lat-o	lat-a	lat-u	= N	lat-em	leci-e	= N
pl.	okn-a	okien-ϕ	okn-om	= N	okn-ami	okn-ach	= N
	lat-a	lat-ϕ	lat-om	= N	lat-ami	lat-ach	= N

II. The table below shows the declension of neuter nouns with the ending *-e* in the nominative sg.

	N	G	D	A	I	L	V
sg.	pol-e	pol-a	pol-u	= N	pol-em	pol-u	= N
	zboże	zboż-a	zboż-u	= N	zboż-em	zboż-u	= N
pl.	pol-a	pól-φ	pol-om	= N	pol-ami	pol-ach	= N
	zboż-a	zbóż-φ	zboż-om	= N	zboż-ami	zboż-ach	= N

III. The table below shows the declension of neuter nouns with the ending *-ę* in the nominative sg.

	N	G	D	A	I	L	V
sg.	ciel-ę	ciel-ęci-a	ciel-ęci-u	= N	ciel-ęci-em	ciel-ęci-u	= N
	źrebi-ę	źrebi-ęci-a	źrebi-ęci-u	= N	źrebi-ęci-em	źrebi-ęci-u	= N
pl.	ciel-ę-ta	ciel-ąt-φ	ciel-ęt-om	= N	ciel-ęt-ami	ciel-ęt-ach	= N
	źrebi-ęt-a	źrebi-ąt-φ	źrebi-ęt-om	= N	źrebi-ęt-ami	źrebi-ęt-ach	= N

IV. List of endings of neuter declension

	sg.	*pl.*
N	-o, -e, -ę	-a
G	-a	-φ, -i, -y
D	-u	-om
A	= N	= N
I	-em	-ami
L	-e, -u	-ach
V	= N	= N

V. Summary of noun inflectional endings: neuter declension

1. Genitive pl.: **-φ**, e.g.: *okien-φ, pól-φ, cieląt-φ*, but nouns ending in *-e* in the nominative sg. have the genitive pl. **-i, -y**, e.g. *narzędzie – narzędz-i, wybrzeże – wybrzeż-y*.

2. The nouns which end in *-um* in the nominative sg. are indeclinable in the singular and declined as follows in the plural:

	N	G	D	A	I	L	V
pl.	lice-a	lice-ów	lice-om	= N	lice-ami	lice-ach	= N

Declension of Nouns – Some Peculiarities

1. Masculine nouns ending in *-a* (*poeta, znawca*) decline in the singular like feminine nouns, and in the plural like masculine nouns.

2. The following nouns are indeclinable: *kakao, boa, menu, salami, jury, alibi*

3. Plural nouns, e.g. *rodzice, państwo, usta, drzwi, nożyce, okulary, fusy, imieniny, perfumy* are declined as follows:

N	G	D	A	I	L	V
pl. skrzypc-e	skrzypc-ów	skrzypc-om	skrzypc-e	skrzypc-ami	skrzypc-ach	skrzypc-e!
pl. obcęg-i	obcęg-ów	obcęg-om	obcęg-i	obcęg-ami	obcęg-ach	obcęg-i!

The Declension of Adjectives

Adjectives are declined by using endings that indicate case, number and gender. In the singular, they occur in three forms e.g. *zdrow-y, zdrow-a, zdrow-e*. In the plural adjectives have two forms: masculine, which describes masculine nouns, e.g.: *zdrow-i mężczyźni, zdrow-i uczniowie*; and non-masculine, which describes feminine, neuter and inanimate masculine nouns, e.g.: *zdrow-e kobiety, zdrow-e cielęta, zdrow-e owoce.*

I. The table below shows the declension of adjectives.

	sg.	*sg.*	*sg.*	*pl.*	*pl.*
	masculine	*feminine*	*neuter*	*masculine*	*non-masculine*
N	tani-i	tani-a	tani-e	tani-i	tani-e
	mił-y	mił-a	mił-e	mil-i	mił-e
G	tani-ego	tani-ej	tani-ego	tan-ich	tan-ich
	mił-ego	mił-ej	mił-ego	mił-ych	mił-ych
D	tani-emu	tani-ej	tani-emu	tan-im	tan-im
	mił-emu	mił-ej	mił-emu	mił-ym	mił-ym
A	tan-i	tani-ą	tani-e	tan-ich	tani-e
	mił-ego	mił-ą	mił-e	mił-ych	mił-e
I	tan-im	tani-ą	tan-im	tan-imi	tan-imi
	mił-ym	mił-ą	mił-ym	mił-ymi	mił-ymi
L	tan-im	tani-ej	tan-im	tan-ich	tan-ich
	mił-ym	mił-ej	mił-ym	mił-ych	mił-ych
V	tan-i!	tani-a!	tani-e!	tan-i!	tani-e!
	mił-y!	mił-a!	mił-e!	mil-i!	mił-e!

II. List of endings of the adjective declension

	sg.	*sg.*	*sg.*	*pl.*	*pl.*
	masculine	*feminine*	*neuter*	*masculine*	*non-masculine*
N	-y, -i	-a	-e	-i, -y	-e
G	-ego	-ej	-ego	-ich, -ych	-ich, -ych
D	-emu	-ej	-emu	-im, -ym	-im, -ym
A	-y, -i, -ego	-ą	-e	-ich, -ych	-e
I	-im, -ym	-ą	-im, -ym	-imi, -ymi	-imi, -ymi
L	-im, -ym	-ej	-im, -ym	-ich, -ych	-ich, -ych
V	= N	= N	= N	= N	= N

III. Summary of inflectional endings of adjectives

1. The differentiation between endings of the same case (e.g. locative sg. masc. has parallel endings *-im, -ym*), depends on the stem of the adjective. An adjective whose stem ends in a soft consonant has *-i* in its ending and *-y* if it ends in a hard consonant.

2. The nominative sg. masc. has the following endings: *-i* for adjectives whose stem ends in a soft consonant *-k, -g, -ch*, e.g.: *tani-i, długi-i; -y* for adjectives whose stem ends in a hard consonant e.g.: *chciw-y*.

3. The accusative sg. of adjectives denoting animate nouns is the same as the genitive e.g. *dobr-ego człowieka*, The accusative sg. of adjectives denoting inanimate nouns is the same as the nominative, e.g. *now-y samochód*.

4. In the nominative pl. masculine, hard consonants change into soft ones: *-py –
-pi, -by – -bi, -wy – -wi, -ny – -ni, -dy – -dzi, -ty – -ci*, e.g.: *równy – równi, garbaty – garbaci*. Additionally, the following consonants change: *-k – -c, -g – -dz, -ch – -s*, e.g.: *wysoki – wysocy, ubogi – ubodzy, cichy – cisi*.

5. Simple adjectives: *zdrów-ɸ, wesół-ɸ, ciekaw-ɸ, pewien-ɸ, gotów-ɸ*, take only the masculine form of the nominative sg., e.g. *Chłopiec jest zdrów*.

IV. Degrees of comparison in adjectives

The comparative is formed by adding the endings *-szy, -si* to the stem of the basic form of the adjective, e.g. sg. *młod-y – młod-szy*, pl. *młod-i – młod-si*. The superlative is formed by adding the prefix *naj-* to the comparative form of the adjective, e.g.: *młodszy – naj-młodszy*.

V. Irregular adjectives:

duży – większy – największy
mały – mniejszy – najmniejszy
dobry – lepszy – najlepszy
zły – gorszy – najgorszy

The Declension of Pronouns

I. The declension of personal pronouns

In the declension of personal pronouns, oblique cases are not formed by using the nominative stem. Within the same case there are variant forms (stressed – longer, and unstressed – shorter), e.g. in the nominative sg. *mnie – mi, tobie – ci*.

N	ja	ty
G	mnie	ciebie
D	mnie, mi	tobie, ci
A	mnie, mię	ciebie, cię
I	mną	tobą
L	mnie	tobie

II. The declension of possessive pronouns

Possessive pronouns e.g. *mój, twój, nasz, wasz* are declined in the same way as adjectives. Oblique cases are not formed by using the nominative stem. Variant forms also occur.

| | sg. | sg. | sg. | pl. | pl. |
	masculine	feminine	neuter	masculine	non-masculine
N	on	ona	ono	oni	one
G	jego, go, niego	jej, niej	jego, go, niego	ich, nich	ich, nich
D	jemu, mu, niemu	jej, niej	jemu, mu, niemu	im, nim	im, nim
A	jego, go, niego	ją, nią	je, nie	ich, nich	je, nie
I	nim	nią	nim	nimi	nimi
L	nim	niej	nim	nich	nich

The Declension of Numerals

I. The numeral *jeden* has the same forms as the personal pronoun *on*. It is declined in the same way as adjectives e.g.: *jeden uczeń, jedna uczennica, jedno dziecko, jedni uczniowie, jedne uczennice.*

II. The numeral *dwa* occurs in three forms: masculine (*dwaj uczniowie*), feminine (*dwie uczennice*) and non-masculine and neuter (*dwa zeszyty*).

III. The numerals from *trzech* to *tysiąc* have only two forms: masculine (*trzej u- czniowie*) and non-masculine (*trzy uczennice, trzy zeszyty*).

IV. Collective numerals, e.g. *dwoje, troje, czworo,* etc. are declined in the same way as neuter nouns in the singular, e.g.: *troj-e ludzi, trojg-a ludzi, trojg-u ludziom, trojgi-em ludzi.*

V. Ordinal numbers, e.g. *pierwszy, drugi, trzeci,* etc. are declined in the same way as adjectives, e.g. *pierwszy uczeń, pierwszego ucznia, pierwszemu uczniowi,* etc.

B. Conjugation

Polish verbs fall into 11 conjugations according to thematic suffixes.

Group I verbs with the thematic suffix *-a-*
e.g. *kochać, biegać, czytać,* the ending of the infinitive is *-ać,*

infinitive	1st pers., sg., present tense	3rd pers., sg., present tense	3rd pers., pl., present tense	imperative	3rd pers., sg., m, f, n, past tense	adverbial simultaneous participle
czyt-a-ć	czyt-a-m	czyt-a	czyt-aj-ą	czyt-aj!	czyt-a-ł(a, -o)	czyt-aj-ąc

In the third person plural present tense, the imperative and the simultaneous participle, the suffix **-a-** undergoes extension to **-aj-**, e.g. *czyt-aj-ą*.

Group II verbs with the thematic suffix **-e-**
e.g. *umieć, rozumieć*, the ending of the infinitive is **-eć**

infinitive	1st pers., sg., present tense	3rd pers., sg., present tense	3rd pers., pl., present tense	impera- tive	3rd pers., sg., m, f, n, past tense	adverbial simulta- neous participle
umi-e-ć	umi-e-m	umie	umi-ej-ą	umi-ej!	umi-a-ł(a, -o)	umi-ej-ąc

In the third person plural present tense, the imperative and the simultaneous participle, the suffix **-e-** undergoes extension to **-ej-**, e.g. *umi-ej-ą*.

Group III verbs with the thematic suffix **-eje-**
e.g. *szaleć, maleć, posmutnieć*, the ending of the infinitive is **-eć**

infinitive	1st pers., sg., present tense	3rd pers., sg., present tense	3rd pers., pl., present tense	impera- tive	3rd pers., sg., m, f, n, past tense	adverbial simulta- neous participle
mal-e-ć	mal-ej-ę	mal-ej-e	mal-ej-ą	mal-ej!	mal-a-ł(a, -o)	mal-ej-ąc

The thematic suffix **-eje-** shortens to **-ej-** before vowels, e.g. *(on) mal-ej-e*; before consonants it takes the following form: **-eje-** e.g. *(ty) mal-eje-sz, (my) mal--eje-my*.

Group IV verbs with the thematic suffix **-uje-**
e.g. *pracować, malować*, the ending of the infinitive is **-ować**

infinitive	1st pers., sg., present tense	3rd pers., sg., present tense	3rd pers., pl., present tense	impera- tive	3rd pers., sg., m, f, n, past tense	adverbial simulta- neous participle
prac-owa-ć	prac-uj-ę	prac-uj-e	prac-uj-ą	prac-uj!	prac-owa-ł(a, -o)	prac-uj-ąc

The thematic suffix **-uje-** gets shortened to **-uj-** before vowels, e.g. *(on) prac--uj-e*.

Group V verbs with the thematic suffix: *-nie-, -nę-* or *-ną-*
e.g. *puchnąć, chudnąć, sunąć*, the ending of the infinitive is *-nąć*

infinitive	1st pers., sg., present tense	3rd pers., sg., present tense	3rd pers., pl., present tense	imperative	3rd pers., sg., m, f, n, past tense	adverbial simultaneous participle
ciąg-ną-ć	ciąg-n-ę	ciąg-nie	ciąg-n-ą	ciąg-nij!	ciąg-ną-ł (-ęła, -ęło)	ciąg-n-ąc
su-ną-ć	su-n-ę	su-nie	su-n-ą	su-ń!	su-ną-ł (-ęła, -ęło)	su-n-ąc
gi-ną-ć	gi-n-ę	gi-nie	gi-n-ą	gi-ń!	gi-ną-ł (-ęła, -ęło)	gi-nąc

Group VI verbs with the thematic suffix: *-i-* or *-y-*
e.g. *topić, mierzyć*, the ending of the infinitive is *-ić, -yć*

infinitive	1st pers., sg., present tense	3rd pers., sg., present tense	3rd pers., pl., present tense	imperative	3rd pers., sg., m, f, n, past tense	adverbial simultaneous participle
top-i-ć	top-i-ę	top-i	top-i-ą	top!	top-i-ł(a, -o)	top-i-ąc
mierz-y-ć	mierz-ę	mierz-y	mierz-ą	mierz!	mierz-y-ł(a, -o)	mierz-ąc

Group VII verbs with the thematic suffix: *-e* in the infinitive, *-i-* or *-y-* in the present tense
e.g. *myśleć, usłyszeć*, the ending of the infinitive is *-ić, -yć*

infinitive	1st pers., sg., present tense	3rd pers., sg., present tense	3rd pers., pl., present tense	imperative	3rd pers., sg., m, f, n, past tense	adverbial simultaneous participle
myśl-e-ć	myśl-ę	myśl-i	myśl-ą	myśl!	myśl-a-ł(a, -o)	myśl-ąc
usłysz-e-ć	usłysz-ę*	usłysz-y*	usłysz-ą*	usłysz!	usłysz-a-ł(a, -o)	–

* forms of the future simple tense

Group VIII verbs with the thematic suffix: *-ywa-, -iwa-*
e.g. *widywać, wymachiwać*, the ending of the infinitive is *-ywać* or *-iwać*,

infinitive	1st pers., sg., present tense	3rd pers., sg., present tense	3rd pers., pl., present tense	imperative	3rd pers., sg., m, f, n, past tense	adverbial simultaneous participle
wid-ywa-ć	wid-uj-ę	wid-uj-e	wid-uj-ą	widuj!	wid-ywa-ł(a, -o)	wid-uj-ąc
wymach-iwa-ć	wymach-uj-ę	wymach-uj-e	wymach-uj-ą	wymach-uj!	wymach-iwa-ł(a,-o)	wymach-uj-ąc

In the present tense verbs have the following suffix *-uje-*, e.g. *(ja) wymach-uj-ę, (ty) wymach-uje-sz*.

Group IX verbs with the thematic suffix: **-a-** in the infinitive, **-e-** in the present tense
e.g. *łapać, pisać, chrapać*, the ending of the infinitive is **-ać**

infinitive	1st pers., sg., present tense	3rd pers., sg., present tense	3rd pers., pl., present tense	impera-tive	3rd pers., sg., m, f, n, past tense	adverbial simulta-neous participle
łap-a-ć	łapi-ę	łapi-e	łapi-ą	łap!	łap-a-ł(a, -o)	łapi-ąc

Group X comprises various verbs: with the thematic suffix: **-a-** in the infinitive, **-e-** in the present tense:
Xa – the stem of the verbs ends in **-i, -y, -u**;
Xb – they have the thematic suffix **-eje-** in the present tense, **-a-** in the past tense and in the infinitive;
Xc – there is a change in the stem from **-n-, -m-** into **-ą-** e.g. *dąć – dmie, tchnąć – tchnie*.

infinitive	1st pers., sg., present tense	3rd pers., sg., present tense	3rd pers., pl., present tense	impera-tive	3rd pers., sg., m, f, n, past tense	adverbial simulta-neous participle
ży-ć	żyj-ę	żyj-e	żyj-ą	żyj!	żył(a, -o)	żyj-ąc
grz-a-ć	grz-ej-ę	grz-ej-e	grz-ej-ą	grzej!	grzał(a, -o)	grz-ej-ąc
dą-ć	dm-ę	dmi-e	dm-ą	dmij!	dął (-ęła, -ęło)	dmi-ąc

Group XI verbs with the thematic suffix: **-e-** in the present tense (*wiezi-e-sz, tłucz-e-my*).
There is no suffix in the infinitive.

infinitive	1st pers., sg., present tense	3rd pers., sg., present tense	3rd pers., pl., present tense	impera-tive	3rd pers., sg., m, f, n, past tense	adverbial simulta-neous participle
wieś-ć	wioz-ę	wiezi-e	wioz-ą	wieź!	wiózł(a, -o)	wioz-ąc
tłuc	tłuk-ę	tłucz-e	tłuk-ą	tłucz!	tłukł(a, -o)	tłuk-ąc

Rules for Forming Conjugations

The Past Simple Tense (the forms are based on the stem of the verb in the past tense)

sg. m, f, n
1. czytał-em, -am
2. czytał-eś, -aś
3. czytał-ф, -a, -o

pl. m, non-m
1. czytali-śmy, czytały-śmy
2. czytali-ście, czytały-ście
3. czytali-ф, czytały-ф

The Present Simple Tense (only imperfect verbs; the forms are based on the stem of the verb in the present tense)

sg.
1. czyta-m
2. czyta-sz
3. czyta-φ

pl.
1. czyta-my
2. czyta-cie
3. czyta-ją

The Future Simple Tense (only perfect verbs; the forms are based on the stem of the verb in the present tense)

sg.
1. przeczyta-m
2. przeczyta-sz
3. przeczyta-φ

pl.
1. przeczyta-my
2. przeczyta-cie
3. przeczyta-ją

The Future Tense type I (only imperfect verbs; the forms are based on the stem of the verb in the past tense)

sg.
1. będ-ę czytać
2. będzie-sz czytać
3. będzie-φ czytać

pl.
1. będzie-my czytać
2. będzie-cie czytać
3. będ-ą czytać

The Future Tense type II

sg. m, f, n
1. będę pisał, -a
2. będziesz pisał, -a
3. będzie pisał, -a, -o

pl. m, non-m
1. będziemy pisali, będziemy pisały
2. będziecie pisali, będziecie pisały
3. będą pisali, będą pisały

Declensional forms of the verb

1. Active and passive participles are declined according to the adjectival declension.
   a) The active participle is formed by adding the following to the stem of the verb in the third person plural of the present tense: the suffix **-ąc-** and the appropriate case ending, e.g. N sg. czytaj-ąc-a kobieta, czytaj-ąc-y chłopiec, G sg. czytaj-ąc-ej kobiety, czytaj-ąc-ego chłopca, etc.
   b) The passive participle is formed by adding the following to the stem of the verb in the past tense: the suffix **-n-, -on-, -t-** and the appropriate case ending, e.g. N sg. czyta-n-a książka, G sg. czyta-n-ej książki, etc.
2. Gerunds are declined according to the noun declension. They are formed by adding the following to the stem: the suffixes **-nie, -(i)enie, -cie, -(i)ęcie, -(ie)nie** and the appropriate case ending, e.g. czyta-nie, macha-nie, widywa-nie, d-ęcie.

Indeclinable forms of the verb

1. Infinitives
2. Adverbial participles
   a) Simultaneous participle – is formed by adding the suffix **-ąc** to the stem of the verb in the 3rd person plural in the present tense, e.g. czytaj-ąc, widz-ąc
   b) Anticipatory participle – is formed by adding the following suffixes to the stem of the verb in the past tense: **-łszy** (if the stem ends in a consonant), e.g. zjad-łszy, podniós-łszy; or **-wszy** (if the stem ends in a vowel), e.g. dojecha-wszy, przeczyta-wszy.
3. Modal verbs, e.g.: trzeba, warto, można, wolno.

Liczebniki – Numerals

Liczebniki główne – Cardinal Numerals

0 *nought*, zero
  telefon: O, zero
1 *one* jeden, jedna, jedno
2 *two* dwa, dwie
3 *three* trzy
4 *four* cztery
5 *five* pięć
6 *six* sześć
7 *seven* siedem
8 *eight* osiem
9 *nine* dziewięć
10 *ten* dziesięć
11 *eleven* jedenaście
12 *twelve* dwanaście
13 *thirteen* trzynaście
14 *fourteen* czternaście
15 *fifteen* piętnaście
16 *sixteen* szesnaście
17 *seventeen* siedemnaście
18 *eighteen* osiemnaście
19 *nineteen* dziewiętnaście
20 *twenty* dwadzieścia
21 *twenty-one* dwadzieścia jeden
22 *twenty-two* dwadzieścia dwa
30 *thirty* trzydzieści
31 *thirty-one* trzydzieści jeden

40 *forty* czterdzieści
41 *forty-one* czterdzieści jeden
50 *fifty* pięćdziesiąt
51 *fifty-one* pięćdziesiąt jeden
60 *sixty* sześćdziesiąt
61 *sixty-one* sześćdziesiąt jeden
70 *seventy* siedemdziesiąt
71 *seventy-one* siedemdziesiąt jeden
80 *eighty* osiemdziesiąt
81 *eighty-one* osiemdziesiąt jeden
90 *ninety* dziewięćdziesiąt
91 *ninety-one* dziewięćdziesiąt jeden
100 *a hundred, one hundred* sto
101 *a/one hundred and one* sto jeden
200 *two hundred* dwieście
300 *three hundred* trzysta
572 *five hundred and seventy-two* pięćset siedemdziesiąt dwa
1000 *a thousand, one thousand* tysiąc
2000 *two thousand* dwa tysiące
5000 *five thousand* pięć tysięcy
1,000,000 *a million, one million* milion
2,000,000 *two million* dwa miliony
1,000,000,000 *a billion, one billion* miliard

Liczebniki porządkowe – Ordinal Numerals

1st *first* pierwszy
2nd *second* drugi
3rd *third* trzeci
4th *fourth* czwarty
5th *fifth* piąty
6th *sixth* szósty
7th *seventh* siódmy
8th *eighth* ósmy
9th *ninth* dziewiąty
10th *tenth* dziesiąty
11th *eleventh* jedenasty
12th *twelfth* dwunasty
13th *thirteenth* trzynasty
14th *fourteenth* czternasty
15th *fifteenth* piętnasty
16th *sixteenth* szesnasty
17th *seventeenth* siedemnasty
18th *eighteenth* osiemnasty
19th *nineteenth* dziewiętnasty
20th *twentieth* dwudziesty
21st *twenty-first* dwudziesty pierwszy
22nd *twenty-second* dwudziesty drugi
23rd *twenty-third* dwudziesty trzeci
30th *thirtieth* trzydziesty
31st *thirty-first* trzydziesty pierwszy
40th *fortieth* czterdziesty

41st *forty-first* czterdziesty pierwszy
50th *fiftieth* pięćdziesiąty
51st *fifty-first* pięćdziesiąty pierwszy
60th *sixtieth* sześćdziesiąty
61st *sixty-first* sześćdziesiąty pierwszy
70th *seventieth* siedemdziesiąty
71st *seventy-first* siedemdziesiąty pierwszy
80th *eightieth* osiemdziesiąty
81st *eighty-first* osiemdziesiąty pierwszy
90th *ninetieth* dziewięćdziesiąty
100th *(one) hundredth* setny
101st *hundred and first* sto pierwszy
200th *two hundredth* dwusetny *lub* dwóchsetny
300th *three hundredth* trzechsetny
572nd *five hundred and seventy-second* pięćset siedemdziesiąty drugi
1000th *(one) thousandth* tysięczny
1950th *nineteen hundred and fiftieth* tysiąc dziewięćset pięćdziesiąty
2000th *two thousandth* dwutysięczny
1,000,000th *millionth* milionowy
2,000,000th *two millionth* dwumilionowy

Ułamki – Fractions

$^1/_2$ *one half* lub *a half* pół *lub* jedna druga

$1^1/_2$ *one and a half* półtora *lub* jeden i jedna druga

$2^1/_2$ *two and a half* dwa i pół *lub* dwa i jedna druga

$^1/_3$ *one third, a third* jedna trzecia

$^2/_3$ *two thirds* dwie trzecie

$^1/_4$ *one a quarter, one fourth* ćwierć *lub* jedna czwarta

$^3/_4$ *three quarters, three fourths* trzy czwarte

$^1/_5$ *one fifth* lub *a fifth* jedna piąta

$3^4/_5$ *three and four fifths* trzy (całe) i cztery piąte

$^5/_8$ *five eighths* pięć ósmych

0.45   (*nought*) *point four five* zero przecinek czterdzieści pięć *lub* czterdzieści pięć setnych

2.5   *two point five* dwa przecinek pięć *lub* dwa i pięć dziesiątych *lub* dwa i pół

once raz
twice dwa razy
three times trzy razy
four times cztery razy
twice as much dwa razy tyle (*przy rzeczownikach niepoliczalnych*)
twice as many dwa razy tyle (*przy rzeczownikach policzalnych*)
firstly, in the first place po pierwsze
secondly, in the second place po drugie
thirdly, in the third place po trzecie

Wykaz angielskich czasowników nieregularnych

Poniższe zestawienie zawiera listę najważniejszych czasowników nieregularnych. W pierwszej kolumnie podano bezokolicznik (infinitive), w drugiej znaczenie (meaning), w trzeciej formę czasu przeszłego (past tense) a w czwartej imiesłów bierny (past participle).

Infinitive	Meaning	Past tense	Past participle
arise	*powstawać*	arose	arisen
awake	*budzić (się)*	awoke	awoken
be	*być*	was *albo* were	been
bear	*nosić/rodzić*	bore	borne/born
beat	*bić*	beat	beaten
become	*stawać się*	became	become
beget	*począć*	begot	begotten
begin	*zaczynać*	began	begun
bend	*zginać (się)*	bent	bent
bet	*zakładać się*	bet *lub* betted	bet *lub* betted
bid[1]	*oferować*	bid	bid
bid[2]	*mówić*	bade *lub* bid	bidden
bind	*wiązać*	bound	bound
bite	*gryźć*	bit	bitten
bleed	*krwawić*	bled	bled
blow	*wiać/dmuchać*	blew	blown
break	*łamać*	broke	broken
breed	*hodować*	bred	bred
bring	*przynosić*	brought	brought
broadcast	*radio i TV: nadawać*	broadcast	broadcast
build	*budować*	built	built
burn	*palić (się)/oparzyć (się)*	burnt *lub* burned	burnt *lub* burned
burst	*pękać*	burst	burst
buy	*kupować*	bought	bought
can	*móc, umieć*	could	–
cast	*rzucać*	cast	cast
catch	*łapać*	caught	caught
choose	*wybierać*	chose	chosen
cling	*przywierać*	clung	clung
come	*przychodzić*	came	come
cost	*kosztować*	cost	cost
creep	*skradać się/pełzać*	crept	crept
cut	*ciąć*	cut	cut
deal	*handlować/zajmować się*	dealt	dealt
dig	*kopać*	dug	dug
dive	*skakać/nurkować*	dived, *AE* dove	dived
do	*robić*	did	done
draw	*ciągnąć/rysować*	drew	drawn
dream	*śnić/marzyć*	dreamt *lub* dreamed	dreamt *lub* dreamed
drink	*pić*	drank	drunk
drive	*prowadzić (pojazd)*	drove	driven
dwell	*mieszkać*	dwelt *lub* dwelled	dwelt *lub* dwelled
eat	*jeść*	ate	eaten
fall	*padać*	fell	fallen
feed	*karmić*	fed	fed
feel	*czuć*	felt	felt
fight	*walczyć*	fought	fought
find	*znajdować*	found	found

fit	*pasować*	fitted, *AE też* fit	fitted, *AE też* fit
flee	*uciekać*	fled	fled
fling	*rzucać*	flung	flung
fly	*latać*	flew	flown
forbid	*zakazywać*	forbade *lub* forbad	forbidden
forecast	*prognozować*	forecast	forecast
foresee	*przewidywać*	foresaw	foreseen
forget	*zapominać*	forgot	forgotten
forgive	*wybaczać*	forgave	forgiven
freeze	*zamarzać/zamrażać*	froze	frozen
get	*dostawać*	got	got, *AE też* gotten
give	*dać/dawać*	gave	given
go	*iść/jechać*	went	gone
grind	*mielić/ostrzyć*	ground	ground
grow	*rosnąć/uprawiać*	grew	grown
hang¹	*wisieć/wieszać*	hung	hung
hang¹	*powiesić (człowieka)*	hanged	hanged
have	*mieć*	had	had
hear	*słyszeć*	heard	heard
hide	*ukrywać (się)*	hid	hidden
hit	*uderzać/trafić*	hit	hit
hold	*trzymać*	held	held
hurt	*boleć/ranić*	hurt	hurt
keep	*trzymać*	kept	kept
kneel	*klęczeć*	knelt, *AM* kneeled	knelt, *AM* kneeled
knit	*robić na drutach*	knitted, knit	knitted, knit
know	*wiedzieć/znać*	knew	known
lay	*kłaść/znosić (jajka)*	laid	laid
lead	*prowadzić*	led	led
lean	*opierać (się)*	leaned, leant	leaned, leant
leap	*skakać*	leapt, *AM* leaped	leapt, *AM* leaped
learn	*uczyć się*	learned, learnt	learned, learnt
leave	*wyjeżdżać/zostawiać*	left	left
lend	*pożyczać (komuś)*	lent	lent
let	*pozwalać*	let	let
lie	*leżeć*	lay	lain
light	*oświetlić/zapalić (się)*	lit, lighted	lit, lighted
lose	*zgubić/przegrać*	lost	lost
make	*robić*	made	made
mean	*znaczyć*	meant	meant
meet	*spotykać (się)*	met	met
mislead	*wprowadzać w błąd*	misled	misled
mistake	*pomylić*	mistook	mistaken
misunder-stand	*źle zrozumieć*	misunderstood	misunderstood
mow	*kosić*	mowed	mown, mowed
outdo	*przewyższać*	outdid	outdone
outgrow	*wyrastać*	outgrew	outgrown
overcome	*pokonać (z czymś)*	overcame	overcome
overdo	*przesadzać (z czymś)*	overdid	overdone
overhear	*przypadkowo usłyszeć*	overheard	overheard
oversleep	*zaspać*	overslept	overslept
overtake	*wyprzedzać*	overtook	overtaken
pay	*płacić*	paid	paid
plead	*błagać*	pleaded, *AM* pled	pleaded, *AM* pled
prove	*udowodnić*	proved	proved, *AM* proven
put	*kłaść/stawiać*	put	put
read	*czytać*	read	read

resit	*ponownie zdawać*	resat	resat
rewind	*przewijać*	rewound	rewound
ride	*jeździć/jechać*	rode	ridden
ring	*dzwonić/telefonować*	rang	rung
rise	*wzrastać/wschodzić*	rose	risen
run	*biec*	ran	run
saw	*piłować*	sawed	sawn, sawed
say	*powiedzieć/mówić*	said	said
see	*widzieć/zobaczyć*	saw	seen
seek	*szukać*	sought	sought
sell	*sprzedawać (się)*	sold	sold
send	*wysyłać*	sent	sent
set	*umieścić/nastawić*	set	set
sew	*szyć/przyszyć*	sewed	sewn, sewed
shake	*trząść (się)*	shook	shaken
shine	*świecić/polerować*	shone, shined	shone, shined
shoot	*strzelać*	shot	shot
show	*pokazywać*	showed	shown
shrink	*kurczyć się*	shrank, shrunk	shrunk
shut	*zamykać (się)*	shut	shut
sing	*śpiewać*	sang	sung
sink	*tonąć/zatopić*	sank	sunk
sit	*siedzieć*	sat	sat
sleep	*spać*	slept	slept
slide	*ślizgać się/przesuwać*	slid	slid
smell	*pachnieć/wąchać*	smelt, *AM* smelled	smelt, *AM* smelled
sow	*siać*	sowed	sown, sowed
speak	*mówić/rozmawiać*	spoke	spoken
spell	*pisać/literować*	spelt, spelled	spelt, spelled
spill	*rozlać (się)*	spilt, *AM* spilled	spilt, *AM* spilled
spin	*wirować/obracać*	spun, span	spun
spit	*pluć*	spat, *AM* spit	spat, *AM* spit
split	*rozczepiać (się)*	split	split
spoil	*psuć/niszczyć/* *rozpieszczać*	spoilt, *AM* spoiled	spoilt, *AM* spoiled
spread	*rozkładać/rozpościerać*	spread	spread
spring	*skoczyć*	sprang, *AM* sprung	sprung
stand	*stać/stawiać*	stood	stood
steal	*kraść*	stole	stolen
stick	*wbijać/przyklejać (się)*	stuck	stuck
sting	*żądlić*	stung	stung
stink	*śmierdzieć*	stank, stunk	stunk
strike	*atakować/uderzać*	struck	struck
strive	*dokładać starań*	strove, strived	striven, strived
swear	*kląć/przysięgać*	swore	sworn
sweep	*zamiatać/zgarniać*	swept	swept
swell	*powiększać (się)/puchnąć*	swelled	swollen, swelled
swim	*płynąć*	swam	swum
swing	*huśtać się/kołysać się*	swung	swung
take	*brać/przyjmować*	took	taken
teach	*uczyć/nauczać*	taught	taught
tear	*rwać/odrywać*	tore	torn
tell	*powiedzieć/opowiadać*	told	told
think	*myśleć*	thought	thought
throw	*rzucać*	threw	thrown
tread	*kroczyć*	trod	trodden, trod
understand	*rozumieć*	understood	understood
undertake	*podejmować się*	undertook	undertaken

undo	*rozpinać*	undid	undone
upset	*sprawić przykrość*	upset	upset
wake	*budzić (się)*	woke, waked	woken, waked
wear	*nosić (ubranie)*	wore	worn
weave	*tkać/wyplatać*	wove	woven
wed	*poślubić*	wedded, wed	wedded, wed
weep	*płakać/łkać*	wept	wept
win	*wygrać/zwyciężyć*	won	won
wind	*nawijać/wić się*	wound	wound
withdraw	*wycofać się*	withdrew	withdrawn
wring	*wykręcać*	wrung	wrung
write	*pisać*	wrote	written

Najważniejsze miary i wagi

Miary długości

1 inch (in) *cal* = 2,54 cm
1 foot (ft) *stopa* = 12 cali = 30,48 cm
1 yard (yd) *jard* = 3 stopy = 91,44 cm
1 (statute) mile *mila* = 1760 jardów = 1,609 km

Lotnictwo i marynarka:

1 nautical mile *mila morska* = 1,852 km

Miary powierzchni

1 square inch (sq in) *cal kwadratowy* = 6,452 cm^2
1 square foot (sq ft) *stopa kwadratowa* = 144 cale kw. = 929,029 cm^2
1 square yard (sq yd) *jard kwadratowy* = 9 stóp kw. = 8361,26 cm^2
1 square mile *mila kwadratowa* = 259 ha = 2,59 km^2

Miary objętości

1 cubic inch (cu in) *cal sześcienny* = 16,387 cm^3
1 cubic foot (cu ft) *stopa sześcienna* = 1728 cali sześciennych = 0,02832 m^3
1 cubic yard *jard sześcienny* = 27 stóp sześciennych = 0,7646 m^3

Brytyjskie miary objętości płynów

1 pint (pt) *pół kwarty* = 0,568 l
1 quart (qt) *kwarta* = 1,136 l
1 gallon (gall) *galon* = 4 kwarty = 4,546 l

Amerykańskie miary objętości płynów

1 pint (pt) *pół kwarty* = 0,4732 l
1 quart (qt) *kwarta* = 0,9464 l
1 gallon (gall) *galon* = 4 kwarty = 3,7853 l
1 barrel petroleum *baryłka* = 42 galony = 158,97 l

Jednostki wagi stosowane w handlu

1 ounce (oz) *uncja* = 28,35 g
1 pound (lb) *funt* = 16 uncji = 453,59 g
1 stone (st) *kamień* = 14 funtów = 6,356 kg
1 hundredweight (cwt) *cetnar*:
BE = 112 funtów = 50,802 kg,
AE = 100 funtów = 45,359 kg
1 long ton *tona angielska* = 20 cetnarów (*BE*) = 1016,05 kg
1 short ton *tona amerykańska* = 20 cetnarów (*AE*) = 907,185 kg
1 metric ton *tona metryczna* = 1000 kg

1 października 1995 r. Wielka Brytania przeszła na system metryczny.
W użyciu pozostaną jednak, przynajmniej przez jakiś czas, pół kwarty (**pint**) w odniesieniu do piwa i mleka oraz mile przy podawaniu odległości na tablicach drogowych.